my BusinessCourse

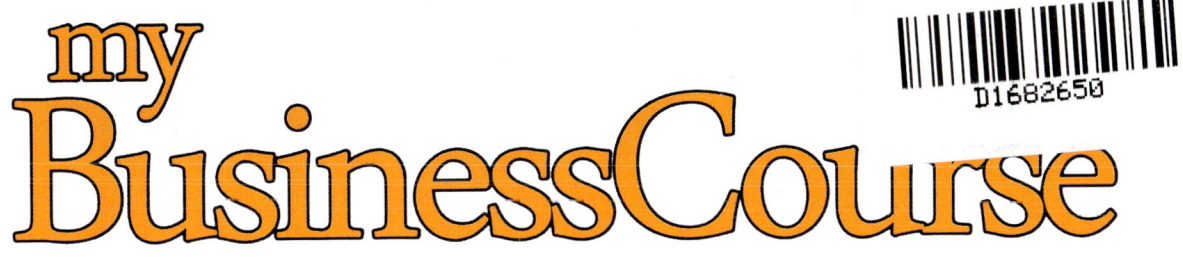

FREE WITH NEW COPIES OF THIS TEXTBOOK*

Scratch here for access code

Scratch here for access code

Start using myBusinessCourse Today: www.mybusinesscourse.com

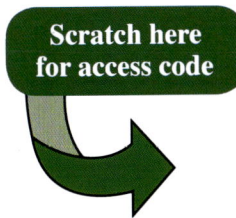

myBusinessCourse is a web-based learning and assessment program intended to complement your textbook and faculty instruction.

Student Benefits

- **eLectures**: These videos review the key concepts of each Learning Objective in each chapter.
- **Guided examples**: These videos provide step-by-step solutions for select problems in each chapter.
- **Auto-graded assignments**: Provide students with immediate feedback on select assignments. (**with Instructor-Led course ONLY**).
- **Quiz and Exam preparation**: myBusinessCourse provides students with additional practice and exam preparation materials to help students achieve better grades and content mastery.

You can access myBusinessCourse 24/7 from any web-enabled device, including iPads, smartphones, laptops, and tablets.

Interactive content that runs on any device.

Built for PCs, iPads, Laptops, Tablets, Smartphones

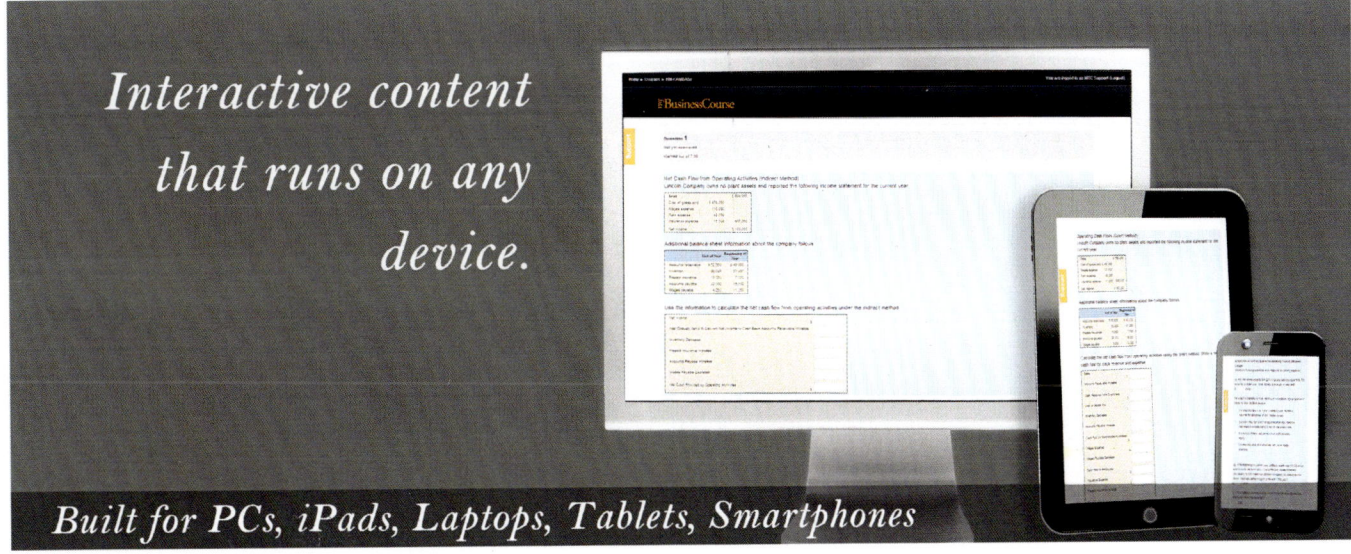

***Each access code is good for one use only.** If the textbook is used for more than one course or term, students will have to purchase additional myBusinessCourse access codes. In addition, students who repeat a course for any reason will have to purchase a new access code. If you purchased a used book and the protective coating that covers the access code has been removed, your code may be invalid.

Access to myBusinessCourse is free ONLY with the purchase of a new textbook.

FIFTH EDITION

Financial & Managerial Accounting for Decision Makers

MICHELLE L. HANLON
Massachusetts Institute of Technology

ROBERT P. MAGEE
Northwestern University

GLENN M. PFEIFFER
Chapman University

SUSAN L. KULP
George Washington University

AMIE L. DRAGOO

To my husband, Chris, and to our children, Clark and Josie.
—MLH

To my wife, Peggy, and our family, Paul and Teisha, Michael and Heather, and grandchildren Sage, Caillean, Rhiannon, Corin, Connor, and Harrison.
—RPM

To my wife, Kathie, and my daughter, Jaclyn.
—GMP

To my parents, Harlene (of blessed memory) and Edwin, my husband, Edoardo, and our children, Geoffrey, Ryan, and Daniella.
—SLK

To my husband, Mike, and to our children, Jake, Justin, Julia, and Josie.
—ALD

Materials from the Certified Management Accountant Examinations, Copyright © 2022 by the Institute of Certified Management Accountants are reprinted and/or adapted with permission.

Photo credits:

Chapter 1: Shutterstock	Chapter 9: Shutterstock	Chapter 17: iStock
Chapter 2: Shutterstock	Chapter 10: iStock	Chapter 18: iStock
Chapter 3: iStock	Chapter 11: Shutterstock	Chapter 19: iStock
Chapter 4: Shutterstock	Chapter 12: Shutterstock	Chapter 20: iStock
Chapter 5: Shutterstock	Chapter 13: Shutterstock	Chapter 21: Shutterstock
Chapter 6: Shutterstock	Chapter 14: Shutterstock	Chapter 22: iStock
Chapter 7: Shutterstock	Chapter 15: iStock	Chapter 23: iStock
Chapter 8: iStock	Chapter 16: Shutterstock	Chapter 24: iStock

Cambridge Business Publishers

Financial & Managerial Accounting for Decision Makers, Fifth Edition, by Michelle L. Hanlon, Robert P. Magee, Glenn M. Pfeiffer, Susan L. Kulp, and Amie L. Dragoo.

COPYRIGHT © 2024 by Cambridge Business Publishers, LLC. Published by Cambridge Business Publishers, LLC. Exclusive rights by Cambridge Business Publishers, LLC, for manufacture and export.

ALL RIGHTS RESERVED. No part of this publication may be reproduced, distributed, or stored in a database or retrieval system in any form or by any means, without prior written consent of Cambridge Business Publishers, LLC, including, but not limited to, in any network or other electronic storage or transmission, or broadcast for distance learning.

Student Edition ISBN: 978-1-61853-564-1

Bookstores & Faculty: To order this book, contact the company via email customerservice@cambridgepub.com or call 800-619-6473.

Students: To order this book, please visit the book's website and order directly online.

Printed in Canada.
10 9 8 7 6 5 4 3 2 1

About the Authors

Michelle L. Hanlon is the Howard W. Johnson Professor at the MIT Sloan School of Management. She earned her doctorate degree at the University of Washington. Prior to joining MIT, she was a faculty member at the University of Michigan. Professor Hanlon has taught undergraduates, MBA students, Executive MBA students, and Masters of Finance students. She has won many awards for her teaching and research, including the 2021 Outstanding Teacher Award, MIT Sloan School, 2020 Presidential Scholar, American Accounting Association, 2020 Distinguished Contribution to Accounting Literature Award, American Accounting Association, 2020 MIT Teaching with Digital Technology Award, and 2013 Jamieson Prize for Excellence in Teaching at MIT Sloan. Professor Hanlon's research focuses primarily on the intersection of financial accounting and taxation. She has published research studies in the *Journal of Accounting and Economics*, the *Journal of Accounting Research*, *The Accounting Review*, the *Review of Accounting Studies*, the *Journal of Finance*, the *Journal of Financial Economics*, the *Journal of Public Economics*, and others. She has won several awards for her research and has presented her work at numerous universities and conferences. Professor Hanlon has served on several editorial boards and currently serves as an editor at the *Journal of Accounting and Economics*. Professor Hanlon is a co-author on four other textbooks—*Financial Accounting, Financial Accounting Using IFRS, Intermediate Accounting,* and *Taxes and Business Strategy*. She has testified in front of the U.S. Senate Committee on Finance and the U.S. House of Representatives Committee on Ways and Means about the interaction of financial accounting and tax policy and international tax policy. She served as a U.S. delegate to the American-Swiss Young Leaders Conference in 2010 and worked as an Academic Fellow at the U.S. House Ways and Means Committee in 2015.

Robert P. Magee is Keith I. DeLashmutt Professor Emeritus of Accounting Information and Management at the Kellogg School of Management at Northwestern University. He received his A.B., M.S., and Ph.D. from Cornell University. Prior to joining the Kellogg faculty in 1976, he was a faculty member at the University of Chicago's Graduate School of Business. For academic year 1980–81, he was a visiting faculty member at IMEDE (now IMD) in Lausanne, Switzerland.

Professor Magee's research focuses on the use of accounting information to facilitate decision-making and control within organizations. He has published articles in *The Accounting Review*, the *Journal of Accounting Research*, the *Journal of Accounting and Economics*, and a variety of other journals. He is the author of *Advanced Managerial Accounting* and co-author (with Thomas R. Dyckman and David H. Downes) of *Efficient Capital Markets and Accounting: A Critical Analysis*. The latter book received the Notable Contribution to the Accounting Literature Award from the AICPA in 1978. Professor Magee has served on the editorial boards of *The Accounting Review,* the *Journal of Accounting Research*, the *Journal of Accounting and Economics,* and the *Journal of Accounting, Auditing and Finance*. From 1994–96, he served as Editor of *The Accounting Review*, the quarterly research journal of the American Accounting Association. He received the American Accounting Association's Outstanding Accounting Educator Award in 1999 and the Illinois CPA Society Outstanding Educator Award in 2000.

Professor Magee has taught financial accounting to MBA and Executive MBA students. He has received several teaching awards at the Kellogg School, including the Alumni Choice Outstanding Professor Award in 2003.

Glenn M. Pfeiffer is the Warren and Doris Uehlinger Professor of Business at the George L. Argyros School of Business and Economics and Provost Emeritus at Chapman University. He received his M.S. and Ph.D. from Cornell University after he earned a bachelors degree from Hope College. Prior to joining the faculty at the Argyros School, he held appointments at the University of Washington, Cornell University, the University of Chicago, the University of Arizona, and San Diego State University.

Professor Pfeiffer's research focuses on accounting and capital markets. He has investigated issues relating to lease accounting, LIFO inventory liquidation, earnings per share, management compensation, corporate reorganization, and technology investments. He has published articles in *The Accounting Review*, *Accounting Horizons*, the *Financial Analysts Journal*, the *International Journal of Accounting Information Systems*, the *Journal of High Technology Management Research*, *Economic Journal*, the *Journal of Accounting Education*, and several other academic journals. In addition, he has published numerous case studies in financial accounting and reporting.

Professor Pfeiffer teaches financial accounting and financial analysis to undergraduate, MBA, and law students. He has also taught managerial accounting for MBAs. He has won several teaching awards at both the undergraduate and the graduate levels.

Susan L. Kulp is Professor of Accountancy at the George Washington University School of Business. She received her Ph.D. at Stanford University. Before joining the George Washington University faculty, Professor Kulp was a faculty member at Harvard Business School.

Professor Kulp's research focuses on performance measurement, incentive, and internal decision-making issues in inter-organizational relationships. The settings that she examines include supply chain relationships, private partnerships, and government entities. Her research highlights the conflicts between inter-organizational contracts and the control systems in place within the partnering firms. She has published research studies in both accounting and operations management journals, including the *Journal of Accounting Research, The Accounting Review, Management Science, Production and Operations Research*, and *Review of Accounting Studies*. Professor Kulp currently serves as a Department Editor at Decision Sciences. In addition to her published research studies, Professor Kulp has published several Harvard Business School cases focused on management control.

Professor Kulp has taught managerial accounting to undergraduate, MBA, online MBA, and executive MBA students. Additionally, she teaches financial accounting to online MBA students. Professor Kulp has won several teaching awards.

Amie L. Dragoo is a Professor of Accounting and Educational Consultant. Former Accounting Department Chair and Associate Professor at Edgewood College, Dr. Dragoo earned her BA and MBA from Michigan State University, and her doctorate from Edgewood College. She holds a CPA license, and for nearly 15 years has been a Becker Professional Education faculty instructor. Prior to her experiences in higher education, she was a senior business assurance associate with PricewaterhouseCoopers LLP (formerly Coopers & Lybrand L.L.P.). Dr. Dragoo has extensive teaching experiences, including courses in Intermediate Accounting I and II, Cost Accounting, Advanced Cost Management, Strategic Financial Management, and other advanced courses in financial and managerial accounting. She has received a number of teaching awards including the School of Business Outstanding Faculty Award and the Estervig-Beaubien Excellence in Teaching and Mentoring Award. She has also worked as an independent consultant, including projects in higher education, and has worked with several corporate clients. Dr. Dragoo's research has been published in the *Journal of Education for Business* and the *Journal of Continuing Higher Education,* and she has contributed to numerous articles published by organizations affiliated with the AICPA. She has been involved in many community-oriented programs, including the Volunteer Income Tax Assistance (VITA) program.

Preface

Welcome to the fifth edition of *Financial & Managerial Accounting for Decision Makers,* and, to the adopters of the previous editions, thank you for contributing to the success of those editions. We wrote this book to equip students with the accounting techniques and insights necessary to succeed in today's business environment. It reflects our combined experience in teaching accounting to college students at all levels. For anyone who pursues a career in business, the ability to read, analyze, and interpret accounting information is an essential skill. *Financial & Managerial Accounting for Decision Makers* is written for future business leaders who want to understand how accounting information is prepared and how the information is used by investors, creditors, financial analysts, and managers. Our goal is to provide the most engaging, relevant, and accessible textbook available.

TARGET AUDIENCE

Financial & Managerial Accounting for Decision Makers is intended for use in an introductory accounting course that combines financial and managerial accounting concepts, at either the undergraduate or the graduate level; one that balances the preparation of accounting information with its analysis and interpretation.

Financial & Managerial Accounting for Decision Makers is real-world oriented and focuses on the most salient aspects of accounting. It teaches students how to read, analyze, and interpret accounting data to make informed business decisions. To that end, it consistently incorporates **real company data**, both in the body of each chapter and throughout the assignment material.

REAL DATA INCORPORATED THROUGHOUT

Today's business students must be skilled in using real financial statements to make business decisions. We feel strongly that the more students are exposed to real financial statements, the more comfortable they become with the differences in financial statements that exist across companies and industries. Through their exposure to various financial statements, students will learn that, while financial statements do not all look the same, they can readily understand and interpret them to make business decisions. Because we update all of the examples throughout the chapters with the most recently available information, students will see the impact of recent events on financial statements, such as the impact of the COVID-19 pandemic. Furthermore, today's students must have the skills to go beyond basic financial statements to interpret and apply nonfinancial disclosures, such as note disclosures and supplementary reports. We expose students to the analysis and interpretation of real company data and nonfinancial disclosures through the use of focus companies in each chapter, the generous incorporation of note disclosures, financial analysis discussions in many chapters, and an abundance of assignments that draw on real company data and disclosures. This analysis extends into managerial accounting topics where real world companies are the basis for hypothetical, yet typical and relevant decision-making scenarios. An ample number of open-ended critical thinking questions are intermingled within the content of each chapter and include suggested solutions.

Focus Companies for Each Chapter

Each chapter's content is explained through the accounting and reporting activities of real companies. Each chapter incorporates a "focus company" for special emphasis and demonstration. The enhanced instructional value of focus companies comes from the way they engage students in real analysis and interpretation. Focus companies were selected based on student appeal and the diversity of industries.

Chapter 1	Nike	Chapter 9	Verizon	Chapter 17	Samsung
Chapter 2	Walgreens	Chapter 10	Deere & Co.	Chapter 18	Ben & Jerry's
Chapter 3	Walgreens	Chapter 11	Pfizer	Chapter 19	Whole Foods
Chapter 4	CVS Health Corporation	Chapter 12	Alphabet, Inc.	Chapter 20	Potbelly
Chapter 5	PepsiCo	Chapter 13	Warby Parker	Chapter 21	Wayfair
Chapter 6	Microsoft Corporation	Chapter 14	Block, Inc.	Chapter 22	Samsonite International S.A.
Chapter 7	Home Depot	Chapter 15	Razor USA, LLC	Chapter 23	Volkswagen
Chapter 8	Procter & Gamble	Chapter 16	Boston Beer	Chapter 24	Amazon

Road Maps

Each chapter opens with a Road Map that identifies each learning objective for the chapter, the related page numbers, the eLecture videos, the reviews, and the assignments. This table allows students and faculty to quickly grasp the chapter content and to efficiently navigate the desired topic.

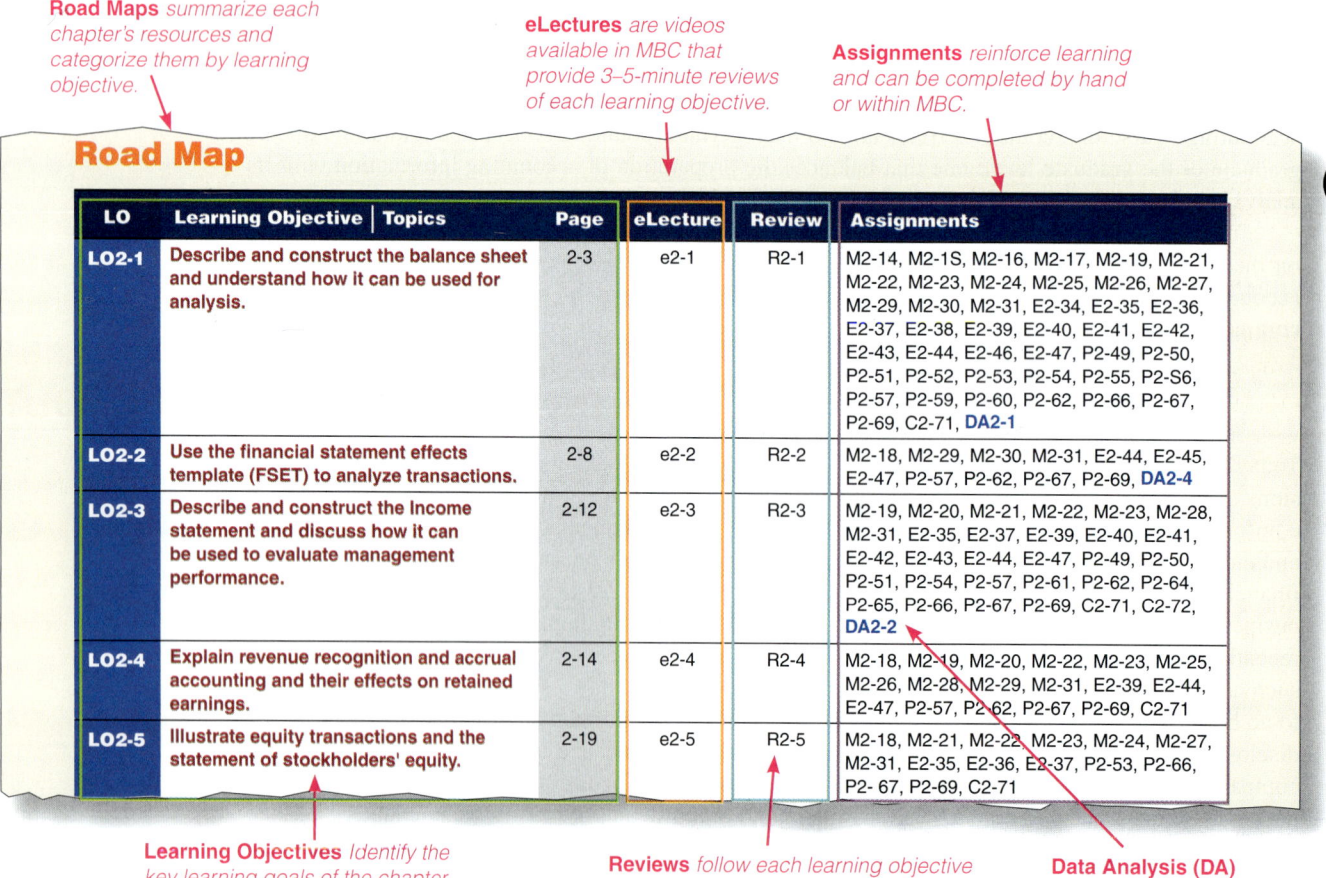

Note Disclosures and Management Disclosures

We incorporate note disclosures and other management disclosures, where appropriate, throughout the book. We explain the significance of the note disclosure and then demonstrate how to use the disclosed information to make managerial inferences and decisions. A representative sample follows.

Disclosure Notes and Interpretations

In its balance sheets, **Microsoft** reports current accounts receivable, net of allowance for doubtful accounts, of $32,011 million at June 30, 2020, and $29,524 million at June 30, 2019. In its MD&A (Management Discussion and Analysis), the company provides the following information.

The allowance for doubtful accounts reflects our best estimate of probable losses inherent in the accounts receivable balance. We determine the allowance based on known trouble accounts, historical experience, and other currently available evidence.

Activity in the allowance for doubtful accounts was as follows:

(In millions) Year Ended June 30	2020	2019	2018
Balance, beginning of period	$434	$397	$361
Charged to costs and other	560	153	134
Write-offs	(178)	(116)	(98)
Balance, end of period	$816	$434	$397

Allowance for doubtful accounts included in our consolidated balance sheets:

June 30	2020	2019	2018
Accounts receivable, net allowance for doubtful accounts	$788	$411	$377
Other long-term assets	28	23	20
Total	$816	$434	$397

Financial Analysis Discussions

Each financial accounting chapter includes a financial analysis discussion that introduces key ratios and applies them to the financial statements of the chapter's focus company. By weaving some analysis into each chapter, we try to instill in students a deeper appreciation for the significance of the accounting methods being discussed. One such analysis discussion follows.

ANALYZING FINANCIAL STATEMENTS

Analysis Objective

We are trying to determine whether Home Depot's sales provide sufficient revenues to cover its operation costs, primarily selling and administrative expenses, after allowing for the costs of acquiring the products and services sold.

LO7-5 Define and interpret gross profit margin and inventory turnover ratios. Use inventory disclosure information to make appropriate adjustments to ratios.

Analysis Tool Gross Profit Margin (GPM) Ratio

$$\text{Gross profit margin} = \frac{\text{Sales revenue} - \text{Cost of goods sold}}{\text{Sales revenue}}$$

Applying the Gross Profit Margin Ratio to The Home Depot.

Fiscal Year Ended

Jan. 28, 2018: $\frac{(\$100{,}904 - \$66{,}548)}{\$100{,}904} = 0.340$ or 34.0%

Feb. 3, 2019: $\frac{(\$108{,}203 - \$71{,}043)}{\$108{,}203} = 0.343$ or 34.3%

Feb. 2, 2020: $\frac{(\$110{,}225 - \$72{,}653)}{\$110{,}225} = 0.341$ or 34.1%

eLecture icons identify topics for which there are instructional videos in **myBusinessCourse** *(MBC).*

Assignments that Draw on Real Data

It is essential for students to be able to apply what they have learned to real financial statements. Therefore, we have included an abundance of assignments in each chapter that draw on recent, real data and disclosures. These assignments are readily identified by an icon in the margin that includes the company's ticker symbol and the exchange on which the company's stock trades. A representative example follows.

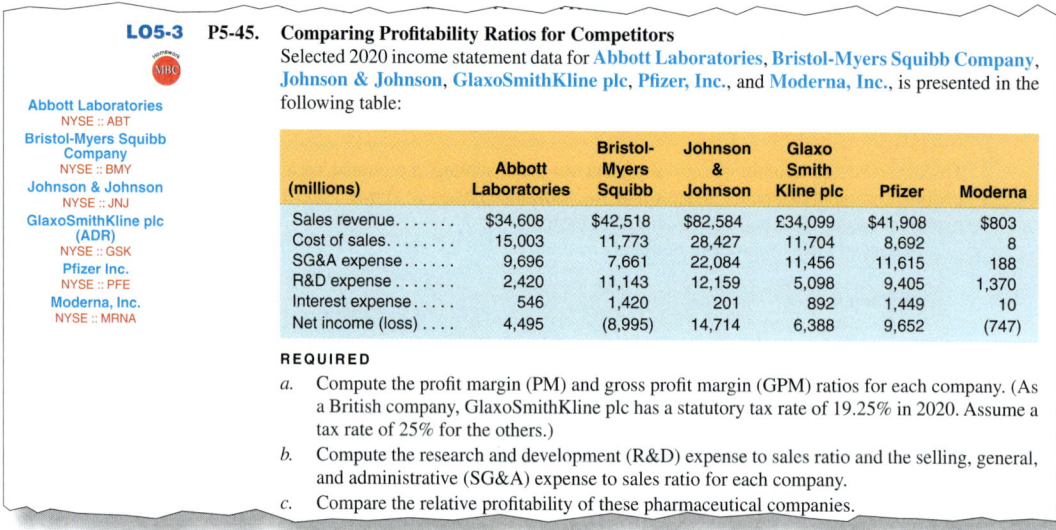

BALANCED APPROACH

As instructors of introductory financial accounting, we recognize that the first financial accounting course serves the general business students as well as potential accounting majors. *Financial & Managerial Accounting for Decision Makers* embraces this reality. This book **balances financial reporting, analysis, interpretation**, and **decision making** with the more standard aspects of accounting such as **journal entries**, **T-accounts**, and the **preparation of financial statements**.

3-Step Process: Analyze, Journalize, Post

One technique we use throughout the book to maintain a balanced approach is the incorporation of a 3-step process to analyze and record transactions. **Step 1** analyzes the impact of various transactions on the financial statements using the financial statement effects template (FSET). **Step 2** records the transaction using journal entries, and **Step 3** requires students to post the journal entries to T-accounts.

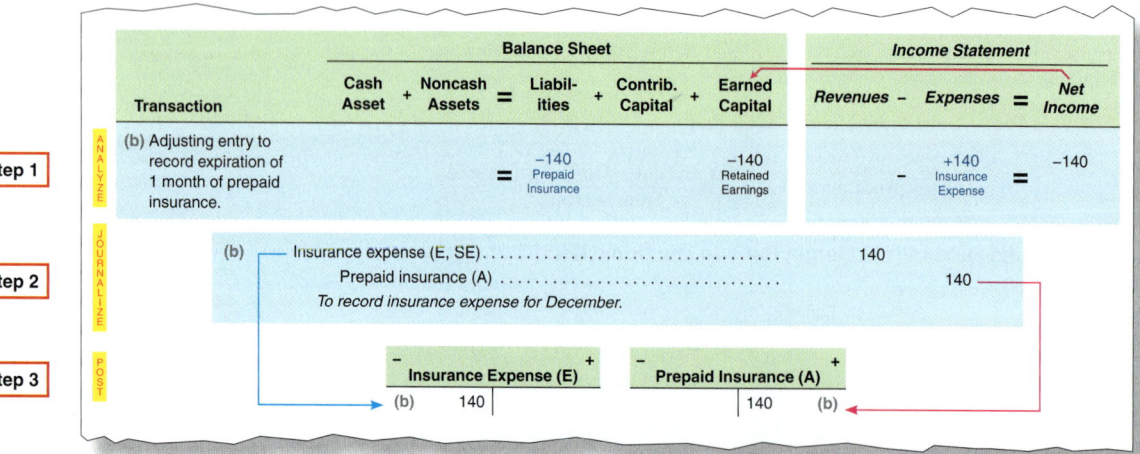

The FSET captures each transaction's effects on the four financial statements: the balance sheet, income statement, statement of stockholders' equity, and statement of cash flows. For the balance sheet, we differentiate between cash and noncash assets to identify the cash effects of transactions. Likewise, equity is separated into the contributed and earned capital components. (The latter includes retained earnings as its major element.) Finally, income statement effects are separated into revenues, expenses, and net income. (The updating of retained earnings is denoted with an arrow line running from net income to earned capital.) The FSET provides a convenient means to represent financial accounting transactions and events in a simple, concise manner for assessing their effects on financial statements. To provide faculty flexibility to tailor instruction, all relevant end of chapter materials can be assigned using the journal entry approach or the FSET approach.

LO4, 5 E6-40. Analysis of Accounts Receivable and Allowance for Doubtful Accounts (FSET)
Steelcase, Inc., reported the following amounts in its 2020 and 2019 10-K reports (years ended February 28, 2020, and February 22, 2019).

Steelcase, Inc.
NYSE :: SCS

($ millions)	2020	2019
From the income statement:		
Revenue	$3,723.7	$3,443.2
From the balance sheet:		
Accounts receivable, net	372.4	390.3
Customer deposits	28.6	20.0
From the disclosure on allowance for doubtful accounts:		
Balance at beginning of period	8.7	11.1
Additions (reductions) charged to income	7.3	5.5
Adjustments or deductions	(6.6)	(7.9)
Balance at end of period	9.4	8.7

a. Report (1) the write-off of accounts receivable as uncollectible in 2020 and (2) the provision for doubtful accounts (bad debt expense) for 2020 using the financial statement effects template.
b. Calculate Steelcase's gross receivables for the years given, and then determine the allowance for doubtful accounts as a percentage of the gross receivables.

Assignments are organized to give instructors the flexibility to assign homework that emphasizes FSET and/or journal entries & T-accounts.

LO4 E6-41. Recording Entries to Adjust the Allowance for Doubtful Accounts
Use the information in E6-40 to complete the following requirements.

a. Prepare the journal entry to record accounts receivable written off as uncollectible in 2020.
b. Prepare the entry to record the provision for doubtful accounts (bad debts expense) for 2020.
c. What effect did these entries have on Steelcase's income for that year?

DATA ANALYTICS & EXCEL SKILL DEVELOPMENT FOR CAREER READINESS

The basics of accounting haven't changed much in hundreds of years, but businesses have experienced significant change in the past decade due to the increased use of new technologies ranging from data analytics and Blockchain to machine learning and artificial intelligence. Technology is rapidly altering how accounting is performed and what can be done with the data once they are collected. In response to the changing demands of the business world, the AACSB has incorporated data analytics requirements within its educational framework. More recently, the AICPA and NASBA have underscored the importance of data analytics by making it a significant element in the CPA Evolution Model Curriculum. The consensus suggests that today's business students need an understanding and working knowledge of data analytics and data visualization to compete for the best jobs. In addition, employers expect prospective employees to be proficient with Excel.

Data Analytics

In recognition of the increasing importance of data analytics and the need for Excel proficiency, the Fifth Edition includes several new features to enhance students' career readiness.

- In many chapters, we use data visualizations to depict financial information. It is important for students to become comfortable interpreting visual depictions of data.

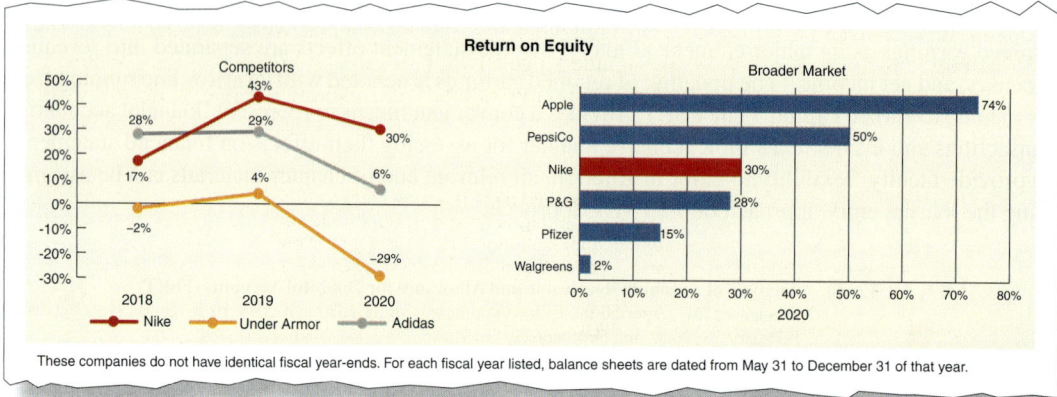

- Each chapter includes assignments that require students to use **Excel** and **Tableau** to hone data analysis and data visualization skills.

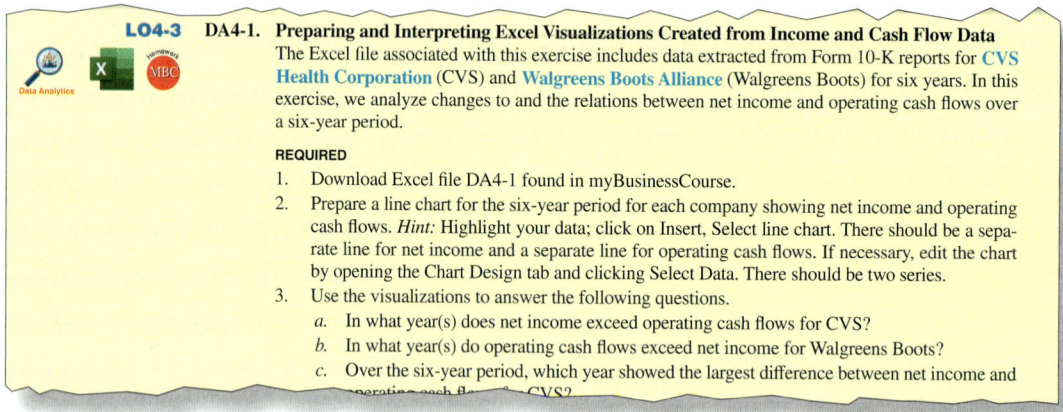

- **Appendix B**, at the end of the book, provides an overview of data analytics, data visualization, and best practices for the effective display of data.

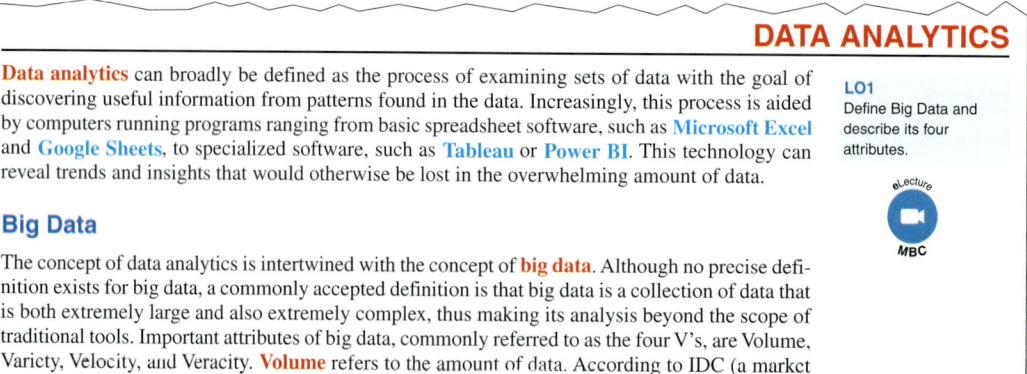

- MBC now contains a series of short videos that demonstrate the basic functions of Excel. These videos can be accessed within MBC as part of your MBC course. In addition, a number of the data analytic problems are accompanied by videos, demonstrating how to complete the assignment or a similar assignment.

Preface xi

INNOVATIVE PEDAGOGY

Business Insights, Critical Thinking, and Decision Making

Students appreciate and become more engaged when they can see the real-world relevance of what they are learning in the classroom. We have included a generous number of current, real-world examples in Business Insight boxes and through critical thinking and decision-making questions. The following is a representative example:

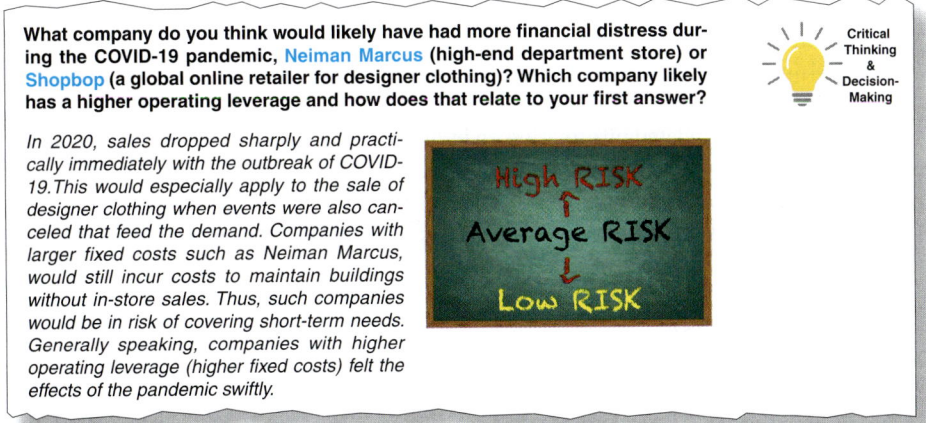

Learning Objective Reviews

Accounting can be challenging—especially for students lacking business experience or previous exposure to business courses. To reinforce concepts presented in each chapter and to ensure student comprehension, we include a review problem at the conclusion of each learning objective. Answers to the review problems are included at the end of the chapter. Each review has a corresponding Guided Example video, available to students in myBusinessCourse (MBC), our online learning and homework system. In addition, each Review is assignable in MBC.

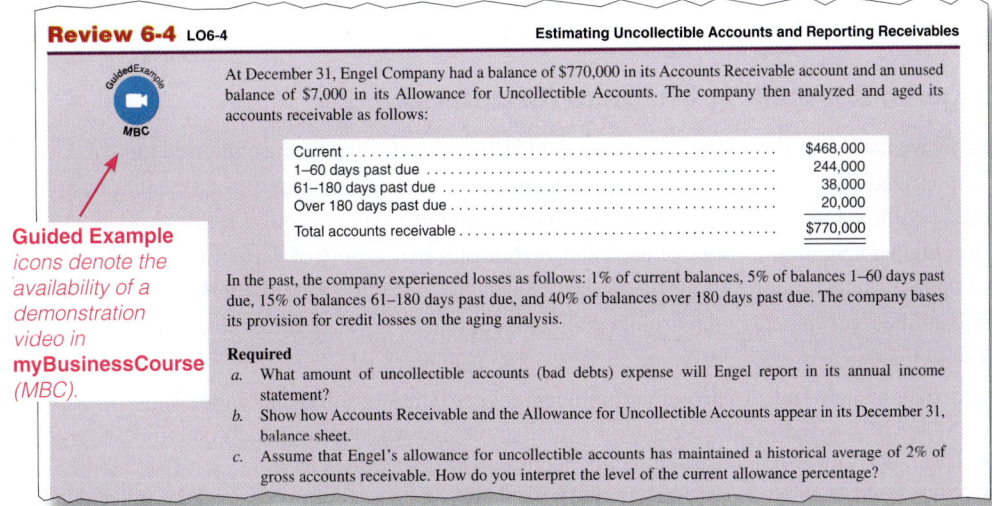

Guided Example icons denote the availability of a demonstration video in myBusinessCourse (MBC).

NEW IN THIS EDITION

Global Changes

New to this edition, we have
- Expanded the coverage, resources, and assignments related to data analytics and Excel skill development in an effort to enhance student career readiness.
- Added a Road Map to each chapter that summarizes the reviews and assignments for each learning objective in the chapter.

- Added review problems to the end of each learning objective, replacing the mid-chapter and end of chapter reviews.
- Updated numbers for examples, illustrations, and assignments that use real data.
- Revised nearly all of the assignments in each chapter with updated data, and in some cases, replaced the chapter's focus company.

Financial Accounting Chapters (1–12)

- **Chapter Updates:** As appropriate, the text and assignments have been updated to reflect the latest FASB standards and other current information:
    - Chapter 4 incorporates restricted cash as part of total cash presented on the statement of cash flows.
    - Chapter 5 includes updated information on industry ratios that is referenced in real life examples not only in this chapter, but throughout the text.
    - Chapter 8 includes a discussion on digital assets with a supporting end of chapter assignment.
    - Chapter 10 discusses the election in lease accounting to not separate lease and non-lease components.
    - Chapter 11 reflects the new guidance on accounting for convertible instruments (including the impact on diluted EPS).
    - Chapter 12 briefly discusses the recording of credit losses on available-for-sale debt securities and new guidance on the amortization of goodwill for private companies.
    - Expanded the FSET presentation in Chapter 4 (transactions that impact the statement of cash flows) and in Chapter 10 (accounting for operating leases by the lessee).
- **Deere & Co.** replaced Delta Air Lines as the focus company of Chapter 10.
- In addition to the chapter-specific changes, there have been several changes that span all financial accounting chapters. Some of these changes include:
    - Expanded all end of chapter materials to allow for the assigning of either the journal entry approach or the FSET approach.
    - Updated note disclosures and other nonfinancial disclosures
    - Updated excerpts from the business and popular press
    - Nearly all of the assignments in each chapter have been revised with updated data or replaced with a new company.

Managerial Accounting Chapters (Chapters 13–24)

In general, we made significant improvements to the flow of each chapter and enhanced topical coverage.

- Emphasized critical thinking required in managerial decision-making through new questions inserted within, and directly related to, the chapter content.
-  Highlighted ESG implications of each chapter's topics in a variety of ways, including new text discussions, critical thinking questions, and end of chapter assignments—all marked with an ESG icon.
- Streamlined, revamped, and rearranged chapter content to improve the chapter flow.
- Revised, enhanced, and added new chapter exhibits and graphics.
- Added many new end-of-chapter assignments (over 80 new assignments in total).
    - Added new assignments to ensure adequate coverage per learning objective.
    - Expanded ethics-related assignments, identified with an ethics icon.
    - Added CMA adapted questions, identified with a CMA icon. Permission has been received from the Institute of Certified Management Accountants to use questions and/or unofficial answers from past CMA examinations.
- Changed many focus companies to increase student interest. We reference the focus company for the vast majority of examples within a chapter for a more consistent presentation. In a similar way, we utilize a *competitor* to the focus company throughout many of the chapter reviews.
- New Chapter Focus Companies

Chapter 13	Warby Parker	**Chapter 20**	Potbelly
Chapter 16	Boston Beer	**Chapter 21**	Wayfair
Chapter 18	Ben & Jerry's	**Chapter 22**	Samsonite International S.A.

Preface xiii

TECHNOLOGY THAT IMPROVES LEARNING AND COMPLEMENTS FACULTY INSTRUCTION

myBusinessCourse is an online learning and assessment program intended to complement your textbook and faculty instruction. Access to **myBusinessCourse** is FREE ONLY with the purchase of a new textbook, but access can be purchased separately.

MBC is ideal for faculty seeking opportunities to augment their course with an online component. MBC is also a turnkey solution for online courses. The following are some of the features of MBC.

95.5% of students who used MBC responded that MBC helped them learn accounting.*

Increase Student Readiness

- **eLectures** cover each chapter's learning objectives and concepts. Consistent with the text and created by the authors, these videos are ideal for remediation and online instruction.
- **Guided Examples** are narrated video demonstrations created by the authors that show students how to solve select problems from the textbook.
- Immediate feedback with **auto-graded homework**.
- **Test Bank** questions that can be incorporated into your assignments.
- Instructor **gradebook** with immediate grade results.

Make Instruction Needs-Based

- Identify where your students are struggling and customize your instruction to address their needs.
- Gauge how your entire class or individual students are performing by viewing the easy-to-use gradebook.
- Ensure your students are getting the additional reinforcement and direction they need between class meetings.

88.3% of students said they would encourage their professor to continue using MBC in future terms.*

Provide Instruction and Practice 24/7

- Assign homework from your Cambridge Business Publishers' textbook and have MBC grade it for you automatically.
- With our videos, your students can revisit accounting topics as often as they like or until they master the topic.
- Make homework due before class to ensure students enter your classroom prepared.
- For an additional fee, upgrade MBC to include the eBook, and you have all the tools needed for an online course.

Integrate with LMS

myBusinessCourse integrates with many learning management systems, including **Canvas**, **Blackboard**, **Moodle**, **D2L**, **Schoology**, and **Sakai**. Your gradebooks sync automatically.

ADDITIONAL RESOURCES

Financial Accounting Bootcamp

This interactive tutorial is intended for use in programs that either require or would like to offer a tutorial that can be used as a refresher of topics introduced in the first financial accounting course. It is designed as an asynchronous, interactive, self-paced experience for students. Available Learning Modules (You Select) follow.

---

* These statistics are based on the results of five surveys in which 4,195 students participated.

1. Introducing Financial Accounting (approximate completion time 2 hours)
2. Constructing Financial Statements (approximate completion time 4 hours)
3. Adjusting Entries and Completing the Accounting Cycle (approximate completion time 4 hours)
4. Reporting and Analyzing Cash Flows (approximate completion time 3.5 hours)
5. Analyzing and Interpreting Financial Statements (approximate completion time 3.5 hours)
6. Excel and Time-Value of Money Basics (approximate completion time 2 hours)

This is a separate, saleable item. Contact your sales representative to receive more information or email customerservice@cambridgepub.com.

For Instructors

myBusinessCourse: An online learning and assessment program intended to complement your textbook and classroom instruction. (See page xiii for more details.) Access to myBusinessCourse is FREE with the purchase of a new textbook but can also be purchased separately.

Solutions Manual: Created by the authors, the *Solutions Manual* contains complete solutions to all the assignment material in the text.

PowerPoint: The PowerPoint slides outline key elements of each chapter.

Test Bank: The Test Bank includes multiple-choice items, short essay questions, and problems.

Website: All instructor materials are accessible via the book's website (password protected) along with other useful links and marketing information. www.cambridgepub.com

For Students

myBusinessCourse: An online learning and assessment program intended to complement your textbook and faculty instruction. (See page xiii for more details.) This easy-to-use program grades assignments automatically and provides you with additional help when your instructor is not available. Access is free with new copies of this textbook. (Look for the page containing the access code towards the front of the book.)

ACKNOWLEDGMENTS

This book has benefited greatly from the valuable feedback of focus group attendees, reviewers, students, and colleagues. We are extremely grateful to them for their help in making this project a success.

Ajay Adhikari	Bruce Busta	Reed Easton	Ling Harris
Hank Adler	Richard J. Campbell	Ellen Engel	David Harvey
Pervaiz Alam	Judson Caskey	Bud Fennema	Rayford Harwell
Kris Allee	Sumantra Chakravarty	Tom Fields	Susan Hass
Bob Allen	Paul Chaney	Mark Finn	Joseph Hatch
Beverley Alleyne	Craig Chapman	Linda Flaming	Haihong He
Samuel Anderson	Sean Chen	David Folsom	Kenneth Henry
Dennis Applegate	Hans Christensen	Elizabeth Foster	Eric Hirst
Elizabeth Arnold	Paul Clikeman	Micah Frankel	Jeffrey Hoopes
Lawrence Aronhime	Daniel Cohen	Henry Friedman	Robert Hoskin
Frances Ayres	John Core	Christina Gehrke	Ying Huang
Paul Bahnson	Erin Cornelsen	George Geis	Marsha Huber
Jan Barton	Steve Crawford	Elisabeth Gilgen	Glenn Huels
Progyan Basu	Somnath Das	Jacqueline Gillette	Richard E. Hurley
Randy Beatty	Angela Davis	Hubert Glover	Robert L. Hurt
James Benjamin	Mark Dawkins	Nancy Goble	Marianne L. James
Anne Beyer	David DeBoskey	Rajul Gokarn	Ross Jennings
Robert Bowen	Mark DeFond	Jeff Gramlich	Jane Jollineau
Kimberly Brickler-Ulrich	Bruce Dehning	Wayne Guay	Chris Jones
Rada Brooks	Bala G. Dharan	Umit Gurun	Januj Juneja
Helen Brubeck	Timothy Dimond	Susan Hamlen	Jane Kennedy
Jacqueline Burke	Joe Dulin	Rebecca Hann	Irene Kim

Jinhwan Kim, Michael Kimbrough, Ken Klein, Allison Koester, Kevin Koharki, Kalin Kolev, Gopal Krishnan, Yingxu Kuang, Susan Kulp, Benjamin Lansford, Stephanie Larocque, Cheol Lee, Zawadi Lemayian, Andrew Leone, Annette Leps, Alina Lerman, Xu Li, Thomas Lin, Brad Lindsey, Thomas J. Linsmeier, Jiangxia Liu, Frank Longo, Barbara Lougee, Luann Lynch, Jason MacGregor, Bill Magrogan, Lois Mahoney, Daphne Main, Cathy Margolin, Maureen Mascha, Dawn Matsumoto, Katie Maxwell, John McCauley, Bruce McClain, Harvey McCown, Katie McDermott, Marc McIntosh, Jeff McMillan, Greg Miller, Jeffrey Miller, Marilyn Misch, Stephen Moehrle, Matt Munson, Mark Myring, Sandeep Nabar, James Naughton, Karen Nelson, Christopher Noe, Walter O'Connor, Jose Oaks, Shailendra Pandit, Simon Pearlman, Marietta Peytcheva, Brandis Phillips, Kristen Portz, Richard Price, S.E.C. Purvis, Kathleen Rankin, Lynn Rees, Susan Riffe, Leslie Robinson, Paulette Rodriguez, Darren Roulstone, Debra Salbador, Anwar Y. Salimi, Haresh Sapra, Robert Scharlach, Steve Sefcik, Timothy Shields, Scott Showalter, Nemit Shroff, Andreas Simon, Robert Singer, Praveen Sinha, David Smith, Eric So, Kathleen Sobieralski, Robin Soffer, Gregory Sommers, Sri Sridharan, Vic Stanton, Jack Stecher, Doug Stevens, Tom Stober, Toby Stock, Phillip Stocken, William Stout, Rob Stussie, Shyam Sunder, Andrew Sutherland, Robert J. Swieringa, Thomas Tallerico, Mary Tarling, Robin Tarpley, Nicole Thibodeau, Patti Tilley, Rodrigo Verdi, Robert Walsh, Isabel Wang, Xue Wang, Rick Warne, Catherine Weber, Joe Weber, Lourdes White, Donna Whitten, Christopher Williams, Gayle Williams, Rahnl Wood, Jia Wu, Jason Xiao, Jennifer Yin, Teri Yohn, Rachel Yoon, Susan Young, Stephen Zeff, Yuping Zhao, Jian Zhou

The author team of this fifth edition would like to acknowledge the contributions of our colleague and friend, Tom Dyckman. Tom is well known in the accounting academy for his scholarship, his teaching, his mentoring, and his service to the field. With this fifth edition, he has chosen to pass the baton to us and enjoy a well-deserved retirement. We wish him and Ann many years in the warmer climes of Florida.

In addition, we are extremely grateful to George Werthman, Lorraine Gleeson, Jocelyn Mousel, Karen Amundson, Rhonda Seelinger, Debbie McQuade, Terry McQuade, and the entire team at Cambridge Business Publishers for their encouragement, enthusiasm, and guidance.

Michelle Hanlon   Robert Magee   Glenn Pfeiffer   Susan Kulp   Amie Dragoo

May 2023

Brief Contents

Chapter	1	Introducing Financial Accounting 1-1	Chapter	15	Cost-Volume-Profit Analysis and Planning 15-1
Chapter	2	Constructing Financial Statements 2-1	Chapter	16	Using Relevant Costs and Differential Analysis for Decision-Making 16-1
Chapter	3	Adjusting Accounts for Financial Statements 3-1	Chapter	17	Product Costing: Job and Process Operations 17-1
Chapter	4	Reporting and Analyzing Cash Flows 4-1	Chapter	18	Activity-Based Costing, Customer Profitability, and Activity-Based Management 18-1
Chapter	5	Analyzing and Interpreting Financial Statements 5-1			
Chapter	6	Reporting and Analyzing Revenues, Receivables, and Operating Income 6-1	Chapter	19	Additional Topics in Product Costing 19-1
			Chapter	20	Decision-Making: Pricing and Product Cost Management 20-1
Chapter	7	Reporting and Analyzing Inventory 7-1			
Chapter	8	Reporting and Analyzing Long-Term Operating Assets 8-1	Chapter	21	Operational Budgeting and Profit Planning 21-1
Chapter	9	Reporting and Analyzing Liabilities 9-1	Chapter	22	Standard Costs and Performance Reports 22-1
Chapter	10	Reporting and Analyzing Leases, Pensions, Income Taxes, and Commitments and Contingencies 10-1	Chapter	23	Performance Measurement Using Segment Reporting, Transfer Pricing, and Balanced Scorecard 23-1
Chapter	11	Reporting and Analyzing Stockholders' Equity 11-1	Chapter	24	Capital Budgeting Decisions 24-1
Chapter	12	Reporting and Analyzing Financial Investments 12-1	Appendix	A	Compound Interest and the Time-Value of Money A-1
Chapter	13	Managerial Accounting: Tools for Decision-Making 13-1	Appendix	B	Data Analytics and Blockchain Technology B-1
Chapter	14	Cost Definitions, Behavior, and Estimation 14-1			Index I-1

Contents

About the Authors iii
Preface v
Brief Contents xvi

Chapter 1
Introducing Financial Accounting 1-1

Demand for Accounting Information 1-3
   Who Uses Financial Accounting Information? 1-4
   Costs and Benefits of Disclosure 1-6
   Review 1-1 Identifying How Financial Statements Are Utilized by Different User Groups 1-6
Business Activities 1-7
   Planning Activities 1-7
   Investing Activities 1-8
   Financing Activities 1-9
   Operating Activities 1-10
   Review 1-2 Applying the Accounting Equation and Computing Financing Proportions 1-10
Financial Statements 1-11
   Balance Sheet 1-11
   Income Statement 1-12
   Statement of Stockholders' Equity 1-13
   Statement of Cash Flows 1-13
   Financial Statement Linkages 1-14
   Information Beyond Financial Statements 1-15
   Review 1-3 Preparing Financial Statements 1-16
Financial Reporting Environment 1-16
   Generally Accepted Accounting Principles 1-17
   Regulation and Oversight 1-17
   Role of the Auditor 1-19
   A Global Perspective 1-19
   Review 1-4 Identifying Roles in the Development and Regulation of Financial Reporting 1-20
Analyzing Financial Statements 1-21
   Profitability Analysis 1-21
   Analysis Objective 1-21
   Credit Risk Analysis 1-23
   Analysis Objective 1-23
   Technology and Accounting 1-24
Organization of the Book 1-24
   Review 1-5 Computing Return on Equity and Debt-to-Equity Ratios 1-25
Appendix 1A: Conceptual Framework for Financial Reporting 1-25
   Objective of Financial Reporting 1-25
   Qualitative Characteristics of Useful Financial Information 1-26
   Enhancing Qualitative Characteristics 1-27
   The Cost Constraint 1-27
   Additional Underlying Basic Assumptions 1-27
   Review 1-6 Identifying Conceptual Framework Topics 1-28
Summary 1-28
Guidance Answers . . . You Make the Call 1-29
Key Ratios 1-30
Multiple Choice 1-30
Data Analytics 1-32
Data Visualization 1-33

Assignments 1-33
Solutions to Review Problems 1-39

Chapter 2
Constructing Financial Statements 2-1

Reporting Financial Condition 2-3
   Assets 2-3
   Liabilities and Equity 2-6
   Review 2-1 Classifying Balance Sheet Accounts 2-8
   Analyzing and Recording Transactions for the Balance Sheet 2-8
   Review 2-2 Using the Financial Statement Effects Template to Analyze Transactions 2-12
Reporting Financial Performance 2-12
   Review 2-3 Preparing an Income Statement 2-13
   Accrual Accounting for Revenues and Expenses 2-14
   Retained Earnings 2-15
   Analyzing and Recording Transactions for the Income Statement 2-16
   Review 2-4 Preparing a Retained Earnings Statement 2-19
Reporting on Equity 2-19
   Analyzing and Recording Equity Transactions 2-19
   Statement of Stockholders' Equity 2-20
   Review 2-5 Preparing a Balance Sheet and a Statement of Stockholders' Equity 2-21
Journalizing and Posting Transactions 2-21
   T-Account 2-21
   Debit and Credit System 2-22
   T-Account with Debits and Credits 2-23
   The Journal Entry 2-23
   Analyze, Journalize, and Post 2-24
   Review 2-6 Reporting Using the FSET and Preparing Journal Entries and the General Ledger 2-29
Analyzing Financial Statements 2-30
   Analysis Objective 2-30
   Review 2-7 Computing Working Capital, Current Ratio, and Quick Ratio 2-32
Summary 2-33
Guidance Answers . . . You Make the Call 2-33
Key Ratios 2-34
Multiple Choice 2-34
Data Analytics 2-35
Data Visualization 2-36
Assignments 2-36
Solutions to Review Problems 2-53

Chapter 3
Adjusting Accounts for Financial Statements 3-1

Accounting Cycle 3-3
Analyzing, Recording, and Posting 3-4
   Review of Accounting Procedures 3-4
   Review of Recording Transactions 3-4
   Review 3-1 Analyzing, Journalizing, and Posting Transactions 3-11
Adjusting the Accounts 3-11

© Cambridge Business Publishers

xvii

xviii Contents

    Preparing an Unadjusted Trial Balance **3-11**
    Types of Adjustments **3-12**
    Ethics and Adjusting Entries **3-18**
  Review 3-2 Record Adjusting Entries and Prepare an Adjusted Trial Balance **3-19**
Constructing Financial Statements from Adjusted Accounts **3-19**
    Preparing an Adjusted Trial Balance **3-19**
    Preparing Financial Statements **3-21**
  Review 3-3 Preparing Financial Statements **3-23**
Closing Temporary Accounts **3-24**
    Closing Process **3-24**
    Closing Steps Illustrated **3-25**
    Preparing a Post-Closing Trial Balance **3-26**
    Subsequent Events **3-26**
Summarizing the Accounting Cycle **3-26**
  Review 3-4 Preparing Closing Entries **3-27**
Financial Statement Analysis **3-27**
    Using Information on Levels and Flows **3-27**
  Review 3-5 Analyzing Changes in Balance Sheet Accounts **3-28**
Summary **3-29**
Guidance Answers . . . You Make the Call **3-29**
Multiple Choice **3-29**
Data Analytics **3-31**
Data Visualization **3-32**
Assignments **3-32**
Solutions to Review Problems **3-50**

Chapter 4
Reporting and Analyzing Cash Flows **4-1**

Purpose of the Statement of Cash Flows **4-3**
    What Do We Mean by "CASH"? **4-3**
    What Does a Statement of Cash Flows Look Like? **4-4**
Framework for the Statement of Cash Flows **4-4**
    Operating Activities **4-5**
    Investing Activities **4-5**
    Financing Activities **4-5**
    Usefulness of Classifications **4-6**
  Review 4-1 Classifying Cash Flows **4-7**
Preparing the Statement of Cash Flows—Operating Activities **4-7**
    Converting Revenues and Expenses to Cash Flows from Operating Activities **4-10**
  Review 4-2 Preparing Operating Activities Section of the Statement of Cash Flows—Direct Method **4-16**
    Reconciling Net Income and Cash Flow from Operating Activities **4-17**
    Cash Flow from Operating Activities Using the Indirect Method **4-18**
  Review 4-3 Reconciling Cash Flows from Operations to Net Income **4-19**
Preparing the Statement of Cash Flows—Investing and Financing Activities **4-19**
    Cash Flows from Investing Activities **4-20**
    Cash Flows from Financing Activities **4-20**
  Review 4-4 Preparing a Complete Statement of Cash Flows **4-22**
Additional Detail in the Statement of Cash Flows **4-23**
    Gains and Losses on Investing and Financing Activities **4-24**
    Noncash Investing and Financing Activities **4-25**
    The Effects of Foreign Currencies on the Statement of Cash Flows **4-27**
    Supplemental Disclosures **4-28**
  Review 4-5 Reconstructing Investing Cash Flows **4-28**
Analyzing Financial Statements **4-29**
    Interpreting Indirect Method Cash from Operations **4-29**
    Analysis Objective **4-29**
    Analysis Objective **4-31**
  Review 4-6 Calculating Ratios to Assess Liquidity and Solvency **4-32**
Appendix 4A: A Spreadsheet Approach to Preparing the Statement of Cash Flows **4-33**
  Review 4-7 Using a Spreadsheet to Create a Statement of Cash Flows **4-35**
Summary **4-35**
Guidance Answers . . . You Make the Call **4-36**
Key Ratios **4-37**
Multiple Choice **4-37**
Data Analytics **4-39**
Data Visualization **4-40**
Assignments **4-40**
Solutions to Review Problems **4-60**

Chapter 5
Analyzing and Interpreting Financial Statements **5-1**

Introduction **5-3**
    Assessing the Business Environment **5-3**
Vertical and Horizontal Analysis **5-4**
  Review 5-1 Preparing Common-Size Income Statements and Balance Sheets **5-6**
Return on Investment **5-8**
    Return on Equity (ROE) **5-8**
    Return on Assets (ROA) **5-8**
    Return on Financial Leverage (ROFL) **5-9**
  Review 5-2 Calculating ROE, ROA, and ROFL **5-10**
    Disaggregating ROA **5-11**
  Review 5-3 Disaggregating the Return on Equity Ratio into Its Components **5-15**
Liquidity and Solvency **5-15**
    Liquidity Analysis **5-17**
    Solvency Analysis **5-19**
    Limitations of Ratio Analysis **5-21**
  Review 5-4 Computing and Interpreting Liquidity and Solvency Ratios **5-23**
Appendix 5A: Analyzing and Interpreting Core Operating Activities **5-23**
  Review 5-5 Measuring the Effects of Operating Activities on ROE **5-25**
Appendix 5B: Financial Statement Forecasts **5-25**
  Review 5-6 Preparing a Forecast Income Statement and Balance Sheet **5-30**
Summary **5-30**
Key Ratios **5-31**
Multiple Choice **5-31**
Guidance Answers . . . You Make the Call **5-32**
Data Analytics **5-33**
Data Visualization **5-35**
Assignments **5-35**
Solutions to Review Problems **5-49**

Chapter 6
Reporting and Analyzing Revenues, Receivables, and Operating Income **6-1**

Reporting Operating Income **6-3**
    Revenue Recognition **6-5**

Review 6-1 Identifying the Steps in the Revenue Recognition Process 6-8
Revenue Recognition Subsequent to Customer Purchase 6-8
Review 6-2 Analyzing Deferred Revenue Charges 6-11
Review 6-3 Recording Revenue Transactions 6-14
Reporting Accounts Receivable 6-14
Determining the Allowance for Uncollectible Accounts 6-15
Reporting the Allowance for Uncollectible Accounts 6-16
Recording Write-Offs of Uncollectible Accounts 6-17
Disclosure Notes and Interpretations 6-19
Review 6-4 Estimating Uncollectible Accounts and Reporting Receivables 6-21
Analyzing Financial Statements 6-22
Net Operating Profit After Taxes (NOPAT) 6-22
Analysis Objective 6-22
Analysis Objective 6-25
Review 6-5 Computing NOPAT, RNOA, NOPM, ART, and ACP 6-26
Earnings Management 6-27
Review 6-6 Identifying the Financial Statement Effect of Managing Earnings 6-28
Appendix 6A: Reporting Nonrecurring Items 6-29
Discontinued Operations 6-29
Exit or Disposal Costs 6-30
Review 6-7 Reporting Nonrecurring Items 6-31
Summary 6-31
Guidance Answers . . . You Make the Call 6-32
Key Ratios 6-33
Multiple Choice 6-33
Data Analytics 6-34
Data Visualization 6-36
Assignments 6-36
Solutions to Review Problems 6-53

Chapter 7
Reporting and Analyzing Inventory 7-1

Reporting Operating Expenses 7-3
Expense Recognition Principles 7-3
Reporting Inventory Costs in the Financial Statements 7-4
Recording Inventory Costs in the Financial Statements 7-5
Inventory and the Cost of Acquisition 7-6
Inventory Reporting by Manufacturing Firms 7-6
Review 7-1 Identifying Inventory Costs 7-7
Inventory Costing Methods 7-7
First-In, First-Out (FIFO) 7-8
Last-In, First-Out (LIFO) 7-9
Inventory Costing and Price Changes 7-11
Average Cost (AC) 7-11
Review 7-2 Accounting for Inventory Using Different Cost Methods 7-12
Lower of Cost or Net Realizable Value 7-13
Review 7-3 Applying the Lower of Cost or Net Realizable Value Rule 7-14
Financial Statement Effects and Disclosure 7-14
Financial Statement Effects of Inventory Costing 7-16
Review 7-4 Interpreting the Effects of Inventory Valuation on Financial Results 7-19
Analyzing Financial Statements 7-20
Analysis Objective 7-20
Analysis Objective 7-21
Review 7-5 Calculating Inventory Ratios 7-25
Appendix 7A: LIFO Liquidation 7-25

Analysis Implications 7-26
Review 7-6 Determining the Financial Statement Impact of LIFO Liquidations 7-27
Summary 7-27
Guidance Answers . . . You Make the Call 7-28
Key Ratios 7-28
Multiple Choice 7-29
Data Analytics 7-30
Data Visualization 7-31
Assignments 7-31
Solutions to Review Problems 7-42

Chapter 8
Reporting and Analyzing Long-Term Operating Assets 8-1

Introduction 8-3
Property, Plant, and Equipment (PPE) 8-3
Determining Costs to Capitalize 8-4
Review 8-1 Determining the Proper Accounting Treatment of Tangible Costs 8-5
Depreciation 8-5
Depreciation Methods 8-6
Changes in Accounting Estimates 8-9
Review 8-2 Accounting for Equipment 8-10
Asset Sales and Impairments 8-10
Note Disclosure 8-12
Review 8-3 Analyzing the Financial Statement Impacts of Disposals and Impairments 8-13
Analyzing Financial Statements 8-13
Analysis Objective 8-13
Analysis Objective 8-14
Cash Flow Effects 8-16
Review 8-4 Analyzing the Effects of Tangible Assets on Financial Statements 8-17
Intangible Assets 8-17
Research and Development Costs 8-17
Patents 8-18
Copyrights 8-19
Trademarks 8-19
Franchise Rights 8-19
Amortization and Impairment of Identifiable Intangible Assets 8-19
Digital Assets 8-21
Goodwill 8-21
Note Disclosures 8-22
Review 8-5 Accounting for Intangible Assets 8-23
Analysis Implications 8-23
Review 8-6 Analyzing the Effects of Intangible Assets and R&D Expense on the Financial Statements 8-24
Summary 8-25
Guidance Answers . . . You Make the Call 8-25
Key Ratios 8-25
Multiple Choice 8-26
Data Analytics 8-27
Data Visualization 8-28
Assignments 8-28
Solutions to Review Problems 8-40

Chapter 9
Reporting and Analyzing Liabilities 9-1

Introduction 9-3
Current Liabilities 9-4
    Accounts Payable 9-4
    Accrued Liabilities 9-6
    Other Current Liabilities 9-10
  Review 9-1 Accounting for Current Operating Liabilities 9-10
    Current Nonoperating (Financial) Liabilities 9-10
  Review 9-2 Accounting for Current Nonoperating Liabilities 9-13
Long-Term Liabilities 9-13
    Installment Loans 9-13
    Bonds 9-15
    Pricing of Bonds 9-15
    Effective Cost of Debt 9-17
  Review 9-3 Computing Bond Issue Price 9-18
    Reporting of Bond Financing 9-18
    Effects of Discount and Premium Amortization 9-20
    The Fair Value Option 9-22
    Effects of Bond Repurchase 9-24
    Financial Statement Disclosure Notes 9-24
    Interest and the Statement of Cash Flows 9-26
    Disclosure of Commitments and Contingencies 9-26
  Review 9-4 Accounting for Long-Term Nonoperating Liabilities 9-27
Analyzing Financial Statements 9-27
    Analysis Objective 9-27
    Debt Ratings and the Cost of Debt 9-29
  Review 9-5 Computing Solvency Ratios 9-31
Summary 9-32
Guidance Answers . . . You Make the Call 9-33
Key Ratios 9-33
Multiple Choice 9-33
Data Analytics 9-34
Data Visualization 9-36
Assignments 9-36
Solutions to Review Problems 9-48

Chapter 10
Reporting and Analyzing Leases, Pensions, Income Taxes, and Commitments and Contingencies 10-1

Introduction 10-3
Leases 10-3
    Lessee Reporting of Leases 10-5
    Lease Disclosures 10-12
  Review 10-1 Accounting for Leases 10-14
Pensions 10-15
    Balance Sheet Effects of Defined Benefit Pension Plans 10-15
    Income Statement Effects of Defined Benefit Pension Plans 10-18
    Note Disclosures—Components of Plan Assets and PBO 10-18
    Note Disclosures—Components of Pension Expense 10-20
    Note Disclosures and Future Cash Flows 10-21
    Other Post-Employment Benefits 10-23
  Review 10-2 Analyzing Pension Disclosures 10-24
Accounting For Income Taxes 10-25
    Book-Tax Differences 10-25
    Revaluation of Deferred Tax Assets and Liabilities Due to a Tax Rate Change 10-31
    Income Tax Disclosures 10-32
    Deferred Taxes in the Statement of Cash Flows 10-35
    Computation and Analysis of Taxes 10-35
  Review 10-3 Accounting for Income Taxes 10-36
Commitments and Contingencies and Other Disclosures 10-36
Analyzing Financial Statements 10-38
    Analysis Objective 10-38
  Review 10-4 Analyzing Commitments and Contingencies 10-39
Summary 10-39
Guidance Answers . . . You Make The Call 10-40
Key Ratios 10-41
Multiple Choice 10-41
Data Analytics 10-42
Data Visualization 10-44
Assignments 10-44
Solutions to Review Problems 10-64

Chapter 11
Reporting and Analyzing Stockholders' Equity 11-1

Introduction 11-3
Contributed Capital 11-4
    Classes of Stock 11-4
    Accounting for Stock Transactions 11-7
  Review 11-1 Accounting for Stock Issuances 11-11
Earned Capital 11-11
    Cash Dividends 11-11
    Stock Dividends and Splits 11-13
    Stock Transactions and the Statement of Cash Flows 11-15
  Review 11-2 Accounting for Cash Dividends, Stock Dividends, and Stock Splits 11-15
    Comprehensive Income 11-16
    Summary of Stockholders' Equity 11-17
Analyzing Financial Statements 11-17
    Analysis Objective 11-17
  Review 11-3 Presenting Other Comprehensive Income 11-19
Earnings Per Share 11-19
    Computation and Analysis of EPS 11-20
  Review 11-4 Computing Basic and Diluted Earnings per Share 11-22
Appendix 11A: Dilutive Securities: Accounting for Convertible Securities, Stock Options, and Restricted Stock 11-22
    Convertible Securities 11-22
    Stock Rights 11-23
    Employee Stock Options 11-24
    Restricted Stock 11-25
  Review 11-5 Accounting for Convertible Debt 11-27
Summary 11-28
Guidance Answers . . . You Make the Call 11-29
Key Ratios 11-29
Multiple Choice 11-29
Data Analytics 11-31
Data Visualization 11-32
Assignments 11-32
Solutions to Review Problems 11-51

Chapter 12
Reporting and Analyzing Financial Investments 12-1

Introduction 12-3
    Review 12-1 Classifying Investments as Passive, Significant, or Controlling 12-5
Fair Value: An Introduction 12-5
    Review 12-2 Classifying Investments Using the Fair Value Hierarchy 12-6
Passive Investments in Debt Securities 12-6
    Acquisition of the Investment 12-6
    Investments Reported at Cost 12-7
    Investments Marked to Fair Value 12-8
    Sale of the Investment 12-8
    Debt Investments Marked to Fair Value 12-9
Passive Investments in Equity Securities 12-12
    Financial Statement Disclosures 12-14
    Potential for Earnings Management 12-16
    Review 12-3 Accounting for Passive Investments 12-17
Investments with Significant Influence 12-17
    Accounting for Investments with Significant Influence 12-18
    Equity Method Accounting and Effects on Ratios 12-20
    Financial Statement Disclosures 12-20
    Review 12-4 Accounting for Investments Using the Equity Method 12-21
Investments with Control 12-22
    Accounting for Investments with Control 12-22
    Reporting of Acquired Assets and Liabilities 12-24
    Noncontrolling Interest 12-28
Financial Statement Analysis 12-30
    Review 12-5 Accounting for a Consolidation 12-31
Appendix 12A: Equity Method Mechanics 12-31
    Review 12-6 Accounting for Equity Investments 12-33
Appendix 12B: Consolidation Accounting Mechanics 12-33
    Review 12-7 Recording a Consolidating Adjustment 12-34
Appendix 12C: Accounting for Investments in Derivatives 12-35
    Review 12-8 Analyzing Derivative Instruments 12-36
Summary 12-37
Guidance Answers . . . You Make the Call 12-39
Multiple Choice 12-39
Data Analytics 12-40
Data Visualization 12-40
Assignments 12-41
Solutions to Review Problems 12-57

Chapter 13
Managerial Accounting: Tools for Decision-Making 13-1

Uses of Accounting Information 13-3
    Financial Accounting 13-3
    Managerial Accounting 13-4
    Review 13-1 Comparison of Financial to Managerial Accounting 13-6
Missions, Goals, and Strategies 13-6
    An Organization's Mission, Goals, and Strategies 13-6
    Strategic Position Analysis 13-8
    Managerial Accounting and Goal Attainment 13-9
    Planning, Organizing, and Controlling 13-10
    Review 13-2 Managerial Accounting Supporting Strategic Position 13-11
Understanding the Value Chain 13-11
    Illustration of the Value Chain 13-12
    Usefulness of a Value Chain Perspective 13-14
    Review 13-3 Classifying Activities Using a Generic Internal Value Chain 13-15
Changing Environment of Business 13-16
    Global Competition and Its Key Dimensions 13-16
    Big Data and Analysis 13-16
    Robotics and Cognitive Technologies 13-17
    Enterprise Risk Management (ERM) 13-17
    Review 13-4 Big Data Analysis and Enterprise Risk Management 13-17
Ethics in Managerial Accounting 13-18
    Ethical Dilemmas 13-18
    Codes of Ethics/Conduct 13-19
Environmental, Social, and Governance Considerations 13-20
    Environmental and Social Considerations 13-20
    Governance Considerations 13-21
    Review 13-5 Corporate Social Responsibility 13-21
Multiple Choice 13-22
Data Analytics 13-22
Data Visualization 13-23
Assignments 13-23
Cases and Projects 13-27
Solutions to Review Problems 13-29

Chapter 14
Cost Definitions, Behavior, and Estimation 14-1

Cost Behavior Analysis 14-3
    Four Basic Cost Behavior Patterns 14-3
    Identifying Cost Behavior Patterns 14-5
    Factors Affecting Cost Behavior Patterns 14-6
    Review 14-1 Identifying Cost Behavior 14-6
    Estimating the Total Cost Function for an Organization or Segment 14-6
    Relevant Range and the Total Cost Function 14-7
    Distinguishing between Total Cost, Variable Cost, and Average Cost 14-9
    Cost Behavior of Committed and Discretionary Fixed Costs 14-11
    Review 14-2 Estimating Costs Using a Linear Total Cost-Estimating Equation 14-12
Analyzing Data for Cost Estimation 14-12
    High-Low Cost Estimation 14-12
    Scatter Diagrams 14-14
    Least-Squares Regression 14-15
    Review 14-3 Cost Estimation 14-18
Additional Issues in Cost Estimation 14-19
    Adapting to Changes in Technology and Prices 14-20
    Responding to Environmental Considerations 14-20
    Matching Activities and Costs 14-20
    Identifying Cost Drivers 14-21
    Review 14-4 Identifying Appropriate Cost Drivers 14-21
Cost Classification and Decision-Making 14-21
    Classifying Costs as Direct or Indirect 14-21
    Combining Cost Behaviors for Decision-Making 14-22

Contents

Review 14-5 Classifying Costs Using Two Classification Systems Simultaneously 14-23
Key Ratios and Equations 14-24
Multiple Choice 14-24
Data Analytics 14-25
Data Visualization 14-28
Assignments 14-29
Solutions to Review Problems 14-38

Chapter 15
Cost-Volume-Profit Analysis and Planning 15-1

Cost-Volume-Profit Analysis 15-3
    Profit Equation 15-3
    Using the Profit Equation in Multiple Scenarios 15-5
  Review 15-1 Determining the Profit Equation 15-6
Contribution Income Statement 15-6
    Analysis Using Contribution Margin (Total, Unit, Ratio) 15-7
  Review 15-2 Preparing a Contribution Income Statement 15-9
Break-Even Point and Profit Planning 15-9
    Determining Break-Even Point and Margin of Safety in Unit Sales 15-9
    Determining Unit Sales at a Target Profit 15-10
    Determining Break-Even in Sales Dollars 15-11
    Determining Sales Dollars at a Target Profit 15-11
    Creating and Analyzing the Cost-Volume-Profit Graph 15-12
    Creating and Analyzing the Profit-Volume Graph 15-13
    CVP Key Assumptions 15-14
  Review 15-3 Applying Cost-Volume-Profit Analysis 15-14
Multiple-Product Cost-Volume-Profit Analysis 15-15
    Determining Break-Even in Unit Sales with Multiple Products 15-15
    Determining Break-Even in Sales Dollars with Multiple Products 15-16
  Review 15-4 Analyzing Profitability of a Multi-Product Firm 15-19
Analysis of Operating Leverage 15-19
  Review 15-5 Applying Operating Leverage Ratio 15-21
Appendix 15A: Cost-Volume-Profit Analysis and Income Taxes 15-21
    Determining Sales at a Target After-Tax Profit 15-22
  Review 15-6 Determining Sales for a Desired After-Tax Profit Amount 15-23
Key Ratios and Equations 15-23
Multiple Choice 15-23
Data Analytics 15-25
Data Visualization 15-26
Assignments 15-26
Solutions to Review Problems 15-38

Chapter 16
Using Relevant Costs and Differential Analysis for Decision-Making 16-1

Identifying Relevant Revenues and Costs 16-3
    Equipment Replacement Decision 16-3
  Review 16-1 Identifying Relevant and Irrelevant Costs 16-7
Preparing and Applying Differential Analysis 16-7
    Equipment Replacement Decision 16-7
  Review 16-2 Preparing a Differential Analysis for a Machine Purchase Decision 16-9
    Evaluating Changes in Profit Plans 16-9

    Evaluating the Effect on the Profit Plan of Discontinuing a Segment 16-11
  Review 16-3 Applying Differential Analysis to Alternative Profit Scenarios 16-11
    Special Orders 16-12
  Review 16-4 Estimating the Profitability of Special Orders 16-14
    Outsourcing Decisions (Make or Buy) 16-14
  Review 16-5 Evaluating an Outsourcing Decision 16-17
    Sell or Process Further 16-17
  Review 16-6 Evaluating Whether to Sell or Process Further 16-19
Appendix 16A: Use of Limited Resources 16-19
    Single Constraint 16-19
    Multiple Constraints 16-20
    Theory of Constraints 16-20
  Review 16-7 Analyzing Profitability Considering a Scarce Resource 16-21
Multiple Choice 16-22
Data Analytics 16-23
Data Visualization 16-24
Assignments 16-25
Solutions to Review Problems 16-41

Chapter 17
Product Costing: Job and Process Operations 17-1

Reporting Inventory Costs in Various Organizations 17-3
    Inventory Categories Reported for Various Types of Organizations 17-3
    Product and Period Cost Reporting Distinction for Manufacturers 17-5
    Three Components of Product Costs 17-6
    Determining Costs of Products Outside of Financial Reporting 17-7
  Review 17-1 Classifying Inventory Costs 17-8
A Closer Look at Manufacturing Overhead 17-8
    Applying Manufacturing Overhead 17-8
  Review 17-2 Applying a Predetermined Overhead Rate 17-11
Job Order Costing for Products and Services 17-11
    Production Planning and Control Process 17-12
    Basic Flow of Costs in Job Order Costing 17-12
    Illustration of Job Order Cost Flows for Samsung 17-14
    Statement of Cost of Goods Manufactured and Cost of Goods Sold 17-18
    Overapplied and Underapplied Overhead 17-19
    Job Costing in Service Organizations 17-21
  Review 17-3 Accounting for Costs of Jobs in a Job Order Costing System 17-22
Process Costing 17-22
    Cost of Production Report Using the Weighted-Average Method 17-23
    First-In, First-Out Process Costing 17-27
    Process Costing in Service Organizations 17-27
  Review 17-4 Accounting for Costs in a Process Costing System 17-28
Appendix 17A: Absorption and Variable Costing 17-28
    Basic Concepts 17-28
    Income Under Absorption and Variable Costing 17-29
    Production Equals Sales: June 17-30
    Production Exceeds Sales: July 17-31
    Sales Exceed Production: August 17-31
    Evaluating Alternatives to Inventory Valuation 17-32

Contents   xxiii

Review 17-5 Computing Inventory Costs Under Absorption and Variable Costing   17-33
Key Ratios and Equations   17-34
Multiple Choice   17-34
Data Analytics   17-35
Data Visualization   17-36
Assignments   17-37
Solutions to Review Problems   17-53

Chapter 18
Activity-Based Costing, Customer Profitability, and Activity-Based Management   18-1

Allocation of Overhead Using Traditional Costing Methods   18-3
   Applying Overhead with a Plantwide Rate   18-3
   Applying Overhead with Departmental Rates   18-5
   Review 18-1 Determining Product Costs Using Traditional Costing   18-7
Concepts Underlying Activity-Based Costing   18-8
   Hierarchy of Activity Costs   18-8
   Summarizing Activity-Based Costing Concepts   18-10
   Review 18-2 Identifying Relevant Cost Drivers   18-10
Applying Activity-Based Costing   18-11
   Illustrating the ABC Product Cost Model   18-11
   Review 18-3 Determining Product Costs Using Activity-Based Costing   18-14
Considerations before Implementing Activity-Based Costing   18-15
   Choosing between Traditional and Activity-Based Costing   18-15
   Limitations of Activity-Based Costing System   18-16
   Challenges of Implementing Activity-Based Costing System   18-16
   Applications of Activity-Based Costing Systems   18-17
   Activity-Based Management   18-18
   Review 18-4 Comparing Product Costs Using Traditional and Activity-Based Costing   18-19
ABC and Customer Profitability Analysis   18-19
   Customer Profitability Profile   18-19
   ABC Customer Profitability Analysis Illustrated   18-20
   Review 18-5 Analyzing Customer Profitability   18-22
Appendix 18A: Profitability Analysis with Activity-Based Cost Drivers   18-22
   Multi-Level Contribution Income Statement   18-22
   Variations in Multi-Level Contribution Income Statement   18-24
   Review 18-6 Performing a Profitability Analysis Using Activity-Based Cost Drivers   18-25
Multiple Choice   18-25
Data Analytics   18-26
Data Visualization   18-27
Assignments   18-28
Solutions to Review Problems   18-46

Chapter 19
Additional Topics in Product Costing   19-1

Allocation of Service Department Costs   19-3
   Reasons for Allocating Service Department Costs   19-4
   The Process of Allocating Service Department Costs   19-4
   Using the Direct Method to Allocate Service Department Costs   19-6
   Comparing the Direct Method to the Step Method   19-7
   Using the Step Method to Allocate Service Department Costs   19-8
   Review 19-1 Allocating Service Department Costs Using the Direct and Step Methods   19-10

The Cost of Excess Capacity   19-11
   Calculating the Overhead Application Rate Under Different Capacity Levels   19-11
   Calculating the Cost of Excess Capacity   19-13
   Managing Excess Capacity   19-13
   Capacity Considerations When Using Dual Overhead Allocation Rates   19-14
   Review 19-2 Managing Excess Capacity   19-14
Just-In-Time (JIT) Inventory Management/Lean Production   19-14
   Characteristics of JIT/Lean Production Approach   19-14
   Performance Evaluation Under JIT/Lean Production Approach   19-17
   Review 19-3 Analyzing Performance in Lean Manufacturing   19-18
Increased Focus on Data-Driven Decision-Making   19-19
   Using Data Effectively   19-19
   Developing Skills for Decision-Making   19-20
   Review 19-4 Discussing Risks and Concerns of Access to Big Data   19-20
Key Ratios and Equations   19-21
Multiple Choice   19-21
Data Analytics   19-22
Data Visualization   19-23
Assignments   19-24
Solutions to Review Problems   19-35

Chapter 20
Decision-Making: Pricing and Product Cost Management   20-1

Cost-Based Pricing   20-3
   Contrasting a Cost-Based Approach to an Economic Approach   20-3
   Cost-Based Approaches to Pricing   20-3
   Review 20-1 Applying Cost-Based Approaches to Pricing   20-7
Price-Based Costing   20-8
   Target Costing: Price-Based Costing   20-8
   Characteristics of Target Costing   20-9
   Review 20-2 Applying Target Costing   20-12
Continuous Improvement   20-12
   Kaizen Costing Approach   20-12
   Review 20-3 Analyzing the Impact of Continuous Improvement Initiatives   20-13
Benchmarking to Improve Performance   20-13
   Applications of Benchmarking   20-14
   Process of Benchmarking   20-14
   Review 20-4 Distinguishing Between Benchmarking and Competitor Research   20-15
Key Ratios and Equations   20-15
Multiple Choice   20-15
Data Analytics   20-16
Data Visualization   20-16
Assignments   20-17
Solutions to Review Problems   20-24

Chapter 21
Operational Budgeting and Profit Planning   21-1

The Budgeting Process   21-3
   Reasons for Budgeting   21-3
   Approaches to Budgeting   21-5

Review 21-1 Applying the Output/Input Approach and Activity-Based Approach to Budgeting 21-7
Master Budget for a Merchandiser 21-8
   Overview of the Master Budget Assembly for a Merchandiser 21-8
   Starting Point: Beginning of Period Balance Sheet 21-10
   Sales Budget 21-11
   Purchases Budget 21-11
   Selling Expense Budget 21-12
   General and Administrative Expense Budget 21-13
   Cash Budget 21-13
   Budgeted Financial Statements 21-15
   Finalizing the Budget 21-16
   Review 21-2 Preparing a Budget for a Merchandising Organization 21-17
Master Budget for a Manufacturer 21-17
   Overview of Master Budget Assembly for a Manufacturer 21-17
   Sales Budget 21-19
   Production Budget 21-19
   Materials Purchases Budget 21-19
   Manufacturing Cost Budget 21-20
   Cash Budget and Financial Statement Budgets 21-20
   Review 21-3 Preparing a Master Budget for a Manufacturer 21-21
Aspects of Budgeting That Impact Behavior and Outcomes 21-22
   Employee Participation in the Budgeting Process 21-22
   Selecting Budgeting Periods 21-23
   Utilizing Forecasts in Budgets 21-23
   Motivating Ethical Behavior in Budget Development 21-24
   Review 21-4 Identifying Aspects of Budget Development Affecting Behavior 21-24
Multiple Choice 21-25
Data Analytics 21-26
Data Visualization 21-27
Assignments 21-28
Solutions to Review Problems 21-43

Chapter 22
Standard Costs and Performance Reports 22-1

Responsibility Accounting 22-3
   Responsibility Accounting and Performance Reporting 22-3
   Performance Reporting and Organization Structures 22-4
   Types of Responsibility Centers 22-5
   Financial and Nonfinancial Performance Measures 22-6
   Review 22-1 Identifying Responsibility Centers 22-7
Performance Reporting for Cost Centers 22-7
   Differentiating a Static Budget from a Flexible Budget 22-7
   Performance Report with a Flexible Budget 22-8
   Standard Costs and Performance Reports 22-10
   Review 22-2 Preparing a Flexible Budget for Performance Reporting 22-11
Variance Analysis for Costs 22-11
   Components of Standard Cost Analysis: Price and Quantity Variances 22-11
   Standard Cost Variance Analysis of Direct Materials 22-11
   Review 22-3 Calculating Standard Cost Variances for Direct Materials 22-14
   Standard Cost Variance Analysis of Direct Labor 22-15
   Review 22-4 Calculating Standard Cost Variances for Direct Labor 22-17
   Standard Cost Variance Analysis of Variable Manufacturing Overhead 22-17
   Overview of Fixed Overhead Variances 22-19
   Review 22-5 Calculating Standard Cost Variances for Variable Manufacturing Overhead 22-20
Revenue Variances and Performance Reporting 22-20
   Performance Report of Sales Department as a Revenue Center 22-20
   Performance Report for Controllable Selling Costs 22-22
   Performance Report of Sales Department as a Profit Center 22-22
   Review 22-6 Calculating Revenue Variances 22-24
Appendix 22A: Fixed Overhead Variances 22-24
   Review 22-7 Calculating Fixed Overhead Budget Variance 22-25
Appendix 22B: Reconciling Budgeted and Actual Income 22-25
   Review 22-8 Reconciling Budgeted and Actual Contribution Margin 22-27
Key Ratios and Equations 22-27
Multiple Choice 22-27
Data Analytics 22-28
Data Visualization 22-29
Assignments 22-30
Solutions to Review Problems 22-43

Chapter 23
Performance Measurement Using Segment Reporting, Transfer Pricing, and Balanced Scorecard 23-1

Segment Analysis and Reporting 23-3
   Preparing Segment Reports 23-3
   Interpreting Segment Reports 23-6
   Review 23-1 Reporting by Segment 23-8
Transfer Pricing 23-8
   Resolving Transfer-Pricing Conflicts 23-8
   Determining Transfer Prices 23-11
   Review 23-2 Analyzing Purchase Decisions with Transfer Pricing 23-14
Investment Center Evaluation Measures 23-14
   Return on Investment 23-14
   Residual Income 23-18
   Economic Value Added 23-19
   Which Measure Is Best? 23-19
   Review 23-3 Computing Return on Investment and Residual Income 23-20
Balanced Scorecard 23-21
   Balanced Scorecard Framework 23-21
   Balanced Scorecard and Strategy 23-25
   Review 23-4 Assigning Metrics to the Balanced Scorecard Categories 23-27
Key Ratios and Equations 23-27
Multiple Choice 23-27
Data Analytics 23-29
Data Visualization 23-30
Assignments 23-31
Solutions to Review Problems 23-45

Chapter 24
Capital Budgeting Decisions 24-1

Long-Range Planning and Capital Budgeting 24-3
   The Capital Budgeting Process 24-4
Capital Budgeting Models That Do Not Consider Time Value of Money 24-6

Predicted Cash Flows **24-6**
Payback Period **24-7**
Accounting Rate of Return **24-8**
Review 24-1 Computing the Payback Period and the Accounting Rate of Return **24-9**
Capital Budgeting Models That Consider Time Value of Money **24-9**
Net Present Value **24-10**
Internal Rate of Return **24-11**
Review 24-2 Calculating Net Present Value and Internal Rate of Return **24-12**
Evaluation of Capital Budgeting Models **24-12**
Advantages and Disadvantages of Capital Budgeting Models **24-13**
Review 24-3 Evaluating Investment Proposals **24-15**
Considering Risks and Relevant Cost Analysis in Capital Budgeting Decisions **24-15**
Evaluating Risk and Uncertainty in Capital Budgeting Decisions **24-15**
Using Differential Analysis in Capital Budgeting Decisions **24-16**
Avoiding Errors in Predicting Differential Costs and Revenues **24-18**
Review 24-4 Considering Nonquantitative Factors in Capital Budgeting Decisions **24-19**
Appendix 24A: Time Value of Money **24-20**
Future Value **24-20**
Present Value **24-20**
Annuities **24-22**
Unequal Cash Flows **24-23**
Deferred Returns **24-23**
Review 24-5 Performing Present Value Calculations Using the Table Approach **24-24**
Appendix 24B: Table Approach to Determining Internal Rate of Return **24-24**
Equal Cash Flows **24-24**
Unequal Cash Flows **24-25**
Review 24-6 Determining the Internal Rate of Return Using the Table Approach **24-26**
Appendix 24C: Taxes in Capital Budgeting Decisions **24-26**
Depreciation Tax Shield **24-26**
Investment Tax Credit **24-28**
Review 24-7 Calculating Net Present Value with the Consideration of Income Taxes **24-28**
Key Ratios and Equations **24-29**
Multiple Choice **24-29**
Data Analytics **24-30**
Data Visualization **24-31**
Assignments **24-32**
Solutions to Review Problems **24-45**

Appendix

Compound Interest and the Time-Value of Money **A-1**

Future Value Concepts **A-2**
Present Value Concepts **A-3**
Present Value of a Single Amount **A-3**
Present Value of an Annuity **A-4**
Installment Loans **A-5**
Bond Valuation **A-5**
Calculating Bond Yields **A-6**
Future Value of Annuities **A-6**
Using Excel to Compute Time-Value **A-7**
Future Value Calculations **A-7**
Present Value Calculations **A-10**
Assignments **A-17**

Appendix

Data Analytics and Blockchain Technology **B-1**

Data Analytics **B-2**
Big Data **B-2**
Types of Data Analytics **B-2**
Data Analytics in the Accounting Profession **B-3**
The Analytics Mindset **B-4**
Data Analytic Tools **B-5**
Data Visualization **B-6**
Blockchain Technology **B-10**
Summary **B-12**
Video Resources for Tableau **B-13**
Assignments **B-13**

Index **I-1**

Chapter 1: Introducing Financial Accounting

LEARNING OBJECTIVES

LO1-1 Identify the users of accounting information and discuss the costs and benefits of disclosure.

LO1-2 Describe a company's business activities and explain how these activities are represented by the accounting equation.

LO1-3 Identify the four key financial statements: balance sheet, income statement, statement of stockholders' equity, and statement of cash flows.

LO1-4 Describe how standardized accounting principles and a regulatory environment are important to financial statement integrity.

LO1-5 Compute two key ratios that are commonly used to assess profitability and risk—return on equity and the debt-to-equity ratio.

LO1-6 Appendix 1A: Explain the conceptual framework for financial reporting.

Learning Objectives identify the key learning goals of the chapter.

Road Maps summarize each chapter's resources and categorize them by learning objective.

Assignments reinforce learning and can be completed by hand or within MBC.

Road Map

LO	Learning Objective / Topics	Page	eLecture	Review	Assignments
LO1-1	Identify the users of accounting information and discuss the costs and benefits of disclosure.	1-3	e1-1	R1–1	M1-25, E1-28, E1-34, C1-49, C1-50, **DA1-1**
LO1-2	Describe a company's business activities and explain how these activities are represented by the accounting equation.	1-7	e1-2	R1–2	M1-19, M1-20, M1-21, E1-27, E1-29, E1-32, E1-33, P1-36, P1-37, P1-38, P1-43, C1-47
LO1-3	Identify the four key financial statements: balance sheet, income statement, statement of stockholders' equity, and statement of cash flows.	1-11	e1-3	R1–3	M1-22, M1-23, M1-24, E1-29, E1-30, E1-31, P1-37, P1-38, P1-39, P1-40, P1-41, P1-42, P1-43, P1-44, P1-45, C1-46, C1-47, C1-49
LO1-4	Describe how standardized accounting principles and a regulatory environment are important to financial statement integrity.	1-16	e1-4	R1–4	M1-26, E1-34, C1-50, **DA1-3**
LO1-5	Compute two key ratios that are commonly used to assess profitability and risk—return on equity and the debt-to-equity ratio.	1-21	e1-5	R1–5	E1-32, E1-33, P1-36, P1-43, P1-44, P1-45, C1-46, C1-47, C1-48, C1-49, **DA1-2**
LO1-6	Appendix 1A: Explain the conceptual framework for financial reporting.	1-25	e1-6	R1–6	E1-35

Learning Objectives identify the key learning goals of the chapter.

eLectures are videos available in MBC that provide 3-5 minute reviews of each learning objective.

Reviews follow each learning objective and require students to apply what they have just learned.
Guided Example videos accompany the Reviews and demonstrate how to solve various types of problems. Reviews are also assignable in MBC.

Data Analysis (DA) exercises using Excel and Tableau are identified with blue font. Exercises are assignable in MBC.

*A **Focus Company** introduces each chapter and illustrates the relevance of accounting in everyday business.*

NIKE
www.Nike.com

Phil Knight majored in accounting and was a member of the track team at the University of Oregon. A few years after graduation, Knight teamed up with his former track coach, Bill Bowerman, to form a business called Blue Ribbon Sports to import, sell, and distribute running shoes from Japan. Blue Ribbon Sports, or BRS as it came to be known, was started on a shoestring—Knight and Bowerman each contributed $500 to start the business. A few years later, BRS introduced its own line of running shoes called Nike. It also unveiled a new logo, the now familiar Nike swoosh. Following the overwhelming success of the Nike shoe line, BRS officially changed its company name to Nike, Inc. Currently, the company is worth more than $120 billion. Knight is the former CEO and the Chairman, Emeritus of Nike, Inc.

Today, Nike, Inc. has sales in almost every country on the planet and, in the fiscal year ended May, 2021, Nike had total revenues of more than $37 billion and income of $2.5 billion. How does someone take a $1,000 investment and turn it into a company whose stock is worth more than $120 billion? Along the way, Nike management made countless decisions that ultimately led the company to where it is today. Each of these decisions involved identifying alternative courses of action and weighing their costs, benefits, and risks in light of the available information.

Accounting is the process of identifying, measuring, and communicating financial information to help people make *economic* decisions. People use accounting information to facilitate a wide variety of transactions, including assessing whether, and on what terms, they should invest in a firm, seek employment in a business, or continue purchasing its products. Accounting information is crucial to any successful business, and without it, most businesses would not even exist.

This book explains how to create and analyze financial statements, an important source of accounting information prepared by companies to communicate with a variety of users. We begin by introducing transactions between the firm and its investors, creditors, suppliers, employees, and customers. We continue by demonstrating how accounting principles are applied to these transactions to create the financial statements. Then we "invert" the process and learn how to analyze the firm's financial statements to assess the firm's underlying economic performance. Our philosophy is simple—we believe it is crucial to have a deep understanding of financial accounting to become critical readers and users of financial statements. Financial statements tell a story—a business story. Our goal is to understand that story and apply the knowledge gleaned from financial statements to make good business decisions.

Sources: Nike.com; Nike, Inc. 10-K Report for the year ended May 31, 2021; *Business Week* (October 2007, August 2009); *Portland Business Journal* (October 2007); *Fortune* (February 2012). For more on Phil Knight and Nike's history, see the book *Shoe Dog* (published by Scribner).

CHAPTER ORGANIZATION

Chapter Organization Charts visually depict the key topics and their sequence within the chapter.

Introducing Financial Accounting

Demand for Accounting Information	Business Activities	Financial Statements	Financial Reporting Environment	Financial Statement Analysis
• Who Uses Financial Accounting Information? • Costs and Benefits of Disclosure	• Planning Activities • Investing Activities • Financing Activities • Operating Activities	• Balance Sheet • Income Statement • Statement of Stockholders' Equity • Statement of Cash Flows • Financial Statement Linkages	• Generally Accepted Accounting Principles • Regulation and Oversight • Role of the Auditor • A Global Perspective • Conceptual Framework (Appendix 1A)	• Profitability Analysis • Credit Risk Analysis

DEMAND FOR ACCOUNTING INFORMATION

LO1-1 Identify the users of accounting information and discuss the costs and benefits of disclosure.

*eLecture icons identify topics for which there are instructional videos in **myBusinessCourse** (MBC). See the Preface for more information on MBC.*

Accounting can be defined as the process of recording, summarizing, and analyzing financial transactions. While accounting information attempts to satisfy the needs of a diverse set of users, the accounting information a company produces can be classified into two categories (see **Exhibit 1.1**):[1]

- **Financial accounting**—designed primarily for decision-makers outside of the company
- **Managerial accounting**—designed primarily for decision-makers within the company

EXHIBIT 1.1 Information Needs of Decision-makers Who Use Financial and Managerial Accounting

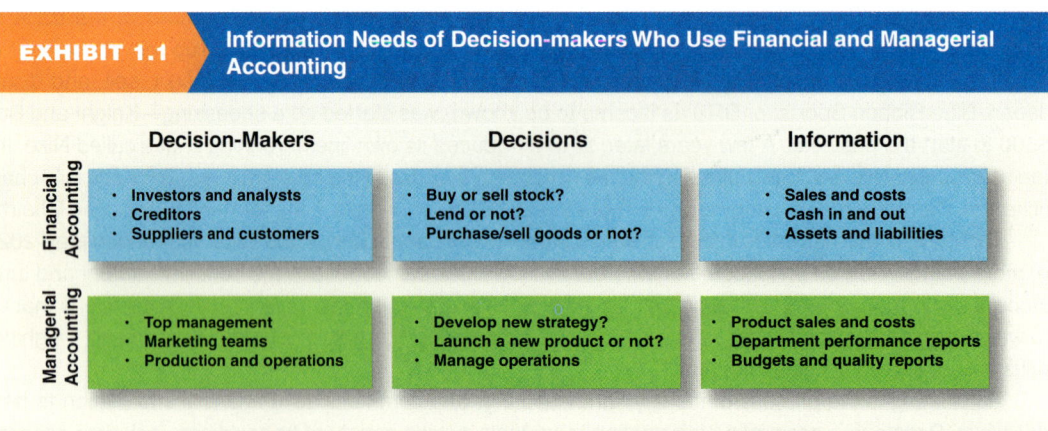

Financial accounting reports include information about company profitability and financial health. This information is useful to various economic actors who wish to engage in contracts with the firm, including investors, creditors, employees, customers, and governments. Managerial accounting information is not reported outside of the company because it includes proprietary information about the profitability of specific products, divisions, or customers. Company managers use managerial accounting reports to make decisions such as whether to drop or add products or divisions, or whether to continue serving different types of customers. The first half of this text focuses on understanding and analyzing financial accounting information.

---

[1] Businesses also have to compute a measure of income for income tax purposes in order to file tax returns in the jurisdictions that require them to file. This book is not about taxation, but we cover the accounting for income taxes in Chapter 10.

Who Uses Financial Accounting Information?

Demand for financial accounting information derives from numerous users including:

- Shareholders and potential shareholders
- Creditors and suppliers
- Managers and directors
- Financial analysts
- Other users

Shareholders and Potential Shareholders Corporations are the dominant form of business organization for large companies around the world, and corporate shareholders are one important group of decision-makers that have an interest in financial accounting information. A **corporation** is a form of business organization that is characterized by a large number of owners who are not involved in managing the day-to-day operations of the company.[2] A corporation exists as a legal entity that issues **shares of stock** to its owners in exchange for cash; therefore, the owners of a corporation are referred to as *shareholders* or **stockholders**.

> **FYI** *features provide additional information that complements the text.*

> **FYI** Shareholders of a corporation are its owners; although managers can own stock in the corporation, most shareholders are not managers.

Because the shareholders are not involved in the day-to-day operations of the business, they rely on the information in financial statements to evaluate management performance and assess the company's financial condition.

In addition to corporations, sole proprietorships, partnerships, and limited liability companies are common forms of business ownership. A **sole proprietorship** has a single owner who typically manages the daily operations. Small family-run businesses, such as corner grocery stores, are commonly organized as sole proprietorships. A **partnership** has two or more owners who are also usually involved in managing the business. Many professionals, such as lawyers and CPAs, organize their businesses as partnerships. Many new businesses today start up as a limited liability company (LLC). An LLC allows for limited liability for the owners similar to a corporation, while allowing for more flexibility and other features that are similar to a partnership.

Most corporations begin as small, privately held businesses (sole proprietorships, partnerships, or an LLC). As their operations expand, however, they require additional capital to finance their growth. One of the principal advantages of a corporation over the other organizational forms of doing business is the ability to raise large amounts of cash by issuing (selling) stock. For example, as Nike grew from a small business with only two owners into a larger company, it raised the funds needed for expansion by selling shares of Nike stock to new shareholders. In the United States, large corporations can raise funds by issuing stock on organized exchanges, such as the **New York Stock Exchange (NYSE)** or **NASDAQ** (which is an acronym for the National Association of Securities Dealers Automated Quotations system). Corporations with stock that is traded on public exchanges are known as *publicly traded corporations* or simply *public corporations*. The raising of capital from a large group of outside shareholders leads to what is known as the separation of ownership and control. For example, as Nike sold more stock, the CEO (Knight) owned a smaller amount of the shares. In cases of such separation, which exists at most publicly traded firms, the information flow from the managers to the shareholders is very important.

Financial statements and the accompanying note disclosures provide information on the risk and return associated with owning shares of stock in the corporation, and they reveal how well management has performed. Financial statements also provide valuable insights into future performance by revealing management's plans for new products, new operating procedures, and new strategic directions for the company as well as for their implementation. Corporate management provides this information because the information reduces uncertainty about the company's future prospects which, in turn, increases the market price of its shares and helps the company raise the funds it needs to grow.

Creditors and Suppliers Few businesses rely solely on shareholders for the cash needed to operate the company. Instead, most companies borrow from banks or other lenders known as **creditors**. Creditors are interested in the potential borrower's ability to repay. They use financial

> **FYI** Financial statements are typically required when a business requests a bank loan. (If the business is very small, then tax returns will often suffice).

---

[2] Most countries have business forms that are similar in structure to those of a U.S. corporation, though they are referred to by different names. For example, while firms that are incorporated in the United States have the extension "Inc." appended to their names, similar firms in the United Kingdom are referred to as a Public Limited Company, which has the extension "PLC."

accounting information to help determine loan terms, loan amounts, interest rates, and collateral. In addition, creditors' loans often include contractual requirements based on information found in the financial statements.

> **Key Terms** are highlighted in bold, red font.

Suppliers use financial information to establish credit sales terms and to determine their long-term commitment to supply-chain relationships. Supplier companies often justify an expansion of *their* businesses based on the growth and financial health of their customers. Both creditors and suppliers rely on information in the financial statements to monitor and adjust their contracts and commitments with a company.

Managers and Directors Financial statements can be thought of as a financial report card for management. A well-managed company earns a good return for its shareholders, and this is reflected in the financial statements. In most companies, management is compensated, at least in part, based on the financial performance of the company. That is, managers often receive cash bonuses, shares of stock, or other *incentive compensation* that is linked directly to the information in the financial statements.

Publicly traded corporations are required by law to have a **board of directors**. Directors are elected by the shareholders to represent shareholder interests and oversee management. The board hires executive management and regularly reviews company operations. Directors use financial accounting information to review the results of operations, evaluate future strategy, and assess management performance.

> **FYI** The Sarbanes-Oxley Act requires issuers of securities to disclose whether they have a code of ethics for the senior officers.

Both managers and directors use the published financial statements of *other companies* to perform comparative analyses and establish performance benchmarks. For example, managers in some companies are paid a bonus for financial performance that exceeds the industry average.

BUSINESS INSIGHT

Court cases involving corporations such as Enron, Tyco, and WorldCom (now MCI) have found executives, including several CEOs, guilty of issuing fraudulent financial statements. These executives have received substantial fines and, in some cases, long jail sentences. These trials have resulted in widespread loss of reputation and credibility among corporate boards.

Financial Analysts Many decision-makers lack the time, resources, or expertise to efficiently and effectively analyze financial statements. Instead, they rely on professional financial analysts, such as credit rating agencies like Moody's investment services, portfolio managers, and security analysts. Financial analysts play an important role in the dissemination of financial information and often specialize in specific industries. Their analysis helps to identify and assess risk, forecast performance, establish prices for new issues of stock, and make buy-or-sell recommendations to investors.

Other Users of Financial Accounting Information External decision-makers include many users of accounting information in addition to those listed above. For example, *prospective employees* often examine the financial statements of an employer to learn about the company before interviewing for or accepting a new job.

Labor unions examine financial statements in order to assess the financial health of firms prior to negotiating labor contracts on behalf of the firms' employees. *Customers* use accounting information to assess the ability of a company to deliver products or services and to assess the company's long-term reliability.

Government agencies rely on accounting information to develop and enforce regulations, including public protection, price setting, import-export, taxation, and various other policies.[3] Timely and reliable information is crucial to effective regulatory policy. Moreover, accounting information is often used to assess penalties for companies that violate regulations.

---

[3] A company's tax returns are distinctly different from its financial statements. Tax returns are prepared for tax authorities in order to comply with income tax rules. The financial statements are prepared to provide information to investors, creditors, and other decision-makers outside of the business.

Costs and Benefits of Disclosure

The act of providing financial information to external users is called **disclosure**. As with every decision, the benefits of disclosure must be weighed against the costs of providing the information.

One reason companies are motivated to disclose financial information to external decision-makers is that it often lowers financing and operating costs. For example, when a company applies for a loan, the bank uses the company's financial statements to help determine the appropriate interest rate. Without adequate financial disclosures in its financial statements, the bank is likely to demand a higher interest rate or perhaps not make the loan at all. Thus, in this setting, a benefit of financial disclosure is that it reduces the company's cost of borrowing.

While there are benefits from disclosing financial information, there are also costs. Besides the obvious cost of hiring accountants and preparing the financial statements, financial disclosures can also result in costs being imposed by competitors. It is common practice for managers to scrutinize the financial statements of competitors to learn about successful products, new strategies, innovative technologies, and changing market conditions. Thus, disclosing too much information can place a company at a competitive disadvantage. Disclosure can also raise investors' expectations about a company's future profitability. If those expectations are not met, they may bring litigation against the managers.

There are also political costs that are potentially associated with accounting disclosure. Highly visible companies, such as defense contractors and oil companies, are often the target of scrutiny by the public and by government officials. When these companies report unusually large accounting profits, they are often the target of additional regulation or increased taxes.

Stock market regulators impose disclosure standards for publicly traded corporations, but the nature and extent of the required disclosures vary substantially across countries. Further, because the requirements only set the minimum level of disclosure, the quantity and quality of information provided by firms will vary. This variation in disclosure ultimately reflects differences among companies in the benefits and costs of disclosing information to the public.

You Make The Call requires you to assume various roles within a business and use your accounting knowledge to address an issue. Solutions are at the end of the chapter.

YOU MAKE THE CALL

You are a Product Manager There is often friction between investors' needs for information and a company's desire to safeguard competitive advantages. Assume that you are the product manager for a key department at your company and you are asked for advice on the extent of information to disclose in the annual report on a potentially lucrative new product that your department has test marketed. What considerations affect the advice you provide and why? [Answer on page 1-29]

Review Problems are self-study tools that require the application of accounting. To aid learning, solutions are provided at the end of the chapter.

Identifying How Financial Statements Are Utilized by Different User Groups LO1-1 **Review 1-1**

For each accounting information user group (1 through 6), determine how it would utilize the financial statements of **Macy's Inc.**, by selecting the relevant task from *a* to *f*.

Guided Example icons denote the availability of a demonstration video in **myBusinessCourse** *(MBC)—see the Preface for more on MBC.*

Accounting Information User Group	Task Aided by Financial Statements
1. ____ Shareholders	a. To assign a rating to Macy's debt, which indicates the chance of default.
2. ____ Creditors	b. To determine whether to lend money to Macy's over a 10-year period.
3. ____ Suppliers	
4. ____ Managers	c. To estimate your year-end bonus based on Macy's financial results.
5. ____ Financial analysts	d. To verify the amount of sales taxes due from Macy's Inc.
6. ____ Government agencies	e. To aid in the decision of whether to buy additional shares of Macy's stock.
	f. As input in a decision to contractually sell a specified quantity of items at a set price to Macy's over the next two years.

Solution on p. 1-39.

BUSINESS ACTIVITIES

LO1-2
Describe a company's business activities and explain how these activities are represented by the accounting equation.

Businesses produce accounting information to help develop strategies, attract financing, evaluate investment opportunities, manage operations, and measure performance. Before we can attempt to understand the information provided in financial statements, we must understand these business activities. That is, what does a business actually do? For example:

- Where does a company such as Nike find the resources to develop new products and open new retail stores?
- What new products should Nike bring to market?
- How much should Nike spend on product development? On advertising? On executive compensation?
- How does Nike's management determine if a product is a success?

Questions such as these define the activities of Nike and other companies.

Exhibit 1.2 illustrates the activities of a typical business. All businesses *plan* business activities, *finance* those activities, *invest* resources in those activities, and then engage in *operating* activities. Companies conduct all these activities while confronting a variety of *external forces,* including competition from other businesses, government regulation, economic conditions and market forces, and changing preferences of customers. The financial statements provide information that helps us understand and evaluate each of these activities.

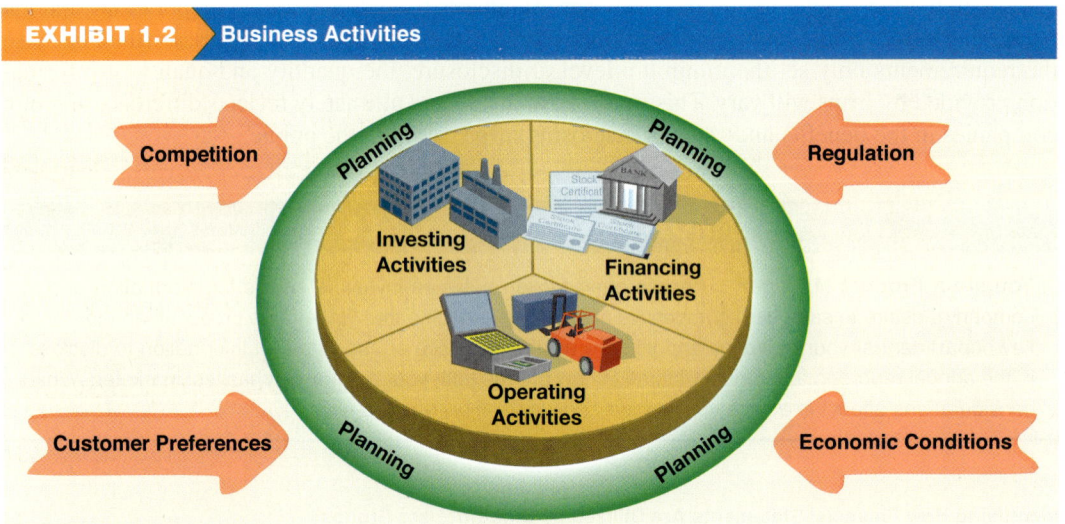

EXHIBIT 1.2 Business Activities

Planning Activities

A company's goals, and the strategies adopted to reach those goals, are the product of its **planning activities**. Nike, for example, states that its mission is "To bring inspiration and innovation to every athlete in the world," adding "If you have a body, you are an athlete." However, in its 2020 annual report to shareholders, for the year ended May 2020, Nike management suggests another goal that focuses on financial success and earning a return for the shareholders.

Excerpts from recent financial statements are used to illustrate and reinforce concepts.

> Our goal is to deliver value to our shareholders by building a profitable global portfolio of branded footwear, apparel, equipment, and accessories businesses. Our strategy is to achieve long-term revenue growth by creating innovative, "must have" products, building deep personal consumer connections with our brands, and delivering compelling consumer experiences through digital platforms and at retail.

As is the case with most businesses, Nike's primary goal is to create value for its owners, the shareholders. How the company plans to do so is the company's **strategy**.

A company's *strategic* (or *business*) *plan* describes how it plans to achieve its goals. The plan's success depends on an effective review of market conditions. Specifically, the company must assess both the demand for its products and services, and the supply of its inputs (both labor and capital). The plan must also include competitive analyses, opportunity assessments, and consideration of business threats. The strategic plan specifies both broad management designs that generate company value and tactics to achieve those designs.

Most information in a strategic plan is proprietary and guarded closely by management. However, outsiders can gain insight into planning activities through various channels, including newspapers, magazines, and company disclosures. Understanding a company's planning activities helps focus accounting analysis and place it in context.

Investing Activities

Investing activities consist of acquiring and disposing of the resources needed to produce and sell a company's products and services. These resources, called **assets**, provide future benefits to the company. Companies differ on the amount and mix of these resources. Some companies require buildings and equipment, while others have abandoned "bricks and mortar" to conduct business through the Internet.

Some assets that a company invests in are used quickly. For instance, a retail clothing store hopes to sell its spring and summer merchandise before purchasing more inventory for the fall and winter. Other assets are acquired for long-term use. Buildings are typically used for several decades. The relative proportion of short-term and long-term investments depends on the type of business and the strategic plan that the company adopts. For example, Nike has relatively few long-term assets because it outsources most of the production of its products to other companies.

The chart in **Exhibit 1.3** compares the relative proportion of short-term and long-term assets held by Nike and seven other companies, several of which are featured in later chapters. Nike has adopted a business model that requires very little investment in long-term resources. A majority of its investments are short-term assets. In contrast, **Verizon**, **PepsiCo**, and **Procter & Gamble** all rely heavily on long-term investments. These companies hold relatively small proportions of short-term assets. This mix of long-term and short-term assets is described in more detail in Chapter 2.

Real Companies and **Institutions** *are highlighted in bold, blue font.*

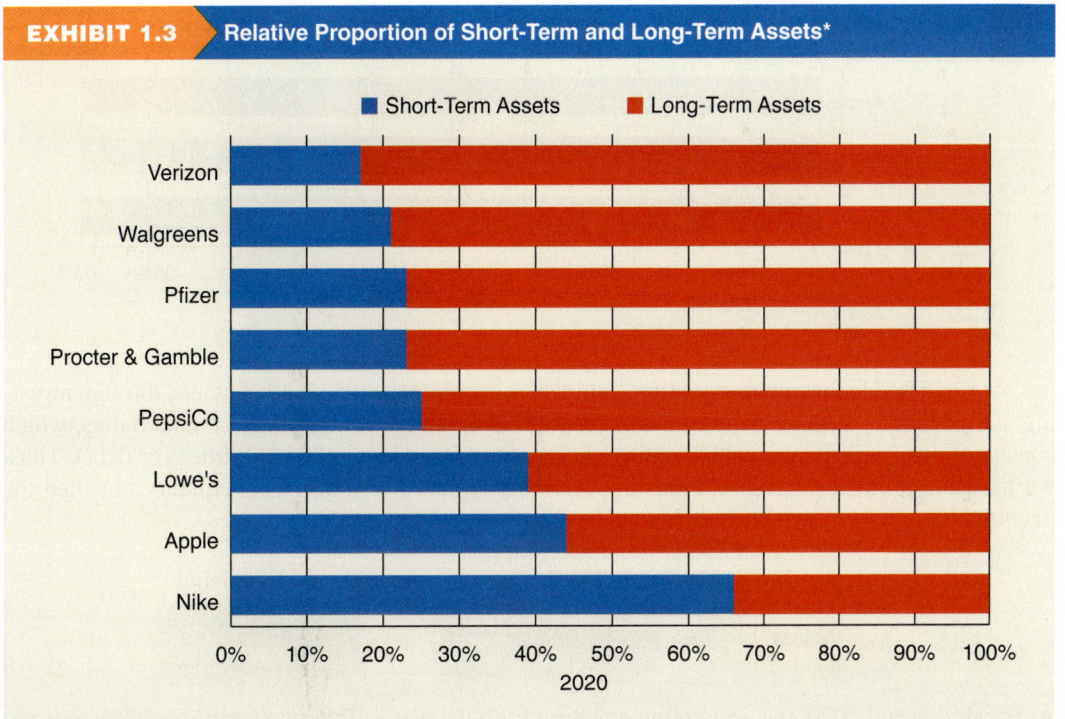

EXHIBIT 1.3 Relative Proportion of Short-Term and Long-Term Assets*

*These companies do not have identical fiscal year-ends. For each fiscal year listed (here and in the exhibits that follow), balance sheets are dated from January 31 to December 31 of that year. For example, Nike's fiscal year-end is May 31, 2020 while PepsiCo's fiscal year-end is December 26, 2020.

Financing Activities

Investments in resources require funding, and **financing activities** refer to the methods companies use to fund those investments. *Financial management* is the planning of resource needs, including the proper mix of financing sources.

Companies obtain financing from two sources: equity (owner) financing and creditor (nonowner) financing. *Equity financing* refers to the funds contributed to the company by its owners along with any income retained by the company. One form of equity financing is the cash raised from the sale (or issuance) of stock by a corporation. *Creditor* (or debt) *financing* is funds contributed by nonowners, which create *liabilities*. **Liabilities** are obligations the company must repay in the future. One example of a liability is a bank loan. We draw a distinction between equity and creditor financing for an important reason: creditor financing imposes a legal obligation to repay, usually with interest, and failure to repay amounts borrowed can result in adverse legal consequences such as bankruptcy. In contrast, equity financing does not impose an obligation for repayment.

Exhibit 1.4 compares the relative proportion of creditor and equity financing for Nike and other companies. PepsiCo uses liabilities to finance 85% of its resources. In contrast, **Walgreens Boots Alliance, Inc.** (Walgreens), relies more heavily on its equity financing, receiving 76% of its financing from creditors. **Pfizer** has the lowest proportion of creditor financing in this sample of companies, with just 59% of its assets financed by nonowners.

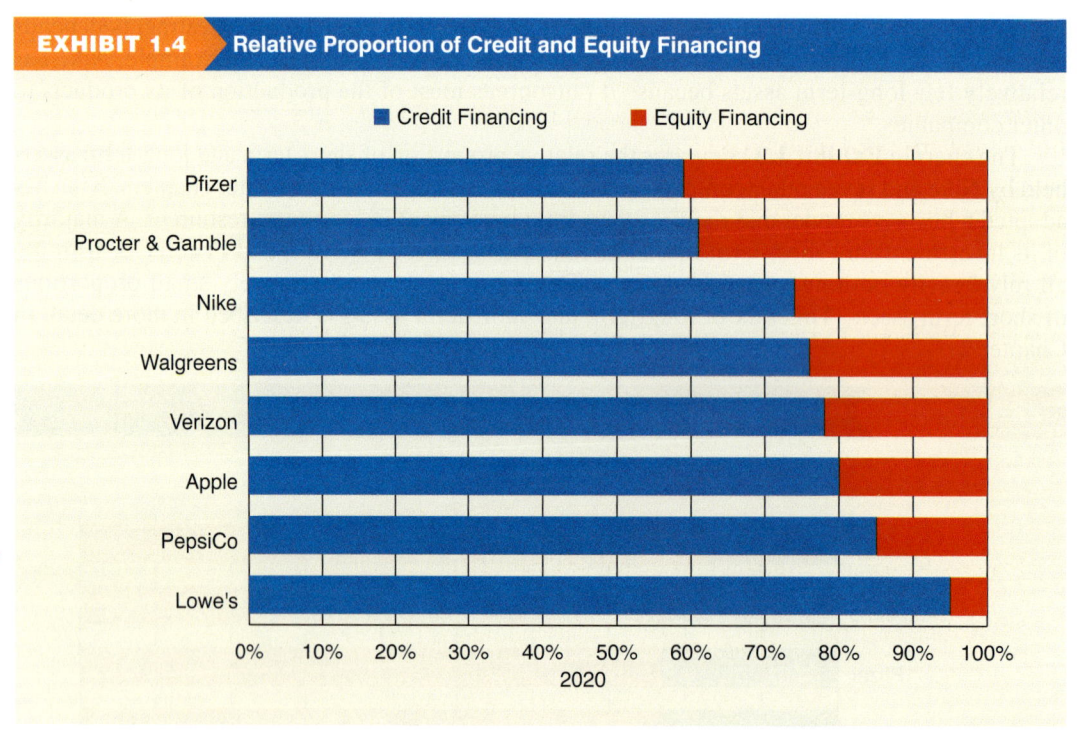

Infographics are used to convey difficult concepts and procedures.

As discussed in the previous section, companies acquire resources, called assets, through investing activities. The cash to acquire these resources is obtained through financing activities, which consist of owner financing, called equity, and creditor financing, called liabilities (or debt). Thus, we have the following basic relationship: *investing equals financing*. This equality is called the **accounting equation**, which is expressed as:

Investing = Financing + Owner Financing

Assets = Liabilities + Equity

At fiscal year-end 2020, the accounting equation for Nike was as follows ($ millions):

$$\$31{,}342 = \$23{,}287 + \$8{,}055$$

By definition, the accounting equation holds for all companies at all times. This relationship is a very powerful tool for analyzing and understanding companies, and we will use it often throughout the text.[4]

Operating Activities

Operating activities refer to the production, promotion, and selling of a company's products and services. These activities extend from a company's input markets, involving its suppliers, and to its output markets, involving its customers. Input markets generate *operating expenses* (or *costs*) such as inventory, salaries, materials, and logistics. Output markets generate *operating revenues* (or *sales*) from customers. Output markets also generate some operating expenses such as for marketing and distributing products and services to customers. When operating revenues exceed operating expenses, companies report *operating income*, also called *operating profit* or *operating earnings*. When operating expenses exceed operating revenues, companies report operating losses.

Revenue is the increase in equity resulting from the sale of goods and services to customers. The amount of revenue is determined *before* deducting expenses. An **expense** is the cost incurred to generate revenue, including the cost of the goods and services sold to customers as well as the cost of carrying out other business activities. **Income**, also called *net income*, equals revenues minus expenses and is the net increase in equity from the company's activities.

$$\text{Income} = \text{Revenues} - \text{Expenses}$$

For fiscal year 2020, Nike reported revenues of over $37 billion, yet its reported income was a fraction of that amount—just over $2.5 billion.

BUSINESS INSIGHT

Each year, *Fortune* magazine ranks the 500 largest corporations in the United States based on total revenues. For 2021, which is based on fiscal 2020 financial results, Nike ranked 85th on the *Fortune 500* list with revenues of over $37 billion. The company also ranked 74th in profits, with net income of approximately $2.5 billion. For comparison, the largest corporation was **Walmart, Inc.**, with revenues of more than $559 billion and $13.5 billion in net income (ranking number 14 in terms of profit). (Source: http://fortune.com/fortune500/list)

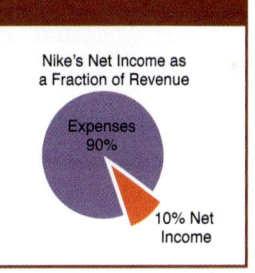

Nike's Net Income as a Fraction of Revenue: Expenses 90%, 10% Net Income

Review 1-2 LO1-2
Applying the Accounting Equation and Computing Financing Proportions

Determine the missing amounts for each year below for Delta Air Lines, Inc., including the percentage of financing provided by owners and creditors.

($ millions)	Assets	Liabilities	Equity	% of Financing Provided by Owners	% of Financing Provided by Creditors
2019	?	$49,174	$15,358	?	?
2018	$60,266	?	$13,687	?	?
2017	$53,671	$41,141	?	?	?

Solution on p. 1-40.

---

[4] There are securities that do not neatly fit into either "debt" or "equity" classification, but rather have characteristics of both. These are known as debt-equity hybrid securities. Their existence does not alter the conceptual idea that assets are financed with debt and equity. A detailed discussion of these is beyond the scope of this textbook, but we describe these briefly in the chapters on debt and equity. For most ratio analyses in this introductory-level textbook, we include all these types of securities as either debt or equity for the sake of simplicity.

FINANCIAL STATEMENTS

LO1-3 Identify the four key financial statements: balance sheet, income statement, statement of stockholders' equity, and statement of cash flows.

Four financial statements are used to periodically report on a company's business activities. These statements are:

- **balance sheet**, which lists the company's investments and sources of financing using the accounting equation;
- **income statement**, which reports the results of operations;
- **statement of stockholders' equity**, which details changes in owner financing;
- **statement of cash flows**, which details the sources and uses of cash.

Exhibit 1.5 shows how these statements are linked across time. A balance sheet reports on a company's position at a point in time. The income statement, statement of stockholders' equity, and the statement of cash flows report on performance over a period of time. The three statements in the middle of **Exhibit 1.5** (period-of-time statements) link the balance sheet from the beginning of a period to the balance sheet at the end of a period. There is a fifth statement, a statement of comprehensive income, but it only comes into play for issues that arise in later chapters.

EXHIBIT 1.5 Financial Statement Links Across Time

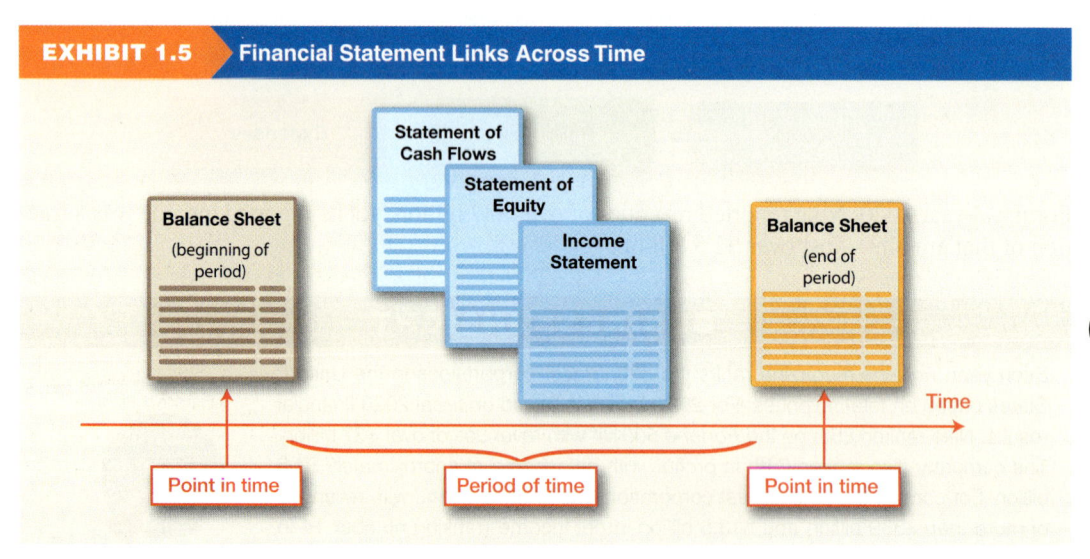

FYI The heading of each financial statement includes who, what, and when.

A one-year, or annual, reporting period is common, which is called the *accounting*, or *fiscal year*. Semiannual, quarterly, and monthly reporting periods are also common. *Calendar-year* companies have a reporting period that begins on January 1 and ends on December 31. **Pfizer**, **Google**, and **Verizon** are examples of calendar-year companies. Some companies choose a fiscal year ending on a date other than December 31. Seasonal businesses, such as retail stores, often choose a fiscal year that ends when sales and inventories are at their lowest level. For example, **Home Depot**, the retail home improvement store chain, ends its fiscal year on the Sunday closest to February 1, after the busy holiday season. Nike has a May 31 fiscal year. The heading of each statement identifies the (1) company name, (2) statement title, and (3) date or time period of the statement.

Balance Sheet

FYI The balance sheet is also known as the statement of financial position and the statement of financial condition.

A **balance sheet** reports a company's financial position at a point in time. It summarizes the result of the company's investing and financing activities by listing amounts for assets, liabilities, and equity. The balance sheet is based on the accounting equation, also called the *balance sheet equation*: Assets = Liabilities + Equity.

Nike's balance sheet for fiscal year 2020, which ended May 31, 2020, is reproduced in a reduced format in **Exhibit 1.6** and reports that assets are $31,342 million, liabilities are $23,287 million, and equity is $8,055 million, where owner financing is the sum of contributed capital of $8,302 million, retained earnings of $(191) million, a deficit, and other equity of $(56) million, a deficit. Thus, the balance sheet equation holds true for Nike's balance sheet: assets equal liabilities plus equity.

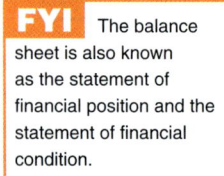

EXHIBIT 1.6 — Balance Sheet ($ millions)

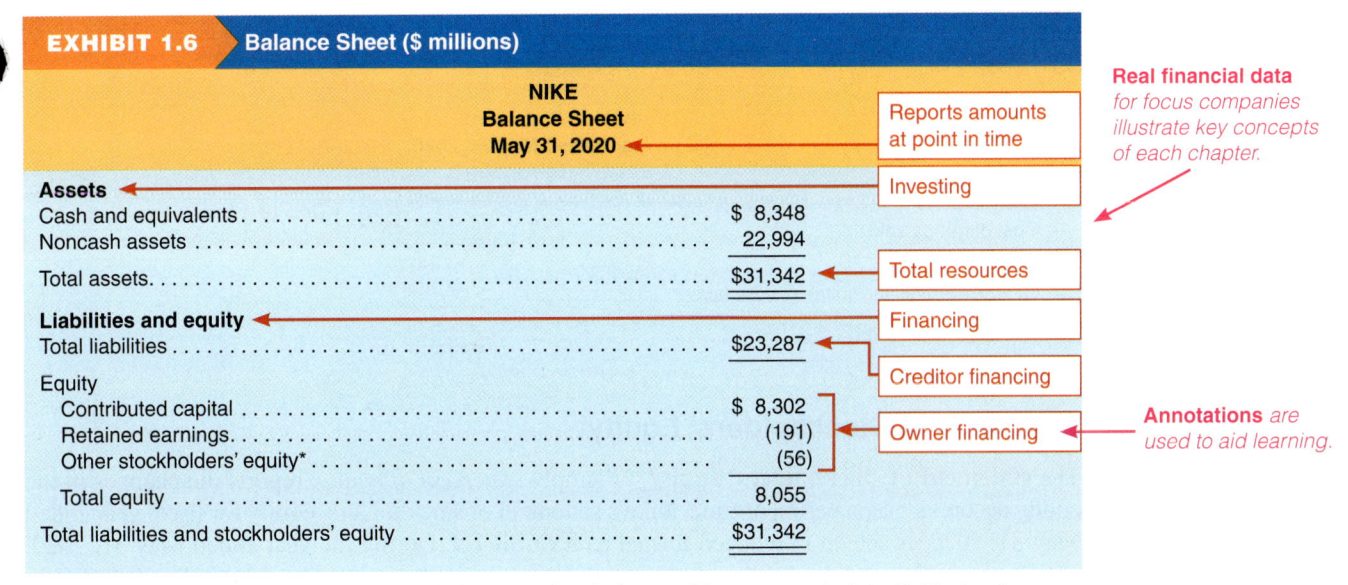

NIKE
Balance Sheet
May 31, 2020 ← Reports amounts at point in time

Assets		← Investing
Cash and equivalents	$ 8,348	
Noncash assets	22,994	
Total assets	$31,342	← Total resources
Liabilities and equity		← Financing
Total liabilities	$23,287	← Creditor financing
Equity		
Contributed capital	$ 8,302	
Retained earnings	(191)	← Owner financing
Other stockholders' equity*	(56)	
Total equity	8,055	
Total liabilities and stockholders' equity	$31,342	

Real financial data for focus companies illustrate key concepts of each chapter.

Annotations are used to aid learning.

* Other stockholders' equity includes accumulated other comprehensive income. Other components of stockholders' equity are discussed in Chapter 11.

Income Statement

The **income statement** reports the results of a company's operating activities over a period of time. It details amounts for revenues and expenses, and the difference between these two amounts is net income. Revenue is the increase in equity that results from selling goods or providing services to customers, and expense is the cost incurred to generate revenue. Net income is the increase in equity *after* subtracting expenses from revenues.

An important difference between the income statement and the balance sheet is that the balance sheet presents the company's position at a *point in time*, for instance December 31, 2020, while the income statement presents a summary of activity over a *period of time*, such as January 1, 2020, through December 31, 2020. Because of this difference, the balance sheet reflects the cumulative history of a company's activities. The amounts listed in the balance sheet carry over from the end of one fiscal year to the beginning of the next fiscal year, while the amounts listed in the income statement do not carry over from one year to the next.

Refer to Nike's income statement for the fiscal year ended May 31, 2020, shown in reduced format as **Exhibit 1.7**. It reports that revenues = $37,403 million, expenses = $34,864 million, and net income = $2,539 million. Thus, revenues minus expenses equals net income for Nike.

For manufacturing and merchandising companies, the **cost of goods sold** is an important expense that is typically disclosed separately in the income statement immediately following revenues. It is also common to report a subtotal for gross profit (also called gross margin), which is revenues less the cost of goods sold. The company's remaining expenses are then reported below gross profit. Nike's income statement is presented in this reduced format in **Exhibit 1.8**.

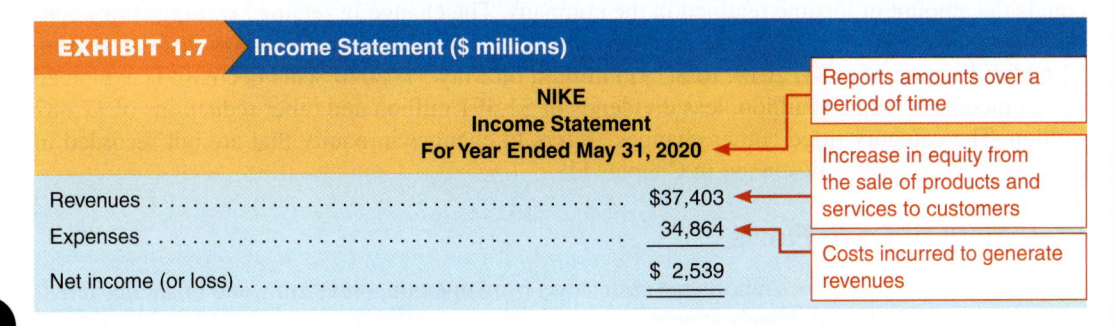

> **FYI** The income statement is also known as a statement of income, statement of earnings, statement of operations, and statement of profit and loss.

> **FYI** The term "gross" refers to an amount before subtractions, such as Gross Sales. An exception is made for the term Gross Profit (Gross Margin), defined as Sales less Cost of Goods Sold (Cost of Sales). When items are subtracted from a gross amount, the term "net" is generally used, as in the case of Net Sales (Gross Sales less returns and other items) or Net Income (Sales less all expenses).

EXHIBIT 1.7 — Income Statement ($ millions)

NIKE
Income Statement
For Year Ended May 31, 2020 ← Reports amounts over a period of time

Revenues	$37,403	← Increase in equity from the sale of products and services to customers
Expenses	34,864	
Net income (or loss)	$ 2,539	← Costs incurred to generate revenues

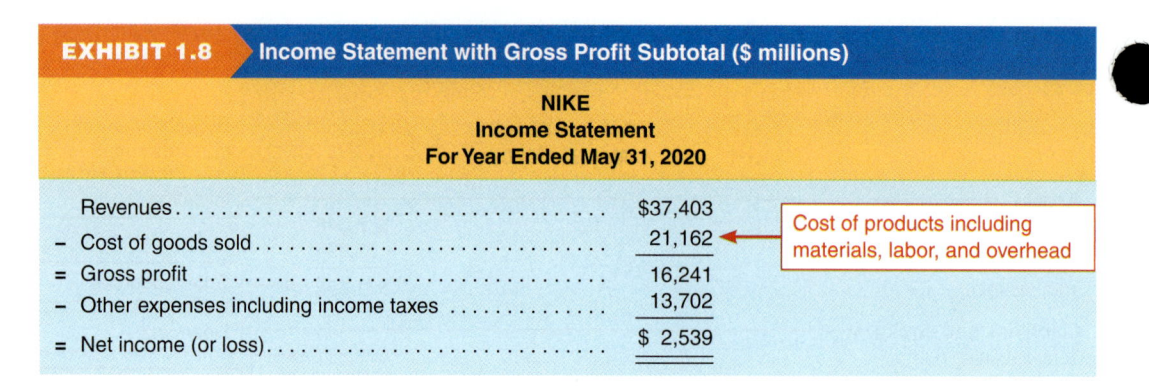

EXHIBIT 1.8 — Income Statement with Gross Profit Subtotal ($ millions)

NIKE
Income Statement
For Year Ended May 31, 2020

	Revenues.................................	$37,403
−	Cost of goods sold.......................	21,162
=	Gross profit.............................	16,241
−	Other expenses including income taxes.....	13,702
=	Net income (or loss)....................	$ 2,539

Cost of products including materials, labor, and overhead

Statement of Stockholders' Equity

The **statement of stockholders' equity**, or simply *statement of equity*, reports the changes in the equity accounts over a period of time. Nike's statement of stockholders' equity for fiscal year ended May 31, 2020, is shown in reduced format as **Exhibit 1.9**. During the year ended May 31, 2020, Nike's equity changed due to share issuance and income reinvestment. The exhibit details and classifies these changes into three categories:

- Contributed capital (includes common stock and additional paid-in capital)
- Retained earnings (includes cumulative net income or loss, and deducts dividends)
- Other stockholders' equity

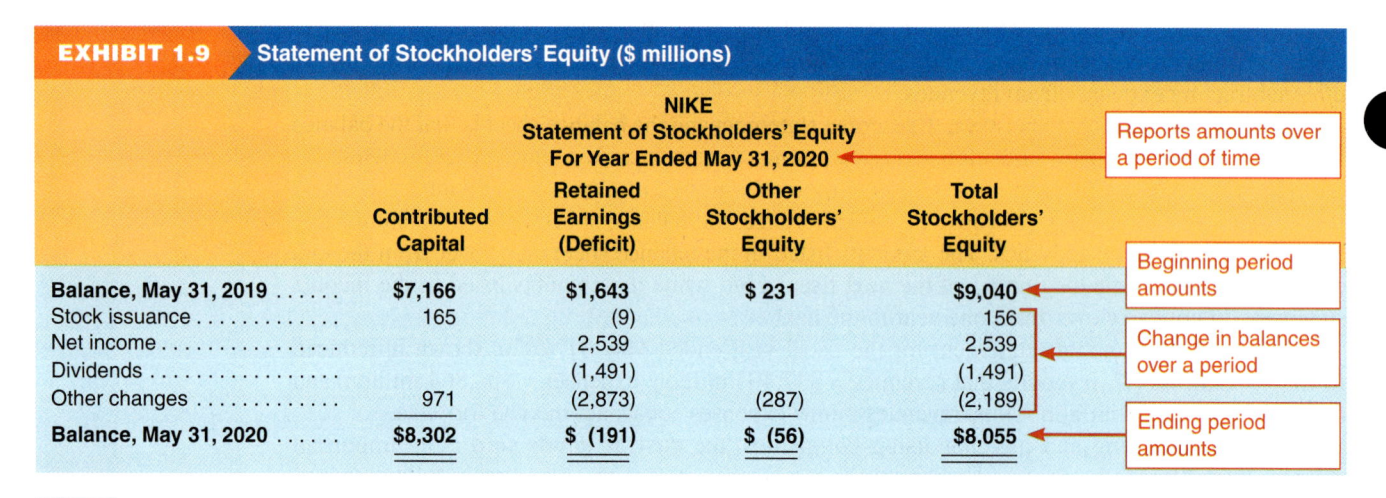

EXHIBIT 1.9 — Statement of Stockholders' Equity ($ millions)

NIKE
Statement of Stockholders' Equity
For Year Ended May 31, 2020

	Contributed Capital	Retained Earnings (Deficit)	Other Stockholders' Equity	Total Stockholders' Equity
Balance, May 31, 2019......	$7,166	$1,643	$ 231	$9,040
Stock issuance.............	165	(9)		156
Net income................		2,539		2,539
Dividends..................		(1,491)		(1,491)
Other changes.............	971	(2,873)	(287)	(2,189)
Balance, May 31, 2020......	$8,302	$ (191)	$ (56)	$8,055

Reports amounts over a period of time
Beginning period amounts
Change in balances over a period
Ending period amounts

FYI Dividends are reported in the statement of equity, and not in the income statement.

Contributed capital represents the net amount received from issuing stock to shareholders (owners). **Retained earnings** (also called *earned capital*) represents the income the company has earned since its inception, minus the dividends it has paid out to shareholders. Thus, retained earnings equals the amount of income retained in the company. The change in retained earnings links consecutive balance sheets through the income statement. Nike's retained earnings decreased from $1,643 million on May 31, 2019, to $(191) million on May 31, 2020. This decrease is explained by net income of $2,539 million, less dividends of $1,491 million and other reductions of $2,882 million. The category titled "other changes" refers to changes in equity that are not recorded in income. This concept is discussed in Chapter 11.

Statement of Cash Flows

FYI Cash is critical to operations because it is necessary for purchasing resources and paying bills.

The **statement of cash flows** reports net cash flows from operating, investing, and financing activities over a period of time. Nike's statement of cash flows for fiscal year ended May 31, 2020, is shown in a reduced format in **Exhibit 1.10**. The statement reports that the cash balance increased by $3,882 million during the fiscal year. Operating activities provided $2,485 million (a cash inflow), investing activities used $1,028 million (a cash outflow), and financing activities provided $2,491 million (a cash inflow). These changes increased Nike's ending balance of cash to $8,348 million.

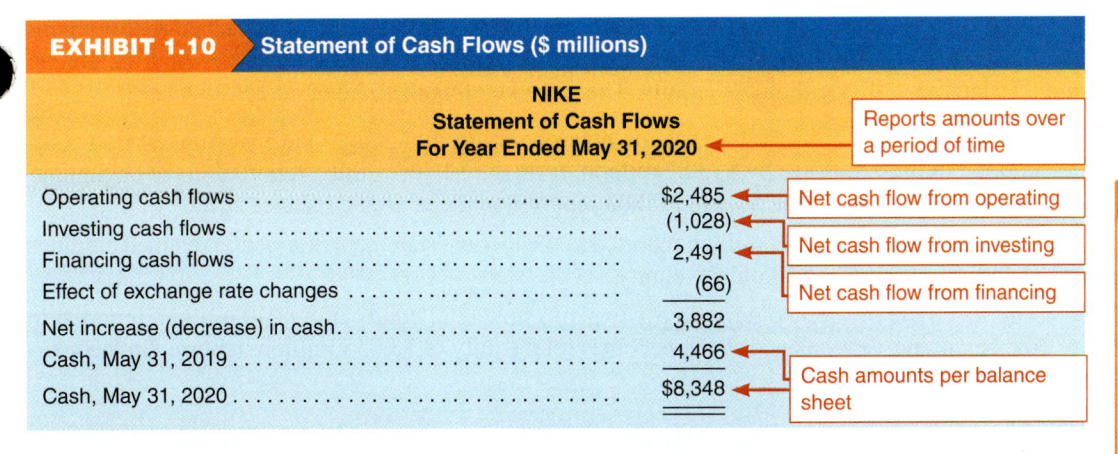

EXHIBIT 1.10 — Statement of Cash Flows ($ millions)

NIKE
Statement of Cash Flows
For Year Ended May 31, 2020 ← Reports amounts over a period of time

Operating cash flows	$2,485 ← Net cash flow from operating
Investing cash flows	(1,028) ← Net cash flow from investing
Financing cash flows	2,491
Effect of exchange rate changes	(66) ← Net cash flow from financing
Net increase (decrease) in cash	3,882
Cash, May 31, 2019	4,466 ← Cash amounts per balance sheet
Cash, May 31, 2020	$8,348

FYI Common formatting for U.S. financial statements includes:
- Dollar sign next to first and last amount listed in a column
- Single underline before a subtraction or addition; double underline after a major total
- Assets listed in order of liquidity, which is nearness to cash
- Liabilities listed in order of due dates

Operating cash flow is the amount of cash generated from operating activities. This amount usually differs from net income due to differences between the time that revenues and expenses are recorded and the time that the related cash receipts and disbursements occur. For example, a company may report revenues for goods sold to customers this period, but not collect the payment until next period. Consistent with most companies, Nike's operating cash flows of $2,485 million do not equal its net income of $2,539 million. **Exhibit 1.11** compares net income and operating cash flows for Nike and several other companies. The exhibit shows that there is large variation across companies in the amount of net income and operating cash flows.

Both cash flow and net income are important for making business decisions. They each capture different aspects of firm performance and together help financial statement users better understand and assess a company's past, present, and future business activities.

EXHIBIT 1.11 — Comparison of Net Income to Operating Cash Flows

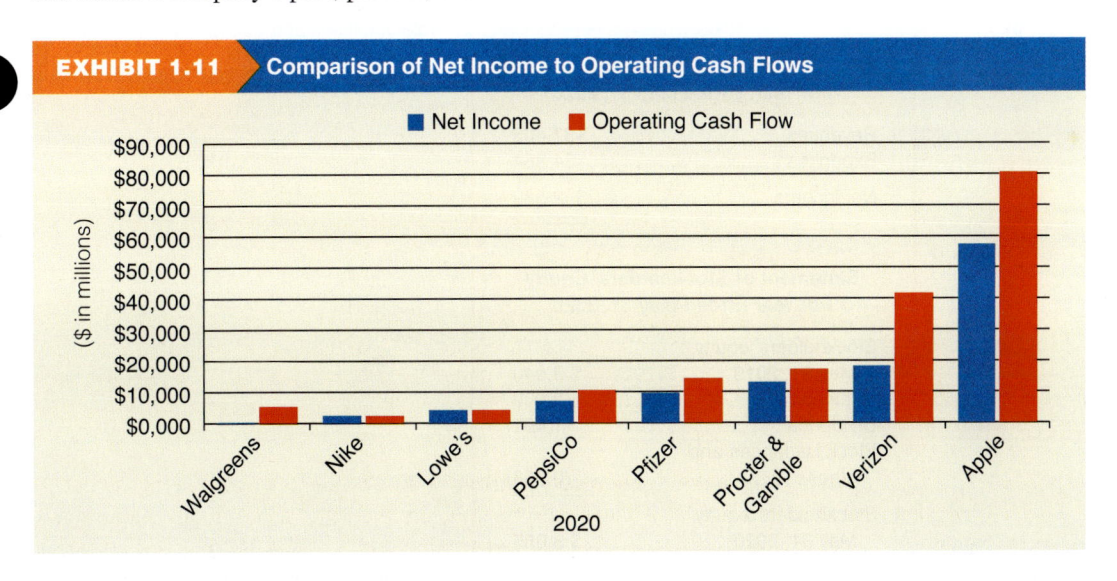

Bar chart (2020, $ in millions) comparing Net Income and Operating Cash Flow for: Walgreens, Nike, Lowe's, PepsiCo, Pfizer, Procter & Gamble, Verizon, Apple.

Financial Statement Linkages

A central feature of the accounting system is the linkage among the four primary statements, referred to as the *articulation* of the financial statements. Three of the key linkages are:

- The statement of cash flows links the beginning and ending cash in the balance sheet.
- The income statement links the beginning and ending retained earnings in the statement of stockholders' equity.
- The statement of stockholders' equity links the beginning and ending equity in the balance sheet.

Exhibit 1.12 demonstrates these links using Nike's financial statements from **Exhibits 1.6** through **1.10**. The left side of **Exhibit 1.12** presents Nike's beginning-year balance sheet for fiscal year 2020 (which is the same as the balance sheet for the end of fiscal year 2019), and the right side presents Nike's year-end balance sheet for fiscal year 2020. These balance sheets report Nike's investing and financing activities at the beginning and end of the fiscal year, two distinct points in time. The middle column of **Exhibit 1.12** presents the three financial statements that report Nike's fiscal year 2020 business activities over time: the statement of cash flows, the income statement, and the statement of stockholders' equity. The three key linkages shown in **Exhibit 1.12** are:

- The statement of cash flows explains how operating, financing, and investing activities increased the cash balance by $3,882 million, from the $4,466 million reported in the beginning-year balance sheet, to the $8,348 million reported in the year-end balance sheet.
- The net income of $2,539 million reported in the income statement is added to retained earnings in the statement of stockholders' equity.
- The statement of stockholders' equity explains how total equity of $9,040 million, reported in the beginning-year balance sheet, becomes total equity of $8,055 million, reported in the year-end balance sheet.

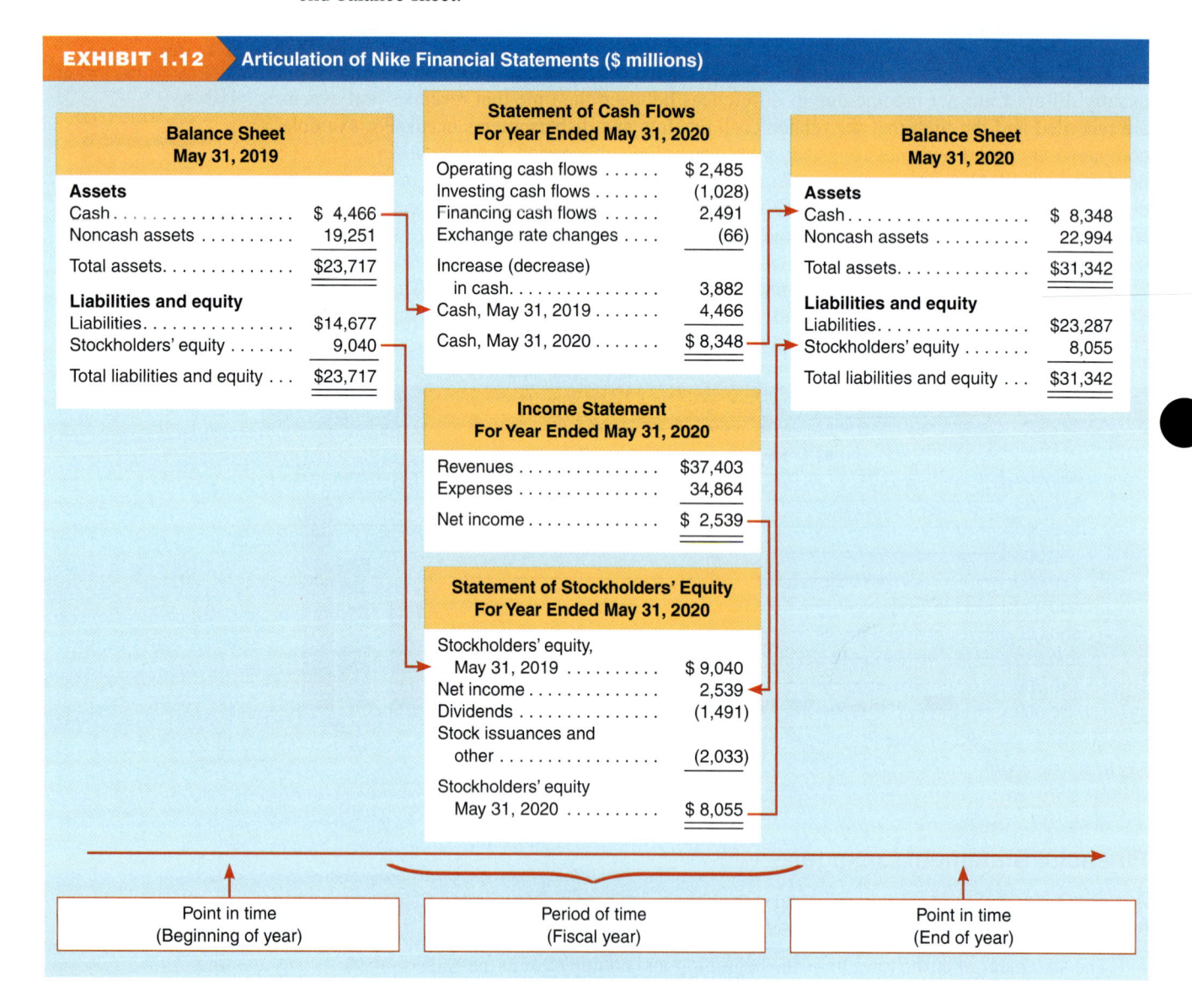

EXHIBIT 1.12 Articulation of Nike Financial Statements ($ millions)

Balance Sheet
May 31, 2019

Assets
Cash.................... $ 4,466
Noncash assets 19,251
Total assets............. $23,717

Liabilities and equity
Liabilities............... $14,677
Stockholders' equity 9,040
Total liabilities and equity ... $23,717

Statement of Cash Flows
For Year Ended May 31, 2020

Operating cash flows ...... $ 2,485
Investing cash flows .... (1,028)
Financing cash flows 2,491
Exchange rate changes .... (66)
Increase (decrease)
 in cash................. 3,882
Cash, May 31, 2019 4,466
Cash, May 31, 2020 .... $ 8,348

Income Statement
For Year Ended May 31, 2020

Revenues $37,403
Expenses 34,864
Net income .... $ 2,539

Statement of Stockholders' Equity
For Year Ended May 31, 2020

Stockholders' equity,
 May 31, 2019 .... $ 9,040
Net income.............. 2,539
Dividends .... (1,491)
Stock issuances and
 other .... (2,033)
Stockholders' equity
 May 31, 2020 .... $ 8,055

Balance Sheet
May 31, 2020

Assets
Cash.................... $ 8,348
Noncash assets 22,994
Total assets............. $31,342

Liabilities and equity
Liabilities............... $23,287
Stockholders' equity 8,055
Total liabilities and equity ... $31,342

Point in time (Beginning of year) — Period of time (Fiscal year) — Point in time (End of year)

Information Beyond Financial Statements

FYI An analysis of a firm's activities requires extensive study of its disclosure notes and the MD&A.

Important information about a company is communicated to various decision-makers through reports other than financial statements. These reports include the following:

- Management Discussion and Analysis (MD&A)
- Independent Auditor Report
- Financial statement disclosure notes

- Regulatory filings, including proxy statements and other SEC filings

We describe and explain the usefulness of these additional information sources throughout the book.

Preparing Financial Statements

LO1-3 Review 1-3

Based in Germany, **Adidas** is one of **Nike**'s primary competitors. It markets athletic shoes and apparel under the Adidas and Reebok brands. It also sells Solomon ski equipment as well as TaylorMade golf equipment. Adidas's financial statements are reported in euros, the currency of the European Union. The statements are also prepared using International Financial Reporting Standards (IFRS). The following information is from the company's December 31, 2019, financial statements (€ millions):

	2019
Cash and cash equivalents	€ 2,220
Cash flow from operations	2,819
Sales revenue	23,640
Stockholders' equity	7,058
Cost of goods sold	11,347
Cash flow used for financing	(2,273)
Total liabilities	13,622
Net other expenses	10,316
Noncash assets	18,460
Cash flow used for investing	(925)
Net income	1,977
Cash, beginning of year	2,629
Effect of exchange rates on cash	(30)

Required

a. Prepare Adidas's balance sheet at December 31, 2019, and its income statement and statement of cash flows for the fiscal year ended December 31, 2019.
b. Compare Adidas's revenue, net income, and cash flow from operations to that of Nike (as reported in this chapter). Assume an exchange rate of €1.00 = $1.12.

Solution on p. 1-40.

FINANCIAL REPORTING ENVIRONMENT

Information presented in financial statements is of critical importance to external decision-makers. Financial statements affect the prices paid for equity securities, such as a company's common stock, and interest rates attached to debt. To the extent that financial performance and condition are accurately communicated to business decision-makers, debt and equity securities are more accurately priced. By extension, financial reporting plays a crucial role in efficient resource allocation within and across economies. Accounting information contributes to the efficient operation of securities markets, labor markets, commodity markets, and other markets.

LO1-4 Describe how standardized accounting principles and a regulatory environment are important to financial statement integrity.

To illustrate, imagine the consequences of a breakdown in the integrity of financial reporting. The Enron scandal provides a case in point. At the beginning of 2001, **Enron** was one of the more, if not the most, innovative and respected companies in the United States. With revenues of over $100 billion and total company value of over $60 billion, it was the fifth largest U.S. corporation based on market value. In October 2001, the company released its third quarter earnings report to the public. Although operating earnings were higher than in previous years, the income statement contained a $1 billion "special charge." Financial analysts began investigating the cause of this charge and discovered that it was linked to related-party transactions and questionable accounting practices. Once it became clear to the capital markets that Enron had not faithfully and accurately reported its financial condition and performance, people became unwilling to purchase its securities. The value of its debt and equity securities dropped precipitously, and the company was unable to obtain the cash needed for operating activities. By the end of 2001, Enron was bankrupt!

Unfortunately, the demise of Enron didn't deter all cases of fraud. For example, **Luckin Coffee**, a China-based company whose shares had been trading on the Nasdaq, agreed to pay $180 million in penalties to the Securities and Exchange Commission (a federal commission described in the next section) in December 2020. The charges relate to a material overstatement of revenues and related expenses in order to falsely report a period of rapid growth. In another case, former executives of **FTE Networks** were charged with fraud by the Securities and Exchange Commission in July 2021. Among the charges were inflating revenue and keeping liabilities off of the balance sheet. These cases illustrate the importance of reliable financial reporting. Accountants recognize the importance of the information that they produce and, as a profession, they agree to follow a set of standards for the presentation of financial statements and the disclosure of related financial information. In the following paragraphs, we discuss these standards, or *principles*, as well as the institutional and regulatory environment in which accountants operate.

Generally Accepted Accounting Principles

Decision-makers who rely on audited financial statements expect that all companies follow similar procedures in preparing their statements. In response to these expectations, U.S. accountants have developed a set of standards and procedures called **generally accepted accounting principles (GAAP)**. GAAP is not a set of immutable laws. Instead, it is a set of standards and accepted practices, based on underlying principles, that are designed to guide the preparation of the financial statements. GAAP is subject to change as conditions warrant. As a result, specific rules are altered or new practices are formulated to fit changes in underlying economic circumstances or business transactions.

Some people mistakenly assume that financial accounting is an exact discipline—that is, companies select the proper standard to account for a transaction and then follow the rules. The reality is that GAAP allows companies considerable discretion in preparing financial statements. The choice of methods often yields financial statements that are markedly different from one company to another in terms of reported income, assets, liabilities, and equity amounts. In addition, financial statements depend on numerous estimates. Consequently, even though two companies may engage in the same transactions and choose the same accounting methods, their financial statements will differ because their managements have made different estimates about such things as the amount to be collected from customers who buy on credit, the length of time that buildings and equipment will be in use, and the future costs for product warranties.

Accounting standard setters walk a fine line regarding choice in accounting. On one hand, they are concerned that management discretion in preparing financial statements will lead to abuse by those seeking to influence the decisions of those who rely on the statements. On the other hand, they are concerned that companies are too diverse for a "one size fits all" financial accounting system. Ultimately, GAAP attempts to strike a balance by imposing constraints on the choice of accounting procedures, while allowing companies some flexibility within those constraints.

YOU MAKE THE CALL

You are a Financial Analyst Accountants, business leaders, and politicians have long debated the importance of considering the **economic consequences** of accounting standards (GAAP). Should accounting standards be designed to influence behavior and affect social or economic change considered by, say, a government body or other interested group? Alternatively, should such standards be designed simply to provide relevant and reliable information on which economic decisions can be made by others with a reasonable degree of confidence? What do you believe the objectives of financial reporting should be? [Answers on page 1-29.]

Regulation and Oversight

Following the U.S. stock market crash of 1929, the United States Congress passed the Securities Acts of 1933 and 1934. These acts were passed to require disclosure of financial and other information about securities being offered for public sale and to prohibit deceit, misrepresentations, and other fraud in the sale of securities. The 1934 Act created the **Securities and Exchange**

Commission (SEC) and gave it broad powers to regulate the issuance and trading of securities. The act also provided that companies with more than $10 million in assets and whose securities are held by more than 500 owners must file annual and other periodic reports, including a complete set of financial statements.

While the SEC has ultimate authority over financial reporting by companies in the United States, it has ceded the task of setting accounting standards to a professional body, the **American Institute of Certified Public Accountants (AICPA)**. Over the years, this process has resulted in three standard-setting organizations.

Currently, accounting standards are established by the **Financial Accounting Standards Board (FASB)**. The FASB is a seven-member board that has the primary responsibility for setting financial accounting standards in the United States. In 2009, the FASB codified the standards into the FASB Accounting Standards Codification. This is now the single source of authoritative, non-governmental U.S. GAAP.

BUSINESS INSIGHT

Accounting can be complicated—but rule-makers are trying to make it a little simpler.
The Financial Accounting Standards Board, which sets accounting rules for U.S. companies, launched the FASB Simplification Initiative in 2014. The objective of the initiative is to make financial reporting a little less complex and reduce costs for companies and their accountants, while maintaining or improving the quality of information reported.

The projects are relatively narrow, straightforward changes in accounting that clearly would help reduce complexity and that the board expects to be able to make relatively quickly, without the years of work that often accompany major revisions in accounting rules.

"Complexity in accounting can be costly to both investors and companies," FASB Chairman Russ Golden said. The simplification initiative, which FASB began in June 2014, "is focused on identifying areas that we can address quickly and effectively, without compromising the quality of information provided to investors."

Besides setting standards for financial accounting, the FASB has developed a framework to form the basis for future discussion of proposed standards and serve as a guide to accountants for reporting information that is not governed by specific standards. A summary of this *Conceptual Framework* is presented in Appendix 1A later in this chapter.

In the wake of the Enron, Tyco, AOL, Global Crossing, Halliburton, Xerox, Adelphia, Bristol-Myers Squibb, and WorldCom scandals, concerns over the quality of corporate financial reporting led Congress to pass the **Sarbanes-Oxley Act** in 2002. The goal of this act—sometimes referred to as SOX—was to increase the level of confidence that external users, particularly investors, have in the financial statements. To accomplish this objective, SOX imposed a number of requirements to strengthen audit committees and improve deficient **internal controls** by:

- increasing management's responsibility for accounting information,
- increasing the independence of the auditors,
- increasing the accountability of the board of directors,
- establishing adequate internal controls (policies and operating processes designed to prevent fraud and protect company resources).

SOX requires that the chief executive officer (CEO) and the chief financial officer (CFO) of a publicly traded corporation personally sign a statement attesting to the accuracy and completeness of financial statements. The prospect of severe penalties is designed to make these managers more vigilant in monitoring the financial accounting process. In addition, SOX established the **Public Company Accounting Oversight Board (PCAOB)** to approve auditing standards and monitor the quality of financial statements and audits.

The Sarbanes-Oxley Act is not without critics. One criticism is that the penalties imposed on management for misstatements or errors are too severe. Some argue that managers have become less forthcoming in their disclosures and more conservative in choosing accounting methods and making accrual estimates to avoid the possibility of heavy fines or criminal charges.

Role of the Auditor

What prevents a company from disclosing false or misleading information? For one thing, the financial statements are prepared by management, and management must take responsibility for what is disclosed. Management's reputation can be severely damaged by false disclosures when subsequent events unfold to refute the information. This situation can adversely affect the firm's ability to compete in capital, labor, and consumer markets. It can also lead to litigation and even criminal charges against management.

Even though management must personally attest to the accuracy and completeness of the financial statements, markets also demand assurances from independent parties. Therefore, the financial statements of publicly traded corporations must be **audited** by an *independent audit firm*. The auditors provide an opinion as to whether the statements *present fairly* and *in all material respects* a company's financial condition and the results of its operations.

The audit opinion is not a guarantee. Auditors only provide reasonable assurance that the financial statements are free of material misstatements. Even so, auditors provide a valuable service. Auditors effectively ensure that the information contained in the financial statements is reliable, thus increasing the confidence of outside decision-makers in the information they use to make investment, credit, and other decisions. Therefore, creditors and shareholders of privately held corporations often demand that the financial statements be audited as well.

Public corporations are required to establish audit committees whose purpose is not to audit but, rather, to appoint the audit firm and ensure that what is learned in the audit is disclosed to the firm's directors and shareholders.

YOU MAKE THE CALL

You are a Member of the Board of Directors   Until recently accounting firms were permitted to earn money for consulting activities performed for clients they audited. Do you see any reason why this might not be an acceptable practice? Do you see any advantage to your firm from allowing such activity? [Answer on page 1-30.]

A Global Perspective

Businesses increasingly operate in global markets. Consumers and businesses with access to the Internet can purchase products and services from anywhere in the world. Products produced in one country are often made with parts and materials imported from many different countries. Businesses outsource parts of operations to other countries to take advantage of better labor markets in those countries. Capital markets are global as well. Corporations whose securities trade on the New York Stock Exchange may also trade on exchanges in London, Toronto, Tokyo, or Hong Kong.

The globalization of capital markets, combined with the diversity of international accounting principles, led to an effort to increase comparability of financial information across countries. The **International Accounting Standards Board (IASB)** oversees the development of accounting standards outside the United States. Over 100 countries, including those in the European Union, require the use of **International Financial Reporting Standards (IFRS)** developed by the IASB.[5] The intention is to unify all public companies under one global set of reporting standards. The remaining major capital markets without an IFRS mandate are the U.S. (with no current plans to adopt), Japan (where voluntary adoption is permitted), and China (where standards are substantially converged and the country has plans to adopt).

Financial statements prepared under IFRS and U.S. GAAP are quite similar, yet important differences remain. For example, balance sheets prepared under IFRS often classify assets in reverse order of liquidity to those prepared under GAAP. Thus, intangible assets are listed first and cash last on the balance sheet. Both approaches require the same basic set of four financial statements, with explanatory disclosure notes. We shall examine some of the more important differences under a Global Perspective heading as they arise in future chapters. Websites maintained by the larger accounting firms as well as both the FASB and IASB provide considerable information.

Global Perspectives *examine issues related to similarities and differences in accounting practices of the U.S. and other countries.*

A GLOBAL PERSPECTIVE

Since 2007, the SEC allows foreign companies to report their financial results using international accounting standards rather than reconciling their financial statements to American rules. While this change made it easier for U.S. investors to purchase securities from around the world, a *New York Times* article referred to a "Tower of Babel in Accounting." The article raises concerns about the difficulty of comparing companies when their financial statements are based on diverse reporting standards. The situation is complicated by the fact that a number of developing countries have reserved the right to adopt exceptions to IFRS when deemed appropriate.

Review 1-4
Identifying Roles in the Development and Regulation of Financial Reporting LO1-4

Match each of the following terms with the most appropriate explanation of its relationship to financial reporting.

Terms: (a) Auditor, (b) FASB, (c) GAAP, (d) Internal controls, (e) Management, (f) PCAOB, (g) SEC

1. ____ Set of authoritative standards and accepted practices that guide the preparation of financial statements in the U.S.
2. ____ Organization that has the ultimate authority over financial reporting.
3. ____ Currently codifies new accounting standards that guide financial reporting.
4. ____ Approves auditing standards and monitors audits of public companies that are required to report annual results.
5. ____ Takes responsibility for the accuracy and completeness of information disclosed in the financial statements.
6. ____ Provides an opinion on the fair presentation of a company's financial reporting.
7. ____ Helps ensure the accuracy of a company's financial reporting through a system of internal monitoring procedures and rules.

Solution on p. 1-40.

---

[5] Because it is international in its scope, the IASB has no legal authority to impose accounting standards on any country. Despite the push for comparability, not everyone is convinced that IFRS will improve the usefulness of accounting information. As one observer put it, "There is a real risk of a veneer of comparability that hides a lot of differences." A number of countries have reserved the right to adopt exceptions to IFRS when they deem them to be appropriate.

ANALYZING FINANCIAL STATEMENTS

*Each chapter includes a section on **Analyzing Financial Statements** to emphasize the use of accounting information in making business decisions.*

LO1-5 Compute two key ratios that are commonly used to assess profitability and risk—return on equity and the debt-to-equity ratio.

The financial statements provide insights into the financial health and performance of a company. However, the accounting data presented in these statements are difficult to interpret in raw form. For example, knowing that Nike's net income was $2,539 million in the fiscal year ended May 2020 is, by itself, not very useful. Similarly, knowing the dollar amount of liabilities does not tell us whether or not Nike relies too heavily on creditor financing.

Financial analysts use a number of tools to help interpret the information found in the financial statements. They look at trends over time and compare one company to another. They calculate ratios using financial statement information to summarize the data in a form that is easier to interpret. Ratios also allow us to compare the performance and condition of different companies even if the companies being compared are dramatically different in size. Finally, ratios help analysts spot trends or changes in performance over time.

Throughout the book, we introduce ratios that are commonly used by financial analysts and other users who rely on the financial statements. Our goal is to develop an understanding of how to effectively use the information in the financial statements, as well as to demonstrate how these statements are prepared. In this chapter we introduce one important measure of **profitability** and one measure of financial **risk**.

Profitability Analysis

Profitability reveals whether or not a company is able to bring its product or service to the market in an efficient manner and whether the market values that product or service. Companies that are consistently unprofitable are unlikely to succeed in the long run.

A key profitability metric for stockholders and other decision-makers is company return on equity. This metric compares the level of net income with the amount of equity financing used to generate that income.

Analysis Objective

We are trying to determine Nike's ability to earn a return for its stockholders.

Analysis Tool   Return on Equity

$$\text{Return on equity} = \frac{\text{Net income}}{\text{Average stockholders' equity*}}$$

*The average is computed by adding the beginning and ending balances of stockholders' equity and dividing by two.

Applying the Return on Equity Ratio to Nike

Fiscal Year Ended May 31:

2018: $\dfrac{\$1,933}{[(\$9,812 + \$12,407)/2]} = 0.174$ or 17.4%

2019: $\dfrac{\$4,029}{[(\$9,040 + \$9,812)/2]} = 0.427$ or 42.7%

2020: $\dfrac{\$2,539}{[(\$8,055 + \$9,040)/2]} = 0.297$ or 29.7%

Guidance   Taken over time, ROE ratios that are over 10% and preferably increasing suggest the company is earning reasonable returns. For firms that are in more risky businesses, such as renewable power, even larger returns on equity would be appropriate, while firms in less risky endeavors, such as large food chains, would not be expected to generate as large returns.

Nike in Context

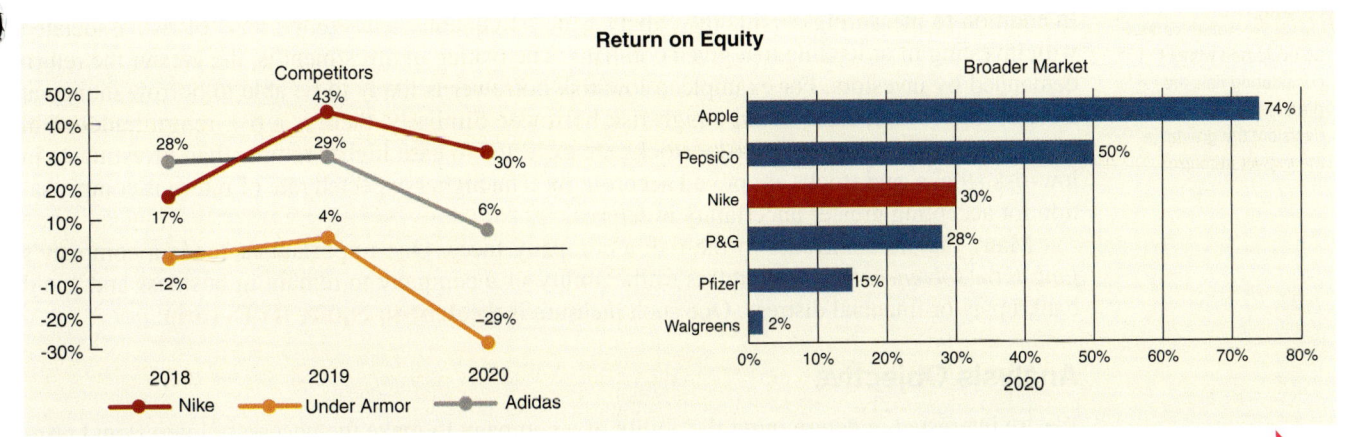

Return on Equity

Competitors:
- Nike: 2018: 17%, 2019: 43%, 2020: 30%
- Under Armor: 2018: -2%, 2019: 4%, 2020: -29%
- Adidas: 2018: 28%, 2019: 29%, 2020: 6%

Broader Market (2020):
- Apple: 74%
- PepsiCo: 50%
- Nike: 30%
- P&G: 28%
- Pfizer: 15%
- Walgreens: 2%

These companies do not have identical fiscal year-ends. For each fiscal year listed, balance sheets are dated from May 31 to December 31 of that year.

Data visualizations are used throughout the text to convey financial information.

Takeaways Over the time period covered by our calculations and by the chart, it is clear that Nike has done very well earning returns for its stockholders. Nike earned an ROE of over 42% for the year ended May 31, 2019 and almost 30% for the year ended May 31, 2020. These are exceptionally high ROE numbers and exceed the returns of its competitors, Adidas and Under Armor. Several new companies have entered the market, and Nike will need to continue developing new products to preserve its market leadership.

Other Considerations As with all ratios, care in their interpretation is essential. First, we need to be careful about comparing companies that operate in different product markets.

Second, regulation, such as applicable tax laws, can be different across countries and over time. In December of 2017 the U.S. enacted a new tax law known as the **Tax Cuts and Jobs Act (TCJA)**. (We discuss the TCJA in more detail in Chapter 10.) Many companies, including Nike, had to account for some of the provisions of the TCJA in the year that contained December 2017—for Nike this is the year that ended May 31, 2018. Nike's tax expense increased significantly, lowering net income. These one-time charges are part of the explanation of the lower ROE in 2018 computed above.[6]

Third, firms with different customer or supplier demographics can also produce different conclusions. Furthermore, different management policies toward assets and liabilities have their own unique effect on ratios across firms. For example, the conversion of inventories to sales can be subject to slowdowns that affect companies differently, within the same industry.

Fourth, these measures can be altered by management decisions designed solely for cosmetic effects such as improving current earnings or an important ratio. Thus, delaying inventory orders or filling sales orders early can lead to increasing net income and ROE in current periods to the detriment of future periods.

Finally, differences in the fiscal year-end of companies can influence a comparison of ROE ratios. If one company's fiscal year ends in May and another company's fiscal year ends in December, economic conditions may change between May and December, creating differences in ROE that are not due to differences in the operations of the two companies. For example, in 2020 the COVID-19 pandemic began to have an impact on businesses in March. The effect of the pandemic on a company's financial statements would depend on when the company's fiscal year ended. A company that had a fiscal year-end on June 30 might show a much different picture than a company with a December 31 fiscal year-end.

---

[6] The TCJA decreased the U.S. corporate statutory tax rate to 21% (from a graduated rate that topped out at 35%). However, the TCJA also required taxation of prior foreign earnings that many companies had not accrued U.S. tax on previously. This was the case for Nike, and it had to accrue a significant amount of U.S. tax (what Nike labels a transition tax in its report), leading to the higher tax expense for 2018. As a ballpark estimation, if we assume the same tax expense as in 2017 for Nike (and adjust earnings and equity accordingly), the ROE would have been 21.5% for 2018.

Credit Risk Analysis

FYI Return cannot be evaluated without considering risk; the greater the risk of any decision, the greater the expected return.

In addition to measuring profitability, analysts also frequently analyze the level of risk associated with investing in or lending to a given company. The riskier an investment is, the greater the return demanded by investors. For example, a low-risk borrower is likely to be able to borrow money at a lower interest rate than would a high-risk borrower. Similarly, there is a risk-return trade-off in equity returns. Investments in risky stocks are expected to earn higher returns than investments in low-risk stocks, and stocks are priced accordingly. The higher expected rate of return is compensation for accepting greater uncertainty in returns.

Many factors contribute to the risk a company faces. One important factor is a company's *long-term solvency*. **Solvency** refers to the ability of a company to remain in business and avoid bankruptcy or financial distress. One such measure is the **debt-to-equity (D/E) ratio**.

Analysis Objective

We are interested in determining the ability of a company to make the necessary interest and principal payments on its debt.

Analysis Tool Debt-to-Equity

$$\text{Debt-to-equity ratio} = \frac{\text{Total liabilities}}{\text{Total stockholders' equity}}$$

Applying the Debt-to-Equity Ratio to Nike

May 31, 2018: $\frac{\$12{,}724}{\$9{,}812} = 1.30$

May 31, 2019: $\frac{\$14{,}677}{\$9{,}040} = 1.62$

May 31, 2020: $\frac{\$23{,}287}{\$8{,}055} = 2.89$

Guidance Solvency is closely related to the extent a company relies on creditor financing. As the amount of creditor financing increases, the possibility of bankruptcy also increases. Short of bankruptcy, a company that has borrowed too much will occasionally find that the required interest payments are hurting the company's cash flow. The debt-to-equity ratio is an important measure used by analysts and others to assess a company's ability to make the necessary interest and principal payments on its debt.

Nike in Context

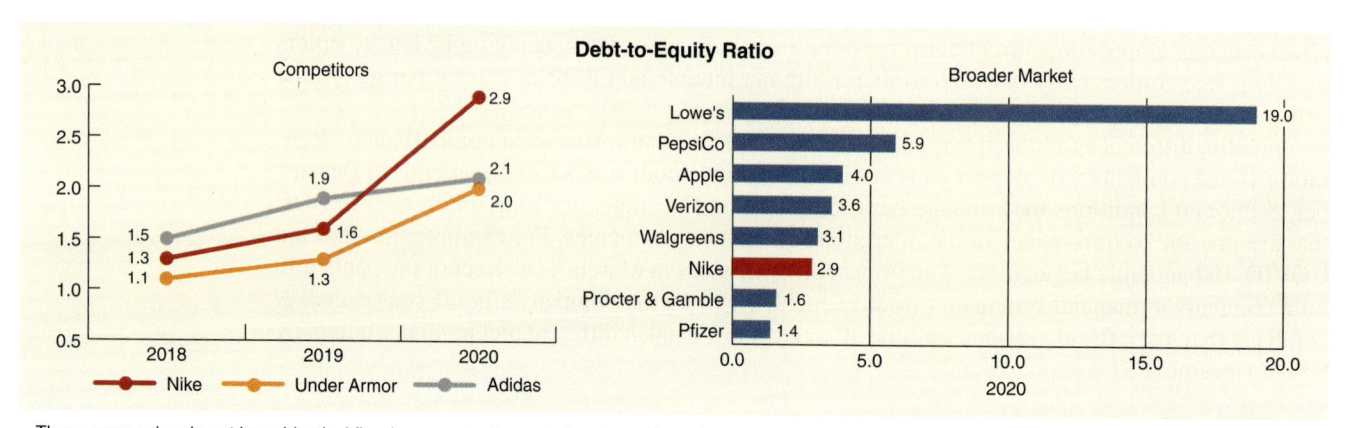

Debt-to-Equity Ratio

Competitors (2018–2020):
- Nike: 1.3 (2018), 1.6 (2019), 2.9 (2020)
- Under Armor: 1.1 (2018), 1.3 (2019), 2.0 (2020)
- Adidas: 1.5 (2018), 1.9 (2019), 2.1 (2020)

Broader Market (2020):
- Lowe's: 19.0
- PepsiCo: 5.9
- Apple: 4.0
- Verizon: 3.6
- Walgreens: 3.1
- Nike: 2.9
- Procter & Gamble: 1.6
- Pfizer: 1.4

These companies do not have identical fiscal year-ends. For each fiscal year listed, balance sheets are dated from January 31 to December 31 of that year.

A debt-to equity ratio of one indicates that the company is using equal parts of debt and equity financing. Nike's debt-to-equity ratio has increased significantly since at least 2012, when it was 0.49.

The appropriate D/E ratio level depends on the nature of the business and will differ appreciably, as can be seen in the chart above. Typically, firms with large long-term commitments often reflected in fixed assets will find it appropriate to raise more capital through borrowing. The amount of debt relative to equity will also mirror the risk tolerance of the firm's management. If management believes it can earn a return above the debt interest cost, borrowing will increase the expected return to the owners.

Takeaways Nike's D/E ratio has increased over the three years presented. Nike's liabilities have been steadily increasing. Yet, stockholders' equity has not increased at the same pace. Indeed, by 2020, Nike has a significantly higher D/E ratio than its closest competitors. As we will discuss in Chapter 5, the ROE ratio discussed earlier and the D/E ratio are closely related. Nike's high ROE, relative to its competitors, can be explained in part by its higher D/E ratio. By relying more on debt financing, Nike is leveraging its profitability resulting in a higher ROE.

Other Considerations Comparisons with other companies in similar lines of business, such as Under Armour and Adidas, are always appropriate. New competitors, such as Quiksilver, could also prove insightful to examine in regard to strategic decisions. In Chapter 9, we will explore the accounting for liabilities in more depth. Balance sheets do not always recognize all obligations of a firm, and a careful reader will examine the disclosure notes to get a more complete picture of financial health in such comparisons. Nike might also consider increasing its debt level if profitable opportunities exist. The company has been, and remains, very successful, but new entrants are emerging indicating there is additional business to be had.

The chart shows that Nike has a similar and somewhat relatively lower D/E ratio when compared to the other companies we show. Procter & Gamble and Pfizer have lower D/Es, but Apple and PepsiCo have higher D/Es. Lowe's D/E is considerably higher than all other comparison companies.

There are other measures of profitability and risk that will be introduced in later chapters. Collectively, these ratios, when placed in the context of the company's business activities, help to provide a clear picture of the *drivers* of a company's financial performance and the factors affecting its financial condition. Understanding these performance drivers and their impact on the financial health of a company is key to effectively using the information presented in the financial statements.

Technology and Accounting

New technological innovations arise frequently, and they often increase the capabilities of businesses and make them more efficient. Recently, data analytics and blockchain technology have emerged as two prominent business-changing innovations. Many companies, including **Amazon** and **Google**, use data analysis throughout their organizations to make business decisions. **Data analytics** can broadly be defined as the process of examining large sets of data with the goal of discovering useful information from patterns found in the data. Business people employing data analytics can glean important insights from large data sets and identify opportunities for growth and operational efficiency. Data analysis has many applications, and you will encounter it in many disciplines beyond accounting.

Blockchain was made famous as the underpinning technology used for digital currencies, such as **Bitcoin** and **Ethereum**. **Blockchain** is a distributed digital ledger that provides a secure means for approved parties to view recorded transactions. This technology has wide-ranging implications for business and is expected to greatly affect the way accountants perform audits.

Understanding what data analytics and blockchain technology are and how they are used is the first step toward developing marketable skills in each area, so we have included examples of each at various points in the book. Each chapter includes data analysis and data visualization assignments. In addition, **Appendix B** at the end of this book provides a more detailed discussion of data analytics.

ORGANIZATION OF THE BOOK

In the pages that follow Chapter 1, we will explore the financial accounting model and how it reflects an organization's activities and events. Chapters 2 and 3 are focused on building the balance sheet and the income statement from transactions and a set of required adjustments. This process requires a structure for "bookkeeping" and an understanding of the basic rules of the accounting language. When do we recognize revenue? When do we recognize an asset? We will look at these questions in a relatively simple setting.

In Chapter 4, we will construct the statement of cash flows. The balance sheet, income statement, and statement of cash flows are all built on the same underlying set of information, and they are each designed to give a different perspective on what's going on in the company. Chapter 5 shows how managers and investors organize financial information using ratios and how managers and investors use those ratios to compare companies and to make forecasts of the future.

While the first five chapters build the financial statement structure and its interpretation, the latter seven chapters are more topical. Accounting is not a cut-and-dried process, and financial reports can be affected by a variety of management decisions. So these seven chapters explore more sophisticated settings and analyses. We will find that financial reports rely on management estimates of future events and that sometimes management has the freedom to choose accounting methods that affect income and assets. And, when accounting practices don't allow reporting discretion, management's choice of transactions can make financial reports look more favorable.

Becoming an effective user of financial information requires an understanding of how the financial reports fit together and a willingness to explore the disclosure notes material to look for useful information. As we progress through *Financial Accounting* together, we will show you how to become a sophisticated reader of financial reports by looking at real companies and real financial statement information.

Review 1-5 LO1-5   Computing Return on Equity and Debt-to-Equity Ratios

Adidas, a major competitor of Nike, markets athletic shoes and apparel under the Adidas and Reebok brands. It also sells Solomon ski equipment and TaylorMade golf equipment. The following information is from Adidas's 2019 financial statements (Adidas's financial statements are reported in Euros, the currency of the European Union):

(millions)	Adidas
Net income (loss) (2019)	€ 1,977
Stockholders' equity (2019 year-end)	7,058
Stockholders' equity (2018 year-end)	6,364
Total liabilities (2019 year-end)	13,622

Required
a. Calculate the 2019 return on equity (ROE) ratio for Adidas.
b. Calculate the 2019 debt-to-equity ratio for Adidas.
c. Compare the profitability and risk of Adidas to that of Nike. Note: In your analysis, compare FY 2020 statements of Nike (12 months ended May 31, 2020) to 2019 statements of Adidas (12 months ended December 31, 2019).

Solution on p. 1-41.

APPENDIX 1A: Conceptual Framework for Financial Reporting

LO1-6 Explain the conceptual framework for financial reporting.

The Financial Accounting Standards Board (FASB) developed a conceptual framework for financial reporting which consists of a system of interrelated objectives that, if met, would help to identify desirable reporting standards. The FASB expects that the Board will most directly benefit from the conceptual framework by using the framework as a common foundation in the development of future standards. Both the IASB and the FASB issued new or amended conceptual frameworks in 2018. In addition, the FASB issued a new Chapter 8: *Notes to Financial Statements* (Statement of Financial Accounting Concepts No. 8). Chapter 8 is primarily about presentation and disclosure. FASB states that the intent is to aid the Board in identifying disclosures to be considered when setting disclosure requirements. The chapter is also intended to help the FASB improve its procedures and promote consistent decision making when determining disclosure requirements.

In this appendix, we focus on the objective for financial reporting as stated in the conceptual framework, as well as the characteristics of financial reporting that determine the degree of success in meeting that objective.

Objective of Financial Reporting

The objective of financial reporting is ***to provide information that is useful to present and potential equity investors, as well as lenders and other creditors, in making decisions about providing resources to the entity.*** The objective suggests that the information that is presented in financial statements is produced to 1) help the firm raise financing by providing information to equity investors and creditors about the financial health and performance of the firm, and 2) provide ongoing information to those deciding whether to buy, sell, or hold equity and debt securities (including whether to settle loans and other types of credit). Information that is intended for investors and creditors may also be useful to other users of the financial statements.

This objective may be met by providing information for the assessment of the amount, timing, and uncertainty of future (net) cash flows to the firm, which enables investors and creditors to assess the amount, timing, and uncertainty of the cash flows that they will receive. The objective of financial reporting is not to provide a value of a firm, but to provide information for users' own assessments of value.

Qualitative Characteristics of Useful Financial Information

The conceptual framework identifies *relevance* and *faithful representation* as two fundamental qualitative characteristics of financial information that are necessary to fulfill the objective described in the previous section. As the conceptual framework states, "Neither a faithful representation of an irrelevant phenomenon, nor an unfaithful representation of a relevant phenomenon, helps users make good decisions." In addition, the conceptual framework identifies several enhancing qualitative characteristics that affect the usefulness of relevant and faithfully represented information. These qualitative characteristics and their relationship to the basic objective are depicted in **Exhibit 1A.1** and discussed below.

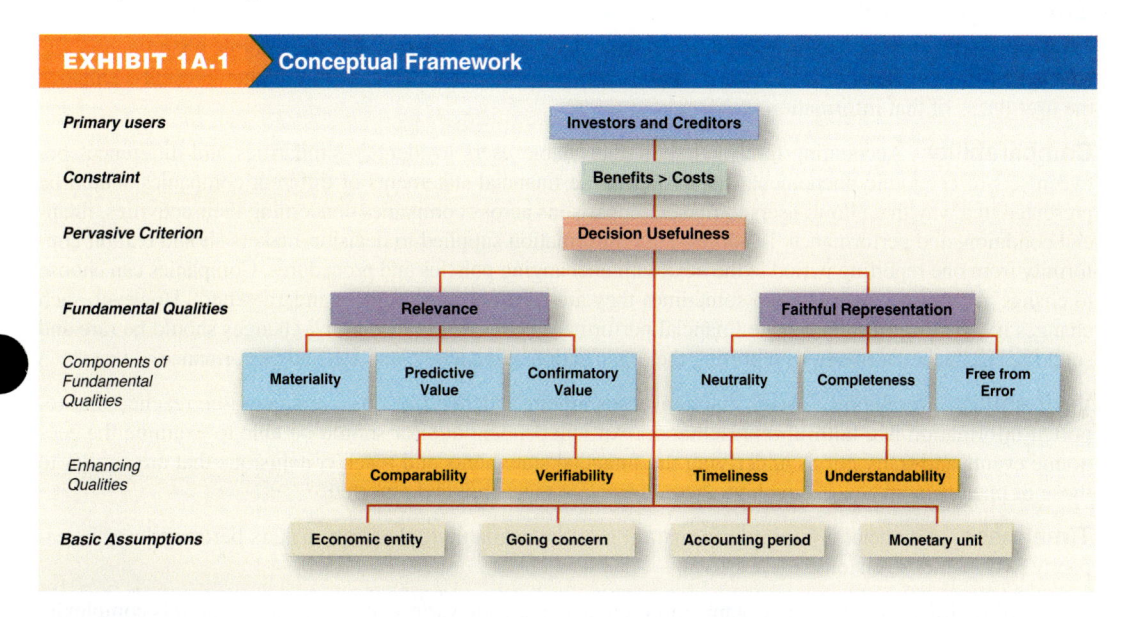

EXHIBIT 1A.1 Conceptual Framework

Primary users	Investors and Creditors
Constraint	Benefits > Costs
Pervasive Criterion	Decision Usefulness
Fundamental Qualities	Relevance / Faithful Representation
Components of Fundamental Qualities	Materiality, Predictive Value, Confirmatory Value / Neutrality, Completeness, Free from Error
Enhancing Qualities	Comparability, Verifiability, Timeliness, Understandability
Basic Assumptions	Economic entity, Going concern, Accounting period, Monetary unit

Relevance To be relevant, accounting information must have the ability to make a difference in a decision. Such information may be useful in making predictions about future performance of a company or in providing confirmatory feedback to evaluate past events.

MATERIALITY Materiality refers to whether a particular amount is large enough or important enough to affect the judgment of a reasonable decision-maker. In practice, materiality is typically judged by the relative size of an item (e.g., relative to total assets, sales revenues, or net income).

PREDICTIVE VALUE Financial information has predictive value if it can be used as an input in the decision processes employed by users to predict future outcomes. The information does not have to be a prediction or forecast itself, but if it can be used by others in making predictions, it has predictive value.

CONFIRMATORY VALUE Financial information has confirmatory value if it provides feedback about previous evaluations.

Faithful Representation In addition to being relevant, financial information must report the economic events that it purports to report. Financial reports describe where an organization is at a point in time and how it arrived at that location from a previous one. To a traveler, a map would provide a faithful representation if the traveler can use the map to discern his or her actual location.

Information is a perfectly faithful representation if it is *complete*, *neutral*, and *free from error*. The objective stated in the conceptual framework does not expect to achieve such perfection, but the requirement of faithful representation for information provides a measuring stick for standard-setters when considering alternative reporting standards.

COMPLETENESS Financial information is complete if it enables the user to understand all the dimensions of an economic phenomenon. Achieving such completeness may require disclosure of additional numerical information (an asset's historical cost and its fair value) or descriptive information (ongoing litigation).

NEUTRALITY While lack of bias is desirable in any reporting system, the effects of financial reports on management and investors create significant incentives to report outcomes and to choose disclosures that portray the firm in a favorable light. In choosing accounting standards, standard-setters aspire to reduce the ability of organizations to bias financial reports and to give financial statement users the ability to identify those biases when they occur.

FREE FROM ERROR Free from error means there are no errors or omissions in the description of the phenomenon and that the process used to produce the reported information has been selected and applied with no errors in the process. A common misconception about accounting is that it consists solely of a historical record of a firm's economic activities. It is such a record, but it is also dependent on management's forecasts of the future. Financial reports are very dependent on forecasts of the future, and forecasts of the future are almost always wrong (though we hope not by much). In this context, "free from error" means that any estimates are described clearly as such, with an explanation of the estimating process.

Enhancing Qualitative Characteristics

For financial information that is relevant to investors and faithfully represents an economic phenomenon, the conceptual framework describes several additional qualitative characteristics that—when present— enhance the usefulness of that information.

Comparability Accounting information should enable users to identify similarities and differences between sets of economic phenomena. For instance, the financial statements of different companies should be presented in a way that allows users to make comparisons across companies concerning their activities, financial condition, and performance. In addition, the information supplied to decision-makers should exhibit conformity from one reporting period to the next with unchanging policies and procedures. Companies can choose to change accounting methods, and sometimes they are required to do so by standard-setters. However, such changes make it difficult to evaluate financial performance over time. Accounting changes should be rare and supported as the better means of reporting the organization's financial condition and performance.

Verifiability Verifiability means that consensus among independent observers could be reached that reported information is a faithful representation. An independent auditor should be able to examine the economic events and transactions underlying the financial statements and reach conclusions that are similar to those of management concerning how these events are measured and reported.

Timeliness Financial reporting information must be available to decision-makers before it loses its capacity to influence decisions.

Understandability Modern organizations engage in a wide variety of transactions, and this complexity can make it difficult for a general user of the financial statements to assess the amount, timing, and uncertainty of the organization's future cash flows. The conceptual framework endeavors to take into consideration the reporting requirements for "users who have a reasonable knowledge of business and economic activities and who review and analyze the information diligently."

The Cost Constraint

Financial reporting requirements impose costs on companies. There are the costs of gathering, processing, and verifying the information, as well as the costs of publicly disclosing information to competitors. These costs are ultimately borne by the companies' investors and should be justified by the benefits of the information produced.

Additional Underlying Basic Assumptions

While not a part of the conceptual framework, four assumptions underlie the preparation of financial statements. Knowing these assumptions is helpful in understanding how the statements are prepared and in interpreting the information reported therein. These assumptions include:

Separate Economic Entity For accounting purposes, the activities of a company are considered independent, distinct, and separate from the activities of its stockholders and from other companies.

Going Concern Companies are assumed to have continuity in that they can be expected to continue in operation over time. This assumption is essential for valuing assets (future benefits) and liabilities (future obligations).

Accounting Period While continuity is assumed, company operations must be reported periodically, normally each fiscal year. Interim reporting periods, such as quarterly or monthly reports, allow companies to supplement the annual financial statements with more timely information.

Monetary Unit The unit of measure is the monetary unit of the country in which the firm's accounting reports are issued. The dollar is the monetary unit in the United States.

YOU MAKE THE CALL

You are the Bank Loan Officer Hertz, the rental car firm, has a fleet of relatively new automobiles that it rents to customers for usually short periods. Suppose that Hertz applied to your bank for a loan and offered their fleet of cars as collateral. Would you, as the loan officer, be satisfied with the value shown on Hertz's balance sheet as a measure of the fleet's value? If not, what value would you prefer, and how might you estimate that value? [Answers on page 1-30.]

Identifying Conceptual Framework Topics LO1-6 **Review 1-6**

The following topics 1 through 5 are discussed in the context of the FASB's conceptual framework.
1. Objective of financial reporting
2. Qualitative characteristics of useful financial information
3. Enhancing qualitative characteristics
4. Cost constraint
5. Accounting assumptions

Required
Listed below are subtopics of the above topics. Match the subtopics *a* through *j* with the topics 1 through 5.

a. ____ Completeness   f. ____ Materiality
b. ____ Cost effectiveness   g. ____ Predictive value
c. ____ Economic entity   h. ____ Provide information to investors and creditors
d. ____ Free from error   i. ____ Timeliness
e. ____ Going concern   j. ____ Verifiability

Solution on p. 1-41.

Summary offers key bullet point takeaways for each Learning Objective.

SUMMARY

Identify the users of accounting information, and discuss the costs and benefits of disclosure. (p. 1-3) **LO1-1**

- There are many diverse decision-makers who use financial information.
- The benefits of disclosure of credible financial information must exceed the costs of providing the information.

Describe a company's business activities, and explain how these activities are represented by the accounting equation. (p. 1-7) **LO1-2**

- To effectively manage a company or infer whether it is well managed, we must understand its activities as well as the competitive and regulatory environment in which it operates.
- All corporations *plan* business activities, *finance* and *invest* in them, and then engage in *operations*.
- Financing is obtained partly from stockholders and partly from creditors, including suppliers and lenders.
- Investing activities involve the acquisition and disposition of the company's productive resources called assets.
- Operating activities include the production of goods or services that create operating revenues (sales) and expenses (costs). Operating profit (income) arises when operating revenues exceed operating expenses.

Identify four key financial statements: balance sheet, income statement, statement of stockholders' equity, and statement of cash flows. (p. 1-11) **LO1-3**

- Four basic financial statements used to periodically report the company's progress are the balance sheet, the income statement, the statement of stockholders' equity, and the statement of cash flows. These statements articulate with one another.
- The balance sheet reports the company's financial position *at a point* in time. It lists the company's asset, liability, and equity items, and it typically aggregates similar items.

- The income statement reports the firm's operating activities to determine income earned, and thereby the firm's performance *over a period* of time.
- The stockholders' equity statement reports the changes in the key equity accounts *over a period* of time.
- The statement of cash flows reports the cash flows into and out of the firm from its operating, investing, and financing sources *over a period* of time.

LO1-4 **Describe how standardized accounting principles and a regulatory environment are important to financial statement integrity. (p. 1-16)**

- Generally Accepted Accounting Principles (GAAP) are established standards and accepted practices designed to guide the preparation of the financial statements.
- While the Securities and Exchange Commission (SEC) has ultimate authority over financial reporting by companies in the United States, it has ceded the task of setting accounting standards to the accounting profession.
- The Financial Accounting Standards Board (FASB) has the primary responsibility for setting financial accounting standards in the United States.
- The Sarbanes-Oxley Act established the Public Company Accounting Oversight Board (PCAOB) to approve auditing standards and monitor the quality of financial statements and audits.
- International Financial Reporting Standards (IFRS) are set by the International Accounting Standards Board (IASB).
- IFRS are an attempt to achieve a greater degree of commonality in financial reporting across different countries.

LO1-5 **Compute two key ratios that are commonly used to assess profitability and risk—return on equity and the debt-to-equity ratio. (p. 1-21)**

- **Return on equity (ROE)**—a measure of profitability that assesses the performance of the firm relative to the investment made by stockholders (equity financing)
- Return on equity (ROE) is an important profitability metric for stockholders.

$$ROE = \frac{\text{Net income}}{\text{Average stockholders' equity}}$$

- **Debt-to-equity ratio (D/E)**—a measure of long-term solvency that relates the amount of creditor financing to the amount of equity financing
- The debt-to-equity ratio is an important measure of long-term solvency, a determinant of overall company risk.

$$D/E = \frac{\text{Total liabilities}}{\text{Total stockholders' equity}}$$

LO1-6 **Appendix 1A: Explain the conceptual framework for financial reporting. (p. 1-25)**

- The conceptual framework includes, among other things, a statement of the *objectives* of financial reporting along with a discussion of the *qualitative characteristics* of accounting information that are important to users.

GUIDANCE ANSWERS... YOU MAKE THE CALL

You are a Product Manager There are at least two considerations that must be balanced—namely, the disclosure requirements and your company's need to protect its competitive advantages. You must comply with all minimum required disclosures. The extent to which you offer additional disclosures depends on the sensitivity of the information; that is, how beneficial it is to your existing and potential competitors. Another consideration is how the information disclosed will affect your existing and potential investors. Disclosures such as this can be beneficial in that they convey the positive investments that are available to your company. Still, there are many stakeholders influenced by your decision, and each must be given due consideration.

You are a Financial Analyst This question has received a lot of discussion from both sides under the title "Economic Consequences." On one side are those who maintain that accounting rules should not only reflect a rule's economic consequences but be designed to facilitate the attainment of a specific economic goal. One example is the case where the oil industry lobbied for an accounting rule that they and others believed would increase the incentive to explore and develop new oil deposits.

Those on the other side of the argument believe that accounting should try to provide data that is objective, reliable, and free from bias without considering the economic consequences of the decisions to be made. They believe that accounting rule makers have neither the insight nor the public mandate to attempt forecasts of the economic effects of financial reporting. Decisions that will affect the allocation of resources or that affect society's social structure should be made only by our elected representatives. While there are substantive points on both sides, we believe that it is the job of accounting rule makers to work toward the objective of financial reporting that reflects economic reality, subject to practical measurement limitations.

You are a Member of the Board of Directors In order to perform a thorough audit, a company's auditors must gain an intimate knowledge of its operations, its internal controls, and its accounting system. Because of this familiarity, the accounting firm is in a position to provide insights and recommendations that another consulting firm might not be able to provide. However, the independence of the auditor is critical to the credibility of the audit, and there is some concern that the desire to retain a profitable consulting engagement might lead the auditors to tailor their audit opinions to "satisfy the customer." Contrary to this concern, however, research finds that there is no evidence that auditors provide more optimistic audit reports for the companies they consult for. Rather, it appears that litigation and reputation concerns are reasonably effective in keeping auditors honest. Nevertheless, recent legislation in the United States now prohibits auditors from performing consulting services for their audit clients.

You are the Bank Loan Officer The value shown on Hertz's books will be the purchase price, though perhaps reduced for the time the fleet has been in use. However, the bank would want to know the current market value of the fleet, not its book value, and the bank would then adjust this market value. The current market value of a single car can be found in used-car market quotes. If the bank ultimately becomes the owner of the fleet, it will need to sell the cars, probably a few at a time through wholesalers. Therefore, the adjusted market value and the book value are likely to differ for several reasons, including:

1. Hertz would have been able to buy the fleet at a reduced value due to buying in large volume regularly (market value lower than used-car quotes).
2. Hertz is likely to have kept the cars in better condition than would the average buyer (market value higher than used-car quotes).
3. The bank would reduce the value by some percentage due to the costs associated with disposing of the fleet (including the wholesaler's discount) and the length of the bank loan (reduction to the value as otherwise determined).

KEY RATIOS

$$\text{Return on equity (ROE)} = \frac{\text{Net income}}{\text{Average stockholders' equity}} \qquad \text{Debt-to-equity (D/E)} = \frac{\text{Total liabilities}}{\text{Total stockholders' equity}}$$

Assignments with the MBC logo in the margin are available in myBusinessCourse. See the Preface of the book for details.

Multiple Choice questions with answers are provided for each chapter.

MULTIPLE CHOICE

1. Which of the following is a potential cost of the public disclosure of accounting information?
   a. Loss of competitive advantage caused by revealing information to competitors.
   b. Potential increased regulation and taxes due to reporting excessive profits in politically sensitive industries.
   c. Raising and then failing to meet the expectations of investors.
   d. All of the above are potential costs of disclosure.

2. Banks that lend money to corporations are considered
   a. creditors.
   b. stockholders.
   c. both *a* and *b* above.
   d. neither *a* nor *b* above.

3. Which of the following financial statements reports the financial condition of a company at a point in time?
   a. the balance sheet
   b. the income statement
   c. the statement of cash flows
   d. the statement of stockholders' equity

4. Which of the following is *not* one of the four basic financial reports?
   a. the balance sheet

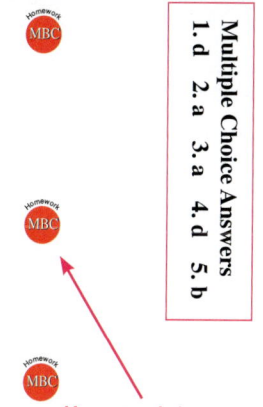

Multiple Choice Answers
1. d 2. a 3. a 4. d 5. b

Homework icons indicate which assignments are available in **myBusinessCourse** (MBC). This feature is only available when the instructor incorporates MBC in the course.

b. the income statement
   c. the statement of stockholders' equity
   d. the notes to the financial statements

5. Which of the following expressions is a correct statement of the accounting equation?
   a. Equity + Assets = Liability
   b. Assets − (Liabilities + Equity) = 0
   c. Liabilities − Equity = Assets
   d. Liabilities + Assets = Equity

Superscript ^{A} denotes assignments based on Appendix 1A.

QUESTIONS

Q1-1. What are the three major business activities of a company that are motivated and shaped by planning activities? Explain each activity.

Q1-2. The accounting equation (Assets = Liabilities + Equity) is a fundamental business concept. Explain what this equation reveals about a company's sources and uses of funds and the claims on company resources.

Q1-3. Companies prepare four primary financial statements. What are those financial statements, and what information is typically conveyed in each?

Q1-4. Does a balance sheet report on a period of time or at a point in time? Also, explain the information conveyed in that report. Does an income statement report on a period of time or at a point in time? Also, explain the information conveyed in that report.

Q1-5. Warren Buffett, CEO of Berkshire Hathaway, and known as the "Sage of Omaha" for his investment success, has stated that his firm is not interested in investing in a company whose business model he does not understand through reading its financial statements. Would you agree? Name several information items (3 or 4) reported in financial statements that corporate finance officers would find particularly relevant in considering whether to invest in a firm.

Q1-6. Does a statement of cash flows report on a period of time or at a point in time? Also, explain the information and activities conveyed in that report.

Q1-7. Explain what is meant by the articulation of financial statements.

Q1-8. The trade-off between risk and return is a fundamental business concept. Briefly describe both risk and return and their trade-off. Provide some examples that demonstrate investments of varying risk and the approximate returns that you might expect to earn on those investments.

Q1-9. Why might a company voluntarily disclose more information than is required by GAAP?

Q1-10. Financial statements are used by several interested stakeholders. Develop a listing of three or more potential external users of financial statements and their applications.

Q1-11. What ethical issues might managers face in dealing with confidential information?

Q1-12. Return on equity (ROE) is an important summary measure of financial performance. How is it computed? Describe what this metric reveals about company performance.

Q1-13. Business decision-makers external to the company increasingly demand more financial information on business activities of companies. Discuss the reasons companies have traditionally opposed the efforts of regulatory agencies like the SEC to require more disclosure.

Q1-14. What are generally accepted accounting principles, and what organization presently establishes them?

Q1-15. What are International Financial Reporting Standards (IFRS)? Why are IFRS needed? What potential issues can you see with requiring all public companies to prepare financial statements using IFRS?

Q1-16. What is the primary function of the auditor? To what does the auditor attest in its opinion?

Q1-17.^{A} What are the objectives of financial accounting? Which of the financial statements satisfies each of these objectives?

Q1-18.^{A} What are the two fundamental qualitative characteristics and the six enhancing qualitative characteristics of accounting information? Explain how each characteristic improves the quality of accounting disclosures.

DATA ANALYTICS

DA1-1. Preparing Data Visualizations in Excel Using Doughnut Charts   **LO1-1**

The Excel file associated with this exercise includes data obtained from the U.S. Bureau of Labor Statistics regarding the employers of (1) accountants and auditors and (2) financial analysts.[7] We will to create a data visualization for each employer group in Excel using a doughnut chart, a form of a pie chart.

REQUIRED

1. Download Excel file DA1-1 found in myBusinessCourse.
2. Create a new row in each dataset for "Other employers."
3. Add the applicable percentage to the new category, "Other employers." *Hint:* When creating a doughnut chart, we are showing proportions of a total. The total of the percentages for each dataset must add up to 100%.
4. Create a doughnut chart for each dataset. *Hint:* Highlight dataset, click on Insert, click on the Pie icon, click Doughnut. Do not include the dataset title when highlighting the dataset.
5. Update the features of your doughnut charts by either choosing one of the chart design templates or updating manually. *Hint:* You can add elements and change the chart style by using the Chart Layouts and Chart Styles tools on the Chart Design tab. The Chart Design tab appears when you click inside a chart.
6. Add percentages to each proportion of the doughnut charts. *Hint:* Right-click on your chart; click on Add data labels. Click on your chart labels to allow editing of color or font size.
7. Calculate the difference between the largest and smallest proportion in the doughnut chart for Dataset A.
8. Calculate the difference between the largest and smallest proportion in the doughnut chart for Dataset B.
9. List any employer categories that overlap between the two occupations.
10. List the formula type associated with the chart. *Hint:* Double-click on the doughnut chart in Dataset A, which will allow the formula to be visible in the formula bar.

DA1-2. Differentiating Between Different Types of Data Analytics   **LO1-5**

For CPAs, we commonly consider four types of data analytics: descriptive analytics, diagnostic analytics, predictive analytics, and prescriptive analytics. To understand the differences between these four types, review Appendix B to this text and refer to *The Next Frontier in Data Analytics* by N. Tschakert, J. Kokina, S. Kozlowski, and M. Vasarhelyi in the *Journal of Accountancy* found at https://www.journalofaccountancy.com/issues/2016/aug/data-analytics-skills.html.

REQUIRED

For each of the following ten examples, indicate which type of data analytics best applies (descriptive, diagnostic, predictive, or prescriptive).

1. Analyzing the trends of collections over the past three years for a customer and using that information to estimate the customer's collection schedule over the upcoming year.
2. Preparing a horizontal analysis, showing changes in expenses over the prior year.
3. Analyzing a significant change in operating expenses over the prior year by drilling down to specific categories that were over budget, down to specific departments, down to specific time periods.
4. An analysis of inventory turns by product in conjunction with an analysis of web clicks for the related product resulted in a list of products to phase out over the next year.
5. Preparing a forecast of sales by major segment using a regression analysis.
6. The relation of a digital marketing campaign and resulting sales is used to budget sales in the following year given the plan for upcoming digital marketing campaigns.
7. An analysis of the relations between the costs of five recent digital marketing campaigns and resulting sales was used to recommend digital marking campaigns to pursue in the future.
8. Preparing monthly unaudited financial statements by department.
9. Examining trends in gross margin at a product level to understand the cause of a drop in overall gross margin.
10. Preparing a data visualization showing how many of the company's current customers are self-employed.

---

[7] Bureau of Labor Statistics, U.S. Department of Labor, Occupational Outlook Handbook, Accountants and Auditors, at https://www.bls.gov/ooh/business-and-financial/accountants-and-auditors.htm (visited August 18, 2021).

DATA VISUALIZATION

LO1-4 DA1-3. Preparing Executive Compensation Visualizations with Tableau: Part I, Part II, Part III
Available in myBusinessCourse, this three-part problem uses Tableau to analyze compensation of chief executive officers and chief financial officers of S&P 500 companies.

Data Visualization Activities are available in myBusinessCourse. These assignments use Tableau Dashboards to expose students to visual depictions of data and introduce students to data analytics through data visualizations. These exercises are easily assignable and auto graded by MBC.

MINI EXERCISES

LO1-2 M1-19. Financing and Investing Relations, and Financing Sources
Total assets of Macy's, Inc. equal $21,172 million, and its equity is $6,377 million. What is the amount of its liabilities? Does Macy's receive more financing from its owners or nonowners, and what percentage of financing is provided by its owners?

LO1-2 M1-20. Financing and Investing Relations, and Financing Sources
Total assets of The Coca-Cola Company equal $86,381 million, and its liabilities equal $65,283 million. What is the amount of its equity? Does Coke receive more financing from its owners or nonowners, and what percentage of financing is provided by its owners?

LO1-2 M1-21. Applying the Accounting Equation and Computing Financing Proportions
Use the accounting equation to compute the missing financial amounts (a), (b), and (c). Which of these companies is more owner-financed? Which of these companies is more nonowner-financed?

($ millions)	Assets	=	Liabilities	+	Equity
Hewlett-Packard Enterprise Company . . .	$54,015.0		$37,919.0		$ (a)
General Mills.	30,806.7		(b)		8,894.1
Harley-Davidson.	(c)		8,724.2		1,804.0

LO1-3 M1-22. Identifying Key Numbers from Financial Statements
Access the most recent 10-K for Apple Inc., at the SEC's EDGAR database for financial reports (www.sec.gov). What are Apple's dollar amounts for assets, liabilities, and equity at September 26, 2020? Confirm that the accounting equation holds in this case. What percent of Apple's assets is financed from creditor financing sources?

LO1-3 M1-23. Verifying Articulation of Financial Statements
Access the 10-K for Nike for the fiscal year ended May 31, 2019, at the SEC's EDGAR database of financial reports (www.sec.gov). Using its consolidated statement of stockholders' equity, prepare a table similar to **Exhibit 1.9** showing the articulation of its retained (reinvested) earnings for the year ended May 31, 2019. Was Nike more or less profitable in the fiscal year ended May 31, 2020, compared to the fiscal year ended May 31, 2019?

Ticker symbols are provided for companies so one can easily obtain additional information.

LO1-3 M1-24. Identifying Financial Statement Line Items and Accounts
Several line items and account titles are listed below. For each, indicate in which of the following financial statement(s) you would likely find the item or account: income statement (IS), balance sheet (BS), statement of stockholders' equity (SE), or statement of cash flows (SCF).

a. Cash asset
b. Expenses
c. Noncash assets
d. Contributed capital
e. Cash outflow for land
f. Retained earnings
g. Cash inflow for stock issued
h. Cash outflow for dividends
i. Net income

LO1-1 M1-25. Ethical Issues and Accounting Choices
Assume that you are a technology services provider and you must decide whether to record revenue from the installation of computer software for one of your clients. Your contract calls for acceptance of the software by the client within six months of installation before payment is due. Although you have not yet received formal acceptance, you are confident that it is forthcoming. Failure to record these revenues will cause your company to miss Wall Street's earnings estimates. What stakeholders will be affected by your decision, and how might they be affected?

M1-26. Internal Controls and Their Importance LO1-4
The Sarbanes-Oxley legislation requires companies to report on the effectiveness of their internal controls. What are internal controls and their purpose? Why do you think Congress felt it to be such an important area to monitor and report?

EXERCISES

E1-27. Applying the Accounting Equation and Assessing Financing Contributions LO1-2
Determine the missing amount from each of the separate situations (a), (b), and (c) below. Which of these companies is more owner-financed? Which of these companies is more creditor-financed?

($ millions)	Assets	=	Liabilities	+	Equity
a. Motorola Solutions, Inc.	$10,642		$?		$ (683)
b. The Kraft Heinz Company	?		49,701		51,749
c. Merck & Co., Inc.	84,397		58,396		?

Motorola Solutions NYSE :: MSI
Kraft Foods NASDAQ :: KHC
Merck & Co. NYSE :: MRK

E1-28. Financial Information Users and Uses LO1-1
Financial statements have a wide audience of interested stakeholders. Identify two or more financial statement users that are external to the company. Specify two questions for each user identified that could be addressed or aided by use of financial statements.

E1-29. Applying the Accounting Equation and Financial Statement Articulation LO1-2, 3
Answer the following questions. (*Hint*: Apply the accounting equation.)

a. **Intel Corporation** had assets equal to $153,091 million and liabilities equal to $72,053 million for a recent year-end. What was the total equity for Intel's business at year-end?
b. At the beginning of a recent year, **JetBlue Airways Corporation**'s assets were $10,959 million, and its equity was $4,685 million. During the year, assets increased $959 million, and liabilities increased $845 million. What was its equity at the end of the year?
c. At the beginning of a recent year, **The Walt Disney Company**'s liabilities equaled $91,132 million. During the year, assets increased by $7,565 million, and year-end assets equaled $201,549 million. Liabilities increased $12,905 million during the year. What were its beginning and ending amounts for equity?

Intel NASDAQ :: INTC
JetBlue Airways NASDAQ :: JBLU
Walt Disney Company NYSE :: DIS

E1-30. Financial Statement Relations to Compute Dividends LO1-3
Colgate-Palmolive Company reports the following balances in its retained earnings.

($ millions)	2019	2018
Retained earnings	$22,501	$21,615

During 2019, Colgate-Palmolive reported net income of $2,367 million.

a. Assume that the only changes affecting retained earnings were net income and dividends. What amount of dividends did Colgate-Palmolive pay to its shareholders in 2019?
b. This dividend amount constituted what percent of its net income?

Colgate-Palmolive NYSE :: CL

E1-31. Calculating Gross Profit and Preparing an Income Statement LO1-3
In 2019, **Colgate-Palmolive Company** reported sales revenue of $15,693 million and cost of goods sold of $6,368 million. Its net income was $2,527 million. Calculate gross profit and prepare an income statement using the format illustrated in **Exhibit 1.8**.

Colgate-Palmolive NYSE :: CL

E1-32. Applying the Accounting Equation and Calculating Return on Equity and Debt-to-Equity Ratio LO1-2, 5
At the end of 2019, **Alphabet, Inc.**, reported stockholders' equity of $201,442 million and total assets of $275,909 million. Its balance in stockholders' equity at the end of 2018 was $177,628 million. Net income in 2019 was $34,343 million.

a. Calculate the return on equity ratio for Alphabet, Inc. for 2019.
b. Calculate its debt-to-equity ratio as of December 31, 2019. (*Hint:* Apply the accounting equation to determine total liabilities.)

Alphabet, Inc. NASDAQ :: GOOG

E1-33. Applying the Accounting Equation and Computing Return on Equity and Debt-to-Equity Ratio LO1-2, 5
At the end of 2019, **Daimler AG**, reported stockholders' equity of €62,841 million and total assets of €302,438 million. Its stockholders' equity at the end of 2018 was €66,053 million. Net income in 2019 was €2,709 million.

Daimler AG OTC :: DDAIF

a. Calculate Daimler's return on equity ratio for 2019.
b. Calculate Daimler's debt-to-equity ratio as of December 31, 2019.

LO1-1, 4 **E1-34.** **Accounting in Society**
Financial accounting plays an important role in modern society and business.

a. What role does financial accounting play in the allocation of society's financial resources?
b. What are three aspects of the accounting environment that can create ethical pressure on management?

LO1-6 **E1-35.**ᴬ **Basic Assumptions, Principles, and Terminology in the Conceptual Framework**
Match each item in the left column with the correct description in the right column.

___ 1. Relevance	a. Refers to whether or not a particular amount is large enough to affect a decision.
___ 2. Verifiability	b. The activities of a business are considered to be independent and distinct from those of its owners or from other companies.
___ 3. Going concern	
___ 4. Materiality	
___ 5. Monetary unit	c. Accounting information should enable users to identify similarities and differences between sets of economic phenomena.
___ 6. Representational faithfulness	
___ 7. Accounting period	d. Financial reporting information must be available to decision-makers before it loses its capacity to influence decisions.
___ 8. Comparability	e. Information is useful if it has the ability to influence decisions.
___ 9. Timeliness	f. Consensus among measures ensures that the information is free of error.
___ 10. Economic entity	g. Accounting information should reflect the underlying economic events that it purports to measure.
	h. The financial reports are presented in one consistent monetary unit, such as U.S. dollars.
	i. A business is expected to have continuity in that it is expected to continue to operate indefinitely.
	j. The life of a business can be divided into discrete accounting periods such as a year or quarter.

PROBLEMS

LO1-2, 5 **P1-36.** **Applying the Accounting Equation and Calculating Ratios**
The following table contains financial statement information for **The Procter & Gamble Company** ($ millions) for the fiscal years ended in June of each year:

Procter & Gamble
NYSE :: PG

Year	Assets	Liabilities	Equity	Net Income
2018	$118,310	$65,427	$?	$ 9,861
2019	?	67,516	47,579	3,966
2020	120,700	?	46,878	13,103

REQUIRED
a. Compute the missing amounts for assets, liabilities, and equity for each year.
b. Compute return on equity for 2019 and 2020. Let's assume that the median ROE for Fortune 500 companies is about 15%. How does P&G compare with this median?
c. Compute the debt-to-equity ratio for 2019 and 2020. Let's assume that the median debt-to-equity ratio for the Fortune 500 companies is 1.8. How does P&G compare to this median?

LO1-2, 3 **P1-37.** **Formulating Financial Statements from Raw Data**
Following is selected financial information from **General Mills, Inc.**, for its fiscal year ended May 31, 2020 ($ millions).

General Mills
NYSE :: GIS

Cash and cash equivalents, end of year	$ 1,677.8
Net cash from operations	3,676.2
Net sales	17,626.6
Stockholders' equity, end of year	8,894.1
Cost of goods sold	11,496.7
Net cash from financing	(1,941.5)
Total liabilities, end of year	21,912.6
Other expenses, including income taxes	3,919.1
Noncash assets, end of year	29,128.9
Net cash from investing	(486.2)
Net income	2,210.8
Effect of exchange rate changes on cash	(20.7)
Cash and cash equivalents, beginning of year	450.0

REQUIRED
a. Prepare an income statement, balance sheet, and statement of cash flows for General Mills, Inc.
b. What portion of the financing is contributed by owners?

P1-38. Formulating Financial Statements from Raw Data   LO1-2, 3

Following is selected financial information from **Abercrombie & Fitch** for its fiscal year ended February 1, 2020 ($ millions).

Abercrombie & Fitch
NYSE :: ANF

Cash asset, end of year	$ 692.2
Cash flows from operations	300.7
Net sales	3,623.1
Stockholders' equity, end of year	1,071.2
Cost of goods sold	1,472.2
Cash flows from financing	(147.9)
Total liabilities, end of year	2,478.5
Other expenses, including income taxes	2,105.9
Noncash assets, end of year	2,857.5
Cash flows from investing	(202.8)
Net income	45.0
Effect of exchange rate changes on cash	(3.6)
Cash asset, beginning of year	745.8

REQUIRED
a. Prepare an income statement, balance sheet, and statement of cash flows for Abercrombie & Fitch.
b. Determine the owner and creditor financing levels.

P1-39. Preparing Comparative Financial Statements from Raw Data   LO1-3

Following is selected financial information for **Tilly's, Inc.**

Tilly's, Inc.
NYSE :: TLYS

($ thousands)	Feb. 1, 2020	Feb. 2, 2019
Cash and cash equivalents	$ 70,137	$ 68,160
Cash flow from operations	36,434	46,743
Cost of goods sold	432,592	417,582
Total liabilities	386,739	129,841
Total assets	546,640	293,168
Cash flow from financing	(27,948)	(25,526)
Sales revenue	619,300	598,478
Cash flow from investing	(6,509)	(6,259)
Other expenses, including income taxes	164,086	155,953

REQUIRED
Prepare balance sheets, income statements, and statements of cash flows for the years ended February 1, 2020 and February 2, 2019.

P1-40. Preparing Comparative Financial Statements from Raw Data   LO1-3

Following is selected financial information for **Tesla, Inc.**

Tesla, Inc.
NASDAQ :: TSLA

($ millions)	Dec. 31, 2019	Dec. 31, 2018
Cash asset	$ 6,783	$ 4,277
Cash flow from operations	2,405	2,098
Cost of goods sold	20,509	17,419
Total liabilities	26,199	23,427
Total assets	34,309	29,740
Cash flow from financing	1,529	574
Sales revenue	24,578	21,461
Cash flow from investing	(1,436)	(2,337)
Other expenses, including income taxes	4,844	5,105
Effect of exchange rate changes on cash	8	(23)

REQUIRED
Prepare balance sheets, income statements, and statements of cash flows for the years ended December 31, 2019 and 2018.

P1-41. Formulating a Statement of Stockholders' Equity from Raw Data   LO1-3

Crocker Corporation began calendar-year 2022 with stockholders' equity of $50,000, consisting of contributed capital of $35,000 and retained earnings of $15,000. During 2022, it issued additional stock for total cash proceeds of $15,000. It also reported $25,000 of net income, of which $12,500 was paid as a cash dividend to shareholders.

LO1-3 P1-42. Formulating a Statement of Stockholders' Equity from Raw Data

DP Systems, Inc., reports the following selected information at December 31, 2022 ($ millions):

Contributed capital, December 31, 2021 and 2022	$ 770
Retained earnings, December 31, 2021	3,412
Cash dividends, 2022	393
Net income, 2022	1,203

REQUIRED

Use this information to prepare its statement of stockholders' equity for 2022.

LO1-2, 3, 5 P1-43. Analyzing and Interpreting Return on Equity

Nokia Corp. manufactures, markets, and sells phones and other electronics. Stockholders' equity for Nokia was €15,401 million in 2019 and €15,371 million in 2018. In 2019, Nokia reported net income of €11 million on sales of €23,315 million.

REQUIRED

a. What was Nokia's return on equity for 2019?
b. Nokia's total assets were €39,128 million at the end of 2019. Compute its debt-to-equity ratio.
c. What were total expenses for Nokia in 2019?

LO1-3, 5 P1-44. Presenting an Income Statement and Computing Key Ratios

Best Buy Co., Inc., reported the following amounts in its February 1, 2020, and February 2, 2019, financial statements.

($ millions)	2020	2019
Sales revenue	$43,638	$42,879
Cost of sales	33,590	32,918
Net income (loss)	1,541	1,464
Total assets	15,591	12,901
Stockholders' equity	3,479	3,306

REQUIRED

a. Prepare an income statement for Best Buy for the year ended February 1, 2020, using the format illustrated in **Exhibit 1.8**.
b. Calculate Best Buy's return on equity for the year ended February 1, 2020.
c. Compute Best Buy's debt-to-equity ratio as of February 1, 2020.

LO1-3, 5 P1-45. Preparing Income Statements and Computing Key Ratios

Facebook, Inc. reported the following amounts in its 2019 and 2018 financial statements.

($ millions)	Dec. 31, 2019	Dec. 31, 2018
Total assets	$133,376	$97,334
Total liabilities	32,322	13,207
Retained earnings	55,692	41,981
Revenue	70,697	55,838
Operating expenses	46,711	30,925
Other expenses, including income taxes	5,501	2,801

REQUIRED

a. Prepare income statements for Facebook for 2019 and 2018. Use the format illustrated in **Exhibit 1.8**.
b. Compute Facebook's return on equity ratio for 2019 and 2018. Facebook's stockholders' equity at the end of 2017 was $74,347 million.
c. Compute Facebook's debt-to-equity ratio for 2019 and 2018.

CASES AND PROJECTS

LO1-3, 5 C1-46. Preparing Comparative Income Statements and Computing Key Ratios

Starbucks Corporation reported the following data in its 2020 and 2019 10-K reports.

($ millions)	Sept. 27, 2020	Sept. 29, 2019
Total assets.	$29,374.5	$19,219.6
Total liabilities	37,173.9	25,450.6
Sales revenue.	23,518.0	26,508.6
Operating expenses	21,956.3	22,430.7
Other expenses, including income taxes	637.0	483.3

REQUIRED

a. Prepare income statements for Starbucks for the years ended September 27, 2020, and September 29, 2019. Use the format illustrated in **Exhibit 1.8**.
b. Compute Starbucks's return on equity ratio for 2020 and 2019. Starbucks stockholders' equity at September 30, 2018, was $1,175.8 million.
c. Compute Starbucks's debt-to-equity ratio for 2020 and 2019.
d. Assume that in 2019, Starbucks reported a lawsuit was in process where plaintiffs allege that Starbucks did not inform customers about the chemical acrylamide in their products (as required by California law). Starbucks did not record a liability (and expense), stating that the loss was possible but not probable. What would Starbucks's ROE have been if it had accrued a $2,000 million litigation liability (and expense)? What effect did this one-time charge have on the company's return on equity ratio? (*Hint:* Compute the ratio and include the litigation charge in other expenses, reduce stockholders' equity, and compare to the ratio computed in *b.*) Ignore tax effects.
e. Assume Starbucks disclosed information about the pending litigation in the disclosure notes to its 2018 financial statements (before the case was settled). Discuss the costs and benefits of disclosing this information in its 2018 annual report.

C1-47. Computing and Interpreting Key Ratios and Formulating an Income Statement LO1-2, 3, 5

Data from the financial statements of **The Gap, Inc.**, and **Nordstrom, Inc.**, are presented below.

The Gap
NYSE :: GPS
Nordstrom
NYSE :: JWN

($ millions)	The Gap	Nordstrom
Stockholders' equity, 2019	$ 3,316	$ 979
Stockholders' equity, 2018	3,553	873
Total assets, 2019.	13,679	9,737
Total assets, 2018.	8,049	7,886
Revenue, 2019	16,383	15,524
Cost of goods sold, 2019	10,250	9,932
Net income, 2019	351	496

REQUIRED

a. Compute the return on equity ratio for The Gap and Nordstrom for 2019. Which company earned the higher return for its shareholders?
b. Compute the debt-to-equity ratio for each company as of 2019. Which company relies more on creditor financing?
c. Prepare a 2019 income statement for each company using the format in **Exhibit 1.8**. For each firm, compute gross profit as a percentage of sales revenue.
d. Based on your answers to questions *a*, *b*, and *c*, compare these two retail companies. What might be the cause of any differences in the ratios that you computed?

C1-48. Computing and Interpreting Key Ratios LO1-5

Data from the financial statements of **JetBlue Airways** and **Southwest Airlines** are presented below.

JetBlue Airways
NASDAQ :: JBLU
Southwest Airlines
NYSE :: LUV

($ millions)	JetBlue Airways	Southwest Airlines
Total liabilities, 2019	$ 7,119	$16,063
Total liabilities, 2018	6,274	16,390
Total assets, 2019.	11,918	25,895
Total assets, 2018.	10,959	26,243
Revenue, 2019	8,094	22,428
Net income, 2019	569	2,300

REQUIRED

a. Compute the return on equity ratio for JetBlue and Southwest for 2019. Which company earned the higher return for its shareholders?

b. Compute the debt-to-equity ratio for each company as of December 31, 2019. Which company relies more on creditor financing?
c. For each firm, compute net income as a percentage of revenue in 2019.
d. Based on your answers to questions *a*, *b*, and *c*, compare these two competitors. What might be the cause of any differences in the ratios that you computed?

LO1-1, 3, 5   **C1-49.**   **Interpreting Financial Statement Information**

Paula Seale is negotiating the purchase of an extermination firm called Total Pest Control. Seale has been employed by a national pest control service and knows the technical side of the business. However, she knows little about accounting data and financial statements. The sole owner of the firm, Meg Krey, has provided Seale with income statements for the past three years, which show an average net income of $86,400 per year. The latest balance sheet shows total assets of $342,000 and liabilities of $54,000. Seale brings the following matters to your attention and requests advice.

1. Krey is asking $360,000 for the firm. She has told Seale that because the firm has been earning 30% on its investment, the price should be higher than the net assets on the balance sheet. (Net assets equal total assets minus total liabilities.)
2. Seale has noticed no salary for Krey on the income statements, even though she worked half-time in the business. Krey explained that because she had other income, the firm only paid $21,600 in cash dividends to Krey (the sole shareholder). If she purchases the firm, Seale will hire a full-time manager for the firm at an annual salary of $43,200.
3. Krey's tax returns for the past three years report a lower net income for the firm than the amounts shown in the financial statements. Seale is skeptical about the accounting principles used in preparing the financial statements.

REQUIRED

a. How did Krey arrive at the 30% return figure in point 1? If Seale accepts Krey's average annual net income figure of $86,400, what would Seale's percentage return be, assuming that the net income remained at the same level and that the firm was purchased for $360,000?
b. Should the dividend to Krey affect the net income reported in the financial statements? What will Seale's percentage return be if she takes into consideration the $43,200 salary she plans to pay a full-time manager?
c. Could there be legitimate reasons for the difference between net income shown in the financial statements and net income reported on the tax returns, as mentioned in point 3? How might Seale obtain additional assurance about the propriety of the financial statements?

LO1-1, 4   **C1-50.**   **Management, Auditing, and Ethical Behavior**

Jackie Hardy, CPA, has a brother, Ted, in the retail clothing business. Ted ran the business as its sole owner for 10 years. During this 10-year period, Jackie helped Ted with various accounting matters. For example, Jackie designed the accounting system for the company, prepared Ted's personal income tax returns (which included financial data about the clothing business), and recommended various cost control procedures. Ted paid Jackie for all these services. A year ago, Ted markedly expanded the business; Ted is president of the corporation and chairs the corporation's board of directors. The board of directors has overall responsibility for corporate affairs. When the corporation was formed, Ted asked Jackie to serve on its board of directors. Jackie accepted. In addition, Jackie now prepares the corporation's income tax returns and continues to advise her brother on accounting matters.

Recently, the corporation applied for a large bank loan. The bank wants audited financial statements for the corporation before it will decide on the loan request. Ted asked Jackie to perform the audit. Jackie replied that she cannot do the audit because the code of ethics for CPAs requires that she be independent when providing audit services.

REQUIRED

a. Why is it important that a CPA be independent when providing audit services?
b. Which of Jackie's activities or relationships impair her independence?

SOLUTIONS TO REVIEW PROBLEMS

Review 1-1

1. e   2. b   3. f   4. c   5. a   6. d

Review 1-2

($ millions)	Assets	Liabilities	Equity	% of Financing Provided by Owners	% of Financing Provided by Creditors
2019	$64,532	$49,174	$15,358	24%	76%
2018	$60,266	$46,579	$13,687	23%	77%
2017	$53,671	$41,141	$12,530	23%	77%

Review 1-3

ADIDAS
Balance Sheet (€ millions)
December 31, 2019

Cash and cash equivalents	€ 2,220	Total liabilities	€13,622
Noncash assets	18,460	Stockholders' equity	7,058
Total assets	€20,680	Total liabilities and stockholders' equity	€20,680

ADIDAS
Income Statement (€ millions)
For Year Ended December 31, 2019

Sales revenue	€23,640
Cost of goods sold	11,347
Gross profit	12,293
Other expenses	10,316
Net income (loss)	€ 1,977

ADIDAS
Statement of Cash Flows (€ millions)
For Year Ended December 31, 2019

Cash flow from operations	€2,819
Cash flow from investing	(925)
Cash flow from financing	(2,273)
Effect of exchange rates on cash	(30)
Net increase (decrease) in cash	(409)
Cash, beginning of year	2,629
Cash, end of year	€2,220

b. Adidas reported revenues of €23,640 million (which is approximately equivalent to $26,477 million) compared to Nike's $37,403 million. Adidas reported net income of €1,977 million ($2,214 million) compared to Nike's $2,539 million. Adidas's operations produced cash flow of €2,819 million ($3,157 million), while Nike's cash flow from operations was $2,485 million. Hence, based on revenues, Nike is a larger company indicated by its substantially larger sales revenue. Its total assets of $31,342 million are also greater than Adidas' total assets of €20,680 million (or $23,162 million). Nike's operating cash flows and income are also larger than those of Adidas.

Review 1-4

1. GAAP 2. SEC 3. FASB 4. PCAOB 5. Management 6. Auditor 7. Internal controls

Review 1-5

a. $\text{ROE} = \dfrac{\text{€}1{,}977}{[(\text{€}6{,}364 + \text{€}7{,}058)/2]} = 0.295 \text{ or } 29.5\%$

b. $\text{Debt-to-equity} = \dfrac{\text{€}13{,}622}{\text{€}7{,}058} = 1.93$

c. One additional benefit to using ratios to analyze financial information is that ratios can be computed for amounts denominated in any currency. Thus, we can compare Adidas and Nike without translating euros into dollars. Adidas's ROE of 29.5% is almost identical to Nike's of 29.7%. This means that both companies earned a very similar return for their stockholders in 2019.

    Adidas's debt-to-equity ratio is 1.93 compared to Nike's 2.89. This means that Nike relies more on debt financing, but again the companies are quite similar. A similar debt-to-equity ratio indicates a similar level of risk associated with an investment in either company.

Review 1-6

a. 2   *b.* 4   *c.* 5   *d.* 2   *e.* 5   *f.* 2   *g.* 2   *h.* 1   *i.* 3   *j.* 3

Chapter 2
Constructing Financial Statements

LEARNING OBJECTIVES

LO2-1 Describe and construct the balance sheet and understand how it can be used for analysis.

LO2-2 Use the financial statement effects template (FSET) to analyze transactions.

LO2-3 Describe and construct the income statement and discuss how it can be used to evaluate management performance.

LO2-4 Explain revenue recognition and accrual accounting and their effects on retained earnings.

LO2-5 Illustrate equity transactions and the statement of stockholders' equity.

LO2-6 Use journal entries and T-accounts to analyze and record transactions.

LO2-7 Compute net working capital, the current ratio, and the quick ratio, and explain how they reflect liquidity.

Road Map

LO	Learning Objective | Topics	Page	eLecture	Review	Assignments
LO2-1	Describe and construct the balance sheet and understand how it can be used for analysis.	2-3	e2-1	R2-1	M2-14, M2-1S, M2-16, M2-17, M2-19, M2-21, M2-22, M2-23, M2-24, M2-25, M2-26, M2-27, M2-29, M2-30, M2-31, E2-34, E2-35, E2-36, E2-37, E2-38, E2-39, E2-40, E2-41, E2-42, E2-43, E2-44, E2-46, E2-47, P2-49, P2-50, P2-51, P2-52, P2-53, P2-54, P2-55, P2-S6, P2-57, P2-59, P2-60, P2-62, P2-66, P2-67, P2-69, C2-71, **DA2-1**
LO2-2	Use the financial statement effects template (FSET) to analyze transactions.	2-8	e2-2	R2-2	M2-18, M2-29, M2-30, M2-31, E2-44, E2-45, E2-47, P2-57, P2-62, P2-67, P2-69, **DA2-4**
LO2-3	Describe and construct the Income statement and discuss how it can be used to evaluate management performance.	2-12	e2-3	R2-3	M2-19, M2-20, M2-21, M2-22, M2-23, M2-28, M2-31, E2-35, E2-37, E2-39, E2-40, E2-41, E2-42, E2-43, E2-44, E2-47, P2-49, P2-50, P2-51, P2-54, P2-57, P2-61, P2-62, P2-64, P2-65, P2-66, P2-67, P2-69, C2-71, C2-72, **DA2-2**
LO2-4	Explain revenue recognition and accrual accounting and their effects on retained earnings.	2-14	e2-4	R2-4	M2-18, M2-19, M2-20, M2-22, M2-23, M2-25, M2-26, M2-28, M2-29, M2-31, E2-39, E2-44, E2-47, P2-57, P2-62, P2-67, P2-69, C2-71
LO2-5	Illustrate equity transactions and the statement of stockholders' equity.	2-19	e2-5	R2-5	M2-18, M2-21, M2-22, M2-23, M2-24, M2-27, M2-31, E2-35, E2-36, E2-37, P2-53, P2-66, P2- 67, P2-69, C2-71
LO2-6	Use journal entries and T-accounts to analyze and record transactions.	2-21	e2-6	R2-6	M2-32, M2-33, E2-45, E2-48, P2-58, P2-63, P2-68, P2-70, **DA2-3**
LO2-7	Compute net working capital, the current ratio, and the quick ratio, and explain how they reflect liquidity.	2-30	e2-7	R2-7	E2-34, E2-36, E2-38, E2-41, E2-42, E2-46, P2-52, P2-55, P2-56, P2-59, P2-60

WALGREENS
www.walgreens.com

More than a hundred years have passed since Charles R. Walgreen, Sr. purchased his first pharmacy in 1901. In that time, the company that bears his name—created via a merger in 2014 of Walgreens and Alliance Boots GmbH—has grown remarkably. As of August 31, 2020, **Walgreens Boots Alliance, Inc.** (hereafter referred to as Walgreens) has a presence in all 50 states, and in more than 15 countries. The company employs roughly 331,000 people (450,000 people if equity method investees are included). The company has more than 13,000 retail locations and has one of the largest global pharmaceutical and wholesale distribution networks. The company continues to grow, adapt, and expand. In July 2020, the Company entered into an agreement with VillageMD to invest $1.0 billion. The Company and VillageMD plan to open 500 to 700 "Village Medical at Walgreens" physician-led primary care clinics in more than 30 U.S. markets.

Still, Walgreens faces a number of challenges. Pharmacy sales constitute a substantial portion of Walgreens' sales, and almost all of those are paid for by a third party. The success of that business depends significantly on factors like the growth of generic pharmaceuticals, legislative changes such as the Affordable Care Act, and the relationships with Pharmacy Benefit Managers. Furthermore, Walgreens faces competition from **CVS Health Corp.** and discount retailers like **Walmart Stores, Inc.**

Of course, the global Coronavirus pandemic presented unprecedented challenges, including store closures, then reduced hours and limited store capacity. Once the vaccines were developed and approved, Walgreens was crucial in the effort to administer the vaccine. The company operated with extended hours, launched mobile vaccine clinics, hosted vaccine clinics in medically underserved areas, and took other actions. As of the time of this writing, Walgreens has administered well over 5 million vaccine doses.

Walgreens has reported profits for many years, though 2020's profit was considerably lower (likely due to the pandemic). As we discovered in Chapter 1, companies like Walgreens prepare financial statements annually. These financial statements allow investors and creditors to assess the impact of changing economic conditions on the company's financial health and performance.

This chapter will introduce and explain financial statements using Walgreens as its prime example. The chapter also introduces some key accounting procedures such as transaction analysis, journal entries, and posting. The general ledger, key accounting assumptions, and basic accounting definitions are also introduced.

Sources: "In the beginning . . ." Walgreens history on the corporate website; Walgreens Boots Alliance, Inc., and Subsidiaries 2020 10-K annual report; Company press releases about vaccine access, *Fortune* magazine, *Wall Street Journal, Chicago Tribune, Bloomberg News* websites.

CHAPTER ORGANIZATION

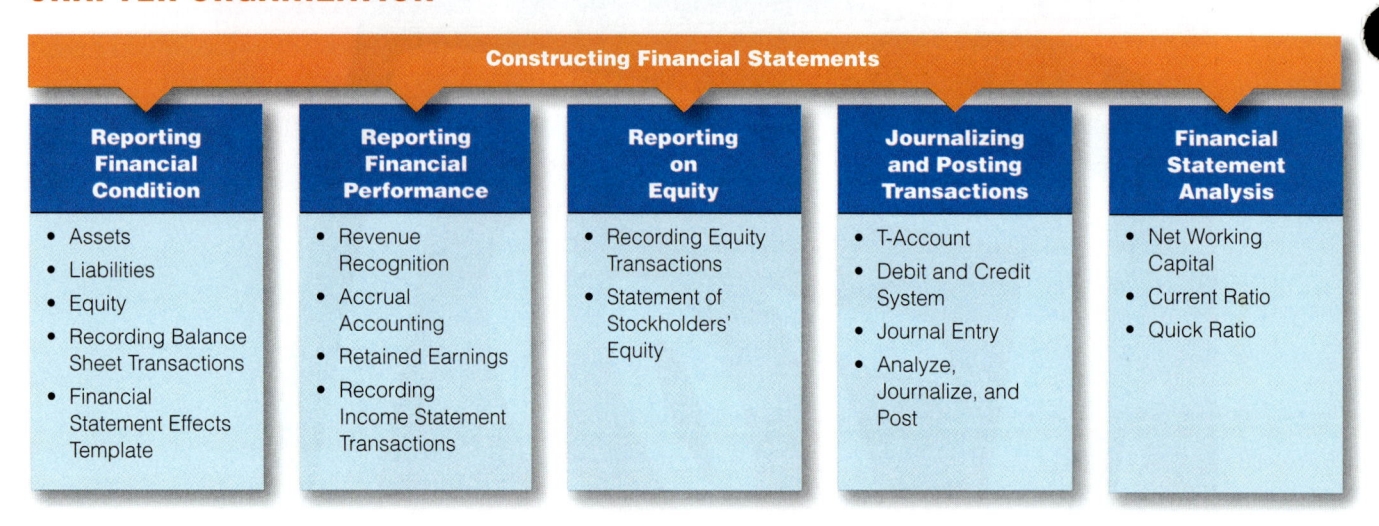

Constructing Financial Statements

Reporting Financial Condition
- Assets
- Liabilities
- Equity
- Recording Balance Sheet Transactions
- Financial Statement Effects Template

Reporting Financial Performance
- Revenue Recognition
- Accrual Accounting
- Retained Earnings
- Recording Income Statement Transactions

Reporting on Equity
- Recording Equity Transactions
- Statement of Stockholders' Equity

Journalizing and Posting Transactions
- T-Account
- Debit and Credit System
- Journal Entry
- Analyze, Journalize, and Post

Financial Statement Analysis
- Net Working Capital
- Current Ratio
- Quick Ratio

In Chapter 1, we introduced the four financial statements—the balance sheet, the income statement, the statement of cash flows, and the statement of stockholders' equity. In this chapter and in Chapter 3, we turn our attention to how the balance sheet and income statement are prepared. The statement of cash flows is discussed in detail in Chapter 4, and the statement of stockholders' equity is discussed in detail in Chapter 11.

REPORTING FINANCIAL CONDITION

LO2-1
Describe and construct the balance sheet and understand how it can be used for analysis.

eLecture
MBC

The balance sheet reports on a company's financial condition and is divided into three components: assets, liabilities, and stockholders' equity. It provides us with information about the resources available to management and the claims against those resources by creditors and shareholders. At the end of August 2020, Walgreens reports total assets of $87,174 million, total liabilities of $66,038 million, and equity of $21,136 million. Drawing on the **accounting equation**, Walgreens' balance sheet is summarized as follows ($ millions).

Assets	=	Liabilities	+	Equity
$87,174	=	$66,038	+	$21,136

The balance sheet is prepared at a *point in time*. It is a snapshot of the financial condition of the company at that instant. For Walgreens, the above balance sheet amounts were reported at the close of business on August 31, 2020. Balance sheet accounts carry over from one period to the next; that is, the ending balance from one period becomes the beginning balance for the next period.

Walgreens' summarized 2020 and 2019 balance sheets are shown in **Exhibit 2.1**. These balance sheets report the assets and the liabilities and shareholders' equity amounts as of August 31, the company's fiscal year-end. Walgreens had $87,174 million in assets at the end of August 31, 2020, with the same amount reported in liabilities and shareholders' equity. Companies report their audited financial results on a yearly basis.[1] Many companies use the calendar year as their fiscal year. Other companies prefer to prepare their yearly report at a time when business activity is at a low level. Walgreens is an example of the latter reporting choice.

Assets

An **asset** is a resource owned or controlled by a company and expected to provide the company with future economic benefits. When a company incurs a cost to acquire future benefits, we say that cost is capitalized and an asset is recorded. An asset must possess two characteristics to be reported on the balance sheet:

---
[1] Companies also report quarterly financial statements, and these are reviewed by the independent accountant, but not audited.

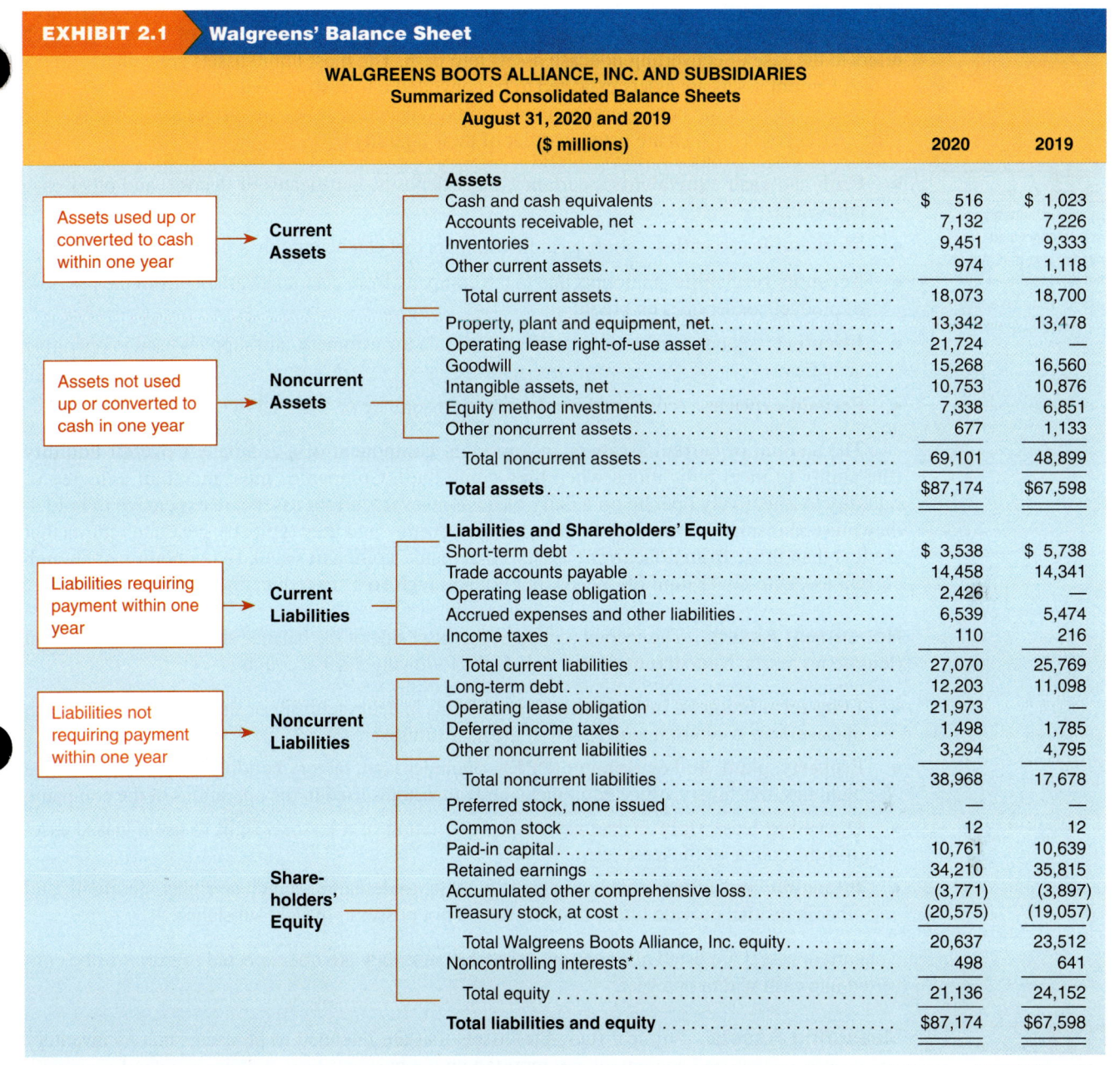

EXHIBIT 2.1 Walgreens' Balance Sheet

WALGREENS BOOTS ALLIANCE, INC. AND SUBSIDIARIES
Summarized Consolidated Balance Sheets
August 31, 2020 and 2019
($ millions)

	2020	2019
Assets		
Cash and cash equivalents	$ 516	$ 1,023
Accounts receivable, net	7,132	7,226
Inventories	9,451	9,333
Other current assets	974	1,118
Total current assets	18,073	18,700
Property, plant and equipment, net	13,342	13,478
Operating lease right-of-use asset	21,724	—
Goodwill	15,268	16,560
Intangible assets, net	10,753	10,876
Equity method investments	7,338	6,851
Other noncurrent assets	677	1,133
Total noncurrent assets	69,101	48,899
Total assets	**$87,174**	**$67,598**
Liabilities and Shareholders' Equity		
Short-term debt	$ 3,538	$ 5,738
Trade accounts payable	14,458	14,341
Operating lease obligation	2,426	—
Accrued expenses and other liabilities	6,539	5,474
Income taxes	110	216
Total current liabilities	27,070	25,769
Long-term debt	12,203	11,098
Operating lease obligation	21,973	—
Deferred income taxes	1,498	1,785
Other noncurrent liabilities	3,294	4,795
Total noncurrent liabilities	38,968	17,678
Preferred stock, none issued	—	—
Common stock	12	12
Paid-in capital	10,761	10,639
Retained earnings	34,210	35,815
Accumulated other comprehensive loss	(3,771)	(3,897)
Treasury stock, at cost	(20,575)	(19,057)
Total Walgreens Boots Alliance, Inc. equity	20,637	23,512
Noncontrolling interests*	498	641
Total equity	21,136	24,152
Total liabilities and equity	**$87,174**	**$67,598**

Annotations:
- Current Assets: Assets used up or converted to cash within one year
- Noncurrent Assets: Assets not used up or converted to cash in one year
- Current Liabilities: Liabilities requiring payment within one year
- Noncurrent Liabilities: Liabilities not requiring payment within one year
- Shareholders' Equity

* Noncontrolling interests arise from the practice of consolidating subsidiaries that are controlled, but not wholly owned. Chapters 11 and 12 provide a brief introduction to this topic.

1. It must be owned or controlled by the company.
2. It must possess probable future benefits that can be measured in monetary units.

The first requirement, that the asset must be owned or controlled by the company, implies that the company has legal title to the asset or has the unrestricted right to use the asset. This requirement presumes that the cost to acquire the asset has been incurred, by paying cash, by trading other assets, or by assuming an obligation to make future payments.

The second requirement indicates that the company expects to receive some future benefit from ownership of the asset. Benefits can be the expected cash receipts from selling the asset or from selling products or services produced by the asset. Benefits can also refer to the receipt of other noncash assets, such as accounts receivable or the reduction of a liability (e.g., when assets are given up to settle debts). It also requires that a monetary value can be assigned to the asset.

Companies acquire assets to yield a return for their shareholders. Assets are expected to produce revenues, either directly (e.g., inventory that is sold) or indirectly (e.g., a manufacturing plant that produces inventories for sale). To create shareholder value, assets must yield resources that are in excess of the cost of the funds utilized to acquire the assets.

Current Assets The assets section of a balance sheet is presented in order of **liquidity**, which refers to the ease of converting noncash assets into cash. The most liquid assets are called **current assets**. Current assets are assets expected to be converted into cash or used in operations within the next year, or within the next operating cycle. Some typical examples of current assets include the following accounts, which are listed in order of their liquidity:

> **FYI** Cash equivalents are short-term, highly liquid investments that mature in three months or less and can be easily converted to cash.

- **Cash** and **cash equivalents**—currency, bank deposits, certificates of deposit, and other cash equivalents;
- **Marketable securities**—short-term investments that can be quickly sold to raise cash;
- **Accounts receivable**—amounts due to the company from customers arising from the past sale of products or services on credit;
- **Inventory**—goods purchased or produced for sale to customers, and supplies used in operating activities;
- **Prepaid expenses**—costs paid in advance for insurance or other services.

The amount of current assets is an important component of a company's overall liquidity (the ability to meet obligations when they come due). Companies must maintain a degree of liquidity to effectively operate on a daily basis. However, current assets are expensive to hold—they must be insured, monitored, financed, and so forth—and they typically generate returns that are less than those from noncurrent assets. As a result, companies seek to maintain just enough current assets to cover liquidity needs, but not so much so as to reduce income unnecessarily.

Noncurrent Assets The second section of the asset side of the balance sheet reports noncurrent (long-term) assets. **Noncurrent assets** include the following asset accounts:

- **Long-term financial investments**—investments in debt securities or shares of other firms that management does not intend to sell in the near future;
- **Property, plant, and equipment (PPE)**—includes land, factory buildings, warehouses, office buildings, machinery, office equipment, and other items used in the operations of the company;
- **Operating lease right-of-use asset**—representation of a lessee's right to use a leased asset over the course of the lease term.
- **Intangible and other assets**—includes patents, trademarks, franchise rights, goodwill, and other items that provide future benefits but do not possess physical substance.

Noncurrent assets are listed after current assets because they are not expected to expire or be converted into cash within one year.

> **FYI** Excluded assets often relate to self-developed, knowledge-based assets, like organizational effectiveness and technology. This is one reason that knowledge-based industries are so difficult to analyze. Yet, excluded assets are presumably reflected in company market values. This fact can explain why the firm's market capitalization (its share price multiplied by the number of shares) is often greater than the book value shown on the balance sheet.

Measuring Assets Physical (tangible) assets that are intended to be used, such as inventory and property, plant, and equipment, are reported on the balance sheet at their **historical cost** (with adjustments for depreciation in some cases). Historical cost refers to the original acquisition cost. The use of historical cost to report asset values rather than market, or fair, value in these cases is because fair value is not often **verifiable**. The historical cost is more verifiable and considered more **representationally faithful** because the acquisition cost (the amount of cash paid to purchase the asset) can be objectively determined and accurately measured. The disadvantage of historical costs is that some assets can be significantly undervalued on the balance sheet. For example, the land in Anaheim, California, on which Disneyland was built more than 65 years ago, was purchased for a mere fraction of its current fair value.

Some assets, such as marketable securities, are reported at current value or **fair value**. The current value of these assets can be easily obtained from online price quotes or from reliable sources such as The Wall Street Journal. Reporting certain assets at fair value increases the **relevance** of the information presented in the balance sheet. Relevance refers to how useful the information is to those who use the financial statements for decision-making. For example, marketable securities are intended to be sold for cash when cash is needed by the company to pay its obligations. Therefore, the most relevant value for marketable securities is the amount of cash that the company would receive if the securities were sold.

Only those asset values that have probable future benefits are recorded on the balance sheet. For this reason, some of a company's most important assets are often not reflected among the reported assets of the company. For example, the well-recognized Walgreens logo does not appear as an asset on the company's balance sheet. The image of Mickey Mouse and that of the Aflac Duck are also absent from **The Walt Disney Company**'s and **Aflac Incorporated**'s balance sheets. Each of these items is referred to as an unrecognized intangible asset. These intangible assets and others, such as the Coke bottle silhouette, the Kleenex name, or a well-designed supply chain, are measured and reported on the balance sheet only when they are purchased from a third party (usually in a merger). As a result, *internally created* intangible assets, such as the Mickey Mouse image, are not reported on a balance sheet, even though many of these internally created intangible assets are of enormous value.

Liabilities and Equity

Liabilities and equity represent the sources of capital to the company that are used to finance the acquisition of assets. **Liabilities** represent the firm's obligations for borrowed funds from lenders or bond investors, as well as obligations to pay suppliers, employees, tax authorities, and other parties. These obligations can be interest-bearing or non-interest-bearing. **Equity** represents capital that has been invested by the shareholders, either directly via the purchase of stock (when issued by the company), or indirectly in the form of earnings that are reinvested in the business and not paid out as dividends (retained earnings). We discuss liabilities and equity in this section.

The liabilities and equity sections of Walgreens' balance sheets for 2020 and 2019 are reproduced in the lower section of **Exhibit 2.1**. Walgreens reports $66,038 million of total liabilities and $21,136 million of equity as of its 2020 fiscal year-end. The total of liabilities and equity equals $87,174—the same as the total assets—because the shareholders have the residual claim on the company.

A liability is a probable future economic sacrifice resulting from a current or past event. The economic sacrifice can be a future cash payment to a creditor, or it can be an obligation to deliver goods or services to a customer at a future date. A liability must be reported in the balance sheet when each of the following three conditions is met:

1. The future sacrifice is probable.
2. The amount of the obligation is known or can be reasonably estimated.
3. The transaction or event that caused the obligation has occurred.

When conditions 1 and 2 are satisfied, but the transaction that caused the obligation has not occurred, the obligation is called an **executory contract** and no liability is reported. An example of such an obligation is a purchase order. When a company signs an agreement to purchase materials from a supplier, it commits to making a future cash payment of a known amount. However, the obligation to pay for the materials is not considered a liability until the materials are delivered. Therefore, even though the company is contractually obligated to make the cash payment to the supplier, a liability is not recorded on the balance sheet. However, information about purchase commitments and other executory contracts is useful to investors and creditors, and the obligations, if material, should be disclosed in the notes to the financial statements. In its annual report, Walgreens reports open inventory purchase orders of $2,227 million at the end of fiscal year 2020.

Current Liabilities Liabilities on the balance sheet are listed according to maturity. Obligations that are due within one year or within one operating cycle are called **current liabilities**. Some examples of common current liabilities include:

- **Accounts payable**—amounts owed to suppliers for goods and services purchased on credit. Walgreens uses another common name for this account—trade accounts payable.
- **Accrued liabilities**—obligations for expenses that have been recorded but not yet paid. Examples include accrued compensation payable (wages earned by employees but not yet paid), accrued interest payable (interest on debt that has not been paid), and accrued taxes (taxes due).
- **Short-term borrowings**—short-term debt payable to banks or other creditors.
- **Operating lease obligation**—an obligation to make payments arising from a lease, measured on a discounted basis. Includes amount scheduled to be repaid within one year.

- **Deferred (unearned) revenues**—an obligation created when the company accepts payment in advance for goods or services it will deliver in the future. The preferred terms for this are contract liability or performance obligation; these are sometimes also called advances from customers or customer deposits.
- **Current maturities of long-term debt**—the current portion of long-term debt that is due to be paid within one year.

Noncurrent Liabilities Noncurrent liabilities (also noncurrent liabilities) are obligations to be paid after one year. Examples of noncurrent liabilities include:

> **FYI** Borrowings are often titled **Notes Payable**. When a company borrows money, it normally signs a promissory note agreeing to pay the money back (including interest)—hence, the title notes payable.

- **Long-term debt**—amounts borrowed from creditors that are scheduled to be repaid more than one year in the future. Any portion of long-term debt that is due within one year is reclassified as a current liability called *current maturities of long-term debt*.
- **Operating lease obligation**—an obligation to make payments arising from a lease, measured on a discounted basis. Includes amounts scheduled to be repaid more than one year in the future.
- **Other long-term liabilities**—various obligations, such as warranty and deferred compensation liabilities and long-term tax liabilities, that will be satisfied at least a year in the future. These items are discussed in later chapters.

Detailed information about a company's noncurrent liabilities, such as payment schedules, interest rates, and restrictive covenants, are provided in the notes to the financial statements.

BUSINESS INSIGHT

How Much Debt Is Reasonable? On August 31, 2020, Walgreens reports total assets of $87,174 million, liabilities of $66,038 ($27,070 current + $38,968 noncurrent) million, and equity of $21,136 million. This means that Walgreens finances 76% of its assets with borrowed funds and 24% with shareholder investment. Liabilities represent claims for fixed amounts, while shareholders' equity represents a flexible claim (because shareholders have a residual claim). Companies must monitor their financing sources and amounts because borrowing too much increases risk, and investors must recognize that companies may have substantial obligations (like Walgreens' inventory purchase commitment) that do not appear on the balance sheet.

Stockholders' Equity Equity reflects capital provided by the shareholders of the company. It is often referred to as a *residual interest*. That is, stockholders have a claim on any assets that are not needed to meet the company's obligations to creditors. The following are examples of items that are typically included in stockholders' equity:

Contributed Capital
- **Common stock**—the capital received from the primary owners of the company. Total common stock is divided into shares. One share of common stock represents the smallest fractional unit of ownership of a company.[2]
- **Additional paid-in capital**—amounts received from the common shareholders in addition to the par value or stated value of the common stock.
- **Treasury stock**—the amount paid for its own common stock that the company has reacquired, which reduces contributed capital.

Earned Capital
- **Retained earnings**—the accumulated earnings that have not been distributed to stockholders as dividends.
- **Accumulated other comprehensive income or loss**—accumulated changes in equity that are not reported in the income statement; discussed in Chapters 11 and 12.

The equity section of a balance sheet consists of two basic components: contributed capital and earned capital. **Contributed capital** is the net funding that a company has received from issuing

---

[2] Many companies' common shares have a par value, but that value has little economic significance. For instance, Walgreens' shares have a par value of $0.01 per share, while the market price of the stock is about $51 at the time of this writing. In most cases, the sum of common stock (at par) and additional paid-in capital represents the value of stockholders' contributions to the business in exchange for shares.

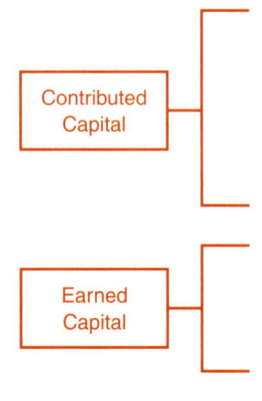

and reacquiring its equity shares. That is, the funds received from issuing shares less any funds paid to repurchase such shares. In 2020, Walgreens' equity section reports $21,136 million in equity. Its contributed capital is a deficit balance of $9,802 million ($12 million in common stock plus $10,761 million in [additional] paid-in capital minus $20,575 million in treasury stock). Note that for Walgreens, their contributed capital is negative because they have repurchased so many shares. This situation is not uncommon.

Earned capital is the cumulative net income (and losses) retained by the company (not paid out to shareholders as dividends). Earned capital typically includes retained earnings and accumulated other comprehensive income or loss. Walgreens' earned capital is $30,439 million ($34,210 million in retained earnings minus $3,771 million in accumulated other comprehensive loss). Other comprehensive income is discussed in Chapters 11 and 12.

RETAINED EARNINGS There is an important relation for retained earnings that reconciles its beginning and ending balances as follows:

> Beginning retained earnings
> + Net income (or − Net loss)
> − Dividends
> = Ending retained earnings

FYI Equity is a term used to describe owners' claims on the company. For corporations, the terms **shareholders' equity** and **stockholders' equity** are also used to describe owners' claims. We use all three terms interchangeably.

This relation is useful to remember, even though there are other items that sometimes affect retained earnings. We revisit this relation after our discussion of the income statement and show how it links the balance sheet and income statement.

Classifying Balance Sheet Accounts

LO2-1 Review 2-1

Assume Schaefer's Pharmacy, Inc., has the following detailed accounts as part of its accounting system. Enter the letter of the balance sheet category A through E in the space next to the balance sheet items numbered 1 through 20. Enter an **X** in the space if the item is not reported on the balance sheet.

A. Current assets
B. Noncurrent assets
C. Current liabilities
D. Noncurrent liabilities
E. Equity
X. Item not reported on balance sheet

_____ 1. Accounts receivable
_____ 2. Short-term notes payable
_____ 3. Land
_____ 4. Retained earnings
_____ 5. Intangible assets
_____ 6. Common stock
_____ 7. Repairs expense
_____ 8. Equipment
_____ 9. Treasury stock
_____ 10. Investments (noncurrent)
_____ 11. Operating lease right-of-use asset
_____ 12. Cash
_____ 13. Buildings
_____ 14. Accounts payable
_____ 15. Prepaid insurance
_____ 16. Borrowings (due in 25 years)
_____ 17. Marketable securities (current)
_____ 18. Inventories
_____ 19. Additional paid-in capital
_____ 20. Unearned revenue

Solution on p. 2-53.

Analyzing and Recording Transactions for the Balance Sheet

The balance sheet is the foundation of the accounting system. Every event, or transaction, that is recorded in the accounting system must be recorded so that the following accounting equation is maintained:

LO2-2 Use the financial statement effects template (FSET) to analyze transactions.

Assets = Liabilities + Equity

We use this fundamental relation throughout the book to help us assess the financial impact of transactions. This is our "step 1" when we encounter a transaction. Our "steps 2 and 3" are to journalize those financial impacts and then post them to individual accounts to emphasize the linkage from entries to accounts. (Steps 2 and 3 are explained later in this chapter.)

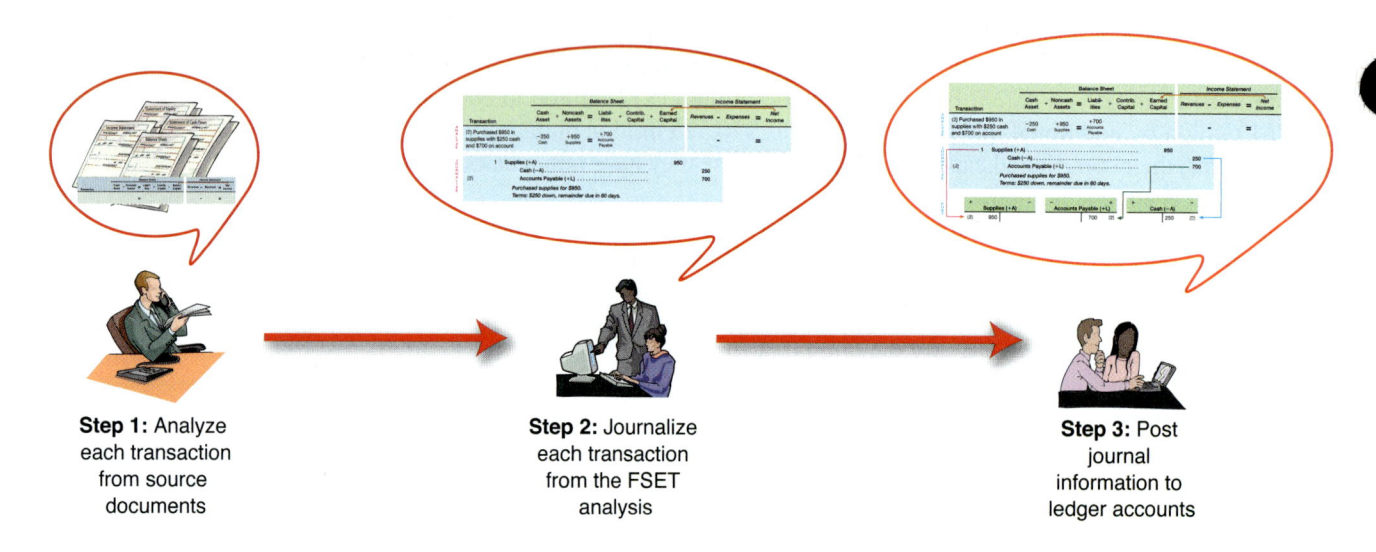

Step 1: Analyze each transaction from source documents

Step 2: Journalize each transaction from the FSET analysis

Step 3: Post journal information to ledger accounts

Financial Statement Effects Template To analyze the financial impacts of transactions, we employ the following **financial statement effects template (FSET)**.

Transaction	Balance Sheet	Income Statement
	Cash Asset + Noncash Assets = Liabilities + Contrib. Capital + Earned Capital	Revenues − Expenses = Net Income
	=	− =

The template accomplishes several things. First and foremost, it captures the transaction that must be recorded in the accounting system. That "recording" function is our focus for the next several pages. But accounting is not just recording financial data; it is also the reporting of information that is useful to financial statement readers. So, the template also depicts the effects of the transaction on the four financial statements: balance sheet, income statement, statement of stockholders' equity, and statement of cash flows. For the balance sheet, we differentiate between cash and noncash assets to identify the cash effects of transactions. Likewise, equity is separated into the contributed and earned capital components. (The latter includes retained earnings as its major element.) Likewise, income statement effects are separated into revenues, expenses, and net income. (The updating of retained earnings is denoted with an arrow line running from net income to earned capital.) Finally, the template proves the accounting equation; transactions must be recorded in a manner such that assets less liabilities equals shareholders' equity. This template provides a convenient means to demonstrate the relationships among the four financial statements and of representing financial accounting transactions and events in a simple, concise manner for analyzing, journalizing, and posting.

The Account An **account** is a mechanism for accumulating the effects of an organization's transactions and events. For instance, an account labeled "Merchandise Inventory" allows a retailer's accounting system to accumulate information about the receipts of inventory from suppliers and the delivery of inventory to customers.

Before a transaction is recorded, we first analyze the effect of the transaction on the accounting equation by asking the following questions:

- What accounts are affected by the transaction?
- What is the direction and magnitude of each effect?

To maintain the equality of the accounting equation, each transaction must affect (at least) two accounts. For example, a transaction might increase assets and increase equity by equal amounts. Another transaction might increase one asset and decrease another asset, while yet another might decrease an asset and decrease a liability. These *dual effects* are what constitute the **double-entry accounting system**.

The account is a record of increases and decreases for each important asset, liability, equity, revenue, or expense item. The **chart of accounts** is a listing of the titles (and identification codes) of all accounts for a company.[3] Account titles are commonly grouped into five categories: assets, liabilities, equity, revenues, and expenses. The accounts for Natural Beauty Supply, Inc. (introduced below), follow:

Assets	Equity
110 Cash	310 Common Stock
120 Accounts Receivable	320 Retained Earnings
130 Other Receivables	**Revenues and Income**
140 Inventory	410 Sales Revenue
150 Prepaid Insurance	420 Interest Income
160 Security Deposit	**Expenses**
170 Fixtures and Equipment	510 Cost of Goods Sold
175 Accumulated Depreciation—Fixtures and Equipment	520 Wages Expense
	530 Rent Expense
Liabilities	540 Advertising Expense
210 Accounts Payable	550 Depreciation Expense—Fixtures and Equipment
220 Interest Payable	
230 Wages Payable	560 Insurance Expense
240 Taxes Payable	570 Interest Expense
250 Gift Card Liability	580 Tax Expense
260 Notes Payable	

Each transaction entered in the template must maintain the equality of the accounting equation, and the accounts cited must correspond to those in its chart of accounts.

Transaction Analysis Using FSET To illustrate the effect of transactions on the accounting equation and, correspondingly, the financial statements, we consider the business activities of Natural Beauty Supply, Inc. Natural Beauty Supply was established to operate as a retailer of organic beauty and health care products, though the owners hoped that they also would become a wholesale provider of such products to local salons. The company began business on November 1, 2021. The following transactions occurred on the first day of business:

(1) Nov. 1 Investors contributed $20,000 cash to launch Natural Beauty Supply, Inc. (NBS), in exchange for 10,000 shares of NBS stock.

(2) Nov. 1 NBS borrowed $5,000 cash from a family member of the company's founders by signing a note. The $5,000 must be paid back on November 30, 2021, with interest of $50.

(3) Nov. 1 NBS arranged to rent a storefront location for six months and began to use the property. The landlord requires payment of $1,500 at the end of each month. NBS paid a $2,000 security deposit that will be returned at the end of the lease.[4]

(4) Nov. 1 NBS purchased, on account (i.e., to be paid later), and received $17,000 of inventory consisting of natural soaps and beauty products.

Let's begin by analyzing the financial statement effects of the first transaction. At the beginning of its life, Natural Beauty Supply has accounts that show no balances, so the financial statements would be filled with zeroes. In the company's very first transaction, shareholders invested $20,000 cash in Natural Beauty Supply, and the company issued 10,000 shares of common stock, which increased equity (contributed capital). This transaction is reflected in the following financial statements effects template.

---

[3] Accounting systems at large organizations have much more detail in their account structures than we use here. The account structure's detail allows management to accumulate information by responsibility center or by product line or by customer.

[4] This lease is for less than one year, so the lease itself will not be accounted for on the balance sheet. Leases are covered more fully in Chapter 10.

Transaction	Balance Sheet						Income Statement		
	Cash Asset	+ Noncash Assets	= Liabilities	+ Contrib. Capital	+ Earned Capital		Revenues −	Expenses =	Net Income
(1) Issue stock for $20,000 cash.	+20,000 Cash		=	+20,000 Common Stock			−	=	

Assets (cash) and equity (common stock) increased by the same amount, and the accounting equation remains in balance (as it always must).

In the second transaction, Natural Beauty Supply borrowed cash by signing a note (loan agreement) with a family member. This transaction increased cash (an asset) and increased notes payable (a liability) by the same amount. The notes payable liability recognizes the obligation to repay the family member.

Transaction	Balance Sheet					Income Statement		
(2) Sign a note and receive $5,000 cash.	+5,000 Cash		= +5,000 Notes Payable				−	=

At this point, Natural Beauty Supply would not record anything for the interest that will eventually be paid. Interest expense occurs with the passage of time, and at the moment of borrowing on November 1, there is no interest obligation to be recognized.

Also on November 1, 2021, Natural Beauty Supply arranged for rental of a location and paid a security deposit that it expects to be returned at a future date. This transaction decreased cash (an asset) and increased security deposits (another asset). We'll assume that Natural Beauty Supply hopes to move to a more upscale location within a year, so the security deposit is considered a current asset.

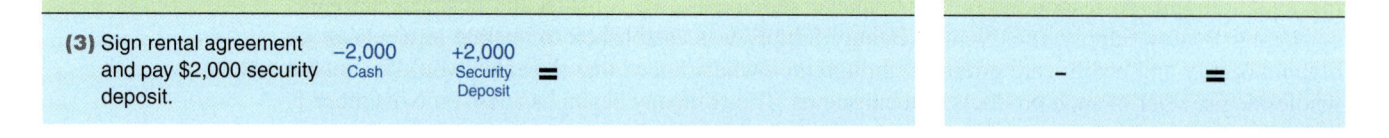

Transaction	Balance Sheet					Income Statement		
(3) Sign rental agreement and pay $2,000 security deposit.	−2,000 Cash	+2,000 Security Deposit	=				−	=

Like the case of interest expense, Natural Beauty Supply would make no entry for rent expense on November 1 because the obligation to pay for the use of the location occurs with the passage of time.

Finally, Natural Beauty Supply purchased and received $17,000 of inventory on credit. This transaction increased inventory (an asset) by $17,000 and increased accounts payable (a liability) by $17,000, recognizing the obligation to the supplier. This transaction is recorded as follows:

Transaction	Balance Sheet					Income Statement		
(4) Purchase $17,000 inventory on account.		+17,000 Inventory	= +17,000 Accounts Payable				−	=

To summarize, the description of each transaction appears in the first column of the template. Then the financial statement effects of that transaction are recorded with a + or a − in the appropriate columns of the template. Under each number, the account title within that column of the balance sheet or income statement is entered. So far, Natural Beauty Supply's activities have not affected the revenue or expense accounts of the income statement.

After each transaction, the equality of the accounting equation is maintained. If we so choose, we can prepare a balance sheet at any time, reflecting the transactions up to that point in time. At the end of the day on November 1, 2021, Natural Beauty Supply's balance sheet appears as follows:

NATURAL BEAUTY SUPPLY, INC.
Balance Sheet
November 1, 2021

Assets		Liabilities and Equity	
Cash	$23,000	Notes payable	$ 5,000
Inventory	17,000	Accounts payable	17,000
Security deposit	2,000	Total current liabilities	22,000
Total current assets	42,000	**Equity**	
		Common stock	20,000
Total assets	$42,000	Total liabilities and equity	$42,000

Using the Financial Statement Effects Template to Analyze Transactions

LO2-2 Review 2-2

Assume that Schaefer's Pharmacy, Inc., enters into the following transactions. Report each of the following transactions in the financial statement effects template.

a. Issued common stock for $20,000 cash.
b. Purchased inventory costing $8,000 on credit.
c. Purchased equipment costing $10,000 for cash.
d. Paid suppliers $3,000 cash for part of the inventory purchased in b.

Solution on p. 2-53.

REPORTING FINANCIAL PERFORMANCE

While balance sheets provide useful information about the structure of a company's resources and the claims on those resources at a point in time, they provide little sense of recent movement or trajectory. The retained earnings balance represents the amount earned (but not paid out in dividends) over the entire life of the company. Looking at the difference between points in time doesn't provide a complete picture about what happened between those points in time. For that perspective, we need the income statement to see whether our business activities generated more resources than they used. For instance, Walgreens' retained earnings decreased by $1,605 million over fiscal year 2020, but that amount does not convey the volume or types of activities that resulted in this decrease.

Walgreens' fiscal year summarized 2020 Statement of Earnings is shown in **Exhibit 2.2**. Walgreens reported net earnings of $424 million on revenues of $139,537 million, or about $0.003 of each revenue dollar ($424 million/$139,537 million). The remaining $0.997 of that revenue dollar relates to costs incurred to generate the revenues, such as the costs of products sold and equipment used, wages, advertising and promotion, interest, and taxes. Interpretation of this $0.003 amount requires further analysis, as shown in Chapter 5, but we can compare it to previous amounts of $0.029 in fiscal year 2019, and $0.038 in fiscal year 2018.

To analyze an income statement, we need to understand some terminology. **Revenues** result in increases in **net assets** (assets minus liabilities) that are caused by the company's transferring goods or services to customers. **Expenses** result from decreases in net assets (assets minus liabilities) that are caused by the company's revenue-generating activities, including costs of products and services sold, operating costs like depreciation, wages and advertising, nonoperating costs like interest on debt and, finally, taxes on income. The difference between revenues and expenses is **net income** when revenues exceed expenses, or **net loss** when expenses exceed revenues. The connection to the balance sheet can be seen in that reporting net income means that revenues exceeded expenses, which in turn means that the company's business activities increased its net assets.

Operating expenses are the usual and customary costs that a company incurs to support its main business activities. These include cost of goods sold expense, selling expenses, depreciation expense, amortization expense, and research and development expense. Not all of these expenses are recognized in the period in which cash is disbursed. For example, depreciation expense is recognized in the time period during which the asset is used, not in the period when it was first acquired in exchange for cash. In contrast, other expenses, such as compensation expense, are

LO2-3 Describe and construct the income statement and discuss how it can be used to evaluate management performance.

FYI The income statement is also called the statement of earnings or the statement of operations or the profit and loss statement. Walgreens uses all three terms (profit, income, and earnings) in Exhibit 2.2.

FYI The terms "revenues" and "sales" are often used interchangeably.

EXHIBIT 2.2 Walgreens' Income Statement

WALGREENS BOOTS ALLIANCE, INC. AND SUBSIDIARIES
Summarized Consolidated Statement of Earnings
Year ended August 31, 2020
($ millions)

Net sales.	$139,537
Cost of sales.	111,520
Gross profit.	28,017
Selling, general and administrative expenses	27,045
Equity earnings in AmerisourceBergen	341
Operating income.	1,312
Interest expense, net	639
Other income	70
Earnings before income tax provision	743
Income tax provision.	360
Post tax earnings from other equity method investments.	41
Net earnings.	424
Net loss attributable to noncontrolling interests*	(32)
Net earnings attributable to Walgreens Boots Alliance, Inc.	$ 456

Per the Walgreens 10-K, certain amounts in the Consolidated Condensed Financial Statements may not add due to rounding.

*Noncontrolling interests arise from the practice of consolidating subsidiaries that are controlled, but not wholly owned. Chapters 11 and 12 provide a brief introduction to this topic.

recognized in the period when the services are performed, which is often before cash is actually paid to employees. Walgreens' operating expenses in 2020 were $138,565 million ($111,520 million + $27,045 million).[5]

Nonoperating revenues and expenses relate to the company's financing and investing activities and include interest revenue and interest expense. Business decision-makers and analysts usually segregate operating and nonoperating activities as they offer different insights into company performance and condition. Walgreens' income statement reports net nonoperating expenses in 2020 of $569 million ($639 million − $70 million), followed by tax expenses of $360 million.

It is helpful to separately identify 1) income from continuing operations and 2) income from nonrecurring items. Many readers of financial statements are interested in forecasting future company performance and focus their analysis on sources of operating income that are expected to *persist* into the future. Nonrecurring revenues and expenses are unlikely to arise in the future and are largely irrelevant to predictions of future performance. Consequently, many decision-makers identify transactions and events that are unlikely to recur and separate them from operating income in the income statement. These nonrecurring items are described in greater detail in Chapter 6.

Review 2-3 LO2-3   Preparing an Income Statement

Assume that Schaefer's Pharmacy, Inc.'s records show the following amounts at December 31. Use this information, as necessary, to prepare its annual income statement. (Ignore income taxes.)

Cash.	$ 3,000	Cash dividends.	$ 1,000
Accounts receivable	12,000	Revenues	45,000
Office equipment	32,250	Cost of goods sold	20,000
Inventory.	26,000	Insurance expense	5,000
Land	10,000	Wages expense	8,000
Accounts payable	7,500	Utilities expense	2,000
Common stock	45,750	Other expenses	4,000

Solution on p. 2-53.

---

[5] Walgreens also reports $341 million in equity earnings in AmerisourceBergen, a company in which Walgreens invested. The operations of AmerisourceBergen are similar enough to Walgreens' operations that they include this as a component of operating income.

Accrual Accounting for Revenues and Expenses

The income statement's ability to measure a company's periodic performance depends on the proper timing of revenues and expenses. Revenue should be recorded when the company has transferred goods or services to customers, in an amount that reflects how much the company expects to be entitled from the transfer—even if there is not an immediate increase in cash. This is called **revenue recognition**, a topic that receives more detailed attention in Chapter 6. Expenses are recognized when assets are diminished (or liabilities increased) as a result of earning revenue or supporting operations, even if there is no immediate decrease in cash. This is called **expense recognition**. **Accrual accounting** refers to this practice of recognizing revenues as goods and services are transferred to customers through the company's operations and recognizing expenses as the assets used and obligations incurred in carrying out those operations.

LO2-4 Explain revenue recognition, accrual accounting, and their effects on retained earnings.

An important consequence of accrual accounting for revenues and expenses is that the balance sheet depicts the resources of the company (in addition to cash) and the obligations that the company must fulfill in the future. Accrual accounting is required under U.S. GAAP (and the International Financial Reporting Standards, IFRS) because it is considered to provide the most useful information for making business decisions and evaluating business performance. (That is not to say that information on cash flows is not important—but it is conveyed by the statement of cash flows discussed in Chapter 4.)

Walgreens' net sales in 2020 were $139,537 million. **Cost of goods sold** (cost of sales) is an expense item in the income statements of manufacturing and merchandising companies. It represents the cost of products that are delivered to customers during the period. The difference between revenues (at selling prices) and cost of goods sold (at purchase price or manufacturing cost) is called **gross profit**. Gross profit for merchandisers and manufacturers is an important number because it represents the remaining income available to cover all of the company's overhead and other expenses (selling, general and administrative expenses, research and development, interest, and so on). Walgreens' gross profit in 2020 is calculated as total net revenues less cost of sales, which equals $28,017 million ($139,537 million − $111,520 million).

The principles of revenue and expense recognition are crucial to income statement reporting. To illustrate, assume a company purchases inventories for $100,000 cash, which it sells later in that same period for $150,000 cash. The company would record $150,000 in revenue when the inventory is delivered to the customer, because at that point, the company has fulfilled its responsibilities in the exchange with the customer. Also assume that the company pays $20,000 cash for sales employee wages during the period. The income statement is designed to tell how effective the company was at generating more resources than it used, and it would appear as follows (ignoring income taxes for the moment):

Revenues	$150,000
Cost of goods sold	100,000
Gross profit	50,000
Wages expense	20,000
Net income (earnings)	$ 30,000

In this illustration, there is a correspondence between each of the revenues/expenses and a cash inflow/outflow within the accounting period. Net income was $30,000, and the increase in cash was $30,000.

However, that need not be the case under accrual accounting. Suppose that the company sells its product on **credit** (also referred to as *on account*) rather than for cash. Does the seller still report sales revenue? The answer is yes. Under GAAP, revenues are reported when a company has transferred goods or services to its customers. This means that the company has satisfied its agreed upon performance obligations—no material contingencies remain. The seller reports an accounts receivable asset on its balance sheet, and revenue can be recognized before cash collection.

Credit sales mean that companies can report substantial sales revenue and assets without receiving cash. When such receivables are ultimately collected, no further revenue is recorded because it was recorded earlier when the revenue recognition criteria were met. The collection

FYI Purchase of inventories on credit or on account means that the buyer does not pay the seller at the time of purchase. The buyer reports a liability (accounts payable) on its balance sheet that is later removed when payment is made. The seller reports an asset (accounts receivable) on its balance sheet until it is removed when the buyer pays.

> **FYI** Sales on credit will not always be collected. The potential for uncollectable accounts introduces additional risk to the firm.

> **FYI** Cash accounting recognizes revenues only when received in cash and expenses only when paid in cash. This approach is not acceptable under GAAP.

of a receivable merely involves the decrease of one asset (accounts receivable) and the increase of another asset (cash), with no resulting increase in net assets.

Next, consider a different situation. Assume that the company sells gift cards to customers for $9,500. Should the $9,500 received in cash be recognized as revenue? No. Even though the gift cards were sold and cash was collected, there has been no transfer of goods or services to the customer. The revenue from gift cards is recognized when the product or service is provided. For example, revenue can be recognized when a customer purchases an item of merchandise using the gift card for payment. Hence, the $9,500 is then recorded as an increase in cash and an increase in *gift card liabilities*, a liability, with no resulting increase in net assets.

The proper timing of revenue recognition suggests that the expenses incurred in generating that revenue be recognized in the same fiscal period. Thus, if merchandise inventory is purchased in one period and sold in another, the cost of the merchandise should be retained as an asset until the items are sold. It would not be proper to recognize expense when the inventory was purchased or the cash was paid. Accurate income determination requires the proper timing of revenue and expense recognition, and the exchange of cash is *not* the essential ingredient.

We have already seen that when a company incurs a cost to acquire a resource that produces benefits in the future (for example, merchandise inventory for future sale), it recognizes an asset. That asset represents costs that are waiting to be recognized as expenses in the future, when these assets are used to produce revenue or to support operations. When inventory is delivered to a customer, we recognize that the asset no longer belongs to the selling company. The inventory asset is decreased, and cost of goods sold is recognized as an expense.

The same principle applies when employees earn wages for work in one period, but are paid in the next period. Wages expense must be recognized when the liability (obligation) is *incurred*, regardless of when they are paid. If the company in the illustration doesn't pay its employees until the following reporting period, it recognizes a wages payable liability of $20,000 and, because this decreases net assets, it would recognize a wage expense of the same amount.

When wages are paid in the next reporting period, both cash and the wages payable liability are decreased. No expense is reported when the wages are paid because the expense is recognized when the employees worked to generate sales in the prior period.

Accrual accounting principles are crucial for reporting the income statement revenues and expenses in the proper period, and these revenues and expenses provide a more complete view of the inflows and outflows of resources (including cash) for the firm. Was an outflow of cash supposed to produce benefits in the current period or in a future period? Was an inflow of cash the result of past operations or current operations? The accrual accounting model uses the balance sheet and income statement to answer such questions and to enable users of financial statements to make more timely assessments of the firm's economic performance.

However, accrual accounting's timeliness requires management to estimate future events in determining the amount of expenses incurred and revenue earned. The precise amount of cash to be received or disbursed may not be known until a later date. In the case of wages, the amount of the accrual is known with certainty. In other cases (e.g., incentive bonuses), it may not and thus require an estimate.

Retained Earnings

Net income for the period is added to the company's retained earnings, which, in turn, is part of stockholders' equity. The linkage between the income statement and the beginning- and end-of-period balance sheets, which we called articulation in Chapter 1, is achieved by tying net income to retained earnings because net income is, by definition, the *change* in retained earnings resulting from business activities during an accounting period. This link is highlighted by the red arrow at the top of the financial statement effects template (FSET).[6] There are typically other adjustments to

---

[6] In the FSET, we show that each transaction that affects the income statement also affects retained earnings. This approach is useful for *analyzing* the effect of the transaction on both the income statement and the balance sheet. However, the impact of net income on retained earnings is *recorded* only once each accounting period, after all of the revenues and expenses have been recorded. This recording procedure is explained later in this chapter and in Chapter 3.

retained earnings. The most common adjustment is for dividend payments to stockholders. **Exhibit 2.3** provides the annual adjustments to retained earnings for Walgreens.

EXHIBIT 2.3 — Walgreens' Retained Earnings Reconciliation

WALGREENS BOOTS ALLIANCE, INC. AND SUBSIDIARIES
Year Ended August 31, 2020
($ millions)

Retained earnings, August 31, 2019	$35,815
Add: Net earnings attributable to Walgreens Boots Alliance, Inc.	456
	36,271
Less: Cash dividends declared	1,618
Less: Adoption of new accounting standard	442
Retained earnings, August 31, 2020	$34,210

Per the Walgreens 10-K, certain amounts in the Consolidated Condensed Financial Statements may not add due to rounding.

Analyzing and Recording Transactions for the Income Statement

Earlier, we introduced the financial statement effects template as a tool to illustrate the effects of transactions on the balance sheet. In this section, we show how this template is used to analyze transactions that may affect the current period's income statement. To do so, we extend our illustration of Natural Beauty Supply (NBS) to reflect the following events in 2021:

(5) Nov. 2   NBS paid $670 to advertise in the local newspaper for November.

(6) Nov. 18   NBS paid $13,300 cash to its suppliers in partial payment for the earlier delivery of inventory.

(7) Nov. —   During the month of November, NBS sold and delivered products to retail customers. The customers paid $7,000 cash for products that had cost NBS $4,000.

(8) Nov. —   During the month of November, sales and deliveries to wholesale customers totaled $2,400 for merchandise that had cost $1,700. Instead of paying cash, wholesale customers are required to pay for the merchandise within ten working days.

(9) Nov. —   NBS employed a salesperson who earned $1,400 for the month of November and was paid that amount in cash.

(10) Nov. 24   NBS received an order from a wholesale customer to deliver products in December. The agreed price of the products to be delivered is $700, and the cost is $450.

(11) Nov. 25   NBS introduced holiday gift certificates, which entitle the recipient to a one-hour consultation on the use of NBS's products. $300 of gift certificates were sold for cash, but none were redeemed before the end of November.

(12) Nov. 30   NBS received $1,450 in partial payment from customers billed in (8).

(13) Nov. 30   NBS repaid the loan and interest in (2).

(14) Nov. 30   NBS paid $1,680 for a twelve-month fire insurance policy. Coverage begins on December 1.

(15) Nov. 30   NBS paid $1,500 to the landlord for November rent.

In the fifth transaction, Natural Beauty Supply gave cash in return for advertising for the month of November. This payment does not create a benefit for future periods, so it does not create an asset. Nor does the payment discharge an existing obligation. Therefore, it decreases NBS's net assets (assets minus liabilities). The purpose of this decrease in net assets is to generate revenues for the company, so it is reported as an expense in the income statement.

We begin by entering the decrease in cash and an increase in expenses. (The minus sign in front of expenses ensures that the accounting equation still holds.) Recording the expense allows the income statement to keep track of the flows of assets and liabilities that result from the company's operations.

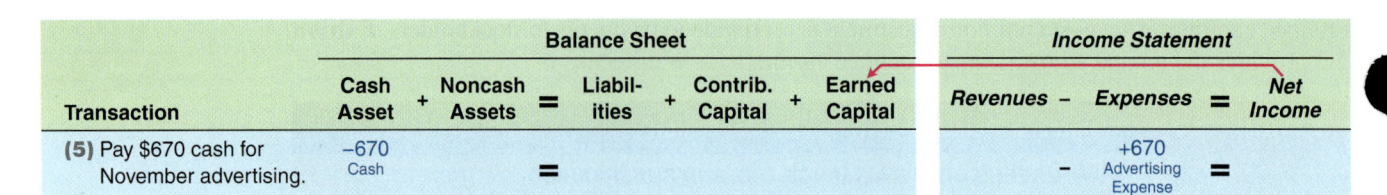

Transaction	Balance Sheet					Income Statement		
	Cash Asset +	Noncash Assets =	Liabilities +	Contrib. Capital +	Earned Capital	Revenues −	Expenses =	Net Income
(5) Pay $670 cash for November advertising.	−670 Cash	=				−	+670 Advertising Expense =	

However, the FSET goes further than recording the accounting entry. It also depicts the effects of the expense on net income and of net income on retained earnings. So, the complete FSET description of transaction (5) is as follows. The FSET uses color to differentiate between the accounting entry (in blue) and the resulting effect on net income and retained earnings (in black).

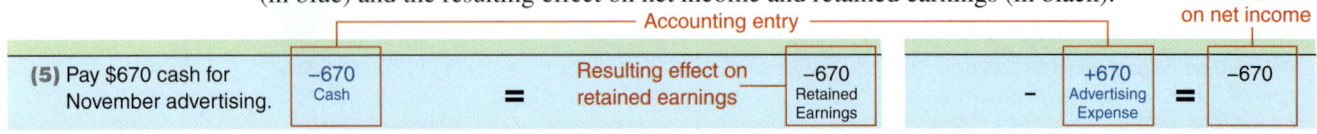

Accounting entry ―――――――――――――――――――――――――― *Resulting effect on net income*

| (5) Pay $670 cash for November advertising. | −670 Cash | = | Resulting effect on retained earnings | | −670 Retained Earnings | − | +670 Advertising Expense = | −670 |

In the sixth transaction, Natural Beauty Supply made a partial payment of $13,300 in cash to the suppliers who delivered inventory on November 1. This transaction decreases cash by $13,300 and decreases the accounts payable liability by $13,300. The income statement is not affected by this payment. The cost of merchandise is reflected in the income statement when the merchandise is sold, not when it is paid for (as we will see shortly).

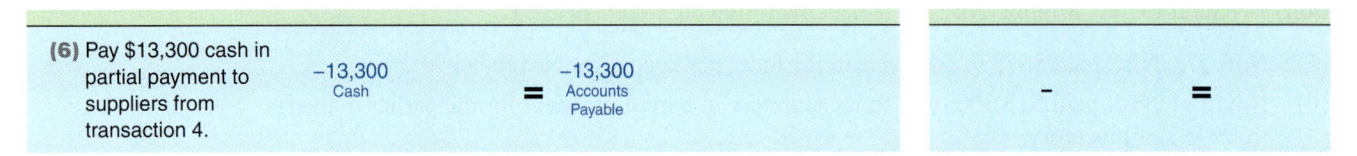

| (6) Pay $13,300 cash in partial payment to suppliers from transaction 4. | −13,300 Cash | = | −13,300 Accounts Payable | | | − | = | |

In transaction seven, Natural Beauty Supply sold and delivered products to customers who paid $7,000 in cash. NBS's transfer of products to customers results in the recognition of revenue in the income statement and an increase in net assets (cash) on the balance sheet. As in transaction 5, the FSET also depicts the impact of these sales on net income and on the retained earnings balance.

| (7a) Sell $7,000 of products for cash. | +7,000 Cash | = | | | +7,000 Retained Earnings | +7,000 Sales Revenue − | = | +7,000 |

At the same time, NBS must recognize that these sales transactions involved an exchange, and cash was received while inventory costing $4,000 was delivered. Transaction (7b) recognizes that NBS no longer has this inventory and that this decrease in net assets produces an expense called cost of goods sold. In this way, the income statement portrays the increases in net assets (revenues) and the decreases in net assets (expenses like cost of goods sold and advertising) from the company's operating activities. (Again, the minus sign in front of all expenses ensures that the accounting equation remains balanced.)

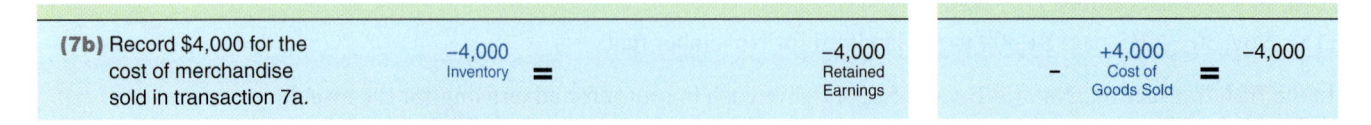

| (7b) Record $4,000 for the cost of merchandise sold in transaction 7a. | | −4,000 Inventory = | | | −4,000 Retained Earnings | − | +4,000 Cost of Goods Sold = | −4,000 |

The eighth transaction is similar to the previous one, except that Natural Beauty Supply's customers will pay for the products ten days after they were delivered. Should NBS recognize revenue on these sales? The products have been delivered, so the revenue has been earned.[7] Therefore, NBS should recognize that it has a new asset—accounts receivable—equal to $2,400, and that it has earned revenue in the same amount. As above, NBS would also record cost of goods sold to recognize the cost of inventory delivered to the customers.

---

[7] In Chapter 6, we consider the possibility that a customer might not pay the receivable. For the time being, we assume that the receivables' collectability is assured.

Transaction	Balance Sheet					Income Statement		
	Cash Asset +	Noncash Assets =	Liabil- ities +	Contrib. Capital +	Earned Capital	Revenues −	Expenses =	Net Income
(8a) Sell $2,400 of products on account.		+2,400 Accounts Receivable =			+2,400 Retained Earnings	+2,400 Sales Revenue	− =	+2,400
(8b) Record $1,700 for the cost of merchandise sold in transaction 8a.		−1,700 Inventory =			−1,700 Retained Earnings	−	+1,700 Cost of Goods Sold =	−1,700

The ninth entry records wage expense. In this case, wages were paid in cash. Cash is decreased by $1,400, and this decrease in net assets results in a recognition of wages expense in the income statement (with resulting decreases in net income and retained earnings).

(9) Record $1,400 in wages to employees.	−1,400 Cash	=			−1,400 Retained Earnings	−	+1,400 Wages Expense =	−1,400

Transaction ten involves a customer order for products to be delivered in December. This transaction is an example of an *executory contract*, which does not require a journal entry (just like Walgreens' open purchase orders for inventory described earlier). NBS does not record revenue because it has not yet delivered the products.

(10) Receive customer order.	Memorandum entry for customer order							

In transaction eleven, Natural Beauty Supply sold gift certificates for $300 cash, but none were redeemed. In this case, NBS has received cash, but revenue cannot be recognized because no goods or services have been transferred to the customers. Rather, NBS has accepted an obligation to provide services in the future when the gift certificates are redeemed. This obligation is recognized as a liability titled Gift Card Liability.

(11) Sell gift certificates for $300 cash.	+300 Cash	=	+300 Gift Card Liability			−	=	

In transaction twelve, NBS received $1,450 cash as partial payment from customers billed in transaction eight. Cash increases by $1,450 and accounts receivable decreases by $1,450. Recall that revenues are recorded when goods or services are transferred to customers (transaction 8), not when cash is received.

(12) Receive $1,450 cash as partial payment from customers billed in transaction 8.	+1,450 Cash	−1,450 Accounts Receivable =				−	=	

In transaction thirteen on November 30, Natural Beauty Supply paid back the family member who had loaned money to the business. The cash payment was the agreed-upon $5,050 ($5,000 principal and $50 interest). The repayment of the principal does not change the net assets of NBS; cash goes down by $5,000, and the note payable liability goes down an equal amount. However, the payment of $50 interest does cause the net assets to decrease, and this net asset decrease creates an interest expense in the income statement.

(13) Pay interest of $50 and repay principal of $5,000.	−5,050 Cash	=	−5,000 Notes Payable		−50 Retained Earnings	−	+50 Interest Expense =	−50

In the fourteenth transaction, NBS paid an annual insurance premium of $1,680 for coverage beginning December 1. NBS will receive the benefits of the insurance coverage in the future, so insurance expense will be recognized in those future periods. At this time, a noncash asset titled prepaid insurance is increased by $1,680, and cash is decreased by the same amount.

Transaction	Balance Sheet					Income Statement		
	Cash Asset	+ Noncash Assets	= Liabilities	+ Contrib. Capital	+ Earned Capital	Revenues	− Expenses	= Net Income
(14) Pay $1,680 for one-year insurance policy.	−1,680 Cash	+1,680 Prepaid Insurance	=				−	=

In the last transaction of the month of November, Natural Beauty Supply paid $1,500 cash to the landlord for November's rent. This $1,500 reduction of net assets is balanced by rent expense in the income statement.

Transaction	Balance Sheet					Income Statement		
(15) Pay $1,500 rent for November.	−1,500 Cash		=		−1,500 Retained Earnings		− +1,500 Rent Expense	= −1,500

We can summarize the revenue and expense entries of these transactions to prepare an income statement for Natural Beauty Supply for the month ended November 30, 2021.

NATURAL BEAUTY SUPPLY, INC.
Income Statement
For Month Ended November 30, 2021

Sales revenue	$9,400
Cost of goods sold	5,700
Gross profit	3,700
Wages expense	1,400
Rent expense	1,500
Advertising expense	670
Operating income	130
Interest expense	50
Net income	$ 80

Review 2-4 LO2-4

Preparing a Retained Earnings Statement

Use the information from Review 2-3 to complete the following requirements. Assume that Schaefer's Pharmacy, Inc., reports the following selected financial information for the year ended December 31.

Retained earnings, Dec. 31	$30,000	Dividends	$ 1,000
Net income	$ 6,000	Retained earnings, Jan. 1	$25,000

a. Prepare the current year retained earnings reconciliation for this company.
b. Suppose that you discover that the company had not recorded digital marketing expense of $750 that had been incurred but was not due to be paid until next year. What impact would this information have on your answer to part *a* (if any)?

Solution on p. 2-54.

REPORTING ON EQUITY

Analyzing and Recording Equity Transactions

LO2-5 Illustrate equity transactions and the statement of stockholders' equity.

Earlier we recorded the effect of issuing common stock on the balance sheet of Natural Beauty Supply. To complete our illustration, we record one final equity transaction: a dividend payment.

(16) Nov. 30   Natural Beauty Supply paid a $50 cash dividend to its shareholders.

To record the dividend payment, we decrease cash and decrease retained earnings.

Transaction	Balance Sheet					Income Statement		
	Cash Asset	+ Noncash Assets	= Liabilities	+ Contrib. Capital	+ Earned Capital	Revenues	− Expenses	= Net Income
(16) Pay $50 cash dividend to shareholders.	−50 Cash		=		−50 Retained Earnings		−	=

No revenue or income is recorded from a stock issuance. Similarly, no expense is recorded from a dividend. This is always the case. Companies cannot report revenues and expenses from capital transactions (transactions with stockholders relating to their investment in the company).

The FSET entries can be accumulated by account to determine the ending balances for assets, liabilities and equity. Natural Beauty Supply's balance sheet for November 30, 2021, appears in **Exhibit 2.4**. The balance in retained earnings is $30 (net income of $80 less the cash dividend of $50).

EXHIBIT 2.4 Natural Beauty Supply's Balance Sheet

NATURAL BEAUTY SUPPLY, INC.
Balance Sheet
November 30, 2021

Assets		Liabilities	
Cash	$ 8,100	Accounts payable	$ 3,700
Accounts receivable	950	Gift card liability	300
Inventory	11,300	Total current liabilities	4,000
Prepaid insurance	1,680	Equity	
Security deposit	2,000	Common stock	20,000
Total current assets	24,030	Retained earnings	30
		Total equity	20,030
Total assets	$24,030	Total liabilities and equity	$24,030

Statement of Stockholders' Equity

The statement of stockholders' equity is a reconciliation of the beginning and ending balances of selected stockholders' equity accounts. The statement of stockholders' equity for Natural Beauty Supply for the month of November is in **Exhibit 2.5**.

EXHIBIT 2.5 Natural Beauty Supply's Statement of Stockholders' Equity

NATURAL BEAUTY SUPPLY, INC.
Statement of Stockholders' Equity
For Month Ended November 30, 2021

	Contributed Capital	Earned Capital	Total Equity
Balance, November 1, 2021	$ 0	$ 0	$ 0
Common stock issued	20,000	—	20,000
Net income	—	80	80
Cash dividends	—	(50)	(50)
Balance, November 30, 2021	$20,000	$30	$20,030

This statement highlights three main changes to Natural Beauty Supply's equity during November.

1. Natural Beauty raised $20,000 in equity capital during the month.
2. Natural Beauty Supply earned net income of $80. That is, its business activities increased the company's net assets by $80 during the month.
3. Natural Beauty Supply declared a $50 cash dividend.

At this point, we can make the important observation that the various financial statements are not the result of independent processes. That is, the process of constructing the income statement is closely tied to the process of constructing the balance sheet. When we think about the fact that revenues reflect how much the company expects to receive from its delivery of goods to customers, and expenses measure the outflow of assets and increases in liabilities resulting from generating revenues and supporting operations, it should be apparent that an error on the income statement will, in all likelihood, lead to an error in the balance sheet. Understanding the connections among the various statements is a key step in becoming an effective reader of financial information.

> ### YOU MAKE THE CALL
>
> **You are an Analyst** Colgate-Palmolive Company reported a balance in retained earnings of $22,501 million on December 31, 2019. This amount compares to $21,615 million one year earlier at the end of 2018. In 2019, Colgate-Palmolive Company reported net income of $2,367 million. Why did the company's retained earnings go up by less than reported net income? [Answer on page 2-33.]

Review 2-5 LO2-5   Preparing a Balance Sheet and a Statement of Stockholders' Equity

Solution on p. 2-54.

a. Use the listing of accounts and figures reported in Review 2-3 along with the ending retained earnings from Review 2-4, part *a* to prepare the December 31 balance sheet for Schaefer's Pharmacy, Inc.
b. Assuming that no new shares of common stock were issued during the year, prepare the company's statement of stockholders' equity for the year.

JOURNALIZING AND POSTING TRANSACTIONS

LO2-6 Use journal entries and T-accounts to analyze and record transactions.

The financial statement effects template is a useful tool for illustrating the effects of a transaction on the balance sheet, income statement, statement of stockholders' equity, and statement of cash flows. However, when representing individual transactions or analyzing individual accounts, the accounting system records information in journal entries (step 2) that are collected in individual accounts. This section introduces the basics of that system. It also introduces the T-account as a useful tool for learning debits and credits and for representing accounts in the ledger (step 3).

T-Account

Accountants commonly use a graphic representation of an account called a **T-account**, so named because it looks like a large T. The typical form of a T-account is:

Account Title	
Debits	Credits
(Dr.)	(Cr.)
Always the left side	Always the right side

FYI Recall that an account is a record of increases and decreases in asset, liability, equity, revenue, or expense items.

One side of the T-account is used to record increases to the account, and the other side is used to record decreases.

Accountants record individual transactions using the journal entry. A **journal entry** is an accounting entry in the financial records (journals) of a company. The journal entry is the *bookkeeping* aspect of accounting. Even if you never make a journal entry for a company, you will interact with accounting and finance professionals who do and who will use this language. Further, journal entries and T-accounts can help in reconstructing transactions and interpreting their financial effects.

Debit and Credit System

Accountants describe increases and decreases in accounts using the terms **debit** and **credit**. The left side of each account is the debit side (abbreviated Dr.), and the right side of each account is the credit side (abbreviated Cr.). In some accounts, increases are recorded on the debit (left) side of the account, and decreases are recorded on the credit (right) side of the account. In other accounts, just the opposite is true—increases are credits and decreases are debits. An easy way to remember what the words "debit" and "credit" reflect is to visualize a balance sheet in "T" account form with assets on the left and liabilities and equity on the right as follows:

Balance Sheet in Accounting Equation Form

Asset Accounts	=	Liability Accounts	+	Equity Accounts
Debit Side Increases / Credit Side Decreases		Debit Side Decreases / Credit Side Increases		Debit Side Decreases / Credit Side Increases

FYI "Debit" and "credit" are accounting terms meaning left and right, respectively.

FYI In our everyday speech, the words "debit" and "credit" are often imbued with value connotations. For example, "To her credit, she took responsibility for the incident." But there are no value connotations within the accounting system. Every good event is recorded with both a debit and a credit, and the same is true for every bad event.

Thus, assets are assigned a *normal debit balance* because they are on the left side. Liabilities and equity are assigned a *normal credit balance* because they are on the right side. So, to reflect an increase in an asset, we debit the asset account. To reflect an increase in a liability or equity account, we credit the account. Conversely, to reflect a decrease in an asset account, we credit it. To reflect a decrease in a liability or equity account, we debit it. (There are exceptions to these normal balances; one case is accumulated depreciation, which is explained in Chapter 3.)

The balance sheet must always balance (assets = liabilities + equity). So too must total debits equal total credits in each journal entry. There can, however, be more than one debit and one credit in an entry. These so-called **compound entries** still adhere to the rule: *total debits equal total credits for each entry*. This important relation is extended below to show the *expanded accounting equation* in T-account form with the inclusion of debit (Dr.) and credit (Cr.) rules. Equity is expanded to reflect increases from stock issuances and revenues and to reflect decreases from dividends and expenses.

FYI The rule that total debits equal total credits for each entry is known as double-entry accounting, or the duality of accounting.

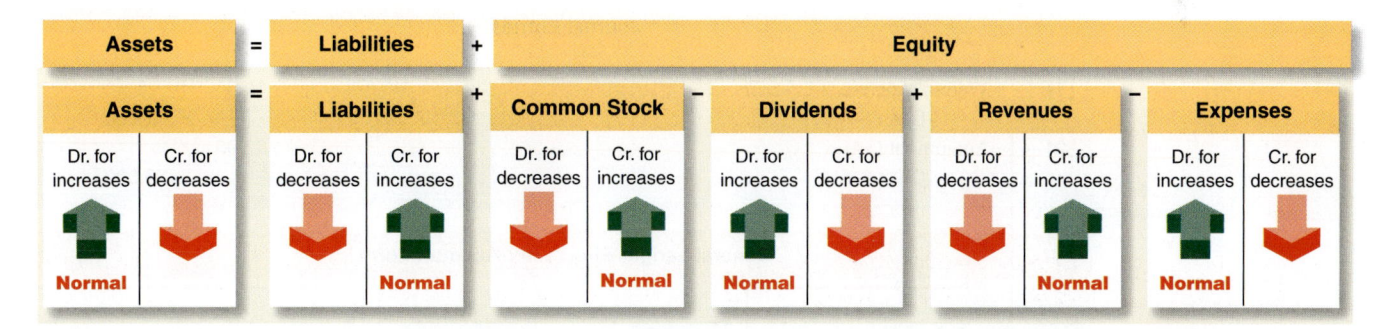

Assets	=	Liabilities	+	Equity

Assets	=	Liabilities	+	Common Stock	−	Dividends	+	Revenues	−	Expenses
Dr. for increases / Cr. for decreases (Normal)		Dr. for decreases / Cr. for increases (Normal)		Dr. for decreases / Cr. for increases (Normal)		Dr. for increases / Cr. for decreases (Normal)		Dr. for decreases / Cr. for increases (Normal)		Dr. for increases / Cr. for decreases (Normal)

Income (revenues less expenses) feeds directly into retained earnings. Also, anything that increases equity is a credit and anything that decreases equity is a debit. So, to reflect an increase in revenues (which increases retained earnings and, therefore, equity), we credit the revenue account, and to reflect an increase in an expense account (which reduces retained earnings and, therefore, equity), we debit it.

FYI The **normal balance** of any account is on the side on which increases are recorded.

To summarize, the following table reflects the use of the terms "debit" and "credit" to reflect increases and decreases to the usual balance sheet and the income statement relations.

	Accounting Relation	Debit	Credit
Balance sheet	Assets (A)	Increase	Decrease
	Liabilities (L)	Decrease	Increase
	Equity (SE)	Decrease	Increase
Income statement	Revenue (R)	Decrease	Increase
	Expense (E)	Increase	Decrease

T-Account with Debits and Credits

To illustrate use of debits and credits with a T-account, we use the Cash T-account for NBS transactions 1, 2, 3, and 4 (see page 2-10 for the transactions). There is a beginning balance of $0 on the left side (which is also the ending balance of the previous period). Increases in cash have been placed on the left side of the Cash T-account, and decreases have been placed on the right side. Transactions (1) and (2) increased the cash balance, while transaction (3) decreased it. Transaction (4) does not involve cash.

The ending balance of cash is $23,000. An account balance is determined by totaling the left side and the right side columns and entering the difference on the side with the larger total. The T-account is an extremely simple record that can be summarized in terms of four elements: beginning balance, additions, subtractions, and ending balance.

	+	Cash (A)	−	
Beg. bal.		0		
(1)		20,000	2,000	(3)
(2)		5,000		
End. bal.		23,000		

Dates and other related data are usually omitted in T-accounts, but it is customary to *key* entries with a number or a letter to identify the similarly coded transaction. The number or letter is keyed to the journal entry (discussed next) that identifies the transaction involved. The type and number of accounts used by a business depend on the complexity of its operations and the degree of detail demanded by managers.

The Journal Entry

FYI We denote the transaction's effect on assets, liabilities, equity, revenues, and expenses in parentheses for each journal entry.

The journal entry records each transaction (step 2) by summarizing the debits and credits. To illustrate the use of journal entries and T-accounts (step 3), assume that Walgreens: (1) Paid employees $1,200 cash wages, recognizing that amount as an expense, and (2) Paid $9,500 cash to acquire equipment. The journal entries and T-accounts reflecting these two transactions follow. The T-accounts can be viewed as an abbreviated representation of the company *ledger*, which is a listing of all accounts and their dollar balances.

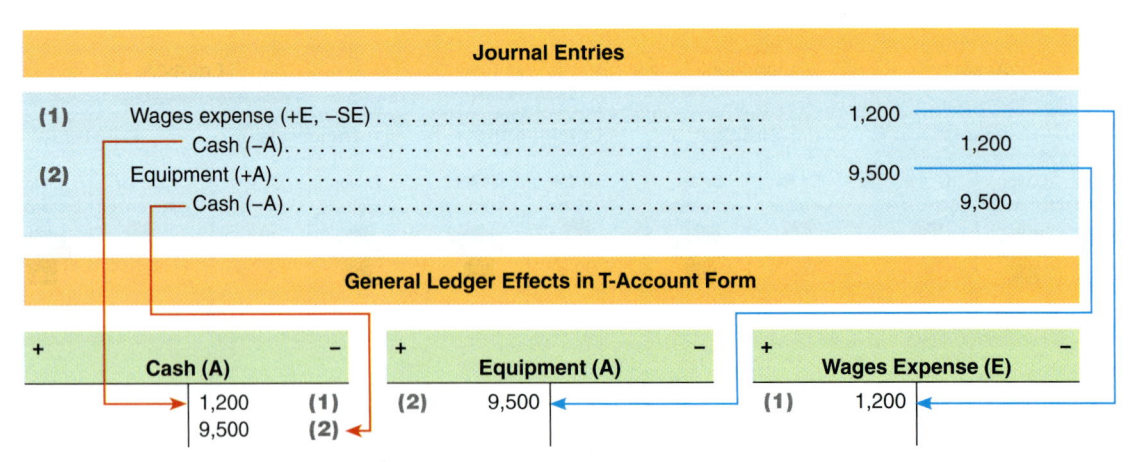

Journal Entries

(1)	Wages expense (+E, −SE)	1,200	
	Cash (−A)		1,200
(2)	Equipment (+A)	9,500	
	Cash (−A)		9,500

General Ledger Effects in T-Account Form

+	Cash (A)	−		+	Equipment (A)	−		+	Wages Expense (E)	−
	1,200	(1)		(2)	9,500			(1)	1,200	
	9,500	(2)								

For journal entries, debits are recorded first followed by credits. Credits are commonly indented. The dollar amounts are entered in both the debit (left) column and the credit (right) column. In practice, recordkeepers also enter the date. An alternative presentation is to utilize the abbreviation *Dr* to denote debits and *Cr* to denote credits that precede the account title. We use the first approach in this book.

Analyze, Journalize, and Post

To illustrate the use of journal entries and T-accounts to record transactions, we return to Natural Beauty Supply and reexamine the same transactions recorded earlier in the financial statement effects template. The following layout illustrates our three-step accounting process of analyzing, journalizing, and posting. The FSET is followed by the journal entry. A debit in the journal entry is posted to the debit side of the relevant T-Account, shown with a blue arrow. A credit in the journal entry is posted to the credit side of the relevant T-Account, shown with a red arrow.

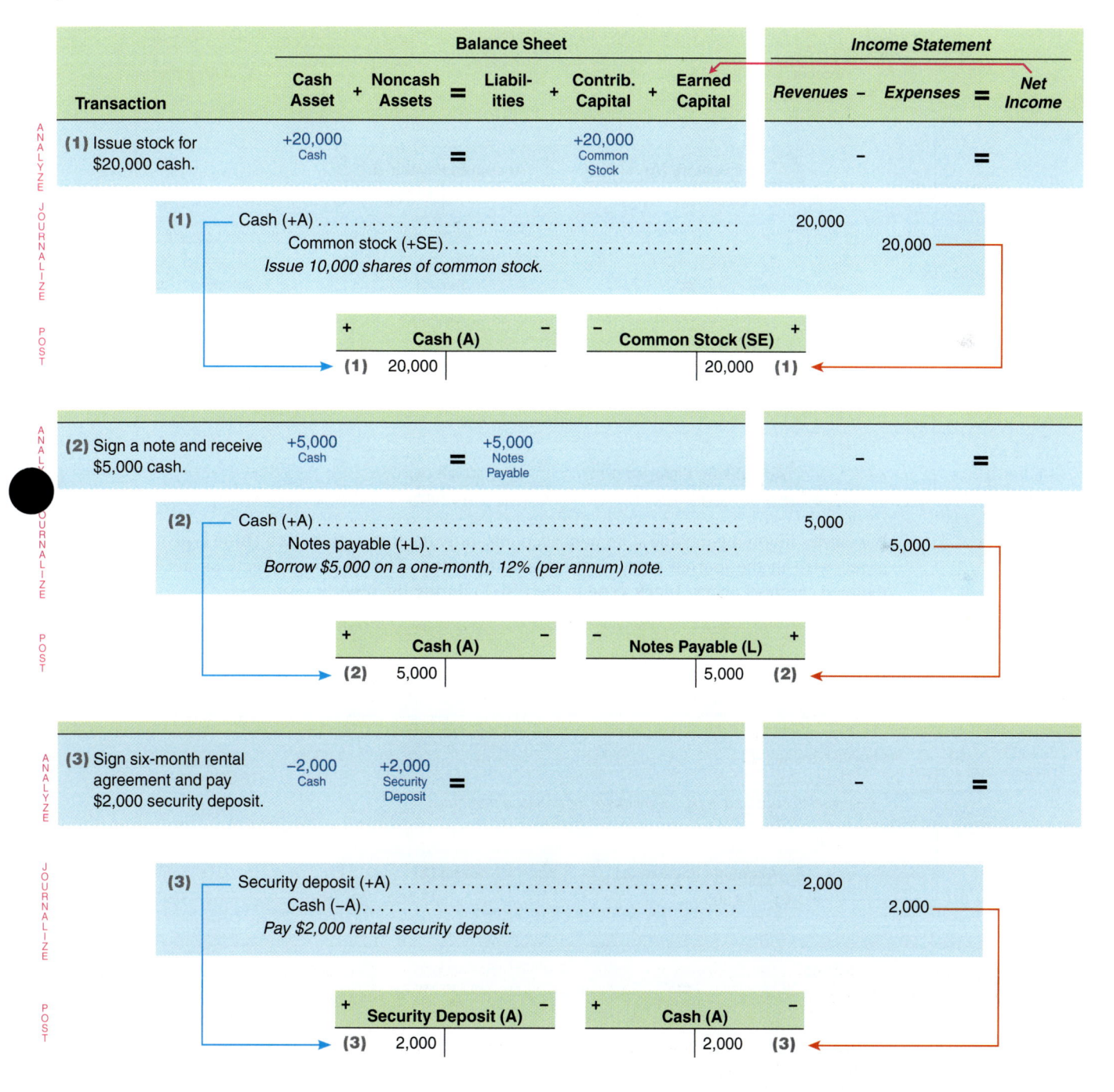

Transaction	Balance Sheet					Income Statement		
	Cash Asset	+ Noncash Assets	= Liabilities	+ Contrib. Capital	+ Earned Capital	Revenues	− Expenses	= Net Income
(1) Issue stock for $20,000 cash.	+20,000 Cash		=	+20,000 Common Stock			−	=

(1) Cash (+A) 20,000
   Common stock (+SE) 20,000
   Issue 10,000 shares of common stock.

+ Cash (A) −		− Common Stock (SE) +	
(1) 20,000			20,000 (1)

Transaction								
(2) Sign a note and receive $5,000 cash.	+5,000 Cash		= +5,000 Notes Payable				−	=

(2) Cash (+A) 5,000
   Notes payable (+L) 5,000
   Borrow $5,000 on a one-month, 12% (per annum) note.

+ Cash (A) −		− Notes Payable (L) +	
(2) 5,000			5,000 (2)

Transaction								
(3) Sign six-month rental agreement and pay $2,000 security deposit.	−2,000 Cash	+2,000 Security Deposit	=				−	=

(3) Security deposit (+A) 2,000
   Cash (−A) 2,000
   Pay $2,000 rental security deposit.

+ Security Deposit (A) −		+ Cash (A) −	
(3) 2,000			2,000 (3)

continued

Chapter 2 Constructing Financial Statements

continued from previous page

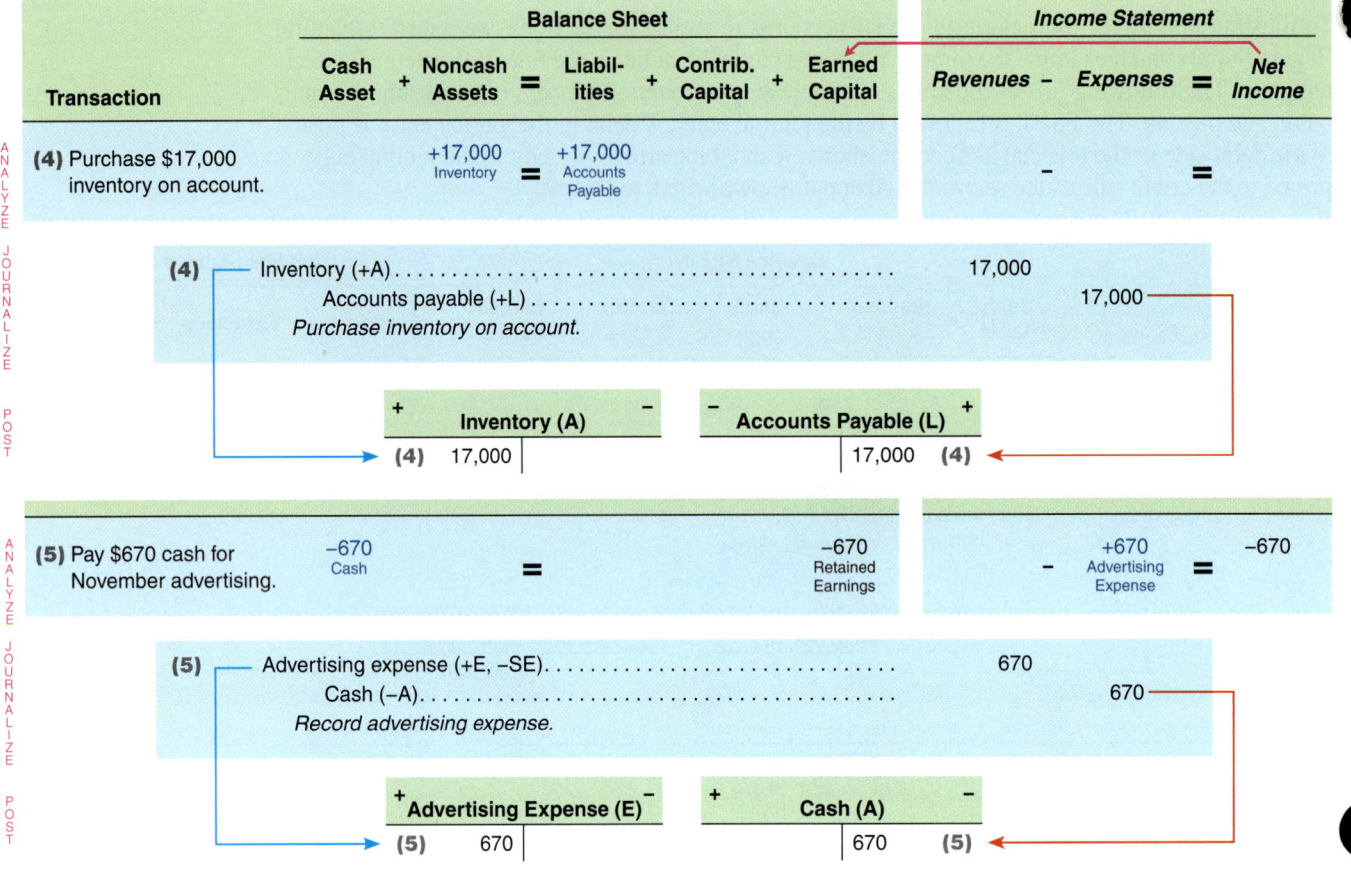

Transaction	Balance Sheet: Cash Asset + Noncash Assets = Liabilities + Contrib. Capital + Earned Capital	Income Statement: Revenues − Expenses = Net Income
(4) Purchase $17,000 inventory on account.	+17,000 Inventory = +17,000 Accounts Payable	− =

(4) Inventory (+A) 17,000
   Accounts payable (+L) 17,000
   Purchase inventory on account.

+ Inventory (A) −	− Accounts Payable (L) +
(4) 17,000	17,000 (4)

Transaction		
(5) Pay $670 cash for November advertising.	−670 Cash = −670 Retained Earnings	+670 Advertising Expense = −670

(5) Advertising expense (+E, −SE) 670
   Cash (−A) 670
   Record advertising expense.

+ Advertising Expense (E) −	+ Cash (A) −
(5) 670	670 (5)

For entries involving income statement accounts, only the transaction itself (**blue type** in the FSET) is recorded in the journal entry and T-account posting. The resulting effects on net income and retained earnings occur (**black type** in the FSET) during the reporting process.

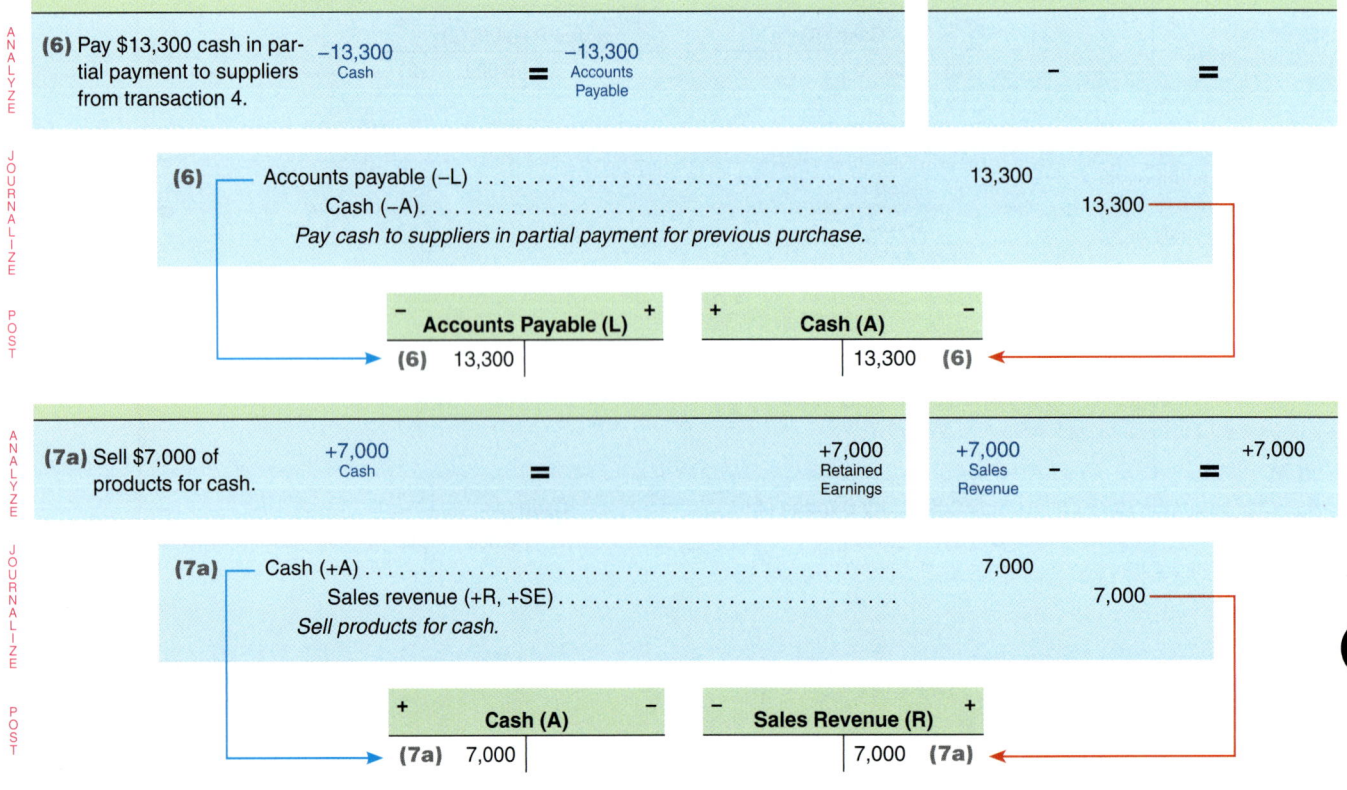

Transaction		
(6) Pay $13,300 cash in partial payment to suppliers from transaction 4.	−13,300 Cash = −13,300 Accounts Payable	− =

(6) Accounts payable (−L) 13,300
   Cash (−A) 13,300
   Pay cash to suppliers in partial payment for previous purchase.

− Accounts Payable (L) +	+ Cash (A) −
(6) 13,300	13,300 (6)

Transaction		
(7a) Sell $7,000 of products for cash.	+7,000 Cash = +7,000 Retained Earnings	+7,000 Sales Revenue − = +7,000

(7a) Cash (+A) 7,000
   Sales revenue (+R, +SE) 7,000
   Sell products for cash.

+ Cash (A) −	− Sales Revenue (R) +
(7a) 7,000	7,000 (7a)

continued

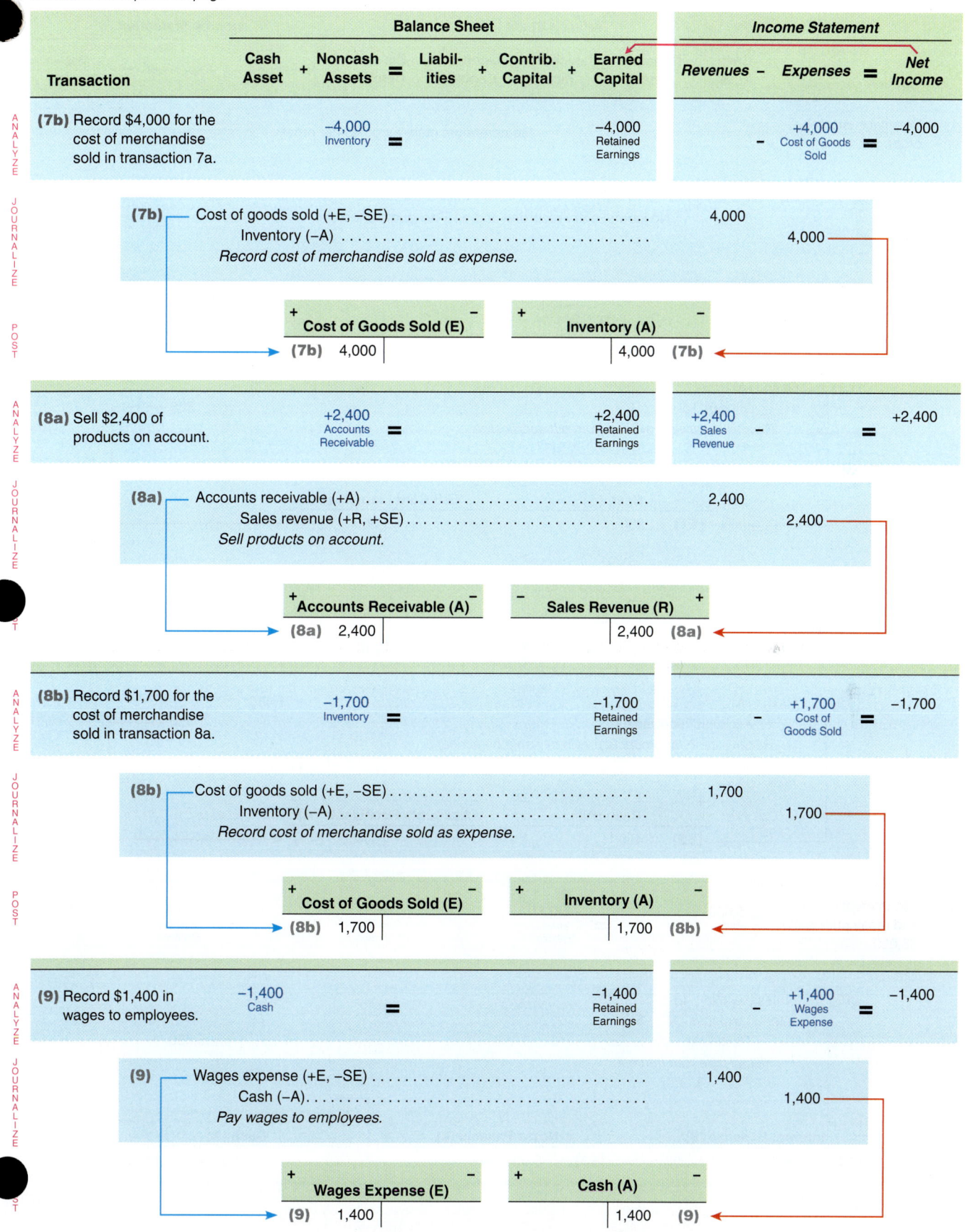

continued from previous page

	Balance Sheet					Income Statement		
Transaction	Cash Asset	+ Noncash Assets	= Liabilities	+ Contrib. Capital	+ Earned Capital	Revenues	− Expenses	= Net Income
(7b) Record $4,000 for the cost of merchandise sold in transaction 7a.		−4,000 Inventory	=		−4,000 Retained Earnings		+4,000 Cost of Goods Sold	−4,000

(7b) Cost of goods sold (+E, −SE) 4,000
 Inventory (−A) 4,000
 Record cost of merchandise sold as expense.

+ Cost of Goods Sold (E) −		+ Inventory (A) −
(7b) 4,000		4,000 (7b)

	Balance Sheet					Income Statement		
(8a) Sell $2,400 of products on account.		+2,400 Accounts Receivable	=		+2,400 Retained Earnings	+2,400 Sales Revenue	−	= +2,400

(8a) Accounts receivable (+A) 2,400
 Sales revenue (+R, +SE) 2,400
 Sell products on account.

+ Accounts Receivable (A) −		− Sales Revenue (R) +
(8a) 2,400		2,400 (8a)

(8b) Record $1,700 for the cost of merchandise sold in transaction 8a.		−1,700 Inventory	=		−1,700 Retained Earnings		+1,700 Cost of Goods Sold	−1,700

(8b) Cost of goods sold (+E, −SE) 1,700
 Inventory (−A) 1,700
 Record cost of merchandise sold as expense.

+ Cost of Goods Sold (E) −		+ Inventory (A) −
(8b) 1,700		1,700 (8b)

(9) Record $1,400 in wages to employees.	−1,400 Cash		=		−1,400 Retained Earnings		+1,400 Wages Expense	= −1,400

(9) Wages expense (+E, −SE) 1,400
 Cash (−A) 1,400
 Pay wages to employees.

+ Wages Expense (E) −		+ Cash (A) −
(9) 1,400		1,400 (9)

continued

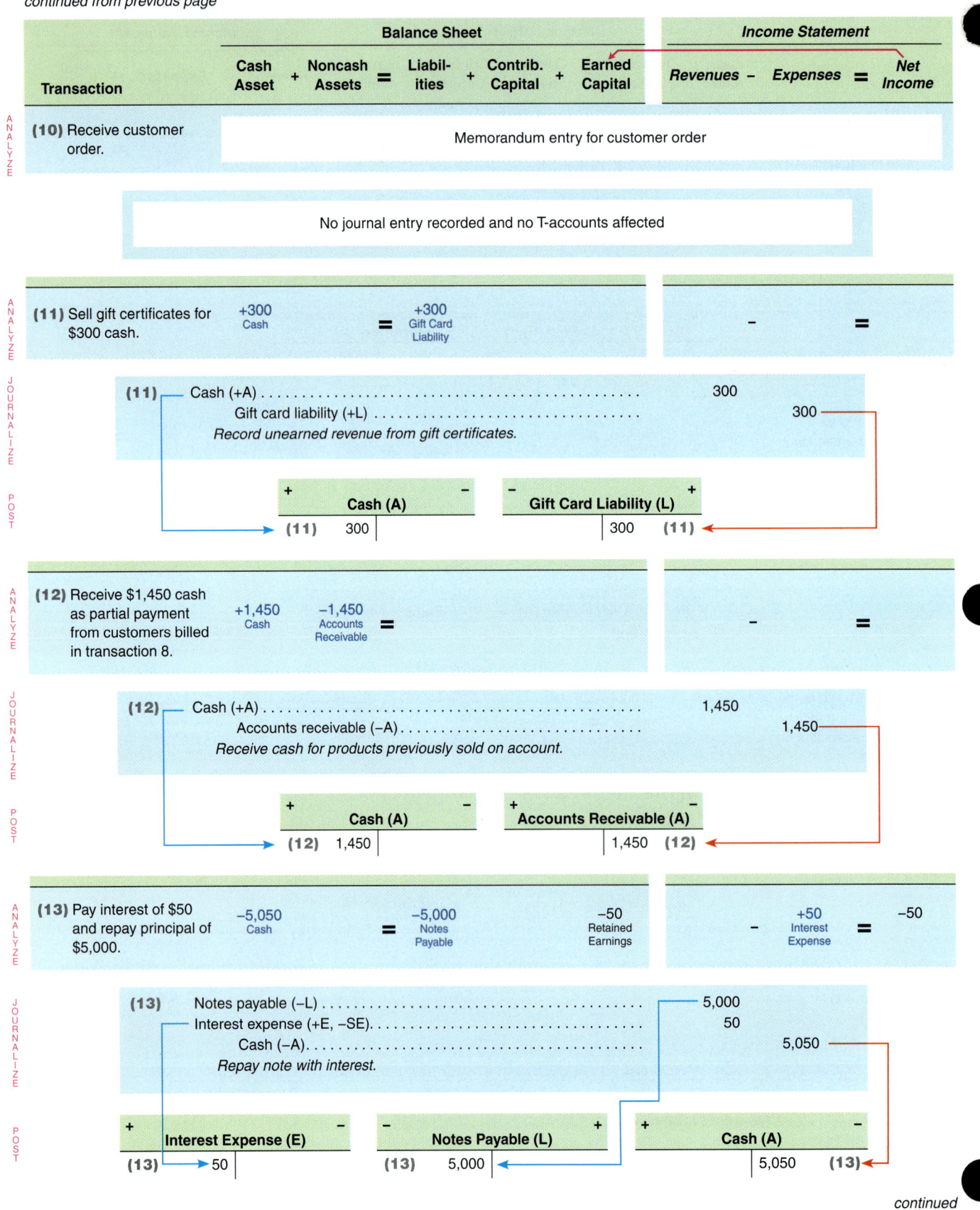

continued from previous page

		Balance Sheet				Income Statement	
Transaction	Cash Asset	+ Noncash Assets	= Liabilities	+ Contrib. Capital	+ Earned Capital	Revenues − Expenses	= Net Income

ANALYZE

(10) Receive customer order.

Memorandum entry for customer order

No journal entry recorded and no T-accounts affected

ANALYZE

(11) Sell gift certificates for $300 cash.

+300 Cash = +300 Gift Card Liability

JOURNALIZE

(11) Cash (+A) 300
      Gift card liability (+L) 300
      Record unearned revenue from gift certificates.

POST

+ Cash (A) −		− Gift Card Liability (L) +	
(11) 300			300 (11)

ANALYZE

(12) Receive $1,450 cash as partial payment from customers billed in transaction 8.

+1,450 Cash −1,450 Accounts Receivable =

JOURNALIZE

(12) Cash (+A) 1,450
      Accounts receivable (−A) 1,450
      Receive cash for products previously sold on account.

POST

+ Cash (A) −		+ Accounts Receivable (A) −	
(12) 1,450			1,450 (12)

ANALYZE

(13) Pay interest of $50 and repay principal of $5,000.

−5,050 Cash = −5,000 Notes Payable   −50 Retained Earnings   +50 Interest Expense = −50

JOURNALIZE

(13) Notes payable (−L) 5,000
      Interest expense (+E, −SE) 50
      Cash (−A) 5,050
      Repay note with interest.

POST

+ Interest Expense (E) −		− Notes Payable (L) +		+ Cash (A) −	
(13) 50		(13) 5,000			5,050 (13)

continued

Transaction	Balance Sheet					Income Statement		
	Cash Asset	+ Noncash Assets	= Liabilities	+ Contrib. Capital	+ Earned Capital	Revenues	− Expenses	= Net Income
(14) Pay $1,680 for one-year insurance policy.	−1,680 Cash	+1,680 Prepaid Insurance	=				−	=

(14) Prepaid insurance (+A).................................... 1,680
    Cash (−A).. 1,680
    Pay insurance premium.

+ Prepaid Insurance (A) −		+ Cash (A) −	
(14) 1,680			1,680 (14)

Transaction	Cash Asset	+ Noncash Assets	= Liabilities	+ Contrib. Capital	+ Earned Capital	Revenues	− Expenses	= Net Income
(15) Pay $1,500 rent for November.	−1,500 Cash		=		−1,500 Retained Earnings		− +1,500 Rent Expense	= −1,500

(15) Rent expense (+E, −SE)............................... 1,500
    Cash (−A).. 1,500
    Record payment of November rent.

+ Rent Expense (E) −		+ Cash (A) −	
(15) 1,500			1,500 (15)

Transaction	Cash Asset	+ Noncash Assets	= Liabilities	+ Contrib. Capital	+ Earned Capital	Revenues	− Expenses	= Net Income
(16) Pay $50 cash dividend to shareholders.	−50 Cash		=		−50 Retained Earnings		−	=

(16) Retained earnings (−SE)............................... 50
    Cash (−A).. 50
    Pay a cash dividend.

− Retained Earnings (SE) +		+ Cash (A) −	
(16) 50			50 (16)

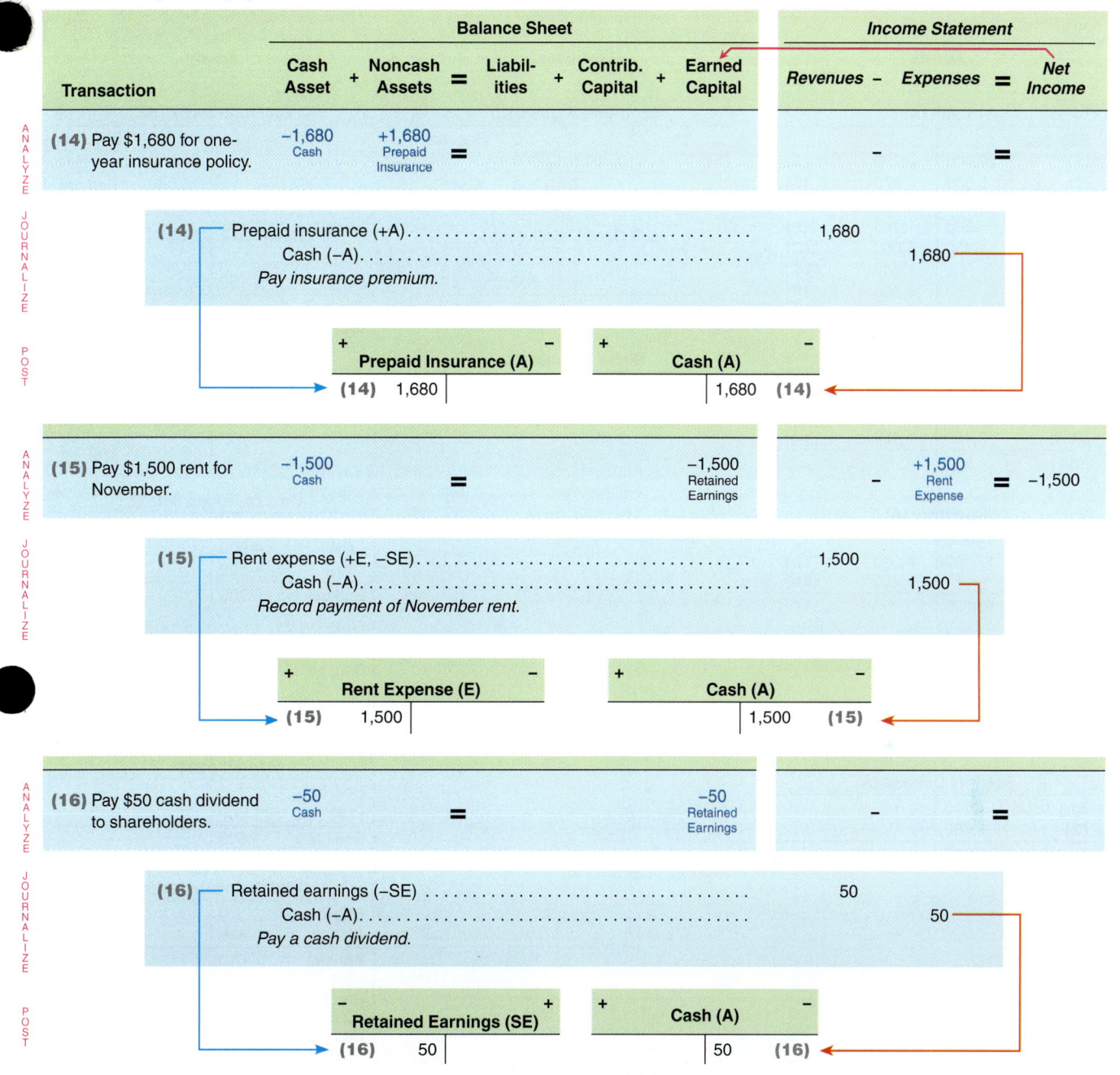

As shown each of the journal entries is posted to the appropriate T-accounts, which represent the general ledger. The complete general ledger reflecting each of these sixteen transactions follows, reflecting how the balance sheet and income statement are produced by the same underlying process. **The dashed line around the six equity accounts indicates those that are reported in the income statement before becoming part of retained earnings.** Each balance sheet T-account starts with an opening balance on November 1 (zero in this case), and the ending balances are the starting balances for December. Income statement T-accounts do not have an opening balance, for reasons we explore in Chapter 3.

As always, we see that: Assets = Liabilities + Equity. Specifically, $24,030 assets ($8,100 + $950 + $11,300 + $1,680 + $2,000) = $4,000 liabilities ($3,700 + $300) + $20,030 equity ($20,000 − $50 + $9,400 − $5,700 − $1,400 − $1,500 − $670 − $50).

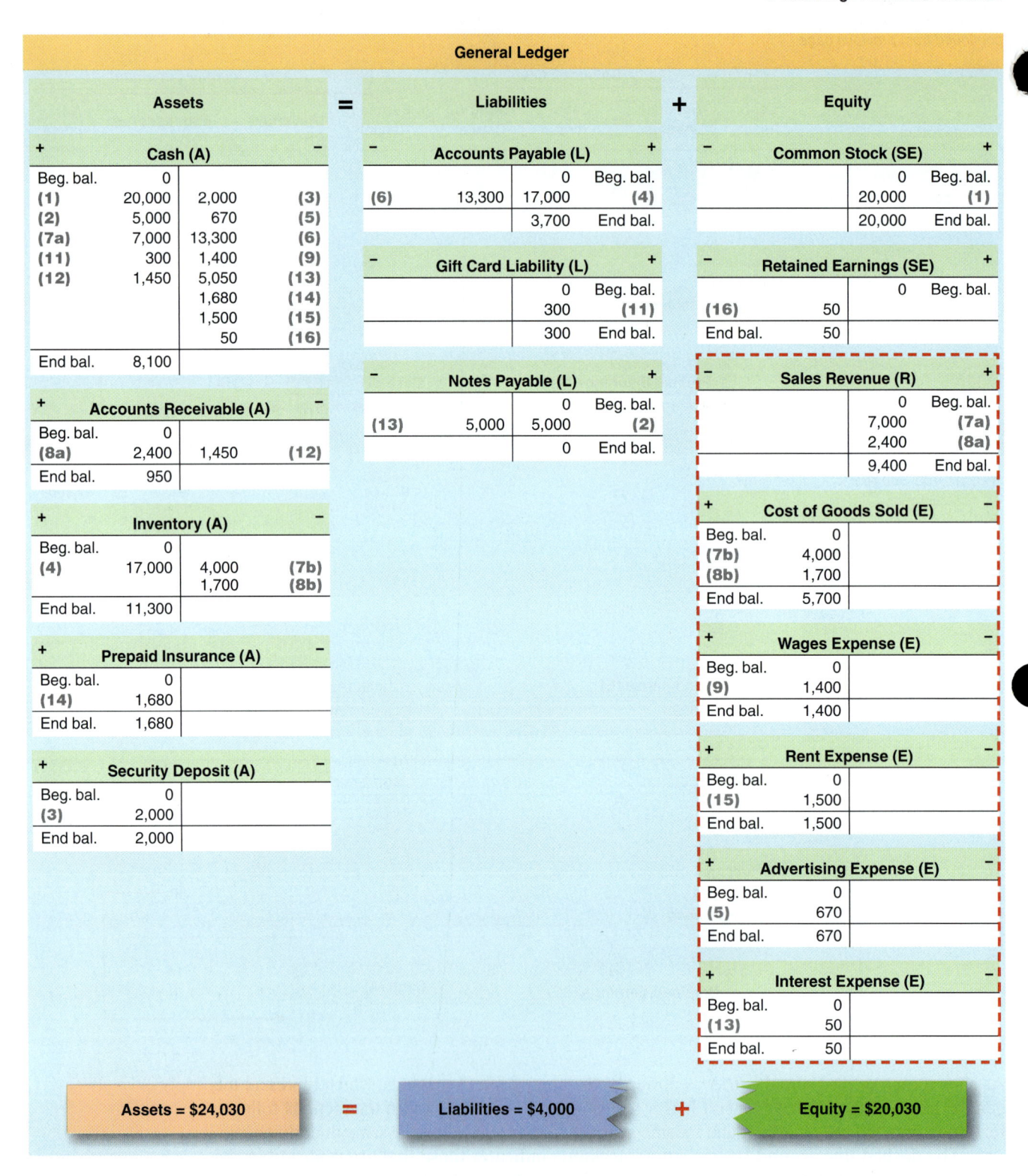

General Ledger

Assets	=	Liabilities	+	Equity

Cash (A) (+/−)
Beg. bal.	0		
(1)	20,000	2,000	(3)
(2)	5,000	670	(5)
(7a)	7,000	13,300	(6)
(11)	300	1,400	(9)
(12)	1,450	5,050	(13)
		1,680	(14)
		1,500	(15)
		50	(16)
End bal.	8,100		

Accounts Receivable (A)
Beg. bal.	0		
(8a)	2,400	1,450	(12)
End bal.	950		

Inventory (A)
Beg. bal.	0		
(4)	17,000	4,000	(7b)
		1,700	(8b)
End bal.	11,300		

Prepaid Insurance (A)
Beg. bal.	0		
(14)	1,680		
End bal.	1,680		

Security Deposit (A)
Beg. bal.	0		
(3)	2,000		
End bal.	2,000		

Accounts Payable (L)
		0	Beg. bal.
(6)	13,300	17,000	(4)
		3,700	End bal.

Gift Card Liability (L)
		0	Beg. bal.
		300	(11)
		300	End bal.

Notes Payable (L)
		0	Beg. bal.
(13)	5,000	5,000	(2)
		0	End bal.

Common Stock (SE)
		0	Beg. bal.
		20,000	(1)
		20,000	End bal.

Retained Earnings (SE)
		0	Beg. bal.
(16)	50		
End bal.	50		

Sales Revenue (R)
		0	Beg. bal.
		7,000	(7a)
		2,400	(8a)
		9,400	End bal.

Cost of Goods Sold (E)
Beg. bal.	0		
(7b)	4,000		
(8b)	1,700		
End bal.	5,700		

Wages Expense (E)
Beg. bal.	0		
(9)	1,400		
End bal.	1,400		

Rent Expense (E)
Beg. bal.	0		
(15)	1,500		
End bal.	1,500		

Advertising Expense (E)
Beg. bal.	0		
(5)	670		
End bal.	670		

Interest Expense (E)
Beg. bal.	0		
(13)	50		
End bal.	50		

Assets = $24,030 = Liabilities = $4,000 + Equity = $20,030

Review 2-6   LO2-6
Reporting Using the FSET and Preparing Journal Entries and the General Ledger

Assume that the following accounts appear in the ledger of M.E. Carter, a financial consultant to companies in the retail sector. Cash; Accounts Receivable; Office Equipment; Prepaid Subscriptions; Accounts Payable; Note Payable; Common Stock; Retained Earnings; Fees Earned; Salaries Expense; Rent Expense; Interest Expense; and Utilities Expense. For each of the following 11 transactions:

continued

continued from previous page

a. Analyze and enter each into the financial statement effects template.
b. Prepare journal entries for each of the transactions, set up T-accounts for each of the ledger accounts, and post the journal entries to those T-accounts—key all entries with the number identifying the transaction.
c. Prepare the general ledger in T-account form, enter the financial effects of all transactions, and determine the ending balance for each account.

(1) M.E. Carter started the firm by contributing $15,500 cash to the business in exchange for common stock.
(2) The firm purchased $10,400 in office equipment, issuing a long-term note payable for $4,400 with the remainder on account.
(3) Paid $700 cash for this period's office rent (on a short-term lease).
(4) Paid $9,600 cash for subscriptions to online financial databases covering the next three periods.
(5) Billed clients $11,300 for services rendered.
(6) Made $1,000 cash payment on account for the equipment purchased in transaction 2.
(7) Paid $2,800 cash for assistant's salary for this period.
(8) Collected $9,400 cash from clients previously billed in transaction 5.
(9) Received $180 invoice for this period's utilities; it is paid early in the next period.
(10) Paid $1,500 cash for dividends to shareholders.
(11) Paid $225 cash for interest on the note payable for the period.

Solution on p. 2-55.

ANALYZING FINANCIAL STATEMENTS

Analysis Objective

We are trying to determine if Walgreens has sufficient funds to pay its short-term debts as they come due. To accomplish this task, we employ several measures of liquidity. We introduce three such measures below to assess liquidity.

LO2-7 Compute net working capital, the current ratio, and the quick ratio, and explain how they reflect liquidity.

Analysis Tool Net Working Capital

$$\text{Net working capital} = \text{Current assets} - \text{Current liabilities}$$

Applying Net Working Capital to Walgreens

2018: $17,846 − $21,667 = $(3,821)
2019: $18,700 − $25,769 = $(7,069)
2020: $18,073 − $27,070 = $(8,997)

Guidance A company's net working capital is determined primarily by the time between paying for goods and employee services and the receipt of cash from sales for cash or on credit. This cycle is referred to as the firm's **cash operating cycle** (see **Exhibit 2.6**). The cash operating cycle can provide additional resources through trade credit financing. For example, inventory is typically bought on credit with terms that allow payment to be deferred for 30 to 90 days without penalty. The delay in payment allows the cash to be invested, thereby increasing the cash to be used in the following operating cycle. Of course, the reluctant supplier of the credit strives to reduce this payment delay, for example, through discounts for early payment.

A company's net working capital is a broad measure including all current assets even though some of them—inventories for one—require time to turn them into cash. Later in the book, we will discover that the accounting for some components of working capital, like inventory, needs to be adjusted with information found in the disclosure notes.

EXHIBIT 2.6 Operating Cycle

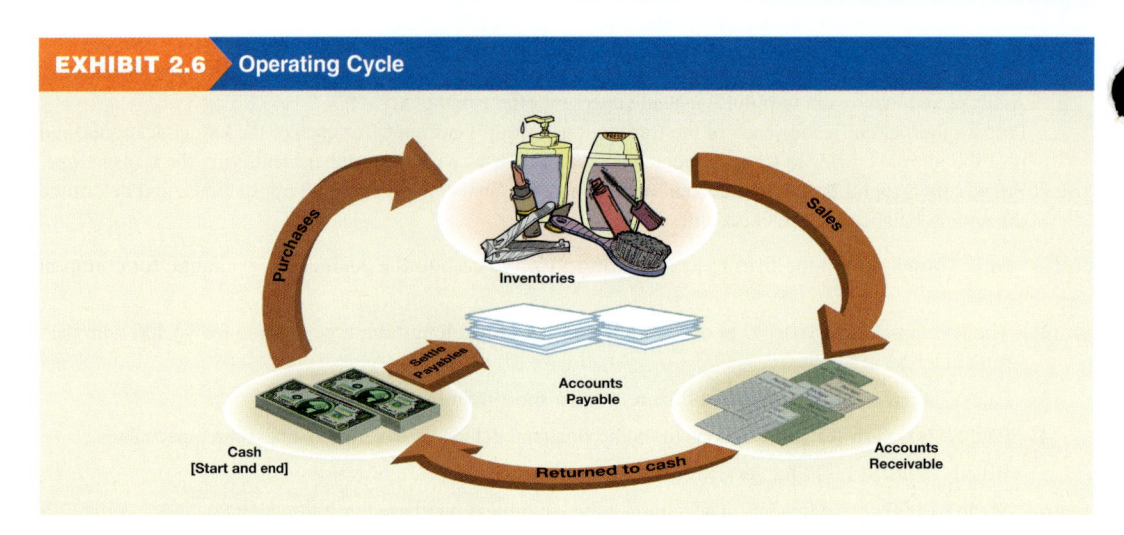

Analysis Tool   Current Ratio

$$\text{Current ratio} = \frac{\text{Current asset}}{\text{Current liabilities}}$$

Applying the Current Ratio to Walgreens

2018: $\dfrac{\$17{,}846}{\$21{,}667} = 0.82$

2019: $\dfrac{\$18{,}700}{\$25{,}769} = 0.73$

2020: $\dfrac{\$18{,}073}{\$27{,}070} = 0.67$

Guidance   The current ratio is just a different form of net working capital and as such simply provides a different viewpoint. Current ratios exceeding one indicate a positive net working capital. However, for firms that find difficulty in predicting sales and collections, a higher current ratio is desirable, as discussed in Chapter 5. Companies generally prefer a current ratio greater than one but less than two. The ratio allows us to discern whether the company is likely to have difficulty meeting its short-term obligations. The current ratio has additional value as a ratio because net working capital depends on the size of the company. This is useful when comparing companies as below.

Walgreens in Context

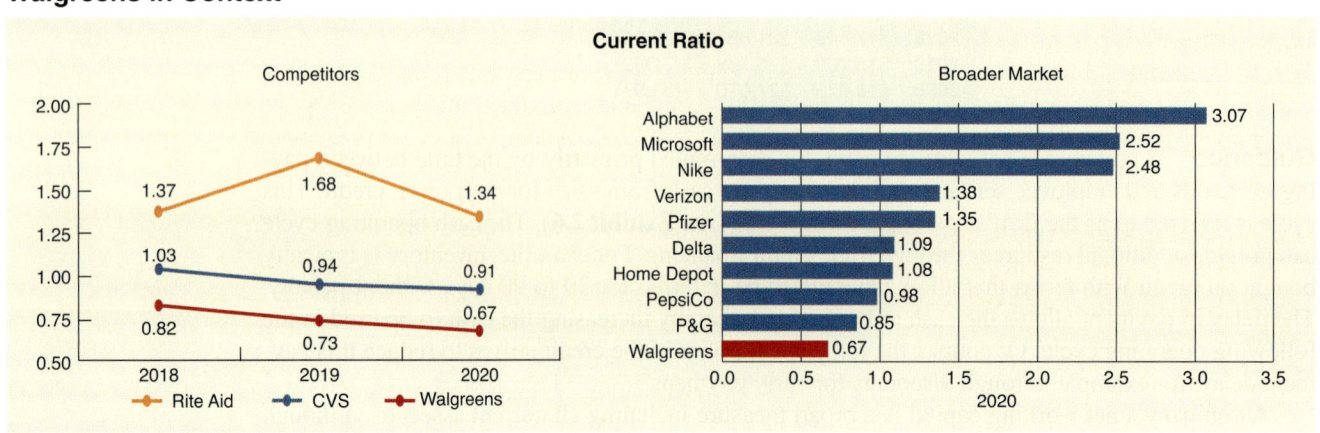

Current Ratio

Competitors:

Company	2018	2019	2020
Rite Aid	1.37	1.68	1.34
CVS	1.03	0.94	0.91
Walgreens	0.82	0.73	0.67

Broader Market (2020):

Company	Current Ratio
Alphabet	3.07
Microsoft	2.52
Nike	2.48
Verizon	1.38
Pfizer	1.35
Delta	1.09
Home Depot	1.08
PepsiCo	0.98
P&G	0.85
Walgreens	0.67

These companies do not have identical fiscal year-ends. For each fiscal year listed, balance sheets are dated from February 2 to December 31 of that year.

Analysis Tool Quick Ratio

$$\text{Quick ratio} = \frac{\text{Cash + Short-term securities + Accounts receivable}}{\text{Current liabilities}}$$

Applying the Quick Ratio to Walgreens

2018: $\dfrac{(\$785 + \$0 + \$6{,}573)}{\$21{,}667} = 0.34$

2019: $\dfrac{(\$1{,}023 + \$0 + \$7{,}226)}{\$25{,}769} = 0.32$

2020: $\dfrac{(\$516 + \$0 + \$7{,}132)}{\$27{,}070} = 0.28$

Guidance The quick ratio is a more restrictive form of the current ratio in that it excludes inventories. Only those assets that are cash, or near cash, are considered in this liquidity measure, making it a more stringent test of liquidity.

Walgreens in Context

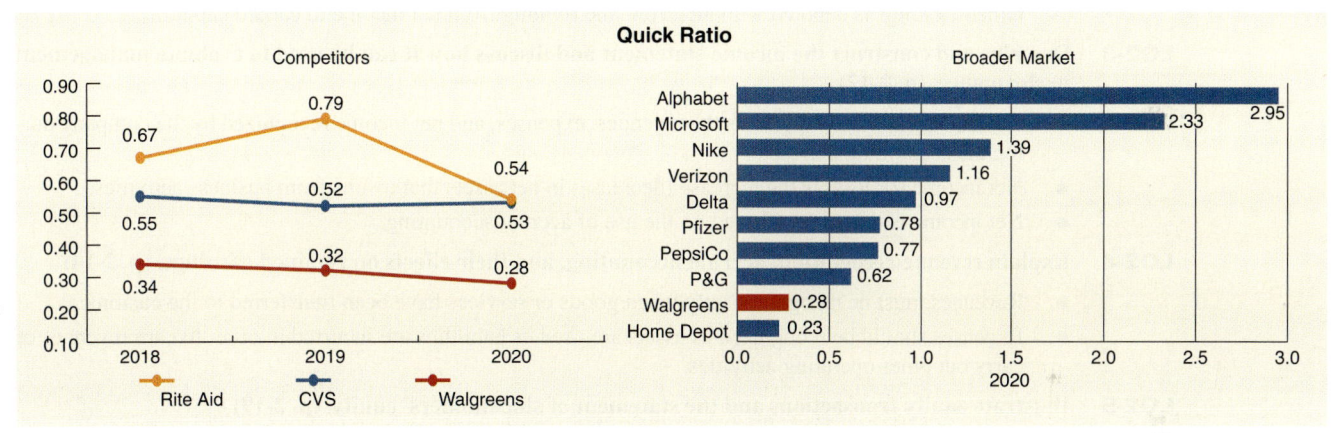

Quick Ratio

Competitors (2018–2020):
- Rite Aid: 0.67 (2018), 0.79 (2019), 0.54 (2020)
- CVS: 0.55 (2018), 0.52 (2019), 0.53 (2020)
- Walgreens: 0.34 (2018), 0.32 (2019), 0.28 (2020)

Broader Market (2020):
- Alphabet: 2.95
- Microsoft: 2.33
- Nike: 1.39
- Verizon: 1.16
- Delta: 0.97
- Pfizer: 0.78
- PepsiCo: 0.77
- P&G: 0.62
- Walgreens: 0.28
- Home Depot: 0.23

These companies do not have identical fiscal year-ends. For each fiscal year listed, balance sheets are dated from February 2 to December 31 of that year.

Takeaways Over the three-year period covered by our calculations, we can see that **Walgreens** is in a relatively weaker position with respect to liquidity compared to its competitors and the broader market. Its net working capital is negative in each of the three years, and has become more negative over this time period. The current and quick ratios have declined over the three years as well. So there may be some cause for concern for Walgreens in terms of liquidity, but this is offset by Walgreens's strong, positive operating cash flow, which will help them meet liquidity needs going forward.

Other Considerations The ratios above tell us about retail pharmacy chains and some other companies in other industries. It is important to note that companies with different operating cycles are likely to exhibit different values at optimal levels of activity. For example, grocery stores will have few current assets but consistent, large operating cash inflows that ensure sufficient liquidity despite current ratios less than one. Additionally, companies that efficiently manage inventories, receivables, and payables can also operate with current ratios less than one. **Walmart Inc.**, for instance, uses its strong market power to extract extended credit terms from suppliers while simultaneously enforcing short payment periods on customers.

Computing Working Capital, Current Ratio, and Quick Ratio LO2-7 **Review 2-7**

Using the information from Review 2-6, compute the following ratios on end-of-year balances for M.E. Carter.

a. Working capital
b. Current ratio
c. Quick ratio

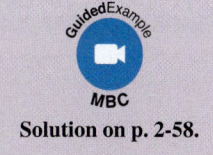

Solution on p. 2-58.

SUMMARY

LO2-1 Describe and construct the balance sheet and understand how it can be used for analysis. (p. 2-3)
- Assets, which reflect investment activities, are reported (in order of their liquidity) as current assets (expected to be used typically within a year) and noncurrent assets.
- Assets are reported at their historical cost and not at market values (with a few exceptions) and are restricted to those that can be reliably measured.
- Not all assets are reported on the balance sheet; a company's self-developed intellectual capital, often one of its more valuable assets, is one example.
- For an asset to be recorded, it must be owned or controlled by the company and carry future economic benefits.
- Liabilities and equity are the sources of company financing; they are ordered by maturity dates.

LO2-2 Use the financial statement effects template (FSET) to analyze transactions. (p. 2-8)
- The FSET captures the effects of transactions on the balance sheet, income statement, statement of stockholders' equity, and statement of cash flows.
- Income statement effects are separated into revenues, expenses, and net income. The updating of retained earnings is denoted with an arrow line running from net income to earned capital.

LO2-3 Describe and construct the income statement and discuss how it can be used to evaluate management performance. (p. 2-12)
- The income statement presents the revenues, expenses, and net income recognized by the company during the accounting period.
- Net income (or loss) is the increase (decrease) in net assets that results from business activities.
- Net income is determined based on the use of accrual accounting.

LO2-4 Explain revenue recognition, accrual accounting, and their effects on retained earnings. (p. 2-14)
- Revenues must be recognized only when goods or services have been transferred to the customer.
- Expenses should be recognized as assets are used or liabilities are incurred in order to earn revenues or carry out other operating activities.

LO2-5 Illustrate equity transactions and the statement of stockholders' equity. (p. 2-19)
- The statement of stockholders' equity reports transactions resulting in changes in equity accounts during the accounting period.
- Transactions between the company and its owners, such as dividend payments, are not reported in the income statement.

LO2-6 Use journal entries and T-accounts to analyze and record transactions. (p. 2-21)
- Transactions are recorded in the accounting system using journal entries.
- Journal entries are posted to a general ledger, represented by "T-accounts."
- Accountants use "debits" and "credits" to record transactions in the accounts.

LO2-7 Compute net working capital, the current ratio, and the quick ratio, and explain how they reflect liquidity. (p. 2-30)
- Net working capital: an indicator of a firm's ability to pay its short-term debts computed as the difference between current assets and current liabilities.
- Current ratio (CR): A measure of liquidity indicating the degree of coverage of current liabilities by current assets.
- Quick ratio (QR): A measure of the ability to cover current liabilities using only cash and cash equivalents (such as money market accounts), short-term securities, and accounts receivable.

GUIDANCE ANSWERS... YOU MAKE THE CALL

You are an Analyst Often, the answer in such a case is dividends. Indeed, in 2019, Colgate-Palmolive Company paid cash dividends of $1,472 million. The net income and dividend payments and, in Colgate-Palmolive's case a $9 million amount classified as "other," account for the change in retained earnings ($22,501 million − $21,615 million = $2,367 million − $1,472 million − $9 million). On occasion, companies pay dividends in excess of their earnings (or pay dividends even when earning losses), resulting in a decrease in retained earnings over the period.

KEY RATIOS

Net working capital = Current assets − Current liabilities

$$\text{Current ratio} = \frac{\text{Current assets}}{\text{Current liabilities}} \qquad \text{Quick ratio} = \frac{\text{Cash + Short-term securities + Accounts receivable}}{\text{Current liabilities}}$$

Assignments with the logo in the margin are available in BusinessCourse.
See the Preface of the book for details.

MULTIPLE CHOICE

1. Which of the following conditions must exist for an item to be recorded as an asset?
    a. Item is not owned or controlled by the company.
    b. Future benefits from the item cannot be reliably measured.
    c. Item must be a tangible asset.
    d. Item must be expected to yield future benefits.

2. Company assets that are excluded from the company financial statements
    a. are presumably reflected in the company's stock price.
    b. include all of the company's intangible assets.
    c. are known as intangible assets.
    d. include investments in other companies.

3. If an asset declines in value, which of the following must be true?
    a. A liability also declines.
    b. Equity also declines.
    c. Either a liability or equity also declines or another asset increases in value.
    d. Neither a nor b can occur.

4. Which of the following is true about accrual accounting?
    a. Accrual accounting requires that expenses always be recognized when cash is paid out.
    b. Accrual accounting is required under GAAP.
    c. Accrual accounting recognizes revenue only when cash is received.
    d. Recognition of a prepaid asset is not an example of accrual accounting.

5. Which of the following options accurately identifies the effects a cash sale of an iPhone has on Apple's accounts?
    a. Accounts receivable increases, sales revenue increases, cost of goods sold increases, and inventory decreases.
    b. Cash increases, sales revenue increases, cost of goods sold decreases, and inventory decreases.
    c. Accounts receivable increases, sales revenue increases, cost of goods sold decreases, and inventory decreases.
    d. Cash increases, sales revenue increases, cost of goods sold increases, and inventory decreases.

Multiple Choice Answers
1. d 2. a 3. c 4. b 5. d

QUESTIONS

Q2-1. The balance sheet consists of assets, liabilities, and equity. Define each category and provide two examples of accounts reported within each category.

Q2-2. Two important concepts that guide income statement reporting are the revenue recognition principle and the expense recognition principle. Define and explain each of these two guiding principles.

Q2-3. GAAP is based on the concept of accrual accounting. Define and describe accrual accounting.

Q2-4. What is the statement of stockholders' equity? What information is conveyed in that statement?

Q2-5. What are the two essential characteristics of an asset?

Q2-6. What does the concept of liquidity refer to? Explain.

Q2-7. What does the term "current" denote when referring to assets?

Q2-8. Assets are often recorded at historical costs even though current market values might, arguably, be more relevant to financial statement readers. Describe the reasoning behind historical cost usage.

Q2-9. Identify three intangible assets that are likely to be excluded from the balance sheet because they cannot be reliably measured.

Q2-10. How does the quick ratio differ from the current ratio?

Q2-11. What three conditions must be satisfied to require reporting of a liability on the balance sheet?

Q2-12. Define net working capital. Explain how increasing the amount of trade credit can reduce the net working capital for a company.

Q2-13. On December 31, Miller Company had $525,000 in total assets and owed $165,000 to creditors. If this corporation's common stock totaled $225,000, what amount of retained earnings is reported on its December 31 balance sheet?

DATA ANALYTICS

LO2-1 DA2-1. Preparing Basic Data Visualization in Excel of the Balance Sheet

The Excel file associated with this exercise includes total liabilities, common stock, and retained earnings balances as of December 31 for Monona Inc. We will prepare data visualizations focusing on how these amounts relate to each other and how the relations are expressed through proportions.

REQUIRED

1. Download Excel file DA2-1 found in myBusinessCourse.
2. Prepare a doughnut chart showing total liabilities, total common stock, and total retained earnings as components of total liabilities plus stockholders' equity. *Hint:* Highlight the dataset and open the Insert tab. Click on the Pie icon in the Charts group and click on Doughnut.
3. Display a percentage label in each section of your chart. *Hint:* Right-click inside the doughnut, select Format data labels, select Percentage. Deselect Value if necessary.
4. List the formula for the chart data range. *Hint:* Click inside the chart. Open the Chart Design tab and click Select Data. The formula is in the Chart data range field.
5. List the percentage amount (or combination of percentage amounts) on the doughnut chart that reflect the stockholders' equity proportion.
6. List the larger percentage: either the total liabilities proportion or the total equity proportion of the pie chart.
7. List the percentage amount (or combination of percentage amounts) on the doughnut chart that reflect the total assets proportion.
8. List the dollar amount of total assets.

LO2-3 DA2-2. Preparing a Basic Data Visualization in Excel to Highlight Changes in Expenses Over Time

The Excel file associated with this exercise includes three years of operating expenses of **Starbucks Corporation** reported in recent reports on Form 10-K. We will use data visualizations to analyze the trends of expenses over this three-year period.

REQUIRED

1. Download Excel file DA2-2 found in myBusinessCourse.
2. Create a data visualization within the worksheet in Excel, through the Sparkline feature: Line option. *Hint:* Highlight the cells with numeric data and click on Insert, click on Sparklines, click on Line. Next, select where to place Sparklines by highlighting the empty cells in the column to the right of your last column of data.
3. Format the Sparklines by adding color markers to the high and low points of your chart and adding thickness to the chart lines. *Hint:* Highlight your Sparkline and under the Sparkline tab, click on High Point and Low Point and choose your desired color scheme from the options listed in the Style Group. To add thickness, click on Sparkline Color and Weight to make an adjustment.
4. Determine which Sparkline (and, thus, pattern of activity) is most similar to the Sparkline for Product and distribution.
5. Determine which Sparkline is most similar to the Sparkline for Store operating expenses.

LO2-6 DA2-3. Explaining the Role of Artificial Intelligence in Accounting

Artificial intelligence (AI) is the simulation of human intelligence through the use of machines. Machines are programmed to sense, recognize speech, problem solve, learn, act, or react. In a post by Nigel Duffy and Karsten Fuser called "Six Ways the CFO Can Use Artificial Intelligence Today" (found at https://www.ey.com/en_us/ai/six-ways-the-cfo-can-use-artificial-intelligence-today), the authors outline several uses of AI. Match a specific example that applies to each of the six uses of AI summarized by the authors.

CATEGORY OF AI USAGE

1. Customer data and predictive behavior
2. Beyond the book value
3. Management of bad debt
4. Fraud
5. Money laundering
6. Taking drudgery out of finance

SPECIFIC EXAMPLE OF AI USAGE

a. ___ Using natural language processing software to review thousands of pages of contracts to identify possible lease agreements.

b. ___ Applying minute-by-minute pricing based upon correlations between customer demographics, type of product, and payment method with the goal of maximizing revenues.

c. ___ Using AI to predict which customers will pay and when they will pay, analyzing data such as the company's credit rating, industry type, purchase history, and contact transactions.

d. ___ A lender assesses the fair value of collateral by assessing thousands of variables including market data and data specific to the collateral.

e. ___ Using AI to analyze trends in all recorded expenses, detecting patterns by certain employees.

f. ___ Classification of suspicious transactions according to the risk that they resulted in illegally obtained money.

DA2-4. Preparing Tableau Visualizations of Basic Financial Information
Available in myBusinessCourse, this problem requires the creation of Tableau visualizations of financial information of S&P 500 companies from balance sheet, income statement and statement of cash flows data.

DATA VISUALIZATION

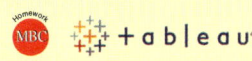

Data Visualization Activities are available in myBusinessCourse. These assignments use Tableau Dashboards to expose students to visual depictions of data and introduce students to data analytics through data visualizations. These exercises are easily assignable and auto graded by MBC.

MINI EXERCISES

M2-14. Determining Retained Earnings and Net Income Using the Balance Sheet
The following information is reported for Kinney Corporation at the end of the year.

Accounts receivable	$ 46,000	Retained earnings	$?
Accounts payable	22,000	Supplies inventory	18,000
Cash	16,000	Equipment	276,000
Common stock	220,000		

a. Compute the amount of retained earnings reported at the end of the year.
b. If the amount of retained earnings at the beginning of the year was $60,000, and $24,000 in cash dividends were declared and paid during the year, what was the company's net income for the year?

M2-15. Applying the Accounting Equation to the Balance Sheet
Determine the missing amount in each of the following separate company cases.

	Assets	Liabilities	Equity
a.	$280,000	$119,000	$?
b.	?	44,800	39,200
c.	130,200	?	72,800

M2-16. Applying the Accounting Equation to the Balance Sheet
Determine the missing amount in each of the following separate company cases.

	Assets	Liabilities	Equity
a.	$300,000	$84,000	$?
b.	?	34,400	8,800
c.	702,400	?	337,600

LO2-1 **M2-17. Applying the Accounting Equation to Determine Unknown Values**
Determine the following for each separate company case:
a. The stockholders' equity of Jensen Corporation, which has assets of $360,000 and liabilities of $260,800.
b. The liabilities of Sloan & Dechow, Inc., which has assets of $494,400 and stockholders' equity of $132,000.
c. The assets of Clem Corporation, which has liabilities of $320,000, common stock of $160,000, and retained earnings of $148,000.

LO2-2, 4, 5 **M2-18. Analyzing Transaction Effects on Equity**
Would each of the following transactions increase, decrease, or have no effect on equity?
a. Paid cash to acquire supplies.
b. Paid cash for dividends to shareholders.
c. Paid cash for salaries.
d. Purchased equipment for cash.
e. Shareholders invested cash in business in exchange for common stock.
f. Rendered service to customers on account.
g. Rendered service to customers for cash.

LO2-1, 3, 4 **M2-19. Identifying and Classifying Financial Statement Items**
For each of the following items, identify whether they would most likely be reported in the balance sheet (B) or income statement (I).

a. Machinery _____   e. Common stock _____   i. Taxes expense _____
b. Supplies expense _____   f. Factory buildings _____   j. Cost of goods sold _____
c. Prepaid advertising _____   g. Receivables _____   k. Long-term debt _____
d. Advertising expense _____   h. Taxes payable _____   l. Treasury stock _____

LO2-3, 4 **M2-20. Computing Net Income**
Healy Corporation recorded service revenues of $200,000 during the year, of which $140,000 were for credit and $60,000 were for cash. Moreover, of the $140,000 credit sales, it collected $40,000 cash on those receivables before year-end. The company also paid $120,000 cash for current year's wages.

a. Compute the company's net income for the year.
b. Suppose you discover that employees had earned an additional $20,000 in wages during the year, but this amount had not been paid. Would annual net income change? If so, by how much?

LO2-1, 3, 5 **M2-21. Classifying Items in Financial Statements**
Next to each item, indicate whether it would most likely be reported on the balance sheet (B), the income statement (I), or the statement of stockholders' equity (SE).

a. Liabilities _____   d. Revenues _____   g. Assets _____
b. Net income _____   e. Stock issuance _____   h. Expenses _____
c. Cash _____   f. Dividends _____   i. Equity _____

LO2-1, 3, 4, 5 **M2-22. Classifying Items in Financial Statements**
For each of the following items, indicate whether it is most likely reported on the balance sheet (B), the income statement (I), or the statement of stockholders' equity (SE).

a. Accounts receivable _____   e. Notes payable _____
b. Prepaid insurance _____   f. Supplies expense _____
c. Net income _____   g. Land _____
d. Stockholders' equity _____   h. Supplies _____

LO2-1, 3, 4, 5 **M2-23. Classifying Items in Financial Statements**
For each of the following items, indicate whether it is most likely reported on the balance sheet (B), the income statement (I), or the statement of stockholders' equity (SE).

a. Cash (year-end balance) _____   e. Dividends _____
b. Advertising expense _____   f. Accounts payable _____
c. Common stock _____   g. Inventory _____
d. Printing fee revenue _____   h. Equipment _____

LO2-1, 5 **M2-24. Determining Company Performance and Retained Earnings Using the Accounting Equation**
Use your knowledge of accounting relations to complete the following table for **L Brands, Inc.** (All amounts are in $ millions.)

L Brands, Inc.
NYSE :: LB

Fiscal Year Ending	February 2, 2019	February 1, 2020
Beginning retained earnings (deficit)	$(1,460)	$(1,482)
Net income (loss)	?	(366)
Dividends paid	(666)	?
Other net changes in retained earnings	0	(2)
Ending retained earnings (deficit)	$(1,482)	$(2,182)

M2-25. Analyzing the Effect of Transactions on the Balance Sheet   LO2-1, 4

Following the example in *a* below, indicate the effects of transactions *b* through *i* on assets, liabilities, and equity, including identifying the individual accounts affected.

    a. Rendered legal services to clients for cash
       ANSWER: Increase assets (Cash)
                   Increase equity (Service Revenues)
    b. Purchased office supplies on account
    c. Issued additional common stock in exchange for cash
    d. Paid amount due on account for office supplies purchased in *b*
    e. Borrowed cash (and signed a six-month note) from bank
    f. Rendered legal services and billed clients
    g. Paid cash to acquire a desk lamp for the office
    h. Paid cash to cover interest on note payable to bank
    i. Received invoice for this period's utilities

M2-26. Analyzing the Effect of Transactions on the Balance Sheet   LO2-1, 4

Following the example in *a* below, indicate the effects of transactions *b* through *i* on assets, liabilities, and equity, including identifying the individual accounts affected.

    a. Paid cash to acquire a computer for use in office
       ANSWER: Increase assets (Office Equipment)
                   Decrease assets (Cash)
    b. Rendered services and billed client
    c. Paid cash to cover rent for this period
    d. Rendered services to client for cash
    e. Received amount due from client in *b*
    f. Purchased an office desk on account
    g. Paid cash to cover this period's employee salaries
    h. Paid cash to cover desk purchased in *f*
    i. Declared and paid a cash dividend

M2-27. Constructing a Retained Earnings Reconciliation from Financial Data   LO2-1, 5

Following is financial information from **Johnson & Johnson** for the year ended December 29, 2019. Prepare the 2019 fiscal-year retained earnings reconciliation for Johnson & Johnson ($ millions).

Johnson & Johnson
NYSE :: JNJ

Retained earnings, Dec. 30, 2018	$106,216	Dividends	$9,917
Net earnings	15,119	Retained earnings, Dec. 29, 2019	?
Other retained earnings changes	(759)		

M2-28. Analyzing Transactions to Compute Net Income   LO2-3, 4

Guay Corp., a start-up company, provided services that were acceptable to its customers and billed those customers for $175,000 in 2021. However, Guay collected only $140,000 cash in 2021, and the remaining $35,000 of 2021 revenues were collected in 2022. Guay employees earned $100,000 in 2021 wages that were not paid until the first week of 2022. How much net income does Guay report for 2021? For 2022 (assuming no new transactions)?

M2-29. Analyzing Transactions Using the Financial Statement Effects Template (FSET)   LO2-1, 2, 4

Report the effects for each of the following independent transactions using the financial statement effects template. If no entry should be made, answer "No entry."

	Balance Sheet	Income Statement
Transaction	Cash Asset + Noncash Assets = Liabilities + Contrib. Capital + Earned Capital	Revenues − Expenses = Net Income
a. Issue common stock for $30,000 cash.	=	− =
b. Pay $3,000 insurance in advance.	=	− =
c. Purchase computer equipment for $10,500 cash.	=	− =
d. Purchase and receive $19,500 of inventory on account (i.e., pay supplier later)	=	− =
e. Pay supplier of inventory in part (d)	=	− =

LO2-1, 2   M2-30. Analyzing Transactions Using the Financial Statement Effects Template (FSET)

Report the effects for each of the following independent transactions using the financial statement effects template. If no entry should be made, answer "No entry."

	Balance Sheet	Income Statement
Transaction	Cash Asset + Noncash Assets = Liabilities + Contrib. Capital + Earned Capital	Revenues − Expenses = Net Income
a. Borrow €28,500 from local bank.	=	− =
b. Pay €4,500 insurance premium for coverage for following year.	=	− =
c. Purchase vehicle for €48,000 cash.	=	− =
d. Purchase and receive €3,750 of office supplies on account (i.e., pay supplier later).	=	− =
e. Place order for €1,500 of additional supplies to be delivered next month.	=	− =

LO2-1, 2, 3, 4, 5   M2-31. Analyzing Transactions Using the Financial Statement Effects Template (FSET)

Report the effects for each of the following independent transactions using the financial statement effects template. If no entry should be made, answer "No entry."

	Balance Sheet	Income Statement
Transaction	Cash Asset + Noncash Assets = Liabilities + Contrib. Capital + Earned Capital	Revenues − Expenses = Net Income
a. Receive merchandise inventory costing $18,000, purchased with cash.	=	− =
b. Sell half of inventory in (a) for $15,000 on credit.	=	− =
c. Place order for $10,000 of additional merchandise inventory to be delivered next month.	=	− =

continued

Transaction	Balance Sheet: Cash Asset + Noncash Assets = Liabilities + Contrib. Capital + Earned Capital	Income Statement: Revenues − Expenses = Net Income
d. Pay employee $8,000 for compensation earned during the month.	=	− =
e. Pay $14,000 rent for use of premises during the month (lease term < 12 months).	=	− =
f. Receive full payment from customer in part (b).	=	− =

M2-32. Journalizing Business Transactions   **LO2-6**
Refer to the transactions in M2-31. Prepare journal entries for each of the transactions (*a*) through (*f*).

M2-33. Posting to T-Accounts   **LO2-6**
Refer to the transactions in M2-31. Set up T-accounts for each of the accounts referenced by the transactions and post the amounts for each transaction to those T-accounts. (The T-accounts will not have opening balances.)

EXERCISES

E2-34. Constructing Balance Sheets and Computing Working Capital   **LO2-1, 7**
The following balance sheet data are reported for Beaver, Inc., on May 31.

Accounts receivable	$27,450	Accounts payable	$ 7,800
Notes payable	30,000	Cash	18,300
Equipment	82,500	Common stock	63,750
Supplies	24,600	Retained earnings	?

Assume that on June 1, only the following two transactions occurred.

June 1   Purchased additional equipment costing $22,500, giving $3,000 cash and a $19,500 note payable.
           Declared and paid a $10,500 cash dividend.

a. Prepare its balance sheet on May 31.
b. Prepare its balance sheet on June 1.
c. Calculate its net working capital on June 1. (Assume that Notes Payable are noncurrent.)

E2-35. Applying the Accounting Equation to Determine Missing Data   **LO2-1, 3, 5**
For each of the four separate situations 1 through 4 that follow, compute the unknown amounts referenced by the letters *a* through *d* shown.

	1	2	3	4
Beginning				
Assets	$50,400	$21,600	$50,400	$ (d)
Liabilities	33,480	9,000	34,200	16,200
Ending				
Assets	54,000	46,800	61,200	72,000
Liabilities	31,140	(b)	27,000	34,200
During Year				
Common Stock Issued	3,600	8,100	(c)	6,300
Revenues	(a)	50,400	32,400	43,200
Expenses	15,300	37,800	19,800	30,600
Cash Dividends Paid	9,000	2,700	1,800	11,700

LO2-1, 5, 7 **E2-36. Preparing Balance Sheets, Computing Income, and Applying the Current and Quick Ratios**

Balance sheet information for Lang Services at the end of Year 2 (the most recent year) and Year 1 is:

	December 31, Year 2	December 31, Year 1
Accounts receivable	$68,400	$52,500
Notes payable	5,400	4,800
Cash	30,000	24,000
Equipment	96,000	81,000
Supplies	14,100	12,600
Accounts payable	75,000	75,000
Stockholders' equity	?	?

a. Prepare Lang Services' balance sheet for December 31 of each year.
b. Lang Services raised $15,000 cash through issuing additional common stock early in Year 2, and it declared and paid a $51,000 cash dividend in December Year 2. Compute its net income or loss for Year 2.
c. Calculate the current ratio and quick ratio for Year 2.
d. Assume the industry average is 1.5 for the current ratio and 1.0 for the quick ratio. Comment on Lang's current and quick ratios relative to the industry.

LO2-1, 3, 5 **E2-37. Constructing Balance Sheets and Determining Income**

Following is balance sheet information for Lynch Services at the end of Year 2 (the most recent year) and Year 1.

	December 31, Year 2	December 31, Year 1
Accounts payable	$ 9,000	$ 13,500
Cash	34,500	30,000
Accounts receivable	63,000	49,500
Land	60,000	60,000
Building	375,000	390,000
Equipment	64,500	67,500
Mortgage payable	135,000	150,000
Supplies	30,000	27,000
Common stock	330,000	330,000
Retained earnings	?	?

a. Prepare balance sheets on December 31 of each year.
b. The firm declared and paid a cash dividend of $15,000 in December Year 2. Compute its net income for Year 2.

LO2-1, 7 **E2-38. Constructing Balance Sheets and Applying the Current and Quick Ratios**

The following balance sheet data are reported for Brownlee Catering on September 30.

Accounts receivable	$ 68,000	Accounts payable	$ 96,000
Notes payable	48,000	Cash	40,000
Equipment	136,000	Common stock	110,000
Supplies inventory	36,000	Retained earnings	?

Assume that on October 1, only the following two transactions occurred:

October 1 Purchased additional equipment costing $44,000, giving $12,000 cash and signing a $32,000 note payable.
Declared and paid a cash dividend of $12,000.

REQUIRED

a. Prepare Brownlee Catering's balance sheet at September 30.
b. Prepare the company's balance sheet at the close of business on October 1.
c. Calculate Brownlee's current and quick ratios on September 30 and October 1. (Assume that Notes Payable are noncurrent.)
d. The October 1 transactions have decreased Brownlee's current and quick ratios, reflecting a decline in liquidity. Identify two transactions that would increase the company's liquidity.

LO2-1, 3, 4 **E2-39. Constructing Financial Statements from Transaction Data**

Yost Corporation commences operations at the beginning of January. It provides its services on credit and bills its customers $45,000 for January sales to be collected in February. Its employees also earn January wages of $18,000 that are not paid until the first of February. Complete the following statements for the month-end of January.

Income Statement		Balance Sheet	
Sales.................................	$	Cash............................	$ 12,000
Wages expense		Accounts receivable	
Net income (loss)	$	Total assets......................	$
		Wages payable.................	$
		Common stock	12,000
		Retained earnings	
		Total liabilities and equity	$

E2-40. Classifying Balance Sheet and Income Statement Accounts LO2-1, 3

Following are selected accounts for **The Procter & Gamble Company** for June 30, 2020.

($ millions)	Amount	Classification
Net sales.......................................	$ 70,950	
Income tax expense	2,731	
Retained earnings	100,239	
Net earnings..................................	13,103	
Property, plant and equipment (net)....	20,692	
Selling, general and administrative expense	19,994	
Accounts receivable.......................	4,178	
Total liabilities................................	73,822	
Stockholders' equity.......................	46,878	
Cost of products sold.....................	35,250	

Procter & Gamble
NYSE :: PG

a. Indicate the appropriate classification of each account as appearing in either its balance sheet (B) or its income statement (I).
b. Using the data, compute the amount that Procter & Gamble reported for total assets.

E2-41. Classifying Balance Sheet and Income Statement Accounts and Computing Current Ratio LO2-1, 3, 7

Shoprite Holdings Ltd is an African food retailer listed on the Johannesburg Stock Exchange. The following accounts are selected from its annual report for the fiscal year ended June 28, 2020. The amounts are in millions of South African rand.

(rand millions)	Amount	Classification
Sales of merchandise.......................	R 156,855	
Depreciation and amortization	5,031	
Reserves (Retained earnings)	13,141	
Property, plant and equipment	18,265	
Cost of goods and services	119,323	
Trade and other payables.................	20,157	
Total assets...................................	82,726	
Total equity...................................	19,994	
Employee benefits expense	12,585	
Total noncurrent assets	42,789	
Total noncurrent liabilities.................	30,159	

Shoprite Holdings Ltd
JSE :: SHP

a. Indicate the appropriate classification of each account as appearing in either its balance sheet (B) or its income statement (I).
b. Using the data, compute Shoprite's total liabilities on June 28, 2020.
c. Calculate Shoprite's current ratio as of June 28, 2020.

E2-42. Classifying Balance Sheet and Income Statement Accounts and Computing Quick Ratio LO2-1, 3, 7

El Puerto de Liverpool (Liverpool) is a large retailer in Mexico. The following accounts are selected from its annual report for the fiscal year ended December 31, 2019. The amounts are in thousands of Mexican pesos.

El Puerto de Liverpool
OTCMKTS :: ELPQF

(pesos thousands)	Amount	Classification
Total revenue	$126,244,910	
Retained earnings	97,320,175	
Inventory	23,340,421	
Administration expenses	34,317,814	
Total assets	200,561,869	
Long-term debt	31,707,410	
Financing costs	6,512,917	
Total current assets	77,082,460	
Total stockholders' equity	109,074,538	
Prepaid expenses	1,804,877	
Total noncurrent liabilities	48,983,414	

    a. Indicate the appropriate classification of each account as appearing in either its balance sheet (B) or its income statement (I).

    b. Determine Liverpool's total liabilities and current liabilities as of December 31, 2019.

    c. Calculate Liverpool's quick ratio as of December 31, 2019. (Assume that Liverpool only has five types of current assets—cash, marketable securities, accounts receivable, inventory, and prepaid expenses.)

LO2-1, 3 E2-43. Classifying Balance Sheet and Income Statement Accounts and Computing Debt-to-Equity

Following are selected accounts for **Kimberly-Clark Corporation** for 2020.

Kimberly-Clark
NYSE :: KMB

($ millions)	Amount	Classification
Net sales	$19,140	
Cost of goods sold	12,318	
Retained earnings	7,567	
Net income	2,352	
Property, plant and equipment, net	8,042	
Marketing research and general expenses	3,632	
Accounts receivable, net	2,235	
Total liabilities	16,626	
Total stockholders' equity	897	

    a. Indicate the appropriate classification of each account as appearing in either its balance sheet (B) or its income statement (I).

    b. Using the data, compute its amounts for total assets and for total expenses.

    c. Compute Kimberly-Clark's debt-to-equity ratio. (Debt-to-equity was defined in Chapter 1.)

LO2-1, 2, 3, 4 E2-44. Analyzing Transactions Using the Financial Statement Effects Template (FSET)

Record the effect of each of the following independent transactions using the financial statements effects template provided. Confirm that Assets = Liabilities + Equity for each transaction.

	Balance Sheet					Income Statement		
Transaction	Cash Asset +	Noncash Assets =	Liabilities +	Contrib. Capital +	Earned Capital	Revenues −	Expenses =	Net Income
(1) Receive €75,000 in exchange for common stock.		=					−	=
(2) Borrow €15,000 from bank.		=					−	=
(3) Purchase €3,000 of supplies inventory on credit.		=					−	=
(4) Receive €22,500 cash from customers for services provided.		=					−	=

continued

continued from previous page

Transaction	Balance Sheet					Income Statement		
	Cash Asset	+ Noncash Assets	= Liabilities	+ Contrib. Capital	+ Earned Capital	Revenues	− Expenses	= Net Income
(5) Pay €3,000 cash to supplier in transaction 3.			=				−	=
(6) Receive order for future services with €5,250 advance payment.			=				−	=
(7) Pay €7,500 cash dividend to shareholders.			=				−	=
(8) Pay employees €9,000 cash for compensation earned.			=				−	=
(9) Pay €750 cash for interest on loan in transaction 2.			=				−	=
Totals			=				−	=

E2-45. Recording Transactions Using Journal Entries and T-Accounts   **LO2-2, 6**

Use the information in Exercise 2-44 to complete the following.

   a. Prepare journal entries for each of the transactions (1) through (9).
   b. Set up T-accounts for each of the accounts used in part *a* and post the journal entries to those T-accounts. (The T-accounts will not have opening balances.)

E2-46. Constructing Balance Sheets and Interpreting Liquidity Measures   **LO2-1, 7**

The following balance sheet data are reported for Bettis Contractors on June 30.

Accounts payable	$ 7,120	Common stock		$80,000
Cash	11,760	Retained earnings		?
Supplies	24,400	Notes payable		24,000
Equipment	78,400	Accounts receivable		7,360
Land	20,000			

Assume that during the next two days only the following three transactions occurred:

July 1 Paid $4,000 cash toward the notes payable owed.
      2 Purchased equipment for $8,000, paying $1,600 cash and a $6,400 note payable for the remaining balance.
      2 Declared and paid a $4,400 cash dividend.

   a. Prepare a balance sheet on June 30.
   b. Prepare a balance sheet on July 2.
   c. Calculate its current and quick ratios on June 30. (Notes payable is a noncurrent liability.)
   d. Assume the industry average is 3.0 for the current ratio and 2.0 for the quick ratio. Comment on Bettis' current and quick ratios relative to the industry.

E2-47. Analyzing Transactions Using the Financial Statement Effects Template (FSET)   **LO2-1, 2, 3, 4**

Record the effect of each of the following independent transactions using the financial statement effects template provided. Confirm that Assets = Liabilities + Equity.

	Balance Sheet						Income Statement		
Transaction	Cash Asset	+ Noncash Assets	= Liabilities	+ Contrib. Capital	+ Earned Capital		Revenues	− Expenses	= Net Income
(1) Receive $80,000 cash in exchange for common stock.			=					−	=
(2) Purchase $8,000 of inventory on credit.			=					−	=
(3) Sell inventory for $12,000 on credit.			=					−	=
(4) Record $8,000 for cost of inventory sold in 3.			=					−	=
(5) Collect $12,000 cash from transaction 3.			=					−	=
(6) Acquire $20,000 of equipment by signing a note.			=					−	=
(7) Pay wages of $4,000 in cash.			=					−	=
(8) Pay $20,000 on a note payable that came due.			=					−	=
(9) Pay $8,000 cash dividend.			=					−	=
Totals			=					−	=

LO2-6 **E2-48. Recording Transactions Using Journal Entries and T-Accounts**
Use the information in Exercise 2-47 to complete the following.

a. Prepare journal entries for each of the transactions 1 through 9.
b. Set up T-accounts for each of the accounts used in part *a* and post the journal entries to those T-accounts. (The T-accounts will not have opening balances.)

PROBLEMS

LO2-1, 3 **P2-49. Comparing Operating Characteristics Across Industries**
Review the following selected income statement and balance sheet data for fiscal years ending in 2019.

Comcast Corporation NASDAQ :: CMCSA
Apple Inc. NASDAQ :: AAPL
Nike, Inc. NYSE :: NKE
Target Corporation NYSE :: TGT
Harley-Davidson, Inc. NYSE :: HOG

($ millions)	Sales	Cost of Sales	Gross Profit	Net Income	Assets	Liabilities	Equity
Comcast Corporation....	$108,942	$ 34,400	$74,542	$13,323	$263,414	$178,168	$85,246
Apple Inc.	260,174	161,782	98,392	55,256	338,516	248,028	90,488
Nike Inc................	39,117	21,643	17,474	4,029	23,717	14,677	9,040
Target Corporation......	78,112	54,864	23,248	3,281	42,779	30,946	11,833
Harley-Davidson Inc.	4,573	3,230	1,343	424	10,528	8,724	1,804

REQUIRED

a. Compare and discuss how these companies finance their operations.
b. Which companies report the highest ratio of income to assets (net income/total assets)? Suggest a reason for this result.
c. Which companies have the highest estimated ROE? Is this result a surprise? Explain.

LO2-1, 3 **P2-50. Comparing Operating Characteristics Within an Industry**
Selected data from **HP Inc.** on October 31, 2020, follow.

HP Inc. NYSE :: HPQ

($ millions)	Sales	Cost of Sales	Gross Profit	Net Income	Assets	Liabilities	Equity
HP Inc.	$56,639	$46,202	$10,437	$2,844	$34,681	$36,909	$(2,228)

REQUIRED

a. Using the data for **Apple Inc.** in P2-49, compare and discuss the two companies on the basis of how they finance their operations.

b. Which company reports the higher ratio of income to assets (net income/total assets)? Suggest a reason for this result.

c. Which firm has the higher gross margin (gross profit as a percentage of sales)? What factors might account for the difference?

P2-51. Comparing Operating Characteristics Within an Industry   LO2-1, 3

Review the following selected income statement and balance sheet data for **Verizon Communications Inc.** as of December 31, 2019.

($ millions)	Sales	Cost of Sales	Gross Profit	Net Income	Assets	Liabilities	Equity
Verizon Communications Inc.	$131,868	$54,726	$77,142	$19,788	$291,727	$228,892	$62,835

REQUIRED

a. Using the data for **Comcast Corporation** in P2-49, compare and discuss how Verizon and Comcast finance their operations.

b. Which company reports the higher ratio of income to assets (net income/total assets)? Suggest a reason for this result.

P2-52. Comparing Operating Structure Across Industries   LO2-1, 7

Review the following selected income statement and balance sheet data from the fiscal years ending in 2020.

($ millions)	Current Assets	Non-current Assets	Total Assets	Current Liab.	Non-current Liab.	Total Liab.	Equity
3M*	$ 14,982	$ 32,362	$ 47,344	$ 7,948	$ 26,465	$ 34,413	$12,931
Abercrombie & Fitch**	1,265	2,284	3,549	815	1,663	2,478	1,071
Apple†	143,713	180,175	323,888	105,392	153,157	258,549	65,339

* Manufacturer of consumer and business products
** Retailer of name-brand apparel at premium prices
† Computer company

REQUIRED

a. Compare and discuss how these companies finance their operations.

b. Which company has the greatest net working capital? Which company has the highest current ratio? Do you have concerns about any firm's net working capital position? Explain.

P2-53. Preparing a Balance Sheet, Computing Net Income, and Understanding Equity Transactions   LO2-1, 5

At the beginning of the year, Barth Company reported the following balance sheet.

Assets		Liabilities and Equity	
Cash	$ 7,200	Accounts payable	$18,000
Accounts receivable	22,050	Equity	
Equipment	15,000	Common stock	71,250
Land	75,000	Retained earnings	30,000
Total assets	$119,250	Total liabilities and equity	$119,250

REQUIRED

a. At the end of the year, Barth Company reported the following assets and liabilities: Cash, $13,200; Accounts Receivable, $27,600; Equipment, $13,500; Land, $75,000; and Accounts Payable, $11,250. Prepare a year-end balance sheet for Barth. (*Hint:* Report equi*Hint:*ty as a single total.)

b. Assuming that Barth did not issue any common stock during the year but paid $18,000 cash in dividends, what was its net income or net loss for the year?
c. Assuming that Barth issued an additional $20,250 common stock early in the year but paid $31,500 cash in dividends before the end of the year, what was its net income or net loss for the year?

LO2-1, 3 **P2-54. Analyzing and Interpreting the Financial Performance of Competitors**

Abercrombie & Fitch Co. and **Nordstrom, Inc.**, are major retailers that concentrate in the higher-end clothing lines. Following are selected data from their 2019 fiscal-year ended February 1, 2020, financial statements:

($ millions)	ANF	JWN
Total liabilities and equity	$3,549	$ 9,737
Net income	45	496
Net sales	3,623	15,132
Total liabilities	2,478	8,758

REQUIRED

a. What is the total amount of assets at (1) ANF and (2) JWN? What are the total expenses for each company (1) in dollars and (2) as a percentage of sales?
b. What is the return on equity (ROE) for (1) ANF and (2) JWN? ANF's total equity at the beginning of 2019 is $1,219 million and JWN's beginning 2019 equity is $873 million. (ROE was defined in Chapter 1.)

LO2-1, 7 **P2-55. Analyzing Balance Sheet Numbers from Incomplete Data and Interpreting Liquidity Measures**

Selected balance sheet amounts for **Kimberly-Clark Corp**, a consumer products company, for four recent years follow:

($ millions)	Current Assets	Non-current Assets	Total Assets	Current Liabilities	Non-current Liabilities	Total Liabilities	Equity
2017	$?	$ 9,940	$15,151	$5,858	$8,350	$14,208	$?
2018	5,041	?	14,518	6,536	?	?	18
2019	5,057	10,226	?	?	8,141	?	223
2020	?	12,349	17,523	6,443	?	16,626	?

REQUIRED

a. Compute the missing balance sheet amounts for each of the four years shown.
b. What types of accounts would you expect to be included in current assets? In noncurrent assets?
c. Calculate Kimberly-Clark's working capital and current ratio for 2019 and 2020.
d. Assume that the industry average is 2.0 for the current ratio. Comment on Kimberly-Clark's liquidity measures relative to the industry.

LO2-1, 7 **P2-56. Analyzing and Interpreting Balance Sheet Data and Interpreting Liquidity Measures**

Selected balance sheet amounts for **Macy's, Inc.**, a retail company, for four recent fiscal years ending in the following calendar years:

($ millions)	Current Assets	Non-current Assets	Total Assets	Current Liabilities	Non-current Liabilities	Total Liabilities	Equity
2017	$7,626	$12,225	$?	$5,647	$9,882	$15,529	$?
2018	?	11,937	19,381	?	8,645	13,720	?
2019	7,445	?	19,194	5,232	?	12,758	6,436
2020	6,810	14,362	?	5,750	?	14,795	?

REQUIRED

a. Compute the missing balance sheet amounts for each of the four years shown.
b. What asset category do you expect to constitute the majority of the company's current assets?
c. Calculate Macy's current ratio for fiscal years 2017 and 2020.
d. If the industry average debt-to-asset ratio is 0.4 and the industry average current ratio for 2020 is 1.8, how would you characterize Macy's financial condition?

P2-57. Analyzing Transactions Using the Financial Statement Effects Template and Preparing an Income Statement (FSET)   **LO2-1, 2, 3, 4**

On December 1, R. Lambert formed Lambert Services, which provides career and vocational counseling services to graduating college students. The following transactions took place during December, and company accounts include the following: Cash, Accounts Receivable, Land, Accounts Payable, Notes Payable, Common Stock, Retained Earnings, Counseling Services Revenue, Supplies Expense, Advertising Expense, Interest Expense, Salary Expense, and Utilities Expense.

1. Raised $21,000 cash through common stock issuance.
2. Paid $2,250 cash for supplies and training materials.
3. Received $1,500 invoice for December advertising expenses.
4. Borrowed $45,000 cash from bank and signed note payable for that amount.
5. Received $3,600 cash for counseling services rendered.
6. Billed clients $20,400 for counseling services rendered.
7. Paid $6,600 cash for secretary salary.
8. Paid $1,110 cash for December utilities.
9. Declared and paid a $2,700 cash dividend.
10. Purchased land for $39,000 cash to use for its own facilities.
11. Paid $300 cash to bank as December interest expense on note payable.

REQUIRED

a. Report the effects for each of the separate transactions 1 through 11 using the financial statement effects template. Total all columns and prove that (1) assets equal liabilities plus equity on December 31, and (2) revenues less expenses equal net income for December.
b. Prepare an income statement for the month of December.

P2-58. Recording Transactions in Journal Entries and T-Accounts   **LO2-6**

Use the information in Problem 2-57 to complete the following requirements.

REQUIRED

a. Prepare journal entries for each of the transactions 1 through 11.
b. Set up T-accounts for each of the accounts used in part *a* and post the journal entries to those T-accounts.

P2-59. Analyzing and Interpreting Balance Sheet Data and Interpreting Liquidity Measures   **LO2-1, 7**

Selected balance sheet amounts for **Apple Inc.**, a retail company, for four recent fiscal years follow:

($ millions)	Current Assets	Non-current Assets	Total Assets	Current Liabilities	Non-current Liabilities	Total Liabilities	Stockholders' Equity
2017	$128,645	$?	$375,319	$?	$140,458	$241,272	$134,047
2018	131,339	234,386	?	116,866	?	258,578	107,147
2019	162,819	175,697	?	?	142,310	248,028	?
2020	?	180,175	323,888	105,392	?	258,549	65,339

Apple Inc.
NYSE :: AAPL

REQUIRED

a. Compute the missing balance sheet amounts for each of the four years shown.
b. What asset category would you expect to constitute the majority of Apple's current assets? Of its long-term assets?
c. Is the company conservatively financed; that is, is it financed by a greater proportion of equity than of debt?
d. Calculate the current ratio for 2017 and 2020.
e. Assume the industry average is 1.0 for the current ratio. Comment on Apple's current ratio relative to the industry.

P2-60. Analyzing Balance Sheet Numbers from Incomplete Data and Interpreting Liquidity Measures   **LO2-1, 7**

Selected balance sheet amounts for **Alibaba Group Holding Ltd**, a China-based online and mobile commerce company, for three recent fiscal years ending March 31 follow:

Alibaba Group Holding Ltd
NYSE :: BABA

(millions of US $)	Current Assets	Non-current Assets	Total Assets	Current Liabilities	Non-current Liabilities	Total Liabilities	Equity
2018	$40,949	$?	$?	$21,651	$?	$44,270	$70,056
2019	?	103,529	143,801	?	22,176	53,120	90,681
2020	?	120,052	185,429	34,159	28,325	?	?

REQUIRED

a. Compute the missing balance sheet amounts for each of the three years shown.
b. What asset category do you expect to constitute the majority of the company's current assets?
c. Calculate Alibaba's current ratio for fiscal years 2018 and 2020.
d. Calculate net working capital for 2018 and 2020.

LO2-3 P2-61. Analyzing and Interpreting Income Statement Data

Selected income statement information for **Nike, Inc.**, a manufacturer of athletic footwear, for four recent fiscal years ending May 31 follows.

Nike, Inc.
NYSE :: NKE

($ millions)	Revenues	Cost of Goods Sold	Gross Profit	Operating Expenses	Operating Income	Other Expenses	Net Income
2017	$34,350	$19,038	$?	$10,563	$4,749	$509	$?
2018	36,397	?	15,956	11,511	4,445	?	1,933
2019	?	21,643	17,474	12,702	4,772	743	?
2020	37,403	21,162	16,241	?	3,115	?	2,539

REQUIRED

a. Compute the missing amounts for each of the four years shown.
b. Compute the gross profit margin (gross profit/sales) for each of the four years and comment on its level and any trends that are evident.
c. What would you expect to be the major cost categories constituting its operating expenses?

LO2-1, 2, 3, 4 P2-62. Analyzing Transactions Using the Financial Statement Effects Template and Preparing an Income Statement (FSET)

On June 1, a group of pilots in Melbourne, Australia, formed Outback Flights by issuing common stock for $25,000 cash. The group then leased several amphibious aircraft and docking facilities, equipping them to transport campers and hunters to outpost camps owned by various resorts in remote parts of Australia. The following transactions occurred during June, and company accounts include the following: Cash, Accounts Receivable, Prepaid Insurance, Accounts Payable, Common Stock, Retained Earnings, Flight Services Revenue, Rent Expense, Entertainment Expense, Advertising Expense, Insurance Expense, Wages Expense, and Fuel Expense.

1. Issued common stock for $25,000 cash.
2. Paid $2,400 cash for June rent of aircraft, dockage, and dockside office. The leases are all for less than 12 months—the company is evaluating the business model before they purchase.
3. Received $800 invoice for the cost of a reception to entertain resort owners in June.
4. Paid $450 cash for June advertising in various sport magazines.
5. Paid $900 cash for insurance premium for July.
6. Rendered flight services for various groups for $11,350 cash.
7. Billed client $1,450 for transporting personnel, and billed various firms for $6,500 in flight services.
8. Paid $750 cash to cover accounts payable.
9. Received $6,600 on account from clients in transaction 7.
10. Paid $8,000 cash to cover June wages.
11. Received $1,750 invoice for the cost of fuel used during June.
12. Declared and paid a $1,500 cash dividend.

REQUIRED

a. Report the effects for each of the separate transactions 1 through 12 using the financial statement effects template. Total all columns and prove that (1) assets equal liabilities plus equity on June 30 and (2) revenues less expenses equal net income for June.
b. Prepare an income statement for the month of June.

P2-63. Recording Transactions in Journal Entries and T-Accounts LO2-6
Use the information in Problem 2-62 to complete the following requirements.

REQUIRED
a. Prepare journal entries for each of the transactions 1 through 12.
b. Set up T-accounts for each of the accounts used in part *a* and post the journal entries to those T-accounts.

P2-64. Analyzing and Interpreting Income Statement Numbers from Incomplete Data LO2-3
Selected income statement information for **Starbucks Corporation**, a coffee-related restaurant chain, for four recent fiscal years follows.

Starbucks Corporation
NASDAQ :: SBUX

($ millions)	Revenues	Cost of Sales	Gross Profit	Operating Expenses	Operating Income	Other Expenses	Net Income
2017	$?	$7,065.8	$15,321.0	$?	$4,134.7	$1,249.8	$?
2018	24,719.5	?	16,788.8	?	?	(634.7)	4,518.0
2019	26,508.6	8,526.9	?	13,903.8	4,077.9	?	3,594.6
2020	?	7,694.9	15,823.1	14,261.4	1,561.7	637.0	?

REQUIRED
a. Compute the missing amounts for each of the four years shown.
b. Compute the gross profit margin (gross profit/sales) for each of the four years and comment on its level and any trends that are evident.
c. What would you expect to be the major cost categories constituting its operating expenses?

P2-65. Analyzing, Reconstructing, and Interpreting Income Statement Data LO2-3
Selected income statement information for **Siemens AG**, a global technology company, for four fiscal years follows:

Siemens AG
OTCMKTS :: SIEGY

(€ millions)	Revenues	Cost of Goods Sold	Gross Profit	Operating Expenses	Operating Income	Other Expense	Net Income
2017	82,863	57,820	25,043	?	7,571	?	6,094
2018	83,044	?	24,863	18,677	?	?	6,120
2019	?	36,848	21,635	15,343	6,292	644	?
2020	57,139	36,953	?	15,147	?	839	4,200

REQUIRED
a. Compute the missing amounts for each of the four years shown.
b. Per the annual report, the company engaged in a restructuring effort effective in 2019 (including changes in reportable segments). Assuming all else constant, what were the effects of the restructuring on the firm's gross profit margin (gross profit/sales)?
c. What would we expect to be the major cost categories constituting Siemens' operating expenses?

P2-66. Preparing the Income Statement, Statement of Stockholders' Equity, and Balance Sheet LO2-1, 3, 5
The records of Geyer, Inc., show the following information after all transactions are recorded for the year.

Notes payable	$ 8,000	Supplies	$12,200
Service fees earned	135,200	Cash	29,600
Supplies expense	19,400	Advertising expense	3,400
Insurance expense	3,000	Salaries expense	60,000
Miscellaneous expense	400	Rent expense (short-term lease)	15,000
Common stock (beg. year)	8,000	Retained earnings (beg. year)	12,400
Accounts payable	3,600		

In addition, Geyer, Inc., raised $2,800 cash through the issuance of additional common stock during this year, and it declared and paid a $27,000 cash dividend near year-end.

REQUIRED
a. Prepare its income statement for the year.
b. Prepare its statement of stockholders' equity for the year.
c. Prepare its balance sheet at December 31.

LO2-1, 2, 3, 4, 5 **P2-67.** **Analyzing Transactions Using the Financial Statement Effects Template and Preparing Financial Statements (FSET)**

Schrand Aerobics, Inc., specializes in offering aerobics classes. On January 1, its beginning account balances are as follows: Cash, $10,000; Accounts Receivable, $10,400; Equipment, $0; Notes Payable, $5,000; Accounts Payable, $2,000; Common Stock, $11,000; Retained Earnings, $2,400; Services Revenue, $0; Insurance Expense, $0; Advertising Expense, $0; Wages Expense, $0; Utilities Expense, $0; Interest Expense, $0. The following transactions occurred during January.

1. Paid $1,200 cash toward accounts payable.
2. Paid $7,200 cash for insurance.
3. Billed clients $23,000 for January classes.
4. Received $1,000 invoice from supplier for T-shirts given to January class members as an advertising promotion.
5. Collected $20,000 cash from clients previously billed for services rendered.
6. Paid $4,800 cash for employee wages.
7. Received $1,360 invoice for January utilities expense.
8. Paid $40 cash to bank as January interest on notes payable.
9. Declared and paid $1,800 cash dividend to stockholders.
10. Paid $8,000 cash on January 31 to purchase sound equipment.

REQUIRED

a. Using the financial statement effects template, enter January 1 beginning amounts in the appropriate columns of the first row. (*Hint:* Beginning balances for columns can include amounts from more than one account.)
b. Report the effects for each of the separate transactions 1 through 10 in the financial statement effects template set up in part *a*. Total all columns and prove that (1) assets equal liabilities plus equity at January 31, and (2) revenues less expenses equal net income for January.
c. Prepare its income statement for January.
d. Prepare its statement of stockholders' equity for January.
e. Prepare its balance sheet at January 31.

LO2-6 **P2-68.** **Recording Transactions in Journal Entries and T-Accounts**

Use the information in Problem 2-67 to complete the following requirements.

REQUIRED

a. Prepare journal entries for each of the transactions 1 through 10.
b. Set up T-accounts, including beginning balances, for each of the accounts used in part *a*. Post the journal entries to those T-accounts.

LO2-1, 2, 3, 4, 5 **P2-69.** **Analyzing Transactions Using the Financial Statement Effects Template and Preparing Financial Statements (FSET)**

Kross, Inc., provides appraisals and feasibility studies. On January 1, its beginning account balances are as follows: Cash, $12,100; Accounts Receivable, $26,700; Notes Payable, $4,500; Accounts Payable, $1,100; Retained Earnings, $22,400; and Common Stock, $10,800. The following transactions occurred during January, and company accounts include the following: Cash, Accounts Receivable, Vehicles, Accounts Payable, Notes Payable, Services Revenue, Rent Expense, Interest Expense, Salary Expense, Utilities Expense, Common Stock, and Retained Earnings.

1. Paid $1,800 cash for January rent (short-term lease < 12 months).
2. Received $15,900 cash on customers' accounts.
3. Paid $900 cash toward accounts payable.
4. Received $2,900 cash for services performed for customers.
5. Borrowed $9,000 cash from bank and signed note payable for that amount.
6. Billed the city $11,200 for services performed, and billed other credit customers for $3,500 in services.
7. Paid $7,200 cash for salary of assistant.
8. Received $800 invoice for January utilities expense.
9. Declared and paid a $10,800 cash dividend.
10. Paid $17,700 cash to acquire a vehicle (on January 31) for business use.
11. Paid $100 cash to bank for January interest on notes payable.

REQUIRED

a. Using the financial statement effects template, enter January 1 beginning amounts in the appropriate columns of the first row. (*Hint:* Beginning balances for columns can include amounts from more than one account.)
b. Report the effects for each of the separate transactions 1 through 11 in the financial statement effects template set up in part *a*. Total all columns and prove that (1) assets equal liabilities plus equity on January 31, and (2) revenues less expenses equal net income for January.
c. Prepare its income statement for January.
d. Prepare its statement of stockholders' equity for January.
e. Prepare its balance sheet at January 31.

P2-70. Recording Transactions in Journal Entries and T-Accounts   **LO2-6**
Use the information in Problem 2-69 to complete the following requirements.

REQUIRED

a. Prepare journal entries for each of the transactions 1 through 11.
b. Set up T-accounts, including beginning balances, for each of the accounts used in part *a*. Post the journal entries to those T-accounts.

CASES AND PROJECTS

C2-71. Constructing Financial Statements from Cash Data   **LO2-1, 3, 4, 5**
Sarah Penney operates the Wildlife Picture Gallery, selling original art and signed prints received on consignment (rather than purchased) from recognized wildlife artists throughout the country. The firm receives a 30% commission on all art sold and remits 70% of the sales price to the artists. All art is sold on a strictly cash basis.

Sarah began the business on March 1. The business received a $15,000 loan from a relative of Sarah to help her get started; it took on a note payable agreeing to pay the loan back in one year. No interest is being charged on the loan, but the relative does want to receive a set of financial statements each month. On April 1, Sarah asks for your help in preparing the statements for the first month.

Sarah has carefully kept the firm's checking account up to date and provides you with the following complete listing of the cash receipts and cash disbursements for March.

Cash Receipts	
Original investment by Sarah Penney	$ 9,750
Loan from relative	15,000
Sales of art	142,500
Total cash receipts	167,250
Cash Disbursements	
Payments to artists for sales made	81,000
Payment of March rent for gallery space	1,350
Payment of March wages to staff	7,350
Payment of airfare for personal vacation of Sarah (vacation will be in April)	750
Total cash disbursements	90,450
Cash balance, March 31	$ 76,800

Sarah also gives you the following documents she has received:

1. A $525 invoice for March utilities; payment is due by April 15.
2. A $2,550 invoice from Careful Express for the shipping of artwork sold in March; payment is due by April 10.
3. Sarah signed a short-term lease for the gallery space; as an incentive to sign the lease, the landlord reduced the first month's rent by 25%; the monthly rent starting in April is $1,800.

In your discussions with Sarah, she tells you that she has been so busy that she is behind in sending artists their share of the sales proceeds. She plans to catch up within the next week.

REQUIRED
From the above information, prepare the following financial statements for Wildlife Picture Gallery: (*a*) income statement for the month of March; (*b*) statement of stockholders' equity for the month of March; and (*c*) balance sheet as of March 31.

LO2-3 C2-72. Financial Records and Ethical Behavior

Andrea Frame and her supervisor are sent on an out-of-town assignment by their employer. At the supervisor's suggestion, they stay at the Spartan Inn (across the street from the Luxury Inn). After three days of work, they settle their lodging bills and leave. On the return trip, the supervisor gives Andrea what appears to be a copy of a receipt from the Luxury Inn for three nights of lodging. Actually, the supervisor indicates that he prepared the Luxury Inn receipt on his office computer and plans to complete his expense reimbursement request using the higher lodging costs from the Luxury Inn.

REQUIRED

What are the ethical considerations that Andrea faces when she prepares her expense reimbursement request?

SOLUTIONS TO REVIEW PROBLEMS

Review 2-1

| 1. A | 2. C | 3. B | 4. E | 5. B | 6. E | 7. X | 8. B | 9. E | 10. B |
| 11. B | 12. A | 13. B | 14. C | 15. A | 16. D | 17. A | 18. A | 19. E | 20. C |

Review 2-2

Balance Sheet

Transaction	Cash Asset	+	Noncash Assets	=	Liabilities	+	Contrib. Capital	+	Earned Capital
(a) Issue common stock for $20,000.	+20,000 Cash			=			+20,000 Common Stock		
(b) Purchase $8,000 of inventory on credit.			+8,000 Inventory	=	+8,000 Accounts Payable				
(c) Purchase equipment for $10,000 cash.	−10,000 Cash		+10,000 Equipment	=					
(d) Pay suppliers $3,000 cash.	−3,000 Cash			=	−3,000 Accounts Payable				
Totals	+7,000		+18,000	=	+5,000		+20,000		

Assets = Liabilities + Equity

Income Statement

Revenues	−	Expenses	=	Net Income
	−		=	
	−		=	
	−		=	
	−		=	

Review 2-3

SCHAEFER'S PHARMACY, INC.
Income Statement
For Year Ended December 31

Revenues		$45,000
Expenses		
Cost of goods sold	$20,000	
Wages expense	8,000	
Insurance expense	5,000	
Utilities expense	2,000	
Other expenses	4,000	
Total expenses		39,000
Net income		$ 6,000

Review 2-4

a.

SCHAEFER'S PHARMACY, INC.
Retained Earnings Reconciliation
For Year Ended December 31

Retained earnings, Jan. 1	$25,000
Add: Net income	6,000
Less: Dividends	(1,000)
Retained earnings, Dec. 31	$30,000

b.

SCHAEFER'S PHARMACY, INC.
Retained Earnings Reconciliation
For Year Ended December 31

Retained earnings, Jan. 1	$25,000
Add: Net income	5,250
Less: Dividends	(1,000)
Retained earnings, Dec. 31	$29,250

Review 2-5

a.

SCHAEFER'S PHARMACY, INC.
Balance Sheet
December 31

Cash	$ 3,000	Accounts payable	$ 7,500
Accounts receivable	12,000		
Inventory	26,000		
Office equipment	32,250	Common stock	45,750
Land	10,000	Retained earnings	30,000
Total assets	$83,250	Total liabilities and equity	$83,250

b.

SCHAEFER'S PHARMACY, INC.
Statement of Stockholders' Equity
For Year Ended December 31

	Contributed Capital	Earned Capital	Total Equity
Balance, January 1	$45,750	$25,000	$70,750
Common stock issued	—	—	0
Net income	—	6,000	6,000
Cash dividends	—	(1,000)	(1,000)
Balance, December 31	$45,750	$30,000	$75,750

Review 2-6

a.

	Balance Sheet					Income Statement		
Transaction	Cash Asset	+ Noncash Assets	= Liabilities	+ Contrib. Capital	+ Earned Capital	Revenues	− Expenses	= Net Income
(1) Issue common stock for cash.	+15,500 Cash		=	+15,500 Common Stock			−	=
(2) Purchase office equipment on account.		+10,400 Office Equipment	= +6,000 Accounts Payable +4,400 Note Payable				−	=
(3) Pay rent expense.	−700 Cash		=		−700 Retained Earnings		− +700 Rent Expense	= −700
(4) Pay for subscriptions in advance.	−9,600 Cash	+9,600 Prepaid Subscriptions	=				−	=
(5) Bill clients for services rendered.		+11,300 Accounts Receivable	=		+11,300 Retained Earnings	+11,300 Fees Earned	−	= +11,300
(6) Pay toward accounts payable.	−1,000 Cash		= −1,000 Accounts Payable				−	=
(7) Pay salary for assistant.	−2,800 Cash		=		−2,800 Retained Earnings		− +2,800 Salaries Expense	= −2,800
(8) Collect cash from clients billed earlier.	+9,400 Cash	−9,400 Accounts Receivable	=				−	=
(9) Recognize utility expense.			= +180 Accounts Payable		−180 Retained Earnings		− +180 Utilities Expense	= −180
(10) Pay cash dividends.	−1,500 Cash		=		−1,500 Retained Earnings		−	=
(11) Pay cash for interest.	−225 Cash		=		−225 Retained Earnings		− +225 Interest Expense	= −225
Totals	9,075	+ 21,900	= 9,580	+ 15,500	+ 5,895	11,300	− 3,905	= 7,395
	Assets		= Liabilities +		Equity			

b.

(1) Cash (+A) 15,500
     Common stock (+SE) 15,500

+ Cash (A) −		− Common Stock (SE) +	
(1) 15,500			15,500 (1)

(2) Office equipment (+A) 10,400
     Accounts payable (+L) 6,000
     Note payable (+L) 4,400

+ Office Equipment (A) −		− Accounts Payable (L) +		− Note Payable (L) +	
(2) 10,400			6,000 (2)		4,400 (2)

continued

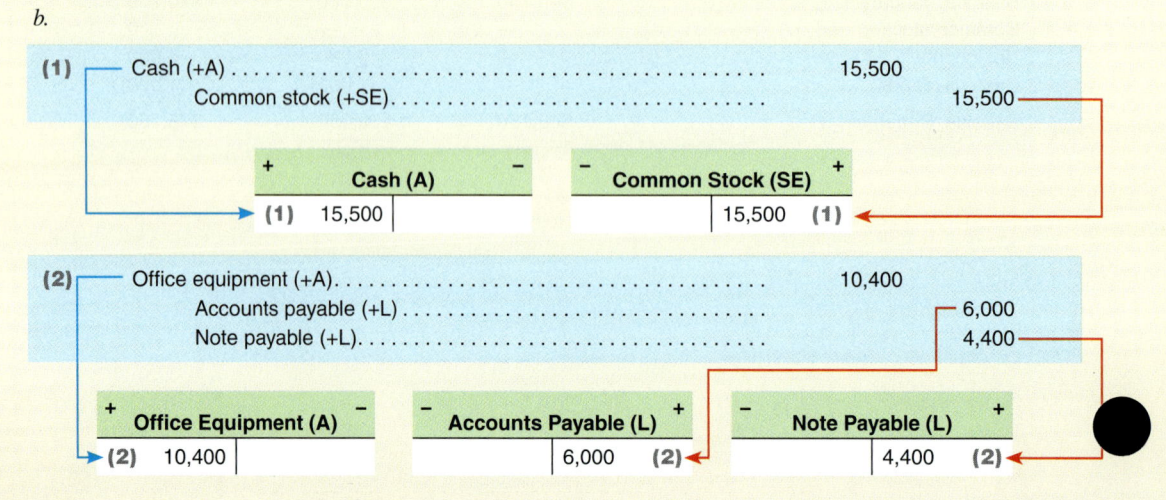

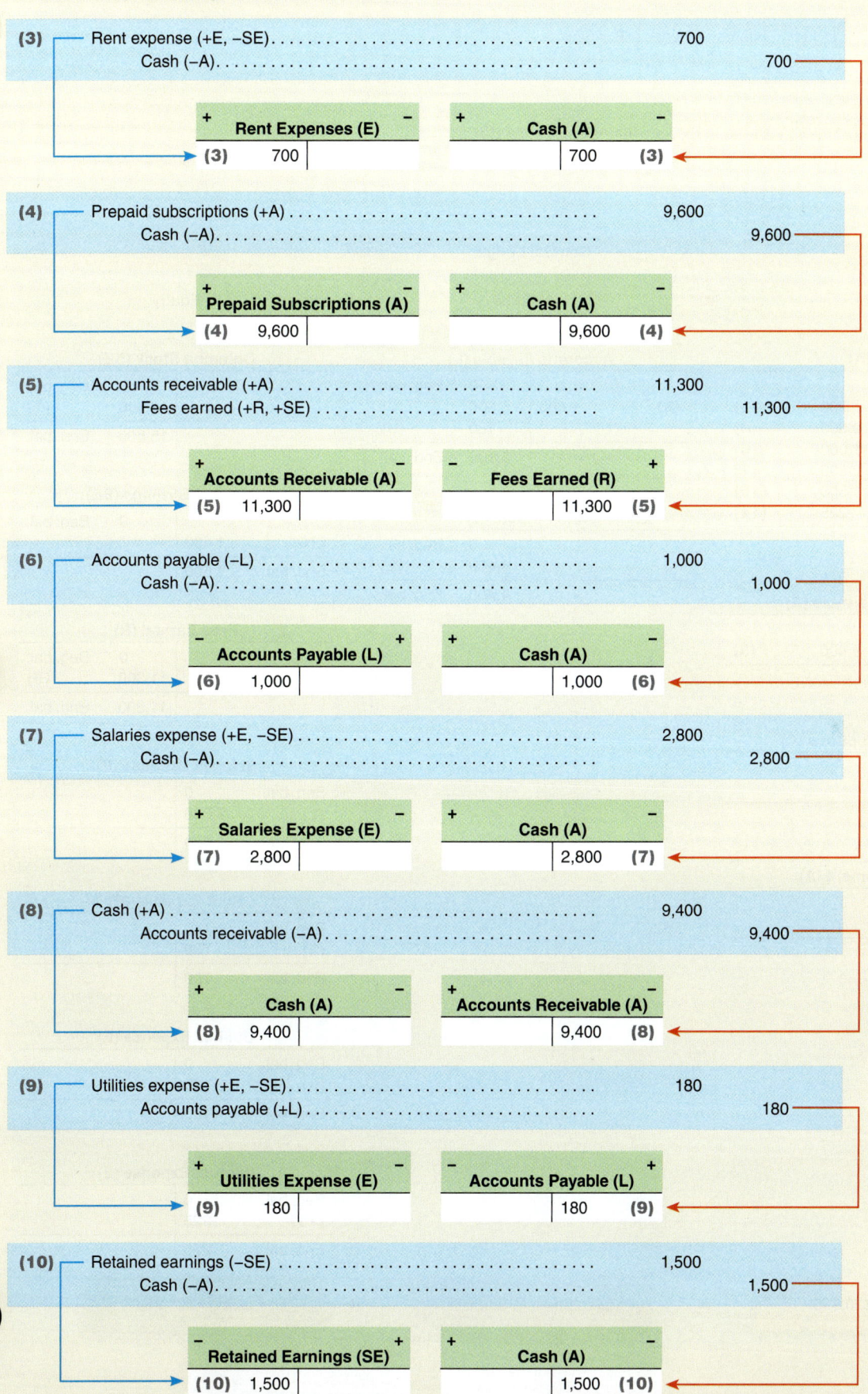

continued from previous page

(3) Rent expense (+E, −SE) 700
      Cash (−A) 700

+ Rent Expenses (E) −	+ Cash (A) −
(3) 700	700 (3)

(4) Prepaid subscriptions (+A) 9,600
      Cash (−A) 9,600

+ Prepaid Subscriptions (A) −	+ Cash (A) −
(4) 9,600	9,600 (4)

(5) Accounts receivable (+A) 11,300
      Fees earned (+R, +SE) 11,300

+ Accounts Receivable (A) −	− Fees Earned (R) +
(5) 11,300	11,300 (5)

(6) Accounts payable (−L) 1,000
      Cash (−A) 1,000

− Accounts Payable (L) +	+ Cash (A) −
(6) 1,000	1,000 (6)

(7) Salaries expense (+E, −SE) 2,800
      Cash (−A) 2,800

+ Salaries Expense (E) −	+ Cash (A) −
(7) 2,800	2,800 (7)

(8) Cash (+A) 9,400
      Accounts receivable (−A) 9,400

+ Cash (A) −	+ Accounts Receivable (A) −
(8) 9,400	9,400 (8)

(9) Utilities expense (+E, −SE) 180
      Accounts payable (+L) 180

+ Utilities Expense (E) −	− Accounts Payable (L) +
(9) 180	180 (9)

(10) Retained earnings (−SE) 1,500
      Cash (−A) 1,500

− Retained Earnings (SE) +	+ Cash (A) −
(10) 1,500	1,500 (10)

continued

continued from previous page

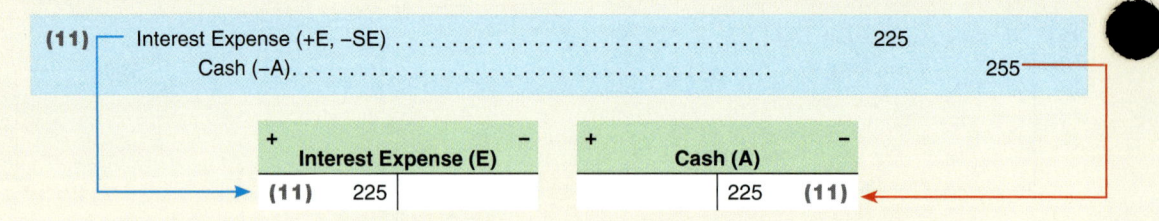

(11) Interest Expense (+E, –SE) 225
     Cash (–A) 255

+ Interest Expense (E) −		+ Cash (A) −	
(11) 225			225 (11)

c.

General Ledger

Assets = Liabilities + Equity

Cash (A)
+		−	
Beg. bal.	0		
(1)	15,500	700	(3)
(8)	9,400	9,600	(4)
		1,000	(6)
		2,800	(7)
		1,500	(10)
		225	(11)
End. bal.	9,075		

Accounts Receivable (A)
+		−	
Beg. bal.	0		
(5)	11,300	9,400	(8)
End. bal.	1,900		

Prepaid Subscriptions (A)
+		−	
Beg. bal.	0		
(4)	9,600		
End. bal.	9,600		

Office Equipment (A)
+		−	
Beg. bal.	0		
(2)	10,400		
End. bal.	10,400		

Accounts Payable (L)
−		+	
		0	Beg. bal.
(6)	1,000	6,000	(2)
		180	(9)
		5,180	End. bal.

Note Payable (L)
−		+	
		0	Beg. bal.
		4,400	(2)
		4,400	End. bal.

Common Stock (SE)
−		+	
		0	Beg. bal.
		15,500	(1)
		15,500	End. bal.

Retained Earnings (SE)
−		+	
		0	Beg. bal.
(10)	1,500		
End. bal.	1,500		

Fees Earned (R)
−		+	
		0	Beg. bal.
		11,300	(5)
		11,300	End. bal.

Salaries Expense (E)
+		−	
Beg. bal.	0		
(7)	2,800		
End. bal.	2,800		

Rent Expense (E)
+		−	
Beg. bal.	0		
(3)	700		
End. bal.	700		

Utilities Expense (E)
+		−	
Beg. bal.	0		
(9)	180		
End. bal.	180		

Interest Expense (E)
+		−	
Beg. bal.	0		
(11)	225		
End. bal.	225		

Assets = $30,975 = Liabilities = $9,580 + Equity = $21,395

Review 2-7
a. Working capital: Current assets ($9,075 + $1,900 + $9,600) − Current liabilities ($5,180) = $15,395
b. Current ratio: $20,575/$5,180 = 4.0
c. Quick ratio: ($9,075 + $1,900)/$5,180 = 2.1

Chapter 3
Adjusting Accounts for Financial Statements

LEARNING OBJECTIVES

LO3-1 Analyze transactions and review the process of journalizing and posting transactions.

LO3-2 Describe the adjusting process and illustrate adjusting entries.

LO3-3 Prepare financial statements from adjusted accounts.

LO3-4 Describe the process of closing temporary accounts.

LO3-5 Analyze changes in balance sheet accounts.

Road Map

LO	Learning Objective | Topics	Page	eLecture	Review	Assignments
LO3-1	Analyze transactions and review the process of journalizing and posting transactions.	3-3	e3-1	R3–1	M3-21, M3-22, M3-23, M3-24, M3-25, M3-26, M3-29, M3-30, M3-34, M3-35, M3-36, M3-37, E3-41, E3-42, E3-45, E3-48, E3-49, P3-51, P3-52, P3-54, P3-56, P3-61, P3-62, P3-63, P3-64, P3-71, P3-74, P3-75, P3-76, C3-78, C3-79, C3-80, C3-81, C3-82, DA3-1
LO3-2	Describe the adjusting process and illustrate adjusting entries.	3-11	e3-2	R3–2	M3-25, M3-26, M3-27, M3-28, M3-29, M3-30, M3-34, M3-35, M3-36, M3-37, E3-39, E3-40, E3-41, E3-42, E3-43, E3-44, E3-45, E3-48, E3-49, P3-51, P3-52, P3-53, P3-54, P3-55, P3-56, P3-57, P3-58, P3-61, P3-62, P3-63, P3-64, P3-65, P3-66, P3-67, P3-68, P3-71, P3-72, P3-73, P3-74, P3-75, P3-76, C3-77, C3-78, C3-79, C3-80, C3-81, C3-82
LO3-3	Prepare financial statements from adjusted accounts.	3-19	e3-3	R3–3	M3-31, E3-50, P3-56, P3-59, P3-68, P3-69, P3-74, P3-76, C3-78, DA3-2, DA3-3
LO3-4	Describe the process of closing temporary accounts.	3-24	e3-4	R3–4	M3-32, M3-33, M3-36, E3-38, E3-41, E3-47, E3-50, P3-56, P3-59, P3-60, P3-68, P3-69, P3-70, P3-74, P3-76, C3-78
LO3-5	Analyze changes in balance sheet accounts.	3-27	e3-5	R3–5	M3-27, M3-28, M3-29, M3-34, E3-43, E3-44, E3-45, E3-46, E3-48, E3-49, P3-51, P3-52, P3-56, P3-67, P3-68, P3-71, P3-72, P3-73, P3-74, P3-75, P3-76, C3-77, C3-78, C3-79, C3-81, C3-82

© Cambridge Business Publishers

WALGREENS
www.walgreens.com

Walgreens Boots Alliance, Inc., is anchored by iconic brands, Walgreens in the United States and Boots in the United Kingdom. The company strives to meet customer needs through many retail locations and digital platforms. The company also works to shape the future of healthcare by bringing more innovative healthcare offerings to customers and patients and by working on government and employer efforts to control healthcare costs.

Walgreen's U.S. retail segment operates 9,021 (as of August 2020) drugstores in 50 states, the District of Columbia, Puerto Rico, and the U.S. Virgin Islands. About 78 percent of the U.S. population lives within five miles of a Walgreens or Duane Reade pharmacy. They sell prescription and non-prescription drugs, as well as a wide assortment of retail products, including health and wellness, beauty, personal care, consumables and general merchandise. Walgreens filled approximately 818 million prescriptions in fiscal 2020, including immunizations.

Because the financial statements should reflect the firm's underlying economic reality, Walgreens' management will need to "adjust" or "update" its financial statements to reflect the changes in its strategy and performance. Accounting adjustments are a key part of creating the financial statements, and they are central to the difference between accrual and cash accounting. While cash accounting only records transactions that involve cash receipts and disbursements, accrual accounting records revenues when they are earned (even if cash has not yet been received) and expenses as they are incurred (regardless of when the cash disbursement associated with that expense is made). The quality, or lack thereof, of the financial statements often hinges on the quality of those adjustments. Thus, understanding how and why accounting adjustments occur is fundamentally important to those who wish to analyze and interpret the financial statements.

This chapter describes the need for adjustments, how they are prepared, their financial statement effect, and the need for ethics and oversight in this process. We illustrate how financial statements are prepared from those adjusted accounts. Then, we end the chapter with the closing process for the financial statements. Such "closing of the books" enables firms to report their performance for the year and then "open the books" anew for the next period.

Sources: United States Segment | Walgreens Boots Alliance About Us | Company & Corporate Info | Walgreens Boots Alliance

CHAPTER ORGANIZATION

Adjusting Accounts for Financial Statements

- **Analyzing and Recording Transactions**
  - Accounting Cycle
  - Review of Analyzing and Journalizing Transactions
- **Adjusting the Accounts**
  - Preparing an Unadjusted Trial Balance
  - Identifying and Recording Adjustments
- **Constructing Financial Statements**
  - Preparing an Adjusted Trial Balance
  - Preparing Financial Statements
- **Closing Temporary Accounts**
  - Performing the Closing Process
  - Preparing a Post-Closing Trial Balance
- **Financial Statement Analysis**
  - Analyzing Changes in Balance Sheet Accounts

The double-entry accounting system introduced in Chapter 2 provides us with a framework for the analysis of business activities, and we use that framework to record transactions and create financial reports. This chapter describes more fully the procedures companies use to account for the operations of a business during a specific time period. All companies, regardless of size or complexity, perform accounting steps, known as the *accounting cycle*, to accumulate and report their financial information. An important step in the accounting cycle is the *adjusting* process that occurs at the end of every reporting period. This chapter focuses on the accounting cycle with emphasis on the adjusting process.

ACCOUNTING CYCLE

LO3-1
Analyze transactions and review the process of journalizing and posting transactions.

Companies engage in business activities. These activities are analyzed for their financial impact, and the results from that analysis are entered into the accounting information system. When management and others want to know where the company stands financially and what its recent performance tells about future prospects, the financial data often require adjustment prior to financial statements being prepared. At the end of this adjustment process, the company *closes the books*. This closing process prepares accounts for the next accounting period.

The process described constitutes the major steps in the **accounting cycle**—a sequence of activities to accumulate and report financial statements. The steps are: analyze, record, adjust, report, and close. **Exhibit 3.1** shows the sequence of major steps in the accounting cycle.

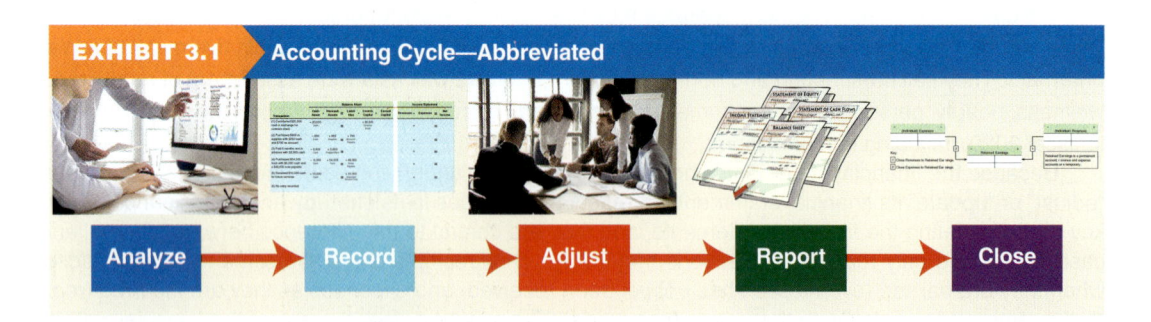

EXHIBIT 3.1 Accounting Cycle—Abbreviated

Analyze → Record → Adjust → Report → Close

The steps in the accounting cycle do not occur with equal frequency. That is, companies analyze and record daily transactions throughout the accounting period, but they adjust and report only when management requires financial statements, often monthly or quarterly, but at least annually. Closing occurs once during the accounting cycle, at the period-end.

The annual (one-year) accounting period adopted by a company is known as its **fiscal year**. Companies with fiscal year-ends on December 31 are said to be on a **calendar year**. About 60% of U.S. companies are on a calendar-year basis. Many companies prefer to have their accounting year coincide with their "natural" year; that is, the fiscal year ends when business is slow. For example,

L Brands, Inc., a specialty retailer, ends its fiscal year on the Saturday nearest January 31. **Starbucks Corporation** ends its fiscal year on the Sunday nearest to September 30. The **Manchester United Ltd.**, a professional soccer team, ends its fiscal year on June 30, during its off-season.

ANALYZING, RECORDING, AND POSTING

The purpose of this section is to (1) review the analysis and recording of transactions as described in Chapter 2, and (2) to extend the Natural Beauty Supply example to illustrate the process of adjusting and closing accounts in the following sections. Natural Beauty Supply's fiscal year-end is December 31.

Review of Accounting Procedures

The **chart of accounts** for Natural Beauty Supply is in **Exhibit 3.2**, and lists the titles and numbers of all accounts found in its general ledger. The account titles are grouped into the five major sections of the general ledger (assets, liabilities, equity, revenues, and expenses). We saw in Chapter 2 that the recording process involves analyzing, journalizing, and posting. The **general journal**, or *book of original entry*, is a tabular record where business activities are captured in debits and credits and recorded in chronological order before they are posted to the general ledger. The word *journalize* means to record a transaction in a **journal**. Each transaction entered in the journal must be stated in terms of equal dollar amounts of debits and credits—the double-entry system at work. The account titles cited must correspond to those in the general ledger (per the chart of accounts).

EXHIBIT 3.2 — Chart of Accounts for Natural Beauty Supply

Assets
- 110 Cash
- 120 Accounts Receivable
- 130 Other Receivables
- 140 Inventory
- 150 Prepaid Insurance
- 160 Security Deposit
- 170 Fixtures and Equipment
- 175 Accumulated Depreciation—Fixtures and Equipment

Liabilities
- 210 Accounts Payable
- 220 Interest Payable
- 230 Wages Payable
- 240 Taxes Payable
- 250 Gift Card Liability
- 260 Notes Payable

Equity
- 310 Common Stock
- 320 Retained Earnings

Revenues and Income
- 410 Sales Revenue
- 420 Interest Income

Expenses
- 510 Cost of Goods Sold
- 520 Wages Expense
- 530 Rent Expense
- 540 Advertising Expense
- 550 Depreciation Expense—Fixtures and Equipment
- 560 Insurance Expense
- 570 Interest Expense
- 580 Tax Expense

After transactions are journalized, the debits and credits in each journal entry are transferred to their related general ledger accounts. This transcribing process is called posting to the general ledger, or simply **posting**. Journalizing and posting occur simultaneously when recordkeeping is automated.

Review of Recording Transactions

In Chapter 2, we recorded the November activities of Natural Beauty Supply (NBS) and created the end-of-November financial statements. As NBS continues its activities into the next month, the end-of-November balance sheet provides the starting point for December. **Exhibit 3.3** provides a summary of Natural Beauty Supply's December 2021 transactions.

EXHIBIT 3.3 — Transactions for Natural Beauty Supply for December 2021

Event	Date	Description
(17)	Dec. 1	NBS signed a three-year note to borrow $11,000 cash from a financial institution. NBS will pay interest on the first business day of every month (starting in January) at the rate of 12% per year or 1% per month. The $11,000 principal is due at the end of three years.
(18)	Dec. 1	NBS purchased and installed improved fixtures and equipment for $18,000 cash.
(19)	Dec. 10	NBS paid $700 to advertise in the local newspaper for December.
(20)	Dec. 20	NBS paid $3,300 cash to its suppliers in partial payment for the delivery of inventory in November.
(21)	Dec. —	During the month of December, NBS sold products costing $5,000 to retail customers for $8,500 cash.
(22)	Dec. —	During the month of December, sales to wholesale customers totaled $4,500 for merchandise that had cost $3,000. Instead of paying cash, wholesale customers are required to pay for the merchandise within ten business days.
(23)	Dec. —	$1,200 of gift cards were sold during the month of December. Each gift card entitles the recipient to a one-hour consultation on the use of NBS' products.
(24)	Dec. —	NBS employed salespersons who were paid $1,625 in cash in December.
(25)	Dec. —	During the month of December, NBS received $3,200 in cash from wholesale customers for products that had been delivered earlier.
(26)	Dec. 28	NBS purchased and received $4,000 of inventory on account.
(27)	Dec. 31	NBS paid $1,500 to the landlord for December rent related to the short-term lease NBS entered into in November.
(28)	Dec. 31	NBS paid $50 cash dividend to its shareholders.

Most of these transactions are similar to those that we analyzed in Chapter 2. Each of the transactions involves an exchange of some kind. Suppliers provide inventory and employees provide labor services in exchange for cash or the promise of future cash payments. Customers receive products in exchange for cash or a promise to pay cash in the future. For each of these items, we analyze, journalize, and post as shown in Chapter 2.

NBS has the opportunity to secure long-term financing from a financial institution and signs a note that must be paid back at the end of three years. Cash increases, and a noncurrent liability increases. Interest payments are made at the start of every month, beginning on January 2, 2022, but no entry is made for interest until time passes and an interest obligation is created.

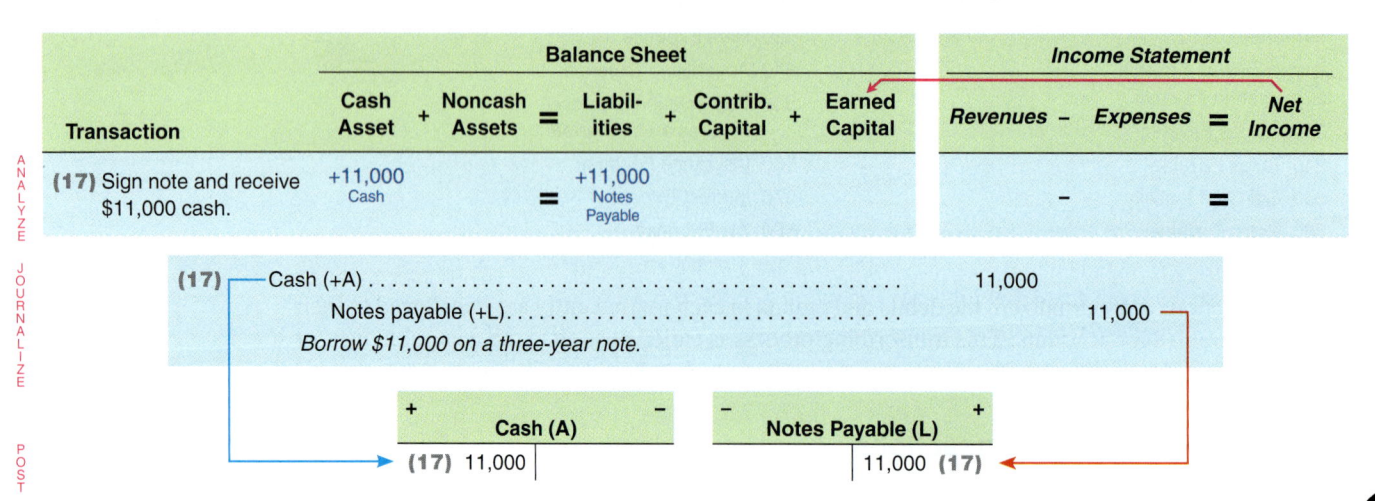

ANALYZE

Transaction	Balance Sheet					Income Statement		
	Cash Asset + Noncash Assets = Liabilities + Contrib. Capital + Earned Capital					Revenues − Expenses = Net Income		
(17) Sign note and receive $11,000 cash.	+11,000 Cash		+11,000 Notes Payable			−		=

JOURNALIZE

(17) Cash (+A) 11,000
      Notes payable (+L) 11,000
      Borrow $11,000 on a three-year note.

POST

+ Cash (A) −		− Notes Payable (L) +	
(17) 11,000			11,000 (17)

NBS pays $18,000 cash to purchase improved fixtures and equipment for its store location. One asset (cash) decreases, while a noncurrent asset (fixtures and equipment) is increased.

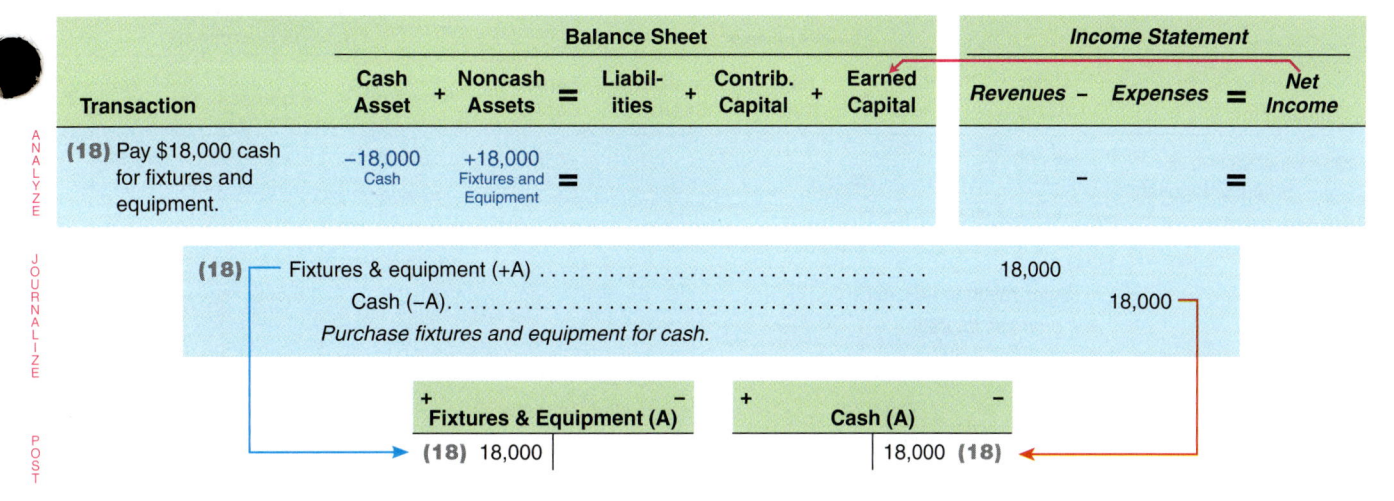

Transaction	Balance Sheet					Income Statement		
	Cash Asset +	Noncash Assets =	Liabilities +	Contrib. Capital +	Earned Capital	Revenues −	Expenses =	Net Income
(18) Pay $18,000 cash for fixtures and equipment.	−18,000 Cash	+18,000 Fixtures and Equipment =				−	=	

(18) Fixtures & equipment (+A) 18,000
     Cash (−A) 18,000
     Purchase fixtures and equipment for cash.

+ Fixtures & Equipment (A) −	+ Cash (A) −
(18) 18,000	18,000 (18)

Transactions (19) and (20) are similar to ones that we saw in Chapter 2. The expenditure for advertising results in an expense that decreases net income and ultimately, retained earnings. The payment to suppliers fulfills (in part) an obligation that appeared in the November 30 balance sheet.

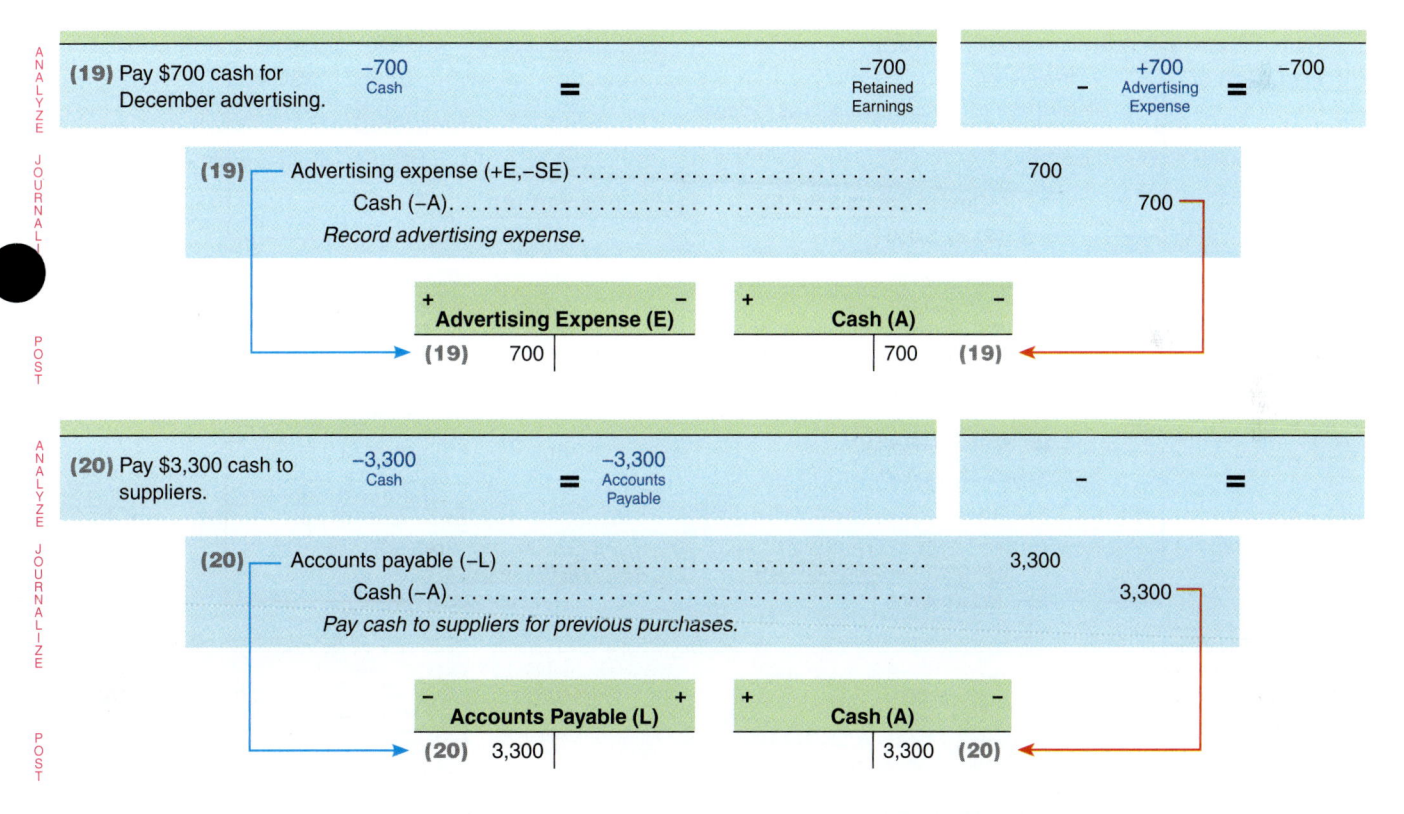

(19) Pay $700 cash for December advertising.	−700 Cash	=			−700 Retained Earnings	−	+700 Advertising Expense =	−700

(19) Advertising expense (+E,−SE) 700
     Cash (−A) 700
     Record advertising expense.

+ Advertising Expense (E) −	+ Cash (A) −
(19) 700	700 (19)

(20) Pay $3,300 cash to suppliers.	−3,300 Cash	=	−3,300 Accounts Payable			−	=	

(20) Accounts payable (−L) 3,300
     Cash (−A) 3,300
     Pay cash to suppliers for previous purchases.

− Accounts Payable (L) +	+ Cash (A) −
(20) 3,300	3,300 (20)

Sales to customers in (21), (22), and (23) are also similar to transactions in Chapter 2, and they are accounted for in similar fashion. Revenue is recognized when products are delivered to customers, rather than when cash is received. When cash is received after delivery, an accounts receivable asset is recorded; when cash is received before delivery, a performance obligation liability is recorded. In this case, NBS uses the account title "Gift Card Liability."[1] Cost of goods sold expense is recognized when the associated revenue is recognized.

---

[1] The Gift Card Liability represents NBS' obligation to deliver services to customers when the gift cards are redeemed. Companies sometimes use the terms "deferred revenue" or "unearned revenue" to refer to these liabilities. We use the preferred terms "performance obligation," "contract liability," or a more descriptive account title such as "Gift Card Liability" wherever possible.

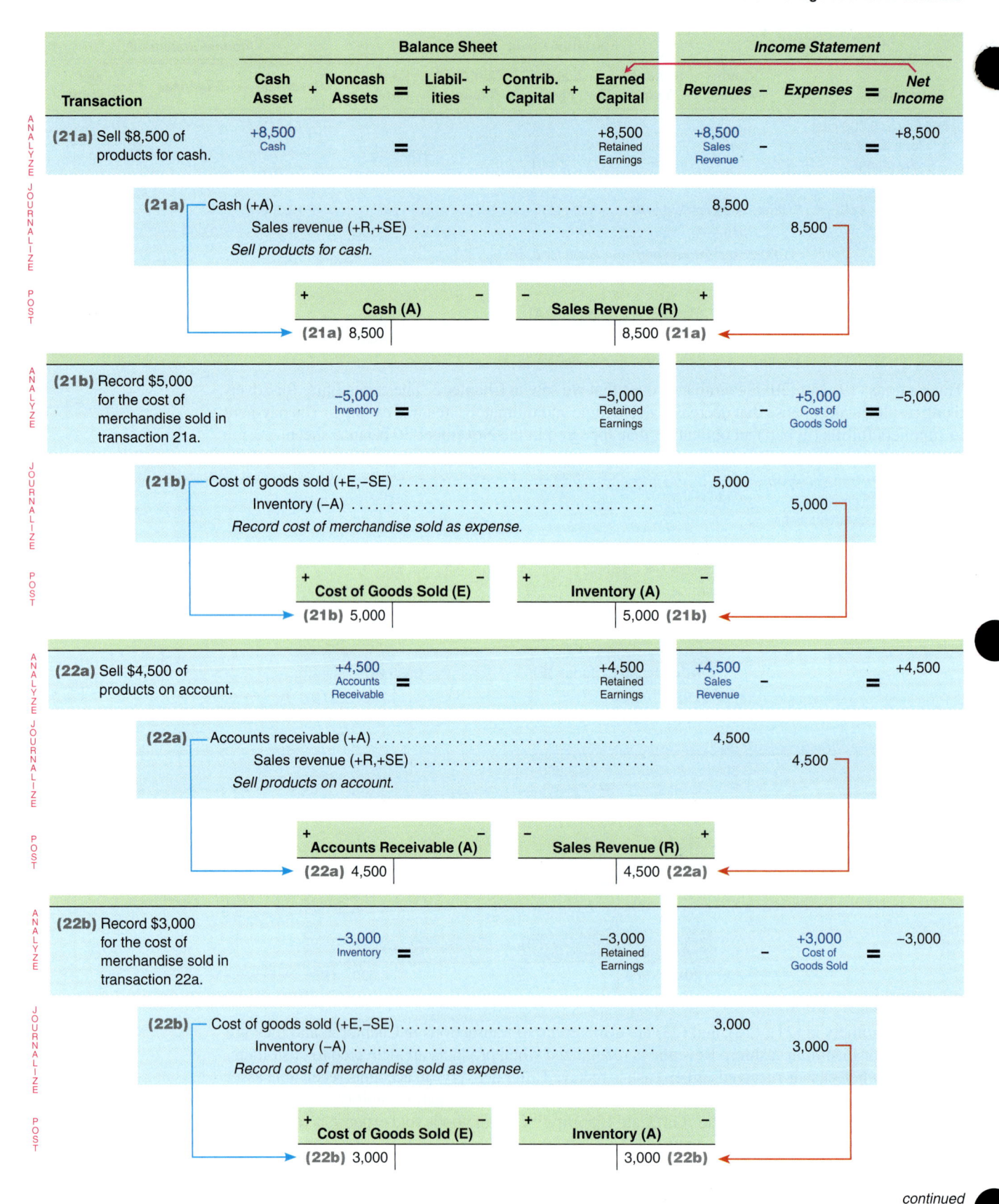

Chapter 3 Adjusting Accounts for Financial Statements

Transaction	Balance Sheet: Cash Asset + Noncash Assets = Liabilities + Contrib. Capital + Earned Capital	Income Statement: Revenues − Expenses = Net Income
(21a) Sell $8,500 of products for cash.	+8,500 Cash = +8,500 Retained Earnings	+8,500 Sales Revenue − = +8,500

(21a) Cash (+A) 8,500
      Sales revenue (+R,+SE) 8,500
Sell products for cash.

+ Cash (A) −	− Sales Revenue (R) +
(21a) 8,500	8,500 (21a)

(21b) Record $5,000 for the cost of merchandise sold in transaction 21a.	−5,000 Inventory = −5,000 Retained Earnings	− +5,000 Cost of Goods Sold = −5,000

(21b) Cost of goods sold (+E,−SE) 5,000
      Inventory (−A) 5,000
Record cost of merchandise sold as expense.

+ Cost of Goods Sold (E) −	+ Inventory (A) −
(21b) 5,000	5,000 (21b)

(22a) Sell $4,500 of products on account.	+4,500 Accounts Receivable = +4,500 Retained Earnings	+4,500 Sales Revenue − = +4,500

(22a) Accounts receivable (+A) 4,500
      Sales revenue (+R,+SE) 4,500
Sell products on account.

+ Accounts Receivable (A) −	− Sales Revenue (R) +
(22a) 4,500	4,500 (22a)

(22b) Record $3,000 for the cost of merchandise sold in transaction 22a.	−3,000 Inventory = −3,000 Retained Earnings	− +3,000 Cost of Goods Sold = −3,000

(22b) Cost of goods sold (+E,−SE) 3,000
      Inventory (−A) 3,000
Record cost of merchandise sold as expense.

+ Cost of Goods Sold (E) −	+ Inventory (A) −
(22b) 3,000	3,000 (22b)

continued

Transaction	Balance Sheet						Income Statement		
	Cash Asset	+ Noncash Assets	= Liabilities	+ Contrib. Capital	+ Earned Capital		Revenues	− Expenses	= Net Income
(23) Sell gift cards for $1,200 cash.	+1,200 Cash		= +1,200 Gift Card Liability					−	=

(23) Cash (+A) 1,200
 Gift Card Liability (+L) 1,200
 Record unearned revenue from gift cards.

+ Cash (A) −	− Gift Card Liability (L) +
(23) 1,200	1,200 **(23)**

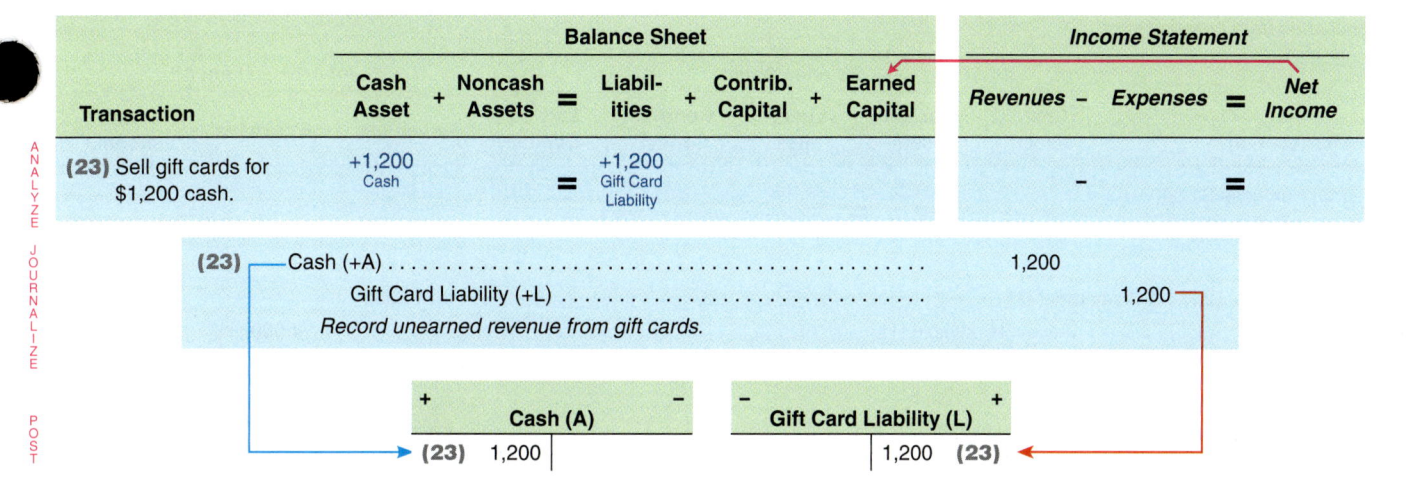

The final five transactions in December also are similar to transactions that NBS had in November. Payment of wages to the employee is reflected in a wage expense. Cash received from wholesale (credit) customers does not cause revenue; rather, the increase in cash is balanced by a decrease in accounts receivable. Purchase of inventory on account does not create an expense—the cost of the inventory is held in the inventory asset account until it is purchased by a customer. Payments to the landlord are balanced by a rent expense in the income statement. The cash dividend to shareholders decreases an asset (cash) and shareholders' equity (retained earnings) but does not affect the income statement.

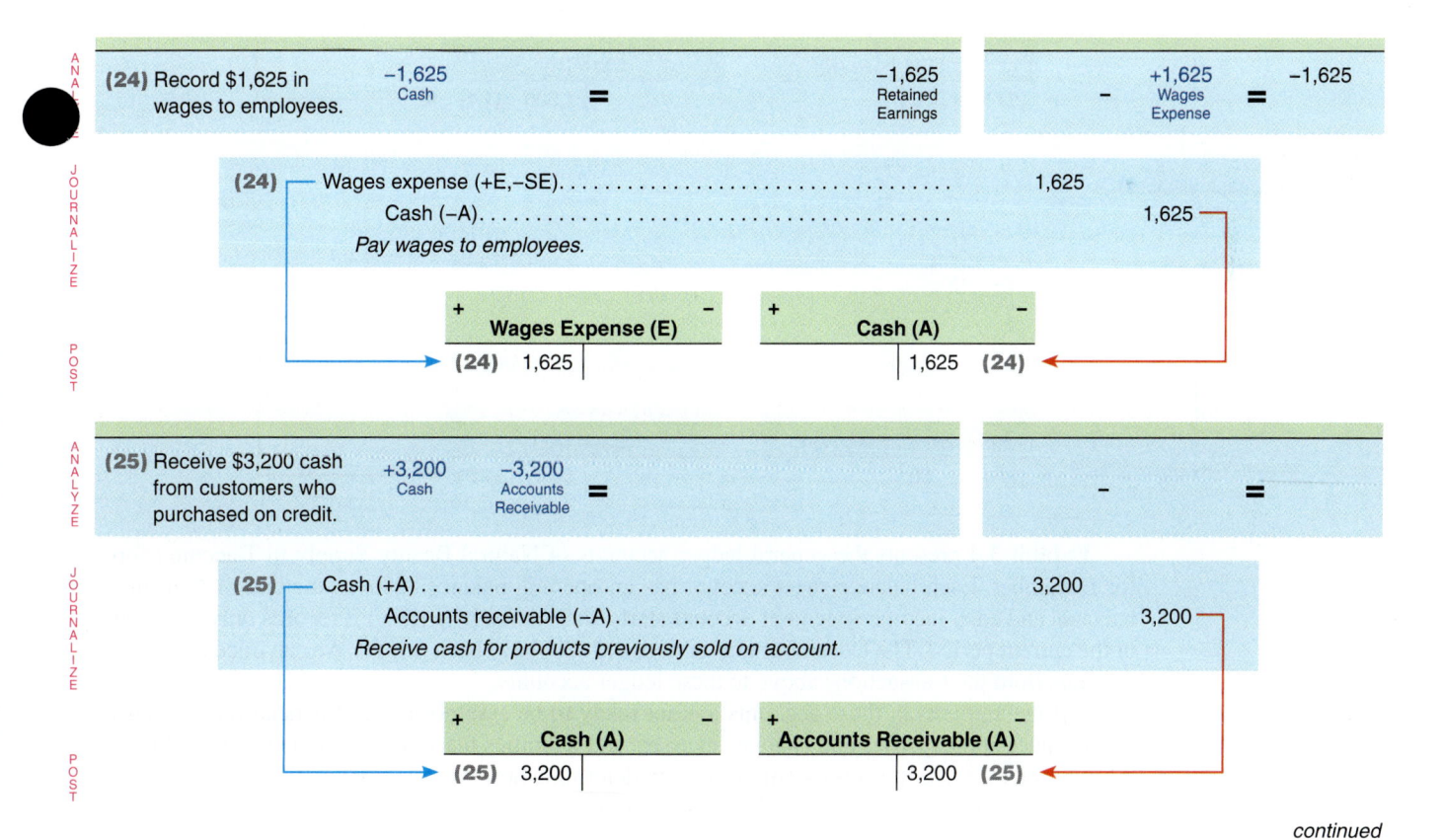

(24) Record $1,625 in wages to employees.	−1,625 Cash	=	−1,625 Retained Earnings	− +1,625 Wages Expense	= −1,625

(24) Wages expense (+E,−SE)..................................... 1,625
 Cash (−A).. 1,625
 Pay wages to employees.

+ Wages Expense (E) −	+ Cash (A) −
(24) 1,625	1,625 **(24)**

(25) Receive $3,200 cash from customers who purchased on credit.	+3,200 Cash	−3,200 Accounts Receivable	=				−	=

(25) Cash (+A)... 3,200
 Accounts receivable (−A)............................... 3,200
 Receive cash for products previously sold on account.

+ Cash (A) −	+ Accounts Receivable (A) −
(25) 3,200	3,200 **(25)**

continued

continued from previous page

Transaction	Balance Sheet					Income Statement		
	Cash Asset	+ Noncash Assets	= Liabilities	+ Contrib. Capital	+ Earned Capital	Revenues	− Expenses	= Net Income
(26) Purchase $4,000 inventory on account.		+4,000 Inventory	+4,000 Accounts Payable					

(26) Inventory (+A) 4,000
      Accounts payable (+L) 4,000
      Purchase inventory on account.

+ Inventory (A) −		− Accounts Payable (L) +
(26) 4,000		4,000 (26)

Transaction	Cash Asset	Noncash Assets	Liabilities	Contrib. Capital	Earned Capital	Revenues	Expenses	Net Income
(27) Pay $1,500 rent for December.	−1,500 Cash				−1,500 Retained Earnings		+1,500 Rent Expense	−1,500

(27) Rent expense (+E,−SE) 1,500
      Cash (−A) 1,500
      Record payment of December rent.

+ Rent Expense (E) −		+ Cash (A) −
(27) 1,500		1,500 (27)

Transaction	Cash Asset	Noncash Assets	Liabilities	Contrib. Capital	Earned Capital	Revenues	Expenses	Net Income
(28) Pay $50 cash dividend to shareholders.	−50 Cash				−50 Retained Earnings			

(28) Retained earnings (−SE) 50
      Cash (−A) 50
      Pay a cash dividend.

− Retained Earnings (SE) +		+ Cash (A) −
(28) 50		50 (28)

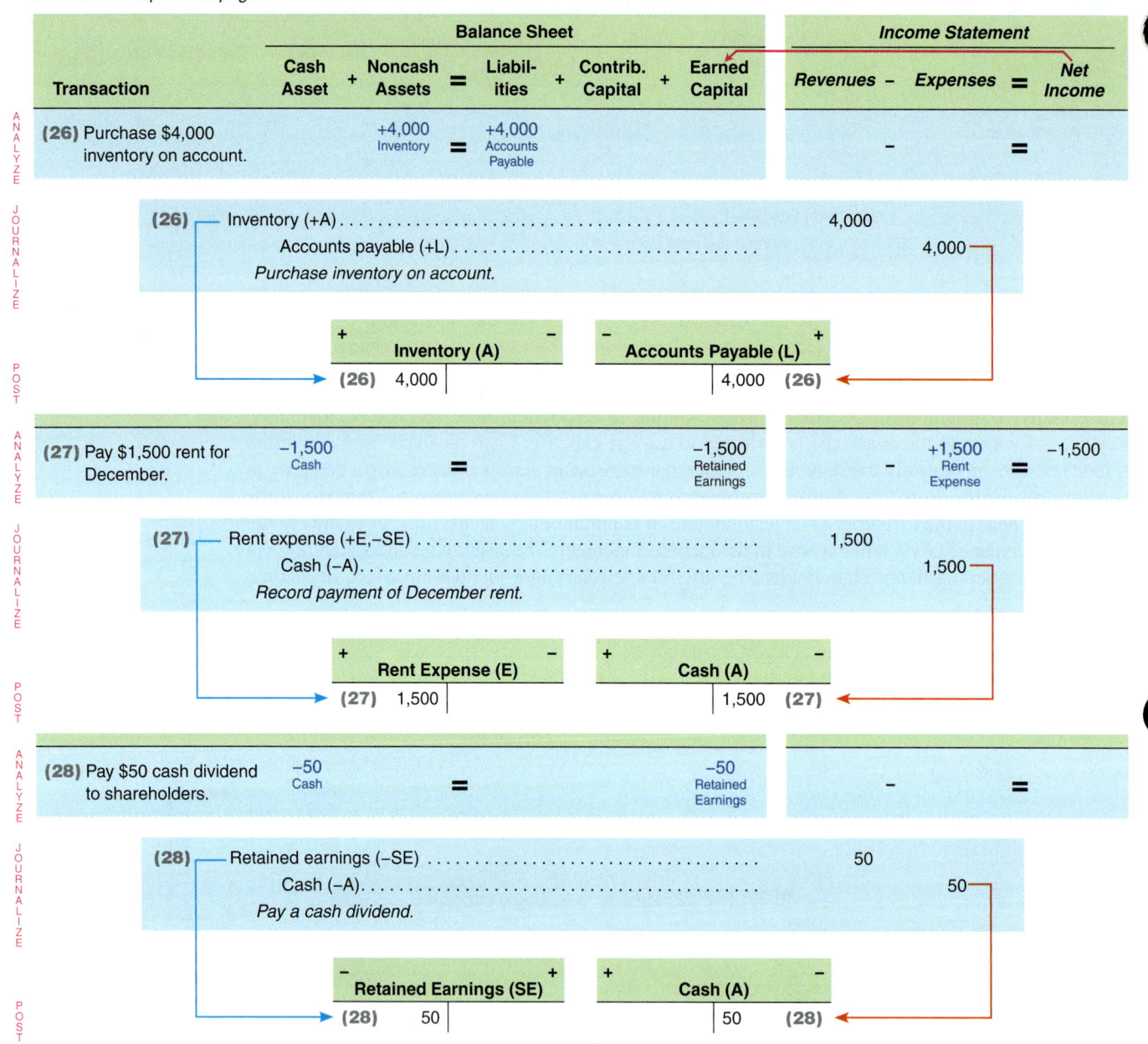

Exhibit 3.4 presents the general ledger accounts of Natural Beauty Supply in T-account form for December. Each balance sheet account has an opening balance equal to the end-of-November balance, and each income statement account starts with a zero balance so it records only the events of the current period. The December transactions (17–28) have been posted. We can trace each of the postings from the transactions above to these ledger accounts.

But the amounts in these accounts are not ready to be assembled into financial reports. There are revenues and expenses and changes in assets and liabilities that occur with the passage of time.[2] Accounting for these items is essential for us to determine how well a company has performed in an accounting period and to assess its financial standing.

---
[2] Natural Beauty Supply's November activities in Chapter 2 were carefully chosen so we could produce financial statements without adjusting entries. But, as **Exhibit 3.1** depicts, the adjusting process is an essential part of the accounting cycle.

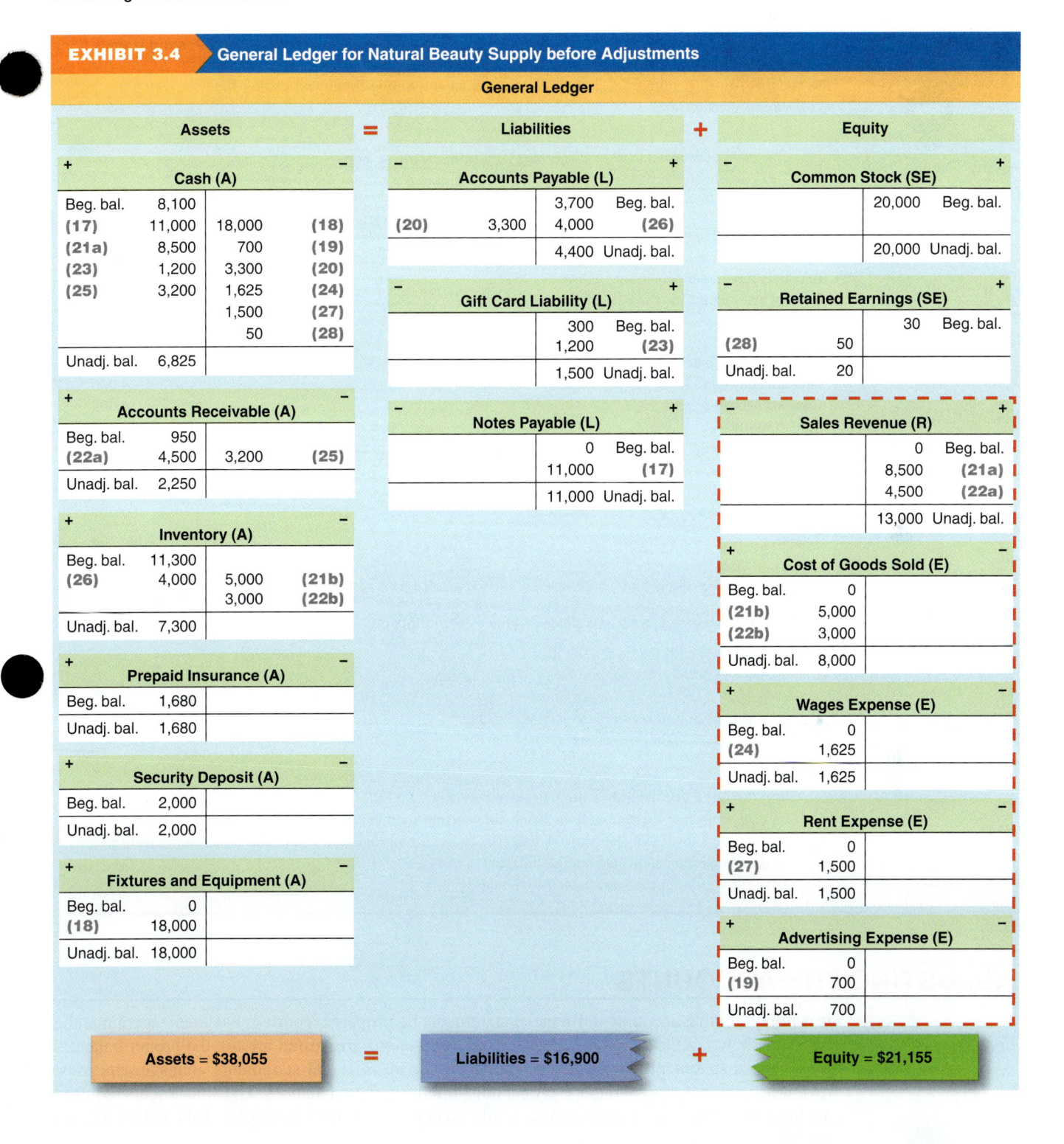

EXHIBIT 3.4 — General Ledger for Natural Beauty Supply before Adjustments

General Ledger

Assets =

Cash (A) (+ / −)

Beg. bal.	8,100		
(17)	11,000	18,000	(18)
(21a)	8,500	700	(19)
(23)	1,200	3,300	(20)
(25)	3,200	1,625	(24)
		1,500	(27)
		50	(28)
Unadj. bal.	6,825		

Accounts Receivable (A)

Beg. bal.	950		
(22a)	4,500	3,200	(25)
Unadj. bal.	2,250		

Inventory (A)

Beg. bal.	11,300		
(26)	4,000	5,000	(21b)
		3,000	(22b)
Unadj. bal.	7,300		

Prepaid Insurance (A)

Beg. bal.	1,680	
Unadj. bal.	1,680	

Security Deposit (A)

Beg. bal.	2,000	
Unadj. bal.	2,000	

Fixtures and Equipment (A)

Beg. bal.	0	
(18)	18,000	
Unadj. bal.	18,000	

Liabilities +

Accounts Payable (L)

		3,700	Beg. bal.
(20)	3,300	4,000	(26)
		4,400	Unadj. bal.

Gift Card Liability (L)

	300	Beg. bal.
	1,200	(23)
	1,500	Unadj. bal.

Notes Payable (L)

	0	Beg. bal.
	11,000	(17)
	11,000	Unadj. bal.

Equity

Common Stock (SE)

20,000	Beg. bal.
20,000	Unadj. bal.

Retained Earnings (SE)

		30	Beg. bal.
(28)	50		
Unadj. bal.	20		

Sales Revenue (R)

0	Beg. bal.
8,500	(21a)
4,500	(22a)
13,000	Unadj. bal.

Cost of Goods Sold (E)

Beg. bal.	0
(21b)	5,000
(22b)	3,000
Unadj. bal.	8,000

Wages Expense (E)

Beg. bal.	0
(24)	1,625
Unadj. bal.	1,625

Rent Expense (E)

Beg. bal.	0
(27)	1,500
Unadj. bal.	1,500

Advertising Expense (E)

Beg. bal.	0
(19)	700
Unadj. bal.	700

Assets = $38,055 = Liabilities = $16,900 + Equity = $21,155

Review 3-1 LO3-1 — Analyzing, Journalizing, and Posting Transactions

Assume that Atwell Laboratories, Inc., operates with an accounting fiscal year ending June 30. Its trial balance as of May 31 is as follows.

ATWELL LABORATORIES, INC.
Trial Balance
May 31

	Debit	Credit
Cash.	$ 500	
Accounts receivable	8,000	
Prepaid insurance.	6,000	
Supplies	30,200	
Equipment	270,000	
Accumulated depreciation—equipment*		$ 60,000
Accounts payable		4,000
Contract liability		4,000
Fees revenue		142,300
Wages expense	54,000	
Rent expense	22,000	
Common stock		120,400
Retained earnings		60,000
Totals	$390,700	$390,700

*Accumulated depreciation, a contra asset account, will be discussed in the next section.

The following five transactions took place in June by the company.

1. Paid $4,000 in cash for wages for June.
2. Received $6,500 in cash for services provided in June.
3. Purchased $1,100 supplies on account.
4. Performed $1,200 of services on account in June.
5. Paid suppliers $2,000 on account.

Required
a. Show the impact of the transactions listed above using the FSET.
b. Show the impact of the transactions listed above using journal entries.
c. Prepare T-accounts with the May 31 balances as beginning balances, enter the transactions from part b, and determine the unadjusted ending balances.
d. Prepare Atwell's June 30 unadjusted trial balance.

Solution on p. 3-50.

ADJUSTING THE ACCOUNTS

LO3-2 Describe the adjusting process and illustrate adjusting entries.

It is important that accounts in financial statements be properly reported. For many accounts, the balances shown in the general ledger after all transactions are posted are not the proper balances for financial statements. So, when it is time to prepare financial statements, management must review account balances and make proper adjustments to these balances. The adjustments required are based on accrual accounting and generally accepted accounting principles. This section focuses on this adjustment process.

Preparing an Unadjusted Trial Balance

The T-accounts in **Exhibit 3.4** show balances for each account after recording all transactions. This set of balances is called an **unadjusted trial balance** because it shows account balances before any adjustments are made. The purpose of an unadjusted trial balance is to be sure the general ledger is in balance before management adjusts the accounts. Showing all general ledger account balances in one place also makes it easier to review accounts and determine which account balances require adjusting. Natural Beauty Supply's unadjusted trial balance at December 31 is shown in **Exhibit 3.5**.

EXHIBIT 3.5 — Unadjusted Trial Balance

NATURAL BEAUTY SUPPLY
Unadjusted Trial Balance
December 31, 2021

	Debit	Credit
Cash	$ 6,825	
Accounts receivable	2,250	
Inventory	7,300	
Prepaid insurance	1,680	
Security deposit	2,000	
Fixtures & equipment	18,000	
Accounts payable		$ 4,400
Gift card liability		1,500
Notes payable		11,000
Common stock		20,000
Retained earnings	20	
Sales revenue		13,000
Cost of goods sold	8,000	
Wages expense	1,625	
Rent expense	1,500	
Advertising expense	700	
Totals	**$49,900**	**$49,900**

FYI Even if the unadjusted trial balance shows an equal amount of debits and credits, this does not mean that the general ledger is correct. Journal entries could have been omitted or falsified, or the accounts used or the amounts involved may have been wrong. Thus, the equality of debits and credits is a necessary, but not a sufficient, condition for the financial statements to be correct.

Types of Adjustments

Accrual adjustments are caused by a variety of accounting practices. There are some revenues and expenses that arise with the passage of time, rather than in a transaction. There are asset and liability values that change over time or that require estimation based on recent events. All of these require adjustments before proper financial statements can be produced.

Adjusting entries have two common characteristics. First, they occur at the end of a reporting period, just before the construction of financial statements. Second, they (almost) never involve cash. Changes in cash require a transaction, and adjusting entries do not involve the recording of transactions.

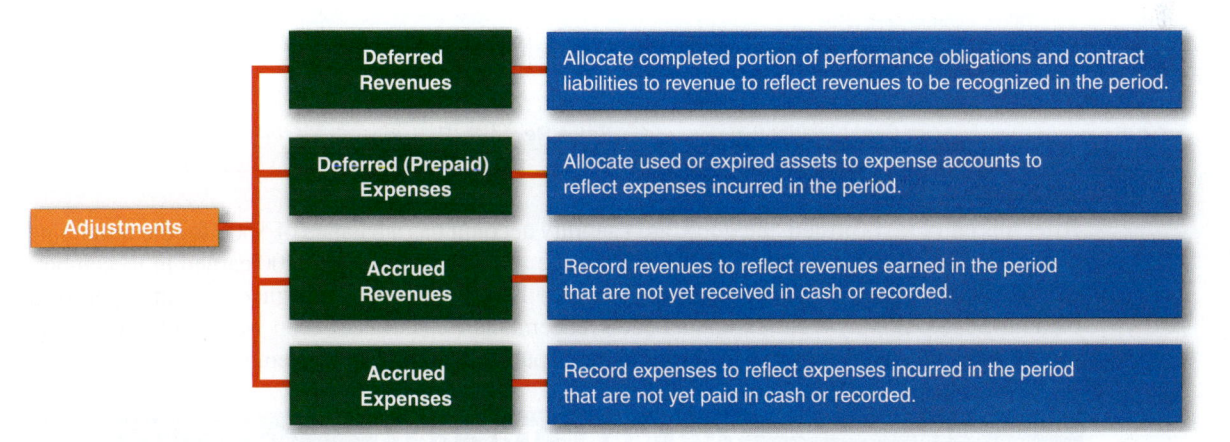

Adjustments

- **Deferred Revenues** — Allocate completed portion of performance obligations and contract liabilities to revenue to reflect revenues to be recognized in the period.
- **Deferred (Prepaid) Expenses** — Allocate used or expired assets to expense accounts to reflect expenses incurred in the period.
- **Accrued Revenues** — Record revenues to reflect revenues earned in the period that are not yet received in cash or recorded.
- **Accrued Expenses** — Record expenses to reflect expenses incurred in the period that are not yet paid in cash or recorded.

Through the course of this book, we will encounter quite a few required adjusting entries, but we will start with four general types of adjustments made at the end of an accounting period.

Journal entries made to reflect these adjustments are known as **adjusting entries**. Each adjusting entry usually affects a balance sheet account (an asset or liability account) and an income statement account (an expense or revenue account). The first two types of adjustments—allocating assets to expense and allocating unearned revenues to revenue—are often referred to as **deferrals**. The distinguishing characteristic of a deferral is that the adjustment deals with an amount previously recorded in a balance sheet account; the adjusting entry decreases the balance sheet account and increases an income statement account. The last two types of adjustments—accruing expenses and accruing revenues—are often referred to as **accruals**. The unique characteristic of an accrual is that the adjustment deals with an amount not previously recorded in any account; this type of adjusting entry increases both a balance sheet account and an income statement account. Both accruals and deferrals allow revenue to be recognized when it is earned and the expenses of the period to reflect asset decreases and liability increases from generating revenues or supporting that period's operations. Let's consider each of these adjustments in more detail.

> **FYI** Chapter 2 explained that revenue recognition is key to determining net income under accrual accounting, which recognizes revenues when services are performed or when goods are sold and recognizes expenses in the period that they help to generate the recorded revenues.

Type 1: Deferred Revenue—Allocating Performance Obligation Liabilities to Revenue Companies often receive fees for products or services before those products or services are rendered. Such transactions are recorded by debiting Cash and crediting a performance obligation liability account for the **deferred revenue** (the account could have other names such as unearned revenue or contract liability). This account reflects the obligation for performing future services or delivering a product in the future. As services are performed or products are delivered, revenue should be recognized. At period-end, an adjusting entry is used to record the revenue in the current accounting period and reduce the liability account that was previously recorded.[3]

DEFERRED REVENUE During November and December, Natural Beauty Supply sold gift cards that entitled the recipient to a one-hour consultation with a salesperson on the use of natural and organic health and beauty products. When the gift cards were purchased, NBS recognized a gift card liability that reflected the obligation to provide these services. During the month of December, gift cards totaling $900 were redeemed. On December 31, Natural Beauty Supply made the adjustment (a) in the following template, journal entry, and T-accounts to recognize the (partial) fulfillment of the obligation and to recognize the $900 of revenue to which it is now entitled. The $900 increase in sales revenue is reflected in net income and carried over to retained earnings.

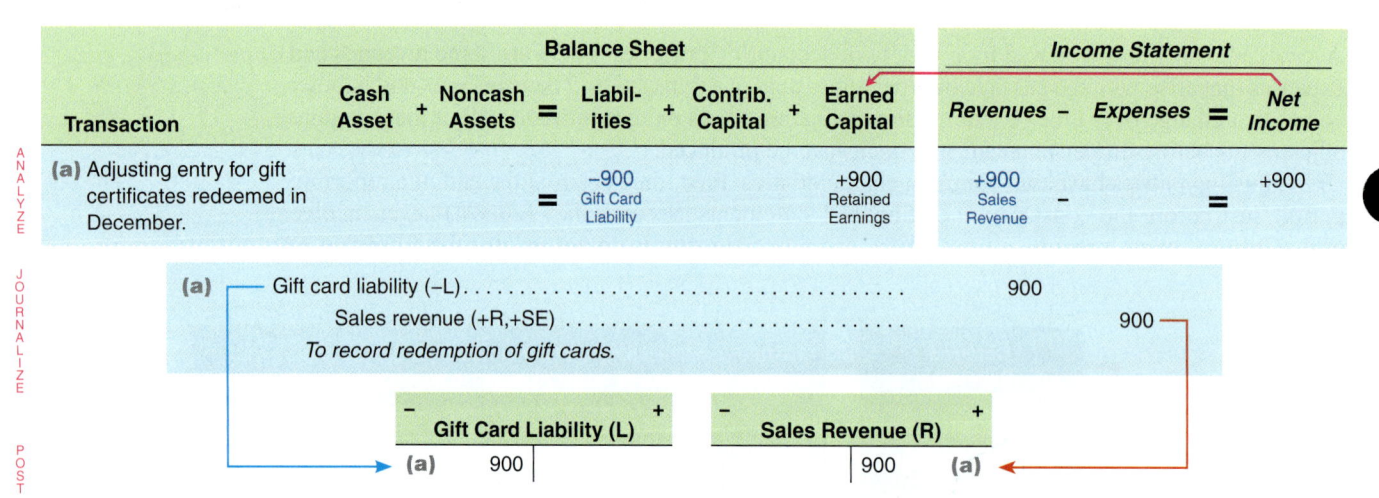

Transaction	Balance Sheet								Income Statement			
	Cash Asset	+	Noncash Assets	=	Liabilities	+	Contrib. Capital	+	Earned Capital	Revenues	− Expenses	= Net Income
(a) Adjusting entry for gift certificates redeemed in December.				=	−900 Gift Card Liability			+	+900 Retained Earnings	+900 Sales Revenue	−	= +900

(a) Gift card liability (−L)... 900
    Sales revenue (+R,+SE)..................................... 900
    To record redemption of gift cards.

− Gift Card Liability (L) +		− Sales Revenue (R) +
(a) 900		900 (a)

After this entry (a) is posted, the Gift Card Liability account has a balance of $600 for the remaining gift certificates outstanding, and the Sales Revenue account reflects the $900 earned in December.

In this case, the cost of the salesperson's time has already been recognized as an expense. If Natural Beauty Supply's gift cards had been redeemable for products, then we would have recognized a Cost of Goods Sold expense for the items purchased with the redeemed certificates.

YOU MAKE THE CALL

You are the Chief Accountant REI requires customers of its travel-vacation business to make an initial deposit equal to $400 when the trip is reserved and to make full payment two months before departure. REI's refunding policy is to return the entire deposit if the customer informs REI of the trip's cancellation three or more months in advance of the trip. REI will refund all but the $400 deposit if the customer cancels between 60 and 90 days prior to the trip or if the customer cancels between 30 and 60 days prior to the trip, REI will retain 50% of the total amount paid. There is no refund if notification occurs within 30 days of the trip. REI's cancellation rate is very low. How should you account for deposits, and when should revenue be recorded? [Answers on page 3-29]

---

[3] Note that there are some conditions under which a contract liability would be recorded even before cash is received from the customer. For example, if the contract is not cancelable and the due date for payment has passed. This is beyond the scope of this book and not common.

Other examples of revenues received in advance include rental payments received in advance by real estate management companies, insurance premiums received in advance by insurance companies, subscription revenues received in advance by magazine and newspaper publishers, and membership fees received in advance by health clubs. In each case, a performance obligation liability account is set up when the advance payment is received. Later, an adjusting entry is made to reflect the revenues earned from the services provided or products delivered during the period.

Type 2: Deferred (Prepaid) Expenses—Allocating Assets to Expenses Many cash outlays benefit several accounting periods. Examples are purchases of buildings, equipment, and supplies; prepayments of advertising; and payments of insurance premiums covering several periods. These outlays are added to (debited to) an asset account when the expenditure occurs. Then at the end of each accounting period, the estimated portion of the outlay that has expired in that period or has benefited that period is transferred to an expense account.

We can usually see when adjustments of this type are needed by inspecting the unadjusted trial balance for costs that benefit several periods. Looking at the December 31 trial balance of Natural Beauty Supply (**Exhibit 3.5**), for example, adjustments are required to record the costs of prepaid insurance and the fixtures and equipment for the month of December.

FYI Many transactions reflected in ledger accounts affect net income of more than one period. Likewise, other events that are not yet recorded in accounts affect the current period's income. The adjusting process identifies these situations to record the proper revenues and expenses in the current period.

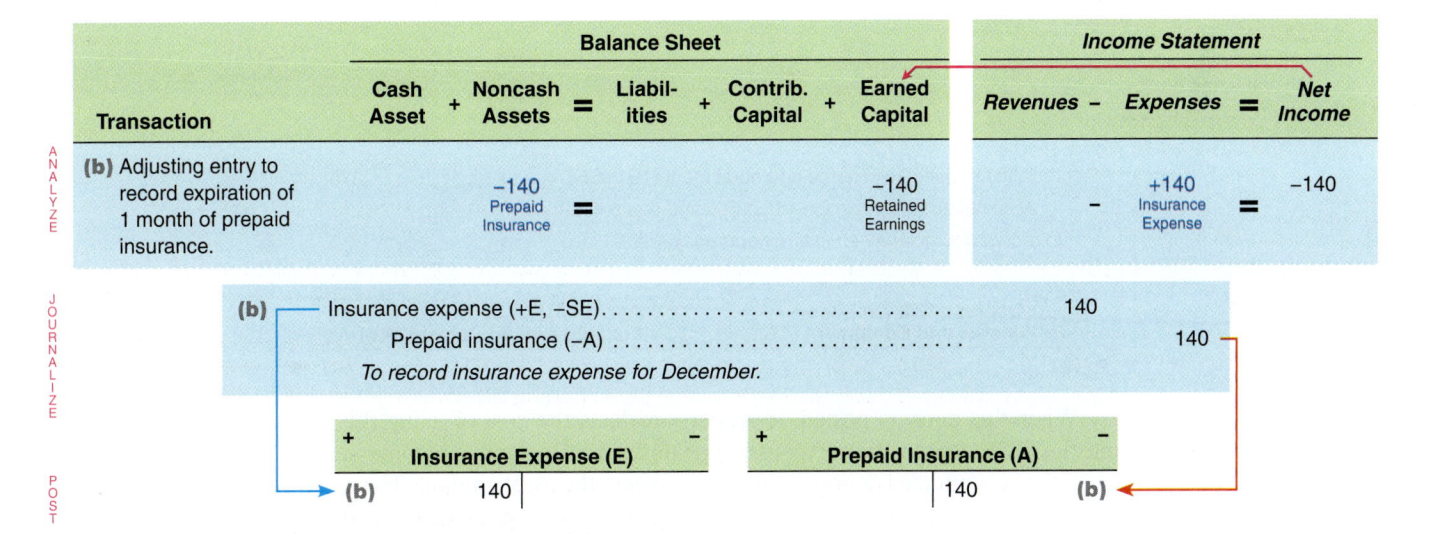

PREPAID INSURANCE On November 30, Natural Beauty Supply paid one year's insurance premium in advance and debited the $1,680 payment to Prepaid Insurance, an asset account. As each day passes and the insurance coverage is being used, insurance expense is being incurred, and the Prepaid Insurance asset is decreasing. It is not necessary to record insurance expense on a daily basis because financial statements are not prepared daily. At the end of an accounting period, however, an adjustment must be made to recognize the proper amount of Insurance Expense for the period and to decrease Prepaid Insurance by that amount. On December 31, one month's insurance coverage has been used up, so Natural Beauty Supply transfers $140 ($1,680/12 months) from Prepaid Insurance to Insurance Expense. This entry is identified as adjustment (b) in the template, journal entry, and T-accounts.

Transaction	Balance Sheet					Income Statement		
	Cash Asset	+ Noncash Assets	= Liabilities	+ Contrib. Capital	+ Earned Capital	Revenues	− Expenses	= Net Income
(b) Adjusting entry to record expiration of 1 month of prepaid insurance.		−140 Prepaid Insurance =			−140 Retained Earnings		− +140 Insurance Expense =	−140

(b) Insurance expense (+E, −SE)..................................... 140
    Prepaid insurance (−A).. 140
    To record insurance expense for December.

+ Insurance Expense (E) −		+ Prepaid Insurance (A) −
(b) 140		140 (b)

The posting of this adjusting entry creates the proper Insurance Expense of $140 for December in the Insurance Expense ledger account and reduces the Prepaid Insurance balance to the (eleven-month) amount that is prepaid as of December 31, which is $1,540.

Examples of other prepaid expenses for which similar adjustments are made include prepaid advertising. When advertising services are purchased in advance, the payment is debited to Prepaid Advertising. At the end of an accounting period, an adjustment is needed to recognize the cost of any of the prepaid advertising used during the period. The adjusting entry debits (increases) Advertising Expense and credits (decreases) Prepaid Advertising.

FYI Contra accounts are used to provide more information to users of financial statements. For example, Accumulated Depreciation is a contra asset reported in the balance sheet that enables users to estimate asset age. For Natural Beauty Supply, the December 31 balance sheet reveals that its Fixtures and Equipment is nearly new as its accumulated depreciation is only $375, which is 1/48 of the $18,000 original cost.

DEPRECIATION The process of allocating the costs of equipment, vehicles, and buildings to the periods benefiting from their use is called **depreciation**. Each accounting period in which such assets are used must reflect a portion of their cost as expense because these assets helped generate revenue or support operations for those periods. This periodic expense is known as *depreciation expense*. Periodic depreciation expense is an estimate. The procedure we use here estimates the annual amount of depreciation expense by dividing the asset cost by its estimated useful life. (We assume that the entire asset cost is depreciated—so-called zero salvage value; later in the book we consider salvage values other than zero.) This method is called **straight-line depreciation** and is used by the great majority of companies in their financial reports.

Expenses are recorded when business activities reduce net assets. But when we record depreciation expense, the asset amount is not reduced directly. Instead, the reduction is recorded in a **contra asset** account (labeled XA in the journal entries and T-accounts) called *Accumulated Depreciation*. **Contra accounts** are so named because they are used to record reductions in or offsets against a related account. The Accumulated Depreciation account normally has a credit balance and appears in the balance sheet as an offset against (or reduction in) the related asset amount. Use of the *contra asset* Accumulated Depreciation allows the original cost of the asset to be reported in the balance sheet, followed (and reduced) by the accumulated depreciation. Let's consider an example.

The fixtures and equipment purchased by Natural Beauty Supply for $18,000 are expected to last for four years. Straight-line depreciation recorded on the equipment is $4,500 per year ($18,000/4 years), or $375 per month ($18,000/48 months). At December 31, Natural Beauty Supply makes adjustment (c), as shown in the following template, journal entry, and T-accounts.

The introduction of contra assets requires a new column in the FSET for these accounts.[4] Increases in a contra asset decrease the net balance of the company's long-term assets. The new column is preceded by a minus sign to indicate that increases in contra assets create a decrease in the asset side of the accounting equation.

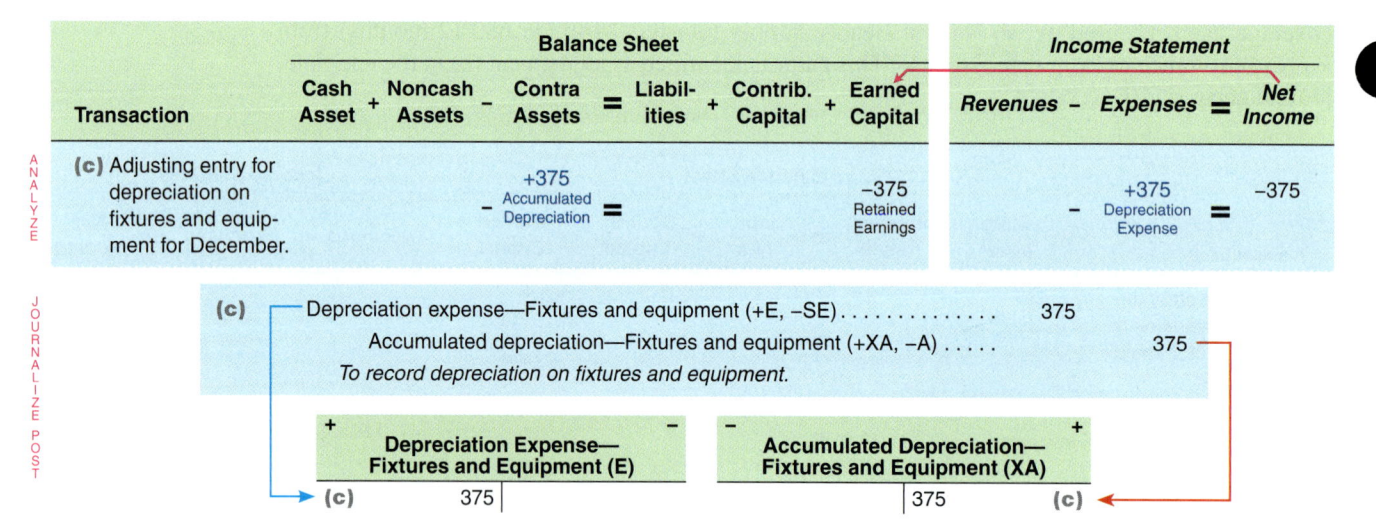

Transaction	Balance Sheet						Income Statement		
	Cash Asset +	Noncash Assets −	Contra Assets =	Liabilities +	Contrib. Capital +	Earned Capital	Revenues −	Expenses =	Net Income
(c) Adjusting entry for depreciation on fixtures and equipment for December.			+375 Accumulated Depreciation =			−375 Retained Earnings		+375 Depreciation Expense =	−375

(c) Depreciation expense—Fixtures and equipment (+E, −SE) 375
         Accumulated depreciation—Fixtures and equipment (+XA, −A)   375
      To record depreciation on fixtures and equipment.

```
     +                                              −
   Depreciation Expense—                    Accumulated Depreciation—
   Fixtures and Equipment (E)               Fixtures and Equipment (XA)
(c)        375                                                375      (c)
```

When this entry is posted, it properly reflects the cost of using this asset during December, and the $375 depreciation expense appears in the December income statement. On the balance sheet, the accumulated depreciation is an offset to the asset amount. The resulting balance (cost less accumulated depreciation), which is the asset's **book value**, represents the unexpired asset cost to be allocated as an expense in future periods. For example, the December 31, 2021, balance sheet reports the equipment with a book value of $17,625, as follows.

Fixtures and equipment	$18,000
Less: Accumulated depreciation	375
Fixtures and equipment, net	$17,625 (book value)

---

[4] Our practice is to include a separate FSET column where contra assets are required, but not to do so all the time. As we progress through the topics in this text, we will also see examples of contra liability accounts and contra equity accounts.

In each subsequent month, $375 is recognized as depreciation expense, and the Accumulated Depreciation contra asset is increased by the same amount (from $375 to $750 to $1,125 and so on). As a result, the book value of the fixtures and equipment is decreased by $375 each month. In Chapter 8, we will see the same principles applied to certain intangible assets.

FYI An increase in the contra asset account Accumulated Depreciation reduces the book value of the asset.

Type 3: Accrued Revenues

Revenue should be recognized when the company has transferred goods or services to customers, and in an amount that reflects the amount to which the company expects to be entitled from the transfer. Yet, a company often provides services during a period that are neither paid for by customers nor billed before the end of the period. Such values should be included in the firm's current period income statement, reflecting the company's fulfillment of its agreement with the customer. To properly account for such situations, end-of-period adjusting entries are made to reflect any revenues or income earned, but not yet billed or received. Such accumulated revenue is often called **accrued revenue** or **accrued income**.

ACCRUED SALES REVENUE/INCOME At the end of December, Natural Beauty Supply learns that its bank has decided to provide interest on checking accounts for small businesses like NBS. Each month, NBS earns interest income based on the average balance in its checking account. The interest is paid into NBS' checking account on the fifth business day of the following month. Based on its average daily balance, NBS earned $30 in interest during December.

In this instance, Natural Beauty Supply does not receive the interest payment until January. Nevertheless, the company earned interest during the month of December. Therefore, it should recognize an interest receivable (or "other receivables") asset and interest income in the income statement. (We could also call this interest revenue, but the term "interest income" is more commonly used for nonfinancial companies.) The entry in the FSET, the journal entry, and the T-account posting is:

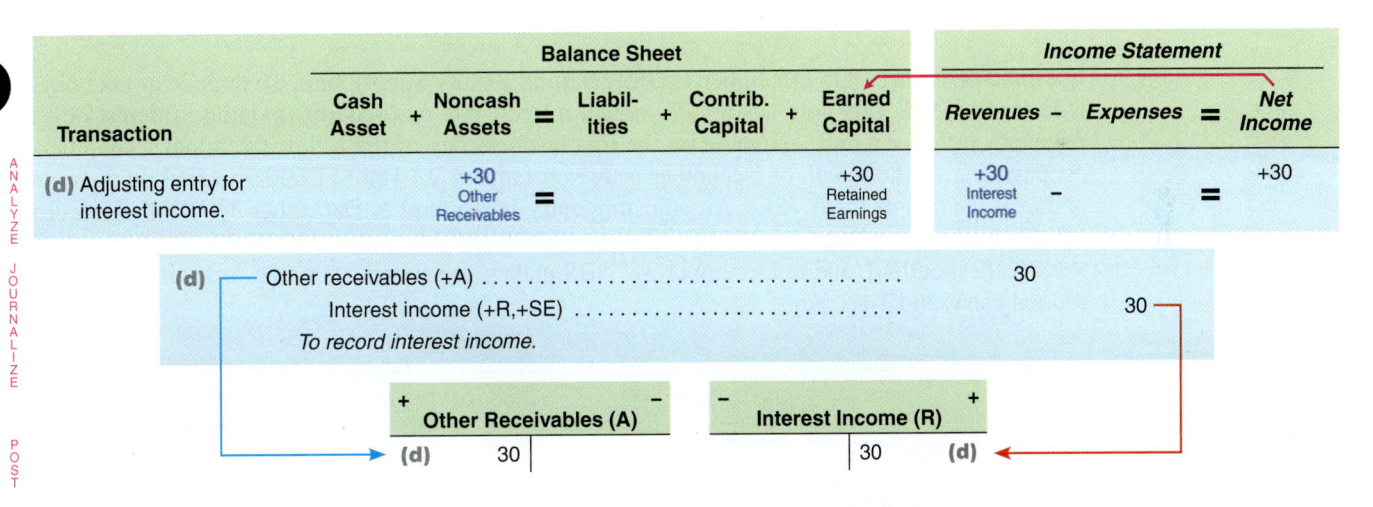

	Balance Sheet					Income Statement		
Transaction	Cash Asset	+ Noncash Assets	= Liabilities	+ Contrib. Capital	+ Earned Capital	Revenues	− Expenses	= Net Income
(d) Adjusting entry for interest income.		+30 Other Receivables	=		+30 Retained Earnings	+30 Interest Income	−	= +30

(d) Other receivables (+A) 30
    Interest income (+R,+SE) 30
    To record interest income.

Other Receivables (A)	Interest Income (R)
(d) 30	30 (d)

Type 4: Accrued Expenses

Companies often incur expenses before paying for them. Wages, interest, utilities, and taxes are examples of expenses that are incurred before cash payment is made. Usually the payments are made at regular intervals of time, such as weekly, monthly, quarterly, or annually. If the accounting period ends on a date that does not coincide with a scheduled cash payment date, an adjusting entry is required to reflect the expense incurred since the last cash payment. Such an expense is referred to as an **accrued expense**. Natural Beauty Supply has three such required adjustments for December 31: one for wages, one for interest, and one for income tax.

ACCRUED WAGES Natural Beauty Supply employees are paid on a weekly basis. Recall that wages of $1,625 were paid during December in transaction 24. However, as of December 31, the company's employees have earned wages of $480 that will be paid in January. Wages expense of $480 must be recorded in the income statement for December because there is now an obligation to compensate employees, who helped generate revenues for December.

Transaction	Balance Sheet					Income Statement		
	Cash Asset +	Noncash Assets =	Liabil- ities +	Contrib. Capital +	Earned Capital	Revenues −	Expenses =	Net Income
(e) Adjusting entry to record wages earned but not yet paid.		=	+480 Wages Payable		−480 Retained Earnings	−	+480 Wages Expense =	−480

(e) Wages expense (+E, −SE) 480
    Wages payable (+L) 480
    To record accrued wages earned for December.

+ Wages Expense (E) −		− Wages Payable (L) +	
(e) 480			480 (e)

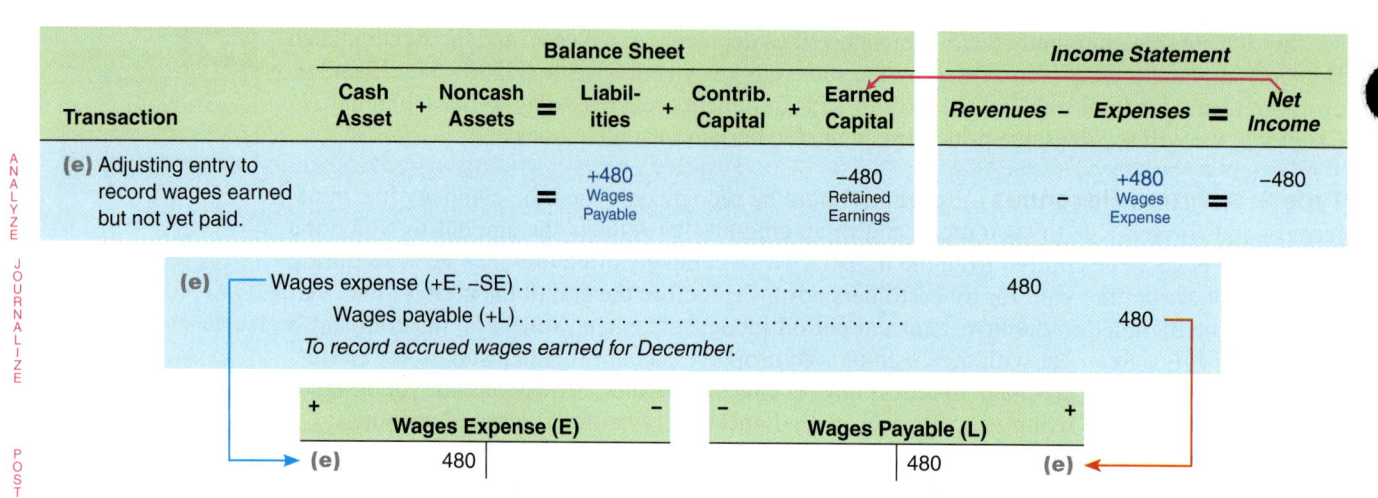

This adjustment enables the firm to reflect as December expense the cost of all wages *incurred* during the month rather than just the wages *paid*. In addition, the balance sheet shows the liability for unpaid wages at the end of the period.

When the employees are paid in January, the following entry is made.

Jan.   Wages payable (−L) 480
         Cash (−A) 480

This entry eliminates the liability recorded in Wages Payable at the end of December and reduces Cash for the wages paid.

ACCRUED INTEREST On December 1, 2021, Natural Beauty Supply signed a three-year note payable for $11,000. This note has a 12% annual interest rate and requires monthly (interest-only) payments (1% per month), payable on the first business day of the following month. (The interest payment for the month of December is due on January 2.) The $11,000 principal on the note is due at the end of three years. An adjusting entry is required at December 31, 2021, to record interest expense for December and to recognize a liability. December's interest is $110 [$11,000 × (12%/12 months)], and at December 31, NBS makes adjustment (f) in the following template, journal entry, and T-accounts.

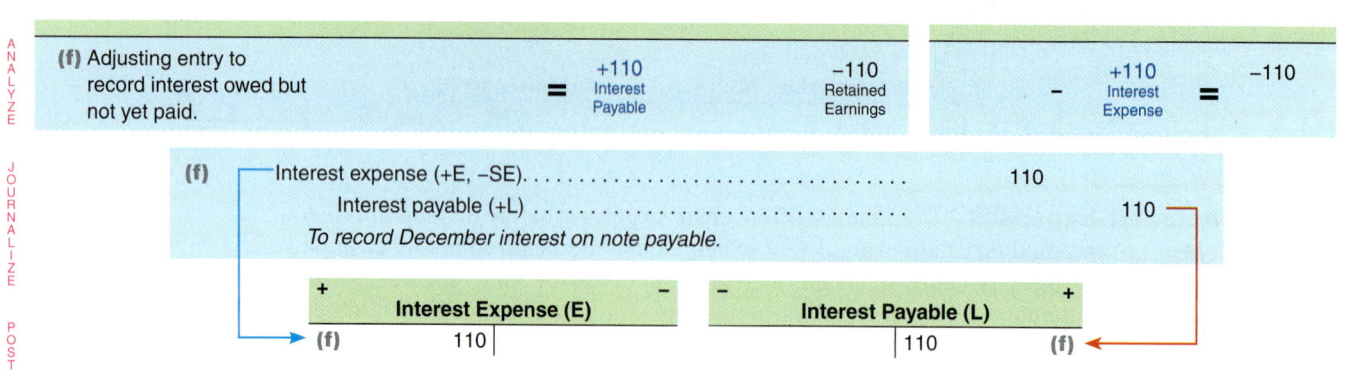

Transaction	Balance Sheet					Income Statement		
(f) Adjusting entry to record interest owed but not yet paid.		=	+110 Interest Payable		−110 Retained Earnings	−	+110 Interest Expense =	−110

(f) Interest expense (+E, −SE) 110
    Interest payable (+L) 110
    To record December interest on note payable.

+ Interest Expense (E) −		− Interest Payable (L) +	
(f) 110			110 (f)

When these entries are posted to the general ledger, the accounts show the correct interest expense for December and the interest liability for one month's interest on the note that has accrued by December 31.

ACCRUED INCOME TAX Describing this at a high level for now (Chapter 10 will cover the topic in more detail), Natural Beauty Supply is required to pay income taxes based on how much it earns. Using an estimated 25% tax rate, income tax expense for December 2021 is $250, computed as ($13,900 sales revenue + $30 interest income − $8,000 cost of goods sold − $1,500 rent expense − $2,105 wages expense − $700 advertising expense − $375 depreciation expense − $140 insurance expense − $110 interest expense) × 25%. Even if the tax payments are not actually made until 2022 (for example, when the company files their tax return), there is an obligation created as a result of the operations in December 2021. Natural Beauty Supply makes adjustment (g) for taxes in the following template, journal entry, and T-accounts.

	Balance Sheet					Income Statement		
Transaction	Cash Asset	+ Noncash Assets	= Liabilities	+ Contrib. Capital	+ Earned Capital	Revenues −	Expenses =	Net Income
(g) Adjusting entry for estimated income tax.		=	+250 Tax Payable		−250 Retained Earnings	−	+250 Tax Expense	= −250

(g) Tax expense (+E, −SE)..................................... 250
       Taxes payable (+L).. 250
       To record estimated income tax for December 2021.

+ Tax Expense (E) −		− Taxes Payable (L) +	
(g) 250			250 (g)

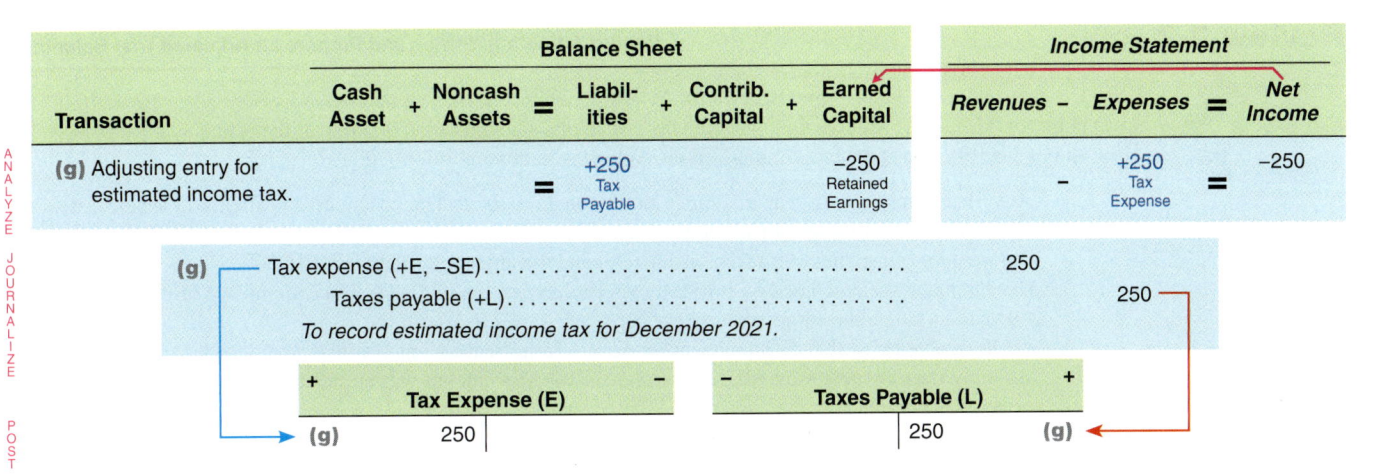

Exhibit 3.6 summarizes the four types of accounting adjustments, the usual journal entries required for each, and their financial impacts on the balance sheet and income statements.

EXHIBIT 3.6 Summary of Accounting Adjustments

Accounting Adjustment	Examples	Adjusting Entry	Financial Effects if *Not* Adjusted — Balance Sheet	Financial Effects if *Not* Adjusted — Income Statement
Deferrals: Deferred revenues	Delivery on advances from clients, gift cards, and subscribers	Dr. Liability Cr. Revenue	Liability overstated Equity understated	Revenue understated
Deferred (Prepaid) Expenses	Expiration of prepaid rent for short-term leases, insurance, and advertising; depreciation of buildings and equipment	Dr. Expense Cr. Asset (or Contra asset)	Asset overstated Equity overstated	Expense understated
Accruals: Accrued revenues	Earned but not received service, sales, and interest revenues	Dr. Asset Cr. Revenue	Asset understated Equity understated	Revenue understated
Accrued expenses	Incurred but unpaid wages, interest, and tax expenses	Dr. Expense Cr. Liability	Liability understated Equity overstated	Expense understated

Ethics and Adjusting Entries

When companies engage in transactions, there is some evidence of the exchange. Cash increases or decreases; asset and liability levels change. Adjusting entries are much more dependent on estimation processes. What was the value of service provided to customers? What obligations have arisen in the past period without a transaction? What is their value? What is the expected useful life of our depreciable assets?

The usefulness of financial performance measures such as net income depends on these questions being answered to the best of management's ability. However, there often are pressures not to provide the most accurate information. For instance, an estimate might convey information about management's strategy that could be used by competitors. Or, the financial community may have set expectations for performance that management cannot meet by executing its current business plan. In these circumstances, managers are sometimes pressured to use the discretion inherent in the reporting process to meet analysts' expectations or to disguise a planned course of action.

The financial reporting environment described in Chapter 1 imposes significant controls on financial reporting because that reporting process is important to the health of the economy.

Managers who do not report accurately and completely are potentially subject to severe penalties. Moreover, adjusting entry estimates have a "self-correcting" character. Underestimating expenses today means greater expenses tomorrow; overestimating revenues today means lower revenues tomorrow.

Review 3-2 LO3-2 — Record Adjusting Entries and Prepare an Adjusted Trial Balance

Use the unadjusted June 30 trial balance for Atwell Laboratories, Inc., completed in Review 3-1 as the starting point for this review. Assume that the company's accounts are adjusted and closed at the company's fiscal year end of June 30. The company summarized the following additional information.

1. Atwell acquired a two-year insurance policy on January 1. The policy covers fire and casualty; Atwell had no coverage prior to January 1.
2. An inventory of supplies was taken on June 30, and the amount available was $6,300.
3. All equipment was purchased on July 1, three years earlier, for $270,000. The equipment's life is estimated at 9 years. Assume the entire asset cost is depreciated over its useful life.
4. Atwell received a $4,000 cash payment on April 1 from Beave Clinic for diagnostic work to be provided uniformly over the next 4 months, beginning April 1. The amount was credited to Contract Liability. The service was provided per the agreement.
5. Unpaid and unrecorded wages at June 30 were $600.
6. Atwell has a short-term rental for $2,000 per month. Atwell has not yet made or recorded the payment for June.

In addition to the unadjusted accounts listed above, Atwell's ledger includes the following accounts, all with zero balances: Insurance Expense; Depreciation Expense; Supplies Expense; Wages Payable; and Rent Payable.

Required

a. Show the impact of the necessary adjusting entries using the FSET.
b. Show the impact of the necessary adjusting entries using journal entries.
c. Prepare T-accounts with the June 30 unadjusted balances as beginning balances and enter the adjusting entries from part b.
d. Prepare Atwell's June 30 adjusted trial balance by entering the adjusting journal entries into the T-accounts.

Solution on p. 3-52.

CONSTRUCTING FINANCIAL STATEMENTS FROM ADJUSTED ACCOUNTS

LO3-3 Prepare financial statements from adjusted accounts

This section explains the preparation of financial statements from the adjusted financial accounts.

Preparing an Adjusted Trial Balance

After adjustments are recorded and posted, the company prepares an adjusted trial balance. The **adjusted trial balance** lists all the general ledger account balances after adjustments. Much of the content for company financial statements is taken from an adjusted trial balance. **Exhibit 3.7** shows the general ledger accounts for Natural Beauty Supply after adjustments, in T-account form.

The adjusted trial balance at December 31 for Natural Beauty Supply is prepared from its general ledger accounts and is in the right-hand two columns of **Exhibit 3.8**. We show the unadjusted balances along with the adjustments to highlight the adjustment process.

EXHIBIT 3.7 — General Ledger for Natural Beauty Supply after Adjustments

General Ledger

Assets = Liabilities + Equity

Assets

Cash (A) + / −
Beg. bal.	8,100		
(17)	11,000	18,000	(18)
(21a)	8,500	700	(19)
(23)	1,200	3,300	(20)
(25)	3,200	1,625	(24)
		1,500	(27)
		50	(28)
Adj. bal.	6,825		

Accounts Receivable (A) + / −
Beg. bal.	950		
(22a)	4,500	3,200	(25)
Adj. bal.	2,250		

Other Receivables (A) + / −
Beg. bal.	0		
(d)	30		
Adj. bal.	30		

Inventory (A) + / −
Beg. bal.	11,300		
(26)	4,000	5,000	(21b)
		3,000	(22b)
Adj. bal.	7,300		

Prepaid Insurance (A) + / −
Beg. bal.	1,680		
		140	(b)
Adj. bal.	1,540		

Security Deposit (A) + / −
Beg. bal.	2,000	
Adj. bal.	2,000	

Fixtures and Equipment (A) + / −
Beg. bal.	0	
(18)	18,000	
Adj. bal.	18,000	

Accumulated Depreciation—Fixtures and Equipment (XA) − / +
		0	Beg. bal.
		375	(c)
		375	Adj. bal.

Liabilities

Accounts Payable (L) − / +
		3,700	Beg. bal.
(20)	3,300	4,000	(26)
		4,400	Adj. bal.

Interest Payable (L) − / +
		0	Beg. bal.
		110	(f)
		110	Adj. bal.

Wages Payable (L) − / +
		0	Beg. bal.
		480	(e)
		480	Adj. bal.

Taxes Payable (L) − / +
		0	Beg. bal.
		250	(g)
		250	Adj. bal.

Gift Card Liability (L) − / +
		300	Beg. bal.
(a)	900	1,200	(23)
		600	Adj. bal.

Notes Payable (L) − / +
		0	Beg. bal.
		11,000	(17)
		11,000	Adj. bal.

Equity

Common Stock (SE) − / +
		20,000	Beg. bal.
		20,000	Adj. bal.

Retained Earnings (SE) − / +
		30	Beg. bal.
(28)	50		
Adj. bal.	20		

Sales Revenue (R) − / +
		0	Beg. bal.
		8,500	(21a)
		4,500	(22a)
		900	(a)
		13,900	Adj. bal.

Interest Income (R) − / +
		0	Beg. bal.
		30	(d)
		30	Adj. bal.

Cost of Goods Sold (E) + / −
Beg. bal.	0	
(21b)	5,000	
(22b)	3,000	
Adj. bal.	8,000	

Wages Expense (E) + / −
Beg. bal.	0	
(24)	1,625	
(e)	480	
Adj. bal.	2,105	

Rent Expense (E) + / −
Beg. bal.	0	
(27)	1,500	
Adj. bal.	1,500	

Advertising Expense (E) + / −
Beg. bal.	0	
(19)	700	
Adj. bal.	700	

Depreciation Expense—Fixtures and Equipment (E) + / −
Beg. bal.	0	
(c)	375	
Adj. bal.	375	

Insurance Expense (E) + / −
Beg. bal.	0	
(b)	140	
Adj. bal.	140	

Interest Expense (E) + / −
Beg. bal.	0	
(f)	110	
Adj. bal.	110	

Tax Expense (E) + / −
Beg. bal.	0	
(g)	250	
Adj. bal.	250	

Assets = $37,570 = Liabilities = $16,840 + Equity = $20,730

EXHIBIT 3.8 — Unadjusted and Adjusted Trial Balances

NATURAL BEAUTY SUPPLY, INC.
Trial Balance
December 31, 2021

	Unadjusted Trial Balance Debit	Unadjusted Trial Balance Credit	Adjustments Debit	Adjustments Credit	Adjusted Trial Balance Debit	Adjusted Trial Balance Credit
Cash	$ 6,825				$ 6,825	
Accounts receivable	2,250				2,250	
Other receivables			(d) $ 30		30	
Inventory	7,300				7,300	
Prepaid insurance	1,680			(b) $ 140	1,540	
Security deposit	2,000				2,000	
Fixtures and equipment	18,000				18,000	
Accumulated depreciation				(c) 375		$ 375
Accounts payable		$ 4,400				4,400
Interest payable				(f) 110		110
Wages payable				(e) 480		480
Taxes payable				(g) 250		250
Gift card liability		1,500	(a) 900			600
Notes payable		11,000				11,000
Common stock		20,000				20,000
Retained earnings	20				20	
Sales revenue		13,000		(a) 900		13,900
Interest income				(d) 30		30
Cost of goods sold	8,000				8,000	
Wages expense	1,625		(e) 480		2,105	
Rent expense	1,500				1,500	
Advertising expense	700				700	
Depreciation expense			(c) 375		375	
Insurance expense			(b) 140		140	
Interest expense			(f) 110		110	
Tax expense			(g) 250		250	
Totals	$49,900	$49,900	$2,285	$2,285	$51,145	$51,145

Preparing Financial Statements

A company prepares its financial statements from the adjusted trial balance (and sometimes other supporting information). The set of financial statements consists of (and is prepared in the order of) the income statement, statement of stockholders' equity, balance sheet, and statement of cash flows. The following diagram summarizes this process.

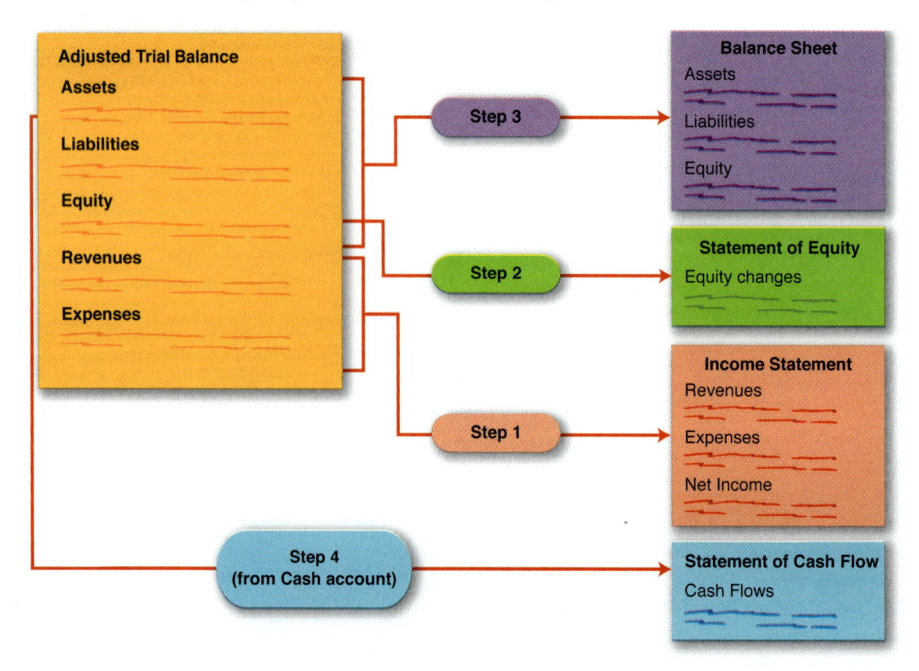

Income Statement The income statement reports a company's revenues and expenses. Natural Beauty Supply's adjusted trial balance contains two revenue/income accounts and eight expense accounts. The revenues and expenses are reported in Natural Beauty Supply's income statement for December, as shown in **Exhibit 3.9**. Its net income for December is $750.

EXHIBIT 3.9 — Income Statement

NATURAL BEAUTY SUPPLY, INC.
Income Statement
For Month Ended December 31, 2021

Sales revenue	$13,900
Cost of goods sold	8,000
Gross profit	5,900
Wages expense	2,105
Rent expense	1,500
Advertising expense	700
Depreciation expense	375
Insurance expense	140
Operating income	1,080
Interest income	30
Interest expense	(110)
Income before tax expense	1,000
Tax expense	250
Net income	$ 750

Statement of Stockholders' Equity The statement of stockholders' equity reports the events causing the major equity components to change during the accounting period. **Exhibit 3.10** shows Natural Beauty Supply's statement of stockholders' equity for December. A review of its common stock account in the general ledger provides some of the information for this statement—namely, its balance at the beginning of the period and stock issuances during the period. The net income (or net loss) amount comes from the income statement. Dividends during the period are reflected in the retained earnings balance from the adjusted trial balance.

EXHIBIT 3.10 — Statement of Stockholders' Equity

NATURAL BEAUTY SUPPLY, INC.
Statement of Stockholders' Equity
For Month Ended December 31, 2021

	Contributed Capital	Earned Capital	Total Equity
Balance, November 30, 2021	$20,000	$ 30	$20,030
Net income	—	750	750
Common stock issued	—	—	—
Cash dividends	—	(50)	(50)
Balances, December 31, 2021	$20,000	$730	$20,730

FYI Financial statements are most commonly prepared for annual and quarterly accounting periods. A request for a bank loan is an example of a situation that can lead to financial statement preparation for a non-accounting period.

Balance Sheet The balance sheet reports a company's assets, liabilities, and equity. The assets and liabilities for Natural Beauty Supply's balance sheet at December 31, 2021, shown in **Exhibit 3.11**, come from the adjusted trial balance in **Exhibit 3.8**. The amounts reported for Common Stock and Retained Earnings in the balance sheet are taken from the statement of stockholders' equity for December (**Exhibit 3.10**).

EXHIBIT 3.11 — Balance Sheet

NATURAL BEAUTY SUPPLY, INC.
Balance Sheet
December 31, 2021

Assets			Liabilities		
Cash		$ 6,825	Accounts payable		$ 4,400
Accounts receivable		2,250	Interest payable		110
Other receivables		30	Wages payable		480
Inventory		7,300	Taxes payable		250
Prepaid insurance		1,540	Gift card liability		600
Security deposit		2,000	Current liabilities		5,840
Current assets		19,945	Notes payable		11,000
Fixtures and equipment	$18,000		Total liabilities		16,840
Less: Accumulated depreciation	375		**Equity**		
Fixtures and equipment, net		17,625	Common stock		20,000
			Retained earnings		730
Total assets		$37,570	Total liabilities and equity		$37,570

Review 3-3 LO3-3

Preparing Financial Statements

Solution on p. 3-54.

Use the adjusted June 30 trial balance for Atwell Laboratories, Inc., completed in Review 3-2 as the starting point for this review.

Required
Prepare the company's June 30 balance sheet and its income statement and statement of stockholders' equity for the year ended June 30.

FYI The income statement, statement of stockholders' equity, and statement of cash flows report on periods of time. These statements illustrate the accounting period concept—the concept that useful statements can be prepared for arbitrary time periods within a company's life span. The purpose of adjusting entries is to obtain useful statements for specific time periods.

Statement of Cash Flows The statement of cash flows is formatted to report cash inflows and outflows by the three primary business activities:

- *Cash flows from operating activities* Cash flows from the company's transactions and events that relate to its primary operations.
- *Cash flows from investing activities* Cash flows from acquisitions and divestitures of investments and long-term assets.
- *Cash flows from financing activities* Cash flows from issuances of and payments toward equity, borrowings, and long-term liabilities.

The net cash flows from these three sections yield the change in cash for the period.

In analyzing the statement of cash flows, we should not necessarily conclude that the company is better off if cash increases and worse off if cash decreases. It is not the cash change that is most important, but the reasons for the change. For example, what are the sources of the cash inflows? Are these sources mainly from operating activities? To what uses have cash inflows been put? Such questions (and their answers) are key to properly using the statement of cash flows. In Chapter 4, we examine the statement of cash flows more closely and answer these questions. The procedures for preparing a statement of cash flows are discussed in the next chapter. For completeness, we present Natural Beauty Supply's statement of cash flows for December in **Exhibit 3.12**.

EXHIBIT 3.12 Statement of Cash Flows

NATURAL BEAUTY SUPPLY, INC.
Statement of Cash Flows
For Month Ended December 31, 2021

Cash Flows from Operating Activities	
Cash received from customers	$12,900
Cash paid for inventory	(3,300)
Cash paid for wages	(1,625)
Cash paid for rent	(1,500)
Cash paid for advertising	(700)
Net cash provided by operating activities	5,775
Cash Flows from Investing Activities	
Cash paid for fixtures and equipment	(18,000)
Net cash used for investing activities	(18,000)
Cash Flows from Financing Activities	
Cash received from loans	11,000
Cash paid for dividends	(50)
Net cash provided by financing activities	10,950
Net change in cash	(1,275)
Cash balance, November 30, 2021	8,100
Cash balance, December 31, 2021	$ 6,825

CLOSING TEMPORARY ACCOUNTS

The chart of accounts contains two different types of accounts. Income statement accounts (revenues, expenses, etc.) are used to measure the net assets generated and used in a specific accounting period. As such, their end-of-period balances are reported in the income statement for that period. We use those balances to construct the statements of stockholders' equity and cash flows. But then these account balances have served their purpose, and we must get them ready to do the same thing for the following accounting period. Specifically, we must set their balances to zero so they can accumulate the revenues and expenses for that following period. For this reason, income statement accounts are called **temporary accounts**. Their end-of-period values do not carry over to the next reporting period.

In contrast, balance sheet account balances do carry over to the next reporting period. For example, the end-of-period balance in accounts receivable is the beginning-of-period balance for the next period. Therefore, balance sheet accounts are referred to as **permanent accounts**.

LO3-4
Describe the process of closing temporary accounts.

Permanent Accounts			Temporary Accounts	
Assets	Liabilities	Equity	Revenues	Expenses
		Contributed capital		
		Retained earnings		

The **closing process** takes the end-of-period balances in the temporary accounts and moves them to a permanent account—the Retained Earnings account. A temporary account is *closed* when an entry is made that changes its balance to zero. The entry is equal in amount to the account's balance but is opposite to the balance as a debit or credit. An account that is closed is said to be closed *to* the account that receives the offsetting debit or credit. Thus, a closing entry simply transfers the balance of one account to another account. When closing entries bring temporary account balances to zero, the temporary accounts are then ready to accumulate data for the next accounting period.

Closing Process

The Retained Earnings account can be used to close the temporary revenue and expense accounts.[5] The entries to close temporary accounts are:

---

[5] *All* revenue and expense accounts are temporary accounts, so they are closed to retained earnings at the end of the reporting period. In addition, companies often use a temporary account entitled Dividends Declared to record the amount of shareholder dividends declared during a reporting period. This account would accumulate a debit balance (because it reduces equity) and is closed to retained earnings at the end of the reporting period.

1. **Close revenue accounts.** Debit each revenue account for an amount equal to its balance, and credit Retained Earnings for the total of revenues.
2. **Close expense accounts.** Credit each expense account for an amount equal to its balance, and debit Retained Earnings for the total of expenses.

After these temporary accounts are closed, the difference equals the period's net income (if revenues exceed expenses) or net loss (if expenses exceed revenues), and that difference is now included in Retained Earnings. The closing process is graphically portrayed as follows.

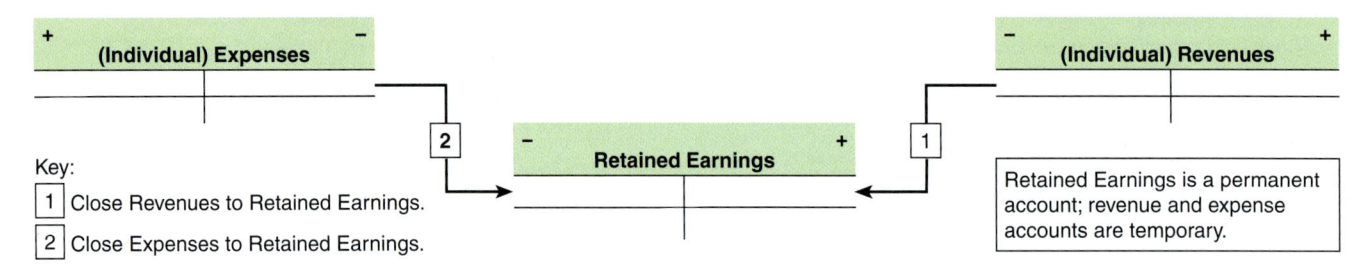

Key:
1. Close Revenues to Retained Earnings.
2. Close Expenses to Retained Earnings.

Retained Earnings is a permanent account; revenue and expense accounts are temporary.

Closing Steps Illustrated

Exhibit 3.13 illustrates the entries for closing revenues and expenses for Natural Beauty Supply. The effects of these entries in T-accounts are shown after the journal entries. (We do not show the financial statement effects template for closing entries because the template automatically closes revenues and expenses to the Retained Earnings account as they occur—see earlier transactions for examples.)

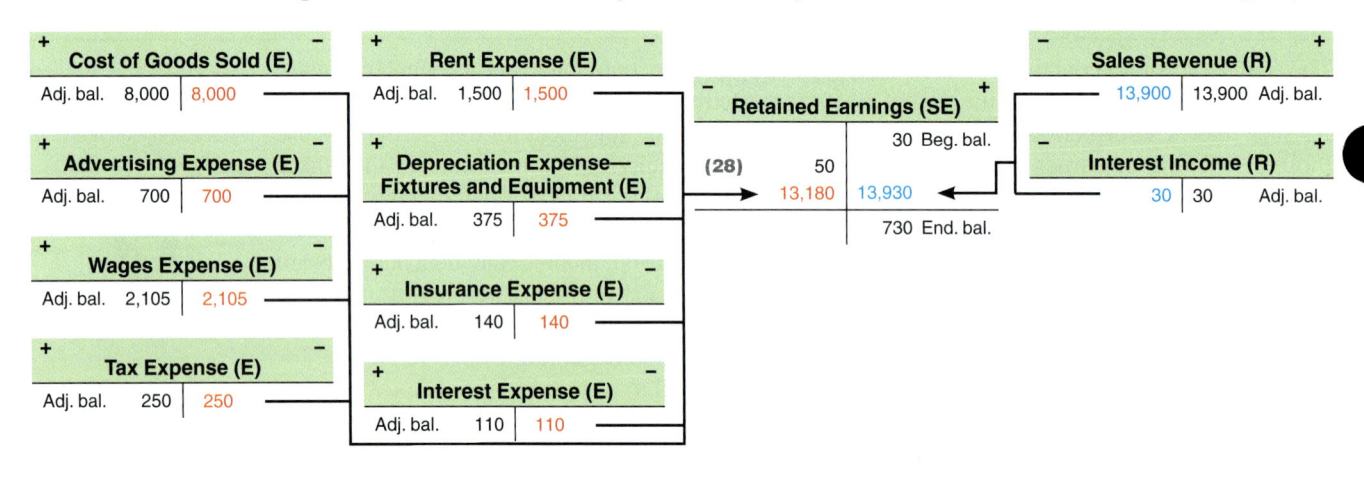

Cost of Goods Sold (E)
Adj. bal. 8,000 | 8,000

Advertising Expense (E)
Adj. bal. 700 | 700

Wages Expense (E)
Adj. bal. 2,105 | 2,105

Tax Expense (E)
Adj. bal. 250 | 250

Rent Expense (E)
Adj. bal. 1,500 | 1,500

Depreciation Expense—Fixtures and Equipment (E)
Adj. bal. 375 | 375

Insurance Expense (E)
Adj. bal. 140 | 140

Interest Expense (E)
Adj. bal. 110 | 110

Retained Earnings (SE)
(28) 50 | 30 Beg. bal.
13,180 | 13,930
 | 730 End. bal.

Sales Revenue (R)
13,900 | 13,900 Adj. bal.

Interest Income (R)
30 | 30 Adj. bal.

EXHIBIT 3.13 — Closing Revenues and Expenses*

1	Dec. 31	Sales revenue (–R)	13,900	
		Interest income (–R)	30	
		Retained earnings (+SE)		13,930
2	Dec. 31	Retained earnings (–SE)	13,180	
		Cost of goods sold (–E)		8,000
		Wages expense (–E)		2,105
		Rent expense (–E)		1,500
		Advertising expense (–E)		700
		Depreciation expense (–E)		375
		Insurance expense (–E)		140
		Interest expense (–E)		110
		Tax expense (–E)		250

* The two entries in this exhibit can be combined into a single entry where the credit (debit) to retained earnings would be net income (loss).

After these two steps, the net adjustment to the Retained Earnings account is a credit equal to the company's net income of $750, computed as $13,930 less $13,180. The Retained Earnings account in this case is increased by $750. We also recall that Natural Beauty Supply paid a cash dividend of $50 (transaction 28), which reduces retained earnings and results in the ending balance of $730.

Preparing a Post-Closing Trial Balance

After closing entries are recorded and posted to the general ledger, all temporary accounts have zero balances. At this point, a **post-closing trial balance** is prepared. A balancing of this trial balance is evidence that an equality of debits and credits has been maintained in the general ledger throughout the adjusting and closing process and that the general ledger is in balance to start the next accounting period. Only balance sheet accounts appear in a post-closing trial balance because all income statement accounts have balances of zero. The post-closing trial balance for Natural Beauty Supply is shown in **Exhibit 3.14**.

EXHIBIT 3.14 Post-Closing Trial Balance

NATURAL BEAUTY SUPPLY, INC.
Post-Closing Trial Balance
December 31, 2021

	Debit	Credit
Cash	$ 6,825	
Accounts receivable	2,250	
Other receivables	30	
Inventory	7,300	
Prepaid insurance	1,540	
Security deposit	2,000	
Fixtures and equipment	18,000	
Accumulated depreciation		$ 375
Accounts payable		4,400
Interest payable		110
Wages payable		480
Taxes payable		250
Gift card liability		600
Notes payable		11,000
Common stock		20,000
Retained earnings		730
Totals	$37,945	$37,945

Subsequent Events

There is usually a few weeks' delay between the end of the fiscal reporting period and the issuing of the financial reports for that period. What happens if a significant event occurs (e.g., a fire at a production facility, an acquisition, etc.) during that interim? Should the previous period's financial statements be changed to reflect the event?

If the event doesn't provide information about the company's condition on the balance sheet date, then the answer is no. So, neither the fire nor the acquisition would be reported in the previous period's financial statements. Such events should be disclosed in a note, if they are material.

SUMMARIZING THE ACCOUNTING CYCLE

The sequence of accounting procedures known as the accounting cycle occurs each fiscal year (period) and represents a systematic process for accumulating and reporting financial data of a company. **Exhibit 3.15** expands on **Exhibit 3.1** to include descriptions of the five major steps in the accounting cycle.

EXHIBIT 3.15 Accounting Cycle

Analyze — Analyze transactions from source documents

Record — Journalize transactions and prepare unadjusted trial balance

Adjust — Journalize adjusting entries and prepare adjusted trial balance

Report — Prepare financial statements

Close — Journalize closing entries and prepare post-closing trial balance

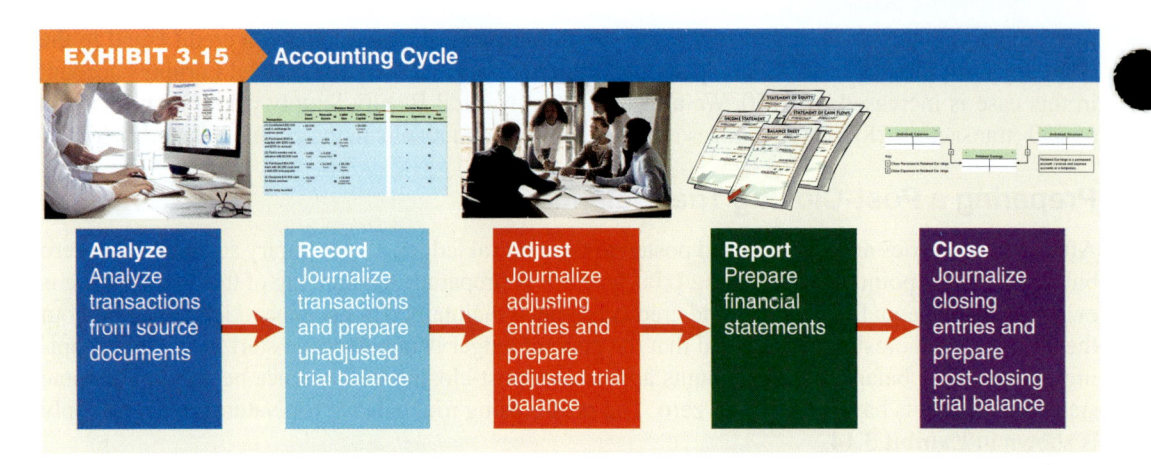

Review 3-4 LO3-4 — Preparing Closing Entries

Use the adjusted June 30 trial balance for Atwell Laboratories, Inc., completed in Review 3-2 as the starting point for this review.

Required

a. Prepare Atwell's closing journal entries.
b. Post entries from part *a* to T-accounts (key the entries).

Solution on p. 3-55.

FINANCIAL STATEMENT ANALYSIS

Using Information on Levels and Flows

LO3-5 Analyze changes in balance sheet accounts.

A careful reader of financial statements must differentiate between those things that depict *levels* and those that depict *flows* or *changes*. The balance sheet portrays levels of resources and claims on those resources at a point in time, and the income statement portrays changes in those levels over a period of time. Knowing how the levels and flows relate to each other can be a very useful tool for analysis.

For instance, suppose that a service business has an inventory of office supplies. On July 1, an inventory count determined that the business has $2,400 of supplies inventory on hand. During the third calendar quarter, there were deliveries of office supplies with a cost of $5,700. And, at the end of the third quarter—on September 30—an inventory count finds $1,900 of supplies on hand. What amount of supplies expense should be recognized for the quarter?

Finding the answer to this question is easier if we recall the transactions that can affect the supplies inventory account, and that these transactions (changes) must lead from the beginning inventory level to the ending inventory level. At present, we know of two such transactions: the purchase of supplies inventory and the usage of supplies inventory.

(a)	Supplies inventory (+A)..	5,700	
	Cash (−A) or Accounts payable (+L)		5,700
	Purchase supplies inventory.		
(b)	Supplies expense (+E, −SE)...................................	?	
	Supplies inventory (−A)		?
	Record expense for supplies used.		

The supplies inventory T-account must look like the following:

	+		−	
	Supplies Inventory (A)			
Beg. bal.	2,400			
(a)	5,700	?		(b)
End. bal.	1,900			

An FSET version of this analysis would look like the following, with the only noncash account being supplies inventory, and assuming that the supplies inventory purchase was made with cash.

	Balance Sheet						Income Statement		
Transaction	Cash Asset	+ Supplies Inventory	= Liabilities	+ Contrib. Capital	+ Earned Capital		Revenues −	Expenses =	Net Income
Beg. bal.		2,400 Supplies Inv							
(a) Purchase office supplies	−5,700 Cash	+5,700 Supplies Inv	=				−	=	
(b) Office supplies taken for use in client service activities		−? Supplies Inv	=		−? Retained Earnings		+?	− Supplies Expense =	−?
End. bal.		1,900 Supplies Inv							

Balancing the account requires that $2,400 + $5,700 − ? = $1,900, and the value that satisfies this condition is $6,200. That amount would be recorded as supplies expense for the quarter.

This application of the account structure is a simple one. But, suppose that a separate source of information (e.g., scanner data) told us that $5,900 in supplies had been taken from inventory for client service activities. When put into the FSET/T-account analysis above, this new fact would imply an additional $300 in supplies had been removed for reasons such as breakage, obsolescence, or pilferage.

As we progress through the topics in future chapters, we will find that accounting reports do not always provide the information that is most useful for assessment of a company's current performance or standing. In those cases, we can often use the more detailed T-accounts and journal entries or the FSET to analyze levels and changes and to develop the numbers that do a better job of answering important questions.

Analyzing Changes in Balance Sheet Accounts

LO3-5 **Review 3-5**

The following excerpts were obtained from the trial balance of Lazer Inc.

	Beg. Bal.	End. Bal.
Accounts receivable	$ 45,000	$ 63,000
Supplies inventory	13,000	12,300
Accounts payable	55,000	65,000
Retained earnings	180,000	187,000

Required
a. If sales on account were $200,000, what were cash collections for the period?
b. If $18,200 of supplies inventory was used during the period, what was the total of supplies inventory purchases for the period?
c. If $160,000 was paid on account for the period, what were the new charges on account this period?
d. If net income for the period was $10,000, what were dividends paid during the period?

Solution on p. 3-56.

SUMMARY

LO3-1 **Analyze transactions and review the process of journalizing and posting transactions. (p. 3-3)**
- The major steps in the accounting cycle are
  a. Analyze   b. Record   c. Adjust   d. Report   e. Close
- Transactions are initially recorded in a journal; the entries are in chronological order, and the journal shows the total effect of each transaction or adjustment.
- Posting is the transfer of information from a journal to the general ledger accounts.

LO3-2 **Describe the adjusting process and illustrate adjusting entries. (p. 3-11)**
- Adjusting entries achieve the proper recognition of revenues and the proper matching of expenses with those revenues; adjustments are summarized as follows.

Adjustment	Adjusting Entry
Adjusting prepaid (deferred) expenses	Increase expense Decrease asset
Adjusting unearned (deferred) revenues	Decrease liability Increase revenue
Accruing expenses	Increase expense Increase liability
Accruing revenues	Increase asset Increase revenue

LO3-3 **Prepare financial statements from adjusted accounts. (p. 3-19)**
- An income statement, statement of stockholders' equity, balance sheet, and statement of cash flows are prepared from an adjusted trial balance and other information.

LO3-4 **Describe the process of closing temporary accounts. (p. 3-24)**
- *Closing the books* means closing (yielding zero balances) revenues and expenses—that is, all temporary accounts. Revenue and expense account balances are transferred (closed) to the Retained Earnings account.

LO3-5 **Analyze changes in balance sheet accounts. (p. 3-27)**
- The combination of balance sheet levels and income statement flows allows a financial statement reader to infer the effects of transactions and adjustments that are not disclosed directly.

GUIDANCE ANSWERS... YOU MAKE THE CALL

You are the Chief Accountant Deposits represent a liability and should be included in REI's current liabilities at the time the cash or check is received. The account that would be used may have several names, including advances, trip deposits, contract liabilities, or performance obligations. Revenue should not be recognized until goods are transferred or services are provided to the customer. In this instance, REI should not recognize revenues until the trip has been completed. It is not unusual for events to occur that result in a refund of some portion or even all of the traveler's total payment. In the present case involving a low cancellation rate, waiting until the trip is over is not only conservative reporting, but is likely more efficient bookkeeping as well.

Assignments with the MBC logo in the margin are available in *my*BusinessCourse.
See the Preface of the book for details.

MULTIPLE CHOICE

1. An end-of-period journal entry made to reflect accrual accounting is called
   a. a posted journal entry.
   b. an adjusting journal entry.
   c. an erroneous journal entry.
   d. a compound journal entry.

2. Posting refers to the process whereby journal entry information is transferred from
   a. journal to general ledger accounts.
   b. general ledger accounts to a journal.
   c. source documents to a journal.
   d. a journal to source documents.

3. Which of the following is an example of an adjusting entry?
   a. Recording the purchase of supplies on account
   b. Recording depreciation expense on a truck
   c. Recording cash received from customers for services rendered
   d. Recording the cash payment of wages to employees

4. A piece of equipment was placed in service on January 1, 2020. The cost of the equipment was $30,000, and it is expected to have no value at the end of its eight-year life. Using straight-line depreciation, what amounts will be seen for depreciation expense and accumulated depreciation for fiscal (and calendar) year 2022?

	Fiscal Year 2022 Depreciation Expense	Fiscal Year-End 2022 Accumulated Depreciation
a.	$ 3,750	$ 3,000
b.	–0–	30,000
c.	3,750	11,250
d.	11,250	11,250

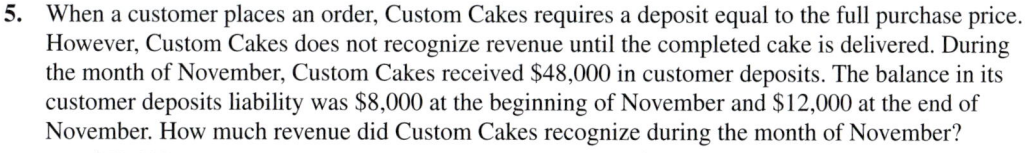

5. When a customer places an order, Custom Cakes requires a deposit equal to the full purchase price. However, Custom Cakes does not recognize revenue until the completed cake is delivered. During the month of November, Custom Cakes received $48,000 in customer deposits. The balance in its customer deposits liability was $8,000 at the beginning of November and $12,000 at the end of November. How much revenue did Custom Cakes recognize during the month of November?
   a. $52,000
   b. $48,000
   c. $44,000
   d. $8,000

Multiple Choice Answers
1. b 2. a 3. b 4. c 5. c

QUESTIONS

Q3-1. What are the five major steps in the accounting cycle? List them in their proper order.

Q3-2. What does the term "fiscal year" mean?

Q3-3. What are three examples of source documents that underlie business transactions?

Q3-4. What is the nature and purpose of a general journal?

Q3-5. Explain the process of posting.

Q3-6. What is an adjusting journal entry?

Q3-7. What is a chart of accounts? Give an example of a coding system for identifying different types of accounts.

Q3-8. Why is the adjusting step of the accounting cycle necessary?

Q3-9. What four different types of adjustments are frequently necessary at the close of an accounting period? Give examples of each type.

Q3-10. On January 1, Prepaid Insurance was debited with the cost of a two-year premium, $2,448. What adjusting entry should be made on January 31 before financial statements are prepared for the month?

Q3-11. What is a contra account? What contra account is used in reporting the book value of a depreciable asset?

Q3-12. A building was acquired on January 1, 2014, at a cost of $3,200,000, and its depreciation is calculated using the straight-line method. At the end of 2018, the accumulated depreciation contra asset for the building is $640,000. What will be the balance in the building's accumulated depreciation contra asset at the end of 2025? What is the building's book value at that date?

Q3-13. The publisher of *International View*, a monthly magazine, received two-year digital subscriptions totaling $12,600 on January 1. (a) What entry should be made to record the receipt of the $12,600? (b) What entry should be made at the end of January before financial statements are prepared for the month?

Q3-14. Globe Travel Agency pays an employee $525 in wages each Friday for the five-day workweek ending on that day. The last Friday of January falls on January 27. What adjusting entry should be made on January 31, the fiscal year-end?

Q3-15. The Bayou Company earns interest amounting to $400 per month on its investments. The company receives the interest every six months, on December 31 and June 30. Monthly financial statements are prepared. What adjusting entry should be made on January 31?

Q3-16. Which groups of accounts are closed at the end of the accounting year?

Q3-17. What are the two major steps in the closing process?

Q3-18. What is the purpose of a post-closing trial balance? Which of the following accounts should *not* appear in the post-closing trial balance: Cash; Unearned Revenue; Prepaid Rent; Depreciation Expense; Utilities Payable; Supplies Expense; and Retained Earnings?

Q3-19. Dehning Corporation is an international manufacturer of films and industrial identification products. Included among its prepaid expenses is an account titled Prepaid Catalog Costs; in recent years, this account's size has ranged between $2,500,000 and $4,000,000. The company states that catalog costs are initially capitalized and then written off over the estimated useful lives of the publications (generally eight months). Discuss the Dehning Corporation's handling of its catalog costs.

Q3-20. At the beginning of January, the first month of the accounting year, the supplies account had a debit balance of $990. During January, purchases of $310 worth of supplies were debited to the account. Although only $750 of supplies were still available at the end of January, the necessary adjusting entry was omitted. How will the omission affect (a) the income statement for January, and (b) the balance sheet prepared at January 31?

DATA ANALYTICS

LO3-1 DA3-1. Matching Chart Types and Aims to Data Measures

In the process of preparing a data visualization, determine which chart would be best suited for each data measure and determine what is the aim of that particular chart. Refer to Appendix B for a description of each chart type.

Data Measure	Chart Type	Aim of Chart
a. Relation of daily clicks on digital ads with daily online sales	__ Bar chart	__ Compare different categories
b. Sales by major city for a company's best-selling product	__ Pie chart	__ Analyze changes over time
c. Level of eight types of digital marketing expenses for the year	__ Line chart	__ Show parts that make up a whole
d. Common stock and retained earnings portions of total equity	__ Scatter plot	__ Show correlation between two variables
e. Ten-year trend in digital marketing expense	__ Map chart	__ Show differences across geographic locations

LO3-3 DA3-2. Preparing Basic Visualization in Excel of Changes in Sales Data Over Time

The Excel file associated with this exercise includes daily sales for the month of December for Strickland Inc. In this exercise, we determine which sales amounts appear to be outliers which means that they differ significantly from the other daily sales amounts.

REQUIRED
1. Download Excel file DA3-2 found in myBusinessCourse.
2. Prepare a line chart for the month of December. *Hint:* Highlight the data and open the Insert tab. Click the Line chart in the Charts group and select one of the 2-D lines. Do not include the column titles or the total row when highlighting the data.
3. Add a trendline to the chart. *Hint:* Right-click on the line in your chart to view the option to add a linear trendline.
4. Describe the position of the trendline on the chart on December 18.
5. List the point(s) (if any) on the chart that are positioned over +/−$1,200 beyond the trendline. *Hint:* Use the gridlines on the chart to help you visually detect outliers.

LO3 DA3-3. Displaying Key Performance Indicators in Excel

A key performance indicator (KPI) is a quantifiable measure used to track a company's overall performance. Managers can create a KPI dashboard, which is a data visualization that displays all indicators in one central location. This allows a manager to conveniently track and monitor key operational data. Information in KPI dashboards may even be updated in real time. For this exercise, we use the data included in the Excel file associated with this exercise for Wakeboards Inc. to create a data visualization (dashboard). Wakeboards Inc. manufactures and sells three types of wakeboards to 50 customers located primarily in oceanside cities in the U.S.

REQUIRED
1. Download Excel file DA3-3 found in myBusinessCourse.
2. Create the following six PivotCharts arranged as one KPI dashboard using the data included in file DA3-3.
   a. Top five customers for Model 1 in a bar chart. *Hint:* Click anywhere inside the data table and open the Insert tab. Click PivotTable in the Tables group. Add the PivotTable to a new worksheet. Drag Customer Name to Rows; Model 1 Sales Units to Values. In the PivotTable,

open the dropdown menu next to RowLabels and select Top 10 in the Values Filter menu. Change to Top 5. Click anywhere inside the PivotTable and open the PivotTable Analyze tab. Click PivotChart in the Tools group. Select Bar. Click inside the bars and click Format Data Labels.

    b. Top five customers for Model 2 in a bar chart. *Hint:* Highlight all cells in the PivotTable created in part *a*. Right-click and select Copy. Move to another location on the same worksheet. Right-click and select Paste. Make the appropriate changes to the second PivotTable.
    c. Top five customers for Model 3 in a bar chart.
    d. Sales in units by model by month in a line chart. *Hint:* Months in Rows; Model 1, 2, and 3 Sales Units fields to Values.
    e. Most recent monthly sales (December) in a pie chart showing the proportion by Model number. *Hint:* Months in Columns; Model 1, 2, and 3 Sales Units fields to Values.
    f. Sales in units by customer by month with a slicer for Customer name and Months. *Hint:* Customer Name and Months fields to Rows; Model 1, 2, and 3 Sales Units fields to Values. Click inside the chart and open the PivotTable Analyze tab. Click Insert Slicer and select Customer Name and Months. Slicers are used to filter the data included in PivotTables.

3. Use the visualizations to answer the following questions.
    a. List the third largest customer for Model 1.
    b. List the first largest customer for Model 2.
    c. List the fifth largest customer for Model 3.
    d. List the peak month for sales of Model 1.
    e. List the quantity of sales in December for Model 2.
    f. List the quantity of sales of Model 1, Model 2, and Model 3 for Marina Inc. in June.

DATA VISUALIZATION

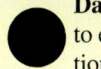

Data Visualization Activities are available in myBusinessCourse. These assignments use Tableau Dashboards to expose students to visual depictions of data and introduce students to data analytics through data visualizations. These exercises are easily assignable and auto graded by MBC.

MINI EXERCISES

M3-21. Recording Transactions in the Financial Statement Effects Template (FSET)   LO3-2

Creative Designs, a firm providing art services for advertisers, began business on June 1. The following transactions occurred during the month of June.

June 1 Anne Clem invested $30,000 cash to begin the business in exchange for common stock.
      2 Paid $2,500 cash for June rent (short-term lease).
      3 Purchased $16,000 of office equipment on account.
      6 Purchased $9,500 of art materials and other supplies; paid $4,500 cash with the remainder due within 30 days.
    11 Billed clients $11,750 for services rendered.
    17 Collected $8,100 cash from clients on their accounts.
    19 Paid $7,500 cash toward the account for office equipment suppliers (see June 3).
    25 Paid $2,200 cash for dividends.
    30 Paid $900 cash for June utilities.
    30 Paid $5,800 cash for June salaries.

REQUIRED

Record the above transactions for June using the financial statement effects template.

M3-22. Journalizing Transactions and Posting to T-Accounts   LO3-1

Use the information from M3-21 to complete the following requirements.
    a. The following accounts in its general ledger are needed to record the transactions for June: Cash; Accounts Receivable; Supplies; Office Equipment; Accounts Payable; Common Stock; Retained Earnings; Service Fee Revenue; Rent Expense; Utilities Expense; and Salaries Expense. Record the above transactions for June in journal entry form.
    b. Set up T-accounts for each of the ledger accounts and post the entries to them (key the numbers in T-accounts by date).

LO3-1 M3-23. Recording Transactions in the Financial Statement Effects Template (FSET)
Minute Maid, a firm providing housecleaning services, began business on April 1. The following transactions occurred during the month of April.

April 1 A. Falcon invested $13,500 cash to begin the business in exchange for common stock.
  2 Paid $4,200 cash for six months' lease on van for the business.
  3 Borrowed $15,000 cash from bank and signed note payable agreeing to repay it in 1 year plus 10% interest.
  3 Purchased $8,200 of cleaning equipment; paid $3,800 cash with the remainder due within 30 days.
  4 Paid $6,400 cash for cleaning supplies.
  7 Paid $500 cash for advertisements to run in newspaper during April.
  21 Billed customers $5,500 for services performed.
  23 Paid $4,400 cash on account to cleaning equipment suppliers (see April 3).
  28 Collected $4,000 cash from customers on their accounts.
  29 Paid $1,500 cash for dividends.
  30 Paid $2,600 cash for April wages.
  30 Paid $1,480 cash to service station for gasoline used during April.

REQUIRED
Record the above transactions for April using the financial statement effects template.

LO3-1 M3-24. Journalizing Transactions and Posting to T-Accounts
Use the information from M3-23 to complete the following requirements.
a. The following accounts in its general ledger are needed to record the transactions for April: Cash; Accounts Receivable; Supplies; Prepaid Van Lease; Equipment; Accounts Payable; Notes Payable; Common Stock; Retained Earnings; Cleaning Fees Earned; Van Fuel Expense; Advertising Expense; and Wages Expense. Record the above transactions for April in journal entry form.
b. Set up T-accounts for each of the ledger accounts and post the entries to them (key the numbers in T-accounts by date).

LO3-1, 2 M3-25. Recording Transactions and Adjustments in the Financial Statement Effects Template (FSET)
Deluxe Building Services offers custodial services on both a contract basis and an hourly basis. On January 1, Deluxe collected $50,250 in advance on a six-month contract for work to be performed evenly during the next six months. Assume that Deluxe closes its books and issues financial reports on a monthly basis.
a. Prepare the entry on January 1 to record the receipt of $50,250 cash for contract work using the financial statements effect template.
b. Prepare the adjusting entry to be made on January 31 for the contract work done during January using the financial statements effect template.
c. At January 31, a total of 45 hours of hourly rate custodial work was unbilled. The billing rate is $19 per hour. Prepare the adjusting entry needed on January 31 using the financial statements effect template. (The firm uses the account Fees Receivable to reflect amounts due but not yet billed.)

LO3-1, 2 M3-26. Journalizing Transactions and Adjusting Accounts
Using the information from M3-25, prepare entries for parts *a*, *b*, and *c* in journal entry form.

LO3-2, 5 M3-27. Adjusting Accounts Using the Financial Statement Effects Template (FSET)
Selected accounts of Ideal Properties, a real estate management firm, are shown below as of January 31 before any adjusting entries have been made.

Unadjusted Account Balances	Debits	Credits
Prepaid insurance	$10,800	
Supplies inventory	2,895	
Office equipment	8,928	
Unearned rent liability		$ 7,875
Salaries expense	4,650	
Rent revenue		22,500

Monthly financial statements are prepared. Using the following information, report the adjusting entries necessary on January 31 using the financial statements effect template.

1. Prepaid Insurance represents a three-year premium paid on January 1.
2. Supplies of $1,275 were still available on January 31.
3. Office equipment—purchased on January 1—is expected to last eight years.
4. On January 1, Ideal Properties collected six months' rent in advance from a tenant renting space for $1,310 per month.
5. Accrued employee salaries of $735 have not been recorded as of January 31.

M3-28. Journalizing Transactions and Adjusting Accounts   LO3-2, 5
Using the information from M3-27, prepare entries for parts 1–5 in journal entry form.

M3-29. Inferring Transactions from Financial Statements (FSET)   LO3-1, 2, 5
El Puerto de Liverpool (Liverpool) is a large retailer in Mexico. The following accounts are selected from its annual report for the fiscal year ended December 31, 2019. For the fiscal year ended December 31, 2019, Liverpool purchased merchandise inventory costing 89,500,425 thousand Mexican pesos. Assume that all purchases were made on account. The following T-accounts reflect information contained in the company's 2019 and 2018 balance sheets in thousands of Mexican pesos.

El Puerto de Liverpool
OTCMKTS :: ELPQF

+	Inventories (A)	−		−	Suppliers (Accounts Payable)	+
12/31/2018 Bal. 20,673,219					23,694,308	12/31/2018 Bal.
12/31/2019 Bal. 23,340,421					22,670,239	12/31/2019 Bal.

a. Prepare the entry using the financial statement effects template to record Liverpool's purchases for the 2019 fiscal year.
b. What amount did Liverpool pay in cash to its suppliers for the fiscal year ended December 31, 2019? Explain. Assume that Suppliers (Accounts payable) is affected only by transactions related to inventory.
c. Prepare the entry using the financial statement effects template to record cost of goods sold for the year ended December 31, 2019.

M3-30. Inferring Transactions from Financial Statements   LO3-1, 2
Using the information from M3-29, prepare entries for parts *a* and *c* in journal entry form.

M3-31. Preparing a Statement of Stockholders' Equity   LO3-3
On December 31, Year 1, the credit balances of the Common Stock and Retained Earnings accounts were $36,000 and $21,600, respectively, for Architect Services Company. Its stock issuances for Year 2 totaled $7,200, and it paid $11,640 cash toward dividends in Year 2. For the year ended December 31, Year 2, the company had net income of $35,880. Prepare a Year 2 statement of stockholders' equity for Architect Services.

M3-32. Applying Closing Procedures   LO3-4
Assume you are in the process of closing procedures for Echo Corporation. You have already closed all revenue and expense accounts to the Retained Earnings account. The total debits to Retained Earnings equal $247,400 and total credits to Retained Earnings equal $277,900. The Retained Earnings account had a credit balance of $79,200 at the start of this current year. What is the post-closing ending balance of Retained Earnings at the end of this current year?

M3-33. Preparing Closing Entries Using Journal Entries and T-Accounts   LO3-4
The adjusted trial balance at December 31 for Smith Company includes the following selected accounts.

Adjusted Account Balances	Debit	Credit
Commissions revenue		$127,350
Wages expense	$54,000	
Insurance expense	2,850	
Utilities expense	12,300	
Depreciation expense	14,700	
Retained earnings		108,150

a. Prepare entries to close these accounts in journal entry form.
b. Set up T-accounts for each of these ledger accounts, enter the balances above, and post the closing entries to them. After these entries are posted, what is the post-closing balance of the Retained Earnings account?

LO3-1, 2, 5 **M3-34. Inferring Transactions from Financial Statements (FSET)**

Amazon.com Inc. is one of the world's leading e-commerce companies, with over $386 billion in revenues for the fiscal year ended December 31, 2020. For the year ended December 31, 2020, Amazon's cost of goods sold was $233,307 million. Assume that all purchases were made on account. The following T-accounts reflect information contained in the company's 2020 and 2019 balance sheets (in millions).

+	Inventories	−		−	Accounts Payable	+
12/31/2019 Bal.	20,497				47,183	12/31/2019 Bal.
12/31/2020 Bal.	23,795				72,539	12/31/2020 Bal.

a. Prepare the entry using the financial statement effects template to record cost of goods sold for the year ended December 31, 2020.
b. Prepare the entry using the financial statement effects template to record Amazon's inventory purchases for the year ended December 31, 2020. (Assume all purchases are made on account.)
c. What amount did Amazon pay in cash to its suppliers for the year ended December 31, 2020?

LO3-1, 2 **M3-35. Inferring Transactions from Financial Statements**

Using the information from M3-34, prepare entries for parts *a* and *b* in journal entry form.

LO3-1, 2, 4 **M3-36. Preparing Entries Across Two Periods**

Hatcher Company closes its accounts on December 31 each year. On December 31, 2021, Hatcher accrued $1,200 of interest income that was earned on an investment but not yet received or recorded. (The investment will pay interest of $1,800 cash on January 31, 2022.) On January 31, 2022, the company received the $1,800 cash as interest on the investment. Prepare journal entries to:

a. Accrue the interest earned on December 31, 2021;
b. Close the Interest Income account on December 31, 2021 (the account has a year-end balance of $4,800 after adjustments); and
c. Record the cash receipt of interest on January 31, 2022.

LO3-1, 2 **M3-37. Inferring Transactions from Financial Statements (FSET)**

Using the information from M3-36, prepare entries for parts *a* and *c* using the financial statement effects template.

EXERCISES

LO3-4 **E3-38. Journalizing and Posting Closing Entries**

The adjusted trial balance as of December 31 for Brooks Consulting Company contains the following selected accounts.

Adjusted Account Balances	Debit	Credit
Service fees		€60,500
Rent expense	€15,600	
Salaries expense	34,200	
Supplies expense	4,200	
Depreciation expense	7,700	
Retained earnings		50,250

a. Prepare entries to close these accounts in journal entry form.
b. Set up T-accounts for each of the ledger accounts, enter the balances above, and post the closing entries to them. After these entries are posted, what is the post-closing balance of the Retained Earnings account?

LO3-2 **E3-39. Preparing Adjusting Entries (FSET)**

For each of the following separate situations, prepare the necessary adjustments using the financial statement effects template.

1. Unrecorded depreciation on equipment is $915.
2. On the date for preparing financial statements, an estimated utilities expense of $585 has been incurred, but no utility bill has yet been received or paid.

3. On the first day of the current period, fees for professional journal subscriptions for four periods were paid and recorded as a $4,200 debit to Prepaid subscriptions and a $4,200 credit to Cash.
4. Nine months ago, the **Hartford Financial Services Group** sold a one-year policy to a customer and recorded the receipt of the premium by debiting Cash for $936 and crediting Contract Liabilities for $936. No adjusting entries have been prepared during the nine-month period. Hartford's annual financial statements are now being prepared.
5. At the end of the period, employee wages of $1,448 have been incurred but not yet paid or recorded.
6. At the end of the period, $450 of interest income has been earned but not yet received or recorded.

Hartford Financial Services Group
NYSE :: HIG

E3-40. Preparing and Journalizing Adjusting Entries   **LO3-2**
Using the information from E3-39, prepare necessary adjustments in journal entry form.

E3-41. Preparing Adjusting and Closing Entries Across Two Periods   **LO3-1, 2, 4**
Norton Company closes its accounts on December 31 each year. The company works a five-day work week and pays its employees every two weeks. On December 31, Norton accrued $6,200 of salaries payable. On January 7 of the following year, the company paid salaries of $15,000 cash to employees. Prepare journal entries to:
a. Accrue the salaries payable on December 31;
b. Close the Salaries Expense account on December 31 (the account has a year-end balance of $275,000 after adjustments); and
c. Record the salary payment on January 7.

E3-42. Preparing Adjusting Entries (FSET)   **LO3-1, 2**
Using the information from E3-41, prepare entries for parts *a* and *c* using the financial statement effects template.

E3-43. Analyzing Accounts Using Adjusted Data   **LO3-2, 5**
Selected T-account balances for Fields Company are shown below as of January 31; adjusting entries have already been posted. The firm uses a calendar-year accounting period but prepares *monthly* adjustments.

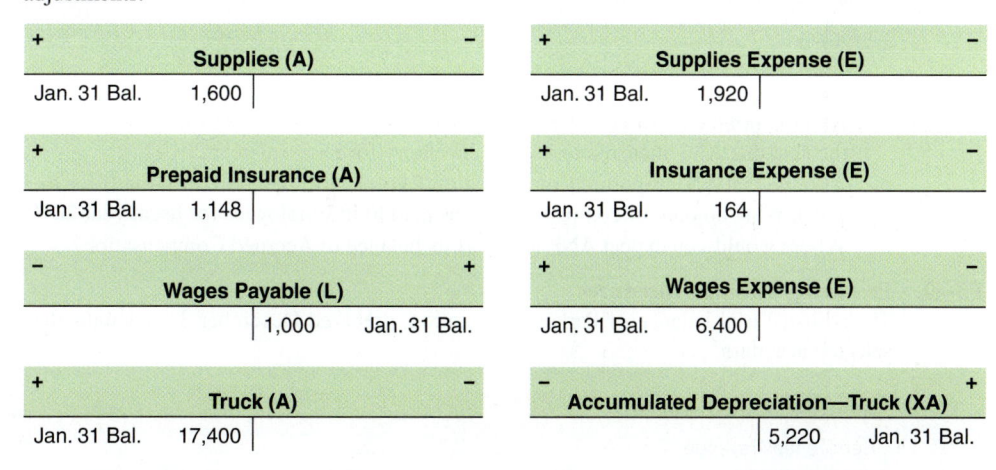

+ Supplies (A) −		+ Supplies Expense (E) −	
Jan. 31 Bal. 1,600		Jan. 31 Bal. 1,920	

+ Prepaid Insurance (A) −		+ Insurance Expense (E) −	
Jan. 31 Bal. 1,148		Jan. 31 Bal. 164	

− Wages Payable (L) +		+ Wages Expense (E) −	
	1,000 Jan. 31 Bal.	Jan. 31 Bal. 6,400	

+ Truck (A) −		− Accumulated Depreciation—Truck (XA) +	
Jan. 31 Bal. 17,400			5,220 Jan. 31 Bal.

a. If the amount in Supplies Expense represents the January 31 adjustment for the supplies used in January, and $1,240 worth of supplies were purchased during January, what was the January 1 beginning balance of Supplies?
b. The amount in the Insurance Expense account represents the adjustment made at January 31 for January insurance expense. If the original insurance premium was for one year, what was the amount of the premium, and on what date did the insurance policy start?
c. If we assume that no beginning balance existed in wages payable or wages expense on January 1, how much cash was paid as wages during January?
d. If the truck has a useful life of five years, what is the monthly amount of depreciation expense, and how many months has Fields owned the truck?

E3-44. Preparing Adjusting Entries (FSET)   **LO3-2, 5**
Jake Thomas began Thomas Refinishing Service on July 1. Selected accounts are shown below as of July 31, before any adjusting entries have been made.

Unadjusted Account Balances	Debit	Credit
Prepaid rent	$8,520	
Prepaid advertising	945	
Supplies inventory	4,500	
Performance obligation liability		$ 900
Refinishing fees revenue		3,750

Using the following information, prepare the adjusting entries necessary on July 31 using the financial statement effects template.

1. On July 1, the firm paid one year's advance rent of $8,520 in cash (assume lease qualifies as short-term).
2. On July 1, $945 cash was paid to the local newspaper for an advertisement to run daily for the months of July, August, and September.
3. Supplies still available at July 31 total $1,650.
4. At July 31, refinishing services of $1,200 have been performed but not yet recorded or billed to customers. The firm uses the account Fees Receivable to reflect amounts due but not yet billed.
5. A customer paid $900 in advance for a refinishing project. At July 31, the project is one-half complete.

LO3-1, 2, 5 **E3-45. Preparing Adjusting Entries**
Use the information from E3-44 to answer the following requirements.
a. Prepare necessary adjustments on July 31 in journal entry form.
b. Set up T-accounts for each of the ledger accounts, enter the balances above, and post the adjusting entries to them.

LO3-5 **E3-46. Inferring Transactions from Financial Statements**
Abercrombie & Fitch Co. (ANF) is a specialty retailer of casual apparel. The following information is taken from ANF's fiscal 10-K report for the fiscal year 2019, which ended February 3, 2020. (All amounts in $ thousands.)

Abercrombie & Fitch Co.
NYSE :: ANF

Selected Balance Sheet Data	February 1, 2020	February 2, 2019
Inventory	$434,326	$437,879
Accrued compensation	58,588	65,156

a. ANF reported Cost of Goods Sold of $1,472,155 (thousand) for its fiscal year 2019. What was the cost that ANF incurred to acquire inventory for its fiscal year 2019?
b. Assume that ANF reported Compensation Expense of $650,000 (thousand) for its fiscal year 2019. What amount of compensation was paid to its employees for fiscal year 2019?
c. Where would you expect ANF to report its balance of Accrued Compensation?

LO3-4 **E3-47. Preparing Closing Procedures**
The adjusted trial balance of Parker Corporation, prepared December 31, contains the following selected accounts.

Adjusted Account Balances	Debit	Credit
Service fees revenue		$74,000
Interest income		1,760
Salaries expense	$33,440	
Advertising expense	3,440	
Depreciation expense	6,960	
Income tax expense	7,920	
Retained earnings		34,160

a. Prepare entries to close these accounts in journal entry form.
b. Set up T-accounts for each of the ledger accounts, enter the balances above, and post the closing entries to them. After these entries are posted, what is the post-closing balance of the Retained Earnings account?

LO3-1, 2, 5 **E3-48. Inferring Transactions from Financial Statements (FSET)**
Ethan Allen Interiors Inc., a leading manufacturer and retailer of home furnishings and accessories, sells products through an exclusive network of approximately 300 design centers. All of Ethan Allen's products are sold by special order. Customers generally place a deposit equal to 25%

Ethan Allen Interiors Inc.
NYSE :: ETH

to 50% of the purchase price when ordering. Orders take 4 to 12 weeks to be delivered. Selected fiscal-year information from the company's balance sheets is as follows ($ thousands):

Selected Balance Sheet Data	2020	2019
Inventories	$126,101	$162,389
Customer deposits and deferred revenues	64,031	56,714

a. In fiscal 2020, Ethan Allen reported total sales revenue of $589,837 (thousand). Assume that the company collected customer deposits equal to $175,000 (thousand) over the year. Prepare entries using the financial statement effects template to record customer deposits and its sales revenue for fiscal year 2020.
b. Ethan Allen's cost of goods sold for 2020 was $266,705 (thousand). Prepare the adjusting entry using the financial statement effects template that it made to record inventory acquisitions.
c. Where would you expect Ethan Allen to report its Customer Deposits?

E3-49. Inferring Transactions from Financial Statements — LO3-1, 2, 5
Use the information from E3-48 to record necessary adjustments in journal entry form for parts a and b.

E3-50. Preparing Financial Statements and Closing Procedures — LO3-3, 4
Solomon Corporation's adjusted trial balance for the year ending December 31 is:

SOLOMON CORPORATION
Adjusted Trial Balance
December 31

	Debit	Credit
Cash	$ 6,000	
Accounts receivable	9,750	
Equipment	117,000	
Accumulated depreciation		$ 21,000
Notes payable		15,000
Common stock		64,500
Retained earnings		18,900
Service fees revenue		106,500
Rent expense	27,000	
Salaries expense	55,650	
Depreciation expense	10,500	
Totals	$225,900	$225,900

a. Prepare its income statement and statement of stockholders' equity for the current year, and its balance sheet for the current year-end. Cash dividends were $12,000, and there were no stock issuances or repurchases.
b. Prepare entries to close its temporary accounts in journal entry form.
c. Set up T-accounts for each of the ledger accounts, enter the balances above, and post the closing entries to them. After these entries are posted, what is the post-closing balance of the Retained Earnings account?

PROBLEMS

P3-51. Recording Transactions and Adjusting Entries Using the Financial Statement Effects Template (FSET) — LO3-1, 2, 5
B. Lougee opened Lougee Roofing Service on April 1. Transactions for April are as follows:

Apr. 1 Lougee contributed $13,800 cash to the business in exchange for common stock.
 1 Paid $3,360 cash for two-year premium toward liability insurance effective immediately.
 2 Paid $7,500 cash for the purchase of a used truck.
 2 Purchased $3,600 of ladders and other equipment; paid $1,200 cash, with the balance due in 30 days.
 5 Purchased $1,400 of supplies on account.
 5 Received an advance of $2,100 cash from a customer for roof repairs to be done during April and May.

Apr. 12 Billed customers $6,600 for roofing services performed.
    18 Collected $5,800 cash from customers on their accounts.
    29 Paid $810 cash for truck fuel used in April.
    30 Paid $120 cash for April digital marketing ads.
    30 Paid $3,000 cash for assistants' wages.
    30 Billed customers $4,800 for roofing services performed.

REQUIRED
a. Record these transactions for April using the financial statement effects template.
b. Supplies still available on April 30 amount to $480; and depreciation for April was $125 on the truck and $75 on equipment; and roofing services were completed by April 30 representing one-fourth of the roofing fees received in advance. Prepare entries to adjust the books for Insurance Expense, Supplies Expense, Depreciation Expense—Trucks, Depreciation Expense—Equipment, and Roofing Fees Revenue using the financial statement effects template.

LO3-1, 2, 5   **P3-52.**   **Journalizing and Posting Transactions, and Preparing a Trial Balance and Adjustments**

REQUIRED
Use the information from P3-51 to complete the following.
a. Set up a general ledger in T-account form for the following accounts: Cash; Accounts Receivable; Supplies; Prepaid Insurance; Trucks; Accumulated Depreciation—Trucks; Equipment; Accumulated Depreciation—Equipment; Accounts Payable; Contract Liability; Common Stock; Roofing Fees Revenue; Fuel Expense; Advertising Expense; Wages Expense; Insurance Expense; Supplies Expense; Depreciation Expense—Trucks; and Depreciation Expense—Equipment.
b. Record these transactions for April in journal entry form.
c. Post these entries to their T-accounts (key numbers in T-accounts by date).
d. Prepare an unadjusted trial balance as of April 30.
e. Prepare the adjusting entries and post the adjusting entries to their T-accounts.

LO3-2   **P3-53.**   **Recording Adjusting Entries Using the Financial Statement Effects Template (FSET)**
SnapShot Company, a commercial photography studio, has just completed its first full year of operations on December 31. General ledger account balances *before* year-end adjustments follow; no adjusting entries have been made to the accounts at any time during the year. Assume that all balances are normal.

Cash	$ 6,450
Accounts receivable	11,400
Prepaid software subscription contract	37,800
Prepaid insurance	8,910
Supplies	12,750
Equipment	68,400
Accounts payable	5,730
Performance obligations	7,800
Common stock	72,000
Photography fee revenue	103,440
Wages expense	33,000
Utilities expense	10,260

An analysis of the firm's records discloses the following.

1. Photography services of $2,775 have been rendered, but customers have not yet paid or been billed. The firm uses the account Fees Receivable to reflect amounts due but not yet billed.
2. Equipment, purchased January 1, has an estimated life of 10 years.
3. Utilities expense for December is estimated to be $1,200, but the bill will not arrive or be paid until January of next year.
4. The balance in Prepaid Software Subscription Contract represents the amount paid on January 1 for a 2-year contract for high-functioning photo editing software and its updates.
5. In November, customers paid $7,800 cash in advance for photos to be taken for the holiday season. When received, these fees were credited to Performance Obligations. By December 31, all of the services related to these fees had been performed.
6. A 3-year insurance premium paid on January 1 was debited to Prepaid Insurance.
7. Supplies available at December 31 are $4,560.
8. At December 31, wages expense of $1,125 has been incurred but not paid or recorded.

REQUIRED
Prepare the company's adjusting entries using the financial statement effects template.

P3-54. Preparing an Unadjusted Trial Balance and Adjustments LO3-1, 2

REQUIRED
Use the information from P3-53 to complete the following.
a. Prove that debits equal credits for SnapShot's unadjusted account balances by preparing its unadjusted trial balance at December 31.
b. Prepare its adjusting entries in journal entry form.
c. Set up T-accounts, enter the balances above, and post the adjusting entries to them.

P3-55. Recording Adjusting Entries Using the Financial Statement Effects Template (FSET) LO3-2

Murdock Carpet Cleaners ended its first month of operations on June 30. Monthly financial statements will be prepared. The unadjusted account balances are as follows.

MURDOCK CARPET CLEANERS Unadjusted Trial Balance June 30	Debit	Credit
Cash	$ 2,950	
Accounts receivable	1,130	
Prepaid insurance	7,740	
Supplies	6,300	
Equipment	11,100	
Accounts payable		$ 1,900
Common stock		5,000
Retained earnings		13,240
Service fees revenue		11,630
Wages expense	2,550	
	$31,770	$31,770

The following information is available.
1. The balance in Prepaid insurance was the amount paid on June 1 for the first four months' insurance.
2. Supplies available at June 30 were $2,050.
3. Equipment, purchased June 1, has an estimated life of five years.
4. Unpaid and unrecorded employee wages at June 30 were $525.
5. Utility services used during June were estimated at $750. A bill is expected early in July.
6. Fees earned for services performed but not yet billed on June 30 were $950. The company uses the account Accounts Receivable to reflect amounts due but not yet billed.

REQUIRED
Prepare its adjusting entries at June 30 using the financial statement effects template.

P3-56. Preparing Adjusting Entries, Financial Statements, and Closing Entries LO3-1, 2, 3, 4, 5

REQUIRED
Use the information from P3-55 to complete the following.
a. Prepare the company's adjusting entries at June 30 in journal entry form.
b. Set up T-accounts, enter the balances above, and post the adjusting entries to them.
c. Prepare its income statement for June and its balance sheet at June 30.
d. Prepare entries to close its temporary accounts in journal entry form.
e. Post the closing entries to the T-accounts.

P3-57. Preparing Adjusting Entries Using the Financial Statement Effects Template (FSET) LO3-2

The following information relates to the December 31 adjustments for Kwik Print Company. The firm's fiscal year ends on December 31.

1. Weekly employee salaries for a five-day week total $3,600, payable on Fridays. December 31 of the current year is a Tuesday.
2. Kwik Print has $40,000 of notes payable outstanding at December 31. Interest of $380 has accrued on these notes by December 31 but will not be paid until the notes mature next year.
3. During December, Kwik Print provided $1,800 of printing services to clients who will be billed on January 2. The firm uses the account Fees Receivable to reflect amounts due but not yet billed.

4. Starting December 1, all maintenance work on Kwik Print's equipment is handled by Richardson Repair Company under an agreement whereby Kwik Print pays a fixed monthly charge of $500. Kwik Print paid six months' service charge in advance on December 1, debiting Prepaid Maintenance for $3,000.
5. The firm paid $1,800 cash on December 15 for a series of radio commercials to run during December and January. One-third of the commercials have aired by December 31. The $1,800 payment was debited to Prepaid Advertising.
6. Starting December 16, Kwik Print rented 400 square feet of storage space from a neighboring business using a short-term lease. The monthly rent of $1.00 per square foot is due in advance on the first of each month. Nothing was paid in December, however, because the neighbor agreed to add the rent for the one-half of December to the January 1 payment.
7. Kwik Print invested $7,500 cash in securities on December 1 and earned interest of $35 on these securities by December 31. No interest payment will be received until January, and the end-of-December market value of the securities remains at $7,500.
8. Annual depreciation on the firm's equipment is $4,350. No depreciation has been recorded during the year.

REQUIRED
Prepare its adjusting entries required at December 31 using the financial statement effects template.

LO3-2 P3-58. Preparing Adjusting Entries

REQUIRED
Use the information from P3-57 to prepare adjusting entries in journal entry form.

LO3-3, 4 P3-59. Preparing Financial Statements and Closing Entries
The following adjusted trial balance is for Trueman Consulting Inc. at December 31. The company had no stock issuances or repurchases during the year.

	Debit	Credit
Cash	$ 1,350	
Accounts receivable	1,635	
Supplies	1,530	
Prepaid insurance	750	
Equipment	3,200	
Accumulated depreciation—equipment		$ 540
Accounts payable		430
Long-term notes payable		3,500
Common stock		500
Retained earnings		1,645
Service fees revenue		29,200
Rent expense	6,000	
Salaries expense	16,700	
Supplies expense	2,350	
Insurance expense	1,625	
Depreciation expense—equipment	360	
Interest expense	315	
	$35,815	$35,815

REQUIRED
a. Prepare its income statement and statement of stockholders' equity for the year and its balance sheet at December 31.
b. Prepare entries to close its accounts in journal entry form.

LO3-4 P3-60. Preparing Closing Entries
The following adjusted trial balance is for Wilson Company at December 31.

	Debit	Credit
Cash	$ 10,200	
Accounts receivable	9,600	
Prepaid insurance	4,320	
Equipment	86,400	
Accumulated depreciation		$ 14,400
Accounts payable		720
Common stock		30,000
Retained earnings		22,920
Service fees revenue		116,640
Miscellaneous income		5,040
Salaries expense	51,360	
Rent expense	16,080	
Insurance expense	2,160	
Depreciation expense	9,600	
Income tax expense	10,560	
Income tax payable		10,560
	$200,280	$200,280

REQUIRED

a. Prepare closing entries in journal entry form.
b. After the firm's closing entries are posted, what is the post-closing balance for the Retained Earnings account?
c. Prepare its post-closing trial balance.

P3-61. Preparing Entries Across Two Periods Using the Financial Statement Effects Template (FSET)   **LO3-1, 2**

The following selected accounts appear in Shaw Company's unadjusted trial balance at December 31, the end of its fiscal year. (All accounts have normal balances.)

Prepaid advertising	$ 1,700	Performance obligations	$ 7,600
Wages expense	61,300	Service fees revenue	121,800
Prepaid insurance	4,800	Rental income	6,900

REQUIRED

a. Prepare its adjusting entries at December 31 using the financial statement effects template and the following additional information.
   1. Prepaid advertising at December 31 is $1,100.
   2. Unpaid and unrecorded wages earned by employees in December are $1,800.
   3. Prepaid insurance at December 31 is $3,200.
   4. Performance obligations represent service fees collected in advance of when the services are provided to customers. Performance obligations at December 31 are $4,200.
   5. Rent revenue of $1,400 owed by a tenant is not recorded at December 31.
b. Prepare entries on January 4 of the following year using the financial statement effects template to record (1) payment of $3,400 cash in wages, which includes the $1,800 accrued at December 31 and (2) cash receipt of the $1,400 rent revenue owed from the tenant.

P3-62. Preparing Entries Across Two Periods   **LO3-1, 2**

REQUIRED

Use the information from P3-61 to prepare journal entries in journal entry form for parts a and b.

P3-63. Recording Transactions and Adjustments Using the Financial Statement Effects Template (FSET)   **LO3-1, 2**

Market-Probe, a market research firm, had the following transactions in June, its first month of operations.

June 1   B. May invested $33,000 cash in the firm in exchange for common stock.
      1   The firm purchased the following: office equipment, $15,360; office supplies, $4,000. Terms are $6,200 cash with the remainder due in 60 days. (Make a compound entry requiring two credits.)
      2   Paid $1,400 cash for June rent owed to the landlord on a short-term lease.
      2   Contracted for three months' advertising in a local newspaper at $400 per month and paid for the advertising in advance.
      2   Signed a six-month contract with a customer to provide research consulting services at a rate of $4,500 per month. Received two months' fees in advance. Work on the contract started immediately.

June 10 Billed various customers $8,100 for services rendered.
12 Paid $5,000 cash for two weeks' salaries (5-day week) to employees.
15 Paid $1,700 cash to employee for travel expenses to conference.
18 Paid $700 cash to post office for bulk mailing of research questionnaire (postage expense).
26 Paid $5,000 cash for two weeks' salaries to employees.
28 Billed various customers $7,300 for services rendered.
30 Collected $10,900 cash from customers on their accounts.
30 Paid $2,100 cash for dividends.

REQUIRED

a. Record these transactions using the financial statement effects template.
b. Prepare adjusting entries using the financial statement effects template that reflect the following information at June 30:
- Office supplies available, $2,100
- Accrued employee salaries, $1,100
- Estimated life of office equipment is 8 years

Adjusting entries must also be prepared for advertising and service fees per information in the June transactions.

LO3-1, 2 **P3-64.** **Journalizing and Posting Transactions, and Preparing a Trial Balance and Adjustments**

REQUIRED
Use the information from P3-63 to complete the following.
a. Set up a general ledger in T-account form for the following accounts: Cash; Accounts Receivable; Office Supplies; Prepaid Advertising; Office Equipment; Accumulated Depreciation—Office Equipment; Accounts Payable; Salaries Payable; Contract Liabilities; Common Stock; Retained Earnings; Service Fees Revenue; Salaries Expense; Advertising Expense; Supplies Expense; Rent Expense; Travel Expense; Depreciation Expense—Office Equipment; and Postage Expense.
b. Record these transactions in journal entry form.
c. Post these entries to their T-accounts (key numbers in T-accounts by date).
d. Prepare an unadjusted trial balance at June 30.
e. Prepare adjusting entries in journal entry form that reflect the following information at June 30:
- Office supplies available, $2,100
- Accrued employee salaries, $1,100
- Estimated life of office equipment is 8 years

Adjusting entries must also be prepared for advertising and service fees per information in the June transactions.
f. Post all adjusting entries to their T-accounts.

LO3-2 **P3-65.** **Preparing Adjusting Entries Using the Financial Statement Effects Template (FSET)**
DeliverAll, a mailing service, has just completed its first full year of operations on December 31. Its general ledger account balances *before* year-end adjustments follow; no adjusting entries have been made to the accounts at any time during the year. Assume that all balances are normal.

Cash	$ 1,900	Accounts payable	$ 4,180
Accounts receivable	4,100	Common stock	7,700
Prepaid advertising	1,380	Mailing fees earned	68,000
Supplies	5,100	Wages expense	31,100
Equipment	33,800	Other compensation expense expense	6,000
Notes payable	6,000	Utilities expense	2,500

An analysis of the firm's records reveals the following.

1. The balance in Prepaid Advertising represents the amount paid for newspaper advertising for one year. The agreement, which calls for the same amount of space and cost each month, covers the period from February 1 of this year to January 31 of the following year. DeliverAll did not advertise during its first month of operations.
2. Equipment, purchased January 1, has an estimated life of eight years.
3. Utilities expense does not include expense for December, estimated at $400. The bill will not arrive until January of the following year.
4. At year-end, employees have earned an additional $1,100 in wages that will not be paid or recorded until January.

5. Supplies available at year-end amount to $1,300.
6. At year-end, unpaid interest of $360 has accrued on the notes payable.
7. The company offers no retirement plan but as part of the compensation contract, the company pays other compensation of $500 per month payable on the first of each month, plus an amount equal to 1/2% of annual mailing fees earned. This is payable within 15 days after the end of the year.

REQUIRED
Prepare adjusting entries using the financial statement effects template.

P3-66. Preparing an Unadjusted Trial Balance and Adjusting Entries — LO3-2

REQUIRED
Use the information from P3-65 to answer the following.
a. Prove that debits equal credits for its unadjusted account balances by preparing its unadjusted trial balance at December 31.
b. Prepare its adjusting entries in journal entry form.
c. Set up T-accounts, enter the balances above, and post the adjusting entries to them.

P3-67. Preparing Adjusting Entries Using the Financial Statement Effects Template (FSET) — LO3-2, 5
Wheel Place Company began operations on March 1 to provide automotive wheel alignment and balancing services. On March 31 the unadjusted balances of the firm's accounts are as follows.

WHEEL PLACE COMPANY
Unadjusted Trial Balance
March 31

	Debit	Credit
Cash	$ 2,280	
Accounts receivable	4,500	
Prepaid insurance	5,700	
Supplies	4,440	
Equipment	43,740	
Accounts payable		$ 3,050
Service contract liability		1,200
Common stock		46,100
Service revenue		14,990
Wages expense	4,680	
Totals	$65,340	$65,340

The following information is available.
1. The balance in Prepaid insurance was the amount paid on March 1 to cover the first 6 months' insurance.
2. Supplies available on March 31 amount to $2,060.
3. Equipment has an estimated life of nine years and a zero salvage value.
4. Unpaid and unrecorded wages at March 31 were $670.
5. Utility services used during March were estimated at $470; a bill is expected early in April.
6. The balance in Service Contract Liability was the amount received on March 1 from a car dealer to cover alignment and balancing services on cars sold by the dealer in March and April. Wheel Place agreed to provide the services at a fixed fee of $600 each month.

REQUIRED
Prepare adjusting entries using the financial statement effects template.

P3-68. Preparing and Posting Adjusting Entries, Preparing Financial Statements, Preparing Closing Entries — LO3-2, 3, 4, 5

REQUIRED
Use the information from P3-67 to answer the following.
a. Prepare its adjusting entries at March 31 in journal entry form.
b. Set up T-accounts, enter the balances above, and post the adjusting entries to them.
c. Prepare its income statement for March and its balance sheet at March 31.
d. Prepare entries to close its temporary accounts in journal entry form and post the closing entries to the T-accounts.

LO3-3, 4 **P3-69. Preparing Financial Statements and Closing Entries**

Trails, Inc., publishes magazines for skiers and hikers. The company's adjusted trial balance for the year ending December 31 is:

TRAILS, INC.
Adjusted Trial Balance
December 31

	Debit	Credit
Cash	$ 5,100	
Accounts receivable	12,900	
Supplies	6,300	
Prepaid insurance	1,395	
Office equipment	99,000	
Accumulated depreciation		$ 16,500
Accounts payable		3,150
Subscription liabilities		15,000
Salaries payable		5,250
Common stock		37,500
Retained earnings		34,830
Subscription revenue		252,450
Advertising revenue		74,550
Salaries expense	150,345	
Printing and mailing expense	128,400	
Rent expense (for a short-term lease)	13,200	
Supplies expense	9,150	
Insurance expense	2,790	
Depreciation expense	8,250	
Income tax expense	2,400	
Totals	$439,230	$493,230

REQUIRED

a. Prepare its income statement and statement of stockholders' equity for the year and its balance sheet at December 31. There were no cash dividends and no stock issuances or repurchases during the year.
b. Prepare entries to close its accounts in journal entry form.

LO3-4 **P3-70. Preparing Closing Entries**

The following adjusted trial balance is for Mayflower Moving Service at December 31.

MAYFLOWER MOVING SERVICE
Adjusted Trial Balance
December 31

	Debit	Credit
Cash	$ 7,600	
Accounts receivable	10,500	
Supplies	4,600	
Prepaid advertising	6,000	
Trucks	56,600	
Accumulated depreciation—trucks		$ 20,000
Equipment	15,200	
Accumulated depreciation—equipment		4,200
Accounts payable		2,400
Service contract liabilities		5,400
Common stock		10,000
Retained earnings		31,100
Service fees revenue		145,000
Wages expense	59,600	
Rent expense	20,400	
Insurance expense	5,800	
Supplies expense	10,200	
Advertising expense	12,000	
Depreciation expense—trucks	8,000	
Depreciation expense—equipment	1,600	
Totals	$218,100	$218,100

REQUIRED

a. Prepare closing entries in journal entry form.

b. After its closing entries are posted, what is the post-closing balance for the Retained Earnings account?
c. Prepare Mayflower's post-closing trial balance.

P3-71. Preparing Entries Across Two Periods Using the Financial Statement Effects Template (FSET) LO3-1, 2, 5
The following selected accounts appear in Zimmerman Company's unadjusted trial balance at December 31, the end of its fiscal year. (All accounts have normal balances.)

Prepaid maintenance	$ 6,750	Commission revenue	$210,000
Supplies	21,000	Wage expense	27,000
Performance obligations	21,250		

Additional information is as follows.

1. On September 1, the company entered into a prepaid equipment maintenance contract. Zimmerman Company paid $6,750 to cover maintenance service for 6 months, beginning September 1. The $6,750 payment was debited to Prepaid Maintenance.
2. Supplies available on December 31 are $8,000.
3. Performance obligations at December 31 are $10,000.
4. Commission revenue where services have been performed but the amounts for which have not yet been billed at December 31 are $7,000. (*Hint:* Debit Commissions Receivable.)
5. Zimmerman Company's compensation plan calls for salary of $2,250 per month payable on the first of each month, plus an annual amount equal to 1% of annual commission revenue. This additional compensation is payable on January 10 of the following year. (*Hint:* Use the adjusted amount of commission revenue in computing the additional compensation.)

REQUIRED
a. Prepare Zimmerman Company's adjusting entries at December 31 using the financial statement effects template.
b. Prepare entries on January 10 of the following year using the financial statement effects template to record (1) the billing of $11,500 in commissions (which includes the $7,000 of commissions not billed at December 31) and (2) the cash payment of the additional compensation owed for the current year. (*Hint for part (1)*: Zimmerman Company has two receivable accounts—Commissions Receivable is used for services performed, but not yet billed, and Accounts Receivable for amounts that are related to services performed and billed to the customer.)

P3-72. Preparing Entries Across Two Periods LO3-2, 5
Use the information from P3-71 to answer the following. Prepare the adjusting entries from part *a* and the transactions in part *b* in journal entry form.

P3-73. Preparing Adjusting Entries (FSET) LO3-2, 5
Fischer Card Shop is a small retail shop. Fischer's balance sheet at year-end 2021 is as follows.

FISCHER CARD SHOP
Balance Sheet
December 31, 2021

Cash		$12,750	Accounts payable	$ 7,800
Inventories		18,000	Wages payable	150
Prepaid insurance		5,700	Total current liabilities	7,950
Total current assets		36,450	Total equity (includes retained earnings)	35,250
Equipment	$11,250		Total liabilities and equity	$43,200
Less accumulated depreciation	4,500			
Equipment, net		6,750		
Total assets		$43,200		

The following information details transactions and adjustments that occurred during 2022.

1. Sales total $218,775 in 2022; all sales were cash sales.
2. Inventory purchases total $114,300 in 2022; at December 31, 2022, inventory totals $21,750. Assume all purchases were made on account.
3. Accounts payable totals $6,150 at December 31, 2022.
4. Annual insurance premiums of $36,000 was paid on March 1, 2022, covering the next 12 months. The balance in prepaid insurance at December 31, 2021, was the balance remaining from the advance premium payment in 2021.

5. Wages are paid every other week on Friday; during 2022, Fischer paid $18,750 cash for wages. At December 31, 2022, Fischer owed employees unpaid and unrecorded wages of $525.
6. Depreciation on equipment totals $2,550 in 2022.

REQUIRED

Prepare any necessary transaction entries for 2022 and adjusting entries at December 31, 2022, using the financial statement effects template.

P3-74. Preparing Adjusting Entries, Financial Statements, and Closing Entries

REQUIRED

Use the information from P3-73 to answer the following.
a. Prepare any necessary transaction entries for 2022 and adjusting entries at December 31, 2022, in journal entry form.
b. Set up T-accounts, enter the balances above, and post the transactions and adjusting entries to them.
c. Prepare its income statement for 2022 and its balance sheet at December 31, 2022.
d. Prepare entries to close its temporary accounts in journal entry form and post the closing entries to the T-accounts.

P3-75. Recording Entries and Adjusting Entries (FSET)

Rhoades Tax Services began business on December 1. Its December transactions are as follows.

Dec. 1 Rhoades invested $50,000 in the business in exchange for common stock.
2 Paid $3,000 cash for December rent to Bomba Realty (short-term lease).
2 Purchased $2,700 of supplies on account.
3 Purchased $23,750 of office equipment, paying $11,750 cash with the balance due in 30 days.
8 Paid $2,700 cash on account for supplies purchased December 2.
14 Paid $2,250 cash for assistant's wages for 2 weeks' work.
20 Performed consulting services for $7,500 cash.
28 Paid $2,250 cash for assistant's wages for 2 weeks' work.
30 Billed clients $18,000 for December consulting services.
31 Paid $4,500 cash for dividends.

Additional information:
1. Supplies available at December 31 are $1,775.
2. Accrued wages payable at December 31 are $675.
3. Depreciation for December is $300.
4. Rhoades has spent 45 hours on an involved tax fraud case in December. When completed in January, his work will be billed at $125 per hour. (The account Fees Receivable is used to reflect amounts earned but not yet billed.)

REQUIRED

Record (a) these transactions and (b) any necessary adjusting entries using the financial statement effects template.

P3-76. Applying the Entire Accounting Cycle

REQUIRED

Use the information from P3-75 to answer the following.
a. Set up a general ledger in T-account form for the following accounts: Cash; Fees Receivable; Supplies; Office Equipment; Accumulated Depreciation—Office Equipment; Accounts Payable; Wages Payable; Common Stock; Retained Earnings; Consulting Revenue; Supplies Expense; Wages Expense; Rent Expense; and Depreciation Expense.
b. Record the above transactions in journal entry form.
c. Post these entries to their T-accounts (key numbers in T-accounts by date).
d. Prepare an unadjusted trial balance at December 31.
e. Journalize the adjusting entries at December 31 in journal entry form, drawing on the information above. Then post adjusting entries to their T-accounts and prepare an adjusted trial balance at December 31.
f. Prepare a December income statement and statement of stockholders' equity and a December 31 balance sheet.
g. Record its closing entries in journal entry form. Post these entries to their T-accounts.
h. Prepare a post-closing trial balance at December 31.

CASES AND PROJECTS

C3-77. Preparing Adjusting Entries (FSET)   **LO3-2, 5**

Seaside Surf Shop began operations on July 1 with an initial investment of $40,000. During the initial 3 months of operations, the following cash transactions were recorded in the firm's checking account.

Cash receipts		Cash payments	
Initial investment by owner	$ 40,000	Rent	$ 19,200
Collected from customers	64,800	Fixtures and equipment	20,000
Borrowed from bank 7/1	8,000	Merchandise inventory	49,600
Total cash receipts	$112,800	Salaries	4,800
		Other expenses	10,400
		Total cash payments	$104,000

Additional information

1. Most sales were for cash; however, the store accepted a limited amount of credit sales; at September 30, customers owed the store $7,200.
2. Rent was paid on July 1 for six months (short-term lease).
3. Salaries of $2,400 per month are paid on the 1st of each month for salaries earned in the month prior.
4. Inventories are purchased for cash; at September 30, inventory worth $16,800 was available.
5. Fixtures and equipment were expected to last five years with zero salvage value.
6. The bank charges 12% annual interest (1% per month) on its bank loan.

REQUIRED

Prepare any necessary adjusting entries at September 30 using the financial statement effects template.

C3-78. Preparing Adjusting Entries, Financial Statements, and Closing Entries   **LO3-1, 2, 3, 4, 5**

REQUIRED

Use the information from C3-77 to answer the following.

a. Prepare any necessary adjusting entries at September 30 in journal entry form.
b. Set up T-accounts and post the adjusting entries to them.
c. Prepare its initial three-month income statement and its balance sheet at September 30. (Ignore taxes.)
d. Analyze the statements from part c and assess the company's performance over its initial three months.

C3-79. Analyzing Transactions, Impacts on Financial Ratios, and Loan Covenants   **LO3-1, 2, 5**

Wyland Consulting, a firm started three years ago by Reyna Wyland, offers consulting services for material handling and plant layout. Its balance sheet at the close of the year is as follows.

WYLAND CONSULTING
Balance Sheet
December 31

Assets			Liabilities	
Cash		$ 5,100	Notes payable	$ 45,000
Accounts receivable		34,315	Accounts payable	6,300
Supplies		19,800	Contract liabilities	16,950
Prepaid insurance		6,750	Wages payable	600
Equipment	$102,750		Total liabilities	68,850
Less: accumulated depreciation	35,960	66,790	**Equity**	
			Common stock	12,000
			Retained earnings	51,905
Total assets		$132,755	Total liabilities and equity	$132,755

Earlier in the year Wyland obtained a bank loan of $45,000 cash for the firm. One of the provisions of the loan is that the year-end debt-to-equity ratio (ratio of total liabilities to total equity) cannot exceed 1.0. Based on the above balance sheet, the ratio at the end of the year is 1.08. Wyland is concerned about being in violation of the loan agreement and requests assistance in reviewing the situation. Wyland believes that she might have overlooked some items at year-end. Discussions with Wyland reveal the following.

1. On January 1 the firm paid a $6,750 insurance premium for 2 years of coverage; the amount in Prepaid Insurance has not yet been adjusted.
2. Depreciation on the equipment should be 10% of cost per year; the company inadvertently recorded 15% for the year.
3. Interest on the bank loan has been paid through the end of the year.
4. The firm concluded a major consulting engagement in December, doing a plant layout analysis for a new factory. The $9,000 fee has not been billed or recorded in the accounts.
5. On December 1, the firm received a $16,950 advance payment from Croy Corporation for consulting services to be rendered over a 2-month period. This payment was credited to the Contract Liabilities account. One-half of this fee was earned by December 31.
6. Supplies costing $7,200 were available on December 31; the company has made no entry in the accounts.

REQUIRED

a. What portion of the company is financed by debt versus equity (called the debt-to-equity ratio and defined in Chapter 1) at December 31?
b. Is the firm in violation of its loan agreement? Prepare computations to support the correct total liabilities and total equity figures at December 31.

LO3-1, 2 **C3-80. Ethics, Accounting Adjustments, and Auditors**

It is the end of the accounting year for Juliet Javetz, controller of a medium-sized, publicly held corporation specializing in toxic waste cleanup. Within the corporation, only Javetz and the president know that the firm has been negotiating for several months to land a large contract for waste cleanup in Western Europe. The president has hired another firm with excellent contacts in Western Europe to help with negotiations. The outside firm will charge an hourly fee plus expenses but has agreed not to submit a bill until the negotiations are in their final stages (expected to occur in another 3 to 4 months). Even if the contract falls through, the outside firm is entitled to receive payment for its services. Based upon her discussion with a member of the outside firm, Javetz knows that its charge for services provided to date will be $150,000. This is a material amount for the company.

Javetz knows that the president wants negotiations to remain as secret as possible so that competitors will not learn of the contract the company is pursuing in Europe. In fact, the president recently stated to her, "Now is not the time to reveal our actions in Western Europe to other staff members, our auditors, or the readers of our financial statements; securing this contract is crucial to our future growth." No entry has been made in the accounting records for the cost of contract negotiations. Javetz now faces an uncomfortable situation. The company's outside auditor has just asked her if she knows of any year-end adjustments that have not yet been recorded.

REQUIRED

a. What are the ethical considerations that Javetz faces in answering the auditor's question?
b. How should Javetz respond to the auditor's question?

LO3-1, 2, 5 **C3-81. Inferring Adjusting Entries from Financial Statements (FSET)**

Lady G's Fashions, a specialty retailer of women's apparel, markets its products through retail stores and catalogs. Selected information from its Year 1 and Year 2 balance sheets is as follows.

Selected Balance Sheet Data ($ thousands)	Year 1	Year 2
Prepaid catalog expenses (asset)	$ 7,788	$ 8,612
Advertising credits receivable	42	1,068
Gift certificate liability	12,216	14,106

The following excerpts are from Lady G's Fashions accompanying note disclosures:
- Catalog costs in the direct segment are considered direct response advertising and as such are capitalized as incurred and amortized over the expected sales life of each catalog, which is generally a period not exceeding six months.
- The Company periodically enters into arrangements with certain national magazine publishers, whereby the Company includes magazine subscription cards in its catalog mailings in exchange for advertising credits or discounts on advertising.

REQUIRED

a. Assume that Lady G's Fashions spent $125,100 to design, print, and mail catalogs in Year 2. Also assume that it received advertising credits of $1,698. Prepare the entry using the financial statement effects template that Lady G's Fashions would have recorded when these costs were incurred.

b. Prepare the adjusting entry using the financial statement effects template that would be necessary to record its amortization of prepaid catalog costs.

c. How do advertising credits expire? Prepare the adjusting entry using both the financial statement effects template that Lady G's Fashions would record to reflect the change in advertising credits.

d. Assume that Lady G's Fashions sold gift certificates valued at $38,350 in Year 2. Prepare the entry using the financial statement effects template that Lady G's Fashions would make to record these sales. Next, prepare the entry using the financial statement effects template that it makes to record merchandise sales to customers who pay with gift certificates.

C3-82. Inferring Adjusting Entries from Financial Statements   LO3-1, 2, 5

REQUIRED

Using the information from C3-81, prepare entries in journal entry form for parts *a* through *d*.

SOLUTIONS TO REVIEW PROBLEMS

Review 3-1

a.

Transaction	Cash Asset	+	Noncash Assets	=	Liabilities	+	Contrib. Capital	+	Earned Capital		Revenues	−	Expenses	=	Net Income
(1) Paid $4,000 for wages	−4,000 Cash			=					−4,000 Retained Earnings			−	+4,000 Wages Expense	=	−4,000
(2) Receipt of $6,500 for services provided.	+6,500 Cash			=					+6,500 Retained Earnings		+6,500 Fees Revenue	−		=	+6,500
(3) Purchase of $1,100 in supplies on account.			+1,100 Supplies	=	+1,100 Accounts Payable							−		=	
(4) Performed $1,200 of services on account.			+1,200 Accounts Receivable	=					+1,200 Retained Earnings		+1,200 Fees Revenue	−		=	+1,200
(5) Paid suppliers $2,000 on account.	−2,000 Cash			=	−2,000 Accounts Payable							−		=	

b.

(1) Wages expense (+E, −SE) 4,000
       Cash (−A)   4,000

(2) Cash (+A) 6,500
       Fees revenue (+R, +SE)   6,500

(3) Supplies (+A) 1,100
       Accounts payable (+L)   1,100

(4) Accounts receivable (+A) 1,200
       Fees revenue (+R, +SE)   1,200

(5) Accounts payable (−L) 2,000
       Cash (−A)   2,000

c.

General Ledger

Assets	=	Liabilities	+	Equity

Cash (A) (+ / −)
Beg. bal.	500	4,000	(1)
(2)	6,500	2,000	(5)
End. bal.	1,000		

Accounts Receivable (A) (+ / −)
Beg. bal.	8,000		
(4)	1,200		
End. bal.	9,200		

Prepaid Insurance (A) (+ / −)
| Beg. bal. | 6,000 | | |
| End. bal. | 6,000 | | |

Supplies (A) (+ / −)
Beg. bal.	30,200		
(3)	1,100		
End. bal.	31,300		

Equipment (A) (+ / −)
| Beg. bal. | 270,000 | | |
| End. bal. | 270,000 | | |

Accumulated Depreciation—Equipment (XA) (− / +)
| | | 60,000 | Beg. bal. |
| | | 60,000 | End. bal. |

Accounts Payable (L) (− / +)
(5)	2,000	4,000	Beg. bal.
		1,100	(3)
		3,100	End. bal.

Contract Liability (L) (− / +)
| | | 4,000 | Beg. bal. |
| | | 4,000 | End. bal. |

Common Stock (SE) (− / +)
| | | 120,400 | Beg. bal. |
| | | 120,400 | End. bal. |

Retained Earnings (SE) (− / +)
| | | 60,000 | Beg. bal. |
| | | 60,000 | End. bal. |

Fees Revenue (R) (− / +)
		142,300	Beg. bal.
		6,500	(2)
		1,200	(4)
		150,000	End. bal.

Rent Expense (E) (+ / −)
| Beg. bal. | 22,000 | | |
| End. bal. | 22,000 | | |

Wages Expense (E) (+ / −)
Beg. bal.	54,000		
(1)	4,000		
End. bal.	58,000		

Assets = $257,500 = **Liabilities = $7,100** + **Equity = $250,400**

d.

ATWELL LABORATORIES, INC.
Unadjusted Trial Balance
June 30

	Debit	Credit
Cash	$ 1,000	
Accounts receivable	9,200	
Prepaid insurance	6,000	
Supplies	31,300	
Equipment	270,000	
Accumulated depreciation—equipment		$ 60,000
Accounts payable		3,100
Contract liability		4,000
Fees revenue		150,000
Wages expense	58,000	
Rent expense	22,000	
Common stock		120,400
Retained earnings		60,000
Totals	$397,500	$397,500

Review 3-2

a.

	Balance Sheet						Income Statement		
Transaction	Cash Asset +	Noncash Assets −	Contra Assets =	Liabilities +	Contrib. Capital +	Earned Capital	Revenues −	Expenses =	Net Income
(1) Adjustment to record insurance expense.		−1,500 Prepaid Insurance	=			−1,500 Retained Earnings		+1,500 Insurance Expense =	−1,500
(2) Adjustment to record supplies expense.		−25,000 Supplies	=			−25,000 Retained Earnings		+25,000 Supplies Expense =	−25,000
(3) Adjustment to record depreciation expense.			+30,000 Accumulated Depreciation —Equipment =			−30,000 Retained Earnings		+30,000 Depreciation Expense =	−30,000
(4) Adjustment to record fees revenue.			=	−3,000 Contract Liability		+3,000 Retained Earnings	+3,000 Fees Revenue −	=	+3,000
(5) Adjustment to record wages expense.			=	+600 Wages Payable		−600 Retained Earnings		+600 Wages Expense =	−600
(6) Adjustment to record rent expense.			=	+2,000 Rent Payable		−2,000 Retained Earnings		+2,000 Rent Expense =	−2,000

b.

(1)	Insurance expense (+E, −SE).................	1,500	
	Prepaid insurance (−A)		1,500
	Record insurance expired $6,000 × (6 months/24 months).		
(2)	Supplies expense (+E, −SE).................	25,000	
	Supplies (−A).........................		25,000
	Record supplies used ($31,300 − $6,300).		
(3)	Depreciation expense (+E, −SE)	30,000	
	Accumulated depreciation—Equipment (+XA, −A)		30,000
	Record depreciation [($270,000 − $0) ÷ 9 years].		
(4)	Contract liability (−L).....................	3,000	
	Fees revenue (+R, +SE)		3,000
	Record fees earned.		
(5)	Wages expense (+E, −SE).................	600	
	Wages payable (+L).....................		600
	Record employee wages incurred.		
(6)	Rent expense (+E, −SE)....................	2,000	
	Rent payable (+L)......................		2,000
	Record rent owed.		

c.

General Ledger

Assets	=	Liabilities	+	Equity

Cash (A)
Unadj. bal. 1,000	
Adj. bal. 1,000	

Accounts Payable (L)
	3,100 Unadj. bal.
	3,100 Adj. bal.

Common Stock (SE)
	120,400 Unadj. bal.
	120,400 Adj. bal.

Accounts Receivable (A)
Unadj. bal. 9,200	
Adj. bal. 9,200	

Contract Liability (L)
	4,000 Unadj. bal.
(4) 3,000	
	1,000 Adj. bal.

Retained Earnings (SE)
	60,000 Unadj. bal.
	60,000 Adj. bal.

Prepaid Insurance (A)
Unadj. bal. 6,000	
	1,500 (1)
Adj. bal. 4,500	

Wages Payable (L)
	0 Unadj. bal.
	600 (5)
	600 Adj. bal.

Fees Revenue (R)
	150,000 Unadj. bal.
	3,000 (4)
	153,000 Adj. bal.

Supplies (A)
Unadj. bal. 31,300	
	25,000 (2)
Adj. bal. 6,300	

Rent Payable (L)
	0 Unadj. bal.
	2,000 (6)
	2,000 Adj. bal.

Insurance Expense (E)
Unadj. bal. 0	
(1) 1,500	
Adj. bal. 1,500	

Equipment (A)
Unadj. bal. 270,000	
Adj. bal. 270,000	

Supplies Expenses (E)
Unadj. bal. 0	
(2) 25,000	
Adj. bal. 25,000	

Accumulated Depreciation—Equipment (XA)
	60,000 Unadj. bal.
	30,000 (3)
	90,000 Adj. bal.

Depreciation Expense (E)
Unadj. bal. 0	
(3) 30,000	
Adj. bal. 30,000	

Rent Expense (E)
Unadj. bal. 22,000	
(6) 2,000	
Adj. bal. 24,000	

Wages Expense (E)
Unadj. bal. 58,000	
(5) 600	
Adj. bal. 58,600	

Assets = $201,000 = Liabilities = $6,700 + Equity = $194,300

d.

ATWELL LABORATORIES, INC.
Adjusted Trial Balance
June 30

	Debits	Credits
Cash	$ 1,000	
Accounts receivable	9,200	
Prepaid insurance	4,500	
Supplies	6,300	
Equipment	270,000	
Accumulated depreciation—equipment		$ 90,000
Accounts payable		3,100
Rent payable		2,000
Wages payable		600
Contract liability		1,000
Fees revenue		153,000
Wages expense	58,600	
Rent expense	24,000	
Insurance expense	1,500	
Supplies expense	25,000	
Depreciation expense	30,000	
Common stock		120,400
Retained earnings		60,000
Totals	$430,100	$430,100

Review 3-3

ATWELL LABORATORIES, INC.
Balance Sheet
June 30

Assets			Liabilities	
Cash		$ 1,000	Accounts payable	$ 3,100
Accounts receivable		9,200	Contract liability	1,000
Prepaid insurance		4,500	Wages payable	600
Supplies		6,300	Rent payable	2,000
Total current assets		21,000	Total current liabilities	6,700
Equipment, original cost	$270,000		**Equity**	
Less accumulated depreciation	90,000	180,000	Common stock	120,400
			Retained earnings	73,900
Total assets		$201,000	Totals liabilities and equity	$201,000

ATWELL LABORATORIES, INC.
Income Statement
For Year Ended June 30

Fees revenue		$153,000
Expenses		
Insurance expense	$ 1,500	
Supplies expense	25,000	
Depreciation expense	30,000	
Rent expense	24,000	
Wages expense	58,600	
Total expense		139,100
Net income		$ 13,900

ATWELL LABORATORIES, INC.
Statement of Stockholders' Equity
For Year Ended June 30

	Common Stock	Retained Earnings	Total
Balance at June 30, prior year	$120,400	$60,000	$180,400
Net Income	—	13,900	13,900
Balance at June 30, current year	$120,400	$73,900	$194,300

Atwell's statement of stockholders' equity is much simpler than the usual statement because we have focused on the adjustment and closing process. In doing so, we did not consider additional activities in which corporations commonly engage, such as paying dividends, issuing stock, and repurchasing stock. (Requirements did not ask for a statement of cash flows. The next chapter is devoted to the statement of cash flows.)

Review 3-4

a.

Retained earnings (–SE)	139,100	
Insurance expense (–E)		1,500
Supplies expense (–E)		25,000
Depreciation expense (–E)		30,000
Rent expense (–E)		24,000
Wages expense (–E)		58,600
Fees revenue (–R)	153,000	
Retained earnings (+SE)		153,000

b.

General Ledger		
Assets =	**Liabilities** +	**Equity**

Cash (A) (+/−)
| Unadj. bal. | 1,000 | |
| Adj. bal. | 1,000 | |

Accounts Payable (L) (−/+)
| | | 3,100 | Unadj. bal. |
| | | 3,100 | Adj. bal. |

Common Stock (SE) (−/+)
| | | 120,400 | Unadj. bal. |
| | | 120,400 | Adj. bal. |

Accounts Receivable (A) (+/−)
| Unadj. bal. | 9,200 | |
| Adj. bal. | 9,200 | |

Contract Liability (L) (−/+)
		4,000	Unadj. bal.
(4)	3,000		
		1,000	Adj. bal.

Retained Earnings (SE) (−/+)
		60,000	Unadj. bal.
(a)	139,100	153,000	(b)
		73,900	Adj. bal.

Prepaid Insurance (A) (+/−)
Unadj. bal.	6,000		
		1,500	(1)
Adj. bal.	4,500		

Wages Payable (L) (−/+)
		0	Unadj. bal.
		600	(5)
		600	Adj. bal.

Fees Revenue (R) (−/+)
		150,000	Unadj. bal.
(b)	153,000	3,000	(4)
		0	Adj. bal.

Supplies (A) (+/−)
Unadj. bal.	31,300		
		25,000	(2)
Adj. bal.	6,300		

Rent Payable (L) (−/+)
		0	Unadj. bal.
		2,000	(6)
		2,000	Adj. bal.

Insurance Expense (E) (+/−)
Unadj. bal.	0		
(1)	1,500	1,500	(a)
Adj. bal.	0		

Equipment (A) (+/−)
| Unadj. bal. | 270,000 | |
| Adj. bal. | 270,000 | |

Supplies Expense (E) (+/−)
Unadj. bal.	0		
(2)	25,000	25,000	(a)
Adj. bal.	0		

Accumulated Depreciation—Equipment (XA) (−/+)
		60,000	Unadj. bal.
		30,000	(3)
		90,000	Adj. bal.

Depreciation Expense (E) (+/−)
Unadj. bal.	0		
(3)	30,000	30,000	(a)
Adj. bal.	0		

Rent Expense (E) (+/−)
Unadj. bal.	22,000		
(6)	2,000	24,000	(a)
Adj. bal.	0		

Wages Expense (E) (+/−)
Unadj. bal.	58,000		
(5)	600	58,600	(a)
Adj. bal.	0		

Assets = $201,000 = **Liabilities = $6,700** + **Equity = $194,300**

Review 3-5

a. $182,000   *b.* $17,500   *c.* $170,000   *d.* $3,000

Chapter 4
Reporting and Analyzing Cash Flows

LEARNING OBJECTIVES

LO4-1 Explain the purpose of the statement of cash flows and classify cash transactions by type of business activity: operating, investing, or financing.

LO4-2 Construct the operating activities section of the statement of cash flows using the direct method.

LO4-3 Reconcile cash flows from operations to net income and use the indirect method to compute operating cash flows.

LO4-4 Construct the investing and financing activities sections of the statement of cash flows.

LO4-5 Examine the sale of investing assets and the disclosure of noncash activities.

LO4-6 Compute and interpret ratios that reflect a company's liquidity and solvency using information reported in the statement of cash flows.

LO4-7 Appendix 4A: Use a spreadsheet to construct the statement of cash flows.

Road Map

LO	Learning Objective | Topics	Page	eLecture	Review	Assignments
LO4-1	Explain the purpose of the statement of cash flows and classify cash transactions by type of business activity: operating, investing, or financing.	4-3	e4-1	R4–1	M4-21, M4-22, M4-23, M4-24, M4-29, C4-58, C4-59
LO4-2	Construct the operating activities section of the statement of cash flows using the direct method.	4-7	e4-2	R4–2	M4-25, M4-27, M4-30, M4-31, E4-34, E4-38, E4-41, E4-43, E4-44, P4-47, P4-49, P4-51, P4-53, C4-59
LO4-3	Reconcile cash flows from operations to net income and use the indirect method to compute operating cash flows.	4-17	e4-3	R4–3	M4-21, M4-23, M4-25, M4-26, M4-27, M4-28, M4-29, E4-35, E4-42, E4-44, P4-45, P4-46, P4-48, P4-50, P4-51, P4-52, P4-53, P4-54, P4-55, P4-56, C4-57, C4-58, C4-59, DA4-1
LO4-4	Construct the investing and financing activities sections of the statement of cash flows.	4-19	e4-4	R4–4	M4-21, E4-39, P4-46, P4-48, P4-50, P4-51, P4-52, P4-53, P4-54, P4-55, P4-56, C4-57, C4-58, C4-59
LO4-5	Examine the sale of investing assets and the disclosure of noncash activities.	4-23	e4-5	R4–5	M4-24, E4-36, E4-37, E4-38, E4-39, P4-48, P4-50, P4-52, P4-53, P4-54, P4-55, C4-57, C4-58, C4-59
LO4-6	Compute and interpret ratios that reflect a company's liquidity and solvency using information reported in the statement of cash flows.	4-29	e4-6	R4–6	E4-32, E4-33, E4-35, E4-43, P4-46, P4-48, P4-50, P4-52, P4-55, P4-56, C4-59, DA4-2
LO4-7	Appendix 4A: Use a spreadsheet to construct the statement of cash flows.	4-33	e4-7	R4–7	E4-42, P4-55

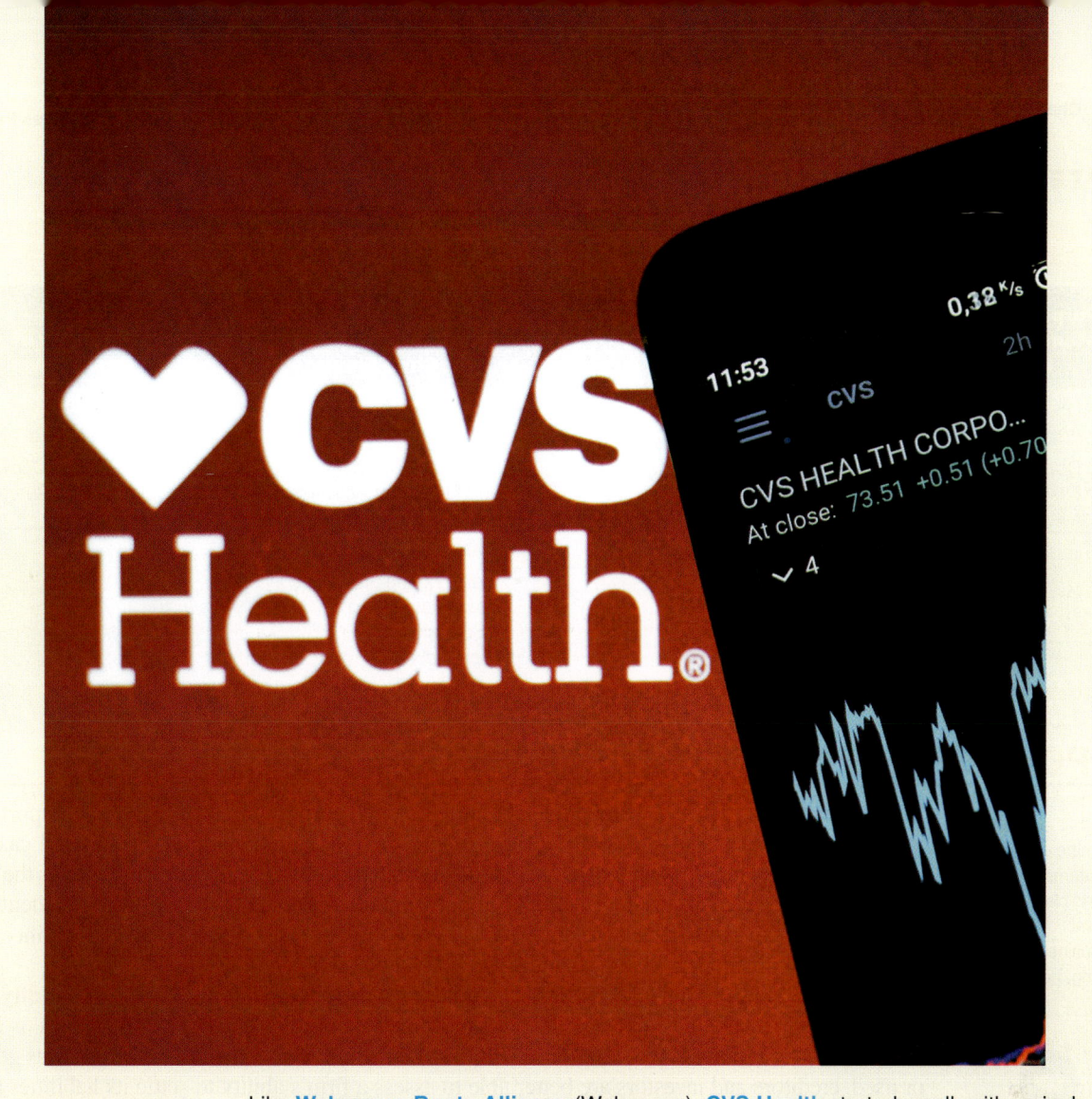

CVS HEALTH CORPORATION

www.cvshealth.com

Like **Walgreens Boots Alliance** (Walgreens), **CVS Health** started small, with a single store in Lowell, Massachusetts, in 1963, where CVS stood for Consumer Value Stores. The company soon grew in number of stores and expanded beyond health and beauty products to include pharmaceuticals. CVS made frequent use of acquisitions to increase the number of stores and the geographic reach of the company. In its 2020 annual report, CVS Health reports that it had more than 9,900 retail locations and almost 300,000 colleagues working at the company.

CVS Health operates at the intersection of two industries—retail and healthcare. In retail, almost all companies are affected by the rapid growth of online retailers and the decline in "bricks and mortar" businesses. And, the political pressure on healthcare costs affects an assortment of parties besides the ultimate consumer—pharmacies, insurance companies, pharmacy benefit managers, and pharmaceutical companies. Over time, CVS Health has expanded beyond its pharmacies into pharmacy benefit management to streamline costs, to provide better service to customers, and to maintain market competitiveness. In November 2018, CVS Health expanded its scope further by acquiring an insurance company, **Aetna, Inc.** The Aetna acquisition further expanded CVS Health's role in the pharmacy market, giving it an opportunity to improve operations and customer service. In addition, analysts suggest the merger provides some protection against online retail companies who might enter the pharmacy market.

However, that acquisition came at a cost, in the form of increased debt service costs and dividends to an increased number of outstanding shareholders. Where do we look to find out how successful CVS Health has been in meeting the challenges of these cost increases in the pandemic environment? For CVS Health, the 2020 statement of cash flows discloses that the company's increased cash inflows enabled it to maintain its dividend and reduce its outstanding debt by a substantial amount.

As we will discover in this chapter, a business must make sure that its cash inflows are adequate to fund new investments, meet obligations to creditors as they come due, and pay dividends to shareholders, in addition to meeting the challenges posed by unforeseen events like the COVID-19 pandemic. Even a profitable company can fail if it does not have a healthy cash flow. We will also discover why it is important to look at the statement of cash flows along with the income statement and balance sheet when trying to assess the financial health of a company.

Sources: CVS Health Corporation, Form 10-K 2020; www.cvshealth.com/about/company-history; "Leveraging cash flow's effect on valuation," *CFO Dive*, cfodive.com May 3, 2021.

CHAPTER ORGANIZATION

Reporting and Analyzing Cash Flows

Purpose of the Statement of Cash Flows
- What Do We Mean by Cash?
- What Does a Statement of Cash Flows Look Like?

Framework for the Statement of Cash Flows
- Operating Activities
- Investing Activities
- Financing Activities
- Usefulness of Classifications

Preparing the Statement of Cash Flows
- Cash Flows from Operating Activities
- Cash Flows from Investing and Financing Activities
- Additional Detail in the Statement of Cash Flows
- Preparing the Statement of Cash Flows Using a Spreadsheet (Appendix 4A)

Analysis of Cash Flows
- Operating Cash Flow to Current Liabilities
- Operating Cash Flow to Capital Expenditures
- Free Cash Flow

PURPOSE OF THE STATEMENT OF CASH FLOWS

LO4-1 Explain the purpose of the statement of cash flows and classify cash transactions by type of business activity: operating, investing, or financing.

In addition to the balance sheet and the income statement, corporations are required to report a statement of cash flows. The **statement of cash flows** tells us how a company generated cash (cash inflows) and how it used cash (cash outflows). The statement of cash flows complements the income statement and the balance sheet by providing information that neither the income statement nor the balance sheet can provide. For instance, slower collection of receivables doesn't affect income, but it does reduce the amount of cash coming into the company.

Understanding the statement of cash flows helps us understand trends in a firm's **liquidity** (ability to pay near-term liabilities and take advantage of investment opportunities), and it helps us assess a firm's **solvency** (ability to pay long-term liabilities). With information about how cash was generated or used, creditors and investors are better able to assess a firm's ability to settle its liabilities and pay dividends to shareholders. A firm's need for outside financing is also better evaluated when using cash flow data. Over time, the statement of cash flows permits users to observe and assess management's investing and financing policies. For example, a business that is not generating enough cash flow internally, i.e., from operations, must get cash from borrowing, issuing shares, or selling off its assets.

The statement of cash flows also provides information about a firm's ability to generate sufficient amounts of cash to respond to unanticipated needs and opportunities. Information about past cash flows, particularly cash flows from operations, helps in assessing a company's financial flexibility. An evaluation of a firm's ability to survive an unexpected drop in demand, for example, should include a review of its past cash flows from operations. The larger these cash flows, the greater is the firm's ability to withstand adverse changes in economic conditions.

So, whether we are a potential investor, loan officer, future employee, supplier, or customer, we greatly benefit from an understanding of the cash inflows and outflows of a company.

What Do We Mean by "CASH"?

FYI A cash equivalent is a short-term, highly liquid investment that is easily converted to cash and is close enough to maturity that its market value is not sensitive to interest rate changes.

The statement of cash flows explains the change in a firm's cash *and* cash equivalents. **Cash equivalents** are short-term, highly liquid investments that are (1) easily convertible into a known cash amount and (2) close enough to maturity that their market value is not sensitive to interest rate changes (generally, investments with remaining maturities of three months or less). Treasury bills, commercial paper (short-term notes issued by corporations), and money market funds are typical examples of cash equivalents.

In some situations, a portion of a company's cash balances may not be immediately available for use. For instance, a lender might require a borrowing company to keep a minimum balance of cash. Such restricted cash is not included in cash and cash equivalents on the balance sheet, but rather in a separate asset account called **restricted cash**, with a note describing the restrictions. For instance, CVS Health reports a balance of cash and cash equivalents of $7,854 million in its balance sheet, plus another $276 million in restricted cash that is included in "other assets."

However, the statement of cash flows describes the total flows of cash, including unrestricted cash and cash equivalents plus restricted cash and cash equivalents, as can be seen at the bottom of **Exhibit 4.1**. The addition of cash equivalents is done because the purchase and sale of investments in cash equivalents are considered to be part of a firm's overall management of cash rather than a source or use of cash. As statement users evaluate and project cash flows, for example, it should not matter whether the cash is readily available in a cash register or safe, deposited in a bank account, or invested in cash equivalents. Consequently, transfers back and forth between a firm's cash on hand, its bank accounts, and its investments in cash equivalents are not treated as cash inflows and cash outflows in its statement of cash flows. When discussing the statement of cash flows, managers generally use the word *cash* rather than the phrases cash, cash equivalents, and restricted cash. We will follow the same practice.

What Does a Statement of Cash Flows Look Like?

Exhibit 4.1 reproduces CVS Health Corporation's statement of cash flows for the fiscal year ended on December 31, 2020. During this fiscal year, CVS Health generated $15,865 million in cash from its operations.

Investing activities used $5,534 million in cash, and financing activities used another $8,155 million of cash. Over the entire year, the company's cash balance increased by $2,176 million and ended the year at $8,130 million on December 31, 2020.

EXHIBIT 4.1 — CVS Health Corporation Statement of Cash Flows

CVS HEALTH CORPORATION
Consolidated Statement of Cash Flows
For the Fiscal Year Ended December 31, 2020

In millions

Cash flows from operating activities	
Cash receipts from customers	$264,327
Cash paid for inventory and prescriptions dispensed by retail network pharmacies	(158,636)
Insurance benefits paid	(55,124)
Cash paid to other suppliers and employees	(29,763)
Interest and investment income received	894
Interest paid	(2,904)
Income taxes paid	(2,929)
Net cash provided by operating activities	15,865
Cash flows from investing activities	
Proceeds from sales and maturities of investments	6,467
Purchases of investments	(9,639)
Purchases of property and equipment	(2,437)
Proceeds from sale-leaseback transactions	101
Acquisitions (net of cash acquired)	(866)
Proceeds from sale of subsidiaries and other assets	840
Net cash used in investing activities	(5,534)
Cash flows from financing activities	
Proceeds from issuance of long-term debt	9,958
Repayments of long-term debt	(15,631)
Derivative settlements	(7)
Dividends paid	(2,624)
Proceeds from exercise of stock options	264
Payments for taxes related to net share settlement of equity awards	(88)
Other	(27)
Net cash used in financing activities	(8,155)
Net increase in cash, cash equivalents, and restricted cash	2,176
Cash, cash equivalents, and restricted cash at the beginning of the period	5,954
Cash, cash equivalents, and restricted cash at the end of the period	**$ 8,130**

FRAMEWORK FOR THE STATEMENT OF CASH FLOWS

The statement of cash flows classifies cash receipts and payments into one of three categories: operating activities, investing activities, or financing activities. Classifying cash flows into these categories identifies the effects on cash of each of the major activities of a firm. The combined effects on cash of all three categories explain the net change in cash for the period. The period's net change in cash is then reconciled with the beginning and ending amounts of cash.

Operating Activities

FYI Cash flows from operating activities (cash flows from operations) refer to cash inflows and outflows directly related to the firm's primary day-to-day business activities.

A company's income statement mainly reflects the transactions and events that constitute its operating activities. The cash effects of these operating transactions and events determine the net cash flow from operating activities. The usual focus of a firm's **operating activities** is on selling goods or rendering services, but the activities are defined broadly enough to include any cash receipts or payments that are not classified as investing or financing activities. For example, CVS Health Corporation reports cash received from customers and for interest. The company paid cash to suppliers (of pharmaceuticals and other items) and employees and tax authorities and to lenders for interest. The following are examples of cash inflows and outflows relating to operating activities.

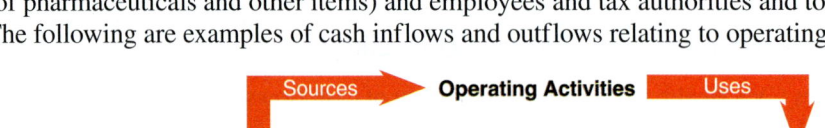

Sources → Operating Activities ← Uses

Cash Inflows
1. Cash receipts from customers for sales made or services rendered (or in anticipation of future deliveries of goods or services).
2. Cash receipts of interest and dividends.[1]
3. Other cash receipts that are not related to investing or financing activities, such as rentals, lawsuit settlements, and refunds received from suppliers.

Cash Outflows
1. Cash payments to employees or suppliers.
2. Cash payments to purchase inventories.
3. Cash payments of interest to creditors.[1]
4. Cash payments of taxes to government.
5. Other cash payments that are not related to investing or financing activities, such as contributions to charity and lawsuit settlements.

Investing Activities

FYI Cash flows from investing activities are cash inflows and outflows related to acquiring or selling productive assets and the investments in securities of other entities.

A firm's transactions involving (1) the acquisition and disposal of property, plant, and equipment (PPE) assets and intangible assets, (2) the purchase and sale of government securities and securities of other companies, including stocks, bonds, and other securities that are not classified as cash equivalents, and (3) the lending and subsequent collection of money constitute the basic components of its **investing activities**. The related cash receipts and payments appear in the investing activities section of the statement of cash flows and, if material in amount, inflows and outflows should be reported separately (not as a net amount). Examples of these cash flows follow:

Sources → Investing Activities ← Uses

Cash Inflows
1. Cash receipts from sales of property, plant, and equipment (PPE) assets and intangible assets.
2. Cash receipts from sales of investments in government securities and securities of other companies (including divestitures).
3. Cash receipts from repayments of loans by borrowers.

Cash Outflows
1. Cash payments to purchase property, plant, and equipment (PPE) assets and intangible assets.
2. Cash payments to purchase government securities and securities of other companies (including acquisitions).
3. Cash payments made to lend money to borrowers.

Financing Activities

FYI Cash flows from financing activities are cash inflows and outflows related to external sources of financing (owners and nonowners).

A firm engages in **financing activities** when it receives cash from shareholders, returns cash to shareholders, borrows from creditors, and repays amounts borrowed. Cash flows related to these

---

[1] Many financial statement readers believe that interest and dividends received should be considered cash inflows from investing activities and that interest payments should be considered cash outflows from financing activities. In fact, when the reporting standard was passed by the Financial Accounting Standards Board, three of the seven members dissented from the standard for this reason (among others). The majority based their decision on "the view that, in general, cash flows from operating activities should reflect the cash effects of transactions and other events that enter into the determination of net income." (Statement of Financial Accounting Standards No. 95, paragraph 88.)

transactions are reported in the financing activities section of the statement of cash flows and again, inflows and outflows should be reported separately (not as a net amount) if material. Examples of these cash flows follow:

Sources → **Financing Activities** ← Uses

Cash Inflows
1. Cash receipts from issuances of common stock and preferred stock and from sales of treasury stock.
2. Cash receipts from issuances of bonds payable, mortgage notes payable, and other notes payable.

Cash Outflows
1. Cash payments to acquire treasury stock.
2. Cash payments of dividends.
3. Cash payments to settle outstanding bonds payable, mortgage notes payable, and other notes payable.

Paying cash to settle such obligations as accounts payable, trade notes payable, wages payable, interest payable, and income tax payable are operating activities, not financing activities, because they are related to the daily operations of the company such as buying and selling inventory. Also, cash received as interest and dividends and cash paid as interest (not dividends) are classified as cash flows from operating activities. However, cash paid to shareholders as dividends is classified as cash flows from financing activities.

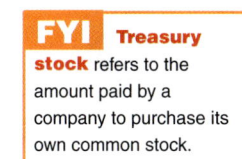

> **FYI** **Treasury stock** refers to the amount paid by a company to purchase its own common stock.

A GLOBAL PERSPECTIVE

Under U.S. accounting principles, payments for interest expense and receipts for interest and dividend income are considered part of cash from operations. International Financial Reporting Standards allow companies to report interest payments as part of either operating activities or financing activities and to report interest and dividend receipts as part of either operating activities or investing activities.

IFRS

Usefulness of Classifications

The classification of cash flows into three categories of activities helps financial statement users interpret cash flow data. To illustrate, assume that Faultless, Inc., Peerless Co., and Dauntless Ltd. each reports a $100,000 cash increase during the current year. Information from their current-year statements of cash flows is summarized in **Exhibit 4.2**.

EXHIBIT 4.2 Summary Information for Three Competitors

	Faultless	Peerless	Dauntless
Net cash provided by operating activities	$100,000	$ 0	$ 0
Cash flows from investing activities			
Sale of property, plant, and equipment	0	100,000	0
Cash flows from financing activities			
Issuance of notes payable	0	0	100,000
Net increase in cash	$100,000	$100,000	$100,000

One of the keys to evaluating a company's worth is estimating its future cash inflows based on the information available. Companies that can generate a stream of future cash inflows are worth more than those with a single cash inflow. In **Exhibit 4.2**, each company's net cash increase was the same, but the source of the increase varied by company. This variation affects the analysis of the cash flow data, particularly for potential creditors who must evaluate the likelihood of obtaining repayment in the future for any funds loaned to the company. Based only on these cash flow data, a potential creditor would feel more comfortable lending money to Faultless than to either Peerless or Dauntless. This choice is because Faultless' cash increase came from its operating activities, and operations tend to be continuing. Both Peerless and Dauntless could only break even on their cash flows from operations. Also, Peerless' cash increase came from the sale of property, plant, and equipment (PPE) assets—a source of cash that is not likely to recur regularly. Dauntless' cash increase came entirely from borrowed funds. This means Dauntless faces additional cash burdens in the future when the interest and principal payments on the note payable become due.

> **BUSINESS INSIGHT**
>
> **Objectivity of Cash** Usefulness of financial statements is enhanced when the underlying data are objective and verifiable. Measuring cash and the changes in cash are among the most objective measurements that accountants make. Thus, the statement of cash flows is arguably the most objective financial statement. This characteristic of the statement of cash flows is welcomed by those investors and creditors interested in evaluating the quality of a firm's income.

Review 4-1 LO4-1 — Classifying Cash Flows

Assume **CVS Health Corporation** executed the following transactions during the year. Indicate whether the transaction creates a cash inflow (In) or outflow (Out). Next, determine how each item should be classified in the statement of cash flows: an operating activity (O), an investing activity (I), or a financing activity (F). For example: $50,000 cash received for the sale of snack foods. Answer: In/O

1. ____ $250,000 cash paid to purchase a warehouse
2. ____ $120,000 cash paid for interest on a loan
3. ____ $850,000 cash paid to employees as wages
4. ____ $20,000,000 cash raised through the issuance of stock
5. ____ $450,000 cash paid to the government for taxes
6. ____ $350,000 cash received as part of a settlement of a legal case
7. ____ $630,000 cash received from the sale of long-term securities
8. ____ $75,000 cash received from the sale of used office equipment
9. ____ $500,000 cash dividend paid to shareholders
10. ____ $90,000 cash received as interest earned on a government bond

Solution on p. 4-60.

PREPARING THE STATEMENT OF CASH FLOWS—OPERATING ACTIVITIES

LO4-2 Construct the operating activities section of the statement of cash flows using the direct method.

In Chapter 3's **Exhibit 3.12**, we presented a statement of cash flows for Natural Beauty Supply (hereafter, NBS) for the month of December 2021. This statement is reproduced in **Exhibit 4.3**. The statement details how NBS' cash balance decreases by $1,275 in December, from $8,100 to $6,825. The statement was prepared by examining all of the cash transactions that occurred during the month and then grouping them according to the type of activity each represents—operating, investing, or financing—as illustrated in the cash T-account below. Transaction (17) was the loan, so that goes in the financing activity section; transaction (18) was the purchase of fixtures and equipment and belongs in the investing activity section; and so on.

	+ Cash (A)			−
	Beg. bal.	8,100		
Operating activities	(21)	8,500	700	(19)
	(23)	1,200	3,300	(20)
	(25)	3,200	1,625	(24)
			1,500	(27)
Investing activities			18,000	(18)
Financing activities	(17)	11,000	50	(28)
	End. bal.	6,825		

An alternative presentation of the transactions affecting cash can be organized by activity using the Financial Statement Effects Template (FSET). Those items involving cash are gathered inside the red box and then categorized according to the type of activity—operating, investing, or financing—that generated them.

Transaction	Balance Sheet					Income Statement		
	Cash asset +	Noncash asset =	Liabil- ities +	Contrib. Capital +	Earned Capital	Revenue -	Expense =	Net income
Beg. Bal.	8,100 Cash							
Operating activities								
(19)	−700 Cash	=			−700 Retained Earnings	−	+700 Advertising Expense	= −700
(20)	−3,300 Cash	=	−3,300 Accts Payable			−	=	
(21)	+8,500 Cash	=			+8,500 Retained earnings	+8,500 Sales Revenue −	=	+8,500
(23)	+1,200 Cash	=	+1,200 Gift Card Liability			−	=	
(24)	−1,625 Cash	=			−1,625 Retained Earnings	−	+1,625 Wage Expense	= −1,625
(25)	+3,200 Cash	−3,200 Accts Receivable =				−	=	
(27)	−1,500 Cash	=			−1,500 Retained Earnings	−	+1,500 Rent Expense	= −1,500
Investing activities								
(18)	−18,000 Cash	+18,000 Fixtures and Equipment =				−	=	
Financing activities								
(17)	+11,000 Cash	=	+11,000 Notes Payable			−	=	
(28)	−50 Cash	=			−50 Retained Earnings	−	=	
End. Bal.	6,825 Cash							

Whether one uses T-accounts or the FSET, the approach to preparing the statement of cash flows is straightforward and doesn't require any additional bookkeeping steps, other than those introduced in Chapters 2 and 3.

However, for many companies, the number and variety of cash transactions that occur each period are so large that such an approach is often impractical. A company with revenues and assets and liabilities in the billions of dollars, like CVS Health, for example, has thousands of cash transactions each day. It has accounts with several different banks in numerous locations and regularly transfers cash from one account to another or back and forth between cash accounts and cash equivalents, as needed. For such a company, simply listing the cash transactions is not practical.

An alternative to this approach of compiling a list of cash flows is to reconcile the information in the income statement and balance sheet to prepare the statement of cash flows. The statement of cash flows complements the balance sheet and the income statement. The balance sheet details the financial position of the company at a given point in time. Comparing two balance sheets prepared at the beginning and at the end of a period reveals changes that transpired during the accounting period. These changes are explained by the income statement and the statement of cash flows. Both the income statement and the statement of cash flows summarize the events and transactions of the business during the accounting period, and as such, provide complementary descriptions of a company's activities. While the statement of cash flows provides information that is not explicitly found in either of the other two statements, it must articulate with the balance sheet and income statement to present a complete picture of company activities.

EXHIBIT 4.3 — NBS Statement of Cash Flows (Direct Method)

NATURAL BEAUTY SUPPLY, INC.
Statement of Cash Flows
For the Month Ended December 31, 2021

Cash Flows from Operating Activities		
Cash received from customers (entries 21, 23, 25)	$12,900	
Cash paid for inventory (entry 20)	(3,300)	
Cash paid for wages (entry 24)	(1,625)	
Cash paid for rent (entry 27)	(1,500)	
Cash paid for advertising (entry 19)	(700)	
Net cash provided by operating activities		$ 5,775
Cash Flows from Investing Activities		
Cash paid for fixtures and equipment (entry 18)	(18,000)	
Net cash used for investing activities		(18,000)
Cash Flows from Financing Activities		
Cash received from loans (entry 17)	11,000	
Cash paid for dividends (entry 28)	(50)	
Net cash provided by financing activities		10,950
Net change in cash		(1,275)
Cash balance, November 30, 2021		8,100
Cash balance, December 31, 2021		$ 6,825

One of the characteristics of the accounting system is that when an entry changes Net Income without a change in Cash, then it must change another account on the balance sheet. And, when an operating cash flow occurs without a change in Net Income, then there must be a change in some other balance sheet account. Therefore, we can start with information from the income statement and then use the balance sheet (and some additional information) to prepare the statement of cash flows. **Exhibit 4.4** presents the income statement and comparative balance sheets for NBS. We will use the data from these financial statements to prepare NBS' reconciliation of Net Income to Cash from Operating Activities.

EXHIBIT 4.4 — NBS Income Statement and Comparative Balance Sheet

NATURAL BEAUTY SUPPLY
Income Statement
For the Month Ended December 31, 2021

Sales revenue		$13,900
Cost of goods sold		8,000
Gross profit		5,900
Operating expenses:		
Rent	$1,500	
Wages	2,105	
Advertising	700	
Depreciation	375	
Insurance	140	
Total operating expenses		4,820
Operating income		1,080
Interest income		30
Interest expense		(110)
Income before taxes		1,000
Income tax expense		350
Net income		$ 650

NATURAL BEAUTY SUPPLY
Comparative Balance Sheets

	12/31/21	11/30/21
Assets:		
Cash	$ 6,825	$ 8,100
Other receivables	30	
Accounts receivable	2,250	950
Inventory	7,300	11,300
Prepaid insurance	1,540	1,680
Security deposit	2,000	2,000
Fixtures and equipment	18,000	
Accumulated depreciation	(375)	
Total assets	$37,570	$24,030
Liabilities:		
Accounts payable	$ 4,400	$ 3,700
Gift card liability	600	300
Wages payable	480	
Interest payable	110	
Taxes payable	350	
Notes payable	11,000	
Stockholders' equity:		
Common stock	20,000	20,000
Retained earnings	630	30
Total liabilities and equity	$37,570	$24,030

Converting Revenues and Expenses to Cash Flows from Operating Activities

We know from Chapter 3 that net income consists of revenues and expenses. We also know that these are often not cash transactions. For example, sales on account will be considered revenue but are not cash inflows until collected. Depreciation is an expense but is not a current-period cash outflow. (The cash outflow presumably occurred when the underlying asset was acquired in a past investing transaction.) We can compute cash flow from operating activities by making adjustments to the revenues and expenses presented in the income statement. The adjustment amounts represent differences between revenues, expenses, gains, and losses recorded under accrual accounting and the related operating cash inflows and outflows. The adjustments are added to or subtracted from net income, depending on whether the related cash flow is more or less than the accrual amount.

Convert Sales Revenues to Cash Received from Customers To illustrate this adjustment procedure for revenues and cash receipts from customers, consider the Chapter 3 transactions and adjusting entry that occurred for NBS in December 2021:

(21) Dec. 20 During the month of December, NBS sold products costing $5,000 to retail customers for $8,500 cash.
(22) Dec. — During the month of December, sales to wholesale customers totaled $4,500 for merchandise that had cost $3,000. Instead of paying cash, wholesale customers are required to pay for the merchandise within ten working days.
(23) Dec. — $1,200 of gift certificates were sold during the month of December. Each gift certificate entitles the recipient to a one-hour consultation on the use of NBS' products.
(25) Dec. — During the month of December, NBS received $3,200 in cash from wholesale customers for products that had been delivered earlier.
(a) Dec. 31 Gift certificates worth $900 were redeemed during the month.

We enter the revenue and cash receipts implications of each of these into the Financial Statement Effects Template (FSET) on the following page. Whenever there is a difference between the revenue recognized and the cash received, that difference affects an operating asset (accounts receivable) or an operating liability (gift card liability). For instance, in transaction (22a), NBS recognizes credit sales revenue. That is, revenue increases, but cash does not, and the accounting equation is kept by increasing accounts receivable, an operating asset. When NBS received cash in advance of revenue recognition, as in transaction (23), the balancing entry is in gift card liability, an operating liability. We will find that when an operating transaction affects cash or income—but not both—the operating assets and operating liabilities serve as a temporary buffer between the two.

The total of each of these columns is given in the last row, and because each individual entry is balanced, the totals are balanced.

Transaction	Balance Sheet					Income Statement		
	Cash Asset	+ Noncash Assets	= Liabilities	+ Contrib. Capital	+ Earned Capital	Revenues	− Expenses	= Net Income
(21a) Sell $8,500 of products for cash.	+8,500 Cash		=		+8,500 Retained Earnings	+8,500 Sales Revenue	−	= +8,500
(22a) Sell $4,500 of products on account.		+4,500 Accounts Receivable	=		+4,500 Retained Earnings	+4,500 Sales Revenue	−	= +4,500
(23) Sell gift certificates for $1,200 cash.	+1,200 Cash		= +1,200 Gift Card Liability				−	=
(25) Receive $3,200 cash from customers who purchased on credit.	+3,200 Cash	−3,200 Accounts Receivable	=				−	=
(a) Adjusting entry for gift certificates redeemed in December.			= −900 Gift Card Liability		+900 Retained Earnings	+900 Sales Revenue	−	= +900
Total changes	+12,900 Cash	+1,300 Accounts Receivable	= +300 Gift Card Liability	+ 0	+ +13,900 Retained Earnings	+13,900 Sales Revenue	− 0	= +13,900

We can see that December's revenue was $13,900, and NBS collected $12,900 from customers during the month. Accounts receivable increased by $1,300 over the month, and gift card liability increased by $300. The FSET maintains the accounting equation at every entry, so we know that the equality will hold for the totals in the last row.

$$\underset{\$12,900}{\text{Cash flow (receipts)}} + \underset{\$1,300}{\text{Change in accounts receivable}} = \underset{\$300}{\text{Change in gift card liability}} + \underset{\$13,900}{\text{Net income (Sales revenue)}}$$

And this relationship can be rewritten as the following:

$$\underset{\$12,900}{\text{Cash flow}} = \underset{\$13,900}{\text{Net income}} - \underset{\$1,300}{\text{Change in accounts receivable}} + \underset{\$300}{\text{Change in gift card liability}}$$

So, when we start with net income and then subtract the change in accounts receivable and add the change in gift card liability, we convert the revenues in net income into the cash receipts from customers needed for cash from operations.

Convert Cost of Goods Sold to Cash Paid for Merchandise Purchased As a second illustration, let's examine the December 2021 transactions involving NBS' inventory and its suppliers (**Exhibit 3.3** in Chapter 3).

(20) Dec. 20 NBS paid $3,300 cash to its suppliers in partial payment for the delivery of inventory in November.

(21) Dec. — During the month of December, NBS sold products costing $5,000 to retail customers for $8,500 cash.

(22) Dec. — During the month of December, sales to wholesale customers totaled $4,500 for merchandise that had cost $3,000. Instead of paying cash, wholesale customers are required to pay for the merchandise within ten working days.

(26) Dec. 28 NBS purchased and received $4,000 of inventory on account.

When a company like NBS purchases inventory for future sale, we know that the purchase will be followed by two events in the normal course of business. One event is that NBS will have to pay the supplier in cash according to the terms of the purchase, resulting in a cash outflow. The other event is the sale of that inventory to a customer of NBS, resulting in a cost of goods sold expense on the income statement. But these two events do not necessarily occur at the same point in time. As we enter these events into the FSET, we see that the differences between cash payments for inventory and cost of goods sold expense are buffered by inventory, an operating asset, and accounts payable, an operating liability.

Transaction	Cash Asset	+	Noncash Assets	=	Liabilities	+	Contrib. Capital	+	Earned Capital	Revenues	−	Expenses	=	Net Income
(20) Pay $3,300 cash to suppliers.	−3,300 Cash			=	−3,300 Accounts Payable						−		=	
(21b) Record $5,000 for the cost of merchandise sold in transaction 21a.			−5,000 Inventory	=					−5,000 Retained Earnings		−	+5,000 Cost of Goods Sold	=	−5,000
(22b) Record $3,000 for the cost of merchandise sold in transaction 22a.			−3,000 Inventory	=					−3,000 Retained Earnings		−	+3,000 Cost of Goods Sold	=	−3,000
(26) Purchase $4,000 inventory on account.			+4,000 Inventory	=	+4,000 Accounts Payable						−		=	
Total changes	−3,300 Cash	+	−4,000 Inventory	=	+700 Accounts Payable	+	0	+	−8,000 Retained Earnings	0	−	+8,000 Cost of Goods Sold	=	−8,000

Again, the FSET keeps the accounting equation with every entry, so we know that the total changes in the last row must also conform to the accounting equation.

$$\text{Cash flow (payments)} + \text{Change in inventory} = \text{Change in accounts payable} + \text{Net income (COGS expense)}$$

$$-\$3,300 + -\$4,000 = \$700 + -\$8,000$$

And this relationship can be written as the following:

$$\text{Cash flow} = \text{Net income} - \text{Change in inventory} + \text{Change in accounts payable}$$

$$-\$3,300 = -\$8,000 - (-\$4,000) + \$700$$

The change in inventory is negative for NBS during December 2021, so when we subtract the change in inventory above, we must subtract a negative number, making a positive adjustment. (That is, −(−$4,000) = +$4,000.) And, when we subtract the change in inventory from net income and add the change in accounts payable to net income, we convert the (minus) cost of goods sold expense to the (minus) payments to suppliers we need for the cash from operations.

Stepping back to look at the big picture, we begin to see a pattern. The cash flow effect of an item is equal to its income statement effect, minus the change in any associated operating asset(s) plus the change in any associated operating liability(ies). That pattern can be confirmed as we look at the remaining necessary adjustments.

Convert Wages Expense to Cash Paid to Employees To determine the adjustment needed for transactions involving employees, we look at the two entries from Chapter 3 related to the wages earned and paid during the month of December 2021.

Transaction	Cash Asset	+	Noncash Assets	=	Liabilities	+	Contrib. Capital	+	Earned Capital	Revenues	−	Expenses	=	Net Income
(24) Record $1,625 in wages to employees.	−1,625 Cash			=					−1,625 Retained Earnings		−	+1,625 Wages Expense	=	−1,625
(e) Adjusting entry to record wages earned but not yet paid.				=	+480 Wages Payable				−480 Retained Earnings		−	+480 Wages Expense	=	−480
Total changes	−1,625 Cash	+	0	=	+480 Wages Payable	+	0	+	−2,105 Retained Earnings	0	−	+2,105 Wages Expense	=	−2,105

Using the same approach as above, the FSET tells us the following about the totals:

$$\text{Cash flow (payments)} = \text{Change in wages payable} + \text{Net income (wage expense),}$$

which can be rewritten as

$$\text{Cash flow} = \text{Net income} + \text{Change in wages payable}$$
$$-\$1,625 = -\$2,105 + \$480$$

NBS recorded more wage expense than it paid to its employees, and that additional expense goes into an operating liability, wages payable. If wages payable had decreased over the period, it would imply that NBS had paid more to its employees than they had earned during the period (perhaps because they were owed compensation from a prior period).

Convert Rent Expense to Cash Paid for Rent and Advertising Expense to Cash Paid for Advertising The December 2021 entries for rent and advertising are presented in the FSET below.

Chapter 4 Reporting and Analyzing Cash Flows

Transaction	Balance Sheet					Income Statement		
	Cash Asset	+ Noncash Assets	= Liabilities	+ Contrib. Capital	+ Earned Capital	Revenues	− Expenses	= Net Income
(19) Pay $700 cash for December advertising.	−700 Cash		=		−700 Retained Earnings		− +700 Advertising Expense	= −700
(27) Pay $1,500 rent for December.	−1,500 Cash		=		−1,500 Retained Earnings		− +1,500 Rent Expense	= −1,500
Total changes	−2,200 Cash	+ 0	= 0	+ 0	+ −2,200 Retained Earnings	0	− +2,200 Advertising and Rent Expense	= −2,200

For these items, the amount paid is exactly equal to the amount recorded as expense, so no adjustment is necessary. The amounts included for advertising and rent in the determination of net income are exactly what we want in the cash from operations. If NBS had paid rent in advance or promised to pay later for its advertising, then operating assets and/or liabilities would have been created, and an adjustment would have been necessary (as we see in the case immediately following).

Other Adjustments There are five more items in NBS' income statement that require adjustment to arrive at the amount of cash from operations for the month of December. Four of these items are insurance expense, interest income, interest expense, and income tax expense. These items involved only adjusting entries during the month of December, so there were no cash flows involved, and we present the adjustments in an abbreviated fashion below.

(b) Adjusting entry to record expiration of 1 month of prepaid insurance.		−140 Prepaid insurance	=		−140 Retained Earnings		− +140 Insurance Expense	= −140
Total changes	0 Cash	+ −140 Prepaid Insurance	= 0	+ 0	+ −140 Retained Earnings	0	− +140 Insurance Expense	= −140

Cash flow + Change in prepaid insurance = Net income, or

Cash flow = Net income − Change in prepaid insurance, or

$0 (zero) = −$140 − (−$140)

| (d) Adjusting entry for interest income earned. | | +30 Other Receivables | = | | +30 Retained Earnings | +30 Interest Income | − | = +30 |
| Total changes | 0 Cash | + +30 Other Receivables | = 0 | + 0 | + +30 Retained Earnings | +30 Interest Income | − 0 | = +30 |

Cash flow + Change in other receivables = Net income, or

Cash flow = Net income − Change in other receivables, or

$0 (zero) = $30 − $30

| (f) Adjusting entry to record interest owed but not yet paid. | | | = +110 Interest Payable | | −110 Retained Earnings | | − +110 Interest Expense | = −110 |
| Total changes | 0 Cash | + 0 | = +110 Interest Payable | + 0 | + −110 Retained Earnings | 0 | − +110 Interest Expense | = −110 |

Cash flow = Change in interest payable + Net income, or

Cash flow = Net income + Change in interest payable, or

$0 (zero) = −$110 + $110

Transaction	Balance Sheet						Income Statement		
	Cash Asset +	Noncash Assets −	Contra Assets =	Liabilities +	Contrib. Capital +	Earned Capital	Revenues −	Expenses =	Net Income
(g) Adjusting entry for estimated income tax.			− =	+350 Taxes Payable		−350 Retained Earnings	−	+350 Tax Expense =	−350
Total changes	0 Cash +	0 −	=	+350 Taxes Payable +	0 +	−350 Retained Earnings	0 −	+350 Tax Expense =	−350

$$\text{Cash flow} = \text{Change in taxes payable} + \text{Net income, or}$$
$$\text{Cash flow} = \text{Net income} + \text{Change in taxes payable, or}$$
$$\$0 \text{ (zero)} = -\$350 + \$350$$

Each of the above four items involved only an adjusting entry (i.e., an entry at the end of the fiscal period). Adjusting entries rarely involve cash, so the adjustment simply cancels out the item in the income statement. We will see more examples in later chapters (e.g., write-downs of physical or intangible assets, restructuring charges, etc.).

Eliminate Depreciation Expense and Other Noncash Operating Expenses
NBS recorded an adjusting entry for depreciation at the end of December 2021 for $375. That entry into the FSET was the following.

Transaction	Balance Sheet						Income Statement		
(c) Adjusting entry for depreciation on fixtures and equipment for December.			+375 Accumulated Depreciation =			−375 Retained Earnings	−	+375 Depreciation Expense =	−375
Total changes	0 Cash +	0 −	+375 Accumulated Depreciation =	0 +	0 +	−375 Retained Earnings	0 −	+375 Depreciation Expense =	−375

We can see that this entry reduced net income by $375, but it had no effect on cash. When we look at the total impact of this entry on the FSET (in the last row), its effect can be written in the following way.

$$\text{Cash flow} - \text{Change in accumulated depreciation (for depreciation expense)} = \text{Net income,}$$

or

$$\text{Cash flow} = \text{Net income} + \text{Depreciation expense}$$
$$\$0 \text{ (zero)} = -\$375 + \$375$$

So, NBS' net income of $650 for December includes a depreciation expense of $375 that did not involve any cash outflow. When we add back depreciation expense (and similar items like amortization expense), we move the net income number one step closer to cash from operations.

Would increasing depreciation expense increase the cash flows from operations? That question is more complex than it initially appears. In Chapter 8, we will find that companies use different depreciation methods for tax reporting and financial reporting, and in Chapter 10 we will see how differences between tax and financial reporting are reconciled. Increasing the tax depreciation expense reduces taxable income and the amount of tax that has to be paid. Increasing depreciation expense in financial reports to shareholders has no effect on the amount of taxes paid and, therefore, no effect on the amount of cash generated.

A General Rule ... with a Note of Caution The relationships illustrated in the above examples suggest a general rule that we can use to prepare the statement of cash flows:

> The difference between a revenue or an expense reported in the income statement and a related cash receipt or expenditure reported in the statement of cash flows will be reflected in the balance sheet as a change in one or more balance sheet accounts.

More specifically, all the above reconciliation adjustments for NBS can be summarized in a pattern:

Net income + Adjustments = Cash from operations

Or, more particularly

$$\text{Net income} + \text{Depreciation expense} - \text{Change in operating assets} + \text{Change in operating liabilities} = \text{Cash from operations}$$

By "operating assets," we mean receivables, inventories, prepaid expenses, and similar assets. "Operating liabilities" refers to accounts and wages payable, accrued expenses, unearned revenues, taxes payable, interest payable, and similar items. Investing assets (like investment securities and property, plant, and equipment) and financing liabilities (like notes payable and long-term debt) would not be included in these adjustments.

Exhibit 4.5 summarizes the basic adjustments needed to convert the revenues, expenses, gains, and losses presented in the income statement to cash receipts and payments presented in the statement of cash flows from operating activities. (The adjustments for nonoperating gains and losses will be discussed shortly.)

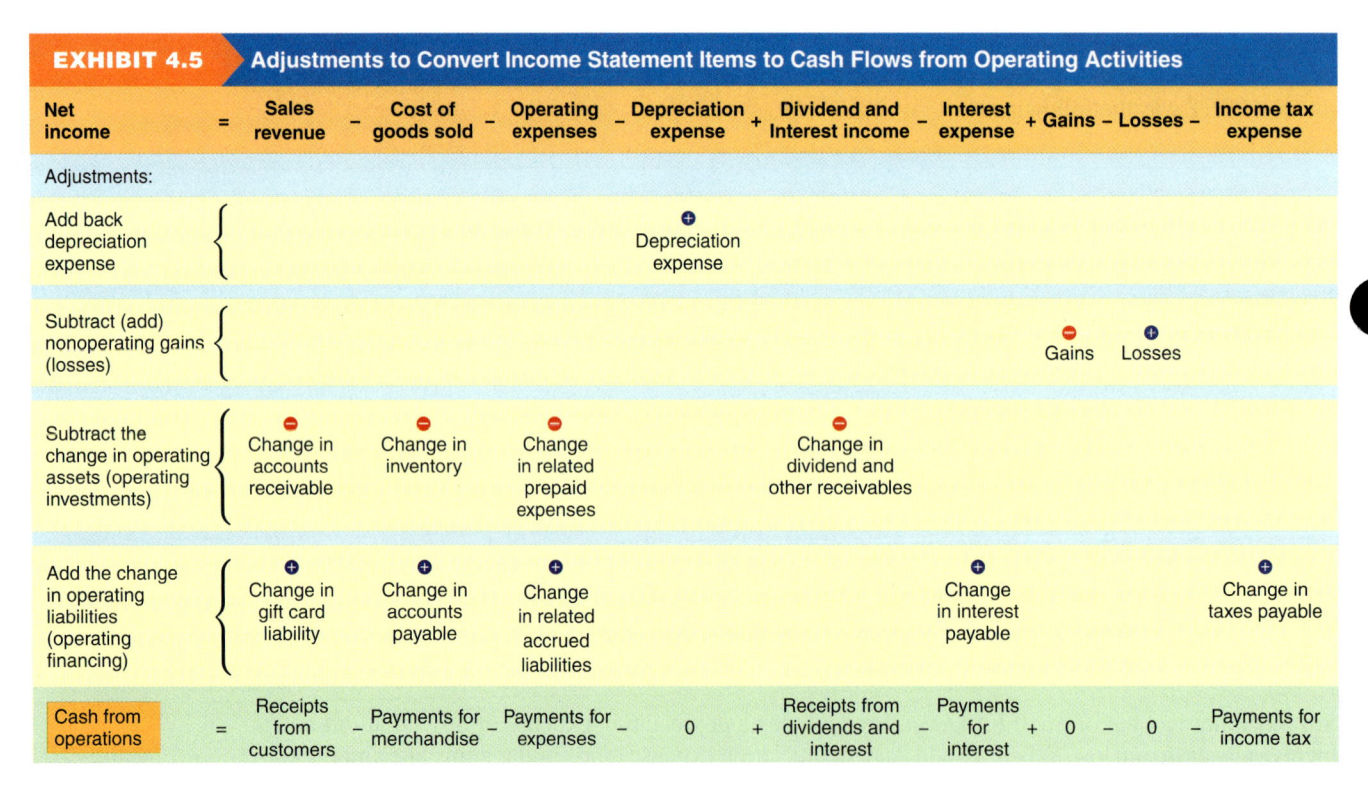

EXHIBIT 4.5 — Adjustments to Convert Income Statement Items to Cash Flows from Operating Activities

Net income	=	Sales revenue	−	Cost of goods sold	−	Operating expenses	−	Depreciation expense	+	Dividend and Interest income	−	Interest expense	+ Gains − Losses −	Income tax expense
Adjustments:														
Add back depreciation expense								(+) Depreciation expense						
Subtract (add) nonoperating gains (losses)													(−) Gains (+) Losses	
Subtract the change in operating assets (operating investments)		(−) Change in accounts receivable		(−) Change in inventory		(−) Change in related prepaid expenses				(−) Change in dividend and other receivables				
Add the change in operating liabilities (operating financing)		(+) Change in gift card liability		(+) Change in accounts payable		(+) Change in related accrued liabilities						(+) Change in interest payable		(+) Change in taxes payable
Cash from operations	=	Receipts from customers	−	Payments for merchandise	−	Payments for expenses	−	0	+	Receipts from dividends and interest	−	Payments for interest	+ 0 − 0 −	Payments for income tax

We have now applied the adjustments to convert each accrual revenue and expense to the corresponding operating cash flow. We use these individual cash inflows and outflows to prepare the operating activities section of the statement of cash flows. The adjustments to convert revenues and expenses to operating cash flows are summarized in **Exhibit 4.6**, and this information can be used to produce NBS' cash from operating activities by using the information in the income statement and balance sheet.

Like all general rules, this one provides useful insights, but it also has limitations. As we learn more and more about business activities and the accounting for them, we find the need for refinements of this general rule. For instance, in Chapter 12, we will see that operating assets and liabilities can increase from acquisitions (an investing activity) as well as from operations. But for the time being, the general rule is a useful way to approach the calculation and interpretation of operating cash flow.

EXHIBIT 4.6 — Converting Revenues and Expenses to Cash Inflows and Outflows from Operating Activity (Natural Beauty Supply)

Net income	=	Sales revenue	+	Interest income	−	Cost of goods sold	−	Wages expense	−	Rent expense	−	Advertising expense	−	Insurance expense	−	Interest expense	−	Depreciation expense	−	Income tax expense
$650	=	$13,900	+	30	−	8,000	−	2,105	−	1,500	−	700	−	140	−	110	−	375	−	350

Adjustments:

Add back depreciation expense: +375 Depreciation expense

Subtract the change in operating assets (operating investments):
- −1,300 Change in accounts receivable
- −30 Change in other receivables
- −(−4,000)* Change in inventory
- −(−140)* Change in prepaid insurance

Add the change in operating liabilities (operating financing):
- +300 Change in gift card liability
- +700 Change in accounts payable
- +480 Change in wages payable
- +110 Change in interest payable
- +350 Change in taxes payable

$5,775	=	$12,900	+	0	−	3,300	−	1,625	−	1,500	−	700	−	0	−	0	−	0	−	0
Cash from operations	=	Receipts from customers	+	Receipts for interest	−	Payments for merchandise	−	Payments to employees	−	Payments for rent	−	Payments for advertising	−	Payments for insurance	−	Payments for interest	−	0	−	Payments for income tax

*When the change in an operating asset is negative, subtracting that negative amount results in a positive adjustment.

Preparing Operating Activities Section of the Statement of Cash Flows—Direct Method
LO4-2 Review 4-2

The income statement and comparative balance sheets for Mug Shots, Inc., (a photography studio) are presented below. Use the information in these financial statements and the frameworks in **Exhibits 4.5** and **4.6** to compute Mug Shots' cash flow from operating activities using the direct method.

MUG SHOTS, INC.
Income Statement
For Month Ended December 31

Revenue		
Sales revenue		$31,000
Expenses		
Cost of goods sold	$16,700	
Wages expense	4,700	
Interest expense	300	
Advertising expense	1,800	
Rent expense	1,500	
Depreciation expense	700	
Total expenses		25,700
Income before taxes		5,300
Income tax expense		1,855
Net income		$ 3,445

MUG SHOTS, INC.
Comparative Balance Sheets

	Dec. 31	Nov. 30
Assets		
Cash	$10,700	$ 5,000
Accounts receivable	2,500	
Inventory	32,300	24,000
Prepaid rent	7,500	9,000
Equipment	30,000	18,000
Accumulated depreciation	(700)	
Total assets	$82,300	$56,000
Liabilities		
Accounts payable	$25,000	$24,000
Interest payable	300	
Wages payable	2,200	
Income tax payable	1,855	
Unearned revenue	500	
Notes payable	30,000	12,000
Equity		
Common stock	20,000	20,000
Retained earnings	2,445	
Total liabilities and equity	$82,300	$56,000

Solution on p. 4-60.

Reconciling Net Income and Cash Flow from Operating Activities

LO4-3 Reconcile cash flows from operations to net income and use the indirect method to compute operating cash flows.

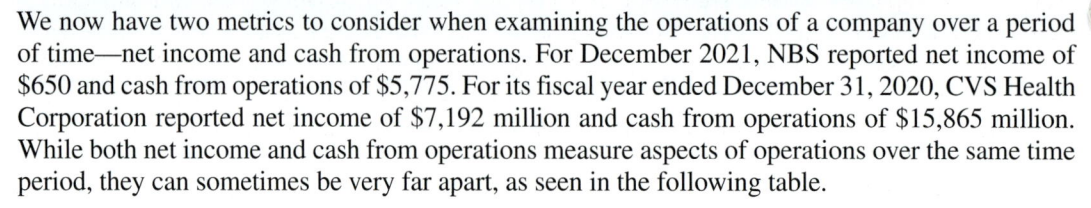

We now have two metrics to consider when examining the operations of a company over a period of time—net income and cash from operations. For December 2021, NBS reported net income of $650 and cash from operations of $5,775. For its fiscal year ended December 31, 2020, CVS Health Corporation reported net income of $7,192 million and cash from operations of $15,865 million. While both net income and cash from operations measure aspects of operations over the same time period, they can sometimes be very far apart, as seen in the following table.

	2020 ($ millions; US$ unless otherwise noted)	
	Net Income	Cash from Operations
Delta Air Lines, Inc.	$(12,385)	$ (3,793)
Southwest Airlines Co.	(3,074)	(1,127)
American Airlines Group, Inc.	(8,885)	(6,543)
Target Corporation	3,281	7,117
Walmart, Inc.	15,201	25,255
Amazon.com, Inc.	21,331	66,064
Alphabet Inc.	40,269	65,124
Facebook, Inc.	29,146	38,747
Tesla, Inc.	862	5,943
BMW Group	€3,857	€13,251
Ford Motor Company	(1,276)	24,269
Toyota Motor Corporation	913	5,764
Carmax, Inc.	888	(237)
AutoNation, Inc.	382	1,208

It would be natural for a financial statement reader to want to understand the source(s) of the differences between net income and cash from operations. So, companies that present their statement of cash flows like CVS Health Corporation must also present a reconciliation of net income to cash from operations. The reconciliation for CVS Health's fiscal year ending December 31, 2020, is in **Exhibit 4.7**.

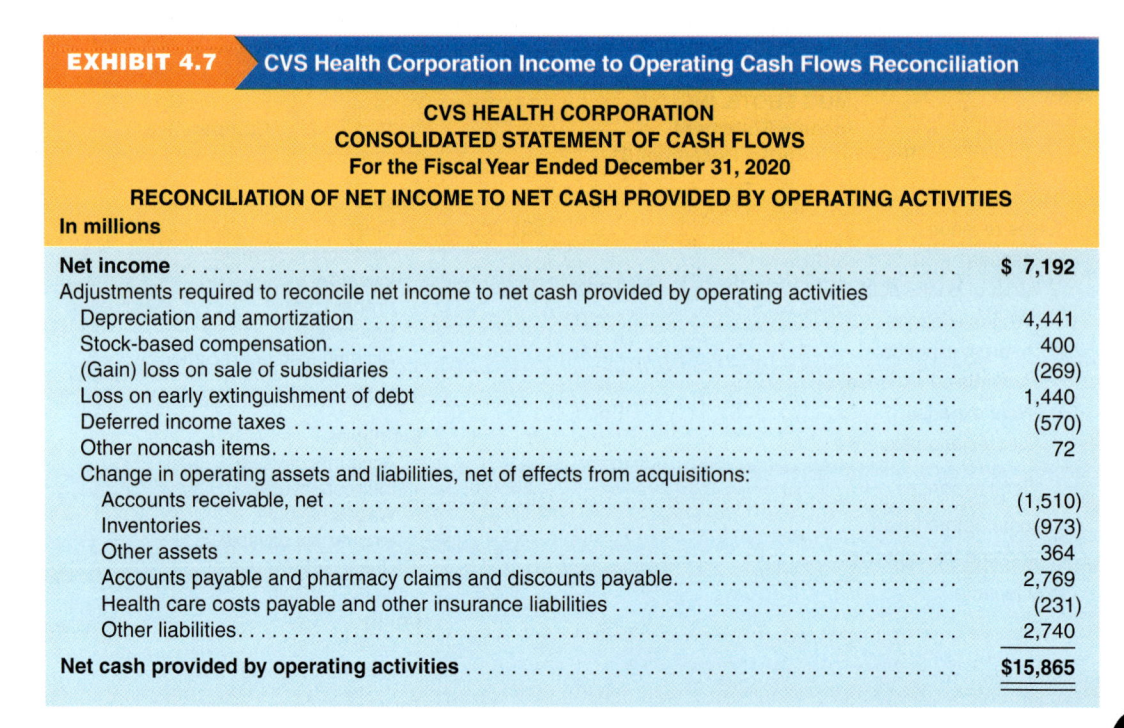

EXHIBIT 4.7 CVS Health Corporation Income to Operating Cash Flows Reconciliation

CVS HEALTH CORPORATION
CONSOLIDATED STATEMENT OF CASH FLOWS
For the Fiscal Year Ended December 31, 2020
RECONCILIATION OF NET INCOME TO NET CASH PROVIDED BY OPERATING ACTIVITIES
In millions

Net income	$ 7,192
Adjustments required to reconcile net income to net cash provided by operating activities	
Depreciation and amortization	4,441
Stock-based compensation	400
(Gain) loss on sale of subsidiaries	(269)
Loss on early extinguishment of debt	1,440
Deferred income taxes	(570)
Other noncash items	72
Change in operating assets and liabilities, net of effects from acquisitions:	
Accounts receivable, net	(1,510)
Inventories	(973)
Other assets	364
Accounts payable and pharmacy claims and discounts payable	2,769
Health care costs payable and other insurance liabilities	(231)
Other liabilities	2,740
Net cash provided by operating activities	**$15,865**

This reconciliation leads to the same number that was presented in the operating section of **Exhibit 4.1**, but in a very different format. How is it produced? It is constructed using the same adjustment process depicted in **Exhibits 4.5** and **4.6**.

CVS Health's reconciliation contains a couple of entries that we did not see for Natural Beauty Supply. A company's income statement may contain gains and losses related to nonoperating activities. Examples include gains and losses from the sale of subsidiaries and the loss on the early extinguishment of debt. Because these gains and losses are included in income but are not related to operating activities, **Exhibit 4.5** shows that we omit them as we convert income statement items to various cash flows from operating activities. The cash flows relating to these gains and losses are reported in the investing activities or financing activities sections of the statement of cash flows. NBS had no nonoperating gains or losses in December, but CVS Health made an adjustment to remove a $269 million gain on the sale of subsidiaries (an investing activity) and a $1,440 million loss on the early extinguishment of debt (a financing activity).

Another adjustment involves stock-based compensation. Corporations often use their common stock to reward employees and to provide incentives for future performance. The value of such grants must be recognized in income as an expense, but it is an expense that does not involve cash. Therefore, the amount expensed—$400 million for CVS Health in 2020—is added back in reconciling net income to cash flow from operations.

CVS Health also makes a negative $570 million adjustment for deferred income taxes. Deferred income taxes occur when companies use different accounting methods for tax and financial reporting and are beyond our scope for the moment. It will be covered later in Chapter 10.

Cash Flow from Operating Activities Using the Indirect Method

Two alternative formats may be used to report the net cash flow from operating activities: the direct method and the indirect method. *Both methods report the same amount of net cash flow from operating activities.* Net cash flows from investing and financing activities are prepared in the same manner under both the indirect and the direct methods; only the format for cash flows from operating activities differs.

For Natural Beauty Supply, we computed cash flow from operating activities using the direct method. The **direct method** presents the components of cash flow from operating activities as a list of gross cash receipts and gross cash payments. This format is illustrated in **Exhibit 4.3** and by CVS Health Corporation's statement in **Exhibit 4.1**.

The direct method is logical and relatively easy to follow. In practice, however, nearly all operating activities sections in the statements of cash flows are presented using what is called the **indirect method**. Under this method, the reconciliation of net income to operating cash flow (e.g., **Exhibit 4.7**) is used for the presentation of cash flow from operations. The cash flow from operations section begins with net income and applies a series of adjustments to net income to convert it to net cash flow from operating activities. However, the adjustments to net income are not cash flows themselves, so the indirect method does not report any detail concerning individual operating cash inflows and outflows. In fact, there are no cash flows in the indirect method operating section of the statement of cash flows, except the subtotal—cash flow from operations. The **Apple Inc.** statement of cash flows on page 4-53 is an example.

While accounting standard-setters prefer the direct method presentation, it is not very popular with reporting companies. In the U.S., surveys have found that fewer than 5% of companies use the direct method presentation. The indirect method is popular because (1) it is easier and less expensive to prepare than the direct method and (2) companies that use the direct method are required to present a supplemental disclosure showing the reconciliation of net income to cash from operations (thus, essentially requiring the company to report both methods for cash from operations). International standard-setters also have stated a preference for the direct method, and its use is more frequent than in the U.S. But the indirect method of presenting cash flow from operations is used by a significant majority of companies.

The procedure for presenting indirect method cash flows from operations uses the same approach that we applied above to convert income statement items to operating cash flows. In fact, the indirect method can be viewed as a "short-cut" calculation of the process shown in **Exhibit 4.5**. That is:

> **Net income ± Adjustments = Cash flow from operating activities**

In **Exhibit 4.5**, revenue and expense components of the income statement are presented in the orange row that totals to net income. The yellow rows list the adjustments, and cash receipts and

FYI Managers can boost declining sales by lengthening credit periods or by lowering credit standards. The resulting increase in accounts receivable can cause net income to outpace operating cash flow. Consequently, many view a large receivables increase as a warning sign.

payments are listed in the green row at the bottom. The total of the green row is cash flow from operating activities. The indirect method skips the listing of individual revenues and expenses and starts with net income. After adjustments, we have total cash flow from operating activities, but not individual receipts and payments.

Cash flow from December's operating activities for NBS is presented using the indirect method in **Exhibit 4.8**. The calculation begins with the December net income of $650 and ends with cash flow from operating activities, $5,775. The total cash flow from operating activities is the same amount as was computed in **Exhibit 4.6** using the direct method. If we compare **Exhibit 4.6** and **Exhibit 4.8**, we see that the two exhibits are very similar. The only difference is that all of the revenues and expenses are listed in the orange row at the top of **Exhibit 4.6**, while **Exhibit 4.8** lists only the total—net income. Similarly, the green row at the bottom of **Exhibit 4.6** lists all of the cash inflows and outflows, while the bottom line of **Exhibit 4.8** lists only the net cash flow from operating activities. In both exhibits, the center rows list the adjustments.

EXHIBIT 4.8 NBS Cash Flow from Operating Activities—Indirect Method

Net income	$ 650
Adjustments:	
Add back depreciation expense	375
Subtract:	
Change in accounts receivable	1,300
Change in other receivables	30
Change in inventory	(4,000)*
Change in prepaid insurance	(140)*
Add:	
Change in gift card liability	300
Change in accounts payable	700
Change in wages payable	480
Change in interest payable	110
Change in taxes payable	350
Total adjustments	5,125
Cash flow from operating activities	$5,775

* When the change in an operating asset is negative, subtracting that negative amount results in a positive adjustment.

Review 4-3 LO4-3   Reconciling Cash Flows from Operations to Net Income

Refer to the financial statements for Mug Shots, Inc., presented in Review 4-2. Compute cash flows from operating activities for Mug Shots, Inc., using the indirect method.

Solution on p. 4-60.

PREPARING THE STATEMENT OF CASH FLOWS—INVESTING AND FINANCING ACTIVITIES

LO4-4 Construct the investing and financing activities sections of the statement of cash flows.

The remaining sections of the statement of cash flows focus on investing and financing activities. Investing activities are concerned with transactions affecting noncurrent (and some current) noncash assets. Financing activities are concerned with raising capital from owners and creditors. The presentation of the cash effects of investing and financing transactions is not affected by the method of presentation (direct or indirect) of cash flows from operating activities.

Accounting standard-setters (both in the United States and International) require that financing and investing items be presented in the statement of cash flows using gross amounts instead of net amounts. In **Exhibit 4.1**, CVS Health reports that it spent $9,639 million in cash to purchase investments in 2020, and it received $6,467 million in cash from the sale and maturities of investments. It would not be acceptable to show the net amount—an outflow of $3,172 million—as a single item unless one of the components is consistently immaterial.

Cash Flows from Investing Activities

Investing activities cause changes in noncash asset accounts. Usually the accounts affected (other than cash) are noncurrent operating asset accounts such as property, plant, and equipment assets and investing assets like marketable securities and long-term financial investments. Cash paid for acquisitions of other companies would be included as well. To determine the cash flows from investing activities, we analyze changes in all noncash asset accounts not used in computing net cash flow from operating activities. Our objective is to identify any investing cash flows related to these changes.

Purchases of noncash assets cause cash outflow. Conversely, a sale of a noncash asset results in cash inflow. This relationship is highlighted in the following decision guide:

Cash flows increase due to:	Cash flows decrease due to:
Sales of assets	Purchases of assets

NBS had only one investing transaction during December—the purchase of fixtures and equipment for $18,000. Any change in the Fixtures and Equipment account in the balance sheet is usually the result of one or both of the following transactions: (1) buying assets, or (2) selling assets.[2] Buying and selling nonoperating assets are classified as investing transactions. NBS' entry to record the purchase of fixtures and equipment for cash is as follows:

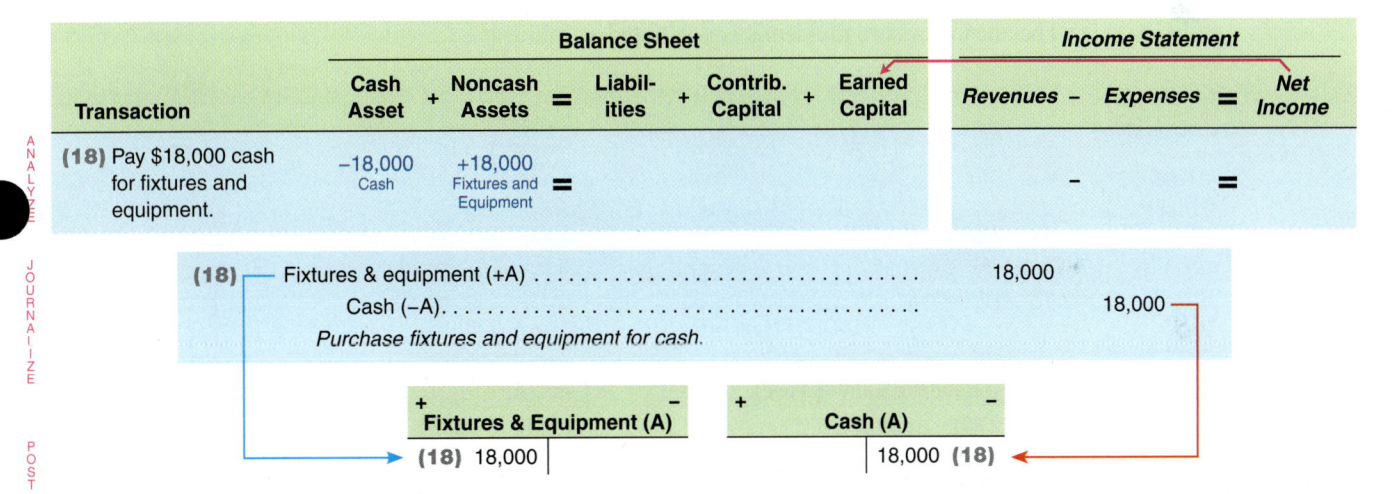

Transaction	Balance Sheet					Income Statement		
	Cash Asset	+ Noncash Assets	= Liabilities	+ Contrib. Capital	+ Earned Capital	Revenues	− Expenses	= Net Income
(18) Pay $18,000 cash for fixtures and equipment.	−18,000 Cash	+18,000 Fixtures and Equipment	=				−	=

(18) Fixtures & equipment (+A) 18,000
     Cash (−A).. 18,000
     Purchase fixtures and equipment for cash.

+ Fixtures & Equipment (A) −	+ Cash (A) −
(18) 18,000	18,000 (18)

The resulting $18,000 cash outflow is listed in the statement of cash flows under cash flow used for investing activities.

Cash Flows from Financing Activities

Financing activities cause changes in financial liabilities and stockholders' equity accounts. Financial liabilities include current liability items like seasonal bank borrowing and the current portion of long-term debt due within the next year, plus noncurrent items like long-term debt issues and longer term borrowing from financial institutions. Cash receipts from the issuance of these liabilities and cash payments to settle outstanding principal balances are considered cash flows from financing activities. Stockholders' equity accounts include contributed capital (common stock, additional paid-in-capital, and treasury stock) and retained earnings. Transactions with shareholders are always considered part of a company's financing activities. This relationship is highlighted in the following decision guide:

Cash flows increase due to:	Cash flows decrease due to:
Taking on a financial liability or issuing shares	Repaying principal on a financial liability or paying dividends to shareholders or making share repurchases

---
[2] The Accumulated Depreciation—Fixtures and Equipment contra-asset account is affected by depreciation expense and selling assets.

NBS had two financing transactions during December. It borrowed $11,000 on a three-year note, resulting in an increase in cash, and it paid $50 in cash dividends to shareholders. The entry to record the $11,000 note is illustrated as:

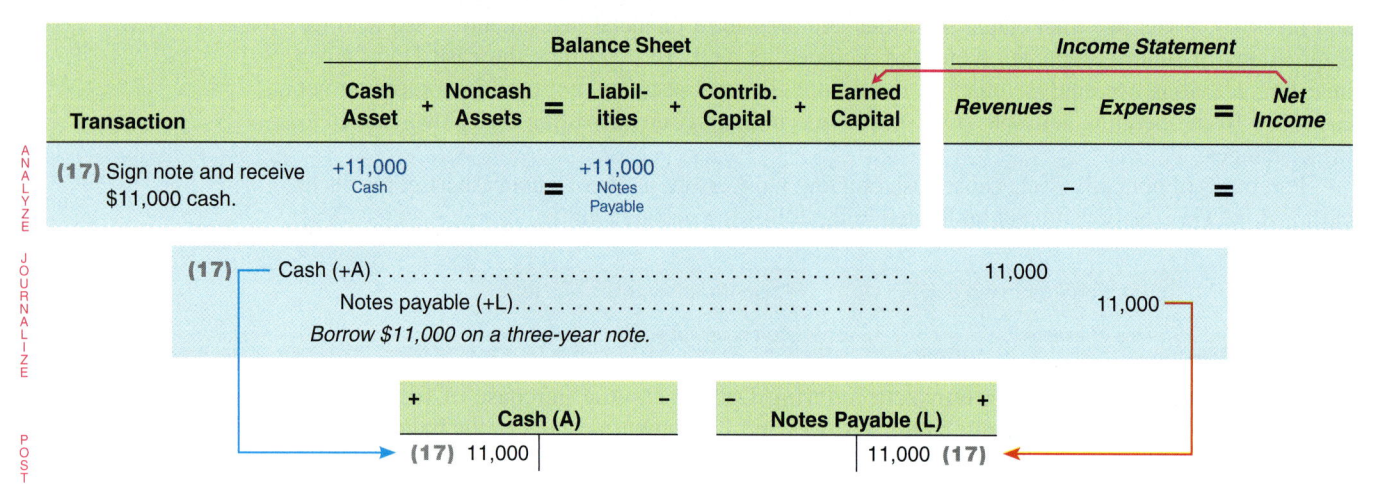

Transaction	Balance Sheet					Income Statement		
	Cash Asset	+ Noncash Assets =	Liabil- ities	+ Contrib. Capital +	Earned Capital	Revenues −	Expenses =	Net Income
(17) Sign note and receive $11,000 cash.	+11,000 Cash		+11,000 Notes Payable					

(17) Cash (+A) 11,000
       Notes payable (+L) 11,000
       Borrow $11,000 on a three-year note.

+ Cash (A) −		− Notes Payable (L) +
(17) 11,000		11,000 **(17)**

The resulting $11,000 cash inflow is listed in the statement of cash flows under cash flow from financing activities.

The entry to record dividends is illustrated as follows:

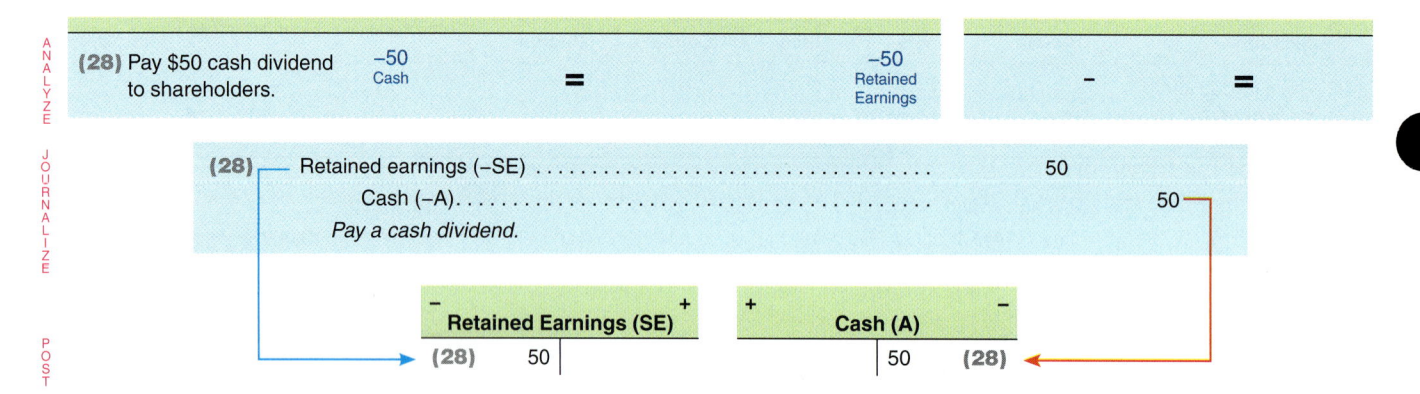

Transaction	Balance Sheet					Income Statement		
(28) Pay $50 cash dividend to shareholders.	−50 Cash	=			−50 Retained Earnings	−	=	

(28) Retained earnings (−SE) 50
       Cash (−A) 50
       Pay a cash dividend.

− Retained Earnings (SE) +		+ Cash (A) −
(28) 50		50 **(28)**

This dividend payment is a financing cash outflow and would be deducted from cash flow from financing activities.

When using the indirect method for the cash flow from operating activities, we should remember that there are some balance sheet accounts that will be affected by more than one type of activity. For instance, the balance in retained earnings will be affected by net income (which is going to appear in the operations section) and shareholder dividends (which will appear in the financing section).

The statement of cash flows lists cash flows from operating activities first (using either the direct or the indirect method), followed by cash flows from investing activities, then cash flows from financing activities. Once all three categories of cash flows have been listed, we total the three amounts to arrive at net cash flow for the period. The final step is to reconcile the cash balance from the beginning of the period to the ending balance. The completed statement of cash flows for NBS using the indirect method for operating cash flows is presented in **Exhibit 4.9**. We see from this statement that operating activities produced a cash inflow of $5,775, while investing activities resulted in a cash outflow of $18,000, and financing activities resulted in a cash inflow of $10,950. The sum of these three amounts ($5,775 − $18,000 + $10,950) equals the change in cash for December of −$1,275 ($6,825 − $8,100).

YOU MAKE THE CALL

You are the Chief Accountant. In its annual report for fiscal year 2020 (ending January 30, 2021), **Kohl's Corporation** reported that its cash used in investing activities decreased by almost 85% from the previous year, in part due to the "sale of real estate." Proceeds for the sale of real estate produced cash inflows of $197 million and gains on sale of $127 million. How would these amounts be reflected in the company's statement of cash flows? [Answer on page 4-36.]

EXHIBIT 4.9 — NBS Statement of Cash Flows—Indirect Method

NATURAL BEAUTY SUPPLY
Statement of Cash Flows
For the Month Ended December 31, 2021

Operating activities:		
Net income		$ 650
Adjustments:		
Add back Depreciation expense		375
Subtract:		
Change in accounts receivable		1,300
Change in other receivables		30
Change in inventory		(4,000)*
Change in prepaid insurance		(140)*
Add:		
Change in gift card liability		300
Change in accounts payable		700
Change in wages payable		480
Change in interest payable		110
Change in taxes payable		350
Total adjustments		5,125
Cash flow from operating activities		$5,775
Investing activities:		
Purchase of fixtures and equipment	(18,000)	
Cash flow used for investing activities		(18,000)
Financing activities:		
Bank note	11,000	
Dividends paid	(50)	
Cash flow from financing activities		10,950
Net decrease in cash		(1,275)
Cash, November 30, 2021		8,100
Cash, December 31, 2021		$ 6,825

*When the change in an operating asset is negative, subtracting that negative amount results in a positive adjustment.

FYI The net cash inflow or outflow for the period is the same amount as the increase or decrease in cash and cash equivalents for the period from the balance sheet.

Preparing a Complete Statement of Cash Flows

LO4-4 Review 4-4

Refer to the financial statements for Mug Shots, Inc., in Review 4-2. Prepare a complete statement of cash flows for December using the indirect method for cash flows from operating activities. Follow the format used in **Exhibit 4.9**.

Solution on p. 4-61.

ADDITIONAL DETAIL IN THE STATEMENT OF CASH FLOWS

LO4-5 Examine the sale of investing assets and the disclosure of noncash activities

There are two additional types of transactions that we must explore to understand the statement of cash flows. The first of these is the sale of investing assets like equipment or an investment security. The transaction itself isn't very complicated, but the use of the indirect method for operating cash flows makes it seem so. And, companies often engage in investing and financing activities that do not involve cash (e.g., acquiring another company through an exchange of stock). This section explores the accounting for these two types of transactions and their effect on the statement of cash flows.

Case Illustration Natural Beauty Supply did not have any disposals of assets or repayments of debt in December 2021, so there is no adjustment to make in this case. However, let's consider the financial statements of One World Café, a coffee shop that is located next door to NBS. The income statement and comparative balance sheet for One World Café are presented in **Exhibit 4.10**. The statement of cash flows is presented in **Exhibit 4.11**.

EXHIBIT 4.10 One World Café Income Statement and Comparative Balance Sheets

ONE WORLD CAFÉ, INC.
Income Statement
For Year Ended December 31, 2021

Revenue		
Sales revenue		$390,000
Expenses		
Cost of goods sold	$227,000	
Wages expense	82,000	
Advertising expense	9,800	
Depreciation expense	17,000	
Interest expense	200	
Loss on sale of plant assets	2,000	
Total expenses		338,000
Income before taxes		52,000
Income tax expense		17,000
Net income		$ 35,000

ONE WORLD CAFÉ, INC.
Comparative Balance Sheets
At December 31

	2021	2020
Assets		
Cash	$ 8,000	$ 12,000
Accounts receivable	22,000	28,000
Inventory	94,000	66,000
Prepaid advertising	12,000	9,000
Plant assets, at cost	208,000	170,000
Less accumulated depreciation	(72,000)	(61,000)
Total assets	$272,000	$224,000
Liabilities		
Accounts payable	$ 27,000	$ 14,000
Wages payable	6,000	2,500
Income tax payable	3,000	4,500
Notes payable	5,000	—
Equity		
Common stock	134,000	125,000
Retained earnings	97,000	78,000
Total liabilities and equity	$272,000	$224,000

For One World Café, creation of the statement of cash flows requires information that cannot be discerned from the income statement and balance sheet. (After all, the statement of cash flows is *supposed* to provide additional information!) In particular, the following events occurred during the year.

- Plant assets were purchased for cash.
- Obsolete plant assets, with original cost of $12,000 and accumulated depreciation of $6,000, were sold for $4,000 cash, resulting in a $2,000 loss.
- Additional common stock was issued for cash.
- Cash dividends of $16,000 were declared and paid during the year.
- One World Café acquired $5,000 of plant assets by issuing notes payable.

Reviewing One World Café's comparative balance sheet, we see that plant assets at cost increased from $170,000 to $208,000, an increase of $38,000. In addition, the accumulated depreciation contra-asset increased by $11,000 from $61,000 to $72,000. However, these are *net* increases, and we need information on the individual components of the increases. Consequently, we need to determine the gross amounts to ensure the statement of cash flows we create properly presents the gross amounts in the investing activities section.

EXHIBIT 4.11 Statement of Cash Flows for One World Café

ONE WORLD CAFÉ, INC.
Statement of Cash Flows
For Year Ended December 31, 2021

Cash flows from operating activities		
Net income		$35,000
Add (deduct) items to convert net income to cash basis		
Add back depreciation		17,000
Add back loss on sale of plant assets		2,000
Subtract change in:		
Accounts receivable		(6,000)*
Inventory		28,000
Prepaid advertising		3,000
Add change in:		
Accounts payable		13,000
Wages payable		3,500
Income tax payable		(1,500)
Net cash provided by operating activities		$44,000
Cash flows from investing activities		
Purchase of plant assets	(45,000)	
Proceeds from sale of plant assets	4,000	
Net cash used for investing activities		(41,000)
Cash flows from financing activities		
Issuance of common stock	9,000	
Payment of dividends	(16,000)	
Net cash flows used for financing activities		(7,000)
Net cash decrease		(4,000)
Cash at beginning of year		12,000
Cash at end of year		$ 8,000

* When the change in an operating asset is negative, subtracting that negative amount results in a positive adjustment.

In addition to the changes in plant assets and accumulated depreciation, notes payable increased by $5,000 in 2021. The best way to fully understand what happened to cause the changes in balance sheet accounts during the year, and the impact of these changes on cash flows, is to "work backward" to reconstruct the investing and financing transactions using journal entries and T-accounts, especially the plant assets and accumulated depreciation accounts.

Gains and Losses on Investing and Financing Activities

The focus of the income statement is on the revenues and expenses that are generated by a company's transactions with customers, suppliers, employees, and other operating activities. But the income statement also contains gains and losses that result from investing or financing transactions. Gains and losses from the sale of investments, property, plant, and equipment, or intangible assets result from investing activities, not operating activities. A gain or loss from the retirement of bonds payable is an example of a financing gain or loss. When these transactions occur, the income statement does not show a revenue and an expense, but rather shows only the net amount as a gain or loss.

The full cash flow effect from these types of events is reported in the investing or financing sections of the statement of cash flows. To illustrate, we record the sale of Old World Café's obsolete plant assets at a loss with the following FSET entry:

	Balance Sheet					Income Statement		
Transaction	Cash Asset +	Noncash Assets −	Contra Asset =	Liabilities +	Contrib. Capital +	Earned Capital	Revenues −	Expenses = Net Income
(1)	+4,000 Cash	−12,000 Plant Assets	−6,000 Accumt Dep'n =			−2,000 Retained Earnings		+2,000 Loss on Sale of Plant Assets = −2,000

Or, using the journal entry and T-accounts shown below.

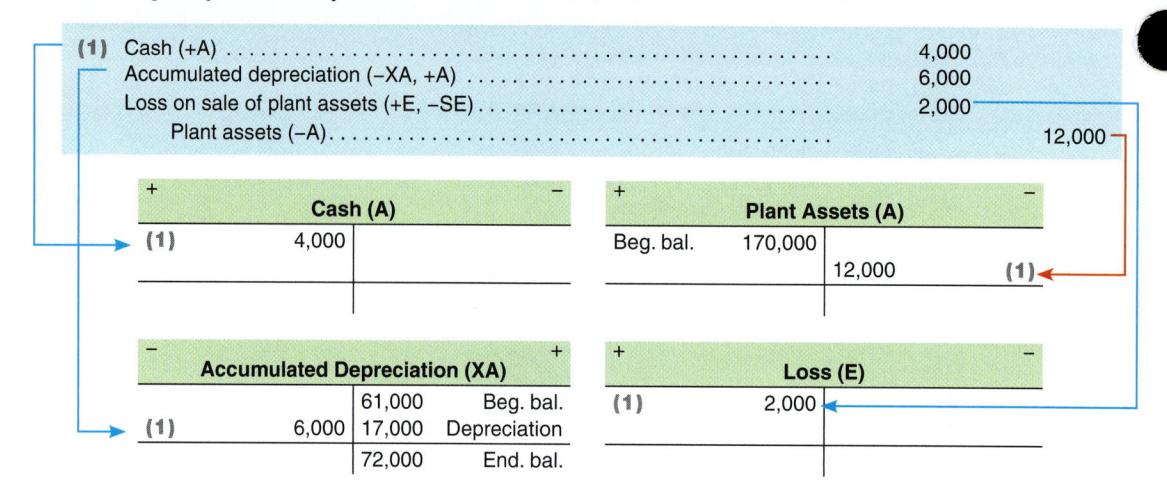

(1) Cash (+A)	4,000	
Accumulated depreciation (−XA, +A)	6,000	
Loss on sale of plant assets (+E, −SE)	2,000	
Plant assets (−A)		12,000

+	Cash (A)	−		+	Plant Assets (A)	−
(1)	4,000			Beg. bal.	170,000	
					12,000	(1)

−	Accumulated Depreciation (XA)	+		+	Loss (E)	−
		61,000 Beg. bal.		(1)	2,000	
(1)	6,000	17,000 Depreciation				
		72,000 End. bal.				

The $4,000 of cash received from this sale should be listed as a cash inflow under cash flows from investing activities, and it can be seen in **Exhibit 4.11**. The $4,000 cash flow is equal to the $6,000 net book value of the plant assets that were sold ($12,000 − $6,000) less the $2,000 loss on the sale.

If we were using the direct method to report the cash flows from operating activities, we wouldn't need to take any additional steps. But an indirect method operating cash flows starts with net income, and Old World Café's net income includes a $2,000 loss from this investing transaction (**Exhibit 4.10**). So, when we add back the investing loss to net income (or subtract an investing gain), we remove the effect of this investing transaction from the determination of cash flows from operating activities. It's one more step in the adjustments that are needed to reconcile net income to the cash flows from operating activities.

In Chapter 9, we will find that companies can experience financing gains (losses) from the early retirement of their debt. These gains and losses appear in the income statement, but they result from financing activities. In an indirect method statement of cash flows, the financing gains (losses) must be subtracted from (added to) net income to determine cash flows from operating activities.

We also see that the accumulated depreciation account started with a credit balance of $61,000, and the obsolete asset sale reduced this by $6,000 to $55,000. But the balance sheet in **Exhibit 4.10** tells us that the ending (credit) balance is $72,000. The difference is due to $17,000 depreciation expense for the year.

YOU MAKE THE CALL

You are the Securities Analyst You are analyzing a company's statement of cash flows. The company extends credit to customers that purchase its products. You see that the company has sold some of its accounts receivable to another company, receiving cash in return. As a result, the sale of receivables is reported as an asset sale, which reduces receivables and yields a gain or loss on sale. This action increases the company's operating cash flows. How should you interpret these items in the statement of cash flows? [Answer on p. 4-37.]

Noncash Investing and Financing Activities

In addition to reporting how cash changed from one balance sheet to the next, cash flow reporting is intended to present summary information about a firm's investing and financing activities. Many of these activities affect cash and are therefore already included in the investing and financing sections of the statement of cash flows. Some significant investing and financing events, however, do not affect current cash flows. Examples of **noncash investing and financing activities** are the issuance of stocks, bonds, or leases in exchange for property, plant, and equipment (PPE) assets or intangible assets; the exchange of long-term assets for other long-term assets; and the conversion of long-term debt into common stock.

To illustrate the effect of noncash transactions on the preparation of the statement of cash flows, consider One World Café's purchase of $5,000 of plant assets that was financed with notes payable. The FSET entry to record the purchase is as follows:

Transaction	Balance Sheet							Income Statement		
	Cash Asset	+ Noncash Assets	− Contra Asset	= Liabilities	+ Contrib. Capital	+ Earned Capital		Revenues	− Expenses	= Net Income
(2)		+5,000 Plant Assets	−	=	+5,000 Notes Payable				−	=

Or, using the journal entry and T-accounts shown below.

(2)	Plant assets (+A)	5,000	
	Notes payable (+L)		5,000

+ Plant Assets (A) −				− Notes Payable (L) +			
Beg. bal.	170,000					0	Beg. bal.
		12,000	(1)			5,000	(2)
(2)	5,000						
						5,000	End. bal.

Because this purchase did not use any cash, it is not presented in the statement of cash flows. Only those capital expenditures that use cash are listed as cash flows from investing activities. That is, cash flows from investing activities should reflect the actual amount of cash spent to purchase plant assets or investment assets.

Noncash investing and financing transactions generally do affect *future* cash flows. Issuing notes payable to acquire equipment, for example, requires future cash payments for interest and principal on the notes and should produce future operating cash flows from the equipment. Alternatively, converting bonds payable into common stock eliminates future cash payments related to the bonds but may carry the expectation of future cash dividends. Knowledge of these types of events, therefore, is helpful to users of cash flow data who wish to assess a firm's future cash flows.

Information on noncash investing and financing transactions is disclosed in a schedule that is separate from the statement of cash flows. The separate schedule is reported either immediately below the statement of cash flows or among the notes to the financial statements.

Solving for Purchases of Plant Assets The remaining entry affecting plant assets is the purchase of plant assets for cash. The amount of plant assets purchased can be determined by solving for the missing amount in the Plant Assets T-account:

+ Plant Assets (A) −			
Beg. bal.	170,000		
		12,000	(1)
(2)	5,000		
(3)	X		
End. bal.	208,000		

Balancing the account requires that we solve for the unknown amount:

$$\$170{,}000 + \$5{,}000 + X - \$12{,}000 = \$208{,}000$$
$$X = \$45{,}000$$

Thus, plant assets costing $45,000 were purchased for cash. This amount is listed as a cash outflow under cash flows for investing activities.

The same analysis can be portrayed using the FSET. The column for Plant assets yields the same $45,000 answer for cash purchases of plant assets.

Transaction	Balance Sheet: Cash Assets + Noncash Assets − Contra Assets = Liabilities + Contrib. Capital + Earned Capital	Income Statement: Revenues − Expenses = Net Income
Beg. Bal.	170,000 Plant Assets	
(1)	+4,000 Cash; −12,000 Plant Assets; −6,000 Accum Dep'n = −2,000 Retained Earnings	+2,000 Loss on Sale of Plant Assets = −2,000
(2)	+5,000 Plant Assets = +5,000 Notes Payable	
(3)	−X Cash; +X Plant Assets =	
End. Bal.	208,000 Plant Assets	

Examining the statement of cash flows for One World Café in **Exhibit 4.11**, we see that two cash flows are listed under investing activities: (1) a $45,000 cash outflow for the purchase of plant assets, and (2) a $4,000 cash inflow from the sale of plant assets. The purchase of plant assets costing $5,000 by issuing notes payable is not listed; nor is the increase in notes payable listed under financing activities.

Appendix 4A at the end of this chapter introduces a spreadsheet approach that can be used to prepare the statement of cash flows. The appendix uses the One World Café financial statements as the illustration.

The Effects of Foreign Currencies on the Statement of Cash Flows

Multinational companies often engage in transactions that involve currencies other than U.S. dollars and may hold assets that were acquired with foreign currencies or liabilities that must be repaid in foreign currencies. Also, part of a company's cash balance may be held in a currency other than dollars. If the company prepares its financial statements in U.S. dollars, these foreign currency amounts must be converted, or *translated*, into dollars before preparing the financial statements. The process of translating transactions based in many currencies into one common currency for financial statement presentation is beyond the scope of an introductory text. However, foreign exchange rates fluctuate, and these fluctuations can have an effect on the statement of cash flows.

The statement of cash flows explains the change in the cash balance during the fiscal year, but part of this change may be due to changes in the dollar value of foreign currencies. This amount is typically small and it is not a cash flow, but it is included in the statement of cash flows so that we can accurately reconcile the beginning balance in cash to the ending balance. The statement of cash flows for **Nike, Inc.**, was summarized in Chapter 1 in **Exhibit 1.10** and is repeated here for illustration. In contrast, CVS Health reported that "the effects of foreign currency remeasurements were not material" for fiscal year 2020.

NIKE
Statement of Cash Flows
For the Year Ended May 31, 2020
($ millions)

Operating cash flows	$2,485
Investing cash flows	(1,028)
Financing cash flows	2,491
Effect of exchange rate changes	(66)
Net increase in cash and cash equivalents	3,882
Cash and equivalents, beginning of year	4,466
Cash and equivalents, end of year	$8,348

Supplemental Disclosures

If the direct method is used in the statement of cash flows, a reconciliation of net income to cash flows from operating activities is also required. If the indirect method is used, two separate supplemental disclosures are required—cash paid for interest and cash paid for income taxes. All companies must disclose the amount and nature of all noncash investing and financing transactions, in addition to the firm's policy for determining which highly liquid, short-term investments are treated as cash equivalents.

One World Café Case Illustration One World Café incurred $200 of interest expense, which was paid in cash. It also reported income tax expense of $17,000 and reported a decrease in income taxes payable of $1,500 ($4,500 − $3,000). Thus, One World Café paid $18,500 ($17,000 + $1,500) in income taxes during 2021. It also had the noncash investment in plant assets costing $5,000, which was financed with notes payable. One World Café would provide the following disclosure:

Supplemental cash flow information	
Cash payments for interest	$ 200
Cash payments for income taxes	18,500
Noncash transaction—investment in plant assets financed with notes payable	5,000

When some portion of a firm's cash and cash equivalent assets is held for a specific purpose and not available for immediate use (i.e., restricted cash), it is reported separately from the balance sheets' cash and cash equivalent amounts. The amount of restricted cash and the nature of the restrictions must be disclosed. However, the beginning and ending cash balances in the statement of cash flows include both unrestricted and restricted cash.

For instance, suppose that Old World Café's new borrowing carried with it a requirement that it keep a minimum cash balance of $500 with the lender. On the balance sheet, the company's ending cash balance would have been $7,500, rather than $8,000, and a $500 asset would appear labeled restricted cash. But for the statement of cash flows, the closing balance would be *Cash and restricted cash* equal to $8,000, and information on the nature of the restrictions should be disclosed in the notes to the financial statements.

Reconstructing Investing Cash Flows — LO4-5 Review 4-5

The balance sheet of Jack's Snacks, Inc., reports the following amounts:

	End-of-Year	Beginning-of-Year
Property, plant, and equipment at cost	$670,000	$600,000
Accumulated depreciation	(150,000)	(140,000)
Property, plant, and equipment, net	$520,000	$460,000

Additional information
During the year, Jack's Snacks disposed of a used piece of equipment. The original cost of the equipment was $80,000 and, at the time of disposal, the accumulated depreciation on the equipment was $60,000. The purchaser of the used piece of equipment paid in cash, and Jack's Snacks reported a gain of $35,000 on the disposal.
All acquisitions of new property, plant, and equipment were paid for in cash.

Required
a. How much cash did Jack's Snacks receive from the used equipment disposal? How would this amount be reported on the statement of cash flows?
b. How much cash did Jack's Snacks spend to acquire new property, plant, and equipment during the year? How would this amount be reported on the statement of cash flows?
c. How much depreciation expense did Jack's Snacks record during the year?
d. Now assume that Jack's Snacks issued common stock (instead of using cash) to acquire the new property, plant, and equipment. How would this transaction be reported on the statement of cash flows?

Solution on p. 4-61.

ANALYZING FINANCIAL STATEMENTS

LO4-6
Compute and interpret ratios that reflect a company's liquidity and solvency using information reported in the statement of cash flows.

Cash is a special resource for companies because of its flexibility. At short notice, it can be used to fulfill obligations and to take advantage of investment opportunities. When companies run short of cash, their suppliers may be reluctant to deliver and lenders may be able to take over control of decision making. In Chapter 2, we introduced the current ratio, which compares the level of current assets to the level of current liabilities at a point in time. But the statement of cash flows gives us the opportunity to compare a company's ongoing cash generating activities to its obligations and to its investment opportunities.

Interpreting Indirect Method Cash from Operations

We want to interpret the cash flows from operations presented using the indirect method.

When companies use the indirect method to present their cash flows from operating activities, it is difficult to interpret the numbers presented to adjust net income to cash from operating activities. For instance, in **Exhibit 4.11**, One World Café reports $6,000 for the change in accounts receivable. Does that mean that the company received cash payments of $6,000 from its customers? It does not! Every item in the reconciliation has to be interpreted relative to the net income at the top. Net income includes revenue of $390,000, and the adjustment addition of $6,000 means that One World Café received payments of $390,000 + $6,000 = $396,000 from its customers.

The $3,500 adjustment for wages payable does not mean that One World Café received payments of $3,500 from its employees. Rather, the company paid its employees $3,500 less than it recognized as wage expense in determining net income. The adjustment for income tax payable was $(1,500), but that doesn't mean that One World Café's tax payments totaled $1,500 for the year. Rather, the $35,000 net income already reflects a charge for tax expense of $17,000, so the adjustment means that One World's payments for income tax totaled $17,000 + $1,500 = $18,500. Depreciation expense is added back not because it increases cash, but because it is an expense that doesn't require a cash outflow.

How should we interpret the changes in operating assets and liabilities? These assets and liabilities are a function of both the scale of the business and the practices of the business. If we're selling to 10% more customers this year, then we would expect an increase in receivables of about 10% over the previous year. If the increase is substantially more than that amount, then there must have been some other change as well. Perhaps increasing sales required that we give more favorable payment terms and customers are taking longer to pay. Such a development could cause an investor to question the "quality" of the company's earnings. If sales are constant and accounts payable are increasing, that may imply that the company is taking longer to pay its suppliers. That change would appear as a positive adjustment in the indirect method cash from operations, but it may indicate an unfavorable development for the company.

The indirect method may also alert us to gains and losses from nonoperating transactions. These gains and losses are often in "other income" in the income statement, and therefore it's easy for a financial statement reader to miss them. The fact that gains must be subtracted and losses must be added back in the indirect cash from operations gives them a prominence that they don't have in the income statement.

Analysis Objective

We are trying to gauge CVS Health Corporations' generation of cash from its operating activities relative to its average short-term obligations found in the balance sheet.

Analysis Tool   Operating Cash Flow to Current Liabilities (OCFCL)

$$\text{Operating cash flow to current liabilities} = \frac{\text{Operating cash flow}}{\text{Average current liabilities*}}$$

*The average is computed by adding the beginning and ending balances of current liabilities and dividing by two.

Applying the Operating Cash Flow to Current Liabilities Ratio to CVS Health Corporation

$$2018: \frac{\$8,865}{\$37,329} = 0.24 \text{ or } 24\%$$

$$2019: \frac{\$12,848}{\$48,656} = 0.26 \text{ or } 26\%$$

$$2020: \frac{\$15,865}{\$57,660} = 0.28 \text{ or } 28\%$$

Guidance CVS Health Corporation's OCFCL is lower than the retail industry average. CVS Health's business is relatively low-margin, which means that it requires a large flow of resources to generate profits and cash from operations, and that large volume of activity results in high levels of current liabilities relative to the cash generated. The OCFCL ratio complements the current ratio and quick ratio introduced in Chapter 2. CVS Health's current ratio is 0.91, also lower than average for the retail industry, and its quick ratio of 0.53 is slightly higher than the industry average.

CVS Health Corporation in Context

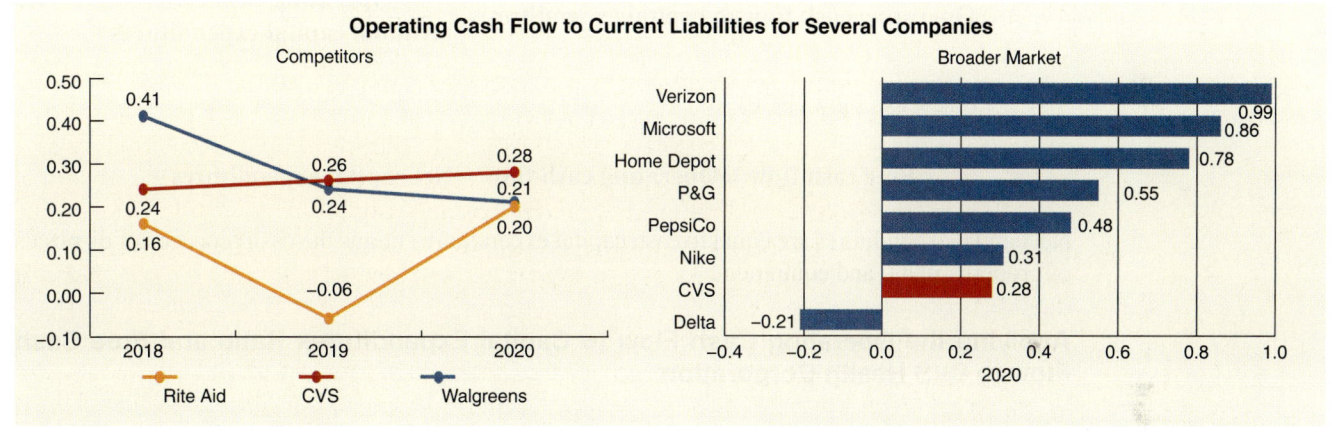

Operating Cash Flow to Current Liabilities for Several Companies

Competitors (2018–2020):
- Rite Aid: 0.16 (2018), −0.06 (2019), 0.20 (2020)
- CVS: 0.24 (2018), 0.26 (2019), 0.28 (2020)
- Walgreens: 0.41 (2018), 0.24 (2019), 0.21 (2020)

Broader Market (2020):
- Verizon: 0.99
- Microsoft: 0.86
- Home Depot: 0.78
- P&G: 0.55
- PepsiCo: 0.48
- Nike: 0.31
- CVS: 0.28
- Delta: −0.21

These companies do not have identical fiscal year-ends. For each fiscal year listed, balance sheets are dated from February 2 to December 31 of that year.

Takeaways Over the past three years, CVS Health's OCFCL ratio has risen steadily and now compares favorably to the two competitors that are included in the chart on the left. Both Walgreen's and Rite Aid's ratios are below the industry average, with Walgreens showing a more stable ratio. Rite Aid is consistently below these other companies. The 2020 increase in CVS Health's OCFCL ratio is largely due to a 23% increase in cash from operations. The comparison of focus companies' OCFCLs in the right-hand chart shows a range from −0.21 for Delta Air Lines to a high of almost one for Verizon. Delta Air Lines was affected significantly by the COVID-19 pandemic, which resulted in an unusual negative value for cash flows from operation. Other than Delta, CVS Health is lower than any of these companies.

Other Considerations There are some transactions that change both the numerator and the denominator, like using cash to pay current operating liabilities. Such a transaction would decrease both the numerator and the denominator, and these changes have an indeterminate effect on the ratio. Paying $100 to a creditor decreases operating cash flow and ending current liabilities by $100, with the average current liabilities decreasing by $50. If the OCFCL is below 2.0 prior to the transaction, it will be even lower after the transaction. If the OCFCL is greater than 2.0 prior to the transaction, it will be even higher after the transaction. Delaying a payment to the creditor would have the opposite effect.

It is also important to take a look at the components of current liabilities. Sometimes there is a large portion of long-term debt that comes due and increases current liabilities for one year. Or, in the case of Delta Air Lines, about 25% of their current liabilities represent unearned revenue from customers who have purchased tickets in advance of travel (like the gift certificates at NBS). For this liability, Delta doesn't have to pay someone; they just need to keep flying.

Analysis Objective

We wish to determine CVS Health's ability to fund the capital expenditures needed to maintain and grow its operations and to make acquisitions.

Does CVS Health generate enough cash from its operations to make its capital investments? If it does not, then the company will have to finance those investments by selling other investments, by borrowing (resulting in future interest costs), by getting cash from shareholders, or by reducing cash balances. If it generates more cash than needed for capital expenditures, then the additional cash can be used to grow the business (e.g., by acquisition) or to distribute cash to investors. Two measures may be used in making this assessment. The first of these measures, operating cash flow to capital expenditures, is a ratio that facilitates comparisons with other companies. The second, free cash flow,[3] is a monetary amount that reflects the funds available for investing in new ventures, buying back stock, paying down debt, or returning funds to stockholders in the form of dividends. The concept is also used in mergers and acquisitions to indicate cash that would be available to the acquirer for investment.

Analysis Tools Operating Cash Flow to Capital Expenditures (OCFCX)

$$\text{Operating cash flow to capital expenditures} = \frac{\text{Operating cash flow}}{\text{Annual capital expenditures}}$$

Free Cash Flow (FCF)

$$\text{Free cash flow} = \text{Operating cash flow} - \text{Net capital expenditures}$$

Net capital expenditures are equal to cash capital expenditures minus the cash proceeds of disposals of property, plant, and equipment.

Applying the Operating Cash Flow to Capital Expenditures Ratio and Free Cash Flow to CVS Health Corporation

	OCFCX		FCF*
2018:	$\frac{\$8,865}{\$2,037}$ = 4.35 or 435%		$8,865 − $2,037 = $6,828
2019:	$\frac{\$12,848}{\$2,457}$ = 5.23 or 523%		$12,848 − $2,457 = $10,391
2020:	$\frac{\$15,865}{\$2,437}$ = 6.51 or 651%		$15,865 − $2,437 = $13,428

*CVS Health did not report proceeds from the sale of property and equipment.

Guidance Operating cash flows to capital expenditures ratios that exceed 1.0 (or free cash flows that are positive) mean that the company can make its capital investments without obtaining additional financing or reducing its cash balances. The excess cash could be used to reduce borrowing, make acquisitions, or it could be returned to shareholders. CVS Health's merger with Aetna in 2018 required more than $40 billion in cash, and CVS Health increased its debt to a level exceeding its long-term target. The company's OCFCX and FCF values have increased significantly across these years, and the company has used this growth in cash flow to repay significant amounts of debt while maintaining dividend payments to shareholders.

---

[3] Free cash flow can be defined in several ways, but it always includes a measure of the cash resources generated by the company's current operations minus a measure of the cash required to sustain those operations. One of the simpler, more common definitions is presented here.

CVS Health Corporation in Context

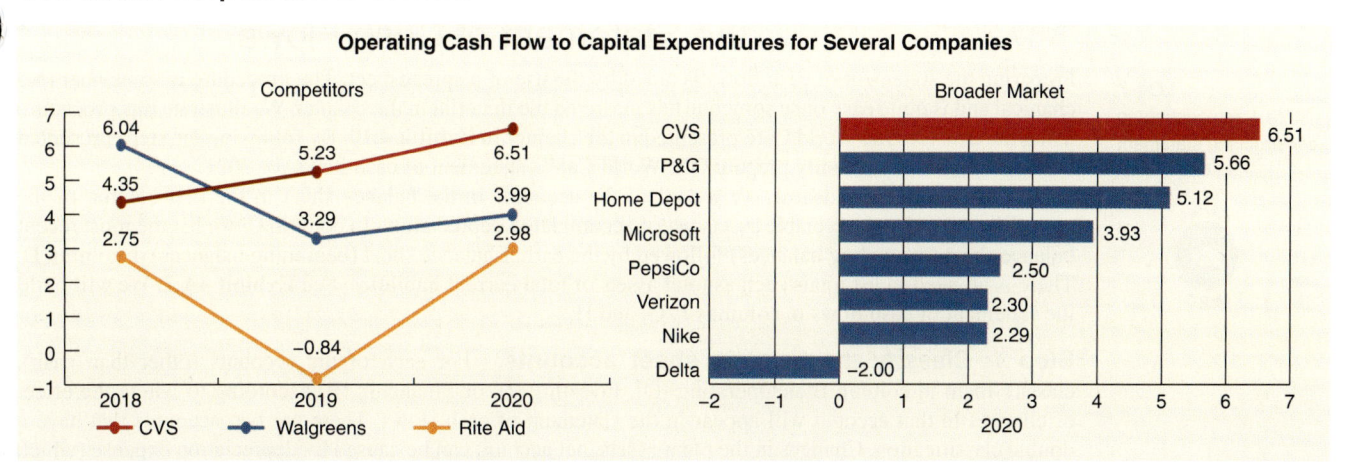

Operating Cash Flow to Capital Expenditures for Several Companies

Competitors chart (2018–2020):
- CVS: 4.35 (2018), 5.23 (2019), 6.51 (2020)
- Walgreens: 6.04 (2018), 3.29 (2019), 3.99 (2020)
- Rite Aid: 2.75 (2018), −0.84 (2019), 2.98 (2020)

Broader Market (2020):
- CVS: 6.51
- P&G: 5.66
- Home Depot: 5.12
- Microsoft: 3.93
- PepsiCo: 2.50
- Verizon: 2.30
- Nike: 2.29
- Delta: −2.00

Takeaways OCFCX increased steadily over the last three years for CVS Health, and its OCFCX is higher than Walgreens and Rite Aid. Like CVS Health, Walgreens and Rite Aid have used the additional cash flow to acquire other businesses and repay long-term debt. But CVS Health's merger with Aetna has resulted in an increase in cash flow from operations that is greater than the increase in capital expenditures. CVS Health has used that growth to repay debt that was used to purchase Aetna, to make new investments, and to maintain dividends to shareholders. The OCFCX values for the focus companies show that many of them—with the exception of Delta—were able to weather the pandemic with cash flows adequate to conduct operations.

Other Considerations Measurement of cash flows is regarded as more objective than measures of income and less dependent on management judgments and estimates. But it may be subject to "lumpy" behavior from management's decisions, particularly for smaller companies. Capital expenditures may differ significantly from year to year if management takes on large, but infrequent, projects. A series of high values of OCFCX followed by a low value might mean deterioration in cash generating performance, but it might also mean that management has been accumulating cash in anticipation of a major project.

RESEARCH INSIGHT

Is the Statement of Cash Flows Useful? Some analysts rely on cash flow forecasts to value common stock. Research shows that both net income and operating cash flows are correlated with stock prices, but that stock prices are more highly correlated with net income than with cash flows. So, do we need both statements? Evidence suggests that by using *both* net income and cash flow information, we can improve our forecasts of *future* cash flows. Also, net income and cash flow together are more highly correlated with stock prices than either net income or cash flow alone. This result suggests that, for purposes of stock valuation, information from the statement of cash flows complements information from the income statement.

Calculating Ratios to Assess Liquidity and Solvency LO4-6 **Review 4-6**

Refer to One World Café's statement of cash flows and comparative balance sheets from **Exhibits 4.10** and **4.11** to complete the following.

Required
1. Calculate the operating cash flow to current liabilities (OCFCL) ratio for One World Café and interpret your findings. Assume that the notes payable are due within the year and are a current liability.
2. Calculate One World Café's operating cash flow to capital expenditures (OCFCX) ratio. What observations can you make about your findings?
3. Calculate the free cash flow (FCF) for One World Café.

Solution on p. 4-63.

APPENDIX 4A: A Spreadsheet Approach to Preparing the Statement of Cash Flows

LO4-7
Use a spreadsheet to construct the statement of cash flows.

Preparing the statement of cash flows is aided by the use of a spreadsheet. The procedure is somewhat mechanical and is quite easy once someone has mastered the material in the chapter. We illustrate this procedure using the data for One World Café presented in the chapter in **Exhibit 4.10**. By following the steps presented below, we are able to readily prepare One World Café's statement of cash flows for 2021.

To set up the spreadsheet, we list all of the accounts in the balance sheet in the first column of the spreadsheet. We list depreciable assets net of accumulated depreciation. In column C, we list the most recent balance sheet (the ending balances) followed by the earlier balance sheet (beginning balances) in column D. There is no need to list totals such as total assets or total current liabilities. See **Exhibit 4A.1**. We will build the statement of cash flows in columns F, G, and H.

Step 1: Classify the balance sheet accounts. For each of the accounts (other than cash), classify them in column B as Operating (O), Investing (I), or Financing (F) according to where the effect of changes in that account will appear in the statement of cash flows. There are two accounts that have a double classification. Changes in the plant assets, net account can be caused by depreciation expense (which will appear in the indirect method cash from operations) and by investing activities, so we label it as (O, I). Changes in the retained earnings account are caused by net income (which appears in the indirect method cash from operations) and dividends, so we label it as (O, F).

For those rows labeled I or F, insert two rows below: one for increases in the account and one for decreases in the account because we must report increases and decreases separately. For plant assets, net, insert three rows below: one for depreciation expense, one for plant asset acquisitions, and one for plant asset sales. For retained earnings, insert two rows below: one for net income and one for dividends.

EXHIBIT 4A.1 — Cash Flow Spreadsheet for One World Café

	A	B	C	D	E	F	G	H	I	J
1		O, I or F?	2021	2020	Change	\multicolumn{3}{c}{Effect of Change on Cash Flow}	No Effect on Cash	Total F, G, H, I
2						Operating	Investing	Financing		
3	**Assets**									
4	Cash...........		8,000	12,000	(4,000)					
5										
6	Accounts receivable.....	O	22,000	28,000	(6,000)	6,000				6,000
7	Inventory.............	O	94,000	66,000	28,000	(28,000)				(28,000)
8	Prepaid advertising.....	O	12,000	9,000	3,000	(3,000)				(3,000)
9	Plant assets, net.......	O,I	136,000	109,000	27,000					
10	Depreciation expense..					17,000				
11	Plant assets purchased..						(45,000)		(5,000)	(27,000)
12	Plant assets sold......					2,000	4,000			
13										
14	**Liabilities**									
15	Accounts payable......	O	27,000	14,000	13,000	13,000				13,000
16	Wages payable........	O	6,000	2,500	3,500	3,500				3,500
17	Income tax payable....	O	3,000	4,500	(1,500)	(1,500)				(1,500)
18	Notes payable.........	F	5,000	—	5,000					
19	New borrowing.......								5,000	5,000
20	Borrowing repayments..									
21										
22	**Shareholders' Equity**									
23	Common stock........	F	134,000	125,000	9,000					
24	New issue of common stock....							9,000		9,000
25	Repurchase of common stock..									
26	Retained earnings......	O,F	97,000	78,000	19,000					
27	Net income..........					35,000				19,000
28	Dividends...........							(16,000)		
29										
30	Totals.............					44,000	(41,000)	(7,000)	—	(4,000)

Step 2: Compute the changes in the balance sheet accounts. Subtract the beginning balances in each account from the ending balances and record these in column E. We highlight the change in the cash balance because this is the amount that we are trying to explain. At this point it is useful to verify that the change in cash is equal to the changes in liabilities plus the changes in stockholders' equity minus the changes in noncash assets:

$$\Delta \text{Cash} = \Delta \text{Liabilities} + \Delta \text{Stockholders' Equity} - \Delta \text{Noncash Assets}$$

In effect, we're going to use changes on the right-hand side of this equation to explain the changes in cash on the left-hand side.

Step 3: Handle the accounts that have single classifications. For those accounts that are operating-only assets (accounts receivable, inventory, prepaid expenses, etc.), we enter in column F the *negative* of the value in column E. The $28,000 increase in inventories in column E results in $(28,000) for the operating cash flows in column F. Changes in assets have the opposite effect on cash. Increases in assets have a negative effect on cash, while decreases in assets lead to positive adjustments to cash.

For those accounts that are operating only liabilities (accounts payable, wages payable, taxes payable, etc.), we enter in column F the value in column E. The $13,000 increase in accounts payable produces a $13,000 entry in column F.

For those accounts that are financing only (notes payable, common stock), we enter in column H the cash effect(s) of the change in column E. For example, we must be aware that the common stock account could have changed due to both issuing stock for cash and repurchasing stock for cash. For One World Café, there was only a $9,000 inflow due to a new stock issue in column H. (We will deal with the notes payable changes in the next step.)

One World Café has no assets that are investing only, but for such accounts (marketable securities, investments, etc.), we would again make entries for increases and decreases separately. And, because these are assets, the change in the balance sheet has the opposite sign of the entry in the cash flow columns. For instance, if One World Café had invested $10,000 in a financial security, its investments asset would increase, and we would put an entry of $(10,000) in column G.

Step 4: Enter the effect of investing/financing transactions that do not involve cash. We know from the information provided about One World Café that it arranged the purchase of $5,000 of plant assets by signing a note payable for the same amount. This transaction affected an investing asset and a financing liability at the same time, and we put the effects into column I. $5,000 is put in the new borrowing row (19), and $(5,000) is put in the plant assets purchased row (11). This transaction will not appear in the statement of cash flows in columns F, G, and H, but it does explain some of the changes in the company's assets and liabilities.

Step 5: Analyze the change in retained earnings. Some accounts require special attention because the change in the account balance involves two types of cash flow effects. For example, the change in retained earnings is actually two changes—net income, which is related to operations, and dividends, which is a financing cash outflow.

One World Café's retained earnings increased by $19,000. It reported net income of $35,000, which is listed as an operating item (because we're using the indirect method), and paid dividends of $16,000, a cash outflow listed under financing activities. For clarity, it is helpful to list each of these changes on a separate line. Thus, we have inserted two lines into the spreadsheet immediately below retained earnings—the first for net income and the second for dividends. The $35,000 inflow and the $16,000 outflow net to $19,000.

Step 6: Analyze the change in plant assets. A change in depreciable assets is actually the result of both operating and investing items. The change in plant assets can be explained by looking at the individual transactions that caused the change. As was the case with retained earnings, it is helpful to list each of these transactions in a separate row in the spreadsheet. Thus, we have inserted three rows into the spreadsheet immediately below the change in plant assets. First, we recall that One World Café reported depreciation expense of $17,000, which reduced its plant assets, net. This is listed in the first row under plant assets as a positive adjustment to cash flow from operations because cash flow effects on the asset side have the opposite sign.

In the next row, we list purchases of plant assets. One World Café purchased plant assets for $45,000 in cash, which is listed under investing as a cash outflow in column F. There was also the $5,000 purchase of plant assets that was financed with notes payable. This transaction did not affect cash, so it's in column I.

In the third row below plant assets, we list the sale of plant assets. One World Café sold plant assets for $4,000 cash, recognizing a loss of $2,000. The loss is listed in the operations column (as a positive adjustment to operating cash flow), and the proceeds from the sale are listed under investing as a cash inflow in column F.

When all of the balance sheet changes have been analyzed, the change for each account should add up to the sum of the effect on operating, investing, and financing cash flows, plus the amount in the "no effect" column. That is, for each change listed in the spreadsheet in column E, we can add columns F, G, H, and I to get the change in the balance sheet account in column J. For retained earnings: $35,000 – $16,000 = $19,000. For assets, the total will be the *negative* of the change. Adding up entries for plant assets: $17,000 – $45,000 – $5,000 + $2,000 + $4,000 = –$27,000, which is minus the amount in column E, row 9.

Step 7: Total the columns. We add up the effects listed in columns F, G, H, and I to get the cash flow subtotals. One World Café had cash flow from operations of $44,000, investing cash flows of −$41,000, and financing cash flows of −$7,000. The total for the "no effect" column (column I) should be $0 because the entries in this column had no effect on cash flow. Finally, we add up these totals to make sure that the cash flow effects equal the change in cash: $44,000 − $41,000 − $7,000 − $0 = −$4,000. If the totals do not add up to the change in cash, then there must be an error in analyzing one or more of the balance sheet changes. For example, if we had forgotten to subtract dividends, then the cash flow effects in columns F, G, and H would not add up to the change in retained earnings listed in column E. Likewise, if we had mistakenly omitted the sale of plant assets, then the change in plant assets would not add up correctly. Totaling the columns and rows is a check to verify that our analysis is complete and correct.

Step 8: Prepare the statement of cash flows. Starting with operating cash flows (column F), we list each of the items in the statement of cash flows. We start with net income and then add depreciation and the loss on the sale of plant assets. Then we list the remaining adjustments, starting with the change in accounts receivable and working down the column. Next, we do the same for the items listed in the investing (column G) and financing (column H) sections of the statement of cash flows. The resulting statement is identical to the statement presented in **Exhibit 4.11**.

Review 4-7 LO4-7

Using a Spreadsheet to Create a Statement of Cash Flows

The comparative balance sheets and income statement information for Rocky Road Bicycles, Inc., are as follows.

ROCKY ROAD BICYCLES, INC.
Comparative Balance Sheets

At December 31	2021	2020
Assets		
Cash	$ 106,000	$ 96,000
Accounts receivable	156,000	224,000
Inventory	752,000	528,000
Prepaid rent	68,000	72,000
Plant assets	1,692,000	1,360,000
Less accumulated depreciation	(562,000)	(488,000)
Total assets	$2,212,000	$1,792,000
Liabilities		
Accounts payable	$ 216,000	$ 112,000
Wages payable	18,000	20,000
Income tax payable	44,000	36,000
Equity		
Common stock	1,142,000	1,000,000
Retained earnings	792,000	624,000
Total liabilities and equity	$2,212,000	$1,792,000

Additional Information

- Rocky Road reported net income of $326,000 in 2021.
- Depreciation expense was $122,000 in 2021.
- Rocky Road sold plant assets during 2021. The plant assets originally cost $88,000, with accumulated depreciation of $48,000, and were sold for a gain of $16,000.
- Rocky Road declared and paid a $158,000 cash dividend in 2021.

Required

Solution on p. 4-64. Use a spreadsheet to create a statement of cash flows for Rocky Road Bicycles, Inc.

SUMMARY

LO4-1 **Explain the purpose of the statement of cash flows and classify cash transactions by type of business activity: operating, investing, or financing. (p. 4-3)**

- The statement of cash flows summarizes information about the flow of cash into and out of the business.
- Operating cash flow includes any cash transactions related to selling goods or rendering services, as well as interest payments and receipts, tax payments, and any transaction not specifically classified as investing or financing.

- Investing cash flow includes acquiring and disposing of plant assets, buying and selling securities, including securities of other companies, and lending and subsequently collecting funds from a borrower.
- Financing cash flow includes all cash received or paid to shareholders, including stock issued or repurchased and dividends paid. In addition, it includes amounts borrowed and repaid to creditors.

Construct the operating activities section of the statement of cash flows using the direct method. (p. 4-7)   **LO4-2**

- The direct method presents net cash flow from operating activities by showing the major categories of operating cash receipts and payments.
- The operating cash receipts and payments are usually determined by converting the accrual revenues and expenses to corresponding cash amounts.

Reconcile cash flows from operations to net income and use the indirect method to compute operating cash flows. (p. 4-17)   **LO4-3**

- Because operating cash flow differs from net income, a reconciliation of these two amounts helps financial statement users understand the sources of this difference.
- The indirect method reconciles net income and operating cash flows by making adjustments for noncash revenues and expenses and changes in balance sheet accounts related to operations.

Construct the investing and financing activities sections of the statement of cash flows. (p. 4-19)   **LO4-4**

- Investing activities capture cash flows from the purchase and disposal of long-term assets such as property, plant, and equipment as well as from the purchase (disposal) of other companies (subsidiaries). Cash flows related to the purchase and disposal of investing assets such as marketable securities and long-term financial investment would be included as well.
- Cash obtained from the issuance of securities or borrowings, and any repayments of debt, are disclosed in the financing section. Cash dividends are also included in this section. Interest payments are included in the operating section of the statement.

Examine the sale of investing assets and the disclosure of noncash activities. (p. 4-23)   **LO4-5**

- Cash receipts from asset disposals are included in the investing section. Because cash receipts include any gain on sale (or reflect any loss), the gain (loss) must be subtracted from (added to) net income in the operating section to avoid double-counting.
- Some events, for example assets donated to the firm, provide resources to the business that are important but which do not involve cash outlays. These events are disclosed separately, along with the statement of cash flows, as supplementary disclosures or in the notes.

Compute and interpret ratios that reflect a company's liquidity and solvency using information reported in the statement of cash flows. (p. 4-29)   **LO4-6**

- Interpreting indirect method cash from operations requires reference to those items that comprise net income. Each adjustment is intended to modify an income statement item to bring it to cash from operations.
- Two ratios of importance that are based on cash flows include:
  - Operating cash flow to current liabilities—a measure of the adequacy of current operations to cover current liability payments.
  - Operating cash flow to capital expenditures—a reflection of a company's ability to replace or expand its activities based on the level of current operations.
- Free cash flow is defined as: Cash flow from operations – Net capital expenditures.
- Free cash flow is a measure of a company's ability to apply its resources to new endeavors.

Appendix 4A: Use a spreadsheet to construct the statement of cash flows. (p. 4-33)   **LO4-7**

- A spreadsheet helps to prepare the statement of cash flows by classifying the effect of each change in the balance sheet as operating, investing, financing, or not affecting cash.
- The spreadsheet approach relies on the key relationship:

  Cash = Liabilities + Stockholders' equity − Noncash assets

GUIDANCE ANSWERS . . . YOU MAKE THE CALL

You are the Chief Accountant In its annual report for fiscal year 2020, Kohl's Corporation would report an increase of $197 million as "proceeds from sale of real estate" in the investing section of its statement of cash flows. The indirect method cash flow from operations of that statement would show an adjustment of a negative $127 million for "Gain on sale of real estate."

You are the Securities Analyst A company's operating activities are the "engine" that produces the cash flows that allow the investment necessary for growth and the funds that may be returned to the sources of capital. Accounting standards say that cash flows from operating activities include cash receipts from sales of goods or services, *including receipts from collection or sale of accounts*. So, receipts from the sale of accounts receivable should be included in cash from operations, along with ordinary cash receipts from customers. However, an analyst should consider the circumstances of the sale of receivables. Is such a sale part of the company's regular practices, enabling it to cut its borrowing or increase its growth? Or, if the sale is a new transaction, does it indicate that the company is having difficulty collecting from its customers or experiencing unusual expenditures or financing problems? Companies will almost always sell receivables at a discount—how much is it giving up to have access to the cash today? Many analysts argue that operating cash flows do not increase as a result of such transactions and that analysts should adjust the statement of cash flows to classify the sale of receivables as a financing activity.

KEY RATIOS

$$\text{Operating cash flow to current liabilities} = \frac{\text{Operating cash flow}}{\text{Average current liabilities}}$$

$$\text{Operating cash flow to capital expenditures} = \frac{\text{Operating cash flow}}{\text{Annual capital expenditures}}$$

$$\text{Free cash flow} = \text{Operating cash flow} - \text{Net capital expenditures}$$

Assignments with the MBC logo in the margin are available in *my*BusinessCourse.
See the Preface of the book for details.

MULTIPLE CHOICE

Multiple Choice Answers
1. a   2. c   3. d   4. c   5. c

1. Which of the following is not disclosed in a statement of cash flows?
   a. A transfer of cash to a cash equivalent investment
   b. The amount of cash at year-end
   c. Cash outflows from investing activities during the period
   d. Cash inflows from financing activities during the period

2. Which of the following events appears in the cash flows from investing activities section of the statement of cash flows?
   a. Cash received from customers
   b. Cash received from issuance of common stock
   c. Cash purchase of equipment
   d. Cash payment of dividends

3. Which of the following events appears in the cash flows from financing activities section of the statement of cash flows?
   a. Cash purchase of equipment
   b. Cash purchase of bonds issued by another company
   c. Cash received as repayment for funds loaned
   d. Cash purchase of treasury stock

4. Tyler Company has a net income of $73,500 and the following related items:

Depreciation expense	$ 7,500
Accounts receivable increase	3,000
Inventory decrease	15,000
Accounts payable decrease	6,000

   Using the indirect method, what is Tyler's net cash flow from operations?
   a. $63,000
   b. $69,000
   c. $87,000
   d. $57,000

5. Refer to information in Review 4-2. Assume that notes payable are not due within the coming year and are classified as a noncurrent liability. The operating cash flow to current liabilities ratio for Mug Shots, Inc., in December is
   a. 6.4%.
   b. 2.9%.
   c. 2.6%.
   d. impossible to determine from the data provided.

Superscript ^A^ denotes assignments based on Appendix 4A.

QUESTIONS

Q4-1. What is the definition of *cash equivalents*? Give three examples of cash equivalents.

Q4-2. Why are cash equivalents included with cash in a statement of cash flows?

Q4-3. What are the three major types of activities classified on a statement of cash flows? Give an example of a cash inflow and a cash outflow in each classification.

Q4-4. In which of the three activity categories of a statement of cash flows would each of the following items appear? Indicate for each item whether it represents a cash inflow or a cash outflow:
   a. Cash purchase of equipment.
   b. Cash collection on loans.
   c. Cash dividends paid.
   d. Cash dividends received.
   e. Cash proceeds from issuing stock.
   f. Cash receipts from customers.
   g. Cash interest paid.
   h. Cash interest received.

Q4-5. Traverse Company acquired a $5,000,000 building by issuing $5,000,000 worth of bonds payable. In terms of cash flow reporting, what type of transaction is this? What special disclosure requirements apply to a transaction of this type?

Q4-6. Why are noncash investing and financing transactions disclosed as supplemental information to a statement of cash flows?

Q4-7. Companies are sometimes required to maintain minimum balances of cash for contractual reasons, making the cash unavailable for general business purposes. How does such an arrangement affect the financial statements of the reporting company?

Q4-8. What is the difference between the direct method and the indirect method of presenting net cash flow from operating activities?

Q4-9. In determining net cash flow from operating activities using the indirect method, why must we add depreciation back to net income? Give an example of another item that is added back to net income under the indirect method.

Q4-10. Vista Company sold for $49,000 cash land originally costing $35,000. The company recorded a gain on the sale of $14,000. How is this event reported in a statement of cash flows using the indirect method?

Q4-11. A firm uses the indirect method. Using the following information, what is its net cash flow from operating activities?

Net income	$132,000
Accounts receivable decrease	19,500
Inventory increase	13,500
Accounts payable decrease	5,250
Income tax payable increase	2,250
Depreciation expense	9,000

Q4-12. What separate disclosures are required for a company that reports a statement of cash flows using the indirect method to report cash flows from operating activities?

Q4-13. If a business had a net loss for the year, under what circumstances would the statement of cash flows show a positive net cash flow from operating activities?

Q4-14. A firm is converting its accrual revenues to corresponding cash amounts using the direct method. Sales on the income statement are $740,000. Beginning and ending accounts receivable on the balance sheet are $46,400 and $35,200, respectively. What is the amount of cash received from customers?

Q4-15. A firm reports $129,000 wages expense in its income statement. If beginning and ending wages payable are $5,850 and $4,200, respectively, what is the amount of cash paid to employees?

Q4-16. A firm reports $51,600 advertising expense in its income statement. If beginning and ending prepaid advertising are $7,200 and $9,120, respectively, what is the amount of cash paid for advertising?

Q4-17. Rusk Company sold equipment for $10,200 cash that had cost $70,000 and had $58,000 of accumulated depreciation. How is this event reported in a statement of cash flows using the direct method to report the operating activities section?

Q4-18. What separate disclosures are required for a company that reports the operating activities section of a statement of cash flows using the direct method?

Q4-19. How is the operating cash flow to current liabilities ratio calculated? Explain its use.

Q4-20. How is the operating cash flow to capital expenditures ratio calculated? Explain its use.

DATA ANALYTICS

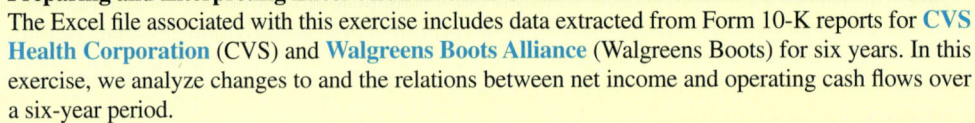

LO4-3 DA4-1. Preparing and Interpreting Excel Visualizations Created from Income and Cash Flow Data

The Excel file associated with this exercise includes data extracted from Form 10-K reports for **CVS Health Corporation** (CVS) and **Walgreens Boots Alliance** (Walgreens Boots) for six years. In this exercise, we analyze changes to and the relations between net income and operating cash flows over a six-year period.

REQUIRED
1. Download Excel file DA4-1 found in myBusinessCourse.
2. Prepare a line chart for the six-year period for each company showing net income and operating cash flows. *Hint:* Highlight your data; click on Insert, Select line chart. There should be a separate line for net income and a separate line for operating cash flows. If necessary, edit the chart by opening the Chart Design tab and clicking Select Data. There should be two series.
3. Use the visualizations to answer the following questions.
    a. In what year(s) does net income exceed operating cash flows for CVS?
    b. In what year(s) do operating cash flows exceed net income for Walgreens Boots?
    c. Over the six-year period, which year showed the largest difference between net income and operating cash flows for CVS?
    d. What is a likely cause of the difference shown between net income and operating cash flows for the year identified in part c?
    e. For Walgreens Boots, in what year were net income and operating cash flows most similar?
    f. For CVS, in what year were net income and operating cash flows most similar?
    g. How would you compare the trend of operating cash flows for CVS vs. Walgreens Boots?

LO4-6 DA4-2. Analyzing Cash Flow Ratio Trends by Industry Segment

The Excel file associated with this exercise includes Compustat data for S&P 500 companies for Year 1 through Year 5. For this exercise, we analyze trends in cash flow ratios by industry segment. The current cash debt coverage ratio is a liquidity ratio that measures whether a company can pay its *current* debts with cash provided from operating activities. The cash debt coverage ratio is a solvency ratio that measures a company's ability to pay *all* debts with cash provided from operating activities. In both cases, an increase in the ratio is generally viewed as favorable because it indicates that the company has a stronger ability to pay off obligations.

PART 1 PREPARING THE DATA
1. Download Excel file DA4-2 found in myBusinessCourse.
2. Format the worksheet as a table. *Hint:* Highlight data in worksheet by clicking on keys Alt and A simultaneously. Select Insert, Table.
3. Sort data in table by Segment and delete all rows in the Financials and Real Estate Segments. Companies in these industries rarely report current assets or liabilities. *Hint:* Because this worksheet is formatted as a table, you can sort by any row using the dropdown at the column head.
4. Add a column to calculate average current liabilities for Years 2 through 5. *Hint:* Use the IF function to calculate the amount (the average current liabilities for that year). If the company name agrees to the company name in the previous cell (Company Name column), then calculate the average; otherwise, put "n/a" in the cell. Year 1 will always be n/a.

5. Copy and Paste Special—Values back into the same cells. This will allow you to sort by other columns in the table without causing a recalculation error. *Hint:* To quickly highlight a long column, double-click on the bottom right corner of the first cell in the column.
6. Add a column to calculate average liabilities for Years 2 through 5. *Hint:* Use similar steps as in part 4.
7. Create a ratio column to calculate the current cash debt coverage ratio and a ratio column to calculate the cash debt coverage ratio. Sort your worksheet in ascending order by each ratio column and eliminate any rows with errors due to incomplete information (such as a Year 1 calculation) or where the answer is zero and it indicates an error or missing information.
8. Eliminate extreme outliers by deleting any company's information where it shows a ratio over +/−60. Be sure to eliminate all years of data of any company considered an outlier.
9. Check your output by answering the following questions:
    a. What is the Current cash debt coverage ratio for XRX for Year 3?
    b. What is the Cash debt coverage ratio for GD for Year 2?
    c. What is Cash flow from operations for HD for Year 5?
    d. How many rows are included for the Materials segment? *Hint:* Sort your worksheet by segment and then by the Materials column and view the "Count" at the bottom right of your screen.

Current Cash Debt Coverage
$$\frac{\text{Cash provided by operating activities}}{\text{Average current liabilities}}$$

Cash Debt Coverage
$$\frac{\text{Cash provided by operating activities}}{\text{Average total liabilities}}$$

PART 2 CREATING A PIVOTTABLE

1. Create a PivotTable showing the average current cash debt coverage ratio and cash debt coverage ratio by segment by year. *Hint:* Drag Year then Segment to Rows and Current cash debt coverage and Cash debt coverage to Values. *Hint:* Right-click on a numeric field, select Value Field Settings, and change to Average.
2. Format your table to show two decimal places. *Hint:* Right-click on any item in the column to format and click on Number Format to update.
3. Eliminate totals from your chart. *Hint:* Click on the Design tab (it will be highlighted when you click anywhere in your PivotTable), Grand totals, Off for rows & columns.
4. Answer the following questions:
    a. Which industry segment has the highest average current cash debt coverage ratio in Year 2?
    b. Which industry segment has the lowest average current cash debt coverage ratio in Year 3?
    c. Which industry segment has the highest average cash debt coverage ratio in Year 5?
    d. Which industry segment has the lowest average cash debt coverage ratio in Year 5?
    e. What company had the largest current cash debt coverage ratio listed in the Telecommunications segment in Year 5? *Hint:* Double-click on the ratio amount in the PivotTable for Telecommunications, Year 5 to open up a new sheet with the supporting detail.

PART 3 PREPARING AND ANALYZING A PIVOTCHART

1. Create a PivotChart of the Cash Debt Coverage Ratio using a line chart.
2. Add a Slicer for Segment. *Hint:* Click inside the chart, click PivotChart Analyze, and click Add Slicer.
3. Describe the trend in each segment from Year 2 through Year 5.

DATA VISUALIZATION

Data Visualization Activities are available in myBusinessCourse. These assignments use Tableau Dashboards to expose students to visual depictions of data and introduce students to data analytics through data visualizations. These exercises are easily assignable and auto graded by MBC.

MINI EXERCISES

M4-21. Identifying the Impact of Account Changes on Cash Flow from Operating Activities (Indirect Method)   **LO4-1, 3, 4**

The following account information was presented as adjustments to net income in the 2019 fiscal year statement of cash flows for **Target Corporation**. Determine whether each item would be a positive adjustment or a negative adjustment to net income in determining cash from operations. ($ millions).

Target
NYSE :: TGT

a. Operating activities increased accounts payable by $140.
b. Operating activities decreased inventories by $505.
c. Early extinguishment of debt resulted in a loss of $10.
d. Depreciation and amortization expense was $2,604.
e. Operating activities decreased other assets by $18.

LO4-1 **M4-22. Classifying Cash Flows**

For each of the items below, indicate whether the cash flow relates to an operating activity, an investing activity, or a financing activity.

a. Cash receipts from customers for services rendered.
b. Sale of long-term investments for cash.
c. Acquisition of plant assets for cash.
d. Payment of income taxes.
e. Bonds payable issued for cash.
f. Payment of cash dividends declared in previous year.
g. Purchase of short-term investments (not cash equivalents) for cash.

LO4-1, 3 **M4-23. Classifying Components of the Statement of Cash Flows**

The following table presents selected items from a recent statement of cash flows of **General Mills, Inc.** For each item, determine whether the amount would be disclosed in the statement of cash flows under operating activities, investing activities, or financing activities. (General Mills uses the indirect method of reporting cash flows from operating activities.)

General Mills, Inc.
NYSE :: GIS

GENERAL MILLS, INC.
Selected Items from Its Statement of Cash Flows

1. Payment of long-term debt
2. Change in receivables
3. Depreciation and amortization
4. Change in prepaid expenses
5. Dividends paid
6. Stock-based compensation
7. Cash received from sales of assets and businesses
8. Net earnings
9. Change in accounts payable
10. Proceeds from common stock issued
11. Purchases of land, buildings, and equipment

LO4-1, 5 **M4-24. Classifying Cash Flows**

For each of the items below, indicate whether it is (1) a cash flow from an operating activity, (2) a cash flow from an investing activity, (3) a cash flow from a financing activity, (4) a noncash investing and financing activity, or (5) none of the above.

a. Paid cash to retire bonds payable at a loss.
b. Received cash as settlement of a lawsuit.
c. Acquired a patent in exchange for common stock.
d. Received advance payments from customers on orders for custom-made goods.
e. Gave large cash contribution to local university.
f. Invested cash in 60-day commercial paper (a cash equivalent).

LO4-2, 3 **M4-25. Reconciling Net Income and Cash Flow from Operations Using FSET**

For the year, Beyer GmbH had the following summary information available concerning its operating activities. The company had no investing or financing activities this year.

1.	Sales of merchandise to customers on credit.	€253,700
2.	Sales of merchandise to customers for cash	45,750
3.	Cost of merchandise sold on credit	160,050
4.	Cost of merchandise sold for cash	31,700
5.	Purchases of merchandise from suppliers on credit.	175,800
6.	Purchases of merchandise from suppliers for cash	23,850
7.	Collections from customers on accounts receivable.	241,700
8.	Cash payments to suppliers on accounts payable	170,100
9.	Operating expenses (all paid in cash)	86,150

REQUIRED

a. Enter the items above into the Financial Statement Effects Template. Under noncash assets, use two separate columns for accounts receivable and inventories. Calculate the totals for each column.
b. What was the company's net income for the year? What was the cash flow from operating activities? (Use the direct method.)
c. Indicate the direction and amounts by which each of the following accounts changed during the year.
  1. Accounts receivable
  2. Merchandise inventory
  3. Accounts payable
d. Using your results above, prepare the operating activities section of the statement of cash flows using the indirect format.

M4-26. Calculating Net Cash Flow from Operating Activities (Indirect Method) LO4-3

The following information was obtained from Galena Company's comparative balance sheets. Assume that Galena Company's annual income statement showed depreciation expense of $12,000, a gain on sale of investments of $13,500, and net income of $67,500. Calculate the net cash flow from operating activities using the indirect method.

	Ending	Beginning
Cash	$ 28,500	$ 13,500
Accounts receivable	66,000	52,500
Inventory	82,500	73,500
Prepaid rent	9,000	12,000
Long-term investments	31,500	51,000
Plant assets	225,000	159,000
Accumulated depreciation	60,000	48,000
Accounts payable	36,000	30,000
Income tax payable	6,000	9,000
Common stock	181,500	138,000
Retained earnings	159,000	136,500

M4-27. Reconciling Net Income and Cash Flow from Operations Using FSET LO4-2, 3

For the year, Riffe Enterprises had the following summary information available concerning its operating activities. The company had no investing or financing activities this year.

1.	Sales of services to customers on credit	$384,600
2.	Sales of services to customers for cash	23,100
3.	Employee compensation earned	263,350
4.	Cash payment in advance to landlord for offices	74,550
5.	Cash paid to employees for compensation	260,800
6.	Rental expense for offices used over the year	58,950
7.	Collections from customers on accounts receivable	362,050
8.	Operating expenses (all paid in cash)	61,400
9.	Depreciation expense	11,500

REQUIRED

a. Enter the items above into the Financial Statement Effects Template. Under noncash assets, use three separate columns for accounts receivable and prepaid rent and the accumulated depreciation contra-asset. Calculate the totals for each column.
b. What was the company's net income for the year? What was the cash flow from operating activities? (Use the direct method.)
c. Indicate the direction and amounts by which each of the following accounts changed during the year.
  1. Accounts receivable
  2. Prepaid rent
  3. Accumulated depreciation
  4. Wages payable
d. Using your results above, prepare the operating activities section of the statement of cash flows using the indirect format.

LO4-3 **M4-28. Calculating Net Cash Flow from Operating Activities (Indirect Method)**

Weber Company had a $16,800 net loss from operations for the year. Depreciation expense for the year was $6,880, and a cash dividend of $4,800 was declared and paid. Balances of the current asset and current liability accounts at the beginning and end of the year follow. Did Weber Company's operating activities for the year provide or use cash? Use the indirect method to determine your answer.

	Ending	Beginning
Cash	$ 2,800	$ 5,600
Accounts receivable	12,800	20,000
Inventory	40,000	42,400
Prepaid expenses	4,800	7,200
Accounts payable	9,600	6,400
Accrued liabilities	4,000	6,080

LO4-1, 3 **M4-29. Classifying Statement of Cash Flows Components and Determining Their Effects**

The following table presents selected items from a recent statement of cash flows of **Nordstrom, Inc.**

a. For each item, determine whether the amount would be disclosed in the statement of cash flows under operating activities, investing activities, or financing activities. (Nordstrom uses the indirect method of reporting.)

b. For each item, determine whether it will appear as a positive or negative in determining the net increase in cash and cash equivalents.

NORDSTROM, INC.
Consolidated Statement of Cash Flows—Selected Items

1. Decrease in accounts receivable
2. Capital expenditures
3. Proceeds from long-term borrowings
4. Increase in deferred income tax net liability
5. Principal payments on long-term borrowings
6. Increase in merchandise inventories
7. Increase in prepaid expenses and other assets
8. Proceeds from issuances under stock compensation plans
9. Increase in accounts payable
10. Net earnings
11. Payments for repurchase of common stock
12. Increase in accrued salaries, wages, and related benefits
13. Cash dividends paid
14. Depreciation and amortization expenses

LO4-2 **M4-30. Calculating Operating Cash Flows (Direct Method)**

Calculate the cash flow for each of the following cases.

a. Cash paid for rent:

Rent expense	$90,000
Prepaid rent, beginning of year	15,000
Prepaid rent, end of year	12,000

b. Cash received as interest:

Interest income	$24,000
Interest receivable, beginning of year	4,500
Interest receivable, end of year	5,550

c. Cash paid for merchandise purchased:

Cost of goods sold	$147,000
Inventory, beginning of year	28,500
Inventory, end of year	33,000
Accounts payable, beginning of year	16,500
Accounts payable, end of year	10,500

M4-31. Calculating Operating Cash Flows (Direct Method) — LO4-2

Chakravarthy Company's current year income statement reports the following:

Sales.	$412,500
Cost of goods sold	275,000
Gross profit.	$137,500

Chakravarthy's comparative balance sheets show the following (accounts payable relate to merchandise purchases):

	End of Year	Beginning of Year
Accounts receivable	$35,500	$30,000
Inventory	54,500	48,000
Accounts payable	15,500	18,500

Compute Chakravarthy's current-year cash received from customers and cash paid for merchandise purchased.

EXERCISES

E4-32. Comparing Firms Using Ratio Analysis — LO4-6

Consider the following 2020 data for several pharmaceutical firms ($ millions). (None of the firms reported the proceeds from disposals of property, plant, and equipment.)

	Average Current Liabilities	Cash from Operations	Expenditures on PPE
Merck & Co., Inc.	$24,774	$10,253	$4,684
Pfizer Inc.	31,612	14,403	2,252
Abbott Laboratories	11,385	7,901	2,177
Johnson & Johnson	39,229	23,536	3,347

Merck & Co. NYSE :: MRK
Pfizer Inc. NYSE :: PFE
Abbott Laboratories NYSE :: ABT
Johnson & Johnson NYSE :: JNJ

a. Compute the operating cash flow to current liabilities (OCFCL) ratio for each firm.
b. Compute the free cash flow for each firm.
c. Comment on the results of your computations.

E4-33. Comparing Firms Using Ratio Analysis — LO4-6

Consider the following data for several firms from 2020 ($ millions):

	Average Current Liabilities	Cash from Operations	Expenditures on PPE	Proceeds from the Sale of PPE
Walmart, Inc.	$77,634	$25,255	$10,705	$321
The Coca-Cola Company	20,787	9,844	1,177	189
Target Corporation	14,751	7,117	3,027	63

Walmart Inc. NYSE :: WMT
The Coca-Cola Company NYSE :: KO
Target Corporation NYSE :: TGT

a. Compute the operating cash flow to current liabilities (OCFCL) ratio for each firm.
b. Compute the free cash flow for each firm.
c. Comment on the results of your computations.

E4-34. Preparing a Statement of Cash Flows (Direct Method) — LO4-2

Use the following information about the annual cash flows of Mason Corporation to prepare a statement of cash flows under the direct method. Refer to **Exhibit 4.3** for the appropriate format.

Cash balance, end of year	$ 9,000
Cash paid to employees and suppliers	111,000
Cash received from sale of land	30,000
Cash paid to acquire treasury stock	7,500
Cash balance, beginning of year	12,000
Cash received as interest	4,500
Cash paid as income taxes	8,250
Cash paid to purchase equipment	66,750
Cash received from customers	145,500
Cash received from issuing bonds payable	22,500
Cash paid as dividends	12,000

LO4-3, 6 **E4-35. Calculating Net Cash Flow from Operating Activities (Indirect Method)**

Lincoln Company owns no plant assets and reported the following income statement for the current year:

Sales		$562,500
Cost of goods sold	$352,500	
Wages expense	82,500	
Rent expense	31,500	
Insurance expense	11,250	477,750
Net income		$ 84,750

Additional balance sheet information about the company follows:

	End of Year	Beginning of Year
Accounts receivable	$40,500	$36,750
Inventory	45,000	49,500
Prepaid insurance	6,000	5,250
Accounts payable	16,500	13,500
Wages payable	6,750	8,250

Use the information to

a. Calculate the net cash flow from operating activities under the indirect method.

b. Compute its operating cash flow to current liabilities (OCFCL) ratio. (Assume current liabilities consist of accounts payable and wages payable.)

LO4-5 **E4-36. Accounting Sleuth: Reconstructing Entries**

Meubles Fischer SA had the following balances for its property, plant, and equipment accounts (in thousands of euros):

	Sept. 30 Year 3	Sept. 30 Year 4
Property, plant, and equipment at cost	€2,000	€2,400
Accumulated depreciation	(700)	(780)
Property, plant, and equipment, net	€1,300	€1,620

During fiscal Year 4, Meubles Fischer acquired €200 thousand in property by signing a mortgage, plus another €600 thousand in equipment for cash. The company also received €200 thousand in cash from the sale of used equipment, and its income statement reveals a €40 thousand gain from this transaction.

a. What was the original cost of the used equipment that Meubles Fischer SA sold during fiscal Year 4?

b. How much depreciation had been accumulated on the used equipment at the time it was sold?

c. How much depreciation expense did Meubles Fischer SA recognize in its fiscal Year 4 income statement?

E4-37. Accounting Sleuth: Reconstructing Entries LO4-5

Kasznik Ltd. had the following balances for its property, plant, and equipment accounts (in millions of pounds):

	Dec. 31 Year 7	Dec. 31 Year 8
Property, plant, and equipment at cost.	£525	£549
Accumulated depreciation	(234)	(249)
Property, plant, and equipment, net	£291	£300

During Year 8, Kasznik Ltd. paid £84 million in cash to acquire property and equipment, and this amount represents all the acquisitions of property, plant, and equipment for the period. The company's income statement reveals depreciation expense of £51 million and a £15 million loss from the disposal of used equipment.

a. What was the original cost of the used equipment that Kasznik Ltd. sold during Year 8?
b. How much depreciation had been accumulated on the used equipment at the time it was sold?
c. How much cash did Kasznik Ltd. receive from its disposal of used equipment?

E4-38. Reconciling Changes in Balance Sheet Accounts LO4-2, 5

The following table presents selected items from the 2020 and 2019 balance sheets and 2020 income statement of **Walgreens Boots Alliance, Inc.**

Walgreens Boots Alliance, Inc.
NYSE :: WBA

WALGREENS BOOTS ALLIANCE, INC. ($ millions)

Selected Balance Sheet Data	2020	2019	Selected Income Statement Data	2020
Inventories	$ 9,451	$ 9,333	Cost of merchandise sold	$111,520
Property and equipment, less accumulated depreciation	13,342	13,478	Depreciation expense*	1,500
Trade accounts payable	14,458	14,341	Net earnings	424
Retained earnings	34,210	35,815		

*Includes amortization on capitalized system development costs and software included in property, plant, and equipment.

a. Compute the cash paid for merchandise inventories in 2020. Assume that trade accounts payable is only for merchandise purchases.
b. Compute the net cost of property acquired in 2020.
c. Compute the cash dividends paid in 2020.

E4-39. Analyzing Investing and Financing Cash Flows LO4-4, 5

During the year, Paxon Corporation's long-term investments account (at cost) increased $30,000, which was the net result of purchasing stocks costing $160,000 and selling stocks costing $130,000 at a $12,000 loss. Also, its bonds payable account decreased $20,000, the net result of issuing $260,000 of bonds and retiring bonds with a book value of $280,000 at an $18,000 gain. What items and amounts appear in the (a) cash flows from investing activities and (b) cash flows from financing activities sections of its annual statement of cash flows?

E4-40. Reconciling Changes in Balance Sheet Accounts LO4-4, 5

The following table presents selected items from the Year 6 (the more recent year) and Year 5 balance sheets and Year 6 income statement of Andrews, Inc.

ANDREWS, INC.

Selected Balance Sheet Data	Year 6	Year 5	Selected Income Statement Data	Year 6
Property and equipment, cost	$1,050,000	$1,041,000	Depreciation expense	$41,600
Accumulated depreciation	815,000	780,000	Gain on sale of property and equipment	600
Retained earnings	215,000	195,000	Net income	34,050

Andrews, Inc., reported expenditures for property and equipment of $12,600 in Year 6. In addition, the company acquired property and equipment valued at $3,000 in a noncash transaction in Year 6.

a. What was the original cost of the property and equipment that Andrews, Inc., sold during Year 6? What was the accumulated depreciation on that property and equipment at the time of sale?
b. Compute the cash proceeds from the sale of property and equipment in Year 6.
c. Prepare the journal entry to describe the sale of property and equipment.
d. Determine the cash dividends paid in Year 6.

LO4-2   E4-41. Calculating Operating Cash Flows (Direct Method)

Calculate the cash flow for each of the following cases.

a. Cash paid for advertising:

Advertising expense	$74,400
Prepaid advertising, beginning of year	13,200
Prepaid advertising, end of year	18,000

b. Cash paid for income taxes:

Income tax expense	$35,000
Income tax payable, beginning of year	8,500
Income tax payable, end of year	5,800

c. Cash paid for merchandise purchased:

Cost of goods sold	$215,000
Inventory, beginning of year	36,000
Inventory, end of year	30,000
Accounts payable, beginning of year	12,000
Accounts payable, end of year	14,500

LO4-3, 4, 7   E4-42.[A] Preparing a Statement of Cash Flows (Indirect Method)

The following financial statements were issued by Hoskins Corporation for the fiscal year ended December 31, Year 8. All amounts are in millions of U.S. dollars.

Balance Sheets

	Dec. 31 Year 7	Dec. 31 Year 8
Assets		
Cash	$ 900	$ 1,650
Accounts receivable	1,800	4,500
Inventory	1,200	1,500
Prepaid expenses	1,200	450
Current assets	5,100	8,100
Property, plant, and equipment at cost	$18,600	$18,300
Less accumulated depreciation	(6,300)	(5,250)
Property, plant, and equipment, net	12,300	13,050
Total assets	$17,400	$21,150
Liabilities and Shareholders' Equity		
Accounts payable	$ 1,200	$ 2,400
Income tax payable	600	300
Short-term debt	3,600	8,100
Current liabilities	5,400	10,800
Long-term debt	3,000	0
Total liabilities	8,400	10,800
Contributed capital	2,400	2,400
Retained earnings	6,600	7,950
Total shareholders' equity	9,000	10,350
Total liabilities and shareholders' equity	$17,400	$21,150

Income Statement	
	Year 8
Sales revenues.	$19,500
Cost of goods sold	10,200
Gross profit.	9,300
Selling, general, and administrative expenses	4,350
Depreciation expense.	1,050
Operating income	3,900
Interest expense.	1,050
Income before income tax expense	2,850
Income tax expense	750
Net income	$2,100

Additional information:

1. During fiscal Year 8, Hoskins Corporation acquired new equipment for $3,600 in cash. In addition, the company disposed of used equipment that had original cost of $3,900 and accumulated depreciation of $2,100, receiving $1,800 in cash from the buyer.
2. During fiscal Year 8, Hoskins Corporation arranged short-term bank financing and borrowed $4,500, using a portion of the cash to repay all of its outstanding long-term debt.
3. During fiscal Year 8, Hoskins Corporation engaged in no transactions involving its common stock, although it did declare and pay in cash a common stock dividend of $750.

REQUIRED

Using the spreadsheet approach from the chapter appendix, prepare a statement of cash flows (all three sections) for Hoskins Corporation's fiscal Year 8, using the indirect method for the cash from operations section.

E4-43. Analyzing Operating Cash Flows (Direct Method)   **LO4-2, 6**
Refer to the information in Exercise 4-35. Calculate the net cash flow from operating activities using the direct method. Show a related cash flow for each revenue and expense. Also, compute its operating cash flow to current liabilities (OCFCL) ratio. (Assume current liabilities consist of accounts payable and wages payable.)

E4-44. Interpreting Cash Flow from Operating Activities   **LO4-2, 3**
Carter Company's income statement and cash flow from operating activities (indirect method) are provided as follows ($ thousands):

Income Statement			Cash Flow from Operating Activities	
Revenue.	$800		Net income	$ 70
Cost of goods sold	430		Plus depreciation expense	140
Gross profit	370			
Operating expenses	220		Operating asset adjustments	
			Less increase in accounts receivable	(50)
Operating income	150		Less increase in inventories	(100)
Interest expense.	50		Less increase in prepaid rent	(10)
Income before taxes	100		Plus increase in accounts payable	130
Income tax expense	30		Plus increase in income tax payable.	10
Net income	$ 70		Cash flow from operating activities.	$190

a. For each of the four statements below, determine whether the statement is true or false.
b. If the statement is false, provide the (underlined) dollar amount that would make it true.
  1. Carter collected $750 from customers in the current period.
  2. Carter paid $0 interest in the current period.
  3. Carter paid $40 in income taxes in the current period.
  4. If Carter increased the depreciation expense (for financial reporting to shareholders) by $100, it would increase its cash from operations by $100.

PROBLEMS

LO4-3 **P4-45. Reconciling and Computing Operating Cash Flows from Net Income**

Petroni Company reports the following selected results for its calendar year.

Net income	$202,500
Depreciation expense	37,500
Gain on sale of assets	7,500
Accounts receivable increase	15,000
Accounts payable increase	9,000
Prepaid expenses decrease	4,500
Wages payable decrease	6,000

REQUIRED

Prepare the operating section only of Petroni Company's statement of cash flows for the year under the indirect method of reporting.

LO4-3, 4, 6 **P4-46. Preparing a Statement of Cash Flows (Indirect Method)**

Wolff Company's income statement and comparative balance sheets follow.

WOLFF COMPANY
Income Statement
For Year Ended December 31, Year 5

Sales		$762,000
Cost of goods sold	$516,000	
Wages expense	103,200	
Insurance expense	9,600	
Depreciation expense	20,400	
Interest expense	10,800	
Income tax expense	34,800	694,800
Net income		$ 67,200

WOLFF COMPANY
Balance Sheets

	Dec. 31 Year 5	Dec. 31 Year 4
Assets		
Cash	$ 13,200	$ 6,000
Accounts receivable	49,200	38,400
Inventory	108,000	72,000
Prepaid insurance	6,000	8,400
Plant assets	300,000	234,000
Accumulated depreciation	(81,600)	(61,200)
Total assets	$394,800	$297,600
Liabilities and Stockholders' Equity		
Accounts payable	$ 8,400	$ 12,000
Wages payable	10,800	7,200
Income tax payable	8,400	9,600
Bonds payable	156,000	90,000
Common stock	108,000	108,000
Retained earnings	103,200	70,800
Total liabilities and equity	$394,800	$297,600

Cash dividends of $34,800 were declared and paid during Year 5. Also in Year 5, plant assets were purchased for cash, and bonds payable were issued for cash. Bond interest is paid semiannually on June 30 and December 31. Accounts payable relate to merchandise purchases.

REQUIRED

a. Compute the change in cash that occurred during Year 5.

b. Prepare a Year 5 statement of cash flows using the indirect method.
c. Compute and interpret Wolff's
  (1) operating cash flow to current liabilities ratio, and
  (2) operating cash flow to capital expenditures ratio.

P4-47. Computing Cash Flow from Operating Activities (Direct Method) — LO4-2

Refer to the income statement and comparative balance sheets for Wolff Company presented in P4-46.

REQUIRED

a. Compute Wolff Company's cash flow from operating activities using the direct method. Use the format illustrated in **Exhibit 4.5** in the chapter.
b. What can we learn from the direct method that may not be readily apparent when reviewing a statement of cash flows prepared using the indirect method?

P4-48. Preparing a Statement of Cash Flows (Indirect Method) — LO4-3, 4, 5, 6

Arctic Company's income statement and comparative balance sheets follow.

ARCTIC COMPANY
Income Statement
For Year Ended December 31, Year 8

Sales.		$582,400
Cost of goods sold	$427,200	
Wages expense	152,000	
Advertising expense	24,800	
Depreciation expense	17,600	
Interest expense	14,400	
Gain on sale of land	(20,000)	616,000
Net loss		$ (33,600)

ARCTIC COMPANY
Balance Sheets

	Dec. 31, Year 8	Dec. 31, Year 7
Assets		
Cash	$ 39,200	$ 22,400
Accounts receivable	33,600	40,000
Inventory	85,600	90,400
Prepaid advertising	8,000	10,400
Plant assets	288,000	177,600
Accumulated depreciation	(62,400)	(44,800)
Total assets.	$392,000	$296,000
Liabilities and Stockholders' Equity		
Accounts payable	$ 13,600	$ 24,800
Interest payable	4,800	—
Bonds payable	160,000	—
Common stock	196,000	196,000
Retained earnings	41,600	75,200
Treasury stock	(24,000)	—
Total liabilities and stockholders' equity	$392,000	$296,000

During Year 8, Arctic sold land for $56,000 cash that had originally cost $36,000. Arctic also purchased equipment for cash, acquired treasury stock for cash, and issued bonds payable for cash in Year 8. Accounts payable relate to merchandise purchases.

REQUIRED

a. Compute the change in cash that occurred during Year 8.
b. Prepare a Year 8 statement of cash flows using the indirect method.
c. Compute and interpret Arctic's
  (1) operating cash flow to current liabilities ratio, and
  (2) operating cash flow to capital expenditures ratio.

LO4-2 P4-49. Computing Cash Flow from Operating Activities (Direct Method)
Refer to the income statement and comparative balance sheets for Arctic Company presented in P4-48.

REQUIRED

a. Compute Arctic Company's cash flow from operating activities using the direct method. Use the format illustrated in **Exhibit 4.5** in the chapter.
b. What can we learn from the direct method that may not be readily apparent when reviewing a statement of cash flows prepared using the indirect method?

LO4-3, 4, 5, 6 P4-50. Preparing a Statement of Cash Flows (Indirect Method)
Dair Company's income statement and comparative balance sheets follow.

DAIR COMPANY
Income Statement
For Year Ended December 31, Year 8

Sales		$525,000
Cost of goods sold	$330,000	
Wages and other operating expenses	71,250	
Depreciation expense	16,500	
Amortization expense	5,250	
Interest expense	7,500	
Income tax expense	27,000	
Loss on bond retirement	3,750	461,250
Net income		$ 63,750

DAIR COMPANY
Balance Sheets

	Dec. 31, Year 8	Dec. 31, Year 7
Assets		
Cash	$ 20,250	$ 13,500
Accounts receivable	39,750	36,000
Inventory	77,250	81,750
Prepaid expenses	9,000	7,500
Plant assets	270,000	252,000
Accumulated depreciation	(65,250)	(63,000)
Intangible assets	32,250	37,500
Total assets	$383,250	$365,250
Liabilities and Shareholders' Equity		
Accounts payable	$ 24,000	$ 19,500
Interest payable	3,000	5,250
Income tax payable	4,500	6,000
Bonds payable	45,000	90,000
Common stock	189,000	171,000
Retained earnings	117,750	73,500
Total liabilities and equity	$383,250	$365,250

During Year 8, the company sold for $12,750 cash old equipment that had cost $27,000 and had $14,250 accumulated depreciation. Also in Year 8, new equipment worth $45,000 was acquired in exchange for $45,000 of bonds payable, and bonds payable of $90,000 were retired for cash at a loss. A $19,500 cash dividend was declared and paid in Year 8. Any stock issuances were for cash.

REQUIRED

a. Compute the change in cash that occurred in Year 8.
b. Prepare a Year 8 statement of cash flows using the indirect method.
c. Prepare separate schedules showing
   (1) cash paid for interest and for income taxes and
   (2) noncash investing and financing transactions.
d. Compute its
   (1) operating cash flow to current liabilities ratio,
   (2) operating cash flow to capital expenditures ratio, and
   (3) free cash flow.

P4-51. Interpreting the Statement of Cash Flows

For this question, refer to the information in **Exhibits 4.1** and **4.7**.

LO4-2, 3, 4
CVS Health Corp.
NYSE :: CVS

a. Based on the information presented in its statement of cash flows, what amount of revenues should CVS Health report in its 2020 income statement?
b. Why is "stock-based compensation" listed under "Adjustments necessary to reconcile net income to net cash provided by operating activities"?
c. Why does CVS Health not list the effect of exchange rate changes on cash and cash equivalents in its statement of cash flows?
d. Using three bullet points, explain what CVS Health did with the nearly $16 billion in cash that was provided by operating activities is 2020.

P4-52. Preparing a Statement of Cash Flows (Indirect Method)

LO4-3, 4, 5, 6

Rainbow Company's income statement and comparative balance sheets follow.

RAINBOW COMPANY
Income Statement
For Year Ended December 31, Year 8

Sales.		$375,000
Dividend income.		7,500
Total revenue		382,500
Cost of goods sold	$220,000	
Wages and other operating expenses	65,000	
Depreciation expense.	19,500	
Patent amortization expense	3,500	
Interest expense.	6,500	
Income tax expense	22,000	
Loss on sale of equipment	2,500	
Gain on sale of investments	(1,500)	337,500
Net income		$ 45,000

RAINBOW COMPANY
Balance Sheets

	Dec. 31, Year 8	Dec. 31, Year 7
Assets		
Cash and cash equivalents	$ 9,500	$ 12,500
Accounts receivable	20,000	15,000
Inventory	51,500	38,500
Prepaid expenses	5,000	3,000
Long-term investments	—	28,500
Land	95,000	50,000
Buildings	222,500	175,000
Accumulated depreciation—buildings	(45,500)	(37,500)
Equipment	89,500	112,500
Accumulated depreciation—equipment	(21,000)	(23,000)
Patents	25,000	16,000
Total assets	$451,500	$390,500
Liabilities and Stockholders' Equity		
Accounts payable	$ 10,000	$ 8,000
Interest payable	3,000	2,500
Income tax payable	4,000	5,000
Bonds payable	77,500	62,500
Preferred stock ($100 par value)	50,000	37,500
Common stock ($5 par value)	189,500	182,000
Paid-in capital in excess of par value—common	66,500	62,000
Retained earnings	51,000	31,000
Total liabilities and equity	$451,500	$390,500

During Year 8, the following transactions and events occurred:

1. Sold long-term investments costing $28,500 for $30,000 cash.
2. Purchased land for cash.
3. Capitalized an expenditure made to improve the building.
4. Sold equipment for $7,000 cash that originally cost $23,000 and had $13,500 accumulated depreciation.

5. Issued bonds payable at face value for cash.
6. Acquired a patent with a fair value of $12,500 by issuing 125 shares of preferred stock at par value.
7. Declared and paid a $25,000 cash dividend.
8. Issued 1,500 shares of common stock for cash at $8 per share.
9. Recorded depreciation of $8,000 on buildings and $11,500 on equipment.

REQUIRED

a. Compute the change in cash and cash equivalents that occurred during Year 8.
b. Prepare a Year 8 statement of cash flows using the indirect method.
c. Prepare separate schedules showing (1) cash paid for interest and for income taxes and (2) noncash investing and financing transactions.
d. Compute its (1) operating cash flow to current liabilities ratio, (2) operating cash flow to capital expenditures ratio, and (3) free cash flow.

LO4-2, 3, 4, 5   **P4-53.**   **Preparing a Statement of Cash Flows (Direct Method)**
Refer to the data for Rainbow Company in Problem 4-52.

REQUIRED

a. Compute the change in cash that occurred in Year 8.
b. Prepare a Year 8 statement of cash flows using the direct method. Use one cash outflow for "cash paid for wages and other operating expenses." Accounts payable relate to inventory purchases only.
c. Prepare separate schedules showing (1) a reconciliation of net income to net cash flow from operating activities and (2) noncash investing and financing transactions.

LO4-3, 4, 5   **P4-54.**   **Interpreting Cash Flow Information**
Apple Inc.
NASDAQ :: AAPL
The 2020 statement of cash flows for **Apple Inc.** is presented below (all $ amounts in millions):

APPLE INC. Consolidated Statement of Cash Flows Year Ended September 30, 2020	
Cash and cash equivalents, beginning of the year	$ 50,224
Operating activities	
Net income	57,411
Adjustments to reconcile net income to cash generated by operating activities:	
Depreciation, and amortization	11,056
Share-based compensation expense	6,829
Deferred income tax expense	(215)
Other	(97)
Changes in operating assets and liabilities:	
Accounts receivable, net	6,917
Inventories	(127)
Vendor nontrade receivables	1,553
Other current and noncurrent assets	(9,588)
Accounts payable	(4,062)
Deferred revenue	2,081
Other current and noncurrent liabilities	8,916
Cash generated by operating activities	80,674
Investing activities	
Purchases of marketable securities	(114,938)
Proceeds from maturities of marketable securities	69,918
Proceeds from sales of marketable securities	50,473
Payments for acquisition of property, plant, and equipment	(7,309)
Payments made in connection with business acquisitions, net	(1,524)
Purchases of nonmarketable securities	(210)
Proceeds from nonmarketable securities	92
Other	(791)
Cash used in investing activities	(4,289)

continued

continued from previous page

Financing activities

Proceeds from issuance of common stock.	880
Payments for taxes related to net share settlement of equity awards.	(3,634)
Payments for dividends and dividend equivalents	(14,081)
Repurchases of common stock.	(72,358)
Proceeds from issuance of term debt, net	16,091
Repayments of term debt	(12,629)
Repayments of commercial paper, net	(963)
Other.	(126)
Cash used in financing activities	(86,820)
Increase (decrease) in cash and cash equivalents	(10,435)
Cash and cash equivalents, end of the year.	$ 39,789
Supplemental cash flow disclosure:	
Cash paid for income taxes, net.	$ 9,501
Cash paid for interest	$ 3,002

REQUIRED

a. Did Apple's accounts receivable go up or down in 2020? Apple reported net sales of $274,515 in its fiscal 2020 income statement. What amount of cash did Apple collect from customers during the year? (Ignore the Vendor nontrade receivables account, which relates to Apple's suppliers.)

b. Apple's cost of goods sold was $169,559 million in 2020. Assuming that accounts payable applies only to the purchase of inventory, what amount did Apple pay to purchase inventory in 2020?

c. At September 30, 2020, Apple reported a balance of $36.8 billion in property, plant, and equipment, net of accumulated depreciation, and its disclosure notes revealed that depreciation expense on property, plant, and equipment was $9.7 billion for fiscal 2020. What was the balance in property, plant, and equipment, net of accumulated depreciation at the end of fiscal 2019?

d. Apple lists stock-based compensation as a positive amount—$11,056 million—under cash flow from operating activities. Why is this amount listed here? Explain how this amount increases cash flow from operating activities.

P4-55.[A] **Preparing the Statement of Cash Flows Using a Spreadsheet**
The table below provides the balance sheets for **Snack Food Inc.** for the fiscal years ended December 31, Year 6 and Year 5.

LO4-3, 4, 5, 6, 7
Snack Food Inc.

	Year Ended	
Consolidated Balance Sheets ($ thousands)	**Year 6**	**Year 5**
Assets		
Cash.	$ 1,610	$ 940
Accounts receivable, net.	8,540	8,870
Inventories	4,590	4,200
Prepaid expenses.	1,030	1,090
Income tax receivable.	20	390
Total current assets.	15,790	15,490
Property, plant, and equipment at cost.	78,560	77,900
Accumulated depreciation.	60,930	58,310
Property, plant, and equipment, net	17,630	19,590
Cash surrender value of life insurance	360	510
Other.	740	780
Total assets	$34,520	$36,370

continued

continued from previous page

Liabilities & stockholders' equity		
Liabilities		
Checks outstanding in excess of bank balances	$ —	$ 860
Accounts payable	3,390	3,240
Salaries payable	100	90
Current portion of long-term debt	670	640
Line of credit outstanding	—	2,260
Other accrued expenses	4,130	4,020
Total current liabilities	8,290	11,110
Note payable to bank, noncurrent	4,290	4,980
Capital lease obligation	170	—
Bonds payable	740	740
Deferred income taxes, net	2,110	2,180
Total liabilities	15,600	19,010
Stockholders' equity		
Common stock at par	7,380	7,380
Additional paid-in capital	5,450	5,250
Retained earnings	16,600	15,240
Treasury shares, at cost	(10,510)	(10,510)
Total stockholders' equity	18,920	17,360
Total liabilities and stockholders' equity	$34,520	$36,370

Additional information (in $ thousands):

1. Net income for Year 6 was $2,550.
2. Depreciation expense for Year 6 was $3,110.
3. Accounts for other assets and for the life insurance asset should be classified as operating.
4. Checks outstanding in excess of bank balances should be treated as an operating liability.
5. During Year 6, Snack Food Inc. sold used property, plant, and equipment, receiving $50 in cash and recognizing a gain of $50.
6. For Year 6, debt proceeds (encompassing the liabilities for current portion of long-term debt, line of credit outstanding, and note payable to bank, noncurrent) were zero and debt repayments were $2,920.
7. During Year 6, Snack Food Inc. acquired a long-term asset in a noncash transaction. At the time of the transaction, the asset and the liability were both valued at $200. The asset is included under property, plant, and equipment in the balance sheet, and it is being depreciated. The associated financial liability is included on the balance sheet under the "capital lease obligation" liability. During Year 6, Snack Food Inc. repaid $30 of principal on this obligation.
8. During Year 6, Snack Food Inc. recognized an expense of $200 for stock-based compensation. The expense increased additional paid-in capital by the same amount.

REQUIRED

a. Set up a spreadsheet to analyze the changes in Snack Food's comparative balance sheets. Use the format illustrated in **Exhibit 4A.1**.
b. Prepare a statement of cash flows (including operations, investing and financing) for Snack Food Inc. for Year 6 using the indirect method for the operating section.
c. Using information in the statement of cash flows prepared in part *b*, compute (1) the operating cash flow to current liabilities ratio and (2) the operating cash flow to capital expenditures ratio.

LO4-3, 4, 6 **P4-56. Managing Cash Flows**

Amazin, Inc., is a specialty online wholesaler that has just completed initial financing and acquired the physical facilities to support its operations. The management team is optimistic about the company's growth opportunities as they begin operations, but they also recognize that there are significant risks for any young company's survival. The current financial condition is shown in the following balance sheet.

Balance Sheet (in $ thousands)	
Assets	
Cash	$ 800
Accounts receivable	—
Property, plant, and equipment at cost	1,200
Total assets	$2,000
Liabilities and shareholders' equity	
Accounts payable	—
Contributed capital	2,000
Retained earnings	—
Total liabilities and shareholders' equity	$2,000

Amazin's management team has "benchmark" financial projections for the first quarter of operation. Revenue is forecasted to be $2,000 thousand in Q1. Cost of goods sold will be 40% of revenue, depreciation will be $150 thousand for the quarter, and selling, general, and administrative expenses (SG&A) will be 30% of revenue. This benchmark case is based on the assumption that customers will pay for purchases in the subsequent quarter, and Amazin, Inc., will be able to delay the payments to suppliers for the same length of time.

Amazin's growth plans will require capital expenditures of $300 thousand in Q1 and subsequent quarters. The dynamic nature of the company's operations means that these physical assets have a useful life of only eight quarters. The family and friends who funded the start-up are expecting dividends equal to 20% of profits. (Taxes may be ignored.)

REQUIRED

a. Produce projected income statement, statement of cash flows, and ending balance sheet for Q1.
b. One team member suggests a more aggressive approach to growth. By increasing SG&A from 30% of revenue to 33%, revenue would increase from $2,000 thousand to $2,400 thousand. What would be the effect of such a change on Amazin's income statement? On its cash flows and financial position?
c. One team member notes that suppliers are not going to be pleased to wait a quarter to be paid. Relative to the benchmark plan, he forecasts that cost of goods sold expense would be lower by 10% if suppliers were paid promptly. What would be the effect of such a change on Amazin's income statement? On its cash flows and financial position?

CASES AND PROJECTS

C4-57. Analyzing a Projected Statement of Cash Flows and Loan Covenants   **LO4-3, 4, 5**

The president and CFO of Lambert Co. will be meeting with their bankers next week to discuss the short-term financing needs of the company for the next six months. Lambert's controller has provided a projected income statement for the next six-month period, and a current balance sheet along with a projected balance sheet for the end of that six-month period. These statements and additional information are presented below ($ millions).

LAMBERT CO. Projected Six-Month Income Statement	
Revenues	$1,200
Cost of goods sold	600
Gross profit	600
Selling and administrative expense	150
Depreciation expense	360
Income before income taxes	90
Income taxes	36
Net income	$ 54

4-57   Chapter 4   Reporting and Analyzing Cash Flows

LAMBERT CO.
Current and Projected Six-Month Balance Sheets

	Current	6-Month Projected
Cash	$ 150	$???
Accounts receivable	540	660
Inventory	600	540
Total current assets	1,290	???
Property, plant, and equipment, cost	1,200	1,500
Less accumulated depreciation	(450)	(660)
Property, plant, and equipment, net	750	840
Total assets	$2,040	$???
Accounts payable	$ 450	$ 540
Income taxes payable	60	30
Short-term borrowing	150	???
Long-term debt	600	540
Total liabilities	1,260	???
Common stock at par	300	375
Retained earnings	480	444
Total liabilities and shareholders' equity	$2,040	$???

Additional Information (already reflected in the projected income statement and balance sheet):
- Lambert's current long-term debt includes $300 that is due within the next six months. During the next six months, the company plans to take advantage of lower interest rates by issuing new long-term debt that will provide $240 in cash proceeds.
- During the next six months, the company plans to dispose of equipment with an original cost of $375 and accumulated depreciation of $150. An appraisal by an equipment broker indicates that Lambert should be able to get $225 in cash for the equipment. In addition, Lambert plans to acquire new equipment at a cost of $675.
- A small issue of common stock for cash ($75) and a cash dividend to shareholders ($90) are planned in the next six months.
- Lambert's outstanding long-term debt imposes a restrictive loan covenant on the company that requires Lambert to maintain a debt-to-equity ratio below 1.75.

REQUIRED

The CFO says, "I would like a clear estimate of the amount of short-term borrowing that we will need six months from now. I want you to prepare a forecasted statement of cash flows that we can take to the meeting next week."

Prepare the required statement of cash flows, using the indirect method to compute cash flow from operating activities. The forecasted statement should include the needed amount of short-term borrowing and should be consistent with the projected balance sheet and income statement, as well as the loan covenant restriction.

LO4-1, 3, 4, 5   **C4-58.   Reconstructing Journal Entries and T-Accounts from Completed Financial Statements**
Lundholm Company's comparative balance sheets, income statement, and statement of cash flows for July are presented below:

LUNDHOLM COMPANY
Comparative Balance Sheets

	July 1	July 31
Cash	$ 900	$ 1,776
Accounts receivable	9,750	10,200
Inventory	3,600	2,700
Prepaid rent	—	600
Current assets	14,250	15,276
Fixtures and equipment at cost	2,850	3,930
Accumulated depreciation	(1,200)	(1,320)
Plant and equipment, net	1,650	2,610
Total assets	$15,900	$17,886

continued

continued from previous page

Accounts payable	$ 4,500	$ 4,650
Salaries and wages payable	150	105
Taxes payable	—	561
Bank loan payable	2,400	—
Current liabilities	7,050	5,316
Long-term loan	—	3,000
Common stock	6,900	6,900
Retained earnings	1,950	2,670
Total liabilities and shareholders' equity	$15,900	$17,886

LUNDHOLM COMPANY
Income Statement
Month Ended July 31

Revenue		$5,700
Operating expenses:		
Cost of goods sold	$2,700	
Salaries and wages	1,050	
Rent	300	
Depreciation	225	
Total operating expenses		4,275
Operating income		1,425
Interest expense		24
Income before taxes		1,401
Income taxes		561
Net income		$ 840

LUNDHOLM COMPANY
Statement of Cash Flows
Month Ended July 31

Operating activities:	
Net income	$ 840
Adjustments:	
Depreciation	225
Increase in accounts receivable	(450)
Decrease in inventory	900
Increase in prepaid rent	(600)
Increase in accounts payable	150
Decrease in salaries and wages payable	(45)
Increase in taxes payable	561
Total adjustments	741
Cash flow from operating activities	1,581
Investing activities:	
Proceeds from disposal of fixtures and equipment	15
Purchases of fixtures and equipment	(1,200)
Cash flow used for investing activities	(1,185)
Financing activities:	
Loan repayment	(2,400)
Proceeds from new loan	3,000
Dividends paid to shareholders	(120)
Cash flow from financing activities	480
Net increase in cash	876
Cash balance, July 1	900
Cash balance, July 31	$1,776

REQUIRED

a. Set up T-accounts and enter beginning and ending balances for each account in Lundholm Company's balance sheet.
b. Provide a set of *summary journal entries* for July that would produce the financial statements presented above. For simplicity, you may assume that all of Lundholm Company's sales are made on account and that all of its purchases are made on account. One such entry is provided as an example.

(1)	Accounts receivable (+A)	5,700	
	Sales revenue (+R, +SE)		5,700

c. Post the journal entries from part *b* to T-accounts and verify ending balances.

LO4-1, 2, 3, 4, 5, 6
Daimler AG
ETR :: DAI

C4-59. Interpreting the Statement of Cash Flows

The statement of cash flows for **Daimler AG** follows:

DAIMLER AG
Consolidated Statement of Cash Flows
Year Ended December 31, 2020 (€ millions)

Profit before income taxes	€ 6,339
Depreciation and amortization/impairments	8,957
Other noncash expense and income	(836)
Gains (−)/losses (+) on disposals of assets	131
Change in operating assets and liabilities	
Inventories	2,039
Trade receivables	1,339
Trade payables	(299)
Receivables from financial services	2,397
Vehicles on operating leases	1,822
Other operating assets and liabilities	653
Dividends received from equity-method investments	1,783
Income taxes paid	(1,993)
Cash provided by operating activities	**22,332**
Additions to property, plant, and equipment	(5,741)
Additions to intangible assets	(2,819)
Proceeds from disposals of property, plant, and equipment and intangible assets	365
Investments in shareholdings	(661)
Proceeds from disposals of shareholdings	259
Acquisition of marketable debt securities and similar investments	(3,792)
Proceeds from sales of marketable debt securities and similar investments	5,941
Other	27
Cash used for investing activities	**(6,421)**
Change in short-term financing liabilities	(3,263)
Additions to long-term financing liabilities	53,713
Repayment of long-term financing liabilities	(59,953)
Dividend paid to shareholders of Daimler AG	(963)
Dividends paid to noncontrolling interests	(282)
Proceeds from issuance of share capital	31
Acquisition of treasury shares	(30)
Cash used for financing activities	**(10,747)**
Effect of foreign exchange rate changes on cash and cash equivalents	(999)
Net increase in cash and cash equivalents	**4,165**
Cash and cash equivalents at the beginning of the period	18,883
Cash and cash equivalents at the end of the period	**€23,048**

REQUIRED

a. Daimler begins its statement of cash flows with before-tax income of €6,339 million, then adds €8,957 million for depreciation and amortization. Why is Daimler adding depreciation and amortization to net income in this computation?

b. Why does Daimler add €131 million of losses on disposals of assets in its indirect method cash flows from operating activities? If these losses are all created by disposals of property, plant, and equipment and intangible assets, what was the book value of the assets Daimler disposed of during fiscal year 2020?

c. Daimler shows a positive €2,039 million for inventories in the statement of cash flows. Does this mean that Daimler paid €2,039 million for inventories in 2020? Explain.

d. Compute Daimler's free cash flow for 2020. How did the company finance its investing activities?

e. Daimler reports a net cash inflow from operating activities of €22,332 million, despite reporting pre-tax income of €6,339 million. What principal activities account for this difference? Does this raise concerns about the health of Daimler AG?

f. Why does Daimler list the "effect of foreign exchange rate changes on cash and cash equivalents" in its statement of cash flows? What does this amount represent?

SOLUTIONS TO REVIEW PROBLEMS

Review 4-1
1. Out/I 2. Out/O 3. Out/O 4. In/F 5. Out/O 6. In/O 7. In/I 8. In/I 9. Out/F 10. In/O

Review 4-2

MUG SHOTS, INC.
Computation of Cash Flow from Operating Activities
For Month Ended December 31

Net income $3,445	=	Sales revenue $31,000	−	Cost of goods sold 16,700	−	Wage expenses 4,700	−	Interest expense 300	−	Advertising expense 1,800	−	Rent expense 1,500	−	Depreciation expense 700	−	Income tax expense 1,855

Adjustments:
Add depreciation expense .... → +700 Depreciation expense

Subtract (add) non-operating gains (losses)

Subtract the change in operating assets (operating investments) ....
- −2,500 Change in accounts receivable
- −8,300 Change in inventory
- −(−1,500) Change in prepaid rent

Add the change in operating liabilities (operating financing) ....
- +500 Change in unearned revenue
- +1,000 Change in accounts payable
- +2,200 Change in wages payable
- +300 Change in interest payable
- +1,855 Change in income tax payable

$700 Cash from operations	=	$29,000 Receipts from customers	−	24,000 Payments for merchandise	−	2,500 Payments for wages	−	0 Payments for interest	−	1,800 Payments for advertising	−	0 Payments for rent	−	0	−	0 Payments for income tax

Review 4-3

MUG SHOTS, INC.
Cash Flow from Operating Activities—Indirect Method

Net income		$3,445
Adjustments:		
Add back depreciation expense	$ 700	
Subtract changes in:		
Accounts receivable	(2,500)	
Inventory	(8,300)	
Prepaid rent	1,500	
Add changes in:		
Unearned revenue	500	
Accounts payable	1,000	
Wages payable	2,200	
Interest payable	300	
Income tax payable	1,855	
Total adjustments		(2,745)
Cash flow from operating activities		$ 700

Review 4-4

MUG SHOTS, INC.
Statement of Cash Flows
For Month Ended December 31

Cash flow from operating activities		
Net income	$ 3,445	
Add back depreciation	700	
Subtract changes in:		
Accounts receivable	(2,500)	
Inventory	(8,300)	
Prepaid rent	1,500	
Add changes in:		
Accounts payable	1,000	
Unearned revenue	500	
Income tax payable	1,855	
Wages payable	2,200	
Interest payable	300	
Net cash provided by operating activities		$700
Cash flow from investing activities		
Purchase of equipment	(12,000)	
Net cash used for investing activities		(12,000)
Cash flow from financing activities		
Bank loan	18,000	
Payment of dividend	(1,000)	
Net cash provided by financing activities		17,000
Net cash increase		5,700
Cash, beginning of period		5,000
Cash, end of period		$10,700

Review 4-5

There are three entries that affected the balance sheet accounts of Property, Plant, and Equipment at cost and Accumulated Depreciation. We know some of the amounts involved, but not all. Let P be the proceeds on the sale of used equipment, let A be the cash spent to acquire new property, plant, and equipment, and let D be the year's depreciation expense. Here are the entries:

a. Disposal—use T-account or FSET

DR Cash (+A)	P	
DR Accumulated depreciation (−XA, +A)	60,000	
CR Property, plant, and equipment at cost (−A)		80,000
CR Gain on equipment disposal (+R, +SE)		35,000

Or

	Balance Sheet						Income Statement		
Transaction	Cash Assets	+ Noncash Assets	− Contra Assets	= Liabilities	+ Contrib. Capital	+ Earned Capital	Revenues −	Expenses =	Net Income
	P Cash	−80,000 PPE at Cost	−−60,000 Accum Dep'n			+35,000 Retained Earnings	+35,000 Gain on Equipment Disposal	−	= +35,000

The value of P must be $55,000 because Jack's Snacks reported a gain of $35,000 on selling an asset with book value of $20,000 (= $80,000 − $60,000). The company would report an inflow of cash of $55,000 in the investing section of the statement of cash flows.

b. Acquisition—use T-account or FSET

DR Property, plant, and equipment at cost (+A)	A	
CR Cash (−A)		A

Or

Transaction	Balance Sheet						Income Statement		
	Cash Assets	+ Noncash Assets	− Contra Assets	= Liabilities	+ Contrib. Capital	+ Earned Capital	Revenues	− Expenses	= Net Income
	−A Cash	+A PPE at Cost		=				−	=

We can determine the cost of acquired assets by looking at the account for Property, Plant, and Equipment at Cost.

+	Property, Plant, and Equipment at Cost (A)	−
Beg. bal.	600,000	
Purchases A	80,000	Disposal
End. bal.	670,000	

Or

Transaction	Balance Sheet						Income Statement		
	Cash Assets	+ Noncash Assets	− Contra Assets	= Liabilities	+ Contrib. Capital	+ Earned Capital	Revenues	− Expenses	= Net Income
Beg. Bal.		600,000 PPE, at cost							
Disposal	+55,000 Cash	−80,000 PPE, at Cost	−−60,000 Accum Dep'n =			+35,000 Retained Earnings	+35,000 Gain on Equipment Disposal	−	= +35,000
Purchase	−A Cash	+A PPE, at Cost	−	=				−	=
End. Bal.		670,000 PPE, at Cost							

The value of A, i.e., the amount spent on acquiring PPE, must have been $150,000. The company would report an outflow of cash of $150,000 in the investing section of the statement of cash flows.

c. Depreciation expense—use T-account or FSET

DR Depreciation expense (+E, −SE) .... D
    CR Accumulated depreciation (+XA, −A)........................... D

Or

Transaction	Balance Sheet						Income Statement		
	Cash Assets	+ Noncash Assets	− Contra Assets	= Liabilities	+ Contrib. Capital	+ Earned Capital	Revenues	− Expenses	= Net Income
			+D Accum Dep'n =			−D Retained Earnings		− +D Dep'n Expense	= −D

We can determine the depreciation expense by looking at the T-account or FSET column for the Accumulated Depreciation contra-asset.

−	Accumulated Depreciation (XA)	+
	140,000	Beg. bal.
Disposal 60,000	D	Deprec. Exp.
	150,000	End. bal.

Or

Transaction	Balance Sheet						Income Statement		
	Cash Assets +	Noncash Assets −	Contra Assets =	Liabilities +	Contrib. Capital +	Earned Capital	Revenues −	Expenses =	Net Income
Beg. Bal.			140,000 Accum Dep'n						
Disposal	+55,000 Cash	−80,000 PPE, at Cost	−−60,000 Accum Dep'n =			+35,000 Retained Earnings	+35,000 Gain on Equipment Disposal	−	= +35,000
Dep'n expense			+D − Accum = Dep'n			−D Retained Earnings	−	+D Dep'n = Expense	−D
End. Bal.			150,000 Accum Dep'n						

The depreciation expense for the year, D, must have been $70,000 because the contra-asset increased by $10,000 even though the disposal decreased it by $60,000.

d. The acquisition of property, plant, and equipment through the issuance of stock would be included in the disclosure notes of the company as a noncash transaction. Neither the investing nor financing sections of the statement of cash flows would be affected by the transaction.

Review 4-6

1. We assume that One World Café's notes payable are classified as current liabilities. If so, current liabilities are $41,000 ($27,000 + $6,000 + $3,000 + $5,000) in 2021 and $21,000 ($14,000 + $2,500 + $4,500) in 2020.
$44,000 / [($41,000 + $21,000)/2] = 1.42
One World Café is generating cash flows from operations in excess of its current liabilities. Assuming that this continues, it should have no difficulty meeting its obligations.

2. $44,000 / $45,000 = 0.98
One World Café spent a little more on plant capacity than it generated through operations. However, for a small business, capital expenditures are often irregular. Thus, this ratio is not alarmingly low.

3. $44,000 − ($45,000 − $4,000) = $3,000.

Review 4-7

Cash Flow Spreadsheet for Rocky Road Bicycles, Inc.

	A	B	C	D	E	F	G	H	I	J
1		O, I, or F?	2021	2020	Change	\multicolumn{3}{c}{Effect of Change on Cash Flow}	No Effect on Cash	Total F, G, H, I
2						Operating	Investing	Financing		
3	**Assets**									
4	Cash.............		106,000	96,000	10,000					
5										
6	Accounts receivable......	O	156,000	224,000	(68,000)	68,000				68,000
7	Inventory........	O	752,000	528,000	224,000	(224,000)				(224,000)
8	Prepaid rent.....	O	68,000	72,000	(4,000)	4,000				4,000
9	Plant assets, net.......	O, I	1,130,000	872,000	258,000					
10	Depreciation expense.......					122,000				
10	Plant assets purchased.......						(420,000)			(258,000)
12	Plant assets sold.........						(16,000)	56,000		
13										
14	**Liabilities**									
15	Accounts payable........	O	216,000	112,000	104,000	104,000				104,000
16	Wages payable........	O	18,000	20,000	(2,000)	(2,000)				(2,000)
17	Income tax payable.......	O	44,000	36,000	8,000	8,000				8,000
18	Notes payable......	F								
19	New borrowing.......									—
20	Borrowing repayments......									
21										
22	**Shareholders' Equity**									
23	Common stock........	F	1,142,000	1,000,000	142,000					
24	New issue of common stock.....							142,000		142,000
25	Repurchase of common stock...									
26	Retained earnings........	O, F	792,000	624,000	168,000					
27	Net income........					326,000				168,000
28	Dividends........							(158,000)		
29										
30	Totals......					390,000	(364,000)	(16,000)	—	10,000

$390,000 - $364,000 - $16,000 = $10,000.

ROCKY ROAD BICYCLES, INC.
Statement of Cash Flows
For Year Ended December 31, 2021

Cash flows from operating activities		
Net income........	$326,000	
Add (deduct) items to convert net income to cash basis		
Depreciation......	122,000	
Gain on sale of plant assets.......	(16,000)	
Accounts receivable......	68,000	
Inventory......	(224,000)	
Prepaid rent......	4,000	
Accounts payable........	104,000	
Wages payable.....	(2,000)	
Income tax payable......	8,000	
Net cash provided by operating activities........		$390,000
Cash flows from investing activities		
Purchase of plant assets......	(420,000)	
Proceeds from sale of plant assets......	56,000	
Net cash used for investing activities........		(364,000)
Cash flows from financing activities		
Issuance of common stock......	142,000	
Payment of dividends......	(158,000)	
Net cash used for financing activities........		(16,000)
Net cash increase........		10,000
Cash at beginning of year........		96,000
Cash at end of year........		$106,000

Chapter 5: Analyzing and Interpreting Financial Statements

LEARNING OBJECTIVES

LO5-1 Prepare and analyze common-size financial statements.

LO5-2 Compute and interpret measures of return on investment, including return on equity (ROE), return on assets (ROA), and return on financial leverage (ROFL).

LO5-3 Disaggregate ROA into profitability (profit margin) and efficiency (asset turnover) components.

LO5-4 Compute and interpret measures of liquidity and solvency.

LO5-5 Appendix 5A: Measure and analyze the effect of operating activities on ROE.

LO5-6 Appendix 5B: Prepare financial statement forecasts.

Road Map

LO	Learning Objective | Topics	Page	eLecture	Review	Assignments
LO5-1	Prepare and analyze common-size financial statements.	5-4	e5-1	R5-1	M5-15, M5-16, M5-19, M5-20, E5-35
LO5-2	Compute and interpret measures of return on investment, including return on equity (ROE), return on assets (ROA), and return on financial leverage (ROFL).	5-8	e5-2	R5-2	M5-14, M5-17, M5-21, M5-22, E5-25, E5-26, E5-27, E5-28, E29, E5-30, E5-31, E5-34, P5-36, P5-38, P5-41, C5-49, DA5-1, DA5-5
LO5-3	Disaggregate ROA into profitability (profit margin) and efficiency (asset turnover) components.	5-11	e5-3	R5-3	M5-14, M5-17, M5-21, M5-22, M5-24, E5-25, E5-27, E5-28, 29, E5-30, E5-31, E5-34, P5-36, P5-38, P5-41, P5-45, P5-46, C5-47, C5-48, C5-49, DA5-4
LO5-4	Compute and interpret measures of liquidity and solvency.	5-15	e5-4	R5-4	M5-18, M5-23, E5-32, E5-33, P5-37, P5-39, P5-42, C5-49, DA5-2, DA5-6
LO5-5	Appendix 5A: Measure and analyze the effect of operating activities on ROE.	5-23	e5-5	R5-5	P5-40, P5-43
LO5-6	Appendix 5B: Prepare financial statement forecasts.	5-25	e5-6	R5-6	E5-35, P5-44, DA5-3

PEPSICO
www.pepsico.com

PepsiCo Chief Executive Officer and Chairman of the Board, Ramon Laguarta, has faced a variety of challenges since he became CEO in 2018. The company operates in very competitive markets for beverages (**The Coca-Cola Company**) and for snack foods (**Kellogg Company**, **Nestlé S. A.**, **Snyder's-Lance, Inc.**). Consumer tastes change constantly, and so a company like PepsiCo must adjust to consumer trends with products that meet changing consumer demands. On August 3, 2021, PepsiCo announced the sale of Tropicana, Naked, and other select juice brands to PAI Partners (a private equity firm), resulting in pre-tax cash proceeds of approximately $3.3 billion. Ramon Laguarta stated that this divestiture will "free us to concentrate on our current portfolio of diverse offerings, including growing our portfolio of healthier snacks, zero-calorie beverages, and products like SodaStream, which are focused on being better for people and the planet."

As is the case in most companies, PepsiCo's management employs a number of financial measures to assess the performance and financial condition of its operating units. These measures include ratios related to profitability and asset utilization as well as return on investment. An analysis of these measures affects significant decisions such as the sale of PepsiCo's juice brands. PepsiCo reported that although its juice businesses delivered approximately $3 billion in net revenue in 2020, its operating profit margins for juice businesses were below PepsiCo's overall operating margin in 2020. Now with a significant cash infusion from the sale, PepsiCo is able to invest in other product offerings that have the potential to be more profitable, while meeting customer demands.

This chapter focuses on the analysis of information reported in the financial statements. We discuss a variety of measures that provide insights into a company's performance to answer questions such as: Is it managed efficiently and profitably? Does it use assets efficiently? Is the performance achieved with an optimal amount of debt? We pay especially close attention to measures of return. In Chapter 1, we introduced one such return metric—namely, return on equity (ROE). In this chapter, we review ROE and add another return metric—return on assets (ROA).

ROE and ROA differ by the use of debt financing, or financial leverage. Companies can increase ROE by borrowing money and using these funds to finance investment in operating assets. However, debt financing can increase company risk and, if not used judiciously, can have a detrimental effect on ROE and even lead to financial distress. In the latter part of this chapter, we examine metrics that measure liquidity and solvency that allow us to assess that risk.

In its shift to healthier snacks, PepsiCo formed a joint venture with **Beyond Meat Inc.**, in 2021 in order to develop and produce snack and beverage products made from plant-based proteins. PepsiCo indicated that the joint venture will allow them the ability to create and scale new snack options. These efforts are being made to meet consumer demands for more nutritious product offerings while PepsiCo scales back from more high-sugar product offerings such as juice drinks.

Sources: PepsiCo annual report 2020; PepsiCo press releases, January 2021, August 2021; *reuters.com*, August 2021

CHAPTER ORGANIZATION

Analyzing and Interpreting Financial Statements

Common-Size Statements
- Vertical Analysis
- Horizontal Analysis

Return on Investment
- Return on Equity
- Return on Assets
- Return on Financial Leverage
- Disaggregating ROA into Profit Margin and Asset Turnover

Liquidity and Solvency
- Short-Term Liquidity: Current Ratio and Quick Ratio
- Long-Term Solvency: Debt-to-Equity and Times Interest Earned
- Limitations of Ratio Analysis

Appendices
- Analyzing Core Operating Activities
- Preparing Financial Statement Forecasts

INTRODUCTION

Companies prepare financial statements to be used. These statements are used by investors who rely on financial statement information to assess investment risk, forecast income and dividends, and estimate value. They are used by creditors to assess credit risk and monitor outstanding loans for compliance with debt covenants. And, as the PepsiCo example illustrates, they are used by management to evaluate the performance of operating units. **Financial statement analysis** identifies relationships between numbers within the financial statements and trends in these relationships from one period to the next. The goal is to help users such as investors, creditors, and managers interpret the information presented in the financial statements.

Financial statement analysis is all about making comparisons. Accounting information is difficult to interpret when the numbers are viewed in isolation. For example, a company that reports net income of $7 million may have had a good year or a bad year. However, if we know that total sales were $100 million, assets total $90 million, and the previous year's net income was $6 million, we have a better idea about how well the company performed. If we go a step further and compare these numbers to those of a competing company or to an industry average, we begin to make an assessment about the relative quality of management, the prospects for future growth, overall company risk, and the potential to earn sustainable returns.

Assessing the Business Environment

Financial statement analysis cannot be undertaken in a vacuum. A meaningful interpretation of financial information requires an understanding of the business, its operations, and the environment in which it operates. That is, before we begin crunching the numbers, we must consider the broader business context in which the company operates. This approach requires starting with the Management's Discussion and Analysis section of the financial reports and asking questions about the company and its business environment, including:

- *Life cycle*—At what stage in its life is this company? Is it a start-up, experiencing the growing pains that often result from rapid growth? Is it a mature company, reaping the benefits of its competitive advantages? Is it in decline?

- *Outputs*—What products does it sell? Are its products new, established, or dated? Do its products have substitutes? Are its products protected by patents? How complicated are its products to produce?

- *Customers*—Who are its customers? How often do customers purchase the company's products? What demographic trends are likely to have an effect on future sales?

- *Competition*—Who are the company's competitors? How is it positioned in the market relative to its competition? Is it easy for new competitors to enter the market for its products? Are its products differentiated from competitors' products? Does it have any cost advantages over its competitors?

- *Inputs*—Who are the company's suppliers? Are there multiple supply sources? Does the company depend on one (or a few) key supply source creating the potential for high input costs?
- *Labor*—Who are the company's managers? How effective are they? Is the company unionized? Does it depend on a skilled or educated workforce?
- *Technology*—What technology does the company employ to produce its products? Does the company outsource production? What transport systems does the company rely on to deliver its products?
- *Capital*—To what extent does the company rely on public markets to raise needed capital? Has it recently gone public? Does it have expansion plans that require large sums of cash to carry out? Is it planning to acquire another company? Is it in danger of defaulting on its debt?
- *Political*—How does the company interact with the communities, states, and countries in which it operates? What government regulations affect the company's operations? Are any proposed regulations likely to have a significant impact on the company?

These are just a few of the questions that we should ask before we begin analyzing a company's financial statements. Ultimately, the answers will help us place our numerical analysis in the proper context so that we can effectively interpret the accounting numbers.

In this chapter, we introduce the tools that are used to analyze and interpret financial statements. These tools include common-size financial statements that are used in vertical and horizontal analysis and ratios that measure return on investment and help to assess liquidity and solvency.

VERTICAL AND HORIZONTAL ANALYSIS

Companies come in all sizes, a fact that presents difficulties when making comparisons between firms and over time. **Vertical analysis** is a method that attempts to overcome this obstacle by restating financial statement information in ratio (or percentage) form. Specifically, it is common to express components of the income statement as a percent of net sales, and balance sheet items as a percent of total assets. This restatement is often referred to as **common-size financial statements**, and it facilitates comparisons across companies of different sizes as well as comparisons of accounts within a set of financial statements.

LO5-1 Prepare and analyze common-size financial statements.

Exhibit 5.1 presents PepsiCo's summarized comparative balance sheets for 2020 and 2019. Next to the comparative balance sheets are common-size balance sheets for the same two years. Vertical analysis helps us interpret the composition of the balance sheet. For example, as of the end of 2020, 24.7% of PepsiCo's assets were current assets and 23.0% were property, plant, and equipment. Intangible assets made up a greater share of the company's total assets. In addition, 85.4% of PepsiCo's total assets were financed with liabilities—up from 81.1% in 2019. Long-term debt obligations were 43.4% of total assets in 2020, but as recently as 2014, long-term liabilities were 33.8% of total assets. This significant change in liabilities can be attributed, in part, to the historically low interest rates of the recent past. Financial statement analysts should be aware of changes that produce significant changes in financial statement relationships. It is not uncommon for companies to use lower-cost debt financing to finance expansion, especially if low stock prices discourage management from issuing common stock. However, increasing debt levels are a concern if profits and cash flows are not growing fast enough to cover the rising interest and principal payments.

In **Exhibit 5.2**, we present PepsiCo's summarized comparative income statements for 2020 and 2019, along with common-size income statements for the same years. Vertical analysis reveals that cost of sales is 45.2% of net revenue, up from 44.9% in 2019. Selling, general, and administrative expenses increased as a percentage of revenue compared to the year before—40.5% versus 39.8%. An increase in selling, general, and administrative expenses could be due to higher marketing and advertising costs, supply chain or distribution improvements, or increased management costs. We also need to recognize the potential higher operating costs that may have been caused by the COVID-19 pandemic in 2020.

EXHIBIT 5.1 PepsiCo Comparative Balance Sheets

PEPSICO, INC.
Balance Sheets and Common-Size Balance Sheets
December 30, 2020 and December 31, 2019

	As Reported ($ millions) 2020	As Reported ($ millions) 2019	As a Percentage of Total Assets 2020	As a Percentage of Total Assets 2019
Assets				
Current assets				
Cash and cash equivalents	$ 8,185	$ 5,509	8.8%	7.0%
Short-term investments	1,366	229	1.5%	0.3%
Accounts and notes receivable, net	8,404	7,822	9.0%	10.0%
Inventories	4,172	3,338	4.5%	4.2%
Prepaid expenses and other current assets	874	747	0.9%	1.0%
Total current assets	23,001	17,645	24.7%	22.5%
Property, plant, and equipment, net	21,369	19,305	23.0%	24.6%
Amortizable intangible assets, net	1,703	1,433	1.8%	1.8%
Goodwill	18,757	15,501	20.2%	19.7%
Other indefinite-lived intangible assets	17,612	14,610	19.0%	18.6%
Investments in noncontrolled affiliates	2,792	2,683	3.0%	3.4%
Deferred income taxes	4,372	4,359	4.7%	5.5%
Other assets	3,312	3,011	3.6%	3.8%
Total assets	$92,918	$78,547	100.0%	100.0%
Liabilities and equity				
Current liabilities				
Short-term debt obligations	$ 3,780	$ 2,920	4.1%	3.7%
Accounts payable and other current liabilities	19,592	17,541	21.1%	22.3%
Total current liabilities	23,372	20,461	25.2%	26.0%
Long-term debt obligations	40,370	29,148	43.4%	37.1%
Deferred income taxes	4,284	4,091	4.6%	5.2%
Other liabilities	11,340	9,979	12.2%	12.7%
Total liabilities	79,366	63,679	85.4%	81.1%
Total equity	13,552	14,868	14.6%	18.9%
Total liabilities and equity	$92,918	$78,547	100.0%	100.0%

Note: Percentages are rounded amounts, and thus, they may not exactly sum to totals and subtotals.

EXHIBIT 5.2 PepsiCo Comparative Income Statements

PEPSICO, INC.
Income Statements and Common-Size Income Statements
Fiscal Years Ended December 30, 2020 and December 31, 2019

	As Reported ($ millions) 2020	As Reported ($ millions) 2019	As a Percentage of Net Revenue 2020	As a Percentage of Net Revenue 2019
Net revenue	$70,372	$67,161	100.0%	100.0%
Cost of sales	31,797	30,132	45.2%	44.9%
Gross profit	38,575	37,029	54.8%	55.1%
Selling, general, and administrative expenses	28,495	26,738	40.5%	39.8%
Operating profit	10,080	10,291	14.3%	15.3%
Other pension and retiree medical benefits expense	117	(44)	0.2%	(0.1)%
Net interest expense and other	(1,128)	(935)	(1.6)%	(1.4)%
Income before income taxes	9,069	9,312	12.9%	13.8%
Provision for taxes	1,894	1,959	2.7%	2.9%
Net income	$ 7,175	$ 7,353	10.2%	10.9%

Horizontal analysis examines changes in financial data across time. Comparing data across two or more consecutive periods is helpful in analyzing company performance and in predicting future performance. **Exhibit 5.3** presents a horizontal analysis of a few selected items from PepsiCo's income statement—revenue, operating income, and net income. The dollar amounts reported in each year from 2016 through 2020 are shown for each item along with a percentage change for each item. The amount of the change for a given year is computed by subtracting the amount for the prior year from the amount for the current year. The change is then divided by the reported amount for the prior year to get the percentage change. For example, PepsiCo's percentage change in net revenue was +4.8% in 2020, computed as follows:

$$+4.8\% = \frac{\$70{,}372 \text{ million} - \$67{,}161 \text{ million}}{\$67{,}161 \text{ million}}$$

Exhibit 5.3 highlights some important information in PepsiCo's income statement. The table shows that revenue per year has been increasing for the last four years. Most recently, revenue increased in 2020 by nearly 5% over 2019 reflecting factors like the increase in snack food sales. Operating profit (operating income) has fluctuated over recent years. Part of the decrease in 2020 the company has attributed to the effects of the COVID-19 pandemic for charges such as projections of customer defaults and incremental frontline incentive pay. Interpreting these numbers requires looking into factors that affect the company but are beyond its control, e.g., fluctuations in raw material prices, international currencies, and the pandemic.

EXHIBIT 5.3 — Horizontal Analysis of Selected Income Statement Items

PEPSICO, INC.
Revenue, Operating Profit, and Net Income
($ millions and percent changes)

	2020	2019	2018	2017	2016[1]
Revenue	$70,372	$67,161	$64,661	$63,525	$62,799
	4.8%	3.9%	1.8%	1.2%	
Operating profit	$10,080	$10,291	$10,110	$10,276	$ 9,804
	−2.1%	1.8%	−1.6%	4.8%	
Net income	$ 7,175	$ 7,353	$12,559	$ 4,908	$ 6,379
	−2.4%	−41.5%	155.9%	−23.1%	

Horizontal analysis is useful in identifying unusual changes that might not be obvious when looking at the reported numbers alone. At the same time, it is important to look at both the percentage change and the reported dollar amount. If a reported amount is close to $0 in one year, the percentage change will likely be very large the following year, even if the amount reported in that year is small. Similarly, if reported earnings is negative one year and positive the next, the percentage change will be negative even though the earnings increased. Horizontal analysis that is based on a denominator that is negative or zero is not meaningful.

Preparing Common-Size Income Statements and Balance Sheets

LO5-1 **Review 5-1**

Following are summarized 2020 and 2019 income statements and balance sheets for The Coca-Cola Company.

Required
Prepare common-size income statements and balance sheets for Coca-Cola. Comment on any noteworthy relationships that you observe.

continued

---

[1] One feature of PepsiCo's annual reporting practices is that its fiscal year is 52 weeks long in most years, but every five or six years, it is 53 weeks long. 2016 was a 53-week year, so the percentage increase in 2017's revenues is really a little better than +1.2%.

THE COCA-COLA COMPANY AND SUBSIDIARIES
Consolidated Statements of Income
($ millions)

Year Ended December 31	2020	2019
Net operating revenues	$33,014	$37,266
Cost of goods sold	13,433	14,619
Gross profit	19,581	22,647
Selling, general, and administrative expenses	9,731	12,103
Other operating charges	853	458
Operating income	8,997	10,086
Interest income	370	563
Interest expense	1,437	946
Equity income (loss)—net	978	1,049
Other income (loss)—net	841	34
Income before taxes	9,749	10,786
Income taxes	1,981	1,801
Consolidated net income	$ 7,768	$ 8,985

THE COCA-COLA COMPANY AND SUBSIDIARIES
Consolidated Balance Sheets
($ millions)

December 31	2020	2019
Assets		
Current assets		
Cash and cash equivalents	$ 6,795	$ 6,480
Short-term investments	1,771	1,467
Marketable securities	2,348	3,228
Trade accounts receivable, net	3,144	3,971
Inventories	3,266	3,379
Prepaid expenses and other assets	1,916	1,886
Total current assets	19,240	20,411
Equity method investments	19,273	19,025
Other investments	812	854
Other assets	6,184	6,075
Deferred income tax assets	2,460	2,412
Property, plant, and equipment, net	10,777	10,838
Trademarks with indefinite lives	10,395	9,266
Goodwill	17,506	16,764
Other intangible assets	649	736
Total assets	$87,296	$86,381
Liabilities and equity		
Current liabilities		
Accounts payable and accrued expenses	$11,145	$11,312
Loans and notes payable	2,183	10,994
Current maturities of long-term debt	485	4,253
Accrued income taxes	788	414
Total current liabilities	14,601	26,973
Long-term debt	40,125	27,516
Other liabilities	9,453	8,510
Deferred income tax liabilities	1,833	2,284
Total liabilities	66,012	65,283
Total equity	21,284	21,098
Total liabilities and equity	$87,296	$86,381

Solution on p. 5-49.

RETURN ON INVESTMENT

Common-size financial statements and percentage changes are useful, but there is a limit to what we can learn from this type of analysis. While vertical and horizontal analysis focuses on relationships within a particular financial statement—either the income statement or the balance sheet—many of the questions that we might ask about a company can be answered only by comparing amounts between statements. For example, return on investment measures are ratios that divide some measure of performance—typically reported in the income statement—by the average amount of investment as reported in the balance sheet.

In this section, we discuss three important return metrics—return on equity (ROE), return on assets (ROA), and return on financial leverage (ROFL). We also examine return on investment in detail by disaggregating ROA into performance drivers that capture profitability and efficiency.

LO5-2 Compute and interpret measures of return on investment, including return on equity (ROE), return on assets (ROA), and return on financial leverage (ROFL).

Return on Equity (ROE)

Return on equity (ROE) is the primary summary measure of company performance and is defined as:

$$\text{ROE} = \frac{\text{Net income}}{\text{Average stockholders' equity}}$$

ROE relates net income to the average investment by shareholders as measured by total stockholders' equity from the balance sheet. The net income number in the numerator measures the performance of the firm for a specific period (typically a fiscal year). Therefore, in order to accurately capture the return for that period, we use the average level of stockholders' equity for the same period as the denominator. The average is computed by adding the beginning and ending stockholders' equity balances and then dividing by two.

ROE	2020	2019	2018	2017	2016
PepsiCo	50.5%	49.9%	98.2%	44.3%	54.9%

FYI Whenever we compare an income statement amount with a balance sheet amount, the balance sheet amount should be the *average* balance for the period (beginning balance plus ending balance divided by 2) rather than the year-end balance.

PepsiCo's ROE was 50.5% in 2020. This return is computed as $7,175 million/[($13,552 million + $14,868 million)/2]. PepsiCo's ROE has been consistently high over the past 5 years, ranging from a low of 44.3% in 2017 to a high of 98.2% in 2018. The 98.2% return in 2018 is something of an anomaly due to the effects of the Tax Cuts and Jobs Act of 2017 (examined in Chapter 10).

ROE is widely used by analysts, investors, and managers as a key overall measure of company performance. Billionaire investor Warren Buffett highlights ROE as part of his acquisition criteria: "businesses earning good returns on equity while employing little or no debt." Companies can use debt to increase their return on equity, but too much debt increases risk because the failure to make required debt payments is likely to yield many legal consequences, including bankruptcy. This is one reason why many analysts focus on returns generated by assets used in operations, rather than on returns produced by increasing the amount of debt financing. Next, we discuss each of these sources of return in more detail.

Return on Assets (ROA)

ROE measures the return on the investment made by the firm's stockholders. In contrast, **return on assets (ROA)** measures the return earned on each dollar that the firm invests in assets. By focusing on the asset side of the balance sheet, ROA captures the returns generated by the firm's operating and investing activities, without regard for how those activities are financed. ROA is defined as:

$$\text{Return on assets (ROA)} = \frac{\text{Earnings without interest expense (EWI)}}{\text{Average total assets}}$$

Average total assets is computed in much the same way that we calculated average stockholders' equity for ROE. We add the beginning and ending balances in total assets and then divide by two. The numerator in this ratio, **earnings without interest expense (EWI)**, is defined to be:

$$\text{Earnings without interest expense (EWI)} =$$
$$\text{Net income} + [\text{Interest expense} \times (1 - \text{Statutory tax rate})]$$

EWI measures the income generated by the firm before taking into account any of its financing costs. Interest costs should be excluded from the ROA calculation so that return is measured without the effect of debt financing. Because interest expense is subtracted when net income is calculated, it must be added back to net income when we compute EWI. However, interest expense is tax deductible and, as such, it reduces the firm's tax obligation. That is, interest expense produces a tax *savings* for the firm. This tax savings is equal to the interest expense times the statutory tax rate. In order to eliminate the full effect of interest cost on EWI, we must add back the interest expense *net* of the resulting tax savings. To accomplish this, we multiply the interest expense by (1 − the statutory tax rate). This amount is then added to net income to get EWI. Thus, we can compute ROA as follows:

$$\text{Return on assets (ROA)} = \frac{\text{Net income} + [\text{Interest expense} \times (1 - \text{Statutory tax rate})]}{(\text{Beginning total assets} + \text{Ending total assets})/2}$$

ROA is an important measure of how well a company's management has utilized assets to earn a profit. If ROA is high, the firm can pay its interest costs to creditors and still have sufficient resources left over to distribute to stockholders as a dividend or to reinvest in the firm.

PepsiCo's ROA was 9.5% in 2020. PepsiCo's return is computed as follows:[2]

$$\text{ROA} = \frac{\$7{,}175 \text{ million} + [\$1{,}252 \text{ million} \times (1 - 0.25)]}{(\$92{,}918 \text{ million} + \$78{,}547 \text{ million})/2} = 9.5\%$$

While PepsiCo reports "Net interest expense and other" on its consolidated statement of income of $1,128 million, the company reports interest expense for 2020 of $1,252 million (a component of this $1,128 million amount) in its 10-K. PepsiCo's return on assets fluctuated from a high of 17.4% in 2018 to a low of 7.4% in 2017, although the 2017 and 2018 figures are affected by the one-time effects of the Tax Cuts and Jobs Act (TCJA) in late 2017.

Return on Financial Leverage (ROFL)

The principal difference between ROE and ROA is the effect that liabilities (including debt financing) have on the return measure. ROA is calculated so that it is independent of financing costs, whereas ROE is computed net of the cost of debt financing. **Financial leverage** refers to the effect that liabilities (including debt financing) have on ROE. A firm's management can increase the return to shareholders (ROE) by effectively using financial leverage. On the other hand, too much financial leverage can be risky. To help gauge the effect that financial leverage has on a firm, the **return on financial leverage (ROFL)** is defined as:

$$\text{ROFL} = \text{ROE} - \text{ROA}$$

This return metric captures the amount of ROE that can be attributed to financial leverage. In the case of PepsiCo, the 2020 ROFL is 41.0% (50.5% − 9.5%). Over the past 5 years, financial leverage has had a significant impact on PepsiCo's ROE performance, as illustrated in **Exhibit 5.4**. The height of each bar in the chart reflects PepsiCo's ROE for that year. Each bar is split into two components—ROA for the same year (the lower portion of each bar) and ROFL (the upper portion of each bar).

---

[2] The statutory federal tax rate for corporations has been 35% (per U.S. tax code) since the early 1990s. Beginning in 2018, the federal income tax rate for corporations was reduced to 21%, with the transition producing many one-time tax expense effects as described above for PepsiCo. To make the mental math simpler, we will use income tax rate approximations of 35% in years prior to 2018 and 25% for years 2018 and thereafter. Most companies provide components of income tax expense as percentages in the income tax note disclosure that may be used for more detailed analysis.

EXHIBIT 5.4 | Contribution of Financial Leverage to PepsiCo's ROE

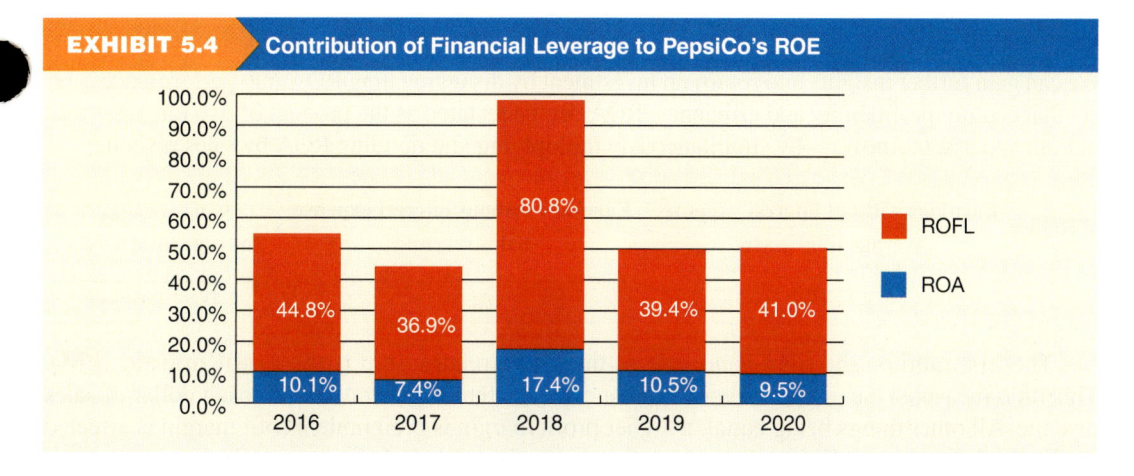

Year	ROA	ROFL
2016	10.1%	44.8%
2017	7.4%	36.9%
2018	17.4%	80.8%
2019	10.5%	39.4%
2020	9.5%	41.0%

In **Exhibit 5.5**, we compare the ROE, ROA, and ROFL of PepsiCo to that of several other companies featured in this text. As in **Exhibit 5.4**, the height of each bar represents the company's ROE for 2020. The lower portion of each bar is the company's ROA, and the upper portion reflects the contribution of financial leverage (ROFL). The chart suggests that PepsiCo's ROE is influenced to a greater extent by financial leverage than the other companies.

EXHIBIT 5.5 | ROE, ROA, and ROFL for PepsiCo and Comparison Companies*

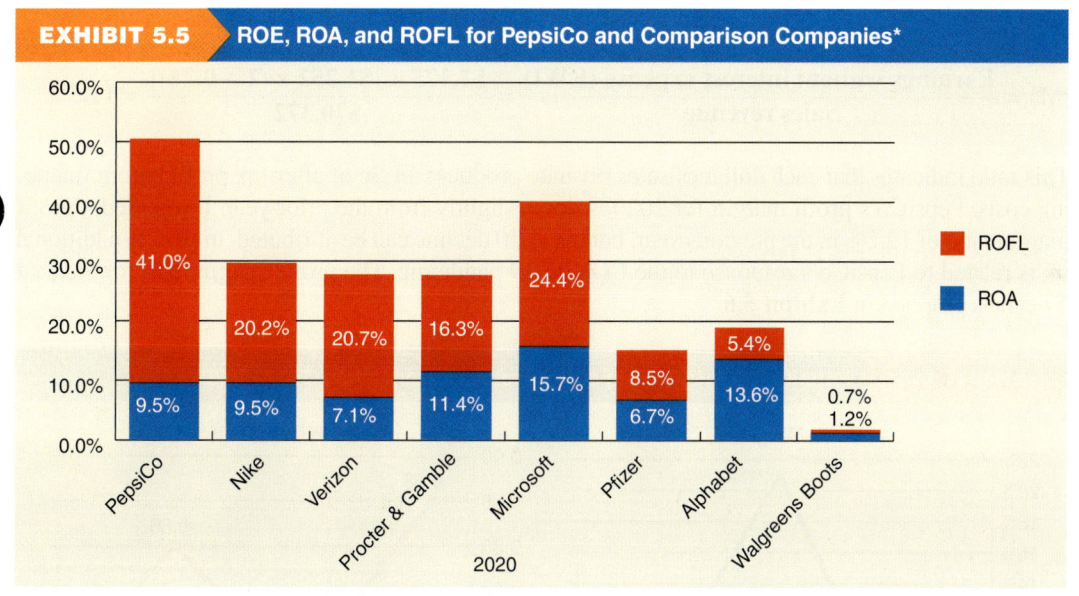

Company	ROA	ROFL
PepsiCo	9.5%	41.0%
Nike	9.5%	20.2%
Verizon	7.1%	20.7%
Procter & Gamble	11.4%	16.3%
Microsoft	15.7%	24.4%
Pfizer	6.7%	8.5%
Alphabet	13.6%	5.4%
Walgreens Boots	1.2%	0.7%

2020

*These companies do not have identical fiscal year-ends; 2020 balance sheets are dated from May 31 to December 31 of 2020.

Later in this chapter, we examine the effects of financial leverage more closely and discuss several ratios that measure liquidity and solvency. These ratios help us to evaluate the risk associated with using financial leverage.

Calculating ROE, ROA, and ROFL LO5-2 **Review 5-2**

Required
Refer to the financial statements for the **Coca-Cola Company** presented in Review 5-1. Calculate Coca-Cola's ROE, ROA, and ROFL for 2020. Assume a 25% statutory tax rate for this year.

Solution on p. 5-50.

Disaggregating ROA

LO5-3 Disaggregate ROA into profitability (profit margin) and efficiency (asset turnover) components.

We can gain further insights into return on investment by disaggregating ROA into performance drivers that capture profitability and efficiency. ROA can be restated as the product of two ratios—profit margin and asset turnover—by simultaneously multiplying and dividing ROA by sales revenue:

$$ROA = \frac{\text{Earnings without interest expense}}{\text{Average total assets}} = \underbrace{\frac{\text{Earnings without interest expense}}{\text{Sales revenue}}}_{\text{Profit Margin}} \times \underbrace{\frac{\text{Sales revenue}}{\text{Average total assets}}}_{\text{Asset Turnover}}$$

The first ratio on the right-hand side of the above relationship is the **profit margin (PM)**. This ratio measures the profit, without interest expense, that is generated from each dollar of sales revenue. All other things being equal, a higher profit margin is preferable. Profit margin is affected by the level of gross profit that the company earns on its sales (sales revenue minus cost of goods sold), which depends on product prices and the cost of manufacturing or purchasing its product. It is also affected by operating expenses that are required to support sales of products or services. These include wages and salaries, marketing, research and development, as well as depreciation and other **capacity costs**. Finally, profit margin is affected by the level of competition, which affects product pricing, and by the company's operating strategy, which affects operating costs, especially discretionary costs such as advertising and research and development.

PepsiCo's profit margin ratio was 11.5% in 2020, computed as follows ($ millions):

$$\text{Profit margin (PM)} = \frac{\text{Earnings without interest expense (EWI)}}{\text{Sales revenue}} = \frac{\$7{,}175 + [\$1{,}252 \times (1 - 0.25)]}{\$70{,}372} = 11.5\%$$

This ratio indicates that each dollar of sales revenue produces 11.5¢ of after-tax profit before financing costs. PepsiCo's profit margin for 2020 is down slightly from the prior year. It reported a profit margin ratio of 12.2% in the previous year, but the 2020 decline can be attributed, in part, to additional costs related to PepsiCo's response to the COVID-19 pandemic. The profit margin ratio for the past 5 years is graphed in **Exhibit 5.6**.

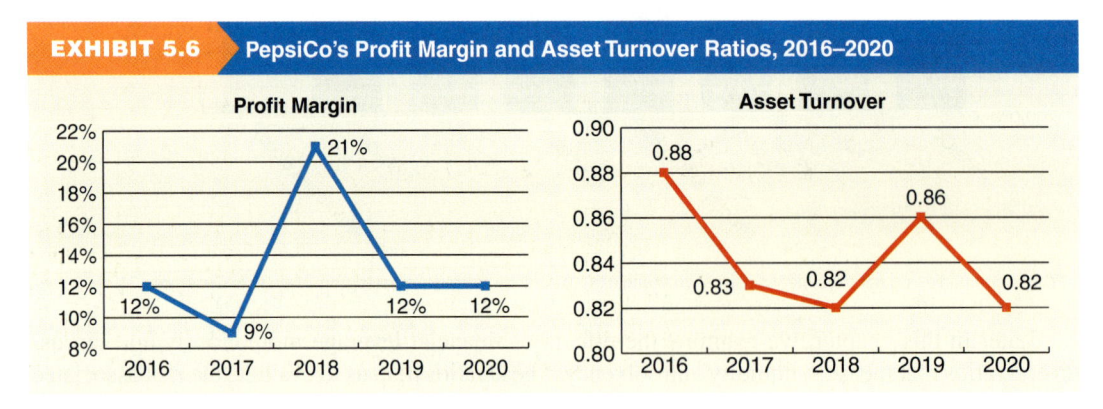

EXHIBIT 5.6 PepsiCo's Profit Margin and Asset Turnover Ratios, 2016–2020

Year	Profit Margin	Asset Turnover
2016	12%	0.88
2017	9%	0.83
2018	21%	0.82
2019	12%	0.86
2020	12%	0.82

The **asset turnover (AT)** ratio reveals insights into a company's productivity and efficiency. This metric measures the level of sales generated by each dollar that a company invests in assets. A high asset turnover ratio suggests that assets are being used efficiently so, all other things being equal, a high asset turnover ratio is preferable. The ratio is affected by inventory management practices, credit policies, and most of all, the technology employed to produce a company's products or deliver its services.

The asset turnover ratio can be improved by increasing the level of sales for a given level of assets or by efficiently managing assets. For many companies, efficiently managing working capital—primarily inventories and receivables—is the easiest way to limit investment in assets and increase turnover. On the other hand, it is usually more difficult to increase asset turnover by managing investment in long-term assets. Capital intensive companies, such as those in the telecommunications or energy production industries, tend to have lower asset turnover ratios (often less than 1.0) because the production technology employed by these firms requires a large investment in property, plant, and equipment. Retail companies, on the other hand, tend to have a relatively small investment in plant assets. As a result, they tend to have higher asset turnover ratios (sometimes over 3.0).[3]

PepsiCo's asset turnover ratio in 2020 is computed as follows ($ millions):

$$\text{Asset turnover (AT)} = \frac{\text{Sales revenue}}{\text{Average total assets}} = \frac{\$70{,}372}{(\$92{,}918 + \$78{,}547)/2} = 0.821$$

The ratio indicates that each dollar of assets generates 82.1¢ in sales revenue each year. Over the past five years, PepsiCo's asset turnover has ranged from 0.821, both in 2020 and 2017, to 0.877 in 2016, as illustrated by the graphic in **Exhibit 5.6**. The 2020 decline in AT results from the larger increase in assets over the prior year relative to the increase in sales revenue over the prior year.

YOU MAKE THE CALL

You are the Entrepreneur You are analyzing the performance of your start-up company. Your analysis of ROA reveals the following (industry benchmarks in parentheses): ROA is 16% (10%), PM is 18% (17%), and AT is 0.89 (0.59). What interpretations do you draw that are useful for managing your company?
[Answer, page 5-32.]

Trade-Off Between Profit Margin and Asset Turnover ROA is the product of profit margin and asset turnover. By decomposing ROA in this way, we can identify the source of PepsiCo's decline in ROA between 2019 and 2020:

	ROA	=	Profit Margin	×	Asset Turnover
2019:	10.5%	=	12.22%	×	0.860
2020:	9.5%	=	11.53%	×	0.821

Between 2019 and 2020, PepsiCo's profit margin declined from 12.22% to 11.53% while, at the same time, asset turnover declined from 0.860 to 0.821. Both ROA and AT decreased in 2020 relative to 2019. These changes are most likely due to the impact of the pandemic. It will be interesting to watch how PepsiCo responds in 2021 and beyond.

Basic economics tells us that any successful business must earn an acceptable return on investment if it wants to attract capital from investors and survive. Yet, there are an infinite number of combinations of asset turnover and profit margin that will yield a given ROA. The trade-off between profit margin and asset turnover is heavily influenced by a company's business model. A company can attempt to increase its ROA by targeting higher profit margins or by increasing its asset turnover. To an extent, this trade-off is the result of strategic decisions made by management. However, to a greater extent, the relative mix of margin and turnover is dictated by the industry in which the company operates. As mentioned earlier, one determinant of a company's profit margin is its competitive environment, while asset turnover is heavily influenced by the production technology employed. For this reason, companies in the same industry tend to exhibit similar combinations of margin and turnover while comparisons between industries can exhibit much greater variation. That is, within a given industry, differences in the mix of profit margin and asset turnover often reflect the specific strategy employed by each individual firm, while variations between industries are caused by differences in the competitive environment and production technology of each industry.

This trade-off is illustrated in **Exhibit 5.7**. The solid curved line represents the median ROA for all companies over the period from 2018–2020. Each point along that curve represents a combination of asset turnover and profit margin that yields the average ROA. Industries that are plotted near the upper-left side of the chart are those that achieve their ROA targets by maintaining a high asset turnover. These industries are often characterized by intense competition and low profit margins. On the other hand, industries in the lower right-hand portion of the chart have lower asset turnover ratios because they typically employ capital-intensive production technologies. At the same time, the competitive environment within these industries allows companies to achieve higher profit margins to offset the lower turnover ratios.

---

[3] Historically, these ratios have also been affected by leasing, the use of contract manufacturers, and other methods of using assets that do not appear on the balance sheet. The new accounting procedures for leasing are discussed in Chapter 10. As of 2019, leasing is no longer a method for off-balance-sheet financing of assets.

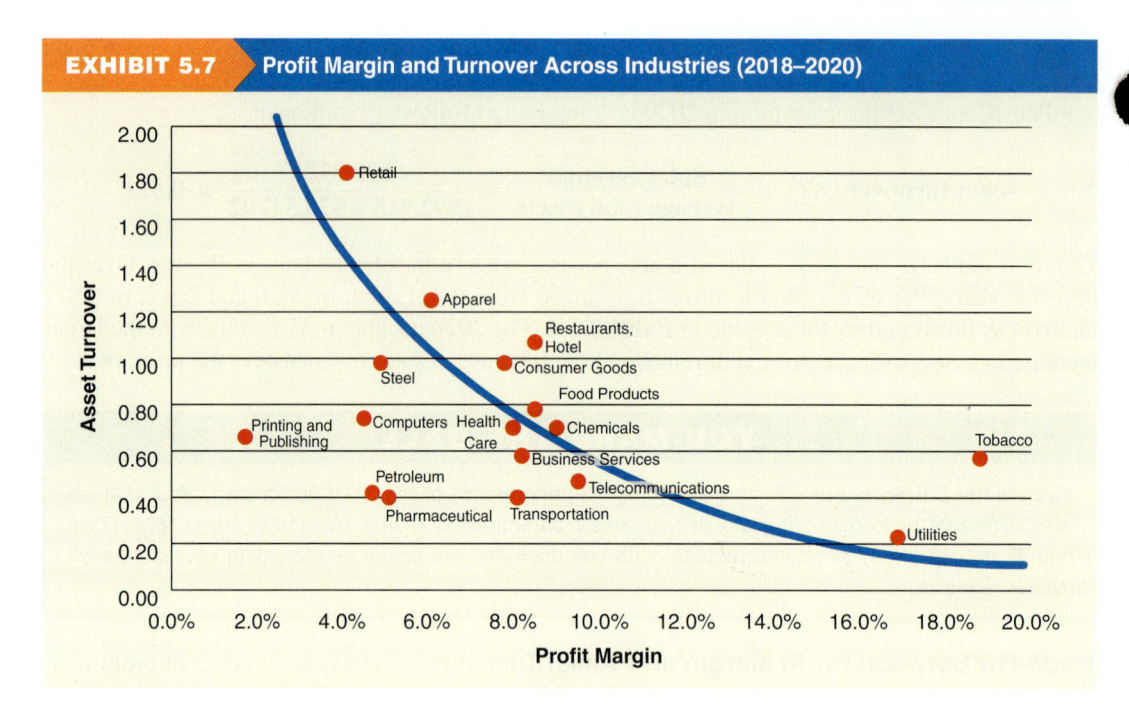

EXHIBIT 5.7 — Profit Margin and Turnover Across Industries (2018–2020)

[Scatter plot of Asset Turnover (y-axis, 0.00 to 2.00) vs. Profit Margin (x-axis, 0.0% to 20.0%) showing industries:
- Retail: ~1.80 turnover, ~4% margin
- Apparel: ~1.25, ~6%
- Restaurants, Hotel: ~1.05, ~9%
- Consumer Goods: ~1.00, ~9%
- Steel: ~1.00, ~4%
- Food Products: ~0.85, ~9%
- Computers: ~0.75, ~5%
- Health Care: ~0.72, ~7%
- Chemicals: ~0.75, ~9%
- Printing and Publishing: ~0.68, ~3%
- Business Services: ~0.60, ~9%
- Tobacco: ~0.60, ~19%
- Petroleum: ~0.45, ~3%
- Pharmaceutical: ~0.43, ~5%
- Transportation: ~0.45, ~8%
- Telecommunications: ~0.48, ~10%
- Utilities: ~0.25, ~17%

with a downward-sloping curve fitted through the points.]

BUSINESS INSIGHT

The DuPont Model   Disaggregation of return on equity (ROE) into three components—profitability, turnover, and financial leverage—was initially introduced by the **E.I. DuPont de Nemours and Company** to aid its managers in performance evaluation. DuPont realized that management's focus on profit alone was insufficient because profit can be increased simply by adding investments in low-yielding, but safe, assets. Further, DuPont wanted managers to think like investors and to manage their portfolio of activities using investment principles that allocate scarce investment capital to competing projects based on a goal of maximizing return on investment.

The basic DuPont model disaggregates ROE as the product of three ratios as follows:

$$\text{ROE} = \underbrace{\frac{\text{Net income}}{\text{Sales}}}_{\text{Net Profit Margin}} \times \underbrace{\frac{\text{Sales}}{\text{Average total assets}}}_{\text{Asset Turnover}} \times \underbrace{\frac{\text{Average total assets}}{\text{Average stockholders' equity}}}_{\text{Financial Leverage}}$$

An important limitation of the DuPont model is that net profit margin is measured using net income in the numerator rather than earnings without interest expense (EWI). This means that this measure of profitability is affected by financial leverage—as financial leverage increases, interest expense increases and the net profit margin decreases. As a consequence, the model fails to adequately separate the effects of operating profitability on ROE from the effects of financial leverage. Despite this limitation, the DuPont model is widely used as a simple, straightforward way to disaggregate ROE.

Further Disaggregation of Profit Margin and Asset Turnover   While disaggregation of ROA into profit margin and asset turnover yields useful insights into the factors driving company performance, analysts, investors, creditors, and managers often disaggregate these measures even further. The purpose of this analysis is to be more precise about the specific determinants of profitability and efficiency.

To disaggregate profit margin (PM), we examine gross profit on products sold and individual expense accounts that contribute to the total cost of operations. The key ratios include the gross profit margin and expense-to-sales ratios. **Gross profit margin (GPM)** is defined as:

$$\text{Gross profit margin (GPM)} = \frac{\text{Sales revenue} - \text{Cost of goods sold}}{\text{Sales revenue}}$$

PepsiCo's GPM is 54.8% ([$70,372 million − $31,797 million]/$70,372 million). That is, just over half (54.8¢) of every sales dollar is gross profit, while slightly less than half (45.2¢) goes to cover the cost of products sold.

Gross profit margin measures the percentage of each sales dollar that is left over after product costs are subtracted. It is easily determined by looking at the common-size income statement. This ratio is discussed in more detail in Chapter 7.

An **expense-to-sales (ETS)** ratio measures the percentage of each sales dollar that goes to cover a specific expense item and is computed by dividing the expense by sales revenue. Expense items that might be examined with ETS ratios include selling, general, and administrative (SG&A) expenses, advertising expense, or research and development (R&D) expense, among others. Which specific ETS ratio is appropriate depends on the company being analyzed. For instance, advertising expense is an important expense item for a consumer products company, such as PepsiCo, while R&D expense is important for an R&D intensive pharmaceutical company, such as Pfizer. Analysts study trends in ETS ratios over time in an effort to uncover clues that might explain changes in profit margin and make predictions about future profitability.

PepsiCo's SG&A ETS ratio is computed by dividing selling, general, and administrative expenses by net revenue. The resulting ETS ratio is 40.5% ($28,495 million/$70,372 million). This ratio indicates that 40.5¢ of every sales dollar goes to pay marketing and administrative costs. This ETS ratio is relatively high because this expense item includes PepsiCo's advertising expenditures. Further analysis of SG&A expenses as described in the notes might look for trends in advertising expenses over time or PepsiCo's expenses relative to competitors.

To disaggregate asset turnover (AT), we examine individual asset accounts and compare them to sales or cost of goods sold. We focus on three specific turnover ratios—accounts receivable turnover (ART), inventory turnover (INVT), and property, plant, and equipment turnover (PPET).

Accounts receivable turnover (ART) is defined as follows:

$$\text{Accounts receivable turnover (ART)} = \frac{\text{Sales revenue}}{\text{Average accounts receivable}}$$

ART measures how many times receivables have been turned (collected) during the period. More turns indicate that accounts receivable are being collected more quickly, while low turnover often indicates difficulty with a company's credit policies. PepsiCo's ART is 8.7 times ($70,372 million/[{$8,404 million + $7,822 million}/2]).

A variation on this measure is days-sales-outstanding = 365/ART = 42.0 for PepsiCo. It implies that—on average—PepsiCo waits 42 days to be paid by its customers. ART is discussed in Chapter 6.

Inventory turnover (INVT) is defined as:

$$\text{Inventory turnover (INVT)} = \frac{\text{Cost of goods sold}}{\text{Average inventory}}$$

INVT measures the number of times during a period that total inventory is turned (sold). A high INVT indicates that inventory is managed efficiently. Retail companies, such as Walmart and Home Depot, focus a great deal of management attention on maintaining a high INVT ratio. PepsiCo's INVT is 8.5 times ($31,797 million/[{$4,172 million + $3,338 million}/2]). A variation on this measure is days-inventory = 365/INVT = 42.9 for PepsiCo. It implies that—on average—PepsiCo's inventory stays in the company for almost 43 days before it's delivered to a customer and becomes cost of goods sold expense. This ratio is discussed further in Chapter 7.

Property, plant, and equipment turnover (PPET) measures the sales revenue produced for each dollar of investment in PP&E. It is computed as the ratio of sales to average PP&E assets:

$$\text{Property, plant, and equipment turnover (PPET)} = \frac{\text{Sales revenue}}{\text{Average PP\&E}}$$

PPET provides insights into asset utilization and how efficiently a company operates given its production technology. PepsiCo's PPET is 3.5 times ($70,372 million/[{$21,369 million + $19,305 million}/2]). This ratio is revisited in Chapter 8.

In the next section, we examine ratios that focus on liquidity and solvency. These ratios help us evaluate the risk associated with debt financing and weigh the costs and benefits of financial leverage. **Exhibit 5.8** presents a schematic summary of the disaggregation of ROE. It identifies the two primary components of ROE—ROA and ROFL—and highlights the disaggregation of ROA into profit margin and asset turnover, along with the drivers of these ratios. In addition, the link between ROFL and liquidity and solvency analysis is highlighted.

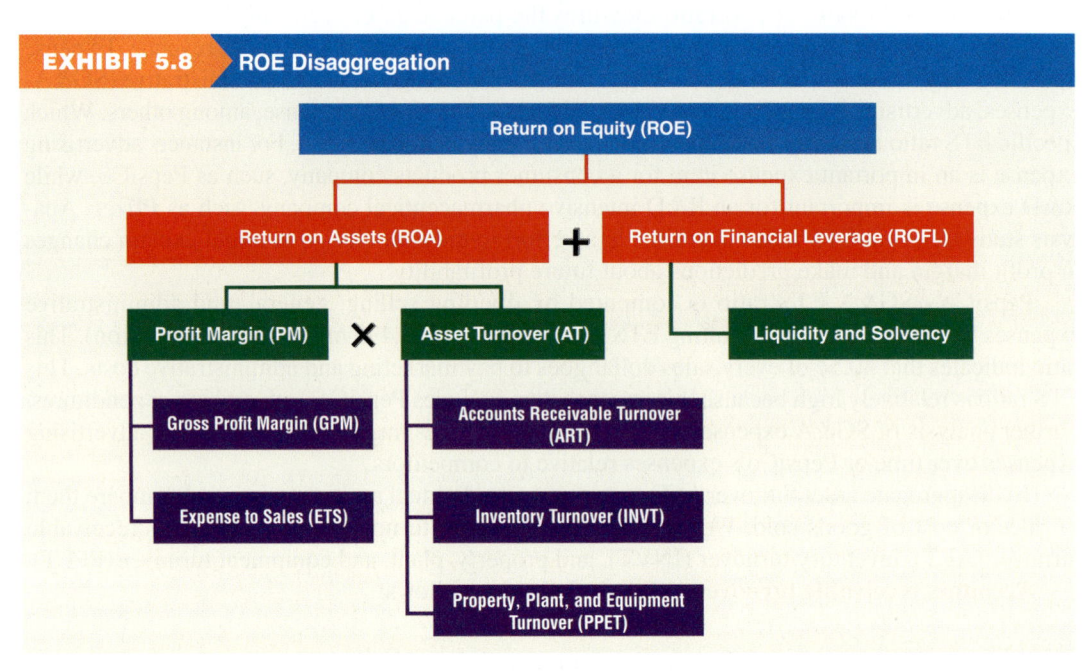

EXHIBIT 5.8 ROE Disaggregation

- Return on Equity (ROE)
  - Return on Assets (ROA) + Return on Financial Leverage (ROFL)
    - Profit Margin (PM) × Asset Turnover (AT)
      - Gross Profit Margin (GPM)
      - Expense to Sales (ETS)
      - Accounts Receivable Turnover (ART)
      - Inventory Turnover (INVT)
      - Property, Plant, and Equipment Turnover (PPET)
    - Liquidity and Solvency

Review 5-3 LO5-3　　Disaggregating the Return on Equity Ratio into its Components

Required
Refer to the financial statements for the Coca-Cola Company presented in Review 5-1.

1. Calculate Coca-Cola's profit margin (PM) and asset turnover (AT) ratios for 2020.
2. Show that ROA = PM × AT using Coca-Cola's financial data.
3. Calculate Coca-Cola's gross profit margin (GPM), accounts receivable turnover (ART), inventory turnover (INVT), and property, plant, and equipment turnover (PPET) ratios for 2020.
4. Evaluate Coca-Cola's ratios in comparison to those of PepsiCo.

Solution on p. 5-50.

LIQUIDITY AND SOLVENCY

LO5-4
Compute and interpret measures of liquidity and solvency.

Companies can use debt to increase financial leverage and boost ROE. The increase in ROE due to the use of debt is called *return on financial leverage (ROFL)*. The primary advantage of debt financing is that it is typically less costly than equity financing for two reasons. For the borrower, interest payments to lenders are tax-deductible, so paying $1 in interest reduces pre-tax income by $1 and reduces tax payments by t, the statutory tax rate. If the tax rate were 25%, the effective cost of $1 in interest to $(1 − 0.25) = $0.75. In addition, lenders require a lower rate of return than shareholders because they are subject to less risk than shareholders. Interest payments have priority over share dividends. And, in the event a firm fails, creditors collect their investment first, while shareholders receive any residual.

Exhibit 5.9 illustrates a comparison between two companies—one (Company A) is financed with 100% equity and the other (Company B) is financed with 50% debt and 50% equity. Both companies have $1,000 in (average) assets and EWI of $100, producing an ROA of 10% ($100/$1,000). Because Company A does not use liability financing, average equity equals average total assets. Also, it reports no interest expense in its income statement, so net income equals EWI. Therefore, for Company A, ROE = ROA, and its ROFL = 0%.

EXHIBIT 5.9 — The Effect of Debt Financing on ROE (ROA > interest rate)

	Company A	Company B
Assets (average)	$1,000	$1,000
EWI	100	100
ROA (EWI/Assets)	10%	10%
Equity (average)	$1,000	$ 500
Debt	0	500
Interest expense (4% of debt)	0	20
Net income (EWI − interest)	100	80
ROE (Net income/equity)	10%	16%
ROFL (ROE − ROA)	0%	6%

In contrast, Company B has $500 of equity financing and $500 of debt financing. It reports interest expense of $20 ($500 × 4%), leaving net income of $80 ($100 − $20). Company B's ROE is 16% ($80/$500), which means that its ROFL is 6% (16% − 10%). Company B has made effective use of debt financing to increase its ROE. As long as a company's ROA is greater than its cost of debt, its ROFL will be positive.[4]

We might further ask: If a higher ROE is desirable, why don't companies use as much debt financing as possible? The answer is that there are risks associated with debt financing. As the amount of debt in a company's balance sheet increases, so does the burden of interest costs on income and debt payments on cash flows. In the best of times, financial leverage increases returns to stockholders (ROE). In contrast, when earnings are depressed, financial leverage has the effect of making a bad year even worse. In the worst case, too much debt can lead to financial distress and even bankruptcy.

To illustrate how debt financing can reduce shareholder returns, **Exhibit 5.10** compares Company A and Company B in a year when reported profits are lower than in the previous example. Both companies have $1,000 in (average) assets, and both report EWI of $30, producing an ROA of 3% ($30/$1,000). Company A does not use liability financing, so its ROE = 3%, and its ROFL = 0%. Because Company B has $500 of equity and $500 of debt, it reports interest expense of $20 ($500 × 4%), leaving net income of $10 ($30 − $20). Company B's ROE is 2% ($10/$500), which means that its ROFL is −1% (2% − 3%). That is, for Company B, the use of financial leverage has a negative effect on ROE. As this example illustrates, whenever ROA is less than the interest rate on the debt, debt financing reduces the return to shareholders.

EXHIBIT 5.10 — The Effect of Debt Financing on ROE (ROA < interest rate)

	Company A	Company B
Assets (average)	$1,000	$1,000
EWI	30	30
ROA (EWI/Assets)	3%	3%
Equity (average)	$1,000	$ 500
Debt	0	500
Interest expense (4% of debt)	0	20
Net income (EWI − interest)	30	10
ROE (Net income/equity)	3%	2%
ROFL (ROE − ROA)	0%	−1%

As a general rule, shareholders benefit from increased use of debt financing provided that the assets financed with the debt earn a return that exceeds the cost of the debt. However, increasing levels of debt result in successively higher interest rates charged by creditors. At some point, the cost of debt exceeds the return on assets that a company can expect from the debt financing. Thereafter, further debt financing does not make economic sense. The market, in essence, places a limit on the amount that a company can borrow.

In addition, creditors usually require a company to execute a loan agreement that places various restrictions on its operating activities. These restrictions, called **covenants**, help safeguard debtholders in the face of increased risk. This occurs because debtholders do not have a voice on the board of directors

---

[4] The interest cost on debt is tax deductible. Therefore, the relevant cost of debt to use to compare to ROA is the after-tax interest rate.

like stockholders do. These debt covenants impose a "cost" on the company beyond that of the interest rate, and these covenants are more stringent as a company increases its reliance on debt financing.

The median ratio of total liabilities to stockholders' equity, which measures the relative use of debt versus equity in a company's capital structure, is approximately 1.5 for large, publicly traded companies. This means that the typical company relies more on debt financing than on equity. However, the relative use of debt varies considerably across industries as illustrated in **Exhibit 5.11**.

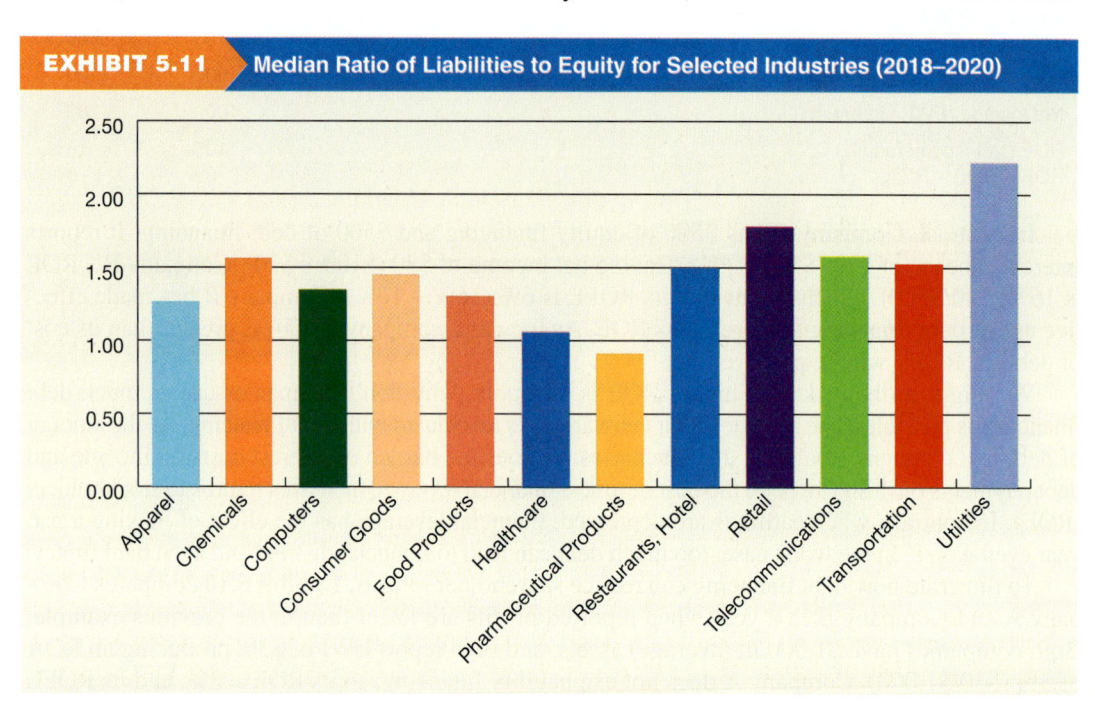

EXHIBIT 5.11 Median Ratio of Liabilities to Equity for Selected Industries (2018–2020)

Companies in the utilities industry have relatively high proportions of debt. Because the utilities industry is regulated, profits and cash flows are relatively certain and stable and, as a result, utility companies can support a higher debt level. The chemicals and telecommunications industries also utilize a relatively high proportion of debt. These industries are not regulated, but their heavy investments in property, plant, and equipment require significant long-term debt. At the lower end of debt financing are pharmaceuticals and apparel companies. Historically, these industries have been characterized by relatively uncertain profits and cash flows. In addition, success in these industries depends heavily on intellectual property and human resources devoted to research and product development. These "assets" do not appear on the balance sheet and cannot be used as collateral when borrowing funds. Consequently, they use less debt in their capital structures.

To summarize, companies can effectively use debt to increase ROE. Although it reduces financing costs, debt increases **default risk**: the risk that the company will be unable to repay debt when it comes due. Because of this risk, analysts carefully examine a company's financial statements to determine if it is using debt financing effectively and judiciously.

The core of our analysis relating to debt is the examination of a company's ability to generate cash to *service* its debt (that is, to make required debt payments of both interest and principal). Analysts, investors, and creditors are primarily concerned about whether the company has sufficient cash available or, alternatively, whether it is able to generate the required cash in the future to cover its debt obligations. The analysis of available cash is called **liquidity analysis**. The analysis of the company's ability to generate sufficient cash in the future is called **solvency analysis** (so named because a bankrupt company is said to be "insolvent").

Liquidity Analysis

Liquidity refers to cash availability: how much cash a company has, and how much it can raise on short notice. The most common ratios used to assess the degree of liquidity are the current ratio and the quick ratio, which were first introduced in Chapter 2, as well as the operating cash flow to current liabilities ratio, which was introduced in Chapter 4. Each of these ratios links required near-term payments to cash available in the near term.

Current Ratio *Current assets* are those assets that a company expects to convert into cash within the next operating cycle, which is typically a year. *Current liabilities* are those liabilities that come due within the next year. An excess of current assets over current liabilities (Current assets − Current liabilities) is known as *net working capital* or simply **working capital**. Positive working capital implies more expected cash inflows than cash outflows in the short run. The **current ratio** expresses working capital as a ratio and is computed as follows:

$$\text{Current ratio (CR)} = \frac{\text{Current assets}}{\text{Current liabilities}}$$

A current ratio greater than 1.0 implies positive working capital. Both working capital and the current ratio consider existing balance sheet data only and ignore cash inflows from future sales or other sources. The current ratio is more commonly used than working capital because ratios allow comparisons across companies of different sizes. Generally, companies prefer a higher current ratio; however, an excessively high current ratio indicates inefficient asset use. Furthermore, a current ratio less than 1.0 is not always problematic for at least two reasons:

1. A cash-and-carry company (like a grocery store) can have little or no receivables (and a low current ratio), but consistently large operating cash inflows ensure the company will be sufficiently liquid. A company can efficiently manage its working capital by minimizing receivables and inventories and maximizing payables. **The Kroger Company** and **Walmart**, for example, use their buying power to exact extended credit terms from suppliers. Consequently, because both companies are essentially cash-and-carry companies, their current ratios are less than 1.0 and both are sufficiently liquid.

2. A service company will typically report little or no inventories among its current assets. In addition, some service companies do not report significant accounts receivable. If short-term borrowings and accrued expenses exceed cash and temporary investments, a current ratio of less than 1.0 would result. **United Airlines Holdings, Inc.**, is an example of such a firm.

The aim of current-ratio analysis is to discern if a company is having, or is likely to have, difficulty meeting its short-term obligations. If a company cannot cover its short-term debts with cash provided by operations, it may need to liquidate current assets to meet its obligations. **PepsiCo**'s current ratio was 0.98 ($23,001 million/$23,372 million) at December 26, 2020. At the end of fiscal year 2019, its current ratio was 0.86 ($17,645 million/$20,461 million).

Quick Ratio The **quick ratio** is a variant of the current ratio. It focuses on quick assets, which are those assets likely to be converted to cash within a relatively short period of time, usually less than 90 days. Specifically, quick assets include cash, short-term securities, and accounts receivable; they exclude inventories and prepaid assets. The quick ratio is defined as follows:

$$\text{Quick ratio (QR)} = \frac{\text{Cash + Short-term securities + Accounts receivable}}{\text{Current liabilities}}$$

The quick ratio reflects on a company's ability to meet its current liabilities without liquidating inventories that could require markdowns. It is a more stringent test of liquidity than the current ratio and may provide more insight into company liquidity in some cases.

At the end of 2020, PepsiCo's quick ratio was 0.77 ([$8,185 million + $1,366 million + $8,404 million]/$23,372 million), which was up from 0.66 in 2019 ([$5,509 million + $229 million + $7,822 million]/$20,461 million). **Exhibit 5.13** shows that the median food products company has a quick ratio well below 1.0, and slightly below PepsiCo's value.

Operating Cash Flow to Current Liabilities The **operating cash flow to current liabilities (OCFCL)** ratio was introduced in Chapter 4 and is defined as follows:

$$\text{Operating cash flow to current liabilities (OCFCL)} = \frac{\text{Cash flow from operations}}{\text{Average current liabilities}}$$

Cash flow from operations is taken directly from the statement of cash flows. It represents the net amount of cash derived from operating activities during the year. Ultimately, the ability of a company to pay its debts is determined by whether its operations can generate enough cash to cover debt payments. Thus, a higher OCFCL ratio is generally preferred by analysts.

PepsiCo reported an OCFCL ratio of 0.48 in 2020 ($10,613 million/[($23,372 million + $20,461 million)/2]). Its 2019 OCFCL ratio was 0.45 ($9,649 million/[($20,461 million + $22,138 million)/2]). PepsiCo's OCFCL ratio has decreased slightly since 2016, though it increased a bit in 2020. The slight increase in 2020 is consistent with increases in the CR and QR. In Chapter 4 we saw that reductions in inventory and receivables increased operating cash flows. As a consequence, the improvement may not be sustainable, and continued improvement is certainly limited. **Exhibit 5.12** provides a plot of all three liquidity ratios over the past 5 years.

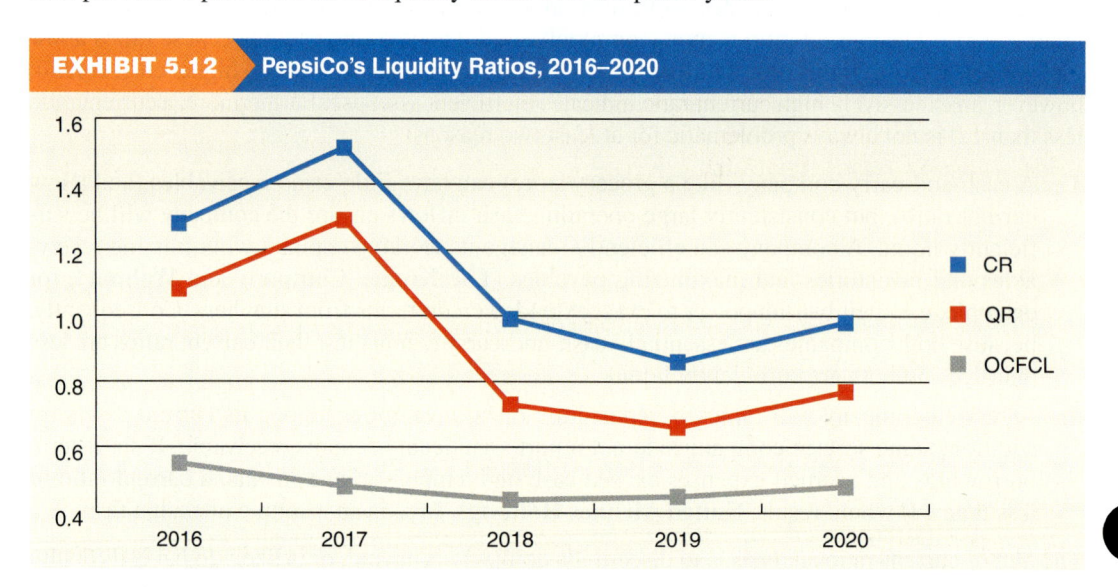

EXHIBIT 5.12 PepsiCo's Liquidity Ratios, 2016–2020

Cash Burn Rate The **cash burn rate (CBR)** is used when a company's free cash flow (cash from operations minus net investments in property, plant, and equipment) is negative. Free cash flow can be negative in a variety of circumstances—for young companies working to become established (e.g., **Tesla**) or for established companies that have run into financial distress (e.g., **Sears**). For 2020, **Blue Apron Holdings, Inc.**, reported that its cash flows used in operations were $5.4 million, and its net investments in property and equipment were $6.0 million, making free cash flow a negative $11.4 million. Blue Apron's cash burn rate would be the following:

$$\text{Cash burn rate} = \text{Free cash flow in the period} \div \text{number of days in the period}$$
$$= -\$11.4 \text{ million} \div 365 \text{ days} = -\$31 \text{ thousand/day}$$

In its efforts to attract and retain subscribers, Blue Apron is using cash at the rate of $31 thousand per day. This represents a significant improvement over the prior years, when the cash burn rate was $59 thousand per day in 2019 and $252 thousand per day in 2018.

Naturally, the interpretation of the cash burn rate depends on the depth of the company's pockets. In its June 30, 2020, balance sheet, Blue Apron reports cash and cash equivalents of $44.1 million, so it would appear that the company can, if necessary, continue on its present course for quite a while. As expected, this cash balance is down from the December 31, 2018, balance of $95.6 million. (We don't calculate PepsiCo's cash burn rate because its free cash flow is positive.)

Solvency Analysis

Solvency refers to a company's ability to meet its debt obligations, including both periodic interest payments and the repayment of the principal amount borrowed. Solvency is crucial because an insolvent company is a failed company. There are two general approaches to measuring solvency. The first approach uses balance sheet data and assesses the proportion of capital raised from creditors. The second approach uses income statement data and assesses the profit generated relative to debt payment obligations. We discuss each approach in turn.

Debt-to-Equity The **debt-to-equity ratio (D/E)**, which was introduced in Chapter 1, is a useful tool for the first type of solvency analysis. It is defined as follows:

$$\text{Debt-to-equity ratio} = \frac{\text{Total liabilities}}{\text{Total stockholders' equity}}$$

This ratio conveys how reliant a company is on creditor financing (which are fixed claims) compared with equity financing (which are flexible or residual claims). A higher ratio indicates less solvency and more risk. PepsiCo's debt-to-equity ratio is 5.9 for 2020 ($79,366 million/$13,552 million). In 2019, its ratio was 4.3 ($63,679 million/$14,868 million). As seen in the chart below, the debt-to-equity ratio declined in 2018, remained steady in 2019, but increased in 2020. Like many large companies, PepsiCo has returned cash to shareholders in the form of dividends and share buybacks and increased debt to take advantage of unusually low interest rates. At some point, the increase in the debt-to-equity ratio may have an impact on PepsiCo's ability to borrow at favorable interest rates. PepsiCo's debt-to-equity ratio is well above the average of approximately 1.31 for other companies in the food industry.

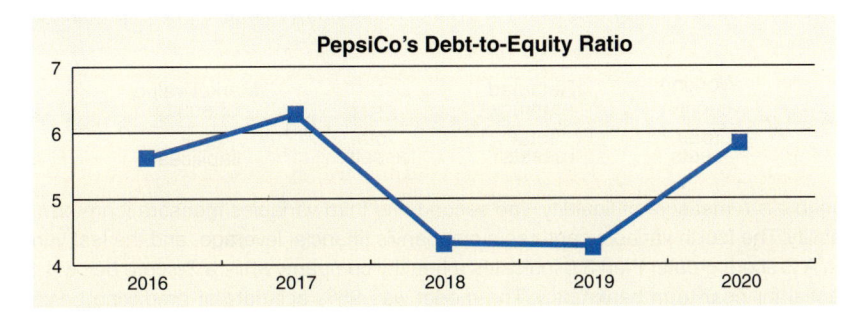

In practice, analysts use a variety of solvency measures that are similar to the debt-to-equity ratio. One variant of this ratio considers a company's *long-term* debt divided by equity. This approach assumes that current liabilities are repaid from current assets (so-called self-liquidating). Thus, it assumes that creditors and stockholders need only focus on the relative proportion of long-term capital.

Times Interest Earned The second type of solvency analysis compares profits to liabilities. This approach assesses how much operating profit is available to cover debt obligations. A common measure for this type of solvency analysis is the **times interest earned (TIE)** ratio (see Chapter 9) defined as follows:

$$\text{Times interest earned} = \frac{\text{Earnings before interest expense and taxes}}{\text{Interest expense}}$$

The times interest earned ratio reflects the operating income available to pay interest expense. The underlying assumption is that only interest needs to be paid because the principal will be refinanced. This ratio is sometimes abbreviated as EBIT/I. The numerator is similar to earnings without interest (EWI), but it is *pretax* instead of after tax.

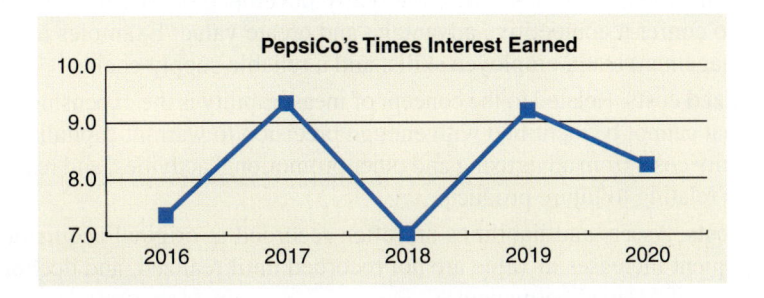

Management wants this ratio to be sufficiently high so that there is little risk of default. PepsiCo's TIE ratio was 8.24 times in 2020 ([$9,069 million + $1,252 million]/$1,252 million), which is down significantly from 9.20 times in 2019 ([$9,312 million + $1,135 million]/$1,135 million). Over the 5-year period between 2016 and 2020, PepsiCo's TIE ratio has ranged from a low of 7.03 in 2018 to a high of 9.34 in 2017. The current level of this ratio suggests that PepsiCo is more than capable of earning income that is sufficient to cover its financing costs.

There are many variations of solvency and liquidity analysis and the ratios used. The basic idea is to construct measures that reflect a company's credit risk exposure. There is not one "best" financial leverage ratio. Instead, as financial statement users, we want to use measures that capture the risk we are most concerned with. It is also important to compute the ratios ourselves to ensure we know what is included and excluded from each ratio.

RESEARCH INSIGHT

Using Ratios to Predict Bankruptcy Several research studies have examined the use of various financial ratios, such as those discussed in this chapter, to predict financial distress of large companies. In a pioneering study, Professor Edward Altman used discriminant analysis to develop a method for scoring a company's credit risk and using that score to predict bankruptcy. Altman's model produced a **Z-score** as follows:

$$Z\text{-score} = 1.2 \times \frac{\text{Working capital}}{\text{Total assets}} + 1.4 \times \frac{\text{Retained earnings}}{\text{Total assets}} + 3.3 \times \frac{\text{EBIT}}{\text{Total assets}} + 0.6 \times \frac{\text{Market value of equity}}{\text{Total liabilities}} + 0.99 \times \frac{\text{Sales}}{\text{Total assets}}$$

The first variable is a measure of liquidity. The second and third variables measure long-term and short-term profitability. The fourth variable captures a company's financial leverage, and the last variable is asset turnover. A Z-score greater than 3.0 indicates a healthy company, while a Z-score below 1.8 suggests a high potential for near-term bankruptcy. The model was 95% accurate at predicting bankruptcy one year in advance and 72% accurate two years in advance. Today, credit scoring models similar to Altman's Z-score are used by nearly all financial institutions and many other businesses to evaluate credit risk. (Altman, E., "Financial Ratios, Discriminant Analysis and the Prediction of Corporate Bankruptcy," *Journal of Finance*, September, 1968.)

Limitations of Ratio Analysis

The quality of financial statement analysis depends on the quality of financial information. We ought not blindly analyze numbers; doing so can lead to faulty conclusions and suboptimal decisions. Instead, we need to acknowledge that current accounting rules (GAAP) have limitations and be fully aware of the company's environment, its competitive pressures, and any structural and strategic changes. **Exhibit 5.13** shows how ratios can differ significantly across industries, so comparisons to companies with similar customers, technologies, and competitive pressures will be most meaningful. Even within industries, there may be differences in strategy that create big differences in ratio values. There can be other factors that limit the usefulness of financial accounting information for ratio analysis.

GAAP Limitations Several limitations in GAAP can distort financial ratios. Limitations include:

1. **Measurability**. Financial statements reflect what can be reliably measured. This results in nonrecognition of certain assets, often internally developed assets, the very assets that are most likely to confer a competitive advantage and create value. Examples are brand name, a superior management team, employee skills, and a reliable supply chain.
2. **Non-capitalized costs**. Related to the concept of measurability is the expensing of costs relating to "assets" that cannot be identified with enough precision to warrant capitalization. Examples are brand equity costs from advertising and other promotional activities, and research and development costs relating to future products.
3. **Historical costs**. Assets and liabilities are often recorded at original acquisition or issuance costs. Subsequent increases in value are not recorded until realized, and declines in value are recognized only if deemed permanent.

Thus, GAAP balance sheets omit important and valuable assets. Our analysis of ROE, including that of liquidity and solvency, must consider that assets can be underreported and that ratios can be distorted. We discuss many of these limitations in more detail in later chapters.

EXHIBIT 5.13 Industry Ratios: Medians of Companies with Market Capitalization > $500 Million (2018–2020)

	ROE	ROA	ROFL	PM	GPM	AT	ART	INVT	PPET	DE	TIE	CR	QR	OCFCL
Apparel	13.1%	7.4%	6.0%	6.2%	50.9%	1.23	9.90	2.84	6.38	1.27	11.02	2.08	0.99	0.47
Business Services	10.7%	4.1%	4.1%	8.3%	53.3%	0.59	5.59	34.60	8.16	1.30	4.08	1.37	1.19	0.35
Chemicals	13.0%	6.2%	6.0%	9.1%	35.0%	0.70	5.91	4.46	2.48	1.58	5.67	1.93	1.12	0.55
Computers	5.7%	3.6%	2.1%	4.6%	42.5%	0.74	4.83	7.47	8.63	1.36	5.80	1.53	1.33	0.34
Consumer Goods	15.1%	7.3%	7.7%	7.8%	47.4%	0.98	8.06	5.09	5.65	1.45	13.07	1.57	0.94	0.48
Food Products	12.1%	6.1%	4.9%	8.6%	34.5%	0.79	12.44	5.73	3.70	1.31	5.90	1.61	0.73	0.59
Healthcare	8.8%	5.8%	2.5%	8.0%	33.0%	0.70	6.38	30.39	4.49	1.07	3.73	1.51	1.19	0.69
Petroleum	4.3%	2.9%	0.8%	4.8%	32.8%	0.43	5.81	11.30	0.82	1.09	3.48	1.35	0.96	0.85
Pharmaceutical	2.8%	2.1%	0.1%	5.2%	70.2%	0.41	5.39	2.34	4.36	0.92	3.04	2.96	2.33	0.38
Printing & Publishing	1.5%	1.3%	0.2%	1.7%	54.1%	0.67	6.08	12.96	6.25	2.15	6.51	1.29	0.84	0.33
Restaurants, Hotel	6.1%	6.6%	2.9%	8.5%	22.1%	1.07	21.71	62.47	2.35	1.51	4.01	0.97	0.78	0.70
Retail	14.2%	6.8%	7.2%	4.1%	31.7%	1.80	41.60	5.60	5.38	1.79	6.66	1.29	0.42	0.46
Steel	8.2%	5.5%	2.2%	5.0%	18.0%	0.98	7.96	5.46	2.42	1.16	5.24	2.12	1.11	0.37
Telecommunications	9.0%	4.1%	3.3%	9.5%	49.9%	0.47	5.27	22.61	1.43	1.60	3.77	1.02	0.78	0.58
Tobacco	15.4%	11.5%	10.0%	18.8%	64.4%	0.57	25.61	2.32	9.07	3.15	8.93	0.99	0.50	0.55
Transportation	11.2%	5.2%	4.0%	8.2%	31.3%	0.41	11.08	30.89	0.57	1.54	3.38	0.96	0.81	0.59
Utilities	9.8%	4.2%	5.6%	16.8%	33.9%	0.24	7.01	13.96	0.34	2.22	2.80	0.69	0.43	0.58
Overall	9.8%	5.1%	3.9%	7.1%	36.9%	0.68	6.90	6.21	3.63	1.33	4.82	1.63	1.05	0.51

Company Changes Many companies regularly undertake mergers, acquire new companies, and divest subsidiaries. Such major operational changes can impair the comparability of company ratios across time. Companies also change strategies, such as product pricing, R&D, and financing. We must understand the effects of such changes on ratios and exercise caution when we compare ratios from one period to the next. Companies also behave differently at different points in their life cycles. For instance, growth companies possess a different profile than do mature companies. Seasonal effects also markedly impact analysis of financial statements at different times of the year. Thus, we must consider life cycle and cyclicality when we compare ratios across companies and over time.

Conglomerate Effects Few companies are pure-play; instead, most companies operate in several businesses or industries. Most publicly traded companies consist of a parent company and multiple subsidiaries, often pursuing different lines of business. PepsiCo reports financial information for six separate business segments. Most heavy equipment manufacturers, for example, have finance subsidiaries, (**Ford Motor Credit Company** and **Caterpillar Financial Services Corporation** are subsidiaries of **Ford** and **Caterpillar**, respectively.) Financial statements of such conglomerates are consolidated and include the financial statements of the parent and its subsidiaries. Consequently, such consolidated statements are challenging to analyze. Typically, analysts break the financials apart into their component businesses and separately analyze each component. Fortunately, companies must report financial information (albeit limited) for major business segments in their 10-Ks.

Means to an End Ratios reduce, to a single number, the myriad complexities of a company's operations. No one number can accurately capture the qualitative aspect of a company. Ratios cannot hope to capture the innumerable transactions and events that occur each day between a company and various parties. Ratios cannot meaningfully convey a company's marketing and management philosophies, its human resource activities, its financing activities, its strategic initiatives, and its product management. In our analysis we must learn to look through the numbers and ratios to better understand the operational factors that drive financial results. Successful analysis seeks to gain insight into what a company is really about and what the future portends. Our overriding purpose in analysis is to understand the past and present to better predict the future. Computing and examining ratios is just one step in that process.

Review 5-4 LO5-4 Computing and Interpreting Liquidity and Solvency Ratios

Refer to the income statements and balance sheets for the Coca-Cola Company presented in Review 5-1 earlier in this chapter.

Required
Compute the following liquidity and solvency ratios for Coca-Cola and interpret your results in comparison to those of PepsiCo.

1. Current ratio
2. Quick ratio
3. Debt-to-equity ratio
4. Times interest earned

Solution on p. 5-50.

APPENDIX 5A: Analyzing and Interpreting Core Operating Activities

LO5-5 Measure and analyze the effect of operating activities on ROE.

In Chapter 4, we analyzed cash flows by grouping them into three categories—operating, investing, and financing. Similarly, the income statement and balance sheet can be formatted to distinguish between operating and nonoperating (investing and financing) activities. In this appendix, we consider the effect of operating activities on the return on investment. The distinction between returns earned from operating activities and those generated by nonoperating activities is important. Operations provide the primary value drivers for stockholders. It is for this reason that many analysts argue that operating activities must be executed successfully if a company expects to remain profitable in the long run.

Operating activities refer to the core transactions and events of a company. They consist of those activities required to deliver a company's products and services to its customers. A company is engaged in operating activities when it conducts research and development, establishes supply chains, assembles administrative support, produces and markets its products, and follows up with after-sale customer service. Although nonoperating activities, namely investing and financing activities, are important and must be managed well, they are not the primary value drivers for investors and creditors.

Operating returns are measured by the **return on net operating assets (RNOA)**. This return metric is defined as follows:

$$\text{RNOA} = \frac{\text{Net operating profit after taxes (NOPAT)}}{\text{Average net operating assets (NOA)}}$$

In order to calculate this ratio, we must first classify the income statement and balance sheet accounts into operating and nonoperating components so that we can assess each separately. First, we will consider operating components of the income statement and the calculation of NOPAT. Then, we consider operating and nonoperating components of the balance sheet and the calculation of NOA.

Reporting Operating Activities in the Income Statement The income statement reports operating activities through accounts such as sales revenue, cost of goods sold, selling, general, and administrative (SG&A) expenses, depreciation, rent, insurance, wages, advertising, and R&D expenses. These activities create the most long-lasting effects on profitability and cash flows. Nonoperating items in the income statement include interest expense on borrowed funds and interest and dividend income on investments as well as gains and losses on those investments.

A commonly used measure of operating income is **net operating profit after taxes (NOPAT)**. NOPAT is calculated as:

$$\text{NOPAT} = \text{Net income} - [(\text{Nonoperating revenues} - \text{Nonoperating expenses}) \times (1 - \text{Statutory tax rate})]$$

NOPAT is an important measure of profitability. It is similar to net income except that NOPAT focuses exclusively on after-tax *operating* performance.

Computation of NOPAT requires that we separate nonoperating revenues and expenses from operating sources of income. Companies often report income from operations as a subtotal (before income taxes) within the income statement. These numbers should be interpreted with caution. Currently, there are no requirements within GAAP that specify which revenue and expense items should be included in operating income. As a consequence, some nonoperating items may be included (as part of SG&A expense, for example). PepsiCo has investments in affiliated companies that distribute its snack foods in certain parts of the world. PepsiCo's income from these investments is included in its SG&A expense in the income statement, but the amount is not disclosed. While this income might appear to be nonoperating, most analysts would argue that this amount should be included in the calculation of NOPAT for PepsiCo because these distribution operations are part of the core operating activities of the business.

The tax rate used to compute NOPAT above is the corporate statutory tax rate. As we have done throughout the book, we use the federal statutory tax rate of 35% for 2017 and earlier and 25% for 2018 and later.[5] PepsiCo's 2020 NOPAT can be computed using this tax rate:

$$\text{NOPAT} = \$7{,}175 \text{ million} - [(\$117 \text{ million} - \$1{,}128 \text{ million}) \times (1 - 0.25)] = \$7{,}933.3 \text{ million}$$

PepsiCo's NOPAT is greater than its net income of $7,175 million in 2020. The difference between net income and NOPAT is the interest expense on its debt, interest income on its investments, as well as other pension and retiree medical benefits income.

Reporting Operating Activities in the Balance Sheet The balance sheet also reflects both operating and nonoperating activities. The asset side of the balance sheet reports resources devoted to operating activities in accounts such as cash, receivables, inventories, property, plant, and equipment, and intangible assets. Among liabilities, accounts payable, accrued expenses, and some long-term liabilities such as deferred compensation and pension benefits arise out of operating activities. In addition, accrued and deferred income taxes are generally considered operating liabilities.

Investments in securities of other companies are usually considered nonoperating. The exception is that some equity-type investments are related to operations. PepsiCo's investment in its snack foods distributors is an example of this type of investment. Equity investments are discussed further in Chapter 12. Among a company's liabilities, short-term and long-term debt accounts are classified as nonoperating. These include accounts such as notes payable, interest payable, current maturities of long-term debt, lease liabilities, and long-term debt.

PepsiCo reported short-term investments of $1,366 million in 2020 ($229 million in 2019), which were nonoperating. It also reported long-term investments in non-controlled affiliates of $2,792 million in 2020 ($2,683 million in 2019). These long-term investments are the aforementioned equity investments in companies distributing PepsiCo's snack foods, and most analysts would consider them to be part of operations. PepsiCo's note disclosures show that its noncurrent Other assets account included nonoperating assets of $493 million in 2020 ($385 million in 2019). Its nonoperating liabilities included short-term debt obligations of $3,780 million in 2020 ($2,920 million in 2019) and long-term debt obligations of $40,370 million in 2020 ($29,148 million in 2019).

By subtracting total operating liabilities from total operating assets, we get **net operating assets (NOA)**.[6] PepsiCo's NOA for 2020 and 2019 is calculated as follows ($ millions):

	2020	2019
Operating assets	$92,918 − $1,366 − $493 = $91,059	$78,547 − $229 − $385 = $77,933
Operating liabilities	$79,366 − $3,780 − $40,370 = $35,216	$63,679 − $2,920 − $29,148 = $31,611
NOA	$55,843	$46,322

Given NOPAT and NOA, we can compute PepsiCo's RNOA as follows:

$$\text{RNOA} = \frac{\text{NOPAT}}{\text{Average NOA}} = \frac{\$7{,}933.3 \text{ million}}{(\$55{,}843 \text{ million} + \$46{,}322 \text{ million})/2} = 15.5\%$$

PepsiCo's ROE was 50.5% in 2020. Its RNOA was 15.5%, which represents 31% of the total return earned by stockholders.

Disaggregating RNOA

We gain further insights into operating returns by disaggregating RNOA into operating profit margin and asset turnover. RNOA can be presented as the product of net operating profit margin (NOPM) and net operating asset turnover (NOAT). We define **net operating profit margin (NOPM)** as the amount of operating profit produced as a percentage of each sales dollar. NOPM is similar to the profit margin (PM) ratio defined in the

---

[5] In the calculation of NOPAT, we want the tax rate used to compute financial accounting income. For total net income, this would be the GAAP effective tax rate (described in Chapter 10). Using the federal statutory tax rate is reasonable when there are no 'permanent differences' (discussed in Chapter 10). However, permanent differences do exist in some cases, and when they do, some nonoperating sources of revenue and expense are not taxed at the statutory rate. For example a significant part of dividend income received from investments of stock of other corporations is excluded from taxable income. A detailed review of the company's tax note is required to attempt to work out whether an effective rate on nonoperating income would be appropriate. We use the statutory rate for simplicity in this introductory book.

[6] Total operating assets can be computed by subtracting nonoperating assets from total assets. Similarly, we can determine operating liabilities either by adding up the operating items or by subtracting the nonoperating items from total liabilities.

chapter, except that it excludes all nonoperating revenues and expenses from the calculation. PepsiCo's NOPM was 11.3% in 2020, computed as:

$$\text{NOPM} = \frac{\text{NOPAT}}{\text{Sales revenue}} = \frac{\$7,933.3 \text{ million}}{\$70,372 \text{ million}} = 11.3\%$$

The ratio indicates that each dollar of sales revenue generated 11.3¢ of after-tax operating profit. PepsiCo's NOPAT is very close to PepsiCo's EWI because the primary nonoperating item in the company's income statement is interest expense. Thus, its NOPM is almost identical to its profit margin of 11.5%.

Net operating asset turnover (NOAT) is defined as the ratio of sales revenue to average net operating assets (NOA). NOAT captures the amount of sales revenue generated by each dollar of net investment in operating assets. PepsiCo's NOAT is 1.38 times, computed as:

$$\text{NOAT} = \frac{\text{Sales revenue}}{\text{Average NOA}} = \frac{\$70,372 \text{ million}}{(\$55,843 \text{ million} + \$46,322 \text{ million})/2} = 1.38$$

This ratio suggests that each dollar of investment in net operating assets generates $1.38 of sales revenue. This ratio is considerably higher than PepsiCo's asset turnover (AT) ratio of 0.821. This difference is caused by the difference between net operating assets (NOA) and total assets. NOAT is computed using average NOA in the denominator rather than average total assets. Thus, nonoperating assets are excluded, and operating assets are presented net of operating liabilities. The resulting denominator is, therefore, considerably smaller.

PepsiCo's RNOA is 15.5%. This return can be disaggregated into the product of NOPM and NOAT as follows:

$$\text{RNOA} = \text{NOPM} \times \text{NOAT}$$
$$15.5\% = 11.27\% \times 1.378$$

Review 5-5 LO5-5

Measuring the Effects of Operating Activities on ROE

Refer to the financial statements of the Coca-Cola Company presented in Review 5-1. For 2020, calculate Coca-Cola's return on net operating assets (RNOA) and then disaggregate RNOA into net operating profit margin (NOPM) and net operating asset turnover (NOAT). Assume a statutory tax rate of 25% and that equity method investments, other assets, and other liabilities are operating items.

Solution on p. 5-51.

APPENDIX 5B: Financial Statement Forecasts

LO5-6
Prepare financial statement forecasts.

The ability to forecast future financial activities is an important aspect of many business decisions. We might, for example, wish to estimate the value of a company's common stock before purchasing its shares. Or, we might want to evaluate the creditworthiness of a prospective borrower. We might also be interested in comparing the financial impact of alternative business strategies or tactics. For each of these decision contexts, a forecast of future earnings and cash flows would be relevant to such an evaluation.

Financial statement forecasts are hypothetical statements prepared to reflect specific assumptions about the company and its transactions. These forecasts are prepared for future periods based on assumptions about the future activities of a business. By varying the assumptions, forecasts of statements allow us to ask "what if" questions about the future activities of the company, the answers to which provide the necessary inputs underlying most business decisions.

In this appendix, we present a common, yet simple method for preparing financial statement forecasts. This method proceeds in seven steps:

1. Forecast sales revenue.
2. Forecast operating expenses, such as cost of goods sold and SG&A expenses.
3. Forecast operating assets and liabilities, including accounts receivable, inventory, property, plant, and equipment, accounts payable, and prepaid and accrued expenses.
4. Forecast nonoperating assets, liabilities, contributed capital, revenues, and expenses.
5. Forecast net income, dividends, and retained earnings.
6. Forecast the amount of cash required to balance the balance sheet.
7. Prepare a statement of cash flows based on the forecasted income statement and balance sheet.

Step 1. Forecast Sales Revenue

The sales forecast is the crucial first step in the preparation of financial statement forecasts because many of the accounts in the income statement and balance sheet depend on their relation to the sales forecast.

The general method for forecasting sales is to assume a revenue growth rate and apply that rate to the current sales revenue amount:

Forecasted revenues = Current revenues × (1 + Revenue growth rate)

A good starting point for estimating the revenue growth rate is the historical rate of sales growth. This is obtained by using data from the horizontal analysis discussed earlier in the chapter. For example, over the past four years, PepsiCo has experienced an average sales growth of 2.9% per year. Once we have this historical rate as a starting point, we can then adjust the growth rate up or down based on other relevant information. For example, we might attempt to answer the following questions:

- How will future sales be affected by economic conditions? What will happen in the economy in the coming year? Do we expect economic growth or a recession? How will economic growth vary in various markets, such as the United States, Europe, Asia, and Latin America? How will foreign currency exchange rates come into play?
- What changes are expected from the company? Are there any new strategic initiatives planned? Is the company planning to open new stores or launch new products, new advertising campaigns, or new pricing tactics? Do we expect any acquisitions of other businesses?
- What changes in the competitive environment do we expect? Are new competitors entering the market? How will existing competitors respond to changes in the company's strategy? How will substitute products affect sales?

To answer each of the above questions, we rely on a variety of information sources, not the least of which is the management's discussion and analysis (MD&A) section of the company's 10-K report. We can also use publicly available information from competitors, suppliers, customers, industry organizations, and government agencies to provide some insight into trends that can have an effect on future revenues. Our objective is to be able to adjust the historical growth rate up or down to reflect the insights we gain from reviewing this additional information. Revenue for 2020 increased by about 4.8% over 2019. Therefore, we forecast the 2021 revenue to be $73,891 million ($70,372 million × 1.05).

Step 2. Forecast Operating Expenses

Given our forecast of sales revenue, we then turn to forecasting operating expenses. We rely on the common-size income statement as a starting point to identify the relationship between operating expense items and sales revenue. That is, we use the expense-to-sales (ETS) ratio for each operating expense item to compute the forecasted expense:

Forecasted operating expense = Forecasted revenues × ETS ratio

While historical ETS ratios provide a good place to start, we may want to adjust these ratios up or down based on observed trends or any additional information that we might have. For example, when we examined PepsiCo's common-size income statements, we learned that cost of goods sold increased to 45.2% of sales in 2020, up from 44.9% in 2019. Will this trend continue into 2021? What are the effects of developments in the sugar market or from tariffs on imported aluminum? What about PepsiCo's cost-cutting efforts over recent years? Or, do we anticipate that this expense item will revert to historical levels in relation to sales? Will the ETS ratios post-pandemic be similar to pre-pandemic levels? As was the case with the sales forecast, there are numerous sources of information that are potentially useful for making adjustments to the historical relationships.

For the purpose of illustration, we assume that 2021 Cost of sales will increase to 45.5% of revenues ($33,990 million) and that Selling, general, and administrative expenses will drop slightly to 40% of revenues in 2021 ($29,556 million).

Step 3. Forecast Operating Assets and Liabilities

The sales forecast can also be used to forecast operating assets and liabilities. The relationship between operating assets and revenues is based on asset turnover analysis. For example, when we compute accounts receivable turnover (ART), sales revenue is divided by average accounts receivable. When forecasting accounts receivable, we assume a relationship between sales revenue and year-end accounts receivable:

$$\text{Forecasted accounts receivable} = \frac{\text{Forecasted sales revenue} \times \text{Reported accounts receivable}}{\text{Reported sales revenue}}$$

PepsiCo reports accounts and notes receivable of $8,404 million in 2020, which is 11.94% of the reported sales revenue of $70,372 million. The forecasted accounts receivable for 2021 is, therefore, $8,823 million ($73,891 million × 11.94%).

The same procedure can be used to forecast other operating assets, such as inventories, prepaid expenses and property, plant, and equipment, as well as operating liabilities such as accounts payable and accrued expenses. Intangible assets, including Goodwill, arise when one company acquires another. Goodwill and some intangibles are not amortized after purchase (more in Chapter 12), but some do get amortized. Forecasting these values requires forecasts of PepsiCo's acquisitions in 2021. For this illustration, we assume no acquisitions in 2021, no impairments of nonamortizable intangibles, and the amortization of intangible assets in 2021 is $90 million, the same as in 2020.

Step 4. Forecast Nonoperating Assets, Liabilities, Revenues, and Expenses

While operating expenses, assets, and liabilities tend to be related to sales revenue, this is typically not the case for nonoperating items. Instead, nonoperating revenues, such as interest and dividend income, tend to be related to investments, while nonoperating expense, namely interest expense, is related to debt financing. As a starting point, we forecast each of these items by assuming no change from the current amounts. For example, PepsiCo reported long-term debt of $40,370 million in 2020 along with short-term obligations of $3,780 million. We forecast the same level of debt financing in 2021. Likewise, net interest expense and other should remain the same at $1,128 million.

There may be information in the notes or in the MD&A section of the 10-K report to suggest other assumptions. For example, the notes typically reveal the amount of long-term debt that will come due in each of the next five years. This information can be used to adjust the balance in short-term obligations because current maturities of long-term debt would be included under this item. Nevertheless, an assumption of no change is a good place to start.

Step 5. Forecast Net Income, Dividends, and Retained Earnings

Once we have forecasts of sales revenue (from step 1), operating expenses (step 2), and nonoperating revenues and expenses (step 4), we can calculate pretax earnings, income tax expense, and net income. Income tax expense is forecasted by multiplying pretax income by the effective tax rate:

Forecasted income tax expense = Forecasted pretax income × Effective tax rate

The **effective tax rate** is the average tax rate applied to pretax earnings and is computed by dividing reported income tax expense by reported pretax earnings. PepsiCo's effective tax rate was 20.9% in 2020 ($1,894 million/$9,069 million). Although this rate can be adjusted up or down based on additional information, we apply a 25% effective tax rate to compute 2021 forecasted income taxes. This assumption results in forecasted income taxes of $2,426 million ($9,704 million × 25%) and forecasted net income of $7,278 million ($9,704 million − $2,426 million). PepsiCo's forecasted 2021 income statement is presented in **Exhibit 5B.1** alongside its 2020 reported income statement.

EXHIBIT 5B.1 PepsiCo Income Statement Forecast

PEPSICO, INC.
2020 Income Statement and 2021 Income Statement Forecast

($ millions)	Forecast 2021	As Reported 2020
Net revenue ($70,372 × 1.05)	$73,891	$70,372
Cost of sales ($73,891 × 0.455)	33,620	31,797
Selling, general, and administrative expenses ($73,891 × 0.40)	29,556	28,495
Operating profit	10,715	10,080
Other pension and retiree medical benefits income/(expense) (no change)	117	117
Net interest expense and other (no change)	(1,128)	(1,128)
Income before income taxes	9,704	9,069
Provision for income taxes ($9,704 × 0.25)	2,426	1,894
Net income	$ 7,278	$ 7,175

Our forecast of dividends relies on the **dividend payout ratio**, defined as dividend payments divided by net income.

Forecasted dividends = Forecasted net income × Dividend payout ratio

PepsiCo paid cash dividends of $5,509 million in 2020, which is 76.8% of its net income of $7,175 million. In 2019, PepsiCo had a dividend payout ratio of 72.1%. Using a dividend payout ratio of 75%, we forecast 2021 dividends to be $5,459 million ($7,278 million × 75%).

Next, we can forecast retained earnings using the forecasts of net income and dividends:

$$\text{Forecasted retained earnings} = \text{Beginning retained earnings} + \text{Forecasted net income} - \text{Forecasted dividends}$$

Throughout this chapter, we have presented PepsiCo's stockholders' equity as a single amount, without separating retained earnings from contributed capital. Contributed capital increases when common stock is issued, and it decreases when common stock is repurchased. PepsiCo has repurchased shares every year for the past eleven years but indicated that it does not expect to repurchase any additional shares in 2021. Thus, total forecasted stockholders' equity in 2021 will equal $15,371, computed as follows:

$$\begin{aligned}\text{Forecasted stockholders' equity} &= \text{Beginning stockholders' equity} + \text{Forecasted net income} - \text{Forecasted dividends}\\ \$15{,}371 \text{ million} &= \$13{,}552 \text{ million} + \$7{,}278 \text{ million} - \$5{,}459 \text{ million}\end{aligned}$$

Step 6. Forecast Cash

If the forecasts of all other components of the balance sheet are in place, we can then forecast the cash balance. This forecast is simply a "plug" amount that makes the balance sheet balance:

$$\text{Forecasted cash} = \text{Forecasted liabilities} + \text{Forecasted stockholders' equity} - \text{Forecasted noncash assets}$$

It is possible that the resulting forecast of cash will be negative or unreasonably small or large. If this occurs, we then revisit steps 4 and 5. If the cash forecast is negative or too low, we adjust our forecast of short-term debt and interest expense to reflect increased borrowing to cover cash needs. If the cash forecast is too large, we can assume that excess cash is invested in marketable securities and increase the amount of interest income. In either case, we then modify our forecast of income taxes, net income, dividends, and retained earnings before recalculating the cash forecast.

PepsiCo's 2021 balance sheet forecast is presented in **Exhibit 5B.2**, alongside the company's 2020 actual balance sheet. The cash balance is forecasted to increase, from $8,185 million in 2020 to $9,725 million in 2021.

EXHIBIT 5B.2 PepsiCo Balance Sheet Forecast

PEPSICO, INC.
2020 Balance Sheet and 2021 Balance Sheet Forecast

($ millions)	Forecast 2021	As Reported 2020
Assets		
Cash and cash equivalents (plug to balance)	$ 9,725	$ 8,185
Short-term investments (no change)	1,366	1,366
Accounts and notes receivable, net ($73,891 × 11.94%)	8,823	8,404
Inventories ($73,891 × 5.93%)	4,382	4,172
Prepaid expenses and other current assets ($73,891 × 1.24%)	916	874
Total current assets	25,212	23,001
Property, plant, and equipment, net ($73,891 × 30.37%)	22,441	21,369
Amortizable intangible assets, net ($1,703 − $90)	1,613	1,703
Goodwill (no change)	18,757	18,757
Other indefinite-lived intangible assets (no change)	17,612	17,612
Investments in noncontrolled affiliates (no change)	2,792	2,792
Deferred income taxes ($73,891 × 6.21%)	4,589	4,372
Other assets ($73,891 × 4.71%)	3,480	3,312
Total assets	$96,496	$92,918
Liabilities and equity		
Short-term obligations (no change)	$ 3,780	$ 3,780
Accounts payable and other current liabilities ($73,891 × 27.84%)	20,571	19,592
Total current liabilities	24,351	23,372
Long-term debt obligations (no change)	40,370	40,370
Deferred income taxes ($73,891 × 6.09%)	4,500	4,284
Other liabilities ($73,891 × 16.11%)	11,904	11,340
Total liabilities	81,125	79,366
Total equity ($13,552 + $7,278 − $5,459)	15,371	13,552
Total liabilities and equity	$96,496	$92,918

Step 7. Prepare the Statement of Cash Flows Forecast

Once we have a forecast of the income statement and balance sheet, we can prepare a forecast of the statement of cash flows using the methods illustrated in Chapter 4. To do so, we need a forecast of depreciation expense (if that item is not explicitly listed as an operating expense in the income statement). The procedure for forecasting depreciation expense is the same as was used for other operating expenses—we simply use the depreciation ETS ratio.

PepsiCo reported depreciation and amortization expense of $2,548 million in 2020, which was 3.62% of sales revenue. Using this ETS ratio, we can forecast depreciation expense of $2,675 million in 2021 ($73,891 million × 3.62%). Using this forecast, along with other items forecasted earlier, we can prepare the statement of cash flows, which is presented in **Exhibit 5B.3**.

Additional Considerations

Forecasts of financial statements are based on a set of assumptions about the future. Any decisions that are based on such statements are only as good as the quality of these assumptions. Therefore, it is important that we appreciate the effect that each assumption has on the forecasted amounts. To this end, it is often helpful to use **sensitivity analysis** to examine the effect of alternative assumptions on the forecasted statements. For example, we might prepare three different forecasted income statements—one using our "most-likely" assumption for the sales forecast, and one each for the "best-case" and "worst-case" scenarios. In some situations, a change in the sales forecast can have a dramatic effect on net income and cash flows, particularly in the presence of large fixed costs. Sensitivity analysis helps to identify these effects before a decision is made so that costly mistakes can be avoided.

It is also important to remember that these statements are predictions about the future and, as such, are bound to be wrong. That is, we expect that there will be **forecast errors**—differences between the forecasted and the actual amounts. The goal of a good forecast is accuracy, which means that we want the forecast errors to be as small as possible. Generating forecasted statements using a computer is relatively easy, and the efficiency and precision of spreadsheet software can provide a false sense of confidence in the numbers. Spreadsheets routinely calculate forecasted amounts to the "nth" decimal place whether or not such precision is justified. However, an amount forecasted to the nearest penny may not be useful if the forecast is off by millions of dollars. It is better to be imprecisely accurate than to be precisely inaccurate.

EXHIBIT 5B.3 PepsiCo Statement of Cash Flow Forecast

PEPSICO, INC.
2021 Statement of Cash Flows Forecast

($ millions)	2021 Forecast
Operating activities:	
Net income	$ 7,278
Adjustments:	
Depreciation and amortization ($73,891 × 3.62%)	2,548
Minus change in accounts and notes receivable	(419)
Minus change in inventories	(210)
Minus change in prepaid expenses and other current assets	(42)
Minus change in deferred income taxes	(217)
Minus change in other assets	(168)
Plus change in accounts payable and other current liabilities	979
Plus change in deferred income taxes	216
Plus change in other liabilities	564
Cash flow from operations	10,529
Investing activities:	
Investment in property, plant, and equipment [$2,548 + ($22,441 − $21,369) + ($1,613 − $1,703)]	(3,530)
Cash used for investing activities	(3,530)
Financing activities:	
Dividends paid	(5,459)
Cash used for financing activities	(5,459)
Net decrease in cash ($10,529 − $3,530 − $5,459)	1,540
Cash and cash equivalents, 2020	8,185
Cash and cash equivalents, 2021	$ 9,725

Preparing a Forecast Income Statement and Balance Sheet

LO5-6 Review 5-6

Refer to the income statements and balance sheets of the Coca-Cola Company presented in Review 5-1.

Required
Make the following assumptions:

- 2021 sales revenue increases 5% from 2020 to $34,665 million.
- Operating expenses increase in 2021 in proportion to sales revenue.
- Operating assets and liabilities increase based on their 2020 relation to sales revenue. Classify "deferred and accrued taxes," "Other assets," and "Other liabilities" as operating.
- Nonoperating revenues, expenses, assets (including investments and intangible assets), and liabilities do not change from 2020 to 2021. Assume no change for equity income or equity method investments.
- Dividend payout is 60% of net income.
- Income tax rate is 25%.

Prepare a forecast income statement and balance sheet for 2021.

Solution on p. 5-51.

SUMMARY

Prepare and analyze common-size financial statements. (p. 5-4) **LO5-1**

- Vertical analysis restates items in the income statement as a percentage of sales revenue and items in the balance sheet as a percentage of total assets.
- Horizontal analysis examines the percentage change from one year to the next for specific items in the income statement and balance sheet.

Compute and interpret measures of return on investment, including return on equity (ROE), return on assets (ROA), and return on financial leverage (ROFL). (p. 5-8) **LO5-2**

- ROE is the primary measure of company performance. It captures the return earned by shareholder investment in the firm.
- ROA measures the return earned on the firm's investment in assets. It is not affected by the way those assets are financed.
- ROFL is the difference between ROE and ROA and measures the effect that financial leverage has on ROE.

Disaggregate ROA into profitability (profit margin) and efficiency (asset turnover) components. (p. 5-11) **LO5-3**

- ROA can be disaggregated as the product of profit margin (PM) and asset turnover (AT).
- PM can be analyzed further by examining the gross profit margin and expense-to-sales ratios.
- AT can be analyzed further by examining accounts receivable turnover (ART), inventory turnover (INVT), and property, plant, and equipment turnover (PPET).
- The trade-off between PM and AT is determined by the company's strategy and its competitive environment.

Compute and interpret measures of liquidity and solvency. (p. 5-15) **LO5-4**

- The current ratio (CR) and quick ratio (QR) measure short-term liquidity by comparing liquid assets to short-term obligations. The operating cash flow to current assets ratio (OCFCL) and the cash burn rate (CBR) relate a company's cash flows to its existing obligations and liquid resources.
- The debt-to-equity ratio (D/E) and times interest earned ratio (TIE) measure long-term solvency by comparing sources of financing and the level of earnings to the cost of debt (interest).

Appendix 5A: Measure and analyze the effect of operating activities on ROE. (p. 5-23) **LO5-5**

- Net operating profit after taxes (NOPAT) measures the portion of income that results from a business' core operating activities.
- Return on net operating assets (RNOA), defined as NOPAT/average net operating assets, measures the return on a company's net investment in operating assets.

Appendix 5B: Prepare financial statement forecasts. (p. 5-25) **LO5-6**

- Financial statement forecasts are prepared for future periods based on assumptions about the future activities of the business.
- Financial statement forecasts can be used to evaluate the effects of alternative actions or assumptions on the financial statements.

KEY RATIOS

RETURN MEASURES

$$\text{Return on equity (ROE)} = \frac{\text{Net income}}{\text{Average stockholders' equity}}$$

$$\text{Earnings without interest expense (EWI)} = \text{Net income} + [\text{Interest expense} \times (1 - \text{Statutory tax rate})]$$

$$\text{Return on assets (ROA)} = \frac{\text{Earnings without interest expense (EWI)}}{\text{Average total assets}}$$

$$\text{Return on financial leverage (ROFL)} = \text{ROE} - \text{ROA}$$

PROFITABILITY RATIOS

$$\text{Profit margin (PM)} = \frac{\text{Earnings without interest expense (EWI)}}{\text{Sales revenue}}$$

$$\text{Gross profit margin (GPM)} = \frac{\text{Sales revenue} - \text{Cost of goods sold}}{\text{Sales revenue}}$$

$$\text{Expense-to-sales (ETS)} = \frac{\text{Individual expense items}}{\text{Sales revenue}}$$

TURNOVER RATIOS

$$\text{Asset turnover (AT)} = \frac{\text{Sales revenue}}{\text{Average total assets}}$$

$$\text{Accounts receivable turnover (ART)} = \frac{\text{Sales revenue}}{\text{Average accounts receivable}}$$

$$\text{Inventory turnover (INVT)} = \frac{\text{Cost of goods sold}}{\text{Average inventory}}$$

$$\text{Property, plant, and equipment turnover (PPET)} = \frac{\text{Sales revenue}}{\text{Average PP\&E}}$$

LIQUIDITY RATIOS

$$\text{Current ratio (CR)} = \frac{\text{Current assets}}{\text{Current liabilities}}$$

$$\text{Quick ratio (QR)} = \frac{\text{Cash} + \text{Short-term securities} + \text{Accounts receivable}}{\text{Current liabilities}}$$

$$\text{Operating cash flow to current liabilities (OCFCL)} = \frac{\text{Operating cash flow}}{\text{Average current liabilities}}$$

$$\text{Cash burn rate} = \frac{\text{Free cash flow in the period}}{\text{Number of days in the period}}$$

SOLVENCY RATIOS

$$\text{Times interest earned (TIE)} = \frac{\text{Earnings before interest expense and taxes (EBIT)}}{\text{Interest expense}}$$

$$\text{Debt-to-equity (D/E)} = \frac{\text{Total liabilities}}{\text{Total stockholders' equity}}$$

Assignments with the MBC logo in the margin are available in *myBusinessCourse*.
See the Preface of the book for details.

MULTIPLE CHOICE

1. Which of the following ratios would not be affected by an increase in cost of goods sold?
   - a. ROA
   - b. INVT
   - c. QR
   - d. PM

2. A company has the following values: PM = 0.07; EWI = $3,770; Average total assets = $74,800. AT equals
   - a. 0.05
   - b. 0.72
   - c. 0.36
   - d. AT is not determinable because its sales are not reported.

3. A company's current ratio is 2 and its quick ratio is 1. What can be said about the sum of the company's cash + short-term securities + accounts receivable?
   a. The sum exceeds the current liabilities.
   b. The sum is equal to the sum of the current liabilities.
   c. The sum is equal to 1/2 of the total current liabilities.
   d. None of the above is correct.

4. A company's interest expense is $250,000 and its net income is $7 million. If the company's effective tax rate is 30%, what is the company's times interest earned (TIE) ratio?
   a. 90
   b. 41
   c. 32
   d. 16

5. If a company's ROFL is negative, which of the following is *not* true?
   a. ROA > ROE
   b. The D/E ratio is negative.
   c. ROA < net interest rate
   d. The company likely has a low TIE ratio.

Multiple Choice Answers
1. c 2. b 3. b 4. b 5. b

GUIDANCE ANSWERS... YOU MAKE THE CALL

You are the Entrepreneur Your company is performing substantially better than its competitors. Namely, your ROA of 16% is markedly superior to competitors' ROA of 10%. However, ROA disaggregation shows that this is mainly attributed to your AT of 0.89 versus competitors' AT of 0.59. Your PM of 18% is essentially identical to competitors' PM of 17%. Accordingly, you will want to maintain your AT because further improvements are probably difficult to achieve. Importantly, you are likely to achieve the greatest benefit with efforts at improving your PM of 18%, which is only marginally better than the industry norm of 17%.

Superscript A(B) denotes assignments based on Appendix 5A (5B).

QUESTIONS

Q5-1. Explain in general terms the concept of return on investment. Why is this concept important in the analysis of financial performance?

Q5-2. (a) Explain how an increase in financial leverage can increase a company's ROE. (b) Given the potentially positive relation between financial leverage and ROE, why don't we see companies with 100% financial leverage (entirely nonowner financed)?

Q5-3. Gross profit margin [(Sales revenue − Cost of goods sold)/Sales revenue] is an important determinant of profit margin. Identify two factors that can cause gross profit margin to decline. Is a reduction in the gross profit margin always bad news? Explain.

Q5-4. Explain how a reduction in operating expenses as a percentage of sales can produce a short-term gain at the cost of long-term performance.

Q5-5. Describe the concept of asset turnover. What does the concept mean, and why is it so important to understanding and interpreting financial performance?

Q5-6. Explain what it means when a company's ROE exceeds its ROA.

Q5-7. What are common-size financial statements? What role do they play in financial statement analysis?

Q5-8. How does a firm go about increasing its AT ratio? What strategies are likely to be most effective?

Q5-9.[A] What is meant by the term "net" in net operating assets (NOA)?

Q5-10. Why is it important to disaggregate ROA into profit margin (PM) and asset turnover (AT)?

Q5-11. What insights do we gain from the graphical relation between profit margin and asset turnover?

Q5-12. Explain the concept of liquidity and why it is crucial to company survival.

Q5-13. Identify at least two factors that limit the usefulness of ratio analysis.

DATA ANALYTICS

LO5-2 **DA5-1. Critically Analyzing a Visualization in Excel**

The financial information in the Excel file associated with this exercise was obtained from 10-K reports for Costco Wholesale Corporation. In this exercise, we examine how changing the starting point (baseline) of the y-axis from 0.0 impacts the chart that is created. The chart that is created for Costco examines return on equity over a five-year period. The return on equity ratio measures the return of the stockholders' investment in the company. An increase in the ratio generally means that the company is more efficiently using its equity to generate profits.

Return on equity
$$\frac{\text{Net income}}{\text{Average stockholders' equity}}$$

REQUIRED

1. Download Excel file DA5-1 found in myBusinessCourse.
2. Calculate the return on equity for Costco for Year 2 through Year 6 in Excel. Carry your answers to three decimal places.
3. Create a line chart showing the return on equity for Year 2 through Year 6. Note that when you use the default setting, the y-axis starts at point 0.0. *Hint:* Highlight data; click Insert, Line. You may need to edit the data selections. Right-click inside the chart, Select Data. The Series (y-axis) should be the ROE; the Category (x-axis) should be Years 2–6.
4. Create a second line chart showing the return on equity for Year 2 through Year 6. For this second chart, change the scale of the y-axis to start at 0.17 and to end at 0.27. *Hint:* Right-click inside the y-axis scale and select Format Axis. Set Minimum bound as 0.17 and Maximum bound as 0.27 on the column chart icon tab.
5. Indicate which of the following descriptions best depicts the trends in Chart 1 and the description that best depicts the trends in Chart 2:
   a. Return on equity increased sharply from Year 2 to Year 4, stabilized for a year and dropped more rapidly in Year 5.
   b. Return on equity gradually increased from Year 2 to Year 4, and remained fairly stable through Year 6.
6. Compute the percentage change in ROE from Year 2 to Year 3, Year 3 to Year 4, Year 4 to Year 5, and Year 5 to Year 6 in Excel.
7. Compare Chart 1 to Chart 2.

LO5-4 **DA5-2. Analyzing the Liquidity of Companies by Industry Segments in Excel**

The Excel file associated with this exercise includes Compustat data for S&P 500 companies for five years. In this exercise, we will prepare the data in the Excel file and convert the information in the data file to a PivotTable. Lastly, we will prepare a PivotChart to discern data trends in liquidity by industry segment, measured through the current ratio.

Current Ratio
$$\frac{\text{Current assets}}{\text{Current liabilities}}$$

REQUIRED

PART 1 PREPARING DATA; CREATING A PIVOTTABLE; MINING DATA

1. Download Excel file DA5-2 found in myBusinessCourse.
2. Add a column to the worksheet in the Excel file that computes the current ratio per each row of data.
3. Sort data in the current ratio column in ascending order to group together rows where errors appear. *Hint:* Use the filter button in the column heading field to sort the data.
4. Identify the industry that had the most instances in which current assets and current liabilities were not provided which resulted in errors in the current ratio column. *Hint:* Use the filter button in the current ratio column heading field and select only those rows with errors (#DIV/0 rows). Then use the filter button in the column heading of the Segment field to sort the column in alphabetical order.
5. Delete all rows in the worksheet where errors appeared in the current ratio calculated cell. *Hint:* Start by clearing the filter in the Current Ratio column. If necessary, re-sort Current Ratio column in ascending order.
6. Create a PivotTable displaying the average current ratio for years 1 through 5 by industry segment. *Hint:* To create a PivotTable, click anywhere inside the table. Open Insert tab and select PivotTable in the Tables group. Add the PivotTable to a new worksheet. Drag Segment to Columns, drag Year to Rows, and drag Current ratio to Values. Select Value Field Settings in the dropdown menu next to Current Ratio in the Values box. Select Average in the Summarize Value Field box.
7. List for each year the industry that has the highest and lowest current ratio.

8. List the company with the highest and lowest current ratio for the Health Care segment in Year 4. *Hint:* Double-click on the average current ratio for Health Care in Year 4 to automatically open up a new sheet that holds the supporting details.

PART 2 CREATING A PIVOTCHART AND ANALYZING TRENDS

1. Create a visualization through a PivotChart in the form of a line chart of the current ratio by industry segment over the five-year period. *Hint:* Click anywhere inside the PivotTable created in Part 1. Open the PivotTable Analyze tab and click PivotChart in the Tools group. Click Line.
2. Based only on the visualization, answer the following questions.
   a. What two industries appear to have had the least fluctuation from year to year?
   b. What three industries appear to have had the most fluctuation from year to year?
3. Describe the trend in liquidity from Year 1 to Year 5 for the Consumer Staples segment.

DA5-3. Forecasting Sales Using Excel   LO5-6

The Excel file associated with this exercise includes weekly data for Clack Inc. including cash sales, number of ad impressions, and number of ad clicks. Ad impressions are the number of times that a digital advertisement is displayed on a person's screen. Ad clicks are the number of times that a user clicks on a digital advertisement. In this exercise, we examine the relation between the number of ad impressions and cash sales and the relation between the number of ad clicks and cash sales. Understanding the relations of ad impressions and ad clicks to cash sales can help us determine if future cash sales can be predicted given future estimates of ad impressions or ad clicks.

REQUIRED

1. Download Excel file DA5-3 found in myBusinessCourse.
2. Create a scatter chart in Excel using the 106 weeks of actual data to determine whether there is a relation between the number of ad impressions and cash sales. *Hint:* Highlight the data to be included in the chart. Use Ctrl to select data in non-contiguous cells. Open the Insert tab and click the Scatter chart in the Charts group.
3. List the category of the x-value and the category of the y-value.
4. Add a trendline to the chart and display the regression equation and R-squared value. *Hint:* Right-click inside the data points on your chart, select Add trendline, check the Display equation on chart, check Display R-squared value on chart.
5. List the R-squared and the equation. *Hint:* The R-squared (a number from 0 to 1) reveals how close the estimated values that make up the trendline correspond to the actual data (portrayed in the scatter plot). The closer the R-squared is to 1, the better the fit of the actual data to the trendline.
6. Create a second scatter chart in Excel using the 106 weeks of actual data to determine whether there is a relation between the number of ad clicks and cash sales.
7. List the category of the x-value and the category of the y-value.
8. Add a trendline to the chart and display the regression equation and R-squared value.
9. List the R-squared and the equation.
10. Determine whether ad impressions or ad clicks are a better indicator of cash sales.
11. Determine the average click-through rate, rounded to four decimal places. *Hint:* The average click-through rate is the ratio of ad clicks to impressions determined from the 106 weeks of actual data provided
12. Estimate ad clicks for Weeks 3 through 14 of Year 3. *Hint:* Use the average click-through rate to estimate ad clicks for the estimated periods.
13. Use the equation with the best fit to the trendline to estimate cash sales for Weeks 3 through 14 of Year 3. List the estimated sales amounts. *Hint:* Estimated cash sales = $x multiplied by predictor (either ad impressions or ad clicks) + fixed cost.

DA5-4. Preparing Tableau Visualizations to Analyze the Use of Assets Through Asset Turnover   LO5-3

Available in myBusinessCourse, this problem uses Tableau to analyze asset utilization of S&P 500 companies in certain segments through the asset turnover ratio.

DA5-5. Preparing Tableau Visualizations to Decompose Return on Equity Using the Dupont Method: Part I, Part II, Part III   LO5-2

Available in myBusinessCourse, this three-part problem uses Tableau to decompose the return on equity ratio of S&P 500 companies using the DuPont method. The final part of the problem includes the creation of an interactive dashboard.

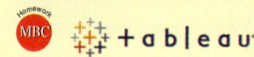

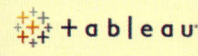

DATA VISUALIZATION

LO5-4 DA5-6. Preparing Tableau Visualizations to Analyze Liquidity Through the Current Ratio
Available in myBusinessCourse, this problem uses Tableau to analyze liquidity of S&P 500 companies through the current ratio. The visualization is exported to PowerPoint for communication purposes.

Data Visualization Activities are available in myBusinessCourse. These assignments use Tableau Dashboards to expose students to visual depictions of data and introduce students to data analytics through data visualizations. These exercises are easily assignable and auto graded by MBC.

MINI EXERCISES

LO5-2, 3   M5-14. Return on Investment, DuPont Analysis, and Financial Leverage

The following table presents selected annual financial information for Sunder Company.

SUNDER COMPANY Selected Annual Financial Data	
Balance Sheet:	
Average total assets	$1,500,000
Average total liabilities	750,000
Average stockholders' equity	750,000
Income statement:	
Sales revenue	$1,500,000
Earnings before interest (net of tax)	30,000
Interest expense (net of tax)	22,500
Net income	7,500

a. Compute Sunder's ROE, ROA, and ROFL for the year.
b. Use the DuPont analysis described in the Business Insight on page 5-13 to disaggregate ROE.
c. How did the use of financial leverage affect Sunder's ROE during the year? Explain.

LO5-1   M5-15. Common-Size Balance Sheets

Following is the balance sheet for **Target Corporation**. Prepare Target's common-size balance sheets as of February 1, 2020, and February 2, 2019.

Target Corporation
NYSE :: TGT

($ millions)	February 1, 2020	February 2, 2019
Assets		
Cash and cash equivalents	$ 2,577	$ 1,556
Inventory	8,992	9,497
Other current assets	1,333	1,466
Total current assets	12,902	12,519
Property and equipment, net	26,283	25,533
Operating lease assets	2,236	1,965
Other noncurrent assets	1,358	1,273
Total assets	$42,779	$41,290
Liabilities and shareholders' investment		
Accounts payable	$ 9,920	$ 9,761
Accrued and other current liabilities	4,406	4,201
Current portion of long-term debt and other borrowings	161	1,052
Total current liabilities	14,487	15,014
Long-term debt and other borrowings	11,338	10,223
Noncurrent operating lease liabilities	2,275	2,004
Deferred income taxes	1,122	972
Other noncurrent liabilities	1,724	1,780
Total noncurrent liabilities	16,459	14,979
Total shareholders' investment	11,833	11,297
Total liabilities and shareholders' investment	$42,779	$41,290

M5-16. Common-Size Income Statements

Following is the income statement for **Target Corporation**. Prepare Target's common-size income statement for the fiscal year ended February 1, 2020.

($ millions)	Fiscal Year Ended February 1, 2020
Sales	$78,112
Cost of sales	54,864
Selling, general, and administrative expenses	16,233
Depreciation and amortization (exclusive of depreciation included in cost of sales)	2,357
Operating income	4,658
Net interest expense	477
Net other (income)/expense	(9)
Earnings from continuing operations before income taxes	4,190
Provision for income taxes	921
Net earnings from continuing operations	3,269
Discontinued operations, net of tax	12
Net earnings	$ 3,281

Target Corporation
NYSE :: TGT

M5-17. Compute ROA, Profit Margin, and Asset Turnover

Refer to the financial information for **Target Corporation**, presented in M5-15 and M5-16.

a. Compute its return on assets (ROA) for the fiscal year ending February 1, 2020. Compute two ROA measures: one using net earnings from continuing operations and one using net earnings. Assume a statutory tax rate of 25%.

b. Disaggregate ROA into profit margin (PM) and asset turnover (AT). Confirm that ROA = PM × AT.

Target Corporation
NYSE :: TGT

M5-18. Analysis and Interpretation of Liquidity and Solvency

Refer to the financial information of **Target Corporation** in M5-15 and M5-16 to answer the following.

a. Compute Target's current ratio and quick ratio on February 1, 2020, and February 2, 2019. Comment on any observed trends.

b. Compute Target's times interest earned for the year ended February 1, 2020, and its debt-to-equity ratios on February 1, 2020, and February 2, 2019. Comment on any trends observed.

c. Summarize your findings in a conclusion about the company's liquidity and solvency. Do you have any concerns about Target's ability to meet its debt obligations?

Target Corporation
NYSE :: TGT

M5-19. Common-Size Balance Sheets

Following is the balance sheet for **3M Company**. Prepare common-size balance sheets for 2020 and 2019.

3M Company
NYSE :: MMM

3M COMPANY AND SUBSIDIARIES

December 31 ($ millions)	2020	2019
Assets		
Current assets		
Cash and cash equivalents	$ 4,634	$ 2,353
Marketable securities—current	404	98
Accounts receivable—net of allowances of $233 and $161	4,705	4,791
Total inventories	4,239	4,134
Prepaids	675	704
Other current assets	325	891
Total current assets	14,982	12,971
Property, plant, and equipment—net	9,421	9,333
Operating lease right of use assets	864	858
Goodwill	13,802	13,444
Intangible assets—net	5,835	6,379
Other assets	2,440	1,674
Total assets	$47,344	$44,659

continued

continued from previous page

3M COMPANY AND SUBSIDIARIES

December 31 ($ millions)	2020	2019
Liabilities and shareholders' equity		
Current liabilities		
Short-term borrowings and current portion of long-term debt	$ 806	$ 2,795
Accounts payable	2,561	2,228
Accrued payroll	747	702
Accrued income taxes	300	194
Operating lease liabilities—current	256	247
Other current liabilities	3,278	3,056
Total current liabilities	7,948	9,222
Long-term debt	17,989	17,518
Pension and postretirement benefits	4,405	3,911
Operating lease liabilities	609	607
Other liabilities	3,462	3,275
Total liabilities	$34,413	$34,533
Total equity	12,931	10,126
Total liabilities and equity	$47,344	$44,659

LO5-1 **M5-20. Common-Size Income Statements**

Following is the income statement for **3M Company**. Prepare common-size income statements for 2020 and 2019.

3M Company
NYSE :: MMM

3M COMPANY AND SUBSIDIARIES

Year Ended December 31 ($ millions)	2020	2019
Net sales	$32,184	$32,136
Operating expenses		
Cost of sales	16,605	17,136
Selling, general, and administrative expenses	6,929	7,029
Research, development, and related expenses	1,878	1,911
Gain on sale of businesses	(389)	(114)
Total operating expenses	25,023	25,962
Operating income	7,161	6,174
Other expense (income), net	450	462
Income before income taxes	6,711	5,712
Provision for income taxes	1,318	1,130
Income of consolidated group	5,393	4,582
Income (loss) from unconsolidated subsidiaries, net of taxes	(5)	—
Net income including noncontrolling interest	$ 5,388	$ 4,582

LO5-2, 3 **M5-21. Compute ROA, Profit Margin, and Asset Turnover**

Refer to the balance sheet and income statement information for **3M Company**, presented in M5-19 and M5-20.

3M Company
NYSE :: MMM

a. Compute 3M's 2020 return on assets (ROA). Interest expense for 2020 (included in "Other expense (income), net") is reported as $529 million. Use 25% as the statutory tax rate.

b. Disaggregate ROA into profit margin (PM) and asset turnover (AT). Confirm that ROA = PM × AT.

LO5-2, 3 **M5-22. Compute ROA, Profit Margin, and Asset Turnover for Competitors**

Selected balance sheet and income statement information from **Urban Outfitters, Inc.**, and **TJX Companies**, clothing retailers in the high-end and value-priced segments, respectively, follows.

Urban Outfitters, Inc.
NASDAQ :: URBN
TJX Companies
NYSE :: TJX

Company ($ millions)	2019 Sales	2019 Earnings Without Interest Expense (EWI)	2019 Total Assets	2018 Total Assets
Urban Outfitters	$ 3,984	$ 169	$ 3,316	$ 2,161
TJX Companies	41,717	3,280	24,145	14,326

a. Compute the 2019 return on assets (ROA) for both companies.

b. Disaggregate ROA into profit margin (PM) and asset turnover (AT) for each company. Confirm that ROA = PM × AT.
c. Discuss differences observed with respect to PM and AT, and interpret these differences in light of each company's business model.

M5-23. Compute and Interpret Liquidity and Solvency Ratios **LO5-4**

Selected balance sheet and income statement information from **Verizon Communications, Inc.**, follows.

Verizon Communications, Inc.
NYSE :: VZ

($ millions)	2020	2019
Current assets	$ 54,594	$ 37,473
Current liabilities	39,660	44,868
Total liabilities	247,209	228,892
Equity	69,272	62,835
Earnings before interest and taxes	28,214	27,463
Interest expense	4,247	4,730
Net cash flow from operating activities	41,768	35,746

a. Compute the current ratio for each year and discuss any change in liquidity. How does Verizon's current ratio compare to the median for the telecommunications industry in **Exhibit 5.13**? What additional information about the numbers used to calculate this ratio might be useful in helping us assess liquidity? Explain.
b. Compute times interest earned, the debt-to-equity, and the operating cash flow to current liabilities ratios for each year and discuss any trends for each. (In 2018, current liabilities totaled $37,930 million.) Compare Verizon's ratios to those that are typical for its industry (refer to **Exhibit 5.13**). Do you have any concerns about the extent of Verizon's financial leverage and the company's ability to meet interest obligations? Explain.
c. Verizon's capital expenditures are expected to remain high as it seeks to respond to competitive pressures to upgrade the quality of its communication infrastructure. Assess Verizon's liquidity and solvency in light of this strategic direction.

M5-24. Computing Turnover Ratios for Companies in Different Industries **LO5-3**

Selected data from 2020 financial statements of **The Procter & Gamble Company**, **CVS Health Corporation**, and **Valero Energy Corporation** are presented below.

The Procter & Gamble Company
NYSE :: PG
CVS Health Corporation
NYSE :: CVS
Valero Energy Corporation
NYSE :: VLO

($ millions)	Procter & Gamble	CVS Health	Valero Energy
Sales	$70,950	$268,706	$64,912
Cost of sales	35,250	163,981	65,652
Average receivables	4,565	20,680	7,549
Average inventories	5,258	18,006	6,526
Average PP&E	20,982	12,325	29,827
Average total assets	117,898	226,582	52,819

a. Compute the asset turnover (AT) ratio for each company.
b. Compute the accounts receivable turnover (ART), inventory turnover (INVT), and PP&E turnover (PPET) for each company.
c. Discuss any differences across these three companies in the turnover ratios computed in a and b.

EXERCISES

E5-25. Compute and Interpret ROA, Profit Margin, and Asset Turnover of Competitors **LO5-2, 3**

Selected 2020 balance sheet and income statement information for **McDonald's Corporation** and **Yum! Brands, Inc.**, follows.

McDonald's Corporation
NYSE :: MCD
Yum! Brands, Inc.
NYSE :: YUM

($ millions)	Sales Revenue	Interest Expense	Net Income	Average Total Assets
McDonald's	$19,208	$1,218	$4,731	$50,069
Yum! Brands	5,652	543	904	5,542

a. Compute the return on assets (ROA) for each company. Use the 25% statutory tax rate.
b. Disaggregate ROA into profit margin (PM) and asset turnover (AT) for each company.
c. Discuss any differences in these ratios for each company. Your interpretation should reflect the distinct business strategies of each company.

LO5-2 E5-26. Compute ROA, ROE, and ROFL and Interpret the Effects of Leverage

Basic income statement and balance sheet information is given below for six different cases. For each case, the assets are financed with a mix of non-interest-bearing liabilities, 10% interest-bearing liability, and stockholders' equity. In all cases, assume the statutory tax rate is 40%.

Case	A	B	C	D	E	F
Average assets............................	$1,500	$1,500	$1,500	$1,500	$1,500	$1,500
Non-interest-bearing liabilities	0	0	0	0	300	300
Interest-bearing liabilities	0	375	750	750	0	450
Average shareholders' equity	1,500	1,125	750	750	1,200	750
Earnings before interest and taxes (EBIT)	180	180	180	120	150	120

a. For each case, calculate the return on equity (ROE), return on assets (ROA), and return on financial leverage (ROFL).
b. Consider cases A, B, and C. How does increasing leverage affect the three ratios? Why does the ROE grow from case A to case C?
c. Consider cases C and D. When does leverage work in favor of shareholders? Does that hold for case E?
d. Case F has two types of liabilities. How does ROA compare to the rate on interest-bearing liabilities? Does leverage work in favor of the shareholders? Why?

LO5-2, 3 E5-27. Compute, Disaggregate, and Interpret Competitors' Rates of Return

Selected balance sheet and income statement information for the drug retailers **CVS Health Corporation** and **Walgreens Boots Alliance** follows. Assume a statutory tax rate of 25%.

CVS Health Corporation
NYSE :: CVS
Walgreens Boots Alliance, Inc.
NASDAQ :: WBA

($ millions)	CVS Health	Walgreens Boots
Sales revenue—2020.....................................	$268,706	$139,537
Interest expense—2020	2,907	639
Net income—2020	7,192	424
Total assets—2020.......................................	230,715	87,174
Total assets—2019.......................................	222,449	67,598
Stockholders' equity—2020	69,701	21,136
Stockholders' equity—2019	64,170	24,152

a. Compute the 2020 return on assets (ROA) for each company.
b. Disaggregate ROA into profit margin (PM) and asset turnover (AT) for each company.
c. Compute the 2020 return on equity (ROE) and return on financial leverage (ROFL) for each company.
d. Discuss any differences in these ratios for each company. Identify the factor(s) that drives the differences in ROA observed from your analyses in parts a through c.

LO5-2, 3 E5-28. Compute, Disaggregate, and Interpret ROE

Selected fiscal year balance sheet and income statement information for the computer chip maker, **Intel Corporation**, follows ($ millions).

Intel Corporation
NASDAQ :: INTC

Balance Sheet Information ($ millions)	2020	2019	2018
Total assets.....................................	$153,091	$136,524	$127,963
Total shareholders' equity.....................	81,038	77,659	74,982

Income Statement Information ($ millions)	2020	2019	2018
Sales revenue...................................	$ 77,867	$ 71,965	$ 70,848
Interest expense................................	629	489	468
Net income.....................................	20,899	21,048	21,053

a. Calculate Intel's return on equity (ROE) for fiscal years 2020 and 2019.
b. Calculate Intel's return on assets (ROA) and return on financial leverage (ROFL) for each year. Is financial leverage working to the advantage of Intel's shareholders? Use a statutory tax rate of 25%.
c. Use the DuPont formulation in the Business Insight on page 5-13 to analyze the variations in Intel's ROE over this period. How does this analysis differ from your answers to a and b above?

LO5-2, 3 E5-29. Return on Investment, Financial Leverage, and DuPont Analysis

The following tables provide information from the recent annual reports of HD Rinker, AG.

Balance Sheets (€ millions)	2022	2021	2020	2019
Total assets	€4,886	€5,161	€5,738	€5,578
Total liabilities	4,776	3,979	3,991	4,078
Total shareholders' equity	110	1,182	1,747	1,500

Income Statements (€ millions) 52 Weeks Ended	2022	2021	2020
Sales revenue	€8,291	€7,690	€6,906
Earnings before interest and income taxes	1,178	1,167	710
Interest expense	197	166	190
Earnings before income taxes	981	1,001	520
Income tax expense	302	357	162
Net earnings	€ 679	€ 644	€ 358

a. Calculate HD Rinker's return on equity (ROE) for fiscal years 2022, 2021, and 2020.
b. Calculate HD Rinker's return on assets (ROA) and return on financial leverage (ROFL) for each year. Is financial leverage working to the advantage of HD Rinker's shareholders? Use a statutory tax rate of 25%.
c. Use the DuPont formulation in the Business Insight on page 5-13 to analyze the variations in HD Rinker's ROE over this period. How does this analysis differ from your answers to *a* and *b* above?

E5-30. **Compute, Disaggregate, and Interpret ROE and ROA** LO5-2, 3
Selected balance sheet and income statement information from **The ODP Corporation** follows ($ millions).

ODP Corp.
NASDAQ :: ODP

Sales 2020	Interest Expense 2020	Net Loss 2020	Total Assets 2020	Total Assets 2019	Stockholders' Equity 2020	Stockholders' Equity 2019
$9,710	$42	$(319)	$5,558	$7,311	$1,880	$2,173

a. Compute the 2020 return on equity (ROE), return on assets (ROA), and return on financial leverage (ROFL). Use 25% as the statutory tax rate.
b. Disaggregate ROA into profit margin (PM) and asset turnover (AT).
c. What inferences do we draw from PM compared to AT? How do these ratios compare to industry medians?

E5-31. **Compute, Disaggregate, and Interpret ROE and ROA** LO5-2, 3
Selected balance sheet and income statement information from the software company, **Intuit Inc.**, follows ($ millions).

Intuit Inc.
NASDAQ :: INTU

Sales 2020	Interest Expense 2020	Net Income 2020	Total Assets 2020	Total Assets 2019	Stockholders' Equity 2020	Stockholders' Equity 2019
$7,679	$14	$1,826	$10,931	$6,283	$5,106	$3,749

a. Compute the 2020 return on equity (ROE), return on assets (ROA), and return on financial leverage (ROFL). Use 25% as the statutory tax rate.
b. Disaggregate the ROA from part *a* into profit margin (PM) and asset turnover (AT).
c. What can we learn by comparing PM to AT? What explanation can we offer for the relation between ROE and ROA observed and for Intuit's use of financial leverage?

E5-32. **Compute and Interpret Liquidity and Solvency Ratios** LO5-4
Selected balance sheet, income statement, and the statement of cash flows information from **Tesla, Inc.**, for 2020 and 2019 follows ($ millions).

Tesla, Inc.
NASDAQ :: TSLA

December 31	2020	2019
Cash and cash equivalents	$19,384	$ 6,268
Net receivables	1,886	1,324
Inventory	4,101	3,552
Other current assets	1,346	959
Current assets	26,717	12,103
Current liabilities	14,248	10,667
Total liabilities	28,418	26,199
Stockholders' equity	23,730	8,110

continued

continued from previous page

Year Ended December 31	2020
Income before income taxes	$1,154
Interest expense	748
Cash flows from operating activities	5,943
Capital expenditures	3,157

a. Compute the current ratio and quick ratio for each year and discuss any trend in liquidity. Do you believe the company is sufficiently liquid? How should the balance in restricted cash affect your analysis?
b. Compute the debt-to-equity ratio for 2020 and 2019 and the times-interest-earned ratio for 2020. Discuss the trend in the debt-to-equity ratio.
c. In 2018, Tesla had a cash burn rate of approximately $8,000 per day. Compute the cash burn rate for 2020. Analyze your results.

LO5-4 E5-33. Compute and Interpret Liquidity and Solvency Ratios

Selected balance sheet and income statement information from **Siemens, AG**, for 2018 through 2020 follows (€ millions).

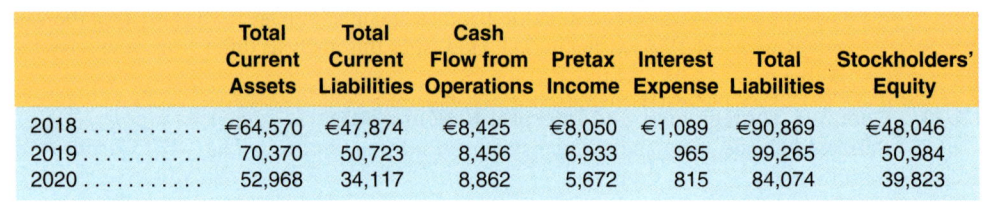

Siemens AG
OTCMKTS :: SIEGY

	Total Current Assets	Total Current Liabilities	Cash Flow from Operations	Pretax Income	Interest Expense	Total Liabilities	Stockholders' Equity
2018	€64,570	€47,874	€8,425	€8,050	€1,089	€90,869	€48,046
2019	70,370	50,723	8,456	6,933	965	99,265	50,984
2020	52,968	34,117	8,862	5,672	815	84,074	39,823

a. Compute the current ratio for each year and discuss any trend in liquidity. Also compute the operating cash flow to current liabilities (OCFCL) ratio for each year. (In 2017, current liabilities totaled €46,077 million.) Do you believe the company is sufficiently liquid? Explain. What additional information about the accounting numbers comprising this ratio might be useful in helping you assess liquidity? Explain.
b. Compute times interest earned and the debt-to-equity ratio for each year and discuss any trends for each.
c. What is your overall assessment of the company's liquidity and solvency from the analyses in a and b? Explain.

LO5-2, 3 E5-34. Compute, Disaggregate, and Interpret ROE and ROA

Income statements for **The Gap, Inc.**, follow, along with selected balance sheet information ($ millions).

The Gap, Inc.
NYSE :: GPS

THE GAP, INC.
Consolidated Statement of Earnings

Fiscal Year Ended	Feb. 1, 2020	Feb. 2, 2019
Net sales	$16,383	$16,580
Cost of goods sold and occupancy expenses	10,250	10,258
Gross profit	6,133	6,322
Operating expenses	5,559	4,960
Operating income	574	1,362
Interest expense	76	73
Interest income	(30)	(33)
Income before income taxes	528	1,322
Income taxes	177	319
Net income	$ 351	$ 1,003

THE GAP, INC.
Selected Balance Sheet Data

	Feb. 1, 2020	Feb. 2, 2019
Merchandise inventories	$ 2,156	$2,131
Total assets	13,679	8,049
Total stockholders' equity	3,316	3,553

a. Compute the return on equity (ROE), return on assets (ROA), and return on financial leverage (ROFL) for the fiscal year ended February 1, 2020. Assume a statutory tax rate of 25%.
b. Disaggregate ROA into profit margin (PM) and asset turnover (AT).
c. Compute the gross profit margin (GPM) and inventory turnover (INVT) ratios for the fiscal year ended February 1, 2020.
d. Assess the Gap's performance. What are the most important drivers of the Gap's success?

E5-35.[B] **Common-Size and Forecast Income Statements**
Refer to the income statements for **The Gap, Inc.**, presented in E5-34.

a. Prepare common-size income statements for fiscal years 2019 (ending February 1, 2020) and 2018 (ending February 2, 2019).
b. Prepare an income statement forecast for the fiscal year 2020 (ending January 30, 2021), based on the following assumptions:
   - Net sales total $14,000 million.
   - Cost of goods sold and occupancy expenses are 62% of sales.
   - Operating expenses total 35% of sales.
   - Interest income and interest expense are unchanged from the 2019 amounts.
   - The Gap's effective tax rate on income before taxes is 25% in 2020.
c. Given the Gap's business strategy, what are the factors that ultimately determine the accuracy of the income statement forecast prepared in b?

PROBLEMS

P5-36. Analysis and Interpretation of Return on Investment for Competitors
Balance sheets and income statements for **Nike, Inc.**, and **Adidas Group** follow. Refer to these financial statements to answer the requirements.

	NIKE, INC. Balance Sheets ($ millions) May 31		ADIDAS GROUP, AG Balance Sheets (€ millions) December 31	
	2020	**2019**	**2019**	**2018**
Assets				
Current assets:				
Cash and cash equivalents	$ 8,348	$ 4,466	€ 2,220	€ 2,629
Short-term investments	439	197	836	548
Accounts receivable, net	2,749	4,272	2,625	2,418
Inventories	7,367	5,622	4,085	3,445
Prepaid expenses and other current assets	1,653	1,968	1,170	773
Total current assets	20,556	16,525	10,934	9,813
Property, plant, and equipment, net	4,866	4,744	2,380	2,237
Operating lease right-of-use assets, net	3,097	—	2,931	—
Goodwill and identifiable intangible assets, net	497	437	2,421	2,285
Deferred income taxes and other assets	2,326	2,011	2,013	1,277
Total assets	$31,342	$23,717	€20,680	€15,612
Liabilities and shareholders' equity				
Current liabilities:				
Short-term debt	$ 251	$ 15	€ 43	€ 66
Accounts payable	2,248	2,612	2,703	2,300
Current portion of operating lease liabilities	445	—	733	—
Accrued liabilities	5,184	5,010	2,437	2,305
Income taxes payable	156	229	618	268
Other current liabilities	—	—	2,219	1,895
Total current liabilities	8,284	7,866	8,754	6,834
Long-term debt	9,406	3,464	1,595	1,609
Operating lease liabilities	2,913	—	2,399	—
Other noncurrent liabilities	2,684	3,347	874	805
Total shareholders' equity	8,055	9,040	7,058	6,364
Total liabilities and shareholders' equity	$31,342	$23,717	€20,680	€15,612

Note: Amounts in the Adidas reports are rounded amounts, and thus, they may not exactly sum to totals and subtotals.

	NIKE, INC. Income Sheets ($ millions) Year Ended May 31		ADIDAS GROUP, AG Income Sheets (€ millions) Year Ended Dec. 31	
	2020	2019	2019	2018
Revenues	$37,403	$39,117	€23,640	€21,915
Cost of sales	21,162	21,643	11,347	10,552
Gross profit	16,241	17,474	12,293	11,363
Total selling and administrative expense	13,126	12,702	9,633	8,995
Operating profit	3,115	4,772	2,660	2,368
Interest expense (income), net	89	49	166	47
Other expense (income), net	139	(78)	(64)	(57)
Income before income taxes	2,887	4,801	2,558	2,378
Income tax expense	348	772	640	669
Net income from continuing operations	2,539	4,029	1,918	1,709
Gain (loss) from discontinued operations, net of tax	—	—	59	(5)
Net income	$ 2,539	$ 4,029	€ 1,977	€ 1,704

REQUIRED

a. Compute return on equity (ROE), return on assets (ROA), and return on financial leverage (ROFL) for Nike and Adidas in the most recent year. The corporate tax rate in Germany, where Adidas is headquartered, is about 30%. Assume a statutory tax rate of 25% for Nike.

b. Disaggregate the ROA's computed into profit margin (PM) and asset turnover (AT) components. Which of these factors drives ROA for each company?

c. Compute the gross profit margin (GPM) and operating expense-to-sales ratios for each company. How do these companies' profitability measures compare?

d. Compute the accounts receivable turnover (ART), inventory turnover (INVT), and property, plant, and equipment turnover (PPET) for each company. How do these companies' turnover measures compare?

e. Nike's fiscal year ends on May 31, 2020, while Adidas' fiscal year ends on December 31, 2019 (a difference of five months). How does this difference affect your analysis of ROE and ROA for these two companies?

f. Nike's financial statements are prepared in accordance with U.S. GAAP, while Adidas, a German company, follows IFRS rules. How does this difference in financial reporting standards affect your comparison of these companies' financial statements?

LO5-4 P5-37. Analysis and Interpretation of Liquidity and Solvency for Competitors

Refer to the financial statements of **Nike** and **Adidas** presented in P5-36.

REQUIRED

a. Compute each company's current ratio and quick ratio for each year. Comment on any changes that you observe.

b. Compute each company's times interest earned ratio and debt-to-equity ratio for each year. Comment on any observed changes.

c. Compare these two companies on the basis of liquidity and solvency. Do you have any concerns about either company's ability to meet its debt obligations?

LO5-2, 3 P5-38. Analysis and Interpretation of Return on Investment for Competitors

Balance sheets and income statements for **The Home Depot, Inc.**, and **Lowe's Companies, Inc.**, follow. Refer to these financial statements to answer the requirements.

($ millions)	HOME DEPOT, INC. Balance Sheets 2/2/20	2/3/19	LOWE'S COMPANIES Balance Sheets 1/31/20	2/1/19
Assets				
Current assets:				
Cash and cash equivalents	$ 2,133	$ 1,778	$ 716	$ 511
Short-term investments	—	—	160	218
Receivables, net	2,106	1,936	—	—
Merchandise inventories	14,531	13,925	13,179	12,561
Other current assets	1,040	890	1,263	938
Total current assets	19,810	18,529	15,318	14,228
Net property and equipment	22,770	22,375	18,669	18,432
Operating lease right-of-use assets	5,595	—	3,891	—
Goodwill	2,254	2,252	303	303
Long-term investments	—	—	372	256
Other assets	807	847	918	1,289
Total assets	$51,236	$44,003	$39,471	$34,508
Liabilities and shareholders' equity				
Current liabilities:				
Short-term debt and current maturities of long-term debt	$ 2,813	$ 1,339	$ 2,538	$ 1,832
Accounts payable	7,787	8,811	7,659	8,279
Accrued salaries and related expenses	1,494	1,506	684	662
Deferred revenue	2,116	1,782	1,219	1,299
Income taxes payable	55	11	—	—
Current operating lease liabilities	828	—	501	—
Other current liabilities	3,282	3,267	2,581	2,425
Total current liabilities	18,375	16,716	15,182	14,497
Long-term debt, excluding current maturities	28,670	26,807	16,768	14,391
Long-term operating lease liabilities	5,066	—	3,943	—
Deferred income taxes	706	491	—	—
Other long-term liabilities	1,535	1,867	1,606	1,976
Total liabilities	54,352	45,881	37,499	30,864
Total shareholders' equity	(3,116)	(1,878)	1,972	3,644
Total liabilities and shareholders' equity	$51,236	$44,003	$39,471	$34,508

($ millions)	HOME DEPOT, INC. Income Statements FY 2019	FY 2018	LOWE'S COMPANIES Income Statements FY 2019	FY 2018
Net sales	$110,225	$108,203	$72,148	$71,308
Cost of sales	72,653	71,043	49,205	48,401
Gross profit	37,572	37,160	22,943	22,908
Operating expenses:				
Selling, general, and administrative	19,740	19,513	15,367	17,413
Depreciation and amortization	1,989	1,870	1,262	1,477
Impairment loss	—	247	—	—
Operating income	15,843	15,530	6,314	4,018
Interest and other (income) expense:				
Interest and investment income	(73)	(77)	—	—
Interest expense	1,201	1,051	691	624
Earnings before provision for income taxes	14,715	14,556	5,623	3,394
Provision for income taxes	3,473	3,435	1,342	1,080
Net earnings	$ 11,242	$ 11,121	$ 4,281	$ 2,314

REQUIRED

a. Compute return on equity (ROE), return on assets (ROA), and return on financial leverage (ROFL) for each company in fiscal year 2019. Assume a statutory tax rate of 25% for these years.

b. Disaggregate the ROA's computed into profit margin (PM) and asset turnover (AT) components. Which of these factors drives ROA for each company?

c. Compute the gross profit margin (GPM) and operating expense-to-sales ratios for each company. How do these companies' profitability measures compare?
d. Compute the accounts receivable turnover (ART), inventory turnover (INVT), and property, plant, and equipment turnover (PPET) for each company. How do these companies' turnover measures compare?
e. Compare and evaluate these competitors' performance in 2019.

LO5-4 **P5-39. Analysis and Interpretation of Liquidity and Solvency for Competitors**
Refer to the financial statements of **Home Depot** and **Lowe's** presented in P5-38.

Home Depot, Inc.
NYSE :: HD
Lowe's Companies, Inc.
NYSE :: LOW

REQUIRED

a. Compute each company's current ratio and quick ratio for each year. Comment on any changes that you observe.
b. Compute each company's times interest earned ratio and debt-to-equity ratio for each year. Comment on any observed changes.
c. Compare these two companies on the basis of liquidity and solvency. Do you have any concerns about either company's ability to meet its debt obligations?

LO5-5 **P5-40.**[A] **Analysis of the Effect of Operations on ROE**
Refer to the financial statements of **Home Depot** and **Lowe's** presented in P5-38.

Home Depot, Inc.
NYSE :: HD
Lowe's Companies, Inc.
NYSE :: LOW

REQUIRED

a. Compute each company's net operating profit after taxes (NOPAT) for fiscal year 2019 and net operating assets (NOA) for fiscal year 2019 and 2018. Classify other assets and other liabilities (both current and noncurrent) as operating assets and liabilities in the balance sheet. Assume a 25% tax rate. *Hint:* The impairment loss is part of operations.
b. Compute each company's return on net operating assets (RNOA) for fiscal year 2019.
c. Compute the fiscal year 2019 net operating profit margin (NOPM) and net operating asset turnover (NOAT) for each company.
d. Compare operating returns for these two companies. How does RNOA compare to ROA? What insights are gained by focusing on operating returns?

LO5-2, 3 **P5-41. Analysis and Interpretation of Profitability**
Balance sheets and income statements for **United Parcel Service, Inc., (UPS)** follow. Refer to these financial statements to answer the following requirements.

United Parcel Service, Inc.
NYSE :: UPS

UNITED PARCEL SERVICE, INC.
Income Statement

Years Ended December 31 ($ millions)	2020	2019	2018
Revenue	$84,628	$74,094	$71,861
Operating expenses:			
Compensation and benefits	44,529	38,908	37,235
Repairs and maintenance	2,365	1,838	1,732
Depreciation and amortization	2,698	2,360	2,207
Purchased transportation	15,631	12,590	13,409
Fuel	2,582	3,289	3,427
Other occupancy	1,539	1,392	1,362
Other expenses	7,600	5,919	5,465
Total operating expenses	76,944	66,296	64,837
Operating profit	7,684	7,798	7,024
Other income and (expense):			
Investment income (expense) and other	(5,139)	(1,493)	(400)
Interest expense	(701)	(653)	(605)
Total other income and (expense)	(5,840)	(2,146)	(1,005)
Income before income taxes	1,844	5,652	6,019
Income tax expense	501	1,212	1,228
Net income	$ 1,343	$ 4,440	$ 4,791

UNITED PARCEL SERVICE, INC.
Balance Sheet

December 31 ($ millions)	2020	2019	2018
Assets			
Current assets:			
Cash and cash equivalents	$ 5,910	$ 5,238	$ 4,225
Marketable securities	406	503	810
Accounts receivable, net	10,750	9,552	8,958
Assets held for sale	1,197	—	—
Other current assets	1,953	1,810	2,217
Total current assets	20,216	17,103	16,210
Property, plant, and equipment, net	32,254	30,482	26,576
Operating lease right-of-use assets	3,073	2,856	—
Goodwill	3,367	3,813	3,811
Intangible assets, net	2,274	2,167	2,075
Investments and restricted cash	25	24	170
Deferred income tax assets	527	330	141
Other noncurrent assets	672	1,082	1,033
Total assets	$62,408	$57,857	$50,016
Liabilities and shareholders' equity			
Current liabilities:			
Current maturities of long-term debt, commercial paper, and finance leases	$ 2,623	$ 3,420	$ 2,805
Current maturities of operating leases	560	538	—
Accounts payable	6,455	5,555	5,188
Accrued wages and withholdings	3,569	2,552	3,047
Self-insurance reserves	1,085	914	810
Accrued group welfare and retirement plan contributions	927	793	715
Other current liabilities	1,797	1,641	1,522
Total current liabilities	17,016	15,413	14,087
Long-term debt and finance leases	22,031	21,818	19,931
Noncurrent operating leases	2,540	2,391	—
Pension and postretirement benefit obligations	15,817	10,601	8,347
Deferred income tax liabilities	488	1,632	1,619
Other noncurrent liabilities	3,847	2,719	2,995
Total liabilities	61,739	54,574	46,979
Total shareowners' equity	669	3,283	3,037
Total liabilities and shareowners' equity	$62,408	$57,857	$50,016

REQUIRED

a. Compute ROA and disaggregate it into profit margin (PM) and asset turnover (AT) for 2020 and 2019. Comment on the drivers of the ROA. Assume a 25% tax rate for this period.
b. Compute any expense to sales (ETS) ratios that you think might help explain UPS' profitability.
c. Compute return on equity (ROE) for 2020 and 2019.
d. Comment on the difference between ROE and ROA. What does this relation suggest about UPS' use of debt?

P5-42. Analysis and Interpretation of Liquidity and Solvency

Refer to the financial information of **United Parcel Service** in P5-41 to answer the following requirements.

REQUIRED

a. Compute its current ratio and quick ratio for 2020 and 2019. Comment on any observed trends.
b. Compute its times interest earned and its debt-to-equity ratios for 2020 and 2019. Comment on any trends observed.
c. Summarize your findings in a conclusion about the company's liquidity and solvency. Do you have any concerns about its ability to meet its debt obligations?

P5-43.[A] Computing and Analyzing Operating Returns

Refer to the financial statements of **United Parcel Service** in P5-41 to answer the following requirements.

REQUIRED

a. Compute net operating profit after taxes (NOPAT) for 2020 and net operating assets (NOA) for 2020 and 2019. Assume a tax rate of 25%.

b. Compute the return on net operating assets (RNOA) for 2020. What percentage of UPS' ROE is generated by operations?
c. Decompose RNOA by computing net operating profit margin (NOPM) and net operating asset turnover (NOAT) for 2020.
d. What can be inferred about UPS from these ratios?

LO5-6 P5-44.[B] **Preparing Financial Statement Forecasts**

Refer to the financial statements of **United Parcel Service** in P5-41 to answer the following requirements. The following assumptions should be useful:

- UPS' sales forecast for 2021 is $90,000 million.
- Operating expenses and operating profits increase in proportion to sales.
- Interest expense is unchanged in 2021, and Investment (income) expense is forecasted to be ($1,500).
- Income taxes are 25% of pretax earnings.
- Marketable securities and Investments and restricted cash are unchanged in 2021, and there are no assets held for sale in 2021; all other assets (except cash) increase in proportion to sales.
- Long-term debt and finance leases, non-current operating leases, current maturities of long-term debt and of operating leases are unchanged in 2021; all other liabilities increase in proportion to sales.
- Dividends are 50% of net income. Income and dividends are the only changes to stockholders' equity in 2021.

REQUIRED

a. Prepare an income statement forecast for 2021.
b. Prepare a balance sheet forecast for 2021.

LO5-3 P5-45. Comparing Profitability Ratios for Competitors

Selected 2020 income statement data for **Abbott Laboratories**, **Bristol-Myers Squibb Company**, **Johnson & Johnson**, **GlaxoSmithKline plc**, **Pfizer, Inc.**, and **Moderna, Inc.**, is presented in the following table:

(millions)	Abbott Laboratories	Bristol-Myers Squibb	Johnson & Johnson	Glaxo Smith Kline plc	Pfizer	Moderna
Sales revenue.......	$34,608	$42,518	$82,584	£34,099	$41,908	$803
Cost of sales........	15,003	11,773	28,427	11,704	8,692	8
SG&A expense......	9,696	7,661	22,084	11,456	11,615	188
R&D expense	2,420	11,143	12,159	5,098	9,405	1,370
Interest expense.....	546	1,420	201	892	1,449	10
Net income (loss)	4,495	(8,995)	14,714	6,388	9,652	(747)

REQUIRED

a. Compute the profit margin (PM) and gross profit margin (GPM) ratios for each company. (As a British company, GlaxoSmithKline plc has a statutory tax rate of 19.25% in 2020. Assume a tax rate of 25% for the others.)
b. Compute the research and development (R&D) expense to sales ratio and the selling, general, and administrative (SG&A) expense to sales ratio for each company.
c. Compare the relative profitability of these pharmaceutical companies.

LO5-3 P5-46. Comparing Profitability and Turnover Ratios for Retail Companies

Selected financial statement data for **Best Buy Co., Inc.**, **The Kroger Co.**, **Nordstrom, Inc.**, **ODP Corp.**, and **Walgreens Boots Alliance, Inc.**, is presented in the following table:

($ millions)	Best Buy	Kroger	Nordstrom	ODP Corp.	Walgreens Boots
Sales revenue........	$43,638.0	$122,286.0	$15,524.0	$9,710.0	$139,537.0
Cost of sales.........	33,590.0	95,294.0	9,932.0	7,578.0	111,520.0
Interest expense......	64.0	603.0	151.0	42.0	639.0
Net income	1,541.0	1,512.0	496.0	(319.0)	424.0
Average receivables ...	1,082.0	1,647.5	163.5	727.0	7,179.0
Average inventories ...	5,291.5	8,293.5	1,949.0	981.0	9,392.0
Average PP&E	2,419.0	21,753.0	4,050.0	627.5	13,410.0
Average total assets ...	14,246.0	41,687.0	8,811.5	6,434.5	77,386.0

REQUIRED

a. Compute return on assets (ROA), profit margin (PM), and asset turnover (AT) for each company. Assume a statutory tax rate of 25%. Discuss the relative importance of PM and AT for each company.
b. Compute accounts receivable turnover (ART), inventory turnover (INVT), and property, plant, and equipment turnover (PPET) for each company. Discuss any difference that you observe.
c. Compute the gross profit margin (GPM) for each company. How does the GPM differ across companies? Does this difference seem to correlate with differences in ART or INVT? Explain.

CASES AND PROJECTS

C5-47. Management Application: Gross Profit and Strategic Management   **LO5-3**

One way to increase overall profitability is to increase gross profit. This can be accomplished by raising prices and/or by reducing manufacturing costs.

REQUIRED

a. Will raising prices and/or reducing manufacturing costs unambiguously increase gross profit? Explain.
b. What strategy might you develop as a manager to (i) yield a price increase for your product or (ii) reduce product manufacturing cost?

C5-48. Management Application: Asset Turnover and Strategic Management   **LO5-3**

Increasing net operating asset turnover requires some combination of increasing sales and/or decreasing net operating assets. For the latter, many companies consider ways to reduce their investment in working capital (current assets less current liabilities). This can be accomplished by reducing the level of accounts receivable and inventories or by increasing the level of accounts payable.

REQUIRED

a. Develop a list of suggested actions to achieve all three of these objectives as manager.
b. Examine the implications of each. That is, describe the marketing implications of reducing receivables and inventories and the supplier implications of delaying payment. How can a company achieve working capital reduction without negatively impacting its performance?

C5-49. Ethics and Governance: Earnings Management   **LO5-2, 3, 4**

Companies are aware that analysts focus on profitability in evaluating financial performance. Managers have historically utilized a number of methods to improve reported profitability that are cosmetic in nature and do not affect "real" operating performance. These are typically subsumed under the general heading of "earnings management." Justification for such actions typically includes the following arguments:

- Increasing stock price by managing earnings benefits shareholders; thus, no one is hurt by these actions.
- Earnings management is a temporary fix; such actions will be curtailed once "real" profitability improves, as managers expect.

REQUIRED

a. Identify the affected parties in any scheme to manage profits to prop up stock price.
b. Do the ends (of earnings management) justify the means? Explain.
c. To what extent are the objectives of managers different from those of shareholders?
d. What governance structure can you envision that might prohibit earnings management?

SOLUTIONS TO REVIEW PROBLEMS

Review 5-1

THE COCA-COLA COMPANY AND SUBSIDIARIES
Consolidated Statements of Income
($ millions)

Year Ended December 31	2020	2019
Net operating revenues	100.0%	100.0%
Cost of goods sold	40.7%	39.2%
Gross profit	59.3%	60.8%
Selling, general, and administrative expenses	29.5%	32.5%
Other operating charges	2.6%	1.2%
Operating income	27.2%	27.1%
Interest income	1.1%	1.5%
Interest expense	4.4%	2.5%
Equity income (loss)—net	3.0%	2.8%
Other income (loss)—net	2.5%	0.1%
Income before taxes	29.4%	29.0%
Income taxes	6.0%	4.8%
Consolidated net income	23.4%	24.2%

THE COCA-COLA COMPANY AND SUBSIDIARIES
Common Size Balance Sheets

December 31	2020	2019
Assets		
Current assets		
Cash and cash equivalents	7.8%	7.5%
Short-term investments	2.0%	1.7%
Marketable securities	2.7%	3.7%
Trade accounts receivable, net	3.6%	4.6%
Inventories	3.7%	3.9%
Prepaid expenses and other current assets	2.2%	2.2%
Total current assets	22.0%	23.6%
Equity method investments	22.1%	22.0%
Other investments	0.9%	1.0%
Other assets	7.1%	7.0%
Deferred income tax assets	2.8%	2.8%
Property, plant, and equipment, net	12.3%	12.5%
Trademarks with indefinite lives	11.9%	10.7%
Goodwill	20.1%	19.4%
Other intangible assets	0.8%	1.0%
Total assets	100.0%	100.0%
Liabilities and equity		
Current liabilities		
Accounts payable and accrued expenses	12.8%	13.1%
Loans and notes payable	2.5%	12.7%
Current maturities of long-term debt	0.6%	4.9%
Accrued income taxes	0.9%	0.5%
Total current liabilities	16.8%	31.2%
Long-term debt	46.0%	31.9%
Other liabilities	10.8%	9.9%
Deferred income taxes	2.1%	2.6%
Total liabilities	75.7%	75.6%
Total equity	24.3%	24.4%
Total liabilities and equity	100.0%	100.0%

Note: Percentages are rounded amounts, and thus, they may not exactly sum to totals and subtotals.

Operating income, income before taxes, and consolidated income as a percentage of sales remained relatively flat from 2019 to 2020. Also, the mix between debt and equity financing changed very little between years (liabilities are approximately 76% of total assets for each year). Current assets as a percentage of total assets dropped slightly from 23.6% in 2019 to 22.0% in 2019 due to a drop in short-term investments and trade accounts receivable as a percentage of total assets in 2020 compared to 2019. The most significant change over the prior year was the increase in long-term debt as a percentage of total assets over the prior year (46% in 2020 vs. 32% in 2019). This caused a drop in current liabilities as a percentage of total assets in 2020 compared to 2019.

Review 5-2

($ MILLIONS)

$$\text{ROE} = \frac{\$7,768}{(\$21,284 + \$21,098)/2} = 0.3666 \text{ or } 36.66\%$$

$$\text{ROA} = \frac{\$7,768 + [\$1,437 \times (1 - 0.25)]}{(\$87,296 + \$86,381)/2} = 0.1019 \text{ or } 10.19\%$$

$$\text{ROFL} = 0.3666 - 0.1019 = 0.2647 \text{ or } 26.47\%$$

Review 5-3

($ MILLIONS)

$$\text{PM} = \frac{\$7,768 + [\$1,437 \times (1 - 0.25)]}{\$33,014} = 0.2679 \text{ or } 26.79\%$$

$$\text{AT} = \frac{\$33,014}{(\$87,296 + \$86,381)/2} = 0.3802 \text{ times}$$

$$26.79\% \times 0.3802 = 10.19\%$$

$$\text{GPM} = \frac{\$33,014 - 13,433}{\$33,014} = 0.5931 \text{ or } 59.31\%$$

$$\text{ART} = \frac{\$33,014}{(\$3,144 + \$3,971)/2} = 9.2801 \text{ times}$$

$$\text{INVT} = \frac{\$13,433}{(\$3,266 + \$3,379)/2} = 4.0430 \text{ times}$$

$$\text{PPET} = \frac{\$33,014}{(\$10,777 + \$10,838)/2} = 3.0547 \text{ times}$$

PepsiCo and Coca-Cola have similar business models, and both companies achieve high returns on the capital invested by their shareholders. PepsiCo has a much higher ROE (51% vs. 37% for Coca-Cola), and Coca-Cola has a slightly higher ROA (10.2% vs. 9.5% for PepsiCo). Most of the cause of the difference in ROE is due to the fact that PepsiCo has a much higher ROFL (41.0% vs. 26.5% for Coca-Cola), caused by its higher use of liabilities as a source of financing. Coca-Cola has a higher GPM and PM, while PepsiCo achieves a higher turnover of total assets. Closer analysis of turnover ratios reveals that ART is similar, implying that they employ similar credit policies. PepsiCo's inventory turns over significantly more quickly than Coca-Cola's inventory, perhaps reflecting differences in their product mix (e.g., PepsiCo's snack foods). This difference plays a significant role in PepsiCo's superior asset turnover. The two companies' PPET ratios are essentially identical, so utilization of fixed assets is not a factor in PepsiCo's higher total asset turnover.

Review 5-4

($ MILLIONS)

$$\text{Current ratio} = \frac{\$19,240}{\$14,601} = 1.318$$

$$\text{Quick ratio} = \frac{\$6,795 + \$4,119 + \$3,144}{\$14,601} = 0.963$$

$$\text{Debt-to-equity ratio} = \frac{\$66,012}{\$21,284} = 3.101$$

$$\text{Times interest earned} = \frac{\$9,749 + \$1,437}{\$1,437} = 7.784$$

Coca-Cola is more liquid than PepsiCo, as indicated by a higher current ratio (1.32 vs. 0.98) and a higher quick ratio (0.96 vs. 0.77). In addition, PepsiCo has a much higher debt-to-equity ratio than Coca-Cola (5.9 vs. 3.1), suggesting that PepsiCo is relying more on debt financing. This is consistent with the higher ROFL ratio computed in Review 5-2. Nevertheless, neither company has significant issues related to solvency. Both report reasonably high times-interest-earned ratios (8.24 for PepsiCo and 7.78 for Coca-Cola).

Review 5-5

($ MILLIONS)

Operating assets:
2020: $87,296 − $4,119 − $812 = $82,365
2019: $86,381 − $4,695 − $854 = $80,832

Operating liabilities:
2020: $66,012 − $2,183 − $485 − $40,125 = $23,219
2019: $65,283 − $10,994 − $4,253 − $27,516 = $22,520

Net operating assets (NOA):
2020: $82,365 − $23,219 = $59,146
2019: $80,832 − $22,520 = $58,312
NOPAT = $7,768 − [($370 − $1,437 + $841) × (1 − 0.25)] = $7,937.5

$$\text{RNOA} = \frac{\$7,937.5}{(\$59,146 + \$58,312)/2} = 13.5\%$$

$$\text{NOPM} = \frac{\$7,937.5}{\$33,014} = 24.04\%$$

$$\text{NOAT} = \frac{\$33,014}{(\$59,146 + \$58,312)/2} = 0.562$$

Review 5-6

THE COCA-COLA COMPANY AND SUBSIDIARIES
Forecasted Statements of Income
($ millions)

Year Ended December 31	2021
Net operating revenues	$34,665 (5% growth)
Cost of goods sold ($34,665 × 40.7%)	14,109
Gross profit	20,556
Selling, general, and administrative expenses ($34,665 × 29.5%)	10,226
Other operating charges ($34,665 × 2.6%)	901
Operating income	9,429
Interest income (unchanged)	370
Interest expense (unchanged)	1,437
Equity income (loss)—net (unchanged)	978
Other income (loss)—net (unchanged)	841
Income from continuing operations before income taxes	10,181
Income taxes from continuing operations ($10,181 × 25%)	2,545
Consolidated net income	$ 7,636

THE COCA-COLA COMPANY AND SUBSIDIARIES
Forecasted Balance Sheet
($ millions)

December 31	2021
Assets	
Current assets	
Cash and cash equivalents	$ 9,662
Short-term investments (unchanged)	1,771
Marketable securities (unchanged)	2,348
Trade accounts receivable, net ($34,665 × 9.5%)	3,293
Inventories ($34,665 × 9.9%)	3,432
Prepaid expenses and other assets ($34,665 × 5.8%)	2,011
Total current assets	22,517
Equity method investments (unchanged)	19,273
Other investments (unchanged)	812
Other assets ($34,665 × 18.7%)	6,482
Deferred income tax assets ($34,665 × 7.5%)	2,600
Property, plant, and equipment, net ($34,665 × 32.6%)	11,301
Trademarks with indefinite lives (unchanged)	10,395
Goodwill (unchanged)	17,506
Other intangible assets (unchanged)	649
Total assets	$91,535
Liabilities and shareholders' equity	
Current liabilities	
Accounts payable and accrued expenses ($34,665 × 33.8%)	$11,717
Loans and notes payable (unchanged)	2,183
Current maturities of long-term debt (unchanged)	485
Accrued income taxes ($34,665 × 2.4%)	832
Total current liabilities	15,217
Long-term debt (unchanged)	40,125
Other liabilities ($34,665 × 28.6%)	9,914
Deferred income taxes ($34,665 × 5.6%)	1,941
Total liabilities	67,197
Total equity [$21,284 + 7,636 − (0.60 × 7,636)]	24,338
Total liabilities and equity	$91,535

Chapter 6
Reporting and Analyzing Revenues, Receivables, and Operating Income

LEARNING OBJECTIVES

LO6-1 Describe and apply the criteria for determining when revenue is recognized.

LO6-2 Illustrate revenue and expense recognition when the transaction involves future deliverables and/or multiple elements.

LO6-3 Illustrate revenue and expense recognition for long-term projects.

LO6-4 Estimate and account for uncollectible accounts receivable.

LO6-5 Calculate return on net operating assets, net operating profit after taxes, return on net operating assets, net operating profit margin, accounts receivable turnover, and average collection period.

LO6-6 Discuss earnings management and explain how it affects analysis and interpretation of financial statements.

LO6-7 Appendix 6A: Describe and illustrate the reporting for nonrecurring items.

Road Map

LO	Learning Objective	Topics	Page	eLecture	Review	Assignments
LO6-1	Describe and apply the criteria for determining when revenue is recognized.	6-5	e6-1	R6-1	M6-14, M6-15, M6-17, E6-28, E6-29, E6-30, E6-31, E6-37, E6-47, E6-48, C6-50, C6-59, C6-61, DA6-1, DA6-2
LO6-2	Illustrate revenue and expense recognition when the transaction involves future deliverables and/or multiple elements.	6-8	e6-2	R6-2	M6-17, M6-26, M6-27, E6-29, E6-30, E6-31, E6-34, E6-35, E6-47, E6-48, E6-49, E6-50, P6-58, C6-59, C6-60, C6-61, C6-62, C6-63
LO6-3	Illustrate revenue and expense recognition for long-term projects.	6-11	e6-3	R6-3	M6-13, M6-16, E6-29, E6-30, E6-31, E6-32, E6-33, P6-52
LO6-4	Estimate and account for uncollectible accounts receivable.	6-14	e6-4	R6-4	M6-18, M6-19, M6-20, M6-21, M6-22, M6-24, M6-25, E6-38, E6-39, E6-40, E6-41, E6-42, E6-43, E6-44, E6-45, P6-54, P6-55, P6-56, P6-57, P6-52, C6-53, DA6-3, DA6-4, DA6-5
LO6-5	Calculate return on net operating assets, net operating profit after taxes, return on net operating assets, net operating profit margin, accounts receivable turnover, and average collection period.	6-22	e6-5	R6-5	M6-21, M6-23, E6-36, E6-40, E6-46, P6-51, P6-54, P6-55, C6-62
LO6-6	Discuss earnings management and explain how it affects analysis and interpretation of financial statements.	6-27	e6-6	R6-6	M6-28, E6-37, P6-53, C6-59, C6-60, C6-61
LO6-7	Appendix 6A: Describe and illustrate the reporting for nonrecurring items.	6-29	e6-7	R6-7	E6-46, P6-51, C6-64

MICROSOFT CORPORATION
www.microsoft.com

Microsoft Corporation has adopted a broad mission—to provide technology that will "empower every person and every organization on the planet to achieve more." To accomplish that objective, the company provides a wide range of software, services, devices, and solutions.

In its early years, Microsoft concentrated on software products—operating systems and productivity tools. Microsoft's current products include operating systems, productivity applications, server and business solution applications, tools to manage servers and to develop software, and video games. The company's products also include personal computers, tablets, and gaming equipment.

The technology industry is notable for quick, substantial changes, with formidable competition. Microsoft has expanded its offerings in cloud computing services that include software, platforms, content, and consulting. The company is one of the world's two largest providers of cloud computing. This service area is where Microsoft is experiencing significant growth. From 2018 to 2020, revenue from products increased by 5%, while revenue from services increased by 63%. But the coronavirus pandemic that appeared in the latter part of the company's 2020 fiscal year has affected some lines of business favorably (e.g., Personal Computing), while others were not (e.g., LinkedIn).

Profitability is the primary measure by which financial statement users gauge a company's success in efficiently offering products and services that receive a favorable response from customers. In this chapter, we focus on how companies report operating income. Operating income is determined by decisions about how and when to recognize revenues and expenses. In addition, the income statement also includes nonrecurring (or transitory) items, such as restructuring charges. Transitory items are often important events reflecting very large dollar amounts and are distinguished by the fact that they are unlikely to recur in subsequent years. Understanding how such nonrecurring items are reported is crucial to interpreting a company's profitability.

Microsoft's performance cannot be measured by profits alone. To control costs and improve operating profits, Microsoft must effectively manage operating assets. For example, accounts receivable is an important operating asset at Microsoft—accounting for almost 20% of its operating assets. By extending credit to customers on favorable credit terms, Microsoft stimulates sales. However, extending credit exposes the company to collectibility risk—the risk that some customers will not pay the amounts owed. In addition, accounts receivable do not earn interest and involve administrative costs associated with billing and collection. Hence, management of receivables is critical to financial success. This chapter describes the reporting of receivables. The reporting of other operating assets is covered in subsequent chapters.

Sources: Microsoft Corporation Annual Report 10-K 2020.

CHAPTER ORGANIZATION

Reporting and Analyzing Revenues, Receivables, and Operating Income

Reporting Operating Income	Reporting Receivables	Analyzing Financial Statements	Further Considerations
• Revenue Recognition • Accounting for Transactions with Future Deliverables • Accounting for Long-Term Projects	• Allowance for Uncollectible Accounts • Disclosures and Interpretations	• Net Operating Profit After Taxes • Return on Net Operating Assets • Net Operating Profit Margin • Accounts Receivable Turnover • Average Collection Period	• Earnings Management • Reporting Nonrecurring Items (Appendix A)

REPORTING OPERATING INCOME

The income statement is the primary source of information about recent company performance. This information is used to predict future performance for investment purposes and to assess the creditworthiness of a company. The income statement is also used to evaluate the quality of management.

This section describes the information reported in the income statement and its analysis implications. The central questions that the income statement attempts to answer are:

- How profitable has the company been recently?
- How did it achieve that profitability?
- Will the current profitability level persist?

To answer these three profitability questions, it is not enough to focus on a company's net income. Rather, we must use the various classifications within the income statement to see how profits were achieved and what the future prospects look like. **Exhibit 6.1** provides a schematic of the primary income statement classifications.

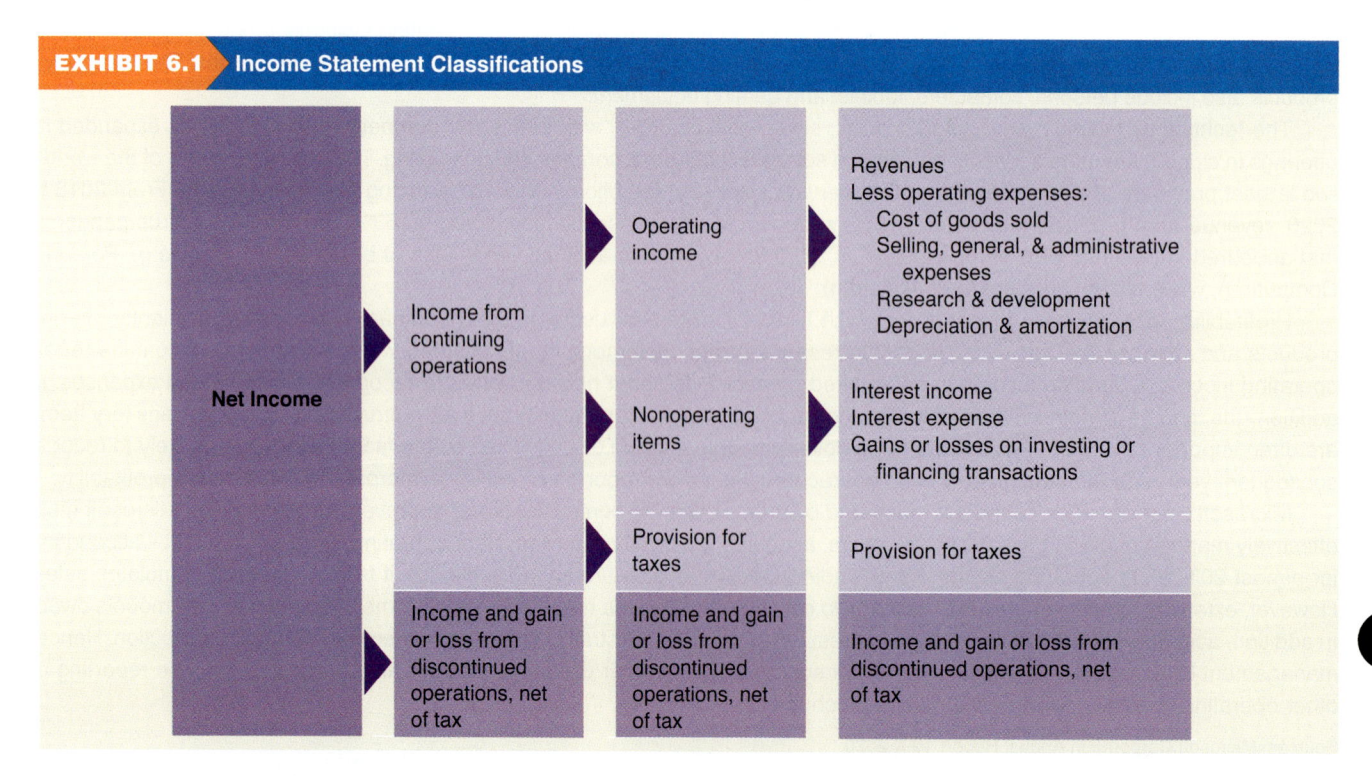

EXHIBIT 6.1 Income Statement Classifications

Net Income	Income from continuing operations	Operating income	Revenues
			Less operating expenses:
			  Cost of goods sold
			  Selling, general, & administrative expenses
			  Research & development
			  Depreciation & amortization

		Nonoperating items	Interest income Interest expense Gains or losses on investing or financing transactions
		Provision for taxes	Provision for taxes
	Income and gain or loss from discontinued operations, net of tax	Income and gain or loss from discontinued operations, net of tax	Income and gain or loss from discontinued operations, net of tax

Operating activities refer to the primary transactions and events of a company. These include the purchase of goods from suppliers, the employment of personnel, the conversion of materials into finished products, the promotion and distribution of goods, the sale of goods and services to customers, and post-sale customer support. Operating activities are reported in the income statement under items such as sales, cost of goods sold, and selling, general, and administrative expenses (including research and development). They represent a company's primary activities, which must be executed successfully for a company to remain consistently profitable.

Nonoperating activities relate to the financial (borrowing) and securities investment activities of a company. These activities are typically reported in the income statement under items such as interest income and expenses, dividend revenues, and gains and losses on sales of securities. Distinguishing income components by operating versus nonoperating is an important part of effective financial statement analysis because operating activities drive company performance. It is of interest, for example, to know whether company profitability results from operating activities or whether poorly performing operating activities are being masked by income from nonoperating activities.

All the line items in income from continuing operations are presented before taxes, with the final line item being provision for income taxes, or tax expense. Microsoft's 2018 provision for income taxes includes the one-time effect of the Tax Cuts and Jobs Act that was enacted at the end of calendar year 2017. The accounting for income taxes is discussed more fully in Chapter 10.

If the company has income or gain/loss items that qualify as discontinued operations, these will be presented after income from continuing operations for the current year and for other income statements presented. Discontinued operations are reported net of income tax expense or benefit. The appendix at the end of this chapter provides a more detailed description of nonrecurring items. Finally, many large corporations report something called **net income attributable to noncontrolling interests**. Such an amount arises when a company consolidates a subsidiary that it controls, but for which it holds less than 100% ownership. This topic is covered in later chapters.

Exhibit 6.2 presents the 2020, 2019, and 2018 income statements (sometimes called statements of operations) for Microsoft Corporation. Microsoft has no discontinued operations during this time period, so income from continuing operations is the same as net income. Like many companies, Microsoft presents operating income as a subtotal in its income statement. Microsoft's operating income is computed by subtracting its total operating expenses (including cost of revenue, research and development, sales and marketing, and general and administrative) from total sales revenues. Nonoperating income and expenses, such as interest income and expense, and other income and expense are added to or deducted from the subtotal for operating income.

FYI When analyzing a company's income statement, it is important to distinguish operating activities from nonoperating activities and recurring activities from nonrecurring activities.

EXHIBIT 6.2 Distinguishing Operating and Nonoperating Sources of Income

MICROSOFT CORPORATION
Income Statements

(In millions, except per share amounts)	2020	2019	2018
Revenue:			
Product	$68,041	$ 66,069	$ 64,497
Service and other	74,974	59,774	45,863
Total revenue	143,015	125,843	110,360
Cost of revenue:			
Product	16,017	16,273	15,420
Service and other	30,061	26,637	22,933
Total cost of revenue	46,078	42,910	38,353
Gross margin	96,937	82,933	72,007
Research and development	19,269	16,876	14,726
Sales and marketing	19,598	18,213	17,469
General and administrative	5,111	4,885	4,754
Operating income	52,959	42,959	35,058
Other income, net	77	729	1,416
Income before income taxes	53,036	43,688	36,474
Provision for income taxes	8,755	4,448	19,903
Net income	$44,281	$ 39,240	$ 16,571

At this time, GAAP does not have specific rules for classifying revenue and expense items as either operating or nonoperating, so management must use judgment in reporting, and financial statement users must be careful to examine each revenue and expense item to determine if it is appropriately listed as part of operating income. Specifically, sales, cost of goods sold, and most selling, general, and administrative expenses are categorized as operating activities. Alternatively, investment-related income from dividends and interest is nonoperating, as is interest expense. Gains and losses on debt retirements and sales of investments are also nonoperating.[1]

While we think of Microsoft as a provider of software, hardware, and services, it had approximately $123 billion (41% of its total assets) invested in financial instruments (mostly government and government-backed securities) at 2020 fiscal year-end. And these assets provided close to $2.7 billion in interest and dividend income for 2020. So, making predictions about Microsoft's profitability for 2021 would be improved by separating the results of its product and service operations from those of its investing activities. In addition, operating income is the normal focus of business unit managers in a company—financing activities and investments in financial instruments and tax administration are usually determined at the central corporate level.

Revenue Recognition

LO6-1
Describe and apply the criteria for determining when revenue is recognized.

eLecture
MBC

Revenue is one of the most important metrics of a company's operating success. The objective of almost all operating activities is to obtain a favorable response from customers, and revenue is a primary indicator of how customers view the company's product and service offerings. Companies can improve profits by reducing costs, but the effects of those improvements are limited unless revenues are increasing. Accordingly, growth in revenue is carefully monitored by management and by investors, as exemplified by the attention given to "same-store sales growth" in the retail industry.[2]

Revenue recognition refers to the timing and amount of revenue reported by the company. The decision of when to recognize revenue depends on certain criteria. Determining whether the criteria for revenue recognition are met is often subjective and requires judgment. Therefore, financial statement readers should pay careful attention to companies' revenue recognition, particularly when companies face market pressures to meet income targets. Indeed, many SEC enforcement actions against companies for inaccurate and sometimes fraudulent financial reporting are for improper (usually premature) revenue recognition.

Sales transactions between companies and their customers generally consist of an exchange in which the company provides a product or a service and, in return, receives a payment (usually, but not necessarily, a payment in cash). For many companies, this is a simple process—the customer walks into the convenience store, selects a soft drink, pays the store clerk for the soft drink, and then consumes the soft drink on the way home. The convenience store's revenue is the amount paid by the customer for the soft drink as the customer walks out with it (minus any sales taxes collected on behalf of government entities).

But other company/customer arrangements can be quite complicated, with delivery of the product and/or service occurring over time and with payments not coinciding with delivery. Revenue is such a vital component of companies' financial results, accounting standard setters formulated a broad principle and a process that is applied to almost all situations. The core principle is the following.

> An entity should recognize revenue to depict the transfer of goods or services to customers in an amount that reflects the consideration to which the entity expects to be entitled in exchange for those goods and services.

---

[1] To further complicate matters, the classification of some items in the income statement as nonoperating is not consistent with their classification in the cash flow statement. Specifically, interest and dividend income and interest expense are classified as operating in the cash flow statement and nonoperating in most income statements. Of course, the distinction between operating and nonoperating items depends on the company's business. For Microsoft, interest income and expense would be classified as nonoperating, but for a financial institution (e.g., a bank), those same items would be considered part of their operations. Purchases and sales of production equipment would be considered nonoperating for Microsoft, but operating for a company in the business of buying and selling used equipment.

[2] For a retail company, sales growth can come from increased sales at existing locations or from sales at recently opened locations—the former coming from customers' increased liking for the company's offerings and the latter coming from increased availability (which costs more to achieve). Quarterly same store sales growth uses only those locations that have been open for the current quarter and the quarter one year prior.

To accomplish this principle, companies follow a five-step process.

Step 1: Identify the contract with a customer.
Step 2: Identify the performance obligations in the contract.
Step 3: Determine the transaction price.
Step 4: Allocate the transaction price (if necessary).
Step 5: Recognize revenue when or as the entity satisfies a performance obligation.

The first step is to determine whether the transaction has commercial substance, that is it changes the future cash flows of the entity.[3] The word "contract" is used here in a general sense—it may refer to a legal document, but it can also reflect an oral agreement or be implied by the entity's (i.e., the seller's) customary business practices. The agreement must create enforceable rights and obligations for the parties.

The second step breaks the contract down into distinct "**performance obligations**" that the entity agrees to perform. Essentially, the entity must determine how many distinct goods and services it has agreed to provide to the customer. These are the "deliverables" for the entity, and the accounting standards require the performance obligations to be distinct from each other. That is, the customer can benefit from each performance obligation on its own or together with readily accessible resources. For instance, if the entity regularly sells the good or service separately, then it can be distinct. For instance, a manufacturer's product warranty is *not* a separate performance obligation if the warranty terms are set to assure the customer that the product will perform as promised. Ford Motor Company's base warranty comes with every vehicle and is not considered a separate performance obligation. On the other hand, a customer may purchase a ticket for travel on an airline, and that purchase would be comprised of transportation services on the scheduled flight *and* frequent flyer miles that can be used for travel in the future. Are the frequent flyer miles a separate performance obligation? The answer is yes, because airlines sell frequent flyer miles separately from travel services.[4] On the other hand, if there are multiple goods and/or services, but they require significant integration or coordination, then there is only one deliverable.

For the third step, the transaction price is the amount of consideration to which the entity expects to be entitled in exchange for transferring promised goods or services.[5] The accounting standard allows for "**variable consideration**," which may include (but is not limited to) price concessions, volume discounts, rebates, refunds, credits, incentives, performance bonuses, and royalties. Determining variable consideration can require significant estimation by the entity's management, and the standard has features that are intended to control undue optimism on the part of management. Consider the following from United Technologies Corporation's 10-K regarding revenue recognition.

> We consider the contractual consideration payable by the customer and assess variable consideration that may affect the total transaction price, including contractual discounts, contract incentive payments, estimates of award fees, unfunded contract value under U.S. Government contracts, and other sources of variable consideration, when determining the transaction price of each contract.
>
> We include variable consideration in the estimated transaction price when there is a basis to reasonably estimate the amount. These estimates are based on historical experience, anticipated performance, and our best judgment at the time.

If there are multiple performance obligations, then Step 4 requires that the transaction price from Step 3 be allocated to these individual performance obligations based on their stand-alone selling prices. This process is simple if stand-alone selling prices are readily available. But if such

---

[3] Suppose Companies A and B each have an inventory of 10,000 units of the same item, with unit costs of $100. They each arrange to sell the inventory to the other for $3 million. Could they each recognize $3 million in revenue and $1 million in cost of goods sold? No, because the transactions leave their future cash flows unaffected, i.e., lacking commercial substance.

[4] If the contract involves providing a series of distinct goods or services that are substantially the same, then the series is treated as a single performance obligation that is satisfied over time. For example, a company might agree to provide nightly cleaning services for an office. While one could treat each day's cleaning as a separate performance obligation, it was deemed easier to view the cleaning contract as a single performance obligation that is fulfilled over time.

[5] Amounts collected for third parties (e.g., sales taxes) are not included in the entity's revenue.

prices do not exist, then the company must estimate the stand-alone selling prices. For example, if the stand-alone selling prices of performance obligations A and B are $150 and $350 respectively, and the entity agrees to deliver them to the customer for a combined price of $400, then it should recognize $120 (= $400 × (150/(150 + 350))) when A is delivered and $280 = $400 × [350/(150 + 350)] when B is delivered.

Finally, Step 5 requires that the entity recognize revenue as it satisfies a performance obligation. A performance obligation is considered to be satisfied when the customer obtains control, i.e., when the customer obtains the ability to direct the use of and obtain substantially all of the remaining benefits of the asset/service that constitutes the performance obligation. In some cases, the customer obtains control over time, but if control does not transfer over time, then it is presumed to transfer at a point in time.

In many instances, the sole performance obligation is to deliver a product or service to the customer. Delivery doesn't refer only to transportation to the customer's location, but rather the transfer of title and the risks and rewards of ownership to the customer. Revenue recognition complications arise if there is uncertainty about collectability or when the sale is contingent on product performance, product approval, or similar contingencies. In some industries, it is standard practice to allow customers to return the product within a specified period of time. When these uncertainties are substantial, companies may have to reconsider the first step in the revenue recognition process. That is, does the delivery have commercial substance?

But for many companies, returns and uncollectible accounts are either immaterial in amount or relatively easy to predict based on history of a large number of similar transactions. The expected returns are estimated and reduce the reported revenue from the sale.

As noted earlier, revenue is a key performance indicator for almost every company, and there exists a wide variety of practices used in formulating a sales contract between a company and its customers. Given that diversity, the process to determine when to recognize revenue and how much revenue to recognize requires substantial judgment on the part of management. Therefore, it's important for the financial statement reader to check the disclosure notes describing a company's practices.

BUSINESS INSIGHT

Performance Obligations and Product Returns at The Gap, Inc. Following is an excerpt from The Gap, Inc.'s accounting policies as reported in its annual financial statements:

> For online sales and catalog sales the Company has elected to treat shipping and handling as fulfillment activities, and not a separate performance obligation. Accordingly, we recognize revenue for our single performance obligation related to online sales and catalog sales at the time control of the merchandise passes to the customer, which is generally at the time of shipment. We also record an allowance for estimated returns based on our historical return patterns and various other assumptions that management believes to be reasonable . . .

The Gap's policy regarding product returns is consistent with GAAP in that expected returns are estimated and deducted from sales at the time that the sale is recorded. This represents the amount to which the company "expects to be entitled" when it makes the sale. If returns cannot be estimated at that point in time, then GAAP would assess that there was not a contract with the customer, and no revenue would be recognized at that point.

The term "delivery" does not refer solely to transportation to the customer's location, but also the transfer of title and of the control of the item's benefits. In a **consignment** sale, a *consignor* delivers product to a *consignee* but retains ownership until the consignee sells the product to the ultimate customer. As long as ownership remains with the consignor, a sale has not taken place. Only when the consignee sells the product should the consignor record the sale revenue. Also at that point, the consignee, who has been acting as an agent for the consignor, will recognize the commission earned (not the full purchase price paid by the ultimate customer).

Identifying the Steps in the Revenue Recognition Process

LO6-1 Review 6-1

Match each of the following descriptions *a* through *e* to each of the step 1 through 5 in the revenue recognition process.

___ a. Requires that a customer obtain control of a promised good/service.
___ b. Determines the amount of consideration expected to be received in exchange for providing a good/service.
___ c. Establishes a contract through a legal document, an oral agreement, or common business practice.
___ d. Requires the determination of actual or estimated standalone selling prices of performance obligations.
___ e. Determines the number of distinct goods/services promised to a customer.

Solution on p. 6-53.

Revenue Recognition Subsequent to Customer Purchase

There are many businesses in which customers purchase a product or a service prior to its delivery. For instance, a customer may pay for a year's subscription to a periodical. The publisher receives the cash at the start of the subscription, but it recognizes revenue as it fulfills its performance obligation to deliver the periodical to the subscriber. Or, a homeowner may pay for the upcoming year's casualty insurance, but the insurance company can only recognize revenue as it fulfills its performance obligation to provide insurance coverage over that year.

In settings where a company's customers pay for the product or service prior to its delivery, the company must recognize a **contract liability**. The term "contract liability" refers to an entity's obligation to transfer goods or services to a customer for which the entity has received consideration (or the amount is due) from the customer. Such contract liabilities are frequently labeled as **unearned revenue** or **deferred revenue**[6] or some other descriptive term. Then this liability is reduced, and revenue recognized, as the performance obligation is fulfilled.

Suppose that on January 1, a subscriber pays $36 for an annual subscription to a monthly magazine. At the time of payment, the publisher would make the following entry:

LO6-2 Illustrate revenue and expense recognition when the transaction involves future deliverables and/or multiple elements.

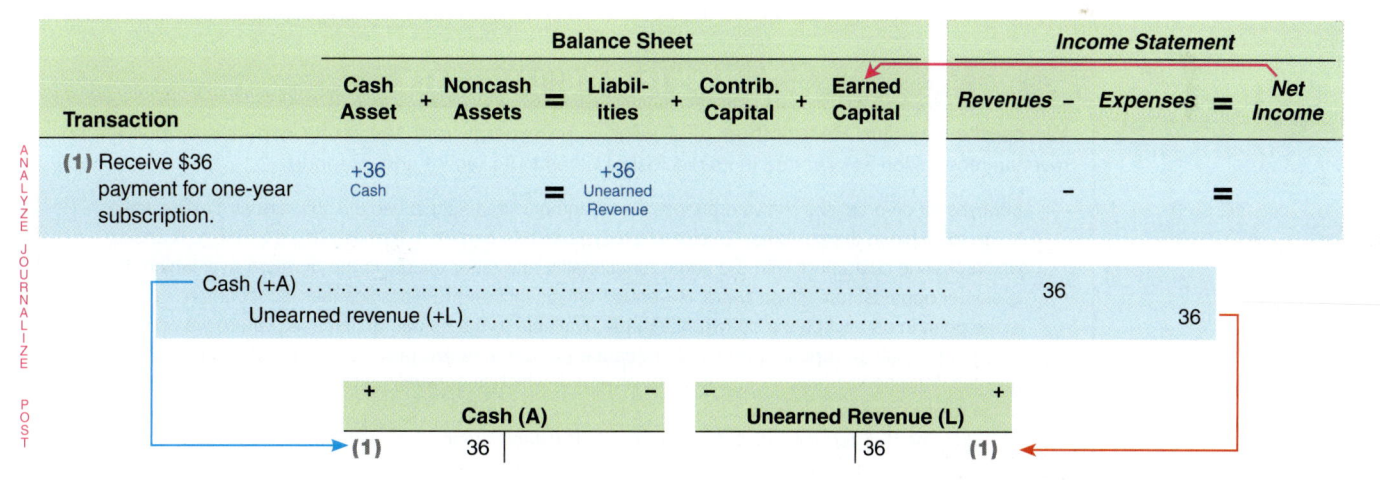

Transaction	Cash Asset	+	Noncash Assets	=	Liabilities	+	Contrib. Capital	+	Earned Capital	Revenues	−	Expenses	=	Net Income
(1) Receive $36 payment for one-year subscription.	+36 Cash			=	+36 Unearned Revenue						−		=	

Cash (+A) 36
    Unearned revenue (+L) 36

+ Cash (A) −		− Unearned Revenue (L) +
(1) 36		36 (1)

The unearned revenue liability represents the publisher's obligation—not to make a payment, but to provide the promised publication. Most liabilities reflect obligations to make a future payment, but unearned revenue is one of a handful of *contract liabilities* that represent an obligation for future performance.

---

[6] The term used for a contract liability may be particular to the company's business. For instance, **Delta Air Lines** shows an Air Traffic Liability of $4,044 million in its December 31, 2020, annual report, which represents customers' purchases of tickets in advance of their flights. **The Allstate Corporation** uses the term *Unearned Premiums*.

On March 31, at the end of its first quarter, the publisher would recognize that three magazines had been delivered to the subscriber, and the publisher has earned three times the monthly revenue of $3, or $9. The entry to recognize this revenue is the following.

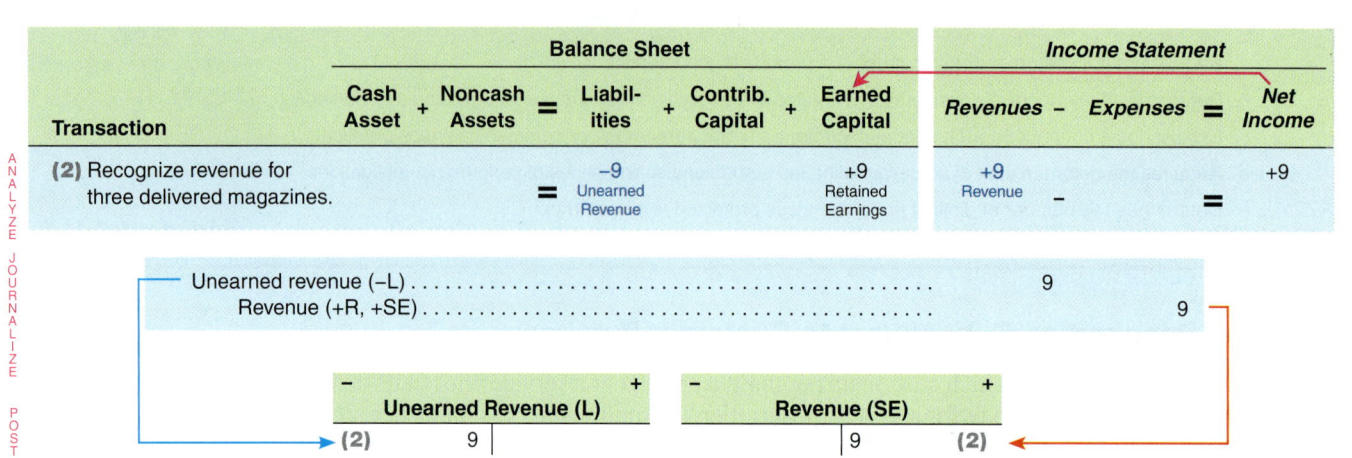

Transaction	Balance Sheet					Income Statement		
	Cash Asset + Noncash Assets	=	Liabilities	+ Contrib. Capital	+ Earned Capital	Revenues −	Expenses =	Net Income
(2) Recognize revenue for three delivered magazines.		=	−9 Unearned Revenue		+9 Retained Earnings	+9 Revenue	−	+9

```
Unearned revenue (−L)..................................................  9
    Revenue (+R, +SE)...................................................      9
```

− Unearned Revenue (L) +	− Revenue (SE) +
(2) 9	9 (2)

The same entries would be made until the subscription expired. In the March 31 balance sheet, the publisher would have an unearned revenue liability of $27, reflecting the remaining obligation for nine months of subscription delivery. And, the quarter's indirect method operating cash flows would include $9 in revenue (in net income) and the $27 increase in unearned revenue liability which, in total, reflect the $36 received from the customer.

Unearned revenue is seen in a growing number of financial statements as companies increase the use of gift cards as well as their promises of future deliveries of products and service due to the changing nature of products and services in the economy and in an effort to build a continuing relationship with their customers. From the point of view of a financial analyst, one implication of revenue deferral is that the change in revenue from one period to the next is not equal to the change in customer purchases over the same period. In the case of our publisher with one-year subscriptions, quarterly revenue is actually a composite of subscriber purchases over the current

BUSINESS INSIGHT

Microsoft's Revenue Recognition Following is an excerpt from Microsoft Corporation's policies on revenue recognition as reported in its disclosure notes to its recent annual report.

> Licenses for on-premises software provide the customer with a right to use the software as it exists when made available to the customer. Customers may purchase perpetual licenses or subscribe to licenses, which provide customers with the same functionality and differ mainly in the duration over which the customer benefits from the software. Revenue from distinct on-premises licenses is recognized upfront at the point in time when the software is made available to the customer. In cases where we allocate revenue to software updates, primarily because the updates are provided at no additional charge, revenue is recognized as the updates are provided, which is generally ratably over the estimated life of the related device or license . . . .
>
> Judgment is required to determine the SSP [Stand-alone Selling Price] for each distinct performance obligation. We use a single amount to estimate SSP for items that are not sold separately, including on-premises licenses sold with SA [Software Assurance] or software updates provided at no additional charge. We use a range of amounts to estimate SSP when we sell each of the products and services separately and need to determine whether there is a discount to be allocated based on the relative SSP of the various products and services.
>
> In instances where SSP is not directly observable, such as when we do not sell the product or service separately, we determine the SSP using information that may include market conditions and other observable inputs. We typically have more than one SSP for individual products and services due to the stratification of those products and services by customers and circumstances. In these instances, we may use information such as the size of the customer and geographic region in determining the SSP.

Microsoft emphasizes that judgment is required at many points in the revenue recognition process, from estimating the total selling price, to identifying distinct performance obligations, to allocating the total price to the performance obligations, and finally recognizing when the performance obligations are fulfilled.

quarter plus the last three quarters and, therefore, not an ideal indicator of how current customers are responding to the publisher's offerings. Both the revenue and unearned revenue accounts need to be analyzed to obtain a complete picture.

A revenue recognition complication arises when an agreement with a customer requires that two or more products or services (i.e., performance obligations) are sold under the same agreement for one lump-sum price. These bundled sales are commonplace in the software industry, where developers sell software, training, maintenance, and customer support in one transaction. In this case, the company must allocate the total consideration to the separate performance obligations based on their stand-alone selling price (estimated, if necessary). Revenue allocated to the performance obligations that have not yet been fulfilled (such as maintenance and customer support) must be deferred, with revenue recognized as those performance obligations are fulfilled in future periods.

To illustrate revenue recognition for a multiple performance obligation arrangement (or bundled sale), assume that Software Innovations, Inc., develops marketing software designed to track customer questions and comments on the Internet and through social media. The software license sells for $125,000 and includes user training for up to 12 individuals and customer support for three years. Software Innovations estimates that the software, if licensed without training or customer support, would sell for $120,000. In addition, it estimates that the value of the user training services, if sold separately, would be $18,000 and the customer support would sell for $12,000. Software Innovations would allocate the $125,000 sales price as illustrated in **Exhibit 6.3**.

EXHIBIT 6.3 Allocation of the Sales Price in a Multiple Performance Obligation Arrangement

Performance Obligation	Estimated Value	Percent of Total Value		Bundle Sales Price		Sales Price Allocated to Each Performance Obligation
Software license	$120,000	80%	×	$125,000	=	$100,000
Training	18,000	12	×	125,000	=	15,000
Customer support	12,000	8	×	125,000	=	10,000
Total	$150,000	100%				$125,000

The sale would be recorded as revenue for the portion that was allocated to software and as deferred (or unearned) revenue for that portion that was allocated to training and customer support:

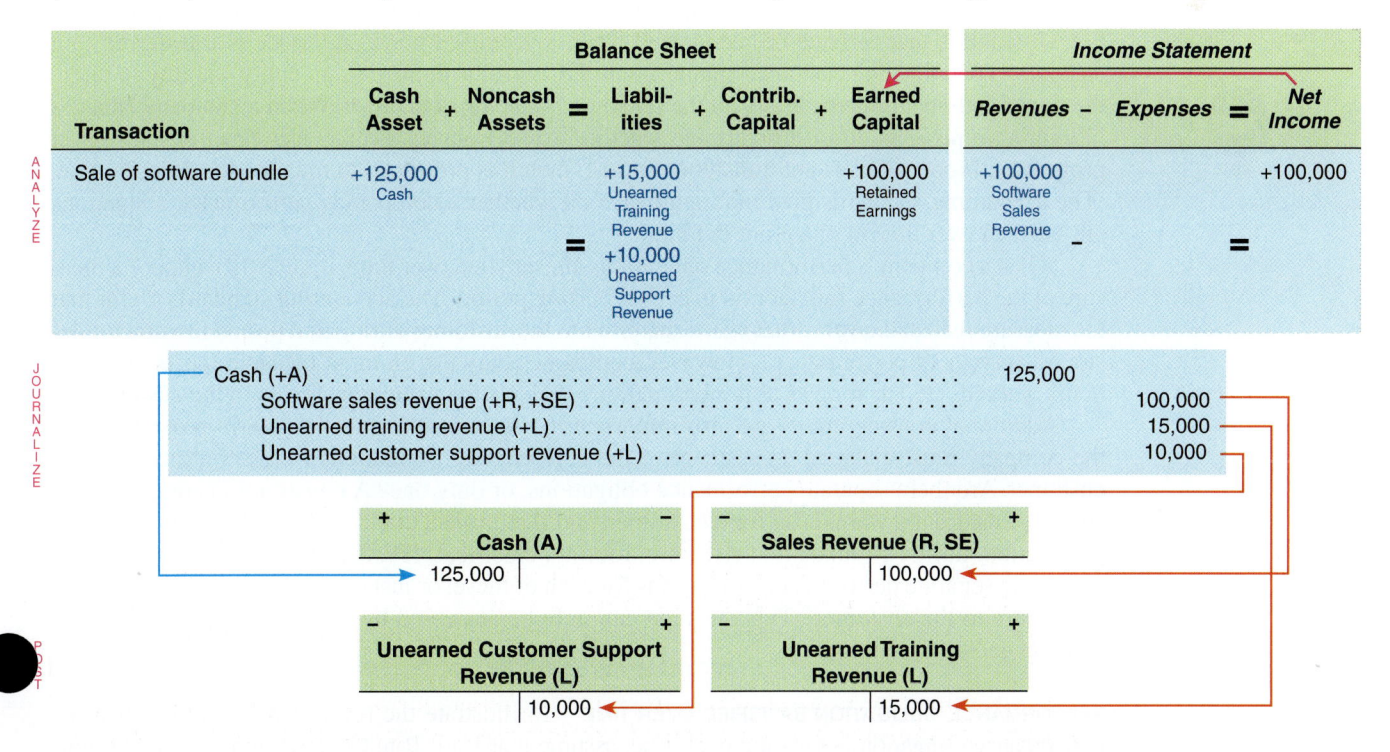

Transaction	Cash Asset	+	Noncash Assets	=	Liabilities	+	Contrib. Capital	+	Earned Capital	Revenues	−	Expenses	=	Net Income
Sale of software bundle	+125,000 Cash				+15,000 Unearned Training Revenue = +10,000 Unearned Support Revenue				+100,000 Retained Earnings	+100,000 Software Sales Revenue	−		=	+100,000

Cash (+A) 125,000
  Software sales revenue (+R, +SE) 100,000
  Unearned training revenue (+L) 15,000
  Unearned customer support revenue (+L) 10,000

+ Cash (A) −		− Sales Revenue (R, SE) +
125,000		100,000

− Unearned Customer Support Revenue (L) +		− Unearned Training Revenue (L) +
10,000		15,000

The unearned training revenue would be recognized as training services are provided. Software Innovations might recognize 1/12 of the $15,000, or $1,250 for each individual trained. The unearned customer support revenue would be recognized over time ($10,000/3 = $3,333 each year).

Review 6-2 LO6-2

Analyzing Deferred Revenue Charges

In its annual report for fiscal year 2020, **Electronic Arts, Inc.**, included the following disclosure in the notes accompanying the financial statements.

> Games with Services. Our sales of Games with Services are evaluated to determine whether the software license, future update rights, and the online hosting are distinct and separable. Sales of Games with Services are generally determined to have three distinct performance obligations: software license, future update rights, and the online hosting.
>
> Since we do not sell the performance obligations on a stand-alone basis, we consider market conditions and other observable inputs to estimate the stand-alone selling price for each performance obligation. For Games with Services, generally 75 percent of the sales price is allocated to the software license performance obligation and recognized at a point in time when control of the license has been transferred to the customer (which is usually at or near the same time as the booking of the transaction). The remaining 25 percent is allocated to the future update rights and the online hosting performance obligations and recognized ratably as the service is provided (over the Estimated Offering Period).

In its income statement for the fiscal year ended March 31, 2020, Electronic Arts reported *Total net revenue* of $5,537 million. At the beginning of that fiscal year, the company had a liability for *Deferred net revenue (online-enabled games)* of $1,100 million. At the end of the fiscal year, that liability was $945 million, a decrease of $155 million.

Required

a. What would cause the *Deferred net revenue (online-enabled gaming)* liability to go down over the fiscal year?
b. What was the amount of online-enabled games purchased by Electronic Arts' customers in the fiscal year ended March 31, 2020? How might that information be useful for a financial statement reader?

Solution on p. 6-53.

LO6-3
Illustrate revenue and expense recognition for long-term projects.

Revenue Recognition for Long-Term Projects Challenges can arise in determining revenue recognition for companies with long-term production/service processes (spanning more than one reporting period), such as consulting firms, construction companies, and defense contractors. GAAP requires that revenue be recognized when a promised good or service is transferred to a customer, i.e., when the customer obtains control. Control is defined as an entity's ability to direct the use of and obtain substantially all the remaining benefits of an asset. When a company engages in long-term projects, it must determine whether it will transfer control over time, as the project progresses. If control does not transfer over time, then it is presumed to transfer at a point in time. (The accounting standards give more guidance on whether a company's performance obligations are satisfied over time or at a point in time.)

When a company's performance obligations are satisfied over time, it must then choose a measure of the performance satisfaction in each reporting period. The accounting standards prefer that the measure reflect the value that was transferred to the customer during that period (contract milestones, surveys of performance). However, companies may use an input measure (costs incurred, hours worked, etc.) as long as that input measure reflects the value transferred to the customer.

Additional considerations are also important in the accounting for long-term projects. First, the company must make an assessment of the performance obligations in the contract with the customer. Are there separate performance obligations, or only one? A construction company may agree to construct a warehouse for a customer, and that project could include several facets—site preparation, utilities, foundation, structure, roofing, electrical, HVAC, and so on. Does the company have separate performance obligations for each of these, or just one—to deliver a functioning warehouse to the customer? This question can only be answered by careful consideration of the contract and the circumstances.

PERFORMANCE OBLIGATION SATISFIED OVER TIME To illustrate the revenue recognition when the performance obligation is satisfied over time, assume that Built-Rite Construction signs a $10 million contract to construct a building for a customer. Built-Rite estimates $7.5 million in construction costs, yielding an expected gross profit of $2.5 million. Based on its review of the contract, Built-Rite determines that the building construction is a single performance obligation satisfied over time. In addition, the construction costs incurred reflect the amount of value transferred to the customer during a reporting period, so Built-Rite can use the "cost-to-cost"[7] measure of performance.

In the first year of construction, Built-Rite incurs $4.5 million in construction costs. The remaining $3.0 million are incurred during the second year. The amount of revenue and gross profit that Built-Rite would report each year (in millions) is illustrated in **Exhibit 6.4**.

EXHIBIT 6.4 Performance Obligation Satisfied over Time Based on Cost-to-Cost

Year	Measure of Value Transferred	Revenue Recognized	Expense Recognized	Gross Profit
1	$4.5/$7.5 = 60%	$10.0 × 60% = $6.0	$4.5	$1.5
2	$3.0/$7.5 = 40%	$10.0 × 40% = 4.0	3.0	1.0
Total	100%	$10.0	$7.5	$2.5

Using this method, Built-Rite would report $1.5 million in gross profit in the first year and $1.0 million in the second year. The timing of revenue and gross profit coincides with the transfer of value to the customer.

When a company's performance obligation is satisfied over time and cost is used to assess performance, it requires an estimate of the total cost to completion. This estimate is initially made at the start of the contract, usually used to bid the contract. However, estimates are inherently prone to error. If total completion costs are underestimated, the percentage of completion is overestimated (the denominator is too small), and too much revenue and gross profit are recognized in the early years of the project. Therefore, the reliability of the reported performance depends on the quality of judgments made by the company's management.

PERFORMANCE OBLIGATION SATISFIED AT A POINT IN TIME In some circumstances, the company will determine that its performance obligation is not satisfied over time, but rather at a point in time. If Built-Rite Construction had determined that its performance obligation to construct the customer's building was not satisfied until delivery of the completed building to the customer, the revenue and gross profit would be reported as in **Exhibit 6.5**.

EXHIBIT 6.5 Performance Obligation Satisfied over Time versus at a Point in Time

	Performance Obligation Satisfied over Time		Performance Obligation Satisfied at a Point in Time	
	Year 1	Year 2	Year 1	Year 2
Revenues	$6.0	$4.0	$0.0	$10.0
Expenses	4.5	3.0	0.0	7.5
Gross profit	$1.5	$1.0	$0.0	$2.5

The total revenue and gross profit are the same under either method. The only difference is in the timing of the income statement reporting. Revenue and gross profit will show more variability when the performance obligation is satisfied at the end of the process.

TIMING DIFFERENCES BETWEEN REVENUES AND CASH RECEIPTS It is very likely that Built-Rite would have received some cash payments from the customer during the construction period, perhaps as advances or based on milestones in the construction process. However, the recognition of revenue is tied to the completion of performance obligations, which may differ from the measures used to determine progress payments. If a company receives payment prior to completion of the performance obligation, then it should recognize a **contract liability**, like deferred revenue or unearned revenue. If the project progress entitles the company to payment, it would also recognize an account receivable.

---

[7] That is, the cost incurred compared to the estimated total cost. This approach is often referred to as "percentage-of-completion."

In addition, the company should recognize revenue in the amount to which it expects to be entitled for completing the performance obligation. So, if a contract includes an incentive payment for timely completion of the project, the company should recognize its estimate of the amount of incentive that it expects to receive, prior to the actual receipt of that payment at the end of the contract. This contract arrangement can result in the company recognizing revenue when it cannot yet send an invoice to the customer. That is, the company is not yet entitled to an unconditional right to future payment. When such revenue is credited, the account debited is referred to as a **contract asset** (sometimes referred to as unbilled receivables). A contract asset represents an amount that the company expects to receive from the customer for performance to date, but for which it is not yet entitled to payment.

As an example, suppose Built-Rite's contract with the customer allows it to bill the customer for half the project once 60% of the work is complete at the end of year 1. The entry made to reflect revenue recognized for year 1 would be the following (all amounts in $ millions):

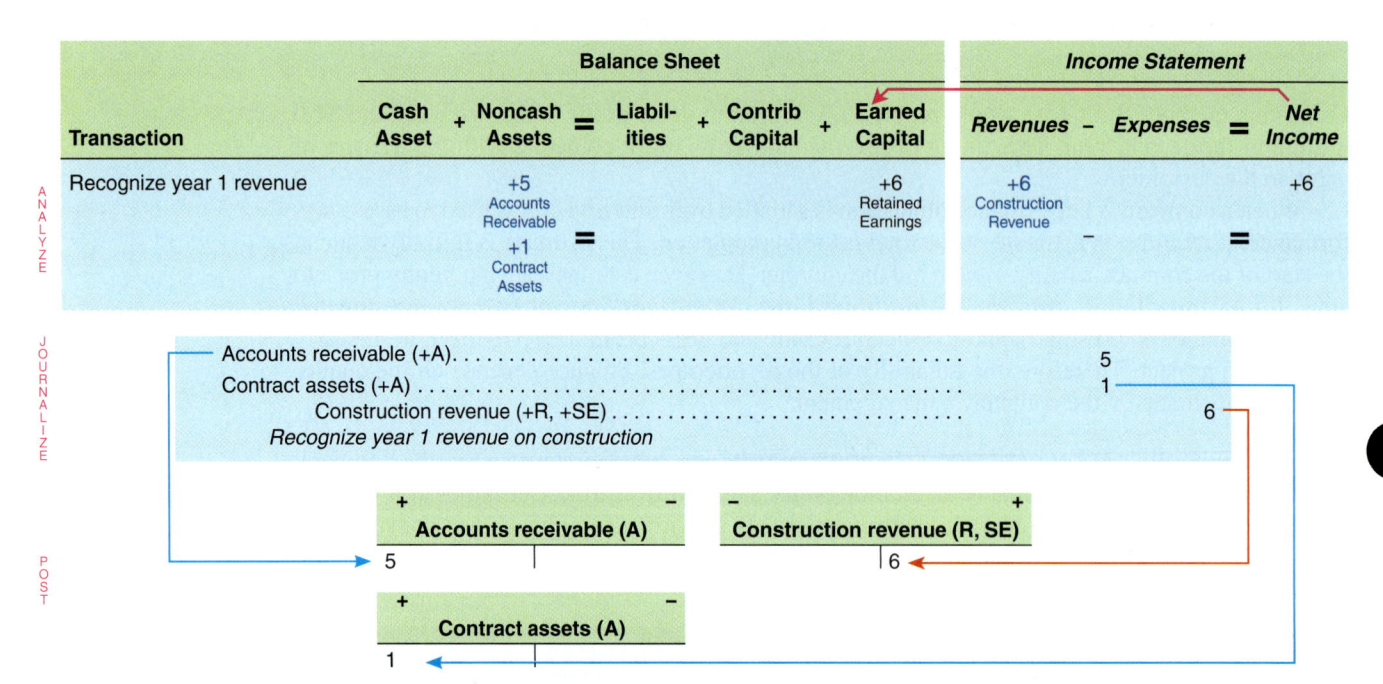

Transaction	Cash Asset	+	Noncash Assets	=	Liabilities	+	Contrib Capital	+	Earned Capital		Revenues	−	Expenses	=	Net Income
Recognize year 1 revenue			+5 Accounts Receivable +1 Contract Assets	=					+6 Retained Earnings		+6 Construction Revenue	−		=	+6

```
Accounts receivable (+A)..................................  5
    Contract assets (+A) ..................................  1
        Construction revenue (+R, +SE)....................       6
    Recognize year 1 revenue on construction
```

+	−		−	+
Accounts receivable (A)			**Construction revenue (R, SE)**	
5				6

+	−
Contract assets (A)	
1	

On completion of the project at the end of year 2, Built-Rite would recognize as revenue the 40% of the project completed. It would bill the customer for this amount *plus* the amount of revenue previously held as contract assets.

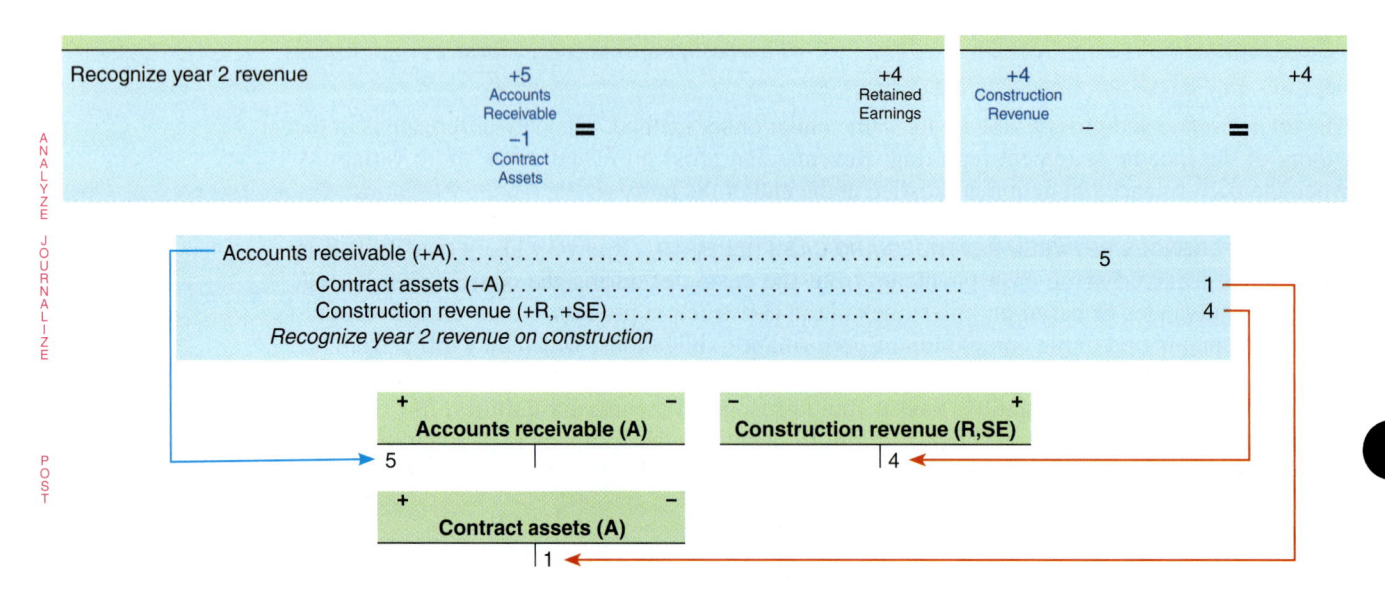

Transaction	Cash Asset	+	Noncash Assets	=	Liabilities	+	Contrib Capital	+	Earned Capital		Revenues	−	Expenses	=	Net Income
Recognize year 2 revenue			+5 Accounts Receivable −1 Contract Assets	=					+4 Retained Earnings		+4 Construction Revenue	−		=	+4

```
Accounts receivable (+A)..................................  5
    Contract assets (−A) ..................................      1
        Construction revenue (+R, +SE)....................       4
    Recognize year 2 revenue on construction
```

+	−		−	+
Accounts receivable (A)			**Construction revenue (R,SE)**	
5				4

+	−
Contract assets (A)	
	1

BUSINESS INSIGHT

Fluor Corporation engages in engineering and construction activities for its customers. The following excerpts from its 2019 10-K are taken from its disclosure note on revenue recognition.

> "We recognize engineering and construction contract revenue over time as we provide services to satisfy our performance obligations. We generally use the cost-to-cost percentage-of-completion measure of progress as it best depicts how control transfers to our clients. The cost-to-cost approach measures progress towards completion based on the ratio of contract cost incurred to date compared to total estimated contract cost. Engineering and construction contracts are generally accounted for as a single unit of account (a single performance obligation) and are not segmented between types of services on a single project . . ."
>
> "The nature of our contracts gives rise to several types of variable consideration, including claims, unpriced change orders, award and incentive fees, liquidated damages, and penalties. We consider variable consideration in the development of our project forecasts so that our forecasted revenue reflects the amount of consideration we expect to be probable of recovering without a significant reversal . . ."

In its December, 31, 2019, balance sheet, Fluor Corporation reports *Contract assets* of $882 million (11.1% of total assets) and *Contract liabilities* of $1,120 million (17.6% of total liabilities). The contract assets represent revenue that has been recognized but not yet billed to the customer. When Fluor bills a customer for an amount that exceeds the recognized revenue, the excess is reported as a contract liability.

Recording Revenue Transactions — LO6-3 **Review 6-3**

Haskins, Inc., has reached an agreement with a customer, Skaife Corporation, to deliver 200 units of a customized product. The standard billing price per unit is $1,000, and there are no discounts. At the time of the agreement on April 6, Skaife Corporation provides a $40,000 cash deposit to Haskins, Inc. Haskins agrees to deliver 120 units to Skaife Corporation on May 31 and, at that time, Haskins can send an invoice for $50,000 to be paid by Skaife Corporation on June 15. The remaining 80 units are to be delivered on July 15, accompanied by an invoice for the remaining amount of the total $200,000 purchase price to be paid on July 31.

Required
Assume that Haskins, Inc., has no uncertainties about its own ability to meet the terms of the contract or about Skaife Corporation's ability and willingness to pay.

a. Report the effects of the above events on Haskins' revenues using the financial statement effects template (leaving out the accounting for Haskins' costs).
b. Prepare journal entries to record the events identified in part a and post to T-accounts.

Solution on p. 6-53.

REPORTING ACCOUNTS RECEIVABLE

Receivables are usually a major part of operating working capital. They must be carefully managed because they represent a substantial asset for most companies. GAAP requires companies to report revenues in the amount to which they expect to be entitled and receivables in the amount to which they have an unconditional right to payment. But the balance sheet value of receivables should be the amount they expect to collect, necessitating an estimation of uncollectible accounts. These estimates determine the amount of receivables reported on the balance sheet as well as revenues and expenses reported on the income statement. Accordingly, it is important that companies accurately assess uncollectible accounts and report them. It is also necessary that readers of financial reports understand management's accounting choices and the effects of those choices on reported balance sheets and income statements.

When companies sell to other companies, they usually do not expect cash upon delivery as is common with retail customers. Instead, they offer credit terms, and the resulting sales are called **credit sales** or *sales on account*.

Companies establish credit policies (to determine which customers receive credit) by weighing the expected losses from uncollectible accounts against the expected profits generated by offering credit. Sellers know that some buyers will be unable to pay their accounts when they become due. Buyers, for example, can suffer business downturns that are beyond their control and which limit their cash available to meet liabilities. They must, then, make choices concerning which of their

LO6-4 Estimate and account for uncollectible accounts receivable.

FYI The phrase "trade receivables" refers to accounts receivable from customers.

FYI Receivables are claims held against customers and others for money, goods, or services.

liabilities to pay. Liabilities to the IRS, to banks, and to bondholders are usually paid because those creditors have enforcement powers and can quickly seize assets and disrupt operations, leading to bankruptcy and eventual liquidation. Buyers also try to cover their payroll because they cannot exist without employees. Then, if there is cash remaining, these customers will pay suppliers to ensure a continued flow of goods.

When a customer faces financial difficulties, suppliers are often the last creditors to receive payment and are often not paid in full. Consequently, there is risk in the collectibility of accounts receivable. This *collectibility risk* is crucial to analysis of accounts receivable.

Accounts receivable are reported on the balance sheet of the seller at **net realizable value**, which is the net amount that the seller expects to collect. Microsoft reports $32,011 million of accounts receivable in the current asset section of its 2020 balance sheet. Its receivables are reported net of allowances for doubtful accounts of $788 million. This means that the total amount owed to Microsoft by customers is $32,799 million ($32,011 million + $788 million), but the company *estimates* that $788 million of these receivables will be uncollectible. Thus, only the net amount that Microsoft expects to collect is reported on the balance sheet.

We might ask why the management of Microsoft would sell to companies from whom they do not expect to collect the amounts owed.[8] The answer is they would not *if* they knew beforehand who those companies were. That is, Microsoft probably cannot identify those companies that constitute the $788 million in uncollectible accounts as of its statement date. Yet, Microsoft knows from past experience that a certain portion of its receivables will prove uncollectible. GAAP requires a company to estimate the dollar amount of uncollectible accounts each time it issues its financial statements (even if it cannot identify specific accounts that are uncollectible) and to report its accounts receivable at the resulting *net realizable value* (total receivables less an **allowance for doubtful (uncollectible) accounts**).

FYI Receivables are classified into three types: (1) current or noncurrent, (2) trade or nontrade, (3) accounts receivable or notes receivable. **Notes receivable** and **notes payable** are discussed in Chapter 9.

Determining the Allowance for Uncollectible Accounts

The amount of expected uncollectible accounts is usually estimated based on an **aging analysis**. When aging the accounts, an analysis of receivables is performed as of the balance sheet date. Specifically, each customer's account balance is categorized by the number of days or months that the related invoices are outstanding. Based on prior experience, assessment of current economic conditions, or other available statistics, uncollectible (bad debt) percentages are applied to each of these categorized amounts, with larger percentages applied to older accounts. The result of this analysis is a dollar amount for the allowance for uncollectible accounts (also called allowance for doubtful accounts) at the balance sheet date.

To illustrate, **Exhibit 6.6** shows an aging analysis for a seller that began operations this year and is owed $100,000 of accounts receivable at year-end. Those accounts listed as current consist of those outstanding that are still within their original credit period. Accounts listed as 1–60 days past due are those 1 to 60 days past their due date. This classification would include an account that is 45 days outstanding for a net 30-day invoice. This same logic applies to all aged categories.

EXHIBIT 6.6 Aging of Accounts Receivable

Age of Accounts Receivable	Receivable Balance	Estimated Percent Uncollectible	Accounts Estimated Uncollectible
Current	$ 50,000	2%	$1,000
1–60 days past due	30,000	3	900
61–90 days past due	15,000	4	600
Over 90 days past due	5,000	8	400
Total	$100,000		$2,900

---

[8] GAAP requires that companies distinguish between amounts that they expected to receive that turned out to be uncollectible and amounts that represent an "implied price concession." For example, suppose a healthcare provider treats an uninsured patient, and the list price of the services is $10,000. But it is common for the healthcare company to accept, say, $1,500 from uninsured patients receiving such services. Should the healthcare company report revenue of $10,000 and $8,500 of bad debt expense? GAAP says that if there is an expectation that the healthcare company will accept the lower amount, then it should recognize $1,500 in revenue, not $10,000.

The calculation illustrated in **Exhibit 6.6** also reflects the seller's experience with uncollectible accounts, which manifests itself in the uncollectible percentages for each aged category. For example, on average, 3% of buyers' accounts that are 1–60 days past due prove uncollectible for this seller. Hence, it estimates a potential loss of $900 for those $30,000 in receivables for that aged category.

One possible means of estimating uncollectible accounts is to use a percentage of sales as an estimate of bad debt expense. That approach might satisfy as an estimate for the forecasting of future period financial statements, but it ignores the actual payments made by customers, making it less accurate and not acceptable under U.S. GAAP.

In the past, investments in many financial instruments were valued at their acquisition cost until there was some evidence that a loss had occurred. Financial standard setters require that companies use a current expected credit loss model (CECL). CECL requires that companies use their historical loss rate, adjusted for current conditions, to value such investments, even at the point of initial investment. The aging-of-accounts described above is one such approach for the valuation of trade receivables and similar instruments.

Reporting the Allowance for Uncollectible Accounts

How does the accounting system record this estimate? The amount that appears in the balance sheet as accounts receivable represents a collection of individual accounts—one or more receivables for each customer. Because we need to keep track of exactly how much each customer owes us, we cannot simply subtract estimated uncollectibles from individual accounts receivable.

In Chapter 3, we introduced contra-asset accounts to record accumulated depreciation. A contra-asset account is directly associated with an asset account but serves to offset the balance of the asset account. To record the estimated uncollectible accounts without disturbing the balance in accounts receivable, we use another contra-asset—the allowance for uncollectible accounts.

To illustrate, we use the data from **Exhibit 6.6**. The summary journal entry to reflect credit sales follows.

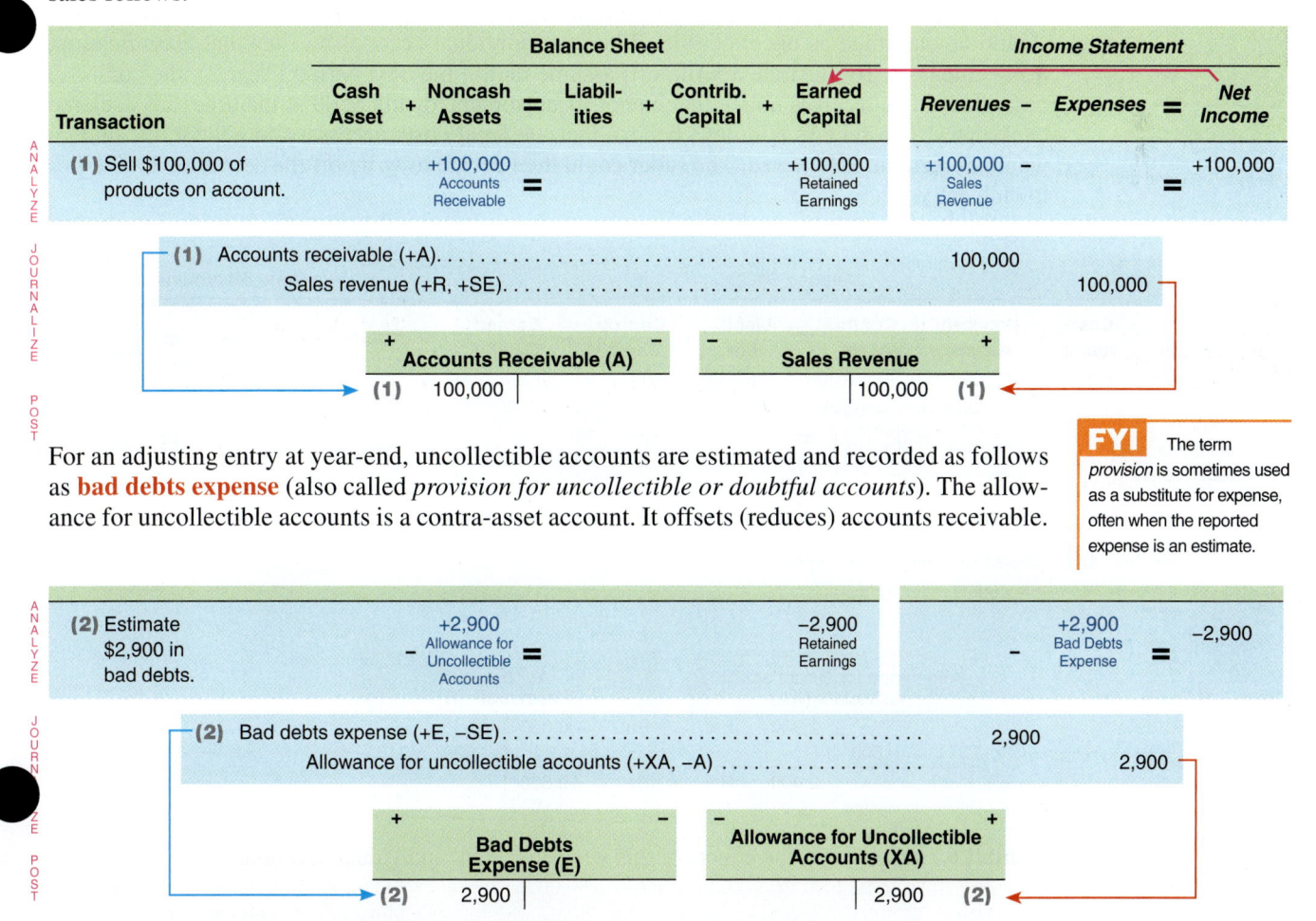

Transaction	Cash Asset	+	Noncash Assets	=	Liabilities	+	Contrib. Capital	+	Earned Capital	Revenues	−	Expenses	=	Net Income
(1) Sell $100,000 of products on account.			+100,000 Accounts Receivable	=					+100,000 Retained Earnings	+100,000 Sales Revenue	−		=	+100,000

(1) Accounts receivable (+A).. 100,000
    Sales revenue (+R, +SE)..................................... 100,000

+ Accounts Receivable (A) −	− Sales Revenue +
(1) 100,000	100,000 (1)

For an adjusting entry at year-end, uncollectible accounts are estimated and recorded as follows as **bad debts expense** (also called *provision for uncollectible or doubtful accounts*). The allowance for uncollectible accounts is a contra-asset account. It offsets (reduces) accounts receivable.

FYI The term *provision* is sometimes used as a substitute for expense, often when the reported expense is an estimate.

Transaction	Cash Asset	+	Noncash Assets	=	Liabilities	+	Contrib. Capital	+	Earned Capital	Revenues	−	Expenses	=	Net Income
(2) Estimate $2,900 in bad debts.			+2,900 Allowance for Uncollectible Accounts	=					−2,900 Retained Earnings		−	+2,900 Bad Debts Expense	=	−2,900

(2) Bad debts expense (+E, −SE)..................................... 2,900
    Allowance for uncollectible accounts (+XA, −A) 2,900

+ Bad Debts Expense (E) −	− Allowance for Uncollectible Accounts (XA) +
(2) 2,900	2,900 (2)

This accounting treatment serves three purposes. First, the balance in accounts receivable is reported in the balance sheet net of estimated uncollectible accounts as follows:

Accounts receivable, net of $2,900 in allowances $97,100

The $97,100 is the estimated net realizable value of the accounts receivable. Second, the original value of accounts receivable is preserved. The individual accounts that add up to the $100,000 in accounts receivable have not been altered. Third, bad debts expense of $2,900, which is part of the cost of offering credit to customers, is recognized against the $100,000 sales generated on credit and reported in the income statement. Bad debts expense is usually included in SG&A expenses.

The allowance for uncollectible accounts is increased by bad debts expense (estimated provision for uncollectibles) and decreased when an account is written off. Because the allowance for uncollectible accounts is a contra-asset account, credit entries increase its balance. The greater the balance in the contra-asset account, the more the corresponding asset account is offset.

BUSINESS INSIGHT

Expense or reduction in revenue? Technically speaking, bad debts expense is not really an expense. It is, instead, a reduction of revenue. Although it is correct under current GAAP to record this item as a subtraction from sales revenue, companies commonly record bad debts expense as part of selling expenses to emphasize that this amount is a cost of offering credit to customers.

Recording Write-Offs of Uncollectible Accounts

Companies have collection processes and policies to determine when an overdue receivable should be classified as uncollectible. When an individual account reaches that classification, it is written off. To illustrate a write-off, assume that in the next period (Year 2), the company described above receives notice that one of its customers, owing $500 at the time, has declared bankruptcy. The seller's attorneys believe that the legal costs necessary to collect the amount would exceed the $500 owed. The seller could then decide to write off the account with the following entry.

Transaction	Balance Sheet						Income Statement		
	Cash Asset	+ Noncash Assets	− Contra Asset	= Liabilities	+ Contrib. Capital	+ Earned Capital	Revenues	− Expenses	= Net Income
(3) Write off $500 in accounts receivable.*		−500 Accounts Receivable	−500 Allowance for Uncollectible Accounts	=				−	=

*There is no effect on accounts receivable, net of the allowance for uncollectible accounts. Consequently, there is no *net* effect on the balance sheet.

(3) Allowance for uncollectible accounts (−XA, +A) 500
    Accounts receivable (−A) 500

Allowance for Uncollectible Accounts (XA)				Accounts Receivable (A)			
−		+		+		−	
		2,900	Bal.	Bal.	100,000		
(3)	500					500	(3)
		2,400	Bal.	Bal.	99,500		

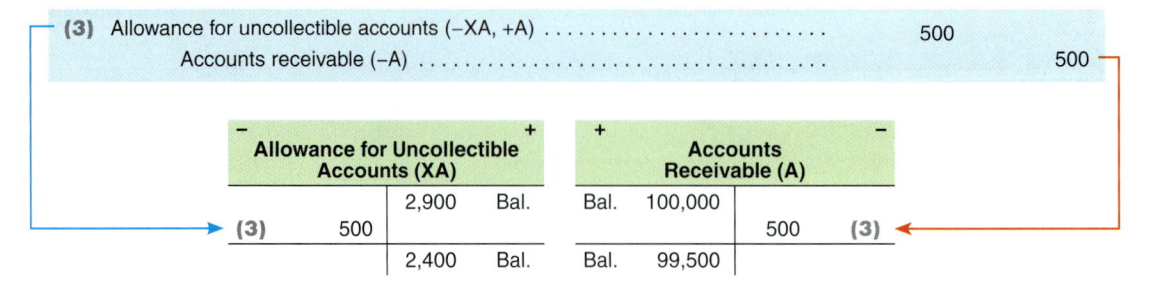

Exhibit 6.7 summarizes the effects of this write-off on the individual accounts.

EXHIBIT 6.7 Effects of an Accounts Receivable Write-Off

	Before Write-Off	Effects of Write-Off	After Write-Off
Accounts receivable	$100,000	$ (500)	$99,500
Less: Allowance for uncollectible accounts	2,900	500	2,400
Accounts receivable, net of allowance	$ 97,100		$97,100

The net amount of accounts receivable that is reported in the balance sheet after the write-off is the same amount that was reported before the write-off. This is always the case. The individual account receivable was reduced and the contra-asset was reduced by the same amount. Also, no entry was made to the income statement. The expense was estimated and recorded in the period when the credit sales were recorded.[9]

To complete the illustration, assume that management's aging of accounts at the end of Year 2 shows that the ending balance in the allowance account should be $3,000, so another $600 should be added to the allowance account at the end of Year 2. This $600 amount would reflect sales made in Year 2, as well as the seller's experience with collections during Year 2. The entry to record the Year 2 provision follows.

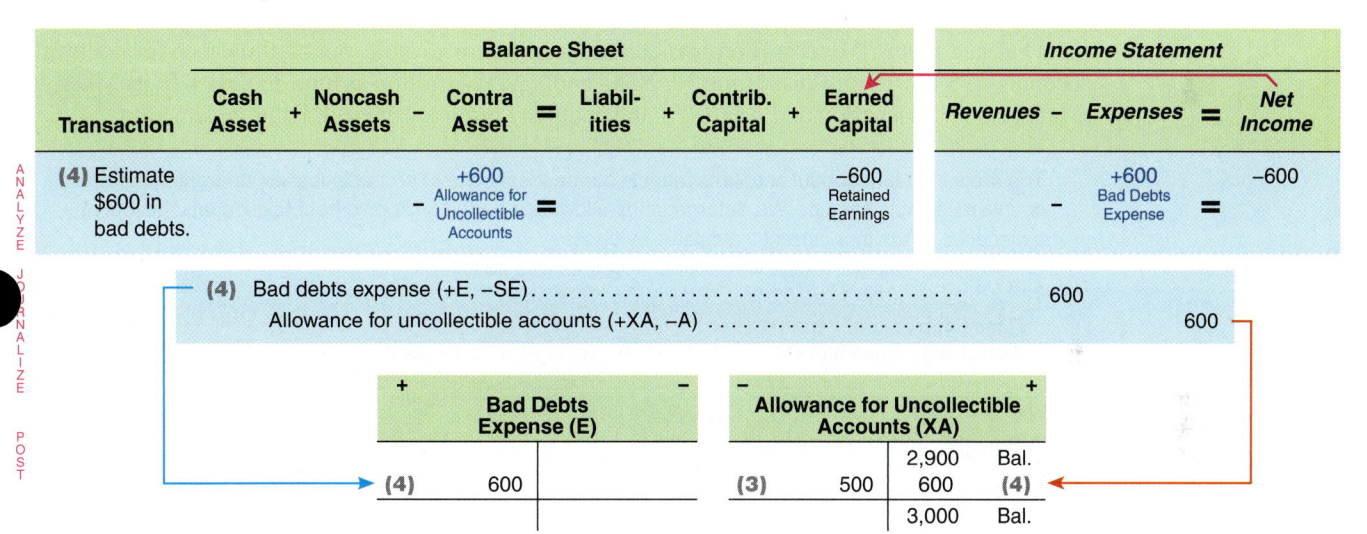

Transaction	Cash Asset	+	Noncash Assets	−	Contra Asset	=	Liabilities	+	Contrib. Capital	+	Earned Capital	Revenues	−	Expenses	=	Net Income
(4) Estimate $600 in bad debts.					+600 Allowance for Uncollectible Accounts						−600 Retained Earnings			+600 Bad Debts Expense		−600

(4) Bad debts expense (+E, −SE) 600
    Allowance for uncollectible accounts (+XA, −A) 600

Bad Debts Expense (E)		Allowance for Uncollectible Accounts (XA)	
(4) 600		(3) 500	2,900 Bal.
			600 (4)
			3,000 Bal.

This entry is the same (albeit with a different dollar amount) as the entry made to record the estimate in Year 1. A reconciliation of allowance for uncollectible accounts for the two years follows.

	Year 1	Year 2
Allowance for uncollectible accounts, beginning balance	$ 0	$2,900
Add: provision for uncollectible accounts (bad debts expense estimate)	2,900	600
Subtract: write-offs of uncollectible accounts receivable	0	(500)
Allowance for uncollectible accounts, ending balance	$2,900	$3,000

To summarize, the *main balance sheet and income statement effects occur when the provision is made to the allowance for uncollectible accounts.* Accounts receivable (net) is reduced, and that reduction is reflected in the income statement as bad debts expense (usually part of selling, general, and administrative expenses). The net income reduction yields a corresponding equity reduction (via reduced retained earnings). Importantly, the main financial statement effects are at the point of *estimation*, not upon the event of *write-off*. In this way, the net accounts receivable reflects the most up-to-date judgments about future customer payments, and bad debts expense is recognized

---

[9] Suppose a previously written off account is unexpectedly paid, often referred to as a *recovery*. If that occurs, the write-off entry (3) is reversed (reinstating the receivable and increasing the allowance), and the payment of this reinstated receivable is accounted for in the usual fashion.

as a cost of achieving the current period's sales and incorporates any changes in management's assessment of the likelihood that customers will pay.

> ### ANALYSIS INSIGHT
>
> In Chapter 4, we looked at the relationship between revenues and cash collected from customers. If a company offers credit to its customer (and receives no payments in advance of sales), then cash collected from customers equals revenue minus the change in accounts receivable. *But* which accounts receivable—gross or net? And what do we do with bad debts and/or write-offs?
>
> The interesting thing about these questions is that there isn't one answer, but two!
>
> Cash received from customers = Revenue − Bad debt expense − Change in Accounts receivable, net,
>
> Or
>
> Cash received from customers = Revenue − Write-offs − Change in Accounts receivable, gross.
>
> Both formulas give the same answer.

Disclosure Notes and Interpretations

In its balance sheets, **Microsoft** reports current accounts receivable, net of allowance for doubtful accounts, of $32,011 million at June 30, 2020, and $29,524 million at June 30, 2019. In its MD&A (Management Discussion and Analysis), the company provides the following information.

The allowance for doubtful accounts reflects our best estimate of probable losses inherent in the accounts receivable balance. We determine the allowance based on known trouble accounts, historical experience, and other currently available evidence.

Activity in the allowance for doubtful accounts was as follows:

(In millions) Year Ended June 30	2020	2019	2018
Balance, beginning of period	$434	$397	$361
Charged to costs and other	560	153	134
Write-offs	(178)	(116)	(98)
Balance, end of period	$816	$434	$397

Allowance for doubtful accounts included in our consolidated balance sheets:

June 30	2020	2019	2018
Accounts receivable, net allowance for doubtful accounts	$788	$411	$377
Other long-term assets	28	23	20
Total	$816	$434	$397

In Microsoft's 10-K report filed with the Securities and Exchange Commission, it discloses that its provision for doubtful accounts (bad debts expense) was $560 million, $153 million, and $134 million in fiscal years 2020, 2019, and 2018, respectively. Based on this information, we could construct a reconciliation of Microsoft's allowance for doubtful accounts (for both current and long-term receivables) as presented in **Exhibit 6.8**.

EXHIBIT 6.8 Reconciliation of Microsoft's Allowance for Doubtful Accounts

Allowance for Doubtful Accounts ($ millions)	
Balance at June 30, 2019	$434
Provision for doubtful accounts	560
Write-offs	(178)
Balance at June 30, 2020	$816

The disclosure notes may also disclose whether or not a company has *pledged* its accounts receivable as collateral for a short-term loan. If this is the case, a short-term loan is presented in the liabilities section of the balance sheet, and a disclosure note explains the arrangement. As an alternative to borrowing, a company may *factor* (or sell) its accounts receivable to a bank or other financial institution. If the receivables have been factored, the bank or other financial institution accepts all responsibility for collection. Consequently, the receivables do not appear on the balance sheet of the selling company because they have been sold.

The reconciliation of Microsoft's allowance account provides insight into the level of its annual provision (bad debts expense) relative to its write-offs. In 2020, Microsoft wrote off $178 million in uncollectible accounts while recording a provision for doubtful accounts (bad debts expense) of $560 million. Because the provision exceeded the write-offs, the total allowance increased from $434 million in 2019 to $816 million in 2020.

Microsoft's bad debts expense (or provision) more than tripled in 2020, though the magnitude is small relative to the size of their sales revenue. The company reported allowance for doubtful accounts of $788 million in 2020 and $411 million in 2019, an increase from 1.4% of accounts receivable to 2.4%. The changes in bad debts expense, both in absolute amount and as a percentage of sales revenue, could be caused by several factors. For example, the creditworthiness of Microsoft's customers may have changed due to the coronavirus pandemic. These changes can be caused by changing economic conditions or changes in Microsoft's credit policies (including collection efforts). Of course, it also could mean that Microsoft expects these changes to occur in the coming months.

The magnitude of Microsoft's uncollectible accounts relative to the company's overall size and profitability makes it an unlikely place for earnings management. But companies in other industries (banking, publishing, retail) often have receivables that require substantial adjustments for expected returns or uncollectible accounts. For instance, the publisher **John Wiley & Sons, Inc.**, reports accounts receivable of $309.4 million in its April 30, 2020, balance sheet, but this amount is net of an allowance for doubtful accounts of $18.3 million. In addition, the company has recognized a print book sales return reserve net liability balance of $19.6 million. So, Wiley only expects to collect about 88% of the amounts it has billed customers. For such companies, modest changes in expectations of returns or collections can have a material effect on reported income. Wiley reports that a 1% change in the estimated return rate would decrease net income by $1.3 million.

Experience tells us that many companies have used the allowance for uncollectible accounts to shift income from one period into another. For instance, a company may overestimate its allowance in some years. Such an overestimation may have been unintentional, or it may have been an intentional attempt to manage earnings by building up a reserve (during good years) that can be drawn down in subsequent periods in order to increase reported income. Such a reserve is sometimes called a **cookie jar reserve**. Alternatively, a company may underestimate its provision in some years. This underestimation may be unintentional, or it may be an attempt to boost earnings to achieve some desired target. Looking at the patterns in the reconciliation of the allowance for uncollectible accounts may provide some indicators of this behavior.[10]

The MD&A section of a company's 10-K report often provides insights into changes in company policies, customers, or economic conditions to help explain changes in the allowance account. Further, the amount and timing of the uncollectible provision is largely controlled by management. Although external auditors assess the reasonableness of the allowance for uncollectible accounts, auditors do not possess the inside knowledge of management and are, therefore, at an information disadvantage, particularly if a dispute arises.

Some insight can be gained by comparing Microsoft's allowance to those of its competitors. **Exhibit 6.9** illustrates that Microsoft's allowance as a percentage of total receivables is at the lower end of other technology companies, **IBM**, **Intuit Inc.**, and **Alphabet Inc.** These percentages increased for all of these companies, probably reflecting the economic upheavals of the coronavirus pandemic.

---

[10] See McNichols, Maureen and G. Peter Wilson, "Evidence of Earnings Management from the Provision for Bad Debts," *Journal of Accounting Research*, Supplement 1988.

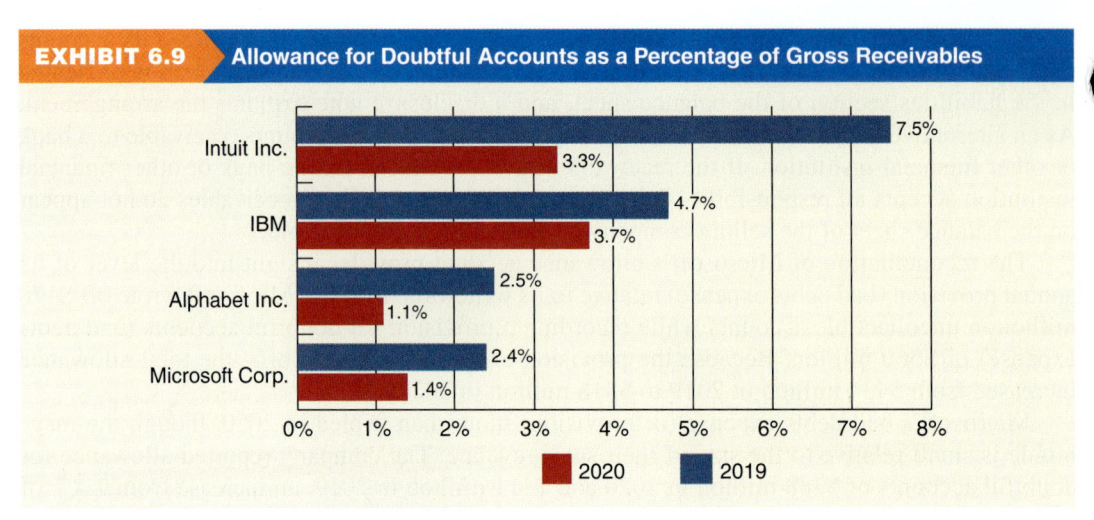

EXHIBIT 6.9 Allowance for Doubtful Accounts as a Percentage of Gross Receivables

Company	2019	2020
Intuit Inc.	7.5%	3.3%
IBM	4.7%	3.7%
Alphabet Inc.	2.5%	1.1%
Microsoft Corp.	2.4%	1.4%

These companies do not have identical fiscal year-ends. For each fiscal year listed above, balance sheets are dated from June 30 to December 31 of that year.

Ultimately, a company makes two representations when reporting accounts receivable (net) in the current asset section of its balance sheet:

1. It expects to collect the asset amount reported on the balance sheet (remember, accounts receivable are reported net of allowance for uncollectible accounts).
2. It expects to collect the asset amount within the next year (implied from its classification as a current asset).

From an analysis viewpoint, we scrutinize the adequacy of a company's provision for its uncollectible accounts. If the provision is inadequate, the cash ultimately collected will be less than what the company is reporting as net receivables.

The financial statement effects of uncollectible accounts are at the point of estimation, not at the time of a write-off. Nevertheless, it is important to remember that management sets the size of the allowance, albeit with auditor assurances.

Review 6-4 LO6-4   Estimating Uncollectible Accounts and Reporting Receivables

At December 31, Engel Company had a balance of $770,000 in its Accounts Receivable account and an unused balance of $7,000 in its Allowance for Uncollectible Accounts. The company then analyzed and aged its accounts receivable as follows:

Current	$468,000
1–60 days past due	244,000
61–180 days past due	38,000
Over 180 days past due	20,000
Total accounts receivable	$770,000

In the past, the company experienced losses as follows: 1% of current balances, 5% of balances 1–60 days past due, 15% of balances 61–180 days past due, and 40% of balances over 180 days past due. The company bases its provision for credit losses on the aging analysis.

Required

a. What amount of uncollectible accounts (bad debts) expense will Engel report in its annual income statement?
b. Show how Accounts Receivable and the Allowance for Uncollectible Accounts appear in its December 31, balance sheet.
c. Assume that Engel's allowance for uncollectible accounts has maintained a historical average of 2% of gross accounts receivable. How do you interpret the level of the current allowance percentage?

continued

continued from previous page

> d. Report the effects for each of the following summary transactions in the financial statement effects template.
>   1. Bad debts expense estimated at the amount determined in part *a*.
>   2. Write off $5,000 in customer accounts.
> e. Prepare journal entries for each transaction in part *d*, and then post the amounts to the appropriate T-accounts.   **Solution on p. 6-54.**

ANALYZING FINANCIAL STATEMENTS

We began this chapter with a discussion of operating income and revenues and proceeded to examine receivables. We now introduce ratios that will aid in our analysis of income, revenue, and receivables. The first ratio is a measure of performance that relates the firm's operating achievements to the resources available. The next ratio, net operating profit margin, relates operating profit to sales. The last two ratios, accounts receivable turnover ratio and the average collection period, aid in the analysis of receivables. Before we discuss these ratios, we examine a commonly used measure of operating profit first introduced in Chapter 5: net operating profit after taxes (NOPAT).

LO6-5 Calculate return on net operating assets, net operating profit after taxes, return on net operating assets, net operating profit margin, accounts receivable turnover, and average collection period.

Net Operating Profit After Taxes (NOPAT)

Net operating profit after taxes (NOPAT) is a widely used measure of operating profitability. NOPAT is calculated as follows:

NOPAT = Net income − [(Nonoperating revenues − Nonoperating expenses) × (1 − Statutory tax rate)]

As described in Appendix A of Chapter 5, we assume that the applicable statutory tax rate on nonoperating revenues and expenses is equal to 25%. To illustrate the calculation of NOPAT, refer to Microsoft's income statement presented in **Exhibit 6.2**. Microsoft reported net income of $44,281 million in 2020. It also reported Other income, net of $77 million. Therefore, Microsoft's NOPAT for 2020 is $44,223 million {$44,281 million − [$77 million × (1 − 0.25)]}. In 2019, Microsoft's NOPAT was $38,693 million {$39,240 million − [$729 million × (1 − 0.25)]}, with the 14% increase in 2020 largely explained by increased demand in Microsoft's products and service (reflected by a 14% increase in sales revenue).

NOPAT is an important measure of profitability. It is similar to net income except that NOPAT focuses exclusively on after-tax operating performance, while net income measures the overall performance of the company and includes both operating and nonoperating components. NOPAT is used as a performance measure by management and analysts alike, and it is also used in a number of ratios, such as the net operating profit margin.

Next, we examine two ratios that allow us to compare operating profitability across firms.

Analysis Objective

We want to gauge the profitability of a company's operations.

Analysis Tool   Return on net operating assets (RNOA).

$$\text{Return on net operating assets (RNOA)} = \frac{\text{NOPAT}}{\text{Average net operating assets}}$$

Applying the Ratio to Microsoft

2018: RNOA = $\frac{\$15{,}509}{\$43{,}796}$ = 0.354 or 35.4%

2019: RNOA = $\frac{\$38{,}693}{\$50{,}469}$ = 0.767 or 76.7%

2020: RNOA = $\frac{\$44{,}223}{\$62{,}292}$ = 0.710 or 71.0%

Microsoft's average total assets for fiscal 2020 total $293,934 ([$301,311 million + $286,556 million]/2), but $122,707 of this amount represents average investments in marketable securities. So, average operating assets are $171,227 million. Microsoft also reports average operating liabilities of $108,935 million. Subtracting this amount from average operating assets gives average net operating assets of $62,292 million.

> **BUSINESS INSIGHT**
>
> **What constitutes "cash," and when is cash operating and when is it nonoperating?** To compute RNOA in this book, we make a simplifying assumption and consider marketable securities and other investments as nonoperating assets, but we consider cash to be an operating asset. This is a matter of judgment for the financial statement user when doing financial statement analysis. The categorization of investment securities as cash or as investments varies across firms. At the end of fiscal 2020, Microsoft had balances of cash and cash equivalents of $13.6 billion and short-term investments of $123.0 billion. But they also disclosed that these amounts—plus cash flow from operations—are expected to be "sufficient to fund our operating activities" and "cash commitments for investing and financing activities," making it difficult to draw a clear distinction between operating and non-operating investments. Other companies include investments in a separate line item on the balance sheet (either in current, long-term assets, or some in each).

Guidance **Return on net operating assets (RNOA)** is conceptually similar to return on assets (ROA) except that it excludes all nonoperating components of income and investment from the calculation. The resulting ratio is a measure of how well the company is performing relative to its core objective. A company can use investments in securities and financial leverage to report a satisfactory level of profit and return overall, even when its primary operating activities are not performing well. RNOA can reveal weaknesses in a company's operating strategy that are not readily apparent from overall measures such as return on equity and return on assets. Microsoft has a very healthy RNOA, though we know that the denominator does not provide an asset value for the company's self-developed intellectual assets. NOPAT grew in 2020, but average net operating assets grew faster, in significant part due to an increase in property and equipment.

Microsoft in Context

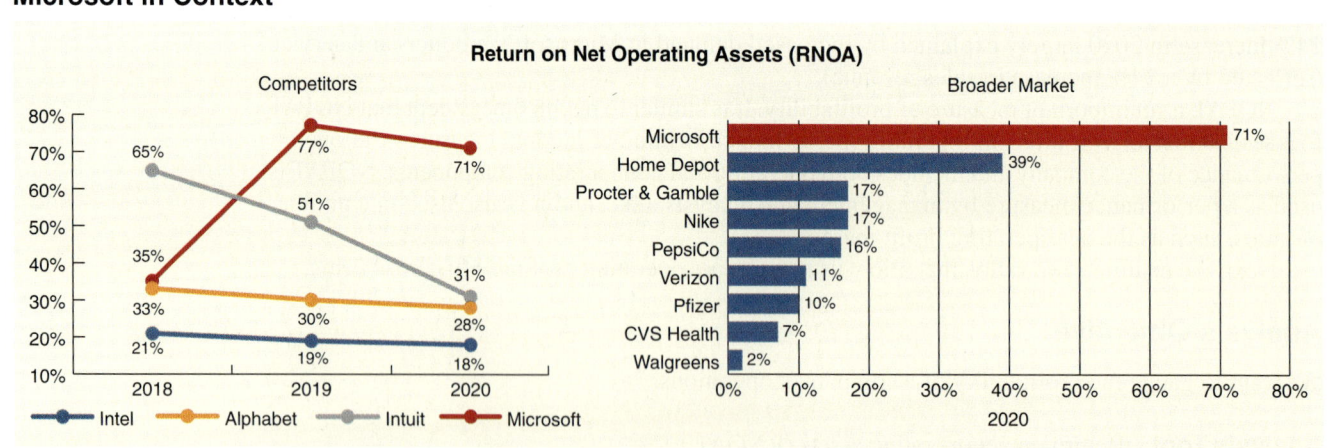

Return on Net Operating Assets (RNOA)

Competitors

Year	Intel	Alphabet	Intuit	Microsoft
2018	21%	33%	65%	35%
2019	19%	30%	51%	77%
2020	18%	28%	31%	71%

Broader Market (2020)

Company	RNOA
Microsoft	71%
Home Depot	39%
Procter & Gamble	17%
Nike	17%
PepsiCo	16%
Verizon	11%
Pfizer	10%
CVS Health	7%
Walgreens	2%

For each fiscal year listed above and in later charts, balance sheets are dated from February 2 to December 31 of that year.

A variation on RNOA is the **return on capital employed**. This ratio examines the return on net operating assets *before* income taxes and is often used to measure performance of business units and division managers within a large organization. Operating managers generally do not have responsibility for income taxes or financing activities. (These functions are typically the responsibility of central management.) Consequently, return on capital employed excludes income taxes and focuses exclusively on the resources made available to the unit manager.

Microsoft does not provide enough information to calculate return on capital employed for individual business units, but we can do so for the company as a whole. From **Exhibit 6.2**, we see that 2020 pretax operating income is $52,959 million. Average net operating assets for 2020, adjusted for income tax assets and liabilities, total $95,930.0 million.[11] Thus, Microsoft's return on capital employed is 55.2% ($52,959 million/$95,930.0 million) for 2020.

Analysis Tool Net operating profit margin (NOPM)

$$\text{Net operating profit margin (NOPM)} = \frac{\text{NOPAT}}{\text{Sales revenue}}$$

Applying the Ratio to Microsoft

2018: NOPM = $\frac{\$15,509}{\$110,360}$ = 0.141 or 14.1%

2019: NOPM = $\frac{\$38,693}{\$125,843}$ = 0.307 or 30.7%

2020: NOPM = $\frac{\$44,223}{\$143,015}$ = 0.309 or 30.9%

Guidance Profit margins are commonly used to compare a company to its competitors and to evaluate the performance of business segments. **Net operating profit margin (NOPM)** is a useful summary measure that focuses on the overall operating profitability of the company relative to its sales revenue.

Microsoft in Context

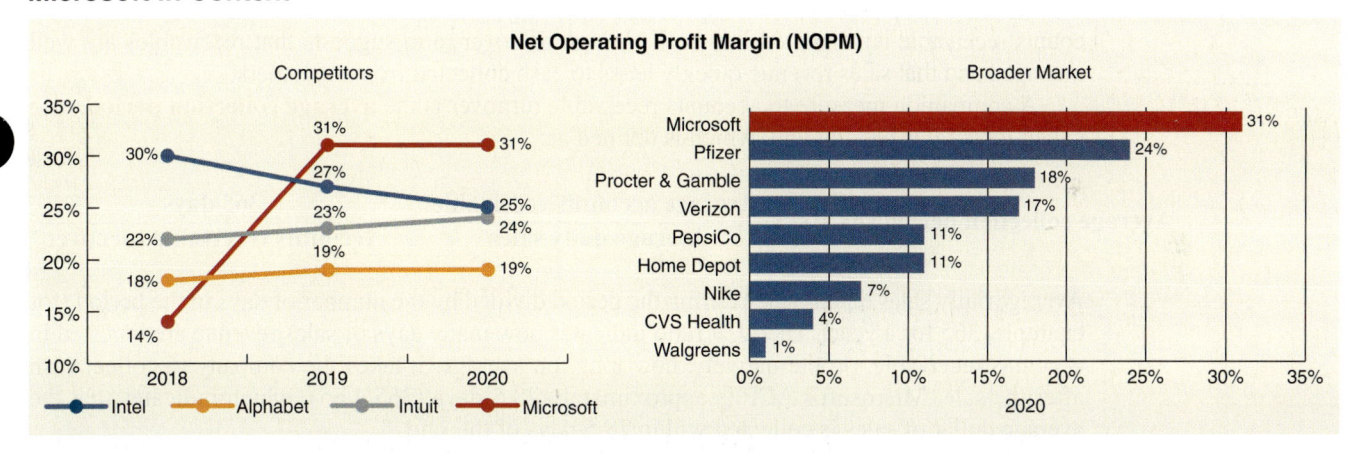

Net Operating Profit Margin (NOPM)

Competitors (2018–2020):
- Intel: 30%, 27%, 25%
- Alphabet: 18%, 19%, 19%
- Intuit: 22%, 23%, 24%
- Microsoft: 14%, 31%, 31%

Broader Market (2020):
- Microsoft: 31%
- Pfizer: 24%
- Procter & Gamble: 18%
- Verizon: 17%
- PepsiCo: 11%
- Home Depot: 11%
- Nike: 7%
- CVS Health: 4%
- Walgreens: 1%

Takeaways Both of Microsoft's return metrics are at the high end of these comparison groups, reflecting returns to its intellectual assets. Retail businesses, such as **Walgreens Boots** and **CVS Health**, tend to have lower operating profit margins than companies in other industries. Retail companies rely more heavily on turnover of operating assets to produce returns, relative to other industries, to achieve a higher value of RNOA. As noted in the introduction, Microsoft's product revenue is not growing, while its service revenue has increased by two-thirds in the past two years. But the margin on its services is significantly lower than the margin on products, so maintaining the same levels of NOPM in the future will be a challenge.

As emphasized in Chapter 5, the calculation of ratios is never the end of the analysis, but rather the beginning. So, the patterns that we see in these ratios should be examined further. For instance, the US Congress enacted a tax reduction at the end of 2017 that had a significant, one-time effect on many companies' tax expense—a topic that we will explore in Chapter 10. Another issue for companies like Microsoft is the recognition of intellectual property assets. In earlier chapters, we explored the differing accounting rules for asset purchases and R&D activities. The former are

---

[11] Because we use operating profit before taxes, accrued income taxes payable, long-term income taxes and deferred income taxes (assets and liabilities) should be excluded when computing net operating assets for this ratio. Microsoft reported average long-term income taxes of $29,522.0 million, average deferred tax liabilities of $218.5 million, and average income taxes payable of $3,897.5 million. Thus, the average net operating assets used to calculate return on capital employed equals $62,292.0 million + ($29,522.0 million + $218.5 million + $3,897.5 million) = $95,930.0 million.

recognized as assets on the balance sheet, while the latter are not—a factor that could influence the denominator in RNOA calculations.

Analysis Objective

We want to evaluate a company's management of its receivables.

Analysis Tool Accounts receivable turnover (ART) and average collection period (ACP)

$$\text{Accounts receivable turnover (ART)} = \frac{\text{Sales revenue}}{\text{Average accounts receivable}}$$

Applying the Accounts Receivable Turnover Ratio to Microsoft

$$2018: \text{ART} = \frac{\$110{,}360}{(\$22{,}431 + \$26{,}481)/2} = 4.51 \text{ times}$$

$$2019: \text{ART} = \frac{\$125{,}843}{(\$26{,}481 + \$29{,}524)/2} = 4.49 \text{ times}$$

$$2020: \text{ART} = \frac{\$143{,}015}{(\$29{,}524 + \$32{,}011)/2} = 4.65 \text{ times}$$

Guidance **Accounts receivable turnover** measures the number of times each year that accounts receivable is converted into cash. A high turnover ratio suggests that receivables are well managed and that sales revenue quickly leads to cash collected from customers.

A companion measure to accounts receivable turnover is the **average collection period**, also called *days sales outstanding*, which is defined as:

$$\text{Average collection period (ACP)} = \frac{\text{Average accounts receivable}}{\text{Average daily sales}} = \frac{365 \text{ days}}{\text{Accounts receivable turnover}}$$

Average daily sales equals sales during the period divided by the number of days in the period (for example, 365 for a year). The ACP ratio indicates how many days of sales revenue are invested in accounts receivable, or alternatively, how long, on average, it takes the company to collect cash after the sale. Microsoft's ACP is approximately 78.5 days (365/4.65), which indicates that the average dollar of sales is collected within 78.5 days of the sale.

Microsoft in Context

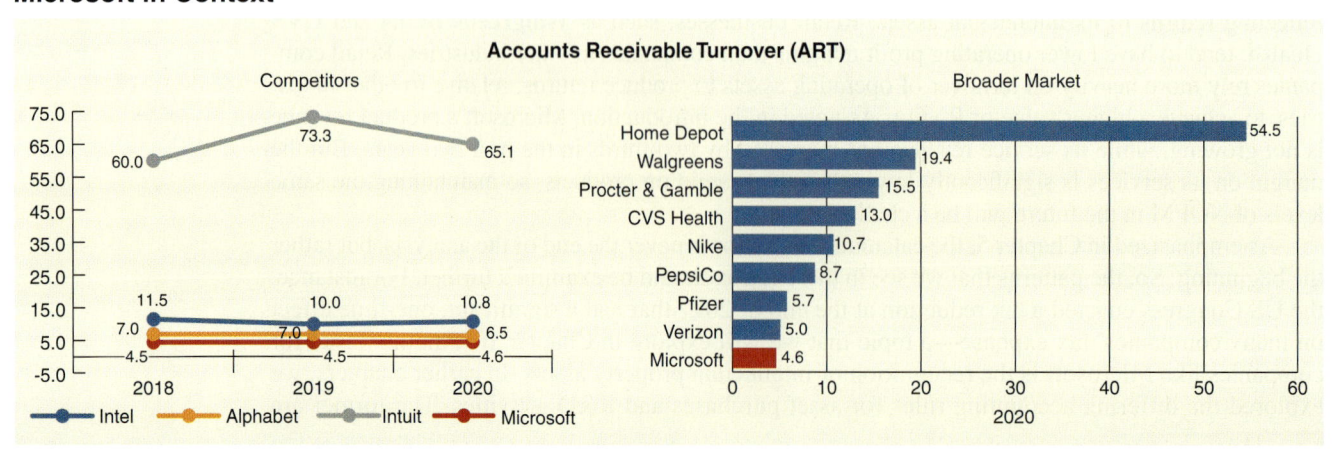

Accounts Receivable Turnover (ART)

Competitors

Year	Intel	Alphabet	Intuit	Microsoft
2018	11.5	7.0	60.0	4.5
2019	10.0	7.0	73.3	4.5
2020	10.8	6.5	65.1	4.6

Broader Market (2020)

Company	ART
Home Depot	54.5
Walgreens	19.4
Procter & Gamble	15.5
CVS Health	13.0
Nike	10.7
PepsiCo	8.7
Pfizer	5.7
Verizon	5.0
Microsoft	4.6

Takeaways The accounts receivable turnover and the average collection period yield valuable insights on at least two dimensions:

1. *Receivables quality.* A change in receivables turnover (and collection period) provides insight into accounts receivable quality. If turnover slows (collection period lengthens), the reason could be deterioration in collectibility of receivables. However, before reaching this conclusion, consider at least three alternative explanations:
   a. A seller can extend its credit terms. If the seller is attempting to enter new markets or take market share from competitors, it may extend credit terms to attract buyers.
   b. A seller can take on longer-paying customers. For example, facing increased competition, many computer and automobile companies began leasing their products, thus reducing the cash outlay for customers and stimulating sales. The change in mix away from cash sales and toward leasing had the effect of reducing receivables turnover and increasing the collection period.
   c. The seller can increase the allowance provision. Receivables turnover is often computed using net receivables (after the allowance for uncollectible accounts). Overestimating the provision reduces net receivables and increases turnover.
2. *Asset utilization.* Asset turnover is an important measure of financial performance, both by managers for internal performance goals, as well as by the market in evaluating companies. High-performing companies must be both efficient (controlling margins and operating expenses) and productive (getting the most out of their asset base). An increase in receivables ties up cash because the receivables must be financed, and slower-turning receivables carry increased risk of loss. One of the first "low-hanging fruits" that companies pursue in efforts to improve asset utilization is efficiency in receivables collection.

Other Considerations Accounts receivable are sometimes used by companies to obtain financing. This is done in one of two ways: (1) the company can use accounts receivable as collateral for a short-term loan in a transaction called *securitization*, or (2) the company can sell its receivables, which is referred to as *factoring*. A thorough discussion of these transactions is beyond the scope of this text. Nonetheless, if a firm uses securitization or factoring of receivables to obtain short-term financing, the amount of accounts receivable listed on the balance sheet is altered which, in turn, affects the ART ratio.

> ### YOU MAKE THE CALL
>
> **You are the Receivables Manager** You are analyzing your receivables turnover report for the period, and you are concerned that the average collection period is lengthening, causing a drop in cash flow from operations. What specific actions can you take to reduce the average collection period?
> [Answers on page 6-32]

Computing NOPAT, RNOA, NOPM, ART, and ACP   LO6-5 **Review 6-5**

The following data were taken from the 2019 10-K reports of **Comcast Corporation** and **Charter Communications**:

($ millions)	Comcast Corp	Charter Communications
Sales revenue	$108,942	$ 45,764
Net income	13,323	1,992
Nonoperating revenues	438	0
Nonoperating expenses	4,567	4,080
Accounts receivable, net (end-of-year)	11,292	2,227
Accounts receivable, net (beginning-of-year)	11,104	1,733
Operating assets (end-of-year)	261,165	148,188
Operating assets (beginning-of-year)	249,538	146,130
Operating liabilities (end-of-year)	70,785	30,299
Operating liabilities (beginning-of-year)	66,123	29,031

continued

Required

a. Compute the following for each company:
   1. Net operating profit after taxes (NOPAT). Assume a 25% statutory tax rate.
   2. Return on net operating assets (RNOA).
   3. Net operating profit margin (NOPM).
   4. Accounts receivable turnover (ART).
   5. Average collection period (ACP).

b. Compare these two companies based on the ratios computed in (a). What inferences can you make about these competitors?

Solution on p. 6-56.

EARNINGS MANAGEMENT

LO6-6 Discuss earnings management and explain how it affects analysis and interpretation of financial statements.

Management choices about transactions, accounting principles, estimates, disclosure, and presentation of income components are an inevitable part of financial reporting. Earnings management occurs when management uses this discretion to mask the underlying economic performance of a company.

There are many motives for earnings management, but these motives generally fall into one of two categories:

1. A desire to mislead some financial statement users about the financial performance of the company to gain economic advantage, or
2. A desire to influence legal contracts that use reported accounting numbers to specify contractual obligations and outcomes.[12]

FYI Earnings management involves earnings quality and management ethics. For the latter, management must consider both legal and personal ethical standards of conduct.

Most earnings management practices relate to aggressive revenue or expense recognition practices. However, financial statement presentation can also be a concern. Below, we identify several examples of potentially misleading reporting.

- *Overly optimistic (or overly pessimistic) estimates.* The use of estimates in accrual accounting is extensive. For instance, revenue recognition requires estimates of things like future discounts and performance awards and the stand-alone value of individual performance obligations. Depreciation expense depends on estimates of useful life, and bad debts expense depends on estimates of future customer payments. Although changes in estimates may be warranted by changes in business conditions, they can have a significant effect on reported net income and, thereby, may provide opportunities for managers to report income that is better (or worse) than it should be.

- *Channel stuffing.* **Channel stuffing** arises when a company uses its market power over customers or distributors to induce them to purchase more goods than necessary to meet their normal needs. Or, the seller may offer significant price reductions to encourage buyers to stock up on its products. Channel stuffing usually occurs immediately before the end of an accounting period and boosts the seller's revenue for that period (while increasing the buyer's inventory). The practice is not illegal, and revenue may be recorded, as long as the transactions meet the necessary criteria for revenue recognition.

- *Strategic timing and disclosure of transactions and nonrecurring gains and losses.* Management has some discretion over the timing of transactions that can affect financial statements. If management has an asset (e.g., a tract of land) with book value less than market value, it can choose when to sell the asset to recognize a gain and maintain steady improvements in net income. This practice is known as **income smoothing**. In some cases, these smoothing effects are reported in combination with other items, making it more difficult to separate recurring amounts from nonrecurring amounts. Or, a company could take a **big bath** by recording a nonrecurring loss in a period of already depressed income. Concentrating bad news in a single period reduces the amount of bad news recognized in other periods. Given adequate disclosure, the astute reader

---

[12] See Healy, Paul M., and James M. Wahlen, "A Review of Earnings Management Literature and Its Implications for Standard Setting," *Accounting Horizons,* December 1999, and Graham, John R., Campbell R. Harvey, and Shiva Rajgopal, "The Economic Implications of Corporate Financial Reporting," *Journal of Accounting & Economics,* December 2005.

of the financial statements will separate nonrecurring income items from persistent operating income, making these income management tactics transparent.

- *Mischaracterizing transactions as arm's-length.* Transfers of inventories or other assets to related entities typically are not recorded until later **arm's-length** sales occur. Sometimes sales are disguised as being sold to unrelated entities to inflate income when (1) the buyer is a related party to the seller, or (2) financing is provided or guaranteed by the seller, or (3) the buyer is a special-purpose entity that fails to meet independence requirements. This financial reporting practice is not consistent with GAAP and may be fraudulent.

> **FYI** An arm's-length transaction is any transaction between two unrelated parties.

The consequence of earnings management is that the usefulness of the information presented in the income statement is compromised. **Quality of earnings** is a term that analysts often use to describe the extent to which reported income reflects the underlying economic performance of a company. Financial statement users must be careful to examine the quality of a company's earnings before using that information to evaluate performance or value its securities.[13]

YOU MAKE THE CALL

You are the Controller While evaluating the performance of your sales staff, you notice that one of the salespeople consistently meets his quarterly sales quotas but never surpasses his goals by very much. You also discover that his customers often return an unusually large amount of product at the beginning of each quarter. What might be happening here? How would you investigate for potential abuse? [Answer on page 6-32]

RESEARCH INSIGHT

Non-GAAP Income Nonrecurring items in income, such as discontinued operations and restructuring charges, make it difficult for investors to determine what portion of income is sustainable into the future. In its 2020 10-K annual report, Microsoft Corporation provided non-GAAP income numbers for 2019 and 2018 (none for 2020). Microsoft's 2019 GAAP numbers included a $2.6 billion tax gain from a one-time transfer of intangible properties for 2019, and the non-GAAP adjustments removed this amount, making non-GAAP net income $2.6 billion lower than GAAP net income. The 2018 adjustment was more substantial. The 2017 Tax Cuts and Jobs Act produced one-time accounting effects for companies like Microsoft. The one-time increase in tax expense was $13.7 billion for Microsoft, resulting in a decrease in net income of 35% from 2017 to 2018. But that $13.7 billion is added to GAAP net income to create a non-GAAP net income that omits this transitory item.

Microsoft has used its non-GAAP adjustments to let financial statement readers see the one-time items affecting its current financial results, but that should not be present in future results. This disclosure should improve forecasts of results for future years. But there may be a temptation for a company to be more strategic in reporting non-GAAP results. Research, however, provides no evidence that more exclusions via non-GAAP income lead to more predictable future cash flows. More important, investors appear to be misled by the exclusions at the time of the non-GAAP income release. The Securities and Exchange Commission has issued Regulation G for non-GAAP disclosures by public companies. Among other requirements, it states that non-GAAP reports be reconciled to the most directly comparable GAAP measure.

Identifying the Financial Statement Effect of Managing Earnings LO6-6 **Review 6-6**

Determine the financial statement impact (overstatement, understatement, or no impact) of each of the following adjustments made by management with the intent to manage earnings. Consider each item separately, and consider the effect only in the period of the adjustment.

continued

---

[13] See Dechow, Patricia, Weili Ge, and Catherine Schrand, "Understanding Earnings Quality: A Review of the Proxies, Their Determinants, and Their Consequences," *Journal of Accounting and Economics*, December, 2010.

continued from previous page

($ millions)		Revenues	Impact on Expenses	Net Income
a.	Increasing the estimate of the useful life of equipment.			
b.	Offering deep discounts in products at year-end, which encourages customers to stock up on product.*			
c.	Expensing in the current year (a pandemic period) amounts prepaid pertaining to maintenance work for the upcoming year.			
d.	Underestimating the expected collectibility of overdue accounts receivable amounts.			
e.	Recognizing sales on products held at a third-party's warehouse, awaiting shipment to customers.*			

Solution on p. 6-56. *Assume selling price exceeds costs.

APPENDIX 6A: Reporting Nonrecurring Items

LO6-7 Describe and illustrate the reporting for nonrecurring items.

In addition to categorizing income statement elements as either operating or nonoperating, it is useful to separate **recurring** components of income from those sources that are **nonrecurring**. Isolating nonrecurring earnings components is useful for two reasons. First, to evaluate company performance or management quality, it is helpful to make comparisons of current performance with prior years and with other companies facing similar economic circumstances. It is easier to make these comparisons if we focus on recurring income components. Nonrecurring income components are likely to be specific to one company and one accounting period, making them irrelevant for comparative purposes. Second, estimation of company value involves forecasts of income and cash flows. Such forecasts are better when we can identify any nonrecurring effects in income and cash flows and then eliminate them from projections. Recurring earnings and cash flows are more **persistent** and, therefore, more useful in estimating company value.

Accounting standards attempt to distinguish some nonrecurring income components. Two of the most common nonrecurring items are:

- **Discontinued operations**—income related to business units that the company has discontinued and sold or plans to sell.
- **Restructuring charges**—expenses and losses related to significant reorganization of a company's operations.

Discontinued Operations

Discontinued operations refer to separately identifiable components of the company that management sells or intends to sell. Recent guidance for discontinued operations (ASU 2014-08) provides that only disposals representing a strategic shift in operations should be reported as discontinued operations. Examples include a disposal of a major geographical segment, a major line of business, or a major equity investment. The new guidance was issued because of concerns that too many disposals of small asset groups were being classified as discontinued operations.

The income or loss of the discontinued operations (net of tax), and the after-tax gain or loss on sale of the unit, are reported in the income statement below income from continuing operations. The segregation of discontinued operations means that its revenues and expenses are *not* reported with revenues and expenses from continuing operations.

To illustrate, assume that Chapman Company's income statement results were the following.

	Continuing Operations	Discontinued Operations	Total
Revenues.	$10,000	$3,000	$13,000
Expenses	7,000	2,000	9,000
Pretax income.	3,000	1,000	4,000
Tax expense (40%).	1,200	400	1,600
Net income	$ 1,800	$ 600	$ 2,400

The reported income statement would then appear with the separate disclosure for discontinued operations (shown in bold, separately net of any related taxes) as follows.

Revenues	$10,000
Expenses	7,000
Pretax income	3,000
Tax expense (40%)	1,200
Income from continuing operations	1,800
Income from discontinued operations, net of income taxes	**600**
Net income	$ 2,400

Revenues and expenses reflect the continuing operations only, and the (persistent) income from continuing operations is reported after deducting the related tax expense. Results from the (transitory) discontinued operations are collapsed into one line item and reported separately net of any related taxes. The same is true for any gain or loss from sale of the discontinued operation's net assets. The net income figure is unchanged by this presentation, but our ability to evaluate and interpret income information is greatly improved.

FYI Income, gains, and losses from discontinued operations are reported separately from other items to alert readers to their transitory nature.

Exit or Disposal Costs

Exit or disposal costs include but are not limited to **restructuring costs**. Exit and disposal costs typically include activities such as consolidating production facilities, reorganizing sales operations, outsourcing product lines, or discontinuing product lines within a business unit or that do not represent a strategic shift in operations. These costs should be separately disclosed if material, but if not material are not required to be shown as a separate line item on the income statement. Often these costs, such as restructuring costs, are material in nature and are shown as a separate line item or are detailed in the notes to the financial statements. These costs are considered transitory because many companies do not engage in restructuring activities every year. As such, these costs should be classified to a transitory category for analysis purposes even though the costs are included in income from continuing operations. Restructuring costs include, but are not limited to, the following types of costs:

1. Employee severance costs
2. Costs to consolidate and close facilities, including asset write-downs

The first of these, **employee severance costs**, represent accrued (estimated) costs for termination of employees as part of a restructuring program. The second part of restructuring costs consists of **asset write-downs**, also called *write-offs* or *charge-offs*. Restructuring activities usually involve closure or relocation of manufacturing or administrative facilities. This process can require the write-down of long-term assets (such as plant assets) and the write-down of inventories that are no longer salable at current carrying costs.

Information summarized from the 2020 10-K financial reports of **GANNETT CO., INC.**:

FYI Management's ability to reduce income using restructuring charges and later reverse some of that charge (creating subsequent period income) reduces earnings quality. U.S. GAAP requires disclosures that enable a financial statement reader to track the restructuring activities and to identify any reversals that occur.

Over the past several years, in furtherance of the Company's cost-reduction and cash-preservation plans, the Company has engaged in a series of individual restructuring programs designed primarily to right-size the Company's employee base, consolidate facilities, and improve operations, including those of recently acquired entities...

Severance and consolidation costs can be summarized as follows for fiscal year 2020 (in $ thousands):

Restructuring charges	Severance and related costs	Facility consolidation and other restructuring-related expenses
Publishing	$55,655	$ 5,197
Digital Marketing Solutions	6,320	343
Corporate and other	24,322	53,894
Total	$86,297	$59,434

The liability for severance and related costs at the end of 2020 is reported as follows (in $ thousands):

Balance at December 31, 2019	$ 30,785
Restructuring provision included in Integration and reorganization costs	86,297
Cash payments	(86,139)
Balance at December 31, 2020	$ 30,943

The restructuring reserve balance is expected to be paid out over the next twelve months.

At the end of fiscal year 2020, GANNETT CO., had an outstanding liability for restructuring costs of $30,943 thousand. That balance represents the costs charged to income prior to December 31, 2020 (but not yet paid) and consists of employee severance and "related" obligations.

RESEARCH INSIGHT

Restructuring Costs and Managerial Incentives Research has investigated the circumstances and effects of restructuring costs. Some research finds that stock prices increase upon announcement of a restructuring as if the market appreciates the company's candor. Research also finds that many companies that reduce income through restructuring costs later reverse those costs, resulting in a substantial income boost for the period of reversal. These reversals often occur when their absence would have yielded an earnings decline. Whether or not the market responds favorably to trimming the fat or simply disregards such transitory items as uninformative, managers have incentives to exclude such income-decreasing items from operating income. These incentives are contractually based, extending from debt covenants and restrictions to managerial bonuses.

YOU MAKE THE CALL

You are the Financial Analyst You are analyzing the financial statements of a company that has reported a large restructuring cost, involving both employee severance and asset write-downs, in its income statement. How do you interpret and treat this cost in your analysis of its current and future period profitability? [Answer on page 6-32]

Review 6-7 LO6-7   Reporting Nonrecurring Items

On April 30 of the current year, Singh Corporation decided to close its operations in Fiji. During the first four months of the year (January through April) these operations had reported a loss of $120,000. Singh paid its employees $12,000 in severance pay. The assets of this operation were sold at a loss of $18,000. The tax rate in Fiji is 30%.

Required
a. If this closure is recorded as discontinued operations, how should it be presented in Singh's income statement?
b. If this closure is classified as a restructuring charge, how would it be presented in Singh's income statement?
c. What would determine whether this event should be reported as discontinued operations or a restructuring charge?

Solution on p. 6-56.

SUMMARY

LO1 Describe and apply the criteria for determining when revenue is recognized. (p. 6-5)
- Revenue is recognized as a company fulfills the performance obligations in its contract with a customer.

LO2 Illustrate revenue and expense recognition when the transaction involves future deliverables and/or multiple elements. (p. 6-8)
- When customers pay prior to the delivery of all elements of the product (or service) package, a contract liability must be recognized.
- When a company recognizes a contract liability, its reported revenue for a period does not coincide with the purchases made by customers in that period.

LO3 Illustrate revenue and expense recognition for long-term projects. (p. 6-11)
- When a company engages in long-term projects, it must determine whether it will transfer control over time, as the project progresses. If it does, then its performance obligation on the contract is fulfilled over time.
- When a company engages in long-term projects, it must determine whether it transfers control over time, as the project progresses. If it does not, then its performance obligation on the contract is fulfilled at a point in time.

- If the long-term project's performance obligations are satisfied over time, the revenue recognition should reflect the value transferred to the customer during the period.

Estimate and account for uncollectible accounts receivable. (p. 6-14)   **LO4**

- Uncollectible accounts are usually estimated by aging the accounts receivable.
- Estimated uncollectible accounts are recorded as a contra-asset called allowance for uncollectible accounts.
- Write-offs of uncollectible accounts are deducted from accounts receivable and from the allowance account.

Calculate return on net operating assets, net operating profit after taxes, return on net operating assets, net operating profit margin, accounts receivable turnover, and average collection period. (p. 6-22)   **LO5**

- Net operating profit after taxes (NOPAT) and the net operating profit margin (NOPM) are measures of the profitability of operating activities.
- Return on net operating assets (RNOA) measures after-tax operating performance relative to available net operating assets; similarly, return on capital employed is a pretax measure that is used to evaluate business unit performance.
- Accounts receivable turnover (ART) and average collection period (ACP) measure the ability of the company to convert receivables into cash through collection.

Discuss earnings management and explain how it affects analysis and interpretation of financial statements. (p. 6-27)   **LO6**

- Earnings management occurs when management uses its discretion to mask the underlying economic performance of a company.
- The consequence of earnings management is that the usefulness of the information presented in the income statement is compromised.

Appendix 6A: Describe and illustrate the reporting for nonrecurring items. (p. 6-29)   **LO7**

- Income or loss from discontinued operations is a transitory (nonrecurring) item that is reported net of income taxes after earnings from continuing operations.
- Restructuring charges include asset write-downs and employee severance costs. Even though these charges are typically reported among earnings from continuing operations, they are classified as transitory for analysis purposes.

GUIDANCE ANSWERS... YOU MAKE THE CALL

You are the Receivables Manager First, you must realize that the extension of credit is an important tool in the marketing of your products, often as important as advertising and promotion. Given that receivables are necessary, there are some methods we can use to speed their collection. (1) We can better screen the customers to whom we extend credit. (2) We can negotiate advance or progress payments from customers. (3) We can use bank letters of credit or other automatic drafting procedures so that billings need not be sent. (4) We can make sure products are sent as ordered to reduce disputes. (5) We can improve administration of past due accounts to provide for more timely notices of delinquencies and better collection procedures.

You are the Controller The salesperson may be channel stuffing or recording sales without a confirmed sales order. The unusual amount of returns suggests that sales revenues are most likely being recognized prematurely. To investigate, you could examine specific sales orders from customers who returned goods early in the following quarter or contact customers directly. Most companies delay bonuses until after an appropriate return period expires and only credit the sales staff with net sales.

You are the Financial Analyst There are two usual components to a restructuring charge: asset write-downs (such as inventories, property, plant, and goodwill) and severance costs. Write-downs occur when the cash flow generating ability of an asset declines, thus reducing its current market value below its book value reported on the balance sheet. Arguably, this decline in cash flow generating ability did not occur solely in the current year and, most likely, has developed over several periods. Delays in loss recognition, such as write-downs of assets, are not uncommon. Thus, prior period income is arguably not as high as reported, and the current period loss is not as great as is reported. Turning to severance costs, their recognition can be viewed as an investment decision by the company that is expected to increase future cash flows (through decreased wages). If this cost accrual is capitalized on the balance sheet, current period income is increased and future period income would bear the amortization of this "asset" to match against future cash flow benefits from severance. This implies that current period income is not as low as reported; however, this adjustment is not GAAP because such severance costs cannot be capitalized. Yet, we can make such an adjustment in our analysis.

KEY RATIOS

Net operating profit after taxes (NOPAT)

NOPAT = Net income − [(Nonoperating revenues − Nonoperating expenses) × (1 − Statutory tax rate)]

Return on net operating assets (RNOA)

$$\text{RNOA} = \frac{\text{NOPAT}}{\text{Average net operating assets}}$$

Accounts receivable turnover (ART)

$$\text{ART} = \frac{\text{Sales revenue}}{\text{Average accounts receivable}}$$

Net operating profit margin (NOPM)

$$\text{NOPM} = \frac{\text{Net operating profit after taxes (NOPAT)}}{\text{Sales revenue}}$$

Average collection period (ACP)

$$\text{ACP} = \frac{\text{Average accounts receivable}}{\text{Average daily sales}} = \frac{365}{\text{Accounts receivable turnover (ART)}}$$

Return on capital employed = $\dfrac{\text{Income from operations before taxes}}{\text{Average net operating assets}}$

Assignments with the MBC logo in the margin are available in myBusinessCourse. See the Preface of the book for details.

MULTIPLE CHOICE

Multiple Choice Answers
1. c
2. b
3. d
4. d
5. a
6. d

1. Which of the following best describes the condition(s) that must be present for the recognition of revenue from a contract with a customer?
   a. Cash payment must have been received from the customer.
   b. All of the performance obligations must be fulfilled.
   c. One of the contract's performance obligations must be fulfilled.
   d. There must be no uncertainty about the amount to be received from the customer.

2. When multiple products or services are bundled and sold for one price, the revenue should be
   a. recognized when the bundle of products or services is sold.
   b. allocated among the distinct performance obligations and recognized as each of these is fulfilled.
   c. deferred until all elements of the bundle are delivered to the customer.
   d. recognized when the customer pays cash for the bundle of products or services.

3. A construction company engages in a contract to build a production facility for a customer. The construction company should recognize revenue as the construction progresses only:
   a. if it receives advance cash payments from the customer.
   b. if it retains title to the project until completion.
   c. if there are no contingent payments (e.g., bonuses, penalties) in the contract with the customer.
   d. if title to the project transfers to the customer as the project progresses.

4. When management selectively excludes some revenues, expenses, gains, and losses from earnings calculated using generally accepted accounting principles, it is an example of
   a. income smoothing.
   b. big bath accounting.
   c. cookie jar accounting.
   d. non-GAAP reporting.

5. If bad debts expense is determined by estimating uncollectible accounts receivable, the entry to record the write-off of a specific uncollectible account would decrease
   a. allowance for uncollectible accounts.
   b. net income.
   c. net book value of accounts receivable.
   d. bad debts expense.

6. If management intentionally underestimates bad debts expense, then net income is
   a. overstated and assets are understated.
   b. understated and assets are overstated.
   c. understated and assets are understated.
   d. overstated and assets are overstated.

Superscript ^A denotes assignments based on Appendix 6A.

QUESTIONS

Q6-1. What is the process that guides firms in the recognition of revenue? What does each of the steps mean? How does this process work for a company like **Abercrombie & Fitch Co.**, a clothing retailer? How would it work for a construction company that builds offices under long-term contracts with developers?

Abercrombie & Fitch
NYSE :: ANF

Q6-2. Why are discontinued operations reported separately from continuing operations in the income statement?

Q6-3. Identify the two typical categories of restructuring costs and their effects on the balance sheet and the income statement.

Q6-4. Explain the concept of a *big bath* and why restructuring costs are often identified with this event.

Q6-5. Why might companies want to manage earnings? Describe some of the tactics that some companies use to manage earnings.

Q6-6. What is the concept of *non-GAAP income* or *pro forma income,* and why has this income measure been criticized?

Q6-7. Why does GAAP allow management to make estimates of amounts that are included in financial statements? Does this improve the usefulness of financial statements? Explain.

Q6-8. How might earnings forecasts that are published by financial analysts encourage companies to manage earnings?

Q6-9. Explain how management can shift income from one period into another by its estimation of uncollectible accounts.

Q6-10. During an examination of Wallace Company's financial statements, you notice that the allowance for uncollectible accounts has decreased as a percentage of accounts receivable. What are the possible explanations for this change?

Q6-11. Under what circumstances would it be correct to say that a company would be better off with more uncollectible accounts?

Q6-12. The FASB allows the aging-of-accounts to report bad debt expense and estimated uncollectibles, but not the percentage-of-sales method. Why?

DATA ANALYTICS

DA6-1. Preparing and Interpreting Sales Data in Excel

Wakeboards Inc. manufactures and sells three types of wakeboards to 50 customers located primarily in oceanside cities in the U.S. The Excel file associated with this exercise contains daily sales data for its three different models over the past year. Using this file, we will drill down to and rank sales by model number, by customer name, by time period.

LO1

PART 1 CREATING PIVOTTABLE ONE

1. Download Excel file DA6-1 found in myBusinessCourse.
2. Prepare a PivotTable showing sales by customer by month. *Hint:* With your cursor on a cell in the worksheet, click on Insert, PivotChart. Drag month into Columns and Customer name into Rows, and desired Model (such as Model 1) into Values.
3. Answer the following questions based upon data in your PivotTable.
    a. How many units of Model 1 did Villager Store purchase for the year?
    b. How many units of Model 1 did Carmel Sports purchase in April?
    c. How many units of Model 2 did West Loop Inc. purchase during the year?
    d. How many units of Model 2 did Marina Inc. purchase in July?
    e. How many units of Model 3 did East Beach purchase in May? What dates were the purchases? *Hint:* Double-click on the total purchases by the customer in May and a worksheet will automatically open with the date details.
4. Apply conditional formatting to the PivotTable, highlighting all monthly orders > 50 units of Model 1. *Hint:* Highlight cells in the month column of the table; then under the Home tab, click on Conditional formatting in the Styles group. Click Highlight cell rules, Greater than and specify your rule.
5. List the companies with four or more orders that are greater than 50 units of Model 1.

PART 2 CREATING PIVOTTABLE TWO

1. Prepare a second PivotTable showing the total sales of Model 1 by month. *Hint:* Drag Months to Columns and Model 1 Sales Units to Values.
2. List the amount of the highest monthly sales and the month in which it occurs.
3. Calculate the number of months where unit sales fall below 500 units.

LO2 DA6-2. Preparing Excel Visualizations to Analyze Industry Trends Over Time

The file associated with this exercise includes data extracted from the Estimates of Monthly Retail and Food Services Sales by Kind of Business obtained at the United States Census Bureau at https://www.census.gov/retail/index.html. In this exercise, we will analyze the trends in sales of *automobile and other motor vehicles* over a five-year period.

REQUIRED

1. Download Excel file DA6-2 found in myBusinessCourse.
2. Transpose the data so that it is shown in a column instead of a long row. *Hint:* Copy, Paste Special, Transpose.
3. Prepare a line chart showing trends in the sales of automobile and other motor vehicle dealers from 2017 to 2021. *Hint:* Highlight data and open Insert tab. Click Line graph in Charts group and select one of the 2-D graphs.
4. Answer the following questions using the visualization for reference.
   a. What was the lowest month of sales during the period of January 2017 to June of 2021?
   b. What was the peak month of sales during the period of January 2017 to June of 2021?
   c. How would you describe the trends in 2020 through the first half of 2021?
   d. What is a likely cause of the low point described in part *a*?

LO4 DA6-3. Preparing Accounts Receivable Aging Using Excel

A review of open invoices of Sketchers Inc. results in a schedule shown in the Excel file associated with this exercise. For this exercise, we convert the list of open invoices into an accounts receivable aging schedule.

PART 1 CLEANING THE DATA

1. Download Excel file DA6-3 found in myBusinessCourse.
2. Separate the items listed in one column in the worksheet into three columns using Text to Columns feature under the Data tab.
3. Determine which method to use to divide the data into columns, delimited or fixed width.
4. List the invoice that required a manual adjustment after applying the Text to columns feature.
5. Create a new column in your worksheet that calculates the number of days the invoices are outstanding. *Hint:* Enter: Dec 31 (the date of reference) in a new cell; next, in a new column, for each invoice, subtract the cell holding each invoice date from the cell holding Dec 31 (using an absolute reference). Add $ before the column and row cell reference in a formula to make it absolute. Absolute references don't change when formulas are copied. Change the format in your new column to Number, if necessary. Add headings to your columns.
6. Determine how many days invoice #204 is outstanding based upon data included in your worksheet.

PART 2 CREATING A PIVOTTABLE

1. Create a PivotTable which results in an aging schedule that lists invoices in categories of (1) less than 30 days due, (2) 31–60 days due, (3) 60–90 days due, and (4) greater than 90 days due. *Hint:* After selecting your data and creating a PivotTable, drag Days outstanding to Rows, and drag Amount to Values. PivotTables are created by highlighting the data, including column titles, and clicking PivotTable on the Insert tab. To group your PivotTable into 30-day increments, right-click on the first column, select Group, and enter 1 for "starting," enter 90 for "ending," and enter 30 for "by." Lastly, drag Invoice to Rows to show invoices within each aging category.
2. Determine the total amount in each category, 1–30, 31–60, 61–90, and >91 based on data in the PivotTable.
3. Determine how many invoices are in the 61–90 day category based on data in the PivotTable. *Hint:* Copy the PivotTable from 1. Remove Invoice number from Rows. Open the dropdown menu next to Sum of Amount in the Values box and select Value Field Settings. Select Count in the Summarize value field by box.
4. Create a new PivotTable, updating the aging categories to show aging categories by 30 days through 180 days past due.

5. Determine the total amount in each category, 1–30, 31–60, 61–90, 91–120, 121–150, 151–180 and >181.
6. Determine how many invoices are in the 151–180 category.

DA6-4. Preparing Tableau Visualizations of Accounting Receivable Aging
Available in myBusinessCourse, this problem uses Tableau to create accounts receivable aging visualizations based on invoice data provided for Hugo Enterprises.

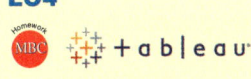

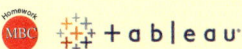

DA6-5. Preparing Tableau Visualizations of Accounting Receivable Aging
Available in myBusinessCourse, this problem uses Tableau to create accounts receivable aging visualizations based on invoice data provided for Javier Enterprises.

DATA VISUALIZATION

Data Visualization Activities are available in myBusinessCourse. These assignments use Tableau Dashboards to expose students to visual depictions of data and introduce students to data analytics through data visualizations. These exercises are easily assignable and auto graded by MBC.

MINI EXERCISES

M6-13. Computing Revenues on Long-Term Projects
In 2021, Bartov Corporation agreed to build a warehouse for $1,900,000. Expected costs for the warehouse follow: 2022, $300,000; 2023, $750,000; and 2024, $375,000. Assume that Bartov completed the warehouse on time and on budget, that Bartov's performance obligation for the warehouse is fulfilled over time and that the costs incurred provide a close approximation of the value conveyed to the customer. Compute revenues, expenses, and income for each year 2022 through 2024.

M6-14. Assessing Revenue Recognition of Companies
Identify and explain when each of the following companies should recognize revenue.

    a. **The GAP Inc.**: The GAP is a retailer of clothing items for all ages.
    b. **Merck & Company Inc.**: Merck engages in the development, manufacturing, and marketing of pharmaceutical products. It sells its drugs to retailers like **CVS Health Corporation** and **Walgreens Boots Alliance, Inc.**
    c. **Deere & Company**: Deere manufactures heavy equipment. It sells equipment to a network of independent distributors, who in turn sell the equipment to customers. Deere provides financing and insurance services both to distributors and to customers.
    d. **Bank of America Corporation**: Bank of America is a banking institution. It lends money to individuals and corporations and invests excess funds in marketable securities.
    e. **Johnson Controls Inc.**: Johnson Controls manufactures products for the U.S. government under long-term contracts.

The GAP Inc.
NYSE :: GPS
Merck & Company Inc.
NYSE :: MRK
CVS Health Corporation
NYSE :: CVS
Walgreens Boots Alliance, Inc.
NYSE :: WBA
Deere & Company
NYSE :: DE
Bank of America Corporation
NYSE :: BAC
Johnson Controls, INC.
NYSE :: JCI

M6-15. Estimating Revenue Recognition with Right of Return
The Unlimited Company offers an unconditional return policy for its retail clothing business. It normally expects 2% of sales at retail selling prices to be returned at some point prior to the expiration of the return period, and returned items cannot be resold. Assuming that it records total sales of $10 million for the current period, how much net revenue would it report for this period?

M6-16. Accounting for Long-Term Contracts
Halsey Building Company signed a contract to build an office building for $20,000,000. The scheduled construction costs follow.

Year	Cost
Year 1	$ 4,500,000
Year 2	7,500,000
Year 3	3,000,000
Total	$15,000,000

The building should be completed in Year 3.

For each year, compute the revenue, expense, and gross profit reported for this construction project under each of the following assumptions:

a. Halsey's performance obligation to build the office building is fulfilled as construction proceeds, and the cost incurred is an accurate reflection of the value transferred to the customer.

b. Halsey's contract does not transfer ownership rights to the customer until the building is completed.

LO1, 2   M6-17. Explaining Revenue Recognition and Bundled Sales

A.J. Smith Electronics is a retail consumer electronics company that also sells extended warranty contracts for many of the products that it carries. The extended warranty provides coverage for three years beyond expiration of the manufacturer's warranty. In 2022, A.J. Smith sold extended warranties amounting to $2,040,000. The warranty coverage for all of these begins in 2023 and runs through 2025. The total expected cost of providing warranty services on these contracts is $600,000 and is expected to be incurred evenly over the three-year warranty period.

a. How should A.J. Smith recognize revenue on the extended warranty contracts? Assume that providing the warranty coverage is considered a single performance obligation that is fulfilled over time.

b. Estimate the revenue, expense, and gross profit reported from these contracts in the year(s) that the revenue is recognized.

c. Also in 2022, as a special promotion, A.J. Smith sold a digital camera (retail price $300), a digital photograph printer (retail price $125), and an extended warranty contract for each (total retail price $75) as a package for a special price of $399. The extended warranty covers the period from 2023 through 2025. The company sold 240 of these camera–printer packages. Compute the revenue that A.J. Smith should recognize in each year from 2022 through 2025.

LO4   M6-18. Reporting Uncollectible Accounts and Accounts Receivables (FSET)

Mohan Company estimates its uncollectible accounts by aging its accounts receivable and applying percentages to various aged categories of accounts. Mohan computes a total of $4,200 in estimated losses as of December 31. Its Accounts Receivable has a balance of $196,000, and its allowance for Uncollectible Accounts has an unused balance of $1,000 before adjustment at December 31.

a. What is the amount of bad debts expense that Mohan will report during the year?

b. Show the effect of the adjustment to the allowance for Uncollectible Accounts in the financial statement effects template.

c. Determine the net amount of accounts receivable reported in current assets at December 31.

LO4   M6-19. Analyzing the Allowance for Uncollectible Accounts Using T-Accounts

Using the information in M6-18, set up T-accounts for both Bad Debt Expense and Allowance for Uncollectible Accounts. Enter any beginning balances and effects from the information provided (including your results from parts *a* and *b*). Explain the numbers for each of your T-accounts.

LO4   M6-20. Explaining the Allowance Method for Accounts Receivable

At a recent board of directors meeting of Ascot, Inc., one of the directors expressed concern over the allowance for uncollectible accounts appearing in the company's balance sheet. "I don't understand this account," he said. "Why don't we just show accounts receivable at the amount owed to us and get rid of that allowance?" Respond to that director's question. Include in your response (a) an explanation of why the company has an allowance account, (b) what the balance sheet presentation of accounts receivable is intended to show, and (c) how the concept of expense recognition relates to the analysis and presentation of accounts receivable.

LO4, 5   M6-21. Analyzing the Allowance for Uncollectible Accounts

Following is the current asset section from the **Ralph Lauren Corporation** balance sheet:

Ralph Lauren Corporation
NYSE :: RL

($ millions)	March 28, 2020	March 30, 2019
ASSETS		
Current assets:		
Cash and cash equivalents.	$1,620.4	$ 584.1
Short-term investments.	495.9	1,403.4
Accounts receivable, net of allowances of $276.2 million and $192.2 million. . .	277.1	398.1
Inventories	736.2	817.8
Income tax receivable.	84.8	32.1
Prepaid expenses and other current assets	160.8	359.3
Total current assets	$3,375.2	$3,594.8

The 2020 allowance consists of $204.7 for returns and $71.5 for uncollectible accounts. The amounts for 2019 were $176.5 and $15.7.

a. Compute the gross amount of accounts receivable for both 2020 and 2019. Compute the percentage of the allowance for uncollectible accounts relative to the gross amount of accounts receivable for each of these years.
b. How do you interpret the change in the percentage of the allowance for uncollectible accounts relative to total accounts receivable computed in part *a*?
c. Ralph Lauren reported net sales of $6,159.8 million in 2020. Compute its accounts receivable turnover and average collection period.

M6-22. Analyzing Accounts Receivable Changes   LO4

The comparative balance sheets of Sloan Company reveal that accounts receivable (before deducting allowances) increased by $21,000 during the year. During the same time period, the allowance for uncollectible accounts increased by $2,940. If sales revenue was $168,000 during the year and bad debts expense was 2% of sales, how much cash was collected from customers during the year?

M6-23. Evaluating Accounts Receivable Turnover for Competitors   LO5

The Procter & Gamble Company and **Colgate-Palmolive Company** report the following sales and accounts receivable balances ($ millions):

Procter & Gamble			Colgate-Palmolive		
Fiscal Year	Net Sales	Accounts Receivable	Fiscal Year	Sales	Accounts Receivable
June 30, 2020	$70,950	$4,178	December 31, 2019	$15,693	$1,440
June 30, 2019	67,684	4,951	December 31, 2018	15,544	1,400

The Procter & Gamble Company
NYSE :: PG

Colgate-Palmolive Company
NYSE :: CL

a. Compute accounts receivable turnover and average collection period for both companies.
b. Identify and discuss a potential explanation for the difference between these competitors' accounts receivable turnover.

M6-24. Analyzing Accounts Receivable Changes (FSET)   LO4

During the year, Grant Corporation recorded credit sales of $2,560,000 and bad debts expense of $33,600. Write-offs of uncollectible accounts totaled $31,200, and one account, worth $9,600 that had been written off in an earlier year, was collected during the year.

a. Report each of the above transactions in the financial statement effects template to show the effect of these entries on the balance sheet and income statement.
b. If net accounts receivable increased by $220,000, how much cash was collected from credit customers during the year? Report the transaction in the financial statement effects template.

M6-25. Recording Accounts Receivable Changes   LO4

Using the information from M6-24:

a. Prepare journal entries to record each of these transactions.
b. If net accounts receivable increased by $176,000, how much cash was collected from credit customers during the year? Prepare a journal entry to record cash collections.
c. Set up T-accounts and post each of the transactions in parts *a* and *b* to them.

M6-26. Analyzing Unearned Revenue Changes   LO2

Finn Publishing Corp. produces a monthly publication aimed at competitive swimmers, with articles profiling current stars of the sport, advice from coaches, and advertising by swimwear companies, training organizations, and others. The magazine is distributed through newsstands and bookstores, and by mail to subscribers. The most common subscription is for twelve months. When Finn Publishing receives payment of an annual subscription, it records an Unearned Revenue liability that is reduced by 1/12th each month as publications are provided.

The table below provides four years of revenues from the income statement and unearned revenue from the balance sheet. (All amounts in $ thousands.)

Fiscal Year	Revenue	Unearned Revenue Liability (End of Year)
Year 1	$72,000	$30,000
Year 2	82,500	36,000
Year 3	93,000	39,000
Year 4	93,000	37,000

a. Calculate the growth in revenue from Year 1 to Year 2, Year 2 to Year 3, and Year 3 to Year 4.
b. Calculate the amount of customer purchases in Year 2, Year 3, and Year 4. Customer purchases are defined as sales made at newsstands and bookstores, plus the amount paid for new or renewal subscriptions. Again, calculate the growth rates from Year 2 to Year 3 and from Year 3 to Year 4.
c. Explain the differences in growth rates between parts *a* and *b* above.

LO2 **M6-27. Applying Revenue Recognition Criteria**

Commtech, Inc., designs and sells cellular phones. The company creates the technical specifications and the software for its products, though it outsources the production of the phones to an overseas contract manufacturer. Commtech has arrangements to sell its phones to the major wireless communications companies who, in turn, sell the phones to end customers packaged with calling plans.

The product life cycle for a phone model is about six months, and Commtech recognizes revenue at the time of delivery to the wireless communications company. The product team for the CD924 model has met to consider a possible modification to the phone. The software team has developed an improved global positioning application for a new phone model, and this application works in the CD924. It could be uploaded to existing phones through the wireless networks.

Marketing's analysis of focus groups and customer feedback is that further sales of the CD924 would be enhanced significantly if the new application were made available. The software engineers have demonstrated that the new GPS application can be successfully sent wirelessly to the CD924.

However, the finance manager points out that Commtech's financial statements have been based on the assumption that the company's phones do not involve multiple performance obligations, like upgrades. All revenue is recognized at the point of sale to the wireless communications companies. Like many communications hardware companies, Commtech has been under pressure to demonstrate its financial performance. Offering an upgrade to the CD924's navigation capabilities would probably be viewed as a significant deliverable in terms of customer value, and the finance manager says that "the accounting won't let us do it."

How should the product team proceed?

LO6 **M6-28. Earnings Management and the Allowance for Doubtful Accounts**

Verdi Co. builds and sells PC computers to customers. The company sells most of its products for immediate payment but also extends credit to some customers. The industry is competitive, and in the most recent year many competitors showed declines in revenue. However, Verdi Co. showed stable revenues. It is later revealed that Verdi Co. made sales and extended credit to customers previously deemed to have credit scores too low for the company to extend credit. The company did not disclose this practice in its financial statements or elsewhere.

a. Explain how this practice would have enabled Verdi Co. to show stable sales.
b. How should Verdi Co. have accounted for these additional sales and related receivables in its financial statements?
c. How would the actions by Verdi Co. in the current period affect financial statements in future periods if the customers cannot pay for the computers they purchased on credit?

EXERCISES

LO1, 2, 3 **E6-29. Assessing Revenue Recognition Timing**

L Brands, Inc.
NYSE :: LB
Boeing Company
NYSE :: BA
United Natural Foods, Inc.
NYSE :: UNFI
Wells Fargo & Company
NYSE :: WFC
Harley-Davidson, Inc.
NYSE :: HOG
Gannett Co., Inc.
NYSE::GCI

Discuss and justify when each of the following businesses should recognize revenues:

a. A clothing retailer like **L Brands, Inc.**
b. A contractor like **The Boeing Company** that performs work under long-term government contracts.
c. An operator of grocery stores like **United Natural Foods, Inc.**
d. A residential real estate developer who constructs only speculative houses and later sells these houses to buyers.
e. A banking institution like **Wells Fargo & Company** that lends money for home mortgages.
f. A manufacturer like **Harley-Davidson, Inc.**
g. A publisher of newspapers like **Gannett Co., Inc.**

LO1, 2, 3 **E6-30. Contract Assets and Liabilities (FSET)**

Haskins, Inc., has reached an agreement with a customer, Skaife Corporation, to deliver 300 units of a customized product. The standard billing price per unit is $1,000, and there are no discounts, so Skaife Corporation will pay $300,000 in total. At the time of the agreement on April 6, Skaife Corporation provides a $60,000 cash deposit to Haskins, Inc. Haskins agrees to deliver 180 units to Skaife Corporation on May 31 and at that time, Haskins can send an invoice for $75,000 to be paid by Skaife Corporation on June 15. The remaining 120 units are to be delivered on July 15, accompanied by an invoice for the remaining amount of the total $300,000 purchase price to be paid on July 31.

REQUIRED
Assume that Haskins, Inc., has no uncertainties about its own ability to meet the terms of the contract or about Skaife Corporation's ability and willingness to pay. Report the events described above in the financial statement effects template (leaving out the accounting for Haskins, Inc.'s costs).

E6-31. Recording Contract Assets and Liabilities
Using the information from E6-30, provide the journal entries to record the events (leaving out the accounting for Haskin, Inc.'s costs).

E6-32. Constructing and Assessing Income Statements for Long-Term Project
Assume that **General Electric Company** agreed in February 2022 to construct an electricity generating facility for **Eversource Energy**, a utility serving the Boston area. The contract price of $600 million is to be paid as follows: $240 million at the time of signing; $120 million on December 31, 2022; and $240 million at completion in May 2023. General Electric incurred the following costs in constructing the power plant: $120 million in 2022, and $360 million in 2023. The construction of the power generating facility is considered to be a single performance obligation.

General Electric Company
NYSE :: GE
Eversource Energy
NYSE :: ES

a. Compute the amount of General Electric's revenue, expense, and income for both 2022 and 2023 assuming that its performance obligation is fulfilled over time and that the costs it incurs are reflective of the value conveyed to Eversource.
b. Compute the amount of GE's revenue, expense, and income for both 2022 and 2023 assuming that its performance obligation to construct the facility is fulfilled at a point in time (at the completion of construction).
c. What performance ratios would be affected by the different contract terms in parts (a) and (b)?

E6-33. Distinct Performance Obligations
Floyd Corporation is a large engineering and construction company that designs and builds office buildings, apartment buildings, distribution warehouses, and other structures for its customers. Projects usually begin with a design and engineering phase, followed by construction of the customer's facility. The design/engineering and construction activities take place in separate divisions of Floyd Corporation, and these two divisions bill separately for their work.

A typical three-year project might have the following pattern of work and billing (in $ millions).

| | Design/Engineering || Construction || Total ||
Year	Cost Incurred	Billings to Customer	Cost Incurred	Billings to Customer	Cost Incurred	Billings to Customer
1.......	$14	$20	$ 0	$ 0	$14	$20
2.......	4	6	30	24	34	30
3.......	2	4	20	36	22	40
Total ...	$20	$30	$50	$60	$70	$90

REQUIRED
a. Assume that Floyd Corporation determines that the work of the design/engineering division and the construction division are separate performance obligations, that these performance obligations are satisfied over time, and that cost incurred is reflective of the value transferred to the customer. For years 1, 2, and 3, determine the amount that Floyd Corporation will recognize in revenue and expense. What is the margin percentage reported in each year?
b. Assume that Floyd Corporation determines that the work of the design/engineering division and the construction division requires too much coordination to be considered separate performance obligations. The combined performance obligation is satisfied over time, and cost incurred is reflective of the value transferred to the customer. For years 1, 2, and 3, determine the amount that Floyd Corporation will recognize in revenue and expense. What is the margin percentage reported in each year?
c. If this is a typical project, how does the performance obligation assessment affect the company's financial statements? For example, how is the debt-to-equity ratio (total liabilities ÷ total shareholders' equity) affected?

LO2 **E6-34. Accounting for Contracts with Multiple Performance Obligations (FSET)**
Amazon.com, Inc., provides the following description of its revenue recognition policies in its second quarter of 2020 10-K report.

> **Revenue**
> Revenue is measured based on the amount of consideration that we expect to receive, reduced by estimates for return allowances, promotional discounts, and rebates. Revenue also excludes any amounts collected on behalf of third parties, including sales and indirect taxes. In arrangements where we have multiple performance obligations, the transaction price is allocated to each performance obligation using the relative stand-alone selling price. We generally determine stand-alone selling prices based on the prices charged to customers or using expected cost plus a margin.
> A description of our principal revenue generating activities is as follows:
>
> *Retail sales*—We offer consumer products through our online and physical stores. Revenue is recognized when control of the goods is transferred to the customer, which generally occurs upon our delivery to a third-party carrier or, in the case of an Amazon delivery, to the customer.
>
> *Third-party seller services*—We offer programs that enable sellers to sell their products in our stores and fulfill orders through us. We are not the seller of record in these transactions. The commissions and any related fulfillment and shipping fees we earn from these arrangements are recognized when the services are rendered, which generally occurs upon delivery of the related products to a third-party carrier or, in the case of an Amazon delivery, to the customer.
>
> *Subscription services*—Our subscription sales include fees associated with Amazon Prime memberships and access to content including digital video, audiobooks, digital music, ebooks, and other non-AWS subscription services. Prime memberships provide our customers with access to an evolving suite of benefits that represent a single stand-ready obligation. Subscriptions are paid for at the time of or in advance of delivering the services. Revenue from such arrangements is recognized over the subscription period.
>
> *AWS*—Our AWS sales arrangements include global sales of compute, storage, database, and other services. Revenue is allocated to services using stand-alone selling prices and is primarily recognized when the customer uses these services, based on the quantity of services rendered, such as compute or storage capacity delivered on-demand. Certain services, including compute and database, are also offered as a fixed quantity over a specified term, for which revenue is recognized ratably. Sales commissions we pay in connection with contracts that exceed one year are capitalized and amortized over the contract term.
>
> *Other*—Other revenue primarily includes sales of advertising services, which are recognized as ads are delivered based on the number of clicks or impressions.

a. What is an "arrangement with multiple performance obligations? How are revenues recognized in such arrangements?

b. Suppose that Amazon.com sells a Fire Tablet with a one-year membership in Amazon Prime. Assume that the device has a stand-alone selling price of $165, and a one-year Prime membership costs $180. Suppose the price charged for the combination is $300, and a customer buys the combination on July 1. What amount of revenue would Amazon recognize in the third calendar quarter (July through September)? How would the remaining revenues be recognized?

c. Report the July 1 transaction described in part b using the financial statement effects template.

LO2 **E6-35. Recording Entries for Contracts with Multiple Performance Obligations**
Referring to the information in E6-34, record the July 1 transaction described in part *b* in journal entry form.

LO5 **E6-36. Computing NOPAT, NOPM, and RNOA**
LVMH Moët Hennessy Louis Vuitton SE (LVMH) is a French multinational luxury goods conglomerate headquartered in Paris. The following information is selected from their 2020 annual report.

(€ millions)	2020	2019
Revenue	44,651	53,670
Operating income	7,972	11,273
Net financial income/(expense)	(608)	(559)
Net income	4,702	7,171
Operating assets	107,932	95,592
Operating liabilities	45,139	45,431

LVMH has an income tax rate of approximately 30%.

a. Compute LVMH's net operating profit after taxes (NOPAT) for 2020 and 2019.
b. Compute LVMH's net operating profit margin (NOPM) for each year.
c. Compute LVMH's return on net operating assets (RNOA) for 2020.

E6-37. Applying Revenue Recognition Criteria LO1, 6

Simpyl Technologies, Inc., manufactures electronic equipment used to facilitate control of production processes and tracking of assets using RFID and other technologies. Since its initial public offering in 1996, the company has shown consistent growth in revenue and earnings, and the stock price has reflected that impressive performance.

Operating in a very competitive environment, Simpyl Technologies provides significant bonus incentives to its sales representatives. These representatives sell the company's products directly to end customers, to value-added resellers, and to distributers.

Consider the four situations below. In each case, determine whether Simpyl Technologies can recognize revenue at this time. Describe the reasons for your judgment.

a. When selling directly to the end customer, Simpyl Technologies requires a sales contract with authorized signatures from the customer company. At the end of Simpyl's fiscal year, sales representative A asks to book revenue from a customer. The customer's purchasing manager has confirmed the intention to complete the purchase, but the contract has only one of the two required signatures. The second person is traveling and will return to the office in a few days (but after the end of Simpyl's fiscal year). The inventory to fulfill the order is sitting in Simpyl's warehouse. Can Simpyl recognize revenue at this time?

b. Sales representative B has an approved contract to deliver units that must be customized to meet the customer's specifications. Just prior to the end of the fiscal year, the uncustomized units are shipped to an intermediate staging area where they will be reconfigured to meet the customer's requirements. Can Simpyl recognize revenue on the basic, uncustomized units at this time?

c. Sales representative C has finalized an order from a value-added reseller who regularly purchases significant volumes of Simpyl's products. The products have been delivered to the customer at the beginning of the fiscal year, and Simpyl Technologies has no further responsibilities for the items. However, the sales representative (with the regional sales manager) is still conducting negotiations with the value-added reseller as to the volume discounts that will be offered for the current year. Can Simpyl recognize revenue on the items delivered to the customer?

d. Sales representative D has finalized an order from a distributor, and the items have been delivered. However, an examination of the distributor's financial condition shows that it does not have the resources to pay Simpyl for the items it has purchased. It needs to sell those items, so the resulting proceeds can be used to pay Simpyl. Can Simpyl recognize revenue on the items delivered to the distributor?

E6-38. Reporting Uncollectible Accounts and Accounts Receivable (FSET) LO4

LaFond Company analyzes its accounts receivable at December 31 and arrives at the aged categories below along with the percentages that are estimated as uncollectible.

Age Group	Accounts Receivable	Estimated Loss %
Current (not past due)	$375,000	0.5%
1–30 days past due	135,000	1.0
31–60 days past due	30,000	2.0
61–120 days past due	16,500	5.0
121–180 days past due	9,000	10.0
Over 180 days past due	6,000	25.0
Total accounts receivable	$571,500	

At the beginning of the fourth quarter, there was a credit balance of $6,525 in the Allowance for Uncollectible Accounts. During the fourth quarter, LaFond Company wrote off $5,745 in receivables as uncollectible.

a. What amount of bad debts expense will LaFond report for the year?
b. What is the balance of accounts receivable that it reports on its December 31 balance sheet?
c. Report (1) the write-off of accounts receivable as uncollectible and (2) bad debt expense calculated in part a using the financial statement effects template.
d. Suppose LaFond wrote off $1,500 more in receivables in the quarter. Or, $1,500 less. How would that affect the bad debt expense for the fourth quarter? How does the aging of accounts deal with the inevitable differences between estimated cash collections and actual cash collections?

LO4 E6-39. Analyzing T-Accounts in Accounting for Uncollectible Accounts
Referring to the information in E6-38, set up T-accounts for both Bad Debts Expense and the Allowance for Uncollectible Accounts. Enter any unadjusted balances along with the dollar effects of the information described (including your results from parts *a* and *b*). Explain the numbers in each of the T-accounts.

LO4, 5 E6-40. Analysis of Accounts Receivable and Allowance for Doubtful Accounts (FSET)
Steelcase, Inc., reported the following amounts in its 2020 and 2019 10-K reports (years ended February 28, 2020, and February 22, 2019).

Steelcase, Inc.
NYSE :: SCS

($ millions)	2020	2019
From the income statement:		
Revenue	$3,723.7	$3,443.2
From the balance sheet:		
Accounts receivable, net	372.4	390.3
Customer deposits	28.6	20.0
From the disclosure on allowance for doubtful accounts:		
Balance at beginning of period	8.7	11.1
Additions (reductions) charged to income	7.3	5.5
Adjustments or deductions	(6.6)	(7.9)
Balance at end of period	9.4	8.7

a. Report (1) the write-off of accounts receivable as uncollectible in 2020 and (2) the provision for doubtful accounts (bad debt expense) for 2020 using the financial statement effects template.
b. Calculate Steelcase's gross receivables for the years given, and then determine the allowance for doubtful accounts as a percentage of the gross receivables.
c. Calculate Steelcase's accounts receivable turnover for 2020. (Use Accounts receivable, net for the calculation.)
d. How much cash did Steelcase receive from customers in 2020?

LO4 E6-41. Recording Entries to Adjust the Allowance for Doubtful Accounts
Use the information in E6-40 to complete the following requirements.

a. Prepare the journal entry to record accounts receivable written off as uncollectible in 2020.
b. Prepare the entry to record the provision for doubtful accounts (bad debts expense) for 2020.
c. What effect did these entries have on Steelcase's income for that year?

LO4 E6-42. Analyzing and Reporting Receivable Transactions and Uncollectible Accounts (Using Percentage-of-Sales Method)
At the beginning of the year, Penman Company had the following (normal) account balances in its financial records:

Accounts receivable	$61,000
Allowance for uncollectible accounts	3,950

During the year, its credit sales were $586,500, and collections on credit sales were $575,000. The following additional transactions occurred during the year:

Feb. 17 Wrote off Nissim's account, $1,800.
May 28 Wrote off White's account, $1,200.
Dec. 15 Wrote off Ohlson's account, $450.
Dec. 31 Recorded the provision for uncollectible accounts at 0.8% of credit sales for the year. (*Hint*: The allowance account is increased by 0.8% of credit sales regardless of any prior write-offs.)

Compute and show how accounts receivable and the allowance for uncollectible accounts are reported in its December 31 balance sheet.

LO4 E6-43. Estimating Bad Debts Expense and Reporting of Receivables (FSET)
At December 31, Sunil Company had a balance of $562,500 in its accounts receivable and an unused balance of $6,300 in its allowance for uncollectible accounts. The company then aged its accounts as follows:

Current	$456,000
0–60 days past due	66,000
61–180 days past due	27,000
Over 180 days past due	13,500
Total accounts receivable	$562,500

The company has experienced losses as follows: 1% of current balances, 5% of balances 0–60 days past due, 15% of balances 61–180 days past due, and 40% of balances over 180 days past due. The company continues to base its provision for credit losses on this aging analysis and percentages.

a. What amount of bad debts expense does Sunil report on its annual income statement?
b. Show how accounts receivable and the allowance for uncollectible accounts are reported in its December 31 balance sheet.
c. Report the increase in bad debt expense calculated in part a using the financial statement effects template.

E6-44. Analyzing T-Accounts in Accounting for Uncollectible Accounts   **LO4**
Using the information from E6-43, set up T-accounts for both Bad Debts Expense and the Allowance for Uncollectible Accounts. Enter any unadjusted balances along with the dollar effects of the information described (including your results from parts a and b in E6-43). Explain the numbers in each of the T-accounts.

E6-45. Estimating Uncollectible Accounts and Reporting Receivables over Multiple Periods   **LO4**
Barth Company, which has been in business for three years, makes all of its sales on credit and does not offer cash discounts. Its credit sales, customer collections, and write-offs of uncollectible accounts for its first three years follow:

Year	Sales	Collections	Accounts Written Off
Year 1	$600,800	$586,400	$4,240
Year 2	700,800	691,200	4,640
Year 3	777,600	750,400	5,200

a. Barth uses the allowance method of recognizing credit losses that provides for such losses at the rate of 1% of sales. (This means the allowance account is increased by 1% of credit sales regardless of any write-offs and unused balances.) What amounts for accounts receivable and the allowance for uncollectible accounts are reported on its balance sheet at the end of Year 3? What total amount of bad debts expense appears on its income statement for each of the three years?
b. Comment on the appropriateness of the 1% rate used to provide for bad debts based on your results in part a. (*Hint*: T-accounts can help with this analysis.)

E6-46.[A] **Evaluating Business Segment Information**   **LO5, 7**
Hewlett-Packard Company reports that its "operations are organized into three segments for financial reporting purposes: Personal Systems, Printing and Corporate Investments" with the last segment encompassing HP Labs and incubation projects. The company provides the following information about these business segments:

Hewlett-Packard
NYSE :: HPQ

($ millions)	2020	2019
Total net revenues		
Personal systems	$38,997	$38,694
Printing	17,641	20,066
Corporate investments	2	2
Earnings (loss) from continuing operations		
Personal systems	2,312	1,898
Printing	2,495	3,202
Corporate investments	(69)	(96)
Total assets		
Personal systems	14,697	14,092
Printing	14,170	14,309
Corporate investments	3	4

a. Calculate the 2020 return on capital employed for each segment. (Base the calculation on total assets instead of net operating assets in the denominator. HP does not disclose operating assets and liabilities by segment.)

b. Which segment is more profitable? Which is growing more quickly?
c. The Corporate Investments segment is dwarfed by the other two reporting segments. Why would HP's management want to keep Corporate Investments separate rather than combining it with one of the others?

E6-47. Analyzing Unearned Revenue Liabilities (FSET)
The **Metropolitan Opera Association, Inc.**, was founded in 1883 and is widely regarded as one of the world's greatest opera companies. The Metropolitan's performances run from September to May, and the season may consist of more than two dozen different operas. Many of the opera's loyal subscribers purchase tickets for the upcoming season prior to the end of the opera's fiscal year-end at July 31. In its annual report, the Metropolitan recognizes a Deferred Revenue liability that is defined in their disclosure notes as follows: "Advance ticket sales, representing the receipt of payments for ticket sales for the next opera season, are reported as deferred revenue in the consolidated balance sheets." Ticket sales are recognized as box office revenue "on a specific performance basis."

Fiscal Year Ended July 31	Revenues (Box Office and Tours)	Deferred Revenue
2019	$85,054	$42,108
2018	86,688	49,615
2017	88,514	42,649
2016	87,582	46,609

a. What revenue recognition principle(s) drive The Metropolitan Opera's deferral of advance ticket purchases?
b. Report (1) ticket sales revenue (box office and tours) for the fiscal year 2019 and (2) advance sales for the fiscal year 2020 season using the financial statement effects template. (Assume that advance ticket sales extend no further than the next year's opera season.)
c. The Metropolitan Opera's season changes every year. At the end of each fiscal year, management of the opera can observe the revenue generated by the season just concluded and its subscribers' enthusiasm for the upcoming season. How might that information be used in managing the organization?

E6-48. Analyzing Unearned Revenue Liabilities
Using the information from E6-47, re-create the summary journal entries to recognize ticket sales revenue (box office and tours) for The Metropolitan Opera's fiscal year 2019 and advance sales for the fiscal year 2020 season. (Assume that advance ticket sales extend no further than the next year's opera season.)

E6-49. Accounting for Membership Fees and Rewards Program (FSET)
BJ's Wholesale Club Holdings, Inc., provides the following description of its revenue recognition policies for membership fees and its reward program.

Performance Obligations
The Company identifies each distinct performance obligation to transfer goods (or bundle of goods) or services. The Company recognizes revenue as it satisfies a performance obligation by transferring control of the goods or services to the customer . . .

Merchandise sales—The Company recognizes sale of merchandise at clubs and gas stations when the customer takes possession of the goods and tenders payment . . .

BJ's Perks Rewards and My BJ's Perks programs—The Company's BJ's Perks® Rewards membership program allows participating members to earn 2% cash back, up to a maximum of $500 per year, on qualified purchases made at BJ's. The Company also offers a co-branded credit card program, the My BJ's Perks® program, which allows My BJ's Perks® Mastercard credit card holders to earn up to 5% cash back on eligible purchases made at BJ's up to 2% cash back on purchases made with the card outside of BJ's. Cash back is in the form of electronic awards issued in $20 increments that may be used online or in-club at the register and expire six months from the date issued.

Earned rewards may be redeemed on future purchases made at the Company. The Company recognizes revenue for earned rewards when customers redeem such rewards as part of a purchase at one of the Company's clubs or the Company's website. The Company accounts for these transactions as multiple element arrangements and allocates the transaction price to separate performance obligations using their relative fair values. The Company includes the fair value of award dollars earned in deferred revenue at the time the award dollars are earned . . .

continued

continued from previous page

> *Membership*—The Company charges a membership fee to its customers. That fee allows customers to shop in the Company's clubs, shop on the Company's website, and purchase gasoline at the Company's gas stations for the duration of the membership, which is generally 12 months. Because the Company has the obligation to provide access to its clubs, website, and gas stations for the duration of the membership term, the Company recognizes membership fees on a straight-line basis over the life of the membership . . .

The following data were extracted from income statement, balance sheet, and disclosure notes of BJ's 10-K annual report for 2020:

($ millions)	Twenty-Six Weeks Ended February 1, 2020
Net sales.	$12,889
Membership fee income	302
Total revenues	$13,191

	February 1, 2020	February 2, 2019
Deferred revenue—membership fees	$144.0	$134.4

a. Explain BJ's accounting for membership fees.
b. Report (1) membership fees collected in cash in the first half of fiscal year 2020 and (2) membership fee revenue recognized over that period using the financial statement effects template.

E6-50. Accounting for Membership Fees and Rewards Program   **LO2**
Using the information from E6-49:

a. Prepare journal entries to record (1) membership fees collected in cash in the first half of fiscal year 2020 and (2) membership fee revenue recognized over that period.
b. Explain BJ's accounting for its BJ's Perks Rewards program that provides 2% cash back, up to a maximum of $500 per year on qualified purchases made at BJ's.

PROBLEMS

P6-51.[A] **Identifying Operating and Nonrecurring Income Components**   **LO5, 7**
The following information comes from recent **DowDuPont, Inc.**, income statements.

DowDuPont Inc.
BYSE :: DWDP

(In millions, except per share amounts) For the Years Ended December 31	2019	2018
Net sales	$42,951	$49,604
Cost of sales	36,657	41,074
Research and development expenses	765	800
Selling, general, and administrative expenses	1,590	1,782
Amortization of intangibles	419	469
Restructuring, goodwill impairment, and asset-related charges—net	3,219	221
Integration and separation costs	1,063	1,179
Equity in earnings (losses) of nonconsolidated affiliates	(94)	555
Sundry income (expense)—net	461	96
Interest income	81	82
Interest expense and amortization of debt discount	933	1,063
Income (loss) from continuing operations before income taxes	(1,247)	3,749
Provision for income taxes on continuing operations	470	809
Income (loss) from continuing operations, net of tax	(1,717)	2,940
Loss from discontinued operations, net of tax	445	1,835
Net income (loss)	$(1,272)	$4,775

REQUIRED

a. Identify the components in its statement that you would consider operating.

b. Identify those components that you would consider nonrecurring.
c. Compute net operating profit after taxes (NOPAT) and net operating profit margin (NOPM) for each year. Use an income tax rate of 25%.

LO3 P6-52. Performance Obligation Fulfilled Over Time
Philbrick Company signed a three-year contract to develop custom sales training materials and provide training to the employees of Elliot Company. The contract price is $1,500 per employee, and the number of employees to be trained is 400. Philbrick can send a bill to Elliot at the end of every training session. Once developed, the custom training materials will belong to Elliot Company, but Philbrick does not consider them to be a separate performance obligation.

The expected number to be trained in each year and the expected development and training costs follow.

	Number of Employees	Development and Training Costs Incurred
Year 1	125	$ 91,000
Year 2	200	112,000
Year 3	75	42,000
Total	400	$245,000

REQUIRED
a. For each year, compute the revenue, expense, and gross profit reported assuming revenue is recognized over time using . . .
   1. the number of employees trained as a measure of the value provided to the customer.
   2. the cost incurred as a measure of the value provided to the customer.
b. Assume that Philbrick's costs are $18,750 to develop the custom training materials at the beginning of the contract and then $500 for each employee trained. Which method do you believe is more appropriate in this situation? Explain.

LO6 P6-53. Incentives for Earnings Management
Harris Corporation pays senior management an annual bonus from a bonus pool. The size of the bonus pool is determined as follows.

Reported Net Income	Bonus Pool
Less than or equal to $12 million	$0
Greater than $12 million, but less than or equal to $24 million	10% of income in excess of $12 million
Greater than $24 million	$1 million

REQUIRED
a. Assume that senior management expects current earnings to be $25 million and next year's earnings to be $22 million. What incentive does management of Harris Corporation have for managing earnings?
b. Assume that senior management expects current earnings to be $20 million and next year's earnings to be $29 million. What incentive does management of Harris Corporation have for managing earnings?
c. Assume that senior management expects current earnings to be $11 million and next year's earnings to be $14 million. What incentive does management of Harris Corporation have for managing earnings?
d. How might the bonus plan be structured to minimize the incentives for earnings management?

LO4, 5 P6-54. Interpreting Accounts Receivable and Uncollectible Accounts (FSET)
Mattel, Inc.
NASDAQ::MAT

Mattel, Inc., designs, manufactures, and markets a broad variety of toy products worldwide that are sold to its customers and directly to consumers. The company's brands include American Girl, Fisher-Price, Hot Wheels, and Barbie. The following information is taken from the company's 10-K annual report for its fiscal year ending December 31, 2019.

($ millions)	2019	2018	2017
Accounts receivable	$954.9	$992.1	$1,150.1
Allowance for doubtful accounts	18.5	22.0	25.4
Accounts receivable, net	936.4	970.1	1,124.7

Activity in the allowance for doubtful accounts for the past three fiscal years is as follows:

($ millions)	2019	2018	2017
Balance at beginning of year	$22.0	$25.4	$21.4
Charged to income	1.0	40.9	17.6
Deductions[a]	4.5	44.3	13.6
Allowance at end of year	18.5	22.0	25.4

[a] Includes write-offs, recoveries of previous write-offs, and currency translation adjustments.

Mattel's revenues were $4,504.6 million and $4,514.8 million for fiscal years 2019 and 2018, respectively.

REQUIRED

a. What amount did Mattel report as accounts receivable, net in its December 31, 2019, balance sheet?
b. Report (1) bad debts expense and (2) write-offs of uncollectible accounts in fiscal 2019 using the financial statement effects template. (Assume that Deductions did not include recoveries or foreign currency adjustments.)
c. Assume that Mattel experienced a $0.5 million recovery of a previously written-off receivable. Report the transaction using the financial statement effects template.
d. Compute the ratio of allowance for doubtful accounts to gross accounts receivable for fiscal 2018 and 2019.
e. Compute Mattel's accounts receivable turnover and average collection period for 2018 and 2019. (Use Accounts receivable, net for the calculation.)
f. What might be the cause of the changes that you observe in parts d and e?

P6-55. Accounting for Receivables and Uncollectible Accounts   LO4

Use the information from P6-54 to complete the following requirements.

a. Prepare journal entries to record bad debts expense and write-offs of uncollectible accounts in fiscal 2019. (Assume that Deductions did not include recoveries or foreign currency adjustments.)
b. Post the entries in part a to T-accounts.
c. Now suppose Mattel experienced a $0.5 million recovery of a previously written-off receivable. How should the company record this recovery?

P6-56. Accounting for Product Returns (FSET)   LO4

In its income statement for fiscal year 2019, **The Gap, Inc.**, reported net sales of $16,383 million and cost of goods sold and occupancy expenses of $10,250 million, resulting in a gross profit of $6,133 million. In its disclosure notes, The Gap reports that "We also record an allowance for estimated merchandise returns based on our historical return patterns and various other assumptions that management believes to be reasonable, which is presented on a gross basis on our Consolidated Balance Sheet."

When The Gap accounts for estimated sales returns, it makes two entries. First, it reduces sales revenue by the returns' expected sales price and recognizes a sales return allowance as a liability for the same amount. Then, The Gap reduces cost of goods sold by the returns' expected cost and recognizes a right of return merchandise asset for that same amount.

At the end of fiscal year 2019, The Gap reported a sales return allowance liability of $74 million and a right of return merchandise asset of $36 million.

REQUIRED

a. What was the estimated gross profit margin on the items The Gap expected to be returned following fiscal year 2019? How does that compare with the gross profit margin reported in the income statement for the first quarter of fiscal year 2019? What might account for the difference?
b. Suppose The Gap sells 150 units of an item for $50 each, and its gross profit on each unit is $20. Further, suppose The Gap expects that 15 of the units will be returned. Using the financial statement effects template, report (1) the sale of 150 units (for cash) along with the expected returns, and (2) the subsequent return of items by 15 customers who receive a cash refund. Assume that the units are undamaged and can be sold to other customers.

P6-57. Accounting for Product Returns   LO4

Use the information from P6-56 part b to complete the following requirements.

a. What entries will be made to record the sale of 150 units (for cash) and the expected returns?

LO2 **P6-58. Analyzing Unearned Revenue Changes**

Take-Two Interactive Software, Inc. (TTWO) is a developer, marketer, publisher, and distributor of video game software and content to be played on a variety of platforms. There is an increasing demand for the ability to play these games in an online environment, and TTWO has developed this capability in many of its products. In addition, TTWO maintains servers (or arranges for servers) for the online activities of its customers.

TTWO considers that its products have multiple performance obligations. The first performance obligation is to provide software to the customer that enables the customer to play the game offline or online. That performance obligation is fulfilled at the point at which the software is provided to the customer. In addition, TTWO's customers benefit from "online functionality that is dependent on our online support services and/or additional free content updates." This second performance obligation is fulfilled over time, and the estimated time period for which an average user plays the software product is judged to be a faithful depiction of the fulfillment of this performance obligation.

At the beginning of fiscal year 2020, TTWO had a deferred net revenue liability of $843,302 thousand. When that fiscal year ended on March 31, 2020, the deferred net revenue liability was $777,784 thousand. Revenue for the fiscal year was $3,088,970 thousand.

REQUIRED
a. What would cause the *deferred net revenue* liability to go down over the quarter?
b. What was the amount of online-enabled games purchased by TTWO's customers in the 2020 fiscal year? Were the purchases greater or less than the revenue recognized in the income statement? How might that information be useful for a financial statement reader?

CASES AND PROJECTS

LO1, 2, 6 **C6-59. Revenue Recognition and Refunds (FSET)**
From the annual 2019 10-K of **Groupon, Inc.**:

> **REVENUE RECOGNITION**
> *Service revenue*
> Service revenue primarily represents the net commissions earned from selling goods or services on behalf of third-party merchants. Those transactions generally involve a customer's purchase of a voucher through one of our online marketplaces that can be redeemed by the customer with a third-party merchant for goods or services (or for discounts on goods or services). Service revenue from those transactions is reported on a net basis as the purchase price collected from the customer less the portion of the purchase price that is payable to the third-party merchant. We recognize revenue from those transactions when our commission has been earned, which occurs when a sale through one of our online marketplaces is completed and the related voucher has been made available to the customer. . . .
>
> *Product revenue*
> We generate product revenue from direct sales of merchandise inventory to customers through our Goods category. For product revenue transactions, we are the primary party responsible for providing the good to the customer, we have inventory risk and we have discretion in establishing prices. As such, product revenue is reported on a gross basis as the purchase price received from the customer. Product revenue, including associated shipping revenue, is recognized when title passes to the customer upon delivery of the product.
>
> *Variable Consideration for Unredeemed Vouchers*
> For merchant agreements with redemption payment terms, the merchant is not paid its share of the sale price for a voucher sold through one of our online marketplaces until the customer redeems the related voucher. If the customer does not redeem a voucher with such merchant payment terms, we retain all of the gross billings for that voucher, rather than retaining only our net commission. We estimate the variable consideration from vouchers that will not ultimately be redeemed using our historical voucher redemption experience and recognize that amount as revenue at the time of sale. We only recognize amounts in variable consideration when we believe it is probable that a significant reversal of revenue will not occur in future periods, which requires us to make significant estimates of future redemptions. . . .

REQUIRED

a. Assume that Groupon sells an Invicta Chronograph watch in its Product marketplace. The price of the watch is $120, and the watch cost Groupon $60. Using the financial statement effects template, illustrate how Groupon would record the sale of the watch.

b. Assume that Groupon sells a restaurant voucher in its Local marketplace. The consumer pays $120, and Groupon will pay the restaurant $60 after the consumer has redeemed the voucher at the restaurant. The consumer has 60 days to redeem the voucher. Using the financial statement effects template, illustrate how Groupon would record the sale of the voucher. Assume that the consumer will redeem the voucher with certainty.

c. Refer to the facts presented in part *b* above. Assume that Groupon estimates that 10% of the Groupon customers will not redeem the voucher within the 60-day period. How does this change the entry in part *b*?

C6-60. Revenue Recognition and Refunds   LO1, 2, 6

Use the information from C6-59, record journal entries to illustrate the transactions in parts *a*, *b*, and *c*.

C6-61. Interpreting Revenue Recognition Policies and Earnings Management   LO1, 2, 6

On May 3, 2021, the Securities and Exchange Commission filed an Accounting and Auditing Enforcement Release (AAER) concerning the sports apparel company, **Under Armour, Inc.** The document contained the following information.

Under Armour, Inc.
NYSE::UAA

> This matter concerns Under Armour's failure to disclose material information about its revenue management practices that rendered statements it made misleading ... Under Armour has emphasized its consistent revenue growth ... For 26 consecutive quarters, beginning in the second quarter of 2010, Under Armour's reported year-over-year revenue growth exceeded 20%, and Under Armour repeatedly highlighted this growth streak in earnings calls and earnings releases.

But starting with the third quarter of 2015, Under Armour's internal revenue forecasts indicated that it would not exceed the growth targets, and the company began a practice of "pull forward," i.e., accelerating the fulfillment of customer orders that were scheduled for a future quarter to allow revenue to be recognized in the current quarter. Sometimes customers were offered price discounts or favorable credit terms. This practice of pulling forward is not in itself illegal, but failure to disclose the practice made the financial statements misleading.

Year	Quarter	Revenue "pulled forward" from succeeding quarter ($ millions)
2015	3rd	$ 45.0
2015	4th	99.0
2016	1st	17.5
2016	2nd	10.0
2016	3rd	65.0
2016	4th	172.0

The table shows the amount of pull forward that was required to meet growth targets, and the practice had grown to the point that the $172 million for the fourth quarter of 2016 represented 13% of its quarterly revenue. Under Armour offered and sold company stock during this period.

Under Armour agreed to a "cease and desist" order from the SEC and a $9 million civil penalty. Shareholder lawsuits are pending at the time of this writing.

REQUIRED

1. Why do companies feel it is so important to meet analyst growth forecasts?
2. If you were an analyst covering Under Armour, how would knowledge of the "pull forward" have affected your assessment of the company?
3. Is a practice of "pull forward" to meet growth forecasts a sustainable one? How can companies like Under Armour prevent earnings management in circumstances such as this?

LO2, 4, 5   **C6-62.**   **Accounting for Doubtful Accounts and Returns (FSET)**

John Wiley and Sons, Inc., publishes books, periodicals, software, and other digital content. Its April 30, 2020, balance sheet reported the following amounts for accounts receivable ($ thousands):

April 30	2020	2019
Accounts receivable, net.	$309,384	$306,631

Wiley's income statement provided the following detail of operating income ($ thousands):

Year Ended April 30	2020	2019
Revenue	$1,831,483	$1,800,069
Costs and Expenses		
Cost of sales	591,024	554,722
Operating and administrative expenses	997,355	963,582
Impairment of goodwill and intangible assets	202,348	0
Restructuring and related charges	32,607	3,118
Amortization of intangibles	62,436	54,658
Operating expenses	$1,885,770	$1,576,080

Wiley normally charges operating and administrative expenses for estimated doubtful accounts. The company provided the following supplemental information concerning doubtful accounts and returns in its disclosure notes ($ thousands):

	Balance at Beginning of Period	Charged to Expenses and Other	Deductions from Reserves	Balance at End of Period
Year ended April 30, 2020				
Allowance for sales returns	$18,542	$48,829	$47,729	$19,642
Allowance for doubtful accounts	14,307	5,470	1,442	18,335
Year ended April 30, 2019				
Allowance for sales returns	$18,628	$37,483	$37,569	$18,542
Allowance for doubtful accounts	10,107	5,279	1,079	14,307

Net sales return reserves are reflected in the following accounts of the Consolidated Statements of Financial Position—increase (decrease):

April 30	2020	2019
Increase in inventories, net	$ 8,686	$ 3,739
Decrease in accrued royalties	(4,441)	(3,653)
Increase in contract liabilities	32,769	25,934
Print book sales return reserve net liability balance	$(19,642)	$(18,542)

REQUIRED

a. Using the financial statement effects template, report bad debts expense and accounts receivable write-offs for 2019 and 2020.
b. Compute the allowance for doubtful accounts as a percentage of accounts receivable. What might account for the change from 2019 and 2020?
c. Wiley has also established an allowance for returns. How do returns differ from doubtful accounts? Under what circumstances might this difference affect the accounting for returns?
d. Calculate the accounts receivable turnover ratio and average collection period for 2020 using net accounts receivable.

LO2, 4   **C6-63.**   **Accounting for Doubtful Accounts and Returns**

Use the information from C6-62 to complete the following requirements.

a. Prepare journal entries to record bad debts expense and accounts receivable write-offs for 2019 and 2020.
b. Post the entries from part a to the Allowance for doubtful accounts T-account.

LO7   **C6-64.**[A]   **Interpreting Restructuring Charges**

The following is from the most recent 10-K report of **3M Company** for the year ended December 31, 2020.

3M COMPANY AND SUBSIDIARIES
Consolidated Statement of Income

(Millions, except per share amounts)	2020
Net sales	$32,184
Operating expenses	
Costs of sales	16,605
Selling, general, and administrative expenses	6,929
Research, development, and related expenses	1,878
Gain on sale of businesses	(389)
Total operating expenses	25,023
Operating income	7,161
Other expense (income), net	450
Income before income taxes	6,711
Provision for income taxes	1,318
Net income including noncontrolling interest	$ 5,393

In its disclosure notes, 3M provided the following information about the gain on sale of businesses in the income statement.

Gain on Sale of Businesses:
During the first quarter of 2020, the Company recorded a pre-tax gain of $2 million ($1 million loss after tax) related to the sale of its advanced ballistic-protection business and recognition of certain contingent consideration. During the second quarter of 2020, the Company recorded a pretax gain of $387 million ($304 after tax) related to the sale of substantially all of its drug delivery business.

In addition, 3M provided information about restructuring charges for fiscal year 2020:

Operational/Marketing Capability Restructuring
In late 2020, 3M announced it would undertake certain actions to further enhance its operations and marketing capabilities to take advantage of certain global market trends while de-prioritizing investments in slower-growth end markets. During the fourth quarter of 2020, management approved and committed to undertake associated restructuring actions impacting approximately 2,100 positions resulting in a pre-tax charge of $137 million. 3M is planning further actions under this initiative primarily in the second half of 2021. This aggregate initiative, spanning 2020 and 2021, is expected to impact approximately 2,900 positions worldwide with an expected pre-tax charge of $250 to $300 million. . . .

Divestiture-Related Restructuring
During the second quarter of 2020, following the divestiture of substantially all of the drug delivery business (see Note 3), management approved and committed to undertake certain restructuring actions addressing corporate functional costs and manufacturing footprint across 3M in relation to the magnitude of amounts previously allocated/burdened to the divested business. These actions affected approximately 1,300 positions worldwide and resulted in a second quarter 2020 pre-tax charge of $55 million, within Corporate and Unallocated. . . .

Other Restructuring
Additionally, in the second quarter of 2020, management approved and committed to undertake certain restructuring actions addressing structural enterprise costs and operations in certain end markets as a result of the COVID-19 pandemic and related economic impacts. These actions affected approximately 400 positions worldwide and resulted in a second quarter 2020 pre-tax charge of $58 million. . . .

REQUIRED

a. Describe where on the income statement the above described restructuring charges and gain on sale of businesses are included.
b. Describe how an analyst of the company should treat these items when making financial statement projections.
c. What incentives might management have to either overstate or understate the above described restructuring charges? Describe how future financial statements would be affected if the costs were overstated or understated when these charges were recorded in 2020.

SOLUTIONS TO REVIEW PROBLEMS

Review 6-1
a. Step 5   b. Step 3   c. Step 1   d. Step 4   e. Step 2

Review 6-2
(All dollar amounts are in millions.)

a. The *Deferred net revenue* liability increases when Electronic Arts sells a game, and it decreases when the company recognizes revenue from providing post-sale services to customers. So a decrease means that the amount sold was less than the amount recognized.

b. Electronic Arts' sales to customers equals its *Total net revenue* plus the change in the *Deferred net revenue* liability, or $5,537 + (−$155) = $5,382. A financial statement reader should recognize that the reported revenues are a weighted average of customer purchases made in the current period and in prior periods. Changes in the deferred revenue liability can be a useful indicator of the revenue in future income statements.

Review 6-3

a.

Transaction	Cash Asset	+	Noncash Assets	=	Liabilities	+	Contrib. Capital	+	Earned Capital	Revenues	−	Expenses	=	Net Income
April 6	+40,000 Cash			=	+40,000 Contract Liability						−		=	
May 31			+50,000 Accounts Receivable +30,000 Contract Assets	=	−40,000 Contract Liability				+120,000 Retained Earnings	+120,000 Revenue	−		=	+120,000
June 15	+50,000 Cash		−50,000 Accounts Receivable	=							−		=	
July 15			+110,000 Accounts Receivable −30,000 Contract Assets	=					+80,000 Retained Earnings	+80,000 Revenue	−		=	+80,000
July 31	+110,000 Cash		−110,000 Accounts Receivable	=							−		=	

b.

April 6

Cash (+A) 40,000
    Contract liability (+L) 40,000
Receive advance payment from customer

+ Cash (A) −		− Contract Liability (L) +
40,000		40,000

May 31

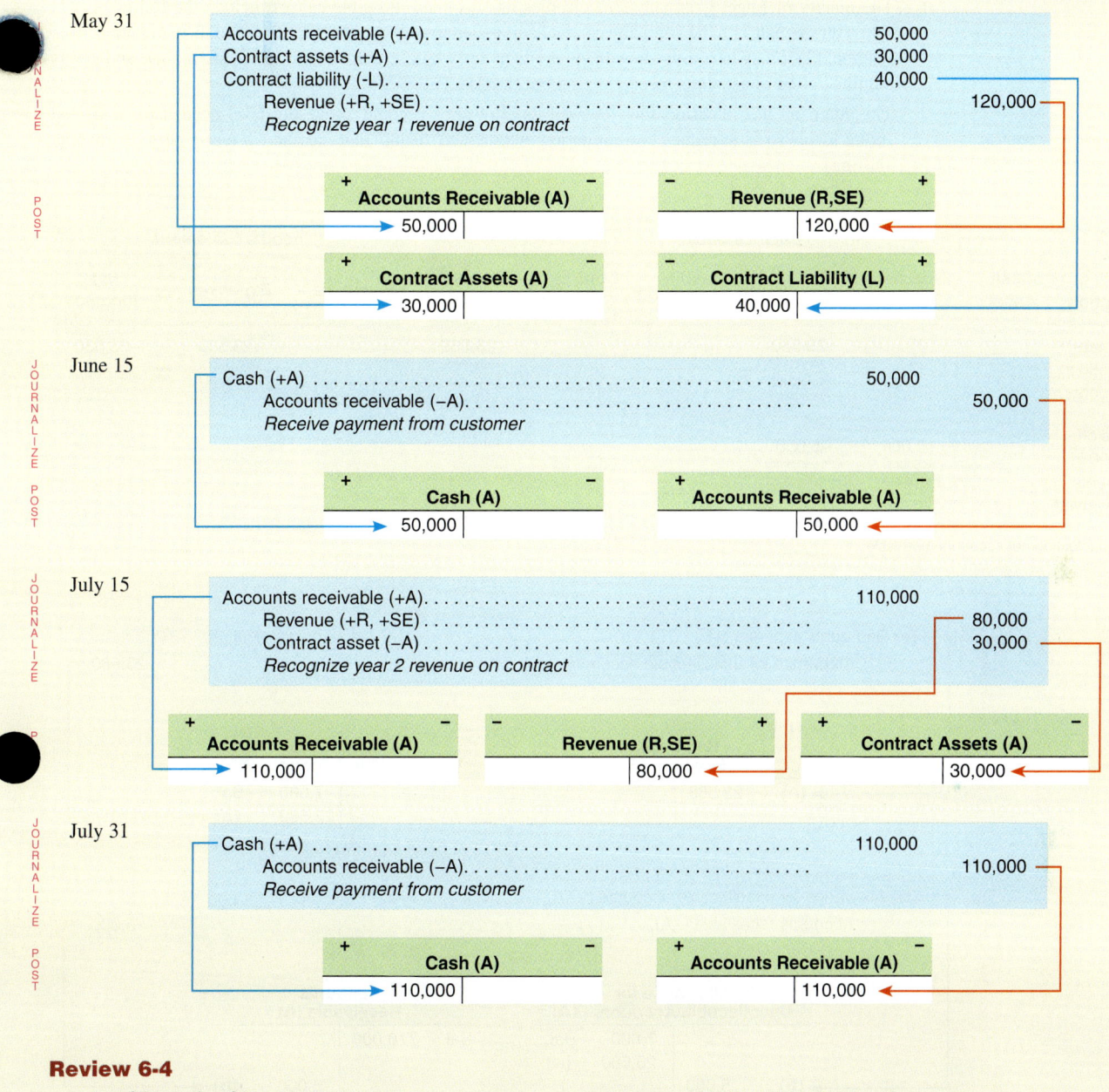

Accounts receivable (+A)	50,000	
Contract assets (+A)	30,000	
Contract liability (-L)	40,000	
Revenue (+R, +SE)		120,000
Recognize year 1 revenue on contract		

+ Accounts Receivable (A) −		− Revenue (R,SE) +
50,000		120,000

+ Contract Assets (A) −		− Contract Liability (L) +
30,000		40,000

June 15

Cash (+A)	50,000	
Accounts receivable (−A)		50,000
Receive payment from customer		

+ Cash (A) −		+ Accounts Receivable (A) −
50,000		50,000

July 15

Accounts receivable (+A)	110,000	
Revenue (+R, +SE)		80,000
Contract asset (−A)		30,000
Recognize year 2 revenue on contract		

+ Accounts Receivable (A) −	− Revenue (R,SE) +	+ Contract Assets (A) −
110,000	80,000	30,000

July 31

Cash (+A)	110,000	
Accounts receivable (−A)		110,000
Receive payment from customer		

+ Cash (A) −		+ Accounts Receivable (A) −
110,000		110,000

Review 6-4

a. As of December 31

Current	$468,000	×	1% =	$ 4,680
1–60 days past due	244,000	×	5% =	12,200
61–180 days past due	38,000	×	15% =	5,700
Over 180 days past due	20,000	×	40% =	8,000
Amount required				$30,580
Unused allowance balance				7,000
Provision				$23,580 Annual bad debts expense

b. Current assets section of balance sheet.

Accounts receivable, net of $30,580 in allowances	$739,420

c. Engel Company has markedly increased the percentage of the allowance for uncollectible accounts to gross accounts receivable—from the historical 2% to the current 4% ($30,580/$770,000). There are at least two possible interpretations:

1. The quality of Engel Company's receivables has declined. Possible causes include the following: (1) sales can stagnate and the company can feel compelled to sell to lower-quality accounts to maintain sales volume; (2) it may have introduced new products for which average credit losses are higher; and (3) its administration of accounts receivable can become lax.
2. The company has intentionally increased its allowance account above the level needed for expected future losses so as to reduce current period income and "bank" that income for future periods (income shifting).

d.

Transaction	Balance Sheet							Income Statement		
	Cash Asset	+ Noncash Assets	− Contra Asset	= Liabilities	+ Contrib. Capital	+ Earned Capital		Revenues	− Expenses	= Net Income
(a) Estimate $23,580 in bad debts.		+23,580	− Allowance for Uncollectible Accounts	=		−23,580 Retained Earnings			− +23,580 Bad Debts Expense	= −23,580
(b) Write off $5,000 in accounts receivable.*		−5,000 Accounts Receivable	− −5,000 Allowance for Uncollectible Accounts	=					−	=

* There is no effect on net accounts receivable.

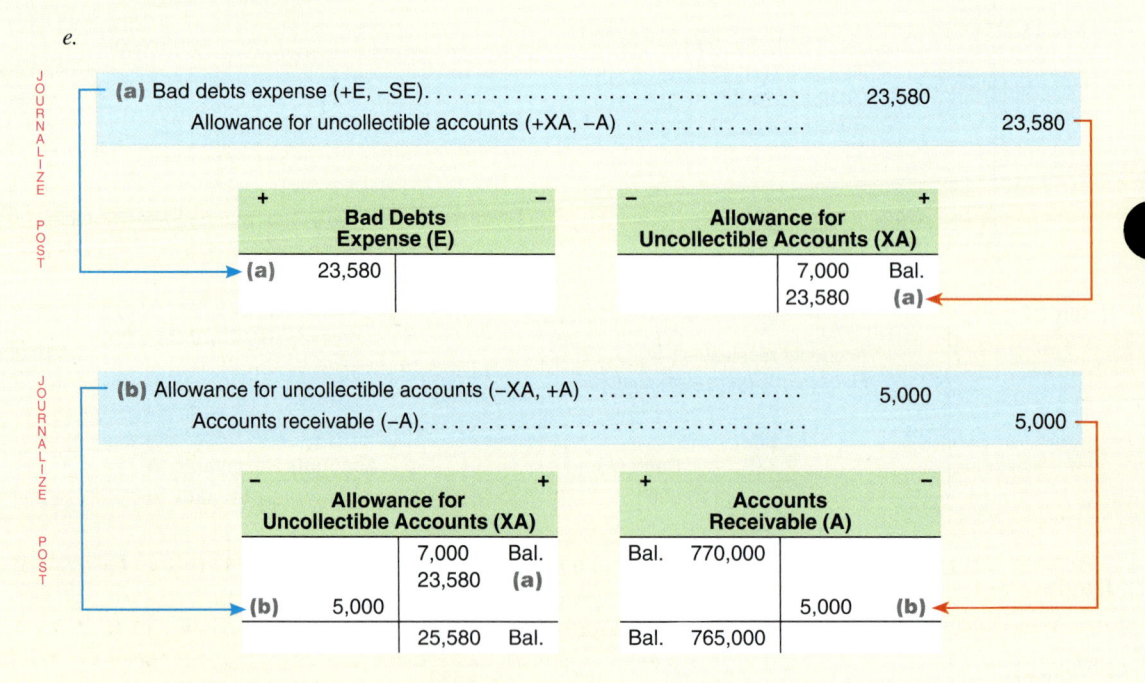

e.

(a) Bad debts expense (+E, −SE) 23,580
  Allowance for uncollectible accounts (+XA, −A) 23,580

+ Bad Debts Expense (E) −		− Allowance for Uncollectible Accounts (XA) +	
(a) 23,580			7,000 Bal.
			23,580 (a)

(b) Allowance for uncollectible accounts (−XA, +A) 5,000
  Accounts receivable (−A) 5,000

− Allowance for Uncollectible Accounts (XA) +		+ Accounts Receivable (A) −	
	7,000 Bal.	Bal. 770,000	
	23,580 (a)		
(b) 5,000			5,000 (b)
	25,580 Bal.	Bal. 765,000	

Review 6-5

a.

($ millions)	Comcast (Xfinity)	Charter Communications
NOPAT	$13,323 − [($438 − $4,567) × (1 − 0.25)] = $16,419.75	$1,992 − [($0 − $4,080) × (1 − 0.25)] = $5,052.00
Average net operating assets	[($261,165 − $70,785) + ($249,538 − $66,123)]/2 = $186,897.5	[($148,188 − $30,299) + ($146,130 − $29,031)]/2 = $117,494.00
Return on net operating assets	$16,419.75/$186,897.5 = 0.088	$5,052.00/$117,494 = 0.043
Net operating profit margin	$16,419.75/$108,942.00 = 0.151	$5,052.00/$45,764 = 0.110
Accounts receivable turnover	$108,942/[($11,292 + $11,104)/2] = 9.73	$45,764/[($2,227 + $1,733)/2] = 23.11
Average collection period	365/9.73 = 37.5 days	365/23.11 = 15.8 days

b. Comcast is considerably bigger, with revenues almost two-and-a-half times of Charter and NOPAT roughly three times bigger. But average operating assets was only about 60% higher. So, it appears that Comcast is able to leverage its size to produce greater returns, in relation to both its operating assets and its revenues. The difference might be ascribed to competitive environment or management capabilities.

There is a significant difference in the companies' handling of receivables, with Charter waiting about 15.8 days to collect, while Comcast is more than twice as long (37.5 days). Both companies collect more quickly than the industry median ART of 5.27 (69.3 days) from Exhibit 5.13.

Review 6-6

	Revenues	Impact on Expenses	Net Income
a.	No impact	Understatement	Overstatement
b.	Overstatement	Overstatement	Overstatement
c.	No impact	Overstatement	Understatement
d.	No impact	Overstatement	Understatement
e.	Overstatement	Overstatement	Overstatement

Review 6-7

a. A loss from discontinued operations of $105,000 would be reported below income from continuing operations. The loss is net of tax and is calculated as follows:
$105,000 = ($120,000 + $12,000 + $18,000) × (1 − 30%).
b. A restructuring charge of $30,000 ($12,000 + $18,000) would be reported as part of operating income. The loss is before taxes. The tax effect of the restructuring charge would be included in the provision for income taxes (income tax expense).
c. Singh could report this loss as discontinued operations only if the closure represented a separate business unit within the company and the closure represents a strategic shift in operations. Otherwise, it must be reported as a restructuring charge.

Chapter 7
Reporting and Analyzing Inventory

LEARNING OBJECTIVES

LO7-1 Interpret disclosures of information concerning operating expenses, including manufacturing and retail inventory costs.

LO7-2 Account for inventory and cost of goods sold using different costing methods.

LO7-3 Apply the lower of cost or net realizable value rule to value inventory.

LO7-4 Evaluate how inventory costing affects management decisions and outsiders' interpretations of financial statements.

LO7-5 Define and interpret gross profit margin and inventory turnover ratios. Use inventory disclosure information to make appropriate adjustments to ratios.

LO7-6 Appendix 7A: Analyze LIFO liquidations and the impact they have on the financial statements.

Road Map

LO	Learning Objective / Topics	Page	eLecture	Review	Assignments
LO7-1	Interpret disclosures of information concerning operating expenses, including manufacturing and retail inventory costs.	7-3	e7-1	R7-1	M7-13, M7-14, M7-I5, M7-16, M7-18
LO7-2	Account for inventory and cost of goods sold using different costing methods.	7-7	e7-2	R7-2	M7-19, M7-20, M7-21, M7-22, M7-23, M7-25, M 7-26, E7-29, E7-30, E7-32, E7-33, E7-34, P7-36, P7-37, P7-39, C7-40, C7-41
LO7-3	Apply the lower of cost or net realizable value rule to value inventory.	7-13	e7-3	R7-3	M7-27, E7-31, DA7-1
LO7-4	Evaluate how inventory costing affects management decisions and outsiders' interpretations of financial statements.	7-14	e7-4	R7-4	M7-19, E7-29, E7-32, E7-33, E7-34, P7-36, P7-37, P7-39, C7-40, C7-41
LO7-5	Define and interpret gross profit margin and inventory turnover ratios. Use inventory disclosure information to make appropriate adjustments to ratios.	7-20	e7-5	R7-5	M7-17, M7-24, E7-28, E7-34, E7-35, P7-36, P7-37, P7-38, C7-40, DA7-2, DA7-3, DA7-4
LO7-6	Appendix 7A: Analyze LIFO liquidations and the impact they have on the financial statements.	7-25	e7-6	R7-6	E7-29, E7-32, E7-33, P7-39, C7-40

HOME DEPOT
www.HomeDepot.com

The Home Depot, Inc., is the world's largest home improvement retailer. At February 2, 2020, the company operated 2,291 retail stores worldwide and reported sales of just over $110 billion. This performance represents the tenth year of increasing revenues.

The One Home Depot strategy focuses on using the digital experience to leverage the capabilities of its more than 400,000 associates and the scale of the company. "Connect stores to online, and online to stores." This approach requires digital tools for associates and customers to connect with products in the stores, as well as improvements in the online customer experience.

A key element of Home Depot's operating strategy is inventory management. Inventory represents one of the largest assets on Home Depot's balance sheet. A typical Home Depot store carries 30,000 to 40,000 products during the year, ranging from garden supplies to hardware and lumber to household appliances. These stores are stocked through a sophisticated logistics program designed to ensure product availability for customers and low supply chain costs. The fiscal 2019 annual report states that the company "continued to focus on optimizing our supply chain network and improving our inventory, transportation and distribution productivity." As of February 2, 2020, the company operated a network of 200 distribution centers and 150 fulfillment centers to facilitate delivery speed. The company also utilizes its retail stores as a network of locations for customers who shop online. Online sales have grown approximately $1 billion in each of the last six years, and more than 50 percent of the time, online customers choose to pick up their order in the company's stores.

In this chapter, we examine the reporting of inventory and cost of goods sold. For most retail and manufacturing businesses, cost of goods sold and the related inventory management costs represent the largest source of expenses in the income statement. Carrying large stocks of inventory is costly for any business. The more that a business can minimize the resources tied up in merchandise or materials, while still meeting customer demand, the more profitable it will be. Moreover, excessive inventory balances can indicate poor inventory management, obsolete products, and weakening sales. We explore accounting methods designed to measure inventory costs and determine cost of goods sold. We also look at measures that help us assess the effectiveness of inventory management practices for companies such as The Home Depot.

Sources: The Home Depot, Inc. 2019–2020 10-K reports; The Home Depot does not end its fiscal year on December 31, but rather on the Sunday closest to January 31. So, "Fiscal Year 2019" actually ended on February 2, 2020. One interesting aspect of this practice is that most of The Home Depot's fiscal years have 52 weeks, but periodically a fiscal year will have 53 weeks. (Fiscal Year 2018 was the most recent year of this event.)

CHAPTER ORGANIZATION

Reporting and Analyzing Inventory

Reporting Operating Expenses
- Expense Recognition
- Recording and Reporting Inventory Costs
- Manufacturing Inventory

Inventory Costing Methods
- FIFO
- LIFO
- Average Cost
- Lower of Cost or NRV

Financial Statement Effects and Disclosure
- Disclosure Notes
- Income Statement Effects
- Balance Sheet Effects
- Cash Flow Effects

Analyzing Financial Statements
- Gross Profit Analysis
- Inventory Turnover
- LIFO Liquidation (Appendix 7A)

REPORTING OPERATING EXPENSES

LO7-1 Interpret disclosures of information concerning operating expenses, including manufacturing and retail inventory costs.

In Chapter 6, we introduced the concept of operating income and discussed issues surrounding revenue recognition and how best to measure and report a company's performance. But the amount of revenue from customers must be interpreted relative to the resources that were required to achieve it. Operating expenses include the costs of acquiring the products (and services) that customers purchase, plus the costs of selling efforts, administrative functions, and any other activities that support the operations of the company. Careful examination of these costs allows financial statement users to judge management's performance, to identify emerging problems, and to make predictions of future performance. For instance, we may address the following questions.

- Are the company's costs of providing products and services increasing or decreasing?
- Is the company able to maintain its margins in the face of changes in costs or competition?
- Does management's ability to judge customer tastes and preferences allow it to avoid overstocks of unpopular inventory and the resulting price discounts that reduce margins?

In this chapter, we begin our examination of operating expenses by studying inventory and cost of goods sold. The reporting of inventory and cost of goods sold is important for three reasons. First, cost of goods sold is often the largest single expense in a company's income statement, and inventory may be one of the largest assets in the balance sheet. Consequently, information about inventory and cost of goods sold is critical for interpreting the financial statements. Second, in order to effectively manage operations and resources, management needs accurate and timely information about inventory quantities and costs. Finally, alternative methods of accounting for inventory and cost of goods sold can distort interpretations of margins and turnovers unless the information in the financial statement disclosure notes is used.

Expense Recognition Principles

In addition to determining when to recognize revenues to properly measure and report a company's performance, we must also determine when to recognize expenses. In general, expenses are recognized when assets are diminished (or liabilities increased) as a result of earning revenue or supporting operations, even if there is no immediate decrease in cash. Expense recognition can be generally divided into the following three approaches.

- **Direct association.** Any cost that can be *directly* associated with a specific source of revenue should be recognized as an expense at the same time that the related revenue is recognized. For a merchandising company (a retailer or a wholesaler), an example of direct association is recognizing cost of goods sold and sales revenue when the product is delivered to the customer. The cost of acquiring the inventory is recorded in the inventory asset account where it remains until the item is sold. At that point, the inventory cost is removed from the inventory asset and transferred to expenses. The future costs of any obligations arising from current revenues should also be estimated and recognized as liabilities and matched as expenses against those revenues. An example of such an expense is expected warranty costs, a topic covered in Chapter 9.

    For a manufacturing company, the accounting system distinguishes between *product costs* and *period costs*. Product costs are incurred to benefit the company's manufacturing activities and include raw materials, production workers and supervisors, depreciation on equipment and facilities, utilities, and so on. Even though some of these costs cannot be directly associated with a unit of production, the accounting system accumulates product costs and assigns them to inventory assets until the unit is sold. All costs not classified as product costs are considered period costs.

- **Immediate recognition.** Many period costs are necessary for generating revenues and income but cannot be directly associated with specific revenues. Some costs can be associated with all of the revenues of an accounting period, but not with any specific sales transaction that occurred during that period. Examples include most administrative and marketing costs. These costs are recognized as expenses in the period when the costs are incurred. Other expense items, such as research and development (R&D) expense, are recognized immediately because of U.S. GAAP requirements.

- **Systematic allocation.** Costs that benefit more than one accounting period and cannot be associated with specific revenues or assigned to a specific period must be allocated across all of the periods benefited. The most common example is depreciation expense. When an asset is purchased, it is capitalized (recorded in an asset account). The asset cost is then converted into an expense over the duration of its useful life according to a depreciation formula or schedule established by management. Depreciation of long-term assets is discussed in Chapter 8.

Inventory and cost of goods sold expense are important for product companies—manufacturers, wholesalers, and retailers. But before turning to an examination of these accounts at The Home Depot, we should recognize that cost of sales expense is also a critical performance component for many service companies, particularly those who engage in projects for their clients and customers. For fiscal 2020, the consulting firm **Accenture PLC** reports revenues of $44.3 billion and cost of services of $30.4 billion; the professional staffing company **Kelly Services, Inc.** reported net service revenues of $4.5 billion and direct costs of services of $3.7 billion; and **Alphabet, Inc.** reported revenue of $136.8 billion and cost of sales of $59.5 billion. While these companies report no inventory, the relationship of revenues to costs of revenues remains important.

Reporting Inventory Costs in the Financial Statements

To help frame our discussion of inventory, **Exhibits 7.1** and **7.2** present information from the current asset section of the balance sheet and the continuing operations section of the income statement for The Home Depot. We highlight merchandise inventories in the balance sheet as well as cost of goods sold in the income statement.

When inventory is purchased or produced, it is capitalized and carried on the balance sheet as an asset until it is sold, at which time its cost is transferred from the balance sheet to the income statement as an expense (cost of goods sold). Cost of goods sold (COGS) is then subtracted from sales revenue to yield **gross profit**:

> **Gross profit = Sales revenue − Cost of goods sold**

The manner in which inventory costs are transferred from the balance sheet to the income statement affects both the level of inventories reported on the balance sheet and the amount of gross profit (and net income) reported on the income statement.

EXHIBIT 7.1 Balance Sheets (Current Assets Only)

THE HOME DEPOT, INC.
Consolidated Balance Sheets

($ millions)	February 2, 2020	January 3, 2019
Assets		
Current assets:		
Cash and cash equivalents	$2,133	$ 1,778
Receivables, net	2,106	1,936
Merchandise inventories	14,531	13,925
Other current assets	1,040	890
Total current assets	$19,810	$18,529

EXHIBIT 7.2 Income Statement

THE HOME DEPOT, INC.
Consolidated Statement of Earnings

($ millions)	Fiscal Year Ended February 2, 2020
Net sales	$110,225
Cost of sales	72,653
Gross profit	37,572
Total operating expenses	21,729
Operating income	15,843
Interest and other, net	1,128
Earnings before provision for income taxes	14,715
Provision for income taxes	3,473
Net earnings	$ 11,242

Recording Inventory Costs in the Financial Statements

To illustrate the inventory purchasing and selling cycle, assume that a start-up company purchases 800 units of merchandise inventory at a cost of $4 cash per unit. We account for this transaction as follows:

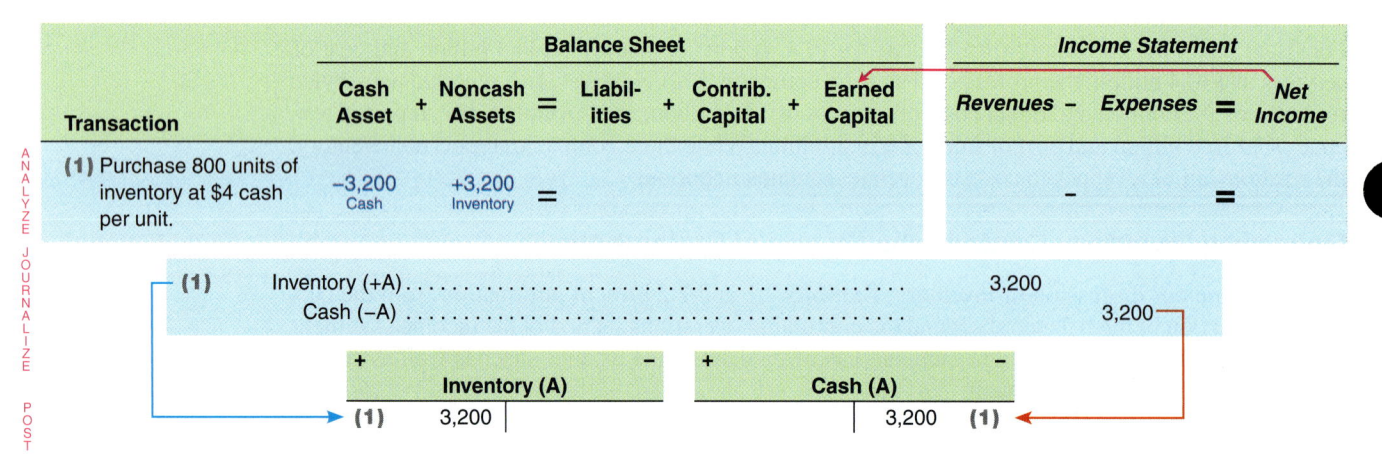

Transaction	Balance Sheet: Cash Asset + Noncash Assets = Liabilities + Contrib. Capital + Earned Capital	Income Statement: Revenues − Expenses = Net Income
(1) Purchase 800 units of inventory at $4 cash per unit.	−3,200 Cash +3,200 Inventory =	− =

(1) Inventory (+A) 3,200
    Cash (−A) 3,200

Inventory (A)
(1) 3,200

Cash (A)
3,200 (1)

Next, assume this company sells 500 of those units for $7 cash per unit. The two following entries are required to record (a) the sales revenue and (b) the expense for the cost of the inventory sold.

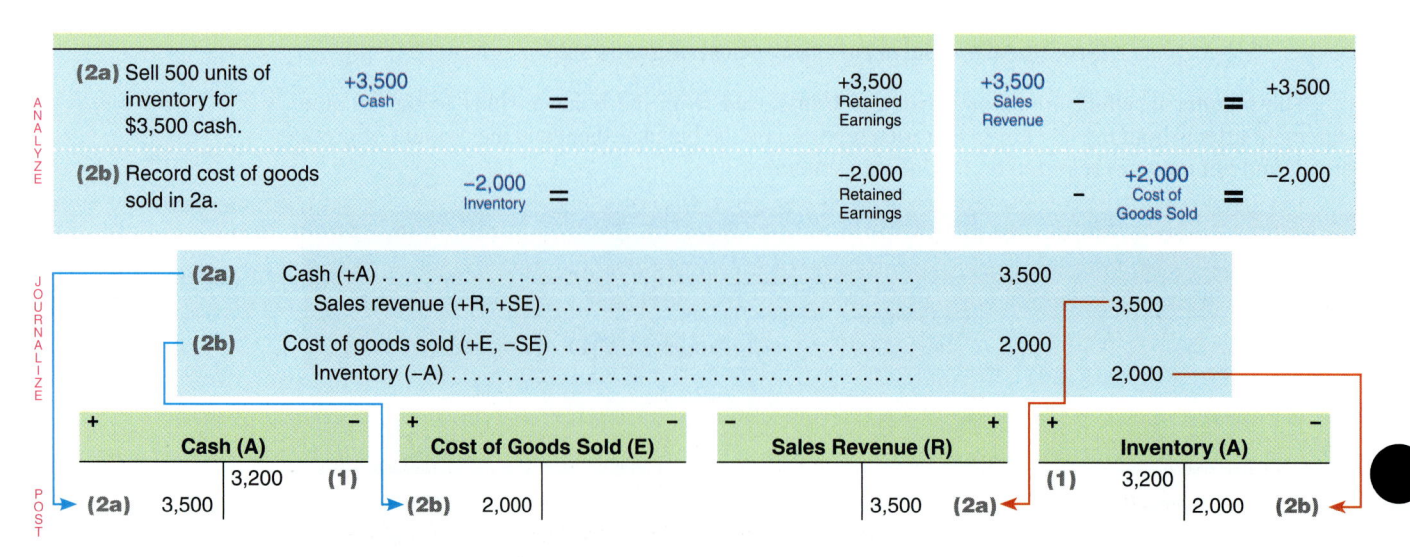

(2a) Sell 500 units of inventory for $3,500 cash.	+3,500 Cash =	+3,500 Retained Earnings	+3,500 Sales Revenue − = +3,500
(2b) Record cost of goods sold in 2a.	−2,000 Inventory =	−2,000 Retained Earnings	− +2,000 Cost of Goods Sold = −2,000

(2a) Cash (+A) 3,500
     Sales revenue (+R, +SE) 3,500

(2b) Cost of goods sold (+E, −SE) 2,000
     Inventory (−A) 2,000

Cash (A)
(1) 3,200
(2a) 3,500

Cost of Goods Sold (E)
(2b) 2,000

Sales Revenue (R)
3,500 (2a)

Inventory (A)
(1) 3,200 | 2,000 (2b)

The gross profit from this sale is $1,500 ($3,500 − $2,000). Also, $1,200 worth of merchandise remains in inventory (300 units × $4 per unit).

Inventory and the Cost of Acquisition

In general, a company should recognize all inventories to which it holds legal title, and that inventory should be recognized at the cost of acquiring the inventory. On occasion, that means that the company will recognize items in inventory that are not on its premises. For instance, if a company purchases inventory from a supplier on an "FOB shipping point" basis, meaning that the purchasing company receives title to the goods as soon as they are shipped by the supplier, the purchasing company should recognize the inventory as soon as it receives notice that the goods have been shipped. A similar situation occurs when a company ships its own products to a customer, but has not yet fulfilled the requirements for recognizing revenue on the shipment. In this case, the cost of the products remains in the selling company's inventory account until revenue (and cost of goods sold) can be recognized.

It is also possible for a company to have physical possession of inventory items, but not to have legal title. **Target Corporation**, for example, reports the following in a recent 10-K.

> **FYI** The term **FOB** ("free on board") **shipping point** means that title passes to the purchaser as soon as it is shipped by the seller. **FOB destination** means that the seller retains title until the item arrives at the purchaser's location.

> We routinely enter into arrangements with vendors whereby we do not purchase or pay for merchandise until the merchandise is ultimately sold to a guest. Under the vast majority of these arrangements, which represent less than 5 percent of consolidated sales, we record revenue and related costs gross. We concluded that we are the principal in these transactions for a number of reasons, most notably because we 1) control the overall economics of the transactions, including setting the sales price and realizing the majority of cash flows from the sale, 2) control the relationship with the customer, and 3) are responsible for fulfilling the promise to provide goods to the customer. Merchandise received under these arrangements is not included in Inventory because the purchase and sale of this inventory are virtually simultaneous.

Inventory is reported in the balance sheet at its cost, including any cost to acquire, transport, and prepare goods for sale. In some cases, determining the cost of inventory requires accounting for various incentives that suppliers offer to purchase more or to pay promptly. If a company qualifies for a supplier's volume discount or rebate, it should immediately recognize the effective reduction in the cost of inventory and cost of goods sold. Or, if the company purchases inventory on credit, suppliers often grant **cash discounts** to buyers if payment is made within a specified time period. Cash discounts are usually established as part of the credit terms and stated as a percentage of the purchase price. For example, credit terms of 1/10, n/30 (one-ten, net-thirty) indicate that a 1% cash discount is allowed if the payment is made within 10 days. If the cash discount is not taken, the full purchase price is due in 30 days. Cash discounts are discussed in greater detail in Chapter 9.

Inventory Reporting by Manufacturing Firms

Retail and wholesale businesses purchase merchandise for resale to customers. In contrast, a manufacturing firm produces the goods it sells. Its inventory reporting is designed to reflect this difference in the nature of its operations.

Manufacturing firms typically report three categories of inventory account:

> **FYI** Only one inventory account appears in the financial statements of a merchandiser. A manufacturer normally has three inventory accounts: Raw Materials, Work-in-Process, and Finished Goods.

- **Raw materials inventory**—the cost of parts and materials purchased from suppliers for use in the production process. When raw materials are used in the production process, the cost of the materials used is transferred from raw materials inventory into the work-in-process inventory account.
- **Work-in-process inventory**—the cost of the inventory of partially completed goods. Work-in-process (abbreviated WIP) includes the materials used in the production of the product as well as labor cost and overhead cost. (Methods by which labor and overhead costs are assigned to products in the WIP account is a *managerial accounting* topic.) When the production process is completed, the **cost of goods produced** is transferred from WIP into the finished goods inventory account.
- **Finished goods inventory**—the cost of the stock of completed product ready for delivery to customers. When finished goods are sold, cost of goods sold is debited and finished goods inventory is credited, much the same as in a retail business.

EXHIBIT 7.3 — Components of Inventory for Pfizer, Inc.

Dec. 31, 2020

Inventories ($ millions):	
Finished goods	$2,878
Work in process	4,430
Raw materials and supplies	738
Total	$8,046

A complete illustration of the accounting process for a manufacturing business is beyond the scope of this text. However, it is useful to understand how these inventory accounts are presented in the financial statements of manufacturing firms. In some cases, each of the three categories of inventory is presented in the balance sheet. Usually, however, the balance sheet only presents the combined total of the three accounts, leaving the detail to be presented in the disclosure notes. **Pfizer, Inc.** reported inventory of $8,046 million in its balance sheet dated December 31, 2020. **Exhibit 7.3** details the components of Pfizer's inventory balance as presented in its 10-K report. It shows that work in process inventory represented the largest portion of the total inventory balance. **Exhibit 7.3** is representative of the note disclosure provided by many manufacturing companies.

BUSINESS INSIGHT

If a manufacturing company has an unexpected buildup of inventory, the interpretation depends on the type of inventory. A larger-than-normal buildup of finished goods would imply that the company was having difficulty getting customers to purchase its products. However, if the buildup is in work-in-process inventory, it might imply a problem with manufacturing processes, particularly if accompanied by a decrease in finished goods inventory.

Review 7-1 LO7-1   Identifying Inventory Costs

Determine whether each cost should be included in the initial measurement of merchandise inventory of the seller. Consider each item separately.

a. _____ Transportation costs incurred by the seller to obtain goods purchased by supplier.
b. _____ Advertising costs incurred to sell the merchandise held for sale.
c. _____ Invoice cost of inventory in-transit from a suppler, shipped FOB shipping point.
d. _____ Sales tax incurred by seller on merchandise purchased.
e. _____ Costs incurred by the seller to ship inventory to the customer, sent FOB shipping point.

Solution on p. 7-42.

INVENTORY COSTING METHODS

LO7-2 Account for inventory and cost of goods sold using different costing methods.

The computation of cost of goods sold is important and is shown in **Exhibit 7.4**.

EXHIBIT 7.4 — Cost of Goods Sold Computation

Beginning inventory value (prior period ending balance sheet)
+ Cost of inventory purchases and/or production
———————————————————————————
Cost of goods available for sale
− Ending inventory value (current period balance sheet)
———————————————————————————
Cost of goods sold (current income statement)

The cost of inventory available at the beginning of a period is a carryover from the ending inventory balance of the prior period. The costs of current period purchases of inventory (or costs of newly manufactured inventories) are added to the costs of beginning inventory on the balance sheet, yielding the total cost of goods (inventory) available for sale. Then, the total cost of goods available either ends up in cost of goods sold for the period (reported on the income statement) or is carried forward as inventory to start the next period (reported on the ending balance sheet). This cost flow is schematically shown in **Exhibit 7.5**.

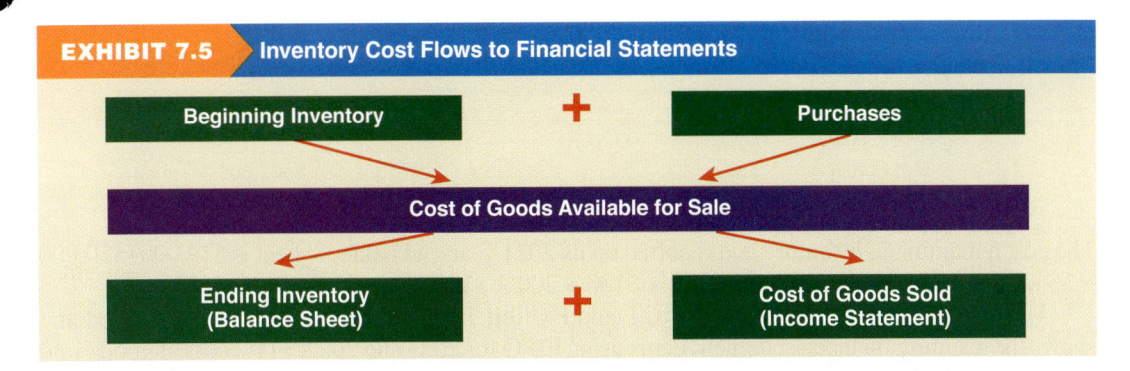

EXHIBIT 7.5 Inventory Cost Flows to Financial Statements

Beginning Inventory + Purchases

Cost of Goods Available for Sale

Ending Inventory (Balance Sheet) + Cost of Goods Sold (Income Statement)

Understanding the flow of inventory costs is important. If the beginning inventory plus all inventory purchased or manufactured during the period is sold, then COGS is equal to the cost of the goods available for sale. However, when inventory remains at the end of a period, companies must identify the cost of those inventories that have been sold and the cost of those inventories that remain.

Most companies will organize the physical flow of their inventories to keep the cost of inventory management low, while minimizing the likelihood of spoilage or obsolescence. However, the accounting for inventory and cost of goods sold does not have to follow the physical flow of the units of inventory, so companies may report using a **cost flow assumption** that does not conform to the actual movement of product through the firm. (For instance, many grocery chains use last-in, first-out to account for inventory costs, but that doesn't mean that they put the newest produce out to sell while keeping the older produce back in the storeroom.)

Illustration To illustrate the possible cost flow assumptions that companies can adopt, assume that **Exhibit 7.6** reflects the inventory records of Butler Company.

EXHIBIT 7.6 Summary Inventory Records for Butler Company

		Number of Units	Cost per Unit	Total Cost	Number of Units	Price per Unit	Total Revenue
January 1, 2021	Beginning inventory...	500	$100	$ 50,000			
2021	Inventory purchased...	200	170	34,000			
	Inventory sold.........				450	$250	$112,500
2022	Inventory purchased...	600	180	108,000			
	Inventory sold.........				500	255	127,500

Butler Company began the period with inventory consisting of 500 units it purchased at a total cost of $50,000 ($100 each). During the two-year period, the company purchased an additional 200 units costing $34,000 and 600 units costing $108,000. The total cost of goods available for sale for this two-year period equals $192,000.

Tracking the number of units available for sale each year and in inventory at the end of each year is simple. However, the changing cost per unit makes it more complicated to determine the cost of goods sold and the ending inventory. The relationships depicted in **Exhibit 7.5** can hold in multiple ways, depending on the cost flow assumption chosen. Three inventory costing methods are acceptable under U.S. GAAP.[1]

First-In, First-Out (FIFO)

The **first-in, first-out (FIFO)** inventory costing method transfers costs from inventory in the order that they were initially recorded. That is, FIFO assumes that the first costs recorded in inventory (first-in) are the first costs transferred from inventory (first-out) to cost of goods sold.

FYI First-in, first-out (FIFO) assumes that goods are used in the order in which they are purchased; the inventory remaining represents the most recent purchases.

---

[1] Of the firms in the Standard and Poor's 500 Index as of March 22, 2021, **13.2%** have a LIFO reserve reported on Compustat in 2019. A few additional firms may be on LIFO but have a zero reserve.

Conversely, the costs of the last units purchased are the costs that remain in inventory at year-end. Applying FIFO to the data in **Exhibit 7.6** means that the costs relating to the 450 units sold are all taken from its *beginning* inventory, which consists of 500 units. The company's 2021 cost of goods sold and gross profit, using FIFO, is computed as follows:

Sales.	$112,500
COGS (450 @ $100 each).	45,000
Gross profit.	$ 67,500

The cost remaining in inventory and reported on its 2021 year-end balance sheet is $39,000 ($50,000 + $34,000 − $45,000; also computed 50 × $100 + 200 × $170).

The same process can be used for 2022, and **Exhibit 7.7** depicts the FIFO costing method and shows the resulting financial statement items using FIFO for 2021 and 2022. FIFO cost of goods sold for 2022 is 50 units at $100 each plus 200 units at $170 each plus 250 units at $180 each, or $84,000. Ending inventory for 2022 is 350 units at $180 each, or $63,000. Over the two-year period, the total cost of goods available for sale of $192,000 is either recognized as cost of goods sold ($45,000 + $84,000 = $129,000) or remains in ending inventory ($63,000).

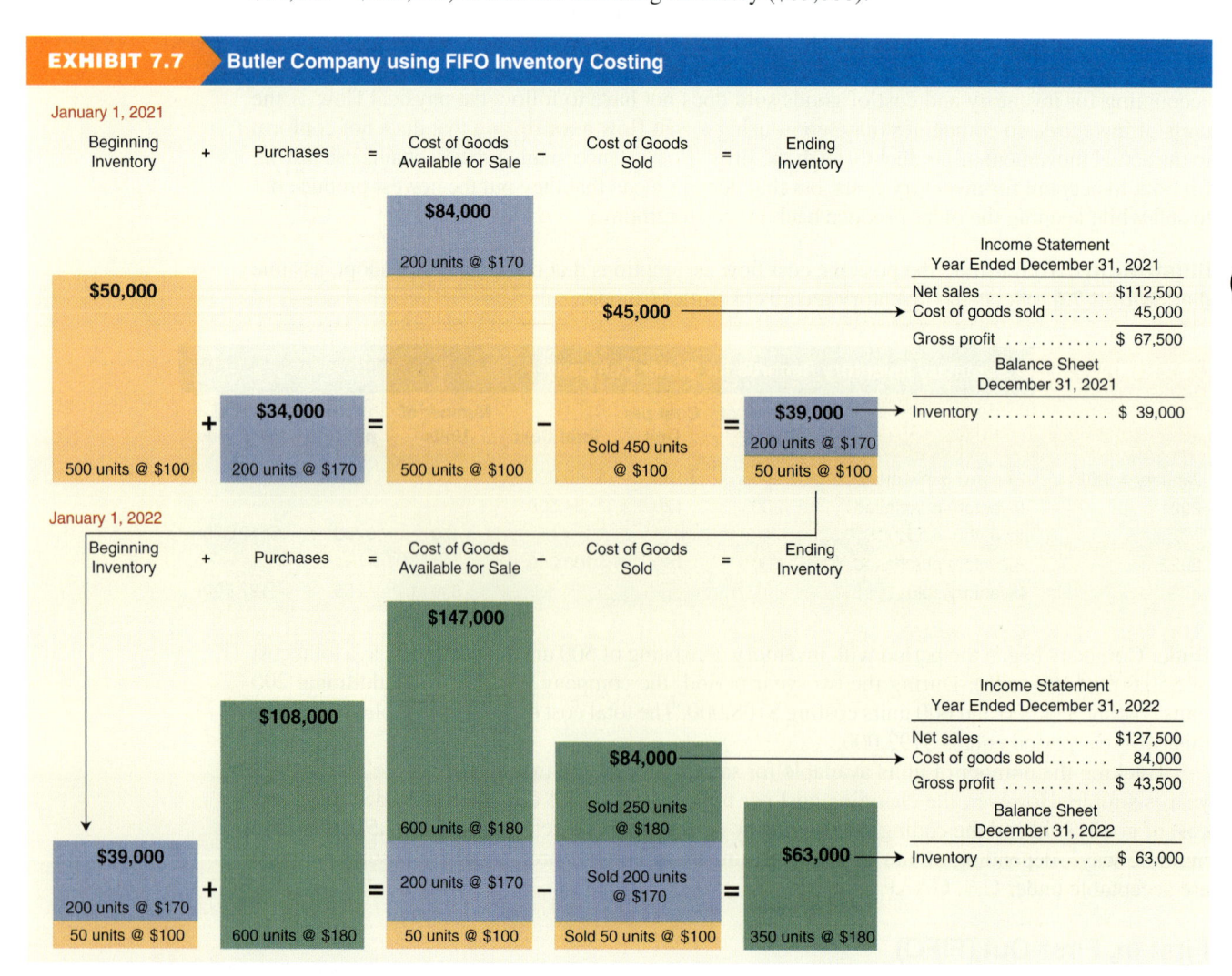

EXHIBIT 7.7 Butler Company using FIFO Inventory Costing

January 1, 2021

Beginning Inventory + Purchases = Cost of Goods Available for Sale − Cost of Goods Sold = Ending Inventory

- Beginning Inventory: $50,000 (500 units @ $100)
- Purchases: $34,000 (200 units @ $170)
- Cost of Goods Available for Sale: $84,000 (500 units @ $100; 200 units @ $170)
- Cost of Goods Sold: $45,000 (Sold 450 units @ $100)
- Ending Inventory: $39,000 (200 units @ $170; 50 units @ $100)

Income Statement Year Ended December 31, 2021
- Net sales $112,500
- Cost of goods sold 45,000
- Gross profit .... $ 67,500

Balance Sheet December 31, 2021
- Inventory .... $ 39,000

January 1, 2022

Beginning Inventory + Purchases = Cost of Goods Available for Sale − Cost of Goods Sold = Ending Inventory

- Beginning Inventory: $39,000 (200 units @ $170; 50 units @ $100)
- Purchases: $108,000 (600 units @ $180)
- Cost of Goods Available for Sale: $147,000 (600 units @ $180; 200 units @ $170; 50 units @ $100)
- Cost of Goods Sold: $84,000 (Sold 250 units @ $180; Sold 200 units @ $170; Sold 50 units @ $100)
- Ending Inventory: $63,000 (350 units @ $180)

Income Statement Year Ended December 31, 2022
- Net sales $127,500
- Cost of goods sold 84,000
- Gross profit .... $ 43,500

Balance Sheet December 31, 2022
- Inventory .... $ 63,000

Last-In, First-Out (LIFO)

FYI Last-in, first-out (LIFO) matches the cost of the last goods purchased against revenue.

The **last-in, first-out (LIFO)** inventory costing method transfers to cost of goods sold the most recent costs that were recorded in inventory. That is, we assume that the most recent costs recorded in inventory (last-in) are the first costs transferred from inventory (first-out). Conversely, the costs of the first units purchased are the costs that remain in inventory at year-end. Butler Company's 2021 cost of goods sold and gross profit, using LIFO, are computed as follows:

Sales.		$112,500
COGS: (200 @ $170 each = $34,000)		
(250 @ $100 each = $25,000).		59,000
Gross profit.		$ 53,500

The cost remaining in inventory and reported on its 2021 balance sheet is $25,000 ($50,000 + $34,000 − $59,000; also computed 250 × $100).

The same process can be used for 2022, and **Exhibit 7.8** depicts the LIFO costing method and shows the resulting financial statement values using LIFO for both years. LIFO cost of goods sold for 2022 is 500 units at $180 each, or $90,000. Ending inventory is 250 units at $100 each plus 100 units at $180 each, or $43,000. Again, the two-year total cost of goods available for sale of $192,000 is either recognized as cost of goods sold ($59,000 + $90,000 = $149,000) or remains in inventory ($43,000).

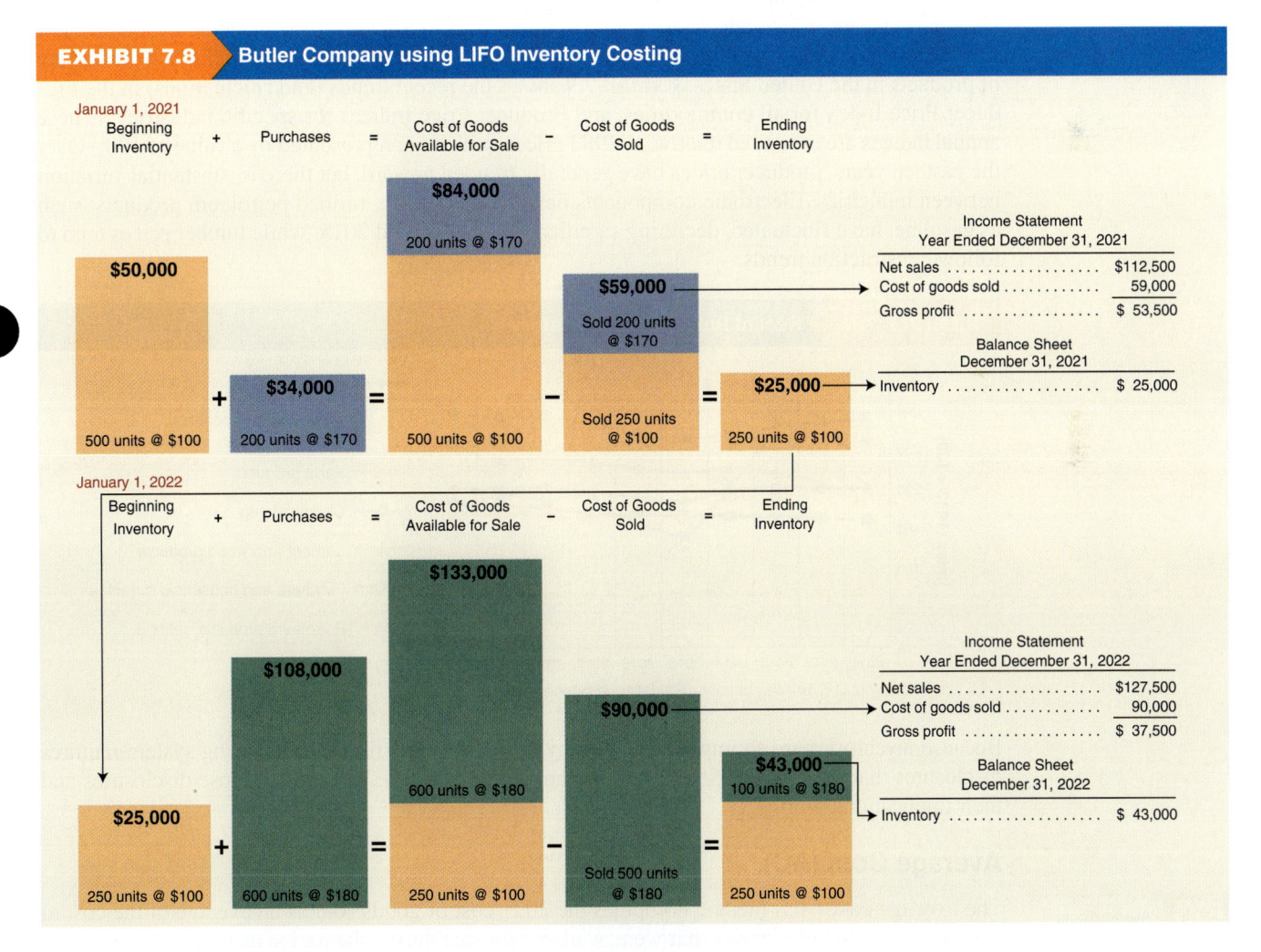

EXHIBIT 7.8 Butler Company using LIFO Inventory Costing

January 1, 2021
Beginning Inventory + Purchases = Cost of Goods Available for Sale − Cost of Goods Sold = Ending Inventory

$50,000 (500 units @ $100) + $34,000 (200 units @ $170) = $84,000 (200 units @ $170 / 500 units @ $100) − $59,000 (Sold 200 units @ $170 / Sold 250 units @ $100) = $25,000 (250 units @ $100)

Income Statement
Year Ended December 31, 2021

Net sales	$112,500
Cost of goods sold	59,000
Gross profit	$ 53,500

Balance Sheet
December 31, 2021

Inventory	$ 25,000

January 1, 2022
Beginning Inventory + Purchases = Cost of Goods Available for Sale − Cost of Goods Sold = Ending Inventory

$25,000 (250 units @ $100) + $108,000 (600 units @ $180) = $133,000 (600 units @ $180 / 250 units @ $100) − $90,000 (Sold 500 units @ $180) = $43,000 (100 units @ $180 / 250 units @ $100)

Income Statement
Year Ended December 31, 2022

Net sales	$127,500
Cost of goods sold	90,000
Gross profit	$ 37,500

Balance Sheet
December 31, 2022

Inventory	$ 43,000

The exhibit shows that **LIFO layers** of inventories added in each year are kept separately. So, the ending inventory in 2022 consists of a pre-2021 layer of 250 units at $100 each plus a 2022 layer of 100 units at $180 each. When unit sales exceed purchases (as we discuss in the appendix), the first costs carried to cost of goods sold are those purchased in the current year, followed by the most recent layer of LIFO inventory and working down to the oldest layers. So, the 2021 beginning inventory value of $100 per unit remains in LIFO inventory as long as there are 250 units remaining at the end of the year. One aspect of this flow assumption is that reported LIFO inventory values can be significantly lower than the current cost of acquiring the same inventory.

LIFO inventory costing is always applied on a periodic, annual basis. This means that Butler's cost of goods sold and ending inventory for 2022 do not depend on the timing of the sales and purchases within the year. Inventory levels might be drawn down below 250 units *during* the year, but the 250 unit LIFO layer at $100 each remains in ending inventory as long as inventory is built up to 250 units by the *end* of the year.

Inventory Costing and Price Changes

There are several important aspects of inventory costing that are illustrated by the Butler Company example. First, both LIFO and FIFO are historical cost methods, though they allocate the costs of inventory differently. All costs are accounted for, but in different ways.

Second, the differences between LIFO and FIFO arise when the costs of inventory change over time. In general, LIFO puts more recent costs into cost of goods sold expense, so LIFO cost of goods sold is higher than FIFO cost of goods sold (and gross profit correspondingly lower) when the costs of inventory are rising over time. This phenomenon can be seen in years 2021 and 2022 for Butler Company. If the costs of inventory are falling, then FIFO cost of goods sold exceeds LIFO cost of goods sold.

One place where we can observe the cost trends of acquiring inventory is in the U.S. Bureau of Labor Statistics' Producer Price Indices. These indices track the costs of producing a wide variety of products in the United States. **Exhibit 7.9** shows the recent trends (and fluctuations) in the Producer Price Index for all commodities, and Producer Price Indices for specific industries. (These annual indices are measured relative to 1982 prices, which are represented by a value of 100.) Over the past ten years, producer prices have generally trended upward, but there is substantial variation between industries. Electronic components have trended down, refined petroleum products, such as gasoline, have fluctuated, declining significantly in 2014 and 2015, while lumber prices tend to follow construction trends.

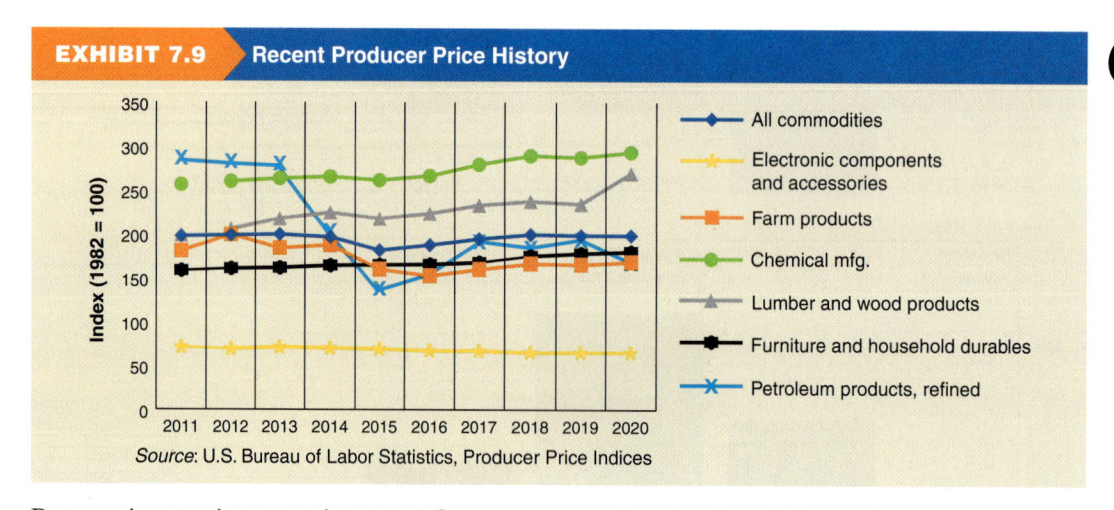

EXHIBIT 7.9   Recent Producer Price History

Source: U.S. Bureau of Labor Statistics, Producer Price Indices

Because inventories are so important for many companies, the financial reporting system requires disclosures that are useful in interpreting financial performance. We turn to those disclosures and their implications shortly.

Average Cost (AC)

The **average cost (AC)** method computes the 2021 cost of goods sold as an average of the cost to purchase all of the inventories that were available for sale during the period as follows:

Sales.	$112,500
COGS (450 @ $120 [{$50,000 + $34,000}/700 units] each)	54,000
Gross profit.	$ 58,500

> **FYI** Average cost values inventory on the basis of the average cost of all similar goods available during the period.

The average cost of $120 per unit is determined from the total cost of goods available for sale divided by the number of units available for sale ($84,000/700 units). The cost remaining in inventory and reported on its 2021 balance sheet is $30,000 ($84,000 − $54,000; also computed 250 × $120).

When average cost is applied to the future years, the beginning inventory balance's average cost is again averaged with the inventory acquisitions made during the year. This new average is used to assign costs to that year's ending inventory and cost of goods sold. For the Butler Company, the average cost is $120 for 2021 and $162.35 (rounded) for 2022. The average cost for 2022 is the opening inventory balance plus the period's purchases ($30,000 + $108,000) divided by the total number of units available for sale (250 + 600). So, 2022 cost of goods sold is 500 units at $162.35 each, and ending inventory is 350 units at that same average cost. **Exhibit 7.10** depicts the average cost method and shows the resulting financial statement values using average cost for both years.

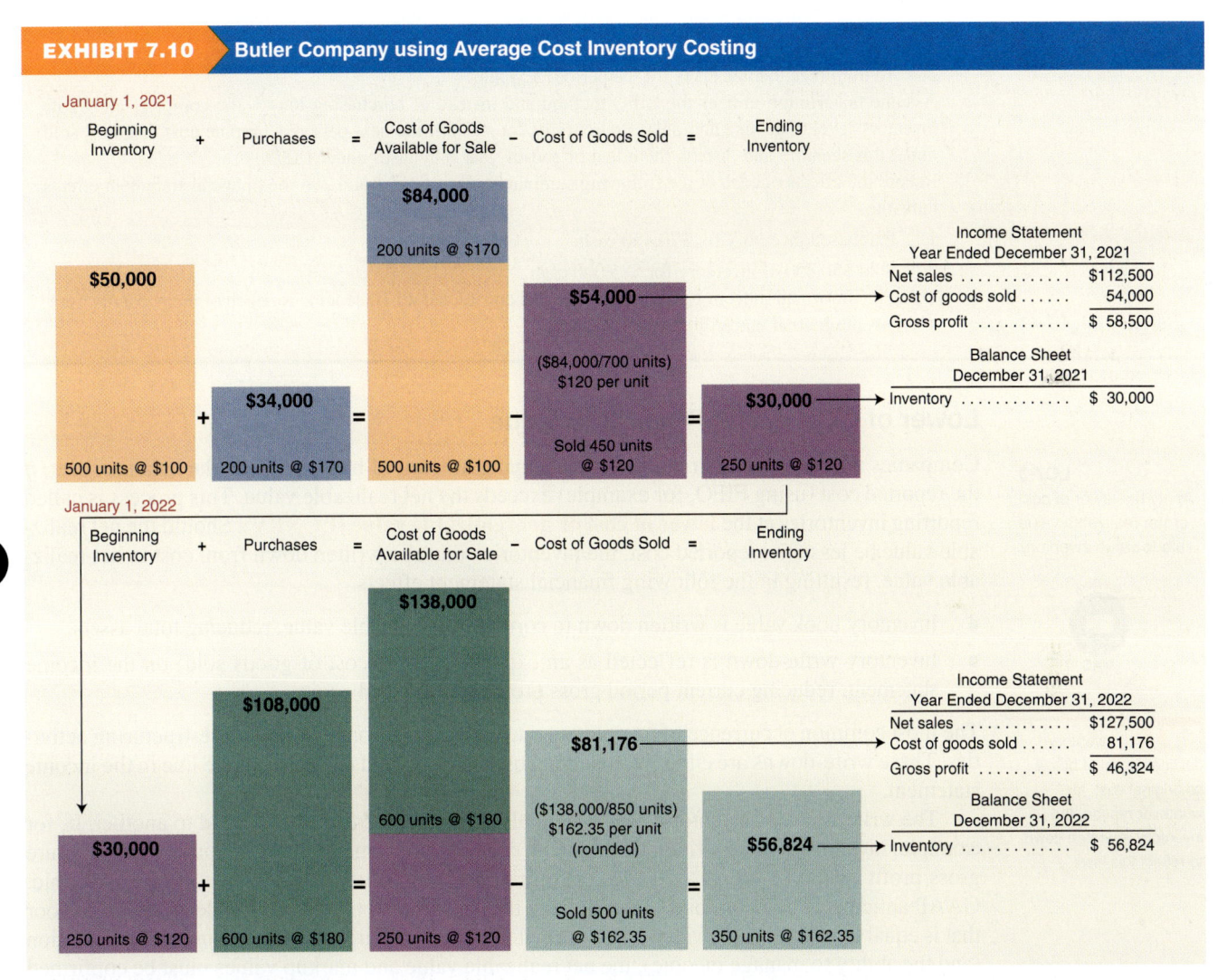

EXHIBIT 7.10 Butler Company using Average Cost Inventory Costing

January 1, 2021

Beginning Inventory + Purchases = Cost of Goods Available for Sale − Cost of Goods Sold = Ending Inventory

- $50,000 (500 units @ $100)
- $34,000 (200 units @ $170)
- $84,000 (500 units @ $100; 200 units @ $170)
- $54,000 — ($84,000/700 units) $120 per unit — Sold 450 units @ $120
- $30,000 (250 units @ $120)

Income Statement
Year Ended December 31, 2021

Net sales	$112,500
Cost of goods sold	54,000
Gross profit	$ 58,500

Balance Sheet
December 31, 2021

Inventory	$ 30,000

January 1, 2022

Beginning Inventory + Purchases = Cost of Goods Available for Sale − Cost of Goods Sold = Ending Inventory

- $30,000 (250 units @ $120)
- $108,000 (600 units @ $180)
- $138,000 (250 units @ $120; 600 units @ $180)
- $81,176 — ($138,000/850 units) $162.35 per unit (rounded) — Sold 500 units @ $162.35
- $56,824 (350 units @ $162.35)

Income Statement
Year Ended December 31, 2022

Net sales	$127,500
Cost of goods sold	81,176
Gross profit	$ 46,324

Balance Sheet
December 31, 2022

Inventory	$ 56,824

Accounting for Inventory Using Different Cost Methods — LO7-2 **Review 7-2**

At the beginning of the current period, Hutton Company holds 1,000 units of its only product with a per-unit cost of $18. A summary of purchases during the current period follows:

	Units	Unit Cost	Cost
Beginning Inventory	1,000	$18.00	$18,000
Purchases: #1	1,800	18.25	32,850
#2	800	18.50	14,800
#3	1,200	19.00	22,800
Goods available for sale	4,800		$88,450

During the current period, Hutton sells 2,800 units.

continued

continued from previous page

Required

a. Assume that Hutton uses the first-in, first-out (FIFO) method. Compute the cost of goods sold for the current period and the ending inventory balance.
b. Assume that Hutton uses the last-in, first-out (LIFO) method. Compute the cost of goods sold for the current period and the ending inventory balance.
c. Assume that Hutton uses the average cost (AC) method. Compute the cost of goods sold for the current period and the ending inventory balance.
d. As manager, which one of these three inventory costing methods would you choose:
   1. To reflect what is probably the physical flow of goods? Explain.
   2. To minimize income taxes for the period? Explain.
e. Assume that Hutton utilizes the LIFO method and instead of purchasing lot #3, the company allows its inventory level to decline and delays purchasing lot #3 until the next period. Compute cost of goods sold under this scenario and discuss the effect of end-of-year purchases under LIFO.
f. Record the effects of each of the following summary transactions 1 and 2 in the financial statement effects template.
   1. Purchased inventory for $70,450 cash.
   2. Sold $50,850 of inventory for $85,000 cash.
g. Using the information from part f, prepare journal entries, set up T-accounts for each of the accounts used, and post the journal entries to those T-accounts.

Solution on p. 7-42.

Lower of Cost or Net Realizable Value

LO7-3 Apply the lower of cost or net realizable value rule to value inventory.

Companies are required to write down the carrying amount of inventories on the balance sheet, *if* the reported cost (using FIFO, for example) exceeds the net realizable value. This process is called reporting inventories at the **lower of cost or net realizable value (LCNRV)**. Should the net realizable value be less than reported cost, the inventories must be written down from cost to net realizable value, resulting in the following financial statement effects.

- Inventory book value is written down to current net realizable value, reducing total assets.
- Inventory write-down is reflected as an expense (part of cost of goods sold) on the income statement, reducing current period gross profit, income, and equity.

FYI If inventory declines in value below its original cost, for whatever reason, the inventory is written down to reflect this loss.

The most common occurrence of inventory write-downs is in connection with restructuring activities. These write-downs are either included in cost of goods sold or on a separate line in the income statement.

The write-down of inventories can potentially shift income from one period to another. If, for example, inventories were written down below current replacement cost (too conservative), future gross profit would be increased as lower future costs would be reflected in cost of goods sold. GAAP anticipates this possibility by requiring that inventories not be written down below a floor that is equal to net realizable value less a normal markup. Although this does allow some discretion (and the ability to manage income), the net realizable value and markup values must be confirmed by the company's auditors.

FYI Standards require the consistent application of costing methods from one period to another.

Illustration To illustrate the lower of cost or net realizable value rule, assume Home Depot has the following items in its current period ending inventory:

Item	Quantity	Cost per Unit	Net Realizable Value	LCNRV per Unit	Total LCNRV
Spools of copper wire.	250	$10	$15	$10	250 × $10 = $2,500
Sheets of wood paneling	500	$ 8	$ 6	$ 6	500 × $ 6 = $3,000

A write-down is not necessary for the spools of copper wire because the net realizable value ($15 per unit) is higher than the acquisition cost ($10 per unit). However, the 500 sheets of wood paneling should be recorded in the current period's ending inventory at the net realizable value of $6 per unit because it is lower than the acquisition cost of $8 per unit. When the net realizable value of inventory declines below its acquisition cost, we must record a write-down. Before the write-down, inventory is recorded at cost of $6,500. With the write-down of $1,000, inventory after the write-down is recorded at LCNRV of $5,500. The effects of this write-down and corresponding journal entries follow:

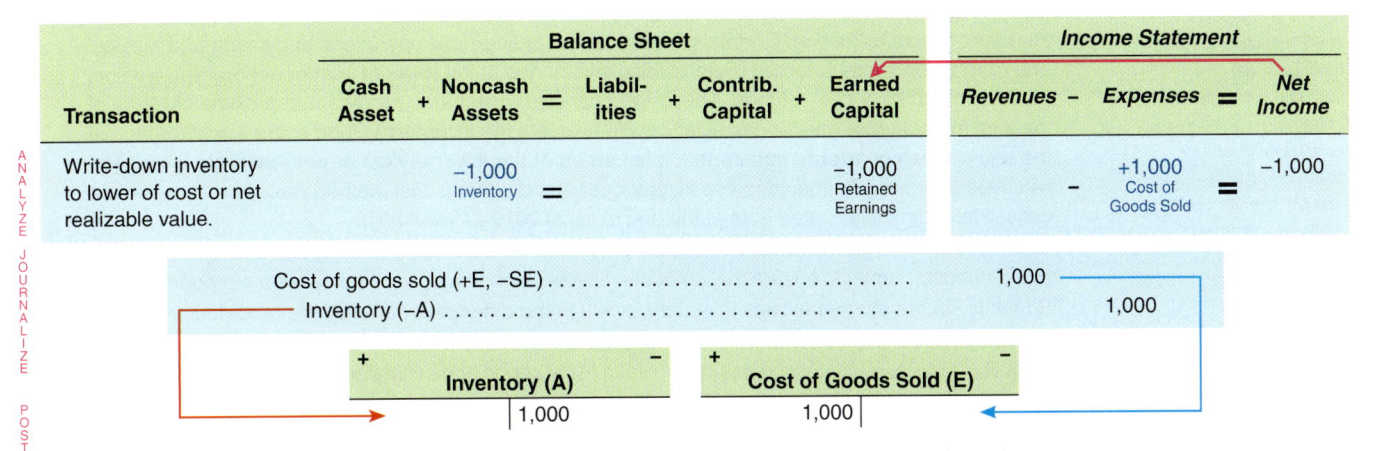

	Balance Sheet					Income Statement		
Transaction	Cash Asset	+ Noncash Assets	= Liabilities	+ Contrib. Capital	+ Earned Capital	Revenues	− Expenses	= Net Income
Write-down inventory to lower of cost or net realizable value.		−1,000 Inventory	=		−1,000 Retained Earnings		+1,000 Cost of Goods Sold	= −1,000

Cost of goods sold (+E, −SE) 1,000
   Inventory (−A) 1,000

+ Inventory (A) −	− Cost of Goods Sold (E) +
1,000	1,000

A GLOBAL PERSPECTIVE

IFRS

Under U.S. GAAP, inventory that has been written down cannot be revalued later at higher levels even if the net realizable value of that inventory increases. IFRS, on the other hand, does allow companies to reverse the write-down of the inventory up to the acquisition cost if market values warrant. The revaluation results in a debit to Inventory and a credit to Cost of Goods Sold. The option to revalue inventory after a write-down differs across countries.

Applying the Lower of Cost or Net Realizable Value Rule

LO7-3 Review 7-3

Venner Company had the following inventory at December 31.

	Quantity	Unit Price Cost	NRV
Fans			
Model X1	300	$18	$19
Model X2	250	22	24
Model X3	400	29	26
Heaters			
Model B7	500	24	28
Model B8	290	35	32
Model B9	100	41	38

Required
1. Determine ending inventory by applying the lower of cost or NRV rule to
   a. Each item of inventory.
   b. Each major category of inventory.
   c. Total inventory.
2. Which of the LCNRV procedures from requirement 1 results in the lowest net income for the year? Explain.

Solution on p. 7-43.

FINANCIAL STATEMENT EFFECTS AND DISCLOSURE

The notes to the financial statements describe, at least in general terms, the inventory accounting method used by a company. To illustrate, The Home Depot reports $14,531 million in merchandise inventory on its February 2, 2020, balance sheet as a current asset. The following note was taken from that 10-K report:

LO7-4 Evaluate how inventory costing affects management decisions and outsiders' interpretations of financial statements.

FYI Standards require financial statement disclosure of (1) the composition of the inventory (in the balance sheet or a separate schedule in the notes), (2) significant or unusual inventory financing arrangements, and (3) inventory costing methods employed (which can differ for different types of inventory).

> The substantial majority of our merchandise inventories are stated at the lower of cost (first-in, first-out) or market, as determined by the retail inventory method, which is based on a number of factors such as markups, markdowns, and inventory losses (or shrink). As the inventory retail value is adjusted regularly to reflect market conditions, inventory valued using the retail method approximates the lower of cost or market. Certain subsidiaries, including retail operations in Canada and Mexico, and distribution centers, record merchandise inventories at the lower of cost or net realizable value, as determined by a cost method. These merchandise inventories represent approximately 29% of the total merchandise inventories balance. We evaluate the inventory valued using a cost method at the end of each quarter to ensure that it is carried at the lower of cost or net realizable value. The valuation allowance for merchandise inventories valued under a cost method was not material to our consolidated financial statements at the end of fiscal 2019 or fiscal 2018.
>
> Independent physical inventory counts or cycle counts are taken on a regular basis in each store and distribution center to ensure that amounts reflected in merchandise inventories are properly stated. Shrink (or in the case of excess inventory, swell) is the difference between the recorded amount of inventory and the physical inventory. We calculate shrink based on actual inventory losses occurring as a result of physical inventory counts during each fiscal period and estimated inventory losses occurring between physical inventory counts. The estimate for shrink occurring in the interim period between physical inventory counts is calculated on a store-specific basis based on recent shrink results and current trends in the business.

This note includes several items that would be of interest to financial statement users:

1. The Home Depot uses the FIFO method to determine the cost of most of its inventory suggesting several methods are likely to be in use.
2. Inventory is reported at the lower of cost or net realizable value, and the amount of write-down (the valuation allowance) was not material at the financial statement date.
3. The company periodically takes a physical count of inventory to identify "shrink." Shrink refers to the loss of inventory due to theft, breakage or damage, spoilage (for perishable goods), or other losses, as well as inaccurate records.

When businesses adjust inventory balances for shrink, the loss is debited to cost of goods sold. Hence, cost of goods sold expense on the income statement includes the actual cost of products sold during the period plus the loss due to shrink as well as losses resulting from lower of cost or market adjustments and discounts lost.

Another illustration of inventory disclosure is taken from the notes of **The Timken Company**. Timken reports an inventory of $841.3 million on its December 31, 2020, balance sheet. The following excerpts were taken from note disclosures in its 2020 10-K report ($ millions):

> **Notes 1 and 7**
> Inventories are valued at the lower of cost or net realizable value, with approximately 61% valued by the FIFO method and the remaining 39% valued by the LIFO method. The majority of the Company's domestic inventories are valued by the LIFO method, while all of the Company's international inventories are valued by the FIFO method.
>
> If all inventories had been valued at FIFO, inventories would have been $172.1 million and $168.9 million greater at December 31, 2020 and 2019, respectively. The Company recognized an increase in its LIFO reserve of $3.2 million during 2020, compared to a decrease in its LIFO reserve of $5.0 million during 2019. Inventory and the allowance for surplus and obsolete inventory increased from 2019 primarily as a result of recent acquisitions.

There are several interesting items disclosed in Timken's note:

1. Timken uses LIFO to report the *majority* of its domestic inventories, while *all* of its international inventories are valued using the FIFO method. Neither U.S. GAAP nor tax authorities such as the IRS require the use of a single inventory costing method. That is, companies are allowed to, and frequently do, use different inventory costing methods for different categories of inventory. In addition, multinational companies may use one costing method in the United States and a different method for foreign inventory stocks.

2. Timken reports inventory values at the lower of cost or net realizable value. The FIFO value differs from the LIFO cost. In 2020, the FIFO cost was $172.1 million higher than the LIFO cost, while in 2019, the FIFO cost was $168.9 million higher than LIFO. Companies using LIFO are required to report the difference between the LIFO cost and current value—determined either as market value or replacement cost or as the FIFO cost. The difference between the ending inventory's FIFO cost (or current cost) and its LIFO cost is called the **LIFO reserve**.

Why do companies disclose such details on inventory, and why is so much attention paid to inventory in financial statement analysis? First, the magnitude of a company's investment in inventory is often large—affecting both balance sheets and income statements. Second, risks of inventory losses are often high, as they are tied to technical obsolescence and consumer tastes. Third, it can provide insight into future performance—both good and bad. Fourth, high inventory levels result in substantial costs for the company, such as:

- Financing costs to purchase inventories (when not purchased on credit)
- Storage costs of inventories (such as warehousing and related facilities)
- Handling costs of inventories (including wages)
- Insurance costs of inventories

Consequently, companies seek to keep inventories at levels that balance these costs against the cost of insufficient inventory (stock-out and resulting lost sales and delays in production, as machines and employees sit idle awaiting inventories to process).

Next, we turn our focus on the effects of the different inventory costing assumptions on the financial statements.

Financial Statement Effects of Inventory Costing

The three inventory costing methods described a few pages earlier yield differing levels of gross profit for our illustrative example, as shown in **Exhibit 7.11**.

We emphasize that, even though the various methods produce different financial statements, the underlying events are the same. That is, different accounting methods can make similar situations seem more different than they really are.

LIFO Reserve Exhibit 7.11 demonstrates one of the income statement/balance sheet links that proves useful in analyzing financial statements. In the beginning inventory for 2021, LIFO and FIFO start from the same point—500 units at $100 each. But during 2021, FIFO would record cost of goods sold that is $14,000 less than LIFO ($45,000 versus $59,000). During 2021, LIFO put $14,000 more into cost of goods sold than FIFO did, but that also means that LIFO put $14,000 less into ending inventory. We can see that the LIFO reserve has grown from zero to $14,000, the same amount. This relationship continues in 2022: the LIFO reserve increased by $6,000 (from $14,000 to $20,000), and the LIFO cost of goods sold was $6,000 greater than the FIFO cost of goods sold ($90,000 versus $84,000). The LIFO reserve equals the ending inventory's FIFO cost less LIFO cost, but it is also the *cumulative* difference between LIFO and FIFO cost of goods sold. The *change* in the LIFO reserve is the difference between LIFO and FIFO cost of goods sold for the current period.

So, if Butler Company chose to report using LIFO, we could estimate what the company's FIFO cost of goods sold would have been by seeing how the LIFO reserve changed.

> **FIFO cost of goods sold = LIFO cost of goods sold − Change in the LIFO reserve**

That relationship proves useful if we want to compare Butler Company's gross profit to that of another company using FIFO. A change in the LIFO reserve also provides some information about how a company's inventory costs changed over the period.

Income Statement Effects The income differences between inventory accounting methods are a function of two factors. First is the speed and direction of inventory cost changes. For Butler Company, inventory costs have increased from $100 per unit to $180 per unit in a two-year period. If costs increased more slowly, the difference between LIFO and FIFO would decrease. And, if costs decreased, the differences would reverse: FIFO cost of goods sold would be greater than LIFO cost of goods sold.

> **FYI** If ending inventory is misstated, then (1) the inventory, retained earnings, working capital, and current ratio in the balance sheet are misstated, and (2) the cost of goods sold and net income in the income statement are misstated.

EXHIBIT 7.11 — Financial Statement Effects of Inventory Costing Methods for Butler Company

		FIFO	LIFO	Average Cost
January 1, 2021	**Balance Sheet**			
	Beginning inventory	$ 50,000	$ 50,000	$ 50,000
	LIFO Reserve	—	—	—
Year Ended 2021	**Income Statement**			
	Revenue	$112,500	$112,500	$112,500
	Cost of goods sold:			
	Beginning inventory	50,000	50,000	50,000
	Add: Purchases	34,000	34,000	34,000
	Goods available for sale	84,000	84,000	84,000
	Subtract: Ending inventory	39,000	25,000	30,000
	Cost of goods sold	45,000	59,000	54,000
	Gross profit	67,500	53,500	58,500
	Selling, general and administrative expenses (assumed number)	10,000	10,000	10,000
	Income before income taxes	57,500	43,500	48,500
	Income tax expense (25%)	14,375	10,875	12,125
	Net income	$ 43,125	$ 32,625	$ 36,375
December 31, 2021	**Balance Sheet**			
	Ending inventory	$ 39,000	$ 25,000	$ 30,000
	LIFO Reserve	—	14,000	—
Year Ended 2022	**Income Statement**			
	Revenue	$127,500	$127,500	$127,500
	Cost of goods sold:			
	Beginning inventory	39,000	25,000	30,000
	Add: Purchases	108,000	108,000	108,000
	Goods available for sale	147,000	133,000	138,000
	Subtract: Ending inventory	63,000	43,000	56,824
	Cost of goods sold	84,000	90,000	81,176
	Gross profit	43,500	37,500	46,324
	Selling, general and administrative expenses (assumed number)	10,000	10,000	10,000
	Income before income taxes	33,500	27,500	36,324
	Income tax expense (25%)	8,375	6,875	9,081
	Net income	$ 25,125	$ 20,625	$ 27,243
December 31, 2022	**Balance Sheet**			
	Ending inventory	$ 63,000	$ 43,000	$ 56,824
	LIFO Reserve	—	20,000	—

The second factor determining the differences is the length of time inventory is held by the company. If Butler Company were able to operate with zero inventory (or at least begin and end the reporting period with zero inventory), the three inventory accounting methods would yield exactly the same cost of goods sold. On the other hand, if inventory must be held for a long period, the differences would increase.

Effects of Changing Costs When the cost of a company's products is changing, management usually makes corresponding changes in the prices it charges for those products. If costs are declining, competitive pressures are likely to push down the prices customers are willing to pay. If costs are increasing, the company will try to increase prices to recover at least some of the greater cost. When costs fluctuate (for example, for a commodity), management may act to cause its prices to fluctuate in an effort to maintain its target profit margin.[2]

---

[2] LIFO has a reporting advantage when inventory costs fluctuate, in that it matches current period costs against current period revenues. For a company that holds one quarter's worth of inventory, FIFO matches the costs from three months ago against current period revenues. Such a "mismatch" might make it difficult for management to convey its success in maintaining its current profit margin.

If costs and prices are rising, then FIFO reports a higher gross margin, because the costs of older, lower-cost inventory are being matched against current selling prices. For tax purposes, the company would prefer to use LIFO because it would decrease gross profit and decrease taxable income. If Butler Company were subject to a 25% income tax rate, the use of LIFO rather than FIFO reduces taxes by $3,500 in 2021 ($14,375 − $10,875 in **Exhibit 7.11**, or 25% of the $14,000 difference in 2021 cost of goods sold) and by $1,500 in 2022 ($8,375 − $6,875 in **Exhibit 7.11**, or 25% of the $6,000 difference in 2022 cost of goods sold). In total over the two years, using LIFO (rather than FIFO) would reduce Butler's tax bill by $5,000 (which equals 25% of the $20,000 LIFO reserve at the end of 2022).

In the United States, LIFO is a popular tax method for accounting for inventories that have an upward trend in costs. But, the Internal Revenue Service has imposed a LIFO conformity requirement. If Butler Company is using LIFO for tax reporting, it must use LIFO for reporting to its shareholders. For inventories with a decreasing trend in costs, FIFO reduces the amount of taxes paid. FIFO is allowed by the Internal Revenue Service, but there is no corresponding conformity requirement for firms that use FIFO.

FYI When a company adopts LIFO in its tax filings, the company is required to use LIFO for reporting to its shareholders (in its 10-K). This requirement is known as the LIFO conformity rule.

Balance Sheet Effects The ending inventory using LIFO for our illustration is less than that reported using FIFO. In prolonged periods of rising costs, using LIFO yields ending inventories that are markedly lower than FIFO. As a result, balance sheets using LIFO do not accurately represent the cost that a company would incur to replace its current investment in inventories.

Timken, for example, reported that the FIFO value of its inventory was $172.1 million higher than the LIFO cost at the end of 2020. That is, the amount presented in its balance sheet was understated (relative to current value) by more than $172 million. For purposes of analysis, the value of the LIFO reserve can be viewed as an *unrealized holding gain*—a gain resulting from holding inventory as prices are rising. That is, there is a holding gain due to rising inventory costs that has not been recorded in the financial statements. This gain is not recognized until the inventory is sold. In its December 31, 2020, balance sheet, Timken reported current assets of $2,000.3 million and current liabilities of $848.0 million, for a current ratio of $2,000.3 ÷ $848.0, or about 2.36. However, Timken's inventory is not reported at an up-to-date amount, while the accounts payable would reflect the current prices owed to suppliers. Therefore, an improved measure of the current ratio would be [$2,000.3 + $172.1] ÷ $848.0, or about 2.56.

In contrast, by assigning the most recently purchased inventory items to ending inventory, FIFO costing tends to approximate current value in the balance sheet. Hence, companies using FIFO tend not to have large unrealized inventory holding gains. However, if prices fall, companies using FIFO are more likely to adjust inventory values to the lower of cost or net realizable value.

FYI Some companies highlight this in their disclosures. For example, another company that uses LIFO, Chevron Corporation, mentions the current ratio effect in the notes to their statements saying "The current ratio was adversely affected by the fact that Chevron's inventories are valued on a last-in, first-out basis."

Cash Flow Effects The increased gross profit using FIFO results in higher pretax income and, consequently, higher taxes payable (assuming FIFO is also used for tax reporting). Conversely, the use of LIFO in an inflationary environment results in a lower tax liability.

Use of LIFO has reduced the dollar amount of Timken inventories by $172.1 million, resulting in a cumulative increase in cost of goods sold and a cumulative decrease in gross profit and pretax profit of that same amount.[3] The decrease in cumulative pretax profits has lowered Timken's tax bill over the life of the company by roughly $43.03 million ($172.1 million × 25% assumed corporate tax rate), which has increased Timken's cumulative operating cash flow by that same amount. The increased cash flow from tax savings is often cited as a compelling reason for management to adopt LIFO.

Adjusting the Balance Sheet to FIFO For analysis purposes, we can use the LIFO reserve to adjust the balance sheet and income statement to achieve comparability between companies that utilize different inventory costing methods. For example, if we wanted to compare Timken with another company using FIFO, we add the LIFO reserve to its LIFO inventory. As explained above, this $172.1 million increase in 2020 inventories increases its cumulative pretax profits by $172.1 million and taxes by $43.03 million. Thus, the balance sheet adjustments involve increasing inventories by $172.1 million, tax liabilities by $43.03 million, and retained earnings by the remaining after-tax amount of $129.07 million (computed as $172.1 million − $43.03 million).

---

[3] Cost of Goods Sold = Beginning Inventories + Purchases − Ending Inventories. Thus, as ending inventories decrease, cost of goods sold increases.

A GLOBAL PERSPECTIVE

One of the important differences in inventory accounting between U.S. GAAP and IFRS is that the latter does not allow the use of last-in, first-out (LIFO) accounting. Only FIFO and Average Cost are allowed for companies reporting under IFRS.

An analyst comparing a U.S. GAAP company to an IFRS company would need to keep an eye on these inventory differences and, when necessary, do the conversions described in the preceding paragraphs. While FIFO firms are not required to disclose what they would have looked like under LIFO, LIFO firms must disclose enough information to do a rough approximation of what they would have looked like under FIFO—making for an improved comparison with an IFRS company.

Adjusting the Income Statement to FIFO To adjust the income statement from LIFO to FIFO, we use the *change* in the LIFO reserve. For Timken, the LIFO reserve changed from $168.9 million in 2019 to $172.1 million in 2020, an increase of $3.2 million. To adjust the income statement to FIFO, we subtract $3.2 million from the cost of goods sold (reported using LIFO) and add the same amount to gross profit and pretax income. To estimate net income, we need to adjust for income taxes. Assuming a corporate tax rate of 25%, the use of LIFO provides Timken with tax savings of additional taxes of $800,000 ($3.2 million × 25%). Thus, 2020 net income using FIFO would be higher by $2.4 million ($3.2 million – $800,000).

RESEARCH INSIGHT

LIFO and Stock Prices The value-relevance of inventory disclosures depends at least partly on whether investors rely more on the income statement or the balance sheet to assess future cash flows. Under LIFO, cost of goods sold reflects current costs, whereas FIFO ending inventory reflects current costs. This implies that LIFO enhances the usefulness of the income statement to the detriment of the balance sheet. This trade-off partly motivates the required LIFO reserve disclosure (the adjustment necessary to restate LIFO ending inventory and cost of goods sold to FIFO).

Research suggests that LIFO-based income statements better reflect stock prices than do pro forma FIFO income statements that are constructed using the LIFO reserve. Research also shows a negative relation between stock prices and LIFO reserve—meaning that higher magnitudes of LIFO reserve are associated with lower stock prices. This is consistent with the LIFO reserve being viewed as an inflation indicator (for either current or future inventory costs) detrimental to company value.

Review 7-4 LO7-4

Interpreting the Effects of Inventory Valuation on Financial Results

Jasmine Company uses the LIFO costing method to value its inventory. The company reported the following information in its Year 2 annual report.

December 31	Year 2	Year 1
Total inventories at FIFO.	$50,000	$60,000
Less LIFO allowance	(15,000)	(12,000)
Total inventories, less allowance	$35,000	$48,000

a. On the company's Year 2 balance sheet, what dollar amount is reported for inventory?
b. Had the company reported inventory under the FIFO method, what dollar amount would be reported on the company's Year 2 balance sheet?
c. If the company reported $100,000 in its Year 2 income statement for cost of goods sold, what is the dollar amount of cost of goods sold under FIFO?

continued

continued from previous page

d. Assuming a 25% tax rate, what is the difference in Year 2 taxes considering the company valued inventory using LIFO (for both financial reporting and tax purposes) instead of FIFO (for both financial reporting and tax purposes)?
e. How do the company's Year 2 results under LIFO compare to results if the company had adopted FIFO instead?

	LIFO compared to FIFO (Higher, lower, same)
1. Ending inventory amount on balance sheet	_____
2. Cost of goods sold on income statement	_____
3. Sales on income statement	_____
4. Gross profit on income statement	_____
5. Amount of taxes paid for the year	_____

Solution on p. 7-44.

ANALYZING FINANCIAL STATEMENTS

Analysis Objective

We are trying to determine whether Home Depot's sales provide sufficient revenues to cover its operation costs, primarily selling and administrative expenses, after allowing for the costs of acquiring the products and services sold.

Analysis Tool Gross Profit Margin (GPM) Ratio

$$\text{Gross profit margin} = \frac{\text{Sales revenue} - \text{Cost of goods sold}}{\text{Sales revenue}}$$

LO7-5 Define and interpret gross profit margin and inventory turnover ratios. Use inventory disclosure information to make appropriate adjustments to ratios.

Applying the Gross Profit Margin Ratio to The Home Depot.

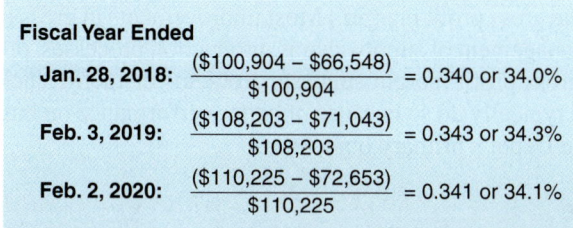

Fiscal Year Ended		
Jan. 28, 2018:	$\dfrac{(\$100{,}904 - \$66{,}548)}{\$100{,}904}$	= 0.340 or 34.0%
Feb. 3, 2019:	$\dfrac{(\$108{,}203 - \$71{,}043)}{\$108{,}203}$	= 0.343 or 34.3%
Feb. 2, 2020:	$\dfrac{(\$110{,}225 - \$72{,}653)}{\$110{,}225}$	= 0.341 or 34.1%

Guidance The gross profit margin is commonly used instead of the dollar amount of gross profit as it allows for comparisons across companies and over time. A decline in GPM is usually cause for concern because it indicates that the company has less ability to pass on to customers increased costs in its products. Because companies try to charge the highest price the market will bear, a decline in GPM is often the result of market forces beyond the company's control. Some possible reasons for a GPM decline are:

- Product line is stale. Perhaps it is out of fashion and the company must resort to markdowns to reduce overstocked inventories. Or, perhaps the product lines have lost their technological edge, yielding reduced demand.

- A change in product mix resulting from a change in buyers' behavior (more generic brands, more necessities, fewer big-ticket items).

- New competitors enter the market. Perhaps substitute products or new technologies are now available from competitors, yielding increased pressure to reduce selling prices.

- General decline in economic activity. Perhaps an economic downturn reduces product demand. The weak housing market during the latter half of the decade likely affected the gross profits of home improvement companies.

- Inventory is overstocked. Perhaps the company overproduced goods and finds itself in an overstock position. This can require reduced selling prices to move inventory.

Takeaways The Home Depot's sales revenue has increased from fiscal year ended January 28, 2018 to fiscal year ended February 2, 2020. It would appear that the company is maintaining its gross profit margin. However, to properly evaluate gross profit margin, it is useful to make comparisons with other companies in the same industry. The left-hand chart below compares The Home Depot's gross profit margin with that of its largest (but smaller) competitor, **Lowe's Companies, Inc.**

Home Depot in Context

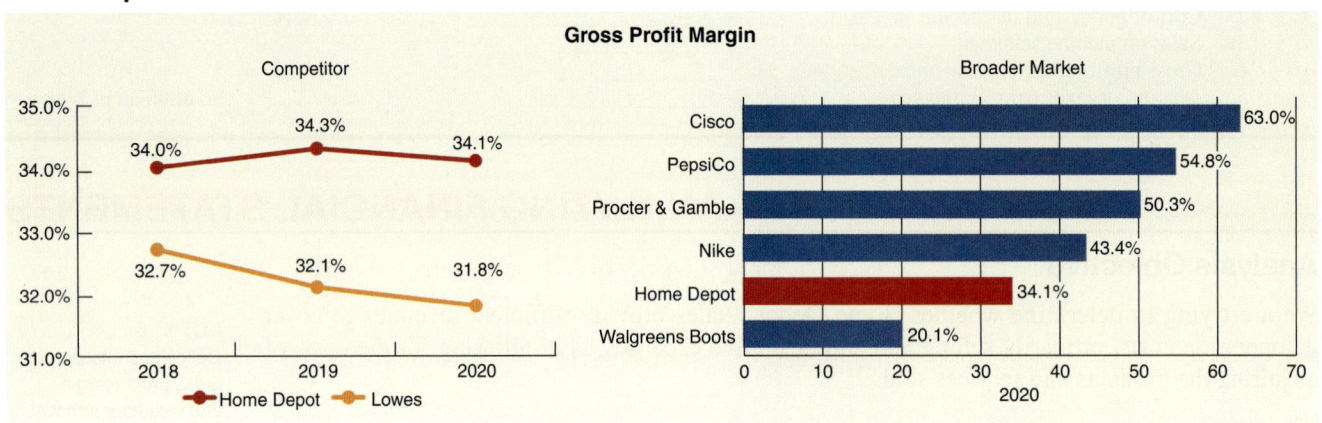

Gross Profit Margin

Competitor

Year	Home Depot	Lowes
2018	34.0%	32.7%
2019	34.3%	32.1%
2020	34.1%	31.8%

Broader Market (2020)

Company	Gross Profit Margin
Cisco	63.0%
PepsiCo	54.8%
Procter & Gamble	50.3%
Nike	43.4%
Home Depot	34.1%
Walgreens Boots	20.1%

As the line chart illustrates, The Home Depot has reported nearly identical, and very stable, gross profit margins in the last three years while Lowe's has reported a decreasing trend in gross profit margins. In addition, in 2020 The Home Depot's sales revenue increased by 1.9%, while Lowe's revenues increased by 1.2%.

Because of competitive pressures, companies rarely have the opportunity to affect gross margin with price increases. (Of course, an astute choice of product offerings is likely to reduce pricing discounts and improve the gross profit margin.) Most improvements in gross margin that we witness are the result of better management of supply chains, production processes, or distribution networks. Similarly, a decline in gross profit margin suggests problems or inefficiencies in these processes. Companies that succeed typically do so because of better performance on basic business processes. This is one of The Home Depot's primary objectives.

Analysis Objective

We wish to determine how quickly inventory passes through the production process and results in sales.

Analysis Tool Inventory Turnover (INVT) Ratio

$$\text{Inventory turnover} = \frac{\text{Cost of goods sold}}{\text{Average inventory}}$$

Applying Inventory Turnover Ratio to Home Depot

Fiscal Year Ended

Jan. 28, 2018: $\dfrac{\$66{,}548}{[(\$12{,}748 + \$12{,}549)/2]} = 5.26$ times per year

Feb. 3, 2019: $\dfrac{\$71{,}043}{[(\$13{,}925 + \$12{,}748)/2]} = 5.33$ times per year

Feb. 2, 2020: $\dfrac{\$72{,}653}{[(\$14{,}531 + \$13{,}925)/2]} = 5.11$ times per year

Home Depot in Context

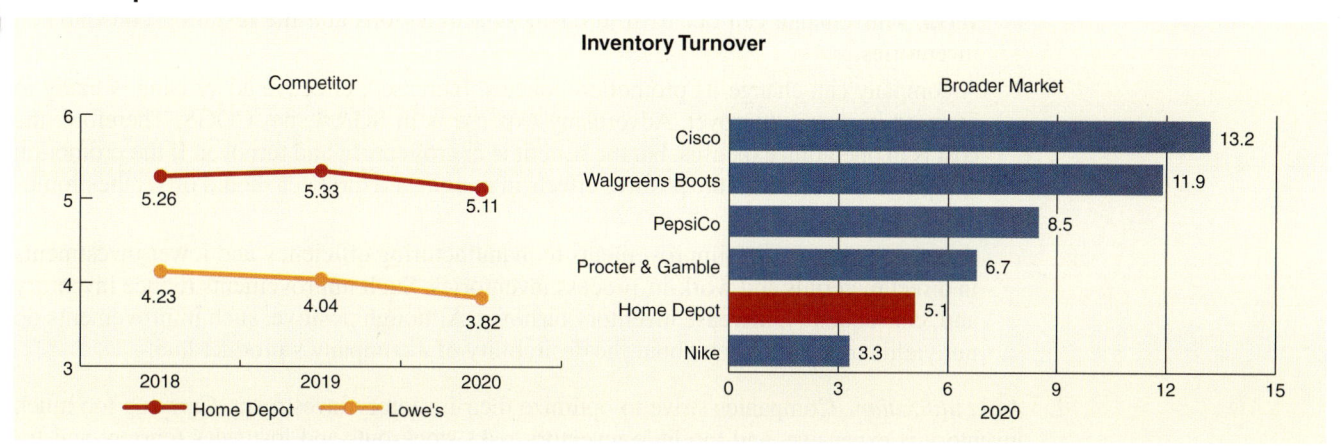

Inventory Turnover

Competitor (Home Depot vs. Lowe's):
- 2018: Home Depot 5.26, Lowe's 4.23
- 2019: Home Depot 5.33, Lowe's 4.04
- 2020: Home Depot 5.11, Lowe's 3.82

Broader Market (2020):
- Cisco: 13.2
- Walgreens Boots: 11.9
- PepsiCo: 8.5
- Procter & Gamble: 6.7
- Home Depot: 5.1
- Nike: 3.3

Cost of goods sold is in the numerator because inventory is reported at cost. The denominator is the average of beginning inventory and ending inventory to recognize growth (or decline) in the company's investment in inventory over the period. Inventory turnover indicates how many times inventory turns (is sold) during a period. More turns indicate that inventory is being sold more quickly.

Analysis Tool Average inventory days outstanding (AIDO), also called *days inventory outstanding*:

$$\text{Average inventory days outstanding} = \frac{\text{Average inventory}}{\text{Average daily cost of goods sold}}$$

Applying Average Inventory Days Outstanding Ratio to Home Depot

Fiscal Year Ended

Jan. 28, 2018: $\dfrac{[(\$12{,}748 + \$12{,}549)/2]}{(\$66{,}548/365)} = 69$ Days

Feb. 3, 2019: $\dfrac{[(\$13{,}925 + \$12{,}748)/2]}{(\$71{,}043/365)} = 69$ Days

Feb. 2, 2020: $\dfrac{[(\$14{,}531 + \$13{,}925)/2]}{(\$72{,}653/365)} = 71$ Days

The Average Inventory Days Outstanding (AIDO) contains the same information as the Inventory Turnover (INVT) ratio, but on a different scale. If a company's INVT goes up (down), its AIDO goes down (up). AIDO = 365÷INVT, or INVT = 365÷AIDO.

Home Depot in Context

The average daily cost of goods sold equals cost of goods sold divided by the number of days in the period (for our example, 365 for a year).

Average inventory days outstanding indicates how long, on average, inventories are on the shelves or in production before being sold. For example, if a retailer's annual cost of goods sold is $1,200 and average inventories are $300, inventories are turning four times and are on the shelves 91.25 days [$300/($1,200/365)] on average. This performance might be an acceptable turnover for the retail fashion industry where it needs to sell out its inventories each retail selling season, but it would not be acceptable for the grocery industry.

Guidance Analysis of inventory turnover is important for at least two reasons:

1. *Inventory quality.* Inventory turnover can be compared with those of prior periods and competitors. Higher turnover is viewed favorably, implying that products are salable, preferably without undue discounting of selling prices, or that production processes are functioning smoothly. Conversely, lower turnover implies that inventory is on the shelves for a longer period of time, perhaps from excessive purchases or production, missed fashion trends or technological advances, increased competition, and so forth. Our conclusions about higher or lower turnover must consider alternative explanations including:

a. Company product mix can change to higher-margin, slower-turning inventories or vice-versa. This change can occur from business acquisitions and the resulting consolidated inventories.

 b. A company can change its promotion policies. Increased, effective advertising is likely to increase inventory turnover. Advertising expense is in SG&A, not COGS. Therefore, the cost is in operating expenses, but the benefit is in gross profit and turnover. If the promotion campaign is successful, the positive effects in margin and turnover should offset the promotion cost in SG&A.

 c. A company can realize improvements in manufacturing efficiency and lower investments in direct materials and work-in-process inventories. Such improvements reduce inventory and, consequently, increase inventory turnover. Although positive, such improvements do not yield any information about the desirability of a company's product line.

2. *Asset utilization.* Companies strive to optimize their inventory investment. Carrying too much inventory is expensive, and too little inventory risks stock-outs and lost sales (current and future). There are operational changes that companies can make to reduce inventory including:

 a. Improved manufacturing processes can eliminate bottlenecks and the consequent build-up of work-in-process inventories.

 b. Just-in-time (JIT) deliveries from suppliers that provide raw materials to the production line when needed can reduce the level of raw materials required.

 c. Demand-pull production, in which raw materials are released into the production process when final goods are demanded by customers instead of producing for estimated demand, can reduce inventory levels. Dell Technologies was founded on a business model that produced for actual, rather than estimated, demand; many of its computers are manufactured after the customer order is received.

3. *Risk.* Reducing inventories reduces inventory carrying costs, thus improving profitability and increasing cash flow (asset reduction is reflected as a cash inflow adjustment in the statement of cash flows). However, if inventories get too low, production can be interrupted and sales lost. The COVID-19 pandemic has highlighted some of the supply chain risks of operations that have minimized inventory.

There is normal tension between the sales side of a company that argues for depth and breadth of inventory and the finance side that monitors inventory carrying costs and seeks to maximize cash flow. Companies, therefore, seek to *optimize* inventory investment, not *minimize* it.

RESEARCH INSIGHT

In a *Wall Street Journal* article, it was reported that in 2013, companies reported deficiencies in their procedures to account for inventory and cost of sales, i.e., internal control weaknesses, so numerous that the category ranked number two in areas with such deficiencies.[5] Recent academic research suggests these deficiencies are important. According to a study of companies over 2004–2009, the evidence is consistent with firms that have inventory-related material weaknesses having systematically lower inventory turnover ratios and being more likely to report inventory impairments relative to firms with effective internal control. In addition, the study shows that firms that fix their internal control weaknesses show improvements in inventory turnover rates.[6]

Takeaways The chart above compares inventory turnover for The Home Depot with that of its chief rival, Lowe's. The Home Depot's inventory turnover and AIDO improved in fiscal year 2019 but then weakened in 2020. Lowe's inventory turnover decreased, year to year, but increases in inventories probably helped it to maintain revenues and gross profit in the changing economic climate.

---

[4] "More Accounting Deficiencies Linked to Inventory," *Wall Street Journal* August 26, 2014.

[5] See Feng, Mei, Chan Li, Sarah E. McVay, and Hollis Skaife, "Does Ineffective Internal Control over Financial Reporting affect a Firm's Operations? Evidence from Firms' Inventory Management." The Accounting Review, March 2015.

When comparing The Home Depot to the broader sample of companies, we can see that The Home Depot is toward the lower end of inventory turnover values. The inventory of technology companies like Cisco is subject to obsolescence and holding inventory reduces its expected value. Walgreen Boots is focused on pharmacy prescriptions, and that inventory has a limited shelf life.

> **YOU MAKE THE CALL**
>
> **You are the Plant Manager** You are analyzing your inventory turnover report for the month and are concerned that the average inventory days outstanding is lengthening. What actions can you take to reduce average inventory days outstanding? [Answer on page 7-28]

Adjusting Turnover Ratios For a company using the last-in, first-out (LIFO) inventory method, it is advisable to make an adjustment before calculating the inventory turnover ratio. LIFO is most commonly used when management has experienced a trend of rising inventory costs. As a result, LIFO puts higher (newer) costs into cost of goods sold and leaves lower (older) costs in inventory. This creates a potential mismatch between the numerator and denominator of the inventory turnover ratio.

For instance, consider Butler Company's 2022 financial information in **Exhibit 7.11**. Measured in physical terms, Butler started 2022 with 250 units, sold 500 units during 2022, and ended 2022 with 350 units. So, the physical inventory turnover would be

$$\text{Physical inventory turnover} = \frac{\text{Units sold}}{\text{Average units held}} = \frac{500}{(250 + 350)/2} = 1.67 \text{ times}$$

However, the 2022 inventory turnover calculated using the LIFO reported numbers does not agree with the physical inventory turnover.

$$\text{LIFO inventory turnover} = \frac{\text{Cost of goods solds}}{\text{Average inventory}} = \frac{\$90,000}{(\$25,000 + \$43,000)/2} = 2.65 \text{ times}$$

Why is the LIFO inventory turnover higher? The distortion occurs because the LIFO cost of goods sold is 500 units valued at $180 each, while the beginning inventory is 250 units valued at $100 each and the ending inventory is 250 units valued at $100 each plus 100 units valued at $180 each. The difference between 1.67 and 2.65 comes about because LIFO causes the value per unit to be higher in the numerator than in the denominator.

A quick fix would be to use the LIFO reserve information to put the beginning and ending inventory values on a more up-to-date basis. LIFO puts the newer costs in cost of goods sold, while FIFO puts the newer costs in inventory. If Butler were using LIFO, we could use the reported inventory balances and the LIFO reserve information to determine that the beginning FIFO inventory would have been $39,000 ($25,000 + $14,000) and the ending FIFO inventory would have been $63,000 ($43,000 + $20,000).

$$\text{Adjusted inventory turnover} = \frac{\text{LIFO cost of goods sold}}{\text{Average FIFO inventory}} = \frac{\$90,000}{(\$39,000 + \$63,000)/2} = 1.76 \text{ times}$$

This adjusted ratio is much closer to what's actually happening to the inventories at Butler Company.

The magnitude of this adjustment can be significant. For instance, **Chevron Corporation** in its 2020 annual report states that its 2020 expense for "Purchased crude oil and products" was $50,488 million. Chevron's balance sheet totals for inventories were $5,848 million at the end of 2019 and $5,676 million at the end of 2020, for an average of $5,762 million. These numbers would give an inventory turnover ratio of $50,488 million ÷ $5,762 million, or 8.76 times, implying that inventory is held less than 42 days on average.

However, we know that the LIFO inventory balances are out of date. Chevron's LIFO reserve disclosure says that the replacement cost of inventories was higher than the reported amounts by $4,513 million at the end of 2019 and $2,749 million at the end of 2020, making the replacement cost of inventories equal to $10,361 million at the end of 2019 and $8,425 million at the end of 2020. The adjusted inventory turnover ratio would be $50,488/[($10,361 + $8,425)/2] = 5.4, implying that inventory is held about 68 days—more than 60% higher than the LIFO measure.

Following a similar line of analysis, it would be possible to construct a FIFO inventory turnover for Chevron, which could be useful in making comparisons to another company that uses IFRS in its financial reports.

Review 7-5 LO7-5 — Calculating Inventory Ratios

Publix Super Markets Inc. reports inventory and cost of goods sold using the last-in, first-out (LIFO) costing method for a "significant portion" of U.S. inventory. The table below presents financial information from its 2020, 2019, and 2018 10-K reports.

($ millions)	2020	2019	2018
Income statement:			
Sales	$44,864	$38,116	$36,094
Cost of goods sold	32,355	27,740	26,311
Gross profit	12,509	10,376	9,783
Balance sheet:			
Inventory	2,034	1,913	1,849
Notes to financial statements:			
LIFO reserve	549	529	489

Required

a. Compute the gross profit margin for each year, 2018 through 2020, and the inventory turnover ratio for 2019 and 2020.
b. What amount for cost of goods sold and gross profit would Publix report in 2019 and 2020 if FIFO were used to assign costs to inventory and cost of goods sold? (Assume that FIFO cost is equal to the current value of Publix's inventory.)
c. Recalculate Publix's inventory turnover ratio for 2019 and 2020 assuming that FIFO had been used to value inventory.

Solution on p. 7-44.

APPENDIX 7A: LIFO Liquidation

LO7-6 Analyze LIFO liquidations and the impact they have on the financial statements.

When companies use LIFO inventory costing, the most recent costs of purchasing inventory are transferred to cost of goods sold, while older costs remain in ending inventory. Each time inventory is purchased at a different price, a new *layer* (also called a **LIFO layer**) is added to the inventory balance. As long as a year's purchases equal or exceed the quantity sold, older cost layers remain in inventory—sometimes for several years. On the other hand, when the quantity sold exceeds the quantity purchased, inventory costs from these older cost layers are transferred to cost of goods sold. This situation is called **LIFO liquidation**. Because these older costs are usually much lower than current replacement costs, LIFO liquidation normally yields a boost to current gross profit as these older costs are matched against current revenues.

To illustrate the effects of LIFO liquidation, we return to the example of Butler Company in **Exhibit 7.6** and add an additional year. At the end of 2022, Butler has 350 units in inventory, 250 at $100 each and 100 at $180 each. Suppose that during 2023, the company purchases 500 units at $190 and sells 650 units at $250. At the end of 2023, Butler will have only 200 units remaining in inventory and, under LIFO, those units will be assigned a cost of $100 each. The determination of cost of goods sold and ending inventory for 2023 can be seen in **Exhibit 7A.1**.

EXHIBIT 7A.1 — Calculation of 2023 LIFO Inventory and Cost of Goods Sold

Beginning Inventory	250 units at $100 each plus 100 units at $180 each	$ 43,000
Purchases	500 units at $190 each	95,000
Cost of goods available for sale		138,000
Ending inventory	200 units at $100 each	20,000
Cost of goods sold	500 units at $190 each plus 100 units at $180 each plus 50 units at $100 each	$118,000

Exhibit 7A.2 portrays graphically that the inventory reduction in 2023 eliminated the LIFO layer added in 2022 and reduced the original LIFO layer from the start of 2021.

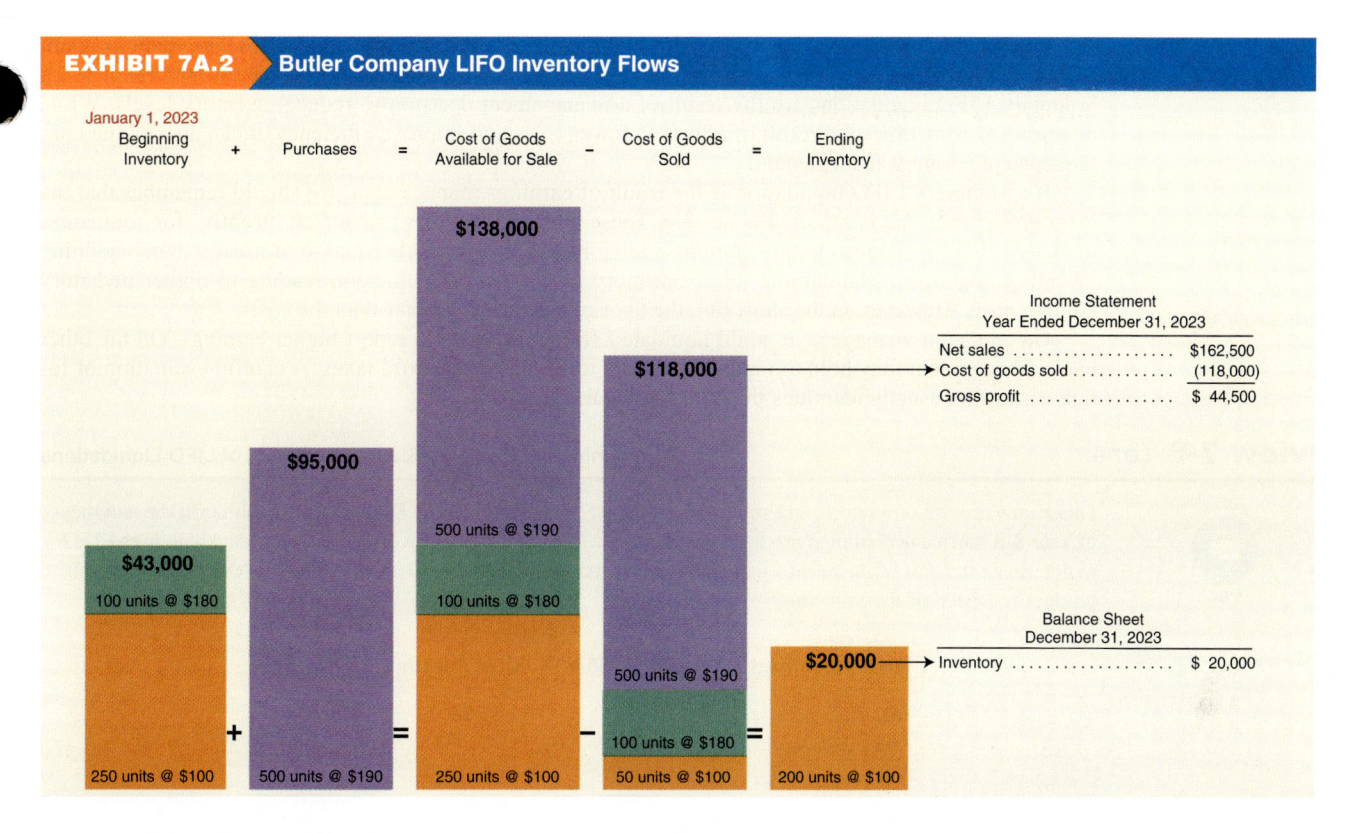

EXHIBIT 7A.2 — Butler Company LIFO Inventory Flows

January 1, 2023

Beginning Inventory + Purchases = Cost of Goods Available for Sale − Cost of Goods Sold = Ending Inventory

$43,000 — 100 units @ $180	
250 units @ $100	
$95,000 — 500 units @ $190	
$138,000 (500 units @ $190; 100 units @ $180; 250 units @ $100)	
$118,000 (500 units @ $190; 100 units @ $180; 50 units @ $100)	
$20,000 — 200 units @ $100	

Income Statement
Year Ended December 31, 2023

Net sales	$162,500
Cost of goods sold	(118,000)
Gross profit	$ 44,500

Balance Sheet
December 31, 2023

Inventory	$ 20,000

What would have happened if Butler had purchased 650 units at $190 in 2023? The ending inventory would have been identical to the beginning inventory. And, the cost of goods sold would have been $123,500 (650 units at $190 each), $5,500 higher than the $118,000 cost of goods sold in **Exhibit 7A.1**. This difference can be attributed to the differences between the current unit cost of inventory ($190) and the old unit costs ($180 and $100) that had been in inventory but are now in cost of goods sold.

Thus, Butler's cost of goods sold has been *reduced* by $5,500 due to the LIFO liquidation, and its gross profit and income before tax have been *increased* by the same amount. If Butler's tax rate were 25%, the net income would be increased by $4,125. This **LIFO liquidation gain** must be disclosed in the company's disclosure notes.

The effect of LIFO liquidation is evident in the following disclosure information from Note 1 to **Kaiser Aluminum Corporation**'s 2020 annual report.

> Inventories. Inventories are stated at the lower of cost or market value. Finished products, work-in-process and raw material inventories are stated on the last-in, first-out ("LIFO") basis. At December 31, 2020 and December 31, 2019, the cost of our inventory on a first-in, first-out ("FIFO") basis, which approximates the current replacement cost, exceeded its stated LIFO value by $8.4 million and $11.9 million, respectively. During the year ended December 31, 2020, we decremented a prior year, lower cost LIFO layer, which resulted in a benefit of $0.2 million. During the year ended December 31, 2019, we decremented a prior year, higher cost LIFO layer which resulted in a charge of $3.6 million. Other inventories are stated on the FIFO basis and consist of operating supplies, which are materials and supplies to be consumed during the production process.

Kaiser reports that reductions in inventory quantities led to the sale (at current selling prices) of products that carried costs from prior years that were less than current costs in 2020 and greater than current costs in 2019. As a result of these inventory reductions, pretax income increased by $0.2 million in 2020 and decreased by $3.6 million in 2019.

Analysis Implications

LIFO liquidation boosts gross profit when older, lower costs are matched against revenues based on current sales prices. This increase in gross profit is transitory. Once an old LIFO layer is liquidated, it can only be replaced at current prices. The transitory boost in gross profit temporarily distorts the gross profit margin (GPM) ratio.

It is important that we ask why the LIFO liquidation happened. Involuntary LIFO liquidations result from circumstances beyond the company's control, such as disruptions in supply due to a natural disaster. Voluntary LIFO liquidations are the result of a management decision to reduce inventory levels. While this result is sometimes the result of efforts to lower costs and improve efficiency, it can also be the consequence of earnings management.

If a voluntary LIFO liquidation is the result of earnings management, we should remember that the extra gross profit that is reported is taxable. These tax consequences provide an incentive for companies to *avoid* LIFO liquidations by maintaining ending inventories at levels equal to or greater than beginning inventory quantities. Maintaining these inventory levels can be inefficient, leading to higher inventory holding costs. However, in the short run, the tax savings can be greater than the costs.

On one hand, management could liquidate LIFO inventories to report higher earnings. On the other hand, management may hold too much inventory to avoid paying extra taxes. A careful evaluation of future cash flows usually identifies the preferred course of action.

Review 7-6 LO7-6 — Determining the Financial Statement Impact of LIFO Liquidations

Dickhaut Corporation imports and sells a product that is produced in the Dominican Republic. In the summer of Year 8, a hurricane disrupted production and affected Dickhaut's supply of this product. Dickhaut uses LIFO to determine the cost of its inventory and cost of goods sold. On January 1, Year 8, Dickhaut's inventory of this product consisted of the following:

Year Purchased	Quantity (units)	Cost Per Unit	Total Cost
Year 6	2,000	$20	$ 40,000
Year 7	3,000	30	90,000
Total	5,000		$130,000

Through mid-December, purchases were limited to 7,000 units, because the cost had increased to $70 per unit. Dickhaut sold 11,500 units during Year 8 at a price of $65 per unit, which significantly depleted its inventory. However, the cost was expected to drop to $55 per unit by early January Year 9.

Required

a. Assume that Dickhaut makes no further purchases during Year 8. Compute its gross profit for Year 8.
b. Assume that Dickhaut purchases 4,500 units for $70 per unit before the end of December Year 8, so that it maintains its balance of inventory at 5,000 units. Compute its gross profit for Year 8.
c. How should Dickhaut disclose the LIFO liquidation if it chooses not to make a year-end purchase?
d. If Dickhaut's corporate tax rate is 25%, should it make a year-end purchase? If so, how many units should the company purchase before December 31, Year 8? Assume that the management of Dickhaut believes it is efficient (in the long run) to carry 5,000 units in inventory.

Solution on p. 7-45.

SUMMARY

LO7-1 Interpret disclosures of information concerning operating expenses, including manufacturing and retail inventory costs. (p. 7-3)

- Inventory is reported in the balance sheet at its cost, including any cost to acquire, transport and prepare goods for sale.
- Manufacturing inventory consists of raw materials, work in process and finished goods. The cost of manufacturing inventory includes the cost of materials and labor used to produce goods, as well as overhead cost.

LO7-2 Account for inventory and cost of goods sold using different costing methods. (p. 7-7)

- FIFO places the cost of the most recent purchases in ending inventory and older costs in the cost of goods sold.
- LIFO places the cost of the most recent purchases in cost of goods sold and older costs in inventory.
- The average cost method computes an average unit cost, which is used to value inventories *and* cost of goods sold.

Apply the lower of cost or net realizable value rule to value inventory. (p. 7-13) **LO7-3**

- If the net realizable value of inventory falls below its cost, the inventory is written down to net realizable value, thereby reducing total assets.
- The loss is added to cost of goods sold and reported in the income statement (unless it is large enough to warrant separate disclosure).

Evaluate how inventory costing affects management decisions and outsiders' interpretations of financial statements. (p. 7-14) **LO7-4**

- When inventory costs are rising, LIFO costing reports higher cost of goods sold and lower income than either FIFO or average costing.
- If LIFO is used for tax reporting, it must be used for financial reporting.
- LIFO distorts the inventory turnover ratio because inventories are often severely undervalued (relative to current cost of goods sold). Management can boost earnings by liquidating these undervalued inventories.
- International Financial Reporting Standards (IFRS) allows FIFO and average costing methods. LIFO is not permitted.

Define and interpret gross profit margin and inventory turnover ratios. Use inventory disclosure information to make appropriate adjustments to ratios. (p. 7-20) **LO7-5**

- Gross profit margin (GPM)—a measure of profitability that focuses on the amount of revenue in excess of cost of goods sold as a percentage of revenue
- Gross profit margin is defined as Gross profit/Sales revenue.
- Inventory turnover (INVT)—a measure of the frequency at which the average balance in inventory is sold each year
- Inventory turnover is defined as Cost of goods sold/Average inventory.
- These ratios provide insight into how efficiently the company is managing inventory.
- Note disclosures enable a financial statement reader to determine the up-to-date costs of LIFO inventories, to estimate what cost of goods sold would have been under FIFO, and to compute an inventory turnover ratio that is not subject to the distortions noted in LO7-4.

Appendix 7A: Analyze LIFO liquidations and the impact they have on the financial statements. (p. 7-25) **LO7-6**

- LIFO liquidation is the result of selling and not replenishing inventory stocks purchased in previous accounting periods.
- When inventory costs are increasing, LIFO liquidation results in higher net income as the unrealized holding gains from LIFO are realized.
- Companies that use LIFO have an incentive to hold inventories to avoid LIFO *liquidation* and the resulting higher income taxes.

GUIDANCE ANSWERS . . . YOU MAKE THE CALL

You are the Plant Manager Companies need inventories to avoid lost sales opportunities; however, there are several ways to minimize inventory needs. (1) We can reduce product costs by improving product design to eliminate costly features not valued by customers. (2) We can use more cost-efficient suppliers, possibly including production in lower wage-rate parts of the world. (3) We can reduce raw material inventories with just-in-time delivery from suppliers. (4) We can eliminate bottlenecks in the production process that increase work-in-process inventories. (5) We can manufacture for orders rather than for estimates of demand to reduce finished goods inventories. (6) We can improve warehousing and distribution to reduce duplicate inventories. (7) We can monitor product sales and adjust product mix as demand changes to reduce finished goods inventories.

KEY RATIOS

Gross profit (GP)

GP = Sales revenue − Cost of goods sold

Inventory turnover (INVT)

$$INVT = \frac{\text{Cost of goods sold}}{\text{Average inventory}}$$

Gross profit margin (GPM)

$$\text{Gross profit margin} = \frac{\text{Sales revenue} - \text{Cost of goods sold}}{\text{Sales revenue}}$$

Average inventory days outstanding (AIDO)

$$AIDO = \frac{\text{Average inventory}}{\text{Average daily cost of goods sold}}$$

MULTIPLE CHOICE

Multiple Choice Answers
1. c 2. c 3. a 4. d 5. b

1. Which of the following is not normally reported as part of total manufacturing inventory cost?
    a. work-in-process
    b. finished goods
    c. property, plant, and equipment
    d. raw materials

2. When the current year's ending inventory amount is overstated, then the
    a. current year's cost of goods sold is overstated.
    b. current year's total assets are understated.
    c. current year's net income is overstated.
    d. next year's income is overstated.

3. In a period of rising prices, the inventory cost allocation method that tends to result in the lowest reported net income is
    a. LIFO.
    b. FIFO.
    c. average cost.
    d. specific identification.

4. Assume that Beyer Corporation has the following initial balance and subsequent purchase of inventory:

Beginning inventory	4,000 units @ $50 each	$200,000
Inventory purchased during the year	10,000 units @ $75 each	750,000
Cost of goods available for sale	14,000 units	$950,000

    During the year, Beyer Corporation sold 12,000 units. Which of the following is not true?
    a. FIFO cost of goods sold would be $800,000.
    b. FIFO ending inventory would be $150,000.
    c. LIFO cost of goods sold would be $850,000.
    d. LIFO ending inventory would be $150,000.

5. Sletten Industries uses the last-in, first-out (LIFO) method of accounting for the inventories of its single product. For the fiscal year, the company reported sales revenue of $160 million and cost of goods sold of $108 million. The following table was reported in the financial statement disclosure notes.

($ millions)	January 1	December 31
Inventory value at LIFO	$20.0	$22.4
LIFO Reserve	11.2	17.6
Inventory value at FIFO	$31.2	$40.0

    If Sletten Industries had used FIFO to account for its inventory, its gross profit for the year would be
    a. $69.6 million.
    b. $58.4 million.
    c. $45.6 million.
    d. $52.0 million.

Superscript ^{A} denotes assignments based on Appendix 7A.

QUESTIONS

Q7-1. Under what circumstances is it justified to include transportation costs in the value of the inventory purchased?

Q7-2. Why do relatively stable inventory costs reduce the importance of management's choice of an inventory costing method?

Q7-3. What is one explanation for increased gross profit during periods of rising inventory costs when FIFO is used?

Q7-4. If inventory costs are rising, which inventory costing method—first-in, first-out; last-in, first-out; or average cost—yields the (a) lowest ending inventory? (b) lowest net income? (c) largest ending inventory? (d) largest net income? (e) greatest cash flow assuming that method is used for tax purposes?

Q7-5. Even though it does not reflect their physical flow of goods, why might companies adopt last-in, first-out inventory costing in periods when costs are consistently rising?

Q7-6. In a recent annual report, Kaiser Aluminum Corporation made the following statement in reference to its inventories: "The Company recorded pretax charges of approximately $19.4 million because of a reduction in the carrying values of its inventories caused principally by prevailing lower prices for alumina, primary aluminum, and fabricated products." What basic accounting principle caused Kaiser Aluminum to record this $19.4 million pretax charge? Briefly describe the rationale for this principle.

Kaiser Aluminum Corporation
NASDAQ :: KALU

Q7-7. Under what conditions would each of the inventory costing methods discussed in the chapter produce the same results?

Q7-8. What is inventory "shrink"? How does a company determine the amount of inventory shrink that may have occurred?

Q7-9. What is a LIFO reserve? How is the LIFO reserve related to unrealized holding gains?

Q7-10. Analysts claim that it is more difficult to forecast net income for a company that uses LIFO. Why might this be true?

Q7-11.[A] LIFO liquidation may be involuntary—that is beyond the control of management. Suggest two situations that might lead to involuntary LIFO liquidation.

Q7-12.[A] LIFO liquidation is often discretionary. What motives might management have to liquidate LIFO inventory?

DATA ANALYTICS

DA7-1. Preparing an Excel Worksheet to Record Inventory at the Lower of Cost or Net Realizable Value

LO7-3

The Excel file associated with this exercise includes a sheet (Inventory Data Sheet) with information regarding Lain Company's inventory including unit cost, cost of disposal, unit selling price, and quantity on hand. A second sheet (Inventory Obsolescence Sheet) includes information about inventory markdowns on the selling price due to obsolescence concerns. In this exercise, we calculate the value of inventory at the lower of cost or net realizable value. In doing so, we first update sales data with the latest inventory obsolescence information using a useful Excel function: VLOOKUP.

REQUIRED

1. Download Excel file DA7-1 found in myBusinessCourse.
2. In the Data-Inventory Obsolescence worksheet, use VLOOKUP to pull in the original selling price from the Data-Inventory worksheet. *Hint:* Use the Item number in the first column as the lookup value, the table in the Inventory Data Sheet for the source to pull from, the column titled Selling price per unit for the source data. This must be an exact match.
3. List the formula that is currently in cell D4 of your Inventory Obsolescence sheet.
4. Calculate the updated selling price, considering the mark-down percentage in the Updated Selling Price per Unit column. Round to two decimal places. What is the updated selling price for Item No.1823555?
5. Using the VLOOKUP function, add the updated selling price from the Data-Inventory Obsolescence worksheet to the Updated Selling Price per Unit column in the Data-Inventory worksheet.
6. Eliminate the errors in the cells in the Updated Selling Price per Unit column on the Data-Inventory worksheet by replacing the error with the original selling price per unit using the IFERROR function. *Hint:* Enclose the formula used in part 5 within the IFERRROR function: replace the error sign with the original selling price per unit.
7. List the formula that is currently in cell G5 of your Inventory Data sheet.
8. For each item, enter the net realizable value in the Net Realizable Value per Unit column.
9. Using an IF statement, calculate the lower of cost per unit or net realizable value per unit in the Lower of Cost or NRV per Unit column. *Hint:* If the cost per unit is less than the net realizable value per unit, show the cost per unit value in the cell; otherwise, show the net realizable value per unit in the cell.
10. Calculate the total inventory value at the lower of cost or net realizable value for each item in the Total Inventory Value column. What is the lower of cost or net realizable value for Item no. 1124503 (in total)? Item no. 1122812 (in total)?
11. List the total inventory value at the lower of cost or net realizable value.

LO7-5 **DA7-2. Preparing Excel Visualizations of Gross Profit Data Over Time**

Financial information for the following five retailers is included in the Excel file associated with this chapter: The Home Depot, Inc. (Home Depot), Lowe's Companies, Inc. (Lowe's), Target Corporation (Target), The ODP Corporation (ODP), and Costco Wholesale Corporation (Costco). In this problem we analyze the gross profit percentage of retail companies with different business models. The gross profit percentage measures a company's ability to cover its operating costs from revenues after allowing for costs of goods and services sold. A gross profit percentage will vary by industry (some industries require extensive manufacturing operations for example) and is also affected by a company's business strategy. For example, a company with a lower gross profit percentage (a grocery store) will make up for profits with higher sales volume. A company with a high gross profit percentage (high-end jewelry store) can afford to sell fewer products when each item has a higher gross profit percentage.

Gross Profit Percentage

$$\frac{\text{Sales revenue} - \text{Cost of goods sold}}{\text{Sales revenue}}$$

REQUIRED
1. Download Excel file DA7-2 found in myBusinessCourse.
2. Calculate the gross profit percentage for each of the three years (with Year 3 being the most recent year).
3. Create a line chart showing the trend of the gross profit percentage for each company over the three-year period.
4. List the companies in order from the highest to the lowest gross profit percentage for each of the three years.
5. Add a trendline to the line chart for each company and forecast one additional period. *Hint:* Right-click on each line in your chart and add trendline. In the format trendline area under Forecast, forward 1 period.
6. List the companies in order from the highest to the lowest gross profit percentage for the forecasted year.
7. Describe the trends in the line chart.
8. Describe the likely source of the difference between the company with the highest gross profit percentage and the lowest gross profit percentage.

LO7-5 **DA7-3. Preparing Tableau Visualizations to Analyze Inventory Management**

Available in myBusinessCourse, this problem uses Tableau to create and analyze visualizations of inventory ratios of certain market segments of S&P 500 companies.

LO7-5 **DA7-4. Preparing Tableau Visualizations to Analyze Gross Profit**

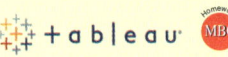

Available in myBusinessCourse, this problem uses Tableau to create and analyze visualizations of gross profit percentages of S&P 500 companies.

DATA VISUALIZATION

Data Visualization Activities are available in myBusinessCourse. These assignments use Tableau Dashboards to expose students to visual depictions of data and introduce students to data analytics through data visualizations. These exercises are easily assignable and auto graded by MBC.

MINI EXERCISES

LO7-1 **M7-13. Recording an Inventory Purchase FSET**

Shields Company has purchased inventories incurring the following costs: (a) the invoice amount of $300, financed through a $250 note with the remainder paid in cash, (b) shipping charges of $15 on account, (c) interest of $5 accrued on the $250 borrowed to finance the purchase, and (d) $4 on account for the cost of moving the inventory to the company's warehouse.

REQUIRED
a. Determine the cost to be assigned to the inventory.
b. Record the transactions using the financial statement effects template.

M7-14. Recording an Inventory Purchase   **LO7-1**

Using the information included in M7-13, record the purchase using "T" accounts.

M7-15. Recording Inventory Costs   **LO7-1**

Schrand Inc., a merchandiser, is requesting help in determining what costs ought to be considered as costs when incurred or treated as inventory costs, which are expensed as COGS. The costs include: sales persons wages, utilities such as heat and light in the store, the floor supervisor's salary, the cost of merchandise to be sold, costs of packaging and shipping to buyers.

REQUIRED

Determine the items above that should be included in inventory.

M7-16. Determining Cost of Goods Sold for a Manufacturing Company   **LO7-1**

Ybarra Products began operations this year. During its first year, the company purchased raw materials costing $100,800 and used $75,600 of those materials in the production of its products. The company's manufacturing operations also incurred labor costs of $69,600 and overhead costs of $33,600. At year-end, Ybarra had $22,800 of partially completed product in work-in-process inventory and $42,000 in finished goods inventory. What was Ybarra Company's cost of goods sold for the year?

M7-17. Calculating Gross Profit Margin   **LO7-5**

Johnson & Johnson reported the following revenue and cost of goods sold information in its 10-K report for 2020, 2019, and 2018.

Johnson & Johnson
NYSE :: JNJ

($ millions)	2020	2019	2018
Sales to customers	$82,584	$82,059	$81,581
Cost of products sold	28,427	27,556	27,091

Compute Johnson & Johnson's gross profit margin for each year.

M7-18. Calculating Effect of Inventory Errors   **LO7-1**

For each of the following scenarios, determine the effect of the error on income in the current period and in the subsequent period. To answer these questions, rely on the inventory equation:

Beginning inventory + Purchases – Cost of goods sold = Ending inventory

a. Porter Company received a shipment of merchandise costing $64,000 near the end of the fiscal year. The shipment was mistakenly recorded at a cost of $46,000.
b. Chiu, Inc., purchased merchandise costing $32,000. When the shipment was received, it was determined that the merchandise was damaged in shipment. The goods were returned to the supplier, but the accounting department was not notified and the invoice was paid.
c. After taking a physical count of its inventory, Murray Corporation determined that it had "shrink" of $25,000, and the books were adjusted accordingly. However, inventory costing $10,000 was never counted.

M7-19. Calculating LIFO, FIFO, Income and Cash Flows   **LO7-2, 4**

An acquaintance has proposed the following business plan to you. A local company requires a consistent quantity of a commodity and is looking for a reliable supplier. You could become that reliable supplier.

The cost of the commodity is expected to rise steadily over the foreseeable future, but the company is willing to pay more than the price that is current at the time. All you would need to do is make an investment, purchase the inventory and then deliver inventory to the company over the following year. One complication is that the commodity is available for purchase only seasonally, so at the end of every year you would need to purchase the supply for the following year. The customer pays promptly on delivery.

An initial cash investment of $136,400 would be used to purchase $110,000 of inventory in December of Year 1. The remaining cash would be held for liquidity needs. In the following year, you would deliver this inventory to the customer. Inventory costs are expected to increase by $22,000 per year, and the customer agrees to pay $33,000 more than the current cost of inventory. So, during Year 2, you would deliver inventory that originally cost $110,000, receive payment of $165,000 and pay $132,000 to purchase inventory for the current year. This pattern would continue in future years, but with annually increasing costs of inventory and corresponding increases in the price charged the customer.

If you accept this proposal, your objective would be to receive $19,800 in dividends (about a 15% return on the $136,400 investment) at the end of each year. Assume your business would have an income tax rate of 40%.

a. Construct a projected balance sheet as of the end of December, Year 1.
b. Construct financial forecasts of income statements, cash flows (direct method) and balance sheets for the next three years (through Year 4). Assume that your business would operate in a tax jurisdiction that requires the use of FIFO for inventory. Would this opportunity meet your financial objective?
c. Suppose that your business would operate in a tax jurisdiction that allowed the use of LIFO for inventory. Would this opportunity meet your financial objective? Why?

LO7-2 M7-20. Computing Cost of Goods Sold and Ending Inventory Under FIFO, LIFO, and Average Cost
Assume that Gode Company reports the following initial balance and subsequent purchase of inventory.

Beginning inventory	2,500 units @ $100 each	$ 250,000
Inventory purchased during the year	5,000 units @ $150 each	750,000
Cost of goods available for sale	7,500 units	$1,000,000

Assume that 4,250 units are sold during the year. Compute the cost of goods sold for the year and the balance reported as ending inventory on its year-end balance sheet under the following inventory costing methods:
a. FIFO
b. LIFO
c. Average cost

LO7-2 M7-21. Inferring Purchases Using Cost of Goods Sold and Inventory Balances FSET
Geiger Corporation, a retail company, reported inventories of $66,000 at the beginning of the year, and $73,000 at the end of the year. The annual income statement reported cost of goods sold of $349,000.
a. Compute the amount of inventory purchased during the year.
b. Record (1) purchases of inventory and (2) cost of goods sold in the financial statement effects template to show the effect of these entries on the balance sheet and income statement.

LO7-2 M7-22. Inferring Purchases Using Cost of Goods Sold and Inventory Balances
Use the information from M7-21 to complete the following.
a. Prepare journal entries to record (1) purchases, and (2) cost of goods sold.
b. Post the journal entries in part *a* to their respective T-accounts.

LO7-2 M7-23. Computing Cost of Goods Sold and Ending Inventory
Bartov Corporation reports the following beginning inventory and purchases for the year:

Beginning inventory	600 units @ $10 each	$ 6,000
Inventory purchased during the year	1,050 units @ $12 each	12,600
Cost of goods available for sale	1,650 units	$18,600

Bartov sells 900 of these units during the year. Compute its cost of goods sold for the year and the ending inventory reported on its year-end balance sheet under each of the following inventory costing methods:
a. FIFO
b. LIFO
c. Average cost

LO7-5 M7-24. Computing and Evaluating Inventory Turnover
Walmart Inc., and **Target Corporation** reported the following in their financial reports:

	Walmart			Target		
($ billions) Fiscal Year	Sales	COGS	Inventory	Sales	COGS	Inventory
2020	$519.9	$394.6	$44.4	$77.1	$54.9	$9.0
2019	510.3	385.3	44.3	74.4	53.3	9.5
2018	495.8	373.4	43.8	71.8	51.1	8.6

a. Compute the 2020 and 2019 inventory turnovers for each of these two retailers.
b. Discuss any changes that are evident in inventory turnover across years and companies from part *a*.
c. Describe ways in which a retailer can improve its inventory turnover. Are there ways to increase inventory turnover that are not beneficial to the company's long-term interests?

M7-25. Inferring Purchases Using Cost of Goods Sold and Inventory Balances (FSET)   **LO7-2**
Penno Company reported ending inventories of $2,945,000 and beginning inventories of $3,223,750. Cost of goods sold totaled $17,848,750 for the year.
a. Calculate inventory purchases for the year.
b. Using the financial statement effects template, show the effects of (a) the purchase of inventory during the year, and (b) cost of goods sold on the balance sheet and income statement.

M7-26. Inferring Purchases Using Cost of Goods Sold and Inventory Balances   **LO7-2**
Use the information from M7-25 to complete the following.
a. Prepare the journal entry to record cost of goods sold.
b. Set up a T-account for inventory and post the cost of goods sold entry from part *a* to this account.
c. Using the T-account from *b*, determine the amount of inventory that was purchased in 2020. Prepare a journal entry to record those purchases.

M7-27. Determining Lower of Cost or Net Realizable Value (NRV)   **LO7-3**
The following data refer to Froning Company's ending inventory.

Item Code	Quantity	Unit Cost	Unit NRV
LXC	84	$45	$48
KWT	295	38	34
MOR	420	22	20
NES	140	27	32

Determine the ending inventory amount by applying the lower of cost or net realizable value rule to (*a*) each item of inventory and (*b*) the total inventory.

EXERCISES

E7-28. Analyzing Inventory and Margin in a Seasonal Business   **LO7-5**
Power Marine Supply, opened its first boating supply store over 30 years ago. Since that time, the company has grown to be one of the largest boating supply companies in the world, with fiscal year 4 revenues in excess of $1,350 million. The accompanying table provides financial information for two recent years. Power Marine Supply's fiscal year is closely aligned with the calendar year. All amounts are in millions.

Time Period	Net Revenues	Cost of Goods Sold	Ending Inventory
Fiscal Year 4	—	—	$428
First quarter Year 5	$ 254	$ 200	514
Second quarter Year 5	506	324	516
Third quarter Year 5	388	276	474
Fourth quarter Year 5	260	204	446
Fiscal Year 5	1,408	1,004	446
First quarter Year 6	260	196	538
Second quarter Year 6	504	324	508
Third quarter Year 6	384	274	464
Fourth quarter Year 6	260	202	424
Fiscal Year 6	1,408	996	424

a. Using the fiscal year (annual) information for Year 5 and Year 6, calculate the gross profit margin and the inventory turnover ratio.
b. Power Marine Supply is in a seasonal business, in which the sales total for the second and third quarters is substantially higher than the sales total for the first and fourth quarters. Calculate the company's gross profit margin by quarter. What do you learn from the seasonal pattern in the gross profit margin?
c. What is the seasonal pattern in inventory balances? What effect does Power Marine Supply's choice of fiscal year-end have on the inventory turnover ratio calculated in *a*?
d. Recalculate Power Marine Supply's inventory turnover ratios for Year 5 and Year 6 using a weighted average of the company's inventory investment over the year.

E7-29.[A] **Applying and Analyzing Inventory Costing Methods**   **LO7-2, 4, 6**
At the beginning of the current period, Chen carried 1,000 units of its product with a unit cost of $20. A summary of purchases during the current period follows:

	Units	Unit Cost	Cost
Beginning Inventory	3,000	$20	$ 60,000
Purchases: #1	5,400	22	118,800
#2	2,400	26	62,400
#3	3,600	29	104,400

During the current period, Chen sold 8,400 units.

a. Assume that Chen uses the first-in, first-out method. Compute its cost of goods sold for the current period and the ending inventory balance.
b. Assume that Chen uses the last-in, first-out method. Compute its cost of goods sold for the current period and the ending inventory balance.
c. Assume that Chen uses the average cost method. Compute its cost of goods sold for the current period and the ending inventory balance.
d. Which of these three inventory costing methods would you choose to:
  1. Reflect what is probably the physical flow of goods? Explain.
  2. Minimize income taxes for the period? Explain.
  3. Report the largest amount of income for the period? Explain.

LO7-2 **E7-30. Computing Cost of Sales and Ending Inventory**
Stocken Company has the following financial records for the current period:

	Units	Unit Cost
Beginning inventory	150	$46
Purchases: #1	975	42
#2	825	38
#3	300	36

Ending inventory at the end of this period is 525 units. Compute the ending inventory and the cost of goods sold for the current period using (a) first-in, first-out, (b) average cost, and (c) last-in, first-out.

LO7-3 **E7-31. Determining Lower of Cost or Net Realizable Value (NRV)**
Crane Company had the following inventory at December 31.

		Unit Price	
	Quantity	Cost	NRV
Desks			
Model 9001	105	$190	$210
Model 9002	70	280	268
Model 9003	30	350	360
Cabinets			
Model 7001	180	60	64
Model 7002	120	95	88
Model 7003	75	130	126

a. Determine the ending inventory amount by applying the lower of cost or net realizable value rule to
  1. Each item of inventory.
  2. Each major category of inventory.
  3. Total inventory.
b. Which of the LCNRV procedures from requirement *a* results in the lowest net income for the year? Explain.

LO7-2, 4, 6 **E7-32.[A] Analyzing Inventory Note Disclosure**
General Motors Corporation reported the following information in its 10-K report:

General Motors
NYSE :: GM

Inventories at December 31 ($ millions)	2008	2007
Productive material, work in process, and supplies	$ 4,849	$ 6,267
Finished product, service parts, etc.	9,426	10,095
Total inventories at FIFO	14,275	16,362
Less LIFO allowance	(1,233)	(1,423)
Total automotive and other inventories, less allowances	$13,042	$14,939

The company reports its inventory using the LIFO costing method during 2007 and 2008.

a. At what dollar amount are inventories reported on its 2008 balance sheet?
b. At what dollar amount would inventories have been reported in 2008 if FIFO inventory costing had been used?
c. What cumulative effect has the use of LIFO had, as of year-end 2008, on GM's pretax income, compared to the pretax income that would have been reported using the FIFO costing method?
d. Assuming a 35% income tax rate, what is the cumulative effect on GM's tax liability as of year-end 2008?
e. In July 2009, GM changed its inventory accounting to FIFO costs. Why do you suppose GM made that choice?

E7-33.[A] **Analyzing of Inventory and Note Disclosure**

The inventory note disclosure from **Deere & Company**'s 2020 10-K follows ($ millions).

LO7-2, 4, 6

Deere & Company
NYSE :: DE

> A majority of inventory owned by Deere & Company and its U.S. equipment subsidiaries are valued at cost, on the "last-in, first-out" (LIFO) basis. Remaining inventories are generally valued at the lower of cost, on the "first-in, first-out" (FIFO) basis, or net realizable value. The value of gross inventories on the LIFO basis at November 1, 2020 and November 3, 2019 represented 52 percent and 55 percent, respectively, of worldwide gross inventories at FIFO value. The pretax favorable income effect from the liquidation of LIFO inventory during 2020 was $33 million. If all inventories had been valued on a FIFO basis, estimated inventories by major classification at November 1, 2020 and November 3, 2019 in millions of dollars would have been as follows:
>
> | ($ million) | 2020 | 2019 |
> |---|---|---|
> | Raw materials and supplies | $1,995 | $2,285 |
> | Work-in-process | 648 | 747 |
> | Finished goods and parts | 4,006 | 4,613 |
> | Total FIFO value | 6,649 | 7,645 |
> | Less adjustment to LIFO value | 1,650 | 1,670 |
> | **Inventories** | **$4,999** | **$5,975** |

We note that not all of Deere's inventories are reported using the same inventory costing method (companies can use different inventory costing methods for different inventory pools).

a. At what dollar amount are Deere's inventories reported on its 2020 balance sheet?
b. At what dollar amount would inventories have been reported on Deere's 2020 balance sheet had it used FIFO inventory costing?
c. What *cumulative* effect has the use of LIFO inventory costing had, as of year-end 2020, on its pretax income compared with the pretax income it would have reported had it used FIFO inventory costing? Explain.
d. Assuming a 25% income tax rate, by what *cumulative* dollar amount has Deere's tax liability been affected by use of LIFO inventory costing as of year-end 2020? Has the use of LIFO inventory costing increased or decreased its cumulative tax liability?
e. What effect has the use of LIFO inventory costing had on Deere's pretax income and tax liability for 2020 (assume a 25% income tax rate)?
f. Deere's 2020 disclosure states: "The pretax favorable income effects from the liquidation of LIFO inventory during 2020 was $33 million." Explain what happened in 2020 with respect to Deere's inventory and why there were favorable income effects.

E7-34. Analyzing Inventories Using LIFO Inventory Disclosure Note

The disclosure note below is from the 2020 10-K report of **Casey's General Stores, Inc.**, an operator of convenience stores ($ thousands).

LO7-2, 4, 5

Casey's General Stores, Inc.
NASDAQ :: CASY

> **Inventories**
> Inventories, which consist of merchandise and fuel, are stated at the lower of cost or market. For fuel, cost is determined through the use of the first-in, first-out (FIFO) method. For merchandise inventories, cost is determined through the use of the last-in, first-out (LIFO) method. The excess of replacement cost over the stated LIFO value was $87,546 and $80,814 at April 30, 2020 and 2019, respectively. There were no material LIFO liquidations during the periods presented. Below is a summary of the inventory values at April 30, 2020 and 2019.

continued

continued from previous page

($ thousands)	Years Ended April 30, 2020	2019
Fuel.	$ 33,695	$ 83,204
Merchandise.	202,312	189,836
Total inventory	$236,007	$273,040

In 2020, Casey's General Stores reported sales revenue of $9,175.3 million and cost of goods sold of $7,030.6 million.

a. Calculate the amount of inventories purchased by Casey's General Stores in 2020.
b. What amount of gross profit would Casey's General Stores have reported if the FIFO method had been used to value all inventories?
c. Calculate the gross profit margin (GPM) as reported and assuming that the FIFO method had been used to value all inventories.

LO7-5 **E7-35. Calculating Gross Profit Margin and Inventory Turnover**

The following table presents sales revenue, cost of goods sold, and inventory amounts for three specialty retailers, **Tiffany & Co.**, **Best Buy**, and **RH**.

Tiffany & Co.
NYSE :: TIF
Best Buy
NYSE :: BBY
RH, Inc.
NYSE :: RH

($ millions)	2020	2019
Tiffany & Co.		
Revenues	$ 4,424	$ 4,442
Cost of goods sold	1,662	1,631
Inventory	2,464	2,428
Best Buy		
Revenues	$43,638	$42,879
Cost of goods sold	33,590	32,918
Inventory	5,174	5,409
RH		
Revenues	$ 2,647	$ 2,506
Cost of goods sold	1,552	1,520
Inventory	439	532

a. Compute the gross profit margin (GPM) for each of these companies for 2020 and 2019.
b. Compute the inventory turnover ratio and the average inventory days outstanding for 2020 for each company.
c. What factors might determine the differences among these three companies' ratios?

PROBLEMS

LO7-2, 4, 5 **P7-36. Analyzing Inventory and Its Disclosure Note**

Caterpillar Inc. and **Komatsu Ltd.** are international manufacturers of industrial and construction equipment. Caterpillar's headquarters is in the United States, while Komatsu's headquarters is in Japan. The following information comes from their recent financial statements.

Caterpillar, Inc.
NYSE :: CAT
Komatsu Ltd. (ADR)
OTC :: KMTUY

Caterpillar—fiscal year ending December 31, 2020 ($ millions)
Cost of goods sold $29,082
Beginning inventory 11,266
Ending inventory 11,402

Komatsu—fiscal year ending March 31, 2020 (¥ millions)
Cost of goods sold ¥1,749,048
Beginning inventory 837,552
Ending inventory 805,309

In its note disclosures, Caterpillar also provides the following information (assume no LIFO liquidation):

Inventories

We state inventories at the lower of cost or net realizable value. We principally determine cost using the last-in, first-out (LIFO) method. The value of inventories on the LIFO basis represented about 60 percent of total inventories at December 31, 2020 and 2019. If the FIFO (first-in, first-out) method had been in use, inventories would have been $2,132 million and $2,086 million higher than reported at December 31, 2020 and 2019, respectively.

REQUIRED

a. Calculate the inventory turnover and average inventory days outstanding ratios for Caterpillar and Komatsu using the information reported in their financial statements. Describe some operational reasons that companies might have differing inventory ratios, even if they are in the same industry.
b. Did the cost of Caterpillar's acquiring (i.e., producing) products go up or down in 2020?
c. Assuming a 25% income tax rate, by what cumulative dollar amount has Caterpillar's tax liability been affected by use of LIFO inventory costing as of fiscal year-end 2020? Has the use of LIFO inventory costing increased or decreased its cumulative tax liability?
d. What effect has the use of LIFO inventory costing had on Caterpillar's pretax income and tax liability for fiscal year 2020? (Assume a 25% tax rate.)
e. In its disclosure notes, Komatsu reports that it "determines cost of work in process and finished products using the specific identification method based on actual costs accumulated under a job-order cost system. The cost of finished parts is determined principally using the first-in, first-out method." What effect does this disclosure note have on your interpretation in question *a* above? Use the information available to make a more appropriate comparison of the two companies' inventory turnover.

P7-37. Analyzing Inventory Disclosure Comparing LIFO and FIFO   **LO7-2, 4, 5**

The current asset section of the 2020 and 2019 fiscal year-end balance sheets of **The Kroger Co.** are presented in the accompanying table:

Kroger
NYSE :: KR

($ millions)	February 1, 2020	February 2, 2019
Current assets		
Cash and temporary cash investments	$ 399	$ 429
Store deposits in-transit	1,179	1,181
Receivables	1,706	1,589
FIFO inventory	8,464	8,123
LIFO reserve	(1,380)	(1,277)
Assets held for sale	—	166
Prepaid and other current assets	522	592
Total current assets	$10,890	$10,803

In addition, Kroger provides the following disclosure note describing its inventory accounting policy (assume the following is their complete disclosure):

Inventories are stated at the lower of cost (principally on a last-in, first-out "LIFO" basis) or market. In total, approximately 91% of inventories in 2019 and 90% of inventories in 2018 were valued using the LIFO method. The remaining inventories, including substantially all fuel inventories, are stated at the lower of cost (on a FIFO basis) or net realizable value. Replacement cost was higher than the carrying amount by $1,380 at February 1, 2020 and $1,277 at February 2, 2019. The Company follows the Link-Chain, Dollar-Value LIFO method for purposes of calculating its LIFO charge or credit.

REQUIRED

a. At what dollar amount does Kroger report its inventory in its February 1, 2020, balance sheet?
b. What is the cumulative effect (through February 1, 2020) of the use of LIFO on Kroger's pretax earnings?
c. Assuming a 25% tax rate, what is the cumulative (through February 1, 2020) tax effect of the use of LIFO to determine inventory costs?
d. Kroger reported net earnings of $1,512 million in its fiscal year 2020 income statement. Assuming a 25% tax rate, what amount of net earnings would Kroger report if the company used the FIFO inventory costing method?

e. Kroger reported merchandise costs (cost of goods sold) of $95,294 million in fiscal year 2020. Compute its inventory turnover for the year.
f. How would the inventory turnover ratio differ if the FIFO costing method had been used?

LO7-5 P7-38. Calculating Gross Profit and Inventory Turnover

The following table presents sales revenue, cost of goods sold, and inventory amounts for three computer/electronics companies, **Samsung Electronics Co.**, **HP Inc.**, and **Apple Inc.**

($ millions)	Fiscal year ending		
Samsung Electronics Co. Ltd. (S. Korean won)	Dec. 31, 2020	Dec. 31, 2019	Dec. 31, 2018
Revenues	236,806,988	230,400,881	243,771,415
Cost of goods sold	144,488,296	147,239,549	132,394,411
Inventory	32,043,145	26,766,464	28,984,704
HP Inc. (US dollar)	Oct. 31, 2020	Oct. 31, 2019	Oct. 31, 2018
Revenues (products only)	56,639	58,756	58,472
Cost of goods sold	46,202	47,586	47,803
Inventory	5,963	5,734	6,062
Apple Inc. (US dollar)	Sept. 26, 2020	Sept. 28, 2019	Sept. 29, 2018
Revenues	274,515	260,174	265,595
Cost of goods sold	169,559	161,782	163,756
Inventory	4,061	4,106	3,956

REQUIRED

a. Compute the gross profit margin (GPM) for each of these companies for all three fiscal years.
b. Compute the inventory turnover ratio and the average inventory days outstanding for each company for the last two fiscal years. (All three firms use FIFO inventory costing.)
c. What factors might determine the differences among these three companies' ratios?

LO7-2, 4, 6 P7-39.[A] Analyzing and Interpreting Inventories and Its Related Ratios and Disclosures

The current asset section from **Seneca Foods Corporation**, a low-cost producer and distributor of quality fruits and vegetables, March 31, 2020 annual report follows:

($ thousands)	March 31, 2020	March 31, 2019
Current Assets		
Cash and cash equivalents	$ 10,702	$ 11,480
Accounts receivable, less allowance for doubtful accounts of $1,598 and $57, respectively	109,802	84,122
Contracts receivable	7,610	—
Assets held for sale-discontinued operations	182	98
Inventories	411,631	501,684
Assets held for sale	—	1,568
Refundable income taxes	4,350	1,221
Other current assets	7,323	3,075
Total current assets	551,600	603,248

Seneca reports the following related to its gross profit:

	Fiscal Years	
($ thousands)	2020	2019
Net sales	$1,335,769	$1,199,581
Cost of sales	1,193,881	1,160,085
Gross profit	$ 141,888	$ 39,496

Seneca further reports the following disclosure note:

11. Inventories

Effective December 30, 2007 (beginning of 4th quarter of Fiscal Year 2008), the Company changed its inventory valuation method from the lower of cost, determined under the FIFO method, or market to the lower of cost, determined under the LIFO method, or market. In the high inflation environment that the Company was experiencing, the Company believed that the LIFO inventory method was preferable over the FIFO method because it better compares the cost of current production to

continued

continued from previous page

current revenue. The effect of LIFO was to increase continuing net earnings by $12.8 million in 2020 and to reduce net earnings by $30.4 million in 2019, compared to what would have been reported using the FIFO inventory method. The increase in earnings per share was $1.38 ($1.37 diluted) in 2020; and a reduction in earnings per share of $3.14 ($3.14 diluted) in 2019. There were LIFO liquidations of $6.6 million in 2020 and $28.7 million in 2019. Most of this LIFO liquidation in 2019 is reported as Discontinued Operations since it related to the Modesto fruit (see Discontinued Operations Note 3). The inventories by category and the impact of using the LIFO method are shown in the following table:

(In thousands)	2020	2019
Finished products	$351,251	$454,920
In process	31,173	42,045
Raw materials and supplies	173,474	166,060
	555,898	663,025
Less excess of FIFO cost over LIFO cost	144,267	161,341
Total inventories	$411,631	$501,684

In prior financial statements, Seneca has stated that it "manages the Company for cash, not reported earnings" and that the "decision to switch to LIFO has turned out to be a very prudent one of the last five years."

a. Compute the ratio of inventories to total current assets for 2020 and 2019. Is the change observed for the ratio a positive development for a company such as Seneca? Explain.
b. Compute inventory turnover for both 2020 and 2019 (2018 ending inventories were $680,828). Interpret and explain the change in inventory turnover as positive or negative for the company.
c. What inventory costing method does Seneca use? What effect has the use of this method (relative to FIFO or LIFO) had on its reported income for 2020 and 2019? Was the result an increase or decrease? Explain.
d. Seneca claims that it manages its company for cash flow. Does its inventory reporting help the Company to do so? How much in taxes has Seneca saved, assuming a 25% tax rate, by the inventory approach it adopted?

CASES AND PROJECT

C7-40.[A] **Analyzing Effects of LIFO on Inventory Turnover Ratios** LO7-2, 4, 5, 6
The current assets of **Exxon Mobil Corporation** follow:

Exxon Mobil Corp.
NYSE :: XOM
BP, p.l.c.
NYSE :: BP

($ millions)	2020	2019
Current assets		
Cash and cash equivalents	$ 4,364	$ 3,089
Notes and accounts receivable, net	20,581	26,966
Inventories:		
Crude oil, products and merchandise	14,169	14,010
Materials and supplies	4,681	4,518
Other current assets	1,098	1,469
Total current assets	$44,893	$50,052

In addition, the following note was provided in its 2020 10-K report:

Inventories. Crude oil, products and merchandise inventories are carried at the lower of current market value or cost (generally determined under the last-in, first-out method—LIFO). Inventory costs include expenditures and other charges (including depreciation) directly and indirectly incurred in bringing the inventory to its existing condition and location. Selling expenses and general and administrative expenses are reported as period costs and excluded from inventory cost. Inventories of materials and supplies are valued at cost or less.

continued

continued from previous page

> **Miscellaneous Financial Information.** In 2020, 2019, and 2018, net income included gains of $41 million, $523 million and $107 million, respectively, attributable to the combined effects of LIFO inventory accumulations and drawdowns. The aggregate replacement cost of inventories was estimated to exceed their LIFO carrying values by $5.4 billion and $9.7 billion at December 31, 2020, and 2019, respectively.

REQUIRED

a. Exxon Mobil reported a pretax loss of $28,883 million in 2020. What amount of pretax earnings would have been reported by the company if inventory had been reported using the FIFO costing method?
b. Exxon Mobil reported cost of goods sold of $94,007 million in 2020. Compute its inventory turnover ratio for 2020 using total inventories.
c. **BP, p.l.c.** (BP) reports its financial information using IFRS. For fiscal year 2020, BP reported cost of goods sold of $132,104 million, beginning inventory of $20,880 million and ending inventory of $16,873 million. Compute BP's inventory turnover ratio for fiscal year 2020.
d. Compare your answers in parts *b* and *c*. BP can't use LIFO to report under IFRS, so revise your calculations in such a way as to find out which company has faster inventory turnover.
e. What is meant by the statement that "2020 net income included gains of $41 million attributable to the combined effects of LIFO inventory accumulations and draw-downs"?

LO7-2, 4 **C7-41. Analyzing Effects of Change from LIFO to FIFO Inventory Costing**

Virco Manufacturing Corp.
NASDAQ :: VIRC

Virco Manufacturing Corp. provided the following note in its annual report for the year ended January 31, 2011:

> On January 31, 2011, the Company elected to change its costing method for the material component of raw materials, work in process, and finished goods inventory to the lower of cost or market using the first-in first-out ("FIFO") method, from the lower of cost or market using the last-in first out ("LIFO") method. The labor and overhead components of inventory have historically been valued on a FIFO basis. The Company believes that the FIFO method for the material component of inventory is preferable as it conforms the inventory costing methods for all components of inventory into a single costing method and better reflects current acquisition costs of those inventories on our consolidated balance sheets. Additionally, presentation of inventory at FIFO aligns the financial reporting with the Company's borrowing base under its line of credit (see Note 3 for further discussion of the line of credit). Further, this change will promote greater comparability with companies that have adopted International Financial Reporting Standards, which does not recognize LIFO as an acceptable accounting method. In accordance with FASB ASC Topic 250, "Accounting Changes and Error Corrections," all prior periods presented have been adjusted to apply the new accounting method retrospectively. In addition, as an indirect effect of the change in our inventory costing method from LIFO to FIFO, the Company recorded additional inventory lower of cost or market expenses and changes in deferred tax assets and income tax expense. The retroactive effect of the change in our inventory costing method...increased the February 1, 2008, opening retained earnings balance by $4.1 million, and increased our inventory and retained earnings balances by $8.5 million and $5.4 million as of January 31, 2009, by $6.9 million and $4.3 million as of January 31, 2010, and by $7.6 million and $4.7 million as of January 31, 2011, respectively.

REQUIRED

a. What do the stated changes in inventory in each year represent (e.g., the $7.6 million in 2011)? Equity? What is the difference between the two?
b. What were Virco's stated reasons for the change to FIFO?
c. In the Annual Report for the year ended January 2010, Virco states the following: "Inventories are stated at the lower of cost or market. Cost is determined using the last-in, first-out ("LIFO") method of valuation for the material content of inventories and the first-in, first-out ("FIFO") method for labor and overhead. The Company uses LIFO as it results in a better matching of costs and revenues." What are some possible motivations behind why Virco changed to the FIFO method of accounting beyond those listed by management?

SOLUTIONS TO REVIEW PROBLEMS

Review 7-1
a. Yes b. No c. Yes d. Yes e. No

Review 7-2

Preliminary computation: Units in ending inventory = 4,800 available − 2,800 sold = 2,000

a. First-in, first-out (FIFO)

Cost of goods sold computation:	Units		Cost		Total
	1,000	@	$18.00	=	$18,000
	1,800	@	$18.25	=	32,850
	2,800				$50,850
Cost of goods available for sale			$88,450		
Less: Cost of goods sold			50,850		
Ending inventory ($22,800 + $14,800)			$37,600		

b. Last-in, first-out (LIFO)

Cost of goods sold computation:	Units		Cost		Total
	1,200	@	$19.00	=	$22,800
	800	@	$18.50	=	14,800
	800	@	$18.25	=	14,600
	2,800				$52,200
Cost of goods available for sale			$88,450		
Less: Cost of goods sold			52,200		
Ending inventory [$18,000 + (1,000 × $18.25)]			$36,250		

c. Average cost (AC)

Average unit cost	= $88,450/4,800	= $18.427
Cost of goods sold	= 2,800 × $18.427	= $51,596
Ending inventory	= 2,000 × $18.427	= $36,854

d.
1. FIFO in most circumstances reflects physical flow. For example, FIFO would apply to the physical flow of perishables and to situations where the earlier items acquired are moved out first because of risk of deterioration or obsolescence.
2. LIFO results in the lowest ending inventory amount during periods of rising costs, which in turn yields the lowest net income and the lowest income taxes.

e. Last-in, first-out with LIFO liquidation

Cost of goods sold computation:	Units		Cost		Total
	800	@	$18.50	=	$14,800
	1,800	@	$18.25	=	32,850
	200	@	$18.00	=	3,600
	2,800				$51,250
Cost of goods available for sale			$65,650		
Less: Cost of goods sold			51,250		
Ending inventory (800 × $18)			$14,400		

The company's LIFO gross profit has increased by $950 ($52,200 − $51,250). This increase is from LIFO liquidation, which is the reduction of inventory quantities that results in matching older (lower) cost layers against current selling prices. The company has, in effect, dipped into lower-cost layers to boost current period profit—all from a simple delay of inventory purchases.

f. Transaction effects shown in the financial statement effects template, journal entries, and T-accounts.

	Balance Sheet					Income Statement		
Transaction	Cash Asset	+ Noncash Assets	= Liabilities	+ Contrib. Capital	+ Earned Capital	Revenues	− Expenses	= Net Income
(1) Purchase $70,450 of inventory.	−70,450 Cash	+70,450 Inventory	=				−	=
(2a) Sell Inventory for $85,000 cash.	+85,000 Cash		=		+85,000 Retained Earnings	+85,000 Sales Revenue	−	= +85,000
(2b) Record cost of goods sold in 2a.		−50,850 Inventory	=		−50,850 Retained Earnings		− +50,850 Cost of Goods Sold	= −50,850

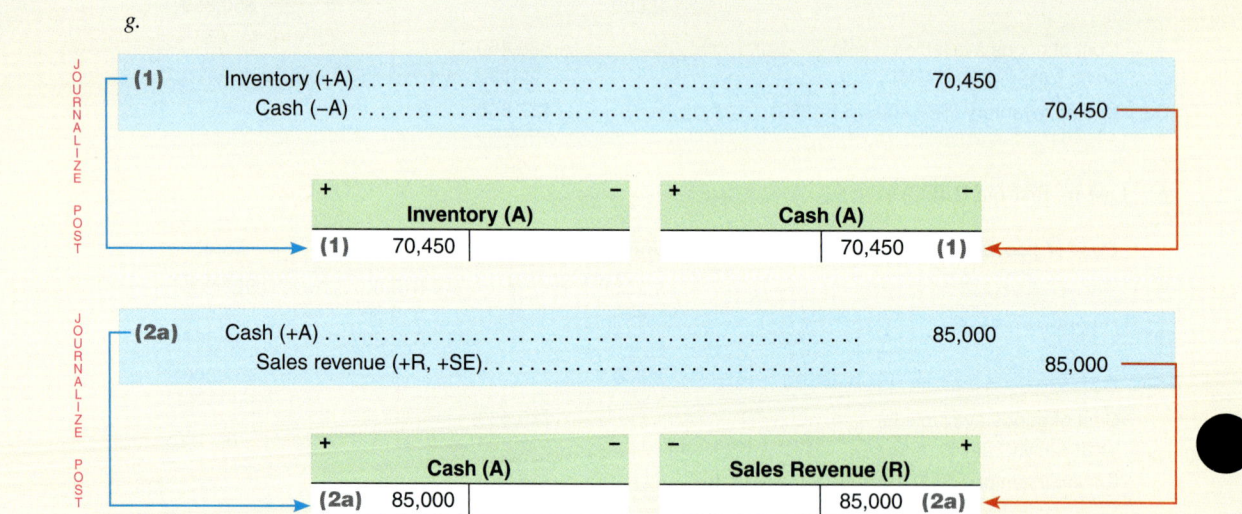

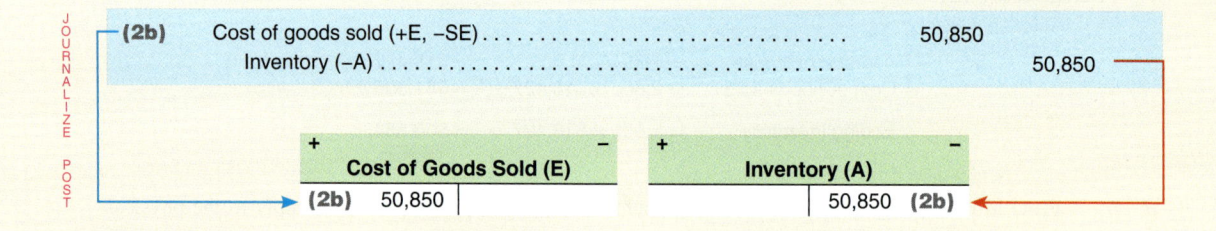

g.

(1) Inventory (+A) 70,450
    Cash (−A) 70,450

+ Inventory (A) −			− Cash (A) +	
(1) 70,450				70,450 (1)

(2a) Cash (+A) 85,000
    Sales revenue (+R, +SE) 85,000

+ Cash (A) −			− Sales Revenue (R) +	
(2a) 85,000				85,000 (2a)

(2b) Cost of goods sold (+E, −SE) 50,850
    Inventory (−A) 50,850

+ Cost of Goods Sold (E) −			+ Inventory (A) −	
(2b) 50,850				50,850 (2b)

Review 7-3

1.

				Inventory Amounts		
Item	Quantity	Cost	NRV	Cost	NRV	LCNRV (by Item)
Fans						
Model X1	300	$18	$19	$ 5,400	$ 5,700	$ 5,400
Model X2	250	22	24	5,500	6,000	5,500
Model X3	400	29	26	11,600	10,400	10,400
Totals				$22,500	$22,100	$21,300
Heaters						
Model B7	500	24	28	$12,000	$14,000	$12,000
Model B8	290	35	32	10,150	9,280	9,280
Model B9	100	41	38	4,100	3,800	3,800
Totals				26,250	27,080	25,080
Totals				$48,750	$49,180	$46,380

a. As shown in this schedule, applying the lower of cost or NRV rule to each item of the inventory results in an ending inventory amount of $46,380.
b. Applying the lower of cost or NRV rule to each major category of the inventory results in an ending inventory amount of $48,350, calculated as follows:

Fans	$22,100
Heaters	26,250
	$48,350

c. As shown in this schedule, applying the lower of cost or NRV rule to the total inventory results in an ending inventory amount of $48,750.

2. The LCM procedure that results in the lowest ending inventory amount also results in the lowest net income for the year (the lower the ending inventory amount, the higher the cost of goods sold). Applying the lower of cost or NRV rule to each item of the inventory results in the lowest net income for the year.

Review 7-4

a. $35,000
b. $50,000
c. $97,000 ($100,000 − ($15,000 − $12,000))
d. $750 ($3,000 × 25%)
e. (1) lower (2) higher (3) same (4) lower (5) lower

Review 7-5

a. The gross profit margin and inventory turnover are calculated as follows:

Gross profit margin
2018: $ 9,783 / $36,094 = 0.271 (or 27.1%)
2019: $10,376 / $38,116 = 0.272 (or 27.2%)
2020: $12,509 / $44,864 = 0.279 (or 27.9%)

Inventory turnover
2019: $27,740/[($1,913 + $1,849)/2] = 14.75 times
2020: $32,355/[($2,034 + $1,913)/2] = 16.39 times

b. Cost of goods sold and gross profit must be adjusted by the change in the LIFO reserve to convert to FIFO.

Cost of goods sold
2019: $27,740 − ($529 − $489) = $27,700
2020: $32,355 − ($549 − $529) = $32,335

Gross profit
2019: $10,376 + ($529 − $489) = $10,416
2020: $12,509 + ($549 − $529) = $12,529

The use of LIFO resulted in a lower cost of goods sold and a higher gross profit in 2019 and 2020 because the LIFO reserve grew larger each year.

c. Restated inventory turnover calculations:

Inventory turnover
2019: $27,700/[($2,442 + $2,338)/2] = 11.6 times
2020: $32,335/[($2,583 + $2,442)/2] = 12.9 times

Because inventory values are higher and cost of goods sold is lower in 2019 and 2020 under FIFO, the inventory turnover ratio is lower when FIFO numbers are used.

Review 7-6

a.

Sales revenue (11,500 × $65)	$747,500
Cost of goods sold (7,000 × $70) + (3,000 × $30) + (1,500 × $20)	610,000
Gross profit	$137,500

b.

Sales revenue (11,500 × $65)	$747,500
Cost of goods sold (11,500 × $70)	805,000
Gross profit	$ (57,500)

c. Dickhaut should report in its disclosure notes that gross profit was increased by $195,000 [$137,500 − $(57,500)] due to LIFO liquidation. It's worth noting that Dickhaut could report any gross profit between $(57,500) and $137,500 by adjusting its end-of-year purchases.

d. The replenishment decision should depend on the cash flows from each alternative over the planning period (until the point where inventory could be replenished next year at $55). The following table looks at three alternatives—no year-end purchase, a year-end purchase of 4,500 units, and a year-end purchase of 1,500 units. The second alternative would retain all the LIFO layers that were in the beginning inventory, while the third alternative would retain only the Year 6 layer at $20 per unit. For this last alternative, cost of goods sold would be $685,000 (8,500 units at $70 each plus 3,000 units at $30 each).

As the table shows, the third alternative is preferred to the second, but the first alternative is preferred over the other two. (Of course, this analysis is based on the assumption that 5,000 units will be held in inventory for the entire planning horizon. If Dickhaut anticipates future inventory reductions, e.g., due to product changes, end-of-year purchases would only defer the payment of taxes and their relative benefits would decrease.)

	No purchase		Purchase 4,500 units		Purchase 1,500 units	
	Income	Cash Flows	Income	Cash Flows	Income	Cash Flows
Revenue	$747,500	$747,500	$747,500	$747,500	$747,500	$747,500
COGS	610,000		805,000		685,000	
Gross profit	137,500		(57,500)		62,500	
Tax (25%)	(34,375)	(34,375)	14,375	14,375	(15,625)	(15,625)
Year-end purchases				(315,000)		(105,000)
Year 9 purchases		(247,500)				(165,000)
Total cash flows		$465,625		$446,875		$461,875

Chapter 8
Reporting and Analyzing Long-Term Operating Assets

LEARNING OBJECTIVES

LO8-1 Determine which costs to capitalize and report as tangible assets and which costs to expense.

LO8-2 Apply different depreciation methods to allocate the cost of assets over time.

LO8-3 Determine the effects of asset sales and impairments on financial statements.

LO8-4 Analyze the effect of tangible assets on key performance measure.

LO8-5 Describe the accounting and reporting for intangible assets.

LO8-6 Analyze the effects of intangible assets on key performance measures.

Road Map

LO	Learning Objective | Topics	Page	eLecture	Review	Assignments
LO8-1	Determine which costs to capitalize and report as tangible assets and which costs to expense.	8-3	e8-1	R 8-1	M8-11, E8-25, E8-26, **DA8-1**
LO8-2	Apply different depreciation methods to allocate the cost of assets over time.	8-5	e8-2	R 8-2	M8-12, M8-13, M8-18, M8-20, M8-21, M8-22, E8-25, E8-26, E8-27, E8-28, E8-29, E8-30, E8-31, E8-32, E8-33, E8-38, E8-39, E8-42, E8-43, **DA8-2**
LO8-3	Determine the effects of asset sales and impairments on financial statements.	8-10	e8-3	R 8-3	M8-14, M8-15, M8-16, M8-17, E8-25, E8-26, E8-28, E8-29, E8-31, E8-42, , E8-43, P8-44, C8-48, C8-49, C8-52, C8-53
LO8-4	Analyze the effect of tangible assets on key performance measures.	8-13	e8-4	R 8-4	M8-23, E8-34, E8-35, E8-40, C8-48, C8-50, **DA8-3**
LO8-5	Describe the accounting and reporting for intangible assets.	8-17	e8-5	R 8-5	M8-19, M8-24, E8-36, E8-37, PB-45, P8-46, P8-47, C8-51
LO8-6	Analyze the effects of intangible assets on key performance measures.	8-23	e8-6	R 8-6	M8-24, E8-41, P8-45, C8-50, C8-51, **DA8-4**

PROCTER & GAMBLE
www.pg.com

The Procter & Gamble Company (P&G) has successfully reinvented itself... again. Founded in 1837 by William Procter and James Gamble, P&G is the largest consumer products company in the world today. P&G markets its products in more than 180 countries, and its annual sales now are in excess of $70 billion, far exceeding competitors such as **Colgate-Palmolive Company** and **Kimberly-Clark Corporation**. P&G has focused on its higher-margin products such as those in beauty care. P&G's advertising budget is approximately a little over 10% of sales, which is about the same percentage as Colgate's and more than twice as large as Kimberly-Clark's.

P&G's financial performance has been impressive. Its return on equity (ROE) in fiscal year 2020 was almost 28%. Although more financially leveraged than the average publicly traded company, there is little need for concern because P&G generates more than $17 billion in operating cash flow, which is more than sufficient to cover its $434 million in interest payments. P&G also returned $15.2 billion to shareholders in dividends and repurchases of its own shares in 2020. (Stock repurchases are covered more fully in Chapter 11.)

P&G has made a priority of focusing on top brands to achieve superior products, packaging, brand communications, retail execution and customer value. P&G's product portfolio consists of numerous well-recognized household brands. Surveys in the business press show that the company is widely admired. A partial listing follows by reportable business segments, including some "Billion Dollar Brands" in each segment:

- **Baby, Feminine & Family Care**—Always, Bounty, Charmin, Pampers, Tampax
- **Beauty**— Head & Shoulders, Olay, Old Spice, Pantene
- **Fabric and Home Care**—Febreze, Cascade, Dawn, Downy, Gain, Tide
- **Grooming**—Braun, Gillette, Venus
- **Health Care**—Crest, Oral-B, Metamucil, Pepto-Bismol

While these brands are well-established, substantial risks exist. In the fiscal 2020 annual report, management states that "Our business model relies on continued growth and success of existing brands and products, as well as the creation of new innovative products. The markets and industry segments in which we offer our products are highly competitive... Our growth strategy is to provide meaningful and noticeable superiority in all elements of our consumer proposition." External risks also exist. For example, in recent years commodity costs have risen rapidly and significantly, and the coronavirus pandemic has disrupted supply chains. Around 55% of the company's business is generated outside North America, and P&G has "on the ground" operations in about 70 countries. Currency exchange rate fluctuations and trade policies can have a disruptive effect on distribution channels and sales growth.

In this chapter, we explore the reporting and analysis of long-term operating assets. In order to maintain growth in sales, income, and cash flows, capital-intensive companies like P&G must be diligent in managing long-term operating assets. As is the case with P&G, many companies have made large investments in innovation and brand value. These investments are not always reflected adequately in the balance sheet. Management's choices and GAAP rules concerning the reporting of long-term operating assets can have a marked impact on the analysis and interpretation of financial statements.

Sources: *Procter & Gamble* 2018 Annual Report and 10-K.

CHAPTER ORGANIZATION

Reporting and Analyzing Long-Term Operating Assets

Property, Plant, and Equipment
- Determining Costs to Capitalize
- Depreciation Methods
- Changes in Accounting Estimates
- Asset Sales and Impairments
- Note Disclosures
- Analysis Implications

Analyzing Financial Statements
- PPE Turnover
- Percent Depreciated Ratio
- Cash Flow Effects

Intangible Assets
- Research and Development Costs
- Patents, Copyrights, Trademarks, and Franchise Rights
- Amortization and Impairment
- Goodwill
- Note Disclosures
- Analysis Implications

INTRODUCTION

LO8-1 Determine which costs to capitalize and report as tangible assets and which costs to expense.

Investments in long-term operating assets often represent the largest component of a company's balance sheet. Effectively managing long-term operating assets is crucial, because these investments affect company performance for several years and are frequently irreversible. To evaluate how well a company is managing operating assets, we need to understand how they are measured and reported.

This chapter describes the accounting, reporting, and analysis of long-term operating assets, including tangible and intangible assets. **Tangible assets** are assets that have physical substance. They are frequently included in the balance sheet as *property, plant, and equipment*, and include land, buildings, machinery, fixtures, and equipment. **Intangible assets**, such as trademarks and patents, do not have physical substance but provide the owner with specific rights and privileges.

Long-term operating assets have two common characteristics. First, unlike inventory, these assets are not acquired for resale. Instead, they are necessary to produce and deliver the products and services that generate revenues for the company. Second, these assets help produce revenues for multiple accounting periods. Consequently, accountants focus considerable attention on how they are reported in the balance sheet and how these costs are transferred over time to the income statement as expenses.

To illustrate the size and importance of long-term operating assets, the asset section (only) of P&G's balance sheet is reproduced in **Exhibit 8.1**. We can see as of June 30, 2020, the end of P&G's fiscal year, P&G's net investment in property, plant, and equipment totaled approximately $20.7 billion, and its intangible assets represent a $63.7 billion investment. Together, these two categories of assets make up about 70% of P&G's total assets.

This chapter is divided into two main sections. The first section focuses on accounting for tangible property, plant, and equipment and the related depreciation expense that is reported each period in the income statement. The second section examines the measurement and reporting of intangible assets.

PROPERTY, PLANT, AND EQUIPMENT (PPE)

For many companies, the largest category of operating assets is long-term property, plant, and equipment (PPE) assets. The size and duration of this asset category raises several important questions, including:

- Which costs should be **capitalized** on the balance sheet as assets? Which should be expensed?
- How should capitalized costs be allocated to the accounting periods that benefited from the asset?
- How should asset sales or significant changes in assets' fair values be reported?

This section explains the accounting, reporting, and analysis of PPE assets and related items.

EXHIBIT 8.1 — Procter & Gamble Balance Sheet (assets only)

($ millions)	June 30 2020	June 30 2019
Assets		
Current assets		
Cash and cash equivalents	$ 16,181	$ 4,239
Available-for-sale investment securities	—	6,048
Accounts receivable	4,178	4,951
Inventories		
Materials and supplies	1,414	1,289
Work in process	674	612
Finished goods	3,410	3,116
Total inventories	5,498	5,017
Prepaid expenses and other current assets	2,130	2,218
Total current assets	27,987	22,473
Property, plant, and equipment, net	20,692	21,271
Goodwill	39,901	40,273
Trademarks and other intangible assets, net	23,792	24,215
Other noncurrent assets	8,328	6,863
Total assets	$120,700	$115,095

Determining Costs to Capitalize

When a company acquires an asset, it must first decide which portion of the cost should be included among the expenses of the current period and which costs should be capitalized as part of the asset and reported in the balance sheet. Outlays to acquire PPE are called **capital expenditures**. Expenditures that are recorded as an asset must possess each of the following two characteristics:

1. The asset is owned or controlled by the company.
2. The asset is expected to provide future benefits.

All normal costs incurred to acquire an asset and prepare it for its intended use should be capitalized and reported in the balance sheet. These costs would include the purchase price of the asset plus any of the following: installation costs, taxes, shipping costs, legal fees, and setup or calibration costs. If owning an asset carries legal obligations at the end of the asset's life (for example, to remove the asset or to perform environmental remediation), the current cost of those obligations should be included in the asset's cost and recognized as a liability at the time the asset is acquired. This cost will be included in the subsequent depreciation of the asset.

Determining the specific costs that should be capitalized requires judgment. There are two important considerations to address when deciding which costs to capitalize. First, companies can only capitalize costs that are *directly linked* to future benefits. Incidental costs or costs that would be incurred regardless of whether the asset is purchased should not be capitalized. Second, the costs capitalized as an asset can be no greater than the expected future benefits to be derived from use of the asset. This requirement means that if a company reports a $200 asset, we can reasonably expect that it will derive at least $200 in expected future cash inflows from the use and ultimate disposition of the asset.

Sometimes, companies construct assets for their own use rather than purchasing a similar asset from another company. In this case, all of the costs incurred to construct the asset—including materials, labor, and a reasonable amount of overhead—should be included in the cost that is capitalized. In addition, in many cases, a portion of the interest expense incurred during the construction period should also be capitalized as part of the asset's cost. This interest is called **capitalized interest**. Capitalizing some of a company's interest cost as part of the cost of a self-constructed asset reduces interest expense in the current period and increases depreciation expense in future periods when the asset is placed in service.

Once an asset is placed in service, additional costs are often incurred to maintain and improve the asset. Routine repairs and maintenance costs are necessary to realize the full potential benefits of ownership of the asset and should be treated as expenses of the period in which the maintenance is performed. However, if the cost can be considered an *improvement or betterment* of the asset, the cost should be capitalized. An improvement or betterment is an outlay that either enhances the usefulness of the asset or extends the asset's useful life beyond the original expectation.

YOU MAKE THE CALL

You are the Company Accountant   Your company has just purchased a plot of land as a building site for an office building. After the purchase, you discover that the building site was once the site of an oil well. Before construction can commence, your company must spend $40,000 to properly cap the oil well and prepare the site to meet current environmental standards. How should you account for the $40,000 cleanup cost? [Answers on page 8-25]

Review 8-1   LO8-1   Determining the Proper Accounting Treatment of Tangible Costs

For each of the following costs incurred by a manufacturer, indicate whether the cost should be capitalized or immediately expensed.

a. Attorney fees for services provided to prepare a contract to purchase a new manufacturing plant
b. Estimated cost of environmental clean-up at the end of the useful life of the new manufacturing plant
c. Cost of repainting the walls of the plant after five years of use of the facilities
d. Cost of an addition to the plant that allows expansion of current production
e. Invoice cost of purchasing new equipment
f. Sales tax paid on equipment purchased
g. Installation costs of new equipment
h. Costs to pay the salaries of employees during the training sessions on the use of the new equipment
i. Payment of insurance premiums to insure against worker accidents pertaining to the use of manufacturing equipment

Solution on p. 8-41.

Depreciation

LO8-2 Apply different depreciation methods to allocate the cost of assets over time.

FYI   Depreciation is a systematic allocation of asset cost over the useful life—not a measure of the change in fair value.

Once an asset has been recorded in the balance sheet, the cost must be transferred over time from the balance sheet to the income statement and reported as an expense. The nature of long-term operating assets is that they benefit more than one period. As a consequence, it is impossible to match a specific portion of the cost *directly* to the revenues of a particular period. Accounting principles require that this expense be recognized as equitably as possible over the asset's useful economic life. Therefore, we rely on a *systematic allocation* to assign a portion of the asset's cost to each period benefited. This systematic allocation of cost is called **depreciation**.

The concept of systematic allocation of an asset's cost is important. When depreciation expense is recorded, the reported value of the asset (also called the *book value* or *carrying value*) is reduced. Naturally, it is tempting to infer that the fair value of the asset is lower as a result. However, this reported value does not reflect the fair value of the asset. The fair value of the asset may decline by more or less than the amount of depreciation expense and can even increase in some periods. Depreciation expense should only be interpreted as an assignment of costs to an accounting period and not a measure of the decline in fair value of the asset.

The amount of cost that is allocated to a given period is recorded as depreciation expense in the income statement with a balancing entry in **accumulated depreciation** in the balance sheet. Accumulated depreciation is a contra-asset account (denoted "XA" in the journal entry). Like all contra-asset accounts, it offsets the balance in the corresponding asset account. To illustrate, assume that Dehning Company purchases a heavy-duty delivery truck for $100,000 and decides to record $18,000 of depreciation expense in the first year of operation. The following entries would be recorded with a cash outflow reflected in the investing section of the statement of cash flows.

The asset would be presented in the balance sheet at period-end at its net book value.

Truck, at cost	$100,000
Less accumulated depreciation	18,000
Truck, net	$ 82,000 (Book Value)

Transaction	Balance Sheet							Income Statement		
	Cash Asset	+ Noncash Assets	− Contra Asset	= Liabilities	+ Contrib. Capital	+ Earned Capital		Revenues	− Expenses	= Net Income
(1) Purchased delivery truck.	−100,000 Cash	+100,000 Truck		=					−	=
(2) Depreciation of delivery truck.			+18,000 Accumulated Depreciation	=		−18,000 Retained Earnings			− +18,000 Depreciation Expense	= −18,000

(1)
Truck (+A) 100,000
    Cash (−A) 100,000

+ Truck (A) −		+ Cash (A) −
(1) 100,000		100,000 (1)

(2)
Depreciation expense (+E, −SE) 18,000
    Accumulated depreciation (+XA, −A) 18,000

+ Depreciation Expense (E) −		− Accumulated Depreciation (XA) +
(2) 18,000		18,000 (2)

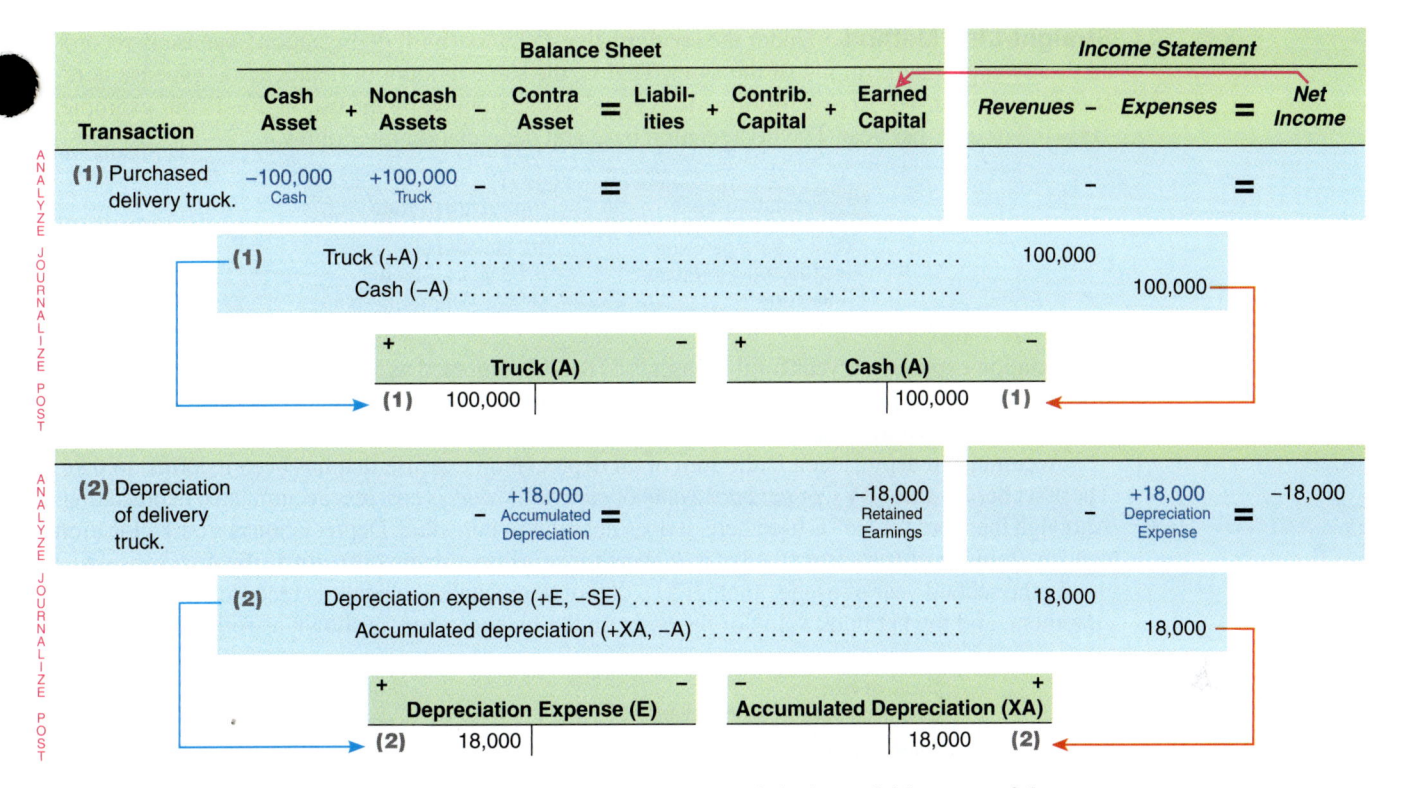

By presenting the information using a contra-asset account, the original acquisition cost of the asset is preserved in the asset account. The net book value of the asset reflects the acquisition cost less the balance in the accumulated depreciation account. The balance in the accumulated depreciation account is the sum of the depreciation expense that has been recorded to date. In a note disclosure accompanying the balance sheet in **Exhibit 8.1**, Procter & Gamble reports that the original cost of its property, plant, and equipment is $43,771 million and the depreciation accumulated as of June 30, 2020, is $23,079 million. The result is a net book value of $20,692 million.

Depreciation Methods

Two estimates are required to compute the amount of depreciation expense to record each period.

1. **Useful life**. The useful life is the period of time over which the asset is expected to provide economic benefits to the company. The useful life is not the same as the physical life of the asset. An asset may or may not provide economic benefits to the company for its entire physical life. This useful life should not exceed the period of time that the company intends to use the asset. For example, if a company has a policy of replacing automobiles every two years, the useful life should be set at no longer than two years, even if the automobiles physically last three years or more.
2. **Residual (or salvage) value**. The residual value is the expected realizable value of the asset at the end of its useful life. This value may be the disposal or scrap value, or it may be an estimated resale value for a used asset.

These factors must be estimated when the asset is acquired. The **depreciation base**, also called the *nonrecoverable cost*, is the portion of the cost that is depreciated. The depreciation base is the capitalized cost of the asset less the estimated residual value. This amount is allocated over the useful life of the asset according to the *depreciation method* that the company has selected.

To illustrate alternative depreciation methods, we return to the example presented earlier. Assume that Dehning Company purchases a delivery truck for $100,000. The company expects the truck to last five years and estimates a residual value of $10,000. The depreciation base is $90,000 ($100,000 − $10,000). We illustrate the three most common depreciation methods:

1. Straight-line method
2. Double-declining-balance method
3. Units-of-production method

Straight-Line Method Under the **straight-line (SL) method**, depreciation expense is recorded evenly over the useful life of the asset. That is, the same amount of depreciation expense is recorded each year. The **depreciation rate** is equal to one divided by the useful life. In our example, 1/5 = 0.2 or 20% per year. The depreciation base and depreciation rate follow.

Depreciation Base	Depreciation Rate
Cost – Salvage value = $100,000 – $10,000 = $90,000	1/Estimated useful life = 1/5 years = 20%

Depreciation expense per year for this asset is $18,000, computed as $90,000 × 20%. For the asset's first full year of usage, $18,000 of depreciation expense is reported in the income statement. At the end of that first year the asset is reported on the balance sheet, as shown earlier in the chapter.

Accumulated depreciation is the sum of all depreciation expense that has been recorded to date. The asset **book value (BV)**, or *net book value* or *carrying value,* is cost less accumulated depreciation. Although the word "value" is used here, it does not refer to fair value. Depreciation is a cost allocation concept (transfer of costs from the balance sheet to the income statement), not a valuation concept.

In the second year of usage, another $18,000 of depreciation expense is recorded in the income statement, and the net book value of the asset on the balance sheet is shown as follows:

Truck, at cost	$100,000
Less accumulated depreciation	36,000
Truck, net	$ 64,000

Accumulated depreciation now includes the sum of the first and second years' depreciation ($36,000), and the net book value of the asset is now reduced to $64,000. After the fifth year, a total of $90,000 of accumulated depreciation will be recorded, yielding a net book value for the truck of $10,000, its estimated salvage value.

Double-Declining-Balance Method GAAP allows companies to use **accelerated depreciation** methods. Accelerated depreciation methods record more depreciation expense in the early years of an asset's useful life and less expense in the later years. The total depreciation expense recorded over the entire useful life of the asset is the same as with straight-line depreciation. The only difference is in the amount of depreciation recorded for any given year.

The **double-declining-balance (DDB) method** is an accelerated depreciation method that computes the depreciation rate as twice the straight-line rate. This double rate is then multiplied by the net book value of the asset, which declines each period as accumulated depreciation increases. For Dehning Company, the depreciation base and the depreciation rate are computed as follows:

Depreciation Base	Depreciation Rate
Net Book Value = Cost – Accumulated Depreciation	2 × SL rate = 2 × 20% = 40%

FYI When calculating DDB depreciation, the depreciation rate is multiplied by the book value; residual value is not subtracted from book value.

The depreciation expense for the first year of usage for this asset is $40,000, computed as $100,000 × 40%. At the end of the first full year, $40,000 of depreciation expense is reported on the income statement (compared with $18,000 under the SL method), and the asset is reported on the balance sheet as follows:

Truck, at cost	$100,000
Less accumulated depreciation	40,000
Truck, net	$ 60,000

In the second year, $24,000 ($60,000 × 40%) of depreciation expense is reported in the income statement, and the net book value of the asset on the balance sheet is shown as follows:

Truck, at cost	$100,000
Less accumulated depreciation	64,000
Truck, net	$ 36,000

The double-declining-balance method continues to record depreciation expense in this manner until the salvage amount is reached, at which point the depreciation process is discontinued. This leaves a net book value equal to the salvage value as with the straight-line method. The DDB depreciation schedule for the life of this asset is illustrated in **Exhibit 8.2**.

EXHIBIT 8.2 Double-Declining-Balance Depreciation Schedule

Year	Book Value at Beginning of Year	Depreciation Expense	Book Value at End of Year
1	$100,000	100,000 × 40% = $40,000	$60,000
2	60,000	60,000 × 40% = 24,000	36,000
3	36,000	36,000 × 40% = 14,400	21,600
4	21,600	21,600 × 40% = 8,640	12,960
5	12,960	12,960 − 10,000 = 2,960*	10,000

*The depreciation expense in the fifth year is not calculated as 40% × $12,960 because the resulting depreciation would reduce the net book value below the $10,000 residual value. Instead, the residual value ($10,000) is subtracted from the remaining book value ($12,960), resulting in depreciation expense of $2,960.

Exhibit 8.3 compares the depreciation expense and net book value for both the SL and the DDB methods. During the first two years, the DDB method yields higher depreciation expense in comparison with the SL method. Beginning in the third year, this pattern reverses and the SL method produces higher depreciation expense. Over the asset's life, the same $90,000 in total depreciation expense is recorded, leaving a residual value of $10,000 on the balance sheet under both methods.

EXHIBIT 8.3 Comparison of Straight-Line and Double-Declining-Balance Depreciation

	Straight-Line		Double-Declining-Balance	
Year	Depreciation Expense	Book Value at End of Year	Depreciation Expense	Book Value at End of Year
1	$18,000	$82,000	$40,000	$60,000
2	18,000	64,000	24,000	36,000
3	18,000	46,000	14,400	21,600
4	18,000	28,000	8,640	12,960
5	18,000	10,000	2,960	10,000
	$90,000		$90,000	

All depreciation methods yield the same salvage value

Total depreciation over asset life is identical for all methods

Units-of-Production Method Under the **units-of-production method**, the useful life of the asset is defined in terms of the number of units of service provided by the asset. For instance, this could be the number of units produced, the number of hours that a machine is operated, or, as with Dehning Company's delivery truck, the number of miles driven. To illustrate, assume that Dehning Company estimates that the delivery truck will provide 150,000 miles of service before it is sold for its residual value of $10,000. The depreciation rate is expressed in terms of a cost per mile driven, computed as follows:

$$\frac{\$100,000 - \$10,000}{150,000 \text{ miles}} = \$0.60 \text{ per mile}$$

If the delivery truck is driven 35,000 miles in year 1, the depreciation expense for that year would be $21,000 (35,000 × $0.60). This method produces an amount of depreciation that varies from year to year as the use of the asset varies.

The units-of-production method is used by companies with natural resources such as oil reserves, mineral deposits, or timberlands. These assets are often referred to as **wasting assets** because the asset is consumed as it is used. The acquisition cost of a natural resource, plus any costs incurred to prepare the asset for its intended use, should be capitalized and reported among PPE assets in the balance sheet.

When the natural resource is used or extracted, inventory is created. The cost of the resource is transferred from the long-term asset account into inventory and, once the inventory is sold, to the income statement as cost of goods sold. The process of transferring costs from the resource account into inventory is called **depletion**.

Depletion is very much like depreciation of tangible operating assets, except that the amount of depletion recorded each period should reflect the amount of the resource that was actually extracted or used up during that period. As a result, depletion is usually calculated using the units-of-production method. The depletion rate is calculated as follows:

$$\text{Depletion rate per unit consumed} = \frac{\text{Acquisition cost} - \text{Residual value}}{\text{Estimated quantity of resource available}}$$

The calculation requires an estimate of the quantity of the resource available, which usually requires the assistance of experts, such as geologists or engineers, who are trained to make these determinations.

Depreciation for Tax Purposes Most companies use the straight-line method for financial reporting purposes and an accelerated depreciation method for tax returns.[1] Governments allow accelerated depreciation, in part, to provide incentives for taxpayers to invest. As a result of the differing depreciation methods used for financial accounting and tax purposes, lower depreciation expense (and higher income) is reported for financial accounting purposes early in the life of an asset relative to tax purposes. Even though this difference reverses in later years, companies prefer to defer the tax payments so that the cash savings can be invested to produce earnings. Further, even with the reversal in the later years of an asset's life, if total depreciable assets are growing at a fast enough rate, the additional first-year depreciation on newly acquired assets more than offsets the lower depreciation expense on older assets, yielding a continuing deferral of taxable income and taxes paid. There are other differences between financial reporting and tax reporting that create issues in determining a company's tax expense. In Chapter 10, we explore these differences further and examine deferred tax liabilities and deferred tax assets.

Changes in Accounting Estimates

The estimates required in the depreciation process are made when the asset is acquired. When necessary, companies can, and do, change these estimates during the useful lives of assets. When either the useful life or residual value estimates change, the change is applied prospectively. That is, companies use the new estimates from the date of the change going forward and do not restate the financial statements of prior periods.

To illustrate, assume that, after three years of straight-line depreciation, Dehning Company decided to extend the useful life of its truck from 5 years to 6 years. From **Exhibit 8.3**, the book value of the delivery truck at the end of the third year is $46,000. The change in estimated useful life would not require a formal accounting entry. Instead, depreciation expense would be recalculated for the remaining three years of the truck's useful life:

$$\frac{\$46,000 - \$10,000}{3 \text{ years}} = \$12,000 \text{ per year}$$

Thus, beginning in year four, depreciation expense of $12,000 (instead of $18,000) would be recorded each year.

---

[1] The U.S. Congress changes allowable tax depreciation methods from time to time. Some investments may qualify for immediate deduction of as much as 100% of the acquisition cost. Another common method is MACRS (Modified Accelerated Cost Recovery System). This method assumes no salvage value, and generally produces depreciation amounts consistent with the double-declining-balance method with a half year of service in the first and last year. When a declining balance method is used with zero salvage, the depreciation schedule must switch after the midpoint of the asset's life to straight-line depreciation of the remaining balance over the remaining life.

Review 8-2 — Accounting for Equipment (LO8-2)

On January 2, Lev Company purchases equipment for use in fabrication of a part for one of its key products. The equipment costs $95,000, and its estimated useful life is five years, after which it is expected to be sold for $10,000.

Required

a. Compute depreciation expense for each year of the equipment's useful life for each of the following depreciation methods:
   1. Straight-line
   2. Double-declining-balance
b. Assume that Lev Company uses the straight-line depreciation method. Show the effects of these entries on the balance sheet and the income statement using the financial statement effects template.
c. Prepare journal entries to record the initial purchase of the equipment on January 2 and the year-end depreciation adjustment on December 31, and post the journal entries to T-accounts.
d. Show how the equipment is reported on Lev's balance sheet at the end of the third year assuming straight-line depreciation.

Solution on p. 8-41.

Asset Sales and Impairments

This section discusses gains and losses from asset sales and computation and disclosure of asset impairments.

Gains and Losses on Asset Sales The gain or loss on the sale (disposition) of a long-term asset is computed as follows:

> **Gain or loss on asset sale = Proceeds from sale − Book value of asset sold**

The book (carrying) value of an asset is its acquisition cost less accumulated depreciation. When an asset is sold, its acquisition cost and related accumulated depreciation are removed from the balance sheet and any gain or loss is reported in income from continuing operations. To illustrate such a transaction, assume that Dehning Company decided to sell the delivery truck after four years of straight-line depreciation (without the aforementioned change in useful life). From **Exhibit 8.3**, we know that the book value of the truck is $28,000 ($100,000 − $72,000). If the truck is sold for $30,000, the entry to record the sale follows.

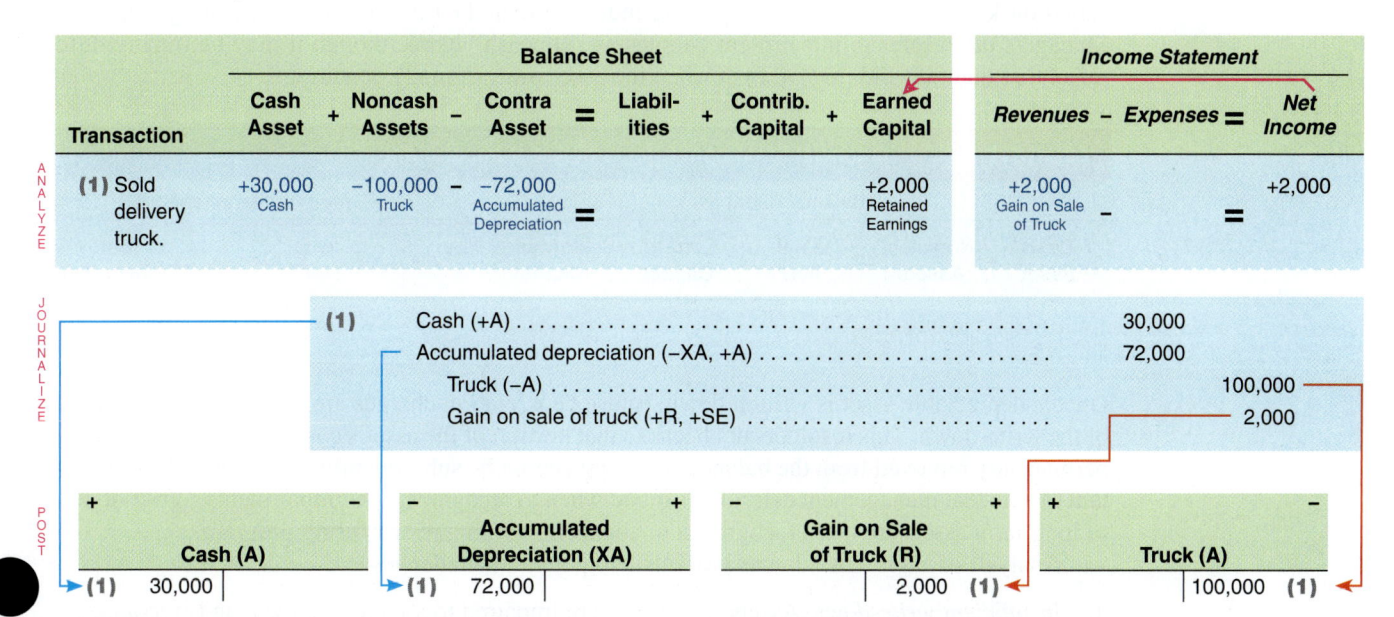

Balance Sheet

Transaction	Cash Asset	+	Noncash Assets	−	Contra Asset	=	Liabilities	+	Contrib. Capital	+	Earned Capital
(1) Sold delivery truck.	+30,000 Cash		−100,000 Truck		−72,000 Accumulated Depreciation	=					+2,000 Retained Earnings

Income Statement

Revenues	−	Expenses	=	Net Income
+2,000 Gain on Sale of Truck			=	+2,000

Journal Entry:

(1) Cash (+A) 30,000
    Accumulated depreciation (−XA, +A) 72,000
        Truck (−A) 100,000
        Gain on sale of truck (+R, +SE) 2,000

T-Accounts:

Cash (A)	Accumulated Depreciation (XA)	Gain on Sale of Truck (R)	Truck (A)
(1) 30,000	(1) 72,000	2,000 (1)	100,000 (1)

Gains and losses on asset sales can be large, and analysts must be aware of these nonrecurring operating income components. Further, if the gains are deemed immaterial, companies often include such gains and losses in general line items of the income statement—often as a component of

LO8-3
Determine the effects of asset sales and impairments on financial statements.

selling, general, and administrative expenses. As described in Chapter 4, the $30,000 increase in cash is an investing cash inflow in the statement of cash flows, and the $2,000 gain would be subtracted from net income in an indirect-method statement of cash flows from operating activities.

Asset Impairments   Property, plant, and equipment assets are reported at their net book values (original cost less accumulated depreciation). This is the case even if fair values of these assets increase subsequent to acquisition. As a result, there can be unrecognized gains hidden in the balance sheet.

However, if fair values of PPE assets subsequently decrease—and it can be determined that the asset value is permanently impaired—then companies must recognize losses on those assets. For assets that the company intends to keep and use, **impairment** is determined by comparing the sum of *expected* future (undiscounted) cash flows from the asset with its net book value. If these expected cash flows are greater than net book value, no impairment is deemed to exist. However, if the sum of expected cash flows is less than net book value, the asset is deemed impaired and it is written down to its current fair value (generally, the discounted present value of those expected cash flows). **Exhibit 8.4** depicts this impairment analysis.

EXHIBIT 8.4   Impairment Analysis of Long-Term Assets

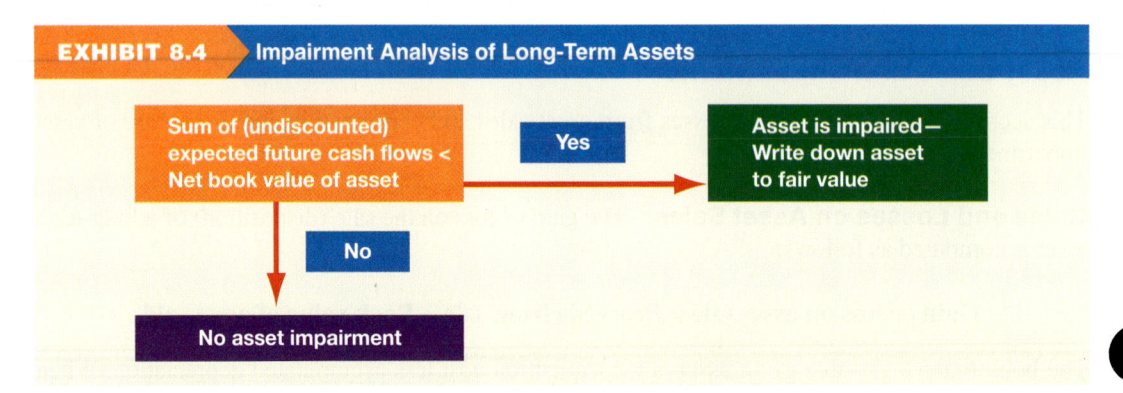

Sum of (undiscounted) expected future cash flows < Net book value of asset
- Yes → Asset is impaired—Write down asset to fair value
- No → No asset impairment

When a company records an impairment charge, assets are reduced by the amount of the write-down and the loss is recognized in the income statement, which reduces current period income. These effects are illustrated in **Exhibit 8.5**. Impairment charges are often included as part of **restructuring costs** along with future costs of workforce reductions. The entry in **Exhibit 8.5** reduces net income but does not affect current cash flows, so the impairment charges would be added back to net income when reporting indirect-method cash flows from operating activities. Managers often refer to impairment charges as "noncash" items, though it may be important to remember that they did involve cash when the asset was originally acquired.

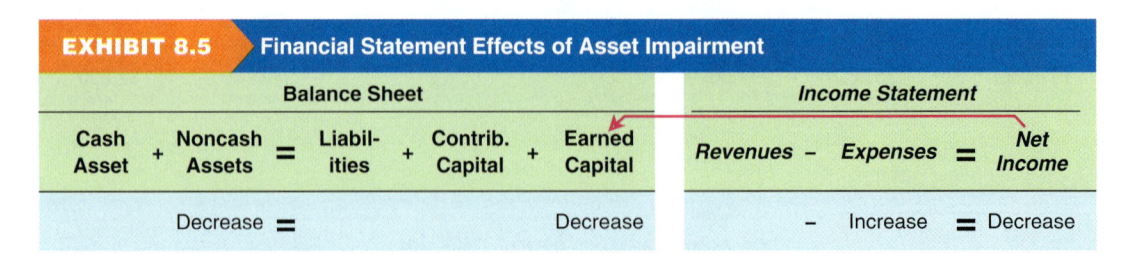

EXHIBIT 8.5   Financial Statement Effects of Asset Impairment

Balance Sheet					Income Statement		
Cash Asset + Noncash Assets = Liabilities + Contrib. Capital + Earned Capital					Revenues − Expenses = Net Income		
Decrease =				Decrease	− Increase = Decrease		

Once a depreciable asset is written down, future depreciation charges are reduced by the amount of the write-down. This result occurs because that portion of the asset's cost that is written down is permanently removed from the balance sheet and cannot be subsequently depreciated. It is important to note that management determines if and when to recognize asset impairments. Write-downs of long-term assets are often recognized in connection with a restructuring program.

Analysis of asset write-downs presents two potential challenges:

1. *Insufficient write-down.* Assets sometimes are impaired to a larger degree than is recognized. This situation can arise if management is overly optimistic about future prospects or is reluctant to recognize the full loss in income. Underestimation of an impairment causes current

income to be overstated and income in future years to be lower relative to income that would have been reported had the impairment been correctly recorded.

2. *Aggressive write-down.* This *big bath* scenario can arise if income is currently and severely depressed by recognizing a larger impairment charge than the actual costs. Management's view is that the market will not penalize the firm for an extra write-off, and that doing so purges the balance sheet of costs that would otherwise reduce future years' income. This leads to income being overstated for several years after the write-down.

Neither of these cases is condoned under GAAP. Yet, because management is estimating future cash flows for the impairment test and such estimates are difficult to verify, it has some degree of latitude over the timing and amount of the write-off and can use that discretion to manage reported income.

Note Disclosure

Procter & Gamble provides the following information in Note 1 of its 2020 Annual Report to describe its accounting for PPE assets.

> **Property, plant, and equipment**
> Property, plant, and equipment is recorded at cost reduced by accumulated depreciation. Depreciation expense is recognized over the assets' estimated useful lives using the straight-line method.
> Machinery and equipment includes office furniture and fixtures (15-year life), computer equipment and capitalized software (3- to 5-year lives), and manufacturing equipment (3- to 20-year lives). Buildings are depreciated over an estimated useful life of 40 years. Estimated useful lives are periodically reviewed and, where appropriate, changes are made prospectively. Where certain events or changes in operating conditions occur, asset lives may be adjusted and an impairment assessment may be performed on the recoverability of the carrying amounts.

The note details P&G's depreciation method (straight-line) and the estimated useful lives of various classes of PPE assets. Later in the notes, the company reports "asset-related costs" of $372 million included in its restructuring charges for the year ended June 30, 2020. The company describes these costs as follows:

> **Asset-related costs**
> Asset-related costs consist of both asset write-downs and accelerated depreciation. Asset write-downs relate to the establishment of a new fair value basis for assets held-for-sale or disposal. These assets were written down to the lower of their current carrying basis or amounts expected to be realized upon disposal, less minor disposal costs. Charges for accelerated depreciation relate to long-lived assets that will be taken out of service prior to the end of their normal service period. These assets related primarily to manufacturing consolidations and technology standardization. The asset-related charges will not have a significant impact on future depreciation charges.

A GLOBAL PERSPECTIVE

International Financial Reporting Standards (IFRS) are very similar to U.S. GAAP in the recognition of asset values when acquired and in the depreciation methods allowed. However, IFRS requires that companies recognize depreciation separately on the significant components of an asset. So, a U.S. company that acquires a building might recognize a single asset and depreciate it over the expected useful life of the building. An IFRS company would be required to recognize a bundle of assets like the structure, the roof, the elevators, the HVAC system, etc. Each of these components would be depreciated separately over its expected useful life, generally producing a more accelerated depreciation expense.

One implication of this difference is that subsequent expenditures might be dealt with differently. The U.S. company that replaces the HVAC system after its expected fifteen-year life would classify the expenditure as a maintenance expense. But the IFRS company would have fully depreciated the original HVAC system, and the new system would be treated as a capital expenditure, creating a new asset.

Review 8-3 LO8-3 — Analyzing the Financial Statement Impacts of Disposals and Impairments

The following three equipment items were purchased at different points in time but were all sold during the current year. Assume all equipment items have a zero salvage value.

Equipment item	Original Cost	Estimated Useful Life	Life at Date of Sale	Cash Sale Price
101	$ 55,000	5 years	36 months	$22,000
220	$ 80,000	8 years	84 months	$12,500
380	$125,000	10 years	48 months	$68,000

a. Using the financial statement effects template, show how the sale of each equipment item affects the balance sheet and income statement. Assume that the company applies the straight-line depreciation method.

b. Instead, assume that Item #380 was not sold. However, the company examined the equipment for impairment and estimates $73,000 in future cash inflows related to the use of the equipment. The fair value of the equipment is determined to be $68,000. Use the financial statement effects template to show the impact of an impairment (if an impairment is required to be recorded).

c. Prepare journal entries required for parts *a* and *b*.

Solution on p.8-41.

ANALYZING FINANCIAL STATEMENTS

LO8-4 Analyze the effects of tangible assets on key performance measures.

Most companies produce their financial performance with their long-term operating assets like property, plant, and equipment and with their intellectual property. Effective use of these assets represents one of the key components of success for companies. In addition, these assets are acquired with the anticipation that they will provide benefits for an extended period of time. They are often expensive relative to their annual benefit, and most of these assets require replenishment on an ongoing basis.

Analysis Objective

We are trying to gauge the effectiveness of Procter & Gamble's use of its physical productive assets.

Analysis Tool PPE Turnover (PPET)

$$\text{PPE Turnover (PPET)} = \frac{\text{Sales revenue}}{\text{Average PPE, net*}}$$

*PPE, net refers to gross PPE less accumulated depreciation.

Applying the PPE Turnover Ratio to Procter & Gamble

2018: $\dfrac{66,832}{(19,893 + 20,600)/2} = 3.30$

2019: $\dfrac{67,684}{(20,600 + 21,271)/2} = 3.23$

2020: $\dfrac{70,950}{(21,271 + 20,692)/2} = 3.38$

Guidance Property, plant, and equipment turnovers vary greatly by industry and are affected by companies' manufacturing strategies, so it is difficult to give specific guidance. In general, a higher ratio is preferred, as it is one significant component of the company's return on assets.

---

[2] See Christensen, Hans B., and Valeri V. Nikolaev, "Does fair value accounting for non-financial assets pass the market test?" *Review of Accounting Studies*, September 2013.

Procter & Gamble in Context

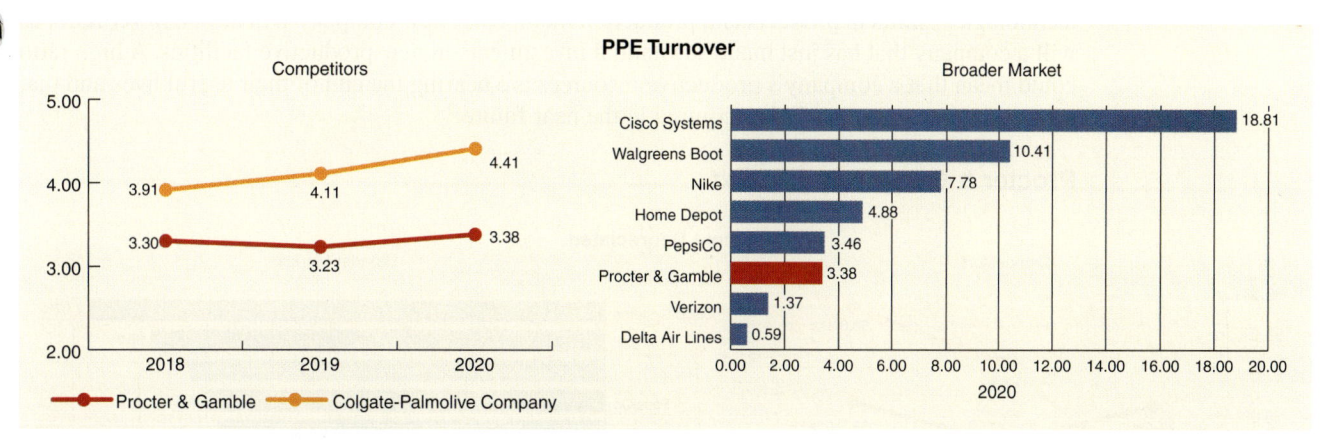

PPE Turnover

Competitors (line chart):
- Procter & Gamble: 2018: 3.30, 2019: 3.23, 2020: 3.38
- Colgate-Palmolive Company: 2018: 3.91, 2019: 4.11, 2020: 4.41

Broader Market (2020):
- Cisco Systems: 18.81
- Walgreens Boot: 10.41
- Nike: 7.78
- Home Depot: 4.88
- PepsiCo: 3.46
- Procter & Gamble: 3.38
- Verizon: 1.37
- Delta Air Lines: 0.59

These companies do not have identical fiscal year ends. For each fiscal year listed above and in later charts, fiscal year-end balance sheet dates range from February 2 to December 31.

Takeaways P&G's fiscal 2020 PPET increased slightly from 2019 PPET, but 2019 PPET decreased slightly from 2018 PPET. Companies prefer that PPET be higher rather than lower, because it implies a lower level of capital investment is required to achieve a given level of sales revenue. P&G's PPET is lower than Colgate-Palmolive, though it is higher than a few others in its industry. We can also see that PPET differs considerably by industry—capital-intensive businesses with long-lived assets like Delta Air Lines and Verizon Communications have a low ratio.

Other Considerations Besides effectiveness of asset usage, PPET depends on a number of factors that affect the denominator and that should be taken into account in interpreting the numbers. First, it reflects the company's manufacturing strategy; a company that outsources its production will have a very high PPET, like Nike. Or, a company that has assets that are more fully depreciated will also report a high PPET. In Chapter 12, we discuss how ratios mixing income statement and balance sheet information can be affected by acquisitions of other companies.

Analysis Objective

We are trying to gauge the age of P&G's long-term tangible operating assets relative to their expected useful lives.

Analysis Tool Percent Depreciated

$$\text{Percent depreciated} = \frac{\text{Accumulated depreciation}}{\text{Cost of depreciable assets}}$$

Applying the Percent Depreciated Ratio to Procter & Gamble Accumulated depreciation can be seen in the balance sheet or note disclosures. The original cost of depreciable assets can be found in the same places. (See **Exhibit 8.1** for P&G's presentation.) Two types of property, plant, and equipment are not depreciated. Land is one type, and the other is construction in progress. Land is not depreciated because it has an indefinite life, and construction in progress is not depreciated until the constructed asset is placed in service. For P&G, the $43,771 million original cost of property, plant, and equipment includes $777 million for land and $2,034 million for construction in progress, which must be removed from the denominator.

2018: $\frac{\$21,247}{\$37,783} = 56.2\%$

2019: $\frac{\$22,122}{\$40,009} = 55.3\%$

2020: $\frac{\$23,079}{\$40,960} = 56.3\%$

Guidance Percent depreciated depends on a company's age and on the occurrence of disruptive technological shifts in products and production methods. A new company will have a lower ratio, as will a company that has just made substantial investments in new productive facilities. A high ratio could mean that a company's productive resources are nearing the end of their useful lives and that substantial investments will be required in the near future.[3]

Procter & Gamble in Context

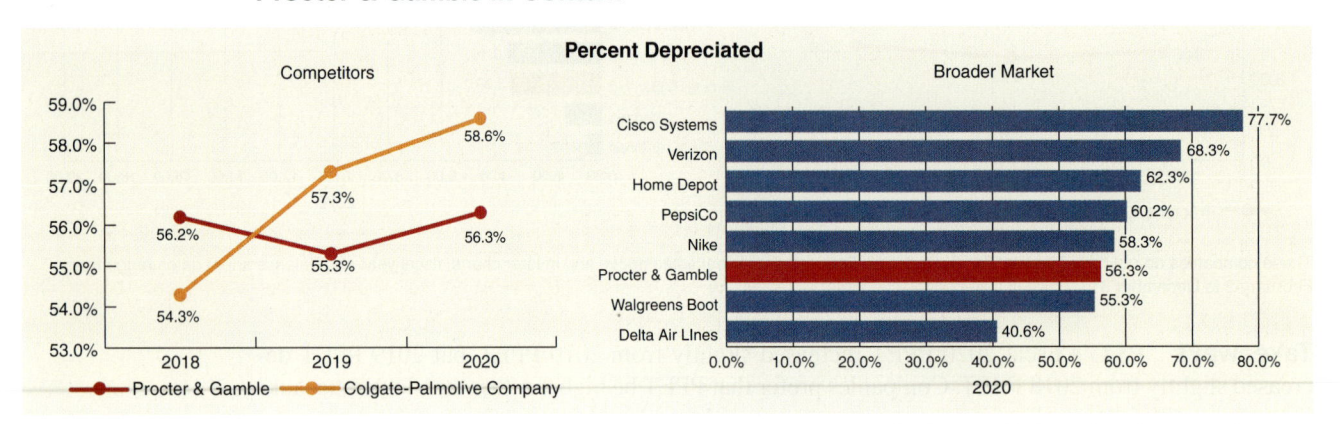

Percent Depreciated

Competitors (Procter & Gamble vs. Colgate-Palmolive Company):
- Procter & Gamble: 2018: 56.2%, 2019: 55.3%, 2020: 56.3%
- Colgate-Palmolive: 2018: 54.3%, 2019: 57.3%, 2020: 58.6%

Broader Market (2020):
- Cisco Systems: 77.7%
- Verizon: 68.3%
- Home Depot: 62.3%
- PepsiCo: 60.2%
- Nike: 58.3%
- Procter & Gamble: 56.3%
- Walgreens Boot: 55.3%
- Delta Air Lines: 40.6%

These companies do not have identical fiscal year ends. For each fiscal year listed above and in later charts, fiscal year-end balance sheet dates range from February 2 to December 31.

Takeaways Both Procter & Gamble and Colgate-Palmolive are mature companies experiencing long-term steady growth. They acquire assets on a continuing basis and, as a result, they have some assets that are brand-new and others that are reaching the end of their productive lives. The net result is that the percent depreciated ratio is approximately 54% to 59% for both companies.

Other Considerations Companies' percent depreciated ratio may differ because they are using different depreciation methods (straight-line or accelerated) or because they have chosen different useful lives for their assets. For instance, one airline depreciates its aircraft over twenty-five years to zero salvage value, while another depreciates its aircraft over fifteen years to ten percent salvage. A percent depreciated ratio of 50% for the first company would mean its average aircraft is 12.5 years old, while the same 50% ratio would imply aircraft that was 8.3 years old for the second company. As a result, it is always advisable to check companies' note disclosures to make sure that the ratios are interpreted correctly.

BUSINESS INSIGHT

Federal authorities arrested **WorldCom, Inc.**'s CEO, Bernie Ebbers, and chief financial officer, Scott Sullivan, in August 2002 for allegedly conspiring to alter the telecommunications giant's financial statements to meet analyst expectations. They were accused of *cooking the books* so the company would not show a loss for 2001 and subsequent quarters.

Specifically, WorldCom incurred large costs in anticipation of an increase in Internet-related business that did not materialize. The executives shifted these costs to the balance sheet and recorded them as PPE, thereby inflating current profitability. By capitalizing these costs (moving them from the income statement to the balance sheet), WorldCom was able to disguise these costs as an asset to be allocated as future costs. Contrary to WorldCom's usual practices and prevailing accounting principles, no support existed for capitalization.

continued

---

[3] Some companies do not provide complete disclosure for this computation. For example, Cisco Systems combines land and buildings in one line item and thus, an external reader of the statements cannot subtract the book value of land from the denominator to compute the percent depreciated accurately.

continued from previous page

Although the WorldCom case also involved alleged fraud, an astute analyst would have suspected something was amiss from analysis of WorldCom's property, plant, and equipment turnover (Sales/Average property, plant, and equipment) as shown below. The decline in turnover reveals that its assets constituted an ever-increasing percent of total sales during 1995 to 2002, by quarter. This finding does not, in itself, imply fraud. It does, however, raise serious questions that should have been answered by WorldCom executives in meetings with analysts.

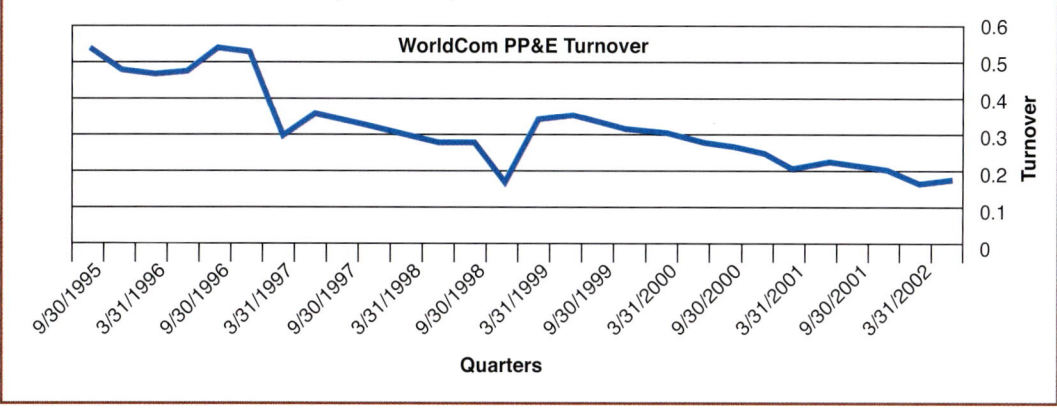

WorldCom PP&E Turnover chart showing declining turnover from ~0.55 in 9/30/1995 to ~0.2 by 3/31/2002, plotted quarterly.

Cash Flow Effects

When cash is involved in the acquisition of plant or equipment, the cash amount is reported as a use of cash in the investment section of the statement of cash flows as discussed in Chapter 4. Any cash received from asset sales is reported as a source of cash. The investing section of Procter & Gamble's 2020 annual report is shown below.

($ millions)	2020
Investing activities.	
Capital expenditures.	$(3,073)
Proceeds from asset sales.	30
Acquisitions, net of cash acquired	(58)
Purchases of short-term investments.	—
Proceeds from sales and maturities of investment securities.	6,151
Change in other investments	(5)
Total investing activities	$ 3,045

In 2020, P&G paid cash of $3,073 million to acquire plant assets and received cash of $30 million on the disposal of plant and equipment. The company also received more than $6 billion cash from the maturities and sales of investment securities. Losses (gains) on these disposal transactions would be added (subtracted) as adjustments in the operating section. Acquisitions of other companies cost $58 million in 2020.

For the Dehning Company delivery truck sale described earlier in this chapter, the investing section of the statement of cash flows would show $30,000 of cash proceeds. The gain on the sale would be subtracted from net income in the operating section. No receivable was involved in the sale.

YOU MAKE THE CALL

You Are the Division Manager You are the division manager for a main operating division of your company. You are concerned that a declining PPE turnover is adversely affecting your division's profitability. What specific actions can you take to increase PPE turnover? [Answers on page 8-25]

Review 8-4 LO8-4 — Analyzing the Effects of Tangible Assets on Financial Statements

American Airlines Group, Inc., reported the following information in its annual 10-K reports for the years 2017 to 2020.

	2020	2019	2018	2017
Sales.	17,337	45,768	44,541	42,622
Operating property and equipment, net	31,669	34,995	34,098	34,156
Accumulated depreciation	16,757	18,659	17,443	15,646
Operating property and equipment*	47,010	51,980	50,263	48,585

* Amount includes flight equipment and ground property and equipment, but excludes equipment purchase deposits.

a. Compute the PPE turnover for 2020, 2019, and 2018. Comment on the trend over time.
b. Calculate the percentage depreciated of American's depreciable assets at the end of fiscal years 2020, 2019, and 2018. Comment on the trend over time.

Solution on p. 8-42.

INTANGIBLE ASSETS

LO8-5 Describe the accounting and reporting for intangible assets.

Intangible assets are assets that lack physical substance but provide future benefits to the owner in the form of specific property rights or legal rights. For many companies, these assets have become an important source of competitive advantage and company value.

For financial accounting purposes, intangible assets are classified as either separately transferable or not separately transferable. Separately transferable intangible assets generally fall into one of two categories. The first category is assets that are the product of contractual or other legal rights. These intangibles include patents, trademarks, copyrights, franchises, license agreements, broadcast rights, mineral rights, and noncompetition agreements. The second category of separately transferable intangible assets includes benefits that are not contractually or legally defined but can be separated from the company and sold, transferred, or exchanged. Examples include customer lists, unpatented technology, formulas, processes, and databases. There are also intangible assets that are not separately transferable, primarily goodwill. Procter & Gamble reports its intangible assets on its 2020 balance sheet in just two categories ($ in millions): Goodwill $39,901; Trademarks and Other Intangible Assets $23,792. A significant portion of these assets resulted from the acquisition of The Gillette Company.

The issues involved in reporting intangible assets are conceptually similar to those of accounting for property, plant, and equipment. We must first decide which costs to capitalize, and then we need to determine how and when those costs will be transferred to the income statement. However, intangible assets often pose a particularly difficult problem for accountants. This problem arises because the benefits provided by these assets are often uncertain and difficult to quantify. In addition, the useful life of an intangible asset is often impossible to estimate with confidence.

As was the case with property, plant, and equipment, intangible assets are either purchased from another individual or company or internally developed. Like PPE assets, the cost of purchased intangible assets is capitalized. Unlike PPE assets, though, we generally do not capitalize the cost of internally developed intangible assets. Research and development (R&D) costs, and the patents and technologies that are created as a result of R&D, serve as useful examples.

Research and Development Costs

R&D activities are a major expenditure for most companies, especially for those in technology and pharmaceutical industries where R&D expenses can exceed 10% of revenues. These expenses include employment costs for R&D personnel, R&D-related contract services, and R&D plant asset costs.

Companies invest millions of dollars in R&D because they expect that the future benefits resulting from these activities will eventually exceed the costs. Successful R&D activities create new products that can be sold and new technologies that can be utilized to create and sustain a competitive advantage. Unfortunately, only a fraction of R&D projects reach commercial production, and it is difficult to predict which projects will be successful. Moreover, it is often difficult to predict when the benefits will be realized, even if the project is successful.

Because of the uncertainty surrounding the benefits of R&D, accounting for R&D activities follows a uniform method—immediate recognition as an expense. This approach applies to all R&D costs incurred prior to the start of commercial production, including the salaries and wages of personnel engaged in R&D activities, the cost of materials and supplies, and the equipment and facilities used in the project. Should any of the R&D activities prove successful, the benefits should result in higher net income in future periods. Costs incurred internally to develop new software products do not satisfy the capitalization requirement of providing expected future profits until the technological feasibility of the product is established. Therefore, until the feasibility requirement can be met, these costs are expensed.

If equipment and facilities are purchased for a specific R&D project and have no other use, their cost is expensed immediately even though their useful life would typically extend beyond the current period. The expensing of R&D equipment and facilities is in stark contrast to the capitalization-and-depreciation of non-R&D plant assets. The expensing of R&D plant assets is mandated unless those assets have alternative future uses (in other R&D projects or otherwise). For example, a general research facility housing multi-use lab equipment should be capitalized and depreciated like any other depreciable asset. However, project-directed research buildings and equipment with no alternate uses must be expensed.

BUSINESS INSIGHT

R&D Costs at Cisco Systems Cisco spends between $6.3 billion and $6.6 billion annually for R&D compared with its revenues of around $49–$52 billion, or about 13%. This level reflects a high percent of revenues devoted to R&D in comparison with nontechnology companies but typifies companies that compete in the high-tech arena. Following is the R&D-expense-to-sales ratio (also called *R&D Intensity*) for Cisco and some related companies.

	2020	2019	2018
Cisco Systems, Inc.	12.87%	12.67%	12.84%
Juniper Networks, Inc.	21.56%	21.50%	21.59%
HP, Inc.	2.61%	2.55%	2.40%

RESEARCH INSIGHT

Research has provided evidence consistent with managers reducing R&D spending when trying to meet certain earnings targets or other earnings goals. Part of this is due to the accounting—research and development costs are expensed immediately, reducing reported earnings in the current period. Thus, although the research and development spending should provide better future performance, it harms current performance leading "myopic" managers to cut back.[4] Recent research also suggests that some firms do not disclose research spending even when it appears that they must have such costs. One theory is that these firms do not want to disclose their research and development spending in order to hide the extent of their costs from their competitors.[5]

Patents

Successful research and development activity often leads a company to obtain a patent for its discoveries. A patent is an exclusive right to produce a product or use a technology. Patents are granted to protect the inventor of the new product or technology by preventing other companies from copying the innovation. The fair value of a patent depends on the commercial success of the product or technology. For example, a patent on the formula for a new drug to treat diabetes could be worth billions of dollars.

---

[4] See Bushee, Brian, "The Influence of Institutional Investors on Myopic R&D Investment Behavior." *Accounting Review*, 1998; Graham, John R., Cam Harvey and Shiva Rajgopal, "The Economic Implications of Corporate Financial Reporting." *Journal of Accounting and Economics*, 2005; and Sloan, Richard and P. Dechow. "Executive Incentives and the Horizon Problem: An Empirical Investigation," *Journal of Accounting and Economics*, 1991, for examples of research on this topic.

[5] See Koh, P.S., and D. M. Reeb. "Missing R&D," *Journal of Accounting and Economics*, 2015.

If a patent is purchased from the inventor, the purchase price is capitalized and reported in the balance sheet as an intangible asset. On the other hand, if the patent is developed internally, only the legal costs and registration fees are capitalized. The R&D cost to develop the new product or technology is expensed as incurred. This accounting illustrates the marked difference between purchased and internally created intangible assets.

Copyrights

A copyright is an exclusive right granted by the government to an individual author, composer, play writer, or similar individual for the life of the creator plus 70 years. Corporations can also obtain a copyright for varying periods set by law. Copyrights, like patents, can be acquired. The acquisition cost would be capitalized and amortized over the expected remaining economic life.

Trademarks

A trademark is a registered name, logo, package design, image, jingle, or slogan that is associated with a product. Many trademarks are easily recognizable, such as the Nike "swoosh," the shape of a Coca-Cola bottle, McDonald's golden arches, and the musical tones played in computer advertisements featuring Intel computer chips. Companies spend millions of dollars developing and protecting trademarks and their value is enhanced by advertising programs that increase their recognition. If a trademark is purchased from another company, the purchase price is capitalized. However, the cost of internally developed trademarks is expensed as incurred. Likewise, all advertising costs are expensed immediately, even if the value of a trademark is enhanced by the advertisement. For these reasons, many trademarks are not presented in the balance sheet.

BUSINESS INSIGHT

Trademarks and Patents at P&G   Procter & Gamble has acquired many of the products it currently markets to consumers. Others were developed internally. The following paragraph from the Management Discussion and Analysis section of P&G's 2020 annual report emphasizes the importance of these intangible assets to the company.

> (Our) trademarks are important to the overall marketing and branding of our products. . . . In part, our success can be attributed to the existence and continued protection of these trademarks, patents, and licenses.

Franchise Rights

A franchise is a contractual agreement that gives a company the right to operate a particular business in an area for a particular period of time. For example, a franchise may give the owner the right to operate a number of fast-food restaurants in a particular geographic region for twenty years. Operating rights and licenses are similar to franchise rights, except that they are typically granted by government agencies. Most franchise rights are purchased and, as a result, the purchase price should be capitalized and presented as an intangible asset in the balance sheet.

Amortization and Impairment of Identifiable Intangible Assets

When intangible assets are acquired and capitalized, a determination must be made as to whether the asset has a definite life. Examples of intangible assets with definite lives include patents and franchise rights. An intangible asset with a definite life must be amortized over the expected useful life of the asset. Amortization is the systematic allocation of the cost of an intangible asset to the periods benefited, similar to depreciation of tangible assets.

Amortization expense is generally recorded using the straight-line method. The expense is included in the income statement as a component of operating income and is often included among selling, general, and administrative expenses. The cost of the intangible asset is presented in the balance sheet net of accumulated amortization.

Amortization   To illustrate, assume that Landsman Company spent $100,000 in early 2022 to purchase a patent. The entry to record the capitalization of this cost follows.

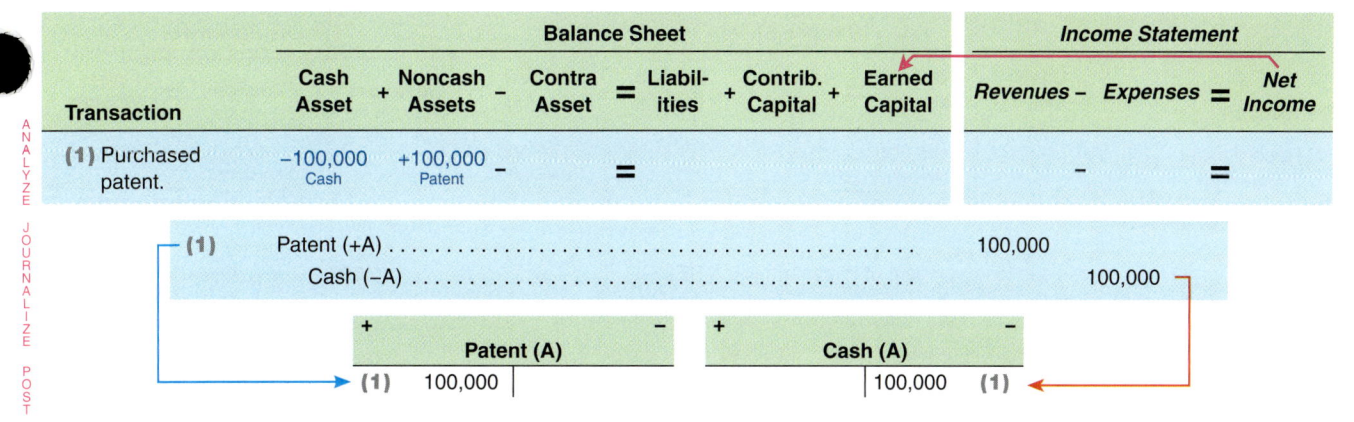

Transaction	Balance Sheet						Income Statement		
	Cash Asset	+ Noncash Assets	− Contra Asset	= Liabilities	+ Contrib. Capital	+ Earned Capital	Revenues −	Expenses =	Net Income
(1) Purchased patent.	−100,000 Cash	+100,000 Patent		=					=

```
(1)  Patent (+A) ..................................... 100,000
         Cash (−A) ..................................         100,000
```

+ Patent (A)		− Cash (A) +	
(1) 100,000			100,000 (1)

Although the patent had a remaining legal life of 12 years, Landsman estimated that the useful life of the patent was 5 years. Thus, the intangible asset has a definite life. The entry to record the annual amortization expense at the end of 2022 follows.

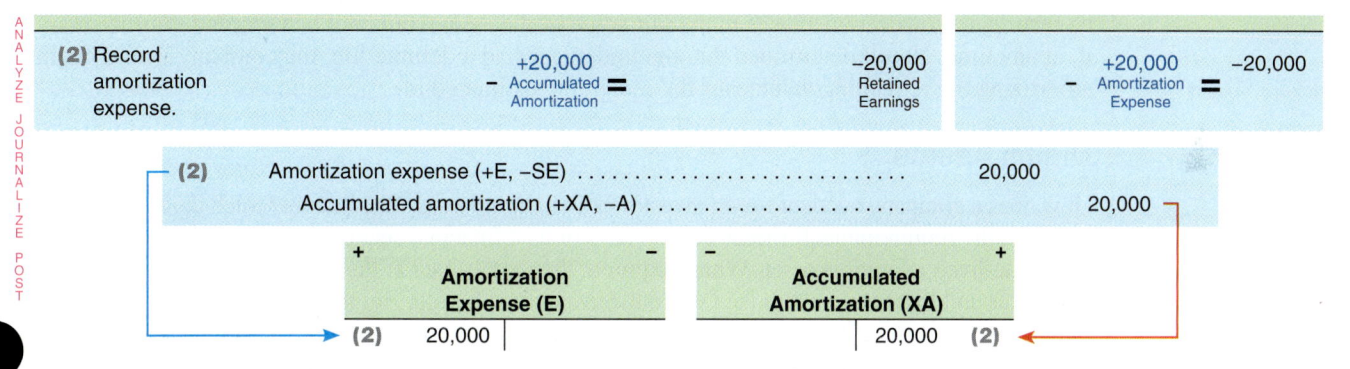

Transaction	Balance Sheet						Income Statement		
(2) Record amortization expense.			+20,000 Accumulated Amortization	=		−20,000 Retained Earnings		+20,000 Amortization Expense =	−20,000

```
(2)  Amortization expense (+E, −SE) ......................  20,000
         Accumulated amortization (+XA, −A) .................         20,000
```

+ Amortization Expense (E) −		− Accumulated Amortization (XA) +	
(2) 20,000			20,000 (2)

Impairment Some transferable intangible assets, such as some trademarks, have indefinite lives. For these assets, the expected useful life extends far enough into the future that it is impossible for management to estimate a useful life. An intangible asset with an indefinite life should not be amortized until the useful life of the asset can be specified. That is, no expense is recorded until management can reasonably estimate the useful life of the asset.

Although intangible assets with indefinite lives are not subject to amortization, they must be tested annually to determine if their value has been impaired. The impairment test for intangibles is slightly different from the impairment test used to evaluate PPE assets. The intangible asset is impaired if the book value of the asset exceeds its fair value and the write-down is equal to the difference between the book value and the fair value.

To illustrate, assume that Norell Company purchased a trademark in 2020 for $240,000 and determined that the intangible asset had an indefinite life. The entry to record the purchase of the trademark follows.

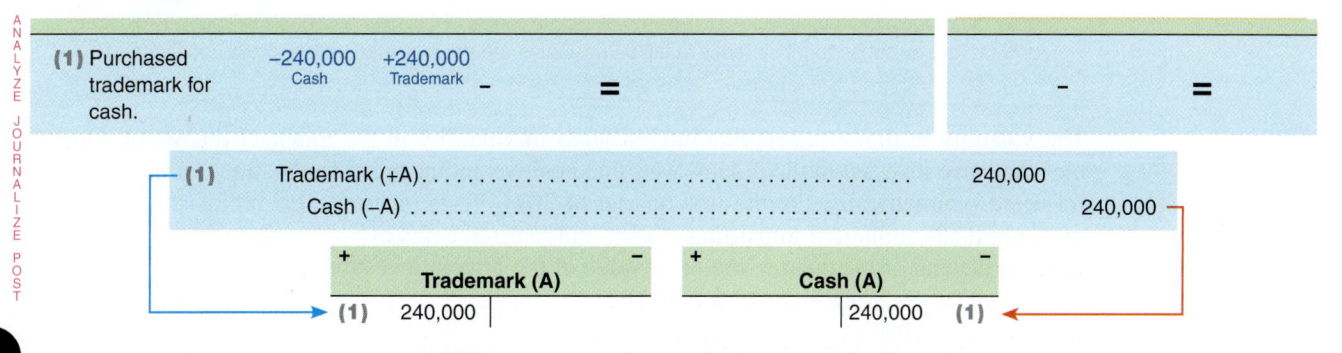

Transaction	Balance Sheet						Income Statement		
(1) Purchased trademark for cash.	−240,000 Cash	+240,000 Trademark		=					=

```
(1)  Trademark (+A) .................................  240,000
         Cash (−A) ..................................         240,000
```

+ Trademark (A) −		− Cash (A) +	
(1) 240,000			240,000 (1)

In 2023, changes in regulations caused Norell to conclude that the value of the trademark had been impaired. They estimated the current fair value was $100,000, resulting in a loss of $140,000 ($240,000 − $100,000). The entry to record the impairment of the trademark would be as follows.

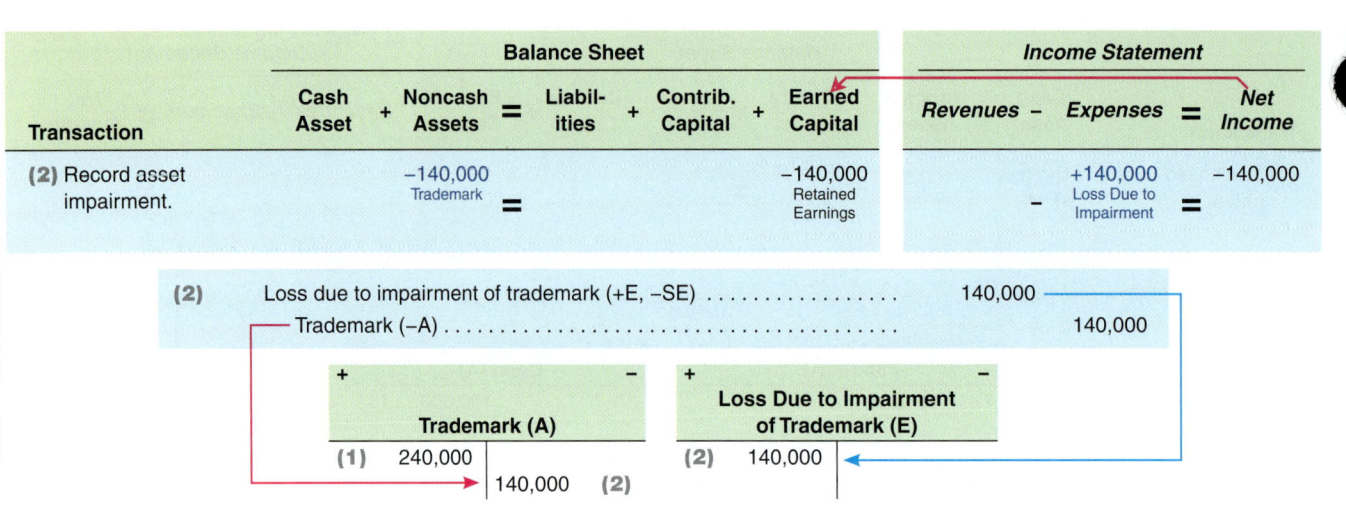

Transaction	Balance Sheet						Income Statement		
	Cash Asset	+ Noncash Assets	= Liabilities	+ Contrib. Capital	+ Earned Capital		Revenues −	Expenses =	Net Income
(2) Record asset impairment.		−140,000 Trademark =			−140,000 Retained Earnings		−	+140,000 Loss Due to Impairment =	−140,000

(2) Loss due to impairment of trademark (+E, −SE) 140,000
      Trademark (−A) 140,000

+ Trademark (A) −		+ Loss Due to Impairment of Trademark (E) −	
(1) 240,000	140,000 (2)	(2) 140,000	

If the value of the trademark subsequently decreases further, additional impairment losses would be recorded. However, increases in the fair value of the asset would not be recorded. Furthermore, if, at any time, Norell determined that the trademark had a definite life, the company would begin amortizing the remaining value over the remaining estimated life.

Digital Assets

How does a company account for an investment in a digital asset, like bitcoin? Such digital assets do not meet the requirements for treatment as cash or as a financial security, so they are considered an indefinite-lived intangible asset. When acquired, they are valued at the cost of acquisition, and realized gains and losses are recognized when the investment is sold. But the asset must be subject to an impairment analysis at the end of a financial reporting period or when there is an indication that the asset has been impaired. It the asset value recovers following an impairment, the asset's book value cannot be written up. The following was reported by Tesla Inc. in its March 31, 2021 10-Q.

> During the three months ended March 31, 2021, we purchased an aggregate of $1.50 billion in digital assets, comprised solely of bitcoin. In addition, during the three months ended March 31, 2021, we began accepting bitcoin as a payment for sales of certain of our products in specified regions, subject to applicable laws... We currently account for all digital assets held as a result of these transactions as indefinite-lived intangible assets in accordance with ASC 350, Intangibles—Goodwill and Other. We have ownership of and control over our bitcoin and we may use third-party custodial services to secure it. The digital assets are initially recorded at cost and are subsequently remeasured on the consolidated balance sheet at cost, net of any impairment losses incurred since acquisition... In determining if an impairment has occurred, we consider the lowest market price of one bitcoin quoted on the active exchange since acquiring the bitcoin. If the then current carrying value of a digital asset exceeds the fair value so determined, an impairment loss has occurred with respect to those digital assets in the amount equal to the difference between their carrying values and the price determined... The impaired digital assets are written down to their fair value at the time of impairment and this new cost basis will not be adjusted upward for any subsequent increase in fair value. Gains are not recorded until realized upon sale(s).

The volatility in digital assets like bitcoin leads to volatility in the financial reports of companies that have invested in them. However, that positive and negative fluctuations in value are not reflected symmetrically. For the first quarter of 2021, Tesla invested $1.5 billion in bitcoin and recognized $27 million of impairment losses and realized gains of $128 million from sales of bitcoin. At the end of the quarter, the book value of the bitcoin investment was $1.33 billion, while the fair value was $2.48 billion, 86% higher.

Goodwill

Goodwill is an intangible asset that is recorded only when one company acquires another company. Goodwill is defined as the excess of the purchase price paid for a company over the fair value of its identifiable net assets (assets minus the liabilities assumed). The identifiable net assets include any identifiable intangible assets acquired in the purchase. Therefore, goodwill can neither be linked to any identifiable source, nor can it be sold or separated from the company. It represents the value of the acquired company above and beyond the specific identifiable assets listed on the balance sheet.

By definition, goodwill has an indefinite life. Once it is recorded in the balance sheet, it is not amortized. Instead, it is subject to an annual impairment test. Goodwill is impaired when the fair value of the acquired business (more specifically, any testable reporting unit) is less than the recorded book value. If this occurs, goodwill is written down to an imputed value. The goodwill write-down (also called a goodwill write-off) results in the immediate transfer of some or all of a company's goodwill book value from the balance sheet to the income statement as an expense. The book value of goodwill is immediately reduced and a corresponding expense is reported in the income statement. Like the impairment write-down of tangible assets, the write-down of goodwill is a discretionary expense whose amount and timing are largely determined by management (with auditor acceptance).

It is commonplace to see goodwill impairment write-downs related to unsuccessful acquisitions, and these usually represent material amounts. For instance, in 2012, Hewlett-Packard wrote down almost $14 billion relating to its 2011 acquisition of Autonomy, a British tech firm, for about $10 billion. Goodwill write-downs are usually nonrecurring but are typically reported by companies in income from continuing operations. For analysis purposes, we normally classify them as operating and nonrecurring.

At the time of this writing, the Financial Accounting Standards Board has tentatively decided to require public companies to amortize goodwill over a ten-year period. Such a change would make the accounting for goodwill similar to that of an intangible asset with a definite life, like a patent.

Note Disclosures

The book value of P&G intangible assets is almost 53% of its total asset value in 2020 (refer to **Exhibit 8.1**). In addition to the amount reported in the balance sheet, P&G provides the following in Notes 1 and 2 that more fully describes its intangible asset accounting.

> **Note 1: Summary of Significant Accounting Policies—**
> **Goodwill and Other Intangible Assets**
> Goodwill and indefinite-lived intangible assets are not amortized, but are evaluated for impairment annually or more often if indicators of a potential impairment are present. Our annual impairment testing of goodwill is performed separately from our impairment testing of indefinite-lived intangible assets.
>
> We have acquired brands that have been determined to have indefinite lives. We evaluate a number of factors to determine whether an indefinite life is appropriate, including the competitive environment, market share, brand history, underlying product life cycles, operating plans, and the macroeconomic environment of the countries in which the brands are sold.
>
> In addition, when certain events or changes in operating conditions occur, an impairment assessment is performed and indefinite-lived assets may be adjusted to a determinable life.
>
> The cost of intangible assets with determinable useful lives is amortized to reflect the pattern of economic benefits consumed, either on a straight-line or accelerated basis over the estimated periods benefited. Patents, technology, and other intangible assets with contractual terms are generally amortized over their respective legal or contractual lives. Customer relationships, brands, and other non-contractual intangible assets with determinable lives are amortized over periods generally ranging from 5 to 30 years. When certain events or changes in operating conditions occur, an impairment assessment is performed and remaining lives of intangible assets with determinable lives may be adjusted.

Procter & Gamble's largest intangible is goodwill ($39.9 billion). The acquisition of Gillette in 2006 resulted in the recognition of $35.3 billion of goodwill, some of which remains as part of goodwill currently on the balance sheet. P&G paid $53.4 billion for Gillette upon acquisition in 2006, and at the time allocated $29.7 billion to other intangibles.

Note 2: Goodwill and Intangible Assets
Identifiable intangible assets were comprised of:

	2020 Gross Carrying Amount	2020 Accumulated Depreciation	2019 Gross Carrying Amount	2019 Accumulated Depreciation
Intangible assets with determinable lives				
Brands	$ 3,820	$ (2,347)	$ 3,836	$ (2,160)
Patents and technology	2,776	(2,513)	2,776	(2,434)
Customer relationships	1,752	(778)	1,787	(691)
Other	143	(92)	145	(91)
Total	$ 8,491	$ (5,730)	$ 8,544	$ (5,376)
Brands with indefinite lives	21,031	—	21,047	—
Total	$29,522	$ (5,730)	$29,591	$ (5,376)

There are two observations that we can make from the above disclosures. First, P&G has purchased a significant amount of intangible assets by acquiring other companies. We can infer this from the large amount of goodwill assets reported in the balance sheet. Second, most of P&G's identifiable intangible assets are trademarks, and most have indefinite lives. Hence, we might expect that the amount of amortization expense in any given year would be small, as indicated by the total in the above table. However, goodwill impairment write-offs could be substantial in any given year.

Review 8-5 LO8-5

Accounting for Intangible Assets

In Year 8, Bowen Company's R&D department developed a new production process that significantly reduced the time and cost required to manufacture its product. R&D costs were $120,000. The process was patented on July 1, Year 8. Legal costs and fees to acquire the patent totaled $12,500. Bowen estimated the useful life of the patent at 10 years.

On July 1, Year 10, Bowen sold the nonexclusive right to use the new process to Kennedy Company for $90,000. Because Bowen retained the patent, the agreement allows Kennedy to use, but not sell, the new technology for a period of 5 years. Both Bowen Company and Kennedy Company have December 31 fiscal years.

On July 1, Year 12, another competitor obtained a patent on a new process that made Bowen's patent obsolete.

Required

a. How should Bowen Company account for the R&D costs? Show the effects of these entries using the financial statement effects template.
b. How should Bowen Company account for legal costs incurred to obtain the patent? Show the effects of these entries using the financial statement effects template.
c. What amount of amortization expense would Bowen record in Year 8? Show the effects of these transactions using the financial statement effects template.
d. How would Kennedy Company record the acquisition of the rights to use the new technology? Show the effects of this transaction using the financial statement effects template.
e. What effect would the new patent registered by the other competitor have on Kennedy Company? Show the effects of this transaction using the financial statement effects template.
f. What effect would the new patent registered by the other competitor have on Bowen Company?
g. Prepare the appropriate journal entries necessary to account for the transactions in parts a, b, c, d, and e and post the entries to T-accounts.

Solution on p. 8-42.

Analysis Implications

LO8-6 Analyze the effects of intangible assets on key performance measures.

Because internally generated intangible assets are not capitalized, an important component of a company's assets is potentially hidden from users of the financial statements. Moreover, differential treatment of purchased and internally created assets makes it difficult to compare companies. If one company generates its patents and trademarks internally, while another company purchases these intangibles, their balance sheets can differ dramatically, even if the two companies are otherwise very similar.

These hidden intangible assets can distort our analysis of the financial statements. For example, when a company expenses R&D costs, especially R&D equipment and facilities that can potentially benefit more than one period, both the income statement and the balance sheet are distorted. Net income, assets, and stockholders' equity are all understated.

The income statement effects may be small if a company regularly purchases R&D assets and the amount of purchases is relatively constant from year to year. Specifically, after the average useful life is reached, say in 5 to 10 years, the expensing of current-year purchases will be approximately the same as the depreciation that would have been reported had the assets been capitalized. Thus, the income statement effect is mitigated. However, the recorded assets and equity are still understated. This accounting produces an upward bias in asset turnover ratios and ROE.

Finally, the statement of cash flows is also affected by the manner in which a company acquires its intellectual assets. A company that generates its patents and trademarks internally recognizes the expenditures as part of cash flow from operating activities. However, a company that purchases its patents and trademarks from an independent party or through acquisitions recognizes the expenditures as part of cash flow from investing activities.

A GLOBAL PERSPECTIVE

Under International Financial Reporting Standards, development costs can be capitalized as intangible assets when specific criteria are met. For instance, the company must be able to demonstrate that it has the ability and the intention to complete the development process and to produce an intangible asset that will generate future benefits through use or sale.

Here is an example from GlaxoSmithKline plc's note disclosures:

Research and development
Research and development expenditure is charged to the income statement in the period in which it is incurred. Development expenditure is capitalised when the criteria for recognising an asset are met, usually when a regulatory filing has been made in a major market and approval is considered highly probable. Property, plant, and equipment used for research and development is capitalised and depreciated in accordance with the Group's policy.

Under IFRS, similar to under U.S. GAAP, goodwill must be periodically evaluated for impairment. The overall concepts are very similar between IFRS and GAAP but the details differ. For example, under IFRS companies are required to compare the recoverable amount (defined as the higher of the fair value or value-in-use) of a cash-generating unit to the carrying value of that unit to determine an impairment loss. Just as under U.S. GAAP, once impaired, goodwill cannot be revalued upward. Although, note that this is different from the treatment of PPE under IFRS, as discussed earlier in the chapter.

Analyzing the Effects of Intangible Assets and R&D Expense on the Financial Statements LO8-6 **Review 8-6**

Selected income statement data for **Bristol-Myers Squibb Company** and **Pfizer, Inc.**, is presented in the following table:

	2020 Bristol-Myers Squibb	2020 Pfizer	2019 Bristol-Myers Squibb	2019 Pfizer	2018 Bristol-Myers Squibb	2018 Pfizer
Sales revenue	$ 42,518	$ 41,908	$ 26,145	$ 41,172	$21,581	$ 40,825
R&D	11,143	9,405	4,871	8,394	4,551	7,760
Other intangible assets	53,243	28,471	63,969	33,936	1,091	35,211
Total assets	118,481	154,229	129,944	167,594	34,986	159,422

a. Compute the percent of net sales that Bristol-Myers Squibb Company and Pfizer, Inc., spent on research and development (R&D) for years 2018, 2019, and 2020.
b. Compute the percent of other intangible assets of total assets for Bristol-Myers Squibb Company and Pfizer, Inc., for years 2018, 2019, and 2020.
c. Comment on any significant trends.

Solution on p. 8-44.

SUMMARY

LO8-1 **Determine which costs to capitalize and report as tangible assets and which costs to expense. (p. 8-3)**
- Tangible assets, including land, buildings, machinery, and equipment, are assets with physical substance and are usually classified as property, plant, and equipment.
- All costs incurred to acquire an asset and prepare it for its intended use should be capitalized and reported in the balance sheet.
- The cost of self-constructed assets should include all costs incurred during construction, including the interest cost of financing the construction.

LO8-2 **Apply different depreciation methods to allocate the cost of assets over time. (p. 8-5)**
- Depreciation methods generally fall into three categories:
  (1) Straight-line depreciation
  (2) Accelerated depreciation, such as the double-declining-balance method
  (3) Units-of-production method

LO8-3 **Determine the effects of asset sales and impairments on financial statements. (p. 8-10)**
- The sale of a long-term asset will result in a gain or loss if the proceeds from the sale are greater than or less than the book value of the asset.
- If the expected benefits (undiscounted cash flows) derived from an asset fall below its book value, the asset is impaired and should be written down to fair value.

LO8-4 **Analyze the effects of tangible assets on key performance measures. (p. 8-13)**
- PPE turnover and long-term asset turnover ratios provide insights into the capital intensity of a company and how efficiently the company is utilizing these investments.
- The ratio of accumulated depreciation divided by the cost of depreciable assets measures the percent depreciated.

LO8-5 **Describe the accounting and reporting for intangible assets. (p. 8-17)**
- Intangible assets are long-term assets lacking in physical substance, such as patents, trademarks, franchise rights, and goodwill.
- For the most part, internally generated intangible assets are not recognized in the balance sheet.
- Intangible assets purchased from other companies are capitalized and presented separately in the balance sheet.
- Intangible assets with definite lives are amortized using the straight-line method.
- Intangible assets with indefinite lives are not amortized, but are checked for impairment.
- Digital assets like cryptocurrencies are treated as intangible assets with indefinite lives.

LO8-6 **Analyze the effects of intangible assets on key performance measures. (p. 8-23)**
- Differential treatment of purchased intangibles and internally generated assets affects financial statement analysis.

GUIDANCE ANSWERS... YOU MAKE THE CALL

You are the Company Accountant Any cost that is necessary in order to bring an asset into service should be capitalized as a part of the cost of the asset. In this case, your company cannot build an office building on this property until the oil well is properly capped. Therefore, the $40,000 cost of capping the oil well should be capitalized as part of the cost of the land.

You are the Division Manager To increase PPE turnover one must either increase sales or reduce PPE assets. The first step is to identify unproductive or inefficiently utilized assets. Unnecessary assets can be sold, and some processes can be outsourced. Also, by reducing downtime, effective maintenance practices will increase asset productivity.

KEY RATIOS

$$\text{PPE Turnover (PPET)} = \frac{\text{Sales revenue}}{\text{Average PPE, net}} \qquad \text{Percent depreciated} = \frac{\text{Accumulated depreciation}}{\text{Cost of depreciable assets}}$$

MULTIPLE CHOICE

1. Burgstahler Corporation bought a lot to construct a new corporate office building. An older building on the lot was razed immediately so that the office building could be constructed. The cost of razing the older building should be
   a. recorded as part of the cost of the land.
   b. written off as a loss in the year of purchase.
   c. written off as an extraordinary item in the year of purchase.
   d. recorded as part of the cost of the new building.

2. The purpose of recording periodic depreciation of long-term PPE assets is to
   a. report declining asset values on the balance sheet.
   b. allocate asset costs over the periods benefited by use of the assets.
   c. account for costs to reflect the change in general price levels.
   d. set aside funds to replace assets when their economic usefulness expires.

3. When the estimate of an asset's useful life is changed,
   a. depreciation expense for all past periods must be recalculated.
   b. there is no change in the amount of depreciation expense recorded for future years.
   c. only depreciation expense for current and future years is affected.
   d. only depreciation expense in the current year is affected.

4. If the sale of a depreciable asset results in a loss, the proceeds from the sale were
   a. less than current fair value.
   b. greater than cost.
   c. greater than book value.
   d. less than book value.

5. Which of the following principles best describes the current method of accounting for research and development costs?
   a. Revenue recognition method
   b. Systematic and rational allocation
   c. Immediate recognition as an expense
   d. Income tax minimization

6. Goodwill should be recorded in the balance sheet as an intangible asset only when
   a. it is sold to another company.
   b. it is acquired through the purchase of another business.
   c. a company reports above-normal earnings for five or more consecutive years.
   d. it can be established that a definite benefit or advantage has resulted from some item such as an excellent reputation for service.

Multiple Choice Answers
1. a 2. b 3. c 4. d 5. c 6. b

QUESTIONS

Q8-1. How should companies account for costs, such as maintenance or improvements, which are incurred after an asset is acquired?

Q8-2. What is the effect of capitalized interest on the income statement in the period that an asset is constructed? What is the effect in future periods?

Q8-3. Why is the recognition of depreciation expense necessary for proper expense recognition?

Q8-4. Why do companies use accelerated depreciation for income tax purposes, when the total depreciation taken over the asset's useful life is identical to straight-line depreciation?

Q8-5. How should a company treat a change in an asset's estimated useful life or residual value? Which period(s)—past, present, or future—is affected by this change?

Q8-6. What factors determine the gain or loss from the sale of a long-term operating asset?

Q8-7. When is a PPE asset considered to be impaired? How is the impairment loss determined?

Q8-8. What is the proper accounting treatment for research and development costs? Why are R&D costs not capitalized under GAAP?

Q8-9. Why are some intangible assets amortized while others are not? What is meant by an intangible asset with an "indefinite life"?

Q8-10. Under what circumstances should a company report goodwill in its balance sheet? What is the effect of goodwill on the income statement?

DATA ANALYTICS

LO8-1 **DA8-1. Preparing an Excel Visualization of Property and Equipment Components Over Time**

The Excel file associated with this exercise includes information regarding **Fastenal Company**'s disclosures on its property and equipment in its Form 10-Ks over a six-year period. For this exercise, we analyze the changes in the composition of property and equipment over time.

REQUIRED
1. Download Excel file DA8-1 found in myBusinessCourse.
2. Create a Stacked Area chart showing the gross balances (before accumulated depreciation) of its property and equipment accounts. *Hint:* Highlight your data and open the Insert tab. Click Recommended Charts in the Charts group. Open the All Charts tab and click Area. Select the Stacked Area chart.
3. Answer the following questions based on the visualization.
    a. In which two years did total property and equipment rise at a slightly faster pace than the other years shown?
    b. From Year 1 to Year 6, which category of property and equipment showed the most growth?
    c. Which category of property and equipment appeared to drop (in proportion to the other categories) from Year 1 to Year 6?
    d. What is the largest category of property and equipment in Year 6?
4. Create two Pie charts, one for Year 1, and one for Year 6, showing gross balances (before accumulated depreciation) of property and equipment accounts.
5. If necessary, add chart titles to state the year. *Hint:* Click inside the chart and open the Chart Design tab. Click Add Chart Element in the Charts Layout group and select Chart Title.
6. Add data labels to the pie charts and edit data labels to only show percentages and not values. *Hint:* Right-click inside the pie and select Format Data Labels. Select Percentages under Label Options in the sidebar. Deselect Value, if necessary.
7. Answer the following questions based on the visualization.
    a. Which component has the highest proportion in Year 1? What is the percentage?
    b. Which component has the highest proportion in Year 6? What is the percentage?
    c. Which component had the greatest increase in proportion of the total from Year 1 to Year 6? What was the percentage difference?
    d. Which component had the greatest decrease in proportion from Year 1 to Year 6? What was the percentage difference?
    e. Which components showed a 2% or less difference in proportion of the total between Year 1 and Year 6?

LO8-2 **DA8-2. Determining the Method Used to Produce a Depreciation Visualization**

The Excel file associated with this exercise includes four charts depicting depreciation under four different methods over the life of a fixed asset with a useful life of five years. In this exercise, we match each depreciation method provided to the appropriate depreciation chart based upon the trend in depreciation over the five-year period.

REQUIRED
1. Download Excel file DA8-2 found in myBusinessCourse.
2. Calculate the fixed asset's original cost if the residual value of the asset is $5,000.
3. Match each of the charts with the depreciation method used: straight-line, sum-of-the-years'-digits, declining-balance, or units-of-production methods.
4. Indicate which chart(s) can be prepared upon purchase of the fixed asset and which chart(s) can only be prepared over time.

LO8-4 **DA8-3. Using Excel Visualizations to Analyze Property and Equipment**

The Excel file associated with this exercise includes data for **Delta Air Lines, Inc.**, as reported in its Form 10-K reports over a 10-year period. The percent depreciated of depreciable fixed assets measures the age of the assets compared to useful life. A company that has made substantial investments in new fixed assets will have a lower ratio compared to a company with fixed assets nearing the end of their useful life. In this exercise, we review the trend of percent depreciated of gross property and equipment for Delta Airlines over a 10-year period.

REQUIRED

1. Download Excel file DA8-3 found in myBusinessCourse.
2. Compute the ratio of accumulated depreciation to gross property and equipment for each year. Assume all assets are depreciable.
3. Prepare the following three charts in Excel.
   - Chart 1: A bar chart showing accumulated depreciation and gross property and equipment per year over the 10-year period.
   - Chart 2: A line chart showing property and equipment additions over the 10-year period, with the earliest year on the left hand side. *Hint:* To reverse the order of the years, right-click inside the horizontal axis. A Format Axis sidebar will appear. Open the bar chart icon tab. Click Categories in reverse order under Axis options.
   - Chart 3: A line chart showing the ratio of accumulated depreciation to gross property and equipment over the 10-year period.
4. Answer the following questions based on your visualizations.
   a. In Chart 1, in what year(s) was the trend of increasing values not evident in the chart?
   b. In Chart 2, what year(s) showed a drop in property and equipment additions?
   c. In Chart 2, what year showed the most significant change?
   d. Describe the trend shown in Chart 3.
   e. What is the likely cause of the increase shown in Year 10 in Chart 3.

Percent Depreciated

$$\frac{\text{Accumulated depreciation}}{\text{Cost of depreciable asset}}$$

DA8-4. Using Excel Visualizations to Analyze Research & Development Expense Trends   LO8-6

The Excel file associated with this exercise includes six years of financial information including research and development (R&D) expense and sales for seven companies in the Health sector. In this exercise, we analyze trends of the ratio of R&D to total sales. An increase in the ratio means that a higher portion of sales was devoted to R&D activities for the period.

REQUIRED

1. Download Excel file DA8-4 found in myBusinessCourse.
2. Calculate in Excel, R&D expense as a percentage of sales for six years for each of the following companies: **Abbott Laboratories**, **Baxter International, Inc.**, **Bristol-Myers Squibb Co.**, **Boston Scientific Corp.**, **Johnson & Johnson**, **Merck & Co.**, and **Pfizer Inc.**
3. Prepare a line chart in Excel showing the trend of R&D expense as a percentage of sales over the six-year period. *Hint:* The vertical axis should be percentages; the horizontal axis should be Year. The series (lines) should be the seven companies. To edit the chart, open the Chart Design Tab and click Select Data. You may need to switch rows/columns.
4. Describe the trend in the chart for each company. *Hint:* Review the trend but also notice the beginning and ending point of your line chart.
5. Indicate which two companies showed the most growth in research as a percentage of sales over the six-year period.

R&D Expense to Sales

$$\frac{\text{R\&D Expense}}{\text{Total Sales}}$$

DATA VISUALIZATION

Data Visualization Activities are available in myBusinessCourse. These assignments use Tableau Dashboards to expose students to visual depictions of data and introduce students to data analytics through data visualizations. These exercises are easily assignable and auto graded by MBC.

MINI EXERCISES

M8-11. Determining Whether to Capitalize or Expense   LO8-1

For each of the following items, indicate whether the cost should be capitalized or expensed immediately:

a. Paid $600 for routine maintenance of machinery
b. Paid $2,700 to rent equipment for two years
c. Paid $1,000 to equip the production line with new instruments that measure quality
d. Paid $10,000 to repair the roof on the building
e. Paid $800 to refurbish a machine, thereby extending its useful life
f. Purchased a patent for $2,500

LO8-2 **M8-12. Computing Depreciation Under Straight-Line and Double-Declining-Balance**

A delivery van costing $27,000 is expected to have a $2,000 salvage value at the end of its useful life of 5 years. Assume that the truck was purchased on January 1, Year 1. Compute the depreciation expense for Year 1 and Year 2 under each of the following depreciation methods:

    a. Straight-line   *b.* Double-declining-balance

LO8-2 **M8-13. Computing Depreciation Under Alternative Methods**

Equipment costing $195,000 is expected to have a residual value of $15,000 at the end of its six-year useful life. The equipment is metered so that the number of units processed is counted. The equipment is designed to process 1,500,000 units in its lifetime. In Year 1 and Year 2, the equipment processed 280,000 units and 205,000 units respectively. Calculate the depreciation expense for Year 1 and Year 2 using each of the following methods:

    a. Straight-line   *c.* Units of production
    b. Double-declining-balance

LO8-3 **M8-14. Recording the Sale of PPE Assets (FSET)**

As part of a renovation of its showroom, O'Keefe Auto Dealership sold furniture and fixtures that were eight years old for $6,000 in cash. The assets had been purchased for $65,000 and had been depreciated using the straight-line method with no residual value and a useful life of ten years.

Show how the sale of the furniture and fixtures affects the balance sheet and income statement using the financial statement effects template.

LO8-3 **M8-15. Recording the Sale of PPE Assets**

Using the information from M8-14, prepare a journal entry to record the sale of furniture and fixtures.

LO8-3 **M8-16. Recording the Sale of PPE Assets (FSET)**

Gaver Company sold machinery that had originally cost $165,000 for $55,000 in cash. The machinery was three years old and had been depreciated using the double-declining-balance method assuming a five-year useful life and a residual value of $11,000.

Using the financial statement effects template, show how the sale of the machinery affects the balance sheet and income statement.

LO8-3 **M8-17. Recording the Sale of PPE Assets**

Using the information from M8-16, prepare a journal entry to record the sale of furniture and fixtures.

LO8-2 **M8-18. Computing Depreciation Under Straight-Line and Double-Declining-Balance for Partial Years**

A machine costing $218,700 is purchased on May 1, Year 1. The machine is expected to be obsolete after three years (36 months) and, thereafter, no longer useful to the company. The estimated salvage value is $8,100. Compute depreciation expense for both Year 1 and Year 2 under each of the following depreciation methods:

    a. Straight-line   *b.* Double-declining-balance

LO8-5 **M8-19. Accounting for Research and Development Under IFRS**

Siemens AG
NYSE :: SI

The following information on **Siemens AG**'s treatment of research and development is extracted from its 2020 financial statements. Siemens AG is an integrated technology company with activities in the fields of industry, energy, and healthcare. The company is incorporated under the laws of Germany and reports using International Financial Reporting Standards (IFRS).

> **Research and development costs**—Costs of research activities are expensed as incurred. Costs of development activities are capitalized when the recognition criteria in IAS 38 are met. Capitalized development costs are stated at cost less accumulated amortization and impairment losses with an amortization period of generally three to ten years.

    a. How does the reporting under IFRS differ from reporting under U.S. GAAP for research and development?
    b. At year-end September 30, 2020, Siemens had a gross carrying amount of Other Intangible Assets of $13.1 billion Euros and accumulated amortization and impairment related to those assets of $8.3 billion Euros. Should the amounts capitalized be tested annually for impairment?

LO8-2 **M8-20. Computing Double-Declining-Balance Depreciation**

DeFond Company purchased equipment for $70,000. For each of the following sets of assumptions, prepare a depreciation schedule (all years) for this equipment assuming that DeFond uses the double-declining-balance depreciation method.

Useful Life	Residual Value
a. Four years	$11,200
b. Five years	4,200
c. Ten years	1,400

M8-21. Computing and Recording Depletion (FSET)   **LO8-2**

The Nelson Oil Company estimated that the oil reserve that it acquired during the year would produce 4.8 million barrels of oil. The company extracted 360,000 barrels the first year, 600,000 barrels the second year, and 720,000 barrels the third year. Nelson paid $40,800,000 for the oil reserve.

a. Compute depletion for each year—Year 1, Year 2, and Year 3.
b. Using the financial statement effects template, report the (i) acquisition of the oil reserve and (ii) depletion for the year.

M8-22. Computing and Recording Depletion   **LO8-2**

Use the information from M8-21 to complete the following.

a. Prepare the journal entries to record (i) the acquisition of the oil reserve and (ii) the depletion for the year.
b. Open T-accounts and post the entries in the accounts.

M8-23. Computing and Comparing PPE Turnover for Two Companies   **LO8-4**

Texas Instruments Incorporated and **Intel Corporation** report the following information:

	Texas Instruments		Intel Corp	
($ millions)	Sales	PPE, Net	Sales	PPE, Net
2020	$14,461	$3,269	$77,867	$56,584
2019	14,383	3,303	71,965	55,386

Texas Instruments Incorporated
NYSE :: TXN
Intel Corporation
NASDAQ :: INTC

a. Compute the 2020 PPE turnover for both companies. Comment on any difference you observe.
b. Discuss ways in which high-tech manufacturing companies like these can increase their PPE turnover.

M8-24. Assessing Research and Development Expenses   **LO8-5, 6**

Abbott Laboratories reports the following income statement (in partial form):

Year Ended December 31 ($ millions)	2020
Net sales	$34,608
Cost of products sold	15,003
Amortization of intangible assets	2,132
Research and development*	2,420
Selling, general, and administrative	9,696
Total operating cost and expenses	29,251
Operating earnings	$ 5,357

Abbott Laboratories
NYSE :: ABT

* including acquired in-process and collaborations R&D

a. Compute the percent of net sales that Abbott Laboratories spends on research and development (R&D). How would you assess the appropriateness of its R&D expense level?
b. Using the financial statement effects template, describe how the accounting for R&D expenditures affects Abbott Laboratories' balance sheet and income statement.

EXERCISES

E8-25. Recording Asset Acquisition, Depreciation, and Disposal (FSET)   **LO8-1, 2, 3**

On January 2, Year 1, Verdi Company acquired a machine for $240,000. In addition to the purchase price, Verdi spent $5,000 for shipping and installation, and $7,000 to calibrate the machine prior to use. The company estimates that the machine has a useful life of five years and residual value of $19,500.

a. Using the financial statement effects template, report the acquisition of the machine.
b. Calculate the annual depreciation expense using straight-line depreciation. Using the financial statement effects template, show how annual depreciation in the first year affects the balance sheet and income statement.

c. On December 31, Year 4, Verdi sold the machine to another company for $35,000. Using the financial statement effects template, show how the sale of the machinery affects the balance sheet and income statement.

LO8-1, 2, 3 **E8-26. Recording Asset Acquisition, Depreciation, and Disposal**
Using the information from E8-25, prepare journal entries for parts *a*, *b*, and *c*.

LO8-2 **E8-27. Computing Straight-Line and Double-Declining-Balance Depreciation**
On January 2, Haskins Company purchased a laser cutting machine for use in fabrication of a part for one of its key products. The machine cost $64,000, and its estimated useful life is five years, after which the expected salvage value is $4,000. Compute depreciation expense for each year of the machine's useful life under each of the following depreciation methods:
  a. Straight-line
  b. Double-declining-balance

LO8-2, 3 **E8-28. Computing Depreciation, Asset Book Value, and Gain or Loss on Asset Sale (FSET)**
Sloan Company uses its own executive charter plane that originally cost $1.2 million. It has recorded straight-line depreciation on the plane for six full years, with an $120,000 expected salvage value at the end of its estimated 10-year useful life. Sloan disposes of the plane at the end of the sixth year.
  a. At the disposal date, what is the (1) accumulated depreciation and (2) net book value of the plane?
  b. Using the financial statement effects template, show how the disposal of the plane affects the balance sheet and income statement, assuming that the sales price is
   1. Cash equal to the book value of the plane.
   2. $300,000 cash.
   3. $900,000 cash.

LO8-2, 3 **E8-29. Computing Depreciation, Asset Book Value, and Gain or Loss on Asset Sale**
Using the information from E8-28, prepare journal entries for the three scenarios in part *b*.

LO8-2 **E8-30. Computing Straight-Line and Double-Declining-Balance Depreciation**
On January 2, Dechow Company purchased a machine to help manufacture a part for one of its key products. The machine cost $196,830 and is estimated to have a useful life of six years, with an expected salvage value of $21,060.
Compute each year's depreciation expense for the first and second year for each of the following depreciation methods.
  a. Straight-line
  b. Double-declining-balance

LO8-2, 3 **E8-31. Computing Depreciation, Asset Book Value, and Gain or Loss on Asset Sale**
Palepu Company owns and operates a delivery van that originally cost $54,400. Straight-line depreciation on the van has been recorded for three years, with a $4,000 expected salvage value at the end of its estimated six-year useful life. Depreciation was last recorded at the end of the third year, at which time Palepu disposed of this van.
  a. Compute the net book value of the van on the sale date.
  b. Compute the gain or loss on sale of the van if its sales price is for:
   1. Cash equal to book value of van.   3. $24,000 cash.
   2. $30,000 cash.

LO8-2 **E8-32. Computing Depreciation and Accounting for a Change of Estimate**
Lambert Company acquired machinery costing $88,000 on January 2. At that time, Lambert estimated that the useful life of the equipment was 6 years and that the residual value would be $12,000 at the end of its useful life. Compute depreciation expense for this asset for the first, second, and third year using the
  a. straight-line method.
  b. double-declining-balance method.
  c. Assume that on January 2 of the third year, Lambert revised its estimate of the useful life to 7 years and changed its estimate of the residual value to $8,000. What effect would this have on depreciation expense in the third year for each of the above depreciation methods?

LO8-2 **E8-33. Computing Depreciation and Accounting for a Change of Estimate**
In January, Rankine Company paid $10,200,000 for land and a building. An appraisal estimated that the land had a fair value of $3,000,000 and the building was worth $7,200,000. Rankine estimated that the useful life of the building was 30 years, with no residual value.
  a. Calculate annual depreciation expense using the straight-line method.

b. Calculate depreciation for the first and second year using the double-declining-balance method.
c. Assume that in the third year, Rankine changed its estimate of the useful life of the building to 25 years. If the company is using the double-declining-balance method of depreciation, what amount of depreciation expense would Rankine record in the third year?

E8-34. Estimating the Percent Depreciated   LO8-4

The property and equipment note disclosure from the **Deere & Company** balance sheet follows ($ millions):

PROPERTY AND DEPRECIATION
A summary of property and equipment at November 1, 2020, in millions of dollars follows:

	2020
Land	$ 282
Buildings and building equipment	4,114
Machinery and equipment	5,936
Dies, patterns, tools, etc.	1,662
All other	1,115
Construction in progress	440
Total at cost	13,549
Less accumulated depreciation	7,771
Property and equipment—net	$ 5,778

Deere & Company
NYSE :: DE

During 2020, the company reported $800 million of depreciation expense.
Estimate the percent depreciated of Deere's depreciable assets. How do you interpret this figure?

E8-35. Computing and Evaluating Receivables, Inventory, and PPE Turnovers   LO8-6

3M Company reports the following financial statement amounts in its 10-K report:

($ millions)	Sales	Cost of Sales	Receivables	Inventories	PPE, Net
2020	$32,184	$16,605	$4,705	$4,239	$9,421
2019	32,136	17,136	4,791	4,134	9,333
2018	32,765	16,682	5,020	4,366	8,738

3M Company
NYSE :: MMM

a. Compute the receivables, inventory, and PPE turnover ratios for both 2020 and 2019. (Receivables turnover and inventory turnover are discussed in Chapters 6 and 7, respectively.)
b. What changes are evident in the turnover rates of 3M for these years? Discuss ways in which a company such as 3M can improve its turnover within each of these three areas.

E8-36. Identifying and Accounting for Intangible Assets   LO8-5

On the first day of the year, Holthausen Company acquired the assets of Leftwich Company, including several intangible assets. These include a patent on Leftwich's primary product, a device called a plentiscope. Leftwich carried the patent on its books for $2,100, but Holthausen believes that the fair value is $280,000. The patent expires in seven years, but competitors can be expected to develop competing patents within three years. Holthausen believes that, with expected technological improvements, the product is marketable for at least 20 years.

The registration of the trademark for the Leftwich name is scheduled to expire in 15 years. However, the Leftwich brand name, which Holthausen believes is worth $700,000, could be applied to related products for many years beyond that.

As part of the acquisition, Leftwich's principal researcher left the company. As part of the acquisition, he signed a five-year noncompetition agreement that prevents him from developing competing products. Holthausen paid the scientist $420,000 to sign the agreement.

a. What amount should be capitalized for each of the identifiable intangible assets?
b. What amount of amortization expense should Holthausen record the first year for each asset?

E8-37. Accounting for Digital Assets   LO8-5

As of the end of its fiscal year, December 31, 2020, **Square, Inc.**, reported an investment in bitcoin valued at $50 million. During the first quarter of 2021, Square made a further investment of $170 million. During the first quarter of 2021, the company "recorded an impairment charge of $19.9 million in the three months ended March 31, 2021 due to the observed market price of bitcoin decreasing below the carrying value during the period."

Square, Inc.
NYSE :: SQ

According to its statement of cash flows for the period, Square, Inc., did not sell off any of its investment in bitcoin during the first quarter of 2021.

REQUIRED

a. What will be the balance of Square's bitcoin investment on March 31, 2021?
b. Square reports that the impairment occurred "during the period" when the market price dropped below the carrying value. At the end of the quarter, the fair value of the bitcoin asset was $472.0 million. How would that affect your answer to part *a*? Why?

LO8-2 E8-38. Computing and Recording Depletion Expense (FSET)

During the year, Eldenburg Mining Company purchased land for $9,000,000 that had a natural resource reserve estimated to be 625,000 tons. Development and road construction costs on the land were $525,000, and a building was constructed at a cost of $62,500. When the natural resources are completely extracted, the land has an estimated residual value of $1,500,000. In addition, the cost to restore the property to comply with environmental regulations is estimated to be $1,000,000. Production in the first and second year was 75,000 tons and 106,250 tons, respectively.

a. Compute the depletion charge for the first and second year.
b. Using the financial statement effects template, report each year's depletion as determined in part *a*.

LO8-2 E8-39. Computing and Recording Depletion

Using the information from E8-38, prepare journal entries to record each year's depletion.

LO8-4 E8-40. Computing and Interpreting Percent Depreciated and PPE Turnover

The following disclosure is from Note 8 to the 2020 10-K of **Tesla, Inc.**:

Tesla, Inc.:
NASDAQ :: ADGF

Note 8—Property, Plant and Equipment, Net

Our property, plant, and equipment, net, consisted of the following (in millions):

	Dec. 31, 2020	Dec. 31, 2019
Machinery, equipment, vehicles, and office furniture	$ 8,493	$ 7,167
Tooling	1,811	1,493
Leasehold improvements	1,421	1,087
Land and buildings	3,662	3,024
Computer equipment, hardware and software	856	595
Construction in progress	1,621	764
	17,864	14,130
Less: Accumulated depreciation	(5,117)	(3,734)
Total	$12,747	$10,396

The summary of significant accounting policies included the following description of Tesla's depreciation policies:

Property, plant, and equipment, net, including leasehold improvements, are recognized at cost less accumulated depreciation. Depreciation is generally computed using the straight-line method over the estimated useful lives of the respective assets, as follows:

Machinery, equipment, vehicles, and office furniture	2 to 12 years
Building and building improvements	15 to 30 years
Computer equipment and software	3 to 10 years

Leasehold improvements are depreciated on a straight-line basis over the shorter of their estimated useful lives or the terms of the related leases.

a. Tesla's revenue totaled $31,536 ($ millions) in 2018. Compute its PPE turnover for the year.
b. Compute the percent depreciated ratio for 2020.
c. Comment on these ratios. What effect does Tesla's depreciation policies have on these ratios?

LO8-6 E8-41. Evaluating R&D Expenditures of Companies

R&D intensity is measured by the ratio of research and development expense to sales revenue. The following table compares the R&D intensity for various companies.

Company	R&D Intensity
Callaway Golf Co.	2.91%
Samsung Electronics Co., Ltd (Korea)	8.96%
Apple, Inc.	6.83%
Intel Corporation	17.41%
Microsoft Corporation	13.47%
Baxter International, Inc.	4.46%
Pfizer, Inc.	22.44%
Merck & Co., Inc.	28.25%
Bayer Group Consolidated (Germany)	17.21%
Syngenta AG (Switzerland)	6.76%
Deere & Company	5.26%

Callaway Golf Co.
NYSE :: ELY
Apple, Inc.
NASDAQ :: AAPL
Samsung Electronics Co., Ltd
KS :: 005930
Intel Corporation
NASDAQ :: INTC
Microsoft Corporation
NASDAQ :: MSFT
Baxter International, Inc.
NYSE :: BAX
Pfizer, Inc.
NYSE :: PFE
Merck & Co., Inc
NYSE :: MRK
Bayer
NYSE :: BAYRY
Syngenta AG
NYSE :: SYT
Deere & Co.
NYSE :: DE

a. Comment on the differences among these companies. To what extent are the differences related to industry affiliation?

b. What other factors (besides industry affiliation) might determine a company's R&D intensity?

E8-42. Computing and Assessing Plant Asset Impairment LO8-2, 3

Zeibart Company purchased equipment for $180,000 on July 1, 2019, with an estimated useful life of 10 years and expected salvage value of $20,000. Straight-line depreciation is used. On July 1, 2023, economic factors cause the fair value of the equipment to decline to $72,000. On this date, Zeibart examines the equipment for impairment and estimates $100,000 in future cash inflows related to use of this equipment.

a. Is the equipment impaired at July 1, 2023? Explain.

b. If the equipment is impaired on July 1, 2023, compute the impairment loss and prepare a journal entry to record the loss.

c. What amount of depreciation expense would Zeibart record for the 12 months from July 1, 2023 through June 30, 2024? Prepare a journal entry to record this depreciation expense. (*Hint*: Assume no change in salvage value.)

E8-43. Computing and Assessing Plant Asset Impairment (FSET) LO8-2, 3

Using the information from E8-42, show how the entries in parts *b* and *c* affect Zeibart Company's balance sheet and income statement by using the financial statement effects template.

PROBLEMS

P8-44. Computing and Recording Proceeds from the Sale of PPE LO8-3

The following information was provided in the 2020 10-K of Hilton Worldwide Holdings, Inc.

Note 7: Property and Equipment ($ millions)

	2020	2019
Property and equipment, gross	$832	$889
Accumulated depreciation and amortization	(486)	(509)
Property and equipment, net	$346	$380

Hilton Worldwide Holdings Inc.
NASDAQ :: HLT

During the year ended December 31, 2020, we recognized $28 million of impairment losses related to property and equipment, including $4 million for finance lease ROU assets, which reduced the gross carrying value of property and equipment by $119 million, including finance lease ROU assets by $42 million, and the accumulated depreciation and amortization by $91 million, including finance lease ROU assets by $38 million.

Note 7 also revealed that depreciation and amortization expense on property and equipment totaled $57 million in 2020. The statement of cash flows reported that expenditures for property and equipment totaled $46 million in 2020 and that there were neither proceeds nor gain or loss on the sale of property and equipment during the year.

REQUIRED

1. Using the information provided, prepare a journal entry or FSET to record:
   a. the acquisition of new property and equipment during the year;
   b. the recording of depreciation and amortization expense for the year;

c. the impairment of the company's property and equipment during the year.
2. Do these entries explain the changes in Hilton's balance sheet accounts for property and equipment? Most of the changes? Would a disposal transaction complete the picture?

LO8-5, 6 P8-45. Analyzing and Assessing Research and Development Expenses

Agilent Technologies, Inc., the high-tech spin-off from HP, Inc., reports the following operating profit for 2020 in its 10-K ($ millions):

Net revenue	
Products.	$3,993
Services and other.	1,346
Total net revenue.	5,339
Costs and expenses	
Cost of products.	1,796
Cost of services and other.	706
Total costs.	2,502
Research and development.	495
Selling, general, and administrative.	1,496
Total costs and expenses	4,493
Income from operations.	$ 846

REQUIRED

a. What percentage of its total net revenue is Agilent spending on research and development?
b. How are its balance sheet and income statement affected by the accounting for R&D costs?
c. In 2003, Agilent's spending on R&D was $1,051 million—17.4% of its total net revenue. What are some possible ways that the company might have reduced its R&D intensity from 2003 to 2020? What are some of the possible implications for the company?

LO8-4 P8-46. Analyzing PPE Accounts and Recording PPE Transactions, Including Discontinued Operations

The 2019 and 2018 income statements and balance sheets (asset section only) for Target Corporation follow, along with its note disclosure describing Target's accounting for property and equipment. Target's statement of cash flows for fiscal 2019 (fiscal year ended February 1, 2020) reported capital expenditures of $3,027 million and disposal proceeds for property and equipment of $63 million. No gain or loss was reported on property and equipment disposals. In addition, Target acquired property and equipment through non-cash acquisitions not reported on the statement of cash flows.

Consolidated Statements of Operations		
($ millions)	2019	2018
Sales.	$77,130	$74,433
Other revenue.	982	923
Total revenues	78,112	75,356
Cost of sales.	54,864	53,299
Selling, general, and administrative expenses	16,233	15,723
Depreciation and amortization		
(exclusive of depreciation included in cost of sales).	2,357	2,224
Operating income.	4,658	4,110
Net interest expense.	477	461
Net other (income)/expense.	(9)	(27)
Earnings from continuing operations before income taxes.	4,190	3,676
Provision for income taxes.	921	746
Net earnings from continuing operations	3,269	2,930
Discontinued operations, net of tax	12	7
Net earnings.	$ 3,281	$ 2,937

Consolidated Statements of Financial Position (Asset Section Only)

($ millions)	February 1, 2020	February 2, 2019
Assets		
Cash and cash equivalents	$ 2,577	$ 1,556
Inventory	8,992	9,497
Other current assets	1,333	1,466
Total current assets	12,902	12,519
Property and equipment		
Land	6,036	6,064
Buildings and improvements	30,603	29,240
Fixtures and equipment	6,083	5,912
Computer hardware and software	2,692	2,544
Construction-in-progress	533	460
Accumulated depreciation	(19,664)	(18,687)
Property and equipment, net	26,283	25,533
Operating lease assets	2,236	1,965
Other noncurrent assets	1,358	1,273
Total assets	$42,779	$41,290

11. Property and Equipment

Property and equipment, including assets acquired under finance leases, is depreciated using the straight-line method over estimated useful lives or lease terms if shorter. We amortize leasehold improvements purchased after the beginning of the initial lease term over the shorter of the assets' useful lives or a term that includes the original lease term, plus any renewals that are reasonably certain at the date the leasehold improvements are acquired. Depreciation expense for 2019, 2018, and 2017 was $2,591 million, $2,460 million, and $2,462 million, respectively, including depreciation expense included in Cost of Sales. For income tax purposes, accelerated depreciation methods are generally used. Repair and maintenance costs are expensed as incurred. Facility pre-opening costs, including supplies and payroll, are expensed as incurred.

We review long-lived assets for impairment when store performance expectations, events, or changes in circumstances—such as a decision to relocate or close a store or distribution center, discontinue a project, or significant software changes—indicate that the asset's carrying value may not be recoverable. We recognized impairment losses of $23 million, $92 million, and $91 million during 2019, 2018, and 2017, respectively . . . Impairments are recorded in Selling, General, and Administrative Expenses.

REQUIRED

a. Prepare journal entries to record the following for fiscal 2019:
  i. Depreciation expense
  ii. Capital expenditures
  iii. Disposal of property, plant, and equipment
  iv. Impairments and write-downs (Assume that impairments and write-downs reduce the property and equipment account, rather than increasing accumulated depreciation.)
b. Estimate the amount of property and equipment that was acquired, if any, through non-cash transactions.

P8-47. Reporting PPE Transactions and Asset Impairment LO8-5

Note B from the fiscal 2018 10-K report of **Williams-Sonoma, Inc.**, (February 3, 2019) follows. Its statement of cash flows reported that the company made capital expenditures of $190,102,000 during fiscal 2018, impaired assets of $9,639,000, and recorded depreciation expense of $182,533,000, excluding amortization of intangibles. In addition, the company reported a loss on the disposal of property and equipment of $570,000.

Williams-Sonoma
NYSE :: WSM

Note B: Property and Equipment
Property and equipment consists of the following:

($ thousands)	Feb. 3, 2019	Jan. 28, 2018
Leasehold improvements	$ 950,259	$ 950,024
Fixtures and equipment	836,400	800,003
Capitalized software	733,941	621,730
Land and buildings	175,181	173,457
Corporate systems projects in progress	39,416	65,283
Construction in progress	7,205	8,615
Total	2,742,402	2,619,112
Accumulated depreciation and amortization	(1,812,767)	(1,686,829)
Property and equipment—net	$ 929,635	$ 932,283

We review the carrying value of all long-lived assets for impairment, primarily at a store level, whenever events or changes in circumstances indicate that the carrying value of an asset may not be recoverable. We review for impairment all stores for which current or projected cash flows from operations are not sufficient to recover the carrying value of the assets. Impairment results when the carrying value of the assets exceeds the estimated undiscounted future cash flows over the remaining useful life. Our estimate of undiscounted future cash flows over the store lease term is based upon our experience, historical operations of the stores, and estimates of future store profitability and economic conditions. The future estimates of store profitability and economic conditions require estimating such factors as sales growth, gross margin, employment rates, lease escalations, inflation on operating expenses, and the overall economics of the retail industry, and they are therefore subject to variability and difficult to predict. If a long-lived asset is found to be impaired, the amount recognized for impairment is equal to the difference between the net carrying value and the asset's fair value.

REQUIRED

Prepare journal entries to record the following for fiscal 2018:

a. Depreciation expense
b. Capital expenditures
c. Impairment of property and equipment (Assume that impairments and write-downs reduce the property and equipment account, rather than increasing accumulated depreciation.)
d. Disposal of property and equipment

CASES AND PROJECTS

LO8-3, 4 C8-48. Interpreting and Reporting Property, Plant, and Equipment (PPE) Expenditures (FSET)

General Mills, Inc.
NYSE :: GIS

General Mills, Inc., is a global consumer foods company. The firm manufactures and sells a wide range of branded products and is a major supplier to the foodservice and baking industries. The company's core product areas are ready-to-eat cereal, super-premium ice cream, convenient meal solutions, and healthy snacking. The following data are taken from the company's 2020 annual report. From the balance sheet:

($ millions)	May 31, 2020	May 26, 2019
Equipment	$ 6,428.0	$ 6,548.3
Buildings	2,412.6	2,477.2
Capitalized software	668.5	631.6
Construction in progress	373.5	343.8
Land	66.1	73.6
Equipment under finance lease	5.8	5.7
Buildings under finance lease	0.3	0.3
Total land, buildings, and equipment	9,954.8	10,080.5
Less accumulated depreciation	(6,374.2)	(6,293.3)
Total	$ 3,580.6	$ 3,787.2

From the income statement ($ millions):

	2020	2019
Net sales.	$17,626.6	$16,865.2

REQUIRED

a. Compute the PPE turnover for 2020. Assuming an average PPE turnover of 4.0 for the company's closest competitors, does General Mills appear to be capital intensive?

b. Calculate the percentage depreciated of General Mills' depreciable assets at the end of fiscal year 2020. What implications might the result suggest for the company's future cash flows?

c. General Mills reported depreciation and amortization (not reported separately) expense of approximately $594.7 million in 2020. Estimate the average useful life of its depreciable assets by dividing average depreciable assets by depreciation expense.

d. During 2020, General Mills purchased $460.8 million of land, buildings, and equipment for cash. Use the financial statement effects template to reflect the asset purchases and the year's depreciation charge.

C8-49. Recording Depreciation and Asset Purchases   LO8-3

Using the information from C8-48, prepare journal entries to record the asset purchases and the year's depreciation expense.

C8-50. Managing Operating Assets to Improve Performance: A Management Application   LO8-4, 6

Return on a company's net operating assets is commonly used to evaluate financial performance. One way to increase performance is to focus on operating assets.

REQUIRED

Indicate how this might be done in relation to the following asset categories. Indicate also any potential problems a given action might create.

a. Receivables
b. Inventories
c. Property, plant, and equipment
d. Intangibles

C8-51. Determining the Effects of Capitalizing Versus Expensing Software Development Costs   LO8-5, 6

The following information is taken from the March 31, 2020, annual report of **Take-Two Interactive Software, Inc.**, a maker and distributor of video games. All amounts are in thousands of U.S. dollars.

Income Statement Information:	2020
Net sales.	$3,088,970
Cost of goods sold	1,542,450
Operating expenses	1,121,253
Income (loss) from operations	$ 425,267

Take-Two Interactive Software, Inc.
NASDAQ :: TTWO

Electronic Arts, Inc.
NASDAQ :: EA

> **Information from the Management Discussion, Balance Sheet and Note 8:**
>
> **Software Development Costs and Licenses**
> Capitalized software development costs include direct costs incurred for internally developed titles and payments made to third-party software developers under development agreements.
>
> We capitalize internal software development costs (including specifically identifiable payroll expense, employee stock-based compensation, and incentive compensation costs related to the completion and release of titles, as well as third-party production and other content costs), subsequent to establishing technological feasibility of a software title. Technological feasibility of a product includes the completion of both technical design documentation and game design documentation. Significant management judgments are made in the assessment of when technological feasibility is established. For products where proven technology exists, this may occur early in the development cycle. Technological feasibility is evaluated on a product-by-product basis. Prior to establishing technological feasibility of a product, we record any costs incurred by third-party developers as research and development expenses . . .

continued

continued from previous page

> Amortization of capitalized software development costs and licenses commences when a product is available for general release and is recorded on a title-by-title basis in cost of goods sold. For capitalized software development costs, annual amortization is calculated using (1) the proportion of current year revenue to the total revenue expected to be recorded over the life of the title or (2) the straight-line method over the remaining estimated life of the title, whichever is greater. For capitalized licenses, amortization is calculated as a ratio of (1) current year revenue to the total revenue expected to be recorded over the remaining estimated life of the title or (2) the contractual royalty rate based on actual net product sales as defined in the licensing agreement, whichever is greater. Amortization periods for our software products generally range from 12 to 36 months.
>
> We evaluate the future recoverability of capitalized software development costs and licenses on a quarterly basis. Recoverability is primarily assessed based on the title's actual performance. For products that are scheduled to be released in the future, recoverability is evaluated based on the expected performance of the specific products to which the cost or license relates. We use a number of criteria in evaluating expected product performance, including historical performance of comparable products developed with comparable technology, market performance of comparable titles, orders for the product prior to its release, general market conditions, and past performance of the franchise. When we determine that capitalized cost of the title is unlikely to be recovered by product sales, an impairment of software development and license costs capitalized is charged to cost of goods sold in the period in which such determination is made.

Capitalized Software Development Costs and Licenses	2020
Beginning balance	$632,316
Additions	131,734
Amortization and write-downs	(321,956)
Ending balance	$442,094

Assume an income tax rate of 25% where necessary.

REQUIRED

You wish to compare the performance of Take-Two with one of its competitors, **Electronic Arts, Inc.** However, Electronic Arts does not capitalize any significant amounts of its software development costs. Estimate Take-Two's 2020 Income from operations if it did not capitalize any software development costs. Briefly explain your adjustment(s).

LO8-3 **C8-52. Analyzing Impairment Charges (FSET)**

The Walt Disney Company
NASDAQ :: DWA

In its fiscal year ended October 3, 2020, **The Walt Disney Company** recorded a loss. Part of this loss was due to impairment charges. In its annual report the company stated:

> *Goodwill and Intangible Asset Impairment*
>
> Our International Channels reporting unit, which is part of the Direct-to-Consumer & International segment, comprises the Company's international television networks. Our international television networks primarily derive revenues from affiliate fees charged to multi-channel video programming distributors (i.e., cable, satellite, telecommunications, and digital over-the-top service providers) (MVPDs) for the right to deliver our programming under multi-year licensing agreements and the sales of advertising time/space on the networks. A majority of the operations in this reporting unit were acquired in the TFCF acquisition, and therefore the fair value of these businesses approximated the carrying value at the date of the acquisition of TFCF.
>
> The International Channels business has been negatively impacted by the COVID-19 pandemic resulting in decreased viewership and lower advertising revenue related to the availability of content, including the deferral of certain live sporting events. The Company's increased focus on DTC distribution in international markets is expected to negatively impact the International Channels business as we shift the primary means of monetizing our film and television content from licensing of linear channels to use on our DTC services because the International Channels reporting unit valuation does not include the value derived from this shift, which is reflected in other reporting units. In addition, the industry shift to DTC, including by us and many of our distributors, who are pursuing their own DTC strategies, has changed the competitive dynamics for the International Channels business and resulted in unfavorable renewal terms for certain of our distribution agreements.
>
> Due to these circumstances, in the third quarter of fiscal 2020, we tested the International Channels' goodwill and long-lived assets (including intangible assets) for impairment . . .

continued

> In the third quarter of fiscal 2020, we recorded a non-cash impairment charge primarily on our MVPD agreement intangible assets of $1.9 billion ... In the third quarter of fiscal 2020, the carrying value of the International Channels exceeded the fair value, and we recorded a non-cash impairment charge of $3.1 billion to fully impair the International Channels reporting unit goodwill. The $1.9 billion impairment of our MVPD relationships and $3.1 billion impairment of goodwill are recorded in "Restructuring and impairment charges" in the Consolidated Statements of Operations.

REQUIRED

a. The Walt Disney Company reported a $1.7 billion pre-tax loss for the fiscal year 2020. What would pre-tax income or loss have been without the above described impairment charges?
b. Show the journal entry for 2020 to record the impairment charges using the financial statement effects template.
c. If circumstances changed in the future and the fair value increased either the MVPD agreement or the goodwill related to the International Channels, could the company reverse a portion of the impairment losses?

C8-53. Analyzing Impairment Charges LO8-3
Using the information from C8-52, prepare journal entries to record the impairment charges.

SOLUTIONS TO REVIEW PROBLEMS

Review 8-1

a. Capitalize   c. Expense   e. Capitalize   g. Capitalize   i. Expense
b. Capitalize   d. Capitalize f. Capitalize   h. Expense

Review 8-2

a1. Straight-line depreciation expense = ($95,000 − $10,000)/5 years = **$17,000 per year**

a2. Double-declining-balance (twice straight-line rate = 2 × (1/5) = 40%)

Year	Book Value × Rate	Depreciation Expense
1	$95,000 × 0.40 =	$38,000
2	($95,000 − $38,000) × 0.40 =	22,800
3	($95,000 − $60,800) × 0.40 =	13,680
4	($95,000 − $74,480) × 0.40 =	8,208
5	($95,000 − $82,688) × 0.40 =	2,312*

*The formula value of $4,925 is not reported because it would depreciate the asset below residual value. Only the $2,312 needed to reach residual value is depreciated.

b.

Balance Sheet

Transaction	Cash Asset	+	Noncash Assets	−	Contra Asset	=	Liabilities	+	Contrib. Capital	+	Earned Capital
(a) Purchased equipment.	−95,000 Cash		+95,000 Equipment			=					
(b) Recorded annual depreciation.					+17,000 Accumulated Depreciation	=					−17,000 Retained Earnings

Income Statement

Revenues	−	Expenses	=	Net Income
	−	+17,000 Depreciation Expense	=	−17,000

c.

(a) Equipment (+A)... 95,000
    Cash (−A)...   95,000

+ Equipment (A) −	+ Cash (A) −
(a) 95,000	95,000 (a)

(b) Depreciation expense (+E, −SE) 17,000
    Accumulated depreciation (+XA, −A)   17,000

+ Depreciation—Expense (E) −	− Accumulated Depreciation (XA) +
(b) 17,000	17,000 (b)

d.
Equipment, cost	$95,000
Less accumulated depreciation	51,000
Equipment, net	$44,000

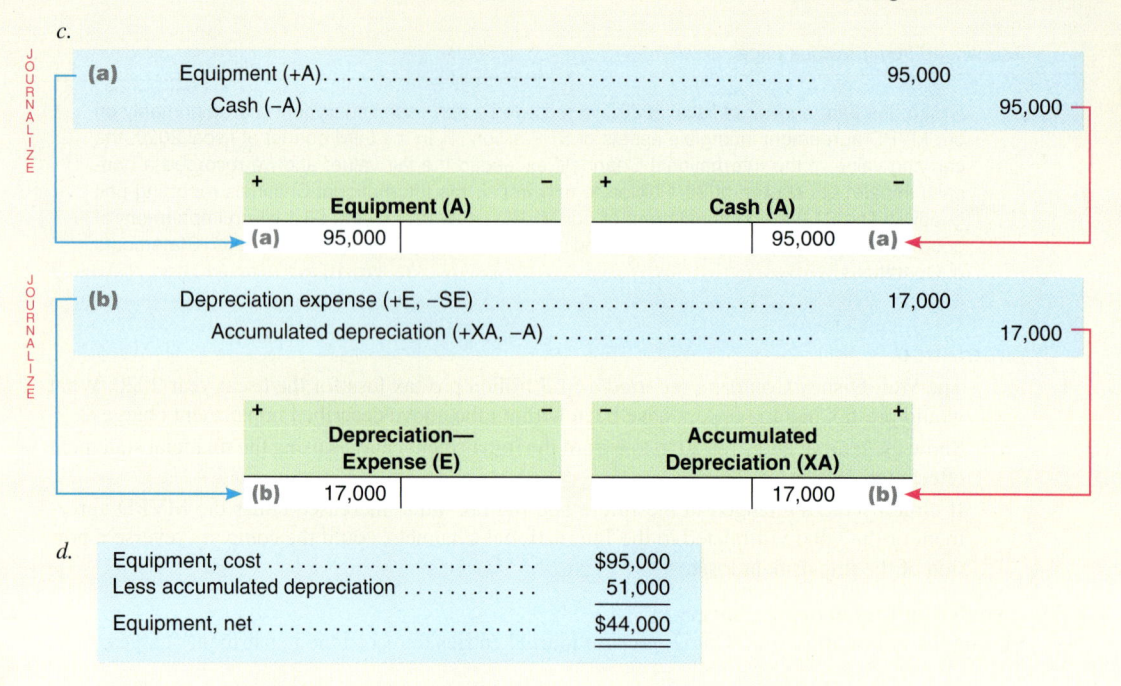

Equipment is reported on Lev's balance sheet at its net book value of $44,000.

Review 8-3

a.

	Balance Sheet							Income Statement		
Transaction	Cash Asset	+ Noncash Assets	− Contra Asset	= Liabilities	+ Contrib. Capital	+ Earned Capital		Revenues	− Expenses	= Net Income
(1) Sold Equipment #101	+22,000 Cash	−55,000 Equipment	−33,000 Accumulated Depreciation	=				−		=
(2) Sold Equipment #220	+12,500 Cash	−80,000 Equipment	−70,000 Accumulated Depreciation	=		+2,500 Retained Earnings		+2,500 Gain on Sale of Equipment	−	= +2,500
(3) Sold Equipment #380	+68,000 Cash	−125,000 Equipment	−50,000 Accumulated Depreciation	=		−7,000 Retained Earnings		−	+7,000 Loss on Sale of Equipment	= −7,000

b.

Transaction	Balance Sheet						Income Statement		
(1) Impairment of Equipment	−7,000 Equipment	−	=			−7,000 Retained Earnings	−	+7,000 Impairment Loss	= −7,000

c.

Cash (+A).. 22,000
Accumulated Depreciation (+XA, −A).......................... 33,000
    Equipment #101 (−A)..   55,000

Cash (+A).. 12,500
Accumulated Depreciation (+XA, −A).......................... 70,000
    Equipment #220 (−A)..   80,000
    Gain on sale of equipment (+R, +SE)   2,500

Cash (+A).. 68,000
Accumulated Depreciation (+XA, −A).......................... 50,000
Loss on sale of equipment (+E, −SE).......................... 7,000
    Equipment #380 (−A)..   125,000

Impairment Loss (+E, −SE) 7,000
    Equipment #380 (−A)..   7,000

Review 8-4

a.

	2020	2019	2018
Sales	$17,337	$45,768	$44,541
Avg PPE, net	$33,332	$34,547	$34,127
PPET	0.52	1.32	1.31

The PPE turnover ratio dropped from a stable 1.3 in 2019 and 2018 to 0.5 in 2020. This was due largely to the sharp drop in revenue due to the pandemic.

While the cost of equipment dropped by 9.5%, sales dropped by 62.1% from 2019 to 2020. This illustrates how an unexpected drop in sales has a significant impact on companies with heavy investments in tangible assets.

b.

	2020	2019	2018
Accumulated depreciation	$16,757	$18,659	$17,443
Cost	$47,010	$51,980	$50,263
% deprec	35.6%	35.9%	34.7%

The percentage of assets remained constant from 2019 to 2020, indicating that assets held are at a similar point in their useful lives. This trend was possible even though average assets decreased by 3.5%, which indicates that some older assets in the mix were replaced with newer assets.

Review 8-5

Transaction	Cash Asset	+	Noncash Assets	−	Contra Asset	=	Liabilities	+	Contrib. Capital	+	Earned Capital	Revenues	−	Expenses	=	Net Income
(a) Record R&D costs as R&D expense.	−120,000 Cash			−		=		+		+	−120,000 Retained Earnings		−	+120,000 R&D Expense	=	−120,000
(b) Record acquisition of patent.	−12,500 Cash	+	+12,500 Patent	−		=		+		+			−		=	
(c) Amortization of patent.				−	+625 Accumulated Amortization	=		+		+	−625 Retained Earnings		−	+625 Amortization Expense	=	−625
(d) Purchased rights to use of patent.	−90,000 Cash	+	+90,000 Technology Rights	−		=		+		+			−		=	
(e) Record impairment of technology rights.			−54,000 Technology Rights	−		=		+		+	−54,000 Retained Earnings		−	+54,000 Loss Due to Impairment	=	−54,000

a. Bowen Company would expense the $120,000 in R&D costs in Year 8.
b. The $12,500 in legal fees to obtain the patent would be capitalized. As a result, the book value of the patent would be $12,500 on July 1, Year 8.
c. Each year, beginning on July 1, Year 8, Bowen would record amortization expense of $1,250 ($12,500/10). For Year 8, six months of amortization expense, or $625, would be recorded ($1,250/2).
d. Because Kennedy purchased the right to use the technology, the purchase price can be capitalized as an intangible asset and amortized over the five-year length of the agreement. Kennedy would record amortization expense of $18,000 ($90,000/5) each year, beginning July 1, 2020. (Bowen would recognize the $90,000 as revenue.)
e. Given that the patent is obsolete, Kennedy Company would record an impairment loss. Kennedy Company would write off the remaining value of the technology agreement, recording an impairment loss of $54,000 [$90,000 − ($18,000 × 2)].
f. Bowen Company would also record an impairment loss. Bowen would write off the unamortized balance in the patent account, resulting in a loss of $7,500 [$12,500 − ($1,250 × 4)].

g.

(a) R&D expense (+E, –SE) 120,000
    Cash (–A) 120,000

+	Research & Development Expense (E)	−		+	Cash (A)	−
(a)	120,000				120,000	(a)

(b) Patent (+A) 12,500
    Cash (–A) 12,500

+	Patent (A)	−		+	Cash (A)	−
(b)	12,500				120,000	(a)
					12,500	(b)

(c) Amortization expense (+E, –SE) 625
    Accumulated amortization (+XA, –A) 625

+	Amortization Expense (E)	−		−	Accumulated Amortization (XA)	+
(c)	625				625	(c)

(d) Technology rights (+A) 90,000
    Cash (–A) 90,000

+	Technology Rights (A)	−		+	Cash (A)	−
(d)	90,000				90,000	(d)

(e) Loss due to impairment of technology rights (+E, –SE) 54,000
    Technology rights (–A) 54,000

+	Loss Due to Impairment of Technology Rights (E)	−		+	Technology Rights (A)	−
(e)	54,000			(d)	90,000	
						54,000 (e)
				Bal.	36,000	

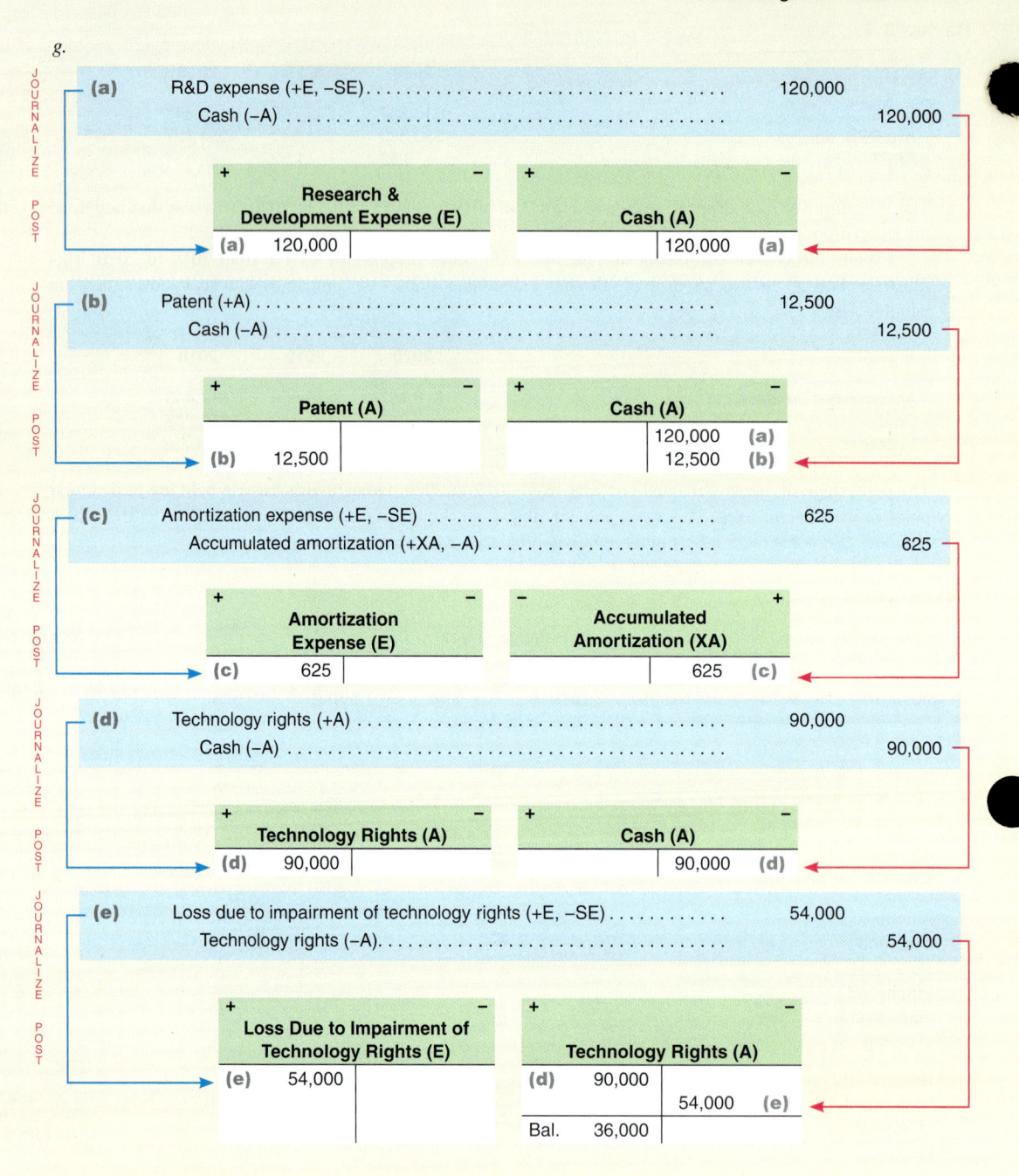

Review 8-6

a.

Bristol-Myers Squibb	Pfizer
2020: 26.21% ($11,143 ÷ $42,518)	2020: 22.44% ($9,405 ÷ $41,908)
2019: 18.63% ($ 4,871 ÷ $26,145)	2019: 20.39% ($8,394 ÷ $41,172)
2018: 21.09% ($ 4,551 ÷ $21,581)	2018: 19.01% ($7,760 ÷ $40,825)

b.

Bristol-Myers Squibb	Pfizer
2020: 44.94% ($53,243 ÷ $118,481)	2020: 18.46% ($28,471 ÷ $154,229)
2019: 49.23% ($63,969 ÷ $129,944)	2019: 20.25% ($33,936 ÷ $167,594)
2018: 3.12% ($ 1,091 ÷ $ 34,986)	2018: 22.09% ($35,211 ÷ $159,422)

c. R&D as a percentage of sales for Bristol-Myers Squibb fluctuated each year, with the most significant increase from 2019 to 2020 as compared to 2018 to 2019. The company reported in its 10-K that this increase was partially due to an acquisition that increased its operations. R&D as a percentage of sales for Pfizer increased each year, with a slightly larger increase from 2019 to 2020 as compared to 2018 to 2019. The company reported in its 10-K that this increase was partially due to costs to co-develop a COVID-19 vaccine. Other intangible assets as a percentage of total assets for Bristol-Myers Squibb increased significantly from 2018 to 2019. The company reported in its 10-K that this increase was largely due to an acquisition that resulted in purchased intangible assets. Other intangible assets as a percentage of total assets for Pfizer decreased each year from 2018 to 2020. The net intangible asset amounts decrease when the decrease due to amortization or impairment charges of existing intangible assets is not outweighed by additions due to purchased intangibles.

Chapter 9
Reporting and Analyzing Liabilities

LEARNING OBJECTIVES

LO9-1 Identify and account for current operating liabilities.

LO9-2 Describe and account for current nonoperating (financial) liabilities.

LO9-3 Explain and illustrate the pricing of long-term nonoperating liabilities.

LO9-4 Analyze and account for financial statement effects of long-term nonoperating liabilities.

LO9-5 Explain how solvency ratios and debt ratings are determined and how they impact the cost of debt.

Road Map

LO	Learning Objective | Topics	Page	eLecture	Review	Assignments
LO9-1	Identify and account for current operating liabilities.	9-4	e9-1	R9-1	M9-18, M9-19, M9-20, M9-21, M9-24, M9-28, M9-38, E9-44, E9-45, E9-46, E9-50, E9-51, P9-64, P9-78, DA9-1
LO9-2	Describe and account for current nonoperating (financial) liabilities.	9-10	e9-2	R9-2	M9-22, M9-23, M9-24, E9-61
LO9-3	Explain and illustrate the pricing of long-term nonoperating liabilities.	9-13	e9-3	R9-3	M9-25, M9-36, M9-37, M9-39, M9-40, M9-41, M9-42, M9-43, E9-47, E9-49, E9-52, E9-53, E9-54, E9-55, E9-56, E9-57, E9-58, E9-59, E9-60, E9-62, P9-65, P9-66, P9-67, P9-68, P9-69, P9-70, P9-71, P9-72, P9-73, P9-74, P9-75, P9-76, P9-77, C9-79, C9-80
LO9-4	Analyze and account for financial statement effects of long-term nonoperating liabilities.	9-18	e9-4	R9-4	M9-26, M9-27, M9-29, M9-30, M9-31, M9-32, M9-33, M9-34, M9-39, M9-40, M9-41, M9-42, E9-47, E9-48, E9-52, E9-53, E9-54, E9-55, E9-56, E9-57, E9-58, E9-59, E9-60, E9-61, E9-62, P9-65, P9-66, P9-67, P9-68, P9-69, P9-70, P9-71, P9-72, P9-73, P9-74, P9-75, P9-76, P9-77, C9-79, C9-80
LO9-5	Explain how solvency ratios and debt ratings are determined and how they impact the cost of debt.	9-27	e9-5	R9-5	M9-25, M9-35, C9-79, C9-80, DA9-2

VERIZON
www.verizon.com

In 2000, **Bell Atlantic Corporation** merged with **GTE** to form **Verizon Communications**, one of the largest telecommunication providers in the world. Verizon's industry is constantly changing and extremely competitive. Hans Vestberg, who became the CEO in 2018, faces the challenging tasks of fending off a host of competitors including **AT&T**, **Comcast**, and **T-Mobile**, as well as dealing with the disruptions like the coronavirus pandemic that lowered revenues and net income for 2020.

In recent years, Verizon has embarked upon a strategic transformation as advances in technology and the pandemic have changed the ways that people communicate in their personal and professional lives. The company has focused on leveraging their network leadership and retaining and growing their customer base while balancing profitability and safety for employees and customers. This strategy requires significant investments in acquiring wireless spectrum, putting the spectrum into service, expanding the fiber optic network that supports wireless and wireline service, maintaining networks, and developing and maintaining database capacity. The company has been a leading developer in fifth generation (5G) wireless technologies. This investment program requires a significant amount of cash ($20 billion annually) at a time when the company is faced with more than $128 billion in outstanding debt (a total liability balance of $247 billion) and $18 billion in employee benefit obligations. Fortunately, Verizon's operating cash flow remains strong at $41 billion in 2020.

Previous chapters focused on the reporting of operating assets, including receivables, inventories, property, plant, and equipment, and intangible assets, along with the related expenses. We now turn our attention to the other side of the balance sheet. Chapter 9 examines how we value liabilities and how debt financing along with the subsequent payment of interest and principal affect the financial statements. We also discuss the required disclosures that enable us to effectively analyze a company's ability to make its liability payments as they mature. Chapter 10 focuses on the reporting for specific types of liabilities, and Chapter 11 examines the reporting of stockholders' equity.

As Verizon faces increased competition from other telecom companies, cable, and Internet providers, it must continue to innovate to maintain its position as an industry leader. This objective will require large investments in technology and infrastructure, only part of which will come from its operating cash flow. The company faces other substantial risks as well, including (1) the threat of cyberattacks, (2) changes in regulation in their industry, (3) technological and business disruptions, and (4) their significant debt burden and possibility of rising interest rates. To be successful, Vestberg will need to manage Verizon's debt burden and efficiently allocate cash resources between strategic investments and debt payments.

Sources: *Verizon* 2020 10-K.

CHAPTER ORGANIZATION

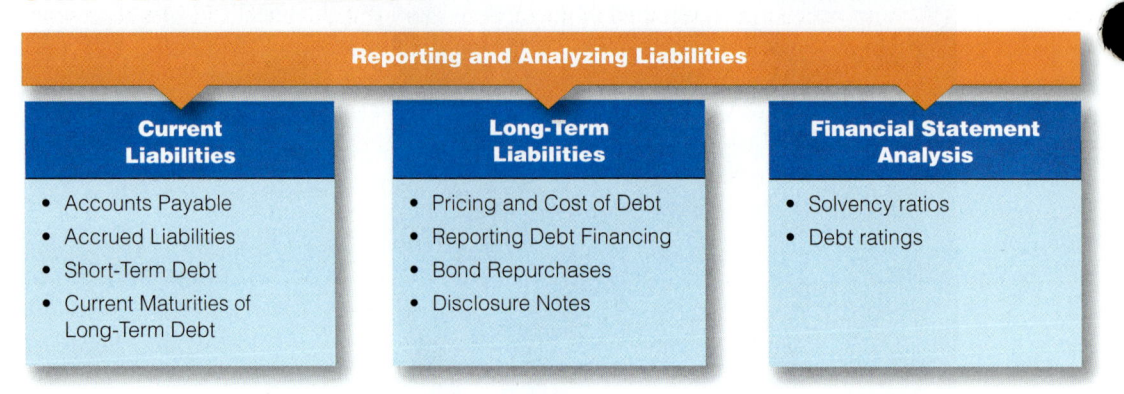

Reporting and Analyzing Liabilities

Current Liabilities
- Accounts Payable
- Accrued Liabilities
- Short-Term Debt
- Current Maturities of Long-Term Debt

Long-Term Liabilities
- Pricing and Cost of Debt
- Reporting Debt Financing
- Bond Repurchases
- Disclosure Notes

Financial Statement Analysis
- Solvency ratios
- Debt ratings

INTRODUCTION

Just as asset disclosures provide us with information on where a company invests its funds, the disclosures concerning liabilities and equity inform us as to how those assets are financed. To be successful, a company must not only invest funds wisely, but be astute in the manner in which it finances those investments.

Companies hope to finance their assets at the lowest possible cost. The cost of financing assets with liabilities is the interest charged by the lender. While many liabilities bear explicit interest rates, many other liabilities (such as accounts payable and accrued liabilities) are non-interest-bearing. This fact does not mean that these liabilities are cost-free. For example, while a supplier may appear to offer interest-free credit terms, the cost of that credit is implicitly included in the price it charges for the goods or services it sells.

Verizon's liabilities and equity, as taken from its 2020 10-K report, are presented in **Exhibit 9.1**. Just as assets are classified as either current or noncurrent, so are liabilities presented in the balance sheet as either current or noncurrent.

Current liabilities, as the name implies, are short-term in nature, generally requiring payment within the coming year. As a result, they are not a suitable source of funding for long-term assets that generate cash flows over several years. Instead, companies often finance long-term assets with long-term liabilities that require payments over several years, so that the cash outflows required by the financing source match the cash inflows produced by the assets to which they relate.

EXHIBIT 9.1 Verizon Communications' Liabilities and Equity

At December 31 ($ millions)	2020	2019
Current liabilities		
Debt maturing within one year	$ 5,889	$ 10,777
Accounts payable and accrued liabilities	20,658	21,806
Current operating lease liabilities	3,485	3,261
Other current liabilities	9,628	9,024
Total current liabilities	39,660	44,868
Long-term debt	123,173	100,712
Employee benefit obligations	18,657	17,952
Deferred income taxes	35,711	34,703
Non-current operating lease liabilities	18,000	18,393
Other liabilities	12,008	12,264
Total liabilities	247,209	228,892
Total equity	69,272	62,835
Total liabilities and equity	$316,481	$291,727

When a company acquires assets and finances them with liabilities, its **financial leverage** increases. Because the magnitude of required liability payments increases with the level of liability financing, those larger payments increase the chance of default should a downturn in business occur. Increasing levels of liabilities make the company riskier to creditors who, consequently, demand a higher return on the financing they provide to the company. The assessment of default risk is part of liquidity and solvency analysis.

This chapter, along with Chapter 10, focuses on liabilities that are reported on the balance sheet and the corresponding interest costs reported in the income statement. All such liabilities represent probable, nondiscretionary, future obligations that are the result of events that have already occurred. Chapter 10 also addresses *off-balance sheet financing*, which encompasses future obligations that are reported in the notes, but not on the face of the balance sheet. An understanding of both on-balance-sheet and off-balance-sheet financing is central to evaluating a company's financial condition and assessing its risk of default.

CURRENT LIABILITIES

Liabilities are separated on the balance sheet into current and noncurrent (long-term). We first focus our attention on current liabilities, which are obligations that must be met (paid) within one year. Most current liabilities, such as those related to utilities, wages, insurance, rent, and taxes, generate a corresponding impact on operating expenses.

LO9-1 Identify and account for current operating liabilities.

Verizon reports three categories of current liabilities: (1) debt maturing within one year, which includes short-term borrowings as well as long-term obligations that are scheduled for payment in the upcoming year, (2) accounts payable and accrued liabilities, and (3) other current liabilities, which consist mainly of customer deposits, dividends declared but not yet paid, and miscellaneous short-term obligations too small to list separately.

It is helpful to separate current liabilities into operating and nonoperating components. These two components primarily consist of:

1. Current operating liabilities
   - **Accounts payable** Obligations to others for amounts owed on purchases of goods and services. These are usually non-interest-bearing.
   - **Accrued liabilities** Obligations for expenses incurred that have not been paid as of the end of the current period. These include, for example, accruals for employee wages earned but yet unpaid, accruals for taxes (usually quarterly) on payroll and current-period profits, and accruals for other liabilities such as rent, utilities, interest, and insurance. Accruals are made to properly reflect the liabilities owed as of the statement date and the expenses incurred in the period. Each one is journalized by a debit to an expense account (an increase in the expense) and a credit to a related liability (an increase in the liability).
   - **Deferred performance liabilities** Obligations that will be satisfied, not by paying cash, but instead, by providing products or services to customers. Examples of deferred performance liabilities include customer deposits, other types of contract liabilities (ASC 606) such as the unconditional right to receive payment from a customer, unearned gift card revenues for retail companies, and liabilities for frequent flier programs offered by airlines.

2. Current nonoperating liabilities
   - **Short-term interest-bearing debt** Short-term bank borrowings and notes expected to mature in whole or in part during the upcoming year.
   - **Current maturities of long-term debt** Long-term borrowings that are scheduled to mature in whole or in part during the upcoming year.

The remainder of this section describes current liabilities.

Accounts Payable

Accounts payable, which are part of current operating liabilities, arise from the purchase of goods and services from others on credit. Verizon reports $20,658 million in accounts payable and accrued liabilities as of December 31, 2020. Its accounts payable represent $6,667 million, or 32%, of this total amount.

Accounts payable are a non-interest-bearing source of financing. Increased payables reduce the amount of net working capital because these payables are deducted from current assets in the computation of net working capital. Also, increased payables improve operating cash flow (because inventories were purchased without using cash). An increase in accounts payable also increases profitability because it causes a reduction in the level of interest-bearing debt that is required to finance operating assets. ROE increases when companies make use of this low-cost financing source. However, management must be careful to avoid excessive "**leaning on the trade**" because short-term income and cash flow gains can result in long-term costs such as damaged supply channels.[1]

When a company purchases goods or services on credit, suppliers often grant **cash discounts** to buyers if payment is made within a specified time period. Cash discounts are usually established as part of the credit terms and stated as a percentage of the purchase price. For example, credit terms of 1/10, n/30 (one-ten, net-thirty) indicate that a 1% cash discount is allowed if the payment is made within 10 days. If the cash discount is not taken, the full purchase price is due in 30 days.

Net-of-Discount Method To illustrate a cash discount, assume that a company purchases 1,000 units of merchandise at $4 per unit on terms of 1/10, n/30. The total purchase price is 1,000 × $4 = $4,000. However, if payment is made within 10 days, the net purchase price would then be $3,960 ($4,000 − $40). While this difference seems like a small amount, consider the cost of not taking the discount. If the discount is missed, the buyer is afforded an extra 20 days to pay for the merchandise, for which it pays a penalty of $40, or $2 per day. Two dollars per day is the equivalent of $730 per year which, in turn, is equivalent to paying interest at an annual rate of 18.4% ($730/$3,960).

When cash discounts are offered, the inventory purchase should be recorded at its cost using the **net-of-discount method**. When the net-of-discount method is used, inventory is capitalized at the net cost, assuming that the discount will be taken by the buyer. Continuing with our example, the following entry would be recorded by the buyer at the time of purchase:

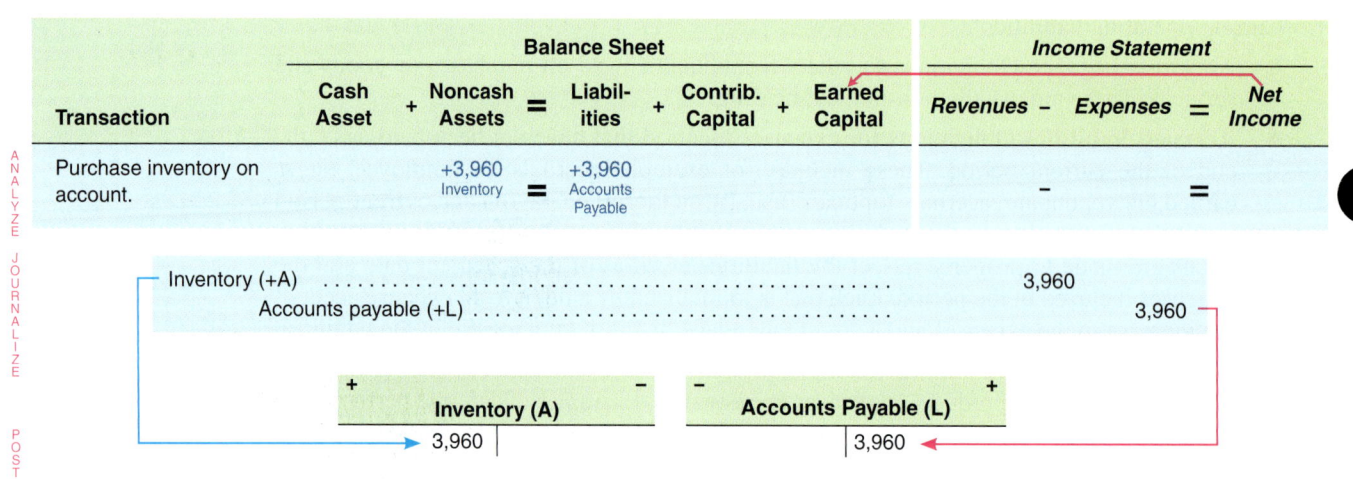

Transaction	Balance Sheet	Income Statement
	Cash Asset + Noncash Assets = Liabilities + Contrib. Capital + Earned Capital	Revenues − Expenses = Net Income
Purchase inventory on account.	+3,960 Inventory = +3,960 Accounts Payable	− =

Inventory (+A) 3,960
    Accounts payable (+L) 3,960

Inventory (A): +3,960
Accounts Payable (L): +3,960

When payment is made within the 10-day discount period, accounts payable is debited and cash is credited:

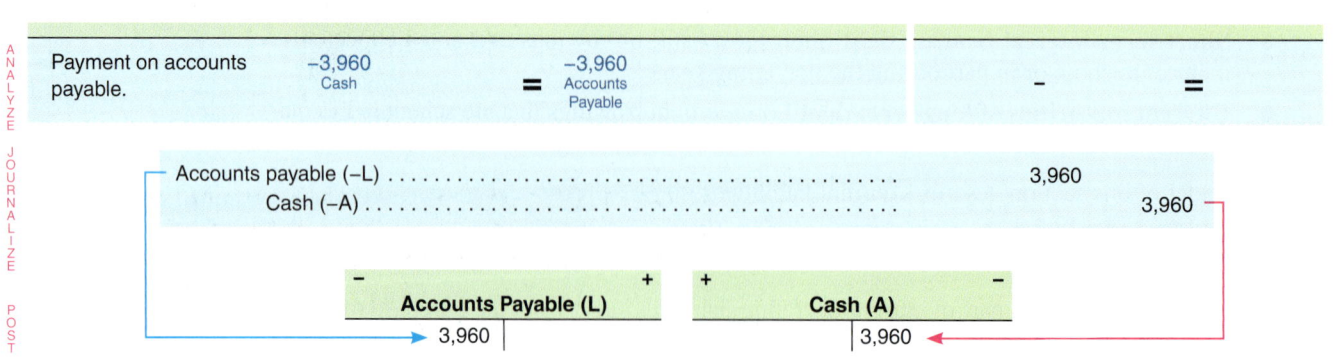

Transaction	Balance Sheet	Income Statement
Payment on accounts payable.	−3,960 Cash = −3,960 Accounts Payable	− =

Accounts payable (−L) 3,960
    Cash (−A) 3,960

Accounts Payable (L): −3,960
Cash (A): −3,960

However, when a discount is missed, the lost discount must be recorded. For example, if full payment is made after the 10-day discount period, the payment is recorded as follows:

---

[1] One must be careful, because excessive delays in the payment of payables can result in suppliers charging a higher price for their goods or, ultimately, refusing to sell to certain buyers. This situation is a hidden "financing" cost that, even though it is not interest, is a real cost.

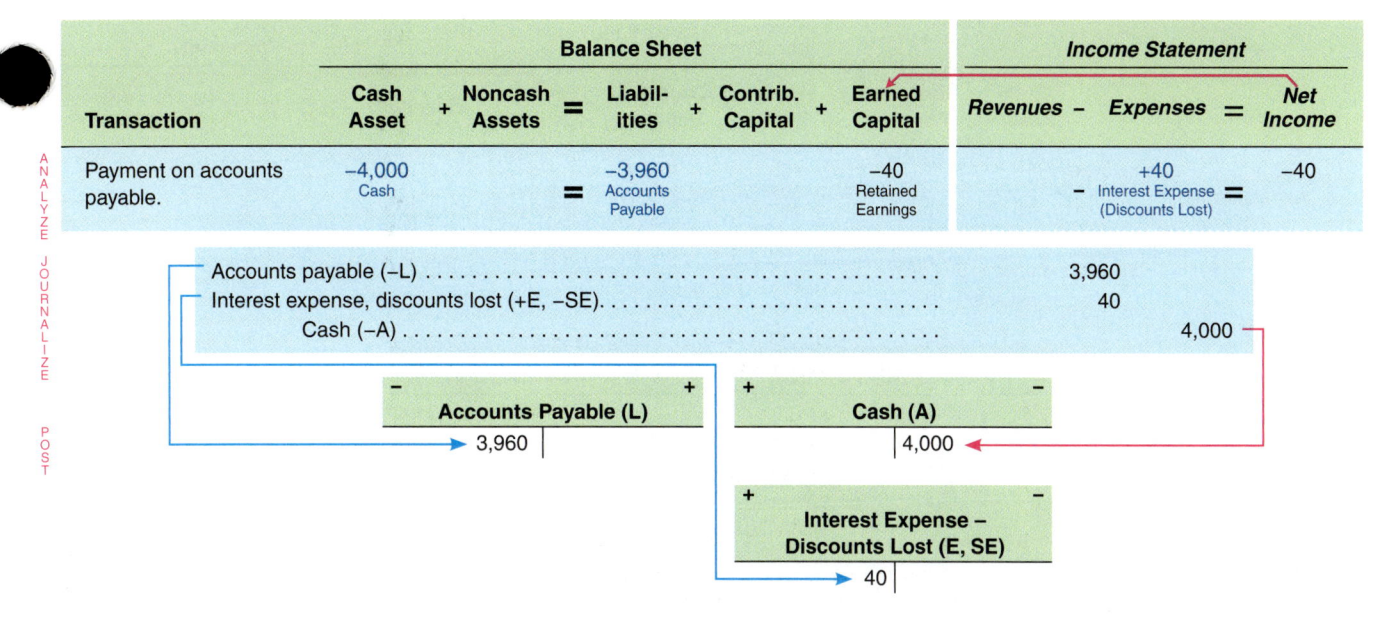

Transaction	Balance Sheet						Income Statement		
	Cash Asset	+	Noncash Assets	=	Liabil- ities	+ Contrib. Capital +	Earned Capital	Revenues − Expenses =	Net Income
Payment on accounts payable.	−4,000 Cash			=	−3,960 Accounts Payable		−40 Retained Earnings	+40 − Interest Expense = (Discounts Lost)	−40

Accounts payable (−L) 3,960
Interest expense, discounts lost (+E, −SE). 40
    Cash (−A) 4,000

Accounts Payable (L)	Cash (A)
3,960 →	4,000 ←

Interest Expense – Discounts Lost (E, SE)
→ 40

The missed discount is an expense in the period when the discount is lost. This serves two purposes. First, discounts lost are not capitalized as part of inventory and are not added to cost of goods sold. Instead, the lost discounts are treated like a finance charge and recorded as an expense of the period when the discount is missed. Second, the net-of-discount method highlights late payments by explicitly keeping a record of lost discounts. Given the high cost of missed cash discounts, most businesses would likely want to minimize the amount of discounts lost. Thus, keeping a record of discounts lost is useful when it comes to managing cash and accounts payable.

Accrued Liabilities

Accrued liabilities are identified at the end of an accounting period to reflect liabilities and expenses that have been incurred during the period but are not yet paid.[2] **Verizon** reports details of its $20,658 million accounts payable and accrued liabilities, including its $6,667 accounts payable, in Note 15 to its 2020 10-K report:

December 31 ($ millions)	2020	2019
Accounts payable	$ 6,667	$ 7,725
Accrued expenses	6,050	5,984
Accrued vacation, salaries and wages	5,057	4,885
Interest payable	1,452	1,441
Taxes payable	1,432	1,771
Total	$20,658	$21,806

Verizon accrues liabilities for the following expenses: miscellaneous accrued expenses, accrued vacation pay, accrued salaries and wages, interest payable, and accrued taxes. These accruals are typical of most companies. The accruals are recognized with a liability on the balance sheet and a corresponding expense on the income statement. This reporting means that liabilities increase, current income decreases, and reported equity decreases. When an accrued liability is ultimately paid, both cash and the liability are decreased (but no expense is recorded because it was recognized previously).

Accounting for Accrued Liabilities The following entries illustrate the accounting for a typical accrued liability, accrued wages:

---
[2] Accruals can also be made for recognition of revenue and a corresponding receivable. An example of this situation would be interest earned but not received on an investment in bonds that is still outstanding at period-end.

	Balance Sheet					Income Statement		
Transaction	Cash Asset	+ Noncash Assets	= Liabilities	+ Contrib. Capital	+ Earned Capital	Revenues	− Expenses	= Net Income
(1) Accrued $75 for employee wages earned.		=	+75 Wages Payable		−75 Retained Earnings		− +75 Wages Expense	= −75

(1) Wages expense (+E, −SE)..................................... 75
    Wages payable (+L).. 75

+ Wages Expense (E) −		− Wages Payable (L) +
(1) 75		75 (1)

Transaction	Cash Asset	+ Noncash Assets	= Liabilities	+ Contrib. Capital	+ Earned Capital	Revenues	− Expenses	= Net Income
(2) Next period's cash payment of wages.	−75 Cash	=	−75 Wages Payable				−	=

(2) Wages payable (−L).. 75
    Cash (−A)... 75

− Wages Payable (L) +		+ Cash (A) −
(2) 75		75 (2)

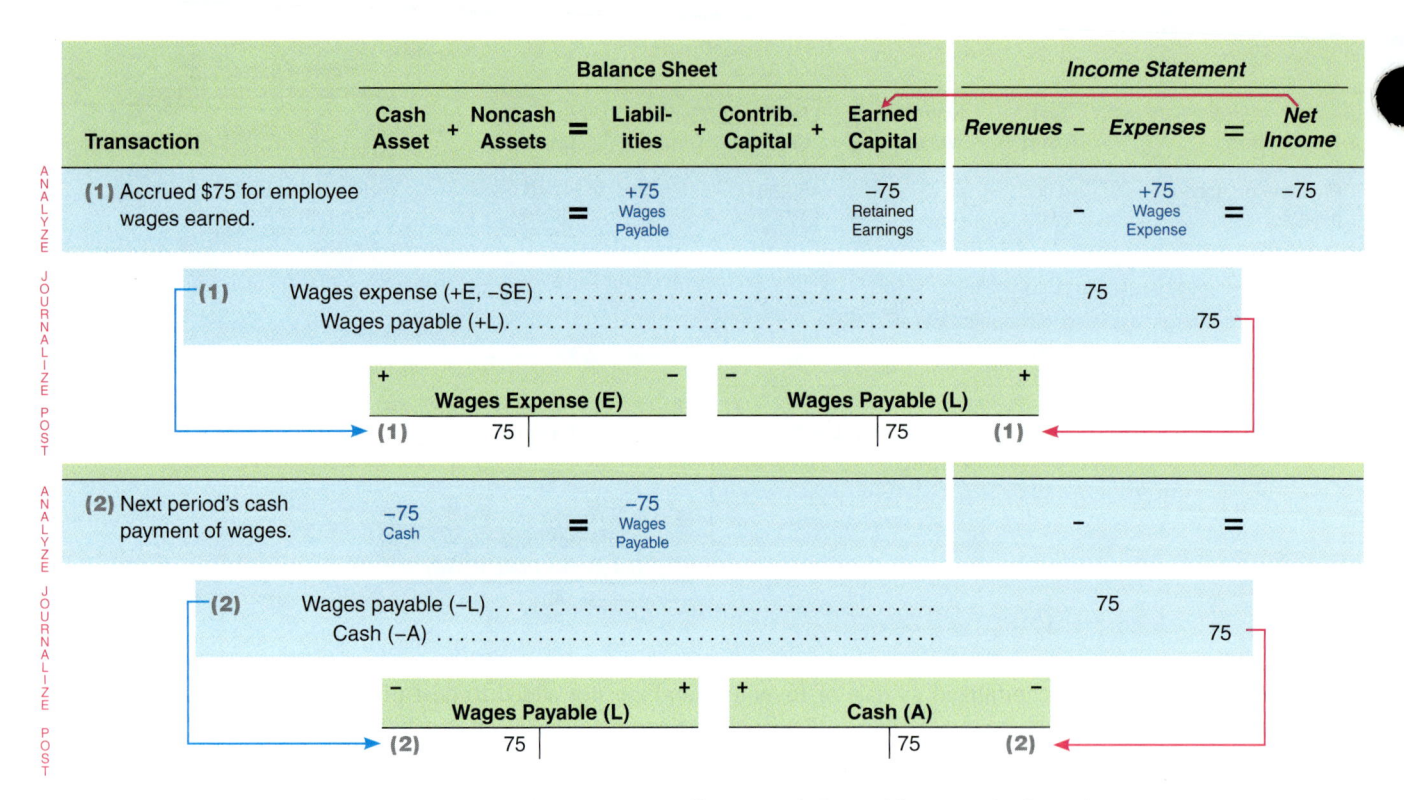

The following financial statement effects result from this accrual of employee wages:

- Employees have worked during a period and have not yet been paid. The effect of this accrual is to increase wages payable on the balance sheet and to recognize wages expense on the income statement. Failure to recognize this liability and associated expense would understate liabilities on the balance sheet and overstate income.

- Employees are paid in the following period, resulting in a cash decrease and a reduction in wages payable. This payment does not result in expense because the expense was recognized in the prior period when incurred.

Contingent Liabilities The accrued wages illustration relates to events that are fairly certain. We know, for example, when wages are incurred but not paid. Other examples of such accruals are rental costs, insurance premiums due but not yet paid, and taxes owed.

Some accrued liabilities, however, are less certain than others. Consider a company facing a lawsuit. Should it record the possible liability and related expense? The answer depends on the likelihood of occurrence and the ability to estimate the obligation. Specifically, if the obligation is *probable* **and** the amount *estimable,* then a company will recognize this obligation, called a **contingent liability**, with a corresponding charge to income. If an obligation is only *reasonably possible,* regardless of the company's ability to estimate the amount, the contingent liability is not reported on the balance sheet and is merely disclosed in the notes to the financial statements (we discuss further below). All other contingent liabilities that are less than reasonably possible are not accrued—disclosure in a note is permitted but not required.

A GLOBAL PERSPECTIVE

Reporting Contingent Liabilities U.S. GAAP and IFRS are similar with respect to reporting accrued liabilities. The one exception is contingencies. IFRS uses the term "provisions" to refer to contingent liabilities that are accrued and reported on the balance sheet, while an obligation that is disclosed in the notes is labeled "contingent liability." Both GAAP and IFRS require accrual of the "best estimate" of the liability. However, if the best estimate of the future payments required to settle the obligation is a range of values, IFRS requires that the midpoint of the range be used as the estimated value of the contingent liability or provision. In the same situation, U.S. GAAP requires that the low end of the range be used, with disclosure of the maximum.

Warranties The revenue recognition standard discussed in Chapter 6 has implications for the accounting for warranty obligations. When a company delivers a product with a warranty, is the warranty simply assurance that the product will function as intended, or should it be considered a separate performance obligation? If it is considered a separate performance obligation, then the company would allocate the purchase price between the product and the warranty and recognize a contract liability at the time of purchase. However, if the warranty is not a separate performance obligation (e.g., it cannot be purchased separately from the product and is intended as assurance that the product will perform as expected), none of the purchase price is allocated to the warranty, and a liability accrual for the warranty obligation must be made at the time of purchase, as mentioned in Chapter 6.

The expected cost of the warranty commitment usually is reasonably estimated at the time of sale based on past experience. GAAP requires manufacturers to record the expected cost of warranties as a liability and to record the related expected warranty expense in the income statement to match against the sales revenue reported for that period.

To illustrate, the effects of an accrual of a $1,000 warranty liability are:

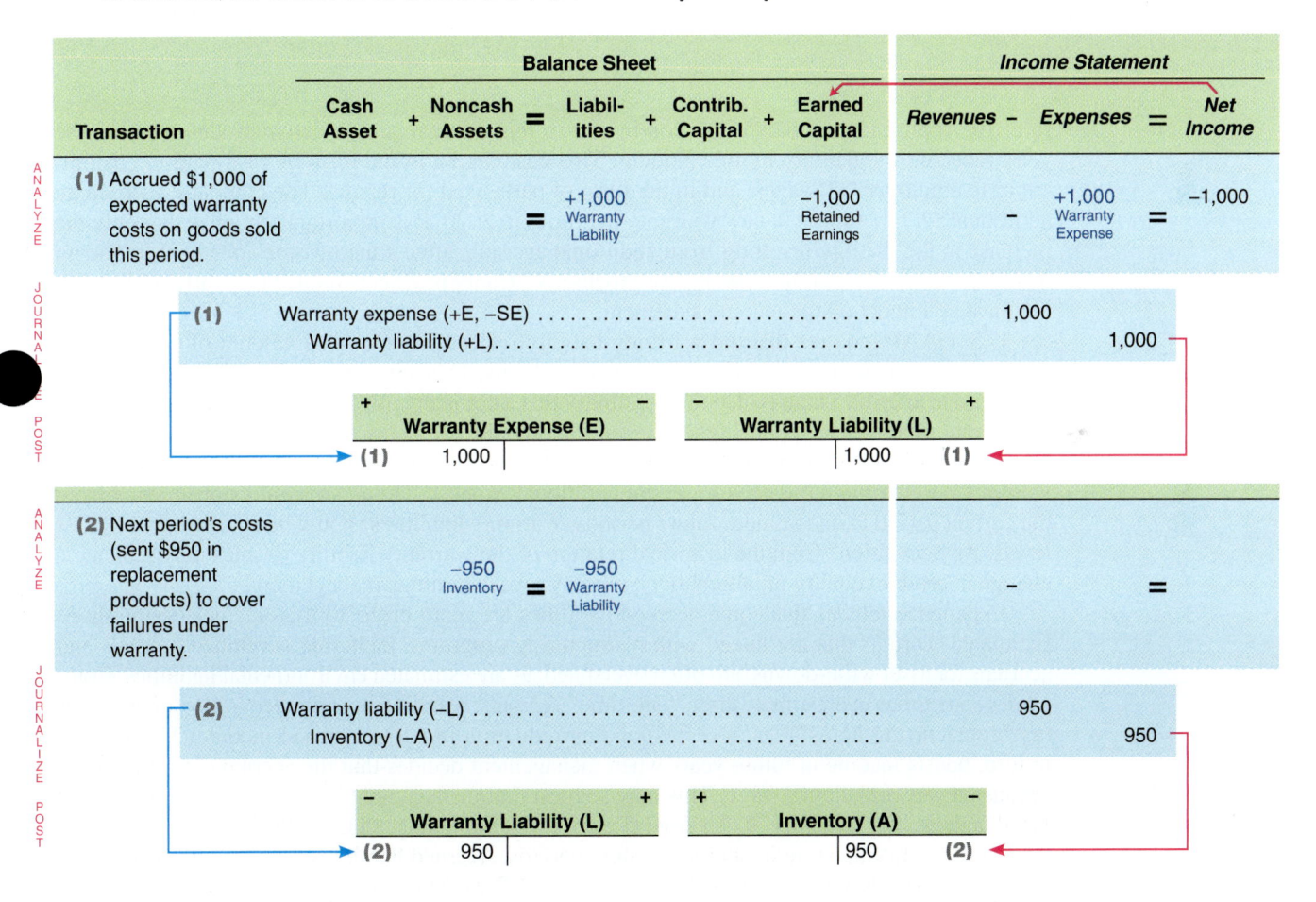

Transaction	Balance Sheet	Income Statement
	Cash Asset + Noncash Assets = Liabilities + Contrib. Capital + Earned Capital	Revenues − Expenses = Net Income
(1) Accrued $1,000 of expected warranty costs on goods sold this period.	+1,000 Warranty Liability = −1,000 Retained Earnings	+1,000 Warranty Expense = −1,000

(1) Warranty expense (+E, −SE) 1,000
    Warranty liability (+L) 1,000

Warranty Expense (E)	Warranty Liability (L)
(1) 1,000	1,000 (1)

Transaction	Balance Sheet	Income Statement
(2) Next period's costs (sent $950 in replacement products) to cover failures under warranty.	−950 Inventory = −950 Warranty Liability	− =

(2) Warranty liability (−L) 950
    Inventory (−A) 950

Warranty Liability (L)	Inventory (A)
(2) 950	950 (2)

Reporting of warranty liabilities has the same effect on financial statements as does the accrual of wages expense in the previous section. That is, a liability is recorded on the balance sheet and an expense is reported in the income statement, reducing income by the warranty accrual. When the defective product is later replaced (or repaired), the liability is reduced together with the cost of the inventory (or other assets) spent to satisfy the claim. (Only a portion of the products estimated to fail does so in the current period; we expect other product failures in future periods. Using methods similar to the aging of accounts in Chapter 6, management monitors this estimate and adjusts it if failure is higher or lower than expected.) As in the accrual of wages, the expense is reported when it is incurred and the liability is estimated at that time, not when payments are made.

Apple Inc. reports $3,354 million of warranty liability in its 2020 balance sheet. The disclosure notes reveal the following additional information:

Several notes are combined below: Accrued Warranty and Indemnification, Warranty, and Warranty Costs The Company offers limited warranties on its new and certified refurbished hardware products and on parts used to repair its hardware products, and customers may purchase extended service coverage, where available, on many of the Company's hardware products. The Company accrues the estimated cost of warranties in the period the related revenue is recognized based on historical and projected warranty claim rates, historical and projected cost per claim, and knowledge of specific product failures outside the Company's typical experience. If actual product failure rates or repair costs differ from estimates, revisions to the estimated warranty liabilities would be required.

Accrued Warranty and Indemnification The following table shows changes in the Company's accrued warranties and related costs for 2020, 2019, and 2018 (in millions):

	2020	2019	2018
Beginning accrued warranty and related costs.	$3,570	$3,692	$3,834
Cost of warranty claims	(2,956)	(3,857)	(4,115)
Accruals for product warranty.	2,740	3,735	3,973
Ending accrued warranty and related costs	$3,354	$3,570	$3,692

In 2020, Apple incurred $2,956 million in cost to replace or repair defective products during the year, reducing the liability by this amount. This cost can be in the form of cash paid to customers or to employees as wages, and in the form of parts used for repairs. The company accrued an additional $2,740 million in new warranty liabilities in 2020. It is important to realize that only the increase in the liability resulting from additional accruals affects the income statement, reducing income through the additional warranty expense. Warranty payments reduce the warranty liability but have no impact on the income statement.

U.S. GAAP requires that the warranty liability reflect the estimated amount of cost that the company expects to incur as a result of warranty claims. This amount is often difficult to estimate and is prone to error. There is also the possibility that a company might intentionally underestimate its warranty liability to report higher current income, or overestimate it so as to depress current income and create an additional liability on the balance sheet that can be used to absorb future warranty costs without the need to record additional expense. Doing so would shift income from the current period to one or more future periods. Warranty liabilities should be compared with sales levels. Any deviations from the historical relation of the warranty liability to sales may indicate a change in product quality or, alternatively, it may reveal earnings management.

Experience tells us that some accrued liabilities are more prone to misstatement than others. Estimated accruals that are linked with restructuring programs, including severance accruals and accruals for asset write-downs, are often overstated, as are estimated environmental liabilities. Companies sometimes overestimate these "one-time" accruals, resulting in early recognition of expenses (as "nonrecurring items") and a corresponding reduction in current period income. This choice, in turn, boosts income in future years when management decides that the accrual can be reversed because it was initially too large. This may suggest that management is conservative and wants to avoid understating liabilities. It can also reflect a desire by management to show earnings growth in the future by shifting current income to future periods. Accrued liabilities set up to smooth income over future periods are called "**cookie jar reserves**." The terms "clearing the decks" and "taking a big bath" have also been applied to such accounting practices.

YOU MAKE THE CALL

You are the Analyst **DowDuPont Inc.** disclosed the following in their 2020 10-K:

Environmental Matters

Accruals for environmental matters are recorded when it is probable that a liability has been incurred and the amount of the liability can be reasonably estimated based on current law and existing technologies. At December 31, 2020, the Company had accrued obligations of $80 million for probable environmental remediation and restoration costs, inclusive of $36 million retained and assumed following the DWDP Distributions and $44 million of indemnified liabilities.

continued

continued from previous page

> What conditions needed to be met before these liabilities could be reported?
> The company then stated that "This is management's best estimate of the costs for remediation and restoration with respect to environmental matters for which the Company has accrued liabilities, although it is reasonably possible that the ultimate cost with respect to these particular matters could range up to $170 million above the amount accrued at December 31, 2020."
> How does this uncertainty affect the company's balance sheet? [Answers on page 9-33]

Other Current Liabilities

Verizon provides more detailed disclosure for the line item on the balance sheet labeled "other" under current liabilities. Here is the table they provide:

Other Current Liabilities	2020	2019
Dividends payable	$2,618	$2,566
Contract liability	4,843	4,651
Other	2,167	1,807
Total	$9,628	$9,024

Contract liability includes advance billings and customer deposits (under ASC 606). Either customers have prepaid for work (i.e., another term for this is deferred revenue), or the unconditional right to payment has occurred according to the contract terms. If the customer has prepaid, cash is increased (debited) and the liability is increased (credited). If the unconditional right to payment has occurred but no payment has been made, then the company increases a receivable (debits a receivable) and increases the liability (credits the liability).

Dividends payable is a liability for dividends that have been declared but not yet paid. There is a liability for the dividends to be paid in this case, but recall dividends are never expensed. The other side of the entry is a decrease to equity (a debit to equity).

Accounting for Current Operating Liabilities — LO9-1 Review 9-1

Part One
On April 12, Waymire Corporation purchased raw materials costing $29,000 on credit. The credit terms were 2/10, n/30.

a. If Waymire paid for the materials on April 19, how much would it pay?
b. Compute the cost of a lost discount as an annual percentage interest rate.

Part Two
The Toro Company reported warranty liabilities of $96,604,000 in its October 31, 2019, balance sheet. On its October 31, 2020, balance sheet, it reported a liability of $107,121,000. It recognized $77,758,000 in net warranty expenses during fiscal year 2020, ending October 31, 2020.

a. What amount of cost did Toro incur to cover warranty claims in 2020?
b. How would the fulfillment of these claims be recorded using the financial statement effects template?
c. Record the entry described in part b in a journal entry.

Toro Company NYSE :: TTC

Solution on p. 9-48.

Current Nonoperating (Financial) Liabilities

Current nonoperating (financial) liabilities include short-term bank loans, the accrual of interest on those loans, and the current maturities of long-term debt. Companies generally try to structure their financing so that debt service requirements (payments) of those financing obligations coincide with the cash inflows from the assets financed. This strategy means that current assets are usually financed with current liabilities and that long-term assets are financed with long-term liability (and equity) sources.

LO9-2 Describe and account for current nonoperating (financial) liabilities.

The use of short-term financing is particularly important for companies that have seasonal sales. To illustrate, a seasonal company's investment in current assets tends to fluctuate during the year, as depicted in the graphic below:

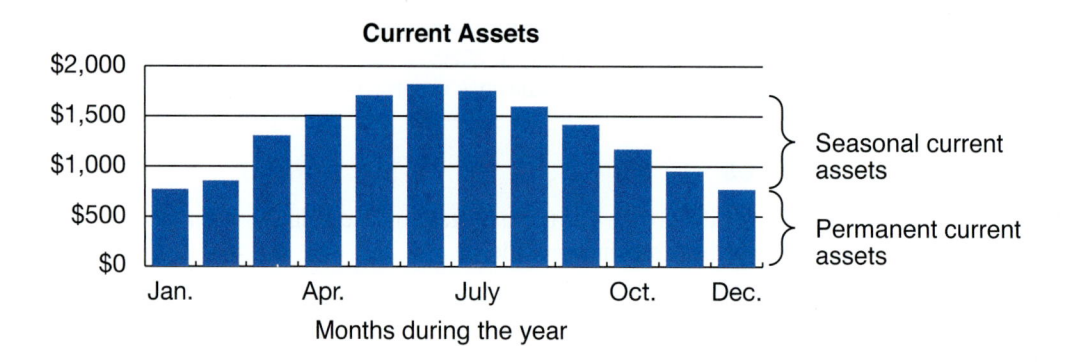

Current Assets

[Bar chart showing monthly current assets from January through December, ranging from about $750 to $1,750, with Seasonal current assets shown above Permanent current assets. X-axis: Months during the year.]

This particular company does most of its selling in the summer months. More inventory is purchased and manufactured in the early spring than at any other time of the year. Sales of the company's manufactured goods are also greater during the summer months, giving rise to accounts receivable that are higher than normal during the summer and fall. The peak working capital level is reached at the height of the selling season and is lowest when the business slows in the off-season. There is a permanent level of working capital required for this business (about $750), and a seasonal component (maximum of about $1,000). Businesses differ in their working capital requirements, but many have permanent and seasonal components.

If a company's working capital needs fluctuate from one season to the next, then the financing needs of the company are also seasonal. Some assets can be financed with short-term operating liabilities. For example, seasonal increases in inventory balances are typically financed with increased levels of accounts payable. However, operating liabilities are unlikely to meet all of the financing needs of a company. Additional financing is provided by short-term interest-bearing debt.

This section focuses on short-term nonoperating liabilities. These include short-term debt and interest as well as current maturities of long-term liabilities.

Short-Term Interest-Bearing Debt Seasonal swings in working capital are often financed with a bank line of credit (short-term debt). In this case the bank provides a commitment to lend up to a given level with the understanding that the amounts borrowed are repaid in full sometime during the year. An interest-bearing note is evidence of such borrowing.

When these short-term funds are borrowed, the cash received is reported on the balance sheet together with an increase in liabilities (notes payable). The note is reported as a current liability because the expectation is that it will be paid within a year. This borrowing transaction has no effect on income or equity, but there will be a financing cash inflow on the statement of cash flows. The borrower incurs (and the lender earns) interest on the note as time passes. U.S. GAAP requires the borrower to accrue the interest liability and the related interest expense each time financial statements are issued.

To illustrate, assume that Verizon borrows $1,000 cash from 1st Bank on January 1. The note bears interest at a 12% annual (3% quarterly) rate, and the interest is payable on the first of each subsequent quarter (April 1, July 1, October 1, January 1). Assuming that Verizon issues calendar-quarter financial statements, this borrowing results in the following financial statement effects for the period January 1 through April 1:

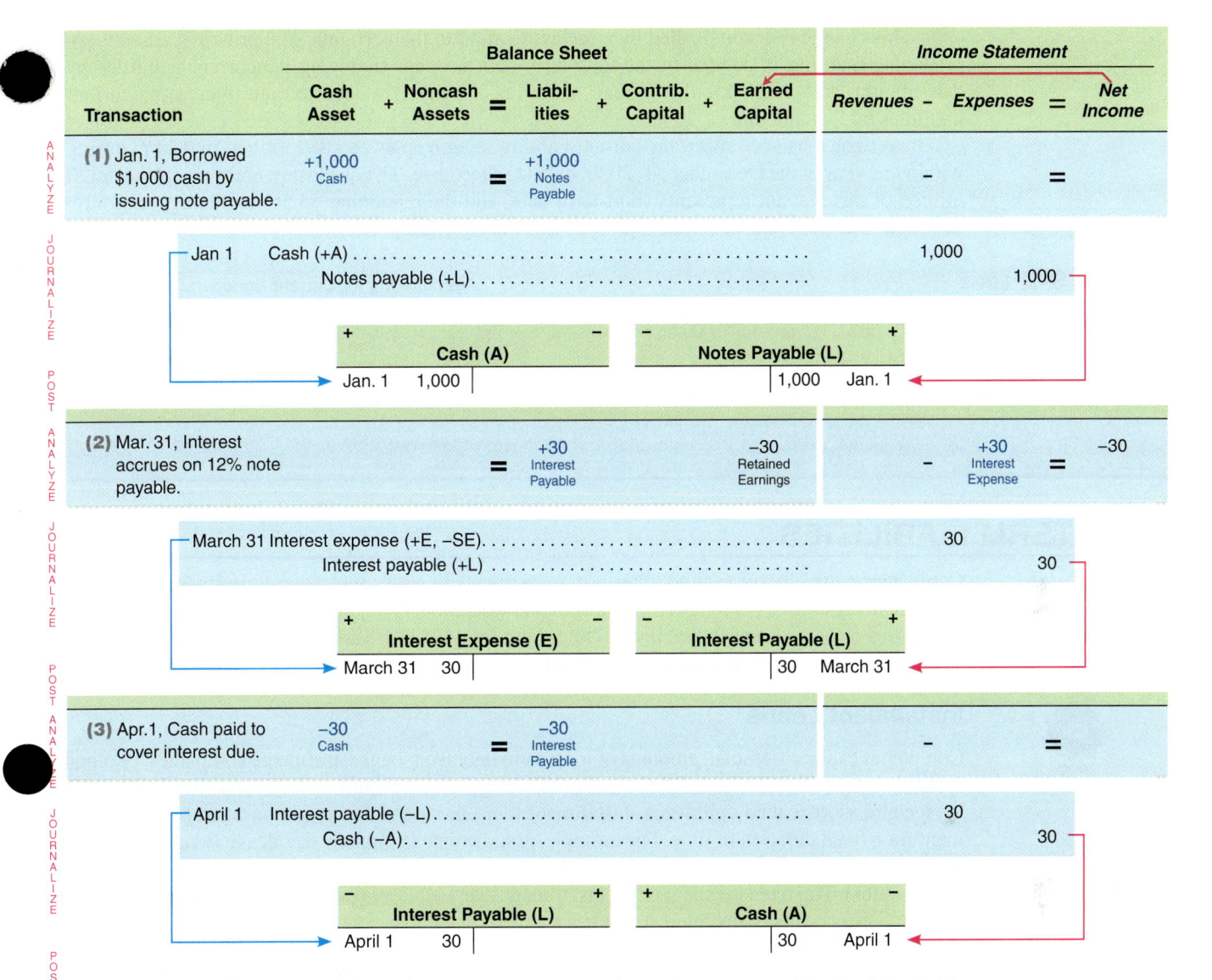

Financial Statement Effects Template

Transaction	Balance Sheet					Income Statement		
	Cash Asset	+ Noncash Assets	= Liabilities	+ Contrib. Capital	+ Earned Capital	Revenues	− Expenses	= Net Income
(1) Jan. 1, Borrowed $1,000 cash by issuing note payable.	+1,000 Cash		= +1,000 Notes Payable				−	=

Jan 1   Cash (+A) 1,000
            Notes payable (+L) 1,000

Cash (A) (+ / −)
Jan. 1   1,000

Notes Payable (L) (− / +)
1,000   Jan. 1

Transaction	Balance Sheet					Income Statement		
(2) Mar. 31, Interest accrues on 12% note payable.			= +30 Interest Payable		−30 Retained Earnings		− +30 Interest Expense	= −30

March 31   Interest expense (+E, −SE) 30
            Interest payable (+L) 30

Interest Expense (E) (+ / −)
March 31   30

Interest Payable (L) (− / +)
30   March 31

Transaction	Balance Sheet					Income Statement		
(3) Apr.1, Cash paid to cover interest due.	−30 Cash		= −30 Interest Payable				−	=

April 1   Interest payable (−L) 30
            Cash (−A) 30

Interest Payable (L) (− / +)
April 1   30

Cash (A) (+ / −)
30   April 1

The January 1 borrowing is reflected by an increase in cash and in notes payable. On March 31, this company issues its quarterly financial statements. Although interest is not paid until April 1, the company has incurred three months' interest obligation as of March 31. Failure to recognize this liability and the expense incurred would not fairly present the financial condition of the company. Accordingly, the quarterly accrued interest is computed as follows:

Interest Expense = Principal × Annual Rate × Portion of Year Outstanding
$$\$30 = \$1,000 \times 12\% \times 3/12$$

The subsequent interest payment on April 1 is reflected in the financial statements as a reduction of cash and a reduction of the interest payable liability accrued on March 31. There is no expense reported on April 1 because it was recorded the previous day (March 31) when the financial statements were prepared; however, the payment of interest would be an operating cash outflow in the statement of cash flows for the quarter beginning April 1. (For fixed-maturity borrowings specified in days, such as a 90-day note, we use a 365-day year for interest accrual computations; see Review 9-2.)

Current Maturities of Long-Term Debt   All companies are required to provide a schedule of the maturities of their long-term debt in the notes to financial statements. Debt payments that must be made during the upcoming 12 months on long-term debt (such as for a mortgage) or the maturity of a bond or note are reported as current liabilities called *current maturities of long-term* debt. This change is accomplished by a reclassification in the accounts. The principal amount approaching maturity is debited to the long-term debt account (reducing noncurrent liabilities by that amount) and credited to the current maturities of long-term debt account (increasing current liabilities by that amount).

In Verizon's balance sheet, the current liability section shows $5,889 million in debt maturing within one year of the December 31, 2020, balance sheet date. The disclosure notes reveal that $320 million of this amount represents short-term debt, and the remaining $5,569 million is long-term debt that must be repaid or refinanced sometime during 2021.

Review 9-2 LO9-2 — Accounting for Current Nonoperating Liabilities

Gigler Company borrowed $10,000 on a 90-day, 6% note payable dated January 15. The bank accrues interest daily based on a 365-day year.

a. Use the financial statement effects template to show the implications (amounts and accounts) of the January 31 month-end interest accrual.
b. Use journal entries and T-accounts to record the month-end interest accrual.

Solution on p. 9-49.

LONG-TERM LIABILITIES

LO9-3 Explain and illustrate the pricing of long-term nonoperating liabilities.

Companies generally try to fund long-term investments in assets with long-term financing. Long-term financing consists of long-term liabilities and stockholders' equity. The remainder of this chapter focuses on long-term debt liabilities. Other long-term liabilities are discussed in Chapter 10, and stockholders' equity is the focus of Chapter 11.

Installment Loans

Companies can borrow small amounts of long-term debt from banks, insurance companies, or other financial institutions. These liabilities are often designed as installment loans and may be secured by specific assets called **collateral**. Installment loans are loans that require a fixed periodic payment for a fixed duration of time. For example, assume that a company decides to finance an office building with a 15-year mortgage requiring 180 equal monthly payments (180 payments = 15 years × 12 months). The fixed payment on an installment loan includes a portion of the principal (i.e., the amount borrowed) plus any interest that has accrued on the loan.

To illustrate the accounting for installment loans, assume that Shevlin Company borrowed $40,000 from 1st Bank on July 1, 2021. The terms of the loan require that Shevlin repay the loan in 12 equal quarterly payments over a three-year period and require 8% interest per year. The quarterly payment is $3,782 and can be calculated using the Table A.3 (page A-22) present value factor for 12 periods (3 years × 4 quarters) and 2% interest (8% per year ÷ 4 quarters) as follows:

$$\text{Present Value} = \text{Payment} \times \text{Present Value Factor}$$

$$\frac{\text{Present Value}}{\text{Present Value Factor}} = \text{Payment}$$

$$\frac{\$40,000}{10.57534} = \$3,782$$

Using a financial calculator, we can compute the payment by letting N be the number of quarters and setting I/Yr equal to the interest rate per quarter. The payment can then be calculated as follows: N = 12; I/Yr = 2; PV = 40,000; FV = 0:

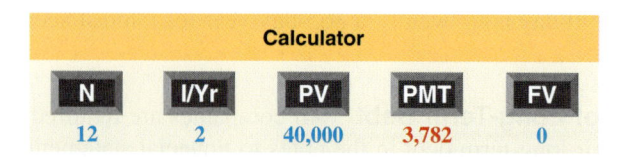

N	I/Yr	PV	PMT	FV
12	2	40,000	3,782	0

Calculator

When Shevlin Company agrees to the loan terms, it receives the loan amount, $40,000 in cash, and incurs a $40,000 liability (installment loan payable). The loan is recorded on July 1 as follows:

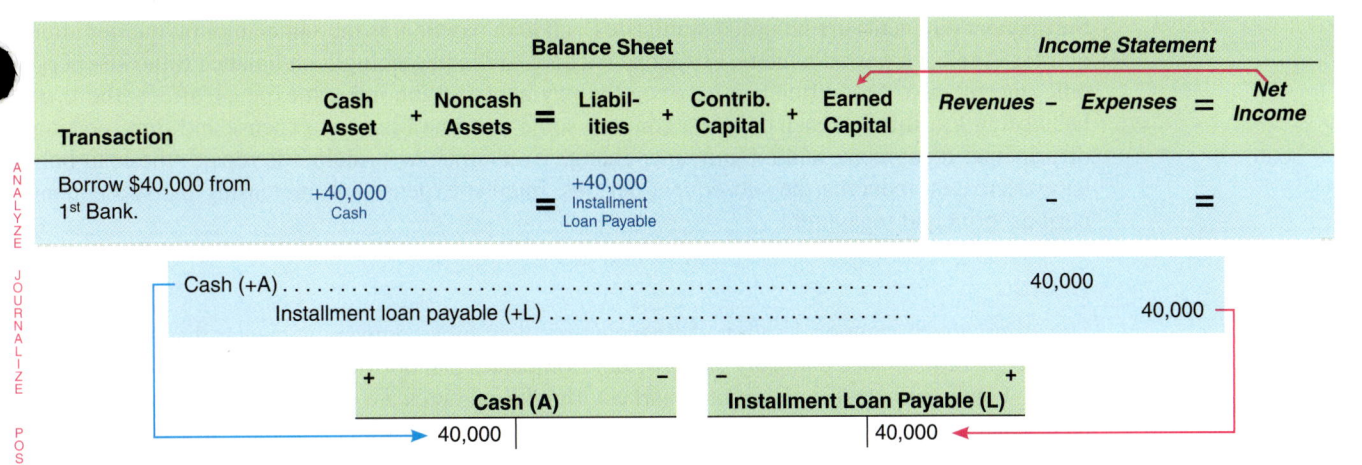

On October 1, 2021, the first payment of $3,782 is due. The payment includes both interest for the three months from July 1 through September 30 and some portion of the original loan amount (the **principal**). The division of the payment between interest and principal is best illustrated using a **loan amortization table**, like the one in **Exhibit 9.2**. (Pages A-14–A-15 in Appendix A demonstrate the use of Excel to calculate the required payment and the amortization table.)

Each payment includes interest and principal. The first loan payment, due on October 1, 2021, is summarized in the second row of the table. Column [B] is the quarterly loan payment. Column [C] is the interest expense, computed by multiplying column [A] by the interest rate (2 percent per quarter). Column [D] is the principal portion of the payment, which is the cash payment (column [B]) less the interest (column [C]). The remaining balance on the loan is in column [E], which is equal to the beginning balance in column [A] less the principal payment from column [D]. The loan balance decreases with each payment until the loan is paid off on July 1, 2024.

EXHIBIT 9.2 Loan Amortization Table

Date	[A] Beginning Balance	[B] Cash Payment	[C] ([A] × interest %) Interest	[D] ([B] − [C]) Principal	[E] ([A] − [D]) Balance
07/01/21					40,000
10/01/21	40,000	3,782	800	2,982	37,018
01/01/22	37,018	3,782	740	3,042	33,976
04/01/22	33,976	3,782	679	3,103	30,873
07/01/22	30,873	3,782	617	3,165	27,708
10/01/22	27,708	3,782	554	3,228	24,480
01/01/23	24,480	3,782	489	3,293	21,187
04/01/23	21,187	3,782	423	3,359	17,828
07/01/23	17,828	3,782	356	3,426	14,402
10/01/23	14,402	3,782	288	3,494	10,908
01/01/24	10,908	3,782	218	3,564	7,344
04/01/24	7,344	3,782	146	3,636	3,708
07/01/24	3,708	3,782	74	3,708	0

The first payment is recorded as follows:

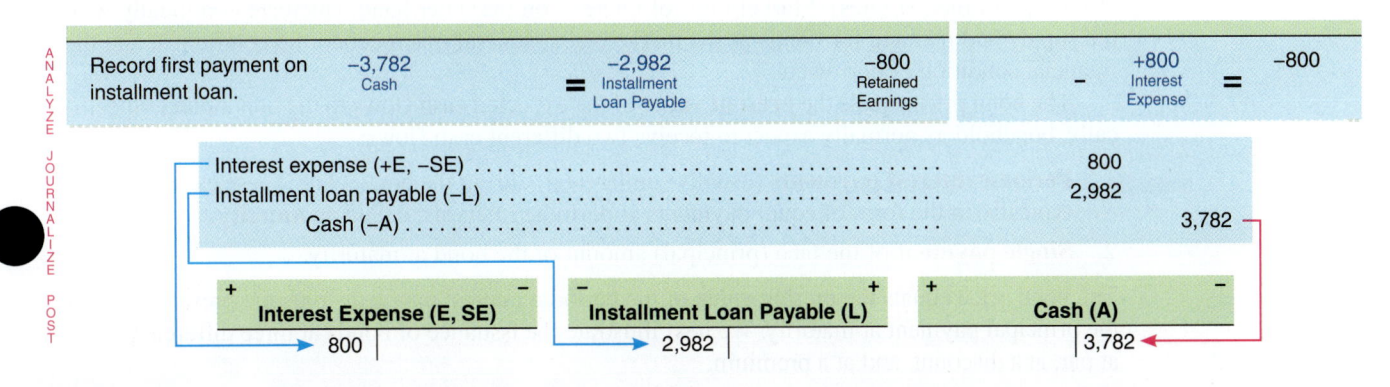

Subsequent payments are recorded similarly. Each loan payment is the same amount, quarter after quarter. And each period's interest expense is equal to the beginning loan balance times the periodic interest rate. Any difference between the payment and the interest expense affects the loan balance. In **Exhibit 9.2**, each payment contains some portion of interest expense and some portion of principal repayment, and the amounts change over time. As principal is repaid, the loan balance decreases, reducing the subsequent periods' interest expense and increasing the subsequent periods' principal repayment.

Bonds

Sometimes the amount or duration of financing required by a company is greater than the amount that a bank or insurance company can provide. Companies can borrow larger amounts of money by issuing bonds (or notes) in the capital markets. Bonds and notes are debt securities issued by companies and traded in the bond markets. When a company issues bonds, it is borrowing money. The investors who buy the bonds are lending money to the issuing company. That is, the bondholders are the company's creditors. Because the bond markets provide companies with access to large amounts of capital, bonds represent a very common, cost-effective source of long-term debt financing.

Bonds and notes are structured like any other borrowing. The borrower receives cash and agrees to pay it back with interest. Generally, the entire **face amount** (principal) of the bond or note is repaid at maturity and interest payments are made (usually semiannually) in the interim.

Companies wishing to raise funds in the bond market normally work with an underwriter (e.g., **Goldman Sachs**) to set the terms of the bond issue. The underwriter sells individual bonds (usually in $1,000 denominations) from this general bond issue to its retail clients, corporations, and professional portfolio managers (e.g., **The Vanguard Group**), and it receives a fee for underwriting the bond issue.

Once issued, the bonds can be traded in the secondary market between investors just like stocks. Market prices of bonds fluctuate daily despite the fact that the company's obligation for payment of principal and interest remains fixed throughout the life of the bond. This occurs because of fluctuations in the general level of interest rates and changes in the financial condition of the borrowing company.

The following sections analyze and interpret the reporting for bonds. We first examine the mechanics of bond pricing. In a subsequent section, we address the accounting for and reporting of bonds.

Pricing of Bonds

Two different interest rates are crucial for understanding how a bond is priced.

- **Coupon (contract** or **stated) rate** The coupon rate of interest is stated in the bond contract. It is used to compute the dollar amount of (semiannual) interest payments that are paid to bondholders during the life of the bond issue.
- **Market (yield) rate** The market rate is the interest rate that investors expect to earn on the investment for this debt security. This rate is used to price the bond issue.

The coupon (contract) rate is used to compute interest payments, and the market (yield) rate is used to price the bond. The coupon rate and the market rate are nearly always different. The coupon rate is fixed prior to issuance of the bond and remains so throughout its life (unless the interest rate "floats" with market rates). Market rates of interest, on the other hand, fluctuate continually with the supply and demand for bonds in the marketplace, general macroeconomic conditions, and the financial condition of borrowers.

The bond price equals the **present value** of the expected cash flows to the bondholder. Specifically, bondholders normally expect to receive two different cash flows:

1. **Periodic interest payments** (usually semiannual) during the bond's life. These cash flows are typically in the form of equal payments at periodic intervals, called an **annuity**.
2. **Single payment** of the face (principal) amount of the bond at maturity.

The bond price equals the present value of the periodic interest payments plus the present value of the principal payment at maturity. We next illustrate the issuance of bonds at three different prices: at par, at a discount, and at a premium.

Bonds Issued at Par When a bond is issued at par, its coupon rate is identical to the market rate. Under this condition, a $1,000 bond sells for $1,000 in the market. To illustrate bond pricing, assume that investors wish to value a bond issue with a face amount of $100,000, a 6% annual coupon rate with interest payable semiannually (3% semiannual rate), and a maturity of 4 years.[3] Investors purchasing this issue receive the following cash flows:

	Number of Payments	Dollars per Payment	Total Cash Flows
Semiannual interest payments......	4 years × 2 = 8	$100,000 × 3% = $ 3,000	$ 24,000
Principal payment at maturity.......	1	$100,000	100,000
			$124,000

Specifically, the bond agreement dictates that the borrower makes 8 semiannual payments of $3,000 each, computed as $100,000 × (6%/2), plus the $100,000 face amount at maturity, for a total of $124,000 in cash flows. Each $1,000 bond in this bond issue provides the bondholder with an annuity of 8 payments of $30 and a principal payment of $1,000 at maturity. For an individual bond, the cash flows total $1,240 (= $30 × 8 + $1,000).

When pricing bonds, the number of periods used for computing the present value is the number of interest (coupon) payments required by the bond. In this case, there are 8 semiannual interest payments required, so we use 8 six-month periods to value the bond. The market interest rate (yield) is 6% per year, which is 3% per six-month period.

The bond price is the present value of the interest annuity plus the present value of the principal payment. Assuming that investors desire a 6% annual market rate (yield), the bond sells for exactly $100,000, which is computed as follows:

	Payment	Present Value Factor[a]	Present Value
Interest.....................	$ 3,000	7.01969[b]	$ 21,059
Principal....................	$100,000	0.78941[c]	78,941
			$100,000

[a] Mechanics of using tables to compute present values are explained in Appendix A at the end of the text. Present value factors are taken from tables provided in Appendix A.
[b] Present value of ordinary annuity for 8 periods discounted at 3% per period.
[c] Present value of single payment in 8 periods, hence discounted at 3% per period.

Because the bond contract pays investors a 6% annual rate when investors demand a 6% market rate, investors purchase these bonds at the **par (face) value** of $1,000 per bond, or $100,000 in total.[4] Using a financial calculator, we can compute the bond value as follows: N = 8; I/Yr = 3; PMT = 3,000; FV = 100,000:

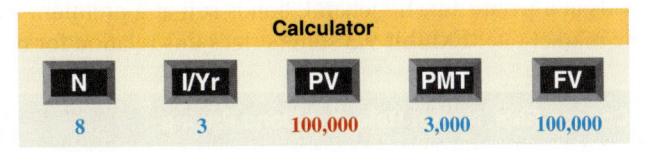

Calculator				
N	I/Yr	PV	PMT	FV
8	3	100,000	3,000	100,000

Bonds Issued at a Discount As a second illustration, assume that market conditions are such that investors demand an 8% annual yield (4% semiannual) for the 6% coupon bond, while all other details remain the same. The bond now sells for $93,267, computed as follows:

	Payment	Present Value Factor	Present Value
Interest.....................	$ 3,000	6.73274[a]	$20,198
Principal....................	$100,000	0.73069[b]	73,069
			$93,267

[a] Present value of ordinary annuity for 8 periods discounted at 4% per period.
[b] Present value of single payment in 8 periods, hence discounted at 4% per period.

---

[3] Semiannual interest payments are typical for bonds. With semiannual interest payments, the issuer pays bondholders two interest payments per year. The semiannual interest rate is the annual rate divided by two.

[4] If we purchase a bond after the semiannual interest date, we must pay accrued interest in addition to the purchase price. This interest is returned to us in the regular interest payment. (This procedure makes the bookkeeping easier for the issuer/underwriter.)

Using a financial calculator, the bond is priced as follows: N = 8; I/Yr = 4; PMT = 3,000; FV = 100,000:

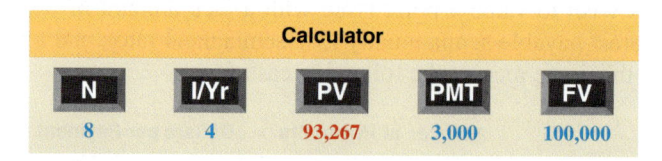

Calculator				
N	**I/Yr**	**PV**	**PMT**	**FV**
8	4	93,267	3,000	100,000

The market price of the bond issue is, therefore, $93,267. The price of each bond in the bond issue is $932.67 (= $93,267/100).

Because the bond carries a coupon rate *lower* than that which investors demand, the bond is less desirable and sells at a **discount**. In general, bonds sell at a discount whenever the coupon rate is less than the market rate.[5]

Bonds Issued at a Premium As a third illustration, assume that investors in the bond market demand a 4% annual yield (2% semiannual) for the 6% coupon bonds, while all other details remain the same. The bond issue now sells for $107,325, computed as follows:

	Payment	Present Value Factor	Present Value
Interest	$ 3,000	7.32548[a]	$ 21,976
Principal	$100,000	0.85349[b]	85,349
			$107,325

[a] Present value of ordinary annuity for 8 periods discounted at 2% per period.
[b] Present value of single payment in 8 periods, hence discounted at 2% per period.

Using a financial calculator, the bond is priced as follows: N = 8; I/Yr = 2; PMT = 3,000; FV = 100,000:

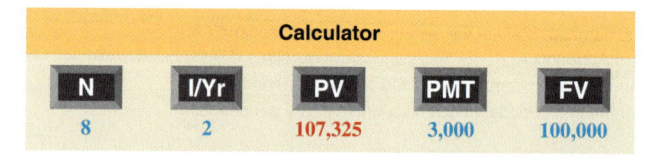

Calculator				
N	**I/Yr**	**PV**	**PMT**	**FV**
8	2	107,325	3,000	100,000

The market price of the bond issue is, therefore, $107,325. The price of each bond in the bond issue is $1,073.25 (= $107,325/100).

Because the bond carries a coupon rate higher than that which investors demand, the bond is more desirable and sells at a **premium**. In general, bonds sell at a premium whenever the coupon rate is greater than the market rate. **Exhibit 9.3** summarizes this relation for bond pricing.

EXHIBIT 9.3 Coupon Rate, Market Rate, and Bond Pricing

Coupon rate > market rate →	Bond sells at a **premium** (above face amount)
Coupon rate = market rate →	Bond sells at **par** (at face amount)
Coupon rate < market rate →	Bond sells at a **discount** (below face amount)

Effective Cost of Debt

When a bond sells for par, the cost to the issuing company is the cash interest paid. In our first illustration where the bond is issued at par, the *effective cost* of the bond is the 6% interest paid by the issuer.

When a bond sells at a discount, the issuer's effective cost consists of two parts: (1) the cash interest paid and (2) the discount incurred. The discount, which is the difference between par and the lower issue price, is a cost that must eventually be reflected in the issuer's income statement

---

[5] Bond prices are often stated in percent form. For example, a bond sold at par is said to be sold at 100 (that is, 100% of its face value, par). The bond sold at $932.67 is said to be sold at 93.267 (93.267% of par, computed as $932.67/$1,000).

as an expense. This fact means that the effective cost of a discount bond is greater than if the bond had sold at par. A discount is a cost and, like any other cost, must eventually be transferred from the balance sheet to the income statement as an expense. In the previous section's discount example, the economic substance is that the bond issuer has not borrowed $100,000 at 6%, but rather $93,267 at 8%.

When a bond sells at a premium, the issuer's effective cost consists of (1) the cash interest paid and (2) a cost reduction due to the premium received. The premium is a benefit that must eventually find its way from the balance sheet to the income statement as a *reduction* of interest expense. As a result of the premium, the effective cost of a premium bond is less than if the bond had sold at par. Effectively, the bond issuer has borrowed $107,325 at 4% in the premium example above.

Bonds are priced to yield the return (market rate) demanded by investors in the bond market, which results in the effective interest rate of a bond *always* equaling the yield (market) rate, regardless of the coupon (stated) rate of the bond. Bond prices are set by the market so as to always yield the rate required by investors based on the terms and qualities of the bond. Companies cannot influence the effective cost of debt by raising or lowering the coupon rate. We discuss the factors affecting the market yield later in the chapter.

The effective cost of debt is ultimately reflected in the amount reported in the issuer's income statement as interest expense. This amount can be, and usually is, different from the cash interest paid. The two are the same only for a bond issued at par. The next section discusses how management reports bonds on the balance sheet and interest expense on the income statement.

Computing Bond Issue Price

LO9-3 **Review 9-3**

On January 2, Randall, Inc., issues $500,000 of 4% bonds that pay interest semiannually and mature in ten years. Compute the bond issue price assuming the following market interest (yield) rate per year compounded semiannually. Consider each case separately.

a. 4%
b. 6%
c. 2%

Solution on p. 9-49.

Reporting of Bond Financing

This section identifies and describes the financial statement effects of bond transactions.

Bonds Issued at Par When a bond sells at par, the issuing company receives the cash proceeds and accepts an obligation to make payments per the bond contract. Specifically, cash is increased and a liability (bonds payable) is increased by the same amount. Using the facts from our earlier illustration, the issuance of bonds at par has the following financial statement effects. (There is no revenue or expense at the date the bond is issued.)

LO9-4
Analyze and account for financial statement effects of long-term nonoperating liabilities.

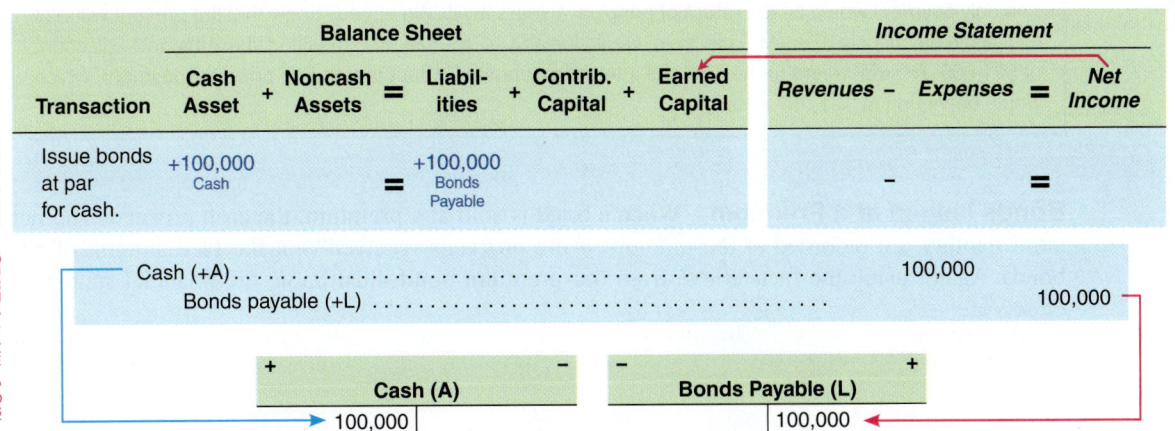

Transaction	Cash Asset	+	Noncash Assets	=	Liabilities	+	Contrib. Capital	+	Earned Capital	Revenues −	Expenses	=	Net Income
Issue bonds at par for cash.	+100,000 Cash			=	+100,000 Bonds Payable					−		=	

Cash (+A) 100,000
    Bonds payable (+L) 100,000

Cash (A) + 100,000
Bonds Payable (L) + 100,000

Bonds Issued at a Discount For the discount bond case, cash is increased by the proceeds from the sale of the bonds, and the liability increases by the same amount. However, the net liability consisting of the two components shown below (including a bond discount contra liability) is reported on the balance sheet.

> **FYI** "Bonds Payable, Net" is a common title reflecting the face value of the bond less the unamortized discount.

Bonds payable, face.	$100,000
Less bond discount.	(6,733)
Bonds payable, net.	$ 93,267

Using the facts above from our bond discount illustration, the financial statement effects follow:

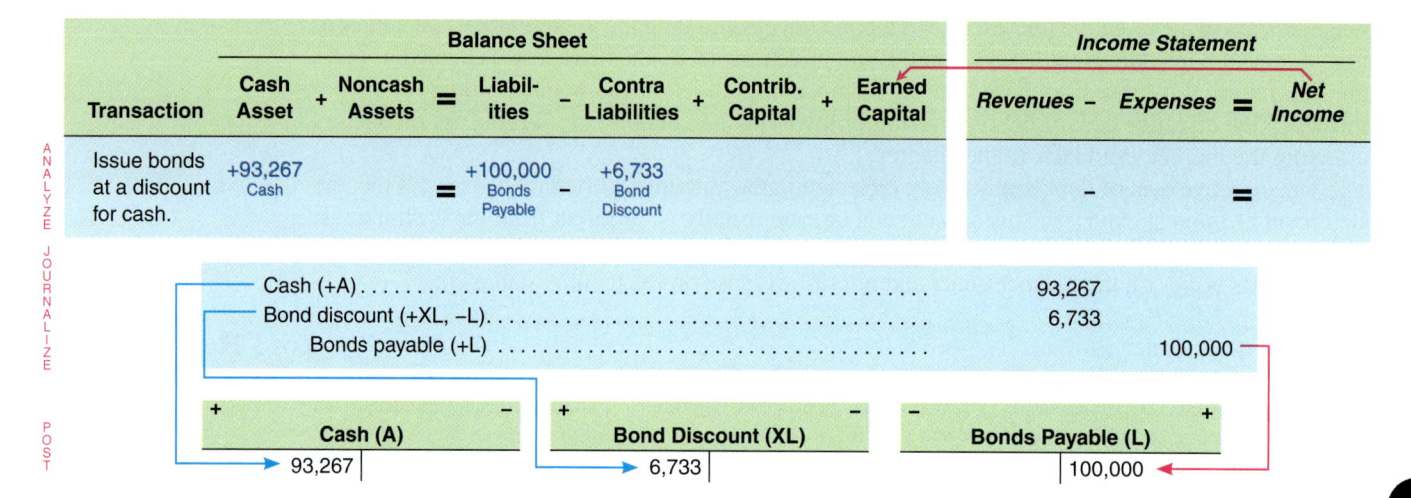

Balance Sheet

Transaction	Cash Asset	+	Noncash Assets	=	Liabilities	–	Contra Liabilities	+	Contrib. Capital	+	Earned Capital
Issue bonds at a discount for cash.	+93,267 Cash			=	+100,000 Bonds Payable	–	+6,733 Bond Discount				

Income Statement

Revenues	–	Expenses	=	Net Income
	–		=	

Cash (+A). 93,267
Bond discount (+XL, –L). 6,733
    Bonds payable (+L) 100,000

+ Cash (A)	– Bond Discount (XL)	– Bonds Payable (L) +
93,267	6,733	100,000

Bonds are reported on the balance sheet net of any discount (or plus any premium). When the bond matures, however, the company is obligated to repay $100,000. Accordingly, at maturity, the bond liability must read $100,000, the amount that is owed. Therefore, between the bond issuance and its maturity, the discount must decline to zero. This reduction of the discount over the life of the bond is called **amortization**. This amortization causes the effective interest expense to be greater than the periodic cash interest payments based on the coupon rate.

> **BUSINESS INSIGHT**
>
> **Zeros and Strips** Zero coupon bonds and notes, called *zeros*, do not carry an explicit coupon rate. However, the pricing of these bonds and notes is done in the same manner as those with coupon rates—the exception is the absence of an interest annuity. This omission means that the price is the present value of just the principal payment at maturity; hence, the bond is sold at a *deep discount*. For example, consider a 4-year, $100,000 zero coupon bond, priced to yield a market rate of 6% that compounds semi-annually. The only payment would be the return of principal 4 years away. We already know that the present value of this single payment is $78,941. This "zero" would initially sell for $78,941, resulting in a substantial discount of $21,059. A "strip" refers to the string of interest payments without the ending principal payment, which would be valued at $21,057 initially.

Bonds Issued at a Premium When a bond is sold at a premium, the cash proceeds and net bond liability are recorded at the amount of the proceeds received (not the face amount of the bond). Again, using the facts above from our premium bond illustration, the financial statement effects are:

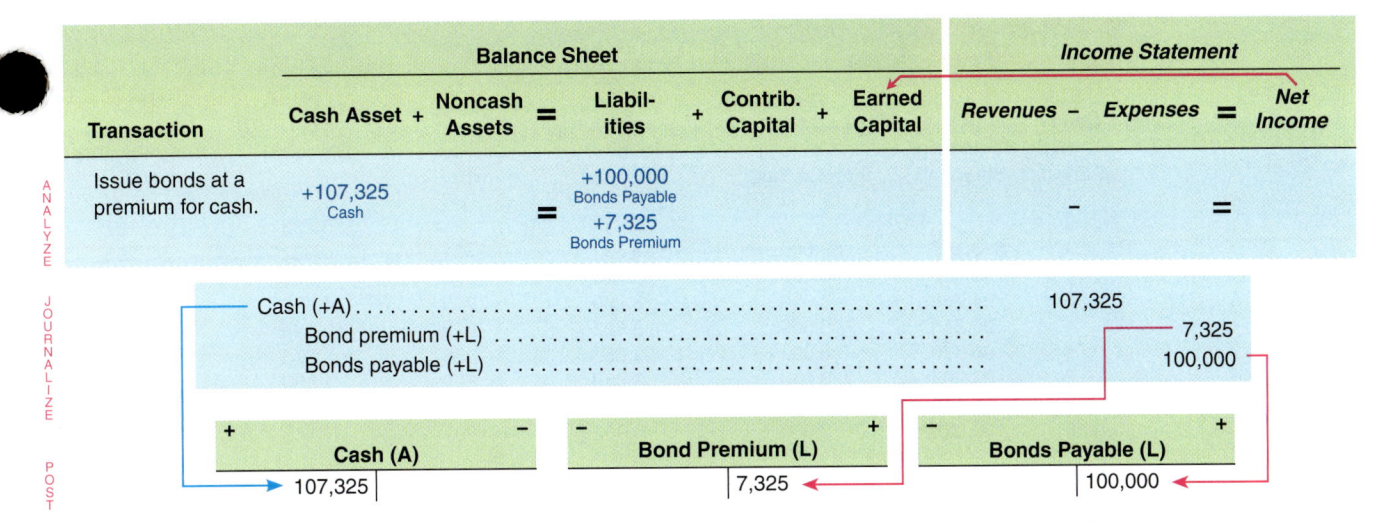

	Balance Sheet						Income Statement		
Transaction	Cash Asset +	Noncash Assets	=	Liabilities	+	Contrib. Capital + Earned Capital	Revenues −	Expenses =	Net Income
Issue bonds at a premium for cash.	+107,325 Cash		=	+100,000 Bonds Payable +7,325 Bonds Premium				−	=

Cash (+A) 107,325
Bond premium (+L) 7,325
Bonds payable (+L) 100,000

Cash (A)	Bond Premium (L)	Bonds Payable (L)
107,325	7,325	100,000

The net bond liability amount reported on the balance sheet, again, consists of two parts:

Bonds payable, face $100,000
Add bond premium 7,325
Bonds payable, net $107,325

The $100,000 must be repaid at maturity, and the premium is amortized to zero over the life of the bond. The premium represents a *benefit,* which yields a *reduction* in interest expense on the income statement.

Effects of Discount and Premium Amortization

The amount of interest expense that is reported on the income statement always equals the loan balance at the beginning of the period (bonds payable, net of discount or premium) times the market interest rate at the time of issue. For bonds issued at par, interest expense equals the cash interest payment. However, for bonds issued at a discount or premium, interest expense reported on the income statement equals interest paid adjusted for the amortization of the discount or premium:

$$\frac{\text{Cash interest paid} + \text{Amortization of discount}}{\text{Interest expense}} \quad \text{or} \quad \frac{\text{Cash interest paid} - \text{Amortization of premium}}{\text{Interest expense}}$$

Specifically, periodic amortization of a discount is added to the cash interest paid to get interest expense for a discount bond. Amortization of the discount reflects the additional cost the issuer incurs from issuance of the bonds at a discount and its recognition, via amortization, as an increase to interest expense. For a premium bond, the premium is a benefit the issuer receives at issuance. Amortization of the premium reduces interest expense over the debt term. Consequently, interest expense on the income statement represents the *effective cost* of debt. (The *nominal cost* of debt is the cash interest paid.) This is true whether the bonds are issued at par, at a discount, or at a premium.

Companies amortize discounts and premiums using the effective interest method. To illustrate, recall the assumptions of the discount bond above—face amount of $100,000, a 6% annual coupon rate payable semiannually (3% semiannual rate), a maturity of 4 years, and a market (yield) rate of 8% annual (4% semiannual). These facts resulted in a bond issue price of $932.67 per bond, or $93,267 for the entire bond issue. **Exhibit 9.4** illustrates a bond discount amortization table for this bond.

EXHIBIT 9.4 — Bond Discount Amortization Table

Semi-Annual Period	[A] Beginning Balance	[B] (Face × coupon%) Cash Interest Paid	[C] ([A] × market%) Interest Expense	[D] ([C] − [B]) Discount Amortization	[E] (Prior bal − [D]) Discount Balance	[F] (Face − [E]) Bond Payable Net
0					$6,733	$ 93,267
1	$93,267	$3,000	$3,731	$731	6,002	93,998
2	93,998	3,000	3,760	760	5,242	94,758
3	94,758	3,000	3,790	790	4,452	95,548
4	95,548	3,000	3,822	822	3,630	96,370
5	96,370	3,000	3,855	855	2,775	97,225
6	97,225	3,000	3,889	889	1,886	98,114
7	98,114	3,000	3,925	925	962*	99,038
8	99,038	3,000	3,962	962	0	100,000

* rounding

The interest period is denoted in the left-most column. Period 0 is the point in time at which the bond is issued. Periods 1–8 are successive six-month interest periods. (Recall, interest is paid semiannually.) Column [B] is cash interest paid, which is a constant $3,000 per period (face amount × coupon rate). Column [C] is interest expense, which is reported in the income statement. This column is computed as the carrying amount of the bond at the beginning of the period (column [A]) multiplied by the 4% semiannual yield rate used to compute the bond issue price. Column [D] is discount amortization, which is the difference between interest expense and cash interest paid. Column [E] is the discount balance, which is the previous balance of the discount less the discount amortization in column [D]. Column [F] is the net bond payable, which is the $100,000 face amount less the unamortized discount from column [E]. Column [A] is the value from the previous period's column [F].

The amortization process continues until period 8, at which time the discount balance is $0 and the net bond payable is $100,000 (the maturity value). An amortization table reveals the financial statement effects of the bond for its duration. Specifically, we see the cash effects in column [B], the income statement effects in column [C], and the balance sheet effects in columns [D], [E], and [F].

To record the interest payment at the end of period 1, we use the values in row 1 of the amortization table. The resulting entry is recorded as follows:

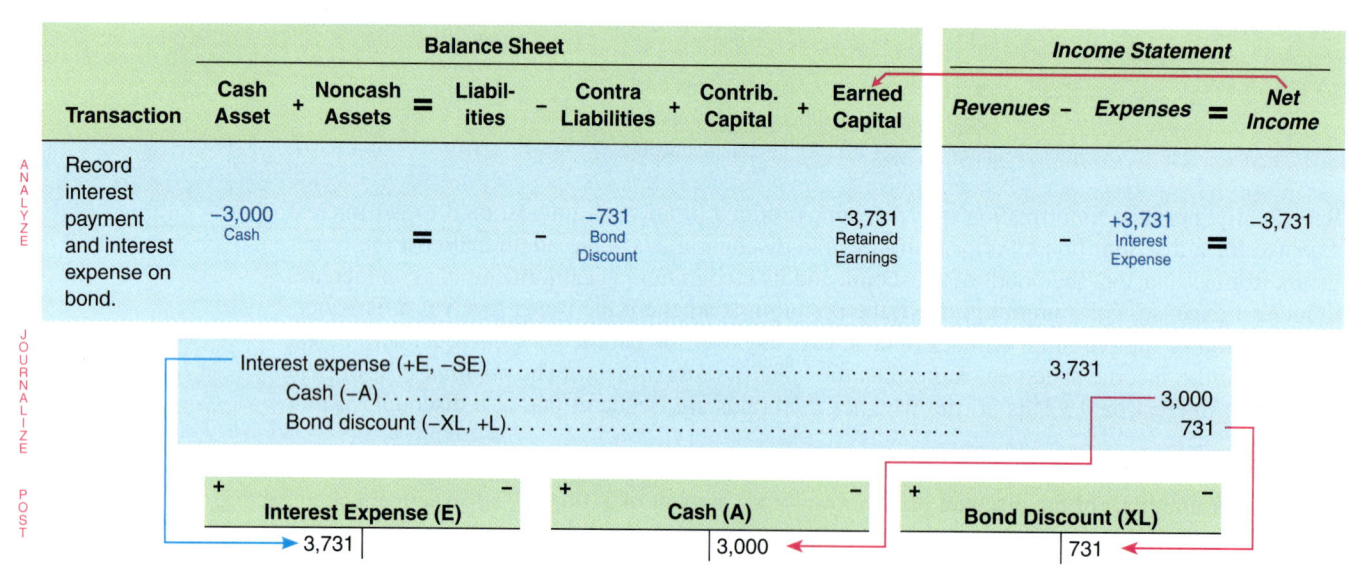

ANALYZE

Transaction	Balance Sheet	Income Statement
	Cash Asset + Noncash Assets = Liabilities − Contra Liabilities + Contrib. Capital + Earned Capital	Revenues − Expenses = Net Income
Record interest payment and interest expense on bond.	−3,000 Cash = −731 Bond Discount −3,731 Retained Earnings	+3,731 Interest Expense = −3,731

JOURNALIZE

Interest expense (+E, −SE) 3,731
    Cash (−A) 3,000
    Bond discount (−XL, +L) 731

POST

+ Interest Expense (E) −	− Cash (A) +	+ Bond Discount (XL) −
3,731	3,000	731

To illustrate amortization of a premium bond, we use the assumptions of the premium bond above—$100,000 face value, a 6% annual coupon rate payable semiannually (3% semiannual rate), a maturity of 4 years, and a 4% annual market (yield) rate (2% semiannual). These parameters resulted in a bond issue price of $1,073.25 per bond or $107,325 for the entire bond issue. **Exhibit 9.5** shows the bond premium amortization table for this bond.

EXHIBIT 9.5 — Bond Premium Amortization Table

Semi-Annual Period	[A] Beginning Balance	[B] (Face × coupon%) Cash Interest Paid	[C] ([A] × market%) Interest Expense	[D] ([B] − [C]) Premium Amortization	[E] (Prior bal − [D]) Premium Balance	[F] (Face + [E]) Bond Payable Net
0					$7,325	$107,325
1	$107,325	$3,000	$2,147	$853	6,472	106,472
2	106,472	3,000	2,129	871	5,601	105,601
3	105,601	3,000	2,112	888	4,713	104,713
4	104,713	3,000	2,094	906	3,807	103,807
5	103,807	3,000	2,076	924	2,883	102,883
6	102,883	3,000	2,058	942	1,941	101,941
7	101,941	3,000	2,039	961	980	100,980
8	100,980	3,000	2,020	980	0	100,000

Interest expense is computed using the same process that we used for discount bonds. The difference is that the yield rate is 4% (2% semiannual) in the premium case. Cash interest paid follows from the bond contract (face amount × coupon rate), and the other columns' computations reflect the premium amortization. After period 8, the premium is fully amortized (equals zero) and the net bond payable balance is $100,000, the amount owed at maturity. The book value of bonds issued at a discount starts below the face value and, over time, increases. The book value of bonds issued at a premium starts above the bonds' face value and, over time, decreases. At maturity, the book value of both types of bonds equals the face value that must be paid to the bondholders. Again, an amortization table reveals the financial statement effects of the bond—the cash effects in column [B], the income statement effects in column [C], and the balance sheet effects in columns [D], [E], and [F].

To record the interest payment at the end of period 1, we, again, use the values in row 1 of the amortization table. The resulting entry is recorded as follows:

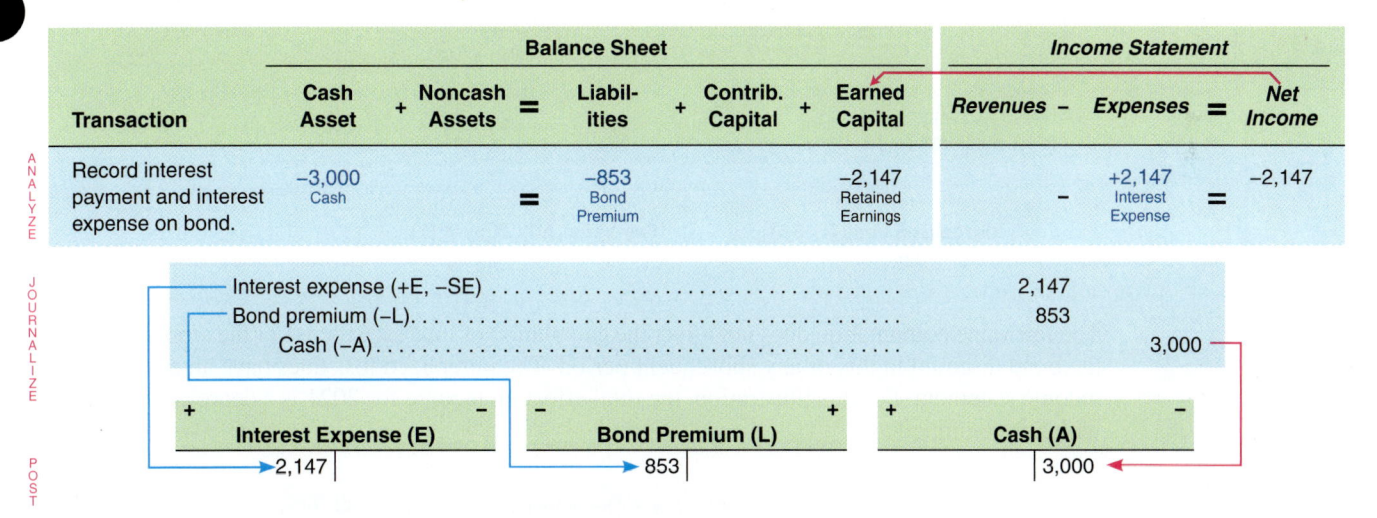

Transaction	Cash Asset	+	Noncash Assets	=	Liabilities	+	Contrib. Capital	+	Earned Capital	Revenues	−	Expenses	=	Net Income
Record interest payment and interest expense on bond.	−3,000 Cash			=	−853 Bond Premium				−2,147 Retained Earnings		−	+2,147 Interest Expense	=	−2,147

Interest expense (+E, −SE) 2,147
Bond premium (−L) 853
  Cash (−A) 3,000

Interest Expense (E) 2,147 | Bond Premium (L) 853 | Cash (A) 3,000

The Fair Value Option

Thus far, we have described the reporting of liabilities at *historical cost*. This means that all financial statement relationships are established on the date that the liability is created and do not subsequently change. For example, the interest rate used to value a bond is the market rate of interest on the date that the bond is issued, and the reported value of the bond is the face value plus the unamortized premium or minus the unamortized discount. Yet, once issued, bonds can be traded in secondary markets. Market interest rates fluctuate and, as a consequence, the market value of a bond is likely to change after the bond is issued.

As an alternative to historical cost, a company may elect to report some or all of its financial liabilities at *fair value*. Moreover, a company may choose to report some of its liabilities at historical cost and others at fair value. It must make this choice at the inception of the liability (e.g., at the time that a bond is issued) and cannot subsequently switch between fair value and historical cost for that liability. If a company elects to report a liability at fair value in its balance sheet, then any changes in fair value are reported as a gain or loss in its income statement. If a liability is to be reported at historical cost, then its fair value is disclosed in the notes.

To illustrate how we report a liability at fair value, we refer to our example of a 4-year, 6% bond issued at a discount to yield 8%. The issue price of this bond is $93,267, and we assume that the bond is issued on June 30, 2021. Six months later, on December 31, the issuing company pays the first of eight coupon payments of $3,000. From **Exhibit 9.4**, we know that after this coupon payment, the bond payable, net of the discount, is equal to $93,998. Now assume that the market value of the bond has increased to $96,943. (This price increase is consistent with a market interest rate that has decreased to 7%.) The bond would now be reported on the balance sheet at a value of $96,943:

Bonds payable	$100,000
Less, unamortized discount	6,002
Bond payable, net (historical cost)	$ 93,998
Plus, fair value adjustment	2,945
Bond payable, net (fair value)	$ 96,943

The increase in the bond's fair value must be added to an account that adjusts the bond payable liability. The balancing entry is included as a loss in the income statement and ends up in retained earnings. The fair value adjustment would be recorded as follows:

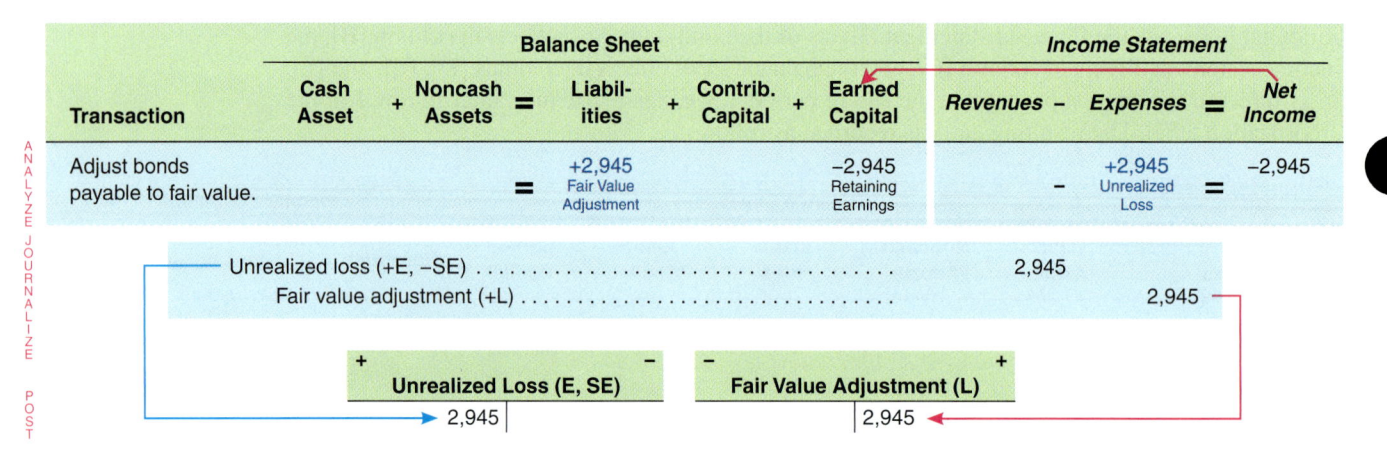

Transaction	Cash Asset	+	Noncash Assets	=	Liabilities	+	Contrib. Capital	+	Earned Capital	Revenues	−	Expenses	=	Net Income
Adjust bonds payable to fair value.				=	+2,945 Fair Value Adjustment				−2,945 Retaining Earnings		−	+2,945 Unrealized Loss	=	−2,945

Unrealized loss (+E, −SE) 2,945
Fair value adjustment (+L) 2,945

Unrealized Loss (E, SE): 2,945
Fair Value Adjustment (L): 2,945

The fair value computation does not affect the calculation of interest expense or the amortization of the bond discount in this or any subsequent period. The unrealized loss does have an effect on the income statement. For this illustration, the total effect on income for 2021 is a decrease of $6,676, which is computed as:

Coupon payment, July 1–December 31	$3,000
Amortization of the bond discount	731
Interest expense	$3,731
Unrealized loss	2,945
Total effect (decrease) on earnings	$6,676

If the fair value of this bond decreases (e.g., because interest rates increase), the fair value adjustment account would be debited and an unrealized gain would be credited and reported in the income statement.[6] We discuss the fair value option further in Chapter 12.

---

[6] In ASC 825, FASB included a requirement that companies separately report in comprehensive income (rather than in net income) the portion of the total change in the fair value of a liability resulting from a change in the instrument-specific credit risk when the entity has elected to value the instrument using the fair-value option. For example, if the entity's own credit quality deteriorates, the company does not report this reduction of the fair value of the liability as income on their income statement, but rather as an item in other comprehensive income.

Effects of Bond Repurchase

Companies can and sometimes do repurchase (also called *redeem*) their bonds prior to maturity. The bond indenture (contract agreement) often includes a **call provision** giving the company the right to repurchase its bond by paying a small premium above face value. Alternatively, the company can repurchase bonds in the open market. When a company uses historical cost to account for its bonds, a bond repurchase usually results in a gain or loss and is computed as follows:

Gain or loss on bond repurchase = Book value of the bond − Repurchase payment

The *book (carrying) value of the bond* is the net amount reported on the balance sheet. If the issuer pays more to retire the bonds than the amount carried on its balance sheet, a loss is reported on its income statement, usually called *loss on bond retirement*. The issuer reports a *gain on bond retirement* if the repurchase price is less than the book value of the bond.

GAAP dictates that any gains or losses on bond repurchases be reported as part of ordinary income unless they meet the criteria for treatment as part of discontinued operations. Relatively few debt retirements meet these criteria and, hence, most gains and losses on bond repurchases are reported as part of income from continuing operations.

The question arises as to how gains and losses on the redemption of bonds should affect our analysis of a company's profitability. Because bonds and notes payable represent nonoperating items, activities including the refunding of bonds and any gain or loss resulting from such activity should be omitted from our computation of net operating profit.

Financial Statement Disclosure Notes

Companies are required to disclose details about their long-term liabilities, including the amounts borrowed under each debt issuance, the interest rates, maturity dates, and other key provisions. Following is Verizon's disclosure in note 7 to its 2020 10-K for its long-term debt ($ millions):

Long-Term Debt
Outstanding long-term obligations as of December 31, 2020 and 2019 are as follows:

At December 31	Maturities	Interest Rates %	2020	2019
Verizon Communications	< 5 Years	0.85–5.51	$ 17,936	$ 19,885
	5–10 Years	1.38–7.75	35,423	30,038
	> 10 Years	1.75–8.95	65,019	47,777
	< 5 Years	Floating	2,917	2,210
	5–10 Years	Floating	941	1,789
Alltel Corporation	5–10 Years	6.80	38	38
	> 10 Years	7.88	58	58
Operating telephone company subsidiaries— debentures	< 5 Years	7.88–8.00	141	141
	5–10 Years	6.00–8.38	317	286
	> 10 Years	5.13–8.75	308	339
GTE LLC	< 5 Years	8.75	141	141
	5–10 Years	6.94	250	250
Other subsidiaries—asset-backed debt	< 5 Years	0.41–3.56	9,414	8,116
	< 5 Years	Floating	1,216	4,277
Finance lease obligations (average rate of 2.5% and 3.2% in 2020 and 2019, respectively)			1,284	1,116
Unamortized discount, net of premium			(6,057)	(4,480)
Unamortized debt issuance costs			(604)	(492)
Total long-term debt, including current maturities			128,742	111,489
Less long-term debt maturing within one year			5,569	10,777
Total long-term debt			$123,173	$100,712

Verizon reported a book value for long-term debt of $128,742 million at year-end 2020. Of this amount, $5,569 million will mature in the next year—hence, its classification as a current liability (current maturities of long-term debt)—and the remainder will mature after 2021. Verizon also reports $6,057 million in unamortized discount (net of unamortized premium) on this debt.

In addition to amounts, rates, and due dates on its long-term debt, Verizon also reports aggregate maturities for the 5 years subsequent to its balance sheet date:

Maturities of Long-Term Debt
Maturities of long-term debt outstanding at December 31, 2020, are as follows ($ millions):

2021	$ 5,227
2022	8,645
2023	7,511
2024	4,286
2025	8,528
Thereafter	93,865

This reporting reveals that Verizon is required to make principal payments of $34,197 million between 2021 and 2025, and $93,865 million thereafter. Such maturities are important, as a company must meet its required payments, negotiate a rescheduling of the indebtedness, or refinance the debt to avoid default. The latter (default) usually has severe consequences, as debt holders have legal remedies available to them that can result in bankruptcy of the company.

Verizon's disclosure on the fair value of its total debt follows:

The fair value of our debt is determined using various methods, including quoted prices for identical debt instruments . . . as well as quoted prices for similar debt instruments with comparable terms and maturities. . . . The fair value of our short-term and long-term debt, excluding finance leases, was as follows ($ millions):

	2020		2019	
At December 31,	Carrying Amount	Fair Value	Carrying Amount	Fair Value
Short-term and long-term debt, excluding finance leases	$127,778	$156,752	$110,373	$129,200

As of December 31, 2020, indebtedness with a book value of $127,778 million had a fair value of $156,752 million, resulting in an unrecognized liability (and loss if the debt is redeemed) of $28,974 million (due mainly to a decline in interest rates subsequent to bond issuance). The justification for not recognizing unrealized gains and losses on the balance sheet and income statement is that such amounts can reverse with future fluctuations in interest rates. Further, because only the face amount of debt is repaid at maturity, unrealized gains and losses that arise during intervening years are not necessarily relevant. (This same logic is used to justify the nonrecognition of gains and losses on held-to-maturity investments in debt securities, a topic covered in Chapter 12.) At this time, Verizon, like most U.S. companies, has elected to report liabilities at historical cost in the financial statements and disclose fair values in the notes.

Sensitivity Analysis
As part of the disclosure, many companies including Verizon also disclose the sensitivity of their estimate of fair value to changes in underlying factors or assumptions. This allows readers to see the effects of changes in assumptions.

The table that follows summarizes the fair values of our long-term debt, including current maturities, and interest rate swap derivatives as of December 31, 2020 and 2019. The table also provides a sensitivity analysis of the estimated fair values of these financial instruments assuming 100-basis-point upward and downward shifts in the yield curve. Our sensitivity analysis does not include the fair

continued

values of our commercial paper and bank loans, if any, because they are not significantly affected by changes in market interest rates.

(dollars in millions) Long-Term Debt and Related Derivatives	Fair Value	Fair Value Assuming + 100 Basis Point Shift	Fair Value Assuming − 100 Basis Point Shift
At December 31, 2020	$155,695	$142,420	$170,423
At December 31, 2019	128,633	119,288	139,980

Interest and the Statement of Cash Flows

GAAP requires that interest payments (and receipts) be included in cash flows from operating activities. For companies using the indirect method for operating cash flows, net income already includes interest expense. Because interest expense does not equal interest payments, the reconciliation of net income to cash flows from operating activities should include an adjustment for any amortization of bond discounts or premiums.

However, interest income and interest expense are typically related to nonoperating assets (investments in securities) and nonoperating liabilities (interest-bearing bonds and notes), respectively. As such, they should be omitted from all computations of net operating profit (as in Appendix A to Chapter 5) and separated from other cash flows when analyzing a company's operations, even though it sometimes requires some digging in the financial statements to determine their magnitudes.

Disclosure of Commitments and Contingencies

All significant contractual commitments must be disclosed in the notes to the financial statements. We discuss this further in Chapter 10.

As discussed above, for contingent liabilities that have a likelihood of occurrence that is probable and the cost that can be estimated, the amount of the liability is recognized on the balance sheet and expensed on the income statement. However, if the liability is only reasonably possible (i.e., less likely than probable), then the liability is disclosed in the notes to the financial statements. If the liability is even less likely to occur than "reasonably possible," then disclosure is permitted but not required.

Many companies are required to include a line item labeled "Commitments and Contingent Liabilities" or some variant of this on the face of the balance sheet.[7] This line item does not have associated amounts on the balance sheet.

The following is Verizon's liability section of the balance sheet, including this line item:

Liabilities and Equity	2020	2019
Current liabilities		
Debt maturing within one year	$ 5,889	$ 10,777
Accounts payable and accrued liabilities	20,658	21,806
Current operating lease liabilities	3,485	3,261
Other	9,628	9,024
Total current liabilities	$ 39,660	$ 44,868
Long-term debt	$123,173	$100,712
Employee benefit obligations	18,657	17,952
Deferred income taxes	35,711	34,703
Non-current operating lease liabilities	18,000	18,393
Other liabilities	12,008	12,264
Total long-term liabilities	$207,549	$184,024
Commitments and Contingencies (Note 16)		

---

[7] Recent SEC guidance (S-X 5-02 (25)) and industrial companies that are SEC registrants include this line item. The SEC requires this caption to appear on the balance sheet whenever a disclosure note bears such a title. If no such disclosure note exists or the only disclosed items are immaterial items, then the caption need not appear on the balance sheet.

Review 9-4 LO9-4

Accounting for Long-Term Nonoperating Liabilities

On January 1, Givoly Company issues $300,000 of 15-year, 10% bonds payable for $351,876, yielding an effective interest rate of 8%. Interest is payable semiannually on June 30 and December 31.

a. Show computations to confirm the issue price of $351,876.
b. Complete the financial statement effects template for (1) bond issuance, (2) semiannual interest payment and premium amortization on June 30, and (3) semiannual interest payment and premium amortization on December 31.
c. Provide Givoly's journal entries and T-accounts for the transactions listed in part b.

Solution on p. 9-49.

ANALYZING FINANCIAL STATEMENTS

LO9-5 Explain how solvency ratios and debt ratings are determined and how they impact the cost of debt.

A major concern of managers and analysts is the solvency of the corporation. In this chapter we revisit two ratios discussed in previous chapters, both of which are designed to measure a firm's solvency. The first ratio is the debt-to-equity ratio (D/E), first introduced in Chapter 1. It measures the extent to which a company relies on debt financing, also known as financial leverage. The second ratio is times interest earned (TIE), which measures the ability of current operations to cover interest costs.

Analysis Objective

We want to gauge the ability of a company to satisfy its long-term debt obligations and remain solvent.

Analysis Tool Debt-to-Equity Ratio

$$\text{Debt-to-equity ratio (D/E)} = \frac{\text{Total liabilities}}{\text{Total stockholders' equity}}$$

Applying the Ratio to Verizon

2018: $\frac{\$210,119}{\$54,710}$ = 3.84 or 384%

2019: $\frac{\$228,892}{\$62,835}$ = 3.64 or 364%

2020: $\frac{\$247,209}{\$69,272}$ = 3.57 or 357%

Guidance A debt-to-equity ratio equal to 1.0 implies that the company is relying on debt and equity financing in equal amounts. As a company's reliance on debt increases and the company's long-term solvency becomes more of a concern, this ratio increases. A debt-to-equity ratio of about 1.3 is about average, though **Exhibit 5.13** (in Chapter 5) shows that the ratio varies by industry, and the median debt-to-equity ratio for telecommunications companies is 1.60.

---

[8] On the balance sheet after "Commitments and contingencies" is what is known as a mezzanine section of the balance sheet (meaning in between the liabilities section and equity section of the balance sheet). This section contains certain types of redeemable preferred stocks, redeemable noncontrolling interests, and some types of convertible notes. These are debt-equity hybrid securities, meaning they have some characteristics of debt and some characteristics of equity. A detailed discussion of each of these securities is outside the scope of this text. For most ratio analysis in this introductory-level textbook, we include all the securities in the mezzanine section as either debt or equity for the sake of simplicity. Analysts or other financial statement users might go into more detail and view some of these securities as debt and some of the securities as equity in their analyses. We note that IFRS does not have a mezzanine section of the balance sheet.

Verizon in Context

Debt-to-Equity Ratio

Competitors

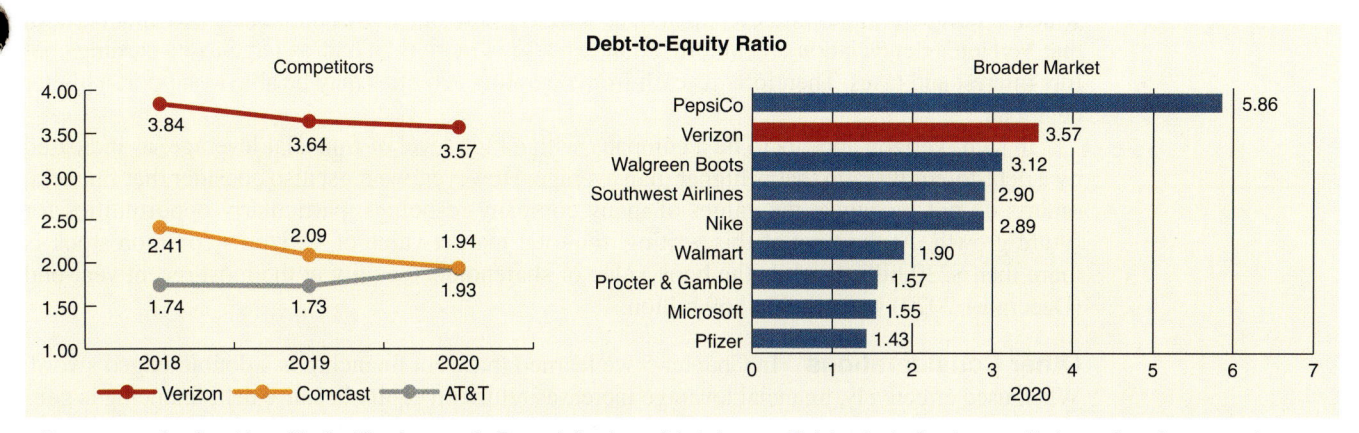

	2018	2019	2020
Verizon	3.84	3.64	3.57
Comcast	2.41	2.09	1.94
AT&T	1.74	1.73	1.93

Broader Market (2020)

PepsiCo	5.86
Verizon	3.57
Walgreen Boots	3.12
Southwest Airlines	2.90
Nike	2.89
Walmart	1.90
Procter & Gamble	1.57
Microsoft	1.55
Pfizer	1.43

These companies do not have identical fiscal year ends. For each fiscal year listed above and in later charts, fiscal year-end balance sheet dates range from January 31 to December 31. For example, Walmart has a fiscal year-end of January 31, 2020, and Pfizer has a fiscal year-end of December 31, 2020.

Analysis Tool Times Interest Earned

$$\text{Times interest earned (TIE)} = \frac{\text{Earnings before interest and taxes}}{\text{Interest expense}}$$

Applying the Ratio to Verizon

2018: $\dfrac{\$24{,}456}{\$4{,}833} = 5.1$ times

2019: $\dfrac{\$27{,}463}{\$4{,}730} = 5.8$ times

2020: $\dfrac{\$28{,}214}{\$4{,}247} = 6.6$ times

Guidance When a company relies on debt financing, it assumes the burden of paying the interest on the debt. The times interest earned ratio measures the burden of interest costs by comparing earnings before interest and taxes (EBIT) to annual interest expense. A high TIE ratio indicates that a company is able to meet its interest costs without adversely affecting profitability. The median TIE for the telecommunications industry is 3.77.

Verizon in Context

Times Interest Earned Ratio

Competitors

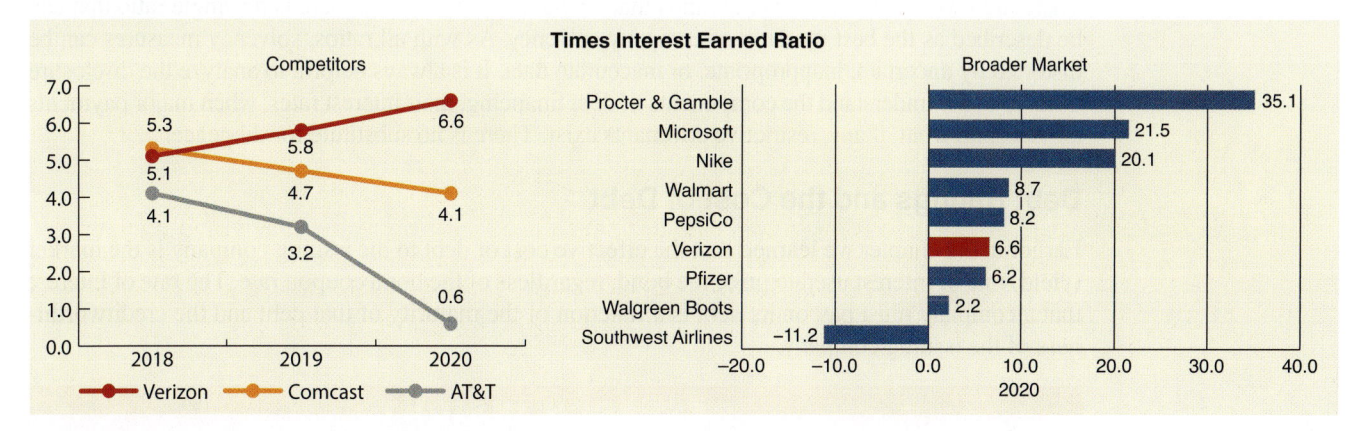

	2018	2019	2020
Verizon	5.1	5.8	6.6
Comcast	5.3	4.7	4.1
AT&T	4.1	3.2	0.6

Broader Market (2020)

Procter & Gamble	35.1
Microsoft	21.5
Nike	20.1
Walmart	8.7
PepsiCo	8.2
Verizon	6.6
Pfizer	6.2
Walgreen Boots	2.2
Southwest Airlines	−11.2

Takeaways Before 2014, Verizon's debt-to-equity ratio was lower than either Comcast or AT&T, two of its competitors. In 2014, Verizon engaged in a transaction to buy out the 45% equity interest of its wireless partner (Vodafone Group Plc) that had the effect of reducing its cash and reducing its shareholders' equity by a substantial amount. Verizon's debt-to-equity ratio increased significantly in 2014; the ratio has been in steady decline ever since. Its times interest earned ratio is lower than the other featured companies in this text, but well in excess of that of its industry and its close competitors. The size of this ratio is driven by two factors—the amount of debt financing, which in turn determines interest expense, as well as profitability. We should also take into account that Verizon's depreciation and amortization expense is more than half as large as its earnings before interest and taxes. Therefore, its cash from operating activities may be able to support a higher debt load.

In sum, Verizon appears to be a company with a high level of financial leverage, as indicated by a debt-to-equity ratio that is higher than average. However, we must also consider that financial reports do not recognize the values of many company resources, particularly opportunities for future growth. At the time of this writing, the total market value of Verizon's common stock is more than $230 billion, while the book value of shareholders' equity at the most recent year-end (December 2020) was roughly $69 billion.

Other Considerations In Chapter 5 we learned that debt financing is a double-edged sword. When used effectively, financial leverage increases return on equity because debt financing is generally less costly than equity financing. However, debt carries with it the risk of **default**, which is the risk that the company will be unable to pay its obligations when they come due (insolvency). To provide some protection against default risk, creditors usually require a company to execute a loan agreement that places restrictions on the company's activities. These restrictions, called covenants, impose indirect costs on a firm beyond the explicit cost of interest, and these indirect costs tend to increase as a company increases its reliance on debt financing. When a company's solvency ratios are close to the limits specified by its covenants, management is more likely to pass up profitable investment opportunities or engage in counterproductive earnings management activities to avoid violating these restrictions.

Walgreens Boots Alliance, Inc., (Walgreens), has several revolving credit facilities with aggregate borrowing capacity of $11.5 billion as of its year-end, August 31, 2020. In a disclosure note and in another section of its 10-K, Walgreens reports:

> Each of the Company's credit facilities described above contain a covenant to maintain, as of the last day of each fiscal quarter, a ratio of consolidated debt to total capitalization not to exceed 0.60:1.00.... The credit facilities contain various other customary covenants. As of August 31, 2020, the Company was in compliance with all such applicable covenants. . . .
>
> If we breach any of these restrictions or covenants and do not obtain a waiver from the lenders, then, subject to applicable cure periods, our outstanding indebtedness could be declared immediately due and payable. This could have a material adverse effect on our business operations and financial condition.

In prior years, the company has also mentioned other covenant restrictions more specifically, such as maintaining a minimum net worth and limitations on the sale of assets and purchases of investment. There are several variations on the ratios that we have discussed, and there is no single ratio that can be described as the best measure of company solvency. As with all ratios, solvency measures can be distorted by uncertain, inappropriate, or inaccurate data. It is always helpful to analyze the disclosure notes to better understand the components of debt financing, their interest rates, when major payments are due, and what, if any, restrictive covenants exist. There is no substitute for diligence.

Debt Ratings and the Cost of Debt

Earlier in the chapter we learned that the effective cost of debt to the issuing company is the market (yield) rate of interest used to price the bond, regardless of the bond coupon rate. The rate of interest that a company must pay on its debt is a function of the maturity of that debt and the creditworthiness of the issuing company.

RESEARCH INSIGHT

Accounting Conservatism and Cost of Debt Research indicates that companies applying more conservative accounting methods incur a lower cost of debt. Research also suggests that while accounting conservatism can lead to lower-quality accounting income (because such income does not fully reflect economic reality), creditors are more confident in the numbers and view them as more credible. Evidence also implies that companies can lower the required return demanded by creditors (the risk premium) by issuing high-quality financial reports that include enhanced note disclosures and detailed supplemental reports.

A company's debt rating, also referred to as credit quality and creditworthiness, is related to default risk. Companies seeking to obtain bond financing from the capital markets normally first seek a rating on their proposed debt issuance from one of several rating agencies, such as **Standard & Poor's**, **Moody's Investors Service**, or **Fitch**. The aim of rating agencies is to rate debt so that its default risk is more accurately determined and priced by the market. Such debt issuances carry debt ratings from one or more of the three large rating agencies, as shown in **Exhibit 9.6**. This exhibit includes the general description attached to the debt for each rating class—for example, AAA is assigned to debt of prime maximum safety (maximum creditworthiness). Bonds with credit ratings below investment grade (below Baa or BBB) are referred to as "high yield" bonds or, more pejoratively, "junk bonds," which may not be purchased by many professionally managed portfolios.[9]

EXHIBIT 9.6 — Corporate Debt Ratings and Descriptions

Moody's	S&P	Fitch	Description
Aaa	AAA	AAA	Prime Maximum Safety
Aa	AA	AA	High Grade, High Quality
A	A	A	Upper-Medium Grade
Baa	BBB	BBB	Lower-Medium Grade
Ba	BB	BB	Non-Investment Grade
B	B	B	Speculative
Caa	CCC	CCC	Substantial Risk
Ca	CC	CC	Extremely Speculative
C	C	C	Exceptionally High Risk
	D		Default

YOU MAKE THE CALL

You are the Vice President of Finance Your company is currently rated BB by credit rating agencies. You are considering possible financial and other restructurings of the company to increase your credit rating. What types of restructurings might you consider? What benefits will your company receive from those restructurings? What costs will your company incur to implement such restructurings? [Answers on page 9-33]

Walgreens provides detailed disclosures about its ratings in its 2020 10-K.

Credit ratings
As of October 14, 2020, the credit ratings of Walgreens Boots Alliance were:

Rating Agency	Long-Term Debt Rating	Commercial Paper Rating	Outlook
Fitch	BBB–	F3	Stable
Moody's	Baa2	P-2	Negative
Standard & Poor's	BBB	A-2	Negative

In assessing the Company's credit strength, each rating agency considers various factors including the Company's business model, capital structure, financial policies, and financial performance. There can be no assurance that any particular rating will be assigned or maintained. The Company's credit ratings impact its borrowing costs, access to capital markets, and operating lease costs. The rating agency ratings are not recommendations to buy, sell, or hold the Company's debt securities or commercial paper. Each rating may be subject to revision or withdrawal at any time by the assigning rating agency and should be evaluated independently of any other rating.

Two years ago, all three ratings agencies gave an outlook of "stable," but Walgreens credit ratings have slipped a little in recent years. Revenues grew by 2% in 2020, while operating income decreased by 74%. The change in accounting for leases caused Walgreens' debt-to-equity ratio to go

---

[9] Standard & Poor's and Fitch modify their ratings to more detail with the addition of a plus (+) or minus (−) sign (e.g., BBB+, BBB, BBB−). Similarly, Moody's uses numerical modifiers within ratings (e.g., Aa1, Aa2, Aa3).

from 1.8 to 3.1. The 2020 ratings above are bordering on the "high yield" range, which could affect the company's ability to access the debt market.

It is these ratings that, in conjunction with the maturity of its bonds, establish the market interest rate and consequent selling price. There are a number of considerations that affect the rating of a bond. **Standard & Poor's** lists the following factors among its credit rating criteria:

Business Risk
- Industry characteristics
- Competitive position (e.g., marketing, technology, efficiency, regulation)
- Management

Financial Risk
- Financial characteristics
- Financial policy
- Profitability
- Capital structure
- Cash flow protection
- Financial flexibility

Rating agencies use a number of accounting ratios to help establish creditworthiness, including measures of liquidity, solvency, and profitability. These ratios are variants of the ratios we describe in Chapter 5 and in this chapter, especially those used to assess solvency.

There are other relevant factors in setting debt ratings, including the following:

- **Collateral** Companies can provide security for debt in the form of mortgages on assets. To the extent debt is secured, the debt holder is in a preferred position vis-à-vis other creditors.

- **Covenants** Debt agreements (indentures) can contain restrictions on the issuing company to protect debt holders. Examples are restrictions on excessive dividend payment, on other company acquisitions, on further borrowing, and on maintaining minimum levels for key liquidity and solvency ratios. These covenants provide debt holders some means of control over the issuer's operations because, unlike equity investors, they do not have voting rights.

- **Options** Debt obligations involve contracts between the borrowing company and debt holders. Options are sometimes written into debt contracts. Examples are options to convert debt into stock (so that debt holders have a stake in value creation) and options allowing the issuing company to repurchase its debt before maturity (usually at a premium).

Review 9-5 LO9-5

Computing Solvency Ratios

Presented below is information reported in the financial statements of Macy's Inc., Nordstrom Inc., and Bed Bath & Beyond, Inc., for the fiscal years ended in February (or March) of 2020 and 2019 ($ millions).

($ million)	Fiscal Year Ended	Income (Loss) before Income Taxes	Interest Expense
Macy's.	Feb. 01, 2020	$ 728	$ 205
Macy's.	Feb. 02, 2019	1,420	261
Nordstrom.	Feb. 01, 2020	682	112
Nordstrom.	Feb. 02, 2019	733	119
Bed Bath & Beyond	Feb. 29, 2020	(764.9)	64.8
Bed Bath & Beyond	Mar. 02, 2019	(156.6)	69.5

a. Compute the times interest earned ratio for each company for the fiscal years ended in 2020 and 2019.
b. Comment on trends in solvency.

Solution on p. 9-50.

SUMMARY

Identify and account for current operating liabilities. (p. 9-4) — **LO9-1**

- Current liabilities are short-term and generally non-interest-bearing; accordingly, firms try to maximize the financing of their assets using these sources of funds.
- ROE increases when firms make use of accounts payable increases to finance operating assets; a firm must avoid excessive "leaning on the trade" for short-term gains that can damage long-term supplier relationships.
- When cash discounts are offered by creditors, companies use the net of discount method to report accounts payable information.
- Accrued liabilities reflect amounts that have been recognized as expenses in the current (or a prior) period, but not yet paid.
- While all accruals result in a liability on the balance sheet and an expense on the income statement, management has latitude in determining (in some cases, estimating) their amount and timing; this discretion offers the opportunity for managing earnings.

Describe and account for current nonoperating (financial) liabilities. (p. 9-10) — **LO9-2**

- Management will generally try to ensure that the debt service on financial (nonoperating) liabilities coincides with the cash flows from the assets financed.
- When large amounts of financing are required for, say, plant and equipment, firms find that bonds, notes, and other forms of long-term financing provide a cost-efficient means of raising capital.

Explain and illustrate the pricing of long-term nonoperating liabilities. (p. 9-13) — **LO9-3**

- The coupon rate indicated on a bond contract determines the periodic interest payment. The required return on any bond called the market (yield or effective) rate is determined by market conditions and rarely equals the coupon (contract) rate. The market rate is used to price the bond and determines the effective cost of the debt to the issuer.
- If the market rate is below the coupon rate, the bond will sell at a premium to its face value, ensuring that the owner of the bond earns only the market rate of interest. If the market rate exceeds the coupon rate, the bond will sell at a discount so that the bond is issued at less than its face value.

Analyze and account for financial statement effects of long-term nonoperating liabilities. (p. 9-18) — **LO9-4**

- A discount for a bond selling below its face value represents additional interest expense over time to the issuer because the issuer received less than face value upon issuance but must pay the holder the face value at the bond's maturity; this discount represents additional interest beyond the coupon payment to the holder. The premium on a bond selling above its face value lowers the interest cost to the issuer.
- Companies may choose to report liabilities at fair value; if the fair value option is elected, changes in fair value are reported as gains and losses in the income statement.[10]
- Gains and losses on bonds repurchased must be reported in operating income, unless they are part of discontinued operations. Such transactions do not represent operating activities, and gains/losses should be removed when determining cash from operations with the indirect method.

Explain how solvency ratios and debt ratings are determined and how they impact the cost of debt. (p. 9-27) — **LO9-5**

- Two debt-related ratios that are particularly useful in evaluating a company's solvency include the debt-to-equity ratio and the times interest earned ratio.
- The market rate of interest to a firm reflects the creditworthiness of the particular issuer. Credit agencies play an important role in this process by issuing debt ratings.
- Borrowing is typically secured by collateral that places the lender in a superior position to other creditors and covenants that put restrictions on the borrower's activities; bonds can also contain options, including those for conversion or repurchase.

---

[10] Unless the change in fair value results from a change in instrument-specific credit risk. If it is caused by instrument-specific credit risk (i.e., a change in fair value because of a change in the credit quality of the issuer), that portion of the change in fair value is reported in other comprehensive income.

GUIDANCE ANSWERS... YOU MAKE THE CALL

You are the Analyst Accrued liabilities must be probable and estimable before they can be reported in the balance sheet. If DowDuPont's environmental costs turn out to be higher than management estimates, it may be understating its liabilities (and overstating equity). As an analyst, if you suspect that DowDuPont's estimate is too low, you should add an additional estimated liability to the company's balance sheet amounts to conduct analysis.

You are the Vice President of Finance The types of restructurings you might consider are those yielding a strengthening of the financial ratios typically used to assess liquidity and solvency by the rating agencies. Such restructurings include inventory reduction to generate cash, the reallocation of cash outflows from investing activities (PPE or intangible assets) to debt reduction, and reducing the cash outflows for repurchases of the company's stock (treasury stock). These actions increase liquidity or reduce financial leverage and, thus, should yield an improved debt rating. An improved debt rating gives the company access to more debt holders, as the current debt rating is below investment grade and is not a suitable investment for many professionally managed portfolios. An improved debt rating also yields a lower interest rate on debt. Offsetting these benefits are costs such as the following: (1) potential loss of sales from inventory stock-outs; (2) potential future cash flow reductions and loss of market power from reduced investing in PPE and intangibles; and (3) possible reductions in share price if shareholders were expecting more cash to be returned in the form of dividends and stock buybacks. All cost and benefits must be assessed before you pursue any restructurings.

KEY RATIOS

$$\text{Debt-to-equity (D/E)} = \frac{\text{Total liabilities}}{\text{Total stockholders' equity}} \qquad \text{Times interest earned (TIE)} = \frac{\text{Earnings before interest and taxes}}{\text{Interest}}$$

Assignments with the MBC logo in the margin are available in *myBusinessCourse*.
See the Preface of the book for details.

MULTIPLE CHOICE

Multiple Choice Answers
1. a 2. b 3. b
4. c 5. a, b, and d

1. Which of the following statements is correct? A decrease in accrued wages liability:
   a. decreases cash flows from operations.
   b. decreases working capital.
   c. increases net income.
   d. increases net nonoperating (financial) assets.

2. On April 1, a firm borrows $18,000 at an annual interest rate of 10% with payments required semiannually on September 30 and March 31. How much interest payable and how much interest expense should appear on the firm's annual report at the end of the firm's fiscal year, December 31?
   a. $1,350 payable and $450 expense.
   b. $450 payable and $1,350 expense.
   c. $900 payable and $900 expense.
   d. $1,350 payable and $900 expense.

3. A firm issues $24,000,000 of 10-year bonds and receives $23.5 million in cash. Which of the following statements is correct?
   a. The bonds do not have a coupon rate because they are zeros.
   b. The market rate exceeds the coupon rate.
   c. The contract rate exceeds the market rate.
   d. The bonds were issued at par.

4. A firm issues $4 million of 10-year, 6% notes with interest paid semiannually. At issuance the firm received $4,654,057 cash reflecting a 4% yield. What is the amount of premium written off against interest expense in the first year the notes are outstanding?
   a. $53,838
   b. $19,622
   c. $54,376
   d. $26,919

5. On May 1 of the current year, Wild, Inc., makes an early repayment of long-term debt due to mature on June 1, two years later. Which of the following ratios for the current year is (are) decreased by this repayment?
   a. Current Ratio
   b. Quick Ratio
   c. Times Interest Earned
   d. Debt-to-Equity

QUESTIONS

Q9-1. What does the term "current liabilities" mean? What assets are usually used to settle current liabilities?

Q9-2. What is the justification for using the net-of-discount method to record inventory purchases when cash discounts are offered?

Q9-3. What is an accrual? How do accruals impact the balance sheet and the income statement?

Q9-4. What is the difference between a bond coupon rate and its market interest rate (yield)?

Q9-5. How does issuing a bond at a premium or discount affect the bond's *effective* interest rate vis-à-vis the coupon (stated) rate?

Q9-6. Why do companies report a gain or loss on the repurchase of their bonds (assuming the repurchase price is different from bond book value)?

Q9-7. How do debt ratings affect the cost of borrowing for a company?

Q9-8. How would you interpret a company's reported gain or loss on the repurchase of its bonds?

Q9-9. What do the following terms mean? (a) bonds payable, (b) call provision, (c) face value, (d) coupon, (e) bond discount, (f) bond premium, and (g) amortization of bond premium or discount.

Q9-10. What are the advantages and disadvantages of issuing bonds rather than common stock?

Q9-11. A $2,500,000 issue of 10-year, 9% bonds was sold at 98 plus accrued interest three months after the bonds were dated. What net amount of cash is received?

Q9-12. How does issuing bonds at a premium or discount "adjust the contract rate to the applicable market rate of interest"?

Q9-13. Regardless of whether premium or discount is involved, what generalization can be made about the change in the book value of bonds payable during the period in which they are outstanding?

Q9-14. If the effective interest amortization method is used for bonds payable, how does the periodic interest expense change over the life of the bonds when they are issued (a) at a discount and (b) at a premium?

Q9-15. How should premium and discount on bonds payable be presented in the balance sheet?

Q9-16. On April 30, one year before maturity, Weber Company retired $400,000 of 9% bonds payable at 101. The book value of the bonds on April 30 was $395,200. Bond interest was last paid on April 30, the date of bond retirement. What is the gain or loss on the retirement of the bonds?

Q9-17. Brownlee Company borrowed money by issuing a 20-year mortgage note payable. The note will be repaid in equal monthly installments. The interest expense component of each payment decreases with each payment. Why?

DATA ANALYTICS

DA9-1. Preparing an Excel Map Visualization of Sales Tax Across States   **LO9-1**

For this exercise, download the Excel file "Table 3: State Tax Collections by State and Type of Tax 2021" obtained at the United States Census Bureau at https://www.census.gov/data/tables/2021/econ/qtax/historical.html. For this exercise, we extract data for *sales and gross receipts taxes by state* for the first quarter of 2021. We then convert the data to a U.S. map chart and analyze the results.

REQUIRED

1. Download Excel file DA9-1 found in myBusinessCourse.
2. Prepare a table by extracting from the U.S. Census Bureau file: General Sales and Gross Receipts Taxes by state for 2021 Q1. You will only be using the General Sales and Gross Receipts data in your analysis. Do not include Washington, D.C. in your table. *Hint:* Eliminate unnecessary data. Then use the Transpose function. (You may want to unmerge cells before transposing the data. After the transposition, you can line up the amounts with the states.) Convert the data to a table as the final step.
3. List the total of the amounts in your table. (Leave the amounts in thousands.)
4. Using the table as a reference, list the states with no tax.
5. Prepare a map chart of the tax by state. *Hint:* Highlight your data; then click on Insert, Maps, and Filled Map. If you're having trouble with the map, try converting the Xs in the Receipts column for states with no taxes to 0s.
6. What is the top and bottom end of the legend automatically prepared for the chart?
7. Answer the following questions using the map visualization:
    a. What three states have the largest tax?

b. Where is there a visible cluster of mid-range taxes on the map if we consider the map in four quadrants?
   c. Where is there the least amount of tax on the map if we consider the map in four quadrants?
8. Is the amount of sales tax dependent only on the volume of sales activity in the state?
9. Does the map visualization provide information on the sales tax rate by state?

LO9-5 DA9-2. Preparing Excel Schedules to Determine Compliance with Debt Agreements

Monroe Inc. (the Company) obtained financing from Pro Bank in Year 8. Associated with the debt agreement are debt covenants, which place restrictions on the Company's activities. The intention of the covenants is to protect the lender (Pro Bank) from a situation where the Company is unable to pay the debt when it is due. A debt agreement will include any debt covenants along with details on any calculations involved. From the debt agreement between Monroe Inc. and Pro Bank, the financial covenants are included below. Key definitions of certain terms are also included.

FINANCIAL COVENANTS

1. Total Leverage Ratio. The Company will not, as of the last day of any fiscal quarter, permit the Total Leverage Ratio to be greater than 2.00 to 1.00.
2. Minimum EBITDA. The Company will not, as of the last day of any fiscal quarter, permit EBITDA, for the period of the quarter ending on or immediately prior to such date to be less than $300 million.
3. Funded Debt. The Company will not, at any time, permit the aggregate outstanding principal amount of all Funded Debt to exceed an amount equal to 10% of the Company's total assets (as determined as of the last day of the most recently ended fiscal quarter for which financial statements have been provided).

DEFINITIONS

- *Total Leverage Ratio:* As of any date of determination, the ratio of (a) Funded Debt on such date to (b) EBITDA for the quarter ending on or immediately prior to such date.
- *EBITDA:* For any period, the sum of the following, for the Company in accordance with GAAP: Net income for such period plus (b) the sum of the following, to the extent deducted in determining net income for such period: (1) income tax expense during such period, (2) interest expense, net of interest income for such period, and (3) amortization and depreciation expense.
- *Funded Debt:* As of the date of determination with respect to the Company, the sum of all liabilities of the Company due to borrowing money.

The Excel file associated with this exercise includes quarterly financial information for Monroe Inc. from Quarter 1 of Year 10 to Quarter 2 of Year 12.

REQUIRED

1. Download Excel file DA9-2 found in myBusinessCourse.
2. Determine the key financial categories needed to determine whether the company is in compliance with the three financial covenants for each quarter presented.
3. Calculate the key financial amounts within the Excel worksheet.
4. Create an IF statement for each financial covenant per quarter that returns a "YES" if the company is in compliance at quarter end, or a "NO" if the company is not in compliance at quarter end.
5. List the formula for the IF statement for Q1 Year 10 for the first financial statement covenant.
6. Add a rule to your IF statement to shade the cell where YES is contained in green and a rule to shade the cell where NO is contained in red. *Hint:* Under the Home tab, click on Conditional formatting, Highlight cell rules, Text that contains, and then set up two rules.
7. Indicate the quarter ends (if any) where the company is not in compliance with the financial covenants.
8. Create *What-if Scenario 1* by duplicating the original schedule created. Assume that Funded Debt was higher by 10% at each quarter-end. Increase interest expense by 10% as well as Funded Debt. Assume no other changes in the financial data provided.
9. Indicate the quarter ends (if any) where the company is not in compliance with the financial covenants based on the schedule created in part 8.
10. Create *What-if Scenario 2* by duplicating the original schedule created. Assume that total assets were lower by 10% each quarter-end. Assume no other changes in the financial data provided.
11. Indicate the quarter ends (if any) where the company is not in compliance with the financial covenants based on the schedule created in part 10.
12. Determine the minimum required net income for each quarter in order to be in compliance with the second financial covenant, using the original data. Use 30% of earnings before tax as an estimate for tax expense. Round tax expense to one decimal place.

13. Determine the quarter where there is the smallest difference between net income reported and the minimum net income required to meet the second financial covenant.

DATA VISUALIZATION

Data Visualization Activities are available in myBusinessCourse. These assignments use Tableau Dashboards to expose students to visual depictions of data and introduce students to data analytics through data visualizations. These exercises are easily assignable and auto graded by MBC.

MINI EXERCISES

M9-18. Recording Cash Discounts (FSET)   LO9-1

On November 15, Shields Company purchased inventory costing $9,300 on credit. The credit terms were 2/10, n/30.

a. Assume that Shields Company paid the invoice on November 23. Using the financial statement effects template, report entries to record the purchase of this inventory and the cash payment to the supplier applying the net-of-discount method.

Transaction	Balance Sheet					Income Statement		
	Cash Asset	+ Noncash Assets	= Liabilities	+ Contrib. Capital	+ Earned Capital	Revenues	− Expenses	= Net Income

b. Compute the cost of a lost discount as an annual percentage rate.

M9-19. Recording Cash Discounts   LO9-1

Using the information from M9-18, complete the following.

a. Prepare journal entries to record the purchase of this inventory and the cash payment to the supplier applying the net-of-discount method.
b. Set up the necessary T-accounts and post the journal entries to the T-accounts.

M9-20. Recording Cash Discounts (FSET)   LO9-1

Schrand Corporation purchased materials from a supplier that offers credit terms of 2/15, n/60. It purchased $10,000 of merchandise inventory from that supplier on January 20.

a. Assume that Schrand Corporation paid the invoice on February 15. Using the financial statement effects template, report the purchase of this inventory and the cash payment to the supplier using the net-of-discount method.
b. Compute the cost of a lost discount as an annual percentage rate.

M9-21. Recording Cash Discounts   LO9-1

Using the information from M9-20, complete the following.

a. Prepare journal entries to record the purchase of this inventory and the cash payment to the supplier applying the net-of-discount method.
b. Set up the necessary T-accounts and post the journal entries to the T-accounts.

M9-22. Analyzing and Computing Financial Statement Effects of Loan Interest (FSET)   LO9-2

Huddart Company gave a creditor a 90-day, 8% note payable for $5,400 on December 16. Record the year-end December 31 accounting adjustment Huddart must make in the financial statement effects template. (Round to the nearest dollar.)

M9-23. Analyzing and Computing Financial Statement Effects of Loan Interest   LO9-2

Using the information from M9-22, complete the following.

a. Prepare the journal entry to record the year-end December 31 accounting adjustment Huddart must make. (Round to the nearest dollar.)
b. Post the journal entry to its respective T-accounts.

M9-24. Analyzing and Determining the Amount of a Liability   LO9-1, 2

For each of the following situations, indicate the liability amount, if any, which is reported on the balance sheet of Hirst, Inc., at December 31.

a. Hirst owes $82,500 at year-end for its inventory purchases.
b. On December 31, Hirst agreed to purchase a $21,000 drill press in January of the following year.

c. During November and December, Hirst sold products to a firm with a 90-day warranty against product failure. Estimated costs in the following year of honoring this warranty are $1,650.
d. Hirst provides a profit-sharing bonus for its executives equal to 5% of its reported pretax annual income. The estimated pretax income for this year is $450,000. Bonuses are not paid until January of the following year.

LO9-3, 5
Microsoft Corporation
NASDAQ :: MSFT

M9-25. Interpreting Relations Between Bond Price, Coupon, Yield, and Rating
In January 2017, **Microsoft Corporation** issued $17 billion of bonds in seven parts, with maturities ranging from 2020 to 2057. The bond issue was rated Aaa by Moody's. Two of the bond offerings are described below.

> Amount: $4 billion; Maturity: February 6, 2027; Coupon: 3.3%; Price: 99.31; Yield: 3.383%.
> Amount: $2 billion; Maturity: February 6, 2057; Coupon: 4.5%; Price: 99.49; Yield: 4.528%.

a. Discuss the relation between the coupon rate, issuance price, and yield for the 2027 issue.
b. Compare the yields on the two bond issues. Why are the yields different when the bond ratings are the same?

LO9-4

M9-26. Determining Gain or Loss on Bond Redemption
On January 1, two years before maturity, Easton Company retired $300,000 of its 8.5% bonds payable at the current market price of 102 (102% of the bond face amount, or $300,000 × 1.02 = $306,000). The bond book value on January 1 was $298,000, reflecting an unamortized discount of $2,000. Bond interest was fully paid and recorded up to the date of retirement. What is the gain or loss on retirement of these bonds?

LO9-4
Pfizer, Inc.
NYSE :: PFE

M9-27. Interpreting Bond Note
In its 2020 10-K, **Pfizer, Inc.**, reported the following maturity schedule for its debt outstanding:

($ millions)	Total	2021	2022–2023	2024–2025	After 2025
Long-term debt, including current portion.......	$39,135	$2,002	$4,346	$3,068	$29,719

a. What did Pfizer, Inc., report in its 2020 balance as the current portion of long-term debt?
b. What implications does the payment schedule have for your evaluation of Pfizer's liquidity and solvency?

LO9-1

M9-28. Classifying Debt Accounts into the Balance Sheet or Income Statement
Indicate the proper financial statement classification (balance sheet or income statement) for each of the following accounts:

a. Gain on Bond Retirement
b. Discount on Bonds Payable
c. Mortgage Notes Payable
d. Bonds Payable
e. Bond Interest Expense
f. Bond Interest Payable (due next period)
g. Premium on Bonds Payable
h. Loss on Bond Retirement

LO9-4

M9-29. Interpreting Bond Note Disclosures
Cencosud SA is a leading Latin American retailer that was listed on the New York Stock Exchange until January 2018. As of December 31, 2017, the company had approximately US$ 4.12 billion in short- and long-term debt. In its last 20-F filing with the Securities and Exchange Commission, Cencosud reports the following:

> Our loan agreements and outstanding bonds contain a number of covenants requiring us to comply with certain financial ratios and other tests. The most restrictive financial covenants under these loan agreements and bonds require us to maintain:
> - a ratio of consolidated Net Financial Debt to consolidated net worth not exceeding 1.2 to 1;
> - a ratio of consolidated Net Financial Debt to EBITDA (as defined in the relevant credit agreements) for the most recent four consecutive fiscal quarters for such period of less than 5.25 to 1;
> - unencumbered assets in an amount equal to at least 120% of the outstanding principal amount of total liabilities;
> - minimum consolidated assets of at least UF 50.5 million[11]; and
> - minimum consolidated net worth of at least UF 28.0 million.
>
> As of the date of this annual report, we are in compliance with all of our loan and debt instruments.

---

[11] "UF" refers to *Unidades de Fomento*. The UF is an inflation-indexed Chilean monetary unit with a value in Chilean pesos that is adjusted daily to reflect changes in the official Consumer Price Index ("CPI").

a. Why do creditors impose restrictive covenants on borrowers?
b. How might restrictive covenants such as these affect management decisions?
c. What implications do these restrictions have on an analysis of the company and its solvency?

M9-30. Analyzing Financial Statement Effects of Bond Redemption (FSET)   LO9-4

Holthausen Corporation issued $500,000 of 11%, 20-year bonds at 108 on January 1, 2016. Interest is payable semiannually on June 30 and December 31. Through January 1, 2022, Holthausen amortized $5,240 of the bond premium. On January 1, 2022, Holthausen will retire the bonds at 103. Record the issue and retirement of these bonds in the financial statement effects template.

M9-31. Analyzing Financial Statement Effects of Bond Redemption   LO9-4

Using the information from M9-30, complete the following.
a. Prepare journal entries to record the issue and retirement of these bonds.
b. Post the journal entries to their respective T-accounts.

M9-32. Analyzing Financial Statement Effects of Bond Redemption   LO9-4

Dechow, Inc., issued $300,000 of 8%, 15-year bonds at 96 on July 1, 2015. Interest is payable semiannually on December 31 and June 30. Through June 30, 2022, Dechow amortized $3,823 of the bond discount. On July 1, 2022, Dechow will retire the bonds at 101. Record the issue and retirement of these bonds in the financial statement effects template. (Assume the June interest expense has already been recorded.)

M9-33. Analyzing Financial Statement Effects of Bond Redemption   LO9-4

Using the information from M9-32, complete the following.
a. Prepare journal entries to record the issue and retirement of these bonds. (Assume the June interest expense has already been recorded.)
b. Post the journal entries to their respective T-accounts.

M9-34. Analyzing and Computing Accrued Interest on Notes   LO9-4

Compute any interest accrued for each of the following notes payable owed by Penman, Inc., as of December 31. (Use a 365-day year.)

Lender	Issuance Date	Principal	Interest Rate (%)	Term
Nissim.	November 21	$25,000	8%	120 days
Klein	December 13	15,000	6	90 days
Bildersee.	December 19	20,000	5	60 days

M9-35. Debt Ratings and Capital Structure   LO9-5

General Mills, Inc., reports the following information in the statement of cash flows for the year ended May 31, 2020:

General Mills, Inc.
NYSE :: GIS

Cash Flows from Financing Activities ($ millions)	Year Ended May 31, 2020
Change in notes payable	$(1,158.6)
Issuance of long-term debt.	1,638.1
Payment of long-term debt.	(1,396.7)
Proceeds from common stock issued on exercised options.	263.4
Purchases of common stock for treasury	(3.4)
Dividends paid	(1,195.8)
Dividends to noncontrolling interests and other, net.	(88.5)
Net cash used by financing activities	$(1,941.5)

a. General Mills reported net income of $2,210.8 million in the year ended May 2020. What effect did these financing cash flows have on General Mills solvency measures for the year? Explain.
b. Would the changes in financing tend to lower or increase the firm's debt rating? (Currently General Mills' long-term debt is rated at upper medium grade.)

M9-36. Computing Bond Issue Price   LO9-3

Bushman, Inc., issues $250,000 of 9% bonds that pay interest semiannually and mature in 10 years. Compute the bond issue price assuming that the bonds' market rate is:
a. 8% per year compounded semiannually.
b. 10% per year compounded semiannually.

LO9-3 **M9-37. Computing Issue Price for Zero-Coupon Bonds**
Baiman, Inc., issues $250,000 of zero-coupon bonds that mature in 10 years. Compute the bond issue price assuming that the bonds' market rate is:

a. 8% per year compounded semiannually.
b. 10% per year compounded semiannually.
c. If prior to the debt issue at 10%, the firm had total assets of $3.5 million and total equity of $1.5 million, what would be the effect of the new borrowing on the financial leverage of the firm?

LO9-1 **M9-38. Financial Statement Effects of Accounts Payable Transactions**
Petroni Company engages in the following sequence of transactions every month:
1. Purchases $450 of inventory on credit.
2. Sells $450 of inventory for $630 on credit.
3. Pays other operating expenses of $165 in cash.
4. Collects $630 in cash from customers.
5. Pays supplier of inventory $450.

a. Create a monthly income statement and statement of operating cash flow (direct method) for four consecutive months.
b. The CFO is disappointed with the cash flows from the business. They do not provide the support for investment and growth that she wants. She proposes delaying supplier payments by a month. That is, each month's inventory purchase will be paid for in the following month. How would this change the monthly income statements and operating cash flows in part *a*? Would it provide the steady flow of cash that the CFO is looking for? Why?

LO9-3, 4 **M9-39. Computing Bond Issue Price and Preparing an Amortization Table in Excel**
On December 31, 2021, Kaplan, Inc., issues $400,000 of 9% bonds that pay interest semiannually and mature in 10 years (December 31, 2031).

a. Using the Excel PV worksheet function, compute the issue price assuming that the bonds' market rate is 8% per year compounded semiannually. (Refer to Appendix A for illustration.)
b. Prepare an amortization table in Excel to demonstrate the amortization of the book (carrying) value to the $400,000 maturity value at the end of the 20th semiannual period. (Refer to Appendix A for illustration.)

LO9-3, 4 **M9-40. Classifying Bond-Related Accounts**
Indicate the proper financial statement classification for each of the following accounts:

Gain on Bond Retirement (material amount)
Discount on Bonds Payable
Mortgage Notes Payable
Bonds Payable
Bond Interest Expense
Bond Interest Payable
Premium on Bonds Payable

LO9-3, 4 **M9-41. Recording and Assessing the Effects of Installment Loans (FSET)**
On December 31, 2021, Thomas, Inc., borrowed $500,000 on a 6%, 15-year mortgage note payable. The note is to be repaid in equal semiannual installments of $25,510 (payable on June 30 and December 31).

Report each of the following transactions using the financial statement effects template: (1) the issuance of the mortgage note payable, (2) the payment of the first installment on June 30, 2022, and (3) the payment of the second installment on December 31, 2022. Round amounts to the nearest dollar.

LO9-3, 4 **M9-42. Recording and Assessing the Effects of Installment Loans**
Using the information from M9-41, complete the following.

a. Prepare journal entries to record each of the transactions.
b. Post the journal entries to their respective T-accounts.

LO9-3 **M9-43. Determining Bond Prices**
Lunar, Inc., plans to issue $500,000 of 6% bonds that will pay interest semiannually and mature in 5 years. Assume that the effective interest rate is 8% per year compounded semiannually. Compute the selling price of the bonds. Use Tables A.2 and A.3 in Appendix A near the end of the book.

EXERCISES

E9-44. Analyzing and Computing Accrued Warranty Liability and Expense — LO9-1

Waymire Company sells a motor that carries a 60-day unconditional warranty against product failure. Waymire estimates that between the sale and lapse of the product warranty, 2% of the 152,000 units sold this period will require repair at an average cost of $50 per unit. The warranty liability for this product had a beginning-of-period balance of $66,000, and $59,000 has already been spent on warranty repairs and replacements during the period.

a. How much warranty expense must Waymire report in its income statement, and what amount of warranty liability must it report on its balance sheet for this year?
b. What analysis issues do we need to consider with respect to the amount of reported warranty liability?
c. What solvency ratios are increased if warranty liabilities rise?

E9-45. Analyzing Contingencies and Assessing Liabilities — LO9-1

The following independent situations represent various types of liabilities. Analyze each situation and indicate which of the following is the proper accounting treatment for each company: (1) record in accounts, (2) disclose in a financial statement note, or (3) neither record nor disclose.

a. A stockholder has filed a lawsuit against Clinch Corporation. Clinch's attorneys have reviewed the facts of the case. Their review revealed that similar lawsuits have never resulted in a cash award, and it is highly unlikely that this lawsuit will either.
b. Foster Company signed a 60-day, 10% note when it purchased (and received) items from another company.
c. The Department of Environment Protection notifies Shevlin Company that a state where it has a plant is filing a lawsuit for groundwater pollution against Shevlin and another company that has a plant adjacent to Shevlin's plant. Test results have not identified the exact source of the pollution. Shevlin's manufacturing process often produces by-products that can pollute groundwater.
d. Sloan Company manufactured and sold products to a retailer that sold the products to consumers. The Sloan Company warranty offers replacement of the product if it is found to be defective within 90 days of the sale to the consumer. Historically, 1.2% of the products are returned for replacement.

E9-46. Analyzing and Computing Accrued Wages Liability and Expense — LO9-1

Demski Company pays its employees on the 1st and 15th of each month. It is March 31, and Demski is preparing financial statements for this quarter. Its employees have earned $40,000 since the 15th of this month and have not yet been paid. How will Demski's balance sheet and income statement change to reflect the accrual of wages that must be made at March 31? What balance sheet and income statement accounts would be incorrectly reported if Demski failed to make this accrual (for each account indicate whether it would be overstated or understated)?

E9-47. Analyzing and Reporting Financial Statement Effects of Bond Transactions (FSET) — LO9-3, 4

On January 1, Hutton Corp. issued $400,000 of 15-year, 11% bonds payable for $503,753, yielding an effective interest rate of 8%. Interest is payable semiannually on June 30 and December 31.

a. Show computations to confirm the issue price of $503,753.
b. Record the bond issuance, semiannual interest payment, and premium amortization on June 30, and semiannual interest payment and premium amortization on December 31 in the financial statement effects template. Use the effective interest rate method.

E9-48. Analyzing and Reporting Financial Statement Effects of Bond Transactions — LO9-4

Using the information from E9-47, complete the following.

a. Prepare journal entries to record the bond issuance, semiannual interest payment, and premium amortization on June 30, and semiannual interest payment and premium amortization on December 31. Use the effective interest rate method.
b. Post the journal entries to their respective T-accounts.

E9-49. Computing the Bond Issue Price — LO9-3

D'Souza, Inc., issues $600,000 of 11% bonds that pay interest semiannually and mature in seven years. Assume that the market interest (yield) rate is 12% per year compounded semiannually. Compute the bond issue price.

LO9-1 **E9-50. Interpreting Warranty Liability Disclosures (FSET)**
The following disclosures were provided by Siemens AG in its 2020 annual report:

Siemens AG
OTCMKTS :: SIEGY

Product-related expenses
Provisions for estimated costs related to product warranties are recorded in line item Cost of sales at the time the related sale is recognized.

Note 18 Provisions

(in millions of €)	Provision for Warranties Year Ended September 30* 2020	2019
Beginning balance	€4,300	€4,575
Additions	633	1,621
Usage	(395)	(1,060)
Reversals	(258)	(1,131)
Translation differences and other	(2,706)	294
Ending balance	€1,574	€4,300

* The company rounds amounts, and thus, they may not exactly sum to totals and subtotals.

a. The provision that Siemens reports is an estimated warranty liability. What would constitute "additions" to the provision in 2020? Using the financial statement effects template, record this addition.
b. What constitutes "usage" of the provision? Besides the provision, what other accounts are likely to be affected by usage? Using the financial statement effects template, record usage of €395 million in 2020.
c. "Reversals" are corrections of previous estimates of warranty obligations. Why would it be useful to report reversals separately from additions?
d. Siemens reported sales revenue of €57,139 million in 2020 and €58,483 in 2019. Calculate the ratio of warranty expense to sales for each year.

LO9-1 **E9-51. Interpreting Warranty Liability Disclosures**
Using the information from E9-50, complete the following.
Prepare the journal entries for (a) additions to the provision and (b) usage of the provision.

LO9-3, 4 **E9-52. Reporting Financial Statement Effects of Bond Transactions (FSET)**
Lundholm, Inc., which reports financial statements each December 31, is authorized to issue $300,000 of 9%, 15-year bonds dated May 1, 2021, with interest payments on October 31 and April 30. Assume the bonds are issued at par on May 1, 2021.
Record the bond issuance, payment of the first semiannual period's interest, and retirement of $100,000 of the bonds at 101 on November 1, 2022, using the financial statement effects template. Assume that interest was paid on October 31, 2022.

LO9-3, 4 **E9-53. Reporting Financial Statement Effects of Bond Transactions**
Using the information from E9-52, complete the following.
a. Prepare journal entries for the transactions described.
b. Post the journal entries to their respective T-accounts.

LO9-3, 4 **E9-54. Reporting Financial Statement Effects of Bond Transactions (FSET)**
On January 1, McKeown, Inc., issued $450,000 of 8%, 9-year bonds for $397,397, yielding a market (yield) rate of 10%. Semiannual interest is payable on June 30 and December 31 of each year.
a. Show computations to confirm the bond issue price.
b. Record the bond issuance, semiannual interest payment, and discount amortization on June 30, and semiannual interest payment and discount amortization on December 31, using the financial statement effects template. Use the effective interest rate.

LO9-3, 4 **E9-55. Reporting Financial Statement Effects of Bond Transactions**
Using the information from E9-54, complete the following.
a. Prepare the journal entries for transactions described in part b.
b. Post the journal entries to their respective T-accounts.

E9-56. Reporting Financial Statement Effects of Bond Transactions (FSET)   **LO9-3, 4**

On January 1, Shields, Inc., issued $500,000 of 9%, 20-year bonds for $549,482, yielding a market (yield) rate of 8%. Semiannual interest is payable on June 30 and December 31 of each year.

   a. Show computations to confirm the bond issue price.

   b. Record the bond issuance, semiannual interest payment, and premium amortization on June 30, and semiannual interest payment and premium amortization on December 31, using the financial statement effects template. Use the effective interest rate method.

E9-57. Reporting Financial Statement Effects of Bond Transactions   **LO9-3, 4**

Using the information from E9-56, complete the following.

   a. Prepare the journal entries for transactions described in part b.

   b. Post the journal entries to their respective T-accounts.

E9-58. Analyzing Bond Pricing, Interest Rates, and Financial Statement Effect of a Bond Issue   **LO9-3, 4**

Following is a price quote for $200 million of 6.55% coupon bonds issued by **Deere & Company** that mature in October 2028:

Ratings/Industry	Issue/Call Information	Coupon/Maturity	Price/YTM
A2/A	Deere & Company	6.550	123.962
Industrial	Non Callable, NYBE, DE	10-01-2028	4.178

This quote indicates that, on this day, Deere's bonds have a market price of 123.962 (123.962% of face value), resulting in a yield of 4.178%.

   a. Assuming that these bonds were originally issued at or close to par value, what does the above market price reveal about the direction that interest rates have changed since Deere issued its bonds? (Assume that Deere's debt rating has remained the same.)

   b. Does the change in interest rates since the issuance of these bonds affect the amount of interest expense that Deere is reporting in its income statement? Explain.

   c. If Deere were to repurchase its bonds at the above market price of 123.962, how would the repurchase affect its current income? Assume that the bonds were issued at face value (100).

   d. Assuming that the bonds remain outstanding until their maturity, at what market price will the bonds sell on their due date of October 1, 2028?

E9-59. Analyzing and Reporting Financial Statement Effects of Bond Transactions (FSET)   **LO9-3, 4**

On January 1, Trueman Corp. issued $400,000 of 20-year, 11% bonds for $369,907, yielding a market (yield) rate of 12%. Interest is payable semiannually on June 30 and December 31.

   a. Confirm the bond issue price.

   b. Record the bond issuance, semiannual interest payment, and discount amortization on June 30, and semiannual interest payment and discount amortization on December 31, using the financial statement effects template. Use the effective interest rate method.

   c. Trueman elected to report these bonds in its financial statements at fair value. On December 31, these bonds were listed in the bond market at a price of 101 (or 101% of par value). Using the financial statement effects template, record the entry to adjust the reported value of these bonds to fair value.

   d. Prepare a table summarizing the effect of these bonds on earnings for the year.

E9-60. Analyzing and Reporting Financial Statement Effects of Bond Transactions   **LO9-3, 4**

Using the information from E9-59, complete the following.

   a. Prepare the journal entries for transactions described in part b.

   b. Post the journal entries to their respective T-accounts.

   c. Prepare the journal entry for the transaction described in part c to adjust the bonds to fair value.

E9-61. Reporting and Interpreting Bond Disclosures   **LO9-2, 4**

The adjusted trial balance for the Hass Corporation at the end of 2021 contains the following accounts:

$ 37,500	Bond Interest Payable
900,000	9% Bonds Payable due 2023
750,000	10% Bonds Payable due 2022
28,500	Discount on 9% Bonds Payable
3,000	Premium on 8% Bonds Payable
250,000	Zero-Coupon Bonds Payable due 2024
150,000	8% Bonds Payable due 2026

LO9-3, 4 **E9-62. Recording and Assessing the Effects of Installment Loans (FSET)**
Prepare the long-term liabilities section of the balance sheet. Indicate the proper balance sheet classification for accounts listed above that do not belong in the long-term liabilities section.

On December 31, Dehning, Inc., borrowed $600,000 on a 6%, 10-year mortgage note payable. The note is to be repaid in equal quarterly installments of $20,056 (beginning March 31). Using the financial statement effects template, report (1) the issuance of the mortgage note payable, (2) the payment of the first installment on March 31, and (3) the payment of the second installment on June 30. Round amounts to the nearest dollar.

LO9-3, 4 **E9-63. Recording and Assessing the Effects of Installment Loans**
Using the information from E9-62, complete the following.
a. Prepare the journal entries for transactions described in E9-62.
b. Post the journal entries to their respective T-accounts.

PROBLEMS

LO9-1 **P9-64. Interpreting Warranty Liability Disclosures**

Hewlett-Packard Enterprise Company
NYSE :: HPQ

Cisco Systems, Inc.
NASDAQ :: CSCO

The following information was extracted from the 10-K reports for the years ended in 2020 for **Hewlett-Packard Enterprise** and **Cisco Systems, Inc.**

($ millions)	Hewlett-Packard Enterprise Company 2020	2019	Cisco Systems, Inc. 2020	2019
Revenue from product sales.	$26,982	$29,135	$49,301	$51,904
Warranty expense.	238	239	561	600
Accrued warranty liability	385	400	331	342

REQUIRED

a. Compute the amount of warranty costs incurred in 2020 for each company. (That is, what amount was spent for warranty repairs and settlements in 2020? Assume no other adjustments to the account are made.)
b. Compare these two companies on the basis of the ratio of warranty expense to sales. What factors might explain any difference that you observe?

LO9-3, 4 **P9-65. Recording and Assessing the Effects of Bond Financing (with Accrued Interest) (FSET)**
Eskew, Inc., which closes its books on December 31, is authorized to issue $250,000 of 6%, 15-year bonds dated May 1, 2021, with interest payments on November 1 and May 1.

REQUIRED
1. Assuming that the bonds were sold at 100 plus accrued interest on October 1, 2021, prepare the necessary entries for items *a–f* below using the financial statement effects template.
    a. The bond issuance.
    b. Payment of the first semiannual period's interest on November 1, 2021.
    c. Accrual of bond interest expense at December 31, 2021.
    d. The adjustment to fair value on December 31, 2021, assuming that Eskew, Inc., elected to use the fair value option. On that date, the bond traded at a price of 98.5 (98.5% of par value) in the bond market. (Assume that the change in fair value results from a change in market interest rates rather than a change in instrument-specific credit risk.)
    e. Payment of the semiannual interest on May 1, 2022. (The firm does not make reversing entries.)
    f. Retirement of $100,000 of the bonds at 101 on May 1, 2026 (immediately after the interest payment on that date). Assume that the fair value adjustment account for the entire issue has a debit balance of $11,250 as of that date. *Hint:* Forty percent of the outstanding bonds were retired in this transaction.
2. Suppose fair value adjustments of bond values were not posted to net income, but rather to other comprehensive income. How would Eskew, Inc.'s December 31, 2021, financial statements change?

LO9-3, 4 **P9-66. Recording and Assessing the Effects of Bond Financing (with Accrued Interest)**
Using the information from P9-65, prepare journal entries for transactions described in parts *a* to *f* of part (1).

P9-67. Interpreting Debt Disclosures on Interest Rates and Expense

Walgreens Boots Alliance, Inc. discloses the following in note 7 in its 10-K relating to its debt:

LO9-3, 4

Walgreens Boots Alliance, Inc.
NYSE :: WBA

In millions	August 31, 2020	August 31, 2019
Short-term debt		
Commercial paper	$ 1,517	$ 2,400
Credit facilities	1,071	1,624
$8 billion note issuance[1]		
2.700% unsecured notes due 2019	—	1,250
£700 million note issuance[1]		
2.875% unsecured Pound sterling notes due 2020	533	—
Other[2]	418	464
Total short-term debt	**$ 3,538**	**$ 5,738**
Long-term debt		
$1.5 billion note issuance[1]		
3.200% unsecured notes due 2030	$ 497	$ —
4.100% unsecured notes due 2050	990	—
$6 billion note issuance[1]		
3.450% unsecured notes due 2026	1,891	1,890
4.650% unsecured notes due 2046	591	591
$8 billion note issuance[1]		
3.300% unsecured notes due 2021	1,248	1,247
3.800% unsecured notes due 2024	1,993	1,992
4.500% unsecured notes due 2034	496	495
4.800% unsecured notes due 2044	1,493	1,492
£700 million note issuance[1]		
2.875% unsecured Pound sterling notes due 2020	—	488
3.600% unsecured Pound sterling notes due 2025	398	365
€750 million note issuance[1]		
2.125% unsecured Euro notes due 2026	891	824
$4 billion note issuance[1]		
3.100% unsecured notes due 2022	1,198	1,197
4.400% unsecured notes due 2042	493	493
Other[4]	24	25
Total long-term debt, less current portion	**$12,203**	**$11,098**

Walgreens Boots also discloses that its interest expense, net was $639 million and it paid interest of $584 million in fiscal 2020.

REQUIRED

a. What was the average interest rate on Walgreens Boots debt in 2020?
b. Does your computation in part *a* seem reasonable given the disclosure relating to specific bond issues? Explain.
c. Why can the amount of interest paid be different from the amount of interest expense recorded in the income statement?

P9-68. Recording and Assessing the Effects of Bond Financing (with Accrued Interest) (FSET)

Petroni, Inc., which closes its books on December 31, is authorized to issue $600,000 of 4%, 20-year bonds dated March 1, 2022, with interest payments on September 1 and March 1.

LO9-3, 4

REQUIRED
Assuming that the bonds were sold at 100 plus accrued interest on July 1, 2022, record each transaction in the financial statement effects template.

a. The bond issuance.
b. Payment of the semiannual interest on September 1, 2022.
c. Accrual of bond interest expense at December 31, 2022.
d. Payment of the semiannual interest on March 1, 2023. (The firm does not make reversing entries.)
e. Retirement of $125,000 of the bonds at 101 on March 1, 2023 (immediately after the interest payment on that date).

P9-69. Recording and Assessing the Effects of Bond Financing (with Accrued Interest)

Using the information from P9-68, complete the following.

LO9-3, 4

a. Prepare journal entries for transactions described in parts *a* to *e*.
b. Post the journal entries to their respective T-accounts.

LO9-3, 4 **P9-70. Preparing an Amortization Schedule and Recording the Effects of Bonds (FSET)**

On December 31, 2021, Kasznik, Inc., issued $480,000 of 4%, 10-year bonds for $442,586, yielding an effective interest rate of 5%. Semiannual interest is payable on June 30 and December 31 each year. The firm uses the effective interest method to amortize the discount.

REQUIRED

a. Prepare an amortization schedule showing the necessary information for the first two interest periods. Round amounts to the nearest dollar.

b. In the financial statement effects template, report (1) the bond issuance on December 31, 2021, (2) bond interest expense and discount amortization at June 30, 2022, and (3) bond interest expense and discount amortization at December 31, 2022.

LO9-3, 4 **P9-71. Recording the Effects of Bonds**

Using the information from P9-70, complete the following.

a. Prepare journal entries for transactions described in part *b*.

b. Post the journal entries to their respective T-accounts.

LO9-3, 4 **P9-72. Preparing an Amortization Schedule and Recording the Effects of Bonds (FSET)**

On April 30 Cheng, Inc., issued $325,000 of 6%, 15-year bonds for $268,801, yielding an effective interest rate of 8%. Semiannual interest is payable on October 31 and April 30 each year. The firm uses the effective interest method to amortize the discount.

REQUIRED

a. Prepare an amortization schedule showing the necessary information for the first two interest periods. Round amounts to the nearest dollar.

b. In the financial statement effects template, report (1) the bond issuance on April 30, (2) the bond interest payment and discount amortization at October 31, (3) the adjusting entry to record bond interest expense and discount amortization at December 31, the close of the firm's accounting year, and (4) the bond interest payment and discount amortization at April 30 of the following year.

LO9-3, 4 **P9-73. Recording the Effects of Bonds**

Using the information from P9-72, complete the following.

a. Prepare journal entries for transactions described in part *b*.

b. Post the journal entries to their respective T-accounts.

LO9-3, 4 **P9-74. Recording and Assessing the Effects of Installment Loans: Semiannual Installments (FSET)**

On December 31, 2021, Wasley Corporation borrowed $300,000 on a 6%, 10-year mortgage note payable. The note is to be repaid with equal semiannual installments, beginning June 30, 2022.

REQUIRED

a. Compute the amount of the semiannual installment payment. Use the appropriate table (in Appendix A near the end of the book) or a financial calculator, and round the amount to the nearest dollar.

b. In the financial statement effects template, report (1) Wasley's borrowing of funds on December 31, 2021, (2) Wasley's installment payment on June 30, 2022, and (3) Wasley's installment payment on December 31, 2022. (Round amounts to the nearest dollar.)

LO9-3, 4 **P9-75. Recording and Assessing the Effects of Installment Loans: Semiannual Installments**

Using the information from P9-74, complete the following.

a. Prepare journal entries for transactions described in part *b*.

b. Post the journal entries to their respective T-accounts.

LO9-3, 4 **P9-76. Recording and Assessing the Effects of Installment Loans: Quarterly Installments (FSET)**

On December 31, 2021, Watts Corporation borrowed $750,000 on an 8%, 5-year mortgage note payable. The note is to be repaid with equal quarterly installments, beginning March 31, 2022.

REQUIRED

a. Compute the amount of the quarterly installment payment. Use the appropriate table (in Appendix A near the end of the book) or a financial calculator, and round amount to the nearest dollar.

b. In the financial statement effects template, report (1) the borrowing of funds by Watts Corporation on December 31, 2021, (2) the installment payment by Watts Corporation on March 31, 2022, and (3) the installment payment by Watts Corporation on June 30, 2022.

P9-77. Recording and Assessing the Effects of Installment Loans: Quarterly Installments   LO9-3, 4
Using the information from P9-76, complete the following.

a. Prepare journal entries for transactions described in part *b*.
b. Post the journal entries to their respective T-accounts.

P9-78. Contingent Liabilities   LO9-1
BP operates off-shore oil drilling platforms, including rigs in the Gulf of Mexico. In April 2010, explosions and a fire on the Deepwater Horizon rig led to the death of 11 crew members and a 200-million-gallon oil spill in the Gulf of Mexico. BP's 2010 annual report included the following description of its contingent liabilities (provision) related to this accident:

BP, PLC
NYSE :: BP

> In estimating the amount of the provision, BP has determined a range of possible outcomes for Individual and Business Claims, and State and Local Claims.... BP has concluded that a reasonable range of possible outcomes for the amount of the provision at December 31, 2010, is $6 billion to $13 billion. BP believes that the provision recorded at December 31, 2010, of $9.2 billion represents a reliable best estimate from within this range of possible outcomes.

REQUIRED

a. BP prepares its financial statements in accordance with IFRS. How did BP report the $9.2 billion estimate in its 2010 financial statements?
b. How would the accounting for this provision differ if BP prepared its financial statements in accordance with U.S. GAAP?

CASES AND PROJECTS

C9-79. Interpreting Debt Disclosures   LO9-3, 4, 5
Comcast Corporation's 2020 income statement and partial balance sheet (liabilities and equity, only) are presented below. In addition, Note 6 pertaining to Comcast's long-term debt obligations is provided. All $ amounts are presented in millions.

Comcast
NASDAQ :: CMCSA

Summarized Consolidated Statement of Income Year Ended December 31 (in millions)	2020	2019
Revenue	$103,564	$108,942
Costs and expenses:		
Programming and production	33,121	34,440
Other operating and administrative	33,109	32,807
Advertising, marketing, and promotion	6,741	7,617
Depreciation	8,320	8,663
Amortization	4,780	4,290
Other operating gains	—	—
Total costs and expenses	86,071	87,817
Operating income	17,493	21,125
Interest expense	(4,588)	(4,567)
Investment and other income (loss), net	1,160	438
Income before income taxes	14,065	16,996
Income tax benefit (expense)	(3,364)	(3,673)
Net income	$ 10,701	$ 13,323

Summarized Consolidated Balance Sheet (Liabilities and Equity only) December 31 (in millions)	2020	2019
Current liabilities:		
Accounts payable and accrued expenses related to trade creditors	$ 11,364	$ 10,826
Accrued participations and residuals	1,706	1,730
Deferred revenue	2,963	2,768
Accrued expenses and other current liabilities	9,617	10,516
Current portion of long-term debt	3,146	4,452
Total current liabilities	28,796	30,292
Long-term debt, less current portion	100,614	97,765
Collateralized obligation	5,168	5,166
Deferred income taxes	28,051	28,180
Other noncurrent liabilities	18,222	16,765
Commitments and contingencies		
Total liabilities	180,851	178,168
Total equity	93,018	85,246
Total liabilities and equity	$273,869	$263,414

Note 6: Long-Term Debt

December 31 (in millions)	Weighted-Average Interest Rate as of December 31, 2020	Weighted-Average Interest Rate as of December 31, 2019	2020[b]	2019[b]
Term loans	2.07%	1.87%	$ 7,641	$ 8,078
Senior notes with maturities of 5 years or less, at face value	3.41%	3.29%	19,190	26,378
Senior notes with maturities between 5 and 10 years, at face value	3.47%	3.74%	23,114	21,683
Senior notes with maturities greater than 10 years, at face value	4.03%	4.54%	54,203	46,653
Other, including finance lease obligations			1,261	1,098
Debt issuance costs, premiums, discounts, fair value adjustments for acquisition accounting and hedged positions, net[a]			(1,649)	(1,673)
Total debt	3.60%[a]	3.78%[a]	103,760	102,217
Less: Current portion			3,146	4,452
Long-term debt			$100,614	$ 97,765

[a] Includes the effects of our derivative financial instruments.

[b] As of December 31, 2020, included in our outstanding debt were foreign currency denominated borrowings with principal amounts of £4.7 billion, €7.3 billion, ¥238.5 billion, and ¥16.4 billion RMB. As of December 31, 2019, included in our outstanding debt were foreign currency denominated borrowings with principal amounts of £4.9 billion, €4.9 billion, ¥267 billion, and ¥9 billion RMB.

> Our senior notes are unsubordinated and unsecured obligations and are subject to parent and/or subsidiary guarantees. As of December 31, 2020 and 2019, our debt had an estimated fair value of $125.6 billion and $115.8 billion, respectively. The estimated fair value of our publicly traded debt was primarily based on Level 1 inputs that use quoted market value for the debt. The estimated fair value of debt for which there are no quoted market prices was based on Level 2 inputs that use interest rates available to us for debt with similar terms and remaining maturities.

Principal Maturities of Debt
December 31 (in millions)

2021	$ 3,133
2022	4,028
2023	3,925
2024	6,746
2025	6,953
Thereafter	80,624

REQUIRED

a. Comcast provided cash flow information revealing that the company paid interest equal to $3,878 million in 2020. Explain why this amount is different from the amount of interest expense reported in its 2020 income statement.

b. Comcast reports its debt using historical cost. What would be the impact on the financial statements if the company elected to report all of its debt at fair value? (Assume no changes to fair values due to changes in instrument-specific credit risk.) Be specific.

c. The financial ratios specified in Comcast's loan agreements include the solvency measures described in this chapter. Calculate Comcast's debt-to-equity ratio and times interest earned for 2020. Explain why creditors might include these ratios in the restrictive covenants of loan agreements.

d. Violation of debt covenants can be a serious event that can impose substantial costs on a company. What actions might management take to avoid violating debt covenants if the company's ratios are near the covenant limits?

e. Explain what type of disclosures are likely present in Note 16—"Commitment and Contingencies," which is represented as a line item on the balance sheet with no amounts.

C9-80. Assessing Debt Financing, Company Interests, and Managerial Ethics   **LO9-3, 4, 5**

Foster Corporation is in the third quarter of the current year, and projections are that net income will be down about $480,000 from the previous year. Foster's return on assets is also projected to decline from its usual 15% to approximately 13%. If earnings do decline, this year will be the second consecutive year of decline. Foster's president is quite concerned about these projections (and his job) and has called a meeting of the firm's officers for next week to consider ways to "turn things around—and fast."

Margot Barth, treasurer of Foster Corporation, has received a memorandum from her assistant, Lorie McNichols. Barth had asked McNichols if she had any suggestions as to how Foster might improve its earnings performance for the current year. McNichols' memo reads as follows:

> As you know, we have $2,400,000 of 4%, 20-year bonds payable outstanding. We issued these bonds 10 years ago at face value, so they have 10 years left to maturity. When they mature, we would probably replace them with other bonds. The economy is expecting a period of greater inflation, and interest rates have increased to about 8%. My proposal is to replace these bonds right now. More specifically, I propose:
>
> 1. Immediately issue $2,400,000 of 20-year, 8% bonds payable. These bonds will be issued at face value.
> 2. Use the proceeds from the new bonds to buy back and retire our outstanding 4% bonds. Because of the current high rates of interest, these bonds are trading in the market at about $1,760,000.
> 3. The benefits to Foster are that (a) the retirement of the old bonds will generate a $640,000 gain for the income statement and (b) there will be an extra $640,000 of cash available for other uses.

Barth is intrigued by the possibility of generating an $640,000 gain for the income statement. However, she is not sure this proposal is in the best long-run interests of the firm and its stockholders.

REQUIRED

a. How is the $640,000 gain calculated from the retirement of the old bonds? Where would this gain be reported in Foster's income statement?

b. Why might this proposal not be in the best long-run interests of the firm and its stockholders?

c. What possible ethical conflict is present in this proposal?

SOLUTIONS TO REVIEW PROBLEMS

Review 9-1

Part One

a. The discount would be $580 ($29,000 × 0.02). Thus, Waymire would pay $28,420 ($29,000 − $580).

b. The cost of the lost discount is $29 per day ($580/20) or $10,585 per year (simple interest). The implicit financing cost of the lost discount is 37.24% ($10,585/$28,420).

Part Two

a. Toro Company incurred $67,241 thousand in warranty claims in 2020 ($000):

$96,604 + $77,758 − warranty claims = $107,121. Warranty claims = $67,241.

b.

Transaction	Balance Sheet					Income Statement		
	Cash Asset	+ Noncash Assets	= Liabilities	+ Contrib. Capital	+ Earned Capital	Revenues	− Expenses	= Net Income
Payment to satisfy warranty claims.	−67,241 Cash		= −67,241 Warranty Liability				−	=

c.

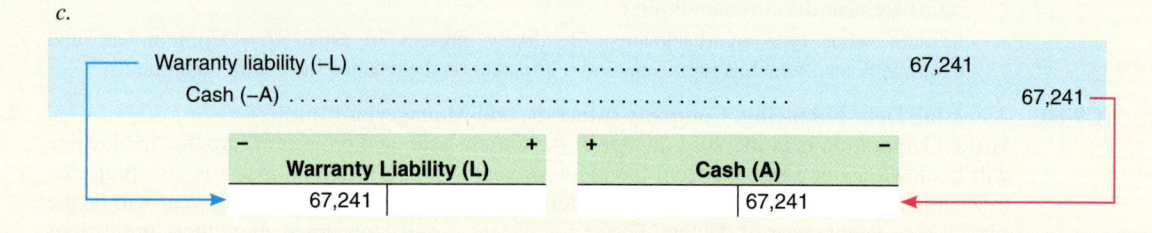

Warranty liability (−L) 67,241
　Cash (−A) 67,241

− Warranty Liability (L)	+	+ Cash (A)	−
67,241			67,241

The credit entry to cash assumes that cash was paid to satisfy the warranty claims. Toro could also have credited wages payable, or parts inventory as needed.

Review 9-2

a. The related journal entry to recognize the accrual of interest is:

Transaction	Balance Sheet					Income Statement		
	Cash Asset	+ Noncash Assets	= Liabilities	+ Contrib. Capital	+ Earned Capital	Revenues	− Expenses	= Net Income
Accrued $26 of interest as of January 31*.			= +26 Interest Payable		−26 Retained Earnings		− +26 Interest Expense	= −26

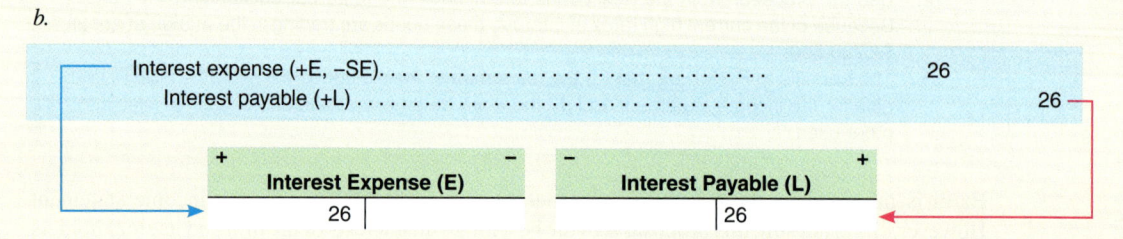

b.

Interest expense (+E, −SE)................................... 26
　Interest payable (+L).. 26

+ Interest Expense (E)	−	− Interest Payable (L)	+
26			26

*Accrued interest for a 16-day period at January 31 = $10,000 × 0.06 × 16/365 = $26.

Review 9-3

The bond issue price:　　a. $500,000　　b. $425,613　　c. $590,228

	N	I/Yr	PV	PMT	FV
a.	20	2.0	**500,000**	10,000	500,000
b.	20	3.0	**425,613**	10,000	500,000
c.	20	1.0	**590,228**	10,000	500,000

Review 9-4

a. Issue price for $300,000, 15-year, 10% semiannual bonds discounted at 8%:

Present value of principal payment ($300,000 × 0.30832)...............	$ 92,496
Present value of semiannual interest payments ($15,000 × 17.29203).....	259,380
Issue price of bonds..	$351,876

b.

Transaction	Balance Sheet					Income Statement		
	Cash Asset	+ Noncash Assets	= Liabilities	+ Contrib. Capital	+ Earned Capital	Revenues	− Expenses	= Net Income
(1) Jan. 1 Issuance.	+351,876 Cash		= +300,000 Bonds Payable +51,876 Bonds Premium				−	=
(2) June 30 Interest and amortization¹.	−15,000 Cash		= −925 Bonds Premium		−14,075 Retained Earnings	+14,075	− +14,075 Interest Expense	= −14,075
(3) Dec. 31 Interest and amortization².	−15,000 Cash		= −962 Bonds Premium		−14,038 Retained Earnings	+14,038	− +14,038 Interest Expense	= −14,038

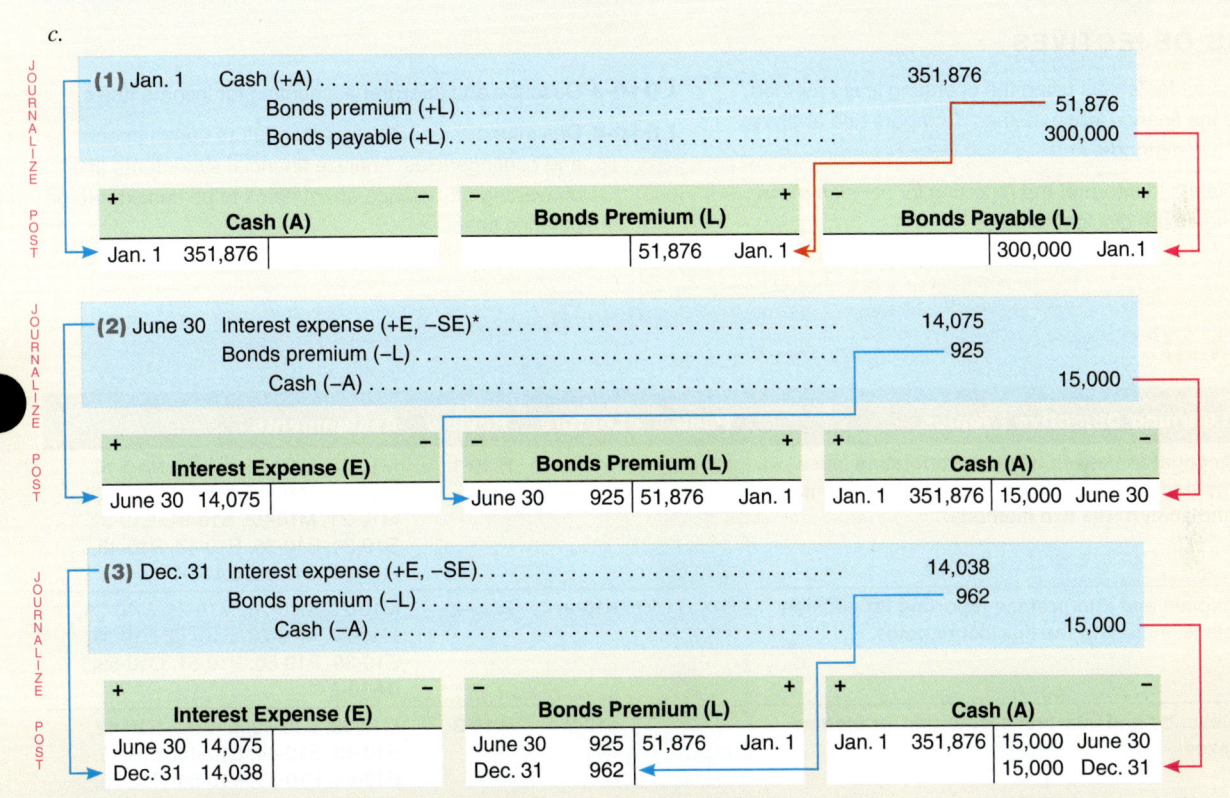

c.

(1) Jan. 1 Cash (+A) 351,876
  Bonds premium (+L) 51,876
  Bonds payable (+L) 300,000

+ Cash (A) −		− Bonds Premium (L) +		− Bonds Payable (L) +
Jan. 1 351,876			51,876 Jan. 1		300,000 Jan.1

(2) June 30 Interest expense (+E, −SE)* 14,075
  Bonds premium (−L) 925
  Cash (−A) 15,000

+ Interest Expense (E) −		− Bonds Premium (L) +		+ Cash (A) −
June 30 14,075		June 30 925	51,876 Jan. 1	Jan. 1 351,876	15,000 June 30

(3) Dec. 31 Interest expense (+E, −SE) 14,038
  Bonds premium (−L) 962
  Cash (−A) 15,000

+ Interest Expense (E) −		− Bonds Premium (L) +		+ Cash (A) −
June 30 14,075		June 30 925	51,876 Jan. 1	Jan. 1 351,876	15,000 June 30
Dec. 31 14,038		Dec. 31 962			15,000 Dec. 31

¹ $300,000 × 0.10 × 6/12 = $15,000 cash payment; 0.04 × $351,876 = $14,075 interest expense; the difference is the bond premium amortization, a reduction of the net bond carrying amount.

² 0.04 × ($351,876 − $925) = $14,038 interest expense. The difference between this amount and the $15,000 cash payment is the premium amortization, a reduction of the net bond carrying amount.

Review 9-5

a.

($ million)	Fiscal Year Ended	Earnings (Loss) before Interest, Tax	Interest Expense	Times Interest Earned
Macy's.............	Feb. 02, 2019	$ 1,681	$ 261	6.4 times
Macy's.............	Feb. 01, 2020	933	205	4.6 times
Nordstrom...........	Feb. 02, 2019	852	119	7.2 times
Nordstrom...........	Feb. 01, 2020	794	112	7.1 times
Bed Bath & Beyond ...	Mar. 02, 2019	(87.1)	69.5	(1.3) times
Bed Bath & Beyond ...	Feb. 29, 2020	(700.1)	64.8	(10.8) times

b. Based on the times interest earned ratio, Macy's and Bed Bath & Beyond's solvency weakened while Nordstrom's solvency slightly weakened in the fiscal year ended in 2020. Relative to each other, Nordstrom's solvency remained stable and was the strongest. Macy's solvency is weaker than Nordstrom's, but with two years of losses, Bed Bath & Beyond clearly has the weakest solvency of the three companies.

Chapter 10
Reporting and Analyzing Leases, Pensions, Income Taxes, and Commitments and Contingencies

LEARNING OBJECTIVES

LO10-1 Account for leases using the operating lease method and the finance lease method. Compare and analyze the two methods.

LO10-2 Explain and interpret the reporting for pension plans, including the disclosure notes.

LO10-3 Describe and interpret accounting for income taxes.

LO10-4 Describe disclosures regarding future commitments and contingencies. Analyze financial statements after converting off-balance-sheet items to be considered on balance sheet.

Road Map

LO	Learning Objective | Topics	Page	eLecture	Review	Assignments
LO10-1	Account for leases using the operating lease method and the finance lease method. Compare and analyze the two methods.	10-3	e10-1	R 10-1	M10-13, M10-14, M1-15, M10-16, M10-17, M10-18, M10-19, M10-20, M10-21, M10-22, E10-31, E10-32, E10-34, E10-35, P10-47, P10-48, C10-59, C10-60, DA10-1
LO10-2	Explain and interpret the reporting for pension plans, including the disclosure notes.	10-15	e10-2	R 10-2	M10-23, M10-24, M10-25, M10-26, M10-27, M10-28, E10-33, E10-38, E10-39, P10-50, P10-51, C10-58, DA10-2
LO10-3	Describe and interpret accounting for income taxes.	10-25	e10-3	R 10-3	M10-30, E10-40, E10-41, E10-42, E10-43, E10-44, E10-45, E10-46, P10-52, P10-53, P10-54, P10-55, P10-56, P10-57, C10-61, C10-62, C10-63, DA10-3
LO10-4	Describe disclosures regarding future commitments and contingencies. Analyze financial statements after converting off-balance-sheet items to be considered on balance sheet.	10-36	e10-4	R 10-4	M10-29, E10-35, E10-36, E10-37, P10-49, C10-59

DEERE & COMPANY
www.Deere.com

Deere & Company has a storied American history. John Deere invented the self-scouring plow in the mid-1800s in Grand Detour, Illinois. His business grew quickly, and he moved to Moline, Illinois, on the Mississippi River for water power and ease of transportation. Today, Deere & Company is a large, multinational corporation and has one of the best-known brands, logos, and slogans: *Nothing runs like a Deere*.

The company makes a wide array of products including lawn mowers, gators, all sizes of tractors used in the agricultural sector, construction equipment, and more. The technological advances have been swift in the industry; for example, Deere produces self-driving tractors and large spraying drones. As of the year-ended November 1, 2020, the company had revenues of $35.5 billion and net income of $2.8 billion. Total assets are $75 billion, and liabilities are $62 billion. Deere employs a large workforce in its manufacturing facilities, and many of the company's employees are covered by a defined benefit pension plan. The company both owns some assets and leases some assets in its operations. In addition, Deere has some commitments that are not required to be on the balance sheet, and the company discloses information about those items so its financial statement users are informed about these future cash commitments. Finally, the company has income tax obligations to many states, the U.S. government, and foreign jurisdictions. We explain the accounting for these items in this chapter.

Source: Deere 2020 10K Report

CHAPTER ORGANIZATION

Reporting and Analyzing Leases, Pensions, and Income Taxes

Leases
- Lessee Reporting of Operating and Finance Leases
- Disclosures
- Analyzing Financial Statements Including the Comparability of Financial Statements

Pensions
- Reporting of Defined Benefit Pension Plans
- Disclosures
- Other Postretirement Benefits

Income Taxes
- Reporting Tax Expense
- Book-Tax Differences
- Disclosures
- Computation and Analysis

INTRODUCTION

Investors, creditors, and other users of financial statements assess the composition of a company's balance sheet and its relation to the income statement. Chapter 6 introduced the concept of earnings quality to refer to the extent to which reported income reflects the underlying economic performance of a company. Similarly, the quality of the balance sheet refers to the extent to which the assets and liabilities of a company are reported in a manner that accurately reflects its economic resources and obligations. For example, in previous chapters, we highlighted the reporting of LIFO inventories and noncapitalized intangible assets to illustrate how some assets can be undervalued or even excluded from the balance sheet.

Financial managers are keenly aware of the importance that financial markets place on the quality of balance sheets. This importance sometimes creates pressure on companies to *window dress* their financial statements in order to report their financial condition and performance in the best possible light. One means of improving the perceived financial condition of the company is by keeping debt off the balance sheet. **Off-balance-sheet financing** refers to financial obligations of a company that are not reported as liabilities in the balance sheet. We note, however, that there are many fewer items that can remain 'off balance sheet' under today's accounting standards relative to the past. It is also important to be cognizant that some items that represent scheduled future cash outflows are required to remain unrecorded, that is 'off balance sheet,' because they do not rise to the level of a liability or cannot be accurately estimated in amount. We discuss off-balance sheet financing in this chapter as well as an analytical procedure for external financial statement users to employ to estimate "as if" balance sheets that include estimates of the off-balance-sheet items.

The first part of this chapter focuses on three common financial obligations (along with any related assets) that companies report in their financial statements—leases, pensions, and income taxes. We discuss other commitments and contingencies and off-balance-sheet financing arrangements at the end of the chapter.

Deere & Company's balance sheet is presented in **Exhibit 10.1**. The amounts reported on Deere's balance sheet related to leases, pensions, taxes, and commitments and contingencies are highlighted.

LEASES

LO10-1
Account for leases using the operating lease method and the finance lease method. Compare and analyze the two methods.

A lease is a contract between the owner of an asset (the **lessor**) and the party desiring to use that asset (the **lessee**). Because this is a private contract between two willing parties, it is governed only by applicable commercial law and can include whatever provisions are negotiated between the parties. The lessor and lessee can be any legal form of organization, including private individuals, corporations, partnerships, and joint ventures.

Leases generally contain the following terms:

- The lessor allows the lessee the unrestricted right to use the asset during the lease term.
- The lessee agrees to make periodic payments to the lessor and to maintain the asset.

EXHIBIT 10.1 — Deere & Company Balance Sheets (excerpts)

DEERE & COMPANY
Consolidated Balance Sheet (excerpts)

As of November 1, 2020, and November 3, 2019 (in millions of dollars)	2020	2019
ASSETS		
Cash and cash equivalents	$ 7,066	$ 3,857
Marketable securities	641	581
Receivables from unconsolidated affiliates	31	46
Trade accounts and notes receivable—net	4,171	5,230
Financing receivables—net	29,750	29,195
Financing receivables securitized—net	4,703	4,383
Other receivables	1,220	1,487
Equipment on operating leases—net	7,298	7,567
Inventories	4,999	5,975
Property and equipment—net	5,817	5,973
Investments in unconsolidated affiliates	193	215
Goodwill	3,081	2,917
Other intangible assets—net	1,327	1,380
Retirement benefits	863	840
Deferred income taxes	1,499	1,466
Other assets	2,432	1,899
Total Assets	**$75,091**	**$73,011**
LIABILITIES AND STOCKHOLDERS' EQUITY		
LIABILITIES		
Short-term borrowings	$ 8,582	$10,784
Short-term securitization borrowings	4,682	4,321
Payables to unconsolidated affiliates	105	142
Accounts payable and accrued expenses	10,112	9,656
Deferred income taxes	519	495
Long-term borrowings	32,734	30,229
Retirement benefits and other liabilities	5,413	5,953
Total liabilities	**62,147**	**61,580**
Commitments and contingencies (Note 21)		
Redeemable noncontrolling interest (Note 5)		14
STOCKHOLDERS' EQUITY		
Total stockholders' equity	12,944	11,417
Total Liabilities and Stockholders' Equity	**$75,091**	**$73,011**

- The legal title to the asset remains with the lessor. At the end of the lease, either the lessor takes physical possession of the asset, or the lessee purchases the asset from the lessor at a price specified in the lease contract.

From the lessor's standpoint, lease payments are set at an amount that yields an acceptable return on investment, commensurate with the credit standing of the lessee. The lessor, thus, obtains a quality investment, and the lessee gains use of the asset.

From the lessee's perspective, the lease serves as a financing vehicle, similar to an intermediate-term secured bank loan. However, there are several advantages to leasing over bank financing:

- Leases often require less equity investment than bank financing. That is, banks often only lend a portion of the asset's cost and require the borrower to make up the difference from its available cash.

- Leases often require payments to be made at the beginning of the period (e.g., the first of the month). However, because leases are contracts between two parties, their terms can be structured in any way to meet their respective needs. For example, a lease can allow variable payments to match seasonal cash inflows of the lessee or have graduated payments for companies in their start-up phase.

- If the lessee requires the use of the asset for only a part of its useful life, leasing avoids the need to sell a used asset.
- Because the lessor retains ownership of the asset, leases provide the lessor with tax benefits such as accelerated depreciation deductions. This fact can lead to lower payments for lessees.

Lessee Reporting of Leases

FASB's Topic 842, *Leases* (hereafter, the lease standard) became effective for public firms with fiscal years and interim periods beginning after December 15, 2018 (the effective date was delayed for private firms to three years later). The standard requires lessees to recognize a **right-of-use asset** and a lease liability for all leases (with the exception, if so elected, of short-term leases) at the commencement date and recognize expenses on their income statements related to the leases. This is a substantial change from the prior standard, in which leases classified as operating leases under the prior accounting standards were "off-balance" sheet—meaning there was no lease asset or lease liability on the balance sheet. Many leases were structured to achieve operating lease classification and, thus, off-balance-sheet financing.

Estimates by the International Accounting Standards Board were that, worldwide, public firms had more than $3 trillion in off-balance-sheet leases before the lease standard took effect.[1] The new accounting standard has significantly changed the balance sheets of lessees.

There are two classifications of leases for lessees: operating leases and finance leases. The main distinction between the categories is that some leases are considered equivalent to a sale/purchase (finance lease), whereas others are not (operating lease). The lease standard requires lessees to record a right-of-use asset and lease liability for *all* leases (with an exception for leases of less than 12 months—also called a short-term lease). However, the income statement treatment is not the same across the two classifications of leases under U.S. GAAP; we discuss the differences below. There are also different lease classifications for the lessor. In fact, you can see that Deere includes within its assets on its balance sheet (see **Exhibit 10-1**) net equipment of $7,298 million that the company, as the lessor, has leased out through operating leases. However, in this text, we focus primarily on the accounting from the lessee's perspective.[2]

An overall summary of lease classification and accounting treatment for lessees is as follows:

		Lessee	
		Finance Lease	
Classification Rule		Accounting	
	Balance Sheet	Income Statement	Cash Flows
Meets at least one of the five lease classification criteria.	Recognize a right-of-use asset and test for impairment. Recognize a lease liability.	Recognize amortization expense on the right-of-use asset (typically straight line over lease term or useful life). Recognize interest expense on the lease liability using the effective interest method.	Interest is operating cash flow; principal is financing.
		Operating Lease	
Classification Rule		Accounting	
	Balance Sheet	Income Statement	Cash Flows
Meets none of the five lease classification criteria.	Recognize a right-of-use asset and test for impairment. Recognize a lease liability.	Recognize lease expense on a straight-line basis as a single line item.	Lease payment is operating cash flow.

Note that finance leases require a recording of interest expense and amortization. The operating leases are expensed on a straight-line basis (rather than high interest costs early in the term of the lease).

---
[1] IFRS Fact Sheet—IFRS 16 Leases

[2] There are classifications of leases for lessors as well: sales-type leases, direct financing leases, and operating leases. The accounting for leases for lessors is essentially unchanged.

The current lease accounting standard is aligned in concept with the current revenue recognition standard that we discussed in Chapter 6. Specifically, the parties need to identify the contract and the consideration. Whether a lease exists is to be determined on the date the contract is signed or authorized (the inception of the lease). The company must determine if the contract is a lease or includes a lease. Next, the consideration for the lease must be determined. Lease payments can consist of five amounts: fixed payments, variable payments, a purchase option, a lease termination penalty, and residual value guarantee. Lease payments are critical because these are the basis for determining the classification of the lease and the amount of the lease liability.

Classification Rules The classification rules are intended to classify leases based on the extent of control of the asset that is passed to the lessee in the contract. If control has passed (the lease meets one of the criteria), the lease is a finance lease. The lease is to be classified (and measurement of the right-of-use asset and lease liability measured) on the lease commencement date (when the asset is available for use). FASB uses five criteria to classify leases; if a lease meets *at least one* of the criteria, it is classified as a finance lease (lessee) and a sales-type lease (lessor).[3] The five criteria, briefly, are as follows:

1. *Ownership transfer*: the lease transfers ownership of the underlying asset to the lessee by the end of the lease term.
2. *Purchase option*: the lease grants the lessee an option to purchase the underlying asset that the lessee is reasonably expected to exercise.
3. *Lease term length*: the lease term is for the major part of the remaining economic life of the underlying asset.
4. *Present value of lease payments*: the present value of the lease payments (and any residual value guaranteed by the lessee that is not already reflected in the lease payments) equals or exceeds substantially all of the fair value of the underlying asset.
5. *Alternative use*: the underlying asset is expected to have no alternative use to the lessor at the end of the lease term.

To illustrate the accounting for the two classifications of leases, we use the following example. Gillette Electronics agrees to lease retail store space in a shopping center. The lease is a 5-year lease with annual payments of $10,000 due at each year-end. (Many leases require payments up front; we generally use end-of-year annual payments in this textbook for simplicity.) Using a 7% interest rate, the present value of the five annual future lease payments equals $41,002, computed as $10,000 × 4.10020 (Appendix A, Table A.3). Using a calculator, the present value of the annual lease payments is computed as follows:[4]

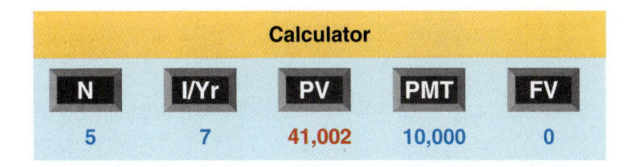

N	I/Yr	PV	PMT	FV
5	7	41,002	10,000	0

Calculator

Finance Lease When the lease is a finance lease, the lessee records a lease liability equal to the present value of the remaining lease payments discounted using the rate implicit in the lease (or if that rate is not available, the lessee's incremental borrowing rate). The lease is recorded on the lease commencement date. In our example, the liability is recorded for $41,002 as follows:

---

[3] Though, the lessor and lease make the determination independently.

[4] The result produced by the financial calculator is actually −41,002. The present value will always have the opposite sign from the payment. So, if the payment is positive, the present value will be negative. **Appendix A** illustrates the use of a financial calculator to compute present values. In this calculation, it is important to set the payments per year (period) to 1 and make sure that the payments are set to occur at the end of each period.

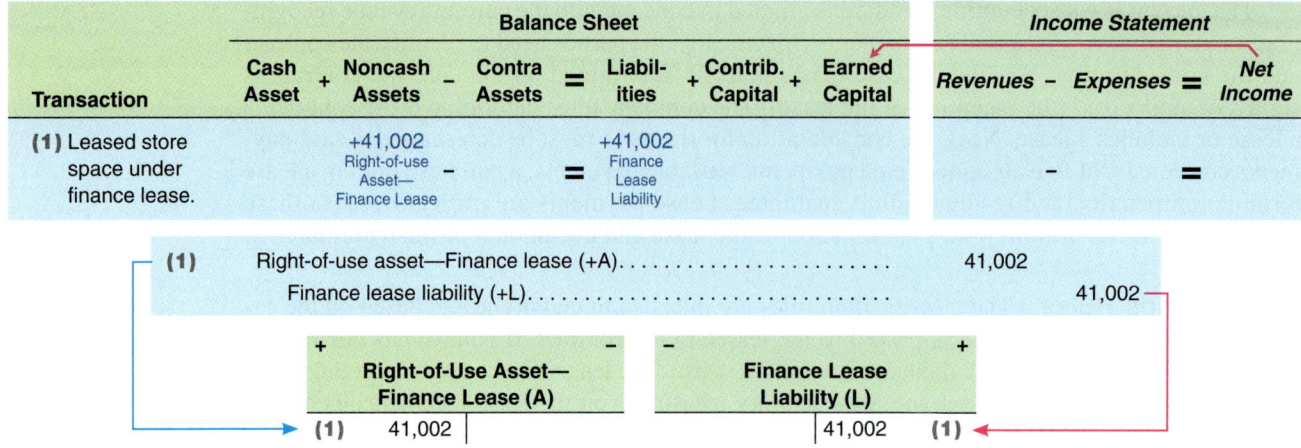

Chapter 10 Reporting and Analyzing Leases, Pensions, Income Taxes

Transaction	Balance Sheet: Cash Asset + Noncash Assets − Contra Assets = Liabilities + Contrib. Capital + Earned Capital	Income Statement: Revenues − Expenses = Net Income
(1) Leased store space under finance lease.	+41,002 Right-of-use Asset—Finance Lease = +41,002 Finance Lease Liability	− =

(1) Right-of-use asset—Finance lease (+A)............... 41,002
Finance lease liability (+L)............................. 41,002

Right-of-Use Asset—Finance Lease (A)	Finance Lease Liability (L)
(1) 41,002	41,002 (1)

The asset is reported among long-term (PPE) assets in the balance sheet, and the liability is reported both in current and long-term debt.

At the end of the first year, two entries are required: one to account for the asset and the other to account for the lease payment. The right-of-use asset must be amortized, similar to how purchased long-term assets must be depreciated. The entry to amortize Gillette's leased asset (assuming straight-line amortization, a useful life of 5 years, and zero residual value [$41,002/5 = $8,200]) is:[5]

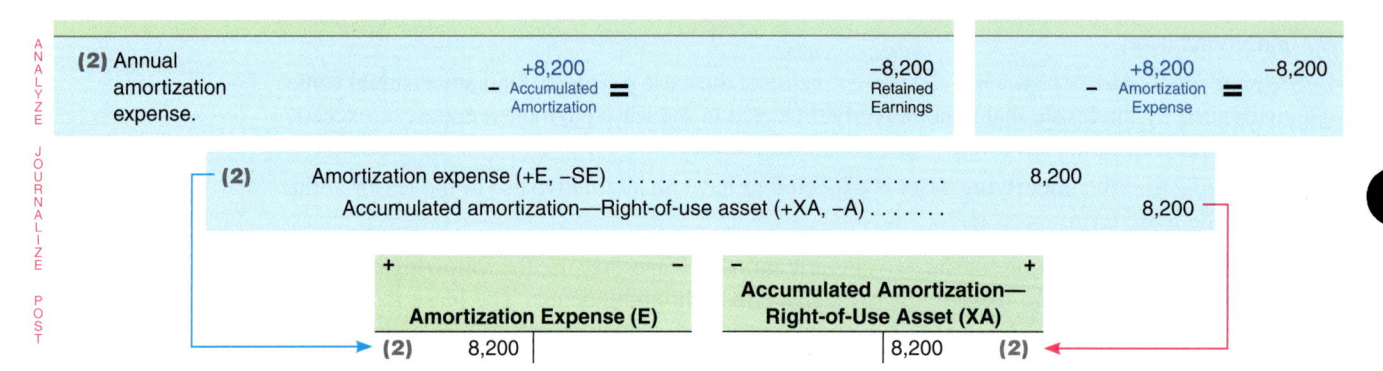

Transaction	Balance Sheet	Income Statement
(2) Annual amortization expense.	+8,200 Accumulated Amortization = −8,200 Retained Earnings	+8,200 Amortization Expense = −8,200

(2) Amortization expense (+E, −SE)............................. 8,200
Accumulated amortization—Right-of-use asset (+XA, −A)....... 8,200

Amortization Expense (E)	Accumulated Amortization—Right-of-Use Asset (XA)
(2) 8,200	8,200 (2)

The second entry is to account for the lease payment. This involves recording the cash payment, recording interest expense, and recording the amount of principal repayment. In our example, we first determine how much of the cash payment is interest and how much is principal repayment.

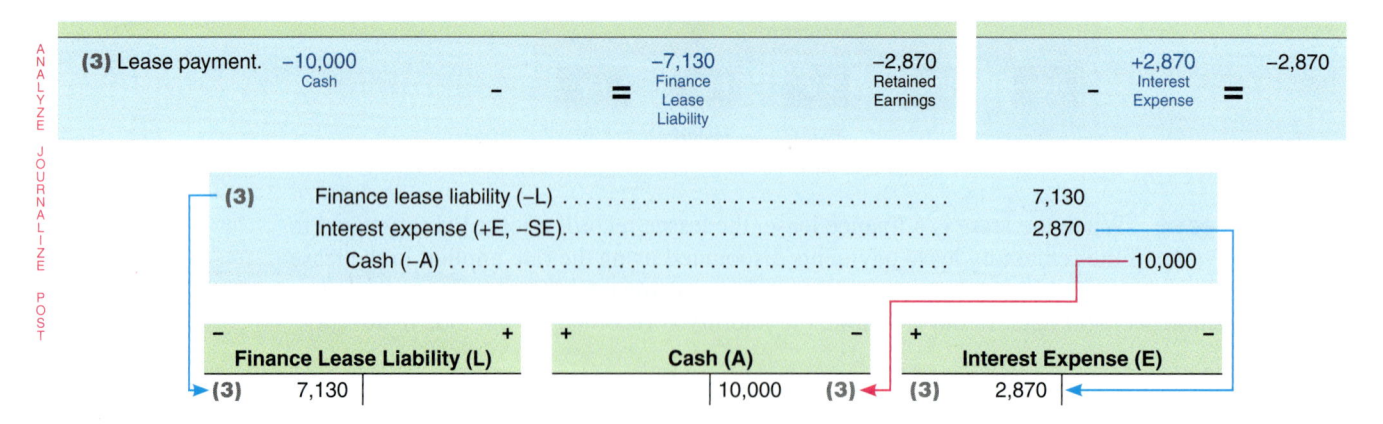

Transaction	Balance Sheet	Income Statement
(3) Lease payment.	−10,000 Cash = −7,130 Finance Lease Liability − 2,870 Retained Earnings	+2,870 Interest Expense = −2,870

(3) Finance lease liability (−L).................................. 7,130
Interest expense (+E, −SE)................................. 2,870
Cash (−A).. 10,000

Finance Lease Liability (L)	Cash (A)	Interest Expense (E)
(3) 7,130	10,000 (3)	(3) 2,870

---

[5] Companies can choose whether to create an accumulated amortization account (contra-asset) or to simply reduce (credit) the right-of-use asset directly.

Interest expense of $2,870 is computed by multiplying the unpaid balance in the lease liability by the interest rate ($41,002 × 7%). The difference between the lease payment and interest expense ($10,000 − $2,870) is the principal repayment, which is recorded as a reduction, or debit, to the lease liability. The year-end balance in the lease liability account is $33,872, calculated as ($41,002 − $7,130).

Exhibit 10.2 presents the amortization table for Gillette's lease liability under the finance lease method. The amortization of finance leases is identical to the amortization of installment loans introduced in Chapter 9.

EXHIBIT 10.2 Amortization Table for a Finance Lease Liability

A Year	B Beginning-Year Lease Liability	C Interest Expense (B × 7%)	D Payment	E Principal Repayment (D − C)	F Ending-Year Lease Liability (B − E)
1	$41,002	$2,870	$10,000	$7,130	$33,872
2	33,872	2,371	10,000	7,629	26,243
3	26,243	1,837	10,000	8,163	18,080
4	18,080	1,266	10,000	8,734	9,346
5	9,346	654	10,000	9,346	0

Operating Lease When the lease is an operating lease, the initial measurement of the right-of-use asset and liability is measured at the same time and in the same manner as we just discussed for finance leases. Gillette will need to prepare an amortization schedule as shown in **Exhibit 10.2** for the operating lease liability. Even though control has not passed to the lessee, the lessee still has a right-of-use asset and an obligation to make lease payments. The difference in accounting occurs subsequent to the initial measurement. Unlike a finance lease, for operating leases an equal amount of expense is recorded each period on the income statement, using the straight-line method for expense recognition.

To illustrate, let's assume the Gillette Electronics lease from our example above is classified as an operating lease. Again, initial measurement is the same as above, and the initial entry is as follows:

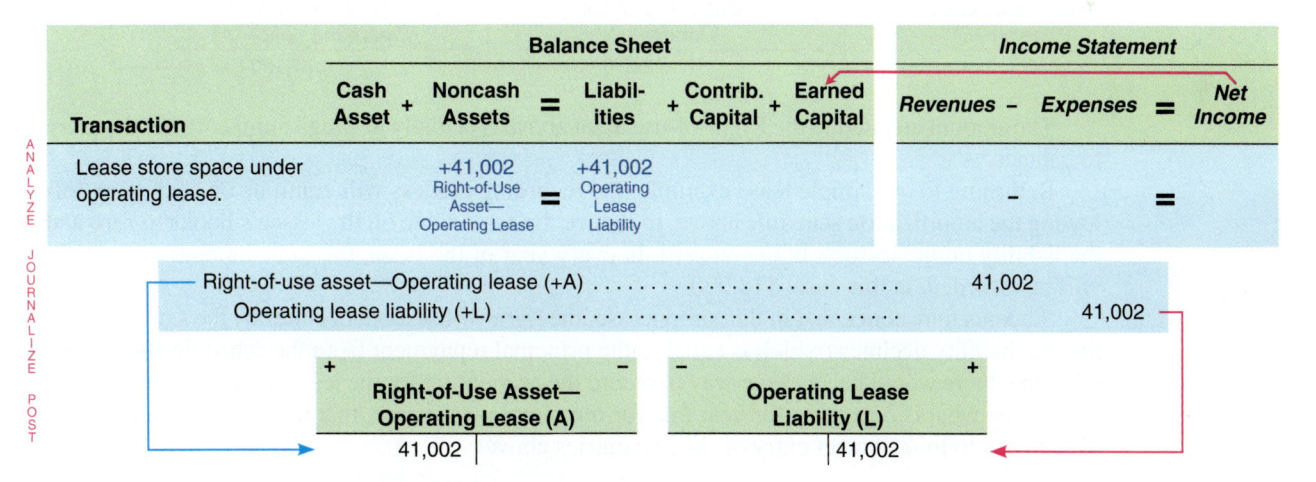

Transaction	Cash Asset	+	Noncash Assets	=	Liabilities	+	Contrib. Capital	+	Earned Capital	Revenues	−	Expenses	=	Net Income
Lease store space under operating lease.			+41,002 Right-of-Use Asset— Operating Lease		+41,002 Operating Lease Liability									

Right-of-use asset—Operating lease (+A) 41,002
    Operating lease liability (+L) 41,002

+ Right-of-Use Asset— Operating Lease (A)	− Operating Lease Liability (L) +
41,002	41,002

At the end of the first year, Gillette will record the straight-line expense amount related to the lease and will record the lease payment in cash. The straight-line expense is computed by taking the total cost of the lease divided by the total number of lease payments. The total cost of the lease in our example is straightforward because this is a simple lease (we briefly discuss more complicated cases below). The total cost of the lease is $50,000, and if we divide by the 5-year term, we obtain $10,000 as the annual straight-line expense amount. As stated above, Gillette still needs to prepare the amortization schedule for the liability. Though no interest expense line item is recorded for the operating lease liability, Gillette needs to compute the "interest" on the lease liability. Gillette also needs to compute the amortization of the right-of-use asset. The amortization is computed as the straight-line expense amount less the computed "interest" amount (though again no actual amortization expense line item or interest expense line item is recorded). The entries to record the payment of the lease payment as well as the recording of the straight-line expense are as follows:

Recording of the lease payment:

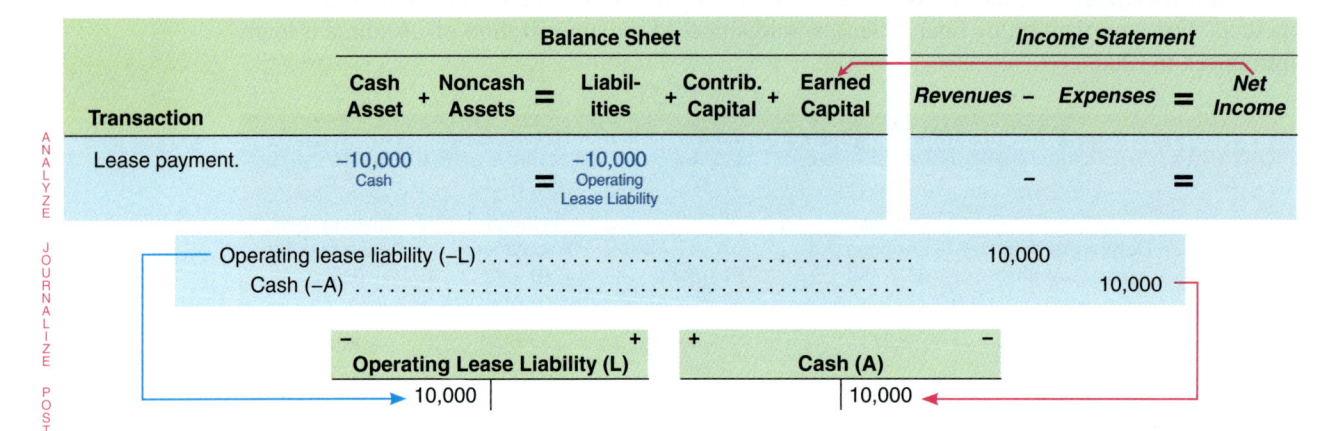

	Balance Sheet					Income Statement		
Transaction	Cash Asset	+ Noncash Assets	= Liabilities	+ Contrib. Capital	+ Earned Capital	Revenues	− Expenses	= Net Income
Lease payment.	−10,000 Cash		−10,000 Operating Lease Liability				−	=

Operating lease liability (−L) 10,000
    Cash (−A) 10,000

− +	+ −
Operating Lease Liability (L)	**Cash (A)**
10,000	10,000

Recording of the straight-line expense:

Transaction	Noncash Assets	= Liabilities	+ Earned Capital	Revenues − Expenses = Net Income
Record lease expense.	−7,130 Right-of-Use Asset— Operating Lease	+2,870 Operating Lease Liability	−10,000 Retained Earnings	+10,000 Operating Lease Expense −10,000

Operating lease expense (+E, −SE) 10,000
    Operating lease liability (+L) 2,870
    Right-of-use asset—Operating lease (−A) 7,130

+ −	− +	+ −
Operating Lease Expense (E)	**Operating Lease Liability (L)**	**Right-of-Use Asset— Operating Lease (A)**
10,000	2,870	7,130

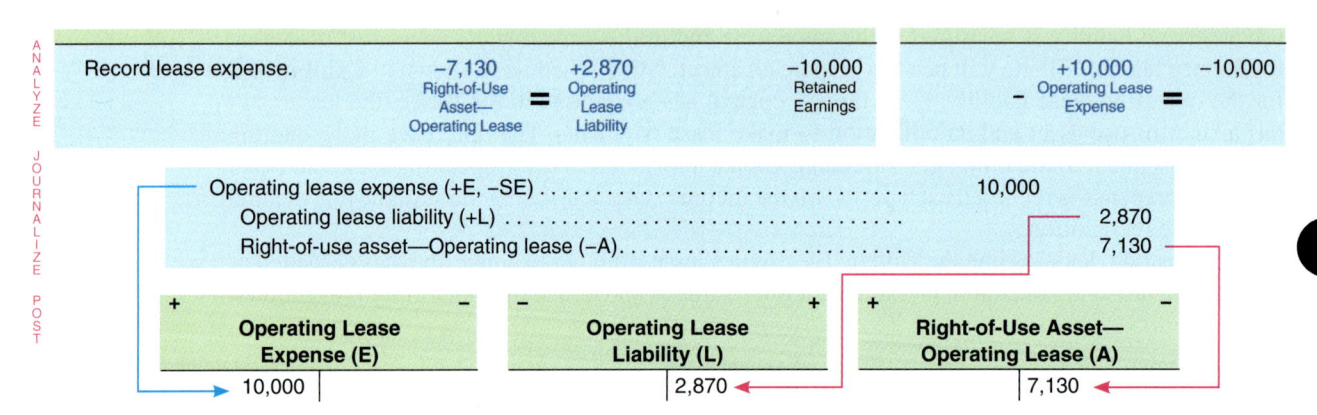

The amount credited to the Right-of-use asset above is actually a "plug" number to get the entry to balance.

Returning to our simple lease example, the recording process will continue on each year, following the amortization schedule above, to reduce the asset value on the lessee's books to zero and the liability on the lessee's books to zero. In every year of the lease, the same amount of expense will be recorded, in this case, $10,000.

Students may notice that in this simple case, the right-of-use asset declines by the same amount that the liability declines (which is equal to the principal repayment from the schedule above) and think that there would be an easier way to record the accounting for the lease. Indeed, an alternative way to see what is occurring for year one for our simple lease case, that may be more obvious to students, is to look at a net entry of the two entries above:

Year 1 net entry:

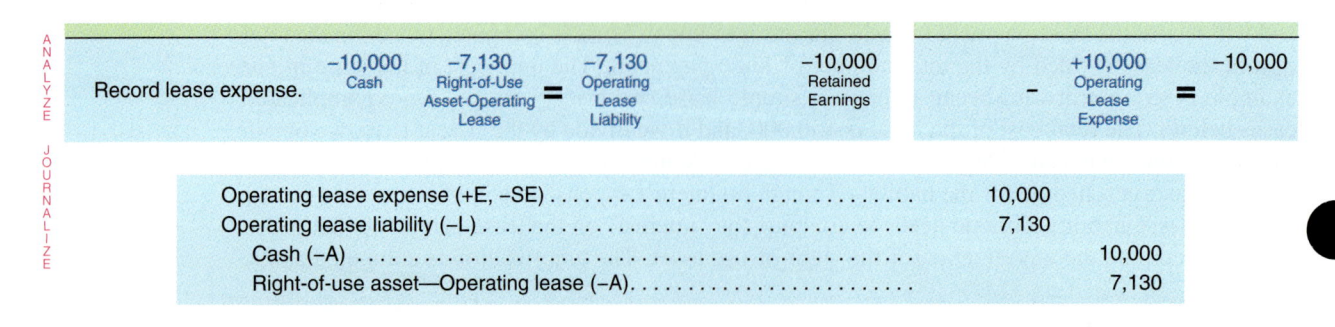

Transaction	Cash Asset	Noncash Assets	= Liabilities	+ Earned Capital	Revenues − Expenses = Net Income
Record lease expense.	−10,000 Cash	−7,130 Right-of-Use Asset-Operating Lease	−7,130 Operating Lease Liability	−10,000 Retained Earnings	+10,000 Operating Lease Expense −10,000

Operating lease expense (+E, −SE) 10,000
Operating lease liability (−L) 7,130
    Cash (−A) 10,000
    Right-of-use asset—Operating lease (−A) 7,130

This is correct in this case, however, this relation—that the decline in the lease liability is the same as the decline in the right-of-use asset—will not always hold. The lease in our case is a simple lease with payments due at the end of the year. If the lease were one with payments due at the beginning of the year, or if the lease were more complex, for example, if it included prepayments, escalation provisions, other required or optional payments, lessee initial direct costs, lease incentives, or other items, then the accounting would be different. In such cases, the decline ("amortization") of the right-of-use asset will not equal reduction of the liability (i.e., the principal repayment). Indeed, in the more complex leases, the right-of-use asset value will not even equal the liability value when the lease commences. As a result, the only way to compute the decline the right-of-use asset value (the "amortization") in more complex cases is as a "plug" number equal to the straight-line expense amount less the computed "interest" amount for the reporting period. In these more complex cases (which are common), the two-entry method originally presented is necessary to correctly record the accounting for the lease.

In year 5 of this lease for Gillette, the entries would be as follows:

Operating lease liability (–L) 10,000	
Cash (–A)	10,000

The entry for the straight-line-expense amount is:

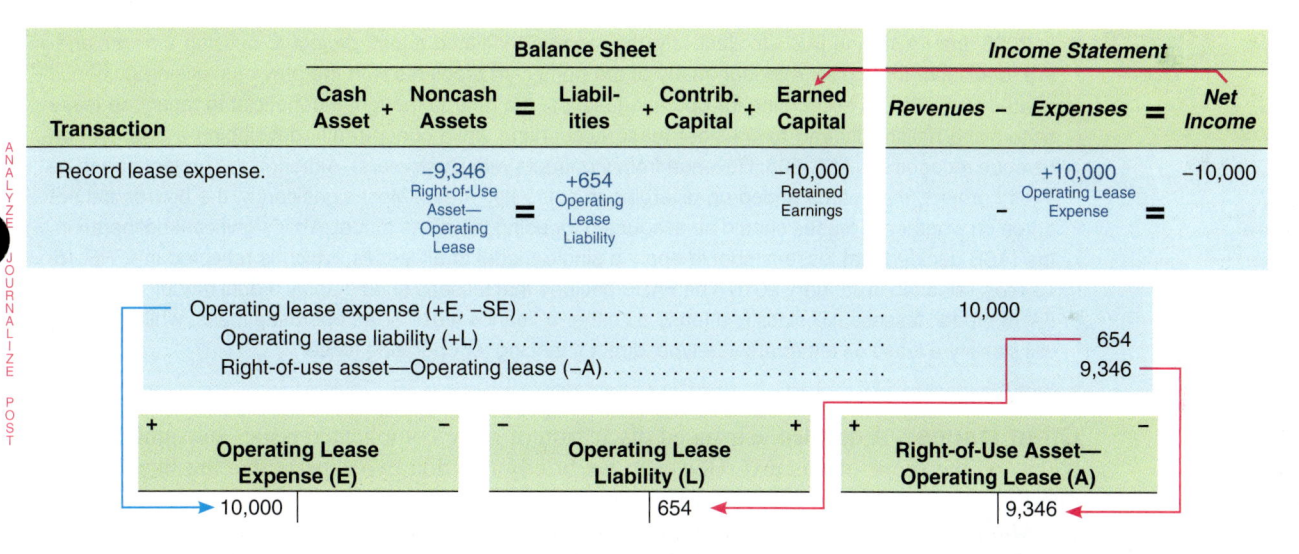

Transaction	Cash Asset	+	Noncash Assets	=	Liabilities	+	Contrib. Capital	+	Earned Capital		Revenues	–	Expenses	=	Net Income
Record lease expense.			−9,346 Right-of-Use Asset— Operating Lease	=	+654 Operating Lease Liability				−10,000 Retained Earnings				+10,000 Operating Lease Expense		−10,000

Operating lease expense (+E, –SE)	10,000	
Operating lease liability (+L)		654
Right-of-use asset—Operating lease (–A).		9,346

+ Operating Lease Expense (E)	− Operating Lease Liability (L)	+ Right-of-Use Asset— Operating Lease (A) −
10,000	654	9,346

Thus, at the end of the lease term, the liability will be zero ($41,002 − $10,000 + $2,870 − $10,000 + $2,371 − $10,000 + $1,837 − $10,000 + 1,266 − $10,000 + $654). The asset also will have a zero balance ($41,002 − $7,130 − $7,629 − $8,163 − $8,734 − $9,346).

Comparison of Operating and Finance Lease Treatment The accounting for operating leases might seem odd in some ways to readers. Gillette is required to compute an "interest" cost using the amortization of the liability table to adjust the lease liability account and to compute the "amortization" of the right-of-use asset to adjust the right-of-use asset account. But there is no interest expense or amortization expense ever recorded in the income statement—only one straight-line Lease Expense. The goal (in the end, anyway) of the standard was to achieve (retain) straight-line expensing for these leases: the related expenses are not greater in the earlier part of the lease relative to the latter part of the lease, as they are with finance lease treatment. For example, even in our simple lease illustration above, the total expense in the first year for Gillette if the lease was a finance lease is $11,070. (Amortization of the right-of-use asset is $8,200, and interest expense is $2,870.) However, with the operating lease classification, the first year expense amount is $10,000. Note that the balance of the asset on the balance sheet differs—the balance of the asset declines faster for the finance lease than the operating lease (i.e., amortization is faster for the finance lease). The balance of the lease liability each year is the same for the finance lease as it is for the operating lease. A full comparison is below:

EXHIBIT 10.3 — Comparison of Expenses and Right-of-Use Asset Balance

	Finance Lease Method					Operating Lease Method		
Year	Interest Expense	Amortization Expense	Total Expense	Right-of-Use Asset Balance End of Year	Operating Lease Liability Balance End of Year	Lease Expense	Right-of-Use Asset Balance End of Year	Operating Lease Liability Balance End of Year
1	$2,870	$ 8,200	$11,070	$32,802	$33,872	$10,000	$33,872	$33,872
2	2,371	8,200	10,571	24,602	26,243	10,000	26,243	26,243
3	1,837	8,200	10,037	16,401	18,080	10,000	18,080	18,080
4	1,266	8,201	9,467	8,200	9,346	10,000	9,346	9,346
5	654	8,201	8,855	0	0	10,000	0	0
Total	$8,998	$41,002	$50,000			$50,000		

Exhibit 10.3 shows how the finance lease method reports a higher total expense (amortization plus interest) in the early years of the lease and a lower total expense in the later years. But the operating lease method reports the same expense every year. Total expense over the 5-year life of the lease is the same under both methods.

A GLOBAL PERSPECTIVE (IFRS)

In 2008, the FASB and IASB (collectively, the "boards") initiated a joint project to develop a new standard to account for leases. Although many of the perceived problems with the previous leasing guidance related to a lessee's accounting for operating leases, the boards thought it beneficial to reflect on lease accounting holistically and to consider lease accounting while concurrently developing a proposal on revenue recognition (ASC 606, Revenue from Contracts with Customers). Although the project began as a joint project, the boards ended up diverging in some key areas. Most significantly, the boards did not agree on whether all leases should be accounted for using the same model. After significant deliberation, the IASB decided that lessees should apply a single model to all leases, which is reflected in *IFRS 16, Leases*, released in January 2016. The FASB decided that lessees should apply a dual model. Under the FASB model, lessees will classify a lease as either a finance lease or an operating lease, while a lessor will classify a lease as either a sales-type, direct financing, or operating lease.

Other Issues A detailed, expanded discussion of more complicated issues surrounding leases is beyond the scope of this text. However, we briefly mention two aspects that are likely to be of interest.

Multiple components: In determining whether a lease exists, management will need to determine if a contract contains a lease. It is possible that a contract could contain both lease and nonlease components and/or multiple lease components. In such a case, consideration in the contract is allocated to the separate components based on relative standalone selling prices.

As a disclosure example of such issues, the following excerpt is from Delta Airlines' 2020 10-K:

> In addition, we have regional aircraft leases that are embedded within our capacity purchase agreements and included in the operating right-of-use ("ROU") asset and lease liability. We allocated the consideration in each capacity purchase agreement to the lease and nonlease components based on their relative standalone value. Lease components of these agreements consist of 125 aircraft as of December 31, 2020, and nonlease components primarily consist of flight operations, in-flight, and maintenance services. We determined our best estimate of the standalone value of the individual components by considering observable information including rates paid by our wholly owned subsidiary, Endeavor Air, Inc., and rates published by independent valuation firms. See Note 12, "Commitments and Contingencies," for additional information about our capacity purchase agreements.

We note that companies can elect a simpler method of not separating the lease and non-lease components in certain cases. For example, Deere & Co., disclose the following:

> The company has elected to combine lease and nonlease components, such as maintenance and utilities costs included in a lease contract, for all asset classes.

Impairment: Lessees need to determine if the leased asset (finance or operating) is impaired. If a lessee records an impairment charge on a right-of-use asset associated with a finance lease, it should revise the amortization expense by calculating a new straight-line amortization based on the revised asset value.

If the lease is an operating lease and the right-of-use asset requires an impairment, once impaired, lease expense will no longer be recognized on a straight-line basis. A lessee should continue to amortize the lease liability using the same effective interest method as before the impairment charge. The right-of-use asset, however, should be subsequently amortized on a straight-line basis.

As can be seen in **Exhibit 10.3** the unamortized value of a right-of-use asset resulting from an operating lease is typically greater than it would have been had the lease been classified as a finance lease. Because of this higher value, a right-of-use asset arising from an operating lease may have a higher risk of impairment.

BUSINESS INSIGHT

A *Wall Street Journal* article discusses an interesting consequence of the new accounting lease standard. The new standard requires companies to collect and disclose lease data to a much greater extent than had been the case previously. While this was a large task for many companies, it provided a more detailed look into their lease spending than they had performed before enabling management to implement cost cutting and achieve greater efficiency. The article provides several examples:

> Tyson Foods Inc. spent about three years analyzing and digitizing its leases to get the comprehensive view of the portfolio required under the new rules. As a result, the Springdale, Ark., meat producer expects to reduce roughly $450 million in lease obligations it has for transportation and material handling equipment and real estate. "The improved visibility gives us a lot better management of our overall lease portfolio," said Brian Martfeld, the company's senior director for controls and automation. CVS Health Corp. spent about $2.5 billion on operating leases in 2017, according to a company spokesman. As it wrangled more than 10,000 lease agreements, the Woonsocket, R.I.-based health-care company found some areas it could trim. "We are considering curtailing the leasing of certain low-dollar equipment in the future," a company spokesman said. "Laptop and desktop computers would be two common examples."

Because many of these leases are long term it may take time to realize the savings.

Source: *Wall Street Journal*, January 22, 2019, "CFOs Uncover Surprise Savings as They Implement New Lease-Accounting Rules"

Lease Disclosures

Deere & Company adopted the new lease standard during the first quarter of 2020. Based on Deere's fiscal year-end, the company was not required to adopt the standard earlier. However, many companies were required or opted to adopt the lease standard earlier than fiscal year 2020, such as Caterpillar Inc. (as of January 1, 2019), American Airlines (as of January 1, 2018), and PepsiCo, Inc. (as of first quarter of 2019).

Deere recognizes operating leases and finance leases as a lessee. Deere discloses that its right-of-use assets and lease liabilities for operating leases and finance leases are embedded in balance sheet accounts shown in Exhibit 10-1. For example, right-of-use assets for operating leases of $324 million are included in the amount of $2,432 million, labeled as "other assets" on the balance sheet. These lease accounts are not stated separately because they are not material to the balance sheet; thus, they do not require separate line items. In the notes to their 2020 financial statements, Deere discloses the following (excerpted and reordered to some extent):

> Lessee
> The company recognizes on the balance sheet a lease liability and a right of use asset for leases with a term greater than one year for both operating and finance leases.
> The amounts of the lease liability and right of use asset are determined at lease commencement and are based on the present value of the lease payments over the lease term. The lease payments are discounted using the company's incremental borrowing rate since the rate implicit in the lease is generally not readily determinable. The company determines the incremental borrowing rate for each lease based primarily on the lease term and the economic environment of the country where the asset will be used,

continued

continued from previous page

adjusted as if the borrowings were collateralized. Leases with contractual periods greater than one year and that do not meet the finance lease criteria are classified as operating leases.

Operating and finance lease right of use assets and lease liabilities follow in millions of dollars:

	2020
Operating leases:	
Other assets	$324
Accounts payable and accrued expenses	305
Finance leases:	
Property and equipment—net	$ 63
Short-term borrowings	21
Long-term borrowings	39
Total finance lease liabilities	$ 60
Weighted-average remaining lease terms:	
Operating leases	5
Finance leases	3
Weighted-average discount rates:	
Operating leases	2.1%
Finance leases	2.2%

The lease expense by type consisted of the following in millions of dollars:

(in millions)	2020
Operating lease expense	$126
Short-term lease expense	23
Variable lease expense	41
Finance lease:	
Depreciation expense	20
Interest on lease liabilities	2
Total lease expense	$212

Cash paid for amounts included in the measurement of lease liabilities follows in millions of dollars:

	2020
Operating cash flows from operating leases	$124
Operating cash flows from finance leases	2
Financing cash flows from finance leases	17

Companies are required to disclose their future lease payments for the next five years and thereafter. Deere & Co. discloses the following:

Operating Leases

Lease payment amounts in each of the next five years at November 1, 2020, follow in millions of dollars:

Due in:	Operating Leases	Finance Leases
2021	$ 90	$22
2022	74	18
2023	52	12
2024	42	5
2025	24	3
Later years	41	2
Total lease payments	323	62
Less imputed interest	18	2
Total minimum lease payments	$305	$60

Notice that the "Total minimum lease payments" is the present value of the lease payments because imputed interest is subtracted. This present value is the liability recorded in the balance sheet as shown in Deere's disclosures above where they show that $305 million is included in "Accounts payable and accrued expenses" in the balance sheet.

Going forward, all firms will report operating leases under this standard. Financial statement users need to be cautious, however, if comparing a year where leases are reported under the new standard to a year where leases are reported under the old standard. For example, 2020 was Deere's first year of adoption so comparing 2020 to 2019 could be misleading because in 2020 the operating lease assets and the associated liabilities are included in the balance sheet and in 2019 the operating lease assets and their associated liabilities are not included in the balance sheet. Many ratios, such as debt-to-equity, debt-to-assets, return-on-assets, and others would be impacted.

Financial statement users could perform better year-over-year analysis in the year of adoption by adjusting the prior year financial statement numbers to 'as if' amounts—'as if' the new standard applied in 2019. We cover this notion of analyzing financial statements after adjusting them such that off-balance sheet debt is treated as if it were on-balance sheet debt below in our discussion of commitments and contingencies.[6]

Leases and the Statement of Cash Flows A lease results in an increase to long-term operating assets and an increase in liabilities. However, in many cases, there is no effect on cash flows at the inception of the lease—see entry (1) on page 10-7. As a consequence, the initial inception of the lease should be reported as a material noncash transaction and not presented in the statement of cash flows under either investing or financing cash flows. Subsequently, the amortization of the leased asset for a finance lease is added (in an indirect method statement of cash flows) to cash flow from operations (an expense that does not require a cash outlay), and the principal portion of the lease payment is treated as debt repayment under cash flows from financing activities. Note that because amortization is added back to earnings to compute operating cash flows in the indirect method Statement of Cash flows, and the principal repayment is a financing cash flow, operating cash flows will likely be higher for a finance lease relative to an operating lease. This is because, again, in the case of the operating lease, the lease expense is in the operating section of the Statement of Cash Flows either as part of net income in an indirect method statement or as a cash outflow in a direct method statement. In a direct method Statement of Cash Flows, the interest on a finance lease is an operating cash flow and the principal repayment is a financing cash flow. For a capital lease when the direct method Statement of Cash Flows is used, the lease payment is shown an operating cash flow.

YOU MAKE THE CALL

You are the CEO While implementing the new lease accounting standard, your CFO gathers more information on your lease contracts than your company has ever had before. What are some decisions and potential outcomes that this information might lead to? [Answer on page 10-40]

Accounting for Leases LO10-1 **Review 10-1**

Assume that **The Gap Inc.** leased a vacant retail space with the intention of opening another store. The lease calls for annual lease payments of $32,000, due at the end of each of the next ten years. Assume the appropriate discount rate is 7%.

continued

---

[6] Estimating the liability and asset amounts for operating leases under the old standard when only the future payments were disclosed and no asset or liability was included in the balance sheet would require the following steps (briefly stated): 1) estimate a discount rate, such as the rate on comparable debt, 2) compute the present value of the disclosed required future lease payments as of the end of the current reporting period, 3) estimate the associated asset value (could do this several ways but most easily one could look at the relative asset to liability ratio of the leases under the new standard), and 4) assume the difference between the 'as if' asset and 'as if' liability under the old standard reduces shareholder equity.

continued from previous page

Part One
First, assume that the lease is treated as a finance lease.
1. Using a financial statement effects template, report the entry that Gap would make to record the commencement of the lease agreement.
2. Using a financial statement effects template, report the entries to record amortization expense and the first lease payment at the end of the first year of the lease.
3. For parts 1 and 2, prepare the journal entries and post to the corresponding T-accounts.

Part Two
Now assume that the lease is treated as an operating lease.
1. Using a financial statement effects template, report the entries necessary for Gap for the first year.
2. For part 1, prepare journal entries and post to the corresponding T-accounts.

Solution on p. 10-64.

PENSIONS

Companies frequently offer retirement or pension plans as a benefit for their employees. There are two general types of pension plans:

1. **Defined contribution plan**. This type of plan is one in which the employer, employee, or both make contributions on a regular basis. Individual accounts are set up for participants. Future benefits are not guaranteed but instead fluctuate on the basis of investment earnings. Following retirement, the employee makes periodic withdrawals from that account. The amount that can be withdrawn is determined by how much is contributed to the plan and the rate of return earned on the investment. A tax-advantaged 401(k) account is a typical example. Under a 401(k) plan, the employee makes contributions that are exempt from federal taxes (as are the returns on the contributions) until they are withdrawn after retirement.

2. **Defined benefit plan**. This type of plan is one in which benefits are defined (promised). Defined benefit plans require the company to make periodic payments to a third party, which then makes payments to an employee after retirement. Retirement benefits are usually based on years of service and the employee's salary, not on the amount invested or the rate of return. It is possible for companies to set aside insufficient funds to cover these obligations. As a result, defined benefit plans can be overfunded or underfunded. (Federal law does set minimum funding requirements.) All pension investments are retained by the third party until paid to the employee. In the event of bankruptcy, employees have the standing of a general creditor, but usually have additional protection from the Pension Benefit Guaranty Corporation (PBGC), an independent agency of the U.S. government funded by premiums paid from the participating companies.

For a defined contribution plan, any company contribution is recorded as an expense in the income statement when the cash is paid or the liability is accrued. A defined benefit plan is more complex. Although the company contributes cash or securities to the pension investment account, the pension obligation is not satisfied until the employee receives pension benefits, which may be many years into the future. This section focuses on how a defined benefit plan is reported in the financial statements and how we assess company performance and financial condition when such a plan exists.

We note that the use of defined benefit plans has declined significantly. Many companies are instead establishing defined contribution plans for employees. For example, as of 2018, IRS data (Form 5500 summary data from the Department of Labor website, so including private companies) reveal that there are 675,007 defined contribution plans covering 105.8 million total, and 83.4 million active, employees compared with 46,869 defined benefit plans covering 34 million total, and 13.1 million active, employees. Many companies disclose that their defined benefit pension plans are closed to new entrants. Despite this decline in the use or contribution to defined benefit plans, such plans still constitute a significant liability for many companies.

Balance Sheet Effects of Defined Benefit Pension Plans

Pension plan assets are primarily investments in stocks and bonds (mostly of other companies, but it is not uncommon for companies to invest pension funds in their own stock). Pension liabilities (called the **projected benefit obligation** or **PBO**) are the company's obligations to pay current and former employees. The difference between the fair value of the pension plan assets and the projected benefit obligation is called the **funded status** of the pension plan. If the PBO exceeds the pension plan assets, the pension is **underfunded**. Conversely, if pension plan assets exceed the PBO, the pension plan is **overfunded**. Under current U.S. GAAP, companies are required to record only the funded status on their balance sheets (that is, the *net* amount, not the pension plan assets and PBO separately), either as an asset if the plan is overfunded, or as a liability if it is underfunded.

Pension plan assets consist of stocks and bonds whose value changes each period in three ways. First, the value of the investments increases or decreases as a result of interest, dividends, and gains or losses on the stocks and bonds held. Second, the pension plan assets increase when the company contributes additional cash or stock to the investment account. Third, the pension plan assets decrease by the amount of benefits paid to retirees during the period. These three changes in the pension plan assets are articulated below.

	Pension Plan Assets
	Pension plan assets, beginning balance
+	Actual returns on investments (interest, dividends, gains and losses)
+	Company contributions to pension plan
−	Benefits paid to retirees
=	Pension plan assets, ending balance

The pension liability, or PBO (projected benefit obligation), is computed as the present value of the expected future benefit payments to employees. The future payments depend on the number of years the employee is expected to work (years of service) and the employee's salary level at retirement. Consequently, companies must estimate future wage increases, as well as the number of employees expected to reach retirement age (or the vesting requirement) with the company. In addition, in order to compute the present value of benefit payments, the company has to estimate how long the plan participants are likely to receive pension benefits following retirement (that is, how long the employee—and often surviving spouse—will live). Once the future retiree pool is determined and the expected future payments under the plan are estimated, the expected payments are then discounted to arrive at the present value of the pension obligation. This is the PBO. A reconciliation of the PBO from beginning balance to year-end balance follows.

	Projected Benefit Obligation
	Projected benefit obligation, beginning balance
+	Service cost
+	Interest cost
+/−	Actuarial losses (gains)
−	Benefits paid to retirees
=	Projected benefit obligation, ending balance

As this reconciliation shows, the balance in the PBO changes during the period for four reasons.

- First, as employees continue to work for the company, their pension benefits increase. The annual **service cost** represents the additional (future) pension benefits earned by employees during the current year.

- Second, **interest cost** accrues on the outstanding pension liability, just as it would with any other long-term liability (see the accounting for bond liabilities in Chapter 9). Because there are no scheduled interest payments on the PBO, the interest cost accrues each year; that is, interest is added to the existing liability.

- Third, the PBO can increase (or decrease) due to **actuarial losses (and gains)**, which arise when companies make changes in their pension plans or make *changes in actuarial assumptions* (including assumptions that are used to estimate the PBO, such as the rate of wage inflation, termination and mortality rates, and the discount rate used to compute the present value of future obligations). For example, if a company increases the discount rate used to compute the present value of future pension plan payments from, say, 8% to 9%, the present value of future benefit payments declines (just like bond prices), and the company records a gain. Conversely, if the discount rate is reduced to 7%, the present value of the PBO increases and a loss is recorded. Other assumptions used to estimate the pension liability (such as the expected wage inflation rate or the expected life span of current and former employees) can create similar actuarial losses or gains.

- Fourth, pension benefit payments to retirees reduce the PBO. (That portion of the liability is now paid.)

Finally, the net pension liability (or asset) that is reported in a company's balance sheet, then, is computed as follows.

Net Pension Asset (or Liability)

Pension plan assets (at fair value)
− Projected benefit obligation (PBO)
─────────────────────────────────
Funded status

If the funded status is positive (assets exceed liabilities), the overfunded pension plan is reported on the balance sheet as an asset, typically called prepaid pension cost. If the funded status is negative (liabilities exceed assets), it is reported as a liability.[7] During the early 2000s, long-term interest rates declined drastically, and many companies lowered their discount rate for computing the present value of future pension payments. Lower discount rates meant higher PBO values. This period also witnessed two bear markets—the "dot com crash" in 2000–2001 and the financial crisis of 2008–2010—and pension plan assets declined in value. The combined effect of the increase in PBO and the decrease in asset values caused many pension funds to become severely underfunded. Willis Towers Watson, a compensation consulting firm, analyzed the Fortune 1000 corporations that sponsor a defined benefit plan (between 350–400 companies) and found that in 2009, aggregate funding was 81% of the projected liability. The companies' funded status was 87% in 2019 and is projected to be 87% for 2020 as well.[8] Deere & Company reported an underfunded pension obligation of $447 million in 2020. This amount was equal to less than 1% of its total assets. Many companies with a defined benefit plan report that their plans are underfunded. The underfunded (overfunded) liability as a percent of total assets for Deere and several other companies is reported in the chart below. One company, Cummins Inc., actually has an overfunded status because plan assets exceed obligations.

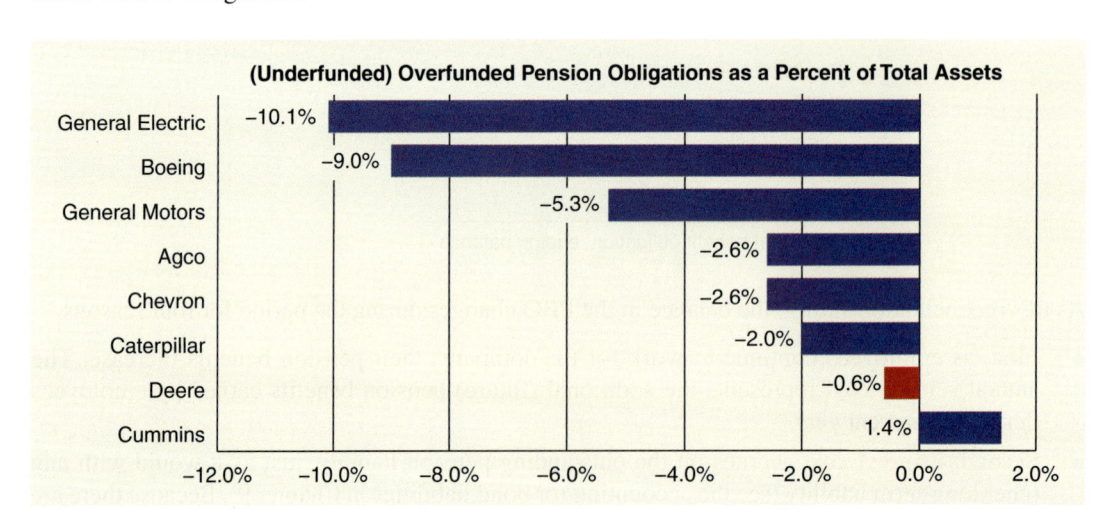

(Underfunded) Overfunded Pension Obligations as a Percent of Total Assets

Company	Percent
General Electric	−10.1%
Boeing	−9.0%
General Motors	−5.3%
Agco	−2.6%
Chevron	−2.6%
Caterpillar	−2.0%
Deere	−0.6%
Cummins	1.4%

---

[7] Companies that have a defined benefit plan typically maintain many pension plans. Some are overfunded and others are underfunded. Current U.S. GAAP requires companies to group all of the overfunded and underfunded plans together and to present a net asset for the overfunded plans and a net liability for the underfunded plans.

[8] Source: https://www.willistowerswatson.com/en-US/News/2021/01/health-of-largest-us-corporate-pension-plans-showed-no-improvement-in-2020

Income Statement Effects of Defined Benefit Pension Plans

In a defined benefit plan, pension expense is not determined by the company's contribution to the pension fund. Instead, net pension expense is computed as follows.

Net Pension Expense
Service cost
+ Interest cost
− *Expected* return on pension plan assets
± Amortization of deferred amounts
Net pension expense

The net pension expense is rarely reported separately on the income statement.

As shown above, the net pension expense has four components. The previous section about the PBO described the first two components: service costs and interest costs. The third component of pension expense relates to the return on pension plan assets, which *reduces* total pension expense. To compute this component, companies use the long-term *expected* rate of return on the pension plan assets, rather than the *actual* return, and multiply that expected rate by the balance in the pension plan assets account. Use of the expected return rather than actual return is an important distinction. Company CEOs and CFOs dislike income variability because they believe that stockholders react negatively to it, so company executives intensely (and successfully) lobbied the FASB to use the more stable expected long-term investment return, rather than the actual return, in computing pension expense. Thus, the pension plan assets' expected return is subtracted to compute net pension expense.

Any difference between the expected and the actual return is accumulated, together with other deferred amounts, off-balance-sheet and reported in the note disclosures. Other deferred amounts include changes in PBO resulting from changes in estimates used to compute the PBO and from amendments to the pension plans made by the company. However, if the deferred amounts exceed certain limits, the excess is recognized on-balance-sheet with a corresponding amount recognized as amortization in the income statement.[9] This amortization is the fourth component of pension expense and can be either a positive or a negative amount depending on the sign of the difference between expected and actual return on plan assets.

> ### YOU MAKE THE CALL
>
> **You are a Consultant to the FASB** The Board has asked your input on whether the assets in the pension fund should be netted against Pension Benefit Obligation (PBO) or whether the pension asset and the pension obligation should be reported separately. How would you advise the Board?
> [Answer on page 10-40]

Note Disclosures—Components of Plan Assets and PBO

GAAP requires extensive disclosures for pensions (and other postretirement benefits that we discuss later). These notes provide details relating to the net pension liability reported in the balance sheet and the components of pension expense reported as part of SG&A expense in the income statement.

Deere & Company indicates in Note 8 to its 2020 10-K that the funded status of its pension plan is $(447) million on December 31, 2020. This means Deere's plan is underfunded. Following are excerpts from the disclosures Deere makes in its pension note (excerpted and reordered to some extent):

---

[9] To avoid amortization, the deferred amounts must be less than 10% of the PBO or pension investments, whichever is less. The excess, if any, is amortized until no further excess remains. When the excess is eliminated (by investment returns or company contributions, for example), the amortization ceases. Alternatively, U.S. GAAP allows for any systematic and rational recognition of gains and losses as a component of net periodic pension cost if the method results in recognition of at least the minimum amortization amount required, is applied consistently, and is applied to all gains and losses on both plan assets and PBOs. Any method that accelerates recognition of gains and losses is generally preferable.

8. PENSION AND OTHER POSTRETIREMENT BENEFITS

The company has several funded and unfunded defined benefit pension plans and other postretirement benefit (OPEB) plans, primarily health care and life insurance plans, covering its U.S. employees and employees in certain foreign countries. The company uses an October 31 measurement date for these plans.

	Pensions 2020	Pensions 2019
Change in benefit obligations		
Beginning of year balance	$(14,250)	$(12,108)
Service cost	(321)	(261)
Interest cost	(347)	(447)
Actuarial gain (loss)	(771)	(2,174)
Benefits paid	749	705
Settlements/curtailments	15	
Foreign exchange and other	(96)	35
End of year balance	(15,021)	(14,250)
Change in plan assets (fair value)		
Beginning of year balance	14,024	12,602
Actual return on plan assets	1,144	2,081
Employer contribution	108	70
Benefits paid	(749)	(705)
Settlements	(12)	
Foreign exchange and other	59	(24)
End of year balance	14,574	14,024
Funded status	$ (447)	$ (226)

The amounts recognized at November 1, 2020, and November 3, 2019, respectively, in millions of dollars consist of the following:

	Pensions 2020	Pensions 2019
Amounts recognized in balance sheet		
Noncurrent asset	$ 863	$ 840
Current liability	(72)	(56)
Noncurrent liability	(1,238)	(1,010)
Total	$ (447)	$ (226)
Amounts recognized in accumulated other comprehensive income—pretax		
Net actuarial loss	$ 4,475	$ 4,312
Prior service cost (credit)	21	32
Total	$ 4,496	$ 4,344

Deere's PBO began in 2020 with a balance of $14,250 million. It increased by the accrual of $321 million in service cost and $347 million in interest cost. During the year, Deere also realized an actuarial loss of $771 million and a loss on foreign exchange and other of $96 million, which increased the pension liability. The PBO decreased as a result of $749 million in benefits paid to retirees and $15 million in settlements, leaving a balance of $15,021 million at year-end.

Pension plan assets began the year with a fair value of $14,024 million, which increased by $1,144 million from investment returns and increased by $108 million from company contributions. The company drew down its investments to make pension payments of $749 million to retirees, and made $12 million in settlements. Finally, plan assets increased for foreign exchange and other of $59 million, leaving the pension plan assets with a year-end balance of $14,574 million. The funded status of Deere's pension plan at year-end is $(447) million ($15,021 million − $14,574 million). The negative balance indicates that its pension plan is underfunded. The PBO and pension plan assets account cannot be separated into operating and nonoperating components; thus, most analysts treat the entire funded status as an operating item (either asset or liability). Deere disclosed that the net $(447) underfunded amount is included in three categories on the balance sheet (**Exhibit 10-1**): as a noncurrent liability ($1,238) and a current liability ($72), offset by a noncurrent asset ($863).

Note Disclosures—Components of Pension Expense

Deere & Company incurred $143 million of pension expense in 2020. Details of this expense are found in its pension note disclosure. Deere reported $160 million in pension cost related to defined contribution plans. In addition, Deere reported its expense (benefit) related to its defined benefit plans as follows ($ millions):

	2020	2019
Pensions		
Service cost	$ 321	$ 261
Interest cost	347	447
Expected return on plan assets	(819)	(802)
Amortization of actuarial loss	256	148
Amortization of prior service cost	13	11
Settlements/curtailments	25	5
Net cost	$ 143	$ 70

Most analysts have long considered the service cost portion of pension expense to be an operating expense, similar to salaries and other benefits. In contrast, the other components were considered nonoperating. The accounting standards require companies to report the service cost component in the same line item as compensation. Meanwhile, the other components of net (benefit) cost are required to be presented outside of income from operations. We note that Deere states that service cost is recorded in the line item "Other operating expenses" in the statement of consolidated income.

> **RESEARCH INSIGHT**
>
> **Valuation of Pension Disclosures** The FASB requires disclosure of the major components of pension cost presumably because it is useful for investors. Pension-related research has examined whether investors assign different valuation multiples to the components of pension cost when assessing company market value. Research finds that the market does, indeed, attach different interpretation to pension components, reflecting differences in information about recurring vs. nonrecurring expenses.

Interest cost is the product of the PBO and the discount rate. This discount rate is set by the company. The expected dollar return on pension assets is the product of the pension plan asset balance and the expected long-run rate of return on the investment portfolio. This rate is also set by the company. Further, the PBO is affected by the expected rate of wage inflation, termination, and mortality rates, all of which are estimated by the company.

U.S. GAAP requires disclosure of several rates used by the company in its estimation of PBO and the related pension expense. Deere discloses the following table in its pension note disclosure:

Weighted-Average Assumptions	2020	2019
Discount rates—service cost	2.9%	4.0%
Discount rates—interest cost	2.7%	4.0%
Rate of compensation increase	3.8%	3.8%
Expected long-term rates of return	6.4%	6.5%
Interest crediting rate—U.S. cash balance plan	2.1%	3.3%

During 2020, Deere decreased its assumed discount rate used to compute the present value of the PBO and service cost. The expected rate of compensation remained constant. Deere decreased its expected long-term rates of returns on plan assets and its interest crediting rate.

Changes in these assumptions have the following general effects on pension expense and, thus, profitability. This table summarizes the effects of increases in the various rates used to compute the pension cost. Decreases have the exact opposite effects of increases. In the computation of the PBO, the higher the discount, the lower the obligation.

Estimate Change	Probable Effect on Pension Expense	Reason for Effect
Discount rate increase	Increases	If the PBO is discounted at a higher rate, the PBO liability will be smaller. This will increase the actuarial gain, which may have to be amortized into pension cost (benefit) over time (along with other items). If the rate used to compute the interest cost increases, then the PBO is multiplied by a higher interest rate, resulting in an increased interest cost component of the pension expense. Often, the interest cost effect dominates.
Investment return increase	Decreases	The dollar amount of expected return on plan assets is the product of the plan assets balance and the expected long-term rate of return. Increasing the return increases the expected return on plan assets, thus reducing pension expense.
Wage inflation increase	Increases	The expected rate of wage inflation affects future wage levels that determine expected pension payments. An increase, thus, increases PBO, which increases both the service and the interest cost components of pension expense.

In the case of Deere, net actuarial losses increased their end-of-year benefit obligation by $771 million in 2020. The company discloses that the loss is due primarily to a decrease in the discount rate used to compute the PBO partially offset by a decrease in mortality assumptions.

BUSINESS INSIGHT

Pension Buyout at GM General Motors' pension obligation was at one time the largest of any company in the world. In 2011, its defined benefit plans were underfunded by $25.4 billion. Because pension fund assets are invested in securities, the underfunded balance can increase if the stock market falls. Analysts argued that the size, risk, and long duration of these obligations depressed GM's credit rating and its stock price.

In an effort to remove some of the projected obligations from its balance sheet, GM offered to buy out the pensions of 42,000 retirees in 2012. The pensions of an additional 76,000 retirees were transferred to Prudential Financial, who will make the annuity payments to the retirees. Although the buyout required an immediate cash payment, the move removed approximately $26 billion of pension obligations from GM's 2012 balance sheet, thus improving solvency ratios. In addition, the reduced obligation means that future income statements will reflect lower pension expense due to reduced interest costs. GM's 2020 financial statement shows that the defined benefit pension plans are still underfunded by $12.4 billion. Note that this is a considerable improvement from 2014, when the plans were underfunded by $24.1 billion. The related pension expense included in the income statement for 2020 was a benefit of $1,023 million.

Note Disclosures and Future Cash Flows

The net periodic defined benefit pension cost for Deere in 2020 is $143 million; this is different from the $108 million in cash that Deere contributed to its defined benefit plans. In addition, Deere paid $160 million into its defined contribution plans. Thus, its total pension cost for 2020 was $303 million ($143 + $160), and its cash contributions totaled $268 million ($108 + $160).

Companies use their pension plan assets to pay pension benefits to retirees. When markets are booming, as was true during the 1990s, pension plan assets can grow rapidly. However, when markets reverse, as in the bear market of the early 2000s and in 2008–2009, the value of pension plan assets can decline. The company's annual pension plan contribution is an investment decision influenced, in part, by market conditions and minimum required contributions specified by law.[10] Companies' cash contributions come from borrowed funds or operating cash flows.

---

[10] The Pension Protection Act of 2006 tightens funding requirements so employers make greater cash contributions to pension funds, closes loopholes that allow companies with underfunded plans to skip cash pension payments, prohibits employers and union leaders from promising extra benefits if pension plans are markedly underfunded, and strengthens disclosure rules to give workers and retirees more information about the status of their pension plan.

RESEARCH INSIGHT

Why Do Companies Offer Pensions? Research examines why companies choose to offer pension benefits. It finds that deferred compensation plans and pensions help align the long-term interests of owners and employees. Research also examines the composition of pension investments. It finds that a large portion of pension fund assets are invested in fixed-income securities, which are of lower risk than other investment securities. This implies that pension assets are less risky than nonpension assets. However, in severe economic downturns, some corporations curtail their pension plan contributions in order to protect cash flow.

Deere paid $749 million in pension benefits to retirees in 2020, yet it contributed only $108 million to pension assets that year. The remaining amount was paid out of available funds in the investment account. Cash contributions to the pension plan assets are the relevant amounts for an analysis of projected cash flows. Benefits paid in relation to the pension liability balance can provide a clue about the need for *future* cash contributions. Companies are required to disclose the expected benefit payments for five years after the statement date and the remaining obligations thereafter. Following is Deere's benefit disclosure statement:

The following table summarizes the benefit payments that are scheduled to be paid in the years ending December 31 ($ millions):

	Pensions
2021	$ 765
2022	724
2023	711
2024	707
2025	699
2026–2030	3,450

Deere's unfunded pension amount increased by roughly $221 million from 2019 to 2020. The company contributed $108 million, and the plan assets had an actual return of $1,144 million. The reason for the increase in the net unfunded balance in its pension plan is from increase in the pension liability essentially because of the actuarial losses. The low interest rate environment we have been in for several years, is keeping the estimated pension liabilities relatively high (because the discounting is at a low rate).

BUSINESS INSIGHT

How Pensions Confound Income Analysis Overfunded pension plans and boom markets can inflate income. Specifically, when the stock market is booming, pension investments realize large gains that flow to income (via reduced pension expense). Although pension plan assets do not belong to shareholders (as they are the legal entitlement of current and future retirees), the gains and losses from those plan assets are reported in income. The following chart plots the funded status of **General Electric Company**'s pension plan together with pension expense (revenue) that GE reported from 2000 to 2020.

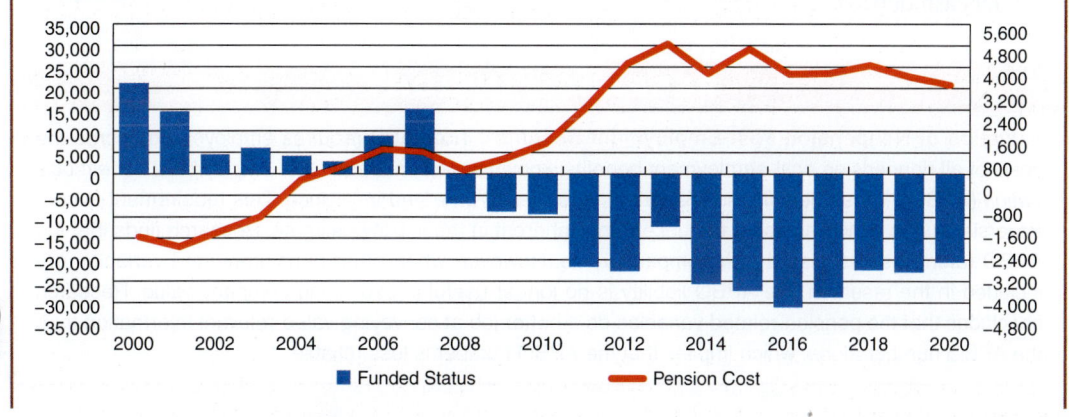

continued

continued from previous page

> GE's funded status was consistently positive (indicating an overfunded plan) until 2008. The degree of overfunding peaked in 1999 at the height of the stock market and began to decline during the bear market of the early 2000s. GE reported pension *revenue* (not expense) during this period. In 2001, GE's reported pension *revenue* was $2,095 million (10.6% of its pretax income). Because of the plan's overfunded status, the expected return and amortization of deferred gains components of pension expense amounted to $5,288 million, far in excess of the service and interest costs of $3,193 million. Since 2004, GE has recorded pension expense (rather than revenue) as the pension plan's overfunding and expected long-term rates of return declined, and in 2008 the funded status turned negative. In 2020, GE reported an unfunded liability of $20.6 billion and a pension expense of roughly $3.6 billion.

One application of the pension note disclosure is to assess the likelihood that the company will be required to increase its cash contributions to the pension plan. This estimate is made by examining the funded status of the pension plan and the projected payments to retirees. For severely underfunded plans, the projected payments to retirees will not be covered by existing pension assets. When this occurs, the company will need to divert operating cash flow from other prospective projects to cover its pension plan. Alternatively, if operating cash flows will not be sufficient, it will likely need to borrow to fund those payments. This decision can be especially troublesome as the debt service payments include interest, thus, effectively increasing the cost of the pension contribution.

Other Post-Employment Benefits

In addition to pension benefits, many companies provide health care and insurance benefits to retired employees. These benefits are referred to as **other post-employment benefits (OPEB)**. These benefits present reporting challenges similar to pension accounting. However, companies most often provide these benefits on a "pay-as-you-go" basis, and it is rare for companies to make contributions in advance for OPEB. As a result, this liability, known as the **accumulated post-employment benefit obligation (APBO)**, is largely, if not totally, unfunded. GAAP requires that the unfunded APBO liability be reported in the balance sheet and the annual service costs and interest costs be accrued as expenses each year. This requirement is controversial for two reasons. First, future health care costs are especially difficult to estimate, so the value of the resulting APBO (the present value of the future benefits) is fraught with error. Second, these benefits are provided at the discretion of the employer and can be altered or terminated at any time. Consequently, employers argue that without a legal obligation to pay these benefits, the liability should not be reported in the balance sheet.

Other post-employment benefits can produce large liabilities. For example, Deere & Company reports underfunded health care and insurance obligations of $3,892 million and a related expense of $198 million in 2020. Our analysis of cash flows related to pension obligations can be extended to other post-employment benefit obligations. For example, in addition to its pension payments, Deere discloses that it is obligated to make health care and insurance payments to retirees totaling $2,947 million over the next 10 years. Our analysis of projected cash flows must consider this potential cash outflow.

RESEARCH INSIGHT

Valuation of Nonpension Post-Employment Benefits The FASB requires employers to accrue the costs of all nonpension post-employment benefits; known as *accumulated post-employment benefit obligation* (APBO). These benefits consist primarily of health care and insurance. This requirement is controversial due to concerns about the uncertainty inherent in the liability estimate. Research finds that the APBO (alone) is associated with company value. However, when other pension-related variables are included in the research, the APBO liability is no longer useful in explaining company value. Research concludes that the pension-related variables do a better job at conveying value-relevant information than the APBO number alone, which implies that the APBO number is less reliable.

A GLOBAL PERSPECTIVE

Pension Fund Status IFRS and U.S. GAAP require companies to report the funded status of their defined benefit pension plans on the balance sheet. IFRS, however, calculates pension expense differently. First, unlike U.S. GAAP, IFRS requires that the expected return on pension assets must be the same rate as the discount rate used to value the PBO. In addition, IFRS recognizes the cost of plan amendments in the income statement immediately, rather than amortizing those costs over the service life of employees. There are also other differences that make direct comparison across IFRS and U.S. GAAP firms difficult.

Analyzing Pension Disclosures

LO10-2 Review 10-2

The following pension data is taken from Note 16 of **The Boeing Company** 10-K report.

($ millions)	2020
Change in Benefit Obligation	
Beginning balance	$77,645
Service cost	3
Interest cost	2,455
Actuarial loss (gain)	7,759
Settlement/curtailment/other	(68)
Gross benefits paid	(5,386)
Exchange rate adjustment	7
Ending balance	$82,415
Change in Plan Assets	
Beginning balance at fair value	$61,711
Actual return on plan assets	9,275
Company contribution	3,013
Settlement payments	(68)
Benefits paid	(5,241)
Exchange rate adjustment	6
Ending balance at fair value	$68,696

Components of Net Periodic Benefit (Income)/Cost	Pension 2020
Service cost	$ 3
Interest cost	2,455
Expected return on plan assets	(3,756)
Amortization of private service credits	(80)
Recognized net actuarial loss/(gain)	1,032
Settlement/curtailment loss/(gain)	9
Net periodic benefit (income)/cost	$ (337)

Required

1. In general, what factors affect a company's pension benefit obligation during a period?
2. In general, what factors affect a company's pension plan investments during a period?
3. What amount is reported on the balance sheet relating to the Boeing Company pension plan?
4. How does the expected return on plan assets affect pension cost?
5. How does Boeing's expected return on plan assets compare with its actual return (in $s) for 2020?
6. How much net pension cost is reflected in Boeing's 2020 income statement?
7. Assess Boeing's ability to meet payment obligations to retirees.

Solution on p. 10-67.

ACCOUNTING FOR INCOME TAXES

LO10-3 Describe and interpret accounting for income taxes.

Companies maintain two sets of books: one for reporting to their shareholders and creditors and one to report to tax authorities. This is not unethical or illegal. In fact, it is often required. Companies with publicly traded securities compute and report financial accounting income under the rules (e.g., GAAP or IFRS) provided by the financial accounting standards setters (e.g., FASB in the United States). As we have discussed, this income computation is done on the accrual basis, and it is meant to provide information about firm performance to outside stakeholders, such as investors and creditors.[11] Companies must also compute taxable income and report the amount on their tax return(s) filed with the tax authorities in the jurisdictions in which they are required to file (e.g., the Internal Revenue Service and state tax authorities in the United States). Taxable income is determined under the rules promulgated by the government of the taxing jurisdiction (e.g., the Internal Revenue Code in the United States). Tax authorities have different objectives from financial accounting standard setters. The tax rules are set in order to raise money to fund government activities, to encourage or discourage certain behaviors, and (hopefully) based on some sense of fairness and equity. In contrast, financial accounting income is meant to provide information about firm performance to investors, creditors, and other stakeholders so that these parties can make informed decisions about such things as investments and loans. The rules and objectives are very different for the two income measures, and as a result, the two resulting income numbers for a company can be very different.

Our objective here is to learn how to determine a corporation's income tax expense that is reported on the income statement for financial accounting purposes. Financial accounting uses accrual accounting; thus, income tax expense is determined using accrual accounting just like all other expenses. As a result, income tax expense on the income statement is not the cash taxes paid for the reporting period. Instead, it is the accrual-based expense measure, meaning it is the total income tax expense related to the financial accounting income reported in the period regardless of whether those income taxes are actually paid in the current period or not. Furthermore, because it is accrual-based, there will be resulting assets and liabilities that need to be accounted for on the balance sheet. These include what are called deferred tax assets and deferred tax liabilities.

The U.S. enacted tax reform through legislation known as the Tax Cuts and Jobs Act (TCJA) in 2017. We provide an overview of the provisions of this legislation where it is relevant for our discussion because the legislation is still affecting and being discussed in many financial statements. One of the key features of the legislation was a reduction in the top statutory corporate income tax rate from 35% to 21%. As mentioned previously early on in the textbook, we employ a 25% rate for our calculations (mainly for ease of mental math but also because raising the rate is being considered).

Book-Tax Differences

There are two general types of differences between taxable income and financial accounting (book) income, also known as book-tax differences: permanent differences and temporary differences.

A difference that would be considered permanent is an item of income or expense that is accounted for differently for book and tax purposes in the current year and never reverses in a future year. A simple example of a permanent difference is interest income on municipal bonds. Municipal bond interest income is included in financial accounting income. However, municipal bond interest is tax exempt at the federal level, meaning it is not included in taxable income. Thus, if a company has municipal bond interest income, its financial accounting income will be higher than its taxable income by the amount of municipal bond interest. This difference will not reverse in the future because the municipal bond interest is never included in taxable income. The accounting for income tax with respect to a permanent difference is straightforward; no deferred tax assets or liabilities are created. Income tax expense is lower (in this case) in the current year as a result of the (explicit) income taxes saved by investing in municipal bonds.

A temporary difference is an item of income or expense that is different between book and taxable income in the current year but will reverse in a future year such that the same amount is included in taxable income and book income over time. Temporary differences are:

1. created by using accrual accounting for book, and cash accounting for tax, and/or
2. created by using different rules for determining the accrual amount for book than for tax.

FYI We use the term "book income" to refer to income before income taxes, as reported in financial statements. "Taxable income" refers to income reported in the income tax return.

---
[11] All companies have to report to tax authorities, but many privately held companies do not have to comply with GAAP.

A common example of a temporary difference is depreciation. For financial accounting purposes, companies often use straight-line depreciation, as discussed in Chapter 8. For U.S. tax purposes, however, companies use an accelerated method of depreciation (the Modified Accelerated Cost Recovery System (MACRS)). Thus, early in an asset's life, tax depreciation will be greater than book depreciation. However, over the life of the asset, the same amount of depreciation will be recorded for book and tax (assuming zero salvage value). This is a temporary difference because tax depreciation is higher earlier on but will be equal to or less than book depreciation in later years in the asset's life. In other words, the book-tax difference will reverse. The computation of the income tax expense is more difficult in this case. We need to account for the taxes due on taxable income (the cash taxes) *and* an accrual of taxes that are known to be due in a future period when the depreciation difference reverses. In other words, total income tax expense is the tax expense related to financial accounting income for the period regardless of whether the taxes are actually paid this year. The accrual for the portion not yet paid creates a **deferred tax liability**—the book-tax difference in this period will lead to higher taxable income relative to book income in the future. This higher relative taxable income means higher cash taxes to be paid in the future—that is, a liability. Furthermore, as part of the TCJA, businesses are now allowed to "fully expense" certain asset purchases (generally with useful lives of 20 years or less) in the first year the asset is put into service. This means that for tax purposes the taxpayer can deduct the entire cost of the qualifying asset as depreciation in the first year. In such cases, the difference between financial accounting treatment and tax treatment is extreme. This full expensing provision is optional to the taxpayer and is currently in the law for assets purchased between December 2017 and December 31, 2022. (The extra [bonus] depreciation phases down for assets purchased after that and will be zero at the start of 2027.) For our purposes, we first provide an example using accelerated depreciation for tax purposes and then modify the example to illustrate what happens when the asset is fully deducted for tax purposes in the first year. The concepts are the same, but the illustration is useful nonetheless.

Example Assume Clark Corporation is in its first year of business. It purchases a piece of equipment that costs $200,000 with a useful life of 4 years and no net salvage value. The firm uses straight-line depreciation for financial reporting purposes and accelerated depreciation under MACRS for tax purposes. (We will use double declining balance depreciation as an approximation for our example.) Comparing the depreciation schedules reveals the following information:

> **FYI** Income tax expense is also titled **provision for income tax**.

Year	Tax Reporting DDB Depreciation	Financial Reporting Straight-Line Depreciation	Tax vs. Book Difference	Cumulative Tax-Book Difference
1............	$100,000	$50,000	$50,000	$50,000
2............	50,000	50,000	0	50,000
3............	25,000	50,000	(25,000)	25,000
4............	25,000	50,000	(25,000)	0

Assume the corporate statutory tax rate is 25%. We expect the tax rate to stay at 25% for the entire 4 years, and that depreciation is the only book-tax difference for the Clark Corporation. The deferred tax liability at the end of each year is the cumulative book-tax difference times the tax rate. The tax rate to be used is the enacted tax rate expected to be in effect when the book-tax difference reverses. The deferred tax expense each period is the current year book-tax difference (which is the change in the cumulative book-tax difference) times the tax rate. The deferred tax liability at the end of each year and the deferred tax expense for each year for Clark Corporation would be:

Year	Cumulative Tax-Book Difference	Tax Rate	Deferred Tax Liability, End of Year	Deferred Tax Expense
1................	$50,000	25%	$12,500	$12,500
2................	50,000	25%	12,500	0
3................	25,000	25%	6,250	(6,250)
4................	0	25%	0	(6,250)

Now assume for illustration that financial accounting earnings each year before depreciation and taxes are $325,000 and there are no other book-tax differences. The yearly calculation of financial reporting and taxable income along with the income tax expense is as follows:

	Tax Reporting			
Year	1	2	3	4
Earnings before depreciation	$325,000	$325,000	$325,000	$325,000
Depreciation deduction	(100,000)	(50,000)	(25,000)	(25,000)
Taxable income	225,000	275,000	300,000	300,000
Tax due on the tax return (@ 25%)	56,250	68,750	75,000	75,000

	Financial Accounting Reporting			
Year	1	2	3	4
Earnings before depreciation	$325,000	$325,000	$325,000	$325,000
Depreciation expense	(50,000)	(50,000)	(50,000)	(50,000)
Earnings before tax	275,000	275,000	275,000	275,000
Tax expense	68,750	68,750	68,750	68,750

The entry to record income tax expense in Year 1 follows using the financial statement effects template and journal entry form. (We show the entries as if the company is paying in cash at the time the entry is recorded. If the company pays in cash at a later time, a short-term liability account, income tax payable, would be credited in the entries below.)

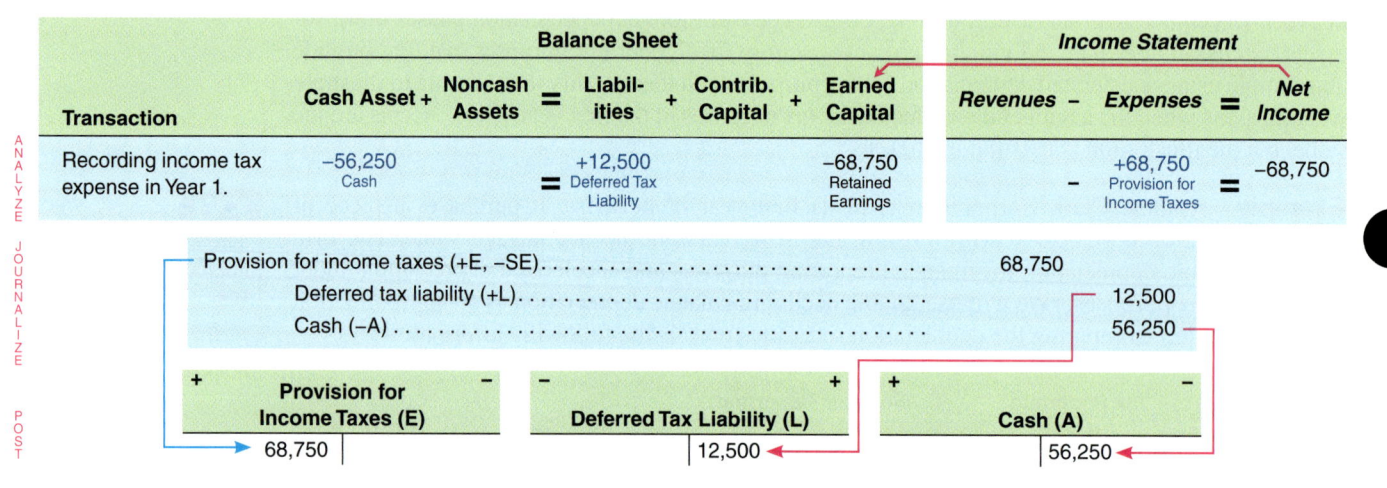

Recording income tax expense in Year 1.

Balance Sheet: Cash Asset −56,250 Cash; Noncash Assets —; = Liabilities +12,500 Deferred Tax Liability; + Contrib. Capital —; + Earned Capital −68,750 Retained Earnings

Income Statement: Revenues − Expenses +68,750 Provision for Income Taxes = Net Income −68,750

Provision for income taxes (+E, −SE)	68,750	
Deferred tax liability (+L)		12,500
Cash (−A)		56,250

Provision for Income Taxes (E): 68,750
Deferred Tax Liability (L): 12,500
Cash (A): 56,250

Clark Corporation would record income tax expense in each of the years of operation. For example, in Year 4, Clark Corporation records its income tax expense as follows:

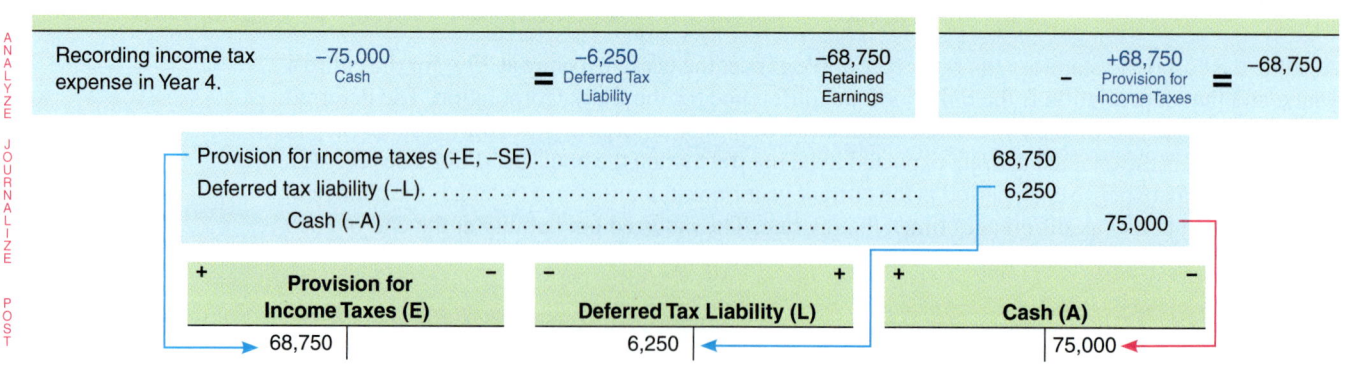

Recording income tax expense in Year 4.

Balance Sheet: Cash Asset −75,000 Cash; = Liabilities −6,250 Deferred Tax Liability; + Earned Capital −68,750 Retained Earnings

Income Statement: Revenues − Expenses +68,750 Provision for Income Taxes = Net Income −68,750

Provision for income taxes (+E, −SE)	68,750	
Deferred tax liability (−L)	6,250	
Cash (−A)		75,000

Provision for Income Taxes (E): 68,750
Deferred Tax Liability (L): 6,250
Cash (A): 75,000

The analysis highlights several facts:

1. Over the 4 years, tax payments to the IRS total $275,000 = $56,250 + $68,750 + $75,000 + $75,000. Total tax expense on the books for the 4 years also equals $275,000 = 4 × $68,750.
2. The timing of the tax payments differs from the tax expense recognized on the books.
3. The deferred tax liability created in the first year is reduced to zero in the 4th year when the useful life of the asset is over.

4. The cash flow takes place consistent with the tax code. The accounting expense amount is an accrual-basis measure.
5. In year 1, the corporation's provision for income tax consists of current income tax expense of $56,250 and deferred income tax expense of $12,500 for the total income tax expense of $68,750. In year 4, the corporation has current income tax expense of $75,000 and deferred income tax expense of $(6,250) for a total income tax expense of $68,750. The total income tax expense is shown on the income statement, and the more detailed breakout into current and deferred expense is disclosed in the notes to the financial statements.

What would occur if Clark Corporation deducted the full cost of the asset for tax purposes under the new rules in the TCJA?

Now we would have the following comparative depreciation schedules:

Year	Tax Reporting Full Deduction	Financial Accounting Reporting Straight-Line Depreciation	Tax vs. Book Difference	Cumulative Tax-Book Difference
1	$200,000	$50,000	$150,000	$150,000
2	0	50,000	(50,000)	100,000
3	0	50,000	(50,000)	50,000
4	0	50,000	(50,000)	0

The deferred tax liability schedule would be as follows:

Year	Cumulative Tax-Book Difference	Tax Rate	Deferred Tax Liability, End of Year	Deferred Tax Expense
1	$150,000	25%	$37,500	$37,500
2	100,000	25%	25,000	(12,500)
3	50,000	25%	12,500	(12,500)
4	0	25%	0	(12,500)

If we assume the same income and facts otherwise, the calculation of taxable income and tax on the tax return is as follows:

	Tax Reporting 1	2	3	4
Earnings before depreciation	$325,000	$325,000	$325,000	$325,000
Depreciation deduction	(200,000)	0	0	0
Taxable income	125,000	325,000	325,000	325,000
Tax due on the tax return (@ 25%)	31,250	81,250	81,250	81,250

Note that the computation of financial accounting income and total tax expense for financial accounting is exactly the same as it was before! Financial accounting depreciation did not change, and neither did total tax expense. What changed is the amount of tax Clark Corporation pays in cash each year versus the amount that is recognized as a deferred tax liability (or reversal of deferred tax liability).

For example, in year 1, the journal entry would be as follows:

Provision for income taxes (+E, –SE)	68,750	
Deferred tax liability (+L)		37,500
Cash (–A)		31,250

Notice that Clark Corporation saves a significant amount of cash taxes in year one between the two different tax treatments of the assets – the tax savings are $25,000 ($56,250 – $31,250; can also compute as additional depreciation deduction of $100,000 multiplied by the tax rate of 25%). However, for financial accounting purposes the deferred tax liability and deferred tax expense must increase because the company needs to account for all the taxes on the reported financial accounting income of $275,000, and that has not changed. Thus, the new tax law saves Clark Corporation cash taxes early in the asset's life and saves Clark Corporation money overall in terms of the time value of money. (Note that Clark Corporation's total cash taxes over the life of the asset did not change.) However, these savings are not reflected on GAAP financial statements because GAAP financial statements are accrual based and do not take the time value of money into account when accounting for income taxes.

> ### RESEARCH INSIGHT
>
> As tax reform was debated over the last decade in the U.S., this issue about the tax versus financial accounting treatment entered into the conversation. The question is whether publicly traded companies, whose financial statements (not tax returns) are the focus of the capital markets, would respond to the tax incentives provided by the immediate expensing of assets. Research suggests that publicly traded companies will respond less than private companies, and maybe less than policymakers would otherwise estimate, because the benefits of the accelerated depreciation, even full expensing, are not reflected on financial statements. One of the authors of this text testified about these issues to both the U.S. House Ways and Means Committee and the Senate Finance Committee. Actual evidence on how companies respond to the TCJA will be forthcoming over time once data are available. However, testing the effects of immediate deducting of asset purchases for tax purposes will be more difficult than it may seem because of confounding factors.

There are also transactions that generate the necessity to record a **deferred tax asset**. For example, bad debts, warranty expense, and many other accrued expenses usually require an associated deferred tax asset to be recorded. For financial accounting purposes, bad debt expense and warranty expense are expensed using management estimates before the receivable actually goes bad and before the warranty costs are actually paid. Again, this is because financial accounting is done on the accrual method and expenses that are associated with the revenue recorded generally are estimated and accrued before they are paid in cash. This is the conservative nature of financial reporting. For tax purposes, these expenses cannot be estimated but instead are deductible generally only when paid. This difference in timing between tax reporting and financial accounting leads to temporary differences where the tax deduction is later in time than the financial accounting expense (opposite of what we just illustrated for depreciation). Because in this case a tax deduction will occur in the future due to a transaction or event in the current period, the company has a deferred tax asset (future benefit) that needs to be recorded.

Temporary book-tax differences also occur with items of revenue. Take, for example, unearned revenue (also called deferred revenue or contract liability) we described in Chapter 6. If a company receives cash in advance of being able to recognize revenue, the company will record unearned revenue (a liability) until the revenue can be recognized. For tax purposes, however, the cash received is generally recorded as income in the period it is received.[12] Thus, there is often a book-tax difference. In this case, the revenue is recorded for tax in an earlier period than for financial accounting, meaning that in some future year(s), taxable income will be less than financial accounting income when the revenue is recognized according to the GAAP rules. That means the company has a deferred tax asset to record in the year the cash is received in the amount of the book-tax difference for revenue times the applicable tax rate.

As a brief example, let's say that the corporation Josie's Jewelry, Inc., makes sales of $100,000 in the current period and estimates and records a bad debt expense of $5,000. This is an expense for financial reporting purposes, but there is no deduction allowed for tax purposes in the current period. The tax deduction is not allowed until the receivable actually goes bad (i.e., is deemed to be uncollectible). Using a tax rate of 25%, Josie's Jewelry would report an increase in a deferred tax asset in the current period of $1,250 ($5,000 × 25%) and a corresponding deferred tax benefit (i.e., a negative deferred tax expense) on the income statement. When the receivable is deemed uncollectible and written off in a future period and the deduction is taken for tax purposes, the corporation will reverse

---

[12] The TCJA codified the principles in a 2004 tax ruling—Revenue Procedure 2004-34. Taxpayers are able to defer income recognition for tax purposes as well as long as the taxpayer is an accrual-basis taxpayer and the income is deferred for financial accounting purposes. The rule is that the taxpayer must recognize the income for tax purposes in gross income in the year of receipt unless they make an election to defer the income. The deferred income must be recognized in the year following the year of receipt (and is accelerated if the taxpayer ceases to exist).

the deferred tax asset to zero (assuming the full $5,000 is the amount that eventually is deducted for tax purposes) and record a $1,250 deferred tax expense. Notice that in this future period, the deduction is taken for tax purposes so the actual tax paid is lower, and thus, current tax expense is lower by $1,250. Thus, the net effect on income in the future period is zero. (Deferred tax expense is higher by $1,250, and current tax expense is lower by $1,250, netting to a zero total effect.) This is correct because the tax benefit was accrued (recognized) in the first period when the revenue was earned, bad debt expense was recorded, and deferred tax asset was established.

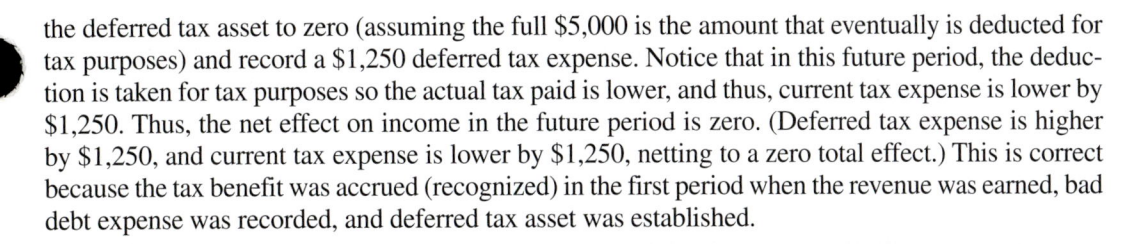

BUSINESS INSIGHT

As part of the TCJA, the United States changed the manner in which the foreign earnings of U.S. businesses are taxed. Previously, the U.S. had a regime that was a worldwide tax system, with deferral. This meant that the U.S. taxed the worldwide earnings of U.S. companies, but the U.S. taxation of certain foreign earnings (i.e., foreign operating earnings of a subsidiary of a U.S. company) was deferred until repatriation to the U.S. When the earnings were repatriated back to the U.S. (e.g., as a dividend to the parent company), then U.S. taxes were due (net of a foreign tax credit). This led to many negative economic consequences, such as U.S. multinational enterprises having an estimated $2 trillion in foreign earnings "locked out" of the U.S. In addition, it led to varied financial accounting outcomes because companies could accrue the U.S. taxes for financial accounting or not accrue the U.S. taxes because of an exception to deferred tax accounting (based on management's plans for the use of the foreign earnings).

The TCJA fundamentally changed the U.S. international tax system. The U.S. now has what some are calling a modified territorial tax system (and some are calling it a sort of worldwide minimum tax system). At a very high level, the new system exempts foreign earnings of U.S. multinationals from U.S. taxation unless the earnings are "high return" earnings in "low tax" jurisdictions, in which case the U.S. will tax those earnings currently (albeit at a lower rate). The system includes other base erosion protections that require companies to compute a type of alternative tax after disallowing certain payments to foreign parties that are considered "base eroding." Much of this is far beyond an introductory accounting textbook; however, one feature that affected financial statements for many multinational companies in 2017 was a mandatory deemed repatriation tax on the accumulated foreign earnings of the company as of the time the TCJA was passed (roughly). As part of the transition to the modified territorial system from the worldwide system, the U.S. required a tax payment on the accumulated earnings at a rate of 15.5% if the earnings were held in cash or cash equivalents, or a rate of 8% if the earnings were in noncash assets. (This tax is sometimes referred to as the transition tax.) This was a mandatory tax but could be paid over installments that stretch eight years. For financial accounting, the standard setters required companies to accrue the tax expense for this tax in the fiscal year containing December 2017, with no discounting for the time value of money, consistent with the rest of the accounting for income taxes.

Because of the variation in the accounting prior to the TCJA, there was some marked variation in terms of the effects of this mandatory tax for financial accounting. If a company had already accrued significant U.S. taxes on its unremitted foreign earnings, the accounting charge for the repatriation tax might not have been very large. Apple, Inc., for example, had substantial unremitted foreign earnings, but had accrued U.S. tax on a portion of these earnings. The accrued U.S. tax, recorded as a deferred tax liability before the TCJA, was $36.4 billion. Apple reports that it owed a deemed repatriation tax of $37.3 billion. Thus, there was very little of the mandatory repatriation tax that needed to have additional U.S. tax expense recorded for financial accounting. On the other hand, Cisco reported that it had $76 billion of unremitted earnings on which it owed a mandatory repatriation tax of $8.1 billion. Cisco did not have any deferred tax liability recorded (meaning no U.S. tax was previously accrued on those earnings). Thus, Cisco had to record all of the $8.1 billion as additional tax expense in their year ended July 28, 2018. The company's effective tax rate for the year was 99.2%!

Net Operating Losses Another book-tax difference is a net operating loss carryover. For tax purposes, corporations can carry over operating losses to future years.[13] Financial accounting does not have such a rule; if a corporation has a loss for financial reporting, the loss is recorded and the corporation starts the next year with a clean slate and measures income for that next year only. Thus,

---

[13] Prior to the TCJA, corporations could carry net operating losses back two years for tax purposes and forward for 20 years. The TCJA changed the rules. Now corporations cannot carry losses (starting with losses generated in 2018) back in time, but can only carry them forward. The TCJA also changes the carryforward period to be indefinite. However, another change in the TCJA is that tax loss carryforwards can only be used to offset 80% of taxable income in the future period. In essence, the concept of allowing loss carryovers for tax purposes approximates an averaging of income over time so companies with volatile income are not required to pay high taxes in years with high income and then get no relief in years with losses. We note that during the COVID-19 pandemic, the U.S. government temporarily made the net operating loss carryover rules more generous.

the net operating loss carryover is a temporary book-tax difference. Because the loss carry over represents future deductions for tax purposes, the company has and must record an increase to deferred tax assets and a deferred tax benefit (i.e., negative deferred tax expense) in the amount of the loss carryover times the tax rate (the enacted tax rate expected to be in effect when the loss carryover will be used to offset taxes). Thus, even though the corporation is not getting the cash benefits of the deduction yet, the accounting rules require the company to accrue the benefit to the current period.

Valuation Allowance After a corporation computes its income tax expense and records its deferred tax assets and liabilities, the corporation has yet another step to complete. The corporation must evaluate the realizability of the deferred tax assets. This means that management must estimate whether the company will have sufficient future taxable income to offset the future deductions represented by the deferred tax assets. If management does not think the company will have enough future taxable income to be able to use all the deferred tax assets, then a contra-asset must be established against the deferred tax assets. Thus, the deferred tax assets on the balance sheet will not be overstated. As an analogy, recall that when a company has accounts receivables, it must evaluate the collectability of those receivables and establish an allowance for doubtful accounts to ensure the accounts receivable asset is not overstated. Similarly, if a corporation has deferred tax assets that management does not expect to be able to use to offset future taxable income, then the company must record a **valuation allowance**. When the contra-asset is recorded, deferred tax expense is increased, which decreases accounting income (and if a valuation allowance is reduced, deferred tax expense is reduced, increasing income). A more detailed discussion is beyond the scope of this text, but net operating losses and associated valuation allowances have been an important part of many companies' accounting for income taxes.

Unrecognized Tax Benefit (Uncertain Tax Positions) Another step in accounting for income taxes is the computation of what is known as an unrecognized tax benefit. Essentially, corporations must estimate what amount tax authorities might assess in additional tax during future audits by the tax authorities (e.g., the IRS). In other words, this is a contingent liability—the corporation might owe more tax if the tax authority disagrees with the tax positions the company has taken on past tax returns. U.S. GAAP requires companies to record additional tax expense for this amount as well as an additional liability. The liability is included in total liabilities on the balance sheet (it is not an off-balance-sheet amount) but is not a separate line item. Details about the account are in the notes to the financial statements.

An example of disclosure about this amount is from Apple, Inc.'s most recent 10-K.

Apple, Inc.
Uncertain Tax Positions
The aggregate changes in the balance of gross unrecognized tax benefits, which excludes interest and penalties, for 2020, 2019, and 2018, is as follows (in millions):

	2020	2019	2018
Beginning balances	$15,619	$9,694	$8,407
Increases related to tax positions taken during a prior year	454	5,845	2,431
Decreases related to tax positions taken during a prior year	(791)	(686)	(2,212)
Increases related to tax positions taken during the current year	1,347	1,697	1,824
Decreases related to settlements with taxing authorities	(85)	(852)	(756)
Decreases related to expiration of statute of limitations	(69)	(79)	—
Ending balances	$16,475	$15,619	$9,694

Revaluation of Deferred Tax Assets and Liabilities Due to a Tax Rate Change

As we have mentioned, deferred tax assets and liabilities are measured using the enacted corporate statutory tax rate expected to be in effect when the deferred tax asset or liability reverses. In addition, as we have also mentioned, the TCJA lowered the U.S. corporate statutory tax rate to 21% from a top rate of 35%. This specific example provides an excellent illustration of the required accounting. When this occurred, companies had to revalue their deferred tax assets and liabilities on their financial statements. For financial accounting, the rules require that the revaluation occur in the period the tax law is enacted, not when it is effective (again, because the rate used to value the deferred tax assets and liabilities is the enacted rate expected to be in effect when the items reverse, not the rate applicable to the current period). Thus, if the company had net deferred tax liabilities, the company would reduce the value of the liability on the balance sheet and record a reduction to deferred tax expense. As a result, accounting income increases (because tax expense is lower). To illustrate a simple case, the Koehler Company had net deferred tax liabilities (meaning deferred tax liabilities in excess of deferred tax assets) of $1 million at the end of 2017 valued at the pre-TCJA tax rate of 35%. The simplest way to think about the tax rate change is that there was a 40% reduction in the tax rate. Thus, Koehler Company is required to devalue its deferred tax liabilities by 40%.[14] In 2017, the company would record the following entry to revalue the deferred tax liabilities at 21% and show the reduction to deferred tax expense:

Deferred tax liability (–L)...	400,000
Deferred tax benefit (–E, +SE)	400,000

The balance sheet equation would be as follows:

Transaction	Balance Sheet					Income Statement		
	Cash Asset +	Noncash Assets	= Liabilities +	Contrib. Capital	+ Earned Capital	Revenues –	Expenses =	Net Income
Revalue deferred tax liabilities for a tax rate change			–400,000 Deferred Tax Liability		+400,000 Retained Earnings		–400,000 Deferred Tax Benefit	+400,000

Conversely, if the company had net deferred tax assets, the company would revalue those assets at the lower rate and increase deferred tax expense. This would result in a higher expense and a "hit" to (a decrease in) accounting earnings.

CVS, one of our focus companies in the text, is a relatively simple company (with little to no foreign operations). Thus, their discussion of this issue is illustrative for our purposes.

The following is a portion of the tax note disclosure in CVS's 2017 10-K:

> On December 22, 2017, the President signed into law the Tax Cuts and Jobs Act (the "TCJA"). Among numerous changes to existing tax laws, the TCJA permanently reduces the federal corporate income tax rate from 35% to 21% effective on January 1, 2018. The effects on deferred tax balances of changes in tax rates are required to be taken into consideration in the period in which the changes are enacted, regardless of when they are effective. As the result of the reduction of the corporate income tax rate under the TCJA, the Company estimated the revaluation of its net deferred tax liabilities and recorded a provisional income tax benefit of approximately $1.5 billion for [the] year ended December 31, 2017. The Company has not completed all of its processes to determine the TCJA's final impact. The final impact may differ from this provisional amount due to, among other things, changes in interpretations and assumptions the Company has made thus far and the issuance of additional regulatory or other guidance. The accounting is expected to be completed by the time the 2017 federal corporate income tax return is filed in 2018.

Income Tax Disclosures

Deere & Company reported income of the consolidated group before income taxes of $3,883 million in 2020. Deere reported an income tax expense of $1,082 million in 2020. In 2019, Deere reported income of consolidated group before income taxes of $4,088 million and income tax expense of $852 million.

To fully understand how income tax expense is determined, we refer to the disclosure notes. Note 9 to Deere's 2020 10-K report contains the table shown in **Exhibit 10.4**.

---

[14] More specifically, the deferred tax liability is $1,000,000 and was computed using a 35% tax rate. Thus, the cumulative book-tax difference was $2,857,143 ($1,000,000/.35). To find the new deferred tax liability, multiply the cumulative book-tax difference by 21%. This yields $600,000 for the new deferred tax liability balance. To get to this balance, the deferred tax liability needs to be reduced by $400,000.

EXHIBIT 10.4 — Deere & Company Income Tax Expense

($ millions)	2020	2019
Current:		
U.S.:		
Federal	$ 400	$ 545
State	53	72
Foreign	640	700
Total current	$1,093	$1,317
Deferred:		
U.S.:		
Federal	$ (68)	$ (345)
State	9	(26)
Foreign	48	(94)
Total deferred	(11)	(465)
Provisions for income taxes	$1,082	$ 852

The income tax expense or benefit reported in the income statement consists of two primary components:

Current tax expense—this can be thought of for our purposes as the amount that has been paid or is payable to tax authorities in the current period. (It also usually contains the income effects of some tax accruals that are beyond the scope of this text.)

Deferred tax expense—this is the effect on tax expense due to changes in deferred tax liabilities and assets. It is the result of temporary differences between the reported income statement and the tax return.

Based on the table shown in **Exhibit 10.4**, Deere reported a tax provision of $1,093 million for current taxes in 2020 and a provision of $1,317 for current taxes in 2019. It also reported a net deferred tax benefit of $11 million in 2020, down from $465 million in 2019.

Companies must also disclose the components of deferred tax assets and liabilities. The components of Deere's deferred tax assets and liabilities are presented in **Exhibit 10.5**.

EXHIBIT 10.5 — Components of Deere & Company's Deferred Income Tax Assets and Liabilities

Deferred income taxes arise because there are certain items that are treated differently for financial accounting than for income tax reporting purposes. An analysis of the deferred income tax assets and liabilities at November 1, 2020, and November 3, 2019, in millions of dollars follows:

	2020 Deferred Tax Assets	2020 Deferred Tax Liabilities	2019 Deferred Tax Assets	2019 Deferred Tax Liabilities
OPEB liabilities	$ 804		$1,015	
Lessor lease transactions		$ 489		$ 599
Tax loss and tax credit carryforwards	937		781	
Accrual for sales allowances	362		518	
Tax over book depreciation		196		339
Goodwill and other intangible assets		368		378
Pension liability – net	316		186	
Allowance for credit losses	81		70	
Accrual for employee benefits	249		207	
Share-based compensation	41		68	
Deferred compensation	40		39	
Lessee lease transactions	56	56		
Other items	366	305	375	311
Less valuation allowances	(858)		(661)	
Deferred income tax assets and liabilities	$2,394	$1,414	$2,598	$1,627

We can reconcile the amounts from this disclosure back to the amounts shown on the balance sheet in **Exhibit 10-1**. The net deferred tax asset on the balance sheet equals $980 million or

$1,499 million − $519 million. The net deferred tax asset in the disclosure above is $980 million or $2,394 − $1,414.[15]

The largest component in the deferred tax asset balance is due to tax loss credits and carry-forwards. A portion of these losses and credits is reported to expire during the years 2021 to 2040, while a portion can be carried forward indefinitely. Notice also that Deere has a large deferred tax asset for pensions and OPEB (other postretirement benefit) plans. As we discussed earlier in the chapter, Deere has a large unfunded pension liability. The company has to record the liability and a pension expense for financial accounting on the accrual basis but does not get a tax deduction until funds are contributed to the plan. Thus, larger expenses have been recorded for book relative to the deductions taken for tax. In the future, this will reverse (assuming Deere eventually funds its pension), and the deductions for tax will be greater than the expenses for book. Thus, Deere has a deferred tax asset. (Again, the total income tax expense is the accrual-basis expense related to financial accounting income, not cash taxes paid.) Deere also recognizes a deferred tax asset for sales allowances. Although an estimate for sales returns, for example, is an expense for financial accounting purposes, it is not deductible for tax purposes unless the allowance is actually granted resulting in a deferred tax asset. Finally, notice the subtraction for the valuation allowance. The company discloses in its 2020 10-K that its deferred tax assets "are regularly assessed for the likelihood of recoverability from estimated future taxable income, reversal of deferred tax liabilities, and tax planning strategies. To the extent the company determines that it is more likely than not a deferred income tax asset will not be realized, a valuation allowance is established." The valuation allowance is 26% and 20% of deferred tax assets (before the allowance) in the years 2020 and 2019, respectively.

In terms of where deferred tax assets and liabilities are reflected on the balance sheet, under the current accounting standards all are recorded in the noncurrent section of the balance sheet. A net amount (asset or liability) is shown.

Companies also report in the disclosure notes a reconciliation of differences between the statutory U.S. tax rate (currently 21%) and the tax expense reported in the income statement. The **effective tax rate** is determined by dividing the provision for income taxes (tax expense) by the income before income taxes. Deere's effective tax rate for 2020 was 27.9% ($1,082 million/$3,883 million: income tax expense/pre-tax accounting income from the income statement). Deere's rate reconciliation lists the principal reasons for the difference between the provision for income taxes calculated using effective tax rate and the U.S. federal statutory income tax rate:

A comparison of the statutory and effective income tax provision and reasons for related differences in millions of dollars follow:

	2020	2019	2018
U.S. federal income tax provision at the U.S. statutory rate (2020 and 2019—21 percent, 2018—23.3 percent)	$ 815	$859	$ 950
Increase (decrease) resulting from:			
Net deferred tax asset remeasurement		6	414
Deemed earnings repatriation tax		(74)	290
Effects of GILTI and FDII	39	(33)	
Other effects of tax reform			42
Differences in taxability of foreign earnings	38	(94)	(92)
Valuation allowance on deferred taxes	139	28	50
Research and business tax credits	(50)	(85)	(43)
State and local income taxes, net of federal income tax benefit	59	47	59
Excess tax benefits on equity compensation	(87)	(40)	(49)
Tax rates on foreign earnings	68	183	44
Unrecognized tax benefits	(32)	(28)	30
Other—net	93	83	32
Provision for income taxes	$1,082	$852	$1,727

---

[15] Readers will note that the asset and liability amounts do not separately, directly tie to the balance sheet, however. It is not clear what classification method Deere is using (but the net amount does tie out). It is possible the company has separated the amounts by jurisdiction, as the GAAP guidance says that an entity shall not offset deferred tax assets and liabilities from different tax jurisdictions. Prior to 2017, companies classified deferred tax assets and liabilities as short term and long term. However, US GAAP changed such that all are now netted and recorded in long term assets or liabilities. We also note that for some companies the disclosures will be impossible to tie to the financial statements at all if, for example, the net amount is small and the company combines with other items into the 'other' category.

Effective tax rates can vary considerably from one company to another due to permanent differences, tax credits, and other factors. A comparison of the effective tax rate for several companies is presented in **Exhibit 10.6**. The leftmost chart shows companies' 2020 ETR split by current and deferred portions of the tax expense. The rightmost chart compares ETRs for companies in 2020 and 2019.

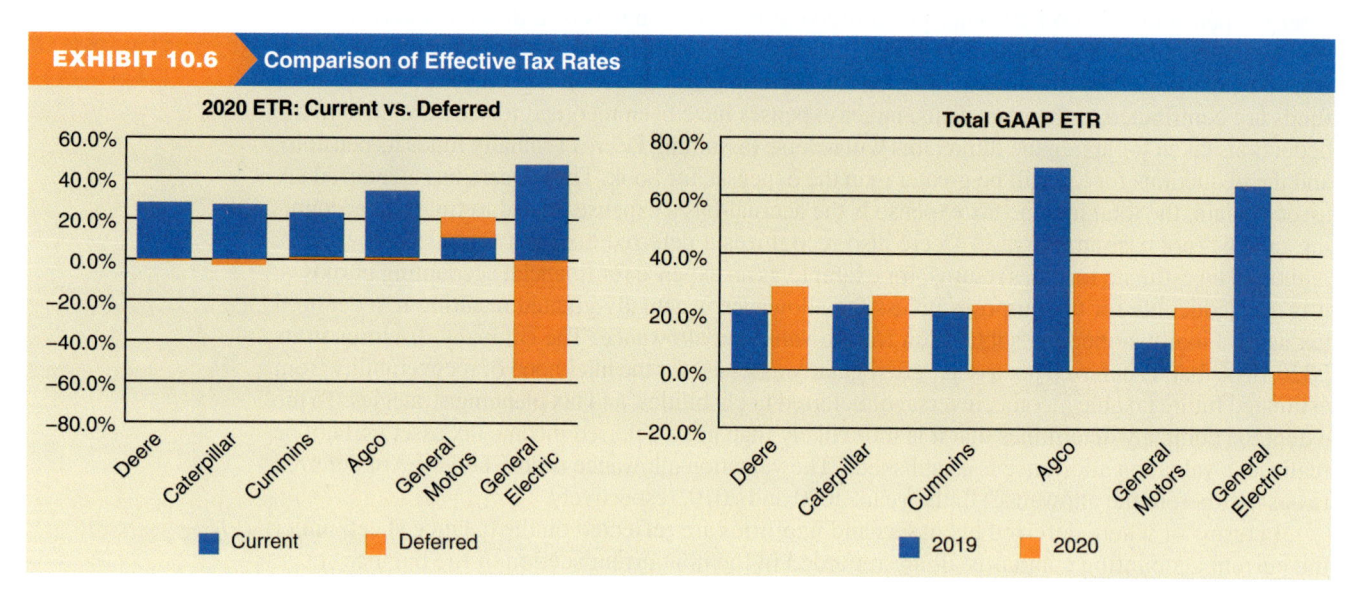

EXHIBIT 10.6　Comparison of Effective Tax Rates

Even though 2020 was the year of the pandemic, the ETRs look quite reasonable, in the range of −10% to +33%. One may wonder why Agco's rate in 2019 was so high. An examination of their 10-K reveals a large impairment charge in 2019. Such a charge would reduce financial accounting income but would not be deductible for tax purposes. Thus, tax expense would not be affected (the numerator) but pre-tax accounting income (the denominator) is lower resulting in a higher effective tax rate (a higher ratio). For GE in 2019 and 2020, it appears from their disclosures that their effective tax rate was significantly impacted by the sale of their BioPharma business. Events such as these in any given year can cause the ETR to be very high or very low but not really indicate a change in tax planning activities. It is important to note again that these rates do not represent cash taxes paid. Thus, even though GE has a negative tax expense in 2020, it does not necessarily mean they received a cash refund of any kind.

Deferred Taxes in the Statement of Cash Flows

Income taxes, including deferred income taxes, are reported in the operating section of the statement of cash flows. When the statement of cash flows is prepared using the direct method, deferred income taxes are excluded from taxes paid in cash. When the indirect (or reconciliation) method is used, the deferred portion of the income tax expense must be added back to net income as an expense not requiring the use of cash. The amount of income taxes paid in cash is then reported at the bottom of the statement of cash flows or in the disclosures.

Computation and Analysis of Taxes

An analysis of deferred taxes can yield useful insights. An increase in deferred tax liabilities indicates that a company is reporting higher profits in its income statement than in its tax return. The difference between reported corporate profits and taxable income increased substantially in the late 1990s, just prior to the stock market decline.

Although an increase in deferred tax liabilities can be the result of legitimate differences between financial reporting standards and tax rules, we must be aware of the possibility that such differences can also be caused by tax avoidance or by earnings management, improper revenue recognition, or other questionable accounting practices. More advanced courses cover the accounting for income taxes in more depth.

> **RESEARCH INSIGHT**
>
> Recent research has studied the accounting for income tax. Several papers have examined whether the overall difference between a company's taxable income and its financial accounting income contains any information about earnings quality. The idea is that if managers use accruals to manage financial accounting earnings upward, taxable income would not likely be similarly managed because there are fewer accruals for tax purposes (e.g., allowance for doubtful accounts, warranty reserves, etc.). The evidence is generally consistent with this hypothesis.[16]

Accounting for Income Taxes   LO10-3 **Review 10-3**

The following note is from the annual report of Adler Corporation.

Note 9: Income Taxes
The provision for income taxes includes the following

($ thousands)	
Current provision	
Domestic	$1,342
Foreign	146
Deferred provision (credit)	
Domestic	960
Foreign	(58)
Total	$2,390

Required

a. (1) What is the amount of income tax expense reported on its income statement? (2) How much of the income tax expense is payable in cash (estimated)? (3) Assuming that the deferred tax liability increased, identify an example that could account for such a change.
b. Prepare the entry, using the financial statement effects template, to record its income tax expense for the year.
c. Prepare the journal entry to record its income tax expense. Post journal entries to the appropriate T-accounts.

Solution on p. 10-67.

COMMITMENTS AND CONTENGENCIES AND OTHER DISCLOSURES

FASB and SEC guidance also require entities to provide additional detail and disclosure about various commitments and contingencies. Often companies will list a line item on the balance sheet "Commitments and Contingencies" with no corresponding amount. **Exhibit 10.1** shows that Deere includes such a line item on their balance sheet.

In the notes to the financial statements, Deere provides disclosure about such items as 1) warranty liability, 2) guarantees to banks related to third-party receivables for the financing of John Deere equipment, 3) commitments for the construction and acquisition of property and equipment, 4) miscellaneous contingent liabilities and 5) unresolved legal actions.

Generally, many of the items in such disclosures are not on the balance sheet as liabilities (though some are); thus, financial statement users need to evaluate how to treat such items. As discussed in the introduction, off-balance-sheet financing refers to financial obligations of a company that are not reported as liabilities in the balance sheet. Off-balance-sheet financing reduces the amount of debt reported on the balance sheet, thereby lowering the company's financial leverage ratios. Additionally, many off-balance-sheet financing techniques (e.g., contract manufacturing) remove assets from the balance sheet, along with the liabilities, without reducing revenues or markedly affecting net income. Such techniques cause operation ratios, such as return on assets (ROA),

LO10-4
Describe disclosures regarding future commitments and contingencies. Analyze financial statements after converting off-balance-sheet items to be considered on balance sheet.

---

[16] See the following studies: 1) Phillips, John, Mort Pincus, and Sonja Rego, "Earnings Management: New Evidence Based on Deferred Tax Expense." *The Accounting Review*, 1999, 2) Lev, Baruch and Doron Nissim, "Taxable Income, Future Earnings, and Equity Values," *The Accounting Review*, October 2004, and 3) Hanlon, Michelle, "The Persistence and Pricing of Earnings, Accruals, and Cash Flows When Firms Have Large Book-Tax Differences," *The Accounting Review*, January 2005.

to appear stronger than they are. Interestingly, the accounting standards have moved many of the "off-balance-sheet" items onto the balance sheet (e.g., parts of pensions, special-purpose entities, and now operating leases). However, there are still some off-balance-sheet items such as contractual obligations that do not meet the FASB definition of a liability. One example is the set of endorsement contract obligations a company such as Nike has when it endorses high-profile athletes.

Nike, Inc., includes the line item "commitments and contingencies" on their balance sheet and discloses the details in a note to their financial statements. Nike also includes a broader disclosure about contractual obligations and off-balance-sheet commitments in the Management Discussion and Analysis section of their annual 10-K. The disclosure in their May 31, 2020, annual report is as follows:

Off-Balance-Sheet Arrangements

In connection with various contracts and agreements, we routinely provide indemnification relating to the enforceability of intellectual property rights, coverage for legal issues that arise and other items where we are acting as the guarantor. Currently, we have several such agreements in place. Based on our historical experience and the estimated probability of future loss, we have determined that the fair value of such indemnification is not material to our financial position or results of operations.

Contractual Obligations

Our significant long-term contractual obligations as of May 31, 2020, and significant endorsement contracts, including related marketing commitments, entered into through the date of this report are as follows:

Description of Commitment (Dollars in millions)	2021	2022	2023	2024	2025	Thereafter	Total
Operating Leases	$ 550	$ 514	$ 456	$ 416	$ 374	$1,474	$ 3,784
Long-Term Debt	289	286	786	275	1,275	11,541	14,452
Endorsement Contracts	1,330	1,471	1,178	1,064	1,135	3,164	9,342
Product Purchase Obligations	4,234	—	—	—	—	—	4,234
Other Purchase Obligations	1,085	345	189	136	127	345	2,227
Transition tax related to the Tax Act	86	86	86	161	215	268	902
Total	$7,574	$2,702	$2,695	$2,052	$3,126	$16,792	$34,941

Note: Footnotes to the tables excluded for brevity.

The endorsement contracts have included contracts with well-known athletes such as Serena Williams, LeBron James, Maria Sharapova, Roger Federer, Tiger Woods, and of course, Michael Jordan. The athletes sign long-term, multimillion dollar contracts to use and promote Nike shoes, apparel, and accessories. These long-term endorsement contracts are just one of Nike's off-balance-sheet obligations.

In the table above, long-term debt, operating leases, and the transition tax related to the Tax Act (discussed previously) are included in the balance sheet. The endorsement contracts, one of the largest items, are not included on the balance sheet as liabilities. If an analyst desires to estimate the associated "as if" liability with such contracts, the following approach could be used. (This process can be used for other off-balance sheet 'liabilities' as long as one has estimates of the future cash outflows.)

1. Estimate a discount rate. One reasonable proxy is the interest rate on Nike's debt, which is roughly 3% per their debt note disclosure.

2. Estimate the future payments and the number of years those payments will be made. One limitation of the above disclosure is that the first five years show the annual payment, but the remaining payments are lumped in a column "thereafter." An estimate of the number of years for the amount in the "thereafter" column can be computed by dividing the amount ($3,164) by the previous year's payment ($1,135). In this case, this estimate yields almost 3 years. To estimate using full years, divide the amount in the "thereafter" column by three and arrive at an estimate of the payment amount for each of the next three years. In this case, it is $1,055 million ($3,164/3).

3. Find the present value of the future payments. The present value of the payments listed above for years 2021 through 2028 (including the estimated payments), at 3% over the 8 years, is roughly $8.3 billion. This can be computed using one of several methods; for example, 1) the

present value tables in Appendix A to find the present value of each payment or 2) Excel's NPV function.

This yields a rough approximation of the "as if" liability related to these payments. However, the associated asset value, if any, for this off-balance-sheet item—the value of advertising through endorsements—is very hard to estimate.

ANALYZING FINANCIAL STATEMENTS

Analysis Objective

We want to assess the effect of financial obligations, including off-balance-sheet commitments, on financial solvency and liquidity.

Analysis Tool Fixed Commitments Ratio

$$\text{Fixed commitments ratio} = \frac{\text{Operating cash flow before fixed commitments}}{\text{Fixed commitments}}$$

Applying the Fixed Commitments Ratio to Deere & Company Some fixed commitments, such as operating lease payments and purchase commitments, are cash outflows that are classified as operating activities in the statement of cash flows. Others (for example, payments due on long-term debt) are classified as financing cash flows, and some can be classified as investing (for example, commitments to purchase plant assets). Deere reports total fixed commitments of $17,562 million in its 10-K report. Of these, $10,926 million is for noninterest payments on long-term debt and finance leases (financing), and $159 is for equipment purchase commitments (investing). Subtracting these amounts leaves the amount of fixed commitments that are part of operating cash flows ($17,562 − $10,926 − $159 = $6,477). To compute the **fixed commitments ratio**, we start with operating cash flows, add back the fixed commitments that are classified as operating, and then divide by the total amount of fixed commitments.

($ millions)	
2018:	$\frac{(\$1{,}822 + \$7{,}023)}{\$20{,}538} = 0.43$
2019:	$\frac{(\$3{,}412 + \$6{,}289)}{\$19{,}544} = 0.50$
2020:	$\frac{(\$7{,}483 + \$6{,}477)}{\$17{,}562} = 0.79$

Guidance A fixed commitments ratio less than 1.0 generally indicates that a company is generating insufficient cash flows from operations to meet its contractual obligations. Some commitments may be met by selling assets or by raising additional financing. For example, when long-term debt comes due, it can be refinanced with new debt if the company is otherwise in sound financial health.

Deere & Company in Context

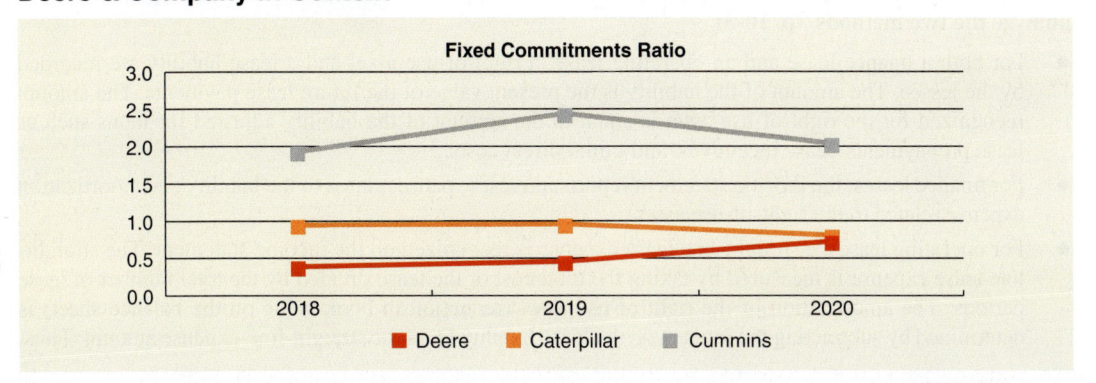

Fixed Commitments Ratio

(Line chart showing Fixed Commitments Ratio for 2018, 2019, 2020 for Deere, Caterpillar, and Cummins.)

Takeaways Deere and Caterpillar are consistently below 1.0 for these three years, which might be a cause for some concern. However, Deere's ratios have increased over the three years suggesting improvement.

The key takeaway from this section is that off-balance sheet obligations can have a significant impact on our analysis and understanding of a company's future obligations, solvency, and liquidity.

Other Considerations The fixed commitments ratio is but one measure of financial solvency and liquidity. It should be used in conjunction with other ratios, such as the debt-to-equity ratio and the current ratio in an effort to gauge the ability of the firm to meet its financial obligations.

Review 10-4 LO10-4   Analyzing Commitments and Contingencies

Cummins Inc. provides the following disclosure in the notes to its 2020 financial statements:

Guarantees and Commitments
Periodically, we enter into guarantee arrangements, including guarantees of non-U.S. distributor financings, residual value guarantees on equipment under operating leases, and other miscellaneous guarantees of joint ventures or third-party obligations. At December 31, 2020, the maximum potential loss related to these guarantees was $44 million.

We have arrangements with certain suppliers that require us to purchase minimum volumes or be subject to monetary penalties. At December 31, 2020, if we were to stop purchasing from each of these suppliers, the aggregate amount of the penalty would be approximately $32 million. Most of these arrangements enable us to secure supplies of critical components. We do not currently anticipate paying any penalties under these contracts.

We enter into physical forward contracts with suppliers of platinum and palladium to purchase certain volumes of the commodities at contractually stated prices for various periods, which generally fall within two years. At December 31, 2020, the total commitments under these contracts were $79 million. These arrangements enable us to guarantee the prices of these commodities, which otherwise are subject to market volatility.

We have guarantees with certain customers that require us to satisfactorily honor contractual or regulatory obligations, or compensate for monetary losses related to nonperformance. These performance bonds and other performance-related guarantees were $100 million at December 31, 2020.

a. How would the following items from the disclosure above be shown on the financial statements?
  1. $44 million of guarantees
  2. $32 million in penalties
  3. $79 million in commitments on contracts
  4. $100 million in performance-related guarantees
b. Compute the present value of the future payments related to purchase commitments of $79 million. (Note: Assume that the amount will be paid evenly over the next two years, with payments made at the end of each year. Assume a discount rate of 4%.)

Solution on p. 10-67.

SUMMARY

LO10-1 **Account for leases using the operating lease method and the finance lease method. Compare and analyze the two methods. (p. 10-3)**

- For both a finance lease and an operating lease, a right-of-use asset and a lease liability are recorded by the lessee. The amount of the liability is the present value of the future lease payments. The amount recognized for the right-of-use asset is equal to the amount of the liability adjusted for items such as lease prepayments, lease incentives, and initial direct costs.
- For finance leases, the income statement reports interest expense related to the liability and amortization expense related to the right-of-use asset.
- For operating leases, a straight-line lease expense is recognized on the income statement. The straight-line lease expense is measured by taking the total cost of the lease divided by the total number of lease periods. The amortization of the right-of-use asset (reduction in book value on the balance sheet) is determined by subtracting the interest on the lease liability from the straight-line-expense amount. Thus,

while the expense is straight-line, a loan amortization table like that used for finance leases is used to determine the reduction in book value of the asset and reduction in liability as payments are made.
- Right-of-use book value declines more quickly with the finance lease method.
- An asset leased using a finance lease will have higher related expenses early in the asset's life relative to an asset leased using an operating lease.
- For companies that utilize operating leases, in order to compare financial statements before and after the new lease standard, an analyst or other financial statement user needs to compute the present value of the future lease payments and treat this present value as an "as-if" liability. In addition, an estimate of the asset would need to be determined.

Explain and interpret the reporting for pension plans, including the disclosure notes. (p. 10-15) **LO10-2**
- Pension and other postretirement obligations represent a large obligation for many companies.
- The projected benefit obligation is the present value of the estimated future benefits that a company expects to pay retired employees.
- The net liability that a company reports on the balance sheet is the projected benefit obligation offset by the plan assets.
- Pension note disclosures provide detailed information about changes in pension obligations, changes in plan assets, and the determinants of pension expense.
- Pension note disclosures provide information allowing us to interpret pension expenses and cash flows.

Describe and interpret accounting for income taxes. (p. 10-25) **LO10-3**
- While income tax expense is reported below income from operations, it is an operating expense. The initial item in an indirect statement of cash flows is net income, which reflects the subtraction of the tax expense.
- Income tax expense is determined as the sum of the tax computed due to the government and the net change in deferred assets and liabilities (and potentially other accruals).
- Deferred taxes occur because of differences between U.S. GAAP reporting and the tax due based on the rules of the tax authority. The former are based on accrual accounting, while the latter are often based on a hybrid accrual and cash-based accounting system.
- Deferred tax assets and liabilities are valued at the enacted tax rate expected to be in effect when the temporary differences between financial accounting and tax bases reverse.

Describe disclosures regarding future commitments and contingencies. Analyze financial statements after converting off-balance-sheet items to be considered on balance sheet. (p. 10-36) **LO10-4**
- Disclosure of future commitments and contingent payments is required.
- Off-balance-sheet financing refers to financial obligations of the company that are not recognized as liabilities in the balance sheet. Recognizing these obligations often requires recognizing off-balance-sheet assets.
- Off-balance-sheet financing improves financial leverage ratios, and the corresponding unrecognized assets improve performance measures.
- Some of these disclosed commitments and contingencies will be recognized on the balance sheet, and some are off-balance-sheet. If the item is off-balance-sheet but an analyst or creditor desires to analyze the company's financials as if the item were treated as a liability, the present value of the future payments should be computed and included in liabilities for analysis purposes.

GUIDANCE ANSWERS... YOU MAKE THE CALL

You are the CEO Normally we think that managers inside the firm have full information about firm activities and performance. However, they likely do not have perfect information. Gathering a new level of data regarding lease contracts and terms may lead corporations to consolidate leases, negotiate better lease terms, or potentially reduce the quantity of assets leased. You, as the CEO, may even decide to invest in machine learning software or textual analysis software to gather more data and help your company be more efficient and cost-effective in setting lease contracts.

You are a Consultant to the FASB Normally accountants do not favor offsetting liabilities against the related assets as is currently the reporting practice required under GAAP for pensions. However, because the pension fund is a separate legal entity, there is a problem with reporting the pension plan assets among the firm's assets. A company does not have unilateral control over a pension trust. It can put assets into the trust but can not easily get them out of the trust. For this reason, the pension assets do not meet the criteria we normally require for recognition. Thus, reporting a net amount (PBO – pension assets) seems the best course of action.

KEY RATIOS

$$\text{Fixed commitments ratio} = \frac{\text{Operating cash flow before fixed commitments}}{\text{Fixed commitments}}$$

$$\text{Effective tax rate} = \frac{\text{Provision for income taxes}}{\text{Income before income taxes}}$$

Assignments with the MBC logo in the margin are available in *my BusinessCourse*. See the Preface of the book for details.

MULTIPLE CHOICE

Multiple Choice Answers
1. a 2. d 3. d 4. b 5. d 6. c 7. c

1. U.S. GAAP requires that certain leases be accounted for as *finance leases*. The reason for this treatment is that this type of lease
   a. is essentially viewed as a sale/purchase.
   b. is an example of form over substance.
   c. provides the use of the leased asset to the lessee for a limited period of time.
   d. is an example of off-balance-sheet financing.

2. For a lease that is accounted for as an operating lease by the lessee, the rent expense should be
   a. allocated and recorded as interest expense and depreciation expense.
   b. allocated and recorded as a reduction in the liability for leased assets and interest expense.
   c. recorded as rent expense with no other entries recorded.
   d. recorded as a straight-line lease expense with associated entries to record the cash payment, reduce the liability, and amortize the right-of-use asset on the balance sheet.

3. The balance sheet liability for a finance lease would be reduced each period by the
   a. lease payment.
   b. lease payment plus the amortization of the related asset.
   c. lease payment less the amortization of the related asset.
   d. lease payment less the periodic interest expense.

4. Which of the following statements characterizes defined benefit pension plans?
   a. The employer's obligation is satisfied by making the necessary periodic contribution.
   b. Retirement benefits are based on the plan's benefit formula.
   c. Retirement benefits depend on how well pension fund assets have been managed.
   d. Contributions are made in equal amounts by employer and employees.

5. When the value of pension plan assets is greater than the projected benefit obligation,
   a. the difference is added to pension expense.
   b. the difference is reported as deferred pension cost.
   c. the difference is reported as a contra equity adjustment.
   d. the pension plan is overfunded.

6. Which of the following is *not* a component of net pension expense?
   a. Interest cost
   b. Expected return on plan assets
   c. Benefits paid to retirees
   d. Amortization of actuarial gains or losses

7. Deferred tax assets and liabilities should be reported using
   a. the tax rate in effect in the current period.
   b. the tax rates management thinks will be passed in the next year.
   c. the enacted tax rate that will be in effect when the temporary differences reverse.
   d. the enacted tax rate that was in effect when the temporary difference was created.

QUESTIONS

Q10-1. Under the lease accounting standard (Topic 842), what are the financial reporting differences between an operating lease and a finance lease? Explain.

Q10-2. Explain the cash flows and Statement of Cash Flow effects of a finance lease and an operating lease.

Q10-3. Is the expense of a lease over its entire life the same whether it is a finance or an operating lease? Explain.

Q10-4. What are the economic and accounting differences between a defined contribution plan and a defined benefit plan?

Q10-5. Under what circumstances will a company report a net pension asset? A net pension liability?

Q10-6. What are the components of pension expense that is reported in the income statement?

Q10-7. What effect does the use of expected returns on pension investments and the deferral of unexpected gains and losses on those investments have on income?

Q10-8. How is the initial valuation determined for lease liability and the right-of-use asset for both an operating lease and a finance lease?

Q10-9. Over what time period should the cost of providing retirement benefits to employees be expensed?

Q10-10. What is the conceptual reason why income tax expense on the income statement is not equal to cash taxes paid?

Q10-11. Under what circumstances would a tax payment be made that also requires the recording of a deferred tax asset or liability?

Q10-12. Explain what an unrecognized tax benefit is and where it is recorded on the balance sheet.

DATA ANALYTICS

DA10-1 Using Excel Visualizations to Analyze the Impact of an Accounting Change

The new lease standard (ASC 842) resulted in significant changes for companies that had large operating lease obligations. Prior to the new lease standard, operating lease obligations were disclosed but a liability was not recorded on the balance sheet. Upon transitioning to the new leasing standard, **Walgreens Boots Alliance, Inc.** (Walgreens Boots) and **Verizon Communications Inc.** (Verizon) disclosed the impact on the beginning balances of the accounting period in which the transition to the new lease standard took place. (The standard was adopted through a modified retrospective approach.)

Information included in the Excel file associated with this exercise was extracted or inferred from disclosures made by Walgreens Boots and Verizon in the year of adoption of the lease standard. Using this data, we calculate ratios before and immediately after the adoption of the lease standard to better understand the impact of the accounting standard on financial statement results.

Total liabilities-to-total assets
$$\frac{\text{Total liabilities}}{\text{Total assets}}$$

Current Ratio
$$\frac{\text{Current assets}}{\text{Current liabilities}}$$

Total liabilities-to-total equity
$$\frac{\text{Total liabilities}}{\text{Total stockholders' equity}}$$

REQUIRED

1. Download Excel file DA10-1 found in myBusinessCourse.
2. Calculate the following ratios in Excel for both companies on the balances shown before and directly after the new lease standard adoption:
    a. Total liabilities-to-total assets
    b. Current ratio
    c. Total liabilities-to-total equity
3. Create a bar chart for each company comparing the three ratios before and after adoption of the new lease standard. For the y-axis, use increments of 0.5 in both charts. Add data labels to the bars. *Hint:* Highlight the data, Insert, Bar. Right-click on the bars and click Add data labels.
4. Indicate which ratio results looked more favorable and which ratio results looked less favorable after adoption of the new lease standard for each company.
5. Answer the following questions:
    a. Did the economics of leasing change the day after the new lease standard became effective?
    b. Would investors or creditors have understood the impact of operating leases on the balance sheet before the adoption of the new lease standard by companies?
    c. Which company showed a more significant relative impact from the adoption of the new lease standard, based on the change in ratios before and after adoption of the new lease standard?
    d. Does the company from your answer to part *c* have the larger liabilities-to-total equity ratio of the two companies before adoption of the new lease standard?
6. Prepare two pie charts in Excel for each company, showing the components of liabilities before and after the adoption of the new lease standard. *Hint:* Add data labels (percentages).
7. Answer the following questions based upon the pie chart visualizations.

a. For Verizon, how many proportions of the pie are there before and after the new lease standard? For Walgreens Boots?
b. What is the difference in the proportion of total current liabilities, long-term debt, long-term operating lease liabilities, and other long-term debt for Verizon after the adoption of the new lease standard? For Walgreens Boots?
c. Why did one company show a larger impact (identified in part *b*) from the adoption of the new lease standard that can be seen in the pie charts?

LO10-2 **DA10-2.** **Analyzing the Trends of Plan Asset and PBO Balances and Service Cost Over Time in Excel**

The **Boeing Company** (Boeing) has sponsored a defined pension benefit plan for many years for its employees. Information obtained from Form 10-K statements over a 10-year period is included in the file associated with this exercise. We analyze the trend of (and the relations between) balances of the PBO and Plan assets over time. We also analyze the trends in service cost over time and determine possible causes of the trends.

REQUIRED

1. Download Excel file DA10-2 found in myBusinessCourse.
2. Prepare a line chart showing the trend of PBO balances and Plan Asset balances over the 10-year period. *Hint:* Highlight data; click Insert, Line.
3. Indicate in which years the plans were overfunded and underfunded.
4. Indicate the year (by visually looking at the chart) where the relation of Plan Assets to PBO differed from the other years most clearly.
5. Describe the trend in the PBO balance over time.
6. Prepare a line chart showing the trend of service cost over the 10-year period.
7. Describe the trend in service cost over time.
8. Answer the following questions based upon the service cost chart.
   a. In what two years did service cost change the most significantly? *Hint:* Use the gridlines in the chart to help you estimate the largest change.
   b. What would be a likely cause of the changes identified in part *a*?
9. Compare and contrast the trend from year 9 to year 10 between the PBO balance and service cost.

LO10-3 **DA10-3.** **Analyzing Excel Visualizations of Deferred Tax Accounts**

The Excel file associated with this exercise includes balance sheet tax account data for two years for 14 large companies in the Consumer Discretionary segment. In this exercise, we analyze trends in the deferred tax allowance as a percentage of the gross deferred tax asset balance. An increase in the percentage means that management expects a larger portion of deferred tax asset to not be realized.

REQUIRED

1. Download Excel file DA10-3 found in myBusinessCourse.
2. Create a schedule in Excel showing each company's deferred tax allowance balance divided by the gross deferred tax asset balance.
3. Sort the data in the table based on the 2020 column data, ordering from largest to smallest, using the Sort function.
4. Create a bar chart visualization showing a bar for 2019 and 2020 for each company. *Hint:* Highlight the data; click Insert, Bar.
5. List the companies in which the ratio did not increase from year 2019 to 2020.
6. List the company that visually showed the largest change in the ratio from 2019 to 2020.
7. What is the most likely reason for the common trend in the ratios from 2019 to 2020?
8. Create a separate schedule in Excel with a column for each company's net deferred tax asset balance and a column for each company's deferred tax liability balance as of 2020.
9. Create a stacked bar chart for each company's net deferred tax asset balance and deferred tax liability balance as of 2020. *Hint:* Select the Insert tab, Recommended charts, and choose the 100% stacked bar chart.
10. Indicate which company has the highest percentage of net deferred tax assets to deferred tax liabilities.
11. Indicate which company has the lowest percentage of net deferred tax assets to deferred tax liabilities.
12. Indicate a factor that could have had a significant impact on the relation of net deferred tax assets to deferred tax liabilities described in part 11.

DATA VISUALIZATION

Data Visualization Activities are available in myBusinessCourse. These assignments use Tableau Dashboards to expose students to visual depictions of data and introduce students to data analytics through data visualizations. These exercises are easily assignable and auto graded by MBC.

MINI EXERCISES

M10-13. Accounting for Leases (FSET) — LO10-1

On January 3, Hanna Corporation signed a lease on a machine for its manufacturing operation and the lease commences on the same date. The lease requires Hanna to make six annual lease payments of $15,000 with the first payment due December 31. Hanna could have financed the machine by borrowing the purchase price at an interest rate of 7%.

a. Using the financial statement effects template, report the entries that Hanna Corporation would make on January 3 and December 31 to record this lease assuming
   i. the lease is reported as an operating lease.
   ii. the lease is reported as a finance lease.
b. Explain how the financial statement effects differ between the two treatments.

M10-14. Accounting for Leases — LO10-2

Using the information from M10-13, prepare the journal entries for part *a* and post to the appropriate T-accounts.

M10-15. Accounting for Leases (FSET) — LO10-1

On July 1, Shroff Company leased a warehouse building under a 10-year lease agreement. The lease requires quarterly lease payments of $5,000. The first lease payment is due on September 30, 2020. The lease was reported as a finance lease using an 8% annual interest rate.

a. Using the financial statement effects template, report the entry to record the commencement of the lease on July 1.
b. Using the financial statement effects template, report the entries that would be necessary on September 30 and December 31.

M10-16. Accounting for Leases — LO10-1

Using the information from M10-15, (1) prepare the journal entries for parts *a* and *b*, and (2) post to the appropriate T-accounts.

M10-17. Accounting for Operating and Finance Leases (FSET) — LO10-1

On January 1, Weber, Inc., entered into two lease contracts. The first lease contract was a six-year lease for computer equipment with $20,000 annual lease payments due at the end of each year. Weber took possession of the equipment on January 1. The second lease contract was a six-month lease, beginning January 1, for warehouse storage space with $1,500 monthly lease payments due the first of each month. Weber made the first month's payment on January 1. The present value of the lease payments under the first contract is $99,359. The present value of the lease payments under the second contract is $8,895.

REQUIRED

a. Assume that the first lease contract is a finance lease. Prepare a financial statement effects template to show the effects of the entry on January 1.
b. Assume the second lease contract is an operating lease. Prepare a financial statement effects template to show the effects of the entry on January 1.

M10-18. Accounting for Operating and Finance Leases — LO10-1

Using the information from M10-17, prepare the journal entries for parts *a* and *b*.

M10-19. Accounting for Operating Leases (FSET) — LO10-1

On January 1 of the current year, Samuels, Inc., purchased a building for $2.5 million to be leased. The building is expected to have a 45-year life with no salvage value. The building was leased immediately by Verdi Corp. (a calendar year-end company) for $162,500 a year payable December 31 of each year. The lease term is five years. The rate of interest implicit in the lease is 7%. The lease is classified as an operating lease.

a. Prepare an amortization schedule of the lease liability.

b. Prepare an amortization schedule for the right-of-use asset.
c. Prepare a financial statement effects template to show the effects of the entries for Verdi Corp. for the current and following year.

LO10-1 **M10-20. Accounting for Operating Leases**
Using the information from M10-19, prepare the journal entries for the current year and the following year.

LO10-1 **M10-21. Accounting for Operating Leases (FSET)**
Redo Mini-Exercise M10-19 but now assume the payments are made on January 1 of each year (including the first year on January 1).

LO10-1 **M10-22. Accounting for Operating Leases**
Redo Mini-Exercise M10-20, but now assume the payments are made on January 1 of each year (including the first year on January 1).

LO10-2 **M10-23. Accounting for Pension Benefits (FSET)**
Bartov Corporation has a defined contribution pension plan for its employees. Each year, Bartov contributes to the plan an amount equal to 4% of the employee payroll for the year. Bartov's current year payroll was $320,000. Bartov also provides a life insurance benefit that pays a $40,000 death benefit to the beneficiaries of retired employees. At the end of the current year, Bartov estimates that its liability under the life insurance program is $500,000. Bartov has assets with a fair value of $140,000 in a trust fund that are available to meet the death benefit payments.

REQUIRED
a. Prepare a financial statement effects template to show the effects of the entry at December 31 to record Bartov's annual defined contribution to a pension trustee who will manage the pension funds for the firm's employees.
b. What amount of liability for death benefit payments must Bartov report in its December 31 balance sheet? Explain.

LO10-2 **M10-24. Accounting for Pension Benefits**
Using the information from M10-23, prepare the journal entry for part a.

LO10-2 **M10-25. Analyzing and Interpreting Pension Disclosures—Expenses and Returns**

Exxon Mobil Corporation
NYSE :: XOM

Exxon Mobil Corporation discloses the following information in its pension note disclosure in its 10-K report:

(In millions)	2020
Service cost	$1,672
Interest cost	1,365
Expected return on plan assets	(1,600)
Amortization of actuarial loss (gain)	726
Amortization of prior service cost	73
Net pension enhancement and curtailment/settlement cost	329
Net periodic pension benefit cost	$2,565

a. How much pension expense does Exxon Mobil Corporation report in its 2020 income statement?
b. What effect does its "expected return on plan assets" have on its reported pension expense? Explain.
c. Explain use of the word "expected" as it relates to results of pension plan investments.

LO10-2 **M10-26. Analyzing and Interpreting Pension Disclosures—Expenses and Returns**

YUM! Brands
NYSE :: YUM

YUM! Brands, Inc., discloses the following pension note disclosure in its 10-K report:

	Pension Benefits	
(In millions)	2020	2019
Service cost	$ 8	$ 6
Interest cost	35	39
Amortization of prior service cost	5	6
Expected return on plan assets	(43)	(44)
Amortization of net loss	14	1
Net periodic benefit cost	$19	$ 8

a. How much pension expense does Yum report in its 2020 income statement?
b. What effect does its "expected return on plan assets" have on its reported pension expense? Explain.
c. Explain use of the word "expected" as it relates to results of pension plan investments.

M10-27. Analyzing and Interpreting Retirement Benefit Disclosure (FSET) **LO10-2**
Abercrombie & Fitch Co. discloses the following disclosure note relating to its retirement plans in its fiscal 2020 10-K report:

Abercrombie & Fitch
NYSE :: ANF

> **16. SAVINGS AND RETIREMENT PLANS:** The Company maintains the Abercrombie & Fitch Co. Savings and Retirement Plan, a qualified plan. All U.S. associates are eligible to participate in this plan if they are at least 21 years of age. In addition, the Company maintains the Abercrombie & Fitch Co. Nonqualified Savings and Supplemental Retirement, composed of two sub-plans (Plan I and Plan II). Plan I contains contributions made through December 31, 2004, while Plan II contains contributions made on and after January 1, 2005. Participation in these plans is based on service and compensation. The Company's contributions to these plans are based on a percentage of associates' eligible annual compensation. The cost of the Company's contributions to these plans was $14.1 million, $14.8 million, and $15.1 million for Fiscal 2020, Fiscal 2019, and Fiscal 2018, respectively.

a. Does Abercrombie have a defined contribution or defined benefit pension plan? Explain.
b. Prepare a financial statement effects template to show the effects of the contributions to its retirement plan for fiscal 2020.
c. How is Abercrombie's obligation to its retirement plan reported on its balance sheet?

M10-28. Analyzing and Interpreting Retirement Benefit Disclosure **LO10-2**
Using the information from M10-27, prepare the journal entry for the company's contributions to its retirement plans in fiscal 2020.

M10-29. Analyzing and Interpreting Disclosures on Contract Manufacturers **LO10-4**
Nike, Inc., reports the following information relating to its manufacturing activities in Part 1 of its 2020 10-K report:

Nike
NYSE :: NKE

> We are supplied by 122 footwear factories located in 12 countries. Virtually all of our footwear is manufactured outside of the United States by over 15 independent contract manufacturers, which often operate multiple factories. The largest single footwear factory accounted for approximately 9% of total fiscal 2020 NIKE Brand footwear production.
> For fiscal 2020, contract factories in Vietnam, Indonesia, and China manufactured approximately 50%, 24%, and 22% of total NIKE Brand footwear, respectively. We also have manufacturing agreements with independent contract manufacturers in Argentina and India to manufacture footwear for sale primarily within those countries. For fiscal 2020, four footwear contract manufacturers each accounted for greater than 10% of footwear production and in the aggregate accounted for approximately 61% of NIKE Brand footwear production.

a. What effect does the use of contract manufacturers have on Nike's balance sheet?
b. Nike executes purchase contracts with its contract manufacturers to purchase their output. How are executory contracts reported under GAAP? Does your answer suggest a possible motivation for the use of contract manufacturing?

M10-30. Computing and Reporting Deferred Income Taxes **LO10-3**
Fisk, Inc., purchased $480,000 of construction equipment on January 1, 2022. The equipment is being depreciated on a straight-line basis over six years with no expected salvage value. MACRS depreciation is being used on the firm's tax returns. At December 31, 2024, the equipment's book value is $240,000, and its tax basis is $138,400. (This is Fisk's only temporary difference.) Over the next three years, straight-line depreciation will exceed MACRS depreciation by $24,800 in 2025, $24,800 in 2026, and $52,000 in 2027. Assume that the income tax rate in effect for all years is 25%.

a. What amount of deferred tax liability should appear in Fisk's December 31, 2024, balance sheet?
b. What amount of deferred tax liability should appear in Fisk's December 31, 2025, balance sheet?
c. What amount of deferred tax liability should appear in Fisk's December 31, 2026, balance sheet?
d. Where should the deferred tax liability accounts be classified in Fisk's balance sheets?

EXERCISES

LO10-1 **E10-31. Account for and Compare Leases Using Finance and Operating Lease Methods (FSET)**
Core Co. leased a piece of manufacturing equipment from E-So Co. with the following terms:

> Annual lease payment: $550,000
> Term of lease: . . . . 5 years
> Interest rate: 4.0%
> Lease commences on January 1, 2023
> Payments are made on December 31 of each year in the lease term

a. Compute the value of the right-of-use asset and the lease liability on the date the lease commences.
b. Prepare a lease liability amortization schedule and right-of-use asset amortization schedule for the lessee.
c. Prepare a financial statement effects template to show the effects for Core Co. for January 1, 2023–December 31, 2024, if the lease is classified as a finance lease.
d. Prepare a financial statement effects template to show the effects for Core Co. for January 1, 2023–December 31, 2024, if the lease is classified as an operating lease.
e. Explain the differences in the operating lease and finance lease treatments for the financial accounting statements including showing the right-of-use asset value over the term of the lease.

LO10-1 **E10-32. Accounting for Leases Using Finance and Operating Lease Methods**
Using the information from E10-31, prepare the journal entries for parts *c* and *d*.

LO10-2 **E10-33. Analyzing and Interpreting Pension Plan Benefit Note Disclosures**

Target
NYSE :: TGT

Target Corporation provides the following note relating to its retirement plans in its 2020 10-K report: (Note the disclosure is excerpted, simplified, and altered for simplicity.)

> **Defined Contribution Plans** Team members who meet eligibility requirements can participate in a defined contribution 401(k) plan by investing up to 80 percent of their eligible earnings, as limited by statute or regulation. We match 100 percent of each team member's contribution up to 5 percent of eligible earnings. Company match contributions are made to funds designated by the participant, none of which are based on Target common stock. Benefits expense related to these matching contributions was $321 million, $278 million, and $215 million as of January 2021, 2020, and 2019 respectively.

a. Does Target have a defined contribution or defined benefit pension plan? Explain.
b. How would Target account for its contributions to its retirement plan?
c. How is Target's obligation to its retirement plan reported on its balance sheet?
d. Do you see any problems for employees in Target's plan?

LO10-1 **E10-34. Analyzing Lease Disclosures Regarding the Adoption of the New Lease Standard and Analyzing Across Companies**

JetBlue Airways Corporation
NASDAQ :: JBLUE

Deere & Company, Inc.
NYSE :: DEL

JetBlue's balance sheet and discussion of the new lease standard is as follows in their 2018 10-K:

(in millions)	2018	2017
Total assets.	$10,426	$9,781
Total liabilities	5,815	5,049
Total equity	4,611	4,732

> In February 2016, the FASB issued ASU 2016-02, *Leases (Topic 842)* of the Codification, which requires lessees to recognize leases on the balance sheet and disclose key information about leasing arrangements. . . . Under the new standard, a lessee will recognize liabilities on the balance sheet, initially measured at the present value of the lease payments, and right-of-use (ROU) assets representing its right to use the underlying asset for the lease term. . . .
> For JetBlue, we believe the most significant impact of the new standard relates to the recognition of new assets and liabilities on our balance sheet for operating leases related to our aircraft, engines, airport terminal space, airport hangars, office space, and other facilities and equipment. Upon adoption, we expect to recognize additional lease assets and lease liabilities ranging from $1.0 billion to $1.4 billion.

1. If JetBlue records $1.2 billion of the operating leases as both an asset and a liability on January 1, 2019, how much will their debt-to-equity ratio from December 31, 2018, change? (Assume no other changes for JetBlue.)
2. If an analyst wants to compare Delta, who adopted in the fourth quarter of 2018, to JetBlue, who is adopting in 2019, what would the analyst need to consider and do?

E10-35. Analyzing and Interpreting Lease Disclosures Prior to and Upon Conversion to the New Lease Standard

LO10-1, 4

Verizon
NYSE :: VZ

Verizon Communications Inc. provides the following balance sheet (excerpted and abbreviated) and discussion and disclosure of leases:

Verizon Communications Inc. and Subsidiaries
2018 Annual Report
Consolidated Balance Sheet information (in millions)

	2018	2017
Total assets.	$248,829	$257,143
Total liabilities	210,119	212,456
Total equity	54,710	44,687

The aggregate minimum rental commitments under noncancelable leases for the periods shown at December 31, 2018, are as follows:

Years	Operating Leases
2019	$ 4,043
2020	3,678
2021	3,272
2022	2,871
2023	2,522
Thereafter	10,207
Total minimum rental commitments	$26,593

The company also discloses the following in the summary of significant accounting policies:

In February 2016, the FASB issued this standard update to increase transparency and improve comparability by requiring entities to recognize assets and liabilities on the balance sheet for all leases, with certain exceptions. In addition, through improved disclosure requirements, the standard update will enable users of financial statements to further understand the amount, timing, and uncertainty of cash flows arising from leases. . . . Upon adoption of this standard, there will be a significant impact in our consolidated balance sheet as we expect to recognize a right-of-use asset and liability related to substantially all operating lease arrangements, which we currently estimate will range between $21.0 billion and $23.0 billion. Verizon's current operating lease portfolio included in this range is primarily comprised of network equipment including towers, distributed antenna systems, and small cells, real estate, connectivity mediums including dark fiber, and equipment leases.

a. As of the end of 2018, what asset amount is included on the balance sheet with respect to operating leases? What amount of liabilities?
b. What amount does Verizon state they need to add to the balance sheet as a right-of-use asset for operating leases and a lease liability for operating leases?
c. If Verizon would have adopted the new lease standard on December 31, 2018, and had determined that the right-of-use lease asset for operating leases and the liability amount were both $22 billion, how would the company's debt-to-equity ratio change? Assume no other changes on the balance sheet. (Note that they would not necessarily be the same amount; we are just assuming the same amount for simplicity.)
d. What do you predict will happen to ratios such as return-on-assets using reported numbers for both before and after the new standard is adopted?

E10-36. Analyzing Commitments and Contingencies

LO10-4

Under Armour, Inc.
NYSE :: UA

Under Armour, Inc., provides the following disclosure in the notes to its 2020 financial statements:

7. Commitments and Contingencies
(excerpts only)

Sports Marketing and Other Commitments

Within the normal course of business, the Company enters into contractual commitments in order to promote the Company's brand and products. These commitments include sponsorship agreements with teams and athletes on the collegiate and professional levels, official supplier agreements, athletic event sponsorships, and other marketing commitments. The following is a schedule of the Company's future minimum payments under its sponsorship and other marketing agreements as of December 31, 2020, as well as significant sponsorship and other marketing agreements entered into during the period after December 31, 2020, through the date of this report:

(In thousands)	
2021	$106,727
2022	85,090
2023	69,454
2024	55,525
2025	32,370
2024 and thereafter	12,453
Total future minimum sponsorship and other payments	$361,619

The amounts listed above are the minimum compensation obligations and guaranteed royalty fees required to be paid under the Company's sponsorship and other marketing agreements. The amounts listed above do not include additional performance incentives and product supply obligations provided under certain agreements. It is not possible to determine how much the Company will spend on product supply obligations on an annual basis as contracts generally do not stipulate specific cash amounts to be spent on products. The amount of product provided to the sponsorships depends on many factors including general playing conditions, the number of sporting events in which they participate, and the Company's decisions regarding product and marketing initiatives. In addition, the costs to design, develop, source, and purchase the products furnished to the endorsers are incurred over a period of time and are not necessarily tracked separately from similar costs incurred for products sold to customers.

a. The above amounts of promised contractual payments to sponsored athletes are not reported on the financial statements. How might financial analysts think about these payments?

b. Compute an estimate of the present value of these payments, using Under Armour's interest rate on its debt, roughly 3%.

LO10-4 **E10-37. Analyzing Commitments and Contingencies**

Apple Inc.
NYSE :: AAPL

Apple Inc. provides the following disclosure in the notes to its 2020 financial statements:

Other Off-Balance-Sheet Commitments

Unconditional Purchase Obligations

The Company has entered into certain off–balance sheet commitments that require the future purchase of goods or services ("unconditional purchase obligations"). The Company's unconditional purchase obligations primarily consist of payments for supplier arrangements, Internet and telecommunication services, intellectual property licenses, and content creation. Future payments under noncancelable unconditional purchase obligations having a remaining term in excess of one year as of September 26, 2020, are as follows (in millions):

2021	$3,476
2022	2,885
2023	1,700
2024	357
2025	104
Thereafter	130
Total	$8,652

Contingencies

The Company is subject to various legal proceedings and claims that have arisen in the ordinary course of business and that have not been fully resolved. The outcome of litigation is inherently uncertain. If one or more legal matters were resolved against the Company in a reporting period for amounts above management's expectations, the Company's financial condition and operating

continued

continued from previous page

> results for that reporting period could be materially adversely affected. In the opinion of management, there was not at least a reasonable possibility the Company may have incurred a material loss, or a material loss greater than a recorded accrual, concerning loss contingencies for asserted legal and other claims, except for the following matters:
>
> **iOS Performance Management Cases**
> Various civil litigation matters have been filed in state and federal courts in the U.S. and in various international jurisdictions alleging violation of consumer protection laws, fraud, computer intrusion, and other causes of action related to the Company's performance management feature used in its iPhone operating systems, introduced to certain iPhones in iOS updates 10.2.1 and 11.2. The claims seek monetary damages and other non-monetary relief. On April 5, 2018, several U.S. federal actions were consolidated through a Multidistrict Litigation process into a single action in the U.S. District Court for the Northern District of California (the "Northern California District Court"). On February 28, 2020, the parties in the Multidistrict Litigation reached a settlement to resolve the U.S. federal and California state class actions. Under the terms of the settlement, which the Northern California District Court preliminarily approved in May 2020, the Company has agreed to pay up to $500 million in the aggregate to certain U.S. owners of iPhones if certain conditions are met. The final amount of the settlement will be determined based on the number of consumers who file valid claims and the attorneys' fee award. However, the Company has agreed to pay at least $310 million to settle the claims. In addition to civil litigation, the Company is also responding to governmental investigations and requests for information relating to the performance management feature. The Company continues to believe that its iPhones were not defective, that the performance management feature introduced with iOS updates 10.2.1 and 11.2 was intended to, and did, improve customers' user experience, and that the Company did not make any misleading statements or fail to disclose any material information. The Company has accrued its best estimate for the ultimate resolution of these matters.

1. Apple discloses that its rate of interest on 5-year debt securities is roughly 2.5%. Compute the present value of the future payments related to their off-balance-sheet purchase obligations. (Note: Assume that the "Thereafter" amount on the table is all paid in 2026.)
2. What would an analyst consider this to be—an asset, a liability, or equity?
3. Has Apple recorded a liability with respect to the litigation and contract for its iOS performance management cases? What amount is recorded, if any?

E10-38. Analyzing and Interpreting Pension Disclosure—Funded and Reported Amounts LO10-2
YUM! Brands, Inc., reports the following pension note disclosure in its 10-K report.

December 27 (in millions)	Pension Benefits 2020
Change in benefit obligation:	
Benefit obligation at beginning of year	$1,015
Service cost	8
Interest cost	35
Plan amendments	1
Special termination benefits	2
Benefits paid	(46)
Settlement payments	—
Actuarial (gain) loss	118
Benefit obligation at end of year	$1,133
Change in plan assets:	
Fair value of plan assets at beginning of year	$ 886
Actual return on plan assets	168
Employer contributions	6
Benefits paid	(46)
Fair value of plan assets at end of year	$1,014
Funded status at end of year	$ (119)

a. Describe what is meant by *service cost* and *interest cost*.
b. What is the source of funds to make payments to retirees?
c. Show the computation of the 2020 funded status for Yum.
d. What net pension amount is reported on its 2020 balance sheet?

LO10-2 **E10-39. Analyzing and Interpreting Pension Disclosures—Funded and Reported Amounts**
Verizon Communications Inc. reports the following pension data in its 2020 10-K report.

At December 31 ($ millions)	Pension 2020
Change in Benefit Obligations:	
Beginning of year	$21,248
Service cost	305
Interest cost	505
Plan amendments	—
Actuarial (gain) loss, net	2,308
Benefits paid	(842)
Settlements paid	(1,288)
End of year	$22,236
Change in Plan Assets:	
Beginning of year	$19,451
Actual return on plan assets	2,750
Company contributions	57
Benefits paid	(842)
Settlements paid	(1,288)
End of year	$20,128
Funded Status—End of year	$ (2,108)

a. Describe what is meant by *service cost* and *interest cost*.
b. What is the source of funds to make payments to retirees?
c. Show the computation of Verizon's 2020 funded status.
d. What net pension amount is reported on its 2020 balance sheet?

LO10-3 **E10-40. Computing and Reporting Deferred Income Taxes (FSET)**
Early in January 2022, Oler, Inc., purchased equipment costing $12,800. The equipment had a 2-year useful life and was depreciated in the amount of $6,400 in 2022 and 2023. Oler deducted the entire $12,800 on its tax return in 2022. This difference was the only one between its tax return and its financial statements. Oler's income before depreciation expense and income taxes was $188,800 in 2022 and $196,000 in 2023. The tax rate in each year was 25%.

REQUIRED
a. What amount of deferred tax liability should Oler report in 2022 and 2023?
b. Prepare the entries to record income taxes for 2022 and 2023 using the financial statement effects template.
c. Repeat requirement *b* if in 2022 the U.S. enacts a permanent tax rate change to be effective in 2023; the rate will increase to 35%.

LO10-3 **E10-41. Computing and Reporting Deferred Income Taxes**
Using the information from E10-40, prepare the journal entries for (i.) part *b* and (ii.) part *c*.

LO10-3 **E10-42. Calculating and Reporting Deferred Income Taxes**
Bens' Corporation paid $18,000 on December 31, 2022, for equipment with a three-year useful life. The equipment will be depreciated in the amount of $6,000 each year. Bens' took the entire $18,000 as an expense in its tax return in 2022. Assume this is the only timing difference between the firm's books and its tax return. Bens' tax rate is 25%.

REQUIRED
a. What amount of deferred tax liability should appear in Bens' 12/31/2022 balance sheet?
b. Where in the balance sheet should the deferred tax liability appear?
c. What amount of deferred tax liability should appear in Bens' 12/31/2023 balance sheet?

LO10-3 **E10-43. Recording Income Tax Expense (FSET)**
Nike, Inc., reports the following tax information in the notes to its 2020 financial report.
Income before income taxes is as follows:

Year Ended May 31 (In millions)	2020	2019	2018
Income before income taxes:			
United States	$2,954	$ 593	$ 744
Foreign	(67)	4,208	3,581
Total income before income taxes	$2,887	$4,801	$4,325

The provision for income taxes is as follows:

Year Ended May 31 (In millions)	2020	2019	2018
Current:			
United States			
Federal	$(109)	$ 74	$1,167
State	81	56	45
Foreign	756	608	533
Total current	728	738	1,745
Deferred:			
United States			
Federal	(231)	(33)	595
State	(47)	(9)	25
Foreign	(102)	76	27
Total deferred	(380)	34	647
Total income tax	$348	$772	$2,392

Nike also states the following:

> The effective tax rate for the fiscal year ended May 31, 2020, was lower than the effective tax rate for the fiscal year ended May 31, 2019, due to increased benefits from discrete items such as stock-based compensation. The foreign earnings rate impact shown above for the fiscal year ended May 31, 2020, includes withholding taxes of 6.5% and held for sale accounting items of 2.9%, offset by a benefit for statutory rate differences and other items of 3.5%. The foreign derived intangible income benefit reflects U.S. tax benefits introduced by the Tax Act for companies serving foreign markets. This benefit became available to the Company as a result of a restructuring of its intellectual property interests. Income tax audit and contingency reserves reflect benefits associated with the modification of the treatment of certain research and development expenditures of 2.9% offset by an increase related to the resolution of an audit by the U.S. Internal Revenue Service ("IRS") and other matters of 1.5%. Included in other is the deferral of income tax effects related to intra-entity transfers of inventory of 2.3% and other items of 0.6%.

a. Record Nike's provision for income taxes for 2020 using the financial statement effects template.
b. Explain how the provision for income taxes affects Nike's financial statements.
c. Calculate and compare Nike's effective tax rate for 2020, 2019, and 2018.

E10-44. Recording Income Tax Expense LO10-3
Using the information from E10-43, record Nike's provision for income taxes for 2020 using journal entries.

E10-45. Recording Income Tax Expense (FSET) LO10-3
Procter & Gamble, Inc. reports the following tax information in its 2020 financial report.

Procter & Gamble, Inc.
NYSE :: PG

Year Ended June 30	2018	2019	2020
Current:			
Federal and state	$4,178	$1,255	$1,558
Foreign	1,131	1,259	1,769
Total	5,309	2,514	3,327
Deferred:			
Federal and state	(1,989)	(296)	39
Foreign	145	(115)	(635)
Total	(1,844)	(411)	(596)
Provisions for income taxes	$3,465	$2,103	$2,731

a. Record P&G's provision for income taxes for 2020 using the financial statement effects template.
b. Explain how the provision for income affects P&G's financial statements.

LO10-3 E10-46. Recording Income Tax Expense
Using the information from E10-45, record P&G's provision for income taxes for 2020 using journal entries.

PROBLEMS

LO10-1 P10-47. Analyzing and Interpreting Leases

United Continental Holdings, Inc.
NASDAQ :: UAL

United Continental Holdings, Inc., did not adopt the new lease standard in 2018 but provides the following disclosure its 2018 10-K report ($ millions).

Consolidated Balance Sheets as of December 31	As Reported 2018	As Reported 2017	New Lease Standard Adjustments 2018	New Lease Standard Adjustments 2017	As Adjusted 2018	As Adjusted 2017
Operating property and equipment:						
Other property and equipment (owned)	$ 7,919	$ 6,946	$(1,041)	$(922)	$ 6,878	$ 6,024
Less-accumulated depreciation and amortization (owned)	(12,760)	(11,159)	140	92	(12,620)	(11,067)
Flight equipment (finance leases)[a]	1,029	1,151	(37)	(211)	992	940
Less-accumulated amortization	(654)	(777)	8	169	(646)	(608)
Operating lease assets						
Flight equipment	—	—	2,380	3,102	2,380	3,102
Other property and equipment	—	—	2,882	2,975	2,882	2,975
Current liabilities:						
Current maturities of finance leases[a]	149	128	(26)	(50)	123	78
Current maturities of operating leases	—	—	719	949	719	949
Other	619	576	(66)	(58)	553	518
Long-term obligations under finance leases[a]	1,134	996	(910)	(766)	224	230
Long-term obligations under operating leases	—	—	5,276	5,789	5,276	5,789

[a] Finance leases, under the New Lease Standard, are the equivalent of capital leases under Topic 840.

> The adoption of the New Lease Standard primarily resulted in the recording of assets and obligations of our operating leases on our consolidated balance sheets. Certain amounts recorded for prepaid and accrued rent associated with historical operating leases were reclassified to the newly captioned Operating lease assets in the consolidated balance sheets. Also, certain leases designated under Topic 840 as owned assets and capitalized finance leases will not be considered assets under the New Lease Standard and will be removed from the consolidated balance sheets, along with the related lease liability.

a. What is the amount United discloses that it would have capitalized for operating leases as right-of-use lease assets for the year ended December 31, 2018?
b. What is the amount of additional liability United discloses that it would have recorded for operating leases had United adopted the new lease standard in 2018?
c. What is the amount of asset under the new lease standard for finance leases? For the lease liability related to finance leases?
d. Why do you think the amount of operating leases is so much greater than finance leases?
e. United reported total assets of $44,792 million, total liabilities of $34,797 million, and total shareholders' equity of $9,995 million. Net income for the year was reported as $2,129 for the year and is essentially unchanged as a result of the new lease standard. Compute the reported return-on-assets and debt-to-equity ratios. Compute the ratios adjusted for the new lease standard, only taking into account the changes for operating leases (ignore all other changes).

LO10-1 P10-48. Analyzing Lease Disclosures

American Airlines Group, Inc.
NASDAQ :: AAL

American Airlines Group, Inc., provides the following disclosures in the notes to their 2020 financial statements (excerpted for brevity):

4. Leases

American leases certain aircraft and engines, including aircraft under capacity purchase agreements. As of December 31, 2020, American had 641 leased aircraft, with remaining terms ranging from less than one year to 12 years.

Supplemental balance sheet information related to leases was as follows (in millions, except lease term and discount rate):

	December 31 2020	December 31 2019
Operating leases:		
Operating lease ROU assets	$7,994	$8,694
Current operating lease liabilities	$1,641	$1,695
Noncurrent operating lease liabilities	6,739	7,388
Total operating lease liabilities	$8,380	$9,083
Finance leases:		
Property and equipment, at cost	$1,021	$ 954
Accumulated amortization	(539)	(447)
Property and equipment, net	$ 482	$ 507
Current finance lease liabilities	$ 100	$ 112
Noncurrent finance lease liabilities	472	558
Total finance lease liabilities	$ 572	$ 670

The components of lease expense were as follows (in millions):

	Year Ended December 31 2020	2019	2018
Operating lease cost	$1,943	$2,012	$1,889
Finance lease cost:			
Amortization of assets	92	79	78
Interest on lease liabilities	38	43	48
Variable lease cost	1,786	2,542	2,353
Total net lease cost	$3,859	$4,676	$4,368

a. What is the right-of-use asset for operating leases as of the end of 2020?
b. What is the net asset recorded for finance leases?
c. What is the lease liability balance for operating leases as of the end of 2020? What does this amount represent?
d. What is the amount of amortization expense recorded in 2020 for finance leases? For operating leases?
e. What is the amount of interest expense recorded in 2020 for finance leases? For operating leases?

P10-49. **Analyze Commitment and Contingency Disclosures** LO10-4

Cisco Systems, Inc., reports the following in the Commitments and Contingencies note to their 10-K for the year ended July 2020.

Cisco Systems, Inc.
NASDAQ :: CSCO

> **Purchase Commitments with Contract Manufacturers and Suppliers**
> We purchase components from a variety of suppliers and use several contract manufacturers to provide manufacturing services for our products. During the normal course of business, in order to manage manufacturing lead times and help ensure adequate component supply, we enter into agreements with contract manufacturers and suppliers that either allow them to procure inventory based upon criteria as defined by us or establish the parameters defining our requirements. A significant portion of our reported purchase commitments arising from these agreements consists of firm, noncancelable, and unconditional commitments. Certain of these purchase commitments

continued

continued from previous page

> with contract manufacturers and suppliers relate to arrangements to secure long-term pricing for certain product components for multi-year periods. In certain instances, these agreements allow us the option to cancel, reschedule, and adjust our requirements based on our business needs prior to firm orders being placed. As of July 25, 2020, and July 27, 2019, we had total purchase commitments for inventory of $4.4 billion and $5.0 billion, respectively.
>
> We record a liability for firm, noncancelable, and unconditional purchase commitments for quantities in excess of our future demand forecasts consistent with the valuation of our excess and obsolete inventory. As of July 25, 2020, and July 27, 2019, the liability for these purchase commitments was $141 million and $129 million, respectively, and was included in other current liabilities.

a. What effect does the use of contract manufacturers have on Cisco's balance sheet?
b. Assuming an interest rate of 4% and payments due in 1 year of $3.4 billion and in years 2-5, $250 million, what is the present value of these commitments as of July 2020?
c. What amount does Cisco state that it has accrued as a liability as of July 2020?

LO10-2 P10-50. Analyzing and Interpreting Pension Disclosures

Hoopes Corporation's December 31, 2022, 10-K report has the following disclosures related to its retirement plans.

> The following table provides a reconciliation of the changes in the pension plans' benefit obligations and fair value of assets over the two-year period ended December 31, 2022, and a statement of the funded status as of December 31, 2022 and 2021 (in millions):
>
> | | Pension Plans | |
> |---|---|---|
> | (in millions) | 2022 | 2021 |
> | **Changes in Projected Benefit Obligation ("PBO")** | | |
> | PBO at beginning of year | $17,381 | $13,260 |
> | Service cost | 625 | 500 |
> | Interest cost | 1,080 | 988 |
> | Actuarial (gain) loss | 2,250 | 3,128 |
> | Benefits paid | (562) | (469) |
> | Other | 72 | (26) |
> | PBO at end of year | $20,846 | $17,381 |
> | **Change in Plan Assets** | | |
> | Fair value of plan assets at beginning of year | $15,954 | $12,974 |
> | Actual return on plan assets | 2,910 | 2,393 |
> | Company contributions | 668 | 1,080 |
> | Benefits paid | (562) | (469) |
> | Other | 38 | (24) |
> | Fair value of plan assets at end of year | $19,008 | $15,954 |
>
> Net periodic benefit cost for the three years ended December 31 were as follows (in millions):
>
> | | Pension Plans | | |
> |---|---|---|---|
> | (in millions) | 2022 | 2021 | 2020 |
> | Service cost | $ 625 | $500 | $ 599 |
> | Interest cost | 1,080 | 988 | 958 |
> | Expected return on plan assets | (1,274) | (1,146) | (1,271) |
> | Recognized actuarial (gains) losses and other | 221 | 28 | (73) |
> | Net periodic benefit cost | $ 652 | $370 | $ 213 |
>
> Weighted-average actuarial assumptions for our primary U.S. pension plans, which represent substantially all of our PBO, are as follows:

continued

continued from previous page

	Pension Plans		
(in millions)	2022	2021	2020
Discount rate used to determine benefit obligation	5.76%	6.37%	7.68%
Rate of increase in future compensation levels used to determine benefit obligation	4.58	4.63	4.42
Expected long-term rate of return on assets	8.00	8.00	8.50

REQUIRED

a. How much pension expense (revenue) does Hoopes report in its 2022 income statement?
b. Hoopes reports a $1,274 million expected return on plan assets as an offset to 2022 pension expense. Approximately, how is this amount computed? What is the actual gain or loss realized on its 2022 plan assets? What is the purpose of using this estimated amount instead of the actual gain or loss?
c. What factors affected its 2022 pension liability? What factors affected its 2022 plan assets?
d. What does the term *funded status* mean? What is the funded status of the 2022 Hoopes retirement plans? What amount of asset or liability does Hoopes report on its 2022 balance sheet relating to its retirement plans?
e. Hoopes decreased its discount rate from 6.37% to 5.76% in 2022. What effect(s) does this have on its balance sheet and its income statement?
f. Hoopes changed its estimate of expected annual wage increases used to determine its defined benefit obligation in 2022. What effect(s) does this change have on its financial statements? In general, how does such a change affect income?

P10-51. Analyzing and Interpreting Pension Disclosures—Funded and Reported Amounts **LO10-2**
Johnson and Johnson reports the following pension note disclosure as part of its 2020 10-K report. Johnson and Johnson NYSE :: JNJ

(in millions)	Pension Benefits 2020
Change in Benefit Obligation:	
Projected benefit obligation—beginning of year	$37,188
Service cost	1,380
Interest cost	955
Plan participant contributions	61
Amendments	(1,780)
Actuarial (gains) losses	5,716
Divestitures and acquisitions	(88)
Curtailments, settlements, and restructuring	(24)
Benefits paid from plan	(1,111)
Effect of exchange rates	1,003
Projected benefit obligation—end of year	$43,300
Change in Plan Assets:	
Plan assets at fair value—beginning of year	$32,201
Actual return on plan assets	5,524
Company contributions	870
Plan participant contributions	61
Settlements	(13)
Divestitures and acquisitions	(84)
Benefits paid from plan assets	(1,111)
Effect of exchange rates	747
Plan assets at fair value—end of year	$38,195
Funded status—end of year	$ (5,105)

a. Describe what is meant by *service cost* and *interest cost*.
b. What is the actual return on pension investments in 2020?
c. Provide an example under which an "actuarial loss," such as the $5,716 million loss that Johnson and Johnson reports in 2020, might arise.
d. What is the source of funds to make payments to retirees?
e. How much cash did Johnson and Johnson contribute to its pension plans in 2020?
f. How much cash did the company pay to retirees in 2020?

g. Show the computation of its 2020 funded status.
h. What net pension amount is reported on its 2020 balance sheet?

LO10-3 P10-52. Interpreting the Income Tax Expense Disclosure

Cummins, Inc., reports the following tax information in its fiscal 2020 financial report.

The provision for income taxes by taxing jurisdiction and by significant component consisted of the following in millions of dollars:

	2020	2019	2018
Current:			
U.S. federal and state	$ 162	$ 288	$ 303
Foreign	358	282	348
Impact of tax law changes	—	—	153
Total current income tax expense	$ 520	$ 570	$ 804
Deferred:			
U.S. federal and state	$ 2	$ (32)	$ (71)
Foreign	22	28	(26)
Impact of tax law changes	(17)	—	(141)
Total deferred income tax expense (benefit)	7	(4)	(238)
Income tax expense	$ 527	$ 566	$ 566
Earnings before taxes on the income statement	$2,338	$2,834	$2,753

REQUIRED

a. What amount of tax expense is reported in Cummins' 2020 income statement? In 2019? In 2018? How much of each year's income tax expense is current tax expense, and how much is deferred tax expense?
b. Compute Cummins' effective tax rate for each year.
c. Assume that Cummins' deferred tax in 2020 is due to deferred tax liabilities. Provide one possible example that would be consistent with this situation.

LO10-3 P10-53. Calculating and Reporting Income Tax Expense (FSET)

Lynch Company began operations in 2022. The company reported $36,000 of depreciation expense on its income statement in 2022 and $39,000 in 2023. On its tax returns, Lynch deducted $48,000 for depreciation in 2022 and $55,500 in 2023. The 2023 tax return shows a tax obligation (liability) of $18,000 based on a 25% tax rate.

REQUIRED

a. Determine the temporary difference between the book value of depreciable assets and the tax basis of these assets at the end of 2022 and 2023.
b. Calculate the deferred tax liability for each year.
c. Calculate the income tax expense for 2023.
d. Record the company's provision for income taxes for 2023 using the financial statement effects template.

LO10-3 P10-54. Calculating and Reporting Income Tax Expense

Using the information from P10-53, prepare the journal entry to record income tax expense for 2023 and post the entry to the appropriate T-accounts.

LO10-3 P10-55. Calculating and Reporting Income Tax Expense (FSET)

Carter Inc. began operations in 2022. The company reported $104,000 of depreciation expense on its 2022 income statement and $102,400 in 2023. Carter Inc. deducted $112,000 for depreciation on its tax return in 2022 and $97,600 in 2023. The company reports a tax obligation of $36,120 for 2023 based on a tax rate of 25%.

REQUIRED

a. Determine the temporary difference between the book value of depreciable assets and the tax basis of these assets at the end of 2022 and 2023.
b. Calculate the deferred tax liability at the end of each year.
c. Calculate the income tax expense for 2023.

d. Record the company's provision for income taxes for 2023 using the financial statement effects template.

P10-56. Calculating and Reporting Income Tax Expense   **LO10-3**
Using the information from P10-55, prepare the journal entry to record income tax expense for 2023 and post the entry to the appropriate T-accounts.

P10-57. Computing and Reporting Deferred Income Taxes   **LO10-3**
Macy's, Inc., reported the following in its fiscal 2017 annual report:

Macy's, Inc.
NASDAQ :: M

> On December 22, 2017, H.R. 1 was enacted into law. This new tax legislation, among other things, reduced the U.S. federal corporate tax rate from 35% to 21% effective January 1, 2018.
>
> In applying the impacts of the new tax legislation to its 2017 income tax provision, the Company remeasured its deferred tax assets and liabilities based on the rates at which they are expected to reverse in the future, which is generally a 21% federal tax rate and its related impact on the state tax rates. The resulting impact was the recognition of an income tax benefit of $571 million in the fourth quarter of 2017. In addition, applying the new U.S. federal corporate tax rate of 21% on January 1, 2018, resulted in a federal income tax statutory rate of 33.7% in 2017. Combining the impacts on the Company's current income tax provision and the remeasurement of its deferred tax balances, the Company's effective income tax rate was a benefit of 1.9% in 2017.
>
> The tax effects of temporary differences that give rise to significant portions of the deferred tax assets and deferred tax liabilities are as follows:

(millions)	Feb. 3, 2018	Jan. 28, 2017
Deferred tax assets		
Postemployment and postretirement benefits	$ 188	$ 405
Accrued liabilities accounted for on a cash basis for tax purposes	218	379
Long-term debt	25	63
Unrecognized state tax benefits and accrued interest	39	76
State operating loss and credit carryforwards	101	79
Other	165	347
Valuation allowance	(65)	(36)
Total deferred tax assets	671	1,313
Deferred tax liabilities		
Excess of book basis over tax basis of property and equipment	(923)	(1,381)
Merchandise inventories	(389)	(604)
Intangible assets	(276)	(380)
Other	(205)	(391)
Total deferred tax liabilities	(1,793)	(2,756)
Net deferred tax liability	$(1,122)	$(1,443)

a. What was the amount of income tax expense or benefit that Macy's reported related to revaluing deferred tax assets and liabilities to the new, lower tax rate?
b. Explain why Macy's reported an income tax *benefit* when it revalued its deferred income tax liabilities and deferred income tax assets to the new, lower tax rate.

CASES AND PROJECTS

C10-58. Analyzing and Interpreting Pension Disclosures   **LO10-2**
DuPont De Nemours, Inc. (abbreviated "DuPont") provides the following disclosures in its 10-K report relating to its pension plans. (Footnotes to the tables excluded for brevity.)

DuPont De Nemours, Inc.
(abbreviated "DuPont")
NYSE :: DD

Net Periodic Benefit Costs for All Significant Plans for the Year Ended December 31	Defined Benefit Pension Plans		
In millions	2020	2019	2018
Net Periodic Benefit Costs:			
Service cost	$ 70	$ 184	$ 651
Interest cost	57	630	1,638
Expected return on plan assets	(110)	(988)	(2,846)
Amortization of prior service credit	(5)	(9)	(24)
Amortization of unrecognized loss (gain)	16	128	649
Curtailment/settlement/other	9	—	(10)
Net periodic benefit costs (credits)—Total	$37	$(55)	$58
Less: Net periodic benefit (credits) costs—discontinued operations	—	(45)	90
Net periodic benefit costs (credits)—Continuing operations	$ 37	$ (10)	$ (32)
Changes in plan assets and benefit obligations recognized in other comprehensive loss (income):			
Net loss (gain)	$ 99	$ 350	$ 1,490
Prior service (credit) cost	—	(65)	34
Amortization of prior service credit	5	3	24
Amortization of unrecognized (loss) gain	(16)	(7)	(649)
Curtailment loss	(4)	(2)	—
Settlement loss	(9)	(2)	2
Effect of foreign exchange rates	21	(2)	1
Total recognized in other comprehensive loss (income)	$ 96	$ 275	$902
Noncontrolling interest	$ 2	$ —	$ —
Total recognized in net periodic benefit costs (credits) and other comprehensive loss (income)	$ 131	$ 265	$ 870

Change in Projected Benefit Obligations of All Plans	Defined Benefit Pension Plans	
In millions	2020	2019
Change in projected benefit obligations:		
Benefit obligations at beginning of year	$4,784	$ 53,014
Service cost	70	184
Interest cost	57	630
Plan participants' contributions	11	11
Actuarial changes in assumptions and experience	298	515
Benefits paid	(268)	(1,247)
Plan amendments	—	(76)
Acquisitions/divestitures/other	—	20
Effect of foreign exchange rates	347	31
Termination benefits/curtailment cost/settlements	(4)	(4)
Spin-off of Dow	—	(29,285)
Spin-off of Corteva	—	(19,009)
Benefit obligations at end of year	$5,295	$ 4,784

Change in Plan Assets and Funded Status of All Plans	Defined Benefit Pension Plans	
In millions	2020	2019
Change in plan assets:		
Fair value of plan assets at beginning of year	$3,757	$ 41,462
Actual return on plan assets	309	1,191
Employer contributions	98	697
Plan participants' contributions	11	11
Benefits paid	(268)	(1,247)
Acquisitions/divestitures/other	—	10
Effect of foreign exchange rates	251	60
Spin-off of Dow	—	(22,626)
Spin-off of Corteva	—	(15,801)
Fair value of plan assets at end of year	$4,158	$ 3,757

Weighted Average Assumptions for All Pension Plans	Benefit Obligations at December 31	
	2020	2019
Discount rate	0.84%	1.21%
Interest crediting rate for applicable benefits	1.25%	1.25%
Rate of compensation increase	3.09%	3.14%
Expected return on plan assets	N/A	N/A

REQUIRED

a. How much pension expense (revenue) does DuPont report in its 2020 income statement?
b. DuPont reports a $110 million expected return on plan assets as an offset to 2020 pension expense. Estimate the rate of return DuPont expected to earn on its plan assets in 2020.
c. What factors affected its 2020 pension liability? What factors affected its 2020 plan assets?
d. What does the term "funded status" mean? What is the funded status of the 2020 DuPont retirement plans at the end of 2020? What amount of asset or liability should DuPont report on its 2020 balance sheet relating to its retirement plans?
e. DuPont changed its discount rate from 1.21% to 0.84% in 2020. What effect(s) does this change have on its balance sheet and its income statement?
f. Suppose DuPont increased its estimate of expected returns on plan assets in 2021. What effect(s) would this increase have on its income statement? Explain.
g. DuPont provides us with its weighted-average discount rate. The company has manufacturing operations in about 40 countries and has roughly 34,000 employees all over the world. Would you expect that the discount rate differed in the United States from the average rate outside the United States? Explain. What would you expect for future compensation levels?

C10-59. Interpreting Finance and Operating Leases (FSET) LO10-1, 4
Target Corporation disclosed the following in the notes to their fiscal year 2020 10-K.

Leases (millions)	Classification	Jan. 30, 2021	Feb. 1, 2020
Assets			
Operating	Operating lease assets	$2,227	$2,236
Finance	Buildings and improvements, net of accumulated depreciation[a]	1,504	1,180
Total leased assets		$3,731	$3,416
Liabilities			
Current			
Operating	Accrued and other current liabilities	$ 211	$ 200
Finance	Current portion of long-term debt and other borrowings	88	67
Noncurrent			
Operating	Noncurrent operating lease liabilities	2,218	2,275
Finance	Long-term debt and other borrowings	1,766	1,303
Total lease liabilities		$4,283	$3,845

Note: We use our incremental borrowing rate based on the information available at commencement date in determining the present value of lease payments.

[a] Finance lease assets are recorded net of accumulated amortization of $550 million and $441 million as of January 30, 2021, and February 1, 2020, respectively.

Lease Cost (millions)	Classification	2020	2019	2018
Operating lease cost[a]	SG&A expenses	$332	$287	$251
Finance lease cost				
Amortization of leased assets	Depreciation and amortization[b]	105	82	65
Interest on lease liabilities	Net interest expense	62	51	42
Sublease income[c]	Other revenue	(11)	(13)	(11)
Net lease cost		$484	$407	$347

[a] 2020 includes $44 million of short-term leases and variable lease costs. Short-term and variable lease costs were insignificant for 2019 and 2018.
[b] Supply chain-related amounts are included in Cost of Sales.
[c] Sublease income excludes rental income from owned properties of $48 million, $48 million, and $47 million for 2020, 2019, and 2018, which is included in Other Revenue.

Maturity of Lease Liabilities (millions)	Operating Leases[a]	Finance Leases[b]	Total
2021	$ 289	$ 152	$ 441
2022	290	159	449
2023	283	158	441
2024	269	155	424
2025	256	154	410
After 2025	1,694	1,687	3,381
Total lease payments	$3,081	$2,465	$5,546
Less: Interest	652	611	
Present value of lease liabilities	$2,429	$1,854	

[a] Operating lease payments include $847 million related to options to extend lease terms that are reasonably certain of being exercised and exclude $231 million of legally binding minimum lease payments for leases signed but not yet commenced.

[b] Finance lease payments include $160 million related to options to extend lease terms that are reasonably certain of being exercised and exclude $1.1 billion of legally binding minimum lease payments for leases signed but not yet commenced.

a. What is the right-of-use asset for operating leases as of the end of fiscal 2020?
b. What is the net asset recorded for finance leases at the end of fiscal 2020?
c. What is the lease liability balance for operating leases as of the end of fiscal 2020? What does this amount represent?
d. What is the amount of amortization expense recorded in 2020 for finance leases?
e. What is the amount of interest expense recorded in 2020 for finance leases?
f. What is recorded on the income statement for operating leases?
g. Assume the lease payment for 2020 for finance leases is $125 million. Report the entries for 2020 (year ended February 2, 2021) for finance leases, using the financial statement effects template.
h. Discuss the implications of the different line items on the income statement for expensing lease costs for both types of leases that Target discloses.
i. Target has reported total assets for 2020 (year ended January 30, 2021) of $51,248, total liabilities of $36,808, and equity of $14,440. Explain the effect on debt-to-equity from having the operating leases "on-balance sheet."

LO10-1 C10-60. Interpreting Finance and Operating Leases
Using the information from C10-59, prepare the journal entries for part g.

LO10-3 C10-61. Interpreting Income Tax Disclosures (FSET)
The following information is taken from **Williams-Sonoma, Inc.**'s 10-K.

Williams-Sonoma
NYSE :: WSM

Note D: Income Taxes

The components of earnings before income taxes, by tax jurisdiction, are as follows:

	Fiscal Year Ended		
(in thousands)	Fiscal 2020 (52 weeks)	Fiscal 2019 (52 weeks)	Fiscal 2018 (53 weeks)
United States	$773,317	$353,215	$333,594
Foreign	121,149	103,806	95,653
Total	$894,466	$457,021	$429,247

continued

continued from previous page

The provision for income taxes consists of the following:

	Fiscal Year Ended		
(in thousands)	Fiscal 2020 (52 weeks)	Fiscal 2019 (52 weeks)	Fiscal 2018 (53 weeks)
Current			
Federal	$171,821	$76,873	$43,745
State	39,498	14,205	15,357
Foreign	15,494	12,438	12,822
Total current	226,813	103,516	71,924
Deferred			
Federal	(7,575)	(606)	23,507
State	(5,997)	(870)	1,562
Foreign	511	(1,081)	(1,430)
Total deferred	(13,061)	(2,557)	23,639
Total provision	$213,752	$100,959	$95,563

In thousands	Jan. 31, 2021	Feb. 2, 2020
Deferred tax (liabilities)		
Operating lease liabilities	$ 319,599	$ 347,693
Compensation	20,852	14,350
Merchandise inventories	20,631	22,311
Gift cards	19,345	19,520
Accrued liabilities	13,451	8,440
Stock-based compensation	9,926	9,860
Loyalty rewards	9,609	5,252
Executive deferred compensation	8,647	7,543
State taxes	7,460	7,546
Federal and state net operating loss	2,609	3,443
Operating lease right-of-use assets	(283,856)	(309,801)
Deferred lease incentives	(31,672)	(46,701)
Property and equipment	(54,724)	(37,309)
Other	(317)	(3,277)
Valuation allowance	(2,819)	(3,648)
Total deferred tax assets, net	$ 58,741	$ 45,222

As of January 31, 2021, we had $38,696,000 of gross unrecognized tax benefits, of which $34,026,000 would, if recognized, affect the effective tax rate.

We accrue interest and penalties related to unrecognized tax benefits in the provision for income taxes. As of January 31, 2021, and February 2, 2020, our accruals for the payment of interest and penalties totaled $8,225,000 and $7,251,000, respectively.

Due to the potential resolution of tax issues, it is reasonably possible that the balance of our gross unrecognized tax benefits could decrease within the next twelve months by a range of $0 to $15,800,000.

We file income tax returns in the U.S. and foreign jurisdictions. We are subject to examination by the tax authorities in these jurisdictions. Our U.S. federal taxable years for which the statute of limitations has not expired are fiscal years 2017 to 2020. Substantially all material states, local and foreign jurisdictions' statutes of limitations are closed for taxable years prior to 2017.

REQUIRED

a. What amount of income tax expense did Williams-Sonoma report for the year ended January 31, 2021?
b. Calculate Williams-Sonoma's effective tax rate for each year reported. In addition, calculate the rate of U.S. federal taxes on U.S. income in the fiscal year ended January 31, 2021.

c. Williams-Sonoma reported income taxes payable of $69,476,000 in its January 31, 2021, balance sheet, and $22,501,000 at February 2, 2020. What amount of income taxes did it pay in cash during the fiscal year ended January 31, 2021?[17]

d. Report the entry to record income tax expense for the fiscal year ended January 31, 2021, using the financial statement effects template.

e. The company reported a net book value of property, plant, and equipment of $873,894,000 on January 31, 2021. Given a tax rate of 21% (assume they are all in the U.S.), what is an estimate of the tax basis of these assets on that date?

f. The company reported $34,988,000 in other long-term liabilities related to deferred compensation obligations on its January 31, 2021, balance sheet. The company provided the following explanation of this asset in Note H to its 10-K:

> We also have a nonqualified executive deferred compensation plan that provides supplemental retirement income benefits for a select group of management. This plan permits eligible employees to make salary and bonus deferrals that are 100% vested. We have an unsecured obligation to pay in the future the value of the deferred compensation adjusted to reflect the performance, whether positive or negative, of selected investment measurement options chosen by each participant during the deferral period.

Explain how this expense results in a temporary difference between tax and financial reporting.

g. Williams-Sonoma has a valuation allowance listed in its schedule of deferred tax assets and liabilities. Briefly and in general explain what a valuation allowance is and how it affects deferred taxes and reported income.

h. In fiscal year 2017, Williams-Sonoma stated that the company recorded a $28.3 million additional tax expense for the remeasurement of deferred tax assets. This remeasurement is related to the drop in the U.S. statutory tax rate of 33.9% to a lower rate of 21%. Explain what this is and why the company had to record this expense.

LO10-3 C10-62. Interpreting Income Tax Disclosures
Using the information from C10-61, prepare the journal entries for part d.

LO10-5 C10-63. Interpreting Income Tax Disclosures

Alphabet Inc.
NASDAQ :: GOOG

Alphabet Inc. reported the following in Note 14 to its 2020 10-K report:

Note 14. Income Taxes
Income from continuing operations before income taxes consists of the following (in millions):

	Year Ended December 31		
	2018	2019	2020
Domestic operations	$15,779	$16,426	$37,576
Foreign operations	19,134	23,199	10,506
Total	$34,913	$39,625	$48,082

	Year Ended December 31		
	2018	2019	2020
Current:			
Federal and state	$2,153	$2,424	$4,789
Foreign	1,251	2,713	1,687
Total	3,404	5,137	6,476
Deferred:			
Federal and state	907	286	1,552
Foreign	(134)	(141)	(215)
Total	773	145	1,337
Provision for income taxes	$4,177	$5,282	$7,813

continued

---

[17] For this problem, assume a simple case. The complicating factors that would change the answer are beyond the scope of this text. For those readers aware of these complicating factors, assume there are no acquisitions of other companies during the year and that Williams-Sonoma has no unrecognized tax benefits.

continued from previous page

Tax Contingencies

We are subject to income taxes in the United States (federal and state) and numerous foreign jurisdictions. Significant judgment is required in evaluating our tax positions and determining our provision for income taxes. During the ordinary course of business, there are many transactions and calculations for which the ultimate tax determination is uncertain. We establish reserves for tax-related uncertainties based on estimates of whether, and the extent to which, additional taxes will be due. These reserves are established when we believe that certain positions might be challenged despite our belief that our tax return positions are fully supportable. We adjust these reserves in light of changing facts and circumstances, such as the outcome of tax audits. The provision for income taxes includes the impact of reserve provisions and changes to reserves that are considered appropriate.

The reconciliation of our tax contingencies is as follows (in millions):

	2018	2019	2020
Gross tax contingencies—January 1	$2,309	$3,414	$3,923
Gross increases to tax positions in prior periods	164	216	88
Gross decreases to tax positions in prior periods	(90)	(181)	(465)
Gross increases to current period tax positions	1,088	707	507
Settlements with tax authorities	(36)	(207)	(1,207)
Lapse of statute of limitations	(21)	(26)	(26)
Gross tax contingencies—December 31	$3,414	$3,923	$2,820

We are under examination, or may be subject to examination, by the Internal Revenue Service ("IRS") for the calendar year 2013 and thereafter. These examinations may lead to ordinary course adjustments or proposed adjustments to our taxes or our net operating losses with respect to years under examination as well as subsequent periods. During Q3 2020, we resolved the audits of tax years 2007 through 2012 with the IRS for amounts that were materially consistent with our accrual. In October 2014, the European Commission opened a formal investigation to examine whether decisions by the tax authorities in Luxembourg with regard to the corporate income tax paid by certain of our subsidiaries comply with European Union rules on state aid. On October 4, 2017, the European Commission announced its decision that determinations by the tax authorities in Luxembourg did not comply with European Union rules on state aid. Based on that decision the European Commission announced an estimated recovery amount of approximately €250 million, plus interest, for the period May 2006 through June 2014, and ordered Luxembourg tax authorities to calculate the actual amount of additional taxes subject to recovery. Luxembourg computed an initial recovery amount, consistent with the European Commission's decision, that we deposited into escrow in March 2018, subject to adjustment pending conclusion of all appeals. In December 2017, Luxembourg appealed the European Commission's decision. In May 2018, we appealed. We believe the European Commission's decision to be without merit and will continue to defend ourselves vigorously in this matter. We are also subject to taxation in various states and other foreign jurisdictions including China, Germany, India, Japan, Luxembourg, and the United Kingdom. We are under, or may be subject to, audit or examination and additional assessments by the relevant authorities in respect of these particular jurisdictions primarily for 2009 and thereafter.

REQUIRED

a. Compute Alphabet's effective tax rate for each year presented. Also, compute Alphabet's domestic tax rate (federal plus state) and its foreign tax rate on income from foreign operations.
b. What is Alphabet's amount of unrecognized tax benefit at the end of 2020? Briefly describe what this is and how it is shown in the company's income statement and balance sheet.

SOLUTIONS TO REVIEW PROBLEMS

Review 10-1

The present value of the lease payments is $224,755, computed as $32,000 × 7.02358 (from Appendix A, Table A-3) or computed using a financial calculator or Excel. At the commencement of the finance lease, The Gap would record a Right-of-Use Asset for the finance lease and a Finance Lease Liability.

The amortization table for the loan is as follows:

Amortization Table for a Lease Liability*

A Year	B Beginning of Year Lease Liability	C Interest Expense (B × 7%)	D Payment	E Principal Payment (D − C)	F Ending-Year Lease Liability (B − E)
1	$224,755	$15,733	$32,000	$16,267	$208,488
2	208,488	14,594	32,000	17,406	191,082
3	191,082	13,376	32,000	18,624	172,458
4	172,458	12,072	32,000	19,928	152,530
5	152,530	10,677	32,000	21,323	131,207
6	131,207	9,184	32,000	22,816	108,391
7	108,391	7,587	32,000	24,413	83,978
8	83,978	5,878	32,000	26,122	57,856
9	57,856	4,050	32,000	27,950	29,906
10	29,906	2,093	32,000	29,907	0

* Small differences due to rounding

Part One

Entry for finance lease treatment—commencement of lease.

Initially, the company records the lease asset and lease liability at the lease commencement. At the end of the first year, Gap would record amortization expense of $22,476 ($224,755/10), interest expense of $15,733 ($224,755 × 0.07; and see table above), and the lease payment.

Transaction	Balance Sheet							Income Statement		
	Cash Asset	+ Noncash Assets	− Contra Assets	= Liabilities	+ Contrib. Capital	+ Earned Capital		Revenues	− Expenses	= Net Income
(1) Lease store space using finance-type lease.		+224,755 Right-of-Use Asset—Finance Lease	−	= +224,755 Finance Lease Liability					−	=
(2a) Annual amortization expense.			+22,476 Accumulated Amortization =			−22,476 Retained Earnings			− +22,476 Amortization Expense	= −22,476
(2b) Lease payment and interest expense.	−32,000 Cash		−	= −16,267 Finance Lease Liability		−15,733 Retained Earnings			− +15,733 Interest Expense	= −15,733

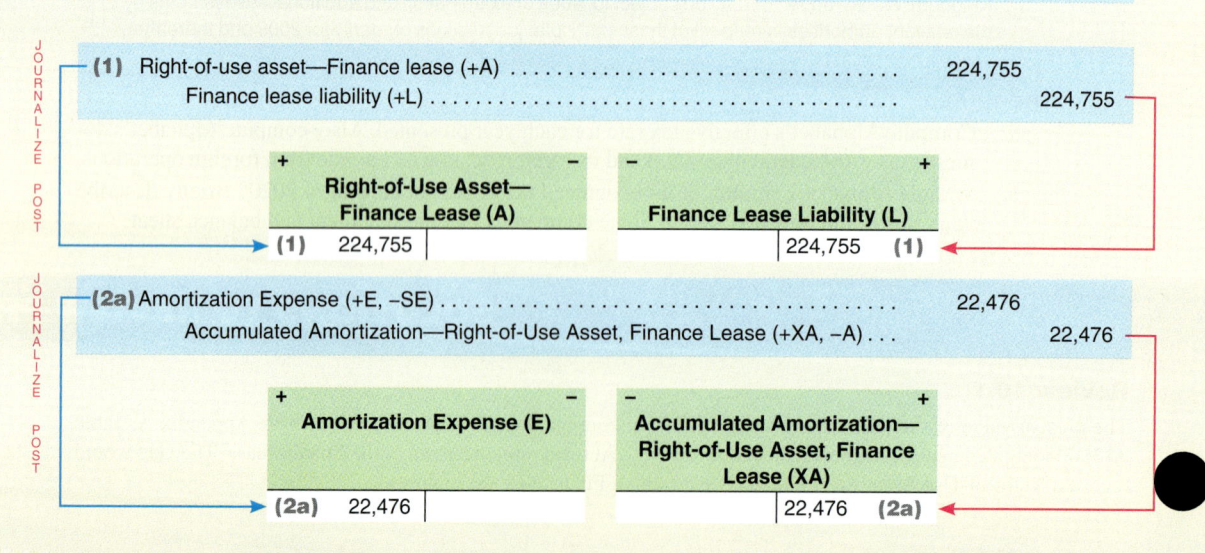

(1) Right-of-use asset—Finance lease (+A) 224,755
    Finance lease liability (+L) 224,755

+ Right-of-Use Asset— Finance Lease (A) −		− Finance Lease Liability (L) +	
(1) 224,755			224,755 (1)

(2a) Amortization Expense (+E, −SE) 22,476
    Accumulated Amortization—Right-of-Use Asset, Finance Lease (+XA, −A) ... 22,476

+ Amortization Expense (E) −		− Accumulated Amortization— Right-of-Use Asset, Finance Lease (XA) +	
(2a) 22,476			22,476 (2a)

(2b) Finance lease liability (−L)				16,267	
Interest expense (+E, −SE)				15,733	
Cash (−A)					32,000

− Finance Lease Liability (L) +		+ Interest Expense (E) −		+ Cash (A) −	
(2b) 16,267		(2b) 15,733			32,000 (2b)

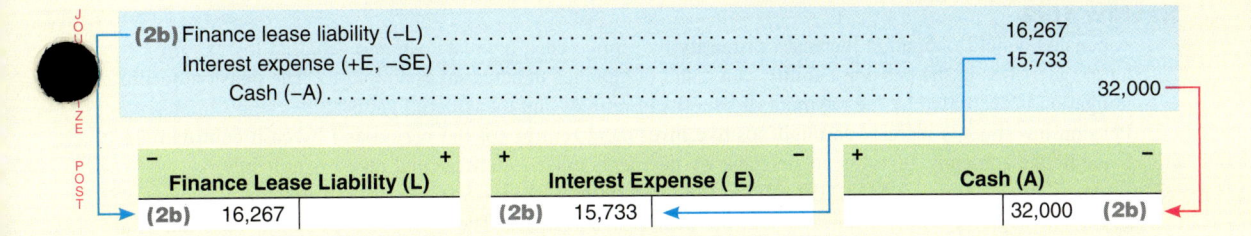

Part Two

If the lease were an operating lease, the entries would be as follows:
(1a) To record lease asset and liability at commencement of lease.
(1b) At the end of the year the lease payment is recorded.
(1c) At the end of the year, the straight-line lease expense is recorded and the balance sheet items are adjusted.

Transaction	Balance Sheet						Income Statement		
	Cash Asset	+ Noncash Assets	− Contra Assets	= Liabilities	+ Contrib. Capital	+ Earned Capital	Revenues	− Expenses	= Net Income
(1a) Lease store space using operating-type lease.		+224,755 Right-of-Use Asset— Operating Lease	−	= +224,755 Operating Lease Liability				−	=
(1b) Lease payment.	−32,000 Cash		−	= −32,000 Operating Lease Liability				−	=
(1c) Record lease expense.		−16,267 Right-of-Use Asset— Operating Lease	−	= +15,733 Operating Lease Liability		−32,000 Retained Earnings		− +32,000 Operating Lease Expense	= −32,000

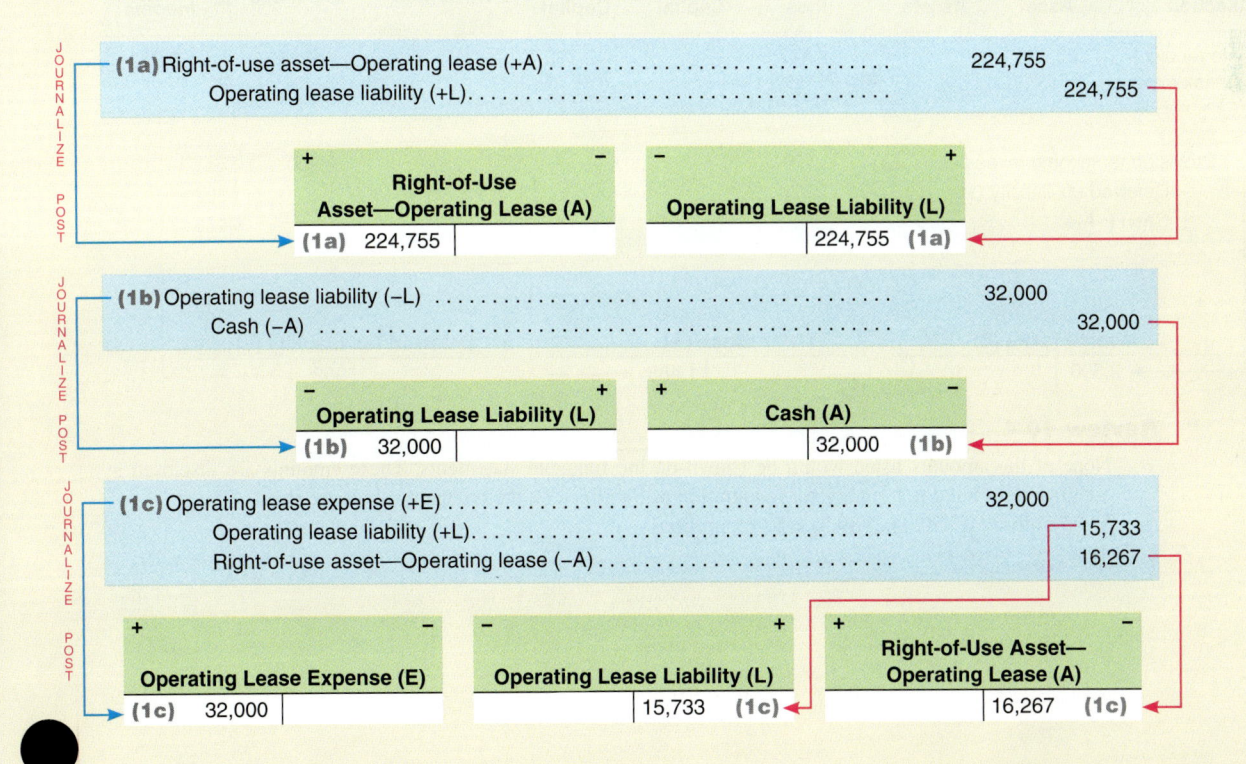

(1a) Right-of-use asset—Operating lease (+A)			224,755	
Operating lease liability (+L)				224,755

+ Right-of-Use Asset—Operating Lease (A) −		− Operating Lease Liability (L) +	
(1a) 224,755			224,755 (1a)

(1b) Operating lease liability (−L)			32,000	
Cash (−A)				32,000

− Operating Lease Liability (L) +		+ Cash (A) −	
(1b) 32,000			32,000 (1b)

(1c) Operating lease expense (+E)			32,000	
Operating lease liability (+L)				15,733
Right-of-use asset—Operating lease (−A)				16,267

+ Operating Lease Expense (E) −		− Operating Lease Liability (L) +		+ Right-of-Use Asset—Operating Lease (A) −	
(1c) 32,000			15,733 (1c)		16,267 (1c)

Review 10-2

1. A pension benefit obligation increases primarily by service cost, interest cost, and actuarial losses. The latter are increases in the pension liability as a result of changes in actuarial assumptions. The pension benefit obligation is decreased by the payment of benefits to retirees and by actuarial gains.
2. Pension investments increase through positive investment returns for the period and by cash contributions made by the company. Investments decrease by payments made to retirees and investment losses.
3. Boeing's funded status is $(13,719) million ($82,415 million PBO − $68,696 million pension assets) as of 2020. The negative amount indicates that the plan is underfunded. Therefore, this amount is reported as a liability on the company's balance sheet.
4. Expected return on plan assets acts as an offset to service cost and interest cost in computing the net pension cost. As the expected return increases (decreases), net pension cost decreases (increases).
5. Boeing's expected return of $3,756 million was less than its actual return of $9,275 million in 2020.
6. Boeing reports net pension income of $337 million due to the expected return on plan assets that more than offset the costs of the plan for the year.
7. Boeing's funded status is negative, indicating an underfunded plan. The company contributed $3,013 million to the pension plan in 2020. The funding status has improved somewhat; for example, in 2019 the plan was underfunded by $(15,934). It is likely that the company will need to increase its future funding levels to cover the plan's requirements. This action is likely to have negative consequences for its ability to fund other operating needs and could damage its competitive position in the future. The company disclosed that most employees have transitioned to defined contribution plans. This is evidenced by the relatively small ($3 million) increase in service cost for the 2020 period. Thus, the company is not materially increasing liabilities based on new commitments but is mainly managing existing obligations from past contracts.

Review 10-3

a.
1. $2,390.
2. $1,488 = $1,342 + $146 is an estimate of the amount currently payable or that has already been paid during the year.
3. The most obvious example would be depreciation allowed by the tax code that exceeded the amount calculated by the straight-line method used for financial accounting.

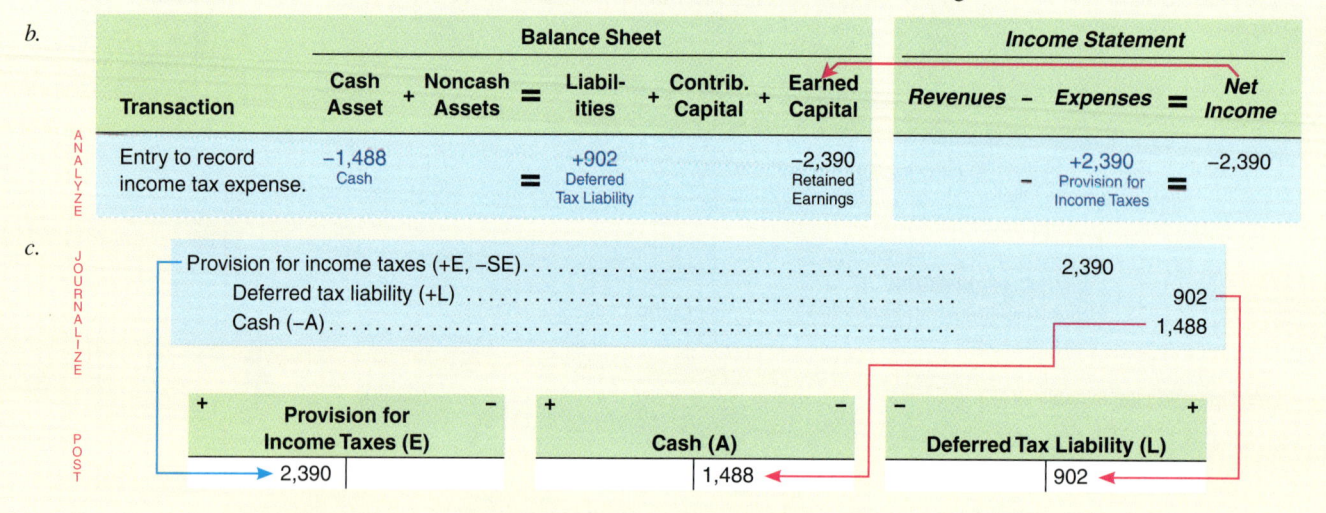

b.

Transaction	Cash Asset	+	Noncash Assets	=	Liabilities	+	Contrib. Capital	+	Earned Capital		Revenues	−	Expenses	=	Net Income
Entry to record income tax expense.	−1,488 Cash			=	+902 Deferred Tax Liability				−2,390 Retained Earnings				+2,390 Provision for Income Taxes	=	−2,390

c.
Provision for income taxes (+E, −SE)............ 2,390
    Deferred tax liability (+L) 902
    Cash (−A)............ 1,488

+ Provision for Income Taxes (E)	− Cash (A)	− Deferred Tax Liability (L) +
2,390	1,488	902

Review 10-4

a. None of the amounts listed would be shown on the financial statements. These amounts are disclosed as contingencies but don't qualify for recognition as liabilities on the company's balance sheet.
b. $74.5 million [PV(0.04,2,-39.5) = $74.5 million]

Chapter 11
Reporting and Analyzing Stockholders' Equity

LEARNING OBJECTIVES

LO11-1 Describe and account for business financing through stock issuances and repurchases.

LO11-2 Describe the effect on equity of earnings, dividends, and stock splits.

LO11-3 Define and illustrate comprehensive income.

LO11-4 Describe and illustrate the basic and diluted earnings per share computations.

LO11-5 Appendix 11A: Analyze the accounting for convertible securities, stock rights, stock options, and restricted stock.

Road Map

LO	Learning Objective | Topics	Page	eLecture	Review	Assignments
LO11-1	Describe and account for business financing through stock issuances and repurchases.	11-3	e11-1	R11-1	M11-19, M11-20, M11-21, M11-22, M11-24, M11-27, M11-42, M11-43, E11-45, E11-46, E11-47, E11-48, E11-49, E11-53, E11-63, E11-65, P11-66, P11-67, P11-68, P11-69, P11-70, P11-71, P11-72, P11-73, P11-74, P11-75, C11-79, C11-80, C11-81, C11-82
LO11-2	Describe the effect on equity of earnings, dividends, and stock splits.	11-11	e11-2	R11-2	M11-23, M11-28, M11-29, M11-30, M11-31, M11-32, M11-33, M11-34, M11-35, M11-36, M11-42, M11-43, E11-50, E11-52, E11-54, E11-55, E11-56, E11-57, E11-58, E11-59, E11-60, E11-61, E11-62, E11-65, P11-66, P11-67, P11-68, P11-69, P11-70, P11-71, P11-72, P11-73, C11-80, C11-81, **DA11-3**
LO11-3	Define and illustrate comprehensive income.	11-16	e11-3	R11-3	M11-22, M11-27, M11-43, E11-49, E11-53, E11-62, E11-63, E11-65, P11-68, P11-74, P11-76
LO11-4	Describe and illustrate the basic and diluted earnings per share computations.	11-19	e11-4	R11-4	M11-25, M11-26, M11-27, M11-37, M11-38, M11-39, M11-42, M11-43, M11-44, E11-49, E11-51, E11-52, E11-61, P11-66, P11-68, P11-70, P11-74, P11-76, C11-81, **DA11-1**
LO11-5	Appendix 11A: Analyze the accounting for convertible securities, stock rights, stock options, and restricted stock.	11-22	e11-5	R11-5	M11-40, M11-41, E11-64, P11-74, P11-76, P11-77, C11-78, C11-82, **DA11-2**

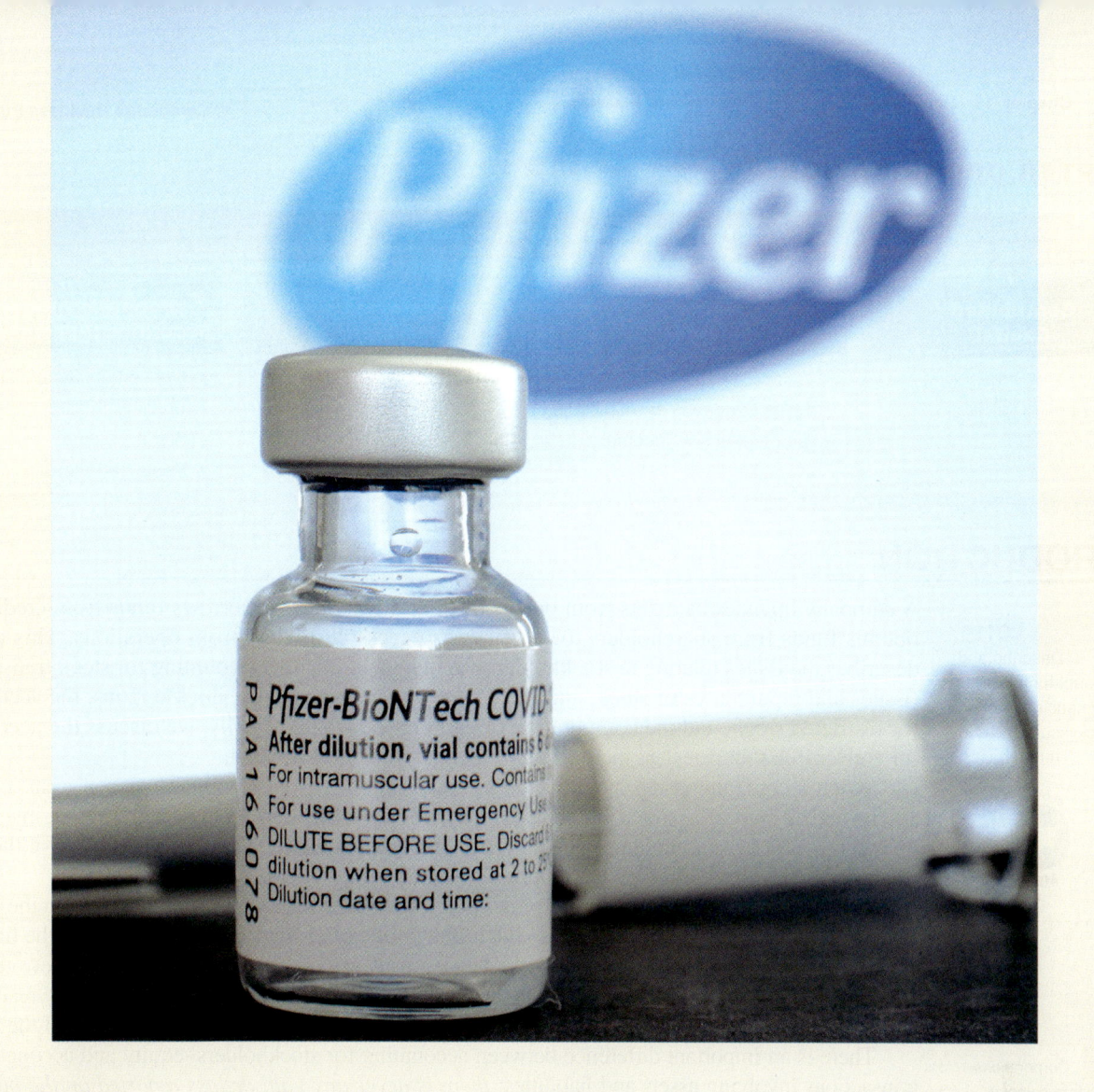

PFIZER
www.pfizer.com

Pfizer Inc. is a research-based, global pharmaceutical company that discovers, develops, manufactures, and markets prescription medicines. Pfizer's 2020 revenues were almost $42 billion. Pfizer was a very well-known company before 2020. With the global pandemic and Pfizer's joint work with BioNTech on one of the widely used COVID-19 vaccines, the company is prominently in the news every day. During 2020, Pfizer spun-off (divested) part of its business. Prior to this, the company had three operating segments. Now the company operates as a single operating segment.

Revenues at pharmaceutical firms are substantially dependent on patent protection following the research and development to discover and produce the drug. As patent protections expire, revenues fall. To counter expiring patents, Pfizer must either acquire companies with innovative drug pipelines (in-process research and development), enter into collaborations to develop drugs with other companies or develop new drugs in-house. To discover new drugs, Pfizer spends sizeable amounts each year on research and development: $8.4 billion in 2019 and $9.4 billion in 2020.

Pfizer must balance the capital needs of its acquisition strategy and its heavy commitment to research and development with the expectations of shareholders. From 2018 to 2020, the company reported $42.9 billion of net cash flow from operating activities, but it also paid $45.5 billion in cash to shareholders in the form of dividends and share repurchases. Other transactions involving shareholders' equity included share-based compensation for employees and conversions of one form of shareholders' equity to another.

This chapter describes the reporting and analysis of equity transactions, including sales and repurchases of stock, dividends, comprehensive income, and convertible securities.

Sources: Pfizer 2020 10-K Report.

CHAPTER ORGANIZATION

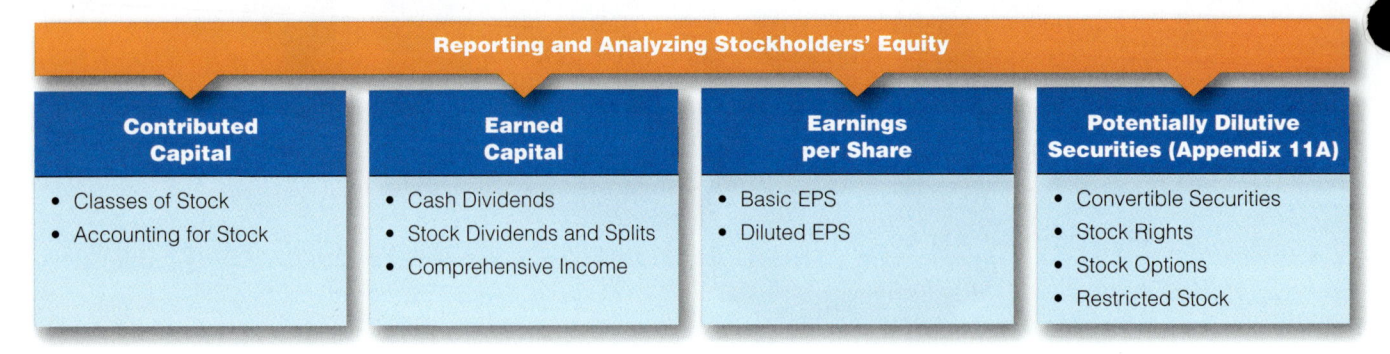

Reporting and Analyzing Stockholders' Equity

Contributed Capital	Earned Capital	Earnings per Share	Potentially Dilutive Securities (Appendix 11A)
• Classes of Stock • Accounting for Stock	• Cash Dividends • Stock Dividends and Splits • Comprehensive Income	• Basic EPS • Diluted EPS	• Convertible Securities • Stock Rights • Stock Options • Restricted Stock

INTRODUCTION

LO11-1 Describe and account for business financing through stock issuances and repurchases.

A company finances its assets from one of three sources: either it borrows funds from creditors, it obtains funds from shareholders, or it reinvests excess cash flow from operations. This chapter describes the issues relating to stockholders' equity, including the accounting for stock transactions (issues and repurchases of stock, and dividends), the accounting for stock options, the accounting for restricted stock, and the computation of earnings per share. Finally, we discuss the accounting for convertible securities, an increasingly prevalent financing vehicle.

When a company issues stock to the investing public, it records the receipt of cash (or other assets) and an increase in contributed capital, a part of stockholders' equity, representing investment in the company by shareholders. The increases in cash and equity equal the issue price of the stock on the issue date multiplied by the number of shares sold.

Contributed capital is accounted for at *historical cost*. Consequently, fluctuations in the market price of the issuer's stock subsequent to the initial public offering do not directly affect the financial statements of the issuing company. These fluctuations are the result of transactions between outside parties not involving the issuer. When and if stock is repurchased and subsequently resold, the issuer's contributed capital decreases (increases) by the current purchase (sales) price of the shares.

FYI Corporations never record gains or losses on the purchase or sale of the company's own stock or the payment of dividends.

There is an important difference between accounting for stockholders' equity and accounting for transactions involving assets and liabilities: *there is never any gain or loss reported on the purchase and sale of the company's own stock or the payment of dividends.* Instead, these "gains and losses" are reflected as increases and decreases in the contributed capital component of the issuing company's stockholders' equity.

This chapter focuses on the two broad categories of shareholder investment: contributed capital and earned capital. **Exhibit 11.1** provides an illustration of this breakdown using Pfizer's stockholders' equity as of December 31, 2020.

EXHIBIT 11.1 Stockholders' Equity from Pfizer's Balance Sheet

Shareholders' Equity (millions except preferred stock issued and per common share data)	Dec. 31, 2020
Contributed capital	
Preferred stock, no par value, at stated value; 27 shares authorized; issued: 2020—0; 2019—431	$ —
Common stock, $0.05 par value; 12,000 shares authorized; issued: 2020—9,407; 2019—9,369	470
Additional paid-in capital	88,674
Treasury stock, shares at cost: 2020—3,840; 2019—3,835	(110,988)
Earned capital	
Retained earnings	96,770
Accumulated other comprehensive loss	(11,688)
Total Pfizer Inc. shareholders' equity	63,238
Equity attributable to noncontrolling interests	235
Total equity	$63,473

Pfizer, like other companies, has two broad categories of stockholders' equity:

1. **Contributed capital** This section reports the proceeds received by the issuing company from original stock issuances. Contributed capital often includes common stock, preferred

stock, and additional paid-in capital. Netted against these capital accounts is treasury stock, the amounts paid to repurchase shares of the issuer's stock from its investors less the proceeds from the resale of such shares. Collectively, these accounts are generically referred to as contributed capital (or *paid-in capital*).

2. **Earned capital** This section consists of (a) retained earnings (or accumulated deficit, if negative), which represent the cumulative income and losses of the company less any dividends to shareholders, and (b) accumulated other comprehensive income (AOCI), which includes changes to equity that are not included in income and are, therefore, not reflected in retained earnings. For Pfizer, AOCI includes foreign currency translation adjustments, changes in market values of derivatives, unrecognized gains and losses on available-for-sale securities, and pension adjustments.

Before turning to a discussion of contributed capital and earned capital, we note one other item in **Exhibit 11.1**—Equity attributable to **noncontrolling interests**. This amount results from the practice of consolidating subsidiaries that are controlled, but not wholly owned, and it represents neither capital contributed to Pfizer nor capital earned by Pfizer's shareholders. Chapter 12 provides a brief introduction to this topic.

CONTRIBUTED CAPITAL

We begin our discussion with contributed capital. Contributed capital represents the cumulative cash inflow that the company has received from the sale of various classes of stock, less the net cash that it has paid out to repurchase its stock from the market.

Pfizer's contributed capital consists of preferred and common stock, additional paid-in capital, less costs of treasury stock (repurchased shares).

Classes of Stock

There are two general classes of stock: preferred and common. The difference between the two lies in the respective legal rights conferred upon each class.

Common Stock Shares of **common stock** represent the primary ownership unit in a corporation. Common stockholders have voting rights that allow them to participate in the governance of the corporation. The total number of common shares is usually presented on the face of the balance sheet. There are three numbers of shares to be aware of:

- The number of **shares authorized** represents the upper limit on the number of shares that the corporation can issue. This number is established in the *articles of incorporation* and can only be increased by an affirmative shareholder vote.
- The number of **shares issued** is the actual number of shares that have been sold to stockholders by the corporation.
- The number of **shares outstanding** is the number of issued shares less the number of shares repurchased as treasury stock.

Pfizer's common stock is described as follows in its 2020 balance sheet (shares in millions):

> Common stock, $0.05 par value; 12,000 shares authorized; issued: 2020—9,407

The Pfizer common stock has the following important characteristics:

- Pfizer common stock has a par value of $0.05 per share. The **par value** is an arbitrary amount set by company organizers at the time of formation. Generally, par value has no substance from a financial reporting or statement analysis perspective. (There are some legal implications, which are usually minor.) Its main impact is in specifying the allocation of proceeds from stock issuances between the two contributed capital accounts on the balance sheet: common stock and additional paid-in capital.
- Pfizer has authorized the issuance of 12,000 million shares. As of December 31, 2020, 9,407 million shares are issued yielding a total par value of $470 million = $0.05 × 9,407 million shares.

When shares are first issued, the number of shares outstanding equals those issued. Any shares subsequently repurchased are subtracted from issued shares to derive outstanding shares.

Some corporations issue multiple classes of stock, with differential voting rights. For instance, **Alphabet Inc.** has Class A common stock with one vote per share, Class B common stock with ten votes per share, and Class C capital stock with no voting rights at all. All shares participate equally in dividends, but this structure has allowed the original management team to raise capital while retaining significant voting rights.

Preferred Stock **Preferred stock** generally has some preference, or priority, with respect to common stock but does not have voting rights. Two typical preferences are:

1. **Dividend preference** Preferred shareholders receive dividends on their shares before common shareholders do. If dividends are not paid in a given year, those dividends are normally forgone. However, some preferred stock contracts include a *cumulative provision* stipulating that any forgone dividends must first be paid to preferred shareholders, together with the current year's dividends, before any dividends are paid to common shareholders.

2. **Liquidation preference** If a company fails, its assets are sold (liquidated), and the proceeds are paid to the creditors and shareholders, in that order. Shareholders, therefore, have a greater risk of loss than do creditors. Among shareholders, the preferred shareholders receive payment in full before any proceeds are paid to common shareholders. This liquidation preference makes preferred shares less risky than common shares. Any liquidation payment to preferred shares is normally at its par value, although it is sometimes specified in excess of par, called a **liquidating value**.

The preferred stock of Pfizer is described in Note 12 to its 2019 10-K:

> The Series A convertible perpetual preferred stock . . . is held by an employee stock ownership plan (Preferred ESOP) Trust and provides dividends at the rate of 6.25%, which are accumulated and paid quarterly. The per-share stated value is $40,300, and the preferred stock ranks senior to our common stock as to dividends and liquidation rights. Each share is convertible, at the holder's option, into 2,574.87 shares of our common stock with equal voting rights. The conversion option is indexed to our common stock and requires share settlement, and, therefore, is reported at the fair value at the date of issuance. We may redeem the preferred stock at any time or upon termination of the Preferred ESOP, at our option, in cash, in shares of common stock, or a combination of both at a price of $40,300 per share.

The preferred stock of Pfizer is described in Note 12 to its 2020 10-K:

> Prior to May 4, 2020, our Series A convertible perpetual preferred stock (the Series A Preferred Stock) was held by an ESOP trust (the Trust). All outstanding shares of Series A Preferred Stock were converted, at the direction of the independent fiduciary under the Trust and in accordance with the certificate of designations for the Series A Preferred Stock, into shares of our common stock on May 4, 2020. The Trust received an aggregate of 1,070,369 shares of our common stock upon conversion, with zero shares of Series A Preferred Stock remaining outstanding as a result of the conversion. In December 2020, we filed a certificate of elimination and a restated certificate of incorporation with the Delaware Secretary of State, which eliminated the Series A Preferred Stock.

Following are several important features of the Pfizer preferred stock:

- As of the end of 2019, the company, had 27 million preferred shares authorized and 431 shares issued. Zero shares are issued as of December 31, 2020, because all preferred shares were converted into common shares. The articles of incorporation set the number of shares authorized for issuance, when that limit is reached, shareholders must approve any increase in authorized shares.

- Pfizer preferred stock has a preference with respect to dividends and liquidation, meaning that preferred shareholders are paid before common shareholders.

- Pfizer preferred stock is convertible into common stock at the option of the holder and at a predetermined exchange rate. A preferred share is convertible, at the holder's option, into common shares. Indeed, on May 4, 2020, all preferred shares outstanding were converted into 1,070,369 common shares.

- In December 2020, the Series A Preferred Stock was eliminated, leaving a zero balance in preferred stock on December 31, 2020.

Pfizer's cumulative preferred shares carried a dividend yield of 6.25%. This dividend yield compared favorably with the $1.52 per share (3.9% yield) paid to its common shareholders (as of December 31, 2019). Generally, preferred stock can be an attractive investment for shareholders seeking higher dividend yields, especially when tax laws wholly or partially exempt such dividends from taxation.

There are additional features sometimes seen in preferred stock agreements:[1]

1. **Call feature** The call feature provides the issuer with the right, but not the obligation, to repurchase the preferred shares at a specified price (also called redeemable preferred stock). This price can vary according to a specified time. A decline in the market rate of interest is one event that can lead to the firm exercising the call provision. While of value to the issuer of the preferred stock, the call provision makes the issue less attractive to potential investors. The result is a lower offering price per share.

2. **Conversion feature** The yield on preferred stock, especially when coupled with a cumulative feature, is similar to the interest rate on a bond or note. Further limited protection is offered because preferred shareholders receive the par value at liquidation like debtholders receive face value. The fixed yield and liquidation value for the preferred stock limit the upside potential return of preferred shareholders. This constraint can be overcome by inclusion of a *conversion feature* that allows preferred stockholders to convert their shares into common shares at their option at a predetermined conversion ratio. Some preferred contracts give the company an option to force conversion.

    The conversion feature causes the shares to be more attractive to potential investors because the preferred stockholders now have the opportunity to share in the fruits of a successful company with the common stockholders. Indeed, the market price of preferred stock tends to reflect the added value of the conversion feature.

3. **Participation feature** Preferred shares sometimes carry a *participation feature* that allows preferred shareholders to share ratably with common stockholders in dividends. The dividend preference over common shares can be a benefit when dividend payments are meager, but a fixed dividend yield limits upside potential if the company performs exceptionally well. This limitation can be overcome with a participation feature.

A GLOBAL PERSPECTIVE

Under IFRS, convertible debt securities are termed compound financial instruments because the conversion feature has a value even if it is not legally detachable for sale. IFRS splits the convertible bonds' value into the separate debt and conversion option values for reporting purposes. GAAP splits the value when the conversion option is determined to be a derivative liability. If the conversion option is determined to be equity, U.S. GAAP does not require bifurcation of the security into separate components. New GAAP rules effective in 2021 make differences between GAAP and IFRS more common (bifurcation less often under GAAP). Another difference is that GAAP has a mezzanine section of the balance sheet between equity and liabilities where securities with both equity and debt features are recorded. IFRS does not allow a mezzanine section of the balance sheet.

---

[1] Preferred shares, in general, are somewhat debt-like. For example, preferred shares have a higher and more certain rate of dividends, approaching something more like interest. In addition, they have preference over common stockholders in the event of bankruptcy. More features can be added to the preferred shares that make them even more debt-like. In some cases, the classification for accounting changes accordingly. For example, if entities have mandatorily redeemable preferred stock that do not contain a conversion option, these securities are to be included as liabilities on the balance sheet, not in equity and not in the mezzanine section of the balance sheet (i.e., the section between the liabilities section and the equity section in the balance sheet). Entities are required to present contingently redeemable preferred stock—meaning redeemable upon the occurrence of an event outside the control of the issuer—and preferred stock that is redeemable at the option of the holder in the mezzanine section of the balance sheet (i.e., the section between the liabilities section and the equity section). The purpose of this classification is to convey to the reader that such a security may not permanently be part of equity and could result in a demand for cash or other assets of the entity in the future. These are the accounting rules, but as discussed elsewhere in the text, analysts and other financial statement users may treat these securities differently than FASB (and may treat some of the securities as debt and some as equity) when conducting ratio-analysis or other evaluations of company performance. For example, in much of the analyses sections of this text, we include these items as either debt or equity: noncontrolling equity interests are included in shareholders' equity, and mezzanine items—redeemable noncontrolling interests in subsidiaries and redeemable preferred stock—are included in equity. But other financial statement users may include them in debt under certain circumstances for analysis purposes.

Accounting for Stock Transactions

We cover the accounting for stock transactions in this section, including the accounting for stock issuances and for stock repurchases.

Stock Issuance Stock issuances, whether common or preferred, yield an increase in both assets and stockholders' equity. Companies use stock issuances to obtain cash and other assets for use in their business.

Stock issuances increase assets (cash) by the number of shares sold multiplied by the issuance price of the stock on the issue date. Equity increases by the same amount, which is reflected in contributed capital accounts. Specifically, assuming the issuance of common stock, the common stock account increases by the number of shares sold multiplied by its par value, and the additional paid-in capital account is increased for the remainder of the purchase price.[2]

> ### BUSINESS INSIGHT
>
> **Airbnb's IPO** In December of 2020, Airbnb offered its shares to the general public for the first time. The first public sale of common stock by a corporation is called an initial public offering, or IPO for short. After the IPO, any offering of stock to the public is called a seasoned equity offering.
>
> The Airbnb IPO was long-awaited by employees who had received equity-based pay and potential new investors alike. The company's stock has a par value of $0.0001. The IPO raised about $3.5 billion with an IPO price of $68 per share. The company stock opened on the Nasdaq at $146 per share. It rose to a high of nearly $220 and as of August, 2021 trades at around $155 per share.

To illustrate, assume that Davis Company issues 10,000 shares of $1 par value common stock at a market price of $43 cash per share. The financial statement effects and entries for this stock issuance follow.

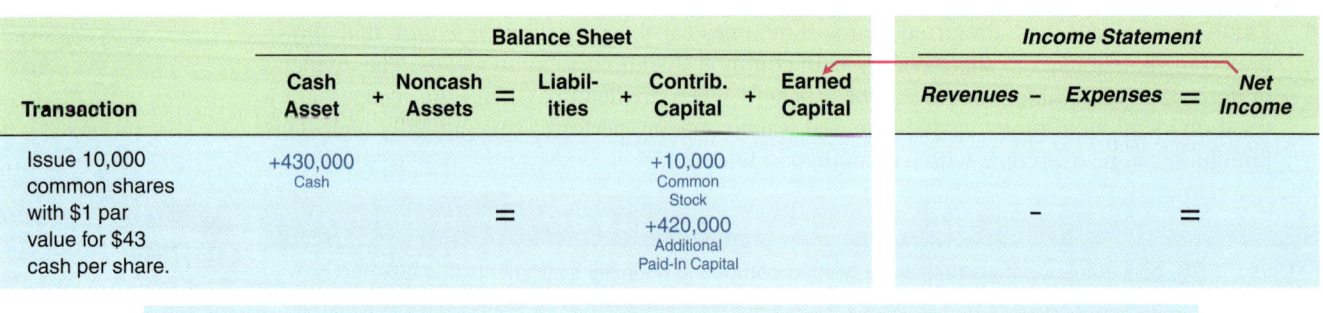

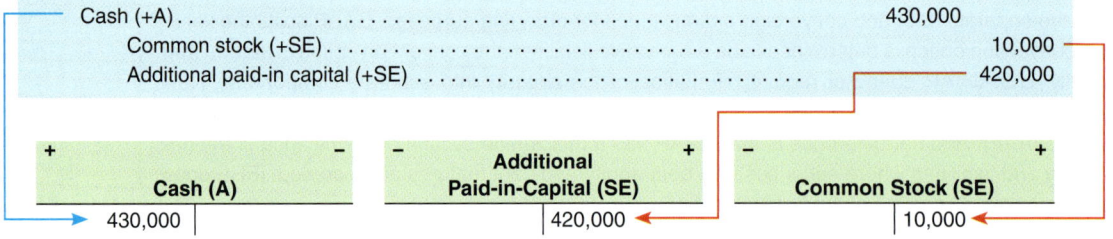

ANALYZE

Transaction	Balance Sheet					Income Statement		
	Cash Asset + Noncash Assets	=	Liabilities	+	Contrib. Capital + Earned Capital	Revenues −	Expenses =	Net Income
Issue 10,000 common shares with $1 par value for $43 cash per share.	+430,000 Cash	=			+10,000 Common Stock +420,000 Additional Paid-In Capital	−		=

JOURNALIZE

Cash (+A) 430,000
    Common stock (+SE) 10,000
    Additional paid-in capital (+SE) 420,000

POST

+ Cash (A) −		− Additional Paid-in-Capital (SE) +		− Common Stock (SE) +
430,000			420,000	10,000

> **FYI** Stock issuance affects the balance sheet, the statement of cash flows, and the statement of stockholders' equity. There is no revenue or gain from stock issuance reported in the income statement.

Specifically, the following financial statement effects of the stock issuance are:

1. Cash increases by $430,000 (10,000 shares × $43 per share) and is reported as a cash inflow from financing activities on the statement of cash flows.
2. Common stock increases by the $10,000 par value of shares sold (10,000 shares × $1 par value).[3]

---

[2] Companies that offer their shares for sale to the general public are called *public corporations*. In a *private company*, ownership is limited to a smaller number of investors, and the stock is not available to the general public. The distinction between public and private corporations should not be confused with media references to the public sector and the private sector. The *public sector* refers to government entities. Virtually all business entities, including public corporations, are considered part of the *private sector*.

[3] Common stock can also be issued as "no par" or as "no par with a stated value." For no par stock, the common stock account is increased by the entire proceeds of the sale, and no amount is assigned to additional paid-in capital. For no par stock with a stated value, the stated value is treated just like par value; that is, common stock is increased by the number of shares multiplied by the stated value, and the remainder is assigned to the additional paid-in capital account.

3. Additional paid-in capital increases by the $420,000 difference between the issue price and par value ($430,000 − $10,000).

Once shares are issued, they are freely traded in the market among investors. The proceeds of those sales and any gains and losses on those sales do not affect the issuing company and are not recorded in its accounting records. Further, fluctuations in the issuing company's stock price subsequent to issuance do not directly affect its financial statements. Hence, the equity section of the balance sheet cannot be used to determine the current market value of the company. The market value (or market capitalization) is given by the product of the number of common shares outstanding times the current per-share market price of the stock.

Pfizer's outstanding common shares, repeated from **Exhibit 11.1**, are (in millions):

Common stock, $0.05 par value; 12,000 shares authorized; issued: 2020—9,407	$ 470
Additional paid-in capital.	88,674

Pfizer's common stock, in the amount of $470 million, equals the number of shares issued multiplied by the common stock's par value: 9,407 million × $0.05 = $470 million.[4] The balance of the proceeds from stock issuances is included in the additional paid-in capital account. Total proceeds from stock issuances are $89,144 ($470 + $88,674) million, or $9.48 per share ($89,144/9,407 million shares).

RESEARCH INSIGHT

Stock Issuance and Stock Returns Seasoned equity offerings are issuances of common stock by firms that already have outstanding shares. On average, stock price declines when a company announces that it will issue additional shares of common stock. Investors infer that issuing common stock rather than debt is an indication that management believes the stock is overvalued in the market, making it a more attractive form of financing. In addition, research has found that companies engage in earnings management around seasoned equity offerings, using both accrual estimates (e.g., underestimating bad debt expense or warranty expense) and real transactions (e.g., cutting R&D or accelerating sales). As a result, both earnings and stock returns decline in subsequent periods.

Stock Repurchase Pfizer provides the following description of its stock repurchase program in notes to its 10-K report.

> We purchase our common stock through privately negotiated transactions or in the open market as circumstances and prices warrant. Purchased shares under each of the share-purchase plans, which are authorized by our BOD, are available for general corporate purposes. In December 2015, the BOD authorized an $11 billion share repurchase program, which was exhausted in the third quarter of 2018. In December 2017, the BOD authorized an additional $10 billion share repurchase program, which was exhausted in the first quarter of 2019. In December 2018, the BOD authorized another $10 billion share repurchase program to be utilized over time and share repurchases commenced thereunder in the first quarter of 2019.
>
> In March 2018, we entered into an accelerated share repurchase agreement (ASR) with Citibank, N.A. to repurchase $4 billion of our common stock pursuant to our previously announced share repurchase authorization. We paid $4 billion and received an initial delivery of 87 million shares of stock at a price of $36.61 per share, which represented approximately 80% of the notional amount of the ASR. In September 2018, the ASR was completed, resulting in Citibank owing us an additional 21 million shares of our common stock. The average price paid for all of the shares delivered under the ASR was $36.86 per share. The common stock received is included in Treasury stock.
>
> In February 2019, we entered into an ASR with Goldman Sachs & Co. LLC to repurchase $6.8 billion of our common stock pursuant to our previously announced share repurchase authorization. We paid $6.8 billion and received an initial delivery of 130 million shares of common stock, which

continued

---
[4] The number of shares issued and the par value of those shares are both rounded to the nearest million.

continued from previous page

represented approximately 80% of the notional amount of the ASR. In August 2019, the ASR with Goldman Sachs & Co. LLC was completed, resulting in Goldman Sachs & Co. LLC owing us an additional 33.5 million shares of our common stock. The average price paid for all of the shares delivered under the ASR was $41.42 per share. The common stock received is included in Treasury stock.

The following table provides the number of shares of our common stock purchased and the cost of purchases under our publicly announced share repurchase plans, including our ASRs [accelerated share repurchase agreements]:

(SHARES IN MILLIONS, DOLLARS IN BILLIONS)	2020	2019[b]	2018[c]
Shares of common stock purchased	—	213	307
Cost of purchase	—	$8.9	$12.2

(a) Represents shares purchased pursuant to the ASR with Goldman Sachs & Co. LLC entered into in February 2019, as well as open market share repurchases of $2.1 billion.

(b) Represents shares purchased pursuant to the ASR with Citibank entered into in March 2018, as well as open market share repurchases of $8.2 billion.

Our remaining share-purchase authorization was approximately $5.3 billion at December 31, 2020.

Pfizer has initiated multiple stock buyback programs over time. One reason a company will repurchase shares is if it feels that the market undervalues them. Management reasons that the repurchase sends a positive signal to the market about the company's financial condition that favorably affects its share price. Recent research provides evidence that share prices generally increase following the announcement of a share repurchase program. Any gain on resale is *never* reflected in the income statement. Instead, the excess of the resale price over the repurchase price is added to additional paid-in capital. GAAP prohibits companies from reporting gains via stock transactions with their own shareholders.

Another reason shares are repurchased is to offset the dilutive effects of an employee stock option program. When employees are compensated with equity-based pay, the number of shares outstanding will increase over time as the shares are given to employees. These additional shares reduce earnings per share and are, therefore, viewed as *dilutive*. In response, many companies repurchase a roughly equivalent number of shares in a desire to keep outstanding shares somewhat constant. Corporations also buy back their own shares in order to concentrate ownership to avoid an unwelcome takeover action. Repurchased shares do not participate in dividends or in shareholder votes.

A stock repurchase has the opposite financial statement effects from a stock issuance. That is, cash is reduced by the price of the shares repurchased (number of shares repurchased multiplied by the purchase price per share), and stockholders' equity is reduced by the same amount. The reduction in equity is achieved by increasing a contra equity account called **treasury stock**. *A contra equity account is a negative equity account with a debit balance,* which reduces stockholders' equity. Thus, when a contra equity account increases, total equity decreases.

Any subsequent reissuance of treasury stock does not yield a gain or loss. Instead, the difference between the proceeds received and the repurchase price of the treasury stock is reflected as an increase or decrease to additional paid-in capital.[5]

To illustrate, assume that 3,000 common shares of Davis Company stock previously issued for $43 are later repurchased for $40. The financial statement effects and entries for this stock repurchase follow.

---

[5] Repurchased shares do not have to be held in treasury but could be retired by the company.

Balance Sheet / Income Statement effects

Transaction	Cash Asset	+	Noncash Assets	=	Liabilities	+	Contrib. Capital	+	Earned Capital	−	Contra Equity		Revenues	−	Expenses	=	Net Income
Repurchase 3,000 common shares for $40 cash per share.	−120,000 Cash			=							+120,000 Treasury Stock		−			=	

Journal entry:

Treasury stock (+XSE, −SE) 120,000
   Cash (−A) 120,000

Treasury Stock (XSE) (+ / −): 120,000
Cash (A) (+ / −): 120,000

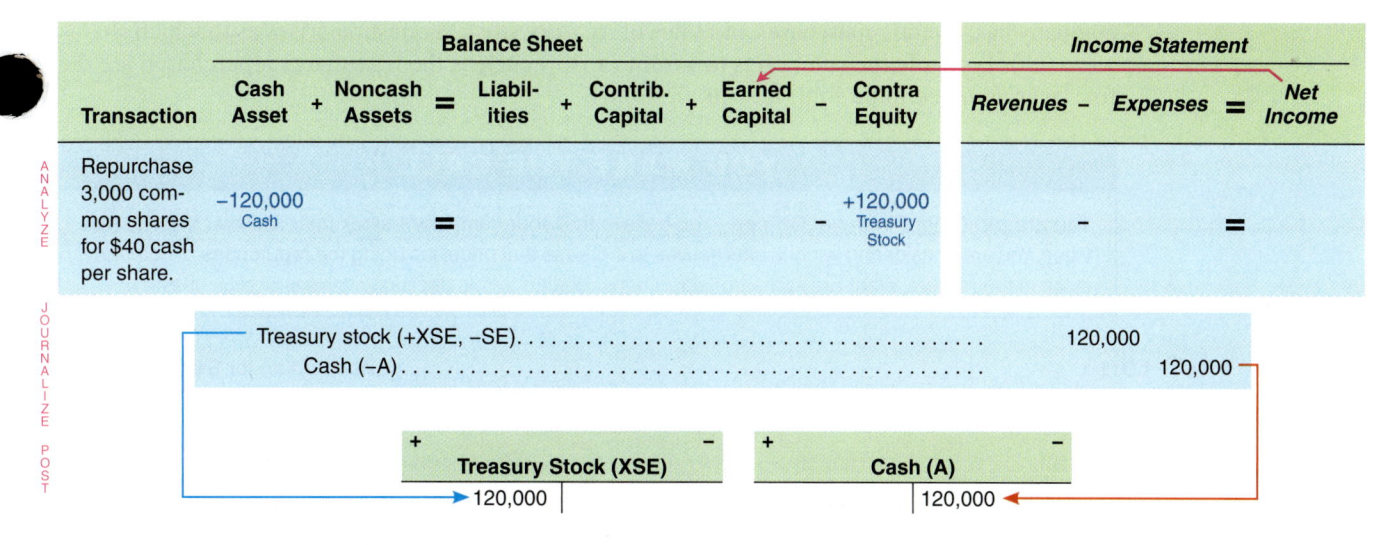

Assets (cash) and equity both decrease. Treasury stock (a contra equity account) increases by $120,000, which reduces stockholders' equity by that same amount.

Assume that these 3,000 shares are then subsequently resold for $42 cash per share. The financial statement effects and entries for this treasury stock sale follow.

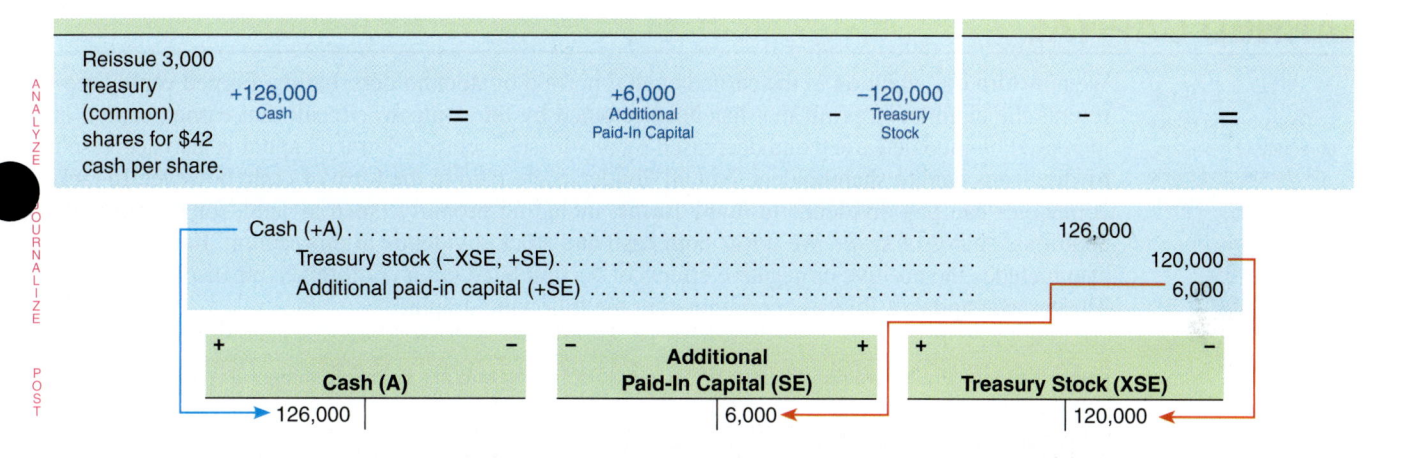

Transaction	Cash Asset	+	Noncash Assets	=	Liabilities	+	Contrib. Capital	+	Earned Capital	−	Contra Equity		Revenues	−	Expenses	=	Net Income
Reissue 3,000 treasury (common) shares for $42 cash per share.	+126,000 Cash			=			+6,000 Additional Paid-In Capital				−120,000 Treasury Stock		−			=	

Journal entry:

Cash (+A) 126,000
   Treasury stock (−XSE, +SE) 120,000
   Additional paid-in capital (+SE) 6,000

Cash (A): 126,000
Additional Paid-In Capital (SE): 6,000
Treasury Stock (XSE): 120,000

Cash assets increase by $126,000 (3,000 shares × $42 per share), the treasury stock account is reduced by the $120,000 cost of the treasury shares issued, and the $6,000 excess (3,000 shares × $2 per share) is reported as an increase in additional paid-in capital.[6] Again, there is no effect on the income statement—companies are prohibited from reporting gains and losses from repurchases and reissuances of their own stock.

The treasury stock section of Pfizer's 2020 balance sheet is reproduced below.

At December 31 (millions)	2020
Treasury stock, shares at cost: 2020—3,840	$(110,988)

Pfizer has repurchased a cumulative total of 3,840 million shares of its common stock for $110,988 million, an average repurchase price of $28.90 per share. This compares with total contributed capital of $89,144 million ($0 million + $470 million + $88,674 million). When a

---

[6] If the reissue price is below the repurchase price, then additional paid-in capital is reduced until it reaches a zero balance, after which retained earnings is reduced.

company has several repurchases and sales of treasury stock, a question arises as to which shares were sold. Typically the solution is to assume a flow such as the first shares repurchased are the first ones assumed to be sold (first-in, first-out).

> ### YOU MAKE THE CALL
>
> **You are the Chief Financial Officer** You believe that your company's stock price is lower than its real value. You are considering various alternatives to increase that price, including the repurchase of company stock in the market. What are some considerations relating to this decision? [Answer on page 11-29]

Review 11-1 LO11-1 — Accounting for Stock Issuances

Plesko Corporation reported the following transactions relating to its stock accounts during the year.

Jan. 15 Issued 10,000 shares of $5 par value common stock at $17 cash per share.
Mar. 31 Purchased 2,000 shares of its own common stock at $15 cash per share.
June 25 Reissued 1,000 shares of its treasury stock at $20 cash per share.

a. Show the financial impact of each transaction using the financial statement effects template.
b. Provide the appropriate journal entry for each transaction, and post the journal entries to the related T-accounts.

Solution on p. 11-51.

EARNED CAPITAL

LO11-2 Describe the effect on equity of earnings, dividends, and stock splits.

We now turn our attention to the earned capital portion of stockholders' equity. Earned capital represents the cumulative profit that has been retained by the company. Recall that earned capital is increased by income earned and decreased by any losses incurred. Earned capital is also decreased by dividends paid to shareholders. Not all dividends are paid in the form of cash, however. In fact, companies can pay dividends in many forms, including property (such as land, for example) or additional shares of stock. We cover both cash and stock dividends in this section. Earned capital also includes the positive or negative effects of accumulated other comprehensive income (AOCI). The earned capital of Pfizer is highlighted in the following graphic:

Shareholders' Equity (millions except preferred stock issued and per common share data)	Dec. 31, 2020
Preferred stock, no par value, at stated value; 27 shares authorized; issued: 2020—0; 2019—431	$ —
Common stock, $0.05 par value; 12,000 shares authorized; issued: 2020—9,407; 2019—9,369	470
Additional paid-in capital	88,674
Treasury stock, shares at cost: 2020—3,840; 2019—3,835	(110,988)
Retained earnings	97,770
Accumulated other comprehensive loss	(11,688)
Total Pfizer Inc. shareholders' equity	63,238
Equity attributable to noncontrolling interests	235
Total equity	$63,473

Cash Dividends

Many companies, but certainly not all, pay dividends. Their reasons for dividend payments are varied. Most dividends are paid in cash on a quarterly basis. The following is a description of Pfizer's dividend policy from its 2020 10-K.

> **Dividends on Common Stock**
> In December 2020, our BOD declared a first-quarter dividend of $0.39 per share, payable on March 5, 2021, to shareholders of record at the close of business on January 29, 2021. The first-quarter 2021 cash dividend will be our 329th consecutive quarterly dividend.

continued

continued from previous page

> Our current and projected dividends provide a return to shareholders while maintaining sufficient capital to invest in growing our business. Our dividends are not restricted by debt covenants. While the dividend level remains a decision of Pfizer's BOD and will continue to be evaluated in the context of future business performance, we currently believe that we can support future annual dividend increases, barring significant unforeseen events. Viatris is expected to begin paying a quarterly dividend in the second quarter of 2021, at which time Pfizer's quarterly dividend is expected to be reduced such that the combined dividend dollar amount received by Pfizer shareholders, based upon the combination of continued Pfizer ownership and approximately 0.124079 shares of Viatris common stock which were granted for each Pfizer share in the spin-off, will equate to Pfizer's dividend amount in effect immediately prior to the initiation of the Viatris dividend.

Outsiders closely monitor dividend payments. It is generally perceived that the level of dividend payments is related to the expected long-term core income. Accordingly, dividend increases are usually accompanied by stock price increases, and companies rarely reduce their dividends unless absolutely necessary. Dividend reductions are, therefore, met with substantial stock-price declines.

BUSINESS INSIGHT

General Electric (GE) was one of the biggest dividend payers in the U.S. However, in 2017, the company cut its dividend in half, from 24 cents/share to 12 cents per share, in an effort to save cash—about $4 billion per year. GE's dividend cut was one of the largest in the history of the S&P 500 and the biggest since the great recession era (2009). Even after this dividend cut, it was projected that about 85% of the company's free cash flow would go toward dividends, which illuminates the change in the company and its business over time. The stock price fell around 7% on the day the dividend cut was announced and almost 6% the next day (though other negative news was simultaneously announced, so not all of the price drop was likely due to the dividend news). In December of 2018, the company slashed the dividend further to only 1 cent per share.

Financial Effects of Cash Dividends Cash dividends reduce both cash and retained earnings by the amount of the cash dividends paid. To illustrate, Pfizer paid over $8.4 billion in 2020 cash dividends on its common and preferred shares (prior to converting the preferred shares). The financial statement effects of this cash dividend payment are reflected as a reduction in assets (cash) and a reduction in retained earnings as follows.

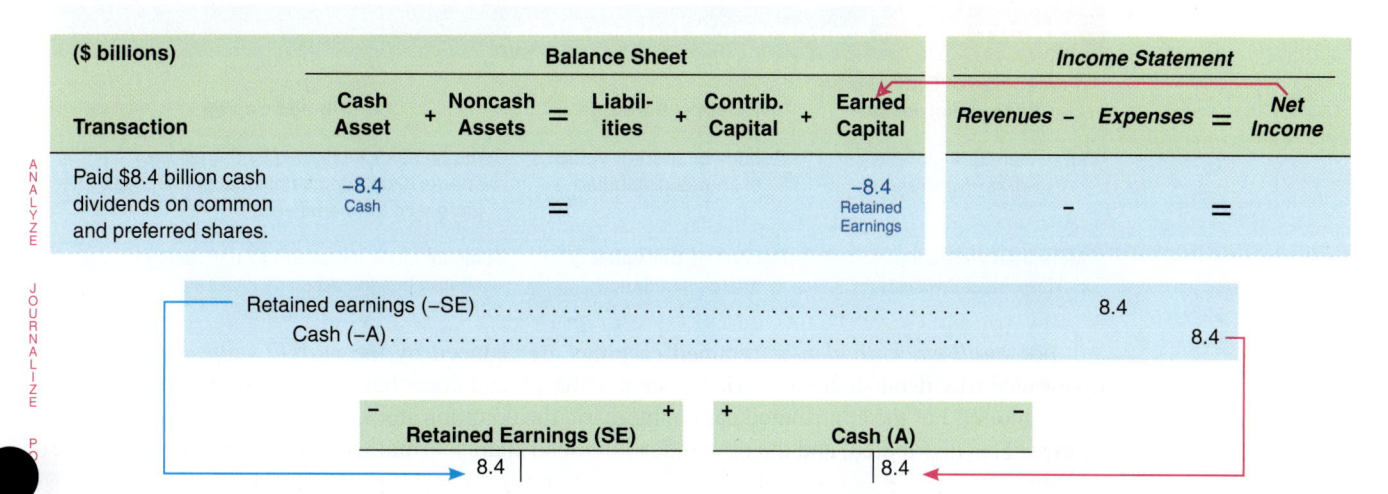

($ billions) Transaction	Cash Asset	+	Noncash Assets	=	Liabilities	+	Contrib. Capital	+	Earned Capital	Revenues	−	Expenses	=	Net Income
Paid $8.4 billion cash dividends on common and preferred shares.	−8.4 Cash			=					−8.4 Retained Earnings				=	

Retained earnings (−SE) 8.4
    Cash (−A) 8.4

Retained Earnings (SE)	Cash (A)
− +	+ −
8.4	8.4

Dividend payments have no effect on profitability. They are a direct reduction to retained earnings (and cash) and bypass the income statement.

Preferred stock dividends have priority over those for common shares, including unpaid prior years' preferred dividends (dividends in arrears) when preferred stock is cumulative. To illustrate, assume that Hanna Company has 15,000 shares of $50 par value, 8% preferred stock outstanding, and 50,000 shares of $5 par value common stock outstanding. During its first three years in business, assume that Hanna declares $20,000 dividends in the first year, $260,000 of dividends in the second year, and $60,000 of dividends in the third year. If the preferred stock is cumulative, the total amount of dividends paid to each class of stock in each of the three years would be:

	Preferred Stock	Common Stock
Year 1		
Current-year dividend ($15,000 × $50 × 8%; but only $20,000 is paid, leaving $40,000 in arrears)	$20,000	
Balance to common		$ 0
Year 2		
Arrearage from Year 1 [($15,000 × $50 × 8%) − $20,000]	40,000	
Current-year dividend ($15,000 × $50 × 8%)	60,000	
Balance to common [$260,000 − ($40,000 + $60,000)]		160,000
Year 3		
Current-year dividend ($15,000 × $50 × 8%)	60,000	
Balance to common		0

Stock Dividends and Splits

Dividends need not be paid in cash. Many companies pay **stock dividends**—that is dividends in the form of additional shares of stock. Companies can also distribute additional shares to their stockholders with a stock split. We cover both of these distributions in this section.

Stock Dividends When dividends are paid in the form of the company's stock, retained earnings are reduced and contributed capital is increased. However, the amount by which retained earnings are reduced depends on the proportion of the outstanding shares distributed to the total outstanding shares on the issue date. **Exhibit 11.2** illustrates two possibilities depending on whether a stock dividend is classified as either a small stock dividend or a large stock dividend. When the additional number of shares issued as a stock dividend is so great that it is likely to have a negative impact on the market price per share of the stock, the dividend must be treated as a large stock dividend. Dividends of less than 20%–25% of the outstanding shares are considered to be small stock dividends, while dividends of more than 20%–25% are classified as large stock dividends.[7]

EXHIBIT 11.2 Analysis of Stock Dividend Effects

Percentage of Outstanding Shares Distributed	Retained Earnings	Contributed Capital
Less than 20%–25% *(small stock dividend)*	Reduce by **market value** of shares distributed	Common stock increased by par value of shares distributed; additional paid-in capital increased for the balance
More than 20%–25% *(large stock dividend)*	Reduce by **par value** of shares distributed	Common stock increased by par value of shares distributed

For *small stock dividends,* retained earnings are reduced by the *market* value of the shares distributed (dividend shares × market price per share), and contributed capital is increased by the same amount. For the contributed capital increase, the common stock is increased by the par value of the shares distributed, and the remainder [dividend shares × (market value per share − par value

---

[7] Standard setters did not want a "bright-line" test and allow facts and circumstances to dictate the treatment between 20% and 25%. The determining factor is the effect on price. For example, if a 25% stock dividend does not affect the stock price, it would be treated as a small stock dividend. Likewise, if a 20% stock dividend does affect price, it would be treated as a large stock dividend for accounting purposes.

per share)] increases additional paid-in capital. For *large stock dividends,* retained earnings are reduced by the *par* value of the shares distributed (dividend shares × par value per share), and common stock is increased by the same amount (no change to additional paid-in capital). A large stock dividend is referred to as a stock split effected in the form of a dividend in the financial statements.

To illustrate the financial statement effects of stock dividends, assume that a company has 1 million shares of $5 par common stock outstanding. It then declares a small stock dividend of 15% of the outstanding shares (1,000,000 shares × 15% = 150,000 shares) when the market price of the stock is $30 per share. This small stock dividend has the following financial statement effects:

Transaction	Balance Sheet					Income Statement		
	Cash Asset	+ Noncash Assets	= Liabilities	+ Contrib. Capital	+ Earned Capital	Revenues	− Expenses	= Net Income
Distribute 150,000 shares as a *small* stock dividend.			=	+750,000 Common Stock +3,750,000 Additional Paid-In Capital	−4,500,000 Retained Earnings	−		=

Retained earnings (−SE) 4,500,000
   Common stock (+SE)   750,000
   Additional paid-in capital (+SE) 3,750,000

− Retained Earnings (SE) +	− Additional Paid-in-Capital (SE) +	− Common Stock (SE) +
4,500,000	3,750,000	750,000

Retained earnings are reduced by $4,500,000, which equals the market value of the small stock dividend (150,000 shares × $30 market price per share). The increase in contributed capital is treated as follows: common stock is increased by the par value of $750,000 (150,000 shares × $5 par value), and the remainder of $3,750,000 increases additional paid-in capital. Similar to cash dividend payments, the stock dividends, whether large or small, never impact income. But unlike cash dividends, stock dividends do not affect the cash flows from financing activities.

Next, assume instead that a company declares a large stock dividend of 70% of the 1 million outstanding common ($5 par) shares when the market price of the stock is $30 per share. This large stock dividend has the following financial statement effects and related entries:

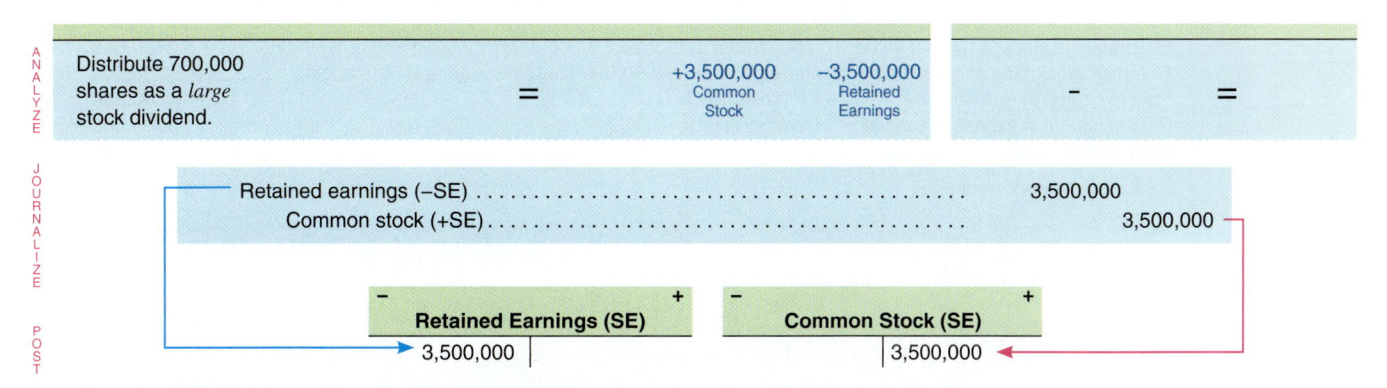

Transaction	Balance Sheet					Income Statement		
Distribute 700,000 shares as a *large* stock dividend.			=	+3,500,000 Common Stock	−3,500,000 Retained Earnings	−		=

Retained earnings (−SE) 3,500,000
   Common stock (+SE) 3,500,000

− Retained Earnings (SE) +	− Common Stock (SE) +
3,500,000	3,500,000

Retained earnings are reduced by $3,500,000, which equals the par value of the large stock dividend (700,000 shares × $5 par value per share). Common stock is increased by the par value of $3,500,000. There is no effect on additional paid-in capital because the dividend is reported at par value.

For both large and small stock dividends, companies are required to show comparable shares outstanding for all prior periods for which earnings per share (EPS) is reported in the statements. The reasoning is that a stock dividend has no effect on the ownership percentage of each common stockholder. As such, to show a dilution in reported EPS would erroneously suggest a decline in profitability when it is simply due to an increase in shares outstanding.

Stock Splits A **stock split** is a proportionate distribution of shares and, as such, is similar in substance to a stock dividend. A typical stock split is 2-for-1, which means that the company distributes one additional share for each share owned by a shareholder. Following the distribution, each investor owns twice as many shares, yet their percentage ownership in the company is unchanged.

A stock split is not a monetary transaction and, as such, there are no financial statement effects. However, companies must disclose the new number of shares outstanding for all periods presented in the financial statements. Further, many states require that the par value of shares be proportionately adjusted as well (for example, halved for a 2-for-1 split).

Stock Transactions and the Statement of Cash Flows

The issuance of common stock, the acquisition of treasury stock, and cash (but not stock) dividends affect the financing section of the statement of cash flows as follows:

Transaction	Effect on Cash Flow from Financing Activities
Issuance of Common Stock	Increase
Acquisition of Treasury Stock	Decrease
Sale of Treasury Stock	Increase
Cash Dividends Paid	Decrease

Stock splits and stock dividends do not influence the statement of cash flows.

Review 11-2 LO11-2   Accounting for Cash Dividends, Stock Dividends, and Stock Splits

Part One
Finn Corporation has outstanding 10,000 shares of $100 par value, 5% preferred stock, and 50,000 shares of $5 par value common stock. During its first three years in business, Finn declared no dividends in the first year, $300,000 of cash dividends in the second year, and $80,000 of cash dividends in the third year.

a. If the preferred stock is cumulative, determine the total amount of dividends paid to each class of stock for each of the three years.
b. If the preferred stock is not cumulative, determine the total amount of dividends paid to each class of stock for each of the three years.

Part Two
The stockholders' equity of Zhang Corporation at December 31 follows.

5% preferred stock, $100 par value, 10,000 shares authorized; 4,000 shares issued and outstanding	$ 400,000
Common stock, $5 par value, 200,000 shares authorized; 50,000 shares issued and outstanding	250,000
Paid-in capital in excess of par value—Preferred stock	40,000
Paid-in capital in excess of par value—Common stock	300,000
Retained earnings	656,000
Total stockholders' equity	$1,646,000

a. The following transactions occurred during the following year. Show the financial impact of each transaction using the financial statement effects template.

   Apr. 1   Declared and issued a 100% stock dividend on all outstanding shares of common stock when the market value of the stock was $11 per share.

   Dec. 7   Declared and issued a 3% stock dividend on all outstanding shares of common stock when the market value of the stock was $7 per share.

   Dec. 31 Declared and paid a cash dividend of $1.20 per share on all outstanding common shares.

b. Provide the appropriate journal entry for each transaction listed in part *a* and post the journal entries to the related T-accounts.
c. Determine the end of year balance in retained earnings if the company reported $288,000 in earnings for the year.
d. If instead of the 100% stock dividend on April 1, the company initiated a 2-for-1 stock split, record the resulting journal entry

Solution on p. 11-52.

Comprehensive Income

Comprehensive income is a more inclusive notion of company performance than net income. It includes all recognized changes in equity that occur during a period except those resulting from contributions by and distributions to owners.

Specifically, comprehensive income includes net income *plus* additional gains and losses not included in the income statement. These additional gains and losses are called *other comprehensive income* and include, for example, foreign currency adjustments, unrealized gains or losses on available-for-sale debt securities, unrealized gains and losses on some derivatives, and adjustments to pension and other benefit plans. Comprehensive income includes the effects on a company of some economic events that are often outside of management's control. Accordingly, some observers assert that net income is a measure of management's performance, while comprehensive income is a measure of company performance.

Comprehensive income can be reported by firms in one of two ways. The first reporting method is to present a statement of comprehensive income that combines net income and other comprehensive income in one statement. Such a statement begins much like any income statement, with revenues, cost of goods sold, operating expenses, and so forth. However, in the statement of comprehensive income, net income is a subtotal, followed by the gains and losses that are classified as other comprehensive income, along with their tax effect. The second reporting approach presents other comprehensive income (after tax) in a separate statement immediately following the income statement. Pfizer follows the second reporting approach. Its statement of comprehensive income is presented in **Exhibit 11.3**.

LO11-3
Define and illustrate comprehensive income.

EXHIBIT 11.3 — Pfizer's 2020 Abridged Consolidated Statement of Comprehensive Income ($ millions)

Net income before allocation to noncontrolling interests		$9,652
Other comprehensive income:		
Foreign currency translation adjustments, net	$ 957	
Reclassification adjustments	(17)	
Unrealized holding gains/(losses) on derivative financial instruments, net	(582)	
Reclassification adjustments for (gains)/losses included in net income	21	
Unrealized holding gains/(losses) on available-for-sale securities, net	361	
Reclassification adjustments for (gains)/losses included in net income	(188)	
Benefit plans: actuarial gains/(losses), net	(1,128)	
Reclassification adjustments related to amortization	276	
Reclassification adjustments related to settlements, net	278	
Other	(189)	
Benefit plans: prior service (costs)/credits and other, net	52	
Reclassification adjustments related to amortization of prior service costs and other, net	(176)	
Tax provision/(benefit) on other comprehensive income/(loss)	(349)	
Total other comprehensive income/(loss)		14
Comprehensive income before allocation to noncontrolling interests		9,666
Less: Comprehensive income attributable to noncontrolling interests		27
Comprehensive income attributable to Pfizer Inc.		$9,639

Unlike net income, other comprehensive income is not closed to retained earnings at the end of each accounting period. Instead, other comprehensive income is closed to a separate earned capital account called **accumulated other comprehensive income** (abbreviated AOCI).

In its 2020 balance sheet, Pfizer reports accumulated other comprehensive loss of $(11,688), compared to $(11,640) in 2019. The $48 decrease from 2019 to 2020 is (almost) equal to the $14 other comprehensive income for 2020 that Pfizer reported in its statement of comprehensive income (**Exhibit 11.3**) less a $71 million loss for the spin-off of the Upjohn Business.[8] (The $9 million difference is due to noncontrolling interests' share of other comprehensive income items. Note also that the noncontrolling interest is $36 million in net income and [$9] million in other comprehensive income for a total of $27, which ties to the amount shown in Exhibit 11.3.)

---

[8] Pfizer reported in its 2020 10-K that "the spin-off also resulted in a net increase to Accumulated other comprehensive loss of $71 million for the derecognition of net gains on foreign currency translation adjustments of $397 million and actuarial losses net of prior service credits associated with benefit plans of $326 million, which were reclassified to Retained earnings."

Summary of Stockholders' Equity

A summary of transactions that affect stockholders' equity is included in the statement of stockholders' equity. This statement reports a reconciliation of the beginning and ending balances of important stockholders' equity accounts. Pfizer's statement of stockholders' equity is shown in **Exhibit 11.4**. Pfizer's statement of shareholders' equity reveals the following key transactions for 2020:

- Total comprehensive income increased shareholders' equity by $9,639 million (net income of $9,616 million plus other comprehensive income of $23 million).
- Dividends to preferred and common shareholders decreased stockholders' equity by $8,571 million.
- Employee share-based compensation increased equity by $1,044 million.
- Conversion of preferred stock into common stock and redemptions decreased the preferred stock account, for a net decrease in stockholders' equity of $1 million.
- The spin-off of the Upjohn business resulted in a decrease in stockholders' equity of $2,015 million.

EXHIBIT 11.4 Pfizer's Stockholders' Equity (December 31, 2020)

(Millions, Except Preferred Shares)	Preferred Stock Shares	Preferred Stock Stated Value	Common Stock Shares	Common Stock Par Value	Additional Paid-In Capital	Treasury Stock Shares	Treasury Stock Cost	Retained Earnings	Accum. Other Comp. Loss	Share-holders' Equity	Non-controlling Interests	Total Equity
Balance December 31, 2019.....	431	$17	9,369	$468	$87,428	(3,835)	$(110,801)	$97,670	$(11,640)	$63,143	$303	$63,447
Net income..................								9,616		9,616	36	9,652
Other comprehensive income/ (loss), net of tax									23	23	(9)	14
Cash dividends declared:												
Common stock								(8,571)		(8,571)		(8,571)
Noncontrolling interests											(91)	(91)
Share-based payment transactions.................			37	2	1,261	(6)	(218)			1,044		1,044
Preferred stock conversions and redemptions.............	(432)	(17)			(15)	1	31			(1)		(1)
Distribution of Upjohn Business ..								(1,944)	(71)	(2,015)	(3)	
Other.......................											(1)	(1)
Balance December 31, 2020.....	—	$—	9,407	$470	$88,674	(3,840)	$(110,988)	$96,770	$(11,688)	$63,238	$235	$63,473

*Amounts may be off by $1 due to rounding.

ANALYZING FINANCIAL STATEMENTS

Analysis Objective

We want to measure the return on investment by common shareholders.

Before getting to the specifics of the performance ratio, we must address a complexity introduced when a company (like Pfizer) has a subsidiary that is not 100% owned. Suppose Company A owns 85% of the common stock of Company B. The remaining 15% of B's shareholders are called a "noncontrolling interest." Company A would be required to incorporate the assets, liabilities, revenues, and expenses of Company B in its reports. As a result, Company A's reported net income would include all the income from both A and B. But then there is an adjustment in which 15% of B's income is subtracted (as "net income attributable to noncontrolling interests"), and the resulting number is "net income attributable to common shareholders." We use this information to develop the following measure of profit that can be attributed to common shareholders of the reporting company.

> Net income
> − Net income attributable to noncontrolling interests
> − Preferred dividends
> **Net income available for common shareholders**

A similar adjustment is required on the balance sheet, where total equity consists of "equity attributable to noncontrolling interests" plus "common shareholders' equity" (as can be seen in **Exhibit 11.4**).

> Total equity
> − Equity attributable to noncontrolling interests
> − Preferred stock equity
> Common shareholders' equity

Analysis Tool Return on Common Equity (ROCE)

$$\text{Return on Common Equity (ROCE)} = \frac{\text{Net income available for common shareholders}}{\text{Average common shareholders' equity}}$$

Applying the Ratio to Pfizer

$$2018: \text{ROCE} = \frac{\$11{,}188 - \$36 - \$19}{[(\$63{,}758 - \$351 - \$19) + (\$71{,}656 - \$348 - \$21)]/2} = 0.165, \text{ or } 16.5\%$$

$$2019: \text{ROCE} = \frac{\$16{,}302 - \$351 - \$19}{[(63{,}447 - \$303 - \$17) + (\$63{,}758 - \$351 - \$19)]/2} = 0.252, \text{ or } 25.2\%$$

$$2020: \text{ROCE} = \frac{\$9{,}652 - \$36 - \$0}{[(\$63{,}473 - \$235 - \$0) + (\$63{,}447 - \$303 - \$17)]/2} = 0.152, \text{ or } 15.2\%$$

Guidance ROCE is similar to ROE except that when we compute ROCE, we remove the effect of noncontrolling interests and preferred stock from both the numerator and the denominator.

Pfizer in Context

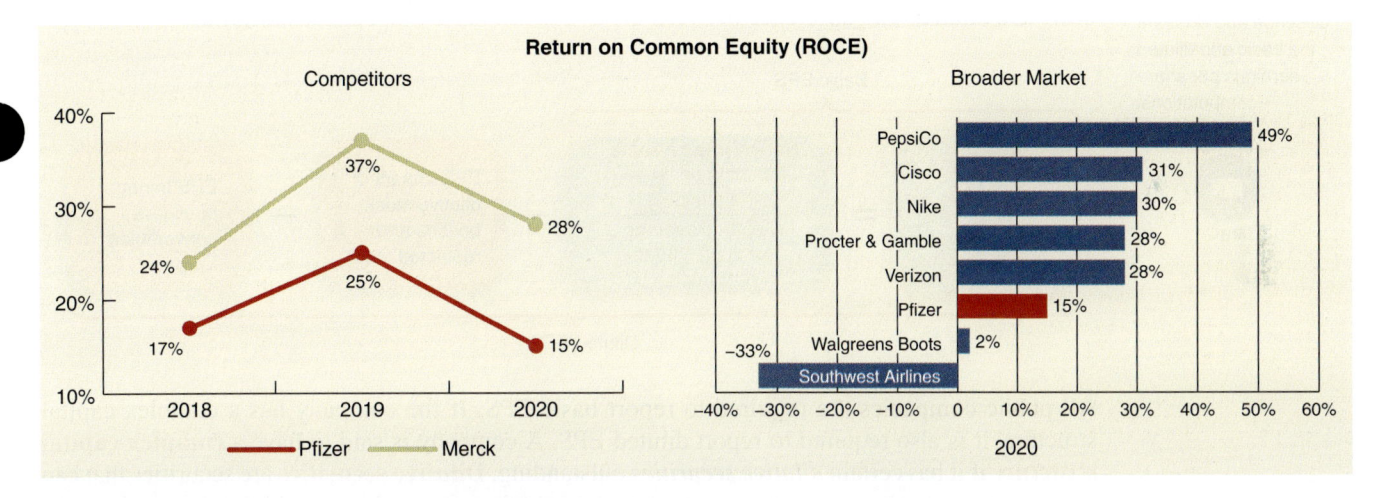

Return on Common Equity (ROCE)

Competitors (Pfizer vs Merck):
- 2018: Pfizer 17%, Merck 24%
- 2019: Pfizer 25%, Merck 37%
- 2020: Pfizer 15%, Merck 28%

Broader Market (2020):
- PepsiCo 49%
- Cisco 31%
- Nike 30%
- Procter & Gamble 28%
- Verizon 28%
- Pfizer 15%
- Walgreens Boots 2%
- Southwest Airlines −33%

Takeaways Neither Pfizer's nor Merck's ROCE has been stable for the past few years. Such volatility can occur from changes in equity, perhaps due to large share repurchases in a year, which decreases equity, or large changes in income, either from operations or one-time items such as gains (losses) on sales of discontinued operations. Pfizer's 2020 ROCE is on the lower end, relative to many of the other focus companies in this textbook.

Many companies have little or no preferred stock or noncontrolling interests. So the difference between return on common equity (ROCE) and return on equity (ROE) will be immaterial for these firms. When preferred stock is present, ROCE is a more accurate measure of return to common shareholders.

Other Considerations In Chapter 5, we learned that ROE can be decomposed into two components: return on assets and return on financial leverage. Differences between firms may reflect a difference in performance, or a difference in the reliance on debt financing. A similar division can be done with ROCE with the caveat that ROCE essentially treats preferred stock as debt rather than equity.

One final point: the financial press sometimes refers to a measure called **book value per share**. This amount is the net book value of the company that is available to common shareholders, defined as: stockholders' equity less preferred stock less equity attributable to noncontrolling interest divided by the number of common shares outstanding (issued common shares less treasury shares). Pfizer's 2020 book value per share is computed as: ($63,473 million − $235 million − $0 million)/(9,407 million shares − 3,840 million shares) = $11.36 book value per common share.

Review 11-3   LO11-3   Presenting Other Comprehensive Income

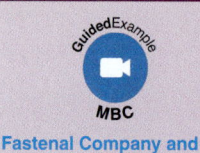

In its 2020 10-K, **Fastenal Company and Subsidiaries** reported the following items ($ millions):

Sales.	$5,647.3
Net earnings.	859.1
Earnings before income taxes	1,132.7
Foreign currency translation adjustment (net of tax)	17.2
Accumulated other comprehensive (loss), Dec. 31, 2020	(21.2)
Accumulated other comprehensive (loss), Dec. 31, 2019	(38.4)
Total stockholders' equity, Dec. 31, 2020	2,733.2

a. Prepare a statement of comprehensive income that would immediately follow the company's income statement.

b. Prepare a reconciliation of accumulated other comprehensive income that would be included as part of the company's statement of stockholders' equity.

Solution on p. 11-53.

Fastenal Company and Subsidiaries
NYSE: FAST

EARNINGS PER SHARE

LO11-4 Describe and illustrate the basic and diluted earnings per share computations.

The income statement reports at least one, and potentially two, earnings per share (EPS) numbers: basic and diluted. The difference between the two measures is illustrated as follows:

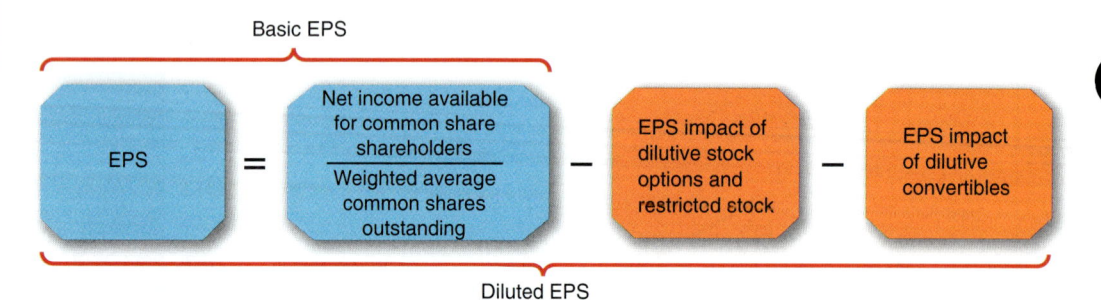

$$\text{EPS} = \underbrace{\frac{\text{Net income available for common share shareholders}}{\text{Weighted average common shares outstanding}}}_{\text{Basic EPS}} - \text{EPS impact of dilutive stock options and restricted stock} - \text{EPS impact of dilutive convertibles}$$

(Diluted EPS)

All public companies are required to report basic EPS. If the company has a complex capital structure, it is also required to report diluted EPS. A company is said to have a **complex capital structure** if it has certain *dilutive securities* outstanding. **Dilutive securities** are securities that can be converted into shares of common stock and would therefore reduce (or dilute) the earnings per share upon conversion. A few of the more prominent types of potentially dilutive securities are:

- Equity-based pay, including stock options and restricted stock
- Convertible debt
- Convertible preferred stock

The Appendix at the end of this chapter details the accounting for these securities. A company with none of these dilutive securities outstanding is said to have a **simple capital structure**.

Basic EPS (BEPS) is computed as earnings available for common shareholders (net income less net income attributable to noncontrolling interests and preferred dividends) divided by the weighted average number of common shares outstanding for the year. (The number of shares is "weighted" by the amount of time each share was outstanding during the year.) The subtraction of net income attributable to noncontrolling interests and preferred stock dividends yields the income per common share available for dividend payments to common shareholders. The preferred dividends are subtracted because this portion of net income does not accrue to the common stockholders.

Computation of **Diluted EPS (DEPS)** reflects the added shares that would have been issued if all "in the money" stock options, unvested restricted stock, and other convertible securities had been exercised at the beginning of the year. When DEPS is calculated, the corporation needs to consider the maximum potential reduction (dilution) of its BEPS that could occur if the conversion of these securities took place. To do so means that only securities that reduce BEPS upon conversion are to be considered converted. The result (DEPS) must be a figure that is lower than BEPS. The actual calculation can be quite complex. This does not detract from the importance of the DEPS value. The diluted earnings per share figure is favored by analysts as a better indicator of performance compared to basic earnings per share. Because reported DEPS never exceeds reported BEPS, the calculation is considered conservative.

Computation and Analysis of EPS

The computation of basic EPS is relatively straightforward, particularly when the firm neither issues nor buys any of its shares during the year. The formula is:

$$\text{Basic EPS (BEPS)} = \frac{\text{Net income available for common shareholders}}{\text{Weighted average number of common shares outstanding}}$$

To illustrate this calculation, assume that United Bridge Corporation reported net income of $200,000 in 2021 and paid $24,000 in preferred dividends. At the beginning of the year, the company had 44,000 shares of common stock outstanding. On June 30 (exactly the midpoint of the year) United Bridge purchased 8,000 shares of stock as treasury stock. Thus, the number of shares outstanding for the first six months of 2021 was 44,000 and, for the second half of the year, the company had 36,000 shares outstanding. The weighted average number of shares outstanding was, therefore, 40,000 [(44,000 + 36,000)/2]. Basic EPS would be calculated as follows:

$$\text{Basic EPS} = \frac{\$200,000 - \$24,000}{40,000 \text{ shares}} = \$4.40 \text{ per share}$$

The computation of diluted EPS is more complex in that it requires adjusting the basic EPS calculation for the effect of dilutive securities. This will typically require adjusting both the numerator and the denominator of the calculation, using the if-converted method.

Diluted earnings per share (DEPS) =

$$\frac{\text{Net income available for common shareholders} + \text{Add-backs}}{\text{Weighted average number of common shares} + \text{Shares of convertible securities and stock options assumed to be converted}}$$

To illustrate, assume that United Bridge Corporation's preferred stock is convertible into 8,000 shares of common stock. To calculate diluted EPS, we must assume that the convertible preferred shares were converted at the beginning of the year. If this had occurred, two things would have been different for United Bridge. First, the weighted average number of shares outstanding would be higher by 8,000 shares. Second, the company would not have paid preferred dividends of $24,000. The resulting calculation would be:

$$\text{Diluted EPS} = \frac{\$200,000}{48,000 \text{ shares}} = \$4.17 \text{ per share}$$

A full description of the procedures for calculating diluted EPS is beyond the scope of this text.[9] However, as the calculation above illustrates, diluted EPS adjusts basic EPS for the effect of dilutive securities. Reported DEPS must be no larger than BEPS to reflect its conservative message.

Pfizer reports both basic and diluted EPS. The table below, drawn from Pfizer's 2020 consolidated income statement, presents its basic and diluted EPS figures.

---

[9] Also, some more complicated securities, including securities in the mezzanine section of the balance sheet, may lead to required adjustments to the numerator of basic EPS at times, and to both the numerator and the denominator of diluted EPS. We note also that while there were previously two methods to compute diluted EPS with respect to convertible instruments; entities may only use one method now under U.S. GAAP. The "if-converted" method is required to be used and the "treasury stock method" should no longer be used (ASU 2020-06). These are beyond the scope of this text, but we note them here for those interested in studying the topic more.

Year Ended December 31	2020	2019
Earnings per common share—basic		
Income from continuing operations attributable to Pfizer Inc. common shareholders	$1.26	$1.95
Income from discontinued operations—net of tax	0.47	0.98
Net income attributable to Pfizer Inc. common shareholders	$1.73	$2.92
Earnings per common share—diluted		
Income from continuing operations attributable to Pfizer Inc. common shareholders	$1.24	$1.91
Income from discontinued operations—net of tax	0.47	0.96
Net income attributable to Pfizer Inc. common shareholders	$1.71	$2.87
Weighted average shares—basic (millions)	5,555	5,569
Weighted average shares—diluted (millions)	5,632	5,675

Several observations should be made regarding Pfizer's EPS disclosures:

1. Pfizer reports basic EPS of $1.73 in 2020 and $2.92 in 2019. Diluted EPS is $0.02 lower and $0.05 lower in 2020 and 2019, respectively, relative to basic EPS. The difference between basic and diluted EPS is caused by the effect of dilutive securities. Specifically, Pfizer has outstanding stock options and convertible preferred stock (in 2019 and part of 2020), and accelerated share repurchase agreements. Most publicly traded companies have at least one type of dilutive security outstanding. The dilutive effect of these securities on Pfizer's EPS is small.

2. The income statement further separates these EPS figures into EPS from continuing operations and EPS from discontinued operations. Discontinued operations resulted in an increase to EPS in both 2020 and 2019. GAAP requires separate reporting of the effects of nonrecurring items on EPS, including discontinued operations (see Chapter 6).

3. Pfizer used weighted average shares outstanding of 5,555 million shares to calculate basic EPS in 2020. This number is not the same as the number of shares outstanding in its December 31, 2020, balance sheet. Nor is it the simple average of the beginning and ending numbers of shares outstanding. The precise number of shares used in the EPS calculations requires knowing exactly when common stock and treasury stock transactions occurred during the year so that the weighted average number of shares outstanding can be calculated. Such detailed information is seldom available in a company's 10-K report.

EPS figures are sometimes used as a method of comparing operating results for companies of different sizes under the assumption that the number of shares outstanding is proportional to the income level (that is, a company twice the size of another will report double the income and will have double the common shares outstanding, leaving EPS approximately equal for the two companies). This assumption is erroneous. Management controls the number of common shares outstanding. Different companies also have different philosophies regarding share issuance and repurchase. For example, consider that most companies report annual EPS of less than $5, while **Berkshire Hathaway Inc.** reported EPS of $26,668 for 2020! The large amount occurs because Berkshire Hathaway has so few common shares outstanding, not necessarily because it has stellar profits.

Most analysts prefer to concentrate their attention on diluted EPS versus basic EPS as the more important measure, but the value of the EPS number is influenced by a number of factors including the number of common shares outstanding. For this reason, comparisons are more useful over time than across firms, but a careful reader should differentiate between EPS growth that comes from increases in the numerator and EPS growth that comes from decreases in the denominator. For these reasons, EPS may be of limited use in evaluating a firm's operational performance.

BUSINESS INSIGHT

It is possible that reported earnings declines but Basic EPS increases. For example, for its year ended July 2020, Cisco Systems, Inc., had a decline in earnings of 3.5% but its basic EPS increased by 2 cents a share. Another example in recent years is Signet Jewelers who one year had a decline in earnings of almost 5% and an increase in Basic EPS of 8%. A similar relation held for IBM in the years 2012–2014. Often this is due to reductions in the number of shares due to share repurchases.

Computing Basic and Diluted Earnings per Share

LO11-4 Review 11-4

Petroni Corporation reported net income of $1,750 million for the year. The weighted average number of common shares outstanding during the year was 760 million shares. Petroni paid $40 million in dividends on preferred stock, which was convertible into 10 million shares of common stock.

a. Calculate Petroni's basic earnings per share.
b. Calculate Petroni's diluted earnings per share.
c. What EPS numbers should Petroni report on its annual income statement?

Solution on p. 11-54.

APPENDIX 11A: Dilutive Securities: Accounting for Convertible Securities, Stock Options, and Restricted Stock

Convertible Securities

Convertible securities are debt and equity securities that provide the holder with an option to convert those securities into other securities. Convertible debentures, for example, are debt securities that give the holder the option to convert the debt into common stock at a predetermined conversion price. Preferred stock can also contain a conversion privilege.

To illustrate, assume 5,000 shares of preferred stock were issued at a stated value of $100 per share, with each share convertible into 12 shares of $5 par value common stock. The appropriate journal entry would be:

LO11-5 Analyze the accounting for convertible securities, stock rights, stock options, and restricted stock.

Cash (+A)	500,000	
Preferred stock (stated value) (+SE)		500,000

Now assume that 2,000 shares are converted to (2,000 × 12) = 24,000 shares of common stock. The appropriate journal entry is:

Preferred stock (stated value) (−SE)	200,000	
Common stock (par $5) (+SE)		120,000
Additional paid-in capital (+SE)		80,000

Conversion privileges offer an additional benefit to the holder of a security. That is, debtholders and preferred stockholders carry senior positions as claimants in bankruptcy and carry a fixed-interest or dividend yield. With a conversion privilege, they can enjoy the residual benefits of common shareholders should the company perform well.

A conversion option is valuable and yields a higher price for the securities than they would otherwise command. However, conversion privileges impose a cost on common shareholders. That is, the higher market price received for convertible securities is offset by the cost imposed on the subordinate (common) securities. Conversion of these securities into common shares dilutes the ownership percentage of existing holders of the firm's common stock.

The accounting for the conversion features at issuance was previously complex at times as GAAP had five models for convertible debt instruments. One model recorded the instrument as a single debt instrument and the other four required separation of the debt instrument and conversion option. Convertible preferred stock was assessed under similar models. Described at a high level here, in 2021, FASB simplified the accounting such that convertible debt will be accounted for at issuance as one security unless the conversion option is required to be accounted for as a derivative security or the convertible debt is issued with a substantial premium for which the premiums are recorded as paid-in capital. If the conversion option is equity, no separation or bifurcation is required. The accounting treatment for convertible preferred stock is similar in the sense that generally only when the conversion feature is required to be accounted for as a derivative will the security be bifurcated for accounting purposes. The new guidance (ASU 2020-06) also requires more disclosures.

When securities are converted, the book value of the converted security is removed from the balance sheet and a corresponding increase is made to contributed capital. To illustrate the most commonly used method, assume that a company has convertible bonds with a face value of $1,000 and an unamortized premium of $100. Its holders convert them into 20 shares of $10 par value common stock. The financial statement effects and related entries of this conversion would be:

Transaction	Balance Sheet					Income Statement		
	Cash Asset +	Noncash Assets =	Liabilities +	Contrib. Capital +	Earned Capital	Revenues –	Expenses =	Net Income
$1,100 book value bonds are converted into 20 common shares of $10 par value.			−1,000 Bonds Payable −100 Bonds Premium	+200 Common Stock +900 Additional Paid-In Capital			−	=

```
Bonds payable (−L) ..................................... 1,000
Bonds premium (−L) .................................... 100
    Common stock (+SE) ............................... 200
    Additional paid-in capital (+SE) .................. 900
```

− Bonds Payable (L) +		− Additional Paid-in Capital (SE) +
1,000		900

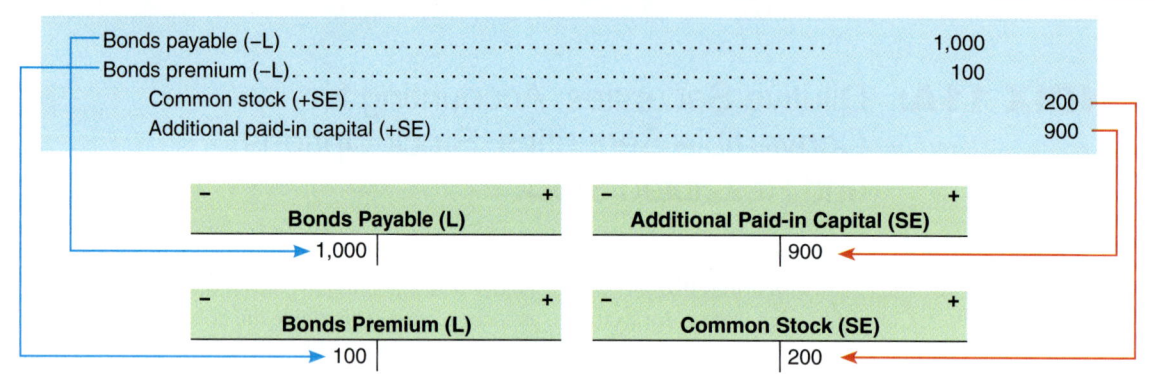

− Bonds Premium (L) +		− Common Stock (SE) +
100		200

The key financial statement effects of this transaction are:

- The bond's face value ($1,000) and unamortized premium ($100) of the bonds are removed from the balance sheet.
- Common stock increases by the par value of the shares issued (20 shares × $10 par = $200), and additional paid-in capital increases for the balance ($900).
- There is no effect on income from this conversion unless an interest accrual is required.

One final note: the potentially dilutive effect of convertible securities is taken into account in the computation of diluted earnings per share (DEPS). Specifically, the diluted EPS computation assumes conversion at the beginning of the year (or when the security is issued if during the year). The earnings available to common shares in the numerator are increased by any forgone after-tax interest expense or preferred dividends, and the additional shares to be issued in the conversion increase the shares outstanding in the denominator.

Stock Rights

Corporations often issue **stock rights** that give the holder an option to acquire a specified number of shares of capital stock under prescribed conditions and within a stated period. The evidence of stock rights is a certificate called a **stock warrant**. Stock rights are issued for several reasons that include the following:

- To compensate outside parties (such as underwriters, promoters, board members, and other professionals) for services provided to the company;
- As a preemptive right that gives existing stockholders the first chance to buy additional shares when the corporation decides to raise additional equity capital through share issuances;
- To enhance the marketability of other securities issued by the company (an example is issuing rights to purchase common stock with convertible bonds).

Stock rights or warrants specify the:

- Number of rights represented by the warrant
- Option price per share (which can be zero)
- Number of rights needed to obtain a share of the stock
- Expiration date of the rights
- Instructions for the exercise of rights

Accounting for stock rights is complex. The goals of this discussion are to understand the essence of stock rights issued to current stockholders.

Stock rights issued to current stockholders have three important dates: (1) Announcement date of the rights offering; (2) Issuance date of the rights; and (3) Expiration date of the rights. Between the announcement date and the issuance date, the price of the stock will reflect the value of the rights. After the issuance date, the shares and the rights trade separately. Shareholders can exercise their rights, sell their stock, or allow the rights to lapse.

To illustrate, assume on December 10, 2021, a company announces the issue of rights to purchase one additional share of its $5 par value common stock for every 10 shares currently held on January 1, 2022. The exercise price per share is $20, and the rights expire September 1, 2022. Assume further that 7,000 of the rights are exercised.

- No recognition is required at the announcement date and at the issuance date.
- The first entry is made when the first stock right is exercised. We give only the summary entry that would be appropriate after September 1, 2022.

Sept 1: To record the issuance of 7,000 shares of common stock on exercise of stock rights:
The financial statement effects and related entries would be (amounts in millions):

Transaction	Cash Asset	+	Noncash Assets	=	Liabilities	+	Contrib. Capital	+	Earned Capital	Revenues	–	Expenses	=	Net Income
Issue 7,000 shares of common stock on exercise of all the stock rights.	+140,000 Cash			=			+35,000 Common Stock +105,000 Additional Paid-In Capital							

Cash (+A) 140,000
    Common stock (+SE) 35,000
    Additional paid-in capital (+SE) 105,000

+ Cash (A) −		− Additional Paid-in-Capital (SE) +		− Common Stock (SE) +
140,000			105,000		35,000

Employee Stock Options

Employee stock options are granted to employees in exchange for service. The option gives the employee the right, but not the obligation, to purchase a share of stock in the future at a price specified today. Generally, options are granted with a strike price (or exercise price) equal to the market price on the date of grant. Stock options are expensed for financial accounting purposes in an amount equal to the fair value of the options on the date of grant. For example, in Note 13 to its 10-K report, Pfizer reported the fair value of stock option grants to be $6.4 million on December 31, 2020 (1.8 million options granted × 3.56 per option).

Stock option grants normally require a vesting period. The **vesting period** is a period of time during which the employee is not allowed to exercise the stock option. For example, a stock option may expire in 5 years and vest over a period of 3 years. Such an option would be exercisable in the fourth or fifth year of its life. Rather than recognizing the entire option value as compensation expense at the time that the option grant is awarded, GAAP requires that the fair value of the option be recorded ratably over the vesting period.

To illustrate stock option accounting, suppose that on January 1, 2021, a company grants options to purchase 200,000 shares to senior management as part of its performance bonus plan. The options are granted with an exercise price of $30 (the current price) and can be exercised after vesting in 2 years. The firm uses an accepted valuation method (not discussed here) to obtain a fair value of $10 per option. The accounting and financial statement effects and related entries for 2021 would be:

    January 1—grant date

The total compensation cost is determined at the grant date, but no journal entry is recorded on the grant date.

    December 31, 2021 and 2022—record compensation expense:

Transaction	Balance Sheet: Cash Asset + Noncash Assets = Liabilities + Contrib. Capital + Earned Capital − Contra Equity	Income Statement: Revenues − Expenses = Net Income
Record compensation expense for 200,000 options granted at $30, valued at $10 per share, vested at 50% per year.	= +1,000,000 Additional Paid-In Capital −1,000,000 Retained Earnings −	+1,000,000 − Compensation Expense = −1,000,000

Dec. 31 Compensation expense (+E, −SE) 1,000,000
          Additional paid-in capital (+SE) 1,000,000

+ Compensation Expense (E) −	− Additional Paid-in Capital (SE) +
Dec. 31 1,000,000	1,000,000 Dec. 31

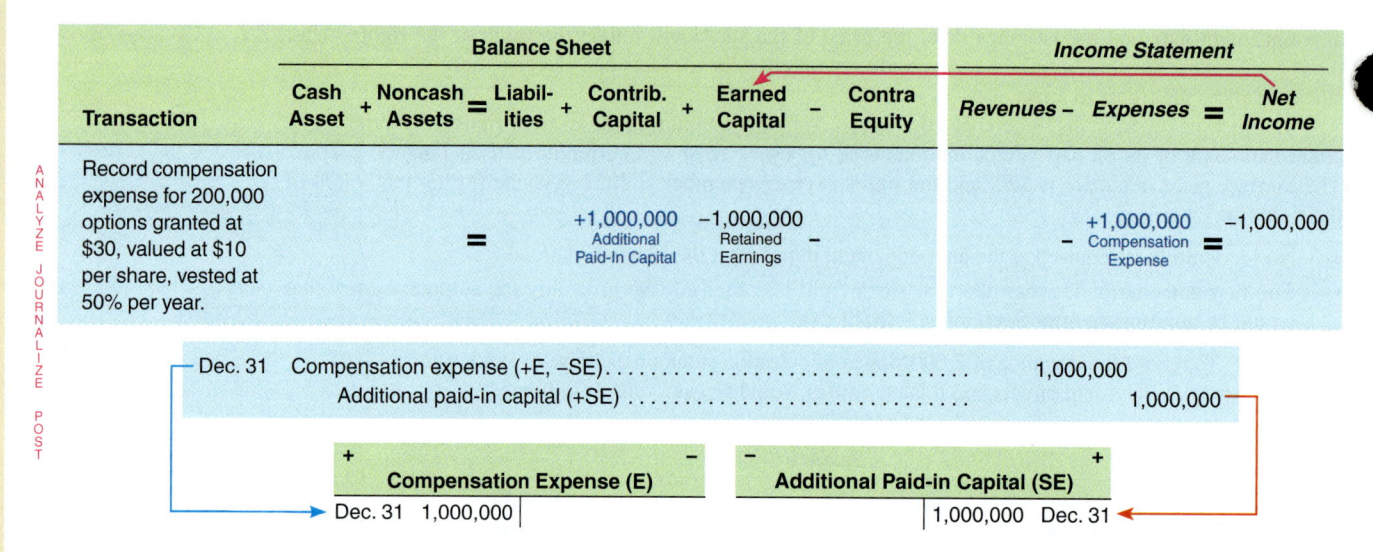

The two entries together bring the total stock-based compensation expense to $2 million. Once vested, the option will not be exercised unless the market price of the common stock exceeds the exercise price. Next, suppose that its stock price rises and all options are exercised on November 15, 2023, with the stock being issued from treasury shares purchased previously at $25. The accounting and financial statement effects follow. In effect, senior management has purchased these shares by contributing $2 million in employment services and $6 million in cash.

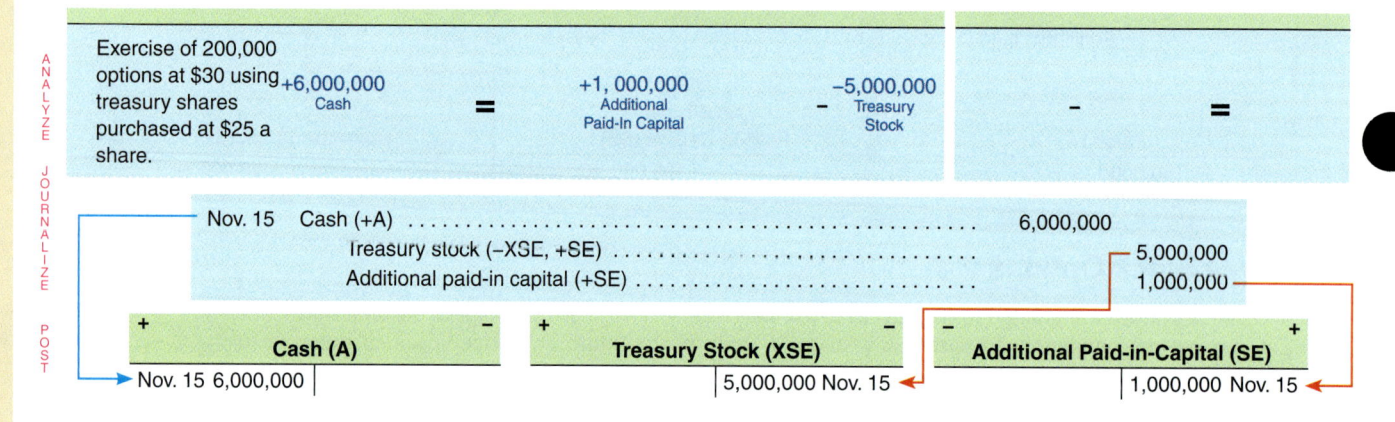

Transaction	Balance Sheet	Income Statement
Exercise of 200,000 options at $30 using treasury shares purchased at $25 a share.	+6,000,000 Cash = +1,000,000 Additional Paid-In Capital − −5,000,000 Treasury Stock	− =

Nov. 15 Cash (+A) 6,000,000
          Treasury stock (−XSE, +SE) 5,000,000
          Additional paid-in capital (+SE) 1,000,000

+ Cash (A) −	+ Treasury Stock (XSE) −	− Additional Paid-in-Capital (SE) +
Nov. 15 6,000,000	5,000,000 Nov. 15	1,000,000 Nov. 15

Restricted Stock

Companies are increasingly moving away from stock options to other types of performance-based pay. One type that is commonly used is restricted stock, either in the form of restricted stock share awards or restricted stock unit awards (which we refer to hereafter as **restricted stock awards (RSAs)** and **restricted stock units (RSUs)** for convenience). Indeed, Pfizer awarded no options under its stock option plan in 2018, 2019, or 2020. In 2020, Pfizer granted $272 million in value of RSUs.

Restricted stock plans give employees shares or rights to shares, but these are restricted (meaning the employee does not have full ownership) until the employee has satisfied vesting requirements. If the employee leaves before the awards vest, the shares or rights would be lost. Pfizer states that it has a three-year vesting period.

While unvested, both RSAs and RSUs are potentially dilutive securities in the calculation of diluted EPS. We note that, generally, unvested RSAs are not included in the calculation of basic EPS, even though as we will see below, the shares are outstanding. (However, sometimes they are considered participating securities and included in the calculation of basic EPS. For example, CISCO excludes them from basic EPS and Facebook includes them.) RSUs are not outstanding shares and are not included in the calculation of basic EPS. RSUs are considered potentially dilutive in the calculation of diluted EPS.

Restricted Stock Award (RSA)

An RSA is a form of equity compensation that transfers stock to the recipient on the date of the grant. It is not an option to buy shares but rather an award of shares. The recipient's rights in shares are restricted until the shares vest.

On the grant date of an RSA, the company increases (debits) a contra-equity account, Unearned Compensation—Equity (also called Deferred Compensation), for the fair value of the shares at the grant date. Common Stock at par and Paid-in Capital in Excess of Par are increased (credited). Over the vesting period, this Unearned Compensation-Equity amount is reversed to Compensation Expense using the straight-line method. Note that compensation is valued at the fair value of the shares at the grant date and is unaffected by any change in stock value during the vesting period.

To illustrate, suppose that on January 1, 2022 a company grants 1,000 shares (RSAs) with a total fair value of $30,000 and a 3-year vesting period. Common stock has a $1 per share par value. The accounting and financial statement effects and related entries on the grant date would be:

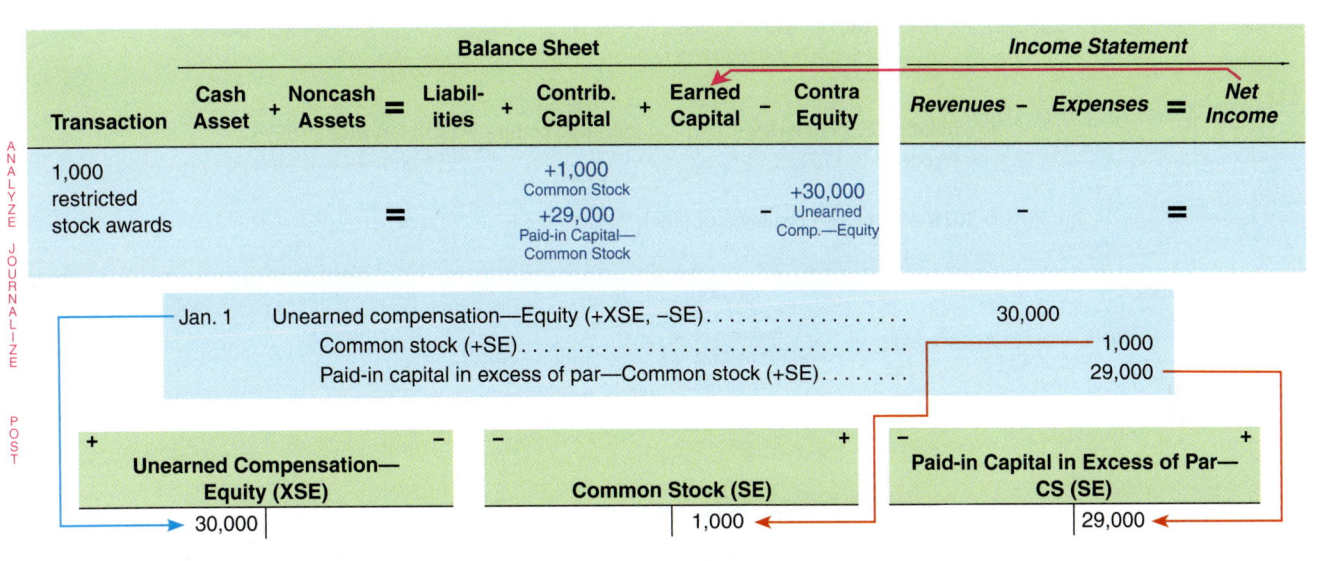

Transaction	Cash Asset	+	Noncash Assets	=	Liabilities	+	Contrib. Capital	+	Earned Capital	−	Contra Equity		Revenues	−	Expenses	=	Net Income
1,000 restricted stock awards				=			+1,000 Common Stock +29,000 Paid-in Capital— Common Stock				+30,000 Unearned Comp.—Equity			−		=	

Jan. 1   Unearned compensation—Equity (+XSE, −SE) 30,000
         Common stock (+SE) 1,000
         Paid-in capital in excess of par—Common stock (+SE) 29,000

+ Unearned Compensation—Equity (XSE) −		− Common Stock (SE) +		− Paid-in Capital in Excess of Par—CS (SE) +
30,000			1,000		29,000

December 31, 2022, 2023, and 2024—To record compensation expense

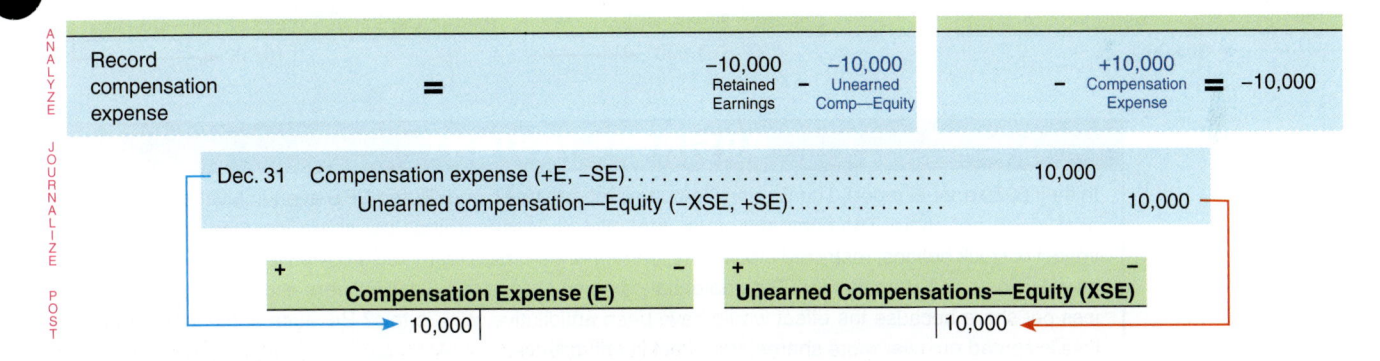

Record compensation expense				=			−10,000 Retained Earnings	−	−10,000 Unearned Comp—Equity				−	+10,000 Compensation Expense	=	−10,000

Dec. 31   Compensation expense (+E, −SE) 10,000
          Unearned compensation—Equity (−XSE, +SE) 10,000

+ Compensation Expense (E) −		− Unearned Compensations—Equity (XSE) +
10,000		10,000

Restricted Stock Unit (RSU)

An RSU is not an actual transfer of stock on the grant date, but rather a commitment to transfer stock once vesting conditions are met. Thus, upon the grant of an RSU, the employee is granted the right to receive a certain number of shares of stock at a future date under certain conditions. There is no issuance of shares on the grant date, in contrast to the RSA discussed above; thus, no accounting entry is required on the grant date. The compensation value is determined at the grant date, however. Over the vesting period as the compensation is earned, the company records Compensation Expense (debit) and increases (credits) an account called Paid-in Capital—Restricted Stock for the proportionate share of the value each reporting period (using the straight-line method). After the employee meets the vesting requirements (the restrictions lapse), the amount from Paid-in Capital—Restricted Stock is transferred to Common Stock at par and Paid-in Capital—Common Stock.

To illustrate, suppose that on January 1, 2022, a company grants 1,000 RSUs. Each RSU may be exchanged for 1 share of $1 par common stock. The fair value of the shares on the grant date is $30, and the requisite service period is 3 years. (Assume no forfeitures and no expectation of forfeitures.) The accounting and financial statement effects and related entries would be:

January 1, 2022—Grant of RSUs
   No entry.

December 31, 2022, 2023, and 2024—To record compensation expense

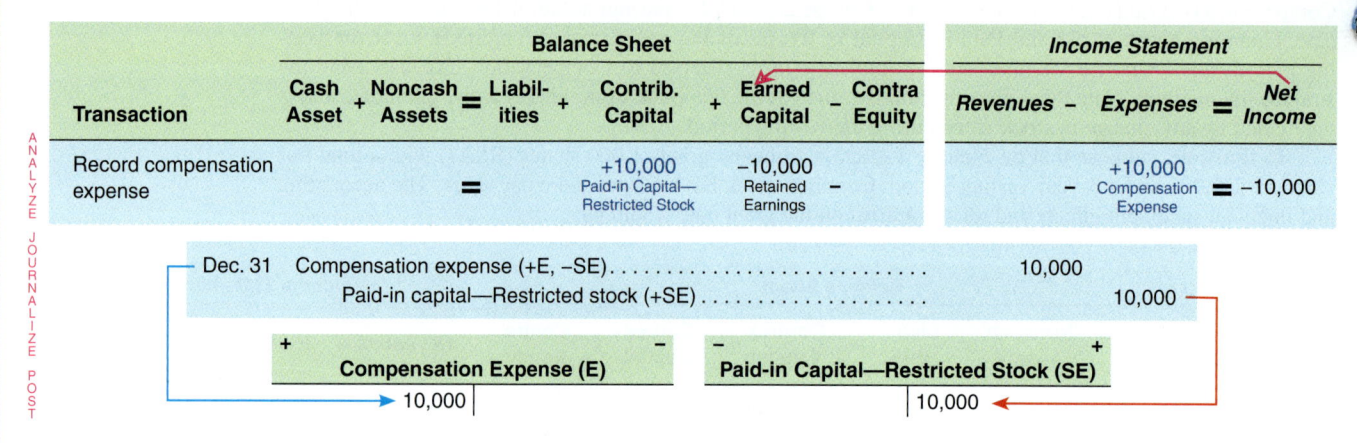

Transaction	Balance Sheet						Income Statement		
	Cash Asset +	Noncash Assets =	Liabilities +	Contrib. Capital +	Earned Capital −	Contra Equity	Revenues −	Expenses =	Net Income
Record compensation expense		=		+10,000 Paid-in Capital—Restricted Stock	−10,000 Retained Earnings	−		+10,000 Compensation Expense	= −10,000

Dec. 31 Compensation expense (+E, −SE)........................... 10,000
        Paid-in capital—Restricted stock (+SE)................... 10,000

+ Compensation Expense (E) −	− Paid-in Capital—Restricted Stock (SE) +
10,000	10,000

January 1, 2022—To record issuance of stock

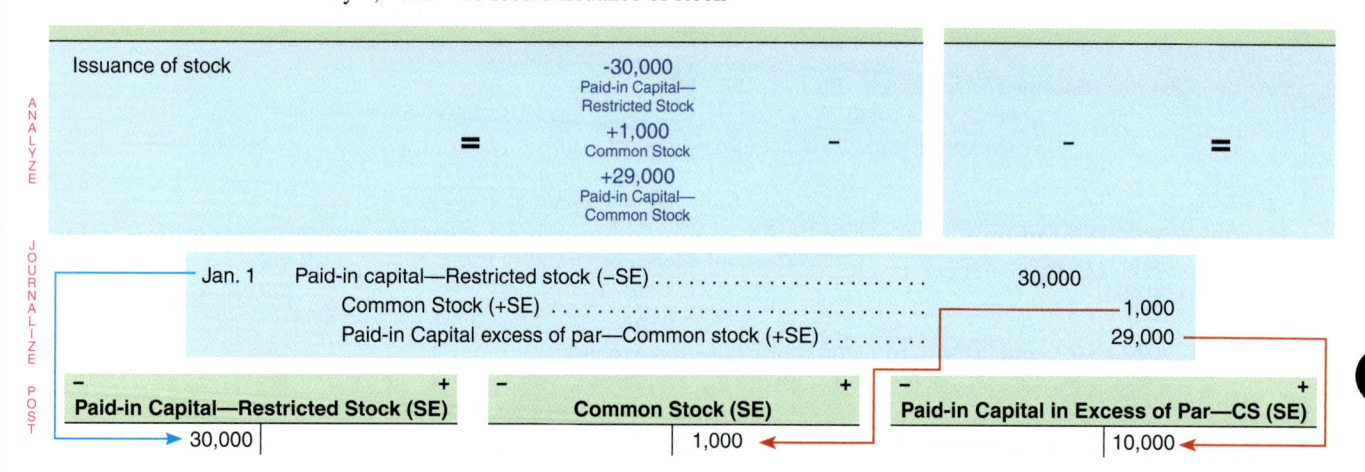

Transaction	Balance Sheet						Income Statement		
Issuance of stock		=		−30,000 Paid-in Capital—Restricted Stock +1,000 Common Stock +29,000 Paid-in Capital—Common Stock	−			−	=

Jan. 1 Paid-in capital—Restricted stock (−SE)........................ 30,000
      Common Stock (+SE) 1,000
      Paid-in Capital excess of par—Common stock (+SE)......... 29,000

− Paid-in Capital—Restricted Stock (SE) +	− Common Stock (SE) +	− Paid-in Capital in Excess of Par—CS (SE) +
30,000	1,000	10,000

BUSINESS INSIGHT

In their 2020 annual report, The Boeing Company, reports basic and diluted EPS at an equivalent amount of ($20.88) per share. The company states that diluted (loss)/earnings per share includes any dilutive impact of stock options, restricted stock units, performance-based restricted stock units, and performance awards. They also state that for 2020, potential common shares of 1.6 million were excluded from diluted loss per share because the effect would have been antidilutive. Why is this? Because of the loss—if the loss is spread out over more shares, the effect is anti-dilutive.

Review 11-5 LO11-5   Accounting for Convertible Debt

Kallapur, Inc., has issued convertible debentures: each $1,000 bond is convertible into 200 shares of $1 par common stock. Assume that the bonds were sold at a discount and that each bond has a current unamortized discount equal to $150.

Required
a. Using the financial statement effects template, illustrate the effects of the conversion of one of its bonds.
b. Prepare journal entries for the transaction assuming conversion of one bond.
c. Post the journal entries to the related T-accounts.

Solution on p. 11-54.

SUMMARY

Describe and account for business financing through stock issuances and repurchases. (p. 11-3) — **LO11-1**

- Contributed capital represents the cumulative cash (or other asset) inflow that the company has received from the sale of various classes of stock, preferred and common.
- Preferred stock receives preference in terms of dividends before common and, if cumulative, receives all dividends not paid in the past before common dividends can be paid. Preferred stock can also be designated as convertible into common stock at the holder's option and at a predetermined conversion ratio. Voting privileges reside only with the common stock.
- Common stock is often repurchased by the firm for use in stock award programs, to signal management confidence in the company, or simply to return cash to shareholders. Repurchased stock is either cancelled or held for reissue. If held for reissue, the repurchase is debited to a contra equity account titled treasury stock.

Describe the effect on equity of earnings, dividends, and stock splits. (p. 11-11) — **LO11-2**

- Earned capital includes retained earnings, which represents the cumulative profit that has been retained by the company. Earned capital is increased by income earned and decreased by losses and dividends declared by the firm. Earned capital also includes the effects of items included in other comprehensive income.
- Dividends in the form of stock decrease retained earnings and increase contributed capital by an equivalent amount.
- A stock split is a proportionate distribution similar in substance to a stock dividend. The new number of shares outstanding must be disclosed. Otherwise, no further accounting is required unless the state of incorporation requires that the par value be proportionally adjusted.

Define and illustrate comprehensive income. (p. 11-16) — **LO11-3**

- Comprehensive income includes several additional items not recognized in net income, including: adjustments for changes in foreign exchange rates, unrealized changes in available-for-sale debt securities, and pension liability adjustments. The concept is designed to highlight impacts on net assets that are beyond management's control.

Describe and illustrate the basic and diluted earnings per share computations. (p. 11-19) — **LO11-4**

- Earnings per share is a closely watched number reported for all publicly traded firms. Basic EPS is computed as the ratio of net income (less preferred dividends and noncontrolling interests) to the weighted average number of outstanding shares for the period. The value of this performance metric is subject to all the difficulties in measuring net income, including the fact that net income can increase due to an acquisition or divestiture that can have no impact on the number of outstanding shares.
- Most analysts are more interested in what is termed diluted earnings per share. This conservative calculation, which, if reported, never exceeds basic EPS, reflects the maximum reduction in basic EPS possible assuming conversion of the convertible securities.
- Stock options that are "in the money" are always dilutive.
- Convertible securities that would be antidilutive are treated as if they were not converted.

Appendix 11A: Analyze the accounting for convertible securities, stock rights, stock options, and restricted stock. (p. 11-22) — **LO11-5**

- Convertible securities are debt and equity instruments, including stock rights, that allow these securities to be exchanged for other securities, typically common stock. The convertible feature adds value to the security to which it is attached.
- Stock options, one form of stock right, allow the holders to exchange them at a specified (strike) price for common stock. This right is valuable and creates an expense when granted to an employee or other individual. Expense recognition is appropriate, using the value obtained by applying an options-pricing model, even though the calculation is not precise. The option will not be exercised unless the market price of the common stock exceeds the strike price.
- Convertible preferred stock and convertible debt securities need to be considered in the calculation of DEPS to the extent conversion reduces reported BEPS.
- Restricted stock awards and restricted stock units are recorded as compensation expense as the vesting period expires (as the employee works over the vesting period).
- Generally, unvested restricted stock awards and restricted stock units are excluded from the denominator of basic EPS. If dilutive, they are taken into account in the calculation of diluted EPS. Once vested, the shares are included in the computation of basic EPS.

GUIDANCE ANSWERS... YOU MAKE THE CALL

You are the Chief Financial Officer Several points must be considered. (1) Treasury shares are likely to prop up earnings per share (EPS). While the numerator (earnings) is likely dampened by the use of cash for the stock repurchase (because the cash cannot be reinvested in operations), EPS is likely to increase because of the reduced shares in the denominator. (2) If the shares are sufficiently undervalued (in management's opinion), the stock repurchase and subsequent resale can provide a better return than some alternative investments. (3) Stock repurchases send a strong signal to the market that management feels its stock is undervalued. This is more credible than merely making that argument with analysts. On the other hand, company cash is diverted from other investments. This is bothersome if such investments are mutually exclusive either now or in the future.

KEY RATIOS

Net income available for common shareholders =
Net income − Net income attributable to noncontrolling interests − Preferred dividends

Common shareholders' equity =
Total equity − Equity attributable to noncontrolling interests − Preferred stock equity

$$\text{Return on Common Equity (ROCE)} = \frac{\text{Net income available for common shareholders}}{\text{Average common shareholders' equity}}$$

$$\text{Basic earnings per share (BEPS)} = \frac{\text{Net income available for common shareholders}}{\text{Weighted average number of common shares outstanding}}$$

Diluted earnings per share (DEPS) =

$$\frac{\text{Net income available for common shareholders + Add-backs}}{\text{Weighted average number of common shares + Shares of convertible securities and stock options assumed to be converted}}$$

Assignments with the MBC logo in the margin are available in myBusinessCourse.
See the Preface of the book for details.

MULTIPLE CHOICE

1. Suppose Pfizer issues 100,000 shares of its common stock, $0.05 par value, to obtain a warehouse and the accompanying land when the price of the stock is $28.00. Which one of the following statements is not true?
   a. The newly acquired assets will increase total assets by $2.8 million.
   b. Retained earnings are unaffected.
   c. The common stock account increases by $5,000.
   d. Total shareholders' equity increases by $2,795,000.

2. Assume Pfizer resells 15,000 shares of its stock that were purchased when the market price of the stock was $25. If the shares are resold for $22, which one of the following statements holds?
   a. Additional paid-in capital decreases by $45,000.
   b. The treasury stock account increases by $45,000.
   c. Additional paid-in capital increases by $45,000.
   d. The treasury stock account decreases by $45,000.

3. Suppose Pfizer declares a 200,000 common stock dividend (par $0.05) when the market value of a share is $30.00. Which one of the following statements is true?
   a. The common stock account increases by $10,000.
   b. Additional paid-in capital decreases by $5.99 million.
   c. Retained earnings increases by $6 million.
   d. Additional paid-in capital increases by $6 million.

Multiple Choice Answers
1. d 2. a 3. a 4. d 5. d

4. Which of the following statements is true?
   a. When a *large stock dividend* is paid, retained earnings are reduced by the market value of the shares distributed.
   b. Neither stock dividends nor stock splits affect basic earnings per share calculations.
   c. A three-for-one stock split increases the total outstanding shares by 300%.
   d. A stock split has no financial statement effects because it is not a monetary transaction.

5. Which of the following statements is not true in relation to diluted EPS (DEPS)?
   a. Stock options that are in the money will always cause DEPS to be less than basic EPS.
   b. Convertible bonds, if dilutive, will cause changes in both the numerator and the denominator of DEPS.
   c. Stock analysts tend to concentrate their attention on DEPS instead of basic EPS.
   d. A company's only equity contract that can lead to dilution is stock options.

QUESTIONS

Q11-1. Define *par value stock*. What is the significance of a stock's par value from an accounting and analysis perspective?

Q11-2. What are the basic differences between preferred stock and common stock? What are the typical features of preferred stock?

Q11-3. What features make preferred stock similar to debt? Similar to common stock?

Q11-4. What is meant by dividend arrearage on preferred stock? If dividends are two years in arrears on $400,000 of 6% preferred stock, and dividends are declared at the end of this year, what amount of total dividends must preferred shareholders receive before any distributions are made to common shareholders?

Q11-5. Distinguish between authorized stock and issued stock. Why might the number of shares issued be more than the number of shares outstanding?

Q11-6. Describe the difference between contributed capital and earned capital. Specifically, how can earned capital be considered as an investment by the company's shareholders?

Q11-7. How does the account "additional paid-in capital" (APIC) arise? What inferences, if any, can you draw from the amount of APIC as reported on the balance sheet relative to the common stock amount in relation to the financial condition of the company?

Q11-8. Define *stock split*. What are the major reasons for a stock split?

Q11-9. Define *treasury stock*. Why might a corporation acquire treasury stock? How is treasury stock reported in the balance sheet?

Q11-10. If a corporation purchases 600 shares of its own common stock at $10 per share and resells them at $14 per share, where would the $2,400 increase in capital be reported in the financial statements? Why is no gain reported?

Q11-11. A corporation has total stockholders' equity of $3,471,000 and one class of $2 par value common stock. The corporation has 375,000 shares authorized; 225,000 shares issued; 195,000 shares outstanding; and 30,000 shares as treasury stock. What is its book value per share?

Q11-12. What is a stock dividend? How does a common stock dividend distributed to common shareholders affect their respective ownership interests?

Q11-13. What is the difference between the accounting for a small stock dividend and the accounting for a large stock dividend?

Q11-14. Employee stock options have a potentially dilutive effect on earnings per share (EPS) that is recognized in the diluted EPS computation. What can companies do to offset these dilutive effects, and how might this action affect the balance sheet?

Q11-15. What information is reported in a statement of stockholders' equity?

Q11-16. What items are typically reported under the stockholders' equity category of other comprehensive income (OCI)?

Q11-17. What is a stock option vesting period? How does the vesting period affect the recognition of compensation expense for stock options?

Q11-18. Describe the accounting for the conversion of a convertible bond to equity. Would this accounting ever result in the recognition of a gain in the income statement?

DATA ANALYTICS

LO11-4 **DA11-1. Analyzing Trends in the Price-to-Earnings Ratio using Excel**

The Excel file associated with this exercise includes market price and ratio information for companies in the S&P 500. (Data obtained from https://datahub.io/core/s-and-p-500-companies#data on August 26, 2021, made available under the Public Domain Dedication and License v1.0 whose full text can be found at: http://opendatacommons.org/licenses/pddl/1.0/.)

For this exercise, we examine trends in the price-to-earnings ratio of S&P 500 companies by industry segment. The price-to-earnings ratio measures the amount an investor is willing to pay per share of stock for each dollar of earnings per share. An increase in this ratio generally means that an investor would have a higher expectation for company profits in the future. In the first analysis, we calculate the average value or mean of the price-to-earnings ratio for each segment. In the second analysis, we calculate the median value of the price-to-earnings ratio for each segment. Lastly, we compare the average and median ratio results and analyze the cause of the differences.

Price-to Earnings Ratio
Market price per share
Earnings per share

REQUIRED

1. Download Excel file DA11-1 found in myBusinessCourse.
2. Create a PivotTable (PivotTable 1) showing the average Price/Earnings ratio by sector. *Hint:* With your cursor in your data, select Insert, PivotChart. Add Sector to Rows and Price/Earnings to Values; select Average for the display of Price/Earnings by right-clicking on an amount in the PivotTable, clicking Value Field Settings, and selecting Average.
3. Remove the grand total row (which is irrelevant for this table). *Hint:* Click on the Design tab, Grand totals, Off for rows & columns.
4. Change display of your data to show two decimal places. *Hint:* Right-click on an amount in the PivotTable, click on number format, and make change.
5. Sort your PivotTable in the order of highest to lowest values. *Hint:* Right-click on an amount in the PivotTable; click Sort, Sort Largest to smallest.
6. Indicate which sector has the highest and which sector has the lowest average price/earnings ratio.
7. Copy original PivotTable, paste below the original to create PivotTable 2, change the calculation of price/earnings to now display maximum value, and sort Price/Earnings values from largest to smallest values. *Hint:* Right-click on an amount in the PivotTable, and click Value Field Settings.
8. Indicate which sector has the highest and which sector has the lowest maximum price/earnings ratio.
9. Copy original PivotTable, paste below PivotTable 2 to create PivotTable 3, change the calculation of price/earnings to now display minimum value, and sort Price/Earnings values from largest to smallest values. *Hint:* Click the i button next to Average of Price/Earnings and select Min.
10. Indicate which sector has the highest and which sector has the lowest minimum price/earnings ratio.
11. Read the following article, "Stuck in the Middle—Mean vs. Median," by Dr. Dieter Schremmer found at the following link: https://www.clinfo.eu/mean-median/.
12. Compute the median value of the Price/Earnings ratio for the Energy sector and for the Industrials sector. *Hint:* Median is not a calculation option within the PivotTables. Instead, double-click on the dollar amount in the PivotTable for Energy to open up a new sheet with the underlying data. In a new cell (at least two rows below the table) calculate the median of the Price/Earnings data: =MEDIAN(xx). Repeat steps for the Industrials sector.
13. Compute the difference between the Maximum Price/Earnings (see PivotTable 2) and the Minimum Price/Earnings (see PivotTable 3) for both sectors: Energy and Industrials.
14. Compare the median values obtained in part 12 to the average values listed in PivotTable 1 and answer the following question: What caused the differences between the mean and median values in your calculations?

LO11-5 **DA11-2. Constructing and Analyzing a Dataset on Share-Based Compensation in Excel**

For this exercise, we create and analyze a dataset in Excel of the changes in the composition of share-based compensation plans (restricted stock unit, performance share, and stock option plans) for **Target Corporation** over a 10-year period.

REQUIRED

1. Download Excel file DA11-2 found in myBusinessCourse.

2. Create a dataset that will provide information on the composition of Target's share-based compensation plans over a 10-year period from fiscal year 2011 to fiscal year 2020.
   - In your dataset, for each of the share-based awards (restricted stock unit, performance share, and stock options) include the following: number of units granted during the year and the unrecognized compensation expense at year-end.
   - Also include in your dataset the total share-based compensation expense included on the income statement for each year and the fair value per unit at grant date of the restricted stock units for each year.
   - *Hints*:
     - This information can be found in the note disclosures in the annual 10-K reports.
     - When collecting your data, note that some amounts are in thousands, and some in millions.
     - Fiscal years end in January or February of the following year; for example, Fiscal Year 2020 ends January 30, 2021.
3. Prepare a line chart in Excel over the 10-year period showing the trends in units granted of the three different types of share-based awards. *Hint:* Highlight data; click Insert, Line. Chart should show the earliest year on the left and the latest year on the right. To change the order, right-click inside the horizontal axis. In the Format Axis sidebar, check Categories in reverse order.
4. Describe the 10-year trend in the data visualization for each of the three awards.
5. Prepare a line chart in Excel showing the trend of share-based compensation expense over the 10-year period.
6. Indicate which year(s) in the data visualization prepared in part 5 showed a highly visible decline in share-based compensation expense.
7. Indicate which year seems to be the start of an increasing trend in the visualization created in part 5.
8. Prepare a line chart in Excel showing the trend of unrecognized share-based compensation expense over the 10-year period for all three share-based plan types.
9. Indicate which share-based plan type in the data visualization prepared in part 8 showed the highest value and lowest value in Fiscal Year 2011, 2015, and 2020.
10. Prepare a schedule for the total fair value of the restricted stock share awards at the date of grant for each of the 10 years. *Hint:* Multiply the number of restricted stock units by the unit price at the date of grant.
11. Indicate which year(s) showed a decrease in total value based on the data visualization prepared in part 10.
12. Describe the trend shown in fair value of restricted stock share awards from fiscal year 2016 to fiscal year 2020.
13. Summarize the result of your analysis.

DA11-3. Preparing Tableau Visualizations to Analyze Dividend Payout Policies Through Ratios   **LO11-2**
Available in myBusinessCourse, this problem uses Tableau to analyze dividend payout policies of S&P 500 companies through the dividend yield and dividend payout ratio.

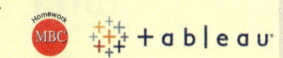

DATA VISUALIZATION

Data Visualization Activities are available in myBusinessCourse. These assignments use Tableau Dashboards to expose students to visual depictions of data and introduce students to data analytics through data visualizations. These exercises are easily assignable and auto graded by MBC.

MINI EXERCISES

M11-19. Analyzing and Identifying Financial Statement Effects of Stock Issuances   **LO11-1**
On June 1, Beatty Corp. issues (*a*) 16,000 shares of $50 par value preferred stock at $68 cash per share, and it issues (*b*) 24,000 shares of $1 par value common stock at $10 cash per share.

a. Do these transactions increase contributed capital or earned capital?
b. What is the effect of these transactions on Beatty Corp.'s income statement?
c. What are the differences between the preferred stock and the common stock issued by Beatty Corp.?

LO11-1 M11-20. Analyzing and Identifying Financial Statement Effects of Stock Issuances (FSET)
On September 1, Magliolo, Inc., (*a*) issues 13,500 shares of $10 par value preferred stock at $48 cash per share and (*b*) issues 90,000 shares of $2 par value common stock at $37 cash per share. Using the financial statement effects template, illustrate the effects of these two issuances.

LO11-1 M11-21. Analyzing and Identifying Financial Statement Effects of Stock Issuances
Using the information from M11-20, answer the following.

a. Prepare the journal entries for the two issuances.
b. Post the journal entries to the related T-accounts.

LO11-1, 3 M11-22. Distinguishing between Common Stock and Additional Paid-in Capital
Following is the stockholders' equity section from the **Cisco Systems, Inc.**, balance sheet (in millions, except par value).

Cisco Systems
NASDAQ :: CSCO

Shareholders' equity	July 25, 2020
Preferred stock, no par value: 5 shares authorized; none issued and outstanding	$ —
Common stock and additional paid-in capital, $0.001 par value: 20,000 shares authorized; 4,237 shares issued and outstanding at July 25, 2020	41,202
Accumulated deficit	(2,763)
Accumulated other comprehensive loss	(519)
Total equity	$37,920

a. For the $41,202 million reported as "common stock and additional paid-in capital," what portion is common stock, and what portion is additional paid-in capital? Explain.
b. The company reported $11.2 billion in net income and $273 million in other comprehensive income for the fiscal year ended July 25, 2020. In what shareholders' equity accounts are these amounts accumulated?

LO11-2 M11-23. Identifying and Analyzing Financial Statement Effects of Stock Issuance and Repurchase (FSET)
On January 1, Bartov Company issues 3,000 shares of $100 par value preferred stock at $250 cash per share. On March 1, the company repurchases 3,000 shares of previously issued $1 par value common stock at $78 cash per share.
Using the financial statement effects template, illustrate the effects of these two transactions.

LO11-1 M11-24. Analyzing and Identifying Financial Statement Effects of Stock Issuance and Repurchase
Using the information from M11-23, answer the following.

a. Prepare the journal entries for the two transactions.
b. Post the journal entries to the related T-accounts.

LO11-4 M11-25. Assessing the Financial Statement Effects of a Stock Split
In its 2020 10-K, **Tesla, Inc.**, included the following information:

Tesla, Inc.
NYSE :: TSLA

> On August 10, 2020, our Board of Directors declared a five-for-one split of the Company's common stock effected in the form of a stock dividend (the "Stock Split"). Each stockholder of record on August 21, 2020 received a dividend of four additional shares of common stock for each then-held share, distributed after close of trading on August 28, 2020. All share and per share amounts presented herein have been retroactively adjusted to reflect the impact of the Stock Split.

Tesla effected this stock split as a large stock dividend. What changes has Tesla made to its balance sheet as a result of this action?

LO11-4 M11-26. Computing Basic and Diluted Earnings per Share
Zeller Corporation began the year with 168,000 shares of common stock and 22,000 shares of convertible preferred stock outstanding. On March 1 an additional 14,000 shares of common stock

were issued. On August 1, another 22,000 shares of common stock were issued. On November 1, 8,400 shares of common stock were acquired for the treasury. The preferred stock has a $2 per-share dividend rate, and each share may be converted into one share of common stock. Zeller Corporation's net income for the year is $701,000.

a. Compute basic earnings per share for the year.
b. Compute diluted earnings per share for the year.
c. If the preferred stock were not convertible, Zeller Corporation would have a simple capital structure. How would this change Zeller's earnings per share presentation?

M11-27. Assessing Common Stock and Treasury Stock Balances   **LO11-1, 3, 4**

Following is the stockholders' equity section from the **Toyota Motor Corporation**'s balance sheet for the 2020 fiscal year, which ended on March 31, 2020.

Toyota Motor Corporation Shareholders' Equity (Millions of Yen)	March 31, 2020
Common stock, no par value: authorized 10,000,000,000 shares in 2019 and 2020; issued: 3,262,997,492 shares at March 31, 2020	¥ 397,050
Additional paid-in capital	489,334
Retained earnings	23,427,613
Accumulated other comprehensive income (loss)	(1,166,273)
Treasury stock, at cost: 496,844,960 shares at March 31, 2020	(3,087,106)
Total Toyota Motor Corporation shareholders' equity	¥20,060,618

Toyota Motor Corporation (ADR) NYSE :: TM

a. Toyota has repurchased 496,844,960 shares that comprise its March 31, 2020, treasury stock account. Compute the number of outstanding shares as of March 31, 2020.
b. Assume that all of this treasury stock had been acquired in one purchase on July 1, 2019. What would have been the effect on the denominator of the basic EPS calculation?
c. The company reported ¥(916,650) in accumulated other comprehensive income (loss) and ¥21,987,515 in retained earnings on March 31, 2019. Given this information, what would the company report as other comprehensive income (loss) for the fiscal year ended March 31, 2020?

M11-28. Identifying and Analyzing Financial Statement Effects of Cash Dividends (FSET)   **LO11-2**

Freid Corp. has outstanding 9,000 shares of $50 par value, 6% preferred stock, and 60,000 shares of $1 par value common stock. The company has $492,000 of retained earnings. At year-end, the company declares and pays the regular $3 per share cash dividend on preferred stock and a $2.20 per share cash dividend on common stock.

Using the financial statement effects template, illustrate the effects of these two dividend payments.

M11-29. Identifying and Analyzing Financial Statement Effects of Cash Dividends   **LO11-2**

Using the information from M11-28, answer the following.

a. Prepare the journal entries for the two dividend payments.
b. Post the journal entries to the related T-accounts.

M11-30. Analyzing and Identifying Financial Statement Effects of Stock Dividends (FSET)   **LO11-2**

Dutta Corp. has outstanding 85,000 shares of $5 par value common stock. At year-end, the company declares and issues a 4% common stock dividend when the market price of the stock is $21 per share.

Using the financial statement effects template, illustrate the effects of this dividend declaration and payment.

M11-31. Analyzing and Identifying Financial Statement Effects of Stock Dividends   **LO11-2**

Using the information from M11-30, answer the following.

a. Prepare the journal entries for the stock dividend declaration and payment.
b. Post the journal entries to the related T-accounts.

M11-32. Analyzing, Identifying, and Explaining the Effects of a Stock Split   **LO11-2**

On September 1, Weiss Company has 225,000 shares of $15 par value ($165 market value) common stock that are issued and outstanding. Its balance sheet on that date shows the following account balances relating to the common stock.

Common stock	$3,375,000
Paid-in capital in excess of par value	2,025,000

On September 2, Weiss splits its stock 3-for-2 and reduces the par value to $10 per share.

a. How many shares of common stock are issued and outstanding immediately after the stock split?
b. What is the dollar balance of the common stock account immediately after the stock split?
c. What is the likely reason that Weiss Company split its stock?

LO11-2 M11-33. Distributing Cash Dividends to Preferred and Common Shareholders

Dechow Company has outstanding 24,000 shares of $50 par value, 6% cumulative preferred stock, and 96,000 shares of $10 par value common stock. The company declares and pays cash dividends amounting to $192,000.

a. If no arrearage on the preferred stock exists, how much in total dividends, and in dividends per share, is paid to each class of stock?
b. If one year's dividend arrearage on the preferred stock exists, how much in total dividends, and in dividends per share, is paid to each class of stock?

LO11-2 M11-34. Analyzing and Preparing a Retained Earnings Reconciliation

Use the following data to prepare the 2022 retained earnings reconciliation for Maffett Company.

Total retained earnings, December 31, 2021	$555,000
Stock dividends declared and paid in 2022	45,000
Cash dividends declared and paid in 2022.	56,000
Net income for 2022	150,000

LO11-2 M11-35. Accounting for Large Stock Dividend and Stock Split (FSET)

Watts Corporation has 32,000 shares of $10 par value common stock outstanding and retained earnings of $656,000. The company declares a 100% stock dividend. The market price at the declaration is $17 per share.

a. Using the financial statement effects template, illustrate the effects of the stock dividend.
b. Assume that the company splits its stock two shares for one share and reduces the par value from $10 to $5 rather than declaring a 100% stock dividend. How does the accounting for the stock split differ from the accounting for the 100% stock dividend?

LO11-2 M11-36. Accounting for Large Stock Dividend and Stock Split

Using the information from M11-35, prepare the general journal entry for the stock dividend in part *a* and stock split in part *b*.

LO11-4 M11-37. Computing Basic and Diluted Earnings per Share

During the year, Park Corporation had 75,000 shares of $10 par value common stock and 15,000 shares of 8%, $50 par value convertible preferred stock outstanding. Each share of preferred stock may be converted into three shares of common stock. Park Corporation's net income was $702,000 for the year.

a. Compute the basic earnings per share for the year.
b. Compute the diluted earnings per share for the year.

LO11-4 M11-38. Computing Earnings per Share

Kingery Corporation began the calendar (and fiscal) year with a simple structure consisting of 47,500 shares of common stock outstanding. On May 1, 12,500 additional shares were issued, and another 2,000 shares were issued on September 1. The company had a net income for the year of $300,000.

a. Compute the earnings per share of common stock.
b. Assume that the company also had 7,500 shares of 6%, $50 par value cumulative preferred stock outstanding throughout the year. Compute the basic earnings per share of common stock.

LO11-4 M11-39. Defining and Computing Earnings per Share

Siemens AG reports the following basic and diluted earnings per share in its 2020 annual report.

(shares in thousands; earnings per share in €)	Year Ended September 30 2020
Income from continuing operations attributable to shareholders of Siemens AG	€ 3,979
Less: Dilutive effect from share-based payment resulting from Siemens Healthineers	3
Income from continuing operations attributable to shareholders of Siemens AG to determine dilutive earnings per share	3,976
Weighted average shares outstanding—basic	806,335
Effect of dilutive share-based payment	11,029
Effective of dilutive warrants	—
Weighted average shares outstanding—diluted	817,364
Basic earnings per share (from continuing operations)	€ 4.93
Diluted earnings per share (from continuing operations)	€ 4.86

a. Describe the accounting definitions for basic and diluted earnings per share.
b. Identify the Siemens numbers that make up both EPS computations.
c. What calculation limits the reported value of diluted EPS?

M11-40.[A] **Analyzing Stock Option Expense for Income (FSET)**   LO11-5

Merck & Co., Inc., reported net income attributable to Merck & Co., Inc., of $7,067 million for the 2020 fiscal year. Its 2020 10-K report contained the following information regarding its stock options.

Merck & Co.
NYSE :: MRK

> Employee stock options are granted to purchase shares of Company stock at the fair market value at the time of grant. These awards generally vest one-third each year over a three-year period, with a contractual term of 7–10 years ... The weighted average exercise price of options granted in 2020 was $77.67 per option ... The weighted average fair value of options granted in 2020 was $9.93 per option.

a. Merck granted 3,564 options to employees in 2020. Using the financial statement effects template, show how the stock option grants would be reported in 2020. (Assume all grants took place on January 1, 2020.)
b. How does the granting of stock options affect EPS?
c. Merck employees exercised 1,685,000 options in 2020, paying a total of $89 million in cash to the company. Using the financial statement effects template, show how these option exercises would be reported in 2020.
d. How does the exercise of stock options affect EPS?

M11-41.[A] **Analyzing Stock Option Expense for Income**   LO11-5
Using the information from M11-40, answer the following.

a. Prepare the journal entry to show how stock option grants would be recorded in 2020.
b. Using a summary journal entry, show how the option exercises described in part c would be recorded in 2020.

M11-42. Examining the Effect of Stock Transactions   LO11-1, 2, 4
Year 1: Noreen Company issues 20,000 shares of its no-par common stock for $30/share in cash.
Year 2: Noreen Company buys 2,000 shares of its no-par common stock for $28/share in cash.
Year 3: Noreen Company declares but has not yet paid a dividend on its no-par common stock of $2 per share. The company's basic earnings per share were $10 in the third year.
   Indicate the effect (increase, decrease, no effect) of each of these stock decisions for each year on the items listed.

Year	Total Assets	Total Liabilities	Total Stockholders' Equity	EPS	Operating Income
1					
2					
3					

LO11-1, 2, 3, 4 **M11-43. Reporting Stockholders' Equity**

Bonner Company began business this year and immediately sold 500,000 common shares for $13,500,000 cash and paid $750,000 in common dividends. At midyear, the firm bought back some of its own shares. The company reports the following additional information at year-end:

Net income...	$3,750,000
Unrealized gain on available-for-sale debt securities..............	$ 66,000
Common stock, at par...................................	$5,000,000
Retained earnings beginning of year........................	$ 0
Common shares authorized...............................	750,000
Common shares outstanding at year's end....................	425,000

a. What was the average sales price of a common share when issued?
b. What is the par value of the common shares?
c. How much is in the Additional paid-in capital account at the end of the year?
d. How much is accumulated other comprehensive income (loss) at the end of the year?
e. Determine the retained earnings amount at the end of the year.
f. How many shares of stock are in the treasury at the end of the year?
g. Compute BEPS.

LO11-4 **M11-44. Analyzing Earnings Per Share Effects of Convertible Securities**

JetBlue Airways Corporation reports the following data in its 2019 10-K. The data relate to the corporation's computation of its earnings per share calculations. (Dollar and share data are in millions.)

JetBlue
NASDAQ :: JBLU

	2019
Net income[(1)]	$ 569
Weighted average basic shares...........................	296.6
Effect of dilutive securities...............................	1.8
Weighted average diluted shares..........................	298.4

[(1)] See JetBlue Airways 2019 10-K

REQUIRED

a. What is the objective behind the calculation of diluted EPS?
b. Calculate JetBlue's basic EPS.
c. Calculate JetBlue's diluted EPS.
d. In a previous year, JetBlue stated that it excluded 6.9 million stock options from the computation of diluted EPS. Under what circumstances would this be appropriate?

EXERCISES

LO11-1 **E11-45. Identifying and Analyzing Financial Statement Effects of Stock Transactions (FSET)**

Lipe Company reports the following transactions relating to its stock accounts.

Feb. 20 Issued 12,000 shares of $1 par value common stock at $25 cash per share.
Feb. 21 Issued 18,000 shares of $100 par value, 8% preferred stock at $250 cash per share.
Jun. 30 Purchased 2,400 shares of its own common stock at $15 cash per share.
Sep. 25 Sold 1,200 shares of the treasury stock at $21 cash per share.

Using the financial statement effects template, illustrate the effects of these transactions.

LO11-1 **E11-46. Identifying and Analyzing Financial Statement Effects of Stock Transactions**

Using the information from E11-45, answer the following.

a. Prepare the journal entries for these transactions.
b. Post the journal entries to the related T-accounts.

E11-47. Analyzing and Identifying Financial Statement Effects of Stock Transactions (FSET) — LO11-1

McNichols Corp. reports the following transactions relating to its stock accounts.

- Jan. 15 Issued 40,000 shares of $5 par value common stock at $17 cash per share.
- Jan. 20 Issued 9,000 shares of $50 par value, 8% preferred stock at $78 cash per share.
- Mar. 31 Purchased 4,500 shares of its own common stock at $20 cash per share.
- June 25 Sold 3,000 shares of the treasury stock at $26 cash per share.
- July 15 Sold the remaining 1,500 shares of treasury stock at $19 cash per share.

Using the financial statement effects template, illustrate the effects of these transactions.

E11-48. Analyzing and Identifying Financial Statement Effects of Stock Transactions — LO11-1

Using the information from E11-47, answer the following.

a. Prepare the journal entries for these transactions.
b. Post the journal entries to the related T-accounts.

E11-49. Analyzing and Computing Average Issue Price and Treasury Stock Cost — LO11-1, 3, 4

Following is the stockholders' equity section from **The Coca-Cola Company** 2020 balance sheet. (All amounts in millions except par value.)

The Coca-Cola Company
NYSE :: KO

The Coca-Cola Company Shareowners' Equity	December 31, 2020
Common stock—$0.25 par value; authorized—11,200 shares; issued—7,040 shares	$ 1,760
Capital surplus	17,601
Reinvested earnings	66,555
Accumulated other comprehensive income (loss)	(14,601)
Treasury stock, at cost—2,738 shares	(52,016)
Equity attributable to shareowners of The Coca-Cola Company	$19,299

a. Compute the number of shares outstanding.
b. At what average price were the Coca-Cola shares issued?
c. At what average cost were the Coca-Cola treasury stock shares purchased?
d. Coca-Cola reported a balance of $(13,544) million in Accumulated other comprehensive income (loss) on December 31, 2019, and Net income attributable to shareowners of the Coca-Cola Company of $7,747 million for 2020. What is (1) comprehensive income and (2) other comprehensive income in 2020?
e. How should treasury stock be treated in calculating EPS?

E11-50. Analyzing and Distributing Cash Dividends to Preferred and Common Stocks — LO11-2

Moser Company began business on March 1, 2021. At that time, it issued 40,000 shares of $60 par value, 5% cumulative preferred stock, and 200,000 shares of $5 par value common stock. Through the end of 2023, there has been no change in the number of preferred and common shares outstanding.

a. Assume that Moser declared and paid cash dividends of $0 in 2021, $270,000 in 2022, and $400,000 in 2023. Compute the total cash dividends and the dividends per share paid to each class of stock in 2021, 2022, and 2023.
b. Assume that Moser declared and paid cash dividends of $0 in 2021, $120,000 in 2022, and $200,000 in 2023. Compute the total cash dividends and the dividends per share paid to each class of stock in 2021, 2022, and 2023.

E11-51. Computing Basic and Diluted Earnings per Share — LO11-4

Soliman Corporation began the year with 50,000 shares of common stock and 15,000 shares of convertible preferred stock outstanding. On May 1, an additional 18,000 shares of common stock were issued. On July 1, 12,000 shares of common stock were acquired for the treasury. On September 1, the 12,000 treasury shares of common stock were reissued. The preferred stock has a $4 per-share dividend rate, and each share may be converted into two shares of common stock. Soliman Corporation's net income is $540,000 for the year.

a. Compute earnings per share for the year.
b. Compute diluted earnings per share for the year.
c. If the preferred stock were not convertible, Soliman Corporation would have a simple capital structure. How would this change Soliman's earnings per share presentation?

LO11-2, 4 **E11-52. Analyzing and Distributing Cash Dividends to Preferred and Common Stocks**

Potter Company has outstanding 12,000 shares of $50 par value, 6% preferred stock, and 40,000 shares of $5 par value common stock. During its first three years in business, it declared and paid no cash dividends in the first year, $225,000 in the second year, and $36,000 in the third year.

    a. If the preferred stock is cumulative, determine the total amount of cash dividends paid to each class of stock in each of the three years.

    b. If the preferred stock is noncumulative, determine the total amount of cash dividends paid to each class of stock in each of the three years.

    c. How should each type of preferred dividends be treated in calculating EPS?

LO11-1, 3 **E11-53. Analyzing and Computing Issue Price, Treasury Stock Cost, Shares Outstanding, and Net Income**

The following is the stockholders' equity section from **Chipotle Mexican Grill, Inc.**'s balance sheet (in thousands, except per share data).

Chipotle Mexican Grill
NYSE :: CMG

Shareholders' Equity	December 31, 2020
Preferred stock, $0.01 par value, 600,000 shares authorized, no shares issued as of December 31, 2020	$ —
Common stock, $0.01 par value, 230,000 shares authorized, and 36,704 shares issued as of December 31, 2020	367
Additional paid-in capital	1,549,909
Treasury stock, at cost, 8,703 common shares at December 31, 2020	(2,802,075)
Accumulated other comprehensive income (loss)	(4,229)
Retained earnings	3,276,163
Total shareholders' equity	$2,020,135

    a. Show the computation to derive the $367 thousand for common stock.

    b. At what average price has Chipotle issued its common stock?

    c. How many shares of Chipotle common stock are outstanding as of December 31, 2020?

    d. At what average cost has Chipotle repurchased its treasury stock as of December 31, 2020?

    e. Give three reasons why a company such as Chipotle would want to repurchase $2,802 million of its common stock.

    f. Chipotle reported a foreign currency translation adjustment, net of tax, of $1,134 thousand and comprehensive income of $356,900 thousand for 2020. What did Chipotle report as net income for the year?

LO11-2 **E11-54. Analyzing and Distributing Cash Dividends to Preferred and Common Stocks**

Skinner Company began business on June 30. At that time, it issued 28,000 shares of $50 par value, 6% cumulative preferred stock, and 100,000 shares of $10 par value common stock. Through the end of Year 3, there has been no change in the number of preferred and common shares outstanding.

    a. Assume that Skinner declared and paid cash dividends of $96,000 in Year 1, $0 in Year 2, and $560,000 in Year 3. Compute the total cash dividends and the dividends per share paid to each class of stock in Year 1, Year 2, and Year 3.

    b. Assume that Skinner declared and paid cash dividends of $0 in Year 1, $168,000 in Year 2, and $239,000 in Year 3. Compute the total cash dividends and the dividends per share paid to each class of stock in Year 1, Year 2, and Year 3.

LO11-2 **E11-55. Analyzing and Identifying Financial Statement Effects of Dividends (FSET)**

Chaney Company has outstanding 20,000 shares of $10 par value common stock. It also has $325,000 of retained earnings. Near the current year-end, the company declares and pays a cash dividend of $1.90 per share and declares and issues a 4% stock dividend. The market price of the stock at the declaration date is $25 per share.

    Using the financial statement effects template, illustrate the effects of these two separate dividends.

LO11-2 **E11-56. Analyzing and Identifying Financial Statement Effects of Dividends**

Using the information from E11-55, answer the following.

    a. Prepare the journal entries for these two separate dividend transactions.

    b. Post the journal entries to the related T-accounts.

E11-57. Identifying and Analyzing Financial Statement Effects of Dividends (FSET) LO11-2
The stockholders' equity of Palepu Company at December 31, 2021, appears below.

Common stock, $10 par value, 300,000 shares authorized; 120,000 shares issued and outstanding	$1,200,000
Paid-in capital in excess of par value	720,000
Retained earnings	450,000

During 2022, the following transactions occurred:

May 12   Declared and issued a 7% stock dividend; the common stock market value was $18 per share.
Dec. 31   Declared and paid a cash dividend of 75 cents per share.

Using the financial statement effects template, illustrate the effects of these transactions.

E11-58. Identifying and Analyzing Financial Statement Effects of Dividends LO11-2
Using the information from E11-57, answer the following.

a. Prepare the journal entries for these transactions.
b. Post the journal entries to the related T-accounts.
c. Prepare a retained earnings reconciliation for 2022 assuming that the company reports 2022 net income of $425,000.

E11-59. Analyzing and Identifying Financial Statement Effects of Dividends (FSET) LO11-2
The stockholders' equity of Kinney Company at December 31, 2021, is shown below:

5% preferred stock, $100 par value, 10,000 shares authorized; 3,500 shares issued and outstanding	$ 350,000
Common stock, $5 par value, 200,000 shares authorized; 45,000 shares issued and outstanding	225,000
Paid-in capital in excess of par value—preferred stock	36,000
Paid-in capital in excess of par value—common stock	270,000
Retained earnings	590,400
Total stockholders' equity	$1,471,400

The following transactions, among others, occurred during 2022.

Apr. 1   Declared and issued a 100% stock dividend on all outstanding shares of common stock. The market value of the stock was $11 per share.
Dec. 7   Declared and issued a 3% stock dividend on all outstanding shares of common stock. The market value of the stock was $14 per share.
Dec. 20   Declared and paid (1) the annual cash dividend on the preferred stock and (2) a cash dividend of 80 cents per common share.

Using the financial statement effects template, illustrate the effects of these transactions.

E11-60. Analyzing and Identifying Financial Statement Effects of Dividends LO11-2
Using the information from E11-59, answer the following.

a. Prepare the journal entries for these transactions.
b. Post the journal entries to the related T-accounts.
c. Prepare a 2022 retained earnings reconciliation assuming that the company reports 2022 net income of $227,700.

E11-61. Analyzing, Identifying, and Explaining the Effects of a Stock Split LO11-2, 4
On March 1 of the current year, Xie Company has 360,000 shares of $20 par value common stock that are issued and outstanding. Its balance sheet shows the following account balances relating to common stock.

Common stock	$7,200,000
Paid-in capital in excess of par value	3,060,000

On March 2, Xie Company splits its common stock 2-for-1 and reduces the par value to $10 per share.

a. How many shares of common stock are issued and outstanding immediately after the stock split?
b. What is the dollar balance in its common stock account immediately after the stock split?
c. What is the dollar balance in its paid-in capital in excess of par value account immediately after the stock split?
d. What is the effect of a stock split on the calculation of EPS?

LO11-2, 3 **E11-62. Analyzing and Computing Dividends, Effect of Options Exercises, and Comprehensive Income**

Following is the stockholders' equity section of the **Intuit Inc.** balance sheet (dollars in millions, except par value; shares in thousands). Changes in the company's outstanding shares are due to (1) treasury share purchases by the company and (2) issues of treasury shares for employee stock options.

Intuit Inc.
NASDAQ :: INTU

Stockholders' Equity ($ millions)	July 31, 2020	July 31, 2019
Preferred stock, $0.01 par value Authorized—1,345 shares total; 145 shares designated Series A; 250 shares designated Series B Junior Participating Issued and outstanding—none	$ —	$ —
Common stock, $0.01 par value Authorized—750,000 shares Outstanding—261,740 shares at July 31, 2020, and 260,180 shares at July 31, 2019	3	3
Additional paid-in capital	6,179	5,772
Treasury stock, at cost	(11,929)	(11,611)
Accumulated other comprehensive loss	(32)	(36)
Retained earnings	10,885	9,621
Total stockholders' equity	$ 5,106	$ 3,749

a. In the fiscal year ended July 31, 2020, Intuit reported net income of $1,826 million. How much did Intuit pay in dividends to its common shareholders?
b. In the fiscal year ended January 31, 2020, Intuit repurchased 1,176 thousand of its common shares. How many shares were issued to employees under stock option plans?
c. Intuit's issuance of shares for stock option plans decreased the Additional paid-in capital balance by $31 million. Was the (average) option exercise price greater or less than the (average) amount Intuit paid to acquire the treasury shares that were reissued?
d. What did Intuit report as comprehensive income in 2020?

LO11-1, 3 **E11-63. Analyzing and Computing Issue Price, Treasury Stock Cost, and Shares Outstanding**

Following is the stockholders' equity section of the **Merck & Co., Inc.**, balance sheet.

Merck & Co.
NYSE :: MRK

Merck & Co., Inc., Stockholders' Equity ($ millions)	Dec. 31, 2020	Dec. 31, 2019
Common stock, $0.50 par value Authorized—6,500,000,000 shares Issued—3,577,103,522 shares in 2020 and 2019	$ 1,788	$ 1,788
Other paid-in capital	39,588	39,660
Retained earnings	47,362	46,602
Accumulated other comprehensive loss	(6,634)	(6,193)
	82,104	81,857
Less treasury stock, at cost: 1,046,877,695 shares in 2020 and 1,038,087,496 shares in 2019	56,787	55,950
Total Merck & Co., Inc., stockholders' equity	$25,317	$25,907

a. Explain the derivation of the $1,788 million in the common stock account.
b. Using December 31, 2020, balances, at what average issue price were the Merck common shares issued?
c. At what average cost was the Merck treasury stock as of December 31, 2020?
d. How many common shares are outstanding as of December 31, 2020?
e. Did Merck report a net other comprehensive income or a net other comprehensive loss in 2020? Compute the amount.

E11-64.[A] **Analyzing the Accounting and Effects of Convertible Securities, Stock Options, and Restricted Stock**

A portion of Note 2: Earnings per Share from **Facebook, Inc.'s** 10-K is as follows:

LO11-5

Facebook, Inc.
NASDAQ :: FB

	2020 Class A Stock	2019 Class A Stock
Basic EPS:		
Numerator		
Net income attributable to common shareholders............	$24,607	$15,569
Denominator		
Weighted ave. shares outstanding........................	2,407	2,404
Basic EPS..	$ 10.22	$ 6.48
Diluted EPS:		
Numerator		
Net income attributable to common shareholders............	$24,607	$15,569
Reallocation of net income as a result of conversion of Class B to Class A common stock......................	4,539	2,916
Net income for diluted EPS.............................	$29,146	$18,485
Denominator		
Number of shares used for basic EPS computation..........	2,407	2,404
Conversion of Class B to Class A common stock............	444	450
Weighted average effect of dilutive RSUs and employee stock options.....................................	37	22
Number of shares used for diluted EPS computation.........	2,888	2,876
Diluted EPS...	$ 10.09	$ 6.43

a. Explain why employee stock options and restricted stock units are adjustments to the denominator for diluted EPS.

b. Facebook computes EPS separately for its Class B shares (not shown here) and states that the computation of the diluted EPS for its Class A stock assumes the conversion of its Class B common stock to Class A common stock. Based on the table above, what were the effects of the assumed conversion?

E11-65. **Interpreting Information in the Statement of Shareholders' Equity**

The 2020 statement of stockholders' equity for **Walt Disney Co.** is presented below. (Disney includes both par value and additional paid-in capital under the heading "Common Stock." Noncontrolling interests have been excluded for simplicity, so the rows may not add up to the total shown. All amounts in millions.)

LO11-1, 2, 3

Walt Disney Co.
NYSE :: DIS

Equity Attributable to Disney

	Shares	Common Stock	Retained Earnings	Accumulated Other Comprehensive Income (Loss)	Treasury Stock	Total Disney Equity
Balance at September 28, 2019....	1,802	$53,907	$42,494	$ (6,617)	$ (907)	$88,877
Comprehensive income (loss) ...	—	—	(2,864)	(1,705)	—	(4,569)
Equity compensation activity.....	8	590	—	—	—	590
Dividends	—	9	(1,596)	—	—	(1,587)
Contributions..................	—	—	—	—	—	—
Adoption of new lease accounting guidance..........	—	—	197	—	—	197
Distributions and other	—	(9)	84	—	—	75
Balance at October 3, 2020	1,810	$54,497	$38,315	$ (8,322)	$ (907)	$83,583

REQUIRED

a. Did Disney issue any additional common shares in fiscal year 2020 (ending on September 29, 2020)?

b. What was Disney's total comprehensive income in fiscal year 2020?

c. According to its statement of cash flows, Disney paid common dividends of $1,587 million in fiscal year 2020. What might be a possible explanation for the fact that dividends reduced retained earnings by $1,596 million?
d. Compute Disney's return on common equity in 2020.

PROBLEMS

LO11-1, 2, 4 **P11-66.** **Analyzing and Identifying Financial Statement Effects of Stock Transactions (FSET)**
The stockholders' equity section of Gupta Company at December 31, 2021, follows.

8% preferred stock, $25 par value, 50,000 shares authorized; 10,200 shares issued and outstanding	$255,000
Common stock, $10 par value, 200,000 shares authorized; 75,000 shares issued and outstanding	750,000
Paid-in capital in excess of par value—preferred stock	102,000
Paid-in capital in excess of par value—common stock	300,000
Retained earnings	405,000

During 2022, the following transactions occurred:

- Jan. 10 Issued 42,000 shares of common stock for $17 cash per share.
- Jan. 23 Purchased 12,000 shares of common stock for the treasury at $19 cash per share.
- Mar. 14 Sold one-half of the treasury shares acquired January 23 for $21 cash per share.
- July 15 Issued 4,800 shares of preferred stock for 192,000 cash.
- Nov. 15 Sold 1,500 of the treasury shares acquired January 23 for $24 cash per share.

REQUIRED

a. Using the financial statement effects template, illustrate the effects of each transaction.
b. Indicate the impact of each transaction on the calculation of basic EPS.
c. Prepare the December 31, 2022, stockholders' equity section of the balance sheet assuming the company reports 2022 net income of $88,500.

LO11-1, 2 **P11-67.** **Analyzing and Identifying Financial Statement Effects of Stock Transactions**
Using the information from P11-66, answer the following.

a. Prepare the journal entries for these transactions.
b. Post the journal entries to the related T-accounts.

LO11-1, 2, 3, 4 **P11-68.** **Analyzing and Identifying Financial Statement Effects of Stock Transactions (FSET)**
The stockholders' equity of Sougiannis Company at December 31 of the prior year follows.

7% preferred stock, $100 par value, 30,000 shares authorized; 7,500 shares issued and outstanding	$ 750,000
Common stock, $15 par value, 150,000 shares authorized; 60,000 shares issued and outstanding	900,000
Paid-in capital in excess of par value—preferred stock	36,000
Paid-in capital in excess of par value—common stock	540,000
Retained earnings	487,500
Total stockholders' equity	$2,713,500

The following transactions, among others, occurred during the current year.

- Jan. 12 Announced a 3-for-1 common stock split, reducing the par value of the common stock to $5 per share. The authorized shares were increased to 450,000 shares.
- Sept. 1 Acquired 15,000 shares of common stock for the treasury at $10 cash per share.
- Oct. 12 Sold 2,250 treasury shares acquired September 1 at $12 cash per share.
- Nov. 21 Issued 7,500 shares of common stock at $11 cash per share.
- Dec. 28 Sold 1,800 treasury shares acquired September 1 at $9 cash per share.

REQUIRED
a. Using the financial statement effects template, illustrate the effects of each transaction.
b. Indicate the impact of each transaction on the calculation of basic EPS.
c. Prepare the December 31 stockholders' equity section of the balance sheet assuming that the company reports net income of $124,500.
d. Compute return on common equity for the year.

P11-69. Analyzing and Identifying Financial Statement Effects of Stock Transactions   **LO11-1, 2**
Using the information from P11-68, answer the following.

a. Prepare the journal entries for these transactions.
b. Post the journal entries to the related T-accounts.

P11-70. Identifying and Analyzing Financial Statement Effects of Stock Transactions (FSET)   **LO11-1, 2, 4**
The stockholders' equity of Verrecchia Company at December 31 of the prior year follows.

Common stock, $5 par value, 280,000 shares authorized; 120,000 shares issued and outstanding	$600,000
Paid-in capital in excess of par value	480,000
Retained earnings	276,800

During the current year, the following transactions occurred.

Jan. 5   Issued 8,000 shares of common stock for $12 cash per share.
Jan. 18   Purchased 3,200 shares of common stock for the treasury at $14 cash per share.
Mar. 12   Sold one-fourth of the treasury shares acquired January 18 for $17 cash per share.
July 17   Sold 400 shares of the remaining treasury stock for $13 cash per share.
Oct. 1   Issued 4,000 shares of 8%, $25 par value preferred stock for $35 cash per share. This is the first issuance of preferred shares from 40,000 authorized shares.

REQUIRED
a. Using the financial statement effects template, illustrate the effects of each transaction.
b. Prepare the December 31 of the current year stockholders' equity section of the balance sheet assuming that the company reports net income of $58,000 for the year.
c. How will each transaction affect the calculation of basic EPS?

P11-71. Identifying and Analyzing Financial Statement Effects of Stock Transactions   **LO11-1, 2**
Using the information from P11-70, answer the following.

a. Prepare the journal entries for these transactions.
b. Post the journal entries to the related T-accounts.

P11-72. Identifying and Analyzing Financial Statement Effects of Stock Transactions (FSET)   **LO11-1, 2**
Following is the stockholders' equity of Dennis Corporation at December 31 of the previous year.

8% preferred stock, $50 par value, 8,000 shares authorized; 5,600 shares issued and outstanding	$ 280,000
Common stock, $20 par value, 40,000 shares authorized; 20,000 shares issued and outstanding	400,000
Paid-in capital in excess of par value—preferred stock	56,000
Paid-in capital in excess of par value—common stock	308,000
Retained earnings	190,400
Total stockholders' equity	$1,234,400

The following transactions, among others, occurred during the current year.

Jan. 15   Issued 800 shares of preferred stock for $62 cash per share.
Jan. 20   Issued 3,200 shares of common stock at $36 cash per share.
May 18   Announced a 2-for-1 common stock split, reducing the par value of the common stock to $10 per share. The authorization was increased to 80,000 shares.
June 1   Issued 1,600 shares of common stock for 48,000 cash.

Sept. 1 Purchased 2,000 shares of common stock for the treasury at $18 cash per share.
Oct. 12 Sold 720 treasury shares at $21 cash per share.
Dec. 22 Issued 400 shares of preferred stock for $59 cash per share.

REQUIRED

Using the financial statement effects template, illustrate the effects of each transaction.

LO11-1, 2 P11-73. Identifying and Analyzing Financial Statement Effects of Stock Transactions

Using the information from P11-72, answer the following.

a. Prepare the journal entries for these transactions.
b. Post the journal entries to the related T-accounts.

LO11-1, 3, 4, 5 P11-74.^A Analyzing and Interpreting Stockholders' Equity and EPS (FSET)

Following is the stockholders' equity section of the balance sheet for **The Procter & Gamble Company** along with selected earnings and dividend data. For simplicity, balances for noncontrolling interests have been left out of income and shareholders' equity information.

Procter & Gamble
NYSE :: PG

($ millions except per share amounts)	2020	2019
Net earnings attributable to Procter & Gamble shareholders	$13,027	$ 3,897
Common dividends	7,551	7,256
Preferred dividends	263	263
Basic net earnings per common share	$ 5.13	$ 1.45
Diluted net earnings per common share	$ 4.96	$ 1.43
Shareholders' equity:		
Convertible class A preferred stock, stated value $1 per share (600 shares authorized)	$ 897	$ 928
Nonvoting class B preferred stock, stated value $1 per share (200 shares authorized)	—	—
Common stock, stated value $1 per share (10,000 shares authorized) shares issued: 2020—4,009.2; 2019—4,009.2	4,009	4,009
Additional paid-in capital	64,194	63,827
Reserve for ESOP debt retirement	(1,080)	(1,146)
Accumulated other comprehensive income (loss)	(16,165)	(14,936)
Treasury stock, at cost (shares held: 2020—1,529.5, 2019—1,504.5)	(105,573)	(100,406)
Retained earnings	100,239	94,918
Shareholders' equity attributable to Procter & Gamble shareholders	$46,521	$47,194

a. Compute the number of shares outstanding at the end of each fiscal year. Estimate the average number of shares outstanding during 2020. How do these two computations compare?
b. Calculate the average cost per share of the shares held as treasury stock at the end of each fiscal year.
c. In 2020, preferred shareholders elected to convert 3.74 million shares of preferred stock ($31 million book value) into common stock. Rather than issue new shares, the company granted to the preferred shareholders 3.74 million common shares held in treasury stock with a total cost of $26 million. Prepare the entry to illustrate how this transaction would have been recorded using the financial statement effects template.
d. P&G has no convertible debt outstanding. What could explain the reported diluted EPS?
e. Calculate P&G's return on common equity (ROCE) for fiscal 2020.

LO11-1 P11-75. Analyzing and Interpreting Stockholders' Equity

Using the information from P11-74, prepare a journal entry to illustrate how the transaction in part c would be recorded.

LO11-3, 4, 5 P11-76.^A Analyzing and Interpreting Equity Accounts and Earnings per Share (FSET)

Alphabet Inc.
NASDAQ :: GOOGL

The 2019 and 2020 statements of stockholders' equity for **Alphabet Inc.** are presented below along with portions on Notes 11 and 13 relating to stockholders' equity and equity-based compensation.

ALPHABET INC.
Consolidated Statements of Stockholders' Equity
(In millions, except per share amounts, which are reflected in thousands)

	Class A and Class B Common Stock, Class C Capital Stock and Paid-in Capital Shares	Amount	Accumulated Other Comprehensive Income (Loss)	Retained Earnings	Total Stock- holders' Equity
Balance as of December 31, 2018	695,556	$45,049	$(2,306)	$134,885	$177,628
Cumulative effect of accounting change	0	0	(30)	(4)	(34)
Common and capital stock issued	8,120	202	0	0	202
Stock-based compensation expense	0	10,890	0	0	10,890
Tax withholding related to vesting of restricted stock units and other	0	(4,455)	0	0	(4,455)
Repurchases of capital stock	(15,341)	(1,294)	0	(17,102)	(18,396)
Sale of interest in consolidated entities	0	160	0	0	160
Net income	0	0	0	34,343	34,343
Other comprehensive income (loss)	0	0	1,104	0	1,104
Balance as of December 31, 2019	688,335	50,552	(1,232)	152,122	201,442
Common and capital stock issued	8,398	168	0	0	168
Stock-based compensation expense	0	13,123	0	0	13,123
Tax withholding related to vesting of restricted stock units and other	0	(5,969)	0	0	(5,969)
Repurchases of capital stock	(21,511)	(2,159)	0	(28,990)	(31,149)
Sale of interest in consolidated entities	0	2,795	0	0	2,795
Net income	0	0	0	40,269	40,269
Other comprehensive income (loss)	0	0	1,865	0	1,865
Balance as of December 31, 2020	675,222	$58,510	$ 633	$163,401	$222,544

Note 11: Stockholders' Equity

Convertible Preferred Stock

Our board of directors has authorized 100 million shares of convertible preferred stock, $0.001 par value, issuable in series. As of December 31, 2019 and 2020, no shares were issued or outstanding.

Class A and Class B Common Stock and Class C Capital Stock

Our board of directors has authorized three classes of stock, Class A and Class B common stock, and Class C capital stock. The rights of the holders of each class of our common and capital stock are identical, except with respect to voting. Each share of Class A common stock is entitled to one vote per share. Each share of Class B common stock is entitled to 10 votes per share. Class C capital stock has no voting rights, except as required by applicable law. Shares of Class B common stock may be converted at any time at the option of the stockholder and automatically convert upon sale or transfer to Class A common stock.

Share Repurchases

In July 2020, the Board of Directors of Alphabet authorized the company to repurchase up to an additional $28.0 billion of its Class C capital stock. The repurchases are being executed from time to time, subject to general business and market conditions and other investment opportunities, through open market purchases or privately negotiated transactions, including through Rule 10b5-1 plans. The repurchase program does not have an expiration date.

During the years ended December 31, 2019 and 2020, we repurchased and subsequently retired 15.3 million and 21.5 million shares of Alphabet Class C capital stock for an aggregate amount of $18.4 billion and $31.1 billion, respectively.

Note 13: Compensation Plans
Stock Plans

Our stock plans include the Alphabet 2012 Stock Plan and Other Bet stock-based plans. Under our stock plans, RSUs and other types of awards may be granted. An RSU award is an agreement to issue shares of our publicly traded stock at the time the award vests. RSUs granted to participants under the Alphabet 2012 Stock Plan generally vest over four years contingent upon employment or service with us on the vesting date.

continued

continued from previous page

As of December 31, 2020, there were 38,777,813 shares of stock reserved for future issuance under our Alphabet 2012 Stock Plan.

Stock-Based Compensation

For the years ended December 31, 2018, 2019, and 2020, total stock-based compensation expense was $10.0 billion, $11.7 billion, and $13.4 billion, including amounts associated with awards we expect to settle in Alphabet stock of $9.4 billion, $10.8 billion, and $12.8 billion, respectively.

For the years ended December 31, 2018, 2019, and 2020, we recognized tax benefits on total stock-based compensation expense, which are reflected in the provision for income taxes in the Consolidated Statements of Income, of $1.5 billion, $1.8 billion, and $2.7 billion, respectively.

For the years ended December 31, 2018, 2019, and 2020, tax benefit realized related to awards vested or exercised during the period was $2.1 billion, $2.2 billion, and $3.6 billion, respectively. These amounts do not include the indirect effects of stock-based awards, which primarily relate to the research and development tax credit.

Stock-Based Award Activities

The following table summarizes the activities for our unvested Alphabet RSUs for the year ended December 31, 2020:

	Unvested Restricted Stock Units	
	Number of Shares	Weighted-Average Grant-Date Fair Value
Unvested as of December 31, 2019	19,394,236	$1,055.22
Granted	12,647,562	1,407.97
Vested	(11,643,670)	1,089.31
Forfeited/canceled	(1,109,335)	1,160.01
Unvested as of December 31, 2020	19,288,793	$1,262.13

The weighted-average grant-date fair value of RSUs granted during the years ended December 31, 2018 and 2019 was $1,095.89 and $1,092.36, respectively. Total fair value of RSUs, as of their respective vesting dates, during the years ended December 31, 2018, 2019, and 2020 were $14.1 billion, $15.2 billion, and $17.8 billion, respectively.

As of December 31, 2020, there was $22.8 billion of unrecognized compensation cost related to unvested employee RSUs. The amount is expected to be recognized over a weighted-average period of 2.6 years.

Note 11. Net Income Per Share (in part)

We compute net income per share of Class A and Class B common stock and Class C capital stock using the two-class method. Basic net income per share is computed using the weighted-average number of shares outstanding during the period. Diluted net income per share is computed using the weighted-average number of shares and the effect of potentially dilutive securities outstanding during the period. Potentially dilutive securities consist of restricted stock units and other contingently issuable shares. The dilutive effect of outstanding restricted stock units and other contingently issuable shares is reflected in diluted earnings per share by application of the treasury stock method. The computation of the diluted net income per share of Class A common stock assumes the conversion of Class B common stock, while the diluted net income per share of Class B common stock does not assume the conversion of those shares.

REQUIRED

a. What is the difference between Alphabet's Class A common stock and its Class B common stock? Why do they have two different classes of common stock? In fiscal year 2014, Alphabet created shares of Class C capital stock, which participate in any common dividends but have no voting rights. What might be the purpose of the Class C stock?

b. Alphabet repurchased some of their Class C shares in 2020. Prepare the journal entry to show the repurchase transaction using the financial statement effects template.

c. Using the information in the notes, estimate the stock-based compensation expense for 2021 related to the 2020 grants of restricted stock units. Show the entry using the financial statement effects template.

d. Alphabet states that there is $22.8 billion of unrecognized compensation cost related to unvested employee RSUs. What are these, and why isn't this a liability on the balance sheet for Alphabet?
e. Alphabet reported net income of $40,269 million in 2020 and basic EPS of $59.15 per share. Estimate the weighted average number of shares used to calculate basic EPS.
f. Assume Alphabet has 15.0 million stock options outstanding at the end of 2020. If all outstanding stock options were exercised in 2020, what would be the impact on Alphabet's basic EPS?
g. Alphabet reported diluted EPS of $58.61 in 2020. What are the primary dilutive securities that Alphabet mentions?

P11-77.[A] Analyzing and Interpreting Equity Accounts   LO11-5
Using the information from P11-76, complete the following.

a. Prepare the journal entry for part *b*.
b. Prepare the journal entry for part *c*.

CASES AND PROJECTS

C11-78.[A] Interpreting Disclosure on Convertible Preferred Securities   LO11-5
On September 30, 2019, **Broadcom, Inc.** issued 4 million shares of 8.00% Mandatory Convertible Stock, Series A, $0.001 par value. The issuance generated revenue of approximately $3,679 million. The company disclosed the following in their 10-K:

Broadcom, Inc.
NASDAQ: AVGO

> The holders of Mandatory Convertible Preferred Stock are entitled to receive, when, as and if declared by our Board of Directors, or an authorized committee thereof, out of funds legally available for payment, cumulative dividends at the annual rate of 8.00% of the liquidation preference of $1,000 per share (equivalent to $80 annually per share), payable in cash or, subject to certain limitations, by delivery of shares of our common stock or any combination of cash and shares of our common stock, at our election; provided, however, that any undeclared and unpaid dividends will continue to accumulate.
>
> Subject to limited exceptions, no dividends may be declared or paid on shares of our common stock, unless all accumulated dividends have been paid or set aside for payment on all outstanding shares of our Mandatory Convertible Preferred Stock for all past completed dividend periods. In the event of our voluntary or involuntary liquidation, dissolution or winding-up, no distribution of our assets may be made to holders of our common stock until we have paid to holders of our Mandatory Convertible Preferred Stock a liquidation preference equal to $1,000 per share plus accumulated and unpaid dividends.
>
> On September 30, 2022, unless earlier converted, each outstanding share of Mandatory Convertible Preferred Stock will automatically convert into shares of our common stock at a rate between the then minimum and maximum conversion rates. At any time prior to September 30, 2022, holders may elect to convert each share of Mandatory Convertible Preferred Stock into shares of our common stock at the then minimum conversion rate. . . . As of November 1, 2020, the minimum conversion rate was 3.0567, and the maximum conversion rate was 3.5729.
>
> We recognized $27 million and $29 million of accrued preferred stock dividends, which were presented as temporary equity in our consolidated balance sheets as of November 1, 2020, and November 3, 2019, respectively.

REQUIRED
a. What is meant by the term "mandatory convertible" prior to the words "preferred stock"?
b. What is reflected on Broadcom's balance sheet at December 31, 2019?
c. The fair market value of a preferred share is $1,422 on December 28, 2020, and the fair value on the date of issue was $1,083. What could account for the substantial increase in the value per share?
d. How should preferred stock be treated in an analysis of a company?
e. Discuss the general effects of the conversion feature on current computations of EPS and also of the future conversion on Broadcom's balance sheet.

C11-79. Identifying Corporate Takeover, Stock Ownership, and Managerial Ethics   LO11-1
Ron King, chairperson of the board of directors and chief executive officer of Image, Inc., is pondering a recommendation to make to the firm's board of directors in response to actions taken by Jack Hatcher. Hatcher recently informed King and other board members that he (Hatcher) had purchased

15% of the voting stock of Image at $12 per share and is considering an attempt to take control of the company. His effort to take control would include offering $16 per share to stockholders to induce them to sell shares to him. Hatcher also indicated that he would abandon his takeover plans if the company would buy back his stock at a price 50% over its current market price of $13 per share.

King views the proposed takeover by Hatcher as a hostile maneuver. Hatcher has a reputation of identifying companies that are undervalued (that is, their underlying net assets are worth more than the price of the outstanding stock), buying enough stock to take control of such a company, replacing top management, and, on occasion, breaking up the company (that is, selling off the various divisions to the highest bidder). The process has proven profitable to Hatcher and his financial backers. Stockholders of the companies taken over also benefited because Hatcher paid them attractive prices to buy their stock.

King recognizes that Image is currently undervalued by the stock market but believes that eventually the company will significantly improve its financial performance to the long-run benefit of its stockholders.

REQUIRED

What are the ethical issues that King should consider in arriving at a recommendation to make to the board of directors regarding Hatcher's offer to be "bought out" of his takeover plans?

LO11-1, 2 **C11-80. Understanding Shareholders' Meeting, Managerial Communications, and Financial Interpretations**

The stockholders' equity section of Pillar Corporation's comparative balance sheet at the end of 2021 and 2022 is presented below. It is part of the financial data just reviewed at a stockholders' meeting.

	December 31, 2022	December 31, 2021
Common stock, $10 par value, 600,000 shares authorized; issued at December 31, 2022, 220,000 shares; 2021, 200,000 shares	$2,200,000	$2,000,000
Paid-in capital in excess of par................	3,660,000	3,300,000
Retained earnings (see Note)	2,368,000	2,260,000
Total stockholders' equity	$8,228,000	$7,560,000

Note: Availability of retained earnings for cash dividends is restricted by $1,600,000 due to a planned plant expansion.

The following items were also disclosed at the stockholders' meeting: net income for 2022 was $976,000; a 10% stock dividend was issued December 14, 2022; when the stock dividend was declared, the market value was $28 per share; the market value per share at December 31, 2022, was $26; management plans to borrow $400,000 to help finance a new plant addition, which is expected to cost a total of $1,840,000; and the customary $1.54 per share cash dividend had been revised to $1.40 when declared and issued the last week of December 2022. As part of its investor relations program, during the stockholders' meeting management asked stockholders to write any questions they might have concerning the firm's operations or finances. As assistant controller, you are given the stockholders' questions.

REQUIRED

Prepare brief but reasonably complete answers to the following questions:

a. What did Pillar do with the cash proceeds from the stock dividend issued in December?
b. What was my book value per share at the end of 2021 and 2022?
c. I owned 6,000 shares of Pillar in 2021 and have not sold any shares. How much more or less of the corporation do I own at December 31, 2022, and what happened to the market value of my interest in the company?
d. I heard someone say that stock dividends don't give me anything I didn't already have. Why did you issue one? Are you trying to fool us?
e. Instead of a stock dividend, why didn't you declare a cash dividend and let us buy the new shares that were issued?
f. Why are you cutting back on the dividends I receive?
g. If you have $1,600,000 put aside in retained earnings for the new plant addition, which will cost $1,840,000, why are you borrowing $400,000 instead of just the $240,000 needed?

C11-81. Assessing Stock Buybacks, Corporate Accountability, and Managerial Ethics   LO11-1, 2, 4

Liz Plummer, vice president and general counsel, chairs the Executive Compensation Committee for Sunlight Corporation. Four and one-half years ago, the compensation committee designed a performance bonus plan for top management that was approved by the board of directors. The plan provides an attractive bonus for top management if the firm's earnings per share grows each year over a five-year period. The plan is now in its fifth year; for the past four years, earnings per share has grown each year. Last year, earnings per share was $1.95 (net income was $5,850,000 and the weighted average common shares outstanding was 3,000,000). Sunlight Corporation has no preferred stock and has had 3,000,000 common shares outstanding for several years. Plummer has recently seen an estimate that Sunlight's net income this year will decrease about 5% from last year because of a slight recession in the economy.

Plummer is disturbed by an item on the agenda for the board of directors meeting on June 20 and an accompanying note from Rob Lundy. Lundy is vice president and chief financial officer for Sunlight. Lundy is proposing to the board that Sunlight buy back 450,000 shares of its own common stock on July 1. Lundy's explanation is that the firm's stock is undervalued now and that Sunlight has excess cash available. When the stock subsequently recovers in value, Lundy notes, Sunlight will reissue the shares and generate a nice increase in contributed capital.

Lundy's note to Plummer merely states, "Look forward to your support of my proposal at the board meeting."

REQUIRED

Why is Plummer disturbed by Lundy's proposal and note? What possible ethical problem does Plummer face when Lundy's proposal is up for a vote at the board meeting?

C11-82.[A] **Redeemable Preferred Shares**   LO11-1, 5

Restaurant Brands International, Inc., reports the following in disclosure Note 13 to their financial statements in their 2017 10-K related to redeemable preferred stock.

Restaurant Brands International Inc.
NYSE :: QSR

> **Note 13**
>
> *Redeemable Preferred Shares*
>
> On December 12, 2014, we issued 68,530,939 Class A 9.0% cumulative compounding perpetual voting preferred shares (the "Preferred Shares") to a subsidiary of Berkshire Hathaway, which were outstanding until the Redemption Date (as defined below). A 9.0% annual dividend accrued on the purchase price of $43.775848 per Preferred Share, and was payable quarterly in arrears, when declared and approved by our board of directors. The Preferred Shares were redeemable at our option on and after December 12, 2017. During 2014, we adjusted the carrying value of the Preferred Shares to their redemption price of $48.109657 per Preferred Share (the "redemption price"). The Preferred Shares were classified as temporary equity while outstanding because redemption was not solely within our control, as the Preferred Shares also contained provisions that allowed the holder to redeem the Preferred Shares for cash beginning in December 2024 or upon a change in control.
>
> On December 12, 2017 (the "Redemption Date"), we redeemed all of the issued and outstanding Preferred Shares for aggregate consideration of $3,115.6 million (the "Redemption Consideration"), consisting of (i) $3,297.0 million, which is the redemption price of $48.109657 per Preferred Share multiplied by the number of Preferred Shares outstanding, plus (ii) $54.0 million of accrued and unpaid preferred dividends up to the Redemption Date, minus (iii) an adjustment of $235.4 million, . . . The $235.4 million adjustment, net of $1.6 million of related transaction costs, is reflected as a $233.8 million increase to net income attributable to common shareholders and common shareholder's equity. . . . Upon redemption, the Preferred Shares were deemed canceled, dividends ceased to accrue, and all rights of the holder terminated.

The company's balance sheet, in part, reflected the following:

Restaurant Brands International Inc. and Subsidiaries
Excerpt from Consolidated Balance Sheet
December 31, 2017 and 2016 (millions of USD)
LIABILITIES, REDEEMABLE PREFERRED SHARES AND SHAREHOLDERS' EQUITY

Current liabilities:		
Accounts and drafts payable	$ 412.9	$ 369.8
Other accrued liabilities	838.2	469.3
Gift card liability	214.9	194.4
Advertising fund liabilities	110.8	83.3
Current portion of long-term debt and capital leases	78.2	93.9
Total current liabilities	1,655.0	1,210.7
Term debt, net of current portion	11,800.9	8,410.2
Capital leases, net of current portion	243.8	218.4
Other liabilities, net	1,455.1	784.9
Deferred income taxes, net	1,508.1	1,715.1
Total liabilities	16,662.9	12,339.3
Redeemable preferred shares; no par value; 68,530,939 shares authorized, issued and outstanding at December 31, 2016	—	3,297.0
Shareholders' equity:		
Common shares, no par value; unlimited shares authorized at December 31, 2017, and December 31, 2016; 243,899,476 shares issued and outstanding at December 31, 2017; 234,236,678 shares issued and outstanding at December 31, 2016	2,051.5	1,955.1
Retained earnings	650.6	445.7
Accumulated other comprehensive income (loss)	(475.7)	(698.3)
Total Restaurant Brands International Inc. shareholders' equity	2,226.4	1,702.5
Noncontrolling interests	2,334.2	1,786.1
Total shareholders' equity	4,560.6	3,488.6
Total liabilities, redeemable preferred shares and shareholders' equity	$21,223.5	$19,124.9

a. Where were the redeemable preferred shares listed on the balance sheet before they were redeemed?

b. What was the aggregate sales price of the redeemable preferred shares in 2014?

c. When issued, $250 million of the issue price was allocated to warrants that were issued as part of the transaction in 2014. Later in 2014, the company adjusted the carrying value of the redeemable preferred shares to their redemption price of $3,297 million. What was the increase in the carrying value of the shares? Where would this have been reported, if at all?

d. If you were an analyst of the company, how would you have viewed these shares?

SOLUTIONS TO REVIEW PROBLEMS

Review 11-1

a.

	Balance Sheet							Income Statement		
Transaction	Cash Asset	+ Noncash Assets	= Liabilities	+ Contrib. Capital	+ Earned Capital	− Contra Equity		Revenues	− Expenses	= Net Income
(1) Jan. 15 Issued 10,000 shares of common stock.	+170,000 Cash		=	+50,000 Common Stock +120,000 Additional Paid-in Capital	−				−	=
(2) Mar. 31 Purchased 2,000 shares of treasury stock.	−30,000 Cash		=			+30,000 − Treasury Stock			−	=

continued

continued from previous page

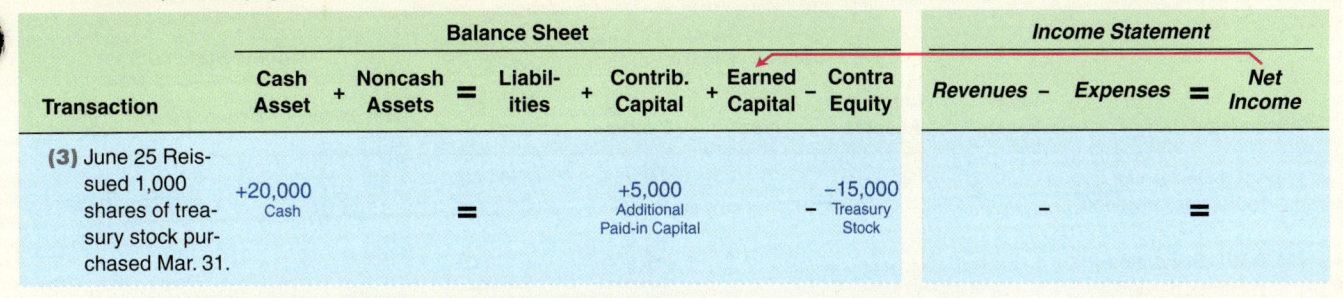

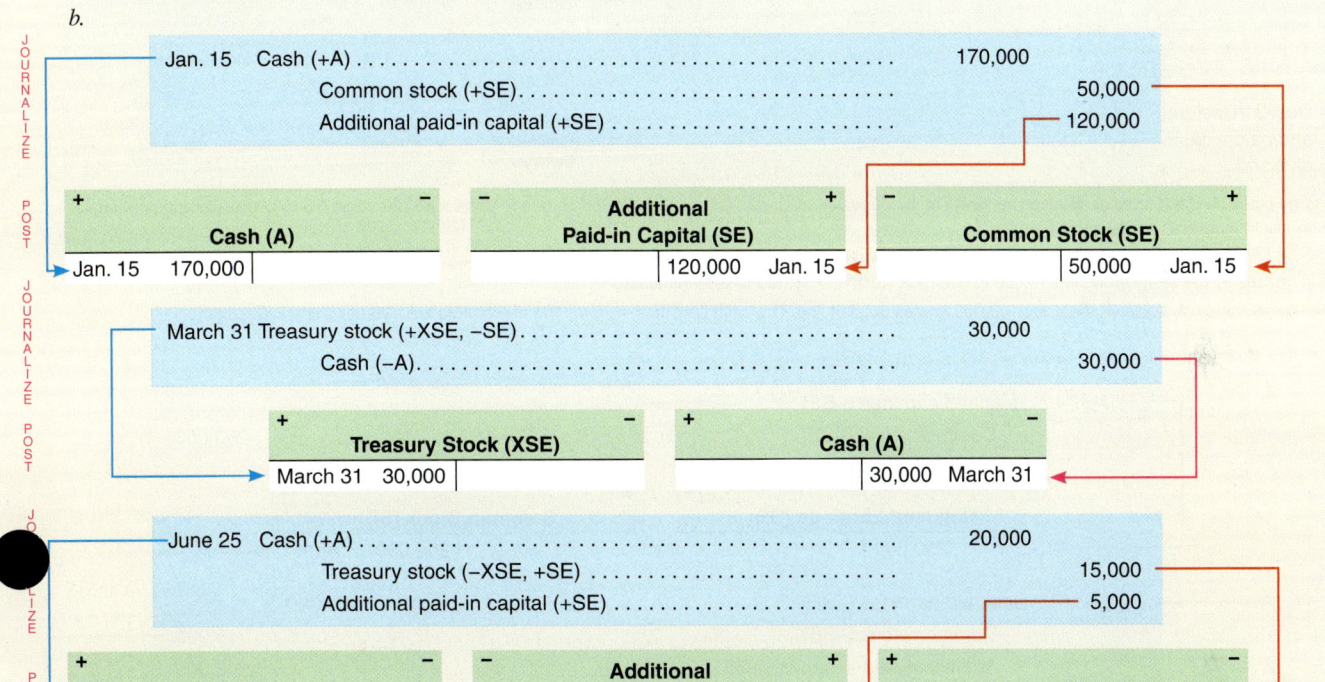

Transaction	Balance Sheet							Income Statement			
	Cash Asset	+ Noncash Assets	= Liabilities	+ Contrib. Capital	+ Earned Capital	− Contra Equity		Revenues	− Expenses	=	Net Income
(3) June 25 Reissued 1,000 shares of treasury stock purchased Mar. 31.	+20,000 Cash		=	+5,000 Additional Paid-in Capital		−15,000 Treasury Stock		−		=	

b.

Jan. 15	Cash (+A)	170,000	
	Common stock (+SE)		50,000
	Additional paid-in capital (+SE)		120,000

Cash (A)		Additional Paid-in Capital (SE)		Common Stock (SE)	
+	−	−	+	−	+
Jan. 15 170,000			120,000 Jan. 15		50,000 Jan. 15

March 31	Treasury stock (+XSE, −SE)	30,000	
	Cash (−A)		30,000

Treasury Stock (XSE)		Cash (A)	
+	−	+	−
March 31 30,000			30,000 March 31

June 25	Cash (+A)	20,000	
	Treasury stock (−XSE, +SE)		15,000
	Additional paid-in capital (+SE)		5,000

Cash (A)		Additional Paid-In Capital (SE)		Treasury Stock (XSE)	
+	−	−	+	+	−
June 25 20,000			5,000 June 25	15,000 June 25	

Review 11-2

PART ONE

a.

	Preferred Stock	Common Stock
Year 1	$0	$0
Year 2		
Arrearage from Year 1 ($1,000,000 × 5%)	50,000	
Current-year dividend ($1,000,000 × 5%)	50,000	
Balance to common		200,000
Year 3		
Current-year dividend ($1,000,000 × 5%)	50,000	
Balance to common		30,000

b.

	Preferred Stock	Common Stock
Year 1	$0	$0
Year 2		
Current-year dividend ($1,000,000 × 5%)	50,000	
Balance to common		250,000
Year 3		
Current-year dividend ($1,000,000 × 5%)	50,000	
Balance to common		30,000

PART TWO

a.

Transaction	Balance Sheet					Income Statement		
	Cash Asset	Noncash Assets	Liabilities	Contrib. Capital	Earned Capital	Revenues	Expenses	Net Income
(1) Apr. 1 Declared a 100% stock dividend.		=		+250,000 Common Stock	−250,000[1] Retained Earnings	−	=	
(2) Dec. 7 Declared a 3% stock dividend.		=		+15,000 Common Stock +6,000 Additional Paid-in Capital	−21,000[2] Retained Earnings	−	=	
(3) Dec. 31 Declared and paid a cash dividend.	−123,600 Cash	=			−123,600[3] Retained Earnings	−	=	

[1] This large stock dividend reduces retained earnings at the par value of shares distributed (50,000 shares × 100% × $5 par value = $250,000). Contributed capital (common stock) increases by the same amount.

[2] This small stock dividend reduces retained earnings at the market value of shares distributed (3% × 100,000 shares × $7 per share = $21,000). Contributed capital increases by the same amount ($15,000 to common stock and $6,000 to paid-in capital).

[3] At the time of the cash dividend, there are 103,000 shares outstanding. The cash paid is, therefore, 103,000 shares × $1.20 per share = $123,600.

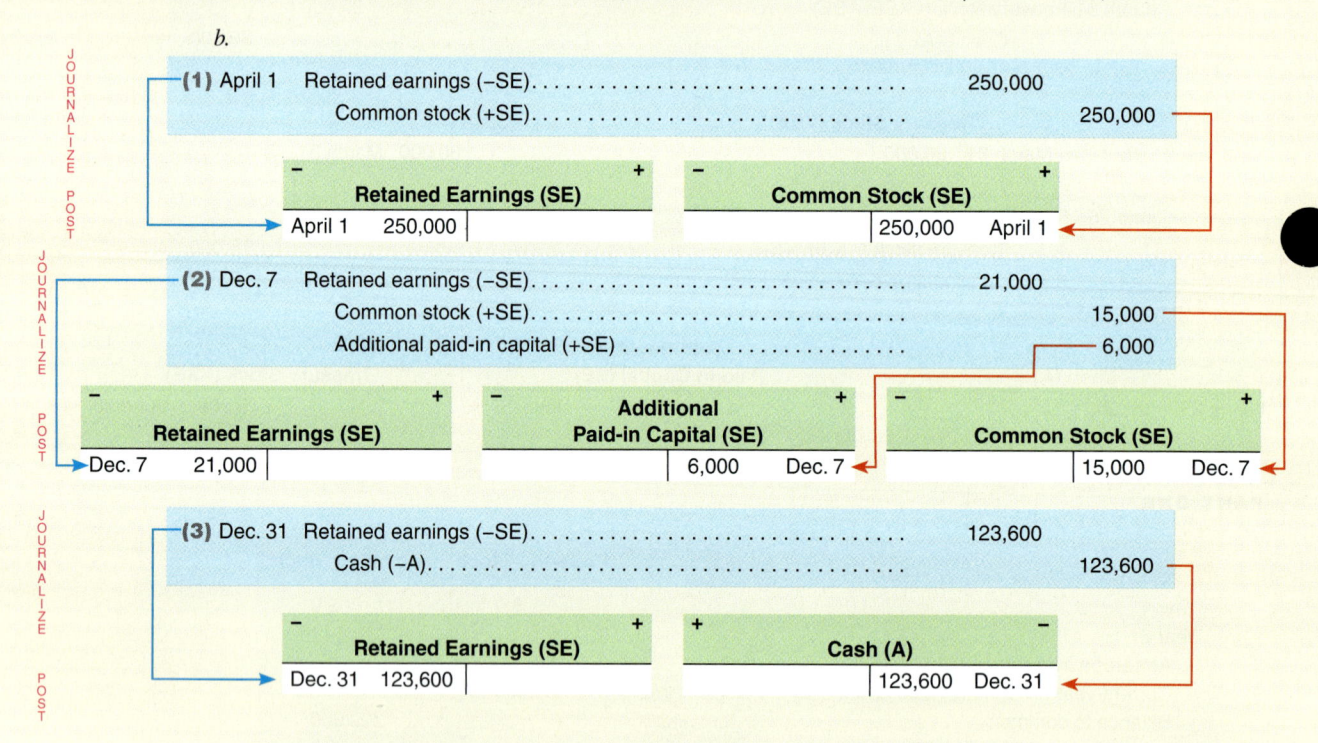

b.

(1) April 1 Retained earnings (−SE)............................. 250,000
              Common stock (+SE)................................   250,000

−	Retained Earnings (SE)	+		−	Common Stock (SE)	+
April 1	250,000				250,000	April 1

(2) Dec. 7 Retained earnings (−SE)............................. 21,000
             Common stock (+SE)................................   15,000
             Additional paid-in capital (+SE)...................   6,000

−	Retained Earnings (SE)	+		−	Additional Paid-in Capital (SE)	+		−	Common Stock (SE)	+
Dec. 7	21,000					6,000	Dec. 7			15,000	Dec. 7

(3) Dec. 31 Retained earnings (−SE)............................. 123,600
              Cash (−A)...   123,600

−	Retained Earnings (SE)	+		+	Cash (A)	−
Dec. 31	123,600				123,600	Dec. 31

c. The ending retained earnings balance is $549,400 ($656,000 − $250,000 − $21,000 − $123,600 + $288,000 = $549,400)

d. If a company initiates a stock split, no journal entry is required.

Review 11-3

a.

Fastenal Company and Subsidiaries
Consolidated Statement of Comprehensive Income
For the Year Ended December 31, 2020 ($ millions)

Net earnings...	$859.1
Other comprehensive income (loss), net of tax:	
Foreign currency translation adjustment, net of tax	17.2
Comprehensive income	$876.3

b.

Accumulated Other Comprehensive Income (Loss) Reconciliation For the Year Ended December 31, 2020 ($ millions)	
Accumulated other comprehensive income (loss), December 31, 2019	$ (38.4)
Other comprehensive income (loss)................................	17.2
Accumulated other comprehensive income (loss), December 31, 2020	$ (21.2)

Review 11-4

a. Basic EPS would be calculated as follows (millions, except per share amount):

$$\text{Basic EPS} = \frac{\$1{,}750 - \$40}{760 \text{ shares}} = \$2.25 \text{ per share}$$

b. Diluted EPS is calculated as follows (millions, except per share amounts):

$$\text{Diluted EPS} = \frac{\$1{,}750}{770 \text{ shares}} = \$2.27 \text{ per share}$$

c. Petroni would only report basic EPS on its income statement. Diluted EPS, as calculated in requirement b, is actually higher than basic EPS because the convertible preferred stock is anti-dilutive. GAAP requires that reported diluted EPS be lower than basic EPS. Consequently, Petroni would not report the diluted EPS number.

Review 11-5

a.

Transaction	Balance Sheet					Income Statement		
	Cash Asset + Noncash Assets	=	Liabilities	− Contra Liabilities	+ Contrib. Capital + Earned Capital	Revenues	− Expenses	= Net Income
Conversion of an $850 book-value bond into 200 common shares of $1 par value.		=	−1,000 Bonds Payable	−150 Bond Discount	+200 Common Stock +650 Additional Paid-In Capital		−	=

b.

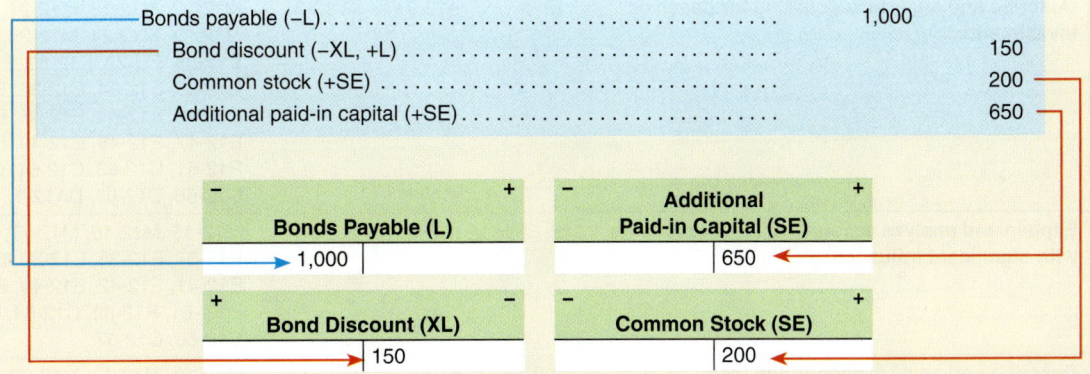

Bonds payable (−L).................................... 1,000
    Bond discount (−XL, +L) 150
    Common stock (+SE) 200
    Additional paid-in capital (+SE)....................... 650

c.

− Bonds Payable (L) +		− Additional Paid-in Capital (SE) +
1,000		650

+ Bond Discount (XL) −		− Common Stock (SE) +
150		200

Chapter 12
Reporting and Analyzing Financial Investments

LEARNING OBJECTIVES

LO12-1 Explain and interpret the three levels of investor influence over an investee—passive, significant, and controlling.

LO12-2 Describe the term "fair value" and the fair value hierarchy.

LO12-3 Describe and analyze accounting for passive investments.

LO12-4 Explain and analyze accounting for investments with significant influence.

LO12-5 Describe and analyze accounting for investments with control.

LO12-6 Appendix 12A: Illustrate and analyze accounting mechanics for equity method investments.

LO12-7 Appendix 12B: Apply consolidation accounting mechanics.

LO12-8 Appendix 12C: Discuss the reporting of derivative securities.

Road Map

LO	Learning Objective | Topics	Page	eLecture	Review	Assignments
LO12-1	Explain and interpret the three levels of investor influence over an investee-passive, significant, and controlling.	12-3	e12-1	R 12-1	M12-11, E12-28, E12-29, E12-30, E12-31, E12-33, E12-34, E12-41, E12-42, E12-43, E12-45, E12-46, E12-47, E12-48, E12-49, E12-50, P12-59, P12-61, P12-62, C12-63, C12-64, C12-65, C12-66, C12-67
LO12-2	Describe the term "fair value" and the fair value hierarchy.	12-5	e12-2	R 12-2	M12-14, E12-49, P12-59, P12-61, C12-66, C12-67
LO12-3	Describe and analyze accounting for passive investments.	12-6	e12-3	R 12-3	M12-12, M12-13, M12-21, M12-22, M12-23, M12-24, M12-25, M12-26, E12-28, EU-29, E12-30, E12-31, E12-33, E12-34, E12-36, E12-41, E12-42, E12-43, E12-45, E12-46, E12-47, E12-48, E12-49, P12-59, P12-61, C12-63, C12-64, C12-65, C12-66, C12-67, **DA12-1**
LO12-4	Explain and analyze accounting for investments with significant influence.	12-17	e12-4	R 12-4	M12-15, M12-16, M12-17, M12-20, E12-37, E12-38, E12-39, E12-40, E12-41, E12-42, E12-49, E12-50, P12-61, P12-62, C12-64, C12-65, C12-66, C12-67
LO12-5	Describe and analyze accounting for investments with control.	12-22	e12-5	R 12-5	M12-18, M12-19, M12-20, M12-27, E12-32, E12-35, E12-44, E12-55, E12-56, P12-60, P12-62, C12-66
LO12-6	Appendix 12A: Illustrate and analyze accounting mechanics for equity method investments.	12-31	e12-6	R 12-6	E12-57, P12-62
LO12-7	Appendix 12B: Apply consolidation accounting mechanics.	12-33	e12-7	R 12-7	E12-51, E12-52, E12-53, E12-54, E12-56, PU-60, P12-62
LO12-8	Appendix 12C: Discuss the reporting of derivative securities.	12-35	e12-8	R 12-8	E12-58

ALPHABET
www.Alphabet.com

When Sergey Brin and Larry Page, Stanford computer science students, started Google Inc., in September, 1998, they were probably unaware that their fortune would be made in the advertising field that now generates nearly all its revenue.

Google went public in August 2004, with an offering price below $100 a share. As of the time of this writing, the stock price is greater than $2,600 and there have been two splits! Alphabet, Inc. (the new parent company name for what was previously Google, Inc.), faces competition in general-purpose search engines from Yahoo, Inc., and Microsoft Corporation, and in social networks from Facebook, Inc., and Twitter, Inc. The company also competes fiercely with Apple Inc., in the mobile applications market. In addition, the company faces legal challenges from competitors and anti-trust investigations in the United States and other countries. Alphabet, Inc., faces substantial scrutiny in international markets. The company faces pressure from its employees' objections to some of its contracts with customers, from privacy concerns of users and regulators, and from customers who object to the placement of their advertisements in proximity to certain types of content.

Alphabet, Inc., addresses these growth challenges in several ways. Roughly 15% of Alphabet's 2020 revenue was spent on research and development to advance the company's provision of cutting-edge products and services to its users and its diversification away from advertising. In addition, Alphabet, Inc., acquires companies with technology that the company can leverage. Most of these acquisitions are small, but Alphabet, Inc., acquired YouTube, Inc., in 2006 for $1.19 billion, DoubleClick, Inc., in 2008 for $3.19 billion, Motorola Mobility Holdings, Inc., in 2012 for $12.4 billion, Waze, in 2013 for over $1 billion, Nest Labs, Inc., in 2014 for roughly $3 billion, an operation of HTC Corporation in 2020 for $1.1 billion to work on hardware development, and Fitbit, in 2021, for approximately $2 billion. In addition to these investments for operating growth, Alphabet, Inc.'s 2020 balance sheet shows that roughly 48% of its reported assets are cash and securities.

As we discuss in this chapter, the accounting method used to report investments depends on the investor company's purpose in making the investment and on the degree of influence or control that the investor company can exert over the investee company (the company whose securities are being purchased). One consequence of these accounting methods is that small changes in the amount invested can produce significant changes in the investor's financial statements.

Sources: Alphabet 2020 10-K report, *Wall Street Journal*, February 5, 2019.

CHAPTER ORGANIZATION

Reporting and Analyzing Financial Investments

Passive Investments	Investments with Significant Influence	Investments with Control	Further Considerations
• Trading Securities • Available-for-Sale Securities • Held-to-Maturity Securities	• Accounting and Reporting • Equity Method and Effects on Ratios	• Accounting and Reporting • Acquired Assets and Liabilities • Accounting for Goodwill • Noncontrolling Interest	• Equity Method Mechanics (Appendix 12A) • Consolidation Accounting Mechanics (Appendix 12B) • Reporting Derivative Securities (Appendix 12C)

INTRODUCTION

LO12-1 Explain and interpret the three levels of investor influence over an investee—passive, significant, and controlling.

Most companies invest in government securities or the securities of other companies. These investments often have the following strategic goals:

- **Short-term investment of excess cash.** Companies often generate excess cash for investment either during slow times of the year (after receivables are collected and before seasonal production begins) or for liquidity needs (such as to counter strategic moves by competitors or to quickly respond to acquisition opportunities).

- **Alliances for strategic purposes.** Companies often acquire an equity interest in other companies for strategic purposes, such as gaining access to their research and development activities, to supply or distribution markets, or to their production and marketing expertise.

- **Market penetration or expansion.** Acquisitions of controlling interests in other companies can achieve vertical or horizontal integration in existing markets or can be avenues to penetrate new and growing markets.

Investments in government securities and in the securities of other companies are usually referred to as **financial investments**. Firms make these investments for different purposes, so accounting for the investments can follow one of five different methods, each of which affects the balance sheet and the income statement differently. To help assimilate the materials in this chapter, Exhibit 12.1 provides a graphical depiction of accounting for financial investments as we will explore it.

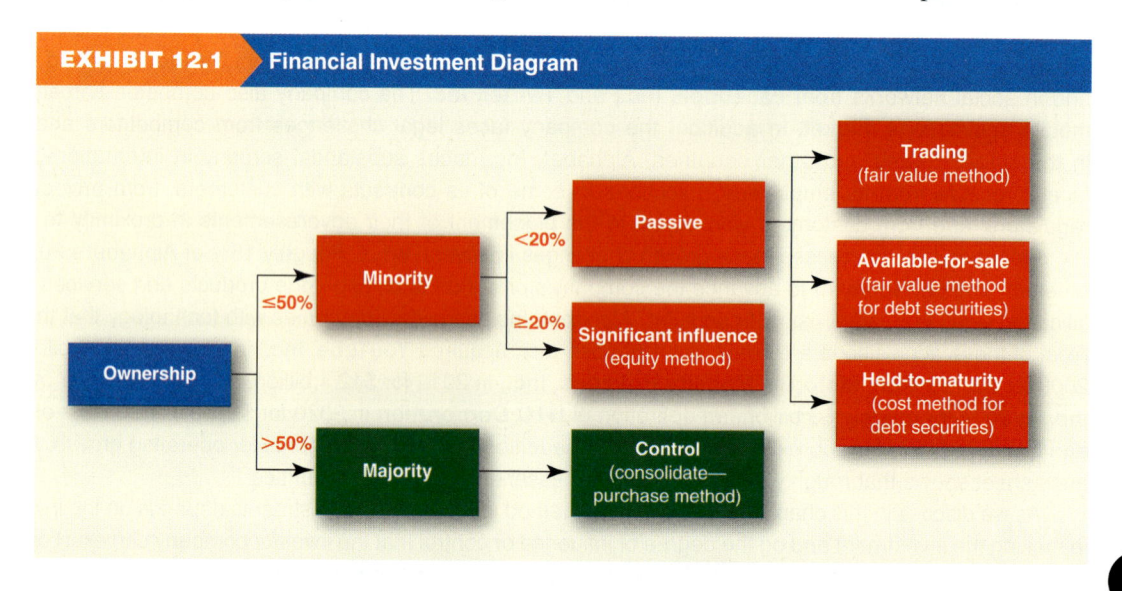

EXHIBIT 12.1 Financial Investment Diagram

Ownership
- ≤50% → Minority
  - <20% → Passive
    - Trading (fair value method)
    - Available-for-sale (fair value method for debt securities)
    - Held-to-maturity (cost method for debt securities)
  - ≥20% → Significant influence (equity method)
- >50% → Majority → Control (consolidate—purchase method)

The degree of influence or control that the investor company (purchaser) can exert over the investee organization (the company or government whose securities are being purchased) determines the accounting method. U.S. GAAP identifies three levels of influence/control:

1. **Passive influence.** In this case, the purchasing company is merely an investor and cannot exert influence over the investee organization. The purchaser's goal for this investment is to realize interest, dividends, and capital gains. Generally, passive investor status is presumed if the investor company owns less than 20% of the outstanding voting stock of the investee. Investments in debt securities, such as bonds or notes of other organizations, are also classified as passive investments.

2. **Significant influence.** An investor company can sometimes exert significant influence over, but not control, the activities of an investee company. This level of influence can result from the percentage of voting stock owned. It also can result from legal agreements, such as a license to use technology, a formula, or a trade secret like production know-how. It also can occur when the investor company is the sole supplier or customer of the investee. Generally, significant influence is presumed if the investor company owns 20% to 50% of the voting stock of the investee.

3. **Controlling influence.** When a company has control over another, it has the ability to elect a majority of the board of directors and, as a result, the ability to determine its strategic direction and hiring of executive management. Control is generally presumed if the investor company owns more than 50% of the outstanding voting stock of the investee company. Control can sometimes occur at less than 50% stock ownership by virtue of legal agreements, technology licensing, or other contractual means.

Once the type of investment and the level of influence/control is determined, the appropriate accounting method is applied, as outlined in **Exhibit 12.2**.

EXHIBIT 12.2 — Investment Type, Accounting Treatment, and Financial Statement Effects

	Accounting	Balance Sheet Effects	Income Statement Effects	Cash Flow Effects
Passive	Trading (Debt or equity investments)	Investment balance reported as end-of-period fair value	Interest and dividend payments from investee are included in income. Capital gain/loss recognized in the period in which it occurs	Purchase/sale of investee yields investing cash flows. Interest and dividend payments received from investee are operating cash inflows
	Available-for-Sale (Debt investments only)	Investment balance reported as end-of-period fair value	Interest payments from investee are included in income. Capital gain/loss recognized when investment sold; interim gain/loss reported as AOCI*	Purchase/sale of investee yields investing cash flows. Interest payments received from investee are operating cash inflows
	Held-to-Maturity (Debt investments only)	Investment balance reported at adjusted acquisition cost	Interest payments from investee are included in income. Capital gain/loss recognized when investment sold	Purchase/sale of investee yields investing cash flows. Interest payments received from investee are operating cash inflows
Significant Influence	Equity Method	Investment balance reflects purchase price and subsequent changes in proportion owned of investee's earned equity	Investor reports income equal to percent owned of investee income. Sale of investee yields gains/losses	Purchase/sale of investee yields investing cash flows. Dividend payments received from investee are operating cash inflows
Control	Consolidation	Balance sheets of investor and investee are presented as if one entity	Income statements of investor and investee are presented as if one entity. Sale of investee yields gains/losses	Purchase/sale of investee yields investing cash flows. Cash flows of investor and investee are presented as if one entity

*AOCI (Accumulated Other Comprehensive Income) is defined in Chapter 11 and discussed further in the following pages.

There are two basic reporting issues with investments: (1) how investment income should be recognized and (2) at what amount (cost or fair value) the investment should be reported on the balance sheet. We next discuss both of these issues under each of the three investment types.

Review 12-1 LO12-1 — Classifying Investments as Passive, Significant, or Controlling

Autos Unlimited Inc., a large auto manufacturer, is considering an investment in one of its suppliers. For each of the separate situations below, determine if the investment by the auto manufacturer should be reported as a passive investment (P), an investment reflecting significant influence (SI), or a controlling interest (C).

1. _____ Autos Unlimited purchases $500,000 of bonds issued by its supplier.
2. _____ Autos Unlimited purchases $5 million of bonds issued by its supplier.
3. _____ Autos Unlimited purchases common stock of its supplier representing 69% of the outstanding common stock of the supplier.
4. _____ Autos Unlimited purchases common stock of its supplier representing 45% of the outstanding common stock of the supplier.
5. _____ Autos Unlimited purchases common stock of its supplier representing 10% of the outstanding common stock of the supplier.

Solution on p. 12-57.

FAIR VALUE: AN INTRODUCTION

LO12-2 Describe the term "fair value" and the fair value hierarchy.

The term **fair value** is finding increasing use in the language of accounting, but it is particularly prevalent in the accounting for financial investments. When an investor purchases a security for $100, the relevance of that acquisition cost fades rather quickly. If the investor considers selling the security a year later, the original $100 cost is much less meaningful than the current price for the security in the markets. Or, if we were to look at the balance sheet of a company, it would be useful to know how much its investments are worth today, rather than what was paid for them at various points in the past.

When accounting requires the use of fair value, U.S. GAAP defines fair value as the amount that an independent buyer would be willing to pay for an asset (or the amount that would need to be paid to discharge a liability) in an orderly transaction. For an asset that is actively traded on financial markets, fair value is the amount that we would receive by selling that asset at the balance sheet date. But fair value is also used when there is no active market for the asset. When Microsoft accounts for its acquisition of LinkedIn, it must report the fair value of the intellectual property that it obtained in that transaction. In such cases, fair value is not "mark-to-market," but rather "mark-to-model." For instance, fair value might be determined by a discounted cash flow analysis as in Chapter 9. U.S. GAAP allows various methods to be used in determining the "most representative" fair value at the appropriate date.

While fair values are often deemed to be more relevant than historical cost, they are also viewed as more subjective—particularly when fair value is determined by reference to a model rather than a liquid market. For this reason, U.S. GAAP requires that firms disclose the methods used to determine fair value for their assets using a **fair value hierarchy**.

Level 1: Values based on quoted prices in active markets for identical assets/liabilities. An example would be a common share of a company traded on an active exchange. For instance, Alphabet, Inc.'s class A common stock closed at a price of $1,739.52 per share on December 31, 2020. That price would be used to determine the fair value of another company's investment in Alphabet, Inc., stock.

Level 2: Values based on observable inputs other than Level 1 (e.g., quoted prices for similar assets/liabilities or interest rates or yield curves). An example would be a bond that is infrequently traded but that is similar to bonds that are actively traded. Moody's rates Alphabet, Inc., bonds at Aa2. Other bonds with that rating would likely have a similar yield, which could be used to compute the present value of the bond payments to estimate the fair value of a bond investment.

Level 3: Values based on inputs observable only to the reporting entity (e.g., management estimates or assumptions). An example would be an operating asset that is judged to be impaired.

Alphabet, Inc.'s use of fair value to report its investments is presented in the coming pages. The purpose of the classification is to provide an assessment of the subjectivity that underlies the numbers in the balance sheet (and sometimes, the income statement), with Level 1 being the least subjective and Level 3 being the most subjective.

In addition, companies have a **fair value option** that provides them with the *option* of using fair value to measure the value of many financial assets and liabilities. This option extends the use of fair value to a wide range of financial assets and liabilities, including accounts and notes receivable, accounts and notes payable, and bonds payable. Other assets that *must* be reported at fair value include (1) investments in other companies' equity securities, (2) derivative securities, such as options, futures, and forward contracts, that are purchased to hedge price, interest rate, or foreign exchange rate fluctuations, (3) long-term assets that are impaired, and (4) inventories that have been written down to fair value based on the lower-of-cost-or-market rule.

Classifying Investments Using the Fair Value Hierarchy

LO12-2 Review 12-2

Indicate the level of the fair value hierarchy (Level 1, Level 2, or Level 3) that is described in the following excerpts from recent 10-K statements of **Pfizer Inc.** and **Coca Cola Company**.

a. Level _____ Investments may include securities that are valued using alternative pricing sources, such as investment managers or brokers, which use proprietary pricing models that incorporate unobservable inputs. (Pfizer 2020 10-K)

b. Level _____ Investments may include individual securities that are valued at the closing price or last trade reported on the major market on which they are traded. (Pfizer 2020 10-K)

c. Level _____ Investments may include corporate bonds, government and government agency obligations, and other fixed income securities valued using bid evaluation pricing models or quoted prices of securities with similar characteristics. (Pfizer 2020 10-K)

d. Level _____ We value assets and liabilities included in this level using dealer and broker quotations, certain pricing models, bid prices, quoted prices for similar assets and liabilities in active markets, or other inputs that are observable or can be corroborated by observable market data. (Coca-Cola Company 2020 10-K)

e. Level _____ Unobservable inputs that are supported by little or no market activity and that are significant to the fair value of the assets or liabilities. This includes certain pricing models, discounted cash flow methodologies, and similar techniques that use significant unobservable inputs. (Coca-Cola Company 2020 10-K)

f. Level _____ The fair values of our investments in debt and equity securities using quoted market prices from daily exchange traded markets are based on the closing price as of the balance sheet date. (Coca-Cola Company 2020 10-K)

Solution on p. 12-57.

PASSIVE INVESTMENTS IN DEBT SECURITIES

LO12-3 Describe and analyze accounting for passive investments.

The term "passive" refers to the investor's role in trying to influence the operations of the investee organization. So, short-term investments of excess cash are typically passive investments, usually in liquid, low-risk securities. In addition, investors seeking trading profits from short-term capital gains would be considered passive investors, even though their trading style may be active. Debt securities have no ownership interest, so they are always passive, and we leave the accounting for passive equity investments for the next section. Passive debt investments can be broadly grouped into two categories: those reported at cost and those reported at fair value. Furthermore, there are two methods for reporting investments at fair value. These alternative treatments are discussed below.

Acquisition of the Investment

When a debt investment is acquired, regardless of the amount purchased, the investment is initially recorded on the balance sheet at its fair value—that is, its price on the date of purchase. This accounting is the same as that for the acquisition of other assets such as inventories or plant assets. Subsequent to acquisition, investments are carried on the balance sheet as current or long-term assets, depending on management's expectations about their ultimate holding period. (The assets are reported as current assets if management expects to dispose of them within one year.)

When investments are sold, any recognized gain or loss on sale usually is equal to the difference between the proceeds received and the book (carrying) value of the investment on the balance sheet. However, there is one passive investment method where that is not true.

To illustrate entries for a passive debt investment, assume that—on January 1 of Year 1—Pownall Company wants to earn a return on a cash balance for which it has no immediate need. King Company has just issued high-quality bonds that mature in five years. Each bond has a face value of $1,000 and an annual coupon rate of interest equal to 10% (paid semi-annually on June 30 and December 31). The bonds have a current market price of $1,000, implying a 10% annual discount rate. At the start of the year, Pownall Company purchases 500 of King Company's bonds for $500,000. The financial statement effects of this transaction for Pownall are the following:

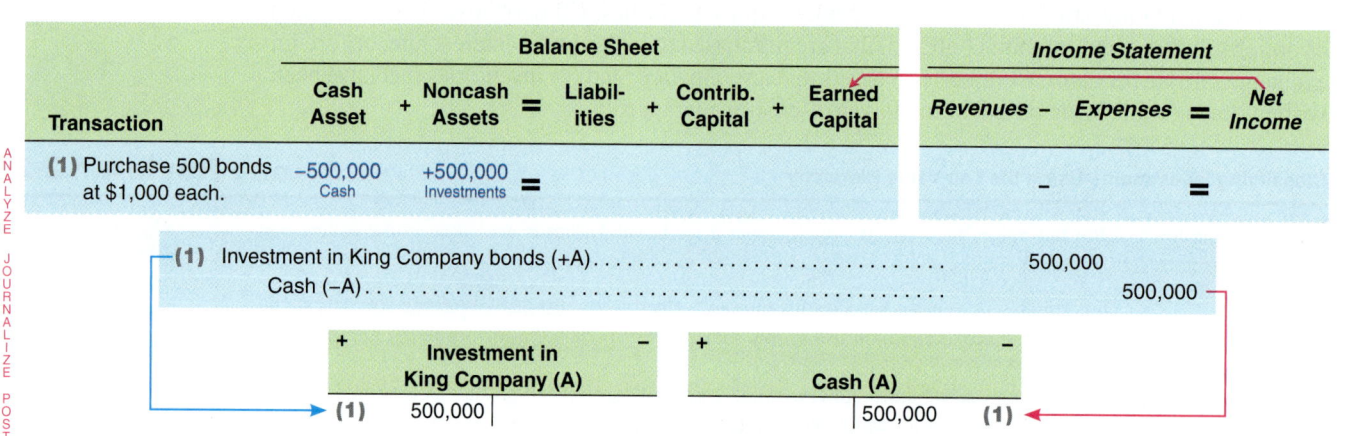

Transaction	Balance Sheet					Income Statement		
	Cash Asset	+ Noncash Assets	= Liabilities	+ Contrib. Capital	+ Earned Capital	Revenues	− Expenses	= Net Income
(1) Purchase 500 bonds at $1,000 each.	−500,000 Cash	+500,000 Investments	=			−		=

(1) Investment in King Company bonds (+A) 500,000
    Cash (−A) 500,000

+ Investment in King Company (A)	− Cash (A)
(1) 500,000	500,000 (1)

While accounting for the initial investment is straightforward, the subsequent reporting can follow one of three paths.

Investments Reported at Cost

When a company purchases a debt security, and it has the positive intent and the ability to hold that security until it matures, the value fluctuations between purchase and maturity are not relevant for financial statement readers. In such cases, these debt securities are classified as **held-to-maturity (HTM)**. **Exhibit 12.3** summarizes the reporting of these securities.

EXHIBIT 12.3

Investment Classification	Reporting of Fair Value Changes	Reporting Interest Received and Gains and Losses on Sale
Held-to-Maturity (HTM)	Fair value changes are not reported in either the balance sheet or the income statement	Reported as other income in income statement

In our illustrative example, we assume (for the moment) that Pownall Company has the ability and the intent to hold the bonds until they mature. For the King Company bonds, Pownall Company's use of the held-to-maturity method would have the following interest income and book value pattern over the five years (mirroring the accounting for a bond from Chapter 9). At the end of each six-month period, Pownall would receive an interest payment of $25,000 and recognize investment income of the same amount. Fluctuations in the market value of King Company bonds are not reflected in the accounting for the investment. At the end of year 5, Pownall would also receive a principal repayment of $500,000.

Year	Beginning Book Value (A)	Interest Income	Interest Received	Principal Payment	Ending Book Value
	(a)	(b) = (a) × 10%/2	(c)		(d) = (a) + (b) − (c)
½	$500,000	$25,000	$25,000	$-0-	$500,000
1	500,000	25,000	25,000	-0-	500,000
1½	500,000	25,000	25,000	-0-	500,000
2	500,000	25,000	25,000	-0-	500,000
2½	500,000	25,000	25,000	-0-	500,000
3	500,000	25,000	25,000	-0-	500,000
3½	500,000	25,000	25,000	-0-	500,000
4	500,000	25,000	25,000	-0-	500,000
4½	500,000	25,000	25,000	-0-	500,000
5	500,000	25,000	25,000	500,000	-0-

Investments Marked to Fair Value

If Pownall Company does not have the ability or the intent to hold the King Company bonds to maturity, then it cannot use the held-to-maturity accounting method. Instead, it must reflect changes in the fair value of those bonds at the end of a reporting period. In this illustration, we assume that Pownall closes its accounts and issues financial statements at the end of every calendar year. At the end of the first six months after the investment, Pownall Company makes the following entry:

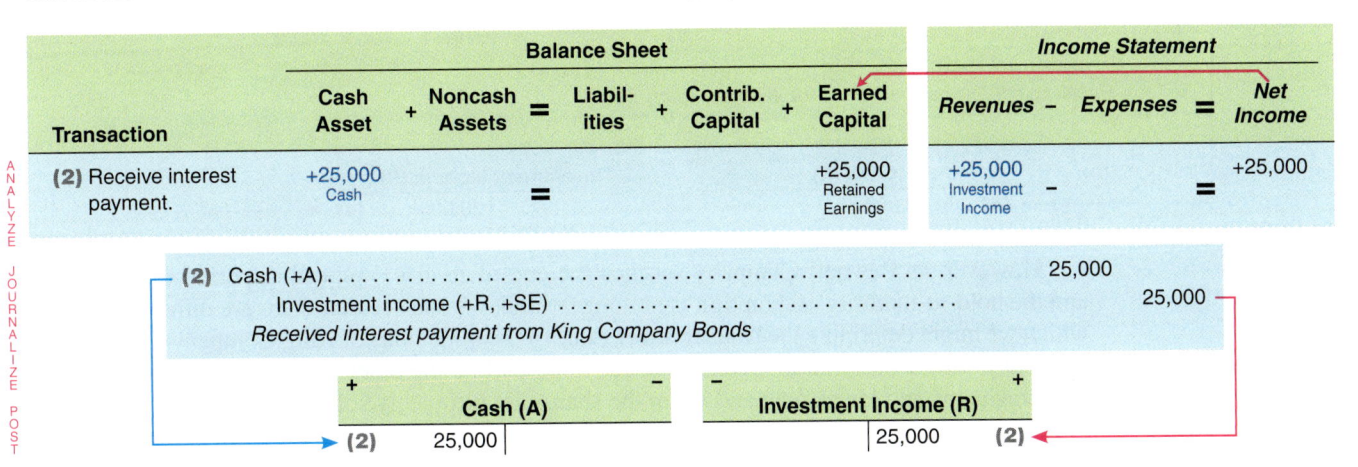

Transaction	Cash Asset	+	Noncash Assets	=	Liabilities	+	Contrib. Capital	+	Earned Capital	Revenues	−	Expenses	=	Net Income
(2) Receive interest payment.	+25,000 Cash			=					+25,000 Retained Earnings	+25,000 Investment Income	−		=	+25,000

(2) Cash (+A) 25,000
    Investment income (+R, +SE) 25,000
    Received interest payment from King Company Bonds

+ Cash (A) −		− Investment Income (R) +
(2) 25,000		25,000 (2)

Sale of the Investment

On July 1, Year 1, an unexpected liquidity need causes Pownall to sell 100 of the 500 bonds for $950 cash per bond. The financial statement effects of this transaction and its related entries for Pownall follow.

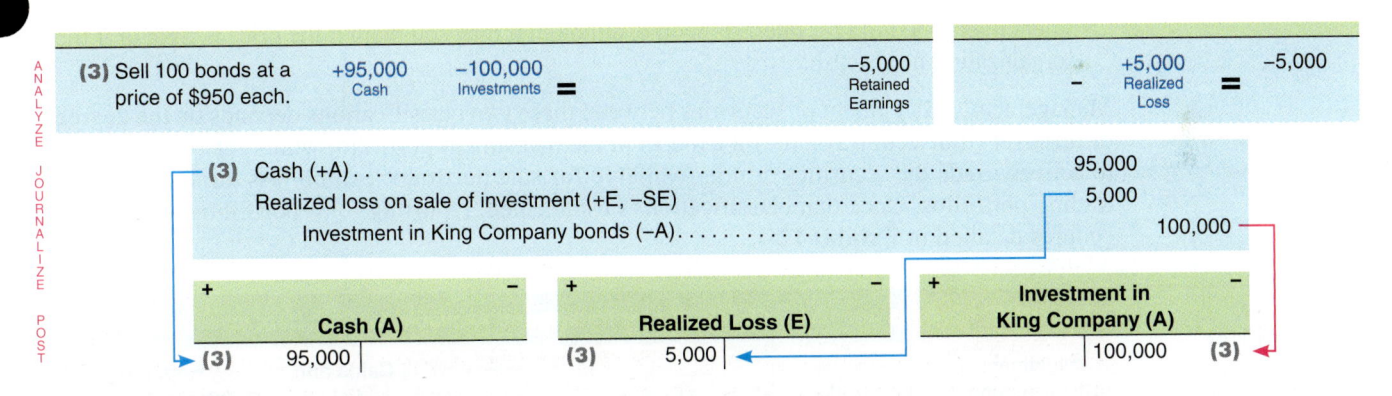

(3) Sell 100 bonds at a price of $950 each.	+95,000 Cash	−100,000 Investments	=			−5,000 Retained Earnings	−	+5,000 Realized Loss	=	−5,000

(3) Cash (+A) 95,000
    Realized loss on sale of investment (+E, −SE) 5,000
    Investment in King Company bonds (−A) 100,000

+ Cash (A) −		− Realized Loss (E) +		+ Investment in King Company (A) −
(3) 95,000		(3) 5,000		100,000 (3)

The gain or loss on sale is reported as a component of *other income,* which is commonly commingled with interest and dividend revenue in the income statement.

On the statement of cash flows, the $500,000 purchase (transaction 1) would be an investing cash outflow, and the $95,000 proceeds (transaction 2) would be an investing cash inflow. If Pownall Company presents its cash flows from operating activities using the indirect method, we would see an addition of the $5,000 loss on sale among the adjustments from net income to cash from operations.

Accounting for the purchase and sale of investments is similar to any other asset. Further, there is no difference in accounting for purchases and sales across the different types of passive investments when those purchases and sales occur in the same reporting period.

Pownall Company continues to receive interest payments from its remaining King Company bonds. On December 31, it would make the following entry:

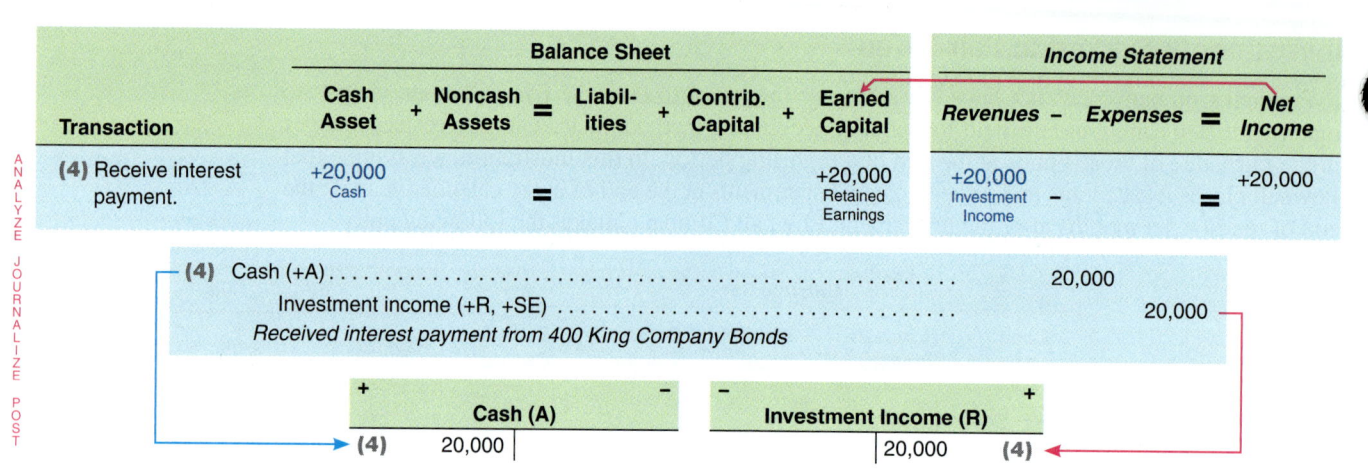

Transaction	Balance Sheet					Income Statement		
	Cash Asset	+ Noncash Assets	= Liabilities	+ Contrib. Capital	+ Earned Capital	Revenues	− Expenses	= Net Income
(4) Receive interest payment.	+20,000 Cash	=			+20,000 Retained Earnings	+20,000 Investment Income	−	= +20,000

(4) Cash (+A) 20,000
    Investment income (+R, +SE) 20,000
    Received interest payment from 400 King Company Bonds

+ Cash (A) −		− Investment Income (R) +
(4) 20,000		20,000 (4)

However, as Pownall Company reaches the end of its fiscal reporting period (a year-end), and the hold-to-maturity assumption is no longer valid, we can see that there are different ways in which we might determine the balance sheet value of the 400 bonds of King Company that Pownall Company still owns. And, that balance sheet value will be the asset's book value going forward, affecting gains and losses now and when the shares are ultimately sold.

Debt Investments Marked to Fair Value

The following two classifications of marketable debt securities require the investment to be reported on the balance sheet at current fair value:

1. **Trading (T) securities.** These are investments in debt securities that management intends to actively buy and sell for trading profits as market prices fluctuate.
2. **Available-for-sale (AFS) securities.** These are investments in debt securities that management intends to hold for interest income, although it may sell them if the price is right or if the organization needs cash.

Management's assignment of securities between these two classifications depends on the degree of turnover (transaction volume) it expects in the investment portfolio, which reflects its intent to actively trade the securities or not. Available-for-sale portfolios exhibit less turnover than do trading portfolios. Once that classification is established, reporting for a portfolio follows procedures detailed in **Exhibit 12.4**.

FYI GAAP permits companies to have multiple portfolios, each with a different classification. Management can change portfolio classification provided it adheres to strict disclosure and reporting requirements if its expectations of turnover change.

EXHIBIT 12.4 — Accounting Treatment for Trading and Available-for-Sale Debt Investments

Investment Classification	Reporting of Fair Value Changes	Reporting Gains and Losses on Sale	Reporting Interest Income
Trading (T)	Balance sheet values are updated to reflect fair value changes; unrealized gains and losses are reported as investment income; affects equity via retained earnings	Gain or loss on sale equals proceeds minus the most recent book (fair) value	Reported as investment income in income statement
Available-for-Sale (AFS)	Balance sheet values are updated to reflect fair value changes; unrealized gains and losses bypass the income statement and are reported directly in the statement of comprehensive income and then in accumulated other comprehensive income (AOCI), a component of equity	Gain or loss on sale equals proceeds minus the original acquisition cost of the investment; any unrealized gains or losses in accumulated other comprehensive income must be eliminated	Reported as investment income in income statement

Both trading (T) and available-for-sale (AFS) investments are reported at fair values on the balance sheet on the statement date. Whether the change in fair value affects current income depends on the investment classification: available-for-sale debt securities have no immediate income effect; trading securities have an income effect. The impact on shareholders' equity is similar for both classifications, with the only difference being whether the change is reflected in retained earnings or in accumulated other comprehensive income (AOCI) in equity. Interest income and any gains or losses on security sales are reported in the investment income section of the income statement for both classifications.

> **FYI** When trading securities are marked-to-fair value, the unrealized gain/loss is recorded as income and reported in the income statement. For available-for-sale investments, unrealized gains/losses are reported as other comprehensive income.

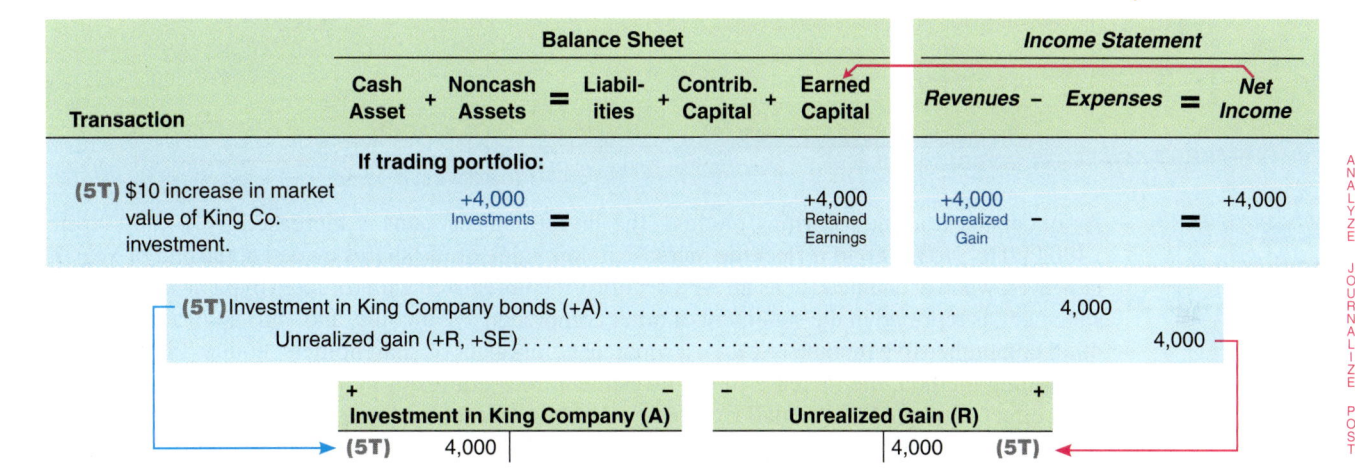

Fair Value Adjustments To illustrate the accounting for changes in fair value subsequent to purchase (and before sale), assume that Pownall's investment in King Co. (400 remaining bonds purchased for $1,000 per bond) could be sold for $1,010 per bond at year-end. The investment must be marked to fair value in an adjusting entry to reflect the $4,000 unrealized gain ($10 per bond increase for 400 bonds).

If the investment is classified as trading securities (T), the entry would be:

Transaction	Balance Sheet					Income Statement		
	Cash Asset	+ Noncash Assets	= Liabilities	+ Contrib. Capital	+ Earned Capital	Revenues	− Expenses	= Net Income
If trading portfolio:								
(5T) $10 increase in market value of King Co. investment.		+4,000 Investments =			+4,000 Retained Earnings	+4,000 Unrealized Gain	−	= +4,000

(5T) Investment in King Company bonds (+A) 4,000
     Unrealized gain (+R, +SE) 4,000

+ Investment in King Company (A)	− Unrealized Gain (R) +
(5T) 4,000	4,000 (5T)

The investment account is increased by $4,000, making the end-of-year book value of Pownall's investment equal to $404,000, its fair value. Total investment income reported on Pownall's income statement would be $44,000, consisting of a realized holding loss of $5,000, interest income of $45,000 (= 500 × 10% × $1,000/2 + 400 × 10% × $1,000/2), and $4,000 in unrealized holding gains. If Pownall is actively trading to achieve capital gains, then this approach seems like the correct way to "keep score."

This entry to adjust the balance sheet to reflect the fair value of the securities is an adjusting entry. It would need to be made at the end of every fiscal period as financial reports are being prepared.

What happens when the securities are subsequently sold? Assume that Pownall Company sells its 400 bonds of King Company for $990 per bond on July 1 of Year 2. Pownall Company would receive the interest payment of $20,000 on June 30 of Year 2, as in transaction (4) above. On July 1, Year 2, Pownall receives $396,000 (= 400 × $990) in cash, and it no longer owns bonds of King Company. When the trading securities method is used, the accounting for the sale of shares is relatively simple:

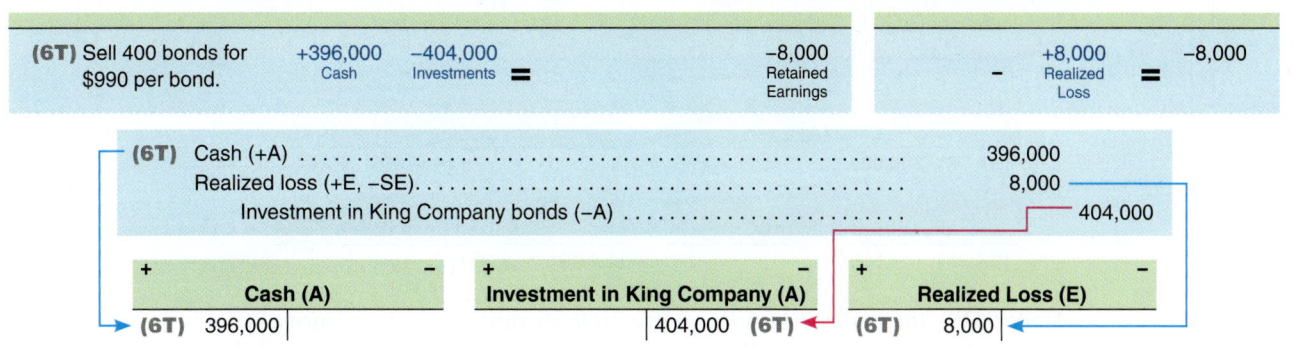

(6T) Sell 400 bonds for $990 per bond.	+396,000 Cash	−404,000 Investments =			−8,000 Retained Earnings		− +8,000 Realized Loss	= −8,000

(6T) Cash (+A) 396,000
     Realized loss (+E, −SE) 8,000
        Investment in King Company bonds (−A) 404,000

+ Cash (A) −	− Investment in King Company (A) +	+ Realized Loss (E) −
(6T) 396,000	404,000 (6T)	(6T) 8,000

Under the trading securities method, holding gains and losses (both realized and unrealized) are recognized in income in the period in which they occur. Holding these 400 bonds caused a holding gain of $4,000 in Year 1 and a holding loss of $8,000 in Year 2. Again, if Pownall Company were actively seeking capital gains, we would say that they were less successful in Year 2 than they had been in Year 1.

Now let's assume that Pownall Company had classified its investment in King Company as available-for-sale (AFS) securities; the end-of-year adjusting entry would be the following:

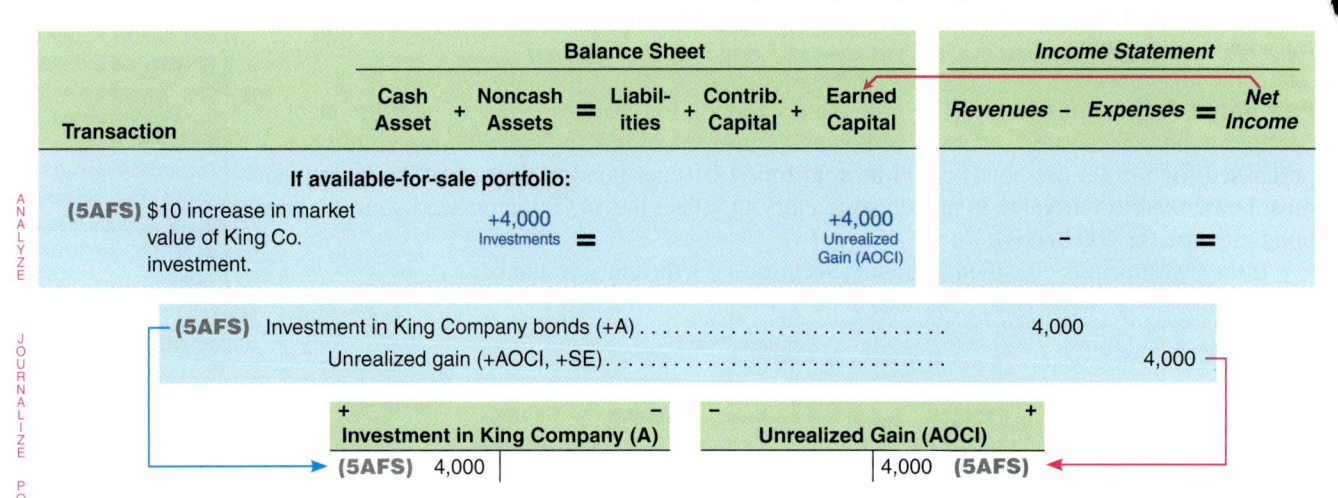

Transaction	Balance Sheet					Income Statement		
	Cash Asset	+ Noncash Assets	= Liabilities	+ Contrib. Capital	+ Earned Capital	Revenues	− Expenses	= Net Income
If available-for-sale portfolio:								
(5AFS) $10 increase in market value of King Co. investment.		+4,000 Investments	=		+4,000 Unrealized Gain (AOCI)		−	=

(5AFS) Investment in King Company bonds (+A) 4,000
        Unrealized gain (+AOCI, +SE) 4,000

+ Investment in King Company (A) −		− Unrealized Gain (AOCI) +	
(5AFS) 4,000			4,000 (5AFS)

As under the trading securities method, the investment account is increased by $4,000 (from $400,000 to $404,000) to reflect the increase in fair value of the shares owned at the end of Year 1. However, when accounted for as an AFS security, the unrealized gain (or loss) bypasses the income statement, is reported in the statement of other comprehensive income, and ends up in accumulated other comprehensive income (AOCI), a separate component of shareholders' equity. In contrast to the trading method, the increase in the investment does not result in an immediate income statement effect. Under AFS, Pownall Company's investment income for Year 1 would reflect only the $5,000 realized loss from the sale of 100 bonds, plus the interest income of $45,000. The $4,000 unrealized gain is reflected in stockholders' equity but not reported on the income statement. In a sense, the balance sheet has been updated to reflect the current values, but the income statement has been left out of the picture for the time being.

When Pownall Company sells the 400 bonds for $396,000 in the subsequent period, the entry under AFS would be the following:

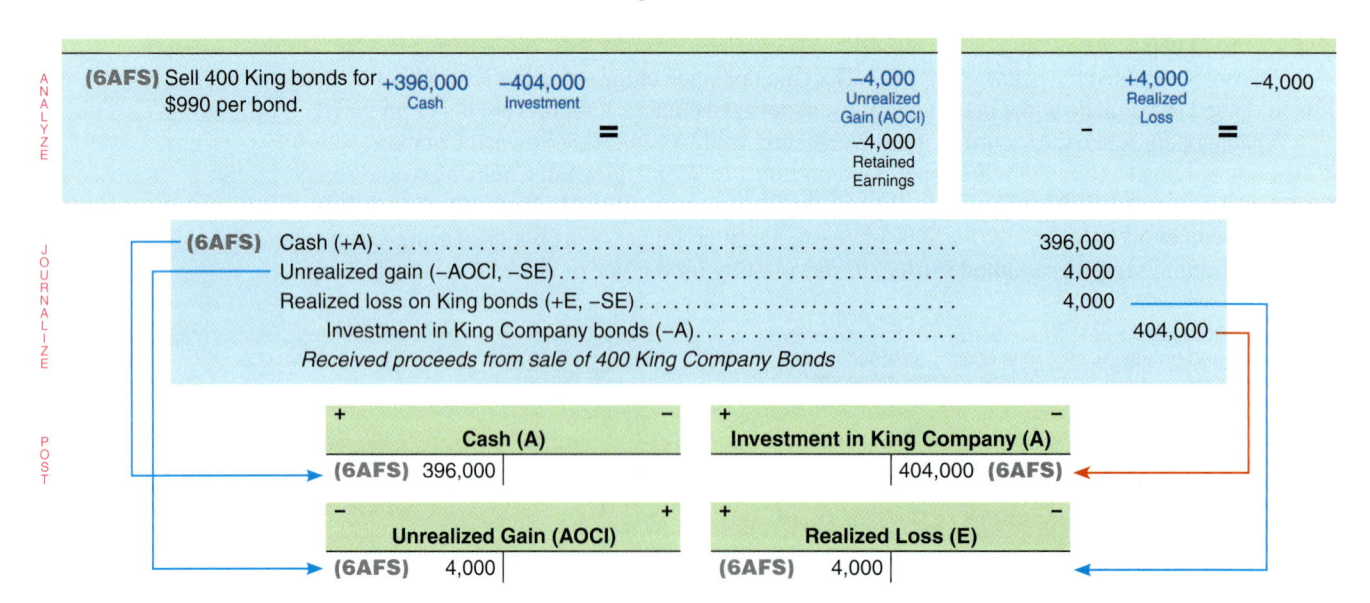

(6AFS) Sell 400 King bonds for $990 per bond.	+396,000 Cash	−404,000 Investment	=	−4,000 Unrealized Gain (AOCI) −4,000 Retained Earnings	+4,000 Realized Loss	−	= −4,000

(6AFS) Cash (+A) 396,000
        Unrealized gain (−AOCI, −SE) 4,000
        Realized loss on King bonds (+E, −SE) 4,000
            Investment in King Company bonds (−A) 404,000
        Received proceeds from sale of 400 King Company Bonds

+ Cash (A) −		+ Investment in King Company (A) −	
(6AFS) 396,000			404,000 (6AFS)

− Unrealized Gain (AOCI) +		+ Realized Loss (E) −	
(6AFS) 4,000		(6AFS) 4,000	

Under AFS, the realized gain (loss) goes into income when the security is sold, and the amount is determined by comparing the amount received when the shares are sold ($990 per bond) to the amount paid for the shares when originally purchased ($1,000 per bond). When the investment is sold, the entry must remove the investment (which was valued at $1,010 per bond at the end of last period) *and* the unrealized holding gain ($10 per bond) that was put into accumulated other comprehensive income when the shares were revalued. Both the Investment in King Company account and the AOCI for King Company have zero balances after this transaction.

The principal difference between trading and available-for-sale accounting for debt securities is in the income statement, as summarized in the following table. Under the trading security method, Pownall Company records income of $44,000 in Year 1 and $12,000 in Year 2. Under available-for-sale, Pownall Company records income that is $4,000 lower in Year 1 and $4,000 higher in Year 2. The total income from the investment in King Company is the same, but the timing is different.

	Income Reported in Income Statement From Investment in King Company Bonds	
	Trading	Available-for-Sale
Year 1		
Interest income	$45,000	$45,000
Realized holding loss	(5,000)	(5,000)
Unrealized holding gain	4,000	—
Total Year 1 investment income	$44,000	$40,000
Year 2		
Interest income	$20,000	$20,000
Realized holding loss	(8,000)	(4,000)
Total year 2 investment income	12,000	16,000
Total investment income—Year 1 plus Year 2	$56,000	$56,000

Because of the difference in the way unrealized gains and losses are reported, the classification of investments as either trading or available-for-sale will have an effect on key ratios that might be used to evaluate the performance of a company. Ratios that use net income in the calculation are affected. Return on equity (ROE), return on assets (ROA), and profit margin (PM) are among those ratios affected. Return on net operating assets (RNOA), which is discussed in Appendix A at the end of Chapter 5, would not be affected by this classification because passive investments would be considered nonoperating assets and excluded from the calculation of net operating assets, and the gains and losses would be excluded from net operating profit after taxes (NOPAT).

Another difference between trading security classification and available-for sale security classification is that under some circumstances, current GAAP requires the recording of an allowance for credit losses on available-for-sale debt securities and the use of the current expected credit loss methodology. This is a recent change to GAAP. A detailed explanation is beyond the scope of an introductory book, thus, we just briefly mention it here. Estimates of expected credit losses are based on historical loss experience as well as on current conditions and reasonable and supportable forecasts. Subsequent to the purchase of the security, changes in expected credit losses are recorded in an allowance for credit losses, a contra-asset account (the investment is not directly written down) and a credit loss expense is recorded in the income statement (or in some cases, Other Comprehensive Income). This treatment maintains the asset at a net realizable value.

PASSIVE INVESTMENTS IN EQUITY SECURITIES

While passive investments in debt securities may be accounted for in three different ways, passive investments in equity securities should be reported based on the trading securities method. That is, passive equity investments should be marked to fair value, and changes in fair value should be reported in the income statement in the period they occur. The available-for-sale method—which lets unrealized holding gains and losses go into AOCI until the security is sold—is not allowed for passive investments in equity securities.

When an equity security is purchased, the cost of the purchase increases (debits) the investment asset. Dividends received are reported as income by the investing company. At the end of every reporting period, the investing company must adjust the investment asset's value to its current fair value. If the value has increased, the change produces an unrealized holding gain in the investing company's income statement. If the investment asset's value has decreased, then marking the asset's value down to fair value produces an unrealized holding loss in the investing company's income statement. Fluctuations in the fair value of an equity security are presented as they occur in the investing company's balance sheet and income statement. When the equity security is sold, the realized holding gain or loss is determined by subtracting the fair value from the investing company's most recent balance sheet from the proceeds of the sale.

In the investing company's statement of cash flows, the original investment would be an investing cash outflow, and the sale proceeds would appear as an investing cash inflow (assuming that the purchase and sale were cash transactions). Cash dividends received would be operating cash inflows (under US GAAP). If the investing company uses the indirect method to report its operating cash flows, it would have to subtract any unrealized holding gain (or add back any unrealized holding loss) that was reporting in its income statement.

As an example, assume that Pownall Company used $50,000 cash to purchase 1,000 common shares of King Company on January 1, Year 1. One thousand shares represent 5% of King's outstanding common stock, so Pownall's investment is considered passive. During Year 1, King pays dividends to its common shareholders equal to $1.50 per share. Assume that King Company shares are traded actively on a national stock exchange. At the end of Year 1, the price for a common share of King Company is $55. Shortly after the end of Year 1, Pownall sells its investment and receives $52,000 in cash. These events would be accounted for in the following way:

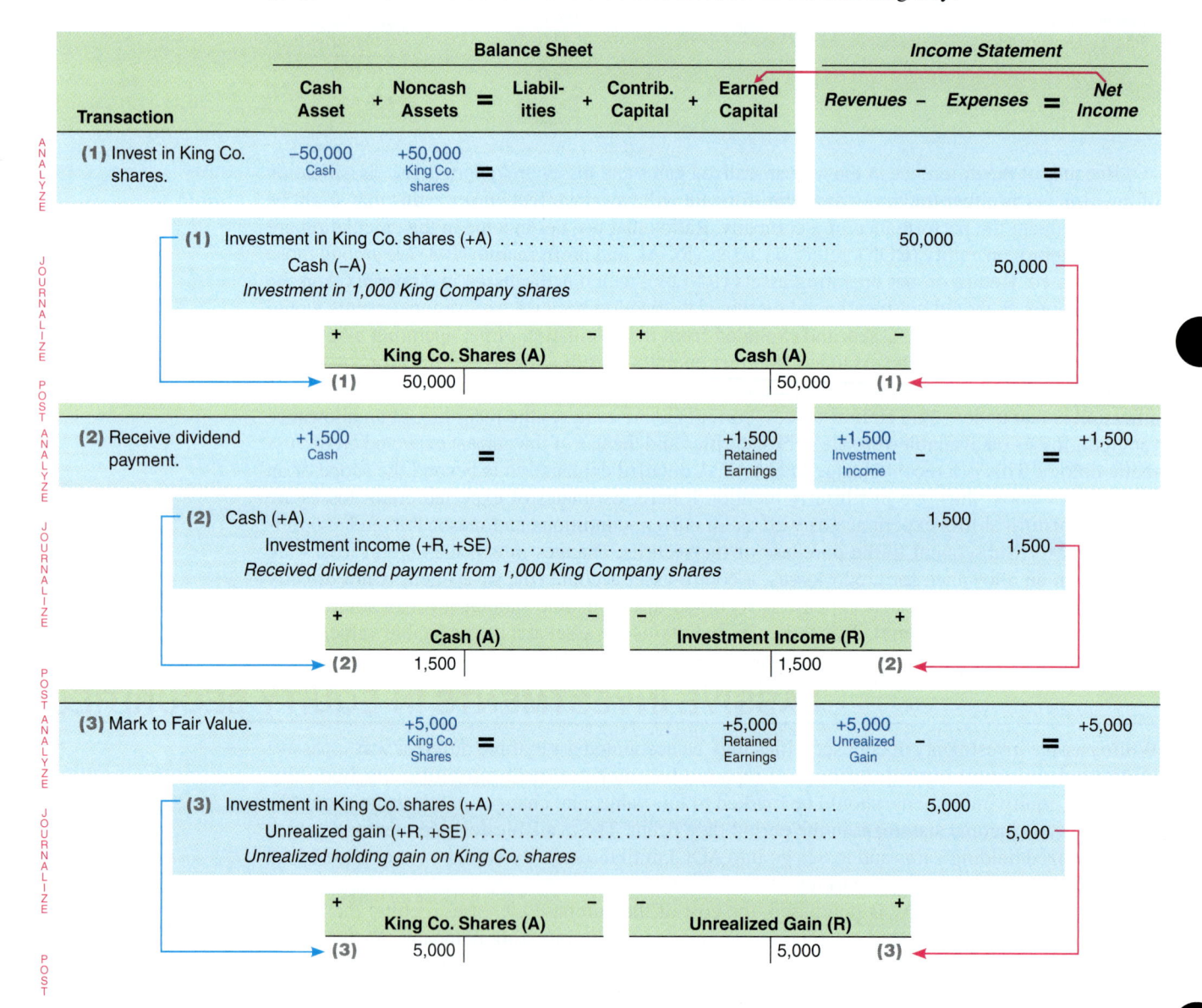

Transaction	Cash Asset	+	Noncash Assets	=	Liabilities	+	Contrib. Capital	+	Earned Capital	Revenues	−	Expenses	=	Net Income
(1) Invest in King Co. shares.	−50,000 Cash		+50,000 King Co. shares	=							−		=	
(2) Receive dividend payment.	+1,500 Cash			=					+1,500 Retained Earnings	+1,500 Investment Income	−		=	+1,500
(3) Mark to Fair Value.			+5,000 King Co. Shares	=					+5,000 Retained Earnings	+5,000 Unrealized Gain	−		=	+5,000

(1) Investment in King Co. shares (+A) 50,000
    Cash (−A) 50,000
    Investment in 1,000 King Company shares

King Co. Shares (A)
(1) 50,000

Cash (A)
| 50,000 (1)

(2) Cash (+A) 1,500
    Investment income (+R, +SE) 1,500
    Received dividend payment from 1,000 King Company shares

Cash (A)
(2) 1,500

Investment Income (R)
| 1,500 (2)

(3) Investment in King Co. shares (+A) 5,000
    Unrealized gain (+R, +SE) 5,000
    Unrealized holding gain on King Co. shares

King Co. Shares (A)
(3) 5,000

Unrealized Gain (R)
| 5,000 (3)

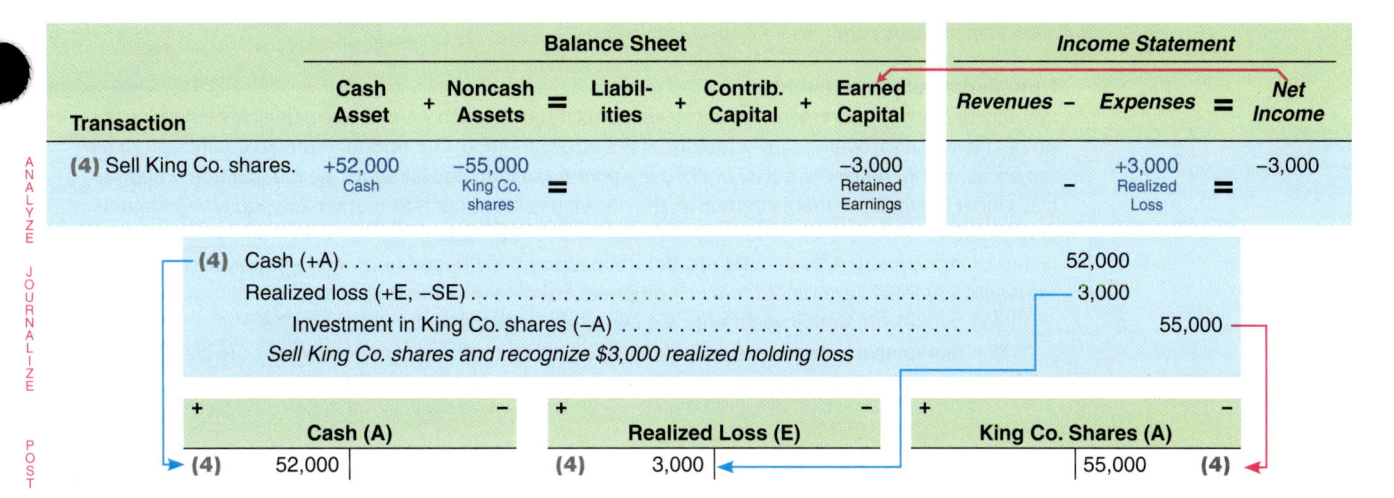

Transaction	Balance Sheet					Income Statement		
	Cash Asset	+ Noncash Assets	= Liabilities	+ Contrib. Capital	+ Earned Capital	Revenues	− Expenses	= Net Income
(4) Sell King Co. shares.	+52,000 Cash	−55,000 King Co. shares	=		−3,000 Retained Earnings		+3,000 Realized Loss	= −3,000

(4) Cash (+A) 52,000
    Realized loss (+E, −SE) 3,000
        Investment in King Co. shares (−A) 55,000
        Sell King Co. shares and recognize $3,000 realized holding loss

Cash (A)	Realized Loss (E)	King Co. Shares (A)
(4) 52,000	(4) 3,000	55,000 (4)

The available-for-sale method is not allowed for equity investments, so the holding gain/loss component of Pownall Company's investment income always reflects the events of that period. There is no opportunity for the investing company to "store up" holding gains or losses and to recognize them at a desired time.

As described earlier, the fair value of financial investments can be determined using a variety of mark-to-market or mark-to-model techniques, including hiring experts in valuation. When those approaches are prohibitively expensive, accounting standard setters also allow a version of a **cost method** for equity investments with no readily determinable fair value. The investing company uses the investment's cost but then adjusts that cost for any impairments and for any observed price changes in orderly transactions for the identical (or similar) investment from the same issuer. This approach—known as the "measurement alternative"—requires the investing company to establish systems to identify such transactions on a continuing basis.

Financial Statement Disclosures

Companies are required to disclose cost and fair value information on their investment portfolios in disclosures to financial statements. **Alphabet, Inc.**, reports its accounting policies for its investments in Note 1 to its 2020 10-K report:

> **Cash, Cash Equivalents, and Marketable Securities**
> We invest all excess cash primarily in government bonds, corporate debt securities, mortgage-backed and asset-backed securities, time deposits, and money market funds.
>
> We classify all marketable debt securities that have stated maturities of three months or less from the date of purchase as cash equivalents and those with stated maturities of greater than three months as marketable securities on our Consolidated Balance Sheets.
>
> We determine the appropriate classification of our investments in marketable debt securities at the time of purchase and reevaluate such designation at each balance sheet date. We have classified and accounted for our marketable debt securities as available-for-sale. After consideration of our risk versus reward objectives, as well as our liquidity requirements, we may sell these debt securities prior to their stated maturities. As we view these securities as available to support current operations, we classify highly liquid securities with maturities beyond 12 months as current assets under the caption marketable securities on the Consolidated Balance Sheets. We carry these securities at fair value, and report the unrealized gains and losses, net of taxes, as a component of stockholders' equity, except for the changes in allowance for expected credit losses, which are recorded in other income (expense), net. For certain marketable debt securities we have elected the fair value option, for which changes in fair value are recorded in other income (expense), net. We determine any realized gains or losses on the sale of marketable debt securities on a specific identification method, and we record such gains and losses as a component of other income (expense), net.
>
> Our investments in marketable equity securities are measured at fair value with the related gains and losses, realized and unrealized, recognized in other income (expense), net.

continued

continued from previous page

> **Non-Marketable Investments**
>
> We account for non-marketable equity investments through which we exercise significant influence but do not have control over the investee under the equity method. Our non-marketable equity securities not accounted for under the equity method are primarily accounted for under the measurement alternative. Under the measurement alternative, the carrying value of our non-marketable equity investments is adjusted to fair value for observable transactions for identical or similar investments of the same issuer or impairment. Adjustments are determined primarily based on a market approach as of the transaction date and are recorded as a component of other income (expense), net.
>
> Non-marketable debt investments are classified as available-for-sale securities.
>
> Non-marketable investments that do not have stated contractual maturity dates are classified as non-current assets on the Consolidated Balance Sheets.

This note reveals that Alphabet, Inc., reports investments in debt securities with maturities of three months or less as cash equivalents. These investments are most likely treated as trading securities, and any changes in their fair value would result in a gain or loss that would be reported in the income statement. Because of the short maturity of these investments, the gains and losses due to changes in fair value are generally very small. Liquid investments in debt securities with longer maturities are reported as marketable securities and classified as available-for-sale. Consistent with this accounting treatment, Alphabet, Inc., notes that its marketable debt securities are carried in the balance sheet at fair value, and it reports the "unrealized gains and losses, net of taxes, as a component of stockholders' equity." Alphabet then states that investments in marketable equity securities are measured at fair value with the related gains and losses recognized in the income statement. The cash, cash equivalents, and marketable securities are presented under current assets in the balance sheet:

December 31 ($ millions)	2020
Cash and cash equivalents	$ 26,465
Marketable securities	110,229
Total cash, cash equivalents, and marketable securities	$136,694

In Note 3 to its 10-K, Alphabet, Inc., provides further information about the composition of its investment portfolio starting with its investments in debt securities.

The following table summarizes Alphabet, Inc.'s debt securities by significant investment categories (in millions):

	As of December 31, 2020					
	Adjusted Cost	Gross Unrealized Gains	Gross Unrealized Losses	Fair Value	Cash and Cash Equivalents	Marketable Securities
Level 2:						
Time deposits[1]	$ 3,564	$ 0	$ 0	$ 3,564	$3,564	$ 0
Government bonds	55,156	793	(9)	55,940	2,527	53,413
Corporate debt securities	31,521	704	(2)	32,223	8	32,215
Mortgage-backed and asset-backed securities	16,767	364	(7)	17,124	0	17,124
Total	$107,008	$1,861	$(18)	$108,851	$6,099	$102,752

[1] The majority of our time deposits are domestic deposits.

A large portion of Alphabet, Inc.'s investment in debt securities is in government bonds. The various types of securities are labeled "Level 2." This label refers to the method used to determine the fair value of each investment. The fair values of the investments listed as Level 2 are determined based on a combination of quoted prices for identical or similar instruments in active markets and models with significant observable market inputs. No portion of Alphabet, Inc.'s debt investments is listed as Level 3. In past years, Alphabet, Inc., had listed Level 3 debt investments representing preferred stock and convertible debt investments that are issued by private companies and have no quoted market prices.

For each type of investment, Alphabet, Inc., reports its cost, its fair value, and the gross unrealized gains and losses; the latter equals the difference between the cost and fair value. Alphabet reports the cost of its debt investments at $107,008 million and its fair value at $108,851 million. The fair value total is then divided into cash and cash equivalents of $6,099 million and marketable securities of $102,752 million. Alphabet accounts for the investments in this table as available-for-sale investments. Alphabet also has about $2 billion of investments in debt securities for which they have elected the fair value option.

In addition to information about its investments in debt securities, Alphabet must report on its equity investments. As seen in the table below, the investments in marketable equity securities are of a much smaller magnitude than the debt securities and are almost all reported using Level 1 fair values. There is no reporting of unrealized holding gains and losses, because equity investments are recorded at fair value, with gains and losses (both realized and unrealized) going through income as they occur.

	As of December 31, 2020	
	Cash and Cash Equivalents	Marketable Equity Securities
Level 1:		
Money market funds	$12,210	$ 0
Marketable equity securities	0	5,470
	12,210	5,470
Level 2:		
Mutual funds	0	388
Total	$12,210	$5,858

Alphabet, Inc., has also invested in nonmarketable equity securities and, at the end of 2020, these securities had a Level 2 or Level 3 fair value totaling $18,893 million.

Potential for Earnings Management

When a company owns an asset with a disparity between its fair value and its book value, there is a potential for "real earnings management" or "transaction smoothing." Real earnings management refers to the use of transactions (rather than estimates) to arrive at an attractive earnings number. Examples from previous chapters would include the liquidation of LIFO inventory or the sale of a fully depreciated physical asset with remaining life. Such transactions would increase reported income and—perhaps—disguise disappointing results in a company's fundamental operations.

These concerns are also relevant in the accounting for financial investments. Suppose financial investments were kept on the books at their original cost. Over time, some would appreciate in value while others would decline. Keeping the investments at cost reduces financial statement usefulness in two ways. First, it fails to keep financial statement readers informed about changes in the company's asset values. Second, it provides management with an earnings management tool. Selling off assets with accumulated gains (losses) would increase (decrease) reported earnings, thereby providing an income smoothing tool that might disguise the company's performance.

The reporting rules for passive investments are designed to limit this sort of problem. For instance, the requirement to mark equity securities to their fair value every reporting period means that holding gains and losses cannot build up over an extended time period. And, on the last day of a reporting period, the holding gain/loss reported in income would be the same—whether the security was sold or not. However, it is still useful for a financial statement reader to identify gains and losses to clarify a company's sources of income. For instance, Alphabet's nonmarketable equity securities' holding gains and losses accounted for a $1.5 billion increase in the company's investment income for 2020.

Fair value fluctuations are ignored for debt securities under the held-to-maturity method. But if a bond is held until its maturity, there will be no gain or loss at that point. The book value and the fair value will coincide. The requirements for using held-to-maturity are that the investing company has both the intent and the ability to hold the debt instrument until it matures, and transfers to another accounting method are generally not permitted.

The available-for-sale method "disconnects" the balance sheet and the income statement, so the balance sheet reports up-to-date values for financial assets, but the unrealized holding gains and losses do not go through the income statement until realized in a transaction. This practice does provide an opportunity for management to affect the current period's income by selling selected securities. Alphabet, Inc., could sell the debt securities with accumulated unrealized holding gains of $1,861 million to increase pre-tax income or sell those with accumulated unrealized holding losses to decrease pre-tax income by $18 million. But limiting this method to debt securities reduces the potential magnitude of these effects, and the financial statement reader can look in the disclosures to find the realized holding gains and losses included in income.

Review 12-3 LO12-3

Accounting for Passive Investments

Part One: Available-for-sale securities
The following investing transactions by Lateral Inc. took place during the current year.

1. On January 1, purchased 500 Pincus Corporation bonds for $470,000 cash. The bonds have a face value of $1,000 each and an annual coupon rate of interest of 6% that is paid semi-annually on June 30 and December 31.
2. On June 30, receive interest of $15,000.
3. On June 30, the fair value of a Pincus Corporation bond is $920.
4. On July 31, all of the Pincus Corporation bonds are sold for $450,000 cash.

Required
Assume Lateral Inc.'s books are closed and financial reports are issued semiannually on June 30 and December 31.
a. Show the effects (amount and account) of the four transactions involving investments in marketable securities classified as available-for-sale in the financial statement effects template.
b. Prepare the journal entries, and post the journal entries to the appropriate T-accounts.

Part Two: Trading securities
Use the same transaction information 1 through 4 from part 1 to answer the following, assuming that the investments are now classified as trading securities.

Required
a. Enter the effects (amount and account) relating to these transactions in the financial statement effects template.
b. Prepare the journal entries, and post the journal entries to the related T-accounts.

Solution on p. 12-57.

INVESTMENTS WITH SIGNIFICANT INFLUENCE

LO12-4
Explain and analyze accounting for investments with significant influence.

Many companies make investments in other companies that yield them significant influence over those other companies. These intercorporate investments are usually made for strategic reasons including:

- **Prelude to acquisition.** Significant ownership can allow the investor company to gain a seat on the board of directors from which it can learn much about the investee company, its products, and its industry.
- **Strategic alliance.** One example of a strategic alliance is an investment in a company that provides critical inputs for the investor's production process or distribution of finished products. This relationship is closer than the usual supplier-buyer relationship, often because the investor company provides trade secrets or technical know-how of its production process.
- **Pursuit of research and development.** Many research activities in the pharmaceutical, software, and oil and gas industries are conducted jointly. The common motivation is to reduce risk or the amount of capital invested by the investor. The investor company's equity investment often carries an option to purchase additional shares or the entire company, which it can exercise if the research activities are fruitful.

A crucial feature in each of these investments is that the investor company has ownership sufficient to exert *significant influence* over the investee company. GAAP requires that such investments be accounted for using the *equity method*.

Significant influence is the ability of the investor to affect the financing or operating policies of the investee. Ownership levels of 20% to 50% of the outstanding common stock of the investee presume significant influence. Significant influence can also exist when ownership is less than 20%. Evidence of such influence can be that the investor company is able to gain a seat on the board of directors of the investee by virtue of its equity investment, or the investor controls technical know-how or patents that are used by the investee, or the investor is able to exert significant influence by virtue of legal contracts between it and the investee. There is growing pressure for determining significant influence by the facts and circumstances of the investment instead of the strict ownership percentage rule reflected in current corporate reporting.

Accounting for Investments with Significant Influence

Investments with significant influence must be accounted for using the **equity method**. The equity method of accounting for investments reports the investment on the balance sheet at an amount equal to the proportion of the investee's equity owned by the investor; hence, the name equity method. (This accounting assumes acquisition at book value. Acquisition at an amount greater than book value is covered in Appendix 12A.) Contrary to passive investments that are reported at fair value, equity method investments increase (decrease) with increases (decreases) in the earned equity of the investee.

Equity method accounting is summarized as follows:

- Investments are initially recorded at their purchase cost.
- Dividends received are treated as a recovery of the investment and, thus, reduce the investment balance. (Unlike passive investments, dividends are *not* reported as income.)
- The investor reports income equal to its proportionate share of the reported income of the investee; the investment account is increased by that income or decreased by its share of any loss.
- The investment is *not* reported at fair value, as is the case with most passive investments.

To illustrate the accounting for investments using the equity method, consider the following scenario: Assume that Alphabet, Inc., acquires a 30% interest in Mitel Networks, a company seeking to develop a new technology in a strategic alliance with Alphabet. At acquisition, Mitel reports $1,000 of stockholders' equity, the book values of its assets and liabilities equal their fair values, and Alphabet purchases its 30% stake for $300. At the first year-end, Mitel reports profits of $100 and pays $20 in cash dividends to its shareholders ($6 to Alphabet). Following are the financial statement effects for Alphabet (the investor company) for this investment using the equity method:

Transaction	Cash Asset	+	Noncash Assets	=	Liabilities	+	Contrib. Capital	+	Earned Capital	Revenues	−	Expenses	=	Net Income
(1) Purchased 30% investment in Mitel for $300 cash.	−300 Cash		+300 Investment in Mitel	=									=	
(2) Mitel reports $100 income.			+30 Investment in Mitel	=					+30 Retained Earnings	+30 Investment Income	−		=	+30
(3) Mitel pays $20 cash dividends, $6 to Alphabet.	+6 Cash		−6 Investment in Mitel	=							−		=	
End. bal. of Alphabet's investment account.			324											

The related journal entries and T-accounts are:

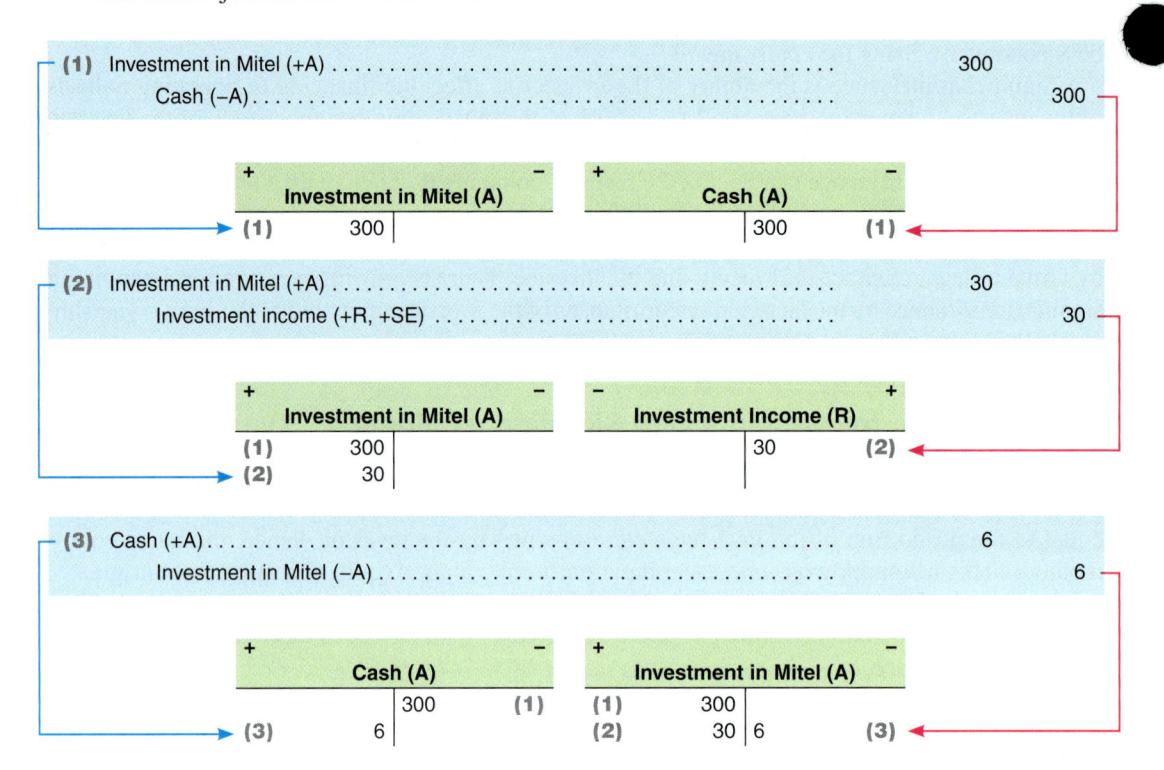

(1) Investment in Mitel (+A) 300
    Cash (−A) 300

+ Investment in Mitel (A) −		+ Cash (A) −	
(1) 300			300 (1)

(2) Investment in Mitel (+A) 30
    Investment income (+R, +SE) 30

+ Investment in Mitel (A) −		− Investment Income (R) +	
(1) 300			30 (2)
(2) 30			

(3) Cash (+A) 6
    Investment in Mitel (−A) 6

+ Cash (A) −		+ Investment in Mitel (A) −	
	300 (1)	(1) 300	
(3) 6		(2) 30	6 (3)

The investment is initially reported on Alphabet's balance sheet at its purchase price of $300, representing a 30% interest in Mitel's equity of $1,000. During the year, Mitel's equity increases to $1,080 ($1,000 plus $100 income and less $20 dividends). Likewise, Alphabet's investment increases by $30 to reflect its 30% share of Mitel's $100 income and decreases by $6 from Mitel's $20 of dividends (30% × $20). After these transactions, Alphabet's investment in Mitel is reported on Alphabet's balance sheet at 30% of $1,080, or $324. Appendix 12A covers the case in which Alphabet might have paid a premium over 30% of the fair value of Mitel's net assets.

On the statement of cash flows, the original investment in Mitel would be seen as a $300 investing cash outflow. The $6 dividend received would be an operating cash inflow. However, the indirect method presentation would start with net income, which includes $30 in income from Mitel. Therefore, a negative $24 adjustment would be necessary (entitled something like "excess of equity income over dividends received") to arrive at the correct operating cash inflow.

Two final points about equity method accounting: First, just as the equity of a company is different from its fair value, so is the balance of the equity investment account different from its fair value. Indeed, there can be a substantial difference between the book value of an investment and its fair value. Second, if the investee company reports income, the investor company also reports income. Recognition of equity income by the investor, however, does not mean that it has received that income in cash. Cash is only received if the investee's directors declare a dividend payment.

FYI Investee dividend-paying ability can be (a) restricted by regulatory agencies or foreign governments, (b) prohibited under debt agreements for highly leveraged borrowers, and/or (c) influenced by directors that the investor does not control.

RESEARCH INSIGHT

Equity Income and Stock Prices The equity method of accounting for investments does not recognize any dividends received from the investee or any fair value changes for the investee in the investor's income until the investment is sold. However, research has found a positive relationship between investors' and investees' stock prices at the time of investees' earnings and dividend announcements. This relationship suggests that the fair value includes information regarding investees' earnings and dividends when assessing the stock prices of investor companies. This finding implies the market looks beyond the book value of the investment account in determining stock prices of investor companies. The finding also reflects the fact that the earnings from the operations of subsidiaries are considered earnings of the parent corporation.

Equity Method Accounting and Effects on Ratios

Under equity method accounting, only the net equity owned is reported on the balance sheet (not the assets and liabilities to which the investment relates), and only the net equity in earnings is reported in the income statement (not the investee's sales and expenses). Both the balance sheet and income statements are, therefore, markedly affected. Further, because the gross assets and liabilities are left off the balance sheet, and because the sales and expenses are omitted from the income statement, several financial ratios are also affected. Some important examples are highlighted:

- **Net operating profit margin** (NOPM = NOPAT/Sales revenue). Many analysts include equity income (sales less expenses) in NOPAT when it relates to operating investments. (For example, when the entities are performing operating activities, such as bottling companies owned by Coca-Cola.) However, the investee's sales are omitted from the investor's sales. The reported NOPM is, thus, *overstated*.

- **Asset turnover ratios** (Sales revenue/Average assets). Because the investee's sales and its assets are omitted from the investor's financial statements, asset turnover ratios such as inventory turnover, receivables turnover, and PPE turnover are affected. The direction of the effect is, however, *indeterminable*.

- **Financial leverage** (Debt-to-equity = Total liabilities/Total stockholders' equity). Financial leverage is *understated* because the liabilities of the investee are omitted from the numerator of the debt-to-equity ratio.

Profitability ratios like ROE and ROA are also affected by the use of equity method investments, though the exact direction would require a careful analysis of the noncontrolling interests described on page 12-28. Analysts frequently adjust reported financial statements for equity investments before conducting their analysis. One approach to adjusting the reported financial statements would be to consolidate the equity method investee with the investor company.

Financial Statement Disclosures

Coca-Cola Company reports its interest in its equity method investees as follows in its 2020 and 2019 financial statements:

Coca-Cola—Financial Statement Effects of Equity Investments		
($ millions)	2020	2019
Balance sheet		
Equity method investments	$19,273	$19,025
Income statement		
Equity income—net	$ 978	$ 1,049
Statement of Cash Flows		
Equity (income) loss, net of dividends	$ (511)	$ (421)

Coca-Cola's equity method investment of $19,273 million represents 22.1% of its total assets of $87,296 million. Its equity income of $978 million is 12.6% of its consolidated net income of $7,768 million. And, while Coca-Cola recognized $978 million in income from its equity investees, $511 million was not received in dividends, meaning that Coca-Cola received $467 million ($978 million – $511 million) in dividends.

Pertinent portions of Note 6 from Coca-Cola's 2020 10-K report are presented below:

> The Company's equity method investments include, but are not limited to, our ownership interests in Coca-Cola European Partners plc ("CCEP"), Monster, AC Bebidas, Coca-Cola FEMSA, Coca-Cola HBC AG ("Coca-Cola Hellenic"), and Coca-Cola Bottlers Japan Holdings Inc. ("CCBJHI"). As of December 31, 2020, we owned approximately 19 percent, 19 percent, 20 percent, 28 percent, 23 percent, and 19 percent, respectively, of these companies' outstanding shares. As of December 31, 2020, our investments in our equity method investees in the aggregate exceeded our proportionate share of the net assets of these equity method investees by $8,762 million. This difference is not amortized.

continued

continued from previous page

A summary of financial information for our equity method investees in the aggregate is as follows (in millions):

Year ended December 31[1]	2020
Net operating revenues	$69,384
Cost of goods sold	41,139
Gross profit	28,245
Operating income	7,056
Consolidated net Income	$ 4,176
Less: Net income attributable to noncontrolling interests	54
Net income attributable to common shareowners	$ 4,122
Company equity income (loss)—net	$ 978

[1] The financial information represents the results of the equity method investees during the Company's period of ownership.

December 31	2020
Current assets	$29,431
Noncurrent assets	67,900
Total assets	$97,331
Current liabilities	20,033
Noncurrent liabilities	33,613
Total liabilities	$53,646
Equity attributable to shareowners of investees	42,622
Equity attributable to noncontrolling interests	1,063
Total equity	$43,685
Company equity method investment	$19,273

One can see that there is a substantial amount of economic activity in these equity method investees relative to that of Coca-Cola. Coca-Cola reports 2020 revenues of $33.0 billion, which is less than half of the $69.4 billion in revenues reported by the equity method investees.

YOU MAKE THE CALL

You are the Chief Financial Officer A substantial percentage of your company's sales are made through a key downstream producer, who combines your product with other materials to make the product that is ultimately purchased by consumers. In the last two years, this downstream producer has been branching out into other products that limit the capacity that can be devoted to your product. As a result, the growth prospects for your company have been diminished. What potential courses of action can you consider? Explain. (Answer on page 12-39.)

Review 12-4 LO12-4   Accounting for Investments Using the Equity Method

Maplewood Inc., completed the following four transactions in the current year for its investments accounted for using the equity method.

1. Purchased 5,000 shares of Hribar common stock at $10 cash per share. These shares reflect 30% ownership of Hribar.
2. Received a $2 per share cash dividend on Hribar common stock.
3. Made an adjustment to reflect $100,000 income reported by Hribar.
4. Sold all 5,000 shares of Hribar common stock for $90,000.

continued

continued from previous page

> **Required**
> a. Show the effects (amount and account) relating to the four transactions in the financial statement effects template.
> b. Prepare the journal entries and post the journal entries to the related T-accounts.
>
> Solution on p. 12-59.

INVESTMENTS WITH CONTROL

If the investor company owns enough of the voting stock of the investee company such that it can exercise control over the investee, it must report **consolidated financial statements**. For example, in Note 1 to its 2020 10-K describing its accounting policies, Alphabet, Inc., reports:

LO12-5
Describe and analyze accounting for investments with control.

> **Basis of Consolidation**
> The consolidated financial statements of Alphabet include the accounts of Alphabet and entities consolidated under the variable interest and voting models. All intercompany balances and transactions have been eliminated.

This statement means that Alphabet, Inc.'s financial statements are an aggregation of those of the parent company and all its subsidiary companies to create the financial statements of the total economic entity. This process involves adding up the separate financial statements, while being careful to remove the effect of transactions between the separate entities.

Accounting for Investments with Control

Accounting for business combinations (acquisitions) can be thought of as requiring one additional step to equity method accounting. Under the equity method, the investment balance represents the proportion of the investee's equity owned by the investor, and the investor company income statement includes its proportionate share of the investee's income. Consolidation accounting (1) replaces the investment balance with the investee's assets and liabilities to which it relates, and (2) replaces the equity income reported by the investor with the investee's sales and expenses to which it relates. Specifically, the consolidated balance sheet includes the gross assets and liabilities of the investee company, and the income statement includes the gross sales and expenses of the investee.

To illustrate, consider the following scenario. Penman Company acquires all of the common stock of Nissim Company by exchanging $3,000 cash for all of Nissim's common stock. Nissim will continue to exist as a separate legal company—a subsidiary of Penman Company, the parent.

In this case, the $3,000 purchase price is equal to the book value of Nissim's stockholders' equity (contributed capital of $2,000 and retained earnings of $1,000), and we assume that the fair values of Nissim's assets and liabilities are the same as their book values. On Penman's balance sheet, the investment in Nissim Co. appears as a financial investment (GAAP only requires consolidation for financial statements issued to the public, not for the internal financial records of the separate companies). Penman records an initial balance in the investment account of $3,000, which equals the purchase price. The balance sheets for Penman and Nissim immediately after the acquisition, together with the required consolidating adjustments (or eliminations), and the consolidated balance sheet that the two companies report are shown in **Exhibit 12.5**.

Penman controls the activities of Nissim, so GAAP requires consolidation of the two balance sheets. That is, Penman must report a balance sheet as if the two companies were one economic entity. For the most part, this process involves adding together the companies' resources and obligations. However, if one company has a claim on the other (e.g., a receivable) and the other company has an obligation to the first (e.g., a payable), the consolidation process must eliminate both the claim and the obligation. In the case of Penman Company and Nissim Company, the consolidated balances for current assets, PPE, and liabilities are the sum of those accounts on each balance sheet. Penman's asset investment in Nissim represents a claim on Nissim Company, and Nissim's stockholders' equity accounts represent an obligation that is held by Penman, and this intercompany claim/obligation must be eliminated to complete the consolidation. This elimination is accomplished by removing the financial investment of $3,000 and removing Nissim's equity to which that investment relates.

EXHIBIT 12.5 Mechanics of Acquisition Accounting (Purchased at Book Value, where Book Values = Fair Values)

	Penman Company	Nissim Company	Consolidating Adjustments*	Consolidated
Current assets	$ 5,000	$1,000		$ 6,000
Investment in Nissim	3,000	0	$(3,000)	0
PPE, net	10,000	4,000		14,000
Total assets	$18,000	$5,000		$20,000
Liabilities	$ 5,000	$2,000		$ 7,000
Contributed capital	10,000	2,000	(2,000)	10,000
Retained earnings	3,000	1,000	(1,000)	3,000
Total liabilities and equity	$18,000	$5,000		$20,000

*The accounting equation remains in balance with these adjustments.

The consolidated balance sheet is shown in the far right column of **Exhibit 12.5**. It shows total assets of $20,000, total liabilities of $7,000, and stockholders' equity of $13,000. Consolidated equity equals that of the parent company—this is always the case when the parent owns 100% of the subsidiary's shares.

Comparing the first and last columns of **Exhibit 12.5** demonstrates the difference between the equity method and consolidation. In the left column, it appears that Penman spent $3,000 to acquire a financial asset. However, in the last column, it appears that Penman spent $3,000 to acquire a "bundle" of assets and liabilities consisting of $1,000 in cash plus $4,000 in PPE minus $2,000 in liabilities. The purchase of the financial asset was the means by which this bundle was acquired. The net value of this bundle is $3,000, so the net assets don't change. But the financial statement reader gets more information about what was acquired.

Penman Company's statement of cash flows would show an investing cash outflow for the acquisition of Nissim Company. However, the outflow is shown net of the cash received in the acquisition, which was $1,000. Therefore, the investing section would have a line item showing something like "Cash paid for acquisitions, net of cash acquired" with an outflow of $2,000.

In addition, the changes in Penman's operating assets and liabilities on this year's balance sheet from last year's balance sheet will no longer match the adjustments for operating assets and liabilities on the indirect method statement of cash flows from operations. For instance, the change in Penman's receivables will be changes due to its own operations (including Nissim after the acquisition) plus any receivables acquired in the Nissim acquisition.

The illustration above assumes that the purchase price of the acquisition equals book value and the fair values of the acquired company's assets and liabilities are equal to their book values. What changes, if any, occur when the purchase price and book value are different? To explore this case, consider an acquisition where purchase price exceeds book value (the typical scenario). This situation might arise, for example, if an investor company believes it is acquiring something of value that is not reported on the investee's balance sheet—such as tangible assets whose fair values have risen above book value, or unrecorded intangible assets like patents or corporate synergies. When an acquisition occurs, all assets and liabilities acquired (both tangible and intangible) must be recognized at their fair value on the consolidated balance sheet.

To illustrate an acquisition where purchase price exceeds book value, assume that Penman Company acquires 100% of Nissim Company for $4,000 instead of the $3,000 purchase price we used in the previous illustration. Also assume that in determining its purchase price, Penman feels that the additional $1,000 ($4,000 vs. $3,000) is justified because (1) Nissim's PPE is worth $300 more than its book value, and (2) Penman expects to realize $700 in additional value from corporate synergies.

The $4,000 investment account reflects two components: the book value acquired of $3,000 (as before) and an additional $1,000 of newly acquired assets. The post-acquisition balance sheets of the two companies, together with the consolidating adjustments and the consolidated balance sheet, are shown in **Exhibit 12.6**.

EXHIBIT 12.6 Mechanics of Acquisition Accounting (Purchased above Book Value)

	Penman Company	Nissim Company	Consolidating Adjustments	Consolidated
Current assets	$ 4,000	$1,000		$ 5,000
Investment in Nissim	4,000	0	$(4,000)	0
PPE, net	10,000	4,000	300	14,300
Goodwill			700	700
Total assets	$18,000	$5,000		$20,000
Liabilities	$ 5,000	$2,000		$ 7,000
Contributed capital	10,000	2,000	(2,000)	10,000
Retained earnings	3,000	1,000	(1,000)	3,000
Total liabilities and equity	$18,000	$5,000		$20,000

The consolidated balances for current assets, PPE, and liabilities are the sum of those accounts on each company's balance sheet. The investment account, however, includes newly acquired assets that must be reported on the consolidated balance sheet. The consolidation process in this case has two steps. First, the $3,000 equity of Nissim Company is eliminated against the investment account as before. Then, the remaining $1,000 of the investment account is eliminated through the adjustments for revised asset and liability balances on the consolidated balance sheet ($300 of PPE and $700 of goodwill not reported on Nissim's balance sheet). Thus, the consolidated balance sheet reflects the book value of Penman and the *fair value* (book value plus the excess of Nissim's fair value over book value) for Nissim Company at the acquisition date.

Reporting of Acquired Assets and Liabilities

Acquisitions are often made at a purchase price in excess of the book value of the acquired company's equity. The excess purchase price must be allocated to all of the assets and liabilities acquired, including those that do not currently appear on the balance sheet of the acquired company. This allocation can be done in three steps:

Step 1: Adjust the book value of all tangible assets acquired and all liabilities assumed to fair value. This adjustment addresses the issue of misvalued assets and liabilities on the acquired firm's balance sheet.

Step 2: Assign a fair value to any identifiable intangible assets. Recall from Chapter 8 that intangible assets are only reported on the balance sheet if they are purchased; internally created intangible assets (other than software) are not capitalized. This step requires the acquiring firm to assign a value to the acquired company's intangible assets, even if those assets are not reported on the acquired firm's balance sheet.

Step 3: Assign the residual amount to goodwill. Goodwill is the excess of the acquisition price over the fair value of identifiable net assets acquired. That is, whatever value cannot be assigned to identifiable tangible and intangible assets is considered goodwill.[1]

The acquiring company is required to disclose relevant information about the allocation of the purchase price in its disclosure notes.

For example, consider Alphabet's reported allocation of its total $2.4 billion purchase price in December 2019 for Looker, a unified platform for business intelligence as reported in Note 8 to its 2019 10-K report:

---

[1] What happens if goodwill is negative? Such a "bargain purchase" is uncommon, because it implies that the "whole" of the acquired company is worth less than the sum of its parts. Therefore, when an acquirer believes that it has made a bargain purchase, it must carefully check its valuation of all the components of the goodwill calculation. If that review confirms that the acquirer has made a bargain purchase, then it recognizes a gain in its income from continuing operations.

> **Note 8. Acquisitions**
> **2019 Acquisitions**
> **Looker**
> In December 2019, we obtained all regulatory clearances necessary to close the acquisition of Looker, a unified platform for business intelligence, data applications, and embedded analytics for $2.4 billion, with integration pending approval from a UK regulatory review. The addition of Looker to Google Cloud is expected to help customers accelerate how they analyze data, deliver business intelligence, and build data-driven applications.
>
> The fair value of assets acquired and liabilities assumed was recorded based on a preliminary valuation and our estimates and assumptions are subject to change within the measurement period. The $2.4 billion purchase price includes our previously held equity interest and excludes post acquisition compensation arrangements. In aggregate, $91 million was cash acquired, $290 million was attributed to intangible assets, $1.9 billion to goodwill, and $48 million to net assets acquired. Goodwill was recorded in the Google segment and primarily attributable to synergies expected to arise after the acquisition. Goodwill is not expected to be deductible for tax purposes.
>
> **Other Acquisitions**
> During the year ended December 31, 2019, we completed other acquisitions and purchases of intangible assets for total consideration of approximately $1.0 billion. In aggregate, $28 million was cash acquired, $282 million was attributed to intangible assets, $904 million to goodwill, and $185 million to net liabilities assumed. These acquisitions generally enhance the breadth and depth of our offerings and expand our expertise in engineering and other functional areas.
>
> Pro forma results of operations for these acquisitions, including Looker, have not been presented because they are not material to the consolidated results of operations, either individually or in the aggregate.
>
> For all intangible assets acquired and purchased during the year ended December 31, 2019, patents and developed technology have a weighted-average useful life of 3.5 years, customer relationships have a weighted average useful life of 6.3 years, and trade names and other have a weighted-average useful life of 4.5 years.
>
> **Pending Acquisition of Fitbit**
> In November 2019, we entered into an agreement to acquire Fitbit, a leading wearables brand, for $7.35 per share, representing a total purchase price of approximately $2.1 billion as of the date of the agreement. The acquisition of Fitbit is expected to be completed in 2020, subject to customary closing conditions, including the receipt of regulatory approvals. Upon the close of the acquisition, Fitbit will be part of Google segment.

Of the approximate $3.4 billion paid for acquisitions during 2019, Alphabet assigned $2.8 billion to goodwill. The remaining $600 million includes $119 million in cash plus $572 million in intangible assets, less $137 million in net liabilities. The $572 million in intangible assets and the $137 million in net liabilities were recorded at fair value at the time of the acquisition.

Alphabet reports its aggregated goodwill separately on its balance sheet but combines its other intangible assets in its balance sheet under the title "Intangible assets, net." Goodwill can only be recognized as an asset in an acquisition and only then in the amount by which the purchase price exceeds the fair value of the identifiable net assets acquired, including all identifiable intangible assets.

For the acquisitions it made in 2019, Alphabet, Inc., estimates customer relationships have a weighted average useful life of 6.3 years. Patents and developed technology have a weighted average useful life of 3.5 years. Tradenames and other intangibles have a weighted average useful life of 4.5 years. These estimated lives determine the annual amortization expense associated with these assets on the firm's financial books. For publicly traded companies, goodwill is not currently amortized under GAAP, but is instead subject to impairment testing and impairment write-downs when appropriate. FASB has been re-evaluating the proper accounting for goodwill. In 2014, the board decided to allow amortization of goodwill for private companies in an effort towards simplicity. In December, 2020 FASB tentatively decided to move to a 10-year amortization period for goodwill for public companies, with impairment testing also required. This 2020 decision is not a rule, but still being worked on and considered by FASB. Below we discuss the current impairment rules. Impairment testing will still be required even if FASB moves to an amortization rule for public company goodwill.[2]

Reporting of Goodwill GAAP requires companies to test goodwill annually for impairment just like any other asset. To begin, the investor company can judge qualitatively—based on economic events and conditions—whether it is more likely than not that the fair value of the subsidiary is less than its book value. If that is not the case (i.e., if fair value exceeds book value), then no further testing is needed.

If it is more likely than not that the subsidiary's fair value is less than its book value (or the investor bypassed the optional qualitative test), then the fair value of that subsidiary is determined and compared with the book value of the parent company's investment account.[3] If the fair value is greater than the investment balance, the investment's goodwill is deemed not to be impaired. If the subsidiary's book value exceeds its fair value, then its goodwill must be written down by the amount of the difference, resulting in an impairment loss that is reported in the consolidated income statement. The impairment loss recognized may not exceed the carrying value of goodwill.

To illustrate the impairment computation, assume that a subsidiary's current book value is reported at $1 million on the parent company's balance sheet, but the subsidiary is found to have a current fair value of $900,000. Under these conditions, goodwill is impaired by $100,000, which is computed as follows.

Fair value of subsidiary	$ 900,000
Minus book value of net assets	(1,000,000)
Impairment loss	$ (100,000)

The financial statement effects and related journal entry and T-accounts are:

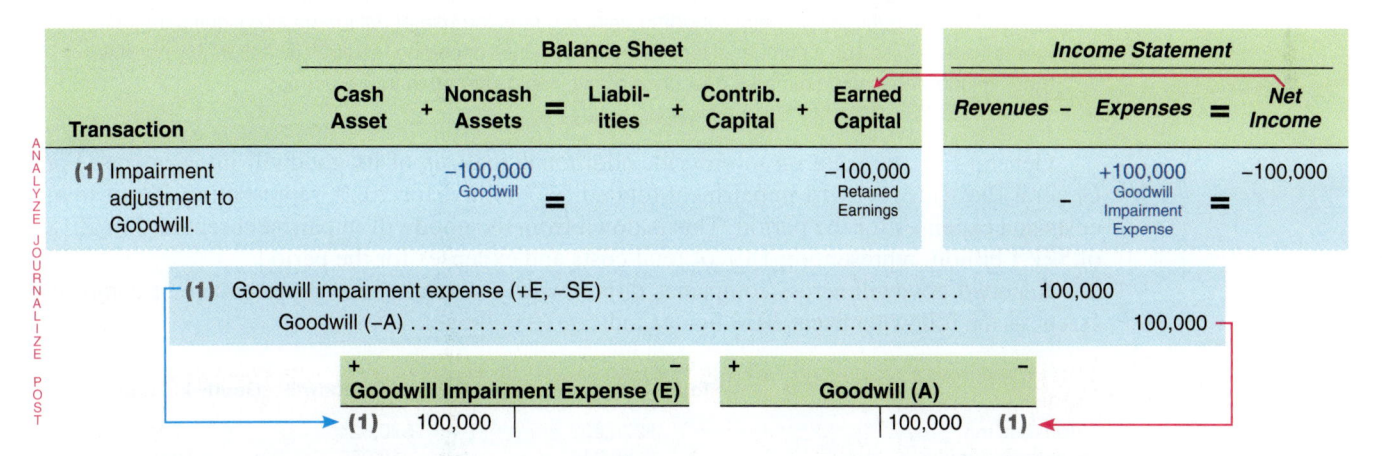

Transaction	Balance Sheet					Income Statement		
	Cash Asset +	Noncash Assets =	Liabilities +	Contrib. Capital +	Earned Capital	Revenues −	Expenses =	Net Income
(1) Impairment adjustment to Goodwill.		−100,000 Goodwill			−100,000 Retained Earnings		+100,000 Goodwill Impairment Expense	−100,000

(1) Goodwill impairment expense (+E, −SE) 100,000
     Goodwill (−A) 100,000

+ Goodwill Impairment Expense (E) −	− Goodwill (A) +
(1) 100,000	100,000 (1)

This analysis of investee company implies that goodwill must be written down by $100,000. The impairment loss is reported as a separate line item in the consolidated income statement. The related note disclosure describes the reasons for the write-down.

General Electric reports the following goodwill impairment in excerpts from its 10-K report for 2020:

---

[2] Whether to amortize goodwill or not is an old debate. Prior to the issuance of Financial Accounting Statement number 141, goodwill was amortized over 40 years.

[3] The fair value of the subsidiary company can be determined using market comparables or another valuation method (such as the discounted cash flow model, residual operating income model, or P/E multiples).

NOTE 8. GOODWILL AND OTHER INTANGIBLE ASSETS
GOODWILL
CHANGES IN GOODWILL BALANCES

(In millions)	Balance at December 31, 2019	Acquisitions	Impairments	Currency Exchange and Other	Balance at December 31, 2020
Power	$ 145	$—	$ —	$ —	$ 146
Renewable Energy	3,290	—	—	111	3,401
Aviation	9,859	—	(877)	266	9,247
Healthcare	11,728	89	—	37	11,855
Capital	839	—	(839)	—	—
Corporate[a]	873	—	—	2	876
Total*	$26,734	$90	$(1,717)	$417	$25,524

* Difference due to rounding.
[a] Corporate balance at December 31, 2020 and 2019 is our Digital business.

In the fourth quarter of 2020, we performed our annual impairment test. Based on the results of this test, the fair values of each of our reporting units exceeded their carrying values.

We continue to monitor the operating results and cash flow forecasts of our Additive reporting unit in our Aviation segment as the fair value of this reporting unit was not significantly in excess of its carrying value. At December 31, 2020, our Additive reporting unit had goodwill of $243 million.

In the second quarter of 2020 we performed an interim impairment test at our Additive reporting unit within our Aviation segment and GECAS reporting unit within our Capital segment, both of which incorporated a combination of income and market valuation approaches. The results of the analysis indicated that carrying values of both reporting units were in excess of their respective fair values. Therefore, we recorded non-cash impairment losses of $877 million and $839 million for the Additive and GECAS reporting units, respectively, in the caption Goodwill impairments in our consolidated Statement of Earnings (Loss). All of the goodwill in Additive was the result of the Arcam AB and Concept Laser GmBH acquisitions in 2016. Of the $839 million of goodwill for GECAS, $729 million arose from the acquisition of Milestone Aviation, our helicopter leasing business, in 2015. After the impairment charges, there was no goodwill remaining in our GECAS reporting unit. . . .

Determining the fair value of reporting units requires the use of estimates and significant judgments that are based on a number of factors including actual operating results. It is reasonably possible that the judgments and estimates described above could change in future periods.

General Electric went on to describe additional analysis of its goodwill impairments. For General Electric, goodwill impairment totaled $1.7 billion for 2020, representing 2% of total costs and expenses for the period. This is down from the goodwill impairment reported in 2018 of $22.1 billion, representing 18% of total costs and expenses for the period.

Reported goodwill across companies differs widely in total and as a percentage of company assets, as the following fiscal 2020 figures indicate ($ millions).

	Total Reported Assets	Reported Goodwill	Goodwill Percentage
Alphabet, Inc.	$275,909	$20,624	7.5%
Facebook, Inc.	159,316	19,050	12.0%
United Airlines, Inc.	52,605	4,523	8.6%
Adobe Inc.	24,284	10,742	44.2%
PepsiCo, Inc.	92,918	18,757	20.2%
The Coca-Cola Company	87,296	17,506	20.1%
The Procter & Gamble Company	120,700	39,901	33.1%
Colgate-Palmolive Company	15,920	3,824	24.0%
Bausch Health Companies Inc.	31,199	13,044	41.8%
Bristol-Myers Squibb Co.	118,481	20,547	17.3%

Reported goodwill is an indicator of whether a company has developed its business opportunities or purchased them and, in the same fashion, reported intangible assets are an indicator of whether a company has acquired its intellectual property in-house or by purchasing it. The purchase of intellectual properties and business opportunities allows a company to react quickly to conditions, but it is often a more expensive way to achieve growth.

> **BUSINESS INSIGHT**
>
> In competitive bidding situations, the winning bidder is likely to be the one who most overvalued the item, a phenomenon known as the "winner's curse." Therefore, acquisition goodwill is viewed with some skepticism by financial analysts. Does the goodwill represent synergies like future cost savings or business opportunities that are available only to the combined companies? Or, does it represent an overpayment?
>
> A *Financial Times* article described multi-billion dollar goodwill impairment charges by General Electric and ascribes a significant portion of these charges to a 2015 acquisition of Alstom in which the $10.1 billion purchase price resulted in $17.3 billion in goodwill. The article said that "the company was so keen to get the deal done that it paid too much."
>
> When companies record a goodwill impairment charge, they often emphasize that the impairment was a "non-cash charge," implying that it is therefore less important. That statement is true as far as the current period is concerned, but acquisitions involve cash or some other item of value. Goodwill impairment requires no current cash outflows, but it does reflect on the wisdom of past cash outflows.
>
> Source: Ed Crooks, "GE's $23 Billion Writedown Is a Case of Goodwill Gone Bad," *Financial Times*, October 3, 2018.

Noncontrolling Interest

Noncontrolling interest represents the equity of shareholders who own a minority of the shares of one or more of the subsidiaries in a consolidated entity. When a company acquires a controlling interest in another company, it must consolidate that subsidiary when preparing its financial statements by reporting all of the subsidiary's assets and liabilities in the consolidated balance sheet and all of the subsidiary's revenues and expenses in the consolidated income statement. This is true even when the controlling parent company acquires less than 100% of the subsidiary. When less than 100% of the subsidiary's shares are acquired, there are two groups of shareholders: the parent company's shareholders and the noncontrolling shareholders who own a minority of the subsidiary's shares. These noncontrolling shareholders have a claim on the net assets and the earnings of the subsidiary company, and this claim is considered part of the consolidated company's shareholders' equity.

To illustrate the reporting of noncontrolling interest, assume that Penman Company acquires 80% of Nissim Company for $2,400 (80% of $3,000). Because Penman must consolidate 100% of the assets and liabilities of Nissim, Penman's equity must increase to maintain the accounting equation. A new equity account titled noncontrolling interests is added to Penman's stockholders' equity. The consolidation worksheet is presented in **Exhibit 12.7**.

EXHIBIT 12.7 Mechanics of Consolidation Accounting
(Less than 100% of Subsidiary Shares Purchased with Fair Values = Book Values)

	Penman Company	Nissim Company	Consolidating Adjustments	Consolidated
Current assets	$ 5,600	$1,000		$ 6,600
Investment in Nissim	2,400	0	$(2,400)	0
PPE, net	10,000	4,000		14,000
Total assets	$18,000	$5,000		$20,600
Liabilities	$ 5,000	$2,000		$ 7,000
Contributed capital	10,000	2,000	$(2,000)	10,000
Retained earnings	3,000	1,000	(1,000)	3,000
Penman shareholders' equity	13,000			13,000
Noncontrolling interests			600	600
Total equity	13,000			13,600
Total liabilities and equity	$18,000	$5,000		$20,600

The contributed capital of the consolidated entity (common stock, additional paid-in capital, treasury stock, etc.) refers to the parent company's shareholders' equity (in this example, Penman Company). The net assets owned by the noncontrolling shareholders are represented in one account, labeled noncontrolling interests, which is considered to be part of shareholders' equity of the consolidated company. Each period, the noncontrolling interests equity account is increased by the noncontrolling shareholders' share of the subsidiary's net income and decreased by any dividends paid to those shareholders.

The consolidated income statement lists total consolidated revenues and expenses and consolidated net income. After net income is computed, the portion of net income that is attributed to noncontrolling interests is subtracted. If the noncontrolling shareholders own 20% of the subsidiary's shares, then 20% of the earnings of the subsidiary are subtracted from the consolidated entity's income statement. (This is not 20% of the consolidated company's earnings, only 20% of the subsidiary's earnings.)

The stockholders' equity section of The Walt Disney Company's 2020 balance sheet is shown as an illustration of the presentation of noncontrolling interests in the balance sheet:

The Walt Disney Company Consolidated Balance Sheet (Stockholders' equity section only) ($ millions)	October 3, 2020
Equity	
Preferred stock	$ —
Common stock, $0.01 par value, authorized—4.6 billion shares, issued—1.8 billion shares	54,497
Retained earnings	38,315
Accumulated other comprehensive loss	(8,322)
Treasury stock, at cost, 19 million shares	(907)
Total Disney shareholders' equity	83,583
Noncontrolling interests	4,680
Total equity	$88,263

Total Disney Company's shareholders' equity is listed at $83,583 million. This is the equity claim of those investors who own shares in Disney. Next, the $4,680 million of noncontrolling interests is listed. This amount represents the share of The Walt Disney Company subsidiaries' net assets that is owned by noncontrolling shareholders (e.g., Hong Kong Disneyland Resort and Shanghai Disney Resort). The final line lists the total equity, which is the sum of Disney's stockholders' equity and the noncontrolling interests.

The Walt Disney Company's income statement presents noncontrolling interests as follows:

The Walt Disney Company Consolidated Income Statement (excerpts) ($ millions)	Year Ended October 3, 2020
Net income (loss)	$(2,474)
Net income from continuing operations attributable to noncontrolling and redeemable noncontrolling interests	(390)
Net income from discontinued operations attributable to noncontrolling interests	—
Net income (loss) attributable to The Walt Disney Company (Disney)	$(2,864)

The Walt Disney Company presents a net loss of $(2,864) million. This is the loss for the consolidated entity, including the share of income for Disney's shareholders as well as that portion that is for the noncontrolling interests. Next, the income attributable to noncontrolling and redeemable noncontrolling interests ($390 million) is subtracted, leaving net loss attributable to Disney's shareholders ($2,864 million).

A GLOBAL PERSPECTIVE

U.S. GAAP and IFRS are very similar in their treatment of the accounting for investments as covered in this chapter. Unlike GAAP, however, IFRS still allows equity investments to be accounted for under available-for-sale. Under this option for equity investments in IFRS, another difference is that the unrealized holding gains and losses remain in AOCI and are never recognized in income.

GAAP uses the term "equity" or "affiliate" to describe an investment involving significant influence (usually between 20% and 50%). IFRS uses the term "associate" to describe such an investment, with the same 20% threshold.

The process of accounting for an acquisition and issuing subsequent consolidated financial statements is very similar to that described in the previous section.

Limitations of Consolidation Reporting Consolidation of financial statements is meant to present a financial picture of the entire set of companies under control of the parent. Because investors typically purchase stock in the parent company and not in the subsidiaries, the view is more relevant than would be one of the parent company's own balance sheet with subsidiaries reported as equity investments. Still, we must be aware of certain limitations that the consolidation process entails:

1. Consolidated income does not imply that cash is received by the parent company and is available for subsidiaries. The parent can only receive cash via dividend payments, and dividend payments may trigger tax obligations. It is readily possible, therefore, for an individual subsidiary to experience cash flow problems even though the consolidated group has strong cash flows. Likewise, debts of a subsidiary are not obligations of the consolidated group. Thus, even if the consolidated balance sheet is strong, creditors of a failing subsidiary are often unable to sue the parent or other subsidiaries to recoup losses.

2. Consolidated balance sheets and income statements are a mix of the subsidiaries, often from different industries. Comparisons across companies, even if in similar industries, are often complicated by the different mix of subsidiary companies. Companies are required to report some financial results for their business segments. For instance, General Electric reports revenues, operating profits, and assets for each of its five operating segments—Power, Renewable Energy, Aviation, Healthcare, and Capital.

3. Segment disclosures on individual subsidiaries are affected by intercorporate transfer-pricing policies that can artificially inflate the profitability of one segment at the expense of another. Companies also have considerable discretion in the allocation of corporate overhead to subsidiaries, which can markedly affect segment and subsidiary profitability.

FINANCIAL STATEMENT ANALYSIS

This section introduces no new ratios, but the topics covered in Chapter 12 do have implications for ratios covered in other chapters. For instance, gains and losses on available-for-sale securities are not recognized in income until those securities are sold. Therefore, management can increase net income by selling securities on which it has gains or decrease net income by selling securities on which it has losses. As a result, management may have a means to smooth the variations in income over time, using gains and losses from previous periods that have nothing to do with current performance. As careful financial statement users, we can read the disclosure notes to find the realized gains and losses included in income for the period.

Financial ratio comparisons are also affected by the percentage ownership of affiliated companies. For instance, suppose Naughton Group has 50% ownership in the company that distributes its products. Chapman Enterprises, a competitor of Naughton, owns 55% of the shares of the company that distributes its products. While the difference between 50% and 55% ownership probably has little economic significance, the accounting reports for Naughton and Chapman will look very different. Naughton's income statement will report only its own revenues and expenses, while Chapman's income statement will report its own revenues and expenses *and* the revenues and expenses of the distribution company (less any intercompany adjustments). Naughton's balance sheet will report its own assets, including its 50% equity in the distributor, while Chapman's balance sheet will report its own assets and liabilities *plus* those of the distribution company. Financial statement readers should interpret comparisons of ratios like PPE Turnover in light of these effects.

A similar "quantum" change in accounting occurs at 20% ownership. There may appear to be little economic difference between owning 19% of a company's shares and owning 20% of those shares. But there is a significant difference in the accounting for those two alternatives, and this difference sometimes affects the choice between a 19% investment and a 20% investment. If the investee is a start-up earning losses, a 20% investment would require the investor to recognize 20% of those losses in its own income. A 19% investment would not recognize any share of the losses, though the fair value fluctuations of the investment will be recognized in income as they occur.

Finally, acquisitions disrupt the usual relationships between income statements and between the income statement and balance sheet items. When one company acquires another, the acquirer consolidates the acquired company as of the date that the deal closes. At that point, it includes the acquired company's assets and liabilities on the consolidated balance sheet, and it begins to report the acquired company's revenues and expenses from that time forward. So, if Hoskin Corp. acquires 100% of Lynch, Inc., on December 31, 2022, how will the inventory turnover ratio be affected? The 2022 cost of goods sold for Hoskin will reflect a year of Hoskin's COGS plus one day of Lynch's COGS. The beginning-of-year inventory will be 100% of Hoskin's inventory at that time, but the end-of-year inventory will be 100% of Hoskin's inventory plus 100% of Lynch's inventory. The inventory turnover ratio is likely to decrease significantly, but that decrease is due to the acquisition, not necessarily a decline in Hoskin's operating performance.

The acquisition's effect on reported sales growth should be carefully examined as well. Suppose that Hoskin Corp and Lynch, Inc., both have a December 31 fiscal year and that Hoskin acquired Lynch on June 30, 2021—halfway through the fiscal year for both companies. When looking at Hoskin's reported revenue and its growth, one should recognize that the 2020 revenues will be Hoskin's alone, and the 2021 revenues will reflect Hoskin's sales plus half a year of Lynch's sales. Finally, the 2022 revenues will reflect a full year of sales for the combined firms. A careful reader of the financial statements should use the disclosure notes to try to separate out the effects of the acquisition from the ongoing, organic performance of the combined company.

Review 12-5 LO12-5

Accounting for a Consolidation

On January 1 of the current year, Bradshaw Company purchased all of the common shares of Dukes Company for $600,000 cash—this is $200,000 in excess of Dukes' book value of its equity. The balance sheets of the two firms immediately after the acquisition follow:

	Bradshaw (Parent)	Dukes (Subsidiary)	Consolidating Adjustments	Consolidated
Current assets	$1,000,000	$100,000		
Investment in Dukes	600,000	—		
PPE, net	3,000,000	400,000		
Goodwill	—	—		
Total assets	$4,600,000	$500,000		
Liabilities	$1,000,000	$100,000		
Contributed capital	2,000,000	200,000		
Retained earnings	1,600,000	200,000		
Total liabilities and equity	$4,600,000	$500,000		

During purchase negotiations, Dukes' PPE was appraised at $500,000, and all of Dukes' remaining assets and liabilities were appraised at values approximating their book values. Also, Bradshaw concluded that payment of an additional $100,000 was warranted because of anticipated corporate synergies.

Required

a. Show the impact of the consolidating adjusting entry in the financial statement effects template.
b. Prepare the appropriate consolidating adjusting journal entry and post the journal entry to the related T-accounts.
c. Prepare the consolidated balance sheet at acquisition.

Solution on p. 12-60.

APPENDIX 12A: Equity Method Mechanics

LO12-6 Illustrate and analyze accounting mechanics for equity method investments.

The appendix provides a comprehensive example of accounting for an equity method investment. Assume that Petroni Company acquires a 30% interest in the outstanding voting shares of Wahlen Company on January 1, 2019, for $234,000 in cash. On that date, Wahlen's book value of equity is $560,000. Petroni agrees to pay $234,000 for a company with a book value of equity equivalent to $168,000 ($560,000 × 30%) because it feels that (1) Wahlen's balance sheet is undervalued by $140,000 (Petroni estimates PPE is undervalued by $50,000 and that Wahlen has unrecorded patents valued at $90,000) and (2) the investment is expected to yield intangible benefits valued at $24,000. (The $140,000 by which the balance sheet is undervalued translates into an investment equivalent of $42,000 [$140,000 × 30%]. This, plus the intangible benefits valued at $24,000, comprises the $66,000 difference between the purchase price [$234,000] and the book value equivalent [$168,000].)

The effect of the investment on Petroni's books is to reduce cash by $234,000 and to report the investment in Wahlen for $234,000. The investment is reported at its fair value at acquisition, just like all other asset acquisitions, and it is reported as a noncurrent asset because the expected holding period of equity method investments is in excess of one year. Subsequent to this purchase there are three main aspects of equity method accounting:

1. Dividends received from the investee are treated as a return *of* the investment rather than a return *on* the investment (investor company records an increase in cash received and a decrease in the investment account).

2. When the investee company reports net income for a period, the investor company reports its proportionate ownership of that income. This amount is usually reported in the investment income section of its income statement. Thus, both income and the investment account increase from equity method income. If the investee company reports a net *loss* for the period, income of the investor company is reduced as well as its investment account by its proportionate share.

3. The investment balance is not marked-to-fair value (market) as with passive investments. Instead, it is recorded at its historical cost and is increased (decreased) by the investor company's proportionate share of investee income (loss) and decreased by any cash dividends received. Unrecognized gains (losses) can, therefore, occur if the fair value of the investment differs from this adjusted cost. (If a decline in value is deemed "other than temporary," then the investment would be written down.)

To illustrate these mechanics, let's return to our illustration and assume that subsequent to acquisition, Wahlen reports net income of $50,000 and pays $10,000 cash dividends. Petroni would reflect these events in the FSET as follows:

Transaction	Cash Asset	+	Noncash Assets	=	Liabilities	+	Contrib. Capital	+	Earned Capital	Revenues	−	Expenses	=	Net Income
(1) Purchase 30% of Wahlen Co. stock.	−234,000 Cash		+234,000 Investment in Wahlen											
(2) Recognize 30% of Wahlen net income.			+15,000 Investment in Wahlen						+15,000 Retained Earnings	+15,000 Investment Income				+15,000
(3) Receive 30% of Wahlen dividends.	+3,000 Cash		−3,000 Investment in Wahlen											

After these entries, the investment balance is $246,000. Petroni has an investing cash outflow of $234,000 and an operating cash inflow of $3,000. Retained earnings increase by $15,000 from recognizing the 30% share of Wahlen's net income.

However, Petroni must also account for the differential values that accounted for the purchase premium. If Wahlen's PPE is undervalued by $50,000 and has an expected remaining life of twenty years, Petroni must depreciate $750 (= 30%*$50,000/20 years) in value for each of the next twenty years. And, if the unrecorded patents have an expected useful life of nine years, Petroni must amortize $3,000 (= 30%*$90,000/9 years) of the investment's value for each of the coming nine years. These amortizations are deducted from the investment income recognized by Petroni. The entries are the following:

Transaction	Cash Asset	+	Noncash Assets	=	Liabilities	+	Contrib. Capital	+	Earned Capital	Revenues	−	Expenses	=	Net Income
(4) Depreciate additional PPE value.			−750 Investment in Wahlen						−750 Retained Earnings	−750 Investment Income				−750
(5) Amortize additional patent assets.			−3,000 Investment in Wahlen						−3,000 Retained Earnings	−3,000 Investment Income				−3,000

A part of the premium paid by Petroni is attributed to items that have definite lives (PPE and patents), and we must account for those amounts in judging the investment's performance. In this case, Petroni records income of $11,250 on its $234,000 investment – $15,000 for its share of Wahlen's income, minus the $3,750 amortization of the premium paid for PPE and patents. The Investment in Wahlen asset has a value of $242,250 ($234,000 + 15,000 − 3,000 − 750 − 3,000) after all entries.

The amount attributed to goodwill is tested for impairment annually, but it is not subject to periodic amortization (under current GAAP, though this may change in the future).

Review 12-6 LO12-6

Accounting for Equity Investments

Harper purchased 35% of the outstanding shares of Maxwell Company on January 1 of the current year for $80,000 in cash. Maxwell's plant assets with a book value of $164,000 were appraised at $170,000, and Maxwell has an unrecorded patent with a fair value of $5,000. All of the remaining assets and liabilities were appraised at values approximating their book values. Assume that the undervalued plant assets have an estimated remaining useful life of 20 years, and the unrecorded patent has a useful life of 5 years. During the year, Maxwell reported net income of $65,000 and paid cash dividends to shareholders totaling $35,000.

Required

a. Prepare the entry to record Harper Company's equity in the earnings of Maxwell Company, including any amortization of the excess of fair value over book value of assets acquired in the financial statement effects template.

b. Prepare the journal entry to record Harper Company's equity in the earnings of Maxwell Company, including any amortization of the excess of fair value over book value of assets acquired.

Solution on p. 12-61.

APPENDIX 12B: Consolidation Accounting Mechanics

LO12-7 Apply consolidation accounting mechanics.

This appendix is a continuation of the example we introduced in Appendix 12A, extended to the consolidation of a parent company and one wholly owned subsidiary. Assume that Petroni Company acquires 100% (rather than 30% as in Appendix 12A) of the outstanding voting shares of Wahlen Company on January 1, 2022. To obtain these shares, Petroni pays $420,000 cash and issues 20,000 shares of its $10 par value common stock. On this date, Petroni's stock has a fair value of $18 per share, and Wahlen's book value of equity is $560,000. Petroni is willing to pay $780,000 ($420,000 plus 20,000 shares at $18 per share) for this company with a book value of equity of $560,000 because it believes Wahlen's balance sheet is understated by $140,000. (Its PPE is undervalued by $50,000, and it has unrecorded patents valued at $90,000.) The remaining $80,000 of the purchase price excess over book value is ascribed to corporate synergies and other unidentifiable intangible assets (goodwill). Thus, the purchase price consists of the following three components:

Investment ($780,000) { Book value of Wahlen ($560,000) / Excess fair value over book ($140,000) / Goodwill ($80,000) }

The investment in Wahlen appears as a financial asset on Petroni's books. This means that at acquisition, Petroni's assets increase by $360,000 (cash decreases by $420,000, and the investments account increases by $780,000), and its equity (contributed capital) increases by the same amount.

The balance sheets of Petroni and Wahlen at acquisition follow, including the adjustments that occur in the consolidation process and the ultimate consolidated balance sheet.

Accounts	Petroni Company	Wahlen Company	Consolidation Adjustments* Entry S	Consolidation Adjustments* Entry A	Consolidated Balance Sheet
Cash	$ 168,000	$ 80,000			$ 248,000
Receivables, net	320,000	180,000			500,000
Inventory	440,000	260,000			700,000
Investment in Wahlen	780,000	0	$(560,000)	$(220,000)	0
Land	200,000	120,000			320,000
PPE, net	1,040,000	320,000		50,000	1,410,000
Patents	0	0		90,000	90,000
Goodwill	0	0		80,000	80,000
Totals	$2,948,000	$960,000			$3,348,000
Accounts payable	$ 320,000	$ 60,000			$ 380,000
Long-term liabilities	760,000	340,000			1,100,000
Contributed capital	1,148,000	80,000	$ (80,000)		1,148,000
Retained earnings	720,000	480,000	(480,000)		720,000
Totals	$2,948,000	$960,000			$3,348,000

*Entry S refers to elimination of subsidiary stockholders' equity, and Entry A refers to adjustment of assets and liabilities acquired.

The initial balance of the investment account at acquisition ($780,000) reflects the $700,000 fair value of Wahlen's net tangible assets and patents ($560,000 book value + $140,000 undervaluation of assets) plus the goodwill ($80,000) acquired. Goodwill is the excess of the purchase price over the fair value of the net assets acquired. It does not appear on Petroni's balance sheet as an explicit asset at this point. It is, however, included in the investment balance and will emerge as a separate asset during consolidation.

The process of completing the initial consolidated balance sheet involves eliminating Petroni's investment account and replacing it with the assets and liabilities of Wahlen Company to which it relates. Recall the investment account consists of three items: the book value of Wahlen ($560,000), the excess of net asset fair value over book value ($140,000), and goodwill ($80,000). The consolidation process eliminates each item as follows:

Entry S: Elimination of Wahlen's book value of equity: Investment account is reduced by the $560,000 book value of Wahlen, and each of the components of Wahlen's equity ($80,000 common stock and $480,000 retained earnings) is eliminated.

Entry A: Elimination of the excess of purchase price over book value: Investment account is reduced by $220,000 to zero. The remaining adjustments increase assets (A) by the additional purchase price paid. PPE is written up by $50,000, and a $90,000 patent asset and an $80,000 goodwill asset are reported.

Stepping back from the consolidation process, we can see its effects by comparing the Petroni Company (parent) balance sheet to the consolidated balance sheet. The Petroni Company balance sheet shows a financial asset valued at $780,000. Consolidation gives us a different perspective. Rather than viewing this as a financial investment, consolidation views the financial investment as the *means* by which Petroni Company acquired a bundle of assets and liabilities. That is, the financial asset of $780,000 has been replaced by Cash ($80,000), Receivables ($180,000), Inventory ($260,000), Land ($120,000), PPE – net ($370,000), Patent ($90,000), Goodwill ($80,000), Payables ($60,000) and Long-term liabilities ($340,000). This bundle has a net value equal to the $780,000, but it provides much more detail about the transaction in which Petroni engaged.

The one part of the balance sheet that is not changed by the consolidation is the shareholders' equity section. The consolidated shareholders' equity accounts are the same as the parent company shareholders' equity accounts when the parent owns 100% of the subsidiary.

Consolidation is similar in successive periods. To the extent that the excess purchase price has been assigned to depreciable assets, or identifiable intangible assets that are amortized over their useful lives, the new assets recognized initially are depreciated. If the PPE value adjustment has an estimated life of 20 years, then the consolidated income statement would include depreciation of 1/20 of this $50,000 each year. Amortization of the $90,000 patent would also appear in the consolidated income statement. Finally, because goodwill is not amortized under GAAP, it remains at its carrying amount of $80,000 on the consolidated balance sheet unless and until it is impaired and written down.

Recording a Consolidating Adjustment

LO12-7 **Review 12-7**

On January 1 of the current year, Harper Company purchased all of the common shares of Maxwell Company for $200,000 cash. Balance sheets of the two firms at the acquisition date follow.

	Harper Company	Maxwell Company	Consolidating Adjustments	Consolidated
Current assets	$ 680,000	$ 48,000		
Investment in Maxwell	200,000	—		
Plant assets, net	1,200,000	164,000		
Goodwill	—	—		
Total assets	$2,080,000	$212,000		
Liabilities	$ 280,000	$ 36,000		
Contributed capital	1,400,000	160,000		
Retained earnings	400,000	16,000		
Total liabilities and equity	$2,080,000	$212,000		

During purchase negotiations, Maxwell's plant assets were appraised at $170,000, and Maxwell had an unrecorded patent with a fair value of $5,000. All of the remaining assets and liabilities were appraised at values approximating their book values. The remaining $13,000 of the purchase price was ascribed to goodwill.

continued

continued from previous page

	Required
Solution on p. 12-61.	a. Prepare the consolidating adjustments and the consolidated balance sheet at acquisition. b. Prepare the journal entry to record the consolidating adjustments at acquisition. c. Record the consolidating adjusting entry in the financial statement effects template.

APPENDIX 12C: Accounting for Investments in Derivatives

LO12-8
Discuss the reporting of derivative securities.

Derivatives refer to financial instruments that are utilized by companies to reduce various kinds of risks. Some examples follow:

- A company expects to purchase raw materials for its production process and wants to reduce the risk that the purchase price increases prior to the purchase.
- A company has an accounts receivable on its books that is payable in a foreign currency and wants to reduce the risk that exchange rates move unfavorably prior to collection.
- A company borrows funds on a floating rate of interest (such as linked to the prime rate) and wants to convert the loan to a fixed rate of interest.

Companies are commonly exposed to these and many similar types of risk. Although companies are generally willing to assume the normal market risks that are inherent in their business, many of these financial-type risks can add variability to income and are uncontrollable. Fortunately, commodities, currencies, and interest rates are all traded on various markets and, further, securities have been developed to manage all of these risks. These securities fall under the label of derivatives. They include forward contracts, futures contracts, option contracts, and swap agreements.

Companies use derivatives to manage many of these financial risks. The reduction of risk comes at a price: the fee that another party (called the counterparty) is charging to assume that risk. Most counterparties are financial institutions, and managing financial risk is their business and a source of their profits. Although derivatives can be used effectively to manage financial risk, they can also be used for speculation with potentially disastrous results. It is for this reason that regulators passed standards regarding their disclosure in financial statements.

Reporting of Derivatives Derivatives work by offsetting the gain or loss for the asset or liability to which they relate. Derivatives thus shelter the company from such fluctuations. For example, if a hedged receivable denominated in a foreign currency declines in value (due to a strengthening of the $US), the derivative security will increase in value by an offsetting amount, at least in theory. As a result, net equity remains unaffected and no gain or loss arises, nor is a loss reported in income.[4]

Although accounting for derivatives is complex, it essentially boils down to this: The derivative contract and the asset or liability to which it relates are both reported on the balance sheet at fair value. The asset and liability are offsetting *if* the hedge is effective and, thus, net equity is unaffected. Likewise, the related gains and losses are largely offsetting, leaving income unaffected. Income is impacted only to the extent that the hedging activities are ineffective or result from speculative activities. It is this latter activity, in particular, that regulators were concerned about in formulating accounting standards for derivatives.

Disclosure of Derivatives Companies are required to disclose both qualitative and quantitative information about derivatives in notes to their financial statements and elsewhere (usually in Management's Discussion and Analysis section). The aim of these disclosures is to inform outsiders about potential risks underlying derivative securities.

Following is **Southwest Airlines Co.**'s disclosures from Note 1 to its 2020 10-K report relating to its use of derivatives.

> **Financial Derivative Instruments**
> The Company accounts for financial derivative instruments at fair value and applies hedge accounting rules where appropriate. The Company utilizes various derivative instruments, including jet fuel, crude oil, unleaded gasoline, and heating oil-based derivatives, to attempt to reduce the risk of its exposure to jet fuel price increases. These instruments are accounted for as cash flow hedges upon proper qualification.

continued

---

[4] Unrealized gains and losses on cash flow and net investment hedges are accumulated in other comprehensive income (OCI) and are not recognized in current income until the time when the hedged item affects earnings (for example, when the commodity is used). Unrealized gains and losses on derivatives classified as *fair value hedges* (such as those relating to interest rate hedges and swaps, and the hedging of asset values such as relating to securities) are recorded in current income on the same line that includes the hedged item's impact on earnings.

continued from previous page

> The Company also has had interest rate swap agreements to convert certain floating-rate debt to a fixed-rate and had interest rate swap agreements to convert portions of its fixed-rate debt to floating rates. The Company has forward-stating interest rate swap agreements, the primary objective of which is to hedge forecasted debt issuances. These interest rate hedges are appropriately designated as cash flow hedges.
>
> Since the majority of the Company's financial derivative instruments are not traded on a market exchange, the Company estimates their fair values. Depending on the type of instrument, the values are determined by the use of present value methods or option value models with assumptions about commodity prices based on those observed in underlying markets.
>
> All cash flows associated with purchasing and selling derivatives are classified as operating cash flows in the Consolidated Statement of Cash Flows, within Changes in certain assets and liabilities. The Company classifies its cash collateral provided to or held from counterparties in a "net" presentation on the Consolidated Balance Sheet against the fair value of the derivative positions with those counterparties. See Note 11 for further information.

Southwest Airlines' derivative use is mainly to hedge against fuel cost. Those hedges act to place a ceiling on fuel cost. The company reports that 77% of its 2020 fuel consumption was covered by hedging activity.

From a reporting standpoint, unrealized gains and losses on these derivative contracts are accumulated in the accumulated other comprehensive income (AOCI) portion of its stockholders' equity until the fuel is consumed. Once that fuel is consumed, those unrealized gains and losses are removed from AOCI, and the gain (loss) on the option is used to offset the loss (gain) on fuel.

Although the fair value of derivatives and their related assets or liabilities can be substantial, the net effect on earnings and stockholders' equity is usually minor because companies are mainly using them as hedges and not as speculative securities. The accounting standards for derivative instruments were enacted in response to a concern that speculative activities were not adequately disclosed. Subsequent to its passage, the financial effects have often appeared modest (with occasional exceptions such as **JP Morgan Chase**'s "London Whale" in 2012). Either these companies were not speculating to the extent expected, or they have since reduced their level of speculation in response to increased scrutiny from better disclosures.

Significant economic disruptions can also impact hedge accounting results. Most recently, for example, during the Coronavirus pandemic, air travel essentially stopped and oil prices plunged. This left many airlines with 'over-hedged' positions. Basically, they hedged more fuel than they ended up using (and fuel was much cheaper than expected as well). For example, British Airways' parent company, International Airlines Group, recorded a €1.325 billion charge, and Air France-KLM recorded a charge of €455 million related to over-hedging.[5] Southwest Airlines disclosed the following in their 2020 10-K: "During 2020, as a result of the drastic drop in demand for air travel due to the COVID-19 pandemic, the Company's forecast for 2020 and 2021 fuel purchases and consumption was significantly reduced, causing the Company to be in an estimated "over-hedged" position for second, third, and fourth quarter 2020, and full year 2021. Therefore, the Company de-designated a portion of its fuel hedges related to these periods, and has reclassified approximately $39 million in losses from AOCI into Other (gains) losses, net, during 2020."

Analyzing Derivative Instruments

LO12-8 Review 12-8

Colgate-Palmolive Company reported the following information regarding its derivative instruments in its 2020 10-K report.

Excerpts from Note 7: Fair Value Measurements and Financial Instruments

> The Company is exposed to market risk from foreign currency exchange rates, interest rates, and commodity price fluctuations. Volatility relating to these exposures is managed on a global basis by utilizing a number of techniques, including working capital management, sourcing strategies, selling price increases, selective borrowings in local currencies and entering into selective derivative instrument transactions, issued with standard features, in accordance with the Company's treasury and risk management policies, which prohibit the use of derivatives for speculative purposes and leveraged derivatives for any purpose. It is the Company's policy to enter into derivative instrument contracts with terms that match the underlying exposure being hedged. Provided below are details of the Company's exposures by type of risk and derivative instruments by type of hedge designation....
>
> The following table presents the location and amount of gains (losses) on hedges recognized on the Company's Consolidated Statements of Income:

continued

---

[5] The Wall Street Journal, May 15, 2020 https://www.wsj.com/articles/overhedging-oil-prices-lands-some-coronavirus-battered-global-airlines-in-further-trouble-11589555843.

	Twelve Months Ended December 31, 2020		
	Cost of Sales	Selling, General, and Administrative Expenses	Interest (Income) Expense, Net
Gain (loss) on hedges recognized in income:			
Interest rate swaps designated as fair value hedges:			
Derivative instrument.	$—	$ —	$(10)
Hedged items.	—	—	10
Foreign currency contracts designated as fair value hedges:			
Derivative instrument.	—	29	—
Hedged items.	—	(29)	—
Foreign currency contracts designated as cash flow hedges:			
Amount reclassified from OCI.	1	—	—
Commodity contracts designated as cash flow hedges:			
Amount reclassified from OCI.	(1)	—	—
Total gain (loss) on hedges recognized in income	$—	$ —	$ —

Required

a. What types of risks would the contracts listed above be designed to hedge against?

b. What is the net gain or loss recognized on the company's 2020 income statement related to the risks described in part a?

Solution on p. 12-62.

SUMMARY

LO12-1 **Explain and interpret the three levels of investor influence over an investee—passive, significant, and controlling. (p. 12-3)**

- Ownership of 20% or less in another corporation is presumed to be a passive investment by the investor.
- Significant influence is assumed to be available to the investor corporation if it owns more than 20% but not over 50% of the outstanding voting stock of the investee corporation.
- Control is generally presumed if the investing firm owns more than 50% of the outstanding voting stock of the investee corporation.

LO12-2 **Describe the term "fair value" and the fair value hierarchy. (p. 12-5)**

- Fair value is the amount that an independent buyer would be willing to pay for an asset (or the amount that would need to be paid to discharge a liability) in an orderly transaction.
- Fair value can be determined by reference to a market price when available, but it may also be determined by other methods (discounted cash flow analysis, pricing of comparable assets, etc.). GAAP defines three levels of fair value determination:
  - Level 1: Values based on quoted prices in active markets for identical assets/liabilities
  - Level 2: Values based on observable inputs other than Level 1 (e.g., quoted prices for similar assets/liabilities or interest rates or yield curves)
  - Level 3: Values based on inputs observable only to the reporting entity (e.g., management estimates or assumptions)
- GAAP requires that companies disclose their fair value determinations in the disclosure notes of their financial statements.

LO12-3 **Describe and analyze accounting for passive investments. (p. 12-6)**

- Ownership of a debt security or 20% or less of the equity of another corporation is treated as a passive investment by the investor. Investing for returns is the objective rather than influencing another corporation's decisions. The investment is reported as a long-term asset only if the intention is to retain the asset for longer than a year. Investments in debt securities are segregated into three types—trading securities, held-to-maturity securities, and securities available-for-sale.
- Debt securities that management intends to hold to maturity are carried at (amortized) cost unless their value is considered impaired, in which case the security is written down. Otherwise changes in fair value are not recognized on the balance sheet or the income statement.

- Debt securities treated as trading securities have an objective of short-term gain and will be converted into cash in a very short period of time. Any trading securities held at the end of an accounting period are marked to their fair value. The value change is recognized as an unrealized gain (or loss) in the income statement.
- Debt securities treated as available-for-sale securities are those that classify as neither held-to-maturity nor trading. Any securities held at the end of an accounting period are also marked to their fair value. However, the value change bypasses the income statement to become part of retained earnings called other comprehensive income. Holding gains and losses are recognized in income when the security is sold.
- Investments in equity securities are always marked to fair value, with holding gains and losses (both realized and unrealized) going through income in the period they occur.
- Gains and losses realized on sale, and dividends on passive investments, are reported as other income in the income statement.

Explain and analyze accounting for investments with significant influence. (p. 12-17)   **LO12-4**

- Significant influence is assumed to be available to the investor corporation if it owns more than 20% but not over 50% of the outstanding voting stock of the investee corporation. Typically, the investment is initially recorded as a long-term asset at the purchase price.
- In the case of significant influence, the equity method of reporting is followed.
- Under the equity method, the investor recognizes its proportionate share of the investee's net income as income and an increase in the investment account. Any dividends received by the investor are treated as a recovery of the investment and reduce the investment balance.

Describe and analyze accounting for investments with control. (p. 12-22)   **LO12-5**

- If a corporation is considered to have control of another corporation, the financial statements of both firms are consolidated and reported as though they were a single entity.
- Control means that the investor has the ability to affect the strategic direction of the investee. Control is generally presumed if the investing firm owns more than 50% of the outstanding voting stock of the investee corporation.
- At the time of the acquisition, acquired assets and liabilities are restated at fair value in the consolidated balance sheet.
- If the purchase price exceeds the fair value of acquired net assets, the remainder is labeled "goodwill." Goodwill is not amortized, but tested for impairment annually. Though, these rules are currently under consideration by FASB, and amortization of goodwill may be required in the future.

Appendix 12A: Illustrate and analyze accounting mechanics for equity method investments. (p. 12-31)   **LO12-6**

- Under the equity method of accounting, neither the investee's assets nor its liabilities are reported on the investor's balance sheet. Only the proportionate investment is reported. Further, only the investor's net equity is reported in income; and the investee's sales and expenses are omitted.
- The result is that revenues and expenses, but not NOPAT, are understated; NOPM (NOPAT/Sales) is overstated; and net operating assets (NOA) are understated. Also, financial leverage is understated. ROE remains unaffected.

Appendix 12B: Apply consolidation accounting mechanics. (p. 12-33)   **LO12-7**

- Identifiable intangible assets (such as patents, trademarks, customer lists) often result from the acquisition of one corporation by another. This is a situation in which the acquirer will have control and consolidation accounting is required.
- Intangibles are valued at the purchase date and then (unless indefinite-lived) amortized over their economic life. Any remaining purchase price not allocated to tangible or identifiable intangible assets is treated as goodwill.
- Goodwill and other indefinite-lived intangibles are not amortized but written down when and if considered impaired. The write-down is an expense of the period. We note again, however, that goodwill accounting is being reviewed by FASB. Private companies are currently allowed to amortize goodwill and amortization is currently under FASB consideration for public companies as well.
- Reports of consolidated corporations are often difficult to understand because they commingle the assets, liabilities, revenues, expenses, and cash flows of several businesses that can be very different.

Appendix 12C: Discuss the reporting of derivative securities. (p. 12-35)   **LO12-8**

- Derivatives refer to financial instruments that are utilized by companies to reduce various kinds of risks.
- Derivatives work by offsetting the gain or loss for the asset or liability to which they relate.
- The accounting for derivatives boils down to this: The derivative contract and the asset or liability to which it relates are both reported on the balance sheet at fair value. The asset and liability are offsetting if the hedge

works. Likewise, the related gains and losses are largely offsetting, leaving income unaffected. For cash flow and net investment hedges, the gains and losses are accumulated in AOCI until the hedged item affects earnings. For fair value hedges, the gains and losses are recorded in the income statement in the same line item as the income effects from the hedged item.

GUIDANCE ANSWERS . . . YOU MAKE THE CALL

You are the Chief Financial Officer When a key component of a company's distribution process begins to turn its attention to other products, it can have a detrimental effect of the prospects for future growth. For instance, the soft-drink companies depend heavily on their bottling companies to get the product to the consumer. In these circumstances, companies may purchase enough shares in the distribution company to exert significant influence (or even control) over the key distributor.

Assignments with the MBC logo in the margin are available in myBusinessCourse.
See the Preface of the book for details.

MULTIPLE CHOICE

Multiple Choice Answers
1. c 2. e 3. a 4. b

1. Corporation A owns 35% of corporation B. This is a case where:
   a. Corporation A controls corporation B.
   b. Corporation A does not control corporation B.
   c. Corporation A has significant influence on corporation B.
   d. Corporation A does not have a significant influence on corporation B.
   e. Both *a* and *c* are correct.

2. In accounting for available-for-sale debt securities, the
   a. securities are reported on the balance sheet at their fair value.
   b. securities are reported at cost.
   c. increases in fair value are reported in income.
   d. increases in fair value are not reported in income.
   e. both *a* and *d* are correct.

3. Which of the following statements is true of investments accounted for under the equity method?
   a. Investor reports its percentage share of the investee's income in its income.
   b. Investor reports dividends received from the investee in its operating income.
   c. Investment is reported at its fair value.
   d. Investment is reported at cost plus any dividends received from the investee.
   e. Investment is reported at fair value less any dividends received from the investee.

4. Which of the following statements is true about goodwill?
   a. Current reporting standards require that goodwill be amortized over its economic life.
   b. Goodwill is written down when the fair value of the investee is less than the book value.
   c. Goodwill can be recognized only when the acquisition price does not exceed the value of the tangible and identifiable intangible assets acquired.
   d. The recording of goodwill can be based on the acquisition of assets such as patents and trademarks.
   e. Goodwill equals retained earnings.

Superscript $^{A\,(B,\,C)}$ denotes assignments based on Appendix 12A (12B, 12C).

QUESTIONS

Q12-1. For investments in debt securities, what measure (fair value or amortized cost) is used for the balance sheet to report (a) trading securities, (b) available-for-sale securities, and (c) held-to-maturity securities?

Q12-2. What is an unrealized holding gain (loss)? Explain. For passive investments in equity securities, how are unrealized holding gains (losses) treated?

Q12-3. Where are unrealized holding gains and losses related to trading securities reported in the financial statements? Where are unrealized holding gains and losses related to available-for-sale debt securities reported in the financial statements?

Q12-4. What does *significant influence* imply regarding financial investments? Describe the accounting procedures used for such investments.

Q12-5. On January 1 of the current year, Yetman Company purchases 40% of the common stock of Livnat Company for $200,000 cash. During the year, Livnat reports $64,000 of net income and pays $48,000 in cash dividends. At year-end, what amount should appear in Yetman's balance sheet for its investment in Livnat?

Q12-6. What accounting method is used when a stock investment represents more than 50% of the investee company's voting stock? Explain.

Q12-7. What is the underlying objective of consolidated financial statements?

Q12-8. Finn Company purchases all of the common stock of Murray Company for $600,000 when Murray Company has $240,000 of common stock and $360,000 of retained earnings. Book values of the assets and liabilities of Murray Company equal their fair values. If a consolidated balance sheet is prepared immediately after the acquisition, what amounts are eliminated in preparing it? Explain.

Q12-9.[B] Bradshaw Company owns 100% of Dee Company. At year-end, Dee owes Bradshaw $150,000. If a consolidated balance sheet is prepared at year-end, how is the $150,000 handled? Explain.

Q12-10. What are some limitations of consolidated financial statements?

DATA ANALYTICS

DA12-1. Using Excel Visualizations to Analyze Changes in Other Comprehensive Income   **LO12-3**

The Excel file associated with this exercise includes data for Amazon.com, Inc., and Apple Inc., as reported in Form 10-Q and 10-K reports over a two-year period ($ millions). In this exercise, we analyze the change in unrealized gains and losses reported in other comprehensive income by quarter over a two-year period for Amazon and Apple.

REQUIRED
1. Download Excel file DA12-1 found in myBusinessCourse.
2. Prepare Waterfall charts in Excel for each year for Amazon and Apple, showing the quarterly change in unrealized gains/losses on securities. *Hint:* Add totals for each year, highlight data, select Insert, Chart, Waterfall.
3. Label the last bar as "total" per the legend. *Hint:* Double-click on bar (last) to open the Format Data Point sidebar. Single-click on the same bar. Check Set as total under Series Options on the bar column icon tab.
4. Indicate how many columns are shown in each chart.
5. Indicate how many orange bars are displayed in each chart. What do the orange bars represent?
6. Indicate how many blue bars are displayed in each chart. What do the blue bars represent?
7. Indicate what type of securities are the source for the gains and losses displayed in the charts.
8. Indicate which chart showed the most volatility over the course of the year. What total amount of gain or loss would be shown on the Form 10-K for that particular year?
9. Indicate whether the trends shown in the charts are similar across companies for each year.
10. Compute the percentage change in the net gain/(loss) from Year 1 to Year 2 for Amazon and for Apple.
11. Indicate why GAAP requires the gains and losses analyzed above to be reported in other comprehensive income rather than net income.

DATA VISUALIZATION

Data Visualization Activities are available in myBusinessCourse. These assignments use Tableau Dashboards to expose students to visual depictions of data and introduce students to data analytics through data visualizations. These exercises are easily assignable and auto graded by MBC.

MINI EXERCISES

LO12-1 **M12-11. Classifying Investments as Passive, Significant, or Controlling**
For each of the situations below, determine if the investment should be reported as a passive investment (P), an investment reflecting significant influence (SI), or a controlling interest (C).

a. _____ Griffin Company purchased 25% of the common stock of Wright, Inc., Griffin is one of several suppliers that Wright, Inc., relies on to supply subcomponents.

b. _____ Dye Corporation purchased 20% of the $40 million bond issue offered by Glover Company.

c. _____ Zhao, Inc., purchased 2,000 shares of Alphabet, Inc., common stock, paying $1.1 million.

d. _____ Watts Corporation purchased 65% of the common stock of Zimmerman, Inc., common stock for cash. Watts and Zimmerman had been engaged in several strategic alliances prior to the purchase.

e. _____ Shevlin, Inc., purchased 15% of Bowen Company's common stock. Shevlin is Bowen Company's largest customer, buying more than 60% of its output.

LO12-3 **M12-12. Interpreting Disclosures of Available-for-Sale Securities**
Use the following year-end note disclosure information from **Cisco Systems, Inc.**'s 2020 10-K report to answer parts *a* and *b*.

Cisco Systems, Inc.
NASDAQ :: CSCO

($ millions)	2020
Amortized cost of available-for-sale debt investments	$17,163
Gross unrealized gains	454
Gross unrealized losses	(7)
Fair value of available-for-sale debt investments	$17,610

a. At what amount is its available-for-sale investments reported on Cisco's 2020 balance sheet? Explain.

b. How is its net unrealized gain of $447 million ($454 million – $7 million) reported by Cisco in its financial statements?

LO12-3 **M12-13. Accounting for Passive Investments in Equity Securities**
Assume that Wu Company purchases 8,500 common shares of Pincus Company for $12 cash per share. Shares of Pincus Company are actively traded. During the year, Wu receives a cash dividend of $1.30 per common share from Pincus, and the year-end market price of Pincus common stock is $13 per share. How much income does Wu report relating to this investment for the year?

LO12-2 **M12-14. Analyzing Disclosures of Investment Securities**
In its June 30, 2020, balance sheet, **Microsoft Corporation** reports short-term investments with a value of $122,951 million. The amount of debt investments excluding the value of derivatives of $35 million is $122,916 million. These debt investments are recognized at fair value, and Microsoft provides information in its disclosure notes related to fair value measurements summarized in the table that follows.

Microsoft Corporation
NASDAQ :: MSFT

June 30, 2020 (In $ millions)	Level 1	Level 2	Level 3	Gross Fair Value
Commercial paper	$ 0	$3,070	$ 0	$ 3,070
Certificates of deposit	0	1,252	0	1,252
U.S. government and agency securities	95,393	1,992	0	97,385
Foreign government bonds	0	6,984	0	6,984
Mortgage- and asset-backed securities	0	4,900	0	4,900
Corporate notes and bonds	0	8,810	58	8,868
Municipal securities	0	366	91	457

a. Explain the differences between the three columns labeled Level 1, Level 2, and Level 3.

b. Are all of these investments "marked-to-fair value"? If not, which ones are not marked-to-fair value? Which investment values do you regard as most subjective? Least subjective?

c. If Microsoft needed to raise cash to take advantage of an investment opportunity, which of these investments do you regard as most liquid (i.e., most easily turned into cash)? Least liquid?

M12-15. Analyzing and Interpreting Equity Method Investments (FSET) LO12-4
Stober Company purchases an investment in Lang Company at a purchase price of $1.5 million cash, representing 30% of the outstanding stock and book value of Lang. During the year, Lang reports net income of $150,000 and pays cash dividends of $60,000. At the end of the year, the fair value of Stober's investment is $1.8 million.

a. At what amount is the investment reported on Stober's balance sheet at year-end?
b. What amount of income from investments does Stober report? Explain.
c. Stober's $300,000 unrealized gain in investment fair value (choose one and explain):
   (1) is not reflected on either its income statement or its balance sheet.
   (2) is reported in its current income.
   (3) is reported on its balance sheet only.
   (4) is reported in its other comprehensive income.
d. Record each of the transactions and events from above in the financial statement effects template.

M12-16. Analyzing and Interpreting Equity Method Investments LO12-4
Using the information from M12-15, answer the following.
a. Prepare journal entries to record the transactions and events.
b. Post the journal entries to their respective T-accounts.

M12-17. Calculating Income for Equity Method Investments LO12-4
Kross Company purchases an equity investment in Penno Company at a purchase price of $6 million, representing 40% of the outstanding stock and book value of Penno. During the current year, Penno reports net income of $720,000 and pays cash dividends of $240,000. At the end of the year, the market value of Kross' investment is $6.5 million. What amount of income does Kross report relating to this investment in Penno for the year? Explain.

M12-18. Computing Consolidating Adjustments and Noncontrolling Interest LO12-5
Philipich Company purchases 80% of Hirst Company's common stock for $480,000 cash when Hirst Company has $240,000 of common stock and $360,000 of retained earnings, and the fair values of Hirst's assets and liabilities equal their book values. If a consolidated balance sheet is prepared immediately after the acquisition, what amounts are eliminated when preparing that statement? What amount of noncontrolling interest appears in the consolidated balance sheet? Where does it appear?

M12-19. Computing Consolidated Net Income LO12-5
Benartzi Company purchased a 90% interest in Liang Company on January 1 of the current year. Benartzi Company had $840,000 net income for the current year *before* recognizing its share of Liang Company's net income. If Liang Company had net income of $210,000 for the year, what is the consolidated net income for the year? How would it be presented?

M12-20. Effect of Investing on Ratios LO12-4, 5
DeFond Company wishes to secure a reliable supply of a key component for its production processes, and its management is considering two alternative investments. Verduzco Company produces exactly the supply that DeFond needs, so DeFond could use cash to purchase 100% of the common stock of Verduzco. Lin Company produces twice as much of the component that DeFond needs, but DeFond could form a joint venture with another company where each would purchase 50% of Lin Company's common stock and each take 50% of Lin Company's output.

The table that follows gives the balance sheet information for all three companies prior to any investment by DeFond. For the questions below, assume that DeFond would be able to purchase shares at the investee companies' book values and that the investee companies' assets and liabilities have fair values equal to their book values.

	DeFond Company	Verduzco Company	Lin Company
Cash	$1,000	$ 125	$ 250
Investment	—	—	—
Noncash assets	2,500	1,125	2,250
Liabilities	2,750	875	1,750
Shareholders' Equity	750	375	750

a. Suppose that DeFond purchases 100% of Verduzco's common stock for $375. Produce the consolidated balance sheet for DeFond immediately after the acquisition.

b. Suppose that DeFond purchases 50% of Lin's common stock for $375. Produce the balance sheet for DeFond immediately after the investment (using the equity method).

c. From a business perspective, either of these investments will accomplish the objective of obtaining a reliable supply of components. How will the financial ratios differ between the two alternatives?

LO12-3

M12-21. Reporting of and Analyzing Financial Effects of Trading (Debt) Securities (FSET)

Hartgraves Company had the following transactions and adjustments related to a bond investment that is a trading security.

Year 1

Oct. 1 Purchased $900,000 face value of Skyline, Inc.'s 7% bonds at 97 plus a brokerage commission of $1,800. The bonds pay interest on September 30 and March 31 and mature in 20 years. Hartgraves Company expects to sell the bonds in the near future.

Dec. 31 Made the adjusting entry to record interest earned on investment in the Skyline bonds.

31 Made the adjusting entry to record the current fair value of the Skyline bonds. At December 31, the fair value of the Skyline bonds was $882,000.

Year 2

Mar. 31 Received the semiannual interest payment on investment in the Skyline bonds.

Apr. 1 Sold the Skyline bond investment for $886,140 cash.

Record each of the transactions in the financial statement effects template.

LO12-3

M12-22. Reporting of and Analyzing Financial Effects of Trading (Debt) Securities

Using the information from M12-21, answer the following.
a. Prepare journal entries to record these transactions.
b. Post the journal entries to their respective T-accounts.

LO12-3

M12-23. Reporting of and Analyzing Financial Effects of Investments in Equity Securities (FSET)

Blouin Company had the following transactions and adjustment related to a stock investment that is a trading security.

Year 1

Nov. 15 Purchased 15,000 shares of Lane, Inc.'s common stock at $17 per share plus a brokerage commission of $1,800. Blouin expects to sell the stock in the near future.

Dec. 22 Received a cash dividend of $1.00 per share of common stock from Lane.

31 Made the adjusting entry to reflect year-end fair value of the stock investment in Lane. The year-end fair value of the Lane common stock is $15.50 per share.

Year 2

Jan. 20 Sold all 15,000 shares of the Lane common stock for $225,000.

Record each of the transactions in the financial statement effects template.

LO12-3

M12-24. Reporting of and Analyzing Financial Effects of Investments in Equity Securities

Using the information from M12-23, answer the following.
a. Prepare journal entries to record these transactions.
b. Post the journal entries from *a* to their respective T-accounts.

LO12-3

M12-25. Reporting of and Analyzing Financial Effects of Available-for-Sale (Debt) Securities (FSET)

Refer to the data for Hartgraves Company in Mini Exercise 12-21. Assume that when the shares were purchased, management did not intend to sell the stock in the near future. Record the transactions and adjustments for Hartgraves Company as an available-for-sale security in the financial statement effects template.

LO12-3

M12-26. Reporting of and Analyzing Financial Effects of Available-for-Sale (Debt) Securities

Using the information from M12-25, answer the following.
a. Prepare journal entries to record these transactions.
b. Post each of the transactions to their respective T-account.

LO12-5

M12-27. Computing Stockholders' Equity in Consolidation

On January 1 of the current year, Halen Company purchased all of the common shares of Jolson Company for $460,000 cash. On this date, the stockholders' equity of Halen Company consisted of $480,000 in common stock and $248,000 in retained earnings. Jolson Company had $280,000 in common stock and $180,000 in retained earnings. What amount of total stockholders' equity appears on the consolidated balance sheet?

EXERCISES

E12-28. Assessing Financial Statement Effects of Trading and Available-for-Sale (Debt) Securities (FSET)   **LO12-1, 3**

Four transactions involving investments in marketable debt securities classified as trading follow.

(1) On July 1, purchased US Treasury Bonds for $610,000 in cash. The bonds have a face value of $600,000 and pay interest semi-annually (June 30 and December 31) at an annual rate of 4.00%.
(2) Received cash interest payment of $12,000 on December 31.
(3) Year-end market price of bonds is $616,000.
(4) Received cash interest payment of $12,000 and sold all bonds on June 30 for $612,000.

a. Record each of the transactions above in the financial statement effects template.
b. Using the same transaction information as above and assuming the investments in marketable securities are classified as available-for-sale, record each of the transactions in the financial statement effects template.

E12-29. Assessing Financial Statement Effects of Trading and Available-for-Sale (Debt) Securities   **LO12-1, 3**

Using the information from E12-28, answer the following.

a. Assuming that the debt securities are classified as trading, (i.) prepare the journal entries to record the four transactions, and (ii.) post the journal entries to their respective T-accounts.
b. Assuming that the debt securities are classified as available-for-sale, (i.) prepare the journal entries to record the four transactions, and (ii.) post the journal entries to their respective T-accounts.

E12-30. Assessing Financial Statement Effects of Passive Investments in Equity Securities (FSET)   **LO12-1, 3**

For the following transactions involving investments in marketable securities, assume that:

1. Ohlson Co. purchases 6,000 common shares of Freeman Co. at $16 cash per share.
2. Ohlson Co. receives a cash dividend of $1.25 per common share from Freeman.
3. Year-end market price of Freeman common stock is $17.50 per share.
4. Ohlson Co. sells all 6,000 common shares of Freeman for $103,680 cash.

Record each of the transactions in the financial statement effects template.

E12-31. Assessing Financial Statement Effects of Passive Investments in Equity Securities   **LO12-1, 3**

Using the information from E12-30, answer the following.

a. Prepare journal entries to record the four transactions.
b. Post the journal entries to their respective T-accounts.

E12-32. Acquisitions and Trend Analysis   **LO12-5**

In its 2018 10-K annual report, **Microsoft Corporation** reported the following revenues:

Microsoft Corporation
NASDAQ :: MSFT

($ millions)	Fiscal Year Ended June 30		
	2018	2017	2016
Total revenues	$110,360	$96,571	$91,154

a. Calculate the yearly revenue growth for this period. Based on this trend, what revenue would you forecast for fiscal year 2019?

In December of 2016 (i.e., almost in the middle of fiscal year 2017, Microsoft completed its $27.0 billion acquisition of LinkedIn Corporation. In the 10-K disclosures for 2018, Microsoft reports

Following are the supplemental consolidated financial results of Microsoft Corporation on an unaudited pro forma basis, as if the acquisition had been consummated on July 1, 2015:

(In millions, except earnings per share) Year Ended June 30	2017	2016
Revenue	$98,291	$94,490

b. How does the acquisition of LinkedIn affect your interpretation of the growth trend in part a?
c. Using the disclosure information, revise the growth calculations to separate the measures of "organic growth" from "purchased growth."

LO12-1, 3 **E12-33. Reporting of and Analyzing Financial Effects of Trading (Debt) Securities (FSET)**
Barclay, Inc., had the following transactions and adjustments related to a bond investment that is classified as a trading security.

Year 1

Nov. 1   Purchased $500,000 face value of Joos, Inc.'s 9% bonds at 102 plus a brokerage commission of $1,500. The bonds pay interest on October 31 and April 30 and mature in 15 years. Barclay expects to sell the bonds in the near future.

Dec. 31   Made the adjusting entry to record interest earned on investment in the Joos bonds.

31   Made the adjusting entry to record the current fair value of the Joos bonds. At December 31, the fair value of the Joos bonds was $502,500.

Year 2

Apr. 30   Received the semiannual interest payment on investment in the Joos bonds.

May 1   Sold the Joos bond investment for $501,500 cash.

Record each of the transactions in the financial statement effects template.

LO12-1, 3 **E12-34. Reporting of and Analyzing Financial Effects of Trading (Debt) Securities**
Using the information from E12-33, answer the following.

a. Prepare journal entries to record these transactions.
b. Post the journal entries to their respective T-accounts.

LO12-5 **E12-35. Reporting of Stockholders' Equity in Consolidation**
Baylor Company purchased 75% of the common stock of Reed Company for $480,000 in cash when the stockholders' equity of Reed Company consisted of $400,000 in common stock and $240,000 in retained earnings. On the acquisition date, the stockholders' equity of Baylor Company consisted of $720,000 in common stock and $352,000 in retained earnings. Prepare the stockholders' equity section in the consolidated balance sheet as of the acquisition date.

LO12-3 **E12-36. Interpreting Note Disclosures for Investments**
CNA Financial Corporation
NYSE :: CNA

CNA Financial Corporation provides the following information from its 2020 10-K report (excerpts from Notes A and B):

Investments
The Company classifies its fixed maturity securities as either available-for-sale or trading, and as such, they are carried at fair value. Changes in fair value of trading securities are reported within Net investment income on the Consolidated Statements of Operations. Changes in fair value related to available-for-sale securities are reported as a component of Other comprehensive income.

Credit Losses
The allowances for credit losses on fixed maturity securities, mortgage loans, reinsurance receivables, and insurance receivables are valuation accounts that are reported as a reduction of a financial asset's cost basis and are measured on a pool basis when similar risk characteristics exist. Management estimates the allowance using relevant available information from both internal and external sources. Historical credit loss experience provides the basis for the estimation of expected credit losses and adjustments may be made to reflect current conditions and reasonable and supportable forecasts. Adjustments to historical loss information are made for any additional factors that come to the Company's attention. This could include significant shifts in counterparty financial strength ratings, aging of past due receivables, amounts sent to collection agencies, or other underlying portfolio changes. Amounts are considered past due when payments have not been received according to contractual terms. The Company also considers current and forecast economic conditions, using a variety of economic metrics and forecast indices. . . .

December 31, 2020 (In millions)	Cost or Amortized Cost	Gross Unrealized Gains	Gross Unrealized Losses	Allowance for Credit Losses[1]	Estimated Fair Value
Fixed maturity securities available-for-sale:					
Corporate and other bonds	$20,792	$3,578	$22	$23	$24,325
States, municipalities, and political subdivisions	9,729	1,863	—	—	11,592
Asset-backed:					
Residential mortgage-backed	3,442	146	1	—	3,587
Commercial mortgage-backed	1,933	93	42	17	1,967
Other asset-backed	2,179	81	9	—	2,251
Total asset-backed	7,554	320	52	17	7,805
U.S. Treasury and obligations of government-sponsored enterprises	339	2	3	—	338
Foreign government	512	32	—	—	544
Redeemable preferred stock	—	—	—	—	—
Total fixed maturity securities available-for-sale	38,926	5,795	77	40	44,604
Total fixed maturity securities trading	27	—	—	—	27
Total fixed maturity securities	$38,953	$5,795	$77	$40	$44,631

[1] As of January 1, 2020, the Company adopted ASU 2016-13, Financial Instruments-Credit Losses (Topic 326): Measurement of Credit Losses on Financial Instruments. The Unrealized OTTI Losses (Gains) column that tracked subsequent valuation changes on securities for which a credit loss had previously been recorded has been replaced with the Allowance for Credit Losses column.

    a. At what amount is its investment portfolio reflected on its balance sheet? In your answer identify its fair value, cost, any unrealized gains and losses, and any allowance for credit losses.

    b. How are its unrealized gains and/or losses reflected in CNA's balance sheet and income statement?

    c. How are any credit losses and the gains and losses realized from the sale of securities reflected in CNA's balance sheet and income statement?

E12-37. Assessing Financial Statement Effects of Equity Method Securities (FSET)   LO12-4

The following transactions involve investments in marketable securities and are accounted for using the equity method.

1. Purchased 18,000 common shares of Barth Co. at $9 cash per share; the shares represent 30% ownership in Barth.
2. Received a cash dividend of $1.25 per common share from Barth.
3. Recorded income from Barth stock investment when Barth's net income is $120,000.
4. Sold all 18,000 common shares of Barth for $180,500.

Record each of the transactions in the financial statement effects template.

E12-38. Assessing Financial Statement Effects of Equity Method Securities   LO12-4

Using the information from E12-37, answer the following.

    a. Prepare journal entries to record these four transactions.
    b. Post the journal entries to their respective T-accounts.

E12-39. Assessing Financial Statement Effects of Equity Method Securities (FSET)   LO12-4

The following transactions involve investments in marketable securities and are accounted for using the equity method.

1. Healy Co. purchases 30,000 common shares of Palepu Co. at $8 cash per share; the shares represent 25% ownership of Palepu.
2. Healy receives a cash dividend of $0.80 per common share from Palepu.
3. Palepu reports annual net income of $240,000.
4. Healy sells all 30,000 common shares of Palepu for $280,000 cash.

Record each of the transactions in the financial statement effects template.

E12-40. Assessing Financial Statement Effects of Equity Method Securities   LO12-4

Using the information from E12-39, answer the following.

    a. Prepare journal entries to record these four transactions.
    b. Post the journal entries to their respective T-accounts.

LO12-1, 3, 4   **E12-41. Assessing Financial Statement Effects of Passive and Equity Method Investments (FSET)**

On January 1, Ball Corporation purchased, as a stock investment, 5,000 shares of Leftwich Company common stock for $15 cash per share. On December 31, Leftwich announced net income of $40,000 for the year and paid a cash dividend of $1.10 per share. At December 31, the market value of Leftwich's stock was $19 per share.

    a. Assume that the stock acquired by Ball represents 15% of Leftwich's voting stock—a passive equity investment. Record each of the following transactions in the financial statement effects template.
        (1) Ball purchased 5,000 common shares of Leftwich at $15 cash per share; the shares represent a 15% ownership in Leftwich.
        (2) Leftwich reported annual net income of $40,000.
        (3) Received a cash dividend of $1.10 per common share from Leftwich.
        (4) Year-end market price of Leftwich common stock is $19 per share.
    b. Assume that Ball's $75,000 investment purchased 30% of Leftwich's voting stock and that Ball accounts for this investment using the equity method since it is able to exert significant influence. For the same four transactions as above, record each of the transactions in the financial statement effects template.

LO12-1, 3, 4   **E12-42. Assessing Financial Statement Effects of Passive and Equity Method Investments**

Using the information from E12-41, answer the following.

For the transactions described in parts *a* and *b*, (i.) prepare journal entries and (ii.) post the journal entries to their respective T-accounts.

LO12-1, 3   **E12-43. Allocation of Acquisition Purchase Price**

In 2017, **Amazon.com, Inc.**, made two significant acquisitions intending to expand the company's retail presence. On May 12, 2017, Amazon acquired Souq Group Ltd. ("Souq"), an e-commerce company, for approximately $583 million, net of cash acquired and on August 28, 2017, acquired Whole Foods Market, a grocery store chain, for approximately $13.2 billion, net of cash acquired. Other acquisitions were also made for consideration of $204 million, making a total of $13,963 million (net of cash acquired) for the year.

From the disclosure in its 2018 10-K, Amazon provides the following information:

The aggregate purchase price of these acquisitions was allocated as follows (in millions):

December 31	2017
Purchase Price	
Cash paid, net of cash acquired.............................	$13,963
Allocation	
Goodwill...	?
Intangible assets:	
Marketing-related.....................................	1,987
Contract-based..	440
Technology-based....................................	166
Customer-related.....................................	54
	2,647
Property and equipment....................................	3,810
Deferred tax assets...	117
Other assets acquired.....................................	1,858
Long-term debt...	(1,165)
Deferred tax liabilities.....................................	(961)
Other liabilities assumed.................................	(1,844)
	$13,963

    a. How are the values in the above table determined?
    b. How much goodwill would Amazon.com recognize from these acquisitions? How will that goodwill be treated in subsequent periods?
    c. Do you think Amazon.com shareholders would prefer to see an allocation that gives a lot of value to separately identifiable assets or an allocation where most of the acquisition price goes to goodwill? Why?

E12-44. Allocation of Acquisition Purchase Price   **LO12-5**

On October 23, 2020, **Gilead Sciences** completed its acquisition of Immunomedics, a company focused on the development of antibody-drug conjugate ("ADC") technology. Immunomedics researches and develops biopharmaceutical products, particularly antibody-based products for patients with solid tumors and blood cancers. The company also manufactures and markets Trodelvy, a Trop-2-directed ADC developed by Immunomedics that is the first ADC the FDA approved for the treatment of adult patients with metastatic triple-negative breast cancer. Immunomedics is a wholly owned subsidiary of Gilead Sciences following the acquisition. Gilead paid $20.6 billion in cash for the stock of Immunomedics.

Gilead Sciences, Inc.
NASDAQ :: GILD

Gilead Sciences's 2020 10-K reports the following for purchase price allocation:

(in millions)	Amount
Cash and cash equivalents	$ 726
Inventories	946
Intangible assets	
Finite-lived intangible asset	4,600
Acquired R&D	15,760
Outlicense contract	175
Deferred income taxes	(4,565)
Liability related to future royalties	(1,100)
Other assets (and liabilities), net	64
Total identifiable net assets	16,606
Goodwill	?

a. How are the values in the above table determined?
b. How much goodwill would Gilead recognize from this acquisition? How will that goodwill be treated in subsequent periods?
c. Do you think Gilead's shareholders would prefer to see an allocation that gives a lot of value to separately identifiable assets or an allocation where most of the acquisition price goes to goodwill? Why?

E12-45. Reporting of and Analyzing Financial Effects of Passive Equity Securities (FSET)   **LO12-1, 3**

Guay Company had the following transactions and adjustment related to a passive equity investment.

Year 1

Nov. 15   Purchased 7,500 shares of Core, Inc.'s common stock at $16 per share plus a brokerage commission of $1,350. Guay Company expects to sell the stock in the near future.
Dec. 22   Received a cash dividend of $1.25 per share of common stock from Core.
      31   Made the adjusting entry to reflect year-end fair value of the stock investment in Core. The year-end market price of the Core common stock is $17.50 per share.

Year 2

Jan. 20   Sold all 7,500 shares of the Core common stock for $129,600.

Record each of the transactions in the financial statement effects template.

E12-46. Reporting of and Analyzing Financial Effects of Passive Equity Securities   **LO12-1, 3**

Using the information from E12-45, answer the following.

a. Prepare journal entries to record these transactions.
b. Post the journal entries to their respective T-accounts.

E12-47. Reporting of and Analyzing Financial Effects of Equity Securities Under International Standards (FSET)   **LO12-1, 3**

Refer to the data for Guay Company in Exercise 12-45. Assume that Guay Company reports under International Financial Reporting Standards (IFRS). Under IFRS, Guay can designate an equity investment for accounting based on FVOCI (fair value—other comprehensive income). While holding the equity investment, dividends are recorded in income and unrealized holding gains and losses go to AOCI, much like AFS securities. However, the difference is that these gains and losses are never recognized in income. Rather, they remain in AOCI. Assume that when the shares were purchased, management designated its investment in Core, Inc., for FVOCI treatment.

a. Record the transactions and adjustments for Guay Company under this assumption in the financial statement effects template.
b. Why might the standard setters have allowed this option to companies reporting under IFRS?

LO12-1, 3 **E12-48. Reporting of and Analyzing Financial Effects of Equity Securities Under International Standards**

Using the information from E12-47, (a) prepare the journal entries and (b) post the journal entries to their respective T-accounts.

LO12-1, 2, 3, 4 **E12-49. Reporting and Interpreting Financial Investment Performance**

Kasznik Company began operations on January 2, and by year-end (December 31) had made the following investments in financial securities. Year-end information on these investments follows.

Investment	Cost or End-of-Year Equity Basis (as appropriate)	Year-End Fair Value	Investment Classification
Common stock of Barth, Inc.	$102,000	$ 97,950	Fair value (Trading)
Common stock of Foster, Inc.	243,750	240,000	Fair value (Trading)
30-Year US Treasury Bond	295,500	288,000	Available-for-sale
10-Year US Treasury Note	235,500	232,050	Available-for-sale
Ertimur, Inc.	150,000	153,600	Equity method
Soliman, Inc.	204,000	199,800	Equity method

a. At what total amount are the trading stock investments reported in the December 31 balance sheet?
b. At what total amount are the available-for-sale debt investments reported in the December 31 balance sheet?
c. At what total amount are the equity method stock investments reported in the December 31 balance sheet?
d. What total amount of unrealized holding gains or unrealized holding losses related to the investments appears in the annual income statement?
e. What total amount of unrealized holding gains or unrealized holding losses related to the investments appears in the stockholders' equity section of the December 31 balance sheet?

LO12-1, 4 **E12-50. Analyzing Equity Method Investment Disclosures**

AT&T, Inc., reports a December 31, 2019, balance of $3,695 million in "Investments in and advances to equity affiliates." Provide the entries for the following events for fiscal year 2020:

AT&T, Inc.
NYSE :: T

a. AT&T's share of income from its affiliates was $95 million.
b. AT&T received dividends and distributions from its affiliates of $133 million during fiscal year 2020.
c. After these events, what should be the balance in AT&T's investments in affiliates account at December 31, 2020? The actual balance was $1,780 million. What might explain any differences between these two values?

LO12-7 **E12-51.[B] Constructing the Consolidated Balance Sheet at Acquisition (FSET)**

On January 1 of the current year, Healy Company purchased all of the common shares of Miller Company for $400,000 cash. Balance sheets of the two firms at acquisition follow.

	Healy Company	Miller Company	Consolidating Adjustments	Consolidated
Current assets	$1,360,000	$ 96,000		
Investment in Miller	400,000	—		
Plant assets, net	2,400,000	328,000		
Goodwill	—	—		
Total assets	$4,160,000	$424,000		
Liabilities	$ 560,000	$ 72,000		
Contributed capital	2,800,000	320,000		
Retained earnings	800,000	32,000		
Total liabilities and equity	$4,160,000	$424,000		

During purchase negotiations, Miller's plant assets were appraised at $340,000; and all of its remaining assets and liabilities were appraised at values approximating their book values. Healy also concluded that an additional $36,000 (in goodwill) demanded by Miller's shareholders was warranted because Miller's earning power was better than the industry average. (1) Prepare the consolidating adjustments, (2) prepare the consolidated balance sheet at acquisition, and (3) record the consolidated transaction in the financial statement effects template.

E12-52.[B] **Recording a Consolidation Adjustment** LO12-7
Using the information from E12-51, (a) prepare the journal entry and (b) post the journal entry to its respective T-accounts.

E12-53.[B] **Constructing the Consolidated Balance Sheet at Acquisition (FSET)** LO12-7
Rayburn Company purchased all of Kanodia Company's common stock for cash on January 1, at which time the separate balance sheets of the two corporations appeared as follows:

	Rayburn Company	Kanodia Company	Consolidating Adjustments	Consolidated
Investment in Kanodia	$ 480,000	—		
Other assets	1,840,000	$560,000		
Goodwill	—	—		
Total assets	$2,320,000	$560,000		
Liabilities	$ 720,000	$128,000		
Contributed capital	1,120,000	240,000		
Retained earnings	480,000	192,000		
Total liabilities and equity	$2,320,000	$560,000		

During purchase negotiations, Rayburn determined that the appraised value of Kanodia's other assets was $576,000; and all of its remaining assets and liabilities were appraised at values approximating their book values. The remaining $32,000 of the purchase price was ascribed to goodwill. (1) Prepare the consolidating adjustments, (2) prepare the consolidated balance sheet at acquisition, and (3) record the consolidated transaction in the financial statement effects template.

E12-54.[B] **Constructing the Consolidated Balance Sheet at Acquisition** LO12-7
Using the information from E12-53, (a) prepare the journal entry and (b) post the journal entry to its respective T-accounts.

E12-55. Assessing Goodwill Impairment LO12-5
On January 1, Engel Company purchases 100% of Ball Company for $23.5 million. At the time of acquisition, Ball's stockholders' equity (and the fair value of its identifiable net assets) is reported at $14.3 million. Engel ascribes the excess of $9.2 million to goodwill. Assume that the fair value of Ball declines to $17.5 million.

a. Provide computations to determine if the goodwill has become impaired and, if so, the amount of the impairment.
b. What impact does the impairment of goodwill have on Engel's financial statements?

E12-56.[B] **Constructing the Consolidated Balance Sheet at Acquisition** LO12-5, 7
Easton Company acquires 100% of the outstanding voting shares of Harris Company on January 1. To obtain these shares, Easton pays $252,000 in cash and issues 6,000 of its $10 par value common stock. On this date, Easton's stock has a fair value of $36 per share, and Harris' book value of stockholders' equity is $336,000. Easton is willing to pay $468,000 for a company with a book value for equity of $336,000 because it believes that (1) Harris buildings are undervalued by $48,000, and (2) Harris has an unrecorded patent that Easton values at $36,000. Easton considers the remaining balance sheet items to be fairly valued (no book-to-fair value difference). The remaining $48,000 of the purchase price excess over book value is ascribed to corporate synergies and other general unidentifiable intangible assets (goodwill). The January 1, 2019, balance sheets at the acquisition date follow:

	Easton Company	Harris Company	Consolidating Adjustments	Consolidated
Cash	$ 100,800	$ 48,000		
Receivables	192,000	108,000		
Inventory	264,000	156,000		
Investment in Harris	468,000	—		
Land	120,000	72,000		
Buildings, net	480,000	132,000		
Equipment, net	144,000	60,000		
Total assets	$1,768,800	$576,000		

continued

continued from previous page

	Easton Company	Harris Company	Consolidating Adjustments	Consolidated
Accounts payable.............	$ 192,000	$ 36,000		
Long-term liabilities	456,000	204,000		
Common stock................	600,000	48,000		
Additional paid-in capital.........	88,800	—		
Retained earnings	432,000	288,000		
Total liabilities & equity..........	$1,768,800	$576,000		

a. Show the breakdown of the investment into the book value acquired, the excess of fair value over book value, and the portion of the investment representing goodwill.
b. Prepare the consolidating adjustments and the consolidated balance sheet. Identify the adjustments by whether they relate to the elimination of stockholders' equity [S] or the excess of purchase price over book value [A].
c. How will the excess of the purchase price over book value acquired be treated in years subsequent to the acquisition?

LO12-6

E12-57.[A] **Accounting for Equity Method Investments**
Refer to the Easton Company acquisition described in E12-56. Instead of a 100% acquisition, assume that Easton purchased 40% of the outstanding shares of Harris Company on January 1 for $187,200 in cash. Also assume that the undervalued buildings have an estimated remaining useful life of 20 years and the unrecorded patent has a useful life of 5 years.

During the year, Harris reported net income of $96,000 and paid cash dividends to shareholders totaling $48,000.

a. Prepare journal entries to record Easton Company's equity in the earnings of Harris Company, including any amortization of the excess of fair value over book value of assets acquired.
b. What is the value of the investment in Harris Company reported on Easton Company's balance sheet as of December 31?

LO12-8

Hewlett Packard Enterprise Company
NYSE :: HPE

E12-58.[C] **Reporting and Analyzing Derivatives**
Hewlett Packard Enterprise Company reports the following information on its cash-flow hedges (derivatives) in comprehensive income (net income plus other comprehensive income) in its 2020 10-K report:

($ millions)	Total
Net earnings...	$(322)
Change in net unrealized gains/(losses) on available-for-sale securities.................	(5)
Change in net unrealized gains/(losses) on cash flow hedges........................	(61)
Change in unrealized components of defined benefit pension plans....................	(99)
Change in cumulative translation adjustment...................................	(12)
Benefit for income taxes..	8
Comprehensive income	$(491)

a. Identify and describe the usual applications for derivatives.
b. How are derivatives and their related assets (and/or liabilities) reported on the balance sheet?
c. By what amount has the unrealized gain or loss on the HPE derivatives affected its current income? What are the analysis implications?

PROBLEMS

LO12-1, 2, 3

Metlife Inc.
NYSE :: MET

P12-59. Analyzing and Interpreting Available-for-Sale Securities Disclosures
Following is a portion of the investments Note 8 from **MetLife Inc.**'s 2020 10-K report. Investment earnings are a crucial component of the financial performance of insurance companies such as MetLife, and investments comprise a large part of its assets. MetLife accounts for its bond investments as available-for-sale securities.

Fixed Maturity Securities Available-for-Sale
The following tables present the fixed maturity securities AFS by sector.

December 31, 2020

(in millions)	Amortized Cost	ACL	Gross Unrealized Gains	Gross Unrealized Losses	Estimated Fair Value
U.S. corporate	$ 79,788	$(44)	$13,924	$ 252	$ 93,416
Foreign government	63,243	(21)	8,883	406	71,699
Foreign corporate	60,995	(16)	8,897	468	69,408
U.S. government and agency	39,094	—	8,095	89	47,100
RMBS	28,415	—	2,062	42	30,435
ABS	16,963	—	231	75	17,119
Municipals	10,982	—	2,746	6	13,722
CMBS	11,331	—	681	102	11,910
Total fixed maturity securities AFS	$310,811	$(81)	$45,519	$1,440	$354,809

December 31, 2019

(in millions)	Amortized Cost	Gains	Temporary Losses	OTTI Losses	Estimated Fair Value
U.S. corporate	$ 79,115	$ 8,943	$ 305	$—	$ 87,753
Foreign government	58,840	8,710	321	—	67,229
Foreign corporate	59,342	5,540	717	—	64,165
U.S. government and agency	37,586	4,604	106	—	42,084
RMBS	27,051	1,535	72	(33)	28,547
ABS	14,547	83	88	—	14,542
Municipals	11,081	2,001	29	—	13,053
CMBS	10,093	396	42	—	10,447
Total fixed maturity securities AFS	$297,655	$31,812	$1,680	$(33)	$327,820

MetLife abbreviates allowance for credit loss as "ACL" and other than temporary impairment as "OTTI."

REQUIRED

a. At what amount does MetLife report its bond investments on its balance sheets for 2020 and 2019?
b. What are its net unrealized gains (losses) for 2020 and 2019? By what amount did these unrealized gains (losses) affect its reported income?
c. What is the difference between *realized* and *unrealized* gains and losses? Are realized gains and losses treated differently in the income statement than unrealized gains and losses? MetLife's 2020 pre-tax income was $6,927 million. What is the maximum amount MetLife could have increased pre-tax income by selling available-for-sale securities on the last day of 2020?
d. Many analysts compute a *mark-to-market investment return* as follows: Net investment income + Realized gains and losses + Change in unrealized gains and losses. Do you think that this metric provides insights into the performance of MetLife's investment portfolio beyond that which is included in GAAP income statements? Explain.

P12-60.B Preparing the Consolidated Balance Sheet LO12-5, 7

On January 1, Gem Company purchased for $490,000 cash a 70% stock interest in Alpine, Inc., which then had common stock of $525,000 and retained earnings of $175,000. Balance sheets of the two companies immediately after the acquisition were as follows:

	Gem	Alpine
Current assets	$ 322,500	$200,000
Stock investment—Controlling (Alpine)	490,000	—
Plant and equipment (net)	331,250	575,000
Total assets	$1,143,750	$775,000
Liabilities	$ 62,500	$ 75,000
Common stock	875,000	525,000
Retained earnings	206,250	175,000
Total liabilities and stockholders' equity	$1,143,750	$775,000

At the time of Gem's investment, the fair values of Alpine's assets and liabilities were equal to their book values.

REQUIRED

Prepare the consolidated balance sheet on the acquisition date; include a column for consolidating adjustments (see **Exhibit 12.7** for guidance).

LO12-1, 2, 3, 4

P12-61. Analyzing and Reporting Debt Investment Performance

Columbia Company began operations in the current year and by year-end (December 31) had made six bond investments. Year-end information on these bond investments follows.

Company	Face Value	Cost or Amortized Cost	Year-End Fair Value	Classification
Ling, Inc.	$150,000	$153,600	$157,950	Trading
Wren, Inc.	375,000	393,750	405,000	Trading
Olanamic, Inc.	300,000	295,500	298,500	Available for sale
Fossil, Inc.	225,000	231,000	240,000	Available for sale
Meander, Inc.	150,000	151,800	153,600	Held to maturity
Resin, Inc.	210,000	204,000	205,500	Held to maturity

REQUIRED

a. At what total amount will the trading bond investments be reported in the December 31 balance sheet?
b. At what total amount will the available-for-sale bond investments be reported in the December 31 balance sheet?
c. At what total amount will the held-to-maturity bond investments be reported in the December 31 balance sheet?
d. What total amount of unrealized holding gains or unrealized holding losses related to bond investments will appear in the annual income statement?
e. What total amount of unrealized holding gains or unrealized holding losses related to bond investments will appear in the stockholders' equity section of the December 31 balance sheet?

LO12-1, 4, 5, 6, 7

Deere & Company
NYSE :: DE

P12-62.[A, B] Analyzing and Interpreting Disclosures on Consolidations

Deere & Company consists of two business units: the equipment operations (parent corporation) and a wholly owned finance subsidiary. These two units are consolidated in Deere's fiscal 2020 10-K report (for the year ended January 31, 2021). Following is a supplemental disclosure that Deere includes in its 10-K report that shows the separate balance sheets of the parent and its subsidiary, as well as consolidating adjustments and the consolidated balance sheet presented to shareholders. This supplemental disclosure is not mandated under GAAP but is voluntarily reported by Deere as useful information for investors and creditors.

Deere & Company
January 31, 2021
Supplemental Consolidating Data

(in millions)	Equipment Operations	Financial Services	Eliminations	Consolidated
Assets				
Cash and cash equivalents	$ 6,074	$ 888		$ 6,962
Marketable securities	8	659		667
Receivables from unconsolidated affiliates. . .	5,151		$ (5,123)	28
Trade accounts and notes receivable—net. . .	900	5,341	(1,204)	5,037
Financing receivables—net	103	29,335		29,438
Financing receivables securitized—net	18	3,913		3,931
Other receivables	1,010	151	(20)	1,141
Equipment on operating leases—net		7,030		7,030
Inventories	5,956			5,956
Property and equipment—net	5,703	38		5,741
Investments in unconsolidated affiliates.	157	21		178
Investment in financial services	5,345		(5,345)	—
Goodwill	3,194			3,194
Other intangible assets—net	1,342			1,342
Retirement benefits	903	60	(57)	906
Deferred income taxes	1,797	51	(292)	1,556
Other assets.	1,485	891	(3)	2,373
Total assets.	$39,146	$48,378	$(12,044)	$75,480

continued

continued from previous page

Deere & Company
January 31, 2021
Supplemental Consolidating Data*

(in millions)	Equipment Operations	Financial Services	Eliminations	Consolidated
Liabilities and stockholders' equity				
Liabilities				
Short-term borrowings	$ 394	$ 8,830		$ 9,224
Short-term securitization borrowings	17	3,952		3,969
Payables to unconsolidated affiliates	119	5,123	$ (5,123)	119
Accounts payable and accrued expenses	8,672	1,959	(1,227)	9,404
Deferred income taxes	394	430	(292)	532
Long-term borrowings	10,139	22,633		32,772
Retirement benefits and other liabilities	5,325	106	(57)	5,374
Total liabilities	25,060	43,033	(6,699)	61,394
Commitments and contingencies				
Redeemable noncontrolling interest				
Stockholders' equity				
Deere stockholders' equity	14,083	5,345	(5,345)	14,083
Non-controlling interests	3			3
Adjusted total stockholders' equity	14,086	5,345	(5,345)	14,086
Total liabilities and stockholders' equity	$39,146	$48,378	$(12,044)	$75,480

* presentation adjusted slightly by authors for simplicity

REQUIRED

a. Does each individual company (unit) maintain its own financial statements? Explain. Why does GAAP require consolidation instead of providing the financial statements of individual companies (units)?s

b. What is the balance of Investments in Financial Services as of January 31, 2021, on the parent's balance sheet (Equipment Operations)? What is the equity balance of the financial services subsidiary to which this relates as of January 31, 2021? Do you see a relationship? Will this relationship always exist?

c. Refer to your answer for *a*. How does the equity method of accounting for the investment in the subsidiary company obscure the actual financial condition of the parent company that is revealed in the consolidated financial statements?

d. Refer to the Consolidating Adjustments column reported—it is used to prepare the consolidated balance sheet. Generally, what do these adjustments accomplish?

e. Compare the consolidated balance of stockholders' equity with the stockholders' equity of the parent company (Equipment Operations). Will the relation that is evident always hold? Explain.

f. Recall that the parent company uses the equity method of accounting for its investment in the subsidiary, and that this account is eliminated in the consolidation process. What is the relation between consolidated net income and the net income of the parent company? Explain.

g. What do you believe is the implication for the consolidated balance sheet if the fair value of the Financial Services subsidiary is greater than the book value of its stockholders' equity?

CASES AND PROJECTS

C12-63. Effect of Investment Accounting on Performance Ratios   LO12-1, 3

Apple Inc.
NASDAQ :: AAPL

Apple Inc., is one of the most successful enterprises of all time. Its computers, tablets, phones, and watches are all highly desired by consumers, and the company's product innovations keep arriving at a steady pace. Apple's financial success can also be attributed to its supply chain management and to its management of its income taxes. Apple has for many years maintained high balances of cash and marketable securities. This was historically partially due to prior tax laws which made it costly to pay dividends from foreign subsidiaries back to the U.S. parent. It is also partially due to other reasons, perhaps that the company desires to maintain sufficient liquidity. In any case, Apple's balance sheet reports substantial investments in marketable securities, as shown in the following:

($ millions)	September 26, 2020	September 28, 2019
Total assets.	$323,888	$338,516
Marketable securities	153,814	157,054
Net operating assets (operating assets – operating liabilities)	23,961	41,481

The following information is taken from the company's fiscal 2020 income statement and disclosure notes:

($ millions)	Year Ended September 26, 2020
Operating income.	$66,288
Other income/(expenses), net*.	803
Income before provision for income tax	67,091
Provision for income tax.	(9,680)
Net income	$57,411

*Apple reported that this amount included interest expense of $2,873 million, interest and dividend income of $3,763, and other income/(expense), net of $(87).

Finally, the following table is taken from Note 2 of Apple's 2020 10-K annual report. The reported numbers are slightly higher than those reported from Apple's balance sheet above because some AFS securities are classified as cash equivalents on the balance sheet, rather than marketable securities.

Fixed-income (debt) investments—AFS:

($ millions)	Adjusted Cost	Unrealized Gains	Unrealized Losses	Fair Value
2020	$189,431	$2,784	$(385)	$191,830
2019	204,977	1,202	(281)	205,898

REQUIRED
a. Calculate Apple's return on assets for fiscal year 2020. Assume an income tax rate of 25%.
b. Calculate Apple's RNOA for 2020. (Refer to Appendix A of Chapter 5 for further discussion.) What factors contribute to this RNOA?
c. What method does Apple use to account for its fixed-income investments? What value is included in its 2020 balance sheet?
d. From its balance sheet, it would appear that a significant portion of Apple's resources are devoted to investing in financial instruments. Calculate the after-tax return to Apple's financial assets. Apple's Statement of Other Comprehensive Income reports an after-tax unrealized holding gain on AFS investments equal to $1,202 million? What would have been Apple's return to financial investments if it had used the trading security method for these investments?

LO12-1, 3, 4 **C12-64. Analyzing Financial Statement Effects of Passive and Equity Investments (FSET)**
On January 2, 2022, Magee, Inc., purchased, as a stock investment, 28,000 shares of Dye, Inc.'s common stock for $21 per share, including commissions and taxes. On December 31, 2022, Dye announced a net income of $392,000 for the year and declared a dividend of 80 cents per share, payable January 15, 2023, to stockholders of record on January 5, 2023. At December 31, 2022, the market value of Dye's stock was $18 per share. Magee received its dividend on January 18, 2023.

REQUIRED
a. Assume that the stock acquired by Magee represents 10% of Dye's voting stock and is classified in the trading category. Prepare all entries appropriate for this investment, beginning with the purchase on January 2, 2022, and ending with the receipt of the dividend on January 18, 2023, using the financial statement effects template.
b. Assume that the stock acquired by Magee represents 40% of Dye's voting stock. Prepare all entries appropriate for this investment, beginning with the purchase on January 2, 2019, and ending with the receipt of the dividend on January 18, 2023, using the financial statement effects template.

LO12-1, 3, 4 **C12-65. Analyzing Financial Statement Effects of Passive and Equity Investments**
Using the information from C12-64, answer the following.

For the transactions described in parts *a* and *b*, (i.) prepare journal entries and (ii.) post the journal entries to their respective T-accounts.

C12-66. Assessing Management Interpretation of Consolidated Financial Statements   **LO12-1, 2, 3, 4, 5**

Demski, Inc., manufactures heating and cooling systems. It has a 75% interest in Asare Company, which manufactures thermostats, switches, and other controls for heating and cooling products. It also has a 100% interest in Demski Finance Company, created by the parent company to finance sales of its products to contractors and other consumers. The parent company's only other investment is a 25% interest in the common stock of Knechel, Inc., which produces certain circuits used by Demski, Inc. A condensed consolidated balance sheet of the entity for the current year follows.

DEMSKI, INC., AND SUBSIDIARIES
Consolidated Balance Sheet
December 31, 2019

Assets		
Current assets		$13,510,000
Stock investment—Influential (Knechel)		1,820,000
Other assets		49,980,000
Excess of cost over equity acquired in net assets of Asare Company		1,190,000
Total assets		$66,500,000
Liabilities and shareholders' equity		
Current liabilities		$ 7,210,000
Long-term liabilities		9,940,000
Shareholders' equity		
Common stock	$35,000,000	
Retained earnings	11,690,000	
Demski, Inc., shareholders' equity	46,690,000	
Noncontrolling interests	2,660,000	
Total shareholders' equity		49,350,000
Total liabilities and shareholders' equity		$66,500,000

This balance sheet, along with other financial statements, was furnished to shareholders before their annual meeting, and all shareholders were invited to submit questions to be answered at the meeting. As chief financial officer of Demski, you have been appointed to respond to the questions at the meeting.

REQUIRED

Answer the following shareholder questions.

a. What is meant by *consolidated* financial statements?

b. Why is the investment in Knechel shown on the consolidated balance sheet, but the investments in Asare and Demski Finance are omitted?

c. Explain the meaning of the asset Excess of Cost over Equity Acquired in Net Assets of Asare Company.

d. What is meant by *noncontrolling interest*, and to what company is this account related?

C12-67. Understanding Intercorporate Investments, Accounting Practices, and Managerial Ethics   **LO12-1, 2, 3, 4**

Gayle Sayres, controller of Nexgen, Inc., has asked her Deputy Controller, Doug Stevens, for suggestions as to how the company can improve its reported financial performance for the year. The company is in the last quarter of the year, and projections to the end of the year show the company will have a net loss of about $320,000 before tax.

"My suggestion," said Stevens, "is that we sell 800 of the 160,000 common shares of Heflin Company that we own. The 160,000 shares give us a 20% ownership of Heflin, and we have been using the equity method to account for this investment. We have owned this stock a long time and the current market value of the 160,000 shares is about $600,000 above our book value for the stock."

"That sale will only generate a gain of about $3,000," replied Sayres.

"The rest of the story," continued Stevens, "is that once we sell the 800 shares, we will own less than 20% of Heflin. We can then reclassify the remaining 159,200 shares from the influential category to the passive equity/fair value category. Then we value the stocks at their current fair value, include the rest of the $600,000 gain in this year's income statement, and finish the year with a healthy net income."

"But," responded Sayres, "we aren't going to sell all the Heflin stock; 800 shares maybe, but certainly not any more. We own that stock because they are a long-term supplier of ours. Indeed, we even have representation on their board of directors. The 159,200 shares do not belong in the passive category."

Stevens rolled his eyes and continued, "The classification of an investment as passive or not depends on management's intent. This year-end we claim it was our intent not to exert influence over Heflin. Next year we change our minds and take the stock out of the trading category. Generally accepted accounting principles can't legislate management intent, nor can our outside auditors read our minds. Besides, why shouldn't we take advantage of the flexibility in GAAP to avoid reporting a net loss for this year?"

REQUIRED

a. Should generally accepted accounting principles permit management's intent to influence accounting classifications and measurements?

b. Is it ethical for Gayle Sayres to implement the recommendation of Doug Stevens?

SOLUTIONS TO REVIEW PROBLEMS

Review 12-1
1. P 2. P 3. C 4. SI 5. P

Review 12-2
a. Level 3 b. Level 1 c. Level 2 d. Level 2 e. Level 3 f. Level 1

Review 12-3

SOLUTION TO PART 1

a.

Transaction	Cash Asset	+	Noncash Assets	=	Liabilities	+	Contrib. Capital	+	Earned Capital	Revenues	−	Expenses	=	Net Income
(1) Purchased 500 Pincus bonds.	−470,000 Cash		+470,000 Investments (AFS)	=							−		=	
(2) Receive $15,000 interest payment from Pincus bonds.	+15,000 Cash			=					+15,000 Retained Earnings	+15,000 Interest Income	−		=	+15,000
(3) June 30 fair value of Pincus bonds is $460,000.			−10,000 Investments (AFS)	=					−10,000 Unrealized Loss (AOCI)		−		=	
(4) On July 31, sell all 500 Pincus bonds for $450,000.	+450,000 Cash		−460,000 Investments (AFS)	=					+10,000 Unrealized Loss (AOCI) −20,000 Retained Earnings		−	+20,000 Realized Loss	=	−20,000

b.

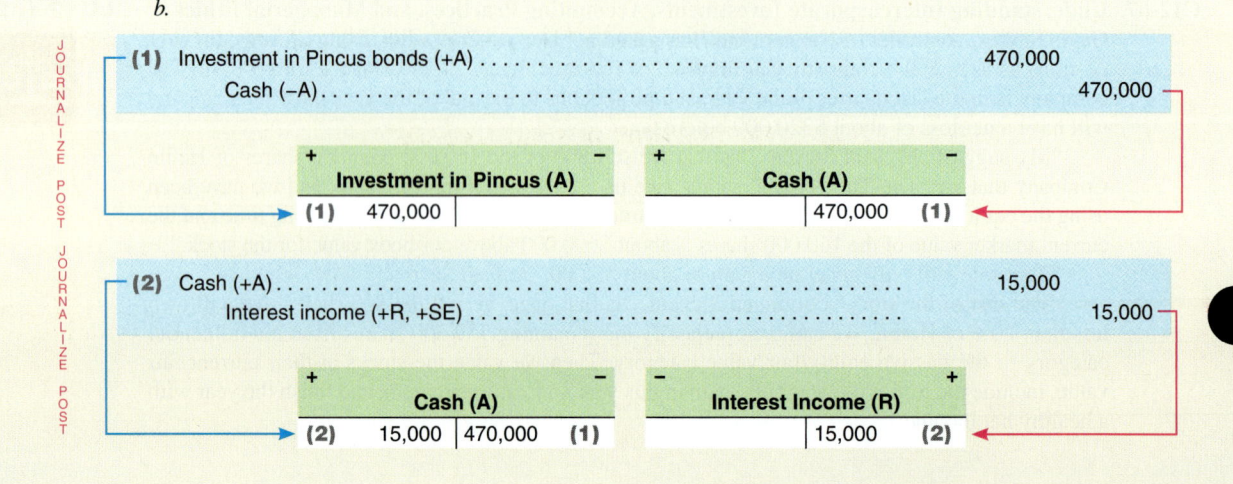

(1) Investment in Pincus bonds (+A) 470,000
    Cash (−A) 470,000

+ Investment in Pincus (A) −		+ Cash (A) −
(1) 470,000		470,000 (1)

(2) Cash (+A) 15,000
    Interest income (+R, +SE) 15,000

+ Cash (A) −	− Interest Income (R) +
(2) 15,000 | 470,000 (1)	15,000 (2)

(3) Unrealized loss (−AOCI, −SE) 10,000
      Investment in Pincus bonds (−A)   10,000

	−	+		+	−
	\multicolumn{2}{c	}{**Unrealized Loss (AOCI)**}	\multicolumn{2}{c	}{**Investment in Pincus (A)**}	
(3)	10,000		(1) 470,000	10,000	(3)

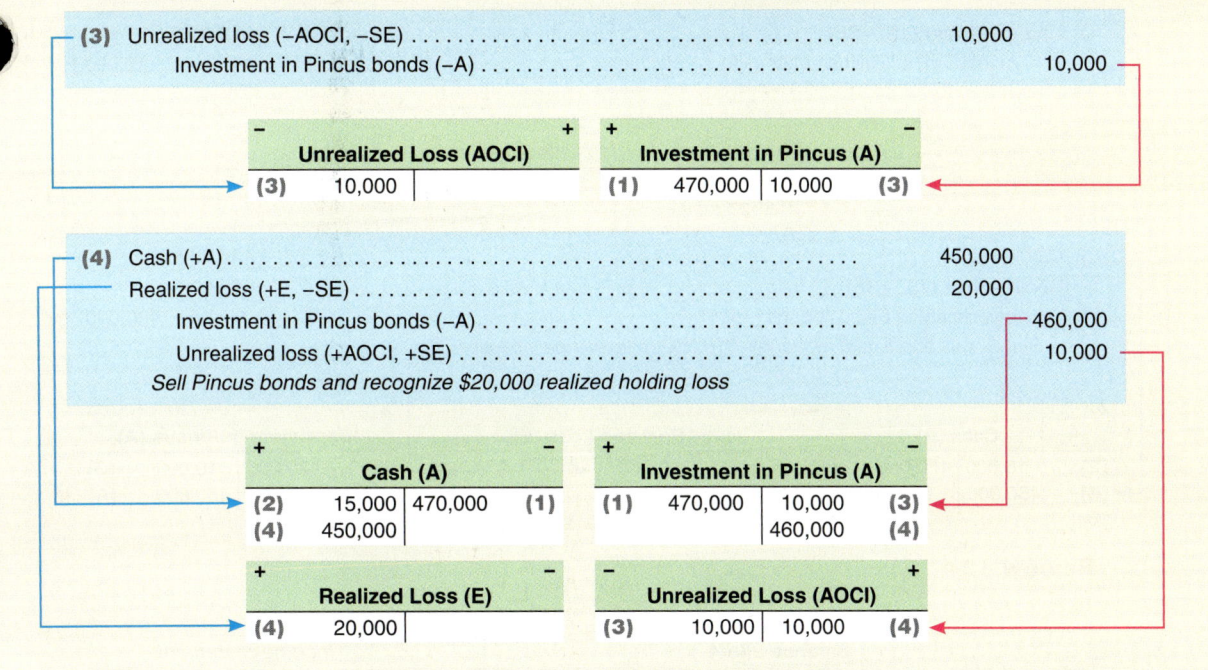

(4) Cash (+A) 450,000
      Realized loss (+E, −SE) 20,000
        Investment in Pincus bonds (−A)   460,000
        Unrealized loss (+AOCI, +SE)   10,000
      Sell Pincus bonds and recognize $20,000 realized holding loss

	+	−		+	−
	\multicolumn{2}{c	}{**Cash (A)**}	\multicolumn{2}{c	}{**Investment in Pincus (A)**}	
(2)	15,000	470,000 (1)	(1) 470,000	10,000	(3)
(4)	450,000			460,000	(4)

	+	−		−	+
	\multicolumn{2}{c	}{**Realized Loss (E)**}	\multicolumn{2}{c	}{**Unrealized Loss (AOCI)**}	
(4)	20,000		(3) 10,000	10,000	(4)

SOLUTION TO PART 2
a.

	Balance Sheet					Income Statement		
Transaction	**Cash Asset** +	**Noncash Assets** =	**Liabil- ities** +	**Contrib. Capital** +	**Earned Capital**	**Revenues** −	**Expenses** =	**Net Income**
(1) Purchased 500 Pincus bonds.	−470,000 Cash	+470,000 Investments (Trading) =				−	=	
(2) Receive $15,000 interest payment from Pincus bonds.	+15,000 Cash	=			+15,000 Retained Earnings	+15,000 Interest Income	−	= +15,000
(3) June 30 fair value of Pincus bonds is $460,000.		−10,000 Investments (Trading) =			−10,000 Retained Earnings	−	+10,000 Unrealized Loss	= −10,000
(4) On July 31, sell all 500 King Co. bonds for $450,000.	+450,000 Cash	−460,000 Investments (Trading) =			−10,000 Retained Earnings	−	+10,000 Realized Loss	= −10,000

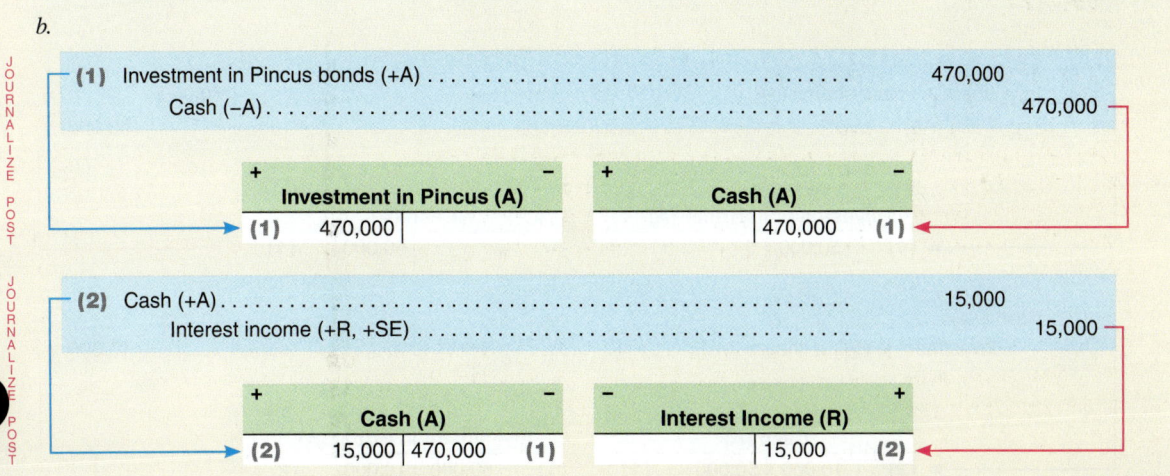

b.

(1) Investment in Pincus bonds (+A) 470,000
      Cash (−A)   470,000

	+	−		+	−
	\multicolumn{2}{c	}{**Investment in Pincus (A)**}	\multicolumn{2}{c	}{**Cash (A)**}	
(1)	470,000			470,000	(1)

(2) Cash (+A) 15,000
      Interest income (+R, +SE)   15,000

	+	−		−	+
	\multicolumn{2}{c	}{**Cash (A)**}	\multicolumn{2}{c	}{**Interest Income (R)**}	
(2)	15,000	470,000 (1)		15,000	(2)

(3) Unrealized loss (+E, −SE) 10,000
      Investment in Pincus bonds (−A) 10,000

+ Unrealized Loss (E) −		+ Investment in Pincus (A) −	
(3) 10,000		(1) 470,000	10,000 (3)

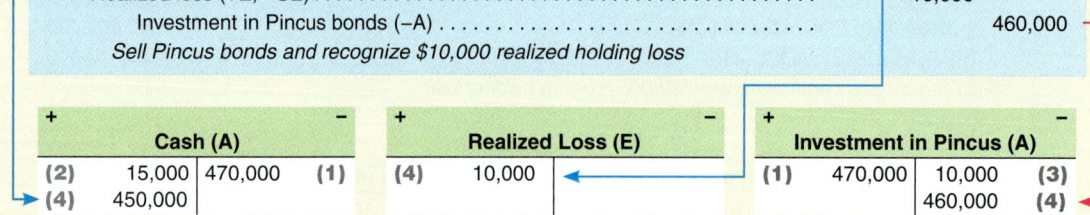

(4) Cash (+A) 450,000
      Realized loss (+E, −SE) 10,000
      Investment in Pincus bonds (−A) 460,000
      Sell Pincus bonds and recognize $10,000 realized holding loss

+ Cash (A) −		+ Realized Loss (E) −		+ Investment in Pincus (A) −	
(2) 15,000	470,000 (1)	(4) 10,000		(1) 470,000	10,000 (3)
(4) 450,000					460,000 (4)

Review 12-4

a.

	Balance Sheet					Income Statement		
Transaction	Cash Asset	+ Noncash Assets	= Liabilities	+ Contrib. Capital	+ Earned Capital	Revenues	− Expenses	= Net Income
(1) Purchased 5,000 Hribar shares at $10 cash per share. These shares reflect 30% ownership of Hribar.	−50,000 Cash	+50,000 Investment in Hribar	=				−	=
(2) Received a $2 per share on cash dividend on Hribar stock.	+10,000 Cash	−10,000 Investment in Hribar	=				−	=
(3) Made an adjustment to reflect $100,000 income reported by Hribar.		+30,000 Investment in Hribar	=		+30,000 Retained Earnings	+30,000 Investment Income	−	= +30,000
(4) Sold all 5,000 Hribar shares for $90,000.	+90,000 Cash	−70,000 Investment in Hribar	=		+20,000 Retained Earnings	+20,000 Gain on Sale	−	= +20,000

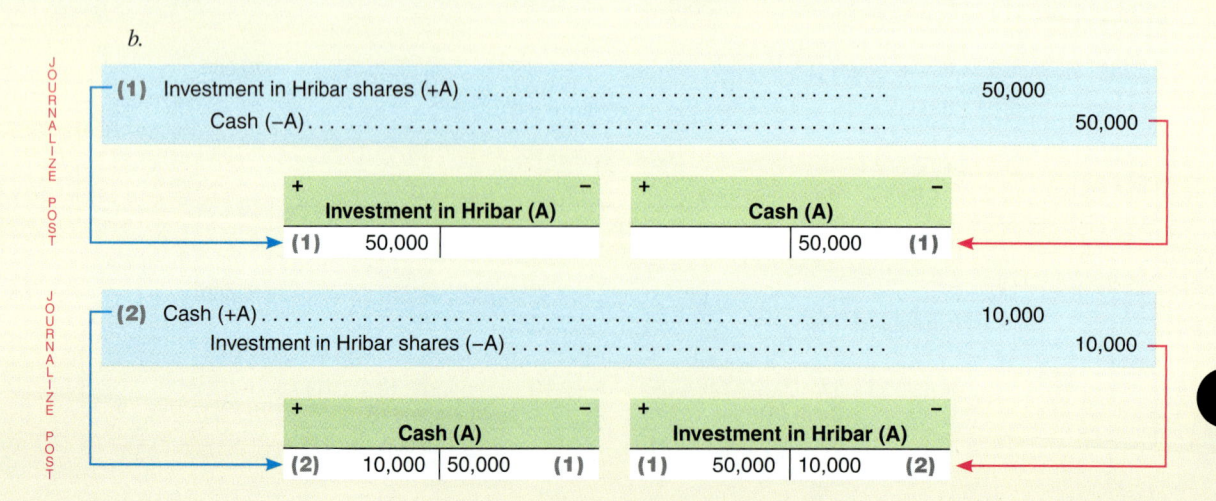

b.

(1) Investment in Hribar shares (+A) 50,000
      Cash (−A) 50,000

+ Investment in Hribar (A) −		+ Cash (A) −	
(1) 50,000			50,000 (1)

(2) Cash (+A) 10,000
      Investment in Hribar shares (−A) 10,000

+ Cash (A) −		+ Investment in Hribar (A) −	
(2) 10,000	50,000 (1)	(1) 50,000	10,000 (2)

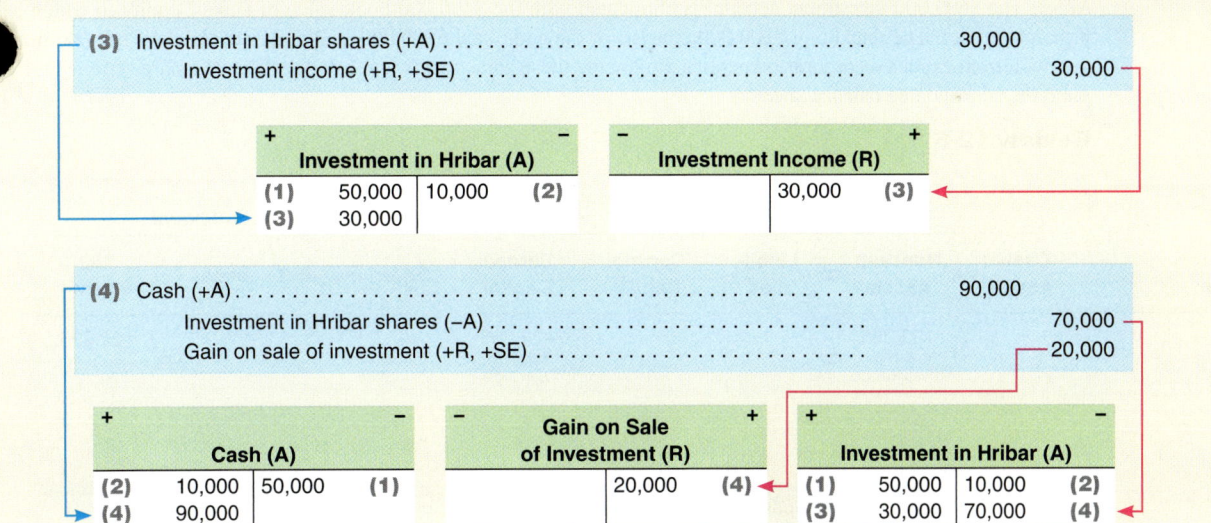

(3) Investment in Hribar shares (+A) 30,000
      Investment income (+R, +SE)   30,000

+ Investment in Hribar (A) −		− Investment Income (R) +	
(1) 50,000	10,000 (2)		30,000 (3)
(3) 30,000			

(4) Cash (+A) 90,000
      Investment in Hribar shares (−A)   70,000
      Gain on sale of investment (+R, +SE)   20,000

+ Cash (A) −		− Gain on Sale of Investment (R) +		+ Investment in Hribar (A) −	
(2) 10,000	50,000 (1)		20,000 (4)	(1) 50,000	10,000 (2)
(4) 90,000				(3) 30,000	70,000 (4)

Review 12-5

a.

	Balance Sheet					Income Statement		
Transaction	Cash Asset	+ Noncash Assets	= Liabilities	+ Contrib. Capital	+ Earned Capital	Revenues −	Expenses =	Net Income
(1) Consolidation adjustment for Bradshaw.		+100,000 PPE, net +100,000 Goodwill −600,000 Investment in Dukes		−200,000 Dukes Common Stock	−200,000 Dukes Retained Earnings	−	=	

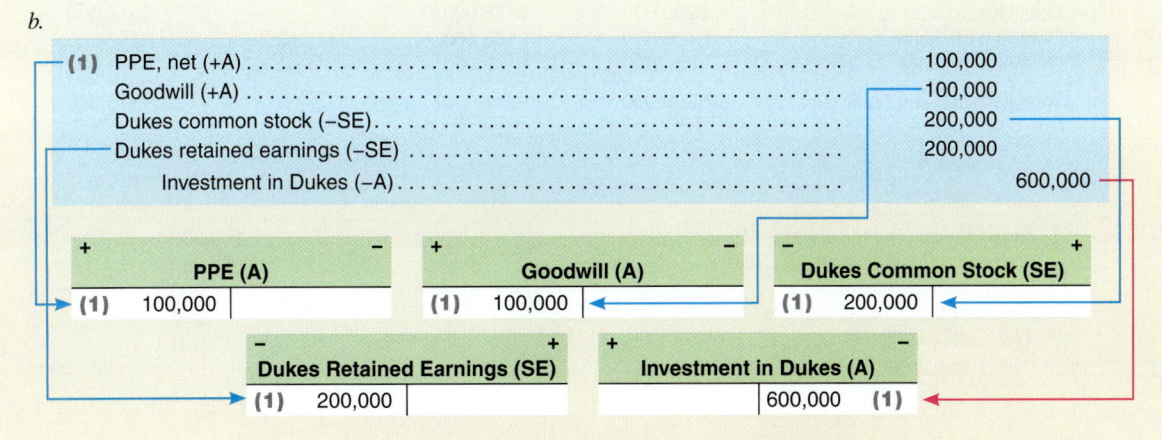

b.

(1) PPE, net (+A) 100,000
      Goodwill (+A) 100,000
      Dukes common stock (−SE)   200,000
      Dukes retained earnings (−SE)   200,000
      Investment in Dukes (−A)   600,000

+ PPE (A) −	+ Goodwill (A) −	− Dukes Common Stock (SE) +
(1) 100,000	(1) 100,000	(1) 200,000

− Dukes Retained Earnings (SE) +	+ Investment in Dukes (A) −
(1) 200,000	600,000 (1)

c.

	Bradshaw (Parent)	Dukes (Subsidiary)	Consolidating Adjustments	Consolidated
Current assets	$1,000,000	$100,000		$1,100,000
Investment in Dukes	600,000	—	$(600,000)	
PPE, net	3,000,000	400,000	100,000	3,500,000
Goodwill	—	—	100,000	100,000
Total assets	$4,600,000	$500,000		$4,700,000
Liabilities	$1,000,000	$100,000		$1,100,000
Contributed capital	2,000,000	200,000	(200,000)	2,000,000
Retained earnings	1,600,000	200,000	(200,000)	1,600,000
Total liabilities and equity	$4,600,000	$500,000		$4,700,000

Notes: The $600,000 investment account is eliminated with the $400,000 book value of Dukes' equity to which it mainly relates. The remaining $200,000 consists of the additional $100,000 in PPE assets and the $100,000 in goodwill from expected corporate synergies. Following these adjustments, the balance sheet items are summed to yield the consolidated balance sheet.

Review 12-6

a.

Transaction	Balance Sheet					Income Statement		
	Cash Asset	+ Noncash Assets	= Liabilities	+ Contrib. Capital	+ Earned Capital	Revenues	− Expenses	= Net Income
		+22,295 Investment in Maxwell Co.	=		+22,295 Retained Earnings	+22,295 Investment Income	−	= +22,295

b.

Investment in Maxwell Company (+A) 22,295
    Investment Income (+R, +SE) 22,295
$22,295 = 35% × ($65,000 − ($6,000/20) − ($5,000/5))

Review 12-7

a.

	Harper Company	Maxwell Company	Consolidating Adjustments	Consolidated
Current assets	$ 680,000	$ 48,000		$ 728,000
Investment in Maxwell	200,000	—	$(200,000)	—
Plant assets	1,200,000	164,000	6,000	1,370,000
Patent	—0	—	5,000	5,000
Goodwill	—	—	13,000	13,000
Total assets	$2,080,000	$212,000		$2,116,000
Liabilities	$280,000	$ 36,000	$ —	$316,000
Contributed capital	1,400,000	160,000	(160,000)	1,400,000
Retained earnings	400,000	16,000	(16,000)	400,000
Total liabilities and equity	$2,080,000	$212,000		$2,116,000

b.

Maxwell contributed capital (−SE) 160,000
Maxwell retained earnings (−SE) 16,000
Plant assets (+A) 6,000
Patent (+A) 5,000
Goodwill (+A) 13,000
    Investment in Maxwell (−A) 200,000

c.

Transaction	Balance Sheet					Income Statement		
	Cash Asset	+ Noncash Assets	= Liabilities	+ Contrib. Capital	+ Earned Capital	Revenues	− Expenses	= Net Income
		+6,000 Plant Assets +5,000 Patent +13,000 Goodwill −200,000 Investment in Maxwell	=	−160,000 Maxwell Contrib. Capital	−16,000 Maxwell Retained Earnings		−	=

Review 12-8

a. The company executes hedging contracts in order to counter market risks. Interest rate swaps are designed to mitigate fluctuations in earnings and cash flows that may result from interest rate volatility. For example, the company states that it "utilizes forward-starting interest rate swaps to mitigate the risk of variability in interest rate for future debt issuances." Foreign currency contracts are designed to mitigate the impact on net income of changes in foreign currency exchange rates. For example, the company states that it hedges "portions of its foreign currency purchases, assets and liabilities arising in the normal course of business…". Commodity contracts are designed to mitigate risks of price changes of materials purchases. The company states that it "is exposed to price volatility related to raw materials used in production, such as essential oils, resins, pulp, tropical oils, tallow, corn, poultry and soybeans."

b. The aim of the company in executing a derivate contract is to offset the gain or loss for the asset or liability to which they relate. This means that the company would be sheltered from losses, but it also would not realize any gains on the held asset or liability. In the table disclosure, it is evident that the gain or loss on a hedged items was completely offset by a corresponding loss or gain of the derivative instrument. The net result is that the income statement reflected no net gain or loss related to the risks outlined in part a.

Chapter 13
Managerial Accounting: Tools for Decision-Making

LEARNING OBJECTIVES

LO13-1 Define managerial accounting, explain its importance, and detail how it differs from financial accounting. (p. 13-3)

LO13-2 Examine how managerial accounting supports and reinforces an organization's mission, goals, and strategies. (p. 13-6)

LO13-3 Explain the importance of viewing the cost of products or services across a value chain. (p. 13-11)

LO13-4 Analyze how trends in the business environment impact the role of managerial accounting. (p. 13-16)

LO13-5 Explain the ethical role of managerial accountants and the increasing emphasis on environmental, social, and governance considerations. (p. 13-18)

Road Map

LO	Learning Objective | Topics	Page	eLecture	Review	Assignments
LO13-1	**Define managerial accounting, explain its importance, and detail how it differs from financial accounting.** Financial Accounting :: Managerial Accounting :: Institute of Management Accountants :: Certified Management Accountant :: Chartered Institute of Management Accountants	13-3	e13–1	R13-1	M13-14, M13-15, M13-16, E13-24
LO13-2	**Examine how managerial accounting supports and reinforces an organization's mission, goals, and strategies.** Mission :: Goal :: Strategy :: Strategic Position :: Cost Leadership :: Product or Service Differentiation :: Market Niche :: Performance Report :: Planning, Organizing, and Controlling :: Organization Chart :: Staff :: Line	13-6	e13–2	R13-2	M13-14, M13-17, M13-18, M13-19, E13-25, E13-26, E13-27, E13-28, C13-34, C13-35, C13-40, DA13-1
LO13-3	**Explain the importance of viewing the cost of products or services across a value chain.** Business Entities :: Processes :: Activities :: Internal Links :: External Links	13-11	e13–3	R13-3	M13-14, M13-20, M13-21, E13-29, E13-30, E13-31, C13-40, C13-41,
LO13-4	**Analyze how trends in the business environment impact the role of managerial accounting.** Global Competition :: Big Data Analysis :: Robotics and Cognitive Technologies :: Artificial Intelligence :: Enterprise Risk Management	13-16	e13–4	R13-4	M13-22, E13-32, DA13-1, DA13-2
LO13-5	**Explain the ethical role of managerial accountants and the increasing emphasis on environmental, social, and governance considerations.** Ethical Dilemmas :: Code of Ethics/Conduct :: Environment :: Sustainability Accounting :: Corporate Social Responsibility :: Corporate Governance and SOX	13-18	e13–5	R13-5	M13-14, M13-23, E13-33, C13-36, C13-37, C13-38, C13-39

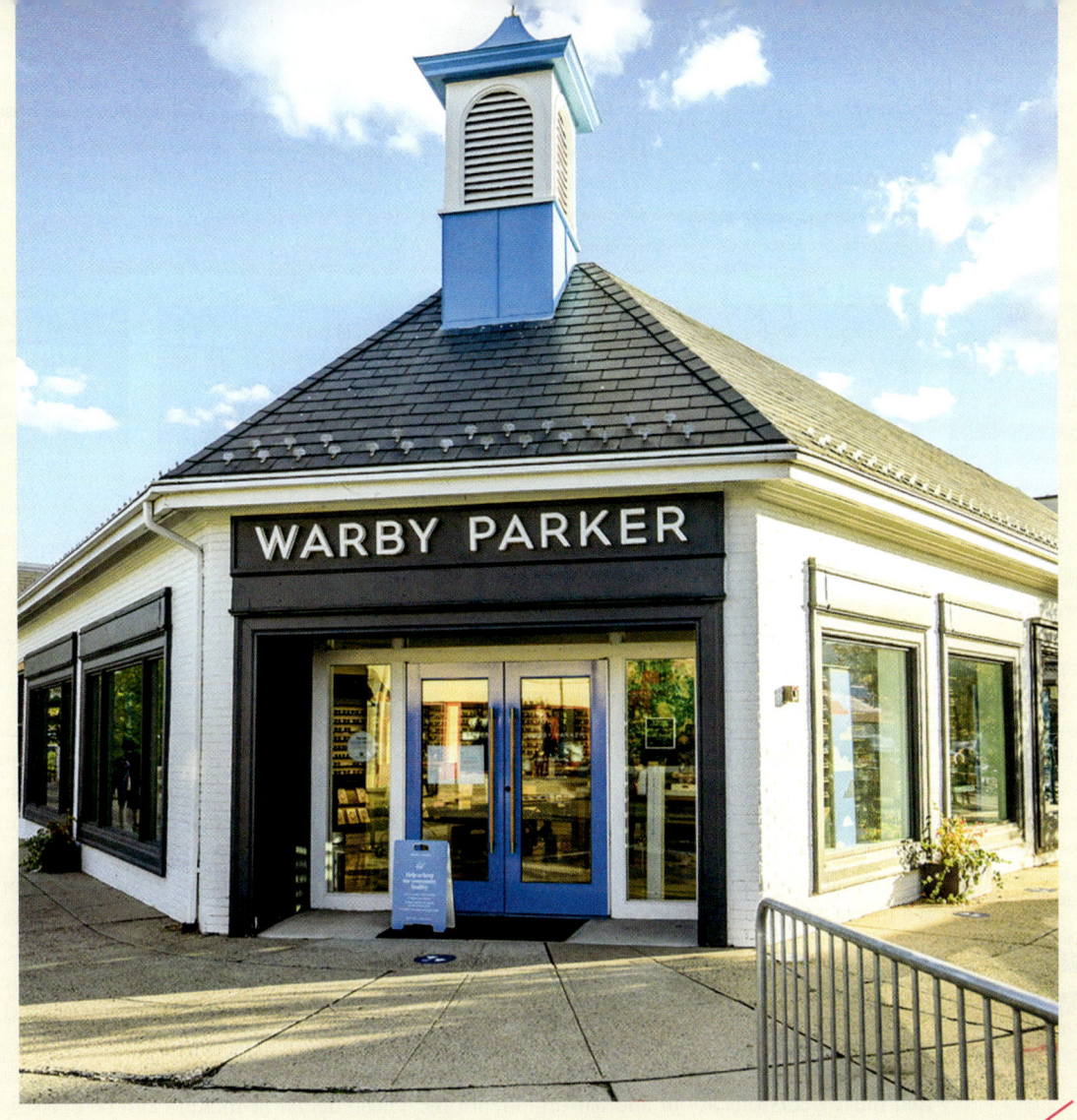

A **Focus Company** *introduces each chapter and illustrates the relevance of managerial accounting in everyday business.*

WARBY PARKER
www.warbyparker.com

The founders of Warby Parker questioned why eyeglasses were prohibitively expensive for many consumers. This led to the launch of Warby Parker, which offers fashionable eyewear to consumers at a significantly lower price than the market. The company strives to demonstrate that "a business can scale, become profitable, and do good in the world—without charging a premium for it."

Among Warby Parker's objectives are profitability, scalability, and social impact. The company uses managerial accounting tools to analyze information, interpret the analyses, define and track performance metrics, and ultimately, to make business decisions. At its start, the company needed to reduce the cost of producing eyewear and/or reduce margins. Managerial accounting techniques help identify and calculate the cost components of producing a pair of eyeglasses. With this information, the company could work toward reducing the highest cost components. Warby Parker identified its suppliers as a main source of costs in the eyewear supply chain. In order to manage these costs, Warby Parker vertically integrated its supply chain. This allowed the company to not only control manufacturing costs, but also influence product quality and fulfillment speed. Given cost accounting information, management can make pricing decisions to achieve a target margin.

Warby Parker can also use managerial accounting to define and track *performance metrics*. In addition to the cost of eyeglasses, management can define performance metrics for its social goals. For example, the company can track the impact of its mission to supply eyewear to the 2.5 billion people who suffer from visual impairments but do not have access to eyewear. By employing data analytic tools, such as those used in managerial accounting, management can make decisions that achieve its goals in the most effective and efficient ways possible.

We begin our exploration of managerial accounting by discussing the differences between managerial and financial accounting. We explore how managerial accounting supports a company's goals and investigate how strategy and operations affect the way organizations use managerial accounting information. Next, we explore how trends in the business environment have increased the need to understand managerial accounting concepts. We also examine the interrelationships among measurement, management, ethics, and environmental, social and governance initiatives.

Sources: Warby Parker Form S-1 and www.warbyparker.com

CHAPTER ORGANIZATION

Managerial Accounting: Tools for Decision-Making

Uses of Accounting Information	Organizations: Missions, Goals, and Strategies	Value Chain	Changing Environment of Business	Ethical, Environmental, Social, and Governance Considerations
• Financial Accounting • Managerial Accounting	• Strategic Position • Managerial Accounting and Goal Attainment • Planning, Organizing, and Controlling	• Illustration of Value Chain • Usefulness of Value Chain	• Global Competition • Big Data and Analysis • Robotics and Cognitive Technologies • Enterprise Risk Management (ERM)	• Ethical Dilemmas • Code of Ethics/Conduct • Corporate Social Responsibility • Corporate Governance

USES OF ACCOUNTING INFORMATION

LO13-1 Define managerial accounting, explain its importance, and detail how it differs from financial accounting.

Managers of organizations such as **Warby Parker** are required to make operational and strategic decisions every day in order to remain competitive in the marketplace. These decisions might involve answering questions such as the following: What is our target market? What products should we offer and at what price? How many employees should we hire? How much should we pay our employees? Which suppliers should we use to fulfill our orders? How much money should we invest in capital resources? Do we accept a new order? How do we reduce the cost of the production process? How can we fulfill our social goals of ensuring access to eyewear while still remaining profitable? And, how will our decisions impact profits? In order to make these decisions and to achieve their organizations' goals, managers must have an understanding of, and access to, timely and reliable information.

Accounting information attempts to satisfy the needs of a variety of individuals and agencies that make decisions about and for organizations. These decision-makers can be classified by their relation to a business as either external users or internal users. **Financial accounting** is designed primarily for decision makers outside of the company, whereas managerial accounting is designed primarily for decision-makers within the company. **Managerial accounting** (also called management accounting) is defined as the activities carried out to provide managers and other employees with accounting information to assist in the formulation and implementation of an organization's strategy. Because there are no official rules, managerial accountants must think critically about the problem that is being raised and how to best provide decision-relevant information.

Financial Accounting

Financial accounting, as discussed in the first half of this text, is an information-processing system that generates general-purpose reports of financial operations (income statement and statement of cash flows) and financial position (balance sheet) for an organization. Although financial accounting is used by decision makers inside and outside the firm, financial accounting typically emphasizes external users, such as security investors, analysts, and lenders. Adding to this external orientation are external financial reporting requirements determined by law and generally accepted accounting principles (GAAP).

Financial accounting is also concerned with keeping records of the organization's assets, revenue generating activities, obligations, and the collection and payment of cash. An organization cannot survive without finalizing sales, converting sales into cash, paying for purchases, meeting payroll, and keeping track of its assets.

UNITED STATES SECURITIES AND EXCHANGE COMMISSION
Washington, D.C. 20549
FORM 10-K

(Mark One)
☒ ANNUAL REPORT PURSUANT TO SECTION 13 OR 15(d) OF THE SECURITIES EXCHANGE ACT OF 1934
For the fiscal year ended December 31, 2021
OR
☐ TRANSITION REPORT PURSUANT TO SECTION 13 OR 15(d) OF THE SECURITIES EXCHANGE ACT OF 1934
For transition period from ___ to ___
Commission File Number 001-40825

Warby Parker Inc.
(Exact name of registrant as specified in its charter)

Delaware — 80-0423634
(State or other jurisdiction of incorporation or organization) — (I.R.S. Employer Identification Number)

233 Spring Street, 6th Floor East, New York, New York — 10013
(Address of registrant's principal executive offices) — (Zip Code)

Registrant's telephone number, including area code (646) 847-7215

Financial Statements

Income Statement	Balance Sheet	Statement of Stockholders' Equity	Statement of Cash Flows
Reports results of operations	Lists assets, liabilities and equity values	Details changes in owner financing	Details sources and uses of cash

Insufficient for Internal Decision-Making Managers often use income statements and balance sheets as a starting point in evaluating and planning the firm's overall activities. Managers learn a great deal by performing a comparative analysis of their firm and competing firms. Corporate goals are often stated using financial accounting numbers such as net income, or ratios such as return on investment and earnings per common share. However, due to GAAP rules, internal decision makers often find the information provided in financial statements of limited value in managing day-to-day operating activities. They often complain that financial accounting information is too aggregated, prepared too late, based on irrelevant past costs, constrained by rules, and not action oriented. For example, the costs of all items produced and sold or all services rendered are summarized in a single line in most financial statements, making it impossible to determine the costs of individual products or services. Financial accounting procedures, acceptable for costing inventories as a whole, often produce misleading information when applied to individual products. The costs of individual products or services are rarely detailed enough in overall financial statements to provide the information needed for product-level decision-making. Financial accounting reports, seldom prepared more than once a month, are not timely enough for use in the management of day-to-day activities that cause excess costs. Financial accounting reports reflect *past* transactions. To make decisions, managers are also concerned with forward-looking information such as predicted costs. While financial accounting information is useful in making some management decisions, its primary emphasis is not on internal decision-making.

Managerial Accounting

As emphasized in our Warby Parker example, managers are constantly faced with the need to understand and control costs, make important product decisions, coordinate resources, and guide and motivate employees. Managerial accounting provides an information framework to organize, evaluate, and report proprietary data in light of an organization's goals and strategies. This information is directed to managers and other employees within the organization to assist in planning activities, controlling costs and behaviors, and making decisions. *Managerial accounting reports should be designed to meet the information needs of internal decision makers.* Top management may need only summary information prepared once a month for each business unit. On the other hand, an engineer responsible for hourly production scheduling may need continuously updated and detailed information concerning the cost of current and alternative ways of producing a product. Managerial accountants often refer to this customization of information as "different costs for different purposes."

With the intensity of competition and the shorter life cycles of new products and services, managerial accounting is crucial to an organization's success. Managerial accountants partner with their co-workers across departments. They assist in identifying, obtaining, and analyzing relevant information required for decision-making. Understanding the financial implications of business decisions is an important part of the decision-making process. The significant differences between financial and managerial accounting are summarized in **Exhibit 13.1**.

> In order to expand sales from a digital focus, Warby Parker has recently opened new brick-and-mortar stores in suburban areas. What type of sales information is needed in order to assess the effectiveness of this decision?
>
> *Sales information reported in its Form 10-K would indicate trends in annual sales from year-to-year, but would be insufficient for a thorough analysis. Alternatively, managerial accounting information could provide sales information by physical store, by month, and even by day. Trends in physical store sales could be compared to trends in digital sales in comparable periods.*

Critical Thinking & Decision-Making

EXHIBIT 13.1 — Differences Between Financial and Managerial Accounting

Financial Accounting	Managerial Accounting
Communicates information primarily to *external* users	Communicates information to *internal* users
Adheres to Generally Accepted Accounting Principles and external standards	Created specifically to answer a business question or as the basis for business decisions
Reports information in aggregated, general purpose financial statements	Creates analyses in aggregate or in detail, depending on the need
Summarizes past decisions and results that can inform the future	Creates accounting data that impacts current and future performance
Focuses on information relevance, reliability, and comparability	Focuses on decision-relevant information
Created and communicated in regulated intervals, such as by quarter or year	Created and communicated as needed for decision-making
Emphasizes objective data	Uses only data relevant to question being analyzed

Managerial accounting information exists to serve the needs of management, in analyzing situations, answering questions, and contributing to solutions. Hence, it should be developed only if the perceived benefits exceed the costs of development and use. Also, while financial measures are often used in managerial accounting, they are not used to the exclusion of other nonfinancial measures. Money is simply a convenient way of expressing events in a form suitable to summary analysis. When this is not possible or appropriate, nonfinancial measures are used. Time, for example, is often an important element of quality or service. Hence, many performance measures focus on time, for example:

- Internet vendors such as UPS and Amazon.com track delivery time.
- Fire departments and police departments measure the response time to emergency calls.
- Airlines, such as Delta Airlines as well as the Federal Aviation Administration, monitor the number of on-time departures and arrivals.

IMA® (Institute of Management Accountants)

No external standards (such as requirements of the Securities and Exchange Commission) are imposed on information provided to internal users. However the IMA®—an association of accountants and financial professionals in business—acts as a guide for defining the role and best practices of managerial accounting. Globally, the IMA supports the profession through research, the CMA® (Certified Management Accountant) program, continuing education, networking, and advocacy of the highest ethical business practices. Recently, the IMA updated its Management Accounting Competency Framework which details skills required by managerial accountants: technical, business, leadership, people, and digital skills. The framework emphasizes the need for managerial accountants to partner in planning and decision-making, create performance management systems, and provide expertise in financial reporting and control.[1] These competencies are discussed in Chapter 19.

The IMA's CMA program credentials managerial accountants. The certification focuses specifically on the competencies required by organizations and CFOs to protect investors and drive business value. The CMA tests professional competencies in budgeting and forecasting, risk management and internal controls, technology and analytics, performance management, corporate finance, professional ethics, and more. CMA-certified professionals work within organizations of all sizes, industries, and types, including manufacturing and services, public and private enterprises, not-for-profit organizations, academic institutions, government entities, and multinational corporations. To become certified, a qualified professional must be a member of IMA, pass a two-part exam, (CMA exam), fulfill a two-year work requirement, stay current through continuing education, and abide by IMA's *Statement of Ethical Professional Practice*. Based on a study cited by the CMA, CMAs have a 55% salary advantage globally. That advantage increases to 70% for CMAs, ages 20–29.[2]

---

[1] http://www.imanet.org/career-resources/management-accounting-competencies

[2] Gregory L. Krippel PhD, and Sheila Mitchell CPA, "The CMA Advantage: An Update," *Strategic Finance*, September 2017, pp. 39–45.

CMA Adapted Questions In the end of chapter assignments, you will see certain problems with a CMA icon, signaling that these are practice questions for the CMA exam. This is another indication that the topics of this text are relevant to practicing professionals working in business today. In fact, there are over 1.4 million accountants and auditors in the U.S., about 75% of which, the IMA estimates work in managerial accounting and academic roles.[3] For more information about the IMA, please visit www.imanet.org.

CIMA (Chartered Institute of Management Accountants)

Another option to obtain additional credentials in the managerial accounting field is through the CGMA (Chartered Global Management Accountant) designation. The CGMA designation is the result of a joint partnership of the American Institute of CPAs (AICPA) and the Chartered Institute of Management Accountants (CIMA). The CGMA exam tests proficiencies in finance, operations, strategy, and management. Candidates are required to be an AICPA member in good standing, pass the CGMA exam, and have a minimum of 3 years of relevant work experience. For more information about the CGMA, please visit www.cgma.org.

> Another option is a certified public accountant (CPA) certificate and license which permits the practice of public accounting. While most states require at least two year of public accounting experience for licensure, many accountants use this experience as a foundation for later careers in managerial accounting. Requirements for the CPA exam can be found at https://us.aicpa.org/becomeacpa/licensure.

Comparison of Financial to Managerial Accounting LO13-1 **Review 13-1**

Bausch & Lomb is an eye care division of Bausch Health that produces many types of contact lenses. Management is contemplating removing one of its brands from the market. To analyze the pros and cons of this decision, management needs managerial accounting information.

Required
Identify relevant *managerial* accounting information from the following list that would be useful in this decision process.

  a. Annual financial statements
  b. The company's strategic sales position
  c. Calculation of the company's earnings per share of common stock
  d. Daily sales by individual brand
  e. Company-wide sales for the first quarter of the year
  f. Report of customer satisfaction survey results by brand.
  g. Detailed cost information by brand.

Solution on p. 13-29.

MISSIONS, GOALS, AND STRATEGIES

An Organization's Mission, Goals, and Strategies

Mission An organization's **mission** is the basic purpose toward which its activities are directed. Warby Parker's mission is to "to inspire and impact the world with vision, purpose, and style (without charging a premium for it)." Warby Parker's ultimate objective is to "provide vision for all." This emphasizes the importance of Warby Parker's social purpose of ensuring that everyone is able to obtain eyeglasses.[4] TED is a nonprofit devoted to spreading ideas, usually in the form of short, powerful talks (18 minutes or less). TED's mission statement found on its website is stated as, "Spread ideas, foster community and create impact."[5] Organizations vary widely in their missions. One benefit of a mission statement is to help focus all the activities of an organization. For instance, the mission of The Coca-Cola Company is stated as follows on the company's website.

LO13-2
Examine how managerial accounting supports and reinforces an organization's mission, goals, and strategies.

> **Our Purpose:**
> Refresh the world. Make a difference.
>
> **Our Vision:**
> Our vision is to craft the brands and choice of drinks that people love, to refresh them in body & spirit. And done in ways that create a more sustainable business and better shared future that makes a difference in people's lives, communities and our planet.[6]

---

[3] https://www.bls.gov/ooh/business-and-financial/accountants-and-auditors.htm#tab-6%20
[4] S-1: https://s28.q4cdn.com/987131352/files/doc_sec/8/24/S-1.pdf
[5] https://www.ted.com/about/our-organization
[6] https://www.coca-colacompany.com/company/purpose-and-vision

The Chairman and CEO of Coca-Cola Company indicated that the company has continued to grow since its inception in 1886 with a purpose to refresh the world and make a difference. This applies beyond a physical sense to include a refreshment in spirit which expands to communities and to the environment in which it operates.[7] Coca-Cola can use its managerial accounting system to help evaluate its success at "making a difference."

We frequently distinguish between organizations on the basis of profit motive. **For-profit organizations** aim to maximize profits, whereas **not-for-profit organizations** maximize the execution of their respective missions. Clearly, the Coca-Cola Company is a for-profit organization, whereas TED and United Way are not-for-profit organizations. (The term *nonprofit* is frequently used to refer to what we have identified as not-for-profit organizations.) Regardless of whether a profit motive exists, organizations must use resources wisely. Every dollar United Way spends for administrative salaries is a dollar that cannot be used to support charitable activities. Not-for-profit organizations, including governments, can go bankrupt if they are unable to meet their financial obligations. All organizations, for-profit and not-for-profit, should use managerial accounting concepts to ensure that resources are used wisely.

Goal A **goal** is a definable, measurable objective. Based on the organization's mission, management sets a number of goals. Ideally, satisfactory performance on the individual goals will lead to achievement of the organization's mission. For-profit organizations have some measure of profitability or shareholder value as one of their stated or implicit goals. The mission of a candle manufacturer located in a small town is to provide quality products in order to increase value for its stakeholders. The company's goals might include earning an annual profit equal to 10% of average total assets, maintaining annual dividends of $2 per share of common stock, developing a customer reputation for above-average quality and service, providing steady employment for area residents, and meeting or exceeding environmental standards.

A clear statement of mission and well-defined goals provide an organization with an identity and unifying purpose, thereby ensuring that all employees are heading in the same direction. Having developed a mission and a set of goals, employees are more apt to make decisions that move the organization toward its defined purpose. Managerial accounting includes the definition, measurement, and analysis of both financial and non-financial information. This information supports managerial decision-making to ensure that a company's actions support its missions and goals.

Strategy A **strategy** is a course of action that will assist in achieving one or more goals. Much of this text will focus on the measurement and control aspects of selecting strategies to achieve goals. For example, if an organization's goal is to improve product quality, possible strategies for achieving this goal include investing in new equipment, implementing additional quality inspections, prescreening suppliers, reducing batch size, redesigning products, training employees, and rearranging the shop floor. Managerial accounting information will assist in determining which of the many alternative strategies for achieving the goal of quality improvement are effective and efficient. The distinction between mission, goals, and strategies is illustrated in **Exhibit 13.2**.

EXHIBIT 13.2 Mission, Goals, and Strategies

Mission	Basic purpose toward which activities are directed, typically ongoing and not precisely measurable. For example, achieving a monetary profit by providing reliable, high-quality voice and data services to customers would be the mission of a cell phone provider.
Goals	Definable, measurable targets or objectives based on the organization's mission. One goal of a cell phone provider might be to increase network speed by 20% for all customers.
Strategies	Courses of action that will assist in achieving one or more goals. The cell phone provider will adopt cost-effective plans to upgrade to the latest generational technology across its footprint.

---

[7] https://www.coca-colacompany.com/content/dam/journey/us/en/our-company/purpose-and-vision/james-quincey-letter-to-employees-coca-cola-company-purpose-dec-2019.pdf

Strategic Position Analysis

In competitive environments, managers must make a fundamental decision concerning their organization's goal for positioning itself in comparison to its competitors. This goal is referred to as the organization's **strategic position**. Much of the organization's strategy depends on this strategic positioning goal. Managerial accounting information helps managers assess the effectiveness of the organization's strategic positioning. Michael Porter, a highly regarded expert on business strategy, has identified three possible strategic positions that lead to business success.[8]

1. **Cost leadership**
2. **Product or service differentiation**
3. **Market niche**

Cost Leadership

According to Porter, cost leadership

> requires aggressive construction of efficient-scale facilities, vigorous pursuit of cost reductions from experience, tight cost and overhead control, avoidance of marginal customer accounts, and cost minimization in areas like R&D [research and development], service, sales force, advertising, and so on. A great deal of managerial attention to cost control is necessary to achieve these aims. Low cost relative to competitors becomes the theme running through the entire strategy, though quality, service, and other areas cannot be ignored.[9]

Achieving cost leadership allows an organization to achieve higher profits selling at the same price as competitors or by allowing the firm to aggressively compete on the basis of price while remaining profitable. One of the first companies to successfully use a cost leadership strategy was **Carnegie Steel Company**.

> Carnegie's operating strategy was to push his own direct costs below his competitors so that he could charge prices that would always ensure enough demand to keep his plants running at full capacity. This strategy prompted him to require frequent information showing his direct costs in relation to those of his competitors. Possessing that information and secure in the knowledge that his costs were the lowest in the industry, Carnegie then mercilessly cut prices during economic recessions. While competing firms went under, he still made profits. In periods of prosperity, when customers' demands exceeded the industry's capacity to produce, Carnegie joined others in raising prices.[10]

Warby Parker and **Southwest Airlines** are current examples of successful businesses competing with a strategy of cost leadership. To succeed at this strategy, an organization must have reliable managerial accounting information including reliable cost information for its products and services. While an organization might compete primarily on the basis of price, management must take care to ensure their products and services adapt to changing customer needs and preferences. Managerial accounting information can help managers analyze the company's market position and measure its success in following its operating strategy.

Product or Service Differentiation

The differentiation strategy focuses on seeking ways to differentiate or distinguish the company from its competitors. One way to differentiate is through high quality service which is an important aspect of the **Chick-fil-A** business model. High quality of service for this fast food chain translates into high efficiency coupled with excellent customer service. In fact, David Farmer, a company vice president, described his mission in an interview as creating "[NASCAR] pit crew efficiency, but where you feel like you just got hugged in the process . . . We'd better not

---

[8] Michael E. Porter, *Competitive Strategy* (New York: The Free Press, 1980), p. 35.

[9] Porter, p. 35.

[10] H. Thomas Johnson and Robert S. Kaplan, *Relevance Lost: The Rise and Fall of Management Accounting* (Boston: Harvard Business School Press, 1987), pp. 33–34.

lose our edge relative to service and hospitality."[11] Managerial accounting information can assist a company like Chick-fil-A in tracking the success of their strategy in sales and profit margins. For example, data collected and analyzed on repeat sales measured through the company's app can detect trends in brand loyalty, a desired outcome of a differentiation strategy.

Market Niche

The third possible strategic position, according to Porter, focuses on a specific market niche such as a buyer group, segment of the product line, or geographic market and

> rests on the premise that the firm is thus able to serve its narrow strategic target more effectively or efficiently than competitors who are competing more broadly. As a result, the firm achieves either differentiation from better meeting the needs of the particular target, or lower costs in serving the target, or both. Even though the focus strategy does not achieve low costs or differentiation for the market as a whole, it does achieve one or both of these positions vis-à-vis its narrow market target.[12]

JOYY Inc. (formerly known as YY Inc.) is following a market niche strategy. JOYY, one of the largest live-streaming companies in the world, has adopted a unique business model in the entertainment market. Instead of generating revenue from advertisers, the company collects fees from users who are allowed to buy gifts for their favorite performers (amateur singers, dancers, and comedians) and purchase virtual goods for use in online games. Users can also pay a monthly subscription fee, which gives them priority entrance to live-streamed performances and access to other enhanced features. To appeal to younger audiences, the company introduced participant-focused live streaming in 2017, where users can interact directly with the performers.[13]

JOYY identified behaviors of its target market, and using managerial accounting information, is adapting its model to better fit its market's needs. JOYY had 3.8 million paying users for livestreaming services in 2021 and reported revenues exceeding $2.6 billion.[14] Managerial accounting helps companies like JOYY understand the cost of delivering their services, and the costs of adapting their business model to access new markets. The success of the strategy is evident in its financial results.

Managerial Accounting and Goal Attainment

A major purpose of managerial accounting is to support the achievement of goals. Hence, determining an organization's strategic position goal has implications for the operation of an organization's managerial accounting system.

Performance Reports Careful budgeting and cost control with frequent and detailed performance reports are critical with a goal of cost leadership. When the product is difficult to distinguish from that of competitors', price is the primary basis of competition. Under these circumstances, everyone in the organization should ensure that product costs are accurately estimated to achieve and maintain the company's cost leadership position. The managerial accounting system should continually compare actual costs with budgeted costs and signal the existence of significant differences. This allows management to immediately respond to cost overruns or to quickly learn about cost savings. Of course, even under different strategic position goals, comparing actual and budget amounts help managers evaluate and learn from current performance. A simplified version of a *performance report* for costs during a budget period is as follows.

Budgeted (planned) Costs	Actual Costs	Deviation from Budget	Percent Deviation
$560,000	$595,000	$35,000 unfavorable	6.25%

---

[11] V. Wong, "Chick-Fil-A Will Soon Be Bigger Than Taco Bell, Burger King, And Wendy's", March 31, 2018, retrieved from https://www.buzzfeednews.com/article/venessawong/chick-fil-a-third-largest-fast-food-chain.

[12] Porter, pp. 38–39.

[13] The Boston Consulting Group, "The 2018 BCG Local Dynamos: Emerging-Market Companies Up Their Game," October 2018

[14] JOYY Inc. Form 20-F: *Annual Report Pursuant to Section 13 or 15(D) of the Securities Exchange Act of 1934* for the fiscal year ended December 31, 2021.

How can managerial accounting support a strategy of product differentiation?

With a strategy of product differentiation, the organization's products are easily distinguishable from those of its competitors, and customers are less sensitive to price. In this case, while managers must understand the financial consequences of their actions, frequent and detailed cost information is less important. Instead, costs should be analyzed from the customer's viewpoint, and the organization should work closely with customers to enhance their perceived value of products or services. The customer may not want a costly feature. Alternatively, the customer may be willing to pay more for an additional feature that requires an increase in operating costs. Managerial accounting can help estimate the profit margin of adding the distinguishing features and also provide an analysis of the estimated demand and pricing of the product or service.

Planning, Organizing, and Controlling

The process of selecting goals and strategies to achieve these goals is often referred to as **planning**. The implementation of plans requires the development of subgoals and the assignment of responsibility to achieve subgoals to specific individuals or groups within an organization. This process of making the organization into a well-ordered whole is called **organizing**. In organizing, the authority to take action to implement plans is delegated to other managers and employees.

Developing an **organization chart** illustrating the formal relationships that exist between the elements of an organization is an important part of organizing. An organization chart for Crown Department Stores is illustrated in **Exhibit 13.3**. The blocks represent organizational units, and the lines represent relationships between the units. Authority flows down through the organization. Top management delegates authority to use resources for limited purposes to subordinate managers who, in turn, delegate to their subordinates more limited authority for accomplishing more structured tasks. Responsibility flows up through the organization. People at the bottom are responsible for specific tasks, but the president is responsible for the operation of the entire organization.

EXHIBIT 13.3 Crown Department Stores' Organization Chart

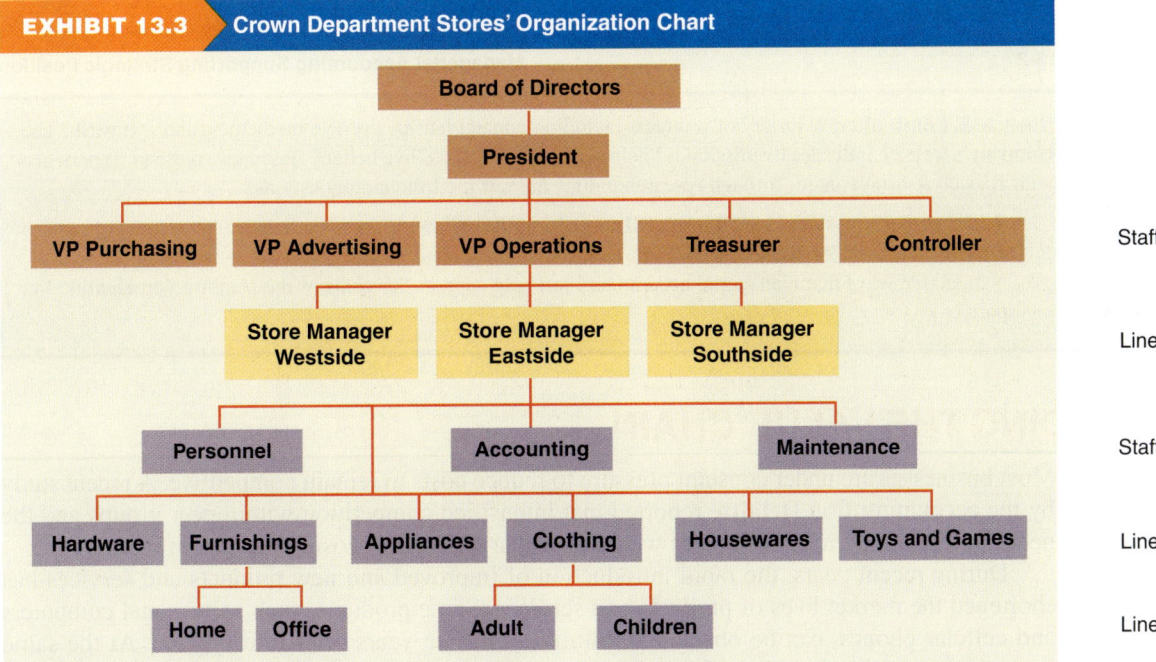

- Board of Directors
- President
- VP Purchasing, VP Advertising, VP Operations, Treasurer, Controller — Staff departments
- Store Manager Westside, Store Manager Eastside, Store Manager Southside — Line departments
- Personnel, Accounting, Maintenance — Staff departments
- Hardware, Furnishings, Appliances, Clothing, Housewares, Toys and Games — Line departments
- Home, Office, Adult, Children — Line departments

A distinction is often made between line and staff departments. *Line departments* engage in activities that create and distribute goods and services to customers. *Staff departments* exist to facilitate the activities of line departments. In **Exhibit 13.3**, we see that Crown Department Stores has two levels of staff organizations—corporate and store. The corporate staff departments are Purchasing, Advertising, Operations, Treasurer, and Controller. Staff departments at the store level are Personnel, Accounting, and Maintenance. All other units are line departments. A change in plans can necessitate a change in the organization. For example, Crown's plan to discontinue the sale of hardware and add an art department during the coming year will necessitate an organizational change.

Controlling is the process of ensuring that results agree with plans with no surprises. A brief example of a performance report for costs was presented previously on page 13-9. In the process of controlling operations, actual performance is compared with plans.

With a cost leadership strategy and long-lived products, if actual results deviate significantly from plans, an attempt is made to bring operations into line with plans, or the plans are adjusted. The original plan is adjusted if it is deemed no longer appropriate because of changed circumstances.

With a differentiation strategy and short-lived products, design and scheduling personnel will consider previous errors in predicting costs as they plan new products and services. Hence, the process of controlling feeds forward into the process of planning to form a continuous cycle coordinated through the managerial accounting system. This cycle is illustrated in **Exhibit 13.4**.

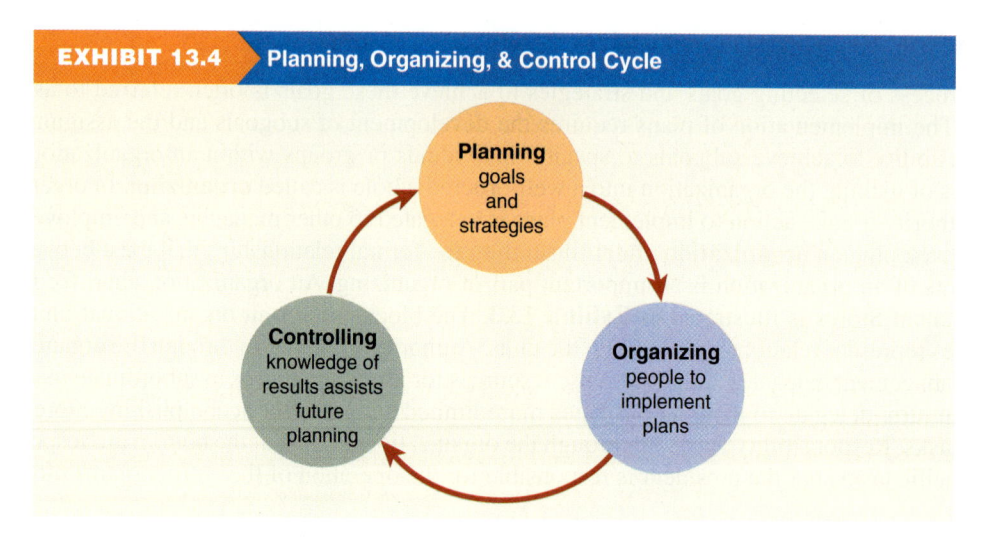

EXHIBIT 13.4 Planning, Organizing, & Control Cycle

- Planning: goals and strategies
- Organizing: people to implement plans
- Controlling: knowledge of results assists future planning

Review 13-2 LO13-2

Managerial Accounting Supporting Strategic Position

Bausch & Lomb offers a variety of products including contact lenses, dry-eye medicines, and eye wash. The company's website indicates its mission is "helping you see better to live better." Based on your own experience with Bausch & Lomb and/or through research online, answer the following questions.

1. Which strategic position does Bausch & Lomb primarily follow: (a) cost leadership, (b) product or service differentiation, or (c) market niche?
2. Name three ways that managerial accountants can help support the goals of the position you identified in part 1.

Solution on p. 13-29.

UNDERSTANDING THE VALUE CHAIN

LO13-3 Explain the importance of viewing the cost of products or services across a value chain.

Most businesses are under constant pressure to reduce costs to remain competitive. A recent study by the accounting firm **Deloitte** reported that intensified competition within peer groups and the need for investment in growth areas were the primary drivers of cost management measures.[15]

During recent years, the rapid introduction of improved and new products and services has shortened the market lives of products and services. Some products, such as personal computers and cellular phones, can be obsolete within two or three years after introduction. At the same time, the increased use of complex automated equipment makes it difficult to change production

---

[15] "Save-to-Transform as a Catalyst for Embracing Digital Disruption," Deloitte's second biennial global cost survey, 2019.

procedures after production begins. Combining short product life cycles with automated production results in an environment where many costs are determined by decisions made before production begins (decisions concerning product design and production procedures).

In responding to these trends, companies are pressured to manage costs and improve efficiencies in order to remain competitive. The cost analyses that inform decision-making should be made within the context of the company's business strategy (discussed in the last section) and in its position in a larger value chain stretching from the development and use of resources to the final consumers.

The **value chain** for a product or service is the set of value-producing activities that stretches from basic raw materials to the final consumer. Each product or service has a distinct value chain, and all entities along the value chain depend on the final customer's perception of the value and cost of a product or service. Theoretically, it is the final customer who ultimately pays all costs and provides all profits to all organizations along the entire value chain. The value chain will not work effectively if costs are not recovered and acceptable profits are not reported within the links in the value chain. Consequently, *the goal of every organization is to maximize the value, while minimizing the cost, of a product or service to final customers*. To this end, all organizations in the value chain should work toward the optimization of the entire value chain, instead of solely focusing on their own organizations.

The value chain provides a viewpoint that encompasses all activities performed to deliver products and services to final customers. Analyzing a value chain from the perspective of the final consumer requires working backward from the end product or service to the basic raw materials entering into the product or service. Analyzing a value chain from the viewpoint of an organization that is in the middle of a value chain requires working forward (downstream) to the final consumer and backward (upstream) to the source of raw materials, also called the supply chain.

Illustration of the Value Chain

Exhibit 13.5 presents the value chain for the outside box packaging of daily contact lenses produced by a third party (**Johnson & Johnson**) but sold by **Warby Parker**. The value chain is presented at three levels, with each successive level containing additional details.

First Level: Business Entities The first level depicts the various business entities in the value chain.

- Timber producers grow the pulp wood (usually pine) used as the basic input into paper products. Some paper companies, such as **International Paper** (the leading producer of paperboard), harvest much of their pulp wood from timberlands that they manage. Other companies, including **Georgia Pacific** (owned by **Koch Industries Inc.**), do not manage their own timberlands, but purchase pulp for their mills on the open market through pulp intermediaries.
- Pulp mills produce the kraft (unbleached) paper used to produce the paperboard. Companies such as **International Paper** and **Georgia Pacific** own pulp mills which produce the kraft paper. Other paperboard manufacturers can purchase pulp and kraft paper from companies such as **Domtar**.
- Paperboard manufacturers perform a laminating process of coating paperboard material used to produce packages for contact lenses. The layers of coating give the top surface a high gloss finish that is water resistant and suitable for multicolor printing.
- The paperboard converter uses manufactured paperboard to print and produce the completed packaging product, the boxes used to package the 24-pack of contact lenses.
- **Johnson & Johnson** purchases the completed paperboard packages from companies like **Graphic Packaging** to package their many different brands of contact lenses.
- The final customer purchases contacts packaged in paperboard packages and uses the package to store the contacts until the 24-pack is used. The packages not only perform a transport and storage function but also serve as an advertising medium by showing the company's logo and brand name.

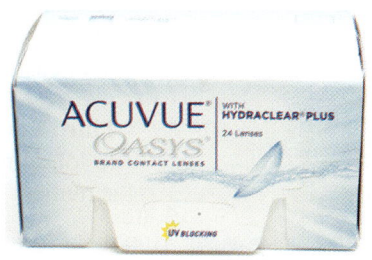

EXHIBIT 13.5 — Value Chain for a Contact Lens Packaging Product

First level: Business Entities

Timber Producer → Pulp Mill → Paperboard Manufacturer → Paperboard Converter → Johnson & Johnson → Final Customer

Second level: Processes

Procurement → Storage → Sell to customer*

Third level: Activities

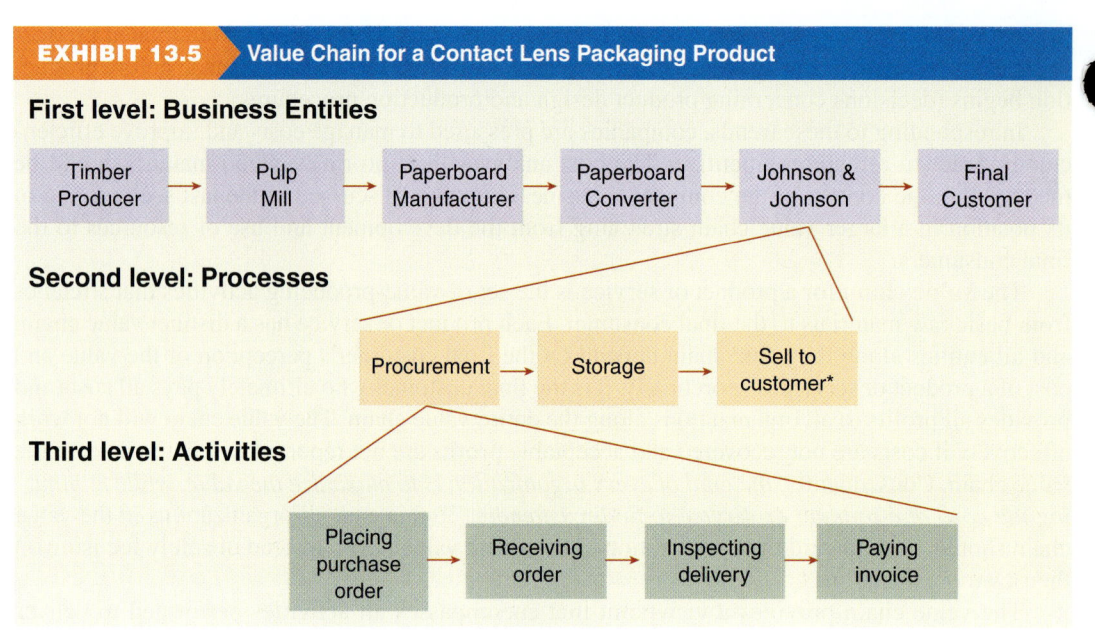

Placing purchase order → Receiving order → Inspecting delivery → Paying invoice

*A portion of sales are sold directly through the Warby Parker website to the customer.

Second Level: Processes To better understand how business entities within the chain add value and incur costs, management might further refine the value chain into **processes**, collections of related activities intended to achieve a common purpose. The second level in **Exhibit 13.5** represents major processes concerning the procurement and sale of Bausch & Lomb products to the final customer. To simplify our illustration, we show only the processes related to the purchase of packaging and the ultimate sales of contacts to customers. These processes include procuring packaging products, storing packaging products, and selling boxes of contacts to the final customers.

Third Level: Activities An **activity** is a unit of work. In the third level of **Exhibit 13.5**, Johnson & Johnson's procurement process of packaging product is further broken up into the following activities:

- *Placing* a purchase order for contact lens packaging material.
- *Receiving* delivery of the contact lens packaging material.
- *Inspecting* the delivery to make sure it corresponds with the purchase order and to verify that the products are in good condition.
- *Paying* for contact lens packaging products acquired after the invoice arrives.

Each of the activities involved in procuring product from a vendor is described by a word ending with *ing*. This suggests that most work activities involve action.

Generic Illustration of an Internal Value Chain

The internal value chain in generic terms, is presented in **Exhibit 13.6**. It reflects the basic components found within most organizations. This generic model, first developed by Michael Porter, is a good starting point in identifying the internal value chain links for a particular organization. The primary processes are made up of five key activities.

- Inbound logistics: Receiving, warehousing and distributing inputs
- Operations: Converting inputs into the finished product/service
- Outbound logistics: Delivering final product/service to the customer
- Marketing and sales: Targeting customer for product/service
- Service: Maintaining the value of the product/service to the customer

Exhibit 13.6 can be used as a guide and then customized to the specific situation. Certain activities might not exist or be more or less prominent in some organizations.

EXHIBIT 13.6 Generic Internal Processes of the Internal Value Chain

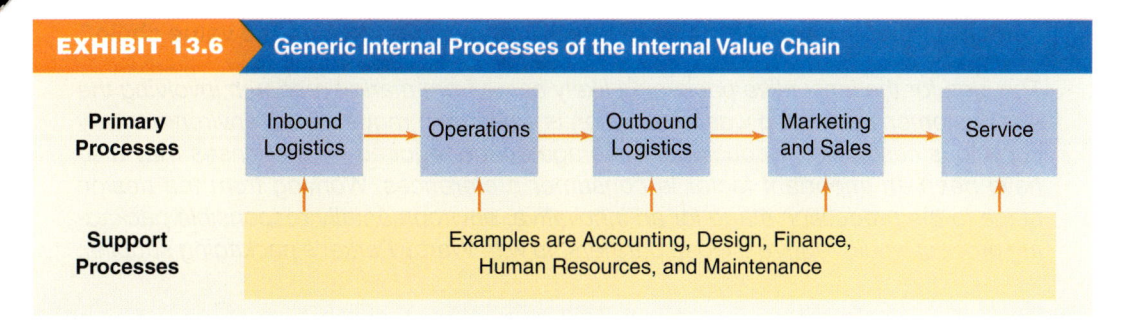

Primary Processes: Inbound Logistics → Operations → Outbound Logistics → Marketing and Sales → Service

Support Processes: Examples are Accounting, Design, Finance, Human Resources, and Maintenance

Usefulness of a Value Chain Perspective

The goal of maximizing final customer value while minimizing final customer cost leads organizations to examine *internal* and *external links* in the value chain rather than the departments, processes, or activities independently. From a value chain perspective, it is total cost across the entire value chain, not the cost of individual businesses, departments, processes, or activities that is most important.

Value Chain Perspective Fosters Supplier–Buyer Partnerships

In the past, relationships between suppliers and buyers were often adversarial. Contact between suppliers and buyers was solely through the selling and purchasing departments. Suppliers attempted merely to meet purchasing contract specifications at the lowest possible cost. Buyers encouraged competition among suppliers with the primary—and often single—goal of obtaining the lowest purchase price.

Exploiting cost reduction and value-enhancing opportunities in the value chain has led many buyers and suppliers to view each other as partners rather than as adversaries. Buyers have reduced the number of suppliers they work with, often developing long-term partnerships with a single supplier. Once they establish mutual trust, both proceed to share detailed information on internal operations and help each other solve problems. Partners work closely to examine mutual opportunities by studying their common value chain. Supplier engineers might determine that a minor relaxation in buyer specifications would significantly reduce supplier manufacturing costs with only minor increases in subsequent buyer processing costs. Working together, they determine how best to modify processes to reduce overall costs and share increased profits.

Companies such as **Hewlett-Packard** and **Boeing** involve suppliers in design, development, and manufacturing decisions. **Motorola Solutions** has even developed a survey asking suppliers to assess Motorola as a buyer. Among other questions, the survey asks sellers to evaluate Motorola's performance in helping them to identify major cost drivers and ways to increase their profitability. These questions represent the concerns of a partner rather than those of an adversary. **Toyota** attributes much of its rapid growth and profitability to virtual integration with suppliers. **Virtual integration** is the use of information technology and partnership concepts to allow two or more entities along a value chain to act as if they were a single economic entity.

Partnerships within the value chain extend to sustainability considerations. As an example, within **Dell Technologies**'s annual **ESG** (environmental, social, and governance) report, the company includes a section on supply chain sustainability. This section details how Dell Technologies partners with thousands of companies in its global supply chain to advance the goal of operating responsibly. The report describes a continuous improvement model consisting of "risk assessment, supplier audits, correction action plans and capability building."[16] Performance metrics and annual results are included for each step.

---

[16] https://www.dell.com/en-us/dt/corporate/social-impact/esg-resources/reports/fy22-esg-report.htm#pdf-overlay=//www.delltechnologies.com/asset/en-us/solutions/business-solutions/briefs-summaries/delltechnologies-fy22-esg-report.pdf

Critical Thinking & Decision-Making

Recently, Warby Parker launched a new proprietary contact brand called Scout. A recent 10-K of Warby Parker indicates that the innovative flat-pack saves space resulting in 80% less packaging than daily contact packs. How might the development of the new packaging have been orchestrated through the value chain?

The idea for the innovative packaging likely came from market research involving the end customer. Packaging waste reduction is a common request from environmentally conscious customers. Reducing the storage space required for the lenses may also have been an important factor in consumer preferences. Working from the design stage to the production stage for an innovative, environmentally responsible packaging product would require a close partnership with Warby Parker's packaging supplier.

Value Chain Perspective Fosters Focus on Core Competencies

Using value chain concepts, relationships with suppliers often begin to represent an extended family, allowing companies to focus on *core competencies*. Core competencies are the products, services, and capabilities of a company that differentiate it from its competitors. Many innovations in supply chain management, as well as new industries and companies, have evolved because of the value chain perspective. For example, a new breed of contract manufacturers, such as Sanmina has emerged. Sanmina promotes itself as an end-to-end solution. It partners with customers across a variety of industries to design and make complex optical, electronic, and mechanical products. This allows Sanmina's customers to focus on marketing and product development while Sanmina focuses on efficient, low-cost manufacturing. Interestingly, because their facilities are available to all innovators with the necessary financing, the emergence of contract manufacturers may speed up innovation.

Applying Value-Added and Value Chain Perspectives

The value chain perspective is often contrasted with a *value-added perspective*. The former concentrates on the entire chain, ensuring that the entire process is efficient and a high quality product is delivered to the end consumer. In contrast, the latter focuses myopically on maximizing the profit of one's own individual organization. Under a value-added perspective, decision makers consider only the cost of resources to their organization and the selling price of products or services to their immediate customers. Using a value-added perspective, the goal is to maximize the value added (the difference between the selling price and costs) by the organization. To do this, the value-added perspective focuses primarily on internal activities and costs. Under a value chain perspective, the goal is to maximize value and minimize cost to final customers, often by developing linkages or partnerships with suppliers and customers.

World-class competitors utilize *both* a value-added and a value chain perspective. These firms always keep the final customer in mind and recognize that the profitability of each entity in the value chain depends on the overall value and cost of the products and services delivered to final customers. Additionally, these firms continue to optimize their own operations and their contribution to the entire value chain.

Review 13-3 LO13-3 Classifying Activities Using a Generic Internal Value Chain

Using Michael Porter's generic model presented in **Exhibit 13.6**, classify each of the following activities of **Bausch & Lomb** (corporate website at https://www.bausch.com) as (a) inbound logistics, (b) operations, (c) outbound logistics, (d) marketing and sales, or (e) service.

_____ 1. Remaking any contact lens item that a customer is not satisfied with at no additional cost to the customer
_____ 2. Distribution of contact lenses through medical clinics.
_____ 3. Offering promotions to customers for specified products.
_____ 4. Sourcing contact lenses from a new supplier.
_____ 5. Increasing the company budget for promotions, advertising, and public relations activities
_____ 6. Maintaining storage sites and regional distribution centers
_____ 7. Investing in innovative equipment to improve the in-house packaging of contact lenses.

Solution on p. 13-29.

CHANGING ENVIRONMENT OF BUSINESS

The changing environment of business includes trends such as the global economic system, big data and predictive analytics, robotics and cognitive technologies, and enterprise risk management (ERM). Additional items such as lean manufacturing will be discussed later in Chapter 19.

LO13-4 Analyze how trends in the business environment impact the role of managerial accounting.

Global Competition and Its Key Dimensions

The move away from isolated national economic systems toward an interdependent global economic system has become increasingly pronounced. This interdependence is made possible by advances in business communications (to move data), technology (to process and analyze data), and transportation (to move products and people).

The labels of origins on goods (Japan, Germany, Canada, Taiwan, China, and so forth) only scratch the surface of existing global relationships. Behind labels designating a product's final assembly point are components from all over the world.

The move toward a global economy has heightened competition and reduced selling prices to such an extent that there is little or no room for error in managing costs or pricing products. Moreover, customers are not just looking for the best price. Well-informed buyers routinely search the world for the product or service that best fits their needs on the three interrelated dimensions of price/cost, quality, and service; hence, these are the three key dimensions of competition. With the increased focus on environmental and social causes, consumers are researching other aspects of companies and products. This includes, for example, the country of origin of component parts, factory labor conditions, factory emissions, and whether or not component parts can be recycled. While we focus the following discussion on price/cost, quality and service, these additional consumer concerns should be kept in mind.

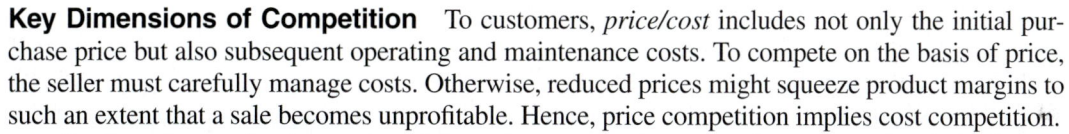

Key Dimensions of Competition To customers, *price/cost* includes not only the initial purchase price but also subsequent operating and maintenance costs. To compete on the basis of price, the seller must carefully manage costs. Otherwise, reduced prices might squeeze product margins to such an extent that a sale becomes unprofitable. Hence, price competition implies cost competition.

Quality refers to the degree to which products or services meet the customer's needs. *Service* includes things such as timely delivery, helpfulness of sales personnel, and subsequent support. In a recent global study of over 19,000 respondents, 50% indicated that they were willing to pay a premium for sustainable brands.[17] This means that an increasingly critical aspect of quality is sustainability.

Managers of successful companies know they compete in a global market with instant communications. Because competition is hungry and always striving to gain a competitive advantage, world-class companies must continuously struggle to improve performance on these three interrelated dimensions: price/cost, quality, and service. Throughout this text, we examine how firms successfully compete on these three dimensions.

Big Data and Analysis

Given recent advancements in technology, there is a vast amount of data available to organizations. However, it can be difficult to turn this data into useful and predictive information. Big data is unique in that it is so large or complex, traditional analysis methods are often inadequate. Due to the changing skills needed for new CMAs related to big data, the CMA exam was recently revised to include a section on technology and analytics. Data and analytics are also tested on all parts of the Certified Public Accountant (CPA) exam. For example, candidates must use data visualizations to identify patterns, trends, and correlations to explain an entity's results.

Organizations are in need of employees who have the abilities to: identify key data trends, perform data mining and extraction, conduct operational and decision analysis, recommend process improvement, and conduct strategic thinking and execution. Preparing and analyzing data visualizations is foundational in developing marketable skills in data analytics. To this end, each chapter includes data analysis and data visualization assignments. In addition, Appendix B at the end of this book provides a more detailed discussion of data analytics.

---

[17] Haller, Karl, Mary Wallace, Jane Cheung, and Sachin Gupta. "Consumers want it all: Hybrid shopping, sustainability, and purpose-driven brands." IBM Institute for Business Value. January 2022, https://ibm.co/2022-consumer-study.

Robotics and Cognitive Technologies

Robotic process automation (RPA) "is an application of technology, governed by business logic and structured inputs, aimed at automating business processes."[18] The U.S. spent over $9.8 billion on robotic equipment in 2020 which accounted for 1.0% of total equipment expenditures that year.[19]

Artificial intelligence (AI) can be defined as technologies that "perform tasks that previously required human intelligence, such as extracting meaning from images, text or speech, detecting patterns and anomalies, and making recommendations, predictions, or decisions."[20] **Cognitive technologies** (or intelligent automation) combine RPA with AI. Examples include machine learning applications that use algorithms to predict what a particular customer is likely to buy and natural language processing chatbots that provide customer support. A specific use in accounting might involve using machine learning applications to predict, based on past performance and current cash flows, when a loan covenant might be breached.[21]

In May 2019, Deloitte surveyed over 500 executives in 26 different countries. Fifty-eight percent of the executives reported that they had either already incorporated or were in the process of incorporating cognitive technologies into their business operations. Increased productivity and cost reduction, greater accuracy, and an improved customer experience were seen as the greatest benefits of the new technologies. Those organizations that had successfully incorporated cognitive technologies reported a 27% reduction in costs with an average payback of nine months.

Incorporating new technologies doesn't come without challenges. Accountants will need to continually develop new skills to meet those challenges. These skills include data strategy and data processing skills, communication skills to convey the meaning of the data, and the ability to implement automation to improve efficiencies such as the implementation of a new managerial reporting process.[22]

Enterprise Risk Management (ERM)

Organizations are constantly faced with uncertainty from the environment, competitors, and other factors that could result in significant risk or loss. The Committee of Sponsoring Organizations (COSO) defines **enterprise risk management (ERM)** as "the culture, capabilities and practices, integrated with strategy-setting and performance, that organizations rely on to manage risk in creating, preserving, and realizing value."[23] The ERM Framework developed by COSO helps companies improve their approach to managing risk. By better understanding the types and potential costs of these risks, managerial accountants can help their organizations devise strategies to better predict and minimize their exposures to risk. In Chapter 21 we will discuss how an organization's budgeting model is used to evaluate the financial impact of a risk and to determine, from a financial perspective, the best response to risk.

Review 13-4 LO13-4 — Big Data Analysis and Enterprise Risk Management

Big data analysis and ERM are of growing interest to leaders of organizations. Discuss briefly how the influence of each might affect the role of managerial accountants.

Solution on p. 13-29.

---

[18] Clint Boulton, "What Is RPA? A Revolution in Business Process Automation," *CIO*, September 2018, https://www.cio.com/article/3236451/what-is-rpa-robotic-process-automation-explained.html

[19] U.S. Census: 2021 Annual Capital Expenditures Survey, https://www.census.gov/programs-surveys/aces/data/tables.2022.List_1970697276.html#list-tab-List_1970697276

[20] Deloitte Insights, "Automation with Intelligence: Reimagining the Organization in the 'Age of With,'" 2019.

[21] Katie Canell, "Accountancy and Technology: The Journey to Cognitive Intelligence," *Accountancy Age*, October 18, 2018.

[22] AICPA-CIMA, "Skills that Help Accounting Professionals Succeed Alongside AI," accessed on March 1, 2023, https://mycareer.aicpa-cima.com/article/accounting-skills-to-succeed-alongside-artificial-intelligence#:~:text=These%20include%20data%20strategy%20and,and%20a%20message%20through%20storytelling.

[23] *Enterprise Risk Management—Integrating with Strategy and Performance,* Committee of Sponsoring Organizations of the Treadway Commission, June 2017.

ETHICS IN MANAGERIAL ACCOUNTING

Ethics deals with the moral quality, fitness, or propriety of a course of action that can injure or benefit people. Ethics goes beyond legality, which refers to what is permitted under the law, to consider the moral quality of an action. Because situations involving ethics are not guided by well-defined rules, they are often subjective.

LO13-5 Explain the ethical role of managerial accountants and the increasing emphasis on environmental, social, and governance considerations.

Ethical Dilemmas

Although some actions are clearly ethical (working a full day in exchange for a full day's pay) and others are clearly unethical (pumping contaminants into an underground aquifer used as a source of drinking water), managers are often faced with situations that do not fall clearly into either category such as the following.

- Accelerating or decelerating shipments at the end of the quarter to meet current earnings forecasts.
- Keeping inventory that is unlikely to be used so as to avoid recording a loss.
- Purchasing supplies from a relative or friend rather than seeking bids.
- Basing a budget on an overly optimistic sales forecast.
- Assigning some costs of Contract A to Contract B to avoid an unfavorable performance report on Contract A.

Many *ethical dilemmas* involve actions that are perceived to have desirable short-run consequences and highly probable undesirable long-run consequences. The ethical action is to face an undesirable situation now to avoid a worse situation later, yet the decision maker prefers to believe that things will work out in the long run, is overly concerned with the consequences of not doing well in the short run, or simply does not care about the future because the problem will then belong to someone else. In a situation that is clearly unethical, the future consequences are known to be avoidable and undesirable. In situations involving questionable ethics, there is some hope that things will work out.

- Next year's sales will more than make up for the accelerated shipments.
- The obsolete inventory can be used in a new nostalgia line of products.
- The relative or friend may charge more but provides excellent service.
- Sales staff will be motivated by corporate optimism.
- Employees will make up for the cost shift by working extra hard and more efficiently with the remaining work on Contract B.

When forced to think about the situation, most employees want to act in an ethical manner. The problem faced by personnel involved in measurement and reporting is that while they may question the propriety of a proposed action, and the arguments may be plausible, they want to be team players, and their careers can be affected by "whistle-blowing." (Whistle-blowing is when an employee reports a wrongdoing by an employer or another employee to an entity such as law enforcement or the company's board of directors.) Of course, careers are also affected when individuals are identified as being involved in unethical behavior.

Theranos is an example of a company engaged in large-scale investor fraud. The founder, Elizabeth Holmes, induced investors with fraudulent claims based on faulty blood-testing technology. For example, Holmes claimed that the company would generate revenues in a future year of $1 billion when she knew revenues would be negligible or modest.[24] Eventually, the company was shut down and the founder was convicted of federal charges.

Major ethical dilemmas can evolve from a series of small compromises, none of which appears serious enough to warrant taking a stand on ethical grounds. **WorldCom** is a notorious case, in which managers deferred expenses inappropriately over several periods to meet profit forecasts, expecting to recognize them at a later time when sales improved. Unfortunately, these small compromises establish a pattern of behavior that is increasingly difficult to reverse. In another example, the **Kraft Heinz Company** agreed to settle charges with the SEC for $62 million. The charges related to an expense management scheme that understated cost of goods sold in certain years.

---

[24] https://www.justice.gov/usao-ndca/pr/theranos-founder-elizabeth-holmes-found-guilty-investor-fraud

While not a case of wide-spread fraud, it illustrates the unethical nature of manipulating financial results to communicate a better financial picture.[25] The key to avoiding these situations is recognizing the early warning signs of situations that involve questionable ethical behavior and taking whatever action is appropriate.

Codes of Ethics/Conduct

Codes of ethics are often developed by professional organizations to increase members' awareness of the importance of ethical behavior and to provide a reference point for resisting pressures to engage in actions of questionable ethics. These professional organizations include the **American Bar Association**, the **American Institute of Certified Public Accountants**, the **American Medical Association**, and the **Institute of Management Accountants** (IMA).

The IMA developed the four standards of ethical conduct for management accountants and financial managers outlined below.[26]

1. **Competence:** Perform their professional duties in accordance with relevant laws, regulations, and technical standards.
2. **Confidentiality:** Refrain from disclosing confidential information acquired in the course of their work except when authorized, unless legally obligated to do so.
3. **Integrity:** Refrain from engaging in or supporting any activity that would discredit the profession.
4. **Credibility:** Communicate information fairly and objectively.

A commitment to ethical professional practice should be guided by these four overarching principles. The IMA also published a Values and Ethics report that explains the steps to establish an ethical culture.[27]

- Define the organization's ethical principles with input from the shareholders, the board of directors, and officers of the organization.
- Develop a code of ethics/conduct that conveys the type of everyday environment that is expected.
- Ensure a commitment to the ethical values by senior management that doesn't allow for deviations for exceptional circumstances.
- Disseminate the completed code of ethics throughout the organization and supplement with training resources.

Many corporations have established codes of ethics. **Hershey**'s has a 30-page published document, "In Good Company," which lists and explains Hershey's code of conduct. One of the important goals of corporate codes of ethics is to provide employees with a common foundation for addressing ethical issues. These codes provide a summary of a company's policies that define ethical standards of employee conduct, and they often include broad philosophical statements about behavior. Hershey's code states, "Our Code is a great resource, but it doesn't cover every situation you may face on the job, so it's important to use good judgment in everything you do and to ask for help if you're ever unsure about the right course of action."[28]

Critical Thinking & Decision-Making

How can management establish an ethical tone in an organization?

Top management can help to set an ethical tone in the organization by ensuring that the company has a code of ethics, demonstrating its support for the code, and, importantly, leading the organization with ethical behavior.

How can pressures for short-run performance lead to ethical dilemmas?

Many ethical dilemmas involve actions that are perceived to have desirable short-run consequences and highly probable undesirable long-run consequences. The ethical action is to face an undesirable situation now to avoid a worse situation later. For

---

[25] https://www.sec.gov/news/press-release/2021-174

[26] IMA, 2017. IMA Statement of Ethical Professional Practice. [ebook] Montvale, NJ: Institute of Management Accountants.

[27] IMA, 2014. IMA Values and Ethics. Montvale, NJ: Institute of Management Accountants.

[28] https://www.thehersheycompany.com/content/dam/hershey-corporate/documents/investors/code-of-conduct-english.pdf

example, an ethical action may result in lower profits now but improved financial results in the future. However, a decision maker's desire to improve short-run performance at the expense of long-run performance can contribute to unethical decision-making.

ENVIRONMENTAL, SOCIAL, AND GOVERNANCE CONSIDERATIONS

Environmental and Social Considerations

To a larger extent in recent years, companies have been pressured by stakeholders to maximize objectives beyond corporate profits. *Specifically, there is increased pressure on companies to prioritize responsible environmental and social practices and to report performance regarding these practices to their stakeholders.* Warby Parker publishes a yearly "Impact Report" to communicate its measures of environmental and social performance. In this report, stakeholders learn about the company's core values and goals and how it measures these goals. The report includes details of its initiatives, such as the company's "Buy a Pair, Give a Pair" initiative. As the pressure to develop and report on social and environmental measures grows, so does the role of managerial accountants. *Managerial accountants play an important role in developing and measuring the impact of ESG initiatives.* The impact of these initiatives can be seen in various aspects of the company including its cost structure, budgets, performance metrics, and operational and strategic decision-making.

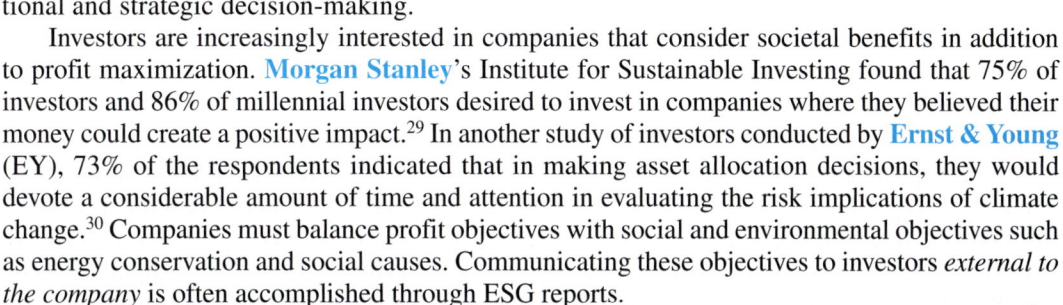

Investors are increasingly interested in companies that consider societal benefits in addition to profit maximization. Morgan Stanley's Institute for Sustainable Investing found that 75% of investors and 86% of millennial investors desired to invest in companies where they believed their money could create a positive impact.[29] In another study of investors conducted by Ernst & Young (EY), 73% of the respondents indicated that in making asset allocation decisions, they would devote a considerable amount of time and attention in evaluating the risk implications of climate change.[30] Companies must balance profit objectives with social and environmental objectives such as energy conservation and social causes. Communicating these objectives to investors *external to the company* is often accomplished through ESG reports.

Managerial accounting includes a variety of models that help managers determine the cost of products and activities, align activities with the company's strategy and objectives, and assess the performance of the activities. These internal company tools can be applied to ESG activities to ensure that all activities are aligned with the company's core values and that such activities show positive results (although the challenge might be measuring performance of any non-financial initiative). Although these models are constantly evolving, they provide a basis for the measurement and communication of ESG initiatives within a company. For example, when evaluating an investment in a factory, Warby Parker must consider not only the initial cash outlay and the asset's life, but also any potential environmental risks and the ultimate disposal of the asset in an environmentally friendly manner.

Being a socially responsible company does not mean abandoning the profit motive or the goal of providing an attractive return to investors. In fact, there is some evidence to support that a commitment to ESG results in *more* revenues for companies. A study of 1,262 large companies from eight major economies indicates that profits for "keen ESG adopters have risen three times faster than those less keen."[31] Social responsibility means that a for-profit company attempts to measure the total benefits and costs of its actions, accepts the responsibility for those actions, and aligns its social impact with its mission. As part of Warbly Parker's mission, it has distributed over 10 million pairs of glass through its buy a pair, give a pair program. In doing so, the company is opening access to corrective eyewear beyond those that can afford to purchase fashionable eyewear. The line between being a competitive organization and being a socially responsible organization is sometimes blurred. For example, many companies offer certain fringe benefits, such as on-site childcare, because it attracts a wider pool of employees; the social advantages of doing so are

---

[29] National Association of State Boards of Accountancy "The Role of Accountants in the Rise of ESG Reporting." https://nasba.org/blog/2022/09/15/the-role-of-accountants-in-the-rise-of-esg-reporting/

[30] EY, "How will ESG Performance Shape Your Future," July 2020, https://assets.ey.com/content/dam/ey-sites/ey-com/en_gl/topics/assurance/assurance-pdfs/ey-global-institutional-investor-survey-2020.pdf.

[31] https://www.internationalaccountingbulletin.com/analysis/4-trillion-increase-in-revenue-for-businesses-placing-greater-importance-on-esg/

a positive externality of this move. Regardless of the motive, managerial accounting tools can be applied to environmental and social initiatives to measure and manage the success of those initiatives.

Governance Considerations

Governance refers to the system of policies, processes, laws, and regulations that affect the way a company is directed and controlled. At the highest level, the system of corporate governance for a company is the responsibility of, including the formation and composition of, the board of directors, but it affects all stakeholders, including employees, creditors, customers, vendors, and the community at large. The large number of corporate failures of the last decade brought the topic of corporate governance to the forefront.

The collapse of **Enron**, along with its independent auditor, **Arthur Andersen**, prompted the U.S. Congress to pass the Sarbanes-Oxley Act of 2002 (or SOX), which was intended to address weaknesses affecting U.S. capital markets. Although SOX deals primarily with issues pertaining to the relationship between publicly traded companies and the capital markets, some of its requirements have become a standard for corporate responsibility and governance affecting both public and private companies, as well as not-for-profit organizations.

SOX consists of 66 sections, including such topics as external auditing standards, auditor conflicts of interest, codes of ethics for financial officers, review of internal controls, and criminal penalties for fraud. Probably the most important provisions of SOX, from a managerial accounting standpoint, are those related to internal control systems. **Internal control systems** generally are made up of the policies and procedures that exist to ensure that company objectives are achieved with regard to (a) effectiveness and efficiency of operations, (b) reliability of financial reporting, and (c) compliance with laws and regulations.

SOX imposes the requirement that CEOs and CFOs annually review and assess the effectiveness of their company's internal controls over financial reporting, and issue a report of their assessment. Although many CEOs and CFOs have argued that the cost of SOX compliance is unjustified by the benefits to investors, research provides evidence that SOX is improving the quality of financial reporting. A team of researchers from Shanghai and Hong Kong have shown that information provided by SOX about internal controls directly influences the pricing of Credit Default Swaps (CDS), a transaction that allows lenders to hedge the risk of their loans. CDS provide the firm's owners with insurance if the firm goes bankrupt, so the connection between information about internal control and the price of this type of insurance suggests that SOX is releasing important information about the way the firm is run.[32]

Even though SOX limits the internal control review to aspects of the system related to financial reporting, in practice there is very little that takes place in any organization that does not impact the financial statements. Therefore, if SOX is resulting in improvements in data that goes into financial reports, it is likely that data supporting managerial accounting is also enhanced by a more reliable internal control system.

Many of the models and processes that we discuss in this text have either a direct or indirect impact on a company's financial statements; hence, they are likely subject to the SOX internal control review. An overlap often exists between the systems that produce the data for the external financial statements and those that produce data for internal decision-making. For example, cost data produced by the product costing system is often used for both financial reporting and managerial decision-making purposes. A more detailed discussion of SOX and internal control systems can typically be found in financial accounting and auditing textbooks.

Review 13-5 LO13-5 — Corporate Social Responsibility

Bausch & Lomb communicates a corporate social responsibility goal of "ensuring affordable access to our products." Provide three examples of how managerial accounting can help support this goal.

Solution on p. 13-30.

---

[32] Dragon Yongjun Tang, Feng Tian, and Hong Yan, "Internal Control Quality and Credit Default Swap Spreads," *Accounting Horizons*, September 2015, Vol. 29, No. 3, pp. 603–629.

MULTIPLE CHOICE

1. Which of the following is not a characteristic of Managerial Accounting? **LO13-1**
   a. No external standards
   b. Reports primarily on past decisions
   c. Provides information for internal users
   d. Information is more detailed

2. A company sells a product that is aimed at the broad mass market but is perceived as unique throughout its industry. The company is earning above average returns on the product. Which one of the following is the **most** appropriate term for the competitive strategy followed by the company? **LO13-2**
   a. Market focus.
   b. Financial leadership.
   c. Cost focus.
   d. Differentiation.

3. Controlling is the process of **LO13-2**
   a. Selecting goals and adopting strategies for achieving them
   b. Delegating authority to others to take action to implement plans
   c. Organizing employees into line and staff functions
   d. Ensuring that results agree with plans

4. In a value chain analysis: **LO13-3**
   a. The links of the chain are the various entities beginning with the producers of raw materials and ending with the final customer
   b. Processes are collections of related activities intended to achieve a common purpose, such as procurement or production
   c. Activities are the units of work that take place within the various processes, such as moving products from one workstation to another
   d. All of the above

5. To improve efficiency, a company is considering utilizing a tool developed by a third party that reviews sales contracts and identifies elements and clauses relevant to revenue recognition. The company is most likely using a tool that is employing **LO13-4**
   a. Business intelligence.
   b. Artificial intelligence.
   c. Blockchain.
   d. Control monitoring.

   CMA adapted

6. Which of the following is not likely to be regarded as an action that has ethical implications in today's business environment? **LO13-5**
   a. Purchasing supplies from a relative or friend rather than seeking bids
   b. Using different depreciation methods for calculating depreciation expense for the financial statements and the income tax return
   c. Failing to recognize obsolete inventory to avoid missing a profit forecast
   d. Shifting costs for one contract to another to make the profits of the contracts line up with initial forecasts

Multiple Choice Answers
1. b 2. d 3. d 4. d 5. b 6. b

DATA ANALYTICS

DA13-1. Analyzing Trends in AI Technology **LO13-4**

Access the **PwC** 2022 AI Business Survey found at https://www.pwc.com/us/en/tech-effect/ai-analytics/ai-business-survey.html and answer the following questions by analyzing the data visualizations included in the report.
   a. What percentage of leaders in companies have been trying to achieve improved decision-making through artificial intelligence (AI) initiatives?
   b. What do business leaders project are the top two and bottom two areas of a business to be supported by AI initiatives?
   c. What are AI simulations? What are the top five ways that leaders project that companies will use AI simulations? Which of these top five areas would managerial accountants likely partner in decision-making?
   d. What top three steps do leaders expect to take to develop and deploy responsible AI systems?
   e. What percentage of company leaders surveyed have already implemented plans to accelerate AI initiatives in order to reduce general hiring needs?

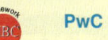

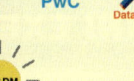

LO13-2, 4

DA13-2. Analyzing Trends in Consumer Behavior

Access the **IBM** Research Insights Report: Consumers Want it All: Hybrid Shopping, Sustainability, and Purpose-Driven Brands at https://www.ibm.com/thought-leadership/institute-business-value/en-us/report/2022-consumer-study and answer the following questions.

a. Referring to the data visualization in Figure 6, what type of consumer represented the largest segment of the population in 2020? In 2022? What implications does this have for companies regarding performance metrics in the area of sustainability?

b. If purpose-driven consumers are likely to pay a premium for products that align with their priorities, what does this imply for companies competing as cost leaders?

c. Why is it important for managerial accountants to understand how product costing is affected by sustainability initiatives?

DATA VISUALIZATION

Data Visualization Activities are available in myBusinessCourse. These assignments use Tableau Dashboards to expose students to visual depictions of data and introduce students to data analytics through data visualizations. These exercises are easily assignable and auto graded by MBC.

QUESTIONS

Q13-1. Contrast financial and managerial accounting on the basis of user orientation, purpose of information, level of aggregation, length of time period, orientation toward past or future, conformance to external standards, and emphasis on objective data.

Q13-2. Distinguish between a mission and a goal.

Q13-3. Describe the three strategic positions that Porter views as leading to business success.

Q13-4. Distinguish between how managerial accounting would support the strategy of cost leadership and the strategy of product differentiation.

Q13-5. Why are the phases of planning, organizing, and controlling referred to as a *continuous cycle*?

Q13-6. What are the relationships among an organization's value chain, processes, and activities?

Q13-7. What should be the goal of every organization along the value chain?

Q13-8. Distinguish between the value-added perspective and the value chain perspective.

Q13-9. Identify three advances that have fostered the move away from isolated national economic systems toward an interdependent global economy.

Q13-10. What are the three interrelated dimensions of today's competition?

Q13-11. How can top management establish an ethical tone in an organization?

Q13-12. Describe how pressures to have desirable short-run outcomes can lead to ethical dilemmas.

Q13-13. Are environmental, social, and governance considerations inconsistent with a company's profit motive?

Assignments with the MBC logo in the margin are available in myBusinessCourse.
See the Preface of the book for details.

MINI EXERCISES

LO13-1, 2, 3, 5

M13-14. Managerial Accounting Terminology

Match the following terms with the best descriptions. Each description is used only once.

TERMS

1. Ethics
2. Mission
3. Controlling
4. Goal
5. Cost drivers
6. Quality
7. Balance sheet
8. Income statement
9. Strategic cost management
10. Financial accounting
11. Managerial accounting
12. Product differentiation

DESCRIPTION
  a. Making decisions concerning specific cost drivers
  b. Factors that influence costs
  c. Reports a company's financial position
  d. Accounting for external users
  e. Increase year 2020 sales by 10% over year 2019 sales
  f. Shows the results of operations for a period of time
  g. The degree to which a new e-book reader meets a buyer's expectations
  h. Used internally to make decisions
  i. The propriety of taking some action
  j. Reduces customer price sensitivity
  k. Basic purpose toward which activities are directed
  l. Comparing the budget with the actual results

M13-15. Financial and Managerial Accounting LO13-1
Indicate whether each phrase is more descriptive of financial accounting or managerial accounting.

  a. May be subjective
  b. Often used to obtain financing
  c. Typically prepared quarterly or annually
  d. May measure time or customer satisfaction
  e. Future oriented
  f. Has a greater emphasis on cost-benefit analysis
  g. Keeps records of assets and liabilities
  h. Highly aggregated statements
  i. Must conform to external standards
  j. Special-purpose reports
  k. Decision-making tool
  l. Income statement, balance sheet, and statement of cash flows

M13-16. Institute of Managerial Accountants LO13-1
What is the role of managerial accounting according to the Institute of Managerial Accountants (IMA), and how does the IMA try to influence the best practices of managerial accountants?

M13-17. Missions, Goals, and Strategies LO13-2
Identify each of the following as a mission, goal, or strategy.

  a. Budget time for study, sleep, and relaxation
  b. Provide shelter for the homeless
  c. Provide an above-average return to investors
  d. Protect the public
  e. Locate fire stations so that the average response time is less than five minutes
  f. Overlap police patrols so that there are always police cars on major thoroughfares
  g. Achieve a 12% market share
  h. Lower prices and costs
  i. Select the most scenic route to drive between Las Vegas and Denver
  j. Graduate from college

M13-18. Line and Staff Organization LO13-2
Presented are the names of several departments often found in a merchandising organization such as Target.

  a. Maintenance
  b. Home Furnishings
  c. Store Manager
  d. Payroll
  e. Human Resources
  f. Advertising

REQUIRED
Identify each as a line or a staff department.

M13-19. Line and Staff Organization LO13-2
Presented are the names of several departments often found in a manufacturing organization such as KraftHeinz.

  a. Manager, Plant 2
  b. Design Engineering
  c. President
  d. Controller
  e. Property Accounting
  f. Sales Manager, District 1

REQUIRED
Identify each as a line or a staff department.

LO13-3 **M13-20. Classifying Activities Using the Generic Internal Value Chain: Aluminum Cable Manufacturer**

Using the generic internal value chain shown in **Exhibit 13.6**, classify each of the following activities of an aluminum cable manufacturer as inbound logistics, operations, outbound logistics, marketing and sales, service, or support.

- a. Advertising in a construction magazine
- b. Inspecting incoming aluminum ingots
- c. Placing bar codes on coils of finished products
- d. Borrowing money to finance a buildup of inventory
- e. Hiring new employees
- f. Heating aluminum ingots
- g. Drawing wire from aluminum ingots
- h. Coiling wire
- i. Visiting a customer to determine the cause of cable breakage
- j. Filing tax returns

LO13-3 **M13-21. Classifying Activities Using the Generic Internal Value Chain: Cable TV Company**

Using the generic internal value chain shown in **Exhibit 13.6**, classify each of the following activities of a cable television company as inbound logistics, operations, outbound logistics, marketing and sales, service, or support.

- a. Installing coaxial cable in the apartment of a new customer
- b. Repairing coaxial cable after a windstorm
- c. Mailing brochures to prospective customers
- d. Discussing a rate increase with members of a regulatory agency
- e. Selling shares of stock in the company
- f. Monitoring the quality of reception at the company's satellite downlink
- g. Preparing financial statements
- h. Visiting a customer to determine the cause of poor-quality television reception
- i. Traveling to a conference to learn about technological changes affecting the industry
- j. Replacing old routers with updated technology

LO13-4 **M13-22. Changing Business Environment**

Identify some trends that should be considered when developing the role and processes of an organization's managerial accounting strategy.

LO13-5 **M13-23. Key Elements of Ethics Policy**

Essential elements in the development of an organization's ethics policy include all of the following except
- a. articulation of organizational values.
- b. input from the board of directors in addition to management and employees.
- c. allowances for exceptional circumstances.
- d. relevance to day-to-day implementation.

CMA adapted

EXERCISES

LO13-1 **E13-24. Financial and Managerial Accounting**

Assume Katie Milling has just been promoted to product manager at **KraftHeinz**. Although she is an accomplished sales representative and well versed in market research, her accounting background is limited to reviewing her paycheck, balancing her checkbook, filing income tax returns, and reviewing the company's annual income statement and balance sheet. She commented that while the financial statements are no doubt useful to investors, she just doesn't see how accounting can help her be a good product manager.

REQUIRED

Based on her remarks, it is apparent that Katie's view of accounting is limited to financial accounting. Explain some of the important differences between financial and managerial accounting and suggest some ways managerial accounting can help Katie be a better product manager.

E13-25. Developing an Organization Chart   **LO13-2**

Develop an organization chart for a three-outlet bakery chain with a central baking operation and deliveries every few hours. Assume the business is incorporated and that the president has a single staff assistant. Also assume that the delivery truck driver reports to the bakery manager.

E13-26. Identifying Monetary and Nonmonetary Performance Measures   **LO13-2**

Identify possible monetary and nonmonetary performance measures for each of the following situations. One nonmonetary measure should relate to quality, and one should relate to time.

a. **Stanford University** wishes to evaluate the success of last year's graduating class.
b. **Good Samaritan Hospital** wishes to evaluate the performance of its emergency room.
c. **Walgreen Boots Alliance** wishes to evaluate the performance of its online order–filling operations.
d. **Marriott International** wishes to evaluate the performance of registration activities at one of its hotels.
e. **United Parcel Service** wishes to evaluate the success of its operations in Knoxville.

Stanford University
Good Samaritan Hospital
Walgreen Boots Alliance
NASDAQ :: WBA
Marriott International
NASDAQ :: MAR
United Parcel Service
NYSE :: UPS

E13-27. Identifying Monetary and Nonmonetary Performance Measures   **LO13-2**

Identify possible monetary and nonmonetary performance measures for each of the following situations. One nonmonetary measure should relate to quality, and one should relate to time.

a. **TDS**'s evaluation of the performance of its Internet service in Chicago.
b. **Comcast**'s evaluation of the performance of new customer cable installations in Springfield.
c. **Asustek Computer**'s evaluation of the performance of its logistical arrangements for delivering computers to its U.S. customers.
d. **Target**'s evaluation of the performance of its website.
e. **Emory University**'s evaluation of the success of its freshman admissions activities.

TDS Inc.
NYSE :: TDS
Comcast
NASDAQ :: CMCSA
Asustek Computer Inc.
Target Corporation
NYSE :: TGT
Emory University

E13-28. Identifying Information Needs of Different Managers   **LO13-2**

Matt Parker operates a number of auto dealerships for **Toyota** and **General Motors**. Identify possible monetary and nonmonetary performance measures for each of the following situations. One nonmonetary measure should relate to quality, and one should relate to time.

a. An individual sales associate.
b. The sales manager of a single dealership.
c. The general manager of a particular dealership.
d. The corporate chief financial officer.
e. The president of the corporation.

Toyota
NYSE :: TM
General Motors
NYSE :: GM

E13-29. Identifying Managerial Accounting Information   **LO13-3**

Considering the environment of **Bausch & Lomb**, select three types of managerial accounting information useful for decision-making. How will this information help management make decisions about its product offering?

Bausch Health
NYSE :: BHC

E13-30. Developing a Value Chain from the Perspective of the Final Customer   **LO13-3**

Prepare a value chain for bottled milk that was purchased for personal consumption at an on-campus cafeteria.

E13-31. Developing a Value Chain: Upstream and Downstream Entities   **LO13-3**

Prepare a value chain for a company that manufactures furniture. Clearly identify upstream and downstream entities in the value chain.

E13-32. Analyzing the Changing Roles of Management Accountants   **LO13-4**

Access the electronic article, "What 2022 Signals for the Management Accounting Profession" by the **Chartered Investment & Management Accountant** (CIMA) Institute at https://www.cima.institute/blog/what-2022-signals-for-the-management-accounting-profession and answer the following questions.

CIMA

REQUIRED

1. What roles should management accountants play in order to stay relevant in the market place? What has caused the evolution in job responsibilities?
2. What are the key drivers of change in management accounting identified in the article?
3. What new skills are required by management accountants?
4. What are four action steps that management accountants can take to remain relevant?
5. Consider the following two task scenarios of management accountants.

a. The accountant reviews sales by product for this month and last month and prepares a variance report showing the percentage change over the prior year. Any changes over 10% from the prior year are highlighted for further analysis by the relevant product managers (outside of accounting). A similar analysis is done each month.
b. Using the sales information for this month and last month, the accountant prepares pivot charts analyzing changes in sales by product, by location, by sales team, by product category, and by age of product. A new pivot chart analysis this month was also prepared by the accountant which compares product sales over the prior month organized by the company's internal product sustainability rating. Significant trends along with potential reasons for the trends were summarized as preparation for a multi-department monthly meeting.

Explain how the two tasks represent how the role of managerial accountants has evolved.

LO13-5

Warby Parker
NYSE :: WRBY

E13-33. Analyzing a Code of Conduct
Access the Investors section of the website for **Warby Parker** at **https://investors.warbyparker.com/overview/default.aspx** and answer the following questions.

REQUIRED
a. Click on the "Governance" link at the top of the page and click on "Governance Documents" and open the "Code of Conduct."
   1. How does the Code of Conduct convey what is expected in the everyday environment?
   2. How does the company allow for anonymous reporting of ethical violations?
   3. How are accounting practices specifically addressed in the Code of Conduct?
b. Instead of clicking on Governance, click on "Impact" and "Impact Report." Open the 2021 Impact Report: Executive Summary" and answer the following questions.
   1. What is the performance metric used to measure the company's vision to provide eyeglasses to all in need?
   2. What is the performance metric used to measure the company's carbon footprint? What parts of the company's carbon footprint are "neutralized?"

CASES AND PROJECTS

LO13-2

C13-34. Goals and Strategies
a. What is your instructor's goal for students in this course? What strategies has your instructor developed to achieve this goal?
b. What is your goal in this course? What strategies will help you achieve this goal?
c. What is your goal for this semester or term? What strategies will help you achieve this goal?
d. What is your next career goal? What strategies will help you achieve this goal?

LO13-2

C13-35 Product Differentiation
You are the owner of Lobster's Unlimited. You have no trouble catching lobsters, but you have difficulty in selling all that you catch. The problem is that all lobsters from all vendors look the same. You do catch high-quality lobsters, but you need to be able to tell your customers that your lobsters are better than those sold by other vendors.

REQUIRED
a. What are some possible ways of distinguishing your lobsters from those of other vendors?
b. Explain the possible results of this differentiation.

LO13-5

C13-36. Ethics and Short-Term Borrowing
Rory, an administrative assistant, is in charge of petty cash for a local law firm. Normally, about $300 is kept in the petty cash box. When Rory is short on cash and needs some for lunch or to pay for childcare, she sometimes takes a few dollars from the box. Because she is in charge of the box, nobody knows that she takes the money, and she always replaces it within a few days.

REQUIRED
a. Is Rory's behavior ethical?
b. Assume that Rory has recently had major problems meeting her bills. She also is in charge of purchasing supplies for the office from petty cash. Last week when she needed $50 for childcare, she falsified a voucher for the amount of $50. Is this behavior ethical?

C13-37. Ethics and Travel Reimbursement

Jake takes many business trips throughout the year. All of his expenses are paid by his company. Last week he traveled to Rio De Janeiro, Brazil, and stayed there on business for five days. He is allowed a maximum of $50 per day for food and $150 per day for lodging. To his surprise, the food and accommodations in Brazil were much less than he expected. Being upset about traveling last week and having to sacrifice tickets he'd purchased to a Cubs baseball game, he decided to inflate his expenses a bit. He increased his lodging expense from $80 per day to $100 per day and his food purchased from $30 per day to $40 per day. Therefore, for the five-day trip, he overstated his expenses by $150 total. After all, the allowance was higher than the amount he spent.

REQUIRED

Assume that the company would never find out that he had actually spent less. Are Jake's actions ethical? Are they acceptable?

C13-38. Ethical Issues with Supplier-Buyer Partnerships

Tory Wopat was excited to learn of her appointment as Circuit Electronics Corporation's sales representative to Household Appliance Inc. For the past four years, Circuit Electronics has supplied all of the electric switches used in Household's washers and dryers. As Circuit Electronics' sales representative, Tory's job involves the following tasks.

1. Working with Household engineers to design electric switches that can be manufactured to meet Household's cost and quality requirements.
2. Assisting Household in resolving any problems related to electric switches.
3. Monitoring the inventory levels of electric switches at Household and placing orders for additional switches when appropriate.

This appointment will require Tory to move to Stuttgart, Germany, for two years. Although Tory has mixed feelings about the move, Tory is familiar with the success of the program in improving Circuit Electronics' financial performance. Tory is also very much aware of the fact that the two previous sales representatives received promotions at the end of their appointments.

As Tory toured the Household factory in Stuttgart with her predecessor, Catherine Bach, Tory's excitement turned to concern. It became apparent that Circuit Electronics had not been supplying Household with the best available switches at the lowest possible costs. Although the switches were adequate, they were more likely to wear out after five or six years of use than would switches currently on the market (and being used by Household's competitors). Furthermore, taking into account the current number of switches in transit by ship from North America to Europe, it also appeared that the inventory level of electric switches would soon be more than enough to satisfy Household's needs for the next four months.

REQUIRED

If you were Tory, what would you do?

C13-39. Expected Values of Questionable Decisions

The members of the jury had to make a decision in a lawsuit brought by the State of Alabama against **Exxon Mobil**. The suit revolved around natural-gas wells that Exxon drilled in state-owned waters. After signing several leases obligating Exxon to share revenues with Alabama, company officials started questioning the terms of the agreement that prohibited deducting several types of processing costs before paying the state royalties.

During the course of the trial, a memo by an in-house attorney of Exxon Mobil came to light. The memo noted that **Royal Dutch Shell**, which had signed a similar lease, interpreted it "in the same manner as the state." The memo then presented arguments the company might use to claim the deduction, estimated the probability of the arguments being successful (less than 50%), and proceeded to consider whether Exxon should obey the law using a cost-benefit analysis. According to the memo, "If we adopt anything beyond a 'safe' approach, we should anticipate a quick audit and subsequent litigation." The memo also observed that "our exposure is 12 percent interest on underpayments calculated from the due date, and the cost of litigation." Deducting the questionable costs did, indeed, result in an audit and a lawsuit.[33]

REQUIRED

If you were a member of the jury, what would you do? Why?

---

[33] Mike France, "When Big Oil Gets Too Slick," *Business Week,* April 9, 2001, p. 70.

LO13-2, 3 C13-40. **Management Decisions**

An avid bicycle rider, you have decided to use an inheritance to start a new business to sell and repair bicycles. Two college friends have already accepted offers to work for you.

REQUIRED
a. What is the mission of your new business?
b. Suggest a strategic positioning goal you might strive for to compete with area hardware and discount stores that sell bicycles.
c. Identify two items that might be long-range goals.
d. Identify two items that might be goals for the coming year.

LO13-2 C13-41. **Success Factors and Performance Measurement**

Three years ago, Vincent Chow completed his college degree. The economy was in a depressed state at the time, and Vincent managed to get an offer of only $35,000 per year as a bookkeeper. In addition to its relatively low pay, this job had limited advancement potential. Since Vincent was enterprising and ambitious, he instead started a business of his own. He was convinced that because of changing lifestyles, a drive-through coffee establishment would be profitable. He was able to obtain backing from his parents to open such an establishment close to the industrial park area in town. Vincent named his business The Cappuccino Express and decided to sell only two types of coffee: cappuccino and decaffeinated.

As Vincent had expected, The Cappuccino Express was very well received. Within three years, Vincent had added another outlet north of town. He left the day-to-day management of each site to a manager and turned his attention toward overseeing the entire enterprise. He also hired an assistant to do the record keeping and other selected chores.[34]

REQUIRED
a. Develop an organization chart for The Cappuccino Express.
b. What factors can be expected to have a major impact on the success of The Cappuccino Express?
c. What major tasks must Vincent undertake in managing The Cappuccino Express?
d. What are the major costs of operating The Cappuccino Express?
e. Vincent would like to monitor the performance of each site manager. What measure(s) of performance should he use?
f. If you suggested more than one measure, which of these should Vincent select if he could use only one?
g. Suppose that last year, the original site had yielded total revenues of $146,000, total costs of $122,000, and hence, a profit of $24,000. Vincent had judged this profit performance to be satisfactory. For the coming year, Vincent expects that due to factors such as increased name recognition and demographic changes, the total revenues will increase by 20% to $175,200. What amount of profit should he expect from the site? Discuss the issues involved in developing an estimate of profit.

SOLUTIONS TO REVIEW PROBLEMS

Review 13-1—Solution
b, d, f, g

Review 13-2—Solution
1. Product/service differentiation
2. Three ways that managerial accountants can help support the goals of product/service differentiation include:
   a. Track customer satisfaction information as it relates to pricing of products in order to determine whether products are priced in line with customers' value perceptions.
   b. Report timely sales data by product type in order to understand and to be able to quickly respond to changes in consumer trends.
   c. Analyze studies of the time it takes for customers to receive their product after an eye examination.

Review 13-3—Solution
1. e   2. c   3. d   4. a   5. d   6. c   7. b

---

[34] Based on Chee W. Chow, "Instructional Case: Vincent's Cappuccino Express—A Teaching Case to Help Students Master Basic Cost Terms and Concepts Through Interactive Learning," *Issues in Accounting Education,* Spring 1995, pp. 173–190.

Review 13-4—Solution
Big Data and Analysis—Given recent advancements in technology, there is a vast amount of data available to organizations. However, it can be difficult to turn this data into useful and predictive information. Organizations are in need of employees who have the abilities to: identify key data trends, perform data mining and extraction, conduct operational and decision analysis, recommend process improvement, and conduct strategic thinking and execution.

ERM—Organizations are constantly faced with uncertainty from the environment, competitors, and other factors that could result in significant risk of loss. By better understanding the types and potential costs of these risks, managerial accountants can help their organizations devise strategies to better predict and minimize exposure to risk.

Review 13-5—Solution
Corporate social responsibility is a balance of the objective of company profitability and of concern for the company's environmental and social impacts. Three examples of how managerial accounting can help support the corporate social responsibility goal of "ensuring affordable access to our products" include:

1. Estimating production adoption percentages in areas with lower economic demographics.
2. Analyzing the average price of products in target areas to ensure affordability.
3. Measuring dollars and products given to non-profit organization that support eye health.

Chapter 14: Cost Definitions, Behavior, and Estimation

LEARNING OBJECTIVES

LO14-1 Define basic cost terms and identify how costs respond to changes in sales volume. (p. 14-3)

LO14-2 Estimate a linear total cost equation. (p. 14-6)

LO14-3 Calculate and compare three analytic approaches to cost estimation. (p. 14-12)

LO14-4 Identify and discuss problems encountered when analyzing data to estimate costs. (p. 14-19)

LO14-5 Define direct cost and indirect cost and discuss using costs for decision-making. (p. 14-21)

Road Map

LO	Learning Objective | Topics	Page	eLecture	Review	Assignments
LO14-1	**Define basic cost terms and identify how costs respond to changes in sales volume.** Cost Behavior :: Variable Cost :: Fixed Cost :: Mixed Cost :: Step Cost :: Factors Affecting Cost Behavior	14-3	e14–1	R14-1	M14-11, M14-12, M14-13, M14-14, E14-17, E14-24, E14-25, E14-26, P14-30
LO14-2	**Estimate a linear total cost equation.** Total Cost Function :: Relevant Range :: Marginal Cost :: Committed and Discretionary Fixed Costs	14-6	e14–2	R14-2	M14-13, M14-14, E14-17, E14-18, E14-19, E14-20, E14-24, E14-25, E14-26, P14-29, P14-31, DA14-1
LO14-3	**Calculate and compare three analytic approaches to cost estimation.** High-Low Cost Estimation :: Scatter Diagrams :: Outlier :: Least Squares Regression :: Coefficient of Determination :: Simple Regression :: Multiple Regression	14-12	e14–3	R14-3	M14-13, M14-14, E14-21, E14-22, E14-23, E14-24, E14-27, P14-29, P14-31, C14-33, DA14-1, DA14-2, DA14-3, DA14-4, DA14-5
LO14-4	**Identify and discuss problems encountered when analyzing data to estimate costs.** Additional Issues :: Changes in Technology and Prices :: Matching Activity and Costs :: Identifying Activity Cost Drivers	14-19	e14–4	R14-4	M14-15, E14-22, E14-23, E14-27, P14-29, P14-31, C14-32, C14-34, DA14-2, DA14-3, DA14-4, DA14-5
LO14-5	**Define direct cost and indirect cost and discuss using costs for decision-making.** Fixed Cost :: Variable Cost :: Direct Cost :: Indirect Cost :: Direct Materials :: Direct Labor :: Manufacturing Overhead :: Combining Cost Behaviors for Decision-Making	14-21	e14–5	R14-5	M14-16, E14-28, P14-30, P14-31, C14-35

© Cambridge Business Publishers

BLOCK, INC.
www.block.xyz

The creators of Twitter, Jack Dorsey and Jim McKelvey, founded **Block, Inc.** (formerly **Square, Inc.**) to address a void in payment processing services for small, portable businesses. Block, Inc. offers over 30 products and services to economically empower individuals, artists, fans, developers, and sellers. The company reports financial information for two operating segments: Square and Cash App. The Square segment processes over $152 billion in transactions each year, comprising over three billion card payments from 526 million payment cards.

The Square segment offers a combination of software, hardware, and financial services products, including credit card readers, online payments apps, and virtual terminals, to help sellers process customer payments. Consider the *chip reader* that sellers use to process credit card payments. The chip reader is a postage stamp-sized card reader that attaches to smartphones. Hardware revenue is earned from the sale of, among other things, chip readers. However, because the hardware is sold to generate revenue on its usage, the hardware is typically sold to customers at a loss.

To manufacture the chip reader, Block incurs direct costs, such as the cost of composite, which can be specifically identified and traced to the chip reader. Block also incurs indirect costs such as rent on a manufacturing facility. Indirect costs are incurred in the production of many products and are allocated to each chip reader in a methodical way. While planning, Block must estimate how many chip readers should be produced based on the expected number of new customers. However, estimating the number of new customers, in advance, is complicated. What methodology would you use to estimate the number of new customers, and based on this estimate, the cost to manufacture the chip readers for those new customers?

The majority of the Square segment's revenues is recognized when merchants process transactions. Estimating the costs associated with processing payments is challenging. What is the make-up of these costs? Do payment processing costs differ based on volume or seasonality? To predict processing costs, we must be able to predict merchant sales volume and the number of transactions. If processing costs vary proportionately with sales activity, the processing costs are referred to as variable costs. What about the costs that do not vary with sales activity, such as salaried engineers? These costs are referred to as fixed costs. As we will see throughout the chapter, many costs are a mixture of variable and fixed costs. Mixed costs present a challenge to companies when estimating future costs. Accurately estimating current product costs and predicting future costs is crucial for financial viability, operational efficiency, and strategic success at Block.

Source: Block, Inc. 2021 10-K Report; www.block.xyz

CHAPTER ORGANIZATION

Cost Definitions, Behavior, and Estimation

Cost Behavior Analysis	Analyzing Data for Cost Estimation	Additional Issues in Cost Estimation	Cost Classification and Decision-Making
• Four Basic Cost Behavior Patterns • Identifying Cost Behavior Patterns • Factors Affecting Cost Behavior Patterns • Total Cost Function for an Organization or Segment • Relevant Range • Total, Variable, and Average Cost • Committed and Discretionary Fixed Costs	• High-Low Cost Estimation • Scatter Diagrams • Least-Squares Regression	• Adapting to changes in Technology and Prices • Responding to Environmental Considerations • Matching Activities and Costs • Identifying Activity Cost Drivers	• Classifying Costs as Direct or Indirect • Combining Cost Behaviors for Decision-Making

COST BEHAVIOR ANALYSIS

LO14-1
Define basic cost terms and identify how costs respond to changes in sales volume.

eLecture
MBC

This chapter introduces **cost behavior**, which refers to the relationship between a given cost item and the quantity of its related cost driver. Cost behavior, therefore, explains how the total amount for various costs responds to changes in a cost driver. To introduce this topic, *we assume that sales in units or dollars (also called sales volume) is the primary cost driver.* In other words, as sales volume increases (decreases), costs go up (down). Understanding cost behavior is essential to understanding and analyzing current costs and estimating future costs. In this chapter, we examine several typical cost behavior patterns and methods for developing cost equations. These concepts help managers make decisions related to production and pricing.

Four Basic Cost Behavior Patterns

Cost Behavior Patterns			
Variable Cost	Fixed Cost	Mixed Cost	Step Cost

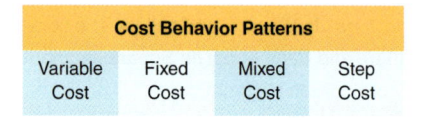

Although there is an unlimited number of ways that costs can respond to changes in sales volume, as a starting point it is useful to classify cost behavior into four categories: **variable cost**, **fixed cost**, **mixed cost**, and **step cost**. Graphs of each are presented in **Exhibit 14.1**. Observe that total cost is measured on the vertical axis, and total sales volume is measured on the horizontal axis.

Let's revisit **Block, Inc.** (Block) focusing on the chip reader. The chip reader is sold to merchants to assist in payment processing. The chip reader is a hardware device that attaches to a smartphone and is made of materials such as plastic. Some items classified as product costs of the chip reader are materials costs, personnel costs, and packaging costs. To manage its growth and pricing strategy for the chip reader, Block must understand its cost structure. This means that Block must understand how costs change as sales volume changes.

1. **Variable costs** change, in total, in direct proportion to changes in the number of units sold. Total variable cost increases as sales volume increases, equaling zero dollars when sales volume is zero and increasing at a constant amount per unit of sales. The higher the variable cost for each unit sold, the steeper the slope (incline) of the line representing total variable cost. The cost of packaging at Block is an example of a variable cost. As more chip readers are sold, total packaging cost increases proportionately. Note however, that per unit variable cost of packaging will remain constant with changes in sales volume.

2. **Fixed costs** do not change in response to a change in sales volume within a specified range of activity. Therefore, a line representing total fixed costs is flat with a slope of zero. Suppose Block employs salaried workers to package the chip readers and prepare the readers for shipment. The salary of these workers does not change with the number of chip readers sold. Workers earn the same salary regardless of whether 10 or 1,000 chip readers are sold. This is an example of a fixed cost, because the personnel cost is unrelated to sales volume.

When discussing fixed costs, we assume that these costs are fixed in the short run and that the company is operating within a specified range of volume called the *relevant range*. While total fixed costs remain constant in the short run, fixed cost per unit varies inversely with sales volume. As sales volume increases (decreases), fixed cost per unit decreases (increases).

3. **Mixed costs** (also known as semivariable costs) contain a fixed and a variable cost element. Total mixed costs are greater than zero (similar to fixed costs) when the sales volume is zero, and they increase in a linear fashion (similar to variable costs) as the sales volume increases. At Block, the cost of electric power is an example of a mixed cost. A minimum level of electricity is required to provide basic lighting (fixed cost), while an increasing amount of electricity is required to manufacture and package the chip readers (variable cost).

4. **Step costs** are constant within a narrow range of sales volume but shift to a higher level when the sales volume exceeds the range. Total step costs increase in a steplike fashion as the sales volume increases. Suppose that one quality control manager is required to conduct quality inspections for every 10,000 chip readers produced and sold in a month. The salary of this manager does not change with sales volume as long as fewer than 10,000 chip readers are produced and sold. However, as soon as demand increases to 10,001 chip readers, Block must hire another quality control manager, thus increasing salary cost. Once again, the cost will be constant until a third manager is required.

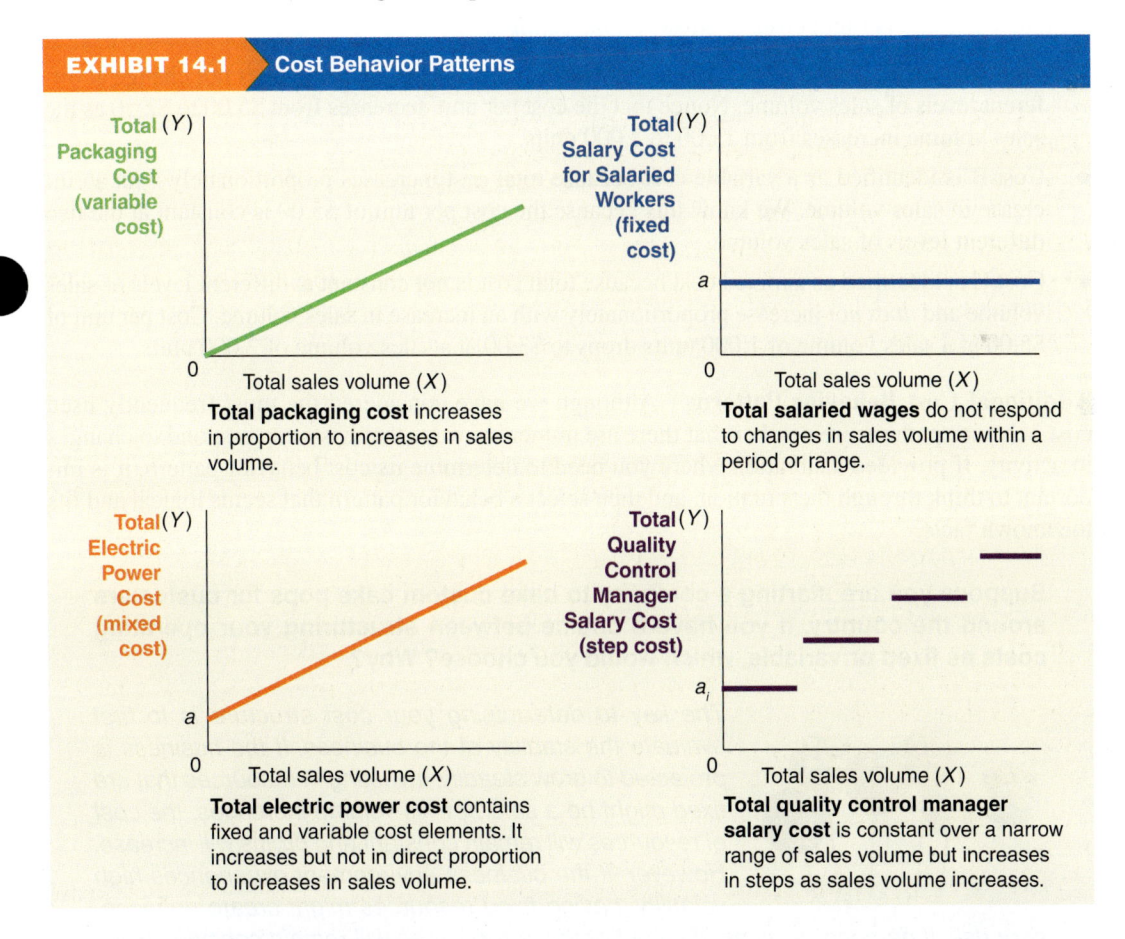

EXHIBIT 14.1 — Cost Behavior Patterns

Total (Y) Packaging Cost (variable cost) vs Total sales volume (X): Total packaging cost increases in proportion to increases in sales volume.

Total (Y) Salary Cost for Salaried Workers (fixed cost) vs Total sales volume (X): Total salaried wages do not respond to changes in sales volume within a period or range.

Total (Y) Electric Power Cost (mixed cost) vs Total sales volume (X): Total electric power cost contains fixed and variable cost elements. It increases but not in direct proportion to increases in sales volume.

Total (Y) Quality Control Manager Salary Cost (step cost) vs Total sales volume (X): Total quality control manager salary cost is constant over a narrow range of sales volume but increases in steps as sales volume increases.

The relationship between total cost (Y axis) and total sales volume (X axis) for the four cost behavior patterns is mathematically expressed, in general terms, as follows, where sales volume represents unit sales.

> Variable cost = Variable cost per unit × Sales volume
> Fixed cost = Total fixed cost within a relevant range
> Mixed costs = Total fixed cost + (Variable cost per unit × Sales volume)
> Step cost = Total fixed cost within a specified range of sales volume

Identifying Cost Behavior Patterns

The following tables show total cost and per unit cost at two different levels of sales volume for three different costs. We assume the company is operating within its relevant range of sales volume.

June Costs at Sales Volume of 1,000 Units	Total Cost	Cost per Unit
Cost A.........	$5,000	$5.00
Cost B.........	5,000	5.00
Cost C.........	5,000	5.00

July Costs at Sales Volume of 2,000 Units	Total Cost	Cost per Unit
Cost A.........	$ 5,000	$2.50
Cost B.........	10,000	5.00
Cost C.........	6,000	3.00

Cost per unit is calculated by dividing total cost by sales volume. We illustrate the cost per unit calculation for Cost A as an example.

$$\text{Cost per Unit of Cost A in June} = \$5{,}000 \text{ total cost}/1{,}000 \text{ units} = \$5.00$$

$$\text{Cost per Unit of Cost A in July} = \$5{,}000 \text{ total cost}/2{,}000 \text{ units} = \$2.50$$

In order to identify whether a cost is fixed, variable, or mixed, it is necessary to review cost patterns for total costs and per unit costs *as sales volume changes*.

- Cost A is easily identified as a fixed cost because the $5,000 total cost does not change at different levels of sales volume. Notice that the cost per unit decreases from $5.00 to $2.50 as the sales volume increases from 1,000 to 2,000 units.

- Cost B is identified as a variable cost because total cost increases proportionately with an increase in sales volume. We know this because the cost per unit of $5.00 is constant at the two different levels of sales volume.

- Cost C is identified as a mixed cost because total cost is *not* constant at different levels of sales volume and *does not* increase proportionately with an increase in sales volume. Cost per unit of $5.00 at a sales volume of 1,000 units drops to $3.00 at a sales volume of 2,000 units.

Additional Cost Behavior Patterns Although we have considered the most frequently used cost behavior patterns, remember that there are numerous ways that costs can respond to changes in activity. If provided a situation where you need to determine its cost behavior pattern, it is important to think through the situation, and then select a behavior pattern that seems logical and fits the known facts.

Critical Thinking & Decision-Making

Suppose you are starting a company to bake custom cake pops for customers around the country. If you have a choice between structuring your operating costs as fixed or variable, which would you choose? Why?

The key to determining your cost structure is to first evaluate the stability of the business. If the business is projected to grow steadily, investing in resources that are fixed might be a safe bet. As volume increases, the cost of resources will remain constant and profits will increase. However, if the business environment experiences high volatility, having fixed resources might create unnecessary risk. If demand declines, the cost of those resources will remain constant. However, if the resources are variable, the costs will adjust as demand fluctuates.

Considering the volatile nature of the market, you determine it would be better for your new baking company to shift costs from fixed to variable. However, you are struggling with the fixed nature of warehouse costs. Is it possible to make warehouse costs a variable cost?

A typical contractual rent payment would be considered a fixed cost. However, to make warehouse costs a variable cost, the company must have the flexibility to scale the warehouse space up or down in relation to sales. **Flexe Inc.** based in Seattle, carved out a niche by offering warehouse space that answers this demand. Flexe rents warehouse space to companies that need space but are not ready to purchase it. Flexe charges by the pallet. For the bakery, if demand increases, more pallet space can be rented. If demand decreases, the bakery can rent less pallet space. In this way, warehouse costs are converted from a fixed cost to a cost that varies with sales (i.e., a variable cost).

Factors Affecting Cost Behavior Patterns

As explained above, the four cost behavior patterns presented are based on the assumption that the number of units sold is the primary cost driver. The implications of this assumption are examined in later chapters.

Another important assumption is that the time period is too short to incorporate structural changes, such as the scale of operations. Although this assumption is useful for short-range planning, for the purpose of developing plans for extended time periods, it is more appropriate to consider possible variations in the size and scope of operations. When this is done, many costs otherwise classified as fixed are better classified as variable. Even the cost of depreciable assets can be viewed as variable if the time period is long enough. For a single month, the straight-line depreciation on Block's machinery is considered a fixed cost. *Depreciation* is the systematic process of allocating the cost of fixed assets to the periods benefiting from their use. However, over a longer time period, Block's sales might fluctuate and its demand for machinery might also change. Consequently, over a multiyear period, depreciation no longer appears fixed or uncorrelated with sales volume.

The total cost function of most organizations has shifted in recent years toward more fixed costs and fewer variable costs, making it increasingly important for organizations to manage their fixed costs. Some organizations have reversed this trend by outsourcing activities, rather than performing the activities internally. This eliminates some fixed costs in exchange for additional variable cost per unit of outsourced activity.

Straight-Line Depreciation:

$$\frac{\text{Cost} - \text{Salvage value}}{\text{Useful Life}}$$

Identifying Cost Behavior

LO14-1 Review 14-1

PayPal, Inc. is a leader in the digital payment industry. The company helps connect merchants and consumers in over 200 markets around the world. Assume PayPal incurs the following costs. Classify each cost as fixed, variable, mixed or step.
  a. Transaction expenses (change as sales revenue changes).
  b. Product manager salary.
  c. Customer support department salaries (temporary positions added as sales reach incremental targets).
  d. Sales team salaries (base amount plus commission based on sales volume).
  e. Product development manager salary.

Solution on p. 14-37.

Estimating the Total Cost Function for an Organization or Segment

Managers are often interested in how total costs respond to a single measure of overall activity, such as units sold or sales revenue. This helps managers to obtain a general understanding of their organization, compare their cost structure to that of different organizations, and perform preliminary planning activities. This overview can be useful, but presenting all costs as a function of a single independent variable (cost driver) is seldom accurate enough to support decisions concerning products, services, or activities. Doing so implies that all an organization's costs can be manipulated by changing a single variable. This is seldom true and we will address this in later chapters.

In developing a total cost function, the independent variable usually represents some measure of the goods or services provided to customers. For Block, the independent variable could be the sales dollars of the transactions it processes in chip readers. Other examples include total student credit hours in a university, total sales revenue in a store, total guest days in a hotel, or total units manufactured in a factory. A cost function that shows the relationship between the independent variable (activity such as sales volume) and the dependent variable (total costs) is illustrated in **Exhibit 14.2**.

LO14-2
Estimate a linear total cost equation.

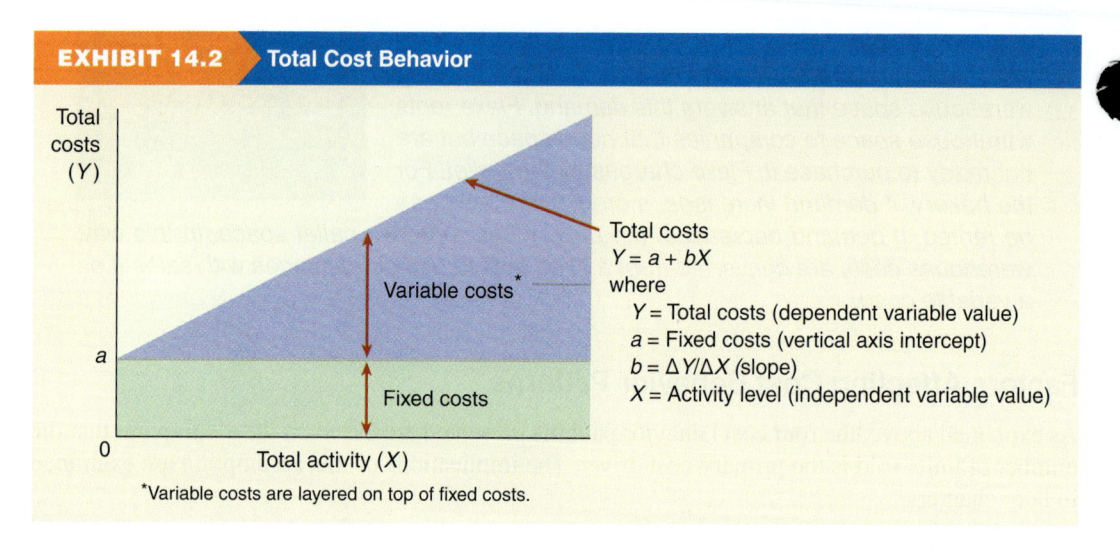

EXHIBIT 14.2 — Total Cost Behavior

Total costs
$Y = a + bX$
where
Y = Total costs (dependent variable value)
a = Fixed costs (vertical axis intercept)
$b = \Delta Y / \Delta X$ (slope)
X = Activity level (independent variable value)

*Variable costs are layered on top of fixed costs.

The equation for total costs is $Y = a + bX$, which can also be stated in general terms as follows.

Total costs = Total fixed costs + (Variable cost per unit × Sales volume)

In situations where the variable, fixed, and mixed costs, and the related cost functions can be determined, a total cost equation can be useful in predicting future costs for various activity levels. For example, assume that one segment of Block incurs fixed costs consisting only of depreciation of its equipment of $4,800 per month. Also assume that the variable cost per unit is $8.50 for every chip reader sold. Therefore, the total cost equation for this segment of Block is:

$$\text{Total costs} = \$4,800 + (\$8.50 \times \text{Sales volume})$$

If the segment expects to sell 1,000 chip readers during July, it can then estimate its total July costs to be:

$$\text{Total cost} = \$4,800 + (\$8.50 \times \$1,000)$$
$$= \$13,300$$

Relevant Range and the Total Cost Function

As mentioned earlier, fixed costs are typically only fixed within a specified range of activity. If companies face extremely high or low demand, they may decide to change fixed resources. This means that the total cost equation is useful for predicting costs in only a limited range of activity. The **relevant range** of a total cost equation is that portion of the range associated with the fixed cost of the current or expected capacity. Suppose for Block, the number of chip readers produced per week depends on the number of machines it operates as shown in the following schedule.

No. of Machines	Chip Readers Produced per Week
1	0 to 50 thousand
2	51 to 100 thousand
3	101 to 150 thousand
4	151 to 200 thousand*

*Relevant range of activity

Assume that the relevant range of activity, given the current fixed cost structure, occurs when production is between 151 and 200 thousand chip readers per week. If Block expects demand and production to exceed 200 thousand per week, it must add another machine. This would change its current total cost equation. Similarly, if Block expects demand and production to decrease, it might eliminate one of the machines, also changing its total cost equation. Thus, the current cost equation is only good for analyzing and predicting costs if the fixed resources remain stable.

Operating Outside of Relevant Range: Impact on Marginal Cost

The use of straight lines in accounting models of cost behavior assumes a linear relationship between sales and cost with each additional unit sale accompanied by a uniform increment in total cost. This uniform increment is known as the *variable cost of one unit*.

Economic models, however, show a nonlinear relationship between activity and cost with each incremental unit of activity being accompanied by a varying increment in total cost. Economists identify the varying increment in total cost as the **marginal cost** *of one unit*. For Block, the marginal cost of one chip reader equals the additional (incremental) cost incurred with each additional chip reader. The nonlinear relationship relates to extra costs incurred at various output levels. For example, when not under pressure, employees might work slower, effectively increasing the production cost. Additionally, extra help might be needed at times to complete the production run, again affecting the marginal cost of production.

It is useful to relate marginal cost to the following three levels of activity.

1. *If production is below the production range for which the facility was designed,* the existence of excess capacity might result in relatively high marginal costs. Having extra time, employees complete assignments at a leisurely pace, increasing the time and the cost to produce each unit above what it would be if employees were more pressed to complete work. Frequent starting and stopping of equipment may also add to costs. For Block:

    Operating level: < 151 thousand chip readers produced per week

2. *Within the production range for which the facility was designed,* activities take place under optimal circumstances and marginal costs are relatively low. For Block:

    Operating level: 151 to 200 thousand chip readers produced per week

3. *If production is above the level for which the facility was designed,* the existence of capacity constraints again results in relatively high marginal costs. Near capacity, employees may be paid overtime wages, less-experienced employees may be used, regular equipment may operate less efficiently, and old equipment with high energy requirements may be placed in service. For Block:

    Operating level: > 200 thousand chip readers produced per week

Based on marginal cost concepts, the economists' short-run total cost function is illustrated in the first graph in **Exhibit 14.3**. To clarify the concept, we use the capacity information for Block. The vertical axis intercept represents fixed costs. In this simple example, our fixed cost is depreciation. Corresponding to the high marginal costs at low levels of activity, the initial slope is quite steep. This represents the extra costs incurred with each unit produced due to,

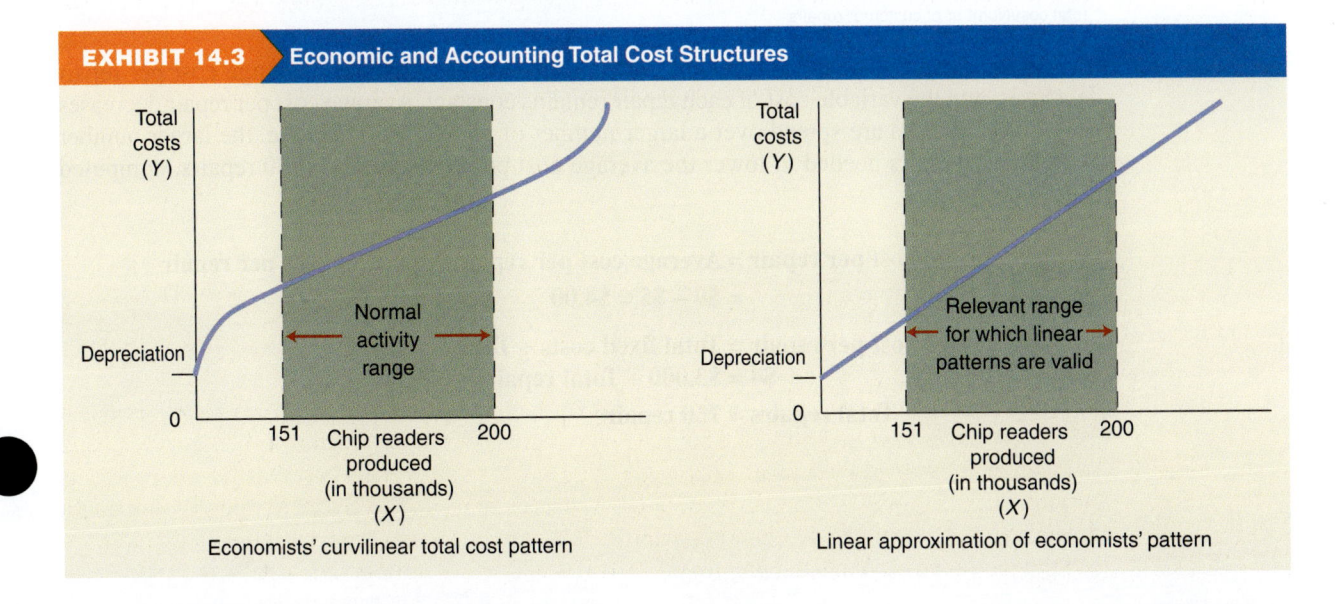

EXHIBIT 14.3 Economic and Accounting Total Cost Structures

Economists' curvilinear total cost pattern

Linear approximation of economists' pattern

for example, less efficient production of the chip readers. In the normal activity range, where marginal costs are relatively low, the slope becomes less steep. This approximates the linear relationship that was discussed earlier in the chapter. For the most part, the variable cost per unit remains constant within the relevant range or normal activity level. Then, corresponding to high marginal costs above the normal activity range, the slope of the economists' total cost function increases again. The increased slope represents the increased production costs due to overtime pay, for example.

If the economists' total cost curve is valid, how can we reasonably approximate it with a straight line? The answer to this question is in the notion of a *relevant range*. A linear pattern may be a poor approximation of the economists' curvilinear pattern over the entire range of possible activity, but a linear pattern as illustrated in the right-hand graph in **Exhibit 14.3** is often sufficiently accurate within the range of probable operations. The range of activity within which a linear cost function is valid is called the relevant range. Linear estimates of cost behavior are valid only within the relevant range. Extreme care must be exercised when making comments about cost behavior outside the relevant range. More sophisticated, nonlinear estimation models are required to estimate the cost effects of actions outside of the relevant range.

Distinguishing between Total Cost, Variable Cost, and Average Cost

Particular care needs to be taken with the vertical axis. So far, all graphs have placed *total* costs on the vertical axis. Miscommunication is likely if one party is thinking in terms of *total* costs while the other is thinking in terms of *variable* or *average* costs. **FIXthat4U** is a smartphone and tablet repair store. Block's chip reader runs off of a smartphone or tablet. Merchants must repair these devices quickly to ensure continued use. Often, companies will use a company like FIXthat4U to ensure a quick, high-quality repair. FIXthat4U's monthly fixed costs include rent and depreciation on tools and furniture. Its variable costs include direct labor and any materials used in the repair, such as new screens. Consider FIXthat4U's following cost function.

Total costs = $3,000 + ($5 × No. of customer repairs)

Total cost, average cost per repair, and variable cost per repair at various levels of activity are provided in the following table and also graphed in **Exhibit 14.4** on the following page.

No. of Customer Repairs	Total Cost	Average Cost per Repair*	Variable Cost per Repair
100	$3,500	$35.00	$5.00
200	4,000	20.00	5.00
300	4,500	15.00	5.00
400	5,000	12.50	5.00
500	5,500	11.00	5.00

* Total cost/Number of customer repairs

As the number of customer repairs increases, total cost increases, average cost per repair decreases, and the variable cost of each repair remains constant. Average cost per repair decreases because fixed costs are spread over a larger number of repairs. For example, the larger number of customer repairs needed to lower the average cost per repair to $9 is 750 repairs, computed as follows.

Fixed cost per repair = Average cost per repair − Variable cost per repair
= $9 − $5 = $4.00

Fixed cost per repair = Total fixed costs ÷ Total repairs
$4 = $3,000 ÷ Total repairs
Total repairs = 750 repairs

EXHIBIT 14.4 Total Cost, Variable Cost per Unit, and Average Cost per Unit

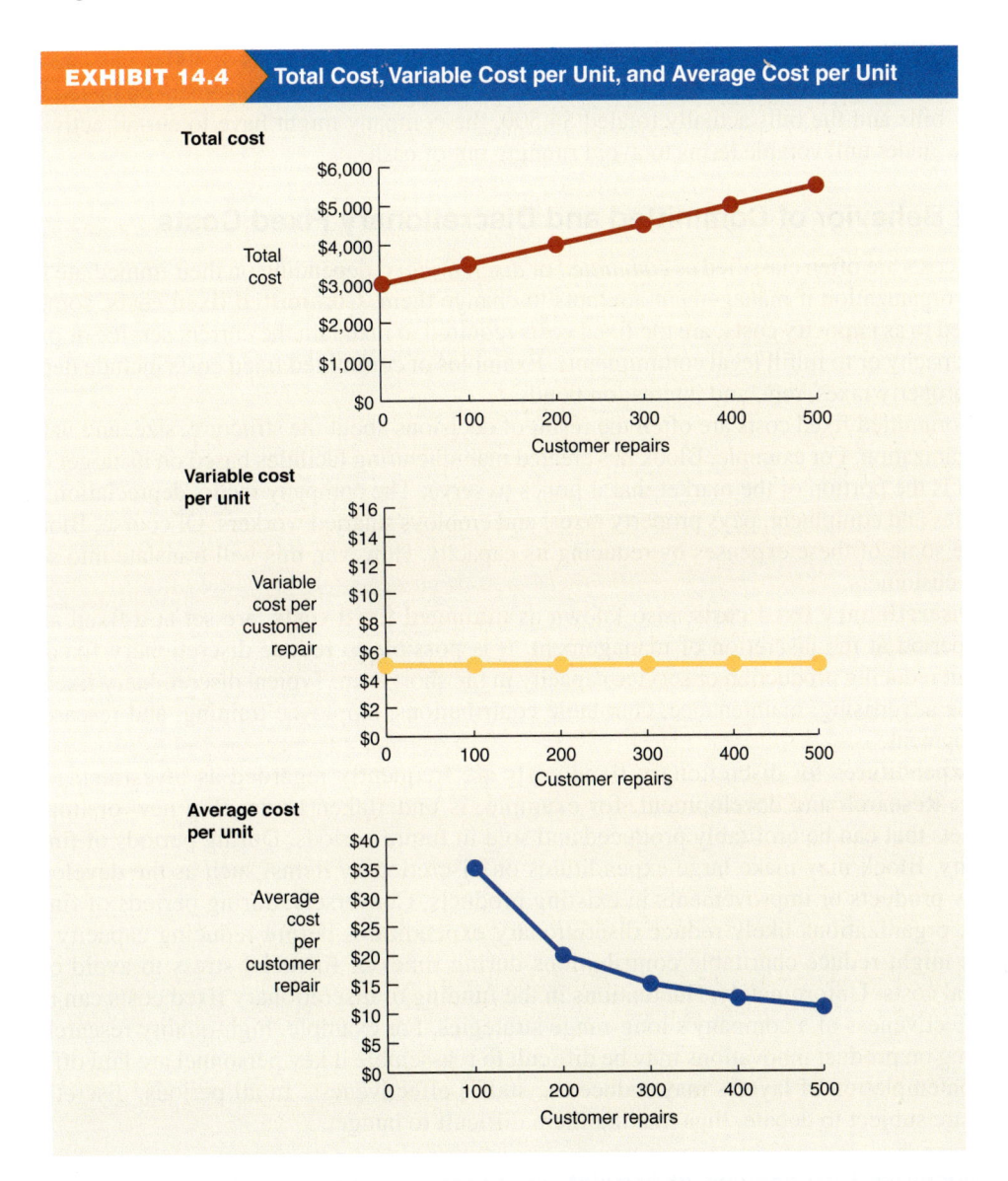

Total cost — Total cost ranges from about $3,000 at 0 customer repairs to about $5,500 at 500 customer repairs, increasing linearly.

Variable cost per unit — Variable cost per customer repair is constant at about $5 across 0 to 500 customer repairs.

Average cost per unit — Average cost per customer repair decreases from about $35 at 100 repairs to about $11 at 500 repairs.

Which cost—total, average, or variable—would you use to determine the minimum price to charge a customer and not be worse off?

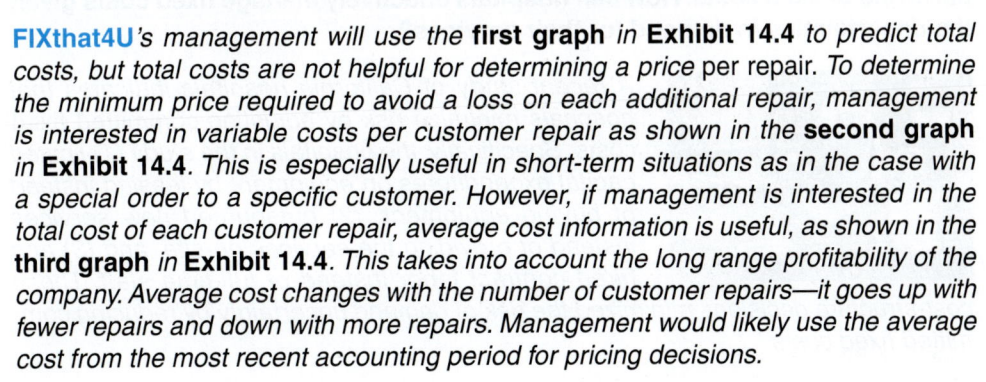

FIXthat4U's management will use the **first graph** in **Exhibit 14.4** to predict total costs, but total costs are not helpful for determining a price per repair. To determine the minimum price required to avoid a loss on each additional repair, management is interested in variable costs per customer repair as shown in the **second graph** in **Exhibit 14.4**. This is especially useful in short-term situations as in the case with a special order to a specific customer. However, if management is interested in the total cost of each customer repair, average cost information is useful, as shown in the **third graph** in **Exhibit 14.4**. This takes into account the long range profitability of the company. Average cost changes with the number of customer repairs—it goes up with fewer repairs and down with more repairs. Management would likely use the average cost from the most recent accounting period for pricing decisions.

Critical Thinking & Decision-Making

Prediction Errors Errors can occur if last period's average costs, perhaps based on a volume of 500 repairs, were used to predict total costs for a future period when the anticipated volume was some other amount, say 300 repairs.

Estimated costs for 300 repairs = $15 × 300 anticipated repair volume = $4,500
Estimated costs for 300 repairs = $̶1̶1̶ × 300 anticipated repair volume = $3,300 **(error)**

Using average costs based on the 500 repairs, the predicted total costs of 300 repairs are underestimated. The prediction error could cause a number of problems. If management budgeted $3,300 to pay bills and the bills actually totaled $4,500, the company might have to curtail activities or borrow under unfavorable terms to avoid running out of cash.

Cost Behavior of Committed and Discretionary Fixed Costs

Fixed costs are often classified as *committed* or *discretionary,* depending on their immediate impact on an organization if management attempts to change them. **Committed fixed costs**, sometimes referred to as **capacity costs**, are the fixed costs required to maintain the current service or production capacity or to fulfill legal commitments. Examples of committed fixed costs include depreciation, property taxes, rent, and interest on bonds.

Committed fixed costs are often the result of decisions about the structure, size, and nature of an organization. For example, Block has created manufacturing facilities based on its target market which is the portion of the market that it hopes to serve. The company incurs depreciation on the facilities and equipment, pays property taxes, and employs salaried workers. Of course, Block can reduce some of these expenses by reducing its capacity. However, this will translate into serving fewer customers.

Discretionary fixed costs, also known as **managed fixed costs**, are set at a fixed amount each period at the discretion of management. It is possible to reduce discretionary fixed costs without reducing production or service capacity in the short term. Typical discretionary fixed costs include advertising, maintenance, charitable contributions, employee training, and research and development.

Expenditures for discretionary fixed costs are frequently regarded as investments in the future. Research and development, for example, is undertaken to develop new or improved products that can be profitably produced and sold in future periods. During periods of financial stability, Block may make large expenditures on discretionary items, such as the development of new products or improvements in existing products. Conversely, during periods of financial stress, organizations likely reduce discretionary expenditures before reducing capacity costs. Block might reduce charitable contributions during times of financial stress to avoid cutting internal costs. Unfortunately, fluctuations in the funding of discretionary fixed costs can reduce the effectiveness of a company's long-range strategies. For example, high-quality research staff working on product innovations may be difficult to reassemble if key personnel are laid off. Even the contemplation of layoffs may reduce the staff's effectiveness. In all periods, discretionary costs are subject to debate, thus making them difficult to budget.

Critical Thinking & Decision-Making

Hospitals face demand uncertainty that increases financial risk. The need for hospital services fluctuates from day-to-day, yet hospitals must incur substantial levels of fixed costs. How can hospitals effectively manage fixed costs given the uncertainties in demand for their services?

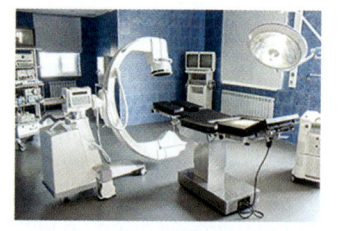

A recent study of California hospitals indicates that hospitals minimize risk by adjusting committed fixed costs. Specifically, the hospitals in the study (1) limited capital expenditures on equipment by leasing instead of buying equipment, (2) outsourced new services instead of providing the services on-site, and (3) and hired contract labor instead of full-time staff. These cost-structure decisions minimized the risk of demand uncertainty by reducing committed fixed costs.[1]

---

[1] Source: Martin Holzhacker, Ranjani Krishnan, and Matthias D. Mahlendorf, "Unraveling the Black Box of Cost Behavior: An Empirical Investigation of Risk Drivers, Managerial Resource Procurement and Cost Elasticity," *The Accounting Review 90*, no. 6 (2015): 2305–2335.

Estimating Costs Using a Linear Total Cost-Estimating Equation

LO14-2 Review 14-2

Assume **PayPal**'s total monthly transaction processing costs are estimated to be $170,000 in fixed costs, plus an additional $0.01 in variable costs per sales dollar. These estimates are valid as long as the total sales through PayPal's system does not exceed $104 million per month.
1. Determine the linear total cost-estimating equation for PayPal.
2. Determine the total monthly cost and the average cost per sales dollar if PayPal expects the following transactions for the month. Consider each scenario separately.
    a. $10 million
    b. $30 million
    c. $100 million
3. Determine the sales volume at which the average cost per sales dollar is $0.015.
4. Assume an alternate cost structure for PayPal where costs are variable: Y = $0.025X. Determine the sales dollars at which the current cost structure becomes preferable (costs less than) the alternate cost structure.

Solution on p. 14-38.

ANALYZING DATA FOR COST ESTIMATION

Cost estimation, the determination of the relationship between a cost driver such as sales volume and cost is an important part of cost management. To properly estimate the relationship between sales and costs, we must be familiar with basic cost behavior patterns and cost-estimating approaches. Costs with a variable or fixed pattern are relatively easy to identify through a review of data trends, inspection of documents, or interviews of employees. For example, employment contracts at Block might reveal that sales personnel are paid 15% of sales as bonuses, indicating that these personnel costs are variable. On the other hand, rental agreements showing stable monthly rent payments on corporate offices indicate rent costs are fixed.

LO14-3 Calculate and compare three analytic approaches to cost estimation.

Mixed costs, which contain fixed and variable cost elements, are more difficult to estimate. According to a basic rule of algebra, two equations are needed to determine two unknowns. Following this rule, at least two observations are needed to determine the variable and fixed elements of a mixed cost. In this section, we illustrate three approaches to estimate the relationship between sales volume and cost: high-low cost estimation, scatter diagrams, and least-squares regression.

Approaches to Cost Estimation

| High-Low Cost Estimation | Scatter Diagrams | Least Squares Regression |

High-Low Cost Estimation

The most straightforward approach to determine the variable and fixed elements of mixed costs is the **high-low method of cost estimation**. This method utilizes data from two time periods, a *representative* high-activity period and a *representative* low-activity period, to estimate fixed and variable costs. Assuming identical fixed costs in both periods, any difference in total costs between these two periods is due entirely to variable costs. The variable cost per unit is found by dividing the difference in total cost by the difference in total activity between the two periods.

$$\text{Variable cost per unit} = \frac{\text{Difference in total cost}}{\text{Difference in activity}}$$

The total variable cost at an activity level is computed by multiplying variable cost per unit by that activity level (either the high or the low activity level). Once total variable cost is determined, fixed cost, which is identical in both periods, is computed by subtracting the total variable cost from the corresponding total cost.

$$\text{Fixed cost} = \text{Total costs} - \text{Variable cost}$$

Assume that Block wants to develop a monthly cost function for one of its chip reader packaging departments. The packaging department incurs costs for each chip reader manufactured and sold. The following observations of a segment are available for the first four months of the year.

		Number of Chip Readers Manufactured and Sold	Packaging Costs
(Low-activity period)	January	6,000	$17,000
	February	9,000	26,000
(High-activity period)	March	12,000	32,000
	April	10,000	20,000

In the four-month period, the low-activity period is January and the high-activity period is March. Using the data for these two months, we solve for variable cost per unit by dividing the difference in total cost by the difference in number of chip readers.

$$\text{Variable cost per unit} = \frac{\text{Difference in total costs}}{\text{Difference in number of chip readers}}$$

$$= \frac{\$32{,}000 - \$17{,}000}{12{,}000 - 6{,}000}$$

$$= \$2.50$$

Next, we estimate total fixed cost by subtracting total variable cost from total cost of *either* the January or March equation.

JANUARY

$$\text{Fixed cost} = \text{Total costs} - \text{Variable cost}$$

$$= \$17{,}000 - (\$2.50 \text{ per chip reader} \times 6{,}000 \text{ chip readers})$$

$$= \$2{,}000$$

or

MARCH

$$\text{Fixed cost} = \$32{,}000 - (\$2.50 \text{ per chip reader} \times 12{,}000 \text{ chip readers})$$

$$= \$2{,}000$$

The cost-estimating equation in algebraic form as introduced in **Exhibit 14.2** is shown for the total packaging department cost.

$$Y = \$2{,}000 + \$2.50X$$

where

X = Number of chip readers

Y = Total costs for the packaging department

Total costs
$Y = a + bX$
where
  Y = Total costs
  a = Fixed costs
  $b = \Delta Y / \Delta X$
  X = Activity level

The concepts underlying the high-low method of cost estimation are illustrated in **Exhibit 14.5**.

EXHIBIT 14.5 — High-Low Cost Estimation

$$\text{Variable cost per unit} = \frac{\text{Difference in total costs}}{\text{Difference in number of chip readers}}$$

$$\text{Fixed cost} = \text{Total cost at either the high or low cost activity level} - \text{Variable cost computed for that level}$$

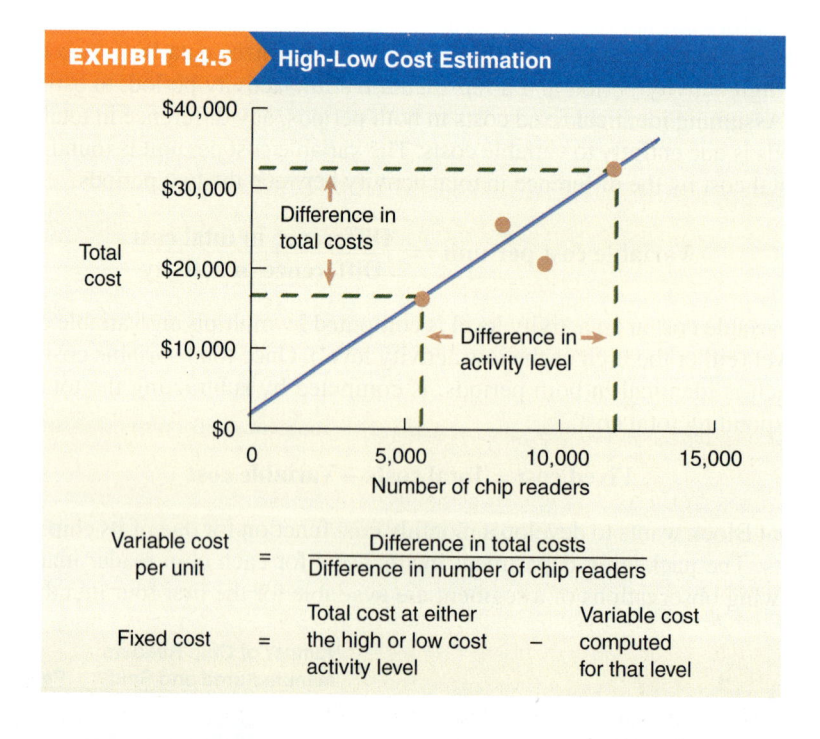

Cost Prediction The forecasting of future costs, called **cost prediction**, is a common purpose of cost estimation. Previously developed estimates of cost behavior through cost estimating equations are often the starting point in predicting future costs. Continuing the Block example, if 5,000 chip readers are budgeted to be sold in June, the predicted June packaging department cost is calculated as follows.

$$Y = \$2,000 + \$2.50X$$
$$= \$2,000 + (\$2.50 \times 5,000)$$
$$= \$14,500$$

Scatter Diagrams

A **scatter diagram** is a graph of past sales activity and cost data, with individual observations represented by dots. Plotting historical cost data on a scatter diagram is a useful approach to cost estimation, especially when used in conjunction with other cost-estimating approaches. A scatter diagram helps in selecting high and low activity levels representative of normal operating conditions. The periods of highest or lowest activity may not be representative because of the cost of overtime, the use of less efficient equipment, strikes, and so forth. If the goal is to develop an equation to predict costs under normal operating conditions, then the equation should be based on *observations of normal operating conditions*.

In **Exhibit 14.6**, we expand our Block example by adding data points for additional months. On the graph, we notice that two observations seem out of place: one is extremely high, and the other is extremely low. When estimating the cost function, we want to eliminate these extreme observations, or **outliers**, from our analysis. A scatter diagram is also useful in determining whether costs can be reasonably approximated by a straight line. One can visually inspect the dots. Is it possible to draw a representative straight-line through the plot of dots, with approximately equal dots on either side of the straight-line? Does your line slope upwards, indicating that costs increase with activity? Using the data in **Exhibit 14.6**, it appears that a line can reasonably be drawn through the cluster of observations, if we do not include the outliers.

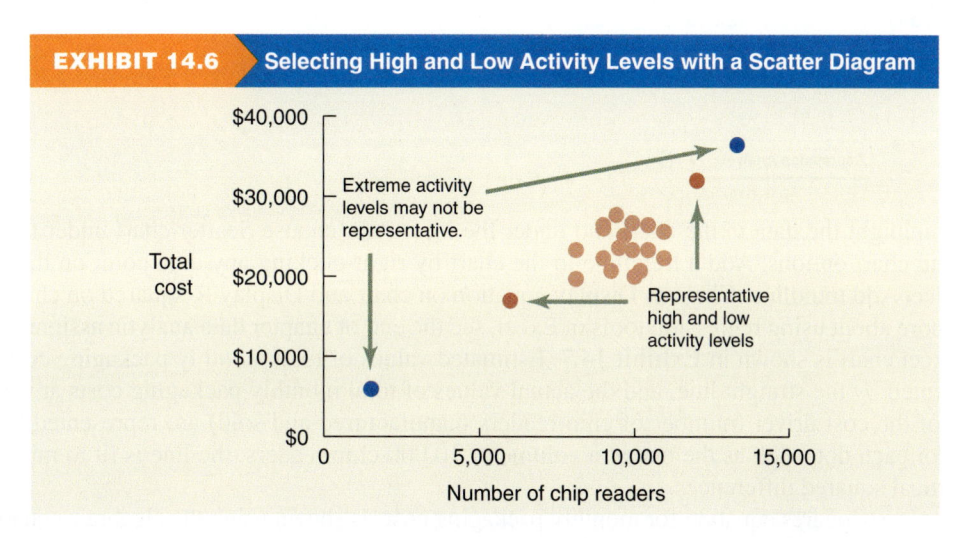

EXHIBIT 14.6 Selecting High and Low Activity Levels with a Scatter Diagram

While a scatter diagram itself may be used to manually draw a line to estimate a cost equation, the scatter diagram is more useful in identifying outliers and in determining whether the cost behavior appears to be predictable (i.e., shows a linear trend). If costs appear to show a linear pattern, an equation for the line can be developed by applying the high-low method to any two points on the line, not considered to be outliers.

Suppose you are the purchasing manager at Block for materials used in the chip reader. You have observed that as the company has increased its sales volume, the total cost to process purchase orders has increased, but not at a constant rate. You would like to estimate the cost to process purchase orders next month. You gather data on purchasing department costs and the number of purchase orders processed for the last eight quarters. How could a scatter diagram assist you in your analysis?

Critical Thinking & Decision-Making

Because costs are not increasing at a constant rate with sales volume, it appears that the cost of purchasing is a mixed cost. Graphing purchasing costs over time using the number of purchase orders as the cost driver can provide quick insights into the cost behavior. The scatter diagram will help identify whether a linear pattern exists indicating that purchasing costs can be predicted by using the number of purchase orders. If a linear pattern does exist, the costs equation can be estimated using the high-low method. After deleting any outliers, the cost equation can be estimated by comparing the highest and lowest points over the period. To continue this analysis, see DA14-5.

Least-Squares Regression

Least-squares regression analysis uses a mathematical approach to fit a cost-estimating equation to the observed data. The least-squares regression analysis creates an equation that minimizes the sum of the vertical squared differences between the estimated and the actual costs at each observation. Each of these differences is an estimating error. A least-squares regression analysis can be completed in **Microsoft Excel®**. To continue with the Block example, first prepare a table in Excel using the data for January through April.

	A	B	C
		Number of Chip Readers	Packaging Costs
January		6,000	$17,000
February		9,000	$26,000
March		12,000	$32,000
April		10,000	$20,000

Next, highlight the data in the chart and under the insert tab, choose Scatter chart under the recommend chart options. Add a trendline to the chart by right-clicking any data point on the chart and select Add trendline. Click on Display equation on chart and Display R-squared on chart. (To learn more about using regression tools in Excel, see the end of chapter data analytic assignments.) The Excel chart is shown in **Exhibit 14.7**. Estimated values of total monthly packaging costs are represented by the straight line, and the actual values of total monthly packaging costs at various levels of the cost driver (number of chip readers manufactured and sold) are represented by the dots. For each dot, such as the one at a volume of 10,000 chip readers, the line is fit to minimize the vertical squared differences.

The least-squares equation for monthly packaging costs is shown using the algebraic equation.

$$Y = \$3,400 + \$2.20X$$

Using the least-squares regression analysis, the predicted June packaging department cost with 5,000 budgeted chip readers is $14,400.

$$Y = \$3,400 + \$2.20X$$
$$= \$3,400 + (\$2.20 \times 5,000)$$
$$= \$14,400$$

Recall that the high-low method predicted June costs of $14,500. Differences between estimation approaches, although small in this case, can vary.

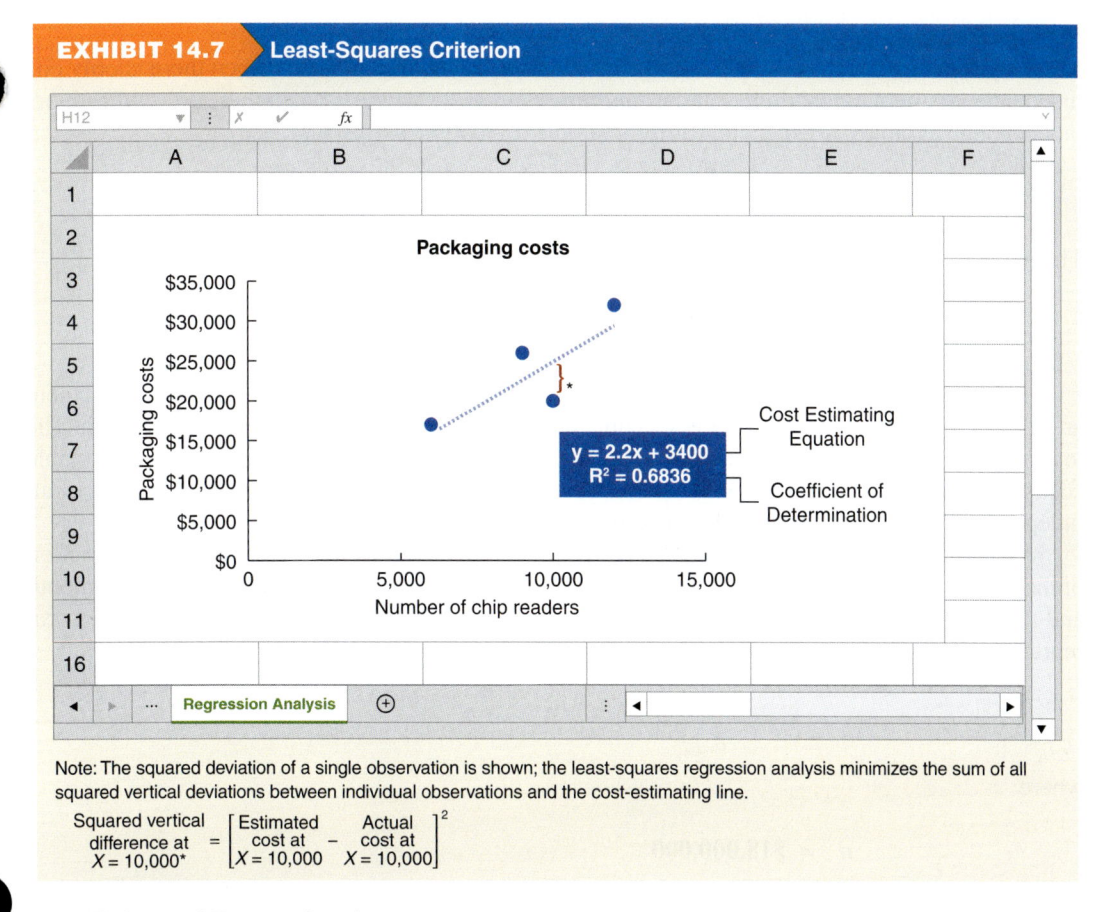

EXHIBIT 14.7 Least-Squares Criterion

[Spreadsheet screenshot showing a scatter plot titled "Packaging costs" with Packaging costs on the y-axis ($0 to $35,000) and Number of chip readers on the x-axis (0 to 15,000). The regression equation is y = 2.2x + 3400 with R² = 0.6836, labeled as "Cost Estimating Equation" and "Coefficient of Determination."]

Note: The squared deviation of a single observation is shown; the least-squares regression analysis minimizes the sum of all squared vertical deviations between individual observations and the cost-estimating line.

$$\text{Squared vertical difference at } X = 10{,}000^* = \left[\text{Estimated cost at } X = 10{,}000 - \text{Actual cost at } X = 10{,}000 \right]^2$$

Coefficient of Determination

Mathematicians regard least-squares regression analysis as superior to both the high-low and the scatter diagram methods. It uses all available data, rather than just two observations, and does not rely on subjective judgment in drawing a line.

In addition to the vertical axis intercept and the slope, the least-squares regression analysis calculates the coefficient of determination. The **coefficient of determination** is a measure of the percent of variation in the dependent variable (such as total packaging department costs), which is explained by variations in the independent variable or variables (such as total chip readers manufactured and sold). Statisticians often refer to the coefficient of determination as R-squared and represent it as R^2.

The coefficient of determination can have values between zero and one, with values close to zero suggesting that the equation is not very useful and values close to one indicating that the equation explains most of the variation in the dependent variable. When choosing between two cost-estimating equations, the one with the higher coefficient of determination is generally preferred. The coefficient of determination for the packaging department cost-estimating equation, determined above using least-squares regression analysis, is 0.6836. This means that approximately 68% of the variation in packaging department costs is explained by the number of chip readers.

Managers, Not Models, Are Responsible for Decision-Making

Although computer programs make least-squares regression analysis easy to use, the generated output should not automatically be accepted as correct. Statistics and other mathematical methods are tools to help managers make decisions. Managers, not mathematical models, are responsible for decisions. Judgment should always be exercised when considering the validity of the least-squares approach, the solution, and the data. If the objective is to predict future costs under normal operating conditions, observations reflecting abnormal operating conditions should be deleted. Also, an examination of the cost behavior pattern to determine whether it is linear is required. Scatter diagrams assist in both of these judgments. Finally, the results should make sense. When the relationships between total cost and several activity drivers are examined, it is possible to have a high R^2 purely by chance. Even though the relationship has a high R^2, if it "doesn't make sense," there is probably something wrong.

Simple Regression and Multiple Regression

Least-squares regression analysis is identified as *simple regression analysis* when there is only one independent variable (cost driver) and as *multiple regression analysis* when there are two or more independent variables. The general form for simple regression analysis is:

$$Y = a + bX$$

The general form for multiple regression analysis is:

$$Y = a + \Sigma b_i X_i$$

In this case, the subscript i is a general representation of each independent variable. When there are several independent variables, i is set equal to 1 for the first, 2 for the second, and so forth. The total variable cost of each independent variable is computed as $b_i X_i$, with b_i representing the variable cost per unit of independent variable X_i. The Greek symbol sigma, Σ, indicates that the costs of all independent variables are summed in determining total variable costs.

As an illustration, assume that Block's costs in the Square segment are expressed as a function of the transactions processed and hardware sold. Assume that fixed costs are $18,000,000 per month and the variable costs are $0.01 per dollar processed and $120 per chip reader. The mathematical representation of monthly costs with two variables is as follows.

$$Y = a + b_1 X_1 + b_2 X_2$$

where

a = $18,000,000
b_1 = $0.01 per dollar processed
b_2 = $120 per chip reader
X_1 = Total sales dollars processed
X_2 = Unit sales of chip readers

During a month if $105 million dollars are processed and 200,000 chip readers are sold, Block's estimated total cost is $43,050,000, calculated as follows.

$$Y = \$18{,}000{,}000 + \$0.01(105 \text{ million}) + \$120(200{,}000)$$
$$= \$43{,}050{,}000$$

In addition to estimating costs, multiple regression analysis can be used to determine the effect of individual product features on the market value of a product or service or the largest drivers of net income or market share. Multiple regression analysis can be performed in Excel or in data analysis applications like Tableau or Python. See the data analytic assignments to practice multiple regression analysis. Step-by-step instructions in Excel are included in the assignments.

Critical Thinking & Decision-Making

While the last example focused on a manufacturer, regression analysis is also applicable to service providers. Consider the owner of a hair salon that would like to estimate costs for the following month. Under what circumstances would a single independent variable of service hours be a sufficient way to estimate costs over the use of a multiple variable regression analysis?

There are a multitude of underlying factors that drive costs. Typically, costs will have many different drivers and will therefore react differently to changes in volume. This can make presenting all costs of an organization as a function of a single independent variable not accurate enough to make specific decisions concerning products, services, or activities.

For a hair salon owner, a single independent variable, such as service hours, may effectively estimate costs if variable costs change in proportion to service hours. Consider an example where the types of service provided are similar and require similar use of resources such as hair products, utilities (water, electricity, etc.). However, if the services provided vary along with the use of resources, results from a multiple regression analysis would be a better predictor of costs. For example, if services included cut and coloring, cost drivers may include service hours and hair product costs.

In our prior examples, we used multiple regression to predict costs, but how can multiple regression be used in predictive analytics to *reduce costs*? Assume a health-insurance company would like to reduce hospital readmission costs for patients recovering from a cardiac event. What type of data could be analyzed that could result in actions that reduce hospital readmission costs?

Kaiser Permanente, a hospital and health-insurance company, has reduced readmission costs by using data to better monitor and assess patients recovering from a cardiac event (i.e., heart attacks, bypass surgery, and heart failure). Patients are given smartwatches to use over an eight-week rehab program. The smartwatch collects data like steps taken and pulse levels. Patients send Kaiser details of exercise sessions and symptoms through a mobile app accessible through their watch. In return, reminders are sent to patients about medication and exercise. If the patient isn't meeting program goals, health providers can follow up with phone calls. Kaiser is also able to use the data collected to determine the most effective program plans. In the first year, readmission rates for participating patients were less than 2%, compared to 10% to 15%, on average, for patients in-clinic rehab programs.[2]

Cost Estimation — LO14-3 Review 14-3

Part One: High-Low Method
Assume that **PayPal** reported the following results for April and May (in thousands).

	April	May
Sales dollars processed	$2,100	$2,700
Transaction processing cost	$1,575	$2,025
Wages and salaries	1,525	1,675
Building rent	1,500	1,500
Depreciation on network equipment	200	200
Utilities	710	770
Supplies	225	255
Miscellaneous	113	131
Total	$5,848	$6,556

Required
a. Create a separate cost equation for each of the following costs: (1) transaction processing cost, (2) wages and salaries, (3) building rent, and (4) total monthly costs. Use the high-low method to create an equation for any mixed cost.
b. Predict total costs for monthly volumes of $1,000 and $2,000 sales dollars processed.
c. Predict the average cost per sales dollar processed at monthly volumes of $1,000 and $2,000 sales dollars processed. Explain why the average costs differ at these two levels of sales dollars processed.

Part Two: Scatter Diagram
Assume that PayPal reported the following monthly results for wages and salaries and sales dollars processed (in thousands).

continued

---
[2] Source: Kayla Matthews, "6 Ways Companies Are Using Data Analytics to Reduce Expenses," *InsideBIGDATA*, February 24, 2019.
Agam Shah, "Kaiser Permanente Bets on Smartwatches to Lower Costs," *Wall Street Journal*, January 15, 2020.

continued from previous page

	Sales Dollars Processed	Wages and Salaries
June	$1,800	$1,243
July	2,400	1,600
August	2,300	1,483
September	2,200	1,435
October	2,400	1,531
November	2,500	1,480
December	2,650	2,010
January	2,500	1,579
February	2,300	1,483
March	2,050	1,363
April	2,100	1,525
May	2,700	1,675

Required

a. Use Excel to create a scatter diagram. Indicate what months (if any) appear to be outliers. *Hint:* Highlight the data to be included in the chart. Open the insert tab and select the Scatter chart in the Charts group.
b. Use the information from *representative* high- and low-volume months to develop a cost-estimating equation for monthly transaction processing costs.
c. What are possible reasons for any outliers?

Part Three: Regression

Assume that PayPal reported the following monthly results for sales dollars processed and total costs per month (in thousands).

	Sales Dollars Processed	Total Costs
June	$1,800	$5,143
July	2,400	6,202
August	2,300	5,992
September	2,200	5,820
October	2,400	6,136
November	2,500	6,175
December	2,650	6,845
January	2,500	6,294
February	2,300	5,997
March	2,050	5,640
April	2,100	5,848
May	2,700	6,556

Required

a. Prepare a scatter plot in Excel in order to determine if there is a relationship between sales dollars processed and total monthly costs. *Hint:* Highlight the data to be included in the chart. Open the insert tab and select the Scatter chart in the Charts group.
b. Add a trendline to the chart and display the regression equation and R^2 value. *Hint:* Right click any of the data points on your chart; select Add trendline and check the Display equation on chart, check Display R^2 value on chart.
c. What does the R^2 indicate about the relationship between sales dollars processed and total monthly costs?
d. Using the cost estimating equation in part b, estimate costs for next month (June) if sales dollars processed is expected to be $2,850.

Solution on p. 14-38.

ADDITIONAL ISSUES IN COST ESTIMATION

LO14-4 Identify and discuss problems encountered when analyzing data to estimate costs.

We previously explained several items to be wary of when developing cost-estimating equations:

- Data that are not based on normal operating conditions (e.g., outliers)
- Nonlinear relationships between total costs and activity
- Obtaining a high R^2 purely by chance

Additional items of concern discussed in this section include:

- Adapting to changes in technology and prices
- Responding to environmental issues
- Matching activities and cost within each observation
- Identifying cost drivers

Adapting to Changes in Technology and Prices

Changes in technology and prices make cost estimation and prediction difficult. Block operates in a rapidly changing environment. As transaction processing evolves, Block must ensure that their cost analyses remain relevant. Care must be taken to ensure that data used in developing cost estimates are based on the existing technology. When this is not possible, professional judgment is required to make the appropriate adjustments.

Only data reflecting a single price level should be used in cost estimation and prediction. If prices have remained stable in the past but then uniformly increase by 20%, cost-estimating equations based on data from previous periods will not accurately predict future costs. In this case, all that is required is a 20% increase in the prediction. Unfortunately, adjustments for price changes are seldom this simple. The prices of various cost elements are likely to change at different rates and at different times. Furthermore, there are probably several different price levels included in the past data used to develop cost-estimating equations. If data from different price levels are used, an attempt should be made to restate them to a single price level.

Responding to Environmental Considerations

Many companies are making investments in new technologies, to reduce negative impacts on the environment, either voluntarily or in response to regulatory requirements. Estimating the impacts of such changes on a company's cost structure is difficult, especially given the uncertainties of new technologies. Carbon pricing is an example of a regulatory approach used widely to address climate issues. Under this approach, companies that emit carbon dioxide (CO_2) are charged a fee. The most significant source of emissions is the combustion of fossil fuels. Under a carbon tax, a price is set per ton of carbon or per ton of CO_2 emitted. Let's assume that Block is subject to a new regulatory carbon tax. Block's current cost structure is as follows for a manufacturing process of chip readers.

$$\text{Total costs} = \$12,200 + (\$4.80 \times \text{Number of chip readers})$$

In the short run, variable cost would increase because the tax increases with carbon usage which is driven by production of chip readers. If the company estimates that the carbon tax will increase variable cost per unit by $0.10 per chip reader, the revised cost estimating equation is as follow.

$$\text{Total costs} = \$12,200 + (\$4.90 \times \text{Number of chip readers})$$

> **Over the long run, how might the cost estimating equation change?**
>
> *In one example, investments in higher efficiency machines could reduce the company's demand for energy for each chip reader produced. This would result in an increase in fixed costs (depreciation on the new equipment) and a decrease in variable costs (carbon taxes and efficiency savings for using the new equipment). Determining the financial impact of different approaches to addressing climate issues requires collaboration of employees with different expertise across a company.*

Critical Thinking & Decision-Making

Matching Activities and Costs

We have been assuming that costs were either variable, responding to changes in sales volume, or fixed. However, sometimes other activities drive costs. The development of accurate cost-estimating equations requires the matching of the cost activities to the related costs within each observation. This accuracy is often difficult to achieve because of the time lag between an activity and the recording of the cost of resources consumed by the activity. For example, current activities usually consume electricity, but an electric bill, that details usage in one month, won't be received and recorded until the next month. Driving an automobile requires routine maintenance for items like lubrication and oil, but the automobile can be driven several weeks or even months before the maintenance is required. Consequently, daily, weekly, and perhaps even monthly observations of miles driven and maintenance costs are unlikely to match the costs of oil and lubrication in the same time period.

In general, the shorter the time period, the higher the probability of error in matching costs and activity. The cost analyst must carefully review the database to verify that activity and cost are matched within each observation. If matching problems are found, it may be possible to adjust the data (perhaps by moving the cost of electricity from one observation to another). Under other circumstances, it may be necessary to use longer periods to more accurately match costs and activity.

Identifying Cost Drivers

When estimating costs in situations where the costs do not vary with sales, we try to find the best proxy for the driver of the costs. For example, is car maintenance best approximated by the miles driven? Identifying the appropriate activity cost driver for a particular cost requires judgment and professional experience.

Consider an example in the auto insurance industry where miles driven are considered to be an indicator of insurance claim costs. Traditionally, insurance premiums were based on an insured party's age, gender, and address. However, by thoroughly analyzing claims data, companies have found that up to 70% of the variation in claims risk relates to the actual number of miles driven.[3] In a sense, the cost of claims is a variable cost that relates to mileage. A new trend in auto insurance is to gather detailed mileage data and to charge drivers a low monthly premium with a variable mileage charge. A pioneer of this approach, **Metromile**, uses a smartphone app and a thumbnail-sized device that users install in their vehicles to gather usage data. Gathering data on mileage allows Metromile to offer substantially lower rates to low-mileage drivers simply by better estimating the cost of insuring each customer. Thus, the more accurate a company's cost information, the more effectively the company can price its products/services.

In general, the cost driver should have a logical, causal relationship with costs. In many cases, the identity of the most appropriate cost driver, such as the miles driven for the cost of automobile gasoline, is apparent. In other situations, where different cost drivers might be used, scatter diagrams and statistical measures, such as the coefficient of determination, are helpful in selecting the cost driver that best explains past variations in cost. If regression analysis is used, the analyst considers the coefficient of determination. In general, a higher coefficient of determination is preferred. The relationship between the cost driver and the cost must seem logical, and relevant data must be available.

Review 14-4 LO14-4 — Identifying Appropriate Cost Drivers

a. Identify potential drivers that would have logical and causal relations with costs in a manufacturing and processing plant.
b. In deciding which activity driver is the most appropriate for a particular manufacturing cost, would the following items make the driver more desirable or less desirable? Consider each scenario separately.
   1. A scatter plot reveals a small dispersion of points around the cost-estimating line.
   2. The coefficient of determination is 0.65, which is less than the coefficient of the other options.
   3. There is a logical relationship between the activity and the cost, but the activity data is not reliably available.
   4. Observations on a scatter plot do not reasonably approximate a straight line.
   5. The cost fluctuates with changes in the level of the activity driver.
   6. The coefficient of determination is 0.88, which is greater than the coefficient of the other options.

Solution on p. 14-40.

COST CLASSIFICATION AND DECISION-MAKING

LO14-5 Define direct cost and indirect cost and discuss using costs for decision-making.

So far, we have focused on classifying costs as fixed or variable in a company's cost structure. In addition to the fixed and variable cost classification, costs can be identified as direct or indirect.

Classifying Costs as Direct or Indirect

A **direct cost** is a cost that is incurred and can be specifically and feasibly traced to a product. For Block, the materials used in the production of the chip reader are direct costs relative to the chip reader. The company knows exactly how much composite, a type of material, is used in each chip reader. The salary of a production engineer who works on all of the Block products is considered an indirect cost relative to the chip reader. The production engineer works on multiple products.

---
[3] Quentin Hardy, "Technology Transforms How Insurers Calculate Risk," *The New York Times*, April 6, 2016.

This means that we cannot specifically and feasibly trace the cost of the engineer to the chip reader. Rather, we will estimate the portion of the engineer's salary that is relevant to the chip reader. In general, multi-use resources are **indirect costs**. Any cost that must be "allocated" or divided based on some proxy is classified as indirect. Indirect costs are often referred to as **overhead**. We will discuss different ways to allocate indirect costs in later chapters.

Over the years, overhead costs have been increasing while direct costs have declined. This is in part due to the recent push for *shared service departments*, which are departments that are created to serve many products and departments throughout the organization. Of course, as overhead increases, the importance of creating a reliable system to allocate these costs to products, divisions, or customers becomes more crucial. Manufacturing costs or product costs are made up of three cost categories.

1. **Direct materials**, the cost of primary raw materials converted into finished goods, have increased slightly over time as organizations purchase components they formerly fabricated. The word "direct" is used to indicate costs that are easily and specifically traced to a finished product or service.
2. **Direct labor**, the wages earned by production employees for the time they spend converting raw materials into finished products, has decreased significantly over time. Employees spend less time physically working on products and more time supporting automated production activities, the cost of which is classified as manufacturing overhead.
3. **Manufacturing overhead**, which includes all manufacturing costs other than direct materials and direct labor, has increased significantly due to automation and technology advances, product diversity, and product complexity. This category reflects all of the indirect costs related to manufacturing.

Because direct materials and direct labor vary directly with the number of units, they are easy to measure. Overhead, an indirect cost, must be allocated to units. With the relatively large size of overhead relative to direct costs, a change in sales volume may *not* be an adequate explanation for changes in costs.

Combining Cost Behaviors for Decision-Making

Two different cost classifications have been presented: fixed vs. variable costs and direct vs. indirect costs. These should not be considered an either/or classification system. Rather, each classification is necessary and useful to managers in various contexts. In fact, it is possible to derive costs that fall into any combination of the two classification systems.

Consider the following cost classifications from the perspective of Block's chip reader. These costs are also illustrated in **Exhibit 14.8**.

- **Direct Variable Cost** The material that is used in each chip reader is a direct cost as it can be specifically traced to the product. Additionally, because the cost of materials increases proportionately with sales, it is a variable cost.
- **Indirect Variable** Electricity can be thought of as a variable cost. (While the cost of electricity could be considered a mixed cost, we simplify the example to consider it a variable cost.) As production and sales increase, electricity increases proportionately. Although there might be a method to trace electricity costs directly to products, it is not a feasible endeavor. Consequently, electricity is considered an indirect variable cost.
- **Direct Fixed** Consider the monthly salary of the product manager of the chip reader. This manager works only on the chip reader, making the salary a direct cost. Additionally, the manager's salary is a fixed cost.
- **Indirect Fixed Costs** Consider the salaried plant manager at the manufacturing plant that produces all of the Square products. The manager's salary is fixed. Because the manager oversees multiple products, the salary is an indirect cost of the chip reader.

Managers consider the classification of costs differently, depending on the question that is being asked or the problem being solved. Unlike financial accounting, managerial accounting does not generally have rules and regulations. Rather, it focuses on thinking critically about the question being asked and using data to answer the question and to make recommendations. The fixed/variable cost dichotomy is typically used when analyzing scenarios that are short-term in nature. For example, how will costs change in the short run if fixed costs increase by 10% and variable cost per unit decrease by 10%? With this information, management can evaluate the impact of the cost changes on profitability.

Considering direct and indirect costs helps with long-run issues. For example, a product manager might want to understand the full cost (i.e., direct and indirect costs) of a product to evaluate the pricing scheme. And while direct costs are easily allocated to products, the process of allocating indirect costs to products requires judgment. The quality of the cost information and the accuracy in how costs are allocated to products/services affects the quality of decisions made by management. As we will see in later chapters, this information is a key ingredient to both operational and strategic decision-making.

EXHIBIT 14.8 Cost Classification Examples

	Direct Cost	Indirect Cost
Variable cost	Materials	Electricity
Fixed cost	Chip reader product manager	Plant manager

Critical Thinking & Decision-Making

For purposes of pricing, is it important for a sales department manager to understand the break out of fixed and variable costs of a newly developed product or is it enough for a sales manager to know how a competing product is priced in the market?

Pricing decisions are complex and take into account many factors. Knowing the competitor's price is important to understanding the perceived value in the market. However, it is also important for the sales department to know if the price will minimally cover all variable costs (at least in the short-term) and average costs (over the long-term). The level of profitability expected on a product will guide many short-term and long-term decisions.

Review 14-5 LO14-5   Classifying Costs Using Two Classification Systems Simultaneously

Consider the following costs for **PayPal**.
1. Corporate headquarters rent.
2. Cost of cybersecurity software to protect all transactions made by a particular customer.
3. Revenue-based commissions paid to executives.
4. Transaction-processing expense that is tied to every sale, based on total sales dollar value.

Required
Relative to the sales dollars processed for a customer account of PayPal, classify each cost activity above as variable or fixed AND direct or indirect.

Solution on p. 14-40.

KEY RATIOS AND EQUATIONS

Variable cost = Variable cost per unit × Sales volume
Fixed cost = Total fixed cost within a relevant range

Mixed costs = Total fixed cost + (Variable cost per unit × Sales volume)
Step cost = Total fixed cost within a specified range of sales volume

Total costs: $Y = a + bX$
Where Y = total costs, a = vertical axis intercept (an approximation of fixed costs), b = slope (an approximation of variable cost per unit of X), and X = value of independent variable.

$$\text{Variable cost per unit} = \frac{\text{Difference in total costs}}{\text{Difference in activity}}$$

Fixed cost = Total cost − Variable cost

General form for simple regression analysis: $Y = a + bX$
Where a = total fixed cost element and b = the variable cost per unit of independent variable X.

General form for multiple regression analysis is: $Y = a + \Sigma b_i X_i$
Where the subscript i is a general representation of each independent variable. When there are several independent variables, i is set equal to 1 for the first, 2 for the second, and so forth. The total variable costs of each independent variable are computed as $b_i X_i$, with b_i representing the variable cost per unit of independent variable X_i. The Greek symbol sigma, Σ, indicates that the costs of all independent variables are summed in determining total variable costs.

Assignments with the MBC logo in the margin are available in BusinessCourse.
See the Preface of the book for details.

MULTIPLE CHOICE

1. A graph of the total cost of ingredients used in **Papa Murphy's** pizzas most closely resembles this total cost behavior pattern: **LO14-1** Papa Murphy's

    a. Variable cost
    b. Fixed cost
    c. Mixed cost
    d. Step cost

2. At a sales volume of 50 units, the average cost is $410 per unit and the variable cost is $10 per unit. Assuming a linear cost behavior pattern, if sales double to 100 units the average cost will be: **LO14-2**

    a. $10
    b. $200
    c. $205
    d. $210

3. Employees of Chelsea, a financial consulting firm, often travel to client sites for project meetings. The firm's business manager is attempting to better understand the costs associated with the employees' company cars. Following is data for the first four months of the year related to miles incurred and costs associated with the cars, including leases, insurance, maintenance, and gas. Use the high-low method to calculate the fixed costs associated with the company cars. **LO14-3**

	Mileage	Costs
Jan.	450	$29,300
Feb.	325	$22,550
Mar.	418	$27,572
Apr.	380	$25,520

    a. $0.54
    b. $3,215
    c. $5,000
    d. $4,500

Multiple Choice Answers
1. a
2. d
3. c
4. b
5. d
6. d
7. c
8. c

LO14-3 4. The relevant range is important in estimating costs because:
   a. In the presence of excess capacity, costs might be understated.
   b. The relevant range best approximates a linear cost function.
   c. The marginal cost of production is constant across the entire cost curve, even outside the relevant range.
   d. When demand exceeds current capacity limits, the marginal cost of an additional unit of production is extremely small.

LO14-3 5. Which of the following is *not* a benefit of least-squares regression analysis as a cost-estimating approach?
   a. Lease-squares regression uses all available data.
   b. Least-squares regression offers statistical measures of the impact of a variable.
   c. Least-squares regression calculates a variable that assesses the amount of variation that is explained.
   d. Least-squares regression results always indicate the cost estimation and solution.

LO14-4 6. Increasing the length of the time period included in each observation of activity and cost will assist in overcoming this possible problem in cost estimation:
   a. Data not based on normal operations
   b. Nonlinear relationship between total costs and activity
   c. Changes in technology or prices
   d. Failure to match activity and costs within each observation

LO14-4 7. Which of the following situations would cause concern when an analyst is developing a cost-estimating equation?
   a. A relatively linear relationship exists between total costs and activity.
   b. The data is based on normal operating conditions.
   c. The industry incurs significant changes in technology.
   d. The cost driver has a logical, causal relationship with costs.

LO14-5 8. **Hasbro** manufactures toys and games for children of all ages. One Hasbro game is the Monopoly brand. Hasbro employs a brand management team focused solely on the Monopoly products. Relative to the Monopoly suite of products, how would you classify the brand management team?

Hasbro
NASDAQ :: HAS

   a. Variable cost / Direct cost
   b. Variable cost / Indirect cost
   c. Fixed cost / Direct cost
   d. Fixed cost / Indirect cost

DATA ANALYTICS

LO14-2, 3 **DA14-1. Selecting a Basis for Predicting Shipping Expenses**

Cambridge Sound sells portable speakers and wireless headphones. In an effort to improve the planning and control of shipping expenses, management is trying to determine which of three variables—units shipped, weight shipped, or sales value of units shipped—has the closest relationship with shipping expenses. The following information is available.

Month	Units Shipped	Weight Shipped (lbs.)	Sales Value of Units Shipped	Shipping Expenses
May	10,000	7,500	$350,000	$38,000
June	12,000	8,760	432,000	42,000
July	15,000	9,200	420,000	50,100
August	20,000	10,500	400,000	72,500
September	12,000	7,600	300,000	41,000
October	8,000	6,000	320,000	35,600

REQUIRED

a. Prepare three scatter plots in Excel showing the relationship between shipping expenses and each of the three variables (units shipped, weight shipped, sales value of units shipped.) *Hint:* Highlight the data to be included in the chart. Open the Insert tab and select the Scatter chart in the Charts group.

b. Using R-squared values, determine which of the three variables has the closest relationship with shipping expenses. *Hint:* Right-click a data point on each scatter chart, select Add trendline, and check the boxes next to Display equation on chart and Display R-squared value on chart.

c. Using the independent variable that appears to have the closest relationship to shipping expenses, develop a cost-estimating equation for total monthly shipping expenses.

d. Use the equation developed in requirement (*b*) to predict total shipping expenses in a month when 14,000 units; weighing 9,380 lbs.; with a total sales value of $420,000 are shipped.

DA14-2. Multiple Regression Analysis for a Special Decision

For billing purposes, assume **Phoenix Family Medical Clinic** classifies its services into one of four major procedures, X1 through X4. Assume that a local business has proposed that Phoenix provide health services to its employees and their families at the following set rates per procedure.

X1	$100	X3	$ 60
X2	200	X4	300

Because these rates are significantly below the current rates charged for these services, management has asked for detailed cost information on each procedure. The following information is available for the most recent 12 months.

		Number of Procedures			
Month	Total Cost	X1	X2	X3	X4
1	$17,250	30	25	155	19
2	18,750	38	30	135	23
3	20,250	50	20	105	38
4	14,250	20	25	90	25
5	15,000	68	15	120	20
6	20,250	90	19	158	14
7	19,125	20	30	143	28
8	16,125	16	30	132	20
9	19,500	60	21	93	35
10	16,500	20	22	75	35
11	17,100	20	18	113	33
12	19,875	72	15	150	30

REQUIRED

a. Use multiple regression analysis to determine the unit cost of each procedure. How much variation in monthly cost is explained by your cost-estimating equation? *Hint:* Under the Data tab, click on Data analysis, Regression, and select the cells for the Y Range and X Range. *Hint:* Use the R^2 value and not the adjusted R^2 value.

b. Evaluate the rates proposed by the local business. Assuming Phoenix has excess capacity and no employees of the local business currently patronize the clinic, what are your recommendations regarding the proposal?

c. Assuming Phoenix is operating at capacity and would have to turn current customers away if it agrees to provide health services to the local business, what are your recommendations regarding the proposal?

Note: Excel's regression tool can be found in the add-in: Analysis Toolpak. To load the add-in, search for "regression" in the Excel Help box and click on Analysis ToolPak add-in.

DA14-3. Cost Estimation, Interpretation, and Analysis

Kendrick Anderson Furniture Maker, LLC creates custom tables in Atlanta. Assume that the following represents monthly information on production volume and manufacturing costs since the company started operations.

	Total Manufacturing Costs	Total Tables Produced	Living Room Tables Produced	Dining Room Tables Produced
Year 1: June	$71,000	110	25	85
July	57,500	90	45	45
August	79,724	130	15	115
September	64,250	95	36	59
October	57,300	76	24	52
November	60,900	92	48	44
December	62,700	105	24	81
Year 2, January	70,130	110	50	60
February	68,400	102	20	82
March	57,400	81	25	56
April	105,790	142	102	40
May	74,750	125	22	103
June	74,290	115	15	100
July	66,500	106	18	88
August	49,888	85	28	57
September	72,668	116	55	61
October	71,700	120	81	39
November	74,200	120	30	90
December	54,900	72	18	54

REQUIRED

a. Use the high-low method to develop a cost-estimating equation for total manufacturing costs driven by total tables produced.
b. In Excel, create a scatter graph of total manufacturing costs and total tables produced. Use the graph to identify any unusual observations. *Hint:* Highlight the data to be included in the chart. Open the insert tab and select the Scatter chart in the Charts group.
c. Excluding any unusual observations, use the high-low method to develop a cost-estimating equation for total manufacturing costs. Comment on the results, comparing them with the results from requirement (*a*).
d. 1. Use simple regression analysis in Excel to develop a cost-estimating equation for total manufacturing costs. *Hint:* Exclude any outlier point(s) identified in part *b*. *Hint:* Under the Data tab, click on Data analysis, Regression, and select the cells for the Y Range and X Range.
   2. How much variation in manufacturing costs is explained by your cost-estimating equation?
   3. What advantages does the simple regression analysis performed in part *d*.1 have in comparison with the high-low method of cost estimation?
   4. Why must analysts carefully evaluate the data used in simple regression analysis?
e. A customer has offered to purchase 50 dining room tables for $452 per table. Management has asked your advice regarding the desirability of accepting the offer. What advice do you have for management? Complete a multiple regression analysis in Excel to support your answer.

LO14-3, 4

DA14-4. Simple and Multiple Regression

Dan Mullen is employed by a mail-order distributor and reconditions used personal computers, routers, and printers. Dan is paid $12 per hour, plus an extra $6 per hour for work in excess of 40 hours per week. The distributor just announced plans to outsource all reconditioning work, so Dan will need to start looking for a new job. Because the distributor is pleased with the quality of Dan's work, he has been asked to enter into a long-term contract to recondition used computers at a rate of $50 per computer, plus all parts. The distributor also offered to rent all necessary equipment to Dan at a rate of $300 per month. Dan has been informed that he should plan on reconditioning as many computers as he can handle, up to a maximum of 20 per week.

Dan has room in his basement to set up a work area, but he is unsure of the economics of accepting the contract, as opposed to working for a local computer repair shop at $14 per hour. Data related to the time spent and the number of units of each type of electronic equipment Dan has reconditioned in recent weeks is as follows.

Week	Printers	Routers	Computers	Total Units	Total Hours
1	3	6	6	15	42
2	0	8	7	15	40
3	3	3	8	14	41
4	1	3	13	17	46
5	10	7	5	22	50
6	4	9	4	17	43
7	4	9	4	17	43
8	4	5	6	15	44
9	1	5	11	17	48
10	7	5	6	18	44
Total				167	441

REQUIRED

Assuming he wants to work an average of 40 hours per week, what should Dan do? Answer the question using (a) an analysis of average time to recondition electronic equipment, (b) simple regression, and (c) multiple regression.

a. Analysis of average time to recondition electronic equipment
   1. What is the average time to repair a piece of electronic equipment based upon the data? How many computers could Dan recondition in a week?
   2. Estimate net profit to recondition desktop computers for a month under the proposed contract. Assume 4 weeks in a month.
   3. What is the net amount that Dan would receive for a month to work at the store?
   4. What should Dan do based on this analysis? Are there any flaws in the analysis?
b. Simple regression
   1. Complete a simple regression analysis (using total units and total hours). *Hint:* Under the Data tab, click on Data analysis, Regression, and select the cells for the *Y* Range and *X*

Range. What is the estimating equation using total units and total hours and what percentage of the variation in total weekly hours is explained by the estimating equation?
   2. How many computers could Dan recondition in a week? Apply the estimating equation from part b. 1, using the time for general electronic repairs to estimate time for computer desktop repairs.
   3. Estimate net profit to recondition desktop computers for a month under the proposed contract.
   4. What should Dan do based on this analysis?
c. Multiple regression
   1. Complete a multiple regression analysis (using total units and total hours). What is the estimating equation for desktop computers using total units and total hours and what percentage of the variation in total weekly hours is explained by the estimating equation?
   2. How many computers could Dan recondition in a week based on this analysis?
   3. Estimate net profit to recondition desktop computers for a month under the proposed contract.
   4. What should Dan do based on this analysis?

DA14-5. Analyzing Data Visualizations: Purchasing Department Costs
Assume you are the purchasing manager at **Block** for materials used in the chip reader. You have observed that as the company has increased its sales volume, the total cost to process purchase orders has increased as well, but not at a constant rate. You would like to estimate the cost to process purchase orders next month. You gather the following data for the last eight quarters.

Quarters	No. of Purchase Orders	Purchase Department Costs
1	8,000	246,686
2	8,160	238,521
3	8,405	247,881
4	8,573	253,340
5	8,763	247,031
6	8,938	260,066
7	9,161	261,603
8	9,344	259,959

REQUIRED
a. Prepare a scatter diagram in Excel that shows the relationship between the number of purchase orders and purchase department costs for the last eight quarters. Based upon the scatter diagram, are purchasing department costs fixed, variable or mixed?
b. Estimate the average purchasing cost per purchase order at the low and high point of purchase orders. Assume no outliers in your analysis.
c. Use the high-low method to develop a cost-estimating equation for total annual operating costs.
d. If purchases for next quarter are expected to be 9,600 units, what are expected purchasing department costs?
e. What is a reason why the total cost to process purchase orders is not increasing at a constant rate? What trend do you expect in the average cost per unit in the purchasing department?

DATA VISUALIZATION

Data Visualization Activities are available in myBusinessCourse. These assignments use Tableau Dashboards to expose students to visual depictions of data and introduce students to data analytics through data visualizations. These exercises are easily assignable and auto graded by MBC.

QUESTIONS

Q14-1. Briefly describe variable, fixed, mixed, and step costs and indicate how the total cost function of each changes as activity increases within a time period.

Q14-2. Why is presenting all costs of an organization as a function of a single independent variable, although useful in obtaining a general understanding of cost behavior, often not accurate enough to make specific decisions concerning products, services, or activities?

Q14-3. Explain the term "relevant range" and why it is important in estimating total costs.

Q14-4. What type of prediction error can occur when average unit costs are used to predict total future costs?

Q14-5. How are variable and fixed costs determined using the high-low method of cost estimation?

Q14-6. Distinguish between cost estimation and cost prediction.

Q14-7. Why is a scatter diagram helpful when used in conjunction with other methods of cost estimation?

Q14-8. Identify two advantages of least-squares regression analysis as a cost-estimating approach.

Q14-9. Why is it important to match activity and costs within each observation? When is this matching problem most likely to exist?

Q14-10. How have direct materials, direct labor, and manufacturing overhead changed as a portion of total manufacturing costs over time? What is the implication of the change in manufacturing overhead for cost estimation?

MINI EXERCISES

LO14-1 **M14-11. Classifying Cost Behavior**

Classify the total costs of each of the following as variable, fixed, mixed, or step. Sales volume is the cost driver.

a. Salary of the department manager
b. Memory chips in a computer assembly plant
c. Real estate taxes
d. Salaries of quality inspectors when each inspector can evaluate a maximum of 1,000 units per day
e. Wages paid to production employees for the time spent working on products
f. Electric power in a factory
g. Raw materials used in production
h. Automobiles rented on the basis of a fixed charge per day, plus an additional charge per mile driven
i. Sales commissions
j. Straight-line depreciation on office equipment

LO14-1 **M14-12. Classifying Cost Behavior**

Classify the total costs of each of the following as variable, fixed, mixed, or step.

a. Straight-line depreciation on a commercial solar system
b. Maintenance costs at a hospital
c. Rent on video conferencing equipment charged as a fixed amount per month, plus an additional charge per hour of technician time
d. Cost of goods sold in a bookstore
e. Salaries paid to temporary college instructors where the number of course sessions varies
f. Lumber used by a home construction company
g. The costs of operating a research department
h. The cost of hiring a dance band for three hours
i. Laser printer paper for a department printer
j. Electric power in a restaurant

LO14-1, 2, 3 **M14-13. Classifying Cost Behavior using Data Visualizations**

For each of the following situations, select the most appropriate cost behavior pattern (as shown in the illustrations following this problem), where the lines represent the cost behavior pattern, the vertical axis represents costs, the horizontal axis represents total volume, and the dots represent actual costs. Each pattern may be used more than once.

a. Variable cost per unit
b. Total fixed costs
c. Total mixed costs
d. Average fixed costs per unit
e. Total current manufacturing costs
f. Average variable costs
g. Total costs when employees are paid $15 per hour for the first 40 hours worked each week and $20 for each additional hour
h. Total costs when employees are paid $15 per hour and guaranteed a minimum weekly wage of $300
i. Total costs per day when a consultant is paid $200 per hour, with a maximum daily fee of $1,000

j. Total variable costs
k. Total costs for salaries of social workers where each social worker can handle a maximum of 25 cases
l. A water bill where a flat fee of $800 is charged for the first 100,000 gallons and additional water costs $0.005 per gallon
m. Total variable costs properly used to estimate step costs
n. Total materials costs
o. Rent on exhibit space at a convention

GRAPHS FOR MINI EXERCISE 14-3

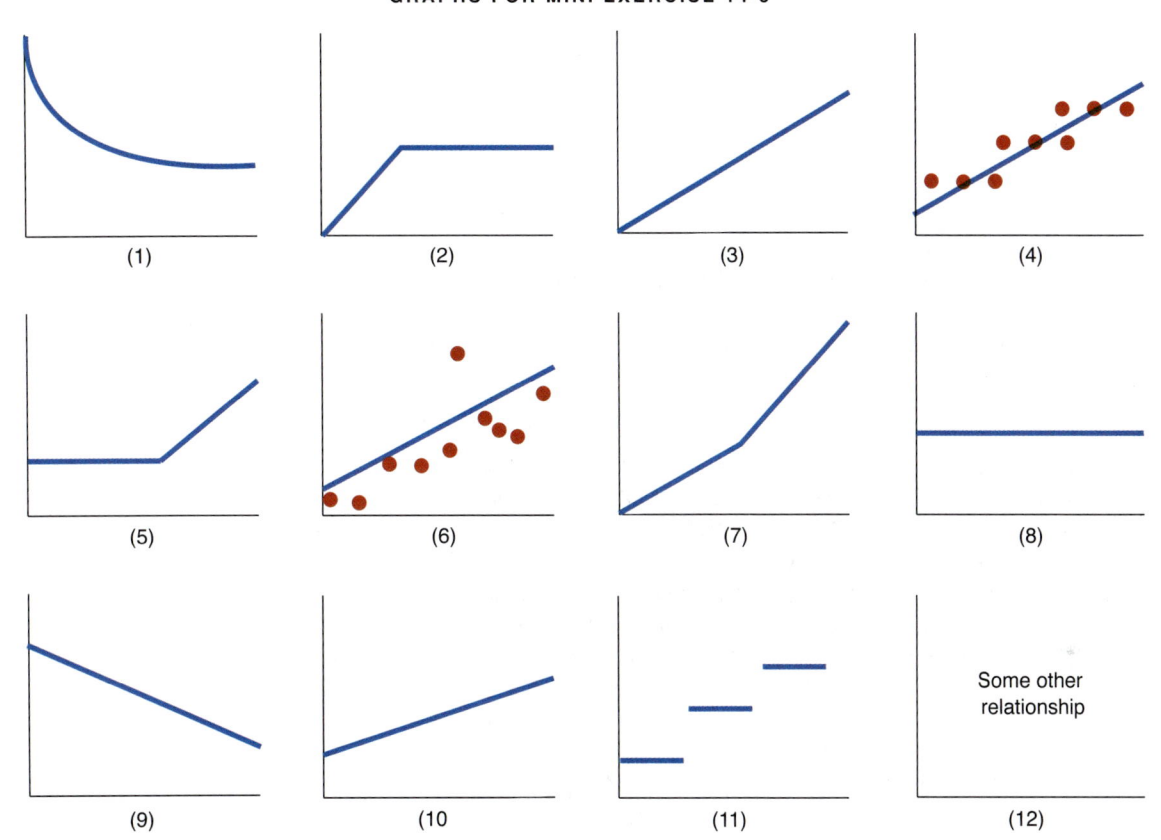

(1) (2) (3) (4)
(5) (6) (7) (8)
(9) (10) (11) (12) Some other relationship

M14-14. Classifying Cost Behavior using Data Visualizations   **LO14-1, 2, 3**

For each of the graphs displayed following this problem, select the most appropriate cost behavior pattern where the lines represent the cost behavior pattern, the vertical axis represents total costs, the horizontal axis represents total volume, and the dots represent actual costs. Each pattern may be used more than once.

a. An online movie streaming site where a flat fee is charged per month for standard movies and an additional $3 fee is charged for each premium movie.
b. Total selling and administrative costs
c. Total labor costs when employees are paid per unit produced
d. Total overtime premium paid to production employees
e. Average total cost per unit
f. Salaries of supervisors when each one can supervise a maximum of 10 employees
g. Total idle time costs when employees are paid for a minimum 40-hour week
h. Materials costs per unit
i. Total sales commissions
j. Electric power consumption in a restaurant
k. Total costs when high volumes of production require the use of overtime and obsolete equipment
l. A realistic linear approximation of actual costs
m. A linear cost estimation valid only within the relevant range

GRAPHS FOR MINI EXERCISE 14-4

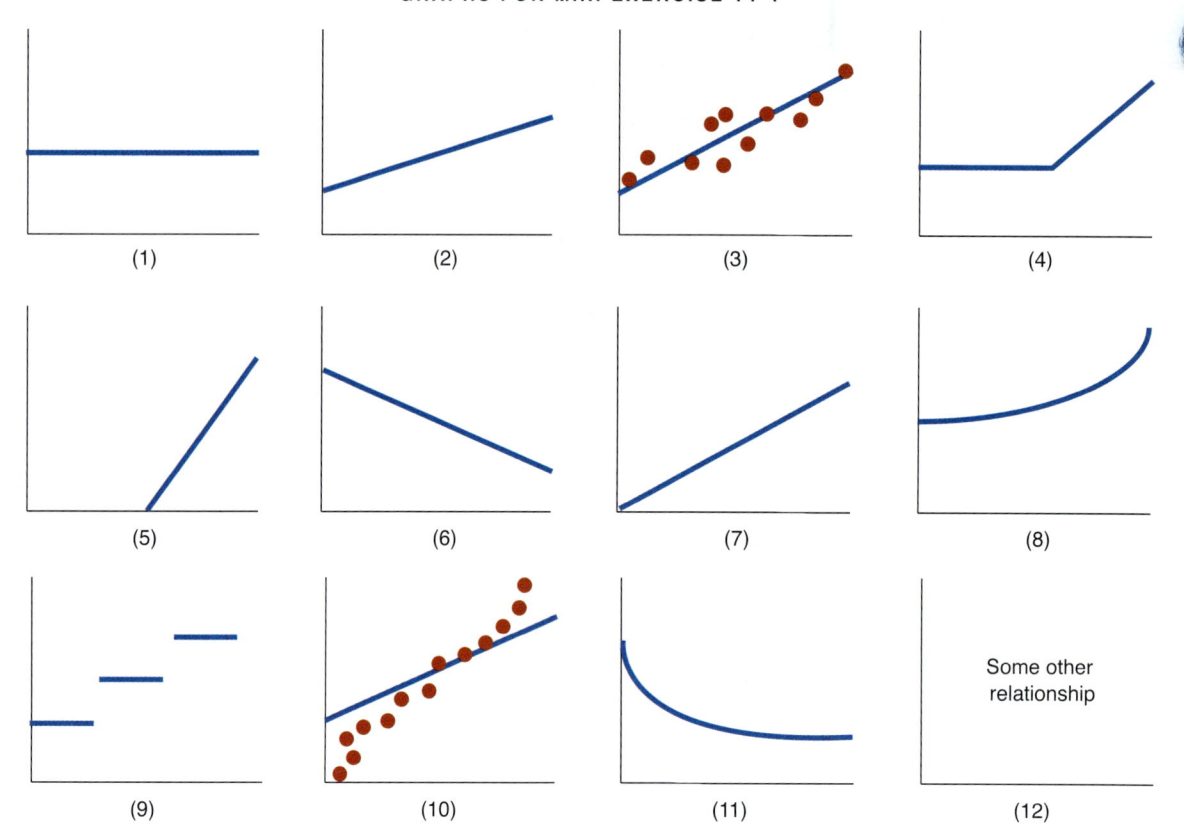

(1) (2) (3) (4)

(5) (6) (7) (8)

(9) (10) (11) (12) Some other relationship

LO14-4 **M14-15. Evaluating Selected Cost Driver**

Assume that a manufacturer of specialized machine parts developed the following total cost-estimating equation for manufacturing costs.

$$Y = \$8,000 + \$1,250 \text{ (actual units)}$$

a. What is total estimated manufacturing costs if 100 units are produced?
b. The company created a scatter diagram of actual units and actual manufacturing costs for the last six months. The company noticed a wide dispersion of observations around the cost-estimating line. What conclusion can be drawn from this analysis?
c. What is a possible reason for why the company changed its total cost-estimating equation to the following?

$$Y = \$8,000 + \$130 \text{ (labor hours)}$$

LO14-5 **M14-16. Classifying Costs**

Blaze Pizza

Consider the pizza chain **Blaze Pizza**. It custom builds and cooks each pizza to order. Items 1–5 represent cost activities associated with a particular store.

1. Pepperoni on the pizza
2. Wood to fuel the fire used to cook the pizzas (assume that ovens are maintained at the same temperature during business hours)
3. Insurance on the building
4. The labor costs for the employee building and cooking each pizza
5. The costs associated with employees taking pizza orders

Relative to the pizzas, classify each cost activity above as variable or fixed AND direct or indirect.

EXERCISES

E14-17. Identifying Cost Behavior — LO14-1, 2 — Subway

Assume a local **Subway** reported the following results for June and July.

	June	July
Sandwiches sold.	160,000	182,000
App and website expense	$ 5,000	$ 5,000
Cost of food sold.	192,000	218,400
Depreciation on equipment.	8,000	8,000
Miscellaneous.	1,500	1,600
Rent on building	4,500	4,500
Salaries expense	155,000	169,000
Supplies	1,250	880
Utilities	1,100	1,200
Total	$368,350	$408,580

REQUIRED

Identify each cost as being fixed, variable, or mixed.

E14-18. Computing Average Unit Costs — LO14-2 — McDonald's NYSE :: MCD

Assume the total monthly operating costs of a **McDonald's** restaurant are:

$$\$40{,}000 + \$0.75X$$

where

$$X = \text{Number of orders}$$

REQUIRED

a. Determine the average cost per order at each of the following monthly volumes: 1,000; 10,000; 50,000; 100,000.

b. Determine the monthly volume at which the average cost per order is $2.35.

E14-19. Automatic vs. Manual Processing — LO14-2 — Bartell's

Bartell's, a Seattle area drug store, operates an in-store printing service for customers with digital cameras. Assume that the current service, which requires employees to download photos from customer cameras, has monthly operating costs of $5,500 plus $0.15 per photo printed. Management is evaluating the desirability of acquiring a machine that will allow customers to download and make prints without employee assistance. If the machine is acquired, the monthly fixed costs will increase to $7,000 and the variable costs of printing a photo will decline to $0.05 per photo.

REQUIRED

a. Determine the total costs of printing 10,000 and 25,000 photos per month:
   1. With the current employee-assisted process
   2. With the proposed customer self-service process

b. Determine the monthly volume at which the proposed process becomes preferable to (i.e., costs less than) the current process.

E14-20. Automatic vs. Manual Processing — LO14-2 — Office Depot NASDAQ :: ODP

Assume **Office Depot** processes 2,500,000 photocopies per month at its service center. Approximately 50% of the photocopies require collating. Collating is currently performed by high school and college students who are paid $10 per hour. Each student collates an average of 5,000 copies per hour. Management is contemplating the lease of an automatic collating machine that has a monthly capacity of 6,000,000 photocopies, with lease and operating costs totaling $3,000, plus $0.05 per 1,000 units collated.

REQUIRED

a. Determine the total costs of collating 1,000,000 and 2,000,000 units per month:
   1. With student help
   2. With the collating machine

b. Determine the monthly volume at which the automatic process becomes preferable to (i.e., costs less than) the manual process.

LO14-3 E14-21. High-Low Cost Estimation

Yellow Corporation
NASDAQ :: YELL

Assume the local **Yellow Corporation** delivery service hub has the following information available about fleet miles and operating costs.

Year	Miles	Operating Costs
Year 1	695,000	$219,500
Year 2	855,000	267,500

REQUIRED

Use the high-low method to develop a cost-estimating equation for total annual operating costs.

LO14-3, 4 E14-22. Scatter Diagrams and High-Low Cost Estimation

Pearle Vision

Assume the local **Pearle Vision** has the following information on the number of sales orders received and order-processing costs.

Month	Sales Orders	Order-Processing Costs
1	3,300	$ 90,970
2	1,650	55,412
3	4,840	132,770
4	3,080	90,090
5	2,530	76,752
6	1,320	47,410
7	2,200	68,750

REQUIRED

a. Use information from the high- and low-volume months to develop a cost-estimating equation for monthly order-processing costs.

b. Plot the data on a scatter diagram. *Hint:* In Excel, highlight the data to be included in the chart. Open the insert tab and select the Scatter chart in the Charts group. Using the information from representative high- and low-volume months, develop a cost-estimating equation for monthly order-processing costs.

c. What factors might have caused the difference in the equations developed for requirements (*a*) and (*b*)?

LO14-3, 4 E14-23. Scatter Diagrams and High-Low Cost Estimation

Coles County Highway Department

From April 1 through October 31, **Coles County Highway Department** hires temporary employees to mow and clean the right-of-way along county roads. Assume that the County Road Commissioner has asked you to help her in determining the variable labor cost of mowing and cleaning a mile of road. The following information is available regarding current-year operations.

Month	Miles Mowed and Cleaned	Labor Costs
April	240	$6,800
May	305	7,680
June	325	8,310
July	275	7,200
August	220	6,550
September	200	5,760
October	75	4,960

REQUIRED

a. Use the information from the high- and low-volume months to develop a cost-estimating equation for monthly labor costs.

b. Plot the data on a scatter diagram. *Hint:* In Excel, highlight the data to be included in the chart. Open the insert tab and select the Scatter chart in the Charts group. Using the information from representative high- and low-volume months, use the high-low method to develop a cost-estimating equation for monthly labor costs.

c. What factors might have caused the difference in the equations developed for requirements (*a*) and (*b*)?

d. Adjust the equation developed in requirement (*b*) to incorporate the effect of an anticipated 5% increase in wages.

LO14-1, 2, 3 E14-24. Cost Behavior Analysis in a Restaurant: High-Low Cost Estimation

Potbelly's
NASDAQ :: PBPB

Assume a **Potbelly's** restaurant has the following information available regarding costs at representative levels of monthly sales (meals served).

	Monthly Sales in Units		
	5,000	7,000	10,000
Cost of food sold.	$ 7,500	$10,500	$15,000
Wages and fringe benefits	5,900	5,940	6,000
Fees paid delivery help.	6,000	8,400	12,000
Rent on building	3,500	3,500	3,500
Depreciation on equipment.	850	850	850
Utilities	600	640	700
Supplies (soap, floor wax, etc.).	400	480	600
Administrative costs	1,200	1,200	1,200
Total	$25,950	$31,510	$39,850

REQUIRED

a. Identify each cost as being variable, fixed, or mixed.
b. Use the high-low method to develop a schedule identifying the amount of each cost that is mixed or variable per unit. Total the amounts under each category to develop an equation for total monthly costs.
c. Predict total costs for a monthly sales volume of 8,500 units.

E14-25. Developing an Equation from Average Costs

Tucker Pup's Pet Resort offers dog boarding services in Chicago. Assume that in March, when dog-days occupancy was at an annual low of 150 days, the average cost per dog-day was $65. In July, when dog-days were at a capacity level of 600, the average cost per dog-day was $20.

REQUIRED

a. Develop an equation for monthly operating costs.
b. Determine the average boarding cost per dog-day at an annual volume of 4,500 dog-days.

E14-26. Pricing Products

Referring to E14-25 to answer the following questions.

REQUIRED

a. What is the minimum price for boarding services where the company would not be worse off?
b. What factors would you consider in setting a price for boarding services?

E14-27. Selecting an Independent Variable: Scatter Diagrams

Brenthaven produces protective cases for mobile technology. The cases are sold internationally, online, and through retail partners. Presented is hypothetical information on production costs and inventory changes for five recent months.

	January	February	March	April	May
Finished goods inventory in units:					
Beginning	20,000	30,000	20,000	5,000	35,000
Manufactured	35,000	45,000	40,000	50,000	60,000
Available	55,000	75,000	60,000	55,000	95,000
Sold	(25,000)	(55,000)	(55,000)	(20,000)	(65,000)
Ending	30,000	20,000	5,000	35,000	30,000
Manufacturing costs	$525,000	$615,000	$550,000	$745,000	$800,000

REQUIRED

a. With the aid of scatter diagrams, determine whether units sold or units manufactured is a better predictor of manufacturing costs. *Hint:* In Excel, highlight the data to be included in the chart. Open the insert tab and select the Scatter chart in the Charts group.
b. Prepare an explanation for your answer to requirement (*a*).
c. Which independent variable, units sold or units manufactured, would be a better predictor of selling costs? Why?

E14-28. Classifying Costs and Decision-Making

In July, Carrie's Rock Walls Inc. completed several projects, one of which was a rock wall for city hall. Costs for the month of July for the company included the following.

	July
Salary of consultant who prepared proposals on all new projects	$4,000
Salary of the designer who prepares designs for all new projects	4,500
City permit for city hall project	40
Cost of brick and mortar for city hall project	6,000
Monthly depreciation on equipment used for project	1,000
Miscellaneous tools (shovel, chisel, etc.) used for projects	6,000
Miscellaneous supplies used during the month on projects	1,400
Salary of rock layer based on hours worked on project	4,500
Gas and maintenance expense on vehicles to transport heavy equipment	500
Rent on office space for designer, consultants, and other personnel	2,000

REQUIRED

a. Relative to the city hall project, classify each of the following costs as variable or fixed AND direct or indirect.
b. Would you recommend that the bid for the city hall job include, at a minimum, only the direct costs, in order for the company to be not worse off? How do the cost classifications impact the pricing decision?

PROBLEMS

LO14-2, 3, 4
Midnight Cookie Company

P14-29. High-Low and Scatter Diagrams with Implications for Regression

Midnight Cookie Company produces and delivers gourmet cookies and ice cream until 1:30 a.m. from its three Seattle area locations. Presented is hypothetical monthly cost and sales information for cookies at one of Midnight's locations.

Month	Sales (Dozens)	Total Costs
January	6,800	$30,650
February	7,800	35,336
March	5,500	29,700
April	1,000	25,000
May	6,100	30,600
June	4,500	28,670

REQUIRED

a. Using the high-low method, develop a cost-estimating equation for total monthly costs.
b. Develop a scatter diagram of all observations for the cookie shop. Select representative high and low values and develop a second cost-estimating equation.
c. Which is a better predictor of future costs? Why?
d. If you decided to develop a cost-estimating equation using least-squares regression analysis, should you include all the observations? Why or why not?
e. Mention two reasons that the least-squares regression analysis is superior to the high-low and scatter diagram methods of cost estimation.

LO14-2, 3, 4, 5
Newman's Own
CT&DM

P14-30. Impact of Investment on Cost-Estimating Equation

Newman's Own manufactures a variety of specialty salad dressings. Assume the following represents general manufacturing costs (manufacturing overhead) for the last twelve months of the year at one production site.

	Total Cases Produced	Total Manufacturing Overhead
January	2,800	$186,000
February	2,700	179,000
March	2,900	192,500
April	3,300	218,500
May	3,200	212,000
June	3,100	206,000
July	2,700	179,500
August	3,100	205,500
September	2,800	186,000
October	2,200	147,000
November	2,700	178,500
December	2,800	186,000

REQUIRED
a. Use the information from the high- and low-volume months to develop a cost-estimating equation for monthly manufacturing costs.
b. What is the average cost per unit on the high- and low-volume month. What causes the difference (if any)?
c. The company plans a significant investment in new equipment next year that will increase capacity from 3,500 cases to 6,000 cases per month. As a result, fixed costs will increase to $20,000 per month. Additionally, the company expects (1) unit variable direct materials to increase by 10% due to rising prices, (2) unit variable direct labor costs to decrease by 30% due to increased automation and (3) unit variable manufacturing overhead costs to remain unchanged. Assume that for the last 12 months, variable costs were made up of following components: direct material (20%), direct labor (50%), and manufacturing overhead (30%).
   1. Estimate costs for a month using the estimating equation from part (a) at a production level of 6,000 cases.
   2. Estimate costs for a month applying the changes in costs described above at a production level of 6,000 cases.
d. Determine the difference between total manufacturing costs and average cost per unit using the original and revised estimating equations from part c. What caused the difference in the results?
e. Other than the cost updates described in part c, what other issue(s) cause the original estimating equation to be inaccurate to predict costs in the following year?

P14-31. Impact of an Unexpected Volume Change on Estimated Costs   LO14-2, 3, 4

Harley-Davidson operates a business segment where it designs, engineers, and manufacturers motorcycles. Assume that monthly overhead costs for one of its plants is estimated by the following cost-estimating equation.

Harley-Davidson
NYSE :: HOG

$$Y = \$325{,}000 + \$215 \text{ (Machine hours)}$$

REQUIRED
a. Compute total monthly manufacturing overhead costs at a level of 1,000 machine hours.
b. What type of cost is overhead: direct or indirect and fixed, variable, or mixed?
c. What would make machine hours a preferable cost driver to labor hours?
d. Assume that an unexpected slow-down in sales caused manufacturing to slow. This caused machine hours to drop by 10%. What is the new estimate of total monthly overhead costs?
e. Assume that the company used average cost per machine hour to estimate manufacturing overhead costs. If the company used the average cost per machine hour calculated from the original cost-estimating equation, what would total manufacturing overhead costs be at a level of 900 machine hours? Why is this amount different from the answer in part d? Which answer is more accurate?

CASES AND PROJECTS

C14-32. Significance of High R^2   LO14-4

Drew Conner had always been suspicious of "newfangled mathematical stuff," and the most recent suggestion of his new assistant merely confirmed his belief that schools are putting a lot of useless junk in students' heads. It seems that after an extensive analysis of historical data, the assistant suggested that the number of pounds of scrap was the best basis for predicting manufacturing overhead. In response to Mr. Conner's rage, the slightly intimidated assistant indicated that of the 35 equations he tried, pounds of scrap had the highest coefficient of determination with manufacturing overhead.

REQUIRED
Comment on Conner's reaction. Is it justified? Is it likely that the number of pounds of scrap is a good basis for predicting manufacturing overhead? Is it a feasible basis for predicting manufacturing overhead?

C14-33. Estimating Machine Repair Costs   LO14-3

In an attempt to determine the best basis for predicting machine repair costs, the production supervisor accumulated daily information on these costs and production over a one-month period. Applying simple regression analysis to the data, she obtained the following estimating equation:

$$Y = \$800 - \$2.60X$$

where

Y = total daily machine repair costs
X = daily production in units

Because of the negative relationship between repair costs and production, she was somewhat skeptical of the results, even though the R^2 was a respectable 0.765.

REQUIRED

a. What is the most likely explanation of the negative variable costs?
b. Suggest an alternative procedure for estimating machine repair costs that might prove more useful in decision-making.

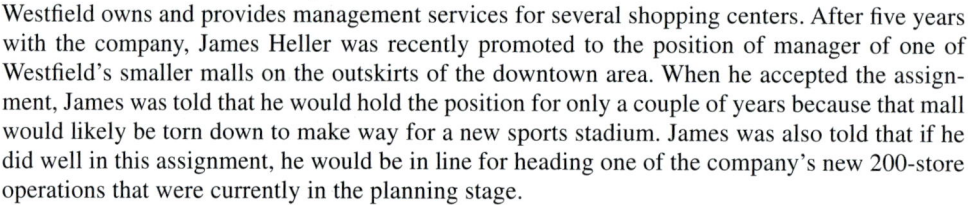

LO14-4 **C14-34. Ethical Problem Uncovered by Cost Estimation**

Westfield owns and provides management services for several shopping centers. After five years with the company, James Heller was recently promoted to the position of manager of one of Westfield's smaller malls on the outskirts of the downtown area. When he accepted the assignment, James was told that he would hold the position for only a couple of years because that mall would likely be torn down to make way for a new sports stadium. James was also told that if he did well in this assignment, he would be in line for heading one of the company's new 200-store operations that were currently in the planning stage.

While reviewing the mall's financial records for the past few years, James observed that last year's oil consumption was up by 8%, even though the number of heating degree days was down by 4%. Somewhat curious, James uncovered the following information:

- The mall is heated by forced-air oil heat. The furnace is five years old and has been well maintained.
- Fuel oil is kept in four 5,000-gallon underground oil tanks. The oil tanks were installed 25 years ago.
- Replacing the tanks would cost $80,000. If pollution was found, cleanup costs could go as high as $2,000,000, depending on how much oil had leaked into the ground and how far it had spread.
- Replacing the tanks would add more congestion to the mall's parking situation.

REQUIRED

What should James do? Explain.

LO14-5 **C14-35. Activity Cost Drivers and Cost Estimation**

Market Street Soup Company produces ten varieties of soup in large vats, several thousand gallons at a time. The soup is distributed to several categories of customers. Some soup is packaged in large containers and sold to college and university food services. Some is packaged in half-gallon or smaller containers and sold through wholesale distributors to grocery stores. Finally, some is packaged in a variety of individual servings and sold directly to the public from trucks owned and operated by Market Street Soup Company. Management has always assumed that costs fluctuated with the volume of soup, and cost-estimating equations have been based on the following cost function:

$$\text{Estimated costs} = \text{Fixed costs} + \text{Variable costs per gallon} \times \text{Production in gallons}$$

Lately, however, this equation has not been a very accurate predictor of total costs. At the same time, management has noticed that the volumes and varieties of soup sold through the three distinct distribution channels have fluctuated from month to month.

REQUIRED

a. What *relevant* major assumption is inherent in the cost-estimating equation currently used by Market Street Soup Company?
b. Provide examples of direct costs, indirect costs, fixed costs, and variable costs for Market Street Soup Company.
c. Suppose you are trying to estimate the total product cost of the half-gallon container of soup. Is it important to understand the direct and indirect costs in addition to the fixed and variable costs? Why?

SOLUTIONS TO REVIEW PROBLEMS

Review 14-1—Solution

Transaction expense is a variable cost. As sales volume increases, transaction expense also increases; this cost changes proportionately with revenue.

Product manager's salary is a fixed cost. Because the salary is constant and does not fluctuate with sales volume, it is a fixed cost.

Customer support salary cost is a step cost. For a given level of sales (and customers), this resource is offered. Within a given range, the resources remains constant. However, if demand surges, the customer support department will add temporary positions in incremental segments.

The salary cost of the sales team is a mixed cost. These professionals are offered a base salary (fixed), as well as a salary component that is tied to sales (variable).

The salary of the product development manager is a fixed cost because the salary does not fluctuate with sales volume.

Review 14-2—Solution

1. Total costs = $170,000 + ($0.01 × Sales dollars)
2. Total costs = $170,000 + ($0.01 × Sales dollars)
    a. $170,000 + ($0.01 × $10 million) = $270,000
       $270,000 / $10 million = $0.027 per sales dollar
    b. $170,000 + ($0.01 × $30 million) = $470,000
       $470,000 / $30 million = $0.016 per sales dollar
    c. $170,000 + ($0.01 × $100 million) = $1,170,000
       $1,170,000 / $100 million = $0.012 per sales dollar
3. $0.015 − $0.01 = $0.005 fixed cost per sales dollar
   $170,000 / $0.005 = $34 million
4. If the cost structures are set equal to each other, to find the sales dollars at which they yield identical costs, we can determine the point at which the current cost structure becomes preferable.

   $0.025X = \$170,000 + 0.01X$
   $0.015X = \$170,000$
   $X = \$11,333,333$

   Beyond sales dollars of $11,333,333, the current cost structure is preferred.

Review 14-3—Solution

(Amounts are in $ thousands, except for per unit amounts)

Part One

a. (1) Transaction processing cost is a variable cost because the cost per unit is the same at both activity levels:
   April: $1,575 Transaction processing cost / $2,100 Sales dollars processed = $0.75
   May: $2,025 Transaction processing cost / $2,700 Sales dollars processed = $0.75

   Cost-estimating equation:

   $$Y = \$0.75X$$

   where X = Sales dollars processed

   (2) Wages and salaries is a mixed cost as shown using the high-low method.

   $$\text{Variable cost per unit} = \frac{\$1,675 - \$1,525}{\$2,700 - \$2,100}$$
   $$= \$0.25$$
   Total fixed cost = $1,525 total cost − ($0.25 × $2,100) variable cost
   $$= \$1,000$$

   Cost-estimating equation:

   $$Y = \$1,000 + \$0.25X$$

   where X = Sales dollars processed

   (3) Building rent is classified as a fixed cost.

   Total fixed cost = $1,500

   Cost-estimating equation:

   $$Y = \$1,500$$

   (4) Total monthly costs follow a mixed cost behavior pattern. Hence, the high-low method is used to estimate the variable and fixed cost components.

   $$\text{Variable cost per unit} = \frac{\$6,556 - \$5,848}{\$2,700 - \$2,100}$$
   $$= \$1.18$$
   Total fixed cost = $5,848 − ($1.18 × $2,100)
   $$= \$3,370$$

Cost-estimating equation:

$$Y = \$3,370 + \$1.18X$$

where X = Sales dollars processed

b. and c.

Sales Dollars Processed	Total Costs	Average Cost per Sales Dollar Processed
$1,000	$3,370 + ($1.18 × $1,000) = $4,550	$\dfrac{\$4,550}{\$1,000}$ = $4.550
$2,000	$3,370 + ($1.18 × $2,000) = $5,730	$\dfrac{\$5,730}{\$2,000}$ = $2.865

The average costs differ at $1,000 and $2,000 sales dollars processed because the fixed costs are being spread over a different amount of sales dollars processed. The larger the sales dollars processed, the smaller the average fixed cost per unit.

Part Two

a.

Wages and Salaries

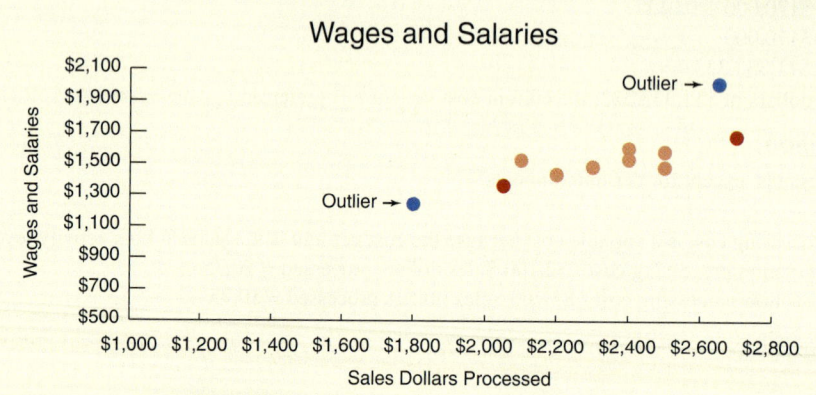

(Scatter plot: Wages and Salaries vs. Sales Dollars Processed. Outliers identified at approximately ($1,800, $1,250) and ($2,600, $1,975).)

Outliers: June and December

b. Representative high and low months are May and March:

$$\text{Variable cost per unit} = \frac{\text{Difference in total costs}}{\text{Difference in dollars processed}} = \frac{(\$1,675 - \$1,363)}{(\$2,700 - \$2,050)} = \$0.48$$

$0.48 × $2,700 = $1,296 total variable costs

$$\underset{\text{(total costs)}}{\$1,675} - \underset{\text{(variable costs)}}{\$1,296} = \$379 \text{ fixed costs}$$

Cost estimating equation:

$$Y = \$379 + \$0.48X$$

c. Number of units processed in June was much lower than other months. A possible reason is a full or partial shut-down, perhaps for a security breach.

Salaries and wages expense were high in the month of December. A possible reason is that annual bonuses were paid in December.

Part Three

a. and *b.*

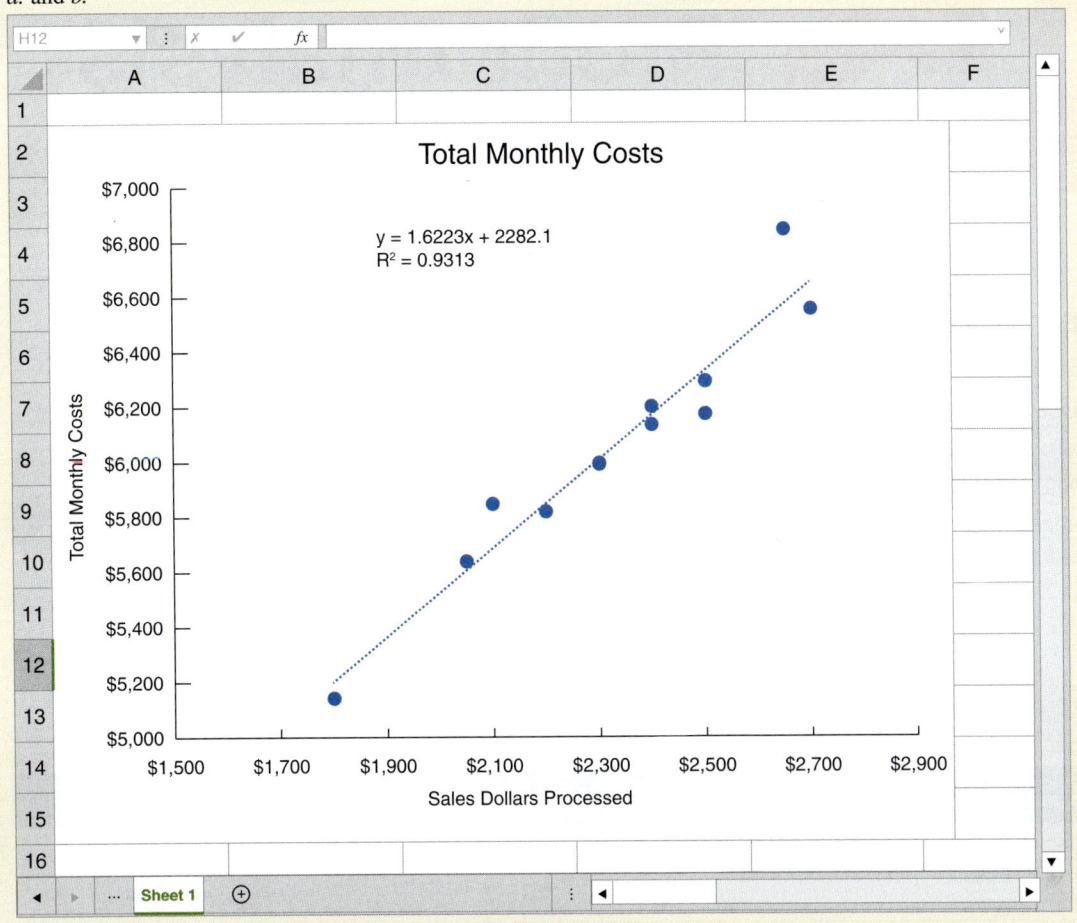

Total Monthly Costs scatter plot with trendline: y = 1.6223x + 2282.1; R² = 0.9313. X-axis: Sales Dollars Processed ($1,500–$2,900). Y-axis: Total Monthly Costs ($5,000–$7,000).

$Y = \$2{,}282.1 + \$1.6223$ (Sales dollars processed); $R^2 = 0.9313$

c. The R^2 indicates that 93% of the variation in monthly costs is explained by sales dollars processed.

d. $Y = \$2{,}282.1 + \$1.6223\ (\$2{,}850) = \$6{,}905.66$

Review 14-4—Solution

a. Some common drivers for stating volume of activity at a manufacturing and processing plant might include direct labor hours, machine hours, units of material produced, and units of finished product. The selection of the most appropriate basis requires judgment and professional experience. The relationship between the cost driver and the cost must seem logical and the data must be available.

b.
1. More desirable
2. Less desirable
3. Less desirable
4. Less desirable
5. More desirable
6. More desirable

Review 14-5—Solution

1. Fixed and Indirect
2. Fixed and Direct
3. Variable and Indirect
4. Variable and Direct

Chapter 15: Cost-Volume-Profit Analysis and Planning

LEARNING OBJECTIVES

LO15-1 Use the profit equation to predict profit. (p. 15-3)

LO15-2 Prepare a contribution income statement. (p. 15-6)

LO15-3 Apply cost-volume-profit analysis to find a break-even point and begin profit planning. (p. 15-9)

LO15-4 Determine the break-even point of a multiple-product firm. (p. 15-15)

LO15-5 Apply the operating leverage ratio to assess opportunities for profit and the risks of loss. (p. 15-19)

LO15-6 Apply cost-volume-profit analysis considering the income tax effect (Appendix 15A). (p. 15-21)

Road Map

LO	Learning Objective / Topics	Page	eLecture	Review	Assignments
LO15-1	**Use the profit equation to predict profit.** CVP Analysis :: Profit Equation :: Profit :: Variable Costs :: Fixed Costs :: Multiple Scenarios	15-3	e15-1	R15-1	M15-11, E15-22, P15-35, P15-45, DA15-2, DA15-3
LO15-2	**Prepare a contribution income statement.** Contribution Income Statement :: Functional Income Statement :: Contribution Margin :: Unit Contribution :: Contribution Margin Ratio :: Sensitivity Analysis	15-6	e15-2	R15-2	M15-12, M15-13, E15-23, E15-26, E15-28, E15-30, E15-32, E15-33, P15-36, C15-46, C15-47
LO15-3	**Apply cost-volume-profit analysis to find a break-even point and begin profit planning.** Break-Even :: Margin of Safety :: Target Profit :: Cost-Volume-Profit Graph :: Profit-Volume Graph :: CVP Key Assumptions	15-9	e15-3	R15-3	M15-14, M15-15, M15-16, M15-17, M15-18, E15-23, E15-24, E15-25, E15-27, E15-28, E15-29, E15-30, E15-32, E15-33, E15-34, P15-35, P15-36, P15-37, P15-38, P15-39, P15-40, P15-41, P15-42, P15-44, P15-45, C15-47, DA15-2, DA15-3
LO15-4	**Determine the break-even point of a multiple-product firm.** Sales Mix Analysis :: Multiple Products :: Break-Even :: Variable Cost Ratio	15-15	e15-4	R15-4	M15-19, E15-31, P15-40, P15-41, P15-42, DA15-1
LO15-5	**Apply the operating leverage ratio to assess opportunities for profit and the risks of loss.** Operating Leverage :: Operating Leverage Ratio :: Sensitivity Analysis	15-19	e15-5	R15-5	M15-20, E15-29, E15-30, P15-36
LO15-6	**Apply cost-volume-profit analysis considering the income tax effect. (Appendix 15A)** After-Tax Profit :: Before-Tax Profit :: Income Tax :: Target After-Tax Profit	15-21	e15-6	R15-6	M15-21, E15-26, P15-43, P15-44

RAZOR USA, LLC

www.razor.com

Since its founding in 2000, **Razor USA, LLC** has "reinvented the wheel." Razor designs, manufactures, and sells a wide array of rideable devices ranging from manual scooters to hoverboards and turbo-powered heel wheels. You can also find Razor e-scooters available to rent in many cities, offering another form of transportation. Since 2000, Razor has sold more than 50 million scooters. The company is viewed as the global expert in scooter innovation.

Razor's creativity and innovation make it well situated for continued success. However, its financial success depends on how it understands its cost structure when making pricing decisions. How much should it charge for its products? How much should it charge for its rentals? How many scooters must Razor sell to break-even in a new product category? What sales dollars must it record to break even as a company? How many hoverboards must it sell to reach a target profit? These are questions that managers within Razor, typically product managers, must answer.

Cost-Volume-Profit (CVP) Analysis involves examining the relations among sales volume, total cost, total revenue, and profit for a time period. Performing CVP analysis requires an understanding of selling prices and the cost structure (i.e., the variable and fixed costs). CVP analysis is widely used to help managers make better decisions regarding existing or proposed products or services. For example, when introducing a new product, the product manager might perform a CVP analysis to assess the probability of hitting a target profit number.

If Razor is to accomplish its goals in the long-run, it must be profitable (i.e., total revenues must exceed total costs). As with all businesses, Razor's manufacturing processes incur materials, labor, and overhead costs. The price of these inputs, as well as the sales price of the products, change over time. By breaking down Razor's costs into its variable and fixed components, the company's managers can perform CVP analyses to determine where to direct their future efforts. In fact, Razor can utilize the tools presented in this chapter to determine how much revenue it must generate to achieve a desired profit. It can also use these tools to perform sensitivity analyses to determine the profitability effect of changes in specific costs, such as materials.

Source: www.razor.com

© Cambridge Business Publishers

CHAPTER ORGANIZATION

Cost-Volume-Profit Analysis and Planning

Cost-Volume-Profit Analysis	Contribution Income Statement	Break-Even Point and Profit Planning	Multiple-Product Cost-Volume-Profit Analysis	Analysis of Operating Leverage	Cost-Volume-Profit Analysis and Income Taxes
• Profit Equation • Multiple Scenarios Using the Profit Equation	• Contribution Income Statement • Analysis Using Contribution (Total, Unit, Ratio) Margin • Sensitivity Analysis	• Break-Even Point • Margin of Safety • Profit Planning • Cost-Volume-Profit Graph • Profit-Volume Graph • CVP Assumptions	• Sales Mix Analysis • Break-Even Point	• Operating Leverage Ratio • Sensitivity Analysis	• Sales at Target After-Tax Profit (Appendix 15A)

COST-VOLUME-PROFIT ANALYSIS

LO15-1 Use the profit equation to predict profit.

In the last chapter, we classified cost behavior as variable, fixed, or mixed. This classification was the basis for tools used to predict future costs at specific sales volume levels under normal operating conditions. In this chapter, we expand our focus beyond costs to include profitability. **Cost-volume-profit (CVP) analysis** is a technique used to examine the relationships among sales volume, total cost, total revenue, and profit for a time period (typically a quarter or year). With CVP analysis, volume refers to a single factor, such as unit sales or dollar sales, that is assumed to correlate with changes in revenue, cost, and profit.

Cost-volume-profit analysis is useful in the early stages of planning because it provides an easily understood framework for discussing planning issues and organizing relevant data. Suppose **Razor USA LLC** (Razor) plans to manufacture an updated electric scooter. The product manager will estimate the revenues and costs expected during the year. With this information, the product manager can assess whether Razor should initiate production and whether the price is adequate. CVP analysis is widely used by for-profit as well as not-for-profit organizations. It is equally applicable to service, merchandising, and manufacturing firms. We begin our analysis by expanding the cost-estimating equation to include profit.

Profit Equation

The profit associated with a product, service, or event is equal to the difference between total sales and total costs as follows.

$$\text{Profit} = \text{Total sales} - \text{Total costs}$$

Sales are a function of the unit selling price (also called selling price per unit) applied to unit sales volume. (For simplicity, other revenues are ignored.) Total costs for a time period are a function of total fixed costs for the period and the unit variable costs (also called variable cost per unit) applied to unit sales volume.

$$\text{Total sales} = \text{Selling price per unit} \times \text{Unit sales}$$

$$\text{Total costs} = \text{Fixed costs} + (\text{Variable cost per unit} \times \text{Unit sales})$$

The equation for profit can then be expanded to include the details of the total sales and total cost equations as follows.

$$\text{Profit} = (\text{Selling price per unit} \times \text{Unit sales}) - (\text{Fixed costs} + [\text{Variable cost per unit} \times \text{Unit sales}])$$

Using information on the selling price, fixed costs per period, and variable cost per unit, this formula is used to calculate or predict profit at any specified sales level.

To illustrate, assume that **Razor**'s only product is a standard kick scooter that it manufactures and sells to merchandisers at $60 per completed scooter. Razor does not maintain inventories of raw materials or finished goods. Instead, newly purchased raw materials are delivered directly to the factory, and finished goods are loaded directly onto trucks for shipment. Razor's variable and fixed costs follow.

1. **Direct materials** refer to the cost of the primary raw materials converted into finished goods. Because the consumption of raw materials increases as the quantity of goods produced and sold increases, *direct materials represents a variable cost.* Razor's raw materials consist primarily of nuts and bolts, rubber wheels, bearings, steel frames, and packaging materials. Assume that all together, these costs are $20 per completed scooter.
2. **Direct labor** refers to wages earned by production employees for the time they spend working on the conversion of raw materials into finished goods. Based on Razor's manufacturing procedures, *direct labor represents a variable cost.* Further assume these costs are $10 per completed scooter.
3. **Variable manufacturing overhead** includes all other variable costs, i.e., indirect costs, associated with converting raw materials into finished goods. Assume Razor's variable manufacturing overhead costs include the costs of lubricants for cutting and packaging machines, electricity to operate these machines, and the cost to move materials between receiving and shipping. These indirect costs are considered variable because they change proportionately with sales volume. These costs are $3 per completed scooter.
4. **Variable selling and administrative costs** include all variable costs other than those directly associated with converting raw materials into finished goods. Assume at Razor, these costs include sales commissions and transportation of finished scooters to merchandisers. These costs are $5 per completed scooter.
5. **Fixed manufacturing overhead** includes all fixed costs associated with converting raw materials into finished goods. Suppose Razor's fixed manufacturing costs include the depreciation, property taxes, and insurance on buildings and machines used for manufacturing, the salaries of manufacturing supervisors, and the fixed portion of electricity used to light the factory. Assume these costs are $35,000 per month.
6. **Fixed selling and administrative costs** include all fixed costs other than those directly associated with converting raw materials into finished goods. These costs include the salaries of Razor's divisional manager and many other staff personnel such as accounting and marketing. Also included are depreciation, property taxes, insurance on facilities used for administrative purposes, and any related utilities costs. Assume these costs are $15,000 per month.

Razor's hypothetical variable and fixed costs are summarized here.

Variable Cost per Scooter			Fixed Costs per Month	
Manufacturing			Manufacturing overhead	$35,000
Direct materials	$20		Selling and administrative	15,000
Direct labor	10		Total	$50,000
Manufacturing overhead	3	$33		
Selling and administrative		5		
Total		$38		

The cost estimation techniques discussed in Chapter 14 can be used to determine many detailed costs. Least-squares regression, for example, might be used to determine the variable and monthly fixed amount of electricity used in manufacturing. Assume Razor manufactures and sells a single product on a continuous basis with all sales to merchandisers under standing contracts. In this case, it is reasonable to assume that in the short run, Razor's total monthly costs respond to the number of scooters sold. Combining all this information, Razor's profit equation is assumed to be:

Profit = ($60 × Number of scooters sold) − ($50,000 + [$38 × Number of scooters sold])

Using this equation, Razor's profit at a volume of 5,400 units is $68,800.

$$\text{Profit} = (\$60 \times 5,400) - (\$50,000 + [\$38 \times 5,400])$$
$$= \$324,000 - (\$50,000 + \$205,200)$$
$$= \$68,800$$

With this basic profit equation, we can estimate profits at different levels of sales volume within a relevant range. What profit will Razor earn at an annual sales volume of 7,000 scooters instead of 5,400 scooters? We can also adjust the assumptions in the profit equation and determine the effect on profit. How will profits change if the selling price of scooters increases by 10% but volume decreases by 5%? Or, how will profits change if the company's cost structure results in an increase in fixed costs and a decrease in variable cost per unit?

Using the Profit Equation in Multiple Scenarios

In our Razor example, we estimated a profit equation based on a single set of revenue and cost assumptions. Next, let's review an example where multiple scenarios are required to provide a more complete picture for the users of the financial information. **Nikola Corporation**'s vision as stated in a recent 10-K is to be the zero-emissions transportation industry leader. Nikola's business units consist of Truck (includes battery electric and hydrogen fuel cell electric trucks) and Energy (includes hydrogen fueling and charging support). As of the publishing date of this text, Nicola has yet to report revenue, but did announce that it had signed purchased orders for a number of zero-emission electric trucks.

The company's journey to market introduction, however, has been marked with irregularities. The company was charged by the SEC (U.S. Securities and Exchange Commission), for making misrepresentations. The SEC outlined a number of false and misleading statements by both Trevor Milton, CEO and then Executive Chairman of the company. One particular disclosure about the Badger (an electric pickup truck) was outlined in the SEC complaint (emphasis added).[1]

The General Motors Partnership. Nikola misled investors by failing to disclose the potential economic impact of the proposed strategic partnership between Nikola and General Motors, pursuant to which General Motors would produce the Badger. In a press release Nikola claimed that it "anticipates saving over $4 billion in battery and powertrain costs over 10 years and over $1 billion in engineering and validation costs." *This claim was misleading because, although Nikola touted potential cost savings, Nikola failed to disclose that unless the market could support a "premium" MSRP price for the Badger, Nikola's internal projections showed that the entire Badger program could potentially generate a net loss of $3.1 billion over six years and threaten Nikola's solvency.* A Nikola executive prepared these internal projections and provided them to Nikola's senior executives and its Board, noting that the projected unit economics from both the "premium" and "market based" pricing approaches. Nevertheless, Nikola went on to tout the discrete potential cost savings associated with one aspect of the program without disclosing the program's overall potential financial impact.

The company claims were based on projections using a technique similar to the profit equation described in this section. So, what went wrong? It appears that the best case scenario estimated the selling price of the trucks in the premium/luxury category. However, if the trucks did not warrant the high MSRP, a significant loss over a six-year period was likely. The company did not disclose the risk of an overall loss under this scenario and therefore was charged with misleading investors.

The cost structure (unit selling price, unit variable cost, and fixed costs) are provided in the examples in this chapter. However, real world examples of forecasting are based on historical information and assumptions about how items will change in the future. It is especially important to understand the assumptions used in start-up companies and with new products that have no historical data to

---

[1] Source: U.S. Securities and Exchange Commission: *In the Matter of Nikola Corporation* (respondent); Administrative Proceeding File No. 3-20687, December 21, 2021.

rely on. Providing different scenarios helps management make informed decisions about the data. For example, developing two profit equations based on two different selling price scenarios provides the users of the information with a best case and worst case scenario. While this may have happened internally at Nikola, the information that was shared with the public did not provide that transparency.

Determining the Profit Equation

LO15-1 **Review 15-1**

Segway manufactures the Ninebot Gokart Pro which it currently sells for $2,000. However, Segway is considering reducing the price to $1,400 in order to spur demand. To minimize inventory, all raw materials are delivered to the factory floor. No raw materials or finished goods inventory is held by the company. Suppose that the Gokart Pro is the only product produced in one factory with the following variable and fixed costs.

Variable Cost per Unit			Fixed Costs per Month	
Manufacturing			Manufacturing overhead............	$ 200,000
Direct materials...............	$125		Selling and administrative..........	800,000
Direct labor...................	50		Total	$1,000,000
Manufacturing overhead........	250	$425		
Selling and administrative........		100		
Total		$525		

Required

a. Determine Segway's profit equation using (1) the current price and (2) the proposed price.
b. Calculate Segway's proposed profit at a volume of 6,200 Gokarts using (1) the current price and (2) the proposed price. Calculate the difference in profits.
c. Assume instead that sales volume is expected to increase by 15% after the price drop. How do your answers to part b change?
d. What information would you want to collect before determining whether or not to recommend a price adjustment?

Solution on p. 15-38.

CONTRIBUTION INCOME STATEMENT

To provide more detailed information on anticipated or actual financial results at a particular sales volume, a **contribution income statement** is often prepared. In a **contribution income statement**, costs are classified according to behavior as variable or fixed, and the **contribution margin** (the difference between total revenues and total variable costs) that goes toward covering fixed costs and providing a profit is emphasized.

LO15-2 Prepare a contribution income statement

Razor's monthly contribution income statement at a volume of 5,400 scooters is shown in **Exhibit 15.1**. Sales ($324,000), variable costs ($205,200), fixed costs ($50,000), and profit ($68,800) amounts match the amounts shown previously in the profit equation. Notice however, that the statement highlights contribution margin, the difference between sales and variable costs of $118,800.

Contribution Income Statement
Sales
(Variable Costs)
Contribution margin
(Fixed costs)
Profit

To the right of Razor's contribution income statement is its functional income statement. A **functional income statement** classifies costs according to function such as manufacturing, selling, and administrative. This is the type of income statement typically included in corporate annual reports. The problem with a functional income statement is the difficulty of relating it to the profit formula in which costs are classified according to behavior rather than function. The relationship among sales volume, cost, and profit is not readily apparent in a functional income statement. This makes it difficult for users to interpret how various changes will impact profitability. Consequently, *we emphasize contribution income statements because they provide more useful information to internal decision makers.*

EXHIBIT 15.1 — Contribution Income Statement vs. Functional Income Statement

RAZOR COMPANY
Contribution Income Statement
For a Monthly Volume of 5,400 Scooters

Sales (5,400 × $60)		$324,000
Less variable costs		
Direct materials (5,400 × $20)	$108,000	
Direct labor (5,400 × $10)	54,000	
Manufacturing overhead (5,400 × $3)	16,200	
Selling and administrative (5,400 × $5)	27,000	(205,200)
Contribution margin		**118,800**
Less fixed costs		
Manufacturing overhead	35,000	
Selling and administrative	15,000	(50,000)
Profit		$ 68,800

RAZOR COMPANY
Functional Income Statement
For a Monthly Volume of 5,400 Scooters

Sales		$324,000
Less cost of goods sold		
Direct materials	$108,000	
Direct labor	54,000	
Variable manufacturing overhead	16,200	
Fixed manufacturing overhead	35,000	(213,200)
Gross profit		110,800
Less other expenses		
Variable selling and administrative	27,000	
Fixed selling and administrative	15,000	(42,000)
Profit		$ 68,800

Critical Thinking & Decision-Making

Suppose the Razor child scooter produces a negative contribution margin. Would you recommend dropping the product? What would you consider in this decision?

The quick answer might be to drop the child scooter. If the contribution margin is negative, the product does not contribute to covering fixed costs. Additionally, the more scooters sold, the larger the loss. Managers might consider how many customers of child scooters become brand loyal and trade-up scooters over time. If this is a large market, it might be beneficial to take a loss on the child scooter knowing that the customers will transition into lifetime customers of highly profitable products.

Analysis Using Contribution Margin (Total, Unit, Ratio)

While the contribution income statement (shown in **Exhibit 15.1**) presents information on total sales revenue, total variable costs, and so forth, it is sometimes useful to present information on a per-unit or portion of sales basis. The following schedule shows contribution margin on a per-unit basis and as a percentage of total sales for Razor based on a monthly predicted sales volume of 5,400 scooters.

	Total	Per Unit	Ratio to Sales
Sales (5,400 units)	$324,000	$60†	1.0000*
Variable costs	(205,200)	38‡	0.6333**
Contribution margin	118,800	$22	0.3667
Fixed costs	(50,000)		
Profit	$ 68,800		

* $324,000/$324,000 = 1.0000   ** $205,200/$324,000 = 0.6333 (rounded)   †$324,000/5,400 = $60   ‡$205,200/5,400 = $38

Total contribution margin is calculated as:

$$\text{Contribution margin} = \text{Sales} - \text{Variable costs}$$
$$= \$324{,}000 - \$205{,}200$$
$$= \$118{,}800$$

Based on sales of 5,400 scooters, Razor earns $324,000 and incurs $205,200 in variable costs. This means that there is $118,800 left to cover fixed costs and to contribute toward profit. The company can use this information, combined with its fixed costs, to project whether it will break-even or earn a profit. Contribution margin is a tool that is frequently used by companies in short-term decision-making. Remember, cost structure is stable in the short-term. However, in the long-term, the cost structure (i.e., the amount of fixed and variable costs) can be altered.

Sensitivity Analysis

Per-unit information assists in short-range planning. The **unit contribution margin** (also called the contribution margin per unit) is the difference between the unit selling price and the unit variable cost. It is the amount, $22 in Razor's case, that each unit contributes toward covering fixed costs and earning a profit.

> Unit contribution margin = Selling price per unit − Variable cost per unit
> = $60 − $38
> = $22

The contribution margin is widely used in **sensitivity analysis** (the study of the responsiveness of a model to changes in one or more of its independent variables such as sales volume). Razor's income statement is an economic model of the firm, and the unit contribution margin indicates how sensitive Razor's income model is to changes in unit sales. In fact, an estimate of the change in profits due to a change in sales volume is readily determinable using the unit contribution margin. For example, *if Razor's sales increase by 100 scooters per month, what is the impact on monthly profits?*

> Change in unit sales × Unit contribution margin = Change in profit
> 100 scooters × $22 = $2,200 (profit increase)

There is no increase in fixed costs, so the new profit level becomes $71,000 ($68,800 + $2,200) per month.

When expressed as a ratio to sales, the sales margin is identified as the **contribution margin ratio**. It is the portion of each dollar of sales revenue that contributed toward covering fixed costs and earning a profit. In the abbreviated income statement above, the portion of each dollar of sales revenue that contributed toward covering fixed costs and earning a profit is 0.3667. This is Razor's assumed contribution margin ratio.

> Contribution margin ratio = Total contribution margin ÷ Sales
> = $118,800 ÷ $324,000
> = 0.3667

The contribution margin ratio can also be used in sensitivity analysis. An estimate of the change in profits due to a change in sales volume is readily determinable using the contribution margin ratio. For example, *if Razor's sales increase by $6,000 per month, what is the impact on monthly profits?*

> Change in sales dollars × Contribution margin ratio = Change in profit
> $6,000 × 0.3667 = $2,200 (profit increase)

The contribution margin ratio is especially useful in situations involving several products or when unit sales information is not available.

Overall, the contribution margin (total, unit, ratio) is a powerful tool that companies use in short-term decision-making. Contribution margin provides insights on the extent to which *projected* sales will cover fixed costs and contribute toward profit. Of course, companies can also estimate the exact point at which they will go from reporting a loss to earning a profit, which we discuss next.

Review 15-2 LO15-2 — Preparing a Contribution Income Statement

Assume **Segway** produces and sells Segway helmets for kids. Further assume Segway offered these helmets at a special price of $40 each. Variable and fixed costs follow.

Variable Cost per Helmet			Fixed Costs per Month	
Manufacturing			Manufacturing overhead...........	$15,000
Direct materials................	$15		Selling and administrative..........	10,000
Direct labor...................	3		Total............................	$25,000
Manufacturing overhead.........	10	$28		
Selling and administrative..........		2		
Total............................		$30		

Suppose in June, Segway produced and sold 3,000 helmets.

Required

Solution on p. 15-39.

a. Prepare a contribution income statement for June.
b. Calculate and explain the relevance of Segway's unit contribution margin and contribution margin ratio.

BREAK-EVEN POINT AND PROFIT PLANNING

LO15-3 Apply cost-volume-profit analysis to find a break-even point and begin profit planning.

The **break-even point** occurs at the unit or dollar sales volume when total revenues equal total costs. The break-even point is of great interest to management. Until break-even sales are reached, a product, service, event, or business segment operates at a loss. Beyond this point, profits are achieved. Also, management often wants to know the **margin of safety**, the amount by which actual or planned sales volume exceeds the break-even point. Other questions of interest include the probability of exceeding the break-even sales volume and the effect of some proposed change on the break-even point.

Determining Break-Even Point and Margin of Safety in Unit Sales

In determining the break-even point, the equation for total sales is set equal to the equation for total costs and then solved for the break-even unit sales volume. Using the general equations for total sales and total costs, the following results are obtained.

Total sales = Total costs
(Selling price per unit × Break-even unit sales) = Fixed costs + (Variable cost per unit × Break-even unit sales)

Solving for the break-even unit sales volume:

(Selling price per unit × Break-even unit sales) − (Variable cost per unit × Break-even unit sales) = Fixed costs
(Selling price per unit − Variable cost per unit) × Break-even unit sales = Fixed costs

$$\text{Break-even unit sales volume} = \frac{\text{Fixed costs}}{\text{Selling price per unit} - \text{Variable cost per unit}}$$

Because the denominator is the unit contribution margin, the break-even point is also computed by dividing fixed costs by the unit contribution margin.

$$\text{Break-even unit sales volume} = \frac{\text{Fixed costs}}{\text{Unit contribution margin}}$$

Based on the information provided about Razor, what is the break-even point for the scooter? With an assumed $22 unit contribution margin and fixed costs of $50,000 per month, Razor's break-even point is 2,273 units per month.

$$\text{Break-even unit sales volume} = \frac{\$50,000}{(\$60 - \$38)} = \frac{\$50,000}{\$22} \approx 2{,}273 \text{ scooters}$$ (Rounded UP to the nearest whole unit)

Note that Razor cannot sell a partial scooter. This means that the break-even point is rounded up to ensure that the profit is greater than or equal to zero. Stated another way, at a $22 per-unit contribution margin, 2,273 units of sales are required to cover $50,000 of fixed costs. With a break-even point of 2,273 units, the monthly margin of safety for a sales volume of 5,400 units is 3,127 units.

> **Margin of safety (units) = Actual (or planned) unit sales − Break-even unit sales**
> = 5,400 − 2,273
> = 3,127 scooters

The expected profit given a margin of safety of 3,127 units is $68,794, calculated as follows.

Expected profit = 3,127 margin of safety in units × $22 contribution margin per unit = $68,794

(The difference between the calculated $68,794 and the profit of $68,800 in **Exhibit 15.1** is due to rounding.) Based on these estimates, it appears that Razor can rely on breaking even on this product in the projected period.

Do all products in a company need to at least break-even? Can you think of a situation in which you might continue to sell an unprofitable product?

There are situations in which a company continues selling products even though the products do not earn positive profits. For example, razors are typically sold at a loss. This is because the corresponding razor blades earn a large profit margin. By selling the initial razor, Gillette, *for example, locks in purchases of the high-margin razor blades. Companies might also sell products at a loss when the products are associated with a specific social endeavor. In such cases, it is crucial that managers understand the cost-volume-profit relationship and ensure that, although one product might not earn a positive profit, the company as a whole is profitable.*

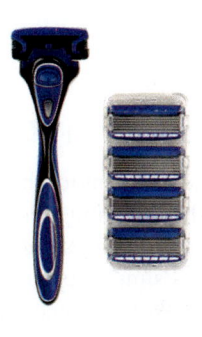

The break-even point concept is applicable to a wide variety of personal situations, such as the decision to buy an electric-powered vehicle. Assume that the incremental cost to purchase an electric vehicle and charge it over a two-year period is $10,000 over a gasoline-fueled vehicle. How many miles would you need to drive to break-even on your purchase, assuming a gas price of $4.00 per gallon and a fuel efficiency of 20 miles per gallon for a gasoline-fueled car? What other factors would you consider in your analysis?

Dividing the fixed costs of $10,000 by $0.20 cost savings per mile ($4.00 ÷ 20), the number of miles at break-even equals 50,000 miles. Further cost factors to include in your analysis may include the difference in maintenance costs per vehicle, tax incentives, cost of public charging stations, and battery disposal costs. Nonfinancial factors may factor in your decision such as the impact of gasoline fueled cars on the environment.

Determining Unit Sales at a Target Profit

Establishing profit objectives is an important part of planning in for-profit and not-for-profit organizations. Profit objectives are stated in many ways. They can be set as a zero profit level, a percentage of last year's profits, a percentage of total assets at the start of the current year, a percentage of donations, or a percentage of owners' equity. They might be based on a profit trend, or they might be expressed as a percentage of sales. The economic outlook for the firm's products as well as anticipated changes in products, costs, and technology are also considered in establishing profit objectives.

Before incorporating profit plans into a detailed budget, it is useful to obtain some preliminary information on the feasibility of those plans. Cost-volume-profit analysis is one way of doing this. By manipulating cost-volume-profit relationships, management can determine the sales volume corresponding to a desired profit. Management might then evaluate the feasibility of this sales volume. If the profit plans are feasible, a complete budget might be developed for this activity level. The required sales volume might be infeasible because of market conditions or because the required volume exceeds production or service capacity, in which case management must lower its profit objective or consider other ways of achieving it. Alternatively, the required sales volume might be less than management believes the firm is capable of selling, in which case, management might raise its profit objective.

Assume that Razor's management desires to know the unit sales volume of scooters required to achieve a monthly profit of $75,000. Using the profit formula, the required unit sales volume is determined by setting profit equal to $75,000 and solving for X, the unit sales.

$$\text{Profit} = \text{Total sales} - \text{Total costs}$$
$$\$75{,}000 = \$60X - (\$50{,}000 + \$38X)$$

Solving for X

$$\$60X - \$38X = \$50{,}000 + \$75{,}000$$
$$X = (\$50{,}000 + \$75{,}000) \div \$22$$
$$= 5{,}682 \text{ units} \text{ (Rounded UP to the nearest whole unit)}$$

The total contribution must cover the desired profit as well as the fixed costs. As shown in the prior calculation, the target sales volume required to achieve a desired profit is computed as the fixed costs plus the desired profit, all divided by the unit contribution margin.

$$\text{Target unit sales volume} = \frac{\text{Fixed costs} + \text{Desired profit}}{\text{Unit contribution margin}}$$

Determining Break-Even in Sales Dollars

The contribution margin ratio can also be used to determine the break-even dollar sales volume. When treating a dollar of sales revenue as a unit, the contribution margin ratio is evaluated. Note that this analysis is analogous to the break-even point analysis that was presented above; dollars of sales simply replaces units of sales.

We previously computed the contribution margin ratio for Razor as 0.3667. This means that Razor has approximately 37 cents left from every sales dollar to cover fixed costs and contribute toward profit. However at break-even, we assume a profit of zero. Similar to the calculation of break-even unit sales, the break-even dollar sales is calculated as follows.

$$\text{Break-even dollar sales volume} = \frac{\text{Fixed costs}}{\text{Contribution margin ratio}}$$

For the Razor scooter,

$$\text{Break-even dollar sales volume} = \frac{\$50{,}000}{0.3667} \approx \$136{,}352 \text{ (Rounded UP to the nearest whole dollar)}$$

To break even, Razor must recognize sales revenues of approximately $136,352. Recall previously that we calculated break-even in units to be 2,273 scooters. This equates to total revenue of 2,273 × $60 = $136,380, with a slight difference from the dollar amount above due to rounding.

Computing break-even in unit sales assumes that pricing is relatively consistent and that an additional sale earns a constant unit contribution margin. The dollar break-even amount does not assume a static or unchanging pricing structure. Rather, it calculates dollars of sales to break even. So, Razor's manager has pricing flexibility as long as the total sales amount equals or exceeds the break-even dollar point.

Determining Sales Dollars at a Target Profit

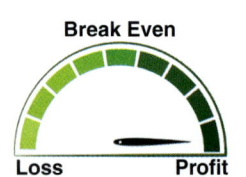

Similarly, computations can be made to find the dollar sales volume required to achieve a desired profit. The following calculation estimates the required dollar sales for Razor to earn a profit of $82,000.

$$\text{Target dollar sales volume} = \frac{\text{Fixed costs} + \text{Desired profit}}{\text{Contribution margin ratio}}$$

For the Razor scooter,

Target dollar sales = ($50,000 + $82,000)/0.3667

= **$359,968** (Rounded UP to the nearest whole dollar)

To achieve a desired profit of $82,000, Razor needs sales of $359,968.

Creating and Analyzing the Cost-Volume-Profit Graph

A **cost-volume-profit graph** illustrates the relationships among sales volume, total revenue, total cost, and profit. Its usefulness comes from highlighting the break-even point and depicting revenue, cost, and profit relationships over a range of activity. This representation allows management to view the relative amount of important variables at any graphed volume. Razor's hypothetical monthly CVP graph is in **Exhibit 15.2**. Total revenues and total costs are measured on the vertical axis, with unit sales measured on the horizontal axis. Separate lines are drawn for total variable costs, total costs, and total revenues. The vertical distance between the total revenue and the total cost lines depicts the amount of profit or loss at a given volume. Losses occur when total revenues are less than total costs (i.e., below the break-even point); profits occur when total revenues exceed total costs (i.e., above the break-even point).

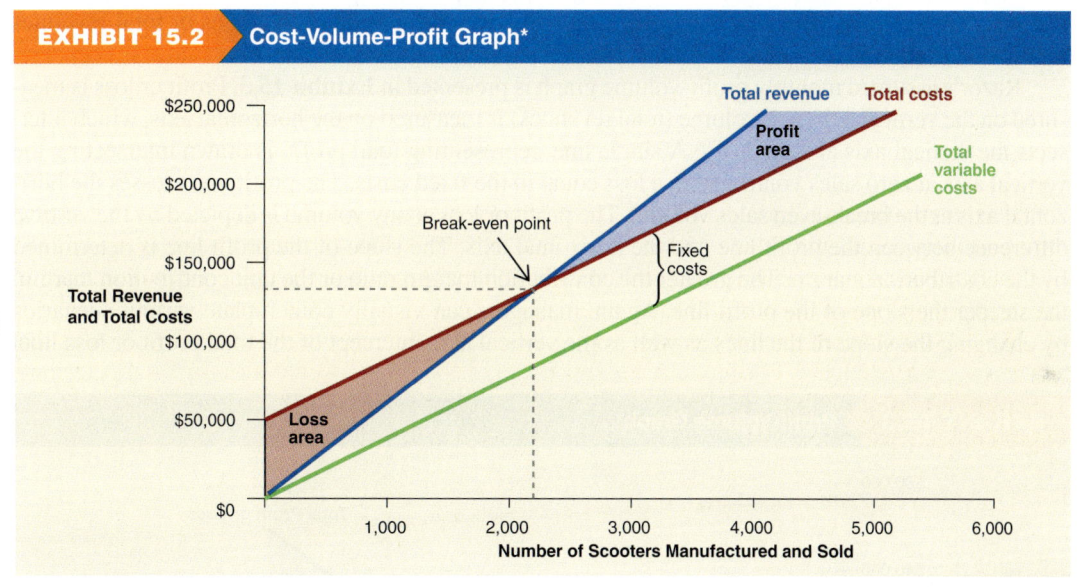

EXHIBIT 15.2 — Cost-Volume-Profit Graph*

* The three lines are developed as follows:
1. **Total variable costs** line is drawn between the origin and total variable costs at an arbitrary sales volume. At 3,000 scooters, total variable costs are $114,000 (3,000 × $38).
2. **Total revenues** line is drawn through the origin and a point representing total revenues at some arbitrary sales volume. At 3,000 scooters, Razor's hypothetical total revenues are $180,000 (3,000 × $60).
3. **Total costs** line is computed by layering fixed costs, $50,000 in this case, on top of total variable costs. This gives a vertical axis intercept of $50,000 and total costs of $164,000 at 3,000 scooters.

The total contribution margin is shown by the difference between the total revenue and the total variable cost lines. Observe that as unit sales increase, the contribution margin first goes to cover the fixed costs. Beyond the break-even point, any additional contribution margin provides a profit.

Sensitivity analyses can be incorporated into graphs by altering the slopes of the various lines as well as the vertical axis intercepts of the total revenue and total cost lines. The various graphs can be compared to evaluate different alternatives.

> **Critical Thinking & Decision-Making**
>
> Let's explore how a start-up technology company could utilize CVP analyses. **Galvani Bioelectronics** is in the preliminary stage of treating illnesses through rice-sized devices that attach to nerve bundles. Many health problems could be solved by implanting and programming these devices to address underlying health problems. The average drug takes 10 years and $2.6 billion to bring to market. Galvani is on track to beat that average with a goal of 7 years for regulatory approval. Unlike traditional drug research where you start from scratch in developing a new drug, the Galvani electronic device could be reprogrammed

for different illnesses. This changes drug therapies from drug problems to software problems.[2] How could Galvani use CVP analyses?

The risk of solvency is significant considering a seven-year or more research phase with no guarantee of a final product to take to market. However, if the technology proves to be viable, the company would have a base of fixed costs (depreciation on technology assets) that would potentially apply to a variety of products. If the treatment became operational and the company met its break-even point, it could see its fixed costs covered and its contribution margin applied more quickly to profits as it rolls out new treatments.

Creating and Analyzing the Profit-Volume Graph

In cost-volume-profit graphs, profits are represented by the difference between total revenues and total costs. When management is primarily interested in the impact of changes in sales volume on profit, a **profit-volume graph** is sometimes used. A profit-volume graph illustrates the relationship between volume and profit. However, it does not show revenues and costs. Profits are read directly from a profit-volume graph, rather than being computed as the difference between total revenues and total costs. Profit-volume graphs are developed by plotting either unit sales or total revenues on the horizontal axis.

Razor's assumed monthly profit-volume graph is presented in **Exhibit 15.3**. Profit or loss is measured on the vertical axis, and volume (total revenues) is measured on the horizontal axis, which intersects the vertical axis at zero profit. A single line, representing total profit, is drawn intersecting the vertical axis at zero sales volume with a loss equal to the fixed costs. The profit line crosses the horizontal axis at the break-even sales volume. The profit or loss at any volume is depicted by the vertical difference between the profit line and the horizontal axis. The slope of the profit line is determined by the contribution margin. The greater the contribution margin ratio or the unit contribution margin, the steeper the slope of the profit line. Again, managers can visually contemplate various scenarios by changing the slope of the lines as well as the vertical axis intercept of the total profit or loss line.

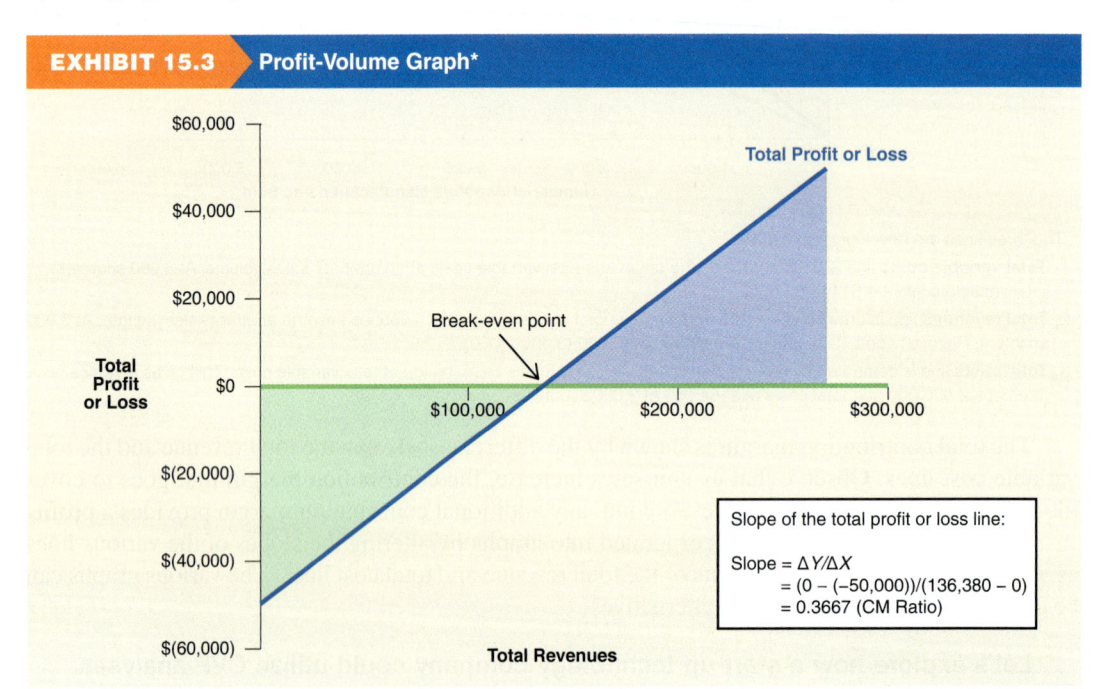

EXHIBIT 15.3 Profit-Volume Graph*

Slope of the total profit or loss line:

Slope = $\Delta Y / \Delta X$
= $(0 - (-50,000))/(136,380 - 0)$
= 0.3667 (CM Ratio)

* The profit line is drawn by determining and plotting profit or loss at two different volumes and then drawing a straight line through the plotted values. Perhaps the easiest values to select are the loss at a volume of zero (with a loss equal to the fixed costs) and the volume at which the profit line crosses the horizontal axis (this is the break-even volume).

---

[2] Sources: Matthew Campbell, "Only One Big Drugmaker Is Working on a Nanobot Cure," Bloomberg Businessweek, June 9, 2016; Ben Hirschler, "GSK and Google Parent Forge $715 million bioelectronic medicines firm," Reuters, August 1, 2016; Andrew Wade, "Nervous Energy: How Bioelectronics is Transforming Healthcare", The Engineer, October 13, 2022.

CVP Key Assumptions

CVP analysis is subject to a number of assumptions. Although these assumptions do not negate the usefulness of CVP models, especially for a single product or service, they do suggest the need for further analysis before plans are finalized. Among the more important assumptions are the following.

1. *All costs are classified as either fixed or variable.* This assumption is most reasonable when analyzing the near future (i.e., within one operating cycle) because, in the long-term, fixed costs are no longer fixed. Although it is possible to classify a large organization's costs as fixed or variable, this works best when analyzing the profitability of a specific event (such as a concert) or the profitability of an organization that produces a single type of product or service on a continuous basis.

2. *The total cost function is linear within the relevant range.* This assumption is often valid within a relevant range of normal operations, but over the entire range of possible activity, changes in efficiency are likely to result in a nonlinear cost function.

3. *The total revenue function is linear within the relevant range.* Unit selling prices are assumed constant over the range of possible volumes. This implies a purely competitive market for final products or services. In some economic models in which demand responds to price changes, the revenue function is nonlinear. Additionally, this structure does not reflect special pricing arrangements such as bulk discounts for large orders. In these situations, the linear approximation is accurate only within a limited range of activity.

4. *The analysis is for a single product, or the sales mix of multiple products is constant.* The *sales mix* refers to the relative portion of unit or dollar sales derived from each product or service and is addressed in the next section. If products have different selling prices and costs, changes in the mix affect CVP model results.

When applied to a single product (such as pounds of potato chips), service (such as the number of vehicles washed), or event (such as the number of tickets sold to a concert), it is reasonable to analyze a single independent variable such as sales volume. The total costs associated with the single product, service, or event during a specific time period are often determined by this single activity cost driver.

Although cost-volume-profit analysis is often used to understand the overall operations of an organization or business segment, accuracy decreases as the scope of operations being analyzed increases. This is because it is difficult to pick specific variables to tie directly to all parts of the operations.

Applying Cost-Volume-Profit Analysis — LO15-3 Review 15-3

Assume **Segway** produces and sells helmets for kids at a sales price of $40. Variable and fixed costs follow.

Variable Cost per Helmet			Fixed Costs per Month	
Manufacturing			Manufacturing overhead............	$15,000
Direct materials................	$15		Selling and administrative..........	10,000
Direct labor	3		Total	$25,000
Manufacturing overhead	10	$28		
Selling and administrative..........		2		
Total		$30		

Suppose in June, Segway produced and sold 3,000 helmets.

Required
a. Prepare a cost-volume-profit graph with unit sales measured on the horizontal axis. Label the revenue line, total cost line, fixed cost line, loss area, profit area, and break-even point. The recommended scale for the horizontal axis is 0 to 5,000 units, and the recommended scale for the vertical axis is $0 to $200,000.
b. Determine Segway's monthly break-even point in units.
c. Determine the monthly dollar sales required for a monthly profit of $5,000.
d. You learn that the direct materials unit price will be higher than $15. How does this impact the various parts of the graph including the break-even point?

Solution on p. 15-40.

MULTIPLE-PRODUCT COST-VOLUME-PROFIT ANALYSIS

Sales mix refers to the relative portion of unit or dollar sales that are derived from each product. One of the limiting assumptions of the basic cost-volume-profit model is that the analysis is for a single product or a constant sales mix. When the sales mix is constant, managers of multiple-product organizations can use the average unit contribution margin, or the average contribution margin ratio, to determine the break-even point or the sales volume required for a desired profit. Often, however, management is interested in the effect of a change in the sales mix rather than a change in the sales volume at a constant mix. In this situation, it is necessary to determine either the average unit contribution margin or the average contribution margin ratio for each alternative mix.

Determining Break-Even in Unit Sales with Multiple Products

Assume that **Razor** sells two types of scooters, the original and the deluxe.

Sales Mix in Units: 1 Original to 1 Deluxe At a 1:1 (one-to-one) unit sales mix in which Razor sells one original scooter for every deluxe scooter, assume the following revenue and cost information is available. To simplify this example, we assume the unit variable costs are the same for all three scooters.

1:1 Sales Mix	Original Scooter	Deluxe Scooter	Average Scooter
Unit selling price.	$40	$120	$80
Unit variable costs	(30)	(30)	(30)
Unit contribution margin	$10	$ 90	$50
Fixed costs per month			$25,000

The average unit contribution margin of $50 in the schedule above is calculated as follows.

$$\text{Average unit contribution margin (1:1 sales mix)} = \frac{(\$10 \times 1 \text{ unit}) + (\$90 \times 1 \text{ unit})}{2 \text{ units}} = \$50$$

At a 1:1 sales mix, assuming fixed costs of $25,000 and an average unit contribution margin of $50, Razor's monthly break-even sales volume is 500 units. The sales mix consists of 250 original scooters and 250 deluxe scooters. The top line in the profit-volume graph shown in **Exhibit 15.4** represents the current sales mix.

> Break-even unit sales volume = Fixed costs ÷ Average unit contribution margin
> = $25,000 ÷ $50
> = 500 units (250 original scooters and 250 deluxe scooters)

Sales Mix in Units: 3 Original to 1 Deluxe Suppose management wants to know the break-even sales volume if the unit sales mix became 3:1. That is, on average, a sale of 4 units contains 3 original scooters and 1 deluxe scooter.

3:1 Sales Mix	Original Scooter	Deluxe Scooter	Average Scooter
Unit selling price.	$40	$120	$60
Unit variable costs	(30)	(30)	(30)
Unit contribution margin	$10	$ 90	$30
Fixed costs per month			$25,000

With no changes in the selling prices or variable costs of individual products, the average contribution margin becomes $30, and the revised break-even sales volume is 834 units, made up of 626 original scooters and 209 deluxe scooters. All answers are rounded up to the nearest whole unit.

Average unit contribution margin (3:1 sales mix) = $\dfrac{(\$10 \times 3 \text{ unit}) + (\$90 \times 1 \text{ unit})}{4 \text{ units}}$ = $30

Break-even unit sales volume = Fixed costs ÷ Average unit contribution margin

= $25,000 ÷ $30

= 834 scooters (626 [834 × 3/4] original scooters and 209 [834 × 1/4] deluxe scooters)

The bottom line in **Exhibit 15.4** represents the revised sales mix. Because a greater portion of the revised sales mix consists of *lower* contribution margin original scooters, the shift in the mix *increases* the break-even point. In other words, Razor is required to sell more scooters to break even because a relatively larger portion of the scooter sales have a lower contribution margin per scooter.

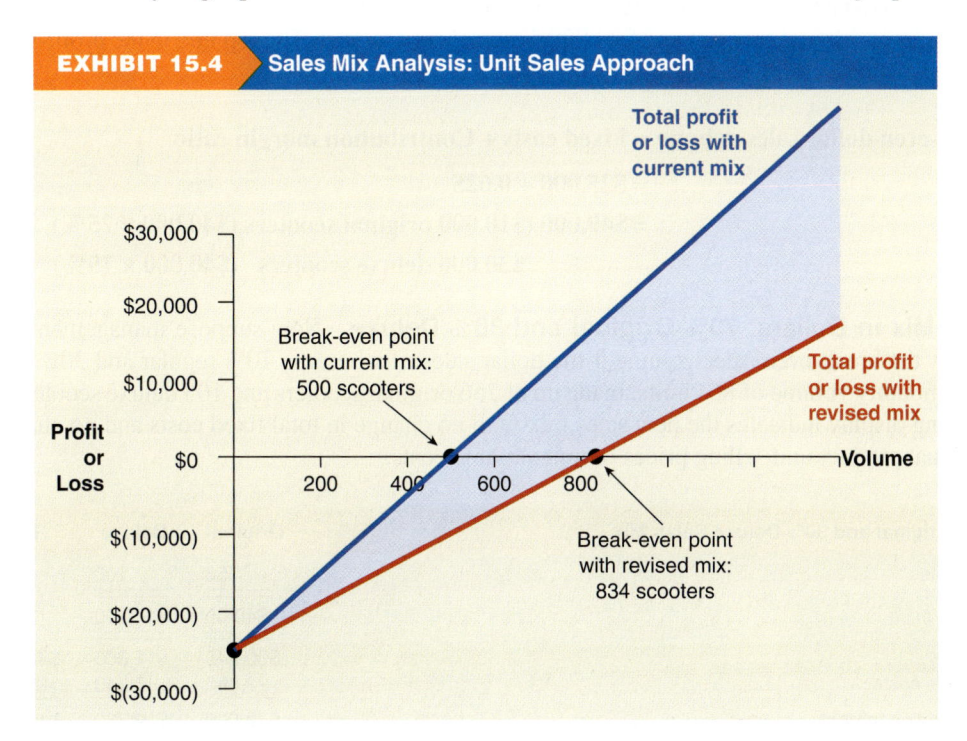

EXHIBIT 15.4 Sales Mix Analysis: Unit Sales Approach

As the manager of a Yeti store, you'd like to understand how sales mix affects your profits. The store's current sales mix is 30% hard coolers and 70% drinkware. Although a much smaller part of the store's sales mix, the hard cooler product line has a larger contribution margin ratio than the drinkware product line. How does this information affect your strategy to increase profitability next year in your store?

Critical Thinking & Decision-Making

Increasing profitability can be achieved in a number of ways. Shifting the sales mix to a higher percentage of hard coolers will result in more profits per sales dollar. Perhaps this can be achieved through target marketing strategies. Profitability can also be achieved with the current sales mix but with an increase in quantity sold of both products.

Determining Break-Even in Sales Dollars with Multiple Products

The preceding analysis focused on units and the average unit contribution margin. An alternative approach focuses on sales dollars and the contribution margin ratio. Following this approach, the sales mix is expressed in terms of sales dollars.

Break Even

Sales Mix in Dollars: 25% Original and 75% Deluxe Assume Razor's current sales dollars are 25% from original scooters and 75% from deluxe scooters. The following display indicates the contribution margin ratios at the current sales mix and monthly volume of 540 units, made up of 270 original scooters and 270 deluxe scooters.

25% Original and 75% Deluxe Sales Mix	Original	Deluxe	Total
Unit sales	270	270	
Selling price	$40.00	$120.00	
Sales	$10,800	$32,400	$43,200
Variable costs	8,100	8,100	16,200
Contribution margin	$ 2,700	$24,300	$27,000
Contribution margin ratio	0.25	0.75	0.625*

* $27,000 ÷ $43,200 = 0.625.

If monthly fixed costs are $25,000, Razor's current break-even sales revenue is $40,000, made up of $10,000 from original scooters and $30,000 from deluxe scooters. The top line in the profit-volume graph shown in **Exhibit 15.5** illustrates the current sales mix.

Break-even dollar sales volume = Fixed costs ÷ Contribution margin ratio

$$= \$25,000 \div 0.625$$
$$= \$40,000 \; (\$10,000 \text{ original scooters } (\$40,000 \times 25\%)$$
$$(\$30,000 \text{ deluxe scooters } \;(\$40,000 \times 75\%)$$

Sales Mix in Dollars: 70% Original and 30% Deluxe Now suppose management wants to know the break-even sales volume if the dollar sales mix became 70% regular and 30% deluxe with a monthly volume of 864 units, made up of 756 original scooters and 108 deluxe scooters. The following display indicates the new sales mix with no change in total fixed costs and no change in individual product unit selling prices or unit variable costs.

70% Original and 30% Deluxe Sales Mix	Original	Deluxe	Total
Unit sales	756	108	
Selling price	$40.00	$120.00	
Sales	$30,240	$12,960	$43,200
Variable costs	22,680	3,240	25,920
Contribution margin	$ 7,560	$ 9,720	$17,280
Contribution margin ratio	0.25	0.75	0.40*

* $17,280 ÷ $43,200 = 0.40

The average contribution margin ratio becomes 0.40 and the revised break-even sales volume is $62,500, made up of $43,750 from original scooters and $18,750 from deluxe scooters.

Break-even dollar sales volume = Fixed costs ÷ Contribution margin ratio

$$= \$25,000 \div 0.40$$
$$= \$62,500 \;(\$43,750 \text{ original scooters } (\$62,500 \times 70\%)$$
$$(\$18,750 \text{ deluxe scooters } \;(\$62,500 \times 30\%)$$

The bottom line in **Exhibit 15.5** represents the revised sales mix. Because a greater portion of the revised mix consists of *lower* contribution margin ratio original scooters, the shift in the mix *increases* the break-even point.

Sales mix analysis is important in multiple-product or multiple-service organizations. Management is just as concerned with the mix of products as with the total unit or dollar sales volume. A shift in the sales mix can have a significant impact on the bottom line. Profits may decline, even when sales increase, if the mix shifts toward products or services with lower unit contribution margins. Conversely, profits may increase, even when sales decline, if the mix shifts toward products or services with higher unit contribution margins. Other things being equal, managers of for-profit organizations strive to increase sales of high-margin products or services.

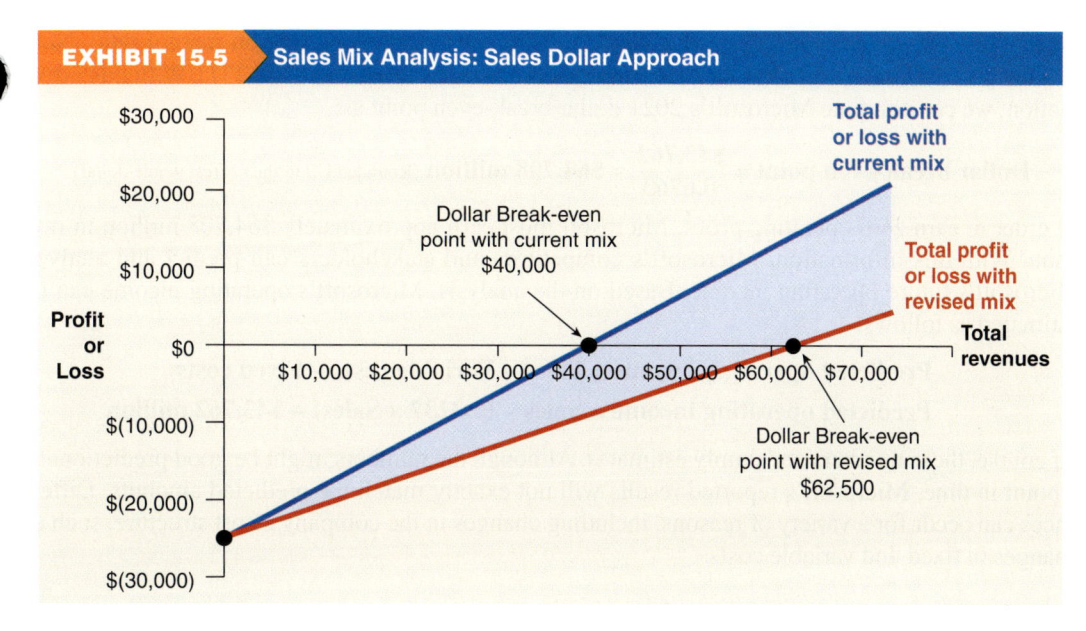

EXHIBIT 15.5 — Sales Mix Analysis: Sales Dollar Approach

Determining Break-Even of a Multi-Product, Public Company

While analysis is commonly used inside organizations to evaluate products and services, it can also be used when analyzing companies externally. For example, Razor might be interested in comparing its cost structure to Segway's cost structure to better understand its competitive position. Because neither company is public, it would be difficult to access the relevant information. However, publicly traded companies are required to disclose financial information. This information can be analyzed to learn about the organization's cost structure.

Microsoft Corporation is a technology company that develops and supports software, services, devices, and solutions. A manager of **Alphabet** might be interested in the cost structure of Microsoft and its dollar break-even point. The following information is from Microsoft's income statement (in millions) for two recent periods

	For the Year Ended	
	June 30, 2021	June 30, 2020
Sales.	$168,088	$143,015
Cost of sales and operating expenses	(98,172)	(90,056)
Operating profit.	$ 69,916	$ 52,959

Using the high-low method (from Chapter 14), we can estimate the cost structure for Microsoft. Based on this estimate, we can better understand the company's cost-volume-profit relationships and forecast profits based on expected sales.

First, calculate the variable costs as a percentage of sales.

$$\text{Variable cost ratio} = \frac{\text{Difference in total costs}}{\text{Difference in Sales}} = \frac{\$98{,}172 - \$90{,}056}{\$168{,}088 - \$143{,}015} = 0.3237$$

Based on this estimate, variable costs are approximately 32.37% of revenues. For every dollar of sales, variable costs are approximately 32 cents. This ratio can be used to estimate Microsoft's total fixed costs. Based on the 2021 information, see the following calculations.

> Annual fixed costs = Total costs − Variable costs
> Annual fixed costs = Total costs − (Sales × 0.3237)
> Annual fixed costs = $98,172 − ($168,088 × 0.3237) = $43,762 million

Thus, Microsoft's estimated cost function is as follows.

> Total annual costs = $43,762 million + (0.3237 × Sales)

To estimate the dollar break-even point for Microsoft, we use the contribution margin ratio. Note that the contribution margin ratio is (1 − variable cost ratio) or 0.6763 (1 − 0.3237). With this information, we can compute Microsoft's 2021 dollar break-even point as:

$$\text{Dollar break-even point} = \frac{\$43{,}762}{0.6763} \approx \$64{,}708 \text{ million} \text{ (Rounded UP to the nearest whole dollar)}$$

In order to earn zero operating profit, Microsoft must earn approximately $64,708 million in revenue. With this information, Microsoft's competitors and stakeholders can predict and analyze Microsoft's future operating income. Based on the analysis, Microsoft's operating income can be estimated as follows.

$$\text{Predicted operating income} = \text{Sales} - \text{Variable costs} - \text{Fixed costs}$$
$$\text{Predicted operating income} = \text{Sales} - (0.3237 \times \text{Sales}) - \$43{,}762 \text{ million}$$

Of course, these numbers are simply estimates. Although the numbers might be good predictions at a point in time, Microsoft's reported results will not exactly match the predicted amounts. Differences can occur for a variety of reasons, including changes in the company's cost structure, such as changes in fixed and variable costs.

Review 15-4 LO15-4   Analyzing Profitability of a Multi-Product Firm

Suppose Segway opens a shop in a Cambridge village shopping center that sells peripherals for their products. Below are the assumed sales and cost data for the shop.

	Seat	Backpack	Phone Holder
Sales price	$120	$80	$30
Variable cost per unit	60	29	12
Fixed costs per month $4,000			

Suppose the company sells each month an average of 25 seats, 40 backpacks, and 60 phone holders.

Required
a. Calculate the current profit, contribution margin ratio, and sales mix based on sales dollars.
b. Using a sales dollar analysis, calculate the monthly break-even point assuming the sales mix does not change.

Solution on p. 15-40.

ANALYSIS OF OPERATING LEVERAGE

LO15-5 Apply the operating leverage ratio to assess opportunities for profit and the risks of loss.

Operating leverage refers to the extent that an organization's costs are fixed. The **operating leverage ratio** is computed as the contribution margin divided by before-tax profit.

$$\text{Operating leverage ratio} = \frac{\text{Contribution margin}}{\text{Before-tax profit}}$$

The rationale underlying this computation is that as fixed costs are substituted for variable costs, the contribution margin as a percentage of income before taxes increases. Hence, a high degree of operating leverage signals the existence of a high portion of fixed costs. For example, a shift from labor-based to automated activities results in a decrease in variable costs and an increase in fixed costs, producing an increase in operating leverage.

Operating leverage is a measure of risk and opportunity. Other things being equal, the higher the degree of operating leverage, the greater the opportunity for profit with increases in sales. Conversely, a higher degree of operating leverage also magnifies the risk of large losses with a decrease in sales. This means that operating leverage is an important consideration when changes in demand, and consequently sales, occur. Higher operating leverage signals a high contribution margin, or low variable costs. In most situations, this also reflects a high fixed cost structure. If prices decline, firms with high operating leverage run the risk of not being able to cover fixed costs. The balance of variable and fixed costs is reflected in the operating leverage ratio.

| | Operating Leverage ||
	High	Low
Profit opportunity with sales increase.	High	Low
Risk of loss with sales decrease.	High	Low

Critical Thinking & Decision-Making

What company do you think would likely have had more financial distress during the COVID-19 pandemic, Neiman Marcus (high-end department store) or Shopbop (a global online retailer for designer clothing)? Which company likely has a higher operating leverage and how does that relate to your first answer?

In 2020, sales dropped sharply and practically immediately with the outbreak of COVID-19. This would especially apply to the sale of designer clothing when events were also canceled that feed the demand. Companies with larger fixed costs such as Neiman Marcus, would still incur costs to maintain buildings without in-store sales. Thus, such companies would be in risk of covering short-term needs. Generally speaking, companies with higher operating leverage (higher fixed costs) felt the effects of the pandemic swiftly.

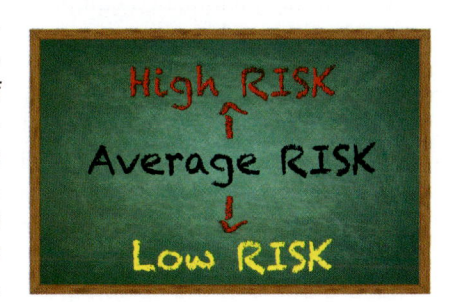

Sensitivity Analysis

In addition to indicating the relative amount of fixed costs in the overall cost structure of a company, the operating leverage ratio can be used to measure the expected change in net income resulting from a change in sales. Consider the following information for **Razor** which compares current and projected results for its original scooter and a new scooter. Assume that the new scooter also sells for $60, but has a different cost structure. The new scooter has a *higher contribution margin and higher fixed costs.* This results in the new scooter having a higher operating leverage ratio than the original scooter (2.35 vs. 1.73).

| | Current || Projected ||
	Razor Original	New Scooter	Razor Original	New Scooter
Unit selling price.	$ 60	$ 60	$ 60	$ 60
Unit variable costs	(38)	(30)	(38)	(30)
Unit contribution margin	$ 22	$ 30	$ 22	$ 30
Unit sales	× 5,400	× 5,400	× 6,048	× 6,048
Contribution margin	$118,800	$162,000	$133,056	$181,440
Fixed costs	(50,000)	(93,200)	(50,000)	(93,200)
Before-tax profit	$ 68,800	$ 68,800	$ 83,056	$ 88,240
Contribution margin	$118,800	$162,000		
Before-tax profit	÷ 68,800	÷ 68,800		
Operating leverage ratio	1.73*	2.35*		
Percent increase in sales			12%	12%
Percent increase in income before taxes			21%*	28%*

*Rounded

Because the fixed costs remain constant, any increase in sales changes revenue and variable costs only. Therefore, the operating leverage ratio multiplied by the percentage change in sales equals the percentage change in profit before taxes. *We expect companies with higher operating leverage ratios to experience higher profit fluctuations when sales volume changes.* In **Razor**'s projected results, both the original and new scooter unit sales are expected to increase 12%, from 5,400 to 6,048 unit sales. Because the new scooter has a higher operating leverage ratio, we expect the new scooter to realize a larger increase in profits as shown in the following calculations.

Operating leverage ratio × Percentage change in sales = Percentage change in before-tax profit

Original scooter: 1.73 × 12% = 21% increase in before-tax profit
New scooter: 2.35 × 12% = 28% increase in before-tax profit

Management is interested in measures of operating leverage to determine how sensitive profits are to changes in sales. Risk-averse managers strive to maintain a lower operating leverage, even if this results in some loss of profits. One way to reduce operating leverage is to use more direct labor and less automated equipment. Another way is to contract outside organizations to perform tasks that could be done internally. While operating leverage is a useful analytic tool, long-run success comes from keeping the overall level of costs down, while providing customers with the products or services they want at competitive prices.

Critical Thinking & Decision-Making

As manager of a division responsible for both production and sales of products, you are looking for ways to increase division profits. You are considering changing your cost structure to include more fixed costs and less variable costs by automating some of the production activities currently performed by people. What are some of the considerations that you should keep in mind as you ponder this decision?

Fixed costs represent a double-edged sword. When a company is growing its sales, fixed costs cause profits to grow faster than sales. However, if a company should experience declining sales, the rate of reduction in profits is greater than the rate of reduction in sales. When sales decline, variable costs decline proportionately, while fixed costs remain the same. For this reason, when a company faces serious declines in sales that are expected to continue, one of the first steps its top management should consider is reducing capacity in order to reduce fixed costs.

Review 15-5 LO15-5

Applying Operating Leverage Ratio

Refer to the information provided In Review 15-4 for Segway to answer the following questions.

Required
a. Calculate Segway's operating leverage ratio.
b. If sales increase by 20%, by how much will before-tax profit be expected to change?
c. If sales decrease by 20%, by how much will before-tax profit be expected to change?

Solution on p. 15-41.

APPENDIX 15A: Cost-Volume-Profit Analysis and Income Taxes

LO15-6
Apply cost-volume-profit analysis considering the income tax effect.

Income taxes are imposed on individuals and for-profit organizations by government agencies. The amount of an individual's or organization's income tax is determined by laws that specify the calculation of taxable income (the income subject to tax) and the calculation of the amount of tax on taxable income. The laws governing the computation of taxable income differ in many ways from the accounting principles that guide the computation of accounting income. Consequently, taxable income and accounting income are seldom the same.

In the early stages of profit planning, income taxes are sometimes incorporated in CVP models by assuming that taxable income and accounting income are identical and that the tax rate is constant. Although these assumptions are seldom true, they are useful for assisting management in developing an early prediction of the sales volume required to earn a desired after-tax profit. Once management has developed a general plan, this early prediction should be refined with the advice of tax experts.

Assuming taxes are imposed at a constant rate per dollar of before-tax profit, income taxes are computed as before-tax profit multiplied by the tax rate. After-tax profit is equal to before-tax profit minus income taxes.

After-tax profit = Before-tax profit − (Before-tax profit × Tax rate)

After-tax profit can also be expressed as before-tax profit times 1 minus the tax rate.

$$\text{After-tax profit} = \text{Before-tax profit} \times (1 - \text{Tax rate})$$

This formula can be rearranged to isolate before-tax profit as follows.

$$\text{Before-tax profit} = \frac{\text{After-tax profit}}{(1 - \text{Tax rate})}$$

Determining Sales at a Target After-Tax Profit

Since all costs and revenues in the profit formula are expressed on a before-tax basis, the most straightforward way of determining the unit sales volume required to earn a desired after-tax profit is to

1. Determine the required before-tax profit.
2. Substitute the required before-tax profit into the profit formula.
3. Solve for the required unit sales volume.

To illustrate, assume that **Razor** is subject to a 40% tax rate and that management desires to earn an after-tax profit of $75,000 for November. First, calculate the before-tax profit as follows.

$$\text{Before-tax profit} = \text{After-tax profit} / (1 - \text{Tax rate})$$
$$= \$75,000/(1 - 0.40)$$
$$= \$125,000$$

Next, calculate the unit sales volume to earn this pre-tax profit of $125,000. Assume as in our previous example that Razor's fixed costs are $50,000 and its unit contribution margin is $22.

$$\text{Target unit sales} = (\text{Fixed costs} + \text{Desired pre-tax profit}) \div \text{Unit contribution margin}$$
$$= (\$50,000 + \$125,000) \div \$22$$
$$= \textbf{7,955 units} \text{ (Rounded UP to the nearest whole unit)}$$

These amounts are verified in **Exhibit 15A.1** as an update to **Exhibit 15.1** to reflect tax.

Another way to remember the computation of before-tax profit is shown on the right side of **Exhibit 15A.1**. The before-tax profit represents 100% of the pie, with 40% going to income taxes and 60% remaining after taxes. Working back from the remaining 60% ($75,000), we can determine the 100% (before-tax profit) by dividing after-tax profit by 0.60.

EXHIBIT 15A.1 — Contribution Income Statement with Income Taxes

RAZOR COMPANY
Contribution Income Statement
Planned for the Month of November

Sales (7,955 × $60)		$477,300	
Less variable costs			
Direct materials (7,955 × $20)	$159,100		
Direct labor (7,955 × $10)	79,550		
Manufacturing overhead (7,955 × $3)	23,865		
Selling and administrative (7,955 × $5)	39,775	(302,290)	
Contribution margin		175,010	
Less fixed costs			
Manufacturing overhead	35,000		
Selling and administrative	15,000	50,000	
Before-tax profit		125,000*	100%
Income taxes ($125,000 × 0.40)		(50,000)	(40)%
After-tax profit		$ 75,000	60%

*Calculated total is $125,010. Difference is due to rounding.

Review 15-6 LO15-6 — Determining sales for a desired after-tax profit amount

Assume **Segway** produces and sells helmets for kids at a sales price of $40. Variable and fixed costs follow.

Variable Cost per Helmet			Fixed Costs per Month	
Manufacturing			Manufacturing overhead............	$15,000
Direct materials................	$15		Selling and administrative..........	10,000
Direct labor...................	3		Total	$25,000
Manufacturing overhead.........	10	$28		
Selling and administrative..........		2		
Total		$30		

Suppose in June, Segway produced and sold 3,000 helmets.

Required

Assuming Segway is subject to a 40% income tax, determine the monthly unit sales required to produce a monthly after-tax profit of $4,500.

Solution on p. 15-41.

KEY RATIOS AND EQUATIONS

Profit = Total sales − Total costs

Total sales = Selling price per unit × Unit sales

Total costs = Fixed costs + (Variable cost per unit × Unit sales)

Profit = (Selling price per unit × Unit sales) − (Fixed costs + [Variable cost per unit × Unit sales])

Unit contribution margin = Selling price per unit − Variable cost per unit

Change in unit sales × Unit contribution margin = Change in profit

$$\text{Contribution margin ratio} = \frac{\text{Revenue} - \text{Variable costs}}{\text{Total sales}}$$

Change in sales dollars × Contribution margin ratio = Change in profit

$$\text{Break-even unit sales volume} = \frac{\text{Fixed costs}}{\text{Selling price per unit} - \text{Variable cost per unit}}$$

$$\text{Break-even unit sales volume} = \frac{\text{Fixed costs}}{\text{Unit contribution margin}}$$

Margin of safety (units) = Actual (or planned) unit sales − Break-even unit sales

$$\text{Target unit sales volume} = \frac{\text{Fixed costs} + \text{Desired profit}}{\text{Unit contribution margin}}$$

$$\text{Break-even dollar sales volume} = \frac{\text{Fixed costs}}{\text{Contribution margin ratio}}$$

$$\text{Target dollar sales volume} = \frac{\text{Fixed costs} + \text{Desired profit}}{\text{Contribution margin ratio}}$$

$$\text{Operating leverage ratio} = \frac{\text{Contribution margin}}{\text{Before-tax profit}}$$

After-tax profit = Before-tax profit × (1 − Tax rate)

MULTIPLE CHOICE

LO15-1 1. With fixed costs of $20,000/month and variable costs of $3/unit, Ace reported a monthly profit of $5,000 at a volume of 12,500 units. The unit selling price was

    a. $1.60   *c.* $4.60

    b. $3.00   *d.* $5.00

2. Presented is information from Wayne's contribution income statement: **LO15-2**

Sales.		$70,000
Less variable costs:		
Manufacturing.	$20,000	
Selling and administrative.	10,000	(30,000)
Contribution margin		40,000
Less fixed costs:		
Manufacturing.	15,000	
Selling and administrative.	8,000	(23,000)
Profit.		$17,000

   With a functional income statement Wayne would have reported a gross profit of
   - a. $35,000
   - b. $40,000
   - c. $47,000
   - d. $50,000

3. Based on the information in question 2, if Wayne had a $5,000 increase in sales, profits would increase by **LO15-2**
   - a. $5,000
   - b. $3,570
   - c. $2,857
   - d. $2,500

4. Penn Company produces a product sold for $40 per unit. Variable and fixed cost information is presented below: **LO15-3**

Variable Cost per Unit		Fixed Costs per Month	
Manufacturing.	$ 8	Manufacturing.	$29,000
Selling and administrative.	2	Selling and administrative.	16,000
Total	$10	Total	$45,000

   The sales volume required for a monthly profit of $36,000 is
   - a. 900 units
   - b. 2,050 units
   - c. 2,700 units
   - d. 3,600 units

5. The Pitch sells 1 select style soccer ball for every 3 classic style balls. The select and classic style balls, respectively, sell for $40 and $20 and have unit variable costs of $20 and $10. Assuming a constant sales mix and total fixed costs for the company of $120,000, the break-even unit sales volume is **LO15-4**
   - a. 7,200
   - b. 384,000
   - c. 9,600
   - d. 9,023

6. Each of the following is true *except*: **LO15-5**
   - a. Operating leverage is a measure of a firm's fixed costs.
   - b. Operating leverage is a measure of risk and opportunity.
   - c. The lower the degree of operating leverage, the greater the opportunity for profit with increases in sales.
   - d. Operating leverage can be used to measure the expected change in net income resulting from a change in sales.

7. Assume a firm has a high operating leverage and sales decrease. Which of the following is true? **LO15-5**
   - a. The firm has a high proportion of variable costs.
   - b. The firm has a high proportion of fixed costs.
   - c. The firm has less opportunity for higher profits with an increase in sales.
   - d. The first has a lower contribution margin compared to a firm with a low operating leverage.

8. Based on the information in question 4, with an income tax rate of 40% the sales volume required for a monthly after-tax profit of $36,000 is **LO15-6**
   - a. 2,000 units
   - b. 3,500 units
   - c. 3,700 units
   - d. 4,500 units

Multiple Choice Answers: 1. d 2. a 3. c 4. c 5. c 6. c 7. b 8. b

DATA ANALYTICS

LO15-4 DA15-1. Analyzing Changes in Product Mix over Time

Fastenal Company
NASDAQ :: FAST

The **Fastenal Company** engages in the wholesale distribution of industrial and construction supplies. The following percentages of sales by product line was included in the 2021 10-K disclosures for Fastenal Company.

Type	Twelve-month Period Ended Dec. 31		
	2021	2020	2019
Other.	3.7%	3.3%	2.9%
Welding supplies	3.8%	3.5%	4.2%
Electrical supplies.	4.3%	4.1%	4.7%
Cutting tools	5.0%	4.7%	5.7%
Material handling	5.6%	5.1%	5.9%
Hydraulics & pneumatics	6.4%	5.9%	6.8%
Janitorial supplies	8.2%	9.8%	7.8%
Tools	8.5%	8.2%	9.9%
Safety supplies	21.2%	25.5%	17.9%
Fasteners	33.3%	29.9%	34.2%
	100.0%	100.0%	100.0%

REQUIRED

a. Prepare a bar chart showing the trend in each product line over the three-year period. *Hint:* Each product line should have 3 bar graphs, one for each year. Based on your bar chart, answer the following questions.
   1. Visually from the bar chart, which product lines are the largest of the ten product lines?
   2. Of the three years 2019, 2020, and 2021, which year visually shows the most change in product mix?
   3. What product lines do you think were most affected by the COVID-19 pandemic in 2020? Why?

b. The company indicated in its 10-K disclosures that the portion of sales attributable to Fasteners has been decreasing for approximately 25 years. The company also indicated that non-fastener products generally carry lower gross profit margins than its Fastener products. Comment on the impact of these trends on the company's profitability.

LO15-1, 3 DA15-2. Determining Fixed vs. Variable Cost Components Using Excel

Genessee Industries introduced a new product last year (6582-D). Although it was very popular, it wasn't very profitable. Management has asked you to provide them with information to help them set a sales price that will provide them with a monthly gross profit of $7,500. (Last year's sales price was $75 per unit.)

You know that the direct costs per unit are $25 for direct materials and $5 for direct labor. You are given information about last year's monthly production levels and manufacturing overhead costs (indirect materials, indirect labor, and other). The Excel file is available on the textbook's website.

REQUIRED

a. Determine the cost formula for 6582-D. Use Excel's regression analysis tool to develop a cost-estimating equation for total fixed and variable manufacturing costs. Use the regression tool three times (once for indirect materials, once for indirect labor, and once for other overhead). Use the information from each analysis, along with the direct cost information to estimate the cost equation. *Hint:* Click on the 95% confidence level box *and* check the box to add a Line fit plot for each indirect cost element to show the relationship in chart form. *Hint:* You may need to change the minimum bound on the horizontal axis to 700 to see the line clearly on each chart.

b. Use the prior year data to create a graph of the various overhead costs by month. Create a Combo chart as follows. *Hint:* Under the Insert tab, click on Create custom combo chart.
   1. The primary vertical axis in dollars, and the secondary vertical axis is units of production. *Hint:* Click the Secondary axis box for units produced.
   2. The horizontal axis is Months.
   3. Units produced should be a Clustered column type; the overhead cost elements should be Line type.
   4. Describe the trend in the overhead components based on a review of your chart.

c. Use Excel's Goal Seek tool to determine the sales price required to meet the $7,500 gross profit goal. Management believes monthly sales in units will average 1,500 next year. Assume the company will not maintain any inventory of finished goods. *Hint:* In a schedule in Excel, enter number of units, variable manufacturing cost per unit, total fixed costs, and a formula for gross profit. Use the Goal Seek tool to find the sales price. Goal Seek is found under the Data tab, and under What-If Analysis.
d. Discuss how Goal Seek (or any other Excel tool) might help management with CVP Analysis.

DA15-3. Determining Fixed vs. Variable Cost Components Using Tableau **LO15-1, 3**
Available in myBusinessCourse, this problem uses Tableau to determine fixed and variable cost components using Tableau.

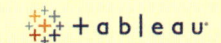

DATA VISUALIZATION

Data Visualization Activities are available in myBusinessCourse. These assignments use Tableau Dashboards to expose students to visual depictions of data and introduce students to data analytics through data visualizations. These exercises are easily assignable and auto graded by MBC.

QUESTIONS

Q15-1. What is cost-volume-profit analysis and when is it particularly useful?

Q15-2. Identify the important assumptions that underlie cost-volume-profit analysis.

Q15-3. When is it most reasonable to use a single independent variable in cost-volume-profit analysis?

Q15-4. Distinguish between a contribution and a functional income statement.

Q15-5. What is the unit contribution margin? How is it used in computing the unit break-even point?

Q15-6. What is the contribution margin ratio and when is it most useful?

Q15-7. How is the break-even equation modified to take into account the sales required to earn a desired profit?

Q15-8. How does a profit-volume graph differ from a cost-volume-profit graph? When is a profit-volume graph most likely to be used?

Q15-9. How are profit opportunities and the risk of losses affected by operating leverage?

Q15-10. What impact do income taxes have on the sales volume required to earn a desired after-tax profit?

Assignments with the MBC logo in the margin are available in myBusinessCourse.
See the Preface of the book for details.

MINI EXERCISES

M15-11. Preparing and Adjusting Profit Equation **LO15-1**
Assume **Strands Salon**, a San Diego hair salon, provides haircuts for $60. Annual fixed costs are $240,000 and the company estimates $15.30 in variable costs per haircut.

REQUIRED
a. Determine the annual profit equation.
b. If the company forecasts that it will provide 9,000 haircuts in the following year, what are estimated profits?
c. How does your answer to part *b* change if fixed costs are expected to increase by 10% and variable cost per unit are expected to increase by $2.34 per haircut?

M15-12. Preparing Contribution Income Statement and Computing Contribution Margin Ratio **LO15-2**
Refer to the initial information in M15-11 to answer the following questions.

REQUIRED
a. Prepare a contribution income statement for the following year assuming the company forecasts that it will provide 9,000 haircuts.
b. Compute the contribution margin ratio.

c. How do your answers to parts *a* and *b* change if fixed costs are expected to increase by 10% and variable cost per unit are expected to increase by $2.34 per haircut?

LO15-2 M15-13. Computing Amounts Based on Analysis of Contribution Margin

	Scenario 1	Scenario 2	Scenario 3	Scenario 4
Sales.............................	$200,000	d. _____	$148,000	l. _____
Variable costs...................	$120,800	e. _____	h. _____	$196,000
Contribution margin	a. _____	$ 3,960	i. _____	m. _____
Fixed costs.....................	$ 12,000	f. _____	j. _____	$ 85,000
Profit...........................	b. _____	$ 2,060	$ 27,996	n. _____
Contribution margin ratio	39.6%	33.0%	k. _____	44.0%
Contribution per unit............	c. _____	$ 2.50	$ 37.37	o. _____
Number of units produced and sold....	4,800	g. _____	800	1,925

LO15-3 M15-14. Computing Break-Even Point, Margin of Safety, Sales at Target Profit

IGK Hair

Assume **IGK Hair**, a Miami hair salon, provides hairstyling services. Annual fixed costs are $225,000, and variable costs are 45% of sales revenue. Last year's revenues totaled $450,000.

REQUIRED
a. Determine its break-even point in sales dollars.
b. Determine last year's margin of safety in sales dollars.
c. Determine the sales dollars required for an annual before-tax profit of $200,000.

LO15-3 M15-15. Cost-Volume-Profit Graph: Identification and Sensitivity Analysis

A typical cost-volume-profit graph is presented below.

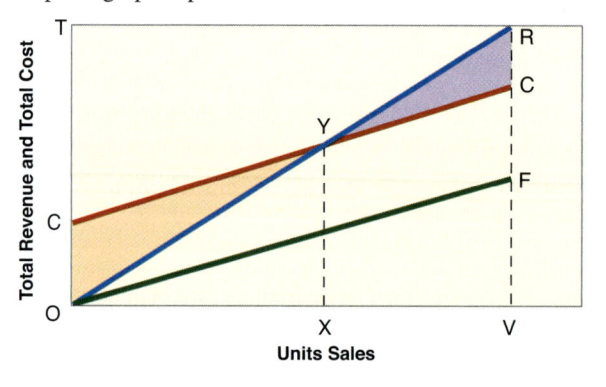

REQUIRED
a. Identify each of the following.
   1. Line OF
   2. Line OR
   3. Line CC
   4. The difference between lines OF and OV at any given number of unit sales
   5. The difference between lines CC and OF at any given number of unit sales
   6. The difference between lines CC and OV at any given number of unit sales
   7. The difference between lines OR and OF at any given number of unit sales
   8. Point X
   9. Area CYO
   10. Area RCY
b. Indicate the effect of each of the following independent events on lines CC, OR, and the break-even point.
   1. A decrease in fixed costs
   2. An increase in unit selling price
   3. An increase in the variable cost per unit
   4. An increase in fixed costs and a decrease in the unit selling price
   5. A decrease in fixed costs and a decrease in the unit variable costs

M15-16. Profit-Volume Graph: Identification and Sensitivity Analysis   **LO15-3**

A typical profit-volume graph follows.

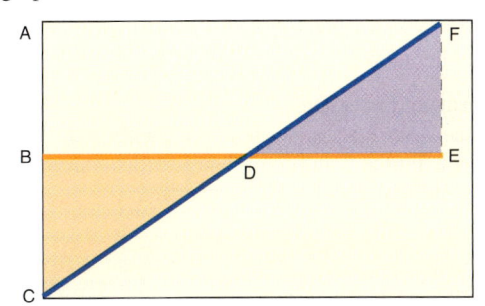

REQUIRED

a. Identify each of the following:

1. Area BDC
2. Area DEF
3. Point D
4. Line AC
5. Line BC
6. Line EF

b. Indicate the effect of each of the following on line CF and the break-even point.

1. An increase in the unit selling price
2. An increase in the variable cost per unit
3. A decrease in fixed costs
4. An increase in fixed costs and a decrease in the unit selling price
5. A decrease in fixed costs and an increase in the variable cost per unit

M15-17. Preparing Cost-Volume-Profit and Profit-Volume Graphs   **LO15-3**

Connie's Pizza

Assume a **Connie's Pizza** shop has the following monthly revenue and cost functions.

Total revenues = $20.00X
Total costs = $35,000 + $6.00X

REQUIRED

a. Prepare a graph (similar to that in **Exhibit 15.3**) illustrating Connie's cost-volume-profit relationships. The vertical axis should range from $0 to $120,000, in increments of $20,000. The horizontal axis should range from 0 units to 6,000 units, in increments of 2,000 units.

b. Prepare a graph (similar to that in **Exhibit 15.4**) illustrating Connie's profit-volume relationships. The horizontal axis should range from 0 units to 6,000 units, in increments of 2,000 units.

c. When is it most appropriate to use a profit-volume graph?

M15-18. Preparing Cost-Volume-Profit and Profit-Volume Graphs   **LO15-3**

Manu's Tacos

Manu's Tacos sells seven different burritos at a fixed price of $9. Assume variable costs are $6 per burrito and fixed operating costs are $120,000 per year.

REQUIRED

a. Determine the annual break-even point in tacos.

b. Prepare a cost-volume-profit graph for the company. Use a format that emphasizes the contribution margin. The vertical axis should vary between $0 and $800,000 in increments of $100,000. The horizontal axis should vary between 0 tacos and 80,000 tacos, in increments of 10,000 tacos. Label the graph in thousands.

c. Prepare a profit-volume graph for the company. The vertical axis should vary between $(150,000) and $150,000 in increments of $50,000. The horizontal axis should vary as described in requirement (b). Label the graph in thousands.

d. Evaluate the profit-volume graph. In what ways is it superior and in what ways is it inferior to the traditional cost-volume-profit graph?

M15-19. Multiple Product Break-Even Analysis   **LO15-4**

Dick's Sporting Goods
NYSE :: DKS
Bauer
Warrior
CCM

Assume **Dick's Sporting Goods** sells three types of youth hockey sticks: **Bauer**, **Warrior**, and **CCM**. Presented is information for Dick's three products.

	Bauer	Warrior	CCM
Unit selling price	$180	$120	$100
Unit variable costs	120	75	60
Unit contribution margin	$ 60	$ 45	$ 40

With monthly fixed costs of $150,000, the company sells two Bauer sticks for each Warrior, and three Warrior for each CCM.

REQUIRED
Determine the number of Warrior sticks sold at the monthly break-even point.

LO15-5
Coffee Bean

M15-20. Computing Operating Leverage
Suppose the **Coffee Bean** has a new shop in a Cambridge village shopping center that sells high-end teas and coffees. Further, suppose it has added smoothie drinks to its product line. Below are the assumed sales and cost data for the company.

	Coffee	Tea	Smoothie
Sales price per (12 oz.) serving	$1.35	$1.25	$1.95
Variable cost per serving	0.60	0.45	0.75
Fixed costs per month $8,000			

Assume that the company sells each month an average of 6,000 servings of coffee, 3,750 servings of tea, and 2,250 servings of smoothies.

REQUIRED
a. Calculate Coffee Bean's operating leverage ratio
b. If sales increase by 20%, by how much will before-tax profit be expected to change?
c. If sales decrease by 20%, by how much will before-tax profit be expected to change?

LO15-6
Dart Container Corp.

M15-21. Determining Sales for a Desired After-Tax Profit
Assume **Dart Container Corp.** produces 16-ounce beverage containers. Further assume that the company sells the cups for $40 per box of 50 containers. Variable and fixed costs follow.

Variable Cost per Box			Fixed Costs per Month	
Manufacturing:			Manufacturing overhead.........	$15,000
Direct materials.........	$15		Selling and administrative........	10,000
Direct labor............	3		Total	$25,000
Manufacturing overhead....	10	$28		
Selling and administrative......		2		
Total		$30		

Suppose in September, the company produced and sold 3,000 boxes of beverage containers.

REQUIRED
Assuming the company is subject to a 40% income tax, determine the monthly unit sales required to produce a monthly after-tax profit of $4,500.

EXERCISES

LO15-1
Picnic Time

E15-22. Preparing a Profit Equation to Predict Future Profits
Picnic Time produces a picnic basket that is sold for $100 per unit. Assume the company produced and sold 4,000 baskets during July. There were no beginning or ending inventories. Variable and fixed costs follow.

Variable Cost per Unit			Fixed Costs per Month	
Manufacturing:			Manufacturing overhead.........	$ 36,000
Direct materials.........	$25		Selling and administrative........	68,000
Direct labor............	15		Total	$104,000
Manufacturing overhead....	5	$45		
Selling and administrative......		4		
Total		$49		

REQUIRED
a. Prepare a monthly profit equation.
b. Determine profit for the month of July using the equation from part a.

c. For August, the company estimates that sales will range between 4,100 on the low-end and 4,400 on the high-end. What is the range of predicted profits?

E15-23. Contribution Income Statement, Graph, and Analysis
Use the information from E15-22 to answer the following questions.

LO15-2, 3
Picnic Time

REQUIRED
a. Prepare a contribution income statement for July.
b. Prepare a cost-volume-profit graph. Label the horizontal axis in units with a maximum value of 8,000. Label the vertical axis in dollars with a maximum value of $1,000,000. Draw a vertical line on the graph for the current (4,000) unit sales level, and label total variable costs, total fixed costs, and total profits at 4,000 units.
c. Determine the break-even point in sales dollars.
d. Suppose the cost of labor is expected to increase next year. How will this affect the break-even point?
e. Determine July's margin of safety in sales dollars.
f. What dollar sales volume is currently required to obtain a before-tax profit of $120,000?

E15-24. Contribution Margin Concepts
DiPinto Electric Guitars & Basses sells musical instruments in Philadelphia. Assume the following information comes from the company's prior year records.

LO15-3
DiPinto Electric Guitars & Basses

	Fixed	Variable	Total
Sales.			$800,000
Costs			
Cost of goods sold		$346,000	
Labor	$180,000	40,000	
Supplies	10,000	4,000	
Utilities	9,000	5,000	
Rent	48,000	—	
Advertising	10,000	—	
Miscellaneous	10,000	5,000	
Total costs	$267,000	$400,000	(667,000)
Net income			$133,000

REQUIRED
a. Determine the annual break-even dollar sales volume.
b. Determine the current margin of safety in dollars.
c. Prepare a cost-volume-profit graph for the guitar shop. Label both axes in dollars with maximum values of $1,000,000. Draw a vertical line on the graph for the current ($800,000) sales level, and label total variable costs, total fixed costs, and total profits at $800,000 sales.
d. What is the annual break-even dollar sales volume if management makes a decision that increases fixed costs by $50,000?

E15-25. Computing Break-Even and Margin of Safety
Assume that last year, **Cliff Consulting**, a firm in Berkeley, CA, had the following contribution income statement.

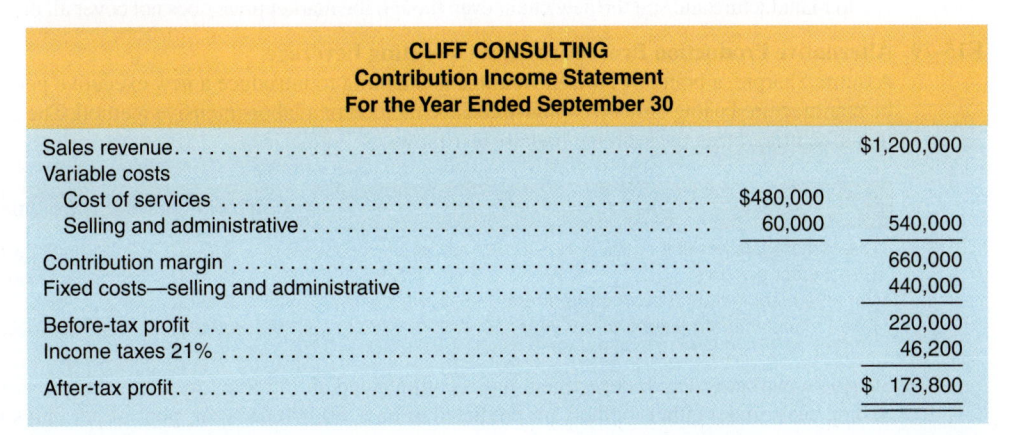

LO15-3
Cliff Consulting

CLIFF CONSULTING
Contribution Income Statement
For the Year Ended September 30

Sales revenue		$1,200,000
Variable costs		
Cost of services	$480,000	
Selling and administrative	60,000	540,000
Contribution margin		660,000
Fixed costs—selling and administrative		440,000
Before-tax profit		220,000
Income taxes 21%		46,200
After-tax profit		$ 173,800

REQUIRED
a. Determine the annual break-even point in sales revenue.
b. Determine the annual margin of safety in sales revenue.
c. What is the break-even point in sales revenue if management makes a decision that increases fixed costs by $80,000?
d. With the current cost structure, including fixed costs of $440,000, what dollar sales revenue is required to provide a before-tax profit of $350,000?
e. Prepare an abbreviated contribution income statement to verify that the solution to requirement *d* will provide the desired before-tax profit.

LO15-2, 6 **E15-26. Computing Sales for a Desired After-Tax Profit**
Cliff Consulting

Using the information from E15-25, answer the following questions.
a. With the current cost structure, including fixed costs of $440,000, what dollar sales revenue is required to provide an after-tax net profit of $250,000?
b. Prepare an abbreviated contribution income statement to verify that the solution to requirement *a* will provide the desired after-tax profit.

LO15-3 **E15-27. Not-for-Profit Applications**
Determine the solution to each of the following independent cases.
a. Collings College has annual fixed operating costs of $20,000,000 and variable operating costs of $2,400 per student. Tuition is $12,000 per student for the coming academic year, with a projected enrollment of 2,000 students. Expected revenues from endowments and federal and state grants total $400,000. Determine the amount the college must obtain from other sources.
b. The Collings College Student Association is planning a fall concert. Expected costs (renting a hall, hiring a band, etc.) are $15,000. Assuming 2,000 people attend the concert, determine the break-even price per ticket. How much will the association lose if this price is charged and only 1,500 tickets are sold?
c. City Hospital has a contract with the city to provide indigent health care on an outpatient basis for $125 per visit. The patient will pay $10 of this amount, with the city paying the balance ($115). Determine the amount the city will pay if the hospital has 5,000 patient visits.
d. A civic organization is engaged in a fund-raising program. On Civic Sunday, it will sell newspapers at $2.50 each. The organization will pay $1.75 for each newspaper. Costs of the necessary permits, signs, and so forth are $750. Determine the amount the organization will raise if it sells 3,000 newspapers.
e. Christmas for the Needy is a civic organization that provides Christmas presents to disadvantaged children. The annual costs of this activity are $10,000, plus $20 per present. Determine the number of presents the organization can provide with $30,000.

LO15-2, 3 **E15-28. Analyzing Sales of Products Below Break-Even**
Men's Wearhouse
IKEA

a. Assume that **Men's Wearhouse**, a high-quality clothing store, intentionally sells ties at a price below the market price, or the price that customers are willing to pay for the ties. The unit selling price is equal to the unit contribution margin. The company incurs a loss on the sale because it does not cover its fixed costs. Why might the company intentionally sell a product below the market price?
b. Assume that **IKEA**, a furniture merchandiser and manufacturer, offers a new chair at market price. The unit selling price is slightly higher than the unit contribution margin. The company incurs a loss on the sale because it does not cover all of its fixed costs. Why might the company continue to manufacture and sell the new chair, even though the market price does not cover all of its costs?

LO15-3, 5 **E15-29. Alternative Production Procedures and Operating Leverage**
Newell Brands
NASDAQ :: NWL

Assume Sharpie, a brand of **Newell Brands**, is planning to introduce a new executive pen that can be manufactured using either a capital-intensive method or a labor-intensive method. The predicted manufacturing costs for each method are as follows.

	Capital Intensive	Labor Intensive
Direct materials per unit	$10.00	$12.00
Direct labor per unit	$ 4.00	$12.00
Variable manufacturing overhead per unit	$ 5.00	$ 2.00
Fixed manufacturing overhead per year	$1,800,000	$500,000

Sharpie's market research department has recommended an introductory unit sales price of $100. Selling costs under either method are predicted to be $250,000 per year, plus $4 per unit sold.

REQUIRED

a. Determine the annual break-even point in units if Sharpie uses the
   1. Capital-intensive manufacturing method.
   2. Labor-intensive manufacturing method.
b. Determine the annual unit volume at which Sharpie is indifferent between the two manufacturing methods.
c. Management wants to know more about the effect of each alternative on operating leverage.
   1. Explain operating leverage and the relationship between operating leverage and the volatility of earnings.
   2. Compute operating leverage for each alternative at a volume of 100,000 units.
   3. Which alternative has the higher operating leverage? Why?
d. Would you select the capital intensive or the labor intensive method? Why?

E15-30. Contribution Income Statement and Operating Leverage   LO15-2, 3, 5
Willamette Valley Fruit Company started as a small cannery-style operation in 1999. The company now processes, on average, 20 million pounds of berries each year. Flash-frozen berries are sold in 30 pound packs to retailers. Assume 650,000 packs were sold for $75 each last year. Variable costs were $42 per pack and fixed costs totaled $14,250,000.

REQUIRED

a. Prepare a contribution income statement for last year.
b. Determine last year's operating leverage.
c. Calculate the percentage change in profits if sales decrease by 10%.
d. Management is considering the purchase of several new pieces of packaging equipment. This will increase annual fixed costs to $15,500,000 and reduce variable costs to $40 per crate. Calculate the effect of this acquisition on operating leverage and explain any change.

E15-31. Multiple Product Break-Even Analysis   LO15-4
TPG Tax & Accounting is a full-service CPA firm located in Apache Junction, Arizona. Assume that tax return services are classified into one of three categories: standard, complex, and full-service (includes end-of-year bookkeeping with tax return preparation). Assume that TPG's fixed costs (rent, utilities, wages, and so forth) totaled $180,000 last year. Additional information from the prior year follows.

	Standard	Complex	Full-Service
Billing rate.............................	$125.00	$250.00	$150.00
Average variable costs	(45.00)	(65.00)	(50.00)
Average contribution margin...........	$ 80.00	$185.00	$100.00
Number of returns prepared............	1,000	200	800

REQUIRED

a. Using sales dollar analysis, determine TPG's break-even dollar sales volume.
b. Determine TPG's margin of safety in sales dollars. *Hint:* Use the weighted average billing rate.
c. Prepare a profit-volume graph for Joe's Tax Service.
d. What will happen to the break-even sales volume if TPG increases the percentage of clients requiring the standard tax preparation?

E15-32. Cost-Volume-Profit Relations: Missing Data   LO15-2, 3
Following are data from four separate companies.

	Case A	Case B	Case C	Case D
Unit sales	2,500	1,600	?	?
Sales revenue.........................	$80,000	?	?	$240,000
Variable cost per unit	$20	$2	$24	?
Contribution margin	?	$1,600	?	?
Fixed costs	$14,000	?	$164,000	?
Net income...........................	?	$900	?	?
Unit contribution margin	?	?	?	$30
Break-even point (units)	?	?	8,000	4,000
Margin of safety (units)...............	?	?	600	2,000

REQUIRED
Supply the missing data in each independent case.

LO15-2, 3 **E15-33. Cost-Volume-Profit Relations: Missing Data**

Following are data from four separate companies.

	Case 1	Case 2	Case 3	Case 4
Sales revenue	$90,000	$150,000	?	?
Contribution margin	$45,000	?	$40,000	?
Fixed costs	$30,000	?	?	?
Net income	?	$15,000	$24,000	?
Variable cost ratio	?	0.40	?	0.60
Contribution margin ratio	?	?	0.25	?
Break-even point (dollars)	?	?	?	$150,000
Margin of safety (dollars)	?	?	?	$125,000

REQUIRED

Supply the missing data in each independent case.

LO15-3 **E15-34. Multiple-Level Break-Even Analysis**

Currently, people retiring at age 67 are entitled to "full" retirement benefits; those retiring at age 62 are eligible for only 70% of "full" benefits. Suppose a person is contemplating retirement at age 62. If the person retires at 67, they will receive $2,265 per month. (Ignore time value of money considerations for this problem.)

REQUIRED

a. How large is the reduction in monthly benefits if a person retires at age 62?
b. What is the break-even age at which the benefits from delaying retirement until age 67 equal the cumulative benefits from retiring at age 62?
c. What would the ultimate decision depend on?

PROBLEMS

LO15-1, 3 **P15-35. CVP Analysis Using Published Financial Statements**

Microsoft
NASDAQ :: MSFT

Condensed data in millions of dollars from **Microsoft**'s 2019 and 2018 income statements follow.

	2019	2018
Revenues	$125,843	$110,360
Total cost of revenues and operating expenses	82,884	75,302
Operating income	$ 42,959	$ 35,058

REQUIRED

a. Develop a profit equation for Microsoft's annual cost of revenues and operating expenses using revenues as the activity.
b. Determine Microsoft's annual break-even point.
c. Predict operating profit for 2020, assuming 2020 sales of $150,000 million.
d. Identify the assumptions required to use the equations and amounts computed above.

LO15-2, 3, 5 **P15-36. Contribution Income Statement, Cost-Volume-Profit Graph**

Jail and Sail:
Alcatraz Tour and Cruise

Jail and Sail: Alcatraz Tour and Cruise provides sunset sightseeing tours of Alcatraz and the San Francisco Bay. Tickets cost $140 each. Assume 2,200 customers were served in July.

Variable Costs per Customer		Fixed Costs per Month	
Admission fees	$60	Operations	$50,000
Overhead	25	Selling and administrative	12,500
Hors d'oeuvres	15		
Selling and administrative	2		
Total	$102	Total	$62,500

REQUIRED

a. Prepare a contribution income statement for July.
b. Determine Jail and Sail's monthly break-even point in units.

c. Determine Jail and Sail's margin of safety in units for July.
d. Determine Jail and Sail's operating leverage ratio.
e. Prepare a cost-volume-profit graph. Label the horizontal axis in units with a maximum value of 4,000. Label the vertical in dollars with a maximum value of $600,000. Draw a vertical line on the graph for the current (2,200) unit level and label total variable costs, total fixed costs, and total before-tax profits at 2,200 units.

P15-37. High-Low Cost Estimation and Profit Planning
Comparative income statements for Bismark Products Inc. follow.

BISMARK PRODUCTS INC.
Comparative Income Statements
For Years Ending December 31

	Year 1	Year 2
Unit sales	6,250	9,375
Sales revenue	$100,000	$150,000
Expenses	(85,000)	(105,000)
Pretax profit (loss)	$ 15,000	$ 45,000

REQUIRED
a. Determine the break-even point in units. *Hint:* Use the high-low cost estimation method to determine variable and fixed cost components (See Chapter 14).
b. Determine the unit sales volume required to earn a pretax profit of $25,000.

P15-38. CVP Analysis and Special Decisions
Smoothie Company produces fruit purees which it sells to smoothie bars and health clubs. Assume the most recent year's sales revenue was $5,800,000. Variable costs were 55% of sales and fixed costs totaled $1,560,000. Smoothie is evaluating two alternatives designed to enhance profitability.
- One staff member has proposed that Smoothie purchase more automated processing equipment. This strategy would increase fixed costs by $250,000 but decrease variable costs to 50% of sales.
- Another staff member has suggested that Smoothie rely more on outsourcing for fruit processing. This would reduce fixed costs by $250,000 but increase variable costs to 60% of sales.

REQUIRED
a. What is the current break-even point in sales dollars?
b. What dollar sales volume is currently required to obtain a before-tax profit of $1,250,000?
c. In the absence of income taxes, at what sales volume will both alternatives (automation and outsourcing) provide the same profit?
d. Briefly describe one strength and one weakness of both the automation and the outsourcing alternatives.

P15-39. Break-Even Analysis in a Not-for-Profit Organization
Melford Hospital operates a general hospital but rents space to separately owned entities rendering specialized services such as pediatrics and psychiatry. Melford charges each separate entity for patients' services (meals and laundry) and for administrative services (billings and collections). Space and bed rentals are fixed charges for the year, based on bed capacity rented to each entity. Melford charged the following costs to Pediatrics this year.

	Patient Services (Variable)	Bed Capacity (Fixed)
Dietary	$ 800,000	
Janitorial		$ 95,000
Laundry	375,000	
Laboratory	600,000	
Pharmacy	460,000	
Repairs and maintenance		40,000
General and administrative		1,750,000
Rent		2,000,000
Billings and collections	400,000	
Total	$2,635,000	$3,885,000

In addition to these charges from Melford Hospital, Pediatrics incurred the following personnel costs.

	Annual Salaries*
Supervising nurses	$135,000
Nurses	270,000
Assistants	240,000
Total	$645,000

* These salaries are fixed within the ranges of annual patient-days considered in this problem.

During the year, Pediatrics charged each patient $400 per day, had a capacity of 80 beds, and had revenues of $8,000,000 for 365 days. Pediatrics operated at 100% capacity on 90 days during this period. It is estimated that during these 90 days, the demand exceeded 100 beds.

Melford will have 20 additional beds available for rent next year. If Pediatrics rents the beds from Melford, the additional rental would proportionately increase Pediatrics' annual fixed charges that are based on bed capacity.

REQUIRED
a. Calculate the minimum number of patient-days required for Pediatrics to break even next year, if the additional beds are not rented. Patient demand is unknown, but assume that revenue per patient-day, cost per patient-day, cost per bed, and salary rates next year will be consistent with the current year.
b. Assume Pediatrics rents the extra 20-bed capacity from Melford during the busy 90-day period. Determine the net increase or decrease in earnings by preparing a schedule of increases in revenues and costs for next year. Assume that patient demand, revenue per patient-day, cost per patient-day, cost per bed, and salary rates remain the same as the current year.

CMA adapted

LO15-3, 4
UCLA Store

P15-40. Multiple-Product Profitability Analysis, Multiple-Level Profitability Analysis
Assume **UCLA Store** sells new college textbooks at the publishers' suggested retail prices and pays the publishers an amount equal to 70% of the suggested retail price. The store's other variable costs average 5% of sales revenue and annual fixed costs amount to $420,000.

REQUIRED
a. Determine the bookstore's annual break-even point in sales dollars.
b. Assuming an average textbook has a suggested retail price of $125, determine the bookstore's annual break-even point in units.
c. UCLA Store is planning to add used book sales to its operations. A typical used book costs the store 25% of the suggested retail price of a new book. The bookstore plans to sell used books for 75% of the suggested retail price of a new book. Assuming unit sales are unchanged, describe the effect on bookstore profitability of shifting sales toward more used and fewer new textbooks.
d. Chicago Publishers produces and sells new textbooks to college and university bookstores. Assume typical project-level costs total $285,000 for a new textbook. Production and distribution costs amount to 20% of the net amount the publisher receives from the bookstores. Textbook authors are paid a royalty of 15% of the net amount received from the bookstores. Determine the dollar sales volume required for Chicago to break even on a new textbook. This is the amount the bookstore pays the publisher, not the bookstore's sales revenue.
e. For a project with predicted sales of 10,000 new books at $125 each, determine
 1. The bookstores' unit-level contribution.
 2. The publisher's project-level contribution.
 3. The author's royalties.

LO15-3, 4
Spalding

P15-41. Multiple-Product Profitability Analysis
Spalding produces acrylic and polycarbonate basketball backboard and rim sets. Assume the following represents sales information for last year.

	Acrylic	Polycarbonate	Total
Units manufactured and sold	2,000	3,500	5,500
Sales revenue	$600,000	$735,000	$1,335,000
Variable costs	346,750	454,250	801,000
Contribution margin	$253,250	$280,750	$ 534,000
Fixed costs			(425,630)
Before-tax profit			108,370
Income taxes (20%)			(21,674)
After-tax profit			$ 86,696

REQUIRED

a. Determine the current break-even point in sales dollars.
b. With the current product mix and break-even point, determine the average unit contribution margin and unit sales.
c. Sales representatives believe that the total sales will increase to 5,750 units, with the sales mix likely shifting to 80% polycarbonate and 20% acrylic over the next few years. Evaluate the desirability of this projection.

P15-42. Multiple-Product Break-Even Analysis

Currently, Corner Lunch Counter sells only Super Burgers for $5.50 each. During a typical month, the Counter reports a profit of $12,125 with sales of $68,750 and fixed costs of $36,000. Management is considering the introduction of a new Super Chicken Sandwich that will sell for $7.00 and have variable costs of $2.50. The addition of the Super Chicken Sandwich will require hiring additional personnel and renting additional equipment. These actions will increase monthly fixed costs by $5,400.

In the short run, management predicts that Super Chicken sales will average 7,500 sandwiches per month. However, almost all short-run sales of Super Chickens will come from regular customers who switch from Super Burgers to Super Chickens. Consequently, management predicts monthly sales revenue from Super Burgers will decline $27,500 (5,000 units). In the long run, management predicts that Super Chicken sales will increase to 9,000 sandwiches per month and that Super Burger sales will increase to 16,000 burgers per month.

REQUIRED

a. Determine each of the following:
   1. The current monthly break-even point in sales dollars.
   2. The short-run monthly profit and break-even point in sales dollars subsequent to the introduction of Super Chickens.
   3. The long-run monthly profit and break-even point in sales dollars subsequent to the introduction of Super Chickens.
b. Based on your analysis, what are your recommendations?

P15-43. Profit Planning with Taxes

Carron Net Company manufactures sports nets for virtually every outdoor sport. Assume Carron sells nets for $50, on average, per unit. Last year, the company manufactured and sold 30,000 nets to obtain an after-tax profit of $275,000. Variable and fixed costs follow.

Variable Cost per Unit		Fixed Costs per Year	
Manufacturing	$20	Manufacturing	$232,250
Selling and administrative	4	Selling and administrative	204,000
Total	$24	Total	$436,250

REQUIRED

a. Determine the tax rate the company paid last year.
b. What unit sales volume is required to provide an after-tax profit of $400,000?
c. If the company reduces the unit variable cost by $4 and increases fixed manufacturing costs by $53,000, what unit sales volume is required to provide an after-tax profit of $400,000?
d. What assumptions are made about taxable income and tax rates in requirements (a) through (c)?

P15-44. CVP Analysis of Alternative Products

Assume **Converse**, a **Nike** company, plans to expand its manufacturing capacity to allow up to 30,000 pairs of a new shoe product each year. Because only one product can be produced, management is deciding between the production of the Roadrunner for backpacking and the Trail Runner for exercising. A marketing analysis indicates Converse could sell between 12,000 and 20,000 pairs of either product.

The accounting department has developed the following price and cost information.

	Product	
	Roadrunner	Trail Runner
Selling price per pair.	$140	$125
Variable costs per pair	$ 80	$ 75
Fixed production costs	$150,000	$100,000

Additional annual facility costs, regardless of product, are estimated at $100,000. Assume Converse is subject to a 20% income tax rate.

REQUIRED

a. Determine the number of pairs of each product that Converse must sell to obtain an after-tax profit of $50,000.
b. Determine the number of pairs of each product Converse must sell to obtain identical before-tax profit.
c. For the solution to requirement (b), calculate Converse's after-tax profit or loss.
d. Which product should Converse produce if both products were guaranteed to sell at least 18,000 pairs? Verify your solution with calculations.
e. How much would the variable costs per pair of the product *not* selected in requirement (d) have to fall before both products provide the same profit at sales of 18,000 pairs? Verify your solution with calculations.

LO15-1, 3 **P15-45. Contribution Margin Analysis – CMA Adapted**

1. Bolger and Co. manufactures large gaskets for the turbine industry. Bolger's per unit sales price and variable costs for the current year are as follows.

Sales price per unit.	$300
Variable cost per unit	210

Bolger's total fixed costs aggregate $360,000. As Bolger's labor agreement is expiring at the end of the year, management is concerned about the effect a new agreement will have on its unit breakeven point. The controller performed a sensitivity analysis to ascertain the estimated effect of a $10 per unit direct labor increase and a $10,000 reduction in fixed costs. Based on these data, it was determined that the breakeven point would

a. decrease by 1,000 units.
b. decrease by 125 units.
c. increase by 375 units.
d. increase by 500 units. **CMA adapted**

2. Wilkinson Company sells its single product for $30 per unit. The contribution margin ratio is 45% and Wilkinson has fixed costs of $10,000 per month. If 3,000 units are sold in the current month, Wilkinson's income would be

a. $30,500.
b. $49,500.
c. $40,500.
d. $90,000. **CMA adapted**

3. Projected sales for a tent manufacturer are $510,000. Each tent sells for $850 and requires $350 of variable costs to produce. The tent manufacturer's total fixed costs are $145,000. The tent manufacturer's margin of safety is

a. 310 units.
b. 710 units.
c. 730 units.
d. 1,310 units. **CMA adapted**

CASES AND PROJECTS

LO15-2 **C15-46. Ethics and Pressure to Improve Profit Plans**

Art Conroy is the assistant controller of New City Muffler, Inc., a subsidiary of New City Automotive, which manufactures tailpipes, mufflers, and catalytic converters at several plants throughout North America. Because of pressure for lower selling prices, New City Muffler has had disappointing financial performance in recent years. Indeed, Conroy is aware of rumblings from corporate headquarters threatening to close the plant.

One of Conroy's responsibilities is to present the plant's financial plans for the coming year to the corporate officers and board of directors. In preparing for the presentation, Conroy was intrigued to note that the focal point of the budget presentation was a profit-volume graph projecting an increase in profits and a reduction in the break-even point.

Curious as to how the improvement would be accomplished, Conroy ultimately spoke with Paula Mitchell, the plant manager. Mitchell indicated that a planned increase in productivity would reduce variable costs and increase the contribution margin ratio.

When asked how the productivity increase would be accomplished, Mitchell made a vague reference to increasing the speed of the assembly line. Conroy commented that speeding up the assembly line could lead to labor problems because the speed of the line was set by union contract. Mitchell responded that she was afraid that if the speedup were opened to negotiation, the union would make a big "stink" that could result in the plant being closed. She indicated that the speedup was the "only way to save the plant, our jobs, and the jobs of all plant employees." Besides, she did not believe employees would notice a 2% or 3% increase in speed. Mitchell concluded the meeting observing, "You need to emphasize the results we will accomplish next year, not the details of how we will accomplish those results. Top management does not want to be bored with details. If we accomplish what we propose in the budget, we will be in for a big bonus."

REQUIRED
What advice do you have for Art Conroy?

C15-47. Cost Estimation and CVP Analysis LO15-3, 5
Presented are the functional income statements of Regional Distribution Inc. for two recent years.

REGIONAL DISTRIBUTION INC.
Functional Income Statements
For Years Ending December 31, Year 1 and Year 2

	Year 1		Year 2	
Sales.		$1,800,000		$1,585,000
Expenses				
Cost of goods sold	$1,350,000		$1,188,750	
Shipping	68,500		65,250	
Sales order processing.	20,650		19,850	
Customer relations	55,000		48,800	
Depreciation	30,000		30,000	
Administrative	90,500	(1,614,650)	90,000	(1,442,650)
Before-tax profit		185,350		142,350
Income taxes (20%)		(37,070)		(28,470)
After-tax profit.		$ 148,280		$ 113,880

REQUIRED
a. Determine Regional Distribution's break-even point in sales dollars.
b. What dollar sales volume is required to earn an after-tax profit of $250,000?
c. Assuming sales of $4,000,000 next year, prepare a budgeted contribution income statement.
d. Discuss the reliability of the calculations in requirements (a–c), including the limitations of the CVP model and how they affect the reliability of the model.

SOLUTIONS TO REVIEW PROBLEMS

Review 15-1—Solution

a. (1) Profit (current price) = $2,000X − ($1,000,000 + $525X)
   where X = Number of scooters

   (2) Profit (proposed price) = $1,400X − ($1,000,000 + $525X)
   where X = Number of scooters

b. (1) Profit (current price)   = ($2,000 × 6,200) − [$1,000,000 + ($525 × 6,200)]
                                                      = $12,400,000 − $4,255,000
                                                      = $8,145,000

   (2) Profit (proposed price) = ($1,400 × 6,200) − [$1,000,000 + ($525 × 6,200)]
                                                        = $8,680,000 − $4,255,000
                                                        = $4,425,000

   Difference in profits   = $3,720,000 (decrease in profits)

c. Profit (current price)   = $8,145,000
   Profit (proposed price)   = ($1,400 × 7,130) − [$1,000,000 + ($525 × 7,130)]
                                                  = $9,982,000 − $4,743,250
                                                   = $5,238,750
   Difference in profits   = $2,906,250 (decrease in profits)

d. Profits are projected to drop, even with a projected increase in volume of 15%, which doesn't support a price drop. However, managers will want to determine how sensitive consumers are to price—would a lesser drop in price still provide an increase in demand? Is the price drop a reaction to competitor pricing? Will an increase in production fall within the relevant range or will the cost structure need to be adjusted? Is it feasible to change the company's cost structure? Given that the operations are profitable, it may be advantageous to shift some variable costs to fixed costs.

Review 15-2—Solution

a.

SEGWAY COMPANY
Contribution Income Statement
For the Month of June

Sales (3,000 × $40)		$120,000
Less variable costs		
Direct materials (3,000 × $15)	$45,000	
Direct labor (3,000 × $3)	9,000	
Manufacturing overhead (3,000 × $10)	30,000	
Selling and administrative (3,000 × $2)	6,000	(90,000)
Contribution margin		30,000
Less fixed costs		
Manufacturing overhead	15,000	
Selling and administrative	10,000	(25,000)
Profit		$ 5,000

b. **Contribution margin per unit = Selling price per unit − Variable cost per unit**
                                                       = $40 − $30
                                                       = **$10 per unit**

    Contribution margin ratio = Unit contribution margin ÷ Selling price per unit
                                                       = $10 ÷ $40
                                                       = **0.25**

For each helmet sold at $40, Segway had $10 more to cover fixed costs and contribute toward profit. Stated another way, 25% of the revenue was left to cover fixed costs and contribute toward profit. In the short-term, as long as there is capacity, Segway should continue producing and selling the helmets.

Review 15-3—Solution

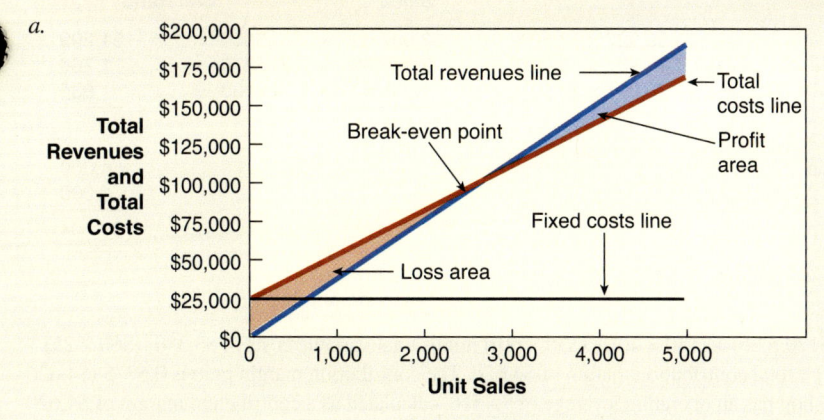

a.

b. $$\text{Break-even sales unit volume} = \frac{\text{Fixed costs}}{\text{Unit contribution margin}}$$

$$= \$25,000 \div \$10$$

$$= 2,500 \text{ units}$$

c. $$\text{Target dollar sales volume} = \frac{\text{Fixed costs} + \text{Desired profit}}{\text{Contribution margin ratio}}$$

$$= (\$25,000 + \$5,000) \div 0.25$$

$$= \$120,000$$

d. If direct materials cost more than anticipated,
   1. The fixed cost line will remain the same
   2. The total cost line will have a steeper slope to reflect the higher variable cost per unit
   3. The break-even point will increase in unit sales because fewer dollars are left from each sale to cover fixed costs.
   4. The loss area will increase due to the higher break-even point.

Review 15-4—Solution

a.

	Seat	Backpack	Phone Holder	Total
Monthly unit sales..........................	25	40	60	
Selling price	$120	$80	$30	
Sales.......................................	$3,000	$3,200	$1,800	$8,000
Variable costs.............................	1,500	1,160	720	3,380
Contribution margin	$1,500	$2,040	$1,080	4,620
Fixed costs				4,000
Before-tax profit				$ 620
Contribution margin (CM) ratio..............	0.5000	0.6375	0.6000	0.5775*
Current sales mix (based on sales dollars)	37.50%	40.00%	22.50%	

*$4,620/$8,000 = 0.5775

b. $$\text{Break-even dollar sales volume} = \frac{\text{Fixed costs}}{\text{Contribution margin ratio}}$$

$$= \frac{\$4,000}{0.5775}$$

$$= \$6,927 \text{ (Rounded UP to the nearest whole dollar)}$$

Proof:		Sales			C/M Ratio
Seat:	$6,927 × 37.50% =	$2,597.63	×	0.5000 =	$1,299
Backpack:	$6,927 × 40.00% =	2,770.80	×	0.6375 =	1,766
Phone Holder:	$6,927 × 22.50% =	1,558.57	×	0.6000 =	935
		$6,927.00			
Total contribution margin					4,000
Fixed costs					4,000
Before-tax profit					$ –0–

Review 15-5—Solution

a. Total sales of $8,000 [($120 × 25) + ($80 × 40) + ($30 × 60)] minus total variable costs of $3,380 [($60 × 25) + ($29 × 40) + ($12 × 60)] = total contribution margin of $4,620. The contribution margin ratio is 0.5775 ($4,620 ÷ $8,000). The Segway shop has an operating leverage of 7.4516, calculated as a contribution margin of $4,620 divided by before-tax profit of $620 ($4,620 − $4,000).

b. If sales dollars increase by 20% to $9,600, before-tax profit should increase by 7.4516 times 20%, or 149%, to $1,544. Because of the leverage caused by fixed costs, a 20% increase in sales results in a 149% increase in before-tax profit.

c. A 20% decrease in sales would result in a 149% decrease in before-tax profit to $(304).

Proof:	20% Sales Increase	20% Sales Decrease
Sales	$9,600	$6,400
CM %	× 0.5775	× 0.5775
Total CM	5,544	3,696
Fixed costs	4,000	4,000
Before-tax profit	$1,544*	$ (304)**

*($1,544 − $620)/$620 = 149% increase in before-tax profit
**(-$304 − $620)/$620 = 149% decrease in before-tax profit

Review 15-6—Solution

$$\text{Target unit sales volume} = \frac{\text{Fixed costs} + \text{Desired before-tax profit}}{\text{Unit contribution margin}}$$

Desired before-tax profit = $4,500 ÷ (1 − 0.40) = $7,500

Target unit sales volume = ($25,000 + $7,500) ÷ $10

= 3,250 units

Chapter 16
Using Relevant Costs and Differential Analysis for Decision-Making

LEARNING OBJECTIVES

LO16-1 Distinguish between relevant and irrelevant revenues and costs. (p. 16-3)

LO16-2 Apply differential analysis to an equipment replacement decision. (p. 16-7)

LO16-3 Apply differential analysis to evaluate changes in profit plans including the discontinuing of a segment. (p. 16-9)

LO16-4 Apply differential analysis to evaluate whether to accept a special order. (p. 16-12)

LO16-5 Apply differential analysis to evaluate outsourcing decisions. (p. 16-14)

LO16-6 Apply differential analysis to evaluate whether to sell or further process a product. (p. 16-17)

LO16-7 Allocate limited resources for purposes of maximizing short-run profit (Appendix 16A). (p. 16-19)

Road Map

LO	Learning Objective | Topics	Page	eLecture	Review	Assignments
LO16-1	**Distinguish between relevant and irrelevant revenues and costs.** Future Revenues :: Outlay Costs :: Sunk Costs :: Sunk Cost Dilemma :: Disposal and Salvage Values :: Opportunity Costs	16-3	e16–1	R16-1	M16-11, M16-12, M16-13, M16-14, M16-15, M16-18, M16-19, M16-20, E16-22, E16-24, E16-25, E16-26, E16-27, E16-28, E16-29, E16-30, P16-34, P16-35, P16-36, P16-37, P16-38, P16-39, P16-40, P16-41, P16-42, C16-43
LO16-2	**Apply differential analysis to an equipment replacement decision.** Differential Cost Analysis :: Full Analysis :: Qualitative Factors	16-7	e16–2	R16-2	M16-13, M16-15, E16-22, P16-34, P16-36, P16-40
LO16-3	**Apply differential analysis to evaluate changes in profit plans including the discontinuing of a segment.** Changes in Profit Plans :: Discontinuing a Segment	16-9	e16–3	R16-3	M16-16, M16-17, E16-23, P16-34, P16-35, P16-39, P16-40, P16-41, P16-42, C16-43
LO16-4	**Apply differential analysis to evaluate whether to accept a special order.** Special Orders :: Relevant Revenue and Costs :: Time Span :: Opportunity Costs :: Qualitative Factors	16-12	e16–4	R16-4	M16-18, E16-24, E16-25, E16-26, P16-37, P16-38, P16-39, P16-40, P16-42, **DA16-1**
LO16-5	**Apply differential analysis to evaluate outsourcing decisions.** Make or Buy :: Opportunity Costs :: Qualitative Factors :: Environmental Factors :: Global Factors	16-14	e16–5	R16-5	M16-19, E16-27, E16-28, E16-29, P16-42, **DA16-3**
LO16-6	**Apply differential analysis to evaluate whether to sell or further process a product.** Single Product Decisions :: Joint Product Decisions	16-17	e16–6	R16-6	M16-20, E16-30, E16-31, P16-42
LO16-7	**Allocate limited resources for purposes of maximizing short-run profit (Appendix 16A).** Single Constraint :: Multiple Constraints :: Theory of Constraints	16-19	e16–7	R16-7	M16-21, E16-32, E16-33, **DA16-2**

BOSTON BEER
bostonbeer.com

Jim Koch founded **The Boston Beer Company** after discovering his great-great grandfather's recipe for Louis Koch Lager. Jim and his co-founder, Rhonda Kallman, introduced Samuel Adams Boston Lager publicly in Boston on Patriot's Day in April 1985. Boston Lager was selected as "The Best Beer in America" in The Great American Beer Festival's Consumer Preference Poll six weeks later. With its introduction, Boston Lager helped start the craft beer revolution. In addition to Samuel Adams, Boston Beer Company's portfolio includes other products such as Dogfish Head and Havana Lager, Angry Orchard Hard Cider, Twisted Tea Hard Iced Tea, and Truly Hard Seltzer.

Recently, Jim Koch announced that the company had a significant amount of excess Truly seltzer inventory. Due to an increased demand, Boston Beer had added capacity and increased inventory levels of raw materials, cans, and flavors. When the market growth unexpectedly slowed, the company found itself with excess inventory that had an expiration date approaching. The company had two options: 1) offer promotions and discounts to increase demand, or 2) dump the excess inventory. The Boston Beer Company executives had to assess the impact of each option on the company, both financially and reputationally. In analyzing the options, only relevant costs related to the decision were considered. For example, if the seltzer was offered at a discount, the company would recognize revenue and incur distribution costs. If the seltzer was disposed of, no incremental revenue would be recognized and no incremental costs would be incurred. But what about any impacts of the decision on the company's reputation? If the product went stale before consumers drank it, the company's reputation for high quality products would be negatively impacted. What if consumers became ill after drinking the beer? Did the company have an ethical obligation to ensure that the beer did not get distributed? If the company dumped the inventory, its reputation would remain intact.

In the end, the company disposed of the excess Truly inventory. After analyzing the different options, the company decided that the reputational risk associated with distributing potentially low-quality product was too high. Consequently, the less "costly" option was to dispose of the excess inventory and take the inventory "hit." This is an example of a decision made by managers after identifying and analyzing cost information and non-quantitative factors. In this chapter, we consider a number of frequently encountered decisions, such as whether to accept or reject a special order, to outsource or make a product, or to sell a product or process it further. Underlying every decision is a review of quantitative and qualitative information.

Although our focus in this chapter is on profit maximization, decisions should not be based solely on this criterion, especially maximizing profit in the short run. Managers must consider the implications decision alternatives have on long-run profit, as well as legal, ethical, social, and other nonquantitative factors. These factors can lead management to select a course of action other than that selected by financial information alone. Furthermore, not-for-profit organizations aim to maximize their missions rather than focusing on profits. When making decisions, the mission must always be front and center.

Sources: Boston Beer Company 2021 10-K and www.bostonbeer.com

CHAPTER ORGANIZATION

Relevant Costs and Benefits for Decision-Making

Identifying Relevant Revenues and Costs
- Relevance of Future Revenues
- Relevance of Outlay Costs
- Irrelevance of Sunk Costs
- Sunk Cost Dilemma
- Relevance of Disposal and Salvage Values
- Relevance of Opportunity Costs

Preparing and Applying Differential Analysis
- Equipment Replacement Decision
- Evaluating Changes in Profit Plans
- Discontinuing of a Segment
- Special Orders
- Outsourcing Decisions (Make or Buy)
- Sell or Process Further

Use of Limited Resources
- Single Constraint
- Multiple Constraints
- Theory of Constraints (Appendix 16A)

IDENTIFYING RELEVANT REVENUES AND COSTS

LO16-1 Distinguish between relevant and irrelevant revenues and costs.

When managers are faced with decisions, they often have access to a large amount of supporting data. However, the vast amount of data available includes information that should not impact decision-making. Identifying which information is pertinent to the decision at hand can be the hardest, yet the most critical part of the process. In decision-making, the key to relevant cost analysis is first to identify the **relevant costs** (future costs that differ among competing decision alternatives) and then to organize them in a manner that clearly indicates how they differ under each alternative. **Irrelevant costs** are those that will be incurred regardless of the path taken. Although these costs will remain and should be analyzed by managers, these costs should not affect the decision. Because the costs are identical between alternatives, irrelevant costs can be ignored for decision-making purposes. Remember, irrelevant costs are irrelevant to the actual decision. However, they are not necessarily irrelevant in the bigger picture of a company's operations. In a similar way, we also determine what *revenues* differ between alternatives. Once we know what costs and revenues differ between the alternatives, we can assess quantitatively which option is more favorable. Let's consider an equipment replacement decision to refine these concepts.

Equipment Replacement Decision

The Boston Beer Company produces and sells Samuel Adams, a craft beer product. The company expects to sell 12,000 cases of beer to retailers during the coming year at a price of $20 per case. Samuel Adams beer is made and bottled on dedicated machines in a plant that produces all Boston Beer products.

The machine used in the manufacture of Samuel Adams beer is two years old and has a remaining useful life of four years. Its purchase price was $90,000 (new), and it has an estimated salvage value of zero dollars at the end of its useful life. Its current book value (original cost less accumulated depreciation) is $60,000, but today, it could only be sold for $35,000.

Variable costs	
Direct materials	$2.50 per case
Conversion*	5.00 per case
Inspection	0.50 per case
Selling and administrative	1.00 per case

*Conversion costs consist of the combined costs of direct labor and manufacturing overhead incurred to convert raw materials to finished goods.

continued

continued from previous page

Fixed costs	
Depreciation on machine	$15,000 per year
Machine maintenance	200 per month
Other overhead	1,000 per month
Selling and administrative	3,450 per month
Common costs	
Administrative salaries	$65,000 per year
Building operations	23,000 per year
Building rent	24,000 per year

Management is evaluating the desirability of replacing the machine with a new machine. The new machine costs $80,000, has a useful life of four years, and a predicted salvage value of zero dollars at the end of its useful life. Although the new machine has the same production capacity as the old machine, its predicted operating costs are lower because it consumes less electricity. Further, because of an artificial intelligence enhanced control system, the new machine allows production of twice as many cases between inspections, and the cost of inspections is lower. The new machine requires only annual, rather than monthly overhauls which lowers machine maintenance costs. Costs for the new machine are predicted as follows.

Variable costs	
Conversion	$4.00 per case
Inspection	$0.15 per case
Fixed costs	
Machine maintenance	$ 200 per year

All other costs and all revenues remain unchanged.

The hypothetical keep-or-replace decision facing Boston Beer's management might be called a **cost reduction proposal** because it is based on the assumption that the organization is committed to an activity and that management desires to minimize the cost of that activity. Here, the two alternatives are either to continue operating with the old machine or to replace it with a new machine.

An analysis of how costs and revenues differ under each alternative assists management in making the best choice. The first objective of this chapter is to study the distinction between relevant and irrelevant items. After evaluating the relevance of each item, we develop an analysis of relevant costs.

Relevance of Future Revenues

Revenues, which are inflows of resources from the sale of goods and services, are relevant to a decision only if they differ between alternatives. In this example, the number of cases of beer sold to retailers does not depend on whether the company purchases the new machine. Because revenues do not change no matter what choice we make, revenues are irrelevant to the decision. Consequently, we ignore revenues in deciding between the two alternatives. Revenues would be relevant if the new machine had greater capacity or if management intended to change the selling price of beer should it acquire the new machine. (The $35,000 disposal value of the old machine is an inflow. However, *revenues* refer to resources from the sale of goods and services to customers in the normal course of business. We include the sale of the old machine under disposal and salvage values.)

Relevance of Outlay Costs

Outlay costs are costs that require *future* expenditures of cash or other resources. Outlay costs that differ under the decision alternatives are relevant to the decision. Outlay costs that do not differ are irrelevant to the decision. In deciding whether to replace the machine, Boston Beer classifies outlay costs as relevant or irrelevant to the decision. The cost of the new machine is a relevant cost as well as the ongoing costs that are expected to change using the new machine. The ongoing costs include conversion costs, inspection, and machine maintenance. The remaining costs are not expected to change with the purchase of the new machine, thus they are considered irrelevant to the machine purchase decision. For the decision of whether to purchase a new machine, the relevant and irrelevant outlay costs are listed in the following table.

Relevant Outlay Costs	Irrelevant Outlay Costs
Cost of New Machine	Direct Materials
Conversion Costs	Depreciation on Machine
Inspection Costs	Other Overhead Costs
Machine Maintenance	Selling and Administrative Costs
	Common Outlay Costs

Note that the irrelevant costs remain real costs that managers need to manage. However, they are considered "irrelevant" at this time because the costs stay constant between the considered alternatives.

Irrelevance of Sunk Costs

Sunk costs result from past decisions that cannot be changed. Suppose we purchased a car for $30,000 five years ago. Today we must decide whether to purchase another car or have major maintenance performed on our current car. In making this decision, the purchase price of our current car is a sunk cost. It is a sunk cost because it happened in the past. We cannot go back and renegotiate the purchase price of the car.

Sunk costs are never relevant. The cost of the old machine is a sunk cost, not a future cost. This cost and the related depreciation result from the past decision to acquire the old machine. Because these costs have already been incurred and cannot be changed, they are considered irrelevant. Sunk costs never differ between alternatives.

If management elects to keep the old machine, its book value will be depreciated over its remaining useful life of four years. However, if management elects to replace the old machine, its book value is written off when it is replaced. Even if management elects to discontinue operations, the book value of the old machine must be written off.

The Sunk Cost Dilemma

Although the book value of the old machine has no economic significance, the accounting treatment of past costs can make it psychologically difficult for managers to regard them as irrelevant. The *sunk cost dilemma* refers to situations in which companies must decide whether to continue with an expensive project, even though it has not achieved targeted results. Too many times, managers continue investing in projects because they have already invested a significant amount. If we assume that management replaces the old machine, a $25,000 accounting loss is recorded in the year of replacement.

Book value	$60,000
Disposal value	(35,000)
Loss on disposal	$25,000

The possibility of recording an accounting loss can create an ethical dilemma for managers. Although an action may be desirable from the long-run viewpoint of the organization, in the short run, choosing the action may result in an accounting loss. A manager might prefer to use the old machine (with lower total profits over the four-year period) as opposed to replacing it and being forced to record a loss on disposal. Although this action may avoid raising troublesome questions for the manager in the near term, the cumulative effect of many decisions of this nature is harmful to the organization's long-run economic health.

From an economic viewpoint, the analysis should focus on future costs and revenues that differ. The decision should not be influenced by sunk costs. In fact, researchers have shown that, far from ignoring sunk costs, many managers increase commitment to a project as sunk costs increase. Experimental research from a team at the University of Melbourne in Australia found that managers' personal motivations interact with the context of the specific project and the related sunk costs. Their study found that individuals who are focused on promotion become increasingly fixated on completion as the end of the project nears. While other managers are able to ignore fixed costs more consistently throughout the project life cycle, those who are focused on promotion are most likely to continue to invest in a project that should be abandoned when the project is close to completion.[1] Although there is no easy solution to this behavioral and ethical problem, managers and management accountants should be aware of its potential impact.

You recently made the decision to purchase an expensive machine for your manufacturing plant. The design of the machine was based on long-established technology. The purchase of this machine was a major decision supported by the chief financial officer, based solely on your recommendation. Shortly after making the purchase, you attend a trade convention where you learn of new technology that essentially renders obsolete the machine you recently purchased. You feel that it may be best for the company to acquire the new technology since most of your competitors will be using it soon. However, you feel that this cannot be done now that you have recently purchased the new machine. What should you consider in making this decision?

This is a decision that has both economic and ethical dimensions. Economically, the cost of the old machine is a sunk cost, since the expenditure to acquire it has already been made. If it can be sold to another company to recover part of the initial cost, that amount would be relevant to the decision regarding the new technology. However, you should ignore the cost of the recently purchased machine and consider only the outlay costs that will differ between keeping the recently purchased machine and purchasing the new technology. In addition, any opportunity costs (described below) that may be involved with disposing of the existing machine and acquiring the new machine should be considered. From an ethical standpoint, managers are often hesitant to recommend an action that reflects poorly on their past decisions. The temptation is to try to justify the past decision. If you have evaluated all of the relevant costs and have considered all of the qualitative issues associated with upgrading the machine, this should be the basis for making your recommendation, not how it might affect your reputation.

Relevance of Disposal and Salvage Values

Boston Beer's assumed revenues (inflows of resources from operations) from the sale of Samuel Adams beer were discussed earlier. The sale of fixed assets is also a source of resources. Because the sale of fixed assets is a *nonoperating item*, cash inflows obtained from these sales are discussed separately in this section.

The disposal value of the old machine is a relevant cash inflow. It is obtained only if the replacement alternative is selected. Any salvage value available at the end of the useful life of either machine is also relevant. A loss on disposal can have a favorable tax impact if the loss can be offset against taxable gains or taxable income. To simplify the analysis, we ignore any tax implications at this point. The tax effects related to capital asset transactions are discussed in Chapter 24.

Relevance of Opportunity Costs

When making a decision between alternative courses of action, accepting one alternative results in rejecting the other alternative(s). Any benefit foregone as a result of rejecting one opportunity in favor of another opportunity is described as an **opportunity cost** of the accepted alternative. For example, if you are employed at a salary of $60,000 per year and you have the opportunity to continue to work or the opportunity to go back to school full-time for two years to earn a graduate degree, the cost of getting the degree includes not only the outlay costs for tuition, books, and so forth, it also includes the salary foregone (or opportunity cost) of $60,000 per year. So, if your tuition and other outlay costs are going to be $25,000 per year for two years, the cost of earning the degree will be $50,000 of outlay costs and $120,000 of opportunity costs, for a total cost of earning the degree of $170,000. Opportunity costs are always relevant in making decisions among competing alternatives because these costs differ between the choices.

The following is a summary of all the relevant and irrelevant costs discussed in this section.

---

[1] Source: Adam P. Barsky and Michael J. Zyphur, "Disentangling Sunk-Costs and Completion Proximity: The Role of Regulatory Focus," *Journal of Experimental Social Psychology* 65 (2016): 105-108.

Relevant Costs		Irrelevant Costs	
Future costs that differ among competing alternatives		Future costs that do not differ among competing alternatives	
Opportunity Costs	**Relevant Outlay Costs**	**Irrelevant Outlay Costs**	**Sunk Costs**
Net benefits foregone of rejected alternatives	Future costs requiring future expenditures that differ	Future costs requiring future expenditures that do not differ	Historical costs resulting from past decisions

Option to Discontinue Operations Although the approach described above is appropriate for many activities, managers should remember that they have another alternative—*discontinue operations*. To simplify the analysis, managers normally do not consider the alternative to discontinue when operations appear to be profitable. However, if there is any doubt about an operation's profitability, this alternative should be considered. Because revenues change if an operation is discontinued, revenues are always relevant whenever this alternative is considered.

Review 16-1 LO16-1   Identifying Relevant and Irrelevant Costs

Anheuser-Busch Inbev NV/SA operates approximately 200 breweries in nearly 50 countries. The company's products include Budweiser products, Stella Artois, Virtue Cider, and Kombrewcha. Assume that Anheuser-Busch is considering the purchase of a new packaging machine. The new machine would replace a labor-intensive process. The cost of the new machine is $1,000,000 and it has an expected useful life of five years. At the end of the five years, the machine is expected to have a residual value of $100,000. The operating cost of the new machine is estimated to be $10,000 per month. Anheuser-Busch believes that it will save $5 of direct labor per month for every case of beer packaged. In addition, one manufacturing manager, with a salary of $6,000 per month, would no longer be needed. The Vice President of Manufacturing earns $10,000 per month. This position is unaffected by the decision to purchase the machine. The new machine will also free up approximately 5,000 square feet of space from the displaced workers. The brewing/manufacturing facility is leased under a 10-year lease with 8 years remaining in the lease term. Additionally, the current lease cost is $1 per square foot per month. Anheuser-Busch has received an offer to rent the excess space to a related company for $3,500 per month.

Required
Classify all of the costs described above as either "relevant" or "irrelevant" to the decision to acquire the new machine.

Solution on p. 16-41.

PREPARING AND APPLYING DIFFERENTIAL ANALYSIS

LO16-2
Apply differential analysis to an equipment replacement decision.

Differential analysis analyzes and compares the relevant revenues and costs in each option for the decision at hand. Irrelevant items are excluded from a differential analysis because they remain constant across alternatives. While these numbers might still be important to managers for other reasons, the numbers are irrelevant to the decision at hand and can be ignored. We will apply differential analysis in management decision-making through the rest of this chapter as outlined below.

Applications of Differential Analysis						
Equipment Replacement Decisions	Evaluating Changes in Profit Plans	Decision to Keep or Drop a Segment	Special Order Decisions	Outsourcing Decisions	Sell or Process Further Decisions	Allocating Limited Resources

Equipment Replacement Decision

A differential analysis of relevant costs for Boston Beer's equipment replacement decision assuming annual production of 12,000 cases of beers is in **Exhibit 16.1**. If the machine is replaced, Boston Beer will purchase the new machine for $80,000 and dispose of the old machine for a $35,000 inflow. In addition, the company will incur $192,000 in conversion costs, $7,200 in inspection costs, and $800 in machine maintenance. The company will expend $245,000, net if it purchases the new machine. If the old machine is kept, the company will continue to incur $240,000 in conversion costs, $24,000 in inspection costs, and $9,600 in machine maintenance costs; keeping the old machine will cost the company $273,600, net. Over the four year period, replacement provides a net advantage of $28,600 ($245,000 − $273,600).

EXHIBIT 16.1 Differential Analysis for Boston Beer's Equipment Replacement

	Four-Year Totals		
	Replace with New Machine	Keep Old Machine	Difference (effect of replacement on income)
Conversion			
Old machine (12,000 cases × $5 × 4 years)		$240,000	
New machine (12,000 cases × $4 × 4 years)	$192,000		($48,000)
Inspection			
Old machine (12,000 cases × $0.50 × 4 years)		24,000	
New machine (12,000 cases × $0.15 × 4 years)	7,200		(16,800)
Machine maintenance			
Old machine ($200 per month × 12 months × 4 years)		9,600	
New machine ($200 per year × 4 years)	800		(8,800)
Disposal of old machine	(35,000)		(35,000)
Cost of new machine	80,000		80,000
Totals	$245,000	$273,600	($28,600)
Advantage of replacement		$28,600	

Differential Analysis vs. Full Analysis An alternative analysis to that presented in **Exhibit 16.1** is to present a *full analysis* of all revenues and costs (relevant and irrelevant) for each alternative in separate columns, such that the bottom line of the analysis is the total profit or loss for each alternative. This method is preferred if the goal is to determine the total profitability of each alternative. Remember, this full analysis will depict revenues and costs that are not affected by the decision (or irrelevant items). Assuming the organization is committed to providing the particular product or service, a differential analysis for a specific decision (as shown in **Exhibit 16.1**) is preferred to a full analysis of all costs and revenues for a number of reasons.

- A differential analysis focuses on only those items that differ, providing a clearer picture of the impact of the decision. This analysis highlights costs that could be avoided by a specific decision, revenues that will be gained or lost, and new costs that might be incurred. Management is less apt to be confused by this analysis than by one that combines relevant and irrelevant items as it highlights the aspects that are most crucial to the decision-making process.
- A differential analysis contains fewer items, making it easier and quicker to prepare. This simplicity focuses managers on what matters most.
- A differential analysis can help to simplify complex situations (such as those encountered by multiple-product or multiple-plant firms), when it is difficult to develop complete firmwide statements to analyze all decision alternatives.

Before preparing a differential analysis for this decision, Boston Beer should reassess the organization's commitment to Samuel Adams. This helps avoid "throwing good money after bad." If Samuel Adams currently had large annual losses, acquiring the new machine would merely reduce total losses over the next four years by $28,600. In this case, discontinuing operations (a third alternative) should also be considered.

Qualitative Factors in Decision-Making

Analytical models, such as differential analysis, are very useful in organizing information for purposes of determining the economics of a decision. However, it is important always to keep in mind that models do not make decisions—managers make decisions. The results of analytical models are an essential and necessary starting point in many decisions, but often there are **qualitative factors** (nonfinancial factors) factors that weigh heavily on a decision that may cause the manager to go against the most economical alternative. There may be human resource, marketing, cultural, logistical, technological, ethical, environmental, or other factors that outweigh the analytics of a decision situation. It is in these situations where managers demonstrate leadership, problem-solving, and executive skill and potential, or the lack thereof.

What qualitative information would Boston Beer want to consider before investing in the new equipment?

Accounting information contributes to decision-making. It offers one perspective on the potential solutions. However, accounting rarely provides clear-cut answers. The accounting information must be combined with other information such as product demand information, pricing information, and alternative production possibilities. Boston Beer might also consider the environmental ramifications of the two machines; does the new machine offer a more sustainable solution?

Review 16-2 LO16-2 — Preparing a Differential Analysis for a Machine Purchase Decision

Refer to the information provided in Review 16-1 for Anheuser-Busch Inbev NV/SA to answer the following questions.

Required

a. Assuming the new machine will be used to produce an average of 5,000 cases of beer per month, prepare a differential analysis of the relevant costs of buying the machine and using it for the next 5 years, versus continuing to use a labor-intensive process.

b. In addition to the quantitative analysis in requirement *a*, what qualitative considerations are important for making the right decision?

Solution on p. 16-41.

LO16-3 Apply differential analysis to evaluate changes in profit plans including the discontinuing of a segment.

Differential analysis is used to provide information for a variety of planning and decision-making situations. Whenever a company faces a decision with multiple options, differential analysis can be used to assess the financial impact of each option. This section illustrates the application of differential analysis to changes in profit plans, including the discontinuing of a segment.

Evaluating Changes in Profit Plans

Recall that Boston Beer collects an average of $20 for every case of Samuel Adams Beer sold. Variable costs (per case) and fixed costs per month are as follows.

Variable Cost per Case		Fixed Costs per Month	
Direct materials	$2.50	Depreciation on machine	$1,250
Conversion	5.00	Machine maintenance	200
Inspection	0.50	Other overhead	1,000
Selling and administrative	1.00	Selling and administrative	3,450
Total	$9.00	Total	$5,900

Based on the above information, the contribution margin is $11 per case of beer ($20 – $9). This represents the amount that is left from each sale to cover fixed costs and contribute toward profit. Boston Beer's hypothetical contribution income statement for April is presented in **Exhibit 16.2**. Assume the April results are based on sales of 1,000 cases.

EXHIBIT 16.2 Contribution Income Statement

BOSTON BEER
Contribution Income Statement
For the Month of April

Revenue (1,000 × $20.00)		$20,000
Less variable costs		
Direct materials (1,000 × $2.50)	$ 2,500	
Conversion (1,000 × $5)	5,000	
Inspection (1,000 × $0.50)	500	
Selling and administrative (1,000 × $1)	1,000	(9,000)
Contribution margin		11,000
Less fixed costs		
Depreciation on machine	1,250	
Machine maintenance	200	
Other overhead	1,000	
Selling and administrative	3,450	(5,900)
Profit		$ 5,100

> **To evaluate the impact of different proposals on profits for Boston Beer, would you use differential analysis or a full analysis approach?**
>
> *Although it is possible to develop a contribution income statement (similar to Exhibit 16.2) for each alternative and compare the profits across statements, this method does not focus managers on the moving pieces of each decision. It is more cumbersome and less intuitive than using differential analysis. Differential analysis focuses only on items that differ between the alternatives.*

Management wants to know the effect that each of the following three mutually exclusive alternatives would have on profits for the month.

1. **The introduction of a bonus program.** For every 100 cases a salesperson sells in one month, the salesperson receives an additional $25. The bonus program is expected to result in a 20% increase in cases sold and a total bonus payout of $300 per month.

Alternative 1	
Profit increase from increased sales (1,000 × 0.20 × $11)	$2,200
Profit decrease from bonus	(300)
Increase in monthly profit	$1,900

   Focusing only on the changes, the proposal to pay bonuses to incentivize sales impacts the revenue as well as employee expenses. The company expects to sell an additional 200 cases (1,000 × 0.20). Remember, each additional case sold will increase the monthly profit by an amount equal to the contribution margin. At a contribution margin of $11 per case, profits will increase by $2,200. Bonuses will increase by the stated $300 for a net increase in profits of $1,900.

2. **Increasing the price of the case of beer by an average of $1.** Increasing the price should result in a monthly drop in sales of 200 cases.

Alternative 2	
Profit decrease from reduced sales price (200 × $11)	$(2,200)
Profit increase from increased price (1,000 − 200 cases) × $1	800
Decrease in monthly profit	$(1,400)

   Due to the price increase, 200 fewer cases of Samuel Adams will be sold. Losing $11 contribution from each case, the brand will earn $2,200 less in profits. This is offset by the increase in price. At $1 more per case, the 800 cases sold will increase profits by $800. Focusing only on these two items, management can assess the impact of the decision as these are the only items that will change with the proposal.

3. **Decreasing the price of beer by an average of $1 per case.** Decreasing the price should result in a monthly increase in sales of 200 cases.

Alternative 3	
Profit increase from increase in sales (200 × $11)	$2,200
Profit decrease from reduced selling price (1,200 × $1)	(1,200)
Increase in monthly profit	$1,000

Profits are expected to increase by $2,200 for the 200 new units sold. This is offset by the $1,200 profit decrease resulting from the reduction in selling price for all units sold. The net profit increase is estimated to be $1,000.

> **What proposal would you recommend that management adopt? Why?**
>
> *Alternative 2 results in a projected profit decrease. Unless there is a business reason to adopt this proposal, it should be dismissed. This leaves management with*

Alternatives 1 and 3, both of which are expected to increase profit. Although it might seem that management should adopt 1 due to the larger profit increase, there might be reasons to adopt alternative 3 as well. At this point, management might want to bring in market, competition and demographic data. How do the company's prices compare to prices of competitors? Is there a reason to decrease the price to spur demand and allow retailers to better promote Samuel Adams? Management should consider the financial impact as well as any qualitative input before making a final decision.

Evaluating the Effect on the Profit Plan of Discontinuing a Segment

One scenario in profit planning explained in an earlier section is to discontinue a segment. In the short-run, differential analysis shows the quantitative effects on profit of discontinuing a segment. Now assume that due to an increase in competition and a decrease in demand, management believes that a drop in the price of Samuel Adams beer of $1 per case is unavoidable. Given the revised selling price and a drop in expected sales volume to 900 units, what is the impact on Boston Beer if the Samuel Adams segment is discontinued? If we assume that the number of units and total fixed costs will not change in the short run, the net effect on profits of Boston Beer are computed as follows.

> **Contribution margin lost = (Sales price per unit − Variable cost per unit) × units**
>
> = ($19 − $9) × 900
>
> = **$9,000 net decrease in overall profits if segment is dropped**

When the contribution margin is positive (negative), the net impact on total profits of dropping a segment is a net decrease (increase). If the Samuel Adams segment is discontinued, the company would lose $9,000 of contribution margin each month that contributes toward fixed costs. In fact, in the short run, the company may opt to continue the segment as long as its contribution margin is positive and is greater than fixed costs that are unavoidable in the short run. In this case, with $5,900 in unavoidable fixed costs, the segment will cover fixed costs as long as the contribution margin per unit is greater than approximately $6.56 ($5,900/900 units). If instead, the company would realize some fixed cost savings (i.e., some of the fixed costs are avoidable in the short run), the *cost savings are deducted from the lost contribution margin to calculate the net effect on profits*. In the long run, segments must be profitable to be viable. However, certain decisions may be made in the short run to allow for time to put into place longer term plans.

Review 16-3 LO16-3   Applying Differential Analysis to Alternative Profit Scenarios

Anheuser-Busch InBev NV/SA brews and distributes Shock Top beer. Suppose each unit (i.e., a six-pack) is sold to retailers for $4.80 each and that manufacturing and other costs are as follows.

Variable Cost per Unit		Fixed Costs per Month	
Direct materials.	$2.00	Factory overhead	$15,000
Direct labor	0.20	Selling and administrative.	5,000
Factory overhead	0.25	Total	$20,000
Distribution	0.05		
Total	$2.50		

The variable distribution costs are for transportation to retailers. Also assume the current monthly production and sales volume is 15,000 and monthly capacity is 20,000 units.

Required
Determine the effect of the following separate situations on monthly profits.

a. A $1.50 increase in the unit selling price should result in an 1,800 unit decrease in monthly sales.
b. A $1.80 decrease in the unit selling price should result in a 6,000 unit increase in monthly sales. However, because of capacity constraints, the last 1,000 units would be produced during overtime, when the direct labor costs increase by 50%.

continued

c. What is the impact on net profits of the company if we assume that the Shock Top segment is discontinued due to declining market conditions that cause the selling price per unit to drop to $3.00? Assume that all fixed costs are unavoidable except for $1,000 in factory overhead. This amount will not continue in the short run if the segment is discontinued, thus it is considered a cost savings if the segment is discontinued. **Solution on p. 16-42.**

Special Orders

On occasion, a company is presented with a proposal to provide products or services to a specific customer under specific conditions. Assume that a not-for-profit is hosting a fundraising dinner, and it would like to purchase Boston Beer products at a reduced rate. Although the fundraiser will offer more than simply Samuel Adams, for this example, let's focus on Samuel Adams. The not-for-profit would like to procure 25 cases of beer for $10 per case (half price). Boston Beer has sufficient capacity to produce and deliver the beverages for the fundraiser. Boston Beer's management wants to know the profit impact of accepting the offer. The following analysis focuses on those costs and revenues that will differ if the offer is accepted.

LO16-4 Apply differential analysis to evaluate whether to accept a special order.

Increase in revenues (25 × $10).................................		$250.00
Increase in costs		
Direct materials (25 × $2.50)................................	$ 62.50	
Conversion (25 × $5)..	125.00	
Inspection (25 × $0.50)......................................	12.50	
Selling and administrative (25 × $1).........................	25.00	225.00
Increase in profits..		$ 25.00

Accepting the offer will result in a profit increase of $25. Although this is a minimal increase, management might consider this to be a great marketing opportunity along with the potential to convert the attendees into future customers. Additionally, it provides $25 more towards covering fixed costs. Finally, management's decision might ultimately depend on the not-for-profit and the mission of the fundraiser. If Boston Beer supports the mission, it might choose to provide the beverages at low, or even negative, profits.

If management were unaware of relevant cost concepts, they might be tempted to compare the special event price of $40 to the average cost of a case of Samuel Adams from the accounting reports. Based on Samuel Adam's hypothetical April contribution income statement in **Exhibit 16.2**, the average cost per case is calculated as follows.

Total variable costs...	$ 9,000
Total fixed costs..	5,900
Total costs...	$14,900
Total cases..	1,000
Average cost per case...	$14.90

Comparing the special event price of $10 per case to the average cost of $14.90, management might conclude the event would result in a loss of $4.90 per case.

It is apparent that the $14.90 figure encompasses all variable and fixed costs, regardless of whether the cost is relevant to the current decision. Fixed costs, however, are not relevant because they are constant, regardless of whether the beverages are supplied for the event. Consequently, only the variable costs are relevant to the decision. Remember, management may not have detailed cost information readily available. Managerial accounting is as much about interpreting data and asking the right questions or getting the right information as it is about creating the analyses. In order to use appropriate information for decision-making purposes, management must first ask for or obtain the specific information needed. *Different configurations of cost information are required for different purposes.* In the absence of specificity of the information needed and a clear understanding of the decision being considered, pertinent relevant information may be missing in the decision process.

Importance of Time Span

The special event is a one-time contract that will use current excess capacity. Consequently, it is appropriate to consider only variable costs to inform the decision-making. What if the not-for-profit wants to sign a multiyear contract to provide 25 cases per month at $10? Under these circumstances, management might consider rejecting the contract. There is a high probability that cost increases would make the order unprofitable in later years. At the very least, management should insist that a cost escalation clause be added to the agreement, specifying that the customer price would increase to cover any cost increases.

Of more concern is the notion that fixed costs are not fixed in the long run. For example, management can replace and upgrade its fixed assets over time. Accordingly, *in the long run, all costs (including costs classified as fixed in a given period) are relevant*. To remain in business in the long run, Boston Beer must replace equipment, pay taxes, pay administrative salaries, and so forth. Consequently, management should consider *all costs,* fixed and variable, in evaluating a long-term contract. Of course, these financial considerations will ultimately be weighed against qualitative arguments, such as the importance of the not-for-profit's mission, to come to a final conclusion.

Full costs include all costs, regardless of their behavior pattern or activity level. The average full cost per unit is sometimes used to approximate long-run variable costs. If accepting a long-term contract increases the monthly production and sales to 1,025 cases of Samuel Adams, the average full cost per case is estimated as follows (amounts are rounded).

Costs per case	
Direct materials.	$ 2.50
Conversion	5.00
Inspection.	0.50
Selling and administrative.	1.00
Depreciation on machine ($1,250/1,025)	1.22
Machine maintenance ($200/1,025).	0.20
Other overhead ($1,000/1,025).	0.98
Selling and administrative ($3,450/1,025).	3.37
Average full cost per case	$14.77

In this case, the estimated long-run variable costs are $14.77 for each case of Samuel Adams. Many managers would say this is the minimum acceptable selling price, especially if the order extends over a long period of time, precluding any compelling, qualitative reason for maintaining the contract.

Opportunity Costs

Because there is excess capacity, there is no alternative use for the capacity in the short run. Consequently, the company is not giving up other sales in order to fulfill the current order. This means that the opportunity cost of accepting the order is zero.

Would your recommendation change if Samuel Adams was operating at capacity?

If Samuel Adam's production was operating at capacity, accepting the special offer would require reducing production for a different customer. Assuming that capacity cannot be easily increased (as is typically the case), Samuel Adams would lose more profitable orders if it accepts the order from the not-for-profit. Customer orders typically have a contribution margin of $11 per case for Samuel Adams. If Samuel Adams works with the not-for-profit, it will lose sales of 25 cases to a more profitable customer. These lost sales equate to the opportunity cost of accepting this order, calculated as follows.

Lost sales, in cases	25
Regular contribution margin per case.	× $11
Opportunity cost of accepting special event.	$275

Because this opportunity cost exceeds the $25 contribution derived from the special event, management might reject the special event. Accepting the event will reduce profits by $250 ($25 contribution − $275 opportunity cost). As discussed previously, there are also qualitative considerations. Even though there is a loss expected from accepting the special event, management might consider this a great marketing opportunity to reach out to new customers and decide that it is worthwhile to accept the order.

Qualitative Factors in Decision-Making

Although an analysis of cost and revenue information may indicate that a special order is profitable (unprofitable) in the short run, management might still reject (accept) the order because of qualitative considerations. Any concerns regarding the order's impact on regular customers might lead management to reject the order even if there is excess capacity. If the order involves a special low price, regular customers might demand a similar price reduction and threaten to take their business elsewhere. Alternatively, management might accept the special order while operating at capacity if they believed there were long-term benefits associated with penetrating a new market. Legal factors must also be considered if the special order is from a buyer who competes with regular customers. The accounting analyses provide valuable information to decision-makers. However, these numbers should never drive decisions in isolation. These analyses must always be combined with a review of qualitative factors before a final decision is made.

Estimating the Profitability of Special Orders — LO16-4 **Review 16-4**

Refer to the information provided in Review 16-3 for **Anheuser-Busch InBev NV/SA** to answer the following questions.

Required
Determine the effect of the following separate situations on monthly profits.

a. A Russian beer distributor has proposed to place a special, one-time order for 4,000 units next month at a reduced price of $4.00 per unit. The distributor would pay all transportation costs. There would be additional fixed selling and administrative costs of $500.

b. An Austrian beer distributor has proposed to place a special, one-time order for 8,000 units at a special price of $4.00 per unit. The distributor would pay all transportation costs. There would be additional fixed selling and administrative costs of $500. Assume overtime production is not possible.

Solution on p. 16-42.

Outsourcing Decisions (Make or Buy)

One of the most common applications of relevant cost analysis involves the make-or-buy decision. Virtually any service, product, or component that can be produced or manufactured internally can also be acquired from an external source. The procurement of services, products, or components from an external source is called **outsourcing**. For example, the management of the bookstore at your college or university may be outsourced to **Barnes and Noble**, and the dining facilities may be outsourced to **Compass Group North America** or **Aramark Corporation**. Similarly, **HP** and **Samsung** actually manufacture very few of the components of their computers. Instead the manufacture of components is outsourced to other firms such as **Intel** for computer chips and **Seagate** for storage devices. Virtually all computer manufacturers, with the exception of **Apple**, outsource their operating systems to **Microsoft**.

Any time you call a customer support call center, the representative reached is likely to be working in a different country. A growing number of companies even outsource employees from employee leasing companies. In the past 25 years, outsourcing of goods and services has expanded exponentially with the emergence of well-trained, low-cost labor forces in China and India and other parts of the world.

As the above discussion reveals, the decision to outsource rather than to produce a service or product internally involves a vast array of qualitative issues. The quantitative issues surrounding the outsourcing (or make-or-buy) decision are often less challenging. To illustrate, we continue the Boston Beer example. Suppose a warehouse facility offers Boston Beer a one-year contract to manage all storage

LO16-5
Apply differential analysis to evaluate outsourcing decisions.

of finished goods for the Samuel Adams brand service at a cost of $1,500 per month. Boston Beer must now decide whether it should continue to store Samuel Adams internally or store the inventory with a third-party warehouse company. Of course, nonquantitative items, such as the storage temperature, will also have to be considered after the financial analysis is complete. An analysis of the decision reveals that if Boston Beer accepts the offer, it will be able to reduce the following costs.

- Conversion costs by $0.20 per case.
- Selling and administrative costs by $400.

A differential analysis of Boston Beer's decision about where to store the Samuel Adams inventory of 1,000 cases is presented in **Exhibit 16.3**.

EXHIBIT 16.3 — Differential Analysis of Outsourcing Decision

	Cost to Do Internally	Cost to Outsource	Difference (income effect of outsourcing)
Cost to outsource storage		$1,500	$(1,500)
Cost to do internally			
Variable costs related to storage ($0.20 × 1,000)	$200		200
Fixed costs related to storage	400		400
Total	$600	$1,500	$ (900)
Advantage of providing service internally		$900	

Again, we only want to focus on the relevant costs—those costs that differ between storing the beer internally or using the warehouse company. If the beer is stored internally, the company incurs incremental variable costs of $0.20 per case and related fixed costs of $400 per month. If outsourced, these costs would be avoided. Consequently, these costs are relevant to the decision. If storage is outsourced, the company will incur warehousing costs of $1,500 per month. The net impact of outsourcing is an increase in warehousing costs of $900.

Opportunity Costs

But what if the building storage capacity created by outsourcing can be used in other ways? Boston Beer runs a philanthropic program, Samuel Adams Brewing the American Dream, to support small business owners in food, beverage, hospitality, and craft brewing. Suppose, a local craft brewer would like to start building inventory of its newest cider, but it does not have storage space. The entrepreneur can afford to pay Boston Beer $925 per month for the storage that will be freed up if the external warehouse is used.

Should Boston Beer outsource its storage and let the craft brewer rent the vacated space? In this case, the storage capacity has an alternative use, and the net cash flow from this alternative use is an opportunity cost of providing the service internally. An updated differential analysis is presented in **Exhibit 16.4**.

EXHIBIT 16.4 — Differential Analysis of an Outsourcing Decision with Opportunity Cost

	Cost to Do Internally	Cost to Outsource	Difference (income effect of outsourcing)
Cost to outsource data storage		$1,500	$(1,500)
Cost to do internally			
Variable costs related to storage ($0.20 × 1,000)	$ 200		200
Fixed costs related to building storage	400		400
Opportunity cost of lost storage revenue	925		925
Total	$1,525	$1,500	$ 25
Advantage of outsourcing		$25	

The financial impact of the decision has shifted. It is now a profitable proposition to outsource storage, even if the net financial benefit is very small. The potential revenue from the entrepreneur can be viewed as an opportunity cost. If Boston Beer does not outsource and free up the storage space, it will not earn the $925 rental fee. The additional $925 shifts the implications of the outsourcing decision. In addition, Boston Beer will be contributing to the mission of its philanthropic endeavors by helping a craft brewer.

> **Outsourcing seems like a lot of effort for an insignificant upside. Would you recommend Boston Beer outsource its storage needs?**
>
> *At this point, management would want to consider qualitative factors. The company has made a commitment to entrepreneurs. Allowing a craft brewer to store beer and grow further is an investment in the entrepreneur. Even if this was a break-even proposition, or even a loss, Boston Beer management would want to consider its philanthropic commitment.*

Qualitative Factors in Decision-Making

Although outsourcing has become widely accepted across virtually all industries, the results of outsourcing are not uniformly positive. Some companies that made a strong commitment to extensive outsourcing have discovered that there are many problems that can occur when they shift key processes and functions to other companies. It is usually easier to make major changes and to correct problems related to in-house functions and processes than for those outsourced to other companies, especially if they are located offshore.

Even if outsourcing appears financially advantageous in the short run, management should not decide to outsource before considering a variety of qualitative risk factors. Is the outside supplier interested in developing a long-term relationship or merely attempting to use some temporarily idle capacity? If so, what will happen at the end of the contract period? Will the supplier continually improve its manufacturing operations in order to remain competitive? Organizations often manufacture products or provide services they can obtain elsewhere in order to control quality, to have an assured supply source, to avoid dealing with a potential competitor, or to maintain a core competency. What impact would a decision to outsource have on the morale of a company's employees? Will it have to rehire laid-off employees after the contract expires? Will the outside supplier meet delivery schedules? Does the supplied part meet quality standards? Will it continue to meet them? What are the environmental impacts of contracting with this supplier? How will this partnership with the supplier impact voluntary or regulatory reporting?

Environmental Factors A qualitative consideration of adding a new supplier is its impact on the environment. A recent new rule of the European Union has increased the number of companies required to publish environmental and social data. While this rule may impact some U.S. based companies that interact with European companies, the U.S. Securities and Exchange Commission is also currently developing new environmental reporting rules. One area of disclosure relates to Scope 3 emissions. (Scope 3 encompasses carbon omissions in a company's value chain, but outside of the company's direct control. Scope 1 includes all direct emissions from the company such as burning gas onsite as a heat source and Scope 2 includes indirect emissions such as the purchase of electricity for the company's use.)

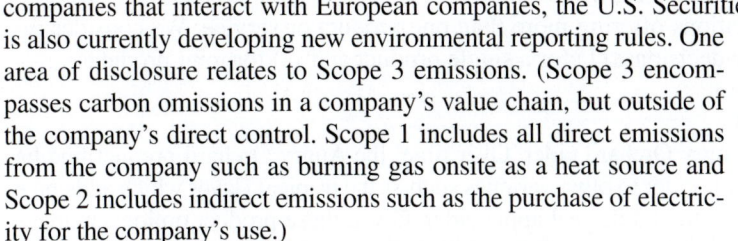

Scope 3 emission requirements includes the disclosure of greenhouse gas emissions that occur from activities of a supplier. Many companies, such as HP, have voluntarily disclosed information on Scope 3 emissions in sustainability reports. In a recent news release, HP shared the results of their research of Scope 3 emissions. HP indicated that their 30 largest partners in their supply chain were responsible for approximately 80% of their Scope 3 emissions.[2] HP

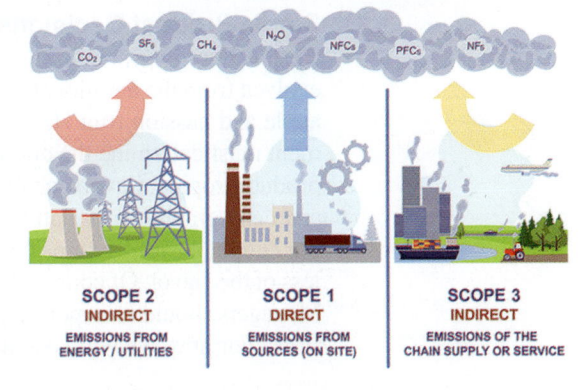

---

[2] Source: J. McCall, "Climate Action for Suppliers Helps Make HP's Supply Chain More Sustainable", News Release by HP Inc., July 14, 2022.

has partnered with their suppliers to reduce Scope 3 emissions in a variety of ways. For example, HP hosts virtual workshops with its suppliers about energy efficiency and renewable energy.

Global Factors The qualitative risk factors including environmental risk factors discussed above are often magnified when a company goes global, either as an outsourcing buyer or provider. Firms are finding that flexibility from outsourcing can come with significant costs, largely in holding the supplier to quality standards. Brent Ahnell, who advises firms on outsourcing, feels that companies regularly forget the risks that they are exposing themselves to when outsourcing. Often firms forget to account for economic, political, and weather hazards that affect their international suppliers.[3] Firms should take care to build redundancy into outsourced supply chains to control disruptions that could come from these sources.

Global outsourcing is often motivated by the desire to get projects completed "on time" and "within budget." Many recommend focusing on core competencies and differentiating factors internally. To continue to innovate and improve products and services, these activities should stay in-house for continued learning and improvement. Outsourcing might be best used for the basics—tasks that offer the organization no competitive advantage. For example, a commodity that can be provided equally by many organizations is a candidate for outsourcing.

Review 16-5 LO16-5   Evaluating an Outsourcing Decision

Refer to the information provided in Review 16-3 for **Anheuser-Busch InBev NV/SA** to answer the following questions.

Required
Determine the effect of the following situation on monthly profits.
  A Mexican farmer has offered a one-year contract to supply grains and hops at a cost of $1.00 per unit. If Anheuser Busch accepts the offer, it will be able to reduce variable manufacturing costs by 40% and rent some of its factory space to another company for $1,000 per month.

Solution on p. 16-43.

Sell or Process Further

LO16-6
Apply differential analysis to evaluate whether to sell or further process a product.

When a product is salable at various stages of completion, management must determine the product's most advantageous selling point. As each stage is completed, management must determine whether to sell the product then or to process it further. For example, petroleum companies have to determine how much crude oil to refine as diesel fuel and how much to process further as gasoline. Management must simultaneously evaluate the financial and market information to determine its desired product mix. These same decisions are made by all organizations offering more than one product or service. We consider two types of sell or process further decisions: (1) for a single product and (2) for joint products.

Single Product Decisions
Boston Beer brews and sells Angry Orchard cider. Over time, the Angry Orchard product line has evolved from the traditional, apple cider to other varieties such as the tropical flavor which adds pineapple and passion fruit flavors to the traditional apple cider. Given these product options, management must determine the optimal selling point of the product. For example, should it continue on to produce tropical flavors, or should it stop with the traditional apple cider. Before considering market and demographic information, the company should start with a financial analysis of the two options. For simplicity, let's assume that the company will sell the same number of 12-packs of bottles, regardless of the flavor. Of course, this is not always the case as product variety might impact sales volume. Managers should incorporate any potential market sales impact into the analysis before making decisions. For now, we will keep it simple to focus on the fundamentals of the analysis.

---
[3] Ben DiPietro, "When Manufacturing Means Building Supply-Chain Resilience," *Wall Street Journal*, October 21, 2015.

	Per 12-Pack Case		
	Traditional Apple	Tropical Flavor	Difference (income effect of tropical flavor)
Selling price	$7	$10	$3
Production costs	(4)	(4)	
Tropical flavor		(1)	(1)
Contribution margin	$3	$ 5	$2
Advantage of tropical flavoring		$2	

The tropical cider flavor contributes $2 more per 12-pack than the traditional apple flavor does. Without considering any additional information related to the market demand and consumer preferences, managers might determine that only the tropical cider should be sold due to its higher contribution margin.

Remember that *all costs incurred prior to the decision point are irrelevant because they are the same for both options*. Given the existence of manufactured, traditional apple cider, the decision alternatives are to sell it now or to add tropical flavoring. A differential analysis for the decision to sell or process further should include only incremental revenues and the incremental costs of further processing as follows.

Increase in revenues		
Sell after tropical flavoring.	$10	
Sell after basic production.	(7)	$3
Additional costs of tropical flavoring		(1)
Advantage of tropical flavoring		$2

In the previous analysis, the revenue earned from traditional apple cider is viewed as an alternative revenue. Managers could also view this revenue as an opportunity cost of selling tropical cider. Because the two products are substitutes, if tropical cider is sold, the company will lose the sale of the traditional apple. The identical solution is obtained if the selling price without tropical flavoring is treated as an opportunity cost as follows.

Revenues after tropical flavoring		$10
Additional costs of tropical flavoring	$1	
Opportunity cost of not selling traditional apple	7	(8)
Advantage of tropical flavoring		$ 2

Joint Product Decisions

Two or more products simultaneously produced by a single process from a common set of inputs are called **joint products**. Joint products are often found in basic industries that process natural raw materials such as grains, dairy, chemicals, meat, petroleum, and wood products. In the petroleum industry, crude oil is refined into fuel oil, gasoline, kerosene, diesel, lubricating oil, and other products.

The point in the process where the joint products become separately identifiable is called the **split-off point**. Materials and conversion costs incurred prior to the split-off point are called **joint costs**. For external reporting purposes, a number of techniques are used to allocate joint costs among joint products. We do not discuss these techniques here (interested students should consult a cost accounting textbook), except to note that none of the methods provide information useful for determining what to do with a joint product once it is produced. Because joint costs are incurred prior to the decision point, they are sunk costs. Consequently, *joint costs are irrelevant to a decision to sell a joint product or to process it further*. The only relevant factors are the alternative costs and revenues subsequent to the split-off point.

Review 16-6 LO16-6
Evaluating Whether to Sell or Process Further

Refer to the information provided in Review 16-3 for Anheuser-Busch InBev NV/SA to answer the following questions. Continue to assume a current monthly production and sales volume of 15,000 units where a unit is considered to be six bottles.

Required

Now assume that the product is currently sold in sets of six bottles (considered one unit) but are unpackaged; that is, they are sold in bulk, in increments of six bottles for $4.80, to retailers who want to sell individual bottles from the refrigerator. Packaging for a six-pack would increase costs by $0.10 per unit (six-pack). However, the six-pack units could then be sold for $5.05. Determine the effect on monthly profits if the company decided to package the six-packs.

Solution on p. 16-43.

APPENDIX 16A: Use of Limited Resources

LO16-7 Allocate limited resources for purposes of maximizing short-run profit.

All of us have experienced time as a limiting or constraining resource. With two exams the day after tomorrow and a paper due next week, our problem is how to allocate limited study time. The solution depends on our objectives, our current status (grades, knowledge, skill levels, and so forth), and available time. Given this information, we devise a work plan to best meet our objectives.

Managers must also decide how to best use limited resources to accomplish organizational goals. A supermarket may lose sales because limited shelf space prevents stocking all available brands of soft drinks. A manufacturer may lose sales because limited machine hours or labor hours prevent filling all orders. An airline may lose sales because it must cancel flights due to staffing shortages. Managers of for-profit organizations will likely find the problems of capacity constraints less troublesome than the problems of excess capacity; nonetheless, these problems are real. Ultimately, the problem often boils down to a product-mix decision, in which we must decide the mix of products or services we are going to offer our customers with the limited resources available to us.

If the limited resource is not a core business activity, it may be appropriate to outsource additional units of the limited resource externally. For example, many organizations have a small legal staff to handle routine activities. If the internal staff becomes fully committed, the organization seeks outside legal counsel.

The long-run solution to the problem of limited resources to perform core activities may be to expand capacity. However, this is usually not feasible in the short run. Economic models suggest that another solution is to reduce demand by increasing the price. Again, this may not be desirable. A hotel or airline, for example, may want to maintain competitive prices. A manufacturer might want to maintain a long-run price to retain customer goodwill to avoid attracting competitors, or to prevent accusations of "price gouging."

Single Constraint

The allocation of limited resources should be made only after a careful consideration of many qualitative factors. The following rule provides a useful starting point in making short-run decisions to best use limited resources: *To achieve short-run profit maximization, a for-profit organization should allocate limited resources in a manner that maximizes the contribution per unit of the limited resource.* Because fixed costs do not change in the short run, we focus on the amount that is left to cover fixed costs and contribute toward profit. Additionally, we want to produce the products that generate the highest contribution using the fewest resources. Remember that this analysis is the starting point. It will ultimately be combined with qualitative information to determine how to best use resources.

Boston Beer's Dogfish Head brand is based in Delaware. Under this brand, the company runs a brewpub, which offers guests a choice of three party packages: Package A (full dinner with multiple drink choices); Package B (light dinner with more limited drink choices); or Package C (Appetizers with limited drink choices). Given recent difficulties staffing its properties, Dogfish Head only has 120 labor hours per week to devote to parties. Information for the three party packages is as follows (note that a unit is one guest).

	Package A	Package B	Package C
Unit selling price	$100	$80	$50
Unit variable costs	(60)	(35)	(25)
Unit contribution margin	$ 40	$45	$25
Hours per unit	4	3	1

Package A carries the highest selling price while Package B has the highest contribution margin. However, given the labor constraint, we want to ensure that we are using staff in the most productive way possible. Consequently, we will calculate the unit margin earned for every hour of labor as follows.

	Package A	Package B	Package C
Unit contribution margin	$40	$45	$25
Hours per unit	÷ 4	÷ 3	÷ 1
Contribution per hour	$10	$15	$25

Following the rule of maximizing the contribution per unit of a single constraining factor (labor hours), Dogfish Head should consider highlighting Package C. Of course, this is based on the financial implications only. We have not yet incorporated demand information for the various packages and the success of the optimization strategy is dependent upon customer demand for Package C. Though Package C offers the highest contribution per hour, it is not helpful to the company if there is no demand for the product. As shown in the following analysis, any other plan would result in lower profits.

	Package A Highest Selling Price per Unit	Package B Highest Contribution per Unit	Package C Highest Contribution per Constraining Factor
Hours available	120	120	120
Hours per unit	÷ 4	÷ 3	÷ 1
Weekly production in units	30	40	120
Unit contribution margin	× $40	× $45	× $25
Total weekly contribution margin	$1,200	$1,800	$3,000

Despite this analysis, management may decide to offer a full product line to satisfy customer demand. However, such decisions sacrifice short-run profits. While there may be support for accepting orders with lower profit margins, the analysis illustrates the trade-offs being made.

Multiple Constraints

Continuing our illustration, assume now that demand for Package C is a second constraint. The maximum weekly demand for the Package C is 90 people, even though the capacity computed in the table above is 120 people each week. In this case, the limited labor resource should first be used to satisfy the demand for Package C, with any remaining capacity going to Package B orders, if possible, which has the next highest contribution per unit of constraining factor. This allocation provides a total weekly contribution of $2,700, illustrated as follows.

Available hours	120
Required for Package C (90 people × 1 hour)	(90)
Hours available for Package B	30
Labor hours per unit	÷ 3
Production of Package B in units	10
Unit contribution margin of Package B	× $45
Contribution from Package B	$ 450
Contribution from Package C ($25 per unit × 90 units)	2,250
Total weekly contribution margin	$2,700

When an organization has alternative uses for several limited resources, such as limited labor hours and limited space, the optimal use of those resources cannot be determined using the rule for short-run profit maximization. In these situations, techniques such as linear programming can be used to assist in determining the optimal mix of products or services.

Theory of Constraints

The **theory of constraints** states that every process has a bottleneck (constraining resource) and that production cannot take place faster than it is processed through that bottleneck. The goal of the theory of constraints is to maximize **throughput** (defined as sales revenue minus direct materials costs) in a constrained environment.[4] For example, if the beer fermentation process has lower capacity, the entire process is limited

---

[4] *The Goal*, by Eliyah M. Goldratt and Jeff Cox, presents the concepts underlying the theory of constraints in the form of a novel.

to the capacity of the fermentation process. Even if the steps before fermentation produce a higher amount, the production process will slow down at fermentation. The theory has several implications for management.

- Management should identify the bottleneck. This is often difficult when several different products are produced in a facility containing many different production activities. One approach is to walk around and observe where inventory is building up in front of workstations. The bottleneck will likely have the largest piles of work that have been waiting for the longest time.
- Management should schedule production to maximize the efficient use of the bottleneck resource. Efficiently using the bottleneck resource might necessitate inspecting all units before they reach the bottleneck rather than after the units are completed. The bottleneck resource is too valuable to waste on units that may already be defective.
- Management should schedule production to avoid a buildup of inventory. Reducing inventory lowers the cost of inventory investments and the cost of carrying inventory. It also assists in improving quality by making it easier to identify quality problems that might otherwise be hidden in large piles of inventory. Reducing inventory will require a change in the attitude of managers who like to see machines and people constantly working. To avoid a buildup of inventory in front of the bottleneck, it may be necessary for people and equipment to remain idle until the bottleneck resource calls for additional input.
- Management should work to eliminate the bottleneck, perhaps by increasing the capacity of the bottleneck resource, redesigning products so they can be produced with less use of the bottleneck resource, rescheduling production procedures to substitute nonbottleneck resources, or outsourcing work performed by bottleneck resources.

The theory of constraints has implications for management accounting performance reports. Keeping people and equipment working on production full-time is often a goal of management. To support this goal, management accounting performance reports have traditionally highlighted underutilization as unfavorable. This has encouraged managers to have people and equipment producing inventory, even if the inventory is not needed or cannot be further processed because of bottlenecks. The theory of constraints suggests that it is better to have nonbottleneck resources idle than it is to have them fully utilized if the production will be piling up waiting for further production. To support the theory of constraints, performance reports should

- Measure the utilization of bottleneck resources
- Measure factory throughput
- Not encourage the full utilization of nonbottleneck resources
- Discourage the buildup of excess inventory

While the theory of constraints is *similar* to our general rule for how to best use limited resources, it emphasizes throughput (selling price minus direct materials) rather than contribution (selling price minus variable costs) in allocating the limited resource. The exclusion of direct labor and variable manufacturing overhead yields larger unit margins, and it may affect resource allocations based on throughput rankings. The result will likely be a reduction in profits from those that could be achieved using our general rule for how to allocate limited resources. Although the theory of constraints has not been widely embraced by companies, many of its users are enthusiastic about its benefits.

Review 16-7 LO16-7

Analyzing Profitability Considering a Scarce Resource

Anheuser-Busch produces three types of products: traditional beer, craft beer, and beyond beer (e.g., seltzer and kombrewcha). The bottling facility is the company's constraining resource. It operates at 90% capacity and management wants to devote the unused capacity to one of the products. The following data represents the current operations.

	Traditional Beer	Craft Beer	Beyond Beer
Per-case data:			
Sales price	$6	$20	$22
Variable cost	2	8	16
Contribution margin	$4	$12	$ 6
Fixed costs*	1	6	2
Net income	$3	$ 6	$ 4

*Allocated on basis of machine hours at $1 per machine hour.

Required

Solution on p. 16-43. Which product should management produce with its extra capacity?

MULTIPLE CHOICE

1. Jabo Inc. is considering a new bifro-spectra machine for its production plant to replace an old machine that originally cost $12,000 and has $9,000 of accumulated depreciation. The new machine can be purchased at a cash cost of $18,000, but the distributor of the new machine has offered to take the old machine in as a trade-in, thereby reducing the cost of the new machine to $16,000. Based only on this information, calculate the total relevant cost of acquiring the new machine. **LO16-1, 2**

    a. $16,000, or the net cash paid to the distributor
    b. $18,000, or the gross cost of the new machine
    c. $19,000, or the net cash paid plus the book value ($3,000) of the old machine
    d. $17,000, or the gross cost of the new machine minus the $1,000 loss on disposing of the old machine

2. Bruno Company is a Rhode Island company that sells a branded product regionally to retail customers in New England. It normally sells its product for $30 per unit; however, it has received a one-time offer from a private-brand company on the West Coast to buy 1,000 units at $19 per unit. Even though the company has excess capacity to produce the units, the president of the company immediately rejected the offer; however, the chief accountant stated that it might be a profitable opportunity for the company, even though $19 is below its unit cost of $21, calculated as follows. **LO16-4**

Direct materials.	$ 9.00
Direct labor.	5.00
Variable overhead.	4.00
Depreciation and other fixed overhead.	3.00
Total unit cost.	$21.00

    Also, the special order will save $1 per unit in packaging costs since the product will be bulk packaged instead of being individually packaged. Calculate the amount of profit or loss per unit if Bruno accepts the special order.

    a. $2 loss
    b. $1 loss
    c. $2 profit
    d. $1 profit

3. Edwards Products has just developed a new product with a manufacturing cost of $30. The Marketing Director has identified three marketing approaches for this new product. **LO16-3**

    Approach X: Set a selling price of $36 and have the firm's sales staff sell the product at a 10% commission with no advertising program. Estimated annual sales would be 10,000 units.
    Approach Y: Set a selling price of $38, have the firm's sales staff sell the product at a 10% commission, and back them up with a $30,000 advertising program. Estimated annual sales would be 12,000 units.
    Approach Z: Rely on wholesalers to handle the product. Edwards would sell the new product to the wholesalers at $32 per unit and incur no selling expenses. Estimated annual sales would be 14,000 units.

    Rank the three alternatives in order of net profit, from highest net profit to lowest.

    a. X, Y, Z.
    b. Y, Z, X.
    c. Z, X, Y.
    d. Z, Y, X. **CMA Adapted**

4. Sitro, LTD had been making a component for one of its products, but is now considering outsourcing the component to a Chinese company, which has offered to sell an unlimited quantity of components for $6 per unit. If Sitro outsources, it could shut down a whole department and rent the building for $2,000 per month. The cost of making the component is $5 per unit, which includes $1.50 of fixed costs, of which only $1.00 per unit can be avoided if the department is shut down. Sitro currently produces about 1,000 units per month. What is the cost advantage or disadvantage of per unit of outsourcing the component? **LO16-5**

    a. $1.00 disadvantage
    b. $1.50 disadvantage
    c. $1.00 advantage
    d. $0.50 advantage

5. Mitrex Company makes a semi-finished machine component for the heavy equipment industry that has a unit contribution margin of $250 to Mitrex. A major customer has been purchasing 100 units per month from Mitrex for many years, but has indicated that it would prefer to purchase them already machined to its specifications. It has offered to pay an additional $50 per unit for the finished units. To meet those specifications, Mitrex would have to rent additional equipment at a cost of $2,000 **LO16-6**

Multiple Choice Answers
1. a 2. c 3. c 4. d 5. a 6. a

per month and incur labor and other direct costs of $15 per unit. Calculate the per-unit advantage or disadvantage of further processing.

a. $15 advantage
b. $35 advantage
c. $50 advantage
d. $15 disadvantage

LO16-7 6. Giko, LTD makes three products (Abba, Babba, and Cabba), all of which use a very rare ingredient called Mecogen. Giko can purchase only 500 ounces of Mecogen per month from its East Asian source. Below are data for the three products:

	Abba	Babba	Cabba
Unit selling price.	$80	$65	$100
Unit variable costs	45	40	60
Unit contribution margin	35	25	40
Mecogen (ounces per unit).	10	15	20

How should Giko allocate the 500 ounces of Mecogen assuming it can sell unlimited quantities of all three produces?

a. All 500 ounces should be allocated to Abba
b. All 500 ounces should be allocated to Babba
c. All 500 ounces should be allocated to Cabba
d. None of the above

DATA ANALYTICS

LO16-4 **DA16-1. Using Data to Analyze Decisions on Special Order**

Kendrick Anderson Furniture Maker, LLC creates custom tables in Atlanta. Assume that you are the product manager for the Living Room Table segment. Your company is planning to meet with a local not-for-profit company that is presenting a proposal for the production of tables for its senior center. Monthly manufacturing costs for the Living Room Table segment are included in the Excel file located in MBC. Assume that the data includes no outliers.

REQUIRED

a. What is the weighted average cost to manufacture a living room table based upon the historical data provided?
b. Using regression analysis, determine the cost-estimating equation to manufacture dining room tables. *Hint:* Under the Data tab, click on Data analysis, Regression, and select the cells for the Y Range and X Range.
c. What is the lowest price that your company would accept without making the company worse off?
d. What other information should you compile in advance of the meeting?

LO16-7 **DA16-2. Using Data to Analyze Decisions on Special Order**

Backyard Helpers, Inc. is a small manufacturing company with 18 different gardening tools in its product line. All of the products are fabricated using the same equipment.

Recently, sales demand has increased. Unfortunately, Backyard Helpers cannot produce enough products with existing equipment to meet that demand. Facilities can be expanded, and new equipment purchased, but it will be at least two years before that happens. The production manager needs to make production scheduling decisions now.

The Excel file available in MBC includes assumed information about demand, sales price, cost, and fabrication time on the shared equipment for each of Backyard Helpers' products.

Maximum machine time is 40,500 minutes per month. The demand for all products is spread equally throughout the month. Fixed costs (manufacturing, selling, and administrative) total $755,750 per month. Backyard Helpers maintains no inventory of finished goods: all units produced are sold during the month.

Note: To add the solver tool in Excel, under the Insert tab, click on Get Add-ins, and search for Solver. After it is added, the link will be available in the menu bar.

REQUIRED

a. Ignore machine time limits in answering the following:
  1. Which product has the highest contribution margin per unit? How many units of that product should be produced each month?
  2. If Backyard could meet demand, what would be the total net operating income per month?
b. If demand was unlimited for all products, which products should Backyard Helpers produce?
c. Given the maximum number of machine minutes per month and the expected demand per month, use Solver in Excel to answer the following questions. To prepare your worksheet to use the Solver tool, add columns with formulas for (1) contribution margin per unit, (2) total

quantity in units, (3) total machine minutes, and (4) total contribution margin. In the Solver tool window, enter the cell that you would like to maximize (*Hint:* It is a single cell), identify the variables (*Hint:* Use quantity in units column) and enter the constraints (*Hint:* There are two constraints relating to demand and machine minutes).

1. How many of the following products should be produced each month?
    i. R25
    ii. JK369
2. Which products would be temporarily eliminated from Backyard Helpers product line under the Excel solution?
3. What is the total net operating income per month given the machine time constraints and the quantities determined by Solver?
4. What is the maximum amount Backyard Helpers should be willing to pay to rent fabrication time from another company? (Assume transportation and other costs would total $50,000.)

d. In Questions c2, you identified products that would be temporarily eliminated if Backyard followed the Excel solution. What reasons, if any, might management have for continuing to produce some of those products even if it means reducing the supply of some of the other products?

DA16-3. Analysis of Scope 3 Emissions Reporting   **LO16-5**
Apple Inc. reports greenhouse gas emissions for Scope 1, Scope 2, and Scope 3. Data on emissions from Apple's 2022 Environment Progress Report are included in an Excel file in MBC.

Apple Inc.
NASDAQ :: AAPL

REQUIRED
a. Prepare a stacked area chart showing the totals only of Scope 1, Scope 2, and Scope 3 greenhouse gas emissions (with the earliest time period on the left). Comment on the relative size of Scope 1, Scope 2, and Scope 3 emissions.
b. Prepare a stacked area chart showing the components of Scope 3 emissions only. Comment on the relative size of the Scope 3 components.
c. Generally speaking, what is the source of the largest component of Scope 3 emissions?
d. What is the general trend in Scope 3 emissions for Apple? What are some significant factors to consider when analyzing the trend in Scope 3 emissions over time?

DATA VISUALIZATION

Data Visualization Activities are available in myBusinessCourse. These assignments use Tableau Dashboards to expose students to visual depictions of data and introduce students to data analytics through data visualizations. These exercises are easily assignable and auto graded by MBC.

QUESTIONS

Q16-1. Distinguish between relevant and irrelevant costs.
Q16-2. In evaluating a cost reduction proposal, what three alternatives are available to management?
Q16-3. When are outlay costs relevant and when are they irrelevant?
Q16-4. Explain the sunk cost dilemma.
Q16-5. Why is a differential analysis of relevant items preferred to a detailed listing of all costs and revenues associated with each alternative?
Q16-6. When are opportunity costs relevant to the evaluation of a special order?
Q16-7. Identify some important qualitative considerations in evaluating a decision to make or buy a part.
Q16-8. In a decision to sell or to process further, of what relevance are costs incurred prior to the decision point? Explain your answer.
Q16-9. How should limited resources be used to achieve short-run profit maximization?
Q16-10. What should performance reports do in support of the theory of constraints?

MINI EXERCISES

LO16-1

Astell&Kern

M16-11. Relevant Cost Terms: Matching

Astell&Kern produces three different versions of high-quality portable digital music players, the A@ultima, A@futura, and A@norma. Assume Astell&Kern is evaluating a proposal that will result in doubling the production of A@futura and discontinuing the production of A@norma. The facilities currently used to produce A@norma will be devoted to the production of A@futura. Furthermore, additional machinery will be acquired to produce A@futura. The production of A@ultima will not be affected. All products have a positive contribution margin.

REQUIRED

Presented below are a number of phrases related to the proposal followed by a list of cost terms. For each phrase, select the most appropriate cost term. Each term is used only once.

PHRASES

1. Cost of equipment to produce A@norma
2. Increased variable costs of A@futura
3. Property taxes on the new machinery
4. Revenues from the sale of A@ultima
5. Increased revenue from the sale of A@futura
6. Contribution margin of A@norma
7. Variable costs of A@ultima
8. Company president's salary

COST TERMS

a. Opportunity cost
b. Sunk cost
c. Irrelevant variable outlay cost
d. Irrelevant fixed outlay cost
e. Relevant variable outlay cost
f. Relevant fixed outlay cost
g. Relevant revenues
h. Irrelevant revenues

LO16-1

Coach
Tapestry, Inc.
NYSE :: TPR

M16-12. Relevant Cost Terms: Matching

Assume **Coach**, owned by **Tapestry, Inc.**, produces and sells 4,000 specialty handbags per month and has the capacity to produce 5,000 units per month. Coach is evaluating a one-time, special order for 2,000 units from Bloomingdales. Accepting the order will increase variable manufacturing costs and certain fixed selling and administrative costs. It will also require the company to forego the sale of 1,000 units to regular customers.

REQUIRED

Presented below are a number of statements related to the proposal followed by a list of cost terms. For each statement, select the most appropriate cost term. Each term is used only once.

STATEMENTS

1. Increased revenues from special order
2. Lost contribution margin from foregone sales to regular customers
3. Revenues from 4,000 units sold to regular customers
4. Variable cost of 4,000 units sold to regular customers
5. Increase in fixed selling and administrative expenses
6. Cost of existing equipment used to produce special order
7. Salary paid to current supervisor who oversees manufacture of special order
8. Increased variable costs of special order

COST TERMS

a. Irrelevant variable outlay cost
b. Irrelevant fixed outlay cost
c. Sunk cost
d. Relevant variable outlay cost
e. Relevant fixed outlay cost
f. Opportunity cost
g. Relevant revenues
h. Irrelevant revenues

LO16-1, 2

City of Hamilton
PJM Interconnection

M16-13. Identifying Relevant Costs and Revenues

The **City of Hamilton** operates a power plant on the Ohio River. The city uses some of this generated electricity to service Hamilton residents and sells the excess electricity to **PJM Interconnection**, manager of a wholesale electricity market serving nearby states. Suppose the city council is evaluating two alternative proposals:

- *Proposal A* calls for replacing the generators used in the plant with more efficient generators that will produce more electricity and have lower operating costs. The salvage value of the old generators is higher than their removal cost.

- *Proposal B* calls for raising the level of the dam to retain more water for generating power and increasing the force of water flowing through the dam. This will significantly increase the amount of electricity generated by the plant. Operating costs will not be affected.

REQUIRED

Presented are a number of cost and revenue items. Indicate in the appropriate columns whether each item is relevant or irrelevant to proposals A and B.

	Proposal A	Proposal B
1. Cost of new furniture for the city manager's office	_____	_____
2. Cost of old generators	_____	_____
3. Cost of new generators	_____	_____
4. Operating cost of old generators	_____	_____
5. Operating cost of new generators	_____	_____
6. The police chief's salary	_____	_____
7. Depreciation on old generators	_____	_____
8. Salvage value of old generators	_____	_____
9. Removal cost of old generators	_____	_____
10. Cost of raising dam	_____	_____
11. Maintenance costs of water plant	_____	_____
12. Revenues from sale of electricity	_____	_____

M16-14. Classifying Relevant and Irrelevant Items

The law firm of **Greenberg Traurig LLP** has been asked to represent a local client. All legal proceedings will be held out of town in Boston.

REQUIRED

Suppose the law firm's accountant has asked you to help determine the incremental cost of accepting this client. Classify each of the following items on the basis of their relationship to this engagement. Items may have multiple classifications.

	Relevant costs		Irrelevant costs	
	Opportunity	Outlay	Outlay	Sunk
1. The case will require three attorneys to stay four nights in a Boston hotel. The predicted hotel bill is $3,600.	___	___	___	___
2. Greenberg Traurig LLP's professional staff is paid $2,000 per day for out-of-town assignments.	___	___	___	___
3. Last year, depreciation on Greenberg Traurig LLP's Philadelphia's office was $25,000.	___	___	___	___
4. Round-trip transportation to Boston is expected to cost $250 per person.	___	___	___	___
5. The firm has recently accepted an engagement that will require several partners to spend two weeks in Chicago. The predicted out-of-pocket costs of this trip are $25,000.	___	___	___	___
6. The firm has a maintenance contract on its computer equipment that will cost $2,200 next year.	___	___	___	___
7. If the firm accepts the client and sends attorneys to Boston, it will have to decline a conflicting engagement in Miami that would have provided a net cash inflow of $15,000.	___	___	___	___
8. The firm's variable overhead is $125 per client hour.	___	___	___	___
9. The firm pays $900 per year for a subscription to a law journal.	___	___	___	___
10. Last year the firm paid $22,500 to increase the insulation in its building.	___	___	___	___

M16-15. Relevant Costs for Equipment Replacement Decision

Urgent Care paid $42,000 for X-ray equipment four years ago. The equipment was expected to have a useful life of 10 years from the date of acquisition with annual operating costs of $25,000. Technological advances have made the machine purchased four years ago obsolete with a zero salvage value. An improved X-ray device incorporating the new technology is available at an initial cost of $50,000 and annual operating costs of $15,000. The new machine is expected to last only six years before it, too, is obsolete. Asked to analyze the financial aspects of replacing the obsolete but still functional machine, an Urgent Care accountant prepared the following analysis. After looking over these numbers, the company's manager rejected the proposal.

Six-year savings [($25,000 – $15,000) × 6]	$ 60,000
Cost of new machine	(50,000)
Undepreciated cost of old machine [($42,000/10) × 6]	(25,200)
Advantage (disadvantage) of replacement	$(15,200)

REQUIRED

Perform an analysis of relevant costs to determine whether the manager made the correct decision. Explain the difference between your analysis and the company's analysis.

LO16-3

M16-16. Applying Differential Analysis to Alternative Profit Scenarios

Epson produces color cartridges for inkjet printers. Suppose cartridges are sold to mail-order distributors for $5.20 each. Total fixed costs per year are $342,000. Variable cost per unit are $1.85 for direct materials, $0.10 for direct labor, $0.30 for factory overhead, and $0.05 for distribution.

The variable distribution costs are for transportation to mail-order distributors. Also assume the current annual production and sales volume is 180,000 and annual capacity is 220,000 units.

REQUIRED

The company would like to increase profitability in the upcoming year. Estimate the effect of the following separate proposals on annual profits.

a. A 15% increase in the unit selling price would likely decrease annual sales by 18,000 units.
b. A 10% decrease in the unit selling price would likely increase annual sales by 20,000 units. However, the additional production will result in machine updates that will increase fixed costs by $2,000.

LO16-3

M16-17. Discontinuing a Segment

Anthropologie, owned by URBN, sells both standard and custom size furniture items. Assume that the contribution income statements for both segments follow.

	Standard	Custom	Total
Sales	$2,000,000	$100,000	$2,100,000
Less variable costs	1,200,000	80,000	1,280,000
Contribution margin	800,000	20,000	820,000
Less fixed costs	600,000	35,000	635,000
Net income (loss)	$ 200,000	$ (15,000)	$ 185,000

Management is considering discontinuing the Custom segment due to the segment's net loss of $15,000. Of the total fixed costs for the Custom segment, $10,000 would not be incurred (a cost saving) if the Custom segment is dropped. Management expects no changes to the sales of the Standard segment if the Custom segment is discontinued.

REQUIRED

If the Custom segment is discontinued, what will be the net effect on the profit of the company?

LO16-1, 4

M16-18. Special Order

VideoSecu produces wall mounts for flat panel television sets. Assume the forecasted income statement for next year is as follows.

VIDEOSECU Budgeted Income Statement For the Year	
Sales ($28 per unit)	$5,600,000
Cost of goods sold ($19 per unit)	(3,800,000)
Gross profit	1,800,000
Selling expenses ($5 per unit)	(1,000,000)
Net income	$ 800,000

ADDITIONAL INFORMATION

(1) Of the production costs and selling expenses, $1,520,000 and $750,000, respectively, are fixed.
(2) VideoSecu received a special order from a hospital supply company offering to buy 10,000 wall mounts for $15. If it accepts the order, there will be no additional fixed selling expenses, and there is currently sufficient excess capacity to fill the order. The company's sales manager argues for rejecting the order because "we are not in the business of paying $19 to make a product to sell for $15."

REQUIRED
a. Do you think the company should accept the special order?
b. Should the decision be based only on the profitability of the sale, or are there other issues that VideoSecu should consider? Explain.

M16-19. Evaluating an Outsourcing Decision

Epson produces color cartridges for inkjet printers. Suppose cartridges are sold to mail-order distributors for $5.20 each. Total fixed costs per year are $342,000. Variable cost per unit are $1.85 for direct materials, $0.10 for direct labor, and $0.30 for factory overhead.

Also assume the current annual production and sales volume is 180,000 and annual capacity is 220,000 units.

REQUIRED
Determine the effect of the following situation on annual profits.

A Guatemalan manufacturer has offered a one-year contract to supply ink for the cartridges (including shipping costs) at a cost of $1.25 per unit. If Epson accepts the offer, it will be able to reduce variable manufacturing costs by 50% and rent some of its factory space to another company for $1,100 per month for 12 months.

M16-20. Sell or Process Further

Assume Beneteau manufactures sailboat hulls at a cost of $7,500 per unit. The hulls are sold to boat-yards for $9,000. The company is evaluating the desirability of adding masts, sails, and rigging to the hulls prior to sale at an additional cost of $2,500. The completed sailboats could then be sold for $10,500 each.

REQUIRED
Determine whether the company should sell sailboat hulls or process them further into complete sailboats. Assume sales volume will not be affected.

M16-21. Analyzing Profitability Considering a Scarce Resource

Assume that Innovative Components Inc. produces only three different types of injection-molded knobs. It produces the Pointer Knob, which is used for on/off devices, the Instrument Knob, which is used for precision adjustment, and the Star Knob, which is used for snowblowers and lawnmowers. The factory machine capacity is the company's constraining resource. It operates at 90% capacity and management wants to devote the unused capacity to one of the products. The following data represents the current operations.

	Pointer Knob	Instrument Knob	Star Knob
Per-case data			
Sales price	$20	$32	$6
Variable cost	8	26	2
Contribution margin	$12	$ 6	$4
Fixed costs*	6	2	1
Net income	$ 6	$ 4	$3

*Allocated on basis of machine hours at $2 per machine hour.

REQUIRED
Which product should management produce with its extra capacity?

EXERCISES

LO16-1, 2
TaylorMade-Adidas Golf Company

E16-22. Applying Differential Analysis to Equipment Replacement Decision

TaylorMade-Adidas Golf Company, a subsidiary of Adidas, manufactures golf clubs using "adjustable weight technology" or AWT. Suppose a European machine company has proposed to sell TaylorMade a new highly automated machine that would reduce significantly the labor cost of producing its golf clubs. The cost of the machine is $3,000,000, and would have an expected life of six years, at the end of which it would have a residual value of 10% of its original cost. The machine has an estimated operating cost of $15,000 per month. The direct labor cost savings per club from using the machine is estimated to be $6 per club, per month. In addition, other fixed overhead costs of $8,000 per month would be eliminated if the new machine is purchased. Also, the new machine would free up about 5,000 square feet of space from the displaced workers. Assume TaylorMade's building is held under a 10-year lease that has eight years remaining. The current lease cost is $1 per square foot per month. TaylorMade has received an offer to rent the excess space to a nearby related company for $3,500 per month for the next two years. (Rental beyond that two year-period is not certain.)

REQUIRED

a. Assuming the new machine would be used to produce an average of 8,000 clubs per month, prepare a differential analysis of the relevant costs of buying the machine and using it for the next six years, versus continuing with the current process. Calculate the net advantage or disadvantage of purchasing the new machine.

b. Suppose the cost of the machine is expected to increase by 5%. If the price increase is in effect, how does your answer to part a change?

LO16-1, 2, 4

E16-23. Applying Differential Analysis to Profitability Scenarios

Assume that Company A and Company B sell a microwave popcorn popper for $20. Although the companies have different cost structures, both companies currently show a profit of $15,000 based on sales of 10,000 units as shown in the following financial statements for the month of June. Both companies hold no inventory and sell contractual orders in the month.

For the month of	Company A June	Company B June
Sales ($20)...	$200,000	$200,000
Variable cost of goods sold ($5.00, $7.50, Company A and B, respectively).............................	50,000	75,000
Variable selling and administrative costs ($2.00, $4.00, Company A and B, respectively)...............	20,000	40,000
Contribution margin	130,000	85,000
Fixed cost of goods sold.........................	75,000	50,000
Fixed selling and administrative costs	40,000	20,000
Profits before-tax	$ 15,000	$ 15,000

REQUIRED

Due to an expected downturn in market conditions, both companies are forecasting the effect on profitability of different scenarios on monthly profit.

a. For each company, determine the impact on monthly profit using differential analysis for each of the following separate scenarios.
   1. Sales volume decreases to 8,000 units for the month for both companies.
   2. Both companies drop the selling price per unit to $18.50 which results in unit sales of 9,000 units for the month.
   3. Both companies drop the selling price per unit to $18.50 which results in unit sales of 9,000 units for the month. In addition, both companies decrease the quality of materials used which drops variable cost of goods sold by $0.20 per unit. Both companies eliminate a part-time administrative position reducing fixed costs by $2,500 per month.

b. Are the companies profitable after cost cutting measures are considered (part a(3))?

c. Even though the reactions of Company A and Company B to declining market condition are similar, why do the financial results differ? Would you suggest additional cost-cutting measures?

E16-24. Special Order

Full Belly Farm grows organic vegetables and sells them to distributors and local restaurants after processing. Assume the farm's leading product for restaurant customers is a mixture of organic green salad ingredients prepared and ready to serve. The company sells a large bag to restaurants for $30. It calculates the variable cost per bag at $20 (including $1 for local delivery), and the average total cost per bag is $24. Growing conditions have been very good this season and Full Belly has extra capacity. A representative of a restaurant association in another city has offered to buy fresh salad stock from the company to augment its regular supply during an upcoming international festival. The restaurant association wants to buy 3,000 bags during the next month for $22 per bag. Delivery to restaurants in the other city will cost the company $0.75 per bag. It can meet most of the order with excess capacity but would sacrifice 200 bags of regular sales to fill this special order. Please assist Full Belly Farm's management by answering the following questions.

REQUIRED

a. Using differential analysis, what is the impact on profits of accepting this one-time special order?
b. What nonquantitative issues should management consider before making a final decision?
c. How would the analysis change if the special order were for 3,000 bags per month for the next five years? Determine the long-term monthly impact on profits from this special order. (Assume there would be no loss of regular sales.)

E16-25. Special Order

Denny's, just off the San Bernardino Freeway in Pomona, California, specializes in a Super Slam breakfast selling for $7. Assume daily fixed costs are $1,575, and variable costs are $5 per meal. With a capacity of 750 meals per day, the restaurant serves an average of 700 meals each day.

REQUIRED

a. Determine the current average cost per meal.
b. A busload of 30 Girl Scouts stops on its way home from the San Bernardino National Forest. The leader offers to bring them in if the scouts can all be served a meal for a total of $195. The owner refuses, saying he would lose $0.75 per meal if he accepted this offer. How do you think the owner arrived at the $0.75 figure? Comment on the owner's reasoning.
c. A local business owner on a break overhears the conversation with the leader and offers the owner a one-year contract to feed 100 of the business owner's employees one meal each day at a special price of $5.50 per meal. Compute the net advantage (disadvantage) of accepting the contract. Should the restaurant owner accept this offer? Why or why not?

E16-26. Special Order: High-Low Cost Estimation

Autoliv produces air bag systems that it sells to automobile manufacturers throughout the world. Assume the company has a capacity of 50 million units per year. Autoliv is currently producing at an annual rate of 40 million units. Assume Autoliv has received an order from a Japanese manufacturer to purchase 100,000 units at $65 each. Budgeted costs for 40 million and 45 million units are as follows.

(in thousands, except costs per unit)	40 Million Units	45 Million Units
Manufacturing costs		
Direct materials	$ 560,000	$ 630,000
Direct labor	220,000	247,500
Factory overhead	1,780,000	1,822,500
Total	2,560,000	2,700,000
Selling and administrative	1,120,000	1,125,000
Total	$3,680,000	$3,825,000
Costs per unit		
Manufacturing	$64.00	$60.00
Selling and administrative	28.00	25.00
Total	$92.00	$85.00

Sales to auto manufacturers are priced at $120 per unit, but the sales manager believes the company should aggressively seek the Japanese business even if it results in a loss of $20 per unit. She believes obtaining this order would open up several new markets for the company's product. The general manager commented that the company cannot tighten its belt to absorb the $2,000,000 loss ($20 × 100,000) it would incur if the order is accepted.

REQUIRED

a. Determine the financial implications of accepting the order. (*Hint:* Use the high-low method to determine variable cost per unit.)

b. How would your analysis differ if the company were operating at capacity? Determine the net advantage or disadvantage of accepting the order under full-capacity circumstances.

LO16-1, 5
HP Inc.
NYSE :: HPQ
Sanmina Corp.
NASDAQ :: SANM

E16-27. Outsourcing (Make-or-Buy) Decision

Assume a division of **HP Inc.** currently makes 50,000 circuit boards per year used in producing diagnostic electronic instruments at a cost of $50 per board, consisting of variable cost per unit of $35 and fixed costs per unit of $15. Further assume **Sanmina Corporation** offers to sell HP the 50,000 circuit boards for $50 each. If HP accepts this offer, the facilities currently used to make the boards could be rented to one of HP's suppliers for $75,000 per year. In addition, $8 per unit of the fixed overhead applied to the circuit boards would be totally eliminated.

REQUIRED

Calculate the net advantage or disadvantage to HP of outsourcing the component from Samina Corporation. Should HP outsource this component from Sanmina Corporation?

LO16-1, 5
Coway

E16-28. Outsourcing (Make-or-Buy) Decision

Coway manufactures a line of room air purifiers. Assume that management is currently evaluating the possible production of an air purifier for automobiles. Based on an annual volume of 50,000 units, the predicted cost per unit of an auto air purifier follows.

Direct materials.	$ 2.50
Direct labor.	2.00
Factory overhead.	12.00
Total.	$16.50

These cost predictions include $450,000 in fixed factory overhead averaged over 50,000 units.

Also assume the completed air purifier units include a battery-operated electric motor, which Coway assembles with parts purchased from an outside vendor for $2.00 per motor. Mini Motor Company has offered to supply an assembled battery-operated motor at a cost of $5.25 per unit, with a minimum annual order of 5,000 units. If Coway accepts this offer, it will be able to reduce the variable labor and variable overhead costs of the auto air purifier by 50%.

REQUIRED

a. Determine whether Coway should continue to make the electric motor or outsource it from Mini Motor Company. Calculate the net advantage or disadvantage of outsourcing the electric motors from Mini Motor Company. (*Hint:* Analyze the relevant costs of making the "motors," not the entire air purifier.)

b. If it could otherwise rent the motor-assembly space for $50,000 per year, should it make or outsource this component? Calculate the net advantage (disadvantage) of outsourcing the motors, assuming the space could be rented.

c. What additional factors should Coway consider in deciding whether to make or outsource the electric motors?

LO16-1, 5

E16-29. Make or Buy

Priya Rahavy, M.D., is a general practitioner whose offices are located in the Lake Forest Professional Building. In the past, Dr. Rahavy has operated her practice with a nurse, a receptionist, and a part-time bookkeeper. Dr. Rahavy, like many small-town physicians, has billed her patients and their insurance companies from her own office. The part-time bookkeeper, who works 20 hours per week, is employed exclusively for this purpose.

North Avenue Physician's Service Center has offered to take over all of Dr. Rahavy's billings and collections for an annual fee of $36,000. If Dr. Rahavy accepts this offer, she will no longer need the bookkeeper. The bookkeeper's wages and fringe benefits amount to $25 per hour, and the bookkeeper works 50 weeks per year. With all the billings and collections done elsewhere, Dr. Rahavy will have three additional hours available per week to see patients. She sees an average of four patients per hour at an average fee of $40 per visit. Dr. Rahavy's practice is expanding, and new patients often have to wait several weeks for an appointment. She has resisted expanding her office hours or working more than 50 weeks per year. Finally, if Dr. Rahavy signs on with the center, she will no longer need to rent a records storage facility for $250 per month.

REQUIRED

Through a relevant cost analysis, calculate the net advantage or disadvantage of outsourcing the bookkeeping. Conduct a relevant cost analysis to determine if it is profitable to outsource the bookkeeping.

E16-30. Sell or Process Further

Ecolab produces cleaning and sanitizing chemicals for commercial markets. Assume the company processes raw material D into joint products E and F. Raw material D costs $8 per liter. It costs $150 to convert 100 liters of D into 60 liters of E and 40 liters of F. Product F can be sold immediately for $40 per liter or processed further into Product G at an additional cost of $12 per liter. Product G can then be sold for $55 per liter.

REQUIRED

Determine whether Product F should be sold or processed further into Product G. Calculate the net advantage or disadvantage of further processing.

E16-31. Sell of Process Further

Rose Hill, a soybean farm in northern Minnesota, has a herd of 25 dairy cows. The cows produce approximately 1,400 gallons of milk per week. The farm currently sells all its milk to a nearby processor for $1.25 per gallon, a significant drop from the $2.00 per gallon they were able to charge five years ago. It costs $1.60 per gallon to produce the milk.

The owners of Rose Hill are deciding whether to sell the dairy cows or expand into the artisan cheese market. Both owners have prior cheese-making experience and they already have all the needed equipment.

It takes 0.8 gallon of milk to make a pound of cheese. Costs to produce a pound of cheese are expected to total $7 per pound. Artisan cheeses are currently selling for $10 per pound at farmer's markets and upscale groceries.

REQUIRED

a. How much incremental profit would Rose Hill recognize if half the milk each week was used to make cheese?
b. How much, in total, would Rose Hill earn each week if half the milk was used to make cheese and half was sold to the processor?
c. How much of the milk would need to be used to make cheese each week in order for Rose Hill to break even on its dairy operations assuming no cows were sold? (*Note:* Any milk not used to make cheese would still be sold to a processor.)
d. What other factors should the owners of Rose Hill consider when deciding whether to sell the dairy cows or expand into cheese-making?

E16-32. Limited Resources

Assume Fender produces only three guitars: the Stratocaster, Telecaster, and Jaguar. A limitation of 960 labor hours per week prevents Fender from meeting the sales demand for these products. Product information is as follows.

	Stratocaster	Telecaster	Jaguar
Unit selling price.	$1,200	$ 900	$1,400
Unit variable costs	(630)	(450)	(850)
Unit contribution margin	$ 570	$ 450	$ 550
Labor hours per unit	15	10	20

REQUIRED

a. Determine the weekly contribution from each product when total labor hours are allocated to the product with the highest
   1. Unit selling price.
   2. Unit contribution margin.
   3. Contribution per labor hour.
   (*Hint:* Each situation is independent of the others.)
b. What generalization can be made regarding the allocation of limited resources to achieve short-run profit maximization?
c. Determine the opportunity cost the company will incur if management requires the weekly production of 15 Jaguars. *Hint:* You want to maximize short-run profit. Determine which guitar is most profitable.
d. Give reasons why a company may not allocate resources in the most economical way in some situations.

E16-33. Limited Resources

Assume Maria Pajet, a regional sales representative for UniTec Systems Inc., has been working about 60 hours per week calling on a total of 85 regular customers each month. Because of family and health considerations, she has decided to reduce her hours to a maximum of 160 per month. Unfortunately, this cutback will require Maria to turn away some of her regular customers or, at least, serve them less frequently than once a month. Maria has developed the following information to assist her in determining how to best allocate time.

	Customer Classification		
	Large Business	Small Business	Individual
Number of customers..................	10	45	100
Average monthly sales per customer.........	$4,000	$2,500	$1,000
Commission percentage..................	5.0%	4.0%	3.0%
Hours per customer per monthly visit.........	4.0	2.5	1.5

REQUIRED
a. Develop a monthly plan that indicates the number of customers Maria should call on in each classification to maximize her monthly sales commissions.
b. Determine the monthly commissions Maria will earn if she implements this plan.
c. Give one or two reasons why Maria might decide not to follow the conclusions of the above analysis entirely.

PROBLEMS

LO16-1, 2, 3

P16-34. Multiple Changes in Profit Plans
In an attempt to improve profit performance, Anderson Company's management is considering a number of alternative actions. An October contribution income statement for Anderson Company follows.

ANDERSON COMPANY
Contribution Income Statement
For Month of October

Sales (12,000 units × $75)................................		$900,000
Less variable costs		
Direct materials (12,000 units × $10)..........................	$120,000	
Direct labor (12,000 units × $10)............................	120,000	
Variable factory overhead (12,000 units × $4).................	48,000	
Selling and administrative (12,000 units × $2)................	24,000	(312,000)
Contribution margin (12,000 units × $49).......................		588,000
Less fixed costs		
Factory overhead..	360,000	
Selling and administrative...................................	240,000	(600,000)
Net income (loss)...		$ (12,000)

REQUIRED
Determine the effect of each of the following separate situations on monthly profit.

a. Purchasing automated assembly equipment, which should reduce direct labor costs by $4 per unit and increase variable overhead costs by $1 per unit and fixed factory overhead by $12,000 per month.
b. Reducing the selling price by $5 per unit. This should increase the monthly sales by 3,000 units. At this higher volume, additional equipment and salaried personnel would be required. This will increase fixed factory overhead by $4,000 per month and fixed selling and administrative costs by $1,800 per month.
c. Buying rather than manufacturing a component of Anderson's final product. This will increase direct materials costs by $5 per unit. However, direct labor will decline $3 per unit, variable factory overhead will decline $1 per unit, and fixed factory overhead will decline $25,000 per month.
d. Increasing the unit selling price by $5 per unit. This action should result in a 2,000-unit decrease in monthly sales.
e. Combining alternatives (a) and (d).

P16-35. Multiple Changes in Profit Plans: Multiple Products LO16-1, 3
Information on Guadalupe Ltd.'s three products follows.

	A	B	C
Unit sales per month.	1,500	1,200	2,000
Selling price per unit.	$20.00	$14.00	$30.00
Variable cost per unit	(22.00)	(10.00)	(18.00)
Unit contribution margin	$ (2.00)	$ 4.00	$12.00

REQUIRED
Determine the effect each of the following situations would have on monthly profits. Each situation should be evaluated separately from all others.

a. Product A is discontinued.
b. Product A is discontinued, and the subsequent loss of customers causes sales of Product B to decline by 150 units.
c. The selling price of A is increased to $25 with a sales decrease of 250 units.
d. The price of Product B is increased to $20 with a resulting sales decrease of 300 units. However, some of these customers shift to Product A; sales of Product A increase by 200 units.
e. Product A is discontinued, and the plant in which A was produced is used to produce D, a new product. Product D has a unit contribution margin of $2. Monthly sales of Product D are predicted to be 1,500 units.
f. The selling price of Product C is increased to $35, and the selling price of Product B is decreased to $10. Sales of C decline by 350 units, while sales of B increase by 400 units.

P16-36. Relevant Costs and Differential Analysis LO16-1, 2
Cornerstone Bank paid $90,000 for a check-sorting machine 10 years ago this month. The machine had an estimated life of 15 years and annual operating costs of $40,000, excluding depreciation. Although management is pleased with the machine, recent technological advances have made check-sorting machines obsolete. Consequently, the machine now has a book value of $30,000, a remaining operating life of five years, and a salvage value of $0.
  The manager of operations is evaluating a proposal to acquire check scanning equipment for all branches. The new equipment would cost $50,000 and reduce annual operating costs to $20,000, excluding depreciation. Because of expected technological improvements, the manager believes the new machine will have an economic life of four years and no salvage value at the end of that life. Prior to signing the papers authorizing the acquisition of the new machine, the president of the bank prepared the following analysis.

Six-year savings [($40,000 − $20,000) × 4 years]	$80,000
Cost of new machine	(50,000)
Loss on disposal of old machine	(30,000)
Advantage (disadvantage) of replacement	$ 0

After looking at these numbers, the manager rejected the proposal and commented that he was "tired of looking at marginal projects. This bank is in business to make a profit, not to break even. If you want to break even, go work for the government."

REQUIRED
a. Evaluate the president's analysis.
b. Prepare a differential analysis of six-year totals for the old and the new machines.
c. Speculate on some limitations of the model or other issues that might be a factor in making a final decision.

P16-37. Special Order LO16-1, 4
Razor USA produces a variety of electric scooters. Assume that Razor has just received an order from a customer (Pulse Cycles) for 500 Power Core scooters. The following price, based on cost plus a 60% markup, has been developed for the order.

Manufacturing costs	
Direct materials.	$11,850
Direct labor	8,500
Factory overhead	15,800
Total	36,150
Markup (60%).	21,690
Selling price	$57,840

Pulse Cycles rejected this price and offered to purchase the 500 scooters at a price of $45,000. The following additional information is available.

- Razor has sufficient excess capacity to produce the scooters.
- Factory overhead is applied on the basis of direct labor dollars.
- Budgeted factory overhead is $8,000,000 for the current year. Of this amount, $6,000,000 is fixed. Of the $15,800 of factory overhead assigned to the Pulse Cycles order, only $3,950 is driven by the special order; $11,850 is a fixed cost.
- Selling and administrative expenses are budgeted as follows.

Fixed.	$3,000,000 per year
Variable.	$10 per unit manufactured and sold

REQUIRED

a. The president of Razor wants to know if he should allow Pulse Cycles to have the scooters for $45,000. Determine the effect on profits of accepting Pulse Cycles' offer.
b. Briefly explain why certain costs should be omitted from the analysis in requirement (*a*).
c. Assume Razor is operating at capacity and could sell the 500 scooters at its regular markup.
  1. Determine the opportunity cost of accepting Pulse Cycles' offer.
  2. Determine the effect on profits of accepting Pulse Cycles' offer.
d. What other factors should Razor consider before deciding to accept the special order?

LO16-1, 4 **P16-38. Special Order**

Every Halloween, Peterson's Ice Cream Shop offers a trick-or-treat package of 25 coupons for $20. The coupons are redeemable by children 12 years or under, for a single-scoop cone, with a limit of one coupon per child per visit. Coupon sales average 600 books per year. The printing costs are $75. A single-scoop cone of Peterson's ice cream normally sells for $2.00. The variable costs of a single-scoop cone are $1.50.

REQUIRED

a. Determine the loss if all coupons are redeemed without any other effect on sales.
b. Assume all coupons will not be redeemed. With regular sales unaffected, determine the coupon redemption rate at which Peterson's will break even on the offer.
c. Assuming regular sales are not affected and one additional single-scoop cone is sold at the regular price each time a coupon is redeemed, determine the coupon redemption rate at which Peterson's will break even on the offer.
d. Determine the profit or loss incurred on the offer if the coupon redemption rate is 60% and:
  1. One-fourth of the redeemed coupons have no effect on sales.
  2. One-fourth of the redeemed coupons result in additional sales of two single-scoop cones.
  3. One-fourth of the redeemed coupons result in additional sales of three single-scoop cones.
  4. One-fourth of the redeemed coupons come out of regular sales of single-scoop cones.

LO16-1, 2, 3, 4, 5 **P16-39. Applications of Differential Analysis**

Moscot

Moscot manufactures high-end sunglasses that it sells in retail shops and online for $310, on average. Assume the following represent manufacturing and other costs.

Variable Cost per Unit		Fixed Costs per Month	
Direct materials.	$ 80	Factory overhead	$450,000
Direct labor	50	Selling and administrative.	375,000
Factory overhead	35	Total	$825,000
Distribution	10		
Total	$175		

The variable distribution costs are for transportation to retail partners. Assume the current monthly production and sales volume is 15,000 units. Monthly capacity is 20,000 units.

REQUIRED

Determine the effect of each of the following separate situations on monthly profits.

a. A $50 increase in the unit selling price should result in a 2,000-unit decrease in monthly sales.
b. A 10% decrease in the unit selling price should result in a 6,000-unit increase in monthly sales. However, because of capacity constraints, the last 1,000 units would be produced during overtime with the direct labor costs increasing by 50%.
c. A British distributor has proposed to place a special, one-time order for 1,000 units at a reduced price of $250 per unit. The distributor would pay all transportation costs. There would be additional fixed selling and administrative costs of $750.
d. A Swiss distributor has proposed to place a special, one-time order for 6,000 units at a special price of $250 per unit. The distributor would pay all transportation costs. There would be additional fixed selling and administrative costs of $1,000. Assume overtime production is not possible.
e. Assume Moscat provides a designer case for each pair of sunglasses that it manufactures. A Chinese manufacturer has offered a one-year contract to supply the cases at a cost of $10 per unit. If Moscat accepts the offer, it will be able to reduce variable manufacturing costs by 5%, reduce fixed costs by $5,000, and rent out some freed-up space for $4,000 per month.
f. The glasses also come with a choice of lens tint. Assume that eliminating that option would reduce variable costs by $5 and eliminate $50,000 in fixed factory overhead. The selling price would likely have to decrease to $290 per unit.

P16-40. Applications of Differential Analysis LO16-1, 2, 3, 4, 5

Adventure Expeditions offers guided back-country hiking/camping trips in British Columbia. Adventure provides a guide and all necessary food and equipment at a fee of $100 per person per day. Adventure currently provides an average of 600 guide-days per month in June, July, August, and September. Based on available equipment and staff, maximum capacity is 750 guide-days per month. Monthly variable and fixed operating costs (valued in Canadian dollars) are as follows.

Variable Cost per Guide-Day		Fixed Costs per Month	
Food	$ 6	Equipment rental	$10,000
Guide salary	20	Administration	12,000
Supplies	4	Advertising	2,500
Insurance	10	Total	$24,500
Total	$40		

REQUIRED

Determine the effect of each of the following situations on monthly profits. Each situation is to be evaluated separately from of all others.

a. A $10 increase in the daily fee should result in a 100-unit decrease in monthly sales.
b. A $10 decrease in the daily fee should result in a 200-unit increase in monthly sales. However, because of capacity constraints, the last 50 guide-days would be provided by subcontracting to another firm at a cost of $50 per guide-day. (The $50 cost includes food, guides, supplies, and insurance.)
c. A French tour agency has proposed to place a special, one-time order for 100 guide-days at a reduced fee of $85 per guide-day. The agency would pay all insurance costs. There would be additional fixed administrative costs of $500.
d. An Italian tour agency has proposed to place a special, one-time order for 300 guide-days next month at a special fee of $80 per guide-day. The agency would pay all insurance costs. There would be additional fixed administrative costs of $500. Assume additional capacity beyond 800 guide-days is not available.
e. An Alberta outdoor supply company has offered to supply all necessary food and camping equipment at $7 per guide-day. This eliminates the current food costs and reduces the monthly equipment rental costs to $8,800.
f. Clients currently must carry a backpack and assist in camp activities such as cooking. Adventure is considering the addition of mules to carry all food and equipment and the hiring of college students to perform camp activities such as cooking. This will increase variable costs by $30 per guide-day and fixed costs by $5,000 per month. However, 600 full-service guide-days per month could now be sold at $150 each.

LO16-1, 3   **P16-41. Continue or Discontinue**

Westview Eye Clinic primarily performs three medical procedures: cataract removal, corneal implants, and laser keratotomy. At the end of the first quarter of this year, Dr. Rajan, president of Westview, expressed grave concern about the cataract sector because it had reported a loss of $150,000. He rationalized that "since the cataract market is losing $150,000, and the overall practice is making $300,000, if we eliminate the cataract market, our total profits will increase to $450,000."

REQUIRED

a. Is the president's analysis correct?
b. Will total profits increase if the cataract section is dropped?
c. Is it possible total profits will decline?
d. Suppose that many of the cataract patients are patients with low income who rely on Westview Eye Clinic for eye care. How would you evaluate the profit objective with an ethical goal of vision for all?

LO16-1, 3, 4, 5, 6   **P16-42. Application of Relevant Costs and Differential Analysis**

1. A company manufactures three products, T1, T2 and T3. Their financial information is shown below.

	T1	T2	T3
Sales	$60,000	$90,000	$24,000
Variable costs	36,000	48,000	15,000
Contribution margin	24,000	42,000	9,000
Fixed costs:			
Avoidable	9,000	18,000	6,000
Unavoidable	6,000	9,000	5,400
Operating income	$ 9,000	$15,000	$ (2,400)

Management is concerned about the financial performance of T3. If the company drops the T3 product line, the operating income will

  a. increase by $2,400.
  b. decrease by $3,000.
  c. increase by $3,000.
  d. decrease by $9,000.

CMA Adapted

2. Johnson Company manufactures a variety of shoes, and has received a special one-time-only order directly from a wholesaler. Johnson has sufficient idle capacity to accept the special order to manufacture 15,000 pairs of sneakers at a price of $7.50 per pair. Johnson's normal selling price is $11.50 per pair of sneakers. Variable manufacturing costs are $5.00 per pair and fixed manufacturing costs are $3.00 a pair. Johnson's variable selling expense for its normal line of sneakers is $1.00 per pair. What would the effect on Johnson's operating income be if the company accepted the special order?

  a. Decrease by $60,000.
  b. Increase by $22,500.
  c. Increase by $37,500.
  d. Increase by $52,500.

CMA Adapted

3. Aril Industries is a multiproduct company that currently manufactures 30,000 units of Part 730 each month for use in production. The facilities now being used to produce Part 730 have fixed monthly overhead costs of $150,000, and a theoretical capacity to produce 60,000 units per month. If Aril were to buy Part 730 from an outside supplier, the facilities would be idle and 40% of fixed costs would continue to be incurred. There are no alternative uses for the facilities. The variable production costs of Part 730 are $11 per unit. Fixed overhead is allocated based on planned production levels.

If Aril Industries continues to use 30,000 units of Part 730 each month, it would realize a net benefit by purchasing Part 730 from an outside supplier only if the supplier's unit price is less than

  a. $12.00.
  b. $12.50.
  c. $13.00.
  d. $14.00.

CMA Adapted

4. A circuit board company conducts a joint manufacturing process to produce 10,000 units of Board A and 10,000 units of Board B. The total joint variable manufacturing cost to produce these two products is $2,000,000. The company can sell all 10,000 units of Board B at the split-off point for $300 per unit, or process Board B further and sell all 10,000 units at $375 per unit. The total additional cost to process Board B further would be $500,000, and all additional

costs would be variable. If the company decides to process Board B further, what effect would the decision have on operating income?

   a. $750,000 decrease in operating income.
   b. $250,000 increase in operating income.
   c. $2,250,000 increase in operating income.
   d. $3,250,000 increase in operating income.

CMA Adapted

CASES AND PROJECTS

C16-43. Assessing the Impact of an Incentive Plan[5]

LO16-1, 3

OVERVIEW
Ladbrecks is a major department store with 50 retail outlets. The company's stores compete with outlets run by companies such as Nordstrom, Macy's, Bloomingdales, and Saks Fifth Avenue. During the early nineties the company decided that providing excellent customer service was the key ingredient for success in the retail industry. Therefore, during the mid 1990s the company implemented an incentive plan for its sales associates in 20 of its stores. Your job is to assess the financial impact of the plan and to provide a recommendation to management to continue or discontinue the plan based on your findings.

INCENTIVES IN RETAIL
The past decade has evidenced a concerted effort by many firms to empower and motivate employees to improve performance. A recent *New York Times* article reported that more and more firms are offering bonus plans to hourly workers. An Ernst and Young survey of the retail industry indicates that virtually all department stores currently offer incentive programs such as straight commissions, base salary plus commission, and quota bonus programs. Although these programs can add to payroll costs, the survey respondents indicated that they believe these plans have contributed to major improvements in customer service.

COMPANY'S BACKGROUND
Ladbrecks was founded by members of the Ladbreck family in the 1880s. The first store opened under the name Ladbreck Dry Goods. Growth was fueled through acquisitions as the industry consolidated during the 1960s. Over this hundred-year period, sales associates were paid a fixed hourly wage. Raises were based on seniority. Sales associates were expected to be neat and courteous to customers. The advent of specialty stores and the stated intention of an upscale west coast retailer to begin opening stores in the Midwest concerned Ladbreck's management. Building on its history of excellence in customer service, the company initiated its performance-based incentive plan to support its stated firm-wide strategy of "customer emphasis" with "employee empowerment." Management expected it to result in further enhancement of customer service and, consequently, in an increase in sales generated at its stores.

INCENTIVE PLAN
The plan was implemented in stores sequentially as company managers intended to examine and evaluate the plan's impact on sales and profitability. Initially, the firm selected one store from a group of similar stores in the same general area to begin the implementation. By the end of 1994, 10 stores had implemented the plan. In 1995, 10 more stores implemented the plan, bringing the total to 20 out of a total of 50.

The performance-based incentive plan is best described as a bonus program. At the time of the plan's implementation, sales associates received little in the form of annual merit increases, and promotions were rare. The bonus payment became the only significant reward for high performance. Each week sales associates are paid a base hourly rate times hours worked. In addition, under the plan sales associates could increase their compensation by receiving a bonus at the end of each quarter. The contract provides sales-force personnel with a cash bonus only if the actual quarterly sales generated by the employee exceed a quarterly sales goal. Individualized pre-specified sales goals were established for each employee based only on the individual's base hourly rate, hours worked, and a multiplier (multiplier = 1/bonus rate). The bonus is computed as a fixed percentage of the excess sales (actual sales minus a pre-specified sales goal) by the employee in a quarter (see Exhibit 16.1).

---

[5] Written to illustrate the use of relevant costs and revenues for Decision-Making. This example is based on an actual company's experience with implementing an incentive plan. The company name and the financial numbers and key ratios have been altered.

$$\text{Employee's Bonus} = 0.08 \times (\text{Employee's actual sales for quarter} - \text{employee's targeted sales for quarter})$$

$$\text{Where employee's targeted sales for quarter} = \text{Employee's hourly wage} \times \text{Hours worked in quarter} \times 12.5$$

Senior managers regarded the incentive plan as a major change for the firm and its sales force. Management expected that the new incentive scheme would motivate many changes in employee behavior that would enhance customer service. Sales associates were now expected to build a client base to generate repeat sales. Actions consistent with this approach include developing and updating customer address lists (including details of their needs and preferences), writing thank you notes, and contacting customers about upcoming sales and new merchandise that matched their preferences.

CONSULTANT'S TASK

Management decided to call you in to provide an independent assessment. While the company thought that sales had increased with the plan's implementation, the human resources department did not know exactly how to quantify the plan's impact on sales and expenses. It suspected that employee salaries, cost of goods sold, and inventory carrying costs, as well as sales, may have changed due to the plan's implementation. You, therefore, requested information on these financial variables.

Sales Analysis: Because each of the 20 stores implemented the plan at different dates, and store sales fluctuated greatly with the seasons and the economy, you could not simply plot store sales. Instead, for each of the 20 stores, you picked another Ladbreck store as a control and computed for 48 months the following series of monthly sales:[6]

$$\text{Percent Change in Sales} = [(\text{Plan Store Sales in Month t} \div \text{Plan Store Sales in Month t-24}) - (\text{Control Store Sales in Month t} \div \text{Control Store Sales in Month t-24})] \times 100$$

The plan's implementation was denoted as month 25, so you had 24 months prior to the plan and 24 months after the plan. Averages were then taken for the 20 stores. If the control procedure worked, then you expected that the first 24 months of the series would fluctuate around zero. The actual results are reported in Figure 1, page 146. Month 25 is denoted as the rollout month, the month the incentive plan began.

Expense Analysis: You then plotted wage expense/sales, cost of goods sold/sales, and inventory turnover for the 20 stores for the 24 months preceding the plan and the first 24 months after plan implementation. After pulling out seasonal effects, these monthly series are presented in Figures 2, 3, and 4. If the plan has no impact on these expenses, then you would expect no dramatic change in the series around month 25.

- Figure 2 plots (wage expense in month t/sales in month t)
- Figure 3 plots (cost of goods sold in month t/sales in month t)
- Figure 4 plots "annual" turnover computed as (12 × cost of goods sold in month t/inventory at beginning of month t)

  For example, if monthly cost of sales is $100 and the annual inventory turnover ratio is 4, it suggests a monthly turnover of 0.333 with the firm holding an average inventory of $300 throughout the year. (Note that a monthly inventory turnover of .333 implies an annual turnover of 4 (from 12 × 0.333).

Financial Report for Store: A typical annual income statement for a pre-plan Ladbreck store before fixed charges, taxes, and incidentals looks as follows.

---

[6] For instance, assume sales for plan store were $2,200 this January and $2,000 two Januarys ago. Also assume that sales in the control store were $4,400 this January and $4,000 two Januarys ago. Percent change = 2,200/2,000 − 4,400/4,000 = 0.

	Total	Percent
Sales.	$10,000,000	100
Cost of goods sold	6,300,000	63
Gross profit.	3,700,000	37
Employee salaries	800,000	8
Profit before fixed charges	$ 2,900,000	29

A store also has substantial charges for rent, management salaries, insurance, etc., but they are fixed with respect to the incentive plan.

REQUIRED

a. Suppose the goal of the firm is to now provide superior customer service by having the sales consultant identify and sell to the specific needs of the customer. What does this goal suggest about a change in managerial accounting and control systems?
b. Provide an estimate of the impact of the incentive plan on sales.
c. Did the sales impact occur all at once, or did it occur gradually?
d. What is the impact of the incentive plan on wage expense as a percent of sales?
e. What is the impact of the incentive plan on cost of goods sold as a percent of sales?
f. What is the impact of incentive plan on inventory turnover (turnover = cost of goods sold ÷ inventory)? [If sales go up, then stores are selling more goods; therefore, more goods need to be on the floor or those goods on floor need to turn over faster.]
g. What is the additional dollar amount of inventory that must be held?
h. Using the information on sales and expenses for a typical store, provide an analysis of the additional store profit contributed by the plan. Assume that it costs 10% a year to carry the added inventory.
i. Look at Exhibit 1, which provides a partial listing of employee pay for one small department within a store. Which "type" of employee is receiving the bonus?
j. Should the company keep the plan? Explain your estimate of the financial impact of the plan and also incorporate any nonfinancial information you feel is relevant in justifying your decision.

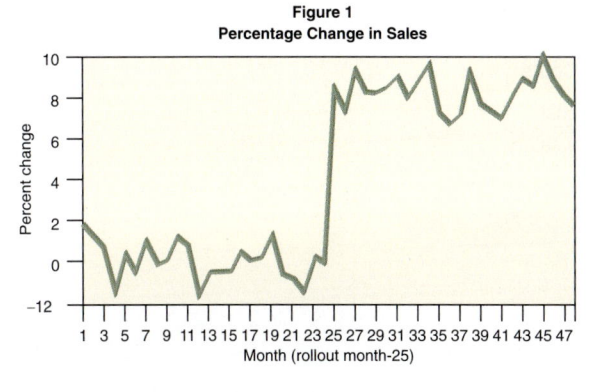

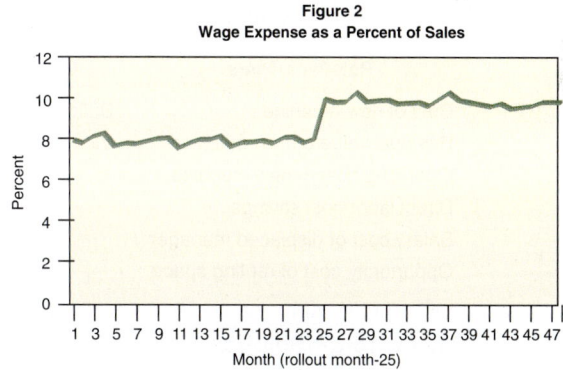

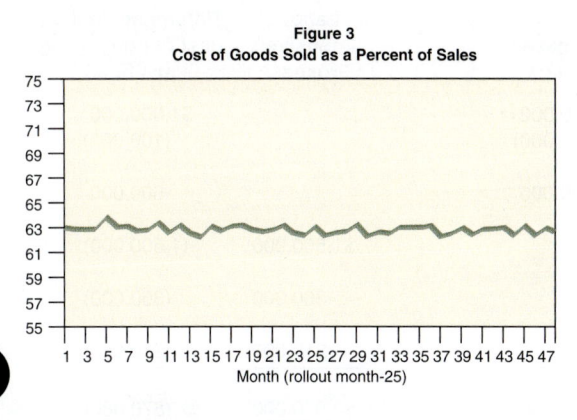

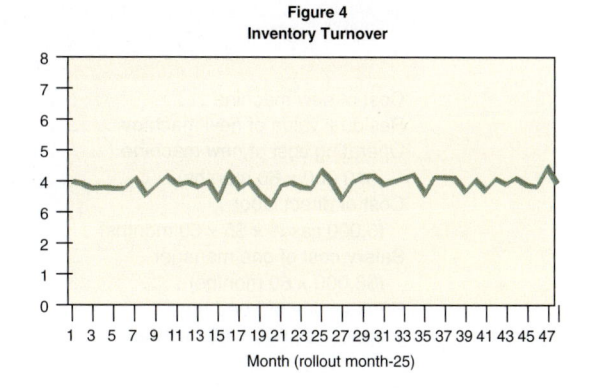

Figure 1
Percentage Change in Sales

Figure 2
Wage Expense as a Percent of Sales

Figure 3
Cost of Goods Sold as a Percent of Sales

Figure 4
Inventory Turnover

EXHIBIT 1 — Wages by subset of employees in Ladbreck's fashion department

Name	Years of Service	Hourly Wage Rate	Hours Worked in Quarter	Regular Pay	Actual Sales for Quarter	Bonus	Total Pay Quarter
Bob Marley	2	4.00	400	1,600	25,000	400	2,000
Jimi Hendrix	16	7.50	440	3,300	41,000	0	3,300
Millie Small	24	9.99	440	4,396	40,000	0	4,396
Al Green	11	6.00	400	2,400	36,000	480	2,880
Bob Dylan	4	5.00	400	2,000	30,000	400	2,400
Janis Joplin	10	6.00	400	2,400	30,000	0	2,400
Wilson Pickett	16	7.50	440	3,300	50,000	700	4,000
Bruce Springsteen	23	9.99	440	4,396	30,000	0	4,396
Michigan & Smiley	13	7.00	400	2,800	38,000	240	3,040
Richie Furay	22	9.90	400	3,960	30,000	0	3,960
John Lennon	5	5.00	400	2,000	34,000	720	2,720
Julio Iglesias	4	5.00	480	2,400	46,000	1,280	3,680
Tommy Petty	11	6.00	400	2,400	36,000	480	2,880
Joan Baez	21	9.90	400	3,960	40,000	0	3,960
Bb King	8	6.00	400	2,400	38,000	640	3,040
Gladys Knight	14	8.00	480	3,840	46,000	0	3,840
Neil Young	15	8.00	480	3,840	36,000	0	3,840
Bo Diddley	4	5.00	400	2,000	30,000	400	2,400

SOLUTIONS TO REVIEW PROBLEMS

Review 16-1—Solution

Relevant Costs	Irrelevant Costs
Cost of new machine	Building lease cost
Residual value of new machine	Vice president's salary
Operating cost of new machine	
Direct labor cost savings	
Salary cost of displaced manager	
Opportunity cost of renting space	

Review 16-2—Solution

a.

	Purchase Machine	Labor Intensive Process	Difference (in total cost of purchasing machine)
Cost of new machine	$1,000,000		$1,000,000
Residual value of new machine	(100,000)		(100,000)
Operating cost of new machine ($10,000 × 60 months)	600,000		600,000
Cost of direct labor (5,000 cases × $5 × 60 months)		$1,500,000	(1,500,000)
Salary cost of one manager ($6,000 × 60 months)		360,000	(360,000)
Rental value of freed-up space ($3,500 × 60 months)		210,000	(210,000)
Total costs	$1,500,000	$2,070,000	$ (570,000)
Advantage of purchasing machine		$570,000	

b. Even though the new machine would save estimated costs of $570,000 over the next five years, there are several qualitative questions that should be answered, including the following:
- Will the new machine provide the same quality product as produced by the current workers?
- How important is it to have a cost structure that includes variable labor costs versus more fixed machine costs? If a business decline should occur, variable costs are often easier to eliminate than fixed costs.
- What is the expected effect on worker morale and community image of eliminating a significant number of jobs in the plant?
- How important is it for the sales staff to be able to promote the product as primarily handmade, versus machine made?
- Can the machine be used to produce other products?

Review 16-3—Solution

Unit selling price	$4.80
Unit variable costs	(2.50)
Unit contribution margin	$2.30

a.

Profit decrease from reduced sales given no changes in prices or costs (1,800 units × $2.30)	$(4,140)
Profit increase from increase in selling price [(15,000 units − 1,800 units) × $1.50]	19,800
Increase in monthly profit	$15,660

b.

Profit increase from increased sales given no changes in prices or costs (6,000 units × $2.30)	$13,800
Profit decrease from reduced selling price of all units [(15,000 units + 6,000 units) × $1.80]	(37,800)
Profit decrease from increased direct labor costs for the last 1,000 units [1,000 units × ($0.20 × 0.50)]	(100)
Decrease in monthly profit	$(24,100)

c. If the segment is discontinued, the net impact on the profit of the company is calculated as follows:

Contribution margin lost = [($3.00 − $2.50) × 15,000] = $7,500
Contribution margin lost − Cost savings (Avoidable fixed costs) = $7,500 − $1,000 = $6,500

In the short run on a monthly basis, the company would incur a loss of $6,500 if the segment was discontinued.

Review 16-4—Solution

a.

Increase in revenues (4,000 units × $4.00)		$16,000
Increase in costs		
Direct materials (4,000 units × $2.00)	$8,000	
Direct labor (4,000 units × $0.20)	800	
Factory overhead (4,000 units × $0.25)	1,000	
Selling and administrative	500	(10,300)
Increase in profits		$ 5,700

b.

Increase in revenues (8,000 units × $4.00)		$32,000
Increase in costs		
Direct materials (8,000 units × $2.00)	$16,000	
Direct labor (8,000 units × $0.20)	1,600	
Factory overhead (8,000 units × $0.25)	2,000	
Selling and administrative	500	
Opportunity cost of lost regular sales [(15,000 units + 8,000 units − 20,000 unit capacity) × $2.30]	6,900	(27,000)
Increase in profits		$ 5,000

Review 16-5—Solution

	Cost to Make	Cost to Buy
Cost to buy		$15,000
Direct materials.	$30,000	18,000
Direct labor	3,000	1,800
Factory overhead	3,750	2,250
Opportunity cost	1,000	
Totals	$37,750	$37,050
Advantage of buying		$ 700

Review 16-6—Solution

Increase in revenues		
Package in six-packs (15,000 units × $5.05)	$75,750	
Sell in bulk (15,000 units × $4.80).	(72,000)	$3,750
Additional packaging costs (15,000 units × $0.10).		(1,500)
Advantage of packaging in six-packs		$2,250

Review 16-7—Solution

Intuition suggests that the extra capacity should be devoted either to produce the Beyond Beer, which has the highest sales price, or the craft beer, which has the highest per-unit contribution margin and net income. However, an analysis of the contribution margin of each product per unit of constraining factor reveals that the traditional beer should receive the extra capacity.

Note that fixed costs are allocated among products on the basis of machine hours—the constraining resource in our example. Furthermore, the unit allocations of fixed costs indicate that the craft beer requires three times as many machine hours as the beyond beer and six times as many as the traditional beer brands. The contribution per unit of machine capacity for each product is as follows.

	Traditional Beer	Craft Beer	Beyond Beer
Contribution margin per case	$4	$12	$6
Divided by units machine capacity required	1	6	2
Contribution margin per unit of machine capacity (the constraining resource)	$4	$ 2	$3

Use of the remaining capacity generates a greater contribution margin if devoted to the traditional beer brands.

Chapter 17

Product Costing: Job and Process Operations

LEARNING OBJECTIVES

LO17-1 Describe how inventory costs are classified for financial reporting in different types of organizations. (p. 17-3)

LO17-2 Apply manufacturing overhead using a predetermined overhead rate. (p. 17-8)

LO17-3 Explain the operation of a job order costing system. (p. 17-11)

LO17-4 Explain the operation of a process costing system. (p. 17-22)

LO17-5 Evaluate the differences between absorption and variable costing income (Appendix 17A). (p. 17-28)

Road Map

LO	Learning Objective | Topics	Page	eLecture	Review	Assignments
LO17-1	**Describe how inventory costs are classified for financial reporting in different types of organizations.** Service Provider :: Merchandiser :: Manufacturer :: Supplies Inventory :: Merchandise Inventory :: Raw Materials :: Work-in-Process :: Finished Goods :: Product Costs :: Period Costs	17-3	e17–1	R17-1	M17-14, M17-15, E17-24, P17-41
LO17-2	**Apply manufacturing overhead using a predetermined overhead rate.** Predetermined Overhead Rates :: Cost Driver :: Overhead Application Base:: Plantwide Rate :: Heterogeneity in Cost :: Heterogeneity in Use	17-8	e17–2	R17-2	M17-16, E17-25, E17-26, E17-28, E17-30, E17-31, E17-32, E17-33, E17-34, E17-35, P17-42, P17-43, P17-44, P17-45, P17-52, C17-53, C17-54
LO17-3	**Explain the operation of a job order costing system.** Job Order Production :: Production Order :: Job Cost Sheet :: Flow of Costs :: Materials Requisition Form :: Work Ticket :: Manufacturing Overhead Applied :: Statement of Cost of Goods Manufactured :: Overapplied and Underapplied Overhead :: Job Costing in a Service Organization	17-11	e17–3	R17-3	M17-17, M17-18, M17-19, M17-20, E17-26, E17-27, E17-28, E17-29, E17-31, E17-32, E17-33, E17-34, E17-35, P17-41, P17-42, P17-43, P17-44, P17-45 P17-52, C17-53, C17-54, **DA17-1, DA17-2**
LO17-4	**Explain the operation of a process costing system.** Cost of Production Report :: Weighted Average Method :: Equivalent Units :: First-In, First-Out :: Process Costing in Service Organizations	17-22	e17–4	R17-4	M17-17, M17-18, M17-21, E17-36, E17-37, P17-46, P17-47, P17-48, P17-52, **DA17-3**
LO17-5	**(Appendix 17A) Evaluate the differences between absorption and variable costing income.** Absorption Costing Income :: Variable Costing Income :: Ending Inventory :: Fixed Manufacturing Costs	17-28	e17–5	R17-5	M17-22, M17-23, E17-38, E17-39, E17-40, P17-49, P17-50, P17-51, C17-55

SAMSUNG
www.samsung.com

The inventory of a manufacturing firm, such as South Korea's **Samsung Electronics**, is complicated because it has many products that are produced using different resources. Let's consider Samsung's smartphones. First, there are several components used in the manufacturing process of a smartphone, including, for example, external cases, batteries, SIM cards, circuit boards, motherboards, speaker assemblies, cameras, flash memory, and controller chips. Of these components, some are purchased from outside vendors, whereas others are made internally by Samsung. In fact, one of Samsung's competitive advantages is that it makes everything from chips to screens in its own factories to control the processing time, technological information and expertise. This allows the company to bring its products to market more quickly than its competitors.

Given that Samsung makes many of its smartphone components internally, the company has raw materials inventory. These are materials that will be transformed during the manufacturing process to become smartphone components. Examples of Samsung's raw materials include steel, glass, chemicals, wood, papers, metals, and polycarbonates. However, Samsung purchases some components from external vendors. As an example, chips for Galaxy S10s come from **Broadcomm**. These components are also considered raw materials inventory until they are requisitioned into the manufacturing process.

Half of Samsung's smartphones (120 million phones per year) are manufactured in two facilities in Vietnam. The other half are manufactured in a single plant in India. Within each factory, employees assemble smartphones at a three-sided workbench that has all the needed tools and raw materials within arm's reach. As raw materials are requisitioned into this part of the facility and direct labor and overhead are added to the raw materials to manufacture the smartphones, these costs are accumulated in another type of inventory account called work-in-process inventory. When the smartphones are completed, they are transferred into a third type of inventory account called finished goods, where they will await sale to a customer. This means that for manufacturing companies, the line item "inventory" on the balance sheet may be the sum of three types of inventory: raw materials inventory, work-in-process inventory, and finished goods inventory.

In this chapter, we explore how the costs of products and services flow through these inventory accounts and how we allocate costs to individual products or services based on those products' or services' consumption of the resources. Sometimes, this allocation is straightforward. For example, we can track the amount of raw materials or direct labor hours that go into a product or service. Other times, however, this allocation is more complicated, such as when multiple products use the same machine as part of the manufacturing process (i.e., overhead or indirect costs).

Sources: Samsung Electronics 2021 10-K, the company's website: www.samsung.com, and Grobart, S. "How Samsung became the world's no. 1 smartphone maker—and its plans to stay on top. Bloomberg." (2013).

CHAPTER ORGANIZATION

Product Costing: Job and Process Operations

Reporting Inventory Costs	Closer Look at Manufacturing Overhead	Job Costing for Products and Services	Process Costing	Absorption and Variable Costing
• Inventory Categories Reported in Various Organization Types • Product and Period Cost Distinctions • Components of Product Costs	• Applying Manufacturing Overhead • Selecting Overhead Allocation Basis • Using Predetermined Overhead Rates • Impact of Changing Cost Structures	• Production Planning and Control Process • Job Costing Illustrated • Overapplied and Underapplied Overhead • Job Costing in Service Organizations	• Cost of Production Report • Weighted Average and First-In, First-Out Process Costing • Process Costing in Service Organizations	• Basic Concepts • Income Under Absorption and Variable Costing • Evaluating Alternatives to Inventory Valuation (Appendix 17A)

REPORTING INVENTORY COSTS IN VARIOUS ORGANIZATIONS

LO17-1
Describe how inventory costs are classified for financial reporting in different types of organizations.

eLecture
MBC

Organizations can be classified as service, merchandising, or manufacturing.

- **Service organizations**, such as **SportClips** hair salons, **Shriners Hospitals for Children**, **The Cheesecake Factory** restaurants, and **Delta Air Lines**, perform services for others.
- **Merchandising organizations**, such as **ModCloth**, **Walmart**, **Urban Outfitters**, and **Best Buy**, buy and sell goods.
- **Manufacturing organizations**, such as **Garmin Ltd.**, **Intel**, and **Hershey**, process raw materials into finished products for sale to others.

Inventory Categories Reported for Various Types of Organizations

The types of inventory categories reported in a company's financial statements depend on whether the company is a service, merchandising, or manufacturing organization. Service organizations typically have a low percentage of their assets invested in inventory, which usually consists only of the supplies needed to facilitate their operations. For example, in its 2022 annual report, **Delta Air Lines** reported *fuel, expendable parts, and supplies inventory* of $1.4 billion which was only 2% of its total assets. In contrast, merchandising organizations usually have a high percentage of their assets invested in inventory. Their largest inventory investment is merchandise purchased for resale, but they also have supplies inventories. For example, in its 2022 annual report, **Best Buy** reported merchandise inventories of $6.0 billion which was 34% of its total assets. Supplies inventory was not reported separately on its balance sheet.

Manufacturing organizations, like merchandisers, have a high percentage of their assets invested in inventories. However, rather than just one major inventory category, manufacturing organizations typically have three: raw materials, work-in-process, and finished goods.

- **Raw materials inventories** contain the physical ingredients and components that will be converted by machines and/or human labor into a finished product. **Samsung Electronics Co., Ltd** (Samsung) owns and stores metal, for example, that is used to manufacture some components of the Samsung Galaxy smartphone. This metal is considered raw materials before it is used in the manufacturing process.

- **Work-in-process inventories** are the partially completed goods that are in the process of being converted into a finished product. In the case of Samsung, smartphones that have been started but are not finished are included in work-in-process inventories.

- **Finished goods inventories** are the completely manufactured products held for sale to customers. The Samsung Galaxy, packed and ready to ship to a retailer or customer, is considered a finished good.

Note that companies might also list inventories that have been purchased and are currently mid-shipment if the company has taken ownership as in the following example. As of December 31, 2022, Samsung reported the following current inventories in the asset section of its balance sheet, making up 11.6% of total assets (in Korean won).

Raw materials and supplies	₩14,979,280 million
Work-in-process	20,077,519 million
Finished goods	16,032,226 million
Materials in transit	1,098,841 million
Total current inventory	₩52,187,866 million

Manufacturing organizations include *manufacturing supplies* in the cost of inventory. However, manufacturing organizations also have *supplies inventories* to facilitate selling and administrative activities. These supplies would typically be included in *other current assets* on the balance sheet.

Exhibit 17.1 illustrates the financial accounting flow of inventory costs in service, merchandising, and manufacturing organizations. In all three types of organizations, the financial accounting system initially records costs of inventories as assets. You may recall from financial accounting that an *asset* is a present right to an economic benefit reported on the balance sheet. When inventories are eventually consumed or sold, inventory costs are recorded as expenses. *Expenses* are outflows from delivering or producing goods or rendering services and are reported on the income statement. Supplies expense represents the value of supplies consumed during the period. *Cost of goods sold* is specific to organizations that sell physical products. Cost of goods sold represents the cost to purchase or manufacture the items that were sold. Inventory and expense are recorded in all types of organizations.

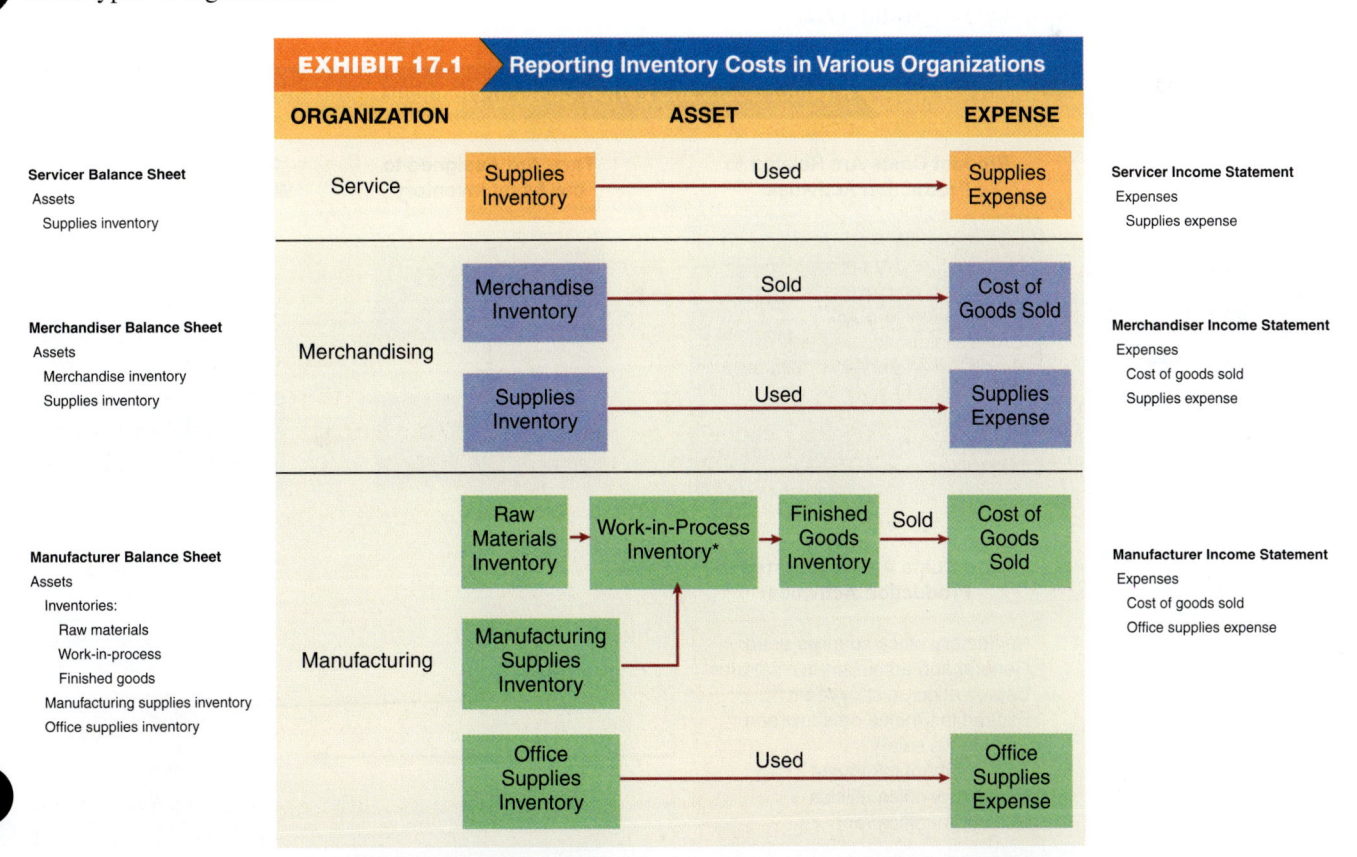

EXHIBIT 17.1 Reporting Inventory Costs in Various Organizations

Servicer Balance Sheet
Assets
  Supplies inventory

Service: Supplies Inventory → Used → Supplies Expense

Servicer Income Statement
Expenses
  Supplies expense

Merchandiser Balance Sheet
Assets
  Merchandise inventory
  Supplies inventory

Merchandising: Merchandise Inventory → Sold → Cost of Goods Sold; Supplies Inventory → Used → Supplies Expense

Merchandiser Income Statement
Expenses
  Cost of goods sold
  Supplies expense

Manufacturer Balance Sheet
Assets
  Inventories:
    Raw materials
    Work-in-process
    Finished goods
  Manufacturing supplies inventory
  Office supplies inventory

Manufacturing: Raw Materials Inventory → Work-in-Process Inventory* → Finished Goods Inventory → Sold → Cost of Goods Sold; Manufacturing Supplies Inventory → (into WIP); Office Supplies Inventory → Used → Office Supplies Expense

Manufacturer Income Statement
Expenses
  Cost of goods sold
  Office supplies expense

*Other costs that are never reported as inventory (direct labor and overhead) also contribute to work-in-process inventory costs.

Critical Thinking & Decision-Making

For Shriners Hospital for Children, what would you expect to see as inventory accounts in its accounting records?

Shriners Hospital is a service organization. It provides specialty medical care to children and families through a system made up of hospitals and clinics. Shriners would maintain a variety of supplies inventory accounts including not only office supplies but also medical supplies such as sutures and bandages.

Most formal inventory costing systems are designed to provide information for general-purpose financial statements. Before the balance sheet and income statement are prepared, the cost of ending inventory and the cost of inventory sold or used during the period must be determined.

Product and Period Cost Reporting Distinction for Manufacturers

In financial reporting for manufacturing organizations, an important distinction is made between the cost of *producing* products and the cost of all other activities such as selling and administration.

Product Costs For financial reporting, all costs incurred in the *manufacturing* of products are called **product costs**. These costs are carried in the accounts as an asset (inventory) until the product is sold, at which time they are recognized as an expense (cost of goods sold). Product costs include the costs of raw materials, production employee salaries and wages, and all other *manufacturing* costs incurred to transform raw materials into finished products.

Period Costs Costs that directly apply to the income statement period (other than costs of goods sold) are called **period costs** and are recognized as expenses when incurred. Period costs include the president's salary, sales commissions, advertising costs, and all other *nonmanufacturing* costs. Costs such as research and development, marketing, distribution, and customer service are important for strategic analyses. However, since these costs are also not incurred in the production process, they are not product costs for *financial reporting purposes*. Product and period costs are illustrated in **Exhibit 17.2**.

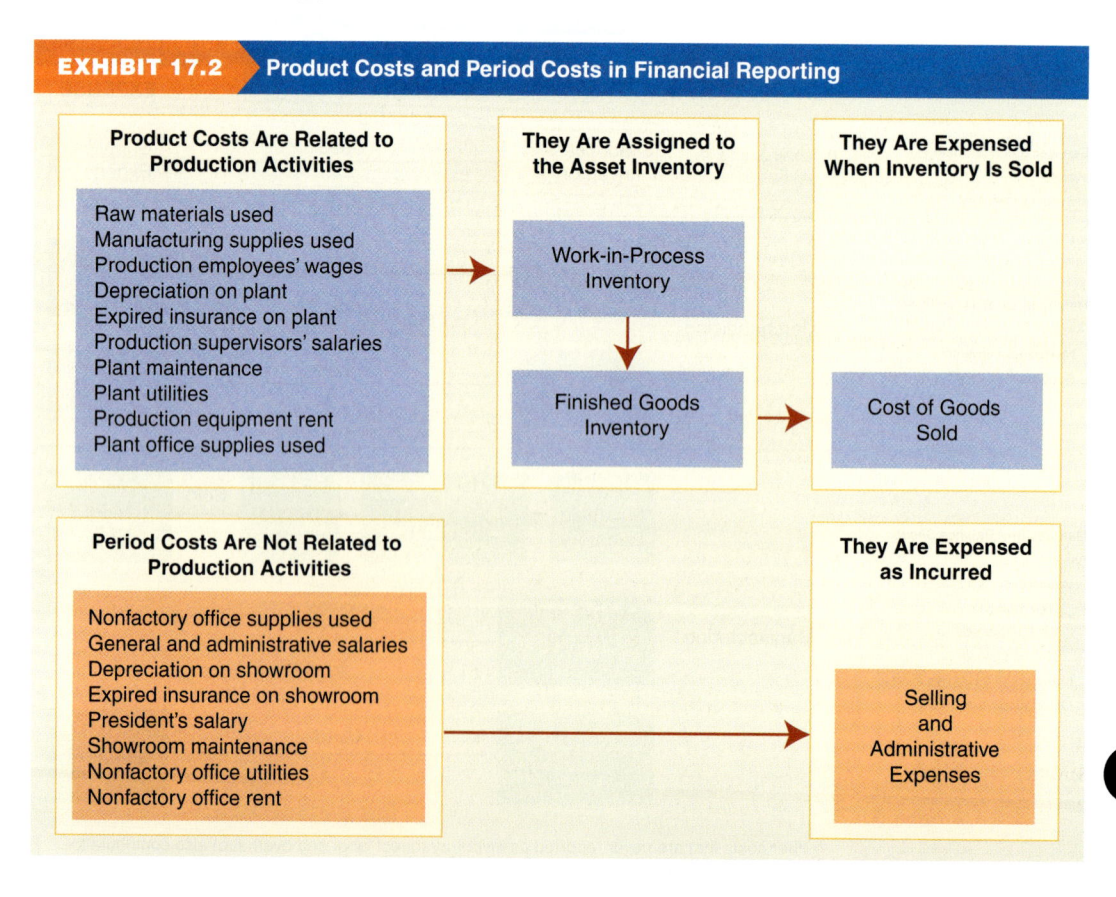

Income Statement
Revenues
Less: Cost of goods sold
Gross profit
Less: Selling and Admin. Exp.
Profit

EXHIBIT 17.2 — Product Costs and Period Costs in Financial Reporting

Product Costs Are Related to Production Activities
- Raw materials used
- Manufacturing supplies used
- Production employees' wages
- Depreciation on plant
- Expired insurance on plant
- Production supervisors' salaries
- Plant maintenance
- Plant utilities
- Production equipment rent
- Plant office supplies used

They Are Assigned to the Asset Inventory
- Work-in-Process Inventory
- Finished Goods Inventory

They Are Expensed When Inventory Is Sold
- Cost of Goods Sold

Period Costs Are Not Related to Production Activities
- Nonfactory office supplies used
- General and administrative salaries
- Depreciation on showroom
- Expired insurance on showroom
- President's salary
- Showroom maintenance
- Nonfactory office utilities
- Nonfactory office rent

They Are Expensed as Incurred
- Selling and Administrative Expenses

To summarize, in the *product cost* versus *period cost* framework of *financial reporting,* costs are classified based on whether or not they are related to the production process. If they are related to the production process, they are product costs; otherwise, they are period costs. In this framework, costs that seem very similar may be treated quite differently. For example, note in **Exhibit 17.2** that the expired cost of insurance on the *plant* is a *product cost,* but the expired cost of insurance on the *showroom* is a *period cost.* The reason is that the plant is used in production, but the showroom is not. This method of accounting for inventory that assigns all production costs to inventory is sometimes referred to as the **absorption cost** (or **full absorption cost**) method because all production costs are said to be fully absorbed into the cost of the product.

Three Components of Product Costs

The manufacture of even a simple product, such as a small wooden table, requires three basic ingredients: materials (wood), labor (the skill of a worker), and production facilities (a building to work in, a saw, and other tools). Corresponding to these three basic ingredients of any product are three basic categories of product costs: direct materials, direct labor, and manufacturing overhead.

In an earlier chapter, we defined and discussed direct materials, direct labor, and manufacturing overhead. Let's revisit these concepts and discuss how they are reflected in inventory costs.

- **Direct materials** are the costs of the primary raw materials converted into finished goods. Examples of primary raw materials include iron ore to a steel mill, coiled aluminum to a manufacturer of aluminum siding, cow's milk to a dairy, logs to a sawmill, and lumber to a builder. For Samsung, raw materials include the glass for screens. The finished product of one firm may be the raw materials of another firm down the value chain. As mentioned earlier, Samsung sources chips for its Galaxy smartphone from Broadcomm. While the chip is a finished product from Broadcomm, it is a raw material used in the phone production process for Samsung.

- **Direct labor** consists of wages earned by *production employees for the time they actually spend working on a product.* The wages of a production line manager for the Samsung Galaxy are a direct labor cost.

- **Manufacturing overhead costs** (also called overhead costs) includes all manufacturing costs other than direct materials and direct labor. Examples of manufacturing overhead are manufacturing supplies, depreciation on manufacturing buildings and equipment, and the costs of plant taxes, insurance, maintenance, security, and utilities. Also included in overhead are production supervisors' salaries and all other manufacturing-related labor costs for employees who do not work directly on the product (such as maintenance, security, and janitorial personnel). Typically, these costs are used in the production process of multiple products. Samsung would likely categorize depreciation on machines, manufacturing supplies, maintenance, and plant utilities as manufacturing overhead. (Manufacturing overhead is also called *factory overhead, burden, manufacturing burden,* and just *overhead.* Merchandising organizations occasionally refer to administrative costs as *overhead.*)

Product Costs
Direct materials
Conversion costs:
 Direct labor
 Manufacturing overhead

Conversion cost consists of the combined costs of direct labor and manufacturing overhead incurred to convert raw materials into finished goods.

Just as raw materials, labor, and production resources are combined to physically produce a finished product, direct materials costs, direct labor costs, and manufacturing overhead costs are accumulated in an accounting system to obtain the total cost of goods produced. **Exhibit 17.3** illustrates that these product costs are accumulated in the *general ledger* in Work-in-Process Inventory (or just Work-in-Process) as production takes place and then are transferred to Finished Goods Inventory when production is completed. (The general ledger within an accounting system holds all of the financial statement accounts such as the inventory accounts.) Product costs are finally assigned to Cost of Goods Sold when the finished goods are sold. (Account titles are capitalized to make it easier to determine when reference is being made to a physical item, such as work-in-process inventory, or to the account, Work-in-Process Inventory, in which costs assigned to the work-in-process inventory are accumulated.)

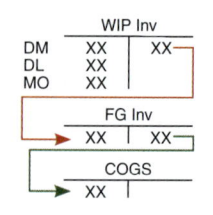

EXHIBIT 17.3 Three Product Cost Components

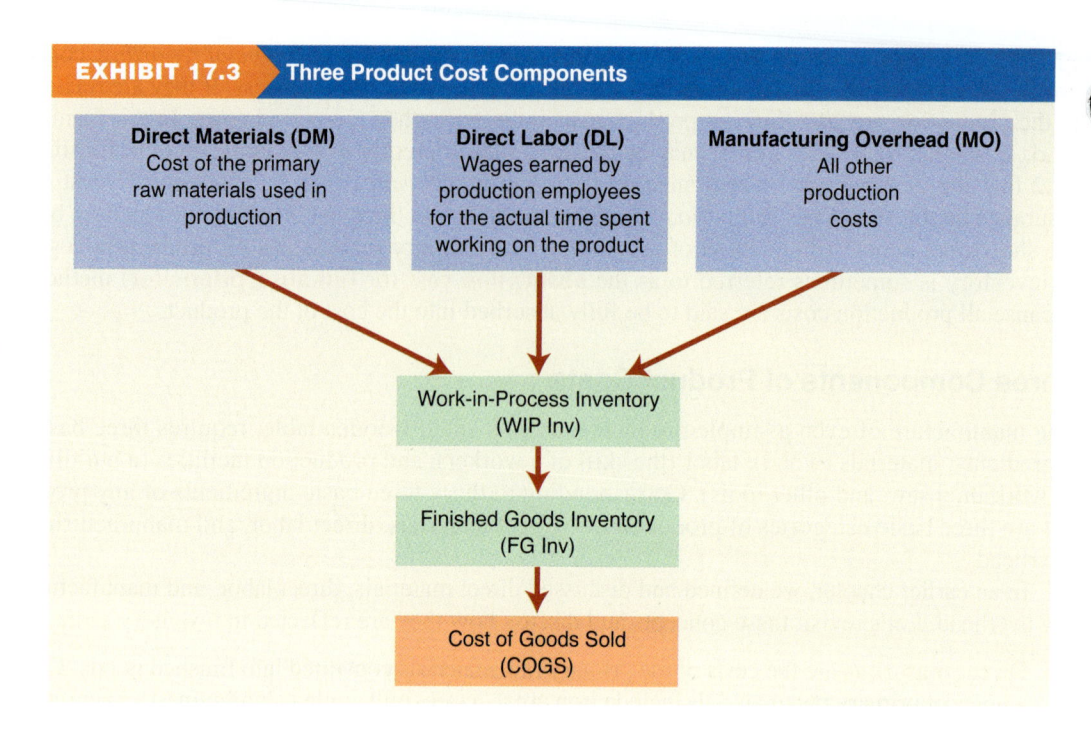

Direct Materials (DM) — Cost of the primary raw materials used in production

Direct Labor (DL) — Wages earned by production employees for the actual time spent working on the product

Manufacturing Overhead (MO) — All other production costs

↓ ↓ ↓

Work-in-Process Inventory (WIP Inv)
↓
Finished Goods Inventory (FG Inv)
↓
Cost of Goods Sold (COGS)

As production occurs, DM, DL, and MO are added to WIP Inv. When the manufacturing process is completed, the value of these items are moved from WIP Inv to FG Inv (red line). Finally, upon sale, the inventory is removed from FG Inv and recorded as COGS (green line).

WIP Inv	
DM XX	XX
DL XX	
MO XX	

FG Inv	
XX	XX

COGS	
XX	

Determining Costs of Products Outside of Financial Reporting

The previous sections describe the financial accounting rules for defining product and period costs for financial statement reporting. Consistency of cost terms makes it possible to compare information across financial statements of different companies. However, this is an example of where financial reporting and managerial reporting diverge. For management accounting purposes, we are less concerned with rules and more concerned with gathering information as the basis for decision-making. Within a company, accountants and managers often use the term product costing to embrace all costs incurred in connection with a product or service throughout the value chain. For operations within a company, determining what costs to include as product costs depends on the decision that is being made.

Critical Thinking & Decision-Making

Let's assume that as an Ikea product manager, you are interested in determining the profitability of a new line of fabric sofas which are manufactured in the U.S. For financial reporting, the product cost of $300 per sofa is easily obtained from the accounting system. Why might you be interested in assigning additional costs to the sofa for your analysis?

Remember that for internal analyses, the strict financial reporting rules of product and period cost distinctions do not apply. To conduct a complete profitability analysis, the product manager will need to gather data for all other costs that relate to the marketing, sales, and distribution of each product, as well as any costs related to providing service to customers who buy the products. For your analysis, you may choose to assign period-type costs to the sofa such as showroom costs, the cost of shipping and installation, and warranty costs which impact the overall profit of the company. Even company-wide sustainability measures could be allocated as a cost to the sofa.

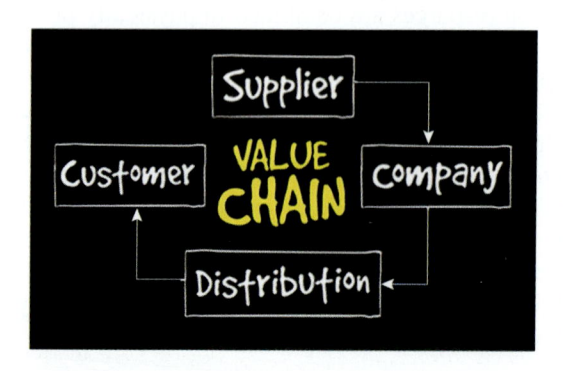

Review 17-1 — Classifying Inventory Costs LO17-1

Below is a list of asset accounts maintained in accounting records.

1. Office supplies inventory.
2. Merchandise inventory.
3. Finished goods inventory.
4. Work-in-process inventory.

Required

a. For each of the asset accounts listed above, answer the following questions.
   1. Identify which organization(s)—Shriners Hospitals for Children, Walmart, or Samsung—is most likely to maintain the account in its records. *Hint:* You may list more than one organization if it is relevant.
   2. Determine where the asset account would be presented in the organization's financial statements.
   3. As each of the above asset accounts is eventually consumed or sold, identify how it would be presented in the organization's financial statements.
b. Identify which organization—Shriners Hospitals for Children, Walmart, or Samsung—is most likely to distinguish between product and period costs. Provide two examples of products costs and two examples of period costs for the company identified.

Solution on p. 17-53.

A CLOSER LOOK AT MANUFACTURING OVERHEAD

The biggest challenge in measuring the cost of a product is determining the amount of overhead incurred to produce it; this is the "problem" of cost accounting. Direct materials cost is driven by the number of raw materials units used. This means that Samsung's chip cost is calculated as the number of chips used multiplied by its cost of each chip. Direct labor cost is driven by the number of directly traceable labor hours worked on the product. The cost is calculated as the production worker's direct labor hours times the hourly rate. But what about manufacturing overhead? Manufacturing overhead often consists of dozens of different cost elements, potentially with many different cost drivers. Electricity cost is based on kilowatt-hours and water cost on gallons used. Depreciation is usually measured in years of service and insurance in premium dollars per thousand dollars of coverage. Supervisors' salaries are typically a fixed amount per month. How do we aggregate these costs and assign them to products in a reasonable way?

LO17-2 Apply manufacturing overhead using a predetermined overhead rate.

Applying Manufacturing Overhead

Historically, accountants have believed that, even when possible, it is not cost effective to try to separately measure the cost incurred for each manufacturing overhead item to produce a unit of finished product. Instead of identifying separate cost drivers for each individual cost component in manufacturing overhead, all overhead costs for a department or plant are frequently aggregated together and assigned to products in a simple way, based on a single cost driver (e.g., direct labor hours or units of production).

If Samsung produced only one product, it would be simple to assign (or apply) overhead to the units produced because it would merely involve dividing total manufacturing overhead cost incurred by the number of units produced to get a cost per unit. For example, if total manufacturing overhead costs were $100,000 for a period when 20,000 Galaxy smartphones were produced, the overhead cost assigned to each phone would be $5 ($100,000 ÷ 20,000).

> **Suppose your company produces two types of products. Each product has a dedicated production line and labor force and there are no shared resources. Will data for decision-making be more accurate if *total manufacturing overhead costs* for the plant are allocated to the two products using a cost driver such as units of production or labor hours?**
>
> *Critical Thinking & Decision-Making*
>
> *In this situation, there are no shared resources. Each product is produced on a dedicated production line so overhead costs such as depreciation on machines are distinct to each product. This means that an allocation of **total overhead** to the two products is not necessary and will not improve the accuracy of the costing of products or the resulting decisions. Instead, the **specific overhead pool** for each product would be assigned to each of the two products in a logical way.*

Selecting a Basis (or Cost Driver) for Assigning Overhead

When allocating overhead costs to products, ideally the allocation will reflect the resources consumed in the production process. The **overhead allocation basis**, or **cost driver**, should have a logical, causal relationship with costs. When multiple products are manufactured in the same facilities, using a simple average of manufacturing overhead cost per unit seldom provides a good estimate of the overhead costs incurred to produce each product. Units requiring extensive manufacturing activity will have too little cost assigned to them, while others requiring only a small amount of manufacturing effort will absorb too much cost. In these cases, units of production is not an appropriate cost driver for manufacturing overhead because it does not reflect the way in which products consume or use manufacturing resources.

To solve this allocation problem, an overhead application base (or cost driver) other than number of units produced is typically used. The overhead application base selected is typically common to all products and has a causal relationship with the incurrence of overhead costs. Although overhead costs are a mixture of fixed and variable costs, the goal is for the driver to proxy for the way in which resources are consumed during production. For example, *machine hours* may be used to assign manufacturing overhead costs if the *number of machine hours used* is believed to be the primary cause of manufacturing overhead cost incurred. Approximating the causal relationship is key to ensuring that the cost system offers information that is useful in decision-making.

Critical Thinking & Decision-Making

Suppose that overhead costs consist primarily of machine and technology costs. Logically, this means that as a product consumes machine and technology resources, the product incurs more costs. However, the cost allocation system bases overhead allocation on direct labor hours because "that is the way it has always been done." How will this affect decision-making based on product costs?

In this situation, all of the costs, including machinery and technology, are aggregated and assigned based on the number of labor hours. However, how many labor hours one product uses is not an indication of its use of machine and technology costs. In fact, a product manufactured with very little labor that uses significant machine and technology resources would be assigned a very small amount of overhead. As a result, any decisions made based on how much a product costs (such as pricing decisions) are apt to be inaccurate. Some products will be assigned costs that are too high while others will not be assigned enough costs. This could cause some products to be priced too high and others too low. To make matters worse, managers may allocate more marketing funds to the product showing higher profitability, when in fact, that product is using more costly resources.

Using Predetermined Overhead Rates

Although some organizations assign actual manufacturing overhead to products at the end of each period (normally a month), two problems often result from measuring product cost using "actual" manufacturing overhead costs.

1. Actual manufacturing overhead cost may not be known until days or weeks after the end of the period, delaying the calculation of unit product cost.
2. Some costs that change seasonally, such as utilities charges, could make the cost of a product produced in one month appear to be greater than that of another month.

To overcome these problems, most firms use a **predetermined manufacturing overhead rate** (also called **predetermined overhead rate**) to assign manufacturing overhead costs to products. A predetermined overhead rate is established, typically as part of the budgeting process, at the start of each year by dividing the *budgeted overhead costs for the year* by the *budgeted volume of the cost driver in the overhead base* for the year. A predetermined overhead rate based on direct labor hours, for example, is computed as follows.

$$\text{Predetermined overhead rate per direct labor hour} = \frac{\text{Budgeted total overhead costs for the year}}{\text{Budgeted total direct labor hours for the year}}$$

It is important to understand the assumptions that underly this predetermined overhead rate. In allocating costs based on direct labor usage, management is assuming that costs are incurred by products in proportion to the way that direct labor is used by products. Thus, when direct labor usage increases, it is assumed that overhead usage increases as well. On the other hand, if management believes machine hours is the major driver of manufacturing overhead, the denominator should be budgeted machine hours.

Using a predetermined overhead rate based on direct labor hours, we compute the assignment of overhead to Work-in-Process Inventory as follows.

$$\text{Manufacturing overhead applied to Work-in-Process Inventory} = \text{Actual direct labor hours} \times \text{Predetermined overhead rate per direct labor hour}$$

To illustrate, assume that at the beginning of the current year, the managers of one of **Samsung**'s plants predicted an activity level of 25,000 direct labor hours with manufacturing overhead totaling $187,500. Using this information, its predetermined overhead rate per direct labor hour for the year would have been computed as follows.

$$\text{Predetermined overhead rate per direct labor hour} = \frac{\$187{,}500}{25{,}000 \text{ direct labor hours}}$$

$$= \$7.50 \text{ per direct labor hour}$$

Thus, for every direct labor hour utilized by a product, it is assigned $7.50 in overhead costs. Products that use more labor hours are assigned more overhead costs and vice versa. If 2,000 direct labor hours were used in September of this year, the applied overhead for September would be $15,000, as shown here.

Applied manufacturing overhead = 2,000 direct labor hours × $7.50 per direct labor hour
= $15,000

Typically, our budgets, or predictions, do not come to fruition exactly as planned. When a predetermined overhead rate is used, monthly variations between actual and applied manufacturing overhead are expected because of changes in costs and monthly activity. As a result, in some months overhead will be "overapplied" as applied overhead exceeds actual overhead. In other months overhead will be "underapplied" as actual overhead exceeds applied overhead. If the beginning-of-the-year estimates are accurate for annual overhead costs and annual activity, monthly over- and underapplied amounts during the year should offset each other by the end of the year. Later in this chapter, we consider accounting for any over- or underapplied manufacturing overhead balance that may exist at the end of the year.

Changing Cost Structures Affect the Basis of Overhead Application

By using a single overhead rate, we assume that variation in the way that products consume overhead costs are proportional to changes in a single cost driver. Historically, a single **plantwide overhead rate** based on direct labor hours was widely used when direct labor was the predominant cost factor in production, and a single pool of manufacturing overhead costs was driven by the utilization of direct labor.

Changes in manufacturing processes have produced major shifts in the composition of conversion costs, resulting in significantly less direct labor and significantly more manufacturing overhead. An example of this shift is the automobile industry where firms such as **Ford** and **Toyota** have spent billions of dollars on robotics and other technologies, thereby reducing direct labor in the production process. In general, the cost system should loosely mimic the production process. If the process becomes more machine-intensive, the cost system should reflect this. This means that direct labor hours are no longer an appropriate basis for assigning manufacturing costs to products in many cases. In others, these changes mean there is no longer a single cost driver that is appropriate for assigning the significantly larger manufacturing overhead pool to products.

Although some companies continue to use a single manufacturing overhead rate because it is convenient, many companies no longer use this approach. Instead, they break down the single pool of overhead costs into multiple overhead cost pools, using an appropriate cost driver for each cost pool. For example, overhead in different departments may be considered different overhead cost pools and relevant cost drivers are determined for each department's overhead cost pool. Multiple overhead cost pool systems range in the types of cost drivers used and the sophistication of the system overall. While the shift toward automation continues, some still struggle with the decision to add a new cost pool and cost driver. For the addition of a cost pool to make a difference in the computed product costs, the system must have:

1. **Heterogeneity in cost**: the resources used in the manufacturing process cost different amounts AND
2. **Heterogeneity in use**: different products use the resources differently.

When both criteria are met, adding a new cost pool and cost driver will change the amounts allocated to products.

Review 17-2 LO17-2

Applying a Predetermined Overhead Rate

Assume that the following predictions were made at the beginning of the year for one of the plants of Intel. Intel is a semi-conductor and chip manufacturer.

Total manufacturing overhead for the year	$40,000,000
Total machine hours for the year	3,200,000

Actual results for February were as follows.

Total manufacturing overhead for the month	$4,410,000
Total machine hours for the month	410,000

Required

a. Determine the predetermined overhead rate per machine hour for the current year.
b. Using the predetermined overhead rate per machine hour, determine the manufacturing overhead applied to Work-in-Process during February.
c. As of February 1, actual overhead was underapplied by $400,000. Determine the cumulative amount of any overapplied or underapplied overhead at the end of February. Why did this occur?

Solution on p. 17-53.

JOB ORDER COSTING FOR PRODUCTS AND SERVICES

LO17-3
Explain the operation of a job order costing system.

Production personnel need to know the specific products to produce on specific machines on a daily or even hourly basis. The detailed scheduling of products on machines is performed by production scheduling personnel. Exactly how production is scheduled depends on whether process manufacturing or job production is used and whether production is in response to a specific customer sales order or for the company's inventory in anticipation of future sales.

In **process manufacturing**, production of identical units is on a *continuous* basis. For example, a production facility is devoted exclusively to one product or to a set of closely related products. Companies where you would likely find a process manufacturing environment include Exxon Mobil and Procter & Gamble. In these settings, products are continuously being manufactured. At any point in time, there are units at each stage in the production process. Process manufacturing is discussed later in this chapter.

In **job production**, also called **job order production** and **job order costing**, products are manufactured in single units or in batches of identical units. Examples of single-unit jobs are found at **Schumacher Homes**, a builder of custom-designed homes, **Bechtel Corporation**, the largest commercial construction company in the U.S., and **Cray Inc.** (a subsidiary of **Hewlett Packard Enterprise**), which manufactures supercomputers. Examples of batches of identical units (multi-unit jobs) are found at **True Religion Brand Jeans**, a clothing manufacturer, and **Herman Miller**, a large producer of office chairs including the ergonomic Aeron model. Of course, the specific products included in different jobs or batches may vary considerably.

Some companies use a combination of process manufacturing and job order production. For example, Samsung might use process manufacturing for screens that are used for many products and devices. However, it might use job order production for specific models of smartphones which are customized for cellular carriers.

In this section, we document the flow of costs through *job order costing* for Galaxy smartphones. We start with the initiation of a sales order for smartphones from a customer to the sale of smartphones to the customer. As we discuss the flow of costs, envision each of the "documents" discussed as digital data in a company's computerized system.

Production Planning and Control Process

Suppose that Samsung receives an order from **Verizon** for customized Galaxy smartphones. The sales department typically receives the order and inputs it into the system. The order initiates the process of production planning and control illustrated in **Exhibit 17.4**. Employees from engineering, scheduling, and accounting contribute to this process.

Engineering Based on an engineering analysis and cost information, the engineering department develops the manufacturing specifications for the Galaxy. First, they create the **bill of materials**, a list that includes both the type of raw materials and the quantity of each material required to produce one smartphone. The engineering team will also detail the **operations list** (sometimes called the **activities list**), which specifies the manufacturing operations and related times required for one unit or batch of smartphones.

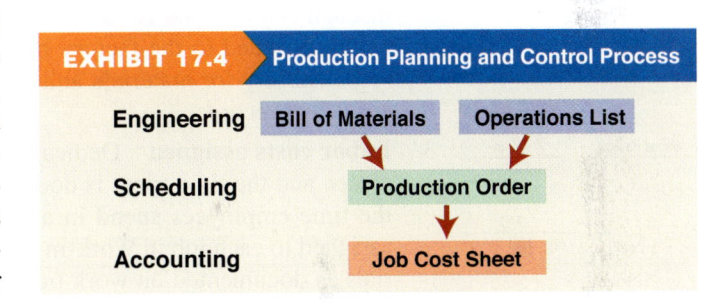

EXHIBIT 17.4 Production Planning and Control Process

Engineering	Bill of Materials	Operations List
Scheduling	Production Order	
Accounting	Job Cost Sheet	

Scheduling Scheduling personnel prepare a production order for each job, based on the information provided from the engineering department. The **production order** contains a job's unique identification number, the number of smartphones to be produced, the raw material requirements, manufacturing operations, as well as the proposed timing of the various operations. The production order serves as authorization for production supervisors to obtain materials from the storeroom and to issue work orders to production employees.

Accounting Once production begins, the accounting department must document and accumulate the costs for Verizon's Galaxy smartphone order. A **job cost sheet** is a document used to accumulate these costs and to monitor the progress of the order. As production occurs, the materials, labor, and machine resources utilized are recorded on the job cost sheet along with the related costs. When Verizon's order is completed, the final cost of the job is determined by totaling the costs on the job cost sheet as illustrated next.

Basic Flow of Costs in Job Order Costing

Exhibit 17.5 shows how inventory costs in a manufacturing organization flow through the financial accounting system. Pay particular attention to the major inventory accounts (Raw Materials, Work-in-Process, and Finished Goods Inventory), the flow of costs between these accounts, and Manufacturing Overhead. Each of the numbered items represents a cost flow affecting an Inventory account, Manufacturing Overhead, or Cost of Goods Sold and is explained below. As an *alternative* *presentation* for illustrating manufacturing costs flows in a job cost system, "T" accounts are shown in the margins for the remainder of this section.

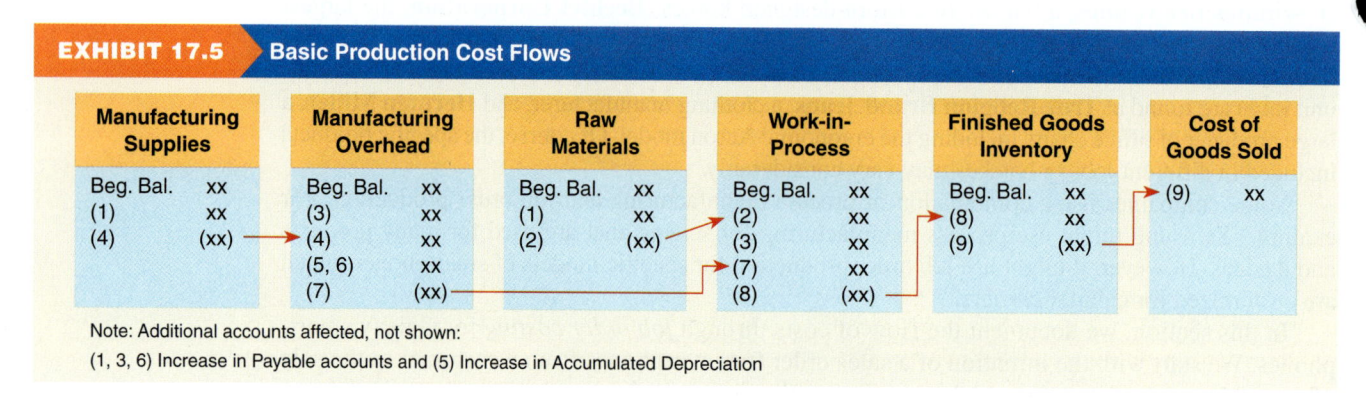

EXHIBIT 17.5 — Basic Production Cost Flows

Manufacturing Supplies	Manufacturing Overhead	Raw Materials	Work-in-Process	Finished Goods Inventory	Cost of Goods Sold
Beg. Bal. xx	Beg. Bal. xx	Beg. Bal. xx	Beg. Bal. xx	Beg. Bal. xx	(9) xx
(1) xx	(3) xx	(1) xx	(2) xx	(8) xx	
(4) (xx)	(4) xx	(2) (xx)	(3) xx	(9) (xx)	
	(5, 6) xx		(7) xx		
	(7) (xx)		(8) (xx)		

Note: Additional accounts affected, not shown:
(1, 3, 6) Increase in Payable accounts and (5) Increase in Accumulated Depreciation

Explanation of Job Order Cost Flows Illustrated in Exhibit 17.5

1. **Raw materials and supplies purchased** When Samsung purchases the glass to use in the smartphone screens and other manufacturing supplies, the costs are recorded in Raw Materials and Manufacturing Supplies, respectively. An increase in Accounts Payable representing the amounts owed to suppliers typically offsets these increases.

2. **Raw materials requisitioned** When the glass is requisitioned to the factory, direct materials costs are transferred from Raw Materials to Work-in-Process. The transfer is initiated through a **materials requisition form** which indicates the type and quantity of each raw material issued to the factory by job number. This form is used to record the transfer of responsibility for materials and also to record materials changes on raw materials and job cost sheet records.

3. **Labor costs assigned** Dedicated employees now work on the glass to transform it into a screen and the time spent is documented on a work ticket. A **work ticket** is used to record the time employees spend in a specific manufacturing operation. *Direct labor* costs are assigned to each job in Work-in-Process based on the time devoted to processing raw materials as documented on work tickets. For example, if a line worker charged 8 hours to Job #101 and earns $20 per hour, $160 would be charged to the Work-in-Process account for Job #101. Indirect labor costs, such as the production manager who oversees both the glass production for this order as well as production of other products, are initially assigned to Manufacturing Overhead. **Indirect labor costs** are labor costs that cannot be traced directly to the finished product (in the case of Samsung, the smartphone).

4–6. **Other indirect costs assigned** Other indirect production-related costs are also assigned to Manufacturing Overhead. For illustration purposes, we use the following indirect cost items: (4) manufacturing supplies, (5) depreciation on factory assets, and (6) miscellaneous items. These items are indirect because they cannot be traced directly to products because the resources are used for multiple jobs. As manufacturing supplies are assigned to manufacturing overhead, the separate Manufacturing Supplies Inventory account is reduced. *Depreciation* is the systematic process of allocating the cost of fixed assets to the periods benefiting from their use. When depreciation of factory assets is assigned to manufacturing overhead, Accumulated Depreciation (a contra account to fixed assets) is increased. Lastly, when miscellaneous items are assigned to manufacturing overhead, Other Payables is increased. Other Payables indicates the amount due for a variety of costs such as repairs and maintenance, utilities, and property taxes. In summary, as indirect costs are incurred by the company, the costs are first assigned to the Manufacturing Overhead account, and not to specific jobs.

7. **Manufacturing overhead applied** Costs assigned to Manufacturing Overhead are periodically reassigned (applied) to Work-in-Process, preferably with the use of a predetermined overhead rate, with drivers such as direct labor hours or machine hours. Samsung might use the $7.50 per direct labor hour calculated in the prior section to apply overhead to the products. Remember, the overhead cost driver is selected to proxy for the way in which

resources are consumed during the production process. Through this process, the incurred indirect costs that were originally assigned to Manufacturing Overhead are now reassigned or applied to specific jobs in the Work-in-Process account.

8. **Costs transferred to finished goods** When products are completed, Samsung's accountant will accumulate product costs on a job cost sheet and transfer the costs from Work-in-Process to Finished Goods Inventory. The costs are still maintained in an inventory account (Finished Goods Inventory) until the products are sold. At this point, the products could be in a warehouse or storage facility.

9. **Costs transferred to cost of goods sold** When the completed products are sold, their costs are transferred from Finished Goods Inventory to Cost of Goods Sold. This means that costs are transferred from an asset account (Finished Goods Inventory) to an expense account (Cost of Goods Sold). The physical goods are no longer in the control of the manufacturer but are in the control of the customer.

Many companies offer consumers the ability to customize their orders while still minimizing product costs. Technological advances have made this possible. As customization and smaller batches become more common, how is the selection of cost systems by companies affected?

Critical Thinking & Decision-Making

The use of job order costing increases with an increase in customization because products are no longer mass produced. Instead, individual orders are considered to be separate jobs as seen in a company like Frilly. **Frilly** *is a contemporary clothing brand meant to "empower you to create a look that is completely yours."[1] Customers select a design and customize it by selecting cuts, fabrics, and details. This made-to-order model helps Frilly minimize waste and pollution associated with producing large, excess inventories. This made-to-order model is used by many companies, including* **Seven Cycles***, a bicycle brand. These companies must estimate costs as accurately as possible to ensure that the company is profitable given the added costs of customization.*

Illustration of Job Order Cost Flows for Samsung

Next we illustrate the nine steps of cost flow outlined previously in a hypothetical example with **Samsung**. We outline the cost flow in August for Samsung's five jobs: **Verizon**, **AT&T**, **T-Mobile**, **Mint Mobile**, and **Cricket**. We use the illustration for the flow of inventory costs outlined in **Exhibit 17.5** to show the flow of costs in our Samsung example. Again, each of the numbered items represents a cost flow affecting an Inventory account, Manufacturing Overhead, or Cost of Goods Sold and are explained next.

Manufacturing Supplies	Manufacturing Overhead	Raw Materials	Work-in-Process	Finished Goods Inventory	Cost of Goods Sold
Beg. Bal. 1,600	Beg. Bal. 0	Beg. Bal. 71,000	Beg. Bal. 109,900	Beg. Bal. 75,000	(9) 214,300
(1) 1,000	(3) 7,200	(1) 30,000	(2) 54,300	(8) 176,800	
(4) (950)	(4) 950	(2) (54,300)	(3) 34,450	(9) (214,300)	
	(5) 2,400		(7) 13,780		
	(6) 3,230		(8) (176,800)		
	(7) (13,780)				

Beginning Inventory Balances

Assume total inventory on August 1 included Raw Materials, $71,000; Work-in-Process, $109,900; and Finished Goods, $75,000. In addition there were manufacturing supplies of $1,600, consisting of various items such as machine lubricant. The August 1 balance in Manufacturing Overhead was $0.

---

[1] Source: Frilly.com accessed on December 16, 2022.

Raw Materials, August 1

Description	Quantity	Unit Cost	Total Cost
Plastic	3,000 cases	$20	$60,000
Glass	100 cases	50	5,000
Metal	20 cases	150	3,000
Adhesive	150 ounces	20	3,000
Total			$71,000

Manufacturing Supplies, August 1

Item	Total Cost
Various	$1,600

Work-in-Process, August 1

Job	Total Cost
AT&T	$58,600
T-Mobile	51,300
Total	$109,900

Finished Goods Inventory, August 1

Job	Total Cost
Verizon	$75,000

Control account and subsidiary ledger Each cost assignment is supported by documented information that is recorded in subsidiary cost system records. For example, the raw materials inventory file contains separate records for each type of raw materials, indicating increases, decreases, and the available balance in both units and costs. Every time there is a change in the Raw Materials Inventory general ledger account, there must be an equal change in one or more individual inventory records. Because of this relationship between the raw materials inventory file and Raw Materials Inventory in the general ledger, Raw Materials Inventory is called a *control account* and the raw materials file of detailed records is called a *subsidiary ledger*. Other general ledger accounts related to the product cost system that have subsidiary files are Work-in-Process, Finished Goods Inventory, and Cost of Goods Sold.

Explanation of Job Order Cost Flows

1. **Raw materials and supplies purchased** Raw materials and manufacturing supplies are purchased on account. The vendor's invoice totals $31,000, including $1,000 of manufacturing supplies and $30,000 of raw materials. The $1,000 of manufacturing supplies increases the Manufacturing Supplies account. The cost of *raw materials* of $30,000 must be assigned to specific raw materials inventory records as shown in the following schedule.

Plastic	850 cases	× $20 =	$17,000
Glass	140 cases	× $50 =	7,000
Metal	40 cases	× $150 =	6,000
Total			$30,000

2. **Raw materials requisitioned** Materials needed to complete Jobs AT&T and T-Mobile are requisitioned. Two new jobs, Mint Mobile and Cricket, were also started and direct materials were requisitioned for them. A total of $54,300 of raw materials was requisitioned as indicated by the following *materials requisition form* which results in a cost transfer from Raw Materials to Work-in-Process.

August	Job AT&T	Job T-Mobile	Job Mint	Job Cricket	Total
Plastic					
975 cases × $20			$19,500		$19,500
955 cases × $20				$19,100	19,100
Glass					
52 cases × $50	$2,600				2,600
30 cases × $50		$1,500			1,500
43 cases × $50			2,150		2,150
20 cases × $50				1,000	1,000
Metal					
12 cases × $150	1,800				1,800
12 cases × $150		1,800			1,800
11 cases × $150			1,650		1,650
14 cases × $150				2,100	2,100
Adhesive					
20 ounces × $20	400				400
15 ounces × $20		300			300
10 ounces × $20			200		200
10 ounces × $20				200	200
Total	$4,800	$3,600	$23,500	$22,400	$54,300

3. **Labor costs assigned** Assume the August payroll was $41,650, including $34,450 for direct labor and $7,200 for indirect labor. The $7,200 of indirect labor increases the Manufacturing Overhead account. Direct labor was assigned to the jobs as shown on the following summary *work ticket* resulting in an increase to the Work-in-Process account.

	Job AT&T	Job T-Mobile	Job Mint	Job Cricket	Total
Direct labor hours	600	900	1,000	945	
Direct labor rate	× $10	× $10	× $10	× $10	
Total	$6,000	$9,000	$10,000	$9,450	$34,450

Note: The $7,200 of indirect labor costs is assigned to products as part of applied overhead.

```
         MO
BB    -0-
(3)  7,200

  Wages Payable
        | 41,650  (3)

       WIP Inv
BB   109,900
(2)   54,300
(3)   34,450
```

4–6. **Other Indirect costs assigned** In addition to indirect labor of $7,200 described above, suppose Samsung incurred the following manufacturing overhead costs.

Manufacturing Supplies (4)	$ 950
Accumulated Depreciation—Factory Assets (5)	2,400
Miscellaneous (Other Payables) (6)	3,230

The total amount of $6,580 ($950 + $2,400 + $3,230) increases Manufacturing Overhead. As indirect costs are incurred by the company, the costs are assigned to the Manufacturing Overhead account, and not to specific jobs. This increase in Manufacturing Overhead affects other accounts: the separate Manufacturing Supplies Inventory account is reduced by $950, Accumulated Depreciation is increased by $2,400 and Other Payables is increased by $3,230.

```
    Mfg Supplies
BB  1,600 | 950  (4)
(1) 1,000 |

   Accum. Depr
        | 2,400  (5)

  Other Payables
        | 3,230  (6)

         MO
BB    -0-
(3)  7,200
(4)    950
(5)  2,400
(6)  3,230
```

7. **Manufacturing overhead applied** Assume manufacturing overhead is applied to jobs using a predetermined rate of $4 per direct labor hour. Assignments to individual jobs are as follows.

	Job AT&T	Job T-Mobile	Job Mint	Job Cricket	Total
Direct labor hours	600	900	1,000	945	
Predetermined overhead rate per labor hour	× $4	× $4	× $4	× $4	
Total	$2,400	$3,600	$4,000	$3,780	$13,780

```
         MO
BB    -0- | 13,780  (7)
(3)  7,200
(4)    950
(5)  2,400
(6)  3,230

       WIP Inv
BB   109,900
(2)   54,300
(3)   34,450
(7)   13,780
```

In this step, cost amounts in Manufacturing Overhead are transferred to Work-in-Process.

```
        WIP Inv
BB  109,900 | 176,800  (8)
(2)  54,300
(3)  34,450
(7)  13,780
     35,630

        FG Inv
BB   75,000
(8) 176,800
```

8. **Costs transferred to finished goods** The jobs for AT&T, T-Mobile, and Mint Mobile are completed with the following costs.

	Job AT&T	Job T-Mobile	Job Mint	Total
Beginning balance, WIP	$58,600	$51,300	$ 0	$109,900
Current costs				
Direct materials (entry 2)	4,800	3,600	23,500	31,900
Direct labor (entry 3)	6,000	9,000	10,000	25,000
Applied overhead (entry 7)	2,400	3,600	4,000	10,000
Total	$71,800	$67,500	$37,500	$176,800

In this step, costs are transferred from Work-in-Process to Finished Goods. Additional analysis for the completed jobs indicates the following.

	Job AT&T	Job T-Mobile	Job Mint
Total cost of job	$71,800	$67,500	$37,500
Units in job	÷ 1,200	÷ 900	÷ 500
Unit cost	$ 59.83	$ 75.00	$ 75.00

```
        FG Inv
BB   75,000 | 214,300  (9)
(8) 176,800
     37,500

        COGS
(9) 214,300
```

9. **Costs transferred to cost of goods sold** The orders for Verizon, AT&T, and T-Mobile are delivered for a sales price of $400,000. Determining the costs transferred from Finished Goods Inventory to Cost of Goods Sold requires summing the total cost of jobs sold.

Job Verizon	$ 75,000
Job A&T	71,800
Job T-Mobile	67,500
Total	$214,300

At this point we can determine the gross profit on the completed jobs.

Sales	$400,000
Cost of goods sold	(214,300)
Gross profit	$185,700

If inventory were produced in anticipation of future sales rather than in response to specific customer orders, it is likely that not all units in a job would be sold at the same time. In this case, the unit cost information is used to determine the amount transferred from Finished Goods Inventory to Cost of Goods Sold.

Exhibit 17.6 shows the cost system records supporting the ending balances in the major inventory accounts and Cost of Goods Sold. Note the importance of the job cost sheets for determining cost transfers affecting Work-in-Process and Finished Goods Inventory. The job cost sheets are also used in determining the ending balances of these accounts.

Samsung's product costing system is adequate for determining the cost for each job for purposes of valuing ending inventories and cost of goods sold in its *external financial statements*. The costing system recognizes the differences in materials costs by carefully tracking each type of material as a separate cost pool. Assuming all direct labor employees are paid the same rate, it is necessary to maintain only one labor cost pool. If we assume that the operations needed to manufacture the smartphone are similar, regardless of style and carrier preferences, we can assume that overhead is proportional to the amount of direct labor used for each job. As a result, even with only one plantwide overhead cost pool applied on the basis of direct labor hours, individual product costs are considered reasonably accurate.

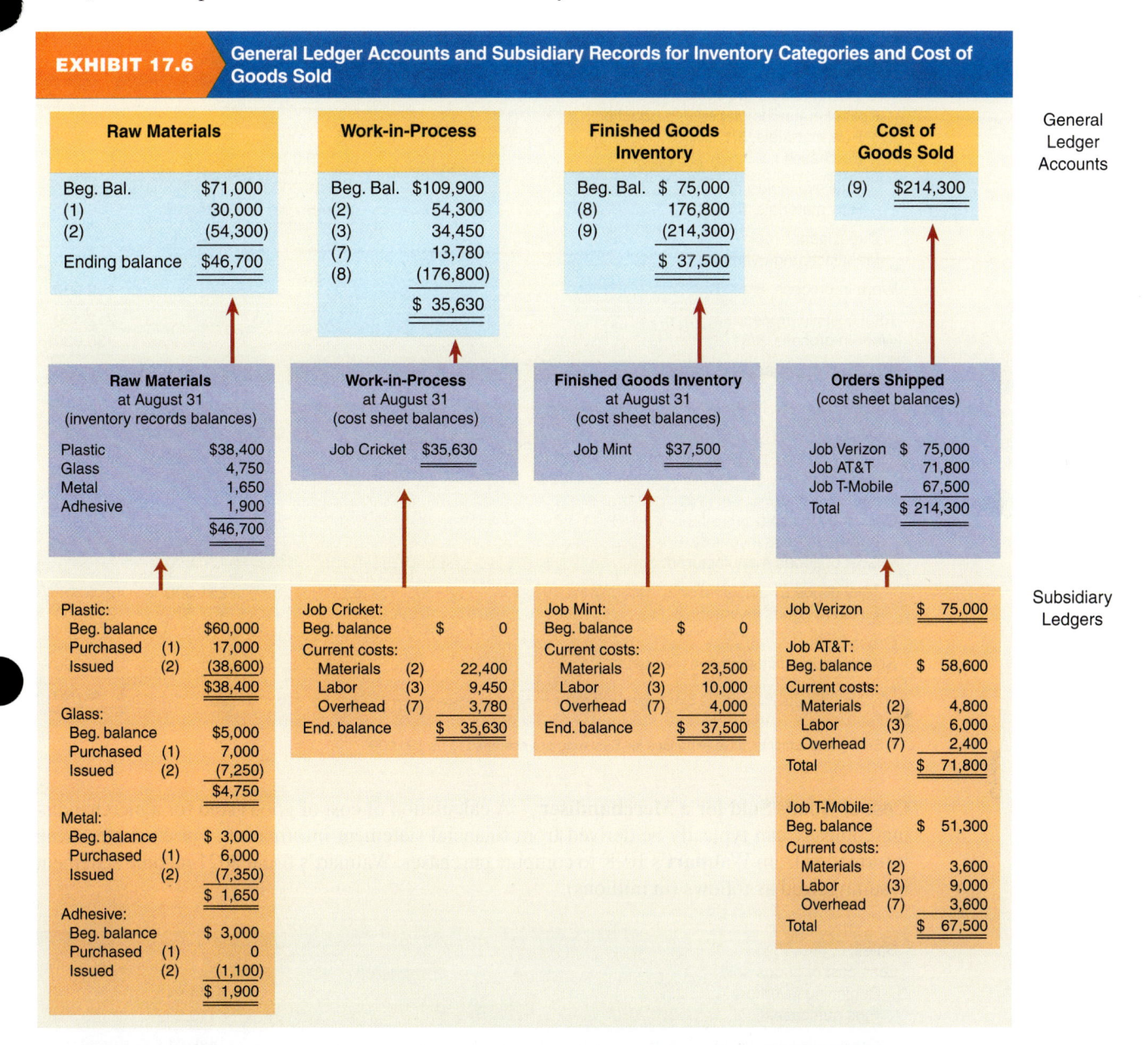

EXHIBIT 17.6 General Ledger Accounts and Subsidiary Records for Inventory Categories and Cost of Goods Sold

General Ledger Accounts

Raw Materials
Beg. Bal.	$71,000
(1)	30,000
(2)	(54,300)
Ending balance	$46,700

Work-in-Process
Beg. Bal.	$109,900
(2)	54,300
(3)	34,450
(7)	13,780
(8)	(176,800)
	$35,630

Finished Goods Inventory
Beg. Bal.	$75,000
(8)	176,800
(9)	(214,300)
	$37,500

Cost of Goods Sold
(9)	$214,300

Subsidiary Ledgers

Raw Materials at August 31 (inventory records balances)
Plastic	$38,400
Glass	4,750
Metal	1,650
Adhesive	1,900
	$46,700

Work-in-Process at August 31 (cost sheet balances)
Job Cricket	$35,630

Finished Goods Inventory at August 31 (cost sheet balances)
Job Mint	$37,500

Orders Shipped (cost sheet balances)
Job Verizon	$75,000
Job AT&T	71,800
Job T-Mobile	67,500
Total	$214,300

Plastic:
Beg. balance		$60,000
Purchased	(1)	17,000
Issued	(2)	(38,600)
		$38,400

Glass:
Beg. balance		$5,000
Purchased	(1)	7,000
Issued	(2)	(7,250)
		$4,750

Metal:
Beg. balance		$3,000
Purchased	(1)	6,000
Issued	(2)	(7,350)
		$1,650

Adhesive:
Beg. balance		$3,000
Purchased	(1)	0
Issued	(2)	(1,100)
		$1,900

Job Cricket:
Beg. balance		$0
Current costs:		
Materials	(2)	22,400
Labor	(3)	9,450
Overhead	(7)	3,780
End. balance		$35,630

Job Mint:
Beg. balance		$0
Current costs:		
Materials	(2)	23,500
Labor	(3)	10,000
Overhead	(7)	4,000
End. balance		$37,500

Job Verizon $75,000

Job AT&T:
Beg. balance		$58,600
Current costs:		
Materials	(2)	4,800
Labor	(3)	6,000
Overhead	(7)	2,400
Total		$71,800

Job T-Mobile:
Beg. balance		$51,300
Current costs:		
Materials	(2)	3,600
Labor	(3)	9,000
Overhead	(7)	3,600
Total		$67,500

While Samsung's assumed costing system may be adequate for financial statement purposes, the data it routinely generates will not provide information for many management decisions. To evaluate product profitability, management needs additional information concerning marketing, distributing, selling, and service costs, which are not included in the product cost system. Furthermore, to answer questions regarding how to best perform operations, a special cost study to obtain relevant information should be performed.

Statement of Cost of Goods Manufactured and Cost of Goods Sold

For *internal reporting purposes*, most manufacturing companies prepare a separate **statement of cost of goods manufactured**, which summarizes the cost of goods completed and transferred into Finished Goods Inventory during the period. Since a manufacturer acquires finished goods from the factory, its cost of goods manufactured is the total cost transferred from Work-in-Process to Finished Goods Inventory during the period. To continue with our example, a statement of cost of goods manufactured and an income statement for Samsung are presented in **Exhibit 17.7** for August.

EXHIBIT 17.7 — Statement of Cost of Goods Manufactured and Income Statement

SAMSUNG
Statement of Cost of Goods Manufactured
August

Current manufacturing costs			
Cost of materials placed in production			
Raw materials, 8/1	$ 71,000		
Purchases	30,000		
Total available	101,000		
Raw materials, 8/31	(46,700)	$ 54,300	
Direct labor		34,450	
Manufacturing overhead		13,780	$102,530
Work-in-process, 8/1			109,900
Total costs in process			212,430
Work-in-process, 8/31			(35,630)
Cost of goods manufactured			**$176,800**

SAMSUNG
Income Statement
August

Sales			$400,000
Cost of goods sold			
Finished goods inventory, 8/1		$ 75,000	
Cost of goods manufactured		**176,800**	
Total goods available for sale		251,800	
Finished goods inventory, 8/31		(37,500)	214,300
Gross profit			185,700
Selling and administrative expenses*			(90,000)
Net income			$ 95,700

* Selling and administrative expenses for Samsung are assumed to be $90,000.

Cost of Goods Sold for a Merchandiser A calculation of cost of goods sold for a merchandising company can typically be derived from financial statement information. For example, using information from Walmart's 10-K to compute purchases, Walmart's fiscal 2021 income statement is summarized as follows (in millions).

Sales		$572,754
Less cost of goods sold		
Beginning inventory	$ 44,949	
Plus purchases	**440,562**	
Goods available for sale	485,511	
Less ending inventory	(56,511)	
Cost of goods sold		(429,000)
Gross profit		143,754
Less selling and administrative expenses		(117,812)
Operating income		$ 25,942

Merchandising organizations modify only one line of this income statement format, changing cost of goods manufactured to purchases.

Overapplied and Underapplied Overhead

In the Samsung example, assume that the predetermined manufacturing overhead rate of $4 per direct labor hour was based on predicted manufacturing overhead for the year of $100,000 and predicted direct labor hours of 25,000.

$$\text{Predetermined overhead rate per direct labor hour} = \frac{\$100{,}000}{25{,}000 \text{ direct labor hours}}$$
$$= \$4.00 \text{ per direct labor hour}$$

Actual overhead = Applied overhead Assume further that it was determined that the company actually incurred $100,000 in manufacturing overhead during the year and that actual direct labor hours for the year were 25,000. Applied manufacturing overhead is computed as follows.

$$\text{Applied manufacturing overhead} = 25{,}000 \text{ direct labor hours} \times \$4.00$$
$$= \$100{,}000$$

The activity in Manufacturing Overhead is summarized as follows.

Manufacturing Overhead	
Beginning balance	$ 0
Actual overhead	100,000
Total	100,000
Applied overhead	(100,000)
Ending balance	$ 0

With identical amounts of actual and applied overhead, the ending balance in Manufacturing Overhead is zero. However, if either the actual overhead cost or the actual level of the production activity base differed from its predicted value, there would be a balance in Manufacturing Overhead representing overapplied or underapplied overhead. Remember, the predetermined overhead rates are based on budgeted or expected numbers. So, in reality, it is likely that these numbers will not be accurate and the company will apply a different amount of overhead than it incurs.

Actual overhead > Applied overhead Assume, for example, that the prediction of 25,000 direct labor hours was correct but that actual overhead cost was $105,000. In this case, Manufacturing Overhead shows a $5,000 positive balance, representing underapplied manufacturing overhead.

Manufacturing Overhead	
Beginning balance	$ 0
Actual overhead	105,000
Total	105,000
Applied overhead	(100,000)
Ending balance	$ 5,000*

* Underapplied; applied costs are less than actual costs.

Actual overhead < Applied overhead If the prediction of 25,000 direct labor hours was correct, but actual manufacturing overhead was only $98,000, Manufacturing Overhead would be overapplied and show a $2,000 negative balance.

Manufacturing Overhead	
Beginning balance	$ 0
Actual overhead	98,000
Total	98,000
Applied overhead	(100,000)
Ending balance	$ (2,000)*

* Overapplied; applied costs are greater than actual costs.

Disposition of Balance in Manufacturing Overhead

If the *prediction* of total manufacturing overhead cost is not accurate, there will be an underapplied or overapplied balance in Manufacturing Overhead at the end of the year. A similar result occurs when the *budgeted* activity level used in computing the predetermined rate differs from the actual activity level. It is not uncommon for such differences to occur. Predictions are exactly that—predictions.

At Interim Month-to-month balances in Manufacturing Overhead are usually allowed to accumulate during the year. In the absence of evidence to the contrary, it is assumed that such differences result from seasonal variations in production or costs or both. However, any year-end balance in Manufacturing Overhead must be eliminated.

At Year-end Theoretically, the disposition of any year-end balance in Manufacturing Overhead should be accomplished in a manner that adjusts every account to what its balance would have been if an actual, rather than a predetermined, overhead rate had been used. This involves adjusting the ending balances in Work-in-Process, Finished Goods Inventory, and Cost of Goods Sold.

However, in most situations, the simple procedure of treating the remaining overhead as an adjustment to Cost of Goods Sold is adequate. Unless there are large ending balances in inventories and a large year-end balance in Manufacturing Overhead, this simple procedure produces acceptable results. Underapplied (Overapplied) overhead requires an adjustment to increase (decrease) Cost of Goods Sold as illustrated in **Exhibit 17.8**.

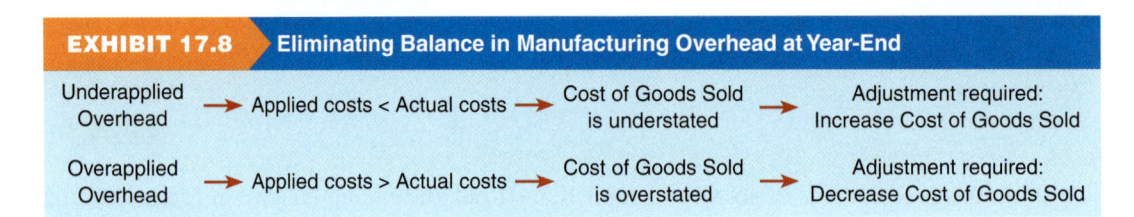

EXHIBIT 17.8 Eliminating Balance in Manufacturing Overhead at Year-End

Underapplied Overhead → Applied costs < Actual costs → Cost of Goods Sold is understated → Adjustment required: Increase Cost of Goods Sold

Overapplied Overhead → Applied costs > Actual costs → Cost of Goods Sold is overstated → Adjustment required: Decrease Cost of Goods Sold

Job Costing in Service Organizations

Service costing, the assignment of costs to services performed, uses job costing concepts to determine the cost of filling customer service orders in organizations such as automobile repair shops, charter airlines, CPA firms, hospitals, and law firms. Many of these organizations bill clients on the basis of resources consumed. Consequently, they maintain detailed records for billing purposes. On the invoice sent to the client, the organization itemizes any materials consumed on the job at a selling price per unit, the labor hours worked on the job at a billing rate per hour, and the time special facilities were used at a billing rate per unit of time. Employees with different capabilities and experience often have different billing rates. In a CPA firm, for example, a partner or a senior manager has a higher billing rate than a staff accountant.

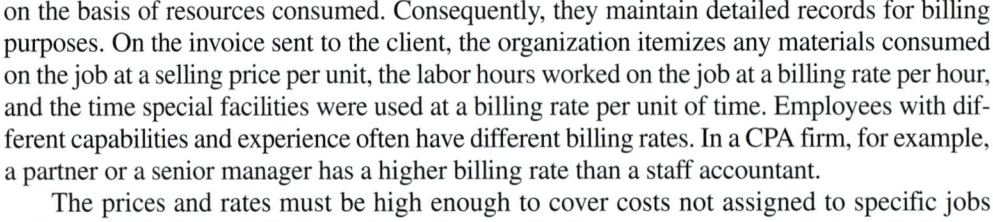

The prices and rates must be high enough to cover costs not assigned to specific jobs and to provide for a profit. To evaluate the contribution to common costs and profit from a job, a comparison must be made between the price charged the customer and the actual cost of the job. This is easily done when the actual cost of resources itemized on the customer's invoice is presented on a job cost sheet. A CPA firm, for example, should accumulate the actual hardware and software costs incurred in an accounting system installation for a client, along with the actual wages earned by employees while working on the job and any related travel costs. Comparing the total of these costs with the price charged, the client indicates the total contribution of the job to common costs and profit.

INVOICE
Sam's Auto Shop
Invoice No. 101
Date: July 1

Parts:	$##
Labor:	
#hours × $50/hour	##
Facilities charge:	##
Total	$##

Reporting Under Job Costing in Service Organizations

Although service organizations may identify costs with individual jobs for management accounting purposes, there is considerable variation in the way job cost information is presented in financial statements. Some organizations report the cost of jobs completed in their income statements using an account such as Cost of Services Provided. They use procedures similar to those outlined in **Exhibit 17.7**. The only major change involves replacing Cost of Goods Sold with Cost of Services Provided.

More often, however, service organizations do not formally establish detailed procedures to trace the flow of service costs. Instead, service job costs are left in their original cost categories such as materials expense, salaries and wages expense, travel expense, and so forth. Because all service costs are typically regarded as expenses rather than product costs, either procedure is acceptable for financial reporting. Regardless of the formal treatment of service costs in financial accounting records and statements, the managers of a well-run service organization need information regarding job cost and contribution. Accurate cost estimation by service firms is especially important when providing unique and customized services to each client. It is imperative to understand the costs of these customized offerings so that the pricing can be formulated accordingly.

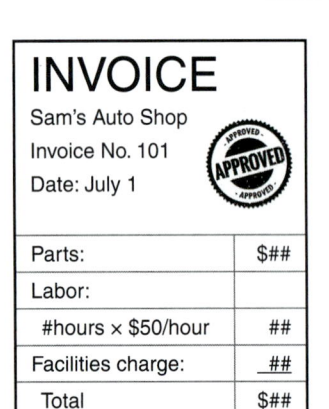

All preceding examples of service costing involve situations in which the order is filled in response to a specific customer request. Job order costing can also be used to determine the cost of making services available even when the names of specific customers are not known in advance and the service is being provided on a speculative basis. A regularly scheduled airline flight, for example, could be regarded as a job. Management is interested in knowing the cost of the job in order to determine its profitability. This is but another example of the versatility of job order costing.

Accounting for Costs of Jobs in a Job Order Costing System — LO17-3 Review 17-3

Assume that **Intel Inc.** has a division that does custom prototypes for large clients. Intel is currently working with **Dell Technologies** on four different prototypes; each prototype has a different job number. Production costs are accounted for using a job cost system. Suppose that at the beginning of June raw materials inventories totaled $7,000; manufacturing supplies amounted to $800; two jobs were in process—Job 225 with assigned costs of $13,750, and Job 226 with assigned costs of $1,800—and there were no finished goods inventories. There was no underapplied or overapplied manufacturing overhead on June 1. The following information summarized June manufacturing activities.

- Purchased raw materials costing $40,000 on account.
- Purchased manufacturing supplies costing $9,000 on account.
- Requisitioned materials needed to complete Job 226. Started two new jobs, 227 and 228, and requisitioned direct materials for them as follows.

Job 226	$ 2,600
Job 227	18,000
Job 228	14,400
Total	$35,000

- Incurred June salaries and wages as follows.

Job 225 (500 hours × $10 per hour)	$ 5,000
Job 226 (1,500 hours × $10 per hour)	15,000
Job 227 (2,050 hours × $10 per hour)	20,500
Job 228 (800 hours × $10 per hour)	8,000
Total direct labor	48,500
Indirect labor	5,000
Total	$53,500

- Used manufacturing supplies costing $5,500.
- Recognized depreciation on factory fixed assets of $5,000.
- Incurred miscellaneous manufacturing overhead cost of $10,750 on account.
- Applied manufacturing overhead at the rate of $5 per direct labor hour.
- Completed Jobs 225, 226, and 227.
- Delivered Jobs 225 and 226 to customers.

Required

a. Prepare (1) tables or (2) "T" accounts showing the flow of costs through the Work-in-Process, Finished Goods, and Cost of Goods Sold accounts.
b. Show the job cost details to support the June 30 balances in Work-in-Process, Finished Goods, and Cost of Goods Sold.
c. Prepare a statement of cost of goods manufactured for June.

Solution on p. 17-54.

PROCESS COSTING

LO17-4 Explain the operation of a process costing system.

A job costing system works well when products are made one at a time (building houses) or in batches of identical items (making blue jeans). However, if products are produced in a continuous manufacturing environment, where production does not have a distinct beginning and ending (producing sheet glass, for example), companies usually use a process costing system.

In job costing, the unit cost is the total cost of the "job" divided by the units produced in the job. Costs are accumulated for each job on a job cost sheet, and those costs remain in Work-in-Process until the job is completed, regardless of how long the job is in progress. A multiple-unit job is not considered completed until all units in the job are finished. The cost is not determined until the job is completed, which will not necessarily coincide with the end of an accounting period. Large jobs (such as construction projects) and jobs started near the end of the period frequently overlap two or more accounting periods.

In process costing, the cost of a single unit is equal to the total product costs assigned to a "process" or "department" during the accounting period (frequently a month) divided by the number of units produced. Since goods in the beginning and ending work-in-process inventory are only partially processed during the period, it is necessary to determine the total production for the period in terms of the *equivalent number* of completed units. The average cost per unit is computed as total product costs divided by the number of equivalent units produced.

A good example of a process costing environment involving continuous production is the soft drink bottling process. At **Coca-Cola**'s bottling facility in Wakefield, England, more than 4,000 twelve-ounce cans and 3,200 varying sized bottles of Coca-Cola can be produced each minute in a continuous process. The process adds the ingredients (concentrate syrup, water, sweetener, and the carbonation agent) at various points in the process.

In a job cost system, job cost sheets are used to collect cost information for each and every job. In a process costing system, cost accumulation requires fewer records because each department's production is treated as the only job worked on during the period. In a department that has just one manufacturing process, process costing is particularly straightforward because the Work-in-Process account is, in effect, the departmental cost record. If a department has more than one manufacturing process, separate records should be maintained for each process.

Cost of Production Report Using the Weighted-Average Method

To illustrate process costing procedures, consider **Samsung**'s smartphone packaging department. Unlike the manufacturing department that tracked costs through job order costing, costs in the highly automated packaging department are hypothetically tracked through process costing. Assume each finished unit requires one unit of raw materials added at the beginning of the manufacturing process. Assumed production and cost data for the month of July for Samsung are as follows.

July Production Data	
Units in process, beginning of period (75% converted)	4,000
Units started	36,000
Completed and transferred to finished goods	35,000
Units in process, end of period (20% converted)	5,000

July Cost Data		
Beginning work-in-process		
Materials costs		$ 16,000
Conversion costs		9,000
Total		$ 25,000
Current manufacturing costs		
Direct materials (36,000 × $4)		$144,000
Conversion costs		
Direct labor	$62,200	
Manufacturing overhead applied	46,700	108,900
Total		$252,900

Developing a cost of production report is a useful way of organizing and accounting for costs in a process costing environment. A **cost of production report**, which summarizes unit and cost data for each department or process for each period, consists of the following sections.

- Summary of units in process
- Equivalent units

- Total cost to be accounted for and cost per equivalent unit
- Accounting for total costs

The cost of production report for Samsung's packaging operations is shown in **Exhibit 17.9**, and its four sections are discussed next.

EXHIBIT 17.9 Cost of Production Report for Process Costing

SAMSUNG PACKAGING
Cost of Production Report
For the Month Ending July 31

Summary of units in process

Beginning	4,000
Units started	36,000
In process	40,000
Completed	(35,000)
Ending	5,000

Equivalent units in process

	Materials	Conversion
Units completed	35,000	35,000
Plus equivalent units in ending inventory	5,000	1,000*
Equivalent units in process	40,000	36,000

Total cost to be accounted for and cost per equivalent unit in process

	Materials	Conversion	Total
Beginning work-in-process	$ 16,000	$ 9,000	$ 25,000
Current cost	144,000	108,900**	252,900
Total cost in process	$160,000	$117,900	$277,900
Equivalent units in process	÷ 40,000	÷ 36,000	
Cost per equivalent unit in process	$ 4.00	$ 3.275	$ 7.275

Accounting for total costs
Transferred out (35,000 × $7.275)			$254,625
Ending work-in-process			
Materials (5,000 × $4.00)	$20,000		
Conversion (1,000 × $3.275)		3,275	23,275
Total cost accounted for			$277,900

* 5,000 units, 20% converted
** Includes direct labor of $62,200 and applied manufacturing overhead of $46,700

Summary of Units in Process

This section of the cost of production report provides a summary of all units in the department during the period—both from an input and an output perspective—regardless of their stage of completion. From an input perspective, total units in process during the period consisted of the following.

Summary of units in process

Beginning	4,000
Units started	36,000
In process	40,000
Completed	(35,000)
Ending	5,000

- Units in process at the beginning of the period, **plus**
- Units started during the period.

From an output perspective, these units in process during the period were either

- Completed and transferred out of the department, **or**
- Still on hand at the end of the period.

In the summary of units in process, all units are treated the same, regardless of the amount of processing that took place on them during the period. The objective here is to account for all discrete units of product in process at any time during the period. In the summary of units in process, 40,000 individual units were in process, including 4,000 partially completed units in the beginning inventory and 36,000 new units started during the month. During the period, 35,000 units were completed, and the remaining 5,000 were still in process at the end of the month.

Equivalent Units in Process

This section of the report translates the number of units in process during the period into equivalent completed units of production. The term **equivalent completed units** refers to the number of completed units that is equal, in terms of production effort, to a given number of partially completed units. For example, 2 units for which 50% of the expected total processing cost has been incurred is the equivalent of 1 completed unit (2 × 0.50).

Frequently, direct materials costs are incurred largely, if not entirely, at the beginning of the process, whereas direct labor and manufacturing overhead costs are added throughout the production process. If direct labor and manufacturing overhead costs are added to the process simultaneously, it is common to treat them jointly as conversion costs. Assume Samsung adds all materials at the beginning of the process; all conversion costs are added evenly throughout the process. Therefore, separate computations are made for equivalent units of materials and equivalent units of conversion. Although the department worked on 40,000 units during the period, the total number of equivalent units in process with respect to conversion costs was only 36,000 units, consisting of 35,000 finished units plus 1,000 equivalent units in ending inventory (5,000 units 20% converted). Because all materials are added at the start of the process, 40,000 equivalent units (35,000 finished and 5,000 in process) were in process during the period with respect to materials costs. The equivalent units calculation of ending inventory is detailed as follows.

Equivalent units in process	Materials	Conversion
Units completed	35,000	35,000
Plus equivalent units in ending inventory	5,000	1,000
Equivalent units in process	40,000	36,000

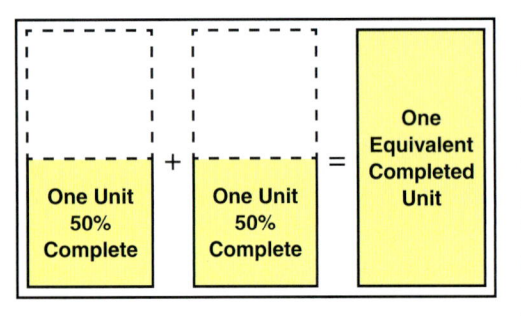

Equivalent Units in Ending Inventory

Materials: 5,000 physical units × 100% materials added = 5,000 equivalent units

Conversion: 5,000 physical units × 20% converted = 1,000 equivalent units

Total Cost to Be Accounted for and Cost per Equivalent Unit in Process

This section of the report summarizes total costs in Work-in-Process during the period and calculates the cost per equivalent unit for materials, conversion, and in total. Total cost consists of the beginning Work-in-Process balance (if any) plus current costs incurred. For our Samsung example, the total cost to be accounted for during July was $277,900, consisting of $25,000 in Work-in-Process at the beginning of the period plus current costs of $252,900 incurred in July. These amounts are broken down between materials costs and conversion costs.

Total cost to be accounted for and cost per equivalent unit in process	Materials	Conversion	Total
Beginning work-in-process	$ 16,000	$ 9,000	$ 25,000
Current cost	144,000	108,900	252,900
Total cost in process	$160,000	$117,900	$277,900
Equivalent units in process	÷ 40,000	÷ 36,000	
Cost per equivalent unit in process	$ 4.00	$ 3.275	$ 7.275

To compute cost per equivalent unit, total cost in process is divided by the equivalent units in process. This is done separately for materials cost and conversion cost. The total cost per equivalent unit is the sum of the unit costs for materials and conversion. Because the number of equivalent units in process was different for materials and conversion, it is not possible to get the total cost per unit by dividing total costs of $277,900 by some equivalent unit amount.

Notice that we make no attempt to account separately for the completed units that came from beginning inventory and those that were started during the current period. This method is called the **weighted average method**, and it simply spreads the combined beginning inventory cost and current manufacturing costs (for materials, labor, and overhead) over the units completed and those in ending inventory on an average basis. For example, the total cost in process for conversion ($117,900) included both beginning inventory cost and current costs; the 36,000 equivalent units in process for conversion included both units from beginning inventory and units started during the current period. Therefore, the average cost per unit of $3.275 is a weighted average cost of the partially completed units in beginning inventory (prior period costs) and units started during the current period. It is not a precise cost per unit for the current period's production activity but an average cost that includes the cost of partially completed units in beginning inventory carried over from the previous period.

Accounting for Total Costs

This section shows the disposition of the total costs in process during the period divided between units completed (and sent to finished goods) and units still in process at the end of the period. As noted in the previous section, total cost in process is $277,900 and each equivalent unit in process has $4.00 of materials cost and $3.275 of conversion costs for a total of $7.275.

		Total
Accounting for total costs		
Transferred out (35,000 × $7.275) . . .		$254,625
Ending work-in-process		
Materials (5,000 × $4.00)	$20,000	
Conversion (1,000 × $3.275)	3,275	23,275
Total cost accounted for		$277,900

Transferred out costs The first step in assigning total costs is to calculate the cost of units transferred out by multiplying the units completed during the period by the total cost per unit. Costs transferred out become finished goods inventory if the product or service is complete or move into the production report of another process (in a multi-process system).

Transferred out costs = 35,000 units × $7.275 total cost per unit
= $254,625

Ending inventory costs This leaves $23,275 ($277,900 − $254,625) to be assigned to *ending Work-in-Process*. To verify that $23,275 is the correct amount of cost remaining in ending Work-in-Process, the materials and conversion costs in ending Work-in-Process are calculated separately. Recall that the 5,000 units in process at the end of the period are 100% completed with materials costs, but only 20% completed with conversion costs. Therefore, in ending Work-in-Process, the materials cost component is computed as follows.

Ending inventory costs
Materials: 5,000 units × $4.000 = $20,000
Conversion: 1,000 units × $3.275 =   3,275
                                   $23,275

Summarizing the Cost of Production Report

The cost of production report summarizes manufacturing costs assigned to Work-in-Process during the period and provides information for determining the transfer of costs from Work-in-Process to Finished Goods Inventory. The supporting documents are similar to those previously illustrated for job costing, except that the single cost of production report replaces all the job cost sheets that flow through a department or process. The flow of costs through Work-in-Process is as follows.

Work-in-Process		
Beginning balance		$ 25,000
Current manufacturing costs		
Direct materials.	$144,000	
Direct labor	62,200	
Applied overhead	46,700	252,900
Total		277,900
Cost of goods manufactured.		(254,625)
Ending balance.		$ 23,275

The reduction in Work-in-Process for the units completed during the period is determined in the cost of production report (see **Exhibit 17.9**). This amount is transferred to Finished Goods Inventory. The $23,275 ending balance in Work-in-Process is also determined in the cost of production report as the amount assigned to units in ending Work-in-Process.

First-In, First-Out Process Costing

Because the costs of materials, labor, and overhead are constantly changing, unit costs are seldom exactly the same from period to period. Therefore, if a unit is manufactured partially in one period and partially in the following period, its actual cost is seldom equal to the unit cost of units produced in either period. An alternative, more precise process costing method is the **first-in, first-out (FIFO) method**. It accounts for unit costs of beginning inventory units separately from those started during the current period. Under this method, the first costs incurred each period are assumed to have been used to complete the unfinished units carried over from the previous period. This means that the cost of the beginning inventory is partially based on the prior period's unit costs and partially based on the current period's unit costs.

Critical Thinking & Decision-Making

In what situations would it make the most sense to use the FIFO method, given the extra costs of tracking information?

In periods with highly variable prices, the difference between the weighted average and FIFO methods will be greater. This means that during inflationary periods, it might be helpful to watch the trends more closely using FIFO. Using the weighted average method during these times will mute the effects because costs are averaged over time. Having less accurate costing from period to period using the weighted average method could impact purchasing decision (such as the purchase of raw materials) and product pricing decisions.

If unit costs are changing from period to period and beginning inventories are large in relation to total production for the period, the FIFO method is more accurate. However, with the current trend toward smaller inventories, the additional effort and cost of the FIFO method may not be justified. Unless stated otherwise, weighted average process costing is used in chapter assignments.

Process Costing in Service Organizations

There are many applications of process costing for service organizations. Process costing in service organizations is similar to that in manufacturing organizations, the primary purpose being to assign costs to cost objects. Generally, the use of process costing techniques for service organizations is easier than for manufacturing organizations because the raw materials element is not necessary. The applications for the labor and overhead costs are similar, if not identical, to those of a manufacturing firm.

Process costing for services is similar to job costing for batches in that an average cost for similar or identical services is determined. There are important differences, though, between batch and process costing. In a batch environment, a discrete group of services is identified, but in a process environment, services are performed on a continuous basis. Batch costing accumulates the cost for a specific group of services as the batch moves through the various activities that make up the service. Process service costing measures the average cost of identical or similar services performed each period (each month) in a department. An example of batch service costing is determining the cost of registering a student at your college during the fall term registration period; an example of process service costing is determining the cost each month of processing a check by a bank. If continuously performed services involved multiple processes, the total cost of the service would be the sum of the costs for each process.

Considerations in Using Process Costing in Service Organizations

After it is determined that process costing would be appropriate for a service activity, the actual decision to use it is generally contingent on two important factors about the items being evaluated. First, is average cost per unit acceptable as an input item to the decision process? For some activities, the answer is obvious. For instance, tracking the actual cost of processing each check through a bank would probably not be as useful as determining the average cost of processing checks for a given period; therefore, average cost is acceptable. For other activities, the answer is more difficult to determine. Should the decision model include average cost per patient-day or actual cost per individual patient? The answer to this depends, of course, on whether the types and costs of patient treatments are similar or vary substantially.

Accounting for Costs in a Process Costing System

LO17-4 Review 17-4

Since there is little product differentiation between a large number of Intel's products, assume it uses a process costing system to determine inventory costs and that production and manufacturing cost data for one year are shown below. Assume that materials are added at the start of production and conversion costs are incurred evenly throughout the period.

Production Data (units)	
Units in process, beginning of period (60% converted)	3,000,000
Units started	27,000,000
Completed and transferred to finished goods	25,000,000
Units in process, end of period (30% converted)	5,000,000

Manufacturing Costs	
Work-in-Process, beginning of period (materials, $468,000; conversion, $252,000)	$ 720,000
Current manufacturing costs	
Raw materials transferred to processing	6,132,000
Direct labor for the period	1,550,000
Overhead applied for the period	3,498,000

Required
Prepare a cost of production report for Intel for the year.

Solution on p. 17-55.

APPENDIX 17A: Absorption and Variable Costing

Product costing for inventory valuation is the link between financial and managerial accounting. Product costing systems determine the cost-based valuation of the manufactured inventories used in making key financial accounting measurements (cost of goods sold and income on the income statement as well as inventory and total assets on the balance sheet). They also provide vital information to managers for setting prices, controlling costs, and evaluating management performance. The influence of financial accounting on product costing systems is apparent in the design of traditional job order and process costing systems. These systems reflect the requirement of financial accounting (i.e., generally accepted accounting principles) that all manufacturing costs be included in inventory valuations for external financial reporting purposes. In these systems, all other costs incurred, such as selling, general, and administrative costs, are treated as expenses of the period. Remember that although we are now focusing on the link between financial and managerial accounting, these two systems do not have to match exactly. The two systems serve different purposes. For external financial reporting, it is important to have consistency across time and companies. For managerial accounting, the information should help managers make decisions. Consequently, the information should be relevant and decision-useful.

LO17-5 Evaluate the differences between absorption and variable costing income.

Basic Concepts

A debate exists over how to treat fixed manufacturing overhead costs in the valuation of inventory. The debate centers around whether fixed costs such as depreciation on manufacturing equipment should be considered an *inventoriable product cost* and treated as an asset cost until the inventory is sold, or as a *period cost* and recorded immediately as an operating expense. **Absorption costing** (also called **full costing**) treats fixed manufacturing overhead as a product cost, whereas **variable costing** (also called **direct costing**) treats it as a period cost. Therefore, fixed manufacturing overhead is recorded initially as an asset (inventory) under absorption costing but as an operating expense under variable costing.

Fixed manufacturing costs:
  Absorption costing treats **fixed manufacturing costs** as **product costs**.
  Variable costing treats **fixed manufacturing costs** as **period costs**.

Since fixed product costs are eventually recorded as expenses under both variable and absorption costing by the time the inventory is sold, why does it matter whether fixed overhead is treated as a product cost or a period cost? It matters because the way it is treated *affects the measurement of income* for a particular period and the valuation assigned to inventory on the balance sheet at the end of the period. Because absorption costing presents fixed manufacturing overhead as a cost per unit rather than a total cost per period, management's perceptions of cost behavior, and decisions based on perceptions of cost behavior, may also be affected.

Inventory Valuations

To illustrate the difference in inventory valuations between absorption and variable costing, assume the following cost data for a single component of a **Samsung** watch at a monthly volume of 4,000 units.

Direct materials.	$ 5 per unit
Direct labor.	2 per unit
Variable manufacturing overhead.	3 per unit
Total variable cost.	$ 10 per unit
Fixed manufacturing overhead.	$8,000 per month

To determine the unit cost of inventory using absorption costing, an average fixed overhead cost per unit is calculated by dividing the monthly fixed manufacturing overhead by the monthly volume. Even though fixed manufacturing overhead is not a variable cost, under absorption costing it is applied to inventory on a per-unit basis, the same as variable costs. At a monthly volume of 4,000 units, Samsung's total component inventory cost per unit is $10 under variable costing and $12 under absorption costing.

	Variable Costing	Absorption Costing
Variable cost per unit	$10	$10
Fixed cost per unit	—	$8,000 ÷ 4,000 = 2
Total cost per unit	$10	$12

The $2 difference in total unit cost is attributed to the treatment of fixed overhead of $8,000 divided by 4,000 units. The difference in the total component inventory valuation on the balance sheet between absorption and variable costing is the number of units in ending inventory times $2. So if 1,000 units are on hand at the end of the month, they are valued at $12,000 if absorption costing is used but at only $10,000 with variable costing.

Income Under Absorption and Variable Costing

The internal income statement formats used for variable and absorption costing are not typically the same. One benefit of variable costing is that it separates costs into variable and fixed costs, making it possible to present the income statement in a contribution format. As illustrated in Chapter 15, in a contribution income statement, variable costs are subtracted from revenues to compute contribution margin. Fixed costs are then subtracted from contribution margin to calculate profit, also called net income or earnings.

When absorption costing is used, the income statement is usually formatted using the functional format, which classifies costs based on cost function, such as manufacturing, selling, or administrative. The functional income statement, used for financial reporting, subtracts manufacturing costs (represented by cost of goods sold) from revenues to calculate gross profit. Selling and administrative costs are then subtracted from gross profit to calculate profit or income.

The contribution format provides information for determining the contribution margin ratio, which is calculated as total contribution margin divided by total sales. It also provides the total amount of fixed costs.

These are the primary items of data needed to determine the break-even point and to conduct other cost-volume-profit analysis (see Chapter 15).

Not only is the income statement format different for absorption and variable costing methods, but also as illustrated in the following hypothetical examples for Samsung, the amount of income reported on the income statement might not be the same because of the difference in the treatment of fixed manufacturing overhead. The following additional information is assumed for the Samsung component examples.

Selling price	$30	per unit
Variable selling and administrative expenses	$3	per unit
Fixed selling and administrative expenses	$10,000	per month

Production Equals Sales: June

Assume Samsung has no component inventory on June 1. Production and sales for the third quarter of the fiscal year ending November 30 are as follows.

Month	Production	Sales
June	3,200 units	3,200 units
July	4,000 units	3,500 units
August	4,000 units	4,500 units
Third quarter	11,200 units	11,200 units

Production and sales both total 3,200 for the month of June. Also, considering the entire third quarter, production and sales in units are equal. A summary of unit production, sales, and inventory levels is presented in **Exhibit 17A.1**. Using previously presented costs and a selling price of $30 per unit, monthly contribution (variable costing) and functional (absorption costing) income statements are presented in **Exhibit 17A.1** parts B and C. An analysis of fixed manufacturing overhead with absorption costing is presented in part D.

EXHIBIT 17A.1 Contribution (Variable Costing) and Functional (Absorption Costing) Income Statements with Variations in Production and Sales

	June (Production equals sales)	July (Production exceeds sales)	August (Sales exceed production)
A. Samsung's Component: Summary of Unit Inventory Changes			
Beginning inventory	0	0	500
Production	3,200	4,000	4,000
Total available	3,200	4,000	4,500
Sales	(3,200)	(3,500)	(4,500)
Ending inventory	0	500	0
B. Contribution (Variable Costing) Income Statements			
Sales ($30/unit)	$96,000	$105,000	$135,000
Less variable expenses			
Cost of goods sold ($10/unit)	32,000	35,000	45,000
Selling & admin. ($3/unit)	9,600	10,500	13,500
Total	(41,600)	(45,500)	(58,500)
Contribution margin	54,400	59,500	76,500
Less fixed expenses			
Manufacturing overhead	8,000	8,000	8,000
Selling & admin.	10,000	10,000	10,000
Total	(18,000)	(18,000)	(18,000)
Net income	$36,400	$ 41,500	$ 58,500

continued

EXHIBIT 17A.1 — Contribution (Variable Costing) and Functional (Absorption Costing) Income Statements with Variations in Production and Sales

continued from previous page

	June (Production equals sales)	July (Production exceeds sales)	August (Sales exceed production)
C. Functional (Absorption Costing) Income Statements			
Sales ($30/unit)	$96,000	$105,000	$135,000
Cost of goods sold (Part D.)	(40,000)	(42,000)	(54,000)
Gross profit	56,000	63,000	81,000
Selling & admin. expenses			
Variable ($3/unit)	9,600	10,500	13,500
Fixed	10,000	10,000	10,000
Total	(19,600)	(20,500)	(23,500)
Net income	$36,400	$42,500	$57,500
D. Analysis of Fixed Manufacturing Overhead under Absorption Costing			
Fixed manufacturing overhead	$8,000	$8,000	$8,000
Units produced	÷ 3,200	÷ 4,000	÷ 4,000
Absorption fixed cost per unit*	$2.50	$2.00	$2.00
Units in ending inventory	× 0	× 500	× 0
Fixed costs in ending inventory	$0	$1,000	$0
Fixed cost of goods sold			
From beginning inventory	$0	$0	$1,000
June (3,200 units × $2.50)	8,000		
July (3,500 units × $2.00)		7,000	
August (4,000 units × $2.00)			8,000
Total fixed	8,000	7,000	9,000
Variable cost of goods sold	32,000	35,000	45,000
Absorption cost of goods sold	$40,000	$42,000	$54,000

* To simplify the illustration, the example does not use a predetermined overhead rate. If a predetermined overhead rate were used, an increase or decrease in the balance of Manufacturing Overhead is treated as an adjustment to ending inventory.

In June, with 3,200 units produced and sold, all $8,000 of fixed manufacturing overhead is deducted as a period cost under variable costing and expensed as part of the cost of goods sold under absorption costing. Since no inventory remained, no costs were deferred.

Production Exceeds Sales: July

July production of 4,000 units exceeded sales of 3,500 units by 500 units. The ending inventory under variable costing consisted of only the variable cost of production, $5,000 (500 × $10). The entire $8,000 of fixed manufacturing overhead is deducted as a period cost.

Under absorption costing, in addition to the variable cost of production, a portion of the fixed manufacturing overhead is assigned to the ending inventory. As shown in the July column of **Exhibit 17A.1**, part D, absorption costing assigns $1,000 of the month's fixed manufacturing overhead to the July ending inventory and $7,000 to the cost of goods sold. Consequently, under absorption costing the July ending inventory is $1,000 higher, the July expenses are $1,000 lower, and the July net income is $1,000 higher than under variable costing.

Sales Exceed Production: August

In August just the opposite of July's situation occurred: sales of 4,500 units exceeded production of 4,000 units by 500 units. The additional units came from the July production. There was no inventory remaining on August 31. Under variable costing all current manufacturing costs (August costs) are expensed either as the variable cost of goods sold or as part of the fixed expense. Additionally, the August variable cost of goods sold includes variable costs assigned the July ending inventory.

Under absorption costing all current month manufacturing costs are expensed as part of the cost of goods sold. Additionally, the cost of goods sold includes the variable and fixed costs assigned the July ending inventory. The inclusion of the July fixed costs caused absorption costing net income to be $1,000 lower than the corresponding variable costing amount.

The above relationships between absorption and variable costing are summarized in **Exhibit 17A.2**.

EXHIBIT 17A.2 — Cost of Production Report for Process Costing

Relationship between period production and sales	Effect on inventory costs	Effect on operating income	Explanation
Production = Sales	No change in inventory costs.	Absorption costing income = Variable costing income.	All current fixed manufacturing costs are expensed under both absorption and variable costing.
Production > Sales	Absorption costing ending inventory > variable costing ending inventory.	Absorption costing income > Variable costing income.	Under absorption costing some current fixed manufacturing costs are assigned to ending inventory. Under variable costing all current fixed manufacturing costs are expensed.
Sales > Production	Absorption costing ending inventory < variable costing ending inventory.	Absorption costing income < Variable costing income.	Under absorption costing fixed manufacturing costs previously assigned to ending inventory are expensed along with current fixed manufacturing costs. Under variable costing only current fixed manufacturing costs are expensed.

Exhibits **17A.1** and **17A.2** reveal several important relationships between absorption costing net income and variable costing net income, as well as the way net income responds to changes in sales and production under both methods.

For each period, the income differences between absorption and variable costing can be explained by analyzing the change in inventoried fixed manufacturing overhead under absorption costing net income. If fixed manufacturing cost per unit remains constant, the following relationship exists.

$$\text{Variable costing net income} + \text{Increase (or minus decrease) in inventoried fixed manufacturing overhead} = \text{Absorption costing net income}$$

Using Samsung's July and August information, the equations are as follows.

July $41,500 + (500 × $2.00) = $42,500 Absorption costing income

August $58,500 − (500 × $2.00) = $57,500 Absorption costing income

For any given time period, regardless of length, if total units produced equals total units sold, net income is the same for absorption costing and variable costing, all other things being equal. Under absorption costing, all fixed manufacturing overhead is released as a product cost through cost of goods sold when inventory is sold. Under variable costing, all fixed manufacturing overhead is reported as a period cost and expensed in the period incurred. As a result, over the life of a product, the income differences within periods are offset since they occur only because of the timing of the release of fixed manufacturing overhead to the income statement.

Evaluating Alternatives to Inventory Valuation

The issue in the variable costing debate is whether or not fixed manufacturing costs add value to products. This is particularly important when we are trying to answer the question "What goes into producing the product and how much does it cost?" Proponents of variable costing argue that these costs do not add value to a product. They believe that fixed costs are incurred to provide the capacity to produce during a given period, and these costs expire with the passage of time regardless of whether the related capacity was used. Variable manufacturing costs, on the other hand, are incurred only if production takes place. Consequently, these costs are properly assignable to the units produced.

Proponents of variable costing also argue that inventories have value only to the extent that they avoid the necessity of incurring costs in the future. Having inventory available for sale avoids the necessity of incurring some future variable costs, but the availability of finished goods inventory does not avoid the incurrence of future fixed manufacturing costs. Proponents conclude that inventories should be valued at their variable manufacturing cost, and fixed manufacturing costs should be expensed as incurred.

Opponents of variable costing argue that fixed manufacturing costs are incurred for only one purpose, namely, to manufacture the product. Because they are incurred to manufacture the product, they should be assigned to the product. It is also argued that in the long run all costs are variable. Consequently, by omitting fixed costs, variable costing understates long-run variable costs and misleads decision makers into underestimating true production costs.

On a pragmatic level, the central arguments for variable costing center around the fact that use of variable costing facilitates the development of contribution income statements and cost-volume-profit analysis. With costs accumulated on an absorption costing basis, contribution income statements are difficult to develop, and cost-volume-profit analysis becomes very complicated unless production and sales are equal.

Finally, fluctuations in inventory levels will impact the results differently under variable and absorption costing. Inventory levels are currently lower than they were at pre-pandemic levels, prior to 2020. However, as of October 2022, the Total Business Inventories to Sales Ratio is 1.33, up from 1.25 from the prior year as shown in **Exhibit 17A.3**. Inventories can build for a number of reasons including an economic slowdown or in the extreme case of a pandemic (resulting in a reduction of sales); or, a positive economic outlook (resulting in aggressive inventory production). As can be seen in the most recent trends, increasing inventory levels create greater financial differences between absorption and variable costing methods. Using absorption costing, the building inventories will result in more fixed manufacturing costs sitting on the balance sheet. Under variable costing, these fixed manufacturing costs will flow through the income statement as an expense in the period of their production.

EXHIBIT 17A.3 Total Business Inventories in Relation to Sales Ratios

Total Business Inventories / Sales Ratios: 2013 to 2022

Source: U.S. Census Bureau, Manufacturing and Trade Inventories and Sales, December 15, 2022.
(Data adjusted for seasonal, holiday and trading day differences but not for price changes)

Review 17-5 LO17-5

Computing Inventory Costs Under Absorption and Variable Costing

Intel has a highly automated assembly line that uses very little direct labor. Therefore, direct labor is part of variable overhead. For October, assume that it incurred the following unit costs.

Direct materials.	$250
Variable overhead.	220
Fixed overhead.	80

The 100 units of beginning inventory for October had an absorption costing value of $45,000 and a variable costing value of $38,000. For October, assume that Intel produced 500 units and sold 540 units.

Required

a. Compute Intel's October amount of ending inventory under both absorption and variable costing if the FIFO inventory method was used.

Solution on p. 17-56.   b. Compute Intel's October Cost of Goods Sold using both the variable and absorption costing methods.

KEY RATIOS AND EQUATIONS

Product costs for financial reporting:
Direct materials costs + Direct labor costs + Manufacturing overhead = Product costs

$$\text{Predetermined overhead rate per direct labor hour} = \frac{\text{Budgeted total overhead costs for the year}}{\text{Budgeted total direct labor hours for the year}}$$

$$\text{Manufacturing overhead applied to Work-in-Process Inventory} = \text{Actual direct labor hours} \times \text{Predetermined overhead rate per direct labor hour}$$

$$\text{Variable costing net income} + \text{Increase (or minus decrease) in inventoried fixed manufacturing overhead} = \text{Absorption costing net income}$$

MULTIPLE CHOICE

1. Which of the following statements best represents manufacturing organizations? **LO17-1**
   a. A manufacturing organization always uses process costing.
   b. A manufacturing organization typically has a low percentage of its assets invested in inventory.
   c. A manufacturing organization typically has three major inventory categories.
   d. A manufacturing organization is the only type of organization that has a cost of goods sold account reported on the income statement.

2. Kay Company's formula for annual manufacturing overhead is: **LO17-2**

   Y = $120,000 + $10X, where X is direct labor dollars

   The predicted activity for the year is 50,000 direct labor hours and the actual activity for January was 4,000 direct labor hours. Using a predetermined overhead rate, the applied January overhead is

   a. $40,000
   b. $49,600
   c. $160,000
   d. $169,600

3. Which of the following statements best represents job order costing? **LO17-3**
   a. Job order costing works best when there is production of identical units on a continuous basis.
   b. Job order costing works best for companies like Kraft Heinz and SanDisk.
   c. In job order costing, scheduling personnel prepare a production order for each job.
   d. In job order costing, a process cost sheet is used to accumulate the costs for each job.

4. Presented is selected information from Took's April income statement and statement of cost of goods manufactured: **LO17-3**

Cost of goods sold	$230,000
Cost of goods manufactured	$210,000
Finished goods inventory, April 30	$ 40,000

   Took's finished goods inventory on April 1 was

   a. $20,000
   b. $40,000
   c. $60,000
   d. $80,000

5. Presented is selected information from Fred's January statement of cost of goods manufactured. **LO17-3**

Predetermined overhead rate	80% of direct labor dollars
Direct materials	$ 60,000
Cost of goods manufactured	$150,000

Multiple Choice Answers
1. c 2. b 3. c 4. c 5. b 6. d 7. a 8. d

Fred's January direct labor was

a. $40,000
b. $50,000
c. $75,000
d. $90,000

LO17-4 6. The beginning inventory consisted of 10,000 units, 30% complete and the ending inventory consisted of 8,000 units, 40% complete. There were 22,000 units started during the period. Determine the equivalent units of conversion in process.

a. 17,800
b. 20,800
c. 25,200
d. 27,200

LO17-4 7. Presented is selected information from Micro Systems cost of production report:

Cost per equivalent unit in process	$ 20
Units completed	30,000
Total costs in process	$664,000
Equivalent units of materials in ending inventory	4,000
Cost per equivalent unit of materials	$ 12

The ending inventory of work-in-process is complete as to materials. The cost of conversion in the ending inventory is

a. $16,000
b. $32,000
c. $48,000
d. $64,000

LO17-5 8. Chandler Company sells its product for $100 per unit. Variable manufacturing costs per unit are $40, and fixed manufacturing costs at the normal operating level of 12,000 units are $240,000. Variable expenses are $16 per unit sold. Fixed administration expenses total $104,000. Chandler had no beginning inventory. During the year, the company produced 12,000 units and sold 9,000. What would the operating income be for Chandler Company for the year using both variable costing and absorption costing?

a. Variable costing $60,000; absorption costing $60,000
b. Variable costing $112,000; absorption costing $52,000
c. Variable costing $112,000; absorption costing $125,000
d. Variable costing $52,000; absorption costing $112,000

DATA ANALYTICS

LO17-3 **DA17-1. Job Profitability Using Excel**

Harvard Products is a job shop (a company that manufactures custom products in small batches). Each batch is managed by one of Harvard's four project managers. Manufacturing facilities are located in Illinois, Wisconsin, Michigan, and Indiana.

Assume the President of Harvard Products has asked for information about costs and profits by job, location, customer, and project manager. A summary of costs (by job) is included in an Excel file available on the textbook's website. *Hint:* Add columns to the Data sheet to separate out account amounts (revenue, direct material, etc.). The IF function is useful here.

REQUIRED
Create PivotTables to answer the following questions.

a. Which customer was the most profitable for Harvard? What was the job number for the most profitable job for that customer? What was the average revenue on jobs for that customer? What was the average revenue for all jobs?

b. Which location was the least profitable (in dollars) for Harvard? What appears to have contributed more to the lower profits at that location – size of jobs (average revenue) or profit margin ratios? Which location had the highest average revenue per job?

c. The President of Harvard Products has decided to give performance bonuses to project managers. Determine which project manager will receive the highest bonus if performance is based on:

1. Average revenue per job?
2. Number of jobs?
3. Total profit?
4. Profit margin ratios?

d. Based solely on the information you have available, would you encourage management to close the facility with the lowest profit margin? Why or why not? Include in your answer the information you might need to have before making a final decision.

DA17-2. Job Profitability Using Tableau
Available in myBusinessCourse, this problem uses Tableau to analyze the profitability of manufacturing jobs and determine how bonus measurements are impacted by the metrics used for assessment.

DA17-3. Analyzing Trends in Manufacturing Costs
A machine parts manufacturer gathered data for its Cutting Department for the last three years. The data includes actual costs and equivalent units for direct materials and conversion costs. The data also includes budget information based on budgeted volume levels. The Excel file is available on the textbook's website. The volume of units in the Cutting Department is relatively consistent from month-to-month. Likewise, costs have remained steady and fairly consistent from year to year. However, a three-year analysis reveals some data points that would be considered outliers.

REQUIRED
Assuming that the company uses process costing to track its manufacturing costs, answer the following questions.

  a. Prepare a stacked column chart of actual total direct materials and actual total conversion costs showing each month over the three-year period. Indicate any months where data points appear to be outliers.

  b. Prepare two clustered column charts, one comparing actual to budgeted direct materials and another comparing actual to budgeted conversion costs. Based on the review of the charts, which outlier(s) appear to be related to a change in volume? What is a possible cause for the change in volume?

  c. Which outlier(s) appear to be due to a change in costs not related to volume? *Hint:* Prepare a chart comparing direct materials and conversion costs per unit to the related budgeted costs per unit. What is a possible cause for the change in costs?

DATA VISUALIZATION

Data Visualization Activities are available in myBusinessCourse. These assignments use Tableau Dashboards to expose students to visual depictions of data and introduce students to data analytics through data visualizations. These exercises are easily assignable and auto graded by MBC.

QUESTIONS

Q17-1. Distinguish among service, merchandising, and manufacturing organizations on the basis of the importance and complexity of inventory cost measurement.

Q17-2. Distinguish between product costing and service costing.

Q17-3. When is depreciation a product cost? When is depreciation a period cost?

Q17-4. What are the three major product cost elements?

Q17-5. How are predetermined overhead rates developed? Why are they widely used?

Q17-6. Briefly distinguish between process manufacturing and job order production. Provide examples of products typically produced under each system.

Q17-7. Briefly describe the role of engineering personnel and production scheduling personnel in the production planning process.

Q17-8. Identify the primary (digital) records involved in the operation of a job cost system.

Q17-9. Describe the flow of costs through the accounting system of a labor-intensive manufacturing organization.

Q17-10. Identify two reasons that a service organization should maintain detailed job cost information.

Q17-11. What are the four major elements of a cost of production report?

Q17-12. What are equivalent completed units?

Q17-13. Under what conditions will equivalent units in process be different for materials and conversion costs?

MINI EXERCISES

LO17-1 M17-14. Classification of Product and Period Costs

Classify the following costs incurred by a manufacturer of golf clubs as product costs or period costs. Also classify the product costs as direct materials or conversion costs.

a. Depreciation on computer in president's office
b. Salaries of legal staff
c. Graphite shafts
d. Plant security department
e. Electricity for the corporate office
f. Rubber grips
g. Golf club heads
h. Wages paid assembly line maintenance workers
i. Salary of corporate controller
j. Subsidy of plant cafeteria
k. Wages paid assembly line production workers
l. National sales meeting in Orlando
m. Overtime premium paid assembly line workers
n. Advertising on national television
o. Depreciation on assembly line

LO17-1 M17-15. Classifying Costs for Various Organization Types

Listed below are seven companies of varying types: service providers, merchandisers, manufacturers, or some combination. Determine which types of inventory that each company would likely track in its accounting records. *Hint:* Access the company's website on the internet for basic company information for any company that is unfamiliar to you.

	Supplies Inventory (non-manufacturing)	Merchandise Inventory	Raw Materials Inventory	Work-in-Process Inventory	Finished Goods Inventory
1. The Walt Disney Company					
2. Deloitte Digital					
3. Thredup Inc.					
4. Adidas AG					
5. Autozone, Inc.					
6. Zevia					
7. Baker McKenzie					

LO17-2 M17-16. Developing and Using a Predetermined Overhead Rate

Assume that the following predictions were made last year for one of the plants of **Milliken & Company**.

Total manufacturing overhead for the year	$15,000,000
Total machine hours for the year	1,200,000

Actual results for February were as follows.

Manufacturing overhead	$1,238,500
Machine hours	98,500

REQUIRED

a. Determine the predetermined overhead rate per machine hour.
b. Using the predetermined overhead rate per machine hour, determine the manufacturing overhead applied to Work-in-Process during February.
c. As of February 1, actual overhead was overapplied by $35,000. Determine the cumulative amount of any overapplied or underapplied overhead at the end of February.

M17-17. Job Order Costing and Process Costing Applications
For each of the following manufacturing situations, indicate whether job order or process costing is more appropriate and why.

a. Manufacturer of chocolate candy bars
b. Manufacturer of carbonated beverages
c. Manufacturer of high-quality men's suits
d. Manufacturer of subway cars
e. Printer of a variety of history books

M17-18. Job Order Costing and Process Costing Applications
For each of the following situations, indicate whether job order or process costing is more appropriate and why.

a. Building contractor for residential dwellings
b. Manufacturer of nylon yarn (single weight) that it sells to fabric-making textile companies
c. Evening gown manufacturer that makes gowns in several different fabrics, colors, styles, and sizes
d. Hosiery mill that manufactures a one-size-fits-all product
e. Vehicle battery manufacturer that has just received an order for 400,000 identical batteries

M17-19. Cost Flow in Job Order Costing
VistaPrint is a company that designs and creates custom marketing products. Assume the company started New Job last month, but completed no units. In the current month of March, the company identified the following cost information.

	New Job
Work-in-process, March 1	$18,500
Finished goods, March 1	$ 8,000
Costs assigned in March:	
Direct materials	12,000
Direct labor	5,000
Manufacturing overhead (applied and actual)	7,500

REQUIRED

a. If ending work-in-process inventory on March 31 is $0, what was cost of goods manufactured for the month of March?
b. If ending finished goods inventory on March 31 is $1,200, what was cost of goods sold?
c. If the manufacturing process is complete for New Job and a total of 1,000 units were produced, what is the total manufacturing cost per unit?

M17-20. Defining Terms in a Manufacturing Environment
Assume **Intel** just received a chip order from Dell Computers. Match the terms with the associated actions and documents of Intel.

a. Process costing
b. Job order costing
c. Production order
d. Job cost sheet
e. Materials requisition
f. Work ticket

___ 1. Intel schedulers use this document to specify the production requirements of a job.
___ 2. Intel uses this accounting system to capture the costs of standard chips that are sold as finished goods continuously.
___ 3. Intel's accountants use this document to accumulate the costs of the job.
___ 4. Intel uses this accounting system to capture the costs of the production of custom-built chips, such as those for the Dell order.
___ 5. Intel employees record the time a job spends in a specific manufacturing operation.
___ 6. This document authorizes the transfer of materials to a job.

M17-21. Process Costing
Snooz makes a single model of its white noise sound machine. Assume the product is produced on a continuous basis in one department. All materials are added at the beginning of production. The total cost per equivalent unit in process in March was $56, consisting of $32 for materials and $24 for conversion. During the month, 12,000 units of product were transferred to finished goods inventory; on March 31, 5,000 units were in process, 10% converted. The company uses weighted average costing.

REQUIRED

a. Determine the cost of goods transferred to finished goods inventory.
b. Determine the cost of the ending work-in-process inventory.
c. What was the total cost of the beginning work-in-process inventory plus the current manufacturing costs?

LO17-5 **M17-22. Absorption and Variable Costing; Inventory Valuation**

Bondware Inc. has a highly automated assembly line that uses very little direct labor. Therefore, direct labor is part of variable overhead. For March, assume that it incurred the following unit costs.

Direct materials.	$450
Variable overhead.	250
Fixed overhead.	550

The 1,200 units of beginning inventory for March had an absorption costing value of $1,500,000 and a variable costing value of $840,000. For March, assume that Bondware Inc. produced 3,000 units and sold 3,500 units.

REQUIRED

Compute Bondware's March amount of ending inventory under both absorption and variable costing if the FIFO inventory method was used.

LO17-5 **M17-23. Absorption and Variable Costing; Cost of Goods Sold**

Use data from Mini Exercise 17-22.

REQUIRED

Compute Bondware's March Cost of Goods Sold using both the variable and absorption costing methods.

EXERCISES

LO17-1 **E17-24. Classifying Costs as Product or Period**

Zevia
NYSE :: ZVIA

Zevia is a beverage company that sells naturally sweetened soft drinks. Zevia manufactures its products in manufacturing facilities in the U.S. and Canada. Classify each of the following assumed costs as product or period for financial reporting purposes.

REQUIRED

1. Costs to lease machines used in manufacturing facilities.
2. Utilities costs of manufacturing facilities.
3. Warehousing costs of packaged beverages ready to be distributed to customers.
4. Cost of stevia, an ingredient of the beverages.
5. Freight costs to deliver stevia to the manufacturing facilities.
6. Freight costs to deliver beverages to customers.
7. Costs for a marketing program for a new beverage product.
8. Cost of aluminum for cans.
9. Research and development costs to find more sustainable packaging solutions.
10. Cost of packaging cans into 12-pack boxes.
11. Advertising cost to sponsor sporting events.
12. Sales commissions.
13. Legal staffing costs.
14. Costs of production line workers in plants.

LO17-2 **E17-25. Classifying Costs as Product or Period**

The process to manufacture custom machine parts involves two departments. Assume that manufacturing overhead is applied using direct labor hours in Department One and machine hours in Department Two. The following annual data was budgeted for the current year.

	Department One	Department Two
Total budgeted manufacturing overhead	$330,000	$504,000
Total budgeted direct labor hours	120,000	4,000
Total budgeted machine hours	8,000	80,000

REQUIRED

a. Determine the applied overhead rate for Department One and the applied overhead rate for Department Two.
b. Job #800 incurred 518 actual direct labor hours (500 in Department One and 18 in Department Two) and 235 actual machine hours (45 in Department One and 190 in Department Two). Determine total overhead applied to Job #800.

c. After year-end, the following actual data was compiled.

	Department One	Department Two
Total actual manufacturing overhead	$340,000	$499,000
Total actual direct labor hours	125,000	4,400
Total actual machine hours	7,800	79,000

Determine total applied overhead and the total amount of over(under) applied overhead for the year for each department.

E17-26. Analyzing Activity in Inventory Accounts

Steger Design makes winter boots and moccasins at its factory in northern Minnesota. Assume the following represents data related to Steger operations last year.

Raw materials used	$400,000
Total manufacturing costs charged to production during the year (includes raw materials, direct labor, and manufacturing overhead applied at a rate of 200% of direct labor costs)	850,000
Cost of goods available for sale	958,000
Selling and general expenses	280,000

	Inventories Beginning	Ending
Raw materials	$110,000	$105,000
Work-in-process	75,000	92,000
Finished goods	125,000	135,000

REQUIRED
Determine each of the following.

a. Cost of raw materials purchased
b. Direct labor costs charged to production
c. Cost of goods manufactured
d. Cost of goods sold

E17-27. Statement of Cost of Goods Manufactured and Income Statement

Information from the records of the Bridgeview Manufacturing Company for August follows.

Sales	$250,000
Selling and administrative expenses	98,600
Purchases of raw materials	32,000
Direct labor	22,000
Manufacturing overhead	38,600

	Inventories August 1	August 31
Raw materials	$ 6,000	$ 6,500
Work-in-process	4,600	5,800
Finished goods	12,000	15,000

REQUIRED
Prepare a statement of cost of goods manufactured and an income statement for August.

E17-28. Statement of Cost of Goods Manufactured from Percent Relationships

Information about Blue Line Products Company for the year ending December 31 follows.

- Sales equal $580,000.
- Direct materials used total $105,000.
- Manufacturing overhead is 200% of direct labor dollars.
- The beginning inventory of finished goods is 25% of the cost of goods sold.
- The ending inventory of finished goods is 1.5 times beginning inventory.
- The gross profit is 20% of sales.
- There is no beginning or ending work-in-process.

REQUIRED
Prepare a statement of cost of goods manufactured for the year. (*Hint:* Prepare an analysis of changes in Finished Goods Inventory.)

LO17-3   E17-29. Account Activity and Relationships

	Case A	Case B	Case C	Case D
Sales	$42,000	$ (b)	$82,500	$ (b)
Direct materials	7,500	31,500	(f)	42,000
Direct labor	3,000	(c)	15,000	(c)
Total direct costs	(a)	48,000	(e)	60,000
Conversion cost	(b)	39,000	(g)	(g)
Manufacturing overhead	4,000	(d)	7,500	(f)
Current manufacturing costs	(c)	(e)	71,250	158,000
Work-in-process, beginning	3,500	15,000	(d)	42,000
Work-in-process, ending	2,500	(f)	15,750	(e)
Cost of goods manufactured	(d)	48,000	(c)	164,000
Finished goods inventory, beginning	4,500	12,000	5,250	24,000
Finished goods inventory, ending	3,000	(g)	6,000	(d)
Cost of goods sold	(e)	52,500	(b)	160,000
Gross profit	(f)	(a)	13,500	30,000
Selling and administrative expenses	10,000	22,500	(a)	(a)
Net income	(g)	33,000	9,000	12,000

REQUIRED

Each case is independent. Solve for missing data in alphabetical order.

LO17-2   E17-30. Developing and Using a Predetermined Overhead Rate: High-Low Cost Estimation

For years, Mattoon Components Company has used an actual plantwide overhead rate and based its prices on cost plus a markup of 30%. Recently the marketing manager, Holly Adams, and the production manager, Sue Walsh, confronted the controller with a common problem. The marketing manager expressed a concern that Mattoon's prices seem to vary widely throughout the year. According to Adams, "It seems irrational to charge higher prices when business is bad and lower prices when business is good. While we get a lot of business during high-volume months because we charge less than our competitors, it is a waste of time to even call on customers during low-volume months because we are raising prices while our competitors are lowering them." Walsh also believed that it was "folly to be so pushed that we have to pay overtime in some months and then lay employees off in others." She commented, "While there are natural variations in customer demand, the accounting system seems to amplify this variation."

REQUIRED

a. Evaluate the arguments presented by Adams and Walsh. What suggestions do you have for improving the accounting and pricing procedures?
b. Assume that the Mattoon Components Company had the following total manufacturing overhead costs and direct labor hours in the last two years.

	Year 1	Year 2
Total manufacturing overhead	$325,000	$380,500
Direct labor hours	34,000	40,000

Use the high-low method (see Chapter 14) to develop a cost-estimating equation for total manufacturing overhead.
c. Develop a predetermined rate for next year, assuming 35,000 direct labor hours are budgeted for next year.
d. Assume that the actual level of activity next year was 36,000 direct labor hours and that manufacturing overhead was $341,550. Determine the underapplied or overapplied manufacturing overhead at the end of the year.
e. Describe two ways of handling any underapplied or overapplied manufacturing overhead at the end of the year.

LO17-2, 3   E17-31. Manufacturing Cost Flows with Machine Hours Allocation

On April 1, Telecom Manufacturing Company's beginning balances in manufacturing accounts and finished goods inventory were as follows.

Raw materials	$35,000
Manufacturing supplies	3,500
Work-in-process	12,000
Manufacturing overhead	0
Finished goods	50,000

During April, Telecom Manufacturing completed the following manufacturing transactions:

1. Purchased raw materials costing $60,000 and manufacturing supplies costing $2,000 on account.
2. Requisitioned raw materials costing $52,000 to the factory.
3. Incurred direct labor costs of $18,000 and indirect labor costs of $6,500.
4. Used manufacturing supplies costing $3,800.
5. Recorded manufacturing depreciation of $11,000.
6. Miscellaneous payables for manufacturing overhead totaled $8,500.
7. Applied manufacturing overhead, based on 2,500 machine hours, at a predetermined rate of $10 per machine hour.
8. Completed jobs costing $90,500.
9. Finished goods costing $95,750 were sold.

REQUIRED

a. Prepare an analysis of the activity in the following accounts: Manufacturing Supplies, Manufacturing Overhead, Raw Materials, Work-in-Process, Finished Goods Inventory, and Cost of Goods Sold.
b. Calculate the balances at the end of April for Work-in-Process Inventory and Finished Goods Inventory.

E17-32. Manufacturing Cost Flows with Machine Hours Allocation Using "T" Accounts   LO17-2, 3

Refer to the information in E17-31 to answer the following questions.

REQUIRED

a. Prepare "T" accounts showing the flow of costs through all manufacturing accounts, Finished Goods Inventory, and Cost of Goods Sold.
b. Calculate the balances at the end of April for Work-in-Process Inventory and Finished Goods Inventory.

E17-33. Service Cost Flows   LO17-2, 3

Cutwater, an advertising agency with offices in San Francisco and New York, develops marketing campaigns for companies in the United States and overseas. To achieve cost control, assume Cutwater uses a job cost system similar to that found in a manufacturing organization. It uses some different account titles:

Account	Replaces
Jobs-in-Process	Work-in-Process
Job Supplies Inventory	Manufacturing Supplies Inventory
Cost of Jobs Completed	Cost of Goods Sold
Accumulated Depreciation, Agency Assets	Accumulated Depreciation, Factory Assets
Production Overhead	Manufacturing Overhead

Cutwater does not maintain Raw Materials or Finished Goods Inventory accounts. Materials, such as props needed for video shoots, are purchased as needed from outside sources and charged directly to Jobs-in-Process and the appropriate job. The April 1 balances were as follows.

Job Supplies Inventory	$ 10,000	
Jobs-in-Process	200,000	
Production Overhead	2,850	underapplied

During April, Cutwater completed the following production transactions:

1. Purchased job supplies costing $4,500 on account.
2. Purchased materials for specific jobs costing $150,000 on account.
3. Incurred direct labor costs of $225,000 and indirect labor costs of $155,000.
4. Used production supplies costing $2,200.
5. Recorded equipment depreciation of $12,000.
6. Incurred miscellaneous payables for production overhead of $78,000.
7. Applied production overhead at a predetermined rate of $100 per production hour, based on 2,500 production hours.
8. Completed jobs costing $622,000.

REQUIRED

a. Prepare an analysis of the activity in the following accounts: Job Supplies Inventory, Production Overhead, Jobs-in-Process, and Cost of Jobs Completed.

b. Calculate the cost incurred as of the end of April for the incomplete jobs still in process.

LO17-2, 3

E17-34. Service Cost Flows Using "T" Accounts

Refer to the information in E17-33 to answer the following questions.

REQUIRED

a. Prepare "T" accounts showing the flow of costs through all service accounts and Cost of Jobs Completed.

b. Calculate the cost incurred as of the end of April for the incomplete jobs still in process.

LO17-2, 3

E17-35. Analyzing Cost Drivers

Plastic Parts is a manufacturer of a large variety of plastic injected molded parts. The company applies total company manufacturing overhead based upon total direct labor hours. The price of each product is computed by taking the product cost per unit and adding a predetermined percentage to arrive at the selling price. Management believes that as long as the selling price is set above the cost for each item, the company's overall profitability will increase over time.

REQUIRED

a. Under what conditions will the process currently used to apply overhead, result in relatively accurate costing?

b. If the current process of applying overhead is determined to be inaccurate, what different options does the company have in applying overhead?

c. Recently, the company has experienced a shift in product mix—while overall sales volume has not decreased, the types of products that customers are selecting have changed. While sales volume in total has remained steady, the company has noticed that overall profits have declined. If we assume that the financial accounting process of applying overhead is providing accurate costing, what else might the company consider when pricing their products?

LO17-4

E17-36. Cost of Production Report: No Beginning Inventories

Port Townsend Paper (PTPC) produces paper by blending recycled corrugated cardboard with other fibers. Assume the following represent production and cost data for October. There was no inventory on hand on October 1.

Units of product started in process during October	20,000 tons
Units completed and transferred to finished goods	19,000 tons
Machine hours operated	3,410
Direct materials costs incurred	$134,000
Direct labor costs incurred	$185,000

Raw materials are added at the beginning of the process for each unit of product produced, and labor and manufacturing overhead are added evenly throughout the manufacturing process. Manufacturing overhead is applied to Work-in-Process at the rate of $50 per machine hour. Units in process at the end of the period were 75% converted.

REQUIRED

Prepare a cost of production report for PTPC for October.

LO17-4

E17-37. Cost of Production Report: No Beginning Inventories

Howell Paving Company manufactures asphalt paving materials for highway construction through a one-step process in which all materials are added at the beginning of the process. During April, the company accumulated the following data in its process costing system.

Production data	
Work-in-process, 4/1	0 tons
Raw materials transferred to processing	35,000 tons
Work-in-process, 4/30 (60% converted)	5,000 tons
Cost data	
Raw materials transferred to processing	$440,000
Conversion costs	
Direct labor cost incurred	$95,000
Manufacturing overhead applied	?

Manufacturing overhead is applied at the rate of $15 per equivalent unit (ton) processed.

REQUIRED

Prepare a cost of production report for April.

E17-38. Absorption and Variable Costing Comparisons: Production Equals Sales   **LO17-6**

Assume that **Smuckers** manufactures and sells 45,000 cases of peanut butter each quarter. The following data are available for the third quarter of the year.

Total fixed manufacturing overhead	$ 675,000
Fixed selling and administrative expenses	1,225,000
Sales price per case	85
Direct materials per case	20
Direct labor per case	10
Variable manufacturing overhead per case	4

The J.M. Smucker Company — NYSE :: SJM

REQUIRED
- a. Compute the cost per case under both absorption costing and variable costing.
- b. Compute net income under both absorption costing and variable costing.
- c. Reconcile any differences in income. Explain.

E17-39. Absorption and Variable Costing Income Statements: Production Exceeds Sales   **LO17-5**

Glenview Company sells its product at a unit price of $20. Unit manufacturing costs are direct materials, $5.00; direct labor, $2.00; and variable manufacturing overhead, $1.00. Total fixed manufacturing costs are $255,000 per year. Selling and administrative expenses are $1.00 per unit variable and $185,000 per year fixed. Though 60,000 units were produced during the year, only 54,000 units were sold. There was no beginning inventory.

REQUIRED
- a. Prepare a functional income statement using absorption costing for the year.
- b. Prepare a contribution income statement using variable costing for the year.

E17-40. Absorption and Variable Costing Comparisons: Sales Exceed Production   **LO17-5**

Wright Development purchases, develops, and sells commercial building sites. As the sites are sold, they are cleared at an average cost of $8,000 per site. Storm drains and driveways are also installed at an average cost of $10,000 per site. Selling costs are 6% of sales price. Administrative costs are $600,000 per year. Two years ago, the company bought 2,000 acres of land for $7,500,000 and divided it into 200 sites of equal size. During that year, 95 sites were sold at an average price of $150,000. Last year, the company purchased and developed another 2,000 acres, divided into 200 sites. The purchase price was again $7,500,000. Sales totaled 250 sites last year at an average price of $150,000.

REQUIRED
- a. Prepare functional income statements using absorption costing for each of the two years.
- b. Prepare contribution income statements using variable costing for each of the two years.

PROBLEMS

P17-41. Cost of Goods Manufactured and Income Statement   **LO17-1, 3**

Following is information from the records of the Savoy Company for July.

Purchases	
Raw materials	$150,000
Manufacturing supplies	2,500
Office supplies	1,000
Sales	583,500
Administrative salaries	46,000
Direct labor	105,000
Production employees' fringe benefits*	10,500
Sales salaries and commissions	45,000
Production supervisors' salaries	10,000
Plant depreciation	12,000
Office depreciation	3,000
Plant maintenance	8,000
Plant utilities	7,500
Office utilities	2,500
Office maintenance	4,200
Production equipment rent	4,000
Office equipment rent	1,000

* Classified as manufacturing overhead

Inventories	July 1	July 31
Raw materials	$25,000	$28,000
Manufacturing supplies	4,000	3,500
Office supplies	1,500	1,000
Work-in-process	18,000	15,000
Finished goods	90,450	88,600

REQUIRED

Prepare a statement of cost of goods manufactured and an income statement. Actual overhead costs are assigned to products.

LO17-2, 3

Bauer Hockey, LLC

P17-42. Cost of Goods Manufactured and Income Statement with Predetermined Overhead and Labor Cost Classifications

Assume information pertaining to **Bauer Hockey** for April of the current year follows.

Sales	$745,500
Purchases	
Raw materials	225,000
Manufacturing supplies	12,000
Office supplies	2,200
Salaries (including fringe benefits)	
Administrative	102,600
Production supervisors	24,500
Sales	105,000
Depreciation	
Plant and machinery	24,000
Office and office equipment	8,000
Utilities	
Plant	15,000
Office	6,000

Inventories	April 1	April 30
Raw materials	$50,350	$52,500
Manufacturing supplies	6,200	7,400
Office supplies	1,800	1,500
Work-in-process	38,500	40,200
Finished goods	90,000	88,000

Additional information follows.

- Manufacturing overhead is applied to products at 125% of direct labor dollars.
- Employee base wages are $15 per hour.
- Employee fringe benefits amount to 20% of the base wage rate. They are classified as manufacturing overhead.
- During April, production employees worked 6,500 hours, including 5,200 regular hours and 400 overtime hours spent working on products. There were 900 indirect labor hours.
- Employees are paid a 50% overtime premium. Any overtime premium is treated as manufacturing overhead.

REQUIRED

a. Prepare a statement of cost of goods manufactured and an income statement for April.
b. Determine underapplied or overapplied overhead for April.
c. Recompute direct labor and actual manufacturing overhead assuming employee fringe benefits for direct labor hours are classified as direct labor.

LO17-2, 3

Custom Crate Engines

P17-43. Actual and Predetermined Overhead Rates

Custom Crate Engines assembles custom designed high-performance engines for classic American cars. Assume the following events occurred during the month of January.

- Materials costing $8,000 were purchased on account.
- Direct materials costing $6,000 were placed in process.
- A total of 450 direct labor hours was charged to individual jobs at a rate of $20 per hour.
- Overhead costs for the month were as follows.

Depreciation on building and equipment	$2,425
Indirect labor	2,700
Utilities	450
Property taxes on automotive shop	375
Insurance on building	350

- There were no jobs in process on January 1.
- On January 31, only one job (A06) was in process with materials costs of $1,800, direct labor charges of $1,000 for 50 direct labor hours, and applied overhead.
- The building and equipment were purchased before operations began and the insurance was prepaid. All other costs will be paid during the following month.

Note: Predetermined overhead rates are used throughout the chapter. An alternative is to accumulate actual overhead costs for the period in Manufacturing Overhead, and apply actual costs at the close of the period to all jobs in process during the period.

REQUIRED

a. Assuming Custom Crate assigned actual monthly overhead costs to jobs on the basis of actual monthly direct labor hours, prepare an analysis of the activity in Work-in-Process for the month of January.
b. Assuming Custom Crate uses a predetermined overhead rate of $15 per direct labor hour, prepare an analysis of Work-in-Process for the month of January. Describe the appropriate treatment of any overapplied or underapplied overhead for the month of January.
c. Assume that utilities and indirect labor are variable costs with respect to direct labor hours and that depreciation and property taxes are fixed costs. Predict the actual overhead rates for months when 250 and 750 direct labor hours are used. Assuming jobs similar to A06 were in process at the end of each month, determine the costs assigned to these jobs.
d. Why do you suppose predetermined overhead rates are preferred to actual overhead rates?

P17-44. Job Costing with Predetermined Overhead Rate   LO17-2, 3

Kubota Corporation manufactures equipment in batches for inventory stock. Assume that Kubota's production costs are accounted for using a job cost system. At the beginning of April raw materials inventories totaled $9,350,000, manufacturing supplies amounted to $1,320,000, and finished goods inventories totaled $6,600,000. Two jobs were in process: Job 522 with assigned costs of $6,440,000 and Job 523 with assigned costs of $2,750,000. The following information summarizes April manufacturing activities.

Kubota
Corporation
OTCMKTS :: KUBTY

- Purchased raw materials costing $27,500,000 on account.
- Purchased manufacturing supplies costing $3,300,000 on account.
- Requisitioned materials needed to complete Job 523. Started two new jobs, 524 and 525, and requisitioned direct materials for them.

Direct materials	
Job 523	$ 3,300,000
Job 524	14,190,000
Job 525	10,560,000
Total	$28,050,000

- Recorded April salaries and wages as follows.

Direct labor	
Job 522 (150,000 hours × $25 per hour)	$ 3,750,000
Job 523 (950,000 hours × $25 per hour)	23,750,000
Job 524 (1,350,000 hours × $25 per hour)	33,750,000
Job 525 (875,000 hours × $25 per hour)	21,875,000
Total direct labor	83,125,000
Indirect labor	7,100,000
Total	$90,225,000

- Used manufacturing supplies costing $2,475,000.
- Recognized depreciation on factory fixed assets of $5,800,000.
- Incurred miscellaneous manufacturing overhead costs of $7,250,000 on account.
- Applied manufacturing overhead at the rate of $6.25 per direct labor hour.
- Completed Jobs 522, 523, and 524.

REQUIRED

Prepare a complete analysis of all activity in Work-in-Process. Be sure to show the beginning and ending balances, all increases and decreases, and label each item. Provide support information on decreases with job cost sheets.

LO17-2, 3   P17-45. Job Costing with Predetermined Overhead Rate

SnoBlo Company manufactures a variety of gasoline-powered snow blowers for discount hardware and department stores. SnoBlo uses a job cost system and treats each customer's order as a separate job. The primary snow blower components (motors, chassis, and wheels) are purchased from three different suppliers under long-term contracts that call for the direct delivery of raw materials to the production floor as needed. When a customer's order is received, a raw materials purchase order is electronically placed with suppliers. The purchase order specifies the scheduled date that production is to begin as the delivery date for motors and chassis; the scheduled date production is to be completed is specified as the delivery date for the wheels. As a consequence, there are no raw materials inventories; raw materials are charged directly to Work-in-Process upon receipt. Upon completion, goods are shipped directly to customers rather than transferred to finished goods inventory. At the beginning of July SnoBlo had the following work-in-process inventories.

Job 365	$ 40,000
Job 366	29,800
Job 367	30,600
Job 368	17,000
Total	$117,400

During July, the following activities took place:
- Started Jobs 369, 370, and 371.
- Ordered and received the following raw materials for specified jobs:

Job	Motors	Chassis	Wheels	Total
366	$ 0	$ 0	$ 1,600	$ 1,600
367	0	0	2,400	2,400
368	0	0	3,050	3,050
369	28,000	10,000	2,100	40,100
370	18,000	7,000	1,800	26,800
371	17,000	7,200	0	24,200
Total	$63,000	$24,200	$10,950	$98,150

- Incurred July manufacturing payroll:

Direct labor	
Job 365	$ 2,450
Job 366	7,600
Job 367	6,500
Job 368	8,300
Job 369	5,850
Job 370	5,050
Job 371	3,000
Total	38,750
Indirect labor	6,850
Total	$45,600

- Incurred additional manufacturing overhead costs for July:

Manufacturing supplies purchased on account and used	$ 5,700
Depreciation on factory fixed assets	11,800
Miscellaneous payables	9,500
Total	$27,000

- Applied manufacturing overhead using a predetermined rate based on predicted annual overhead of $405,000 and predicted annual direct labor of $450,000.
- Completed and shipped Jobs 365 through 370.

REQUIRED

Prepare a complete analysis of all activity in Work-in-Process. Be sure to show the beginning and ending balances, all increases and decreases, and label each item. Provide support information on decreases with job cost sheets.

P17-46. Weighted Average Process Costing

Minot Processing Company manufactures one product on a continuous basis in two departments, Processing and Finishing. All materials are added at the beginning of work on the product in the Processing Department. During November, the following events occurred in the Processing Department.

Units started	20,000 units
Units completed and transferred to Finishing Department	21,000 units

Costs assigned to processing	
Raw materials	$350,000
Manufacturing supplies used	25,000
Direct labor costs incurred	182,000
Supervisors' salaries	15,000
Other production labor costs	18,000
Depreciation on equipment	12,000
Other production costs	95,000

Additional information follows.
- Minot uses weighted average costing and applies manufacturing overhead to Work-in-Process at the rate of 90% of direct labor cost.
- Ending inventory in the Processing Department consists of 3,000 units that are one-fourth converted.
- Beginning inventory contained 4,000 units, one-half converted, with a cost of $57,950 ($34,000 for materials and $23,950 for conversion).

REQUIRED

a. Prepare a cost of production report for the Processing Department for November.
b. Prepare an analysis of all changes in Work-in-Process.

P17-47. Weighted Average Process Costing

Assume that **JIF**, which is part of **The J.M. Smucker Company**, processes its only product, 12-ounce jars of peanut butter, in a single process and uses weighted average process costing to account for inventory costs. All materials are added at the beginning of production. Assume the following inventory, production, and cost data are provided for September.

Production data	
Beginning inventory (25% converted)	200,000 units
Units started	600,000 units
Ending inventory (75% converted)	225,000 units

Manufacturing costs	
Beginning inventory in process	
Materials cost	$182,000
Conversion cost	44,600
Raw materials cost added at beginning of process	578,000
Direct labor cost incurred	401,900
Manufacturing overhead applied	446,000

REQUIRED

a. Prepare a cost of production report for September.
b. Prepare a statement of cost of goods manufactured for September.

P17-48. Weighted Average Process Costing with Error Correction

Capital Manufacturing Company began operations on December 1. On December 31 a new accounting intern was assigned the task of calculating and costing ending inventories.

The intern estimated that the ending work-in-process inventory was 40% complete as to both materials and conversion, resulting in 6,000 equivalent units of materials and conversion. The ending work-in-process was then valued at $60,000, including $30,000 for materials and $30,000 for conversion. A subsequent review of the intern's work revealed that although the materials portion of the ending inventory was correctly estimated to be 40% complete, the units in ending inventory, on average, were only 25% complete as to conversion.

REQUIRED
a. Determine the number of units in the ending inventory.
b. How many equivalent units of conversion were in the ending inventory?
c. What cost per unit did the intern calculate for conversion?
d. Assuming 12,000 units were completed during the month of December, determine the correct cost per equivalent unit. (*Hint:* Find the total conversion costs in process.)
e. Determine the corrected cost of the ending inventory.
f. By how much was the cost of goods manufactured misstated as a result of the intern's error? Indicate whether the cost of goods manufactured was overstated or understated.

LO17-5 **P17-49. Absorption and Variable Costing Comparisons**

Otabo is a shoe manufacturer. Assume the company is concerned with changing to the variable costing method of inventory valuation for making internal decisions. Functional income statements using absorption costing for January and February follow.

OTABO
Functional (Absorption Costing) Income Statements
For January and February

	January	February
Sales (10,000 units)	$800,000	$800,000
Cost of goods sold	(490,000)	(586,000)
Gross profit	310,000	214,000
Selling and administrative expenses	(235,000)	(235,000)
Net operating income	$ 75,000	$ (21,000)

Production data follow.

Production units	12,000	8,000
Variable costs per unit	$25	$25
Fixed overhead costs	$288,000	$288,000

The preceding selling and administrative expenses include variable costs of $2 per unit sold.

REQUIRED
a. Compute the absorption cost per unit manufactured in January and February.
b. Explain why the net operating income for January was higher than the net operating income for February when the same number of units was sold in each month.
c. Prepare contribution income statements for both months using variable costing.
d. Reconcile the absorption costing and variable costing net operating income figures for each month. (Start with variable costing net operating income.)

LO17-5 **P17-50. Absorption and Variable Costing Comparisons**

Red Arrow Blueberries manufactures blueberry jam. Because of bad weather, its blueberry crop was small. The following data have been gathered for the summer quarter of last year.

Beginning inventory (cases)	0
Cases produced	8,000
Cases sold	7,000
Sales price per case	$115
Direct materials per case	$25
Direct labor per case	$40
Variable manufacturing overhead per case	$10
Total fixed manufacturing overhead	$192,000
Variable selling and administrative cost per case	$2
Fixed selling and administrative cost	$38,000

REQUIRED
a. Prepare a functional income statement for the quarter using absorption costing.
b. Prepare a contribution income statement for the quarter using variable costing.
c. What is the value of ending inventory under absorption costing?
d. What is the value of ending inventory under variable costing?
e. Reconcile the difference in ending inventory under absorption costing and variable costing.

P17-51. Variable and Absorption Costing with High-Low Cost Estimation and CVP Analysis Including Taxes   LO17-5

Presented are the Charger Company's functional income statements for January and February.

CHARGER COMPANY
Functional (Absorption Costing) Income Statements
For the Months of January and February

	January	February
Production and sales	35,000	40,000
Sales Revenue	$2,450,000	$2,800,000
Cost of goods manufactured and sold	(1,470,000)	(1,540,000)
Gross profit	980,000	1,260,000
General and administrative expenses	(650,000)	(650,000)
Net operating income	330,000	610,000
Income taxes at 0.21	(69,300)	(128,100)
Net income after taxes	$ 260,700	$ 481,900

REQUIRED
a. Using the high-low method (see Chapter 14), develop a cost-estimating equation for total monthly manufacturing costs.
b. Determine Charger Company's monthly break-even point.
c. Determine the unit sales required to earn a monthly after-tax income of $600,000.
d. Prepare a January contribution income statement using variable costing.
e. If the January net income amounts differ using absorption and variable costing, explain why. If they are identical, explain why.

P17-52. Job Order and Process Costing Analysis   LO17-2, 3, 4

1. A company uses a predetermined overhead rate to allocate its overhead costs. The manufacturing process requires the use of machining equipment, which is a primary driver of overhead. The actual factory overhead amount is $450 for Department A, Job 120 as of the end of the year. Production costs are shown below.

Estimated annual overhead for all departments	$220,000
Expected annual machine hours for all departments	20,000
Actual machine hours for Department A, Job 120	32
Actual labor hours for Department A, Job 120	21

The overhead cost for Department A, Job 120 is

a. $98 overapplied.
b. $98 underapplied.
c. $219 overapplied.
d. $219 underapplied.   **CMA Adapted**

2. Baldwin Printing Company uses a job order costing system and applies overhead based on machine hours. A total of 150,000 machine hours have been budgeted for the year. During the year, an order for 1,000 units was completed and incurred the following.

Direct material costs	$1,000
Direct labor costs	1,500
Actual overhead	1,980
Machine hours	450

The accountant calculated the inventory cost of this order to be $4.30 per unit. The annual budgeted overhead in dollars was

a. $577,500.
b. $600,000.
c. $645,000.
d. $660,000.   **CMA Adapted**

3. Mack Inc. uses a weighted-average process costing system. Direct materials and conversion costs are incurred evenly during the production process. During the month of October, the following costs were incurred.

Direct material	$39,700
Conversion costs	70,000

The work-in-process inventory as of October 1 consisted of 5,000 units, valued at $4,300, that were 20% complete. During October, 27,000 units were transferred out. Inventory as of October 31 consisted of 3,000 units that were 50% complete. The weighted-average inventory cost per unit completed in October was

a. $3.51.
b. $3.88.
c. $3.99.
d. $4.00.

CMA Adapted

CASES AND PROJECTS

LO17-2, 3 **C17-53. Cost Data for Financial Reporting and Special Order Decisions**

Harman Greeting Card Company produces a full range of greeting cards sold through pharmacies and department stores. Each card is designed by independent artists. A production master is then prepared for each design. The production master has an indefinite life. Product designs for popular cards are deemed to be valuable assets. If a card sells well, many batches of the design will be manufactured over a period of years. Hence, Harman Greeting maintains an inventory of production masters so that cards may be periodically reissued. Cards are produced in batches that may vary by increments of 1,000 units. An average batch consists of 10,000 cards. Producing a batch requires placing the production master on the printing press, setting the press for the appropriate paper size, and making other adjustments for colors and so forth. Following are facility-, product-, batch-, and unit-level cost information. Note: These terms are defined in Chapter 18.

Product design and production master per new card	$ 3,500
Batch setup (typically per 10,000 cards)	300
Materials per 1,000 cards	150
Conversion per 1,000 cards	200
Shipping (per batch)	15
Selling and administrative	
Companywide	306,000
Per product design marketed	675

Information from previous year:

Product designs and masters prepared for new cards	125
Product designs marketed	150
Batches manufactured	800
Cards manufactured and sold	8,000,000

REQUIRED

You may need to review materials in Chapter 16 to complete the requirements.

a. Describe how you would determine the cost of goods sold and the value of any ending inventory for financial reporting purposes. (No computations are required.)
b. You have just received an inquiry from **Walgreens** department stores to develop and manufacture 10 special designs for sale exclusively in Walgreens stores. The cards would be sold for $3.00 each, and Walgreens would pay Harman Greeting $0.70 per card. The initial order is for 30,000 cards of each design. If the cards sell well, Walgreens plans to place additional orders for these and other designs. Because of the preestablished sales relationship, no marketing costs would be associated with the cards sold to Walgreens. How would you evaluate the desirability of the Walgreens proposal?
c. Explain any differences between the costs considered in your answer to requirement (a) and the costs considered in your answer to requirement (b).

C17-54. Continue or Discontinue: Plantwide Overhead with Labor- and Machine-Intensive Operations **LO17-2, 3**

When Dart Products started operation five years ago, its only product was a radar detector known as the Bear Detector. The production system was simple, with Bear Detectors manually assembled from purchased components. With no ending work-in-process inventories, unit costs were calculated once a month by dividing current manufacturing costs by units produced.

Last year, Dart Products began to manufacture a second product, code-named the Lion Tamer. The production of Lion Tamers involves both machine-intensive fabrication and manual assembly. The introduction of the second product necessitated a change in the firm's simple accounting system. Dart Products now separately assigns direct material and direct labor costs to each product using information contained on materials requisitions and work tickets. Manufacturing overhead is accumulated in a single cost pool and assigned on the basis of direct labor hours, which is common to both products. Following are last year's financial results by product.

	Bear Detector		Lion Tamer	
Sales				
Units	7,500		3,000	
Dollars	$750,000		$450,000	
Cost of goods sold				
Direct materials	$165,000		$97,500	
Direct labor	281,250		90,000	
Applied overhead	393,750		126,000	
Total		(840,000)		(313,500)
Gross profit		$(90,000)		$136,500

Management is concerned about the mixed nature of last year's financial performance. It appears that the Lion Tamer is a roaring success. The only competition, the Nittney Company, has been selling a competing product for considerably more than Dart's Lion Tamer; this company is in financial difficulty and is likely to file for bankruptcy. The management of Dart Products attributes the Lion Tamer's success to excellent production management. Management is concerned, however, about the future of the Bear Detector and is likely to discontinue that product unless its profitability can be improved. You have been asked to help with this decision and have obtained the following information:
- The labor rate is $15 per hour.
- Dart has two separate production operations, fabrication and assembly. Bear Detectors undergo only assembly operations and require 2.5 assembly hours per unit. Lion Tamers undergo both fabrication and assembly and require 1.5 fabrication hours and 0.5 assembly hour per unit.
- The annual Fabricating Department overhead cost function is:

$$\$184{,}500 + \$6 \text{ (labor hours)}$$

- The annual Assembly Department overhead cost function is:

$$\$62{,}250 + \$12 \text{ (labor hours)}$$

REQUIRED

You may need to review materials in Chapters 15 and 16 to complete this case. Evaluate the profitability of Dart's two products and make any recommendations you believe appropriate.

C17-55. Absorption Costing and Performance Evaluation **LO17-5**

On July 2, Maddon Financial acquired 90% of the outstanding stock of Kluber Industries in exchange for 2,000 shares of its own stock. Maddon Financial has a reputation as a "high flier" company that commands a high price-to-earnings ratio because its management team works wonders in improving the performance of ailing companies.

At the time of the acquisition, Kluber was producing and selling at an annual rate of 100,000 units per year. This is in line with the firm's average annual activity. Fifty thousand units were produced and sold during the first half of the year.

Immediately after the acquisition Maddon Financial installed its own management team and increased production to practical capacity. One-hundred thousand units were produced during the second half of the year.

At the end of the year, the new management declared another dramatic turnaround and a $100,000 cash dividend when the following set of income statements was issued:

KLUBER INDUSTRIES
Income Statement
For the first and second half of the year

	First	Second	Total
Sales.	$2,800,000	$2,800,000	$5,600,000
Cost of goods sold*	(2,400,000)	(1,400,000)	(3,800,000)
Gross profit.	400,000	1,400,000	1,800,000
Selling and administrative expenses	(400,000)	(800,000)	(1,200,000)
Net income	$ 0	$ 600,000	$ 600,000

* Absorption costing with any underabsorbed or overabsorbed overhead written off as an adjustment to cost of goods sold. Kluber applies manufacturing overhead using a predetermined overhead rate based on predicted annual fixed overhead of $2,000,000 and annual production of 200,000 units.

REQUIRED

As the only representative of the minority interest on the board of directors, evaluate the performance of the new management team.

SOLUTIONS TO REVIEW PROBLEMS

Review 17-1—Solution

a. 1. **Office supplies inventory**

   Each of the organizations would likely maintain an office supplies inventory account in its accounting records. Samsung might include the term "office" in order to distinguish it from manufacturing supplies. Office supplies will typically be included in the balance sheet classification of "other current assets." As the office supplies are consumed, they will move to the income statement and be classified as supplies expense.

   2. **Merchandise inventory**

   Merchandise inventory is an inventory account in the current asset section of the balance sheet of a merchandising company like Walmart. As the inventory is sold, it moves to the income statement and is reported as a cost of goods sold expense.

   3. **Finished goods inventory**

   Finished goods inventory is an inventory account in the current asset section of the balance sheet of a manufacturer like Samsung. As the inventory is sold, it moves to the income statement and is reported as a cost of goods sold expense.

   4. **Work-in-process inventory**

   Work-in-process inventory is an inventory account in the current asset section of the balance sheet of a manufacturer like Samsung. As the work-in-process inventory is completed, it moves on to the finished goods inventory account in the current asset section of the balance sheet. Then, as discussed above, as the finished goods inventory is sold, it moves to the income statement and is reported as a cost of goods sold expense.

b. A manufacturer, such as Samsung, will distinguish between product and period costs. Samsung's product costs include costs of sales (direct materials, direct labor and overhead) and its period costs include selling and administrative expenses (salaries, commissions, depreciation, amortization, advertising, etc.).

Review 17-2—Solution

a. Predetermined overhead rate per machine hour = $40,000,000/3,200,000 = $12.50
b. Applied overhead = $12.50 × 410,000 = $5,125,000

c.
Actual overhead	$4,410,000
Applied overhead	(5,125,000)
Overapplied overhead for February	(715,000)
Underapplied overhead, February 1	400,000
Overapplied overhead, end of February	$ (315,000)

Intel allocated more overhead to products during the month than was actually incurred. As a result, the products will appear more costly than reality. During the year, this might even out because in later months, actual overhead may exceed applied overhead. It is not unusual for overhead costs to be incurred at different rates during the year.

Review 17-3—Solution

a. 1. Table Format

Work-in-Process		Finished Goods Inventory		Cost of Goods Sold	
Beg. Bal.	$15,550	Beg. Bal.	$ —	COGS	$48,150
Direct materials	35,000	Cost of goods manuf.	96,900		
Direct labor	48,500	Cost of goods sold	(48,150)		
Applied overhead	24,250	End. Bal.	$48,750		
Cost of goods manuf.	(96,900)				
End. Bal.	$26,400				

2. T-Account Format

Work-in-Process

Balance, June 1	15,550	96,900	Cost of Goods Manufactured in June
Direct materials	35,000		
Direct labor	48,500		
Applied overhead	24,250		
Balance, June 30	26,400		

Finished Goods Inventory

Balance, June 1	–0–	48,150	Cost of jobs sold in June
Cost of goods manufactured in June	96,900		
Balance, June 30	48,750		

Cost of Goods Sold

Cost of jobs sold in June	48,150	

b. Job in Work-in-Process at June 30:

	Job 228
Direct materials	$14,400
Direct labor	8,000
Applied overhead (800 × $5)	4,000
Total	$26,400

Job in Finished Goods at June 30:

	Job 227
Direct materials	$18,000
Direct labor	20,500
Applied overhead (2,050 × $5)	10,250
Total	$48,750

Jobs sold in June:

	Job 225	Job 226	Total
Costs assigned from prior period	$13,750	$ 1,800	$15,550
June Costs: Direct materials	–0–	2,600	2,600
Direct labor	5,000	15,000	20,000
Applied overhead (500 & 1,500 × $5)	2,500	7,500	10,000
Total	$21,250	$26,900	$48,150

c. Statement of cost of goods manufactured for June:

INTEL, INC.
Statement of Cost of Goods Manufactured
June

Current manufacturing costs			
Cost of materials placed in production			
Raw materials, 6/1	$ 7,000 ^		
Purchases	40,000 ^		
Total available	47,000		
Raw materials, 6/30	(12,000)	$35,000 ^	
Direct labor		48,500	
Manufacturing overhead applied		24,250 *	$107,750
Work-in-process, 6/1			15,550 **
Total costs in process			123,300
Work-in-process, 6/30			(26,400)***
Cost of goods manufactured			$ 96,900

*Manufacturing Overhead Applied

Job 225:	500 hrs. × $5 =	$ 2,500
Job 226:	1,500 hrs. × $5 =	$ 7,500
Job 227:	2,050 hrs. × $5 =	$10,250
Job 228:	800 hrs. × $5 =	$ 4,000
		$24,250

**Work-in-process, 6/1

Job 225:	$13,750^
Job 226:	$ 1,800^
	$15,550

***Work-in-process, 6/30 (see part b.)

^ Given

Review 17-4—Solution

INTEL, INC.
Cost of Production Report
For the Year

Summary of units in process

Beginning	3,000,000
Units started	27,000,000
In process	30,000,000
Completed	(25,000,000)
Ending	5,000,000

Equivalent units in process	Materials	Conversion
Units completed	25,000,000	25,000,000
Plus equivalent units in ending inventory	5,000,000	1,500,000
Equivalent units in process	30,000,000	26,500,000

continued

continued from previous page

Total costs to be accounted for and cost per equivalent unit in process	Materials	Conversion	Total
Work-in-Process, beginning	$ 468,000	$ 252,000	$ 720,000
Current cost	6,132,000	5,048,000	11,180,000
Total cost in process.	$ 6,600,000	$ 5,300,000	$11,900,000
Equivalent units in process.	÷ 30,000,000	÷26,500,000	
Cost per equivalent unit in process	$0.22	$0.20	$0.42
Accounting for total costs			
Transferred out (25,000,000 × $0.42).			$10,500,000
Work-in-Process, ending			
Materials (5,000,000 × $0.22).		$ 1,100,000	
Conversion (1,500,000 × $0.20).		300,000	1,400,000
Total cost accounted for			$11,900,000

Review 17-5—Solution

a.   Ending inventory = 100 beginning inventory + 500 produced − 540 sold = 60 units

    Absorption costing
       Direct materials ($250 × 60). $15,000
       Variable overhead ($220 × 60)   13,200
       Fixed overhead ($80 × 60)   4,800
       Total. $33,000

    Variable costing
       Direct materials ($250 × 60). $15,000
       Variable overhead ($220 × 60)   13,200
       Total. $28,200

b.   Absorption costing
      Beginning inventory . . . . $ 45,000
      Production
         Direct materials (500 × $250). $125,000
         Variable overhead (500 × $220) 110,000
         Fixed overhead (500 × $80)   40,000   275,000
      Goods available for sale   320,000
      Less ending inventory ($275,000/500 × 60)   33,000
      Cost of goods sold $287,000

    Variable costing
      Beginning inventory . . . . $ 38,000
      Production
         Direct materials (500 × $250). $125,000
         Variable overhead (500 × $220) 110,000   235,000
      Goods available for sale   273,000
      Less ending inventory ($235,000/500 × 60)   28,200
      Cost of goods sold $244,800

Chapter 18
Activity-Based Costing, Customer Profitability, and Activity-Based Management

LEARNING OBJECTIVES

LO18-1 Review the allocation of overhead to products using traditional plantwide and departmental overhead rates. (p. 18-3)

LO18-2 Explain the concept of activity-based costing. (p. 18-8)

LO18-3 Perform product costing using activity-based costing method. (p. 18-11)

LO18-4 Assess a move from traditional to activity-based costing and other activity-based costing implementation considerations. (p. 18-15)

LO18-5 Analyze customer profitability using activity-based costing. (p. 18-19)

LO18-6 Perform profitability analysis with activity-based cost drivers (Appendix 18A). (p. 18-22)

Road Map

LO	Learning Objective | Topics	Page	eLecture	Review	Assignments
LO18-1	**Review the allocation of overhead to products using traditional plantwide and departmental overhead rates.** Plantwide Overhead Rate :: Single Cost Pool :: Departmental Overhead Rates :: Multiple Cost Pools :: Cost Cross-Subsidization	18-3	e18–1	R18-1	M18-17, E18-23, E18-24, E18-25, E18-26, E18-27, E18-28, P18-34, P18-35, P18-36, P18-37, P18-38, C18-43, C18-44, C18-45, **DA18-1, DA18-2**
LO18-2	**Explain the concept of activity-based costing.** Unit-Level Activity :: Batch-Level Activity :: Product-Level Activity :: Facility-Level Activity :: Cost of Resources :: Activity Pools :: Cost Objects	18-8	e18–2	R18-2	M18-10, M18-11, M18-12, M18-13, E18-19, E18-20, E18-21, P18-37, P18-39, P18-40, C18-43, C18-44, C18-45, **DA18-1**
LO18-3	**Perform product costing using activity-based costing method.** Two-Stage, Activity-Based Cost Model :: Total Activity Cost :: Activity Cost Driver :: Unit Activity Rate :: Cost Cross-Subsidization	18-11	e18–3	R18-3	M18-15, M18-16, M18-17, E18-22, E18-24, E18-25, E18-26, E18-27, E18-28, P18-33, P18-34, P18-35, P18-36, P18-37, P18-38, P18-39, P18-40, C18-43, C18-44, C18-45, **DA18-1, DA18-2**
LO18-4	**Assess a move from traditional to activity-based costing and other activity-based costing implementation considerations.** Traditional vs. ABC Methods :: Limitations of ABC :: Implementation Challenges :: Time-Driven ABC :: Activity-Based Management	18-15	e18–4	R18-4	E18-27, E18-28, E18-28, P18-33, P18-34, P18-35, P18-36, P18-37, P18-38, P18-40, C18-43, C18-44, C18-45, **DA18-2**
LO18-5	**Analyze customer profitability using activity-based costing.** Customer Profitability Profile :: Customer Profitability Analysis	18-19	e18–5	R18-5	M18-14, M18-18, E18-26, E18-29, E18-30. P18-41
LO18-6	**Perform profitability analysis with activity-based cost drivers (Appendix 18A).** Profitability Analysis:: Multi-Level Contribution Income Statement :: Cost Hierarchy and Contribution Income Statement	18-22	e18–6	R18-6	E18-31, E18-32, P18-42

UNILEVER
www.unilever.com

Consider the Anglo-Dutch company **Unilever**, one of the largest fast-moving consumer goods (FMCG) companies in the world, focused on "making sustainable living commonplace." More than 3.4 billion people in approximately 190 countries use Unilever products each day. The company operates through three divisions. The largest (by revenue) is Beauty & Personal Care, followed by Foods & Refreshment, and then Home Care. Unilever's over 400 household brands include Ben & Jerry's, Dove Beauty Products, Vaseline, and Seventh Generation.

Overall, Unilever focuses on developing products that meet the consumer demand for more natural products and purpose-driven brands. In fact, one of its strategic goals is to create brands that can be seen as a force for good: brands that are associated with a mission, a purpose, and innovation. Its goal is to create value not only for its shareholders, but also for its employees, consumers, customers, suppliers, business partners, and society.

With more than 400 brands, many in the same product category, Unilever plans production and fulfillment in a way that minimizes its costs, by taking advantage of shared resources and economies of scale where possible. For example, Unilever produces many frozen dessert brands, including Ben and Jerry's, Magnum, and Breyer's Ice Cream. To assess the profitability of Ben and Jerry's Chocolate ice cream, it must determine the resources consumed in producing and distributing this particular type of ice cream. The allocation method derived must make intuitive sense. It must mirror (in a general way), the manufacturing process. How do you allocate the cost of a plant manager? What about the cost of the freezer truck? How many different cost pools should be used? For each cost pool, which cost driver best represents the manner in which resources are consumed?

When we break down costs and then allocate those costs to products or brands, we provide the basis by which a company such as Unilever can make broad strategic and operational changes to its business. This chapter will demonstrate how to develop and implement costing systems based on resource consumption, which provide more accurate cost information as the basis for decision-making.

Source: Company's website at www.unilever.com.

CHAPTER ORGANIZATION

Activity-Based Costing, Customer Profitability, and Activity-Based Management

Allocation of Overhead Using Traditional Costing Methods	Concepts Underlying Activity-Based Costing	Applying Activity-Based Costing	Considerations before Implementing Activity-Based Costing	ABC and Customer Profitability Analysis	Profitability Analysis with Activity-Based Drivers
• Applying Overhead with Plantwide Rate • Applying Overhead with Departmental Rates	• Hierarchy of Activity Costs • Summarizing Activity-Based Costing Concepts	• Illustrating the ABC Product Cost Model • Two-Stage, Activity-Based Allocation Process • Estimation of Product Costs	• Choosing between Traditional and Activity-Based Costing • Limitations of ABC System • Challenges of Implementing ABC System • Applications of ABC Systems • Activity-Based Management	• Customer Profitability Profile • ABC Customer Profitability Analysis Illustrated	• Multi-Level Contribution Income Statement • Variations in Multi-Level Contribution Income Statement (Appendix 18A)

ALLOCATION OF OVERHEAD USING TRADITIONAL COSTING METHODS

LO18-1
Review the allocation of overhead to products using traditional plantwide and departmental overhead rates.

What are appropriate prices for **Unilever**'s various products? What are the current resources that contribute to Unilever's costs? Does each resource and activity add value for Unilever's customers? Which customers contribute the most to Unilever's profitability, and which customers are unprofitable?

In a competitive business environment, it is imperative that a firm understands its costs in order to make good business decisions. It has become increasingly difficult to appropriately link overhead (indirect) costs to the products and services they support. Overhead costs have increased as a proportion of total product costs over time given the move toward shared services. This means that a growing pool of overhead costs must be allocated to products and services for the purpose of decision-making. In this section, we start with a review of the traditional costing model where overhead costs are allocated to products using (1) a plantwide predetermined overhead rate and (2) departmental predetermined overhead rates. In later sections, we will compare these traditional methods to an alternative costing method, *activity-based costing*.

Applying Overhead with a Plantwide Rate

In Chapter 17, we assumed that manufacturing overhead was allocated to products using a plantwide manufacturing overhead rate. It was assumed that, for example, each hour of labor worked on products caused manufacturing overhead to be incurred. In that case, all manufacturing costs were assumed to be driven by one factor, direct labor hours. To illustrate, assume that **Ben & Jerry's**, a division of **Unilever**, produces two ice cream products, Non-Dairy Cookie Dough and Frozen Yogurt (Fro-Yo) Cookie Dough. The Non-Dairy product has been facing intense competition from other producers in the ice cream market, as the demand for non-dairy substitutes has been increasing.

Each product is worked on in two departments, Blending and Packaging. Both Blending and Packaging operations are highly automated. In fact, the Packaging department is assumed to be fully automated, incurring only machine hours and no labor hours. As a result, the most common element of both products is machine hours in Blending and Packaging.

If you were to select one plantwide cost driver, what would it be given the information provided thus far for the Ben & Jerry's division?

Given that the Blending and Packaging operations are highly automated, a cost driver related to machine operations would likely show a causal relation to overhead costs. Without any additional information, a cost driver of machine hours appears to be a good option because it assigns more costs to products that spend more time in the machines.

The products are produced in large, 1,000-gallon batches. Assume the Non-Dairy ice cream requires 3 machine hours per batch and the Fro-Yo product requires 2 machine hours per batch. Suppose for July, 232 batches of Non-Dairy product and 400 batches of Fro-Yo product were produced, with expected total plantwide manufacturing overhead of $187,000 and 1,496 total machine hours. Assuming costs are allocated based on machine hours, the plantwide overhead rate for July is calculated as $125 per machine hour as follows.

Total plantwide manufacturing overhead	$187,000
Total plantwide machine hours	÷ 1,496
Plantwide overhead rate per machine hour	$ 125

Assigning $125 to each machine hour used is the simplest method of assigning manufacturing overhead to the products. Overhead is considered *one cost pool* and it is allocated using *one cost driver* as shown in **Exhibit 18.1**.

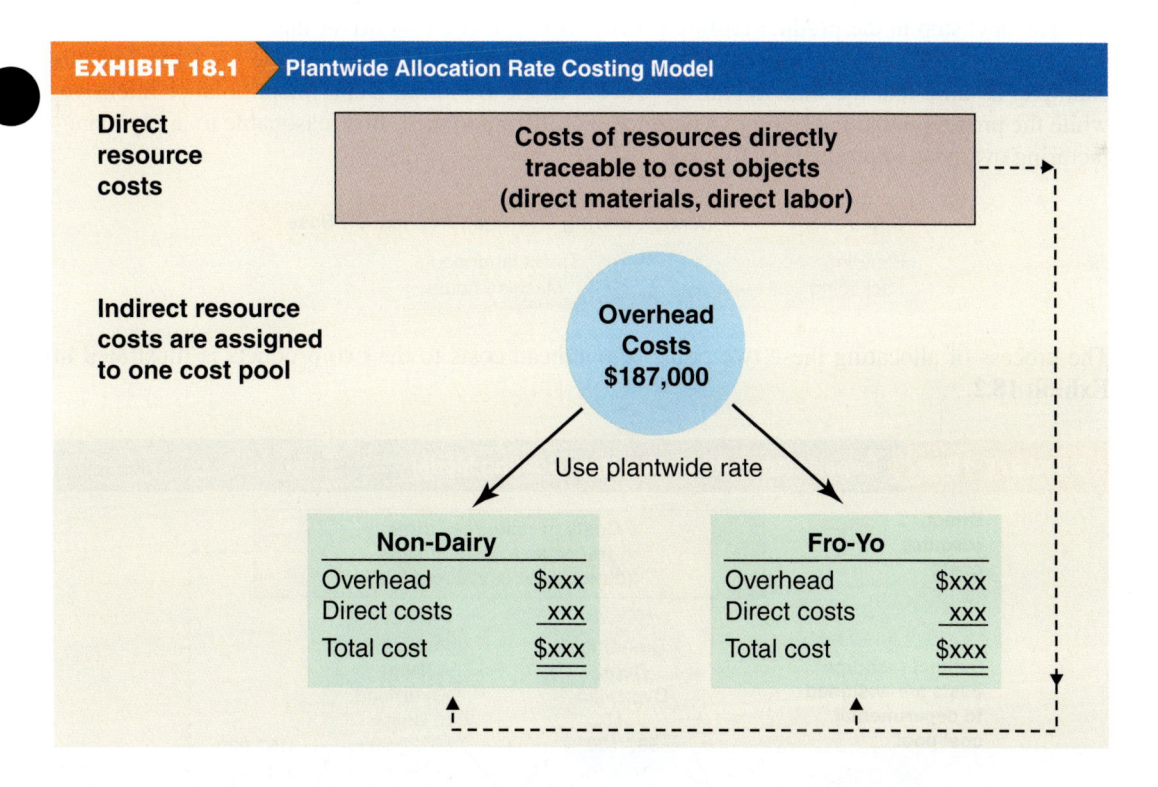

EXHIBIT 18.1 — Plantwide Allocation Rate Costing Model

Direct resource costs: Costs of resources directly traceable to cost objects (direct materials, direct labor)

Indirect resource costs are assigned to one cost pool: Overhead Costs $187,000

Use plantwide rate

Non-Dairy		Fro-Yo	
Overhead	$xxx	Overhead	$xxx
Direct costs	xxx	Direct costs	xxx
Total cost	$xxx	Total cost	$xxx

The allocation of overhead through a plantwide rate assumes that Blending and Packaging resources are consumed in proportion to the time spent in machinery. If this assumption is valid, this simple system will allocate costs in a reasonable way. Below is the calculation of costs for the Non-Dairy and Fro-Yo products using the current system. Note that the Non-Dairy product will be assigned overhead based on 3 machine hours of usage at $125 per hour (i.e., $375), and Fro-Yo will be assigned overhead based on 2 machine hours of usage at $125 per hour (i.e., $250). Under the current system, assuming the direct materials and direct labor usage presented below, the total cost per batch of Non-Dairy is $610 and the total cost per batch of Fro-Yo is $400.

	Cost per Batch	
	Non-Dairy	Fro-Yo
Direct materials.	$125	$120
Direct labor.	110	30
Manufacturing overhead		
Non-Dairy: 3 machine hours × $125.	375	
Fro-Yo: 2 machine hours × $125.		250
Total cost per batch	$610	$400

A plantwide overhead allocation method is often used in situations where companies produce only one product in a plant, or where multiple products are very similar in regard to the cost and use of resources. If multiple products are produced that consume varying levels of resources in multiple production departments, departmental overhead allocation rates will produce a more accurate allocation of overhead costs to the various products.

Applying Overhead with Departmental Rates

For Ben & Jerry's to establish separate overhead allocation rates for each of its two production departments, it is first necessary to assign the $187,000 of total overhead costs for the plant to the two production departments. Some of the $187,000 is directly assignable to the departments. For example, the departmental supervisors' salaries could be directly assignable to the departments. Other manufacturing overhead costs, such as support costs for maintenance, payroll, and so forth, are allocated to the production departments. Assume that after these allocations, the total costs assigned to the departments are $59,100 for Blending and $127,900 for Packaging, which totals $187,000.

The next step in the product costing process is to select a cost driver that reflects the manner in which resources are consumed and then assign the departmental costs to the products. For this example, assume that the manufacturing process in the Blending Department is labor intensive, while the process in the Packaging Department is fully automated. It is reasonable to apply manufacturing overhead to products as follows.

Department	Manufacturing Overhead Application Base
Blending	Direct labor hours
Packaging	Machine hours

The process of allocating these two pools of overhead costs to the two products is illustrated in **Exhibit 18.2**.

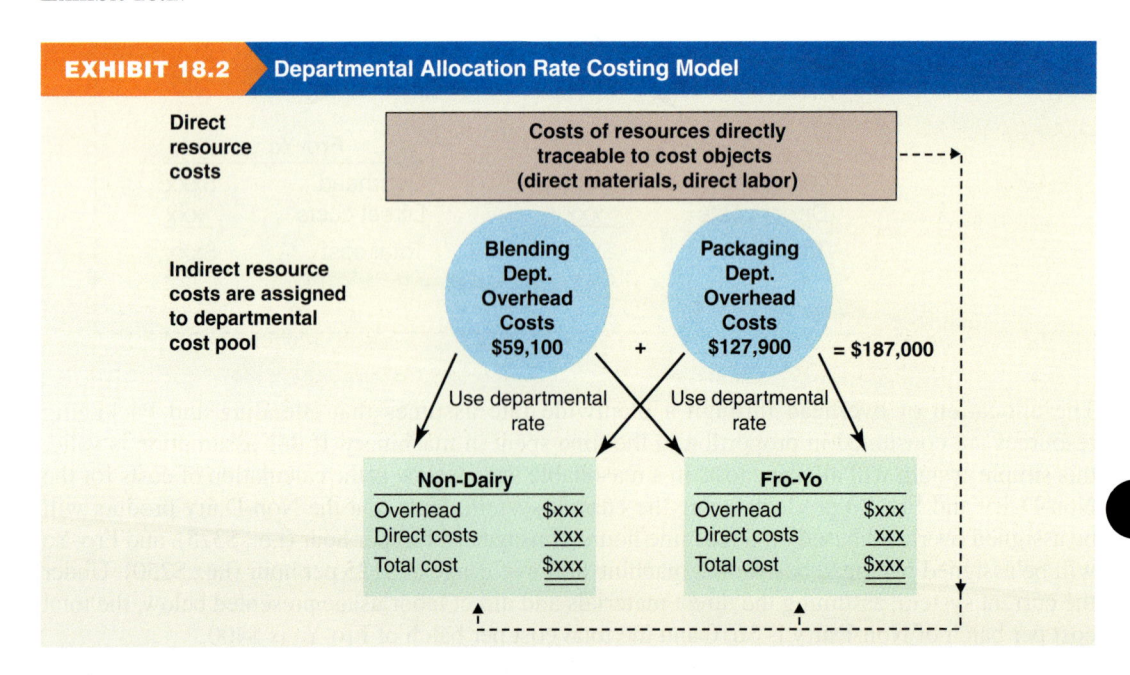

EXHIBIT 18.2 Departmental Allocation Rate Costing Model

Direct resource costs: Costs of resources directly traceable to cost objects (direct materials, direct labor)

Indirect resource costs are assigned to departmental cost pool:
Blending Dept. Overhead Costs $59,100 + Packaging Dept. Overhead Costs $127,900 = $187,000

Use departmental rate

Non-Dairy		Fro-Yo	
Overhead	$xxx	Overhead	$xxx
Direct costs	xxx	Direct costs	xxx
Total cost	$xxx	Total cost	$xxx

During the month of July, 500 direct labor hours are expected to be worked in Blending, and 800 machine hours are expected to be used in Packaging. Using these amounts, the departmental overhead rates for July are calculated as follows.

Department manufacturing overhead rates for July	Blending	Packaging
Total department manufacturing overhead (direct plus allocated department costs)	$59,100	$127,900
Quantity of overhead application base		
Direct labor hours	÷ 500	
Machine hours		÷ 800
Department manufacturing overhead rates	$118.20	$159.875
	Per direct labor hour	Per machine hour

Next assume the following direct labor and machine hours per batch were incurred for the month of July for the two products as follows.

	Non-Dairy	Fro-Yo
Blending		
Machine hours per batch	2.00	0.58
Direct labor hours per batch	1.00	0.67
Packaging		
Machine hours per batch	1.00	1.42

Using the same direct costs from the previous example and applying overhead using departmental rates, the total cost per batch of Non-Dairy is $513 and the total cost per batch of Fro-Yo is $456.

	Cost per Batch	
Total costs per batch for July using department rates	Non-Dairy	Fro-Yo
Direct materials	$125	$120
Direct labor	110	30
Manufacturing overhead		
Blending: 1.00 labor hour × $118.20	118	
0.67 labor hours × $118.20		79
Packaging: 1.00 machine hour × $159.875	160	
1.42 machine hours × $159.875		227
Total cost per batch	$513	$456

Allocating manufacturing overhead costs based on departmental rates (rather than on a plant-wide rate of $125 per machine hour) causes a shift in costs from Non-Dairy (decreases from $610 to $513 per batch) to Fro-Yo (increases from $400 to $456 per batch).

Why do you think the cost of Non-Dairy decreases while the cost of Fro-Yo increases with the change in cost system?

*Recall from Chapter 17 that adding a cost pool will make a difference in unit costs if there is **heterogeneity in cost** (resources used in the manufacturing process cost different amounts) and there is **heterogeneity in use** (different products use different resources). Both are true in this case: Fro-Yo uses more Packaging resources and less Blending resources and the resources cost different amounts per batch. Because the resources cost a different amount, the product that uses more expensive resources will be allocated more costs when using departmental rates. Although Fro-Yo uses less overall machine hours, it uses more machine hours in the more costly department of Packaging. Therefore, using departmental rates, Fro-Yo is allocated more packaging costs consistent with its use of more packaging resources.*

Critical Thinking & Decision-Making

Assume that a competitor offered to sell a competing product to one of Ben & Jerry's current Non-Dairy customers for $525. How does Ben & Jerry's cost system potentially affect any pricing decisions Ben & Jerry's makes based upon the competitive market place?

The per-batch costs with departmental overhead allocation rates are substantially different from the per-batch costs when using plantwide rates. In fact, the cost of Non-Dairy is slightly below the competitor's bid of $525 instead of being higher than the competitor's bid using plantwide overhead allocation. Ben & Jerry's could potentially lose a customer if its selling price of the Non-Dairy was calculated using the $610 amount as a starting point (before markup). This illustrates how crucial the cost system is to the decision-making process.

By creating separate manufacturing overhead cost allocation pools, allocation bases, and overhead application rates for Blending and Packaging, it is possible to recognize overhead cost differences in various products based on differences in Blending Department labor hours used and Packaging Department machine hours used for each product. In most multiproduct manufacturing environments, this approach represents a cost system improvement over using a single, plantwide overhead rate, and it reduces the likelihood of **cost cross-subsidization**, which occurs when one product is assigned too much cost as a result of another being assigned too little cost.

In the Ben & Jerry's hypothetical example, we see that departmental overhead rates provide more accurate costing than plantwide overhead rates. Will it be beneficial to further break down overhead cost pools into more overhead pools with more cost drivers?

We could continue to break down the overhead cost pools into multiple cost pools if it results in more accurate and decision-useful information. For example, if one machine is used selectively and is very expensive to operate, the machine might be its own overhead cost pool. However, judgment is required to determine how sophisticated a system should be based on the cost of monitoring and using the system vs. the benefits (e.g., better decision-making) derived. Adding more cost pools does not come without a price—identifying cost pools, tracking cost pools, tracking cost drivers, and allocating overhead for multiple pools requires company resources. This means that if a plantwide overhead rate provides sufficient information for decision-making, a company may opt to use a plantwide rate even if it is less accurate.

Multiple overhead rates may improve product costing results for many organizations by better reflecting how costs are consumed, and in fact may be satisfactory. However, this method does not attempt to reflect the actual activities used in producing the different products which can provide additional information for decision-making as discussed in the next section.

Review 18-1 LO18-1

Determining Product Costs Using Traditional Costing

Assume that Nestlé's Purina division has the following predicted indirect costs and cost driver for the year.

	Overhead Costs	Machine Hours
Formulation Department.....	$120,000	10,000
Packaging Department......	$ 55,000	5,000

Suppose Purina's divisional manager is trying to evaluate the company's product mix strategy regarding two of its dog foods, Dog Chow and Purina One. The company has been using a plantwide overhead rate based on machine hours but is considering switching to departmental rates. The production manager has provided the following data for the production of a batch of 100 cases (i.e., 12 bags) for each of these models.

continued

continued from previous page

	Dog Chow	Purina One
Direct materials cost	$12,000	$18,000
Direct labor cost	$5,000	$4,000
Machine hours (Formulation)	500	700
Machine hours (Packaging)	200	100

Required
a. Determine the cost of one case each of Dog Chow and Purina One, assuming a plantwide overhead rate is used based on total machine hours.
b. Determine the cost of one case of Dog Chow and Purina One, assuming departmental overhead rates are used. Overhead is assigned based on machine hours in both departments.

Solution on p. 18-46.

CONCEPTS UNDERLYING ACTIVITY-BASED COSTING

If overhead costs are low in comparison to other costs and if factories produce few products in large production runs, the use of an overhead rate based on direct labor hours or machine hours may be adequate. However, with large overhead cost pools, more varied products, and increased competition, a traditional, unit-based costing system might not adequately reflect how resources are consumed.

Activity-based costing (ABC) involves determining the cost of activities and tracing their costs to cost objects on the basis of the cost object's utilization of units of activity. Activities can be thought of as specific units of work performed, that consume costly resources as part of the production or service process. The cost driver relates to the performance of activities; it reflects how costs are consumed. Typically, we think of activities in terms of actions. For **Ben & Jerry's**, the activities might include placing orders for ingredients, receiving the ingredients, and moving the ingredients to the mixing machines. Of course, figuring out the activities (cost pools) and selecting an appropriate cost driver is not an easy task.

Hierarchy of Activity Costs

The ABC framework was developed by Cooper and Cooper and Kaplan.[1,2] Although it was originally applied to primarily manufacturing situations, it is now used in every industry including service and not-for-profit.

Hierarchy of Costs for Manufacturers When using ABC in a manufacturing setting, activities are initially classified into four categories.

1. A **unit-level activity** is performed for each unit of product produced. Adding labeling to each individual carton of Ben & Jerry's Non-Dairy product is considered a unit-level activity. The associated cost driver selected might even be the number of units if each unit consumes an equal amount of resources.

2. A **batch-level activity** is performed for each batch of product produced. A batch is a number of identical units produced at the same time. At Ben & Jerry's, batch-level activities include setting up the machines to mix the ingredients in an identical manner, moving the entire batch between workstations (i.e., mixing, bottling, labeling, and shipping), and inspecting the first unit in the batch to verify that the machines are set up correctly. These costs occur when a new batch is initiated. Thus, the selected cost driver might be the number of batches.

3. A **product-level activity** is performed to support the production of each different type of product. At Ben & Jerry's, product-level activities for a specific type of Non-Dairy product include initially deriving the recipe, producing and maintaining the exact ingredients and proportions, and determining manufacturing operations for the specific flavor. The product-level activities occur once for every type of Non-Dairy product. Consequently, the variety, or number of different flavors might be an appropriate cost driver.

---
[1] Robin Cooper, "Cost Classification in Unit-Based and Activity-Based Manufacturing Cost Systems," *Journal of Cost Management*, Fall 1990, pp. 4–14.
[2] Robin Cooper and Robert S. Kaplan, "Profit Priorities from Activity-Based Costing," *Harvard Business Review*, May–June 1991, pp. 130–135.

4. A **facility-level activity** is performed to maintain general manufacturing capabilities. At Ben & Jerry's, facility-level activities include plant management, building maintenance, property taxes, and electricity required to sustain the manufacturing plant. Facility costs occur at a higher level. These might be allocated to products or left at an administrative level.

Several additional examples of the costs driven by activities at each level are presented in **Exhibit 18.3**.

EXHIBIT 18.3 — Hierarchy of Activity Costs

Activity Level	Reason for Activity	Examples of Activity Cost
1. Unit level	Performed for each unit of product produced or sold	• Cost of raw materials • Cost of inserting a component • Utilities cost of operating equipment • Some costs of packaging • Sales commissions
2. Batch level	Performed for each batch of product produced or sold	• Cost of processing sales order • Cost of issuing and tracking work order • Cost of equipment setup • Cost of moving batch between workstations • Cost of inspection (assuming same number of units inspected in each batch)
3. Product level	Performed to support each different product that can be produced	• Cost of product development • Cost of product marketing such as advertising • Cost of specialized equipment • Cost of maintaining specialized equipment
4. Facility level	Performed to maintain general manufacturing capabilities	• Cost of maintaining general facilities such as buildings and grounds • Cost of nonspecialized equipment • Cost of maintaining nonspecialized equipment • Cost of real property taxes • Cost of general advertising • Cost of general administration such as the plant manager's salary

When using a cost hierarchy for analyzing and estimating costs, total costs are broken down into the different cost levels in the hierarchy, and a separate cost driver is determined for each level of cost. For example, using the above hierarchy, the costs that are related to the number of units produced (such as direct materials or direct labor) may have direct labor hours or machine hours as the cost driver. On the other hand, batch costs may be driven by the number of setups of production machines, or the number of times materials are moved from one machine to another. Other costs may be driven by the number of different products produced. Facility-level costs are generally regarded as fixed costs and do not vary unless capacity is increased or decreased.

The manufacturing hierarchy presented is but one of many possible ways of classifying activities and their costs. Classification schemes should be designed to fit the organization and meet user needs.

Hierarchy of Costs for Merchandisers or Sales Divisions A merchandising organization or the sales division of a manufacturing organization might use the following hierarchy.

1. **Unit-level activity**: performed for each unit sold.
2. **Order-level activity**: performed for each sales order.
3. **Customer-level activity**: performed to obtain or maintain each customer.
4. **Facility-level activity**: performed to maintain the general sales or store function.

This classification scheme assists in answering questions concerning the cost of individual orders or individual customers.

Hierarchy of Costs for Sellers to Distinct Market Segments If an organization sells to distinct market segments (for profit, not for profit, and government), the cost hierarchy can be modified as follows.

1. Unit-level activity
2. Order-level activity
3. Customer-level activity
4. **Market-segment-level activity**: performed to obtain or maintain operations in a segment.
5. Facility-level activity

The market-segment-level activities and their related costs differ with each market segment. This classification scheme assists in answering questions concerning the profitability of each segment.

Hierarchy of Costs for Sellers of Unique Projects Finally, an organization that completes unique projects for different market segments (such as buildings for **IBM** and the **U.S. Department of Defense**) can use the following hierarchy to determine the profitability of each segment.

1. **Project-level activity**: performed to support the completion of each project.
2. Market-segment-level activity
3. Facility-level activity

The possibilities are endless. The important point is that both the cost hierarchy and the costs included in the hierarchy should be tailored to meet the specific circumstances of an organization and the interests of management.

Summarizing Activity-Based Costing Concepts

Once the activities are identified, the costs of the activities can be assigned to cost objects. This process is summarized in the following two statements and illustrations.

1. Activities performed to fill customer needs consume resources that cost money.

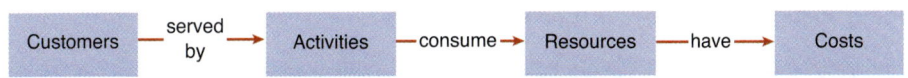

   Customers —served by→ Activities —consume→ Resources —have→ Costs

2. The cost of resources consumed by activities should be assigned to cost objects on the basis of the units of activity consumed by the cost object.

   Costs of Resources —assigned to→ Activity Pools —reassigned to*→ Cost Objects

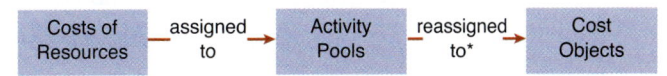

   *Based on units of activity utilized by the cost object.

The cost object is typically a product or service provided to a customer. Depending on the information needs of decision makers, the cost object might even be the customer as we will discuss later in this chapter.

To summarize, activity-based costing is a system of analysis that identifies and measures the cost of key activities, and then traces these activity costs to products or other cost objects based on the quantity of activity consumed by the cost objects. ABC is based on the premise that activities drive costs and that costs should be assigned to products (or other cost objects) in proportion to the volume of activities they consume. The key insight is that not all costs are unit-based. Each cost pool should be classified at its appropriate cost level in the cost system. Although activity cost analysis is most often associated with product costing, it offers many benefits for controlling and managing costs, as we will see later in this chapter.

Identifying Relevant Cost Drivers

LO18-2 **Review 18-2**

Nestlé has produced over 2,000 brands in categories including baby food, cereals, drinks, and petcare. The baby food category includes Gerber, a trusted name in baby wellness since 1927, and Cerelac, instant, easy-to-digest cereals produced since 1949. Suppose these two products are produced in one factory. Each time the production line produces a line/flavor of food, the production line must be set up according to the specs. The production run is then started. Once the ingredients are mixed, the food must be packaged. The packaging machine is programmed to run based on the number of units; more units require more packaging resources. For each production run, the quality assurance team tests a percentage of the units produced. After passing the quality inspection, the packaged food is sent to the shipping department. The entire production run is loaded onto trucks. Although larger runs might take longer to load, the difference in timing is negligible.

continued

continued from previous page

Required
Below is a list of activities performed in the production process for Nestlé. Determine an appropriate cost driver that might be used for each activity.

Activities
_____ 1. Production line setup
_____ 2. Food production
_____ 3. Food packaging
_____ 4. Quality testing
_____ 5. Shipping

Solution on p. 18-47.

APPLYING ACTIVITY-BASED COSTING

LO18-3 Perform product costing using activity-based costing.

As illustrated in an earlier section, traditional costing considers the cost of a product to be its direct costs for materials and labor plus some allocated portion of manufacturing overhead, using overhead rates typically based on direct labor or machine hours (i.e., unit level drivers). Activity-based costing is based on the notion that companies incur costs because of the activities they conduct in pursuit of their goals and objectives, and these activities are not necessarily unit-based. For example, various activities take place to produce a particular product, such as setting up, maintaining or monitoring the machines to make the product, physically moving raw materials and work in process, and so forth. Each of these activities has a cost; therefore, the total cost of producing a product using ABC is the sum of the direct materials and direct labor costs of that product, plus the cost of other activities conducted to produce that product.

Illustrating the ABC Product Cost Model

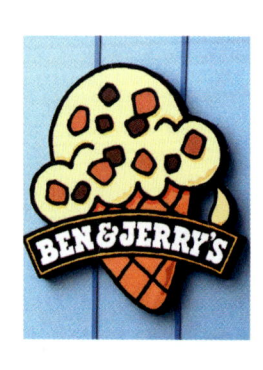

Continuing with the Ben & Jerry's hypothetical example, Blending and Packaging have overhead costs of $59,100 and $127,900, respectively. Overhead costs in the Blending and Packaging departments consist of two types of costs: direct department costs and allocated costs from other support departments. *Direct department overhead costs* are costs that are incurred directly by the department such as supervisory wages. *Allocated support costs* are costs allocated from other departments (specifically, support services, engineering, and buildings and grounds) that provide services to both Blending and Packaging.

- **Direct Department Overhead Costs** Assume that the direct department overhead costs in Blending of $25,000 were driven primarily by labor hours, whereas direct department overhead costs in Packaging of $105,000 were driven primarily by machine hours.

- **Allocated Support Costs** It was also determined that each component of support services, engineering, and buildings and grounds represents a separate activity cost pool, and that these costs totaling $57,000 support both the Blending and Packaging Departments. Therefore, these costs should be assigned to the products based on specific cost drivers rather than a single department cost driver.

In total, $187,000 ($25,000 + $105,000 + $57,000) in costs still need to be allocated to products. The total overhead costs are not changing from our prior examples. All that changes at this point is the amount allocated to each product. These are only accounting changes. To change the total cost of $187,000, management must change the manner in which products are made or decrease the resources being used.

Two-Stage, Activity-Based Allocation Process

The two-stage ABC product cost model is illustrated in **Exhibit 18.4** for the example of Ben & Jerry's.

- **First Stage** The first stage includes the assignment of support costs (indirect resource costs) to activity cost pools. In this case there are six activity cost pools. Note that this is a complicated task. To identify the activities, and narrow them into relatively homogenous cost pools requires detailed analyses. Typically, the process begins with a thorough walk-through of the manufacturing process, from start to finish.

- **Second Stage** The second stage assigns those activity cost pools to products Non-Dairy and Fro-Yo.

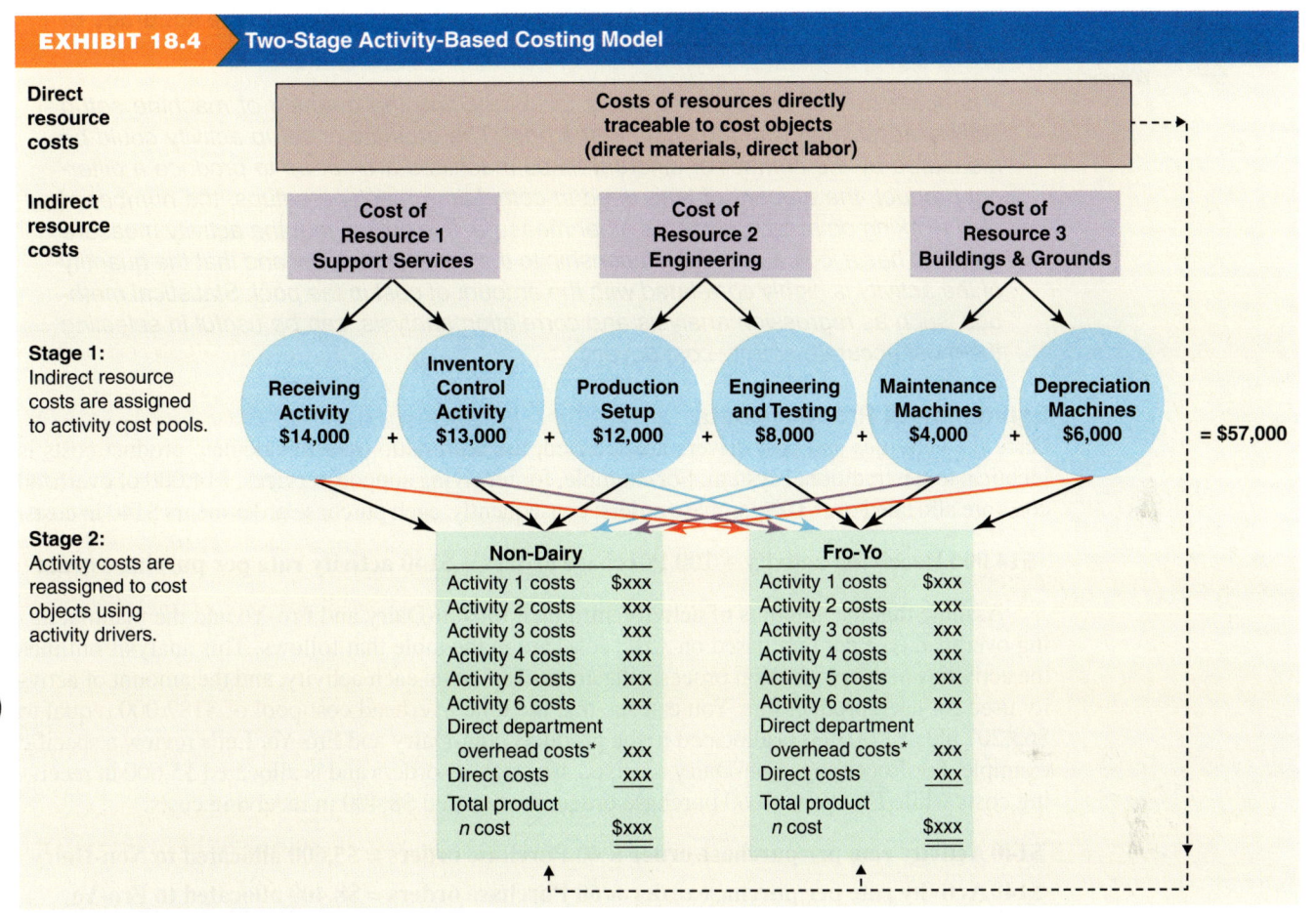

EXHIBIT 18.4 Two-Stage Activity-Based Costing Model

Direct resource costs: Costs of resources directly traceable to cost objects (direct materials, direct labor)

Indirect resource costs:
- Cost of Resource 1 — Support Services
- Cost of Resource 2 — Engineering
- Cost of Resource 3 — Buildings & Grounds

Stage 1: Indirect resource costs are assigned to activity cost pools.

Receiving Activity $14,000 + Inventory Control Activity $13,000 + Production Setup $12,000 + Engineering and Testing $8,000 + Maintenance Machines $4,000 + Depreciation Machines $6,000 = $57,000

Stage 2: Activity costs are reassigned to cost objects using activity drivers.

Non-Dairy		Fro-Yo	
Activity 1 costs	$xxx	Activity 1 costs	$xxx
Activity 2 costs	xxx	Activity 2 costs	xxx
Activity 3 costs	xxx	Activity 3 costs	xxx
Activity 4 costs	xxx	Activity 4 costs	xxx
Activity 5 costs	xxx	Activity 5 costs	xxx
Activity 6 costs	xxx	Activity 6 costs	xxx
Direct department overhead costs*	xxx	Direct department overhead costs*	xxx
Direct costs	xxx	Direct costs	xxx
Total product n cost	$xxx	Total product n cost	$xxx

*Direct department overhead costs are allocated to the two products in the same way as illustrated earlier in the chapter with multiple departmental rates.

Notice in **Exhibit 18.4** that direct product costs, such as direct materials and direct labor, are directly assigned to products and are excluded from the activity cost pools. Direct department overhead costs are allocated based on department rates and are also excluded from the activity cost pools. The remaining indirect product costs are assigned to products via six activity cost pools.

The following is a detailed analysis of overhead cost data and cost drivers for July's operations.

Overhead Activity	Total Activity Cost	Activity Cost Driver	Quantity of Activity	Unit Activity Rates
Direct departmental overhead costs				
Blending	$ 25,000	Labor hours	500	$ 50.000
Packaging	105,000	Machine hours	800	131.250
Common overhead costs				
Support Services				
Receiving	14,000	Purchase orders	100	140.000
Inventory control	13,000	Units produced	632	20.570
Engineering Resources				
Production setup	12,000	Production runs	20	600.000
Engineering and testing	8,000	Machine hours	1,496	5.348
Building and Grounds				
Maintenance, machines	4,000	Machine hours	1,496	2.674
Depreciation, machines	6,000	Units produced	632	9.494
Total	$187,000			

The most critical step in ABC is identifying activities and determining cost drivers. The activity cost driver for a particular cost (or cost pool) is the characteristic selected for measuring the quantity of the activity for a particular period of time.

> **Critical Thinking & Decision-Making**
>
> **Assume Ben & Jerry's establishes an activity cost pool for machine setups. What are possible cost drivers for this cost pool and how could the accuracy of the cost drivers be verified?**
>
> *It is necessary to select some basis for measuring the quantity of machine setup activity associated with the costs in the pool. The quantity of setup activity could be measured by the number of different times machines are set up to produce a different product, the amount of time used in completing machine setups, the number of staff working on setups, or some other measure. It is critical that the activity measure selected has a logical, causal relationship to the costs in the pool and that the quantity of the activity is highly correlated with the amount of cost in the pool. Statistical methods, such as regression analysis and correlation analysis, can be useful in selecting the most accurate activity cost drivers.*

Estimation of Product Costs

Once the activities and cost drivers are selected, the arithmetic used to calculate product costs is identical to the traditional system. For example, for receiving support services, $14,000 of overhead costs are allocated over 100 purchase orders; consequently, each purchase order incurs $140 in costs.

$14,000 Receiving activity ÷ 100 Purchase orders = $140 activity rate per purchase order

Assume that the amounts of activity attributed to Non-Dairy and Fro-Yo and the manufacturing overhead cost per unit based on ABC costs are in the table that follows. This analysis outlines the activities in the production process, the amount spent on each activity, and the amount of activity used for each product line. You can see that the total overhead cost pool of $187,000 (equal to $63,207 plus $123,793) is allocated to the products Non-Dairy and Fro-Yo. Let's review a specific example. For Receiving, Non-Dairy received 40 purchase orders and is allocated $5,600 in receiving costs while Fro-Yo with 60 purchase orders is allocated $8,400 in receiving costs.

$140 Activity rate per purchase order × 40 Purchase orders = $5,600 allocated to Non-Dairy
$140 Activity rate per purchase order × 60 Purchase orders = $8,400 allocated to Fro-Yo

	Non-Dairy		Fro-Yo	
Activity (cost per unit of driver activity)	Quantity of Activity	Cost of Activity	Quantity of Activity	Cost of Activity
Blending ($50.00 per labor hour)	232	$11,600	268	$ 13,400
Packaging ($131.25 per machine hour)	232	30,450	568	74,550
Receiving ($140.00 per order)	40	5,600	60	8,400
Inventory control ($20.57 per batch produced)	232	4,772	400	8,228
Production setup ($600.00 per run)	5	3,000	15	9,000
Engineering and testing ($5.348 per machine hour)	696	3,722	800	4,278
Maintenance, machines ($2.674 per machine hour)	696	1,861	800	2,139
Depreciation, machines ($9.494 per batch produced)	232	2,202	400	3,798
Total manufacturing overhead product cost		$63,207		$123,793
Batches produced		÷ 232		÷ 400
Manufacturing overhead cost per batch of product		$ 272		$ 309
Direct materials cost per batch of product		125		120
Direct labor cost per batch of product		110		30
Total cost per batch using ABC		$ 507		$ 459

> **Critical Thinking & Decision-Making**
>
> **As a manager reviewing the information in the table above, how might the data on production setup affect your decisions regarding cost control?**

The data indicates that it costs $600 to set up the machines for each production run. Due to the high cost, it might be beneficial to combine some production runs or minimize the amount of time spent setting up production. The ABC information offers managers better insight into what is driving costs.

The following table summarizes the total product costs for Ben and Jerry's two products using the three different overhead cost assignment methods.

	Non-Dairy	Fro-Yo
Plantwide overhead rate	$610	$400
Departmental overhead rates	513	456
ABC	507	459

Cost cross-subsidization ABC often reveals product cross-subsidization problems. This is when ABC produces costs for some products that are higher, and costs for other products that are lower, than costs produced by traditional costing methods. For example, the cost of Fro-Yo (Non-Dairy) is higher (lower) under ABC than under traditional costing. Failing to assign and allocate costs by activity results in Non-Dairy subsidizing Fro-Yo. This can lead to ineffective business decisions such as product pricing decisions. With an actual per-batch cost for Non-Dairy of $507, rather than $513 or $610, the company has more latitude to compete on price with other companies in its competitive market and remain profitable. Inaccurate costing can affect management's assessment of product profitability and its decisions regarding which products to continue to produce and which products to discontinue. Flawed product costing information can cause management mistakenly to decide to keep products that are losing money and discontinue products that are profitable. Using a plantwide or departmental overhead allocation method could have led Ben & Jerry's management to shift its emphasis from the Non-Dairy to the Fro-Yo market, a decision that could have been a poor decision for the company.

Can you think of a reason to maintain products that have a high cost to produce and must be sold at a slim (or negative) margin?

There are often strategic reasons to maintain products; the cost analysis does not provide the full picture. For example, the company may want to expand their customer base by attracting new customers with lower-priced items. If new customers become familiar with the company's product lines, perhaps they will buy other products with profitable margins. For example, grocery stores will often advertise items that are loss leaders in order to attract customers into their stores. Once in the store, the customers will likely purchase other items with profitable margins. Another reason to maintain low margin products is if these products have a social value. Companies might elect to offer such products at a low price to achieve a social mission.

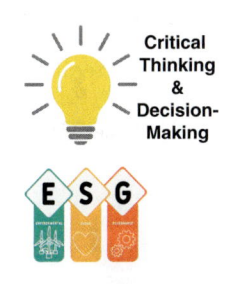

Determining Product Costs Using Activity-Based Costing — LO18-3 Review 18-3

Assume that **Nestlé**'s Purina division has the following predicted indirect costs and cost drivers for the year for the given activity cost pools.

	Formulation Department	Packaging Department	Cost Driver
Maintenance	$ 20,000	$10,000	Machine hours
Materials handling	30,000	15,000	Material moves
Machine setups	70,000	5,000	Machine setups
Inspections	—	25,000	Inspection hours
	$120,000	$55,000	

The following activity predictions were also made for the year.

continued

continued from previous page

	Formulation Department	Packaging Department
Machine hours	10,000	5,000
Materials moves	3,000	1,500
Machine setups	700	50
Inspection hours	—	1,000

It is assumed that the cost per unit of activity for a given activity does not vary between departments.

Suppose Purina's divisional manager is trying to evaluate the company's product mix strategy regarding two of its dog foods, Dog Chow and Purina One. The company has been using a plantwide overhead rate based on machine hours but is considering switching to activity-based rates. The production manager has provided the following data for the production of a batch of 100 cases (i.e., 12 bags) for each of these models.

	Dog Chow	Purina One
Direct materials cost	$12,000	$18,000
Direct labor cost	$5,000	$4,000
Machine hours (Formulation)	500	700
Machine hours (Packaging)	200	100
Materials moves	30	50
Machine setups	5	9
Inspection hours	30	60

Solution on p. 18-47. Determine the cost of one case of Dog Chow and Purina One, assuming activity-based overhead rates are used for maintenance, materials handling, machine setup, and inspection activities.

CONSIDERATIONS BEFORE IMPLEMENTING ACTIVITY-BASED COSTING

LO18-4
Assess a move from traditional to activity-based costing and other activity-based costing implementation considerations.

In previous sections, we examined traditional costing methods and the activity-based costing method. While the product costs may differ under different costing systems, what are other considerations for companies choosing to implement an activity-based costing system?

Choosing between Traditional and Activity-Based Costing

Procedurally, ABC is not a new method for assigning costs to cost objects. Traditional costing systems have used a two-stage allocation model (similar to the ABC model) to assign costs to cost pools (such as departments) and subsequently assign those cost pools to products using an allocation base. In most traditional costing systems, overhead is assigned to one or more cost pools based on departments and functional characteristics (such as labor-related, machine-related, and space-related costs) and then reassigned to products using a unit-level allocation base such as direct labor hours, direct labor dollars, or machine hours. ABC is different in that it divides the overall manufacturing processes into activities or steps. ABC accumulates costs in cost pools for the major activities and then assigns the costs of these activities to products or other cost objects that benefit from these activities. *Conceptually,* ABC is different because of the way it views the operations of the company; *procedurally,* it uses a methodology that has been around for a long time.

Challenges The challenge in using ABC is specifying the model; that is, determining how many activity pools should be established for a given cost measurement purpose, which costs should be assigned to each activity pool, and the appropriate activity driver to use in each pool. Specifying the model also includes determining the cost drivers for assigning indirect resource costs to the various activity cost pools.

Cost benefit analysis When evaluating whether to implement an ABC model, management must weigh the value of more accurate information against the administrative efforts of producing it. This can be complicated by the fact that it is often more difficult to measure the benefits of a process than it is to measure tangible costs. For example, how do we identify and measure *better decision-making*? Further, once a company makes the decision to implement an ABC system, it also needs to assess the level of accuracy it wants the system to provide. In his article, "Implementing

Activity-Based Costing," Gary Cokins emphasizes that the "quest for perfection is expensive," and that a reasonable level of accuracy might be sufficient.[3] The goal of the cost system is not to measure costs as accurately as possible; this is too expensive and potentially, not attainable. Rather, the goal of the cost system is to develop a relatively simple system that will be used by managers throughout the organization. The system should mimic the company's economic process at a high level, reflecting major resources and the costs of consuming these resources; it need not reflect every item individually. Remember, the goal is better decision-making, not perfect information.

Cost cross-subsidization The distortion in product costs or cost cross-subsidization for Ben & Jerry's from using traditional cost systems based on plantwide or departmental rates, while hypothetical, is not uncommon. Studies have shown that distortions of this type occur regularly in traditional systems in which a significant variation exists in the volume and complexity of products and services produced.[4] As companies evolve and become more sophisticated, management often forgets to update its cost system; consequently, the cost systems, and the information produced, become obsolete. Traditional systems tend to overcost high-volume, low-complexity products, and they tend to undercost low-volume, high-complexity products. These studies also indicate that the typical amount of overcosting is up to 200% for high-volume products with low complexity and that the typical undercosting can be more than 1,000% for low-volume, highly complex products. In companies with a large number of different products, traditional costing can show that most products are profitable. After changing to ABC, however, these companies might find that 10% to 15% of the products are profitable while the remainder are unprofitable. Adopting ABC often leads to increased profits merely by changing the product mix to minimize the number of unprofitable products.

Limitations of Activity-Based Costing System

Of course, ABC is more complicated than simply adding columns to a spreadsheet. The reality is that ABC adoption in the United States never reached predicted levels. Let's review some of the limitations of activity-based costing.

- **Full analysis includes nonmanufacturing costs** For the sake of simplicity, the Ben & Jerry's hypothetical example used in this chapter was limited to manufacturing cost considerations. A complete analysis would also require considerations of nonmanufacturing costs, such as marketing, distribution, and customer service, before a final determination of product profitability could be made.
- **Unit-based system is less complex** ABC will never be perfect, and many organizations find it difficult to determine the relation between how resources are consumed and the production output. It is sometimes easier to implement and explain a unit-based system.
- **Costs may not exceed benefits** The complexity of having numerous, complicated cost pools might not be worth it. ABC is most beneficial when large dollar amounts are at stake (coined the "Willie Sutton rule" by ABC creators). Organizations should not implement a sophisticated, costly system unless it will add new information and affect decisions.
- **New information may not add value** To the extent that products, customers, and/or processes are homogenous and similar, a sophisticated system will only add complexity without adding new information.
- **Improvements require real change** Remember that overhead is comprised of both variable and fixed costs. In most cases, overhead is dominated by fixed costs. Consequently, reductions in activities will not necessarily lead to lower costs. Managers will have to interpret the ABC information and make real changes (e.g., eliminating fixed resources) in order to lower costs.

Challenges of Implementing Activity-Based Costing System

Several challenges in the implementation of Activity-based costing are outlined as follows.

- **Management reporting system vs. Financial reporting system** Most companies initially do not abandon their traditional cost system and move to a system that uses ABC for management and

---
[3] Gary Cokins, "Implementing Activity-Based Costing" (Institute of Management Accountants, 2014).
[4] Gary Cokins, Alan Stratton, and Jack Helbling, *An ABC Manager's Primer* (Montvale, NJ: Institute of Management Accountants, 1993).

financial reporting purposes because financial statements must withstand the scrutiny of auditors and tax authorities. This scrutiny typically implies more demands on the cost accounting system for consistency, objectivity, and uniformity than required when the system is used only for management purposes.

Obtaining user buy-in ABC systems must be built facility by facility rather than being embedded in a software program that can be used by all facilities within the company.[5] The ABC system is more complicated and less standardized. Consequently, it can be difficult to get buy-in from groups that will either use the system or be evaluated based on the system (e.g., division profitability, production planning, etc.). Lack of buy-in to the system can halt it from being fully implemented and successful.

Choosing number of cost pools Although an ABC system may be complex, it merely mirrors the complexity of an organization's design, manufacturing, and distribution systems. If a firm's products are diverse and its production and distribution procedures complex, the ABC system will also be complex. However, if its products are homogeneous and its production environment relatively simple, its ABC system should also be relatively simple. Even in highly complex manufacturing environments, ABC systems usually have no more than 10 to 20 cost pools. Many ABC experts in practice have observed that creating a large number of activity cost pools for a given costing application normally does not significantly improve cost accuracy above that of a smaller number of cost pools.

Applications of Activity-Based Costing Systems

In addition to using ABC for product costing purposes, other important uses for ABC have also been found. One of the most useful applications for ABC discussed in the next section is in evaluating customer costs and distribution channel costs. Other applications include costing administrative functions such as processing accounts receivable or accounts payable; costing the process of hiring and training employees; and costing such menial tasks as processing emails. Any process, function, or activity performed in an organization, whether it is related to production, marketing and sales, finance and accounting, human resources, or even research and development, is a candidate for ABC analysis. In short, almost any cost object that has more than an insignificant amount of indirect costs can be more effectively measured using ABC. One refinement of ABC is using time as a cost driver in place of a complex system as described in the next section.

Time-Driven Activity-Based Costing

ABC's complexity is both a strength and a weakness. To successfully implement ABC, an organization must be able to model and measure its production process in great detail. In many industries, this is close to impossible and has hindered the implementation of ABC. Kaplan and his colleagues introduced a refinement to ABC, **Time-Driven Activity-Based Costing (TDABC)**.[6] Rather than defining complex sets of activities and their rates, TDABC uses historical data to estimate two relationships—the cost of each resource and the amount of time each unit or customer spends with each resource. For example, a hospital might characterize the patient and diagnoses as the unit of analysis. The system would calculate the cost of each resource used in treatment and the amount of time the patient spends with each resource.

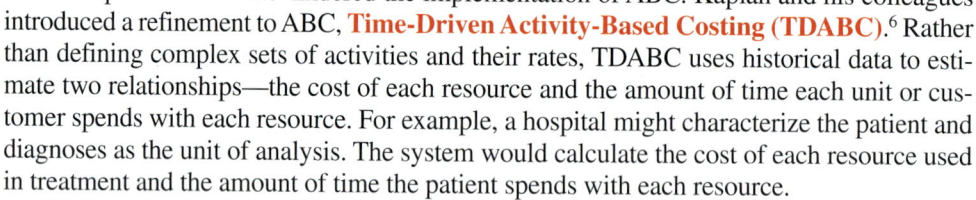

These estimated relationships allow hospitals and other organizations to implement ABC without fully characterizing their activities. In this way, the hospitals (or other organizations) can focus on the resources that are particularly costly or problematic. Using TDABC helps minimize the implementation issues discussed in this chapter while bringing some of the benefits of ABC to organizations.

In practice, the cost calculation within a TDABC system is similar to the ABC system. However, rather than selecting specific drivers for each activity, costs are measured for each unit of time. Suppose that Ben & Jerry's Blending department's capacity is 14,000 minutes during the month. The cost of operating the blending department is $25,000. With this information, we can calculate the capacity cost rate as $2.00 per minute as follows.

Capacity cost rate = $28,000 blending cost pool ÷ 14,000 minutes = $2.00 per minute

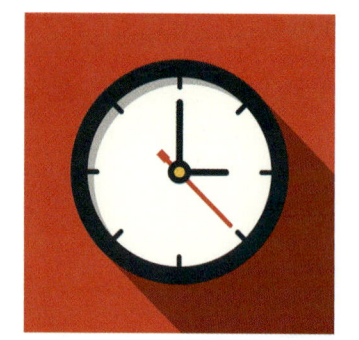

---
[5] Robert S. Kaplan and Robin Cooper, *Cost and Effect* (Boston: Harvard Business School Press, 1998), p. 105.
[6] Robert Kaplan and Michael Porter, "The Big Idea: How to Solve the Cost Crisis in Health Care," *Harvard Business Review*, September 2011.

This number represents the cost of each minute of task in the blending department. For each step in the blending process, Ben & Jerry's will calculate the cost driver based on how long the step takes. Suppose that the first step is to add ingredients to the machinery, and it takes 20 minutes to gather and add the ingredients each time a production run is initiated. Assuming there are 5 production runs for Non-Dairy and 15 production runs for Fro-Yo, assigned costs for adding ingredients costs would be calculated as follows.

$$\text{Non-Dairy: 5 production runs} \times 20 \text{ minutes} \times \$2.00 \text{ per minute} = \$200$$
$$\text{Fro-Yo: 15 production runs} \times 20 \text{ minutes} \times \$2.00 \text{ per minute} = \$600$$

The reports that are generated through a TDABC system are intuitive and useful to management. Rather than looking at activities with various drivers, everything is displayed in terms of minutes. In addition to the cost driver rate and the total cost assigned to the various products or services, managers will be able to identify the number of minutes spent on each of the various steps and the total number of minutes on the steps, by product and in total. Because everything is stated in units of time, managers can easily compare the efficiencies of the various tasks.

Activity-Based Management

In the early development of ABC, it was discovered that a by-product of accurately measuring costs using ABC is that management invariably gains a much better understanding of the processes and activities that are used to create products or services. Although ABC could be justified on the basis of its value as a tool in helping produce more accurate cost measurements for various cost objects, its *greatest potential value may be in its by-products*.

The access to ABC data enables managers to engage in **activity-based management (ABM)**, defined as the identification and selection of activities to maximize the value of the activities while minimizing their cost from the perspective of the final consumer. In other words, ABM is concerned with how to efficiently and effectively manage activities and processes to provide value to the final consumer. Defining processes and identifying key activities helps management better understand the business and to evaluate whether activities being performed add value to the customer. ABM focuses managerial attention on what is most important among the activities performed to create value for customers. This approach to viewing a product enables management to evaluate the importance of each of the activities consumed in making a product and the associated cost of the activity. Possibly some activities can be eliminated or a lower cost activity substituted for a more costly one without reducing the quality or performance of the product.

> **You have heard about companies that have adopted ABC and experienced significant differences in product costs compared with previous cost calculations using traditional costing methods. Consequently, you were surprised when your newly implemented ABC system provided product costs that were almost identical to those from the old costing system. You are, therefore, thinking about abandoning the ABC system, since it is quite costly to maintain. Should you abandon your ABC system?**
>
> *It may not be the right decision to abandon the ABC system because there are many benefits to using ABC other than just calculating product costs. Indeed, in cases where companies produce multiple products that are fairly homogeneous in terms of the use of resources, ABC may not produce more accurate costs than traditional methods. However, there are many uses of ABC information beyond just calculating the cost of products. Having detailed information about activities and their costs helps companies manage those activities. Identifying key activities and measuring their costs often cause companies to improve processes, outsource activities that are currently performed internally, and/ or eliminate unnecessary activities. Activity cost information can also be used to identify best practices within an organization, or to benchmark internal activity costs with other organizations.*

Review 18-4 LO18-4 — Comparing Product Costs Using Traditional and Activity-Based Costing

Guided Example — MBC

Refer to Review 18-1 and Review 18-3 to obtain unit product costs for Dog Chow and Purina One under the traditional and activity-based costing methods.

Required

Based on your calculations, compare and contrast the case costs of Dog Chow and Purina One using the plant-wide, department, and activity-based rates to assign manufacturing overhead.

Solution on p. 18-48.

ABC AND CUSTOMER PROFITABILITY ANALYSIS

LO18-5 Analyze customer profitability using activity-based costing.

eLecture — MBC

One of the most beneficial applications of activity-based costing is in the analysis of customer profitability. Companies that have a large number of diverse customers also usually have widely varied profits from serving those customers. Similar to products, some customers might demand lots of services while others are relatively easy to serve. Many companies never attempt to calculate the profit earned from individual customers. They merely assume that if they are selling products above their costs, and that overall the company is earning a profit, then each of the customers must be profitable. Unfortunately, the cost incurred to sell goods and provide services to individual customers is not usually proportionate with the gross profits generated by those sales. Customers with high sales volume are not necessarily the most profitable. Profitability of individual customers depends on whether the gross profits from sales to those customers exceed the customer-specific costs of serving those customers. Some customers are simply more costly than others, and some may even be unprofitable, and the unprofitable customers are eating away at the total profits of the company. In an ideal world, only profitable customers would be retained, and unprofitable customers would be either converted to a profitable status or they would be dropped as customers, unless there is a strategic reason for maintaining the relationship.

Customer Profitability Profile

If a company knows the amount of profits (or losses) generated by each of its customers, a **customer profitability profile** can be prepared similar to the one illustrated in **Exhibit 18.5**.

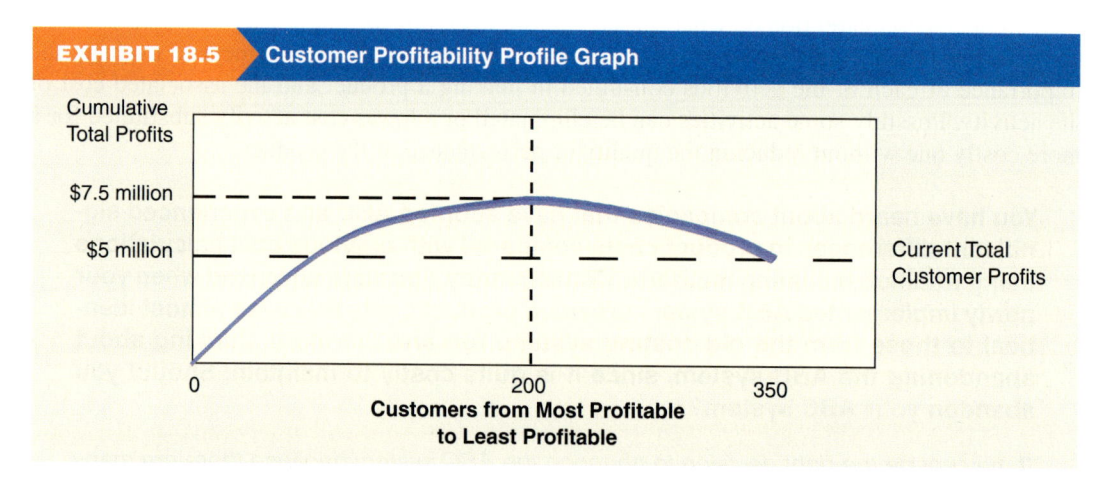

EXHIBIT 18.5 — Customer Profitability Profile Graph

A graph with "Cumulative Total Profits" on the y-axis and "Customers from Most Profitable to Least Profitable" on the x-axis. The curve rises from 0, peaks at $7.5 million at 200 customers, then declines to $5 million (Current Total Customer Profits) at 350 customers.

Suppose the local division of Ben & Jerry's has 350 customers and has current total profits of $5 million, but only 200 of its customers are profitable. Cumulative profits reach $7.5 million when the 200th customer is added to the graph, but the 201st through the 350th customers cause cumulative profits to decline to $5 million because they are unprofitable. Once a company has profitability data on each of its customers (or categories of customers), only then can it proceed to try to move them toward profitability, or seek to terminate the relationship with those customers. Just as we saw that ABC provided a model for producing more accurate product cost data, ABC is also a valuable tool for generating customer profitability data. ABC information offers insight into how to improve the customer relationships. For example, it might highlight the expensive ordering behavior of one of its customers. In this way, ABC helps create a path for improvement.

ABC Customer Profitability Analysis Illustrated

Let's assume that **Unilever** has built a solid and growing customer base, but it continues to invest significant time and expense servicing customers. Clients range from small clients ordering in small quantities to large conglomerates with sophisticated warehouses. Some customers require a lot of "hand-holding" with frequent visits, emails and calls. These customers tend to purchase frequently in small amounts, often requiring repackaging. Other customers require little attention and support, and many of them purchase in large amounts once a year.

Although the company is profitable, management believes that profits could be higher if sales and other customer-related costs could be decreased. Unilever's accountant has decided to conduct a customer profitability analysis using activity-based costing. As a first step, the accountant determined that there were five primary activities related to serving customers: visits to customers by sales representatives, remote contacts (phone, email), processing and shipping of customer orders, repackaging, and billing and collection. After extensive analysis, including numerous interviews and statistical analyses of activity and cost data, the accountant determined the following cost drivers and cost per unit of activity for the five customer-related activities.

Activity	Activity Cost Driver	Unit Activity Rate
Visits to customers	Visits	$800
Remote contacts	Number of contacts	75
Processing & shipping	Customer orders	450
Repackaging	Number of requests	250
Billing & collection	Invoices	90

After collecting activity driver data on each of these activities for its customers, the accounting group prepared the customer activity cost and profitability analysis presented in **Exhibit 18.6** for a sample of its customers (in terms of sales dollars) in the order of greatest to least profit for the most recent year. Note that the calculations are identical, in nature, to those performed when calculating the cost of products.

EXHIBIT 18.6 Unilever

Customer Activity Cost and Profitability Analysis

	Seattle Supplies & Food	NY Quick Market	Sensational Sundries	Gulf Coast Convenience	Consolidated Markets	Total
Customer Activity Cost Analysis						
Activity Cost Driver Data						
Visits to customers	3	5	4	1	1	
Remote contacts	5	7	8	2	3	
Processing & shipping	3	3	5	4	1	
Repackaging	0	2	3	0	0	
Billing & collection	3	3	5	4	1	
Customer Activity Cost						
Visits to customers	$ 2,400	$ 4,000	$ 3,200	$ 800	$ 800	
Remote contacts	375	525	600	150	225	
Processing & shipping	1,350	1,350	2,250	1,800	450	
Repackaging	0	500	750	0	0	
Billing & collection	270	270	450	360	90	
Total activity costs	$ 4,395	$ 6,645	$ 7,250	$ 3,110	$ 1,565	
Customer Profitability Analysis						
Customer sales	$17,500	$20,000	$12,000	$15,000	$16,250	$80,750
Less cost of goods sold	10,500	12,000	7,200	9,000	9,750	48,450
Gross profit on sales	7,000	8,000	4,800	6,000	6,500	32,300
Less activity costs	4,395	6,645	7,250	3,110	1,565	22,965
Customer profitability	$ 2,605	$ 1,355	$ (2,450)	$ 2,890	$ 4,935	$ 9,335
Customer profitability ratio*	14.9%	6.8%	(20.4%)	19.3%	30.4%	11.6%

* Customer profitability ÷ Sales

Analyzing Customer Profitability

Unilever's results show an overall 40% gross profit ratio (Gross profit of $32,300 divided by Sales of $80,750), and a combined net profitability of 11.6% of sales (Profit of $9,335 divided by Sales of $80,750). However, all customers are not equally profitable. The high level of support required by NY Quick Market and Sensational Sundries resulted in a net customer loss from sales to Sensational Sundries and only a 6.8% customer profitability ratio for NY Quick Market. Armed with the information in the customer activity cost and profitability analysis, Unilever can take proactive steps to increase its overall profitability ratio.

Drop a Customer   An obvious option would be to try to terminate its relationship with Sensational Sundries since the company is clearly losing money on that customer. Let's assume that Sensational Sundries was terminated as a customer, and that all of the cost of goods sold and activity costs associated with Sensational Sundries could be avoided by the termination. Unilever's total profit would increase to $11,785 resulting in a profitability ratio on the remaining four customers of 17.1%.

	Current Results	Sensational Sundries	Results After Dropping Customer
Sales	$80,750	$12,000	$68,750
Cost of goods sold	48,450	7,200	41,250
Activity costs	22,965	7,250	15,715
Customer profitability	$ 9,335	$ (2,450)	$11,785
Customer profitability ratio	11.6%	(20.4)%	17.1%

Reduce activity costs   A more proactive approach would be to focus efforts on reducing support activities without reducing customer sales. For example, Unilever could work to reduce high support activities of repackaging, frequent visits, and remote contacts at NY Quick Market and Sensational Sundries. This could result in maintaining the current level of gross profit, but generating a significantly higher level of total net customer profitability.

Charge for extra services   Another option would be to charge for the extra services demanded. Similar to the discussion about products subsidizing other products, Unilever might be in a situation where some customers are subsidizing other customers. In order to change behavior, Unilever could share the ABC information with its customers and begin charging for excess services. In this way, Unilever will maintain its relationships and customers can select which services are necessary.

Other considerations   Two caveats should be considered when using activity cost data to manage customer profitability. First, there may be justifiable reasons (such as having a new customer that requires a high level of early-stage support, trying to penetrate a new geographic market, or existing relationships with other more profitable customers) for keeping customers that have lower profitability, or even customers that are not profitable. If so, these customers should be managed intensely to attempt to reduce the activities devoted to their support. Another caveat is that eliminating a customer may not immediately translate into an immediate reduction of activity costs. Some activity costs may not have a variable cost behavior pattern, and eliminating customers may merely create excess capacity in the short term. Managers must then work to either fill the capacity with other business or eliminate the excess capacity. Of course, these decisions should not be made in a vacuum. These decisions require conversations across many departments, using the information from the ABC system as one input into the conversation. Customer profitability analysis is increasing in use across organizations. Banks were an early adopter, calculating the cost of customers and the pricing structure. This analysis detailed the cost related to customers who do business with tellers in a branch vs. those who banked fully online. Many fee structures exist based on these analyses.

Critical Thinking & Decision-Making

Changes in distribution have altered the business model and cost structure of the software industry. Software used to be distributed by physical discs, in a standardized process. With the rise of the internet and cloud-based computing, the software industry's business model is rapidly changing. Oracle switched its business from traditional software-as-product to software-as-service and platform-as-service. Cloud-based and license support service business now represents the majority of Oracle's revenues. Would ABC and customer profitability analysis be beneficial to Oracle?

In the new offerings, Oracle provides both the products as well as hardware and networking support on a subscription basis. Because each customer has different service needs and different demand for storage and support, it could be helpful to determine the drivers of customer profitability. ABC is particularly useful in this situation where the units sold offer an incomplete picture of the costs of serving the client.

Analyzing Customer Profitability LO18-5 **Review 18-5**

Suppose **Nestlé** offers customized display delivery and installation services to its customers. Although the displays are often customized with logos and branding, the work that goes into the display delivery and installation projects is fairly standardized and routine. As a result, the pricing is standardized for all customers. While the company is profitable overall, the CFO thinks the net margins should be higher. The CFO is concerned that customer support costs are eating up some of the margin and has decided to do a customer profitability analysis based on the five different types of customers. The following data for the most recent period have been collected to support the analysis.

Support Activity	Driver	Cost per Driver Unit
A. Minor visits for maintenance and upgrades	Hours on jobs	$160
B. Visits to customer	Number of visits	$300
C. Communication	Number of calls	$ 50

Customer Group	Activity A	Activity B	Activity C	Profit Before Support Costs
1	69	25	128	$80,000
2	141	42	205	85,000
3	74	19	99	83,000
4	61	28	106	90,000
5	136	39	189	78,000

Required

a. Calculate customer profit and the ratio of support costs to profit before support costs for each customer group.
b. Comment on the usefulness of this type of analysis. What reasonable actions might the company take as a result of this analysis?

Solution on p. 18-48.

APPENDIX 18A: Profitability Analysis with Activity-Based Cost Drivers

A major limitation of cost-volume-profit analysis and the related contribution income statement discussed in Chapter 15 is the exclusive use of unit-level activity cost drivers. Even when multiple products are considered, the CVP approach either restates volume in terms of an average unit or in terms of a dollar of sales volume. Additionally, CVP analysis does not consider other categories of cost drivers.

Profitability analysis examines the relationships among revenues, costs, and profits. We now expand profitability analysis to incorporate *activity-based cost drivers*. While the addition of multiple levels of cost drivers makes it difficult to develop graphical relationships (illustrating the impact of cost driver changes on revenues, costs, and profits), it is possible to modify the traditional contribution income statement to incorporate a hierarchy of cost drivers. The expanded framework is not only more accurate, but it encourages management to ask important questions concerning costs and profitability.

LO18-6
Perform profitability analysis with activity-based cost drivers.

Multi-Level Contribution Income Statement

To illustrate the use of profitability analysis with unit and nonunit cost drivers, assume **Anthropologie**, a multiple-product merchandising organization, has the following cost hierarchy.

Unit-level activities	
Cost of goods sold	$0.80 per sales dollar
Order-level activities	
Cost of processing order	$20 per order
Customer-level activities	
Mail, phone, sales visits, recordkeeping, etc.	$200 per customer per year
Facility-level costs	
Depreciation, manager salaries, insurance, etc.	$120,000 per year

Assume that Anthropologie is subject to a 40% income tax rate and has the following plans for next year.

Sales	$3,000,000
Number of sales orders	3,200
Number of customers	400

While Anthropologie's plans could be summarized in a functional income statement, we have previously considered the limitations of such statements for management. Contribution income statements are preferred because they correspond to the cost classification scheme used in CVP analysis. In this case, Anthropologie's cost structure (unit level, order level, customer level, and facility level) does not correspond to the classification scheme used in traditional contribution income statements (variable and fixed). The problem occurs because traditional contribution income statements consider only unit-level cost drivers. When a larger set of unit and nonunit cost drivers is used for cost analysis, an expanded contribution income statement should be used for profitability analysis.

A hypothetical multi-level contribution income statement for Anthropologie is presented in **Exhibit 18A.1**. Costs are separated using a cost hierarchy and there are several contribution margins, one for each level of costs that responds to a short-run change in activity. Suppose that in the case of Anthropologie, the contribution margins are at the unit level, order level, and customer level. Because the facility-level costs do not vary with short-run variations in activity, the final customer-level contribution goes to cover facility-level costs and to provide for a profit. If a company had a different activity cost hierarchy, it would use a different set of contribution margins.

EXHIBIT 18A.1 Multi-Level Contribution Income Statement with Taxes

ANTHROPOLOGIE
Multi-Level Contribution Income Statement
For Next Year

Sales	$3,000,000
Less unit-level costs	
Cost of goods sold ($3,000,000 × 0.80)	(2,400,000)
Unit-level contribution margin	**600,000**
Less order-level costs	
Cost of processing order (3,200 orders × $20)	(64,000)
Order-level contribution margin	**536,000**
Less customer-level costs	
Mail, phone, sales visits, recordkeeping, etc. (400 customers × $200)	(80,000)
Customer-level contribution margin	**456,000**
Less facility-level costs	
Depreciation, manager salaries, insurance, etc.	(120,000)
Before-tax profit	336,000
Income taxes ($336,000 × 0.40)	(134,400)
After-tax profit	$ 201,600

A number of additional questions of interest to management can be formulated and answered using the multi-level hierarchy. Consider the following examples.

- Holding the number of sales orders and customers constant, what is the break-even dollar sales volume? The answer is found by treating all other costs as fixed and dividing the total nonunit-level costs by the unit-level contribution margin ratio. Here the contribution margin ratio indicates how many cents of each sales dollar is available for profits and costs above the unit level.

$$\text{Unit-Level Break-Even Point in Dollars with No Changes in Other Costs} = \frac{\left(\text{Current Order-Level Costs} + \text{Current Customer-Level Costs} + \text{Facility-Level Costs}\right)}{\text{Contribution Margin Ratio}}$$

$$= (\$64{,}000 + \$80{,}000 + \$120{,}000) \div 0.20^*$$
$$= \$1{,}320{,}000$$

* $600,000/$3,000,000 = 0.20

- What order size is required to break even on an individual order? Answering this question might help management to evaluate the desirability of establishing a minimum order size. To break even, each order must have a unit-level contribution equal to the order-level costs. Any additional contribution is used to cover customer- and facility-level costs and provide for a profit.

$$\text{Break-even order size} = \$20 \div (1 - 0.80)$$
$$= \$100$$

- What sales volume is required to break even on an average customer? Answering this question might help management to evaluate the desirability of retaining certain customers. Based on the preceding information, an average customer places 8 orders per year (3,200 orders ÷ 400 customers). With costs of $20 per order and $200 per customer, the sales to an average customer must generate an annual contribution of $360. Sales volume to break-even is calculated as follows.

$$\text{Break-even sales for average customer} = \text{Fixed costs/Contribution margin ratio}$$
$$= ([\$8 \text{ orders} \times \$20 \text{ per order}] + \$200)/(1 - 0.80)$$
$$= \$1{,}800$$

Management might consider discontinuing relations with customers with annual purchases of less than this amount. Alternatively, they might inquire as to whether such customers could be served in a less costly manner.

The concepts of multi-level break-even analysis and profitability analysis are finding increasing use as companies such as **FedEx**, **Best Buy**, and **Bank of America** strive to identify profitable and unprofitable customers. At FedEx, customers are sometimes rated as "the good, the bad, and the ugly." FedEx strives to retain the "good" profitable customers, turn the "bad" into profitable customers, and ignore the "ugly" who seem unlikely to become profitable.

Variations in Multi-Level Contribution Income Statement

Classification schemes should be designed to fit the organization and user needs. In this chapter, when analyzing the costs of a manufacturing company, we used a manufacturing cost hierarchy. While formatting issues can seem mundane and routine, format is important because the way information is presented encourages certain types of questions while discouraging others. Hence, management accountants must inquire as to user needs before developing management accounting reports, just as users of management accounting information should be knowledgeable enough to request appropriate information and know whether the information they are receiving is the information they need. While the amount of available data is seemingly endless, the most important issues involve identifying the important questions and presenting information to address those questions.

In the case of Anthropologie, we used a customer cost hierarchy with information presented in a single column. A multiple-column format is also useful for presenting and analyzing information. Assume that Anthropologie's management believes that the differences between the in-store and internet-based markets are such that these markets could be better served with separate marketing activities. They would have two market segments, one for the in-store customers and one for internet-based customers, resulting in the following cost hierarchy.

1. Unit-level activities
2. Order-level activities
3. Customer-level activities
4. Market segment activities
5. Facility-level activities

One possible way of presenting Anthropologie's hypothetical multi-level income statement with two market segments is shown in **Exhibit 18A.2**. The details underlying the development of this statement are not presented. In developing the statement, we assume the mix of units sold, their cost structure, and the costs of processing an order are unchanged. Finally, we present new market segment costs and assume that the addition of the segments allows for some reduction in previous facility-level costs.

The information in the total column is all that is required for a multi-level contribution income statement. The information in the two detailed columns for the government and private segments can, however, prove useful in analyzing the profitability of each. Observe that the facility-level costs, incurred for the benefit of both segments, are not assigned to specific segments. Depending on the nature of the goods sold, it may be possible to further analyze the profitability of each product (or type of product) sold in each market segment. The profitability analysis of business segments is more closely examined in Chapter 23.

EXHIBIT 18A.2 — Multi-Level Contribution Income Statement with Segments and Taxes

ANTHROPOLOGIE
Multi-Level Contribution Income Statement
For Next Year

	In-Store Segment	Internet Segment	Total
Sales.	$1,500,000	$2,000,000	$3,500,000
Less unit-level costs			
Cost of goods sold (0.80)	(1,200,000)	(1,600,000)	(2,800,000)
Unit-level contribution margin	300,000	400,000	700,000
Less order-level costs			
Cost of processing order			
(1,000 × $20; 3,000 × $20)	(20,000)	(60,000)	(80,000)
Order-level contribution margin	280,000	340,000	620,000
Less customer-level costs			
Mail, phone, sales visits, recordkeeping, etc.			
(150 × $200, 300 × $200)	(30,000)	(60,000)	(90,000)
Customer-level contribution margin	250,000	280,000	530,000
Less market segment-level costs	(80,000)	(20,000)	(100,000)
Market segment-level contribution	$170,000	$260,000	430,000
Less facility-level costs			
Depreciation, manager salaries, insurance, etc.			(90,000)
Before-tax profit			340,000
Income taxes ($340,000 × 0.40)			(136,000)
After-tax profit			$204,000

Review 18-6 LO18-6 — Performing a Profitability Analysis Using Activity-Based Cost Drivers

7-Eleven operates a number of convenience stores worldwide. Assume that an analysis of operating costs, customer sales, and customer patronage reveals the following.

Fixed costs per store	$80,000/year
Variable cost ratio	0.80
Average sale per customer visit	$17.00
Average customer visits per week	1.50
Customers as portion of city population	0.05

Required
Solution on p. 18-48. Determine the city population required for a single 7-Eleven to earn an annual profit of $40,000.

MULTIPLE CHOICE

LO18-2

1. A company's operations include a high-level of fixed costs and produce a variety of products. What type of costing system should be recommended?
   a. Job-order costing
   b. Process costing
   c. Process value analysis
   d. Activity-based costing **CMA adapted**

LO18-1

2. Marko Company produces two products, Xeon and Zeon, in a small manufacturing plant which had total manufacturing overhead of $45,000 in January and used 600 direct labor hours. The factory has two departments, Preparation, which incurred $25,000 of manufacturing overhead, and Processing which incurred $20,000 of manufacturing overhead. Preparation used 400 hours of direct labor and Processing used 160 machine hours. During January, 300 direct labor hours were used in making 100 units of Xeon, and 300 were used in making 100 units of Zeon. If Marko uses a plantwide rate based on direct labor hours to assign manufacturing costs to products, the total manufacturing overhead assigned to each unit of Xeon and Zeon in January were

Multiple Choice Answers
1. d 2. b 3. b 4. d 5. a 6. c

a. $22,500 for Xeon and $22,500 for Zeon
b. $225 for Xeon and $225 for Zeon
c. $25,000 for Xeon and $20,000 for Zeon
d. $107.14 for Xeon, and $42.86 for Zeon

3. Refer to the previous question. Assume that instead of using a plantwide overhead rate, Marko used departmental rates based on direct labor hours for the Preparation Department and machine hours for the Processing Department. The departmental overhead rates for the Preparation and Processing Departments were **LO18-1**

   a. $75 per direct labor hour for both Preparation and Processing
   b. $62.50 per direct labor hour for Preparation, and $125 per machine hour for Processing
   c. $125 per direct labor hour for Preparation, and $62.50 per machine hour for Processing
   d. $80.35 per direct labor hour for Preparation, and $80.35 per machine hour for Processing

4. Refer to the previous questions regarding Marko Company. Assume that Xeon used 175 direct labor hours and Zeon used 225 direct labor hours in the Preparation Department. Also, assume that Xeon used 100 machine hours and Zeon used 60 machine hours in the Processing Department. The overhead costs assigned to each unit of Xeon and Zeon were **LO18-1**

   a. $253.50 for Xeon and $196.50 for Zeon
   b. $62.50 for Xeon and $125 for Zeon
   c. $215.63 for Zeon and $215.63 for Xeon
   d. $234.38 for Xeon and $215.63 for Zeon

5. Refer to the previous questions regarding Marko Company. Assume that Marko used an ABC product costing system and that its total manufacturing overhead costs of $45,000 were assigned to the following ABC cost pools: **LO18-3**

Material inspections & preparation ($20,000)...........	$20 per pound of raw materials
Material moves ($5,000)........	$50 per move
Machine setups ($6,000)	$300 per setup
Machine operations ($14,000)	$87.50 per machine hour

   Xeon and Zeon used the following quantities of the four activity drivers:

	Xeon	Zeon
Pounds of raw materials....	500	500
Material moves........	60	40
Setups	12	8
Machine hours	100	60

   The overhead costs assigned to each unit of Xeon and Zeon were
   a. $253.50 for Xeon and $196.50 for Zeon
   b. $62.50 for Xeon and $125 for Zeon
   c. $215.63 for Xeon and $234.63 for Zeon
   d. $234.38 for Xeon and $215.63 for Zeon

6. Assume that Arco, Inc. has three activity pools which have the following costs: Machine Setups, $30,000; Material Moves, $45,000; and Machine Operations, $28,000. The activity cost drivers (and driver quantity) for the three pools are, respectively, number of setups (200), number of material moves (450), and number of machine hours (350). Product XJ3 used the following quantity of activity drivers to produce 100 units of final product: 25 setups, 40 material moves, and 75 machine hours. The total ABC cost and unit ABC cost assigned to Product XJ3 is **LO18-3**

   a. $103,000 total ABC cost and $1,030 unit ABC cost
   b. $103,000 total ABC cost and $103 unit ABC cost
   c. $13,750 total ABC cost and $137.50 unit ABC cost
   d. $3,300 total ABC cost and $330 unit ABC cost

DATA ANALYTICS

DA18-1. Activity-Based Costing Using Excel **LO18-1, 2, 3**

Assume Kirkland Industries (a contract assembly manufacturer) has decided to adopt activity-based costing techniques to determine its manufacturing overhead rates. The production manager has identified three activities (materials movement, assembly, and packaging/shipping) and a number of possible activity measures (# of jobs, direct labor hours, machine hours, # of boxes shipped, and # of components used). Working together, the production and accounting managers have used historical data from 2014 to 2021 to determine total activity costs by month. Those results are included in a data file on the textbook's website. The workbook also includes totals for the various activity measures from the same 2014–2021 period.

Budgeted overhead dollars and activities for the year are as follows.

Budgeted Overhead		Budgeted Measures	
Materials movement	$1,080,000	No. of jobs	480
Assembly	$1,950,000	Direct labor hours	16,000
Packaging/Shipping	$1,584,000	Machine hours	7,800
		No. of boxes shipped	48,000
		No. of components used	4,000,000

Note: *If the Analyze section does not appear, you will need to load the Analysis ToolPak. Click the File tab, click Options, and click Add-Ins. Make sure Excel Add-ins appears in the Manage field. Check the Analysis ToolPak option and click OK.*

REQUIRED

a. Use the correlation tool in Excel to determine which measure should be used for each activity. *Hint:* The correlation tool can be found on the *Data Analysis* menu in the *Analyze* section of the Data tab in Excel. *Hint:* Open the Correlation Tool and highlight the data. If the first row is highlighted, check the box for Labels in first row. From your results, determine which variable has the highest correlation value for each of the three overhead categories.

b. Using the measures identified in part *a*, determine the activity rates for allocating manufacturing overhead to jobs.

c. What would the predetermined rate be if direct labor hours were used to allocate all manufacturing overhead costs?

d. Assume Kirkland had a job that required 36 direct labor hours, 16 machine hours, 1,875 components, and 68 boxes. How much manufacturing overhead would be applied to that job under ABC? How does that compare to the amount applied if direct labor hours were used to allocate overhead? What might account for the difference?

LO18-1, 3, 4 **DA18-2. Analyzing Product Costs Using Different Overhead Application Methods**

Analyze the results of E18-24 by completing the following analyses in Excel.

a. Create pie charts of the product costs of Job 845 for each part *b* (activity-based costing), part *c* (departmental overhead allocation), and part *d* (plantwide overhead allocation) of E18-24. In each pie chart, include total direct materials, total direct labor, and total overhead costs. Display proportions in percentages. *Hint:* Right-click inside the pie and select Format Data Labels. Select Percentages under Label Options in the sidebar. Deselect Value, if necessary.

b. Describe the differences in the charts in part *a*. How might the charts impact a manager's assessment of product costs under the different methods.

c. Create pie charts showing the components of overhead of Job 845 for each part *b*, *c*, and *d*. Display proportions as values.

d. Which chart in part *c* provides a better management tool for decision-making? Why?

e. Create one bar chart comparing applied overhead in total for each part *b*, *c*, and *d*.

f. How do the differences shown in the bar chart affect the costing of the other jobs of the company?

DATA VISUALIZATION

Data Visualization Activities are available in myBusinessCourse. These assignments use Tableau Dashboards to expose students to visual depictions of data and introduce students to data analytics through data visualizations. These exercises are easily assignable and auto graded by MBC.

QUESTIONS

Q18-1. Summarize the concepts underlying activity-based costing in two sentences.

Q18-2. What steps are required to implement the two-stage activity-based costing model?

Q18-3. Define activity cost pool, activity cost driver, and cost per unit of activity.

Q18-4. Name two possible activity cost drivers for each of the following activities: maintenance, materials movement, machine setup, inspection, materials purchases, and customer service.

Q18-5. What is the premise of activity-based costing for product costing purposes?

Q18-6. In what ways does ABC product costing differ from traditional product cost methods?

Q18-7. Explain why ABC often reveals existing product cost cross-subsidization problems.

Q18-8. How can ABC be used to improve customer profitability analysis?

Q18-9. Explain activity-based management and how it differs from activity-based costing.

MINI EXERCISES

M18-10. Activities and Cost Drivers   LO18-2

For each of the following activities, select the most appropriate cost driver. Each cost driver may be used only once.

Activity		Cost Driver
1. Pay vendors	a.	Number of different kinds of raw materials
2. Evaluate vendors	b.	Number of classes offered
3. Inspect raw materials	c.	Number of tables
4. Plan for purchases of raw materials	d.	Number of employees
5. Packaging	e.	Number of operating hours
6. Supervision	f.	Number of units of raw materials received
7. Employee training	g.	Number of moves
8. Clean tables	h.	Number of vendors
9. Machine maintenance	i.	Number of checks issued
10. Move in-process product from one workstation to the next	j.	Number of customer orders

M18-11. Activities and Cost Drivers   LO18-2

For each of the following activities, select the most appropriate cost driver. Each cost driver may be used only once.

Activity		Cost Driver
1. Pay vendors	a.	Number of different raw material items
2. Receive material deliveries	b.	Number of classes offered
3. Inspect raw materials	c.	Number of machine hours
4. Plan for purchases of raw materials	d.	Number of employees
5. Packaging	e.	Number of maintenance hours
6. Supervision	f.	Number of units of raw materials received
7. Employee training	g.	Number of new customers
8. Operating machines	h.	Number of deliveries
9. Machine maintenance	i.	Number of checks issued
10. Opening accounts at a bank	j.	Number of customer orders

M18-12. Developing a List of Activities for Baggage Handling at an Airport   LO18-2
Southwest Airlines
NYSE :: LUV

Assume you have been asked to determine the activities involved in the baggage-handling process of Southwest Airlines' Chicago-Midway hub. Prior to conducting observations and interviews, you decide that a list of possible activities would help you to better observe key activities and ask meaningful questions.

REQUIRED

For incoming aircraft only, develop a sequential list of baggage-handling activities. Your list should contain between 8 and 10 activities.

M18-13. Stage 1 ABC at a College: Assigning Costs to Activities   LO18-2
University of Texas

Assume an accounting professor at the University of Texas devotes 60% of her time to teaching, 30% of her time to research and writing, and 10% of her time to service activities such as committee work and curriculum development. The professor teaches two semesters per year. During each semester, she teaches one section of an introductory financial accounting course (with a maximum enrollment of 60 students) and one section of a graduate financial accounting course (with a maximum enrollment of 30 students). Including course preparation, classroom instruction, and appointments with students, each course requires an equal amount of time. The accounting professor is paid $150,000 per year.

REQUIRED

Determine the activity cost of instruction per student in both the introductory and the graduate financial accounting courses.

LO18-5
Charlie's Produce

M18-14. Stage 2 ABC for a Wholesale Company

Charlie's Produce is a West Coast distributor of fresh produce. Assume the following information represents activity costs for the Los Angeles distribution center.

Activity	Cost per Unit of Activity Driver
Customer relations	$110.00 per customer per month
Selling	0.05 per sales dollar
Accounting	7.50 per order
Warehousing	0.60 per case shipped
Packing	0.30 per case shipped
Shipping	0.05 per pound shipped

The following information pertains to June operations for the Los Angeles distribution center of Charlie's Produce.

Number of orders	3,220
Sales revenue	$2,150,000
Cost of produce sold	$1,405,000
Number of customers	432
Cases shipped	57,850
Pounds shipped	1,250,000

REQUIRED

Determine the profitability of sales in the Los Angeles distribution center for June.

LO18-3

M18-15. Stage 2 ABC for Manufacturing: Reassigning Costs to Cost Objects

Woodland Corporation has developed the following activity cost information for its manufacturing activities.

Activity	Activity Cost
Machine setup	$120.00 per batch
Movement	15.00 per batch move
	0.10 per pound, per move
Drilling	6.00 per hole
Welding	4.00 per inch
Shaping	22.00 per hour
Assembly	18.00 per hour
Inspection	2.00 per unit

Filling an order for a batch of 125 fireplace inserts (each insert weighing 50 pounds) required the following.

- Four batch moves
- Three sets of inspections
- Drilling eight holes in each unit
- Completing 100 inches of welds on each unit
- Forty-five minutes of shaping for each unit
- One hour of assembly per unit

REQUIRED

Determine the activity cost of converting the raw materials into 125 fireplace inserts.

LO18-3
The Vollrath Company

M18-16. Two-Stage ABC for Manufacturing

Vollrath Manufacturing, a division of **The Vollrath Company**, manufactures restaurant equipment. Assume the company has determined the following activity cost pools and cost driver levels for the year.

Activity Cost Pool	Activity Cost	Activity Cost Driver
Machine setup	$750,000	18,750 setup hours
Material handling	121,600	3,800 tons of materials
Machine operation	552,500	16,250 machine hours

The following data are for the production of single batches of two products, Equipment Stands and Charbroilers during the month of August.

	Equipment Stands	Charbroilers
Units produced	100	50
Machine hours	8	25
Direct labor hours	400	1,200
Direct labor cost	$10,000	$30,000
Direct materials cost	$48,000	$125,000
Tons of materials	4	14
Setup hours	6	36

REQUIRED
Determine the unit costs of Equipment Stands and Charbroilers using ABC.

M18-17. Two-Stage ABC for Manufacturing
Assume **Sherwin-Williams**, a large paint manufacturer, has determined the following activity cost pools and cost driver levels for the latest period.

LO18-1, 3

Sherwin-Williams
NYSE :: SHW

Activity Cost Pool	Activity Cost	Activity Cost Driver
Machine setup	$ 210,000	3,500 setup hours
Material handling	468,000	6,500 material moves
Machine operation	1,026,270	12,670 machine hours

The following data are for the production of single batches of two of its products, Cashmere and Emerald.

	Cashmere	Emerald
Gallons produced	20,000	25,000
Machine hours	100	120
Setup hours	24	26
Material moves	35	40

REQUIRED
a. Determine the batch and unit overhead costs per gallon of Cashmere and Emerald considering overhead costs as one cost pool allocated using machine hours.
b. Determine the batch and unit overhead costs per gallon of Cashmere and Emerald using ABC.

M18-18. Customer Profitability Analysis
Elite Services, Inc. provides residential painting services for three home building companies, Brookside, Edgewater, and Hillrose, and it uses a job costing system for determining the costs for completing each job. The job cost system does not capture any cost incurred by Elite for return touchups and refinishes after the homeowner occupies the home. Elite paints each house on a square footage contract price, which includes painting as well as all refinishes and touchups required after the homes are occupied. Each year, the company generates about one-third of its total revenues and gross profits from each of the three builders. The Elite owner has observed that the builders, however, require substantially different levels of support following the completion of jobs. The following data have been gathered.

LO18-5

Support Activity	Driver	Cost per Driver Unit
Major refinishes	Hours on jobs	$150
Touchups	Number of visits	$100
Communication	Number of calls	$ 30

Builder	Major Refinishes	Touchups	Communication
Brookside	120	260	900
Edgewater	70	205	530
Hillrose	80	220	590

REQUIRED

Assuming that each of the three customers produces gross profits of $150,000, calculate the profitability from each builder after taking into account the support activity required for each builder.

EXERCISES

LO18-2

E18-19. Assigning Costs to Products

Nestlé is the world's largest food and beverage company. It has more than 2,000 brands and is sold in 186 countries worldwide. In a competitive business environment, it is imperative that Nestlé understand its costs in order to make good business decisions. These decisions might include: What are appropriate prices for Haagen-Dazs and Dreyers pints of ice cream? What current activities contribute to a firm's costs and are used in producing pints of Dreyers and Haagen-Dazs? What shared resources are used by these two brands? Which brand of ice cream contributes the most to profitability?

REQUIRED

Discuss some of the factors that make it increasingly difficult for Nestlé to accurately assign costs to the ice cream brands.

LO18-2

E18-20. Identifying Relevant Cost Drivers

Mobile Health Screening (MHS) offers onsite general health screening services for a flat rate of $35 per screening. MHS typically provides its services to businesses that offer fitness and health programs as a benefit to their employees. A representative of MHS arrives at a business early in the morning and sets up a room with the necessary equipment and supplies. The rooms are stocked with kits based on the expected number of participants. MHS sees participating employees throughout the day and screens for basic health measures such as blood pressure, weight, blood screening, and health behaviors. MHS sends samples to an outside lab for testing. MHS then compiles the results of all the tests and provides employees access to their individual results via a logon identification and password on the website. Participating employees may consult with a physician with questions on test results. Physicians are contracted by MHS and paid for time spent with the participants.

REQUIRED

For MHS, match each of the six activities to a likely related cost driver. A cost driver may be used more than once.

Activities	Cost Drivers
____ 1. Room setup	a. Number tests
____ 2. Reception and admission of participating employees	b. Number of participating employees
____ 3. Administration of tests	c. Number of minutes of consultation services
____ 4. External lab processing	
____ 5. Compiling, processing, and electronic posting of test results	
____ 6. Consultations with MHS physician	

LO18-2

E18-21. Stage 1 ABC for a Machine Shop: Assigning Costs to Activities

As the chief engineer of a small fabrication shop, Christine Sanders refers to herself as a "jack-of-all-trades." When an order for a new product comes in, Christine must do the following:

1. Design the product to meet customer requirements.
2. Prepare a bill of materials (a list of materials required to produce the product).
3. Prepare an operations list (a sequential list of the steps involved in manufacturing the product).

Each time the foundry manufactures a batch of the product, Christine must perform these activities:

1. Schedule the job.
2. Supervise the setup of machines that will work on the job.
3. Inspect the first unit produced to verify that it meets specifications.

Christine supervises the production employees who perform the actual work on individual units of product. She is also responsible for employee training, ensuring that production facilities are in proper operating condition, and attending professional meetings. Christine's estimates (in percent) of time spent on each of these activities last year are as follows.

Designing product.	15%
Preparing bills of materials.	5
Preparing operations lists.	9
Scheduling jobs	12
Supervising setups.	6
Inspecting first units	7
Supervising production.	25
Training employees.	8
Maintaining facility	3
Attending professional meetings	10
	100%

REQUIRED

Assuming Christine Sanders' salary is $115,000 per year, determine the dollar amount of her salary assigned to unit-, batch-, product-, and facility-level activities. (You may need to review Chapter 18 before answering this question.)

E18-22. Two-Stage ABC for Manufacturing   LO18-3

Thornton Company has determined its activity cost pools and cost drivers to be the following.

Cost pools	
Setup.	$ 55,000
Material handling.	10,050
Machine operation	242,400
Packing.	67,200
Total indirect manufacturing costs.	$374,650
Cost drivers	
Setups.	550
Material moves	670
Machine hours	20,200
Packing orders	1,400

One product made by Thornton, metal casements, used the following activities during the period to produce 500 units.

Setups	45
Material moves.	112
Machine hours	2,400
Packing orders	195

REQUIRED

a. Calculate the cost per unit of activity for each activity cost pool for Thornton Company.
b. Calculate the manufacturing overhead cost per metal casement manufactured during the period.

E18-23. Calculating Manufacturing Overhead Rates   LO18-1

Windsor Company accumulated the following data from last year's operations.

Milling Department manufacturing overhead	$450,000
Finishing Department manufacturing overhead	$150,000
Machine hours used	
Milling Department	15,000 hours
Finishing Department	5,000 hours
Labor hours used	
Milling Department	2,000 hours
Finishing Department	2,000 hours

In the Milling department, grooves are cut into aluminum and steel rods using computer-controlled equipment. In the Finishing department, the rods are individually cleaned and polished.

REQUIRED

a. Calculate the plantwide manufacturing overhead rate using machine hours as the allocation base.
b. Calculate the plantwide manufacturing overhead rate using direct labor hours as the allocation base.
c. Calculate department overhead rates using machine hours in Milling and direct labor hours in Finishing as the allocation bases.
d. Calculate department overhead rates using direct labor hours in Milling and machine hours in Finishing as the allocation bases.
e. Which of these allocation systems seems to be the most appropriate? Explain.

LO18-1, 3 **E18-24. Calculating Activity-Based Costing Overhead Rates, Plantwide Overhead Rate, and Departmental Overhead Rates**

Assume that manufacturing overhead for Windsor Company in the previous exercise consisted of the following activities and costs.

Setup (2,500 setup hours)	$125,000
Production scheduling (150 batches)	75,000
Production engineering (20,000 machine hours)	265,000
Supervision (4,000 direct labor hours)	85,800
Machine maintenance (1,025 repair requests)	49,200
Total activity costs	$600,000

The following additional data were provided for Job 845.

Direct materials costs	$1,450
Direct labor cost (5 Milling direct labor hours; 15 Finishing direct labor hours)	$ 500
Setup hours	2 hours
Production scheduling	1 batch
Machine hours used (15 Milling machine hours; 5 Finishing machine hours)	20 hours
Machine maintenance	1 repair request

REQUIRED

a. Calculate the cost per unit of activity driver for each activity cost category.
b. Calculate the cost of Job 845 using ABC to assign the overhead costs.
c. Calculate the cost of Job 845 using the plantwide overhead rate based on machine hours calculated in the previous exercise.
d. Calculate the cost of Job 845 using a machine hour departmental overhead rate for the Milling Department and a direct labor hour overhead rate for the Finishing Department (see E18-23).

LO18-1, 3 **E18-25. Activity-Based Costing and Traditional Costs Compared**
Conair Corporation

Cuisinart, a Conair Corporation, manufactures outdoor gas cookers and charcoal smokers. Assume that Cuisinart only makes a single model of each product and that the following information pertains to the total manufacturing costs for the products in the current month.

	Gas Cooker	Charcoal Smoker
Units	4,000	3,500
Number of batches	80	35
Number of machine hours	16,000	3,000
Direct materials	$225,500	$108,500
Direct labor	$100,683	$50,341

Manufacturing overhead follows.

Activity	Cost	Cost Driver
Materials acquisition and inspection	$ 50,100	Amount of direct materials cost
Product assembly	123,500	Number of machine hours
Scheduling	15,180	Number of batches
	$188,780	

REQUIRED

a. Determine the total and per-unit costs of manufacturing the Gas Cooker and Charcoal Smoker for the month, assuming all manufacturing overhead related to these two products is assigned on the basis of direct labor dollars.

b. Determine the total and per-unit costs of manufacturing the Gas Cooker and Charcoal Smoker for the month, assuming manufacturing overhead is assigned using activity-based costing.

E18-26. Activity-Based Costing Versus Traditional Costing   LO18-1, 3, 4

Refer to the previous exercise in E18-25 for Cuisinart.

REQUIRED

a. Comment on the differences between the solutions to requirements (a) and (b). Which is more accurate? What errors might managers make if all manufacturing overhead costs are assigned on the basis of direct labor dollars?

b. Cuisinart's manufacturing process has become increasingly automated over the past few years. Discuss how this will likely impact its ability to accurately measure product costs.

c. Comment on the adequacy of the preceding data to meet management's needs.

E18-27. Traditional Product Costing versus Activity-Based Costing   LO18-1, 3, 4

Assume that Panasonic Corporation has determined its estimated total manufacturing overhead cost for one of its plants to be $436,000, consisting of the following activity cost pools for the current month.

Activity Centers	Activity Costs	Cost Drivers	Activity Level
Assembly setups	$124,000	Setup hours	4,000
Materials handling	57,000	Number of moves	600
Assembly	225,000	Assembly hours	12,500
Maintenance	30,000	Maintenance hours	1,200
Total	$436,000		

Total direct labor hours used during the month were 16,000. Panasonic produces many different electronic products, including the following two products produced during the current month.

	Model X301	Model Z205
Units produced	2,000	2,000
Direct materials costs	$18,550	$18,550
Direct labor costs	$5,000	$5,000
Direct labor hours	200	200
Setup hours	30	60
Materials moves	75	150
Assembly hours	500	750
Maintenance hours	25	45

REQUIRED

a. Calculate the total per-unit cost of each model using direct labor hours to assign manufacturing overhead to products.

b. Calculate the total per-unit cost of each model using activity-based costing to assign manufacturing overhead to products.

c. Comment on the accuracy of the two methods for determining product costs.

d. Discuss some of the strategic implications of your answers to the previous requirements.

E18-28. Traditional Product Costing versus Activity-Based Costing   LO18-1, 3, 4

Ridgeland Inc. makes backpacks for large sporting goods chains that are sold under the customers' store brand names. The Accounting Department has identified the following overhead costs and cost drivers for next year.

Overhead Item	Expected Costs	Cost Driver	Maximum Quantity
Setup costs	$175,000	Number of setups	1,750
Ordering costs	120,000	Number of orders	15,000
Assembly	910,000	Number of machine hours	14,000
Finishing	208,000	Number of direct labor hours	104,000

The following data are for two recently completed jobs.

	Job 201	Job 202
Cost of direct materials.	$12,000	$14,000
Cost of direct labor.	$20,500	$40,000
Number of units completed.	1,000	850
Number of setups.	15	18
Number of orders.	200	100
Number of machine hours.	200	225
Number of direct labor hours.	820	1,600

REQUIRED

a. Determine the unit cost for each job using a traditional plantwide overhead rate based on machine hours.
b. Determine the unit cost for each job using ABC. (Round answers to two decimal places.)
c. As the manager of Ridgeland, is there additional information that you would want to help you evaluate the pricing and profitability of Jobs 201 and 202?
d. Assuming the company has been using the method required in part *a,* how should management react to the findings in part *b?*

LO18-5 E18-29. Customer Profitability Analysis

Leahy Inc. has 10 customers that account for all of its $1,472,000 of net income. Its activity-based costing system is able to assign all costs, except for $200,000 of general administrative costs, to key activities incurred in connection with serving its customers. A customer profitability analysis based on activity costing produced the following customer profits and losses.

Customer	
#1	$ 350,000
#2	262,000
#3	(75,000)
#4	240,000
#5	50,000
#6	375,000
#7	(100,000)
#8	325,000
#9	225,000
#10	(180,000)
Total	$1,472,000

REQUIRED
Prepare a customer profitability profile like the one in **Exhibit 18.6**.

LO18-5 E18-30. Customer Profitability Analysis

Refer to the previous exercise E18-29 for Leahy Inc.

REQUIRED

a. If Leahy were to notify customers 3, 7, and 10 that it will no longer be able to provide them services in the future, will that increase company profits by $355,000? Why or why not?
b. What is the primary benefit of preparing a customer profitability analysis?

LO18-6 E18-31. Customer-Level Planning

Circle K, a company of **Alimentation Couche-Tard**, operates a number of convenience stores worldwide. Assume that an analysis of operating costs, customer sales, and customer patronage reveals the following.

Fixed costs per store	$125,000
Variable cost ratio.	0.60
Average sale per customer visit	$10.00
Average customer visits per week	2.00
Customers as portion of city population.	0.05

REQUIRED
Determine the city population required for a single Circle K to earn an annual profit of $75,000.

E18-32. Multiple-Level Break-Even Analysis   LO18-6

Kucera Associates provides marketing services for a number of small manufacturing firms. Kucera receives a commission of 10% of sales. Operating costs are as follows.

Unit-level costs	$0.05 per sales dollar
Sales-level costs	$400 per sales order
Customer-level costs	$1,000 per customer per year
Facility-level costs	$75,000 per year

REQUIRED

a. Determine the minimum order size in sales dollars for Kucera to break even on an order.
b. Assuming an average customer places five orders per year, determine the minimum annual sales required to break even on a customer.
c. What is the average order size in (b)?
d. Assuming Kucera currently serves 100 customers, with each placing an average of five orders per year, determine the minimum annual sales required to break even.
e. What is the average order size in (d)?
f. Explain the differences in the answers to (a), (c), and (e).

PROBLEMS

P18-33. Two-Stage ABC for Manufacturing with ABC Variances   LO18-3, 4

Meade Manufacturing developed the following activity cost pool information for its current year manufacturing activities.

	Budgeted Activity Cost	Activity Cost Driver at Practical Capacity
Purchasing and materials handling	$ 475,000	950,000 kilograms
Setup	225,000	1,500 setups
Machine operations	1,540,000	14,000 machine hours
First unit inspection	280,000	1,600 batches
Packaging	100,000	200,000 units

Actual production information for three of Meade's products during the year is as follows.

	Standard Product A	Standard Product B	Specialty Products
Units	35,000	15,000	10,000
Batches	140	50	400
Setups*	150	45	800
Machine hours	1,200	650	800
Kilograms of raw materials	175,000	65,000	95,000
Direct materials costs	$58,000	$44,350	$27,000
Direct labor costs	$95,500	$64,900	$45,000

* Some products require setups on two or more machines.

REQUIRED

a. Determine the unit cost of each product for Meade Manufacturing under activity-based costing.
b. Explain why the unit cost of the specialty products is so much higher than the unit cost of Standard Product A or Standard Product B.

P18-34. ABC—A Service Application   LO18-1, 3, 4

Grand Haven is a senior living community that offers a full range of services including independent living, assisted living, and skilled nursing care. The assisted living division provides residential space, meals, and medical services (MS) to its residents. The current costing system adds the cost of all of these services (space, meals, and MS) and divides by total resident days to get a cost per resident day. Recognizing that MS tends to vary significantly among the residents, Grand Haven's accountant recommended that an ABC system be designed to calculate more accurately the cost of MS provided to residents. She decided that residents should be classified into four categories (A, B,

C, D) based on the level of services received, with group A representing the lowest level of service and D representing the highest level of service. Two cost drivers being considered for measuring MS costs are number of assistance calls and number of assistant contacts. A contact is registered each time an assistance professional provides medical services or aid to a resident. The accountant has gathered the following data for the most recent annual period.

Resident Classification	Annual Resident Days	Annual Assistance Hours	Number of Assistance Contacts
A	18,000	9,100	27,000
B	10,000	22,500	31,000
C	5,500	23,000	27,500
D	3,000	18,400	24,000
	36,500	73,000	109,500

Other data
Total cost of medical services for the period $4,927,500
Total cost of meals and residential space $2,591,500

REQUIRED (ROUND ANSWERS TO THE NEAREST DOLLAR):
a. Determine the total cost of a resident day using the current system.
b. Determine the ABC cost of a resident day for each category of residents using assistance hours as the cost driver for medical services and resident days as the cost driver for meals and residential space.
c. Determine the ABC cost of a resident day for each category of residents using assistance contacts as the cost driver for medical services and resident days as the cost driver for meals and residential space.
d. Which cost driver do you think provides the more accurate measure of the cost per day for a Grand Haven resident?

LO18-1, 3, 4
Molitor Financial Group

P18-35. ABC Costing for a Service Organization
Molitor Financial Group is a full-service residential mortgage company in the Chicago area that operates in a very competitive market. Assume management is concerned about operating costs associated with processing mortgage applications and has decided to install an ABC costing system to help them get a handle on costs. Although labor hours seem to be the primary driver of the cost of processing a new mortgage, the labor cost for the different activities involved in processing new loans varies widely. The Accounting Department has provided the following data for the company's five major cost pools for the current year.

Activity Cost Pools		Activity Drivers	
Taking customer applications	$ 306,000	Time—assistant managers	3,600 hours
Conducting credit investigations	378,000	Time—credit managers	5,400 hours
Underwriting	405,000	Time—Underwriting Department	5,400 hours
Preparing loan packages	594,000	Time—Processing Department	10,800 hours
Closing loans	396,000	Time—Legal Department	3,600 hours
	$2,079,000		28,800 hours

During the year, the company processed and issued 900 new mortgages, two of which are summarized here with regard to activities used to process the mortgages.

	Loan 7023	Loan 8955
Application processing hours	2.00	4.00
Credit investigating hours	3.00	5.00
Underwriting hours	6.00	6.00
Processing hours	9.00	18.00
Legal hours	4.00	6.00
Total hours	24.00	39.00

REQUIRED

a. Determine the cost per unit of activity for each activity cost pool.
b. Determine the cost of processing loans 7023 and 8955.
c. Determine the cost of preparing loans 7023 and 8955 assuming that an average cost per hour for all activities is used.
d. Compare and discuss your answers to requirements (b) and (c).

P18-36. Activity-Based Costing in a Service Organization   LO18-1, 3, 4

Banctronics Inc. has 10 automatic teller machines (ATMs) spread throughout the city maintained by the ATM Department. You have been assigned the task of determining the cost of operating each machine. Management will use the information you develop, along with other information pertaining to the volume and type of transactions at each machine, to evaluate the desirability of continuing to operate each machine and/or changing security arrangements for a particular machine.

The ATM Department consists of a total of six employees: a supervisor, a head cashier, two associate cashiers, and two maintenance personnel. The associate cashiers make between two and four daily trips to each machine to collect and replenish cash and to replenish supplies, deposit tickets, and so forth. Each machine contains a small computer that automatically summarizes and reports transactions to the head cashier. The head cashier reconciles the activities of the two associate cashiers to the computerized reports. The supervisor, who does not handle cash, reviews the reconciliation. When an automatic teller's computer, a customer, or a cashier reports a problem, the two maintenance employees and one cashier are dispatched immediately. The cashier removes all cash and transaction records, and the maintenance employees repair the machine.

Maintenance employees spend all of their time on maintenance-related activities. The associate cashiers spend approximately 25% of their time on maintenance-related activities and 75% on daily trips. The head cashier's time is divided, with 60% directly related to daily trips to each machine and 40% related to supervising cashiers on maintenance calls. The supervisor devotes 20% of the time to daily trips to each machine and 80% to the equal supervision of each employee. Cost information for a recent month follows.

Salaries	
Supervisor	$ 8,000
Head cashier	6,000
Other ($3,000 each for other cashiers; $3,500 each for maintenance employees)	13,000
Lease and operating costs	
Cashiers' service vehicle	2,400
Maintenance service vehicle	4,800
Office rent and utilities	12,000
Machine lease, space rent, and utilities ($2,000 each machine)	20,000
Total	**$66,200**

Related monthly activity information for this month follows.

Machine	Daily Trips	Maintenance Call Hours
1	40	22
2	50	20
3	40	18
4	80	20
5	40	22
6	80	18
7	80	24
8	30	14
9	20	16
10	40	16
Total	500	190

Additional information follows:
- The office is centrally located with about equal travel time to each machine.
- Maintenance hours include travel time.
- The cashiers' service vehicle is used exclusively for routine visits.
- The office space is divided equally between the supervisor and the head cashier.

REQUIRED

a. Determine the monthly operating costs of machines 7 and 8 when cost assignments are based on the number of machines.
b. Determine the activity cost of a routine trip and a maintenance hour for the month given. Round answers to the nearest cent.
c. Determine the operating costs assigned and reassigned to machines 7 and 8 when activity-based costing is used.
d. How can ABC cost information be used by Banctronics Inc. to improve the overall management of monthly operating costs?

LO18-1, 2, 3, 4

P18-37. Product Costing: Plantwide Overhead versus Activity-Based Costing

Sterling Industries produces machine parts as a contract provider for a large manufacturing company. Sterling produces two particular parts, shafts and gears. The competition is keen among contract producers, and Sterling's top management realizes how vulnerable its market is to cost-cutting competitors. Hence, having a very accurate understanding of costs is important to Sterling's survival.

Sterling's president, Sheila Hudson, has observed that the company's current cost to produce shafts is $23.35, and the current cost to produce gears is $14.30. She indicated to the controller that she suspects some problems with the cost system because Sterling is suddenly experiencing extraordinary competition on shafts, but it seems to have a virtual corner on the gears market. She is even considering dropping the shaft line and converting the company to a one-product manufacturer of gears. She asked the controller, George Coleman, to conduct a thorough cost study and to consider whether changes in the cost system are necessary. The controller collected the following data about the company's costs and various manufacturing activities for the most recent month.

	Shafts	Gears
Production units	50,000	18,000
Selling price	$34.95	$25.50
Overhead per unit (based on direct labor hours)	$12.50	$6.25
Materials and direct labor cost per unit	$10.85	$8.05
Number of production runs	20	30
Number of purchasing and receiving orders processed	50	98
Number of machine hours	43,000	6,500
Number of direct labor hours	25,000	4,500
Number of engineering hours	2,500	2,500
Number of material moves	62	33

The controller was able to summarize the company's total manufacturing overhead into the following pools.

Setup costs	$ 40,000
Machine costs	198,000
Purchasing and receiving costs	218,300
Engineering costs	209,000
Materials handling costs	72,200
Total	$737,500

REQUIRED

a. Calculate Sterling's current plantwide overhead rate based on direct labor hours.
b. Verify Sterling's calculation of overhead cost per unit of $12.50 for shafts and $6.25 for gears.
c. Calculate the manufacturing overhead cost per unit for shafts and gears using activity-based costing, assuming each of the five cost pools represents a separate activity pool. Use the most appropriate activity driver for assigning activity costs to the two products.
d. Comment on Sterling's current cost system and the reason the company is facing fierce competition for shafts but little competition for gears.

LO18-1, 3, 4
Newman's Own

P18-38. Multiple Cost Drivers

Newman's Own manufactures a variety of specialty salad dressings. Production runs are both high-volume and low-volume activities, depending on customer orders. Assume the following represents general manufacturing costs (manufacturing overhead) and each cost's related activity cost driver for Newman's Own.

Level	Total Cost	Units of Cost Driver
Unit.	$600,000	20,000 machine hours
Batch	40,000	400 customer orders
Product.	84,000	15 products

The lime vinaigrette dressing required 1,000 machine hours to fill 60 customer orders for a total of 4,000 cases.

REQUIRED

a. Assuming all manufacturing overhead is estimated and predicted on the basis of machine hours, determine the predicted total overhead costs to produce the 4,000 cases of lime vinaigrette.
b. Assuming manufacturing overhead is estimated and predicted using separate rates for machine hours, customer orders, and products (a multiple-level cost hierarchy), determine the predicted total overhead costs to produce the 4,000 cases of lime vinaigrette.
c. Calculate the error in predicting manufacturing overhead using machine hours versus using multiple cost drivers. Indicate whether the use of only machine hours results in overpredicting or underpredicting the costs to produce 4,000 cases of lime vinaigrette.
d. Looking just at batch level costs, calculate the error in predicting those costs using machine hours versus using customer orders. Indicate whether the use of only machine hours results in overpredicting or underpredicting the batch-level costs to produce 4,000 cases of lime vinaigrette.
e. Looking just at product-level costs, calculate the error in predicting those costs using machine hours versus using number of products. Indicate whether the use of only machine hours results in overpredicting or underpredicting the product-level costs to produce 4,000 cases of lime vinaigrette.

P18-39. Unit and Batch Level Cost Drivers   LO18-2, 3

Kentucky Fried Chicken (a reportable operating segment of **Yum Brands Inc.**), a fast-food restaurant, serves fried chicken. Assume the managers are considering an "all you can eat" promotion and want to know the costs before setting a price. Each batch must be 50 pieces. The chicken is pre-cut by the chain headquarters and sent to the stores in 10-piece bags. Each bag costs $5. Preparing a batch of 50 pieces of chicken with KFC's special coating takes one employee two hours. The current wage rate is $10 per hour. Another cost driver is the cost of putting fresh oil into the fryers. New oil, costing $9, is used for each batch.

REQUIRED

a. Determine the cost of preparing one batch of 50 pieces.
b. If management projects that it will sell 150 pieces of fried chicken, determine the total cost and the cost per piece.
c. If management estimates the sales to be 350 pieces, determine the total costs.
d. How much will the batch costs increase if the government raises the minimum wage to $12 per hour?
e. If management decided to increase the number of pieces in a batch to 100, determine the cost of preparing 350 pieces. Assume that the batch would take twice as long to prepare, pay rate stays at $10 per hour, and management wants to replace the oil after 100 pieces are cooked. Assume no change in expected sales volume. Note that only full batches can be prepared.
f. Should management increase the batch size to 100? Why or why not?

P18-40. Analyzing and Applying Activity-Based Costing – CMA adapted   LO18-2, 3, 4

1. All of the following are likely to be used as a cost allocation base in activity-based costing except the
    a. number of different materials used to manufacture the product.
    b. units of materials used to manufacture the product.
    c. number of vendors supplying the materials used to manufacture the product.
    d. cost of materials used to manufacture the product.

CMA adapted

2. Pelder Products Company manufactures two types of engineering diagnostic equipment used in construction. The two products are based upon different technologies, x-ray and ultra-sound, but are manufactured in the same factory. Pelder has computed the manufacturing cost of the x-ray and ultra-sound products by adding together direct materials, direct labor, and overhead cost applied based on the number of direct labor hours. The factory has three overhead departments that support the single production line that makes both products. Budgeted overhead spending for the departments is as follows.

	Department			
	Engineering design	**Material handling**	**Setup**	**Total**
	$6,000	$5,000	$3,000	$14,000

Pelder's budgeted manufacturing activities and costs for the period are as follows.

	Product	
Activity	**X-Ray**	**Ultra-Sound**
Units produced and sold....................................	50	100
Direct materials used	$5,000	$8,000
Direct labor hours used	100	300
Direct labor cost	$4,000	$12,000
Number of parts used..	400	600
Number of engineering changes	2	1
Number of product setups	8	7

What is the budgeted cost to manufacture one ultra-sound machine using the activity-based costing method?

CMA adapted

3. The Chocolate Baker specializes in chocolate baked goods. The firm has long assessed the profitability of a product line by comparing revenues to the cost of goods sold. However, Barry White, the firm's new accountant, wants to use an activity-based costing system that takes into consideration the cost of the delivery person. Listed below are activity and cost information relating to two of Chocolate Baker's major products.

	Muffins	**Cheesecake**
Revenue..	$53,000	$46,000
Cost of goods sold	26,000	21,000
Delivery Activity		
Number of deliveries..	150	85
Average length of delivery	10 Minutes	15 Minutes
Cost per hour for delivery.................................	$20.00	$20.00

REQUIRED

a. Using activity-based costing, determine the profitability of muffins.
b. Using activity-based costing, determine the profitability of cheesecakes.

CMA adapted

LO18-5 **P18-41. Customer Profitability Analysis**

Remington Aeronautics LTD is a British aeronautics subcontract company that designs and manufactures electronic control systems for commercial airlines. The vast majority of all commercial aircraft are manufactured by **Boeing** in the U.S. and **Airbus** in Europe; however, there is a relatively small group of companies that manufacture narrow-body commercial jets. Assume for this exercise that Remington does contract work for the two major manufacturers plus three companies in the second tier.

Because competition is intense in the industry, Remington has always operated on a fairly thin 20% gross profit margin; hence, it is crucial that it manage nonmanufacturing overhead costs effectively in order to achieve an acceptable net profit margin. With declining profit margins in recent years, Remington Aeronautics' CEO, John Remington, has become concerned that the cost of obtaining contracts and maintaining relations with its five major customers may be getting out of hand. You have been hired to conduct a customer profitability analysis.

Remington Aeronautics' nonmanufacturing overhead consists of $2 million of general and administrative (G&A) expense (including, among other expenses, the CEO's salary and bonus and the cost of operating the company's corporate jet) and selling and customer support expenses of $3.15 million (including 5% sales commissions and $750,000 of additional costs).

The accounting staff determined that the $750,000 of additional selling and customer support expenses related to the following four activity cost pools.

Activity	Activity Cost Driver	Cost per Unit of Activity
1. Sales visits	Number of visit days	$1,000
2. Product adjustments	Number of adjustments	1,600
3. Phone and email contacts	Number of calls/contacts	100
4. Promotion and entertainment events	Number of events	3,000

Financial and activity data on the five customers follow (Sales and Gross Profit data in millions).

Customer	Sales	Gross Profit	Activity 1	Activity 2	Activity 3	Activity 4
A	$19	$3.8	90	10	160	21
B	14	2.8	105	20	200	20
C	5	1.0	95	18	100	17
D	6	1.2	30	8	35	12
E	4	0.8	30	4	25	14
	$48	$9.6	350	60	520	84

In addition to the above, the sales staff used the corporate jet at a cost of $1,000 per hour for trips to customers as follows.

Customer A	16 hours
Customer B	32 hours
Customer C	8 hours
Customer D	0 hours
Customer E	5 hours

The total cost of operating the airplane is included in general and administrative expense; none is included in selling and customer support costs.

REQUIRED

a. Prepare a customer profitability analysis for Remington Aeronautics that shows the gross profits less all expenses that can reasonably be assigned to the five customers.
b. Now assuming that the remaining general and administrative costs are assigned to the five customers based on relative sales dollars, calculate net profit for each customer.
c. Discuss the merits of the analysis in part *a* versus part *b*.

P18-42. Multi-Level Profitability Analysis

AccuMeter manufactures and sells its only product (Z1) in lot sizes of 1,000 units. Because of this approach, lot (batch)-level costs are regarded as variable for CVP analysis. Presented is sales and cost information for the year:

Sales revenue (75,000 units at $65)	$4,875,000
Direct materials (75,000 units at $20)	1,500,000
Processing (75,000 units at $15)	1,125,000
Setup (150 lots at $2,500)	375,000
Batch movement (150 lots at $500)	75,000
Order filling (150 lots at $250)	37,500
Fixed manufacturing overhead	1,000,000
Fixed selling and administrative	450,000

REQUIRED

a. Prepare a traditional contribution income statement in good form.
b. Prepare a multi-level contribution income statement in good form. (*Hint:* First determine the appropriate cost hierarchy.)
c. What is the current contribution per lot (batch) of 1,000 units?
d. Management is contemplating introducing a limited number of specialty products. One product would sell for $80 per unit and have direct materials costs of $35 per unit. All other costs and all production and sales procedures will remain unchanged. What lot (batch) size is required for a contribution of $800 per lot?

CASES AND PROJECTS

LO18-1, 2, 3, 4   **C18-43. Designing an ABC System for a Country Club**

The Reserve Club is a traditional private golf and country club that has three different categories of memberships: golf, tennis & swimming, and social. Golf members have access to all amenities and programs in the club, Tennis & Swimming members have access to all amenities and programs except use of the golf course, and Social members have access to only the social activities of the club, excluding golf, tennis, and swimming. All members have clubhouse privileges, including use of the bar and restaurant, which is operated by an outside contractor. During the past year, the average membership in each category, along with the number of club visits during the year, was as follows.

	Members	Visits
Golf	500	15,000
Tennis & Swimming	110	2,200
Social	250	5,000

Some members of the club have been complaining that heavy users of the club are not bearing their share of the costs through their membership fees. Dess Rosmond, General Manager of the Reserve Club, agrees that monthly fees paid by the various member groups should be based on the annual average amount of cost-related activities provided by the club for the three groups, and he intends to set fees on that basis for the coming year. The annual direct costs of operating the golf course, tennis courts, and swimming pool have been calculated by the club's controller as follows.

Golf course	$1,250,000
Swimming pool	75,000
Tennis courts	45,000

The operation of the bar and restaurant and all related costs, including depreciation on the bar and restaurant facilities, are excluded from this analysis. In addition to the above costs, the club incurs general overhead costs in the following amounts for the most recent (and typical) year.

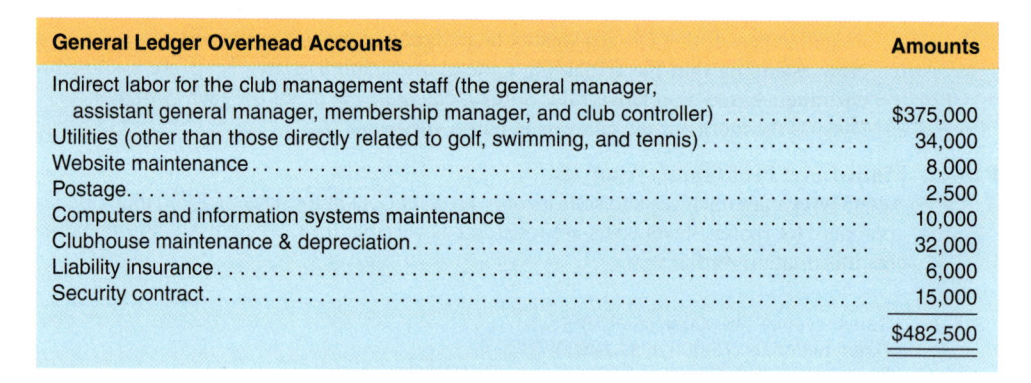

General Ledger Overhead Accounts	Amounts
Indirect labor for the club management staff (the general manager, assistant general manager, membership manager, and club controller)	$375,000
Utilities (other than those directly related to golf, swimming, and tennis)	34,000
Website maintenance	8,000
Postage	2,500
Computers and information systems maintenance	10,000
Clubhouse maintenance & depreciation	32,000
Liability insurance	6,000
Security contract	15,000
	$482,500

Dess believes that the best way to assign most of the overhead costs to the three membership categories is with an activity-based system that recognizes four key activities that occur regularly in the club:

- Recruiting and providing orientation for new members
- Maintaining the membership roster and communicating with members
- Planning, scheduling, and managing club events
- Maintaining the financial records and reporting for the club

REQUIRED

a. Identify and explain which overhead costs can reasonably be assigned to one or more of the four key activities, and suggest a basis for making the assignment.
b. Identify a cost driver for each activity cost pool that would seem to be suitable for assigning the activity cost pool to the three membership categories.
c. Suggest a method for assigning any overhead costs to the three membership categories that cannot reasonably be assigned to activity pools.
d. Comment on the suitability of ABC to this cost assignment situation.

C18-44. Product Costing: Department versus Activity-Based Costing for Overhead

LO18-1, 2, 3, 4

Advertising Technologies, Inc. (ATI) specializes in providing both published and online advertising services for the business marketplace. The company monitors its costs based on the cost per column inch of published space printed in print advertising media and based on the cost per minute of online advertising time delivered on "The AD Line," a computer-based, online advertising service. ATI has one new competitor, Tel-a-Ad, in its local online advertising market; and with increased competition, ATI has seen a decline in sales of online advertising in recent years. ATI's president, Robert Beard, believes that predatory pricing by Tel-a-Ad has caused the problem. The following is a recent conversation between Robert and Jane Minnear, director of marketing for ATI.

Jane: I just received a call from one of our major customers concerning our advertising rates on "The AD Line" who said that a sales rep from another firm (it had to be Tel-a-Ad) had offered the same service at $1 per minute, which is $0.75 per minute less than our price.

Robert: It's costing about $1.40 per minute to produce that product. I don't see how they can afford to sell it so cheaply. I'm not convinced that we should meet the price. Perhaps the better strategy is to emphasize producing and selling more published ads, which we're more experienced with and where our margins are high and we have virtually no competition.

Jane: You may be right. Based on a recent survey of our customers, I think we can raise the price significantly for published advertising and still not lose business.

Robert: That sounds promising; however, before we make a major recommitment to publishing, let's explore other possible explanations. I want to know how our costs compare with our competitors. Maybe we could be more efficient and find a way to earn a good return on online advertising.

After this meeting, Robert and Jane requested an investigation of production costs and comparative efficiency of producing published versus online advertising services. The controller, Tim Gentry, indicated that ATI's efficiency was comparable to that of its competitors and prepared the following cost data.

	Published Advertising	Online Advertising
Estimated number of production units	100,000	5,000,000
Selling price	$210	$1.75
Direct product costs	$10,500,000	$2,500,000
Overhead allocation*	$5,100,000	$4,500,000
Overhead per unit	$51	$0.90
Direct costs per unit	$105	$0.50
Number of customers	90,000	12,500
Number of salesperson days	14,250	1,750
Number of art and design hours	17,500	2,500
Number of creative services subcontract hours	50,000	12,500
Number of customer service calls	36,000	4,000

* Based on direct labor costs

Upon examining the data, Robert decided that he wanted to know more about the overhead costs since they were such a high proportion of total production costs. He was provided the following list of overhead costs and told that they were currently being assigned to products in proportion to direct labor costs.

Selling costs	$4,200,000
Visual and audio design costs	1,700,000
Creative services costs	2,950,000
Customer service costs	750,000

REQUIRED

Using the data provided by the controller, prepare analyses to help Robert and Jane in making their decisions. (*Hint:* Prepare cost calculations for both product lines using ABC to see whether there is any significant difference in their unit costs.) Should ATI switch from the fast-growing, online advertising market back into the well-established published advertising market? Does the charge of predatory pricing seem valid? Why are customers likely to be willing to pay a higher price to get published services? Do traditional costing and activity-based costing lead to the same conclusions?

LO18-1, 2, 3, 4   **C18-45. Unit-Level and Multiple-Level Cost Assignments with Decision Implications**

CarryAll Company[7] produces briefcases from leather, fabric, and synthetic materials in a single production department. The basic product is a standard briefcase made from leather and lined with fabric. CarryAll has a good reputation in the market because the standard briefcase is a high-quality item that has been produced for many years.

Last year, the company decided to expand its product line and produce specialty briefcases for special orders. These briefcases differ from the standard in that they vary in size, contain both leather and synthetic materials, and are imprinted with the buyer's logo (the standard briefcase is simply imprinted with the CarryAll name in small letters). The decision to use some synthetic materials in the briefcase was made to hold down the materials cost. To reduce the labor costs per unit, most of the cutting and stitching on the specialty briefcases is done by automated machines, which are used to a much lesser degree in the production of the standard briefcases. Because of these changes in the design and production of the specialty briefcases, CarryAll management believed that they would cost less to produce than the standard briefcases. However, because they are specialty items, they were priced slightly higher; standards are priced at $30 and specialty briefcases at $32.

After reviewing last month's results of operations, CarryAll's president became concerned about the profitability of the two product lines because the standard briefcase showed a loss while the specialty briefcase showed a greater profit margin than expected. The president is wondering whether the company should drop the standard briefcase and focus entirely on specialty items. Units and cost data for last month's operations as reported to the president are as follows.

	Standard	Specialty
Units produced	10,000	2,500
Direct materials		
Leather (1 sq. yd. × $15.00; ½ sq. yd. × $15.00)	$15.00	$ 7.50
Fabric (1 sq. yd. × $5.00; 1 sq. yd. × $5.00)	5.00	5.00
Synthetic		5.00
Total materials	20.00	17.50
Direct labor (½ hr. × $12.00; ¼ hr. × $12.00)	6.00	3.00
Manufacturing overhead (½ hr. × $8.98; ¼ hr. × $8.98)	4.49	2.25
Cost per unit	$30.49	$22.75

Manufacturing overhead is applied on the basis of direct labor hours. The rate of $8.98 per direct labor hour was calculated by dividing the total overhead ($50,500) by the direct labor hours (5,625). As shown in the table, the cost of a standard briefcase is $0.49 higher than its $30 sales price; the specialty briefcase has a cost of only $22.75, for a gross profit per unit of $9.25. The problem with these costs is that they do not accurately reflect the activities involved in manufacturing each product. Determining the costs using ABC should provide better product costing data to help gauge the actual profitability of each product line.

The manufacturing overhead costs must be analyzed to determine the activities driving the costs. Assume that the following costs and cost drivers have been identified:

- The Purchasing Department's cost is $6,000. The major activity driving these costs is the number of purchase orders processed. During the month, the Purchasing Department prepared the following number of purchase orders for the materials indicated.

Leather	20
Fabric	30
Synthetic material	50

- The cost of receiving and inspecting materials is $7,500. These costs are driven by the number of deliveries. During the month, the following number of deliveries were made.

Leather	30
Fabric	40
Synthetic material	80

- Production line setup cost is $10,000. Setup activities involve changing the machines to produce the different types of briefcases. Each setup for production of the standard briefcases requires one hour; each setup for specialty briefcases requires two hours. Standard briefcases are produced in batches

---
[7] The CarryAll Company case, prepared by Professors Harold Roth and Imogene Posey, was originally published in the *Management Accounting Campus Report*.

of 200, and specialty briefcases are produced in batches of 25. During the last month, there were 50 setups for the standard item and 100 setups for the specialty item.
- The cost of inspecting finished goods is $8,000. All briefcases are inspected to ensure that quality standards are met. However, the final inspection of standard briefcases takes very little time because the employees identify and correct quality problems as they do the hand cutting and stitching. A survey of the personnel responsible for inspecting the final products showed that 150 hours were spent on standard briefcases and 250 hours on specialty briefcases during the month.
- Equipment-related costs are $6,000. Equipment-related costs include repairs, depreciation, and utilities. Management has determined that a logical basis for assigning these costs to products is machine hours. A standard briefcase requires 1/2 hour of machine time, and a specialty briefcase requires 2 hours. Thus, during the last month, 5,000 hours of machine time relate to the standard line and 5,000 hours relate to the specialty line.
- Plant-related costs are $13,000. These costs include property taxes, insurance, administration, and others. For the purpose of determining average unit costs, they are to be assigned to products using machine hours.

REQUIRED
a. Using activity-based costing concepts, what overhead costs should be assigned to the two products?
b. What is the unit cost of each product using activity-based costing concepts?
c. Reevaluate the president's concern about the profitability of the two product lines.
d. Discuss the merits of activity-based management as it relates to CarryAll's ABC cost system.

C18-46. Ethics and Cost Allocation LO18-4
A consulting firm offers services to both a governmental contractor and private organizations. The government typically absorbs all of the firm's reported costs plus a prenegotiated margin. The private contracts typically are arranged as fixed fee contracts. The consulting firm is contemplating moving to an ABC costing system, but management believes that this will result in a reallocation of costs from the government contract to the private contracts. Should the consulting firm move forward with the updated ABC system?

SOLUTIONS TO REVIEW PROBLEMS

Review 18-1—Solution

a. Plantwide overhead rate = Total manufacturing overhead ÷ Total machine hours
= ($120,000 + $55,000) ÷ (10,000 + 5,000)
= $175,000 ÷ 15,000
= $11.67 per machine hour

	Dog Chow	Purina One
Product costs per unit		
Direct materials.	$12,000	$18,000
Direct labor	5,000	4,000
Manufacturing overhead		
500 + 200 = 700 machine hours × $11.67	8,169	
700 + 100 = 800 machine hours × $11.67		9,336
Total cost per batch	$25,169	$31,336
Number of units per batch	÷ 100	÷ 100
Cost per case	$251.69	$313.36

b. Departmental overhead rates = Total departmental overhead ÷ Dept. allocation base
Formulation = $120,000 ÷ 10,000 machine hours
= $12 per machine hour
Packaging = $55,000 ÷ 5,000 machine hours
= $11 per machine hour

	Dog Chow	Purina One
Product costs per unit		
Direct materials...	$12,000	$18,000
Direct labor...	5,000	4,000
Manufacturing overhead		
Formulation Department		
500 machine hours × $12..................	6,000	
700 machine hours × $12..................		8,400
Packaging Department		
200 machine hours × $11..................	2,200	
100 machine hours × $11..................		1,100
Total cost per batch...	$25,200	$31,500
Number of units per batch................................	÷ 100	÷ 100
Cost per case...	$252.00	$315.00

Review 18-2—Solution

Answers may vary but likely activities and related drivers might include:
- Production line setup/number of production runs
- Food production/time in production
- Food packaging/units produced
- Quality testing/number of units or number of batches of units
- Shipping/number of production runs

Review 18-3—Solution

Activity-based overhead rates = Activity cost pool ÷ Activity cost driver
Maintenance = $30,000 ÷ 15,000 machine hours
= $2 per machine hour
Materials handling = $45,000 ÷ 4,500 materials moves
= $10 per materials move
Machine setups = $75,000 ÷ 750 setups
= $100 per machine setup
Inspections = $25,000 ÷ 1,000 inspection hours
= $25 per inspection hour

	Dog Chow	Purina One
Product costs per unit		
Direct materials...	$12,000	$18,000
Direct labor...	5,000	4,000
Manufacturing overhead		
Maintenance activity		
700 machine hours × $2....................	1,400	
800 machine hours × $2....................		1,600
Materials handling activity		
30 materials moves × $10...................	300	
50 materials moves × $10...................		500
Machine setups activity		
5 machine setups × $100...................	500	
9 machine setups × $100...................		900
Inspections activity		
30 inspection hours × $25..................	750	
60 inspection hours × $25..................		1,500
Total cost per batch...	$19,950	$26,500
Number of units per batch................................	÷ 100	÷ 100
Cost per unit...	$199.50	$265.00

Review 18-4—Solution

Following is a summary of product costs for Dog Chow and Purina One assigning overhead costs based on a plantwide rate, department rates, and activity-based rates.

	Dog Chow	Purina One
Plantwide rate	$251.69	$313.36
Department rates	$252.00	$315.00
Activity-based rates	$199.50	$265.00

Changing from a plantwide rate to department rates had little effect on unit costs because the department rates per machine hour are close to the plantwide rate per machine hour. Based on machine hours, both departments have similar cost structures.

When using activity-based rates, however, the cost of these two products drops dramatically because they use only a small portion (less than 2%) of the activities of materials handling (80 of 4,500) and setup (14 of 750). Neither a plantwide rate nor department rates recognize this fact, resulting in a large amount of cost cross-subsidization of other products by Dog Chow and Purina One for these costs. Although this problem did not include cost analysis of the other products, it shows that they are less profitable and that Dog Chow and Purina One are much more profitable than management previously thought.

Review 18-5—Solution

a. Activity A—Minor visits – maintenance and upgrades
   Activity B—Visits to customers
   Activity C—Communications via phone

Activity	1	2	3	4	5
A (@ $160)	$11,040	$22,560	$11,840	$ 9,760	$21,760
B (@ $300)	7,500	12,600	5,700	8,400	11,700
C (@ $50)	6,400	10,250	4,950	5,300	9,450
Total support costs	$24,940	$45,410	$22,490	$23,460	$42,910
Profit before support costs	80,000	85,000	83,000	90,000	78,000
Customer profits	$55,060	$39,590	$60,510	$66,540	$35,090
Ratio of support costs to profit before support costs	31%	53%	27%	26%	55%

b. This analysis is beneficial to Nestlé because it shows that Groups 2 and 5 are outliers among the five customer groups in terms of support services required. Groups 2 and 5 are significantly larger consumers of activities for all three of the support activities. Note also that Group 4 customers are relatively light users of minor systems maintenance, and Group 3 are relatively light users of phone communications. Calculating the ratio of total support costs to profit before support costs provides additional insight into the relative profitability of the customer groups. All five customer groups are profitable; however, this analysis provides useful information for improving profits by working with Groups 2 and 5 to control support activities and related costs and attempt to bring their support costs in line with the other customer groups.

Review 18-6—Solution

Weekly contribution per average customer:
$17 sales per visit × (1 − 0.80) contribution ratio × 1.50 visits = $5.10
Annual contribution per customer = $5.10 × 52 weeks = $265.20
Customers required for desired profit = ($80,000 + $40,000)/$265.20 = 453 (rounded up to the next whole number)
Required population = 453 customers/0.05 customers in population = 9,060

Chapter 19: Additional Topics in Product Costing

LEARNING OBJECTIVES

LO19-1 Describe the allocation of service department costs under the direct and step methods. (p. 19-3)

LO19-2 Calculate and explain the cost of excess capacity. (p. 19-11)

LO19-3 Describe the JIT/Lean Production Approach. (p. 19-14)

LO19-4 Explain managerial accountants' focus on data-driven decision-making. (p. 19-19)

Road Map

LO	Learning Objective | Topics	Page	eLecture	Review	Assignments
LO19-1	**Describe the allocation of service department costs under the direct and step methods.** Producing Department :: Operating Department :: Service Department :: Interdepartmental Services :: Shared Services Department :: Direct Method :: Step Method	19-3	e19–1	R19-1	M19-17, M19-18, M19-19, E19-24, E19-25, E19-26, E19-27, P19-35, P19-36, P19-37, P19-38, P19-39, P19-40
LO19-2	**Calculate and explain the cost of excess capacity.** Theoretical Capacity :: Actual Capacity :: Practical Capacity :: Cost of Excess Capacity :: Dual Rates	19-11	e19–2	R19-2	M19-20, E19-28, P19-41, P19-42
LO19-3	**Describe the JIT/Lean Production Approach.** Just-In-Time :: Lean Production :: Cycle Time :: Materials-Push System :: Materials-Pull System :: Inventory Turnover :: Gross Margin Return on Inventory Investment :: Cycle Efficiency :: Backflush Costing	19-14	e19–3	R19-3	M19-21, M19-22, E19-29, E19-30, E19-31, E19-32, P19-43, P19-44, C19-45, C19-46, **DA19-1**
LO19-4	**Explain managerial accountants' focus on data-driven decision-making.** Data-Driven Decision-Making :: Correlation :: Causation :: CGMA Competency Framework :: Digital Skills	19-19	e19–4	R19-4	M19-23, E19-33, E19-34, **DA19-2, DA19-3**

WHOLE FOODS
www.wholefoodsmarket.com

Whole Foods, a subsidiary of **Amazon.com, Inc.** (hereafter referred to as Amazon), tried to shed its nickname "Whole Paycheck" for years without success. However, since being purchased by Amazon, attitudes about the company have improved, according to **YouGov**, a market research company. The main reasons for the change in perception include: expanded grocery delivery, online ordering, price cuts on selected items, and regular discounts for Amazon's Prime members.

To increase grocery delivery and online ordering volume, Whole Foods has been expanding, geographically, into areas previously unserved. Leasing and startup costs can be minimized by looking at sites previously occupied by struggling retailers like Sears and Kmart. These larger sites can also be used to accommodate Amazon delivery and pickup for online orders.

To maintain profitability while cutting prices, Whole Foods has been moving away from local vendors and stocking larger national brands, including its own brand, **365 Everyday Value**®. Private labels typically have higher profit margins due to their lower costs. Besides the sale of 365 products at Whole Foods, 365 products are one of the best-selling private label brands on Amazon.com.

A grocery operation has numerous support departments—areas that are necessary to the operation of the store, but not directly attributable to any one product or group of products. Examples of support departments include human resources, accounting, and custodial services. Whole Foods must develop a system of service cost allocation that will minimize distortions in profitability across grocery departments. The company must also operate as efficiently as possible. However, that efficiency shouldn't come at the expense of the quality that has become Whole Foods' bedrock.

The last, but perhaps most important factor for the profitability of a company is how well it manages its inventory. Holding inventory is costly due to storage and insurance costs; and in the case of a grocer, perishable inventory is prone to spoilage and waste. This chapter discusses how companies, such as Whole Foods, assign the cost of their internal service departments to their products, and the benefits of adopting a lean operations philosophy in managing their inventory levels.

Sources: today.yougov.com and www.wholefoodsmarket.com

CHAPTER ORGANIZATION

Additional Topics in Product Costing

Allocation of Service Department Costs	The Cost of Excess Capacity	Just-In-Time (JIT) Inventory Management/Lean Production	Increased Focus on Data-Driven Decision-Making
• Reasons for Allocating Service Department Costs • The Process of Allocating Service Department Costs • Direct Method • Comparing the Direct Method to the Step Method • Step Method	• Capacity Levels • Calculating the Cost of Excess Capacity • Managing Excess Capacity • Capacity Considerations When Using Dual Rates	• Characteristics of JIT/Lean Production Approach • Performance Evaluation Under JIT/Lean Production Approach	• Using Data Effectively • Developing Skills for Decision-Making

ALLOCATION OF SERVICE DEPARTMENT COSTS

LO19-1
Describe the allocation of service department costs under the direct and step methods.

In Chapter 17, we discussed two basic methods (job order costing and process costing) for accumulating, measuring, and recording the costs of producing goods (and in some cases, services). In Chapter 18, we discussed both traditional and activity-based methods for assigning indirect costs to products and to services. We now look in more detail at assigning indirect costs of service departments to producing, operating, or other service departments.

A department typically falls into one of the following three categories.

- *Production departments* (also called *producing departments*) actually perform work on a product.
- *Operating departments* provide services.
- *Support departments*, such as payroll, human resources, information technology, security, and facilities, provide support services for production, operating and other service departments. These support departments are typically called **service departments**.

Service departments, which are considered essential elements in the overall business process, do not work directly on a "product" or "service" but provide auxiliary support to other departments. In addition to providing support for production and operating departments, some service departments also provide services to other service departments. Services provided by one service department to other service departments are called **interdepartmental services**. For example, **Amazon**'s payroll and personnel departments could provide services to production departments and other service departments, whereas engineering may provide services to only the production departments.

Recently, there has been a trend toward wider implementation of **shared services departments**. In a shared services model, support services across a company's different business components are consolidated into one support function to increase efficiencies and decrease overall company costs. This means, for example, that Amazon could have an information technology department that serves Whole Foods and other companies owned by Amazon such as **Zappos** and **Wag**. In a recent example, **Verizon** announced a move toward a new central support services operation in order to drive efficiencies. Examples of its shared services include supply chain, fleet, and global technology solutions.[1] In another example, **Energizer Holdings, Inc.**'s operating model includes both standalone and shared service functions between product segments. Its shared services include sales, marketing, human resources, technology and finance.[2] In summary, the total cost of goods and services includes the costs incurred within production or operating departments, as well as the cost of services received from service departments.

---
[1] Young, Richard," Verizon announces organization evolution to accelerate efficiency and growth", Verizon, Oct. 11, 2022. https://www.verizon.com/about/news/verizon-announces-organization-evolution-accelerate-efficiency-and-growth

[2] Energizer Holdings, Inc.'s 2022 10-K

Reasons for Allocating Service Department Costs

Determining Cost of Inventory for Financial Reporting The product costing system for a manufacturer must include a policy for assigning to products the cost of services received from service departments. Suppose Whole Foods uses one company-wide overhead rate in costing its proprietary product line. (We assume for illustration purposes in our hypothetical examples in this chapter, that Whole Foods manufactures its proprietary product line.) The costs of all service departments utilized in manufacturing would be included in a single cost pool, allocated to products using one cost driver such as direct labor hours. If Whole Foods uses departmental overhead rates, service department costs are allocated to the production departments that utilize their services, and the allocated service department costs are added to the indirect manufacturing costs incurred within the department to arrive at total departmental overhead. Departmental overhead is allocated to products using cost drivers. In either case, *the cost of inventory and cost of goods sold include the allocated costs of service departments that are part of indirect manufacturing costs.*

Determining Cost of Products/Services for Managerial Purposes The computation of product or service costs has many implications for manufacturers, merchandisers, and service providers. For example, pricing decisions are often based on the cost of a product or service, as well as the product's consumer demand and price elasticity. (Price elasticity describes the sensitivity of price to volume changes and is discussed further in Chapter 22.) Consider a veterinarian office that allocates administration service department costs to routine wellness and urgent care in order to price services more accurately. Prices should be set to not only recover the costs of medical care and supplies, but of administrative costs such as scheduling, billing, and accounting.

In some scenarios when a company is reimbursed for its incurred costs plus a margin, the calculation of product costs impacts the revenue and/or cash received by an organization. Emory University, a major research university, encounters numerous situations where the cost allocation system can substantially impact the university's financial well-being. For example, governmental and private insurance systems typically reimburse costs of services provided to patients in the hospitals and clinics of Emory University. These reimbursements are typically based on costs incurred while offering medical services. Additionally, research grants are often awarded and disbursed based on incurred costs. It is crucial that the cost system properly accounts for all costs incurred to treat patients and or conduct research. Failing to properly allocate service department costs can result in large revenue losses to Emory since reimbursement is based, in part, on the amount of allocated costs. During economic recessions, it is even more important to accurately measure the indirect service department costs to ensure maximum cost recovery.

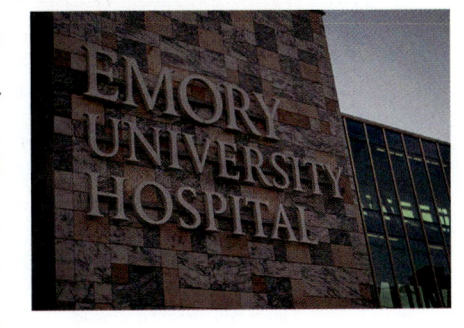

> **Suppose you are looking at the cost of operating one Whole Foods store in Washington, D.C. Should the cost of service departments always be allocated to the store?**
>
> *The cost analysis depends on the decision being made. If you are interested in analyzing the full cost of operating the Whole Foods in Washington, D.C., and comparing it to other stores, you would include the cost of service departments like information technology and human resources. However, if you are trying to calculate how much the company will save if it closes the Washington, D.C., store, the analysis would differ. In this case, you would only look at relevant or avoidable costs. Consequently, if the information technology costs at Amazon would remain constant, regardless of the status of the store, you would not include an allocation of information technology costs in the analysis.*

Critical Thinking & Decision-Making

The Process of Allocating Service Department Costs

To illustrate service department cost allocations, suppose the Whole Foods Division of Amazon has two producing departments for its proprietary product line (Mixing and Bottling), three service departments (Support Services, Engineering Resources, and Buildings and Grounds), and three product groups (beverages; sauces and marinades; and jams, jellies and nut butters). The service departments and their respective service functions and cost allocation bases are as follows.

Department	Service Functions	Allocation Base
Support Services	Receiving and inventory control	Total amount of department capital investment
Engineering Resources	Production setup and engineering and testing	Number of employees
Buildings and Grounds	Machinery maintenance and depreciation	Amount of square footage occupied

Difficulty in choosing an allocation base for service department costs is not uncommon. For example, Whole Foods may have readily determined the appropriate allocation bases for the Engineering Resources and the Buildings and Grounds departments but may have found the choice for Support Services to be less clear. Perhaps after conducting correlation studies, the most equitable base for allocating Support Services costs to other departments was determined to be total capital investment in the departments. Capital investments could include items such as computer-tracking equipment, both manual and automated forklifts, and other material-moving equipment.

Department Costs	
Direct	**Indirect**
Includes direct costs and indirect costs distinctive to the department	Includes costs allocated or reassigned to the department

A **direct department cost** is a cost assigned directly to a department (production, operating, or service) when it is incurred. For a producing department, direct department costs include both *direct* product costs (direct materials and direct labor) as well as *indirect* product costs (such as indirect labor and indirect materials) incurred distinctly within a department. An **indirect department cost** is a cost allocated to a department as a result of an indirect allocation, or reassignment from another department.

Assume direct department costs and allocation base information used to illustrate Whole Foods's July service department cost allocations are summarized as follows.

	Direct Department Costs	Number of Employees		Amount of Square Footage Occupied		Total Amount of Department Capital Investment	
Service departments							
Support Services	$ 27,000	15	15%	4,000	8%	—	—
Engineering Resources	20,000	—	—	2,000	4	$ 45,000	8%
Buildings and Grounds	10,000	5	5	—	—	50,000	9
Producing departments							
Mixing	40,000*	24	24	11,000	22	180,000	33
Bottling	90,000*	56	56	33,000	66	270,000	50
	$187,000	100	100%	50,000	100%	$545,000	100%

*Direct department overhead

The preceding information omitted the amount of capital investment in Support Services, the number of employees in Engineering Resources, and the amount of square footage used by Buildings and Grounds. These data were omitted because a department does not allocate costs to itself; it allocates costs only to the departments it serves.

Two methods commonly used for service department cost allocations—direct and step—are discussed in this section. Each of these methods eventually results in all service department costs being assigned to the producing departments. Once this is done, Whole Foods can use either department overhead rates or activity-based costing to further assign the indirect costs that are accumulated in the producing departments to the actual product groups. Remember that if Whole Foods were to use a plantwide overhead rate to allocate indirect costs, the service department costs would not be allocated to the producing departments. Instead, they would be added to the single plantwide indirect cost pool and allocated directly to the products.

Critical Thinking & Decision-Making

When would it be appropriate for Whole Foods to allocate shared services costs to departments using one plantwide cost pool?

Using one cost pool is simple and is appropriate at times. If the shared services are consumed in proportion to the cost driver used to compute the plantwide overhead rate, then using one cost pool and including the costs of shared services within that single cost pool might be appropriate.

Using the Direct Method to Allocate Service Department Costs

The **direct method** allocates all service department costs based only on the amount of services provided to the producing departments. **Exhibit 19.1** shows the flow of costs using the direct method. All arrows depicting the cost flows extend directly from service departments to producing departments. Under the direct method there are no cost allocations *between* the service departments. After the costs are allocated from the service departments to the Mixing and Bottling departments, the costs are then allocated to the product groups based on the amount of resources used in the production of each product group. For example, after the final allocation, the cost of beverages will include a share of Mixing and Bottling costs. Within those costs are allocated costs from the service departments.

EXHIBIT 19.1 Flow of Costs—Direct Method

Service Departments: Support Services | Engineering Resources | Buildings and Grounds

Producing Departments: Mixing | Bottling

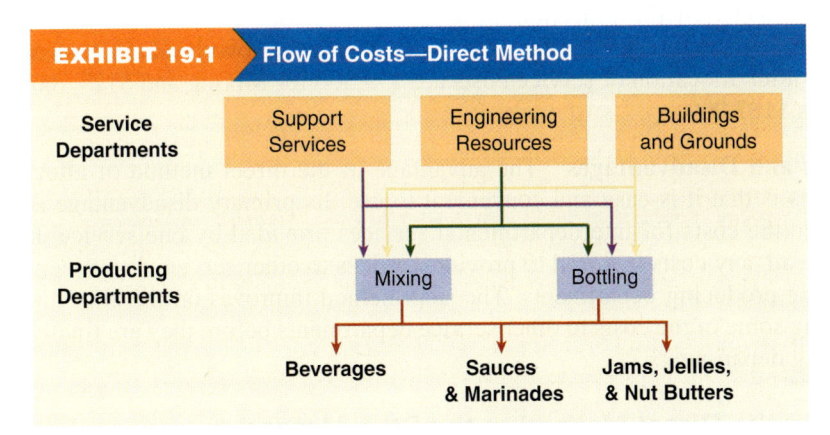

Products: Beverages | Sauces & Marinades | Jams, Jellies, & Nut Butters

Exhibit 19.2 shows the service department cost allocations using the direct method. This method is similar to the costing systems discussed in earlier chapters.

EXHIBIT 19.2 Service Department Cost Allocations—Direct Method

	Total	Mixing	Bottling
Support Services Department			
Allocation base (capital investment)	$450,000	$180,000	$270,000
Amount per dollar of department capital investment	$0.06		
Cost allocations	$ 27,000	$ 10,800	$ 16,200
Engineering Resources Department			
Allocation base (number of employees)	80	24	56
Cost per employee	$250		
Cost allocations	$ 20,000	$ 6,000	$ 14,000
Buildings and Grounds Department			
Allocation base (square footage occupied)	44,000	11,000	33,000
Amount per square foot occupied	$0.22727		
Cost allocations	$ 10,000	$ 2,500	$ 7,500

Cost Allocation Summary

	Support Services	Engineering Resources	Buildings and Grounds	Mixing	Bottling	Total
Department cost before allocations	$27,000	$20,000	$10,000	$40,000	$ 90,000	$187,000
Cost allocations						
Support Services	(27,000)			10,800	16,200	0
Engineering Resources		(20,000)		6,000	14,000	0
Buildings and Grounds			(10,000)	2,500	7,500	0
Department costs after allocations	$ 0	$ 0	$ 0	$59,300	$127,700	$187,000

Notice the allocation base used to allocate costs from the three support departments. Only amounts relating to the *producing departments* are considered in the allocation base. For Engineering Resources, 80 employees are in the allocation base (24 in Mixing and 56 in Bottling). Engineering Resource costs of $20,000 are spread over 80 employees which means $250 will be allocated for each employee. The allocation calculations follow for Engineering Resources (other departments would follow similar calculations).

Engineering Resources Cost Allocation
Mixing: $20,000/80 = $250 × 24 = $6,000
Bottling: $20,000/80 = $250 × 56 = $14,000

Note that you would calculate the same allocations if you based it on a percentage of the driver in each division rather than an overhead rate. However, the overhead rate is important to calculate as it offers additional information about the cost of an underlying product or service.

The cost allocation summary at the bottom of **Exhibit 19.2** shows that all service department costs have been allocated, decreasing the service department costs to zero and increasing the mixing and bottling overhead balances by the amounts of the respective allocations. Also, total costs are not affected by the allocations. The total of $187,000 was merely redistributed so that all costs are reassigned to the departments. Total department overhead costs of the producing departments after allocation of service costs are $59,300 for Mixing and $127,700 for Bottling which equals $187,000.

Advantages and Disadvantages The advantage of the direct method of allocating shared services costs is that it is easy and convenient to use. Its primary disadvantage is that it does not recognize the costs for interdepartmental services provided by one service department to another. Instead, any costs incurred to provide services to other service departments are passed directly to the producing departments. The step method improves on the allocation procedure by redirecting some of the costs to other service departments before they are finally allocated to the producing departments.

Comparing the Direct Method to the Step Method

The **step method** gives partial recognition of interdepartmental services by using a methodology that allocates the service department costs *sequentially* both to the remaining service departments and the producing departments. This method acknowledges that service departments use each other's services. For example, Buildings and Grounds of Whole Foods might use Support Services. Consequently, Buildings and Grounds should be allocated costs from Support Services. Any indirect costs allocated to a service department in this process are added to that service department's direct costs to determine the total costs to allocate to the remaining departments. Through this procedure, all service department costs are assigned to the producing departments and ultimately to the products.

Simplified Example: Direct Method vs. Step Method

Before returning to the Whole Foods example, let's look at a simpler example to illustrate some differences between the direct and step methods. Assume that Prestige Company has two service departments, S1 and S2, and two producing departments, P1 and P2, that provide services as follows.

Provider of Services	Receiver of Services			
	S1	S2	P1	P2
S1	0%	0%	70%	30%
S2	50%	0%	25%	25%

Direct Method If the direct method is used to allocate service department costs to the producing departments, S2 total costs of $100,000 will be allocated equally to the producing departments because they use the same amount of S2 services (25% each). The direct method allocation follows. (Although not illustrated, allocating S1 costs would follow a similar procedure.)

Direct Method	S2	P1	P2
S2 costs before allocation	$100,000		
Allocation of S2 to P1 and P2	$(100,000)	$50,000	$50,000
Department costs after allocation of S2 costs	$ 0	$50,000	$50,000

Does the direct method provide an equitable allocation of S2 costs?

The entire $100,000 is divided equally between the two producing departments, each being allocated $50,000, with no allocation to S1. However, S2 provides half of its services to the other service department (S1), which, in turn, provides the majority of its services to P1. This allocation would underestimate costs for P1 and overestimate costs for P2 because it doesn't take into account P1's share of S2 services that are used by S1.

Step Method Consider the following alternative allocation of the $100,000 of S2 costs that takes into account interdepartmental services. First, the $100,000 of S2 costs is allocated to each of the other departments in proportion to the amount of services provided to them by S2.

$$\text{S2 costs allocated to S1: } 50\% \times \$100,000 = \$50,000$$
$$\text{S2 costs allocated to P1: } 25\% \times \$100,000 = \$25,000$$
$$\text{S2 costs allocated to P2: } 25\% \times \$100,000 = \$25,000$$

Next, the $50,000 allocated to S1 from S2 is reallocated to the producing departments in proportion to the amount of services provided to them by S1.

$$\text{S1 costs allocated to P1: } 70\% \times \$50,000 = \$35,000$$
$$\text{S1 costs allocated to P2: } 30\% \times \$50,000 = \$15,000$$

In this scenario, the $100,000 of S2 costs is ultimately allocated $60,000 to P1 and $40,000 to P2.

Step Method	S1	S2	P1	P2
S2 costs before allocation		$100,000		
Step 1:				
Allocate S2 costs to S1, P1, and P2.............	$50,000	$(100,000)	$25,000	$25,000
Step 2:				
Reallocate S1 costs to P1 and P2	(50,000)	0	35,000	15,000
Department costs after allocation of S2 costs	$ 0	$ 0	$60,000	$40,000

This calculation shows only the ultimate allocation of S2 costs. Of course, any S1 direct department costs would also have to be allocated to P1 and P2 on a 70:30 basis. If interdepartmental services are ignored as shown earlier under the direct method, P1 is allocated only $50,000 of S2 costs. By considering interdepartmental services, P1 is allocated $60,000. Certainly, a more accurate measure of both the direct services and indirect services received by P1 from S2 is $60,000, not $50,000.

Is the step method always better than the direct method? If not, when is the direct method preferable?

If all of the producing departments are similar in the way in which they utilize shared services, the more sophisticated step method will not add new information. However, if, as in this case, the producing departments use shared services differently, the step method will provide a more accurate cost allocation and minimize cost cross-subsidization.

Using the Step Method to Allocate Service Department Costs

The step method is illustrated graphically in **Exhibit 19.3** for Whole Foods. Notice the sequence of the allocations: first, Engineering Resources, second, Support Services, and third, Buildings and Grounds.

EXHIBIT 19.3 — Flow of Costs—Step Method

Service Departments: Engineering Resources → Support Services → Buildings and Grounds

Producing Departments: Mixing, Bottling → Products

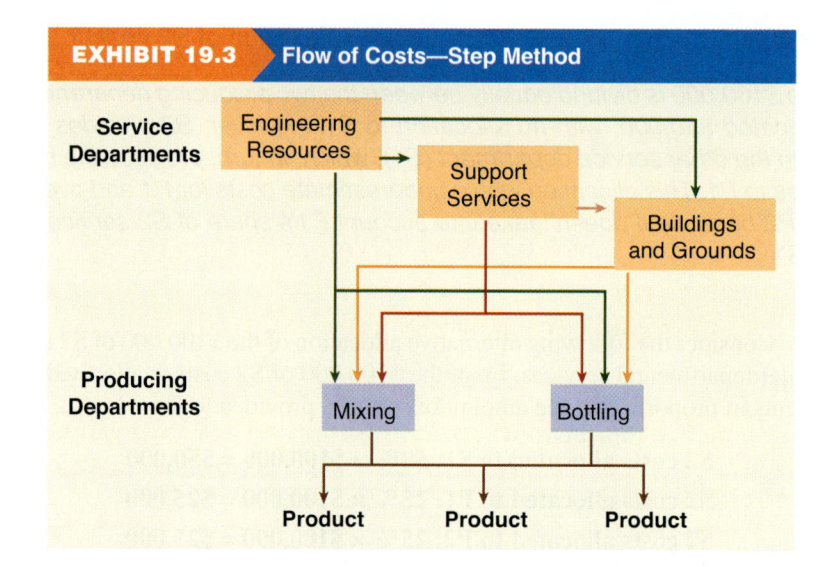

When using the step method, the sequence of allocation is typically based on the relative percentage of services provided to other service departments, **with the largest provider of interdepartmental services allocated first and the smallest provider of interdepartmental services allocated last.** For Whole Foods, Engineering Resources is allocated first because, of the three service departments, it provides the largest percentage (20%) of its services to other service departments: 15% to Support Services and 5% to Buildings and Grounds (see previous cost allocation data on page 19-5). Buildings and Grounds is allocated last because it provides the least amount (12%) of its services to other service departments: 8% to Support Services and 4% to Engineering Resources. The service department cost allocations for Whole Foods using the step method are shown in **Exhibit 19.4**. Note that the total cost of $187,000 has not changed: only the allocation between products has changed.

EXHIBIT 19.4 — Service Department Cost Allocations—Step Method

	Total	Support Services	Buildings and Grounds	Mixing	Bottling
Engineering Resources Department					
Allocation base (number of employees)	100	15	5	24	56
Allocation per employee	$200				
Cost allocations	$20,000	$3,000	$1,000	$4,800	$11,200
Support Services Department					
Allocation base (capital investment)	$500,000		$50,000	$180,000	$270,000
Allocation per dollar of investment	$0.06				
Cost allocations	$30,000*		$3,000	$10,800	$16,200
Buildings and Grounds Department					
Allocation base (square footage occupied)	44,000			11,000	33,000
Allocation per square foot	$0.318				
Cost allocations	$14,000**			$3,500	$10,500

Cost Allocation Summary

	Engineering Resources	Support Services	Buildings and Grounds	Mixing	Bottling	Total
Department costs before allocations	$20,000	$27,000	$10,000	$40,000	$90,000	$187,000
Cost allocations						
Engineering Resources	(20,000)	3,000	1,000	4,800	11,200	—
Support Services		(30,000)	3,000	10,800	16,200	—
Buildings and Grounds			(14,000)	3,500	10,500	—
Department costs after allocations	$0	$0	$0	$59,100	$127,900	$187,000

*$27,000 Direct Support Services cost + $3,000 Allocated Engineering Resources cost = $30,000

**$10,000 Direct Buildings and Grounds cost + $1,000 Allocated Engineering Resources cost + $3,000 Allocated Support Services cost = $14,000

Notice the allocation base used to allocate costs from the three support departments under the step method. Now the amounts relating to *producing* and *service* departments are considered in the allocation base. For Engineering Resources, 100 employees are in the allocation base (15 + 5 + 24 + 56). The allocation calculations follow for Engineering Resources (other departments would follow similar calculations).

Engineering Resources Cost Allocation

Support Services:	$20,000/100 = $200 × 15 = $ 3,000
Buildings and Grounds:	$20,000/100 = $200 × 5 = $ 1,000
Mixing:	$20,000/100 = $200 × 24 = $ 4,800
Bottling:	$20,000/100 = $200 × 56 = $11,200

Why is the change in the allocated costs to Mixing and Bottling minimal ($59,300 vs. $59,100 and $127,700 vs. $127,900) when comparing the direct method to the step method?

In this scenario, Mixing and Bottling departments use the different shared services in similar proportions. Because of this, the difference between the direct and step methods is minimal. In these situations, managers should determine whether the more accurate cost estimate is worth the extra effort. Whether a company should use the direct method or the step method, depends on the extensiveness of interdepartmental services and how evenly those services are used by the producing departments.

Suppose you are developing a cost system for Target and your goal is to calculate the cost of the regional distribution centers. After creating a flowchart of shared services, you realize that some service departments only provide services to the distribution centers, whereas others provide services to distribution centers and other service departments. You would like to use the method that provides reliable cost measurements to be used in decision-making, but without creating more costs than the benefits derived. Which method do you recommend?

When designing a cost allocation system, you must weigh the benefits derived from more informed decision-making with the costs of designing and operating the system. Additionally, usability is key in the design. The system must be comprehensible and usable to stakeholders throughout the organization. For this system design, consider how the information will be used and the level of accuracy that is required. If the information need only be approximately correct, a simpler system might be preferred. For the service departments that only work with producing departments, a direct method is adequate. However, for the service departments that serve each other as well as the producing departments, the step method should be considered. If usage proportions are relatively consistent across producing departments for each service, the direct method might be sufficient. If a large amount of heterogeneity exists in the way that the shared services are used by producing departments, a more complex method is probably a better choice.

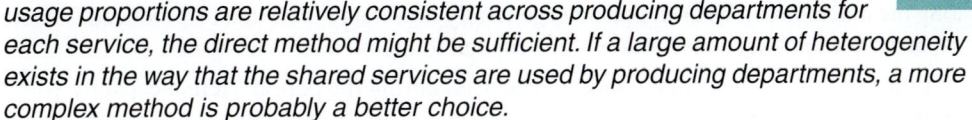

Allocating Service Department Costs Using the Direct and Step Methods — LO19-1 Review 19-1

Suppose a Target retail store is organized into four departments: Apparel, Household Products, Administrative Services, and Facilities Services. The first two departments are the primary producing departments. The last two departments provide services to the producing departments as well as to each other. Top management has decided that, for internal reporting purposes, the cost of service department operations should be allocated to the producing departments. Administrative Services costs are allocated on the basis of the number of employees, and Facilities Services costs are allocated based on the amount of square footage of floor space occupied. Hypothetical data pertaining to the cost allocations for February are as follows.

continued

continued from previous page

Department	Direct Department Cost	Number of Employees	Square Footage Occupied
Apparel	$ 60,000	15	15,000
Household Products	50,000	9	7,500
Administrative Services	18,000	3	2,500
Facilities Services	12,000	2	1,000
Total	$140,000	29	26,000

Required

a. Determine the amount of service department costs to be allocated to the producing departments under the *direct method* of service department cost allocation, and total costs for each producing department.
b. Determine the percentage of total Administrative Department services that was provided to the Facilities Department.
c. Determine the percentage of total Facilities Department services that was provided to the Administrative Department.
d. Determine the amount of service department costs to be allocated to the producing departments under the *step method* of service department cost allocation, and total costs for each producing department.

Solution on p. 19-35.

THE COST OF EXCESS CAPACITY

LO19-2 Calculate and explain the cost of excess capacity.

As we discussed previously, the overhead allocation rate is calculated by taking total overhead costs divided by an estimated overhead allocation base (such as machine hours). However, we have not considered up to this point, how the total overhead allocation base (i.e., cost driver) is derived. For example, the total number of machine hours could be based on total expected machine hours under *ideal* conditions, or total expected machine hours under *typical* conditions. We will consider in this section how the estimate of the overhead allocation base affects product costing for internal purposes as well as decisions based upon this cost information. Remember that product cost information for internal purposes aids management in controlling costs and improving profitability. This information is not reported outside of the company and thus does not follow financial reporting rules for product costing described in the last chapter.

Calculating the Overhead Application Rate Under Different Capacity Levels

Selecting the amount of a cost driver requires an understanding of the types of capacity numbers that could be utilized.

Levels of Capacity: Theoretical Capacity | Actual Capacity | Practical Capacity

- **Theoretical capacity** is the production quantity, or units, that can be packaged by the machine under ideal conditions. In some cases, capacity can be defined instead as the number of minutes that a machine can run efficiently. This ties indirectly to the number of production units because how long the machine can be used indicates generally how many units can be produced. Theoretical capacity does not account for downtime related to maintenance or repairs.

- **Actual capacity** is the actual quantity produced during the period. Actual capacity will likely be different from the plan due to unforeseen events such as a change in product demand in the period.

- **Practical capacity** adjusts theoretical capacity to reflect normal downtime and the organization's production plans.

Consider Whole Foods's production of its proprietary brand of flour tortillas. The tortillas are sold in bags of six, and Whole Foods has a machine for packaging bread products in plastic. The tortillas, as well as other bread products, are packaged on this machine.

Theoretical capacity

Most agree that theoretical capacity should not be used to allocate costs. Theoretical capacity is unattainable. Basing the overhead allocation base on theoretical capacity results in an unrealistically high denominator in the overhead rate calculation. Suppose that the bread packaging machine costs $15,000 per month to run. During August, the machine can run for 30,000 minutes per month if everything operates exactly to plan under ideal operating conditions. The company allocates overhead based on minutes processed which means the allocation base is equal to 30,000 minutes. Therefore, the overhead allocation rate will be $0.50 per minute.

$$\$15{,}000 \text{ Overhead costs} \div 30{,}000 \text{ minutes} = \$0.50 \text{ overhead cost per minute}$$

When using theoretical capacity, is the overhead allocation rate too high or too low? How will this impact the allocation of the packaging machine costs?

Because theoretical capacity will never be attained, using 30,000 minutes per month overestimates the machine's capacity. Consequently, the overhead allocation rate is too low. At $0.50 per minute, the $15,000 will not be fully allocated to bread products because the full 30,000 minutes will not be accounted for. As a result, all of the unit product costs will look too low because the packaging costs are underestimated. Additionally, the company will need to account for the underapplied overhead balance.

Actual capacity

Instead, the organization can base the cost driver used in the overhead allocation rate calculation on *actual capacity*. Suppose that only 20,000 minutes of machine time was utilized during August. This means that tortillas will be allocated $0.75 for every minute that these products use the machine.

$$\$15{,}000 \text{ Overhead costs} \div 20{,}000 \text{ minutes} = \$0.75 \text{ overhead cost per minute}$$

This is higher than the rate using the theoretical capacity, as expected.

What happens in September if machine time utilized was 23,000 minutes instead of 20,000 minutes?

If September actual capacity is higher than August, the denominator will increase (from 20,000 minutes to 23,000 minutes). With a higher denominator, the overhead allocation rate will decrease, and fewer costs will be allocated for every minute of machine use. Even though Whole Foods might aim to use the packaging machine 20,000 minutes each month, this will probably not come to fruition perfectly. Each time machine usage changes, the allocation rate will change when the denominator is based on actual capacity.

When using actual capacity, the overhead application rate could change each month. Does that mean that the economics behind the packaging of tortillas change each month?

If no changes were made to the packaging process or the machine, the economics have not changed. Theoretically, the cost of operating the machine is the same; only the output and minutes used by the machine have changed due to changes in demand which affect production. The inconsistencies in costs from month to month make it difficult for managers to make decisions based on the cost information.

Practical capacity

Often, companies will base the cost driver in the denominator of the overhead allocation rate on *practical capacity*. Practical capacity reflects the company's plan for the use of the resource. Whole Foods would determine how many minutes per month on average, it will use the packaging machine during the year. The same average minutes amount is used in the denominator in the overhead allocation rate each month. This is analogous to adopting a straight-line depreciation policy in financial accounting: the cost of a fixed asset is depreciated at a constant rate. Suppose Whole Foods expects to operate the machine for 25,000 minutes each month under normal conditions. The overhead allocation using practical capacity, is $0.60 per minute.

$15,000 Overhead costs ÷ 25,000 minutes = $0.60 overhead cost per minute

Using practical capacity has benefits over actual capacity. First, as long as Whole Foods does not alter its plan for using the packaging machine, the overhead allocation rate will remain constant. This means that the unit costs of products will not fluctuate from month to month. Second, it does not hide the cost of excess or unused capacity as explained in the following section.

Calculating the Cost of Excess Capacity

Continuing with the Whole Foods example, let's assume that the company bases its overhead application rate on practical capacity ($0.60 overhead cost per minute), but production falls short due to labor shortages. This means that there will be unallocated costs due to the machine not running at the expected level (or number of minutes). Suppose the machine only operated for 20,000 minutes. The difference of 5,000 minutes (25,000 – 20,000) is **excess capacity**. Excess capacity is the unused or idle capacity during a period of time. Since the $15,000 of overhead cost is allocated based on the practical capacity, there will be 5,000 minutes that are not accounted for. In this case, managers should (1) recognize that there was excess or idle capacity this month and (2) determine the cost of that excess capacity. Excess capacity is treated as a separate cost pool in the following analysis.

Cost Object	Minutes Used	Cost per Minute	Allocated Cost
Products (tortillas and other breads)	20,000	$0.60	$12,000
Excess Capacity	5,000	0.60	3,000
Total	25,000		$15,000

Notice that when using practical capacity, unit overhead cost remains constant at $0.60 per minute from month to month. This differs from the actual capacity example where the unit cost rose to $0.75 in August. In that case, the cost of the excess capacity is "hidden" within the new unit cost of $0.75. Alternatively when practical capacity is used, the cost of excess capacity is identifiable. Given this information, management of Whole Foods can track excess capacity from month to month and make decisions to ensure that capacity is optimized in the future.

Managing Excess Capacity

Once the information about excess capacity is revealed in a transparent manner, decisions can be made to manage capacity. Of course, the final actions will depend on the answers to a few questions. Why does the capacity exist? Who should be held accountable for the excess capacity, if anyone? Are there long-term plans for the excess capacity?

Suppose Whole Foods expects the packaging machine to have excess capacity now, but it plans to fill the excess capacity over time, as demand increases. This situation is analogous to new companies that must set up facilities before full demand is realized. In this setting, no particular product or service is responsible for the excess capacity; rather, it is part of the growing process. However, management can track excess capacity over time to see if trends indicate a decline in excess capacity due to increases in product demand that materialize.

> **Critical Thinking & Decision-Making**
>
> **The tortilla production manager is frustrated by the excess capacity due to the labor shortage. Should the production manager be held accountable for the excess capacity issues? Are there cases where the product manager should work with other departments within the company to address the labor issue?**
>
> *Determining who is responsible for staffing the manufacturing line and determining the cause of the labor shortage would help determine who is responsible for the labor shortage. Is the labor shortage due to turnover related to conditions in the plant or inadequate training? Is the labor shortage a pervasive issue in the region that is not particular to the plant? Have alternative staffing agencies or different employee pools been considered? Is the employee pay competitive within the market? In order to address the issue, the production manager may need to work with departments across the company to address the problem including human resources and accounting.*

Capacity Considerations When Using Dual Overhead Allocation Rates

When allocating department costs, it can be useful to provide separate allocations for fixed costs and variable costs. This first requires the separation of indirect costs into the categories of fixed costs and variable costs, which is not always practical to do. Separately analyzing costs, however, results in cost allocations that more accurately reflect the factors that drive costs. Capacity most often drives fixed costs, whereas some type of actual activity usually drives variable costs. *Dual rates involve establishing separate bases for allocating fixed and variable costs.*

It is important to remember the relationship between capacity and cost when selecting the allocation method. Total variable costs change as output changes. Fixed costs, however, are the same whether the output is at or below capacity. Fixed costs should usually be allocated based on practical capacity.

Dual rates can be used in conjunction with the direct or step methods discussed in the last section. Fixed costs based on practical capacity eliminate the possibility that the amount of the cost allocation to one department is affected by the level of services utilized by other departments. When fixed service department costs are allocated based on the user department's practical capacity, managers of the user departments are charged for that capacity whether they use it or not, and their use of services has no effect on the amount of costs allocated to other departments. A benefit of this allocation system is that it reduces the temptation for managers to avoid or delay services to minimize fixed cost allocations to their departments.

The allocation methods and bases may be different for variable and fixed costs. Because this exercise could be cumbersome and challenging, it might not be practical to separate fixed and variable costs within the overhead costs. Dual rates are examined in more detail in most cost accounting texts.

Managing Excess Capacity LO19-2 **Review 19-2**

> **Target** recently launched Kona Sol, a swimwear brand. Production occurs primarily in the late fall and early winter months to prepare for vacation and swim season, which starts in spring. To accommodate the production of the swimwear line within the tight timeline, Target purchased additional machinery to ensure that the production runs for the other clothing products would not be impacted. The annual manufacturing overhead cost related to the new machinery is $132,000. The practical capacity of the new machinery is 4,400 machine hours for the year. However, because of the seasonal nature of demand, Kona Sol utilizes half of the capacity of the machinery for the year, resulting in significant excess capacity.
>
> **Required**
> a. Calculate the cost of the excess capacity for the year.
> b. Should the Kona Sol division be responsible for the related costs?
>
> Solution on p. 19-36.

JUST-IN-TIME (JIT) INVENTORY MANAGEMENT/LEAN PRODUCTION

Previously, our discussions about inventories have centered around how to measure the cost of products. A related issue is how to manage the production process and physical inventory levels.

LO19-3
Describe the JIT/Lean Production Approach.

Characteristics of JIT/Lean Production Approach

Just-in-time (JIT) inventory management is a comprehensive inventory management philosophy that stresses policies, procedures, and attitudes by managers and other workers, which result in the efficient production of high-quality goods while maintaining the minimum level of inventories. JIT is often described simply as an inventory model that maintains only the level of inventories required to meet current production and sales requirements, but it is, in reality, much more than that. The key elements of the JIT philosophy, which has come to be known as the **lean production** philosophy, include increased coordination throughout the value chain, reduced inventory, reduced production times, increased product quality, and increased employee involvement and empowerment. From an environmental viewpoint, JIT aims to eliminate waste through lower inventories and continuously improved processes. Coordination across the value chain requires that managers consider their suppliers' and customers' strategies, goals, and objectives if they hope to compete successfully in a global marketplace.

The concept of a JIT/lean approach is that in a manufacturing environment, the customers pull the production through the system with customer orders. Instead of the business making the decisions of what and when to produce, the customer does. JIT/lean production is a system aimed at reducing or eliminating waste, increasing cost efficiency, and securing a competitive advantage. Accordingly, it emphasizes a nimble production process with small lot sizes, short setup and change-over times, effective and efficient quality controls, a minimum number of bottlenecks and backups, and maximum efficiency of people. We will focus next on how a successful adoption of the JIT/lean approach results in minimized inventory levels, reduced cycle time, and simplified bookkeeping.

Minimized Materials Inventory Levels

The JIT/lean approach to reducing incoming materials includes these elements:

1. Developing long-term relationships with a limited number of vendors.
2. Selecting vendors on the basis of service and material quality, as well as price.
3. Establishing procedures for key employees to order materials for current needs directly from approved vendors.
4. Accepting vendor deliveries directly to the shop floor, and only as needed.

When fully implemented, these steps minimize or eliminate many materials inventories. Sufficient materials would be on hand to meet only immediate needs, and the materials inventories in the manufacturing setting are located on the shop floor. To achieve this reduction, vendors and buyers must work as a team, and key employees must be involved in decision-making. The goal of the JIT approach to purchasing is not to shift materials carrying costs to vendors. Purchasers' scheduling information is provided to vendors so that vendors also can reduce inventories and minimize costs by manufacturing in small batches as needed. Further, vendors are more confident of future sales.

Maintaining a limited number of vendors also creates risks. Toyota has faced a number of supply disruptions over the years. A massive earthquake affected 660 of its suppliers. Since this occurrence, Toyota has managed supply disruption risk, partially by ensuring suppliers come from a diverse set of locations.[3]

Reduced Cycle Time and Work-In-Process Inventory Levels

Reducing the total time required to complete one unit of a product, or the **cycle time**, is the key to reducing work-in-process inventories and is central to a lean production approach.

$$\text{Cycle time} = \text{Setup time} + \text{Processing time} + \text{Movement time} + \text{Waiting time} + \text{Inspection time}$$

In a manufacturing organization, cycle time is composed of the time needed for setup, processing, movement, waiting, and inspection. *Of the five elements of cycle time, only processing time adds value to the product.* Because of this, it is important in a JIT/lean system to minimize time spent in non-value-added activities.

- **Setup time** is the time required to prepare equipment to produce a specific product, or to change from producing one product to another product.
- **Processing time** is the time spent working on units.
- **Movement time** is the time units spend moving between work or inspection stations.
- **Waiting time** is the time units spend in temporary storage waiting to be processed, moved, or inspected.
- **Inspection time** is the amount of time it takes units to be inspected.

Cycle time can be reduced by moving from a materials-push to a materials-pull approach to production. Under a traditional **materials-push system**, employees work to reduce the pile of inventory

---

[3] Source: Yoko Kubota, "Japan Earthquakes Rattle Toyota's Vulnerable Supply Chain," *Wall Street Journal*, April 19, 2016. Link: http://www.wsj.com/articles/japan-earthquakes-rattle-toyotas-supply-chain-1460986805

building up at their workstations. Workers at each station remove materials from an in-process storage area, complete their operation, and place the output in another in-process storage area. Hence, they *push* the work to the next workstation. Inventories are large enough to allow for variations in processing speeds, for discarding defective units without interrupting production, and for machine downtime.

Under a **materials-pull system** (often called a **Kanban system**[4]), employees at each station work to provide inventory for the next workstation only as needed, which minimizes levels of work-in-process inventory. In fact, the building of excess inventories is strictly prohibited. When the number of units in inventory reaches a specified limit, work at the station stops until workers at a subsequent station pull units from the in-process storage area. Hence, the *pull* of inventory by a subsequent station authorizes production to continue.

A pull system's low inventory levels require a team effort. To avoid idle time, processing speeds must be balanced and equipment must be kept in good repair. Quality problems are identified immediately, and the low inventory levels require immediate correction of quality problems. To make a pull system work, management must accept the notion that it is better to have employees idle than to have them building excess inventory. A pull system also requires careful planning by management and active participation in decision-making by employees.

Minimized Finished Goods Inventory Levels

Finished goods inventory can be reduced by reducing cycle time and by better predicting customer demand for finished units. Lowering cycle times reduces the need for speculative inventories. If finished goods can be replenished quickly, the need diminishes for large inventory levels to satisfy customer needs and to provide for unanticipated fluctuations in customer orders. Anticipating customers' demand for goods can be improved by adopting a value chain approach to inventory management by which the manufacturer or supplier is working as a partner with its customers to meet their inventory needs. This frequently involves having online computer access to customers' inventory levels on a real-time basis and being able to synchronize changes in production with changes in customers' inventory levels as they occur.

Sharing this type of information obviously requires an enormous amount of mutual trust between a manufacturer or supplier and its customers, but it is becoming increasingly common among world-class organizations. An example of this type of vendor-customer relationship is the relationship between **Procter & Gamble**, one of the world's largest consumer products companies, and its largest customer, **Walmart**. By having access to Walmart's computer inventory system, Procter & Gamble is better able to determine and fill Walmart's specific needs for products, such as disposable diapers.

As with anything, managers should have contingency plans. As we have seen, sudden spurts of demand can cause short-term supply issues for companies that operate in systems with minimal inventory and minimal slack. **Forever 21** recently asked a bankruptcy court to approve plans to sell most of its assets. Inventory management was one of the causes for the company's decline. The company ordered too much inventory one year and too little the next. Excess inventory was sent to store managers who ended up returning the items to distribution centers when styles changed. Furthermore, inventory shortages required replacement stock to be shipped overnight, and errors were made in the choice of items sent to specific stores (e.g., out-of-season items). Both errors resulted in increased shipping costs. The company's failure to manage its inventories in light of anticipated industry changes contributed to its failure.[5]

Simplified Recordkeeping Under JIT/Lean Production Approach

Lean production and JIT enable significant reductions in the number of accounting transactions required for purchasing and production activities. This results in cost savings by shifting accounting resources from recordkeeping to the development of more useful activity cost data.

Reduces Raw Material Transactions   In a traditional accounting system, every purchase results in the preparation of several documents. Additional documents are prepared for the issuance of raw materials to the factory. JIT, on the other hand, attempts to minimize inventory levels and stresses

---

[4] *Kanban*, the Japanese word for *card*, is a system created in Japan that originally used cards to indicate that a department needed additional components.

[5] Sources: Susan Berfield, Eliza Ronalds-Hannon, and Lauren Coleman-Lochner, "The Failure of the Forever 21 Empire," *Bloomberg Businessweek*, January 17, 2020. Eliza Ronalds-Hannon, "Forever 21 Proposed Auction to Keep Fashion Chain in Business," *Bloomberg*, January 30, 2020.

long-term relationships with a limited number of vendors who have demonstrated their ability to provide quality raw materials on a timely basis, as well as at a competitive price. Under a JIT inventory system, a company often has standing purchase orders for specified materials from specified vendors at specified prices. Production personnel are authorized to requisition materials directly from authorized vendors, who deliver limited quantities of materials as needed directly to the shop floor. Production personnel verify receipt of the raw materials. Periodically, each vendor sends an invoice for several shipments, which the company acknowledges and pays.

Eliminates Tracking of Costs through Inventory Accounts Under JIT, ending inventories can be nonexistent, or so small that the costs assigned to them are insignificant in comparison with the costs assigned to Cost of Goods Sold. In this case, it makes little sense to track product costs through several inventory accounts. Instead of using a traditional product cost accounting system (as illustrated in Chapter 17), firms that have implemented JIT often use what is sometimes referred to as a backflush approach. Under **backflush costing**, all costs of direct materials, direct labor, and manufacturing overhead are assigned as incurred to Cost of Goods Sold. If there are no inventories on hand at the end of the period, no additional steps are required. However, if there are inventories on hand at year-end, costs are backed out of Cost of Goods Sold and assigned to the appropriate inventory accounts.

Let's assume that **Whole Foods** manufactures its proprietary bread products using a JIT/Lean production approach. Under this approach, the company manufactures and ships products based only upon orders. Thus, it holds no finished goods inventory and there is minimal product in process at the end of a workday. Raw material purchase orders based on bread orders are automatically sent to a set of core vendors who ship the necessary raw materials within two days. This approach reduces the risk of spoilage of raw materials and bread products. Information for the month of August is summarized below.

Raw materials costs incurred	$180,000
Conversion costs incurred	$200,000
Units in process during the month	250,000

Under the backflush method, Cost of Goods Sold would increase during the month by $380,000 ($180,000 + $200,000). If we assume that ending inventory balances of Raw Materials, Work-in-Process, and Finished Goods are all $0 at month-end, no other adjustments are necessary. However, if inventory does exist, the cost of the inventory is backed out of Cost of Goods Sold and recorded in the relevant inventory accounts.

Performance Evaluation Under JIT/Lean Production Approach

The selection of performance measures used by a company should align with the company's goals and objectives. In accordance with the goal of eliminating inventory and reducing cycle time, JIT supportive performance measures emphasize inventory turnover, cycle time, and cycle efficiency.

Assume that a department of Whole Foods that produces bread products is following the JIT/lean production approach and would like to measure its performance. Using the following information, we will compute (1) inventory turnover in units, (2) inventory turnover in dollars, (3) gross margin return on inventory investment, and (4) cycle efficiency. The inventory data provided relates to finished goods inventory.

Annual Demand in Units	Cost of Goods Sold	Average Inventory in Units	Average Inventory in Dollars	Sales in Dollars	Processing Time in Minutes	Cycle Time in Minutes
18,000	$35,100	1,500	$2,775	$55,000	2.20	8.20

Inventory Turnover in Units When applied to a specific item of raw materials or finished goods, **inventory turnover** is computed as the annual demand in units divided by the average inventory in units.

$$\text{Inventory turnover (in units)} = \frac{\text{Annual demand in units}}{\text{Average inventory in units}} = \frac{18,000}{1,500} = 12.0$$

The selection of performance measures used by a company should align with the company's goals and objectives. Progress toward the goal of reducing inventory is measured by comparing successive inventory turnover ratios. Whole Foods could measure its inventory turnover in recent years and compare it to the current level of 12.0. Generally, the higher the inventory turnover, the better as this would indicate that average inventory is being sold more times per year as a result of increased demand and/or decreased inventory.

Inventory Turnover in Dollars When measured with inventory dollars instead of inventory units, inventory turnover can be used as a measure of the organization's overall success in reducing inventory, or in increasing sales in relation to inventories. This financial measure can be derived directly from a firm's financial statements.

$$\text{Inventory turnover (in dollars)} = \frac{\text{Cost of goods sold}}{\text{Average inventory (in dollars)}} = \frac{\$35,100}{\$2,775} = 12.6$$

For Whole Foods, the measure is similar to the inventory turnover in units because the average unit cost of finished goods inventory is similar to the unit cost of items sold during the year.

Gross Margin Return on Inventory Investment Another ratio often used to monitor the effectiveness of inventory levels in retail organizations, such as **Whole Foods**, is gross margin return on inventory investment (GMROI), calculated as follows. (Gross margin is another term for gross profit.)

$$\text{GMROI} = \frac{\text{Gross margin (in dollars)}}{\text{Average inventory (in dollars)}} = \frac{(\$55,000 - \$35,100)}{\$2,775} = 7.2$$

The GMROI indicates the margin earned for each dollar of inventory. Gross margin is calculated for Whole Foods by taking sales of $55,000 minus cost of goods sold of $35,100. The resulting gross margin of $19,900 is divided by average inventory of $2,775 to arrive at the GMROI. Whole Food's GMROI indicates a gross margin of $7.20 for each dollar of inventory. With JIT, the goal is to maximize this number, earning a higher margin per unit of inventory.

Cycle Efficiency Cycle efficiency is computed as the ratio of processing time to total cycle time.

$$\text{Cycle efficiency} = \frac{\text{Processing time}}{\text{Cycle time}} = \frac{2.20}{8.20} = 0.27$$

The highest cycle efficiency possible is always sought. Only processing time adds value to the product; hence, the time required for all other activities should be driven toward zero. The use of flexible manufacturing systems, properly sequencing jobs, and properly placing tools will minimize setup time. If the shop floor is optimally arranged, workers pass products directly from one workstation to the next. If production is optimally scheduled, inventory will not wait in temporary storage between workstations. If raw materials are of high quality and products are manufactured so that they always conform to specifications, separate inspection activities can be minimized.

If all non-value-added activities are eliminated, this ratio equals one. With a current cycle efficiency of 0.27, Whole Foods would want to analyze the time components and strive to decrease non-value-added time. It is difficult to eliminate all of the extra activities. However, companies would like to see the cycle efficiency moving toward one.

Analyzing Performance in Lean Manufacturing   LO19-3 **Review 19-3**

Assume **Target** is trying to decide which automated production line to use to produce its Up & Up sandwich bags. Suppose the two best systems under consideration have the following estimated performance characteristics, based on minutes per 1,000 bags produced.

continued

continued from previous page

	System A	System B
Setup time	25	10
Movement time from start to finish	10	14
Waiting time	3	16
Inspection time	5	7
Processing time	40	30
Total time in minutes	83	77

Required

Solution on p. 19-36.

a. Determine the cycle time per batch for each system. How do you interpret these results?
b. Determine the cycle efficiency for each system. Describe the differences between these two systems.
c. Assuming Target is a "lean" manufacturer, what improvements may be possible in the two systems?

INCREASED FOCUS ON DATA-DRIVEN DECISION-MAKING

LO19-4
Explain managerial accountants' focus on data-driven decision-making.

Increased access to data is changing the landscape of managerial accounting. Business leaders should be able to increasingly rely on data to answer difficult questions. Which products or services are most profitable? What is driving the cost of the products and how can we work to decrease the costs? What are the ideal prices to charge for our services? Which manufacturing process is the most efficient? When business leaders can rely on data to answer these types of questions, they can then focus efforts on understanding which questions to ask. What is our business's core competency? What is our organization's strategic position (as discussed in Chapter 13)? Which products or services should we offer, or in which markets should we compete?

Using Data Effectively

In order to rely on data, it must be accurate and timely. Costing models, such as ABC and the step method, can help provide more accurate information on product costs. In fact, the *linear algebra method* could provide even more accuracy than the step method because it uses a series of linear algebraic equations to allocate service department costs both interdepartmentally and to the producing departments. (This method is covered in most cost accounting courses.) However, the accuracy of this data relies on management choosing relevant activity cost pools and cost drivers, and reasonable additional assumptions. Further, employees throughout the organization must understand and support the costing model. The concept of GIGO (garbage in, garbage out) refers to the idea that incorrect information going into a system results in incorrect data coming out. The system does not magically fix the information.[6] Therefore, the first step in using data analytics effectively is having managers that think critically, understanding both the business and the underlying data used in decision-making.

Even when analysts have reliable and timely data, there are risks associated with data-driven decision-making. A common issue is the misunderstanding of correlation versus causation. **Correlation** is a statistical measure describing the magnitude and direction of a relationship between at least two variables. **Causation** indicates that one variable is caused by another variable. The idea behind big data analytics is to uncover hidden patterns and correlation among activities, and then to use this information to make decisions and to predict outcomes.[7] Often, just because there is a high correlation between two events, does not mean that one *caused* the other. Using this information to then extrapolate further outcomes will be inaccurate. An example often referenced to demonstrate this issue is the windmill. The faster the windmill rotates, the more wind can be observed. Can we conclude that windmills cause wind? As ice cream sales increase, the rate of drowning

---
[6] Rod Koch, "Big Data or Big Empathy," *Strategic Finance*, December 1, 2015.

[7] http://www.sas.com/en_us/insights/analytics/big-data-analytics.html

increases. Does ice cream consumption cause drowning? These examples make it fairly obvious that one event does not cause the other, even though they are correlated. However, as managers are inundated with data, it may not always be so easy to understand the distinction between correlation and causation, resulting in poor decision-making.

Developing Skills for Decision-Making

As the environment changes in terms of the availability of managerial accounting information, so too do the skills required of managerial accountants. The CGMA (Chartered Global Management Accountant) competency framework illustrated in **Exhibit 19.5** assists management accountants in understanding the skills needed to be trusted finance and business strategists. Finance professionals require *technical skills* such as the recording of costs and determining product pricing, subjects that are discussed in this text and in advanced cost accounting texts. *Business skills* require a basic understanding of a company's operations and performance measures. With this knowledge, accountants can implement a company's strategies and eventually advise on strategic options. Beyond the more technical aspects of accounting and business, softer skills are required including *people skills* such as negotiation and communication and *leadership skills* such as team building and coaching. Lastly, an essential competency relates to *digital skills* which includes digital literacy and data analytics. While digital skills is listed as a separate skill, it also affects the other knowledge areas. Importantly, the framework is guided by the need for *ethics, integrity, and professionalism*.

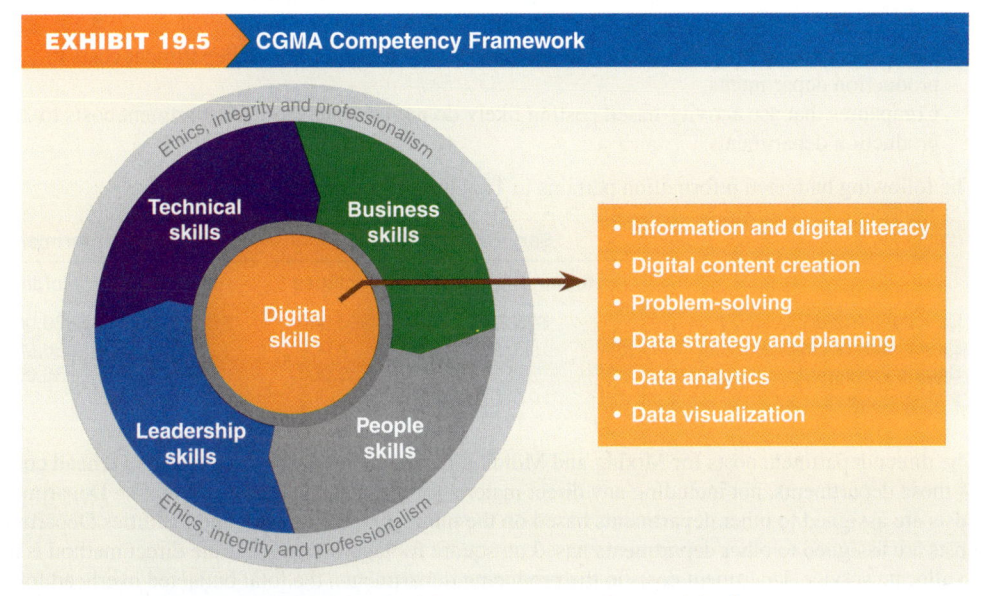

EXHIBIT 19.5 | CGMA Competency Framework

Ethics, integrity and professionalism

- Technical skills
- Business skills
- Digital skills
- Leadership skills
- People skills

- Information and digital literacy
- Digital content creation
- Problem-solving
- Data strategy and planning
- Data analytics
- Data visualization

Source: https://www.cgma.org/resources/tools/cgma-competency-framework.html

The accounting data and related analyses are just part of the story. To make decisions, managers must include qualitative information (e.g., demographics), capabilities, and strategic position, for example. Additionally, it must then be communicated to set the company up for success. This requires a team that is interdisciplinary and can understand the information and data analyses.

Discussing Risks and Concerns of Access to Big Data   LO19-4 **Review 19-4**

Increased access to data can help business leaders make better and more timely decisions. This can also allow them to focus more of their efforts toward more strategic analysis and thinking. Even though there are many benefits to the increasing availability of data, there are also risks and concerns. Consider **Target**. Target collects a large amount of data on everything from its own production process to consumer demographics and behaviors.

Required
Discuss some accompanying risks and concerns of Target's access to big data.   **Solution on p. 19-37.**

KEY RATIOS AND EQUATIONS

$$\text{Inventory turnover} = \frac{\text{Annual demand in units}}{\text{Average inventory in units}}$$

$$\text{Inventory turnover} = \frac{\text{Cost of goods sold}}{\text{Average inventory (in dollars)}}$$

$$\text{Gross margin return on inventory investment} = \frac{\text{Gross margin (in dollars)}}{\text{Average inventory (in dollars)}}$$

$$\frac{\text{Cycle}}{\text{time}} = \frac{\text{Setup}}{\text{time}} + \frac{\text{Processing}}{\text{time}} + \frac{\text{Movement}}{\text{time}} + \frac{\text{Waiting}}{\text{time}} + \frac{\text{Inspection}}{\text{time}}$$

$$\text{Cycle efficiency} = \frac{\text{Processing time}}{\text{Cycle time}}$$

MULTIPLE CHOICE

Multiple Choice Answers
1. d 2. a 3. c 4. c
5. b 6. d 7. d 8. c

LO19-1 1. Which of the following statements regarding production and service department costs is incorrect?
   a. For a production department, direct department costs include both direct and indirect product costs.
   b. An indirect department cost is a cost assigned to a department as a result of a reassignment from another service department.
   c. Companies that use departmental overhead rates likely allocate service department costs to production departments.
   d. Companies that use activity-based costing likely do not allocate service department costs to production departments.

LO19-1 2. The following budgeted information pertains to Trawbing Company.

	Service Departments		Producing Departments	
	Human Resources	Facilities	Mixing	Molding
Direct department costs	$75,000	$50,000	$520,000	$860,000
Direct labor hours	6,000	4,000	20,000	36,000
Square footage	2,000	3,000	24,000	36,000
# of employees	3	2	18	12

The direct department costs for Mixing and Molding represent the direct department overhead costs of those departments, not including any direct material or direct labor. Human Resource Department costs are assigned to other departments based on the number of employees, and Facilities Department costs are assigned to other departments based on square footage occupied. If the direct method is used to allocate service department costs to the producing departments, the total budgeted overhead for the Molding Department after service department costs are allocated is
   a. $920,000.00
   b. $585,000.00
   c. $584,062.50
   d. $920,937.50

LO19-1 3. Refer to the previous question. If the step method is used to allocate service departments to the producing departments, the total budgeted overhead for the Mixing Department after service department costs are allocated is (round all calculations to two decimal places)
   a. $920,000.00
   b. $585,000.00
   c. $584,062.50
   d. $920,937.50

LO19-1 4. Refer to question 2. Assume that the Molding Department uses a predetermined overhead rate for assigning overhead costs to products based on budgeted total overhead after service department costs are allocated using the direct allocation method. The predetermined overhead rate for the Molding Department is (round all calculations to two decimal places)
   a. $26.88 per direct labor hour
   b. $23.89 per direct labor hour
   c. $25.56 per direct labor hour
   d. $29.25 per direct labor hour

LO19-2 5. Keane Corp. purchased a machine to be used in the operations of three products. All of the products are new, and the company is not sure when the machine will be operated fully. Under perfect conditions, the machine can operate 670 hours per month. Given current demand, Keane expects to run the machine 350 hours per month during the next six–twelve months. Eventually, the machine will operate 500 hours per month. The cost of the machine is budgeted to be $2,010,000 per year. How much machine cost should Keane allocate (i.e., what is the overhead allocation rate per hour)?

a. $479 per hour
b. $335 per hour
c. $250 per hour
d. None of the above

6. The key elements of JIT/lean production include which of the following? **LO19-3**
   a. Increased coordination throughout the value chain
   b. Reduced inventories and production times
   c. Increased product quality and employee empowerment
   d. All of the above are elements of JIT/lean production.

7. Topaz Company sold and produced 40,000 units of product at a cost of $1,200,000 for a sales price of $60 per unit during the most recent year. Throughout the year its average inventory was 4,000 units with an average cost of $120,000. Based on this information, which of the following cannot be determined about Topaz's inventory management performance? **LO19-3**
   a. Topaz's inventory turnover in units was 10 times.
   b. Topaz's gross margin return on average inventory investment was 1,000%.
   c. Topaz's inventory turnover in dollars was 10 times.
   d. Topaz's production cycle efficiency was 100%.

8. Which of the following is not a characteristic of a business environment with increasing availability of data? **LO19-4**
   a. There is potential risk of misinterpretation between correlation and causation.
   b. It is increasingly important that data be accurate and timely.
   c. There is decreasing reliance on the softer skills such as strategic analysis and communication.
   d. The largest technical skills talent gaps occur in areas of identifying key data trends and data mining and extraction.

DATA ANALYTICS

DA19-1. Using Tableau to Analyze Inventory **LO19-3**
You recently joined the Coca-Cola Company (in the consumer staples segment) as a cost accountant. You have learned of the importance of a company being able to sell its products in a timely fashion, and that the ratio of days sales in inventory provides this useful information. You decide a dashboard would be helpful in seeing if this ratio is improving or declining in the consumer discretionary and the consumer staples segments between 2017 and 2018. You will later compare your company results to this industry data. You build two sheets that are included in the dashboard. The first sheet shows the level of the ratio for each segment for the two years in question. The second sheet shows the change in the ratio between the two years. (Data is included in MBC.)

REQUIRED
Has the ratio days sales in inventory improved or declined in the consumer discretionary and the consumer staples segments between 2017 and 2018. By how much?

DA19-2. Correlation vs. Causation **LO19-4**
Assume that you are a cost accountant working with a plant that manufacturers machinery components. You have noticed that quality costs (including inspection costs and costs of reworking rejected parts) have increased over the last year. Overhead costs for the plant are allocated using a single overhead cost pool and a single cost driver. In order to better understand the increase in quality costs, you first identified a pool of quality costs over the past year ranging from approximately $17,200 to $24,600. You prepared the following data visualization showing the relationship between units of products produced and quality costs.

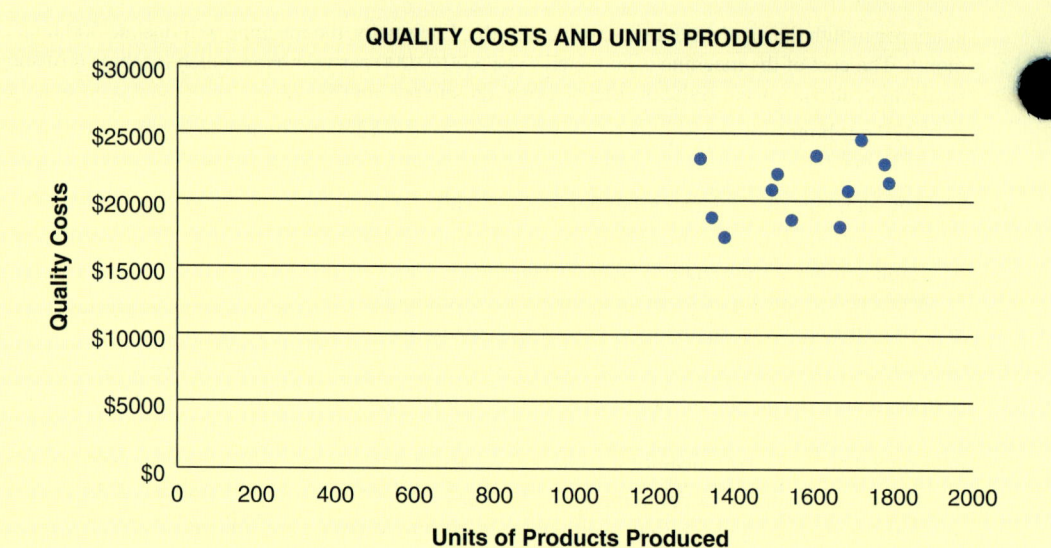

QUALITY COSTS AND UNITS PRODUCED

[Scatter plot: Quality Costs ($0–$30000) vs. Units of Products Produced (0–2000). Data points cluster between 1300–1800 units and $17000–$24000.]

REQUIRED

a. Explain whether or not quality costs correlate with units produced.
b. Explain the factors you would consider in determining whether or not, units produced cause quality costs.
c. After discussions with production workers on the factory floor, you determine that the number of line setups may impact the number of rejected parts (the more setups, the more rejects). How might this information affect (a) additional data visualizations that you develop and (b) your understanding of correlation and causation of quality costs?

LO19-4 DA19-3. Analyzing Inventory Turnover Ratio

Applying data visualization techniques for existing data sets is a proficiency included in the CGMA Competency Framework. Creating data visualizations under best practices is essential in communicating an accurate message to your audience.

Review the following data visualizations for Company A and Company B over the last three years. Assume that both companies adopted lean manufacturing techniques that resulted in an increase in inventory turnover over a three-year period.

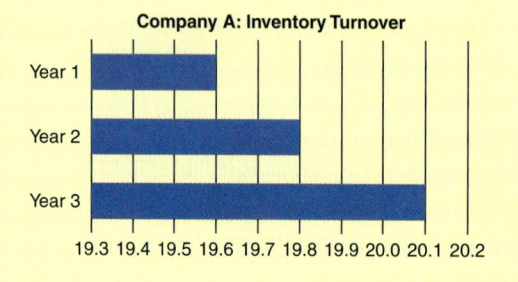

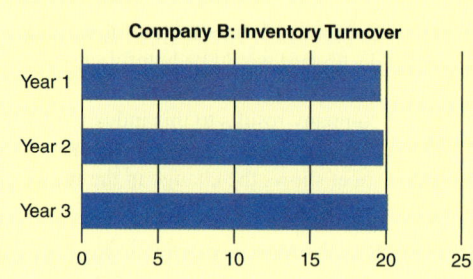

[Bar chart — Company A: Inventory Turnover, scale 19.3–20.2, showing Year 1, Year 2, Year 3]

[Bar chart — Company B: Inventory Turnover, scale 0–25, showing Year 1, Year 2, Year 3]

REQUIRED

Which company showed a more favorable impact on inventory turnover over the three-year period when lean manufacturing methods were adopted? Explain your answer. *Hint:* Review the *Data Visualization* report issued by the IMA found at https://www.imanet.org/research-publications/statements-on-management-accounting/data-visualization

DATA VISUALIZATION

Data Visualization Activities are available in myBusinessCourse. These assignments use Tableau Dashboards to expose students to visual depictions of data and introduce students to data analytics through data visualizations. These exercises are easily assignable and auto graded by MBC.

QUESTIONS

Q19-1. What are two reasons for allocating service department costs?

Q19-2. Distinguish between the following sets of terms:
   a. Direct product costs and indirect product costs.
   b. Direct department costs and indirect department costs.

Q19-3. Define the terms direct cost and indirect cost.

Q19-4. Differentiate between cost assignment and cost allocation.

Q19-5. Explain how a cost item can be both a direct cost and an indirect cost.

Q19-6. What is the primary advantage of separately allocating fixed and variable indirect costs?

Q19-7. Define interdepartmental services.

Q19-8. To what extent are interdepartmental services recognized under the direct and step methods of service department cost allocation?

Q19-9. Is it feasible to assign interdepartmental services to production departments using ABC?

Q19-10. What are the major elements of the JIT/lean approach?

Q19-11. Describe the difference between a materials-push system and a materials-pull system.

Q19-12. Describe the process of backflush costing.

Q19-13. What elements of the JIT approach contribute to reducing materials inventories?

Q19-14. Define and identify the elements of cycle time. Which of these elements adds value to the product?

Q19-15. Explain briefly how JIT/lean production benefits organizations that take a value-chain approach to management.

Q19-16. What are the competencies in the CGMA Framework?

Assignments with the MBC logo in the margin are available in *BusinessCourse*.
See the Preface of the book for details.

MINI EXERCISES

M19-17. Allocating Service Department Costs Using the Direct Method
Adam Corporation manufactures computer tables and has the following budgeted indirect manufacturing cost information for next year.

	Support Departments		Operating Departments		
	Maintenance	Systems	Machining	Fabrication	Total
Budgeted overhead	$360,000	$95,000	$200,000	$300,000	$955,000
Support work furnished					
From Maintenance		10%	50%	40%	100%
From Systems	5%		45%	50%	100%

If Adam uses the direct method to allocate support department costs to production departments, what is the total overhead (rounded to the nearest dollar) for the Machining Department to allocate to its products?

CMA adapted

M19-18. Indirect Cost Allocation: Direct Method
Charlie Manufacturing Company has two production departments, Melting and Molding. Direct general plant management and plant security costs benefit both production departments. Charlie allocates general plant management costs on the basis of the number of production employees and plant security costs on the basis of space occupied by the production departments using the direct method of overhead allocation. In November, the following overhead costs were recorded.

Melting Department overhead	$500,000
Molding Department overhead	400,000
General plant management	200,000
Plant security	100,000

Other pertinent data follow.

	Melting	Molding
Number of employees.	60	40
Space occupied (square feet).	20,000	80,000
Machine hours	1,056	3,200
Direct labor hours	10,560	7,200

REQUIRED

a. Prepare a schedule allocating general plant management costs and plant security costs to the Melting and Molding departments using the direct method.
b. Determine the total departmental overhead costs for the Melting and Molding departments.
c. Assuming the Melting Department uses machine hours and the Molding Department uses direct labor hours to apply overhead to production, calculate the overhead rate for each production department.

LO19-1 **M19-19. Interdepartmental Services: Step Method**

ABC Manufacturing Company reports the following information for its two service departments and two producing departments.

	Receiver of Services			
Provider of Services	**Service A**	**Service B**	**Producing A**	**Producing B**
Service A	0%	0%	60%	40%
Service B	40%	0%	30%	30%

REQUIRED

Using the step method, prepare a schedule for ABC Manufacturing Company allocating the service department costs (Departments A and B) to the producing departments (Departments A and B). Assume that total costs for Service Department A are $160,000 and total costs for Service Department B are $320,000.

LO19-2 **M19-20. Computing Cost of Excess Capacity**

Assume that **Ford Motor Company** has experienced plant shut down periods this year due to supply chain issues. Because of excessive delays in receiving parts from suppliers, the company was forced to run less production time than budgeted. The practical capacity of machines in one of its assembly departments is 6,000 hours for the year. However, actual hours for the year were only 4,800. If the budgeted overhead cost pool is $888,000, what is the cost of excess capacity for the year?

LO19-3 **M19-21. Inventory Ratio Calculations**

Dell Technologies reported the following data for Year 8 and Year 9 (in millions).

Inventory	
February 3, Year 7	$ 2,538
February 2, Year 8	2,678
February 1, Year 9	3,649
Cost of products sold	
Year ended February 2, Year 8	$51,433
Year ended February 1, Year 9	57,889
Gross margin	
Year ended February 2, Year 8	$ 9,818
Year ended February 1, Year 9	13,398

REQUIRED

a. Calculate the inventory turnover ratio for the years ended in February of Year 8 and February of Year 9.
b. Calculate the gross margin return on inventory investment for the years ended in February of Year 8 and February of Year 9.

LO19-3 **M19-22. Distinguishing Lean Production from a Traditional Inventory Model**

For each of the statements a–g below, identify which of the following two concepts is more relevant.
1. An element of lean production and just-in-time inventory management

2. An element of a traditional inventory model that focuses on maintaining specified levels of inventory

_____ a. Nimble production process with small lot sizes and short setup and changeover times
_____ b. Material-push system
_____ c. Reduction of cycle time
_____ d. Finished goods inventory is stored in warehouses until needed.
_____ e. Selecting vendors on the basis of service and material quality, as well as price
_____ f. Accepting vendor deliveries directly to the shop floor, and only as needed
_____ g. Employees at each station work to provide inventory for the next workstation only as needed.

M19-23. Determining Appropriate Data Visualizations for Different Scenario
Applying data visualization techniques for existing data sets is a proficiency included the CGMA Competency Framework. Determine an appropriate chart to create for each of the following separate situations according to best practices. Refer to information in the *Data Visualization* report issued by the IMA found at https://www.imanet.org/research-publications/statements-on-management-accounting/data-visualization. Choose from bar chart, bubble chart, line graph, pie chart, scatter chart, and tree map. Use each chart only once.

1. To illustrate the proportions of five different components of overhead costs to total overhead costs.
2. To illustrate the proportions of 25 different components of overhead costs to total overhead costs.
3. To show the trend in monthly costs of five different overhead cost pools over a one-year period.
4. To compare the annual costs of five different overhead cost pools (making up the total of overhead) for the current year.
5. To highlight correlation between a potential cost driver (number of deliveries) and costs of deliveries.
6. To highlight correlation between a potential cost driver (number of deliveries) and costs of deliveries along with the amount of time spent on deliveries.

EXERCISES

E19-24. Allocating Service Department Costs Using the Direct Method: Allocation Basis Alternatives
Assume **Genzink Steel**, a metal fabrication company, has two producing departments, P1 and P2, and one service department, S1. Estimated overhead costs per month are as follows.

P1	$2,000,000
P2	750,000
S1	1,000,000

Other data follow:

	P1	P2
Number of employees	50	30
Production capacity (units)	75,000	20,000
Space occupied (square feet)	57,600	22,400
Five-year average percent of S1's service output used	60%	40%

REQUIRED

a. For each of the following allocation bases, determine the total estimated overhead cost for P1 and P2 after allocating S1 cost to the producing departments.
 1. Number of employees
 2. Production capacity in units
 3. Space occupied
 4. Five-year average percentage of S1 services used
 5. Estimated overhead costs (Round your answer to the nearest dollar.)

b. For each of the five allocation bases, explain the circumstances (including examples) under which each allocation base might be most appropriately used to allocate service department cost in a manufacturing plant such as Genzink Steel. Also, discuss the advantages and disadvantages that might result from using each of the allocation bases.

LO19-1 **E19-25. Interdepartmental Services: Direct Method**

Wilhelm Manufacturing Company has five operating departments, two of which are producing departments (P1 and P2) and three of which are service departments (S1, S2, and S3). All costs of the service departments are allocated to the producing departments. The following table shows the distribution of services from the service departments.

	\multicolumn{5}{c}{Services Provided to}
Services provided from	S1	S2	S3	P1	P2
S1	—	10%	20%	28%	42%
S2	5%	—	15%	52%	28%
S3	7%	3%	—	27%	63%

The direct operating costs of the service departments are as follows.

S1	$150,000
S2	80,000
S3	106,000

REQUIRED

Using the direct method, prepare a schedule allocating the service department costs to the producing departments.

LO19-1 **E19-26. Interdepartmental Services: Step Method**

Refer to the data in Mini Exercise E19-25. Using the step method, prepare a schedule for Wilhelm Manufacturing Company allocating the service department costs to the producing departments. (Round calculations to the nearest dollar.)

LO19-1 **E19-27. Interdepartmental Services: Step Method**

Assume that Wilson's, a department store in Massachusetts, allocates the costs of the Personnel and Payroll departments to three retail sales departments, Housewares, Clothing, and Toys. In addition to providing services to the operating departments, Personnel and Payroll provide services to each other. Wilson's allocates Personnel Department costs on the basis of the number of employees and Payroll Department costs on the basis of gross payroll. Cost and allocation information for June is as follows.

	Personnel	Payroll	Housewares	Clothing	Toys
Direct department cost	$25,000	$30,340	$50,174	$60,830	$45,156
Number of employees	3	5	12	20	10
Gross payroll	$12,960	$17,280	$36,000	$43,200	$34,560

REQUIRED

a. Determine the percentage of total Personnel Department services that was provided to the Payroll Department.
b. Determine the percentage of total Payroll Department services that was provided to the Personnel Department.
c. Prepare a schedule showing Personnel Department and Payroll Department cost allocations to the operating departments, assuming Wilson's uses the step method. (Round calculations to the nearest dollar.)

LO19-3 **E19-28. Excess Capacity**

Assume **Marriott International** just opened a new hotel in Bethesda, MD. The hotel has 245 rooms, or 89,425 room-nights per year. The hotel was built with the aim that it would be 90% occupied during the spring and summer months, and it would be at a much lower capacity of 50% during the remaining portion of the year. The cost of the building cleaning and maintenance is estimated to be $28,000,000 per year.

a. Calculate the practical capacity of the hotel.
b. Calculate the cost per room night of cleaning and maintenance.
c. Calculate the cost of excess capacity for the year.
d. Should the division or customers be accountable for the cost of excess capacity? If so, how?

LO19-3 **E19-29. Backflush Costing Method in a JIT/Lean Environment**

Johanna Computer manufactures laptop computers under its own brand, but acquires all the components from outside vendors. No computers are assembled until the order is received online from customers, so there is no finished goods inventory. When an order is received, the bill of materials required to fill the order is prepared automatically and sent electronically to the various vendors. All components are received from vendors within three days, and the completed order is shipped to the customer immediately when completed, usually on the same day the components are received from vendors. The number of units in process at the end of any day is negligible.

The following data are provided for the most recent month of operations.

Actual components costs incurred	$1,200,000
Actual conversion costs incurred	$1,850,000
Units in process, beginning of month	0
Units started in process during the month	4,000
Units in process, end of month	0

REQUIRED

a. Assuming Johanna uses traditional cost accounting procedures:
  1. How much cost was charged to Work-in-Process during the month?
  2. How much cost was charged to cost of goods sold during the month?
b. Assuming Johanna is a lean production company and uses the backflush costing method:
  1. How much cost was charged to Work-in-Process during the month?
  2. How much cost was charged to cost of goods sold during the month?

E19-30. Inventory Management Metrics

Large retailers like **Costco** and **Target** typically use gross margin ratio (gross margin ÷ sales), inventory turnover (sometimes referred to as inventory turns), and gross margin return on investment (GMROI) to evaluate how well inventory has been managed. The goal is to maximize profits while minimizing the investment in inventory. The following data is for four scenarios, a base scenario (A) followed by three modifications (B, C, and D) to the base scenario.

Costco
NASDAQ :: COST
Target
NYSE :: TGT

	Scenario A	Scenario B	Scenario C	Scenario D
Sales	$50,000	$75,000	$60,000	$50,000
Cost of goods sold	35,000	35,000	30,000	35,000
Gross profit	$15,000	$40,000	$30,000	$15,000
Average inventory	$ 6,000	$ 6,000	$ 6,000	$ 4,000

REQUIRED
For each scenario calculate the gross margin percent, the inventory turnover, and GMROI.

E19-31. Evaluating Inventory Management Metrics
Refer to E19-30.

REQUIRED

a. For Scenarios B through D, explain what change occurred relative to Scenario A to cause GMROI to change. For example, was the change in GMROI caused by a change in inventory turns, a change in gross margin percent, or by reducing inventory levels?
b. What general conclusions can be made from the calculations and observations regarding the factors that influence GMROI?

E19-32. Cycle Efficiency

Clarion Scooters, Inc. runs one 8-hour shift per day. Three different machines are used in the production of electric scooters, Clarion's sole product.

The operations manager at Clarion is looking at ways to be more efficient and has gathered the following information.

Manufacturing time per batch of 50 scooters	
Function	**Time**
Actual processing time on the machines for one batch of scooters	3.75 hours
Time spent moving a batch of scooters from one station to the next	2 hours
Time spent on quality control testing, per batch	45 minutes
Time spent setting up equipment, for batch processing	30 minutes

The operations manager also noted that, on average, there was about one hour of downtime per batch. (Downtime occurred when employees were unavailable to move or test the scooters.)

REQUIRED
a. What is the cycle time per batch, in hours?
b. What is Clarion's cycle efficiency?
c. What are some practical steps Clarion could take to improve its efficiency?

LO19-4

E19-33. Technical Skills Gap

Assume Katie Dempsey works as a recruiter, placing accounting and finance professionals. Katie's current project is to fill an open managerial accounting position at **PepsiCo.** Identify the technical skills that Katie will be looking for in the applicant's resume and application materials that will likely lead to success in the position. Do you think these skills will be difficult to find in candidates? If so, what are some ways PepsiCo might be able to develop these skills in-house?

LO19-4

E19-34. Researching the CGMA Competencies for Management Accountants

Access the **CGMA (Chartered Global Management Accountant)** Competency Framework at **https://www.aicpa.org/resources/article/cgma-competency-framework** in order to answer the following questions.

REQUIRED
a. List the competencies under each major skill category.
b. What are the four levels of proficiency levels for a competency? How does each proficiency level match to an expected staffing level within an organization?
c. What is the difference between the competencies of data analytics and data visualization at the foundational level of proficiency?
d. Consider the requirements of DA19-2. What CGMA competencies would you as the cost accountant draw upon in order to follow through with the steps identified in the scenario?

PROBLEMS

LO19-1

P19-35. Selecting Cost Allocation Bases and Direct Method Allocations

Seattle Company has three producing departments (P1, P2, and P3) for which direct department costs are accumulated. In January, the following indirect costs of operation were incurred.

Plant manager's salary and office expense	$20,500
Plant security	6,000
Plant nurse's salary and office expense	7,000
Factory depreciation (building)	20,000
Equipment depreciation	15,000
Machine maintenance	7,000
Plant cafeteria cost subsidy	5,000
Total	$80,500

The following additional data have been collected for the three producing departments.

	P1	P2	P3
Number of employees	20	30	10
Space occupied (square feet)	12,000	6,000	6,000
Direct labor hours	3,400	5,000	1,600
Machine hours	1,500	600	900
Number of nurse office visits	25	20	5

REQUIRED
a. Group the indirect cost items into cost pools based on their common basis for allocation. Identify the most appropriate allocation basis for each cost pool and determine the total January costs in the pool. (*Hint:* A cost pool may consist of one or more cost items.)
b. Allocate the cost pools directly to the three producing departments using the allocation bases selected in requirement (*a*).
c. How much indirect cost would be allocated to each producing department if Seattle Company was using a plantwide rate based on direct labor hours? Based on machine hours?
d. Comment on the benefits of allocating costs in pools compared with using a plantwide rate.

P19-36. Evaluating Allocation Bases and Direct Method Allocations LO19-1

Brahtz Company has two service departments, Maintenance and Information Technology (IT), that serve two producing departments, Mixing and Packaging. The following data have been collected for these departments for the current year.

	IT	Maintenance	Mixing	Packaging
Direct department costs	$210,000	$185,000	$1,200,000	$550,000
Number of employees			40	20
Number of ethernet connections			50	30
Number of maintenance hours used			1,500	1,000
Number of maintenance orders			120	180

REQUIRED

a. Using the direct method, allocate the service department costs under the following independent assumptions:
   1. IT costs are allocated based on the number of employees, and Maintenance costs are allocated based on the number of maintenance hours used.
   2. IT costs are allocated based on the number of ethernet connections served, and Maintenance costs are allocated based on the number of maintenance orders.

b. Comment on the reasonableness of the bases used in the calculations in requirement (a). What considerations should determine which bases to use for allocating IT and Maintenance costs?

P19-37. Cost Reimbursement and Step Allocation Method LO19-1

Hope Clinic is a not-for-profit outpatient facility that provides medical services to both fee-paying patients and low-income government-supported patients. Reimbursement from the government is based on total actual costs of services provided, including both direct costs of patient services and indirect operating costs. Patient services are provided through two producing departments, Medical Services and Ancillary Services (includes X-ray, therapy, etc.). In addition to the direct costs of these departments, the clinic incurs indirect costs in two service departments, Administration and Facilities. Administration costs are allocated first based on the number of full-time employees, and Facilities costs are then allocated based on space occupied. Costs and related data for the current month are as follows.

	Administration	Facilities	Medical Services	Ancillary Services
Direct costs	$65,000	$30,750	$745,700	$350,000
Number of employees	6	4	8	4
Amount of space occupied (square feet)	2,000	600	7,500	2,500
Number of patient visits	—	—	7,975	3,000

REQUIRED

a. Using the step method, prepare a schedule allocating the common service department costs to the producing departments.
b. Determine the amount to be reimbursed from the government for each low-income patient visit.

P19-38. Budgeted Service Department Cost Allocation: Pricing a New Product LO19-1

Fit & Active Company is adding a new diet food concentrate called Body Fit & Healthy to its line of bodybuilding and exercise products. A plant is being built for manufacturing the new product. Management has decided to price the new product based on a 100% markup on total manufacturing costs. A direct cost budget for the new plant projects that direct department costs of $7,152,500 will be incurred in producing an expected normal output of 750,000 pounds of finished product. In addition, indirect costs for Administration and Technical Support will be shared by Body Fit & Healthy with the two exercise products divisions, Commercial Products and Retail Products. Budgeted annual data to be used in making the allocations are summarized here.

	Administration	Technical Support	Commercial Products	Retail Products	Body Fit & Healthy
Number of employees	10	4	70	60	20
Amount of technical support time (hours)	690	—	1,840	1,610	460

Direct costs are budgeted at $750,000 for the Administration Department and $500,000 for the Technical Support Department.

REQUIRED

a. Using the step method, determine the total direct and indirect costs of Body Fit & Healthy. (Administration costs are allocated based on number of employees; Technical Support costs are allocated based on technical support time.)
b. Determine the selling price per pound of Body Fit & Healthy. (Round calculations to the nearest cent.)

LO19-1

P19-39. Allocation and Responsibility Accounting

Assume that **Timberland Company**, owned by **VF Corp.**, uses a responsibility accounting system for evaluating its managers and that abbreviated performance reports for the company's three divisions for the month of March are as follows (amounts in thousands).

	Total	East	Central	West
Operating income before service department cost allocations	$480,000	$200,000	$170,000	$110,000
Less allocated costs:				
Information Technology	(250,000)	(96,154)	(76,923)	(76,923)
Personnel	(160,000)	(71,111)	(53,333)	(35,556)
Division income (loss)	$ 70,000	$ 32,735	$ 39,744	$ (2,479)

The West Division manager is very disturbed over his performance report and recent rumors that his division may be closed because of its failure to report a profit in recent periods. He believes that the reported profit figures do not fairly present operating results because his division is being unfairly burdened with service department costs. He is particularly concerned over the amount of Information Technology costs charged to his division. He believes that it is inequitable for his division to be charged with approximately one-third of the total cost when it is using only 20% of the services. He believes that the Personnel Department's use of the Information Technology Department should also be considered in the cost allocations. Cost allocations were based on the following distributions of service provided.

	Services Receiver				
Services Provider	Personnel	Computer Services	East	Central	West
Information Technology	35%	—	25%	20%	20%
Personnel	—	10%	40%	30%	20%

REQUIRED

a. What method is the company using to allocate Personnel and Information Technology costs?
b. Recompute the cost allocations using the step method. (Round calculations to the nearest dollar.)
c. Revise the performance reports to reflect the cost allocations computed in requirement (b).
d. Comment on the complaint of the West Division's manager. Are there established rules on what method should be used to allocate costs? How does the choice of a cost allocation base result in an ethical dilemma for the top management of the divisions?

LO19-1

P19-40. Allocating Service Department Costs: Direct and Step Methods; Department and Plantwide Overhead Rates

Assume that **Brown Jordan**, a manufacturer of fine casual outdoor furniture, allocates Human Resources Department costs to the producing departments (Cutting and Welding) based on number of employees; Facilities Department costs are allocated based on the amount of square footage occupied. Direct department costs, labor hours, and square footage data for the four departments for October are as follows.

	Human Resources	Facilities	Cutting	Welding
Direct department overhead costs	$150,000	$450,000	$2,662,500	$1,102,500
Number of employees	12	20	60	90
Number of direct labor hours	—	—	12,000	15,000
Amount of square footage	15,000	4,500	225,000	75,000

Assume that two jobs, A1 and A2, were completed during October and that each job had direct materials costs of $3,000. Job A1 used 75 direct labor hours in the Cutting Department and 25 direct labor hours in the Welding Department. Job A2 used 25 direct labor hours in the Cutting Department and 75 direct labor hours in the Welding Department. The direct labor rate per hour, including benefits, is $50 in both departments.

REQUIRED
a. Find the cost of each job using a plantwide rate based on direct labor hours.
b. Find the cost of each job using department rates with *direct* service department cost allocation.
c. Find the cost of each job using department rates with *step* service department cost allocation.
d. Explain the differences in the costs computed in requirements (a)–(c) for each job. Which costing method is best for product pricing and profitability analysis?

P19-41. Dual Allocation Approach and Charging for Services
Assume that the Maintenance Department of one of **Embassy Suites** properties, a **Hilton Worldwide** franchise has fixed costs of $750,000 a year. It also incurs $75 in out-of-pocket expenses for every hour of work. During the year the Rooms Department used 35,000 maintenance hours. The Food and Beverage (F&B) Department used 15,000 maintenance hours. When the Maintenance Department was established, the Rooms and F&B departments estimated they would need 35,000 and 25,000 maintenance hours, respectively. It turns out F&B cut back on maintenance hours used to ensure it would meet its budget.

REQUIRED
a. Calculate the amount of Maintenance Department costs to allocate to Rooms and F&B based entirely on actual usage.
b. Calculate the amount of Maintenance Department costs to allocate to Rooms and F&B using a dual allocation approach where fixed cost is allocated based on estimated capacity needed and variable cost is allocated based on actual usage.
c. Which of the two methods applied in parts *a* and *b* is more fair to the two departments?
d. Assume that the Maintenance Department allocates costs to the producing departments using a user charge. What amount would you suggest for the user charge? Is it a good idea to use a user charge for allocating costs?

P19-42. Dual Allocation Approach and Charging for Services
Ecoclock manufactures four environmentally friendly consumer products, and the firm is organized as four operating centers, each responsible for a single product. The main mechanism of each product is the same and requires an identical initial processing step, although subsequent processing for each product is very different. Ecoclock's management has decided to centralize the initial processing function and purchase new equipment that has a 40,000 unit annual practical capacity. For budgeting and costing purposes, the initial processing function will be assigned to a new center, Center E. Shown below is the budgeted production for the product centers.

	Annual Production
Center A	5,000
Center B	7,500
Center C	4,000
Center D	6,000

A large part of the managers' compensation is derived from bonuses that they receive for meeting or exceeding cost targets. The managers of centers A through D each agree that they should be charged with the variable costs per unit that are delivered by Center E. However, they disagree about the allocation of the fixed costs of Center E, primarily because they believe that the new equipment has a much larger capacity than is necessary and they do not want to be charged with the cost of the unused capacity. The fixed costs for Center E total $150,000, while the variable cost per unit is $6.

REQUIRED
a. Assume fixed costs are allocated based on the proportion of units produced by each center. What is Center D's per unit cost?
b. What would be Center A's per unit cost if Center E's fixed costs are allocated based on practical capacity?
c. Although allocating Center E's fixed costs on a per-unit produced basis seems equitable, the manager of Center C is worried about Center B reducing the number of units produced. Calculate Center C's per unit cost with no change in production.
d. If Center B reduces the number of units produced to 5,000, will Center C's cost increase or decrease and by how much?
e. The center managers are concerned that being charged for unused capacity will impact their bonus. Explain how company management could alleviate the concerns.
f. Identify three additional measures that could be used to evaluate manager performance.

CMA adapted

LO19-3 **P19-43. JIT/Lean Production and Product Costing**

Presented is information pertaining to the standard or budgeted unit cost of a product manufactured in a JIT/Lean Production environment at CNN Systems Inc.

Direct materials.	$30
Conversion	60
Total	$90

All materials are added at the start of the production process. All raw materials purchases and conversion costs are directly assigned to Cost of Goods Sold. At the end of the period, costs are backed out and assigned to Raw Materials in Process (only for materials still in the plant) and Finished Goods Inventory (for materials and conversion costs for completed units). Costs assigned to inventories are based on the standard or budgeted cost multiplied by the number of units in inventory. Conversion costs are assigned to inventories only for fully converted units. Since inventory levels tend to be small in this JIT environment, partially completed units are assigned no conversion costs. CNN Systems had no beginning inventories on August 1. During the month, it incurred the following manufacturing-related costs.

Purchase of raw materials on account	$500,000
Factory wages	100,000
Factory supervision salaries	25,000
Facilities costs	75,000
Factory supplies purchased	15,000
Depreciation	35,000

The end-of-month inventory included raw materials in process of 150 units and finished goods of 250 units. One hundred units of raw materials were 0% converted; the other 50 units averaged 40% converted.

REQUIRED

a. Calculate the total cost debited to Cost of Goods Sold during August.
b. Calculate the balances in Raw Materials in Process, Finished Goods Inventory, and Cost of Goods Sold at the end of August.
c. Assuming that August is a typical month, is it likely that using the company's shortcut backflush accounting procedures will produce misleading financial statements? Explain.

LO19-3 **P19-44. Just-in-Time Performance Evaluation**

To control operations, Sirius Company makes extensive and exclusive use of financial performance reports for each department. Although all departments have been reporting favorable cost variances in most periods, management is perplexed by the firm's low overall return on investment. You have been asked to look into the matter. Believing the purchasing department is typical of the company's operations, you obtained the following information concerning the purchases of parts for a product it started producing five years ago.

Year	Purchase Price Variance	Quantity Used (units)	Average Inventory (units)
Year 1	$ 1,500 F	10,000	1,500
Year 2	10,500 F	15,000	2,500
Year 3	12,000 F	17,500	3,000
Year 4	20,000 U	12,500	2,500
Year 5	8,000 F	18,000	2,250
Current year	9,500 F	14,500	2,900

REQUIRED

a. Compute the inventory turnover for each year. What conclusions can be drawn from a yearly comparison of the purchase price variance and the inventory turnover?
b. Identify problems likely to be caused by evaluating purchasing only on the basis of the purchase price variance.
c. Offer whatever recommendations you believe appropriate.

CASES AND PROJECTS

C19-45. Materials Push and Materials Pull Systems LO19-3

Data Storage Inc. produces three models of external storage devices for personal computers. Each model is produced on a separate assembly line. Production consists of several operations in separate work centers. Because of a high demand for Data's products, management is most interested in high-production volume and operating efficiency. Each work center is evaluated on the basis of its operating efficiency. To avoid idle time caused by defective units, variations in machine times, and machine breakdowns, significant inventories are maintained between each workstation.

At a recent administrative committee meeting, the director of research announced that the firm's engineers have made a dramatic breakthrough in designing a low-cost, read/write optical storage device. Data Storage's president is very enthusiastic, and the vice president of marketing wishes to add an assembly line for optical storage devices as soon as possible. The equipment necessary to manufacture the new product can be purchased and installed in less than 60 days. Unfortunately, all available plant space is currently devoted to the production of conventional storage devices, and expansion is not possible at the current plant location. It appears that adding the new product will require dropping a current product, relocating the entire operation, or manufacturing the optical storage devices at a separate location.

The vice president of marketing is opposed to dropping a current product. The vice president of finance is opposed to relocating the entire operation because of financing requirements and the associated financial risks. The vice president of production is opposed to splitting up production activities because of the loss of control and the added costs for various types of overhead.

REQUIRED

Explain how switching to a materials-pull (Kanban) system can help solve Data Storage's space problems while improving quality and cycle time. Describe how a materials pull system works and the changes required in management attitude toward inventory and efficiency to make it work.

C19-46. Product Costing Using Activity-Based Costing and Just-in-Time: A Value Chain Approach LO19-3

Wearwell Carpet Company is a small residential carpet manufacturer started by Don Stegall, a longtime engineer and manager in the carpet industry. Stegall began Wearwell in the early 1990s after learning about ABC, JIT, total quality management, and several other manufacturing concepts being used successfully in Japan and other parts of the world. Although it was a small company, he believed that with his many years of experience and by applying these advanced techniques, Wearwell could very quickly become a world-class competitor.

Stegall buys dyed carpet yarns for Wearwell from three different major yarn manufacturers with which he has done business for many years. He chose these companies because of their reputation for producing high-quality products and their state-of-the-art research and development departments. He has arranged for two carpet manufacturing companies to produce (tuft) all of his carpets on a contractual basis. Both companies have their own brands, but they also do contract work for other companies. For each manufacturer, Stegall had to agree to use the full output of one manufacturing production line at least one day per month. Each production line was dedicated to producing only one style of carpet, but each manufacturer had production lines capable of running each type of carpet that Wearwell sold.

Stegall signed a contract with a large transport company (CTC), which specializes in carpet-related shipping, to pick up and deliver yarn from the yarn plants to the tufting mills. This company will then deliver the finished product from the tufting mills to Wearwell's ten customers, which are carpet retailers in the ten largest residential building markets in the country. These retailers pay the shipping charges to have the carpets delivered to them. Wearwell maintains a small sales staff (which also doubles as a customer service staff) to deal with the retailers and occasionally with the end customers on quality problems that arise.

Wearwell started selling only one line of carpet, a medium-grade plush, but as new carpet styles were developed, it added two additional lines, a medium-grade berber carpet and a medium-grade textured carpet. Three colors are offered in each carpet style. By selling only medium grades with limited color choices, Stegall felt that he would reach a very large segment of the carpet market without having to deal with a large number of different products. As textured (trackless) carpets have become more popular, sales of plush have diminished substantially.

REQUIRED

a. Describe the value chain for Wearwell Carpet Company and identify the parties who compose this value chain.

b. Identify and discuss the cost categories that would be included in the cost of the product for financial reporting purposes.
c. Identify and discuss the cost categories that would be included in the cost of the product for pricing and other management purposes.
d. Discuss some of the challenges that Stegall will have trying to apply JIT to regulate the levels of control at Wearwell. Suggest changes that might be necessary to make JIT work.
e. Does Wearwell seem to be an appropriate setting for implementing ABC? If so, what are likely to be the most important activities and related cost drivers?

SOLUTIONS TO REVIEW PROBLEMS

Review 19-1—Solution
Service Department Cost Allocation
a. Direct Method

	Total	Apparel	Household Products
Administrative Services Department			
Allocation base (number of employees)	24	15	9
$ per employee	$ 750		
Cost allocation	$18,000	$11,250	$6,750
Facilities Services Department			
Allocation base (square footage)	22,500	15,000	7,500
$ per square foot	$ 0.533		
Cost allocation	$12,000	$ 8,000	$4,000

Cost Allocation Summary

	Administrative	Facilities	Apparel	Household Products	Total
Departmental costs before allocation	$18,000	$12,000	$60,000	$50,000	$140,000
Cost allocations					
Administrative	(18,000)	—	11,250	6,750	0
Facilities	—	(12,000)	8,000	4,000	0
Departmental costs after allocation	$ 0	$ 0	$79,250	$60,750	$140,000

b. and c.

Allocation Sequence

	Administrative	Facilities
Allocation base	Number of employees	Amount of square footage
Total base for other service and producing departments (a)	26	25,000
Total base for other service departments (b)	2	2,500
Percent of total services provided to other service departments (b ÷ a)	7.7%	10.0%
Order of allocation	Second	First

d. *Step Method*

Step Allocations

	Total	Administrative	Apparel	Household Products
Facilities Services Department				
Allocation base (square footage)	25,000	2,500	15,000	7,500
$ per square foot	$ 0.48			
Cost allocation	$12,000	$1,200	$ 7,200	$3,600
Administrative Services Department				
Allocation base (number of employees)	24	—	15	9
$ per employee	$ 800			
Cost allocation ($18,000 + $1,200)	$19,200	—	$12,000	$7,200

Cost Allocation Summary

	Facilities	Administrative	Apparel	Household Product	Total
Departmental costs before allocation	$12,000	$18,000	$60,000	$50,000	$140,000
Cost allocations					
Facilities	(12,000)	1,200	7,200	3,600	0
Administrative	—	(19,200)	12,000	7,200	0
Departmental costs after allocations	$ 0	$ 0	$79,200	$60,800	$140,000

Review 19-2—Solution

a.

Cost object	Machine Hours Used	Cost per Machine Hour	Allocated Cost
Products (swim suits)	2,200	$30	$ 66,000
Excess capacity	2,200	30	66,000
Total	4,400		$132,000

The cost of the excess capacity is $66,000.

b. Kona Sol is a seasonal product. Consequently, there are high demand and low demand times. In managing this product, the facilities are set up to accommodate the high demand time periods. As a result, excess capacity exists during the low demand times. Because the capacity is developed around the Kona Sol product, the excess capacity will be allocated to this product line. The cost of excess capacity should be detailed separately so that managers can develop plans to fill this capacity with other products or ensure that the cost of capacity is covered by the product line through volume or price.

Review 19-3—Solution

a. Cycle time is the total time required to produce one batch, including both value-added and non-value-added activities: System A = 83; System B = 77. System B has a quicker cycle overall as the cycle time is 77 rather than 83. Assuming this is the only basis for decision-making, Target would prefer System B as long as quality is upheld.

b. The cycle efficiency is the percent of total time used in value-added activities. In this case, only the processing time is adding value to the product. Cycle efficiency: System A = 40/83 = 0.48; System B = 30/77 = 0.39. System A is more efficient as a higher proportion of the total time is spent on processing. Assuming that this is the only difference, Target management would like a system that minimizes non-value added activities.

c. In a lean environment, management and all employees involved will be seeking ways to reduce the cycle time while maintaining a high-quality product. For A, the company could reduce non-value-added time, especially setup time. The company should also evaluate why the processing time is higher than in System B. For B, the most likely opportunity for significant reduction is to reduce the large amount of movement and waiting time. If these components of total cycle time can be reduced, B becomes even more attractive.

Review 19-4—Solution

Students will have a variety of answers. Here are a few possible responses.

1. The data must be timely and reliable. Incorrect or misleading data can result in bad information and lead to Target managers making incorrect and poor decisions.
2. Softer skills such as communication and collaboration and partnering are also of growing importance as Target focuses more on the need to communicate and execute business strategies.
3. Analysts must be careful when drawing conclusions based on data. Often, events may seem to be linked when there may be no causal relationship driving the correlation. The cause may be inverted as in the windmill example. The machine does not cause the wind, but the wind causes the windmill to move. Or there may be additional factors to consider as in the ice cream/drowning relationship. The missing link here is that higher temperatures likely lead to more swimming and therefore, more drowning, and higher temperatures also lead to more ice cream consumption. Target must discuss the data analyses with a cross-functional group. This will allow for a full discussion of the data and potential interpretations.

Chapter 20
Decision-Making: Pricing and Product Cost Management

LEARNING OBJECTIVES

LO20-1 Apply cost-based approaches to pricing. (p. 20-3)

LO20-2 Explain target costing and discuss its advantages and disadvantages. (p. 20-8)

LO20-3 Explain the continuous improvement costing approach. (p. 20-12)

LO20-4 Explain how benchmarking is used to improve performance. (p. 20-13)

Road Map

LO	Learning Objective | Topics	Page	eLecture	Review	Assignments
LO20-1	**Apply cost-based approaches to pricing.** Economic Approach :: Cost-Based Pricing :: Single-Product Companies :: Multiple-Product Companies :: Markup on Cost Base	20-3	e20–1	R20-1	M20-10, M20-11, M20-12, E20-17, E20-18, E20-19, E20-20, E20-21, P20-25, P20-29, P20-30, C20-32, **DA20-1**
LO20-2	**Explain target costing and discuss its advantages and disadvantages.** Target Cost :: Cost Management Approach :: Design for Manufacture :: Product Development Stage	20-8	e20–2	R20-2	M20-13, M20-14, E20-22, E20-23, P20-26, C20-31, C20-32
LO20-3	**Explain the continuous improvement costing approach.** Kaizen Costing :: Continuous Improvement :: Production Stage	20-12	e20–3	R20-3	M20-18, E20-23, P20-27, P20-28
LO20-4	**Explain how benchmarking is used to improve performance.** Benchmarking :: Best Practices :: Setting Goals	20-13	e20–4	R20-4	M20-16, E20-24

POTBELLY
www.potbelly.com

Potbelly Corporation originated as a small antique store in Chicago. The original owner began offering toasty warm sandwiches to customers to increase sales. Almost by accident, the antique shop was transformed; customers frequented the store to eat and enjoy the featured live music rather than to purchase antiques. Despite many competitors in the area, Potbelly gained popularity, acquiring a loyal and growing following.

Potbelly opened its second shop in 1997. Continuing expansion, Potbelly went public in 2013. It currently operates 384 company shops in 31 states and the District of Columbia, and franchises 45 shops. Potbelly shops are fairly concentrated, with 69% of shops located in five states and the District of Columbia. Despite the good news and strong growth, Potbelly has recently reported large losses due to the COVID-19 pandemic. However, in 2022, the company reported profits and is renewing its growth strategy primarily in franchise development, while closing underperforming company shops.

Potbelly competes in the restaurant industry and faces significant competition from restaurants, convenience stores, meal delivery kit services, and more recently, food delivery services from a wide variety of restaurants due to COVID-19. The company believes that it competes "primarily based on product quality, restaurant concept, service, convenience, value perception and price." As new competitors, like meal delivery kit services, enter the industry, Potbelly must adapt to compete in a profitable manner.

However, how does Potbelly collect and analyze data to ensure profitability growth? To stay competitive, Potbelly must ensure quality food at a great value. The company is prioritizing low-cost, high-return opportunities to drive traffic to its shops as well as initiatives that focus on increasing margins at the shops. Cost analysis discussed in previous chapters as well as cost-based decision-making techniques discussed in this chapter will help Potbelly's management make informed decisions. Strategic cost management techniques, such as target costing and continuous improvement costing, represent important concepts for product management professionals involved in the development, manufacture, and marketing of products and services. Virtually all such techniques are grounded in the notion of managing the value chain. This chapter examines pricing, the interrelation between price and cost, and the role of benchmarking in meeting customer needs at the lowest possible price. The managerial tools discussed throughout this chapter will help Potbelly management continue to develop, produce, and market its products in a highly competitive industry.

Source: Potbelly 2022 10-K

CHAPTER ORGANIZATION

Pricing and Other Product Management Decisions

Cost-Based Pricing
- Contrasting a Cost-Based Approach to an Economic Approach
- Cost-Based Approaches to Pricing

Price-Based Costing
- Target Costing
- Characteristics of Target Costing

Continuous Improvement
- Kaizen Costing Approach
- Characteristics of Kaizen Approach

Benchmarking to Improve Performance
- Applications of Benchmarking
- Process of Benchmarking

COST-BASED PRICING

LO20-1 Apply cost-based approaches to pricing.

Pricing products and services is one of the most important and complex management decisions because it affects the entire value chain. Each partner determines the price of its product/service to charge to the next organization in the value chain. Ultimately, each individual pricing decision in the value chain affects the final selling price to the consumer.

Pricing decisions directly affect not only the salability of individual products or services, but the profitability, and even the survival, of the organization as a whole. Many economists have spent their entire careers examining the foundations of pricing. To respond to the needs of pricing hundreds or thousands of individual items, managers have developed pricing guidelines that are typically based on costs. More recently, global competition has turned cost-based approaches upside down. Managers of world-class organizations increasingly start with a price that customers are willing to pay and then determine allowable costs.

Contrasting a Cost-Based Approach to an Economic Approach

In economic models, a firm has a *profit-maximizing goal and known cost and revenue functions.* Typically, increases in sales quantity require reductions in selling prices, causing *marginal revenue* (the varying increment in total revenue derived from the sale of an additional unit) to decline as sales increase. Increases in production cause an increase in *marginal cost* (the varying increment in total cost required to produce and sell an additional unit of product). In economic models, profits are maximized at the sales volume at which marginal revenues equal marginal costs. Firms continue to produce as long as the marginal revenue derived from the sale of each additional unit exceeds the marginal cost of producing that unit.

Economic models provide a useful framework for considering pricing decisions. The ideal price is the one that will lead customers to purchase all units a firm can provide up to the point at which the last unit has a marginal cost exactly equal to its marginal revenue.

Despite their conceptual merit, economic models are seldom used for day-to-day pricing decisions. Perfect information and an indefinite time period are required to achieve equilibrium prices at which marginal revenues equal marginal costs. Additionally, the market does not always act rationally as assumed by the economic models. *In the short run, most for-profit organizations attempt to achieve a target profit rather than a maximum profit.* One reason for this is an inability to determine the single set of actions that will lead to profit maximization. Furthermore, managers are more apt to strive to satisfy a number of goals (such as profits for investors, job security for themselves and their employees, and being a socially responsible corporate citizen) than to strive for the maximization of a single profit goal. In any case, to maximize profits, a company's management would have to know the cost and revenue functions of every product the firm sells. For most firms, this information cannot be developed at a reasonable cost. As a result, firms often resort to a pricing method that is based on the estimated costs of the products.

Cost-Based Approaches to Pricing

Although cost is not the only consideration in pricing, it has traditionally been the most important for several reasons.

- *Cost data are typically available.* When hundreds or thousands of different prices must be set in a short time, cost could be the only feasible basis for product pricing.
- *Cost-based prices are defensible.* Managers threatened by legal action or public scrutiny feel secure using cost-based prices. They can argue that prices are set in a manner that provides a "fair" profit.
- *Revenues must exceed costs if the firm is to remain in business.* In the long run, total sales must exceed total costs for the organization. In general, each product should be priced to exceed the full production cost. However, there are always exceptions such as products sold through strategic partnership agreements, bundled products, or products sold at a loss that lead to other, more profitable purchases.

Cost-based pricing is illustrated in **Exhibit 20.1**. The process begins with market research to determine customer wants. Additionally, research will be completed to assess *how* customers want products to be produced. Often, customers are willing to pay more to companies that produce in a sustainable manner or donate a portion of proceeds to a specific cause or mission. If the product requires components to be designed and produced by vendors, the process of obtaining prices can be time consuming. When some costs, such as those fixed costs at the facility level, are not assigned to specific products, a markup is added to cover these costs. An additional markup is added to achieve a desired profit. The selling price is then set as the sum of the assigned costs, the markup to cover unassigned costs, and the markup to achieve the desired profit.

EXHIBIT 20.1 Cost-Based Pricing for a New Product

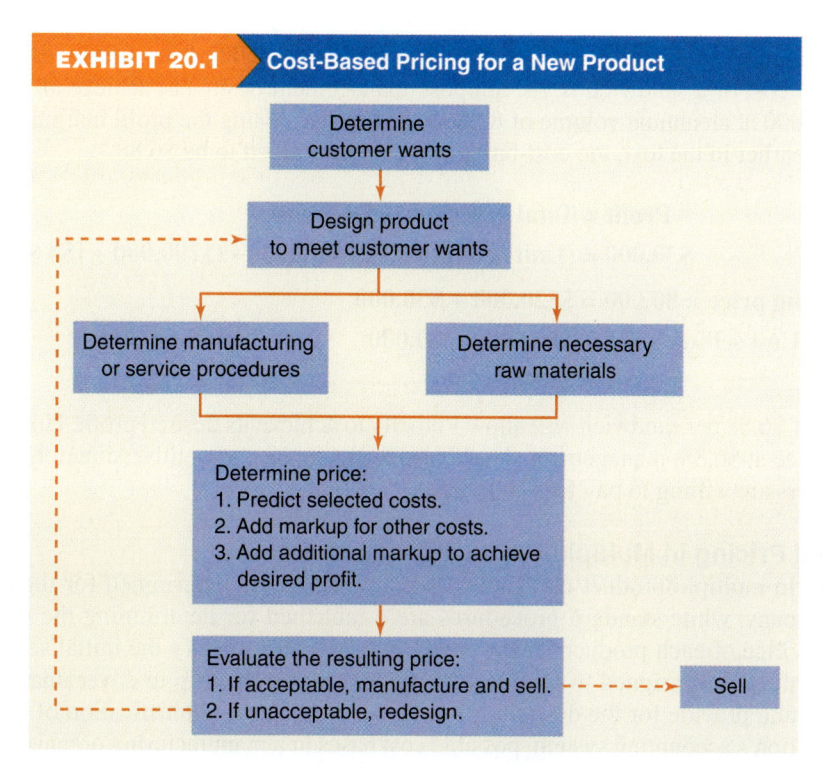

- Determine customer wants
- Design product to meet customer wants
- Determine manufacturing or service procedures
- Determine necessary raw materials
- Determine price:
  1. Predict selected costs.
  2. Add markup for other costs.
  3. Add additional markup to achieve desired profit.
- Evaluate the resulting price:
  1. If acceptable, manufacture and sell. → Sell
  2. If unacceptable, redesign.

The proposed selling price should be evaluated with regard to competitive information and what customers are willing to pay. If the price is acceptable, the product or service is produced. If the price is too high, the product might be redesigned, manufacturing procedures might be changed, and different types of materials might be considered until either an acceptable price is achieved or it is determined that the product cannot be produced at an acceptable price.

In times of high inflation, sellers pay higher prices for materials, merchandise and services that often must be passed on to the consumer in order for the seller to remain profitable. What are some ways that companies can maintain profits in periods of rising prices without raising the *posted* selling price of the product or service?

Critical Thinking & Decision-Making

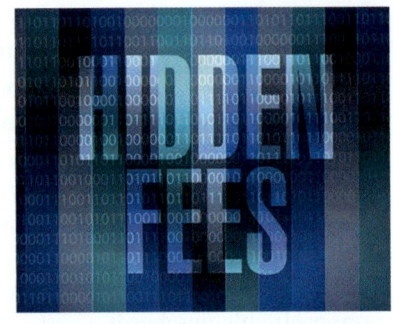

Rising prices affect businesses and consumers. In order to avoid an increase to the posted price of a product or service, businesses will find other ways to maintain margins without turning away price-conscious customers. Even though the consumer pays more in the end, the posted price does not show an increase. For example, food items are sold in smaller package sizes, new add-on fees are applied to a purchase, hotel rooms sheets are only changed between guests, or add-on free services are canceled. In 2021, Walt Disney's *Disney World in Orlando canceled its free airport shuttles and* Harley Davidson *charged dealers a materials surcharge fee which dealers passed on to customers.*[1] *Kleenex boxes that used to contain 65 tissues now only hold 60 tissues and yogurt has shrunk from 5.3 ounces to 4.5 ounces.*[2] *These examples highlight ways in which companies indirectly increase selling prices in response to rising costs.*

Cost-Based Pricing in Single-Product Companies

Implementing cost-based pricing in a single-product company is straightforward if everything is known but the selling price. In this case, all known data are entered into the profit formula, which is then solved for the variable price. Assume that Potbelly sells one type of sandwich. Assume that a single Potbelly's location's annual fixed facility-level costs are $200,000 and the unit cost of a sandwich is $4. Suppose management desires to achieve an annual profit of $30,000 at an annual volume of 80,000 sandwiches. Using the profit margin formula presented earlier in the text, the cost-based price is determined to be $6.88.

$$\text{Profit} = \text{Total revenues} - \text{Total costs}$$

$$\$30{,}000 = (\text{Unit selling price} \times 80{,}000) - (\$200{,}000 + [\$4 \times 80{,}000])$$

$$\text{Unit selling price} \times 80{,}000 = \$520{,}000 + \$30{,}000$$

$$\text{Unit selling price} = \$550{,}000 \div 80{,}000$$

$$= \$6.88$$

A price of $6.88 per sandwich will allow Potbelly to achieve its desired profit. However, before setting the price at $6.88, management should also evaluate the competitive situation and consider what customers are willing to pay for sandwiches.

Cost-Based Pricing in Multiple-Product Companies

In multiple-product companies, desired profits are determined for the entire company, while standard procedures are established for determining the initial selling price of each product. These procedures typically specify the initial selling price as the costs assigned to products or services plus a markup to cover unassigned costs and provide for the desired profit. Depending on the sophistication of the organization's accounting system, possible cost bases in a manufacturing organization include markups based on a *combination of cost behavior and function*. The possible cost bases include the following:

- Direct materials costs
- Variable manufacturing costs
- Total variable costs (manufacturing, selling, and administrative) and
- Full manufacturing costs.

Regardless of the cost base, the general approach to developing a markup is to recognize that the markup must be large enough to provide for costs not included in the base plus the desired profit.

---

[1] Gasparro, A., Rubin, G., "The Hidden Ways Companies Raise Prices," The Wall Street Journal, February 12, 2022.
[2] "'Shrinkflation' accelerates globally as manufacturers quietly shrink package sizes", June 8, 2022, found at https://www.npr.org/2022/06/08/1103766334/shrinkflation-globally-manufacturers-shrink-package-sizes.

$$\text{Markup on cost base} = \frac{\text{Costs not included in the base} + \text{Desired profit}}{\text{Costs included in the base}}$$

This approach is for long-run pricing in which the aim is to cover all costs and generate a profit for the organization. First we illustrate a pricing decision with total variable costs as the cost base, followed by an example with full manufacturing costs as the cost base.

Markup based on total variable costs When the markup is based on total variable costs, it must be large enough to cover all fixed costs and the desired profit. Assume that the predicted annual variable and fixed costs for one of **Potbelly**'s regions are as follows.

Variable		Fixed	
Manufacturing.	$600,000	Manufacturing.	$300,000
Selling and administrative.	200,000	Selling and administrative.	100,000
Total	$800,000	Total	$400,000

Furthermore, assume that Potbelly's region has total assets of $1,250,000. Management believes that an annual return of 16% on total assets is an appropriate target. A 16% return translates into a desired annual profit of $200,000.

$$\text{Annual return on assets} \times \text{Total assets} = \text{Desired annual profit}$$
$$16\% \times \$1{,}250{,}000 = \$200{,}000$$

Assuming all cost predictions are correct, obtaining a profit of $200,000 requires a 75% markup on total variable costs.

$$\text{Markup on total variable costs} = \frac{\text{Fixed costs} + \text{Desired profit}}{\text{Total variable costs}}$$
$$= \frac{\$400{,}000 + \$200{,}000}{\$800{,}000}$$
$$= 0.75$$

If the predicted variable costs for the tuna sandwich is $3.25, the initial unit selling price for the tuna sandwich is $5.69.

$$\text{Unit selling price} = \$3.25 + (\$3.25 \times 0.75)$$
$$= \$5.69$$

Markup based on full manufacturing costs When the markup is based on full manufacturing costs, it must be large enough to cover selling and administrative expenses and to provide for the desired profit. Again, it is necessary to determine the desired profit and predict all costs for the pricing period. The initial prices of individual products are then determined as their unit manufacturing costs plus the markup. For Potbelly, the markup on manufacturing costs would be 55.6%.

$$\text{Markup on full manufacturing costs} = \frac{\text{Selling and administrative costs} + \text{Desired profit}}{\text{Total manufacturing costs}}$$
$$= \frac{(\$200{,}000 + \$100{,}000) + \$200{,}000}{\$900{,}000}$$
$$= 0.556$$

If the predicted full manufacturing costs for the turkey sandwich is $5.25, the initial unit selling price for the turkey sandwich is $8.17.

$$\text{Unit selling price} = \$5.25 + (\$5.25 \times 0.556)$$
$$= \$8.17$$

Cost-Based Pricing for Special Orders

Many organizations use cost-based pricing to bid on unique projects called *special orders*. If the special order requires dedicated assets, the acquisition of new fixed assets, or an investment in employee training, the desired profit on the special order should allow for an adequate return on the dedicated assets or additional investment.

Critical Thinking & Decision-Making

Suppose Potbelly is approached to provide in-house catering for an organization. The client would like Potbelly to provide employee lunches one day per week throughout the year. What should Potbelly consider in pricing this special order?

Potbelly should consider the variable cost of the sandwiches and the number of sandwiches to be served. In addition to this, Potbelly should consider any incremental investments needed to serve this client. Will Potbelly have to hire and train dedicated staff? What are the additional incremental costs such as transportation costs? What is the desired profit for the special order?

Critique of Cost-Based Pricing

Cost-based pricing has four major drawbacks.

1. Cost-based pricing requires accurate cost assignments. If costs are not accurately assigned, some products could be priced too high, losing market share to competitors. Other products could be priced too low, gaining market share but being less profitable than anticipated.
2. The higher the portion of unassigned costs, the greater is the likelihood of over- or under-pricing individual products.
3. Cost-based pricing assumes that goods or services are relatively scarce and, generally, customers who want a product or service are willing to pay the price.
4. In a competitive environment, cost-based approaches can increase the time and cost of bringing new products to market. Ultimately, management must decide if the information derived from the system is worth the extra time it takes to obtain the information. If managers are able to make better decisions that lead to profitable results, it might be worth it.

Cost-based pricing became the dominant approach to pricing during an era when products were relatively long-lived and there was relatively little competition. While cost-based pricing reflects the need to recover costs and earn a return on investment, and is easily justified, cost-based prices might not be competitive. Competition puts intense downward pressure on prices and removes slack from pricing formulas. There is little margin for error in pricing. In a highly competitive market, small variations in pricing make significant differences in success.

Review 20-1 LO20-1 — Applying Cost-Based Approaches to Pricing

Assume that Portillo's, a restaurant chain serving iconic Chicago street food, has the following current year contribution income statement.

PORTILLO'S Contribution Income Statement For Year Ended December		
Sales (82,000 units at $6.50 per unit)		$533,000
Less variable costs		
Manufacturing	$ 90,000	
Selling and administrative	45,000	(135,000)
Contribution margin		398,000
Less fixed costs		
Manufacturing	246,000	
Selling and administrative	124,000	(370,000)
Net income		$ 28,000

continued

continued from previous page

Assume Portillo's has total assets of $1,000,000 and management desires an annual return of 10% on total assets.

Required
a. Determine the dollar amount by which Portillo's exceeded or fell short of the desired annual rate of return for the year.
b. Given the current sales volume and cost structure, determine the unit selling price required to achieve an annual profit of $50,000.
c. Given your answer to requirement (b) and the current sales volume and cost structure, determine (1) sales as a percentage of variable manufacturing costs and (2) the markup as a percentage of variable manufacturing costs, to achieve an annual profit of $50,000.
d. Restate your answer to requirement (c) for the markup as a percentage of variable manufacturing costs, dividing into two separate markup percentages.
   1. The markup on variable manufacturing costs required to cover unassigned costs.
   2. The additional markup on variable manufacturing costs required to achieve an annual profit of $50,000.

Solution on p. 20-24.

PRICE-BASED COSTING

Economists argue that cost-based prices are not realistic, because in the real world prices are determined by the confluence of supply and demand. However, when a new product is introduced into the market for which there is no previously existing supply or demand, there has to be a starting point. As discussed in the last section, cost has often been the baseline for determining initial selling prices. All too often, however, companies introduce new products into the market based on what the designers and engineers "think" the market wants (or based on inadequate market research). Only later, do they find out that either the market does not want the product, or it is not willing to buy the new product at a price sufficient to cover its cost plus an acceptable profit to the producer. This often leads to costly redesign, or in many cases, complete abandonment of the product, typically resulting in substantial financial losses. An alternative to this approach is target costing.

LO20-2 Explain target costing and discuss its advantages and disadvantages.

Target Costing: Price-Based Costing

Toyota, which has pioneered many innovations in manufacturing systems, adopted and expanded *price-based costing*, referred to as **target costing**. Toyota determined that before a new product is introduced into the market, it must be able to be produced at a cost that will make it profitable when sold at a price acceptable to customers. The acceptable selling price to the marketplace determines the acceptable cost of producing the product. If the acceptable cost, given the expected price and target profit, cannot be attained, management will rethink the launch of the product. Target costing reverses the direction of decision-making. Rather than starting with cost and calculating a price, managers start with the price and work backwards to estimate the acceptable cost.

Target costing starts with determining what customers are willing to pay for a product or service and then subtracts a desired profit on sales to determine the allowable, or target, cost of the product or service.

Target cost = Estimated selling price − Desired profit

This target cost is then communicated to a cross-functional team of employees representing such diverse areas as marketing, product design, manufacturing, and management accounting. Reflecting value chain concepts and the notion of partnerships up and down the value chain, suppliers of raw materials and components are often included in the teams. Through collaborative planning, the target costing team is challenged to design a product that meets customer price, function, and quality requirements while providing a desired profit. Its job is not completed until the target cost is met, or a determination is made that the product or service cannot be profitably introduced under the current circumstances.

Exhibit 20.2 provides an overview of target costing. What happens if the target cost cannot be achieved? In this case, management must assess whether the product is still worthwhile. Should the selling price or desired profit be adjusted? Are the resources better used on a different product? Of course, the entire team will also contribute to making this decision. Even at this early stage, abandoning a product is a difficult decision.

EXHIBIT 20.2 Target Costing in a Competitive Environment

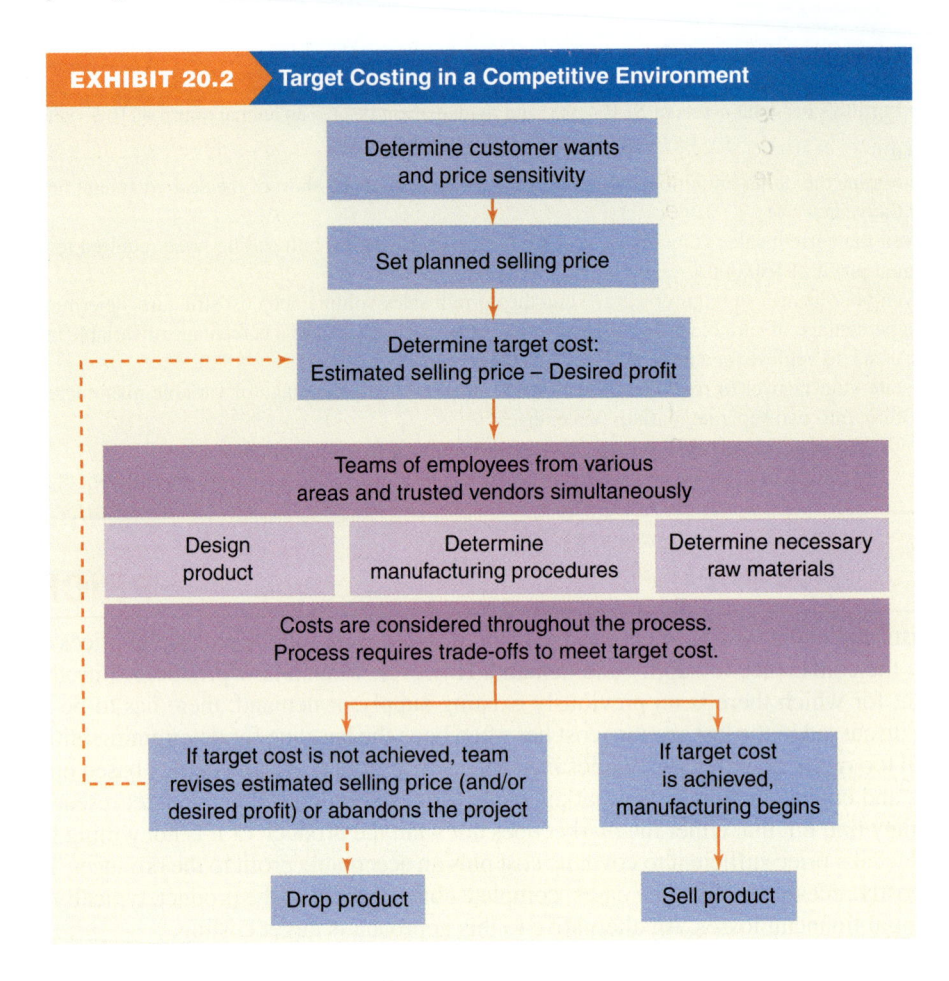

```
Determine customer wants
and price sensitivity
          ↓
Set planned selling price
          ↓
Determine target cost:
Estimated selling price – Desired profit
          ↓
Teams of employees from various
areas and trusted vendors simultaneously
  [Design product]  [Determine manufacturing procedures]  [Determine necessary raw materials]
Costs are considered throughout the process.
Process requires trade-offs to meet target cost.
          ↓
  ┌──────────────────────────┴──────────────────────────┐
If target cost is not achieved, team            If target cost
revises estimated selling price (and/or          is achieved,
desired profit) or abandons the project       manufacturing begins
          ↓                                            ↓
    Drop product                                 Sell product
```

Characteristics of Target Costing

Target costing has a number of signature characteristics that differentiates it from traditional costing approaches. Target costing requires a proactive management approach, encourages design for manufacture, reduces time to market for new products, depends upon alternative cost information, and requires coordinated efforts.

Requires a Proactive Cost Management Approach

Although a formula can be used to determine a markup on cost, it is not possible to develop a formula indicating how to achieve a target cost. Hence, target costing is not a technique. It is more a philosophy or an approach to pricing and cost management. It takes a proactive approach to cost management, reflecting the belief that costs are best managed by decisions made during *product development*. This contrasts with the more passive cost-plus belief that costs result from design, procurement, and manufacture. Target costing helps orient employees toward the final customer by reinforcing the notion that all departments within the organization and all organizations along the value chain must work together. Target costing also empowers employees who will be assigned the responsibility for carrying out activities necessary to deliver a product or service with the authority to determine what activities will be selected.

Critical Thinking & Decision-Making

How are supplier price agreements a form of cost management that is beneficial to the target costing approach in the service industry?

Creating and meeting cost targets in an age of global supply and distribution as well as a time of shortages and transportation issues are challenging. **Potbelly** *manages its cost targets using fixed pricing protocols (and other protocols) where a vendor price is mutually agreed upon and does not change over a specified time period. A fixed price* *protocol helps Potbelly predict and plan more effectively. Potbelly's procurement group has also established a contingency plan to ensure that products can be procured at competitive prices and in a timely manner should its regular suppliers face an unforeseen issue. The combination of up-front pricing protocols with its vendor partners and proactive contingency planning help Potbelly to obtain products at competitive prices, and in line with costs developed through a target costing approach.*

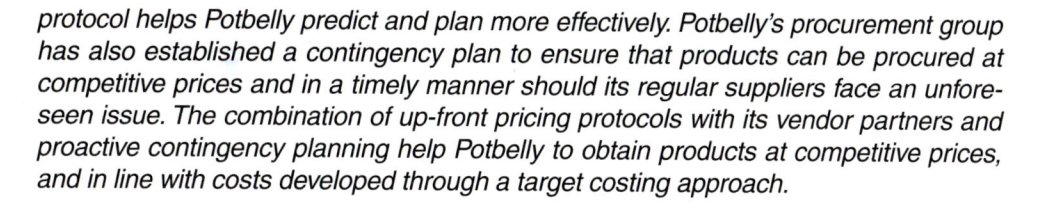

Encourages Design for Manufacture

In the absence of a target costing approach, design engineers are apt to focus on incorporating leading-edge technology and the maximum number of features in a product. Target costing keeps the customer's function, quality, and price requirements in the forefront at all times. If customers do not want leading-edge technology (which could be expensive and untested) or extra product features, they will resist paying for them. Focusing on achieving a target cost keeps design engineers tuned in to the requirements of the final customer.

A target costing approach also forces design engineers to explicitly consider the costs of manufacturing and servicing a product while it is being designed. This is known as **design for manufacture**. Minor changes in design that do not affect the product's functioning can often produce dramatic savings in manufacturing and servicing costs. Examples of design for manufacture include the following.

- Using molded plastic parts to avoid assembling several small parts.
- Designing two parts that must be fit together so that joining them in the correct manner is obvious to assembly workers.
- Placing an access panel in the side of an appliance so service personnel can make repairs quickly.
- Using standard-size parts to reduce inventory requirements, to reduce the possibility of assembly personnel inserting the incorrect part, and to simplify the job of service personnel.
- Using manufacturing procedures that are common to other products.

The successful implementation of target costing requires employees from all involved disciplines to be familiar with costing concepts and the notions of value-added and non-value-added activities. When considering the manufacturing process, team members should minimize non-value-added activities such as movement, storage, inspection, and setup. They should also select the lowest-cost value-added activities that do the job properly. Design for manufacture truly is a collaborative and creative process.

> **As head of new product development for your electronics company, you are concerned that so many of the ideas for new products coming from your research and development group are not succeeding in the market. Many recent attempts to take new products to market have failed, not because of technological deficiencies in the products, but because the market would not support the high prices for new products that were necessary to produce a satisfactory profit. What should you do to try to reverse this trend of new product failures?**

You should consider adopting target costing methods for new product development. Great product research ideas are successful only when they translate into products that can be produced and sold for an acceptable profit. Creating and producing new products before determining what the customer wants and is willing to pay often leads to failure. Target costing avoids this issue because a product is only produced if it has features and a selling price that are acceptable to potential customers, and its production costs allow the seller to make an acceptable profit.

Reduces Time to Market for New Products

By designing a product to meet a target cost (rather than evaluating the marketability of a product at a cost-plus price and having to recycle the design through several departments), target costing reduces the time required to introduce new products. Involving vendors in target costing design teams makes the vendors aware of the necessity of meeting a target cost. This facilitates the concurrent engineering of components to be produced outside the organization and reduces the time required to obtain components.

How can target costing reduce time to introduce new products in a service organization such as Potbelly?

Rather than planning a new sandwich in isolation, the food development team can work with the procurement team to ensure that ingredients can be purchased to achieve a target cost. Working together will reduce the back-and-forth discussions and allow the menu to be adapted in a more timely manner.

Depends upon Alternative Cost Information

Implementing target costing requires detailed information on the cost of alternative activities. This information allows decision makers to select design and manufacturing alternatives that best meet function and price requirements. Detailed databases of cost information for various manufacturing variables are used in designing products and selecting processes to meet target costs. Along with costs, sustainability considerations about the different material components and required processes is useful for weighing different options. For example, how are alternative material components sourced, transported, packaged, handled, used, and retired? What are the related environmental implications?

How can alternative cost information be utilized in target costing for Potbelly in developing a new sandwich?

Suppose that a new sandwich option at Potbelly requires avocado and cheese. Knowing that the cost of avocados has been increasing, management might make the decision to minimize the cost of the other ingredients to ensure that the target cost is achieved. A detailed cost list of the various cheese options helps the team make this trade-off in an informed manner.

Requires Coordinated Efforts

Limitations of target costing are employee and supplier attitudes and the many meetings required to coordinate product design and to select manufacturing processes. All people involved must have a basic understanding of the overall processes required to bring a product to market and an appreciation of the cost consequences of alternative actions. They must also respect, cooperate, and communicate with other team members and be willing to engage in a negotiation process involving trade-offs. This process can be even more difficult when outside vendors become a part of the coordination process. See **Exhibit 20.3** for an evaluation of target costing.

EXHIBIT 20.3 — Advantages and Disadvantages of Target Costing

Advantages
- Takes proactive approach to cost management.
- Orients organization toward customer.
- Breaks down barriers between departments.
- Enhances employee awareness and empowerment.
- Fosters partnerships with suppliers.
- Minimizes non-value-added activities.
- Encourages selection of lowest-cost value-added activities.
- Reduces time to market.

Disadvantages
- To be effective, requires the development of detailed cost data.
- Requires all involved to have a basic understanding of business processes.
- Requires many meetings for coordination.

How can ESG considerations be factored into the target costing approach in new product development?

First, the company can determine how sustainability features affect the customer's perceived value of the product as well as the estimated selling price. For example, the selling price may be increased if customers are willing to pay more for sustainable features.

After the target cost is calculated, the product can be designed in a way to minimize its carbon footprint within the cost constraints. Product development should consider ESG implications of materials used, sourcing options, production processes, energy usage, packaging options, product usage and disposal. More specifically, could existing tooling be used in manufacturing instead of creating special tooling which impacts the carbon footprint? What are the greenhouse gas emissions under alternative manufacturing processes? What is the cost of using biodegradable ink for packaging? What are the product recycling options? Incorporating sustainable discussions in the design stage, allows for more efficient and cost effective implementation of sustainability initiatives.

Applying Target Costing   LO20-2 **Review 20-2**

The **Portillo's** menu does not contain plant-based meat substitutes. However, the company believes that there is a demand for plant-based products, such as burgers. Based on market research, Portillo's does not think that its customer base will pay more than $6 for a plant-based burger. Additionally, given its reputation, the plant-based burger must be made from high-quality ingredients.

Required
a. How would Portillo's determine whether a target cost can be achieved?
b. What should Portillo's do if the estimated cost to produce the product exceeds the target cost?

Solution on p. 20-25.

CONTINUOUS IMPROVEMENT

Kaizen Costing Approach

In the previous sections, we focused on the pricing of new products, where changes could be made to affect the *planned* manufacturing process. But what about a situation where a company has an established product and wishes to make the product more profitable? **Continuous improvement (Kaizen) costing** calls for establishing cost reduction targets for products or services that an organization is currently providing to customers. Developed in Japan, this approach to cost management is often referred to as *Kaizen costing.* Kaizen means "continuous improvement" in Japanese. Continuous improvement costing begins where target costing ends. Target costing takes a proactive approach to cost management during the conception, design, and preproduction stages of a product's life. Continuous improvement costing takes a proactive approach to cost management during the *production stage* of a product's life.

LO20-3
Explain the continuous improvement costing approach.

Time →
Conception Design Preproduction	Production
Target costing	Continuous improvement costing

Calculating and Achieving Continuous Improvement Targets   Continuous improvement costing establishes a specific target to be achieved during the production stage. Basically, the mathematics of the concept is quite simple, but its implementation is difficult. Assume that **Potbelly** wanted to reduce the cost of food handling in each of its stores, and management set a target reduction of 2% of each year's expected cost. If a given store had current annual merchandise handling costs of $25,000 and expects an increase in the next year due to a 10% estimated growth rate over the current year, the budget for the next year would be $26,950. The budget for next year based on growth is $27,500 less the continuous improvement factor of 0.02.

Expected costs for next year: $25,000 × 1.10 = $27,500
Budgeted costs for next year under Kaizen costing: $27,500 × 0.98 = $26,950

Like target costing, Kaizen costing should be viewed as a serious attempt to make processes more efficient, while maintaining or improving quality, thereby making the company more competitive and profitable. In Kaizen costing, cost reductions can be achieved *internally* through continuous redesign and improved internal processes. Cost reductions can be achieved *externally* by working with vendors to improve their designs and processes. Kaizen is a team effort involving everyone who has an influence on costs. Kaizen is typically found in companies that have adopted a lean production philosophy. When sophisticated cost systems, such as ABC, are employed, the information provided can offer insight into how to approach the cost reduction exercise.

Successful companies use continuous improvement costing to avoid complacency. Competitors are constantly striving to win market share through better quality or lower prices. **Hewlett-Packard** studied **Epson** to determine its strengths and weaknesses. To fend off competition, prices and costs must be continuously reduced. To maintain its competitive position, Hewlett-Packard has reduced the list price of the basic inkjet printer from nearly $400 when first introduced to less than $50 today. This could not have been done without continuous reductions in costs.

Utilizing Performance Reports The "Toyota Way" describes **Toyota's** method to set Kaizen cost reduction targets for each cost element, including purchased parts per car, direct materials per car, labor hours per car, and office utilities. *Performance reports* developed at the end of each month compare targeted and actual cost reductions. If actual cost reductions are more than the targeted cost reductions, the results are favorable. If the actual cost reductions are less than the targeted cost reductions, the results are unfavorable.

Because cost reduction targets are set before it is known how they will be achieved, continuous improvement costing can be stressful to employees. A critical element in motivating employee cooperation in continuous improvement costing, is to avoid using performance reports to place blame for failure. The proper response to a performance report that falls short of its target is to analyze the situation, learn from the performance, ask for assistance, and make changes to improve future results.

Review 20-3 LO20-3 — Analyzing the Impact of Continuous Improvement Initiatives

Portillo's sells "unrivaled Chicago street food" in its restaurants. In its Skokie store, the actual costs per customer for the last two years were as follows:

	Year 1	Year 2
Direct materials		
Ingredients	$ 4.50	$ 4.40
Packaging	0.66	0.57
Direct labor	16.00	15.00
Indirect manufacturing costs		
Fixed	3.00 (100,000 customers)	2.85 (120,000 customers)

The company has used target costing in the past but has not been able to meet the very competitive pricing. Beginning in Year 2, the company implemented a continuous improvement program that requires cost reduction targets.

Required
If continuous improvement (Kaizen) costing sets a target of a 5% reduction of the Year 1 variable costs per customer, how successful was Portillo's Skokie store in meeting its per customer cost reduction targets in Year 2? Assume that the company sets a target for fixed costs to remain constant in total. Support your answer with appropriate computations.

Solution on p. 20-25.

BENCHMARKING TO IMPROVE PERFORMANCE

LO20-4 Explain how benchmarking is used to improve performance.

When **Potbelly's** studies its food equipment manufacturers to evaluate and compare their strengths and weakness, it is engaging in *benchmarking*, a practice that has been around for centuries. Not only is it used in business, but benchmarking is also used in education (grading) and athletics. In recent years, however, as globalization and increased competitiveness have forced businesses to more aggressively compete on the bases of cost, quality, and service, benchmarking has become more formalized and transparent. No longer regarded as spying, **benchmarking** is now a systematic approach to identifying the best practices to help an organization take action to improve performance.

Applications of Benchmarking

The formalization of benchmarking is largely attributed to a book written decades ago by Robert Camp of Xerox. Since then, many managers have come to believe that benchmarking is a requirement for success. Although benchmarking can focus on anything of interest, it typically deals with target costs for a product, service, or operation, customer satisfaction, quality, inventory levels, inventory turnover, cycle time, and productivity. *Internal* benchmarking compares performance within a company. For example, sustainability performance metrics in one division could be compared to sustainability performance metrics in another division of the company. *External* benchmarking focuses on the study of competitors. However, benchmarking efforts can even be expanded to the study of companies in different fields. For example, an electronics company like Samsung may benchmark its order fulfillment processes against Amazon, or a grocery company like the Kroger Company may benchmark its inventory management processes against an apparel company like Gap.

In considering how to go about benchmarking, an organization must be careful because it must consider nonfinancial limitations. No single numerical measurement can completely describe the performance of a complex device, such as a microprocessor or a cellular phone, but benchmarks can be useful tools for comparing different products, components, and systems. The only accurate way to measure the performance of a given product is to test it against other products while performing the exact same activity.

Benchmarking can be applied to activity on a company's website. Understanding how a company is competing within an industry is an indication of company performance. For example, benchmarking reports in Google Analytics or Semrush allow a company to track and measure its website metrics compared to industry averages. Examples of metrics include the number of new users to a site and the average session duration. Are advertising campaigns drawing in new customers at a faster rate than its competitors? What is the company's average session duration compared to the industry? The results could provide information on customer preferences, customer satisfaction, effectiveness of advertising expenditures, and more. As in all cases of benchmarking, it is important to understand the context of the data in order to accurately assess the results.

A benchmark is, at most, only one type of information that an organization can use during the purchasing or manufacturing process. To get a true picture of the performance of a component or system being considered, the organization should consult industry sources, publicly available research reports, and even government publications of related information.

Process of Benchmarking

Benchmarking provides measurements that are useful in setting goals. It can lead to dramatic innovations, and it can help overcome resistance to change. When presented with a major cost reduction target, employees often believe they are being asked to do the impossible. Benchmarking can be a psychological tool that helps overcome resistance to change by showing how others have already met the target.

Although each organization has its own approach to benchmarking, the following six steps are typical.

1. Decide what to benchmark.
2. Plan the benchmark project.
3. Understand your own performance.
4. Study others.
5. Learn from the data.
6. Take action.

Let's assume that Potbelly wanted to compare its customer ordering process against its competitors through benchmarking. How could this process improve the performance and profitability of Potbelly?

By comparing performance measures of Potbelly shops to that of its competitors, Potbelly can determine its relative strengths and weaknesses. For example, Potbelly

could compare performance measures of speed and accuracy of order taking for person-to-person ordering and kiosk ordering to its competitors. Improvements made to Potbelly shops based on the benchmarking process could improve internal performance (increase speed and accuracy of ordering taking). The improvements could result in higher customer satisfaction, translating into higher repeat sales, and thus increased profitability.

Review 20-4 LO20-4 — Distinguishing Between Benchmarking and Competitor Research

iSixSigma provides information on the Lean Six Sigma process (method to improve business processes) and training and tools for Six Sigma certifications. The associated website specifically provides resources on the purpose and use of benchmarking.

Required

a. Visit: https://www.isixsigma.com/methodology/benchmarking/understanding-purpose-and-use-benchmarking/. Identify five differences between benchmarking and competitor research.
b. Assume that Portillo's implemented a menu change last year, adding plant-based burger products made from high-quality ingredients. The company is considering both competitor research and strategic benchmarking in order to improve its new product. How would the process differ between the two options?

Solution on p. 20-26.

KEY RATIOS AND EQUATIONS

$$\text{Markup on cost base} = \frac{\text{Costs not included in the base} + \text{Desired profit}}{\text{Costs included in the base}}$$

MULTIPLE CHOICE

Multiple Choice Answers
1. a   2. a   3. b   4. c
5. b   6. c   7. d

LO20-1 1. Innovators, Inc. launched is first product ten years ago. The initial price was relatively high, which yielded a high profit margin. The market for the product is now becoming very competitive, and demand for the product is slowing. What pricing strategy should the company follow for the product based on the current market conditions?

a. Because of the increased competition, the product's price should be decreased.
b. Pricing for the product should be at its highest level to recoup its innovation R&D.
c. The company should sell the product below cost so that it can force competitors out of the market.
d. Prices should be held steady with only inflation adjustments.

CMA adapted

LO20-1 2. In a cost-based pricing model, the markup percentage is determined by an equation that

a. Has the cost base in the denominator and any remaining costs plus the desired profit in the numerator
b. Has variable costs plus fixed costs in the denominator and total profit in the numerator
c. Always has only variable costs in the numerator
d. Always has desired profit as part of the denominator

LO20-1 3. Brown Company makes profits with varying pricing structures, but it wants to determine the minimum markup percentage for all products based on manufacturing costs that will ensure that it does not fall below the break-even point. It has estimated the following costs for the coming year for its planned production of all products.

Variable manufacturing costs	$600,000
Fixed manufacturing costs	200,000
Selling expenses	100,000
Administrative expenses	150,000

The markup percentage required for Brown Company to break even is

a. 320%
b. 31.25%
c. 75%
d. Cannot be determined unless desired profit is known

4. Electronics Inc. is considering producing a new MP3 player that will offer several new features, including wireless earphones and wireless download of music and videos from any computer to the device. After much market research, it has determined that the appropriate target price for the new product is $90. To achieve its normal minimum profit margin of 20%, Electronics must be able to produce the product at a maximum total cost of

    a. $108
    b. $70
    c. $72
    d. $18

    LO20-2

5. Orange Inc. produces electronic devices such as computers and cell phones. It has recently introduced a digital reader, called the e-pad, but realizes that to compete effectively in the future, it must be able to lower the cost of production and the selling price. The current cost per unit for producing the e-pad is $138, and Orange is estimating inflation on e-pad components and supplies purchased externally to be 1.5% in the coming year. In the most recent period, these items had a cost of $74. Despite these cost increases, Orange has adopted a Kaizen cost improvement model that targets a 5% cost decrease. Orange's Kaizen cost target (rounded to two decimal places) for the e-pad is

    a. $131.11
    b. $132.15
    c. $133.07
    d. $130.05

    LO20-3

6. Typical characteristics of benchmarking include each of the following except

    a. Planning the benchmarking project
    b. Understanding your own performance
    c. Focusing on performance measures
    d. Studying others

    LO20-4

7. Retail Partners Inc., which operates eight discount store chains, is seeking to reduce the costs of its purchasing activities through reengineering and a heavier use of electronic data interchange (EDI). Which of the following benchmarking techniques would be appropriate in this situation?

    I. A comparison of the purchasing costs and practices of each of Retail Partners' store chains to identify their internal "best in class."
    II. A comparison of the practices of Retail Partners to those of Discount City, another retailer, whose practices are often considered "best in class."
    III. A comparison of the practices of Retail Partners to those of Capital Airways, an international airline, whose practices are often considered "best in class."
    IV. An in-depth review of a retail trade association publication on successful electronic data interchange applications.

    a. II and IV only
    b. I and II only
    c. I and IV only
    d. I, II, III, and IV

    LO20-4

    CMA

    CMA adapted

DATA ANALYTICS

DA20-1. Analyzing Pricing Trends

Access the data file for **UPS (United Parcel Service Inc.)** on the textbook's website with select information for the three quarters ended 2021 and 2022.

LO20-1

REQUIRED

a. Prepare line charts for each of the following.
   1. Average revenue per piece for the first three quarters of 2021
   2. Average revenue per piece for the first three quarters of 2022
   3. Average daily package volume for the first three quarters of 2021
   4. Average daily package volume for the first three quarters of 2022
b. Describe the trends in average revenue per piece over time and average daily package volume over time.
c. Sales for the nine months ended September 30, 2022, were up 4.2% from the same period in the prior year. What does this indicate about the company's pricing strategy in 2022?

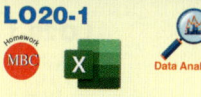

DATA VISUALIZATION

Data Visualization Activities are available in myBusinessCourse. These assignments use Tableau Dashboards to expose students to visual depictions of data and introduce students to data analytics through data visualizations. These exercises are easily assignable and auto graded by MBC.

QUESTIONS

Q20-1. Why are economic models seldom used for day-to-day pricing decisions?

Q20-2. Identify three reasons that cost-based approaches to pricing have traditionally been important.

Q20-3. Identify four drawbacks to cost-based pricing.

Q20-4. How does target costing differ from cost-based pricing?

Q20-5. Why is cost-based pricing more a technique, and target costing is more a philosophy? Which approach takes a more proactive approach to cost management?

Q20-6. How do the cost-based approaches differ in single-product companies as compared to multi-product companies?

Q20-7. What is the relationship between target costing and continuous improvement (Kaizen) costing?

Q20-8. How are performance reports used to measure results in continuous improvement (Kaizen) costing?

Q20-9. What advantage is derived from benchmarking against firms other than competitors?

Assignments with the MBC logo in the margin are available in myBusinessCourse.
See the Preface of the book for details.

MINI EXERCISES

LO20-1
Sue Bee Honey

M20-10. Product Pricing: Single Product

Sue Bee Honey is one of the largest processors of its product for the retail market. Assume that one of its plants has annual fixed costs totaling $16,317,500, of which $5,250,500 is for administrative and selling efforts. Sales are anticipated to be 950,000 cases a year. Variable costs for processing are $35 per case, and variable selling expenses are 10% of selling price. There are no variable administrative expenses.

REQUIRED

If the company desires a pretax profit of $9,000,000, what is the selling price per case?

LO20-1
Pinkberry

M20-11. Product Pricing: Single Product

Assume that you plan to open a Pinkberry frozen yogurt franchise at a local shopping mall. Fixed operating costs for the year are projected to be $144,500. Variable costs per serving include the cost of the ice cream and cone, $1.50, and a franchise fee payable to Pinkberry, $0.20. A market analysis prepared by Pinkberry indicates that annual sales should total 130,000 servings.

REQUIRED

Determine the price you should charge for each serving to achieve a $125,000 pretax profit for the year.

LO20-1

M20-12. Product Pricing

A few years ago, Hotel Klingerhoffer, a large hotel chain, announced that because occupancy rates had declined during the previous quarter, it was raising room rates to cover the cost of its increase in vacant rooms. Although not referring to accounting or economics, several business journalists during the week following the announcement questioned the basis for the rate increases. One stated that "Hotel Klingerhoffer increases rates of vacant rooms."

REQUIRED

a. Did the journalist mean that vacant rooms would be more expensive? Explain.
b. Do you think Hotel Klingerhoffer's action to raise room rates was based on economics, accounting, or both?

LO20-2

M20-13. Determining Target Cost

Latest Toys Inc. developed an idea for a new toy with a projected life cycle of two years. This means that the toy would not be sold beyond a two-year period. Revenues for the two-year period are estimated to be $500,000, based upon the estimated sales quantities and unit selling price. The required profits for the two-year period are 20% of sales.

REQUIRED

a. What is the target cost for the two-year period?
b. In order to achieve the target cost, what activities will be performed by the multi-department target cost team?

M20-14. Determining Target Cost

Stellantis has been conducting early-stage research on hydrogen-powered automobiles and is nearing the point where product development will begin. In order to determine the feasibility of the product, assume Chrysler has conducted market research. Research indicates the price target for the product must be no more than $35,000 if it is to appeal to a large enough market segment to sell 150,000 automobiles in the first year of production. The CFO has indicated that the new product must meet a 15% minimum profit margin requirement.

REQUIRED

a. Calculate the target cost per unit to produce the hydrogen-powered automobile.
b. If the company cannot achieve the 15% profit margin requirement, but can come close, should Stellantis continue to produce the car given the environmental benefits?
c. One of the researchers realizes that the margin will be less than the 15% minimum profit margin requirement. However, the researcher believes that the automobile would be beneficial to society. Given the inherent error implicit in cost measurement, should the researcher intentionally underestimate the cost of the automobile in order to ensure that the automobile is produced?

M20-15. Determining Target Cost

Access the article "Creating a Culture of Continuous Improvement" in the Harvard Business Review (May 24, 2019) which describe the continuous improvement process in the health care industry found at https://hbr.org/2019/05/creating-a-culture-of-continuous-improvement. Use the information in the article to answer the following question: Identify and briefly explain the four practices that can help sustain a culture of continuous improvement.

M20-16. Benchmarking

Your company is developing a new product for the 3D printing industry. You have talked to several material vendors about being able to supply quality components for the new product. The product designers are satisfied with the company's ability to make the product in the current facilities. Numerous potential customers also have been surveyed, and most have indicated a willingness to buy the product if the price is competitive.

REQUIRED
What are some means of benchmarking the development and production of your new product?

EXERCISES

E20-17. Product Pricing: Single Product

Presented is the current year contribution income statement of Grafton Products.

GRAFTON PRODUCTS
Contribution Income Statement
For Year Ended December 31

Sales (15,000 units)		$2,625,000
Less variable costs		
Cost of goods sold	$1,275,000	
Selling and administrative	150,000	(1,425,000)
Contribution margin		1,200,000
Less fixed costs		
Manufacturing overhead	685,000	
Selling and administrative	330,000	(1,015,000)
Net income		$ 185,000

Next year, Grafton expects an increase in variable manufacturing costs of $10 per unit and in fixed manufacturing costs of $30,000.

REQUIRED

a. If sales for next year remain at 15,000 units, what price should Grafton charge to obtain the same profit as last year?
b. Management believes that sales can be increased to 18,000 units if the selling price is lowered to $165. Is this action desirable? (Use the cost data from part *a*.)
c. After considering the expected increases in costs, what sales volume is needed to earn a pretax profit of $200,000 with a unit selling price of $165?

LO20-1 **E20-18. Cost-Based Pricing and Markups with Variable Costs**

Computer Consultants provides computerized inventory consulting. The office and computer expenses are $830,000 annually and are not assigned to specific jobs. The consulting hours available for the year total 18,000, and the average consulting hour has $40 of variable costs.

REQUIRED
a. If the company desires a profit of $250,000, what should it charge per hour?
b. What is the markup on variable costs if the desired profit is $322,000?
c. If the desired profit is $100,000, what is the markup on variable costs to cover (1) unassigned costs and (2) desired profit?

LO20-1 **E20-19. Computing Markups**

The predicted annual costs for Mighty Motors are as follows.

Manufacturing Costs		Selling and Administrative Costs	
Variable.	$250,000	Variable.	$250,000
Fixed.	350,000	Fixed.	550,000

Average total assets for the year are predicted to be $7,500,000.

REQUIRED
a. If management desires a 10% rate of return on total assets, what are the markup percentages based on total variable costs and based on total manufacturing costs?
b. If the company desires an 8% rate of return on total assets, what is the markup percentage on total manufacturing costs for (1) unassigned costs and (2) desired profit?

LO20-1 **E20-20. Product Pricing: Two Products**

Assume **Spindrift Beverage Co.** manufactures two products, flavored water and carbonated water, both on the same assembly lines and packaged 30 cans per pack. The predicted sales are 150,000 packs of flavored water and 500,000 packs of carbonated water. The predicted costs for the year are as follows.

	Variable Costs	Fixed Costs
Materials.	$4,000,000	$1,560,000
Other.	2,000,000	2,052,500

Flavored water uses 25% of the materials costs and 10% of the other costs. Carbonated water uses 75% of the materials costs and 90% of the other costs. The management of Spindrift desires an annual profit of $450,000.

REQUIRED
a. What price should Spindrift charge for each pack if management believes the carbonated water sells for twice the price of flavored water?
b. What is the total profit per product using the selling prices determined in part *a*?

LO20-1 **E20-21. Product Pricing: Two Products**

Refer to the previous exercise, E20-20. Based on your calculations of the selling price and profit for flavored water and carbonated water, how should **Spindrift** evaluate the status of these two products? Should either flavored water or carbonated water be discontinued? What additional information does the management of Spindrift need in order to make an appropriate judgment on the future status of these two products?

LO20-2 **E20-22. Target Costing**

Assume **Champion Power Equipment** wants to develop a new log-splitting machine for rural homeowners. Market research has determined that the company could sell 7,500 log-splitting machines per year at a retail price of $1,200 each. An independent digital catalog company would handle sales for an annual fee of $12,000 plus $75 per unit sold. The cost of the raw materials required to produce the log-splitting machines amounts to $200 per unit.

REQUIRED
If company management desires a return equal to 30% of the final selling price, what is the target conversion and administrative cost per unit? *Hint*: The target unit cost will only or should only include conversion costs and remaining or additional sales and administrative costs.

E20-23. Continuous Improvement (Kaizen) Costing
LO20-2, 3

Safety Manufacturing Inc. summarized its manufacturing costs for the prior year based on production of 10,000 units.

	Prior Year
Direct material costs.	$250,000
Direct labor costs	85,000
Indirect manufacturing costs.	235,000

REQUIRED

a. The company is interested in adopting a continuous improvement (Kaizen) costing approach. At what stage in a product's life cycle is continuous improvement costing adopted? How does your answer differ under target costing?

b. If the company sets a 4% per unit cost reduction target for all costs, what is the target cost per unit for direct materials, direct labor, and indirect manufacturing costs?

c. In what ways can the company meet its target cost goals? What risks does the company face if the target reduction goals are too aggressive?

E20-24. Target Costing
LO20-4

The virtual help center for digital scanning equipment produced by High-Tech Company processes 1.2 million customer inquiries per year. Roughly 50% of the time, the chatbot can successfully resolve the customer question without the help of a live agent. Live agents are paid $22 per hour and stay on a call for six minutes on average. After High-Tech Company engaged in process benchmarking, the need for live agent intervention dropped by 15%.

REQUIRED

a. What was the annual salary cost of the live agents prior to benchmarking?

b. What is the annual salary cost of the live agents after benchmarking? What is the cost savings in one year?

c. To determine the success (or failure) of the benchmarking process, what other financial and nonfinancial items would you consider?

PROBLEMS

P20-25. Product Pricing: Two Products
LO20-1

Macquarium Inc. provides computer-related services to its clients. Its two primary services are web page design (WPD) and Internet consulting services (ICS). Assume that Macquarium's management expects to earn a 35% annual return on the assets invested. Macquarium has invested $6 million since its opening. The annual costs for the coming year are expected to be as follows.

	Variable Costs	Fixed Costs
Consulting support .	$250,000	$1,750,000
Sales and administration	150,000	850,000

The two services expend about equal costs per hour, and the predicted hours for the coming year are 15,000 for WPD and 25,000 for ICS.

REQUIRED

a. If markup is based on variable costs, how much revenue must each service generate to provide the profit expected by corporate headquarters? What is the anticipated revenue per hour for each service? *Hint:* Start by determining the markup rate.

b. If the markup is based on total costs, how much revenue must each service generate to provide the expected profit?

c. Explain why answers in requirements (a) and (b) are either the same or different.

d. Comment on the advantages and disadvantages of using a cost-based pricing model.

P20-26. Target Costing
LO20-2

Ericsson is a large global company providing cloud-based engineering software for large companies. Assume that it is developing a new software system for smaller, private companies. To attract small companies, Ericsson must keep the price low without giving up too many of the features of larger systems. Assume that a marketing research study conducted on the company's behalf found that the software set-up price range must be $50,000 to $75,000. Management has determined a target price to be $65,000. The company's minimum profit percentage of sales is normally 15%, but the company is willing to reduce it to 12% to get the new product on the market. The fixed costs for the first year are anticipated to be $8,000,000. If sales reach 400 installations, the company needs to know how much it can spend on variable costs, which are primarily related to installation.

REQUIRED
a. What is the amount of total cost allowed if the 12% profit target is allowed and the 400 installations sales target is met? Show the amount for fixed and for variable costs.
b. What is the amount of total costs allowed if the 15% normal profit target is desired at the 400 installations sales target? Show the amount for fixed and for variable costs.
c. Discuss the advantages of using a target costing model versus using cost-based pricing.

LO20-3 **P20-27. Continuous Improvement (Kaizen) Costing**
Samira Company does contract manufacturing of commercial video cameras. At its Pacific plant, cost control has become a concern of management. The actual costs per unit for the previous two years were as follows.

	Year 1		Year 2	
Direct materials				
Plastic case	$ 5.10		$ 4.75	
Lens set	12.00		10.90	
Electrical component set	8.30		7.00	
Film track	10.50		10.05	
Direct labor	48.00	(1.6 hours)	45.00	(1.5 hours)
Indirect manufacturing costs				
Variable	5.60		5.00	
Fixed	16.00	(100,000 unit base)	12.75	(120,000 unit base)

The company manufactures all of the camera components except the lens sets, which it purchases from several vendors. The company has used target costing in the past but has not been able to meet the very competitive global pricing. Beginning in Year 2, the company implemented a continuous improvement program that requires cost reduction targets.

REQUIRED
a. If continuous improvement (Kaizen) costing sets a target of a 10% reduction of the first year cost base, how successful was the company in meeting the per unit cost reduction targets in the second year? Support your answer with appropriate computations.
b. Evaluate and discuss Samira's use of Kaizen costing.

LO20-3 **P20-28. Continuous Improvement (Kaizen) Costing**
General Electric (NYSE :: GE)
Assume that GE Capital, a division of **General Electric**, has been displeased with the costs of servicing its consumer loans. Assume that it has decided to implement a Kaizen-based cost improvement program. For the current year, GE Capital incurred the following costs ($ millions).

Loan processing	$12,500
Customer relations	2,800
Printing, mailing, and postage	550

For the next two years, GE Capital expects an increase in consumer loans of 8% annually with related increases in costs.

REQUIRED
a. If the company has a continuous improvement goal of 4% each year, develop a budget for the next two years for the consumer loan department.
b. Identify some possible ways that GE Capital can achieve the Kaizen costing goal.
c. Discuss the potential benefits and limitations of GE's Kaizen costing model.

LO20-1 **P20-29. Price Setting: Multiple Products**
Tech Com's predicted variable and fixed costs for next year are as follows.

	Variable Costs	Fixed Costs
Manufacturing	$405,000	$ 424,200
Selling and administrative	102,000	594,000
Total	$507,000	$1,018,200

Tech Com is a small company producing a wide variety of computer devices. Per-unit manufacturing cost information about one of these products, a webcam, is as follows.

Direct materials.	$8
Direct labor.	4
Manufacturing overhead	
Variable.	3
Fixed.	6
Total manufacturing costs.	$21

Variable selling and administrative costs for the webcam are $4 per unit. Management has set a target profit for next year of $300,000.

REQUIRED
a. Determine the markup percentage on variable costs required to earn the desired profit.
b. Use the variable cost markup to determine a suggested selling price for the webcam.
c. For the webcam, break the markup on variable costs into separate parts for fixed costs and profit. Explain the significance of each part.
d. Determine the markup percentage on manufacturing costs required to earn the desired profit.
e. Use the manufacturing costs markup to determine a suggested selling price for the webcam.
f. Evaluate the variable and the manufacturing cost approaches to determine the markup percentage.

P20-30. Price Setting: Multiple Products LO20-1

Pipestem Golf produces a wide variety of golfing equipment. In the past, product managers set prices using their professional judgment. Samuel Snead, the new controller, believes this practice has led to the significant underpricing of some products (with lost profits) and the significant overpricing of other products (with lost sales volume). You have been asked to assist Snead in developing a corporate approach to pricing. The output of your work should be a cost-based formula that can be used to develop initial selling prices for each product. Although product managers are allowed to adjust these prices to meet competition and to take advantage of market opportunities, they must explain such deviations in writing. The following cost information from the current year accounting records is available.

	Manufacturing Costs	Selling and Administrative Costs
Variable.	$335,000	$ 55,000
Fixed.	245,000	365,000

During the year, Pipestem Golf reported earnings of $200,000. However, the controller believes that proper pricing should produce earnings of at least $250,000 on the same sales mix and unit volume. Accordingly, you are to use the preceding cost information and a target profit of $250,000 in developing a cost-based pricing formula. Selling and administrative expenses are not currently associated with individual products. However, you have obtained the following unit production cost information for the TW Irons.

Variable manufacturing costs	$145
Fixed manufacturing costs	105
Total.	$250

REQUIRED
a. Determine the standard markup percentage for each of the following cost bases. Round answers to two decimal places.
   1. Full costs, including fixed and variable manufacturing costs, and fixed and variable selling and administrative costs.
   2. Manufacturing costs plus variable selling and administrative costs.
   3. Manufacturing costs.
   4. Variable costs.
   5. Variable manufacturing costs.
b. Explain why the markup percentages become progressively larger from requirement (a), parts (1) through (5).
c. Determine the initial price of a set of TW Irons using the manufacturing cost markup and the variable manufacturing cost markup.
d. Do you believe the controller's approach to product pricing is reasonable? Why or why not?

CASES AND PROJECTS

LO20-2 **C20-31. Target Costing**

The president of Houston Electronics was pleased with the company's newest product, the next generation smart watch. Based on development costs and predictions of sales volume, manufacturing costs, and distribution costs, the cost-based price of the new smart watch was determined to be $425. Following a market-skimming strategy, management set the initial selling price at $525. The marketing plan was to reduce the selling price by $50 during each of the first two years of the product's life to obtain the highest contribution possible from each market segment.

The initial sales of the smart watches were strong, and Houston Electronics found itself adding second and third production shifts. Although these shifts were expensive, at a selling price of $525, the product had ample contribution margin to remain highly profitable. The president was talking with the company's major investors about the desirability of obtaining financing for a major plant expansion when the bad news arrived. A foreign company had announced that it would shortly introduce a similar product that would incorporate new design features and sell for only $350. The president was shocked. "Why," she remarked, "it costs us $375 to put a complete unit in the hands of customers."

REQUIRED

How could the foreign competitor profitably sell a similar product for less than the manufacturing costs to Houston Electronics? What advice do you have for the president concerning the smart watches? What advice would you have to help the company avoid similar problems in the future?

LO20-1, 2 **C20-32. Comparing Markup Pricing and Target Costing**

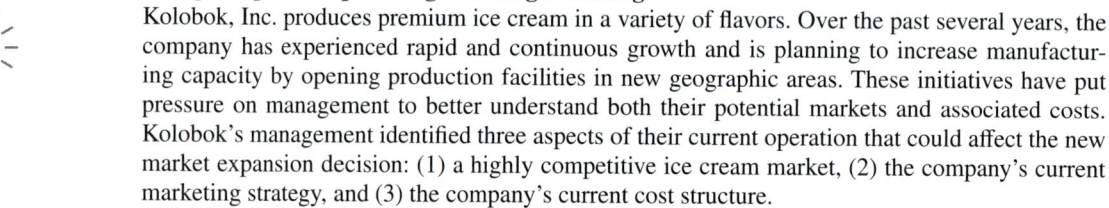

Kolobok, Inc. produces premium ice cream in a variety of flavors. Over the past several years, the company has experienced rapid and continuous growth and is planning to increase manufacturing capacity by opening production facilities in new geographic areas. These initiatives have put pressure on management to better understand both their potential markets and associated costs. Kolobok's management identified three aspects of their current operation that could affect the new market expansion decision: (1) a highly competitive ice cream market, (2) the company's current marketing strategy, and (3) the company's current cost structure.

Since the company began operations, Kolobok has used the markup approach for establishing prices for six-gallon containers of ice cream. The product prices include the cost of materials and labor, a markup for profit and overhead cost (a standard $20), and a market adjustment. The market adjustment is used to appropriately position a variety of products in the market. The goal is to price the products in the middle of comparable ice creams offered by competitors while maintaining high quality and high differentiation. Sales for the year based on Kolobok's markup pricing are presented below by product.

Product	Material and Labor	Markup	Market Adjustment	Unit Price	Boxes Sold	Total Materials & Labor	Total Sales
Vanilla	$29.00	$20.00	$1.00	$50.00	10,200	$ 295,800	$ 510,000
Chocolate	28.00	20.00	7.00	55.00	12,500	350,000	687,500
Caramel	26.00	20.00	2.00	48.00	12,900	335,400	619,200
Raspberry	27.00	20.00	2.00	49.00	13,600	367,200	666,400
Total					49,200	$1,348,400	$2,483,100

For the year, Kolobok's before-tax return on sales was 7%. The company's overhead expenses were $500,000, selling expenses $250,000, administrative expenses $180,000, and interest expenses were $30,000. Kolobok's marginal tax rate is 30%.

Kolobok is considering replacing markup pricing with target costing and has prepared the table below to better compare the methods. Kolobok tries to appeal to the top 30% of the retail sales customers, including restaurants and cafes. In positioning Kolobok's products, three dimensions are considered: price, quality, and product differentiation. Accordingly, there are three main competitors in the market as follows.

Competitor A – Low cost, low quality, high standardization
Competitor B – Average cost, moderate quality, average differentiation
Competitor C – High cost, high quality, high differentiation

Product	Competitor A Pricing	Competitor B Pricing	Competitor C Pricing	Kolobok Target Prices
Vanilla..................	$49	$55	$55	$53
Chocolate..............	50	53	56	53
Caramel................			51	50
Raspberry..............		51	52	50

Kolobok has also been reviewing its purchasing, manufacturing, and distribution processes. Assuming that sales volumes will not be affected by the new target prices, the company believes that improvements will yield a $125,000 decrease in labor expense and a 25% reduction in overhead expense.

REQUIRED

1. Describe target costing.
2. Analyze and compare the two alternative pricing methods: markup pricing and target costing.
3. Assuming that the sales volumes will not be affected by the new product pricing based on target costing and that the process improvements will be implemented, calculate Kolobok's before-tax return on sales using the proposed target prices.
4. Recommend which pricing method (markup or target) Kolobok should use in the future and explain why.

CMA adapted

SOLUTIONS TO REVIEW PROBLEMS

Review 20-1—Solution

a.

Desired annual profit ($1,000,000 × 0.10)	$100,000
Actual profit...	(28,000)
Amount actual profit fell short of achieving the desired return	$ 72,000

b.

Predicted costs			
Variable..		$135,000	
Fixed...		370,000	$505,000
Desired profit			50,000
Required revenue..			$555,000
Unit sales			÷ 82,000
Required unit selling price..			$ 6.77

c.

1. Sales/Variable manufacturing costs .... $555,000 ÷ $90,000 = 617%

2.
Variable selling and administrative.................	$ 45,000	
Fixed costs.......................................	370,000	
Desired profit	50,000	$465,000
Variable manufacturing costs		÷90,000
Markup as a percent of variable manufacturing costs ...		517%

d. Detail of markup on variable manufacturing costs.

1.	Unassigned costs		
	Variable selling and administrative	$ 45,000	
	Fixed costs	370,000	$415,000
	Variable manufacturing costs		÷90,000
	Markup on variable manufacturing costs to cover unassigned costs		461%
2.	Desired profit		$ 50,000
	Variable manufacturing costs		÷90,000
	Additional markup on variable manufacturing costs to achieve desired profit		56%

Note: 461% + 56% = 517%

Review 20-2—Solution

a. Management has decided that a plant-based burger should be added. However, to develop and sell the new item effectively, a cross-functional team must be employed, combining marketing, menu development, chefs, management accounting, and external vendors. The task is to determine how best to develop a delicious plant-based burger that meets customer price and quality requirements while providing the desired profit.

b. If the team's initial cost estimates are too high, they should explore every possibility, including redeveloping the recipe, using ingredients from existing products, partnering with plant-based manufacturers, or finding lower-cost vendors. If it is finally determined that the target cannot be reached, then management has to decide if it is willing to go forward with the product with a lower than desired initial profit margin. In some cases, managers will proceed with the idea that additional cost savings will be found (using Kaizen costing methods) after the product is in production. Other times, managers may decide not to pursue the new product. For **Portillo's**, management might decide to move forward with a lower margin if it is believed that the new menu item will attract more customers who will also buy more profitable products at the same time.

Review 20-3—Solution

Item	Year 1	× Target %	Year 2 Target	Year 2 Actual	Variance
Direct materials (per unit)					
Ingredients	$ 4.50	0.95	$ 4.275	$ 4.40	$0.125 U
Packaging	0.66	0.95	0.627	0.57	0.057 F
Direct labor (per unit)	16.00	0.95	15.200	15.00	0.200 F
Indirect mfg (in total)					
Fixed costs	$300,000	1.00	$300,000	$342,000	$42,000 U

The company made progress during Year 2 with positive results for packaging direct materials and for direct labor. The unfavorable variance for ingredients requires more consideration since they are vendor purchased. Possibly new vendors can be found, or current vendor contracts can be renegotiated. Was the increase unavoidable due to external pressures and inflation? Are there other ways, such as adjusting recipes, to address the increasing costs?

The fixed manufacturing costs also need attention. The total fixed costs increased from $300,000 (100,000 × $3) to $342,000 (120,000 × $2.85), exceeding the target of $300,000. If the costs are fixed, why did they increase? Did increased production or other factors cause the increase in fixed costs over the prior year? If the increase was volume driven, maybe some of the costs are not fixed and should be reassigned as variable costs.

Review 20-4—Solution

a. According to iSixSigma.com, neither approach is superior to the other. Which approach to use will depend on an organization's available time and resources. Differences between the two methods identified by iSixSigma.com include the following.

Differences Between Benchmarking and Competitor Research	
Benchmarking	**Competitor Research**
Focuses on best practices	Focuses on performance measures
Strives for continuous improvement	Bandage or quick fix
Partnering to share information	Considered corporate spying by some
Needed to maintain a competitive edge	Simply a "nice to have"
Adapting based on customer needs after examination of the best	Attempting to mirror another company/process

Source: https://www.isixsigma.com/methodology/benchmarking/understanding-purpose-and-use-benchmarking/

b. If the company chooses to perform competitor research, it would obtain sample products from its competitors for comparison purposes. The company would obtain nutritional information and other publicly available product information. It could host focus groups asking customers questions who have frequented its restaurant and those of its competitors.

On the other hand, with strategic benchmarking, the goal is to identify world-class performance by working with a partner. For example, Portillo's could partner with a company that is not a direct competitor, but offers plant-based burgers, such as a high-end restaurant. The benchmarking process includes establishing objectives, documenting the current process, determining metrics and what to benchmark, and collecting data at the partner's site through a coordinated visit.

Chapter 21

Operational Budgeting and Profit Planning

LEARNING OBJECTIVES

LO21-1 Describe the purpose of budgeting and its basic approaches. (p. 21-3)

LO21-2 Explain the relationships among elements of a master budget and develop a basic master budget. (p. 21-8)

LO21-3 Develop elements of a basic master budget for a manufacturer. (p. 21-17)

LO21-4 Analyze the relationship between budget development and employee behavior. (p. 21-22)

Road Map

LO	Learning Objective | Topics	Page	eLecture	Review	Assignments
LO21-1	**Describe the purpose of budgeting and its basic approaches.** Management by Exception :: Risk Management :: Output/Input :: Activity Based :: Incremental :: Zero-Based	21-3	e21–1	R21-1	M21-17, M21-18, E21-24, E21-25, E21-26, E21-27, **DA21-3**
LO21-2	**Explain the relationships among elements of a master budget and develop a basic master budget.** Master Budget :: Sales Budget :: Purchases Budget :: Selling Expense Budget :: General and Administrative Expenses Budget :: Cash Budget :: Budgeted Financial Statements :: Finalizing the Budget	21-8	e21–2	R21-2	M21-19, M21-20, E21-28, E21-29, E21-30, E21-31, E21-32, E21-33, E21-34, E21-35, P21-39, P21-40, P21-41, P21-42, P21-43, P21-44, P21-45, P21-46, P21-47, **DA21-1**, **DA21-2**
LO21-3	**Develop elements of a basic master budget for a manufacturer.** Sales Budget :: Production Budget :: Purchases Budget :: Manufacturing Cost Budget :: Cash Budget :: Financial Statement Budget	21-17	e21–3	R21-3	M21-21, M21-22, E21-36, E21-38, P21-43, P21-44, P21-45, P21-46, P21-47, **DA21-3**
LO21-4	**Analyze the relationship between budget development and employee behavior.** Imposed Budget :: Participative Budget :: Budgetary Slack :: Life-Cycle Budgeting :: Rolling Budget :: Forecasts :: Ethical Behavior	21-22	e21–4	R21-4	M21-23, E21-37, P21-46, C21-48, C21-49, C21-50, C21-51, **DA21-1**, **DA21-2**

WAYFAIR
www.wayfair.com

Experienced executives understand that budgeting is the lifeblood of a business enterprise. A budget quantitatively reflects the strategy and priorities of an organization and is the mechanism by which it plans its operations for the upcoming quarter, year, or decade. It is the way an organization communicates those plans and coordinates employees' efforts. A budget can even alert management to risks such as staff shortages, cash deficits, and excess capacity. Given the importance of budgeting, it is interesting that, more likely than not, a budget will not be 100% accurate. Actual results rarely equal forecasted results. When the actual results are known, the budget is part of a feedback loop used to evaluate past operations. Companies, small and large, rely on budgets to manage operations.

Wayfair offers an online destination for the home. The company sells more than thirty-three million products from more than 23,000 suppliers. Wayfair has built its reputation by offering customers sophisticated browsing, a wide array of merchandise, easy product searching, and competitive pricing. Wayfair can offer a wide selection of products at various price points because it holds minimal inventory. Products are shipped from Wayfair's suppliers, with many products flowing through the Wayfair logistics (transportation) system. Wayfair contends that significant investment in its logistics system has allowed for faster delivery, reduced damages in transit, and decreased reliance on third parties.

Wayfair prepares a "master budget," which serves as a guide for the company's operations. The first step in preparing the master budget is to budget or forecast sales revenue and the remaining budgets build off of the sales budget. Thus, starting with an accurate sales forecast is essential to the budgeting process. Developing an accurate sales budget is challenging, especially when faced with unforeseen events. For example, with an increase in the demand for outdoor living products due to the pandemic, Wayfair experienced an unusually profitable year in 2020. How should Wayfair calculate a revenue budget going forward if it believes prior year results were primarily caused by a unique event?

Wayfair also develops an expense budget for everything from cost of goods sold to labor to selling expenses. How will budgeted expenses be affected by sales volume increases (decreases) and anticipated cost increases (decreases)? Wayfair will likely need budgets under best and worst case scenarios to help determine proper pricing and to plan for needed resources. Artificial intelligence tools can be used to produce multiple scenarios with ranges of outcomes by detecting patterns and trends from relevant data. Wayfair's management can then analyze the budget scenarios to determine the greatest risks that it faces. For example, if a profit is forecasted, but wages are being renegotiated, at what point would higher wages eliminate profit?

Wayfair is a growing, dynamic company. As it evolves, it will also have to budget and manage its cash flows and capital investments. Having a good idea/product is the first step. However, management must have enough cash to pay the bills, while still planning for large expenditures along the way. The budgeting techniques discussed in this chapter will aid in planning and managing Wayfair's operations in the face of constantly changing business conditions.

CHAPTER ORGANIZATION

Operational Budgeting and Profit Planning

The Budgeting Process	Master Budget for a Merchandiser	Master Budget for a Manufacturer	Aspects of Budgeting That Impact Behavior and Outcomes
• Reasons for Budgeting • Approaches to Budgeting	• Overview of Master Budget Assembly for a Merchandiser • Starting Point: Beginning of Period Balance Sheet • Sales Budget • Purchase Budget • Selling Expense Budget • General and Administrative Expense Budget • Cash Budget • Budgeted Financial Statements • Finalizing the Budget	• Overview of Master Budget Assembly for a Manufacturer • Sales Budget • Production Budget • Purchases Budget • Manufacturing Cost Budget • Cash Budget • Financial Statement Budget	• Employee Participation in the Budgeting Process • Selecting Budgeting Periods • Utilizing Forecasts in Budgets • Motivating Ethical Behavior in Budget Development

THE BUDGETING PROCESS

LO21-1 Describe the purpose of budgeting and its basic approaches.

A **budget** is a formal plan of action, or roadmap, expressed in monetary terms. A budget is influenced by a company's strategies and priorities for the upcoming periods. In this chapter, we illustrate a *master budget* for a merchandiser followed by a manufacturer. A master budget is an organization-wide set of budgets. Managers frequently regard budgeting as a time-consuming task that diverts attention from current problems. Indeed, the development of an effective budget is a difficult job that can often consume many people for months. It is also a necessary one. Organizations that do not plan are likely to wander aimlessly and ultimately succumb to the swirl of current events. The formal development of a budget helps to ensure both success and survival. This is especially true for start-up companies. Budgets are often the first official control system that managers install in new organizations. Budget models are also used to analyze and prepare for various business risks. Although it sometimes feels that the budgeting process is diverting employees from everyday work responsibilities, in fact, the budget is one of the critical tools used to manage the company and ensure that everyone is aligned.

Reasons for Budgeting

The budgeting process formalizes the planning process. It also promotes communication and coordination, provides a guide to action and a basis for evaluation, and aids in risk management.

Formalizes the Planning Process Formal budgeting procedures require people to think about the future. Without the discipline of formal planning procedures, busy operating managers would not find time to plan. Immediate needs would consume all available time. Formal budgeting procedures, with specified deadlines, force managers to plan for the future by making the completion of the budget a priority. Budgeting moves an organization from an informal "reactive" style to a formal "proactive" style of management. As a result, management and other employees spend less time solving unanticipated problems and more time on positive measures and preventative actions.

Budgets are typically prepared over various lengths of time. While a quarterly or annual budget may seem to be standard, most companies will extend budgeting out to even five or ten years. This allows management to plan for the short term and long term. While a long-range budget will be less accurate, it will be adjusted as new information is learned and strategies are fine-tuned.

Promotes Communication and Coordination When operating responsibilities are divided, it is difficult to synchronize activities. Production must know what marketing intends to sell. Purchasing and personnel must know the factory's material and labor requirements. The treasurer must plan to ensure the availability of cash to support receivables, inventories, and capital expenditures. Budgeting forces managers of these diverse functions to communicate their plans and coordinate their activities. It helps ensure that plans are feasible and synchronized. Can Wayfair's purchasing department obtain enough outdoor dining sets to support projected sales this year? What type of advertising campaign will Wayfair run? How will the campaign impact sales of the various products? The final version of the budget emerges after an extensive (often lengthy) process of communication and coordination.

Provides a Guide to Action and Basis of Evaluation Once the budget has been finalized, the various operating managers know what is expected of them, and they can set about doing it. If employees do not have a guide to action, their efforts could be wasted on unproductive or even counterproductive activities.

After employees accept the budget as a guide to action, they can be held responsible for their portion of the budget. When results do not agree with plans, managers attempt to determine the cause of the divergence. This information is then used to adjust operations or to modify plans. More generally, budgeting is an important part of **management by exception**, whereby management directs attention only to those activities not proceeding according to plan. Without the budget, management might spend an inordinate amount of time seeking explanation of past activities and not enough time planning future activities.

Aids in Risk Management The models used for budgeting are also used in managing risk. **Risk** is the danger that things will not go according to plan. Although some risk results from anticipated events having a positive impact, such as an increase in sales volume or selling prices, risk is more typically associated with events that have a negative impact, like a work stoppage at a key supplier, a supply-chain delay, a fire, or hackers shutting down a retail website for an extended period of time.

Risk management (also called enterprise risk management) is the process of identifying, evaluating, and planning possible responses to risks that could impede an organization from achieving its plans. It also involves monitoring the sources of risk. An organization's budget model can be used to evaluate the financial impact of a risk and to determine, from a financial perspective, the best response to a risk. The performance evaluation procedures considered in Chapter 22, if completed on a timely basis, assist in monitoring risk.

Exhibit 21.1 reflects a proposed approach to risk management. This process begins with managers identifying the major risks of the company and the related implications. Wayfair faces the risk of failing to acquire new customers or retaining its current customers. Failure to acquire or retain customers could affect the company's operating results and profitability. Once various scenarios of different customer levels are modeled, management can determine what to do next. For example, the company could increase advertising to ensure better market penetration or maintain advertising and accept the risk of customer loss. After determining a risk response, management will continuously monitor new customer acquisition. If it trends downward, management might decide to alter its approach. Combining the budget with this approach to risk, management is equipped to react in a timely manner and minimize any downside implications.

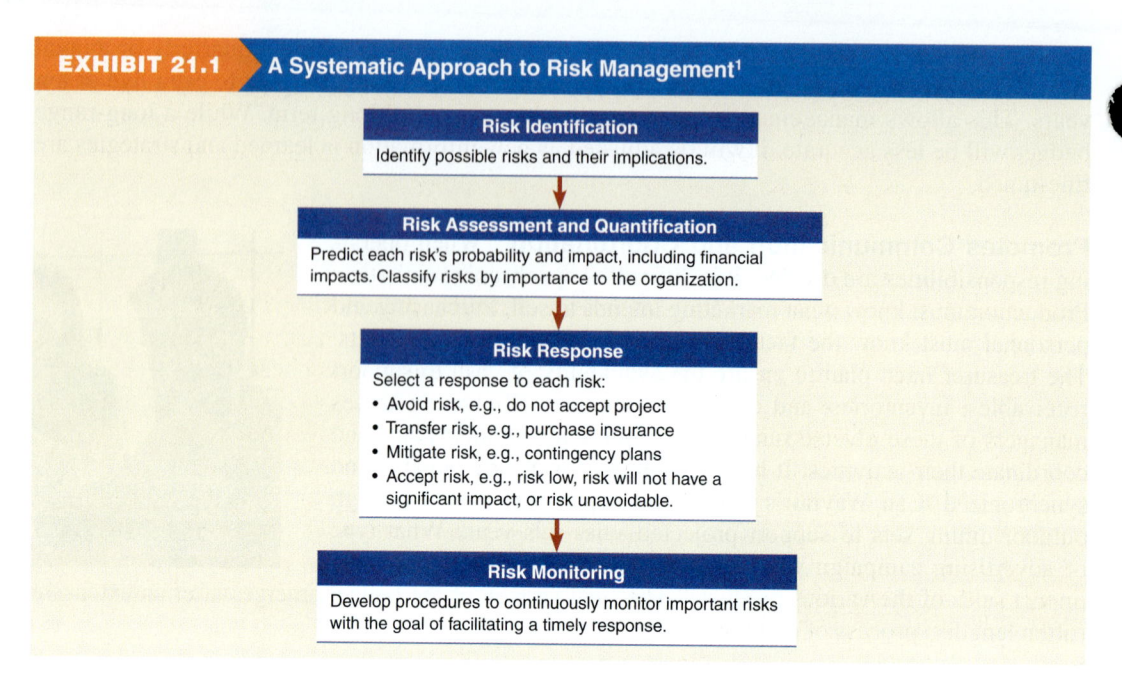

EXHIBIT 21.1 A Systematic Approach to Risk Management[1]

Risk Identification
Identify possible risks and their implications.

Risk Assessment and Quantification
Predict each risk's probability and impact, including financial impacts. Classify risks by importance to the organization.

Risk Response
Select a response to each risk:
- Avoid risk, e.g., do not accept project
- Transfer risk, e.g., purchase insurance
- Mitigate risk, e.g., contingency plans
- Accept risk, e.g., risk low, risk will not have a significant impact, or risk unavoidable.

Risk Monitoring
Develop procedures to continuously monitor important risks with the goal of facilitating a timely response.

Approaches to Budgeting

Before an organization can develop a master budget, management must decide which approaches to budget planning will be used for the various revenue and expenditure activities and organizational units. Widely used planning approaches to budgeting include the output/input, activity-based, incremental, and zero-based budgeting approaches. More than one approach is often used within the same organization. As with any decision-making tool, there are pros and cons to each method. Furthermore, budgeting and performance are often tied to resource allocation decisions, performance measurement, and incentive compensation.

Budgeting Approaches

| Output/Input Approach | Activity-Based Approach | Incremental Approach | Zero-Based Budgeting |

Output/Input Approach The **output/input approach** budgets physical inputs and costs as a function of planned unit-level activities. This approach is often used for service, merchandising, manufacturing, and distribution activities that have defined relationships between effort and accomplishment. Assume that a supplier of Wayfair manufactures coffee tables that require 2 pounds of direct materials (i.e., wood) that cost $5 per pound, and the planned production volume is 25 tables. The budgeted inputs for direct materials are 50 pounds of wood.

$$25 \text{ tables} \times 2 \text{ pounds per table} = 50 \text{ pounds}$$

The budgeted cost for direct materials is $250.

$$50 \text{ pounds} \times \$5 \text{ per pound} = \$250$$

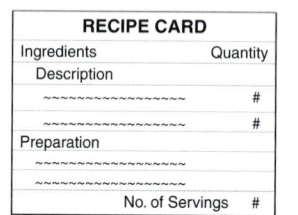

In a similar way, direct labor is budgeted based on direct labor hours required per table and manufacturing overhead is applied based on a volume-based cost driver such as the amount of direct labor hours. The budgeted inputs are a function of the planned outputs, similar to cooking where the amount of ingredients needed depends on the recipe and the number of servings that you are preparing. The output/input approach starts with the planned outputs and works backward to budget the inputs. It is difficult to use this approach for costs that do not respond to changes in unit-level cost drivers. Furthermore, this method depends on the accuracy of the sales predictions.

RECIPE CARD

Ingredients	Quantity
Description	
~~	#
~~	#
Preparation	
~~	
~~	
No. of Servings	#

Critical Thinking & Decision-Making

Suppose the sales and marketing personnel of **Wayfair**'s supplier in the prior example are compensated based on total sales relative to budgeted sales. What impact, if any, might this have on the budgeting process?

---

[1] Source: Alan J. Chilcott, "Risk Management—A Developing Field of Study and Application," *Cost Engineering*, September 9, 2010, pp. 21–26; Neville Turbit, "Basics of Managing Risk," The Project Perfect White Paper Collection, www.projectperfect.com.au.

If sales and marketing personnel are evaluated and rewarded based on performance relative to budget, the staff might underestimate sales. If this is the case, the sales of tables will be underestimated. This, in turn, will cause wood purchases to be underestimated. If manufacturing plans production and orders materials based on the budget, this could result in manufacturing shortages and delays.

Activity-Based Approach The **activity-based approach** is a type of output/input method, but it reduces the distortions in the transformation through *emphasis on the expected cost of the planned activities* that will be consumed for a process, department, service, product, or other budget objective. It is an approach based on the activity-based costing system. Overhead costs are budgeted on the basis of the cost objective's (i.e., the table's) anticipated consumption of activities, not based only on some broad-based cost driver such as direct labor hours or machine hours.

The amount of each activity cost driver used by each budget objective (for example, Wayfair's table) is determined and multiplied by the cost per unit of the activity cost driver. The result is an estimate of the costs of each product or service based on cost drivers, such as assembly-line setup or inspections, as well as the traditional volume-based drivers such as direct labor hours or units of direct materials consumed. Continuing with the Wayfair supplier example, let's assume that 1,000 coffee tables are budgeted to be produced during the period, with budgeted costs of $10,000 in direct materials and $2,000 in direct labor. Manufacturing overhead is applied under activity-based costing using the following budgeted information.

Material inspections	2,000 pounds	@ $4 per pound	= $ 8,000
Material setups	5 setups	@ $280 per set up	= 1,400
Machine operations	250 machine hours	@ $100 per machine hour	= 25,000
Total applied manufacturing overhead			$34,400

The budgeted cost per table is $46.40, computed as follows.

($10,000 direct materials + $2,000 direct labor + $34,400 overhead) ÷ 1,000 tables = $46.40 per table

Activity-based budgeting predicts costs of budget objectives by adding all costs of the activity cost drivers that each product or service is budgeted to consume. In evaluating the proposed budget, management would focus their attention on identifying the optimal set of activities rather than just the output/input relationships.

Incremental Approach The **incremental approach** budgets costs for a coming period as a dollar or percentage change from the amount budgeted for (or spent during) some previous period. This approach is often used when the relationships between inputs and outputs are weak or nonexistent. For example, it is difficult to establish a clear relationship between sales volume and advertising expenditures. Consequently, the budgeted amount of advertising for a future period is often based on the budgeted or actual advertising expenditures in a previous period. If Wayfair's budgeted advertising expenditures for last year were $200,000, the budgeted expenditures for this year would be some increment, say 5%, above $200,000.

$200,000 prior year budget × 1.05 = $210,000 current year budget

In evaluating the proposed current year budget, management would accept the $200,000 base and focus attention on justifying the increment. Wayfair is assuming that advertising will be approximately the same and increase due to, for example, inflation. The incremental approach might also be used in companies that are relatively stable and constant. In this situation, companies expect the costs relative to revenues to be fairly consistent.

The incremental approach is widely used in government and not-for-profit organizations. In seeking a budget appropriation, a manager using the incremental approach need only justify proposed expenditures *in excess of the previous budget*. The primary advantage of the incremental approach is that it simplifies the budget process by considering only the increments in the various budget items. A major disadvantage is that existing waste and inefficiencies could escalate year after year. There is never a chance to go back and start from scratch.

In the incremental approach, companies often base the current budget on *previous year's actual spending*. In this case, managers are incentivized to spend the entire budgeted amount, even if not necessary. If managers' spending is under budget, they risk being allotted a smaller budget in the future.

Zero-Based Budgeting Some organizations, especially units of government, employ zero-based budgeting. Under **zero-based budgeting** every dollar of expenditure must be justified. *Zero-based budgeting aims to develop realistic estimates. By starting at zero spending, managers must justify the existence and priority of projected spending.* The essence of zero-based budgeting is breaking an organizational unit's total budget into program packages with related costs. Management then ranks all program packages on the basis of the perceived benefits in relation to their costs. Program packages are then funded for the budget period using this ranking. High-ranking packages are most likely to be funded and low-ranking packages are least likely to be funded.

Critical Thinking & Decision-Making

How does a company incorporate uncertainty in budgeting?

While some items in a budget are often predictable, such as depreciation or rent, other items are not. A sales budget depends on many things outside of the control of the seller such as competition, economic conditions, and changes in consumer preferences. Costs of purchased products and services can also vary with overall economic conditions and supply changes. In response to this uncertainty, companies must develop different budget scenarios and establish trigger points which would prompt certain actions. In each scenario, managers alter key assumptions and determine the impact on the budget. For example, assume that Wayfair faced significant supply delays due to a global supply chain shortage. If actual units purchased fell to a certain level, this would trigger a move to a scenario budget that modeled a contraction in the business. Using the new budget is more relevant as it outlines a strategy for the company to remain profitable under the current conditions.

Review 21-1 LO21-1

Applying the Output/Input Approach and Activity-Based Approach to Budgeting

Overstock.com is an online retailer of price-competitive furnishings and accessories that works with many vendors who manufacture products. Assume that Overstock.com manufactures a limited number of products including two types of night lights, standard and rechargeable. Suppose last period, Overstock.com produced 18,000 units of standard and 45,000 units of rechargeable at a total unit cost of $38 for standard and $32 for rechargeable. Assume estimated overhead costs of $408,500 for the next period include the cost of assembly-line setups, engineering and maintenance, and inspections. Total estimated assembly hours are 50,000 hours; therefore, the estimated overhead cost per assembly hour is $8.17. Other predicted data for the next period follow.

	Standard	Rechargeable
Direct materials (per unit)...	$20.00	$14.50
Direct labor hours of assembly time (per unit)	0.5	0.8
Assembly labor cost (per hour).....................................	$18	$18
Total estimated production (in units)................................	20,000	50,000
Total setup hours	1,000	1,500
Total engineering and maintenance hours	500	600
Total inspections...	650	580
Setup cost (per setup hour)	$25	$25
Engineering and maintenance (per engineering and maintenance hour) ...	$35	$35
Inspection cost (per inspection)	$250	$250

continued

continued from previous page

Required
a. Calculate Overstock.com's budgeted cost per unit to produce standard and rechargeable night lights during the next period, assuming it uses an output/input approach and budgets overhead cost based only on assembly hours.
b. Repeat *a*, assuming Overstock.com uses an activity-based approach and budgets overhead cost based on budgeted activity costs.

Solution on p. 21-43.

MASTER BUDGET FOR A MERCHANDISER

Overview of the Master Budget Assembly for a Merchandiser

LO21-2 Explain the relationships among elements of a master budget and develop a basic master budget.

The culmination of the budgeting process is the preparation of a **master budget** for the entire organization that considers all interrelationships among organizational units. The master budget groups together all budgets and supporting schedules and coordinates all financial and operational activities, placing them into an organization-wide set of budgets for a given time period.

Because it explicitly considers organizational interrelationships, the master budget is more complex than budgets developed for products, services, organizational units, or specific processes. The elements of the master budget depend on the nature of the business, its products or services, processes and organization, and management needs.

Operating Cycle Modeled in the Master Budget A major goal of developing a master budget is to ensure the smooth functioning of a business throughout the budget period and the organization's operating cycle. As shown in **Exhibit 21.2**, the operating cycle involves the conversion of cash into other assets, which are intended to produce revenues in excess of their costs. The cycle generally follows a path from cash, to inventories, to receivables (via sales or services), and back to cash. There are, of course, intermediate processes such as the purchase or manufacture of inventories, payments of accounts payable, and the collection of receivables. The master budget is merely a detailed model of the firm's operating cycle that includes all internal processes.

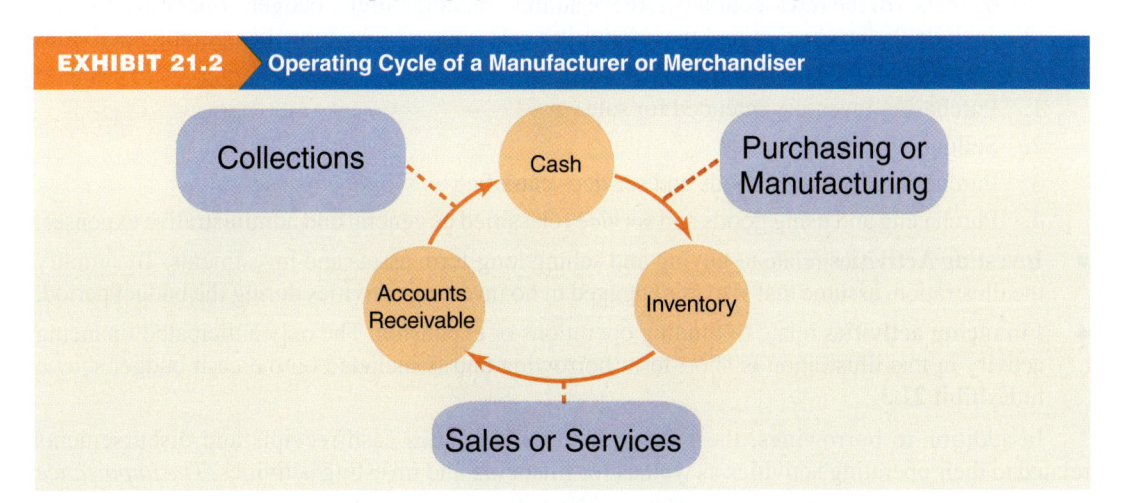

EXHIBIT 21.2 Operating Cycle of a Manufacturer or Merchandiser

Collections → Cash → Purchasing or Manufacturing → Inventory → Sales or Services → Accounts Receivable → Collections

Assembly of the Master Budget Most for-profit organizations begin the budgeting process with the development of the *sales budget* and conclude with the development of *budgeted financial statements*. **Exhibit 21.3** depicts the annual master budget assembly process in a retail merchandising organization like Wayfair. To illustrate the procedures involved in budget assembly, a hypothetical monthly budget for the second quarter of the year is developed for Wayfair. The assembly sequence follows the overview illustrated in **Exhibit 21.3**. Each element of the budget process in **Exhibit 21.3** (with the exception of special budgets) is illustrated in a separate exhibit. Because of the numerous elements in the budget process illustrated for Wayfair, you will find it useful to refer to **Exhibit 21.3** often.

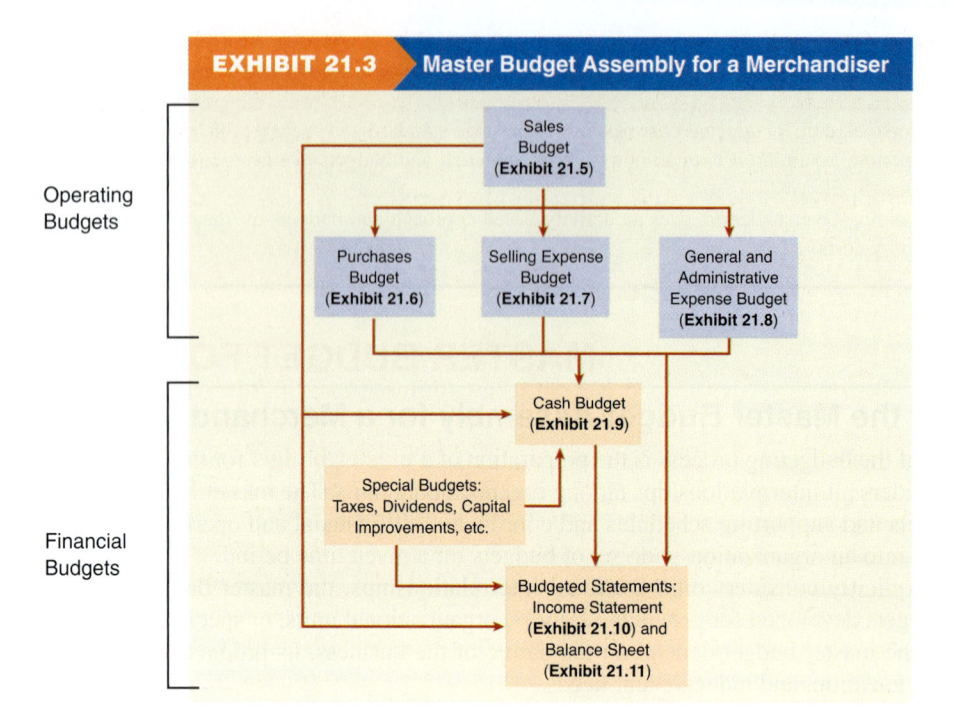

EXHIBIT 21.3 Master Budget Assembly for a Merchandiser

Operating Budgets
- Sales Budget (Exhibit 21.5)
  - Purchases Budget (Exhibit 21.6)
  - Selling Expense Budget (Exhibit 21.7)
  - General and Administrative Expense Budget (Exhibit 21.8)

Financial Budgets
- Cash Budget (Exhibit 21.9)
- Special Budgets: Taxes, Dividends, Capital Improvements, etc.
- Budgeted Statements: Income Statement (Exhibit 21.10) and Balance Sheet (Exhibit 21.11)

Operating, Investing and Financing Activities in the Master Budget The activities of a business can be summarized under three broad categories: operating activities, investing activities, and financing activities.

- **Operating activities** are the normal profit-related activities performed in conducting the daily affairs of an organization. The corresponding budgets are called the **operating budgets** which concern the development of detailed plans to guide operations throughout the budget period. In **Exhibit 21.3**, these include the sales, purchases, selling expense and general and administrative budgets. (In the next section where we address manufacturer's budgets, operating budgets also include the production and manufacturing cost budgets.) Assume the operating activities of Wayfair include the following.
  1. Purchasing inventory intended for sale.
  2. Selling goods or services.
  3. Purchasing and using goods and services classified as selling expenses.
  4. Purchasing and using goods and services classified as general and administrative expenses.
- **Investing Activities** relate to buying and selling long-term assets and investments. To simplify the illustration, assume that Wayfair engaged in no investing activities during the budget period.
- **Financing activities** relate to funding operations or expansion. The only anticipated financing activity in this illustration is short-term borrowing and is included on the cash budget shown in **Exhibit 21.3**.

In addition to borrowings, the cash budget also includes cash receipts and disbursements related to their operating activities as well as for financing and investing activities. *The importance of cash planning makes the cash budget a vital part of the total budget process.* Management must, for example, be aware in advance of the need to borrow funds and have some idea when borrowed funds can be repaid. A budget with positive income indicates that the business can move forward and generate a profit. On the other hand, a cash budget will indicate the viability of the organization or project. Will the company be able to pay its bills and keep the lights on? Both positive income and adequate cash management are essential for organizational success. Great ideas will not survive without cash to fund it. Cash rich organizations will not succeed without sales growth due to, for example, innovation and new product offerings.

The final step in the master budget is the development of the budgeted financial statements which summarize the results of the preceding budgets. Once it is determined that the master budget is a viable path forward, the financial statement budget information will be combined with qualitative data to determine whether the company *should* move forward in the proposed direction.

There are two important questions that managers should ask in the budgeting process. The first is whether the budget proposal is feasible. "Can we do it?" The second question is whether the budget proposal is acceptable. "Should we do it?" If Wayfair's budget assumes that it can borrow a significant amount on a line of credit during each quarter, when might this not be feasible? If Wayfair's budget also assumes expansion into physical store locations, why might this not be acceptable?

Critical Thinking & Decision-Making

Management must determine whether a budget is feasible and then whether it is acceptable. A reason why the Wayfair budget may not be feasible is if the company is at risk of being denied funding by a financial institution. Consider that Wayfair Inc. reported losses in recent years which could affect its ability to obtain financing. Without financing, many items on the budget, such as assumptions for purchases of merchandise and capital expenditures, would be impacted. Wayfair's budget may not be acceptable to the company if physical store expansion is not in line with the company's strategy or if the projected returns are not acceptable. If the company is primarily an online retailer, does it have the expertise to successfully expand its physical footprint? Are the projected returns large enough to offset the risks to expand? The company must consider both financial and nonfinancial factors when making a decision on whether to move forward with a budget scenario.

Starting Point: Beginning of Period Balance Sheet

The hypothetical balance sheet for April 1, the start of the second quarter, is presented in **Exhibit 21.4**. Note that we simplified the presentation and numbers in the financial statements to focus on the budgeting process. It contains information used as a starting point in preparing the various budgets. To reduce complexity, we use the *output/input approach* to budget variable costs and assume that the budgets for other costs were previously developed using the *incremental approach*. Budgets to be prepared include those for sales, purchases, selling expense, general and administrative expense, and cash. As you work through each section, think about the assumptions that are needed to create the

EXHIBIT 21.4 — Initial Balance Sheet

Wayfair Inc.
Balance Sheet
April 1

Assets			
Current assets			
Cash		$ 15,000	
Accounts receivable, net		59,200	
Merchandise inventory		157,000	$231,200
Fixed assets			
Buildings and equipment	$460,000		
Less accumulated depreciation	(124,800)	335,200	
Land		60,000	395,200
Total assets			$626,400
Liabilities and Stockholders' Equity			
Current liabilities			
Accounts payable		$ 84,000	
Taxes payable*		35,000	$119,000
Stockholders' equity			
Capital stock		350,000	
Retained earnings		157,400	507,400
Total liabilities and stockholders' equity			$626,400

*Assume quarterly income taxes are paid within 30 days of the end of each quarter.

Beginning of the period balance sheet

The balance sheet at the beginning of the budgeted period contains information used as a starting point in preparing the various budgets.

budget and which employees/departments are involved in the budgeting process. Also, remember that the budget is just an estimate. It is the best guess given current information. Although the budget is rarely, if ever, spot-on, it is a useful guide to operations and management of the organization.

Sales Budget

The **sales budget** includes a forecast of sales revenue.

> **Critical Thinking & Decision-Making**
>
> **What information is needed to create the sales budget? Who in the organization contributes to the formulation of this estimate?**
>
> *As we know from financial accounting, sales revenue is the basis for formulating the income statement. This number, at its core, is derived from the product of the number of units expected to be sold and the expected sales price. This information is typically created by the sales and marketing department, based on historical data and data that provides insights on future trends.*

Because sales drive almost all other activities in a for-profit organization, the sales budget is the first budget created in the budgeting process. Managers use the best available information to accurately forecast future market conditions. These forecasts, along with information on merchandise availability, marketing plans, and expected pricing policies, should lead to the most dependable sales budget. Assume the sales budget of Wayfair is in **Exhibit 21.5**.

Sales budget
The sales budget is the first budget created in the budgeting process.

EXHIBIT 21.5 Sales Budget

WAYFAIR INC.
Sales Budget
For the Second Quarter Ending June 30

	April	May	June	Quarter Total	July
Sales............	$190,000	$228,000	$250,000	$668,000	$309,000

The information in the sales budget along with predictions of the expected portion of cash sales and the timing of collections from credit sales are used to calculate cash receipts (See **Exhibit 21.9**). In the event of a projected cash shortfall, management could consider ways to increase cash sales or to accelerate the collection of receipts from credit sales.

Purchases Budget

The **purchases budget** indicates the materials that must be acquired to meet sales needs and ending inventory requirements. It can be referred to as a merchandise budget if it contains only purchases of merchandise for sale. (For a manufacturer, the purchases budget would include raw materials costs as illustrated in the next section.) The purchases budget, shown in **Exhibit 21.6**, includes only purchases of merchandise. The purchases budget is based on the sales budget combined with the current inventory position.

In reviewing Wayfair's purchases budget, note the following.

- Because Wayfair sells a wide variety of items, the purchases budget is expressed in terms of sales dollars, with the assumed cost of merchandise averaging 60% of the selling price. Management also keeps detailed records for budgeting the number of units of items carried. An organization that only sold a small number of items might present the sales budget in units as well as dollars. For larger organizations like Wayfair, supporting this forecast will be detailed budgets by product type, such as for outdoor furniture and lighting.

- The budget assumes management desires to have 50% of the inventory needed to fill the following month's sales in stock at the end of the previous month. This is a policy and/or assumption that is adjusted based on, for example, product availability, storage facility accessibility, and storage costs.

- To provide for a possible delay in the receipt of inventory and to meet variations in customer demand, the budget assumes that Wayfair maintains an additional base inventory of $100,000.

- The total inventory needs equal current sales plus desired ending inventory, including the base inventory.
- Budgeted purchases are computed as total inventory needs less the beginning inventory.

EXHIBIT 21.6 Purchases Budget

WAYFAIR INC.
Purchases Budget
For the Second Quarter Ending June 30

	April	May	June	Quarter Total	July
Budgeted sales (Exhibit 21.5)	$190,000	$228,000	$250,000	$668,000	$309,000
Current cost of goods sold*	$114,000	$136,800	$150,000	$400,800	
Desired ending inventory**	168,400	175,000	192,700	192,700	
Total needs	282,400	311,800	342,700	593,500	
Less beginning inventory***	(157,000)	(168,400)	(175,000)	(157,000)	
Purchases	$125,400	$143,400	$167,700	$436,500	

*Cost of goods sold is 60% of selling price (i.e. for April: $190,000 × 60% = $114,000).
**Fifty percent of inventory required for next month's budgeted sales plus base inventory of $100,000.
   April: ($228,000 May sales × 0.60 cost × 0.50 desired ending inventory) + $100,000 = $168,400
   May: ($250,000 June sales × 0.60 cost × 0.50 desired ending inventory) + $100,000 = $175,000
   June :($309,000 July sales × 0.60 cost × 0.50 desired ending inventory) + $100,000 = $192,700
***Note that monthly beginning inventory is the same as previous month's ending inventory.

Purchases budget
The purchases budget indicates the merchandise that must be acquired to meet sales needs and ending inventory requirements.

The information in the purchases budget and the information on expected timing of payments for purchases are used to budget cash disbursements for purchases (See **Exhibit 21.9**). In the event of a projected cash shortfall, management can consider ways to delay the purchase of inventory or the payment for inventory purchases.

Selling Expense Budget

The **selling expense budget** presents the expenses the organization plans to incur in connection with sales and distribution. In the selling expense budget, **Exhibit 21.7**, the budgeted variable selling expenses are determined as a percentage of budgeted sales dollars. The budgeted fixed selling expenses are based on amounts obtained from the manager of the sales department. To simplify the presentation of the cash budget, the budget assumes Wayfair pays its selling expenses in the month they are incurred.

EXHIBIT 21.7 Selling Expense Budget

WAYFAIR INC.
Selling Expense Budget
For the Second Quarter Ending June 30

	April	May	June	Quarter Total
Budgeted sales (Exhibit 21.5)	$190,000	$228,000	$250,000	$668,000
Variable selling expenses				
Setup/Display (1% sales)	$ 1,900	$ 2,280	$ 2,500	$ 6,680
Commissions (2% sales)	3,800	4,560	5,000	13,360
Miscellaneous (1% sales)	1,900	2,280	2,500	6,680
Total	7,600	9,120	10,000	26,720
Fixed selling expenses				
Advertising	2,250	2,250	2,250	6,750
Office	1,250	1,250	1,250	3,750
Miscellaneous	1,000	1,000	1,000	3,000
Total	4,500	4,500	4,500	13,500
Total selling expenses	$ 12,100	$ 13,620	$ 14,500	$ 40,220

Selling expense budget
The selling expense budget presents the expenses the organization plans to incur in connection with sales and distribution.

General and Administrative Expense Budget

The **general and administrative expense budget** presents the expenses the organization plans to incur in connection with the general administration of the organization. Sources of these expenses include the accounting department, the technology center, and the president's office. Wayfair's assumed general and administrative expense budget is presented in **Exhibit 21.8**.

> **General and administrative expense budget**
>
> The general and administrative expense budget presents the expenses the organization plans to incur in connection with the general administration of the organization.

EXHIBIT 21.8 General and Administrative Expense Budget

WAYFAIR INC.
General and Administrative Expense Budget
For the Second Quarter Ending June 30

	April	May	June	Quarter Total
General and administrative expenses				
Compensation	$25,000	$25,000	$25,000	$75,000
Insurance	2,000	2,000	2,000	6,000
Depreciation	2,000	2,000	2,000	6,000
Utilities	3,000	3,000	3,000	9,000
Miscellaneous	1,000	1,000	1,000	3,000
Total general and administrative expenses	$33,000	$33,000	$33,000	$99,000

The depreciation of $2,000 per month is a noncash item and is not carried forward to the cash budget. No *variable* general and administrative costs are included for simplicity. We will assume that most expenditures categorized as general and administrative are related to top-management operations that do not vary with unit-level cost drivers. To simplify the presentation of the cash budget (presented next), the budget assumes that general and administrative expenses, except depreciation, are paid in the month they are incurred.

Cash Budget

The **cash budget** summarizes all cash receipts and disbursements expected to occur during the budget period. Cash is critical to survival. Income is like food, and cash is like water. Food is necessary to survive and prosper over time, but you can get along without food for a short period of time. You cannot survive very long without water. Hence, cash budgeting is very important, especially in a small business where cash receipts from sales often lag behind purchases of inventory. Preparing a cash budget is an important factor in determining whether a budget is *feasible*. Without cash on hand to pay bills, the company could go bankrupt despite a great product or service. Cash budgeting is particularly important in seasonal businesses. Managers of seasonal businesses must plan cash receipts and cash payments strategically, to ensure that cash is on hand when needed.

Critical Thinking & Decision-Making

Can you think of an example of a seasonal business that plans cash inflows strategically?

One example is the sports industry. Season ticket sales typically occur in advance of the season. This cash inflow helps pay expenses later, at a time when there would otherwise be no cash inflow. A cash budget assists managers in planning how the cash received early on will be used to pay for expenses in later months.

After an organization makes sales predictions, it uses information regarding credit terms, collection policy, and prior collection experience to develop a cash collections budget. Collections on sales normally include receipts from the current period's sales and collections from sales of prior periods. An allowance for bad debts, which reduces each period's collections, is also predicted. Other items often included are cash sales, sales discounts, allowances for volume discounts, and seasonal changes of sales prices and collections. Wayfair's assumed cash budget is in **Exhibit 21.9**.

EXHIBIT 21.9 Cash Budget

WAYFAIR INC.
Cash Budget
For the Second Quarter Ending June 30

	April	May	June	Quarter Total
Budgeted sales (**Exhibit 21.5**)	$190,000	$228,000	$250,000	$668,000
Cash balance, beginning	$ 15,000	$ 15,770	$ 44,850	$ 15,000
Collections on sales				
Cash sales (50% sales)	95,000	114,000	125,000	
Credit sales				
Current month (25% credit sales)	23,750	28,500	31,250	
Prior month (74% credit sales)	59,200*	70,300	84,360	
Total	177,950	212,800	240,610	631,360
Cash available for operations	192,950	228,570	285,460	646,360
Disbursements				
Purchases (**Exhibit 21.6**)				
Current month (20% purchases)	25,080	28,680	33,540	
Prior month (80% purchases)	84,000**	100,320	114,720	
Total	109,080	129,000	148,260	386,340
Selling expenses (**Exhibit 21.7**)	12,100	13,620	14,500	40,220
General and administrative expenses				
(**Exhibit 21.8**, excluding depreciation)	31,000	31,000	31,000	93,000
Taxes (**Exhibit 21.4**)	35,000			35,000
Total	(187,180)	(173,620)	(193,760)	(554,560)
Excess (deficiency) cash available over disbursements	5,770	54,950	91,700	91,800
Short-term financing***				
New loans	10,000			10,000
Repayments		(10,000)		(10,000)
Interest	—	(100)	—	(100)
Net cash from financing	10,000	(10,100)	—	(100)
Cash balance, ending	$ 15,770	$ 44,850	$ 91,700	$ 91,700

*April 1 accounts receivable.
**April 1 accounts payable.
***Loans are obtained in $1,000 increments at the start of the month to maintain a minimum balance of $15,000 at all times. Repayments are made at the end of the month, as soon as adequate cash is available. Assume interest of 12% per year (1% per month) is paid when the loan is repaid.

> **Cash budget**
> The cash budget summarizes all cash receipts and disbursements expected to occur during the budget period.

Note the following important points.

- Management estimates that one-half of all sales are for cash and the other half are on the company's credit card. (When sales are on bank credit cards, the collection is immediate, less any bank fee. However, the budget assumes customer charges using Wayfair's credit card are collected by the company from the customer.) Twenty-five percent of the credit card sales are collected in the month of sale, and 74% are collected in the following month. Bad debts are budgeted at 1% of credit sales. This resource flow is graphically illustrated as follows.

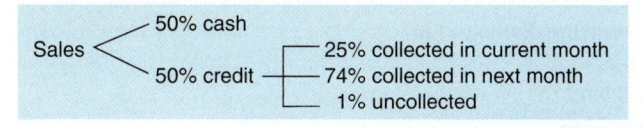

```
                    50% cash
Sales <
                    50% credit ─┬─ 25% collected in current month
                                ├─ 74% collected in next month
                                └─ 1% uncollected
```

- The budget assumes payments for purchases are made 20% in the month purchased and 80% in the next month.
- Information on cash expenditures for selling expenses and for general and administrative expenses is based on budgets for these items. The monthly cash expenditures for general and administrative expenses are $31,000 rather than $33,000. The $2,000 difference relates to depreciation, which does not require the use of cash.
- The budget assumes Wayfair's income taxes are determined on the basis of predicted taxable income following IRS rules. Estimated tax payments are made during the month following the end of each quarter. Hence, the taxes payable on April 1 are paid during April.

- The cash budget shows cash operating deficiencies and surpluses expected to occur at the end of each month. This is used to plan for borrowing and loan payment.
- The budget assumes the cash maintenance policy for Wayfair specifies that a minimum balance of $15,000 is to be maintained.
- The budget assumes Wayfair has a line of credit with a bank, with any interest on borrowed funds computed at the simple interest rate of 12.0% per year, or 1.0% per month. All necessary borrowing is assumed to occur at the start of each month in increments of $1,000. Repayments including interest are assumed to occur at the end of the month.
- The cash budget indicates Wayfair needs to borrow $10,000 in April. The $10,000 plus interest is repaid in May.

If Wayfair had any cash disbursements for dividends or capital expenditures, they would be included in the cash budget. These items, along with information on income taxes, would be shown in special budgets.

Budgeted Financial Statements

The preparation of the master budget culminates in the preparation of budgeted financial statements. **Budgeted financial statements** are pro forma statements that reflect the "as-if" effects of the budgeted activities on the actual financial position of the organization. That is, the statements reflect the results of operations assuming all budget predictions are correct. Of course, we know that these numbers are most likely not correct but rather, are the best guess of the future given the vast amount of qualitative and quantitative information available to organizations.

The budgeted income statement can follow the functional format traditionally used for financial accounting or the contribution format introduced in Chapter 15. In either case, the balance sheet amounts reflect the corresponding budgeted entries.

Exhibit 21.10 presents the budgeted income statement for the quarter ending June 30. If all predictions made in the budgets leading up to the financial statement budget are correct, Wayfair will produce a net income of $51,540 for the quarter. Almost every item on the budgeted income statement comes from one of the budget schedules.

EXHIBIT 21.10 — Budgeted Income Statement

WAYFAIR INC.
Budgeted Income Statement
For the Second Quarter Ending June 30

Sales (**Exhibit 21.5**)		$668,000
Cost of goods sold*		
Beginning inventory (**Exhibit 21.4**)	$157,000	
Purchases (**Exhibit 21.6**)	436,500	
Cost of merchandise available	593,500	
Ending inventory (**Exhibit 21.6**)	(192,700)	(400,800)
Gross profit		267,200
Other expenses		
Bad debts (1% of credit sales)**	3,340	
Selling (**Exhibit 21.7**)	40,220	
General and administrative (**Exhibit 21.8**)	99,000	(142,560)
Income from operations		124,640
Interest expense (**Exhibit 21.9**)		(100)
Net income from operations		124,540
Tax expense***		(73,000)
Net income		$ 51,540

*Also computed as sales × 0.60
**$668,000 × 0.50 credit sales × 0.01 bad debts
***Provided by accounting

The budgeted balance sheet, presented in **Exhibit 21.11**, shows Wayfair's financial position as of June 30, assuming that all budget predictions are correct. Sources of the budgeted balance sheet data are included as part of the exhibit.

EXHIBIT 21.11 — Budgeted Balance Sheet

WAYFAIR INC.
Balance Sheet
June 30

Assets			
Current assets			
Cash (**Exhibit 21.9**)		$ 91,700	
Accounts receivable, net*		92,500	
Merchandise inventory (**Exhibits 21.6** and **21.10**)		192,700	$376,900
Fixed assets			
Buildings and equipment (**Exhibit 21.4**)	$460,000		
Less accumulated depreciation			
(**Exhibit 21.4** plus depreciation **Exhibit 21.8**)	(130,800)	329,200	
Land (**Exhibit 21.4**)		60,000	389,200
Total assets			$766,100
Liabilities and Stockholders' Equity			
Current liabilities			
Accounts payable**		$134,160	
Taxes payable (**Exhibit 21.10**)		73,000	$207,160
Stockholders' equity			
Capital stock (**Exhibit 21.4**)		350,000	
Retained earnings (**Exhibit 21.4** plus net income **Exhibit 21.10**)		208,940	558,940
Total liabilities and stockholders' equity			$766,100

*June credit sales collected in July, $250,000 × 0.50 × 0.74 = $92,500.
**June purchases paid in July, $167,700 × 0.80 = $134,160.

Is the budgeting process as straight-forward as arithmetic in a spreadsheet?

Preparing the spreadsheet is the easy part of the budgeting process. Deriving the assumptions from various divisions throughout the organization is the challenge. Underlying every number is a series of assumptions. Developing the underlying assumptions, such as market demand and ensuring that the assumptions are reasonable, is the tough part. When developing, analyzing, or using a budget, we must always start by critically examining the assumptions used.

Critical Thinking & Decision-Making

Finalizing the Budget

After studying the Wayfair example, you might conclude that developing the master budget is the end of a mechanical process. That is not the case. Understanding the basics of budget assembly is just the start.

Before finalizing the budget, the following questions must be addressed.

- **Is the proposed budget feasible? Or, can we do it?**
- **Is the proposed budget acceptable? Or, should we do it?**

To be feasible, the organization must be able to implement the proposed budget. Are there any constraints that would prevent the company from achieving its budgetary objectives? Without the assumed line of credit, Wayfair's budget is not feasible because the company would run out of cash sometime in April. Knowing this, management can take timely corrective action. Possible actions include obtaining equity financing, issuing long-term debt, or reducing the amount of inventory on hand at the end of each quarter. Other constraints that would make the budget infeasible include the availability of merchandise and, in the case of a manufacturing organization, production capacity.

Once management determines that the budget is feasible, they still need to determine if it is acceptable. Should the company move forward using the budget as a guide? To evaluate acceptability, management might consider various financial ratios such as return on assets. They might compare the return provided by the proposed budget with past returns, industry averages, or some organizational goal. Furthermore, is this strategically the right path for the organization? Should the company move in the proposed direction? To fully evaluate the acceptability of the budget, the quantitative data will be combined with qualitative data to evaluate whether the company should move in the strategic direction outlined by the budget.

Review 21-2 LO21-2   Preparing a Budget for a Merchandising Organization

For **Overstock.com**, suppose the following information is available for April for its two products, loofahs and bath bombs. The division that carries these two products is preparing a budget for the month. For simplicity, assume that these are the only two products sold by the division.

Estimated sales
- Bath Bombs .... 160,000 bath bombs at $10 each
- Loofahs .... 240,000 loofahs at $5 each

Estimated costs
- Bath Bomb .... $8 per bath bomb
- Loofah .... $2 per loofah

	Beginning	Ending
Desired inventories (in units)		
Bath Bombs	10,000	12,000
Loofahs	4,000	5,000

Assumed financial information follows.
- Beginning cash balance is $400,000.
- Purchases of merchandise are paid 60% in the month of purchase and 40% in the following month. Purchases totaled $1,800,000 in March and are estimated to be $2,000,000 in May.
- Employee wages and salaries are paid for in the current month. Employee expenses for April totaled $156,000.
- Selling expenses are paid in the next month. The accounts payable amount for these expenses from March is $80,000 and for May will be $90,000. April's selling expenses total $80,000.
- Sales are on credit and are collected 70% in the current period and the remainder in the next period. March's sales were $3,000,000, and May's sales are estimated to be $3,200,000. Bad debts average 1% of sales.
- General and administrative expenses total $450,000, including $40,000 of depreciation. Assume any amounts due are paid in the current month.
- All unit costs for April are the same as they were in March.

Required
Prepare the following for April.

Solution on p. 21-43.
a. Sales budget in dollars.
b. Purchases budget
c. Cash budget
d. Budgeted income statement.

MASTER BUDGET FOR A MANUFACTURER

LO21-3
Develop elements of a basic master budget for a manufacturer.

Overview of Master Budget Assembly for a Manufacturer

The importance of inventory in various organizations was introduced in Chapter 17 where **Exhibit 17.1** summarized inventory and related expense accounts for service, merchandising, and manufacturing organizations. Recall that most service organizations have a low percentage of their assets invested in inventory, typically consisting of the supplies needed to facilitate operations. In contrast, merchandising organizations usually have a high percentage of their total assets invested in inventory, with the largest inventory investment in merchandise purchased for resale. The preceding illustration of the development of a master budget was for a merchandising organization. In this section, we will illustrate development of a master budget for a manufacturing organization. We will contrast the assembly of a budget for a merchandiser in **Exhibit 21.3** with the assembly of a budget for a manufacturer in **Exhibit 21.12** through our hypothetical budget of Wayfair that follows.

EXHIBIT 21.12 Master Budget Assembly for a Manufacturer

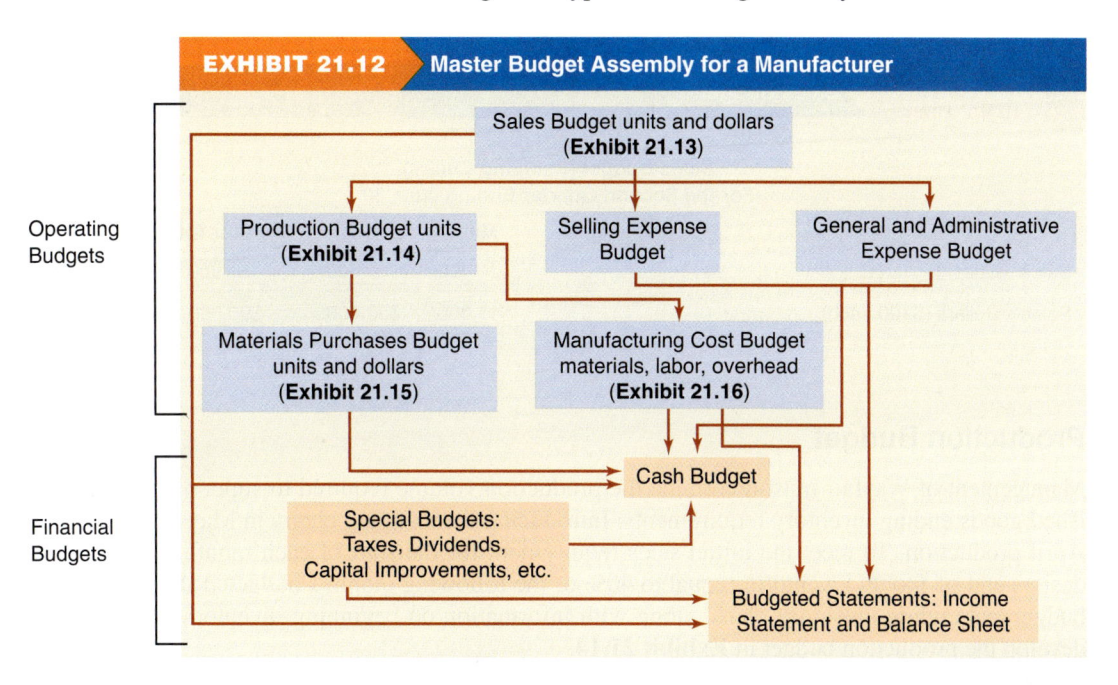

Operating Budgets:
- Sales Budget units and dollars (Exhibit 21.13)
- Production Budget units (Exhibit 21.14)
- Selling Expense Budget
- General and Administrative Expense Budget
- Materials Purchases Budget units and dollars (Exhibit 21.15)
- Manufacturing Cost Budget materials, labor, overhead (Exhibit 21.16)

Financial Budgets:
- Cash Budget
- Special Budgets: Taxes, Dividends, Capital Improvements, etc.
- Budgeted Statements: Income Statement and Balance Sheet

Continuing our Wayfair example, assume that management is considering the option of manufacturing a high-quality, all-weather camping chair as an alternative to purchasing a similar item from an outside vendor. Unit variable and monthly fixed cost estimates associated with the manufacture of the chair follow.

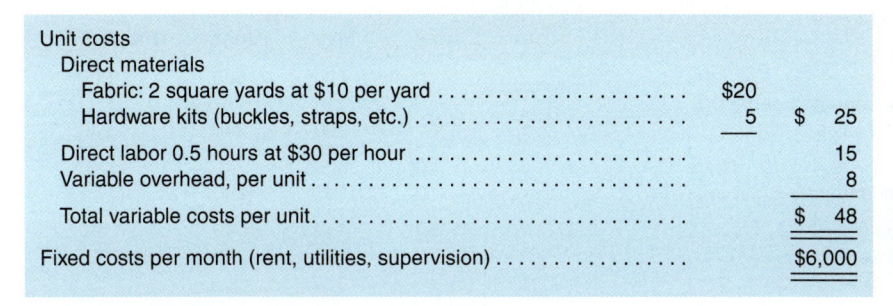

Unit costs		
Direct materials		
Fabric: 2 square yards at $10 per yard	$20	
Hardware kits (buckles, straps, etc.)	5	$ 25
Direct labor 0.5 hours at $30 per hour		15
Variable overhead, per unit		8
Total variable costs per unit		$ 48
Fixed costs per month (rent, utilities, supervision)		$6,000

Because management anticipates an average monthly production volume of 500 camping chairs, the average fixed cost per unit, a predetermined overhead rate, is $12.

$6,000 budgeted fixed costs ÷ 500 average production volume = $12 fixed cost per unit

For budgeting purposes, management uses a budgeted amount per unit of product (i.e., also called a standard cost), for valuing inventories and forecasting cost of goods sold. The standard cost of a camping chair is $60.

Direct materials	$25
Direct labor	15
Variable overhead	8
Fixed overhead	12
Standard cost	$60

Sales Budget

Management, planning to introduce this new product in May, developed the sales budget shown in **Exhibit 21.13**. In this case, because unit information is necessary to determine production requirements, the sales budget is expressed in units as well as dollars.

> **Manufacturing sales budget**
>
> Because unit information is necessary to determine production requirements, the sales budget is expressed in units as well as dollars.

EXHIBIT 21.13   Sales Budget

WAYFAIR INC.
Sales Budget (Camping Chairs)
For the Second Quarter Ending June 30

	April	May	June	Quarter Total	July
Sales—Units	0	400	500	900	600
Sales—Dollars ($100 each)	0	$40,000	$50,000	$90,000	$60,000

Production Budget

Management of Wayfair must determine the production volume required to support sales and finished goods ending inventory requirements. Introducing the camping chairs in May requires some April production. To meet the initial sales requirement for the start of each month, management desires end-of-month inventories equal to 40% of the following month's budgeted sales. The sales budget and ending inventory plans, along with information on beginning inventories, are used to develop the production budget in **Exhibit 21.14**.

> **Production budget**
>
> The sales budget and ending inventory plans, along with information on beginning inventories, are used to develop the production budget.

EXHIBIT 21.14   Production Budget

WAYFAIR INC.
Production Budget (Camping Chairs)
For the Second Quarter Ending June 30

	April	May	June	Quarter Total
Budgeted sales	0	400	500	900
Desired ending inventory 40% following month sales	160	200	240	240
Total requirements	160	600	740	1,140
Less beginning inventory	0	(160)	(200)	0
Budgeted production	160	440	540	1,140

Materials Purchases Budget

The production budget, along with information on beginning inventories of raw materials and planned ending inventory levels (for simplicity, assume month-end requirements of 500 square yards of fabric and 200 kits), is then used to budget the purchases in **Exhibit 21.15** for raw materials in units and dollars.

EXHIBIT 21.15 — Materials Purchases Budget

WAYFAIR INC.
Materials Purchases Budget
For the Second Quarter Ending June 30

	April	May	June	Quarter Total
Fabric				
Current needs (2 yards per unit)	320	880	1,080	2,280
Desired ending inventory (500 yards)	500	500	500	500
Total requirements	820	1,380	1,580	2,780
Less beginning inventory	(0)	(500)	(500)	(0)
Fabric purchases in yards	820	880	1,080	2,780
Assembly kits				
Current needs (1 per unit)	160	440	540	1,140
Desired ending inventory (200 kits)	200	200	200	200
Total requirements	360	640	740	1,340
Less beginning inventory	(0)	(200)	(200)	(0)
Kit purchases in units	360	440	540	1,340
Purchases (Dollars)				
Fabric at $10 per yard	$ 8,200	$ 8,800	$10,800	$27,800
Kits at $5 each	1,800	2,200	2,700	6,700
Total materials purchases in dollars	$10,000	$11,000	$13,500	$34,500

Materials Purchases Budget

The production budget, along with information on beginning inventories of raw materials and planned ending inventory levels, is then used to budget the purchases for raw materials in units and dollars.

Manufacturing Cost Budget

In addition to a selling expense budget and a general and administrative expense budget, management needs also to develop a manufacturing cost budget, which is similar in design to a statement of cost of goods manufactured (see **Exhibit 17.7**) except that it is prepared in advance of production rather than after production. The production budget, along with standard variable and predicted fixed cost information, are used to develop the manufacturing cost budget in **Exhibit 21.16**.

EXHIBIT 21.16 — Manufacturing Cost Budget

WAYFAIR INC.
Manufacturing Cost Budget
For the Second Quarter Ending June 30

	April	May	June	Quarter Total
Direct materials				
Fabric used in production (production × 2 yards × $10)	$ 3,200	$ 8,800	$10,800	$22,800
Kits used in production (production × 1 kit × $5)	800	2,200	2,700	5,700
Total	4,000	11,000	13,500	28,500
Direct labor (production × 1/2 hour × $30)	2,400	6,600	8,100	17,100
Manufacturing overhead				
Variable ($8 per unit)	1,280	3,520	4,320	9,120
Fixed	6,000	6,000	6,000	18,000
Total	7,280	9,520	10,320	27,120
Total manufacturing costs	$13,680	$27,120	$31,920	$72,720

Manufacturing Cost Budget

The production budget, along with standard variable and predicted fixed cost information, is also used to develop the manufacturing cost budget.

Cash Budget and Financial Statement Budgets

The cash budget and the budgeted financial statements for Wayfair with the manufacturing of the camping chairs are not presented because they do not require the introduction of new topics. Keep in mind that the cash budget will include disbursements for purchases shown in **Exhibit 21.15** (rather than materials used in production) and for direct labor, variable overhead, and fixed overhead shown in **Exhibit 21.16**. A budgeted functional income statement using absorption costing will include the predicted cost of goods sold for camping chairs at a $60 standard cost per unit. A contribution income statement using variable costing would include the cost of goods sold for the camping chairs at a $48 standard cost per unit with all fixed manufacturing costs expensed in the period incurred. Finally, the budgeted balance sheet will include standard costs of any June raw materials (500 square yards at $10 per yard and 200 kits at $5 each), work in process (none), and finished goods. Any unpaid liabilities for purchases of raw materials, direct labor, and manufacturing overhead would also be shown under current liabilities. Note that completing the cash budget and the budgeted statements requires information on the estimated timing of payments for the purchases of raw materials, direct labor, and manufacturing overhead.

Review 21-3 LO21-3 — Preparing a Master Budget for a Manufacturer

Assume **Overstock.com** manufactures and sells two industrial products in a single plant. Suppose a new manager wants to have quarterly budgets and has prepared the following information for the first quarter of the year.

Budgeted sales

Trimmer	60,000 at $100 each
Chainsaw	40,000 at $125 each

Budgeted inventories

	Beginning	Ending
Trimmer, finished	20,000 units	25,000 units
Chainsaw, finished	8,000 units	10,000 units
Metal, direct materials	32,000 pounds	36,000 pounds
Plastic, direct materials	29,000 pounds	32,000 pounds
Handles, direct materials	6,000 each	7,000 each

Standard variable costs per unit

	Trimmer		Chainsaw	
Direct materials				
Metal	5 pounds × $8.00	$40.00	4 pounds × $8.00	$32.00
Plastic	3 pounds × $5.00	15.00	3 pounds × $5.00	15.00
Handles	1 handle × $3.00	3.00		
Total		58.00		47.00
Direct labor	2 labor hours × $12.00	24.00	3 labor hours × $16.00	48.00
Variable manufacturing overhead	2 labor hours × $1.50	3.00	3 labor hours × $1.50	4.50
Total		$85.00		$99.50

Assume fixed manufacturing overhead is $214,000 per quarter (including noncash expenditures of $156,000) and is allocated on total units produced. Financial information follows.

- Beginning cash balance is $1,800,000.
- Sales are on credit and are collected 50% in the current period and the remainder in the next period. Last quarter's sales were $8,400,000. There are no bad debts.
- Purchases of direct materials and labor costs are paid for in the quarter acquired.
- Manufacturing overhead expenses are paid in the quarter incurred.
- Selling and administrative expenses are all fixed and are paid in the quarter incurred. They are budgeted at $340,000 per quarter, including $90,000 of depreciation.

Required

For the first quarter of the year, prepare the following.

  a. Sales budget in dollars.
  b. Production budget in units.
  c. Purchases budget.
  d. Manufacturing cost budget.
  e. Cash budget.
  f. Budgeted contribution income statement. (*Hint:* See Chapter 15.)

Solution on p. 21-44.

ASPECTS OF BUDGETING THAT IMPACT BEHAVIOR AND OUTCOMES

Organizations are composed of individuals who perform a wide variety of activities in pursuit of the organization's goals. To accomplish these goals, management must recognize that how budgets are developed, implemented, and used has an impact on the behavior of the organization's employees. This means that budgeting can lead to positive or negative behavioral reactions of employees.

Many blame budgeting for bad outcomes in the form of employee behavior. However, often the problems occur due to the way in which the budget is implemented or used; it is a flaw in the process, not in the budget itself. The budget has many roles in organizations, such as resource allocation, planning, coordination, communication, control, motivation, and performance evaluation. These roles and related goals might conflict with each other at times and, consequently, lead to positive outcomes in some aspects but undesired outcomes in other aspects. Due to the many uses of budgets, the process of budgeting becomes tricky to manage.

LO4 Analyze the relationship between budget development and employee behavior.

Employee Participation in the Budgeting Process

Budgeting should be used to promote productive employee behavior directed toward meeting the organization's goals. The budgeting system should be set up in a way that avoids motivating employees to report bias numbers during the budgeting process. While no two organizations use exactly the same budgeting procedures, two approaches to employee involvement in budgeting represent possible end points on a continuum. These approaches are sometimes referred to as top-down and bottom-up methods.

With a **top-down** or **imposed budget**, top management identifies the primary goals and objectives for the organization and communicates them to lower management levels. Because relatively few people are involved in top-down budgeting, an imposed budget saves time. It also minimizes the slack that managers at lower organizational levels are sometimes prone to build into their budgets. However, this nonparticipative approach to budgeting can have undesirable motivational consequences. Personnel who do not participate in budget preparation might lack a commitment to achieve their part of the budget. Furthermore, information typically resides at lower levels in the organization. By not including all levels of employees in the budgeting process, this information might be lost, resulting in less accurate budgets.

> **Suppose you are the CFO of a high-growth enterprise in a competitive industry. You would like to formalize the financial planning process in order to increase operating efficiencies of your company. You are leaning toward a top-down budgeting process because you feel that the financial staff has the most expertise and a solid understanding of the business. Do you have concerns about excluding the lower-level managers from the budgeting process?**
>
> *The top-down approach might produce an effective set of benchmarks. However, it might not maximize the benefits of budgeting. If managers will be evaluated relative to budgeted numbers, their involvement is crucial to their adoption and acceptance of the numbers. A top-down budget is less likely to be embraced by managers.*

With a **bottom-up** or **participative budget**, managers at all levels—and in some cases, even nonmanagers—are involved in budget preparation. Budget proposals originate at the lowest level of management possible and are then integrated into the proposals for the next level, and so on, until the proposals reach the top level of management, which completes the budget. It is not uncommon for larger companies to have a *financial planning department* or a *budget committee* responsible for the review, analysis, compilation, and approval of the various budgets. This process still allows for a participative budgeting process in that each department can submit budget proposals with changes made through a collaborative process. Furthermore, companies with strong governance will have a committee on the Board of Directors that reviews and approves the budget. In addition to the numbers presented, the Board committee will ensure that the strategy implicit in the budget is consistent with the intended direction of the company. The role of a budget committee is discussed further in Chapter 24.

Participation helps ensure that important issues are considered, the information is added at each level of the organization, and that employees understand the importance of their roles in meeting the organization's goals. It also provides opportunities for problem solving and fosters employee commitment to agreed-upon goals. Hence, budget predictions are likely to be more accurate, and the people responsible for the budget are more likely to strive to accomplish its objectives. These self-imposed budgets reinforce the concept of participative management and should strengthen the overall budgeting process.

Participative approaches to budgeting have a few disadvantages. Because they require the involvement of many people, the preparation period is longer than that for an imposed budget. Another disadvantage is the tendency of some managers to intentionally understate revenues or overstate expenses to provide **budgetary slack**. A manager might do this to reduce a concern regarding unfavorable performance reviews or to make it easier to obtain favorable performance reviews. This behavior is often exacerbated when managers are rewarded based on performance relative to the budget. If a department consistently produces favorable results versus budget with little apparent effort, this might be a symptom of budgetary slack.

Is budgetary slack a desirable feature? Can it be prevented?

Budgetary slack is not desirable because it undermines the budgeting process. It is difficult to prevent, but it can be reduced if the budgeting process adequately reflects an understanding of human behavior, provides a proper model for evaluations and control, allows inputs at each budget level (but with proper oversight), and holds each manager accountable for the results.

Selecting Budgeting Periods

Although most organizations use a one-year budget period, many organizations also budget for shorter and longer periods. In fact, most organizations have multiple budgets, varying in time periods and in detail. For example, the current period budget might be very detailed while the five-year budget focuses on a few, high-level numbers. The time-frame of budgets utilized by management for evaluation of performance can impact employee behavior. Does management emphasize meeting short-term over long-term budget goals? Are there key items in the long-term budget that guide the overall business strategy? Do the budgets extend out far enough into the future to impact important decisions made today? In addition to fixed-length budget periods, two other types of budget periods commonly used are life-cycle budgeting and continuous budgeting.

When a fixed time period is not particularly relevant to planning, an organization can use **life-cycle budgeting**, which involves developing a budget for a project's entire life. An ice cream vendor at the beach might develop a budget for the season. A general contractor might budget costs for the entire (multiple-year) time required to construct a building. Life cycle budgeting is specific to the product or service of interest. Different companies might use different horizons for different products due to life cycle differences.

Under **continuous budgeting**, the budget (sometimes called a **rolling budget**) is based on a moving time frame. For example, an organization on a continuous four-quarter budget system adds a quarter to the budget at the end of each quarter of operations, thereby always maintaining a budget for four quarters into the future. Under this system, plans for a full year into the future are always available, whereas under a fixed annual budget, operating plans for a full year ahead are available only at the beginning of the budget year. Because managers are constantly involved in this type of budgeting, the budget process becomes an active and integral part of the management process. Managers are forced to be future oriented throughout the year rather than focused on budgeting just once each year.

Utilizing Forecasts in Budgets

Budget preparation requires the development of a variety of forecasts. The sales forecast is based on a variety of interrelated factors such as historical trends, product innovation, general economic conditions, industry conditions, and the organization's strategic position for competing on the basis of price, product differentiation, or market niche. Many organizations first determine the industry forecast for a given product or service and then extract from it their sales estimations.

Although the sales forecast is primary to most organizations, there are many other forecasts of varying importance that must be made, including (a) the collection period for sales on account, (b) percent of uncollectible sales on account, (c) cost of materials, supplies, utilities, and so forth, (d) employee turnover, (e) time required to perform activities, (f) interest rates, and (g) development time for new products or services.

Budgets incorporate multiple assumptions based on information that is gathered from a variety of people and sources. Each assumption might turn out to be inaccurate by a small or large degree. Managers can react more swiftly to changes from the forecasts if uncertainty is built into the budget development process. When manager alter key assumptions, especially as they relate to forecasted data, they can assess the impact on the budget. This process prepares employees to more efficiently and effectively respond to change.

Motivating Ethical Behavior in Budget Development

Because most wrongful activities related to budgeting are unethical, rather than illegal, organizations often have difficulty dealing with them. However, when managers' actions cross the gray area between ethical and fraudulent behavior, organizations are not reluctant to dismiss employees or even pursue legal actions against them.

Although most managers have a natural inclination to be conservative in developing their budgets, at some level the blatant padding or building slack into the budget becomes unethical. In an extreme case, it might even be considered theft if an inordinate level of budgetary slack creates favorable performance variances that lead to significant bonuses or other financial gain for the manager. Another form of falsifying budgets occurs when managers include expense categories in their budgets that are not needed in their operations and subsequently use the funds to pad other budget categories. The deliberate falsification of budgets is unethical behavior and is grounds for dismissal in most organizations. Organizations must ensure that systems are in place to minimize unethical behavior.

How can management motivate employees to participate in the budget planning process in an ethical manner?

Participation in the budget process helps encourage employees to adhere to the budget, enhance pride in achieving the budget, and increase employee loyalty. The budget should be used to emphasize the importance of the budget, encourage participation, emphasize top management's support of the budgeting process, allow flexibility in changing the budget, and educate employees about the budgeting process.

Critical Thinking & Decision-Making

Identifying Aspects of Budget Development Affecting Behavior LO21-4 Review 21-4

Items 1 though 4 represent different aspects in the development of budgets.
1. Budgetary Slack
2. Participative Budget
3. Top-down Budget
4. Life-Cycle Budgeting

Required
Identify a term above that most appropriately describes each of the scenarios below.

_____ a. Overstock's marketing department is asked to provide an estimate as to how much it will spend on print ads during the next fiscal year.

_____ b. Overstock's marketing department provides a budget amount for print ads for the next fiscal year that includes the expected expenditures plus 10% to account for uncertainty.

_____ c. Overstock is only planning to sell patio furniture for the summer season. It developed a budget to estimate how much it will make during the upcoming summer season.

_____ d. During the height of the pandemic, Overstock's chief officers prepared a revised quarterly budget and forwarded it to all departments.

Solution on p. 21-47.

MULTIPLE CHOICE

Multiple Choice Answers
1. c   2. a   3. d   4. b   5. c
6. b   7. a   8. b   9. c   10. b

LO21-1   **1.** Each of the following is a true statement regarding the budgeting process, except
     a. The budget is the basis for evaluating performance.
     b. Budgets represent a guide for accomplishing goals and objectives.
     c. The budget is developed by the finance team and its primary purpose is to predict costs.
     d. An organization's budget model can be used to evaluate the financial impact of a risk.

LO21-1   **2.** The major objectives of budgeting are to
     a. foster the planning of operations, provide a framework for performance evaluation, and promote communication and coordination among the organization's segments.
     b. foster the planning of operations, facilitate the identification of blame for missed budget predictions, and ensure goal congruence between superiors and subordinates.
     c. define responsibility centers, provide a framework for performance evaluation, and promote communication and coordination among the organization's segments.
     d. define responsibility centers, facilitate the identification of blame for missed budget predictions, and ensure goal congruence between superiors and subordinates.

CMA adapted

LO21-1   **3.** All of the following are advantages of the use of budgets in a management control system except that budgets
     a. force management planning.
     b. provide performance criteria.
     c. promote communication and coordination within the organization.
     d. limit unauthorized expenditures.

CMA adapted

LO21-2   **4.** Budgeted sales of the East End Burger Joint for the first quarter of the year are as follows.

January	$50,000
February	60,000
March	68,000

The cost of sales averages 40% of sales revenue and management desires ending inventories equal to 25% of the following month's sales. Assuming the January 1 inventory is $5,000, the January purchases budget is
     a. $19,000   c. $31,000
     b. $21,000   d. $69,000

LO21-2   **5.** Syracuse Distribution's sales budget for the first quarter follows.

January	$250,000
February	300,000
March	290,000

All sales are on account (credit) with 50% collected in the month of sale, 30% collected in the month after sale, and 20% collected in the second month after sale. There are no uncollectible accounts. The March cash receipts are
     a. $140,000   c. $285,000
     b. $235,000   d. None of the above

LO21-2   **6.** Refer to question 5 and determine the accounts receivable at the end of March.
     a. $147,000   c. $235,000
     b. $205,000   d. $285,000

LO21-2   **7.** A company is developing its budget for the upcoming month. The financial planning department has developed the following range of sales activity and the associated probabilities for each level of budgeted sales.

Sales Estimate	Probability
$120,000	25%
$170,000	40%
$200,000	35%

The company's cost of goods sold averages 80% of sales, and the relationship is expected to remain consistent in the next fiscal year. What is the expected value of the company's budgeted cost of goods sold?

a. $134,400
b. $136,000
c. $168,000
d. $170,000

CMA adapted

8. Presented is selected second quarter budget data for the Arnold Company. **LO21-3**

	Sales
April	20,000 units
May	30,000 units
June	36,000 units

Additional information:
- Each unit of finished product requires three pounds of raw materials.
- Arnold maintains ending finished goods inventories equal to 20% of the following month's budgeted sales.
- Arnold maintains raw materials inventories equal to 25% of the following month's budgeted production.
- April 1 inventories are in line with Arnold's inventory policy.

Arnold's budgeted purchases (in pounds) for April are

a. 66,000 pounds
b. 72,900 pounds
c. 89,400 pounds
d. None of the above

9. Presented is additional information for the Arnold Company (refer to question 8): **LO21-3**
   - Price per pound of raw materials — $20
   - Direct labor per unit of finished product — 0.40 hours at $25 per hour
   - Total monthly factory overhead — $200,000 + $10 per direct labor hour

Arnold's total manufacturing cost budget for April is

a. $880,000
b. $1,680,000
c. $1,828,000
d. $1,966,000

10. A company pays its production manager an annual bonus based on how well the manager performs against the production department's annual budgets. The production manager has been overestimating budgeted costs the past few years in order to obtain a higher bonus payment. The production manager's actions are best described as **LO21-4**

a. motivating employee effort.
b. building budgetary slack.
c. balancing production costs.
d. setting budgeted performance.

CMA adapted

DATA ANALYTICS

DA21-1. Forecasting Using Excel **LO21-2, 4**

Melton Manufacturing opened in January 2023. Sales have increased significantly in the first two years of operations, and management is now looking to expand production capacity. To finance the purchase of a new factory, they would need to either raise capital or borrow funds. They have asked you to make some projections for the next year of operations. They intend to share these with potential investors and lenders. Information about unit sales, sales revenues, and net profits for the past two years is included in the file available on the textbook's website. A video demonstrating Excel tools used to answer the questions in this problem is also available on the website.

REQUIRED

1. Create three line graphs in Excel (one for units sold, one for sales revenue, and one for net operating income). Add trendlines to all graphs.
   a. Extend the trendline out for 12 months.
   b. Use the Polynomial (Order 2) trendline option for all charts
   c. To see how closely the trendline matches the data, check the Display R-squared value on chart box. The closer the R-square value is to 1, the better the match.

2. Create the same three graphs using the Forecast Sheet tool (line charts) in Excel. *Hint:* The Forecast Sheet tool is found under the Data tab. Highlight data to analyze, click on Forecast sheet, and click on Options to make the following adjustments.
   a. Set the Forecast End to 12/1/2025.
   b. Use an 85% Confidence Interval.
   c. Check the Include forecast statistics box.
   d. Leave remaining defaults as is.
3. Use the trendline graphs to determine: (*Hint:* To help identify the answers, display gridlines. Consider changing vertical axis bounds.)
   a. Expected unit sales in October 2025
   b. Expected sales revenue in June 2025
   c. Expected net profits in December 2025
4. Use the Forecast sheets to determine:
   a. Range of expected unit sales in October 2025 (Upper to lower Confidence bounds)
   b. Expected sales revenue in June 2025 (Upper to lower Confidence bounds)
   c. Range of expected net profits in December 2025 (Upper to lower Confidence bounds)
5. To evaluate the Forecast sheets, rerun the forecasts. This time change the Forecast Start date to 1/1/2024 to see what the model would have predicted for 2024. (Leave the confidence level at 85%.) Compare the forecasted results for 2024 to the actual results for 2024. Were the predictions higher or lower than the actual results? What could have caused the differences?

LO21-2, 4 **DA21-2. Forecasting Using Tableau**
Available in myBusinessCourse, this problem uses Tableau to forecast sales and net profits.

LO21-1, 2 **DA21-3. Analyzing Revenue Budget Data**
Access the data file from the **Connecticut Office of the State Comptroller** available on the textbook website and answer the following questions.

REQUIRED
a. Prepare a PivotChart showing the revenue actual totals by revenue category in a bar chart. *Hint:* With your cursor on a cell in the worksheet, click on Insert, PivotChart. Drag Revenue category into Axis (Rows) and Actual Amount into Values. Right click on chart to Select a new chart type and choose Bar chart.
b. Add two chart slicers: one for Fiscal Year and one for Fund type in order to capture data only for 2022 and for General fund. Add data labels to columns. *Hint:* Under the "PivotChart Analyze" label, select Insert slicer and select Fiscal year. Repeat steps but now select Fund type. To add data labels, with cursor on a bar (make sure all bars are highlighted), right click and select Add data labels.
c. Sort bar chart from the largest expenditure to the smallest.
d. Using your data visualization, answer the following questions.
   1. What are the top three revenue sources and dollar amounts for the General fund in 2022?
   2. What is the dollar amount of revenue for the category "Cigarettes and Tobacco"?
   3. Display the amounts as a percentage of the grand total. Starting from the category with the highest percentage, what categories make up 94.46% of the total? *Hint:* Open the dropdown menu next to the amount field in the Values section. Select Value Field Settings and open the Show values as tab. Select % of Grand Total.
e. Create a revenue budget for 2023 using the incremental approach: increase each 2022 category by 2% as the basis for your 2023 revenue budget. Round the amounts to millions of dollar. *Hint:* Create an Excel worksheet using the data from your summary table. Arrange your budget from the largest to the smallest dollar amounts.
f. What are some strengths and weaknesses of using the incremental approach to budgeting?

DATA VISUALIZATION

Data Visualization Activities are available in myBusinessCourse. These assignments use Tableau Dashboards to expose students to visual depictions of data and introduce students to data analytics through data visualizations. These exercises are easily assignable and auto graded by MBC.

QUESTIONS

Q21-1. Does budgeting require formal or informal planning? What are some advantages of this style of management?

Q21-2. Identify the advantages and disadvantages of the incremental approach to budgeting.

Q21-3. Explain zero-based budgeting.

Q21-4. How does activity-based budgeting predict a cost objective's budget?

Q21-5. Explain the continuous improvement concept of budgeting.

Q21-6. Which budget brings together all other budgets? How is this accomplished?

Q21-7. What budgets are normally used to support the cash budget? What is the net result of cash budget preparations?

Q21-8. Define *budgeted financial statements*.

Q21-9. After a budget is drafted but before it is finalized, what considerations should management make?

Q21-10. Identify the two budgets that are part of the master budget of a manufacturing organization but not part of the master budget of a merchandising organization.

Q21-11. Contrast the top-down and bottom-up approaches to budget preparation.

Q21-12. Is budgetary slack a desirable feature? Can it be prevented? Why or why not?

Q21-13. Why are annual budgets not always desirable? What are some alternative budget periods?

Q21-14. Explain how continuous budgeting works.

Q21-15. In addition to the sales forecast, what forecasts are used in budgeting?

Q21-16. Why should motivational considerations be a part of budget planning and utilization? List several ways to motivate employees with budgets.

Assignments with the MBC logo in the margin are available in BusinessCourse. See the Preface of the book for details.

MINI EXERCISES

M21-17. Output/Input Budget — LO21-1

Vinyard Clinic has the following resource input information available for a routine physical examination.
- Each exam normally requires 0.75 hour of examining room time, including
  - 30 minutes of nursing services,
  - 15 minutes of physician services.
- Each exam also utilizes one package of examination supplies costing $50 each.
- Including benefits, physicians earn $90/hour and nurses earn $35/hour.
- Variable overhead is budgeted at $15 per examining room hour and fixed overhead is budgeted at $8,000 per month.

REQUIRED

a. Prepare an output/input budget for October when 500 routine examinations are planned.

b. Discuss some of the likely benefits to Vinyard Clinic of dedicating time to go through the budgeting process.

M21-18. Incremental Budget — LO21-1

Wood County uses an incremental approach to budgeting. The current year cash budget for the Wood County Department of Motor Vehicles is presented as follows.

Supplies	$ 12,000
Temporary and seasonal wages	32,000
Wages of full-time employees	200,000
Supervisor salaries	60,000
Rent	48,000
Insurance	16,000
Utilities	10,000
Miscellaneous	9,600
Contingencies and equipment	25,000
Total	$412,600

REQUIRED

Prepare an incremental cash budget for next year, assuming the planned total budget increase is 3%. Budget details include a budget increment for salaries and wages of 3%, no change in rent, and 2.5% increases in the budget for supplies and miscellaneous. Utility companies have received approvals for rate increases amounting to 2% and insurance companies have announced an increase in premiums of 4%. (*Hint:* The Contingencies and equipment budget is a plug.)

LO21-2 **M21-19. Purchases Budget in Units and Dollars**

Thunder Road Guitars specializes in vintage, used, and rare guitars. Assume budgeted sales for the first six months of the year are as follows.

Month	Unit Sales	Month	Unit Sales
January	15	April	18
February	12	May	22
March	16	June	20

Beginning inventory for the year is 7 units. The budgeted inventory at the end of a month is 50% of units to be sold the following month. Purchase price per unit is $800.

REQUIRED

Prepare a purchases budget in units and dollars for each month, January through May.

LO21-2 **M21-20. Cash Budget**

Patrick's Retail Company is planning a cash budget for the next three months. Estimated sales revenue is as follows.

Month	Sales Revenue	Month	Sales Revenue
January	$250,000	March	$400,000
February	350,000	April	375,000

All sales are on credit; 75% is collected during the month of sale, and 25% is collected during the next month. Cost of goods sold is 70% of sales. Payments for merchandise sold are made in the month following the month of sale. Operating expenses total $125,000 per month and are paid during the month incurred. The cash balance on February 1 is estimated to be $55,000.

REQUIRED

Prepare monthly cash budgets for February, March, and April.

LO21-3 **M21-21. Production and Purchases Budgets in Units**

At the end of business on June 30, the PE Rug Company had 35,000 square yards of rugs and 100,000 pounds of raw materials on hand. Budgeted sales for the third quarter are as follows.

Month	Sales
July	50,000 sq. yards
August	35,000 sq. yards
September	42,000 sq. yards
October	48,000 sq. yards

The PE Rug Company wants to have sufficient square yards of finished product on hand at the end of each month to meet 60% of the following month's budgeted sales and sufficient pounds of raw materials to meet 40% of the following month's production requirements. Seven pounds of raw materials are required to produce one square yard of carpeting.

REQUIRED

Prepare a (1) production budget for the months of July, August, and September and (2) a purchases budget in units for the months of July and August.

LO21-3 **M21-22. Manufacturing Cost Budget**

Assume Carolina Table, a furniture manufacturer located in South Carolina, produces a conference table with the following standard costs.

Unit costs		
Direct materials		
Wood: 24 square feet at $35	$840	
Hardware kits (screws, etc.)	20	$ 860
Direct labor 0.75 hours at $40 per hour		30
Variable overhead, per unit		25
Total variable costs per unit		$ 915
Fixed costs per month (rent, utilities, supervision)		$91,250

Management plans to produce 250 units in April.

REQUIRED
Prepare a manufacturing cost budget for April.

M21-23. Identifying Types and Characteristics of Budgets

Gap Inc. has several subsidiary companies including **Gap**, **Banana Republic**, **Old Navy**, and **Athleta**. Identify one of the following terms that most appropriately describes each of the hypothetical six scenarios below. Use each term only once.

Terms: budget with budgetary slack, life-cycle budget, participative budget, rolling budget, top-down budget, unethical budget

1. Athleta developed a new style of travel waist bag that has an expected life-cycle of only two years. For production planning purposes, management developed a two-year sales budget for the new product.
2. Individual Athleta store managers submitted individual store sales budget estimates for next year to the corporate managers of the Athleta subsidiary. Sales budgets were reviewed and were determined to be reasonably attainable. Corporate managers from the Athleta subsidiary met with other subsidiary managers in San Francisco to finalize the sales budget for Gap Inc.
3. Individual Athleta store managers submitted individual store sales budget estimates for next year to the corporate managers of the Athleta subsidiary. Sales budgets were reviewed and for one store, were determined to be extremely understated. Corporate managers of Athleta reviewed the outlier and determined that the understatement was deliberate.
4. Individual Athleta store managers submitted individual store sales budget estimates for next year to the corporate managers of the Athleta subsidiary. Sales budgets were reviewed and for a few stores, were determined to be easily attainable, if not understated. Corporate managers of Athleta reviewed these budgets with the individual store managers and adjustments were made.
5. A sales budget for the Athleta subsidiary for next year was prepared at Gap Inc.'s corporate headquarters in San Francisco and communicated to the Athleta subsidiary.
6. Athleta prepared a 12-month budget for the current year. On January 31, management finalized a budget for the month of January of the following year in order to still have budgetary information for the next full twelve months.

EXERCISES

E21-24 Discussing the Benefits of Budgeting

Assume Mark Fisher was recently hired as an intern at **Overstock.com, Inc.**, an online retailer of price-competitive furnishings and accessories. After recently finishing a course in management accounting, Mark asks his manager if he can see a copy of the current year's operating budget. His manager replies that as a newly publicly-traded company, they are too busy focusing on day-to-day operations to take the time to create a budget.

REQUIRED
Discuss some ways that an operating budget might benefit Overstock.com, Inc.

E21-25. Activity-Based Budget

Highland Industries has the following budget information available for February.

Units manufactured.	25,000
Factory administration	$145,000
Assembly	¼ hour per unit × $20
Direct materials.	3 pounds per unit × $6
Inspection.	$40 per batch of 1,000 units
Manufacturing overhead.	$8 per unit
Product development	$50,000
Setup cost.	$100 per batch of 1,000 units

REQUIRED

a. Use activity-based costing to prepare a manufacturing cost budget for February. Clearly distinguish between unit, batch, product, and facility-level costs.
b. The operating managers at Highland Industries are concerned that the budgeting process is too time-consuming and diverts attention from their current day-to-day responsibilities. Discuss the reasons that Highland should continue budgeting.

LO21-1 E21-26. Product and Department Budgets Using Activity-Based Approach

The following data are from the general records of the Loading Department of Jonah Freight Company for November.

- Cleaning incoming trucks, 30 minutes.
- Obtaining and reviewing shipping documents for loading truck and instructing loaders, 15 minutes.
- Loading truck, 1 hour.
- Cleaning shipping dock and storage area after each loading, 15 minutes.
- Employees perform both cleaning and loading tasks and are currently averaging $25 per hour in wages and benefits.
- The supervisor spends 15% of her time overseeing the cleaning activities; 35% overseeing various loading activities; and the remainder of her time making general plans and managing the department. Her current salary is $6,000 per month.
- Other overhead of the department amounts to $12,000 per month, 30% for cleaning, 65% for loading, and 5% for administration.

REQUIRED

Prepare an activities budget for cleaning and loading in the Loading Department for November, assuming 20 working days and the loading of an average of 25 trucks per day.

LO21-1 E21-27. Activity-Based Budgeting

Assume Mountain View Hospital uses an activity-based budgeting approach for all costs except physician care. Some of the patients are treated in the emergency room as outpatients. Others are admitted to the hospital for additional tests and treatments. Its emergency room has three activity areas with cost drivers as follows.

1. *Reception*—paperwork of incoming patients. Cost driver is the number of forms completed.
2. *Treatment*—initial diagnosis and treatment of patients. Cost driver is the number of diagnoses treated.
3. *Cleaning*—general cleaning plus preparing treatment facilities for next patient. Cost driver is the number of people visiting the emergency room.

		Budgeted Amount of Cost Driver	
Activity Area	**Cost Driver Rates**	**Outpatients**	**Admitted Patients**
Reception.	$ 20	9,200 forms	8,800 forms
Treatment.	175	4,600 diagnoses	2,200 diagnoses
Cleaning.	30	4,500 people	3,000 people

REQUIRED

a. Prepare the total budgeted cost for each activity.
b. How might you adjust the budget approach if you found that outpatients were kept in the emergency room for one hour on average while admitted patients remained for two hours?
c. What advantage does an activity-based approach have over the hospital's former budgeting method of basing the next year's budget on the last year's actual amount plus a percentage increase?

E21-28. Sales Budget

Honolulu Shirt Shop has very seasonal sales. Assume that for next year management is trying to decide whether to establish a sales budget based on average sales or on sales estimated by quarter. The unit sales for next year are expected to be 5% higher than current year sales. Unit shirt sales by quarter for this year were as follows.

	Children's	Women's	Men's	Total
Winter quarter.	80	80	140	300
Spring quarter.	180	120	160	460
Summer quarter.	500	600	260	1,360
Fall quarter.	120	160	160	440
Total.	880	960	720	2,560

Children's T-shirts sell for $10 each, women's sell for $15, and men's sell for $18.

REQUIRED

Assuming a 5% increase in sales, prepare a sales budget for each quarter of the year using the following:
a. Average quarterly sales. (*Hint:* Winter quarter children's shirts are 231 [880 × 1.05 ÷ 4].)
b. Actual quarterly sales. (*Hint:* Winter quarter children's shirts are 84 [80 × 1.05].)
c. Suggest advantages of each method.

E21-29. Cash Budget & Short-Term Financing

Presented are partial October, November, and December cash budgets for Holiday Events.

HOLIDAY EVENTS
Partial Cash Budgets

	October	November	December	Total
Cash balance, beginning	$ 25,000	$?	$?	$?
Collections on sales	100,000	90,000	140,000	?
Cash available for operations	?	?	?	?
Disbursements for operations	(115,000)	(110,000)	(115,000)	?
Ending cash before borrowings or replacements	?	?	?	?
Short-term finance:				
New loans	?	?	?	?
Repayments	?	?	?	?
Interest	?	?	?	?
Cash balance, ending	$?	$?	$?	$?

Loans are obtained in increments of $1,000 at the start of each month to maintain a minimum end-of-month balance of $12,000. Interest is 1% simple interest (no compounding) per month, payable when a loan payment is made. Repayments are made as soon as possible, subject to the minimum end-of-month balance.

REQUIRED

Complete the short-term financing section of the cash budget.

E21-30. Purchases and Cash Budgets

On July 1, MTC Wholesalers had a cash balance of $125,000 and accounts payable of $160,000, and Inventory of $78,000. Actual sales for May and June, and budgeted sales for July, August, September, and October are as follows.

Month	Actual Sales	Month	Budgeted Sales
May.	$250,000	July.	$260,000
June	225,000	August	240,000
		September	270,000
		October.	275,000

All sales are on credit with 60% collected during the month of sale, 30% collected during the next month, and 10% collected during the second month following the month of sale. Cost of goods sold averages 60% of sales revenue. Ending inventory is one-half of the next month's predicted cost of sales. The other half of the merchandise is acquired during the month of sale. All purchases are paid for in the month after purchase. Operating costs are estimated at $95,000 each month and are paid during the month incurred.

REQUIRED

Prepare purchases and cash budgets for July, August, and September.

LO21-2 **E21-31. Cash Receipts**

The sales budget for Andrew Inc. is forecasted as follows.

Month	Sales Revenue
May..........	$150,000
June..........	175,000
July..........	160,000
August........	200,000

To prepare a cash budget, the company must determine the budgeted cash collections from sales. Historically, the following trend has been established regarding cash collection of sales.

- 60% in the month of sale.
- 20% in the month following sale.
- 15% in the second month following sale.
- 5% uncollectible.

The company gives a 2% cash discount for payments made by customers during the month of sale. The accounts receivable balance on April 30 is $85,000, of which $25,000 represents uncollected March sales and $60,000 represents uncollected April sales. (*Hint:* For collections of March and April receivables, start by determining total sales for the month. Assume the normal sales pattern.)

REQUIRED

Prepare a schedule of budgeted cash collections from sales for May, June, and July. Include a three-month summary of estimated cash collections.

LO21-2 **E21-32. Cash Disbursements**

Assume Stimson Lumber, headquartered in Portland, Oregon, is in the process of preparing its budget for next year. Cost of goods sold has been estimated at 60% of sales. Lumber purchases and payments are to be made during the month preceding the month of sale. Wages are estimated at 20% of sales and are paid during the month of sale. Other operating costs amounting to 5% of sales are to be paid in the month following the month of sale. Additionally, a monthly lease payment of $10,000 is paid for computer services. Sales revenue is forecast as follows.

Month	Sales Revenue
February........	$340,000
March..........	420,000
April...........	440,000
May............	520,000
June...........	480,000
July...........	560,000

REQUIRED

Prepare a schedule of cash disbursements for April, May, and June.

LO21-2 **E21-33. Cash Disbursements**

Assume that Ringwood Manufacturing manages its cash flow from its home office. Ringwood controls cash disbursements by category and month. In setting its budget for the next six months, beginning in July, it used the following managerial guidelines.

Category	Guidelines
Purchases...........	Pay 60% in current month and 40% in following month.
Payroll.............	Pay half in current and half in following month.
Loan payments......	Pay total amount due each month.

Predicted activity for selected months follow.

Category	May	June	July	August
Purchases............	$75,000	$80,000	$70,000	$85,000
Payroll..............	45,000	40,000	50,000	45,000
Loan payments.......	15,000	15,000	15,000	15,000

REQUIRED
Prepare a schedule showing cash disbursements by account for July and August.

E21-34. Budgeted Income Statement

Quality Wool Company, a merchandising company, is developing its master budget for next year. The income statement for the current year is as follows.

QUALITY WOOL COMPANY Income Statement For Year Ending December 31	
Gross sales.	$1,200,000
Less uncollectible accounts	(26,000)
Collected sales.	1,174,000
Cost of goods sold	(780,000)
Profit before operating expense	394,000
Operating expenses (including $15,000 depreciation).	(206,000)
Income before tax.	$ 188,000

The following are management's goals and forecasts for next year.

1. Selling prices will increase by 3%, and sales volume will increase by 5%.
2. The cost of merchandise will increase by 2%.
3. All operating expenses are fixed. Price increases for operating expenses will be 4%. The company uses straight-line depreciation.
4. The estimated uncollectibles are 2% of budgeted sales.

REQUIRED
Prepare a budgeted functional income statement for next year.

E21-35. Budgeted Income Statement with CVP

Assume **Barnes & Noble** is planning a budget for one of its stores. The estimate of sales revenue is $2,000,000 and the cost of goods sold is 70% of sales revenue. Depreciation on the office building and fixtures is budgeted at $36,000. Salaries and wages are budgeted at $375,000. Advertising has been budgeted at $12,000, and other operating costs should amount to $15,000. Income tax is estimated at 20% of operating income.

REQUIRED
a. Prepare a budgeted income statement for next year.
b. Assuming management desired an after-tax income of $150,000, determine the necessary sales volume.

E21-36. Production and Purchases Budgets

At the beginning of October, Comfy Cushions had 3,400 cushions and 8,500 pounds of raw materials on hand. Budgeted sales for the next three months are as follows.

Month	Sales
October.	11,000 cushions
November.	12,000 cushions
December.	10,000 cushions

Comfy Cushions wants to have sufficient raw materials on hand at the end of each month to meet 20% of the following month's production requirements and sufficient cushions on hand at the end of each month to meet 30% of the following month's budgeted sales. Four pounds of raw materials, at a standard cost of $1.10 per pound, are required to produce each cushion.

REQUIRED
a. Prepare a production budget for October and November.
b. Prepare a purchases budget in units and dollars for October.

E21-37. Distinguishing Between Budgetary Slack and Unethical Behavior

Refer to the information in E21-36 but also assume that the sales budget for October through December for Comfy Cushions was finalized by the sales manager. The bonus structure for the sale staff is determined based on performance compared to budget. For example, a full bonus is earned if the sales department sells cushions equal to 100% of the budget.

REQUIRED

a. Explain how the bonus structure at Comfy Cushions could encourage budgetary slack?
b. In reviewing the monthly budgets, let's assume that the president of the company determined that the December sales budget of 10,000 cushions was understated and a more realistic estimate of sales is 11,000. Is the behavior of the sales staff considered to be unethical?

LO21-3

Advance Drainage Systems, Inc.
NYSE :: WMS

E21-38. Production and Purchases Budgets

Advance Drainage Systems produces thermoplastic corrugated pipe. Assume budgeted unit sales for one of its products (a 12" by 20-ft pipe) over the next several months are as follows.

Month	Sales
September	3,000
October	2,500
November	1,500
December	500

At the beginning of September, 850 units of finished goods were in inventory. During the final third of the year, as road construction declines, plans are to have an inventory of finished goods equal to 30% of the following month's sales. Each unit of finished goods requires 70 pounds of raw materials at a cost of $1.50 per pound. Management wishes to maintain month-end inventories of raw materials equal to 40% of the following month's needs. Sixty thousand pounds of raw materials were on hand at the start of September.

REQUIRED

a. Prepare a production budget for September, October, and November.
b. Prepare a purchases budget in units and dollars for September and October.

PROBLEMS

LO21-2

ODP Corporation
NASDAQ :: ODP

P21-39. Cash Budget

Assume all **ODP Corporation** stores do cash budgeting every quarter. One store is planning its cash needs for the third quarter of the year, and the following information is available to assist in preparing a cash budget. Budgeted income statements for July through October are as follows.

	July	August	September	October
Sales	$45,000	$52,000	$60,000	$75,000
Cost of goods sold	23,500	25,500	30,500	35,000
Gross profit	21,500	26,500	29,500	40,000
Less other expenses				
Selling	6,000	8,000	8,500	10,500
Administrative	9,100	10,500	8,500	9,400
Total	(15,100)	(18,500)	(17,000)	(19,900)
Net income	$ 6,400	$ 8,000	$12,500	$20,100

Additional information follows:

1. Other expenses, which are paid monthly, include $3,500 of depreciation per month.
2. Sales are 44% for cash and 56% on credit.
3. Credit sales are collected 50% in the month of sale, 35% one month after sale, and 15% two months after sale. May sales were $40,000, and June sales were $42,000.
4. Merchandise is paid for 50% in the month of purchase; the remaining 50% is paid in the following month. Accounts payable for merchandise at June 30 totaled $12,000.
5. The store maintains its ending inventory levels at 30% of the cost of goods to be sold in the following month. The inventory at June 30 is $7,600.
6. An equipment note of $10,000 per month is being paid through August.
7. The store must maintain a cash balance of at least $10,000 at the end of each month. The cash balance on June 30 is $10,000.
8. The store can borrow from its bank as needed. Borrowings and repayments must be in multiples of $100. All borrowings take place at the beginning of a month, and all repayments are

made at the end of a month. When the principal is repaid, interest on the repayment is also paid. The interest rate is 6% per year.

REQUIRED

a. Prepare a monthly schedule of budgeted operating cash receipts for July, August, and September.
b. Prepare a monthly purchases budget and a schedule of budgeted cash payments for purchases for July, August, and September.
c. Prepare a monthly cash budget for July, August, and September. Show borrowings from the store's bank and repayments to the bank as needed to maintain the minimum cash balance.

P21-40. Cash Budget LO21-2

The Williams Supply Company sells for $50 one product that it purchases for $20. Budgeted sales in total dollars for the year are $3,000,000. The sales information needed for preparing the July budget follows.

Month	Sales Revenue
May	$175,000
June	240,000
July	295,000
August	320,000

Account balances at July 1 include these.

Cash	$125,000
Merchandise inventory	47,200
Accounts receivable (sales)	84,530
Accounts payable (purchases)	47,200

The company pays for one-half of its purchases in the month of purchase and the remainder in the following month. End-of-month inventory must be 40% of the budgeted sales in units for the next month. A 2% cash discount on sales is allowed if payment is made during the month of sale. Experience indicates that 60% of the billings will be collected during the month of sale, 25% in the following month, 12% in the second following month, and 3% will be uncollectible. Total budgeted selling and administrative expenses (excluding bad debts) for the fiscal year are estimated at $1,200,000, of which three-fourths is fixed expense (inclusive of a $36,000 annual depreciation charge). Fixed expenses are incurred evenly during the year. The other selling and administrative expenses vary with sales. Expenses are paid during the month incurred.

REQUIRED

a. Prepare a schedule of estimated cash collections for July.
b. Prepare a schedule of estimated July cash payments for purchases. *Hint:* Start by doing a purchase budget.
c. Prepare schedules of July selling and administrative expenses, separately identifying those requiring cash disbursements.
d. Prepare a schedule of cash receipts over disbursements assuming no equipment purchases or loan payments.

P21-41. Budgeting Purchases, Revenues, Expenses, and Cash in a Service Organization LO21-2

Wauconda Medical Center is located in a summer resort community. During the summer months (June through August), the center operates an outpatient clinic for the treatment of minor injuries and illnesses. The clinic is administered as a separate department within the hospital. It has its own staff and maintains its own financial records. All patients requiring extensive or intensive care are referred to other hospital departments.

An analysis of past operating data for the outpatient clinic reveals the following.

- Staff: Seven full-time employees with total monthly salaries of $42,000. On a monthly basis, one additional staff member is hired for every 500 budgeted patient visits in excess of 3,000, at a cost of $7,000 per month.
- Facilities: Monthly facility costs, including depreciation of $2,500, total $15,000.
- Supplies: The supplies expense averages $20 per patient visit. The center maintains an end-of-month supplies inventory equal to 10% of the predicted needs of the following month, with a minimum ending inventory of $4,000, which is also the desired inventory at the end of August.
- Additional variable patient costs, such as medications, are charged directly to the patient by the hospital pharmacy.

- Payments: All staff and maintenance expenses are paid in the month the cost is incurred. Supplies are purchased at cost directly from the hospital with an immediate transfer of cash from the clinic cash account to the hospital cash account.
- Collections: The average bill for services rendered is $75. Of the total bills, 40% are paid in cash at the time the service is rendered, 10% are never paid, and the remaining 50% are covered by insurance. In the past, insurance companies have disallowed 30% of the claims filed and paid the balance two months after services are rendered.
- May 30 status: At the end of May, the clinic had $15,000 in cash and supplies costing $5,000.

Budgeted patient visits for next summer are as follows.

Month	Patient Visits
June	3,000
July	3,500
August	4,500

REQUIRED

Complete the following requirements for the Wauconda Outpatient Clinic.

a. Prepare a supplies purchases budget for June, July, and August with a total column.
b. Prepare a revenue and expense budget for June, July, and August with a total column.
c. Prepare a cash budget for June, July, and August with a total column. (*Hint:* See requirement *d.*)
d. Is the cash budget for the annual summer outpatient clinic feasible? If not, make appropriate recommendations for management's consideration.

LO21-2 P21-42. Developing a Master Budget for a Merchandising Organization

Assume **Nordstrom** prepares budgets quarterly. The following information is available for use in planning the second quarter budgets for one of its stores.

NORDSTROM
Balance Sheet
March 31

(in thousands)

Assets		Liabilities and Stockholders' Equity	
Cash	$ 2,525	Merchandise purchases payable	$ 2,400
Accounts receivable	2,040	Dividends payable	710
Inventory	3,400	Stockholders' equity	8,005
Prepaid insurance	150		
Fixtures	3,000		
Total assets	$11,115	Total liabilities and equity	$11,115

Actual and forecasted sales for selected months in the upcoming year are as follows.

Month (in thousands)	Sales Revenue
January	$2,600
February	2,700
March	3,000
April	3,600
May	3,800
June	3,500
July	3,200
August	4,000

Monthly operating expenses (in thousands) are as follows.

Wages and salaries	$750
Depreciation	75
Advertising	55
Other costs	350

Cash dividends for the store of $710 thousand are declared during the third month of each quarter and are paid during the first month of the following quarter. Operating expenses, except insurance, rent, and depreciation are paid as incurred. The prepaid insurance is for five more months. Cost of goods sold is equal to 60% of sales. Ending inventories are sufficient for 150% of the next month's cost of sales. Purchases during any given month are paid in full during the following month. Cash sales account for 50% of the revenue. Of the credit sales, 60% are collected in the next month and 40% are collected in the month after. Money can be borrowed and repaid in multiples of $100 thousand at an interest rate of 12% per year. The company desires a minimum cash balance of $2 million on the first of each month. At the time the principal is repaid, interest is paid on the portion of principal that is repaid. All borrowing is at the beginning of the month, and all repayment is at the end of the month. Money is never repaid at the end of the month it is borrowed.

REQUIRED

a. Prepare a purchases budget for each month of the second quarter ending June 30.
b. Prepare a cash receipts schedule for each month of the second quarter ending June 30. Do not include borrowings.
c. Prepare a cash disbursements schedule for each month of the second quarter ending June 30. Do not include repayments of borrowings.
d. Prepare a cash budget for each month of the second quarter ending June 30. Include budgeted borrowings and repayments.
e. Prepare an income statement for each month of the second quarter ending June 30.
f. Prepare a budgeted balance sheet as of June 30.

P21-43. Developing a Master Budget for a Manufacturing Organization

Cubs Incorporated manufactures a product with a selling price of $75 per unit. Units and monthly cost data follow.

Variable	
Selling and administrative.............................	$ 3 per unit sold
Direct materials...	15 per unit manufactured
Direct labor...	5 per unit manufactured
Variable manufacturing overhead.......................	7 per unit manufactured
Fixed	
Selling and administrative.............................	$160,000 per month
Manufacturing (including depreciation of $15,000).....	150,000 per month

Cubs Inc. pays all bills in the month incurred. All sales are on account with 50% collected the month of sale and the balance collected the following month. There are no sales discounts or bad debts.

Cubs Inc. desires to maintain an ending finished goods inventory equal to 40% of the following month's sales and a raw materials inventory equal to 20% of the following month's production. January 1 inventories are in line with these policies.

Actual unit sales for December and budgeted unit sales for January, February, and March are as follows.

CUBS INCORPORATED
Sales Budget
For the Months of January, February, and March

Month	December Actual	January Budget	February Budget	March Budget
Sales—Units......................	10,000	12,000	11,500	12,500
Sales—Dollars	$750,000	$900,000	$862,500	$937,500

Additional information
- The January 1 beginning cash is projected as $10,000.
- For the purpose of operational budgeting, units in the January 1 inventory of finished goods are valued at variable manufacturing cost.
- Each unit of finished product requires one unit of raw materials.
- Cubs Inc. intends to pay a cash dividend of $15,000 in January

REQUIRED

a. A production budget for January and February.
b. A purchases budget in units for January.
c. A manufacturing cost budget for January.
d. A cash budget for January.
e. A budgeted contribution income statement for January.

LO21-2, 3 **P21-44. Risk Management in a Manufacturing Organization**

REQUIRED

Continuing problem P21-43, management is concerned that their supplier of raw materials will have a strike. Determine the budget implications if management plans to increase the January-end raw materials inventory to 150% of February's production needs. Offer any recommendations you believe appropriate.

LO21-2, 3 **P21-45. Developing a Master Budget for a Manufacturing Organization: Challenge Problem**

Computer Accessories Inc. assembles a computer networking device from kits of imported components. You have been asked to develop a quarterly and annual operating budget and pro forma income statements for next year. You have obtained the following information.

Beginning-of-year balances			
Cash	$ 75,000		
Accounts receivable (previous quarter's sales)	$245,000		
Raw materials	950 kits		
Finished goods	1,500 kits		
Accounts payable (materials)	$125,000		
Borrowed funds	$ 30,000		
Desired end-of-year inventory balances			
Raw materials	1,000 kits		
Finished goods	1,600 kits		
Desired end-of-quarter balances			
Cash	$ 30,000		
Raw materials as a portion of the following quarter's production	0.20		
Finished goods as a portion of the following quarter's sales	0.30		
Manufacturing costs			
Standard cost per unit	Units	Unit price	Total
Raw materials	1 kit	$75.00	$75.00
Direct labor hours at rate	0.50 hour	$30.00	15.00
Variable overhead/labor hour	0.50 hour	$ 5.00	2.50
Total standard variable cost			$92.50
Fixed cost per quarter			
Cash	$110,000		
Depreciation	15,000		
Total	$125,000		
Selling and administrative costs			
Variable cost per unit	$8.00		
Fixed costs per quarter			
Cash	$150,000		
Depreciation	7,500		
Total	$157,500		
Interest rate per quarter	0.015		
Portion of sales collected			
Quarter of sale	0.70		
Subsequent quarter	0.29		
Bad debts	0.01		
Portion of purchases paid			
Quarter of purchase	0.60		
Subsequent quarter	0.40		
Unit selling price	$225.00		

Sales forecast

Quarter	First	Second	Third	Fourth
Unit sales	4,400	4,600	4,500	4,800

Additional information
- All cash payments except purchases are made quarterly as incurred.
- All borrowings occur at the start of a quarter.
- All repayments on borrowings occur at the end of a quarter.
- At the time the principal is repaid, interest is paid on the portion of principal that is repaid.
- Borrowings and repayments may be made in any amount.

REQUIRED
a. A sales budget for each quarter and the year.
b. A production budget for each quarter and the year.
c. A purchases budget for each quarter and the year.
d. A manufacturing cost budget for each quarter and the year.
e. A selling and administrative expense budget for each quarter and the year.
f. A cash budget for each quarter and the year.
g. A pro forma contribution income statement for each quarter and the year.

P21-46. Budgeting practices and processes   LO21-2, 3, 4

The executives at Stark Inc., a plumbing supply manufacturer, recently reviewed production capacity for the upcoming year and set production budgets. Based on the number of units that they expected to produce, they budgeted sales and set sales targets for each of their retail locations. They did not ask for the input of the individual store managers as they believed that they had sufficient information and they wanted to ensure that the store targets were not easily attainable. When the actual sales numbers started to come in, they were much lower than the budget. In investigating the variance, the company found that one location had a new competitor that had opened just down the street, and another had significant road construction that impeded the traffic flow and cut down on customers. There were also some new products on the market that were cutting into the company's market share. Because of the missed sales budget, the company had over-produced resulting in excess inventory.

REQUIRED
1. Explain the role of a sales budget in the development of the annual profit plan.
2. Identify four factors that should be considered when preparing a sales forecast.
3. Which two factors did management fail to consider in this scenario and what was the impact?
4. Discuss top-down and bottom-up budgets and identify which type is described in the scenario.
5. Identify and describe two best practice guidelines for the budget process.
6. Identify and describe four characteristics that define a successful budgeting process.
7. Discuss the financial impact of excess inventory.

CMA adapted

P21-47. Developing a Master Budget   LO21-2, 3

Great Rivers International is a global company operating mainly in North America, Europe, and Asia. Two years ago, the company decided to enter the African market through its subsidiary in Africa, Nile River Company. Nile River Company has just completed building its pharmaceutical plant in Africa. The total project cost was $26.1 million, as shown below.

Building.	$10.0 million
Machinery and equipment	15.0 million
Furniture and fixtures	0.5 million
Vehicles	0.2 million
Working capital	0.4 million
Total	$26.1 million

Next year will be the first year of operation for Nile River Company after almost two years being in a development stage. The company has formulated its strategic plan and an operational plan for next year. Management intends to translate the operational plan into a master budget. The finance manager at Nile River Company is responsible for all planning and budgeting activities in the company. Next year's master budget will be the first master budget to be prepared for Nile River Company.

REQUIRED
1. Define the master budget and outline the process that should be followed in order to prepare the master budget at Nile River Company.
2. Identify the components of the sales budget. Explain the interrelationships of the sales budget with the other components of the master budget.
3. Assume that the company is expecting to sell 10,000 units of product during its first year of operation and that the expected annual sales growth is 5% during the second year of operation. Assume further that the first year's desired ending inventory is 30% of the following year's sales. What will be the budgeted production quantity during the first year of operation? Show your calculations.
4. Other than sales, identify two other budgets that should be prepared in order to compute budgeted net operating income.
5. Identify and explain three characteristics of a successful budgeting process.

CMA adapted

CASES AND PROJECTS

LO21-4 **C21-48. Behavioral Implications of Budgeting**

Cindy Jones, controller of Systematic Designs, believes that effective budgeting greatly assists in meeting the organization's goals and objectives. She argues that the budget serves as a blueprint for the operating activities during each reporting period, making it an important control device. She believes that sound management evaluations can be based on the comparisons of performance and budgetary schedules and that employees respond more favorably when they participate in the budgetary process. Kevin Dobbs, treasurer of Systematic Designs, agrees that budgeting is essential for overall organization success, but he argues that human resources are too valuable to spend much time planning and preparing the budgetary process. He thinks that the roles people play in budgetary preparation are not important in the final analysis of a budget's effectiveness.

REQUIRED

Contrast the participative versus imposed budgeting concepts and indicate how the ideas of Jones and Dobbs fit the two categories.

LO21-4 **C21-49. Behavioral Considerations and Budgeting**

Anthony Wagner, the controller in the Division of Transportation for the state, recognizes the importance of the budgetary process for planning, control, and motivation purposes. He believes that a properly implemented participative budgeting process for planning purposes and a management by exception reporting procedure based on that budget will motivate his subordinates to improve productivity within their particular departments. Based on this philosophy, Wagner has implemented the following budget procedures.

- An appropriation target figure is given to each department manager. This amount is the maximum funding that each department can expect to receive in the next fiscal year.
- Department managers develop their individual budgets within the following spending constraints as directed by the controller's staff.
    1. Expenditure requests cannot exceed the appropriation target.
    2. All fixed expenditures should be included in the budget; these should include items such as contracts and salaries at current levels.
    3. All government projects directed by higher authority should be included in the budget in their entirety.
- The controller consolidates the departmental budget requests from the various departments into one budget that is to be submitted for the entire division.
- Upon final budget approval by the legislature, the controller's staff allocates the appropriation to the various departments on instructions from the division manager. However, a specified percentage of each department's appropriation is held back in anticipation of potential budget cuts and special funding needs. The amount and use of this contingency fund are left to the discretion of the division manager.
- Each department is allowed to adjust its budget when necessary to operate within the reduced appropriation level. However, as stated in the original directive, specific projects authorized by higher authority must remain intact.
- The final budget is used as the basis of control for a management by exception form of reporting. Excessive expenditures by account for each department are highlighted on a monthly basis. Department managers are expected to account for all expenditures over budget. Fiscal responsibility is an important factor in the overall performance evaluation of department managers.

Wagner believes that his policy of allowing the department managers to participate in the budget process and then holding them accountable for their performance is essential, especially during these times of limited resources. He also believes that department managers will be positively motivated to increase the efficiency and effectiveness of their departments because they have provided input into the initial budgetary process and are required to justify any unfavorable performances.

REQUIRED

a. Explain the operational and behavioral benefits that generally are attributed to a participative budgeting process.
b. Identify deficiencies in Wagner's participative budgetary policy for planning and performance evaluation purposes. For each deficiency identified, recommend how the deficiency can be corrected.

CMA adapted

C21-50. Budgetary Slack with Ethical Considerations

Karen Bailey was promoted to department manager of a production unit in Parkway Industries three years ago. She enjoys her job except for the evaluation measures that are based on the department's budget. After three years of consistently poor annual evaluations based on a set annual budget, she has decided to improve the evaluation situation. At a recent budget meeting of junior-level managers, the topic of budgetary slack was discussed as a means to maintain some consistency in budgeting matters. As a result of this meeting, Bailey decided to take the following steps in preparing the upcoming year's budget.

1. Use the top quartile for all wage and salary categories.
2. Select the optimistic values for the estimated production ranges for the coming year. These are provided by the marketing department.
3. Use the average of the three months in the current year with poorest production efficiency as benchmarks of success for the coming year.
4. Base equipment charges (primarily depreciation) on replacement values furnished by the purchasing department.
5. Base other fixed costs on current cost plus an inflation rate estimated for the coming year.
6. Use the average of the 10 newly hired employees' performance as a basis of labor efficiency for the coming year.

REQUIRED

a. For each item on Bailey's list, explain whether it will create budgetary slack. Use numerical examples as necessary to illustrate.
b. Given the company's use of static budgets as one of the performance evaluation measures of its managers, can the managers justify the use of built-in budgetary slack?
c. What would you recommend as a means for Bailey to improve the budgeting situation in the company? Provide some specific examples of how the budgeting process might be improved.

C21-51. Budgetary Slack with Ethical Considerations

Norton Company, a manufacturer of infant furniture and strollers, is in the initial stages of preparing the annual budget for next year. Scott Ford recently joined Norton's accounting staff and is interested to learn as much as possible about the company's budgeting process. During a recent lunch with Marge Atkins, sales manager, and Pete Granger, production manager, Ford initiated the following conversation.

Ford: Since I'm new around here and am going to be involved with the preparation of the annual budget, I'd be interested to learn how the two of you estimate sales and production numbers.

Atkins: We start out very methodically by looking at recent history, discussing what we know about current accounts, potential customers, and the general state of consumer spending. Then we add that usual dose of intuition to come up with the best forecast we can.

Granger: I usually take the sales projections as the basis for my projections. Of course, we have to make an estimate of what this year's closing inventories will be, which is sometimes difficult.

Ford: Why does that present a problem? There must have been an estimate of closing inventories in the budget for the current year.

Granger: Those numbers aren't always reliable since Marge makes some adjustments to the sales numbers before passing them on to me.

Ford: What kind of adjustments?

Atkins: Well, we don't want to fall short of the sales projections, so we generally give ourselves a little breathing room by lowering the initial sales projection anywhere from 5% to 10%.

Granger: So, you can see why this year's budget is not a very reliable starting point. We always have to adjust the projected production rates as the year progresses; of course, this changes the ending inventory estimates. By the way, we make similar adjustments to expenses by adding at least 10% to the estimates; I think everyone around here does the same thing.

REQUIRED

a. Marge Atkins and Pete Granger have described the use of budgetary slack.
   1. Explain why Atkins and Granger behave in this manner, and describe the benefits they expect to realize from the use of budgetary slack.
   2. Explain how the use of budgetary slack can adversely affect Atkins and Granger.
b. As a management accountant, Scott Ford believes that the behavior described by Marge Atkins and Pete Granger could be unethical and that he might have an obligation not to support this behavior. Explain why the use of budgetary slack could be unethical.

CMA adapted

SOLUTIONS TO REVIEW PROBLEMS

Review 21-1—Solution

a. Under the output/input approach, the output of units dictates the expected cost inputs. Here budgeted overhead costs are based on the number of budgeted assembly hours.

	Standard	Rechargeable
Direct materials (20,000 × $20)	$400,000	
(50,000 × $14.50)		$ 725,000
Direct assembly labor (20,000 × 0.5 × $18)	180,000	
(50,000 × 0.8 × $18)		720,000
Overhead (20,000 × 0.5 × $8.17)	81,700	
(50,000 × 0.8 × $8.17)		326,800
Total budgeted cost	$661,700	$1,771,800
Unit Cost	$33.085	$35.436

b. Under the activity-based approach, budgeted overhead costs are based on expected activities to produce the products, not only on assembly hours.

	Standard	Rechargeable
Direct materials (20,000 × $20)	$400,000	
(50,000 × $14.50)		$ 725,000
Direct assembly labor (20,000 × 0.5 × $18)	180,000	
(50,000 × 0.8 × $18)		720,000
Setup (1,000 hours × $25)	25,000	
(1,500 hours × $25)		37,500
Engineering and Maintenance (500 hours × $35)	17,500	
(600 hours × $35)		21,000
Inspections (650 inspections × $250)	162,500	
(580 inspections × $250)		145,000
Total budgeted cost	$785,000	$1,648,500
Unit cost	$39.25	$32.97

Review 21-2—Solution

a.

OVERSTOCK.COM
Sales Budget
For Month of April

	Units	Price	Sales
Bath bomb	160,000	$10	$1,600,000
Loofah	240,000	5	1,200,000
Total			$2,800,000

b.

OVERSTOCK.COM
Purchases Budget
For Month of April

	Bath bombs	Loofahs	Total
Units			
Sales needs	160,000	240,000	
Desired ending inventory	12,000	5,000	
Total	172,000	245,000	
Less beginning inventory	(10,000)	(4,000)	
Purchases (in units)	162,000	241,000	
Purchases (in dollars)	$1,296,000	$482,000	$1,778,000

c.

OVERSTOCK.COM
Cash Budget
For Month of April

Cash balance, beginning		$ 400,000
Collections on sales		
Current month's sales ($2,800,000 × 0.70).	$1,960,000	
Previous month's sales ($3,000,000 × 0.29).	870,000	2,830,000
Cash available from operations		3,230,000
Less budgeted disbursements		
March purchases ($1,800,000 × 0.40)	720,000	
April purchases ($1,778,000 × 0.60).	1,066,800	
Wages and salaries.	156,000	
Selling (March)	80,000	
General and administrative ($450,000 − $40,000 depreciation)	410,000	(2,432,800)
Cash balance, ending.		$ 797,200

d.

OVERSTOCK.COM
Budgeted Income Statement
For Month of April

Sales (sales budget).			$2,800,000
Costs of merchandise sold			
Bath bombs (160,000 × $8)	$1,280,000		
Loofahs (240,000 × $2).	480,000	$1,760,000	
Wages and salaries	156,000		
Selling.	80,000		
Bad debt ($2,800,000 × 1%)	28,000		
General and administrative.	450,000	714,000	(2,474,000)
Net income			$ 326,000

Review 21-3—Solution

a.

OVERSTOCK.COM
Sales Budget
For First Quarter

	Units	Price	Sales
Trimmer.	60,000	$100	$ 6,000,000
Chainsaw	40,000	125	5,000,000
Total			$11,000,000

b.

OVERSTOCK.COM
Production Budget
For First Quarter

	Trimmers	Chainsaws
Budget sales.	60,000	40,000
Plus desired ending inventory	25,000	10,000
Total inventory requirements	85,000	50,000
Less beginning inventory	(20,000)	(8,000)
Budgeted production	65,000	42,000

c.

OVERSTOCK.COM
Purchases Budget
For First Quarter

	Trimmers	Chainsaws	Total
Metal purchases			
Production units (production budget)	65,000	42,000	
Metal (pounds)	× 5	× 4	
Production needs (pounds)	325,000	168,000	493,000
Desired ending inventory (pounds)			36,000
Total metal needs (pounds)			529,000
Less beginning inventory (pounds)			(32,000)
Purchases needed (pounds)			497,000
Cost per pound			× $8
Total metal purchases			$3,976,000
Plastic purchases			
Production units (production budget)	65,000	42,000	107,000
Plastic (pounds)			× 3
Production needs (pounds)			321,000
Desired ending inventory (pounds)			32,000
Total plastic needs (pounds)			353,000
Less beginning inventory (pounds)			(29,000)
Purchases needed (pounds)			324,000
Cost per pound			× $5
Total plastic purchases			$1,620,000
Handle purchases			
Production units (production budget)	65,000		65,000
Handles			× 1
Production needs			65,000
Desired ending inventory			7,000
Total handle needs			72,000
Less beginning inventory			(6,000)
Purchases needed			66,000
Cost per handle			× $3
Total handle purchases			$ 198,000
Total purchases			
Metal			$3,976,000
Plastic			1,620,000
Handles			198,000
Total purchases			$5,794,000

d.

OVERSTOCK.COM Manufacturing Cost Budget For First Quarter	Trimmers	Chainsaws	Total
Direct materials			
Metal			
Production units (production budget)	65,000	42,000	
Metal per unit of product (pounds)	× 5	× 4	
Production needs for metal (pounds)	325,000	168,000	
Unit cost	× $8	× $8	
Cost of metal issued to production	$2,600,000	$1,344,000	$3,944,000
Plastic			
Production units (production budget)	65,000	42,000	
Plastic (pounds)	× 3	× 3	
Production needs for plastic (pounds)	195,000	126,000	
Unit cost	× $5	× $5	
Cost of plastic issued to production	$ 975,000	$ 630,000	1,605,000
Handles			
Production units (production budget)	65,000		
Handles	× 1		
Production needs for handles	65,000		
Unit cost	× $3		
Cost of handles issued to production	$ 195,000		195,000
Total			5,744,000
Direct labor			
Budgeted production	65,000	42,000	
Direct labor hours per unit	× 2	× 3	
Total direct labor hours	130,000	126,000	
Labor rate	× $12	× $16	
Labor expenditures	$1,560,000	$2,016,000	3,576,000
Manufacturing overhead			
Variable manufacturing overhead			
Direct labor hours	130,000	126,000	
Variable manufacturing overhead rate	× $1.50	× $1.50	
Total variable overhead	$ 195,000	$ 189,000	384,000
Fixed manufacturing overhead			214,000
Total			$9,918,000

e.

OVERSTOCK.COM Cash Budget For First Quarter		
Cash balance, beginning		$ 1,800,000
Collections on sales		
Current quarter's sales ($11,000,000 × 0.50)	$5,500,000	
Previous quarter's sales ($8,400,000 × 0.50)	4,200,000	9,700,000
Cash available from operations		11,500,000
Less budgeted disbursements		
Materials (purchases budget)	5,794,000	
Labor (manufacturing cost budget)	3,576,000	
Manufacturing overhead (manufacturing cost budget)		
([$384,000 + $214,000] − $156,000 noncash)	442,000	
Selling and administrative ($340,000 − $90,000 depreciation)	250,000	(10,062,000)
Cash balance, ending		$ 1,438,000

f.

OVERSTOCK.COM Contribution Income Statement For First Quarter		
Sales (sales budget)...		$11,000,000
Less variable cost of goods sold		
Trimmers (60,000 × $85.00).................................	$5,100,000	
Chainsaws (40,000 × $99.50)................................	3,980,000	(9,080,000)
Contribution margin		1,920,000
Less fixed costs		
Manufacturing overhead......................................	214,000	
Selling and administrative expenses............................	340,000	(554,000)
Net income..		$ 1,366,000

Review 21-4—Solution

a. 2   *b.* 1   *c.* 4   *d.* 3

Chapter 22
Standard Costs and Performance Reports

LEARNING OBJECTIVES

LO22-1 Explain responsibility accounting. (p. 22-3)

LO22-2 Prepare a performance report for a cost center using a flexible budget. (p. 22-7)

LO22-3 Formulate and interpret direct materials cost variances. (p. 22-11)

LO22-4 Formulate and interpret direct labor cost variances. (p. 22-15)

LO22-5 Formulate and interpret overhead cost variances. (p. 22-17)

LO22-6 Calculate revenue variances and prepare a performance report for a revenue center. (p. 22-20)

LO22-7 Formulate and interpret fixed overhead cost variances (Appendix 22A). (p. 22-24)

LO22-8 Reconcile budgeted and actual income (Appendix 22B). (p. 22-25)

Road Map

LO	Learning Objective | Topics	Page	eLecture	Review	Assignments
LO22-1	**Explain responsibility accounting.** Performance Reports :: Management by Exception :: Controllable Costs :: Uncontrollable Costs :: Organization Structure :: Cost Center :: Profit Center :: Investment Center :: Financial and Nonfinancial Performance Measures	22-3	e22–1	R22-1	M22-16, E22-27, P22-46, P22-47, C22-49, C22-51, **DA22-1**
LO22-2	**Prepare a performance report for a cost center using a flexible budget.** Static Budget :: Flexible Budget :: Flexible Budget Variance :: Activity Variance :: Static Variance :: Standard Cost	22-7	e22–2	R22-2	M22-17, E22-28, E22-29, E22-30, P22-38, P22-42, P22-43, P22-47, P22-48. C22-50, C22-51, **DA22-2**
LO22-3	**Formulate and interpret direct materials cost variances.** Components of Standard Cost Analysis :: Materials Price Variance :: Materials Quantity Variance :: Interpreting Material Variances	22-11	e22–3	R22-3	M22-18, M22-19, E22-31, E22-32, E22-34, P22-39, P22-40, P22-41, P22-42, P22-43, P22-44, P22-47, P22-48, C22-51
LO22-4	**Formulate and interpret direct labor cost variances.** Labor Rate Variance :: Labor Efficiency Variance :: Interpreting Labor Variances	22-15	e22–4	R22-4	M22-20, M22-21, E22-31, E22-32, E22-34, E22-34, P22-39, P22-40, P22-41, P22-42, P22-43, P22-44, P22-47, P22-48, C22-51
LO22-5	**Formulate and interpret overhead cost variances.** Variable Overhead Spending Variance :: Variable Overhead Efficiency Variance :: Interpreting Variable Overhead Variances :: Fixed Overhead Budget Variance	22-17	e22–5	R22-5	M22-22, E22-33, E22-34, P22-40, P22-41, P22-42, P22-43, P22-44, P22-47, P22-48, C22-51
LO22-6	**Calculate revenue variances and prepare a performance report for a revenue center.** Revenue Variance :: Sales Price Variance :: Sales Volume Variance :: Controllable Selling Costs :: Net Sales Volume Variance :: Net Sales Department Variance	22-20	e22–6	R22-6	M22-23, E22-35, P22-46, P22-47, P22-48
LO22-7	**Formulate and interpret fixed overhead cost variances (Appendix 22A).** Fixed Overhead Budget Variance :: Standard Fixed Overhead Rate :: Fixed Overhead Volume Variance	22-24	e22–7	R22-7	M22-24, M22-25, E22-36, P22-45, P22-47, P22-48
LO22-8	**Reconcile budgeted and actual income (Appendix 22B).** Contribution Format :: Assigning Variances to Responsibility Centers :: Reconciliation of Budgeted and Actual Income	22-25	e22–8	R22-8	M22-26, E22-37, P22-46, P22-47, P22-48, C22-52

SAMSONITE INTERNATIONAL S.A.
https://www.samsonite.com

In the last chapter, we discussed how budgeting was critical to planning within a business. But planning is only half of the story. At the end of the period, the operating results are compared to the budget. By evaluating the differences between the budgeted and the actual results, a manager can identify areas of the business that need attention and learn from areas of the business that performed well. We call these differences *budget variances*, and a thorough analysis of these variances aids the manager in controlling the human and physical resources of the business and planning for the future.

To effectively control the business through variance analysis, it is important that the lines of responsibility are clearly defined among the managers. Managers (and the people who evaluate their results) need to understand who is responsible for revenues, costs, profits, capital investments, or some combination of those elements. This assignment of responsibility prevents managers from "passing the buck" when something goes wrong. Consider the case of Samsonite. Samsonite is the world's largest travel luggage company, currently listed on the Stock Exchange of Hong Kong Limited. The company was founded over 100 years ago in Denver, Colorado. The company's focus is on premium quality luggage that is durable. Samsonite designs, manufactures, sources, and distributes its products.

Managers at Samsonite can analyze performance through variance analysis to assess where the company is excelling and where the company is falling short. Some of the variances relate to usage or efficiency, while others relate to the dollar amount spent on a resource. For example, Samsonite could use more or less materials than expected and the price paid could differ from expectations. Production workers could work more or less hours than expected and wages paid could be more or less than planned. Variance analysis can be extended to other areas such as transportation, selling expenses, and overhead costs.

Managers prefer timely notification of potential variances so they still have time to "right the ship" before the end of the reporting period. In this chapter, we focus on performance assessment and variance analysis.

Source: www.samsonite.com

CHAPTER ORGANIZATION

Standard Costs and Performance Reports

Responsibility Accounting
- Responsibility Accounting and Performance Reporting
- Performance Reporting and Organization Structures
- Types of Responsibility Centers
- Financial and Nonfinancial Performance Measures

Performance Reporting for Cost Centers
- Differentiating a Static Budget from a Flexible Budget
- Performance Report with a Flexible Budget
- Standard Costs and Performance Reports

Variance Analysis for Costs
- Components of Standard Cost Analysis
- Variance Analysis of Direct Materials
- Variance Analysis of Direct Labor
- Variance Analysis of Variable Manufacturing Overhead
- Overview of Fixed Overhead Variances

Revenue Variances and Performance Reporting
- Performance Report of Sales Department as a Revenue Center
- Performance Report for Controllable Selling Costs
- Performance Report of Sales Department as a Profit Center

Additional Topics in Standard Costing
- Establishing and Using Fixed Overhead Variances (Appendix 22A)
- Reconciling Budgeted and Actual Income (Appendix 22B)

RESPONSIBILITY ACCOUNTING

LO22-1 Explain responsibility accounting.

Management accounting tools aid in the assessment of the performance of the firm as a whole and all of its various components. Feedback in the form of performance reports is essential if the benefits of budgeting and other types of planning are to be fully realized. To control current operations and to improve future operations, managers must know how actual results compare with the current budget. These performance reports should be prepared in accordance with the concept of **responsibility accounting**, which is the structuring of performance reports addressed to individual (or group) members of an organization to emphasize the factors they control. Of course, it is difficult to fully assess factors that are under one's control, but the performance reports are a good place to start.

Responsibility Accounting and Performance Reporting

Performance reports that include comparisons of actual results with plans or budgets serve as assessment tools and attention-directors to help managers control activities. These reports start a conversation about performance during the period: what went wrong? What went well? What are contributing factors to the performance? These reports help managers form basic questions that are used to further analyze performance. According to the concept of *management by exception,* the absence of significant differences indicates that activities are proceeding as planned, whereas the presence of significant differences indicates a need to either take corrective action or revise plans. These evaluations and actions are made within the framework of an organization's overall mission, goals, and strategies.

> **Critical Thinking & Decision-Making**
>
> **Should we always ignore small or zero differences between actual and budgeted performance? Why or why not?**
>
> *Just because there is no difference between actual and budgeted results does not mean that no problems (or big wins) occurred during the period. The zero difference might be the aggregation of two large, offsetting differences. Sometimes, it is worth investigating high-level differences that are small, especially if the qualitative information and/or your instinct signal that there is more to the story.*

Distinguishing Controllable from Uncontrollable Costs Responsibility accounting reports are customized to emphasize the activities of specific organizational units. For example, a performance report addressed to the head of a production department contains manufacturing costs *controllable* by the department head. This report should not contain costs (such as advertising, sales commissions, or the president's salary) that the head of the production department cannot control. Including *noncontrollable* costs in the report distracts the manager's attention from the controllable costs, thereby diluting a manager's efforts to deal with controllable items. In practice, defining controllable costs is complicated due to the many interdependencies that occur within organizations. There is much debate about which costs are uncontrollable and whether these costs should be eliminated from performance evaluations.

Should excess costs due to the pandemic be classified as uncontrollable in manager performance evaluations?

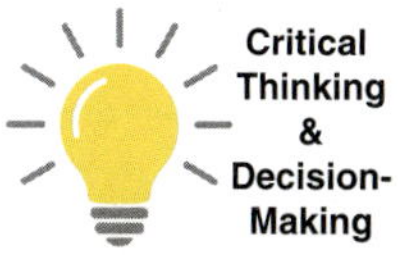

If managers are shielded from pandemic effects, we might eliminate the motivation for managers to work hard in the face of a challenge. However, holding them responsible for pandemic losses might seem unfair since they cannot control world health. The trick is to balance unfair evaluations with the goal of encouraging managers to think outside of the box in the face of challenging circumstances. For example, during the Covid pandemic, some restaurants quickly shifted to take-out and delivery options or even to the sale of meal kits. Some manufacturing companies pivoted to products that they did not normally manufacture such as hand sanitizer and respirator masks.

Minimizing Incentives for Unethical Behavior   If too much pressure is placed on managers to meet performance targets, they may take actions that are not in the best interest of the organization. Bonuses, promotions, and stock performance are often tied to accounting numbers. Where there are incentives for performance, there are incentives for unethical practices.

Channel stuffing, as *Business Insider*'s Jim Edwards says, is the "oldest—and worst—trick in the book." Channel stuffing occurs when a company ships more product to retailers than they need, and then records these increased shipments as sales. The immediate effect is that revenue goes up, but this technique almost always backfires. In the following period, the retailers have more than enough inventory, and revenues fall again. At this point the game is up, unless the company turns to more fraudulent methods. Often, firms will take the excess inventory back as sales returns and maintain the overshipping, thus increasing sales but also increasing refund liability. This is a red flag for the SEC. **Diageo**, maker of Johnny Walker and Smirnoff, was investigated by the SEC for just this impropriety. It is important for firms to monitor this sort of behavior.[1]

The designers of an organization's responsibility accounting system need to be aware of the potential pressures that such a system can place on managers. The decision-making model of the organization should be such that managers are not influenced to make undesirable decisions just to receive bonuses or promotions. Of course, this is easier said than done. When designing the systems, managers must try to predict human behavior, such as channel stuffing. It is then up to management to alter the performance measurement system, or create another control system, to minimize the deceptive behaviors.

Performance Reporting and Organization Structures

All areas of authority and responsibility within an organization must be clearly defined before a responsibility accounting system can be implemented. Organization charts and other documents should be examined to determine an organization's authority and responsibility structure. **Organization structure** is the arrangement of lines of authority and responsibility within an organization. These structures vary widely. Some companies have functional-based structures along the lines of marketing, production, research, and so forth. Others use products, services, customers, or geography as the basis of organization. For Samsonite, the company could be organized by function, such as marketing and operations. Alternatively, it could be organized geographically, based on region. When an attempt is made to implement a responsibility accounting system, management could find instances of overlapping duties, authority not commensurate with responsibility, and expenditures for which no one appears responsible. The identification and resolution of these problems can be a major benefit of implementing a responsibility accounting system.

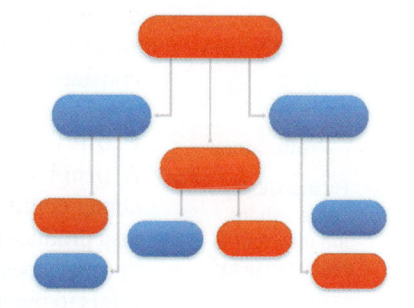

[1] "What Is Channel Stuffing and How Might It Affect Your Business?" PwC Fraud Academy Blog, May 12, 2016; Jim Edwards, "The SEC Wants to Know If Diageo Used the Oldest—and Worst—Trick in the Book to Fudge Its Numbers," *Business Insider*, July 24, 2015.

Although performance reports can be developed for areas of responsibility as narrow as a single worker, the basic responsibility unit in most organizations begins with the department and progresses to division and corporate levels. In manufacturing plants, separate performance reports may be prepared for each production and service department, and then summarized into a performance report for all manufacturing activities. In large universities, reports may be prepared for individual departments such as history, philosophy, and English, and then summarized into a performance report of a college, such as Liberal Arts, and ultimately aggregated into the performance of the university as a whole.

Types of Responsibility Centers

Responsibility centers can be classified as cost centers, revenue centers, profit centers, or investment centers.

Cost Center

Cost Center
Responsibility center where the manager is responsible only for costs.

A **cost center** manager is only responsible for costs; there is no revenue responsibility. A cost center can be as small as a segment of a department or large enough to include a major aspect of the organization, such as all manufacturing activities. Typical examples of cost centers include the following.

Organization	Cost Center
Manufacturing plant	Tooling department
	Assembly activities
Retail store	Inventory control function
	Maintenance department
Hospital	Radiology
	Emergency room
College	History department
	Registrar's office
City government	Public safety (police and fire)
	Road maintenance

Samsonite could classify its repairs and maintenance department for its manufacturing plants as a cost center. The department does not "sell" its services. Instead, it exists to ensure that other departments can operate effectively. This department incurs costs, with no revenues. Consequently, it will be measured and evaluated based on the costs incurred and potentially, the quality of the service it provides.

Revenue Center

Revenue Center
Responsibility center where the manager is focused only on revenues.

A **revenue center** manager is responsible for the generation of sales revenues. Even though the basic performance report of a revenue center emphasizes sales, revenue centers are likely to be assigned responsibility for the controllable costs they incur in generating revenues. If revenues and costs are evaluated separately, the center has dual responsibility as a revenue center and as a cost center. If controllable costs are deducted from revenues to obtain some bottom-line contribution, the center is, in fact, being treated more like a profit center than a revenue center. Samsonite might treat the sales department as a revenue center. If the sales department is only responsible for ensuring sales targets are met without worrying about the associated costs, the sales department is considered a revenue center.

Profit Center

Profit Center
Responsibility center where the manager is responsible for revenues and costs.

A **profit center** manager is responsible for revenues, costs, and the resulting profits. A profit center could be an entire organization, but it is more frequently a segment of an organization such as a product line, marketing territory, or store. In the context of performance evaluation, the word "profit" does not necessarily refer to the bottom line of an income statement. Instead, it typically refers to the profit center's contribution to common corporate costs and profit. Profit is computed as the center's revenues less all costs directly associated with operating the center. Profit is analogous to the terms operating income or division income. Having limited authority regarding the size of total assets, the profit center manager is *not* held responsible for the relationship between profits and assets. Samsonite could establish profit centers by product line, such as its hardside luggage collection and softside luggage collection.

In recent years many hospitals have been treating critical care and clinical service departments as profit centers to encourage physician chiefs to manage their departments as small businesses. However, profit centers may be a poor fit for health care. Dr. David Young contends that there are problems with profit-based performance evaluation in hospitals. For example, departments vary in their profitability for fundamental reasons unrelated to performance. Cardiovascular surgery will be more profitable than pediatrics due to the fundamental structure of health care rather than solely due to performance.[2] Management must ensure that treating health care departments as profit centers, encourages behavior that is aligned with the overall strategy and goals of the hospital.

Investment Center

An **investment center** manager is responsible for the relationship between its profits and the total assets invested in the center. Investment center managers have a high degree of organization autonomy. In general, management of an investment center is expected to earn a target profit per dollar invested. Investment center managers are evaluated on the basis of how well they use the total resources entrusted to their care to earn a profit. An investment center is the broadest and most inclusive type of responsibility center. Managers of these centers have more authority and responsibility than other managers and are primarily responsible for planning, organizing, and controlling firm activities. Because of their authority regarding the size of corporate assets, they are held responsible for the relationship between profits and assets. Investment centers are discussed further in Chapter 23.

> **Investment Center**
> Responsibility center where the manager is responsible for the relationship between profits and total assets invested.

Financial and Nonfinancial Performance Measures

This chapter's emphasis is on financial performance reports. Dollar-based financial reports have several advantages over other performance measures. Their "bottom line" impact is readily apparent. If actual fixed costs exceed budgeted fixed costs by $10,000, the before-tax income of an organization is $10,000 less than it would be without the extra fixed costs. Additionally, because dollars are additive and applicable to all organizational units, financial measures are easily summarized, compared, and reported up the organization chart.

It is important to keep in mind that although financial measures may indicate results are not in accordance with the budget, they do not indicate the root cause of financial deviations. *The identification and analysis of the root cause of financial deviations require asking questions and, frequently, the use of nonfinancial data.* Managers and employees at lower levels of the organization are often better served by performance reports focusing on data directly related to their job, such as units processed or customers served per hour. Examples of nonfinancial performance measures include defects per thousand units in a manufacturing plant, average and longest waiting time in a restaurant, nursing staff hours per patient day in a hospital, response time for a fire department, and customer satisfaction at a retail store or bank. Companies might also measure ESG-related activities such as carbon emissions, energy consumption, and waste disposal to ensure that their divisions are meeting established standards.

> **What do you think are some nonfinancial measures used by Southwest Airlines, a Dallas, Texas based airlines, to evaluate its performance?**
>
> *Although financial performance is critical to Southwest Airlines' top management and is still used to evaluate managers, aircraft, and routes, the focus for the evaluation should also include nonfinancial measures. The company's annual sustainability report highlights a number of nonfinancial measures including the following.* 
> - *Hours of training by employees*
> - *Customer satisfaction scores*
> - *Percentage of reported flight operations arriving on-time*
> - *Employee volunteer hours*
> - *Scope 2 emissions*

---

[2] David W. Young, "Profit Centers in Clinical Care Departments an Idea Whose Time Has Gone: A Case Can Be Made for Converting a Hospital's Clinical Care Departments from Profit Centers into Standard Expense Centers," *Healthcare Financial Management* (March 2008): 66+. Academic OneFile. Web. July 25, 2016.

By tracking these performance measures over time and against internal and external benchmarks, the company can determine the success or setbacks of their current operations and make adjustments going forward.

When organizations seek to improve financial performance beyond what is possible with current products, procedures, or services, the initial focus is most often on nonfinancial measures. **Trader Joe's** grocery stores might benchmark the length of their cash-register waiting times against **Whole Foods**'. Differences discovered in wait time may be a leading indicator of financial differences between the two companies. A leading indicator provides information *before* financial indicators can be summarized or are known. This concept is discussed further in the next chapter.

Review 22-1 LO22-1   Identifying Responsibility Centers

Eli's Cheesecake is a family-owned business based out of Chicago, IL. Eli's operates its corporate office, bakery, retail store, and café from one location on the west side of the city and recently opened a Cheesecake Café at Chicago's O'Hare Airport.

Required
Peruse Eli's website at http://www.elicheesecake.com to become more familiar with the company. Listed below are likely reporting centers for Eli's. Identify the type of responsibility center that would most likely be assigned to each reporting center: (1) cost center, (2) revenue center, (3) profit center, or (4) investment center.

_____ Bakery
_____ Accounting department
_____ Product line—Original Plain Cheesecake
_____ Human resources department
_____ Cheesecake Café at O'Hare Airport

Solution on p. 22-41.

PERFORMANCE REPORTING FOR COST CENTERS

Differentiating a Static Budget from a Flexible Budget

LO22-2
Prepare a performance report for a cost center using a flexible budget.

A budget that is based on a prediction of sales and production, typically prepared before the start of the period, is called a **static budget**. The master budget explained in Chapter 21 is a static budget. Budgets can also be set for a series of possible production and sales volumes, or budgets can be adjusted to a particular level of production after the fact (i.e. after the period has ended). These budgets, based on cost-volume relationships, are called **flexible budgets**. Flexible budgets are used to determine what costs should be for a specific level of activity.

Budgets	
Static	Flexible
Budget based on predicted sales and production levels	Budget based on actual sales and production levels

Financial performance reports for cost centers include a comparison of actual and budgeted costs and identify the difference as a **variance**. *Allowed* costs in performance reports are the flexible budget amounts for the actual level of activity. Variances are labeled as favorable or unfavorable based on their impact on income. Variances that increase income are labeled as *favorable* and variances that decrease income are labeled as *unfavorable*. Extrapolating to costs, the variance is favorable if actual costs are less than budgeted costs and unfavorable if actual costs are more than budgeted costs. Holding everything else constant, lower (higher) costs result in higher (lower) income; thus, the variance is favorable (unfavorable). These comparisons are made in total and individually for each type of controllable cost assigned to a cost center.

How is artificial intelligence affecting variance analysis?

Critical Thinking & Decision-Making

Artificial intelligence automates aspects of the process of variance analysis. Technology allows automated examination of data of a company in order to identify trends that are odd or different than expected. Automating the data analysis process allows all of a company's transactions to be considered, not just the top-level

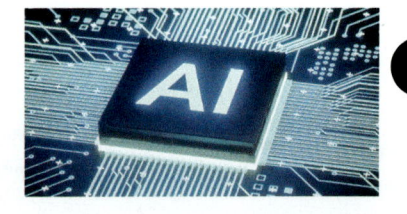

numbers that come out in the initial variance analysis.[3] Such tools find patterns that raise suspicion. Suspicious patterns can be as simple as sales clustered just before the quarter-end and expenses clustered just after. These tools do the work of combing through a company's data for suspicious patterns, but it remains the job of management accountants and auditors to determine whether the patterns are operational or fraudulent.

Next we prepare a hypothetical variance analysis for **Samsonite**'s production department, considered to be a cost center. If Samsonite plans production of 10,000 luggage bags at a cost of materials of $10 per bag for July, its static budget for materials is $100,000. If Samsonite actually produces 11,000 luggage bags in July, the flexible budget will reflect this actual production level at a budgeted cost per unit of $10 to arrive at a flexible budget of $110,000. Let's assume $108,000 was the actual spending for July. A variance analysis comparing the static budget, flexible budget, and the actual spending amounts follows.

Budget Item	Static Budget	Flexible Budget	Actual
Materials.........................	$100,000 (10,000 bags × $10)	$110,000 (11,000 bags × $10)	$108,000

$10,000 U $2,000 F

$8,000 U

In total, the production department of Samsonite spent $8,000 more than was originally budgeted (i.e., $108,000 actual amount − $100,000 static budget amount).

Should the production manager be held responsible for the overspending of $8,000?

The primary reason for the overspending is because Samsonite produced more luggage bags than originally predicted. Of course, producing 11,000 bags will cost more than producing 10,000 bags. The production manager should not be penalized because of the need to produce more bags. Consequently, the production manager is better evaluated based on what actually happened which is reflected in a flexible budget based on 11,000 bags. The difference between the flexible budget and the actual budget shows that the production manager spent $2,000 less than the amount that was forecasted to be spent for 11,000 bags. This is a favorable variance because costs are under budget which means that income is over budget. The next step is to understand what the production manager did to save this money.

Critical Thinking & Decision-Making

Performance Report with a Flexible Budget

As illustrated in the last example, if activity changes (for example, number of bags produced), the entity's financial responsibility for costs should be based on the actual level of activity. This means that the flexible budget is tailored, after the fact, to the actual level of activity. This distinction between planned and actual activity makes it possible to analyze two types of variances that comprise the total variance (also called the *static variance*).

- A **flexible budget variance** is computed for each cost as the difference between the actual cost and the flexible budget cost. This amount reflects the discrepancies in the internal costs, assuming a comparable level of activity. This means that any variance is due to cost differences, such as material price changes, but not due to sales volume changes.

- An **activity variance** is computed for each cost as the difference between the static budget cost and the flexible budget cost. These variances are due to changes in volume levels such as sales or production volumes.

---

[3] Michael Rapoport, "Auditing Firms Count on Technology for Backup," *Wall Street Journal*, March 7, 2016.

For a complete example of a flexible budget, let's continue the **Samsonite** production department example. Assume that Samsonite produces only one luggage bag. Also assume the company has only three departments: production, sales, and administration. The standards for the production department follow. For this example, variable overhead is applied based upon the quantity of direct materials required for planned production.

> Variable costs
>   Direct materials—2 pounds per bag at $5 per pound, or $10 per bag
>   Direct labor—0.25 hour per bag at $24 per hour, or $6 per bag
>   Variable overhead—2 pounds of direct material per bag at $4 per pound, or $8 per bag
> Fixed costs—$52,000

If management plans to produce 10,000 luggage bags in July, the budgeted costs are $292,000.

SAMSONITE
Manufacturing Cost Budget
For Month of July

Manufacturing costs	
Variable costs	
Direct materials (10,000 bags × 2 pounds × $5)	$100,000
Direct labor (10,000 bags × 0.25 hours × $24)	60,000
Variable overhead (10,000 bags × 2 pounds × $4)	80,000
Fixed costs	52,000
Total	$292,000

Assume that Samsonite produced 11,000 bags in July rather than 10,000 bags as budgeted. Examples of a performance report for July based on static and flexible budgets are presented in **Exhibit 22.1**.

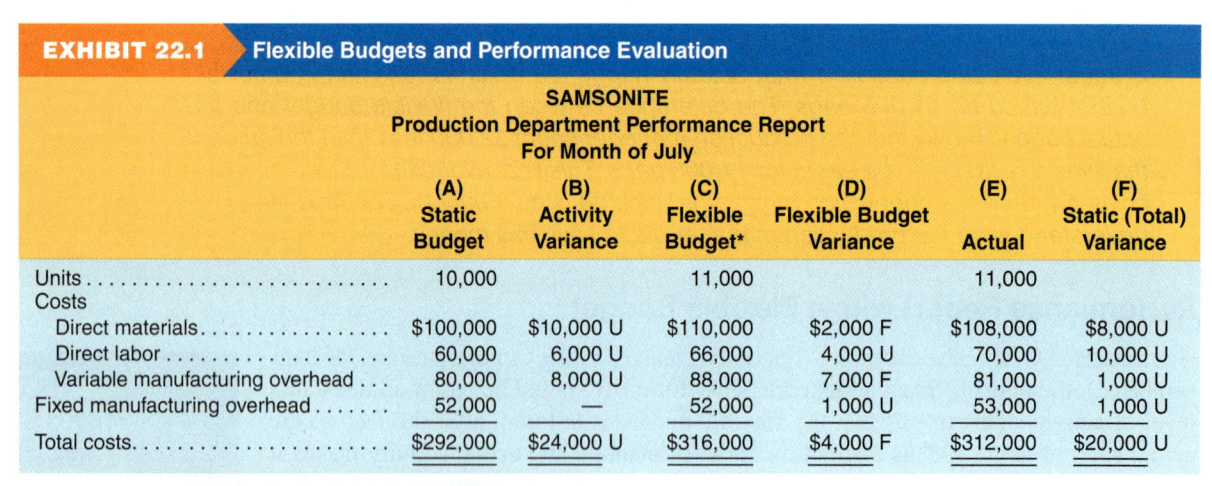

EXHIBIT 22.1   Flexible Budgets and Performance Evaluation

SAMSONITE
Production Department Performance Report
For Month of July

	(A) Static Budget	(B) Activity Variance	(C) Flexible Budget*	(D) Flexible Budget Variance	(E) Actual	(F) Static (Total) Variance
Units	10,000		11,000		11,000	
Costs						
Direct materials	$100,000	$10,000 U	$110,000	$2,000 F	$108,000	$8,000 U
Direct labor	60,000	6,000 U	66,000	4,000 U	70,000	10,000 U
Variable manufacturing overhead	80,000	8,000 U	88,000	7,000 F	81,000	1,000 U
Fixed manufacturing overhead	52,000	—	52,000	1,000 U	53,000	1,000 U
Total costs	$292,000	$24,000 U	$316,000	$4,000 F	$312,000	$20,000 U

* Flexible budget manufacturing costs: (Actual bags × Budgeted cost per bag)
Direct materials (11,000 bags × 2 pounds × $5) = $110,000
Direct labor (11,000 bags × 0.25 labor hour × $24) = $66,000
Variable overhead (11,000 bags × 2 pounds × $4) = $88,000

Static Variance When the production department's performance is evaluated by comparing the original static budget for 10,000 bags (Column A) with the actual results (Column E) for 11,000 bags, the costs all appear unfavorable (or higher). This is represented in the Static Variance (Column F). However, this difference includes both the differences due to the increase in bags as well as any changes in the efficiency of the department (e.g., the cost of materials). Ideally, managers would want to understand the effects of these differences separately.

Flexible Budget Variance The flexible budget adjusts for any change in bags produced. Consequently, the flexible budget reflects what would have been budgeted had the actual production volume been known. This means that variable costs are adjusted for the change in volume but the fixed costs remain the same. For example, the budget for direct materials cost increases to $110,000 (11,000 bags × 2 pounds × $5) while the budget for fixed manufacturing overhead costs remains the same at $52,000.

When the production department's financial performance is evaluated by comparing actual costs (Column E) with costs allowed in a flexible budget (Column C), the results are mixed. Direct materials have a $2,000 favorable variance and variable overhead has a $7,000 favorable variance. Direct labor has a $4,000 unfavorable variance and fixed costs have a $1,000 unfavorable variance. The net flexible budget variance is $4,000 favorable, a substantial difference from the static budget variance of $20,000 unfavorable.

Activity Variance Note that the difference between the original budget and the flexible budget, called the activity variance, reflects differences that are driven entirely by changes in production. When bags increase, variable costs will also increase (by definition), causing unfavorable variances.

Benefits of a Flexible Budget Flexible budget variances provide a much better indicator of performance than static budget variances that do not consider the increased level of production (11,000 bags rather than 10,000 bags). When production exceeds the planned level, the static budget variances are usually unfavorable. Likewise, when actual production is substantially below the planned level of activity, the static variances are usually favorable. This is by definition since all variable costs will change proportionately with production level. While it is important to isolate and determine the cause of any variation between planned and actual production, the financial-based performance report is not the appropriate place to mix volume-created variances with those related to the actual production levels. The flexible budget analysis as shown in **Exhibit 22.1**, allows management to make this distinction.

Standard Costs and Performance Reports

A **standard cost** indicates what it should cost to provide an activity or produce one batch or unit of product under planned and efficient operating conditions. In a standard costing environment, the flexible budget is based on standard unit costs. Traditionally, standard costs have been developed from an engineering analysis or from an analysis of historical data adjusted for expected changes in the product, production technology, or costs. When standards are developed using historical data, management must be careful to ensure that past inefficiencies are excluded from current standards.

Standard Cost Development and Impact on Human Behavior To obtain the full benefit of standard costs, the standards must be based on realistic expectations. The management of Samsonite might set their standards for direct labor at 0.22 hours per bag rather than at the expected 0.25 hours per bag, hoping that employees will strive toward the lower time and, consequently, the lower cost of $5.28 ($24 × 0.22). The use of tight standards often causes planning and behavioral problems because management expects them to result in unfavorable variances. Accordingly, tight standards should not be used to budget input requirements and cash flows because management expects to incur more labor costs than the standards allow. The use of tight standards can have undesirable behavioral effects if employees find that a second set of standards is used in the "real" budget or if they are constantly subject to unfavorable performance reports. These employees could come to distrust the entire budgeting and performance evaluation system, or they may quit trying to achieve any of the organization's standards.

Tight standards are more likely to occur in an imposed budget than in a participation budget. In a participation budget, the risk may be in *overstating* the costs required to produce a product. Loose standards may fail to properly motivate employees and can make the company uncompetitive due to costs that are higher than competitors'.

Review 22-2 LO22-2 — Preparing a Flexible Budget for Performance Reporting

Suppose you receive the following performance report from the accounting department for your first month as bakery manager for Eli's Cheesecake. Your supervisor, the vice president of manufacturing, has concerns that the report for March does not provide an accurate picture of your performance in the area of cost control.

	Budget	Actual	Variance
Units	5,200	5,000	
Costs			
Direct materials	$ 104,000	$104,125	$ 125 U
Direct labor	78,000	82,400	4,400 U
Variable manufacturing overhead			
Category 1	31,200	31,000	200 F
Category 2	20,800	18,000	2,800 F
Fixed manufacturing overhead	39,000	42,000	3,000 U
Total costs	$273,000	$277,525	$4,525 U

Required

Solution on p. 22-44. Prepare a revised budget using the format illustrated in **Exhibit 22-1** to better reflect your performance.

VARIANCE ANALYSIS FOR COSTS

Components of Standard Cost Analysis: Price and Quantity Variances

LO22-3 Formulate and interpret direct materials cost variances.

To use and interpret standard cost variances properly, managers must understand the processes and activities that drive costs. Cost variances are merely signals. They do not explain why costs differ from expectations. Underlying causes of variances must be investigated before final judgment is passed on the effectiveness and efficiency of an operation or activity. **Standard cost variance analysis** is a systematic approach to examining *flexible budget variances*.

Price and Quantity Variances Standard cost variance analysis identifies the general causes of the total flexible budget variance by breaking it into separate price and quantity variances for each production component.

Two possible reasons that actual cost could differ from flexible budget cost for a given amount of output produced are (1) a difference between actual and standard prices paid for the production components—the price variance—and (2) a difference between the actual input quantity used for production and the standard input quantity allowed for the production components—the *input quantity variance*. Variances have different names for different cost categories as follows.

Cost Category	Price Variance Name	Quantity Variance Name
Direct materials	Materials price variance	Materials quantity variance
Direct labor	Labor rate variance	Labor efficiency variance
Variable overhead	Variable overhead spending variance	Variable overhead efficiency variance

Fixed overhead is excluded from the unit standard costs because, within the relevant range of normal activity, it does not vary with the volume of production. To facilitate product costing, however, many organizations develop a standard fixed overhead cost per unit.

Standard Cost Variance Analysis of Direct Materials

For Samsonite, we analyze the flexible budget cost variances for materials, labor, and variable overhead, beginning in this section with materials. Our illustration is based on the following hypothetical July activity and costs of Samsonite's production department.

SAMSONITE
Actual Manufacturing Costs
For Month of July*

Actual bags completed..	11,000
Manufacturing costs	
Unit level costs	
Direct materials (24,000 pounds × $4.50).........................	$108,000
Direct labor (2,800 hours × $25.00)	70,000
Variable overhead	81,000
Fixed overhead costs	53,000
Total	$312,000

Establishing Standards for Direct Materials

The two basic elements contained in the standards for direct materials are the *standard price* and the *standard input quantity*. Recall from the previous section that we identified the standards for direct materials for Samsonite as follows.

Direct materials—2 pounds per bag at $5 per pound, or $10 per bag

Standard direct materials price per unit The standard price (i.e., $5 per pound) indicates how much an organization should pay for each input unit of direct materials. It includes all reasonable costs necessary to acquire the materials. These costs include the invoice price of materials, less planned discounts plus freight, insurance, special handling, and any other costs related to the acquisition of the materials.

Standard input quantity per unit The standard input quantity (i.e., 2 pounds per bag) indicates the quantity of direct materials that the company should use to produce one unit of finished product. This amount should include the amount dictated by the physical characteristics of the process and the product, plus a reasonable allowance for normal spoilage, waste, and other inefficiencies. The input quantity standard can be determined by an engineering analysis, professional judgment, or by averaging the actual amount used for several periods. Caution should be taken in using an average of actual past materials usage as a standard quantity because it could include excessive waste and inefficiencies.

How does the input quantity concept apply to a recipe for baking cupcakes?

Think of the standard input quantity as analogous to a recipe. A cupcake recipe presents the number of cups of flour used to produce a specific number of cupcakes. The flour to cupcake ratio represents the input quantity of flour used to produce one cupcake. Keep in mind that the input quantity is separate from the sales quantity; the sales quantity relates to outputs and the input quantity relates to inputs. The number of cupcakes baked and sold is the sales quantity and the amount of flour used is the input quantity.

Critical Thinking & Decision-Making

Computing Direct Materials Variances

- The **materials price variance** is the difference between the actual material cost and the standard cost of actual material inputs.
- The **materials quantity variance** is the difference between the standard cost of actual materials inputs and the flexible budget cost of materials.

The flexible budget cost represents the amount of inputs that should have been used for the actual output produced. Computation of the direct materials variances for **Samsonite** follow.

Standard Cost Variance Analysis		
Input component: Direct materials		**Output: 11,000 Bags**
Actual Cost	**Standard Cost of Actual Inputs**	**Flexible Budget Cost**
Actual quantity (AQ)... 24,000 Actual price (AP)...... × $4.50 **$108,000**	Actual quantity (AQ)... 24,000 Standard price (SP)... × $5.00 **$120,000**	Standard quantity allowed (SQ)... 22,000* Standard price (SP)............ × $5.00 **$110,000**
	Materials price variance $12,000 F	Materials quantity variance $10,000 U
	Total flexible budget materials variance $2,000 F	

*11,000 bags × 2 pounds per bag

Materials Price Variance Samsonite had a favorable materials price variance of $12,000 because the actual cost of materials purchased and used ($108,000) was less than the standard cost of actual materials purchased and used ($120,000). Using the formula approach, the materials price variance equals the actual quantity (AQ) purchased and used times the difference between the actual price (AP) and the standard price (SP). Samsonite paid $0.50 per pound below the standard price for 24,000 pounds for a total savings of $12,000.

$$\text{Materials price variance} = AQ(AP - SP)$$
$$= 24{,}000(\$4.50 - \$5.00)$$
$$= 24{,}000 \times \$0.50$$
$$= \$12{,}000 \text{ F}$$

Materials Quantity Variance The unfavorable quantity variance of $10,000 occurred because the standard cost of actual materials used, $120,000 (24,000 × $5), was higher than the cost of materials allowed by the flexible budget, $110,000 (22,000 × $5). *A total of 22,000 pounds of materials is allowed to produce 11,000 units of finished outputs. This is computed as 11,000 finished bags times 2.0 pounds of direct materials per bag.* Using the formula approach, the materials quantity variance equals the standard price (SP) per pound times the difference between the number of pounds actually used (AQ) and the number of pounds allowed (SQ).

$$\text{Materials quantity variance} = SP(AQ - SQ)$$
$$= \$5(24{,}000 - 22{,}000)$$
$$= \$5 \times 2{,}000$$
$$= \$10{,}000 \text{ U}$$

Interpreting Direct Materials Variances

By the end of the period, managers should instinctively understand the organization's performance and the main drivers of performance. However, after computing variances, managers are in a better position to analyze their business's results and to make better and more relevant decisions. Variance analysis offers a systematic way of analyzing performance changes, in dollars. This analysis provides the basis of conversations about performance and future improvements.

Favorable materials price variance A favorable materials price variance indicates that the employee responsible for materials purchases paid less per unit than the price allowed by the standards. This could result from receiving discounts for purchasing more than the normal quantities, effective bargaining by the employee, purchasing substandard-quality materials, purchasing from a distress seller, or other factors. Ordinarily, when a favorable price variance is reported, the employee's performance is interpreted as favorable. However, if the favorable price variance results from the purchase of materials of lower than standard quality or from a purchase in more than desirable quantities, the employee's performance would be questionable. *Thus, favorable does not always equate to good and unfavorable does not always equate to bad.* The variance is a starting point; management must investigate the underlying causes of the discrepancies and any externalities on other parts of the business. All large variances, including favorable variances, should be thoroughly investigated for causes and corrections. Managers might also want to investigate zero variances. Zero variances might indicate opposite, offsetting variances that are concerning.

Unfavorable materials price variance An unfavorable materials price variance means that the purchasing employee paid more per unit for materials than the price allowed by the standards. This could be caused by failure to buy in sufficient quantities to receive normal discounts, purchase of higher-quality materials than called for in the product specifications, failure to place materials orders on a timely basis, failure to bargain for the best available prices, or other factors. An unfavorable variance does not always mean that the employee performed unfavorably. Many noncontrollable factors can impact the purchasing function, including unanticipated price increases, the need to increase production to meet unanticipated sales, and supply chain problems such as a work stoppage at a vendor.

Favorable materials quantity variance A favorable materials quantity variance means that the actual quantity of direct materials used was less than the quantity allowed for the units produced. This could result from factors such as less materials waste than allowed by the standards, better than expected machine efficiency, direct materials of higher quality than required by the standards, and more efficient use of direct materials by employees.

Unfavorable materials quantity variance An unfavorable materials quantity variance occurs when the quantity of direct materials used exceeds the quantity allowed for the units produced. This could result from incurring more waste than provided for in the standards, poorly maintained machinery requiring larger amounts of direct materials, direct materials of lower quality than required by the standards, or poorly trained employees who were unable to use the materials at the level of efficiency required by the standards. The variance calculation is a starting point; it is now up to management to combine the variance analysis with qualitative data and conversation to develop a story of operations for the period. With the full story, management can develop a plan to improve next period.

Due to supply shortages and inflation, the cost of ingredients for restaurants has increased. In order to avoid passing the increased cost to customers, restaurants have decided to decrease portions. How will these two events impact the variance analysis?

It is likely that the cost increase was not predicted. Consequently, the materials price variance will be unfavorable, reflecting the increased cost of ingredients. With the smaller portions, restaurants will show a favorable materials quantity variance as fewer ingredients were used in each item (i.e., fewer inputs for every output). Although this might not be perceived as a good thing by customers, the materials quantity variance will be classified as favorable.

Calculating Standard Cost Variances for Direct Materials   LO22-3 **Review 22-3**

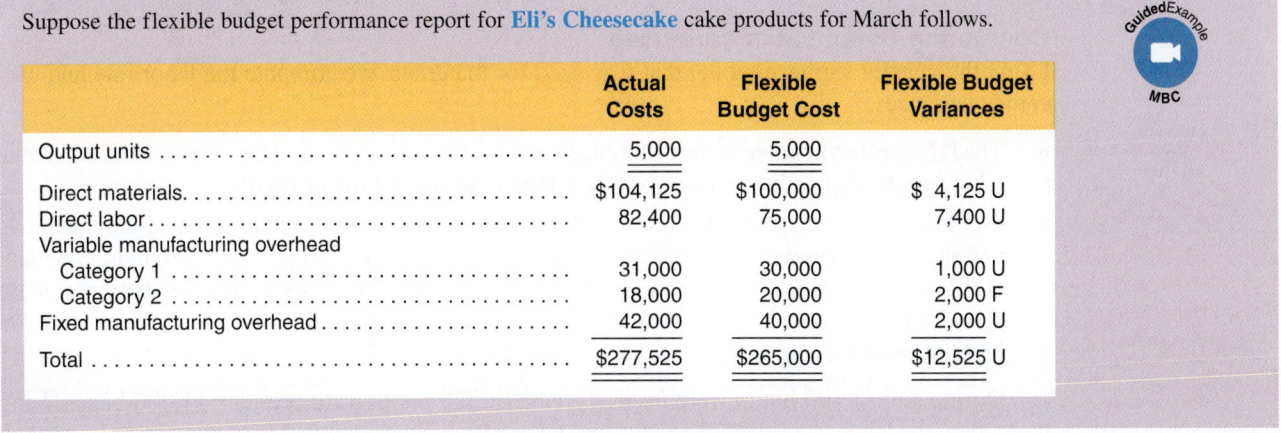

Suppose the flexible budget performance report for **Eli's Cheesecake** cake products for March follows.

	Actual Costs	Flexible Budget Cost	Flexible Budget Variances
Output units	5,000	5,000	
Direct materials	$104,125	$100,000	$ 4,125 U
Direct labor	82,400	75,000	7,400 U
Variable manufacturing overhead			
Category 1	31,000	30,000	1,000 U
Category 2	18,000	20,000	2,000 F
Fixed manufacturing overhead	42,000	40,000	2,000 U
Total	$277,525	$265,000	$12,525 U

continued

The standard unit cost for cheesecakes follows.

Direct materials (4 pounds × $5.00 per pound)	$20
Direct labor (1.25 hours × $12.00 per hour)	15
Variable overhead, Category 1 (1.25 hours × $4.80)	6
Variable overhead, Category 2 ($4 per finished cake)	4
Total standard variable cost per unit	$45

Actual cost of materials is based on 21,250 pounds of direct materials purchased and used at $4.90 per pound; actual cost of assembly is based on 7,000 labor hours. Variable overhead is applied on labor hours for Category 1 and finished units for Category 2.

Required

a. Calculate all standard cost variances for direct materials.

Solution on p. 22-44.   *b.* As the manager of Eli's, name two possible reasons for each variance.

Standard Cost Variance Analysis of Direct Labor

We continue with the **Samsonite** example to now explain labor variances.

Establishing Standards for Direct Labor   To evaluate management performance in controlling labor costs, it is necessary to determine the *standard labor rate* for each hour allowed and the *standard time allowed* to produce a unit. Recall from a previous section that we identified the standards for direct labor for Samsonite as follows.

Direct labor—0.25 hour per bag at $24 per hour, or $6 per bag

Standard direct labor rate per unit   Setting labor rate standards (i.e., $24 per hour) can be quite simple or extremely complex. If all employees have the same wage rate, determining the standard cost is relatively easy: simply adopt the normal wage rate as the standard labor rate. If there are variations in employee wage rates, the standard labor rate should be based on the expected mix of employee wage rates.

Standard time allowed per unit   The standard labor time per unit (i.e., 0.25 hour per bag) can be determined by an engineering approach or an empirical observation approach. When using an engineering approach, industrial engineers ascertain the amount of time required to produce a unit of finished product by applying time and motion methods or other available techniques. Normal operating conditions are assumed in arriving at the labor standard. Therefore, allowances must be made for normal machine downtime, employee personal breaks, and so forth. Under the empirical approach, the average time required to produce a unit under normal operating conditions is used as a basis for the standard.

Computing Direct Labor Variances

Using the general variance model that was used for materials, we compute the labor rate and efficiency variances.

- The **labor rate variance** is the difference between the actual cost and the standard cost of actual labor inputs. Typically, we think of labor units in terms of time or hours.
- The **labor efficiency variance** is the difference between the standard cost of actual inputs and the flexible budget cost for labor. In this calculation, the output units are held constant, at the actual output level. The analysis compares how many labor hours, for example, were actually used versus how many labor hours were budgeted to be used to produce a specific level of outputs.

During July, 2,800 hours were used at a cost of $25 per hour to produce 11,000 bags. Using these data, the labor rate (price) variance and labor efficiency (quantity) variance can be computed as shown in the following illustration.

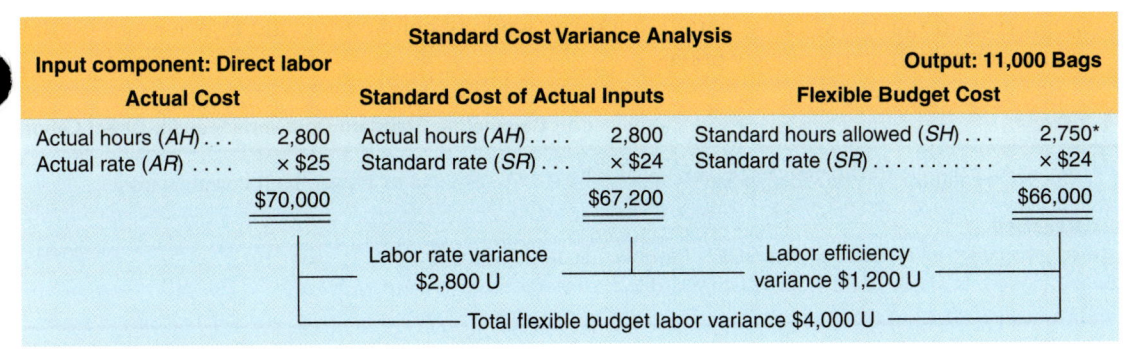

| Standard Cost Variance Analysis ||||
| Input component: Direct labor ||| Output: 11,000 Bags |
Actual Cost	Standard Cost of Actual Inputs		Flexible Budget Cost
Actual hours (AH)... 2,800 Actual rate (AR) .... × $25 **$70,000**	Actual hours (AH).... 2,800 Standard rate (SR)... × $24 **$67,200**		Standard hours allowed (SH)... 2,750* Standard rate (SR).......... × $24 **$66,000**

Labor rate variance $2,800 U — Labor efficiency variance $1,200 U

Total flexible budget labor variance $4,000 U

*11,000 bags × 0.25 hours per bag

Labor Rate Variance Using the formula approach, the labor rate variance equals the actual number of hours used times the difference between the actual rate and the standard rate.

$$\text{Labor rate variance} = AH(AR - SR)$$
$$= 2{,}800(\$25 - \$24)$$
$$= 2{,}800 \times \$1$$
$$= \$2{,}800 \text{ U}$$

This computation of the labor rate variance shows that the company paid $1 more than the standard rate for each of the 2,800 hours worked.

Labor Efficiency Variance Since 11,000 units of product were finished during the period and 0.25 hour of labor was allowed for each bag, the total number of standard hours allowed was 2,750 (11,000 bags × 0.25 hour). Using the formula approach, the labor efficiency variance equals the standard rate times the difference between the actual labor hours and the standard hours allowed.

$$\text{Labor efficiency variance} = SR(AH - SH)$$
$$= \$24(2{,}800 - 2{,}750)$$
$$= \$24 \times 50$$
$$= \$1{,}200 \text{ U}$$

Samsonite's labor efficiency variance indicates that the company used 50 more labor hours than allowed. By itself, this inefficiency caused an unfavorable variance of $1,200.

Interpreting Direct Labor Variances

The possible explanations for labor rate variances are rather limited.

Unfavorable labor rate variance An unfavorable labor rate variance can be caused by the use of higher-paid laborers than the standards provided. An increase in wage rates not reflected in the standards can also cause an unfavorable labor rate variance.

Favorable labor rate variance A favorable labor rate variance occurs if lower-paid workers were used or if actual wage rates declined. Paying higher or lower wages, by itself, does not indicate whether the company was effective or not. More investigation is needed to understand, for example, the quality of the work of the personnel.

Unfavorable labor efficiency variance An unfavorable labor efficiency variance occurs when the actual labor hours exceed the number of hours allowed for the actual output. This could be caused by using poorly trained workers or poorly maintained machinery or by the use of low-quality materials. Low employee morale and generally poor working conditions could also adversely affect labor efficiency.

Favorable labor efficiency variance A favorable labor efficiency variance occurs when the actual labor hours are less than the number of hours allowed for the actual output. This above-normal efficiency can be caused by the company's use of higher-skilled (and higher-paid) workers, better machinery, or higher-quality direct materials than the standards require. High employee morale, improved job satisfaction, or generally improved working conditions could also account for the above-normal efficiency of the workers.

Review 22-4 LO22-4 — Calculating Standard Cost Variances for Direct Labor

Refer to the information provided in Review 22-3 for **Eli's Cheesecake** to answer the following questions.

Required

Solution on p. 22-45.
a. Calculate all standard cost variances for direct labor.
b. As the manager of Eli's, name two possible reasons for each variance.

LO22-5 Formulate and interpret overhead cost variances.

The traditional unit-level approach to cost estimation, budgeting, and variance analysis *separates overhead costs into fixed and variable elements*. This separation is necessary because fixed costs are primarily driven by factors related to capacity and variable costs are primarily driven by factors related to volume. The primary focus of this section is on variable overhead variances.

Standard Cost Variance Analysis of Variable Manufacturing Overhead

Because it includes many heterogeneous costs, manufacturing overhead poses a unique problem in establishing standards for the standard quantity and the standard price of inputs. This is similar to the problem of assigning overhead costs to products. Direct materials have a natural physical measure of quantity such as tons, barrels, pounds, and liters. Similarly, labor or assembly is measurable in hours or minutes. However, no single quantity measure is common to all overhead items. Overhead is a cost group that can simultaneously include costs measurable in hours, pounds, liters, and kilowatts.

Establishing Standards for Variable Manufacturing Overhead The most frequent approach to dealing with the problem of multiple quantity measures in variable manufacturing overhead is to use a *single surrogate* (or substitute) measure to represent the quantity of all items in a given group. Typical substitute measures include machine hours, units of finished product, direct labor hours, and direct labor dollars. The variable overhead standard is then stated in terms of this surrogate measure. The measure used, in most cases, will be the same measure that is used to allocate overhead costs to products.

Computing Variable Overhead Variances

- The **variable overhead spending variance** is the difference between the actual variable overhead cost and the standard variable overhead cost for the actual inputs of the surrogate measure.
- The **variable overhead efficiency variance** is the difference between the standard variable overhead cost for the actual inputs of the surrogate measure and the flexible budget cost allowed for variable overhead based on actual outputs.

Actual cost Assume for **Samsonite**, the actual variable overhead in July was $81,000. This represents the actual cost of overhead items such as indirect materials and indirect labor.

Standard cost of actual inputs Pounds of materials is Samsonite's surrogate measure for quantity for variable overhead allowed and used. This means that the standard costs allowed for variable overhead varies with the pounds of direct materials allowed. Hence the standard cost of actual inputs is calculated as actual pounds of direct materials (AQ) times the standard variable overhead rate per pound (SR).

$$\text{Standard cost of actual inputs} = (AQ \times SR)$$
$$= 24{,}000 \times \$4$$
$$= \$96{,}000$$

Flexible budget cost The direct materials allowed (SQ) is equal to the actual number of bags produced multiplied by the pounds of direct materials allowed per bag (11,000 bags × 2 pounds). The allowed quantities are multiplied by the standard variable overhead rate (SR). The resulting variable overhead flexible budget cost is $88,000.

$$\text{Flexible budget cost} = (SQ \times SR)$$
$$= 22{,}000 \times \$4$$
$$= \$88{,}000$$

Using these data, the calculations for the variable overhead spending (price) variance and the variable overhead efficiency (quantity) variance follow.

Standard Cost Variance Analysis

Input component: Variable overhead   **Output: 11,000 Bags**

Actual Cost	Standard Cost of Actual Inputs	Flexible Budget Cost
$81,000	Actual pounds (AQ) .... 24,000 Standard rate (SR) ..... × $4 Total $96,000	Pounds allowed (SQ) .... 22,000* Standard rate (SR) .... × $4 Total $88,000

Variable overhead spending variance **$15,000 F**

Variable overhead efficiency variance **$8,000 U**

Total flexible budget variable overhead variance **$7,000 F**

*11,000 bags × 2 lbs.

Variable Overhead Spending Variance The company reported a $15,000 favorable variable overhead spending variance because actual spending was less than the standard cost of actual inputs. Using the formula approach, the variable overhead spending variance equals the difference between actual cost and the standard cost of actual inputs.

$$\text{Variable overhead spending variance} = \text{Actual cost} - (AQ \times SR)$$
$$= \$81{,}000 - (24{,}000 \times \$4)$$
$$= \$15{,}000 \text{ F}$$

Variable Overhead Efficiency Variance Using the formula approach, the variable overhead efficiency variance equals the standard rate times the difference between the actual quantity and the allowed quantity.

$$\text{Variable overhead efficiency variance} = SR(AQ - SQ)$$
$$= \$4(24{,}000 - 22{,}000)$$
$$= \$8{,}000 \text{ U}$$

This approach emphasizes that the 2,000 extra pounds used should have increased variable overhead by $8,000 at the standard rate of $4 per pound.

Interpreting Variable Overhead Variances

Favorable variable overhead spending variance A favorable variable overhead spending variance encompasses all factors that cause actual expenditures to be less than the amount expected for the actual inputs of the measurement base, including consumption and payment.

Unfavorable variable overhead spending variance Conversely, an unfavorable variable overhead spending variance results when the actual expenditures are more than expected for the inputs of the measurement base. This is caused by consuming more overhead items than expected, or by paying more than the expected amount for overhead items consumed, or by both. Thus, the term *spending variance* is often used instead of *price variance*. The key to understanding the variable overhead spending variance is recognizing that the amount of variable overhead cost allowed is determined by the level of the surrogate measurement base used. The surrogate base is typically selected to be consistent with the activity drivers in the cost allocation system. Any deviation from this spending budget causes a spending variance to occur.

Analyzing variable overhead efficiency variance The variable overhead efficiency variance measures the difference between the standard variable overhead cost for the actual quantity of the surrogate measurement base and the standard variable overhead cost for the allowed quantity of the surrogate measurement base. This variance measures the amount of variable overhead that should have been saved (or incurred) because of the efficient (or inefficient) use of the surrogate measurement base. It provides no information about the degree of efficiency in using variable overhead items such as indirect materials and indirect labor.

> **Critical Thinking & Decision-Making**
>
> **Your company has had a practice for many years of budgeting variable overhead costs based on direct labor hours. The managerial accountants have argued that if direct labor hours are controlled, variable overhead costs will also be in control since direct labor hours drive variable overhead costs. You (and your plant managers) have become skeptical of this policy because in recent years variable overhead variances have been erratic—sometimes large favorable amounts and other times large unfavorable amounts. You are beginning to plan for the coming budget year. How do you think you should budget variable overhead and evaluate managers who control these costs?**
>
> *It appears that direct labor hours may no longer be a reliable basis for budgeting variable overhead in your company. If actual variable overhead costs do not appear to correlate closely with direct labor hours, this could be an indication that the components of variable overhead have changed since direct labor hours was selected as the cost driver. Your cost accountants should consider other unit-level cost drivers for budgeting variable overhead costs. An activity-based costing method using multiple overhead cost pools with separate cost drivers might provide a more reliable basis for budgeting and controlling variable overhead costs.*

Overview of Fixed Overhead Variances

By definition, the quantity of goods and services classified as fixed expenditures is not expected to change in proportion to short-run changes in the level of production. For example, in the short run, the production level does not affect the amount of depreciation on buildings, the number of fixed salaried employees, or the amount of real property subject to property taxes. Whether Samsonite produces 10,000 or 15,000 luggage bags, the same quantity of fixed overhead is expected to be incurred, as long as the production level is within the relevant range of activity provided by the current fixed overhead items. Therefore, an efficiency variance is not computed for fixed overhead costs.

Even though the components of fixed overhead are not expected to be affected by the output level in the short run, the actual amount spent for fixed overhead items can differ from the amount budgeted. For example, higher than budgeted supervisors' salaries could be paid, there may be unanticipated increases in property taxes or insurance premiums, and the cost of leased facilities may increase. Fixed overhead costs in excess of the amount budgeted are reflected in the fixed overhead budget variance. The **fixed overhead budget variance** is, simply, the difference between budgeted and actual fixed overhead. Using the assumed fixed costs of Samsonite as an example, the fixed overhead budget variance is $1,000 unfavorable.

> **Fixed overhead budget variance = Actual fixed overhead − Budgeted fixed overhead**
> = $53,000 − $52,000
> = $1,000 U

The fixed overhead budget variance is always the same as the total fixed overhead flexible budget variance. Because budgeted fixed overhead is the same for all outputs within the relevant range, the budget variance explains the total flexible budget variance between actual and allowed fixed overhead. Similar to variable overhead, fixed overhead variances can be caused by a combination of price and quantity factors. Fixed overhead variances are examined further in Appendix 22A.

Review 22-5 — Calculating Standard Cost Variances for Variable Manufacturing Overhead *LO22-5*

Refer to the information provided in Review 22-3 for **Eli's Cheesecake** to answer the following question.

Required
Calculate all standard cost variances for variable manufacturing overhead.

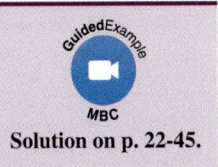

Solution on p. 22-45.

REVENUE VARIANCES AND PERFORMANCE REPORTING

The financial performance reports for *revenue centers* include a comparison of actual and budgeted revenues. Controllable costs can be deducted from revenues to obtain some bottom-line contribution margin. (Recall that contribution margin is equal to revenues minus variable costs.) If the center is then evaluated on the basis of this contribution, it is being treated as a *profit center*. Analogous to the earlier variances discussed, the total revenue variance will be decomposed into a variance that is caused by a change in selling price and a variance caused by a change in the sales quantity (also called sales volume).

LO22-6 Calculate revenue variances and prepare a performance report for a revenue center.

Performance Report of Sales Department as a Revenue Center

Assume that **Samsonite**'s July sales budget called for selling 10,000 bags at $40.00 each. If Samsonite actually sold 11,000 bags at $38.50 each, the total revenue variance is $23,500 favorable.

Actual revenues (11,000 × $38.50)	$423,500
Budgeted revenues (10,000 × $40)	(400,000)
Revenue variance	$ 23,500 F

Computing Revenue Variances

The **revenue variance** is the difference between the budgeted sales volume at the budgeted selling price and the actual sales volume at the actual selling price. Samsonite's actual revenues exceeded budgeted revenues. Higher revenues lead to increased income, which is favorable. Thus, Samsonite's total revenue variance is favorable. It can be presented as follows.

> **Revenue variance = (Actual volume × Actual price) − (Budgeted volume × Budgeted price)**

The separate impact of changing prices and volume on revenue is analyzed with the sales price and sales volume variances.

- The **sales price variance** indicates the impact of the change in sales price per unit on revenues, assuming there was no change in the quantity of units sold.
- The **sales volume variance** indicates the impact of the change in sales volume on revenues, assuming there was no change in selling price.

Revenue Variance Analysis Output: 11,000 Bags

Actual Revenue	Flexible Budget	
Actual selling price .... $ 38.50	Budgeted selling price ... $ 40.00	Budgeted selling price ... $ 40.00
Actual sales volume ... × 11,000	Actual sales volume ..... × 11,000	Budgeted sales volume ... × 10,000
$423,500	$440,000	$400,000

Sales price variance $16,500 U

Sales volume variance $40,000 F

Total revenue variance $23,500 F

Sales Price Variance The sales price variance is computed as the change in selling price times the actual sales volume.

Sales price variance = (Actual selling price − Budgeted selling price) × Actual sales volume

For Samsonite, the sales price variance for July follows.

$$\text{Sales price variance} = (\$38.50 - \$40.00) \times 11{,}000 \text{ bags}$$
$$= \$16{,}500 \text{ U}$$

Sales Volume Variance The sales volume variance indicates the impact of the change in sales volume on revenues, assuming there was no change in selling price. The sales volume variance is computed as the difference between the actual and the budgeted sales volume times the budgeted selling price.

Sales volume variance = (Actual sales volume − Budgeted sales volume) × Budgeted selling price

For Samsonite, the sales volume variance for July follows.

$$\text{Sales volume variance} = (11{,}000 \text{ bags} - 10{,}000 \text{ bags}) \times \$40$$
$$= \$40{,}000 \text{ F}$$

The net of the sales price and the sales volume variances is equal to the revenue variance.

Sales price variance.	$16,500 U
Sales volume variance	40,000 F
Revenue variance.	$23,500 F

Interpreting Revenue Variances

Interpretation of these variances is subjective. In this case, we could say that if the increase in sales volume had not been accompanied by a decline in selling price, revenues would have increased $40,000 instead of $23,500. The $1.50 per unit decline in selling price cost the company $16,500 in revenues. Alternatively, we might note that a $1.50 reduction in the unit selling price was more than offset by an increase in sales volume. An economic analysis could explain the relationship as volume being sensitive to price (*price elasticity*).

In any case, variances are merely signals that actual results are not proceeding according to plan. They help managers identify potential problems and opportunities. An investigation into their cause(s) could even indicate that a manager who received a favorable variance was doing a poor job, whereas a manager who received an unfavorable variance was doing an outstanding job. Consider Samsonite's favorable revenue variance. This occurred because actual sales exceeded budgeted sales by 1,000 bags (10%), which on the surface indicates good performance. But what if the total market for the company's products exceeded the company's forecast by 15%? In this hypothetical case, Samsonite's sales volume falls below its expected percentage share of the market. The favorable variance could occur (despite a poor marketing effort) because of strong customer demand that competitors could not fill.

Application of Revenue Variance Analysis Variance analysis can also be used by external analysts to assess the impact of various policies or economic changes. To understand the impact of California's Hospital Fair Pricing Act (CHFPA), Professor Ge Bai of Washington and Lee University applied variance analysis to California hospitals' expense recovery data.[4] Expense recovery is simply the rate at which the hospital is able to recover the costs of serving a patient by collecting from insurers. The CHFPA stipulates that hospitals can only charge low-income, uninsured patients Medicare rates for services. The act also makes it more difficult to collect payment from these patients. Dr. Bai's study shows that the CHFPA decreases the rate of expense recovery from low-income patients and increases the share of these patients in the health-care system, consistent with the aims of the CHFPA. His study also shows that hospitals appear to be offsetting the cost of

---

[4] Ge Bai, "Applying Variance Analysis to Understand California Hospitals' Expense Recovery Status by Patient Groups," *Accounting Horizons,* Vol. 30, No. 2 (June 2016): pp. 211–223.

treating more low-income patients at lower rates by collecting more aggressively from both public programs and from private insurance companies.

Performance Report for Controllable Selling Costs

Controllable costs should also be considered when evaluating the overall performance of revenue centers. A failure to consider costs could encourage uneconomic selling practices, such as excessive advertising and entertaining, and spending too much time on small accounts. The controllable costs of revenue centers include variable and fixed selling costs. These costs are sometimes further classified into order-getting and order-filling costs.

- **Order-getting costs** are incurred to obtain customers' orders (for example, advertising, salespersons' salaries and commissions, travel, telephone, and entertainment).
- **Order-filling costs** are distribution costs incurred to place finished goods in the hands of purchasers (for example, storing, packaging, and transportation).

The performance of a revenue center in controlling costs can be evaluated with the aid of a flexible budget prepared for the actual level of activity. Assume that Samsonite's July budget for the sales department calls for variable costs of $5 per bag sold and fixed costs of $10,000. If the actual variable and fixed selling expenses for July are $65,000 and $9,500, respectively, the total cost variances assigned to the sales department, detailed in **Exhibit 22.2**, are $9,500 unfavorable. In evaluating the sales department's performance as both a cost center and a revenue center, management should consider these cost variances as well as the revenue variances.

EXHIBIT 22.2 Sales Department Performance Report for Controllable Costs

SAMSONITE
Sales Department Performance Report for Controllable Costs
For Month of July

	Actual	Flexible Budget*	Flexible Budget Variance
Bags	11,000	11,000	
Selling expenses			
Variable	$65,000	$55,000	$10,000 U
Fixed	9,500	10,000	500 F
Total	$74,500	$65,000	$ 9,500 U

*Flexible budget formulas:
Variable selling expenses ($5 per bag)
Fixed selling expenses ($10,000 per month)

Performance Report of Sales Department as a Profit Center

Even though we have computed revenue and cost variances for Samsonite's sales department, we are still left with an incomplete picture of this revenue center's performance. Is the sales department's performance best represented by the $23,500 favorable revenue variance, by the $9,500 unfavorable cost variance, or by the net favorable variance of $14,000 ($23,500 F − $9,500 U)? Actually, it is inappropriate to attempt to obtain an overall measure of the sales department's performance by combining these separate revenue and selling cost variances. The combination of revenue and cost variances is appropriate only for a profit center; so far, we have left out one important cost that must be assigned to the sales department before it can be treated as a profit center. That cost is the *standard variable cost of goods sold.*

Computing the Net Sales Department Variance

As a profit center, the sales department acquires units from the production department and sells them outside the firm. Its total responsibilities include revenues, the standard variable cost of goods sold, and actual selling expenses. The sales department is assigned the *standard,* rather than the *actual, variable cost of goods sold.* Because the sales department does not control production activities, it should not be assigned actual production costs. Doing so results in passing the production department's variances on to the sales department. Fixed manufacturing costs are not assigned to the sales department because short-run variations in sales volume do not normally affect the total amount of these costs.

Net Sales Volume Variance To evaluate the sales department as a profit center, the net sales volume variance must be computed. The **net sales volume variance** indicates the impact of a change in sales volume on the contribution margin given the budgeted selling price *and* the standard variable costs. Thus, the *net sales volume variance* differs from the *sales volume variance*. It is computed as the difference between the actual and the budgeted sales volume times the budgeted unit contribution margin.

Net sales volume variance = (Actual volume − Budgeted volume) × Budgeted unit contribution margin

Using the $40 budgeted selling price, the standard unit variable manufacturing costs, and the standard unit variable selling expenses, the budgeted unit contribution margin is $11.00.

Sales.		$40.00
Direct materials.	$10.00	
Direct labor.	6.00	
Variable manufacturing overhead.	8.00	
Selling.	5.00	(29.00)
Contribution margin		$11.00

The net sales volume variance is computed as follows.

Net sales volume variance = (11,000 − 10,000) × $11.00

= $11,000 F

As a profit center, the sales department has responsibility for the sales price variance, the net sales volume variance, and any cost variances associated with its operations. As shown in **Exhibit 22.3**, the sales department variances, as a profit center, net to $15,000 unfavorable.

EXHIBIT 22.3 Sales Department Profit Center Performance Report

SAMSONITE
Sales Department Profit Center Performance Report
For Month of July

Sales price variance (see page 22-20).	$16,500 U
Net sales volume variance (see calculation above).	11,000 F
Selling expense variance (see page 22-22).	9,500 U
Sales department variances, net.	$15,000 U

Interpreting the Net Sales Department Variance

In an attempt to improve their overall performance, managers often commit themselves to unfavorable variances in some areas, believing that these variances will be more than offset by favorable variances in other areas. When the sales department is evaluated as a revenue center, the favorable sales volume variance more than offsets the price reductions and the higher selling expenses. The more complete evaluation of the sales department as a profit center (with a $15,000 unfavorable variance) gives a very different impression than the evaluation of the sales department as a pure revenue center (with a $23,500 favorable variance) or as a revenue center responsible only for its own direct costs with net favorable variances of $14,000, computed as $23,500 F minus $9,500 U. This analysis helps managers ensure that too much is not being invested into the push for sales. The performance reports of all the organization's responsibility centers are summarized to reconcile budgeted and actual income in Appendix 22B.

Calculating Revenue Variances

LO22-6 Review 22-6

Presented is assumed information for the month of March pertaining to cheesecakes sold by Eli's cheesecake.

	Budget	Actual
Unit sales	5,200	5,000
Selling price per unit	$70	$72

Required
a. Compute the revenue, sales price, and the sales volume variances.
b. What do you learn about the price elasticity of the cheesecakes?

Solution on p. 22-45.

APPENDIX 22A: Fixed Overhead Variances

The total fixed manufacturing overhead variance is comprised of two variances: the fixed overhead budget variance and the fixed overhead volume variance. We introduced the fixed budget variance in a previous section. We will review this variance using the Samsonite example and also explain the fixed overhead volume variance in this section. Both variances for Samsonite are illustrated in the following variance analysis schedule.

LO22-7 Formulate and interpret fixed overhead cost variances.

Standard Cost Variance Analysis

Input component: Fixed manufacturing overhead		Output: 11,000 Bags
Actual Cost	Budgeted Cost	Budgeted Cost Assigned
		Standard hours allowed (SH) . . . 4,400†
		Standard rate (SR) . . . . × $13
$53,000	$52,000	$57,200

Fixed overhead budget variance $1,000 U
Fixed overhead volume variance $5,200 F‡
Total fixed manufacturing overhead variance $4,200 F

† 11,000 bags × 0.40
‡ Also computed as: (4,400 allowed hours − 4,000 budget hours) × $13 standard rate per hour

Fixed Overhead Budget Variance By definition, the quantity of goods and services purchased by fixed expenditures is not expected to change in proportion to short-run changes in the level of production. For example, in the short run, the production level does not affect the amount of depreciation on buildings, the number of fixed salaried employees, or the amount of real property subject to property taxes.

Even though the components of fixed overhead are not expected to be affected by the production activity level in the short run, the actual amount spent for fixed overhead items can differ from the amount budgeted. For example, higher than budgeted supervisors' salaries could be paid, insurance premiums may increase unexpectedly, and price increases could cause the amounts paid for equipment to be higher than expected. Fixed overhead costs in excess of the amount budgeted are reflected in the fixed overhead budget variance. Samsonite's fixed overhead budget variance was previously determined as follows.

Fixed overhead budget variance = Actual fixed overhead − Budgeted fixed overhead

= $53,000 − $52,000
= $1,000 U

The fixed overhead budget variance is always the same as the total fixed overhead flexible budget variance. Because budgeted fixed overhead is the same for all outputs within the relevant range, the budget variance explains the total flexible budget variance between actual and allowed fixed overhead.

Fixed Overhead Volume Variance Recall that predetermined overhead rates are computed by dividing the predicted overhead costs for the period by the predicted activity of the period. The motivation for using a standard fixed overhead rate is the same as the motivation for using a predetermined overhead rate; namely, quicker product costing and assigning identical fixed costs to identical products, regardless of when they are produced during the year.

When a standard fixed overhead rate is used, total fixed overhead costs assigned to production behave as variable costs. As production increases, the total fixed overhead assigned to production increases. Because total budgeted fixed overhead does not vary, differences arise between budgeted and assigned fixed overhead, and managers often inquire about the cause of the differences.

The standard fixed overhead rate is computed as the budgeted fixed costs divided by some budgeted standard level of activity. Assume Samsonite applies fixed manufacturing overhead on the basis of machine hours and that 0.40 machine hours are allowed to produce one bag. Further assume that the budgeted production is 10,000 bags per month, a level that allows 4,000 (10,000 × 0.40) machine hours. The standard fixed overhead rate per machine hour is $13.

> **Standard fixed overhead rate = Budgeted total fixed overhead ÷ Budgeted activity level**
> = $52,000 ÷ 4,000 hours
> = $13 per machine hour

The total fixed overhead assigned to production is computed as the standard rate of $13 multiplied by the standard hours allowed for the units produced. Note that assigned fixed overhead cost equals budgeted fixed overhead only if the allowed activity equals the budgeted activity of 4,000 hours. If less than 4,000 hours are allowed, the fixed overhead assigned to production is less than the $52,000 budgeted. If more than 4,000 hours are allowed, the fixed overhead assigned to production is more than the amount budgeted.

Even though budgeted fixed overhead is not affected by production below or above 4,000 hours, the fixed overhead assigned to production increases at the rate of $13 per allowed machine hour. The difference between budgeted fixed overhead and fixed overhead assigned to production is called the **fixed overhead volume variance**. This variance is sometimes referred to as the **capacity variance**, a term that emphasizes the maximum output of an operation. The fixed overhead volume variance indicates neither good nor poor performance. Instead, it indicates the difference between the activity allowed for the actual output and the budget level used as the denominator in computing the standard fixed overhead rate. If fewer hours are assigned than expected, it indicates that excess capacity is present. Managers can evaluate how much excess capacity exists and the best way to fill the capacity.

To explain the difference between actual fixed overhead and fixed overhead assigned to production, two fixed overhead variances are computed: the fixed overhead budget variance and the fixed overhead volume variance. As previously explained, the fixed overhead budget variance represents the difference between actual fixed overhead and budgeted fixed overhead. The fixed overhead budget variance is caused by a combination of price and quantity factors related to the use of fixed overhead goods and services (e.g., depreciation, insurance, supervisors' salaries). The $1,000 unfavorable budget variance for Samsonite was caused either by using higher quantities of fixed overhead goods and services, or by paying higher prices than expected for those items, or both.

The fixed overhead volume variance represents the difference between budgeted and assigned fixed overhead and is caused by a difference between the activity level allowed for the actual output and the budgeted activity used in computing the fixed overhead rate. For Samsonite, actual July output of 11,000 bags resulted in 4,400 allowed machine hours and applied fixed overhead of $57,200 (11,000 bags × 0.40 hours × $13).

> **Fixed overhead volume variance = Budgeted fixed overhead − Budgeted fixed overhead assigned**
> = $52,000 − $57,200
> = $5,200 F

The $5,200 favorable fixed overhead volume variance indicates that the activity level allowed for the actual output was more than the budgeted activity level. As previously stated, this variance ordinarily cannot be used to control costs. If the budgeted activity is based on production capacity, an unfavorable variance alerts management that facilities are underutilized, and a favorable variance alerts management that facilities are utilized above their expectations.

Review 22-7 LO22-7 — Calculating Fixed Overhead Budget Variance

Assume that **Eli's Cheesecake** uses a standard cost system. The monthly fixed overhead budget is $39,000 for a planned output of 5,200 cheesecakes. For March, the actual fixed cost was $42,000 for 5,000 cheesecakes.

Required
a. Determine the fixed overhead budget variance.
b. If fixed overhead is applied on a per-cheesecake basis, determine the volume variance.

Solution on p. 22-46.

APPENDIX 22B: Reconciling Budgeted and Actual Income

LO22-8
Reconcile budgeted and actual income.

Using a contribution format, it is possible to reconcile the difference between budgeted and actual net income for an entire organization. This is done by assigning all costs and revenues to responsibility centers and summarizing the financial performance of each responsibility center. **Samsonite**'s budgeted and actual income statements, in a contribution format, for July are presented in **Exhibit 22B.1**.

EXHIBIT 22B.1 — Budgeted and Actual Income Statements: Contribution Format

SAMSONITE
Budgeted Income Statement
For Month of July

Sales (10,000 bags × $40)			$400,000
Less variable costs			
Variable cost of goods sold			
Direct materials (10,000 bags × $10)	$100,000		
Direct labor (10,000 bags × $6)	60,000		
Manufacturing overhead (10,000 bags × $8)	80,000	$240,000	
Selling (10,000 bags × $5)		50,000	(290,000)
Contribution margin			110,000
Less fixed costs			
Manufacturing overhead		52,000	
Selling		10,000	
Administrative		4,000	(66,000)
Budgeted net income			$ 44,000

Actual Income Statement
For the Month of July

Sales (11,000 bags × $38.50)			$423,500
Less variable costs			
Variable cost of goods sold			
Direct materials	$108,000		
Direct labor	70,000		
Manufacturing overhead	81,000	$259,000	
Selling		65,000	(324,000)
Contribution margin			99,500
Less fixed costs			
Manufacturing overhead		53,000	
Selling		9,500	
Administrative		3,800	(66,300)
Net income			$ 33,200

We have assumed Samsonite contains three responsibility centers: a production department, a sales department, and an administration department. Earlier in the chapter, we discussed both the production and the sales department variances. The sales department's variances in **Exhibit 22.3** net to $15,000 U and the production department's variances in **Exhibit 22.1** net to $4,000 F. Next, we assume that the administration department which incurs nonoperating expenses, had a budgeted amount of $4,000 while the actual amount spent was $3,800. Because the administration department which incurs nonoperating expenses, is a discretionary cost center, this variance of $200 ($3,800 actual − $4,000 budget) is best identified as being under budget (labeled as favorable). By assigning all variances to these three responsibility centers, the reconciliation of budgeted and actual income is as shown in **Exhibit 22B.2**.

EXHIBIT 22B.2 — Reconciliation of Budgeted and Actual Income

SAMSONITE
Reconciliation of Budgeted and Actual Income
For Month of July

Budgeted net income	$44,000
Sales department variances (**Exhibit 22.3**)	15,000 U
Production department variances (**Exhibit 22.1**)	4,000 F
Administration department variances ($3,800 actual − $4,000 budgeted)	200 F
Actual net income	$33,200

Review 22-8 LO22-8 — Reconciling Budgeted and Actual Contribution Margin

Assume that Eli's Cheesecake operates in three responsibility centers: a production department, a sales department, and an administration department. Use the information from the earlier reviews in this chapter for information on both the production and the sales department variances for the month of March. Next, assume that the administration department had a budgeted fixed amount of $36,000 while the actual amount spent was $38,000.

Required
a. Prepare a budgeted income statement (static budget) and an actual income statement for the month of March in the contribution margin format.
b. Reconcile the budgeted and actual income in part *a* with the sales, production, and administrative expense variances discussed in this and prior reviews in this chapter for Eli's Cheesecake.

Solution on p. 22-46.

KEY RATIOS AND EQUATIONS

Materials price variance = Actual quantity (Actual price − Standard price)
Materials quantity variance = Standard price (Actual quantity − Standard quantity)
Labor rate variance = Actual hours (Actual rate − Standard rate)
Labor efficiency variance = Standard rate (Actual hours − Standard hours)
Standard variable overhead cost of actual inputs = (Actual quantity × Standard variable overhead rate)
Flexible variable overhead budget cost = (Standard quantity × Standard variable overhead rate)
Variable overhead efficiency variance = Standard rate (Actual quantity − Standard quantity)
Fixed overhead budget variance = Actual fixed overhead − Budgeted fixed overhead
Revenue variance = (Actual volume × Actual price) − (Budgeted volume × Budgeted price)
Sales price variance = (Actual selling price − Budgeted selling price) × Actual sales volume
Sales volume variance = (Actual sales volume − Budgeted sales volume) × Budgeted selling price
Net sales volume variance = (Actual volume − Budgeted volume) × Budgeted contribution margin
Standard fixed overhead rate = Budgeted total fixed overhead ÷ Budgeted activity level

MULTIPLE CHOICE

Multiple Choice Answers
1. b 2. a 3. b 4. a 5. d 6. b 7. d

LO22-1 1. Which of the following statements least describes characteristics of an investment center?
  a. It is responsible for the relationship between its profits and the total assets invested in the center.
  b. It is most frequently a segment of an organization such as a product line, marketing territory, or store.
  c. It is expected to earn a target profit per dollar invested.
  d. It is the broadest and most inclusive type of responsibility center.

LO22-2 2. Presented is an abbreviated performance report for the month of July.

	Actual	Budget	Variance
Units	5,500	5,000	
Costs:			
Direct materials	$ 45,500	$ 40,000	$ 5,500 U
Direct labor	181,500	150,000	31,500 U
Variable manufacturing overhead	208,000	160,000	48,000 U
Fixed manufacturing overhead	125,000	120,000	5,000 U
Total costs	$560,000	$470,000	$90,000 U

The total flexible budget variance is
  a. $55,000 Unfavorable
  b. $90,000 Unfavorable
  c. $50,000 Favorable
  d. $55,000 Favorable

Note: Questions 3, 4, and 5 analyze the flexible budget cost variances from question 2.

LO22-3 3. The following additional information is available for the materials costs in question 2:
  - Standard cost per unit produced: 2 liters @ $4.00 per liter
  - Actual use of raw materials 13,000 liters @ $3.50 per liter

The materials price and materials quantify variances are

a. $5,500 F materials price variance and $8,000 U materials quantity variance
b. $6,500 F materials price variance and $8,000 U materials quantity variance
c. $6,500 F materials price variance and $12,000 U materials quantity variance
d. None of the above

4. The following additional information is available for the labor costs in question 2. **LO22-4**

   - Standard cost per unit of product 1.5 direct labor hours @ $20 per labor hour
   - Actual use of direct labor is 8,250 hours @ $22 per hour

   The labor rate and the labor efficiency variances are

   a. $16,500 U labor rate variance and $0 labor efficiency variance
   b. $16,500 F labor rate variance and $0 labor efficiency variance
   c. $16,500 U labor rate variance and $15,000 U labor efficiency variance
   d. None of the above

5. The following additional information is available for the variable overhead costs in question 2: **LO22-5**

   - Standard cost per unit of product 2 liters of direct materials @ $16 per liter
   - Actual use of direct materials was 13,000 liters and actual variable overhead was $208,000

   The variable overhead spending and variable overhead efficiency variances are

   a. $32,000 U spending and $0 efficiency
   b. $32,000 U spending and $16,000 U efficiency
   c. $16,000 U spending and $32,000 U efficiency
   d. $0 spending and $32,000 U efficiency

6. Budgeted June sales of the Tack Shop include 100 western saddles at $650 each. Actual sales were 90 saddles at $725 each. The June sales price and sales volume variances for western saddles are **LO22-6**

   a. $250 F sales price variance and $10 U sales volume variance
   b. $6,750 F sales price variance and $6,500 U sales volume variance
   c. $7,500 F sales price variance and $6,500 U sales volume variance
   d. None of the above

7. Cordell Company uses a standard cost system. On January 1 of the current year, Cordell budgeted fixed manufacturing overhead cost of $600,000 and production at 200,000 units. During the year, the firm produced 190,000 units and incurred fixed manufacturing overhead of $595,000. The production volume variance for the year was **LO22-7**

   a. $5,000 unfavorable
   b. $10,000 unfavorable
   c. $25,000 unfavorable
   d. $30,000 unfavorable

   CMA adapted

DATA ANALYTICS

DA22-1. Budget Variance Analysis Using Excel: Management by Exception **LO22-1**

Preston Township's City Council will be evaluating costs incurred in the various city departments at its next meeting. In total, costs exceeded budgeted amounts in the prior year by $576,277. The Council president has asked for information about actual vs. budgeted costs by department and by expense type to help in the evaluation process. Transaction and budget information is included in the file available on the textbook's website. A video demonstrating Excel tools used to answer the questions in this problem is also available on the website.

REQUIRED

1. Create two PivotTables.
   a. One for actual costs by department and expense type.
   b. One for budgeted costs by department and expense type.
2. Create two Budget Variance reports (one for variances by department and one for variances by expense type).
   - Both reports should link actual and budget data from the PivotTables. *Hint:* Before copying the formula linking your report to the PivotTable down the column of your report, you must change the reference in your formula from the name in the cell to the cell address (A5, for example). *Hint:* When linking the data, you'll discover one referencing error due to a difference in account names. The referencing error can be resolved either by updating the account name in one of the data files or by using a hard reference to the desired data cell.

- The reports should include columns for budgeted amounts, actual amounts, variance (in dollars), and variance (in percent). Show the unfavorable dollar variances as negative numbers, favorable variances as positive numbers. Show all percent variances as positive numbers. *Hint:* Use the ABS function in Excel in the formula to calculate percent variances.

3. Use the PivotTable and the variance reports to answer the following questions:
   a. Which department experienced the greatest variance between budgeted and actual cost (in dollars)? Which expense type in that department accounted for the largest share of the variance? *Hint:* Filter your PivotTables to update the variance reports.
   b. Which expense type had the highest unfavorable variance (in dollars)? Which department had the highest unfavorable variance in that expense type? Which expense type had the highest favorable variance (in dollars)? Which department had the highest favorable variance in that expense type?
   c. Which department had the highest percentage variance? Which type of expense was most over or under budget in that department? Which expense type had the highest percentage variance? Which department was most over or under budget in that expense type?
   d. Schools had the largest budget. Does it appear that the budget dollars were well managed? Explain your answer.
4. In general, should the council members be more concerned about the departments or expense types with the highest unfavorable dollar variances or the highest unfavorable percentage variances? Should the council members be concerned about departments or expense types with favorable variances? Explain your answers.

LO22-2

DA22-2. Using a Flexible Budget to Illustrate Best and Worst Case Scenarios
Refer to the data in Problem 22-38 to answer the following questions.

REQUIRED
a. Assume that budgeted selling prices for regular and deluxe packs are $60 and $90 respectively. The company expects to sell all of the products produced for the period. Management estimates that the best case scenario is that regular units increase by 10% and deluxe units increase by 20%. Management estimates that the worst case scenario is that regular units decrease by 10% and deluxe unit decrease by 15%. Create a schedule in Excel showing the contribution margin at budget, best, and worst case scenarios for regular and deluxe product.
b. Create a stacked column chart showing contribution margin of regular and deluxe products at budget, best case, and worst case. In what $10,000 range does the top of each bar fall under?
c. How could calculating a best and worst case scenario assist management in planning?

DATA VISUALIZATION

Data Visualization Activities are available in myBusinessCourse. These assignments use Tableau Dashboards to expose students to visual depictions of data and introduce students to data analytics through data visualizations. These exercises are easily assignable and auto graded by MBC.

QUESTIONS

Q22-1. What is responsibility accounting? Why should noncontrollable costs be excluded from performance reports prepared in accordance with responsibility accounting?

Q22-2. How can responsibility accounting lead to unethical practices?

Q22-3. Responsibility accounting reports must be expanded to include what nonfinancial areas? Give some examples of nonfinancial measures.

Q22-4. What is a cost center? Give some examples.

Q22-5. How is a cost center different from either an investment or a profit center?

Q22-6. What problems can result from the use of tight standards?

Q22-7. What is a standard cost variance, and what is the objective of variance analysis?

Q22-8. Standard cost variances can usually be broken down into two basic types of variances. Identify and describe these two types of variances.

Q22-9. Identify possible causes for (1) a favorable materials price variance; (2) an unfavorable materials price variance; (3) a favorable materials quantity variance; and (4) an unfavorable materials quantity variance.

Q22-10. How is standard labor time determined? Explain the two ways.

Q22-11. In the standard cost system, what is the appropriate treatment of a change in wage rates (per new labor union contract) that dominate the cost of labor?

Q22-12. Explain the difference between the revenue variance and the sales price variance.

Q22-13. Explain the net sales volume variance and list its components.

Q22-14. Explain the difference between how the *actual costs* and the *standard cost of actual inputs* are computed in variable overhead analysis.

Q22-15. Explain what the net sales volume variance measures.

Assignments with the MBC logo in the margin are available in *my*BusinessCourse. See the Preface of the book for details.

MINI EXERCISES

M22-16. Flexible Budgets and Performance Evaluation — LO22-1

For each of the following organizational units, indicate whether the unit would be most likely classified as a cost center, revenue center, profit center, or investment center.

REQUIRED
a. Hospital-owned gift shop
b. Laundry unit for a luxury hotel
c. Ticket office of a national baseball team
d. A retail clothing company owned by a parent company
e. Virtual technology help desk for a university
f. Thrift store owned by an animal shelter

M22-17. Flexible Budgets and Performance Evaluation — LO22-2

Presented is the January performance report for the Production Department of Nowwhat Company.

NOWWHAT COMPANY
Production Department Performance Report
For Month of January

	Actual	Static Budget
Volume	50,000	46,000
Manufacturing costs		
Direct materials	$130,500	$124,200
Direct labor	118,000	105,800
Variable overhead	72,000	69,000
Fixed overhead	252,000	250,000
Total	$572,500	$549,000

REQUIRED
a. Evaluate the performance report.
b. Prepare a more appropriate performance report. *Hint:* Use the format in **Exhibit 22.1**.

M22-18. Materials Variances — LO22-3

Dark Wind manufactures decorative metal house number plaques that have a standard materials cost of three pounds of direct materials at $4.00 per pound. During September, 17,500 pounds of direct materials purchased costing $4.25 per pound were used in making 6,000 house number plaques.

REQUIRED
Determine the materials price and quantity variances.

M22-19. Materials Variances — LO22-3 — Pearle Vision

Assume that **Pearle Vision** uses standard costs to control the materials in its made-to-order sunglasses. The standards call for 3 ounces of material for each pair of lenses. The standard cost per ounce of material is $12. During July, the Santa Clara location produced 6,000 pairs of sunglasses and used 17,750 ounces of materials. The cost of the materials during July was $12.25 per ounce, and there were no beginning or ending inventories.

REQUIRED
a. Determine the flexible budget materials cost for the completion of the 6,000 pairs of glasses.
b. Determine the actual materials cost incurred for the completion of the 6,000 pairs of glasses and compute the total materials variance.

c. How much of the total variance was related to the price paid to purchase the materials?
d. How much of the difference between the answers to requirements (a) and (b) was related to the quantity of materials used?

LO22-4 **M22-20.** **Direct Labor Variances**

Advanced Micro Devices develops high-performing computing products. Assume one of its microprocessors has a standard labor time of 0.25 hours and a standard labor rate of $20 per hour. During February, the following activities pertaining to direct labor for the microprocessor were recorded.

Direct labor hours used	64,000
Direct labor cost	$1,248,000
Units of the microprocessor manufactured	250,000

REQUIRED
a. Determine the labor rate variance.
b. Determine the labor efficiency variance.
c. Determine the total flexible budget labor cost variance.

LO22-4 **M22-21.** **Significance of Direct Labor Variances**

Chipper Company's April budget called for labor costs of $192,000. Because the actual labor costs were exactly $192,000, management concluded there were no labor variances.

REQUIRED
Comment on management's conclusion.

LO22-5 **M22-22.** **Variable Overhead Variances**

Assume that the best cost driver that **Sony Group Corporation** has for variable manufacturing overhead in the assembly department is machine hours. During April, the company budgeted 585,000 machine hours and $4,972,500 for its Texas plant's assembly department. The actual variable overhead incurred was $5,002,500, which was related to 575,000 machine hours.

REQUIRED
a. Determine the variable overhead spending variance.
b. Determine the variable overhead efficiency variance.

LO22-6 **M22-23.** **Sales Variances**

Presented is information pertaining to an item sold by Wheeping Creek General Store.

	Actual	Budget
Unit sales	650	600
Unit selling price	$38	$40
Unit variable costs	31	32
Unit contribution margin	$ 7	$ 8
Revenues	$24,700	$24,000
Variable costs	20,150	19,200
Contribution margin at standard costs	$ 4,550	$ 4,800

REQUIRED
Compute the revenue, sales price, and the sales volume variances.

LO22-7 **M22-24.** **Fixed Overhead Variances**

Assume that **ExxonMobil** uses a standard cost system for each of its refineries. For the Houston refinery, the monthly fixed overhead budget is $9,900,000 for a planned output of 6,000,000 barrels. For September, the actual fixed cost was $10,115,000 for 5,950,000 barrels.

REQUIRED
a. Determine the fixed overhead budget variance.
b. If fixed overhead is applied on a per-barrel basis, determine the volume variance.

LO22-7 **M22-25.** **Fixed Overhead Variances**

Tazer Inc. summarized the following production information for the most recent year.

Budgeted fixed overhead costs in total	$62,400	Actual fixed overhead costs in total	$68,900
Budgeted direct labor hours	5,200	Actual output of final units	9,900
Budgeted direct labor hours per unit	0.50		

REQUIRED

If fixed manufacturing overhead is applied on the basis of direct labor hours, compute (a) the fixed overhead budget variance and (b) the fixed overhead volume variance. Indicate whether each variance is favorable or unfavorable.

M22-26. Reconciling Budgeted and Actual Net Income   **LO22-8**

Assume that **New Balance**, a privately owned company, summarized the following information for a division that produces soccer shoes.

	February
Net sales department variance	$32,500 F
Net production department variance	24,500 U
Net administration department variance	8,800 U

REQUIRED

If the company's budgeted income is $45,000 for February, determine the actual income (loss) for the month.

EXERCISES

E22-27. Differentiating Responsibility Centers   **LO22-1**

Assume that you arrive at the airport of the city of your vacation destination. For transportation to your hotel, you board a shuttle bus. Under differing scenarios, explain how this service could be viewed as part of a (1) cost center, (2) profit center, and (3) investment center.

E22-28. Elements of a Flexible Budget   **LO22-2**

Presented are partial flexible cost budgets for various levels of output.

	Rate per Unit	Units		
		5,000	7,500	10,000
Direct materials	a.	$20,000	b.	c.
Direct labor	d.	e.	11,250	f.
Variable overhead	$2	g.	h.	i.
Fixed overhead		j.	k.	l.
Total		m.	n.	$140,000

REQUIRED

Solve for items "a" though "n."

E22-29. Computing Activity Variance and Flexible Budget Variance   **LO22-2**

Burt's Bees, owned by the **Clorox Company**, manufacturers a number of skin products. Assume that the company compiled the following budgeted manufacturing cost information for a line of lip balm.

Budgeted Costs	
Variable costs	
Direct materials	$6.00 per case
Direct labor	$3.00 per case
Variable overhead	$10.00 per case
Fixed costs	$160,000

Management budgets production of 10,000 cases for the month of June but actually produced 9,500 cases. Actual costs were as follows: direct materials, $58,000 , direct labor, $28,000 ; variable overhead $105,000; and fixed costs, $158,000.

REQUIRED

a. Prepare a variance analysis using the format illustrated in **Exhibit 22.1**
b. Analyze the activity variances and the flexible budget variances.

E22-30. Preparing a Flexible Budget for Performance Reporting   **LO22-2**

Suppose you receive the following performance report from the accounting department for your first month as plant manager for a new company. Your supervisor, the vice president of manufacturing, has concerns that the report does not provide an accurate picture of your performance in the area of cost control.

	Actual	Budgeted	Variance
Units	10,000	12,000	2,000 U
Costs			
Direct materials	$ 299,000	$ 360,000	$ 61,000 F
Direct labor	345,500	432,000	86,500 F
Variable manufacturing overhead	180,000	216,000	36,000 F
Fixed manufacturing overhead	375,000	360,000	15,000 U
Total costs	$1,199,500	$1,368,000	$168,500 F

REQUIRED
Prepare a variance analysis using the format illustrated in **Exhibit 22.1**.

LO22-3, 4 **E22-31. Computing Materials and Labor Variances**

General Mills Inc
NYSE :: GIS

In March, assume that **General Mills Inc.** purchased milk to use in the production of Yoplait yogurt. During March, General Mills manufactured 4,500 containers of yogurt for commercial use. The following information is available about standard and actual quantities and costs. There were no beginning or ending materials inventories.

	Standard for One Unit	Actual Usage for March
Direct materials	4.2 pounds @ $1.1 per pound	20,100 pounds @ $1.0 per pound
Direct labor	0.2 hour @ $16 per DLH	1,280 DLHs @ $16.50 per DLH

REQUIRED
a. Compute the materials price variance and the materials quantity variance.
b. Compute the labor rate, labor efficiency, and total labor variance.

LO22-3, 4 **E22-32. Computation of Variable Cost Variances**

The following information pertains to the standard costs and actual activity for Repine Company for September.

Standard cost per unit	
Direct materials	3 units of material A × $8.00 per unit
	2 units of material B × $4.00 per unit
Direct labor	2 hours × $15.00 per hour
Activity for September	
Materials purchased and used	
Material A	6,430 units × $7.80 per unit
Material B	3,950 units × $4.50 per unit
Direct labor used	4,100 hours × $15.50 per hour
Production output	2,000 units

There were no beginning direct materials inventories.

REQUIRED
a. Determine the materials price and quantity variances.
b. Determine the labor rate and efficiency variances.

LO22-4, 5 **E22-33. Elements of Labor and Variable Overhead Variances**

Chelsea Fabricating applies variable overhead to products on the basis of standard direct labor hours. Presented is selected information for last month when 25,000 units were produced.

	Direct Labor	Variable Overhead
Actual cost	a.	f.
Standard hours/unit	b.	b.
Actual hours (total)	12,000	12,000
Standard rate/hour	$25.00	$15.00
Actual rate	$25.50	
Flexible budget	$312,500	$187,500
Labor rate or variable overhead spending variance	c.	g.
Efficiency variances	d.	h.
Total flexible budget variance	e.	$5,000 U

REQUIRED

Solve for items "a" through "h."

E22-34. Causes of Standard Cost Variances (Comprehensive) LO22-3, 4, 5

Following are 10 unrelated situations that would ordinarily be expected to affect one or more standard cost variances.

1. A salaried production supervisor is given a raise, but no adjustment is made in the labor cost standards.
2. The materials purchasing manager gets a special reduced price on raw materials by purchasing a train carload. A warehouse had to be rented to accommodate the unusually large amount of raw materials. The rental fee was charged to Rent Expense, a fixed overhead item.
3. An unusually hot August caused the company to use 30,000 kilowatts more electricity than provided for in the variable overhead standards.
4. The local electric utility company raised the charge per kilowatt-hour. No adjustment was made in the variable overhead standards.
5. The plant manager traded in his leased company car for a new one in July, increasing the monthly lease payment by $85.
6. A machine malfunction on the assembly line (caused by using cheap and inferior raw materials) resulted in decreased output by the machine operator and higher than normal machine repair costs. Repairs are treated as variable overhead costs.
7. Two assembly workers retired after 20 years on the job. They were replaced by two young apprentices.
8. An announcement that vacation benefits had been increased resulted in improved employee morale. Consequently, raw materials pilferage and waste declined, and production efficiency increased. Employee benefits are charged to overhead.
9. The plant manager reclassified her secretary to administrative assistant and gave him an increase in salary.
10. A union contract agreement calling for an immediate 4% increase in production worker wages was signed. No changes were made in the standards.

REQUIRED

For each of these situations, indicate by letter which of the following standard cost variances would be affected. More than one variance will be affected in some cases.

a. Materials price variance.
b. Materials quantity variance.
c. Labor rate variance.
d. Labor efficiency variance.
e. Variable overhead spending variance.
f. Variable overhead efficiency variance.
g. Fixed overhead budget variance.

E22-35. Sales Variances LO22-6

Assume that **Casio Computer Company, LTD.** sells G-Shock for $50 during August as a back-to-school special. The normal selling price is $100. The standard variable cost for each device is $35. Sales for August had been budgeted for 500,000 units nationwide; however, due to the uptick in the economy, sales came in at 525,000.

REQUIRED

Compute the revenue, sales price, sales volume, and net sales volume variances. *Hint:* Compute the variances using the normal selling price as the standard.

E22-36. Fixed Overhead Variances LO22-7

Petra Company uses standard costs for cost control and internal reporting. Fixed costs are budgeted at $125,000 per month at a normal operating level of 25,000 units of production output. During October, actual fixed costs were $122,000, and actual production output was 24,000 units.

REQUIRED

a. Determine the fixed overhead budget variance.
b. Assume that the company applied fixed overhead to production on a per-unit basis. Determine the fixed overhead volume variance.
c. Was the fixed overhead budget variance from requirement (*a*) affected because the company operated below the normal activity level of 25,000 units? Explain.
d. Explain the possible causes for the volume variance computed in requirement (*b*). How is reporting of the volume variance useful to management?

E22-37. Reconciling Budgeted and Actual Contribution Margin LO22-8

The following information pertains to Midstate Supply Company for the month of November.

Static Budget	Units	Unit Price	Total
Sales	1,000	$300	$300,000
Variable manufacturing costs	1,000	$100	100,000
Variable selling costs	1,000	$50	50,000
Contribution margin			$150,000

Actual Results	Units	Unit Price	Total
Sales	1,400	$275	$385,000
Variable manufacturing costs	1,400	$110	154,000
Variable selling expense	1,400	$45	63,000
Contribution margin			$168,000
Variance between static budget and actual results:			$ 18,000 F

REQUIRED

a. Prepare a schedule for November showing actual results, a flexible budget, and the static budget.

b. Calculate the following variances for the month of November using information from part (a) where applicable and reconcile to the total variance of $18,000. Which variance(s) are due to differences in units from budget and which variance(s) are due to differences of unit dollar amounts from budget?
  1. Sales price variance
  2. Net sales volume variance
  3. Variable manufacturing cost flexible budget variance
  4. Variable selling expense flexible budget variance

c. If the company had two responsibility centers, sales and production, how would the variances be allocated to the centers?

PROBLEMS

LO22-2 P22-38. Multiple Product Performance Report

Case Products manufactures two models of cell phone cases: regular and deluxe. Presented is standard cost information for each model, sold to retailers in packages of 6 units.

Cost Components for a Pack	Regular			Deluxe		
Direct materials						
Plastic sheets	3 sheets × $12	=	$36.00	5 sheets × $12	=	$60.00
Assembly kit		=	5.00		=	5.00
Direct labor	0.5 hour × $20	=	10.00	0.75 hour × $20	=	15.00
Variable overhead	0.5 labor hr. × $5	=	2.50	0.75 labor hr. × $5	=	3.75
Total			$53.50			$83.75

Budgeted fixed manufacturing overhead is $46,000 per month. During July, the company produced 8,000 regular and 3,500 deluxe packs of cell phone cases while incurring the following manufacturing costs.

Direct materials	$561,300
Direct labor	130,800
Variable overhead	34,625
Fixed overhead	48,150
Total	$774,875

REQUIRED
Prepare a flexible budget performance report for the July manufacturing activities.

P22-39. Variance Computations and Explanations LO22-3, 4

Tarptent manufactures camping tents from a lightweight synthetic fabric. Assume the company's two-person tent has a standard materials cost of $60, consisting of 4 yards of fabric at $15 per yard. The standards call for 1.5 hours of assembly at $20 per hour. The following data were recorded for October, the first month of operations to produce 1,200 tents.

Fabric purchased and used in production	4,850 yards × $14.50 per yard
Direct labor used	1,850 hours × $19.50 per hour

REQUIRED

a. Compute all standard cost variances for materials and labor.
b. Give one possible reason for each of the preceding variances.
c. Determine the standard variable cost of the 1,200 tents produced, separated into direct materials and labor.

P22-40. Determining Unit Costs, Variance Analysis, and Interpretation LO22-3, 4, 5

Nestlé, manufacturer of Purina Dog Chow, produces its product in 500-bag batches. Assume the standard batch consists of 10,000 pounds of direct materials at $0.25 per pound, 16 direct labor hours at $15 per hour, and variable overhead cost (based on machine hours) at the rate of $20 per hour with 10 machine hours per batch. The following variable costs were incurred for the last 500-bag batch produced.

Direct materials	10,250 pounds costing $2,255 were purchased and used
Direct labor	15 hours costing $231
Variable overhead	$215
Machine hours used	9.5 hours

REQUIRED

a. Determine the actual and standard variable costs per bag of dog food produced, separated into direct materials, direct labor, and variable overhead.
b. For the last 500-bag batch, determine the standard cost variances for direct materials, direct labor, and variable overhead.
c. Explain the possible causes for each of the variances determined in requirement (b).

P22-41. Computation of Variances and Other Missing Data LO22-3, 4, 5

The following data for Bernie Company pertain to the production of 1,000 units of Product X during December. Selected data items are omitted.

Direct materials (all materials purchased were used during period)
    Standard cost per unit: (a) pounds at $3.20 per pound
    Total actual cost: (b) pounds costing $10,626
    Standard cost allowed for units produced: $9,600
    Materials price variance: (c)
    Materials quantity variance: $704 U

Direct labor
    Standard cost: 2.5 hours at $12.00
    Actual cost per hour: $12.25
    Total actual cost: (d)
    Labor rate variance: (e)
    Labor efficiency variance: $144 F

Variable overhead
    Standard costs: (f) hours at $4.00 per direct labor hour
    Actual cost: $10,600
    Variable overhead spending variance: (g)
    Variable overhead efficiency variance: (h)

REQUIRED

Complete the missing amounts lettered (a) through (h).

LO22-2, 3, 4, 5   **P22-42.**   **Flexible Budgets and Performance Evaluation**

Kathy Vanderbosch, supervisor of housecleaning for Hotel Valhalla, was surprised by her summary performance report for March given below.

HOTEL VALHALLA
Housekeeping Performance Report
For the Month of March

Actual	Budget	Variance	%Variance
$260,708	$252,000	$8,708 U	3.456% U

Kathy was disappointed. She thought she had done a good job controlling housekeeping labor and towel usage, but her performance report revealed an unfavorable variance of $8,708. She had been hoping for a bonus for her good work, but now expected a series of questions from her manager.

The cost budget for housekeeping is based on standard costs. At the beginning of a month, Kathy receives a report from Hotel Valhalla's Sales Department outlining the planned room activity for the month. Kathy then schedules labor and purchases using this information. The budget for the housekeeping was based on 8,000 room nights. Each room night is budgeted based on the following standards for various materials, labor, and overhead.

Shower supplies	4 bottles @ $0.50 each
Towels*	1 @ $4.00
Laundry	8 lbs. @ $0.25 a lb.
Labor	¾ hour @ $15.00 an hour
VOH	$3.00 per labor hour
FOH	$10 a room night (based on 8,000 room nights)

*Replacements for towels evaluated by housekeeping as inappropriate for cleaning and reuse.

With 8,600 room nights sold, actual costs and usage for housekeeping during April were

$14,620 for 36,550 bottles of shower supplies.
$32,121 for 7,740 towels.
$20,898 for 69,660 lbs. of laundry.
$91,504 for 6,020 labor hours.
$19,565 in total VOH.
$82,000 in FOH.

REQUIRED

a. Develop a complete budget column for the above performance report presented to Kathy. Break it down by expense category. The following format, with additional lines for expense categories, is suggested.

Account	Actual	Budget	Variance
Shower Supplies.	$ 14,620	?	?
⋮	⋮	⋮	⋮
Total	$260,708	$252,000	$8,708 U

b. Evaluate the usefulness of the cost center performance report presented to Kathy.
c. Prepare a more logical performance report where standard allowed is based on actual output. Also, split each variance into its price/rate/spending and quantity/efficiency components (except fixed of course). The following format, with additional lines for expense categories, is suggested.

Account	Actual	Flexible Budget	Total Variance	Price/Rate/ Spending Variance	Quantity/ Efficiency Variance
Shower Supplies.	$ 14,620	?	?	?	?
⋮	⋮	⋮	⋮		
Total	$260,708	?	?		

d. Explain to Kathy's boss what your report suggests about Kathy's department performance.
e. Identify additional nonfinancial performance measures management might consider when evaluating the performance of the housekeeping department and Kathy as a manager.

P22-43. Flexible Budget Performance Evaluation with Process Costing LO22-2, 3, 4, 5

The Evanston Company produces a single product on a continuous basis. During January, 2,000 units were completed. The July 31 ending work-in-process inventory contained 500 units, 50% complete as to materials and 25% complete as to conversion.

Evanston uses standard costs for planning and control. The following standard costs are based on a monthly volume of 2,000 equivalent units with fixed manufacturing overhead budgeted at $80,450 per month.

Direct materials [(3 square meters per unit × $12.00 per meter) × 2,000]	$72,000
Direct labor [(2 hours per unit × $22.00 per hour) × 2,000]	88,000
Variable overhead [(2 hours per unit × $5.00 per hour) × 2,000]	20,000
Fixed manufacturing overhead	80,450

Actual July production costs were as follows.

Direct materials	$ 80,525
Direct labor	95,250
Manufacturing overhead	101,165

REQUIRED

a. Determine the equivalent units of materials and conversion manufactured during July using the weighted average method.

b. Based on the July equivalent units of materials and conversion, prepare a July performance report for the Evanston Company. *Hint:* Combine variable and fixed manufacturing overhead data in the report.

c. Explain the treatment of overhead in the July performance report.

P22-44. Measuring the Effects of Decisions on Standard Cost Variances (Comprehensive) LO22-3, 4, 5

The following five unrelated situations affect one or more standard cost variances for materials, labor (assembly), and overhead:

1. Sally Smith, a production worker, announced her intent to resign to accept another job paying $1.75 more per hour. To keep Sally, the production manager agreed to raise her salary from $12 to $14 per hour. Sally works an average of 175 regular hours per month.

2. At the beginning of the month, a supplier of a component used in our product notified us that, because of a minor design improvement, the price will be increased by 10% above the current standard price of $125 per unit. As a result of the improved design, we expect the number of defective components to decrease by 50 units per month. On average, 1,200 units of the component are purchased each month. Defective units are identified prior to use and are not returnable.

3. In an effort to meet a deadline on a rush order in Department A, the plant manager reassigned several higher-skilled workers from Department B, for a total of 360 labor hours. The average salary of the Department B workers was $2.15 more than the standard $11.00 per hour rate of the Department A workers. Since they were not accustomed to the work, the average Department B worker was able to produce only 24 units per hour instead of the standard 36 units per hour. (Consider only the effect on Department A labor variances.)

4. Robbie Wallace is an inspector who earns a base salary of $2,000 per month plus a piece rate of 40 cents per bundle inspected. His company accounts for inspection costs as manufacturing overhead. Because of a payroll department error in June, Robbie was paid $1,500 plus a piece rate of 60 cents per bundle. He received gross wages totaling $2,100. *Hints:* Robbie's compensation has both fixed and variable components.

5. The materials purchasing manager purchased 5,000 units of component K2X from a new source at a price $20 below the standard unit price of $200. These components turned out to be of extremely poor quality with defects occurring at three times the standard rate of 6%. The higher rate of defects reduced the output of workers (who earn $12 per hour) from 20 units per hour to 16 units per hour on the units containing the discount components. Each finished unit contains one K2X component. To appease the workers (who were irate at having to work with inferior components), the production manager agreed to pay the workers an additional $0.50 for each of the components (good and bad) in the discount batch. Variable manufacturing overhead is applied at the rate of $6.00 per direct labor hour. The defective units also caused a 25-hour increase in total machine hours. The actual cost of electricity to run the machines is $2.00 per hour.

REQUIRED

For each of the preceding situations, determine which standard cost variance(s) will be affected, and compute the amount of the effect for one month on each variance. Indicate whether the effect is favorable or unfavorable. Assume that the standards are not changed in response to these situations. (Round calculations to two decimal places.)

LO22-7 **P22-45.** **Fixed Overhead Budget and Volume Variance**

Four-Leaf Clover Company assigns fixed overhead costs to inventory for external reporting purposes by using a predetermined standard overhead rate based on direct labor hours. The standard rate is based on a normal activity level of 30,000 standard allowed direct labor hours per year. There are five standard allowed hours for each unit of output. Budgeted fixed overhead costs are $420,000 per year. During the prior year, the company produced 5,800 units of output, and actual fixed costs were $425,000.

REQUIRED

a. Determine the standard fixed overhead rate used to assign fixed costs to inventory.
b. Determine the amount of fixed overhead assigned to inventory during the year.
c. Determine the fixed overhead budget variance.

LO22-1, 6, 8 **P22-46.** **Profit Center Performance Report**

Bach Tunes is a classical music retailer specializing in the Internet sale of digital albums of the works of J. S. Bach. Although prices vary with album popularity and number of songs, the digital albums sell for an average of $12 each and Bach Tunes pays a fixed royalty of $5.75 per digital album. With the exception of royalty fees, the operating costs of Bach Tunes are fixed. Presented are budgeted and actual income statements for the month of September.

BACH TUNES Budgeted and Actual Contribution Statements For Month of September		
	Actual	Budget
Unit sales	7,500	8,000
Unit selling price.	$12.50	$12.00
Sales revenue.	$93,750	$96,000
Cost of goods sold	(43,125)	(46,000)
Gross profit.	50,625	50,000
Operating costs	(34,700)	(35,000)
Contribution to corporate costs and profits.	$15,925	$15,000

REQUIRED

Compute variances to assist in evaluating the performance of Bach Tunes as a profit center. What was the likely cause of the shortfall in sales revenue?

LO22-1, 2, 3, 4, 5, 6, 7, 8

Falafel, Inc.

P22-47. **Profit Center Performance Report**

Falafel, Inc. operates fast-food restaurants in Washington, DC. Its main product is a serving of falafel that requires ground chick peas (direct material) and food preparation (direct labor). Assume the April budget for Falafel Inc.'s Georgetown restaurant was

- Sales 24,000 servings at $4.25 each
- Standard food cost of $0.50 per serving (1/4 pound @ $2.00 per pound)
- Standard direct labor of $0.60 per serving (1/25th hour @ $15.00 per hour)
- Fixed occupancy expenses (equipment and rent) of $7,500

Actual April performance of the Georgetown restaurant was

- Sales 26,000 servings at $4.50 each
- Food cost of $14,820 for 7,800 pounds
- Direct labor cost of $19,240 for 1,300 hours
- Fixed occupancy expenses of $7,200

In early May, the manager received the following financial performance report.

FALAFEL, INC.—GEORGETOWN
Performance Report
For the Month of April

	Actual	Budgeted	Variance
Revenues	$117,000	$102,000	$15,000 F
Food Cost	(14,820)	(12,000)	2,820 U
Labor Cost	(19,240)	(14,400)	4,840 U
Occupancy	(7,200)	(7,500)	300 F
Profit	$ 75,740	$ 68,100	$ 7,640 F

REQUIRED

a. Partition variance into variances for 1) selling price and net sales volume, 2) food variances for price and quantity, and 3) labor variances for rate and efficiency.

b. Using the results of your analysis, prepare an alternative reconciliation of budgeted and actual profit. Be sure to include the occupancy variance. *Hint:* The net variance in your revised reconciliation will still be $7,640 F.

c. Explain why the total variances for sales, food, and labor in your reconciliation differ from those originally presented to the restaurant manager.

P22-48. Comprehensive Performance Report

Instant Computing is a contract manufacturer of laptop computers sold under brand named companies. Presented are Instant's budgeted and actual contribution income statements for October. The company has three responsibility centers: Production, Selling and Distribution, and Administration. Production and Administration are cost centers while Selling and Distribution is a profit center.

INSTANT COMPUTING
Budgeted Contribution Income Statement
For Month of October

Sales (2,000 × $400)			$800,000
Less variable costs			
Variable cost of goods sold			
Direct materials (2,000 × $60)	$120,000		
Direct labor (2,000 × $40)	80,000		
Manufacturing overhead (2,000 × $20)	40,000	$240,000	
Selling and Distribution (2,000 × $45)		90,000	(330,000)
Contribution margin			470,000
Less fixed costs			
Manufacturing overhead		160,000	
Administrative		125,000	
Selling and Distribution		75,000	(360,000)
Net income			$110,000

INSTANT COMPUTING
Actual Contribution Income Statement
For Month of October

Sales (2,250 × $385)			$866,250
Less variable costs			
Cost of goods sold			
Direct materials	$139,500		
Direct labor	85,500		
Manufacturing overhead	43,875	$268,875	
Selling and Distribution		105,750	(374,625)
Contribution margin			491,625
Less fixed costs			
Manufacturing overhead		168,000	
Administrative		135,000	
Selling and Distribution		74,600	(377,600)
Net income (loss)			$114,025

REQUIRED

a. Prepare a performance report for Production that compares actual and allowed costs.
b. Prepare a performance report for Selling and Distribution that compares actual and allowed costs.
c. Determine the sales price and the net sales volume variances.
d. Prepare a report that summarizes the performance of Selling and Distribution.
e. Determine the amount by which Administration was over or under budget.
f. Prepare a report reconciling budgeted and actual net income. Your report should focus on the performance of each responsibility center.

CASES AND PROJECTS

LO22-1

C22-49. Discretionary Cost Center Performance Reports

TruckMax had been extremely profitable, but the company has been hurt in recent years by competition and a failure to introduce new consumer products. Three years ago, Tom Lopez became head of Consumer Products Research (CPR) and began a number of product development projects. Under his leadership the group had good ideas that led to the introduction of several promising products. Nevertheless, when financial results for Lopez's second year were reviewed, CPR's report revealed large unfavorable variances leading management to criticize Lopez for poor cost control. Management was quite concerned about cost control because profits were low, and the company's cash budget indicated that additional borrowing would be required to cover out-of-pocket costs. Because of his inability to exert proper cost control, Lopez was relieved of his responsibilities last year, and Gabriella Garcia became head of Consumer Products Research. Garcia vowed to improve the performance of CPR and scaled back CPR's development activities to obtain favorable financial performance reports.

By the end of this year, the company had improved its market position, profitability, and cash position. At this time, the board of directors promoted Garcia to president, congratulating her for the contribution CPR made to the revitalization of the company, as well as her success in improving the financial performance of CPR. Garcia assured the board that the company's financial performance would improve even more in the future as she applied the same cost-reducing measures that had worked so well in CPR to the company as a whole.

REQUIRED

a. For the purpose of evaluating financial performance, what responsibility center classification should be given to the Consumer Products Research Department? What unique problems are associated with evaluating the financial performance of this type of responsibility center?
b. Compare the performances of Lopez and Garcia in the role as head of Consumer Products Research. Did Garcia do a much better job, thereby making her deserving of the promotion? Why or why not?

LO22-2

C22-50. Developing Cost Standards for Materials and Labor

After several years of operating without a formal system of cost control, DeWalt Company, a tools manufacturer, has decided to implement a standard cost system. The system will first be established for the department that makes lug wrenches for automobile mechanics. The standard production batch size is 100 wrenches. The actual materials and labor required for eight randomly selected batches from last year's production are as follows.

Batch	Materials Used (in pounds)	Labor Used (in hours)
1	504.0	10.00
2	508.0	9.00
3	506.0	9.00
4	521.0	5.00
5	516.0	8.00
6	518.0	7.00
7	520.0	6.00
8	515.0	8.00
Average	513.5	7.75

Management has obtained the following recommendations concerning what the materials and labor quantity standards should be:

- The manufacturer of the equipment used in making the wrenches advertises in the toolmakers' trade journal that the machine the company uses can produce 100 wrenches with 500 pounds of direct materials and 5 labor hours. Company engineers believe the standards should be based on these facts.
- The accounting department believes more realistic standards would be 505 pounds and 5 hours.
- The production supervisor believes the standards should be 512 pounds and 7.75 hours.
- The production workers argue for standards of 522 pounds and 8 hours.

REQUIRED

a. State the arguments for and against each of the recommendations, as well as the probable effects of each recommendation on the quantity variance for materials and labor.

b. Which recommendation provides the best combination of cost control and motivation to the production workers? Explain.

C22-51. Behavioral Effect of Standard Costs   LO22-1, 2, 3, 4, 5

Merit Inc. has used a standard cost system for evaluating the performance of its responsibility center managers for three years. Top management believes that standard costing has not produced the cost savings or increases in productivity and profits promised by the accounting department. Large unfavorable variances are consistently reported for most cost categories, and employee morale has fallen since the system was installed. To help pinpoint the problem with the system, top management asked for separate evaluations of the system by the plant manager, the controller, and the human resources director. Their responses are summarized here.

Plant Manager—The standards are unrealistic. They assume an ideal work environment that does not allow materials defects or errors by the workers or machines. Consequently, morale has gone down and productivity has declined. Standards should be based on expected actual prices and recent past averages for efficiency. Thus, if we improve over the past, we receive a favorable variance.

Controller—The goal of accounting reports is to measure performance against an absolute standard and the best approximation of that standard is ideal conditions. Cost standards should be comparable to "par" on a golf course. Just as the game of golf uses a handicap system to allow for differences in individual players' skills and scores, it could be necessary for management to interpret variances based on the circumstances that produced the variances. Accordingly, in one case, a given unfavorable variance could represent poor performance; in another case, it could represent good performance. The managers are just going to have to recognize these subtleties in standard cost systems and depend on upper management to be fair.

Human Resources Director—The key to employee productivity is employee satisfaction and a sense of accomplishment. A set of standards that can never be met denies managers of this vital motivator. The current standards would be appropriate in a laboratory with a controlled environment but not in the factory with its many variables. If we are to recapture our old "team spirit," we must give the managers a goal that they can achieve through hard work.

REQUIRED

Discuss the behavioral issues involved in Merit Inc.'s standard cost dilemma. Evaluate each of the three responses (pros and cons) and recommend a course of action.

LO22-8   C22-52.   Evaluating a Companywide Performance Report

Mr. Chandler, the production supervisor, bursts into your office, carrying the company's prior year performance report and thundering, "There is villainy here, sir! And I shall get to the bottom of it. I will not stop searching until I have found the answer. Why is Mr. Richards so down on my department? I thought we did a good job last year. But Richards claims my production people and I cost the company $11,700. I plead with you, explain this performance report to me." Trying to calm Chandler, you take the report from him and ask to be left alone for 15 minutes. The report is as follows.

DICKENS COMPANY, LIMITED
Performance Report
For the Prior Year

	Actual	Budget	Variance
Unit sales	9,000	7,500	
Sales	$526,500	$450,000	$ 76,500 F
Less manufacturing costs			
Direct materials	42,750	37,500	5,250 U
Direct labor	19,350	15,000	4,350 U
Manufacturing overhead	192,100	190,000*	2,100 U
Total	(254,200)	(242,500)	(11,700) U
Gross profit	272,300	207,500	64,800 F
Less selling and administrative expenses			
Selling (all fixed)	52,750	50,000	2,750 U
Administrative (all fixed)	54,785	50,000	4,785 U
Total	(107,535)	(100,000)	(7,535) U
Net income	$164,765	$107,500	$ 57,265 F
Performance summary			
Budgeted net income			$107,500
Sales department variances			
Sales revenue	$ 76,500 F		
Selling expenses	2,750 U	$ 73,750 F	
Administration department variances		4,785 U	
Production department variances		11,700 U	57,265 F
Actual net income			$164,765

*Includes fixed manufacturing overhead of $160,000.

REQUIRED

a. Evaluate the performance report. Is Mr. Richards correct, or is there "villainy here"?
b. Assume that the sales department is a profit center and that the production and administration departments are cost centers. Determine the responsibility of each for cost, revenue, and income variances, and prepare a report reconciling budgeted and actual net income. Your report should focus on the performance of each responsibility center.

SOLUTIONS TO REVIEW PROBLEMS

Review 22-1—Solution

There is some discretion as to how each of the reporting units below would be classified by Eli's. However, likely classifications would be as follows:

- **Bakery**—Cost Center: In this case, the bakery is the "manufacturing facility." Typically, a manufacturing facility is a cost center. The bakery is responsible for producing high-quality products in the most cost-effective way possible.
- **Accounting**—Cost Center
- **Product line/Original Plain Cheesecake**—Profit Center: Typically, a product line is a profit center. The product manager of the Original Plain Cheesecake is likely responsible for the revenues, costs, and resulting profits of his or her product line. A product line is not typically an investment center as many

of the production assets are shared with other products; therefore, any decisions regarding the overall bakery assets will be made at a higher level in the organization.

Human resources—Cost Center

Cheesecake Café at O'Hare Airport—Investment Center: The Café at O'Hare will have separate assets such as a display case, cash register, and refrigerators. It will be responsible for attractive displays and customer service. So it is likely that the Café will be evaluated based on its target profit per dollar invested.

Review 22-2—Solution

The performance report prepared by the accounting department was based on a "static" budget. A better basis for evaluating your performance is to compare actual performance with a flexible budget. By dividing the budgeted variable costs amounts by 5,200 units, the budgeted unit variable costs amounts can be determined as follows:

Direct materials.	$104,000 ÷ 5,200 = $20.00 per unit
Direct labor.	$ 78,000 ÷ 5,200 = $15.00 per unit
Variable manufacturing overhead	
Category 1	$ 31,200 ÷ 5,200 = $ 6.00 per unit
Category 2	$ 20,800 ÷ 5,200 = $ 4.00 per unit

Using these budgeted unit values, a flexible budget can be prepared as follows.

	Static Budget	Activity Variance	Flexible Budget	Flexible Budget Variance	Actual	Static (total) Variance
Units	5,200		5,000		5,000	
Costs						
Direct materials	$104,000	$4,000 F	$100,000	$4,125 U	$104,125	$125 U
Direct labor	78,000	3,000 F	75,000	7,400 U	82,400	4,400 U
Variable manufacturing overhead						
Category 1	31,200	1,200 F	30,000	1,000 U	31,000	200 F
Category 2	20,800	800 F	20,000	2,000 F	18,000	2,800 F
Fixed manufacturing overhead	39,000	—	39,000	3,000 U	42,000	3,000 U
Total costs	$273,000	$9,000 F	$264,000	$13,525 U	$277,525	$4,525 U

The plant did not produce the number of units originally budgeted. Therefore, from a cost control standpoint, a flexible budget is a better basis for evaluating performance because it compares the actual cost of producing 5,000 units with a budget also based on 5,000 units. Based on the flexible budget, your performance is unfavorable; however, it is much less favorable than it appeared using a static budget.

Review 22-3—Solution

a.

Standard Cost Variance Analysis

Input component: Direct materials **Output: 5,000 units**

Actual Cost	Standard Cost of Actual Inputs	Flexible Budget Cost
Actual quantity (AQ) 21,250	Actual quantity (AQ) 21,250	Standard quantity allowed (SQ) 20,000*
Actual price (AP) .... × $4.90	Standard price (SP) .... × $5.00	Standard price (SP) .... × $5.00
$104,125	$106,250	$100,000

Materials price variance $2,125 F

Materials quantity variance $6,250 U

Total flexible budget materials variance $4,125 U

*5,000 units × 4 pounds per unit produced

b. Eli's purchased ingredients for less than expected. However, more ingredients were used per cheesecake than anticipated. It might be that the purchasing department was very effective and negotiated a good price while the production department had a lot of waste. Alternatively, the purchasing department might have purchased low-quality ingredients. Because the ingredients were lower quality, the production department was unable to use everything, resulting in waste.

Review 22-4—Solution

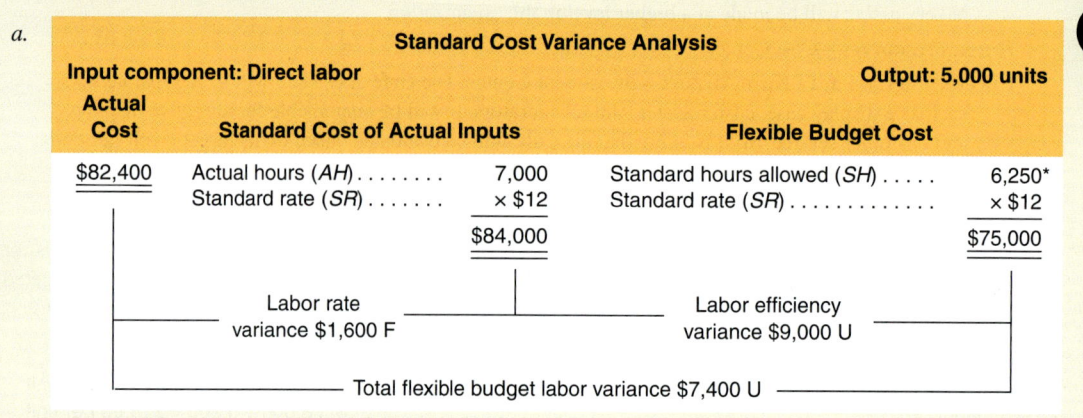

a.

Standard Cost Variance Analysis
Input component: Direct labor   **Output: 5,000 units**

Actual Cost	Standard Cost of Actual Inputs		Flexible Budget Cost	
$82,400	Actual hours (AH)	7,000	Standard hours allowed (SH)	6,250*
	Standard rate (SR)	× $12	Standard rate (SR)	× $12
		$84,000		$75,000

Labor rate variance $1,600 F   Labor efficiency variance $9,000 U

Total flexible budget labor variance $7,400 U

*5,000 units × 1.25 hours per unit

b. The labor rate variance is favorable which means that the company paid less in labor costs than expected. This could be due to less overtime charged by workers or the use of more temporary workers. The labor efficiency variance was unfavorable which means that the hours incurred were more than the standard allowed. This could be due to the use of temporary workers that lacked experience causing activities to take longer or could be due to machinery downtime which caused idle time for laborers.

Review 22-5—Solution

Standard Cost Variance Analysis
Input component: Variable overhead   **Output: 5,000 units**

Actual Costs		Standard Cost of Actual Inputs		Flexible Budget Cost	
Category 1	$31,000	Actual labor hours.	7,000	Standard hours allowed	6,250
Category 2	18,000	Standard rate	× $4.80	Standard rate	× $4.80
Total.	$49,000	Driver total.	$33,600	Driver total.	$30,000
		Finished units	5,000	Finished units	5,000
		Standard rate	× $4.00	Standard rate	× $4.00
		Driver total	$20,000	Driver total	$20,000
		Total.	$53,600	Total.	$50,000

Variable overhead spending variance $4,600 F   Variable overhead efficiency variance $3,600 U

Total flexible budget variable overhead variance $1,000 F

Review 22-6—Solution

a.   Revenue variance   = (AQ × AP) − (BQ × BP)
                                   = (5,000 × $72) − (5,200 × $70)
                                   = $4,000 U

    Sales price variance   = (AP − BP) × AQ
                                     = ($72 − $70) × 5,000
                                     = $10,000 F

    Sales volume variance   = (AQ − BQ) × BP
                                     = (5,000 − 5,200) × $70
                                     = $14,000 U

b. Eli's increased the price for cheesecakes this period. However, the sales quantity decreased. This indicates that the cheesecakes seem to be price elastic as there is a negative change in quantity that resulted from the price increase.

Review 22-7—Solution

a.

Actual fixed overhead cost	$42,000
Budgeted fixed overhead cost	39,000
Fixed overhead budget variance	$ 3,000 U

b.

Fixed overhead rate = $39,000/5,200 = $7.50 per unit

Budgeted fixed overhead cost	$39,000
Applied fixed overhead (5,000 units × $7.50)	37,500
Volume variance	$ 1,500 U

Review 22-8—Solution

Budgeted Income Statement (Static)
For Month of March

Sales ($70 × 5,200)	$364,000
Less variable costs	
Variable cost of goods sold	
Direct materials	104,000
Direct labor	78,000
Manufacturing overhead	
Category 1	31,200
Category 2	20,800
Contribution margin	130,000
Less fixed costs	
Manufacturing overhead	39,000
Administrative expenses	36,000
Budgeted net income	$ 55,000

Actual Income Statement
For Month of March

Sales ($72 × 5,000)	$360,000
Less variable costs	
Variable cost of goods sold	
Direct materials	104,125
Direct labor	82,400
Manufacturing overhead	
Category 1	31,000
Category 2	18,000
Contribution margin	124,475
Less fixed costs	
Manufacturing overhead	42,000
Administrative expenses	38,000
Budgeted net income	$ 44,475

Reconciliation of Budgeted and Actual Income

Budgeted net income	$55,000
Sales department variance*	5,000 F
Production department variance (See Review 22-2)	(13,525) U
Administrative expense variance ($38,000 − $36,000)	(2,000) U
Actual net income	$ 44,475

*$10,000 F sales price variance + $5,000 U net sales volume variance calculated as
[(5,200 − 5,000) × ($130,000/5,200)] = $5,000 U

Chapter 23

Performance Measurement Using Segment Reporting, Transfer Pricing, and Balanced Scorecard

LEARNING OBJECTIVES

LO23-1 Describe how segment reports are used to measure performance. (p. 23-3)

LO23-2 Explain why transfer pricing is necessary in a performance measurement system and assess alternative transfer-pricing methods. (p. 23-8)

LO23-3 Determine and analyze performance measures for investment centers. (p. 23-14)

LO23-4 Describe the balanced scorecard as a comprehensive performance measurement system. (p. 23-21)

Road Map

LO	Learning Objective / Topics	Page	eLecture	Review	Assignments
LO23-1	**Describe how segment reports are used to measure performance.** Strategic Business Segment :: Segment Reports :: Single-Level Reporting :: Multilevel Segment Reporting :: Segment Margin :: Segment Income :: Common Segment Costs :: Avoidable Common Costs :: Discontinuing a Segment	23-3	e23–1	R23-1	M23-15, M23-16, E23-24, P23-33, P23-34, P23-35, P23-36, P23-42, DA23-1, DA23-2, DA23-3
LO23-2	**Explain why transfer pricing is necessary in a performance measurement system and assess alternative transfer-pricing methods.** Transfer-Pricing Conflicts :: Market Price :: Variable Costs :: Variable Costs Plus Opportunity Costs :: Absorption Cost Plus Markup :: Negotiated Prices :: Dual Prices	23-8	e23–2	R23-2	M23-17, M23-18, M23-19, E23-25, E23-26, E23-27, P23-39, P23-40, P23-42, C23-43, C23-44, C23-45
LO23-3	**Determine and analyze performance measures for investment centers.** Return on Investment :: Investment Center Income :: Investment Center Asset Base :: Valuation Issues :: Residual Income :: Economic Value Added	23-14	e23–3	R23-3	M23-20, M23-21, E23-28, E23-29, E23-30, P23-37, P23-38, P23-39, P23-42
LO23-4	**Describe the balanced scorecard as a comprehensive performance measurement system.** Balanced Scorecard Framework :: Financial :: Customer :: Internal Processes :: Learning and Growth :: Cost of Quality :: Prevention Costs :: Appraisal Costs :: Internal Failure Costs :: External Failure Costs :: ESG Considerations :: Strategy	23-21	e23–4	R23-4	M23-22, M23-23, E23-31, E23-32, P23-41, P23-42

VOLKSWAGEN
www.volkswagenag.com

On the shores of the Mittelland Canal, in the shadow of Wolfsburg Castle, stands the 70 million square-foot factory of **Volkswagen** (VW). Along with employing 65,000 workers and utilizing 5,000 robots, VW's presence is felt throughout the region from the Volkswagen Arena to the VW-owned Ritz Carlton to Autostadt, VW's sprawling theme park houses the most popular car museum in the world, the ZeitHaus. But VW's products go beyond its flagship brand to include Skoda, Seat, Cupra, Audi, Lamborghini, Bentley, Porsche, Ducati, and Volkswagen Commercial Vehicles. VW also has manufacturing or assembly plants in 31 different countries in Europe, the Americas, Africa, and Asia.

How do the executives of VW set strategy for a company that has many different divisions, produces over 8.2 million units per year and employs over 672 thousand people? Given the company's diversity by product line and geographic region, preparing VW's financial and operating reports by segment assists VW managers in determining where the company should expand or contract its operations. However, the sheer complexity and volume of the company's business make the allocation of common costs across segments a difficult proposition.

One of VW's initiatives to manage the business across product and geographic lines is the introduction of modular tool-kit assemblies. This system allows the company to build all of its vehicles using four basic setups: a different tool kit for small, midsize, sports, or large/SUV vehicles. Doing this allows VW to standardize its engineering platforms and reduce inventory costs by using shared components wherever possible. With standardization comes an increase in transfers of components across product line and geographic divisions. However, what is the correct "price" to charge between internal divisions? The "selling" division would like to maximize its divisional performance by charging the highest price possible on the transfer, while the "buying" division would prefer to minimize its costs by paying the lowest price possible to the selling division. Which transfer price best represents the performance of the divisions *and* is optimal for the organization as a whole?

In this chapter, we discuss how companies can better measure and manage performance. We explain the ways that an organization evaluates strategic business segments and ensures corporate alignment. We also consider transfer pricing and some of the problems that occur when one segment provides goods or services to another segment in the same organization.

Sources: Volkswagen 2021 annual report and the company's website.

CHAPTER ORGANIZATION

Performance Measurement Using Segment Reporting, Transfer Pricing, and Balanced Scorecard

Segment Analysis and Reporting	Transfer Pricing	Investment Center Evaluation Measures	Balanced Scorecard
• Preparing Segment Reports • Interpreting Segment Reports	• Resolving Transfer-Pricing Conflicts • Determining Transfer Prices	• Return on Investment • Residual Income • Economic Value Added • Which Measure Is Best?	• Balanced Scorecard Framework • Balanced Scorecard and Strategy

SEGMENT ANALYSIS AND REPORTING

LO23-1 Describe how segment reports are used to measure performance.

A **strategic business segment** has its own mission and set of goals. Its mission influences the decisions that top managers make in both short-run and long-run situations. The organization structure dictates to a large extent the type of financial segment reporting and other measures used to evaluate the segment and its managers. In **decentralized organizations**, for example, the reporting units (typically called *divisions*) normally are quasi-independent companies, often having their own information technology system, cost accounting system, and administrative and marketing staffs.

Examples of strategic business segments include the **Porsche division of Volkswagen** and the Asia Pacific Group of **The Coca-Cola Company**. Sometimes companies establish segments within segments such as at Coca-Cola, whose Asia Pacific Group has separate business units for individual countries (Japan, Korea, etc.). In organizations, such as Volkswagen and Coca-Cola, upper management needs to create a control structure to ensure that accurate information about performance is communicated up the organizational structure. Often, management sets specific performance and profitability objectives for each segment and allows the manager of the segment the decision-making freedom to achieve those objectives. Mechanisms are created to ensure the timely and accurate flow of information. Additionally, top management will meet with segment managers to discuss performance.

Although segment reports are normally produced to coincide with managerial lines of responsibility, some companies also produce segment reports for smaller slices of the business that do not represent separate responsibility centers. These parts of the business are not significant enough to be identified as "strategic" business units as defined, but management could want information about them on a continuing basis. For example, management may even track the performance of a unit as small as a product or product line.

For example, **Volkswagen Group** has two divisions: the Automotive Division and the Financial Services Division. Financial reports are prepared for each of these units. Within the Automotive Division is the Passenger Cars Business Area. This area has eight brands. Volkswagen Group can also prepare segment reports on each of these brands to better understand the relative contribution of each.

The point is that segment reporting is not constrained by lines of responsibility. A segment report can be prepared for any part of the business for which management believes more detailed information is useful in managing that portion of the business. There are no rules that govern internal reporting. Rather, management should create and analyze segment information in ways that best support management decision-making.

Preparing Segment Reports

Segment reports are income statements for portions or segments of a business. Segment reporting is used primarily for internal purposes, although generally accepted accounting principles also require some disclosure of segment information for public corporations. Even though there are many different types of segment reports, at least three steps are basic to the preparation of all segment reports:

1. Identify the segments,
2. Assign direct costs to segments, and
3. Allocate indirect costs to segments.

The format of segment income statements varies depending on the approach adopted by a company for reporting income statements internally. The income statement formats illustrated earlier in this text, specifically, the *functional format* and the *contribution format*, can be used for segment reporting. Data availability can, however, dictate the format used. Regardless of the format adopted, it is essential that costs be separable into those directly traceable to the segments (i.e., direct costs) and those not directly traceable to segments (i.e., indirect costs or overhead). See **Exhibit 23.1**, below, for how the three steps above can be incorporated in the development of segment income. This process is analogous to earlier discussions about allocating costs to products to determine product profitability. Now, the cost object is the segment rather than the product.

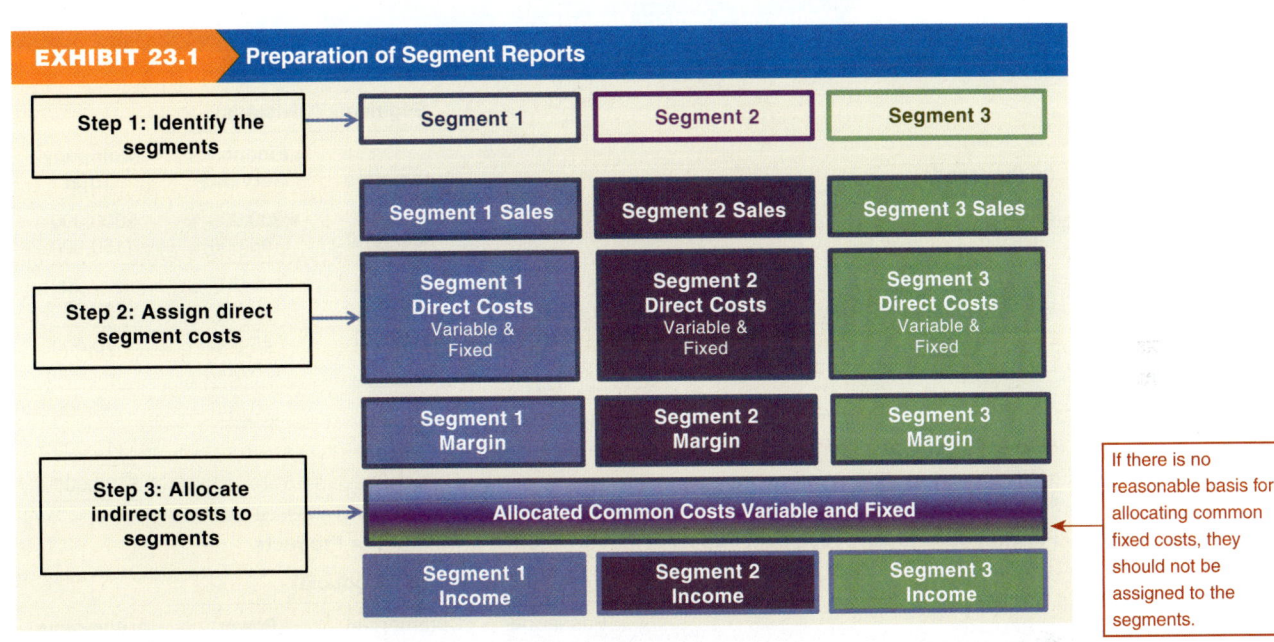

EXHIBIT 23.1 Preparation of Segment Reports

Step 1: Identify the segments	Segment 1	Segment 2	Segment 3
	Segment 1 Sales	Segment 2 Sales	Segment 3 Sales
Step 2: Assign direct segment costs	Segment 1 Direct Costs — Variable & Fixed	Segment 2 Direct Costs — Variable & Fixed	Segment 3 Direct Costs — Variable & Fixed
	Segment 1 Margin	Segment 2 Margin	Segment 3 Margin
Step 3: Allocate indirect costs to segments	Allocated Common Costs Variable and Fixed		
	Segment 1 Income	Segment 2 Income	Segment 3 Income

If there is no reasonable basis for allocating common fixed costs, they should not be assigned to the segments.

Determining the segment reporting structure is often a more difficult decision than choosing the format for the segment income statements. Companies must decide whether to structure segment reporting along the lines of responsibility reporting, and whether segment reports will be prepared only on one level or on several levels.

Single-Level Segment Reporting Approach

Under a *single-level segment* reporting approach, the total income of the segment is broken down using one measure, such as geographical area. To illustrate, we now assume that **Volkswagen** has two divisions, three product lines, and two geographic territories. Volkswagen's two divisions include the Automotive Division and the Financial Services Division. Further assume Volkswagen's three main automotive product lines are passenger cars, commercial vehicles, and power engineering. The company is organized into two geographic territories, Europe and International. If Volkswagen were using only a single-level segment reporting approach for all three groupings, one report would show the total company income statement broken down into the two divisions, a second report would show the total company income statement broken down into the three product lines, and a third report would show the total company income statement broken down into the two geographic territories.

Multilevel Segment Reporting Approach

If top management of Volkswagen wants to know how much a particular product line is contributing to the income of one of the two divisions or how much income a particular product line in one of its two geographic territories contributes, it is necessary to follow a *multilevel segment reporting approach*. Since we are assuming that Volkswagen sells three products and operates through two divisions in two territories, many combinations of divisions, products, and territories could be used in structuring the company's multilevel segment reporting. The goal is not to slice and dice the revenue and cost data in as many ways as possible but to provide useful and meaningful information to management. Therefore, deciding what type of reporting structure is most useful in managing the company is important.

This decision will be constrained to a great extent by data availability and cost. If there were no data constraints, Volkswagen could look at the company's net income for every possible combination of division, product, and territory. The more data required to support a reporting system, however, the more costly it is to maintain the system, so management must determine the value and the cost of the additional information and make an appropriate cost-benefit judgment. The ultimate goal is to aggregate data in a way that impacts decision-making. Consequently, management might eliminate analyses that would not impact the decision at hand.

Exhibit 23.2 illustrates a hypothetical *multilevel* segment report for Volkswagen.

EXHIBIT 23.2 — Multilevel Segment Reports

Panel A: First-Level Segment Report of Volkswagen—For Divisions

(in thousands)	Automotive	Financial Services	Company Total
Sales	$100,000	$200,000	$300,000
Less direct variable costs	(55,000)	(95,000)	(150,000)
Contribution margin	45,000	105,000	150,000
Less direct fixed costs	(20,000)	(60,000)	(80,000)
Division margin	25,000	45,000	70,000
Less allocated segment costs	(10,000)	(25,000)	(35,000)
Division income	$ 15,000	$ 20,000	35,000
Less unallocated common costs			(12,000)
Net income			$ 23,000

Panel B: Second-Level Segment Report of the Automotive Division—For Products

(in thousands)	Passenger Cars	Commercial Vehicles	Power Engineering	Automotive Total
Sales	$30,000	$40,000	$30,000	$100,000
Less direct variable costs	(15,000)	(19,000)	(21,000)	(55,000)
Contribution margin	15,000	21,000	9,000	45,000
Less direct fixed costs	(9,000)	(4,000)	(2,000)	(15,000)
Product margin	6,000	17,000	7,000	30,000
Less allocated segment costs	(5,000)	(4,000)	(1,000)	(10,000)
Product income	$ 1,000	$13,000	$ 6,000	20,000
Less unallocated common costs				(5,000)
Automotive Division income				$ 15,000

Panel C: Third-Level Segment Report of the Passenger Cars Product Line in the Automotive Division—For Geographic Territories

(in thousands)	Europe	International	Passenger Cars Total
Sales	$20,000	$10,000	$30,000
Less direct variable costs	(11,000)	(4,000)	(15,000)
Contribution margin	9,000	6,000	15,000
Less direct fixed costs	(3,000)	(4,000)	(7,000)
Territory margin	6,000	2,000	8,000
Less allocated segment costs	(2,000)	(3,000)	(5,000)
Territory income	$ 4,000	$(1,000)	3,000
Less unallocated common costs			(2,000)
Passenger cars income			$ 1,000

Allocated common segment costs are incurred for the common benefit of all related segments and can be reasonably allocated to segments.

The multilevel segment report shown in **Exhibit 23.2** is divided into three sections.

- **Panel A** illustrates a first-level report in which the total company income statement is segmented into the two divisions, Automotive and Financial Services.
- **Panel B** shows a second-level report in which the Automotive Division's segment income statement is broken down into its three product lines, passenger cars, commercial vehicles, and power engineering. When moving to a second-level report, costs that are direct at the first-level may not be directly traceable at a subsequent level. For example, $5,000 of the direct fixed costs at the division level (Panel A) were not directly traceable to products (Panel B) and thus became an unallocated common cost.
- **Panel C** provides a third-level income statement for the Automotive Division's passenger car product line sales in each of the company's two geographic territories, the Europe and International territories.

The example in **Exhibit 23.2** shows only part of the segment reports for Volkswagen. The complete three-level set of segment reports would also break down the Financial Services Division into its product lines and all passenger car product lines for both divisions into geographic territories.

In the Volkswagen example in **Exhibit 23.2**, the first reporting level is the company's divisions, its second reporting level is product lines, and the third is geographic territories. Another approach could be to structure the segment reports with product lines as the first level, geographic territories as the second level, and divisions as the third level. Still another approach would be to make product lines the first level, divisions the second level, and geographic territories the third level.

Regardless of how many different ways the company segments the income statements, at least one set of segment reports follows the company's responsibility reporting system. Therefore, one of the segment reports has the operating divisions as the first level. If each division has a product manager for each product, the division segment reports are broken down by products. Finally, if each product within each division has a territory manager, the product segment reports are broken down by territories.

Format of Segment Reports

While the format and labels of segment reports can vary, we describe typical components. **Exhibit 23.2** reports costs in four categories: direct variable costs, direct fixed costs, allocated common costs, and unallocated common costs. *Direct variable costs* vary in proportion to the level of sales and are subtracted from sales in calculating contribution margin. These costs are all defined analogous to our earlier definition. However, the cost object is now the segment rather than a specific product. **Direct segment fixed costs** are nonvariable costs directly traceable to the segments incurred for the specific benefit of the respective segments. **Segment margin** equals the contribution margin minus the direct segment fixed costs. In **Exhibit 23.2**, Volkswagen's segment margins are referred to as *division margins, product margins,* and *territory margins.* Segment margins represent the amount that a segment contributes directly to the company's profitability in the short run.

Segment Report
Sales
(Direct variable costs)
Contribution margin
(Direct segment fixed costs)
Segment margin
Allocated common segment costs
Segment income

Common segment costs are incurred for the common benefit of all related segments shown on a segment income statement. In some cases, allocating some common costs is reasonable. For example, if segments share common space, allocating all space-related costs to the segments based on building space occupied could be appropriate. In **Exhibit 23.2**, these **allocated common segment costs** are called *allocated segment costs*. If management believes that the common cost should be absorbed by the higher level, and not by the segment (e.g., the salary of an executive), it should not be allocated to the segment. In Panel C of **Exhibit 23.2**, if advertising costs to promote the company's passenger car products on national television could not be reasonably allocated to the two geographic territories, they would be charged to the passenger car product line as an *unallocated common cost*, not to the individual territories.

If some portion of common costs can be reasonably allocated to the segments, those allocated costs are subtracted from the segment margins to determine segment income. Hence, **segment income** represents all revenues of the segment minus all costs directly or indirectly charged to it.

Interpreting Segment Reports

To properly interpret segment income, we should ask whether segment income represents the amount by which net income of the company will change if that segment is discontinued. For example, does it mean that if the Automotive Division stops selling passenger cars in the International territory, Volkswagen's net income will increase by $1 million?

Answering this question depends on whether the costs allocated to the segments are *avoidable*. **Avoidable common costs** are allocated common costs that eventually can be avoided (that is, can be eliminated) if a segment is discontinued. If all allocated common costs are avoidable, the effect of discontinuing the segment on corporate profitability equals the amount of segment income. In most cases, the short-term impact of discontinuing a segment equals the segment margin because fixed costs are difficult to adjust in the short run. Over time, the company should be able to adjust fixed costs, such as capacity, and eliminate some, or possibly all, of the allocated common costs or find productive uses for the resources in other segments of the business. The unallocated common costs cannot be changed readily in the short term or the long term without causing major disruptions to the company and its strategy. Therefore, over the long term, the impact of discontinuing a segment should be, approximately, its segment income.

If Volkswagen discontinues selling passenger cars in the International territory (see **Exhibit 23.2**, Panel C), the short-term effect on the company's profits will probably be a $2 million reduction of profits, which equals the International territory's margin. The revenues and costs that make up the International territory margin would all be lost if passenger car sales were discontinued in the International territory, but the $3 million of common costs allocated to the International territory would continue, at least in the short term. Over the long term, however, after adjusting the capacity for selling this product in the International territory and eliminating the $3 million of allocated common costs, the effect of discontinuing passenger cars in the International territory on profits should be an increase of about $1 million, which is the amount of the segment loss for passenger cars in the International territory.

To summarize, generally, *segment margin is relevant for measuring the short-term effects of decisions to continue or discontinue a segment. However, segment income is relevant for measuring the long-term effects of decisions to continue or discontinue.* Even absent any decision to continue or discontinue a segment, the segment reporting is very informative. It helps management assess the relative profitability of various segments and helps with resource allocation decisions among divisions.

Why would an established company strategically shift from organizing segments geographically to organizing by product line?

Very few automakers have sold 10 million vehicles in a year. Toyota struggled after it hit this mark. Senior executives at Toyota expressed concern that this scale of production, sales, and distribution was difficult to manage. In order to remain nimble and competitive, Toyota reorganized operations, shifting from a geographic organization to one based on product lines. Toyota President Akio Toyoda said "We can't talk about our future without finding new ways to do our jobs." Analysts who cover the auto industry felt that this attitude was key to Toyota's ability to adjust more swiftly to challenges such as recalls and natural disasters.[1] One of the key ways that this new structure helped is by streamlining Toyota's product lines. For example, what Japanese and American customers recognized as the Prius C was marketed in Europe as the Aqua. This geographical focus served Toyota well as it grew, but there were gains to be had by simplifying the product lines. This simplification was made possible partially due to the size of the company, but also due to the global familiarity with Toyota vehicles. All companies should be prepared to modify internal structures as they evolve.

---

[1] Naomi Tajitsu, "Toyota Shakes Up Corporate Structure to Focus on Product Lines," *Reuters*, March 2, 2016. Yoko Kubota, "Toyota Plans Organizational Shake-Up," *Wall Street Journal*, February 29, 2016.

Reporting by Segment

LO23-1 Review 23-1

Refer to the Volkswagen power engineering product line in the Automotive Division in Panel B of **Exhibit 23.2** to answer the following questions.

Required
a. If the power engineering product line is dropped, in the short run, what is the impact on Automotive Division Income?
b. Assume the additional hypothetical information provided below for the power engineering product line in the Automotive Division (in thousands).

Sales—Europe territory	$12,000
Sales—International territory	18,000
Direct fixed cost—Europe territory	500
Direct fixed cost—International territory	800
Allocated segment costs—Europe territory	200
Allocated segment costs—International territory	600

Prepare a geographic territory segment report of the power engineering product line. Assume variable costs are always the same percent of sales for power engineering products.
c. Explain why the total of the Territory Margins for geographic segments of the power engineering product line does not equal the product margin of the power engineering product segment in Panel B of **Exhibit 23.2**.

Solution on p. 23-45.

TRANSFER PRICING

To determine whether each division is achieving its organizational objectives, managers must be accountable for the goods and services they acquire, both externally and internally. When goods or services are exchanged internally between segments of a decentralized organization, the way that the transferor and the transferee will report the transfer must be determined, either by negotiations between the two segments or by corporate policy. A **transfer price** is the internal value assigned a product or service that one division provides to another. The transfer price is recognized as revenue by the division providing goods or services and as expense (or cost) by the division receiving them. Transfer-pricing transactions normally occur between profit or investment centers rather than between cost centers of an organization. However, managers often consider cost allocations between cost centers as a type of transfer price. The focus in this section is on transfers between responsibility centers that are evaluated based on profits (called profit centers).

LO23-2
Explain why transfer pricing is necessary in a performance measurement system and assess alternative transfer-pricing methods.

Resolving Transfer-Pricing Conflicts

The desire of the selling and buying divisions of the same company to maximize their individual performance measures often creates transfer-pricing conflicts within an organization. Obviously, the buying division wants a low price (to minimize costs) and the selling division would like a high price (to maximize profits). As illustrated in the prior section, performance of segments is affected by revenue and costs of segments. Acting as independent units, divisions could take actions that are not in the best interest(s) of the organization as a whole, such as purchasing parts externally when the company produces plenty internally at a lower cost. This is because the autonomous divisions are focused on the performance of their own division, and not on the company as a whole. The three examples that follow illustrate the need for organizations to maintain a *corporate* profit-maximizing viewpoint while attempting to allow *divisional* autonomy and responsibility.

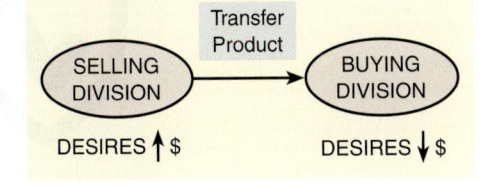

Example One: External Price < Internal Transfer Price
Suppose Volkswagen's divisions transfer products and product components to each other. Suppose the Monitors and Displays (M&D) segment within the Automotive Division manufactures two products, the basic mount and advanced mount. It sells the basic mount externally for $50 per unit and transfers the advanced mount internally for $60 per unit. The costs associated with the two hypothetical products follow.

Monitors and Displays Segment	Product	
	Basic	Advanced
Variable costs		
Direct materials	$15	$14
Direct labor	5	10
Variable manufacturing overhead	5	16
Selling	4	0
Fixed costs		
Fixed manufacturing overhead	6	15
Total	$35	$55

An external company has just proposed to supply an advanced mount substitute product to the Volkswagen passenger car brands at a price of $52. From the corporate viewpoint, this is merely a make or buy decision. The relevant costs are the differential outlay costs of the alternative actions. Assuming that the fixed manufacturing costs of the M&D Segment are unavoidable, the relevant costs of this proposal from an *overall, corporate* perspective are as follows.

Buy		$52
Make		
Direct materials	$14	
Direct labor	10	
Variable manufacturing overhead	16	(40)
Advantage of producing product internally		$12

From the corporate viewpoint, the best decision is for the product to be transferred since the relevant cost is $40 rather than to buy it from an external source for $52. However, the decision for the managers of the various passenger car brands is basically one of cost minimization assuming there is no quality difference: buy from the source that charges the lowest price. If the M&D Segment is not willing to transfer the advanced mount at a price of $52 or less, purchasing from the external supplier maximizes the profits of the passenger car brands. Of course, corporate management could intervene and require the internal transfer even though it would hurt M&D Segment's profits.

Critical Thinking & Decision-Making

When Volkswagen passenger car brand segments weigh the $60 internal purchase of the advanced mount against the $52 substitute product purchase from an external supplier, how does quality of products impact the decision?

The managers certainly are concerned about the quality of the goods. If the $52 product does not meet quality standards, the passenger car brand managers might decide to buy from the M&D Division at the higher price. A lower quality of materials can have a number of negative effects, such as an increase in material waste and excess labor costs, that could impact segment profitability. A negative impact on profitability due to purchasing lower quality goods could offset cost savings from buying the less expensive product.

Example Two: External Price < Internal Transfer Price with an External Sales Option

Consideration For the second example, assume that the M&D Segment has the option to sell an equivalent amount of the advanced mounts externally for $60 per unit instead of selling internally at a discounted price. Now the decision for M&D's management is simple: sell to the external buyer at $60 per unit. From the corporate viewpoint, it is also best for the M&D Segment to sell to the external buyer for $60 and for the passenger car brands to purchase from the external provider for $52.

Example Three: External Price < Internal Transfer Price with an Opportunity Cost

Consideration To examine a slightly different transfer-pricing conflict, assume that the M&D Segment can sell all the basic mounts that it can produce (it is operating at capacity). Also assume that there is no external market for the advanced mount, but there is a one-to-one trade-off between the production of the two mounts, which use equal amounts of the M&D Segment's limited capacity. (In other words, another basic mount can be made for every advanced mount not made by the M&D Segment.)

The corporation still regards this as a make or buy decision, but the costs of producing the advanced mounts have changed. The cost of the advanced mount now includes an outlay cost and an opportunity cost. The advanced mount's opportunity cost is the net benefit foregone if the M&D Segment's limited capacity is used to produce the advanced mount rather than the basic mount. This analysis is analogous to the relevant cost and opportunity cost analyses presented in an earlier chapter. The only difference is that we are now comparing internal and external transfers.

Selling price of basic mount		$50
Outlay costs of basic mount		
Direct materials	$15	
Direct labor	5	
Variable manufacturing overhead	5	
Variable selling	4	(29)
Opportunity cost of making advanced mount		$21

The outlay cost of the advanced mount is its variable cost of $40 ($14 + $10 + $16), as previously computed. Accordingly, the relevant costs in the make or buy decision are as follows.

Make		
Outlay cost of the advanced mount	$40	
Opportunity cost of the advanced mount	21	$61
Buy		(52)
Advantage of outsourcing		$ 9

From the corporate viewpoint, the passenger car brands should purchase advanced mounts from the outside supplier for $52 because in this case it costs $61 to make the product, considering the opportunity cost. If there were no outside suppliers, the corporation's relevant cost of manufacturing the advanced mounts would be $61. This is another way of saying that the passenger car brands should not acquire advanced mounts internally unless its revenues cover all outlay costs (including the $40 in the M&D Segment) and provide a contribution of at least $21 ($61 − $40). From the corporate viewpoint, the relevant costs in make or buy decisions are the external price, the outlay costs to manufacture, and the opportunity cost to manufacture. The opportunity cost is zero if there is excess capacity because no current production is sacrificed to produce additional units.[2]

Summary of the Advanced Mount Purchase Decision

	External Price	Internal Price	Relevant Cost	External Market	Opportunity Cost	Preferred Choice of Division	Preferred Choice of Company
Example One	$52	$60	$40	No	No	External purchase	Internal transfer
Example Two	$52	$60	$40	$60	No	External purchase	External purchase
Example Three	$52	$60	$61	No	Yes	External purchase	External purchase

In all three examples, the internal buyer would opt for the external purchase of $52 because the price is less than the internal transfer price of $60. However, from an *overall company perspective*, an internal transfer is preferable in Example One because the relevant cost is less than the external price and there is no external buyer willing to pay the higher price of $60 (or more). These examples highlight that there are a number of factors affecting the transfer decision and that the option preferable

---

[2] Setting of transfer prices can have additional economic impacts when divisions are in different countries with different tax rates. In practice, the tax rates are the first factor that impacts transfer prices in order to maximize after-tax corporate profit. The tax impact of transfer pricing however, is beyond the scope of this textbook and is covered in more advanced courses.

to the internal buyer may not be the decision that is in the best interest of the company. In the next section, we present common transfer price methods and how they impact individual segment profitability and overall company profitability.

Determining Transfer Prices

As illustrated, the transfer price of goods or services can be subject to much controversy when autonomous units are assessed on their individual unit's performance. The most widely used and discussed transfer prices are covered in this section. Although a price must be agreed upon for each item or service transferred between divisions, the selection of the pricing method depends on many factors. The conditions surrounding the transfer determine which one of the alternative methods is selected.

Although no method is likely to be ideal, one should be adopted and then used to evaluate the performance of the various segments or divisions. In considering each method, observe that each transfer results in a revenue entry on the supplier's books and a cost entry on the receiver's books.

Transfer Price Options					
Market Price	Variable Cost	Variable Cost + Opportunity Cost	Absorption Cost + Markup	Negotiated Price	Dual Prices

Market Price

When there is an existing market with established prices for an intermediate product and the transfer actions of the company will not affect prices, market prices are ideal transfer prices. If divisions are free to buy and sell outside the firm, the use of market prices preserves divisional autonomy and leads divisions to act in a manner that maximizes corporate goal congruence. Unfortunately, not all product transfers have equivalent external markets. Furthermore, the divisions should carefully evaluate whether the market price is competitive or controlled by one or two large companies. When substantial selling expenses are associated with outside sales, many firms specify the transfer price as market price less selling expenses. This is because the internal sale may not require the incurrence of costs to get and fill the order.

Critical Thinking & Decision-Making

If the selling division has excess capacity, should it insist on charging no less than the market price, even if it results in lost internal sales?

Excess Capacity

While the market price appears to be a fair price, the selling division should not stick to this price at all costs. If there is excess capacity, the incremental cost of selling internally is the variable costs of the units. Consequently, the selling division is better off making the sale, as long as the price exceeds variable costs, even if it falls below market prices.

To illustrate the impact of selling expenses using the Volkswagen example, assume that the basic mount can be sold externally at $50 per unit or transferred internally to a different segment. Under most situations, the M&D Division will never sell the basic mount for less than $50, and the other segments will likewise never pay more than $50 for it. However, if any variable expenses related to marketing and shipping can be eliminated by divisional transfers, these costs are generally subtracted from the competitive market price. In our illustration in which variable selling expenses are $4 for the basic mount, the transfer price could be reduced to $46 ($50 − $4). A price between $46 and $50 would probably be better than either extreme price. To the extent that these transfer prices represent a nearly competitive situation, the profitability of each division can then be fairly evaluated.

Variable Cost

If excess capacity exists in the supplying division, establishing a transfer price equal to variable costs leads the purchasing division to act in a manner that is optimal from the corporation's viewpoint. The buying division has the corporation's variable cost as its own variable cost as it enters the external market. Unfortunately, establishing the transfer price at variable cost causes the supplying division to report zero profits or a loss equal to any fixed costs. If excess capacity does not exist, establishing a transfer price at variable cost would not lead to optimal action because the supplying division would have to forgo external sales that include a markup for fixed costs and profits. If the advanced mount could be sold externally for $60, the M&D Segment would not want to transfer the advanced mount to any internal passenger car brand for a $40 transfer price based on the following variable costs.

Direct materials.	$14
Direct labor.	10
Variable manufacturing overhead.	16
Total variable costs.	$40

The M&D Segment would much rather sell outside the company for $60, which covers variable costs and provides a profit contribution margin of $20.

Selling price of advanced mount	$60
Variable costs.	(40)
Contribution margin	$20

Variable Cost Plus Opportunity Cost

From the corporation's viewpoint, variable cost plus the opportunity cost is the optimal transfer price. Because all relevant costs are included in the transfer price, the purchasing division is led to act in a manner optimal for the overall company, whether or not excess capacity exists.

With excess capacity in the supplying division, the transfer price is the variable cost per unit. Without excess capacity, the transfer price is the sum of the variable and opportunity costs. Following this rule in the previous example, if the M&D Segment had excess capacity, the transfer price of the advanced mounts would be set at its variable costs of $40 per unit. At this transfer price, the passenger car brands would buy the advanced mount internally, rather than externally at $52 per unit. If the M&D Division cannot sell the advanced mount externally but can sell all the basic mounts it can produce and is operating at capacity, the transfer price per unit would be set at $61, the sum of the advanced mount's variable and opportunity costs ($40 + $21). (Refer back two pages.) At this transfer price, the passenger car brands would buy advanced mounts externally for $52. In both situations, the management of the passenger car brands has acted in accordance with the corporation's profit-maximizing goal.

There are two problems, however, with this method. First, when the supplying division has excess capacity, establishing the transfer price at variable cost causes the supplying division to report zero profits or a loss equal to any fixed costs; the division is no worse off, but it is also no better off. Second, determining opportunity costs when the supplying division produces several products is difficult. If the problems with the previously mentioned transfer-pricing methods are too great, three other methods can be used: absorption cost plus markup, negotiated prices, and dual prices.

Absorption Cost Plus Markup

According to absorption costing, all variable and fixed manufacturing costs are product costs. Pricing internal transfers at absorption cost eliminates the supplying division's reported loss on each product that can occur using a variable cost transfer price. Absorption cost plus markup provides the supplying division a contribution toward unallocated costs.

> **Under the absorption cost plus markup method, why should costs be defined as standard costs instead of as actual costs?**
>
> *Defining costs at standard prevents the supplying division from passing on the cost of inefficient operations to other divisions, and it allows the buying division to know its cost in advance of purchase.*

Critical Thinking & Decision-Making

In this method, *all costs* of the supplying division become variable costs of the purchasing division. This might deter the purchasing divisions from proceeding with the internal transfer. Even though cost-plus transfer prices may not maximize company profits, they are widely used. Their popularity stems from several factors, including ease of implementation, justifiability, and perceived fairness. Once everyone agrees on absorption cost plus markup pricing rules, internal disputes are minimized.

Negotiated Price

Negotiated transfer prices are used when the supplying and buying divisions independently agree on a price. As with market-based transfer prices, negotiated transfer prices are believed to preserve divisional autonomy. Of course, the strength of the negotiators will have a large impact on the outcome of the negotiations. Negotiated transfer prices can lead to some suboptimal decisions, but this is regarded as a small price to pay for other benefits of decentralization. When some companies use negotiated transfer prices, they establish arbitration procedures to help settle disputes between divisions. However, the existence of an arbitrator with any real or perceived authority reduces divisional autonomy.

Negotiated prices should have market prices as their ceiling and variable costs as their floor. Although frequently used when an external market for the product or component exists, the most common use of negotiated prices occurs when no identical-product external market exists. Negotiations could start with a floor price plus add-ons such as overhead and profit markups or with a ceiling price less adjustments for selling and administrative expenses and allowances for quantity discounts.

Dual Prices

Dual prices exist when a company allows a difference in the supplier's and receiver's transfer prices for the same product. This method should minimize internal disagreements of division managers and problems of conflicting divisional and corporate goals. The supplier's transfer price normally approximates market price, which allows the selling division to show a "normal" profit on items that it transfers internally. The receiver's price is usually the internal cost of the product or service, calculated as variable cost plus opportunity cost. This ensures that the buying division will make an internal transfer when it is in the best interest of the company to do so.

Summary

In most cases, a market-based transfer price achieves the optimal outcome for both the divisions and the company as a whole. An exception occurs when a division is operating below full capacity and has no alternative use for its excess capacity. In this case, it is best for the corporation to have an internal transfer. Thus, to ensure that the receiving division makes an internal transfer, the company must require the internal transfer as long as its price does not exceed the established market rate. The only time an external price is more attractive when excess capacity exists is when the external price is below the variable cost of the providing internal division, and that scenario is highly unlikely.

The ideal transfer-pricing arrangement is seldom the same for both the providing and receiving divisions for every situation. In these cases, what is good for one division is likely not to be good for the other division, resulting in no transfer, even though a transfer could achieve corporate goals. These conflicts are sometimes overcome by having a higher-ranking manager impose a transfer price and insist that a transfer be made. Managers in organizations that have a policy of decentralization, however, often regard these orders as undermining their autonomy. Therefore, the imposition of a price could solve the corporate profit optimization problem but create other problems regarding the company's organization strategy. Transfer pricing thus becomes a problem with no ideal solutions.

The previous discussion has focused on the challenges of establishing transfer prices that motivate managers to make decisions that are beneficial to their divisions as well as the overall company. However, research concluded that there are often price benefits when dealing with outside vendors, if the company has the option of acquiring the goods or services internally. Suppliers might be more willing to negotiate lower prices when aware of transfer-pricing problems within the purchasing firm.[3]

---

[3] Anil Arya and Brian Mittendorf, "Interacting Supply Chain Distortions: The Pricing of Internal Transfers and External Procurement," *The Accounting Review*, May 2007.

Analyzing Purchase Decisions with Transfer Pricing LO23-2 **Review 23-2**

> **Toyota Motor Corporation** has an Apparel Division that is currently producing and selling 200,000 hats per year but has a capacity of 300,000 hats. The variable costs of each hat are $16, and the annual fixed costs are $1,350,000. The hats sell for $24 on the open market. The company's Lexus Division wants to buy 100,000 hats at $13.50 each. The Apparel Division manager refuses the order because the price is below variable cost. The Lexus Division manager argues that the order should be accepted because it will lower the fixed cost per hat from $6.75 to $4.50.
>
> **Required**
> a. Should the Lexus Division order be accepted? Why or why not?
> b. From the viewpoints of the Apparel Division and the company, should the order be accepted if the manager of the Lexus Division intends to sell each hat on the outside market for $44 after incurring additional costs of $10 per hat?
> c. What action should the company take, assuming it believes in divisional autonomy?
>
> Solution on p. 23-46.

INVESTMENT CENTER EVALUATION MEASURES

It is often difficult to select performance measures that reflect the actions and performance of the division, are measurable, and are aligned with firm objectives. Suppose you need to evaluate both an investment center and its managers. Three measures of investment center performance, return on investment, residual income, and economic value added, are discussed in the following sections. Several supporting components of these measures that help clarify the applications are also presented. In Chapter 21, we distinguished operating activities from nonoperating activities: investing and financing activities. We can similarly separate operating and nonoperating items for performance measurement. In this case, all measures would be adjusted to yield operating sales, operating assets, operating income, and so forth. Then, the following analysis would apply to those operating metrics and would reflect the operating performance of each center.

LO23-3 Determine and analyze performance measures for investment centers.

Investment Center Measures

| Return on Investment | Residual Income | Economic Value Added |

Return on Investment

Return on investment (ROI) is a measure of the earnings per dollar of investment. If financing decisions are not a responsibility of the division manager but are made at the corporate level, all effects of financing should be removed from the performance measure. Hence, the corporation's investment in the division equals the division's asset base. The return on investment of an investment center is computed by dividing the income of the center by its asset base (usually average total assets for the time period of the investment center income).

$$\text{ROI} = \frac{\text{Investment center income}}{\text{Investment center asset base}}$$

ROI can be disaggregated into investment turnover times the return-on-sales ratio.

$$\text{ROI} = \text{Investment turnover} \times \text{Return-on-sales}$$

where

$$\text{Investment turnover} = \frac{\text{Sales}}{\text{Investment center asset base}}$$

and

$$\text{Return-on-sales} = \frac{\text{Investment center income}}{\text{Sales}}$$

When investment turnover is multiplied by return-on-sales, the product is the same as investment center income divided by investment center asset base. However, the disaggregation offers the managers more information about the center's performance.

$$\text{ROI} = \frac{\text{Sales}}{\text{Investment center base}} \times \frac{\text{Investment center income}}{\text{Sales}} = \frac{\text{Investment center income}}{\text{Investment center asset base}}$$

An interesting implication of this model is that management can work toward increasing ROI through initiatives that improve investment turnover, while also taking steps to manage return-on-sales. Focusing on each of the drivers of ROI provides opportunities for management to improve financial results.

Preparing an ROI Report Based on Past Performance To illustrate the computation and use of ROI, suppose the following information is available concerning the operations of **Audi** for a single year.

Division	Asset Base	Sales	Divisional Income
Sedan	$8,000,000	$12,000,000	$1,440,000
Hatchback	4,000,000	8,000,000	960,000
SUV	7,500,000	5,000,000	1,650,000
Convertible	3,800,000	5,700,000	1,026,000

Using this information and the preceding equations, a set of performance measures is shown in **Exhibit 23.3**. To illustrate, the Sedan Division earned a return on its investment base of 18%.

$$\text{ROI} = \frac{\text{Sales}}{\text{Investment center asset base}} \times \frac{\text{Investment center income}}{\text{Sales}}$$

$$= \frac{\$12,000,000}{\$8,000,000} \times \frac{\$1,440,000}{\$12,000,000}$$

$$= 1.50 \times 0.12$$

$$= 0.18 \text{ or } 18\%$$

Using such an analysis, the company has three measurement criteria with which to evaluate the performance of the Sedan Division: (1) ROI, (2) investment turnover, and (3) return-on-sales. Management might focus on one of these metrics more than the others if it is more aligned with the company's strategy. Or, management might only analyze ROI, and let the divisions achieve their goals in any way possible.

EXHIBIT 23.3 Performance Evaluation Data

AUDI
Performance Measures
For Year Ending June 30

	Investment Turnover	×	Return-on-Sales	=	ROI
Operating unit					
Sedan	1.50		0.12		0.18
Hatchback	2.00		0.12		0.24
SUV	0.67		0.33		0.22
Convertible	1.50		0.18		0.27
Company performance criteria					
Projected minimums	1.20		0.15		0.18

Assume that for the year, Audi chose to evaluate its divisions based on company ROI and its interrelated components of investment turnover and return-on-sales. Because each division is different in size, the company evaluation standard is not a simple average of the divisions but is based on the desired relationships between assets, sales, and income.

Based on ROI, the Convertible Division had the best performance, the Hatchback Division excelled in investment turnover, and the SUV Division had the highest return-on-sales. From **Exhibit 23.3**, the Convertible Division had the best year because it was the only division that exceeded each of the company's performance criteria. Each division equaled or exceeded the minimum ROI established by the company for the year, even though the component criteria of ROI were not always achieved. Management might want to dig deeper to better understand why the targets were not met in all cases.

To properly evaluate each division, the company should study the underlying components of ROI. For the Sedan Division, management would want to know why the minimum investment turnover was exceeded while the return-on-sales minimum was not. The Sedan Division could have incurred higher unit costs by producing inefficiently. As a result of inefficient production, the return-on-sales declined to a point below the minimum desired level. Evaluating a large operating division based on one financial indicator is difficult. Remember that even the disaggregated metrics are still at a high level. Management will want to investigate components of ROI at a deeper level to fully understand the trends.

> **How is ROI of a segment of a company that sells parts internally impacted by transfer pricing policies? How is the ROI of the buying segment impacted?**
>
> *The transfer pricing policy utilized by a company impacts the sales price of goods transferred within the company. Thus, the selling price impacts the selling segment's ROI which is based on the sales of the segment. This could be further complicated if compensation of management of the segment is also tied to the performance results of the segment. On the other hand, the income of the buying segment would be impacted. The purchase price impacts cost of goods sold which affects segment income.*

Critical Thinking & Decision-Making

Preparing an ROI Report for Planning A similar analysis of ROI and its components is useful for planning for the future. In developing plans for the next year, management wants to know the possible effect of changes in the major elements of ROI for the Sedan Division. **Sensitivity analysis** can be used to predict the impact of changes in sales, the investment center asset base, or the investment center income.

Assuming the investment asset base is unchanged, a projected ROI can be determined for the Sedan Division for a sales goal of $16,000,000 and an income goal of $1,600,000.

$$\text{ROI} = \frac{\text{Sales}}{\text{Investment center asset base}} \times \frac{\text{Investment center income}}{\text{Sales}}$$

$$= \frac{\$16,000,000}{\$8,000,000} \times \frac{\$1,600,000}{\$16,000,000}$$

$$= 2.0 \times 0.10$$

$$= 0.20 \text{ or } 20\%$$

ROI would increase from 18% to 20%, even though the return-on-sales is expected to decrease from 12% to 10%. The expected change in turnover from 1.5 to 2.0 would more than offset the reduced return-on-sales. Sensitivity analysis can involve changing only one factor or a combination of factors in the ROI model. When more than one factor is changed, it is important to analyze exactly how much change is caused by each factor.

Measures such as ROI, investment turnover, and return-on-sales mean little by themselves. They take on meaning only when compared with an objective, a trend, another division, a competitor, or an industry average. Many businesses establish minimum ROIs for each of their divisions, expecting them to attain or exceed this minimum return. The salaries, bonuses, and promotions of division managers can be tied directly to their division's ROI. Without other evaluation techniques, managers often strive for ROI maximization, sometimes to the long-run detriment of the entire organization. As with all performance measures, management must create systems to minimize poor decision-making and conflicting incentives.

Determining Investment Center Income

Despite the relevance and conceptual simplicity of ROI, a division's ROI cannot be determined until management decides how to measure divisional income and investment of the investment center. Divisional income equals divisional revenues less divisional operating expenses. Determining divisional revenues is usually a relatively easy task since revenues are typically generated and recorded at the division level, but determining total operating expenses for divisions is more complicated. Because many expenses are incurred at the corporate level for the common benefit of the various operating divisions and to support corporate headquarters operations (i.e., indirect costs), the cost allocation issues discussed earlier in this chapter and book affect investment center income.

Direct division expenses are always included in division operating expenses, but there are conflicting viewpoints about how to deal with common corporate expenses. As stated earlier in this chapter, in corporate annual reports, many companies are required to provide segment revenues and expenses segmented by product lines, geographic territories, customer markets, and so on. Companies also show operating income for their various segments in their annual reports, but they include a category called *corporate* or *unallocated* for company expenses that cannot be reasonably attributed to the various segments activities. ("Unallocated" typically includes costs for corporate staffs, certain goodwill write-offs, and nonoperational gains and losses.) For example, the Volkswagen Motor Corp's 2021 annual report includes the following breakdown of its operating income by segments (stated in millions of Euro).

Note that unallocated costs are contained within the *reconciliation* line.

Passenger cars.	14,614 euro
Commercial vehicles	134
Power engineering	45
Financial services.	6,045
Reconciliation	(1,563)
Total operating income	19,275 euro

Uncontrollable Corporate Costs For internal segment reporting, some companies do not allocate corporate costs that cannot be associated closely with individual segments. Other companies insist on allocating all common corporate costs to the operating divisions to emphasize that the company does not earn a profit until revenues have covered all costs. Some top managers believe that since only operating divisions produce revenues, they should also bear all costs, including corporate costs. These managers want to ensure that the sum of the division income for the various segments equals the total income for the company.

Division managers do not control corporate costs; therefore, these costs are seldom relevant in evaluating a division manager's performance. To deal with this conflict, some companies allocate some, or possibly all, common corporate costs in reporting segment operating income, but for ROI calculation purposes exclude allocated corporate costs that are not closely associated with the divisions. These companies include in the ROI calculation costs that represent an identifiable benefit to the divisions but not general corporate costs that provide no identifiable benefits to the divisions. In practice, the treatment of corporate costs for division performance evaluation varies widely.

Determining Investment Center Asset Base

Because the primary purpose for computing ROI is to evaluate the effectiveness of a division's operating management in using the assets entrusted to them, most organizations define *investment* as the average total assets of a division during the evaluation period. For most companies, the *investment base* is defined as each division's operating assets. These normally include those assets held for productive use, such as accounts receivable, inventory, and plant and equipment. Nonproductive assets, such as land for a future plant site, are not included in the investment base of a division but in the investment base for the company. The investment base can also be measured as operating assets less current operating liabilities (net operating assets). Operating liabilities are obligations directly related to normal business operations, such as accounts payable and accrued liabilities.

General corporate assets allocated to divisions should not be included in their bases. Although the divisions might need additional administrative facilities if they were truly independent, they have no control over the headquarters' facilities. The joint nature and use of corporate facility-level expenses make any allocation arbitrary.

Other Valuation Issues in Computing Return on Investment

Once divisional investment and income have been operationally defined and ROI computations have been made, the significance of the resulting ratios can still be questioned. Return on investment can be overstated in terms of constant dollars because inflation and arbitrary inventory and depreciation procedures cause an undervaluation of the inventory and fixed assets included in the investment center asset base. Asset measurement is particularly troublesome if inventories are valued at last-in, first-out (LIFO) cost or if fixed assets were acquired many years ago. For example, a division manager could hesitate to replace an old, inefficient asset with a new, efficient one because the replacement could lower income and ROI through an increased investment base and increased depreciation. Thus, the manager is making short-sighted decisions to maximize performance measurement rather than investing in the future success of the organization.

To improve the comparability between divisions with old and new assets when computing ROI, some firms value assets at original cost rather than at net book value (cost less accumulated depreciation). This procedure does not reflect inflation, however. An old asset that cost $120,000 ten years ago is still being compared with an asset that costs $200,000 today. A better solution could be to value old assets at their replacement cost, although replacement costs are often difficult to determine.

> **Division managers in your company are evaluated primarily based on division return on investment. You recently received financial reports for your division and discovered that the ROI for your division was 14.5%; whereas, the target ROI for your division set by the CFO and the CEO was 15%. What action can you take to try to avoid missing your performance target for the next period?**
>
> *Critical Thinking & Decision-Making*

ROI is primarily a measure of the profitability of a division's assets, which is in turn a measure of how effectively the investment in assets was used to generate sales, and how profitable those sales were. ROI is driven by investment (or asset) turnover (which is division sales divided by assets) and return on sales (which is division net income divided by division sales). Therefore, increasing ROI is similar to a simultaneous balancing act involving controlling sales, expenses, and asset investment. You can increase ROI by increasing sales more than expenses, while holding asset investment constant, or by other combinations of these three variables that ultimately increase ROI. If you adjust one of these variables, at the same time you must keep your eye on the other two variables or you may not achieve your goal of increasing ROI.

Residual Income

Residual income is an often-mentioned alternative to ROI for measuring investment center performance. **Residual income** is the excess of investment center income over the minimum rate or dollar of return. The *minimum rate of return* represents the rate that can be earned on alternative investments of similar risks, which is the opportunity cost of the investment. The *minimum dollar return* is computed as a percentage of the investment center's asset base.

> **Residual Income**
> = Investment center income − Minimum dollar return on investment
> = Investment center income − (Minimum percentage return × Investment center's asset base)

When residual income is the primary basis of evaluation, the management of each investment center is encouraged to maximize residual income rather than ROI. We can again measure assets, sales, income, and so forth, as excluding all nonoperating components; similarly, the investment base can be measured as operating assets less operating liabilities.

To illustrate the computation, assume that Volkswagen requires a minimum return of 12% on each division's investment base. The residual income of Scania buses, a division of Volkswagen, with an annual net operating income of $2,000,000 and an investment base of $15,000,000 is $200,000 as computed here.

Division income	$2,000,000
Minimum return ($15,000,000 × 0.12)	(1,800,000)
Residual income	$ 200,000

Economic Value Added

A variation of residual income, referred to as **economic value added** or **EVA®**, is also often used as a basis for evaluating investment center performance. (The term EVA is a registered trademark of the financial consulting firm of Stern Stewart and Company.) EVA measures residual income earned on all funds committed long term to the organization by lenders (debt) or shareholders (equity). The key differences from the residual income approach, as discussed in the previous section, are the use of after-tax income and an organization's weighted average cost of capital. EVA can be calculated as follows.

> **EVA = Income after tax − [(Total assets − Current liabilities) × Weighted average cost of capital]**

Weighted average cost of capital is an average of the after-tax cost of all long-term borrowing and the cost of equity.[4] Economic value is added only if a division's taxable income exceeds its net cost of investing.

Using the preceding situation, assume that the company has a cost of capital of 10%, $1,800,000 in current liabilities, and a 30% tax rate. The economic value added is $80,000, computed as follows.

Scania income after taxes ($2,000,000 × 0.70)	$1,400,000
Cost of capital employed [($15,000,000 − $1,800,000) × 0.10]	(1,320,000)
Economic value added	$ 80,000

In calculating EVA, users often ignore any accounting principles that are viewed as distorting the measurement of wealth creation. In practice, EVA consultants have identified up to 150 different adjustments to GAAP income and equity that could be made to restore equity and income to their true economic values. Most companies use no more than about five adjustments (such as the capitalization of research and development cost, recognition of the market value of certain assets, and the elimination of goodwill write-offs). This process ignores the accounting rules that do not reflect the underlying economics of the transactions and business.

EVA provides a good operational metric for assessing managers' performance in terms of maximizing the market value of the company over time. It is a model that can be used to guide managerial action. Companies that use EVA for evaluating performance use it in making a broad range of decisions such as evaluating capital expenditure proposals, adding or dropping a product line, or acquiring another company. Only alternatives that provide economic value are accepted.

Which Measure Is Best?

Many executives view residual income or EVA as a better measure of managers' performance than ROI. They believe that residual income and EVA encourage managers to make profitable investments that managers might reject if being measured exclusively by ROI.

To illustrate, assume that three **Volkswagen** car brands have an opportunity to make an investment of $100,000 that requires $10,000 of additional current liabilities and that will generate a return of 20%. The manager of Volkswagen is evaluated using ROI, the manager of Audi is evaluated using residual income, and the manager of Porsche is evaluated using economic value added. The current ROI of each division is 24%. Each division has a current income of $120,000, a minimum return of 18% on invested capital, and a cost of capital of 14%. If each division has a current investment base of $500,000, current liabilities of $40,000, and a tax rate of 30%, the effect of the proposed investment on each division's performance is as follows.

---

[4] Weighted average cost of capital computations are covered in introductory corporate finance textbooks.

	Current	+	Proposed	=	Total
Volkswagen					
Investment center income/Asset base	$120,000 / $500,000		$20,000 / $100,000		$140,000 / $600,000
ROI	24%		20%		23.3%
Audi					
Asset base	$500,000		$100,000		$600,000
Investment center income	$120,000		$20,000		$140,000
Minimum return (0.18 × base)	(90,000)		(18,000)		(108,000)
Residual income	$30,000		$2,000		$32,000
Porsche					
Assets	$500,000		$100,000		$600,000
Current liabilities	(40,000)		(10,000)		(50,000)
Evaluation base	$460,000		$90,000		$550,000
Investment center income	$120,000		$20,000		$140,000
Income taxes (30%)	(36,000)		(6,000)		(42,000)
Income after taxes	84,000		14,000		98,000
Cost of capital (0.14 × base)	(64,400)		(12,600)		(77,000)
Economic value added	$19,600		$1,400		$21,000

The Volkswagen manager will not want to make the new investment because it reduces the current ROI from 24% to 23.3%. This is true, even though the company's minimum return is only 18%. Not wanting to explain a decline in the division's ROI, the manager will probably reject the opportunity even though it could have benefited the company as a whole.

The Audi manager will probably be happy to accept the new project because it increases residual income by $2,000. Any investment that provides a return more than the required minimum of 18% will be acceptable to the Audi manager. Given a profit maximization goal for the organization, the residual income method is preferred over ROI evaluations because it encourages division managers to accept all projects with returns above the 18% cutoff. The same is true for the Porsche manager, although the EVA increase is not as high as that of the residual income because it has a different base.

The primary disadvantage of the residual income and EVA methods as comparative evaluation tools is that they measure performance in absolute dollars rather than percentages. Although they can be used to compare period-to-period results of the same division or with similar-size divisions, they cannot be used effectively to compare the performance of divisions of substantially different sizes. For example, the residual income of a multimillion dollar sales division should be higher than that of a half-million-dollar sales division. Because most performance evaluations and comparisons are made between units or alternative investments of different sizes, ROI continues to be extensively used.

Computing Return on Investment and Residual Income — LO23-3 **Review 23-3**

Toyota, a decentralized automobile company, has three divisions: Toyota, Lexus, and Powertrain. Assume corporate management desires a minimum return of 15% on its investments and has a 20% tax rate. Suppose the divisions' current results follow (in thousands).

Division	Income	Investment
Toyota	$30,000	$200,000
Lexus	50,000	250,000
Powertrain	22,000	100,000

The company is planning an expansion project next year that will cost $50,000,000 and return $9,000,000 per year.

continued

continued from previous page

Required
a. Compute the ROI for each division for the current year.
b. Compute the residual income for each division for the current year.
c. Rank the divisions according to their ROI and residual income.
d. Assuming that other income and investments will remain unchanged, determine the ROI of the project by itself. What is the effect on ROI and residual income, if the new project is added to each division?

Solution on p. 23-46.

BALANCED SCORECARD

LO23-4 Describe the balanced scorecard as a comprehensive performance measurement system.

Financial metrics only tell part of the story. Typically, financial analysis is the first step. The quantitative information must then be combined with qualitative measures to evaluate managerial performance. This section examines a popular method of performance evaluation using *both* financial and nonfinancial information, the balanced scorecard.

We might ask: why not use just financial measures?

- First, no single financial measure captures all performance aspects of an organization. More than one measure must be used.

- Second, financial measures have reporting time lags that could hinder timely decision-making. Nonfinancial measures are *leading indicators* of performance that can often provide information before financial indicators.

- Third, financial measures might not accurately capture the information needed for current decision-making because of the delay that sometimes occurs between making financial investments and receiving their results. For example, building a new nuclear power plant can take several years with the investment in total assets increasing the entire time without generating any revenues.

Balanced Scorecard Framework

Comprehensive performance measurement systems are one suggested solution. The basic premise is to establish a relevant set of key performance indicators to monitor performance. The **balanced scorecard** is a performance measurement system that includes financial and operational measures related to a firm's goals and strategies. The balanced scorecard aims to translate strategy into a system of related metrics. The goal is for the company to succeed at its strategy by improving on the metrics included in the balanced scorecard. The balanced scorecard comprises several categories, or perspectives, of measurements, the most common of which include the following.

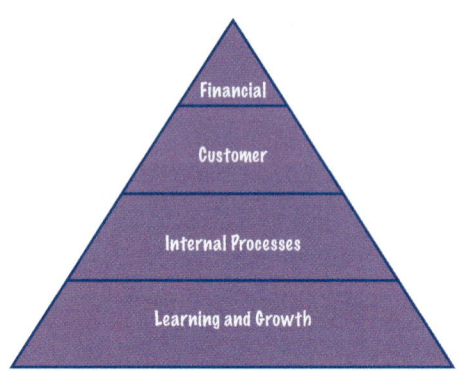

- Financial: Measures the company's financial performance
- Customer: Reflects the customer's view of the company
- Internal processes: Measures the effectiveness of the company's operations
- Learning and growth (also called innovation and learning): Reflects the willingness of employees to improve and create company value

A balanced scorecard is typically a set of reports required of operating units in an organization. Many companies develop strategy maps that detail the ways in which measures of innovation and learning lead to improvements in internal process metrics, which lead to an improvement in customer perception. This increase in customer perception impacts sales, which ultimately improves shareholder value. When managers arrange the metrics in map form, employees are better able to visualize how their actions result in company success.

Balanced Scorecard Illustrations

For example, **Volkswagen** might have a balanced scorecard that looks something like the one in **Exhibit 23.4** for the division that manufactures and sells spare parts. This balanced scorecard uses four categories for evaluation and includes financial and nonfinancial information. Each category being monitored has information from the previous period and the standard related to the category. The report should always include the current period, at least one previous period, and some standard. Each department manager should provide documentation and an appropriate explanation as to the change in measurements during the reporting period.

EXHIBIT 23.4 — Balanced Scorecard Illustration

	Standard	Prior Period	Current Period
Financial			
Cash flow	$ 25,000	$ 28,000	$ 21,000
Return on investment (ROI)	0.18	0.22	0.19
Sales	$4,400,000	$4,494,000	$4,342,000
Customer			
Average customers per hour	75	80	71
Number of customer complaints per period	22	21	17
Number of sales returns per period	10	8	5
Internal Processes			
Parts sold/produced per day ratio	0.96	0.93	0.91
Daily units lost (broken, misplaced, etc.)	25	32	34
Employee turnover per period	0.10	0.07	0.00
Learning and Growth			
New products introduced during period	1	1	0
Products discontinued during period	1	1	1
Number of sales promotions	3	3	2
Special offers, discounts, etc.	4	5	3

In making assessments with the evaluation categories, it is important to consider both trailing and leading performance measures. **Trailing measures** look backward at historical data while **leading measures** provide some idea of what to expect currently or in the near future. For example, in the financial category, ROI is a trailing indicator while a budget of production units and costs for the next period is a leading indicator. In the customer category, the number of sales invoices per store might tell us whether each store is maintaining its customer base (a trailing indicator) while the number of product complaints per 1,000 invoices might be a leading indicator of customer satisfaction, quality control problems, and future sales. The power of the balanced scorecard (or other similar methodologies) lies in the linkages between metrics over time. For example, a drop in the number of product complaints today, could favorably impact customer perception, and ultimately sales in the future.

Not-for-profit balanced scorecard application The use of balanced scorecard systems to monitor and assess managerial and organizational performance is increasing worldwide. For example, the **Department of Education** applies a modified version of the balanced scorecard to universities. The College Scorecard was developed to help prospective students evaluate universities before applying. Like all balanced scorecard approaches, the efficacy of the College Scorecard depends on how well what is measured reflects the underlying economics of the business or organization, which is reflected in both the praise and criticism of the College Scorecard.[5] Proponents of the scorecard point to measurement of alumni debt and salaries as powerful reflections of important economic realities that prospective students should consider. Critics of the College Scorecard note that the data in the Scorecard does not allow students to compare themselves by major. A history major considering two schools can only compare average students at the two schools, not history majors at the two schools. Critics also point to the fact that the scorecard only considers full-time students who start and finish at the same school.

---

[5] Peter McPherson and Andrew Kelly, "The College Scorecard Strikes Out," *Wall Street Journal*, March 16, 2015. Jonathan Rothwell, "Understanding the College Scorecard," *Brookings*, September 28, 2015.

Considerations in Using the Balanced Scorecard Approach

With all balanced scorecard approaches to performance evaluation, two essential considerations underpin success. First, the scorecard must be based on a clear understanding of the business activity. Second, the limitations of what can be measured should be carefully considered. Users of the scorecard approach must be careful to craft measurements that accurately reflect the underlying value creation process.

A balanced scorecard gives management a perspective of the organization's performance on a recurring set of criteria. Since each reporting unit knows what reports are expected, no one is surprised by changing monthly requests for data. Because the multiple perspectives provide management a broad analysis of the organization's performance, it allows them to determine how and where the goals and objectives are either being achieved or not achieved. Management can look at the links between the metrics to see *why* high-level goals were not achieved. For example, was there a lack of new product introductions last quarter that resulted in lower sales this quarter?

For most management teams, the balanced scorecard highlights trade-offs between measures. For example, a substantial increase in customer satisfaction can result in a short-run decrease in ROI because the extra effort to please customers is expensive, thereby reducing current ROI. However, the goal is that the investment in customer satisfaction will lead to increased future ROI. A balanced scorecard can be filtered down the organization with successively lower-level operating units having their own scorecards that mimic those of the higher-level units. This provides all levels of management an opportunity to evaluate operations from more than just a financial perspective.

As with all management tools and techniques, the use of the balanced scorecard must be incorporated with the other information sources within the organization. Just as the accounting information system cannot stand alone in managing a business, neither can the balanced scorecard. Some areas could need extensive accounting information in great detail to make the best possible decision while other areas need great detail in production or service integration to be at the right place at the right time. By using a multifaceted approach to managing, the organization should be able to better establish an operating strategy that coincides with its overall goals and objectives.

Internal Measure: Cost of Quality

A focus on quality is a way to increase the effectiveness of the company's operations. Thus, a type of internal processes measure found on a balanced scorecard is focused on improving product and service quality. For example, an internal process measure could be to decrease quality defects. Managing the costs of quality is a way to impact quality defects.

Costs of quality can be classified into four categories.

- **Prevention costs** are incurred for activities that preclude product defects resulting from dysfunctional processing. Prevention activities include improved production equipment, worker training, and engineering and product modeling.

- **Appraisal costs** are incurred to monitor and compensate for mistakes not eliminated through prevention activities. Organizational spending for prevention and appraisal activities will reduce failure costs.

- **Internal failure costs** are expenditures, such as scrap or rework, incurred to remedy defective units before they are shipped to customers.

- **External failure costs** are expenditures for items, such as warranty work, customer complaints, litigation, and defective product recalls, that are incurred after a faulty unit of product has been shipped to (or an improper service has been performed for) the customer.

Total quality costs can also be classified as compliance (or assurance) and noncompliance (or quality failure). The **cost of compliance** equals the sum of prevention and appraisal costs. Compliance costs are incurred to reduce or eliminate the present and future costs of failure; thus, expenditures for compliance are proactive. Furthermore, effective investments in prevention activities can even minimize the costs of appraisal. The **cost of noncompliance** results from production imperfections and is equal to internal and external failure costs. **Exhibit 23.5** provides specific examples of each type of quality cost.

A **cost of quality report** summarizes the categories of quality costs for a period. Theoretically, if prevention and appraisal costs were prudently incurred, failure costs would become $0. However, because prevention and appraisal costs must still be incurred to identify and reduce failures, total quality costs can never actually be zero. Total company costs decline, rather than increase, as an organization makes quality improvements. It seems that it is the lack of high quality, rather than the pursuit of high quality, that is expensive. Understanding the types and causes of quality costs helps managers prioritize improvement projects and provide feedback that supports and justifies improvement efforts. These efforts could ultimately have a positive impact on the internal processes section of the balanced scorecard.

EXHIBIT 23.5 Types of Quality Costs

Cost of Compliance		Costs of Noncompliance	
Prevention Costs	**Appraisal Costs**	**Internal Failure Costs**	**External Failure Costs**
Quality training of employees	Quality inspections	Reworking products	Handling of complaints
Quality product design	Testing equipment	Scrap and waste	Warranty processing
Developing product specifications	Automating processes	Rescheduling production and setup	Repairing or replacing returns
Testing and adjusting equipment	Reporting defects	Experiencing unplanned downtime in production	Litigating warranty claims

Considering the manufacturing of a passenger car for Volkswagen, which costs of quality would you expect to be incurred (a) only before or during production and (b) only after the sale of the car?

Before Production	During Production	After Production	After Sale

a (Before Production, During Production, After Production)   b (After Sale)

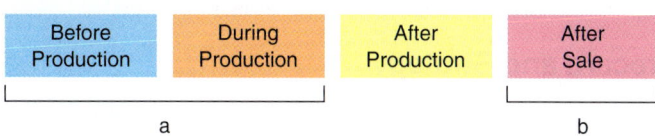

Prevention costs incur before the product is complete (a). The goal is to prevent a defect from happening. External failure costs, by definition, incur after the sale of the car (b). This is the worst case scenario and can come in the form of a recall. The timing of the other two quality costs differ, but take place before the sale of the car. Appraisal costs incur anytime before the sale of the car. For example, quality audits can take place along the manufacturing process, up to the time the car is sold to the customer. Internal failure costs incur after production starts but before the sale of the product. For example, a part within the car may needed to be reworked due to machine or human error.

ESG Considerations in Balance Scorecard

As shown in many sections throughout this text, ESG considerations influence many aspects of a corporation's strategy. This means that environmental, social, and governance factors will likely impact all four sections of a company's balanced scorecard.

Kaplan and McMillan describe a re-imagining of the balanced scorecard to be successful in the new inclusive ecosystem where companies work collaboratively with multiple players to implement strategies that benefit participants in the system where the company operates.[6]

- The financial perspective is replaced with positive impact outcomes to emphasize not only financial metrics, but also environmental and social benefits.
- The customer perspective, which is single entity-based, is replaced with a stakeholder perspective, to encompass other entities such as inhabitants of the city where a corporation is based.
- The internal processes perspective is replaced with sustainable and innovative processes to emphasize the achieving of internal operations while still achieving ESG initiatives.
- The learning and growth perspective is replaced with key enablers and resources in order to reflect the diverse capabilities required for the successful implementation of strategy.

---

[6] Kaplan, R., and David McMillan. "Reimagining the balanced scorecard for the ESG era." *Harv. Bus. Rev* 3 (2021).

Regardless of whether the components of the balanced scorecard are redesigned, ESG considerations can be incorporated into each section. In fact, companies that fail to embrace ESG initiatives risk losing capital funding tied to ESG performance measures, unmet expectations of stakeholders, and decreasing market share since many customers are now influenced by ESG policies.[7] Examples of ESG metrics are included in **Exhibit 23.6**.

EXHIBIT 23.6 ESG Considerations in the Balanced Scorecard

Finance
Level of investment in sustainable processes and product design
Percentage of revenue from sustainable products
Amount of federal subsidies used for environmental projects
Cost of data breaches due to cybersecurity issues

Customers
Measuring customer satisfaction related to ESG considerations
Percentage of sales of sustainable products
Employee hours devoted to initiatives supporting communities where the company resides

Internal Processes
Percentage of water recycled
Measuring energy consumption, kWh/year
Percentage of recycled materials used
Measuring CO_2 emissions
Percentage of suppliers that comply with the company's sustainability standards

Learning and Growth
Hours of female involvement in executive training initiatives
Number of hours of training in engineering on product design with environmental considerations
Number of workplace injuries
Dollars spent on employee educational reimbursement

Balanced Scorecard and Strategy

When a balanced scorecard system is fully utilized to monitor and evaluate an organization's progress, it becomes a system for operationalizing the organization's strategy. *Strategy*, as discussed in Chapter 13, is a course of action that will assist a company in achieving one or more goals. Having a goal to maximize shareholder value or generate a certain income does not constitute a strategy. Maximizing shareholder value can be an overarching corporate goal, but it will not likely be realized without a well-developed strategy that identifies and establishes a balanced set of goals on various dimensions of performance.

A balanced scorecard can be the primary vehicle for translating strategy into action and establishing accountability for performance. The balanced scorecard identifies the areas of managerial action that are believed to be the drivers of corporate achievement. If the corporate goal is to increase ROI or residual income, the balanced scorecard should include key performance indicators that drive these measures.

Critical Thinking & Decision-Making

How is a balanced scorecard similar to the key performance indicators the manager of a professional baseball team uses in setting goals and evaluating progress?

The manager of the New York Yankees *does not just tell players and managers at the beginning of the baseball season that the team's goal is to win the World Series or even a certain number of ball games. The win-loss record is only one metric used to set goals and evaluate performance for a baseball team. The manager looks at many different drivers of success related to hitting, pitching, and fielding, including the earned-run averages of the pitchers, the batting and on-base averages of hitters, the number of errors per game by fielders, and the number of bases stolen by base runners. At the end of the season, the manager measures success not just by whether the*

---
[7] Mezzio, Steven S., et al. "ESG Integration and Small Business." *The CPA Journal* 92.7/8 (2022): 18–27.

Yankees won the World Series, but also by the batting average, number of home runs, and number of bases stolen by individual players, and whether or not a team member won a Golden Glove award or the Cy Young award. These are all measures by which to evaluate achievement and strategic accomplishment. By achieving the goals for each of these areas of the game, the win-loss ratio will take care of itself. If the win-loss results are not acceptable, then the manager adjusts his strategic goals with respect to the key performance indicators (or the manager is dismissed).

Like a baseball team, a company can use a balanced scorecard to develop performance metrics for managers from the top of the company to the lowest-level department. The scorecard becomes a vehicle for communicating the factors that are key to the success of managers, factors that upper management will monitor in evaluating the success of lower managers in carrying out the corporate strategy. To make balanced scorecards more user friendly, several companies use performance monitoring **dashboards**, which are computer-generated graphics that present scorecard results using graphics, some of which mimic the instrument displays on an automobile dashboard. Companies also use a *strategy map* that illustrates the four levels of metrics and how the metrics relate to each other. Volkswagen discloses the nine key performance metrics used to implement and monitor its strategy implementation in its annual report. These comprise a mix of financial and nonfinancial metrics, including, for example, deliveries to customers, sales revenue, research and development costs in relation to sales revenue, and operating results.

BUSINESS INSIGHT

Balanced Scorecard Dashboard The following dashboard provides information about an organization in an "at-a-glance" format. Many software companies now provide utilities for generating dashboards from SAP, Excel, QuickBooks, and other databases. The following is an example of a dashboard with drill-down capabilities, designed by Moss Adams for assessment of financial performance. Within the dashboard, clicking on a visual provides additional data, allowing for a more detailed level of analysis. The categories can be revised to meet the needs of management. For example, key indicators of each part of a company's balanced scorecard can be represented on its dashboard.

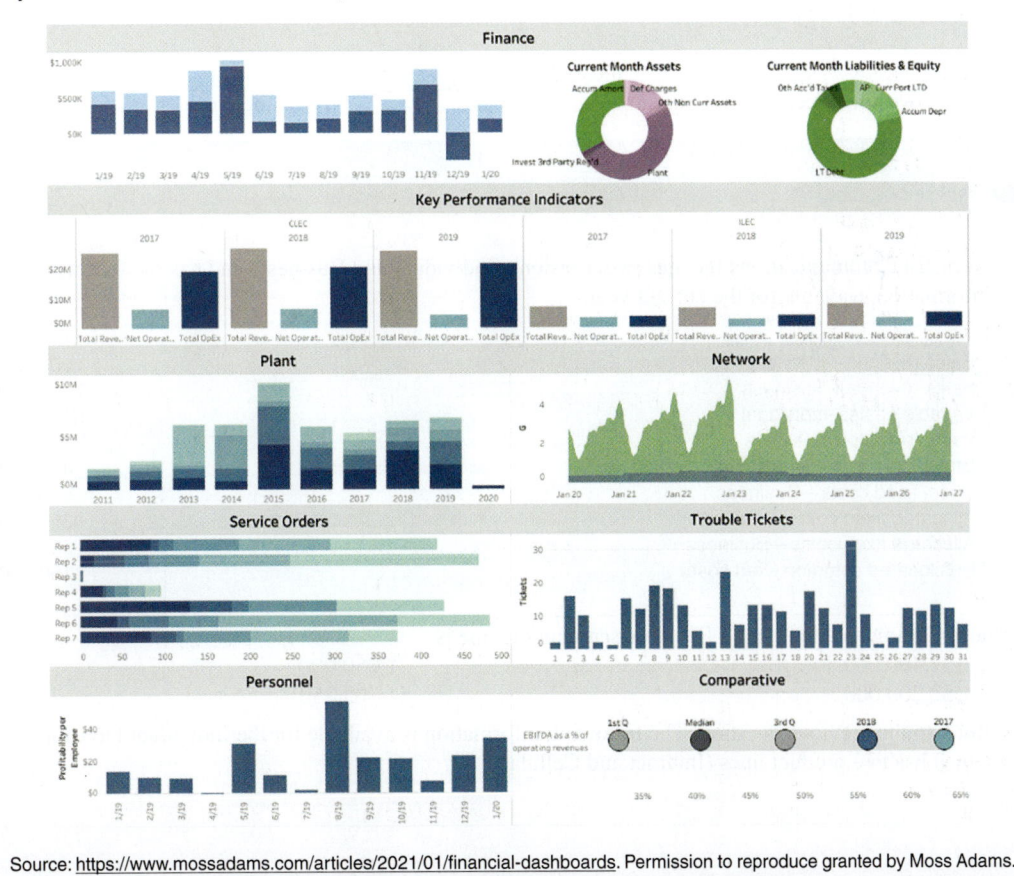

Source: https://www.mossadams.com/articles/2021/01/financial-dashboards. Permission to reproduce granted by Moss Adams.

Review 23-4 LO23-4 — Assigning Metrics to the Balanced Scorecard Categories

The following alphabetically ordered list of financial and nonfinancial performance metrics is provided for Toyota.

Average call wait	Job offer acceptance rate	Net profit margin
Average customer survey rating	Market share	Number of complaints
Employee turnover ratio	New customer count	Number of defects reported
Expense as a % of revenue	New customer sales value	Service error rate
Expense variance %	New product acceptance rate	Time to market on new products
Fulfillment %	New product revenue	Unique repeat customer count
Headcount growth	New product ROI	Year-over-year revenue growth
Industry quality rating	Net profit	

Required

a. Assign the above metrics to the four balanced scorecard categories of (1) Financial Success, (2) Customer Satisfaction and Brand Improvement, (3) Business Process Improvement, (4) Learning and Growth of Motivated Workforce.

b. Comment on the use of balanced scorecard versus a single financial measure such as ROI or EVA.

Solution on p. 23-47.

KEY RATIOS AND EQUATIONS

$$\text{Return on investment} = \frac{\text{Investment center income}}{\text{Investment center asset base}}$$

$$\text{Return on investment} = \text{Investment turnover} \times \text{Return-on-sales}$$

$$\text{Investment turnover} = \frac{\text{Sales}}{\text{Investment center asset base}}$$

$$\text{Return-on-sales} = \frac{\text{Investment center income}}{\text{Sales}}$$

$$\text{Return on investment} = \frac{\text{Sales}}{\text{Investment center asset base}} \times \frac{\text{Investment center income}}{\text{Sales}} = \frac{\text{Investment center income}}{\text{Investment center asset base}}$$

MULTIPLE CHOICE

Multiple Choice Answers
1. c   2. d   3. a   4. c   5. a   6. d   7. b

LO23-1 1. Northern Communications Inc. has two divisions (Individual and Business) and has the following information available for the current year.

Sales revenue—Individual	$3,000,000
Sales revenue—Business	5,000,000
Variable costs—Individual	1,200,000
Variable costs—Business	2,250,000
Direct fixed costs—Individual	400,000
Direct fixed costs—Business	550,000
Allocated fixed costs—Individual	250,000
Allocated fixed costs—Business	350,000
Unallocated common fixed costs	150,000

Northern Communications Inc.'s Business segment income is
 a. $2,400,000
 b. $2,200,000
 c. $1,850,000
 d. $1,765,250

LO23-1 2. Refer to the previous question. The following information is available for the Individual Division, which has two product lines (Internet and Cellular).

Sales revenue—Internet	$1,200,000
Sales revenue—Cellular	1,800,000
Variable costs—Internet	680,000
Variable costs—Cellular	520,000
Direct fixed costs—Internet	150,000
Direct fixed costs—Cellular	250,000
Allocated fixed costs—Internet	100,000
Allocated fixed costs—Cellular	150,000
Unallocated common fixed costs	125,000

The product margin for Internet is
 a. $270,000
 b. $170,000
 c. $520,000
 d. $370,000

3. Varcore Inc. is currently acquiring a key component from its sister company, Farcore Inc., at a transfer price of $10 per unit. Farcore's variable cost of purchasing the unit is $4, and its fixed cost per unit is $3 per unit. Farcore does not have any excess capacity and can sell all it makes to external customers at $10 per unit. Varcore has been offered a price of $9 per unit for the component from another vendor and is insisting that Farcore reduce its price to $9. Which of the following statements below is false regarding this scenario? **LO23-2**

   a. Varcore should not accept the outside offer because the variable cost of purchasing it inside is only $4 per unit.
   b. Varcore should purchase the unit externally because the internal cost of purchasing the unit internally is a variable cost of $4 per unit plus an opportunity cost of $6 per unit, or $10.
   c. The company will be better off if Farcore rejects Varcore's demand and instead sells the units that Varcore would buy to outside customers.
   d. Since Farcore is operating at full capacity and has other external customers ready to purchase additional units, the best transfer price is its regular market price.

4. Shealy's Lawn and Garden Supply Company has recently acquired a lawn sod company that grows turf grasses for lawns. Previously, Shealy's was purchasing sod from other suppliers at 50 cents per square foot. The new sod division, which has substantial excess capacity, is able to produce grass sod at a cost of 35 cents per square foot, including direct materials and direct labor cost of 25 cents, variable overhead of 5 cents, and fixed overhead of 5 cents per square foot. The supply division manager argues that the transfer price should be no more than 35 cents per square foot. What transfer price between the sod and the supply divisions will lead the manager of the supply division to act in a manner that will maximize company profits? **LO23-2**
   a. 50 cents
   b. 25 cents
   c. 30 cents
   d. 35 cents

5. SGA Inc., a division of AGS Inc., had sales of $4,000,000, total assets of $2,000,000, and net income of $400,000. Senior management of AGS Inc. has set a target minimum rate of return for SGA Inc. of 18%. Calculate SGA's residual income. **LO23-3**
   a. $40,000
   b. $36,000
   c. $72,000
   d. None of the above

6. Which of the following is not one of the four most common categories of measurement presented in a balanced scorecard? **LO23-4**
   a. Financial
   b. Internal processes
   c. Innovation and learning
   d. External processes

7. When measuring the cost of quality, the cost of inspecting incoming raw materials is a(n) **LO23-4**
   a. prevention cost.
   b. appraisal cost.
   c. internal failure cost.
   d. external failure cost.

CMA adapted

DATA ANALYTICS

LO23-1

DA23-1. Segment Profitability Reports Using Excel

Southern Comforts Inc. is a department store chain with stores in North Carolina, Tennessee, Kentucky, and West Virginia. Its corporate headquarters are located in Charlotte, North Carolina. In the past, the store owners only received financial reports for the company operations overall. They have recently asked for reports of costs and profitability by segment (location and department). Southern Comforts' locations include the four stores (Charlotte, Nashville, Virginia Beach, and Louisville) and the corporate office (Charlotte HQ). Departments include the product lines (Men's, Women's, Kids, Shoes, and Home) and the overhead expense types (Facilities, Labor, and Other). Provided is an Excel file that includes Southern Comfort transactions for the year. The first step is to make sure the data is in the form needed by separating revenue transactions from expense transactions (all transactions are currently in the Transactions column). After the data is in a useful format, we will then use the data to analyze profitability by store.

PART 1 PREPARING THE DATA

1. Download Excel file found in myBusinessCourse.
2. Add two new column headers, Revenues and Expenses.
3. Convert the schedule to a table. *Hint:* Click on any cell in the data; click on Insert, Table. Check the My table has headers box.
4. Use the IF function to add data to the Revenues column and Expenses column. *Hint:* In F2, enter =IF(E2>0,E2," "). The formula will be copied down to all cells in the Revenues column. Enter the formula to identify expenses in G2.
5. Add a new column after Month and call it Month Name.
6. Use the TEXT function to convert the date format to a text format. *Hint:* =TEXT(cell reference,"mmmm")—returns a full month name, as January–December.

PART 2 CREATING PIVOTTABLES

1. Create PivotTable 1 on a new worksheet showing revenues, expenses, and net income per store. *Hint:* To change from Count of to Sum of, open the dropdown menu next to the fields in Values. Select Value Field Settings and click Sum in the Summarize value field by box. Drag Store to Rows and Revenue and Expenses to Values (change to "sum of"). Create a calculated field for net income by clicking on PivotTable Analyze, Fields, Items & Sets, and Calculated fields. The formula for net income will be Revenues + Expenses because expenses are negative numbers.
2. Indicate which store was the most profitable (in dollars)? What was the store's net income?
3. Indicate which store had the most revenue? What was the store's revenue?
4. Create PivotTable 2 showing revenues by store by month. *Hint:* Drag Store to Columns and Month Name to Rows, and Revenues to Values (change to "sum of").
5. Indicate which month had the highest revenue. What was the amount?
6. Duplicate PivotTable 2 (called PivotTable 2A) on the same worksheet and display each amount in a column as a percentage of the total of that column in this new table. *Hint:* Click on Sum of Revenues in Values and select Value Field Settings. Open the Show Values As tab and select % of Column Total.
7. Identify what percentage of total sales occurred during the month indicated in part 5. Round percentage to two decimal places.
8. Create PivotTable 3 showing net income by month.
9. Indicate which month was the least profitable (in dollars). What was the net income that month?
10. Create PivotTable 4 showing gross profit by month and by store. *Hint:* Create a PivotTable showing net income by store. Drag Month Name to Columns, Store to Rows, Net income to Values. Click anywhere inside the PivotTable and open the PivotTable Analyze tab. Click Insert Slicer and select Department. Use the slicer to include the retail departments only (Mens, Womens, Kids, Shoes, and Home). After the overhead expense categories are removed, the "net income" amount will equal gross margin (sales minus the direct costs for each retail department).
11. List the total gross margin (in dollars) for 2020. Which store had the highest gross margin (in dollars)? List the amount of gross margin in dollars.
12. Create PivotTable 5 showing department cost categories by store. *Hint:* Drag Department to Columns, Store to Rows, Expenses (sum of) to Values.

13. Indicate which store had the highest labor costs and which store had the highest facilities cost. List the dollar amounts.

PART 3 SUMMARIZING RESULTS
1. For the two stores with the largest sales, compute the gross profit percentage (gross profit/sales), labor as a percentage of total sales, facilities as a percentage of total sales, and other as a percentage of total sales. *Hint:* Use data from the various PivotTables to calculate the expense percentages.
2. Indicate which of the two stores in Question 1 had the (a) lowest gross profit, (b) highest percentage of labor over sales, (c) highest percentage of facilities over sales, and (d) the highest percentage of other items over sales.

DA23-2. Segment Profitability Reports Using Tableau
Available in myBusinessCourse, this problem uses Tableau to analyze the profitability of segments.

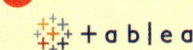

DA23-3. Segment Analysis
Refer to the data in P23-33 to answer the following questions.

REQUIRED
a. Prepare a column chart using information in part *a*, showing sales and income for each of the 3 product segments.
b. Prepare a column chart using information in part *b*, showing sales and income for each of the 3 territories.
c. Prepare a column chart using information in part *c*, showing sales and income for the Americas territory for the 3 product segments.
d. Calculate the profit margin percentage (margin/sales) for each segment in each of the 3 charts.
e. Using the 3 charts created above, answer the following questions.
   1. In reviewing the first chart, what conclusions do you draw on sales per product segment and profitability per product segment?
   2. In reviewing the second chart, what conclusions do you draw about profitability across territories?
   3. Comparing the third chart to the first chart, what conclusions do you draw that make the trends shown in the Americas product segments different from overall company product segment trends?
   4. Pick one product segment or territory segment from Chart 1 or 2 and make a case for why the company would want to invest resources in that segment.

DATA VISUALIZATION

Data Visualization Activities are available in myBusinessCourse. These assignments use Tableau Dashboards to expose students to visual depictions of data and introduce students to data analytics through data visualizations. These exercises are easily assignable and auto graded by MBC.

QUESTIONS

Q23-1. What is the relationship between segment reports and reports of operating results by product?
Q23-2. What is a business segment? How is it determined?
Q23-3. Can a company have more than one type of first-level statement in segment reporting?
Q23-4. Explain the relationships between any two levels of statements in segment reporting.
Q23-5. Distinguish between direct and indirect segment costs.
Q23-6. What types of information are needed before management should decide to drop a segment?
Q23-7. In what types of organizations and for what purpose are transfer prices used?
Q23-8. What problems arise when transfer pricing is used?

Q23-9. When do transfer prices lead to suboptimization? How can suboptimization be minimized? Can it be eliminated? Why or why not?

Q23-10. For what purpose do organizations use return on investment? Why is this measure preferred to net income?

Q23-11. What advantages do residual income and EVA have over ROI for segment evaluations?

Q23-12. Contrast the difference between residual income and EVA.

Q23-13. Explain how a balanced scorecard helps with the evaluation process of internal operations.

Q23-14. How can a balanced scorecard be used as a strategy implementation tool?

Assignments with the MBC logo in the margin are available in *my*BusinessCourse.
See the Preface of the book for details.

MINI EXERCISES

LO23-1 M23-15. Multiple Levels of Segment Reporting
Connect Inc. manufactures three different lines of medical devices: critical care, hospital care, and surgical care. Each of the product lines is produced in all of the company's three plants: Beckley, Huntington, and Charleston. Marketing efforts of the company are divided into five regions: East, West, South, North, and Central.

REQUIRED

a. Develop a reporting schematic that illustrates how the company might prepare single-level reports segmented on three different bases.

b. Develop a segment reporting schematic that has three different levels. Be sure to identify each segment's level. Briefly explain why you chose the primary-level segment.

LO23-1 M23-16. Income Statements Segmented by Products
Francisco Consulting Firm provides three types of client services in three health-care-related industries. The income statement for July is as follows.

FRANCISCO CONSULTING FIRM
Contribution Income Statement
For Month of July

Sales.		$820,000
Less variable costs.		(580,750)
Contribution margin		239,250
Less fixed expenses		
Service	$85,600	
Selling and administrative.	70,400	(156,000)
Net income		$ 83,250

The sales, contribution margin ratios, and direct fixed expenses for the three types of services are as follows.

	Hospitals	Physicians	Nursing Care
Sales.	$340,000	$205,000	$275,000
Contribution margin ratio	25%	35%	30%
Direct fixed expenses of services.	$ 36,500	$ 8,500	$ 18,750
Allocated common fixed services expense.	$ 8,500	$ 2,500	$ 4,000

REQUIRED
Prepare income statements segmented by client categories. Include a column for the entire firm in the statement.

LO23-2 M23-17. Internal or External Acquisitions: No Opportunity Costs
The Van Division of Travel Vans Corporation has offered to purchase 48,000 wheels from the Wheel Division for $80 per wheel. At a normal volume of 320,000 wheels per year, production costs per wheel for the Wheel Division are as follows.

Direct materials	$20
Direct labor	12
Variable overhead	8
Fixed overhead	25
Total	$65

The Wheel Division has been selling 320,000 wheels per year to outside buyers at $100 each. Capacity is 400,000 wheels per year. The Van Division has been buying wheels from outside suppliers at $95 per wheel.

REQUIRED

a. Should the Wheel Division manager accept the offer? Show computations.
b. From the standpoint of the company, will the internal sale be beneficial?

M23-18. Transfer Prices at Full Cost with Excess Capacity: Divisional Viewpoint   LO23-2

Karakomi Cameras Inc. has a Disposables Division that produces a camera that sells for $10 per unit in the open market. The cost of the product is $5.50 (variable manufacturing of $3.00, and fixed manufacturing of $2.50). Total fixed manufacturing costs are $100,000 at the normal annual production volume of 40,000 units. The Overseas Division has offered to buy 10,000 units at the full cost of $5.50. The Disposables Division has excess capacity, and the 10,000 units can be produced without interfering with the current outside sales of 40,000 units. The total fixed cost of the Disposables Division will not change.

REQUIRED

Explain whether the Disposables Division should accept or reject the offer. Show calculations.

M23-19. Transfer Pricing with Excess Capacity: Divisional and Corporate Viewpoints   LO23-2

Assume **Art.com** has a Print Division that is currently producing 150,000 prints per year but has a capacity of 200,000 prints. The variable costs of each print are $30, and the annual fixed costs are $1,650,000. The prints sell for $44 in the open market. The company's Retail Division wants to buy 50,000 prints at $20 each. The Print Division manager refuses the order because the price is below variable cost. The Retail Division manager argues that the order should be accepted because it will lower the fixed cost per print from $11 to $8.25.

REQUIRED

a. Should the Retail Division order be accepted? Why or why not?
b. From the viewpoints of the Print Division and the company, should the order be accepted if the manager of the Retail Division intends to sell each print in the outside market for $40 after incurring additional costs of $5 per print?
c. What action should the company take, assuming it believes in divisional autonomy?

M23-20. ROI and Residual Income: Impact of a New Investment   LO23-3

The Stallion Division of Motortown Motors had an operating income of $805,000 and net assets of $3,500,000. Motortown Motors has a target rate of return of 20%.

REQUIRED

a. Compute the return on investment.
b. Compute the residual income.
c. The Stallion Division has an opportunity to increase operating income by $165,000 with an $800,000 investment in assets.
   1. Compute the Stallion Division's return on investment if the project is undertaken. (Round your answer to three decimal places.)
   2. Compute the Stallion Division's residual income if the project is undertaken.

M23-21. ROI: Fill in the Unknowns   LO23-3

Provide the missing data in the following situations.

	Eastern Division	Western Division	Southern Division
Sales	?	$8,000,000	?
Net operating income	$250,000	$600,000	$1,080,000
Operating assets	?	?	$3,000,000
Return on investment	20%	15%	?
Return on sales	5%	?	6%
Investment turnover	?	?	6

LO23-4 **M23-22. Selection of Balanced Scorecard Items**

The Worldwide Auditors' Association is a professional association. Its current membership totals 65,400 worldwide. The association operates from a central headquarters in New Zealand but has local membership units throughout the world. The local units hold monthly meetings to discuss recent developments in accounting and to hear professional speakers on topics of interest. The association's journal, *Worldwide Auditor,* is published monthly with feature articles and topical interest areas. The association publishes books and reports and sponsors continuing education courses. A statement of revenues and expenses follows.

WORLDWIDE AUDITORS' ASSOCIATION
Statement of Revenues and Expenses
For Year Ending November 30
($ in thousands)

Revenues		$50,702
Expenses		
Salaries	$28,050	
Other personnel costs	5,872	
Occupancy costs	5,545	
Reimbursement to local units	2,536	
Other membership services	1,200	
Printing and paper	383	
Postage and shipping	165	
General and administrative	845	44,596
Excess of revenues over expenses		$ 6,106

Additional information follows:

- Membership dues are $480 per year, of which $100 is considered to cover a one-year subscription to the association's journal. Other benefits include membership in the association and unit affiliation.
- One-year subscriptions to *Worldwide Auditor* are sold to nonmembers for $120 each. A total of 10,000 of these subscriptions was sold. In addition to subscriptions, the journal generated $500,000 in advertising revenue. The cost per magazine was $50.
- A total of 30,000 technical reports was sold by the Books and Reports Department at an average unit selling price of $110. Average costs per publication were $36.
- The association offers a variety of continuing education courses to both members and nonmembers. During the year, the one-day course, which cost participants an average of $600 each, was attended by 25,600 people. A total of 3,800 people took two-day courses at a cost of $1,000 per person.
- General and administrative expenses include all other costs incurred by the corporate staff to operate the association.
- The organization has net capital assets of $87,230,000 and had an actual cost of capital of 6%.

REQUIRED

a. Give some examples of key financial performance indicators (no computations needed) that could be part of a balanced scorecard for the IAA.
b. Give some examples of key customer and operating performance indicators (no computations needed) that could be part of a balanced scorecard for IAA.

LO23-4 **M23-23. Identifying Costs of Quality**

A company is currently performing a cost of quality analysis of one of its facilities. The following are costs compiled by the facility accountant.

Inspection	$1,500
Warranty repair	2,800
Testing of new materials	400
Product testing	950
Spoilage	645
Scrap	150
Preventive equipment maintenance	590
Liability claims	1,870
Rework	1,285

Calculate the company's prevention costs, appraisals costs, internal failure costs, and external failure costs.

EXERCISES

E23-24. Income Statements Segmented by Territory LO23-1
Assume Pentel has two product lines. The September income statements of each product line and the company are as follows.

PENTEL OF AMERICA, LTD
Product Line and Company Income Statements
For Month of September

(in thousands)	Pens	Pencils	Total
Sales	$60,000	$60,000	$120,000
Less variable expenses	(27,000)	(27,000)	(54,000)
Contribution margin	33,000	33,000	66,000
Less direct fixed expenses	(16,000)	(14,000)	(30,000)
Product margin	$17,000	$19,000	36,000
Less common fixed expenses			(15,500)
Net income			$20,500

Pens and pencils are sold in two sales regions, West and East, as follows.

(in thousands)	West	East
Pen sales	$35,000	$25,000
Pencil sales	20,000	40,000
Total sales	$55,000	$65,000

The common fixed expenses (in thousands) are traceable to each territory as follows.

West fixed expenses	$ 5,500
East fixed expenses	6,500
Home office administration fixed expenses	3,500
Total common fixed expenses	$15,500

The direct fixed expenses of pens, $16,000, and of pencils, $14,000, cannot be identified with either territory. The company's accountants were unable to allocate any of the common fixed expenses to the various segments.

REQUIRED
Prepare income statements segmented by territory for September, including a column for the entire firm.

E23-25. Appropriate Transfer Prices: Opportunity Costs LO23-2
Olam International Limited sources and processes agricultural products including edible nuts and spices. Assume the company recently acquired a peanut-processing company that has a normal annual capacity of 180,000 bushels and that sold 125,000 bushels last year at a price of $35 per bushel. The purpose of the acquisition is to furnish peanuts for a new peanut butter plant, which needs 75,000 bushels of peanuts per year. It has been purchasing peanuts from suppliers at the market price. Production costs per bushel of the peanut-processing company are as follows.

Direct materials	$9
Direct labor	4
Variable overhead	2
Fixed overhead at normal capacity	10
Total	$25

Management is trying to decide what transfer price to use for sales from the newly acquired Peanut Division to the Peanut Butter Division. The manager of the Peanut Division argues that $35, the market price, is appropriate. The manager of the Peanut Butter Division argues that the cost price of $25 (or perhaps even less) should be used since fixed overhead costs should be recomputed. Any output of the Peanut Division up to 180,000 bushels that is not sold to the Peanut Butter Division could be sold to regular customers at $35 per bushel.

REQUIRED

a. Compute the annual gross profit for the Peanut Division using a transfer price of $35.
b. Compute the annual gross profit for the Peanut Division using a transfer price of $25.
c. What transfer price(s) will lead the manager of the Peanut Butter Division to act in a manner that will maximize company profits?

LO23-2 E23-26. Negotiating a Transfer Price with Excess Capacity

The Foundry Division of Findlay Pumps Inc. produces metal parts that are sold to the company's Assembly Division and to outside customers. Operating data for the Foundry Division for the current year are as follows.

	To the Assembly Division	To Outside Customers	Total
Sales			
600,000 parts × $8.00	$4,800,000		
400,000 parts × $9.00		$3,600,000	$8,400,000
Variable expenses at $3.75	(2,250,000)	(1,500,000)	(3,750,000)
Contribution margin	2,550,000	2,100,000	4,650,000
Fixed expenses*	(1,350,000)	(900,000)	(2,250,000)
Net income	$1,200,000	$1,200,000	$2,400,000

*Allocated on the basis of unit sales.

The Assembly Division has just received an offer from an outside supplier to supply parts at $5.50 each. The Foundry Division manager is not willing to meet the $5.50 price. She argues that it costs her $6.00 per part to produce and sell to the Assembly Division, so she would show no profit on the Assembly Division sales. Sales to outside customers are at a maximum, 400,000 parts.

REQUIRED

a. Verify the Foundry Division's $6 unit cost figure.
b. Should the Foundry Division meet the outside price of $5.50 for Assembly Division sales? Explain.
c. Could the Foundry Division meet the $5.50 price and still show a net profit for sales to the Assembly Division? Show computations.

LO23-2 E23-27. Dual Transfer Pricing

The Athens Company has two divisions, Alpha and Delta. Delta Division produces a product at a variable cost of $12 per unit, and sells 200,000 units to outside customers at $20 per unit and 60,000 units to Alpha Division at variable cost plus 50%. Under the dual transfer price system, Alpha Division pays only the variable cost per unit. Delta Division's fixed costs are $575,000 per year. After further processing, Alpha sells the 60,000 units to outside customers at $40 per unit. Alpha has variable costs of $11 per unit, in addition to the costs from Delta Division. Alpha Division's annual fixed costs are $380,000. There are no beginning or ending inventories.

REQUIRED

a. Prepare the income statements for the two divisions and the company as a whole.
b. Why is the income for the company less than the sum of the profit figures shown on the income statements for the two divisions? Explain.

LO23-3 E23-28. ROI and Residual Income: Basic Computations

Watkins Associated Industries

Watkins Associated Industries is a privately held conglomerate. Assume that the company uses return on investment and residual income as two of the evaluation tools for division managers. The company has a minimum desired rate of return on investment of 15%. Selected operating data for three of the divisions of the company follow.

	Trucking Division	Seafood Division	Construction Division
Sales	$6,450,000	$1,845,000	$5,200,000
Operating assets	3,750,000	580,000	1,750,000
Net operating income	525,000	116,000	385,000

REQUIRED

a. Compute the return on investment for each division. (Round answers to three decimal places.)
b. Compute the residual income for each division.

E23-29. ROI and Residual Income: Assessing Performance   **LO23-3**
Refer to the computations in the previous exercise E23-28. Assess the performance of the division managers, basing your conclusions on ROI. Assess the performance of the division managers, basing your conclusions on residual income. Which manager is doing the best job?

E23-30. ROI, Residual Income, and EVA with Different Bases   **LO23-3**
Envision Company has a target return on capital of 10%. In evaluating operations, management looks at book values (GAAP compliant) and current values. Current values reflect management's estimates of asset values. The following financial information is available for October ($ thousands).

	Cloud Storage Division (Value Base)		Consulting Division (Value Base)		Venture Capital Division (Value Base)	
	Book	Current	Book	Current	Book	Current
Sales............	$200,000	$200,000	$450,000	$450,000	$625,000	$625,000
Pretax income......	35,000	37,200	37,000	38,500	63,000	43,200
Operating assets ...	250,000	310,000	185,000	175,000	700,000	720,000
Current liabilities....	30,000	30,000	20,000	20,000	65,000	65,000

REQUIRED

a. Compute the return on investment using both book and current values for each division. (Round answers to three decimal places.) For ROI calculations, Envision uses operating assets as the investment base.
b. Compute the residual income for both book and current values for each division.
c. Compute the economic value-added income for both book and current values for each division if the tax rate is 20% and the weighted average cost of capital is 8%.
d. Does book value or current value provide a better basis for performance evaluation? Which division do you consider the most successful?

E23-31. Balanced Scorecard Preparation   **LO23-4**
The following information is in addition to that presented in exercise M23-22 for the Worldwide Auditors' Association. In the budget for the current year, the organization had set a membership goal of 75,000 members with the following anticipated results.

Worldwide Auditors' Association
Planned Revenues and Expenses
For Year Ending November 30

($ in thousands)

Revenues...		$54,436
Expenses		
Salaries..	28,000	
Other personnel costs.................................	7,000	
Occupancy costs.....................................	6,000	
Reimbursement to local units	2,500	
Other membership services	1,500	
Printing and paper....................................	500	
Postage and shipping.................................	300	
General and administrative............................	1,000	46,800
Excess of revenues over expenses		$ 7,636

Additional information follows:
- One-year subscriptions to *Worldwide Auditor* were anticipated to be 8,000 units.
- Advertising revenue was budgeted at $450,000. Each magazine was budgeted at a cost of $48.
- A total of 25,000 technical reports was anticipated at an average price of $100 with average costs of $36.

- The budgeted one-day courses had an anticipated attendance of 25,000 with an average fee of $600. The two-day courses had an anticipated attendance of 5,000 with an average fee of $1,000 per person.
- The organization began the year with net capital assets of $84,100,000 with a planned cost of capital of 6%.

REQUIRED

a. Prepare a balanced scorecard for IAA for November with calculated key performance indicators presented in two columns for planned performance and actual performance—include key financial, customer, and operating performance indicators.
b. Which of the evaluation areas you selected indicated success and which indicated failure?
c. Give some explanations of the successes and failures.

LO23-4 E23-32. Explaining Trends in Costs of Quality

Harmon's Hardware has gathered the following data on its quality costs for Year 1 and Year 2.

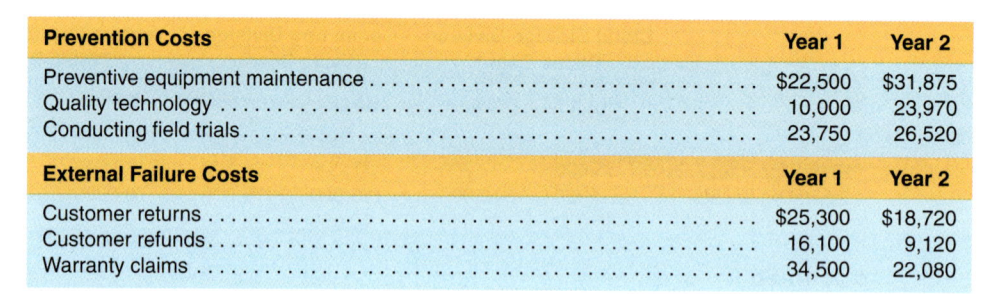

Prevention Costs	Year 1	Year 2
Preventive equipment maintenance	$22,500	$31,875
Quality technology	10,000	23,970
Conducting field trials	23,750	26,520

External Failure Costs	Year 1	Year 2
Customer returns	$25,300	$18,720
Customer refunds	16,100	9,120
Warranty claims	34,500	22,080

REQUIRED

a. Compute the percentage change in cost of quality categories of prevention and external failures from Year 1 to Year 2.
b. Explain the reasons for the trends that you identified in part a.

PROBLEMS

LO23-1 P23-33. Multiple Segment Reports

Worldwide Communications, Incorporated, sells power supply products throughout the world in three sales territories: Europe, Asia, and the Americas. For July, all $1,045,000 of administrative expense is traceable to the territories, except $200,000, which is common to all units and cannot be traced or allocated to the sales territories. The percentage of product line sales made in each of the sales territories and the assignment of traceable fixed expenses follow.

	Sales Territory			
	Europe	Asia	The Americas	Company
Motors	40%	35%	25%	100%
Generators	35%	35%	30%	100%
Power distribution	10%	15%	75%	100%
Fixed administrative expense	$350,000	$275,000	$220,000	$845,000
Fixed selling expense	$155,000	$175,000	$550,000	$880,000

The manufacturing takes place in one large facility with three distinct manufacturing operations. Selected product-line cost data follow.

	Motors	Generators	Power Distribution	Company
Variable cost per unit	$ 15	$ 850	$ 1,950	
Depreciation and supervision	60,000	175,000	275,000	$ 585,000*
Other mfg. overhead (common)				650,000
Fixed administrative expense (common)				1,045,000
Fixed selling expense (common)				880,000

*Includes common costs of $75,000

The unit sales and selling prices for each product follow.

	Unit Sales	Selling Price
Motors.	6,500	$ 25
Generators	1,500	1,900
Power distribution	2,500	3,500

REQUIRED

a. Prepare an income statement for July segmented by product line. Include a column for the entire firm.

b. Prepare an income statement for July segmented by sales territory. Include a column for the entire firm.

c. Prepare an income statement for July by product line for The Americas sales territory. Include a column for the territory as a whole. Products are manufactured in a single facility. Although depreciation and supervision are allocated by product line, those costs are not allocated by territory.

d. Discuss the value of multilevel segment reporting as a managerial tool. Compare and contrast the benefits of the reports generated in parts a, b, and c.

P23-34. Segment Reporting and Analysis

The Essential Baking Company bakes artisan loaves, baguettes, and rolls and sells them in cities throughout the Northwest. Assume the following March income statement was prepared for the stores located in Seattle and Portland.

THE ESSENTIAL BAKING COMPANY
Territory Income Statements
For Month of March

(in thousands)	Seattle	Portland	Total
Sales	$8,400	$6,800	$15,200
Cost of goods sold	(4,796)	(3,894)	(8,690)
Gross profit	3,604	2,906	6,510
Selling and administrative expenses	(2,755)	(2,155)	(4,910)
Net income	$ 849	$ 751	$ 1,600

Sales and selected variable expense data are as follows.

	Products		
	Loaves	Baguettes	Rolls
Fixed baking expenses	$ 565	$ 450	$410
Variable baking expenses as a percentage of sales	50%	50%	40%
Variable selling expenses as a percentage of sales	10%	20%	20%
City of Seattle, sales (in thousands)	$3,800	$2,650	$1,950
City of Portland, sales (in thousands)	$3,250	$2,150	$1,400

The fixed selling expenses were $1,440 for March, of which $860 was a direct expense of the Seattle market and $580 was a direct expense of the Portland market. Fixed administrative expenses were $1,135, which management has decided not to allocate when using the contribution approach.

REQUIRED

a. Prepare a segment income statement showing the margin for each territory (city) for March. Include a column combining the two territories.

b. Prepare segment income statements showing the product margin for each product. Include a column for the combined products.

c. If the rolls line is dropped and fixed baking expenses do not change, what is the product margin for loaves and baguettes?

d. What other type of segmentation might be useful to The Essential Baking Company. Explain.

P23-35. Segment Reporting and Analysis

Business Book Publishers, Inc., has prepared income statements segmented by divisions, but management is still uncertain about actual performance. Financial information for May is given as follows.

	Textbook Division	Professional Division	Company Total
Sales	$150,000	$307,500	$457,500
Less variable expenses			
Manufacturing	24,000	153,750	177,750
Selling and administrative	7,500	15,375	22,875
Total	(31,500)	(169,125)	(200,625)
Contribution margin	118,500	138,375	256,875
Less direct fixed expenses	(15,000)	(150,000)	(165,000)
Net income	$103,500	$ (11,625)	$ 91,875

Management is concerned about the Professional Division and requests additional analysis. Additional information regarding May operations of the Professional Division is as follows.

	Professional Division		
	Accounting Books Segment	Executive Books Segment	Management Books Segment
Sales	$105,000	$105,000	$97,500
Variable manufacturing expenses as a percentage of sales	60%	40%	50%
Other variable expenses as a percentage of sales	5%	5%	5%
Direct fixed expenses	$37,500	$55,100	$37,500
Allocated common fixed expenses	$ 3,000	$ 1,500	$ 4,500

The professional accounting books are sold to auditors and controllers. The current information on these markets is as follows.

	Accounting Books Segment		
	Auditors Market	Controllers Market	Total
Sales	$22,500	$82,500	$105,000
Variable manufacturing expenses as a percentage of sales	60%	60%	—
Other variable expenses as a percentage of sales	5%	5%	—
Direct fixed expenses	$11,250	$22,500	$33,750
Allocated common fixed expenses	$ 1,125	$ 1,500	$ 2,625

REQUIRED

a. Prepare an income statement segmented by product for the Professional Division. Include a column for the division as a whole.
b. Prepare an income statement segmented by market for the Accounting Books Segment of the Professional Division.
c. Evaluate which Accounting Books Segment the Professional Division should keep or discontinue in the short run.
d. What is the correct long-run decision? Explain fully, including any possible risks associated with your recommendation.

LO23-1 **P23-36.** **Segment Reports and Cost Allocations**

All Things Greek Inc. has three sales divisions. One of the key evaluation inputs for each division manager is the performance of his or her division based on division income. The division statements for August are as follows.

	Alpha	Beta	Gamma	Total
Sales	$250,000	$300,000	$275,000	$825,000
Cost of sales	139,500	165,000	158,250	462,750
Division overhead	39,000	45,000	41,250	125,250
Division expenses	(178,500)	(210,000)	(199,500)	(588,000)
Division contribution	71,500	90,000	75,500	237,000
Corporate overhead	(41,000)	(49,000)	(45,000)	(135,000)
Division income	$ 30,500	$ 41,000	$ 30,500	$102,000

The Gamma manager is unhappy that his profitability is the same as that of the Alpha Division and 74% that of the Beta Division when his sales are halfway between these two divisions. The manager knows that his division must carry more product lines because of customer demands, and many of these additional product lines are not very profitable. He has not dropped these marginal product lines because of idle capacity; all of the products cover their own variable costs. After analyzing the product lines with the lowest profit margins, the divisional controller for Gamma provided the following to the manager.

Sales of marginal products		$55,000
Cost of sales	$34,100	
Avoidable fixed costs	13,500	47,600
Product margin		$ 7,400

Although these products were 20% of Gamma's total sales, they contributed only about 10% of the division's profits. The controller also noted that the corporate overhead allocation was based on relative sales proportions and the allocation would decrease if the weak product line was dropped.

REQUIRED

a. Prepare a set of segment statements for August assuming that all facts remain the same except that Gamma's weak product lines are dropped and corporate overhead is allocated as follows: Alpha, $43,800; Beta, $52,600; and Gamma, $38,600. Does the Gamma Division appear better after this action? What will be the responses of the other two division managers?

b. Suggest improvements for All Things Greek's reporting process that will better reflect the actual operations of the divisions. Keep in mind the utilization of the reporting process to assist in the evaluation of the managers. What other changes could be made to improve the manager evaluation process?

P23-37. **ROI, Residual Income, and EVA: Impact of a New Investment** LO23-3
EEG Inc. is a decentralized organization with four autonomous divisions. The divisions are evaluated on the basis of the change in their return on invested assets. Operating results in the Commercial Division for the year follow.

EEG INC.—COMMERCIAL DIVISION Income Statement For Year Ending December 31	
Sales	$3,000,000
Less variable expenses	(1,550,000)
Contribution margin	1,450,000
Less fixed expenses	(1,200,000)
Net operating income	$ 250,000

Operating assets for the Commercial Division currently average $2,500,000. The Commercial Division can add a new product line for an investment of $400,000. Relevant data for the new product line are as follows.

Sales	$625,000
Variable expenses (% of sales)	60%
Fixed expenses	$220,000
Increase in current liabilities	$ 18,000

REQUIRED

a. Determine the effect on ROI of accepting the new product line. (Round calculations to three decimal places.)
b. If a return of 6% is the minimum that any division should earn and residual income is used to evaluate managers, would this encourage the division to accept the new product line? Explain and show computations.
c. If EVA is used to evaluate managers, should the new product line be accepted if the weighted average cost of capital is 6% and the income tax rate is 20%?

LO23-3   **P23-38.**   **Valuing Investment Center Assets**

Six Flags Entertainment Corp operates theme parks in the United States, Mexico, and Europe. One of its first theme parks, Six Flags over Georgia, was built in the 1960s in Atlanta on a large tract of land that has appreciated enormously over the years. Although most of the rides and other attractions have a fairly short life, some of the major buildings that are still in use on the property have been fully depreciated since they were built. Assume that Six Flags over Georgia operates as an investment center with total assets that have a book value of $75 million and current liabilities of $5 million. Assume also that in the current year, this particular theme park had sales of $65 million and pretax division income of $12 million. The replacement cost of all the assets in this park is estimated to be $115 million. The company has a 20% tax rate and a target return of 10% and a cost of capital of 6%.

REQUIRED

a. Calculate the ROI, residual income, and EVA for Six Flags over Georgia using asset book value in the valuation basis for the investment center asset base.
b. Repeat requirement (a) using replacement cost as the investment center asset value.
c. Which valuation, accounting book value, or replacement cost do you think the company uses to evaluate the managers of its various theme parks? Discuss.

LO23-2, 3   **P23-39.**   **Transfer Pricing with and without Capacity Constraints**

Elise Carpets Inc. has just acquired a new backing division that produces a rubber backing, which it sells for $3.75 per square yard. Sales are about 1 million square yards per year. Since the Backing Division has a capacity of 1.5 million square yards per year, top management is thinking that it might be wise for the company's Tufting Division to start purchasing from the newly acquired Backing Division. The Tufting Division now purchases 350,000 square yards per year from an outside supplier at a price of $3.50 per square yard. The current price is lower than the Backing division's $3.75 price as a result of the large quantity discounts. The Backing Division's cost per square yard follows.

Direct materials.	$1.25
Direct labor.	0.50
Variable overhead.	0.15
Fixed overhead (1,000,000 level).	0.85
Total cost	$2.75

REQUIRED

a. If both divisions are to be treated as investment centers and their performance evaluated by the ROI formula, what transfer price would you recommend? Why?
b. If fixed costs are assumed not to change, determine the effect on corporate profits of making the backing.
c. Based on your transfer price, would you expect the ROI in the Backing Division to increase, decrease, or remain unchanged? Explain.
d. What would be the effect on the ROI of the Tufting Division using your transfer price? Explain.
e. Assume that the Backing Division is now selling 1.5 million square yards per year to retail outlets. What transfer price would you recommend? What will be the effect on corporate profits?
f. If the Backing Division is at capacity and decides to sell to the Tufting Division for $3.50 per square yard, what will be the effect on the company's profits?
g. Suppose that the Backing Division is in a lower tax locale. Should this difference in tax rates affect the pricing decision?
h. What are the ethical considerations when making the pricing decision?

P23-40. Transfer Pricing and Special Orders   **LO23-2**

Washington State Products has several manufacturing divisions. The Seattle Division produces a component part that is used in the manufacture of electronic equipment. The cost per part for July is as follows.

Variable cost	$150
Fixed cost (at 3,000 units per month capacity)	90
Total cost per part	$240

Some of Seattle Division's output is sold to outside manufacturers, and some is sold internally to the Redmond Division. The price per part is $375. The Redmond Division's cost and revenue structure follow.

Selling price per unit		$1,500
Less variable costs per unit		
Cost of parts from the Seattle Division	$375	
Other variable costs	550	(925)
Contribution margin per unit		575
Less fixed costs per unit (at 2,000 units per month)		(175)
Net income per unit		$ 400

The Redmond Division received a one-time order for 500 units. The buyer wants to pay only $750 per unit.

REQUIRED

a. From the perspective of the Redmond Division, should the $750 price be accepted? Explain.
b. If both divisions have excess capacity, would the Redmond Division's action benefit the company as a whole? Explain.
c. If the Redmond Division has excess capacity but the Seattle Division does not and can sell all of its parts to outside manufacturers, what would be the advantage or disadvantage of accepting the 500 unit order at the $750 price to the Redmond Division?
d. To make a decision that is in the best interest of the company, what transfer-pricing information does the Redmond Division need?

P23-41. Balanced Scorecard   **LO23-4**

Assume **Chase Bank** recently decided to adopt a balanced scorecard system of performance evaluation. Below is a list of primary performance goals for four major performance categories that have been identified by corporate management and the board of directors.

JPMorgan Chase & Co.
NYSE :: JPM

1. Financial Perspective—Maintain and grow the bank financially
    a. Increase customer deposits
    b. Manage financial risk
    c. Provide profits for the stockholders
2. Customer Perspective—Maintain and grow the customer base
    a. Increase customer satisfaction
    b. Increase number of depositors and customer retention
    c. Increase quality of deposits
3. Internal Perspective—Improve internal processes
    a. Achieve best practices for processing transactions
    b. Improve employee satisfaction
    c. Improve employee promotion opportunities
4. Learning and Innovation—Improve market differentiation
    a. Beat competitors in introducing new products
    b. Become first mover in establishing customer benefit for customers
    c. Become recognized as an innovator in the industry

REQUIRED

a. For each of the 12 goals above, suggest at least one measure of performance to measure the achievement of the goal.

b. At what level of the organization should the balanced scorecard be implemented as a means of evaluating performance? Explain.

LO23-1, 2, 3, 4 **P23-42. Analyzing Various Performance Scenarios—CMA Adapted**

1. A retail company has three segments with total operating income of $500,000. Selected financial information for Segment 1 is presented below.

	Segment 1
Unit sales	28,000
Sales revenue	$700,000
Cost of sales	420,000
Administrative expenses	144,000
Commissions	14,000
Rent	140,000
Salaries	32,000

- Administrative expenses are allocated to the three segments equally.
- Commissions are paid to the salespersons in each segment based on 2% of gross sales.
- The company rents the entire building and allocates the rent to the three segments based on the square footage occupied by each.
- Salaries represent payments to the employees in the segment.

The controller has expressed concern about the operating loss for Segment 1 and has suggested that it be closed. If the segment is closed, none of the employees would be retained. Should the company drop Segment 1?

CMA adapted

2. Morrison's Plastics Division, a profit center, sells its products to external customers as well as to other internal profit centers. Which one of the following circumstances would justify the Plastics Division selling a product internally to another profit center at a price that is below the market-based transfer price?
   a. The buying unit has excess capacity.
   b. The selling unit is operating at full capacity.
   c. Routine sales commissions and collection costs would be avoided.
   d. The profit centers' managers are evaluated on the basis of unit operating income.

CMA adapted

3. A company's management is planning on making an investment of UAE Dirham (AED) 1,000,000 to establish a new division in the United Arab Emirates. The new division is expected to generate sales of AED 720,000 and net income of AED 250,000 in Year 1. If the company's required rate of return is 10%, what is the division's residual income in Year 1?

CMA adapted

4. A sign of the successful implementation of a balanced scorecard is the presence of cause-and-effect relationships. An example of this success for a hotel is meeting the target of:
   a. decreasing a customer's check-in time, which causes an increase in the number of implemented employee suggestions.
   b. increasing employee training hours, which causes employee compensation to increase.
   c. increasing profit, which causes an increase in employee job satisfaction ratings.
   d. receiving more 5-star ratings from customers, which causes an increase in profit.

CMA adapted

CASES AND PROJECTS

LO23-2 **C23-43. Transfer Price Decisions**

IBM Corporation
NYSE :: IBM

Assume the Consulting Division of **IBM Corporation** is often involved in assignments for which IBM computer equipment is sold as part of a systems installation. The Computer Equipment Division is frequently a vendor of the Consulting Division in cases for which the Consulting Division purchases the equipment from the Computer Equipment Division. The Consulting Division does not view itself as a sales arm of the Computer Equipment Division but as a strong competitor to the major consulting firms of information systems. The Consulting Division's goal is to maximize its profit contribution to the company, not necessarily to see how much IBM equipment it can sell. If the Consulting Division is truly an autonomous investment center, it has the freedom to purchase equipment from competing vendors if the consultants believe that a competitor's products serve the needs of a client better than the comparable IBM product in a particular situation.

REQUIRED

a. In this situation, should corporate management be concerned about whether the Consulting Division sells IBM products or those of other computer companies? Should the Consulting Division be required to sell only IBM products?
b. Discuss the transfer-pricing issues that both the Computer Equipment Division manager and the Consulting Division manager should consider. If top management does not have a policy on pricing transfers between these two divisions, what alternative transfer prices should the division managers consider?
c. What is your recommendation regarding how the managers of the Consulting and Computer Equipment Divisions can work together in a way that will benefit each of them individually and the company as a whole?

C23-44. **Transfer Pricing at Absorption Cost**   LO23-2

The Injection Molding Division of Universal Sign Company produces molded parts that are sold to the Sign Division. This division uses the parts in constructing signs that are sold to various businesses. The Molding Division contains two operations, injection and finishing. The unit variable cost of materials and labor used in the injection operation is $150. The fixed injection overhead is $1,200,000 per year. Current production (20,000 units) is at full capacity. The variable cost of labor used in the finishing operation is $24 per part. The fixed overhead in this operation is $600,000 per year. The company uses an absorption-cost transfer price. The price data for each operation presented to the Sign Division by the Molding Division follow.

Injection		
Variable cost per unit.	$150	
Fixed overhead cost per unit ($1,200,000 ÷ 40,000 units)	30	$180
Finishing		
Labor cost per unit	24	
Fixed overhead cost per unit ($600,000 ÷ 40,000 units).	15	39
Total cost per unit.		$219

An outside company has offered to lease machinery to the Sign Division that would perform the finishing portion of the parts manufacturing for $400,000 per year. With the new machinery, the labor cost per part would remain at $24. If the Molding Division transfers the units for $180, the following analysis can be made.

Current process		
Finishing process costs (40,000 × $39)		$1,560,000
New process		
Machine rental cost per year.	$400,000	
Labor cost ($24 × 40,000 units)	960,000	1,360,000
Savings.		$ 200,000

The manager of the Sign Division wants approval to acquire the new machinery.

REQUIRED

a. How would you advise the company concerning the proposed lease?
b. How could the transfer-pricing system be modified or the transfer-pricing problem eliminated?

C23-45. **Transfer-Pricing Dispute**   LO23-2

MBR Inc. consists of three divisions that were formerly three independent manufacturing companies. Bader Corporation and Roper Company merged several years ago, and the merged corporation acquired Mitchell Company a year later. The name of the corporation was subsequently changed to MBR Inc., and each company became a separate division retaining the name of its former company.

The three divisions have operated as if they were still independent companies. Each division has its own sales force and production facilities. Each division management is responsible for sales, cost of operations, acquisition and financing of divisional assets, and working capital management. The corporate management of MBR evaluates the performance of the divisions and division management on the basis of return on investment.

Mitchell Division has just been awarded a contract for a product that uses a component manufactured by the Roper Division and also by outside suppliers. Mitchell used a cost figure of $3.80 for the component manufactured by Roper in preparing its bid for the new product. Roper supplied this cost figure in response to Mitchell's request for the average variable cost of the component; it represents the standard variable manufacturing cost and variable selling and distribution expenses.

Roper has an active sales force that is continually soliciting new prospects. Roper's regular selling price for the component Mitchell needs for the new product is $6.50. Sales of this component are expected to increase. The Roper management has indicated, however, that it could supply Mitchell the required quantities of the component at the regular selling price less variable selling and distribution expenses. Mitchell's management has responded by offering to pay standard variable manufacturing cost plus 20%.

The two divisions have been unable to agree on a transfer price. Corporate management has never established a transfer-pricing policy because interdivisional transactions have never occurred. As a compromise, the corporate vice president of finance suggested a price equal to the standard full manufacturing cost (i.e., no selling and distribution expenses) plus a 15% markup. The two division managers have also rejected this price because each considered it grossly unfair.

The unit cost structure for the Roper component and the three suggested prices follow.

Standard variable manufacturing cost	$3.20
Standard fixed manufacturing cost	1.20
Variable selling and distribution expenses	0.60
	$5.00
Regular selling price less variable selling and distribution expenses ($6.50 − $0.60)	$5.90
Standard full manufacturing cost plus 15% ($4.40 × 1.15)	$5.06
Variable manufacturing plus 20% ($3.20 × 1.20)	$3.84

REQUIRED

a. What should be the attitude of the Roper Division's management toward the three proposed prices?
b. Is the negotiation of a price between the Mitchell and Roper Divisions a satisfactory method of solving the transfer-pricing problem? Explain your answer.
c. Should the corporate management of MBR Inc. become involved in this transfer-price controversy? Explain your answer.

CMA adapted

SOLUTIONS TO REVIEW PROBLEMS

Review 23-1—Solution

a. In the short run, the Automotive Division income would decrease by the product margin of power engineering or $7 million (see Exhibit 23.2 Panel B).

b.

(in thousands)	Europe	International	Power Engineering Total
Sales	$12,000	$18,000	$30,000
Less direct variable costs	(8,400)	(12,600)	(21,000)
Contribution margin	3,600	5,400	9,000
Less direct fixed costs	(500)	(800)	(1,300)
Territory margin	3,100	4,600	7,700
Less allocated segment costs	(200)	(600)	(800)
Territory income	$ 2,900	$ 4,000	6,900
Less unallocated common costs			(900)
Power engineering income			$ 6,000

c. The Product Margin for the power engineering product line in Panel B was $7 million and reflected $2 million of direct fixed costs that were attributable to that product line in the Automotive Division. However, when the power engineering product segment income statement is further segmented into geographic segments, only $1.3 million of the $2 million could be directly traced to the two geographic territories. Therefore, $700,000 of costs that were direct costs at the product segment level became common costs (either allocated or unallocated) at the territory segment level. This reflects the general notion that as segmentation is extended down to lower and lower levels, the total amount of common costs increases and direct costs decrease. Hence, segmentation rarely is extended to more than three levels.

Review 23-2—Solution

a. No.

	Current Sales	Proposed Sales
Selling price	$ 24.00	$ 13.50
Variable costs	(16.00)	(16.00)
Unit contribution margin	$ 8.00	$ (2.50)
Unit sales	× 200,000	× 100,000
Contribution margin	$1,600,000	$(250,000)

Currently, the division is making $250,000 on 200,000 hats ($1,600,000 − $1,350,000 fixed costs); but under the proposal, with a $250,000 negative contribution, it would revert to a break-even situation.

Current contribution margin		$1,600,000
Fixed costs	$1,350,000	
Loss on special order	250,000	(1,600,000)
Net income		$ 0

As a general rule, a project should never be undertaken if the contribution margin is negative.

b. What the Lexus Division does with the hats after receiving them is of no concern to the Apparel Division. Hence, the Apparel Division would still object to a transfer price of $13.50. However, for the company, the proposal does have a contribution of $18 per unit ($44 − $16 − $10). Consequently, the order is desirable from the viewpoint of the company.

c. If the company believes in autonomous divisions, it should not require the Apparel Division to sell, nor should it dictate a higher transfer price. On the other hand, the company may want to create incentives to encourage (but not require) the two division managers to reach some compromise transfer price that would increase the contribution and profits of both divisions, and the company as a whole.

Review 23-3—Solution
(in thousands)

a.
$$\text{Return on investment} = \frac{\text{Investment center income}}{\text{Investment center asset base}}$$

Toyota = $30,000 ÷ $200,000
= 0.15 or 15%

Lexus = $50,000 ÷ $250,000
= 0.20 or 20%

Powertrain = $22,000 ÷ $100,000
= 0.22 or 22%

b. Residual income = Investment center income − (Minimum return × Investment center asset base)

Toyota = $30,000 − (0.15 × $200,000)
= $0.00

Lexus = $50,000 − (0.15 × $250,000)
= $12,500

Powertrain = $22,000 − (0.15 × $100,000)
= $7,000

c. ROI ranks the Powertrain Division first, Lexus second, and Toyota third. Residual income ranks Lexus first, the Powertrain Division second, and Toyota third. Because the investments for each division are different, it is somewhat misleading to rank the divisions according to residual income. Lexus had the highest residual income, but it also had the largest investment. The Powertrain Division's residual income was 56% of Lexus's income, but it had only 40% of the investment of Lexus. This fact, along with the best ROI ranking, probably justifies the Powertrain Division being evaluated as the best division of Toyota.

d. Return on investment:

$$\text{Investment} = \$9,000 \div \$50,000$$
$$= 0.18 \text{ or } 18\%$$
$$\text{Toyota} = (\$30,000 + \$9,000) \div (\$200,000 + \$50,000)$$
$$= 0.156 \text{ or } 15.6\%$$
$$\text{Lexus} = (\$50,000 + \$9,000) \div (\$250,000 + \$50,000)$$
$$= 0.1967 \text{ or } 19.67\%$$
$$\text{Powertrain} = (\$22,000 + \$9,000) \div (\$100,000 + \$50,000)$$
$$= 0.2067 \text{ or } 20.67\%$$

ROI will increase for Toyota but decrease for Lexus and the Powertrain division, even though the project's ROI of 18% exceeds the company's minimum return of 15%.

Residual income:

$$\text{Toyota} = (\$30,000 + \$9,000) - [0.15 \times (\$200,000 + \$50,000)]$$
$$= \$1,500$$
$$\text{Lexus} = (\$50,000 + \$9,000) - [0.15 \times (\$250,000 + \$50,000)]$$
$$= \$14,000$$
$$\text{Powertrain} = (\$22,000 + \$9,000) - [0.15 \times (\$100,000 + \$50,000)]$$
$$= \$8,500$$

Because the project's ROI exceeds the company's minimum return, the residual income of all divisions will increase.

Review 23-4—Solution

a. Financial Success
   Expense as a % of revenue
   Expense variance %
   New product ROI
   Net profit
   Net profit margin
   Year-over-year revenue growth
   New product revenue

   Customer Satisfaction and Brand Improvement
   Number of complaints
   Market share
   Average customer survey rating
   New customer count
   New customer sales value
   Unique repeat customer count

   Business Process Improvement
   Average call wait
   Service error rate
   Fulfillment %
   Industry quality rating
   New product acceptance rate
   Number of defects reported
   Time to market on new products

Learning and Growth of Motivated Workforce
    Employee turnover ratio
    Headcount growth
    Job offer acceptance rate

Note that some of the key performance indicators could be included in more than one category. For example New Product ROI is an indicator of the success of introducing new products, but it is also an indicator of financial success.

b. The balanced scorecard has been quite successful in helping companies to better focus managers' attention on the factors that drive ultimate success. If only a general performance metric such as ROI or EVA is used to evaluate performance, managers are left on their own to figure out for themselves the components of managerial performance that drive improvements in the overall indicator. The balanced scorecard provides a framework and structure for carefully thinking about the key performance indicators that drive ultimate success. Once top management has identified the key performance indicators with input from all levels, some or all of the indicators can be used to evaluate managers and employees throughout the organization.

Chapter 24
Capital Budgeting Decisions

LEARNING OBJECTIVES

LO24-1 Explain the capital budgeting process and analyze decisions using models such as payback period and accounting rate of return, that do not consider the time value of money. (p. 24-3)

LO24-2 Analyze capital budgeting decisions, using models such as net present value and internal rate of return, that consider the time value of money. (p. 24-9)

LO24-3 Evaluate the strengths and weaknesses of alternative capital budgeting models. (p. 24-12)

LO24-4 Evaluate risk and use differential analysis in capital budgeting decisions. (p. 24-15)

LO24-5 Compute basic present value cash flow amounts (Appendix 24A). (p. 24-20)

LO24-6 Determine internal rate of return using present value tables (Appendix 24B). (p. 24-24)

LO24-7 Determine the net present value of investment proposals with consideration of taxes (Appendix 24C). (p. 24-26)

Road Map

LO	Learning Objective | Topics	Page	eLecture	Review	Assignments
LO24-1	**Explain the capital budgeting process and analyze decisions using models such as payback period and accounting rate of return, that do not consider the time value of money.** Capital Expenditures :: Capital Budgeting :: Budget Committee :: Post-Audit Process :: Payback Period :: Accounting Rate of Return	24-3	e24–1	R24-1	M24-13, M24-14, M24-15, M24-16, E24-23, E24-24, E24-25, E24-27, E24-28, E24-29, E24-30, P24-32, P24-33, P24-34, P24-38, C24-41, C24-43, C24-46, C24-47
LO24-2	**Analyze capital budgeting decisions, using models such as net present value and internal rate of return, that consider the time value of money.** Net Present Value :: Table Approach :: Spreadsheet Approach :: Internal Rate of Return :: Cost of Capital	24-9	e24–2	R24-2	M24-19, M24-20, E24-23, E24-24, E24-25, E24-26, E24-27, E24-28, E24-29, E24-30, P24-32, P24-33, P24-34, P24-35, P24-36, P24-37, C24-41, C24-42, C24-44, C24-45, C24-46, C24-47, **DA24-1, DA24-2**
LO24-3	**Evaluate the strengths and weaknesses of alternative capital budgeting models.** Strength and Weaknesses of Each Approach :: Multiple Investment Criteria :: Nonfinancial Measures	24-12	e24–3	R24-3	M24-21, E24-30, P24-32, P24-34, C24-44
LO24-4	**Evaluate risk and use differential analysis in capital budgeting decisions.** Evaluating Risk :: Sensitivity Analysis :: Relevant Costs :: Differential Analysis :: Avoiding Errors	24-15	e24–4	R24-4	M24-22, E24-27, E24-28, E24-29, P24-34, P24-35, P24-36, P24-37, C24-42, C24-43, C24-44, C24-45, C24-46, C24-47, **DA24-1, DA24-2**
LO24-5	**Compute basic present value cash flow amounts (Appendix 24A).** Future Value :: Present Value :: Annuities :: Unequal Cash Flows :: Deferred Returns	24-20	e24–5	R24-5	M24-17, M24-18
LO24-6	**Determine internal rate of return using present value tables (Appendix 24B).** Equal Cash Flows :: Unequal Cash Flows	24-24	e24–6	R24-6	M24-19, M24-20, E24-23, E24-24, E24-25, E24-30, P24-33, P24-34, C24-44
LO24-7	**Determine the net present value of investment proposals with consideration of taxes (Appendix 24C).** Depreciation Tax Shield :: Investment Tax Credit	24-26	e24–7	R24-7	E24-31, P24-38, P24-39, P24-40, C24-41, C24-45

AMAZON
www.amazon.com

Seattle-based **Amazon.com Inc.** started out as an online bookseller in 1995 and quickly expanded its product offerings. Ten years later, the company introduced two-day free shipping with an Amazon Prime membership, which would become a signature offering. Over time, Amazon's products expanded to include services such digital music and books, streaming movie and video game services, as well as a full range of web services including cloud storage and block chain. Amazon also purchased Whole Foods in 2017 and opened its first Amazon Fresh store in 2020 which competes more competitively on price.

Today, Amazon sells more goods online than all other Internet retailers, including **ODP Corporation**, **Apple**, **Walmart**, and **Best Buy**. Amazon's meteoric rise was no doubt fueled by well-chosen capital investments, including its distribution center that enables quick deliveries and its website infrastructure that highlights customer-centric features such as the first shopping carts, one-click buying, email purchase confirmations, and post-shipping follow-ups. Over the years Amazon has kept its prices low by leveraging its purchasing volume, thereby staving off its competition. To maintain its position, Amazon has forgone profits in favor of continual improvement of its business model. In an effort to gain more control over its fulfillment process, Amazon has invested billions of dollars in warehouses and inventory management information systems. As a result, Amazon has been able to offer expedited shipping on its orders since 2005.

All of the new products and services described above required investments of significant financial resources. Amazon's management team needed to tread carefully in evaluating these investments. When faced with a new investment decision, Amazon's managers should be asking themselves these questions: How will we finance these investments, and at what cost can we raise the needed funds? What tax deductions or incentives might defray some of the costs of these investments? How long before these investments recover their initial costs through increased revenues? Do our estimates consider increases in operating costs? In other words, Amazon needs to determine which capital investments will ultimately have a net positive effect on operating results. However, even the most careful planning cannot prevent all investment failures. Consider that Amazon discontinued the Fire Phone, an android-based smartphone in 2015, just over one year after its introduction or the video game Crucible, that was canceled within months of its introduction in 2020. These examples illustrate the importance of effective management tools to help companies determine whether or not to invest in new product ideas/services. It also emphasizes the underlying risk in capital budgeting decisions.

This chapter will detail important tools that managers can use to increase the probability that their capital investments will be sound. We introduce important capital budgeting concepts and models, and explain the proper use of accounting data in these models.

Sources: Amazon.com, Inc. 2022 annual report and Gartenberg, C. "Bezos' Amazon: From bookstore to backbone of the internet." *The Verge* 3 (2021).

CHAPTER ORGANIZATION

Capital Budgeting Decisions

Long-Range Planning and Capital Budgeting	Capital Budgeting Models That Do Not Consider the Time Value of Money	Capital Budgeting Models That Consider the Time Value of Money	Evaluation of Capital Budgeting Models	Considering Risks and Relevant Cost Analysis in Capital Budgeting Decisions	Additional Considerations
• Capital Budgeting Process	• Predicted Cash Flows • Payback Period • Accounting Rate of Return	• Net Present Value • Internal Rate of Return	• Advantages and Disadvantages of Capital Budgeting Models • Criteria for Evaluation	• Evaluating Risk and Uncertainty • Using Differential Analysis • Avoiding Predicting Errors	• Time Value of Money (Appendix 24A) • Table Approach to Determining Internal Rate of Return (Appendix 24B) • Taxes in Capital Budgeting Decisions (Appendix 24C)

LONG-RANGE PLANNING AND CAPITAL BUDGETING

LO24-1
Explain the capital budgeting process and analyze decisions using models such as payback period and accounting rate of return, that do not consider the time value of money.

Capital expenditures are investments of financial resources in projects to develop or introduce new products or services, to expand current production or service capacity, or to change current production or service facilities. Capital expenditures are made with the expectation that the new product, process, or service will generate future financial inflows that exceed the initial costs. Capital expenditure decisions are made infrequently but once made are difficult to change. They commit the organization to the use of certain facilities and activities to satisfy customer needs. In making large capital expenditure decisions, such as for **Amazon**'s warehouse facilities, management is risking the future existence of the company.

Although capital expenditure decisions are fraught with risk, management accounting provides the concepts and tools needed to organize information, compare alternatives, and help with decision-making. This systematic organization and analysis is the essence of capital budgeting. **Capital budgeting** is a process that involves identifying potentially desirable projects for capital expenditures, evaluating capital expenditure proposals, and selecting proposals that meet minimum criteria. A number of quantitative models are available to assist managers in evaluating capital expenditure proposals.

The best capital budgeting models are conceptually similar to the short-range planning models used in Chapters 15 and 16. They all emphasize cash flows and focus on future costs (and revenues) that differ among decision alternatives. The major difference is that capital budgeting models involve cash flows over several years, whereas short-range planning models involve cash flows for a year or less. Most planning beyond the next budget year is called *long-range planning*. When the cash flows associated with a proposed activity extend over several years, an adjustment is necessary to compare cash flows that are expected to occur at different points in time. The *time value of money concept* explains why monies received or paid at different points in time must be adjusted to comparable values.

Increased uncertainty and business alternatives add to the difficulty of planning as the horizon lengthens. Even though long-range planning is difficult and involves uncertainties, management must make long-range planning and capital expenditure decisions based on the answers to many questions. How will the decisions be made? Will they be made on the basis of the best information available? Will managers ensure that capital expenditure decisions align with the organization's long-range goals? Will the potential consequences, both positive and negative, of capital expenditures be considered? Will important alternative uses of the organization's limited financial resources be considered in a systematic manner? Will managers be held accountable for the capital expenditure programs they initiate? The alternative to a systematic approach to capital budgeting is the haphazard expenditure of resources on the basis of a hunch, immediate need, or persuasion—without accountability by the person(s) making the decisions.

The Capital Budgeting Process

The steps of an effective capital budgeting process are outlined in **Exhibit 24.1**. A basic requirement for a systematic approach to capital budgeting is a defined mission, a set of long-range goals, and a business strategy. These elements provide focus and boundaries that reduce the types of capital expenditure decisions management considers. If, for example, one of **Amazon**'s goals is low-cost leadership, it should only consider proposals that will further this goal. Proposals that will result in higher prices will be immediately dismissed.

EXHIBIT 24.1 Capital Budgeting Procedures

- Identify potential capital expenditures
- Determine whether a proposed expenditure fits mission, goals, and business strategy
- Perform preliminary data gathering and analysis using capital budgeting models
- Increase analytical rigor and required level of approval as importance and size of project increase
- Develop implementation plans for approved projects
- Monitor implementation and revise implementation of project as required
- Conduct a post audit review to assign responsibility and improve future planning

A more detailed or refined business strategy will likewise guide capital expenditure decisions. If **Amazon** is following a strategy to obtain technological leadership in distribution, it might consider a proposal to meet customer needs by investing in new innovative distribution facilities but would not consider a proposal to purchase and refurbish used (but seemingly cost-efficient) equipment for their distribution facilities.

Sometimes, decisions seem at odds with a company's business strategy. **Consumers Energy**, a public utility in Michigan serving 6.7 million people, has plans to spend $25 billion before 2030 to replace aging gas and electric equipment with solar panels, wind turbines, and large-scale battery storage units. In the 18 months it took the company to complete the study of renewable energy sources, solar prices had fallen 30%. The initial costs of solar technologies were now more competitive with the costs of natural gas plants than initially forecasted. The company is also working to help customers reduce their electricity consumption through the use of smart thermostats and smart meters.[1] The focus on reducing consumption of Consumers' primary source of revenue may seem counterintuitive, but the company believes the switch to renewable energy sources, along with better management of energy demand, will ultimately result in higher profits. Most capital budgeting decisions are about deciding to spend money to make money. The decision by Consumers to budget for energy efficiency was about spending money to save money and reduce its carbon emissions.

Capital Budget Approval Process

Management should also develop procedures for the review, evaluation, approval, and post-audit of capital expenditure proposals. In a large organization, a **capital budgeting committee** that provides guidance to managers in the formulation of capital expenditure proposals is key to these procedures. This committee reviews, analyzes, and approves or rejects major capital expenditure proposals. Major projects often require the approval of top management and even the board of directors. The capital budgeting committee should include persons knowledgeable in

- capital budgeting models,
- financing alternatives and costs,
- operating procedures,

---
[1] Katherine Blunt, "How A Utility's Counterintuitive Strategy Might Fuel A Greener Future," *Wall Street Journal*, February 8, 2020.

- cost estimation and prediction methods,
- research and development efforts,
- the organization's goals and basic strategy, and
- the expectations of the organization's stockholders or owners.

A management accountant who is generally an expert in data collection, retrieval, and analysis is normally part of the capital budgeting committee. For example, accountants can collect data on alternative proposals and analyze the alternative proposals under sets of different assumptions.

Not all capital expenditure proposals require committee approval or are subject to formal evaluation. With the approval of top management, the committee might provide guidelines indicating the type and dollar amount of capital expenditures that managers at each level of the organization can make without formal evaluation or committee approval, or both. The guidelines might state that expenditures of less than $20,000 do not require committee approval and that only expenditures of more than $100,000 must be evaluated using capital budgeting models.

Typically, managers at higher levels have greater discretion in making capital expenditures. In a college or university, a department chairperson could have authority to purchase office and instructional equipment with a maximum limit of $10,000 per year. A dean may have authority to renovate offices or classrooms with a maximum limit of $50,000 per year, but the conversion of the power plant from one fuel source to another at a cost of $400,000 could require the formal review of a capital budgeting committee and final approval of the board of trustees. Similarly, employees at different levels within Amazon (or other companies) will have limited authority to approve expenditures.

Capital Budget Post-Audit Process

The post-audit of approved capital expenditure proposals is an important part of a well-formulated approach to capital budgeting. A *post-audit* involves the development of project performance reports comparing planned and actual results (i.e., variance analysis). Project performance reports should be provided to the manager who initiated the capital expenditure proposal, the manager assigned responsibility for the project (if a different person), the project manager's supervisor, and the capital budgeting committee. These reports help keep the project on target (especially during the initial investment phase), identify the need to reevaluate the project if the initial analysis was in error or significant environmental changes occur, and improve the quality of investment proposals. When managers know they will be held accountable for the results of projects they initiate, they are likely to put more care into the development of capital expenditure proposals and take a greater interest in approved projects. Problems can occur when decision makers are rewarded for undertaking major projects but are not held responsible for the consequences that occur several years later. It is important to tie performance measurement and incentives to all phases of the project to ensure alignment of manager performance with project goals and company strategies.

A post-audit review of approved projects also helps the capital budgeting committee do a better job in evaluating new proposals. The committee might learn how to adjust proposals for the biases of individual managers, learn of new factors that should be considered in evaluating proposals, and avoid the routine approval of projects that appear desirable by themselves but are related to larger projects that are not meeting management's expectations.

You have recently accepted the position of VP of finance for a rapidly growing biotech company. Last year the company made capital expenditures of $10 million and you anticipate that annual capital expenditures will exceed $30 million in a couple of years. You believe it is time to develop a more formal approach to making capital expenditure decisions. Where do you begin?

There is no single correct response to this question. It is useful to start by learning how other companies in similar circumstances handle capital expenditure decisions. This might be done through personal contacts or through professional organizations, such as the Financial Executives International. Another starting point might be the formation of a small capital budgeting committee, which could be expanded as necessary once formal procedures were in place. Early tasks of the committee might

include developing guidelines for the size of expenditures at various organizational levels subject to committee review and developing guidelines for the criteria used in formal reviews. You would want to ensure that the CEO is in agreement with these proposals. If the company has a board of directors, you would also want some mutual understanding of the board's role in the approval of capital expenditures. Finally, you would want to make clear the importance of a post-audit review.

CAPITAL BUDGETING MODELS THAT DO NOT CONSIDER TIME VALUE OF MONEY

The capital budgeting process described in the last section requires an analysis of potential capital projects as part of the approval process. The capital budgeting models presented in this chapter have gained wide acceptance by for-profit and not-for-profit organizations. Keep in mind that while the models provide data for investment decisions, managers are needed to determine the assumptions used in the models and to interpret the results. Models that do not consider the time value of money, called *nondiscounting models,* are often used as initial screening devices for potential projects. Further, nondiscounting models remain entrenched in small businesses. We consider two nondiscounting models, the *payback period* and the *accounting rate of return* in this section. Discounting models are discussed in a later section.

Capital Budgeting Models (No time value of money)	
Payback Period	Accounting Rate of Return

Predicted Cash Flows

The focus of capital budgeting models is on cash receipts and cash disbursements that differ, in timing and amounts, under decision alternatives. It is often convenient to distinguish between the following three phases of a project's cash flows.

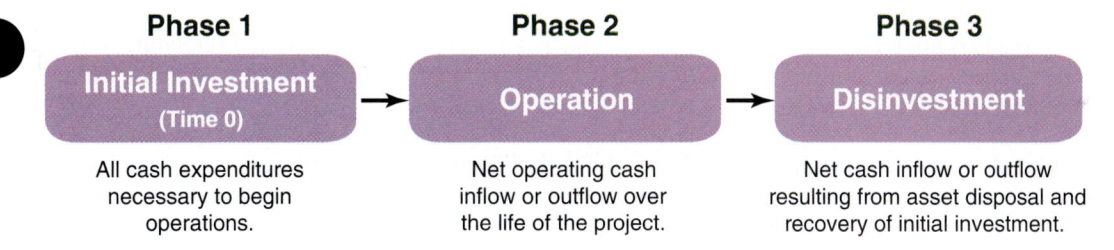

Phase 1 — Initial Investment (Time 0) → **Phase 2** — Operation → **Phase 3** — Disinvestment

- Phase 1: All cash expenditures necessary to begin operations.
- Phase 2: Net operating cash inflow or outflow over the life of the project.
- Phase 3: Net cash inflow or outflow resulting from asset disposal and recovery of initial investment.

- **Phase 1** All cash expenditures necessary to begin operations are classified as part of the project's *initial investment phase.* Expenditures to acquire property, plant, and equipment are part of the initial investment. Less obvious, but equally important, are expenditures to acquire working capital to purchase inventories and recruit and train employees. Although the initial investment phase often extends over many years, in our examples, we assume that the initial investment takes place at a single point in time.

- **Phase 2** Cash receipts from sales of goods or services, as well as normal cash expenditures for materials, labor, and other operating expenses, occur during the operation phase. The *operation phase* is typically broken down into one-year periods. For each period, operating cash expenditures are subtracted from operating cash receipts to determine the net operating cash inflow or outflow for the period.

- **Phase 3** The *disinvestment phase* occurs at the end of the project's life when assets are disposed of for their salvage value and any initial investment of working capital is recovered. Also included are any expenditures to dismantle facilities and dispose of waste. Although this phase might extend over many years, in our examples, we assume disinvestment takes place at a single point in time.

To illustrate the analysis of a project's cash flows, suppose Amazon is approached by one of its Whole Foods stores to expand its operations to include pizzas-to-go. The primary investment relates to equipment including a pizza oven. The predicted cash flows associated with the project, which has an expected life of five years, are presented in **Exhibit 24.2**. Note that the exhibit highlights the cash flows associated with the three phases of cash flows.

EXHIBIT 24.2 — Analysis of a Project's Predicted Cash Flows

Phase 1

Initial investment (at time 0)
Equipment	$ (90,554)
Inventories and other working capital	(4,000)
Total investment cash outflow	**$ (94,554)**

Phase 2

Operation (per year for 5 years)
Sales		$ 175,000
Cash expenditures		
Food	$47,000	
Labor	65,000	
Supplies	9,000	
Utilities	8,000	
Advertising	4,000	
Miscellaneous	12,000	(145,000)
Net annual cash inflow		**$ 30,000**

Phase 3

Disinvestment (at the end of 5 years)
Sale of equipment	$ 8,000
Recovery of investment in inventories and other working capital	4,000
Total disinvestment cash inflow	**$ 12,000**

Payback Period

The **payback period** is the time required to recover the initial investment in a project. The payback decision rule states that acceptable projects must have less than some maximum payback period designated by management. Payback emphasizes management's concern with liquidity and the need to minimize risk through a rapid recovery of the initial investment. It is frequently used for small expenditures having such obvious benefits that the use of more sophisticated capital budgeting models is not required or justified. The payback period is also a good, initial screening tool for larger expenditures. Its simplicity allows it to be used more readily by smaller companies without sophisticated financial resources.

Payback with Predicted Equal Annual Cash Flows When a project is expected to have equal annual net operating cash inflows, its payback period is computed as follows:

$$\text{Payback period} = \frac{\text{Initial investment}}{\text{Annual net operating cash inflows}}$$

The company expects to invest $94,554 into the store and earn $30,000 per year as cash inflows. The payback period of 3.15 is calculated as follows.

$$\text{Payback period} = \frac{\$94,554}{\$30,000} = 3.15$$

Thus, if the assumptions hold true, it will take 3.15 years for Amazon to recoup its investment.

Payback with Predicted Unequal Annual Cash Flows Determining the payback period for a project having unequal cash flows is slightly more complicated. Assume that **Amazon** is evaluating a capital expenditure proposal to open a new Whole Foods store that requires an initial investment of $50,000,000. Because the store is located in a new area, it is more difficult to project cash inflows. In addition, management expects cash flow amounts to be *inconsistent* over time. Amazon expects the following net annual cash inflows.

Year	Net Cash Inflow
1	$15,000,000
2	25,000,000
3	40,000,000
4	20,000,000
5	10,000,000

To compute the payback period, we must determine the net unrecovered investment amount at the end of each year. The *net unrecovered investment* amount is equal to the initial investment minus the accumulated net cash inflow. At the point where the initial investment is fully recovered, the net unrecovered investment amount is equal to zero. In the year of full recovery, the net cash inflows are assumed to occur evenly and are prorated based on the unrecovered investment at the start of the year. Full recovery of Amazon's investment proposal is expected to occur in Year 3. More specifically, $10,000,000 of the total cash inflows of $40,000,000 is needed in Year 3 to complete the recovery of the initial investment.

Year	Net Cash Inflow	Unrecovered Investment
0	$ 0	$50,000,000
1	15,000,000	35,000,000
2	25,000,000	10,000,000
3	40,000,000	0

The payback period of this investment is 2.25 years, calculated as follows.

Full years (Year 1 and Year 2)	= 2.00 years
Partial Year 3 = $10,000,000 ÷ $40,000,000	= 0.25 year
Total payback period = 2.0 + 0.25	= 2.25 years

This project is acceptable if management specified a maximum payback period of three years. Because the net cash inflows of Years 4 and 5 occur after the payback period, they are ignored.

The payback period method is simple to compute. The result can be easily compared to the maximum payback period designated by management. It doesn't preclude a company from also using more sophisticated models, but if a payback period is excessively long, management might decide to reject the proposal without doing more analysis.

Accounting Rate of Return

The **accounting rate of return** is the average annual increase in net income that results from the acceptance of a capital expenditure proposal divided by either the initial investment or the average investment in the project. This method differs from other capital budgeting models in that it focuses on accounting income rather than on cash flow. In most capital budgeting applications, accounting net income is approximated as net cash inflow from operations minus expenses not requiring the use of cash, such as depreciation. *Depreciation* is the systematic and rational allocation of plant asset cost over the plant asset's estimated useful life.

Accounting Rate of Return on Initial Investment Consider Amazon's capital expenditure proposal, with cash flows outlined in **Exhibit 24.2**. The equipment costs $90,554 and has a salvage value of $8,000 at the end of five years, resulting in an average annual increase in net income of $13,489.

Annual net cash inflow from operations	$30,000
Less average annual depreciation [($90,554 − $8,000) ÷ 5]	(16,511)
Average annual increase in net income	$13,489

Considering the investment in inventories and other working capital, the initial investment is $94,554 ($90,554 + $4,000), and the *accounting rate of return on initial investment* is calculated as:

$$\frac{\text{Accounting rate of return}}{\text{on initial investment}} = \frac{\text{Average annual increase in net income}}{\text{Initial investment}} = \frac{\$13,489}{\$94,554} = 0.1427$$

Accounting Rate of Return on Average Investment Amazon can expect to earn approximately 14%, per year, on the investment. Amazon can also calculate the return on the average investment. The average investment is computed as the initial investment plus the expected value of any disinvestment (which is the book value of the asset at the end of the investment's life), all divided by 2. For the hypothetical Amazon example, average investment is calculated as follows.

$$\text{Average investment} = \frac{\text{(Initial investment + Expected value of disinvestment)}}{2} = \frac{[\$94{,}554 + (\$8{,}000 + \$4{,}000)]}{2} = \$53{,}277$$

The *accounting rate of return on average investment* is 25.32%, computed as follows.

$$\frac{\text{Accounting rate of return}}{\text{on average investment}} = \frac{\text{Average annual increase in net income}}{\text{Average investment}} = \frac{\$13{,}489}{\$53{,}277} = 0.2532$$

When using the accounting rate of return, management specifies either the initial investment or average investment plus some minimum acceptable rate. Management rejects capital expenditure proposals with a lower accounting rate of return but accepts proposals with an accounting rate of return higher than or equal to the minimum.

Critical Thinking & Decision-Making

Suppose you own a bakery and are considering purchasing an additional commercial oven. Would you analyze this decision using the payback period or the accounting rate of return?

If you are looking for a quick screening tool, the payback method works well. If sales for the bakery are increasing and are expected to continue to increase into the near future, a relatively quick payback period for the oven may be a sufficient analysis to support the investment. If the payback period is longer than expected and closer to the maximum acceptable payback period, you would probably want to perform further analysis, such as the computation of the accounting rate of return.

Review 24-1 LO24-1   Computing the Payback Period and the Accounting Rate of Return

One of **Costco Wholesale Corporation**'s stores is considering investing in new equipment. The following chart presents estimates related to the investment.

Initial investment	
Depreciable assets	$27,740
Working capital	3,000
Operations (per year for 4 years)	
Cash receipts	25,000
Cash expenditures	15,000
Disinvestment	
Salvage value of plant and equipment	2,000
Recovery of working capital	3,000

Required

a. Compute the payback period.
b. Compute the accounting rate of return on initial investment and on average investment.
c. Would you suggest that Costco invest in the new equipment? Why or why not?

Solution on p. 24-45.

CAPITAL BUDGETING MODELS THAT CONSIDER TIME VALUE OF MONEY

LO24-2
Analyze capital budgeting decisions, using models such as net present value and internal rate of return, that consider the time value of money.

While useful under certain circumstances, the payback method and the accounting rate of return do not consider the time value of money. Our primary focus in this section is on the *net present value* and the *internal rate of return models*, which better reflect economics because they consider the time value of money. Although we briefly consider the cost of financing capital expenditures, we leave a detailed treatment of this topic, as well as a detailed examination of the sources of funds for financing investments, to books on financial management.

Capital Budgeting Models (Time value of money)

Net Present value	Internal Rate of Return

Net Present Value

A project's **net present value**, usually computed as of the time of the initial investment, is the present value of the project's net cash inflows from operations and disinvestment less the amount of the initial investment. Appendix 24A contains an introduction to the time value of money, including net present value fundamentals. In computing a project's net present value, the cash flows occurring at different points in time are adjusted for the time value of money using a **discount rate** that is the minimum rate of return required for the project to be acceptable. Projects with positive net present values (or values at least equal to zero) are acceptable because the project's expected return exceeds the company's discount rate. Projects with negative net present values are unacceptable because the project's expected return is *less than* the company's discount rate. The effect of income tax on the net present value calculation is addressed in Appendix 24C. Two methods to compute net present value follow.

Table Approach

Assuming that management uses a 12% discount rate, the net present value of the proposed investment for Amazon is shown in **Exhibit 24.3** (a) to be $20,398. Since the net present value is more than zero, the investment by Amazon is expected to provide a return greater than the discount rate of 12%.

EXHIBIT 24.3 — Net Present Value of a Project's Predicted Cash Flows

(a) Table approach:

	Predicted Cash Inflows (outflows) (A)	Year(s) of Cash Flows (B)	12% Present Value Factor (C)	Present Value of Cash Flows (A) × (C)
Initial investment	$(94,554)	0	1.00000	$(94,554)
Operation	30,000	1–5	3.60478	108,143
Disinvestment	12,000	5	0.56743	6,809
Net present value of all cash flows				$ 20,398

(b) Spreadsheet approach:

Input:

	A	B
1	Year of cash flow	Cash flow
2	1	$30,000
3	2	30,000
4	3	30,000
5	4	30,000
6	5	42,000
7	Present value	=NPV(0.12,B2:B6)
8	Initial investment at time 0	(94,554)
9	Net present value	=B7+B8

Output:

	A	B
1	Year of cash flow	Cash flow
2	1	$ 30,000
3	2	30,000
4	3	30,000
5	4	30,000
6	5	42,000
7	Present value	$114,952.41
8	Initial investment at time 0	(94,554.00)
9	Net present value	$ 20,398.41

We can verify the amounts and computations in **Exhibit 24.3** (a). Start by tracing the cash flows back to **Exhibit 24.2**. Next, determine the 12% present value factors by referring to **Exhibits 24A.1** and **24A.2** in Appendix 24A. The initial investment is assumed to occur at a single point in time (identified as time 0), the start of the project. In net present value computations, all cash flows are restated in terms of their value at time 0. Hence, time 0 cash flows have a present value factor of 1. To simplify computations, all other cash flows are assumed to occur at the end of years 1 through 5, even if they occurred during the year. Although further refinements could be made to adjust for cash flows occurring throughout each year, such adjustments are seldom necessary. Observe that net operating cash inflows are treated as an *annuity*, whereas cash flows for the initial investment and disinvestment are treated as *lump-sum amounts*. If net operating cash flows varied from year to year, we would treat each year's cash flow as a separate amount.

Spreadsheet Approach

Visit https://office.live .com/start/Excel.aspx for free access to Microsoft Excel Online by creating a Microsoft account.

Spreadsheet software contains functions that compute the present value of a series of cash flows. With this software, simply enter a column or row containing the net cash flows for each period and the appropriate formula. The discount rate of 0.12 is entered as part of the formula. Sample spreadsheet input to determine the net present value of the proposed investment by Amazon is shown on the left in **Exhibit 24.3** (b). The spreadsheet output is shown on the right, in **Exhibit 24.3** (b).

Two cautionary notes when using the spreadsheet approach to calculate net present value follow.

1. The spreadsheet formula for the net present value assumes that the first cash flow occurs at time "1," rather than at time "0." Hence, we cannot include the initial investment in the data set analyzed by the spreadsheet formula when computing the net present value. Instead, the initial investment is subtracted from the present value of future cash flows.

2. Arrange the cash flows subsequent to the initial investment from *top* to bottom in a column, or *left* to right in a row in your spreadsheet.

Internal Rate of Return

The **internal rate of return (IRR)**, often called the **time-adjusted rate of return**, is the discount rate that equates the present value of a project's cash inflows with the present value of the project's cash outflows. It is the discount rate that results in a project's net present value equaling zero.

All practical applications of the IRR model use a calculator or spreadsheet. Thus, we illustrate determining an IRR with a spreadsheet. A table approach to determining a project's internal rate of return is illustrated in Appendix 24B of this chapter.

Within a spreadsheet program, simply enter a column or row containing the net cash flows for each period and the appropriate formula. Spreadsheet input for Amazon's investment proposal is shown in **Exhibit 24.4**. The spreadsheet formula for the IRR assumes that the first cash flow occurs at time "0."

The spreadsheet approach requires an initial prediction or guess of the project's internal rate of return. Although the closeness of the prediction to the final solution affects computational speed, for textbook examples almost any number can be used. We use an initial estimate of 0.08 in all illustrations. Because the IRR formula assumes that the first cash flow occurs at time 0, the initial investment is included in the data analyzed by the IRR formula. Again, we must order the cash flows from top to bottom in a column or left to right in a row. As shown on the right column in **Exhibit 24.4**, the spreadsheet program computes the IRR as 20%.

EXHIBIT 24.4 Spreadsheet Approach to Determining Internal Rate of Return

Input:

	A	B
1	Year of cash flow	Cash flow
2	0	$(94,554)
3	1	30,000
4	2	30,000
5	3	30,000
6	4	30,000
7	5	42,000
8	IRR	=IRR(B2:B7,0.08)*

Output:

	A	B
1	Year of cash flow	Cash flow
2	0	$(94,554)
3	1	30,000
4	2	30,000
5	3	30,000
6	4	30,000
7	5	42,000
8	IRR	0.20

*The formula is "=IRR(Input data range, guess)." The guess, which is any likely rate of return, is used as an initial starting point in determining the solution. We use 0.08 in all illustrations.

The calculated internal rate of return is compared to the discount rate established by management to evaluate investment proposals. If the proposal's IRR is greater than or equal to the discount rate established by management, the project is acceptable; if it is less than the discount rate established by management, the project is questionable. Because Amazon has a 12% discount rate, the project is acceptable using the IRR model. (Note that if Amazon's discount rate was 20% instead, the net present value of this current proposal would be zero.)

Although a project's IRR should be compared to the discount rate established by management, such a discount rate is often unknown. In these situations, computing the IRR still provides insights into a project's profitability.

Does the ease of using Excel to calculate NPV and IRR for an investment proposal turn a capital budgeting decision into a quick, objective process?

Although spreadsheet programs quickly and accurately perform tedious computations, computational ease increases the opportunity for inappropriate use. The ability to plug numbers into Excel and obtain an output labeled NPV or IRR could mislead the unwary into believing that capital budgeting models are easy to use and provide an objective answer. This is not true. Training and professional judgment are required to identify relevant costs and other assumptions, to implement procedures to obtain relevant cost information, and to make a good decision once results are available. Capital budgeting models are merely decision aids to a subjective process. Managers, not models, make the decisions.

Critical Thinking & Decision-Making

Cost of Capital Used As the Discount Rate When discounting models are used to evaluate capital expenditure proposals, management must determine the discount rate (1) used to compute a proposal's net present value or (2) used as the standard for evaluating a proposal's IRR. An organization's cost of capital is often used as this discount rate. The **cost of capital** is the average rate an organization pays to its creditors and shareholders to obtain the resources necessary to make investments. The cost of capital is the minimum return acceptable for investment purposes. Any investment proposal not expected to yield this minimum rate should normally be rejected. Because of difficulties encountered in determining the cost of capital, many organizations adopt a discount rate or a target rate of return without complicated mathematical analysis. Procedures for determining the cost of capital are covered in finance books.

Review 24-2 — Calculating Net Present Value and Internal Rate of Return — LO24-2

Consider again, **Costco**'s investment proposal.

Initial investment	
Depreciable assets	$27,740
Working capital	3,000
Operations (per year for 4 years)	
Cash receipts	25,000
Cash expenditures	15,000
Disinvestment	
Salvage value of plant and equipment	2,000
Recovery of working capital	3,000

Required
Determine each of the following.
a. Net present value at a 10% discount rate.
b. Internal rate of return. (Refer to Appendix 24B if using the table approach.)

Solution on p. 24-45.

EVALUATION OF CAPITAL BUDGETING MODELS

As a single criterion for evaluating capital expenditure proposals, capital budgeting models that consider the time value of money are superior to models that do not consider it. This means that the net present value and the internal rate of return would be preferable to the payback method and the accounting rate of return. However, each method has a slightly different purpose and can be useful depending on the context of the situation.

LO24-3 Evaluate the strengths and weaknesses of alternative capital budgeting models.

Advantages and Disadvantages of Capital Budgeting Models

Payback Period The payback model concerns merely how long it takes to recover the initial investment from a project, yet investments are not made with the objective of merely getting the money back. Indeed, not investing has a payback period of 0. Investments are made to earn a profit. Hence, what happens after the payback period is more important than is the payback period itself. The payback period model, when used as the sole investment criterion, has a fatal flaw in that it fails to consider cash flows *after the payback period*. Despite this flaw, payback is a rough-and-ready approach to getting a handle on investment proposals. Sometimes a project is so attractive using payback as a screening tool that, when its payback period is considered, no further analysis is necessary.

Accounting Rate of Return vs. Net Present Value Unlike the payback method, the accounting rate of return considers the proposal's profitability. Using the accounting rate of return, a project that merely returns the initial investment will have an average annual increase in net income of 0 and an accounting rate of return of 0. The problem with the accounting rate of return is that it fails to consider the timing of cash flows. It treats all cash flows within the life of an investment proposal equally despite the fact that cash flows occurring early in a project's life are more valuable than cash flows occurring late in a project's life. Early period cash flows can earn additional profits by being invested elsewhere. Consider the two investment proposals summarized in **Exhibit 24.5**. Both have an accounting rate of return of 5%, but Project A is superior to Project B because most of its cash flows occur in the first two years. Because of the timing of the cash flows when discounted at an annual rate of 10%, Project A has a net present value of $1,120 while Project B has a negative net present value of $(10,928).

> **Critical Thinking & Decision-Making**
>
> **In this case, the return of the project with the positive net present value exceeded the company's discount rate while the return of the project with the negative net present value did not exceed the company's discount rate. If instead, both net present value amounts were positive, would the project with the highest net present value always be the more favorable option?**
>
> *While this will likely be the case, it may not always be the case. For example, there may be nonfinancial factors that come into play that make the project with the lower net present value more favorable such as less uncertainties in the time required for project implementation or an environmental goal such as the use of solar energy for production. Also, comparing the net present value of two projects with different initial investment levels can be more complicated. If two projects required different initial investments, let's say $1 million vs. $250,000, the company may choose the project with the lower initial investment, even if its net present value is lower. This example emphasizes the importance in evaluating the results from capital budgeting models and not treating the results as objective answers.*

EXHIBIT 24.5 Evaluating Capital Budgeting Models with Differences in Cash Flow Timing

Accounting rate of return analysis of Projects A and B

	Project A	Project B
Predicted net cash inflow from operations		
Year 1	$ 50,000	$ 10,000
Year 2	50,000	10,000
Year 3	10,000	50,000
Year 4	10,000	50,000
Total	120,000	120,000
Total depreciation	(100,000)	(100,000)
Total net income	$ 20,000	$ 20,000
Project life	÷ 4 years	÷ 4 years
Average annual increase in net income	$ 5,000	$ 5,000
Initial investment	÷ 100,000	÷ 100,000
Accounting rate of return on initial investment	0.05	0.05

continued

continued from previous page

EXHIBIT 24.5 Evaluating Capital Budgeting Models with Differences in Cash Flow Timing

Net present value analysis of Project A

	Predicted Cash Inflows (outflows)	Year(s) of Cash Flows	10% Present Value Factor	Present Value of Cash Flows
Initial investment.	$(100,000)	0	1.00000	$(100,000)
Operation	50,000	1–2	1.73554	86,777
Operation	10,000	3–4	3.16987 – 1.73554	14,343
Net present value of all cash flows.				$ 1,120

Net present value analysis of Project B

	Predicted Cash Inflows (outflows)	Year(s) of Cash Flows	10% Present Value Factor	Present Value of Cash Flows
Initial investment.	$(100,000)	0	1.00000	$(100,000)
Operation	10,000	1–2	1.73554	17,355
Operation	50,000	3–4	3.16987 – 1.73554	71,717
Net present value of all cash flows.				$ (10,928)

Net Present Value vs. Internal Rate of Return The net present value and the internal rate of return models both consider the time value of money and all project cash flows. They almost always provide the same evaluation of individual projects whose acceptance or rejection will not affect other projects. Both methods use the company's discount rate in determining whether to accept or reject a project. The net present value method uses the discount rate to discount the project's expected cash flows. When the internal rate of return is calculated, it is compared to the company's discount rate. However, a key difference in the methods relates to the assumptions on reinvestment of a project's net cash inflows. The net present value model assumes that all net cash inflows are immediately reinvested elsewhere at the discount rate. The internal rate of return model assumes that all net cash inflows are immediately reinvested elsewhere at the project's internal rate of return. This may not be the case, especially when the project's internal rate of return is high.

Let's assume that the internal rate of return on a project is 20% and the company's discount rate is 10%. The built in assumption of the internal rate of return is that predicted project cash inflows are reinvested immediately at the internal rate or return, which in this case is 20%. Does the company have other opportunities to invest at 20% when its discount rate is only 10%? Consequently, when funds received from a project can only be reinvested elsewhere at the cost of capital, the net present value method is superior. See **Exhibit 24.6** for a summary of the advantages and disadvantages of the capital budgeting models discussed in this chapter.

EXHIBIT 24.6 Advantages and Disadvantages of Capital Budgeting Models

PAYBACK	ACCOUNTING RATE OF RETURN
⊕ Quick and easy screening tool	⊕ Does not require complicated calculations
⊕ Focuses on liquidity concerns	⊕ Measures project profitability
⊖ Does not measure project profitability	⊕ Considers project accounting (GAAP) income
⊖ Does not consider time value of money	⊖ Does not consider time value of money
⊖ Does not consider cash flows after payback	⊖ Does not focus on project cash flows

NET PRESENT VALUE	INTERNAL RATE OF RETURN
⊕ Considers all project cash flows	⊕ Considers all project cash flows
⊕ Considers time value of money	⊕ Considers time value of money
⊖ Assumes immediate reinvestment of project net cash inflows elsewhere at a single discount rate, which may not be possible	⊖ Assumes immediate reinvestment of project net cash inflows elsewhere at the project's internal rate of return, which may not be possible
⊖ Requires complicated calculations and analysis	⊖ Requires complicated calculations and analysis

Using Multiple Investment Criteria to Evaluate Projects

Using multiple capital budgeting models In performing this initial screening, management can use a single capital budgeting model or multiple models, including some we have not discussed. Management might specify that proposals must be in line with the organization's long-range goals and business strategy, have a maximum payback period of three years, have a positive net present value when discounted at 14%, and have an initial investment of less than $500,000. The maximum payback period might be intended to reduce risk, the present value criterion might be to ensure an adequate return to investors, and the maximum investment size might reflect the resources available for investment.

Considering nonfinancial measures Nonquantitative factors such as market position, operational performance improvement, and strategy implementation often play a decisive role in management's final decision to accept or reject a capital expenditure proposal that has passed the initial screening. More recently, managers consider ESG metrics to a greater extent. The impact of the project on, for example, gas emissions might impact management's evaluation of the project. ESG goals and metrics should be considered when making capital investment decisions. Also important at this point are top management's attitudes toward risk and financing alternatives, their confidence in the professional judgment of other managers making investment proposals, their beliefs about the future direction of the economy, and their evaluation of alternative investments.

In the next section, we will focus on evaluating risk and uncertainty in capital budgeting, differential analysis of project cash outflows, and avoiding errors in predicting differential costs and revenues.

Review 24-3 LO24-3   Evaluating Investment Proposals

Costco Warehouse is considering three different unrelated capital investments. Presented is information pertaining to each investment proposal.

	Proposal A	Proposal B	Proposal C
Initial investment....................................	$45,000	$45,000	$45,000
Cash flow from operations			
Year 1	40,000	22,500	45,000
Year 2	5,000	22,500	
Year 3	22,500	22,500	

Required
a. Rank these investment proposals using the payback period, the accounting rate of return on initial investment, and the net present value criteria. Assume that the organization's cost of capital is 10%.
b. Explain the difference in rankings. Which investment would you recommend?

Solution on p. 24-46.

CONSIDERING RISKS AND RELEVANT COST ANALYSIS IN CAPITAL BUDGETING DECISIONS

LO24-4
Evaluate risk and use differential analysis in capital budgeting decisions.

The capital budgeting models discussed do not make investment decisions. Rather, they help managers separate capital expenditure proposals that meet certain criteria from those that do not. Managers can then focus on those proposals that pass the initial screening.

Evaluating Risk and Uncertainty in Capital Budgeting Decisions

All capital expenditure proposals involve risk, including risk related to the following.

- Cost of the initial investment.
- Time required to complete the initial investment and begin operations.
- Whether the new facilities will operate as planned.
- Life of the facilities.
- Customers' demand for the product or service.
- Final selling price.
- Operating costs.
- Disposal values.

Projected cash flows (such as those summarized for the Amazon proposal in **Exhibit 24.2**) are based on management's best predictions. Although these predictions are likely to reflect the professional judgment of economists, marketing personnel, engineers, and accountants, they are far from certain. For example, managers might be overly optimistic with their predictions, and they are sometimes tempted to modify predictions to justify capital expenditures. Perhaps they are interested in personal rewards. They might also want to avoid a loss of prestige or employment for themselves or to keep a local facility operating for the benefit of current employees and the local economy. Unfortunately, if a major expenditure does not work out, not only the local plant but also the entire company could be forced out of business. For example, under pressure to increase current sales, automobile leasing companies could be tempted to overstate cash receipts during the disinvestment phase of a lease.

Managers should use **sensitivity analysis** to understand how changes in the assumptions and forecasts alter the implications derived from the capital expenditure analysis. Managers will re-evaluate the proposal, changing the various assumptions by small amounts, to understand how the projections change. It is important for managers to remember that capital budgeting decisions may be impacted by global factors such as exchange rate fluctuations and political instability.

Many techniques have been developed to assist in the analysis of the risks inherent in capital budgeting. Suggested approaches include the following.

- *Adjust the discount rate for individual projects based on management's perception of the risks associated with a project.* A project perceived as being almost risk free might be evaluated using a discount rate of 12%; a project perceived as having moderate risk may be evaluated using a discount rate of 16%; and a project perceived as having high risk might be evaluated using a discount rate of 20%.

- *Compute several internal rates of return and/or net present values for a project.* For example, a project's net present value might be computed three times: first assuming the most optimistic projections of cash flows; second assuming the most likely projections of cash flows; and third assuming the most pessimistic projections of cash flows. The final decision is then based on management's attitudes toward risk. A project whose most likely outcome is highly profitable would probably be rejected if its pessimistic outcome might lead to bankruptcy.

- *Subject a capital expenditure proposal to sensitivity analysis*, a study of the responsiveness of a model's dependent variable(s) to changes in one or more of its independent variables. Management might want to know, for example, the minimum annual net cash inflows that will provide an internal rate of return of 12% with other cost and revenue projections being as expected.

Using Differential Analysis in Capital Budgeting Decisions

All previous examples assume that capital expenditure proposals produce additional net cash inflows, but this is not always the case. Units of government and not-for-profit organizations might provide services that do not produce any cash inflows. For-profit organizations might be required to make capital expenditures to maintain product quality or to bring facilities up to environmental or safety standards. In these situations, it is impossible to compute a project's payback period, accounting rate of return, or internal rate of return. It is possible, however, to compute the present value of all life-cycle costs associated with alternative ways of providing the service or meeting the environmental or safety standard. Here, the alternative with the smallest negative net present value is preferred unless there is a strategic reason to select a different path or other complicating factors to consider.

Capital expenditure proposals to reduce operating costs by upgrading facilities might not provide any incremental cash inflows. Again, we can use a total cost approach and calculate the present value of the costs associated with each alternative, with the *low-cost alternative being preferred.* Alternatively, we can perform a differential analysis of cash flows and, treating any reduced operating costs as if they were cash inflows, compute the net present value or the internal rate of return of the cost reduction proposal. Recall from Chapter 16 that a relevant cost analysis focuses on the costs that differ under alternative actions. Once the differential amounts have been determined, they can be adjusted for the time value of money. To illustrate the differential approach, we revisit the Boston Beer example introduced in Chapter 16.

Differential Analysis of Predicted Project Cash Outflows Let's again assume **Boston Beer** produces a variety of craft beer products, including 12,000 cases of Samuel Adams per year. Further assume the machine currently used in manufacturing Samuel Adams is two years old and has a remaining useful life of four years. It cost $90,000 and has an estimated salvage value of zero dollars at the end of its useful life. Its current book value (original cost less accumulated depreciation) is $60,000, but its current disposal value (resale value) is only $35,000.

Management is evaluating the desirability of replacing the machine with a new machine. The new machine costs $80,000, has a useful life of four years, and a predicted salvage value of zero dollars at the end of its useful life. Although the new machine has the same productive capacity as the old machine, its predicted operating costs are lower because it requires less electricity. Furthermore, because of an artificial intelligence enhanced control system, the new machine will require less frequent and less expensive inspections. Finally, the new machine requires less maintenance.

An analysis of the cash flows associated with this cost reduction proposal, separated into the three phases of the project's life, are presented in **Exhibit 24.7**. Because the proposal does not have a disposal value, this portion of the analysis could have been omitted. (A detailed explanation of the relevant costs included in this analysis is in **Exhibit 16.1** in Chapter 16.) Assuming that Boston Beer has a discount rate of 12%, the proposal's net present value (computed in **Exhibit 24.8**) is $10,887. The proposal is acceptable because the net present value is a positive amount.

EXHIBIT 24.7 Differential Analysis of Predicted Cash Flows of Samuel Adams Machine

	Keep Old Machine (A)	Replace with New Machine (B)	Difference (cash flow effect of replacement) (A) − (B)
Initial investment			
Cost of new machine		$80,000	$(80,000)
Disposal value of old machine		(35,000)	35,000
Net initial investment			$(45,000)
Annual operating cash savings			
Conversion			
Old machine (12,000 cases × $5)	$60,000		
New machine (12,000 cases × $4)		$48,000	$12,000
Inspection			
Old machine (12,000 cases × $0.50)	6,000		
New machine (12,000 cases × $0.15)		1,800	4,200
Machine maintenance			
Old machine ($200 per month × 12 months)	2,400		
New machine ($200 per year)		200	2,200
Net annual cost savings			$18,400
Disinvestment at end of life			
Old machine	$ 0		
New machine		$ 0	

One Year Totals

EXHIBIT 24.8 Differential Analysis of Predicted Cash Flows of Samuel Adams Machine

	Predicted Cash Inflows (outflows) (A)	Year(s) of Cash Flows (B)	12% Present Value Factor (C)	Present Value of Cash Flows (A) × (C)
Initial investment	$(45,000)	0	1.00000	$(45,000)
Operation	18,400	1–4	3.03735	55,887
Disinvestment	0	4	0.63552	0
Net present value of all cash flows				$ 10,887

Your company is considering an investment in solar panels to power its manufacturing plant. You would like to prepare a differential analysis on purchasing the solar panels compared to the company's current reliance on fossil fuel power plants. What type of information will you need for your analysis?

Your differential analysis will first calculate the cost of the initial investment in solar panels, less (plus) any disposal value (cost) of equipment. Next, the annual cost savings in using solar power over fossil fuels will be estimated. The cost savings will be discounted to the present value using the company's discount rate, and from that amount, the initial investment will be subtracted. Variables that may impact the calculation include the following. What percentage of energy needs is planned with solar? Are there offsetting governmental solar subsidies? What is the annual cost of maintaining solar panels and what is the estimated useful life of the solar panels? How long is the installation process? What is the reliability factor of the solar panels and will alternate energy sources be required? What is the cost to insure the solar system? Will there still be unavoidable utility charges after converting to solar?

Avoiding Errors in Predicting Differential Costs and Revenues

Selecting proper capital budgeting alternatives and accurately predicting the cash flows associated with each alternative are critical to the capital budgeting process. A flawed analysis could result in management accepting inferior proposals or missing out on profitable proposals. Three types of errors to avoid are (1) investing in unnecessary or overly complex equipment, (2) overestimating cost savings, and (3) underestimating incremental sales or cost savings.

Investing in Unnecessary or Overly Complex Equipment

A common error is to simply compare the cost associated with the current inefficient way of doing things with the predicted cost of performing the identical operations with more modern equipment. Although capital budgeting models might suggest that such investments are justifiable, the result could be the costly and rapid completion of non-value-added activities. Consider the following examples.

- Suppose Boston Beer invests in an automated system to speed the movement of work in process between workstations without first evaluating the plant layout. Boston Beer is still unable to compete with other companies having better organized plants that allow lower cycle times, lower work-in-process inventories, and lower manufacturing costs. Management should have evaluated the plant layout before investing in new equipment. They may have found that rearranging the factory floor would have reduced materials movement and eliminated the need for the investment.

- Boston Beer invests in an automated warehouse to permit the rapid storage and retrieval of products while competitors work to eliminate excess inventory. Boston Beer is left with large inventories and a large investment in the automated warehouse while competitors, not having to earn a return on similar investments, are able to charge lower prices. Management should have evaluated the need for current inventory levels and perhaps shifted to a just-in-time approach to inventory management before considering the investment in an automated warehouse.

- Boston Beer hires staff to perform quality inspections while competitors implement total quality management and seek to eliminate the need for quality inspections. While defective products or services are now identified before they affect customers, they still exist. Furthermore, the company has higher expenditures than competitors, resulting in a less competitive cost structure. The inspections might not have been needed if management had shifted from inspecting for conformance to an emphasis on "doing it right the first time."

- Boston Beer invests in its automated assembly line to more efficiently produce its Samuel Adams product. The company's main competitor captures additional costs savings by integrating more advanced artificial intelligence in its assembly line system to detect quality issues. Although the cost of producing the Samuel Adams product might be lower, the company's cost structure is still not competitive.

All of these examples illustrate the limitations of capital budgeting models and the need for good judgment. *In the final analysis, managers, not models, make decisions.* Management must carefully evaluate the situations and determine whether they have considered the proper alternatives and all important cash flows.

Overestimating Cost Savings

When a number of activities drive manufacturing overhead costs, estimates of overhead cost savings based on a single activity cost driver can significantly overestimate cost savings. Assume, for example, that Boston Beer, which utilizes both machine-intensive and labor-intensive operations, develops a cost-estimating equation for overhead with labor as the only independent variable. Because of this, all overhead costs are allocated based on labor. The predicted cost savings can be computed as the sum of predicted reductions in labor plus predicted reductions in overhead. The predicted reductions in overhead are computed as the overhead per direct labor dollar or labor hour multiplied by the predicted reduction in direct labor dollars or labor hours. Because a major portion of the overhead is driven by factors other than direct labor and/or is fixed, reducing direct labor will not provide the predicted savings. Capital budgeting models might suggest that the investment is acceptable, but the models are based on inaccurate cost data.

Underestimating Incremental Sales or Cost Savings

Underestimating incremental sales In evaluating proposals for investments in new equipment, management often assumes that the baseline for comparison is the current sales level, but this might not be the case. If competitors are investing in equipment to better meet customer needs and to reduce costs, a failure to make similar investments might result in uncompetitive prices and declining, rather than steady, sales. Hence, the baseline for sales without the investment is overstated, and the incremental sales of the investment is understated. Not considering the likely decline in sales understates the incremental sales associated with the investment and biases the results against the proposed investment.

Underestimating cost savings Investments in manufacturing technologies, such as flexible manufacturing systems (FMS) and computer integrated manufacturing (CIM), do more than simply allow the efficient production of current products. Flexible manufacturing systems are designed to easily adapt to changes in the type and quantity of the product being manufactured. In computer integrated manufacturing, companies can use computers to not only manage what equipment does but also manage the flow of materials and inventory levels. Such investments also make possible the rapid, low-cost switching to new products. The result is expanded sales opportunities.

Such investments might also produce cost savings further down the value chain, either within or outside the company. Boston Beer's decision to acquire a new machine might have the unanticipated consequence of reducing customer quality complaints or increasing sales because customers are attracted to a higher-quality product.

Unfortunately, because such opportunities are difficult to quantify, they are often ignored in the evaluation of capital expenditure proposals. The solution to this dilemma involves the application of management's professional judgment, a willingness to take risks based on this professional judgment, and recognition that certain investments transcend capital budgeting models in that they involve strategic as well as long-range planning. At this level of planning, qualitative decisions concerning the nature of the organization are at least as important as quantified factors.

Review 24-4 LO24-4   Considering Nonquantitative Factors in Capital Budgeting Decisions

Costco Wholesale is considering making a capital investment in new sorting machinery at the distribution center. Costco's finance team assessed the investment using the net present value model and predicts the investment will generate a positive net present value cash flow over the life of the asset.

Required
Identify and discuss additional factors that Costco's management should consider after the initial screening of the capital investment, before making a final evaluation of the investment.

Solution on p. 24-47.

APPENDIX 24A: Time Value of Money

When asked to choose between $500 today or an IOU for $500 to be paid one year later, rational decision makers choose the $500 today. Two reasons for this involve the *time value of money* and the *risk*. A dollar today is worth more than a dollar tomorrow or at some future time. Having a dollar provides flexibility. It can be spent, buried, or invested in a number of projects. If invested in a savings account, it will amount to more than one dollar at some future time because of the effect of interest. The interest paid by a bank (or borrower) for the use of money is analogous to the rent paid for the use of land, buildings, or equipment. Furthermore, we live in an uncertain world, and, for a variety of reasons, the possibility exists that an IOU might not be paid.

LO24-5 Compute basic present value cash flow amounts.

Future Value

Future value is the amount that a current sum of money earning a stated rate of interest will accumulate to at the end of a future period. Suppose we deposit $500 in a savings account at a financial institution that pays interest at the rate of 10% per year. At the end of the first year, the original deposit of $500 will total $550 ($500 + ($500 × 0.10) or $500 × 1.10), the original $500 plus the $50 earned in interest. If we leave the $550 for another year, the amount will increase to $605 ($550 × 1.10). It can be stated that $500 today has a future value in one year of $550, or conversely, that $550 one year from today has a present value of $500. Interest of $55 ($605 − $550) was earned in the second year, whereas interest of only $50 was earned in the first year. This happened because interest during the second year was earned on the principal plus interest from the first year ($550). When periodic interest is computed on principal plus prior periods' accumulated interest, the interest is said to be *compounded*. Compound interest is used throughout this text.

To determine future values at the end of one period (usually a year), multiply the beginning amount (present value) by 1 plus the interest rate. When multiple periods are involved, the future value is determined by repeatedly multiplying the beginning amount by 1 plus the interest rate for each period. When $500 is invested for two years at an interest rate of 10% per year, its future value is computed as $500 × 1.10 × 1.10. The following equation is used to figure future value.

$$fv = pv(1 + i)^n$$

where:

fv = future value amount
pv = present value amount
i = interest rate per period
n = number of periods

For our $500 deposit, the equation becomes:

$$fv \text{ of } \$500 = pv(1 + i)^n$$
$$= \$500(1 + 0.10)^2$$
$$= \$605$$

In a similar manner, once the interest rate and number of periods are known, the future value amount of any present value amount is easily determined.

Present Value

Present value is the current worth of a specified amount of money to be received at some future date at some interest rate. Solving for pv in the future value equation, the new present value equation is determined as follows.

$$pv = \frac{fv}{(1 + i)^n}$$

Using this equation, the present value of $8,800 to be received in one year, discounted at 10%, is computed as follows.

$$pv \text{ of } \$8,800 = \frac{\$8,800}{(1 + 0.10)^1}$$
$$= \frac{\$8,800}{(1.10)}$$
$$= \$8,000$$

Thus, when the discount rate is 10%, the present value of $8,800 to be received in one year is $8,000. The present value equation is often expressed as the future value amount times the present value of $1.

$$pv = fvn \frac{\$1}{(1 + i)^n}$$

Using the equation for the present value of $1, the present value of $8,800 to be received in one year, discounted at 10%, is computed as follows.

$$pv \text{ of } \$8,800 = \$8,800 \times \frac{\$1}{(1 + 0.10)^1}$$
$$= \$8,800 \times 0.90909$$
$$= \$8,000$$

The present value of $8,800 two periods from now is $7,273, computed as [$8,800 ÷ (1.10)²] or [$8,800 × $1 ÷ (1.10)²].

If a calculator or spreadsheet program is not available, present value computations can be done by hand. Tables, such as **Exhibit 24A.1** for the present value of $1 at various interest rates and time periods, can be used to simplify hand computations.

EXHIBIT 24A.1 — Present Value of $1

Present value of $1 = $\frac{1}{(1 + i)^n}$

Discount rate (*i*)

Periods (n)	4%	6%	8%	10%	12%	14%	16%	18%	20%	22%	24%	26%	28%
1	0.96154	0.94340	0.92593	0.90909	0.89286	0.87719	0.86207	0.84746	0.83333	0.81967	0.80645	0.79365	0.78125
2	0.92456	0.89000	0.85734	0.82645	0.79719	0.76947	0.74316	0.71818	0.69444	0.67186	0.65036	0.62988	0.61035
3	0.88900	0.83962	0.79383	0.75131	0.71178	0.67497	0.64066	0.60863	0.57870	0.55071	0.52449	0.49991	0.47684
4	0.85480	0.79209	0.73503	0.68301	0.63552	0.59208	0.55229	0.51579	0.48225	0.45140	0.42297	0.39675	0.37253
5	0.82193	0.74726	0.68058	0.62092	0.56743	0.51937	0.47611	0.43711	0.40188	0.37000	0.34111	0.31488	0.29104
6	0.79031	0.70496	0.63017	0.56447	0.50663	0.45559	0.41044	0.37043	0.33490	0.30328	0.27509	0.24991	0.22737
7	0.75992	0.66506	0.58349	0.51316	0.45235	0.39964	0.35383	0.31393	0.27908	0.24859	0.22184	0.19834	0.17764
8	0.73069	0.62741	0.54027	0.46651	0.40388	0.35056	0.30503	0.26604	0.23257	0.20376	0.17891	0.15741	0.13878
9	0.70259	0.59190	0.50025	0.42410	0.36061	0.30751	0.26295	0.22546	0.19381	0.16702	0.14428	0.12493	0.10842
10	0.67556	0.55839	0.46319	0.38554	0.32197	0.26974	0.22668	0.19106	0.16151	0.13690	0.11635	0.09915	0.08470
11	0.64958	0.52679	0.42888	0.35049	0.28748	0.23662	0.19542	0.16192	0.13459	0.11221	0.09383	0.07869	0.06617
12	0.62460	0.49697	0.39711	0.31863	0.25668	0.20756	0.16846	0.13722	0.11216	0.09198	0.07567	0.06245	0.05170
13	0.60057	0.46884	0.36770	0.28966	0.22917	0.18207	0.14523	0.11629	0.09346	0.07539	0.06103	0.04957	0.04039
14	0.57748	0.44230	0.34046	0.26333	0.20462	0.15971	0.12520	0.09855	0.07789	0.06180	0.04921	0.03934	0.03155
15	0.55526	0.41727	0.31524	0.23939	0.18270	0.14010	0.10793	0.08352	0.06491	0.05065	0.03969	0.03122	0.02465
16	0.53391	0.39365	0.29189	0.21763	0.16312	0.12289	0.09304	0.07078	0.05409	0.04152	0.03201	0.02478	0.01926
17	0.51337	0.37136	0.27027	0.19784	0.14564	0.10780	0.08021	0.05998	0.04507	0.03403	0.02581	0.01967	0.01505
18	0.49363	0.35034	0.25025	0.17986	0.13004	0.09456	0.06914	0.05083	0.03756	0.02789	0.02082	0.01561	0.01175
19	0.47464	0.33051	0.23171	0.16351	0.11611	0.08295	0.05961	0.04308	0.03130	0.02286	0.01679	0.01239	0.00918
20	0.45639	0.31180	0.21455	0.14864	0.10367	0.07276	0.05139	0.03651	0.02608	0.01874	0.01354	0.00983	0.00717

Using the factors in **Exhibit 24A.1**, the present value of any future amount can be determined. For example, with an interest rate of 10%, the present value of the following future amounts to be received in one period are as follows.

Future Value Amount		Present Value Factor of $1		Present Value
$ 100	×	0.90909	=	$ 90.91
628	×	0.90909	=	570.91
4,285	×	0.90909	=	3,895.45
9,900	×	0.90909	=	8,999.99

To further illustrate the use of **Exhibit 24A.1**, consider the following application. Suppose Amazon wants to invest its surplus cash at 12% to have $10,000 to pay off a long-term note due at the end of five years. **Exhibit 24A.1** shows that the present value factor of $1, discounted at 12% per year for five years, is 0.56743. Multiplying $10,000 by 0.56743, the present value is determined to be $5,674.

$$pv \text{ of } \$10,000 = \$10,000 \times \text{Present value factor for } \$1$$
$$= \$10,000 \times 0.56743$$
$$= \$5,674$$

Therefore, if Amazon invests $5,674 today, it will have $10,000 available to pay off its note in five years.

Managers also use present value tables to make investment decisions. Assume that Amazon can make an investment that will provide a cash flow of $12,000 at the end of eight years. If the company demands a rate of return of 14% per year, what is the most it will be willing to pay for this investment? From **Exhibit 24A.1**, we find that the present value factor for $1, discounted at 14% per year for eight years, is 0.35056.

$$pv \text{ of } \$12,000 = \$12,000 \times \text{Present value factor for } \$1$$
$$= \$12,000 \times 0.35056$$
$$= \$4,207$$

If the company demands an annual return of 14%, the most it would be willing to invest today is $4,207.

Annuities

Not all investments provide a single sum of money. Many investments provide periodic cash flows called *annuities*. An **annuity** is a series of equal cash flows received or paid over equal intervals of time. Suppose that $100 will be received at the end of each of the next three years. If the discount rate is 10%, the present value of this annuity can be determined by summing the present value of each receipt.

$$\text{Year 1 } \$100 \times \$1 \div (1 + 0.10)^1 = \$ \ 90.90$$
$$\text{Year 2 } \$100 \times \$1 \div (1 + 0.10)^2 = \ \ \ 82.65$$
$$\text{Year 3 } \$100 \times \$1 \div (1 + 0.10)^3 = \ \ \ 75.13$$
$$\text{Total} \ldots\ldots\ldots\ldots\ldots\ldots \ \$248.68$$

Alternatively, the following equation can be used to compute the present value of an annuity with cash flows at the end of each period.

$$pva = \frac{a}{i} \times \left[1 - \frac{1}{(1+i)^n}\right]$$

where:

pva = present value of an annuity (also called the annuity factor)
i = prevailing rate per period
n = number of periods
a = annuity amount

This equation was used to compute the factors presented in **Exhibit 24A.2** for an annuity amount of $1.

EXHIBIT 24A.2 Present Value of an Annuity of $1

Present value of an annuity of $1 = $\frac{1}{i} \times \left[1 - \frac{1}{(1+i)^n}\right]$

Discount rate (*i*)

Periods (n)	4%	6%	8%	10%	12%	14%	16%	18%	20%	22%	24%	26%	28%
1	0.96154	0.94340	0.92593	0.90909	0.89286	0.87719	0.86207	0.84746	0.83333	0.81967	0.80645	0.79365	0.78125
2	1.88609	1.83339	1.78326	1.73554	1.69005	1.64666	1.60523	1.56564	1.52778	1.49153	1.45682	1.42353	1.39160
3	2.77509	2.67301	2.57710	2.48685	2.40183	2.32163	2.24589	2.17427	2.10648	2.04224	1.98130	1.92344	1.86844
4	3.62990	3.46511	3.31213	3.16987	3.03735	2.91371	2.79818	2.69006	2.58873	2.49364	2.40428	2.32019	2.24097
5	4.45182	4.21236	3.99271	3.79079	3.60478	3.43308	3.27429	3.12717	2.99061	2.86364	2.74538	2.63507	2.53201
6	5.24214	4.91732	4.62288	4.35526	4.11141	3.88867	3.68474	3.49760	3.32551	3.16692	3.02047	2.88498	2.75938
7	6.00205	5.58238	5.20637	4.86842	4.56376	4.28830	4.03857	3.81153	3.60459	3.41551	3.24232	3.08331	2.93702
8	6.73274	6.20979	5.74664	5.33493	4.96764	4.63886	4.34359	4.07757	3.83716	3.61927	3.42122	3.24073	3.07579
9	7.43533	6.80169	6.24689	5.75902	5.32825	4.94637	4.60654	4.30302	4.03097	3.78628	3.56550	3.36566	3.18421
10	8.11090	7.36009	6.71008	6.14457	5.65022	5.21612	4.83323	4.49409	4.19247	3.92318	3.68186	3.46481	3.26892
11	8.76048	7.88687	7.13896	6.49506	5.93770	5.45273	5.02864	4.65601	4.32706	4.03540	3.77569	3.54350	3.33509
12	9.38507	8.38384	7.53608	6.81369	6.19437	5.66029	5.19711	4.79322	4.43922	4.12737	3.85136	3.60595	3.38679
13	9.98565	8.85268	7.90378	7.10336	6.42355	5.84236	5.34233	4.90951	4.53268	4.20277	3.91239	3.65552	3.42718
14	10.56312	9.29498	8.24424	7.36669	6.62817	6.00207	5.46753	5.00806	4.61057	4.26456	3.96160	3.69485	3.45873
15	11.11839	9.71225	8.55948	7.60608	6.81086	6.14217	5.57546	5.09158	4.67547	4.31522	4.00129	3.72607	3.48339
16	11.65230	10.10590	8.85137	7.82371	6.97399	6.26506	5.66850	5.16235	4.72956	4.35673	4.03330	3.75085	3.50265
17	12.16567	10.47726	9.12164	8.02155	7.11963	6.37286	5.74870	5.22233	4.77463	4.39077	4.05911	3.77052	3.51769
18	12.65930	10.82760	9.37189	8.20141	7.24967	6.46742	5.81785	5.27316	4.81219	4.41866	4.07993	3.78613	3.52945
19	13.13394	11.15812	9.60360	8.36492	7.36578	6.55037	5.87746	5.31624	4.84350	4.44152	4.09672	3.79851	3.53863
20	13.59033	11.46992	9.81815	8.51356	7.46944	6.62313	5.92884	5.35275	4.86958	4.46027	4.11026	3.80834	3.54580

The present value of an annuity of $1 per period for three periods discounted at 10% per period is as follows.

$$\text{pva of } \$1 = \frac{1}{0.10} + \left[1 - \frac{1}{(1 + 0.10)^3}\right]$$

$$= 2.48685$$

Using this factor, the present value of a $100 annuity can be computed as $100 × 2.48685, which yields $248.689. To determine the present value of an annuity of any amount, the annuity factor for $1 can be multiplied by the annuity amount.

To further illustrate the use of **Exhibit 24A.2**, assume that Amazon is considering an investment in a piece of equipment that will produce net cash inflows of $2,000 at the end of each year for five years. If the company's desired rate of return is 12%, an investment of $7,210 will provide such a return:

$$\text{pva of } \$2{,}000 = \$2{,}000 \times \begin{array}{l}\text{Present value for an annuity of \$1}\\ \text{for five periods discounted at 12\%}\end{array}$$

$$= \$2{,}000 \times 3.60478$$
$$= \$7{,}210$$

Here, the $2,000 annuity is multiplied by 3.60478, the factor for an annuity of $1 for five periods found in **Exhibit 24A.2**, discounted at 12% per period.

Another use of **Exhibit 24A.2** is to determine the amount that must be received annually to provide a desired rate of return on an investment. Assume that Amazon invests $33,550 in a piece of machinery and desires a return of the investment plus interest of 8% in equal year-end payments for 10 years. The minimum amount that must be received each year is determined by solving the equation for the present value of an annuity.

$$\text{pva} = a \times (\text{pva of } \$1)$$

$$a = \frac{\text{pva}}{\text{pva of } \$1}$$

From **Exhibit 24A.2**, we see that the 8% factor for 10 periods is 6.71008. Dividing the $33,550 investment by 6.71008, the required annuity is computed to be $5,000.

$$a = \frac{\$33{,}550}{6.71008}$$
$$= \$5{,}000$$

Unequal Cash Flows

Many investment situations do not produce equal periodic cash flows. When this occurs, the present value for each cash flow must be determined independently because the annuity table can be used only for equal periodic cash flows. **Exhibit 24A.1** is used to determine the present value of each future amount separately. To illustrate, assume that Amazon wishes to contract with a new designer who has a significant Twitter following. Management believes this designer will return incremental cash flows to Amazon at the end of each of the next three years in the amounts of $2,500,000, $4,000,000, and $1,500,000. Because Amazon is unsure as to whether the designer's influence will be sustainable, it plans to sign a contract with the designer for only three years. If the company requires a minimum return of 14% on their investment, how much would they be willing to pay for the contract?

To solve this problem, it is necessary to determine the present value of the expected future cash flows. Here we use **Exhibit 24A.1** to find the $1 present value factors at 14% for Periods 1, 2, and 3. The cash flows are then multiplied by these factors.

Year	Annual Cash Flow		Present Value of $1 at 14%		Present Value Amount
1	$2,500,000	×	0.87719	=	$2,192,975
2	4,000,000	×	0.76947	=	3,077,880
3	1,500,000	×	0.67497	=	1,012,455
Total					$6,283,310

The total present value of the cash flows for the three years, $6,283,310, represents the maximum amount Amazon would be willing to pay for the contract.

Deferred Returns

Many times, organizations make investments for which they receive no cash until several periods have passed. The present value of an investment discounted at 12% per year, which has a $2,000 return only at the end of Years 4, 5, and 6, can be determined as follows.

Year	Amount	Present Value of $1 at 12%		Present Value Amount
1	$ 0 ×	0.89286	=	$ 0
2	0 ×	0.79719	=	0
3	0 ×	0.71178	=	0
4	2,000 ×	0.63552	=	1,271
5	2,000 ×	0.56743	=	1,135
6	2,000 ×	0.50663	=	1,013
Total				$3,419

Computation of the present value of the deferred annuity can also be performed using the annuity tables if the cash flow amounts are equal for each period. The present value of an annuity for six years minus the present value of an annuity for three years yields the present value of an annuity for Years 4 through 6.

Present value of an annuity for 6 years at 12%: $2,000 × 4.11141 = ... $8,223
Present value of an annuity for 3 years at 12%: 2,000 × 2.40183 = ... (4,804)
Present value of the deferred annuity... $3,419

Performing Present Value Calculations Using the Table Approach

LO24-5 Review 24-5

Using the tables in Appendix 24A of this chapter, determine the answers to each of the following separate situations.

a. The future value in two years of $2,000 deposited today in a savings account with interest compounded annually at 6%.
b. The present value of $8,000 to be received in four years, discounted at 12%.
c. The present value of an annuity of $2,000 per year for five years discounted at 14%.
d. An initial investment of $32,010 is to be returned in eight equal annual payments. Determine the amount of each payment if the interest rate is 12%.
e. A proposed investment will provide cash flows of $20,000, $8,000, and $6,000 at the end of Years 1, 2, and 3, respectively. Using a discount rate of 20%, determine the present value of these cash flows.
f. Find the present value of an investment that will pay $5,000 at the end of Years 10, 11, and 12. Use a discount rate of 14%.

Solution on p. 24-47.

APPENDIX 24B: Table Approach to Determining Internal Rate of Return

We consider the use of present value tables to determine the internal rate of return of a series of cash flows with (1) equal net cash flows after the initial investment and (2) unequal net cash flows after the initial investment.

LO24-6 Determine internal rate of return using present value tables.

Equal Cash Flows

An investment proposal's internal rate of return is easily determined when a single investment is followed by a series of equal annual net cash flows. The general relationship between the initial investment and the equal annual cash inflows is expressed as follows:

$$\text{Initial investment} = \text{Present value factor for an annuity of \$1} \times \text{Annual net cash inflow}$$

Solve for the appropriate present value factor as follows.

$$\text{Present value factor for an annuity of \$1} = \frac{\text{Initial investment}}{\text{Annual net cash inflows}}$$

Once the present value factor is calculated, use Exhibit 24A.2 and go across the row corresponding to the expected life of the project until a table factor equal to or closest to the project's computed present value factor is found. The corresponding percentage for the present value factor is the proposal's internal rate of return. If a table factor does not exactly equal the proposal's present value factor, a more accurate answer can be obtained by interpolation (which is not discussed in this text).

To illustrate, assume that the Amazon proposed investment described in **Exhibit 24.2** has a zero disinvestment value. The proposal's present value factor is 3.15180.

$$\text{Present value factor for an annuity of \$1} = \frac{\text{Initial investment}}{\text{Annual net cash inflows}}$$

$$= \frac{\$94{,}554}{\$30{,}000}$$

$$= 3.15180$$

Using **Exhibit 24A.2**, go across the row for five periods; the closest table factor is 3.12717, which corresponds to an internal rate of return of 18%.

Unequal Cash Flows

If periodic cash flows subsequent to the initial investment are unequal, the simple procedure of determining a present value factor and looking up the closest corresponding factor in **Exhibit 24A.2** cannot be used. Instead, a trial-and-error approach must be used to determine the internal rate of return.

The first step is to select a discount rate estimated to be close to the proposal's IRR and to compute the proposal's net present value. If the resulting net present value is zero, the selected discount rate is the actual rate of return. However, it is unlikely that the first rate selected will be the proposal's IRR. If the computation results in a positive net present value, the actual IRR is higher than the initially selected rate. In this case, the next step is to compute the proposal's net present value using a higher rate. If the second computation produces a negative net present value, the actual IRR is less than the selected rate. Therefore, the actual IRR is between the first and the second rates. This trial-and-error approach continues until a discount rate is found that equates the proposal's cash inflows and outflows. For Amazon's investment proposal outlined in **Exhibit 24.2**, the details of the trial-and-error approach are presented in **Exhibit 24B.1**.

EXHIBIT 24B.1 — Internal Rate of Return with Unequal Cash Flows

First trial with a 24% discount rate

	Predicted Cash Inflows (outflows) (A)	Year(s) of Cash Flows (B)	24% Present Value Factor (C)	Present Value of Cash Flows (A) × (C)
Initial investment	$(94,554)	0	1.00000	$(94,554)
Operation	30,000	1–5	2.74538	82,361
Disinvestment	12,000	5	0.34111	4,093
Net present value of all cash flows				$ (8,100)

Second trial with a 16% discount rate

	Predicted Cash Inflows (outflows) (A)	Year(s) of Cash Flows (B)	16% Present Value Factor (C)	Present Value of Cash Flows (A) × (C)
Initial investment	$(94,554)	0	1.00000	$(94,554)
Operation	30,000	1–5	3.27429	98,229
Disinvestment	12,000	5	0.47611	5,713
Net present value of all cash flows				$ 9,388

Third trial with a 20% discount rate

	Predicted Cash Inflows (outflows) (A)	Year(s) of Cash Flows (B)	20% Present Value Factor (C)	Present Value of Cash Flows (A) × (C)
Initial investment	$(94,554)	0	1.00000	$(94,554)
Operation	30,000	1–5	2.99061	89,718
Disinvestment	12,000	5	0.40188	4,823
Net present value of all cash flows				$ (13)

In **Exhibit 24B.1** the first rate produced a negative net present value, indicating that the proposal's IRR is less than 24%. To produce a positive net present value, a smaller rate was selected for the second trial. Since the second rate produced a positive net present value, the proposal's true IRR must be between 16% and 24%. The 20% rate selected for the third trial produced a net present value of $(13) which is approximately zero, indicating that this is the proposal's IRR.

Determining the Internal Rate of Return Using the Table Approach

LO24-6 Review 24-6

The internal rate of return is often referred to as the time-adjusted rate of return. It is the discount rate that equates the present value of a project's cash inflows with the present value of the project's cash outflows.

Required
Using the information provided in Review 24-2, determine the internal rate of return of the project using the table approach.

Solution on p. 24-47.

APPENDIX 24C: Taxes in Capital Budgeting Decisions

To focus on capital budgeting concepts, we deferred consideration of the impact of taxes. Because income taxes affect cash flows and income, their consideration is important in evaluating investment proposals in for-profit organizations.

The cost of investments in plant and equipment is not deducted from taxable revenues in determining taxable income and income taxes at the time of the initial investment. Instead, the amount of the initial investment is deducted as depreciation over the operating life of an asset. To focus the impact of taxes on cash flows, assume the following:

LO24-7
Determine the net present value of investment proposals with consideration of taxes.

- Revenues and operating cash receipts are the same each year.
- Depreciation is the only noncash expense of the project.

Depreciation Tax Shield

Depreciation does not require the use of cash (the funds were spent at the initial investment), but depreciation is said to provide a "tax shield" because it reduces cash payments for income taxes. Because depreciation expense reduces taxable income, it reduces the tax payment required. The **depreciation tax shield** is the reduction in taxes due to the deductibility of depreciation from taxable revenues. The depreciation tax shield is computed as follows.

Depreciation tax shield = Depreciation × Tax rate

The value of the depreciation tax shield is illustrated using Amazon's capital expenditure proposal summarized in **Exhibit 24.2**. Amazon's annual straight-line depreciation is $16,511. With an assumed tax rate of 34%, the annual depreciation tax shield is $5,614.

$$\text{Straight-line depreciation} = \frac{\text{(Initial investment} - \text{Disposal value)}}{\text{Useful life}} = \frac{(\$90,554 - \$8,000)}{5} = \$16,511$$

Tax shield = Depreciation × Tax rate = $16,511 × 34% = $5,614

The increase in annual cash flows provided by the depreciation tax shield is illustrated in **Exhibit 24C.1**. Examine this exhibit, paying particular attention to the lines for depreciation, income taxes, and net annual cash flow.

The U.S. Tax Code contains guidelines concerning the depreciation of various types of assets. (Analysis of these guidelines is beyond the scope of this text.) Tax guidelines allow organizations a choice in tax depreciation procedures between straight-line depreciation and an accelerated depreciation method detailed in the Tax Code. Because of the time value of money, profitable businesses should usually select the tax depreciation procedure that provides the earliest depreciation. To illustrate the effect of accelerated depreciation on taxes and capital budgeting, we use double-declining balance depreciation rather than the accelerated method detailed in the Tax Code. When making capital expenditure decisions, managers should, of course, refer to the most current version of the Tax Code to determine the specific depreciation guidelines in effect at that time.

Exhibits 24C.2 and **24C.3** illustrate the effect of two alternative depreciation procedures, straight-line and double-declining balance, on the net present value of Amazon's proposed investment. Under the *double-declining balance method*, companies depreciate an asset at double, or 2 times the straight-line rate. In this case with an asset with a five-year useful life, the straight-line rate is 1/5 per year. Thus, the double-declining balance rate is calculated as follows.

Double declining balance rate = 2 × straight-line rate = 2 × 1/5 = 2/5 per year.

The cash flows for this investment were presented in **Exhibit 24.2**, and the effect of taxes on the investment's annual cash flows were examined in **Exhibit 24C.1**. Ignoring taxes, the investment was shown (in **Exhibit 24.3**) to have a positive net present value of $20,398 at a discount rate of 12%. With taxes, the investment has a positive net present value of $3,866 using straight-line depreciation and $6,082 using double-declining balance depreciation. Although taxes and cash flows are identical over the entire life of the project, the use of double-declining balance depreciation for taxes results in a higher net present value because it results in lower cash expenditures for taxes in the earlier years of an asset's life.

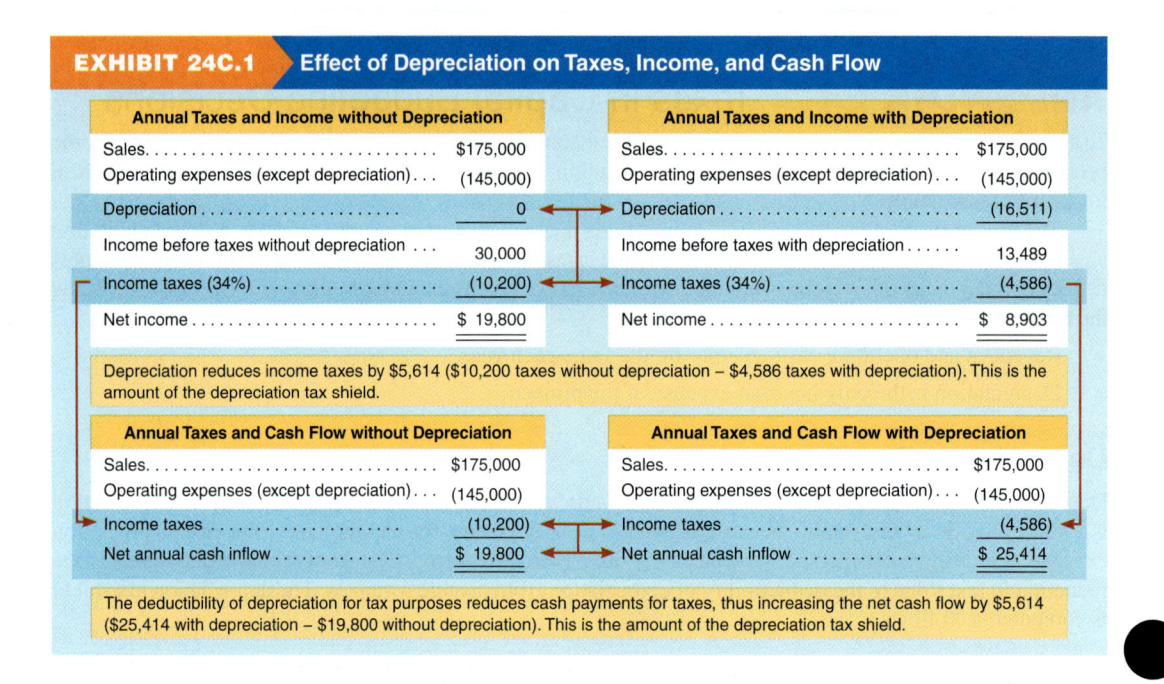

EXHIBIT 24C.1 — Effect of Depreciation on Taxes, Income, and Cash Flow

Annual Taxes and Income without Depreciation

Sales	$175,000
Operating expenses (except depreciation)	(145,000)
Depreciation	0
Income before taxes without depreciation	30,000
Income taxes (34%)	(10,200)
Net income	$ 19,800

Annual Taxes and Income with Depreciation

Sales	$175,000
Operating expenses (except depreciation)	(145,000)
Depreciation	(16,511)
Income before taxes with depreciation	13,489
Income taxes (34%)	(4,586)
Net income	$ 8,903

Depreciation reduces income taxes by $5,614 ($10,200 taxes without depreciation − $4,586 taxes with depreciation). This is the amount of the depreciation tax shield.

Annual Taxes and Cash Flow without Depreciation

Sales	$175,000
Operating expenses (except depreciation)	(145,000)
Income taxes	(10,200)
Net annual cash inflow	$ 19,800

Annual Taxes and Cash Flow with Depreciation

Sales	$175,000
Operating expenses (except depreciation)	(145,000)
Income taxes	(4,586)
Net annual cash inflow	$ 25,414

The deductibility of depreciation for tax purposes reduces cash payments for taxes, thus increasing the net cash flow by $5,614 ($25,414 with depreciation − $19,800 without depreciation). This is the amount of the depreciation tax shield.

EXHIBIT 24C.2 — Analysis of Capital Expenditures Including Tax Effects: Straight-Line Depreciation

	Predicted Cash Inflows (outflows) (A)	Year(s) of Cash Flows (B)	12% Present Value Factor (C)	Present Value of Cash Flows (A) × (C)
Initial investment				
Equipment	$(90,554)	0	1.00000	$ (90,554)
Inventory and other working capital	(4,000)	0	1.00000	(4,000)
Operations				
Annual taxable income without depreciation	30,000	1–5	3.60478	108,143
Taxes on income without depreciation ($30,000 × 0.34)	(10,200)	1–5	3.60478	(36,769)
Depreciation tax shield*	5,614	1–5	3.60478	20,237
Disinvestment				
Sale of equipment	8,000	5	0.56743	4,539
Inventory and other working capital	4,000	5	0.56743	2,270
Net present value of all cash flows				$ 3,866

*Computation of depreciation tax shield:

Annual straight-line depreciation	$16,511
Tax rate	× 0.34
Depreciation tax shield	$ 5,614

EXHIBIT 24C.3 — Analysis of Capital Expenditures Including Tax Effects: DDB Depreciation

	Predicted Cash Inflows (outflows) (A)	Year(s) of Cash Flows (B)	12% Present Value Factor (C)	Present Value of Cash Flows (A) × (C)
Initial investment				
Equipment	$(90,554)	0	1.00000	$(90,554)
Inventory and other working capital	4,000	0	1.00000	(4,000)
Operations				
Annual taxable income without depreciation	30,000	1–5	3.60478	108,143
Taxes on income without depreciation ($30,000 × 0.34)	(10,200)	1–5	3.60478	(36,769)
Depreciation tax shield*				
Year 1	12,315	1	0.89286	10,996
Year 2	7,389	2	0.79719	5,890
Year 3	4,434	3	0.71178	3,156
Year 4	2,660	4	0.63552	1,690
Year 5	1,270	5	0.56743	721
Disinvestment				
Sale of equipment	8,000	5	0.56743	4,539
Inventory and other working capital	4,000	5	0.56743	2,270
Net present value of all cash flows				**$ 6,082**

*Computation of depreciation tax shield:

Year	Depreciation Base† (A)	Annual Rate (B)	Annual Depreciation (C) = (A) × (B)	Tax Rate (D)	Tax Shield (E) = (C) × (D)
1	$90,554	2/5	$36,222	0.34	$12,315
2	54,332	2/5	21,733	0.34	7,389
3	32,599	2/5	13,040	0.34	4,434
4	19,559	2/5	7,824	0.34	2,660
5	11,735	balance	3,735	0.34	1,270

†The depreciation base is reduced by the amount of all previous depreciation. The annual rate is twice the straight-line rate. For simplicity, we depreciated the remaining balance in the fifth year and did not switch to straight-line depreciation when the straight-line amount exceeds the double-declining balance amount. This would happen in the fourth year, when $19,559 ÷ 2 = $9,780. Although the depreciable base excludes the predicted disposal value of $8,000, under double-declining balance depreciation, an asset is only depreciated down to its disposal value. Hence, Year 5 depreciation is computed as the $11,735 depreciable base minus the $8,000 disposal value.

Investment Tax Credit

From time to time, for the purpose of stimulating investment and economic growth, the U.S. federal government has implemented an investment tax credit. An **investment tax credit** reduces taxes in the year a new asset is placed in service by some stated percentage of the cost of the asset. In recent years tax credits, such as the credits for purchasing hybrid automobiles, have been used to stimulate investments that reduce the emission of greenhouses gases. Typically, this is done without reducing the depreciation base of the asset for tax purposes. An investment tax credit reduces cash payments for taxes and, hence, is treated as a cash inflow for capital budgeting purposes. This additional cash inflow increases the probability that a new asset will meet a taxpayer's capital expenditure criteria.

Calculating Net Present Value with the Consideration of Income Taxes LO24-7 **Review 24-7**

Assume that **Costco Wholesale** is considering a proposal to change the company's manual design system to a computer-aided design system to aid in developing various store layouts. The new system is expected to save 9,000 design hours per year; an operating cost savings of $45 per hour. The annual cash expenditures of operating the new system are estimated to be $200,000. The new system would require an initial investment of $550,000. The estimated life of this system is five years with no salvage value. The tax rate is 35%, and Costco uses straight-line depreciation for tax purposes. Costco has a cost of capital of 14%.

Required
a. Compute the annual after-tax cash flows related to the new design system.
b. Determine the project's net present value.

Solution on p. 24-48.

KEY RATIOS AND EQUATIONS

$$\text{Payback period} = \frac{\text{Initial investment}}{\text{Annual operating cash inflows}}$$

$$\text{Accounting rate of return on initial investment} = \frac{\text{Average annual increase in net income}}{\text{Initial investment}}$$

$$\text{Accounting rate of return on average investment} = \frac{\text{Average annual increase in net income}}{\text{Average investment}}$$

$$\text{Depreciation tax shield} = \text{Depreciation} \times \text{Tax rate}$$

$$fv = pv(1 + i)^n$$

Where: fv = future value amount, pv = present value amount, i = interest rate per period, n = number of periods.

$$pv = \frac{fv}{(1 + i)^n}$$

Where: fv = future value amount, pv = present value amount, i = interest rate per period, n = number of periods.

$$pva = \frac{a}{i} \times \left[1 - \frac{1}{(1 + i)^n}\right]$$

Where: pva = present value of an annuity, i = prevailing rate per period, n = number of periods, a = annuity amount.

$$\text{Present value factor for an annuity of \$1} = \frac{\text{Initial investment}}{\text{Annual net cash flows}}$$

MULTIPLE CHOICE

LO24-1 1. Which of the following statements is not a characteristic of an effective capital budgeting process?
   a. Requires an adjustment to make cash flows comparable when they are expected to occur at different points in time.
   b. Develops implementation plans for approved projects.
   c. All projects should be required to go through formal review of a capital budgeting committee.
   d. Conducts a post audit review to assign responsibility and improve future planning.

Use Exhibits 24A.1 and 24A.2 in Appendix 24A to answer questions 2, 3, and 4.

LO24-2 2. Max is considering an investment proposal that requires an initial investment of $91,100, has predicted cash inflows of $30,000 per year for four years and no salvage value. At a discount rate of 10% the projects net present value is

   a. $3,996
   b. $20,486
   c. $24,486
   d. $95,096

LO24-2 3. The internal rate of return of the investment proposal presented in question 2 is

   a. 8%
   b. 10%
   c. 12%
   d. Less than 8%

LO24-2 4. The Pepper Shop is evaluating a capital expenditure proposal with the following predicted cash flows:

Initial investment	$(40,000)
Operations, each year for four years	15,000
Salvage	5,000

At a discount rate of 12%, the project's net present value is

   a. $2,383
   b. $5,560
   c. $8,738
   d. $20,740

Multiple Choice Answers
1. c 2. a 3. c 4. c 5. d 6. b 7. c 8. c 9. b 10. c 11. c

5. The payback period of the investment proposal presented in question 4 is **LO24-1**

    a. $270,000
    b. $170,000
    c. $520,000
    d. $370,000

6. The accounting rate of return on the initial investment presented in question 4 is **LO24-1**

    a. 0.125
    b. 0.156
    c. 0.219
    d. 0.375

7. Foggy Products is evaluating two mutually exclusive projects, one requiring a $4 million initial outlay and the other a $6 million outlay. The Finance Department has performed an extensive analysis of each project. The chief financial officer has indicated that there is no capital rationing in effect. Which of the following statements are correct? **LO24-3**

    I. Both projects should be rejected if their payback periods are longer than the company standard.
    II. The project with the highest Internal Rate of Return (IRR) should be selected (assuming both IRRs exceed the hurdle rate).
    III. The project with the highest positive net present value should be selected.
    IV. Select the project with the smaller initial investment, regardless of which evaluation method is used.

    a. I, II, and IV only.
    b. I, II and III only.
    c. I and III only.
    d. II and III only.

    CMA adapted

8. Each of the following statements is true regarding capital budgeting decisions, except **LO24-4**

    a. Capital expenditure proposals involve risk.
    b. A common error is to invest in unnecessary or overly complex equipment.
    c. Capital budgeting models cannot be relied on when a project is projected to have cash flows over a period of time greater than three years.
    d. When a number of activities drive manufacturing overhead costs, estimates of overhead cost based on a single activity driver can significantly overestimate cost savings.

9. Compute the present value of an investment at 10% per year, which has a $3,000 return only at the end of Years 3, 4, and 5. **LO24-5**

    a. $11,372
    b. $6,166
    c. $16,579
    d. $13,066

10. Assume that the Yogurt Shoppe has a proposed investment of $68,500 with a zero disinvestment value. The life of the investment is expected to be five years and the annual net cash inflows are expected to be $20,000. Determine the investment proposal's IRR using the tables in Appendix 24A. **LO24-6**

    a. 18%
    b. 16%
    c. 14%
    d. 12%

11. For a typical $120,000 investment in equipment with a five-year life and no salvage value, determine the present value of the tax shield using straight-line depreciation. Assume an income tax rate of 21% and a discount rate of 16%. **LO24-7**

    a. $24,000
    b. $8,400
    c. $16,502
    d. $30,511

DATA ANALYTICS

DA24-1. Use a Sensitivity Analysis to Adjust Discount Rate in NPV **LO24-2, 4**
Refer to the data in P24-32 to answer the following questions.

REQUIRED

a. Prepare a table in Excel to compute the net present value for each proposal, A, B and C. In your formulas, reference the discount rate used for all of your calculations to a single cell. Hint: By referencing all of your calculations to a single cell, you can easily develop a sensitivity analysis by changing the discount rate in that cell and the output (net present value) will update automatically.

b. Prepare a new table listing the discount rate from 5% to 20% along with the net present value for each proposal, A, B, and C. Hint: Using the table from part a, enter each percentage. Take the results and copy and paste values into the new table.

c. Prepare a line chart showing the net present value of proposals A, B, and C with discount rates ranging from 5% to 20%.
d. Using the chart in part c, answer the following questions.
1. Which project has the highest net present value for each interest rate in your chart?
2. Which project has the lowest net present value for each interest rate in your chart?
3. Using only the chart and no additional calculations, what is the approximate internal rate of return for each project?
4. Does the net present value increase or decrease as the interest rate changes? Why?
5. How does this sensitivity analysis take into account the risk of the investment? Should each project be discounted at the same interest rate?
6. What's the highest discount rate that generates a net present value for all proposals that's not a negative amount?
7. Based on the net present value, which proposal would you recommend, assuming that you must choose one?

DA24-2. Use a Sensitivity Analysis to Adjust Cash Flows in NPV
Refer to the data in P24-32 to answer the following questions.

REQUIRED
a. Prepare a table in Excel to compute the net present value for Proposal A and consider this the *likely* scenario. Next, prepare an optimistic and pessimistic scenario. For the *optimistic* scenario, increase each cash inflow by 10% and for the *pessimistic* scenario, decrease each net cash inflow by 10%.
b. Prepare a bar chart showing the net present value for the likely, optimistic, and pessimistic scenarios.
c. Using the chart in part b, answer the following questions.
1. Indicate whether any of the three scenarios meet the screening test based on net present value.
2. Would you recommend that the company move forward with proposal A?

DATA VISUALIZATION

Data Visualization Activities are available in myBusinessCourse. These assignments use Tableau Dashboards to expose students to visual depictions of data and introduce students to data analytics through data visualizations. These exercises are easily assignable and auto graded by MBC.

QUESTIONS

Q24-1. What is the relationship between long-range planning and capital budgeting?

Q24-2. What tasks are often assigned to the capital budgeting committee?

Q24-3. What purposes are served by a post-audit of approved capital expenditure proposals?

Q24-4. Into what three phases are a project's cash flows organized?

Q24-5. What weakness is inherent in the payback period when it is used as the sole investment criterion?

Q24-6. What weakness is inherent in the accounting rate of return when it is used as an investment criterion?

Q24-7. State three alternative definitions or descriptions of the internal rate of return.

Q24-8. Why is the cost of capital an important concept when discounting models are used for capital budgeting?

Q24-9. Why are the net present value and the internal rate of return models superior to the payback period and the accounting rate of return models?

Q24-10. State two basic differences between the net present value and the internal rate of return models that often lead to differences in the evaluation of competing investment proposals.

Q24-11. Identify several nonquantitative factors that are apt to play a decisive role in the final selection of projects for capital expenditures.

Q24-12. In what way does depreciation affect the analysis of cash flows for a proposed capital expenditure?

MINI EXERCISES

M24-13. Identifying Terms Relevant to Capital Budgeting Decisions   LO24-1

Below is a list of terms relevant to capital budgeting decisions.

1. Capital budgeting
2. Capital expenditures
3. Time value of money concept
4. Long-range planning
5. Post audit

REQUIRED

For each of the statements below, select the most relevant term from the above list. Each term above may be used more than once.

___ a. An investment of funds in a project to develop a new product.
___ b. Process that involves identifying desirable projects, evaluating proposals, and selecting proposals that meet minimum criteria.
___ c. Involves the development of project performance reports comparing planned and actual results.
___ d. Concepts and tools that organize information and evaluate alternatives.
___ e. Explains why monies received or paid at different points in time must be adjusted to comparable values.
___ f. Requires an adjustment to make cash flows comparable when they are expected to occur at different points in time.
___ g. Planning beyond the next budget year.
___ h. Helps the capital budgeting committee do a better job in evaluating new proposals.

M24-14. Payback Period and Accounting Rate of Return: Equal Annual Operating Cash Flows without Disinvestment   LO24-1

Juliana is considering an investment proposal with the following cash flows.

Initial investment—depreciable assets	$74,250
Net cash inflows from operations (per year for 5 years)	16,500
Disinvestment	0

REQUIRED

a. Determine the payback period.
b. Determine the accounting rate of return on initial investment.
c. Determine the accounting rate of return on average investment.

M24-15. Payback Period and Accounting Rate of Return: Equal Annual Operating Cash Flows with Disinvestment   LO24-1

Minn is considering an investment proposal with the following cash flows.

Initial investment—depreciable assets	$227,500
Net cash inflows from operations (per year for 10 years)	32,500
Disinvestment—depreciable assets	22,750

REQUIRED

a. Determine the payback period.
b. Determine the accounting rate of return on initial investment.
c. Determine the accounting rate of return on average investment.

M24-16. Payback Period and Accounting Rate of Return: Equal Annual Operating Cash Flows with Disinvestment   LO24-1

Roopali is considering an investment proposal with the following cash flows.

Initial investment—depreciable assets	$100,000
Initial investment—working capital	20,000
Net cash inflows from operations (per year for 5 years)	24,000
Disinvestment—depreciable assets	20,000
Disinvestment—working capital	20,000

REQUIRED

a. Determine the payback period.
b. Determine the accounting rate of return on initial investment.
c. Determine the accounting rate of return on average investment.

LO24-2, 5   **M24-17.**   **Time Value of Money: Basics**

Using the equations and tables in Appendix 24A of this chapter, determine the answers to each of the following independent situations.

a. The future value in two years of $5,000 deposited today in a savings account with interest compounded annually at 4%.
b. The present value of $15,000 to be received in four years, discounted at 10%.
c. The present value of an annuity of $2,500 per year for five years discounted at 12%.
d. An initial investment of $69,845 is to be returned in eight equal annual payments. Determine the amount of each payment if the interest rate is 8%.
e. A proposed investment will provide cash flows of $20,000, $25,000, and $30,000 at the end of Years 1, 2, and 3, respectively. Using a discount rate of 6%, determine the present value of these cash flows.
f. Find the present value of an investment that will pay $3,000 at the end of Years 10, 11, and 12. Use a discount rate of 8%.

LO24-2, 5   **M24-18.**   **Time Value of Money: Basics**

Using the equations and tables in Appendix 24A of this chapter, determine the answers to each of the following independent situations.

a. The future value in three years of $8,900 invested today in a certificate of deposit with interest compounded annually at 6%.
b. The present value of $12,000 to be received in five years, discounted at 6%.
c. The present value of an annuity of $25,000 per year for four years discounted at 8%.
d. An initial investment of $66,200 is to be returned in six equal annual payments. Determine the amount of each payment if the interest rate is 10%.
e. A proposed investment will provide cash flows of $10,000, $7,500, and $5,000 at the end of Years 1, 2, and 3, respectively. Using a discount rate of 14%, determine the present value of these cash flows.
f. Find the present value of an investment that will pay $15,000 at the end of Years 8, 9, and 10. Use a discount rate of 16%.

LO24-2, 6   **M24-19.**   **NPV and IRR: Equal Annual Net Cash Inflows**

Kailey James Company is evaluating a capital expenditure proposal that requires an initial investment of $30,723, has predicted cash inflows of $5,000 per year for 10 years, and has no salvage value.

REQUIRED

a. Using a discount rate of 8%, determine the net present value of the investment proposal.
b. Determine the proposal's internal rate of return. (Refer to Appendix 24B if you use the table approach.)
c. What discount rate would produce a net present value of zero?

LO24-2, 6   **M24-20.**   **NPV and IRR: Equal Annual Net Cash Inflows**

Spotify Technology SA   NYSE :: SPOT

Assume Spotify is evaluating a capital expenditure proposal that requires an initial investment of $294,800, has predicted cash inflows of $67,750 per year for six years, and has no salvage value.

REQUIRED

a. Using a discount rate of 12%, determine the net present value of the investment proposal.
b. Determine the proposal's internal rate of return. (Refer to Appendix 24B if you use the table approach.)
c. What discount rate would produce a net present value of zero?

LO24-3   **M24-21.**   **Identifying Characteristics of Different Capital Budgeting Models**

For each of the following statements that describe a capital budgeting model, indicate to which method, or methods, the statement applies. Choose from payback, accounting rate of return, net present value, and internal rate of return.

REQUIRED

1. Does not consider net cash flows after the initial investment is recovered.
2. Provides the rate that results when a project's net present value is equal to zero.

3. Considers GAAP income related to a project rather than cash flows.
4. Considers all project's net cash flows.
5. Does not take into account the time value of money.
6. Assumes that net cash inflows are reinvested at the project's specific rate of return.

M24-22. Using Sensitivity Analysis for Risk Assessment LO24-4
Assume that **PepsiCo** is considering an upgrade to its manufacturing facilities with an initial cost of $2,800,000. The upgrade is predicted to result in net cash inflows over a ten-year period of $500,000 annually. The company's discount rate is 8%. In performing a sensitivity analysis to adjust for perceived risks of the project, three alternative scenarios are under consideration where one variable is adjusted, and the remaining facts do not change from the original scenario.

PepsiCo
NASDAQ :: PEP

- New scenario 1: The discount rate was adjusted up to 14%.
- New scenario 2: The number of years of cash flows is adjusted down to 8 years.
- New scenario 3: The cash flows were adjusted down by 15%.

REQUIRED
a. Compute the net present value under the original scenario.
b. Compute the net present value under the three proposed scenarios.
c. Rank the four options (original and three new scenarios) in order from the smallest net present value result to the largest net present value amount.

EXERCISES

E24-23. Payback, NPV and IRR: Unequal Annual Net Cash Inflows LO24-1, 2, 6
Assume that **Tesla Inc.** is evaluating a capital expenditure proposal that has the following predicted cash flows.

Tesla Inc.
NASDAQ :: TSLA

Initial investment.	$(160,000)
Operation	
Year 1	42,000
Year 2	95,000
Year 3	65,000
Salvage.	0

REQUIRED
a. Determine the payback period. (The company uses a payback period of three years or less when screening new projects.)
b. Using a discount rate of 10%, determine the net present value of the investment proposal.
c. Determine the proposal's internal rate of return. (Refer to Appendix 24B if you use the table approach to use a trial-and-error approach.)
d. Should the company make the investment?
e. What nonfinancial ESG considerations should Tesla take into account assuming sustainability is integrated into its overall corporate strategy?

E24-24. NPV and IRR: Unequal Annual Net Cash Inflows LO24-1, 2, 6
Rocky Road Company is evaluating a capital expenditure proposal that has the following predicted cash flows.

Initial investment.	$(85,000)
Operation	
Year 1	30,500
Year 2	60,000
Year 3	31,000
Salvage.	0

REQUIRED
a. Determine the payback period.
b. Using a discount rate of 12%, determine the net present value of the investment proposal.
c. Determine the proposal's internal rate of return. (Refer to Appendix 24B if you use the table approach to use a trial-and-error approach.)

LO24-1, 2, 6   **E24-25.**   **Payback Period, IRR, and Minimum Cash Flows**

The management of Mohawk Limited is currently evaluating the following investment proposal.

	Time 0	Year 1	Year 2	Year 3	Year 4
Initial investment..............	$210,000	—	—	—	—
Net operating cash inflows.....	—	$70,000	$70,000	$70,000	$70,000

REQUIRED

a. Determine the proposal's payback period.
b. Determine the proposal's internal rate of return. (Refer to Appendix 24B if you use the table approach.)
c. Given the amount of the initial investment, determine the minimum annual net cash inflows required to obtain an internal rate of return of 14%.

LO24-2   **E24-26.**   **Time-Adjusted Cost-Volume-Profit Analysis**

Assume **The Hershey Company** is considering the desirability of producing a new chocolate candy called Pleasure Bombs. Before purchasing the new equipment required to manufacture Pleasure Bombs, the company performed the following analysis.

Unit selling price...	$2.50
Variable manufacturing and selling costs...........................	(1.85)
Unit contribution margin..	$0.65
Annual fixed costs	
Depreciation (straight-line for 5 years)........................	$ 62,000
Other (all cash)..	48,500
Total...	$110,500

Annual break-even sales volume = $110,500 ÷ $0.65 = 170,000 units

Because the expected annual sales volume is 200,000 units, Hershey decided to undertake the production of Pleasure Bombs. This required an immediate investment of $310,000 in equipment that has a life of four years and no salvage value. After four years, the production of Pleasure Bombs will be discontinued.

REQUIRED

a. Evaluate the analysis performed by the company.
b. If Hershey has a time value of money of 8%, should it make the investment with projected annual sales of 200,000 units?
c. Considering the time value of money, what annual unit sales volume is required to break even? *Hint:* Refer to Chapter 15 to review break-even analysis.

LO24-1, 2, 4   **E24-27.**   **Payback Period and IRR of a Cost Reduction Proposal—Differential Analysis**

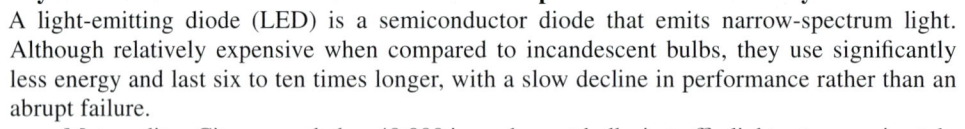

A light-emitting diode (LED) is a semiconductor diode that emits narrow-spectrum light. Although relatively expensive when compared to incandescent bulbs, they use significantly less energy and last six to ten times longer, with a slow decline in performance rather than an abrupt failure.

    Metropolitan City currently has 40,000 incandescent bulbs in traffic lights at approximately 6,000 intersections. It is estimated that replacing all the incandescent bulbs with LEDs will cost $17.7 million. However, the investment is also estimated to save the city $4.42 million per year in energy costs.

REQUIRED

a. Determine the payback period of converting Metropolitan City traffic lights to LEDs.
b. If the average life of an incandescent streetlight is one year and the average life of an LED street-light is seven years, should the city finance the investment in LEDs at an interest rate of 5% per year? Justify your answer.

LO24-1, 2, 4   **E24-28.**   **Payback Period and NPV of a Cost Reduction Proposal—Differential Analysis**

Hermione decided to purchase a new automobile. Being concerned about environmental issues, she is leaning toward the hybrid rather than the gasoline only model. Nevertheless, as a new business school graduate, she wants to determine if there is an economic justification for purchasing the hybrid, which costs $2,200 more than the regular model. She has determined that city/highway combined gas mileage of the hybrid and regular models are 40 and 30 miles per gallon respectively. Hermione anticipates she will travel an average of 15,000 miles per year for the next several years.

REQUIRED

a. Determine the payback period of the incremental investment if gasoline costs $2.60 per gallon.
b. Assuming that Hermione plans to keep the car about six years and does not believe there will be a trade-in premium associated with the hybrid model, determine the net present value of the incremental investment at 6% time value of money.
c. Determine the cost of gasoline required for a payback period of four years.
d. At $4.00 per gallon, determine the gas mileage required for a payback period of four years.

E24-29. Payback Period and NPV of Alternative Automobile Purchase

Wendy Li decided to purchase a new Honda Accord. Being concerned about environmental issues, she is leaning toward a Honda Accord Hybrid rather than the completely gasoline-powered LX model. Nevertheless, she wants to determine if there is an economic justification for purchasing the Hybrid, which costs $2,000 more than the LX. Based on a mix of city and highway driving, she predicts that the average gas mileage of each car is 48 MPG for the Hybrid and 30 MPG for the LX. Wendy also anticipates she will drive an average of 15,000 miles per year and that gasoline will cost an average of $2.50 per gallon over the next four years. She also plans to replace whichever car she purchases at the end of four years when the resale values of the Hybrid and the LX are predicted to be $12,500 and $9,000 respectively.

REQUIRED

a. Determine the payback period of the incremental investment associated with purchasing the Hybrid.
b. Determine the net present value of the incremental investment associated with purchasing the Hybrid at a 8% time value of money.
c. Determine the cost of gasoline required for a payback period of two and a half years on the incremental investment.
d. Identify other factors Wendy should consider before making her decision.

E24-30. Analyze Capital Projects and Provide Recommendations

Randolph Inc. is considering the following three capital project proposals.

	Proposal A	Proposal B	Proposal C
Initial investment.	$250,000	$200,000	$100,000
Annual net cash flows.	$ 75,000	$ 63,000	$ 40,000
Disinvestment.	$ 0	$ 0	$ 0
Life	5 years	4 years	3 years

The company initially screens projects considering (1) a payback period of 2.5 years or less and (2) a positive net present value using a discount rate of 10%.

REQUIRED

a. Compute the payback period for each proposal and determine whether each proposal passes the initial screening based on your results.
b. Compute the net present value for each proposal and determine whether each proposal passes the initial screening based on your results.
c. Provide a recommendation on whether to invest in proposal A, B, or C based only on the company's screening considerations.
d. First, calculate the internal rate of return of each proposal. Next, provide a recommendation on whether to invest in proposal A, B, or C based on the company's screening considerations, the internal rate of return of each proposal, and assuming that the company must choose one of the projects to pursue.

E24-31. Time-Adjusted Cost-Volume-Profit Analysis with Income Taxes

Assume the same facts as given in Exercise E24-26 for Hershey.

REQUIRED

With a 20% tax rate and a 8% time value of money, determine the annual unit sales required to break even on a time-adjusted basis. Assume straight-line depreciation is used to determine tax payments.

PROBLEMS

LO24-1, 2, 3 **P24-32.** **Ranking Investment Proposals: Payback Period, Accounting Rate of Return, and Net Present Value**

Presented is information pertaining to the cash flows of three mutually exclusive investment proposals.

	Proposal A	Proposal B	Proposal C
Initial investment...........................	$100,000	$100,000	$100,000
Cash flow from operations			
Year 1	60,000	25,000	110,000
Year 2	40,000	40,000	—
Year 3	35,000	70,000	—
Disinvestment...............................	0	0	0

REQUIRED

a. Determine the payback period, the accounting rate of return on initial investment, and the net present value, assuming a discount rate of 12%, for each of the three proposals.
b. Rank these investment proposals using the payback period, the accounting rate of return on initial investment, and the net present value criteria. Assume that the organization's cost of capital is 12% and that all investments are in depreciable assets.
c. Explain the difference in rankings. Which investment would you recommend?

LO24-1, 2, 6 **P24-33.** **Cost Reduction Proposal: IRR, NPV, and Payback Period**

PA Chemical currently discharges liquid waste into Pittsburgh's municipal sewer system. However, the Pittsburgh municipal government has informed PA that a surcharge of $6 per thousand cubic liters will soon be imposed for the discharge of this waste. This has prompted management to evaluate the desirability of treating its own liquid waste.

A proposed system consists of three elements. The first is a retention basin, which would permit unusual discharges to be held and treated before entering the downstream system. The second is a continuous self-cleaning rotary filter required where solids are removed. The third is an automated neutralization process required where materials are added to control the alkalinity-acidity range.

The system is designed to process 700,000 liters a day. However, management anticipates that only about 350,000 liters of liquid waste would be processed in a normal workday. The company operates 300 days per year. The initial investment in the system would be $1,500,000, and annual operating costs are predicted to be $280,000. The system has a predicted useful life of 10 years and a salvage value of $100,000.

REQUIRED

a. Determine the project's net present value at a discount rate of 14%.
b. Determine the project's approximate internal rate of return. (Refer to Appendix 24B if you use the table approach.)
c. Determine the project's payback period.
d. Suppose that the PA Chemical determines that it might be easier (in many ways) to use the municipal sewer system. However, management knows that installing its own system is more effective in treating waste and ensuring that harmful chemicals do not ultimately enter the water supply. How should this information enter management's decision-making?

LO24-1, 2, 3, 4, 6 **P24-34.** **Analyze Capital Projects and Provide Recommendations**

Macro Solutions Inc., a hardware manufacturer, has experienced rapid growth. Macro is considering two new capital expenditure projects and has a cost of capital of 10%. Project A requires an investment of $155,000 and Project B requires an investment of $240,000. Wendy Alexander, CFO of Macro, has been asked to analyze both projects and provide a recommendation. She has compiled the following data.

	Project A Cash Flows	Project B Cash Flows
Year 1	$43,000	$60,000
Year 2	43,000	60,000
Year 3	43,000	60,000
Year 4	43,000	60,000
Year 5	43,000	60,000

REQUIRED

1. Calculate the internal rate of return (IRR) for each project.
2. Based on the IRR of each project, and a capital rationing constraint of $275,000, what recommendations should Alexander make regarding the projects?
3. If Macro has no capital rationing constraints, what recommendation should Alexander make regarding the projects?
4. Calculate the payback period for both projects. Assuming a four-year maximum payback requirement and no other constraint, what recommendation should Alexander make?
5. Identify and explain two advantages of using net present value (NPV) over IRR and one advantage of using IRR over NPV
6. Identify and explain three weaknesses of the payback method.
7. Define and explain sensitivity analysis. Explain two ways Alexander can use sensitivity analysis to further evaluate proposed projects.

CMA adapted

P24-35. NPV Total and Differential Analysis of Replacement Decision
Assume Mitsubishi Chemical is evaluating a proposal to purchase a new compressor that would cost $200,000 and have a salvage value of $20,000 in five years. Mitsubishi's cost of capital is 16%. It would provide annual operating cash savings of $22,500, as follows.

	Old Compressor	New Compressor
Salaries	$60,000	$75,000
Supplies	12,000	7,500
Utilities	23,000	15,000
Cleaning and maintenance	35,000	10,000
Total cash expenditures	$130,000	$107,500

If the new compressor is purchased, Mitsubishi will sell the old compressor for its current salvage value of $60,000. If the new compressor is not purchased, the old compressor will be disposed of in five years at a predicted scrap value of $6,000. The old compressor's present book value is $85,000. If kept, the old compressor will require repairs one year from now predicted to cost $75,000.

Required

a. Use the total cost approach to evaluate the alternatives of keeping the old compressor and purchasing the new compressor. Indicate which alternative is preferred.
b. Use the differential cost approach to evaluate the desirability of purchasing the new compressor.

P24-36. NPV Total and Differential Analysis of Replacement Decision
Assume Pinstripes Cleaning and Restoration, near Dallas, Texas, must either have a complete overhaul of its current dry-cleaning system or purchase a new one. Its cost of capital is 16%. The following cost projections have been developed.

	Old System	New System
Purchase cost (new)	$85,000	$90,000
Remaining book value	17,000	
Overhaul needed	25,000	
Annual cash operating costs	60,850	40,200
Current salvage value	12,000	
Salvage value in 5 years	4,500	10,000

If Pinstripes keeps the old system, it will have to be overhauled immediately. With the overhaul, the old system will have a useful life of five more years.

Required
a. Use the total cost approach to evaluate the alternatives of keeping the old system and purchasing the new system. Indicate which alternative is preferred.
b. Use the differential cost approach to evaluate the desirability of purchasing the new system.

LO24-2, 4   P24-37.   NPV Differential Analysis of Replacement Decision
The management of Dusseldorf Manufacturing Company is currently evaluating a proposal to purchase a new, innovative drill press as a replacement for a less efficient piece of similar equipment, which would then be sold. The cost of the equipment, including delivery and installation, is $320,000. If the equipment is purchased, Dusseldorf will incur a $10,000 cost in removing the present equipment and revamping service facilities. The present equipment has a book value of $150,000 and a remaining useful life of 10 years. Because of new technical improvements that have made the present equipment obsolete, it now has a disposal value of only $70,500. Management has provided the following comparison of manufacturing costs.

	Present Equipment	New Equipment
Annual production (units)	500,000	500,000
Annual costs		
Direct labor (per unit)	$0.15	$0.08
Overhead		
Depreciation (10% of asset's book value)	$15,000	$32,000
Other	$84,600	$42,500

Additional information follows.
- Management believes that if the current equipment is not replaced now, it will have to wait 10 years before replacement is justifiable.
- Both pieces of equipment are expected to have a negligible salvage value at the end of 10 years.
- Management expects to sell the entire annual production of 500,000 units.
- Dusseldorf's cost of capital is 14%.

Required
Evaluate the desirability of purchasing the new equipment.

LO24-7   P24-38.   NPV with Income Taxes: Straight-Line versus Accelerated Depreciation
Carl William, Inc. is a conservatively managed boat company whose motto is, "The old ways are the good ways." Management has always used straight-line depreciation for tax and external reporting purposes. Although they are reluctant to change, they are aware of the impact of taxes on a project's profitability.

REQUIRED
For a typical $200,000 investment in equipment with a five-year life and no salvage value, determine the present value of the advantage resulting from the use of double-declining balance depreciation as opposed to straight-line depreciation. Assume an income tax rate of 21% and a discount rate of 20%. Also assume that there will be a switch from double-declining balance to straight-line depreciation in the fourth year.

LO24-1, 7   P24-39.   Payback Period and NPV: Taxes and Straight-Line Depreciation
Assume that Regional Design Company is evaluating a proposal to change the company's manual design system to a computer-aided design (CAD) system. The proposed system is expected to save 12,000 design hours per year; an operating cost savings of $65 per hour. The annual cash expenditures of operating the CAD system are estimated to be $600,000. The CAD system requires an initial investment of $200,000. The estimated life of this system is five years with no salvage value. The tax rate is 21%, and the company uses straight-line depreciation for tax purposes. The company has a cost of capital of 14%.

Required
a. Compute the annual after-tax cash flows related to the CAD project.
b. Compute each of the following for the project:
   1. Payback period.
   2. Net present value.

P24-40. NPV: Taxes and Accelerated Depreciation

Assume the same facts as given in P24-39, except that management intends to use double-declining balance depreciation with a switch to straight-line depreciation (applied to any undepreciated balance) starting in Year 4.

Required
Determine the project's net present value.

CASES AND PROJECTS

C24-41. Payback, ARR, and IRR: Evaluating the Sale of Government Assets (Requires Spreadsheet)

In 2008 the City of Chicago agreed to lease 35,000 parking meters to a Morgan Stanley–led partnership for a one-time sum of $1.15 billion. The lease extends to the year 2083. The lease has been criticized as an example of "one-shot" deals arrived at behind closed doors to balance a current budget at the expense of future generations. Some have observed that deals such as this are akin to individuals using their retirement savings to meet current needs, instead of planning for the future. "These deals are rarely done under the light of public scrutiny," says Richard G. Little, director of the Keston Institute for Public Finance at the University of Southern California. "Often the facts come out long after the deal is done."

Since the lease was signed, helped by parking-fee hikes, the partnership has earned a profit before taxes and depreciation of $0.80 per dollar of revenue. In 2010, total revenues over the 75-year life of the lease were projected to be $11.6 billion.

Defending the city's action, Gene Saffold, Chicago's chief financial officer, stated that "The concession agreement was absolutely the best deal for Chicagoans. … The net present value of $11.6 billion in revenue over the life of the 75-year agreement is consistent with $1.15 billion.[2]

Required
Evaluate the 75-year lease and determine if the projected revenues are consistent with the initial investment. To simplify your analysis, assume equal revenues and operating costs in all periods, no investment required in working capital, and no salvage value at the end of the lease. Use a corporate tax rate of 34% (in effect in 2008) in your calculations. Suggested elements of your solution include the following:
a. Determine the payback period in the absence of taxes.
b. Determine the accounting rate of return on the initial investment in the absence of taxes.
c. Determine the accounting rate of return on the initial investment using 34% as the tax rate.
d. Determine the internal rate of return in the absence of taxes.
e. Determine the internal rate of return using 34% as the tax rate.
f. Summary of analysis and conclusions.

C24-42. Determining Terms of Automobile Leases (Requires Spreadsheet)

Avant-Garde Motor Company has asked you to develop lease terms for the firm's popular Avant-Garde Challenger, which has an average selling price (new) of $25,000. You know that leasing is attractive because it assists consumers in obtaining new vehicles with a small down payment and "reasonable" monthly payments. Market analysts have told you that to attract the widest number of young professionals, the Challenger must have an initial down payment of no more than $500, monthly payments of no more than $400, and lease terms of no more than five years. When the lease expires, Avant-Garde will sell the used Challengers at the automobile's resale market price at that time. It is difficult to predict the future price of the increasingly popular Challenger, but you have obtained the following information on the average resale prices of used Challengers.

Age	Resale Price
1 year	$21,000
2 years	18,000
3 years	17,000
4 years	15,500
5 years	13,000

Avant-Garde's cost of capital is 12% per year, or 1% per month.

---
[2] "Windfall for Investors, A Loss for the Windy City," *Bloomberg Businessweek*, August 29, 2010, pp. 44–45; Ianthe Jeanne Dugan, "Facing Budget Gaps, Cities Sell Parking, Airports, Zoo," *Wall Street Journal*, August 23, 2010, pp. A1, A12.

Required

a. With the aid of Excel, develop a competitive and profitable lease payment program. Assuming a $500 down payment, calculate the program's monthly payments for two-, three-, four-, and five-year leases. Assume the down payment and the first lease payment are made immediately and that all subsequent lease payments are made at the start of the month. [*Hint:* PMT (rate,nper,pv,fv,type), where rate = the time value of money; nper = the number of periods; pv = the present value; fv = the future value; and type = 0 (when the payment is at the end of the period) or 1 (when the payment is at the beginning of the period). For monthly payments, rate should be set at the annual rate divided by 12, and nper should be set at the number of months in the lease. Here, fv is the salvage value.]

b. Reevaluate the lease program assuming a down payment of $1,000.

c. Reevaluate the lease program assuming a down payment of $500 and a $1,000 increase in salvage values.

d. Reevaluate the lease program assuming a down payment of $1,000 and a $1,000 increase in salvage values.

e. What is your final recommendation? What risks are associated with your recommendation? Are there any other actions to consider?

LO24-1, 4   C24-43.   Evaluating Data and Using Payback Period for an Investment Proposal

To determine the desirability of investing in a larger computer monitor (as opposed to the typical monitor that comes with a new personal computer), researchers developed an experiment testing the time required to perform a set of tasks. The tasks included the following:

- Setting up a meeting using electronic mail.
- Reviewing meeting requests.
- Checking an online schedule.
- Embedding a video file into a document.
- Searching a customer database to find a specific set of contracts.
- Copying a database into a spreadsheet.
- Modifying a slide presentation.

The researchers assumed this was a typical set of tasks performed by a manager. They determined that there was a 9% productivity gain using the larger monitor. One test manager commented that the largest productivity gain came from being able to have multiple applications open at the same time and from being able to view several files at once.

Required

Accepting the 9% productivity gain as accurate, what additional information is needed to determine the payback period of an investment in a larger monitor that is to be used by a manager? Make any necessary assumptions and obtain whatever data you can (perhaps from computer component advertisements) to determine the payback period for the proposed investment.

LO24-2, 3, 4, 6   C24-44.   IRR and NPV with Performance Evaluation Conflict

Pepperoni Pizza Company owns and operates fast-service pizza parlors throughout North America. The firm operates on a regional basis and provides almost complete autonomy to the manager of each region. Regional managers are responsible for long-range planning, capital expenditures, personnel policies, pricing, and so forth. Each year the performance of regional managers is evaluated by determining the accounting return on fixed assets in their regions; a return of 16% is expected. To determine this return, regional net income is divided by the book value of fixed assets at the start of the year. Managers of regions earning a return of more than 18% are identified for possible promotion, and managers of regions with a return of less than 14% are subject to replacement.

Mr. Light, with a degree in hotel and restaurant management, is the manager of the Northeast region. He is regarded as a "rising star" and will be considered for promotion during the next two years. Light has been with Pepperoni for a total of three years. During that period, the return on fixed assets in his region (the oldest in the firm) has increased dramatically. He is currently considering a proposal to open five new parlors in the Boston area. The total project involves an investment of $1,000,000 and will double the number of Pepperoni pizzas sold in the Northeast region to a total of 600,000 per year. At an average price of $9 each, total sales revenue will be $5,400,000.

The expenses of operating each of the new parlors include variable costs of $5 per pizza and fixed costs (excluding depreciation) of $175,000 per year. Because each of the new parlors has only a five-year life and no salvage value, yearly straight-line depreciation will be $40,000 [($1,000,000 ÷ 5 parlors) ÷ 5 years].

Required

a. Evaluate the desirability of the $1,000,000 investment in new pizza parlors by computing the internal rate of return and the net present value. Assume a time value of money of 16%. (Refer to Appendix 24B if you use the table approach.)

b. If Light is shrewd, will he approve the expansion? Why or why not? (Additional computations are suggested.)

C24-45. NPV and Project Reevaluation with Taxes, Straight-Line Depreciation   LO24-2, 4, 7

Last year, the Bayside Chemical Company prepared the following analysis of an investment proposal for a new manufacturing facility.

	Predicted Cash Inflows (outflows) (A)	Year(s) of Cash Flows (B)	12% Present Value Factor (C)	Present Value of Cash Flows (A) × (C)
Initial investment				
Fixed assets	$(810,000)	0	1.00000	$ (810,000)
Working capital	(100,000)	0	1.00000	(100,000)
Operations				
Annual taxable income without depreciation	310,000	1–5	3.60478	1,117,482
Taxes on income ($310,000 × 0.21)	(65,100)	1–5	3.60478	(234,671)
Depreciation tax shield	34,020*	1–5	3.60478	122,635
Disinvestment				
Site restoration	80,000	5	0.56743	(45,394)
Tax shield of restoration ($80,000 × 0.21)	16,800	5	0.56743	9,533
Working capital	100,000	5	0.56743	56,743
Net present value of all cash flows				$ 116,328

*Computation of depreciation tax shield:

Annual straight-line depreciation ($810,000 ÷ 5)	$162,000
Tax rate	× 0.21
Depreciation tax shield	$ 34,020

Because the proposal had a positive net present value when discounted at Bayside's cost of capital of 12%, the project was approved; all investments were made at the end of the year. Shortly after production began this year, a government agency notified Bayside of required additional expenditures totaling $300,000 to bring the plant into compliance with new federal emission regulations. Bayside has the option either to comply with the regulations by the end of the year, or to sell the entire operation (fixed assets and working capital) for $350,000. The improvements will be depreciated over the remaining four-year life of the plant using straight-line depreciation. The cost of site restoration will not be affected by the improvements. If Bayside elects to sell the plant, any book loss can be treated as an offset against taxable income on other operations. This tax reduction is an additional cash benefit of selling.

Required

a. Should Bayside sell the plant or comply with the new federal regulations? To simplify calculations, assume that any additional improvements are paid for on the last day of the current year.

b. Would Bayside have accepted the proposal at the beginning of the year if it had been aware of the forthcoming federal regulations?

c. Do you have any suggestions that might increase the project's net present value? (No calculations are required.)

C24-46. Post-Audit and Reevaluation of Investment Proposal: NPV   LO24-1, 2, 4

Anthony Company's capital budgeting committee is evaluating a capital expenditure proposal for the production of an upgraded webcam to be sold as an add-on feature for personal computers. The proposal calls for an independent contractor to construct the necessary facilities by December 31 of the current year at a total cost of $350,000. Payment for all construction costs will be made on that date. An additional $75,000 in cash will also be made available on December 31 of the current year, for working capital to support sales and production activities.

Management anticipates that the upgraded webcam has a limited market life; there is a high probability that within six years all new PCs will have advanced the current webcam offering. Accordingly, the proposal specifies that production will cease after six years. The investment in working capital will be recovered on that date, and the production facilities will be sold for $80,000. Predicted net cash inflows from operations for the next six years are as follows.

20X1	$125,000
20X2	125,000
20X3	125,000
20X4	60,000
20X5	60,000
20X6	60,000

Anthony Company has a time value of money of 14%. For capital budgeting purposes, all cash flows are assumed to occur at the end of each year.

Required

a. Evaluate the capital expenditure proposal using the net present value method. Should Anthony accept the proposal?

b. Assume that the capital expenditure proposal is accepted, but construction delays caused by labor problems and difficulties in obtaining the necessary construction permits delay the completion of the project. Payments totaling $250,000 were made to the construction company on December 31 of the current year. However, completion is now scheduled for December 31, 20X1, and an additional $150,000 will be required to complete construction. If the project is continued, the additional $150,000 will be paid at the end of 20X1, and the plant will begin operations on January 1, 20X2.

Because of the cost overruns, the capital budgeting committee requests a reevaluation of the project, before agreeing to any additional expenditures. After much effort, the following revised predictions of net operating cash inflows are developed.

20X2	$150,000
20X3	125,000
20X4	60,000
20X5	60,000
20X6	60,000

The working capital investment and disinvestment and the plant salvage values have not changed, except that the cash for working capital would now be made available on December 31, 20X1. Use the net present value method to reevaluate the initial decision to accept the proposal. Given the information currently available about the project, should it have been accepted? (*Hint:* Determine the net present value as of December 31 of the current year assuming management has not committed Anthony to the proposal.)

c. Given the situation that exists in early 20X1, should management continue or cancel the project? Assume that the facilities have a current salvage value of $95,000. (*Hint:* Assume that the decision is being made on January 1, 20X1.)

LO24-1, 2, 4   C24-47.   Post-Audit and Reevaluation of Investment Proposal: IRR

Throughout his four years in college, Ronald King worked at the local Beef Burger Restaurant in College City. Although the working conditions were good and the pay was not bad, Ron believed he could do a much better job of managing the restaurant than the current owner-manager. In particular, Ron believed that the proper use of marketing campaigns and sales incentives, such as selling a second burger for a 25% discount, could increase annual sales by 40%.

Just before graduation Ron inherited $600,000 from his great uncle. He seriously considered buying the restaurant. It seemed like a good idea because he liked the town and its college atmosphere, knew the business, and always wanted to work for himself. He also knew that the current owner wanted to sell the restaurant and retire to Florida. As part of a small business management course, Ron developed the following income statement for the restaurant's prior year operations.

BEEF BURGER RESTAURANT: COLLEGE CITY
Income Statement
For Prior Year Ended December 31

Sales.		$495,000
Expenses		
Cost of food.	$165,000	
Supplies	22,000	
Employee expenses	154,000	
Utilities	30,800	
Property taxes.	22,000	
Insurance	11,000	
Advertising	8,800	
Depreciation	66,000	479,600
Net income		$ 15,400

Ron believed that the cost of food and supplies were all variable, the employee expenses and utilities were one-half variable and one-half fixed last year, and all other expenses were fixed. If Ron purchased the restaurant and followed through on his plans, he believed there would be a 40% increase in unit sales volume and all variable costs. Of the fixed costs, only advertising would increase by $10,000. The use of discounts and special promotions would, however, limit the increase in sales revenue to only 30% even though sales volume increased 40%.

Required

a. Determine
  1. The current annual net cash inflow.
  2. The predicted annual net cash inflow if Ron executes his plans and his assumptions are correct.
b. Ron believes his plan would produce equal net cash inflows during each of the next 15 years, the period remaining on a long-term lease for the land on which the restaurant is built. At the end of that time, the restaurant would have to be demolished at a predicted net cost of $88,000. Assuming Ron would otherwise invest the money in stock expected to yield 12%, determine the maximum amount he should pay for the restaurant.
c. Assume that Ron accepts an offer from the current owner to buy the restaurant for $450,000. Unfortunately, although the expected increase in sales volume does occur, customers make much more extensive use of the promotions than Ron had anticipated. As a result, total sales revenues are 8% below projections. Furthermore, to improve employee attitudes, Ron gave a 10% raise immediately after purchasing the restaurant. Reevaluate the initial decision using the actual sales revenue and the increase in labor costs, assuming conditions will remain unchanged over the remaining life of the project. Was the investment decision a wise one?
d. Ron can sell the restaurant to a large franchise operator for $350,000. Alternatively, he believes that additional annual marketing expenditures and changes in promotions costing $25,000 per year could bring the sales revenues up to their original projections, with no other changes in costs. Should Ron sell the restaurant or keep it and make the additional expenditures? Assume that Ron has just purchased the restaurant and his original assumptions remain unchanged; however, he immediately gave his employees a 10% raise.

SOLUTIONS TO REVIEW PROBLEMS

Review 24-1—Solution

Basic computations:

Initial investment	
Depreciable assets	$(27,740)
Working capital	(3,000)
Total	$(30,740)
Operation	
Cash receipts	$ 25,000
Cash expenditures	(15,000)
Net cash inflow	$ 10,000
Disinvestment	
Sale of depreciable assets	$ 2,000
Recovery of working capital	3,000
Total	$ 5,000

a. Payback period = $30,740 ÷ $10,000
 = 3.074 years

b. Accounting rate of return on initial and average investments:

Annual net cash inflow from operations	$10,000
Less average annual depreciation [($27,740 − $2,000) ÷ 4]	(6,435)
Average annual increase in net income	$ 3,565

$$\text{Accounting rate of return on initial investment} = \frac{\$3,565}{\$30,740}$$

$$= 0.1160 \text{ or } 11.6\%$$

$$\text{Average investment} = (\$30,740 + \$5,000) \div 2$$

$$= \$17,870$$

$$\text{Accounting rate of return on average investment} = \frac{\$3,565}{\$17,870}$$

$$= 0.1995 \text{ or } 19.95\%$$

c. Based on the information provided, management would likely invest in the new equipment. For machinery, a payback period of approximately three years seems reasonable. We would expect this equipment to be operable longer than three years. Additionally a 20% return on the average investment also is favorable. Before making a final decision, we would want to compare this return to the average return on Costco's other long-term assets to ensure that it is comparable. We would also want to know if Costco had a maximum payback period expected on new equipment purchases.

Review 24-2—Solution

a. Net present value at a 10% discount rate:

	Predicted Cash Inflows (outflows) (A)	Year(s) of Cash Flows (B)	10% Present Value Factor (C)	Present Value of Cash Flows (A) × (C)
Initial investment	$(30,740)	0	1.00000	$(30,740)
Operation	10,000	1–4	3.16987	31,699
Disinvestment	5,000	4	0.68301	3,415
Net present value of all cash flows				$ 4,374

b. Internal rate of return:
Using a spreadsheet, the proposal's internal rate of return is readily determined to be 16%.

	A	B
1	Year of cash flow	Cash flow
2	0	$(30,740)
3	1	10,000
4	2	10,000
5	3	10,000
6	4	15,000
7	IRR	0.16

Review 24-3—Solution

a.

	Proposal A	Proposal B	Proposal C
Payback period	2 years	2 years	1 year
Accounting rate of return			
Total increase in income before depreciation	$67,500	$67,500	$45,000
Total depreciation	(45,000)	(45,000)	(45,000)
Total increase in income	$22,500	$22,500	$0
Life in years	÷ 3	÷ 3	÷ 1
Average annual increase in net income	$7,500	$7,500	$0
Initial investment	÷45,000	÷45,000	÷45,000
Accounting rate of return	0.1667	0.1667	0.0

Net present value at 10%:

Year	Factor	Present Values Proposal A	Proposal B	Proposal C
1	0.90909	$36,363.60	$20,454.53	$40,909.05
2	0.82645	4,132.25	18,595.13	
3	0.75131	16,904.48	16,904.48	
Total		57,400.33	55,954.14	40,909.05
Initial investment		(45,000.00)	(45,000.00)	(45,000.00)
Net present value		$12,400.33	$10,954.14	$ (4,090.95)

Rankings:

	Proposal A	Proposal B	Proposal C
Payback	2–3	2–3	1
Accounting rate of return	1–2	1–2	3
Net present value	1	2	3

b. While the accounting rate of return and the net present value criteria consider profitability, payback considers only the time required to recover the investment. Proposal C provides for the shortest payback; hence, it ranks first using the payback criterion even though Proposal C does not provide a profit.

Proposals A and B have identical total cash flows over their lives; hence, they have identical accounting rates of return. However, the timing of their cash flows differs. Because Proposal A has higher early-period cash flows, its net present value is higher than that of Proposal B. Of the three criteria used, only net present value considers both profitability and the timing of cash flows. Plus, the initial investment is the same for all options, thus, we would recommend Proposal A.

Review 24-4—Solution

In making the final decision to accept or reject a capital expenditure proposal that has passed the initial screening, nonquantitative factors should also be considered. Very important at this point are management's attitudes toward risk and financing alternatives, their confidence in the professional judgment of managers making investment proposals, their beliefs about the future direction of the economy, and their evaluation of alternative investments.

Specific to Costco's investment decision, their management might consider factors such as the following:

- Will new models of the equipment be available in the next few years that will be more efficient and/or safer?
- How is the economy and do they expect to be able to sustain the number of products that they have had in recent years?
- How likely is it that they will see a decline in number and variety of products going through the distribution center?
- Are there any other revenue-generating investments that might be a better alternative?

Review 24-5—Solution

a. fv = $2,247

   or

   $2,000/0.89000 = $2,247

b. pv = $8,000 × 0.63552
       = $5,084

c. pva = $2,000 × 3.43308
        = $6,866

d. a = $32,010/4.96764
      = $ 6,444

e.

Year	Cash Flow		Present Value at 20%		Present Value Amount
1	$20,000	×	0.83333	=	$16,667
2	8,000	×	0.69444	=	5,556
3	6,000	×	0.57870	=	3,472
Total					$25,695

f.
Present value of an annuity for 12 years at 14% ($5,000 × 5.66029)............ $28,301
Present value of an annuity for 9 years at 14% ($5,000 × 4.94637)............. (24,732)
Present value of the deferred annuity................................... $ 3,569

Review 24-6—Solution

Based on the solution of Review 24-2, the net present value of this project using a discount rate of 10% is $4,374. Because the proposal has a positive net present value when discounted at 10%, its internal rate of return must be higher than 10%. Through a trial-and-error approach, the internal rate of return is determined to be 16%.

	Predicted Cash Inflows (outflows) (A)	Year(s) of Cash Flows (B)	16% Present Value Factor (C)	Present Value of Cash Flows (A) × (C)
Initial investment	$(30,740)	0	1.00000	$(30,740)
Operation	10,000	1–4	2.79818	27,982
Disinvestment	5,000	4	0.55229	2,761
Net present value of all cash flows				$ 3

Review 24-7—Solution

a.

Operating cost savings (9,000 hours × $45)	$405,000
Operating costs of CAD/CAM system	(200,000)
Before-tax cash savings	205,000
Income taxes without tax shield at 35%	(71,750)
Depreciation tax shield [($550,000/5 years) × 0.35]	38,500
Relevant annual after-tax cash flow	$171,750

b.

	Design System
Present value of annuity ($171,750 × 3.43308)	$589,632
Initial investment	(550,000)
Net present value	$ 39,632

Appendix A

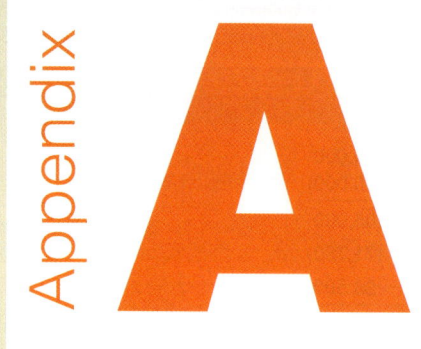

Compound Interest and the Time-Value of Money

Suppose you were lucky enough to hold a winning lottery ticket that allowed you to choose when you would receive your prize. Most of us would answer: Now! But let's say this ticket gave you the option of receiving $20,000 now, or $24,000 two years from now. Which would you choose?

Of course, $24,000 is better than $20,000. But the choice is not that simple. If you take the $20,000 today, you can buy a new car, pay next semester's tuition, or invest the money in the stock market. If you wait, you'll receive the larger prize, but you may have to take the bus for the next two years, postpone your college studies, or pass up on a great investment opportunity.

This is the essence of what is called the **time-value of money**. A dollar received today is worth more than a dollar received two years in the future. Having cash in our possession gives us the opportunity to spend or invest that cash today. Cash received in the future cannot be spent or invested today.[1]

The easiest way to illustrate the time-value of money is to assume that we collect the $20,000 cash prize today and invest it in a money-market account that guarantees a 10% return on our investment. In one year, the investment would be worth $22,000—which is the original $20,000 investment plus $2,000 interest ($20,000 × 10%). At the end of two years, the investment would be worth $24,200 [= $22,000 + ($22,000 × 10%) = $22,000 × 1.10].

In the second year, the investment earns a return of $2,200, which is $22,000 × 10%. The interest earned in the second year is greater than the interest earned in year one because the interest earned in the first year earns interest in year two. This interest earned on interest is called **compound interest**. As interest accumulates on an investment, both the original investment and the accumulated interest will earn a return in subsequent periods. Interest calculated on the original investment, but not on interest accrued in prior periods, is called **simple interest**.

This Appendix explains and illustrates the concepts of time-value of money and compound interest. It is divided into three sections. The first two address future value concepts and present value concepts, respectively. In the last section, we illustrate the use of spreadsheet software to compute present and future values.

---

[1] The time-value of money is primarily due to lost opportunities. However, the risk associated with some future cash flows will influence our assessment of their time-value. That is, there may be some uncertainty associated with a future payment. For instance, in our lottery ticket example, there may be a possibility that the payer could default on the $24,000 payment. Risk is reflected in time-value calculations by using higher interest rates for risky cash flows.

FUTURE VALUE CONCEPTS

As illustrated above, $20,000 invested today to earn a return of 10% per year will accumulate interest and be worth $24,200 in two years. The $24,200 is referred to as the *future value* of $20,000 because it represents what $20,000 invested today at 10% would be worth two years in the future. The **future value** of any amount is the amount that an investment is worth at a given future date if invested at a given rate of compound interest.

Assume that we allow our $20,000 investment to continue to earn interest for three years. The interest will continue to compound and the future value will continue to grow. This is illustrated in **Exhibit A.1**.

EXHIBIT A.1 — Future Value of $20,000

Initial investment	$20,000
Interest earned in year 1 (initial investment × 10%)	2,000
Investment plus accumulated interest (future value) in 1 year	22,000
Interest earned in year 2 (year 1 amount × 10%)	2,200
Investment plus accumulated interest (future value) in 2 years	24,200
Interest earned in year 3 (year 2 amount × 10%)	2,420
Investment plus accumulated interest (future value) in 3 years	$26,620

As **Exhibit A.1** illustrates, the future value of $20,000 invested for three years at 10% per year is $26,620. This can be calculated as $26,620 = \$20,000 \times 1.10 \times 1.10 \times 1.10 = \$20,000 \times (1.10)^3$. Similarly, if the interest rate is 8%, the future value is $25,194 = \$20,000 \times (1.08)^3$. That is, to determine the future value of an amount *n* periods in the future, we multiply the present value by one plus the interest rate, raised to the nth power:

$$\text{Future Value} = \text{Present Value} \times (1 + \text{interest rate})^n$$

The future value of any amount depends on two factors: time and rate. That is, how many periods (e.g., years or months) into the future do we want to project the future value, and what rate of return (or interest rate) do we use? There are two simple methods that we can use to obtain future values. The first method uses tables presented at the end of this Appendix. **Table A.1** presents the future value of a single amount. To use the table, move across the top of the table to choose the appropriate interest rate, and then move down the column to choose the number of periods in the future. **Table A.1** shows that future value increases as the number of periods and as the interest rate increase.

For example, if we move across the top to the 10% column and then down to period 3, **Table A.1** provides a value of 1.33100. This is the future value of $1 in three periods at 10% interest per period and is called the **future value factor**. If we want to calculate the future value of $20,000, we multiply the *future value factor* from **Table A.1** by $20,000:

Initial Amount	×	Future Value Factor	=	Future Value
$20,000	×	1.33100	=	$26,620

The future value can also be calculated using a financial calculator. Financial calculators require four inputs to calculate a fifth value, which is the solution. We illustrate the use of a calculator with the following graphic:

Calculator

N	I/Yr	PV	PMT	FV
3	10	20,000	0	**26,620**

On the financial calculator, N is the number of periods (3), I/Yr is the interest rate per period (10), PV is the current, or present, value ($20,000), PMT refers to a periodic payment (0 in our example), and FV is the future value. Because we are calculating the future value in this illustration, that value is highlighted in red as the solution.[2]

Whether we use the tables at the end of the Appendix or a financial calculator, it is important to recognize that these computations are based on an interest rate *per period*. Most interest rates are stated on an annual, or *per year*, basis. However, for compound interest calculations, a period need not be equal to a year.

---

[2] Actually, most calculators return a solution of −26,620. The calculator interprets the PV as an investment (cash out) and FV as the return (cash in). So, if PV is entered as a positive amount, then FV will come back negative, and vice versa.

Therefore, we must always be careful to adjust our interest rate *per year* to the appropriate interest rate *per period* and use the corresponding number of time periods in our calculations.

To illustrate, assume that our $20,000 investment paid 8% annual interest, *compounded quarterly*. Although the interest rate is quoted as 8% *per year*, the rate is actually 2% every three-month *period* (=8%/4). Hence, in three years, we would have twelve periods. To determine the future value, we would go down the 2% column in **Table A.1** to the 12-period row to get a future value factor of 1.26824.

$$\text{Initial Amount} \times \text{Future Value Factor} = \text{Future Value}$$
$$\$20{,}000 \times 1.26824 = \$25{,}365$$

Alternatively, using the financial calculator:

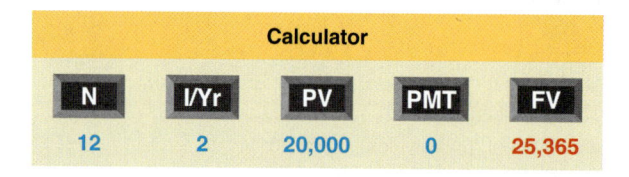

Calculator				
N	I/Yr	PV	PMT	FV
12	2	20,000	0	25,365

That is, the future value of $20,000 invested for three years at 8%, compounded quarterly, is $25,365.

PRESENT VALUE CONCEPTS

The concept of *present value* is the inverse of future value. Rather than determining how much an amount today is worth in the future, present value determines how much a future amount is worth today. The **present value** of an amount is the value *today* of a cash flow occurring at a future date given a rate of compound interest. As was the case with future value, present values depend on two factors: time and rate.

Present value is a particularly useful concept because it allows us to compare cash flows occurring at different times in the future. We can do this because we can calculate the value of each cash flow at a common point in time—today. For example, let's say we want to compare two investments. Investment A pays $15,000 in two years. Investment B pays $16,000 in three years. We cannot compare these two investments directly, because the payoffs occur in different amounts at different times in the future.[3] However, we can determine how much each payoff is worth today. If the appropriate interest rate is 8%, the present value of Investment A is $12,860 and the present value of Investment B is $12,701. (We demonstrate how to compute these amounts below.) Hence, Investment A is worth more today than Investment B. By determining the value of each cash payoff at the same point in time (today), we can easily compare the alternatives.

Present Value of a Single Amount

To determine the present value of a single cash payment occurring one period in the future, we simply divide the future cash flow by one plus the interest rate (the interest rate is also called the **discount rate**):[4]

$$\text{Present Value} = \frac{\text{Future Value}}{(1 + \text{discount rate})}$$

If the cash flow occurs *n* periods in the future, we rearrange the equation from the previous page and divide by one plus the discount rate raised to the nth power:

$$\text{Present Value} = \frac{\text{Future Value}}{(1 + \text{discount rate})^n}$$

---

[3] The reason that this comparison is difficult is that Investment A pays a return in two years, while Investment B doesn't pay a return until year 3. One way to understand this complexity is to ask: What will happen to the cash earned on Investment A during the third year? Or, alternatively, if we invest the return on Investment A for an additional year, how much would we earn after three years? By comparing present values, we are implicitly assuming that any cash payoffs from either investment could be reinvested at the rate of return used to calculate the present value.

[4] The term "discount rate" is often used when referring to present values. This is because when future cash flows are valued using present value calculations, the present value is always less than the future cash amount. Hence, we say that the future value is "discounted" to the present value using the "discount rate."

There are two simple methods for obtaining the present value of a single cash flow occurring at any date in the future. The first method relies on **Table A.2** at the end of this Appendix. We use **Table A.2** in the same way we used **Table A.1** to calculate future values. First, we choose the column representing the appropriate discount rate, and then we move down the column to select the number of periods in the future. The value in the table is the **present value factor**, which decreases as the number of periods and the interest rate increase. We then multiply the future amount by the *present value factor* to get the present value.

For example, consider Investment A. From **Table A.2**, the present value factor for 8% and two periods is 0.85734. The present value of $15,000 received in two years, discounted at 8% per year, is calculated as follows:

Future Amount	×	Present Value Factor	=	Present Value
$15,000	×	0.85734	=	$12,860

The present value can also be computed using a financial calculator. In this case, N=2; I/Yr = 8; PMT = 0; FV = 15,000 and PV is our answer (highlighted in red).

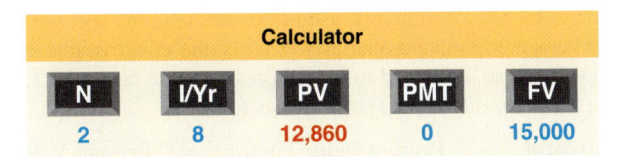

Calculator

N	I/Yr	PV	PMT	FV
2	8	12,860	0	15,000

By similar means we can compute the present value of Investment B. The present value factor for 8% and three periods is 0.79383. The present value of $16,000 received in three years, discounted at 8% per year is:

Future Amount	×	Present Value Factor	=	Present Value
$16,000	×	0.79383	=	$12,701

Or, using the financial calculator, we get the same answer as follows:

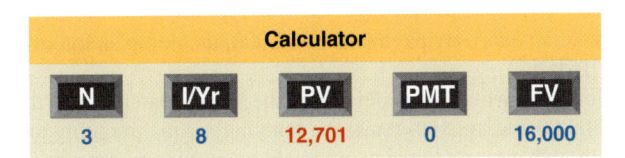

Calculator

N	I/Yr	PV	PMT	FV
3	8	12,701	0	16,000

Present Value of an Annuity

Sometimes, we are faced with determining the present value of a series of regular, equal payments, called an **annuity**. For example, let's say we have an investment that pays $7,000 each year for the next three years. We can calculate the present value of each payment and then sum the results to get the present value of the entire annuity. Assume the appropriate discount rate is 6% per year. From **Table A.2**, the present value factors for a 6% discount rate are 0.94340 for one period, 0.89000 for two periods, and 0.83962 for three periods. The calculation of the present value is presented in **Exhibit A.2** (rounded to the nearest whole dollar):

EXHIBIT A.2 Present Value of an Annuity of 3 Payments of $7,000 Discounted at 6%

	Future Payment	×	Present Value Factor	=	Present Value
1	$7,000		0.94340		6,604
2	7,000		0.89000		6,230
3	7,000		0.83962		5,877
					$18,711

While this method of computing the present value of an annuity is accurate, it can be tedious for annuities with many cash payments. **Table A.3** at the end of this Appendix presents present value factors for annuities of various lengths. This table is used in the same way as **Table A.2**: first we choose the column reflecting our discount rate, and then we choose the row representing the number of payments. From **Table A.3**, the present value factor for an annuity of three payments discounted at 6% is 2.67301. To calculate the present value of an annuity, we multiply the periodic payment by the present value factor:

Payment	×	Present Value Factor	=	Present Value
$7,000	×	2.67301	=	$18,711

Or alternatively, using a financial calculator, we enter N=3, I/Yr=6, PMT=7,000, FV=0, and the solution is the PV, highlighted in red:

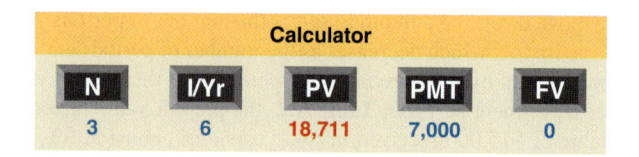

Calculator
N	I/Yr	PV	PMT	FV
3	6	18,711	7,000	0

Installment Loans

One useful application of the present value of an annuity is to value an *installment loan*. An **installment loan** is a loan that requires a series of equal payments, or installments, each of which includes interest and some of the original principal. Assume that we take out a bank loan requiring 12 quarterly payments of $2,000 and an annual interest rate of 8%. When working with annuities, a period is the time between payments, and the number of payments is the number of periods we use in our calculations. Because the payments are made quarterly, the 8% annual rate is compounded quarterly. That is, the effective interest rate is 2% per quarter. To calculate the loan amount, we use **Table A.3** to get the present value factor for 12 payments discounted at 2%, and then multiply the factor by our $2,000 payment, as follows:

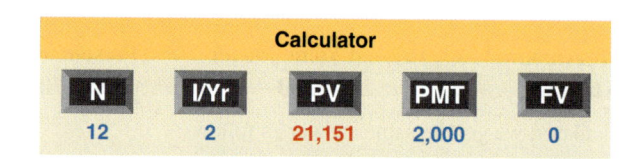

Payment	×	Present Value Factor	=	Present Value
$2,000	×	10.57534	=	$21,151

Calculator
N	I/Yr	PV	PMT	FV
12	2	21,151	2,000	0

That is, if we agreed to make 12 quarterly payments of $2,000, including an interest charge of 2% per quarter, we could borrow $21,151.

A more common calculation would be to determine the loan payment given the amount borrowed. For example, if we borrow $30,000 and agree to repay the loan in 24 equal monthly payments at a 12% annual interest rate (1% per month), what monthly payment would we need to make to repay the loan plus interest? To compute the payment, we divide the present value (the loan amount) by the present value factor from **Table A.3** (1%, 24 periods) as follows:

Present Value	÷	Present Value Factor	=	Payment
$30,000	÷	21.24339	=	$1,412.20

Using a financial calculator, we can calculate the payment (PMT) directly, given the other inputs:

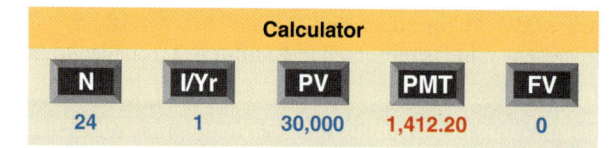

Calculator
N	I/Yr	PV	PMT	FV
24	1	30,000	1,412.20	0

Bond Valuation

From Chapter 9, we know that a typical corporate bond has a face value of $1,000 and pays periodic interest payments every six months based on the stated (or coupon) interest rate. That is, the face value and the stated rate of a bond allow us to lay out the cash flows that will be paid to the bondholder. We also know that bonds are valued using the market interest rate, which may be different from the stated rate.

Bonds represent a combination of an annuity of the periodic interest payments and a single future payment of the face value, or principal payment, sometimes called a **balloon payment**. In order to value a bond, we must calculate the present value of each of these two components. Let's assume that we wish to value a $1,000, 5-year, 7% bond that pays a semi-annual coupon payment. The face value is $1,000, and the semi-annual payment is $35 (= $1,000 × 7%/2). Let's assume a market interest rate (yield) of 8% (which is 4% every six months). The bond is valued as the sum of two parts:

1. Use **Table A.2** to compute the value of the principal (balloon) payment.
2. Use **Table A.3** to compute the value of the annuity of interest (coupon) payments.

This calculation is illustrated in **Exhibit A.3**:

EXHIBIT A.3 Calculating a Bond Value Using Present Value Tables (4%, 10 periods)

	Cash Flow	×	Present Value Factor	=	Present Value
Face value: 1 payment of $1,000 at the end of 5 years (Table A.2—4%, 10 periods)	$1,000	×	0.67556	=	$675.56
Semi-annual coupon payments: 10-payment annuity of $35 every six months (Table A.3—4%, 10 periods)	$35	×	8.11090	=	283.88
					$959.44

The bond value can also be calculated using a financial calculator, with the following inputs: N=10; I/Yr=4; PMT=35; FV=1,000. The solution is the PV:

Calculator

N	I/Yr	PV	PMT	FV
10	4	959.45	35	1,000

The calculator automatically adds the present value of the annuity (10 payments of $35) to the present value of the single amount ($1,000 principal value) to get the bond value. That is, the market is willing to invest $959.45 in a $1,000, 5-year, 7% bond that pays interest semi-annually, and this amount is what would be received in proceeds from issuing the bond. The difference between $1,000 and $959.45 can be attributed to the difference between the 7% coupon rate of interest and the 8% required by investors.

Calculating Bond Yields

Sometimes we know the future cash payments and the present value of those payments, but not the discount rate used to compute the present value. This would be useful, for example, if we knew the price of a bond but wanted to determine the yield.

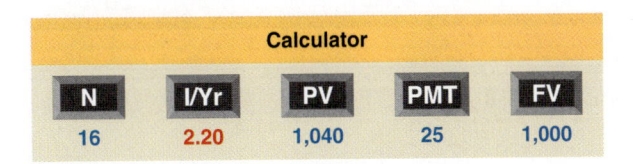

To illustrate the calculation of a bond yield, assume that we have a $1,000, 8-year, 5% bond that is currently priced at 104 (104% of par value or $1,040). The semiannual interest payment is $25 (= $1,000 × 5%/2), and the principal amount of $1,000 is due in 8 years (16 semiannual periods). We input the following values: N=16; PV=1,040; PMT=25; FV=1,000. The solution is returned by pressing the I/Yr button:

Calculator

N	I/Yr	PV	PMT	FV
16	2.20	1,040	25	1,000

In this case, the calculator returns a solution of 2.20%. This is the interest rate *per period* that discounts the future payments on the bond to the present value of $1,040. Because each period is six months, we must double this rate to get the bond yield (or market rate of interest), which is always quoted on an annual basis. Thus, the yield on this bond is 4.4% (= 2.2% × 2).[5]

Future Value of Annuities

On occasion, we may have a future funding target that will be met by making period payments. For instance, we may wish to accumulate a down payment for a residence or accumulate a retirement balance to draw upon in future years. For this analysis, we must examine the future value created by an annuity, i.e., a series of payments.

Suppose we wish to accumulate a down payment by making quarterly payments into an account that earns 4% per year (1% per quarter). Payments of $2,000 would be made at the beginning of each quarter and

---

[5] Technically, in order to obtain the result illustrated here, the amounts for PMT and FV must be entered with the same sign, but the PV amount must be entered with the opposite sign. For example, if we enter PV = −1,040, PMT = 25 and FV = 1,000, we would get the result above.

would continue for five years. How much would accumulate over the five years? The future value of each payment can be determined using **Table A.1**, but **Table A.4** accumulates the amounts in a convenient format. An annuity of $2,000 per quarter for 20 quarters at 1% per period would produce a future value of:

Payment	×	Future Value Factor	=	Future Value
$2,000	×	22.2392	=	$44,478.40

This analysis would also allow for testing the sensitivity of the amount to various factors. For instance, making payments for 6 years would increase the balance to $54,486.40. Investing in an account that provided 2% interest per quarter would accumulate $49,566.60 after five years.

USING EXCEL TO COMPUTE TIME-VALUE

Spreadsheet software, such as Microsoft Excel, is extremely useful for performing a variety of time-value calculations. In this section, we illustrate a few of the features of Excel.

Future Value Calculations

Calculating future value in Excel is straightforward by using the formula for future value or using the function wizard feature. Assume we wish to compute the future value of $12,000 invested today at 6% interest for four years. The formula for this calculation is:

$$=12000*1.06\wedge4$$

Excel returns the value 15149.72. An alternative method of making this calculation is by using the function wizard. The function wizard is accessed by clicking on the *fx* icon in the formula bar at the top of the spreadsheet.

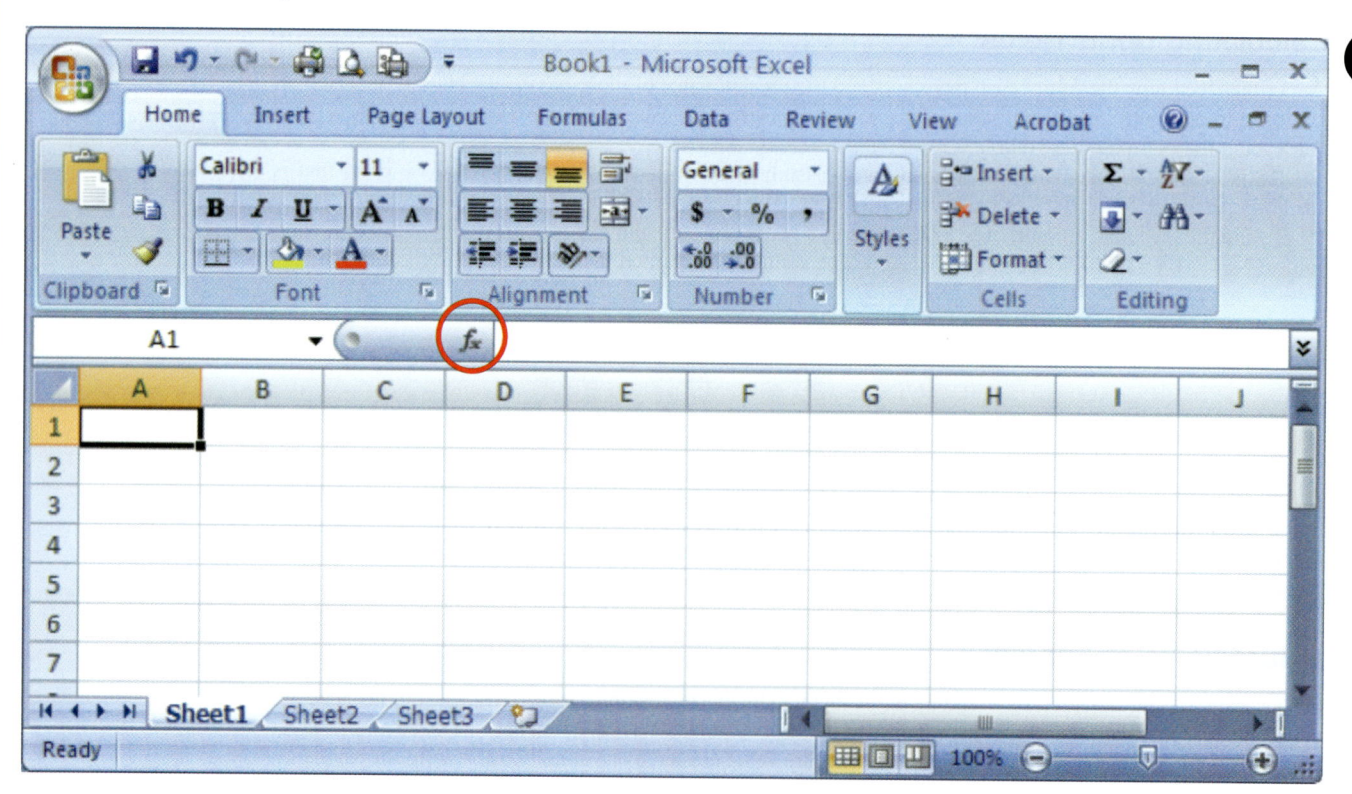

Clicking on the *fx* icon opens a dialog box that offers a variety of built-in functions. The dialog box appears as follows:

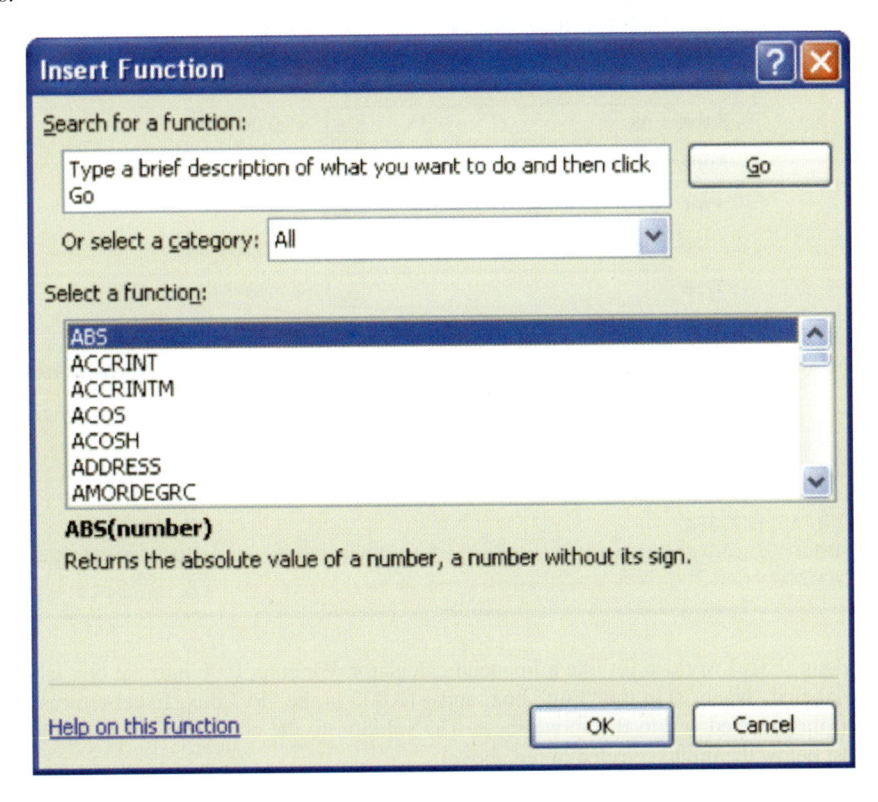

The user can scroll through the long list of built-in Excel functions or customize the search by selecting a category of functions. In the screen shot below, the category of functions described as "Financial" is selected. Scrolling through the list, we select the FV function (for future value).

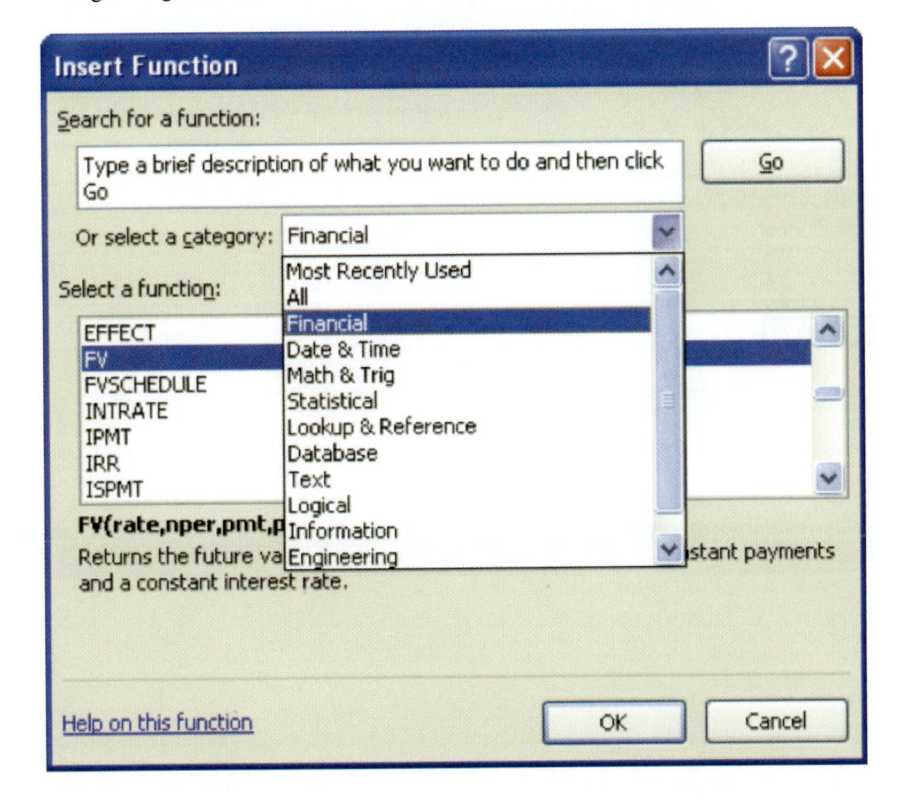

Once the FV function is selected, a new dialog box appears:

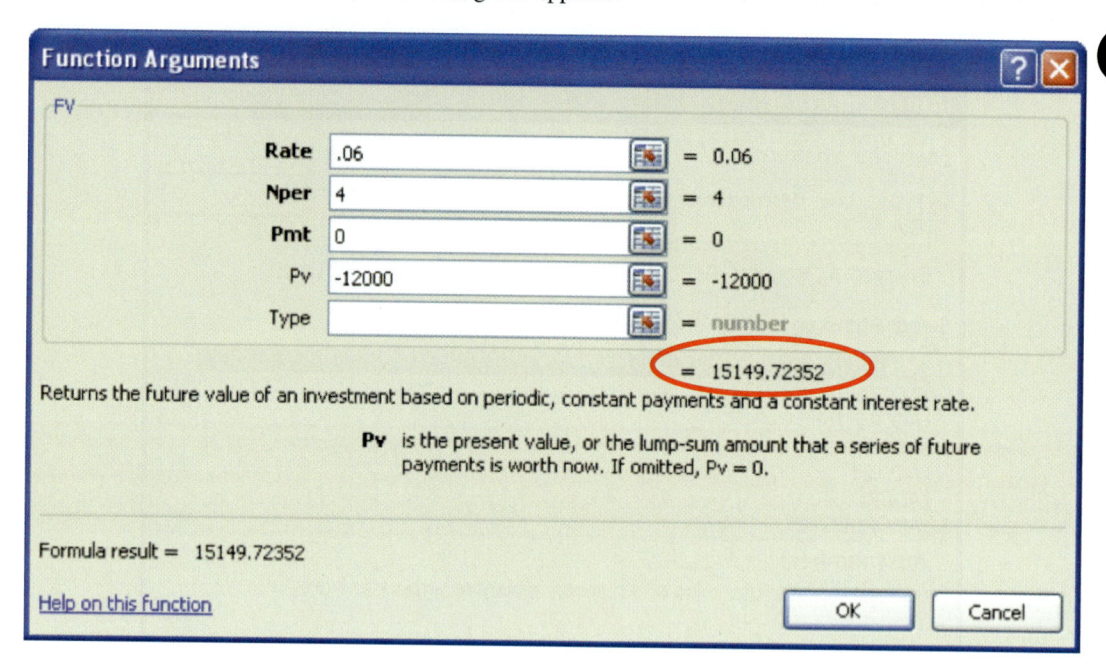

Function Arguments

FV

Rate .06 = 0.06
Nper 4 = 4
Pmt 0 = 0
Pv -12000 = -12000
Type = number

= 15149.72352

Returns the future value of an investment based on periodic, constant payments and a constant interest rate.

Pv is the present value, or the lump-sum amount that a series of future payments is worth now. If omitted, Pv = 0.

Formula result = 15149.72352

Help on this function   OK   Cancel

At this point, Excel works a lot like a financial calculator. We enter 0.06 into the box labeled "Rate," 4 in the box labeled "Nper," 0 in the "Pmt" box, and −12,000 in the "Pv" box. Excel returns the value of $15,149.72 in the selected cell in the spreadsheet. The solution to the calculation is also presented in the dialog box just below the inputs (circled in red above).

One advantage of Excel is that it allows the user to enter cell locations as function arguments in the dialog box. This can be useful if we wish to gauge the impact of changing an argument. For instance, we could enter the following in a spreadsheet:

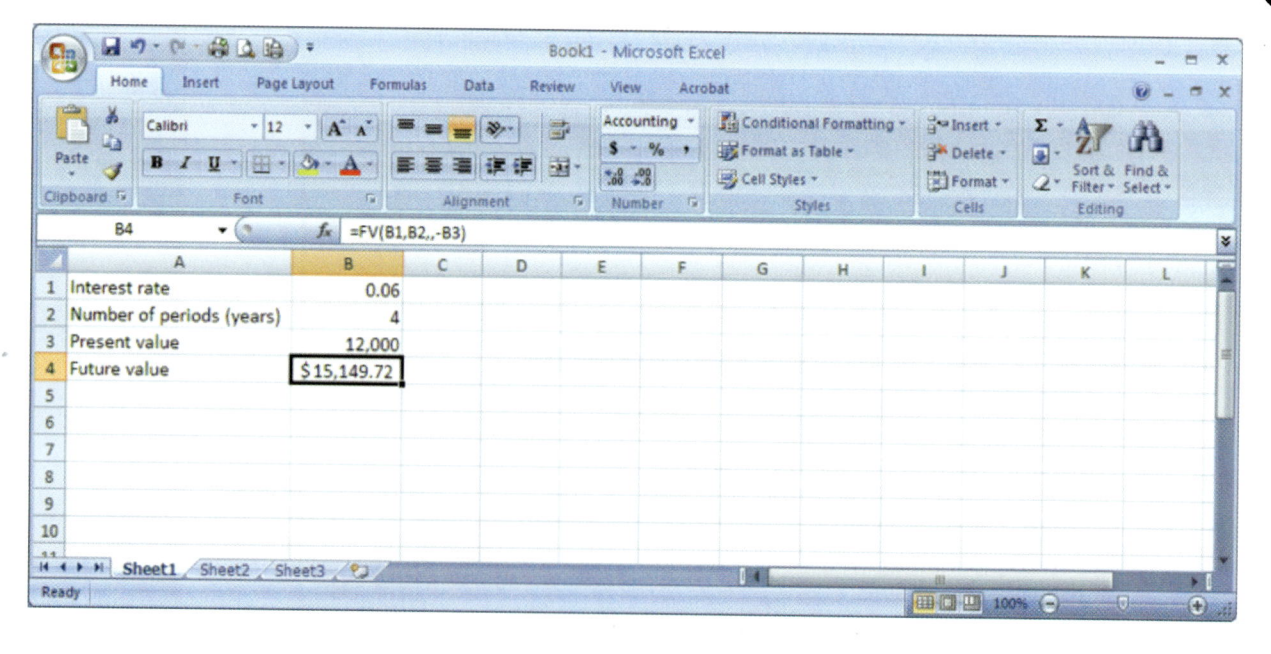

B4: =FV(B1,B2,,-B3)

	A	B
1	Interest rate	0.06
2	Number of periods (years)	4
3	Present value	12,000
4	Future value	$15,149.72

The amount presented as the "Future value" is actually returned by the dialog box below:

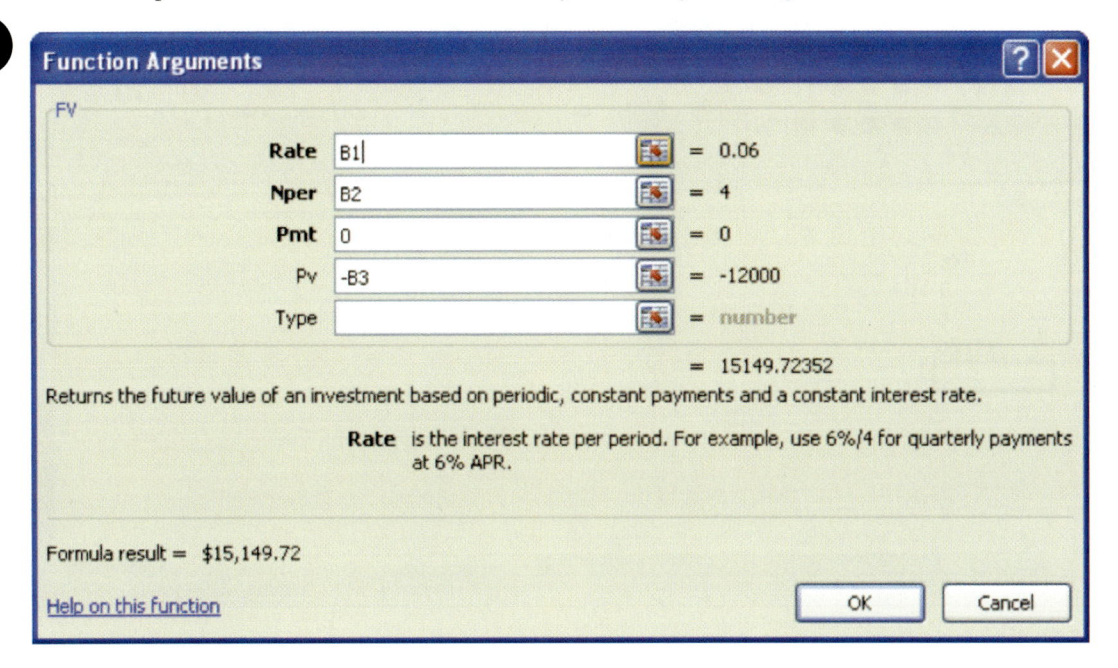

Function Arguments

FV
- Rate: B1 = 0.06
- Nper: B2 = 4
- Pmt: 0 = 0
- Pv: -B3 = -12000
- Type: = number

= 15149.72352

Returns the future value of an investment based on periodic, constant payments and a constant interest rate.

Rate is the interest rate per period. For example, use 6%/4 for quarterly payments at 6% APR.

Formula result = $15,149.72

Help on this function   OK   Cancel

When we enter cell locations (e.g., "B1") in the boxes for function arguments, the function wizard uses the value in that cell as the argument. The benefit of this is that we can now change an argument and recalculate the future value without revisiting the function wizard dialog box. For example, let's say we wish to determine what the future value of our investment would be if we held our investment for five years instead of four years. We simply replace the "4" in cell B2 with a "5" as follows:

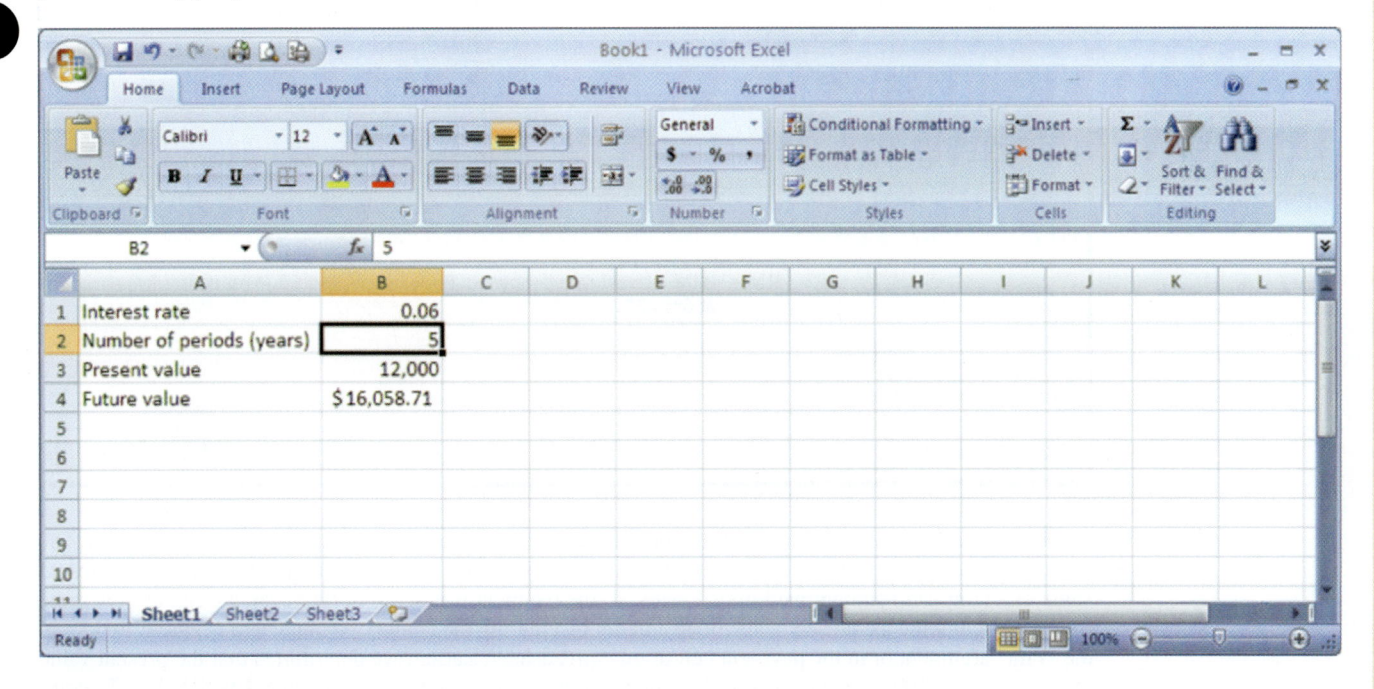

	A	B
1	Interest rate	0.06
2	Number of periods (years)	5
3	Present value	12,000
4	Future value	$16,058.71

Excel automatically returns the value of $16,058.71 as the future value (cell B4).

Present Value Calculations

Computing present value is as straightforward as future value. The function to use is "PV" for present value. Let's assume we wish to calculate the present value of $15,000 that we expect to receive in two years discounted at 8% per year. Earlier, we determined that the present value is $12,860. To make this calculation using Excel, we enter each of the arguments in the spreadsheet as follows:

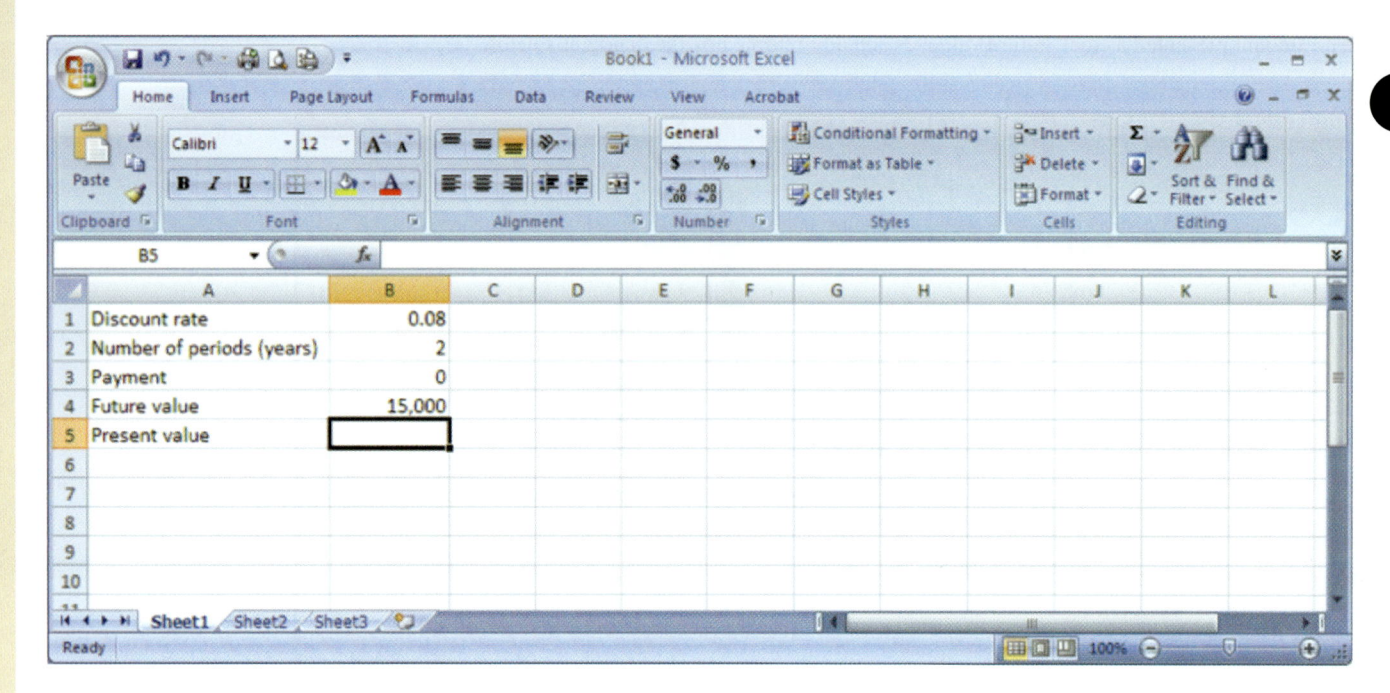

We then use the function wizard to access the "PV" function:

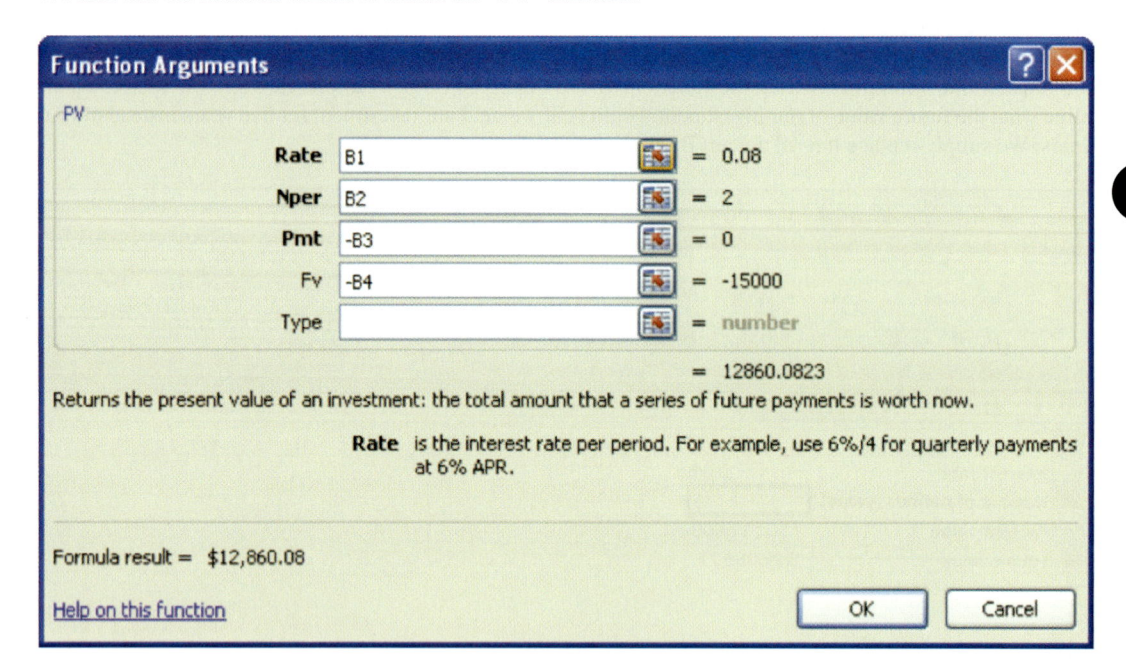

The PV function is similar to the FV function. The amount returned is the present value of $12,860.08. The "Pmt" argument in the PV function is used for annuity payments. In this example, we wanted the present value of a lump-sum amount paid in two years, so the payment was set to 0. However, we can use the same function to compute the present value of an annuity by entering the annuity payment as a negative amount in the "Pmt" argument or in the payment cell of our spreadsheet. Earlier, we determined that the present value of a series of $7,000 payments received annually for three years and discounted at 6% is $18,711. To compute this amount using Excel, we list the payment (Pmt) as 7,000 and the future value (FV) as 0:

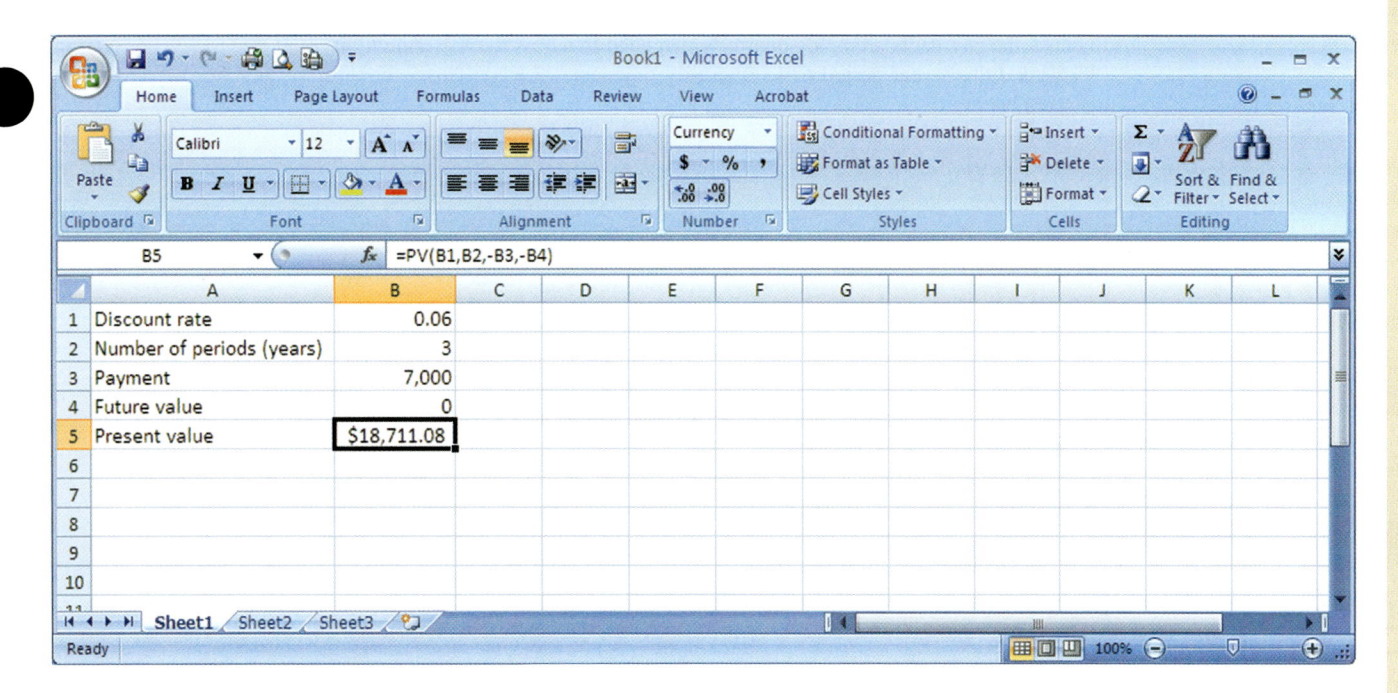

	A	B
1	Discount rate	0.06
2	Number of periods (years)	3
3	Payment	7,000
4	Future value	0
5	Present value	$18,711.08

B5: =PV(B1,B2,-B3,-B4)

Similarly, our installment loan that requires 12 quarterly payments of $2,000 at 8% interest per year (2% per quarter) would have a present value of $21,150.68, which is computed as follows:

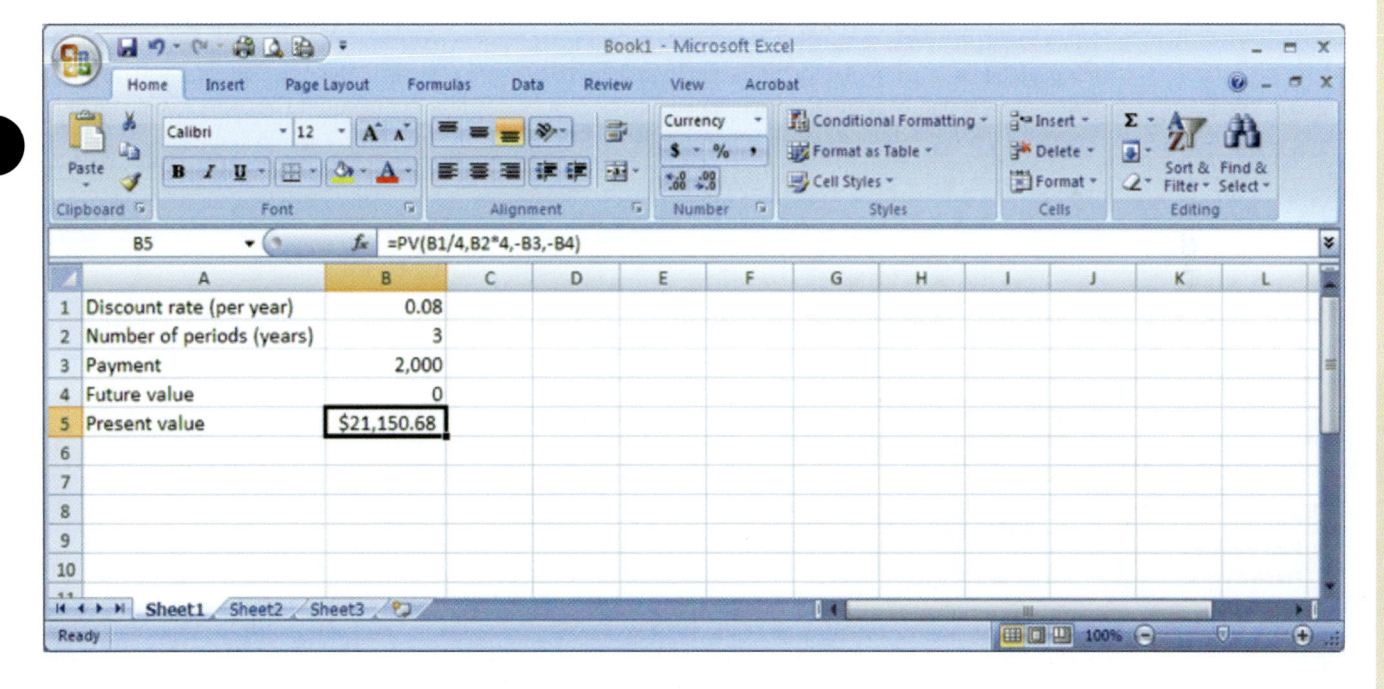

	A	B
1	Discount rate (per year)	0.08
2	Number of periods (years)	3
3	Payment	2,000
4	Future value	0
5	Present value	$21,150.68

B5: =PV(B1/4,B2*4,-B3,-B4)

Because the payments are made quarterly, we need to adjust the 8% annual discount rate to 2% per quarter (8%/4) and the 3-year period to 12 quarterly payments (3 × 4). This is done in the function wizard, as illustrated below:

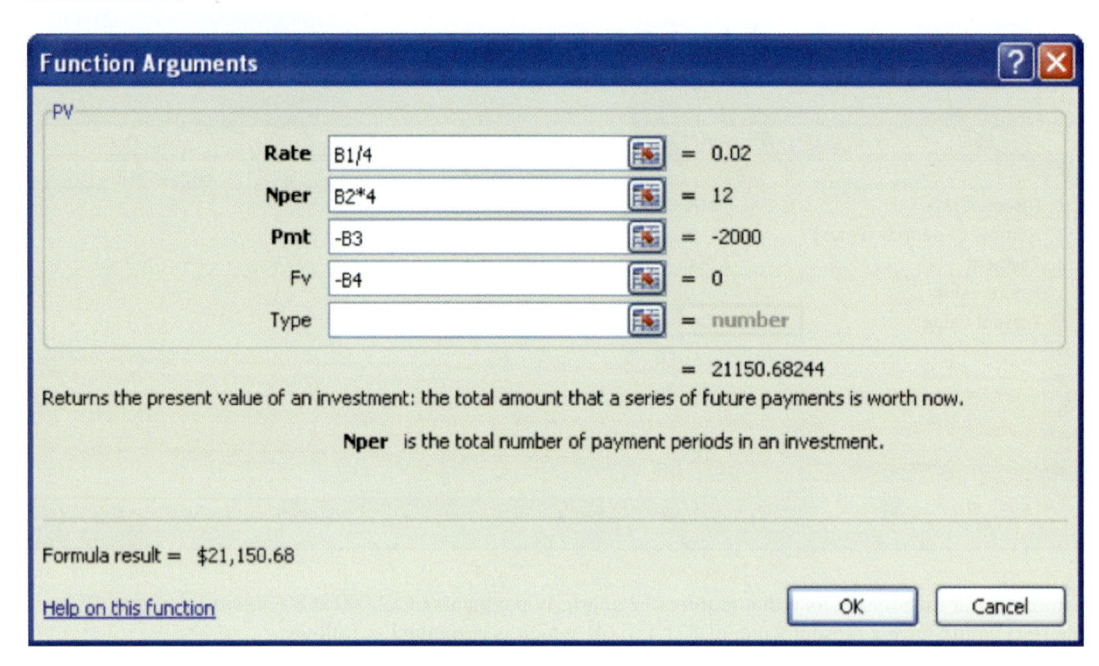

Function Arguments

PV

Rate	B1/4	= 0.02
Nper	B2*4	= 12
Pmt	-B3	= -2000
Fv	-B4	= 0
Type		= number

= 21150.68244

Returns the present value of an investment: the total amount that a series of future payments is worth now.

Nper is the total number of payment periods in an investment.

Formula result = $21,150.68

Help on this function

Another function that is very useful for installment loans is the "PMT" function. This function calculates the payment required to pay off an installment loan. Earlier, we calculated the payment on a $30,000 loan requiring 24 monthly payments at an annual interest rate of 12% (1% per month) to be $1,412.20 per month. Using the PMT function in Excel, we get the same result:

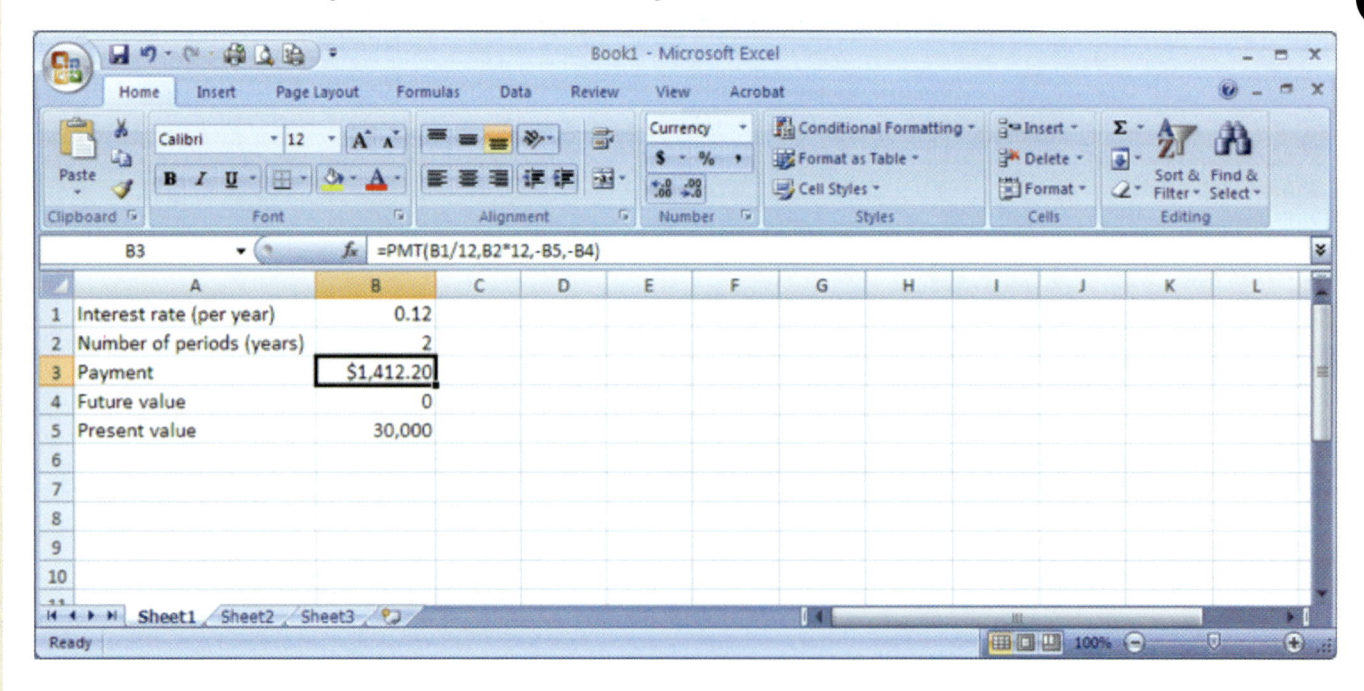

B3   fx =PMT(B1/12,B2*12,-B5,-B4)

	A	B
1	Interest rate (per year)	0.12
2	Number of periods (years)	2
3	Payment	$1,412.20
4	Future value	0
5	Present value	30,000

Here we need to divide the annual interest rate by 12 and multiply the number of years by 12 in order to allow for monthly compounding.

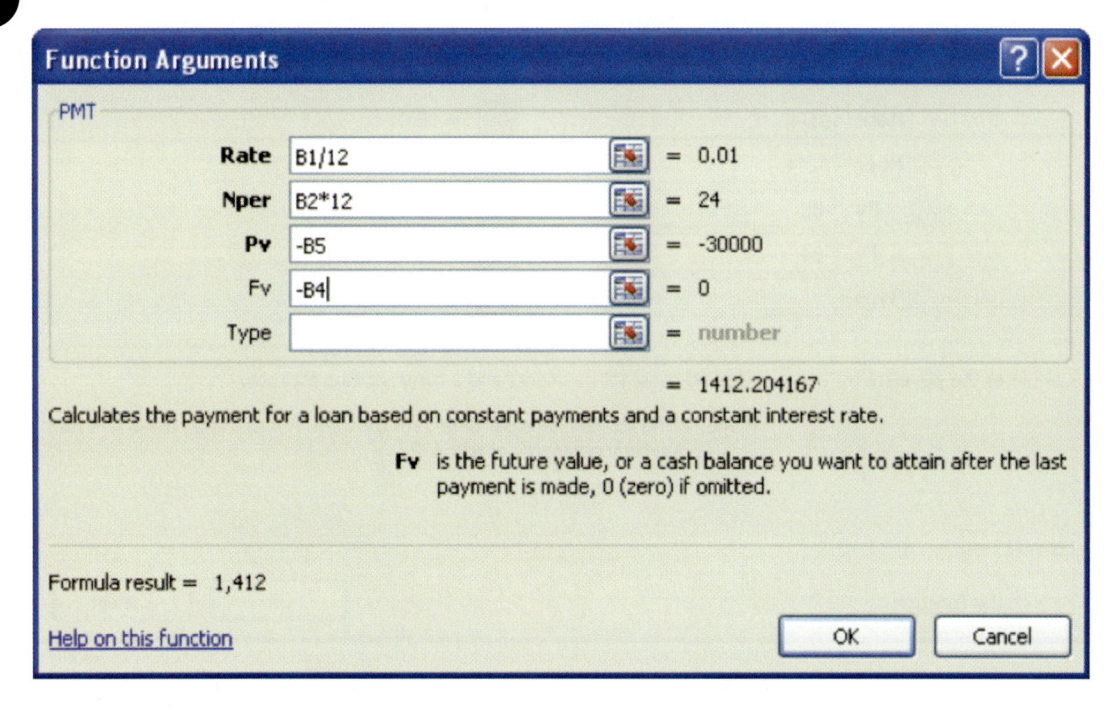

Function Arguments

PMT

- Rate: B1/12 = 0.01
- Nper: B2*12 = 24
- Pv: -B5 = -30000
- Fv: -B4 = 0
- Type: = number

= 1412.204167

Calculates the payment for a loan based on constant payments and a constant interest rate.

Fv is the future value, or a cash balance you want to attain after the last payment is made, 0 (zero) if omitted.

Formula result = 1,412

Help on this function

Excel is very useful for setting up loan amortization tables. These tables lay out the loan payments and calculate the interest and principal included in each payment. To illustrate, assume we borrow $5,000 at 4% annual interest and agree to repay the loan in 8 quarterly payments (four payments per year for two years). The quarterly payment is $653.45, calculated as follows:

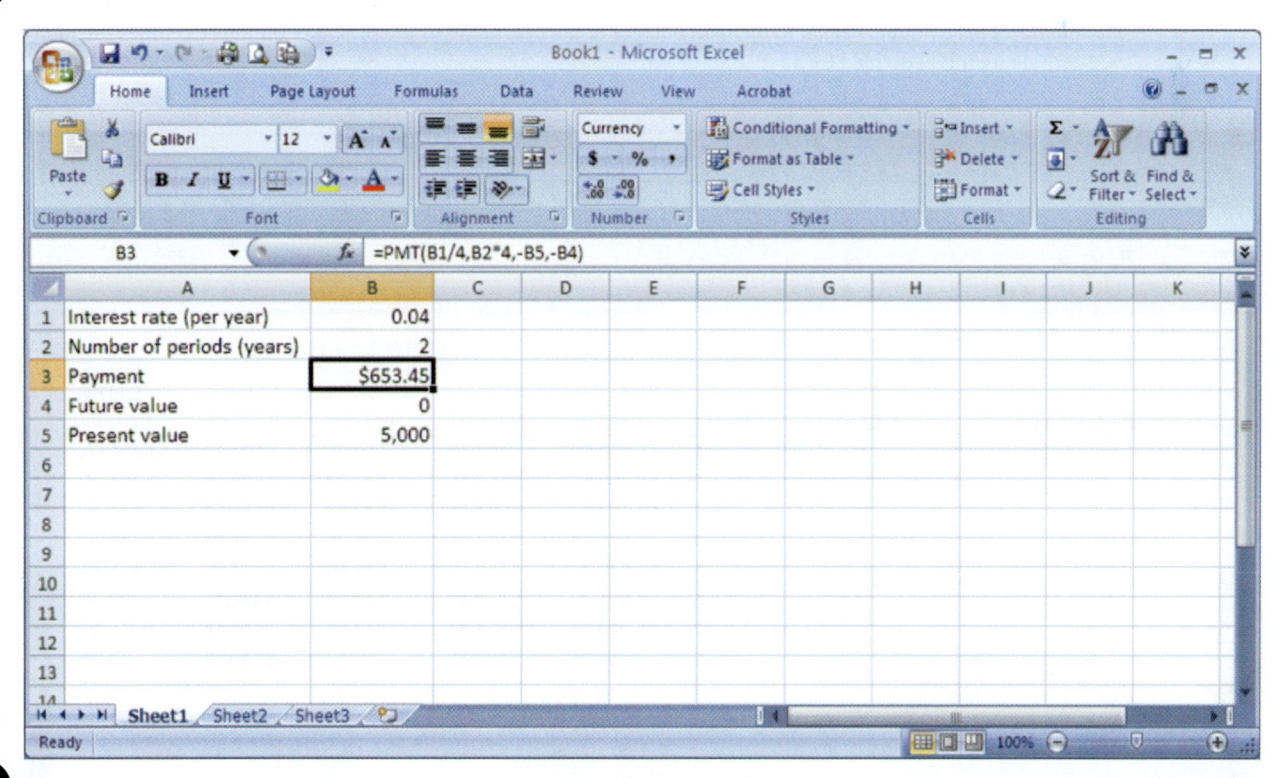

B3 =PMT(B1/4,B2*4,-B5,-B4)

	A	B
1	Interest rate (per year)	0.04
2	Number of periods (years)	2
3	Payment	$653.45
4	Future value	0
5	Present value	5,000

The function box appears as follows:

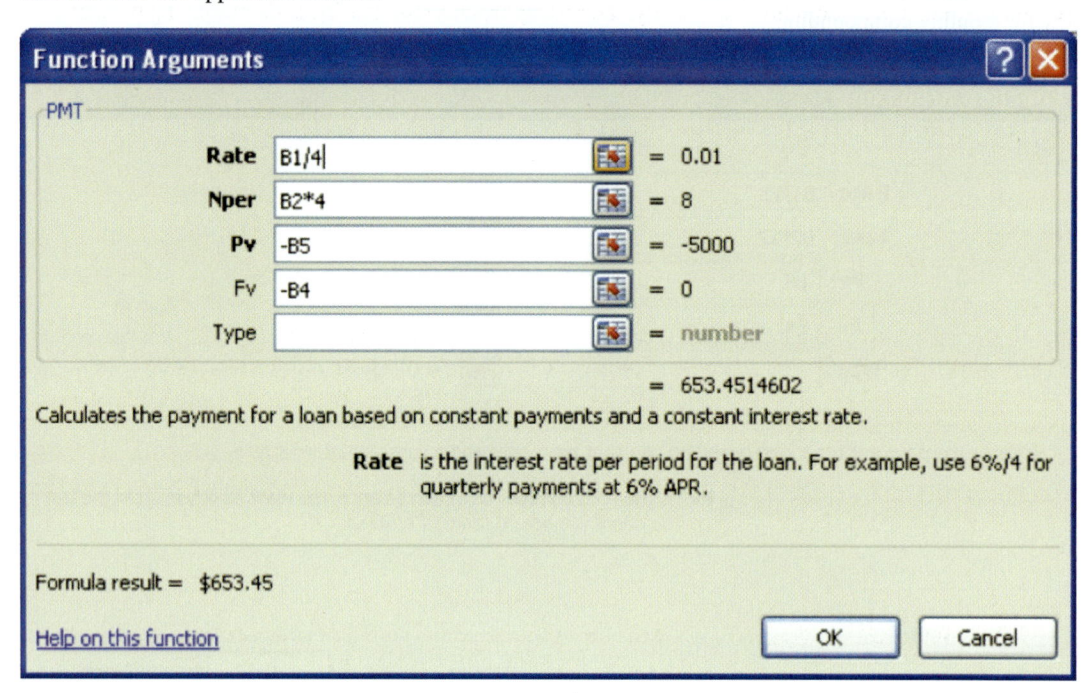

Function Arguments

PMT

Rate	B1/4	=	0.01
Nper	B2*4	=	8
Pv	-B5	=	-5000
Fv	-B4	=	0
Type		=	number

= 653.4514602

Calculates the payment for a loan based on constant payments and a constant interest rate.

Rate is the interest rate per period for the loan. For example, use 6%/4 for quarterly payments at 6% APR.

Formula result = $653.45

Help on this function [OK] [Cancel]

The loan amortization table can be set up on the same worksheet or in a separate sheet linked to the payment calculation. Here we use the same worksheet.

The first column [D] lists the period (1 through 8). In the second column [E], we list the loan balance at the beginning of each period. For the first period, the beginning balance is the loan amount of $5,000. Thereafter, the beginning balance is set equal to the ending balance from the previous period, which is in column [I]. Column [F] lists the quarterly payment of $653.45. In column [G], we compute the interest each quarter. This amount is equal to the loan balance at the beginning of the period (Column [E]) times the interest rate (cell B1) divided by 4.

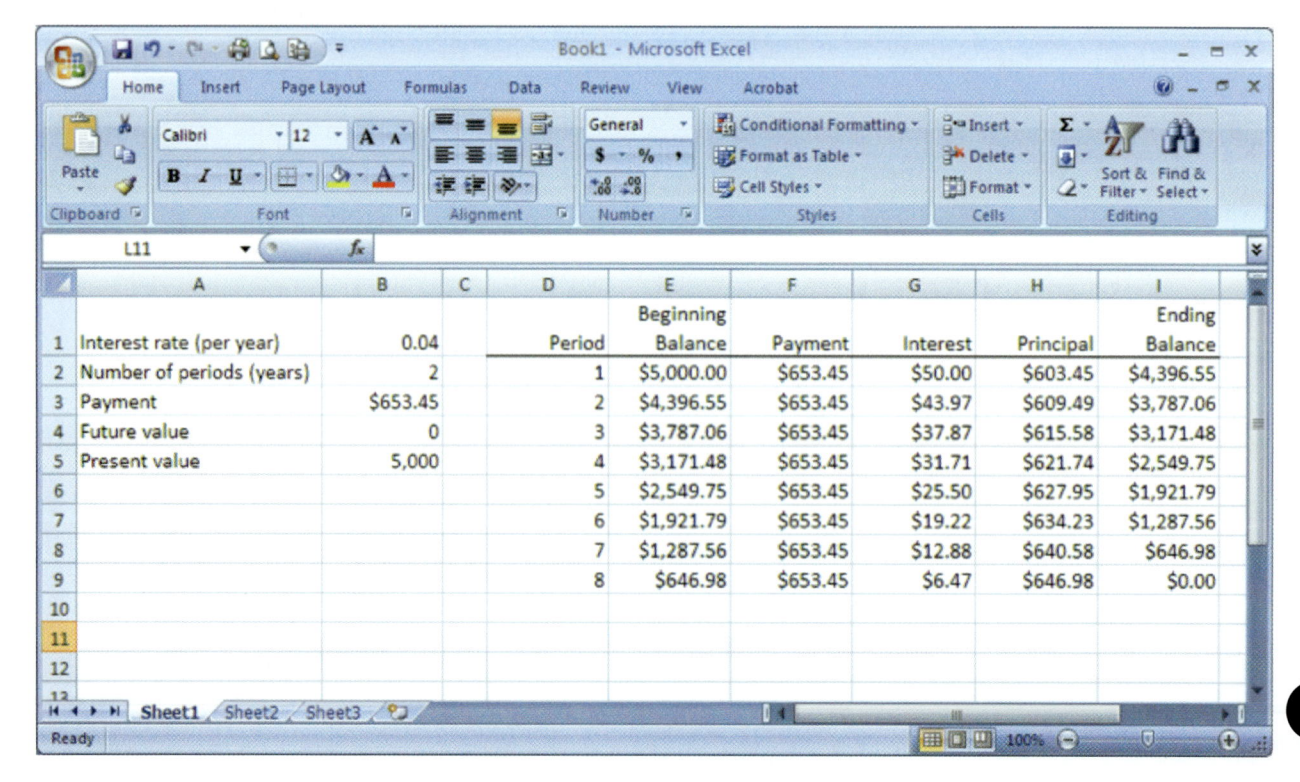

	A	B	D	E	F	G	H	I
				Beginning				Ending
1	Interest rate (per year)	0.04	Period	Balance	Payment	Interest	Principal	Balance
2	Number of periods (years)	2	1	$5,000.00	$653.45	$50.00	$603.45	$4,396.55
3	Payment	$653.45	2	$4,396.55	$653.45	$43.97	$609.49	$3,787.06
4	Future value	0	3	$3,787.06	$653.45	$37.87	$615.58	$3,171.48
5	Present value	5,000	4	$3,171.48	$653.45	$31.71	$621.74	$2,549.75
6			5	$2,549.75	$653.45	$25.50	$627.95	$1,921.79
7			6	$1,921.79	$653.45	$19.22	$634.23	$1,287.56
8			7	$1,287.56	$653.45	$12.88	$640.58	$646.98
9			8	$646.98	$653.45	$6.47	$646.98	$0.00

In column [H] we compute the principal component of each payment. This amount is the payment (column [F]) minus the interest (column [G]). Finally, the ending balance (column [I]) is the beginning balance (column [E]) minus the principal (column [H]). Note that the ending balance in period 8 is $0. (The loan has been completely paid off.)

Loan amortization tables are especially useful for accountants because the table computes the amounts we enter for each payment. To illustrate, to record the original $5,000 loan, we make the following journal entry:

Cash (+A)...	5,000.00	
Loan payable (+L)		5,000.00

Now, each period, we make a loan payment of $653.45, and that payment is part interest expense and part loan principal. To determine the split between interest and principal, we consult the loan amortization table. For instance, in period 1, the payment is split as $50.00 of interest and $603.45 of principal. To record this payment, we would make the following journal entry:

Interest expense (+E, −SE)	50.00	
Loan payable (−L)...................................	603.45	
Cash (−A)		653.45

Finally, Excel allows us to easily compute the present value of a series of irregular cash flows. To do this we use the NPV function. (NPV stands for *Net Present Value*.) To compute NPV we need a series of cash flows at regular time intervals, such as one payment per year. If we skip a period, we must enter a 0 for that period. The cash flows can be a mixture of positive and negative cash flows (for instance, receipts and payments). In the following spreadsheet, we present a series of seven cash flows and calculate the present value of these payments discounted at 5% using the NPV function.

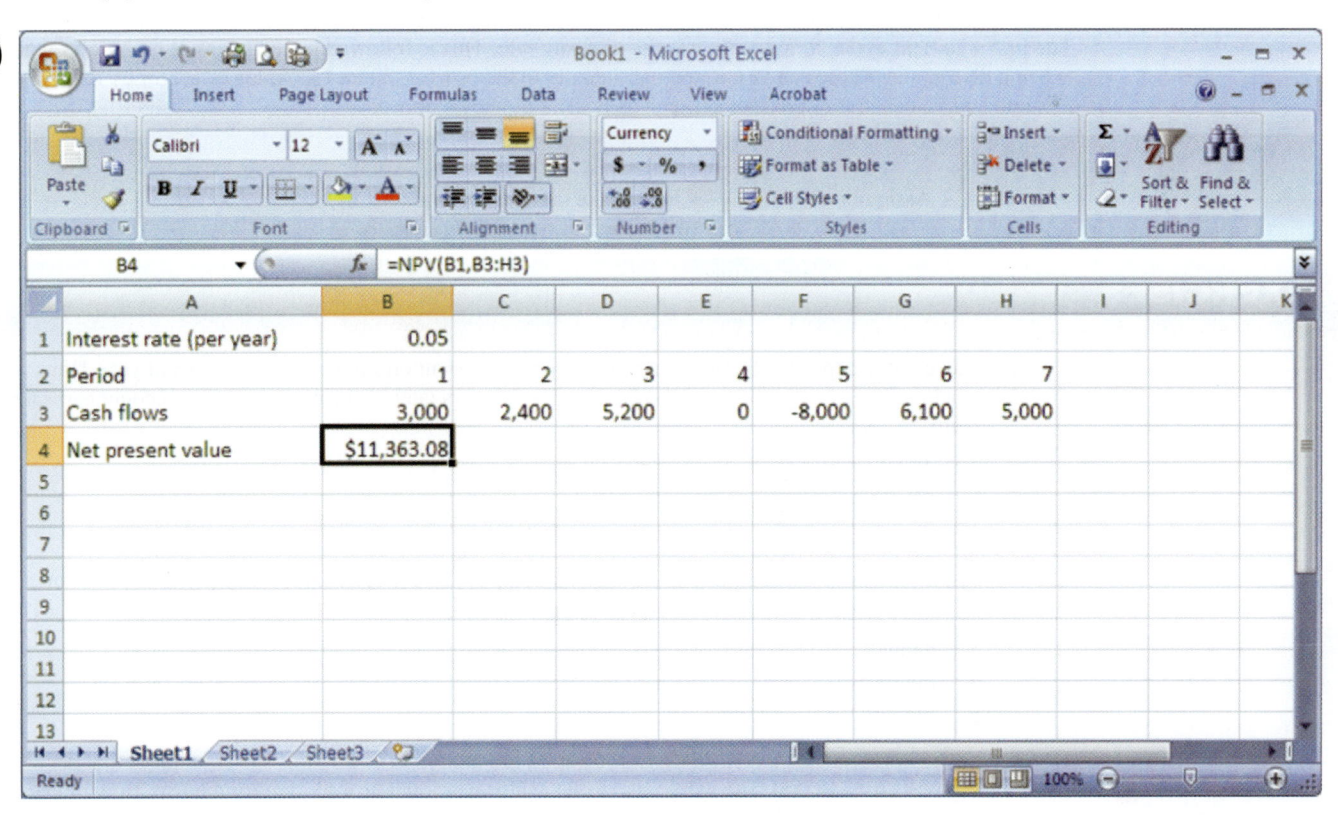

	A	B	C	D	E	F	G	H
1	Interest rate (per year)	0.05						
2	Period	1	2	3	4	5	6	7
3	Cash flows	3,000	2,400	5,200	0	-8,000	6,100	5,000
4	Net present value	$11,363.08						

Formula in B4: =NPV(B1,B3:H3)

The spreadsheet shows a net present value of $11,363.08. The function wizard dialog box for the NPV function is presented below:

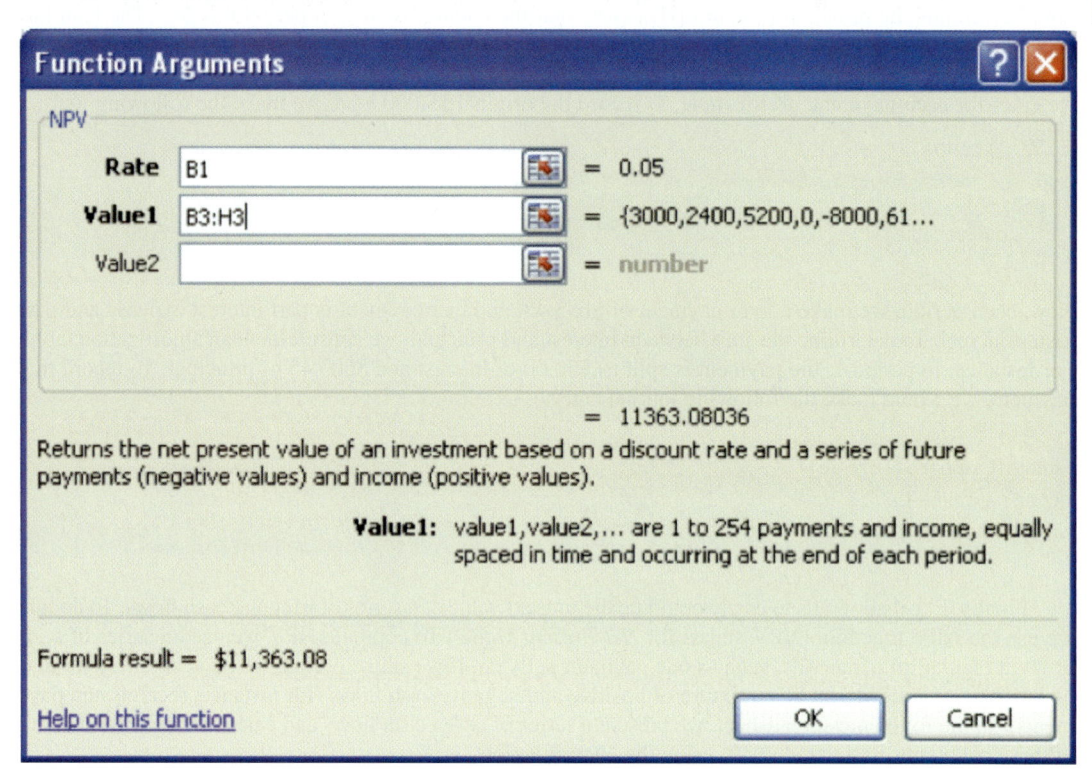

The first argument in the NPV function is the discount rate. This is followed by the series of cash flows that is being discounted. These can be entered individually in the box for "Value1," "Value2," etc. or by referring to a range of values in the spreadsheet, such as B3:H3, as shown above.

Assignments with the MBC logo in the margin are available in myBusinessCourse. See the Preface of the book for details.

EXERCISES

EA-1. Dawn Riley deposited $6,000 in a money market account on January 2 of the current year. How much will her savings be worth on January 2, six years later, if the money market account earns a return of

 a. 4%?
 b. 6%?
 c. 8%?

EA-2. Jason Shields invested $4,800 in an account that pays a 12% return. How much will the account be worth in four years if the interest is compounded

 a. annually?
 b. quarterly?
 c. monthly?

EA-3. Leslie Porter is planning a trip to Europe upon graduation in two years. She anticipates that her trip will cost $18,000. She would like to set aside an amount now to save for the trip. How much should she set aside if her savings earns 4% interest compounded quarterly?

EA-4. Matt Wilson has an investment opportunity that promises to pay him $30,000 in four years. He could earn 6% if he invested his money elsewhere. What is the maximum amount that he should be willing to invest in this opportunity?

EA-5. Robert Smith purchased a used car for $16,000. To pay for his purchase, he borrowed $14,000 from a local bank at 12%. The loan requires that Robert repay the loan by making 36 monthly payments. How much will Robert have to pay each month to repay the loan?

EA-6. Refer to Exercise EA-5. How much interest will Robert Smith pay as part of his first monthly payment?

EA-7. Sandy Nguyen just graduated from college and has $50,000 in student loans. The loans bear interest at a rate of 8% and require quarterly payments.

    a. What amount should Sandy pay each quarter if she wishes to pay off her student loans in six years?

    b. Sandy can only afford to pay $1,800 per quarter. How long will it take Sandy to repay these loans?

EA-8. In 2022, Cart Inc. adopted a plan to accumulate funds for environmental remediation beginning July 2, 2027 at an estimated cost of $30 million. Cart plans to make five equal annual payments into a fund earning 6% interest compounded annually. The first deposit is scheduled for July 1, 2022. Determine the amount of the required annual deposit.

EA-9. On May 1, 2022, Ott, Inc., sold merchandise to Fox Inc. Fox signed a noninterest bearing note requiring payment of $50,000 annually for 7 years. The first payment is due May 1, 2023. The prevailing rate for similar notes on that date is 9%. What amount should Ott, Inc., report as revenue in 2022 and 2023?

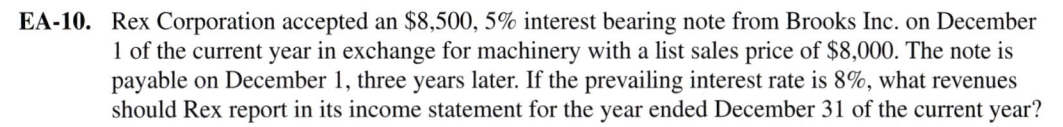

EA-10. Rex Corporation accepted an $8,500, 5% interest bearing note from Brooks Inc. on December 1 of the current year in exchange for machinery with a list sales price of $8,000. The note is payable on December 1, three years later. If the prevailing interest rate is 8%, what revenues should Rex report in its income statement for the year ended December 31 of the current year?

EA-11. Rye Company is considering purchasing a new machine with a useful life of ten years, at which time its salvage value is estimated to be $60,000. Management estimates a net increase in operating cash inflow due to the new machine at $240,000 per year. What is the maximum amount the company should be willing to pay for the machine if the relevant cost of capital associated with this type of investment is 12%?

EA-12. Debra Wilcox won $10 million in the California lottery. She must choose how she wants the prize to be paid to her. First, Debra can elect to receive 26 annual payments, with the first payment due immediately. Second, she can elect to receive a single payment immediately for the entire amount. However, if she elects the single payment option, the winning prize is reduced to one-half the winnings ($5 million). Which option should Debra choose if her cost of capital (discount rate) is

    a. 8%?

    b. 4%?

    c. What rate would make Debra indifferent between these two options?

EA-13. Linda Reed, an executive at VIP Inc., has earned a performance bonus. She has the option of accepting $30,000 now or $50,000 5 years from now. What would you advise her to do? Explain and support with calculations.

EA-14. On September 1 of the current year, Luft, Inc., deposited $320,000 in a debt retirement fund. The company needs $764,000 cash to settle a maturing debt September 1, eight years later. What is the minimal rate of compound interest required to ensure the debt will be paid when due?

EA-15. Wolf Inc. establishes a construction fund on July 1, 2022, by making a single deposit of $280,000. At the end of each year, Wolf will deposit an additional $45,000. The fund guarantees a 12% return each year. How much will be in the fund on June 30, 2026?

EA-16. Sylvia Owen, owner of I-Haul Trucking, is considering expanding operations from Seattle to the Portland area. Expansion is estimated to cost $15 million, including the required new facilities and additional trucks. Sylvia has elected to finance the expansion by borrowing from her local bank at a yearly interest rate of 10%. She has agreed to repay the loan in twenty equal payments over a 10-year period to begin in six months. (Payments will be made at the end of every half-year period.)

    a. What will Sylvia's periodic payments be?

    b. How much of her first payment will be interest expense?

c. Assume that after five years, Sylvia decided to pay off the loan early. How much would she owe at that time?

EA-17. On November 1 of the current year, Ybarra Construction Company issued $180,000 of 5-year bonds that pay interest at an annual rate of 5%. The interest payments are due every six months. (That is, the interest is compounded semi-annually.) At the end of the five-year period, Ybarra must pay the bond holders a balloon payment of $180,000.

a. What would the issue price of the bonds be if the prevailing interest rate is (i) 4%? (ii) 6%?
b. Compute the market price of these bonds on November 1, two years later assuming that the prevailing market interest rate at that time is 8%.

EA-18. On August 1 of the current year, Paradise Airlines agreed to lease a passenger jet from Boeing Corporation. The 20-year lease requires an annual payment of $550,000. If Paradise were to purchase the jet, it could borrow the necessary funds at a 9% interest rate.

a. What is the present value of the lease payments if the first payment is due on August 1 of the current year?
b. What is the present value of the lease payments if the first payment is due on August 1, one year later?

EA-19. Burnham Corporation is comparing two alternatives for leasing a machine.

Alternative A is a lease that requires six annual payments of $12,000, with the first payment due immediately.

Alternative B is a lease that requires two payments of $16,500 and three payments of $13,500, with the first payment due one year from now.

a. Which alternative should Burnham choose if the relevant discount rate is 5%?
b. Which alternative should Burnham choose if the relevant interest rate is 7%?

EA-20. On January 2, DeSantis Company is comparing two alternatives for leasing a machine.

Alternative A is a lease that requires 24 quarterly payments of $2,000, with the first payment due on March 31.

Alternative B is a lease that requires five annual payments of $10,000, with the first payment due on December 31.

Which alternative should DeSantis choose if the appropriate discount rate is 8% compounded quarterly?

EA-21. Despite his relative youth, Samuel Hunter has started planning for his retirement. At present, he has $3,000 he can invest, and he believes that he will be able to invest that amount each year for the next 39 years—40 contributions in total.

a. If his investment earns 4% per year for the 40 years, how much will Samuel have accumulated at the end of 40 years?
b. If Samuel delays investing for 10 years, how will that affect the balance accumulated at the end of 40 years?
c. If Samuel begins investing now and finds an investment earning 5% per year for 40 years, how much more will he have accumulated than if he earns 4%?

EA-22. Janice Utley is saving for a real estate investment. If she invests $1,500 now and then at the beginning of each of the next 35 months (36 months in total) at an interest rate of 1% per month, what will be the investment balance at the end of month 36?

TABLE A.1 — Future Value of Single Amount

$f = (1 + i)^t$

Interest Rate

Period	0.01	0.02	0.03	0.04	0.05	0.06	0.07	0.08	0.09	0.10	0.11	0.12
1	1.01000	1.02000	1.03000	1.04000	1.05000	1.06000	1.07000	1.08000	1.09000	1.10000	1.11000	1.12000
2	1.02010	1.04040	1.06090	1.08160	1.10250	1.12360	1.14490	1.16640	1.18810	1.21000	1.23210	1.25440
3	1.03030	1.06121	1.09273	1.12486	1.15763	1.19102	1.22504	1.25971	1.29503	1.33100	1.36763	1.40493
4	1.04060	1.08243	1.12551	1.16986	1.21551	1.26248	1.31080	1.36049	1.41158	1.46410	1.51807	1.57352
5	1.05101	1.10408	1.15927	1.21665	1.27628	1.33823	1.40255	1.46933	1.53862	1.61051	1.68506	1.76234
6	1.06152	1.12616	1.19405	1.26532	1.34010	1.41852	1.50073	1.58687	1.67710	1.77156	1.87041	1.97382
7	1.07214	1.14869	1.22987	1.31593	1.40710	1.50363	1.60578	1.71382	1.82804	1.94872	2.07616	2.21068
8	1.08286	1.17166	1.26677	1.36857	1.47746	1.59385	1.71819	1.85093	1.99256	2.14359	2.30454	2.47596
9	1.09369	1.19509	1.30477	1.42331	1.55133	1.68948	1.83846	1.99900	2.17189	2.35795	2.55804	2.77308
10	1.10462	1.21899	1.34392	1.48024	1.62889	1.79085	1.96715	2.15892	2.36736	2.59374	2.83942	3.10585
11	1.11567	1.24337	1.38423	1.53945	1.71034	1.89830	2.10485	2.33164	2.58043	2.85312	3.15176	3.47855
12	1.12683	1.26824	1.42576	1.60103	1.79586	2.01220	2.25219	2.51817	2.81266	3.13843	3.49845	3.89598
13	1.13809	1.29361	1.46853	1.66507	1.88565	2.13293	2.40985	2.71962	3.06580	3.45227	3.88328	4.36349
14	1.14947	1.31948	1.51259	1.73168	1.97993	2.26090	2.57853	2.93719	3.34173	3.79750	4.31044	4.88711
15	1.16097	1.34587	1.55797	1.80094	2.07893	2.39656	2.75903	3.17217	3.64248	4.17725	4.78459	5.47357
16	1.17258	1.37279	1.60471	1.87298	2.18287	2.54035	2.95216	3.42594	3.97031	4.59497	5.31089	6.13039
17	1.18430	1.40024	1.65285	1.94790	2.29202	2.69277	3.15882	3.70002	4.32763	5.05447	5.89509	6.86604
18	1.19615	1.42825	1.70243	2.02582	2.40662	2.85434	3.37993	3.99602	4.71712	5.55992	6.54355	7.68997
19	1.20811	1.45681	1.75351	2.10685	2.52695	3.02560	3.61653	4.31570	5.14166	6.11591	7.26334	8.61276
20	1.22019	1.48595	1.80611	2.19112	2.65330	3.20714	3.86968	4.66096	5.60441	6.72750	8.06231	9.64629
21	1.23239	1.51567	1.86029	2.27877	2.78596	3.39956	4.14056	5.03383	6.10881	7.40025	8.94917	10.80385
22	1.24472	1.54598	1.91610	2.36992	2.92526	3.60354	4.43040	5.43654	6.65860	8.14027	9.93357	12.10031
23	1.25716	1.57690	1.97359	2.46472	3.07152	3.81975	4.74053	5.87146	7.25787	8.95430	11.02627	13.55235
24	1.26973	1.60844	2.03279	2.56330	3.22510	4.04893	5.07237	6.34118	7.91108	9.84973	12.23916	15.17863
25	1.28243	1.64061	2.09378	2.66584	3.38635	4.29187	5.42743	6.84848	8.62308	10.83471	13.58546	17.00006
26	1.29526	1.67342	2.15659	2.77247	3.55567	4.54938	5.80735	7.39635	9.39916	11.91818	15.07986	19.04007
27	1.30821	1.70689	2.22129	2.88337	3.73346	4.82235	6.21387	7.98806	10.24508	13.10999	16.73865	21.32488
28	1.32129	1.74102	2.28793	2.99870	3.92013	5.11169	6.64884	8.62711	11.16714	14.42099	18.57990	23.88387
29	1.33450	1.77584	2.35657	3.11865	4.11614	5.41839	7.11426	9.31727	12.17218	15.86309	20.62369	26.74993
30	1.34785	1.81136	2.42726	3.24340	4.32194	5.74349	7.61226	10.06266	13.26768	17.44940	22.89230	29.95992
31	1.36133	1.84759	2.50008	3.37313	4.53804	6.08810	8.14511	10.86767	14.46177	19.19434	25.41045	33.55511
32	1.37494	1.88454	2.57508	3.50806	4.76494	6.45339	8.71527	11.73708	15.76333	21.11378	28.20560	37.58173
33	1.38869	1.92223	2.65234	3.64838	5.00319	6.84059	9.32534	12.67605	17.18203	23.22515	31.30821	42.09153
34	1.40258	1.96068	2.73191	3.79432	5.25335	7.25103	9.97811	13.69013	18.72841	25.54767	34.75212	47.14252
35	1.41660	1.99989	2.81386	3.94609	5.51602	7.68609	10.67658	14.78534	20.41397	28.10244	38.57485	52.79962
36	1.43077	2.03989	2.89828	4.10393	5.79182	8.14725	11.42394	15.96817	22.25123	30.91268	42.81808	59.13557
37	1.44508	2.08069	2.98523	4.26809	6.08141	8.63609	12.22362	17.24563	24.25384	34.00395	47.52807	66.23184
38	1.45953	2.12230	3.07478	4.43881	6.38548	9.15425	13.07927	18.62528	26.43668	37.40434	52.75616	74.17966
39	1.47412	2.16474	3.16703	4.61637	6.70475	9.70351	13.99482	20.11530	28.81598	41.14478	58.55934	83.08122
40	1.48886	2.20804	3.26204	4.80102	7.03999	10.28572	14.97446	21.72452	31.40942	45.25926	65.00087	93.05097

TABLE A.2 — Present Value of Single Amount

$p = 1/(1 + i)^t$

Interest Rate

Period	0.01	0.02	0.03	0.04	0.05	0.06	0.07	0.08	0.09	0.10	0.11	0.12
1	0.99010	0.98039	0.97087	0.96154	0.95238	0.94340	0.93458	0.92593	0.91743	0.90909	0.90090	0.89286
2	0.98030	0.96117	0.94260	0.92456	0.90703	0.89000	0.87344	0.85734	0.84168	0.82645	0.81162	0.79719
3	0.97059	0.94232	0.91514	0.88900	0.86384	0.83962	0.81630	0.79383	0.77218	0.75131	0.73119	0.71178
4	0.96098	0.92385	0.88849	0.85480	0.82270	0.79209	0.76290	0.73503	0.70843	0.68301	0.65873	0.63552
5	0.95147	0.90573	0.86261	0.82193	0.78353	0.74726	0.71299	0.68058	0.64993	0.62092	0.59345	0.56743
6	0.94205	0.88797	0.83748	0.79031	0.74622	0.70496	0.66634	0.63017	0.59627	0.56447	0.53464	0.50663
7	0.93272	0.87056	0.81309	0.75992	0.71068	0.66506	0.62275	0.58349	0.54703	0.51316	0.48166	0.45235
8	0.92348	0.85349	0.78941	0.73069	0.67684	0.62741	0.58201	0.54027	0.50187	0.46651	0.43393	0.40388
9	0.91434	0.83676	0.76642	0.70259	0.64461	0.59190	0.54393	0.50025	0.46043	0.42410	0.39092	0.36061
10	0.90529	0.82035	0.74409	0.67556	0.61391	0.55839	0.50835	0.46319	0.42241	0.38554	0.35218	0.32197
11	0.89632	0.80426	0.72242	0.64958	0.58468	0.52679	0.47509	0.42888	0.38753	0.35049	0.31728	0.28748
12	0.88745	0.78849	0.70138	0.62460	0.55684	0.49697	0.44401	0.39711	0.35553	0.31863	0.28584	0.25668
13	0.87866	0.77303	0.68095	0.60057	0.53032	0.46884	0.41496	0.36770	0.32618	0.28966	0.25751	0.22917
14	0.86996	0.75788	0.66112	0.57748	0.50507	0.44230	0.38782	0.34046	0.29925	0.26333	0.23199	0.20462
15	0.86135	0.74301	0.64186	0.55526	0.48102	0.41727	0.36245	0.31524	0.27454	0.23939	0.20900	0.18270
16	0.85282	0.72845	0.62317	0.53391	0.45811	0.39365	0.33873	0.29189	0.25187	0.21763	0.18829	0.16312
17	0.84438	0.71416	0.60502	0.51337	0.43630	0.37136	0.31657	0.27027	0.23107	0.19784	0.16963	0.14564
18	0.83602	0.70016	0.58739	0.49363	0.41552	0.35034	0.29586	0.25025	0.21199	0.17986	0.15282	0.13004
19	0.82774	0.68643	0.57029	0.47464	0.39573	0.33051	0.27651	0.23171	0.19449	0.16351	0.13768	0.11611
20	0.81954	0.67297	0.55368	0.45639	0.37689	0.31180	0.25842	0.21455	0.17843	0.14864	0.12403	0.10367
21	0.81143	0.65978	0.53755	0.43883	0.35894	0.29416	0.24151	0.19866	0.16370	0.13513	0.11174	0.09256
22	0.80340	0.64684	0.52189	0.42196	0.34185	0.27751	0.22571	0.18394	0.15018	0.12285	0.10067	0.08264
23	0.79544	0.63416	0.50669	0.40573	0.32557	0.26180	0.21095	0.17032	0.13778	0.11168	0.09069	0.07379
24	0.78757	0.62172	0.49193	0.39012	0.31007	0.24698	0.19715	0.15770	0.12640	0.10153	0.08170	0.06588
25	0.77977	0.60953	0.47761	0.37512	0.29530	0.23300	0.18425	0.14602	0.11597	0.09230	0.07361	0.05882
26	0.77205	0.59758	0.46369	0.36069	0.28124	0.21981	0.17220	0.13520	0.10639	0.08391	0.06631	0.05252
27	0.76440	0.58586	0.45019	0.34682	0.26785	0.20737	0.16093	0.12519	0.09761	0.07628	0.05974	0.04689
28	0.75684	0.57437	0.43708	0.33348	0.25509	0.19563	0.15040	0.11591	0.08955	0.06934	0.05382	0.04187
29	0.74934	0.56311	0.42435	0.32065	0.24295	0.18456	0.14056	0.10733	0.08215	0.06304	0.04849	0.03738
30	0.74192	0.55207	0.41199	0.30832	0.23138	0.17411	0.13137	0.09938	0.07537	0.05731	0.04368	0.03338
31	0.73458	0.54125	0.39999	0.29646	0.22036	0.16425	0.12277	0.09202	0.06915	0.05210	0.03935	0.02980
32	0.72730	0.53063	0.38834	0.28506	0.20987	0.15496	0.11474	0.08520	0.06344	0.04736	0.03545	0.02661
33	0.72010	0.52023	0.37703	0.27409	0.19987	0.14619	0.10723	0.07889	0.05820	0.04306	0.03194	0.02376
34	0.71297	0.51003	0.36604	0.26355	0.19035	0.13791	0.10022	0.07305	0.05339	0.03914	0.02878	0.02121
35	0.70591	0.50003	0.35538	0.25342	0.18129	0.13011	0.09366	0.06763	0.04899	0.03558	0.02592	0.01894
36	0.69892	0.49022	0.34503	0.24367	0.17266	0.12274	0.08754	0.06262	0.04494	0.03235	0.02335	0.01691
37	0.69200	0.48061	0.33498	0.23430	0.16444	0.11579	0.08181	0.05799	0.04123	0.02941	0.02104	0.01510
38	0.68515	0.47119	0.32523	0.22529	0.15661	0.10924	0.07646	0.05369	0.03783	0.02673	0.01896	0.01348
39	0.67837	0.46195	0.31575	0.21662	0.14915	0.10306	0.07146	0.04971	0.03470	0.02430	0.01708	0.01204
40	0.67165	0.45289	0.30656	0.20829	0.14205	0.09722	0.06678	0.04603	0.03184	0.02209	0.01538	0.01075

TABLE A.3 Present Value of Ordinary Annuity

$p = \{1 - [1/(1 + i)^t]\}/i$

Period	0.01	0.02	0.03	0.04	0.05	0.06	0.07	0.08	0.09	0.10	0.11	0.12
1	0.99010	0.98039	0.97087	0.96154	0.95238	0.94340	0.93458	0.92593	0.91743	0.90909	0.90090	0.89286
2	1.97040	1.94156	1.91347	1.88609	1.85941	1.83339	1.80802	1.78326	1.75911	1.73554	1.71252	1.69005
3	2.94099	2.88388	2.82861	2.77509	2.72325	2.67301	2.62432	2.57710	2.53129	2.48685	2.44371	2.40183
4	3.90197	3.80773	3.71710	3.62990	3.54595	3.46511	3.38721	3.31213	3.23972	3.16987	3.10245	3.03735
5	4.85343	4.71346	4.57971	4.45182	4.32948	4.21236	4.10020	3.99271	3.88965	3.79079	3.69590	3.60478
6	5.79548	5.60143	5.41719	5.24214	5.07569	4.91732	4.76654	4.62288	4.48592	4.35526	4.23054	4.11141
7	6.72819	6.47199	6.23028	6.00205	5.78637	5.58238	5.38929	5.20637	5.03295	4.86842	4.71220	4.56376
8	7.65168	7.32548	7.01969	6.73274	6.46321	6.20979	5.97130	5.74664	5.53482	5.33493	5.14612	4.96764
9	8.56602	8.16224	7.78611	7.43533	7.10782	6.80169	6.51523	6.24689	5.99525	5.75902	5.53705	5.32825
10	9.47130	8.98259	8.53020	8.11090	7.72173	7.36009	7.02358	6.71008	6.41766	6.14457	5.88923	5.65022
11	10.36763	9.78685	9.25262	8.76048	8.30641	7.88687	7.49867	7.13896	6.80519	6.49506	6.20652	5.93770
12	11.25508	10.57534	9.95400	9.38507	8.86325	8.38384	7.94269	7.53608	7.16073	6.81369	6.49236	6.19437
13	12.13374	11.34837	10.63496	9.98565	9.39357	8.85268	8.35765	7.90378	7.48690	7.10336	6.74987	6.42355
14	13.00370	12.10625	11.29607	10.56312	9.89864	9.29498	8.74547	8.24424	7.78615	7.36669	6.98187	6.62817
15	13.86505	12.84926	11.93794	11.11839	10.37966	9.71225	9.10791	8.55948	8.06069	7.60608	7.19087	6.81086
16	14.71787	13.57771	12.56110	11.65230	10.83777	10.10590	9.44665	8.85137	8.31256	7.82371	7.37916	6.97399
17	15.56225	14.29187	13.16612	12.16567	11.27407	10.47726	9.76322	9.12164	8.54363	8.02155	7.54879	7.11963
18	16.39827	14.99203	13.75351	12.65930	11.68959	10.82760	10.05909	9.37189	8.75563	8.20141	7.70162	7.24967
19	17.22601	15.67846	14.32380	13.13394	12.08532	11.15812	10.33560	9.60360	8.95011	8.36492	7.83929	7.36578
20	18.04555	16.35143	14.87747	13.59033	12.46221	11.46992	10.59401	9.81815	9.12855	8.51356	7.96333	7.46944
21	18.85698	17.01121	15.41502	14.02916	12.82115	11.76408	10.83553	10.01680	9.29224	8.64869	8.07507	7.56200
22	19.66038	17.65805	15.93692	14.45112	13.16300	12.04158	11.06124	10.20074	9.44243	8.77154	8.17574	7.64465
23	20.45582	18.29220	16.44361	14.85684	13.48857	12.30338	11.27219	10.37106	9.58021	8.88322	8.26643	7.71843
24	21.24339	18.91393	16.93554	15.24696	13.79864	12.55036	11.46933	10.52876	9.70661	8.98474	8.34814	7.78432
25	22.02316	19.52346	17.41315	15.62208	14.09394	12.78336	11.65358	10.67478	9.82258	9.07704	8.42174	7.84314
26	22.79520	20.12104	17.87684	15.98277	14.37519	13.00317	11.82578	10.80998	9.92897	9.16095	8.48806	7.89566
27	23.55961	20.70690	18.32703	16.32959	14.64303	13.21053	11.98671	10.93516	10.02658	9.23722	8.54780	7.94255
28	24.31644	21.28127	18.76411	16.66306	14.89813	13.40616	12.13711	11.05108	10.11613	9.30657	8.60162	7.98442
29	25.06579	21.84438	19.18845	16.98371	15.14107	13.59072	12.27767	11.15841	10.19828	9.36961	8.65011	8.02181
30	25.80771	22.39646	19.60044	17.29203	15.37245	13.76483	12.40904	11.25778	10.27365	9.42691	8.69379	8.05518
31	26.54229	22.93770	20.00043	17.58849	15.59281	13.92909	12.53181	11.34980	10.34280	9.47901	8.73315	8.08499
32	27.26959	23.46833	20.38877	17.87355	15.80268	14.08404	12.64656	11.43500	10.40624	9.52638	8.76860	8.11159
33	27.98969	23.98856	20.76579	18.14765	16.00255	14.23023	12.75379	11.51389	10.46444	9.56943	8.80054	8.13535
34	28.70267	24.49859	21.13184	18.41120	16.19290	14.36814	12.85401	11.58693	10.51784	9.60857	8.82932	8.15656
35	29.40858	24.99862	21.48722	18.66461	16.37419	14.49825	12.94767	11.65457	10.56682	9.64416	8.85524	8.17550
36	30.10751	25.48884	21.83225	18.90828	16.54685	14.62099	13.03521	11.71719	10.61176	9.67651	8.87859	8.19241
37	30.79951	25.96945	22.16724	19.14258	16.71129	14.73678	13.11702	11.77518	10.65299	9.70592	8.89963	8.20751
38	31.48466	26.44064	22.49246	19.36786	16.86789	14.84602	13.19347	11.82887	10.69082	9.73265	8.91859	8.22099
39	32.16303	26.90259	22.80822	19.58448	17.01704	14.94907	13.26493	11.87858	10.72552	9.75696	8.93567	8.23303
40	32.83469	27.35548	23.11477	19.79277	17.15909	15.04630	13.33171	11.92461	10.75736	9.77905	8.95105	8.24378

TABLE A.4 — Future Value of Annuity Paid at Beginning of Period

$$FVAD = \left[\frac{(1+i)^n - 1}{i}\right] \times (1+i)$$

Interest Rate

Period	0.01	0.02	0.03	0.04	0.05	0.06	0.07	0.08	0.09	0.10	0.11	0.12
1	1.0100	1.0200	1.0300	1.0400	1.0500	1.0600	1.0700	1.0800	1.0900	1.1000	1.1100	1.1200
2	2.0301	2.0604	2.0909	2.1216	2.1525	2.1836	2.2149	2.2464	2.2781	2.3100	2.3421	2.3744
3	3.0604	3.1216	3.1836	3.2465	3.3101	3.3746	3.4399	3.5061	3.5731	3.6410	3.7097	3.7793
4	4.1010	4.2040	4.3091	4.4163	4.5256	4.6371	4.7507	4.8666	4.9847	5.1051	5.2278	5.3528
5	5.1520	5.3081	5.4684	5.6330	5.8019	5.9753	6.1533	6.3359	6.5233	6.7156	6.9129	7.1152
6	6.2135	6.4343	6.6625	6.8983	7.1420	7.3938	7.6540	7.9228	8.2004	8.4872	8.7833	9.0890
7	7.2857	7.5830	7.8923	8.2142	8.5491	8.8975	9.2598	9.6366	10.0285	10.4359	10.8594	11.2997
8	8.3685	8.7546	9.1591	9.5828	10.0266	10.4913	10.9780	11.4876	12.0210	12.5795	13.1640	13.7757
9	9.4622	9.9497	10.4639	11.0061	11.5779	12.1808	12.8164	13.4866	14.1929	14.9374	15.7220	16.5487
10	10.5668	11.1687	11.8078	12.4864	13.2068	13.9716	14.7836	15.6455	16.5603	17.5312	18.5614	19.6546
11	11.6825	12.4121	13.1920	14.0258	14.9171	15.8699	16.8885	17.9771	19.1407	20.3843	21.7132	23.1331
12	12.8093	13.6803	14.6178	15.6268	16.7130	17.8821	19.1406	20.4953	21.9534	23.5227	25.2116	27.0291
13	13.9474	14.9739	16.0863	17.2919	18.5986	20.0151	21.5505	23.2149	25.0192	26.9750	29.0949	31.3926
14	15.0969	16.2934	17.5989	19.0236	20.5786	22.2760	24.1290	26.1521	28.3609	30.7725	33.4054	36.2797
15	16.2579	17.6393	19.1569	20.8245	22.6575	24.6725	26.8881	29.3243	32.0034	34.9497	38.1899	41.7533
16	17.4304	19.0121	20.7616	22.6975	24.8404	27.2129	29.8402	32.7502	35.9737	39.5447	43.5008	47.8837
17	18.6147	20.4123	22.4144	24.6454	27.1324	29.9057	32.9990	36.4502	40.3013	44.5992	49.3959	54.7497
18	19.8109	21.8406	24.1169	26.6712	29.5390	32.7600	36.3790	40.4463	45.0185	50.1591	55.9395	62.4397
19	21.0190	23.2974	25.8704	28.7781	32.0660	35.7856	39.9955	44.7620	50.1601	56.2750	63.2028	71.0524
20	22.2392	24.7833	27.6765	30.9692	34.7193	38.9927	43.8652	49.4229	55.7645	63.0025	71.2651	80.6987
21	23.4716	26.2990	29.5368	33.2480	37.5052	42.3923	48.0057	54.4568	61.8733	70.4027	80.2143	91.5026
22	24.7163	27.8450	31.4529	35.6179	40.4305	45.9958	52.4361	59.8933	68.5319	78.5430	90.1479	103.6029
23	25.9735	29.4219	33.4265	38.0826	43.5020	49.8156	57.1767	65.7648	75.7898	87.4973	101.1742	117.1552
24	27.2432	31.0303	35.4593	40.6459	46.7271	53.8645	62.2490	72.1059	83.7009	97.3471	113.4133	132.3339
25	28.5256	32.6709	37.5530	43.3117	50.1135	58.1564	67.6765	78.9544	92.3240	108.1818	126.9988	149.3339
26	29.8209	34.3443	39.7096	46.0842	53.6691	62.7058	73.4838	86.3508	101.7231	120.0999	142.0786	168.3740
27	31.1291	36.0512	41.9309	48.9676	57.4026	67.5281	79.6977	94.3388	111.9682	133.2099	158.8173	189.6989
28	32.4504	37.7922	44.2189	51.9663	61.3227	72.6398	86.3465	102.9659	123.1354	147.6309	177.3972	213.5828
29	33.7849	39.5681	46.5754	55.0849	65.4388	78.0582	93.4608	112.2832	135.3075	163.4940	198.0209	240.3327
30	35.1327	41.3794	49.0027	58.3283	69.7608	83.8017	101.0730	122.3459	148.5752	180.9434	220.9132	270.2926
31	36.4941	43.2270	51.5028	61.7015	74.2988	89.8898	109.2182	133.2135	163.0370	200.1378	246.3236	303.8477
32	37.8690	45.1116	54.0778	65.2095	79.0638	96.3432	117.9334	144.9506	178.8003	221.2515	274.5292	341.4294
33	39.2577	47.0338	56.7302	68.8579	84.0670	103.1838	127.2588	157.6267	195.9823	244.4767	305.8374	383.5210
34	40.6603	48.9945	59.4621	72.6522	89.3203	110.4348	137.2369	171.3168	214.7108	270.0244	340.5896	430.6635
35	42.0769	50.9944	62.2759	76.5983	94.8363	118.1209	147.9135	186.1021	235.1247	298.1268	379.1644	483.4631
36	43.5076	53.0343	65.1742	80.7022	100.6281	126.2681	159.3374	202.0703	257.3759	329.0395	421.9825	542.5987
37	44.9527	55.1149	68.1594	84.9703	106.7095	134.9042	171.5610	219.3159	281.6298	363.0434	469.5106	608.8305
38	46.4123	57.2372	71.2342	89.4091	113.0950	144.0585	184.6403	237.9412	308.0665	400.4478	522.2667	683.0102
39	47.8864	59.4020	74.4013	94.0255	119.7998	153.7620	198.6351	258.0565	336.8824	441.5926	580.8261	766.0914
40	49.3752	61.6100	77.6633	98.8265	126.8398	164.0477	213.6096	279.7810	368.2919	486.8518	645.8269	859.1424

TABLE A.5 — Present Value of an Annuity Paid at Beginning of Period:

$$PVAD = \left[\frac{1 - 1(1 + i)^n}{i}\right] \times (1 + i)$$

Interest Rate

Period	0.02	0.03	0.04	0.05	0.06	0.07	0.08	0.09	0.10	0.11	0.12	0.15
1	1.00000	1.00000	1.00000	1.00000	1.00000	1.00000	1.00000	1.00000	1.00000	1.00000	1.00000	1.00000
2	1.98039	1.97087	1.96154	1.95238	1.94340	1.93458	1.92593	1.91743	1.90909	1.90090	1.89286	1.86957
3	2.94156	2.91347	2.88609	2.85941	2.83339	2.80802	2.78326	2.75911	2.73554	2.71252	2.69005	2.62571
4	3.88388	3.82861	3.77509	3.72325	3.67301	3.62432	3.57710	3.53130	3.48685	3.44371	3.40183	3.28323
5	4.80773	4.71710	4.62990	4.54595	4.46511	4.38721	4.31213	4.23972	4.16987	4.10245	4.03735	3.85498
6	5.71346	5.57971	5.45182	5.32948	5.21236	5.10020	4.99271	4.88965	4.79079	4.69590	4.60478	4.35216
7	6.60143	6.41719	6.24214	6.07569	5.91732	5.76654	5.62288	5.48592	5.35526	5.23054	5.11141	4.78448
8	7.47199	7.23028	7.00205	6.78637	6.58238	6.38929	6.20637	6.03295	5.86842	5.71220	5.56376	5.16042
9	8.32548	8.01969	7.73274	7.46321	7.20979	6.97130	6.74664	6.53482	6.33493	6.14612	5.96764	5.48732
10	9.16224	8.78611	8.43533	8.10782	7.80169	7.51523	7.24689	6.99525	6.75902	6.53705	6.32825	5.77158
11	9.98259	9.53020	9.11090	8.72173	8.36009	8.02358	7.71008	7.41766	7.14457	6.88923	6.65022	6.01877
12	10.78685	10.25262	9.76048	9.30641	8.88687	8.49867	8.13896	7.80519	7.49506	7.20652	6.93770	6.23371
13	11.57534	10.95400	10.38507	9.86325	9.38384	8.94269	8.53608	8.16073	7.81369	7.49236	7.19437	6.42062
14	12.34837	11.63496	10.98565	10.39357	9.85268	9.35765	8.90378	8.48690	8.10336	7.74987	7.42355	6.58315
15	13.10625	12.29607	11.56312	10.89864	10.29498	9.74547	9.24424	8.78615	8.36669	7.98187	7.62817	6.72448
16	13.84926	12.93794	12.11839	11.37966	10.71225	10.10791	9.55948	9.06069	8.60608	8.19087	7.81086	6.84737
17	14.57771	13.56110	12.65230	11.83777	11.10590	10.44665	9.85137	9.31256	8.82371	8.37916	7.97399	6.95423
18	15.29187	14.16612	13.16567	12.27407	11.47726	10.76322	10.12164	9.54363	9.02155	8.54879	8.11963	7.04716
19	15.99203	14.75351	13.65930	12.68959	11.82760	11.05909	10.37189	9.75563	9.20141	8.70162	8.24967	7.12797
20	16.67846	15.32380	14.13394	13.08532	12.15812	11.33560	10.60360	9.95012	9.36492	8.83929	8.36578	7.19823
21	17.35143	15.87747	14.59033	13.46221	12.46992	11.59401	10.81815	10.12855	9.51356	8.96333	8.46944	7.25933
22	18.01121	16.41502	15.02916	13.82115	12.76408	11.83553	11.01680	10.29224	9.64869	9.07507	8.56200	7.31246
23	18.65805	16.93692	15.45112	14.16300	13.04158	12.06124	11.20074	10.44243	9.77154	9.17574	8.64465	7.35866
24	19.29220	17.44361	15.85684	14.48857	13.30338	12.27219	11.37106	10.58021	9.88322	9.26643	8.71843	7.39884
25	19.91393	17.93554	16.24696	14.79864	13.55036	12.46933	11.52876	10.70661	9.98474	9.34814	8.78432	7.43377

Appendix B: Data Analytics and Blockchain Technology

Road Map

	Learning Objectives	Page	eLecture
1	Define Big Data and describe its four attributes.	B-2	e.1
2	Identify and define the four types of data analytics.	B-2	e.1
3	Describe the use of data analytics within the accounting profession.	B-3	e.2
4	Describe the analytics mindset.	B-4	e.3
5	Describe data visualization best practices.	B-6	e.4
6	Describe how blockchain technology works and its use within the accounting profession.	B-10	e.5

DATA ANALYTICS

Data analytics can broadly be defined as the process of examining sets of data with the goal of discovering useful information from patterns found in the data. Increasingly, this process is aided by computers running programs ranging from basic spreadsheet software, such as **Microsoft Excel** and **Google Sheets**, to specialized software, such as **Tableau** or **Power BI**. This technology can reveal trends and insights that would otherwise be lost in the overwhelming amount of data.

LO1 Define Big Data and describe its four attributes.

Big Data

The concept of data analytics is intertwined with the concept of **big data**. Although no precise definition exists for big data, a commonly accepted definition is that big data is a collection of data that is both extremely large and also extremely complex, thus making its analysis beyond the scope of traditional tools. Important attributes of big data, commonly referred to as the four V's, are Volume, Variety, Velocity, and Veracity. **Volume** refers to the amount of data. According to IDC (a market intelligence company), there were 33 available zettabytes of data globally in 2018. IDC predicted that the amount of data would increase to 175 zettabytes by 2025. (Just so you know, there are 21 zeros in one zettabyte.) Total amounts of data are growing because we are creating more data (through new technologies) and because we are able to store more data (using cloud storage services like Amazon Web Services [AWS] and Microsoft Azure). Massive data sets can't be managed on a single machine. They must be stored in clusters over multiple physical or virtual machines.

Variety refers to the source of data. Data can be structured, semi-structured, or unstructured. Structured data can be contained in rows and columns and stored in spreadsheets or relational databases. Although most accounting data is structured, it is estimated that less than 20 percent of all data is structured.

Unstructured data cannot be easily contained in rows and columns and is, therefore, difficult to search and analyze. Photos, video and audio files, and social media content are examples of unstructured data.

Semi-structured data has characteristics of both structured and unstructured data. It may include some defining details but doesn't completely conform to a rigid structure. For example, the words in an email are unstructured data. The email date and the addresses of the sender and the recipient are structured data. Artificial intelligence algorithms are used to process unstructured and semi-structured data in a way that makes the information useable.

Velocity refers to the speed at which the data is being produced. The amount of data is not only growing; it's growing exponentially as more people gain internet access, and more technology is created that connects humans to machines and machines to machines. Collecting and translating data (especially unstructured data) into usable information is complicated by how quickly new data is generated.

Veracity refers to the quality of the data. Data quality can be negatively affected by untrustworthy data sources, inconsistent or missing data, statistical biases, and human error. The veracity of unstructured data is especially difficult to determine. Machine learning, a type of artificial intelligence based on the idea that systems can learn from data and can identify patterns, is often used to assess data quality.

In summary, a set of data would be considered "big data" if:

- The data set is too large to be managed by traditional methods.
- The data set includes a variety of types of data (structured, semi-structured, and unstructured).
- The amount of data in the data set is expanding rapidly.
- The accuracy and reliability of the data may be uncertain.

Types of Data Analytics

Data analytics can be categorized into four main types, ranging in sophistication from relatively straightforward to very complex. The first category is **descriptive analytics**, which describes what has happened over a given period of time. Simple examples include determining sales trends over a period of time and the relative effectiveness of various social media promotions based on

LO2 Identify and define the four types of data analytics.

click-through rates. Microsoft Excel and other spreadsheet programs include built-in functions that greatly simplify performing descriptive analytics.

Diagnostic analytics focuses more on why something occurred. This data analytics technique is used to monitor changes in data and often includes a certain amount of hypothesizing: Did the marketing campaign lead to the increase in sales? Did changing the beverage items affect food choices? Did the opening of competing restaurants negatively impact sales growth? Diagnostic analytics is useful because past performance is often a reliable predictor of future outcomes and can greatly aid in planning and forecasting.

Whereas descriptive and diagnostic analytics use data to try to understand what happened and why, **predictive analytics** uses data to try to determine what *will* happen. The movie *Moneyball* made the general manager of the Oakland Athletics, Billy Beane, famous for using predictive analytics to make personnel decisions in professional baseball. In his evaluation of baseball players, Beane used data to predict player performance so he could assemble the team with the greatest likelihood of winning the World Series. Banks also use predictive analytics to identify and prevent fraudulent transactions by monitoring customer credit card transactions and red flagging those that deviate from a customer behavior profile that was developed from previous transaction and geographic data.

Prescriptive analytics moves beyond what is going to happen to suggesting a course of action for what *should* happen to optimize outcomes. The forecasts created using predictive analytics can be used to make recommendations for future courses of action. For example, if we own a sports bar and determine there is a high likelihood of our local sports team winning the championship this year, we should expand the bar area and add more big-screen televisions to maximize revenues. **Exhibit B.1** summarizes the four types of data analytics.

EXHIBIT B.1 — The Four Types of Data Analytics

Type of Data Analytics	Purpose	Example
Descriptive	To explain what happened	What were sales by month last year?
Diagnostic	To understand why it happened	Did the new advertising campaign cause sales to increase last quarter?
Predictive	To predict what will happen	Does this credit card charge deviate (amount, location, etc.) from past purchases by this credit card holder?
Prescriptive	To determine what should happen	How many servers should be on the schedule for game nights?

Data Analytics in the Accounting Profession

LO3 Describe the use of data analytics within the accounting profession.

Accountants are already preparing descriptive analytic reports regularly. Comparative income statements, sales reports by location, inventory valuation reports, and ratio calculations (average collection periods, days' sales in inventory, etc.) are all examples of descriptive analytics.

Budget variance reports and segment reports by region or product line prepared by accountants can be used for diagnostic analytics. Accountants may also work with sales and production managers to analyze the reasons behind changes in operating results. A distributor might want to know how much of the increase in overall sales last year was caused by the transfer of two of its representatives to other sales regions. A grocery store manager might want to know if the winter storm last month impacted sales in all or just some of the various departments. A production manager might work with the accounting department to determine any correlation between equipment repair costs and the number of units produced over the last two years.

Data analytics should not be limited to only descriptive and diagnostic analysis. Accountants can provide even more value by employing predictive and prescriptive analytics. Accountants can obtain data from a variety of company sources, including enterprise resource planning systems, customer relationship management systems, and point-of-sale systems, to aid them in obtaining insight into future outcomes and providing guidance for future actions. The area of credit granting provides an example. Predictive analytics can help compute credit scores to predict the likelihood of future payments. As a result, prescriptive analytics can aid in suggesting terms for granting credit. Predictive analytics can also be used to help analyze outstanding accounts receivables and determine estimated credit losses based on how much time has elapsed since the credit sale took place.

Many other opportunities exist for accountants to utilize data analytics. Tax accountants can apply data analysis to unique tax issues to suggest optimal tax strategies. Accountants serving as investment advisors can use big data to find patterns in consumer behavior that others can use to build analytic models for identifying investment opportunities.

Perhaps no area of accounting can benefit more from an understanding of data analytics than auditing. Auditors employ data analytics to shift from the sample-based audit model to one based on continuous modeling of much larger data sets. This allows auditors to identify the riskiest areas of an audit by focusing on outliers and exceptions.

The major accounting firms have fully embraced the power of data analytics. **Pricewaterhouse-Coopers** (PWC), **Deloitte**, **Ernst & Young** (EY), and **KPMG** all devote significant staffing resources to provide data analytics services to their clients. These firms claim they can help their clients optimize their data assets to aid in faster and better decisions. For example, PWC provides a flowchart starting with the building of a data foundation and applies advanced analytics to improving business performance, ultimately leading to opportunities for innovation.

While computers and software are instrumental in the entire process, the human element is the most critical factor in the success of any data analytics program. One commonality among surveys of top company managers is the value placed on data analytics for the company's future. Another commonality is the need for professionals trained in data analytics to help the company attain its goals.

DATA ANALYTICS IN ACCOUNTING

Benford's Law provides an example of how data analytics has been used to uncover fraud in a national call center. Forensic accountants utilized their knowledge of Benford's Law to form evidence of a problem by observing patterns in the data. According to Benford's Law, in any list of financial transactions, the number one should occur as the first digit 30.1 percent of the time, with each successive number occurring as the first digit in lesser percentages, with the number nine occurring less than 5 percent of the time. Forensic accountants examined issued refunds and noticed an excessively high occurrence of the number four. The forensic accountants learned that the company had a policy that required supervisor approval of refunds that exceeded $50. The accountants were able to identify a small group of operators who had been issuing fraudulent refunds to family, friends, and themselves. These fraudulent $40 refunds totaled several hundred thousand dollars.

In order to be useful, data needs to be analyzed. Technology has provided the analyst with powerful tools that allow big data to provide insights that would not have been possible in the past. Still, the most important tool in the analytics toolkit comes from the analyst. Without critical thinking and good judgement, the value would remain locked within the data.

The Analytics Mindset[1]

The analytics mindset consists of a four-step process of (1) asking the right questions; (2) extracting, transforming, and loading the necessary data; (3) applying appropriate data analytics techniques; and (4) interpreting and presenting the results. **Exhibit B.2** summarizes the steps and requirements of an analytics mindset.

Note that while technology is imbedded in this process, the process still begins and ends with the human element of asking the right questions and interpreting the results. Nothing is more critical than the first step of knowing what to ask. The right questions guide the process to find the right data to analyze and interpret.

LO4 Describe the analytics mindset.

---

[1] The analytics mindset discussed here is an approach developed by the Ernst & Young Foundation.

EXHIBIT B.2	Steps of an Analytics Mindset
Steps in the Analytics Mindset	**Requirements**
Ask the right questions	Understand the objectives of the end user
	Understand the underlying business processes
Extract, transform, and load the data	Know what to ask for
	Manage the data security
	Transform the data into the required format
	Cleanse the data for completeness and accuracy
Apply the appropriate analytics techniques	Determine whether the need is for a confirmatory or an exploratory approach
Interpret and present the results	Use appropriate critical judgement regarding what you see
	Visually display the results in a format that is easy to understand without unnecessary clutter

Asking the right questions requires a few prerequisites. First, you need to know the audience that the analysis is for and what their objectives are. Next, you need to understand the context underlying the problem. For example, to analyze a marketing question you should understand the industry characteristics and the consumer demographics. Without this knowledge, you may not select the correct indicators to analyze.

Along with knowing the right questions to ask, an analytical mindset requires you to form an idea of what to expect from the data. For example, when analyzing inventory salability, you would expect to see certain associated movements in sales and receivables.

After your questions are formed, you need to determine the data needed to aid in finding answers to those questions. This requires a knowledge of the data characteristics of the four V's previously mentioned. With this knowledge you can begin the data extraction process. Here you will need to know what data to ask for, how to manage data security, and what form the data will take.

Once you have the data, you will need to transform it into a format suitable for analysis. This is often referred to as data cleaning. Data is rarely found in the form of a nicely organized Excel spreadsheet. Rather, the data will often need to be converted into a proper format and tested for completeness and accuracy. Further, unnecessary data should be removed from the data set.

The data should then be loaded into the proper analysis tool, such as **Tableau** or Microsoft's **Power BI**. Once loaded, the data should again be cleansed to be sure it is ready for analysis in the chosen software.

It is necessary to determine the appropriate technique to analyze the data within the analysis tool. There are a multitude of ways that the data can be analyzed. Possible choices include computing ratios between associated measures, identifying trends among various measures, creating comparisons between dates, and sorting measures. The proper technique to use will be guided by the questions being asked.

In your interpretation of the data, you should ask yourself what do you see and is this what you expected? In other words, do these results make sense or did the results create new questions that require further analysis?

Eventually, the results must be packaged into a presentation that can be shared with the intended audience. Software such as Tableau, Power BI, or Excel can greatly enhance these presentations through their ability to create **visualizations** and **dashboards**. These visualizations can take many forms, from simple tables to bar or pie charts, to more sophisticated scatter plots, map charts, heat maps, and more. Dashboards are created by combining multiple visualizations. Interactive dashboards allow users to filter out or drill down on content included in the charts and tables, on demand.

Data Analytic Tools

Technologies used by organizations to analyze data and communicate information to users are known as Business Intelligence (BI) tools. Data warehousing (data storage), data mining (extracting usable insights from data), and reporting and querying software are all BI tools.

Excel and Tableau are two popular BI tools that you will be using in the exercises and problems at the end of this Appendix.

Although Excel and Tableau can be used in similar ways, there are some important differences. Excel is a software application that is used for creating, organizing, and analyzing data. Tableau is a data visualization tool. Although calculations can be performed in Tableau, those calculations are made to create new fields for use in visualizations, not as support for accounting transactions. For example, Excel might be used to calculate sales commission amounts, which are then inputted into the accounting system. Tableau would not be used for that purpose.

Users in both Excel[2] and Tableau can

- Connect with different data sources
- Create visualizations and dashboards
- Work with big data sets

Tableau has much stronger interactivity tools and a more comprehensive selection of chart options. Excel generally has more flexibility and more extensive analytics tools.[3]

Python and **R** are popular programming languages that are used for data analysis, particularly when working with big data sets. Although these are programming languages and not application software (Business Intelligence tools), they are relatively easy to code compared to other languages and can be used to write software programs that perform powerful data analyses and visualizations.

ACCESSING EXCEL AND TABLEAU

Excel, if not available to you through your school, can be accessed for free by creating a Microsoft account at https://office.live.com/start/Excel.aspx. A free version of Tableau (Tableau Public) is available to you at https://public.tableau.com/en-us/s/. Tableau Public has most of the functions of Tableau Desktop (the full version). However, you can't save your workbooks locally if you're using Tableau Public. Instead, all workbooks are saved online and are accessible to any Tableau user unless you elect to hide your visualizations. Hiding visualizations is done in Settings after you've registered for Tableau on the Tableau website. Walk-through videos are available for every exercise and problem at cambridgepub.com. Tableau tutorial videos are available at https://www.tableau.com/learn/training/.

Data Visualization

As noted previously, the final step in the analytics mindset is to present your results. This is often done in the form of a visualization. While it is possible to present results as a bunch of tables full of numbers, visualizations with imagery are often a far better means to convey the raw numbers. Visualizations can be thought of as a blending of the art of design with the science of data.

There is an unlimited number of ways that data can be presented; however, certain best practices exist that can serve as a guide when building a visualization. For example, the exact same data on GDP levels are shown in the three charts in **Exhibit B.3**, but each displays the data differently. The table presents the raw data; however, the reader cannot easily rank the different economies. The two bar charts both show the same data; however, the one all in blue makes it far easier to compare economies by showing the data in sorted order. Also, note that adding multiple colors to the other bar chart does nothing to aid the reader, rather it just adds confusion.

Visualizations can be divided into two primary categories, exploratory and explanatory. **Exploratory visualizations** are meant to allow the reader to explore the data presented in order to do additional analysis. Exploratory visualizations would normally include interactive tools like filters that allow the user to change the level of data displayed. This can be useful when the problem is not clearly defined, and the reader wishes to gain a further understanding of the data.

In contrast to exploratory visualizations, **explanatory visualizations** are used to convey information to the audience. A classic example of such a visualization was prepared in 1854 by the British physician Dr. John Snow. Dr. Snow plotted cholera deaths in central London on a map that also showed the location of water pumps. The visualization identified the relationship between these

LO5
Describe data visualization best practices.

---

[2] Full functionality in Excel is only available if you have Excel 2010 or newer and you are running a 64-bit version of Windows. To determine the version of Windows on your computer, go to Settings>System>About. The version will be listed in the Device specifications section.

[3] Pan and Blankley, Excel vs. Tableau: See your data differently, *Journal of Accountancy*, February 29, 2020.

EXHIBIT B.3 Different Displays of the Same Data

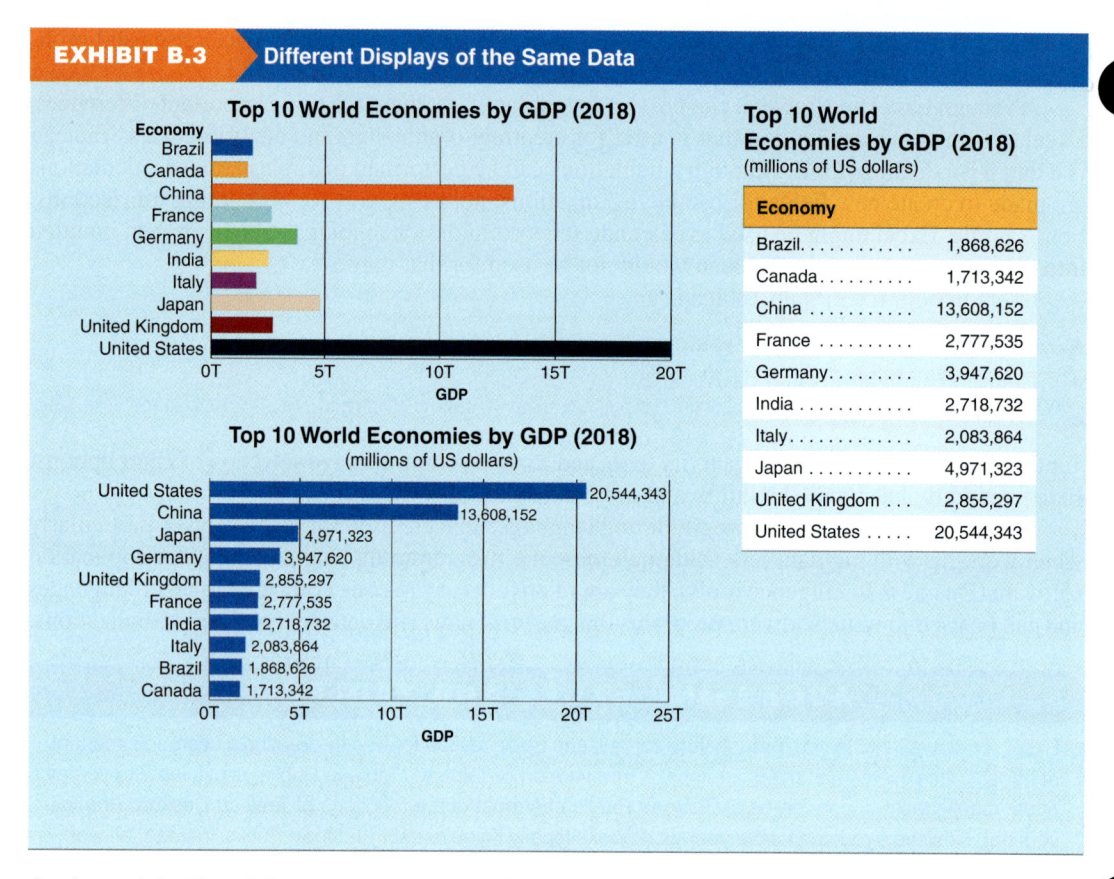

Top 10 World Economies by GDP (2018)

[Bar chart showing GDP by economy: Brazil, Canada, China, France, Germany, India, Italy, Japan, United Kingdom, United States, with GDP from 0T to 20T]

Top 10 World Economies by GDP (2018) (millions of US dollars)

Economy	
Brazil	1,868,626
Canada	1,713,342
China	13,608,152
France	2,777,535
Germany	3,947,620
India	2,718,732
Italy	2,083,864
Japan	4,971,323
United Kingdom	2,855,297
United States	20,544,343

Top 10 World Economies by GDP (2018) (millions of US dollars)

- United States: 20,544,343
- China: 13,608,152
- Japan: 4,971,323
- Germany: 3,947,620
- United Kingdom: 2,855,297
- France: 2,777,535
- India: 2,718,732
- Italy: 2,083,864
- Brazil: 1,868,626
- Canada: 1,713,342

deaths and the Broad Street water pump and lead to a change in the water and waste systems. Dr. Snow's visualization is shown in **Exhibit B.4**.

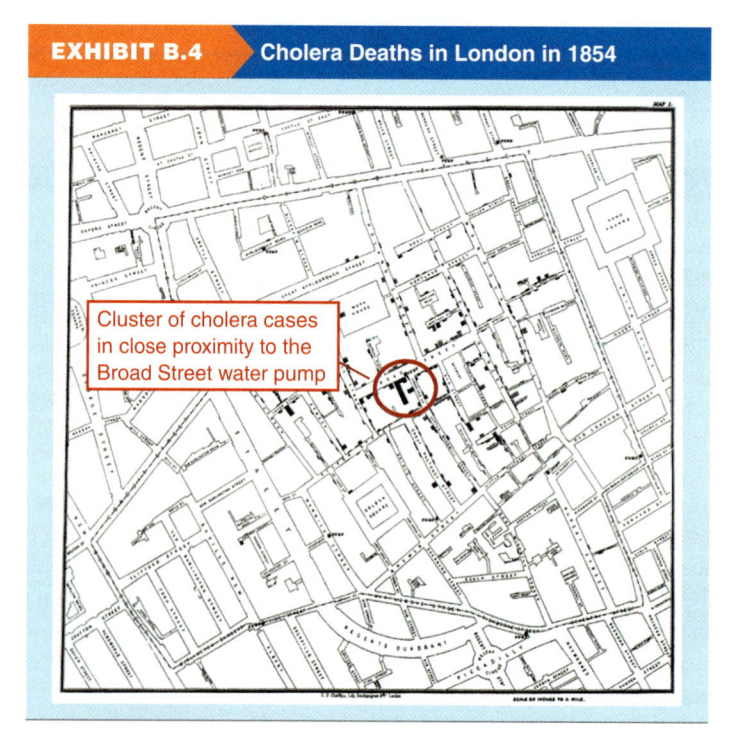

EXHIBIT B.4 Cholera Deaths in London in 1854

[Map of London showing cholera deaths with annotation: "Cluster of cholera cases in close proximity to the Broad Street water pump"]

Good visualization design can be enhanced by considering how our brains process visual details such as form, position, and color.

For example, items that are different from the rest become the focus of attention as shown in **Exhibit B.5**. An item that is longer, wider, or in a different orientation will stand out, as will an item that is of a different size, shape, in a different position, or has a different hue or intensity of color.

EXHIBIT B.5 Displays that Emphasize How Differences Focus Our Attention

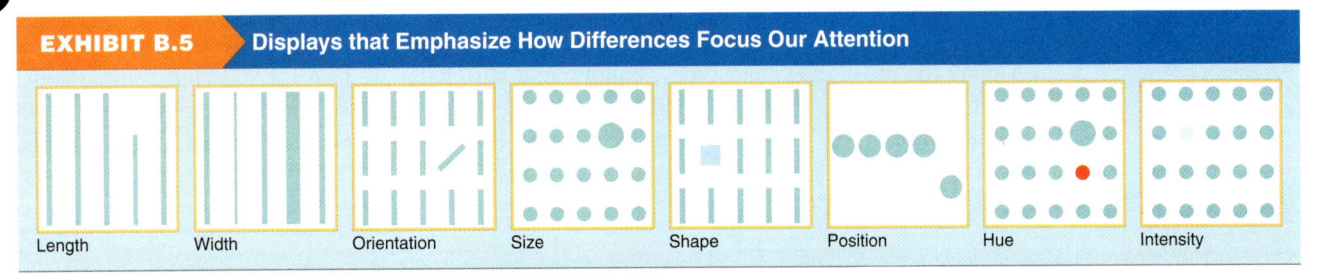

Length | Width | Orientation | Size | Shape | Position | Hue | Intensity

While the use of color can help an item to stand out, it is important to use color correctly. The use of too much color can add to visual clutter. And it's important that color is used consistently, such as always representing a certain year or category. The choice of color is also important since color can convey meanings that differ from one culture to another. For example, red may mean good luck, and green may mean jealousy.

Good visualization design requires the removal of items that detract from the message that we are trying to communicate. **Visual clutter** confuses the audience and lessens the chance that they will be able to easily understand the information that is being conveyed. The concept that less is more is the essence of the visualization design principles developed by Edward Tufte, a statistician and professor emeritus at Yale University. Tufte uses the term chart-junk to refer to any unnecessary or confusing elements included in information displays. His principles show that "excellence in statistical graphics consists of ideas communicated with clarity, precision and efficiency."[4]

Exhibit B.6 illustrates **Tufte's principles**. Note in the first visualization all of the visual clutter only serves to distract the audience from seeing the main point that the United States is the largest economy based on its GDP. Now notice how much cleaner the second visualization is after removing the distracting yellow background, the color coding of each economy, the redundant labeling, and the unnecessary grid lines.

EXHIBIT B.6 Illustration of Tufte's Principles

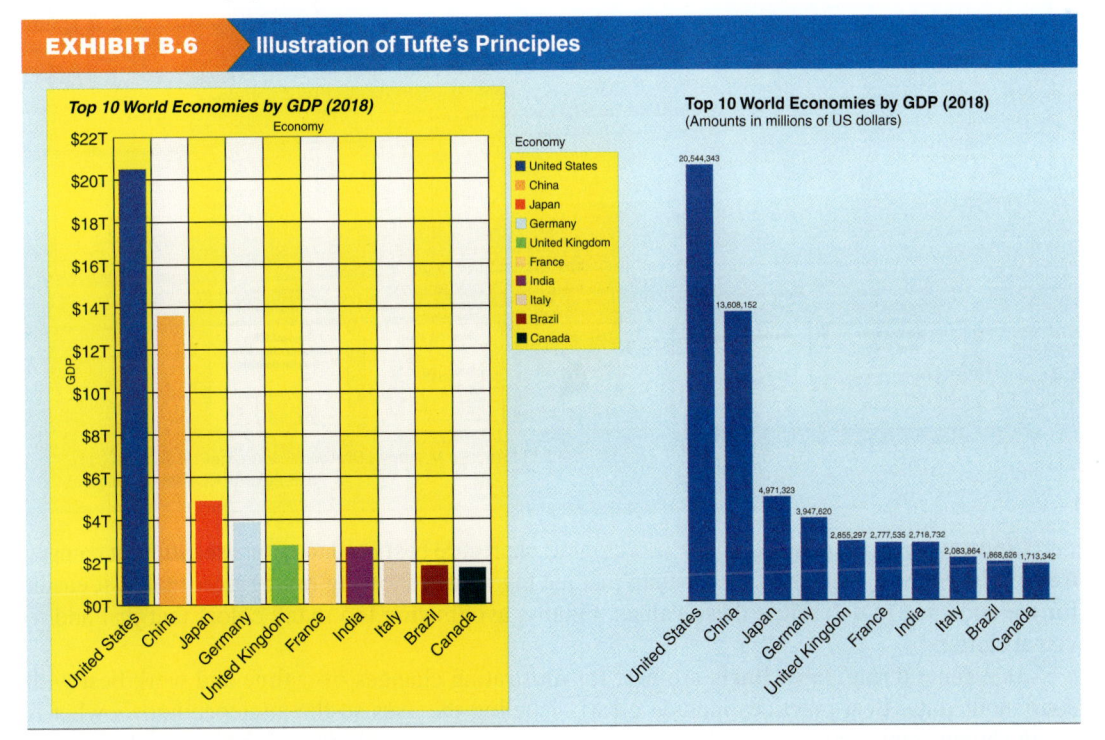

Good visualization construction also involves choosing the most effective chart type depending on what information is being presented.

---
[4] E.R. Tufte, *The Visual Display of Quantitative Information* (Graphics Press, Cheshire, CT 2001).

The starting point for all of the visualizations we will be discussing is a simple table of data. While the table is excellent for looking up values and can precisely communicate numerical values, visualizations in the form of charts provide the audience an easier method to see what the analyst is attempting to convey.

Among the most used chart types, column and bar charts are best for showing comparisons, line charts are useful for showing trends, pie charts are typically used for showing how individual parts make up a whole, and scatter plots are best for showing relationships and distributions. **Exhibit B.7**, reprinted with permission from the author, provides an excellent tool to help in choosing the correct chart type.[5]

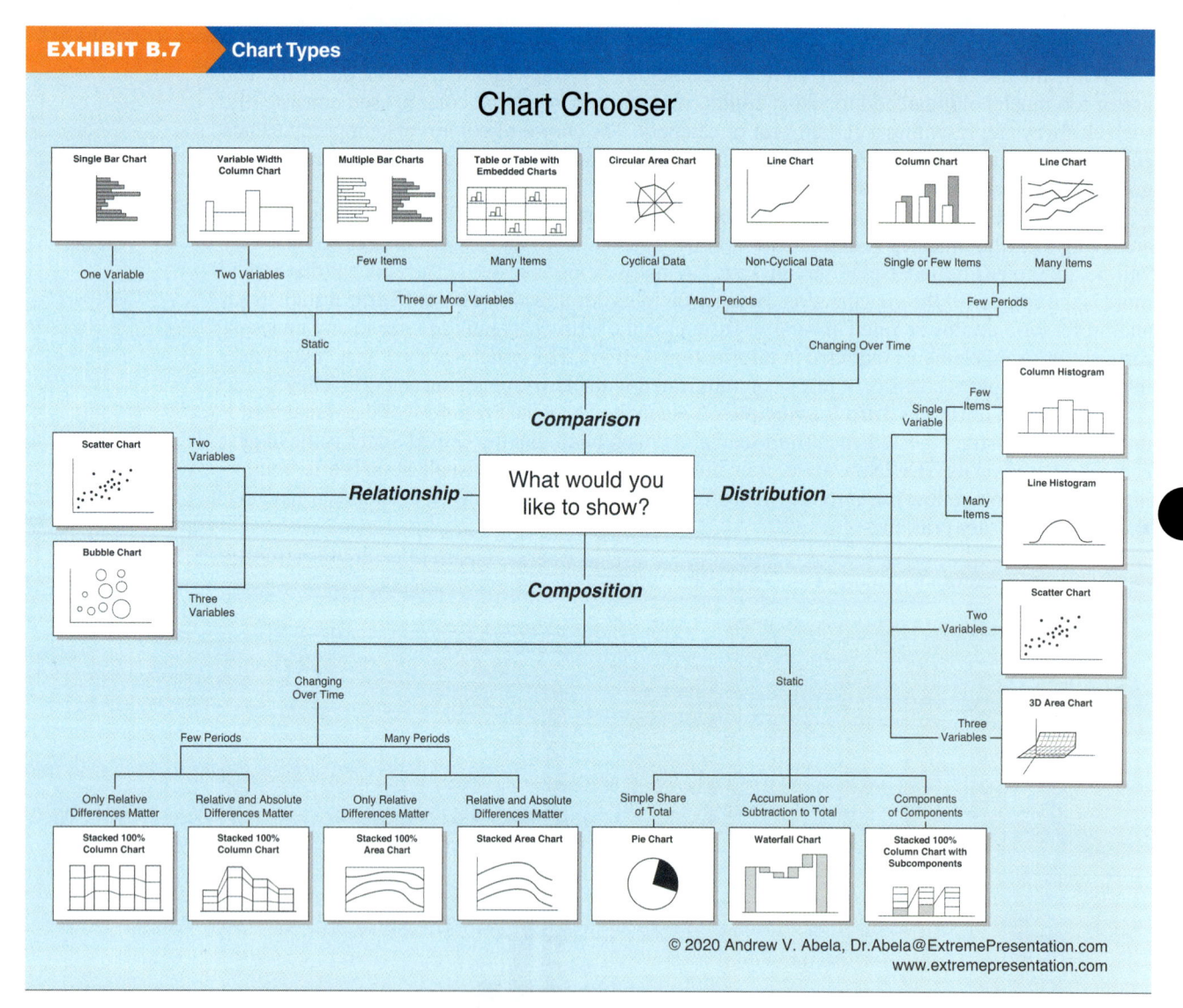

EXHIBIT B.7 | Chart Types

Chart Chooser

© 2020 Andrew V. Abela, Dr.Abela@ExtremePresentation.com
www.extremepresentation.com

Column (vertical) charts and **bar** (horizontal) charts are best used to compare different categories. Adding labels to the bars rather than just having values showing on the axes makes it easier for the audience to determine these values. Finally, avoid using too many colors that just add to visual clutter.

As a general rule, **line charts** are best for illustrating changes over time and work best with continuous data. Best practices include clearly labeling the axes so the audience knows what is being shown, removing excess clutter such as grid lines and redundant labeling, and avoiding comparing more than five to seven lines.

Pie charts are best used to show parts of a whole. Be sure the parts add up to 100 percent. Pie charts work best when there are just a few categories. If there are many categories of similar size,

---
[5] Abela, Andrew V. (2013). *Advanced Presentations by Design: Creating Communication that Drives Action*. John Wiley & Sons.

consider using a bar or column chart instead. Finally, avoid the temptation to get "fancy" with 3-D imagery and tilting the pie chart.

Scatter plots are useful if the goal is to show correlations between two variables. They are also useful for showing data distributions and clustering, which can identify anomalies and outliers. A **bubble chart** can extend the capability of a scatter plot by adding an additional dimension through changing the size of each bubble in the scatter plot. The more data that is included in a scatter plot or bubble chart, the better are the comparisons that can be made. If the elements being graphed are distributed over a very wide range, the horizontal axis can be converted from a linear to a logarithmic scale (where the numbers on the horizontal axis increase by multiples of a number). Bubble charts should use only circles rather than other shapes. Bubble charts should be scaled based on the area of the circle and not the diameter.

A **map chart** is a good choice if the data being conveyed in the visualization includes geographic locations. Map charts are best at showing relative differences in numerical values among geographic locations rather than precise differences since the values are usually portrayed as differences in a color gradient.

There are several general rules to follow regardless of the chart type. The following list was found from a search of best practices for data visualization charts.[6]

- Time axis. When using time in charts, set it on the horizontal axis. Time should run from left to right. Do not skip values (time periods), even if there are no values.
- Proportional values. The numbers in a chart (displayed as bar, area, bubble, or other physically measured element in the chart) should be directly proportional to the numerical quantities presented.
- Visual clutter. Remove any excess information, lines, colors, and text from a chart that do not add value.
- Sorting. For column and bar charts, to enable easier comparison, sort your data in ascending or descending order by the value, not alphabetically. This applies also to pie charts.
- Legend. You don't need a legend if you have only one data category.
- Labels. Use labels directly on the line, column, bar, pie, etc., whenever possible, to avoid indirect look-up.
- Colors. In any chart, don't use more than six colors.
- Colors. For comparing the same value at different time periods, use the same color in a different intensity (from light to dark).
- Colors. For different categories, use different colors. The most widely used colors are black, white, red, green, blue, and yellow.
- Colors. Keep the same color palette or style for all charts in the series and the same axes and labels for similar charts to make your charts consistent and easy to compare.

BLOCKCHAIN TECHNOLOGY

Blockchain technology differs from the traditional accounting ledger in a fundamental way that has immense implications for the accounting profession. A traditional ledger system is a closed system controlled at a centralized location with individuals at the centralized location responsible for the maintenance and integrity of the ledger. In contrast, a blockchain is an open, decentralized ledger, where the ledger is distributed across multiple computers called **nodes**. The blockchain ledger is managed autonomously by the distributed nodes such that data is authenticated by mass collaboration rather than by a central authority. Each node on the blockchain maintains a complete copy of all past transactions that have been added to the ledger. Thus, by comparing to the other nodes' copies, the ledger is continuously synchronized. Unlike traditional accounting ledgers, none of the nodes has any special rights that differ from those of the other nodes.

Blockchains get their name because new ledger data are periodically bundled into blocks, which are then added to previous blocks to form a chain. Each block can contain a cryptocurrency exchange, as is the case with **Bitcoin**, but other possibilities include sales transactions, equity

LO6
Describe how blockchain technology works and its use within the accounting profession.

---

[6] https://eazybi.com/blog/data_visualization_and_chart_types/

trades, loan payments, election votes—pretty much any contract transaction. In addition, the block contains a **time stamp** and a **hash #**, which together form a cryptographic signature associated with the previous blocks. This time stamp and hash make the blockchain essentially tamper-proof because the blocks cannot be changed without the change being apparent to all other nodes. While the chain propagates in only a single chronological order, it can be audited in both directions. **Exhibit B.8** is a visual depiction of the blockchain process.

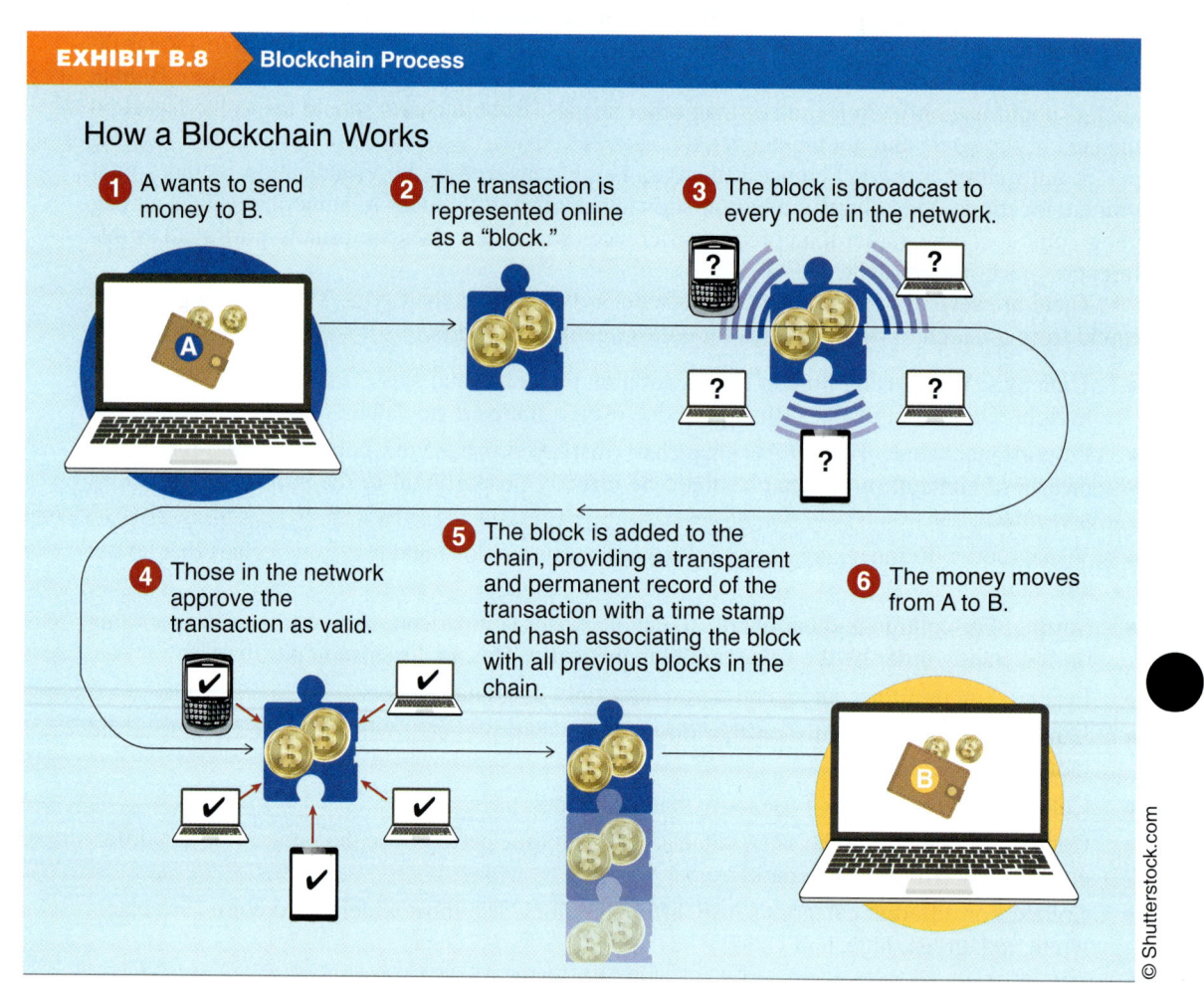

EXHIBIT B.8 Blockchain Process

How a Blockchain Works

1. A wants to send money to B.
2. The transaction is represented online as a "block."
3. The block is broadcast to every node in the network.
4. Those in the network approve the transaction as valid.
5. The block is added to the chain, providing a transparent and permanent record of the transaction with a time stamp and hash associating the block with all previous blocks in the chain.
6. The money moves from A to B.

© Shutterstock.com

The accounting profession has seen changes arising from a vast array of technological innovations, from computer spreadsheets to general ledger software to enterprise resource systems. Blockchain technology represents another innovation in the way accounting is and will be performed. The invention of double-entry accounting, the bedrock of financial accounting, allowed managers to trust their own financial recordkeeping. Unfortunately, the same level of trust does not exist with outsiders, which is why companies rely on independent auditors for an opinion on the integrity of an entity's financial statements. These audits are often very time consuming and costly.

Accountants working in the traditional centralized-ledger environment are likely to spend a large amount of time reconciling accounts and amounts. This involves comparing balances at their company with external documents from outside entities, including banks, brokerages, and business partners, among others. In addition to the time-consuming process of acquiring all the needed sources of information and performing the comparisons, additional time and effort are often needed to reconcile any differences. In a blockchain's distributed ledger system, all node participants can continually confirm all transactions, greatly reducing the effort involved in periodic reconciliations.

Accountants working in the traditional environment are expected to produce internal, ad hoc reports. This often requires considerable effort reconciling internal documents, perhaps from multiple departments or divisions. In a blockchain environment, accountants spend far less time verifying transactional data, freeing up time for more valuable advisory activities.

As a final example of the many ways blockchain technology will change the way accountants work, consider the traditional closing of the books at the end of each period. Instead of needing to acquire the necessary data, verify its accuracy, and make all the necessary adjustments, one could envision a far more automated process with the use of blockchain technology. Financial statements could be updated continuously from data provided by the blockchain, making the period-ending closing process much less time consuming.

Blockchain technology is widely viewed as the next major step in financial accounting. Instead of keeping separate records documenting each transaction, transactions can be written directly into the decentralized ledger. Thus, each transaction is distributed and cryptographically signed to ensure against later falsification or destruction. This has the potential to allow auditors to automatically verify much of the data in a traditional audit, freeing them to provide value in more important areas, such as the analysis of complex transactions or operational efficiencies.

Some accountants may worry that these evolving technologies will diminish the need for accountants. If history is any indication, the opposite is likely. The accountant's role in the financial process will certainly change, but this change will be evolution, not extinction. Information will still need to be interpreted and categorized before entering the blockchain, and this is where future accountants will provide their value. The Big Four accounting firms realize this and are at the forefront in research on how blockchain technology will be used.

SUMMARY

Define Big Data and describe its four attributes. (p. B-2) — **LO1**
- Big data is a collection of data that is both extremely large and also extremely complex, thus making its analysis beyond the scope of traditional tools.
- The four attributes of Big Data are volume, variety, velocity, and veracity.

Identify and define the four types of data analytics. (p. B-2) — **LO2**
- Data analytics can broadly be defined as the process of examining sets of data with the goal of discovering useful information from patterns found in the data.
- Data analytics can be categorized into four types: descriptive, diagnostic, predictive, and prescriptive.

Describe the use of data analytics within the accounting profession. (p. B-3) — **LO3**
- Many accountants are already performing descriptive and diagnositc data analytics.
- Accountants can add value by performing predictive and prescriptive data analytics.
- The large accounting firms have devoted large resources to data analytics.
- Being well trained in data analytics is important for future accountants.

Describe the analytics mindset. (p. B-4)
- Analytics is the process of deriving value from the data.
- An analytics mindset requires critical thinking and judgement.
- The four steps of the analytics mindset include (1) asking the right questions; (2) extracting, transforming, and loading the data; (3) applying the proper analytics techniques; and (4) interpreting and presenting the results.

Describe data visualization best practices. (p. B-6) — **LO5**
- Form, position, and color can be used to have elements stand out without any conscious effort by the audience.
- Tufte's principles of design emphasize the elimination of visual clutter that serves to distract from the ability of a visualization to convey its message.
- Use of the proper chart type can help the intended audience to visualize comparisons, compositions, distributions, and relationships in the data.

Describe how blockchain technology works and its use within the accounting profession. (p. B-10) — **LO 6**
- A blockchain represents a decentralized ledger system and each decentralized computer on the blockchain is called a node.

- Unlike a traditional ledger system where authority for maintenance and integrity rests at a centralized location, each node on the blockchain has the same rights as each other node.
- Each block in the blockchain contains information, such as transaction details, along with a time stamp and a hash linking the block to previous blocks in a chronological order.
- Blockchains are essentially tamperproof because alteration to a block by a node would be apparent to every other node on the blockchain.
- Blockchain technology represents another innovation that will change the way accountants perform their work. Blockchain technology will fundamentally change the way audits are performed, and greatly reduce the time and effort spent on tasks, such as reconciling source documents, producing ad hoc reports, and performing period-ending book closings.

VIDEO RESOURCES FOR TABLEAU

Many assignments require the use of Tableau. For anyone new to Tableau, the following videos are recommended. In addition to these videos, Tableau offers many more free training videos on its website under the learning tab.

A general introduction to the software. (25 minutes). https://www.tableau.com/learn/tutorials/on-demand/getting-started?playlist=484034

An introduction to the Tableau interface. (4 minutes). https://www.tableau.com/learn/tutorials/on-demand/tableau-interface?playlist=484034

Gaining an understanding of relationships in order to connect to outside data. Stop at 14 minutes and 33 seconds. https://www.tableau.com/learn/tutorials/on-demand/relationships?playlist=484036

A general introduction to visual analytics. (6 minutes). https://www.tableau.com/learn/tutorials/on-demand/getting-started-visual-analytics?playlist=484037

How to use sorting. (5 minutes). https://www.tableau.com/learn/tutorials/on-demand/sorting?playlist=484037

An introduction to filtering. (2 minutes). https://www.tableau.com/learn/tutorials/on-demand/ways-filter?playlist=484037

A deeper look at filtering. (7 minutes). https://www.tableau.com/learn/tutorials/on-demand/using-filter-shelf?playlist=484037

Using interactive filters. (4 minutes). https://www.tableau.com/learn/tutorials/on-demand/interactive-filters?playlist=484037

An introduction to formatting. (7 minutes). https://www.tableau.com/learn/tutorials/on-demand/formatting?playlist=484037

The formatting pane. (7 minutes). https://www.tableau.com/learn/tutorials/on-demand/formatting-pane?playlist=484037

An introduction to calculation in Tableau. (3 minutes). https://www.tableau.com/learn/tutorials/on-demand/getting-started-calculations?playlist=484040

Calculation syntax in Tableau. (4 minutes). https://www.tableau.com/learn/tutorials/on-demand/calculation-syntax?playlist=484040

MULTIPLE CHOICE

LO 1 1. Which of the following are four characteristics of big data?
   a. Volume, variety, vagueness, veracity
   b. Volume, variety, velocity, veracity
   c. Volume, validate, velocity, veracity
   d. Volume, variety, velocity, vulnerability

LO 2 2. Which of the following are the four categories of data analytics?
   a. Descriptive, diagnostic, predictive, prescriptive
   b. Expressive, diagnostic, predictive, prescriptive
   c. Descriptive, analytical, predictive, prescriptive
   d. Descriptive, diagnostic, prognostic, prescriptive

3. What is the correct order of the steps in the analytics mindset?
   a. Extract, transform, and load the data; ask the right questions; apply the proper analytics techniques; interpret and present the results.
   b. Ask the right questions; extract, transform, and load the data; apply the proper analytics techniques; interpret and present the results.
   c. Ask the right questions; extract, transform, and load the data; interpret and present the results; apply the proper analytics techniques.
   d. Ask the right questions; apply the proper analytics techniques; extract, transform, and load the data; interpret and present the results.

4. Charts are used in visualizations to convey the following primary types of information:
   a. comparisons, compositions, distributions, and relationships.
   b. comparisons, historical, distributions, and relationships.
   c. comparisons, compositions, forecasts, and relationships.
   d. geographical, compositions, distributions, and relationships.

5. Which of the following statements is not true regarding the use of color in a chart?
   a. Use at most six different colors in a chart.
   b. To show changes in an item over time use a color gradient rather than different colors.
   c. Always use color in a chart to differentiate items.
   d. Use the same color palette in a chart series.

6. The glue that binds blocks in a blockchain consists of what?
   a. Time stamps
   b. Sequential numbering
   c. Regulatory approval
   d. Hashes
   e. Both *a.* and *d.*

DATA ANALYTICS AND DATA VISUALIZATIONS

Data Analytics and Data Visualization Activities are available in myBusinessCourse. These assignments use **Excel** and **Tableau** to expose students to visual depictions of data and to introduce students to data analytics. These exercises are easily assignable and auto graded by MBC.

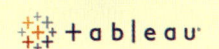

Index

A

absorption costing, 17-28–17-29, 23-12–23-13
   alternatives to inventory valuation, 17-32–17-33
   income under, 17-29–17-31
   production exceeds sales, 17-31
   sales exceed production, 17-31–17-32
absorption cost, 17-6
accelerated depreciation, 8-7
Accenture PLC, 7-4
accounting, 2-14
   accrual, 2-14
      for revenues and expenses, 2-14–2-15
   defined, 1-2, 1-3
   estimates, changes in, 8-9
   information, 1-3
      costs and benefits of disclosure, 1-6
      users of, 1-4–1-5
   for investments
      with control, 12-22–12-30
      in derivatives, 12-35–12-36
      with significant influence, 12-17–12-22
accounting cycle, 3-3–3-4
   steps in, 3-3e
   See also adjusting accounts for financial statements
accounting equation, 1-9–1-10, 2-3
accounting information
   financial accounting, 13-3–13-4
   managerial accounting, 13-4–13-6
accounting rate of return, 24-8–24-9, 24-13–24-14
   net present value vs., 24-13
accounts, 2-9–2-10. *See also specific accounts*
accounts payable, 2-6, 9-4–9-6
accounts receivable, 2-5, 6-14–6-15
   aging of, 6-15e
   uncollectible accounts
      determining allowance for, 6-15–6-16
      footnote disclosures and interpretations, 6-19–6-21
      reporting allowance for, 6-16–6-17
      recording write-offs of, 6-17–6-19
accounts receivable turnover (ART), 5-14, 6-25
accrual accounting, 2-14
   for revenues and expenses, 2-14–2-15
accrual adjustments, 3-12
accruals, 3-12
accrued expenses, 3-16
accrued income. *See* accrued revenues
accrued income tax, 3-17–3-18
accrued interest, 3-17
accrued liabilities, 2-6, 9-4, 9-6–9-10
   accounting for, 9-6–9-7
   contingent liabilities, 9-7
   warranties, 9-8–9-9
accrued revenues, 3-16
accrued sales revenue/income, 3-16
accrued wages, 3-16–3-17
accumulated depreciation, 3-15, 8-5
accumulated other comprehensive income (AOCI), 2-7, 11-16
accumulated other comprehensive loss, 2-7
accumulated post-employment benefit obligation (APBO), 10-23
acquired assets, 12-24–12-28
acquisition of investment, 12-6–12-7
activities list, 17-12
activity, 13-13
activity-based approach, 21-6
activity-based cost drivers, 18-22
activity-based costing (ABC)
   and activity-based management, 18-18
   applications of systems, 18-17–18-18
   challenges of implementing, 18-16–18-17
   and customer profitability analysis
      customer profitability profile, 18-19
      illustrated, 18-20–18-22
   hierarchy of activity costs, 18-8–18-10
   limitations of, 18-16
   product cost model, 18-11–18-15
   summarizing concepts, 18-10–18-11
   time-driven, 18-17–18-18
   traditional and, 18-15–18-16
   two-stage, 18-11–18-12
activity-based management (ABM), 18-18
activity cost drivers, identifying, 14-21
activity costs, hierarchy of, 18-8–18-10, 18-9e
activity variance, 22-10
actual capacity, 19-11, 19-12
actuarial losses (and gains), 10-16
additional paid-in capital, 2-7
Adidas, 1-16, 1-25
adjusted trial balance, 3-19
adjusting accounts for financial statements
   accounting cycle, 3-3–3-4, 3-27e
   adjusting accounts, 3-11
      adjustments, types of, 3-12–3-18
      ethics and adjusting entries, 3-18–3-19
      unadjusted trial balance, 3-11
   analyzing and recording transactions
      accounting procedures, 3-4
      recording transactions, 3-4–3-10
   constructing financial statements
      adjusted trial balance preparation, 3-19
      financial statements preparation, 3-21–3-24
      financial statement analysis, 3-27–3-28
      temporary accounts, closing, 3-24–3-26
adjusting entries, 3-12
Adler Corporation, 10-36
administrative costs, 15-4
advertising expense, to cash paid for advertising, 4-12–4-13
Aetna, Inc., 4-2
Aflac Incorporated, 2-6
aggressive write-down, 8-12
aging analysis, 6-15
Airbnb, 11-7
Alliance Boots GmbH, 2-2
allocated common costs, 23-6, 23-7
allocated segment costs, 23-6
allocated support costs, 18-11
allowance for doubtful (uncollectible) accounts
   determining, 6-15–6-16
   footnote disclosures and interpretations, 6-19–6-21
   reporting, 6-16–6-17
   write-offs, 6-17–6-19
allowed costs, 22-7
Allstate Corporation, 6-8
Alltel Corporation, 9-2
Alphabet, Inc., 6-20, 7-4, 11-5, 12-2, 12-14, 15-18e
   accounting for investments with significant influence, 12-17–12-22
   debt securities, 12-14
Amazon.com, Inc., 1-24, 13-5, 19-2–19-4, 20-14, 24-2–24-4, 24-7, 24-23, 24-26
American Bar Association, 13-19
American Institute of Certified Public Accountants (AICPA), 1-18, 13-6, 13-19
American Medical Association, 13-19
amortization, 9-19
   discount and premium, effects of, 9-20–9-22
   of identifiable intangible assets, 8-19–8-20
analysis implications, 8-23–8-24
Andersen, Arthur, 13-21
Anheuser-Busch Inbev NV/SA, 16-7, 16-9, 16-11, 16-14, 16-17, 16-19, 16-21
annuity, 9-15, 24-10, 24-22–24-23, 24-22e
Anthropologie, 18-23, 18-25

Apple Inc., 4-18, 9-8, 16-14, 24-2
    uncertain tax positions, 10-31
appraisal costs, 23-23
Aramark Corporation, 16-14
arm's-length, 6-28
articulation of financial statements, 1-14
artificial intelligence (AI), 13-17
asset, 1-8
    acquired, 12-24–12-28
    characteristics, 2-3–2-4
    current, 2-5
    defined, 2-3
    measuring, 2-5–2-6
    noncurrent, 2-5
    right-of-use, 10-5
    short-term and long-term, 1-8e
    See also specific assets
asset-related costs, 8-12
asset sales, 8-10–8-11
    gains and losses on, 8-10–8-11
asset turnover (AT), 5-11–5-12, 12-20
    disaggregation of, 5-13–5-15
    profit margin and, 5-12
asset utilization, 6-26
asset write-downs, 6-30
    analysis of, 8-11–8-12
AT&T, 9-2, 17-14
Atwell Laboratories, Inc., 3-27
Audi, 23-15
auditor, role of, 1-19
available-for-sale (AFS) securities, 12-9, 12-15
average collection period (ACP), 6-25
average cost (AC), 7-11–7-12, 14-9–14-11
average inventory days outstanding (AIDO), 7-22
average total assets, 5-9
avoidable common costs, 23-7

B

backflush costing, 19-17
bad debts expense, 6-16
balance sheet, 1-11, 1-12e, 5-5e
    in accounting equation form, 2-22
    adjusting to FIFO, 7-18
    Coca-Cola Company, 5-7
    comparative, 4-9e
    Deere & Company, 10-4e
    effecting inventory costing, 7-18
    effects of defined benefit pension plans, 10-15–10-17
    equation, 1-11
    Home Depot, Inc., 7-4e
    Natural Beauty Supply Inc., 2-12e, 2-20e, 3-23e
    Nike, Inc., 1-11, 1-12e
    One World Café, 4-23e
    PepsiCo, 5-5e
    preparation from adjusted accounts, 3-22
    Procter & Gamble Company, 8-4e
    reporting financial condition, 2-3–2-4
    reporting operating activities in, 5-24
    transactions, analyzing and recording, 2-8–2-12
    Walgreens Boots Alliance, Inc., 2-4e
balanced scorecard, 23-21–23-26
    dashboard, 23-26
    framework, 23-21–23-25
    and strategy, 23-25–23-26
balloon payment, A-5
bank financing, leasing over, 10-4
Bank of America, 18-24
bar, B-9
Barnes & Noble, 16-14
basic earnings per share (BEPS), 11-19
batch-level activity, 18-8
Bausch & Lomb, 13-6, 13-11, 13-15
Bausch Health, 13-6
Bechtel Corporation, 17-12
Bell Atlantic Corporation, 9-2
Ben & Jerry's, 18-3–18-5, 18-7–18-8, 18-13, 18-16
benchmarking, 20-13
    applications of, 20-14
    process of, 20-14–20-15
Benford's Law, B-4
Berkshire Hathaway Inc., 11-21
Best Buy, 17-3, 18-24, 24-2
Beyond Meat Inc., 5-2
big bath, 6-27
big data, 13-17, 19-20
bill of materials, 17-12
Bitcoin, 1-24, B-10
Block, Inc., 14-2, 14-3
blockchain, 1-24, B-10–B-12
Blue Apron Holdings, Inc., 5-19
board of directors, 1-5
Boeing Company, 10-24, 13-14
bonds, 9-15
    financing, reporting of, 9-18–9-20
    issued at discount, 9-16–9-17, 9-21e
    issued at par, 9-16
    issued at premium, 9-17, 9-22e
    pricing, 9-15–9-17, 9-17e
    repurchase, 9-24
book of original entry, 3-4
book-tax differences, 10-25–10-31
book value (BV), 3-15, 8-5, 8-7
    of bond, 9-24
    per share, 11-18
Boston Beer Company, The, 16-2, 16-3, 16-10, 16-16, 24-17–24-19
    contribution income statement, 16-9e
    differential analysis for, 16-8e
bottom-up budget, 21-22
break-even point, 15-9
    and margin of safety
        cost-volume-profit graph, 15-12–15-13
        profit-volume graph, 15-13
    in sales dollars, 15-11
    sales dollars at target profit, 15-11–15-12
    in unit sales, 15-9–15-10
    unit sales at target profit, 15-10–15-11
    multiple-product cost-volume-profit analysis
        in sales dollars with multiple products, 15-16–15-19
        in unit sales with multiple products, 15-15–15-16
    in sales dollars, 15-11
Bristol-Myers Squibb Company, 8-24
Broadcomm, 17-2
bubble chart, B-10
budgetary slack, 21-23
budgeted financial statements, 21-15–21-16
budgeting, 21-3
    activity-based approach, 21-6
    for communication and coordination, 21-4
    developing honesty in, 21-24
    development and manager behavior
        budgeting periods, 21-23
        employee participation, 21-22–21-23
        ethics, 21-24
        forecasts, 21-23–21-24
    development in manufacturing organizations
        cash budget and financial statement budgets, 21-20–21-21
        manufacturing cost budget, 21-20
        production budget, 21-19
    guide to action and basis of evaluation, 21-4
    incremental approach, 21-6–21-7
    master budget, 21-8–21-10
        budgeted financial statements, 21-15–21-16
        cash budget, 21-13–21-15
        finalizing, 21-16–21-17
        general and administrative expense budget, 21-13, 21-13e
        period balance sheet, beginning of, 21-10–21-11
        purchases budget, 21-11–21-12
        sales budget, 21-19
        selling expense budget, 21-12
    for objectives, 21-6
    output/input approach, 21-5–21-6
    periods, 21-23
    for planning, 21-3–21-4
    in risk management, 21-4–21-5
    for uncertainty, 21-7
    zero-based budgeting, 21-7–21-8
Built-Rite Construction, 6-11–6-13
business activities, 1-7, 1-7e
    financing activities, 1-9–1-10
    investing activities, 1-8
    operating activities, 1-10
    planning activities, 1-7–1-8
business environment, assessing, 5-3–5-4
business skills, for decision-making, 19-20

Note: Exhibits included in the index with *e* following the page numbers.

Butler Company
    average cost, 7-11–7-12, 7-12e
    financial statement effects of inventory costing methods, 7-17e
    first-in, first-out, 7-8–7-9, 7-9e
    last-in, first-out, 7-10, 7-10e
    LIFO inventory and cost of goods sold, 7-25e
    summary inventory records for, 7-8e

C

calendar year, 1-11, 3-3
California's Hospital Fair Pricing Act (CHFPA), 22-21
call feature, 11-6
call provision, 9-24
capacity costs, 5-11, 14-11. *See also* committed fixed costs
capacity variance, 22-25
capital budgeting, 24-2
    additional aspects
        differential analysis of predicted project cash outflows, 24-17–24-18
        evaluating risk, 24-15–24-16
        multiple investment criteria, 24-15
        predicting differential costs and revenues, 24-18–24-19
    approval process, 24-4–24-5
    evaluation of models, 24-12–24-15
        advantages and disadvantages of, 24-13–24-15
    long-range planning and, 24-3–24-6
    models considering time value of money
        cost of capital, 24-12
        internal rate of return, 24-11–24-12
        net present value, 24-14
        payback period, 24-27–24-28
        predicted cash flows, 24-26–24-27
    models do not considering time value of money
        accounting rate of return, 24-8–24-9
        payback period, 24-7–24-8
    procedures, 24-4e
    to save money, 24-4
    table approach for internal rate of return
        equal cash flows, 24-24–24-25
        unequal cash flows, 24-23
    taxes in
        depreciation tax shield, 24-26–24-28
        investment tax credit, 24-28
    time value of money
        annuities, 24-22–24-23
        deferred returns, 24-23–24-24
        future value, 24-20
        present value, 24-20–24-22, 24-22e
        unequal cash flows, 24-25–24-26
capital budgeting committee, 24-4
capital expenditures, 8-4, 24-3
    analysis of, 24-27, 24-28e
capital markets, globalization of, 1-20

capitalized cost, 8-3
capitalized interest, 8-4
Carnegie Steel Company, 13-8
carrying value, 8-5, 8-7
cash, 2-5, 5-28
cash accounting, 2-15
cash budget, 21-13–21-15
cash burn rate (CBR), 5-19
cash discounts, 7-6, 9-5
cash dividends, 11-11–11-13
    financial effects of, 11-12–11-13
cash equivalents, 2-5, 4-3
cash flows
    equal, 24-24–24-25
    unequal, 24-23
cash operating cycle, 2-30, 2-31e
    effecting inventory costing, 7-18
    preparation from adjusted accounts, 3-23
    preparation of, 5-29
cash receipts, revenues and, 6-12–6-13
Caterpillar Financial Services Corporation, 5-22
causation, 19-19
Certified Management Accountant, 13-5
channel stuffing, 6-27, 22-4
Chapman Enterprises, 12-30
chart of accounts, 2-10, 3-43-3-44e
Charter Communications, 6-26
Chartered Global Management Accountant (CGMA) competency framework, 19-20, 19-20e
Chartered Institute of Management Accountants (CIMA), 13-6
Cheesecake Factory, The, 17-3
Chevron Corporation, 7-24
Chick-fil-A, 13-8, 13-9
Cisco Systems, 8-18
    multilevel segment reporting approach, 23-4–23-6
Clark Corporation, 10-26–10-29
close expense accounts, 3-25
close revenue accounts, 3-25
closing process, temporary accounts, 3-24–3-25
Coca-Cola Company, 5-2, 5-10, 5-15, 5-23, 8-19, 12-6, 12-20, 13-6, 17-23, 23-3
    balance sheets, 5-7
    financial statement effects of equity investments, 12-20–12-22
    income statements, 5-7
codes of ethics/conduct, 13-19–13-20
coefficient of determination, 14-16
cognitive technologies, 13-17
Colgate-Palmolive Company, 8-2, 8-14–8-15, 12-36
collateral, 9-13, 9-31
collectibility risk, 6-15
column, B-9
Comcast Corporation, 6-26, 9-2
commitments and contingencies, disclosure of, 9-26–9-27, 10-36–10-38

committed fixed costs, 14-11
Committee of Sponsoring Organizations (COSO), 13-17
common segment costs, 23-6
common-size financial statements, 5-4. *See also* financial statement, analysis
common stock, 2-7
    dividends on, 11-11–11-12
communication, budgeting and, 21-4
company changes, 5-22
comparability, 1-27
Compass Group North America, 16-14
completeness, 1-27
complex capital structure, 11-19
compound entries, 2-22
compound interest, A-1
comprehensive income, 11-16
comprehensive performance measurement systems, 23-21
computer integrated manufacturing (CIM), 24-19
confirmatory value, 1-26
conglomerate effects, 5-22
conservative accounting methods, 9-29
consignment sale, 6-7
consolidated financial statements, 12-22
    basis of, 12-22
    limitations of, 12-30
    mechanics, 12-31–12-33
consolidation accounting mechanics, 12-28e, 12-31–12-33
constructing financial statements
    from adjusted accounts
        adjusted trial balance preparation, 3-19
        financial statements preparation, 3-21–3-24
    equity, reporting on
        equity transactions, 2-19–2-20
        statement of stockholders' equity, 2-20–2-21
    financial condition reporting
        assets, 2-3–2-6
        balance sheet transactions, 2-8–2-12
        liabilities and equity, 2-6–2-8
    financial performance reporting, 2-12–2-13
        accrual accounting for revenues and expenses, 2-14–2-15
        income statement transactions, 2-16–2-19
        retained earnings, 2-15–2-16
    financial statements analysis
        current ratio, 2-31
        net working capital, 2-30
        quick ratio, 2-32
    journalizing and posting transactions
        analyze, journalize, and post, 2-24–2-29
        debit and credit system, 2-22
        journal entry, 2-23

Note: Exhibits included in the index with *e* following the page numbers.

constructing financial statements, *(continued)*
    journalizing and posting transactions, *(continued)*
        T-account, 2-21
        T-account with debits and credits, 2-23
Consumers Energy, 24-4
contingent liabilities, 9-7
continuous budgeting, 21-23
continuous improvement, 20-12–20-13
contra accounts, 3-15
contra asset, 3-15
contra equity account, 11-9
contract asset, 6-13
contract liability, 6-8, 6-12
contractual obligations, 10-37
contributed capital, 2-7–2-8, 11-3–11-4
    accounting for stock transactions, 11-7–11-11
    classes of stock
        common stock, 11-4–11-5
        preferred stock, 11-5–11-6
contribution income statement, 15-6–15-7
    contribution margin, 15-7–15-9
    functional income statement vs., 15-7e
    with income taxes, 15-22e
contribution margin, 15-6–15-9
contribution margin ratio, 15-8
control account, 17-15
controllable costs, 22-22
controlling, 13-10–13-11
controlling influence, 12-4
    investments with
        accounting for, 12-22–12-24
            noncontrolling interest, 12-28–12-30
            reporting of acquired assets and liabilities, 12-24–12-28
conversion cost, 17-6
conversion feature, 11-6
convertible securities, 11-22–11-23
cookie jar reserve, 6-20, 9-9
copyrights, 8-19
corporate governance, 13-21
corporate social responsibility, 13-21
corporation, 1-4
correlation, 19-19
cost-based pricing
    critique of, 20-7
    economic approach, 20-3
    multiple-product companies, 20-5–20-6
    new product, 20-4e
    pricing, 20-3–20-8
    single-product companies, 20-5
    special orders, 20-7
cost behavior
    basic patterns, 14-3–14-4
    committed and discretionary fixed costs, 14-11–14-12
    factors affecting patterns, 14-6
    relevant range, 14-7–14-9
    total cost function, 14-6–14-7
cost benefit analysis, 18-15–18-16
cost center, 22-5
    performance reporting
        flexible budgets, 22-7–22-8
        standard costs and performance reports, 22-10–22-11
cost cross-subsidization, 18-7, 18-16
cost drivers, 13-14, 17-9
    identifying activity, 14-21
    profitability analysis with unit and nonunit, 18-22–18-25
cost estimation, 14-12
    changes in technology and prices, 14-20
    high-low, 14-12–14-14
    identifying activity cost drivers, 14-21
    least-squares regression, 14-15–14-19
    matching activity and costs, 14-20–14-21
    scatter diagrams, 14-14–14-15
cost flow assumption, 7-8
cost leadership, 13-8
cost method, 12-14
cost of acquisition, inventory and, 7-6
cost of capital, 24-12
cost of compliance, 23-23
cost of debt, 9-29–9-31
cost of goods produced, 7-6
cost of goods sold, 1-12, 2-14, 7-7, 7-7e, 17-4, 17-18–17-19
    convert to cash paid for merchandise purchased, 4-11–4-12
cost of noncompliance, 23-23
cost of production report, 17-23–17-26, 17-32e
cost of quality report, 23-24
cost prediction, 14-13
cost reduction proposal, 16-4
cost savings
    overestimating, 24-19
    underestimating, 24-19
cost-volume-profit (CVP) analysis, 15-3
    break-even point and margin of safety
        cost-volume-profit graph, 15-12–15-13
        margin of safety in unit sales, 15-9–15-10
        profit-volume graph, 15-13
        in sales dollars, 15-11
        sales dollars at a target profit, 15-11–15-12
        unit sales at target profit, 15-10–15-11
    contribution income statement, 15-6–15-7
        contribution margin, 15-7–15-9
        functional income statement vs., 15-7e
    and income taxes, 15-21–15-22
    key assumptions, 15-14
    multiple-product
        break-even in sales dollars with multiple products, 15-16–15-19
        break-even in unit sales with multiple products, 15-15–15-16
    operating leverage, 15-19–15-21
    profit equation, 15-3–15-5
        in multiple scenarios, 15-5–15-6
cost-volume-profit graph, 15-12–15-13
Costco Wholesale Corporation, 24-9, 24-15, 24-19, 24-28
costing methods
    inventory, 7-7–7-8
        average cost, 7-11–7-12
        first-in, first-out, 7-8–7-9
        inventory costing and price changes, 7-11
        last-in, first-out, 7-9–7-11
        lower of cost or net realizable value, 7-13–7-14
costs to capitalize, 8-4–8-5
coupon (contract/stated) rate, 9-15, 9-17e
covenants, 5-16, 9-31
COVID-19 pandemic, 1-22, 4-2, 20-2
Cray Inc., 17-12
credit, 2-14
    risk analysis, 1-23–1-24
    sales, 6-14
creditors, 1-4–1-5
    (or debt) financing, 1-9, 1-9e
Cricket, 17-14
Crown Department Stores, 13-10
Cummins Inc., 10-39
current asset, 2-5, 5-18
current liabilities, 2-6–2-7, 5-18
    accounts payable, 9-4–9-6
    accrued liabilities, 9-6–9-10
    nonoperating (financial), 9-10–9-13
    others, 9-10
current maturities of long-term debt, 2-7, 9-4, 9-12–9-13, 9-25
current ratio (CR), 2-31, 5-18
current tax expense, 10-33
customer-level activity, 18-9
customer profitability analysis
    customer profitability profile, 18-19
    illustrated, 18-20–18-22
customer profitability profile, 18-19
CVS Health Corp., 2-2, 2-32, 4-2, 4-7, 6-24
    financial statements analysis
        free cash flow, 4-31
        operating cash flow to capital expenditures, 4-31–4-32
        operating cash flow to current liabilities, 4-29–4-30
        reconciliation of net income and cash flow from operating activities, 4-17–4-18, 4-17e
        statement of cash flows, 4-4e
cycle efficiency, 19-18
cycle time, 19-15

Note: Exhibits included in the index with *e* following the page numbers.

D

dashboards, 23-26, B-5
data analytics, 1-24
    accounting profession, B-3–B-4
    analytics mindset, B-4–B-5
    big data, B-2
    data analytic tools, B-5–B-6
    data visualization, B-6–B-10
    types of, B-2–B-3
Dauntless Ltd., 4-6e
Davis Company, 11-7, 11-9
days inventory outstanding. *See* average inventory days outstanding
debt financing, 1-9, 1-9e, 5-16e
debt securities, passive investments in, 12-6–12-12
    acquisition of investment, 12-6–12-7
    debt investments marked to fair value, 12-9–12-12
    investments marked to fair value, 12-8
    investments reported at cost, 12-7
    sale of investment, 12-8–12-9
debt system, 2-22
debt-to-equity (D/E) ratio, 9-27
    to Nike, 1-23–1-24
    solvency analysis, 5-20
decentralized organizations, 23-3
Deere & Company, 10-2
    balance sheets of, 10-4e
    components of deferred income taxes assets and liabilities, 10-33e
    financial statements analysis, 10-38–10-39
    footnote disclosures
        of leases, 10-12–10-14
        pensions, 10-18–10-23
    income tax expense, 10-32–10-35
    underfunded pension obligations, 10-16
default, 9-29
    risk, 5-17
deferrals, 3-12
deferred performance liabilities, 9-4
deferred returns, 24-23–24-24
deferred revenues, 2-7, 3-13–3-14
deferred tax assets, 10-29
    in cash flow statement, 10-35
    computation and analysis of, 10-35
    revaluation due to tax rate change, 10-31–10-32
deferred tax expense, 10-33
deferred tax liability, 10-26
    revaluation due to tax rate change, 10-31–10-32
defined benefit pension plan, 10-15
    balance sheet effects of, 10-15–10-17
    income statement effects of, 10-18
defined contribution pension plan, 10-15
definite life, 8-19
Dehning Company, 8-5–8-10, 8-16
Dell Inc., 7-23
Dell Technologies, 13-14, 17-22

Deloitte, 13-11, 13-17, B-4
Delta Air Lines, 6-8, 8-14, 13-5, 17-3
Department of Education, 23-22
departmental allocation rate costing model, 18-5e
depletion, 8-9
depreciation, 3-15, 8-5–8-6
    accelerated, 8-7
    accumulated, 8-5, 3-15
    straight-line, 3-15
    methods, 8-6–8-9
        double-declining-balance method, 8-7–8-8
        straight-line method, 8-7
        units-of-production method, 8-8–8-9
    for tax purposes, 8-9
depreciation base, 8-6
depreciation expense, eliminating, 4-14–4-15
depreciation rate, 8-7
depreciation tax shield, 24-26–24-28, 24-27e
derivatives
    accounting for investments in, 12-35–12-36
    disclosure of, 12-35–12-36
    reporting of, 12-35–12-36
descriptive analytics, B-2
design for manufacture, 20-10
Diageo, 22-4
diagnostic analytics, B-3
differential analysis
    limited resources, use of
        multiple constraints, 16-20
        single constraint, 16-19–16-20
        theory of constraints, 16-20–16-21
    predicted project cash outflows, 24-17–24-18
    preparing and applying
        equipment replacement decision, 16-7–16-9
        outsourcing decisions, 16-14–16-17
        profit plan of discontinuing, 16-11–16-12
        profit plans, changes in, 16-9–16-11
        sell or process further, 16-17–16-9
        special orders, 16-12–16-14
differential costs, predicting, 24-18–24-19
digital skills, for decision-making, 19-20
diluted earnings per share (DEPS), 11-19–11-20
dilutive securities, 11-19
    convertible securities, 11-22–11-23
    restricted stock, 11-25–11-27
    stock options, 11-24–11-25
    stock rights, 11-23–11-24
direct association, 7-3–7-4
direct cost, 14-21
direct costing. *See* variable costing
direct department cost, 19-5
direct department overhead costs, 18-11
direct fixed, 14-22

direct labor (DL), 14-22, 15-4, 17-6
    standards for, 22-15–22-17
    variances, 22-15
        interpreting, 22-16
direct materials (DM), 14-22, 15-4, 17-6
    standards for, 22-11–22-15
    variances, 22-15–22-17
        interpreting, 22-13–22-15
direct method, 4-18, 19-6–19-7
    advantages and disadvantages, 19-7
    step method vs., 19-7–19-8
direct segment fixed costs, 23-6
direct variable cost, 14-22, 23-6
directors, 1-5
disclosure, costs and benefits of, 1-6
discontinued operations, 6-29
discount
    amortization, 9-20–9-22
    bonds issued at, 9-16-17, 9-19
    cash, 7-6, 9-5
    net-of-discount method, 9-5–9-6
    rate, 24-10, 24-22, A-3
discretionary fixed costs, 14-11–14-12
disinvestment phase of cash flows, 24-6
disposal value, 16-6
dividends, 5-27–5-28
    cash, 11-11–11-13
    on common stock, 11-11–11-12
    large stock, 11-14
    payout ratio, 5-27
    preference, 11-5
    small stock, 11-13
    stock, 11-13–11-14
division margins, 23-6
divisions, 23-3
Domtar, 13-12
double-declining-balance (DDB) method, 8-7–8-8, 24-26
    straight-line (SL) method vs., 8-8e
double-entry accounting system, 2-9
DoubleClick, Inc., 12-2
DowDuPont Inc., 9-9
dual overhead allocation rates, 19-14
dual prices, 23-13
DuPont Model, The, 5-13

E

earned capital, 2-8, 11-4
    cash dividends, 11-11–11-13
    comprehensive income, 11-16
    stock dividends and splits, 11-13–11-14
    stock transactions and the cash flows statement, 11-15
    See also retained earnings
earnings management, 6-27–6-29
    potential for, 12-16–12-17
earnings per share (EPS), 11-19–11-20
    computation and analysis of, 11-20–11-21
earnings without interest expense (EWI), 5-9

economic consequences, 1-17
economic value added (EVA), 23-19
effective cost of debt, 9-17–9-18, 9-20
effective tax rate, 5-27, 10-34, 10-35e
E.I. DuPont de Nemours and Company, 5-13
Electronic Arts, Inc., 6-11
Eli's Cheesecake, 22-7, 22-11, 22-14–22-15, 22-17, 22-20, 22-24–22-25
Emory University, 19-4
employee benefit plans, 10-18
employee participation, 21-22–21-23
employee severance costs, 6-30
employee wages, accrual of, 9-7
ending inventory costs, 17-26
Energizer Holdings, Inc., 19-3
Engel Company, 6-21–6-22
Enron, 1-5, 1-16, 13-21
enterprise risk management (ERM), 13-17.
  See also risk
environmental/social considerations, 13-20–13-21
Epson, 20-13
equal cash flows, 24-24–24-25
equity, defined, 2-6
equity financing, 1-9, 1-9e
equity income, 12-19
equity method accounting
  and effects on ratios, 12-20
  mechanics, 12-31–12-33
equity securities, passive investments in, 12-12–12-17
  financial statement disclosures, 12-14–12-16
  potential for earnings management, 12-16–12-17
equivalent completed units, 17-25
Ernst & Young (EY), 13-20, B-4
ESG, 13-14
Ethereum, 1-24
ethics
  and adjusting entries, 3-18–3-19
  in budgeting, 21-24
  in managerial accounting, 13-18–13-20
    codes of ethics/conduct, 13-19–13-20
    corporate governance, 13-21
excess capacity cost
  calculating, 19-13
  managing, 19-13
  overhead application rate
    calculating, 19-11–19-13
    dual, 19-14
executory contract, 2-6, 2-18
exit/disposal costs, 6-30
expected cash flows, 24-14
expense recognition principles, 2-14, 7-3–7-4
expense-to-sales (ETS), 5-14
expenses, 1-10, 2-12, 5-26
  accrual accounting for, 2-14–2-15
  converting to cash flows, 4-12–4-14

explanatory visualizations, B-6
external failure costs, 23-23
Exxon Mobil, 17-11
EY, 13-20

F

face amount, 9-15
Facebook, Inc., 12-2
facility-level activity, 18-9
factoring, 6-26
fair value, 2-5, 12-5–12-6
  adjustments, 12-10–12-12
  debt investments marked to, 12-9–12-12
  hierarchy, 12-5
  investments marked to, 12-9–12-12
  option, 9-22–9-23, 12-6
faithful representation, 1-26–1-27
Fastenal Company and Subsidiaries, 11-19
Faultless, Inc., 4-6e
favorable materials price variance, 22-13–22-14
favorable materials quantity variance, 22-14
favorable variable overhead spending variance, 22-18
Federal Aviation Administration, 13-5
FedEx, 18-24
finance lease, 10-6–10-8
  criteria for, 10-6
  liability, amortization table for, 10-8e
  operating lease vs., 10-10–10-11
financial accounting, 1-3–1-28, 1-3e, 13-3–13-4
  accounting information, 1-3
    costs and benefits of disclosure, 1-6
    users of, 1-4–1-5
  business activities, 1-7, 1-7e
    investing activities, 1-8
    financing activities, 1-9–1-10
    operating activities, 1-10
    planning activities, 1-7–1-8
  financial statements, 1-11, 1-11e
    balance sheet, 1-11, 1-12e
    financial statement linkages, 1-14–1-15
    income statement, 1-12, 1-12–1-13e
    statement of cash flows, 1-13–1-14, 1-14e
    statement of stockholders' equity, 1-13, 1-13e
  financial statements analysis
    credit risk analysis, 1-23–1-24
    profitability analysis, 1-21–1-22
    technology and accounting, 1-24
  managerial accounting vs., 13-5e
Financial Accounting Standards Board (FASB), 1-18, 1-20, 1-25, 10-5
financial analysts, 1-5
financial condition reporting
  assets, 2-3–2-6
  balance sheet transactions, analyzing and recording, 2-8–2-12
  liabilities and equity, 2-6–2-8

Financial Executives International, 24-5
financial information
  qualitative characteristics of, 1-26–1-27
  enhancing, 1-27
financial investments, 12-3
  accounting for investments in derivatives, 12-35–12-36
  consolidation accounting mechanics, 12-31–12-33
  defined, 12-3
  equity method mechanics, 12-31–12-33
  fair value, 12-5
  financial statement analysis, 12-30–12-31
  investments with control
    accounting for investments with control, 12-22–12-30
    noncontrolling interest, 12-28–12-30
    reporting of acquired assets and liabilities, 12-24–12-28
  investments with significant influence
    accounting for investments with significant influence, 12-17–12-22
    equity method accounting and effects on ratios, 12-20
    financial statement disclosures, 12-20–12-22
  passive investments in debt securities, 12-6–12-12
    acquisition of investment, 12-6–12-7
    debt investments marked to fair value, 12-9–12-12
    investments marked to fair value, 12-9–12-12
    investments reported at cost, 12-7
    sale of investment, 12-8–12-9
  passive investments in equity securities, 12-12–12-17
    financial statement disclosures, 12-14–12-16
    potential for earnings management, 12-16–12-17
  strategic goals, 12-3
financial leverage, 5-9, 9-3, 12-20
financial management, 1-9
financial performance reporting, 2-12–2-13
  accrual accounting for revenues and expenses, 2-14–2-15
  income statement transactions, analyzing and recording, 2-16–2-19
  retained earnings, 2-15–2-16
financial reporting
  conceptual framework for
    additional underlying basic assumptions, 1-27–1-28
    cost constraints, 1-27
    enhancing qualitative characteristics, 1-27
    qualitative characteristics of useful financial information, 1-26–1-27

Note: Exhibits included in the index with *e* following the page numbers.

financial reporting, *(continued)*
  environment
    generally accepted accounting principles, 1-17
    global perspective, 1-19–1-20
    regulation and oversight, 1-17–1-18
    role of auditor, 1-19
  management reporting vs., 18-16–18-17
  objective of, 1-25–1-26
financial statement, 1-11, 1-11e
  analysis, 3-27–3-28, 5-3
  assumptions underlie preparation of, 1-27–1-28
  balance sheet, 1-11, 1-12e
  budgeted, 21-15–21-16
  business environment, assessing, 5-3–5-4
  consolidated, 12-22
  core operating activities
    balance sheet, reporting operating activities in, 5-24
    income statement, reporting operating activities in, 5-23–5-24
    RNOA, disaggregating, 5-24–5-25
  disclosures
    Alphabet, Inc., 12-14
    Coca-Cola Company, 12-20–12-22
  effecting inventory costing, 7-16–7-19
    adjusting balance sheet to FIFO, 7-18
    adjusting income statement to FIFO, 7-19
    balance sheet, 7-18
    cash flow, 7-18
    changing costs, 7-17–7-18
    income statement, 7-16–7-17
    LIFO reserve, 7-16
  effects and disclosure, 7-14–7-16
  effects of stock issuance, 11-7–11-8
  financial statement linkages, 1-14–1-15
  forecasts, 5-25–5-29
  horizontal analysis, 5-6
  income statement, 1-12, 1-12–1-13e
  inventory costs in
    recording, 7-5–7-6
    reporting, 7-4, 7-5e
  linkages, 1-14–1-15
  liquidity analysis
    cash burn rate, 5-19
    current ratio, 5-18
    operating cash flow to current liabilities, 5-18–5-19
    quick ratio, 5-18
  ratio analysis limitations
    company changes, 5-22
    conglomerate effects, 5-22
    GAAP limitations, 5-21–5-22
    means to an end, 5-22
  return on investment
    disaggregating ROA into profit margin and asset turnover, 5-11–5-15
    return on assets, 5-8–5-9, 5-10e
    return on equity, 5-8, 5-10e
    return on financial leverage, 5-9–5-10, 5-10e
  solvency analysis
    debt-to-equity, 5-20
    times interest earned, 5-20–5-21
  statement of cash flows, 1-13–1-14, 1-14e
  statement of stockholders' equity, 1-13, 1-13e
  vertical analysis, 5-4
financial statement effects template (FSET), 2-9, 2-10, 2-17, 2-24
financing activities, 1-9–1-10, 4-5–4-6, 4-20–4-21, 21-9–21-10
  gains and losses on, 4-24–4-25
  noncash investing and, 4-25–4-27
finished goods inventories, 7-6, 17-4
Finn Corporation, 11-15
first-in, first-out (FIFO), 7-8–7-9, 17-26
  adjusting balance sheet to, 7-18
  adjusting income statement to, 7-19
fiscal year, 1-11, 3-3
Fitbit, 12-2
Fitch, 9-30
fixed commitments ratio, 10-38
fixed costs, 14-3–14-4
  committed and discretionary, 14-11–14-12
fixed manufacturing overhead, 15-4
fixed overhead variance, 22-19–22-20, 22-24–22-25
fixed overhead volume variance, 22-25
fixed selling and administrative costs, 15-4
FIXthat4U, 14-9, 14-10
Flexe Inc., 14-6
flexible budgets, 22-7–22-8
  development of, 22-10–22-11
  performance report, 22-8–22-10, 22-9e
  variance, 22-8, 22-10
flexible manufacturing systems (FMS), 24-19
Fluor Corporation, 6-14
footnote disclosures
  components of plan assets and PBO, 10-18–10-20
  components of pension expense, 10-20–10-21
  financial statement, 9-24–9-25
  and future cash flows, 10-21–10-23
  intangible assets, 8-22–8-23
  and interpretations, accounts receivable, 6-19–6-21
  of leases, 10-12–10-14
  other post-employment benefits, 10-23
  property, plant, and equipment assets, 8-14
  valuation of pension, 10-20
for-profit organizations, 13-7
Ford Motor Credit Company, 5-22, 17-10
  forecasts, 21-23–21-24
  financial statement, 5-25
    cash, 5-28
    errors, 5-29
    net income, dividends, and retained earnings, 5-27–5-28
    nonoperating assets, liabilities, revenues and expenses, 5-27
    operating assets and liabilities, 5-26–5-27
    operating expenses, 5-26
    preparing cash flow statement, 5-29
    sales revenue, 5-25–5-26
foreign currencies, effect on statement of cash flows, 4-27
Forever 21, 19-16
Fortune (magazine), 1-10
franchise rights, 8-19
free cash flow (FCF), 4-31
free from error, 1-27
free on board (FOB) destination, 7-6
free on board (FOB) shipping point, 7-6
Frilly, 17-14
Frozen Yogurt (Fro-Yo) Cookie Dough, 18-3–18-4
FTE Networks, 1-16
full absorption cost, 17-6
full costs, 16-13, 17-28. *See also* absorption costing
functional income statement, 15-6
  contribution income statement vs., 15-7e
funded status, 10-16
future cash flows, footnote disclosures and, 10-21–10-23
future revenues, 16-4
future value, 24-20, A-2–A-3, A-2e
future value calculations, A-7–A-10
future value factor, A-2

G

gain on bond retirement, 9-24
Galvani Bioelectronics, 15-12
Gannett Co., Inc., 6-30
Gap Inc., 10-14, 20-14
  performance obligations and product returns at, 6-7
Garmin Ltd., 17-3
general and administrative expense budget, 21-13, 21-13e
General Electric (GE), 10-22, 11-12, 12-26, 12-30
general journal, 3-4
General Motors Co. (GM), pension obligation, 10-21
generally accepted accounting principles (GAAP), 1-17
  accelerated depreciation methods, 8-7
  accounting for share repurchases, 11-9
  accumulated postemployment benefit obligation, 10-23
  asset value recognition, 8-12
  contingent liabilities reporting, 9-7
  fair value, defined, 12-5

generally accepted accounting principles (GAAP), *(continued)*
   footnote disclosures for pensions, 10-18
   influence/control, levels of, 12-3–12-4
   interest and statement of cash flows, 6-3
   inventory, 7-15, 7-19
   gains or losses on bond repurchases, 9-24
   goodwill, 8-24, 12-26–12-28
   limitations of ratio analysis, 5-21–5-22
   pension fund status, 10-24
   revenue recognition, 6-11
   revenue reporting, 2-14
   warranty liability, 9-9
Georgia Pacific, 13-12
gift card liabilities, 2-15
Gigler Company, 9-13
Gillette Electronics, 10-6–10-8, 15-10
goals, 13-7
   attainment, 13-9–13-10
Goldman Sachs, 9-15
goodwill, 8-21–8-22
   and indefinite-lived intangible assets, 8-22
   and intangible assets, 8-23
   reporting of, 12-26–12-28
Google Analytics, 20-14
Google Inc., 1-11, 1-24, 12-2
Google Sheets, B-2
governance, 13-21
government agencies, 1-5
Graphic Packaging, 13-12
gross margin return on inventory investment (GMROI), 19-18
gross profit, 2-14, 7-4
gross profit margin (GPM) ratio, 5-13, 7-20–7-21
GTE, 9-2

H

Hanna Company, 11-13
Harley Davidson, 20-5
hash #, B-11
Haskins, Inc., 6-14
held-to-maturity (HTM), 12-7, 12-8
Herman Miller, 17-12
Hershey, 13-19, 17-3
Hertz, 1-28
heterogeneity in cost, 17-11, 18-6
heterogeneity in use, 17-11, 18-6
Hewlett-Packard Company (HP, Inc.), 8-18, 13-14, 16-14, 17-12, 20-13
high-low method of cost estimation, 14-12–14-14
"high yield" bonds, 9-30
historical cost, 2-5, 5-21–5-22, 9-22, 11-3
Home Depot, Inc., 1-11, 5-14, 7-2, 7-15
   balance sheets, 7-4e
   financial statements analysis
      average inventory days outstanding, 7-22
      gross profit margin ratio, 7-20–7-21

inventory turnover ratio, 7-21–7-22, 7-24
   income statement, 7-5e
horizontal analysis, 5-6
HTC Corporation, 12-2
Hutton Company holds, 7-12–7-13

I

IBM, 6-20, 18-10
ideal transfer-pricing arrangement, 23-13
identifiable intangible assets, 8-20–8-21
identifiable net assets, 8-22
IKEA, 17-7
IMA, 13-5
immediate recognition, 7-4
imposed budget, 21-22
incentive compensation, 1-5
income, defined, 1-10
income smoothing, 6-27
income statement, 1-11, 1-12, 1-12–1-13e, 5-5e, 6-3–6-5
   adjusting to FIFO, 7-19
   budgeted and actual, 22-25–22-27, 22-26e
   classifications, 6-3e
   Coca-Cola Company, 5-7
   effecting inventory costing, 7-16
   effects of defined benefit pension plans, 10-18
   Home Depot, Inc., 7-5e
   Microsoft Corporation, 6-4–6-5, 6-4e
   Natural Beauty Supply Inc., 2-19e, 3-22e, 4-9e, 4-13–4-14
   One World Café, 4-23e
   PepsiCo, 5-5e
   preparation from adjusted accounts, 3-18, 3-22
   reporting operating activities in, 5-23–5-24
   statement of cost of goods manufactured and, 17-19e
   transactions, analyzing and recording, 2-16–2-19
income taxes
   accounting for, 10-25–10-36
   book-tax differences, 10-25–10-31
   deferred tax assets
      in cash flow statement, 10-35
      computation and analysis of, 10-35
      and liabilities, 10-31–10-32
   disclosures, 10-32–10-35
incremental approach, 21-6–21-7
independent audit firm, 1-19
indirect costs, 14-22
indirect department cost, 19-5
indirect fixed costs, 14-22
indirect labor costs, 17-13
indirect method, 4-18–4-19
   interpreting cash flows from operations using, 4-29
indirect variable, 14-22
initial investment phase of cash flows, 24-6

inspection time, 19-15
installment loans, 9-13–9-15
Institute of Management Accountants (IMA), 13-5, 13-19
insufficient write-down, 8-11–8-12
intangible assets, 2-5, 8-3
   analysis implications, 8-23–8-24
   copyrights, 8-19
   footnote disclosures, 8-22–8-23
   franchise rights, 8-19
   goodwill, 8-21–8-22
   identifiable, amortization and impairment of, 8-19–8-21
   patents, 8-18–8-19
   research and development costs, 8-17–8-18
   trademarks, 8-19
Intel Inc., 8-19, 16-14, 17-3, 17-11, 17-22, 17-28, 17-33
interdepartmental services, 19-3
interest
   cost, 10-16
   and statement of cash flows, 9-26
internal control systems, 13-21
internal controls, 1-18
internal failure costs, 23-23
internal rate of return (IRR), 24-11–24-12, 24-14
   models, 24-14
   table approach to, 24-24–24-26
International Accounting Standards Board (IASB), 10-5, 1-20, 1-25
International Financial Reporting Standards (IFRS), 1-20, 11-6
   asset value recognition, 8-12
   contingent liabilities reporting, 9-7
   convertible debt securities, 11-6
   goodwill, 8-24, 12-26–12-28
   inventory, 7-14, 7-19
   pension fund status, 10-24
International Paper, 13-12
Intuit Inc., 6-20
inventoriable product cost, 17-28
inventory, 2-5
   and cost of acquisition, 7-6
   costing methods, 7-7–7-8
      average cost, 7-11–7-12
      financial statement effects of, 7-16–7-19
      first-in, first-out, 7-8–7-9
      inventory costing and price changes, 7-11
      last-in, first-out, 7-9–7-11
      lower of cost or net realizable value, 7-13–7-14
   financial statements analysis
      average inventory days outstanding, 7-22
      gross profit margin ratio, 7-20–7-21
      inventory turnover ratio, 7-21–7-23
   financial statement effects and disclosure, 7-14–7-16

Note: Exhibits included in the index with e following the page numbers.

inventory, *(continued)*
   operating expenses
      expense recognition principles, 7-3–7-4
      reporting inventory costs in financial statements, 7-4, 7-5–7-6, 7-5e
   reporting by manufacturing firms, 7-6–7-7
inventory cost, for financial reporting, 19-4
inventory turnover, 19-17
   in Dollars, 19-18
   in Units, 19-17–19-18
inventory turnover (INVT) ratio, 5-14, 7-21–7-23
   analysis of, 7-22–7-23
investing activities, 1-8, 4-5, 4-19–4-20, 21-9
   gains and losses on, 4-24–4-25
investing equals financing, 1-9
investment base, 23-17
investment center, 22-6
investment center asset base, 23-17
investment center evaluation measures, 23-14–23-21
   economic value added, 23-19
   investment center asset base, 23-17
   investment center income, 23-17
   other valuation issues, 23-18
   residual income, 23-18–23-19
   return on investment, 23-14–23-18
investment center income, 23-17
investment(s)
   accounting
      with control, 12-22–12-30
      in derivatives, 12-35–12-36
      with significant influence, 12-17–12-22
   defined, 23-14
investment tax credit, 24-28
irrelevant costs, 16-3, 16-7
iSixSigma, 20-15

J

Jack's Snacks, Inc., 4-28
job cost sheet, 17-12
job costing, 17-11–17-12
   basic flow of, 17-12–17-14
   overapplied and underapplied overhead, 17-19–17-21
   production planning and control process, 17-12
   for Samsung, 17-14–17-18
   in service organizations, 17-21–17-22
   statement of cost of goods manufactured and cost of goods sold, 17-18–17-19
job order costing, 17-12
job order production, 17-12
job production, 17-12
John Wiley & Sons, Inc., 6-20
Johnson & Johnson, 13-12
joint costs, 16-18

joint products, 16-18
Josie's Jewelry, Inc., 10-29
journal, 3-4
journal entry, 2-21, 2-23
journalizing and posting transactions
   analyze, journalize, and post, 2-24–2-29
   debit and credit system, 2-22
   journal entry, 2-23
   T-account, 2-21
      with debits and credits, 2-23
JOYY Inc., 13-9
JP Morgan Chase, 12-36
Juniper Networks, Inc., 8-18
junk bonds, 9-30
just-in-time inventory (JIT) management/ lean production approach
   characteristics of, 19-14–19-17
   minimized finished goods inventory levels, 19-16
   minimized materials inventory levels, 19-15
   performance evaluation under, 19-17–19-19
   reduced cycle time and work-in-process inventory levels, 19-15–19-16
   simplified recordkeeping under, 19-16–19-17

K

Kaiser Aluminum Corporation, 7-26
Kaiser Permanente, 14-18
Kaizen costing approach, 20-12
Kallapur, Inc., 11-27
Kanban system, 19-16
Kellogg Company, 5-2
Kelly Services, Inc., 7-4
Kimberly-Clark Corporation, 8-2
King Company
   acquisition of investment, 12-7
   fair value adjustments, 12-10–12-12
   investments marked to fair value, 12-12
   investments reported at cost, 12-7
   passive investments in equity securities, 12-12–12-17
   sale of investment, 12-9
Koch Industries Inc., 13-12
Koehler Company, 10-32
Kohl's Corporation, 4-22
Kona Sol, 19-14
KPMG, B-4
Kraft Heinz Company, 13-18
Kroger Company, The, 5-18, 20-14

L

L Brands, Inc., 3-4
labor efficiency variance, 22-15
labor rate variance, 22-15
labor unions, 1-5
Landsman Company, 8-19–8-20
large stock dividends, 11-14
last-in, first-out (LIFO), 7-9–7-11

liquidation, 7-25–7-26
leadership skills, for decision-making, 19-20
leading measures, 23-22
lean production approach, just-in-time inventory (JIT) management and
   characteristics of, 19-14–19-17
   minimized finished goods inventory levels, 19-16
   minimized materials inventory levels, 19-15
   performance evaluation under, 19-17–19-19
   reduced cycle time and work-in-process inventory levels, 19-15–19-16
   simplified recordkeeping under, 19-16–19-17
leaning on trade, 9-5
leases, 10-3–10-5
   and cash flow statement, 10-14
   footnote disclosures of, 10-12–10-14
   lessee reporting of, 10-5–10-6
      classification rules, 10-6
      comparison of operating and finance lease treatment, 10-10–10-11
      finance lease, 10-6–10-8
      operating lease, 10-8–10-10
      other issues, 10-11–10-12
least-squares regression analysis, 14-15–14-19
   Coefficient of Determination, 14-16
   managers, not models, are responsible, 14-16
   simple and multiple regression, 14-17–14-19
lessee, 10-3
   lease classification and accounting treatment for, 10-5
   reporting of leases, 10-5–10-6
      classification rules, 10-6
      comparison of operating and finance lease treatment, 10-10–10-11
      finance lease, 10-6–10-8
      operating lease, 10-8–10-10
      other issues, 10-11–10-12
lessor, 10-3
liabilities, 1-9, 5-26–5-27, 12-24–12-28
   current, 2-6–2-7
      accounts payable, 9-4–9-6
      accrued liabilities, 9-6–9-10
      nonoperating (financial), 9-10–9-13
      others, 9-10
   financial statements analysis, 9-27
      debt ratings and cost of debt, 9-29–9-31
      debt-to-equity ratio, 9-27
      times interest earned, 9-28
   long-term liabilities, 9-13
      bond repurchase, 9-24
      bonds, 9-15
      disclosure of commitments and contingencies, 9-26–9-27

Note: Exhibits included in the index with *e* following the page numbers.

liabilities, *(continued)*
   long-term liabilities, *(continued)*
      discount and premium amortization, 9-20–9-22
      effective cost of debt, 9-17–9-18
      fair value option, 9-22–9-23
      financial statement footnotes, 9-24–9-25
      installment loans, 9-13–9-15
      interest and statement of cash flows, 9-26
      pricing of bonds, 9-15–9-17
      reporting of bond financing, 9-18–9-20
   noncurrent, 2-7
licenses, 8-19
life-cycle budgeting, 21-23
LIFO layer, 7-10, 7-25
LIFO liquidation gain, 7-26
LIFO reserve, 7-16
line charts, B-9
line departments, 13-10–13-11
linear algebra method, 19-19
liquidating value, 11-5
liquidation preference, 11-5
liquidity, 2-5, 4-3, 5-17
   analysis
      cash burn rate, 5-19
      current ratio, 5-18
      operating cash flow to current liabilities, 5-18–5-19
      quick ratio, 5-18
loan amortization table, 9-14, 9-14e
long-range planning, and capital budgeting, 24-3–24-6
long-term debt, 2-7
   current maturities of, 9-4, 9-12–9-13, 9-25
long-term financial investments, 2-5
long-term liabilities, 2-7, 9-13
   bond repurchase, 9-24
   bonds, 9-15
   disclosure of commitments and contingencies, 9-26–9-27
   discount and premium amortization, 9-20–9-22
   effective cost of debt, 9-17–9-18
   fair value option, 9-22–9-23
   financial statement footnotes, 9-24–9-25
   installment loans, 9-13–9-15
   interest and statement of cash flows, 9-26
   pricing of bonds, 9-15–9-17
   reporting of bond financing, 9-18–9-20
long-term operating assets
   financial statements analysis
      cash flow effects, 8-16
      percent depreciated, 8-14–8-15
      PPE turnover, 8-13–8-14
   intangible assets
      analysis implications, 8-23–8-24
      copyrights, 8-19
      footnote disclosures, 8-22–8-23
      franchise rights, 8-19
      goodwill, 8-21–8-22
      identifiable, amortization and impairment of, 8-19–8-21
      patents, 8-18–8-19
      research and development costs, 8-17–8-18
      trademarks, 8-19
   property, plant, and equipment, 8-3
      accounting estimates, changes in, 8-9
      asset sales and impairments, 8-10–8-12
      costs to capitalize, 8-4–8-5
      depreciation, 8-6
      depreciation methods, 8-6–8-9
      footnote disclosure, 8-12
long-term projects, revenue recognition for, 6-11–6-13
loss on bond retirement, 9-24
lower of cost or net realizable value (LCNRV), 7-13–7-14
Lowe's Companies, Inc., 7-21, 7-21e
Luckin Coffee, 1-16
lump-sum amounts, 24-10

M

Macy's Inc., 1-6
managed fixed costs. *See* discretionary fixed costs
management by exception, 21-4, 22-3
management reporting vs. financial reporting, 18-16–18-17
manager behavior
   budgeting development and budgeting periods, 21-23
   employee participation, 21-22–21-23
   ethics, 21-24
   forecasts, 21-23–21-24
managerial accounting, 1-3, 1-3e
   accounting information
      financial accounting, 13-3–13-4
      managerial accounting, 13-4–13-6
   changing environment of business
      big data and analysis, 13-16
      enterprise risk management, 13-17
      global competition/key dimensions, 13-16
      robotics and cognitive technologies, 13-17
   ethics in, 13-18–13-20
      codes of ethics/conduct, 13-19–13-20
      corporate governance, 13-21
   financial accounting vs., 13-5e
   and goal attainment, 13-9–13-10
   mission and goals, 13-6–13-7
   planning, organizing, and controlling, 13-10–13-11
   strategic position analysis, 13-8–13-9
   planning, organizing, and controlling, 13-11e
managers, 1-5
Manchester United Ltd., 3-4
manufacturing costs budget, 21-17–21-18, 22-9e
manufacturing firms, inventory reporting by, 7-6–7-7
manufacturing organizations, 17-3
manufacturing overhead (MO), 14-22
   applying, 17-8–17-11
   predetermined overhead rates, 17-9
   selecting basis, 17-9
manufacturing overhead costs, 17-6
map chart, B-10
margin of safety, 15-9
   break-even point and cost-volume-profit graph, 15-12–15-13
   profit-volume graph, 15-13
   in sales dollars, 15-11
   sales dollars at target profit, 15-11–15-12
   in unit sales, 15-9–15-10
   unit sales at target profit, 15-10–15-11
marginal cost, of one unit, 14-8
mark-to-market technique, 12-5, 12-14
mark-to-model technique, 12-14
market (yield) rate, 9-15, 9-17e
Market Niche, 13-19
market price, 23-11
market-segment-level activity, 18-10
market value, 11-14
marketable securities, 2-5
Marko Company, 18-25
markup pricing, 23-13
master budget, 21-8–21-10
   budgeted financial statements, 21-15–21-16
   cash budget, 21-13–21-15
   finalizing, 21-16–21-17
   general and administrative expense budget, 21-13
   purchases budget, 21-19–21-20
   sales budget, 21-19
   selling expense budget, 21-12
materiality, 1-26
materials price variance, 22-12, 22-13
materials-pull system, 19-16–19-15
materials quantity variance, 22-12, 22-13
materials requisition form, 17-13
McDonald's, 8-19
MCI Communications Corp., 1-5
measurability, 5-21
measurement alternative approach, 12-14
measuring asset, 2-5–2-6
merchandising organizations, 17-3
Metromile, 14-21
Microsoft Corporation, 6-2, 12-2, 15-18e, 16-14
   allowance for doubtful accounts, 6-19–6-21, 6-19e
   financial statements analysis, 6-22

Note: Exhibits included in the index with *e* following the page numbers.

Microsoft Corporation, *(continued)*
  financial statements analysis, *(continued)*
    accounts receivable turnover, 6-25
    average collection period, 6-25
    net operating profit after taxes, 6-22
    net operating profit margin, 6-24
    return on net operating assets, 6-23
  income statements, 6-4–6-5, 6-4e
  revenue recognition, 6-9
Microsoft Excel, 14-15, B-2
minimum dollar return, 23-18
minimum rate of return, 23-18
Mint Mobile, 17-14
mission, 13-6–13-7
Mitel Networks, 12-18
mixed costs, 14-3, 14-4
ModCloth, 17-3
Modified Accelerated Cost Recovery System (MACRS), 10-26
Moneyball, B-3
Moody's investment services, 1-5, 9-30
Morgan Stanley, 13-20
Motorola Mobility Holdings, Inc., 12-2
Motorola Solutions, 13-14
movement time, 19-15
Mug Shots, Inc., 4-16, 4-22
multilevel contribution income statement, 18-22–18-24
  variations in, 18-24–18-25
multilevel segment reporting approach, 23-4–23-6
multiple investment criteria, 24-15
multiple-product cost-volume-profit analysis
  break-even
    in sales dollars with multiple products, 15-16–15-19
    in unit sales with multiple products, 15-15–15-16
multiple regression analysis, 14-17–14-19

N

National Association of Securities Dealers Automated Quotations system (NASDAQ), 1-4
Natural Beauty Supply Inc. (NBS)
  accounts for, 2-10–2-11
  accrued expenses, 3-16
  accrued revenues, 3-16
  adjusted trial balances, 3-21e
  balance sheet, 2-12e, 2-20e, 3-23e
  chart of accounts for, 3-4, 3-4e
  closing revenues and expenses, 3-25e
  comparative balance sheet, 4-9e
  deferred revenue, 3-13–3-14
  equity transactions, analyzing and recording, 2-19–2-20
  general ledger after adjustments, 3-20e
  general ledger before adjustments, 3-10e
  income statement, 2-19e, 3-22e, 4-9e, 4-13–4-14
  transactions, analyzing and recording, 2-16–2-19
  journalizing and posting transactions, 2-24–2-29, 3-4–3-9, 3-5e
  net income and cash flow from operating activities, 4-16
  post-closing trial balance, 3-26e
  prepaid expenses, 3-14–3-16
  revenues and expenses to cash flows from operating activities, 4-10–4-16, 4-16e
  statement of cash flows, 3-24e
    direct method, 4-9e
    indirect method, 4-19e, 4-22e
    from financing activities, 4-20–4-21
    from investing activities, 4-20
  statement of stockholders' equity, 2-20, 2-20e, 3-22e
  temporary accounts, closing, 3-25–3-26
  unadjusted trial balance, 3-12e, 3-21e
negotiated transfer prices, 23-13
Neiman Marcus, 15-19
Nest Labs, 12-2
Nestlé, 5-2, 18-7–18-8, 18-10–18-11, 18-14, 18-22
net assets, 2-12
net book value, 8-7
net income, 1-10, 2-12, 5-27–5-28
  attributable to noncontrolling interests, 6-4
  from operating activities, 4-17–4-18
net loss, 2-12
net-of-discount method, 9-5–9-6
net operating asset (NOA), 5-24
net operating asset turnover (NOAT), 5-25
net operating losses, 10-30–10-31
net operating profit after taxes (NOPAT), 5-23–5-24, 6-22
net operating profit margin (NOPM), 5-24–5-25, 6-24, 12-20
net present value, 24-10–24-11
  internal rate of return vs., 24-14
net realizable value, 6-15
net sales volume variance, 22-23
net unrecovered investment, 24-28
net working capital, 2-30, 5-18
neutrality, 1-27
New York Stock Exchange (NYSE), 1-4
New York Times, 1-20
New York Yankees, 23-25
Nike, Inc., 1-2, 1-16, 4-27, 8-19
  articulation of financial statements, 1-14–1-15, 1-15e
  balance sheet, 1-11, 1-12e
  debt-to-equity ratio to, 1-23–1-24
  income statement, 1-12, 1-12–1-13e
  net income to operating cash flows, 1-14e
  return on equity to, 1-22
  statement of cash flows, 1-13–1-14, 1-14e, 4-27
  statement of stockholders' equity, 1-13, 1-13e
Nikola Corporation, 15-5
Nissim Company, 12-24
  mechanics of acquisition accounting, 12-22–12-24, 12-23–12-24e, 12-28e
nodes, B-10
non-capitalized costs, 5-21
Non-Dairy Cookie Dough, 18-3–18-4
non-GAAP income, 6-28
noncash investing and financing activities, 4-25–4-27
noncash operating expenses, 4-14–4-15
noncontrolling interest, 11-4, 12-28–12-30
noncurrent asset, 2-5
noncurrent liabilities, 2-7
nondiscounting models, 24-6
nonoperating activities, 6-4
nonoperating revenues and expenses, 2-13
nonpension post-employment benefits, 10-23
nonrecurring income components, 6-29
  discontinued operations, 6-29
  exit/disposal costs, 6-30
Norell Company, 8-20
normal credit balance, 2-22
normal debit balance, 2-22
not-for-profit organizations, 13-7
notes payable, 6-15
notes receivable, 6-15

O

Oakland Athletics, B-3
ODP Corporation, 24-2
off-balance-sheet financing, 10-3
  arrangements, 10-37
One World Café, 4-23–4-24, 4-28
  gains and losses on investing and financing activities, 4-24–4-25
  income statement and comparative balance sheets, 4-23e
  noncash investing and financing activities, 4-25–4-27
  statement of cash flow for, 4-24e
    spreadsheet approach to, 4-33–4-35, 4-33e
operating activities, 1-10, 6-4, 21-9
  reporting in balance sheet, 5-24
  reporting in income statement, 5-23–5-24
  RNOA, disaggregating, 5-24–5-25
  statement of cash flows, 4-5, 4-7–4-9
    converting revenues and expenses, 4-10–4-16
    reconciling net income and, 4-17–4-18
    using indirect method, 4-18–4-19

operating assets, 5-26–5-27. *See also* long-term operating assets
operating budgets, 21-4
operating cash flow, 1-14
operating cash flow to capital expenditures (OCFCX), 4-31–4-32
operating cash flow to current liabilities (OCFCL), 4-29–4-30, 5-18–5-19
operating departments, 19-3
operating earnings, 1-10
operating expenses (or costs), 1-10, 2-12, 5-26
   expense recognition principles, 7-3–7-4
   inventory costs in financial statements
      reporting, 7-4, 7-5e
      recording, 7-5–7-6
   noncash, 4-14–4-15
operating income, 1-10, 6-3–6-5
   revenue recognition, 6-5–6-7
      for long-term projects, 6-11–6-13
      subsequent to customer purchase, 6-8–6-13
operating lease, 10-8–10-10
   finance lease vs., 10-10–10-11
operating lease obligation, 2-6–2-7
operating leverage, 15-19–15-21
operating leverage ratio, 15-19
operating liabilities, 5-26–5-27
operating profit, 1-10
operating revenues (or sales), 1-10
operating rights, 8-19
operation phase of cash flows, 24-6
operations list, 17-12
opportunity costs, 16-6, 16-15–16-16
options, 9-31
Oracle, 18-21
order-filling costs, 22-22
order-getting costs, 22-22
order-level activity, 18-9
organization chart, 13-10
organization structures, 22-4–22-5
organizing, 13-10–13-11
other post-employment benefits (OPEB), 10-23
outlay costs, 16-4–16-5
outliers, 14-14
output/input approach, 21-5–21-6
outsourcing, 16-14
overestimating cost savings, 24-19
overfunded, 10-16
overhead, 14-22
overhead allocation basis, 17-9
overhead application rate
   calculating, 19-11–19-13
   dual, 19-14
overhead costs. *See* manufacturing overhead costs
Overstock.com, 21-7–21-8, 21-17, 21-21

P

paid-in capital, 11-26. *See also* contributed capital
par (face) value, 11-4, 11-14
   bonds issued at, 9-16, 9-18
participation feature, 11-6
participative budget, 21-22
partnership, 1-4
passive influence, 12-4
passive investments
   in debt securities, 12-6–12-12
      acquisition of investment, 12-6–12-7
      debt investments marked to fair value, 12-9–12-12
      investments marked to fair value, 12-12
      investments reported at cost, 12-7
      sale of investment, 12-8–12-9
   in equity securities, 12-12–12-17
      financial statement disclosures, 12-14–12-16
      potential for earnings management, 12-16–12-17
patents, 8-18–8-19
payback period, 24-7–24-8, 24-13
PayPal, Inc., 14-6, 14-12, 14-18, 14-23
Peerless Co., 4-6e
Penman Company, 12-28
   acquisition accounting mechanics, 12-23–12-24e, 12-28e
Pension Benefit Guaranty Corporation (PBGC), 10-15
pension expense, components of, 10-20–10-21
pension plan assets, 10-15–10-16
   components of, 10-18–10-20
Pension Protection Act of 2006, 10-21
pensions
   confounding income analysis, 10-22–10-23
   defined benefit plan, 10-15
      balance sheet effects of, 10-15–10-17
      income statement effects of, 10-18
   defined contribution plan, 10-15
   footnote disclosures
      components of plan assets and PBO, 10-18–10-20
      components of pension expense, 10-20–10-21
      and future cash flows, 10-21–10-23
      other post-employment benefits, 10-23
people skills, for decision-making, 19-20
PepsiCo, 1-8, 5-2, 5-18, 24-34
   accounts receivable turnover, 5-14
   asset turnover ratio, 5-11–5-12, 5-11e
   balance sheets, 5-5e
   balance sheet forecast, 5-28e
   debt-to-equity ratio, 5-20
   financial statement forecasts, 5-26–5-29
   gross profit margin, 5-13
   horizontal analysis, 5-6, 5-6e
   income statements, 5-5e
   income statement forecast, 5-27e
   inventory turnover, 5-14
   liquidity ratios, 5-19, 5-19e
   net operating asset, 5-24
   net operating asset turnover, 5-25
   net operating profit after taxes, 5-23–5-24
   net operating profit margin, 5-25
   operating cash flow to current liabilities, 5-18–5-19
   profit margin ratio, 5-11, 5-11e
   property, plant, and equipment turnover, 5-14
   quick ratio, 5-18
   return on assets, 5-8–5-9, 5-10e
   return on equity, 5-8, 5-10e
   return on financial leverage, 5-9–5-10, 5-10e
   statement of cash flow forecast, 5-29e
   times interest earned, 5-21
   vertical analysis, 5-4
percent depreciated, 8-14–8-15
percentage of sales, 6-16
performance measures, financial and nonfinancial, 22-6–22-7
performance obligations, 6-6–6-7
   allocation of sales price in, 6-10e
   satisfied at point in time, 6-12
   satisfied over time, 6-11–6-12
performance report, 13-11
   cost center, 22-5
   flexible budgets, 22-7–22-8
   standard costs and performance reports, 22-10–22-11
   and organization structures, 22-4–22-5
   revenue center, 22-5, 22-20–22-22
      controllable costs, 22-22
      as profit centers, 22-22–22-24
period costs, 7-3–7-4, 17-5, 17-5e
periodic interest payments, 9-15
permanent accounts, 3-24
Pfizer Inc., 1-9, 1-11, 5-14, 7-7, 7-7e, 8-24, 11-2, 12-6
   cash dividends, 11-11–11-13
   common stock, 11-4–11-5
   comprehensive income, 11-16, 11-16e
   earnings per share, 11-21
   financial statements analysis, 11-17–11-19
   return on common equity, 11-18
   preferred stock, 11-5–11-6
   stock issuance, 11-8
   stockholders' equity, 11-3e, 11-17e
   stock repurchase, 11-8–11-11
physical (tangible) assets, 2-5
pie charts, B-9
planning, 13-10–13-11
   activities, 1-7–1-8
plant assets, 4-25–4-27
plantwide allocation rate costing model, 18-4e, 18-5
plantwide overhead rate, 17-10
Plesko Corporation, 11-11
Porsche division of Volkswagen, 23-3

post-audit, 24-5–24-6
post-closing trial balance, 3-26
posting, 3-4. *See also* journalizing and posting transactions
Potbelly Corporation, 20-2, 20-5–20-7, 20-9, 20-11–20-13, 20-14–20-15
potential shareholders, 1-4
Power BI, B-2, B-5
Pownall Company
  acquisition of investment, 12-7
  fair value adjustments, 12-10–12-12
  investments marked to fair value, 12-8
  investments reported at cost, 12-7
  passive investments in equity securities, 12-12–12-17
  sale of investment, 12-9
PPE turnover (PPET), 8-13–8-14
practical capacity, 19-11, 19-12–19-13
predetermined manufacturing overhead rate, 17-9
predetermined overhead rate. *See* predetermined manufacturing overhead rate
predictive analytics, B-3
predictive value, 1-26
preferred stock, 11-5–11-6. *See also specific entries*
premium
  amortization, 9-20–9-22
  bonds issued at, 9-17, 9-19–9-20
prepaid expenses, 2-5, 3-14–3-16
prepaid insurance, 3-14
prescriptive analytics, B-3
present value, 9-15, 24-20–24-22, 24-22e, A-3–A-7
  annuity, A-4–A-5
  bond valuation, A-5–A-6
  calculating bond yields, A-6
  future value of annuities, A-6–A-7
  installment loan, A-5
  single amount, A-3–A-4
present value calculations, A-10–A-16
prevention costs, 23-23
price-based costing
  cost of alternative activities, 20-11
  design for manufacture, 20-10
  new products, reduces time to market for, 20-10–20-11
  proactive cost management approach, 20-9
  requires coordinated efforts, 20-11–20-12
  target costing, 20-8–20-9
price changes, inventory costing and, 7-11
price/cost, 13-16
PricewaterhouseCoopers (PWC), B-4
pricing products/services, 20-3
principal, 9-14
process costing, 17-22–17-23
  cost of production report using weighted-average method, 17-23–17-26

first-in, first-out process costing, 17-27
  process costing in service organizations, 17-27–28
process manufacturing, 17-11
processing time, 19-15
Procter & Gamble Company (P&G), 1-8, 8-2, 17-11, 19-16
  balance sheet, 8-4e
  financial statements analysis
    cash flow effects, 8-16
    percent depreciated, 8-14–8-15
    PPE turnover, 8-13–8-14
    footnote disclosure, 8-12
Producer Price Indices, 7-11
producing departments. *See* production departments
product costing, 7-3–7-4, 17-5, 17-5e, 19-4
  ABC model, 18-11–18-15
  absorption and variable costing, 17-28–17-29
    alternatives to inventory valuation, 17-32–17-33
    income under, 17-29–17-31
    production exceeds sales, 17-31
    sales exceed production, 17-31–17-32
  data-driven decision-making
    developing skills for, 19-20
    using effective data, 19-19–19-20
  excess capacity cost
    calculating, 19-13
    considerations when using dual overhead allocation rates, 19-14
    managing, 19-13
    overhead application rate, calculating, 19-11–19-13
  job costing, 17-11–17-12
    basic flow of, 17-12–17-14
    overapplied and underapplied overhead, 17-19–17-21
    production planning and control process, 17-12
    for Samsung, 17-14–17-18
    in service organizations, 17-21–17-22
    statement of cost of goods manufactured and cost of goods sold, 17-18–17-19
  just-in-time inventory management/lean production
    characteristics of, 19-14–19-17
    performance evaluation under, 19-17–19-19
  manufacturing overhead
    applying, 17-8–17-11
    predetermined overhead rates, 17-9
    selecting basis, 17-9
  process costing, 17-22–17-23
    cost of production report using weighted-average method, 17-23–17-26
    first-in, first-out process costing, 17-27

process costing in service organizations, 17-27–28
  reporting inventory costs, 17-4e
    costs of products outside of financial reporting, 17-7–17-8
    inventory categories, types of, 17-3–17-5
    product and period cost reporting, 17-5–17-6
    product costs, components of, 17-6, 17-7e
  service department costs, allocation of, 19-3
    direct method to, 19-6–19-7
    direct vs. step method, 19-7–19-8
    process of, 19-4–19-5
    reasons for, 19-4
    step method to, 19-8–19-11
product development, 20-9
product-level activity, 18-8
product margins, 23-6
production budget, 21-19
production departments, 19-3
production order, 17-12
product/service differentiation, 13-8–13-9
profit center, 22-5–22-6
  revenue center as, 22-22–22-24
profit margin (PM), 5-11, 12-12
  and asset turnover, 5-12
  disaggregation of, 5-14–5-15
profit planning
  break-even point and cost-volume-profit graph, 15-12–15-13
  margin of safety in unit sales, 15-9–15-10
  profit-volume graph, 15-13
  in sales dollars, 15-11
  sales dollars at a target profit, 15-11–15-12
  unit sales at target profit, 15-10–15-11
  changes in, 16-9–16-11
  discontinuing, 16-11–16-12
profit-volume graph, 15-13
profitability analysis, 1-21–1-22, 18-22
  with unit and nonunit cost drivers, 18-22–18-23
  multilevel contribution income statement, 18-22–18-24
  variations in, 18-24–18-25
project-level activity, 18-10
projected benefit obligation (PBO), 10-16
  components of, 10-18–10-20
property, plant, and equipment (PPE) assets, 2-5, 8-3
  accounting estimates, changes in, 8-9
  asset sales and impairments, 8-10–8-12
  costs to capitalize, 8-4–8-5
  depreciation, 8-6
    methods, 8-6–8-9
    footnote disclosure, 8-12

Note: Exhibits included in the index with *e* following the page numbers.

property, plant, and equipment turnover (PPET), 5-14
prospective employees, 1-5
Prudential Financial, 10-21
Public Company Accounting Oversight Board (PCAOB), 1-18
public corporations, 1-4
publicly traded corporations, 1-4
Publix Super Markets Inc., 7-25
purchases budget, 21-19–21-20
Python/R, B-6

Q

qualitative factors, 16-8, 16-14, 16-16
quality, 13-16
quality of earnings, 6-28
quick ratio (QR), 2-32, 5-18

R

ratio analysis limitations
    company changes, 5-22
    conglomerate effects, 5-22
    GAAP limitations, 5-21–5-22
    means to an end, 5-22
raw material transactions, 19-16–19-17
raw materials inventories, 17-3, 7-6
Razor USA, LLC, 15-2–15-4, 15-6–15-7, 15-15, 15-20, 15-22
real earnings management, 12-16
receivables quality, 6-26
reconciling budgeted and actual income, 22-25–22-27, 22-26e
recording transactions, review of, 3-4–3-10
recurring components, 6-29
redeem, 9-24
relevance, 1-26, 2-5
relevant costs, 16-3, 16-7
    disposal and salvage values, 16-6
    future revenues, 16-4
    opportunity costs, 16-6
    outlay costs, 16-4–16-5
    sunk cost dilemma, 16-5–16-6
    sunk costs, 16-5
relevant range, 14-7–14-9
rent expenses, 4-12–4-13
reporting inventory costs, 17-4e
    costs of products outside of financial reporting, 17-7–17-8
    inventory categories, types of, 17-3–17-5
    product and period cost reporting, 17-5–17-6
    product costs, components of, 17-6, 17-7e
research and development costs, 8-17–8-18
residual (or salvage) value, 8-6
residual income, 23-18–23-19
residual interest, 2-7
responsibility accounting, 22-3
    financial and nonfinancial performance measures, 22-6–22-7

performance reporting and organization structures, 22-4–22-5
responsibility centers
    cost center, 22-5
    investment center, 22-6
    profit center, 22-5–22-6
    revenue center, 22-5
responsibility centers
    cost center, 22-5
    investment center, 22-6
    profit center, 22-5–22-6
    revenue center, 22-5
restricted stock, 11-25–11-27
    award, 11-25–11-26
    unit, 11-26–11-27
restructuring costs, 6-29–6-30, 8-11
retained earnings, 1-13, 2-7–2-8, 2-15–2-16, 5-27–5-28
return on assets (ROA), 5-2, 5-8–5-9, 5-10e, 12-12
    disaggregating, 5-11–5-15
return on capital employed, 6-23
Return on Common Equity (ROCE), 11-18
return on equity (ROE), 5-2, 5-8, 5-10e, 12-12
    disaggregation, 5-15e
    effect of debt financing on, 5-16e
    to Nike, 1-22
return on financial leverage (ROFL), 5-9–5-10, 5-10e, 5-15
return on investment (ROI), 23-14–23-18
    return on assets, 5-8–5-9, 5-10e
        disaggregating, 5-11–5-15
    return on equity, 5-8, 5-10e
    return on financial leverage, 5-9–5-10, 5-10e
return on net operating assets (RNOA), 5-24–5-25, 6-23, 12-12
    disaggregating, 5-24–5-25
revenues, 1-10, 2-12, 5-27, 16-4
    accrual accounting for, 2-14–2-15
    and cash receipts, 6-12–6-13
    converting to cash flows, 4-12–4-14
    expense/reduction in, 6-17
    recognition, 2-14, 6-5–6-7
        for long-term projects, 6-11–6-13
        subsequent to customer purchase, 6-8–6-13
    variance, 22-20–22-22
    See also specific revenues
revenue center, 22-5, 22-20–22-22
    controllable costs, 22-22
    as profit centers, 22-22–22-24
right-of-use asset, 10-5
risk, 21-4
    evaluating, 24-15–24-16
    management, budgeting in, 21-4
Rite Aid Corporation, 2-32
robotic process automation (RPA), 13-17
Rocky Road Bicycles, Inc., 4-35
rolling budget, 21-23

S

sale of investment, 12-8–12-9
sales budget, 21-19
sales department profit center performance report, 22-23e
sales mix, 15-15, 15-16e, 15-18e
sales on account, 6-14
sales price variance, 22-21
sales revenue, 5-25–5-26
    convert to cash receipts from customers, 4-10–4-11
sales volume variance, 22-21
salvage value, 16-6
Samsonite, 22-2, 22-8, 22-9, 22-11–22-13, 22-15, 22-19, 22-25
Samsung, 16-14, 20-14
Samsung Electronics, 17-2, 17-3, 17-8, 17-10, 17-14–17-18, 17-23–17-24, 17-29
Sanmina, 13-15
Sarbanes-Oxley Act of 2002 (SOX), 1-5, 1-18, 13-21
scatter diagrams, 14-14–14-15
scatter plots, B-10
Schumacher Homes, 17-12
Scope 3 emission requirements, 16-16
Seagate, 16-14
Sears, 5-19
seasoned equity offering, 11-7
Securities Acts of 1933 and 1934, 1-17–1-18
Securities and Exchange Commission (SEC), 1-17–1-18, 13-5
securitization, 6-26
segment income, 23-6
segment margin, 23-6
segment reporting, 23-3–23-8
    format of, 23-6
    interpreting segment reports, 23-6–23-8
    multilevel segment reporting approach, 23-4–23-6
    preparation of, 23-3–23-23-6, 23-4e
    single-level segment reporting approach, 23-4
    strategic business segments and, 23-3
Segway, 15-6, 15-9, 15-14, 15-19, 15-21
self-liquidating, 5-20
selling expense budget, 21-12
Semrush, 20-14
sensitivity analysis, 5-29, 9-25, 15-8, 15-20, 23-16, 24-16
service costing, 10-16, 17-21, 19-4
service department, 19-3
    cost allocation of, 19-3
        direct method to, 19-6–19-7
        direct vs. step method, 19-7–19-8
        process of, 19-4–19-5
        reasons for, 19-4
        step method to, 19-8–19-11
service organizations, 17-3
setup time, 19-15

Note: Exhibits included in the index with e following the page numbers.

Seven Cycles, 17-14
7-Eleven, 18-25
shared services departments, 19-3
shareholders, 1-4
shares authorized, 11-4
shares issued, 11-4
shares of stock, 1-4
shares outstanding, 11-4
Shevlin Company, 9-13
Shopbop, 15-20
short-term borrowings, 2-6
short-term interest-bearing debt, 9-4, 9-11–9-12
Shriners Hospital for Children, 17-3, 17-5, 17-8
significant influence, 12-4
   investments with
      accounting for, 12-17–12-22
      equity method accounting and effects on ratios, 12-20
      financial statement disclosures, 12-20–12-22
simple capital structure, 11-19
simple interest, A-1
simple regression analysis, 14-17–14-19
single-level segment reporting approach, 23-4
single payment, 9-15
small stock dividends, 11-13
Snyder's-Lance, Inc., 5-2
Software Innovations, Inc., 6-10–6-11
sole proprietorship, 1-4
solvency, 1-23, 4-3, 5-19
   analysis, 5-19
      debt-to-equity, 5-20
      times interest earned, 5-20–5-21
Southwest Airlines Co., 12-35, 13-8, 22-6
split-off point, 16-18
SportClips, 17-3
spreadsheet approach, 24-11, 24-11e
Square, Inc., 14-2
staff departments, 13-10–13-11
Standard & Poor's, 9-30–9-31
standard cost variance analysis, 22-11–22-15
standard costs, 22-10
   analysis, components of, 22-11
   and performance reports, 22-10–22-11
   variance analysis, 22-11
standard labor rate, 22-15
standard price, 22-12
standard quantity, 22-12
standard time allowed, 22-15
standard variable cost of goods sold, 22-22
Starbucks Corporation, 3-4
statement of cash flows, 1-11, 1-13–1-14, 1-14e, 4-3, 8-16, 9-26, 11-15
   classifications of, 4-6–4-7
   deferred tax assets in, 10-35
   effects of foreign currencies on, 4-27
   financing activities, 4-5–4-6, 4-20–4-21
      gains and losses on, 4-24–4-25

   noncash investing and, 4-25–4-27
financial statements analysis
   free cash flow, 4-31
   interpreting indirect method cash from operations, 4-29
   operating cash flow to capital expenditures, 4-31–4-32
   operating cash flow to current liabilities, 4-29–4-30
   framework for, 4-4–4-7
   investing activities, 4-5, 4-19–4-20
      gains and losses on, 4-24–4-25
   leases and, 10-14
   operating activities, 4-5, 4-7–4-9
      converting revenues and expenses to, 4-10–4-16
      reconciling net income and cash flow, 4-17–4-18
      using indirect method, 4-18–4-19
   purpose of, 4-3–4-4
   spreadsheet approach to preparing, 4-33–4-35
   supplemental disclosures, 4-28
statement of cost of goods manufactured, 17-18–17-19
statement of stockholders' equity, 1-11, 1-13, 1-13e
   constructing, 2-20–2-21
   preparation from adjusted accounts, 3-22
static budget, 22-7–22-8
static variance, 22-9
step costs, 14-3–14-4
step method to, 19-8–19-11
   direct method vs., 19-7–19-8
Stern Stewart and Company, 23-19
stock dividends, 11-13–11-14
stock issuance, 11-7–11-8
stock options, 11-24–11-25
stock prices, 12-19
stock repurchase, 11-8–11-11
stock returns, 11-8
stock rights, 11-23–11-24
stock splits, 11-15
stock transactions, 11-15
   accounting for, 11-7–11-11
stock warrant, 11-23
stockholders, 1-4
stockholders' equity, 2-7–2-8
   contributed capital, 11-3–11-4
      accounting for stock transactions, 11-7–11-11
      classes of stock, 11-4–11-6
   dilutive securities
      convertible securities, 11-22–11-23
      restricted stock, 11-25–11-27
      stock options, 11-24–11-25
      stock rights, 11-23–11-24
   earned capital, 11-4
      cash dividends, 11-11–11-13
      comprehensive income, 11-16
      stock dividends and splits, 11-13–11-15

      stock transactions and the cash flows statement, 11-15
   earnings per share, 11-19–11-20
      computation and analysis of, 11-20–11-21
      financial statements analysis, 11-17–11-19
      return on common equity, 11-18
   Pfizer Inc., 11-3e
   summary of, 11-17
straight-line (SL) method, 8-7
   double-declining-balance (DDB) method vs., 8-8e
straight-line depreciation, 3-15, 24-26–24-28, 24-27e
strategic (or business) plan, 1-8
strategic business segment, 23-3
   preparation of, 23-4e
   multilevel segment reporting approach, 23-4–23-6
   segment reporting and, 23-3
      interpreting segment reports, 23-6–23-8
strategic position analysis, 13-8–13-9
strategic thinking, 13-16
strategy, 1-7, 13-7
strips, 9-19
subsidiary ledger, 17-15
sunk costs, 16-5
   dilemma, 16-5–16-6
supplemental disclosures, statement of cash flows, 4-28
suppliers, 1-5
support departments, 19-3
systematic allocation, 7-4
   of asset's cost, 8-5

T

T-account, 2-21
   with debits and credits, 2-23
T-Mobile, 9-2, 17-14
table approach, 24-10
   for determining internal rate of return, 24-24–24-26
Tableau, B-2, B-5
tangible assets, 8-3
Target Corporation, 7-6, 19-10, 19-14, 19-18–19-20
Tax Code, 24-26
Tax Cuts and Jobs Act (TCJA), 1-22, 10-25, 10-30, 10-32
taxes
   in capital budgeting decisions
      depreciation tax shield, 24-26–24-28, 24-27e
      investment tax credit, 24-28
technical skills, for decision-making, 19-20
technology and accounting, 1-24
TED, 13-6, 13-7
temporary accounts, closing, 3-24–3-26
territory margins, 23-6

Tesla Inc., 5-19, 8-21
theoretical capacity, 19-11–19-12
theory of constraints, 16-20–16-21
Theranos, 13-18
365 Everyday Value, 19-2
throughput, 16-20
time-adjusted rate of return. *See* internal rate of return
Time-Driven Activity-Based Costing (TDABC), 18-17
time stamp, B-11
time value of money, 24-3, 24-6–24-9, A-1
   annuities, 24-22–24-23
   capital budgeting models considering cost of capital, 24-12
      expected cash flows, 24-14
      internal rate of return, 24-11–24-12
      net present value, 24-10–24-11
   capital budgeting models do not considering
      accounting rate of return, 24-8–24-9
      payback period, 24-7–24-8
   deferred returns, 24-23–24-24
   future value, 24-20
   present value, 24-20–24-22, 24-22e
   unequal cash flows, 24-25–24-26
timeliness, 1-27
times interest earned (TIE), 5-20–5-21, 9-28
top-down budget, 21-22
Toro Company, 9-10
total costs, 14-9–14-11
   function, 14-6–14-7
total liabilities, median ratio of, 5-17
Tower of Babel in Accounting, 1-20
Toyota Motor Corporation, 13-14, 17-10, 20-13, 23-7, 23-14, 23-20
trade-off, between profit margin and asset turnover, 5-12
trade receivables, 6-14
trademarks, 8-19
Trader Joe's, 22-7
trading (T) securities, 12-9
traditional costing methods
   overhead with departmental rates, 18-5–18-8
   overhead with plant-wide rate, 18-3–18-5
trailing measures, 23-22
transaction
   determination of
      market price, 23-11
   journalizing and posting
      accounting procedures, review of, 3-4
      analyze, journalize, and post, 2-24–2-29
      debit and credit system, 2-22
      journal entry, 2-23
      recording transactions, review of, 3-4–3-10
      T-account, 2-21
      T-account with debits and credits, 2-23

transfer pricing, 23-8
   determination of
      absorption cost plus markup, 23-12–23-13
      dual prices, 23-13
      negotiated prices, 23-13
      variable costs, 23-11–23-12
      variable costs plus opportunity costs, 23-12
   resolving transfer-pricing conflicts, 23-8–23-11
transferred out costs, 17-26
treasury stock, 2-7, 4-6, 11-9
True Religion Brand Jeans, 17-12
Tufte's principles, B-8
Twitter, Inc., 12-2, 14-2
Tyco, 1-5

U

unadjusted trial balance, 3-11, 3-12e
unallocated common costs, 23-6, 23-7
uncertain tax positions, 10-31
underestimating incremental sales/cost savings, 24-19
underfunded, 10-16
understandability, 1-27
unearned revenue, 6-8–6-10
unequal cash flows, 24-23, 24-25–24-26
unfavorable labor efficiency variances, 22-16
unfavorable labor rate variance, 22-16
unfavorable materials price variance, 22-14
unfavorable materials quantity variance, 22-14–22-15
Unilever, 18-2, 18-3, 18-20
unit contribution margin, 15-8
unit-level activity, 18-8, 18-9
United Airlines Holdings, Inc., 5-18
United Way, 13-7
units-of-production method, 8-8–8-9
unrealized holding gain, 7-18
unrecognized tax benefit, 10-31
UPS, 13-5
Urban Outfitters, 17-3
U.S. Bureau of Labor Statistics, 7-11
U.S. Department of Defense, 18-10
useful life, 8-6

V

valuation allowance, 10-31
value chain, 13-12
Vanguard Group, 9-15
variable costing, 14-3, 14-9–14-11, 17-28–17-29, 23-11–23-12
   alternatives to inventory valuation, 17-32–17-33
   income under, 17-29–17-31
   of one unit, 14-8
   plus opportunity costs, 23-12
   production exceeds sales, 17-31
   sales exceed production, 17-31–17-32

variable manufacturing overhead, 15-4
variable overhead
   efficiency variance, 22-18
   spending variance, 22-18
   standards for, 22-17–22-19
   variances, 22-18
      interpreting, 22-18–22-19
variable selling and administrative costs, 15-4
variance, 22-8
variance analysis for costs
   fixed overhead variances, 22-19–22-20, 22-24–22-25
   reconciling budgeted and actual income, 22-25–22-27, 22-26e
   standard cost analysis, components of, 22-11
   standards for direct labor, 22-15
   standards for direct materials, 22-12
   standards for variable overhead, 22-17–22-19
variety, B-2
velocity, B-2
veracity, B-2
verifiability, 1-27
Verizon Communications, 1-8, 1-11, 8-14, 9-2, 17-12, 17-14, 19-3
   accounts payable, 9-4–9-6
   accrued liabilities, 9-6–9-10
   financial statements analysis, 9-27
      debt-to-equity ratio, 9-28
      debt ratings and cost of debt, 9-29–9-31
      times interest earned, 9-28
   financial statement footnotes, 9-24–9-25
   liabilities and equity, 9-3e
   nonoperating (financial), 9-10–9-13
vertical analysis, 5-4, 5-5e
vesting period, 11-24
virtual integration, 13-14
visual clutter, B-8
visualizations, B-5
Volkswagen (VW), 23-2–23-4, 23-8–23-9, 23-19, 23-22
volume, B-2

W

Wag, 19-3
wage expenses, 4-12
waiting time, 19-15
Walgreens Boots Alliance, Inc., 1-9, 2-2, 2-32, 3-2, 4-2, 6-24, 9-29
   balance sheet, 2-4e
   earned capital, 2-8
   financial condition reporting, 2-3–2-8
   financial performance reporting, 2-12–2-16
   financial statements analysis
      current ratio, 2-31
      net working capital, 2-30
      quick ratio, 2-32

Walgreens Boots Alliance, Inc., *(continued)*
    income statement, 2-13e
    retained earnings reconciliation, 2-16e
Wall Street Journal, 2-5, 7-23, 10-12
WalMart Stores, Inc., 1-10, 2-2, 2-32, 5-14, 5-18, 17-3, 17-8, 17-19, 19-16, 24-2
Walt Disney Company, The, 2-6, 20-5
Warby Parker, 13-2–13-4, 13-6, 13-8, 13-12, 13-15, 13-20
warranties, 9-8–9-9
wasting assets, 8-9
Wayfair, 21-2, 21-5, 21-7, 21-8, 21-10
Waymire Corporation, 9-10
Waze, 12-2
weighted average cost of capital, 23-19

Weighted-Average Method, 17-23–17-26
whistle-blowing, 13-18
Whole Foods, 19-2, 19-4–19-5, 19-17–19-18, 22-7
Willis Towers Watson, 10-17
Winner's curse, 12-28
work-in-process inventory, 7-6, 17-3
work ticket, 17-13
working capital, 5-18
WorldCom, Inc., 1-5, 8-15, 13-18
write-offs, 6-17–6-19. *See also* asset write-downs

X

Xerox, 20-14

Y

Yahoo, Inc., 12-2
Yeti, 15-16
YouGov, 19-2
YouTube, Inc., 12-2
YY Inc., 13-9

Z

Zappos, 19-3
zero-based budgeting, 21-7–21-8
zeros, 9-19
Zhang Corporation, 11-15

Note: Exhibits included in the index with *e* following the page numbers.

Notes

Note: Exhibits included in the index with *e* following the page numbers.